PELHAM PUBLIC
LIBRARY
PELHAM, NY

D0161328

THE BIOGRAPHY BOOK

A Reader's Guide to Nonfiction, Fictional, and Film Biographies of More Than 500 of the Most Fascinating Individuals of All Time

Daniel S. Burt

Oryx Press

2001

The rare Arabian Oryx is believed to have inspired the myth of the unicorn. This desert antelope became virtually extinct in the early 1960s. At that time several groups of international conservationists arranged to have 9 animals sent to the Phoenix Zoo to be the nucleus of a captive breeding herd. Today the Oryx population is over 1,000 and nearly 500 have been returned to reserves in the Middle East.

© 2001 by Daniel S. Burt
Published by The Oryx Press
An imprint of Greenwood Publishing Group, Inc.
88 Post Road West
Westport, CT 06881-5007
(203) 226-3571
(800) 225-5800
http://www.oryxpress.com

All rights reserved. No part of this publication may be reproduced or transmitted in any form or by any means, electronic or mechanical, including photocopying, recording, or by any information storage and retrieval system, without permission in writing from Greenwood Publishing Group, Inc.

Published simultaneously in Canada
Printed and Bound in the United States of America

∞ The paper used in this publication meets the minimum requirements of American National Standard for Information Science—Permanence of Paper for Printed Library Materials, ANSI Z39.48, 1984.

Library of Congress Cataloging-in-Publication Data

Burt, Daniel S.
    The biography book: a reader's guide to nonfiction, fictional, and
film biographies of more than 500 of the most fascinating individuals of all time /
by Daniel S. Burt.
        p. cm.
Includes bibliographical references and indexes.
ISBN 1-57356-256-4 (alk. Paper)
1. Biography—Bibliography.   I. Title.
Z5301 B96 2001
[CT104]
016.92—dc21   00-010116

CONTENTS

INTRODUCTION

This reference volume is intended to serve the general reader by identifying and assessing the biographical materials available on the most written-about historical figures. That biographies remain one of the most popular literary genres is evident by the large number published each year. It is the exception for any historical figure of even modest accomplishments not to be examined by a biographer, and the notion of a definitive or final word on such figures as Lincoln, Napoleon, or Elizabeth I is challenged by an almost continual stream of yearly reassessments.

Readers of biography are increasingly able to be viewers as well, of documentary and dramatic profiles in films and television. The popular appeal of the lives and times of others is clear from the success of Arts & Entertainment Channel's nightly series "Biography." Cable television's highest-rated program, "Biography" has spawned its own Web site, a Saturday program for kids, and a monthly magazine devoted to biographical profiles.

Readers can also find versions of biographies in the fiction section of libraries and bookstores. Published in 1999 alone were fictional lives of such figures as Joe McCarthy (William F. Buckley's *Redhunter*), Joseph Stalin (Richard Lourie's *The Autobiography of Joseph Stalin*), George Washington (William Martin's *Citizen Washington*), William Shakespeare (Robert Nye's *The Late Mr. Shakespeare*), Warren G. Harding (Martin Blinder's *Fluke*), and Benedict Arnold (John Ensor Harr's *Dark Eagle*). There were also dozens of novels that featured interesting presentations of the lives and characters of historical figures, such as Crazy Horse in Dan O'Brien's *The Contract Surgeon*, Hitler in Ron Hansen's *Hitler's Niece*, Samuel Pepys in Ferdinand Mount's *Jem (and Sam)* and Sara George's *The Journal of Mrs. Pepys*, and Douglas MacArthur in James H. Webb's *The Emperor's General*.

Yet with all this biographical material to choose from, readers have few reference tools to assist them in sorting through what's available, and no single volume that brings together a wide range of important historical figures and biographical nonfiction, fiction, and film.

This book is designed to assist readers in identifying biographical books and films available on a particular individual and to help judge whether a title is of interest or will meet the reader's specialized or general interest.

Selection

The first step in the preparation of this book was to determine which historical figures should be included. Since the biographies of living figures are still evolving and any assessment is, therefore, incomplete and tentative, only the deceased were considered. I selected those individuals for whom the reader had the most biographical choices and, therefore, the most need for assistance. Included in this volume, therefore, are over 500 of the most written-about historical figures as determined from the number of titles on each in typical library holdings. Instead of relying on numbers from the subject headings of the Library of Congress, I ranked my list based on data from the state of Connecticut's libraries. Connecticut's well-funded library system offers a fair, representative sample with its mix of urban and suburban and large and small public and university libraries. The individuals who made the final cut have had at least 30 books produced on some aspect of their lives, work, or achievement.

It is often a judgment call identifying whether a book serves a significant biographical as opposed to a historical or critical focus, and I have tried to select those books for review that at least offer as much about a figure's life as his or her achievements, significance, or influence. Not every biographical title on each figure, however, was finally included. This reader's guide is not intended as a scholarly annotated bibliography. Rather, the listings are meant to reflect what most readers could expect to find or at least easily retrieve from their linked library systems through interlibrary loan. Obscure or antiquated titles that now have little more than historical interest, because they have been superseded by subsequent research, have been omitted unless they continue to be important biographical sources.

Organization

No individual could possibly have the expertise to canvass such a large selection of figures and works without relying on the views of others. In the assessment of titles, I have tried to reflect critical consensus, derived from contemporary reviews and later expert assessments of the value of particular works. Space consideration forced each entry to be brief, but I have tried to indicate the scope of each book as well as its strengths and weaknesses and to provide readers with a sense of what they can expect from a particular title, whether, for example, a book is a full-length biography or a more specialized study of an aspect of the individual's life, and what if any bias or limitations affect a biography's reliability and usefulness.

I have organized the coverage of each figure into sections beginning with available autobiographical material ("Autobiography and Primary Sources"), including memoirs, collections of letters, diaries, and interviews, and essential documentary evidence. I have followed this section with those biographies judged the best in the field ("Recommended Biographies"), books considered standard or definitive or which have, because of a particular viewpoint or interpretation, exerted the strongest impact on how we view a particular figure. The titles that follow these recommendations ("Other Biographical Studies") are, in most cases, also extremely valuable and should not be overlooked. In most cases they lack the comprehensiveness of the recommended biographies and are more general introductory overviews or offer a more specialized look at a narrower aspect of a figure's life. Many were not included in the recommended section not because they are weak books, but because I felt it would be helpful to single out a smaller number of titles for special attention in an attempt to suggest what books, given a reader's limited time, interest, or inclination, should not be missed.

Nonfictional biographies are followed whenever available with those fictional biographies in which novelists dramatically present significant portions of an individual's life ("Biographical Novels"). Freed from a more restrictive obligation to the evidence in nonfictional biographies, the fictional biographer is able to offer a more creative, imaginative interpretation in the same ways in which a historical novel differs from a historical text. Long criticized for the liberties taken and resulting distortions, the fictional biography continues to attract readers and some distinguished writers, and for those interested in a particular historical figure this genre should not be overlooked or underestimated in its capacity both to entertain and to enlighten. Included as well is a sampling of those novels in which the historical figure appears as a character ("Fictional Portraits"). This category identifies the most elusive biographical information, since sometimes a figure appears only briefly in such a novel, and that appearance is rarely recorded. Additional titles can be found in the excellent listings *Historical Figures in Fiction* by Donald K. Hartman and Gregg Sapp (Oryx Press, 1994), *World Historical Fiction* and *American Historical Fiction* by Lynda G. Adamson (Oryx Press, 1999), or in my own book *What Historical Novel Do I Read Next?* (Gale Research, 1997).

I have also selected the best available biographies for middle grade (ages 9–12) and young adult (ages 13–17) readers, limited by space to a maximum of three to four titles ("Recommended Juvenile Biographies"). In many cases biographies listed here are also useful introductions for the adult general reader. Young adult and middle grade material is indicated in the text by the abbreviations MG and YA.

Biographical plays as well as documentary and dramatic films are also listed ("Biographical Films and Theatrical Adaptations"). Plays are listed at the beginning of the section, followed by documentary and fictional films; I have selected those that feature more than a cameo appearance by a particular historical figure. For the buff or enthusiast who wishes to view every possible dramatic interpretation of a figure there are several electronic databases from which to choose to locate every appearance, including more obscure and mainly unavailable titles. One of the best is the Internet Movie Database (http://www.us.imdb.com). I have emphasized films available on video.

Each entry concludes with any available biographical reference guides— chronologies, collections of biographical essays and recollections, encyclopedias, and sourcebooks. These materials are excellent complements or supplements to more standard biographical approaches. Many include valuable bibliographical information directing readers to additional works on a particular figure.

I hope that this arrangement is a useful, informative, and interesting one in helping readers find and appreciate the wealth of biographical material that exists on particular individuals. Included are not only the most fascinating historical figures but also some of the best biographies ever written.

Acknowledgments

My own biography during the nearly two years of labor to complete this project is marked by the many courtesies and assistance I have received from a variety of individuals. I would like to acknowledge publicly the generosity and patience of the staffs at the Eldredge Public Library, Chatham, Massachusetts, and Russell Library in Middletown, Connecticut. My thanks to Ed Rubacha and his fellow reference librarians at Wesleyan University's Olin Library. Thanks as well to Krishna Winston for her sympathy, counsel, and hospitality and to Ed Knappman for his always sensible advice. My largest debt is to my wife, Debby Felder, who has helped more than any other in seeing this project to completion.

THE BIOGRAPHY BOOK

1. ABIGAIL ADAMS
1744–1818

One of the most distinguished and influential first ladies in U.S. history, Abigail Adams was also one of the most important women in early American history. The wife of the second and mother of the sixth president, Adams was at the center of American political life through the United States' formative years, and she provides in her letters a vivid reflection of social history from a revealing female perspective.

Autobiography and Primary Sources

The primary source for modern biographies of Abigail Adams are the extensive Adams Papers slowly being edited and published in their entirety. Completed volumes include *The Adams Family Correspondence* 4 vols. (Cambridge, Massachusetts: Harvard University Press, 1963–1973), edited by L.H. Butterfield, as well as a briefer selection of letters, also edited by Butterfield, *The Book of Abigail and John: Selected Letters of the Adams Family, 1762–1784* (Cambridge, Massachusetts: Harvard University Press, 1975. 411pp.).

Recommended Biographies

Akers, Charles W. *Abigail Adams: An American Woman*. Boston: Little, Brown, 1980. 207pp. The first biography of Abigail Adams to appear after the Adams family papers were opened to scholars, this account captures the paradoxes in Adams's character, particularly concerning her feminism, and offers revelations about Adams absent from earlier biographies. However, many aspects of Adams's complex life and times are sacrificed or superficially treated to fit the exigencies of a compact, short biography.

Levin, Phyllis L. *Abigail Adams: A Biography*. New York: Saint Martin's, 1987. 575pp. The most comprehensive and detailed account of Adams for readers of all levels, the book is excellent on Adams's relationships, her visit to Europe, her youth, and her old age. Scrupulous in her documentation, Levin footnotes almost every paragraph. However, more interpretation rather than accumulation of data and paraphrased letters by and to Adams

would have better assisted Levin's intention to reconstruct the complex character of her subject.

Withey, Lynne. *Dearest Friend: A Life of Abigail Adams*. New York: Free Press, 1981. 369pp. The biography's strengths rest in the historical and cultural contexts Withey provides and her willingness to present Adams with her paradoxes and ambivalences intact, shaped by the contradictions of her times and the role of women Adams struggled equally to expand and maintain.

Other Biographical Studies

Bobbé, Dorothie. *Abigail Adams: The Second First Lady*. New York: Minton Balch, 1929. 336pp. This admiring early biography is marred by sentimentality and melodrama, avoids unflattering aspects of Adams's life and character, and employs undocumented, invented dialogue. It is best on period fashion and lifestyle.

Gellis, Edith B. *Portia: The World of Abigail Adams*. Bloomington: Indiana University Press, 1992. 227pp. This fascinating biographical study sees Adams in the context of eighteenth-century ideas and recent feminist thought that focuses on relationships and power, patriarchy, and individualism in the context of Adams's eighteenth-century world. Critics have asserted that Gellis's approach reconceptualizes and revolutionizes the very notion of biography; others have noted some questionable assumptions about the veracity of certain historical truths about women.

Nagel, Paul C. *The Adams Women: Abigail and Louisa Adams, Their Sisters and Daughters*. New York: Oxford University Press, 1987. 310pp. Centering on the biographical data of the Adams family, Nagel provides an extensive portrait of how American women actually lived and thought between 1750 and 1850. The minutia of Abigail Adams's daily life are fully captured.

Whitney, Janet. *Abigail Adams*. Boston: Little, Brown, 1947. 347pp. At its best in its historical reconstruction, the author's portrait of Adams is marred by an overly enthusiastic advocacy of Adams's feminism, which other biographers have qualified, as well as imagined, undocumented conversations.

Biographical Novels

Stone, Irving. *Those Who Love*. Garden City, New York: Doubleday, 1965. 662pp. Tracing the married and political lives of John and Abigail Adams from their courtship to Adams's election as president, the novel shows Abigail Adams as her husband's true partner. The period background is convincing, with the essential elements of the Adamses' story faithfully depicted.

Fictional Portraits

Abigail Adams appears as a character in a number of historical fictions on the American Revolution and the early years of the United States, no doubt because of her colorful character and her proximity to the great events and figures of the times. The most interesting portraits can be found in the following:

Byrd, Max. *Jefferson: A Novel*. New York: Bantam, 1993. 424pp. Jefferson's service as ambassador to the court of Louis XVI is chronicled from the perspective of his secretary with intimate glimpses of those such as Abigail Adams who were important role players.

Chase-Riboud, Barbara. *Sally Hemings*. New York: Viking, 1979. 348pp. This controversial novel is based on the long-held suspicion that Thomas Jefferson had an affair with his slave Sally Hemings who bore him children. Their affair is dramatized over a 38-year period with historical figures such as Abigail Adams brought on for their perspectives.

Recommended Juvenile Biographies

Bober, Natalie. *Abigail Adams: Witness to a Revolution*. New York: Atheneum, 1995. 248pp. YA. Interweaving excerpts from Adams's correspondence into a coherent, award-winning biography, Bober creates a complex portrait as well as a detailed eighteenth-century background showing her subject as the product of her times.

Meeker, Clare Hodgson. *Partner in Revolution: Abigail Adams*. New York: Benchmark, 1998. 118pp. MG. Beautifully illustrated and reliable, Meeker's biography is valuable as both a biographical study and a depiction of the American Revolution and the formative years of the United States.

Osborne, Angela. *Abigail Adams.* New York: Chelsea House, 1989. 111pp. MG. Part of the American Women of Achievement series, this detailed and well-illustrated summary of Adams's life and times focuses on her role as a women's rights advocate.

Biographical Films and Theatrical Adaptations

Gibson, William. *American Primitive: The Words of John and Abigail Adams Put into a Sequence for the Theater, with Addenda in Rhyme.* New York: Atheneum, 1972. 115pp. Gibson's script for the theater derives its dialogue from letters written between 1774 and 1777 on both domestic and political affairs.

The Adams Chronicles (1975). Director: Paul Bogart. This popular PBS series dramatizes four generations of the Adams family in an entertaining and mostly reliable fashion. George Grizzard plays John Adams and Kathryn Walker portrays Abigail Adams.

Shepherd, Jack. *The Adams Chronicles: Four Generations of Greatness* (Boston: Little, Brown, 1975. 448pp.). This is the companion book to the PBS series.

Liberty! The American Revolution (1997). Directors: Ellen Hovde and Muffie Meyer. This PBS documentary series features actors portraying the principals in dramatic readings from their letters and speeches. Abigail Adams is played by Donna Murphy. The companion volume is written by Thomas J. Fleming (New York: Viking, 1997. 394pp.). Video.

1776 (1972). Director: Peter H. Hunt. The film version of the Broadway musical comedy by Sherman Edwards and Peter Stone that opened in 1969 concerns the first Continental Congress and the signing of the Declaration of Independence. Abigail Adams, played by Virginia Vestoff, delivers her famous "Remember the Ladies" comments to her husband (William Daniels). Video.

See also John Adams; John Quincy Adams

2. JOHN ADAMS
1735–1826

Second president of the United States John Adams has been called the "Atlas of the Revolution" for his determined leadership in the conflict and the formation of the American government. A member of the drafting committee that produced the Declaration of Independence, Adams served as a diplomat in France and was one of the negotiators of the Treaty of Paris that ended the Revolutionary War. Vice president under George Washington, Adams succeeded him in 1796 for a single term marked by crisis, conflict, and ideological clashes between the more conservative Adams and his longtime friend and nemesis Thomas Jefferson.

Autobiography and Primary Sources

Diary and Autobiography of John Adams. 4 vols. L.H. Butterfield, ed. Cambridge, Massachusetts: Harvard University Press, 1961. Part of the mas-

sive Adams Papers series, Adams's autobiography was intended for his family but was never finished. In three long sections, the first deals with his boyhood and early legal and political career, the second and third his diplomatic experiences. Readers interested in the primary sources for biographies of John Adams should consult

The Adams Family Correspondence in four volumes (Cambridge, Massachusetts: Harvard University Press, 1963–1973), edited by L.H. Butterfield, and a briefer collection, also edited by Butterfield, *The Book of Abigail and John: Selected Letters of the Adams Family, 1762–1784* (Cambridge, Massachusetts: Harvard University Press, 1975. 411pp.).

John Adams: A Biography in His Own Words. James Bishop Peabody, ed. New York: Newsweek, 1973. 416pp. Based on the Adams Papers, Peabody organizes Adams's letters, diaries, and memoir into a succinct account of Adams's career and attitudes.

Recommended Biographies

Ellis, Joseph J. *Passionate Sage: The Character and Legacy of John Adams.* New York: W.W. Norton, 1993. 277pp. Lacking the coverage of a full biography, Ellis's meditative study focuses instead on the latter part of Adams's life and challenges previous negative valuation of Adams's character and accomplishments, helping to restore a balanced view of Adams and an appreciation for his contribution and ideas.

Ferling, John E. *John Adams: A Life.* Knoxville, University of Tennessee Press, 1992. 535pp. Ferling's life of John Adams is the most comprehensive and authoritative single-volume biography. The author makes a case that Adams was a better diplomat and president than previous scholars have judged. The book achieves not only a stimulating account of Adams life, career, and achievement but an absorbing picture of America and Europe during his lifetime.

Smith, Page. *John Adams.* New York: Doubleday, 1962. 2 vols. Among the first biographies to make use of the extensive Adams Papers, this remains the definitive account, comprehensively chronicling Adams's long career, complex character, and thought in the context of his times. Winner of the Kenneth Roberts Memorial Award.

Other Biographical Studies

Adams, John Quincy, and Charles Francis Adams. *The Life of John Adams.* Philadelphia: Lippincott, 1871. Reprint ed. New York: Chelsea House, 1980. 2 vols. Written by Adams's son and grandson, this biography focuses on several crises in Adams's political life. Aiming at objectivity, the pair neglect their extensive personal family knowledge which might have provided a more intimate and human portrait.

Bowen, Catherine Drinker. *John Adams and the American Revolution.* Boston: Little, Brown, 1950. 699pp. Treating Adams's younger years from 1745 to 1776, this sympathetic account restores considerable credit to Adams for his role in the Revolution, but its reliability is compromised by fanciful,

undocumented conversations that cause it to resemble a fictional biography.

Chinard, Gilbert. *Honest John Adams.* Boston: Little, Brown, 1933. 359pp. A readable early biography that helped to revive Adams's reputation, this is a sympathetic portrait that captures the complexity of Adams's ideas as well as his wit and warmth, at odds with the view of the dour and glacial figure of earlier studies.

Shaw, Peter. *The Character of John Adams.* Chapel Hill: University of North Carolina Press, 1975. 324pp. Shaw attempts to explain Adams's contradictory character in the context of the times and values that shaped him. The result is a heightened appreciation of the complexity of Adams's personality and an explanation of his behavior as a man and politician.

Readers also should consult these studies on the Adams family:

Nagel, Paul C. *Descent from Glory: Four Generations of the John Adams Family.* New York: Oxford University Press, 1983. 400pp. A fact-filled family history, this account locates the source of John Adams's development in his domestic affairs.

Russell, Francis. *Adams: An American Dynasty.* New York: American Heritage, 1976. 374pp. This is a reliable overview of the generational history of the Adams clan.

Shepherd, Jack. *The Adams Chronicles: Four Generations of Greatness.* Boston: Little, Brown, 1975. 448pp. The companion volume to the popular PBS series that aired in the 1970s.

Biographical Novels

Stone, Irving. *Those Who Love.* Garden City, New York: Doubleday, 1965. 662pp. The novel traces the married and political lives of John and Abigail Adams from their courtship to Adams's election as president. Based on extensive research, Stone manages a very human portrait of Adams and his relationship with his wife.

Fictional Portraits

John Adams makes cameo appearances in a number of historical novels set during the Revolutionary period. The most interesting portraits occur in the following novels:

Byrd, Max. *Jefferson: A Novel.* New York: Bantam, 1993. 424pp. Jefferson's service as ambassador to the court of Louis XVI is chronicled from the perspective of his secretary with Jefferson's relationship to his nemesis John Adams glimpsed.

Chase-Riboud, Barbara. *Sally Hemings.* New York: Viking, 1979. 348pp. This controversial novel is based on the long-held, unproven suspicion that Thomas Jefferson had an affair with his slave Sally Hemings, who bore him children. The stolid John Adams provides a contrast with the more flamboyant and morally tortured Jefferson.

Wyckoff, Nicholas. *The Braintree Mission.* New York: Macmillan, 1957. 184pp. This what-if speculation imagines what might have happened had George III been persuaded to moderate his attitude toward the American colonies and elevated several colonists to seats in the House of Commons. At the center of the action is John Adams's behind-the-scenes diplomatic maneuvering.

Recommended Juvenile Biographies

Brill, Marlene Torg. *John Adams: Second President of the United States.* Chicago: Childrens Press, 1987. 98pp. MG. A reliable summary of Adams's career, this biography provides a worthy introduction to its subject, covering the childhood, adolescence, political career, and family life of the second president, liberally illustrated with a helpful chronology of American history.

Dwyer, Frank. *John Adams.* New York: Chelsea House, 1989. 109pp. MG. World Leaders Past & Present series entry in which the history and culture of colonial New England are explored along with a balanced account of Adams's life, character, and career.

Falkner, Leonard. *John Adams: Reluctant Patriot of the Revolution.* Englewood Cliffs, New Jersey: Prentice-Hall, 1969. 144pp. MG. Falkner's thoughtful treatment of Adams's complex temperament and motivation makes this life one of the more challenging and sophisticated treatments for younger readers.

Biographical Films and Theatrical Adaptations

Gibson, William. *American Primitive: The Words of John and Abigail Adams Put into a Sequence for the Theater, with Addenda in Rhyme.* New York: Atheneum, 1972. 115pp. Gibson's theatrical script derives its dialogue from letters written between 1774 and 1777 on both domestic and political affairs.

The Adams Chronicles (1975). Director: Paul Bogart. This popular PBS series dramatizes four generations of the Adams family in an entertaining and mostly reliable fashion. George Grizzard portrays John Adams. Video.

Liberty! The American Revolution (1997). Directors: Ellen Hovde and Muffie Meyer. This PBS documentary series features actors portraying the principals in dramatic readings from their letters and speeches. John Adams is played by Peter Donaldson. The companion volume is written by Thomas J. Fleming (New York: Viking, 1997. 394pp.). Video.

1776 (1972). Director: Peter H. Hunt. This film version of the Broadway musical comedy by Sherman Edwards and Peter Stone that opened in 1969 concerns the first Continental Congress and the signing of the Declaration of Independence. William Daniels portrays John Adams, the ideological and temperamental foil to the more liberal and mercurial Thomas Jefferson (Ken Howard). Video.

See also Abigail Adams; John Quincy Adams

3. JOHN QUINCY ADAMS
1767–1848

Sixth president of the United States and son of John and Abigail Adams, John Quincy Adams served as an ambassador to Prussia, Russia, and Great Brit-

ain, was a U.S. senator and secretary of state under President Monroe, and helped to shape the Monroe Doctrine. President from 1825 to 1829, Adams became the only former president to return as a congressman, where he had a long tenure from 1831 to 1848, throughout which he spoke out against slavery.

Autobiography and Primary Sources

The essential primary material for any biographer of John Quincy Adams is his voluminous diary which he kept from the age of eleven and is slowly being edited and published as part of the Adams Papers series. So far, two volumes have appeared covering the years 1779 to 1788 (Cambridge, Massachusetts: Harvard University Press, 1981). A condensed, single-volume edition, *Diary of John Quincy Adams, 1794–1845* (New York: Scribner, 1951. 585pp.) is available, edited by Allan Nevis. See also *Memoirs of John Quincy Adams: Comprising Portions of His Diary from 1795 to 1848* (Philadelphia: Lippincott, 1874–1877) in 12 volumes, edited by Charles Francis Adams.

Recommended Biographies

Bemis, Samuel Flagg. *John Quincy Adams and the Foundations of American Foreign Policy.* New York: Knopf, 1949. 588pp. and *John Quincy Adams and the Union.* New York: Knopf, 1954. 546pp. Bemis's two-volumes still constitutes the definitive account of Adams's public career. A model of biographical research and analysis, Bemis's work is unfortunately thin on Adams's presidency and personal life.

Nagel, Paul C. *John Quincy Adams: A Public Life, a Private Life.* New York: Knopf, 1997. 464pp. The best available one-volume biography, Nagel's account is the first to draw upon Adams's complete diary and manages to portray both the events of a crowded public life and Adams's inner resources and conflicts, penetrating Adams's notorious "iron mask" of cold aloofness. Critics of the book have complained of the lack of interpretation at the expense of the author's extensive chronicling of events.

Other Biographical Studies

East, Robert A. *John Quincy Adams: The Critical Years, 1785–1794.* New York: Bookman, 1962. 588pp. Adams's youth from his entering Harvard to his selection as a diplomatic envoy to Holland is depicted in a revealing treatment of Adams's maturation under severe family pressures.

Hargreaves, Mary W.M. *The Presidency of John Quincy Adams.* Lawrence: University Press of Kansas, 1985. 398pp. This is the best account of the Adams administration, though critics have questioned the book's overly sympathetic view.

Hecht, Marie B. *John Quincy Adams: A Personal History of an Independent Man.* New York: Macmillan, 1972. 682pp. This examination of the private side of Adams sacrifices reliability by an overly sympathetic approach and an uncritical reliance on the Adams Papers.

Lipsky, George A. *John Quincy Adams: His Theory and Ideas.* New York: Crowell, 1950. 347pp.

This intellectual biography concentrates on Adams's attitude toward government, slavery, federal power, and foreign affairs.

Parsons, Lynn H. *John Quincy Adams.* Madison, Wisconsin: Madison House, 1998. 284pp. An effective one-volume popular biography, the book treats the essential outline and qualities of Adams's career and character without the ponderous accumulation of detail that glazes the eye of the casual reader.

Richards, Leonard L. *The Life and Times of Congressman John Quincy Adams.* New York: Oxford University Press, 1986. 245pp. Adams's congressional career is the focus with helpful insights about the antislavery movement. Adams's role is clearly placed in the context of his times.

Russell, Greg. *John Quincy Adams and the Public Virtue of Diplomacy.* Columbia: University of Missouri Press, 1995. 295pp. This study of Adams's diplomatic career brings together his literary, philosophical, and political career in an analysis of Adams's political thinking that explains his policies.

Shepherd, Jack. *Cannibals of the Heart: A Personal Biography of Louisa Catherine and John Quincy Adams.* New York: McGraw-Hill, 1980. 440pp. This is an intimate look at Adams's troubled marriage and relationship with his son.

Fictional Portraits

While no full-scale fictional biography has been written about John Quincy Adams, he does appear in several novels dramatizing his role in defense of the slaves seized aboard the *Amistad.*

Chase-Riboud, Barbara. *Echo of Lions.* New York: Morrow, 1989. 381pp. The author's fictionalized meeting between John Quincy Adams and the slave leader Cinque was the basis for a charge of plagiarism brought against the Spielberg film. This imagined scene, like others in the book, shapes the facts in the *Amistad* case into a powerful drama more concerned with essential truths rather than historical accuracy.

Pate, Alexs. *Amistad.* New York: Signet, 1997. 316pp. Based on the screenplay by David Franzoni and Steven Zaillan of the Steven Spielberg film, this fictionalization deepens the movie treatment by dramatizing the emotions and internal confusion of the slaves. As in the film, Adams's involvement and speeches partially distort historical facts in service of the drama.

Pesci, David. *Amistad: The Thunder of Freedom.* New York: Marlowe, 1997. 292pp. Pesci's treatment of the *Amistad* rebellion and trial is closer to the historical truth, though speculation and surmise are employed throughout. Adams's role, in particular, is more in line with the facts than other treatments.

Recommended Juvenile Biographies

Coelho, Tony. *John Quincy Adams.* New York: Chelsea House, 1990. 111pp. MG. Entry in the World Leaders Past & Present series thoughtfully explores the character similarities and differences between Adams and his father, as well as John Quincy Adams's young adulthood, political career, the pros and cons of his presidency, and his role in the *Amistad* slave rebellion case.

Greenblatt, Miriam. *John Quincy Adams: 6th President of the United States*. Ada, Oklahoma: Garrett, 1990. 120pp. MG. This is a straightforward, informative introduction to Adams's accomplishments.

Kent, Zachary. *John Quincy Adams: Sixth President of the United States*. Chicago: Childrens Press, 1987. 98pp. MG. Highlights are sketched in this brief, informative volume, tracing the whole of Adams's life, with the primary focus on his achievements.

Biographical Films and Theatrical Adaptations

Amistad (1997). Director: Steven Spielberg. This account of slave mutiny aboard the *Amistad* features Anthony Hopkins in the role of John Quincy Adams arguing the slaves' case before the Supreme Court. Dramatically intense, the film takes considerable liberties with the facts surrounding Adams's involvement. Video.

The Adams Chronicles (1975). Director: Paul Bogart. This popular PBS series dramatizes four generations of the Adams family in an entertaining and mostly reliable fashion. David Birney plays the young John Quincy Adams and William Daniels plays Adams in maturity. Video.

Shepherd, Jack. *The Adams Chronicles: Four Generations of Greatness* (Boston: Little, Brown, 1975. 448pp.) is the book that accompanied the series.

Other Sources

Parsons, Lynn H. *John Quincy Adams: A Bibliography*. New York: Greenwood, 1993. 240pp. This bibliography provides a guide to the works on Adams's life and career.

See also Abigail Adams; John Adams

4. JANE ADAMS
1860–1935

American social worker, Addams founded Hull-House in Chicago, one of the first social settlements in the United States, which served as a community center for the poor and an important center for social reform activities. Addams was a leader in the woman suffrage and pacifist movements. She received the Nobel Peace Prize in 1931.

Autobiography and Primary Sources

Jane Addams's recollections have been published in two well-known volumes. *Twenty Years at Hull-House* (New York: Macmillan, 1910. 462pp.) describes her childhood, education, and experiences leading up to founding Hull-House and its first two decades.

Second Twenty Years at Hull-House (New York: Macmillan, 1930. 413pp.) chronicles the years 1910–1929 and includes Addams's involvement with the International League for Peace and Freedom and the furor caused by her opposition to World War I. Throughout her memoirs, Addams

takes liberties with the facts, but her insights remain revealing and essential sources to understand Addams's evolution and attitudes.

Recommended Biographies

Davis, Allen F. *American Heroine: The Life and Legend of Jane Addams*. New York: Oxford University Press, 1973. 339pp. The most comprehensive and authoritative account to date, Davis's biography goes beyond the image of Addams as reformist heroine to create a credible portrait of a more complex and flawed figure than conventionally shown.

Diliberto, Gioia. *A Useful Woman: The Early Life of Jane Addams*. New York: Scribner, 1999. 318pp. Tracing Addams's life through the end of the nineteenth century, the author provides a sensitive and subtle guide to Addams's complex character and formative development.

Linn, James Weber. *Jane Addams: A Biography*. New York: Appleton-Century, 1935. 457pp. Written with the approval of Addams, this biography by her nephew is valuable for its insights and anecdotes about Addams's personal life, although Addams's role in selecting the material from which the biography was based places its overall reliability into question, not so much for what is included but what was excluded or ignored.

Other Biographical Studies

Farrell, John C. *Beloved Lady: A History of Jane Addams's Ideas on Reform and Peace*. Baltimore: Johns Hopkins University Press, 1967. 272pp. Relying on impressive research using primary materials from Addams's voluminous writings, speeches, and papers, Farrell provides a detailed intellectual history that uses her ideas to interpret and explain her actions.

Levine, Daniel. *Jane Addams and the Liberal Tradition*. Madison: State Historical Society of Wisconsin, 1971. 277pp. In this intellectual biography Levine's thesis is that Jane Addams is a pivotal figure in the transformation of America from a rural and agricultural society to an urban, industrial one who prepared the way for the New Deal and the modern welfare state.

Fictional Portraits

Mark, Grace. *The Dream Seekers*. New York: Morrow, 1992. 412pp. Set during the 1893 Chicago World's Fair, the novel follows the stories of a socialite and the daughter of an immigrant that involves actual events, such as the Pullman Strike, and actual historical figures, such as Jane Addams, Eugene V. Debs, and Clarence Darrow, to create a believable period drama.

Recommended Juvenile Biographies

Kittredge, Mary. *Jane Addams*. New York: Chelsea House, 1988. 111pp. MG. Part of the American Women of Achievement series, the book covers both Addams's career as a social reformer and a peace activist who became "one of the most hated women in America." This is a balanced and honest portrayal.

Meigs, Cornelia. *Jane Addams, Pioneer for Social Justice*. Boston: Little, Brown, 1970. 274pp. YA. This extensive biography is an excellent and well-written account of Addams's career, appropriate for very good middle-grade readers, young adults, and even adults. Covering the whole of Addams life, the book also provides the historical context surrounding her many achievements.

Wise, Winifred. *Jane Addams of Hull-House*. New York: Harcourt, Brace, 1935. 255pp. MG. Written with the approval of Jane Addams, the book concentrates on her youth and experiences at Hull-House. Wise's treatment is interesting in reflecting the version of the reformer's story that Addams herself wanted young people to appreciate.

5. ALBERT, PRINCE CONSORT OF QUEEN VICTORIA
1819–1861

The son of Ernest I, duke of Saxe-Coburg-Gotha, Albert married Queen Victoria in 1840. Initially unpopular in Britain, he eventually earned the respect of the nation for his strength of character and devotion to the queen and to their children. A liberal and progressive by temperament, Albert was nevertheless a staunch supporter of royal power and privilege who exerted considerable influence on the queen and affected British policy behind the scenes, particularly in the Trent Affair (1861) when his moderation helped avert war with the United States. Albert's death in 1861 caused Victoria, who lived until 1901, to go into a long period of mourning and withdrawal from public life that was only gradually ended.

Autobiography and Primary Sources

Readers interested in examining primary source material can consult the following volumes of correspondence and speeches: *Letters of the Prince Consort* (New York: Dutton, 1938. 381pp.) and *The Principal Speeches and Addresses of His Royal Highness the Prince Consort* (London: J. Murray, 1862. 268pp.).

Recommended Biographies

James, Robert Rhodes. *Prince Albert: A Biography*. New York: Knopf, 1983. 299pp. In the author's reassessment, Albert is depicted as a man of considerable intellect and complexity, one of the most accomplished and influential of Britain's royal figures. Based on new materials uncovered from the royal archives, James provides a dramatic and overall balanced portrait that is neither too flattering nor dismissive.

Weintraub, Stanley. *Uncrowned King: The Life of Prince Albert*. New York: Free Press, 1997. 478pp. In the most comprehensive, modern biography, Weintraub probes the hidden role of Albert as husband and political figure, providing illuminating details of the private life and daily routine of the royal couple from previously unexplored sources. Albert is shown as distinctly human, not the paragon of past interpretations, and the book's unsentimentalized version of the couple's love is a refreshing antidote to earlier versions. Weintraub's balanced assessment may well become the definitive study of Albert.

Other Biographical Studies

Bennett, Daphne. *King Without Crown*. Philadelphia: Lippincott, 1977. 430pp. Bennett's comprehensive life depicts a complex Albert, an astute politician and sensitive lover of art and music whose liberal instincts were at war with his firm belief in the monarchy who was the real genius behind Victoria's throne.

Bernardy, Françoise de. *Albert and Victoria*. New York: Harcourt, Brace, 1953. 341pp. Bernardy, a French historian, offers an assessment of the prince from a decidedly European perspective, seeing him as a person of importance. The author asserts that she has drawn on new source material. Unfortunately, the book lacks footnotes or a bibliography to trace her sources.

Bolitho, Hector. *Albert, Prince Consort*. Indianapolis: Bobbs-Merrill, 1965. 250pp. Bolitho's first biography, *Albert the Good*, was published in 1932 and has been substantially rewritten here to incorporate subsequently uncovered sources. Still very much an admirer of the prince whom he describes as "a remarkable, essentially good man," Bolitho's flattery gets in the way of an objective rendering, and his treatment of the British political scene is cursory.

Chancellor, Frank. *Prince Consort*. New York: Dial Press, 1931. 308pp. Chancellor began the process of critical reassessment of the prince, attempting to find the middle ground between Victorian adulation and Strachey's caustic diminishment. He attempts to clear away many misconceptions and chronicles the undisputed facts. The result is a portrait of Albert avoiding any idealized aura but still granting him considerable virtues and importance.

Duff, David. *Victoria and Albert*. New York: Taplinger, 1972. 319pp. Duff's study of the courtship and 22-year marriage of the queen and the prince is very much in the Lytton Strachey debunking, revisionist mode, questioning whether theirs was in fact a great love affair. In making his case, the author indulges in many speculative flights of fancy.

Eyck, Frank. *The Prince Consort: A Political Biography*. Boston: Houghton Mifflin, 1959. 269pp. Drawing on the Royal Archive at Windsor and the Ducal Archive at Coburg, this is neither a formal biography nor the story of a royal marriage. Eyck instead focuses on Albert as a political force who helped ensure the survival of constitutional monarchy in Britain and whose death had a dramatic, negative impact on developments in German and European history.

Fulford, Roger. *The Prince Consort*. London: Macmillan, 1949. 292pp. Written by an admirer and apologist of the monarchy, the book gives Albert almost full credit for rescuing the British crown from the depths it had sunk to under Victoria's two uncles. In the author's view, Albert shaped Victoria's character and asserted such an influential role over the era that it could be described as the Albertian Age. Using documents from the royal archives and Victoria's unpublished journals, Fulford marshals his evidence to counter antipathy toward Albert.

Grey, Charles. *The Early Years of His Royal Highness the Prince Consort*. New York: Harper, 1867. 371pp. Asserting its royal authorization with the phrase, "compiled under the direction of Her majesty," Grey's chronicle of Albert's boyhood and youth lacks objectivity or a willingness to reveal anything unflattering. The book is of mainly historical interest, however, in its establishing Albert as a mythical icon.

Hobhouse, Hermione. *Prince Albert: His Life and Work*. London: Hamish Hamilton, 1983. 182pp. This generously illustrated visual biography summarizes the details of Albert's life and emphasizes his considerable contributions to British national life during the period.

Hough, Richard. *Victoria and Albert*. New York: Saint Martin's, 1996. 224pp. Prolific popular historian and British royal watcher, Hough presents a joint biography of Queen Victoria and her husband intended as a corrective to the often misunderstood popular image of the queen and the prince. Utilizing Victoria's letters and diaries to bring to life the most famous marriage of the era, Hough arranges a straightforward, factual narrative that offers few interpretative insights but achieves a balanced view that is neither too saccharine nor too acid in its treatment.

Martin, Theodore. *The Life of His Royal Highness the Prince Consort*. London: Smith, Elder, 1876-80. 5 vols. Martin's massive official life of the prince remains important as a repository of useful documents and sources.

Pound, Reginald. *Albert: A Biography of the Prince Consort*. New York: Simon & Schuster, 1974. 378pp. Using hitherto neglected or underutilized papers by ministers and politicians, such as Peel, Gladstone, Aberdeen, and Russell, the author stresses Albert's role in the development of Victorian culture and imperial affairs and achieves a balanced and complex political portrait. Critics have detected a patchwork quality to the narrative that relies less on interpretation and more on scissors and paste in recording letters and documents.

Richardson, Joanna. *Victoria and Albert*. New York: Quadrangle, 1977. 239pp. Lavishly illustrated, Richardson's study of the royal marriage focuses primarily on Albert and his complex role as husband and consort, revealing the inevitable strains it caused.

Strachey, Lytton. *Queen Victoria*. 1921. Reprint ed. New York: Harcourt, Brace, 1978. 434pp. Strachey's masterful portrait of the queen also includes a sharply detailed biographical sketch of Albert that established the revisionist depiction of a dour and extremely limited man, very much at odds with the idealized Victorian saint. Although more balanced studies are no doubt closer to the truth, Strachey's highly entertaining and vivid analysis is not to be missed.

Tisdall, E.E.P. *Restless Consort: The Invasion of Albert the Conqueror*. New York: Stanley Paul, 1952. 203pp. This popular narrative account lacks documentation for its many anecdotes and reconstructed conversations, critical objectivity, and much in-depth analysis of either the prince or the era.

Wilson, A.N. *Eminent Victorians*. New York: W.W. Norton, 1990. 240pp. Based on a BBC television series, this collection of brief biographical profiles, including a balanced assessment of Prince Albert, counters Strachey's cynical view with a restoration of stature for a number of Victorian figures.

Biographical Novels

Anthony, Evelyn. *Victoria and Albert*. New York: Crowell, 1958. 312pp. The novel looks at the famous royal marriage with a controversial portrait of Albert, who does not claim Victoria's blind allegiance to him. The historical background is well developed.

Plaidy, Jean. *The Queen's Husband*. New York: Putnam, 1978. 382pp. The details of the private lives of the royal family are carefully and plausibly presented, well within the bounds of what we know for sure about Victoria and Albert. The author's *Victoria Victorious* (New York: Putnam, 1985. 569pp.) provides Victoria's autobiographical perspective on their relationship.

Whittle, Tyler. *Albert's Victoria*. New York: Saint Martin's, 1972. 263pp. The second volume of the author's trilogy on the life and reign of Victoria concerns her married years. The account is based on fact, and the minor liberties taken to bridge gaps in the documentary evidence are within historical probability.

Fictional Portraits

Wilkins, William Vaughan. *Consort for Victoria*. Garden City, New York: Doubleday, 1959. 284pp. This tale of blackmail and conspiracy involves an attempt to suggest that Prince Albert was illegitimate. The plot shows how the scheme was foiled using authentic period elements. The author's *Seven Tempests* (New York: Macmillan, 1942. 458pp.) employs Prince Albert in a fanciful adventure plot in which the prince bests King Leopold of Belgium.

Biographical Films and Theatrical Adaptations

Albert has been portrayed as a supporting character in a number of dramas concerning Queen Victoria and Edward VII, including the following:

Housman, Laurence. *Victoria Regina*. New York: Scribner, 1935. 469pp. This volume brings together the author's Palace Plays that look at Victoria's reign and marriage. In the playwright's view, Victoria is the irresistible headstrong force meeting the immovable scholarly and reserved Albert. However, the prince emerges with a refreshing sense of humor.

Norris, Kathleen. *Victoria: A Play in Four Acts and Twelve Scenes*. Garden City, New York: Doubleday, 1934. 140pp. This closet drama of dramatic episodes from Queen Victoria's life lacks a unifying dramatic principle and fails to rise much beyond a sketch.

Edward the King (1975). Director: John Garrie. The life and short reign of Edward VII is chronicled with his relationship with his parents detailed. Robert Hardy portrays Prince Albert, Annette Crosbie is Queen Victoria, and Timothy West is the Prince of Wales and later king. Video.

Victoria Regina (1961). Director: George Schaefer. This made-for-television film tells the story of Victoria's reign in a series of vignettes from her ascension to the throne in 1837 through the celebration of her Diamond Jubilee. Julie Harris stars as Victoria with James Donald as Prince Albert. Video.

See also Edward VII; Victoria

6. LOUISA MAY ALCOTT
1832–1888

An American writer and the author of *Little Women* (1868), one of the most well-known children's books of all time, Alcott was the daughter of educator and philosopher Bronson Alcott and was mainly taught by him. Her letters to her family while serving as a nurse during the Civil War were published as *Hospital Sketches* (1863); her first novel was *Moods* (1864). Other enduring children's books by Alcott include *Little Men* (1871), *Jo's Boys* (1886), *Eight Cousins* (1875), and *Rose in Bloom* (1876).

Autobiography and Primary Sources

Her Life, Letters, and Journals. Ednah D. Cheney, ed. 1889. Reprint ed. New York: Chelsea House, 1980. 404pp. Cheney, an Alcott friend, supplies her affectionate recollections as well as an important selection of letters and journal extracts, the originals of which have disappeared.

Hospital Sketches. Boston: Redpath, 1863. 102pp. Alcott records her experiences as a nurse during the Civil War in this moving account.

The Journals of Louisa May Alcott. Joel Myerson and Daniel Sheahy, eds. Boston: Little, Brown, 1989. 356pp. The editors have collected the extant diaries, journals, and notes to form a continuous chronological record of Alcott's life from 1843 to her death. This important collection reveals Alcott's state of mind and attitudes toward major events in her life.

Selected Letters of Louisa May Alcott. Joel Myerson and Daniel Sheahy, eds. Boston: Little, Brown, 1987. 352pp. A collection of the most important of Alcott's surviving letters, the writer reveals herself as very different from her public persona in her correspondence. Includes a biographical introduction by Madeleine B. Stern.

Recommended Biographies

Bedell, Madelon. *The Alcotts: Biography of a Family.* New York: C.N. Potter, 1980. 400pp. Bedell's group portrait of the Alcott family follows their lives and activities up to 1854 and provides a corrective view to those accounts that have equated the idealized March family with Louisa's own. The book is an insightful look at the author's formative years and her family circle.

Saxton, Martha. *Louisa May: A Modern Biography of Louisa May Alcott.* Boston: Houghton Mifflin, 1977. 428pp. Saxton's is the leading scholarly biography that supplies a far darker and more complex, nuanced view of Alcott's family life and the writer's personality and relationships than previously suggested. In Saxton's provocative view, Alcott was divided between her need for her father's approval and her own need to rebel against social constraints.

Stern, Madeleine B. *Louisa May Alcott.* Norman: University of Oklahoma Press, 1950. 424pp. The first well-documented biography, Stern's narrative account is reliable and informative, covering the full range of Alcott's life and works. Despite lapses into sentimentality and a lack of objectivity, particularly regarding Bronson Alcott, the book is a highly readable, dramatic treatment that serves as a useful overview for the general reader.

Other Biographical Studies

Anthony, Katharine. *Louisa May Alcott.* New York: Knopf, 1938. 304pp. Anthony's is the first study to look critically at the Alcott family and the darker side of the writer's background and domestic experience. Anthony's often tentative psychological interpretation is more controversial than convincing, with conjecture substituting for compelling evidence.

Elbert, Sarah. *A Hunger for Home: Louisa May Alcott and Little Women.* New Brunswick, New Jersey: Rutgers University Press, 1984. 278pp. Elbert presents Alcott's life and writing in a feminist context, examining the conflict between domesticity and the desire for full individuality. The book is particularly strong on Alcott's relationship with her mother.

Worthington, Marjorie. *Miss Alcott of Concord: A Biography.* Garden City, New York: Doubleday, 1958. 330pp. A highly sympathetic and often sentimental account of Alcott's life and literary career in which excerpts from the writer's letters and journals are supplemented with fictionalized conjectures.

Fictional Portraits

Jakes, John. *Love and War.* San Diego: Harcourt, Brace, 1984. 1,019pp. In this installment of Jakes's family saga, the Civil War period is chronicled with appearances by a host of historical figures, including Alcott.

Recommended Juvenile Biographies

Burke, Kathleen. *Louisa May Alcott.* New York: Chelsea House, 1988. 111pp. MG/YA. Burke's is a sound, straightforward summary of Alcott's life, character, and career.

Johnston, Norma. *Louisa May: The World and Work of Louisa May Alcott.* New York: Four Winds Press, 1991. 239pp. MG/YA. Johnston emphasizes the physical, emotional, and intellectual stresses on the Alcott family, showing how Louisa coped with them in her writing and life.

Meigs, Cornelia. *Invincible Louisa: The Story of the Author of Little Women.* Boston: Little, Brown, 1933. 260pp. YA. Meigs's Newbery Award-winning biography rivals most adult treatments in its comprehensiveness and skill.

7. ALEXANDER I
1777–1825

Czar of Russia from 1801 to 1825, Alexander I introduced a number of liberal reforms during the early years of his reign. In 1805 he joined the coalition against Napoleon, but after Russia's defeat at Austerlitz and Freidland, Alexander formed an alliance with France that was broken by Napoleon's invasion. Alexander's defeat of the French made him one of the most powerful rulers in Europe. After 1812, preoccupied with a mystical Christianity, Alexander became increasingly conservative and repressive. His death was surrounded in mystery and rumor that he escaped to Siberia to live as a hermit.

Recommended Biographies

Hartley, Janet M. *Alexander I.* New York: Longman, 1994. 256pp. In the Profiles in Power series this straightforward, competent study attempts to resolve the contradictions in Alexander's character and policies by establishing the principles that governed his domestic and foreign policies. Hartley argues, contrary to others, that Alexander did in fact remain broadly consistent with them throughout his reign.

McConnell, Alan. *Tsar Alexander I: Paternalistic Reformer.* New York: Crowell, 1970. 232pp. In a concise summary of Alexander's development and reign, McConnell challenges both excessively heroic and negative interpretations of Alexander for a more balanced, human portrait that turns on the impact of his father's murder in shaping his ideas and policies. Includes a useful survey of available biographical and critical studies of Alexander and the period.

Palmer, Alan W. *Alexander I: Tsar of War and Peace.* New York: Harper & Row, 1974. 487pp. Palmer comes closest to writing the definitive study with thorough documentation from a wide range of sources and an impressive grasp of the period, producing a well-written and highly detailed perspective on the elusive and contradictory czar that can be enjoyed by the general reader.

Other Biographical Studies

Almedingen, E.M. *The Emperor Alexander I.* New York: Vanguard, 1964. 257pp. In this study, intended for a popular audience, the author attempts to solve the various enigmas surrounding Alexander with only partial success. She is best on the relationship between Alexander and his wife.

Cate, Curtis. *The War of Two Emperors.* New York: Random House, 1985. 487pp. The author provides a reliable introduction to the French invasion of Russia in 1812 and Alexander's role in the conflict.

Paléologue, Maurice. *The Enigmatic Tsar.* New York: Harper, 1937. 325pp. Paléologue's study is far more critical than other interpretations and focuses much of its attention on Alexander's various romances.

Strakhovsky, Leonid I. *Alexander I of Russia: The Man Who Defeated Napoleon.* New York: W.W. Norton, 1947. 302pp. Convinced that Alexander did not die in 1825 but lived incognito in Siberia until 1864, Strakhovsky focuses much of his attention to proving his hypothesis, which most scholars have rejected as fanciful and has caused some libraries to catalog the biography as historical fiction.

Troyat, Henri. *Alexander of Russia: Napoleon's Conqueror.* New York: Dutton, 1982. 335pp. A master of biographical narrative with a flair for revealing detail, Troyat creates a mainly reliable account that will appeal to the general reader interested in following a clear trail through the maze of ambiguity and complexity surrounding Alexander and his period.

Biographical Novels

Anthony, Evelyn. *Far Flies the Eagle.* New York: Crowell, 1955. 270pp. Describing her work as "animated history," blending imagination and historical fact, Anthony dramatizes Alexander's life from his treaty with Napoleon in 1807 until his death in an unconventional portrait of the czar as a worthy adversary in the diplomatic and military struggle with Napoleon. The rush of great events allows for only quick character sketches with complexity simplified for dramatic effect and often breathlessly romantic portrayals.

Blech, William James. *The Angel: A Novel Based on the Life of Alexander I of Russia.* Garden City, New York: Doubleday, 1950. 438pp. A full-scale, cradle-to-grave fictional biography, the novel makes a heroic attempt to solve the riddle of Alexander and resolve his various contradictions. Unfortunately, the accumulation of incidents fails to be synthesized into a satisfying narrative pattern, and the author relies on the imagination when sources fail to provide a sufficiently colorful answer.

Sava, George. *The Emperor Story: A Historical Romance.* London: Faber and Faber, 1959. 285pp. Recounting the reign of Alexander I, the novel combines historical fact with the legends that have grown around the czar, treated as truth.

Fictional Portraits

Harrod-Eagles, Cynthia. *Anne.* New York: Saint Martin's, 1991. 631pp. The first volume of the author's Kirov Saga is set during the Napoleonic Wars and features cameos by historical figures, including Alexander.

Komroff, Manuel. *Feast of Jesters.* New York: Farrar, Straus, 1947. 305pp. Set amidst the glitter and intrigue of the Congress of Vienna, convened to redraw the map of Europe after the defeat of Napoleon, a troupe of French actors and others, including Alexander, come to Vienna with various motives. The novel is best on reconstructing the atmosphere of the period and its portraits of several major and minor players.

Krasnov, Peter N. *Napoleon and the Cossacks.* New York: Duffield & Green, 1931. 593pp. The author, who commanded a Siberian Cossack regiment, dramatizes the events of Napoleon's invasion seen through the eyes of a young Cossack and

a Russian aristocrat, with authentic period detail and an interesting account of the conflict between Napoleon and Alexander.

Michael, Prince of Greece. *Sultana.* New York: Harper & Row, 1983. 448pp. This is the fictional memoir of the actual Aimee Dubuc de Riverie who was abducted by pirates and sold into the sultan's Turkish harem, became the mother of the heir, and had love affairs with both Napoleon and Alexander.

Pilgrim, David. *So Great a Man.* New York: Harper, 1937. 463pp. Covering a 10-month period between 1808 and 1809, the fictional story used to animate the historical events involves a young Frenchman charged with escorting Napoleon's mistress from Warsaw to Paris. He becomes a page in the Emperor's household and a witness of the leading figures of the period.

Tolstoy, Leo. *War and Peace.* 1869. Various editions. In Tolstoy's massive and masterful historical and domestic panorama, Alexander I, like Napoleon, shares the stage with the interconnected story of the Rostovs, Bezuhovs, and Bolkonskys. Alexander is shown reviewing his troops before Austerlitz, in conference with Napoleon, and reacting to the French invasion.

Waldeck, R.G. *Lustre in the Sky.* Garden City, New York: Doubleday, 1946. 434pp. At the center of this novel about the Congress of Vienna is the wily French ambassador Talleyrand who maneuvers for power in the new world order after Napoleon's fall and embarks on an affair with his own niece. Although there are a number of historical inaccuracies, the novel does provide interesting portraits of Alexander and Metternich.

See also Napoleon Bonaparte

8. ALEXANDER THE GREAT
356–323 B.C.

King of Macedon and conqueror of much of Asia and the Mediterranean world before he died at the age of 33, Alexander was the son of Philip II of Macedon and succeeded him to the throne in 336 B.C. after receiving a classical education under the tutelage of Aristotle. In 334, Alexander crossed the Hellespont against the Persians in one of the greatest military conquests of all time. When his conquest ended, Alexander controlled more than two million square miles of territory (two-thirds of the known world) as far east as Afghanistan and Northern India.

Recommended Biographies

Fox, Robin Lane. *The Search for Alexander.* New York: Dial Press,1974. 568pp. Writing on an epic scale, Fox brilliantly, if at times somewhat romantically and eccentrically, fills in the gaps from the lack of eyewitness accounts of Alexander's adventures. The book's disadvantages—an unclear connection between the text and its sources, a hard-to-follow chronology, and an index restricted to proper names—are offset by Fox's wide-ranging erudition, sharp judgment, and painterly skill in describing scenes and characters.

Green, Peter. *Alexander of Macedon: 365–323 B.C.: A Historical Biography.* Berkeley: University of California Press, 1991. 585pp. Green portrays Alexander as a complex personality and single-minded general whose absolute power corrupted him absolutely. This scrupulous and accurate recreation of the spirit of the times is especially recommended for those interested in military and ancient history.

Hammond, N.G.L. *The Genius of Alexander the Great.* Chapel Hill: University of North Carolina Press, 1997. 224pp. Distilling a lifetime of scholarship into a brief summary for the general reader, Hammond is clearly an Alexander partisan, and he portrays him as a charismatic leader, while minimizing unflattering details. This compact study is best as a summary of the facts and of military history rather than for insights into Alexander's personality.

Other Biographical Studies

Ancient Greek writers Plutarch and Arrian wrote early biographies of Alexander. The former's account is the most vivid; while the latter's is likely the most accurate. The Roman historian Quintus Curtius Rufus also produced a history of Alexander that remains of interest, particularly because of its influence in the Middle Ages as a source for the many epics and legends created around Alexander. Briant, Pierre. *Alexander the Great: Man of Action- Man of Spirit.* New York: Abrams, 1996. 175pp. Lavishly illustrated, this is a straightforward, though brief, account of Alexander's military campaigns that also does not neglect the inner man.

O'Brien, John Maxwell. *Alexander the Great: The Invisible Enemy: A Biography.* New York: Routledge, 1992. 336pp. O'Brien bases his controversial assessment of Alexander's character and career on the role of alcohol in his life.

Renault, Mary. *The Nature of Alexander.* New York: Pantheon, 1975. 240pp. This is an insightful nonfictional supplement to the author's fictional Alexander trilogy exploring his nature and character.

Wood, Michael. *In the Footsteps of Alexander the Great: A Journey from Greece to Asia.* Berkeley: University of California, 1997. 256pp. Wood offers an interesting approach in this history of Alexander, combining a biographical study with an account of tracing Alexander's entire route of conquest by a film crew in preparation for a television series.

Biographical Novels

Druon, Maurice. *Alexander the God.* New York: Scribner, 1954. 319pp. Cast in the form of a fictional memoir of Alexander's soothsayer, Aristander, this is a biographical account of Alexander's career and military campaigns with an emphasis on Alexander's compulsions and fixation with his own divinity. The novel mixes fact and fiction and invents scenes and dialogue, though plausibly.

Eiker, Karl V. *Star of Macedon.* New York: Putnam, 1957. 376pp. Told from the perspective of his slave, Gyges, this is an intimate and human portrait of the leader in which surmises and interpretations often predominate over documented fact.

Gerson, Noel B. *The Golden Lyre.* Garden City, New York: Doubleday, 1963. 335pp. This romanticized treatment of the career of Alexander spans the decade 338-328 B.C. Although much of the account is grounded in fact, the author admits to making equal use of legend and his own imagination.

Kazantzakis, Nikos. *Alexander the Great.* Athens: Ohio University Press, 1982. 222pp. Originally written for young readers, the novel is appropriate for adults as well, presenting the life and exploits of Alexander from age 15 to his death. Blending the historical and legendary, the author's account is very much in the heroic mode with Alexander's flaws largely ignored.

Lamb, Harold. *Alexander of Macedon: The Journey to the World's End.* Garden City, New York: Doubleday, 1946. 402pp. This is a detailed recreation of the journeys of the Macedonians with a psychological portrait of their commander. There is no distortion of fact, but the author's interpretations of motive and temperament are open to question.

Marshall, Edison. *The Conqueror: A Novel of Alexander the Great.* Garden City, New York: Doubleday, 1962. 396pp. Alexander recollects the stages of his extraordinary career from his schooling to his end when madness and hubris mar his great achievements in a believable portrait of a flawed, complex leader.

Payne, Robert. *Alexander the God.* New York: A.A. Wyn, 1954. 307pp. Covering the period of Alexander's military campaigns from his conquest of Tarsus to his death in Babylon, the plot focuses on the romance between Alexander and Thaissa, an Athenian flute girl, whom Alexander elevates as his mistress-queen. Legend as well as fact are woven into the narrative.

Renault, Mary. *Alexander Trilogy.* Renault's remarkable trilogy traces the career and legacy of Alexander beginning with *Fire from Heaven* (New York: Pantheon, 1969, 375pp.) that covers his childhood to his succession to the throne at the age of 20 after the murder of his father. In *The Persian Boy* (New York: Pantheon, 1972. 419pp.) the male courtesan and eunuch Bagoas offers his perspective on Alexander's last seven years. In *Funeral Games* (New York: Pantheon, 1981. 335pp.), although Alexander dies early on in the narrative, his departed presence is still the center of this story of the scramble for power that fills the vacuum left by Alexander's death. The novels blend the known with the imagined, and there are few historical novelists better at creating believable, reliable period backgrounds.

Wassermann, Jakob. *Alexander in Babylon.* Chicago: Ziff-Davis, 1949. 167pp. The novel dramatizes the last two years of Alexander's life with him shown slowly slipping into obsession and madness. The general course of historical events is mainly followed, but the characterizations are less reliable as historical portraits than case histories.

Fictional Portraits

Apostolou, Anna. *A Murder in Macedon: A Mystery of Alexander the Great.* New York: Saint Martin's, 1997. 256pp. This historical mystery features the actual murder of Philip II in which Alexander must fight for his rights as heir, prove his own innocence, and solve the crime. A sequel, *A Murder in Thebes* (New York: Saint Martin's, 1998. 240pp.) continues Alexander's story as conqueror and sleuth.

Bova, Ben. *Orion and the Conqueror.* New York: Tor, 1994, 350pp. This time-travel adventure deals with the court of Philip II and the succession conflict and the relationship between Alexander and his parents.

De Camp, L. Sprague. *An Elephant for Aristotle.* Garden City, New York: Doubleday, 1958. 360pp. Alexander appears as part of a comic adventure that imagines what might have happened if Alexander had decided to present Aristotle with the first elephant brought from India to Greece.

Tarr, Judith. *Lord of the Two Lands* New York: T. Doherty, 1993. 317pp. This historical fantasy involves Alexander in actual campaigns against the Persians as well as more supernatural conflicts.

Recommended Juvenile Biographies

Ash, Maureen. *Alexander the Great: Ancient Empire Builder.* Chicago: Childrens Press, 1991. 128pp. MG. A lively and lavishly illustrated biography of Alexander from his boyhood through his conquests, and early death, the book balances stories and legends with recorded accounts. Ash includes useful information on Greek and Near Eastern culture as well as a timeline and glossary of terms.

Green, Robert. *Alexander the Great.* New York: F. Watts, 1996. 63pp. MG. This concise and straightforward summary describes Alexander's life, campaigns, influence on the ancient world, and mythological status.

Stewart, Gail. *Alexander the Great.* San Diego: Lucent Books, 1994. 127pp. MG/YA. A highly readable, balanced, and informative account of Alexander's career and historical background. Illustrated with a helpful chronology.

Biographical Films and Theatrical Adaptations

Alexander the Great (1956). Director: Robert Rosen. This lavish Hollywood CinemaScope production with an impressive cast is disappointingly flat and fails to capture the epic sweep of Alexander's campaigns or the complexity of his personality. Richard Burton portrays Alexander. Video.

Conquerors (1997). Directors: Nigel Maslin and Robert Marshall. Film profiles of four great leaders: Peter the Great, Napoleon, Alexander the Great, and Suleyman. Video.

In the Footsteps of Alexander the Great (1998). Producer: Rebecca Dobbs. Michael Wood retraces Alexander's route of conquest in a multipart series combining history, biography, and travelogue. The companion volume to the series is discussed above. Video.

9. SUSAN B. ANTHONY
1820–1906

American social reformer and leader of the woman suffrage movement, Anthony was a resolute pioneer of women's equality and social causes, including temperance and abolition. With Elizabeth Cady Stanton, whom she met in 1851, Anthony was the principal organizer and ideological voice of the National Woman Suffrage Association that they formed in 1869. Anthony led a group of women to the polls in Rochester, New York, in 1872 to test the franchise for women under the Fourteenth Amendment. Her arrest, trial, and sentence of a fine that she refused to pay became a model for other suffrage protests. Although she did not live to see women gain the vote, Anthony's single-minded advocacy of equal justice for women has been credited with helping to win social and political gains for women and launching the women's movement in the twentieth century.

Autobiography and Primary Sources

While Anthony produced no explicit memoir of her life and career, the massive six-volume *History of Woman Suffrage* (1881–1922. Reprint ed. New York: Arno Press, 1969), which documents through letters, speeches, reminiscences, and conference papers the suffrage movement and Anthony's involvement, is very much the record Anthony wanted preserved. The project was directed by Anthoy until her death and completed by her authorized biographer, Ida Husted Harper.

Interested readers should also consult *Elizabeth Cady Stanton, Susan B. Anthony: Correspondence, Writings, Speeches.* edited by Ellen C. DuBois (New York: Schocken, 1981. 212pp.) for insights into their partnership and for the restoration of many letters that had been previously expurgated.

Recommended Biographies

Anthony, Katharine. *Susan B. Anthony: Her Personal History and Her Era.* Garden City, New York: Doubleday, 1954. 521pp. This well-written life captures both Anthony's strengths and heroism but also does not avoid shortcomings or the tensions in her relationships. The biographer achieves what her subtitle asserts: both a psychologically valid look at the private Anthony and her public battles.

Barry, Kathleen. *Susan B. Anthony: A Biography of a Singular Feminist.* New York: New York University Press, 1988. 426pp. This scholarly and authoritative study is dominated by the author's feminist interpretation that attempts to show the various stages in Anthony's development, challenging the predominant notions of male and female roles and power. The effect is a transformation of the documentary story created by Anthony and Harper into a new stimulating relevance.

Harper, Ida Husted. *Life and Work of Susan B. Anthony.* 1898–1908. Reprint ed. Salem, New Hampshire: Ayer, 1983. 3 vols. 1633pp. Harper, Anthony's authorized biographer, had direct access to the massive archive Anthony collected in her Rochester attic as well as a close relationship with her subject that she used to advantage in this detailed, accurate, chronological record meant to present a polished, public view of Anthony's achievements. Although clearly biased in Anthony's favor, Harper's life has provided the basis for most subsequent biographies and remains an invaluable resource.

Other Biographical Studies

Dorr, Rheta Childe. *Susan B. Anthony: The Woman Who Changed the Mind of a Nation.* 1928. Reprint ed. New York: AMS Press, 1970. 367pp. An admiring popular biography, Dorr's life adds colorful detail to the material from Harper's biography to enhance the drama of Anthony's story, often sentimentally and uncritically.

Lutz, Alma. *Susan B. Anthony: Rebel, Crusader, Humanitarian.* Boston: Beacon Press, 1959. 340pp. This workmanlike and well-documented account is best in capturing the nineteenth-century social scene and in humanizing previous views of Anthony as a monolithic saint. The disagreements and splits among the various reformers working for the advancement of women are often tedious, however, with chronicling predominating over needed interpretation.

Sherr, Lynn. *Failure Is Impossible: Susan B. Anthony in Her Own Words.* New York: Times Books, 1995. 382pp. Using excerpts from Anthony's speeches and letters, connected by biographical essays by ABC's *20/20* correspondent, Sherr, the book provides a helpful introduction to Anthony and her struggle that challenges the conception of a dour and solemn crusader.

Ward, Geoffrey, and Ken Burns, et al. *Not for Our Selves Alone: The Story of Elizabeth Cady Stanton & Susan B. Anthony.* New York: Knopf, 1999. 272pp. This companion volume of Burns's PBS documentary offers a dual visual biography of the pair's life and times.

Fictional Portraits

Malm, Dorothea. *The Woman Question.* New York: Appleton-Century, 1957. 277pp. In this amusing look at domestic customs and the burgeoning women's rights movement that culminates in the first Women's Rights Convention in 1853, actual figures such as Lucretia Mott, Lucy Stone, and Susan B. Anthony interact with an activist teacher from Connecticut whose advanced social views disrupt her family.

McCall, Dan. *Beecher: A Novel.* New York: Dutton, 1979. 214pp. Based on one of America's greatest scandals in the nineteenth century in which celebrated minister Henry Ward Beecher was accused of seducing the wife of his protégé, the novel dramatizes Beecher's trial with a large cast of characters, including Susan B. Anthony.

Recommended Juvenile Biographies

Kendall, Martha E. *Susan B. Anthony: Voice for Women's Voting Rights.* Springfield, New Jersey: Enslow, 1997. 128pp. MG. This fact-filled account portrays Anthony as a visionary who pioneered a new role for women, showing her Quaker roots, her education, and her various campaigns for women's property rights, suffrage, and the right to divorce.

Levin, Pamela. *Susan B. Anthony: Fighter for Women's Rights.* New York: Chelsea House, 1993. 79pp. MG. Basic, informative, if sometimes choppy biography that depicts Anthony's early and family life but glosses over her adult character to focus on her struggle to achieve abolition and voting rights for women. Includes some dialogue, many well-chosen quotes, a helpful chronology, and glossary of terms.

Weisberg, Barbara. *Susan B. Anthony: Woman Suffragist.* New York: Chelsea House, 1988. 111pp. The focus here is on Anthony's struggles for women's rights and suffrage, helpfully serving as both an introduction to Anthony the person and the early women's movement.

Biographical Films and Theatrical Adaptations

Thomson, Virgil. *The Mother of Us All.* New York: Music Press, 1947. 157pp. Thomson's opera, with a libretto by Gertrude Stein that was her last completed work, shows Anthony unhistorically debating Daniel Webster, crusading for women's rights, and assessing her contributions. Thomson's musical accompaniment of Stein's freewheeling inventions is a pastiche of American musics, fitted to Anthony as a symbol of the American spirit.

A&E Biography Video: Susan B. Anthony: Rebel for the Cause (1995). Director: Adam Freedman. This is a reliable documentary look at Anthony and the struggle for women's rights, combining archival photographs, dramatic re-creations, and interviews. Video.

Not for Our Selves Alone: The Story of Elizabeth Cady Stanton & Susan B. Anthony (1999). Director: Ken Burns. This film portrait documents the history of the women's rights movements using archival material and actors reading from Anthony and Stanton's works. Video.

10. SAINT THOMAS AQUINAS
ca. 1225–1274

Italian theologian and philosopher, known as the Angelic Doctor, Thomas Aquinas entered the Dominican order and studied in Paris with Albertus Magnus. He was advisor to the papal court (1252-1269) and organized a house of studies in Naples. His most important work is *Summa theologica* (1267-1273), a systematic exposition of theology that uses Aristotelian logic to examine the existence of God. He was canonized in 1323 and proclaimed a Doctor of the Church in 1567.

Autobiography and Primary Sources

The Life of Saint Thomas Aquinas: Biographical Documents. Kenelm Foster, ed. Baltimore: Helicon Press, 1959. 172pp. The editor selects from various documentary evidence and contemporaneous accounts a plausible view of Aquinas's life story derived from the earliest historical sources.

Recommended Biographies

Bourke, Vernon J. *Aquinas's Search for Wisdom.* Milwaukee: Bruce, 1965. 244pp. In alternating chapters, Bourke's study chronicles both the events of Aquinas's life and the development of his thought. Erudite but not inaccessible for the nonspecialist, Bourke's is a scholarly work that ably illuminates the historical Aquinas, while avoiding speculation and reliance on legend to fill in the gaps in the record.

Chesterton, G.K. *Saint Thomas Aquinas.* New York: Sheed & Ward, 1933. 248pp. Chesterton's modest aim in his brief introductory study of Aquinas's life and philosophy was to lead "those who have hardly even heard of Saint Thomas Aquinas to read about him in better books." There are, however, few better books on the theologian. Witty and perceptive, Chesterton captures Aquinas's personality and the conditions that make his development a compelling human drama.

Torrell, Jean-Pierre. *Saint Thomas Aquinas.* Washington, DC: Catholic University of America Press, 1996–1999. 2 vols. Torrell's is a scholarly review of Aquinas's life and work with the first volume devoted exclusively to a chronological summary of the saint's activities and development. Volume two considers the philosophical and theological impact of his ideas.

Weisheipl, James A. *Friar Thomas D'Aquino: His Life, Thought, and Work.* Garden City, New York: Doubleday, 1974. 464pp. Comprehensive and readable, Aquinas's life is chronicled in terms of an excellent examination of his era that explains both the man and his ideas. A work of considerable research and learning, Weisheipl's study assumes considerable familiarity with medieval thought and culture, but the rewards for the less-than-casual reader are considerable.

Other Biographical Studies

Petitot, Hyacinthe. *The Life and the Spirit of Thomas Aquinas.* Chicago: Priory Press, 1966. 174pp. First published in French in 1926, Petitot's study is an intellectual biography that relates the development of Aquinas's ideas to his historical background. The book helpfully illuminates the connections between the experiences of Aquinas's life and the intellectual ferment of his era and his quest to reconcile his faith and his intellect.

Pieper, Josef. *Guide to Thomas Aquinas.* New York: Pantheon, 1972. 181pp. Pieper's guide to the origin, development, and influence of Aquinas's thoughts is a demanding, scholarly exegesis more for the specialist than for the general reader. The reader with sufficient breadth of knowledge in ancient and medieval philosophy to follow Pieper's logic about the nature of Aquinas's ideas and their originality will experience a refreshing and contrary view of the man and his achievement.

Vaughan, Roger W.B. *The Life and Labours of Saint Thomas Aquin.* New York: Catholic Publication Society, 1890. 2 vols. Vaughan's massive compendium of early source material is fashioned into a detailed narrative account. Mixing fact and legend, Vaughan's effort stands somewhere between reliable history and historical fiction.

Biographical Novels

Carroll, Malachy G. *Time Cannot Dim.* Chicago: Regnery, 1955. 202pp. Carroll's fictionalized biography is an earnest and reverent tribute that commits a number of factual errors.

De Wohl, Louis. *The Quiet Light.* Philadelphia: Lippincott, 1950. 317pp. Aquinas's life is chronicled in an idealized and romanticized portrait that does touch on the highlights of his career.

Other Sources

Kretzmann, Norman, and Eleanore Stump, eds. *The Cambridge Companion to Aquinas.* New York: Cambridge University Press, 1993. 302pp. This selection of essays gives the reader a strong sense of modern scholarship on Aquinas's life and ideas.

11. BENEDICT ARNOLD
1741–1801

American Revolutionary general, Benedict Arnold was one of colonial America's military heroes, winning fame and promotion in action against the British at Fort Ticonderoga (1775), in the failed invasion of Canada (1775), and in engagements on Lake Champlain (1776) and in Connecticut. His brilliant leadership during the Battle of Saratoga (1778) played a decisive part in the American victory. In 1780, in command of West Point, Arnold arranged to surrender the fort to the British in exchange for money and a commission. The plot was discovered and foiled, but Arnold escaped, serving with the British army in Connecticut and Virginia, before going into exile in Britain and Canada. Although he was described by Washington as "the bravest of the brave," Arnold's military achievement has been overshadowed by his treachery as the most vilified figure in American history and his name synonymous with treason and betrayal.

Recommended Biographies

Randall, Willard S. *Benedict Arnold: Patriot and Traitor.* New York: Morrow, 1990. 667pp. Meticulously researched and drawing on new material never before presented, this is a definitive study that does justice to Arnold's strengths and tragic failings. The sources are woven into a brisk and captivating narrative, complete with the author's skill in capturing scenes and characters in a few vivid phrases.

Wallace, Willard M. *Traitorous Hero: The Life and Fortunes of Benedict Arnold.* New York: Harper, 1954. 394pp. Scholarly and authoritative, this judicious and penetrating biography balances Arnold's positives and negatives, while providing a psychological analysis of Arnold and his motives that goes well beyond earlier simplistic and obvious explanations for his tragic fall without invalidating or distorting what we know for certain.

Other Biographical Studies

Arnold, Isaac N. *The Life of Benedict Arnold: His Patriotism and His Treason.* Chicago: A.G. McClurg, 1880. 444pp. Arnold's early attempt to balance the depiction of Arnold and grant his considerable achievement to the American cause provoked a storm of protest branding the author as an Arnold apologist. The author's work, however, established the context and pattern for subsequent biographies and remained the standard work until the 1950s. It is still a readable and useful account.

Boylan, Brian R. *Benedict Arnold: The Dark Eagle.* New York: W.W. Norton, 1973. 266pp. This radically revisionist study presents Arnold as one of the Revolution's greatest heroes and justifies his treason as a morally responsible act of a man convinced that the ideals of the Revolution had been betrayed and the war was unwinnable. Boylan's simplistic thesis uncritically accepts Arnold's own justification for his actions and overly reflects his own era's moral ambivalence under the pressure of the Vietnam War.

Brandt, Clare. *The Man in the Mirror: A Life of Benedict Arnold.* New York: Random House, 1994. 360pp. Locating the cause of Arnold's treason in overreaching ambition and social and personal insecurities, Brandt offers an absorbing psychological study that reveals the man behind the legend who was brought down by self-delusion and a reckless unconcern for anyone but himself. Brandt provides a useful lens to examine Arnold's career coherently, though sometimes the theory drives the events, and the psychological insights lack subtlety.

Flexner, James T. *The Traitor and the Spy: Benedict Arnold and John André.* New York: Harcourt, Brace, 1953. 431pp. This dual biography of Arnold and John André provides a good introduction and guide to the labyrinth of Arnold's intrigue. At the core of Flexner's analysis is the fatal relationship of Arnold, André, and Arnold's second wife Peggy Shippen, as Arnold's treason is depicted as a dramatic human story.

Martin, James Kirby. *Benedict Arnold, Revolutionary Hero: An American Warrior.* New York: New York University Press, 1997. 535pp. Debunking much of the popular mythology associated with Arnold, this revisionist account suggests that Arnold was a victim of his own inept political skills and wounded by the lack of appreciation by his colleagues. Martin refuses to distort Arnold's character and contributions as earlier biographers have done to prove their case of villainy and meticulously details Arnold's military service. Somewhat heavy-handed in pressing his thesis, the biography does offer a more humanized portrait of a complex individual.

Van Doren, Carl. *The Secret History of the American Revolution.* 1941. Reprint ed. Clifton, New Jersey, A. M. Kelly, 1973, 534pp. Although not strictly speaking a biography, the book, which concentrates on the Arnold conspiracy, provides essential source material, including the Arnold-André correspondence and British commander Sir Henry Clinton's narrative account of the conspiracy.

Biographical Novels

Bailey, Anthony. *Major André.* New York: Farrar, Straus, 1987. 200pp. The Arnold conspiracy is shown from the perspective of British spy John André prior to his execution. The novel captures André's personality and the incident with sophistication and perceptiveness.

Callahan, North. *Peggy.* New York: Cornwall, 1983. 241pp. Arnold is shown from the perspective of the woman he marries, Margaret Shippen.

Gessner, Robert. *Treason.* New York: Scribner, 1944. 383pp. Exploring the motivation behind Arnold's treason, the conspiracy is narrated partly from the perspective of a young aide whose initial hero worship must be painfully reassessed. Faithful to the facts, the novel treats Arnold sympathetically without apologizing for his betrayal.

Harr, John Ensor. *Dark Eagle: A Novel of Benedict Arnold and the American Revolution.* New York: Viking, 1999. 544pp. In a wide-ranging, comprehensive, and balanced treatment of Arnold's life and military career, Harr neither whitewashes Arnold's failings nor diminishes his considerable achievements. The novel is packed with vividly created battle scenes and convincing portraits of a large cast of historical figures.

Hough, Frank O. *Renown.* New York: Carrick & Evans, 1938. 497pp. In this sympathetic account of the career of Benedict Arnold, he emerges as a brilliant and courageous, though frustrated leader whose betrayal is mitigated by a certain nobility of purpose. Inventing only conversations, the novel keeps close to the known facts, though the novel's interpretation of Arnold and his motives is questionable.

Partington, Norman. *The Sunshine Patriot: A Novel of Benedict Arnold.* New York: Saint Martin's, 1975. 221pp. These fictional memoirs of Lord Cornwallis tell the story of Benedict Arnold from a decidedly sympathetic British perspective. In all important respects the book does not distort historical facts, but its interpretation is questionable.

Roberts, Kenneth. *Arundel.* Garden City, New York: Doubleday, 1930. 632pp; *Rabble in Arms.* Garden City, New York: Doubleday, 1933. 870pp. Both are classic historical novels that depict Arnold's epic march through the Maine wilderness to Quebec in 1775, the disastrous retreat, the naval engagement in Lake Champlain, and the climactic Saratoga campaign. In these historically accurate novels, Arnold emerges as a genuine hero despite his later betrayal.

Spicer, Bart. *Brother to the Enemy.* New York: Dodd, Mead, 1958. 308pp. Based on an actual incident recounted in the memoirs of Light-Horse Harry Lee, the novel describes the effort to recapture Arnold after he has joined the British by John Champe pretending to be a deserter. The facts of the Champe incident are considerably heightened to serve the adventure.

Vail, Philip. *The Twisted Saber: A Biographical Novel of Benedict Arnold.* New York: Dodd, Mead, 1963. 310pp. Tracing Arnold's life and military career, particularly his campaigns in Quebec, Saratoga, and Ticonderoga, the novel attempts to solve the enigma of his character and the motive for his treason. Vail, a pseudonym for the prolific historical fiction writer Noel B. Gerson, preserves the basic facts but invents episodes and dialogue.

Wolf, William J. *Benedict Arnold: A Novel.* Ashfield, Massachusetts: Paideia, 1990. 413pp. Carrying Arnold's story beyond his treason through his years in exile, nearly all the significant episodes of his life are narrated in a masterful handling of the facts through the perspective of a colleague who discovers that Arnold is both more evil than he thought and a better human being than his contemporaries could or would acknowledge.

Fictional Portraits

Benedict Arnold is surpassed only by George Washington as the most popular character for fiction writers in novels of the American Revolution, and the Arnold conspiracy is the central incident in a number of historical novels. Some of the best include the following:

Haines, Edwin. *The Exquisite Siren.* New York: Lippincott, 1938. 444pp. The novel looks at the Arnold conspiracy from the perspective of his second wife, Peggy Shippen, and her secret love for John André. Much of the plot is fanciful and does not reflect the actual events of the case.

Lancaster, Bruce. *The Secret Road.* Boston: Little, Brown, 1952. 259pp. Artfully blending fact and fiction, the novel dramatizes the role of the American secret service in uncovering Arnold's plot to surrender West Point.

Longstreet, Stephen. *Eagles Where I Walk.* Garden City, New York: Doubleday, 1961. 477pp. This second volume of a trilogy concerning a young surgeon in Washington's army dramatizes the New York campaign and the Arnold conspiracy, combining fact and the imagination.

Rinaldi, Ann. *Finishing Becca: A Story of Peggy Shippen and Benedict Arnold.* New York: Harcourt, Brace, 1994. 362pp. This young adult novel will interest older readers as well in its story of Peggy Shippen's maid who finds herself involved in the conspiracy.

Taylor, David. *Storm the Last Rampart.* Philadelphia: Lippincott, 1960. 384pp. Covering the American Revolution's pivotal year of 1780, the novel dramatizes the Arnold conspiracy as seen by a fictional spy and a tavern maid. Although the central story and characters are invented, the framework is historically accurate.

Recommended Juvenile Biographies

Alderman, Clifford. *The Dark Eagle: The Story of Benedict Arnold.* New York: Macmillan, 1976. 136pp. MG. Historical novelist Alderman dramatizes Arnold's life and treachery in a very well-written character-driven account that also presents a vivid picture of Revolutionary America.

Fritz, Jean. *Traitor: The Case of Benedict Arnold.* New York: Putnam, 1981. 191pp. MG. In Fritz's compelling and eloquent study, Arnold's need to prove his courage and gain recognition leads to his downfall. This well-written, thorough account is both filled with historical information and entertaining, placing the facts in a fictional framework that does not sacrifice accuracy.

Wade, Mary D. *Benedict Arnold.* New York: F. Watts, 1994. 64pp. MG. Although the text is brief, the author includes several excerpts from original

sources and an afterword that clarifies the fate of Arnold, his wife, and Major André. Helpfully illustrated, this is an objective introduction to the subject.

Biographical Films and Theatrical Adaptations

A&E Biography Video: Benedict Arnold: Triumph and Treason (1975). Producer: Eric Lindstrom. Setting out to solve the mystery of Arnold's betrayal, this documentary looks at his youth and military career, uncovering greed and envy as the motives for his treason. Video.

The Scarlet Coat (1955). Director: John Sturges. With Robert Douglas in the role of Arnold, this is a fast-paced costume adventure based on the Arnold conspiracy with a fictional story mostly predominating over a factual view.

Other Sources

Gocek, Matilda A. *Benedict Arnold: A Reader's Guide and Bibliography.* Monroe, New York: Library Research, 1973. 28pp. This is a useful reference guide to works on Benedict Arnold.

12. MATTHEW ARNOLD
1822–1888

English poet and critic, Arnold was the son of renowned educator Dr. Thomas Arnold and was educated at Rugby and Oxford. He worked as a school inspector (1851–1886) and was professor of poetry at Oxford (1857–1867). His poetry and criticism advocated a new cultural climate in which intellectual perfection would overtake narrow nineteenth-century middle-class provincialism. His works include *Empedocles on Etna* (1852), *New Poems* (1867), *Culture and Anarchy* (1869), and *Literature and Dogma* (1873).

Autobiography and Primary Sources

Letters of Matthew Arnold. Cecil Y. Lang, ed. Charlottesville: University Press of Virginia, 1996–1998. 3 vols. The definitive scholarly edition of Arnold's letters have reached 1870 in a superbly edited and informative series that is an indispensable biographical source.

Letters of Matthew Arnold 1848–1888. G.W.E Russell, ed. New York: Macmillan, 1895. 2 vols. Made up chiefly of letters to his family, Russell's early collection provided a groundbreaking view of Arnold's life, character, and ideas.

Selected Letters of Matthew Arnold. Clifton Machann and Forrest D. Burt, eds. Ann Arbor: University of Michigan Press, 1993. 350pp. A collection of 216 letters grouped chronologically and covering four stages of Arnold's life from 1844 to his death. Includes 49 previously unpublished letters.

Recommended Biographies

Hamilton, Ian. *A Gift Imprisoned: The Poetic Life of Matthew Arnold.* New York: Basic Books, 1999. 241pp. Hamilton's critical biography is a lucid and revealing account of Arnold's poetic genius and the

personal and biographical factors that caused him to turn away from poetry. Ably blending astute criticism with a firm grasp of Arnold's character and biography, Hamilton supplies an often moving account of a great writer's battle with himself over the proper purpose of his genius.

Honan, Park. *Matthew Arnold: A Life.* New York: McGraw-Hill, 1981. 496pp. Based on a large amount of previously unpublished materials, Honan's is one of the fullest accounts available of Arnold's life and times, essential for the scholar but not beyond the reach and enjoyment of the general reader. Arnold is shown in relation to his family and times and emerges as a sympathetic and compelling human figure.

Machann, Clifton. *Matthew Arnold: A Literary Life.* New York: St. Martin's, 1998. 177pp. The author explores how Arnold's poetry and prose grew out of his personal, social, and professional life. Arnold's relationship with his father, the poet Arthur Hugh Clough, and the mysterious Marguerite of the Switzerland poems are examined afresh with insights that illuminate the development and coherence of the writer's sensibility and works.

Murray, Nicholas. *A Life of Matthew Arnold.* New York: St. Martin's, 1997. 400pp. Murray counters conventional depictions of Arnold's life and character with a rousing reassessment, drawing on Lang's edition of the letters and fresh research. Murray stresses Arnold's outsider's status as an ironic critic of Victorian values and a dynamic figure very different from his aloof and austere image.

Trilling, Lionel. *Matthew Arnold.* New York: W.W. Norton, 1939. 465pp. Trilling's intellectual biography sets out "to show the thought of Matthew Arnold in its complex unity and to relate it to the historical and intellectual events of his time." Although based exclusively on published sources, the book succeeds in forming a coherent biography of Arnold's mind that has not been surpassed by subsequent critical examinations.

Other Biographical Studies

Chambers, E.K. *Matthew Arnold: A Study.* Oxford: Clarendon Press, 1947. 144pp. Chambers's is a remarkably succinct, knowledgeable biographical study that can serve the general reader as a basic overview of Arnold's life.

Kingsmill, Hugh. *Matthew Arnold.* New York: Dial Press, 1928. 317pp. Described by one contemporary reviewer as "one prolonged sneer," Kingsmill's debunking portrait is a frustratingly disjointed mixture of biographical details, epigrams, and critical analysis, more a series of essays than a sustained view of Arnold's life and work, and too unsympathetic and self-centered to be of much use.

Neiman, Fraser. *Matthew Arnold.* New York: Twayne, 1968. 190pp. Neiman's critical biography chronicles Arnold's life up to his major works and then shifts to mainly an analysis of his intellectual development and what his works reveal about the nature of the man.

Paul, Herbert. *Matthew Arnold.* New York: Macmillan, 1902. 188pp. Paul, a friend of the poet, provides a straightforward chronological account of Arnold's life and work.

Rowse, A.L. *Matthew Arnold: Poet and Prophet.* London: Thames and Hudson, 1976. 208pp. Rowse stresses Arnold's Celtic background and the influence of his mother in this critical biography that also emphasizes Arnold's contributions to education.

Russell, G.W.E. *Matthew Arnold.* New York: Scribner, 1904. 265pp. The editor of the first collection of Arnold's letters supplies this succinct biographical portrait that still serves as a brief and informed introductory study.

Saintsbury, George. *Matthew Arnold.* New York: Dodd, Mead, 1899. 232pp. Written 11 years after Arnold's death, Saintsbury's critical assessment of the writer's life and work represents a contemporary's valuation, showing a preference for Arnold's poetry over his prose.

Biographical Novels

MacDonald, Isobel. *The Buried Self.* London: P. Davies, 1949. 238pp. Chronicling the important years in Arnold's life between 1848 and 1851, this biographical novel attempts a personal context for Arnold's development as a writer, documenting the experiences that resulted in his poems.

13. KEMAL ATATURK
1881–1938

Founder of modern Turkey, Kemal Ataturk was born Mustapha Kemal in Thessaloniki. Educated at a military academy, he joined the Young Turks, a liberal movement to establish a constitutional government for the Ottoman Empire. During World War I, Ataturk's leadership stiffened Turkish resistance to the allied invasion at Gallipoli. In 1919 he organized the Turkish Nationalist party and opposed Allied control, expelling the Greeks from Anatolia in 1922 when he abolished the sultanate and created an independent and sovereign Turkey. He served as president of the Turkish republic for four terms by a unanimous parliament and set in motion a program of internal reform and Westernization. Ruthless in prosecuting extremists, including Islamic conservatives, Ataturk was nonetheless held in high regard as the creator of the modern Turkish state.

Recommended Biographies

Kinross, Patrick Balfour. *Ataturk: A Biography of Mustafa Kemal, Father of Modern Turkey.* New York: Morrow, 1965. 615pp. This is still one of the most comprehensive and balanced portrait available, in which every phase of Ataturk's career is brought into sharp focus. However, the biography lacks detailed source references and the chapters on the final years of Ataturk's life seem hurried and disorganized. Very much a book on Ataturk's life rather than his times, readers may need to consult historical works on modern Turkey to supplement Kinross's account.

MacFie, A.L. *Ataturk.* New York: Longman, 1994. 217pp. Part of the Profiles in Power series, this is a succinct account of the man in the context of his times and is useful for the reader with a limited grasp of the historical events that Ataturk dominated.

Mango, Andrew. *Ataturk: The Biography of the Founder of Modern Turkey.* Woodstock, New York: Overlook Press, 2000. 666pp. Mango's is an informed and balanced, full-length portrait that succeeds in tracing Ataturk's rise to power and often ruthless hold on it, revealing a complex man of both high ideals and personal limitations. The book should remain the definitive modern study of Ataturk's life and career for some time to come.

Other Biographical Studies

Armstrong, H.C. *Gray Wolf, Mustafa Kemal: An Intimate Study of a Dictator.* New York: Minton, Balch, 1933. 298pp. Despite the book's subtitle, this is a more impressionistic than an intimate study. Written in a semi-fictional style and the first to reveal Ataturk's scandalous private life, the view is unsparing in its criticism of Ataturk's morals, while recognizing his abilities as a soldier and statesman. The major compensation is the author's expert knowledge of Turkey that creates a plausible background.

Froembgen, Hanns. *Kemal Ataturk: A Biography.* New York: Hillman-Curl, 1937. 285pp. This popular, semi-fictionalized life is too admiring of everything about Ataturk to provide the reader with much criticism or analysis of motive or behavior. The book also contains several inaccuracies.

Mikusch, Dagobert von. *Mustapha Kemal: Between Europe and Asia: A Biography.* Garden City, New York: Doubleday, 1931. 380pp. Written by an eyewitness and a friend of Ataturk, this is a partisan's interpretation that still mentions Ataturk's faults and shortcomings. Best as a straightforward narrative account of events, the study is lacking in many psychological insights.

Volkan, Vamik D., and Norman Itzkowitz. *The Immortal Ataturk: A Psychobiography.* Chicago: University of Chicago Press, 1984. 374pp. Containing much original material, this analysis, written by a historian and a psychoanalyst, respectively, traces the development of Ataturk's "grandiose self," which is regarded as his basic character trait, from his childhood.

Walker, Barbara. *To Set Them Free: The Early Years of Mustafa Kemal Ataturk.* Grantham, New Hampshire: Tompson & Rutter, 1981. 96pp. Providing the fullest account of Ataturk's boyhood and youth, this analysis seeks to explain his development and essential character as it is revealed by his early experiences. Uses invented dialogue based on the speaker's acknowledged sentiments.

Wortham, Hugh E. *Mustapha Kemal of Turkey.* Boston: Little, Brown, 1931. 251pp. A short historical biography for the general reader, the book was the first reasonably complete account of Ataturk's remarkable career, and Wortham puts the various phases of his life into a comprehensive whole.

Biographical Novels

Brock, Roy. *Ghost on Horseback: The Incredible Ataturk.* New York: Duell, Sloan and Pearce, 1954. 408pp. Although sometimes cataloged as nonfiction, the author himself describes his book as a historical novel, and the romanticized and fictional elements justify the description. Brock dwells at great lengths on Ataturk's sins and violent behavior and ignores many of his constructive achievements. The book will appeal to readers who like history dramatized and crammed with imagined details.

Gavin, Catherine. *The House of War.* New York: Morrow, 1970. 350pp. Detailing the war for Turkish independence and Ataturk's great victory over the Greeks, the novel constructs a fictional romance between Ataturk and an American journalist's wife to offer a different side of the brilliant military commander. Despite this invention, the period atmosphere is convincing, and the portrait of Ataturk is plausible.

Fictional Portraits

Bridge, Ann. *The Dark Moment.* New York: Macmillan, 1952. 337pp. Based on the rise of modern Turkey in the years before, during, and after World War I, the novel tells the story of an English girl who falls in love with Ataturk. Clearly written by a partisan, the novel diminishes Ataturk's faults and Turkey's crimes against the Greeks, but is strongest in its period painting.

Reinhardt, Richard. *The Ashes of Smyrna.* New York: Harper & Row, 1971. 481pp. Set during the Greco-Turkish War (1919–1922) and concerning the battle for Smyra, the novel details the conflict between a Greek and Turkish family with a glimpse of Ataturk. Solidly researched, the novel captures with authority the battles and intrigues of the war and Ataturk's role in it.

Recommended Juvenile Biographies

Heller, Deane Fons. *Hero of Modern Turkey: Ataturk.* New York: J. Messner, 1972. 190pp. YA. Mainly a laudatory account, best on Ataturk's leadership and administration.

Lengyel, Emil. *They Called Him Ataturk.* New York: J. Day, 1962. 192pp. YA. This is an informative and highly readable account that brings the man vividly to life. Will appeal to the serious student of history.

Tachau, Frank. *Kemal Ataturk.* New York: Chelsea House, 1987. 111pp. MG/YA. A solid, objective entry in the World Leaders Past and Present series, the book traces the events in Ataturk's life and the historical background that shaped him and that he helped to transform.

14. W.H. AUDEN
1907–1973

Poet and critic Wystan Hugh Auden was one of the major figures of twentieth-century English literature. Born in York, England, he lived in Germany during the early days of Nazism and was a stretcher-bearer for the Republicans during the Spanish Civil War. After living for a time in the United States, he became professor of poetry at Oxford (1956–1961). His works cover a broad range of subjects and include *The Age of Anxiety* (1947) and *The Shield of Achilles* (1955). He also collaborated on dramas and opera librettos.

Recommended Biographies

Carpenter, Humphrey. *W.H. Auden: A Biography.* Boston: Houghton Mifflin, 1981. 495pp. Carpenter's is a detailed chronological study that establishes Auden's essential biographical record. Judicious and balanced in its approach, the book is filled with glimpses of Auden that collectively form a convincing and compelling portrait.

Davenport-Hines, Richard. *Auden.* New York: Pantheon, 1995. 406pp. Relying mainly on Auden's journals, letters, poetry, and prose, the author creates a thorough, intimate, and convincing portrait. Acknowledging his debt to Carpenter's life, Davenport-Hines explains that he "was free to write a biography that is more thematic, or selectively emphatic." The theme that unites the author's portrait is Auden's capacity for love, traced through his relationships and his poetry.

Mendelson, Edward. *Early Auden.* New York: Viking, 1981. 407pp; *Later Auden.* New York: Farrar, Straus, 1999. 570pp. Auden's literary executor provides a history and interpretation of Auden's writings rather than a conventional biographical study. Although leaving unsaid the full story of Auden's relationships, the two volumes trace with skill and insight the writer's artistic development. Volume one follows Auden's career up to 1939, with volume two on the American years.

Other Biographical Studies

Clark, Thekla. *Wystan and Chester: A Personal Memoir of W.H. Auden and Chester Kallman.* New York: Columbia University Press, 1996 130pp. Clark details her relationship with Auden and his companion, Chester Kallman, from the 1950s in a fond but not uncritical series of recollections with a number of insightful recollected conversations.

Farnan, Dorothy J. *Auden in Love.* New York: Simon & Schuster, 1984. 253pp. Farnan focuses on Auden's relationship with Chester Kallman based on her firsthand knowledge of both men, letters, and interviews with members of the Auden-Kallman circle. Sometimes the chronology is confused and Auden at times shifts to a supporting role, but the book offers a revealing treatment of this important aspect of Auden's life.

Johnson, Wendell S. *W.H. Auden.* New York: Continuum, 1990. 175pp. Johnson's is a short and simplified introduction to Auden's life and work. An opening biographical sketch is supplemented by personal anecdotes and a record of the writer's relationships and literary works.

Miller, Charles H. *Auden: An American Friendship.* New York: Scribner, 1983. 180pp. Based on journals kept by the author recording his contact with Auden at the University of Michigan in the 1940s and his continuing friendship until the poet's death, Miller supplies a convincing portrait of Auden at home, at work, and in conversation assembled from mostly trivial details.

Osborne, Charles. *W.H. Auden: The Life of a Poet.* New York: Harcourt, Brace 1979. 336pp. Osborne's is a highly readable full-length portrait, taking advantage of the author's personal acquaintance with Auden. Although lacking in interpretive skill, the book serves as an interesting collection of anecdotes and a reasonably complete chronicle of Auden's life and career.

Page, Norman. *Auden and Isherwood: The Berlin Years.* New York: Saint Martin's, 1999. 212pp. Page's joint biographical portrait of Auden and Isherwood discusses both men and their time in Berlin between 1928 and 1933. Based on Auden's unpublished diaries, the book provides a revealing look at both men in their historical context.

Rowse, A.L. *The Poet Auden: A Personal Memoir.* London: Methuen, 1987. 138pp. Rowse's informal recollections of Auden as an undergraduate at Oxford and their later acquaintance are the basis for this odd memoir of a man the author knew only in passing and whom he does not seem to like. Mixing biography and criticism, Rowse reveals as much about himself as his subject.

Fictional Portraits

Cross, Amanda. *Poetic Justice.* New York: Knopf, 1970. 224pp. Cross's witty academic mystery features a sleuth who is enthralled by Auden's poetry, and the poet himself is an unwitting participant in the novel's detections.

Other Sources

Spender, Stephen, ed. *W.H. Auden: A Tribute.* New York: Macmillan, 1975. 255pp. In a valuable source for primary biographical information, this volume collects the reminiscences of a wide circle of Auden's intimates, including his brother, schoolmates, collaborators, and friends, along with a collection of photos spanning the poet's life.

15. JOHN JAMES AUDUBON
1785–1851

An ornithologist and artist celebrated for his paintings of bird life, Audubon was born in Santo Domingo (Haiti) and educated in France. After immigrating to the United States in the early 1800s, he worked as a portrait painter, drawing teacher, and conducted (1823-1828) a private school in Louisiana with his wife, although his main occupation was the observation of birds. Audubon is best known for his *The Birds of America* (1827-1838). He also produced other illustrated works on American natural history.

Autobiography and Primary Sources

Audubon, by Himself: A Profile of John James Audubon from Writings. Alice Ford, ed. Garden City, New York: Natural History Press, 1969. 276pp. Using extracts from Audubon's writings (some of which are rewritten), the editor has arranged a self-portrait, including the artist's first attempt to draw, his observations on America in the early 1800s, and his travels into the wilderness and abroad.

Selected Journals and Other Writings. Ben Forkner, ed. New York: Penguin, 1996. 573pp. Although many of Audubon's letters and journals have disappeared, this collection brings together an important selection of his writings, affording the reader a glimpse of Audubon's life, views, and work habits.

Writings and Drawings. New York: Library of America, 1999. 942pp. This recent collection of Audubon's works includes important letters and extracts from his memoirs and journals. Included as well are 45 color sketches.

Recommended Biographies

Adams, Alexander B. *John James Audubon: A Biography.* New York: Putnam, 1966. 510pp. Adams's is, along with Ford's, the fullest and most authoritative modern biographical portrait available, well-documented, and balanced in its assessment of both Audubon's achievements and his flaws.

Ford, Alice. *John James Audubon.* Norman: University of Oklahoma Press, 1964. 488pp. Ford's biography, the result of extensive research among Audubon's private papers, uncovers new material and corrects a number of fabrications perpetrated by the artist and his family. Reliable as a factual record of Audubon's activities, the book is less sure-handed in synthesizing the amassed data into a compelling and coherent character portrait.

Other Biographical Studies

Arthur, Stanley C. *Audubon: An Intimate Life of the American Woodsman.* New Orleans: Harmanson, 1937. 517pp. Arthur provides a chronicle of Audubon's life from extracts of his letters and diaries and the testimony of those who knew the naturalist. The book is chiefly valuable as a repository of important primary and secondary materials on Audubon.

Chancellor, John. *Audubon.* New York: Viking, 1978. 224pp. Chancellor's is a more readable chronological, illustrated narrative derived from Herrick's more scholarly account. The book offers an accurate summary of the major events in Audubon's life as well as an assessment of his work.

Forshay, Ella M. *John James Audubon.* New York: Abrams, 1997. 160pp. This beautifully illustrated oversized volume accompanies its many illustrations with a biographical profile of Audubon's life and development as an artist and naturalist.

Herrick, Francis. *Audubon the Naturalist: A History of His Life and Time.* 1917. Revised ed. New York: Appleton-Century, 1938. 2 vols. Long established as the standard source on Audubon's life, Herrick is generally reliable on the details of Audubon's life and career but a lack of critical objectivity limits the book's usefulness as an interpretive account of his character.

Biographical Novels

Kennedy, Lucy. *Mr. Audubon's Lady.* New York: Crown, 1957. 343pp. Audubon's personality and activities are shown from the perspective of his long-suffering wife. The dramatization of their marriage and collaboration is based on journals, letters, and the records of the Audubon family.

Recommended Juvenile Biographies

Anderson, Peter. *John James Audubon: Wildlife Artist.* New York: F. Watts, 1995. 63pp. MG. Part of acclaimed First Book series, this is an informative and visually pleasing introduction to Audubon's life and artistic career.

Kastner, Joseph. *John James Audubon*. New York: Abrams, 1992. 92pp. MG/YA. Part of the excellent First Impressions series, this is a lively summary of Audubon's career drawn from his writings. Illustrated with reproductions in color.

Kendall, Martha E. *John James Audubon*. Brookfield, Connecticut: Millbrook Press, 1993. 48pp. MG. Kendall traces Audubon's life from his childhood through his eventual success as an artist and naturalist in a brief but informative biography.

Biographical Films and Theatrical Adaptations

West, Jessamyn. *A Mirror for the Sky*. New York: Harcourt, Brace, 1948. 155pp. West's opera script based on Audubon's life covers a 30-year period in a series of colorful but ultimately unconvincing scenes.

Iron Mistress (1952). Director: Gordon Douglas. A western adventure dramatizing the life of frontiersman Jim Bowie (Alan Ladd) features an appearance by Audubon, played by George Voskovec.

16. SAINT AUGUSTINE
354–430

Theologian and Latin Christian, Augustine is considered second only to Saint Paul in his influence on Christianity as one of the principle founders of Western theology. Raised a Christian by his devoted mother, Saint Monica, Augustine gave up his religion when he went to school in Carthage and indulged in a misspent youth that produced an illegitimate son. His *Confessions* (ca. 400), a classic of Christian mysticism and faith, recounts his conversion struggles. He embraced Christianity in 387 and, against his will, became a priest and spent the rest of his life in Hippo as its bishop. Augustine died during the siege of Hippo by the Vandals.

Autobiography and Primary Sources

The Confessions (trans. Henry Chadwick. New York: Oxford University Press, 1991. 311pp.) is the essential starting point for all biographies of Augustine, and his conversion story provides more intimate knowledge about him than any other figure in antiquity. However, this classic work is not an autobiography in the modern sense but a recollection of his early life in the context of his conversion, as much a lyrical and devotional reflection of his faith as an individual's memoir.

Recommended Biographies

Brown, Peter. *Augustine of Hippo*. Berkeley: University of California Press, 1967. 463pp. Brown's scholarly yet readable life is the most thorough and authoritative study yet written on the entirety of Augustine's career and the culture and personal impulses that formed his ideas. Brown combines a sensitivity with a fidelity to the texts and events to form a model, definitive biographical account.

Wills, Garry. *Saint Augustine*. New York: Viking, 1999. 176pp. Despite its brevity, this is a subtle and informative interpretation of Augustine's life and work and a ringing defense of some of the many charges that have been leveled at him. By showing Augustine in the context of his times, Wills argues that the theologian becomes "more surprising than most people realize—more interesting, more original."

Other Biographical Studies

Bentley-Taylor, D. *Augustine: Wayward Genius*. Grand Rapids, Michigan: Baker Book House, 1981. 272pp. An accessible introduction to Augustine's theology, the book is slanted in favor of portraying Augustine as an evangelical Christian, which limits its effectiveness and reliability.

Bonner, Gerald. *St. Augustine of Hippo*. Philadelphia: Westminster Press, 1963. 428pp. This intellectual biography focuses on the development of Augustine's theology, written for both the student of theology and the general reader interested in the history of ideas. This is by far the best book focusing on the origin and development of Augustine's ideas.

Chabannes, Jacques. *St. Augustine*. Garden City, New York: Doubleday, 1963. 239pp. A brief, popular life of Augustine, the book is marred by novelistic touches and sentimentality, and is closer to hagiography than to a reliable, documented account.

Guardini, Romano. *The Conversion of Augustine*. Westminster, Maryland: Newman Press, 1960. 258pp. Concerned with the struggle toward faith revealed in the *Confessions*, Guardini provides a dramatic account of Augustine's intellectual and spiritual conflict that adds dimension to Augustine's own depiction.

Meer, Frederick van der. *Augustine the Bishop: Life and Work of a Father of the Church*. London: Sheed & Ward, 1961. 679pp. Devoted to Augustine's life after his conversion, this is a precise and detailed portrait of the man, his times, and his congregation. The author's examination of church life at Hippo is soundly based on solid evidence, diligently assembled.

O'Meara, John J. *The Young Augustine: The Growth of St. Augustine's Mind Up to His Conversion*. New York: Longmans, 1954. 215pp. Concentrating on the personal development that led to Augustine's Christian faith, this is a useful supplement to the *Confessions*.

Scott, T. Kermit. *Augustine: His Thought in Context*. New York: Paulist Press, 1995. 253pp. A useful and accessible introduction, the book places the life and teachings of Augustine in the context of his region and times.

Smith, Warren T. *Augustine: His Life and Thought*. Atlanta: John Knox Press, 1980. 215pp. This devotional appreciation written for a lay person, despite its avowed intention to show Augustine's life as the working of grace, does not violate biographical facts and provides an accessible, though limited, brief life.

Biographical Novels

Coray, Henry W. *Son of Tears: A Novel on the Life of Saint Augustine*. New York: Putnam, 1957. 316pp. Dramatizing the career of Augustine, the novel depicts his defiance of his mother, his youthful sensual and philosophical experimentation, his conversion, and his years as the bishop of Hippo in an account that is scrupulous in its research and documentation.

De Wohl, Louis. *The Restless Flame*. Philadelphia: Lippincott, 1951. 284pp. Using the *Confessions* as its primary source, the novel dramatizes the story of Augustine's youth, conversion, and years of devotion in a moving, though at times breathlessly sentimental, depiction.

Warner, Rex. *The Converts: A Historical Novel*. Boston: Little, Brown, 1967. 337pp. The early years of Augustine before his conversion are seen through the journal account of a friend who records Augustine's struggle with himself and his domineering mother before embracing Christianity. The novel is effective in evoking the era and maintains the essential details of Augustine's story.

Fictional Portraits

Gaarder, Jostein. *That Same Flower: Floria Aemilia's Letter to Saint Augustine*. New York: Farrar, Straus, 1988. 256pp. This inventive and provocative philosophical novel in epistolary form imagines Augustine's former mistress, constructed from passing references in Augustine's writings. The novel consists of a long, grief-stricken letter from Floria Aemilia to Augustine after he has abandoned her for his ascetic faith. Gaarder offers an interesting alternative view of the *Confessions*.

White, Helen Constance. *The Four Rivers of Paradise*. New York: Macmillan, 1955. 246pp. In this romantic tale a young man journeys to Rome prior to Alaric's invasion. He is on hand for the sack of Rome and meets Saint Jerome and Augustine who help set him on a religious path. More atmospheric than reliable as history, a strong devotional tone dominates the presentation.

Recommended Juvenile Biographies

Hansel, Robert R. *The Life of Saint Augustine*. New York: F. Watts, 1968. 116pp. MG. In this rare treatment of Augustine for younger readers, the author provides a useful introduction to his life and times.

Other Sources

Fitzgerald, Allan, et al., eds. *Augustine through the Ages: An Encyclopedia*. Grand Rapids, Michigan: William B. Eerdmans, 1999. 902pp. This is an extensive reference guide to Augustine's life, thoughts, and influence.

17. AUGUSTUS
63 BC–AD 14

The first Roman emperor and the founder of Roman imperial system, Augustus, born Gaius Octavius, was the grandson of the sister of Julius Caesar, who made him his heir. With Caesar's murder, Augustus aligned himself with Marc Antony and Lepidus to defeat the conspiracy led by Brutus at Philippi. At Actium, Augustus defeated Antony and Cleopatra and consolidated his power. Named emperor in 28 BC, Augustus reigned during a period of unprecedented prosperity and cultural achievement, secured by the Pax Romana and the stability that Augustus supplied as one of Rome's greatest rulers.

Autobiography and Primary Sources

Augustus's own catalog of the achievements of his reigns are collected in the *Res Gestae* (London: Oxford University Press, 1967. 90pp.).

Recommended Biographies

Buchan, John. *Augustus*. Boston: Houghton Mifflin, 1937. 379pp. Buchan's account of Augustus's life, character, and history of his times superseded all previous works on the subject and remains one of the most authoritative and thorough portraits. Vividly written with a flair for the dramatic, Buchan's book clearly shows the author's sympathy for his subject and asserts a number of debatable assessments about Augustus's character, but the framework is sound.

Southern, Pat. *Augustus*. New York: Routledge, 1998. 336pp. Tracing the life, works, and times of the emperor chronologically, Southern presents events as they occurred from Augustus's point of view in a crisply written, concise, and well-researched biography. Augustus emerges as an extraordinary man who transformed the Roman Republic into the Roman Empire.

Other Biographical Studies

Grabsky, Phil. *I, Caesar: Ruling the Roman Empire*. Parkwest, New York: BBC Books, 1998. 256pp. Written for the general reader, this companion book for a television history series traces the rise and fall of the Roman Empire through the lives of several emperors, including Augustus. Sweeping generalizations sometimes lead the author into errors of fact and some long-outmoded interpretations.

Jones, A.H.M. *Augustus*. New York: W.W. Norton, 1971. 196pp. Part of the Ancient Culture and Society series, this is a useful introduction to Augustus and his times by an authority on both.

Massie, Allan. *The Caesars*. New York: F. Watts, 1984. 233pp. Massie's introduction for general readers of the lives of first Roman emperors has the merits of succinctness and the exposure of many commonly held misconceptions.

Shotter, David. *Augustus Caesar*. New York: Routledge, 1991. 98pp. This brief study repeats the traditional two-part division in viewing Augustus between the brutal rise to power of the immature Octavius and the benign emperor, surpressing anything that does not fit this pattern. The author's simplistic and dogmatic approach limits its reliability and usefulness.

Biographical Novels

Birkenfeld, Günther. *Augustus*. New York: Liveright, 1935. 396pp. Although the novel blends invented scenes and dialogue with much conjecture, the author accurately portrays the era and the temperament of the emperor.

Graves, Robert. *I, Claudius*. New York: Modern Library, 1934. 427pp. Graves's groundbreaking historical novel is written in the form of a memoir by Claudius who provides a detailed, insider's view of the reigns of Augustus, Tiberius, and Caligula. Graves interweaves primary sources and conjecture into memorable reconstruction of Roman life and attitudes, describing a very modern story of the corruption of power. Scholars may question many of Graves's portraits, but readers will be spellbound.

Massie, Allan. *Augustus*. New York: Carroll & Graf, 1986. 381pp. First published in the United States as *Let the Emperor Speak*, this is a first-person narrative in which Augustus describes his career. Solidly researched, the novel is convincing in its reconstruction of events and Augustus's character.

Williams, John. *Augustus*. New York: Viking, 1972. 305pp. Told in the form of letters, journals, and memoirs by Augustus and his contemporaries, the novel presents a multidimensional portrait of Augustus and his reign. The novel's primary documents are invented; the chronology has been modified, and facts have been changed or invented.

Fictional Portraits

Duggan, Alfred. *Three's Company*. London: Faber and Faber, 1956. 286pp. The author looks at the shaky triumvirate of Antony, Octavius, and Lepidus, formed to punish Julius Caesar's murderers. Interestingly, Dugan concentrates on Lepidus, the least known of the trio, whose career is chronicled as a capable man pushed beyond the limits of his abilities by historical events.

Recommended Juvenile Biographies

Nardo, Don. *The Age of Augustus*. San Diego: Lucent Books, 1997. 112pp. MG. Although not strictly a biography, this valuable, well-documented, and balanced study describes the politics, culture, religion, and society during the reign of Augustus that helpfully reflects the emperor's accomplishments.

Stearns, Monroe. *Augustus Caesar: Architect of Empire*. New York: F. Watts, 1972. 183pp. MG/YA. Stearns places Augustus in the context of his times with revealing details about both the man and his era.

Walworth, Nancy Z. *Augustus Caesar*. New York: Chelsea House, 1989. 111pp. MG/YA. This detailed, account of Augustus's life explores his character and achievement, both the positives and the negatives, as contrasted with other prominent Roman leaders during the time of the Republic and the early empire.

Biographical Films and Theatrical Adaptations

Warner, Francis. *Virgil and Caesar: A Play*. Chester Springs, Pennsylvania: Dufour Editions, 1993. 95pp. Warner's verse drama explores the tension between Augustus's worldly rule and pragmatic politics with the vision of Rome's idealistic poet. The action opens in 29 BC and ends in 19 BC with Virgil's death.

Cleopatra (1963). Director: Joseph L. Mankeiwicz. This lavish Hollywood epic dwarfs its historical characters with spectacle. Roddy McDowall portrays Augustus as the nemesis in the romance between Antony and Cleopatra. Only Rex Harrison as Julius Caesar manages any depth and believability in his characterization. Video.

I, Claudius (1980). Director: Herbert Wise. The acclaimed BBC series based on Robert Graves's novels is remarkably faithful to his intimate portrait of a dysfunctional first family of Imperial Rome, absolutely corrupted by power. Brian Blessed portrays Augustus under the thumb of the monstrous Livia. Video.

See also Cleopatra; Julius Ceasar

18. MARCUS AURELIUS
AD 121–180

A Roman emperor and Stoic philosopher, Marcus Aurelius succeeded his uncle Antoninus Pius (161). His reign was spent defending the empire against Parthians, Germans, and Britons. He worked to improve living conditions for the poor and lessened the brutality of gladiatorial contests. However, he savagely persecuted the Christians, whom he viewed as natural enemies of Rome. His *Meditations* expresses his philosophy.

Autobiography and Primary Sources

The Meditations of Marcus Aurelius Antoninus. New York: Oxford University Press, 1998. 224pp. Written during his military campaign against barbarian invaders, Marcus Aurelius's musings by a man trained in the Stoic philosophy offer a revealing glimpse of the complex character of the Roman emperor.

Recommended Biographies

Birley, Anthony. *Marcus Aurelius: A Biography*. 1966. Revised ed. New Haven, Connecticut: Yale University Press, 1987. 320pp. Birley's is the most complete, modern biographical study. The first half deals with Marcus Aurelius's formative years; the second concerns his reign. The book relies on Marcus Aurelius's own words and relates his activities to the customs of the age.

Other Biographical Studies

Farquharson, A.S.L. *Marcus Aurelius: His Life and World*. New York: W. Salloch, 1951. 154pp. Not a chronological biography but a series of appreciative essays on various aspects of Marcus Aurelius's life, times, and ideas. Farquharson, a devoted specialist, displays the result of his considerable research.

Grant, Michael. *The Roman Emperors: A Biographical Guide to the Rulers of Imperial Rome 31 BC–AD 476*. New York: Scribner, 1985. 367pp. Grant provides 92 capsule biographies of the Roman emperors with an outline of the political and military events of each reign.

Sedgwick, Henry D. *Marcus Aurelius*. New Haven, Connecticut: Yale University Press, 1921. 309pp. Based on Marcus Aurelius's letters, Sedgwick focuses on the Roman emperor's character and ideas, his inner life and moral influences.

Biographical Novels

Gibbs, Willa. *A Fig in Winter*. New York: Morrow, 1963. 370pp. Events from the reign of Marcus Aurelius are described from the perspective of his personal slave in an authentic recreation of the period, with much of the characteristics of Aurelius based on his *Meditations*.

Fictional Portraits

Burns, Ron. *Roman Nights*. New York: Saint Martin's, 1991. 340pp. Burns's clever period mystery involves a lawyer who serves Emperor Marcus Aurelius who is plunged into the violence of the era and tries to halt the onrush of anarchy and the dissolution of the empire.

Pater, Walter. *Marius the Epicurean*. 1885. Reprint ed. New York: Dutton, 1963. 267pp. Pater's influential literary and philosophical classic shows the young Marius developing a workable synthesis of mysticism, epicureanism, and Christianity. Historians have criticized Pater's facts, but most grant his mastery of the spirit of the times.

Pilpel, Robert H. *Between Eternities*. San Diego: Harcourt, Brace, 1985. 559pp. Roman life during the second century is presented in the fictional journal of Lucius Celer, whose patron was Marcus Aurelius. Celer recalls his past experiences and his present difficulties with Aurelius's son, whom Celer opposed as the emperor's successor.

Biographical Films and Theatrical Adaptations

The Fall of the Roman Empire (1964). Director: Anthony Mann. Lavish, big-budget epic on the reign of Marcus Aurelius, with Alec Guinness a standout as the emperor. Co-starring James Mason, Stephen Boyd, Omar Sharif, and Christopher Plummer. Video.

19. JANE AUSTEN
1775–1817

English novelist Jane Austen was a clergyman's daughter whose comedies of manner concern what she knew best: the customs of country gentry families. Although all of her novels describe courtships and end in marriage, Austen never shared the fate of her heroines. Instead, she lived a quiet, largely uneventful life among her large family, protecting her anonymity as the author of six novels—*Sense and Sensibility* (1811), *Pride and Prejudice* (1813), *Mansfield Park* (1814), *Emma* (1815), and *Northanger Abbey* and *Persuasion* (1818)—regarded as some of the finest in literature.

Autobiography and Primary Sources

The major source for all subsequent biographies of Jane Austen are her remarkable letters. See *Jane Austen's Letters*. Deirdre Le Faye, ed. (New York: Oxford University Press, 1995. 643pp.). In addition, *Jane Austen: A Family Record*, revised edition, edited by Deirdre Le Faye (New York: Macmillan, 1989. 323pp.) is a valuable source for primary material on Jane Austen's life and family background.

Recommended Biographies

Chapman, R.W. *Jane Austen: Facts and Problems*. Oxford: Clarendon Press, 1948. 224pp. Thorough and assiduous in his presentation, Chapman, the editor of standard editions of Austen's novels, lays out the essential data of what is known for certain about Austen's life, with sensible interpretations when called for that convinces by the depth of his research and solid knowledge of his subject and her era.

Honan, Park. *Jane Austen: Her Life*. New York: Saint Martin's, 1988. 452pp. The first to make full use of Austen material that has come to light in this century, Honan creates a richly detailed family, political, and historical context for Austen's life. Unfortunately, he tries to penetrate the novelist's placid, domestic routine with imagined scenes that ultimately fail to come to life. Honan's account is best for its fresh insights and astute critical analysis of the novels.

Nokes, David. *Jane Austen: A Life*. New York: Farrar, Straus, 1997. 512pp. Nokes's revisionist account offers a strikingly alternative view of the novelist by rejecting previous efforts to paint Austen as flawless. This is a refreshing human portrait, unfortunately overbalanced frequently by questionable speculation, even though Nokes's psychological probing is acute.

Tomalin, Claire. *Jane Austen: A Life*. New York: Knopf, 1997. 341pp. Tomalin provides a straightforward account of Austen's life and works that expertly places the novelist in her social setting. If the author fails to reach the psychological depths of Nokes's analysis, she stays closer to what we know for certain about her subject.

Other Biographical Studies

Austen-Leigh, J.E. *A Memoir of Jane Austen*. 1869. Reprint ed. Oxford: Clarendon Press, 1926. 235pp. Despite an attempt to protect his aunt's reputation and that of his family, Austen-Leigh's account remains important in establishing a believable framework for a portrait of the novelist in the context of her family relationships and attitudes.

Austen, W., and R.A. Austen. *Jane Austen: Her Life and Letters*. 1913. Revised ed. Deirdre Le Faye, ed. Boston: G.K. Hall, 1989. 326pp. Descendants of Austen-Leigh, the authors attempt to correct errors in his works by relying principally on the letters and incorporating subsequent research. Long regarded as authoritative, the book has been superseded by more recent biographies.

Cecil, David. *A Portrait of Jane Austen*. New York: Hill & Wang, 1979. 208pp. Lavishly illustrated, this brief account displays the author's balanced and sensible judgment and masterful command of the period.

Fergus, Jan. *Jane Austen: A Literary Life*. New York: Saint Martin's, 1994. 208pp. Concentrating on Austen the literary artist, this is a valuable study of the conditions surrounding the production of her novels and the evolution of her craft.

Halperin, John. *The Life of Jane Austen*. Baltimore: Johns Hopkins University Press, 1984. 399pp. Although thorough and often penetrating, Halperin's account is often marred by the author's focus on her resentments and domestic failures and his speculative attempt to uncover autobiographical clues from Austen's highly polished art.

Hodge, Jane Aiken. *Only a Novel: The Double Life of Jane Austen*. New York: Coward-McCann, 1972. 252pp. In this assiduous, well-researched biography, the author attempts to reconcile Austen's uneventful life with the genius of her novels in a thesis that shows a divided life of a spinster and aunt, condemned to her lot by her wit and propensity to satire, and her private life as novelist and artist. Unfortunately, many of Hodge's contentions are speculative.

Jenkins, Elizabeth. *Jane Austen: A Biography*. 1949. Reprint ed. New York: Minerva Press, 1969. 410pp. In a sensible, readable, and carefully documented study, Jenkins provides a faithful portrait within the limitations of the known facts, set against a background crafted with elaborate care. The author is wisely skeptical about the amount of autobiographical connections to be detected in the novels. Although she breaks no new ground, Jenkins offers a meticulous presentation that does not pretend to offer a single key to unlock the hidden depths of Austen's genius.

Laski, Marghanita. *Jane Austen*. New York: Thames and Hudson, 1986. 144pp. An illustrated biography, this is a useful introduction to Austen's work, life, and times.

Myer, Valerie Grosvenor. *Jane Austen: Obstinate Heart*. New York: Arcade, 1997. 268pp. Like the other recent lives of the novelist, Myer allows for an unflattering dimension of Austen's personality. Drawing on memoirs from friends and acquaintances and the surviving letters, the author stitches together a reliable account of Austen's family life, social scene, and literary pursuits, but fails to arrive at a satisfactory inner view to justify her contention that Austen's obstinate heart led to her failure to marry and formed the core of her artistic genius.

Tucker, George Holbert. *Jane Austen the Woman: Some Biographical Insights*. New York: St. Martin's, 1994. 268 pp. Less a narrative than a reference guide to Austen's life, Tucker focuses on the woman rather than the author and provides previously unpublished biographical material uncovering a network of family connections and relationships.

Wilks, Brian. *Jane Austen*. New York: Hamlyn, 1978. 144pp. In this illustrated biography, Austen is allowed to tell her own story through excerpts from her letters.

Biographical Novels

Ashton, Helen. *Parson Austen's Daughter*. New York: Dodd, Mead, 1949. 337pp. Family papers, letters, and biographies are woven into a fictional account of Jane Austen's life. The author invents little here and stays within the confines of what is known about the novelist. Recommended for its vivid depiction of the customs, clothing, and pastimes of the period.

Corringham, Mary. *I, Jane Austen: A Re-creation in Rime Royal Based on the Letters of Jane Austen, Her Novels and the Comments of Her Biographers*. London: Routledge, 1971. 84pp. Although not technically a novel, this curious poetic treatment of

Austen's life and observations is a unique homage to the author and a fictional imagining of her perspective.

Gould, Jean. *Jane.* Boston: Houghton Mifflin, 1947. 248pp. This fictionalized biography written for young adults draws from the letters and other sources for its incidents and is a satisfactory introduction to Austen, her career, and times for any reader.

Fictional Portraits

Barron, Stephanie. *Jane and the Unpleasantness at Scargrave Manor.* New York: Bantam, 1996. 289pp.; *Jane and the Man of the Cloth.* New York: Bantam, 1997. 274pp.; *Jane and the Wandering Eye.* New York: Bantam, 1998. 262pp.; *Jane and the Genius of the Place.* New York: Bantam, 1999. 290pp. Barron's entertaining mystery series employs Austen as a sleuth in incidents loosely based on events or situations in the novelist's life.

Wilson, Barbara Ker. *Antipodes Jane: A Novel of Jane Austen in Australia.* New York: Viking, 1985. 329pp. This intriguing, though farfetched, what-if novel imagines a visit by Jane Austen to Australia in the early 1800s. The novel provides Austen's imagined perspective on frontier life as correspondences are worked out between well-ordered Georgian society and the former penal colony.

Recommended Juvenile Biographies

Brown, Ivor. *Jane Austen and Her World.* New York: H.Z. Walck, 1966. 44pp. YA. A short, absorbing, if slightly formal, illustrated portrait of Austen's life that also examines her times and the social contexts for her novels.

Le Faye, Deirdre. *Jane Austen.* New York: Oxford University Press, 1998. 128pp. MG/YA. By a distinguished Jane Austen scholar and part of the British Library Writers' Lives series, this is a thorough and engaging, sophisticated look at the author, her life, and her era.

Biographical Films and Theatrical Adaptations

Jane Austen: A Concise Biography (1993). Director: Malcolm Hossick. This documentary traces the life and literary career of Jane Austen using photographs and views of places associated with her life. Video.

Jane Austen's Life, Society, and Works (1997). Director: Liam Dale. Three videotapes look at Jane Austen's biography, historical and cultural background, and novels featuring sites associated with the novelist. Video.

Other Sources

Grey, J. David. *The Jane Austen Companion.* New York: Macmillan, 1986. 511pp. Grey's is a detailed reference guide to all aspects of Austen's life and works.

Copeland, Edward, and Juliet McMaster, eds. *The Cambridge Companion to Jane Austen.* New York: Cambridge University Press, 1997. 251pp. A comprehensive and up-to-date guide to the works of Jane Austen in the context of her contemporary world and present-day critical views, the book also provides a chronology with biographical information.

Pinion, F.B. *A Jane Austen Companion.* New York: Saint Martin's, 1973. 342pp. A useful reference source on details on Austen's life and novels, including an alphabetical listing of the people and places in the fiction.

Poplawski, Paul. *A Jane Austen Encyclopedia.* Westport, Connecticut: Greenwood, 1998. 411pp. An accurate, comprehensive, and detailed guide to Austen's life and works, this reference guide provides a chronology outlining the principal events of her life and hundreds of alphabetically arranged entries that identify characters, discuss works and themes, and synthesize the criticism devoted to her writings.

Tyler, Natalie C. *The Friendly Jane Austen: A Well-Mannered Introduction to a Lady of Sense & Sensibility.* New York: Viking, 1999. 304pp. Tyler's lively guide to Austen's life and works is a browser's delight, mixing a chronological account with period and critical insights.

B

20. JOHANN SEBASTIAN BACH
1685–1750

German composer and organist, Bach is regarded by many as one of the greatest and most influential composers in Western music. In 1708 he was court organist and chamber musician at Weimar where he became concert master in 1714. In 1723 he took the important post of music director of the church of Saint Thomas in Leipzig where he remained until his death. Most of his work was written for church ceremony, and with it he perfected the art of polyphonic baroque music. Best known during his lifetime as an organist, few of Bach's many works were published before his death, and his music was neglected until the nineteenth century when he was recognized by such composers as Mendelssohn and Schumann as a musical genius.

Autobiography and Primary Sources

Readers interested in consulting primary sources regarding Bach should see *The New Bach Reader* Hans T. David, Christoph Wolff, and Arther Mendel, eds. (New York: W.W. Norton, 1998. 512pp.). This informative documentary collection brings together essential original source materials, such as Bach's letters, the entire first full-length biography of Bach by Johann Nikolaus Forkel, published in 1802, and recollections by Bach's contemporaries.

Recommended Biographies

Boyd, Malcolm. *Bach.* New York: Schirmer Books, 1997. 279pp. This highly acclaimed study alternates biographical chapters with commentary on Bach's works, demonstrating how circumstances helped shape his music. This is a skillful, sensitive treatment of Bach's life and the development of his genius.

Spitta, Philip. *Johann Sebastian Bach.* 1884–1885. Reprint ed. New York: Dover, 1992. 3 vols. Spitta's massive study is a detailed and authoritative analysis of Bach's life and musical development. Although some of the data has been updated and corrected by modern scholars, Spitta's compendium remains an essential reference for the reader with more than a casual interest in Bach.

Wolff, Christoph. *Johann Sebastian Bach: The Learned Musician.* New York: W.W. Norton, 2000. 544pp. The recognized modern expert on the composer has crafted a learned and sensitive intellectual biography that incorporates the best modern scholarship into a convincing, human portrait of Bach. The book traces the connections between Bach's life and his music in the broader context of his times. Highly readable and particularly insightful on Bach the musician, this biography will likely be regarded as the standard life for some time to come.

Other Biographical Studies

Bettmann, Otto L. *Johann Sebastian Bach as His World Knew Him.* New York: Birch Lane Press, 1995. 235pp. The founder of the Bettmann Archive and a lifelong Bach enthusiast provides an informative biography of the master organized alphabetically by topic that serves as a helpful introduction to the composer and a delight for the browser.

Geiringer, Karl. *Johann Sebastian Bach: The Culmination of an Era.* New York: Oxford University Press, 1966. 352pp. A basic, one-volume interpretive study, the book includes many discoveries about Bach's life and music uncovered by modern scholarship and is reliable both in its biographical findings and its assessment of Bach's genius in the context of his times.

Headington, Christopher. *Johann Sebastian Bach: An Essential Guide to His Life and Works.* London: Trafalgar Square, 1997. 112pp. This compact, basic introduction to Bach and his music is part of a British series to enhance the appreciation of radio listeners and is a good choice for a brief volume for the nonspecialist.

Neumann, Werner. *Bach: A Pictorial Biography.* New York: Viking, 1961. 143pp. Neumann provides a biographical sketch to accompany the visual record of Bach and his environment. The general reader will find this a satisfying introduction.

Schweitzer, Albert. *J.S. Bach.* 1911. Reprint ed. New York: Dover, 1966. 2 vols. Schweitzer's influential study is dominated by his attempt to connect Bach's music with his life in an approach that modern musicologists have demonstrated as limited and restrictive.

Terry, Charles Sanford: *Bach: A Biography.* London: Oxford University Press, 1928. 292pp. In Terry's detailed investigation of the biographical record, he neglects an appreciation of Bach's music for a vivid chronicle of his career, shaped into a human story that sheds new light on Bach's family and ancestors.

Wohlfarth, Hannsdieter. *Johann Sebastian Bach.* Philadelphia: Fortress Press, 1985. 120pp. This succinct illustrated profile of Bach's life and accomplishments is a worthy, brief introduction for the general reader.

Wolff, Christoph, et al., eds. *The New Grove Bach Family.* New York: W.W. Norton, 1983. 372pp. A modern equivalent to the exhaustive nineteenth-century work of Spitta, this volume reflects the latest biographical research that has revised many of Spitta's findings and is regarded as the authoritative source on a wide range of subjects concerning Bach's life and musical accomplishments.

Biographical Novels

Meynell, Esther. *The Little Chronicle of Magdalena Bach.* New York: Frederick Ungar, 1970. 245pp. Bach's homelife is described from the perspective of his adoring wife.

Recommended Juvenile Biographies

Dowley, Tim. *Bach.* New York: Omnibus Press, 1983. 144pp. YA. For the musically inclined and those interested in musical history or history in general, this straightforward, somewhat dry account of the composer's life and European society traces Bach's struggle to create his works in a climate of petty court politics. Illustrated throughout with drawings and musical scores.

Vernon, Roland. *Introducing Bach.* Englewood Cliffs, New Jersey: Silver Burdett, 1996. 32pp. MG. Offering a useful and entertaining introduction to the man and his music, this informative short study examines the childhood and early musical training of the German composer, as well as the influences and historical elements that shaped his adult life.

Westcott, Frederick. *Bach.* New York: H.Z. Walck, 1967. 96pp. YA. The problems and challenges of a professional musician in Germany during the period is revealingly traced as Bach is placed in the context of his society and time.

Biographical Films and Theatrical Adaptations

John Sebastian Bach (1989). Director: Hans Conrad Fischer. Presents the life and works of Bach with musical excerpts of his most famous compositions. Video.

John Sebastian Bach (1996). Director: Malcolm Hossick. Part of the Famous Composer series providing a concise biography with a musical overview. Video.

The Joy of Bach (1978). Director: Paul Lammers. Dramatizes scenes from Bach's life, interspersed with performances of his music. Filmed on location at sites associated with the composer. Video.

J. S. Bach: A Documentary Portrait (1987). Producer: Films for the Humanities. This documentary film provides a helpful visual record of the places associated with the composer and documents the highlights of Bach's life. Video.

Other Sources

Boyd, Malcolm, and John Butt, eds. *J.S. Bach.* New York: Oxford University Press, 1999. 480pp. Nine hundred alphabetically arranged entries cover details of Bach's life, family, pupils, patrons, individual works, as well as musical and technical terms. A thematic overview lists entries by topic.

Butt, John, ed. *The Cambridge Companion to Bach.* New York: Cambridge University Press, 1997. 326pp. This is an informative collection of essays by various scholars on different aspects of Bach's life, career, and music.

21. FRANCIS BACON
1561–1626

English philosopher, essayist, and statesman, Francis Bacon is one of the towering figures of the Elizabethan and Jacobean periods. He was knighted in 1603, became attorney general in 1613, lord keeper in 1617, and lord chancellor in 1618. After 1621, Bacon's career as a public servant ended, and he spent the rest of his life writing in retirement. Bacon's application of the inductive method was his greatest contribution to philosophy and scientific thought, causing him to be commonly regarded as one of the founders of the scientific revolution.

Recommended Biographies

Jardine, Lisa, and Alan Stewart. *Hostage to Fortune: The Troubled Life of Francis Bacon.* London: Gollancz, 1998. 637pp. This is the best modern assessment of Bacon's life and career that reflects recent scholarship and a balanced interpretation and should remain the definitive life for some time to come.

Spedding, James. *An Account of the Life and Times of Francis Bacon.* Boston: Houghton Mifflin, 1878. 2 vols. The editor of the seven-volume *Letters and Life of Francis Bacon* (1861–1874), Spedding has written the most comprehensive Bacon biography that still is preeminent in its exhaustive scholarship. Despite a clear sympathy for his subject, Spedding manages an impressive analysis

of the various political and cultural factors that shaped Bacon's career and thinking.

Zagorin, Perez. *Francis Bacon.* Princeton, New Jersey: Princeton University Press, 1998. 286pp. Combining keen scholarship and psychological insight, Zagorin's intellectual biography concentrates on Bacon as philosopher and thinker. The various threads of Bacon's complex personality and career are woven together comprehensively to bring out the richness, scope, and greatness of his accomplishments and character.

Other Biographical Studies

Anderson, Fulton. *Francis Bacon: His Career and His Thought.* Los Angeles: University of Southern California, 1962. 367pp. An incisive and scholarly work, Anderson's account attempts to unite Bacon the thinker and statesman, relating certain of Bacon's opinions to traditional and contemporary ideas.

Bevan, Bryan. *The Real Francis Bacon: A Biography.* London: Centaur Press, 1960. 303pp. Drawing on the Lambeth Palace Library holdings of the papers of Anthony Bacon, this popular account concentrates on Bacon's relationships, with the controversial suggestion of Bacon's homosexuality.

Bowen, Catherine Drinker. *Francis Bacon: The Temper of a Man.* Boston: Little, Brown, 1963. 245pp. Setting out to solve the enigma of Bacon's personality rather than offering a full-scale summation of his life and work, the author arranges his career into a five-act drama that serves to animate the human side of a towering and often intimidating figure.

Crowther, James G. *Francis Bacon: The First Statesman of Science.* London: Cresset Press, 1960. 362pp. The book examines Bacon's career from the context of his contribution to science. It succeeds in its goal, but the focus does not allow a full and balanced appreciation of Bacon's entire career.

Du Maurier, Daphne. *Golden Lads: Sir Francis Bacon, Anthony Bacon, and Their Friends.* Garden City, New York: Doubleday, 1975. 251pp. Bacon's family history is the focus here in a lively narrative that draws on the appropriate primary and secondary sources. *The Winding Stair: Francis Bacon, His Rise and Fall* (Garden City, New York: Doubleday, 1977. 224pp.) covers the last 25 years of Bacon's life in a popular account that is best on his personal life and marriage. Du Maurier fails to explore the factors that led to his fall and makes no assessment of his literary or philosophical accomplishments. Du Maurier's credibility is undermined by her tentative defense of Bacon's authorship of some of Shakespeare's plays.

Epstein, Joel J. *Francis Bacon: A Political Biography.* Athens: Ohio University Press, 1977. 187pp. Epstein's focus is Bacon's political career and the evolution of his political ideas, showing how his principles helped shape his fortunes. Although restricted to a single dimension, Epstein's study is still useful as a framework for viewing his entire career.

Farrington, Benjamin. *Francis Bacon: Pioneer of Planned Science.* New York: Praeger, 1963.

122pp. One of the Pathfinder Biographies series, this is a short, succinct introduction to Bacon that covers the highlights of his entire career with an emphasis on the development of his scientific thought.

Macaulay, Thomas Babington. *Lord Bacon.* 1852. Reprint ed. London: Longmans, 1914. 252pp. Macaulay reacted to Basil Montagu's defense of Bacon with this biographical essay that shows a far more flawed and morally dubious figure. Both Macaulay and Montagu can still be read profitably for their marking out the two sides in the controversy over Bacon's character.

Marwell, Jonathan. *The Trials of Counsel: Francis Bacon in 1621.* Detroit: Wayne State University Press, 1976. 236pp. Beginning with the climax of Bacon's political career, this study interprets Bacon's earlier experiences as a courtier and minister, tracing both his rise and fall in a useful though somewhat discursive analysis.

Mathews, Nieves. *Francis Bacon: The History of a Character Assassination.* New Haven, Connecticut: Yale University Press, 1996. 592pp. The author provides an exhaustive analysis of the various controversies that have surrounded Bacon and have formed his reputation.

Montagu, Basil. *The Life of Francis Bacon.* 1834. Reprint ed. Kila, Montana: Kessinger, 1995. 498pp. The first scholarly biography of Bacon, Montagu's account is that of a Bacon partisan, and the author assembles an elaborate defense for all of history's charges against Bacon.

Fictional Portraits

Eckerson, Olive. *My Lord Essex.* New York: Holt, 1955. 397pp. The rise and fall of the Earl of Essex is dramatized with Bacon's moral crisis of whether to turn on his friend. This is an impressive re-creation of the period and the Essex affair.

Garrett, George. *Death of the Fox.* Garden City, New York: Doubleday, 1971, 739pp. The execution of Sir Walter Raleigh is the occasion for a series of interior monologues, including one of Sir Francis Bacon, Raleigh's bitter nemesis. Garrett is a master of historical recreation and intriguing animation of historical figures.

Tranter, Nigel. *Unicorn Rampant.* London: Hodder and Stoughton, 1984. 351pp. The novel captures life in the court world of James I in 1617, including a revealing portrait of Francis Bacon.

Other Sources

Peltonen, Markku, ed. *The Cambridge Companion to Bacon.* New York: Cambridge University Press, 1996. 376pp. For the nonspecialist this is a convenient interpretive guide to Bacon's writings on science, his theories, moral and political philosophy, and legacy by leading experts. For advanced students and specialists the volume reflects recent scholarship on Bacon.

22. GEORGE BALANCHINE
1904–1983

A major Russian-born twentieth-century choreographer who founded the modern American classical ballet style, Balanchine was a principal dancer and choreographer with Diaghilev's Ballet Russe (1824–1924) and after moving (1933) to the United States was director of ballet for the Metropolitan Opera House (1934–1937) and cofounder (1934) of the School of American Ballet. From 1948 he was artistic director and principal choreographer for the New York City Ballet. He created more than 200 ballets, including *Borrée Fantastique*, *Don Quixote*, and *Slaughter on Tenth Avenue* for the musical *On Your Toes*.

Autobiography and Primary Sources

Balanchine's Complete Stories of the Great Ballets. 1954. Revised ed. Garden City, New York: Doubleday, 1977. 902pp. This revealing volume of Balanchine's reflections on the history of the ballet includes some autobiographical commentary and insights on dancers and choreography.

Recommended Biographies

Buckle, Richard, and John Taras. *George Balanchine, Ballet Master: A Biography.* New York: Random House, 1988. 409pp. The authors present an objective, balanced treatment of Balanchine's career that is well researched, using the insights of many of the choreographer's associates through interviews.

Taper, Bernard. *Balanchine: A Biography.* 1963. Revised ed. Berkeley: University of California Press, 1985. 448pp. First published in 1963 and twice revised and expanded with new material covering Balanchine's last years, Taper's is a detailed account that, if it never fully resolves the enigma of the choreographer's character, offers numerous examples of his many sides, his creative genius, and his personal contradictions.

Other Biographical Studies

Danilova, Alexandra. *Choura: The Memoirs of Alexandr Danilova.* New York: Knopf, 1986. 213pp. The memoirs of Balanchine's mistress records her lifelong friendship from their years together as classmates at the Maryinsky Ballet School and their time in Diaghilev's company in Europe following the Russian Revolution. Danilovna makes many perceptive comments on Balanchine's artistry and personality.

Geva, Tamara. *Split Seconds: A Remembrance.* New York: Harper & Row, 1972. 358pp. Balanchine's first wife offers the story of her life as a ballerina growing up in Russia. Although Balanchine appears late in her story, Geva's insights into their life together are absorbing and revealing on the details of Balanchine's early career and the impact of the Russian Revolution.

Kirstein, Lincoln. *The New York City Ballet.* New York: Knopf, 1973. 261pp. Kirstein's illustrated account of the history of the New York City Ballet which he founded with Balanchine in 1934 is an invaluable record. Written in the form of diary entries

with commentary, this is an excellent reference source to track Balanchine's career up to 1973.

McDonagh, Don. *George Balanchine.* Boston: Twayne, 1983. 201pp. McDonagh's introduction to Balanchine's work includes biographical data on his early years in Russia and analysis of selected Balanchine ballets to identify his creative method, development, and achievement. The book includes a reliable chronology and helpful photographs.

Recommended Juvenile Biographies

Kristy, Davida. *George Balanchine: American Ballet Master.* Minneapolis: Lerner, 1996. 128pp. MG. Covering Balanchine's life from his Russian childhood, this is an informative, highly readable biography that traces how the choreographer become one of the dominant forces in dance.

Other Sources

Mason, Francis. *I Remember Balanchine: Recollections of a Ballet Master by Those Who Knew Him.* New York: Doubleday, 1991. 604pp. The testimony of 84 associates, ranging from various colleagues and dancers to his doctors during his final years provides multiple perspectives on Balanchine's character and genius.

23. HONORÉ DE BALZAC
1799–1850

French writer, Balzac is considered one of the giants in the history of the novel. He began his career writing sensational fiction under a pseudonym. Legendary for his productiveness and oversized appetites, Balzac during the last two decades of his life produced the vast cycle of novels and short stories collectively titled *La Comédie humaine*, an epic reproduction of French society of his time. Despite a tendency toward melodrama and often a lax literary style, Balzac's greatness rests with his great power of observation and invention that has gained him the reputation as one of the founders of the modern novel.

Autobiography and Primary Sources

Letters to His Family 1809–1850. Walter Scott Hastings, ed. Princeton, New Jersey: Princeton University Press, 1934. 511pp. This collection of 190 letters candidly reveal Balzac's ambitions, egotism, vanity, and determination, providing an essential glimpse of the writer's character.

Recommended Biographies

Hunt, Herbert J. *Honoré de Balzac: A Biography.* 1957. Reprint ed. New York: Greenwood, 1969. 198pp. Hunt, one of the foremost authorities on Balzac's works, draws on his considerable research in this concise and balanced portrait. A reader interested in a succinct and scrupulous biography of Balzac could not find a better one than this one.

Maurois, André. *Prometheus: The Life of Balzac.* New York: Harper & Row, 1966. 573pp. A masterful literary biography, the book shapes Balzac's life and career into a comprehensive, vivid narrative. Maurois's analysis of the structure and unity

of *Comedie humaine* is a model of incisive criticism. Scholars may quibble over Maurois's occasional lapses into hyperbole and distortions of fact, however.

Robb, Graham. *Balzac: A Life.* New York: W.W. Norton, 1994. 521pp. This vivid and readable summation of Balzac's amazing career and peculiar genius is thoughtful and informed, constructed like a detective story probing incidents for the clues to unlocking Balzac's essence. Although some of Robb's interpretations, for example, Balzac's alleged homosexual tendencies, are debatable, on the whole the biography is balanced and accomplished in charting in human terms Balzac's gigantic appetites and achievements.

Other Biographical Studies

Bertault, Philippe. *Balzac and the Human Comedy.* New York: New York University Press, 1963. 212pp. Bertault's critical study of Balzac's art is one of the best volumes available integrating his career, temperament, and literary genius.

Festa-McCormack, Diana. *Honoré de Balzac.* Boston: Twayne, 1979. 187pp. This critical study includes a useful chronology and annotated bibliography as well as a reading of Balzac's works that describes the development of his genius and does not neglect his personality or circumstances.

Gerson, Noel B. *The Prodigal Genius: The Life and Times of Honoré de Balzac.* Garden City, New York: Doubleday, 1972. 355pp. A popular account drawn from existing biographies, written by a man whose own prolific production approached that of Balzac himself, the emphasis is on colorful, at times sensationalized, drama rather than careful, detailed analysis.

Pritchett, V.S. *Balzac.* New York: Knopf, 1973. 272pp. Pritchett's workmanlike and sensible appreciation intended for the nonspecialist has the advantage of a fellow novelist's perspective. The high points here, however, are the lavish illustrations.

Zweig, Stefan. *Balzac.* New York: Viking, 1946. 404pp. Incomplete at the time of Zweig's death, the biography was completed by his literary executor, Richard Friedanthal. Zweig provides a dynamic introduction to Balzac that hides none of his weaknesses. However, the absence of an index or any critical apparatus of documentation limits the book's usefulness and reliability.

Biographical Novels

Gorham, Charles. *Wine of Life: A Novel about Balzac.* New York: Dial Press, 1958. 598pp. The author captures Balzac's violent energy and entire incredible story believably, sticking close to the biographical facts.

Fictional Portraits

McConnor, Vincent. *I Am Vidocq.* New York: Dodd, Mead, 1985. 385pp. Set in Paris during 1823, the novel follows the investigations of the renowned chief of the Surete, Francois Eugene Vidocq, with appearances by Balzac and Dumas.

24. P.T. BARNUM
1810–1891

American showman and circus impresario Phineas Taylor Barnum worked as a salesman and as manager of a boarding house before causing a sensation with his first exhibit (1835), a self-proclaimed 161-year-old African American woman. In New York City he opened (1842) the American Museum, which featured such exhibits as Siamese twins Chang and Eng and General Tom Thumb, and engaged Swedish singer Jenny Lind for a U.S. tour. In 1881 Barnum's traveling circus show merged with James A. Bailey's circus to become the famous Barnum and Bailey "Greatest Show on Earth."

Autobiography and Primary Sources

Selected Letters of P.T. Barnum. A.H. Saxon, ed. New York: Columbia University Press, 1983. 351pp. Saxon has selected 303 of the best of Barnum's letters covering most of his lifetime and offering a glimpse of his personality, business and family relations, and his ideas on many subjects.

Struggles and Triumphs. Carl Bode, ed. New York: Penguin, 1981. 394pp. Barnum produced three versions of his life story in 1855, 1869, and 1884. A final posthumous edition with a concluding chapter by his wife was published in 1893. This edited version is a convenient source for Barnum's recollections of his long career.

Recommended Biographies

Kunhardt, Philip B. Jr., Philip B. Kunhardt III, and Peter W. Kunhardt. *P.T. Barnum: America's Greatest Showman.* New York: Knopf, 1995. 358pp. This lavishly illustrated companion volume to the Kunhardts' documentary film chronicles Barnum's remarkable career in a straightforward, objective manner, drawing on archival material and more than 1,000 unpublished letters.

Saxon, A.H. *P.T. Barnum: The Legend and the Man.* New York: Columbia University Press, 1989. 437pp. Written by the recognized expert on Barnum, Saxon's scholarly and authoritative study is the most objective and comprehensive available, derived almost exclusively from primary sources, including diaries, contracts, and 4,000 letters written by or to Barnum. Both the public and private Barnum is displayed, offering a far more complex portrait than other treatments.

Other Biographical Studies

Adams, Bluford. *E Pluribus Barnum: The Great Showman and the Making of U.S. Popular Culture.* Minneapolis: University of Minnesota Press, 1997. 249pp. Assuming a basic familiarity with Barnum's life and career, Adams concentrates on Barnum as a cultural phenomenon, tracing how he shaped his image and his shows to appeal to a changing American social scene.

Harris, Neil. *Humbug: The Art of P.T. Barnum.* Boston: Little, Brown, 1973. 337pp. Harris examines Barnum's publicity techniques while offering a social analysis of nineteenth-century America, making a strong case for the cultural influences that helped shape Barnum and contributed to his successes.

Root, Harvey W. *The Unknown Barnum.* New York: Harper, 1927. 376pp. Although describing the highlights of Barnum's career, the book focuses on his personality and the lesser-known aspects of his life, including his journalistic career, his political career as mayor of Bridgeport, Connecticut, and his social reform efforts.

Wallace, Irving. *The Fabulous Showman: The Life and Times of P.T. Barnum.* New York: Knopf, 1959. 279pp. Wallace's anecdotally rich and entertaining biography is a vivid synthesis of many sources, highlighting both Barnum's career and personal life. Less an interpretation than a dramatic presentation of both the familiar and lesser-known details of the Barnum legend.

Biographical Novels

Trell, Max. *The Small Gods and Mr. Barnum.* New York: McCall, 1971. 230pp. Barnum's promotional skills are documented in this novel that mixes fact and fancy.

Thorp, Roderick. *Jenny and Barnum: A Novel of Love.* Garden City, New York: Doubleday, 1981. 375pp. Based on fact but with invented scenes and dialogue, the novel dramatizes the relationship between Barnum and the Swedish soprano, Jenny Lind.

Fictional Portraits

Idell, Albert E. *Rogers' Folly.* Garden City, New York: Doubleday, 1957. 328pp. A family saga and social chronicle are woven around Barnum's activities, particularly his bringing of the famous elephant, Jumbo, to New York.

Recommended Juvenile Biographies

Andronik, Catherine M. *Prince of Humbug: The Life of P.T. Barnum.* New York: Atheneum, 1994. 136pp. MG/YA. Using quotations from Barnum's autobiography, this is an informative and entertaining summary of the showman's many ventures, his successes and failures.

Fleming, Alice M. *P.T. Barnum: The World's Greatest Showman.* New York: Walker, 1993. 160pp. MG/YA. Barnum's several careers and promotional techniques are covered in this biography that is particularly good on the nineteenth-century social milieu.

Tompert, Ann. *The Greatest Showman on Earth: A Biography of P.T. Barnum.* Minneapolis: Dillon Press, 1987. 120pp. MG/YA. Tompert traces the main outlines of Barnum's private and public life in a competent, generally reliable biography.

Biographical Films and Theatrical Adaptations

Bramble, Mark. *Barnum: A Musical Suggested by the Life of P.T. Barnum.* Garden City, New York: Doubleday, 1980. 77pp. The script for the Broadway musical. A performance is available on tape as *Barnum* (1991) (Director: Terry Hughes) with Michael Crawford in the lead. Video.

A&E Biography Video: P.T. Barnum: American Dreamer (1994). Director: Andrea Black. A documentary portrait of Barnum's life and career using stills, early newsreels, and interviews with modern circus performers. Depicts Barnum's little-known forays into politics, publishing, and land development. Video.

Barnum (1986). Director: Lee Phillips. Barnum's life story is dramatized based on his autobiography. Starring Burt Lancaster in the title role. Video.

The Mighty Barnum (1934). Director: Walter Lang. Wallace Beery stars in the title role in a largely fictional biography. With Adolphe Menjou as Bailey, Virginia Bruce as Jenny Lind, and Janet Beedner as Nancy Barnum.

P.T. Barnum (1999). Director: Simon Wincer. Beau Bridges stars as the promoter in this made-for-television biography showing both his public career and private family tragedies. Video.

P.T. Barnum: America's Greatest Showman (1995). Director: Peter W. Kunhardt. A documentary look at Barnum's life and impact on American popular culture. Video.

25. BÉLA BARTÓK
1881–1945

A Hungarian composer who greatly influenced twentieth-century music, Bartok achieved an original modern style by combining folk elements, atonality, and traditional techniques. He was also a virtuoso pianist and taught piano at the Royal Academy, Budapest. His works include concertos, sonatas, a set of progressive piano studies, *Mikrokosmos* (1926–1939), orchestra works such as *Music for Strings, Percussion, and Celesta* (1936), and six string quartets.

Autobiography and Primary Sources

Béla Bartók: His Life in Pictures and Documents. Ferenc Bónis, ed. New York: Belwin Mills, 1972. 259pp. This collection of photographs and other documentary evidence, including programs and manuscripts, is a useful reference source. Includes a brief, competent introductory biographical profile.

Béla Bartók Letters. János Demény, ed. New York: St. Martin's, 1971. 466pp. Divided into chronological sections, the 298 letters show Bartók's development as a pianist, composer, and musicologist, ending with the years of exile in America. No other source takes the reader deeper into the mind of the composer.

Recommended Biographies

Chalmers, Kenneth. *Béla Bartók.* New York: Chronicle Books, 1995. 240pp. Chalmers's is a reliable and informative biographical portrait that covers the highlights of composer's life, musical career, and development in a useful introduction for the general reader.

Griffiths, Paul. *Bartók.* London: Dent, 1984. 224pp. Intermingling biographical and musical discussion, Griffiths's is a thorough assessment of the full range of the composer's musical achievement. Adept at using Bartók's own words whenever possible to characterize his methods and intentions, Griffiths's is a thoughtful critical biography for the specialist but not inaccessible for the informed, general reader.

Stevens, Halsey. *The Life and Music of Béla Bartók*. New York: Oxford University Press, 1953. 366pp. Stevens's biography and critical study has long held sway as the standard treatment of the composer's life and work. The first half of the book is devoted to Bartók's life in a clear, reliable chronological account; the second half looks at the music by genre.

Ujfalussy, József. *Béla Bartók*. Boston: Crescendo Publishing, 1972. 459pp. The author provides an insider's view of Bartók's Hungarian background and the political and social impact on his life and career, as well as a detailed account of the composer's field work collecting folksongs.

Other Biographical Studies

Fassett, Agatha. *Béla Bartók: The American Years*. New York: Dover, 1970. 367pp. Limited to Bartók's years of exile in America, Fassett's is a personal record of the composer's final period full of heartfelt appreciation that at times overwhelms the book's factual accuracy.

Helm, Everett. *Bartók*. New York: Crowell, 1972. 80pp. Helm's brief illustrated volume serves as an introductory overview of Bartók's life and work.

Lesznai, Lajos. *Bartók*. New York: Octagon, 1973. 219pp. Lesznai's critical biography devotes most of its coverage to the composer's life up to the 1920s, emphasizing Bartók's musicological research in Hungary, Rumania, Turkey, and North Africa, with the music analyzed in nontechnical terms. An extensive chronology relates the events of Bartók's life to those of contemporary musicians.

Milne, Hamis. *Bartók: His Life and Times*. New York: Hippocrene Books, 1982. 112pp. Milne's is another brief, illustrated introductory account incorporating modern scholarship and recent critical appraisals.

Biographical Films and Theatrical Adaptations

After the Storm: The American Exile of Béla Bartók (1989). Director: Donald Sturrock. Covers the years 1940 to 1945. Video.

Other Sources

Gillies, Malcolm. *The Bartók Companion*. Portland, Oregon: Amadeus Press, 1994. 586pp. This collection of 38 essays covers his major works and his efforts to collect Eastern European and North African folk music.

Gillies, Malcolm. *Bartók Remembered*. New York: W.W. Norton, 1991. 238pp. The book provides numerous excerpts from the recollections of those who knew the composer personally, including his mother, two wives, sons, conductors, students, and musicians. Features an extensive chronology and a many photographs.

Laki, Peter, ed. *Bartók and His World*. Princeton, New Jersey: Princeton University Press, 1995. 314pp. Several leading scholars consider various aspects of the composer's life and music, providing

a convenient way for the reader to become acquainted with current scholarship.

26. CLARA BARTON
1821–1912

Clara Barton nursed in army camps and under fire during the Civil War and earned the sobriquet of "the Angel of the Battlefield." During the Franco-Prussian War she worked behind the German lines for the International Red Cross. In 1881 Barton organized the American Red Cross, which she headed until 1904, personally supervising aid to victims of flood, fire, and conflict in the United States, Armenia, and Cuba. She was throughout her life a social reformer, committed to woman suffrage and equal rights.

Autobiography and Primary Sources

Barton's three autobiographical accounts, *The Red Cross in Peace and War*. 1899 (Washington, DC: American Historical Press, 1899. 703pp.); *A Story of the Red Cross*. 1904. Reprint ed. (New York: Airmont, 1968. 128pp.); *The Story of My Childhood*. 1907. Reprint ed. (New York: Arno Press, 1980. 125pp.), alter and shape details and events to produce the positive image she wanted presented to the public and should be read more for her perspective than a factual and reliable chronicle of her life and career.

Recommended Biographies

Oates, Stephen B. *A Woman of Valor: Clara Barton and the Civil War*. New York: Free Press, 1995. 527pp. Concentrating on Barton's life during the Civil War years, there are few better writers who can capture the immediacy and horror of battle. Barton's nursing experiences are brought to vivid life, but a full appreciation of her motives and temperament needs a wider context of the pre- and postwar years. The book will be particularly enjoyed by Civil War buffs.

Pryor, Elizabeth Brown. *Clara Barton: Professional Angel*. Philadelphia: University of Pennsylvania Press, 1987. 444pp. The most comprehensive and authoritative study of Barton, her career, and times, which deserves to be considered definitive. Drawing on new sources and recently discovered diary and papers found behind a wall of Barton's Maryland home, Pryor penetrates the legend to reveal a complex, flawed, though unquestionably heroic, individual whose achievements takes on added significance and understanding when treated with honesty and candor.

Ross, Ishbel. *Angel of the Battlefield: The Life of Clara Barton*. New York: Harper, 1956. 305pp. Meticulously researched, this is a vivid account of Barton's career and a portrait of a restless and ambitious figure.

Other Biographical Studies

Barton, William E. *Life of Clara Barton*. 1922. Reprint ed. New York: AMS Press, 1969. 2 vols. This authorized biography written by Barton's favorite cousin is based on her journals, unpublished autobiographical account of her girlhood and teaching

experiences, letters, and official and personal records Barton collected throughout her lifetime. The author is not indiscriminate in his admiration but analyzes Barton's character with her faults and mistakes mentioned, if readily forgiven.

Burton, David Henry. *Clara Barton: In the Service of Humanity*. Westport, Connecticut: Greenwood, 1995. 176pp. A concise, interpretative account that chronicles Barton's career. Her heroism and generosity are balanced against self-centeredness and sensitivity to slights in a portrait that manages both sympathy and candor.

Dulles, Foster Rhea. *The American Red Cross: A History*. 1950. Reprint ed. Westport, Connecticut: Greenwood, 1971. 554pp. This objective and balanced history of the American Red Cross from its founding in 1881 through World War II presents detailed information on Barton's role in its growth. Not just a laudatory treatment, this account is critical of the limitations of the founder.

Epler, Percy H. *The Life of Clara Barton*. New York: Macmillan, 1915. 438pp. A sympathetic though candid portrait, Epler's early biography takes advantage of conversations with Barton and eyewitness evidence. More recent source material has made much of the book now obsolete.

Fictional Portraits

Allis, Marguerite. *The Bridge*. New York: Putnam, 1949. 307pp. In this novel concerning town rivalries brought on by the construction of a railroad bridge in Connecticut, both Clara Barton and Dorothea Dix appear in their nursing roles during the Civil War.

Jakes, John. *Homeland*. New York: Doubleday, 1993. 785pp. and *The Titans*. New York: Pyramid, 1976. 638pp. Clara Barton is included in Jake's crowded cast of historical personages who make cameo appearances in his family chronicles.

Jones, Douglas C. *Remember Santiago*. New York: Holt, 1988. 354pp. Events of the Spanish-American War from the invasion of Cuba to the storming of San Juan Hill are depicted, with an appearance by Clara Barton in an unusual non-Civil War setting.

Recommended Juvenile Biographies

Dubowski, Cathy E. *Clara Barton: Healing the Wounds*. Englewood Cliffs, New Jersey: Silver Burdett, 1991. 122pp. MG. Part of the History of the Civil War series, this account concentrates on Barton's war experiences, but does summarize her youth and later Red Cross work. Solidly researched, the book is vivid and informative.

Stevenson, Augusta. *Clara Barton: Founder of the American Red Cross*. New York: Macmillan, 1982. 192. MG. The focus is on the youth of Clara Barton in an account that is believable and effective in introducing the historical context for Barton's achievements.

Tilton, Rafael. *The Importance of Clara Barton*. San Diego: Lucent Books, 1995. 112pp. MG/YA. Tilton's documentary account of Barton's achievement does not gloss over human imperfections for a balanced, sympathetic, though honest, appreciation.

Whitelaw, Nancy. *Clara Barton: Civil War Nurse.* Springfield, New Jersey: Enslow, 1997. 128pp. MG/YA. This is a preferred volume for readers seeking a more sophisticated portrait but reluctant to attempt an adult biography. The author uses quotes and other sources to document her narrative, with historical events helpfully explained.

27. CHARLES BAUDELAIRE
1821–1867

French poet and critic, Baudelaire is one of the great figures of French literature and an originator of symbolism in his influential volume, *Les Fleurs du mal (The Flowers of Evil).* Published in 1857, the volume with its theme of the inseparable connection between beauty and corruption was condemned as obscene. As a critic, Baudelaire was responsible for resuscitating the reputation of Edgar Allan Poe. A collection of prose poems, *Petits Poèmes en prose*, was published posthumously in 1869. T.S. Eliot praised Baudelaire as "the greatest exemplar in modern poetry in any language."

Autobiography and Primary Sources

Readers interested in primary sources should consult *The Letters of Charles Baudelaire to His Mother, 1833–1866* (New York: Haskell House, 1971. 302pp.); *Letters from His Youth* (Garden City, New York: Doubleday, 1970, 143pp.); *Selected Letters of Charles Baudelaire: The Conquest of Solitude.* Rosemary Lloyd, ed. (Chicago: University of Chicago Press, 1986. 268pp.); and *The Essence of Laughter, and Other Essays, Journals, and Letters.* Peter Quennell, ed. (New York: Meriden 1956. 223pp.).

Baudelaire: A Self-Portrait. Lois Boe Hyslop, ed. New York: Oxford University Press, 1957. 259pp. Through selected letters Hyslop fashions a revealing autobiographical portrait.

Recommended Biographies

Pichois, Claude. *Baudelaire.* New York: Penguin, 1989. 430pp. Taking advantage of the most recent scholarship and the discovery of new letters and documents, Pichois's exhaustive scholarly study is now the most authoritative source for reliable information and insightful interpretations.

Richardson, Joanna. *Baudelaire.* New York: Saint Martin's, 1994. 602pp. In the author's massive, well-documented analysis, Richardson sets out to reveal the enigmas of the poet, finding a man divided against himself, unable to resist carnal desires yet feeling degraded by them, and locked in a destructive relationship with his mother who abandoned him. Although Richardson's diagnosis of Baudelaire's traumas are at times reductive, the book offers insightful revelations at all the stages of the poet's life.

Starkie, Enid. *Baudelaire.* 1933. Revised ed. New York: New Directions, 1958. 622pp. When it first appeared in 1933, Starkie's massive, detailed study helped establish Baudelaire's reputation outside of France. Her revision in 1958, making use of subsequently uncovered material, made the book the definitive biography up to that point. New letters and

documents that have been since uncovered have dates Starkie's account somewhat, but the book remains thorough and essentially reliable, though marred by evident hero worship.

Other Biographical Studies

Burton, Richard D. E. *Baudelaire in 1859: A Study in the Sources of Poetic Creativity.* New York: Cambridge University Press, 1988. 213pp. The author looks at the poet during his three-month stay with his mother at Honfleur as a turning point and the basis for his literary blossoming. Although the book's focus is narrow, the insights provided are essential for an appreciation of Baudelaire's poetic development.

De Jonge, Alex. *Baudelaire, Prince of Clouds: A Biography.* New York: Paddington Press, 1976. 240pp. This is a somewhat superficial treatment that never penetrates very far beneath the surface of events or the poet's extravagances. A clear Baudelaire partisan, De Jonge is merciless on perceived slights inflicted by others.

Hemmings, F.W.J. *Baudelaire the Damned.* New York: Scribners, 1982. 251pp. Hemming's psychological study attributes Baudelaire's peculiarities and obsession to a religious mania in this revealing portrait.

Hyslop, Lois Boe. *Baudelaire: Man of His Time.* New Haven, Connecticut: Yale University Press, 1957. 207pp. This volume helpfully places Baudelaire in the context of his times and deals with his relations with his contemporaries.

Morgan, Edwin. *Flower of Evil: A Life of Charles Baudelaire.* 1943. Reprint ed. Freeport, New York: Books for Libraries Press, 1970. 189pp. This short critical biography is useful as a compact introduction to Baudelaire's life and poetic development.

Sartre, Jean-Paul. *Baudelaire.* New York: New Directions, 1950. 192pp. Originally written as an introduction to an edition of Baudelaire's diaries and letters, Sartre's existential essay offers a number of intriguing psychological insights, though Sartre's evident hostility to the poet imbalances his treatment.

Williams, Roger L. *The Horror of Life: Charles Baudelaire, Jules de Goncourt, Gustave Flaubert, Guy de Maupassant, Alphonse Daudet.* Chicago: University of Chicago Press, 1980, 381 pp. The author's study of the effects of syphilis on five French authors meticulously examines Baudelaire's medical history with revealing insights to help explain the poet's physical and emotional torments.

Biographical Novels

Wagner, Geoffrey. *Wings of Madness: A Novel of Charles Baudelaire.* San Bernardino, California: Borgo Press, 1978. 224pp. Written by a translator of Baudelaire's poetry, the novel presents a fictional narrative of the poet's life that tries to supply biographical contexts for the poems. It offers a number of highly unusual surmises concerning Baudelaire's relationship with Jean Duval and Apollonie Sabatier.

White, Charles W. *The Midnight Gardener: A Novel about Baudelaire.* New York: Harper, 1948. 367pp. The novel covers the life and literary career

of Baudelaire from his youth to the eve of his departure for Brussels where he died. While the novel observes the main facts of Baudelaire's life and times, the interpretations are often overly psychoanalytical and debatable.

Fictional Portraits

Perowne, Barry. *A Singular Conspiracy.* Indianapolis: Bobbs-Merrill, 1974. 209pp. Imaginatively filling in the gap in Edgar Allan Poe's whereabouts in 1844, the author sends him to Paris where he meets Baudelaire. Together they join forces to free Baudelaire's inheritance from his stepfather. This is an ingenious speculation of what might have happened had the two writers met.

28. AUBREY BEARDSLEY
1872–1898

English illustrator and writer and a leader of the Aesthetic movement, Beardsley is known for his graphic style consisting of sharp black-and-white contrasts, flowing lines, and detailed patterning. He was art editor of the *Yellow Book* magazine, edited the periodical, *The Savoy*, and his distinctive illustrations appeared in such works as Oscar Wilde's *Salomé* (1894) and an edition of Alexander Pope's *Rape of the Lock* (1896). Ravaged by tuberculosis, he died at the age of 26. A collection of his fiction, *Under the Hill*, was published in 1904.

Autobiography and Primary Sources

The Letters of Aubrey Beardsley. John Duncan, ed. Rutherford, New Jersey: Fairleigh Dickinson University Press, 1970. 472pp. This collection of the artist's letters covers his life from the age of six to his death organized into chronological sections with insightful biographical introductions for each.

Recommended Biographies

Benkovitz, Miriam J. *Aubrey Beardsley: An Account of His Life.* New York: Putnam, 1981. 226pp. Benkovitz's is a careful factual treatment of Beardsley's life that concentrates on the artist's most productive period from 1894 to 1898. The book features a balanced evaluation of Beardsley's character, asserting nothing that cannot be proven, and a vivid depiction of his family and social circle.

Fletcher, Ian. *Aubrey Beardsley.* Boston: G.K. Hall, 1987. 206pp. Beardsley's life and career both as an artist and a writer are examined in this comprehensive and balanced critical study. Unfortunately without illustrations, the book should be complemented by one of several collections of the artist's works.

Sturgis, Matthew. *Aubrey Beardsley: A Biography.* Woodstock, New York: Overlook Press, 1999. 404pp. The author, an expert on the English Decadents of the 1890s, has written the most comprehensive biography of the artist to date. Extensively researched and drawing on fresh, untapped sources, Sturgis's highly detailed portrait succeeds in placing the artist squarely in his times, tracing the influences of the Pre-Raphaelite and Aesthetic movements on Beardsley's artistic development and showing how the artist manufactured and manipulated his public image.

Weintraub, Stanley. *Aubrey Beardsley: Imp of the Perverse*. University Park: Pennsylvania State University Press, 1976. 292pp. Incorporating new documentary evidence uncovered since his 1967 biography, Weintraub offers a reassessment that is more focused on uncovering Beardsley's personality behind his work and activities.

Weintraub, Stanley. *Beardsley: A Biography*. New York: G. Braziller, 1967. 285pp. Weintraub takes a life-and-times approach in a chronological account of Beardsley's career. The book is well documented and informed, with all the major events of the artist's life narrated with skill and the literary sources for Beardsley's work expertly traced.

Other Biographical Studies

Brophy, Brigid. *Black and White: A Portrait of Aubrey Beardsley*. New York: Stein and Day, 1969. 95pp. Brophy's critical and biographical essay reviews the artist's life and work, drawing connections between the two by a study of the iconography of 44 of Beardsley's designs.

Brophy, Brigid. *Beardsley and His World*. New York: Harmony, 1976. 128pp. Less focused on a critical examination of Beardsley's work than her earlier book, Brophy concentrates more on the artist's life in this illustrated biography. The basic facts of Beardsley's career are supplemented with psychological conjectures on the connection between his experiences and his artistic genius.

Calloway, Stephen. *Aubrey Beardsley*. New York: Abrams, 1998. 224pp. The writer, a curator of the Victoria and Albert Museum, provides an insightful critical study of the artist's career related to his cultural milieu and his influences. Includes drawings, illustrations, and photographs of Beardsley's circle.

Easton, Malcolm. *Aubrey and the Dying Lady: A Beardsley Riddle*. Boston: Godine, 1972. 272pp. In a psychological analysis, the author examines the artist's sexuality, threading gossip, circumstantial evidence, and conjecture to suggest the artist's homosexuality, transvestitism, and incestuous relationship with his sister Mabel. Only occasionally convincing, the book is a highly speculative, though ingenious, exploration of the deeper recesses of Beardsley's obsessions.

Raby, Peter. *Aubrey Beardsley and the Nineties*. London: Trafalgar Square, 1998. 120pp. Raby places Beardsley's life and artistic career in the context of his age, along with numerous reproductions from his works.

Reade, Brian. *Beardsley*. New York: Viking, 1967. 372pp. This comprehensive collection of Beardsley's graphic work features an informative biographical and analytical essay that touches on psychological and sexual issues of the artist's relationship with his mother and sister and homosexuality.

Fictional Portraits

Berkman, Ted. *To Seize the Passing Dream: A Novel of Whistler, His Women, and His World*. Garden City, New York: Doubleday, 1972. 431pp.

This biographical novel of James MacNeil Whistler features appearances by a number of his associates, including Wilde, Swinburne, Toulouse-Lautrec, Degas, and Beardsley.

Other Sources

Langenfeld, Robert, ed. *Reconsidering Aubrey Beardsley*. Ann Arbor, Michigan: UMI Research Press, 1989. 508pp. This annotated bibliography of works on Beardsley includes an opening series of essays on the artist's life, art, and times.

29. SAMUEL BECKETT
1906–1989

Anglo-French playwright and novelist, Beckett's intense and darkly comic writing has defined the modern literary landscape in the twentieth century. Born in Dublin, Beckett permanently settled in France in 1937 where he fought in the French Resistance during World War II. His most famous work, *Waiting for Godot*, is one of the most important and influential modern plays, an absurd, though touchingly human, dramatization of futility and angst.

Recommended Biographies

Cronin, Anthony. *Samuel Beckett: The Last Modernist*. New York: HarperCollins, 1997. 645pp. Using Beckett's letters, early fiction, and the author's own acquaintance with his subject and mutual friends, this close-up study of Beckett's life and times challenges earlier depictions of a philosophical recluse to show a much more benign and engaging personality, made accessible to the general reader by the author's vivid narrative and deft characterization.

Knowlson, James. *Damned to Fame: The Life of Samuel Beckett*. New York: Simon & Schuster, 1996. 800pp. This long-anticipated authorized biography by one of the world's leading Beckett scholars takes full advantage of unprecedented access to letters, notebooks, and Beckett himself in a series of interviews conducted before his death. The result is a comprehensive, detailed, and most likely definitive biography of Beckett. It is invaluable for the scholar and absorbing for the general reader curious about the personal dimension of the reclusive and seemingly impenetrable modernist.

Other Biographical Studies

Bair, Dierdre. *Samuel Beckett: A Biography*. Revised ed. New York: Summit Books, 1990. 736pp. First published in 1978, Bair's critical biography, written against the wishes of Beckett with limited access to source materials, has served, despite its considerable shortcomings, as the standard work on the writer until Knowlson. Bair represents Beckett as neurotic, cold, and hermitic, a characterization that later biographers have modified.

Gordon, Lois G. *The World of Samuel Beckett: 1906–1946*. New Haven, Connecticut: Yale University Press, 1996. 262pp. Gordon traces Beckett's life and career from his birth until at age 40, he began to find himself as a writer, exploring his life within a larger historical context. In

Gordon's view, Beckett was not a fragile and isolated loner but a sensitive and courageous man "marked by and responsive to the world." Gordon's viewpoint is as refreshing and ultimately moving as it is revealing.

O'Brein, Eoin. *The Beckett Country: Samuel Beckett's Ireland*. New York: Arcade, 1993. 432pp. Tracing the impact of his native Ireland on the formation of Beckett's ideas and art, this intriguing and well-illustrated volume documents Beckett's Irish haunts and their references in his works.

Other Sources

Pilling, John, ed. *The Cambridge Companion to Beckett*. New York: Cambridge University Press, 1994. 249pp. This collection of critical essays by various scholars includes a chronology of Beckett's life and discussions of various aspects of his life and career.

30. LUDWIG VAN BEETHOVEN
1770–1827

A German composer, Beethoven has been universally recognized as one of the world's greatest music geniuses. Born in Bonn, Germany, a child piano prodigy, Beethoven first visited Vienna in 1787 where he impressed Mozart and was invited to become Haydn's student. In 1801, Beethoven was afflicted with deafness which by 1817 became total, preventing public performances, but his creativity was unaffected. A prolific composer in various genres, Beethoven created music of an unsurpassed depth and emotional intensity.

Autobiography and Primary Sources

Readers interested in approaching Beethoven through primary sources have a number of useful choices including

Hamburger, Michael, ed. *Beethoven: Letters, Journals, and Conversations*. London: Thames and Hudson, 1990. 281pp. This volume collects important documents of Beethoven and his contemporaries contained in the "conversation books" his guests used while visiting the composer after he became deaf.

Sonneck, Oscar G., ed. *Beethoven: Impressions by Contemporaries*. New York: Dover, 1995. 231pp. Arranged chronologically, this compilation brings together diary and memoir accounts of Beethoven for a fully realized picture of Beethoven and his times.

Tyson, Alan, and Joseph Kerman. *The New Grove Beethoven*. New York: W.W. Norton, 1983. 216pp. An excellent entry in the Grove series, this volume succinctly organizes the essential primary material upon which a full understanding of Beethoven's life and career depends.

Recommended Biographies

Kinderman, William. *Beethoven*. Los Angeles: University of California Press, 1995. 374pp. Drawing on the most recent research, Kinderman's analytical study provides both a vivid portrait of Beethoven and an insightful guide to his music, although some of the technical musical analysis may prove too formidable for the untrained, general reader.

Solomon, Maynard. *Beethoven.* 1977. Revised ed. New York: Schirmer, 1998. 554pp. Solomon's psychoanalytic biography traces the personal themes in Beethoven's life that affected his compositions. The author devotes a considerable portion of his study to the detective work that uncovered conclusively the identity of Beethoven's "Immortal Beloved." Based on previously unpublished letters and documents, the book is comprehensive and revealing.

Thayer, Alexander W. *Thayer's Life of Beethoven.* Revised and edited by Elliot Forbes. Princeton, New Jersey: Princeton University Press, 1964. 2 vols. 1141pp. Thayer's massive study remains a fundamental source for Beethoven scholars and subsequent biographers, collecting important source materials. Largely neglecting musical analysis, Thayer concentrates on placing Beethoven in the context of his times.

Other Biographical Studies

Cooper, Martin. *Beethoven: The Last Decade 1817–27.* New York: Oxford University Press, 1970. 483pp. The focus here is on Beethoven's final, troubled decade in an insightful analysis that brings together the composer's personal crises and musical achievements.

Johnson, Stephen. *Ludwig van Beethoven: An Essential Guide to His Life and Works.* London: Trafalgar Square, 1997. 112pp. Part of a helpful English series to aid radio listeners, this short guide provides a lively, though basic, introduction to Beethoven.

Kendall, Alan. *The Life of Beethoven.* New York: Hamlyn, 1978. 144pp. This illustrated biography is the best of several available that offers a comprehensive and balanced account of Beethoven's life and career.

Knight, Frida. *Beethoven and the Age of Revolution.* New York: International, 1974. 206pp. Placing his music squarely in the context of his times, Knight's study is a revealing historical and cultural biography, an essential complement to more psychological accounts.

Landon, H.C. Robbins. *Beethoven: His Life, Work, and World.* New York: Thames and Hudson, 1993. 248pp. Landon places Beethoven clearly in his era at the center of the musical and social life of Vienna to form a useful introduction to the subject.

Marek, George. *Beethoven: Biography of a Genius.* New York: Funk & Wagnalls, 1969. 696pp. Marek's comprehensive life concentrates on the man, not his music. Based principally on Thayer's pioneering study, supplemented with new evidence, Beethoven is placed in the social, cultural, and political contexts of his times, and his relationships with family and friends, erratic behavior, and the personal tragedy of his deafness are well documented.

Schlosser, Johann Aloys. *Beethoven: The First Biography, 1827.* Portland, Oregon: Amadeus Press, 1996. 196pp. Published only a few months after the composer's death, this biography of Beethoven has essential firsthand information as well as distortions of fact. In this edition, Beethoven scholar Barry Cooper puts Schlosser's work in perspective and clarifies inaccuracies.

Schlinder, Anton. *Beethoven as I Knew Him: A Biography.* 1840. Reprint ed. Donald MacArdle, ed. Chapel Hill: University of North Carolina Press, 1966. 545pp. Schlinder is principally responsible for establishing the myth of Beethoven as a romantic hero. Despite distortions of fact to polish Beethoven's image and the author's own prestige, Schlinder's book contains essential and unique facts about the composer and his music.

Biographical Novels

Brenner, Jacques. *Nephew to the Emperor: A Novel Based on the Life of Beethoven.* Cleveland: World, 1959. 190pp. Beethoven is seen from the perspective of his nephew who is left in the care of the 40-year-old bachelor Beethoven. The author has drawn extensively on Beethoven's letters and conversation books to establish its authenticity.

Chotzinoff, Samuel. *Eroica: A Novel Based on the Life of Ludwig van Beethoven.* New York: Simon & Schuster, 1930. 312pp. In a series of episodes treated with remarkable fidelity to the facts, the novel develops an intimate portrait of Beethoven that allows for his defects. All the important episodes in Beethoven's life are represented in a treatment closer to that of a biography than a novel.

Pidoll, Carl von. *Eroica: A Novel about Beethoven.* New York: Vanguard, 1957. 218pp. Narrated by a friend of Beethoven from his arrival in Vienna, this fictional biography captures the life and musical accomplishments of Beethoven and the effects of his deafness. Impeccably researched, the novel stays within the actual facts of Beethoven's biography.

Recommended Juvenile Biographies

Autexier, Philippe A. *Beethoven: The Composer as Hero.* New York: Abrams, 1992. 143pp. YA. This sophisticated chronicle of Beethoven's career places his musical achievement in the context of his times and personal turmoil.

Balcavage, Dynise. *Ludwig van Beethoven: Composer.* New York: Chelsea House, 1996. 119pp. MG/YA. This is an informative, full-length biographical profile, balancing the important public events in Beethoven's life with details about his private life.

Thompson, Wendy. *Ludwig von Beethoven.* New York: Viking, 1991. 48pp. MG/YA. Part of the Composer's World series, Beethoven's career is detailed in this lavishly illustrated biography that includes extracts from the composer's finest works in simple keyboard arrangements.

Biographical Films and Theatrical Adaptations

Beethoven (1997). Director: Malcolm Hossick. This documentary summarizes the life and work of Beethoven with performances. Video.

Beethoven: A Portrait (1985). Director: Nicholas Vaznyi. Narrated by Anthony Quayle, the film provides the story of Beethoven's life in a psychological portrait with views of landmarks in Bonn, Vienna, and the Rhine countryside. Video.

Beethoven's Great Love (1936). Written and directed by French cinematic master Abel Gance with a vivid intensity, the film captures the composer's artistic and personal struggles underscored with impressionistic imagery and expressionistic use of sound. Harry Bauer plays Beethoven. Video.

Beethoven Lives Upstairs (1989). Director: David Devine. In a sensitive film treatment set in nineteenth-century Vienna, a 10-year-old boy reacts to the family's new tenant, Ludwig van Beethoven (Neil Munro), and gradually appreciates the genius of his music and its personal cost. Video.

Beethoven's Nephew (1985). Director: Paul Morrissey. The film treats the composer's relationship with his nephew as a subject for farce. There is little here that is either convincing or reliable historically. Wolfgang Reichmann portrays Beethoven. Video.

Immortal Beloved (1994). Director: Bernard Rose. In this intriguing and visually stunning film, the mystery of the identity of the "immortal beloved" referred to in a letter found after Beethoven's death leads to flashbacks dramatizing the composer's life and loves. Considerable liberties with the facts prevent the film from being viewed as a faithful account, but Gary Oldman as Beethoven is well cast as the tortured genius. Isabella Rosselini co-stars. Video.

Other Sources

Arnold, Denis, and Nigel Fortune, eds. *The Beethoven Reader.* New York: W.W. Norton, 1971. 542pp. A compendium of essays by distinguished scholars on various aspects of Beethoven's life and work, this volume provides new facts and fresh views of the man and his genius.

Cooper, Barry, ed. *The Beethoven Compendium: A Guide to Beethoven's Life & Music.* New York: Thames and Hudson, 1992. 350pp. Written by four leading Beethoven scholars reflecting the latest research, this reference guide provides a calendar of Beethoven's life and works, a who's who of his associates, biographical and musical source material, and sections on his daily routine, beliefs and opinions, and historical and musical background.

Nettl, Paul. *The Beethoven Encyclopedia: His Life and Art from A to Z.* New York: Carol, 1994. 325pp. An alphabetical reference guide to every aspect of Beethoven's life, career, and associates, this useful volume features a detailed chronology.

Stanley, Glenn, ed. *The Cambridge Companion to Beethoven.* New York: Cambridge University Press, 2000. 325pp. Reflecting recent developments in musicology and theory, this collection of critical essays examines Beethoven's music and the personal and historical context in which it was composed and received.

31. ALEXANDER GRAHAM BELL
1847–1922

Second only to Thomas Edison as the greatest modern inventor, Scottish-born scientist Alexander Graham Bell is known chiefly for his development of the telephone. However, his interests and contributions in phonetics, acoustics, the education of the deaf, aviation, architectural engineering, animal husbandry, and genetics are also significant. His early studies of speech and sound and work as an instructor of the deaf, which he considered his true life's work, led to his invention of the telephone in 1876.

Recommended Biographies

Bruce, Robert V. *Alexander Graham Bell and the Conquest of Solitude.* Boston: Little, Brown, 1973. 564pp. Regarded as the definitive, scholarly biography, Bruce's study takes advantage of full access to Bell's personal papers and is the best choice for a comprehensive and authoritative examination of Bell's professional and personal life.

Mackay, James A. *Alexander Graham Bell: A Life.* New York: Wiley, 1997, 320pp. Mackay's biography offers new information about the inventor's early life and relationships, helpfully tracing his fascination with science and the roots of his altruism. Mackay's study is a worthy successor and complement to Bruce's authoritative biography.

Other Biographical Studies

Costain, Thomas B. *The Chord of Steel: The Story of the Invention of the Telephone.* Garden City, New York: Doubleday, 1960. 192pp. Although the focus here is limited to Bell's development of the telephone, Costain's popular account does reveal details about Bell's residence in Canada.

Grosvenor, Edwin, Morgan Wesson, and Robert V. Bruce. *Alexander Graham Bell: The Life and Times of the Man Who Invented the Telephone.* New York: Abrams, 1997. 304pp. This superbly illustrated biography provides a useful, succinct overview of Bell's career and achievements.

Mackenzie, Catherine D. *Alexander Graham Bell: The Man Who Contracted Space.* Boston: Houghton Mifflin, 1928. 382pp. Written by Bell's personal secretary, this biographical sketch rather than a full-scale, scholarly study is informed by her firsthand contact but is unsatisfactory as a balanced and detached analysis of Bell and his career.

Fictional Portraits

McMahon, Thomas. *Loving Little Egypt.* New York: Viking, 1987. 273pp. This comic fantasy follows the adventures of a prodigy who creates an underground telephone network among the blind nationwide. His discovery pits him against Thomas Edison and Alexander Graham Bell for control of science. Most of the plot contrivances and many of the inventions attributed to Bell and Edison are fanciful.

Recommended Juvenile Biographies

Davidson, Margaret. *The Story of Alexander Graham Bell: Inventor of the Telephone.* New York:

Dell, 1989. 100pp. MG. Part of the Famous Lives series, this biography traces Bell's career from childhood and emphasizes not only his invention of the telephone but his lifelong interest in helping the deaf.

Lewis, Cynthia Copeland. *Hello, Alexander Graham Bell Speaking: A Biography.* Minneapolis: Dillon Press, 1991. 64pp. MG. Less than a full-scale biography, Lewis focuses on Bell's invention of the telephone, but the salient features of Bell's life and career are highlighted in a highly readable factual profile.

Matthews, Tom. *Always Inventing.* Washington, DC: National Geographic Society, 1999. 64pp. MG. This visually inviting large format book offers a biographical portrait along with many photographs, drawings, and pages from Bell's original notebooks.

Pasachoff, Naomi E. *Alexander Graham Bell: Making Connections.* New York: Oxford University Press, 1996. 144pp. YA. In a well-written and engaging narrative, the author surveys Bell's life and career with several helpful insets that explain the principles of acoustics, electromagnetism, and the workings of the telephone.

Biographical Films and Theatrical Adaptations

A&E Biography Video: Alexander Graham Bell: Voice of Invention (1996). Producer: Rick Davis. This documentary goes beyond Bell's invention of the telephone to his other considerable accomplishments. Contrary to other heroic and simplistic portraits, Bell is shown as wracked with self-doubt and possessing a strong competitive streak, tempered by his driving passion to enable the deaf to communicate. Video.

The Sound and the Silence (1993). Director: John Kent Harrison. This Canadian/New Zealand biopic is a detailed and authentic presentation of Bell's motivation to invent the telephone that grew out of his personal connection with the deaf. John Bach stars as the inventor; Elizabeth Quinn portrays Mabel Bell. Video.

The Story of Alexander Graham Bell (1939). Director: Irving Cummings. Hollywood's version of Alexander Graham Bell's career is depicted with Don Ameche in the title role and Henry Fonda as the earnest Watson in this lavish and sometimes inaccurate dramatization. Video.

32. DAVID BEN-GURION
1886–1973

Polish-born Israeli statesman, Ben-Gurion was one of the principal founders of the modern state of Israel. An active Zionist during World War I, Ben-Gurion cooperated with the British in the struggle to create an independent Jewish state in Palestine, but after World War II led the political struggle against them and authorized the sabotage activities of the Hebrew resistance, heading the defense effort in 1947–1948. Ben-Gurion became the first prime minister of Israel, a post he held from 1948 to 1953, and again from 1955 to 1963.

Autobiography and Primary Sources

Ben-Gurion: In His Own Words. Amram Ducovny, ed. New York: Fleet, 1968. 152pp. The author stitches together various material from Ben-Gurion's published works to capture his perspective on his life and career.

Israel: A Personal History. New York: Funk & Wagnalls, 1971. 862pp. Tracing the modern development of Israel from the early Zionist movement to Ben-Gurion's retirement in the 1960s, the volume also relates his own story and the forces and personalities that shaped the Jewish state. Unfortunately, Ben-Gurion sidesteps controversies, plays down his own role, and provides few insights into the inner man.

Memoirs. Compiled by Thomas R. Bransten. New York: World, 1970. 216pp. Based on a series of interviews with Ben-Gurion during the filming of the documentary *Forty-Two Six* on his life and times, Ben-Gurion's words are arranged into a chronological narrative.

Recommended Biographies

Bar-Zohar, Michael. *Ben-Gurion: The Armed Prophet.* Englewood Cliffs, New Jersey: Prentice-Hall, 1968. 296pp. Drawing on extensive sources, including Ben-Gurion's diaries, notebooks, and official papers, this is an informative, journalistic treatment of Ben-Gurion's life and career, written by an admirer. Unfortunately the book lacks documentation for scholarly purposes.

Kurzman, Dan. *Ben-Gurion: Prophet of Fire.* New York: Simon & Schuster, 1983. 544pp. Written by an award-winning foreign correspondent, this is the best full-length study of Ben-Gurion yet published. Synthesizing multiple sources, including interviews with Ben-Gurion's associates and political rivals, the book forms a sympathetic multidimensional appreciation that does not overlook Ben-Gurion's weaknesses and inconsistencies.

Teveth, Shabtai. *Ben-Gurion: The Burning Ground: 1886–1948.* Boston: Houghton Mifflin, 1987. 967pp. Almost exclusively a political portrait that ends on the eve of the establishment of the state of Israel, this is the best analysis of the stages leading up to Israeli independence in English, groundbreaking in its thoroughness and synthesis of multiple sources.

Other Biographical Studies

Avi-hai, Avraham. *Ben-Gurion, State Builder: Principles and Pragmatism 1948-63.* New York: Wiley, 1974. 354pp. Not a chronological summary, the book looks thematically at Ben-Gurion's rise to power, his impact on defense, foreign policy, and Arab relationships. Clearly an enthusiastic admirer, Avi-Hai shapes his portrait through a sometimes too narrow theory of leadership analysis contrasting Ben-Gurion's ideals and pragmatic political actions.

Edelman, Maurice. *David: The Story of Ben-Gurion.* New York: Putnam, 1965. 214pp. A brief but vivid biography, Edelman's account lacks the dimensions of a full-scale portrait and is superficial in its treatment of the complexity of the political scene.

Litvinoff, Barnett. *Ben-Gurion of Israel.* New York: Praeger, 1955. 273pp. In the first close to full-scale treatment, the author chronicles Ben-Gurion's early life in the Russian pale, his struggles as a laborer in Palestine, and the complexity of Zionist politics over a 20-year period that finally led to the fulfillment of Ben-Gurion's dream of an independent Israel. This is a competent and informative summary of Ben-Gurion up to 1948 and his early years as prime minister.

Saint John, Robert. *Ben-Gurion: A Biography.* Garden City, New York: Doubleday, 1971. 360pp. Written by a journalist who interviewed Ben-Gurion several times, this is a lively, often revealing character study, first published in 1959 as *Ben-Gurion: The Biography of an Extraordinary Man,* and expanded to cover the last years of Ben-Gurion's life.

Fictional Portraits

Wouk, Herman. *The Hope.* Boston: Little, Brown, 1993. 693pp. A panoramic novel of the history of modern Israel covers the period from the War of Independence to the Six-Day War. A fictional story concerning four Israeli army officers connects with a number of historical personages, including David Ben-Gurion.

Recommended Juvenile Biographies

Saint John, Robert. *Ben-Gurion: Builder of Israel.* Garden City: Doubleday, 1961. YA. 185pp. Reworking his 1959 adult biography for younger readers, the author maintains his vivid and informative style that helpfully puts Ben-Gurion's achievements in a proper historical and cultural context.

Silverstein, John J. *David Ben-Gurion.* New York: F. Watts, 1988. 128pp. MG/YA. An entry in the well-regarded Impact Biographies series, this detailed biography traces the career of a zealous but compassionate leader, a visionary with unmatched practical skills for political organization. Very much a heroic portrait, the book does provide a helpful explanation of the tangled political situation that Ben-Gurion mostly dominated.

Vail, John J. *David Ben-Gurion.* New York: Chelsea House, 1987. 112pp. MG/YA. Part of the World Leaders Past & Present series, this is an informative summary of Ben-Gurion's life and career that clarifies the often confusing political struggle he faced.

Biographical Films and Theatrical Adaptations

Ben-Gurion (1978). Director: Terence Smith. Narrated by Henry Fonda, this film portrait describes Ben-Gurion's role in the creation of Israel. Video.

Ben-Gurion (1996). Producer: Films for the Humanities. A brief though informative documentary portrait. Video.

Hanna's War (1988). Director: Menchem Golan. Based on the true story of Hungarian freedom fighter Hanna Senesh who volunteered for a suicide mission behind German lines in World War II, the film also offers a rare glimpse of Ben-Gurion (Shimon Finkel) prior to 1948. Video.

The House on Garibaldi Street (1979). Director: Peter Collinson. In this television dramatization of the capture of Eichman, Ben-Gurion is portrayed by English actor Leo McKern. Video.

A Woman Called Golda (1982). Director: Alan Gibbon. Chronicling the life and career of Golda Meir, this television drama depicts Ben-Gurion in his youth and maturity, played by actors David De Keyser and Barry Foster. Video.

33. HECTOR BERLIOZ
1803–1869

A French Romantic composer of dramatic and descriptive works whose ideas of orchestration influenced many later composers, Berlioz studied at the Paris Conservatory and later was librarian there. In 1830 his *Symphonie fantastique* was performed in Paris and he received the prestigious Prix de Rome. Berlioz's works include the choral symphony *Romeo and Juliet*, the concert opera *The Damnation of Faust*, the nonliturgical oratorio *The Childhood of Christ*, and a requiem.

Autobiography and Primary Sources

The Memoirs of Hector Berlioz. David Cairns, ed. New York: W.W. Norton, 1975. 636pp. Begun in 1848, Berlioz fashioned his memoirs from letters, essays, and sections from earlier autobiographical fragments, tied together with additional commentary. Completed in 1856 and published after the conductor's death, the *Memoirs* is regarded as a literary and musical classic.

Selected Letters of Berlioz. Hugh Macdonald, ed. New York: W.W. Norton, 1997. 479pp. In a representative sampling of 481 of the composer's more than 4,000 surviving letters, this collection covers the whole of Berlioz's life, touching on both personal and professional matters with such correspondents as Wagner, Liszt, Goethe, Balzac, Flaubert, Napoleon III, and Queen Victoria. Berlioz's literary skill is as impressive as his musical talent.

Recommended Biographies

Barzun, Jacques. *Berlioz and the Romantic Century.* Boston: Little, Brown, 1950. 2 vols. Reissued as *Berlioz and His Century: An Introduction to the Age of Romanticism.* Cleveland: World, 1956. 448pp. Barzun's massive effort to document the life of the composer retains its importance as a reference source and provocative critical assessment. As much about the era as the man and his work, Barzun's study is a monumental appreciation. In the words of one reviewer, "One feels that all the composer ever said and did, and everything that has been said and done about him, has found its way into this work."

Bloom, Peter. *The Life of Berlioz.* New York: Cambridge University Press, 1998. 211pp. Part of the Musical Lives series, this is a succinct biographical portrait that places Berlioz firmly in his intellectual, artistic, and political context, while offering an astute analysis of the composer's musical development. Serves as an excellent accessible overview for the student and the general reader.

Cairns, David. *Berlioz.* Berkeley: University of California Press, 1989-2000. 2 vols. Cairns's two-volume study is a highly detailed and balanced narrative account of Berlioz's life that incorporates new documentary sources and modern research. Cairns creates a highly readable, convincing portrait, the first choice for the reader looking for an integrated study of both the man and his music.

Holoman, D. Kern. *Berlioz.* Cambridge, Massachusetts: Harvard University Press, 1989. 687pp. In a beautifully illustrated biography, Holoman chronicles Berlioz's personal and family life, his intellectual and artistic development, as well as an analysis of his compositions and his work as a conductor and critic.

Other Biographical Studies

Clarson-Leach, Robert. *Berlioz: His Life and Times.* New York: Hippocrene, 1983. 124pp. This is an illustrated introduction to Berlioz's life, work, and era that serves as a useful overview for the general reader.

Crabbe, John. *Hector Berlioz: Rational Romantic.* New York: Taplinger, 1980. 143pp. Billed by its author as "a first venture into a new sort of biography," Crabbe's study dispenses with a conventional chronological arrangement to examine the composer's ideas, beliefs, and feelings to uncover the source of his creative genius. Berlioz's life and work is also related to the social, political, religious, literary, and philosophical influences, forming an interior, developmental biography of the mind. Readers are assumed to have a basic familiarity with the facts of the composer's life.

Elliot, John H. *Berlioz.* New York: Dutton, 1938. 243pp. After an initial chapter outlining the historical background of Berlioz's life, the book offers a straightforward, chronological account of the composer's life and work, followed by a critical assessment.

MacDonald, Hugh. *Berlioz.* London: Dent, 1982. 261pp. Part of the Master Musician series, MacDonald's study combines an impressively compressed life of the composer with an extensive analysis of his work.

Turner, W.J. *Berlioz: The Man and His Work.* 1934. Reprint ed. New York: Vienna House, 1974. 374pp. The first full-length study in English, Turner's account is now dated and superseded by subsequent scholarship on both Berlioz's life and work.

Wotton, Tom S. *Hector Berlioz.* London: Oxford University Press, 1935. 224pp. Although not informed by the source material subsequently uncovered, Wotton's is a sensible early critical study by a recognized expert on the composer. Wotton's views on Berlioz's achievement and development are convincing, but the book does assume the reader's familiarity with the composer's life and work.

Biographical Novels

Kenyon, Frank W. *Passionate Rebel: The Story of Hector Berlioz.* New York: Dodd, Mead, 1972. 255pp. Kenyon observes the basic factual framework with some surmises and imagined scenes and dialogue to chronicle Berlioz's life.

Fictional Portraits

Hersey, John. *Antonietta*. New York: Knopf, 1991. 304pp. Hersey's inventive 300-year "biography" of a Stradivarius violin comes into the possession of Berlioz.

Rousselot, Jean. *Hungarian Rhapsody: The Life of Franz Liszt*. New York: Putnam, 1961. 248pp. This fictional biography shows Liszt's association with a number of leading musical figures, including Berlioz.

Biographical Films and Theatrical Adaptations

Berlioz (1984). Director: Herbert Chappell. This film portrait discusses the events of the composer's life and his influence. His *Symphonie fantastique* is performed by the London Symphony. Video.

Lisztomania (1975). Director: Ken Russell. Russell's extravaganza on the life of Franz Liszt (Roger Daltry) includes an appearance by Berlioz (Murray Melvin). Video.

34. SARAH BERNHARDT
1844–1923

French actress, born Rosine Bernard, Sarah Bernhardt can legitimately be considered the first theatrical superstar, the most famous actress of her era. With the Comédie Française from 1872 to 1880 she was acclaimed for her portrayal of Phèdre and Doña Sol in Hugo's *Hernani*. In 1880 she began tours of Europe and the United States and managed several theaters. She appeared in silent films and continued to perform, despite illness and an amputated limb, until her death.

Autobiography and Primary Sources

Bernhardt's own autobiographical accounts of her life and acting career provide fascinating, though often unreliable, insights, and readers should approach them with caution, more as a gauge of her attitudes than as a factual record.

Memories of My Life. New York: Appleton, 1907. 456pp. Although not trustworthy in all its details, Bernhardt's whimsical and rhapsodical reflections are rich in minor details and provide insights into an eccentric and versatile woman.

The Art of the Theatre. 1924. Reprint ed. New York: B. Blom, 1969. 224pp. Dictated during her last months, the volume is a lively, chatty blend of anecdotes and reminiscences that is interesting for its reflection of Bernhardt's views and personality.

The Memoirs of Sarah Bernhardt. Sandy Lesberg, ed. New York: Peeples Press, 1977. 256pp. Although these recollections go no further than 1888 and omit a great deal, Bernhardt does provide insights on her childhood and reveals her dedication, eccentricities, vanities, and insecurities. Includes her novella, *In the Clouds*, an account of her balloon ascent in 1877.

My Double Life: The Memoirs of Sarah Bernhardt. Victoria Larson, ed. Albany: State University Press of New York, 1999. 345pp. This is a modern translation and abridgement of Bernhardt's volumes of recollections that includes helpful background notes by the editor.

Recommended Biographies

Gold, Arthur, and Robert Fizdale. *The Divine Sarah: A Life of Sarah Bernhardt*. New York: Knopf, 1991. 353pp. Using never-before published letters, including private correspondence with Bernhardt's lovers, friends, and her son, this is a comprehensive and lively portrait of the legendary actress that authoritatively balances sympathy and candor.

Richardson, Joanna. *Sarah Bernhardt and Her World*. New York: Putnam, 1977. 232pp. Richardson's study is the first serious study of the actress by an objective writer who tries to penetrate the various legends that have obscured a true examination. The Bernhardt that emerges is multifaceted and complex.

Other Biographical Studies

Baring, Maurice. *Sarah Bernhardt*. 1934. Reprint ed. Westport, Connecticut: Greenwood, 1970. 162pp. The most famous of the early biographies of Bernhardt, Baring avoids the actress' failures but offers firsthand appreciation of her performances and details of his acquaintance with Bernhardt.

Emboden, William. *Sarah Bernhardt*. New York: Macmillan, 1975. 176pp. Emboden's illustrated life features the largest collection of photographs of the actress. The author's judgment at various points is questionable and features a revisionist view of Bernhardt's later acting career.

Row, Arthur. *Sarah the Divine*. New York: Comet Press, 1957. 169pp. Written by a onetime actor with and former press agent for Bernhardt, Row's short life provides a number of insightful sketches but does not reach a full and comprehensive portrait that transcends the biographer's adoration.

Skinner, Cornelia Otis. *Madame Sarah*. Boston: Houghton Mifflin, 1975. 356pp. This lively and balanced life benefits from being written by a gifted actress whose special insights into the theater adds considerably to an appreciation of Bernhardt's career and achievement.

Taranow, Gerda. *Sarah Bernhardt: The Art Within the Legend*. Princeton, New Jersey: Princeton University Press, 1972. 287pp. Less a biographical study than an exhaustive analysis of Bernhardt's acting skills, the book examines each of the actress's histrionic elements (voice, pantomime, gesture, and spectacle) and shows how she adapted past practices to her strengths and weaknesses. The author assumes a great deal of familiarity with the dates and details of Bernhardt's career.

Verneuil, Louis. *The Fabulous Life of Sarah Bernhardt*. 1942. Reprint ed. Westport, Connecticut: Greenwood, 1972. 312pp. Written by the husband of Bernhardt's granddaughter, who wrote the last two original plays the actress performed and was her daily companion in her final years, this intimate look at Bernhardt is adoring but frank in its details of her everyday dealings at the end of her life.

Biographical Novels

Sagan, Françoise. *Dear Sarah Bernhardt*. New York: Seaver Books, 1988. 232pp. Sagan casts her biographical study in the form of an imaginary correspondence between herself and the actress, providing Bernhardt with an intimate, first-person voice as she reflects on her career, lovers, motherhood, money, and fame. Though often inexact in its facts, the book succeeds in capturing Bernhardt's wit, spirit, and a version of her essence.

Gross, Joel. *Sarah*. New York: Morrow, 1987. 340pp. This fictional chronicle of Sarah Bernhardt's life and career attempts with some success to penetrate the legend to reach a more human portrait of the actress.

Fictional Portraits

Douglas, Carole Nelson. *Good Morning, Irene*. New York: Tor, 1991. 374pp. and *Irene at Large*. New York: Tor, 1992. 381pp. Douglas's mystery series features Irene Adler, opera singer and amateur sleuth, whose path crosses those of such historical figures as Bernhardt, Oscar Wilde, and Bram Stoker. The scenes of Paris during the era are well developed and convincing.

Lovesey, Peter. *Bertie and the Crime of Passion*. New York: Mysterious Press, 1995. 244pp. In the author's amusing series of historical mysteries featuring Edward, Prince of Wales, as sleuth, Bertie is in Paris investigating a murder at the Moulin Rouge with Sarah Bernhardt as his assistant and Toulouse-Lautrec as the crime scene sketch artist. Lovesey's exuberate fancy is anchored by authentic period details.

Soares, Jo. *A Samba for Sherlock*. New York: Pantheon, 1997. 271pp. Bernhardt, on tour in Brazil, invites Sherlock Holmes to investigate the disappearance of a Stradivarius violin in this period mystery.

Stubbs, Jean. *Eleanora Duse*. New York: Stein and Day, 1970. 320pp. In this documentary novel chronicling the career of Bernhardt's rival for acting preeminence, Eleanora Duse, Bernhardt is glimpsed. The author has invented events and conversations.

Recommended Juvenile Biographies

Hope, Charlotte. *The Young Sarah Bernhardt*. New York: Roy, 1966. 143pp. MG. This somewhat old-fashioned fictionalized narrative of Bernhard's childhood up to her first stage performance in 1862 offers a brief chronology of her later career in an epilogue. More inspiring than reliable.

Noble, Iris. *Great Lady of the Theatre: Sarah Bernhardt*. New York: J. Messner, 1960. 192pp. YA. This full and comprehensive appreciatory biography penetrates the legends to capture both the actress' struggles and triumphs. Partly fictionalized, the book's sources are woven into a dramatic and vivid narrative.

Biographical Films and Theatrical Adaptations

The Incredible Sarah (1976). Director: Richard Fleischer. Glenda Jackson stars as Bernhardt who is more flamboyant than convincing in this dramatically vivid but psychologically thin presentation. A novelization of the filmscript is available with the same title by Alan Arnold (New York: New American Library, 1976. 186pp.). Video.

35. LEONARD BERNSTEIN
1918–1990

An American composer, conductor, and pianist, Bernstein was one of the twentieth-century's most versatile musical figures. He was soloist and conductor with many orchestras in the United States and abroad, and was musical director (1958–1970) of the New York Philharmonic Symphony Orchestra. His works include the symphonies *The Age of Anxiety* (1949) and *Kaddish* (1963), the ballet *Fancy Free* (1944), and the musicals *On the Town* (1944), *Candide* (1956), and *West Side Story* (1957). His multiperformer theater piece *Mass* (1971) was performed at the opening of the Kennedy Center in Washington, DC.

Recommended Biographies

Burton, Humphrey. *Leonard Bernstein.* New York: Doubleday, 1994. 594pp. Granted exclusive access to the Bernstein archives as well as full cooperation from the Bernstein family, Burton's is the most comprehensive and authoritative chronicle of Bernstein's activities available. Although Burton does not gloss over Bernstein's failures and flaws, a very strong defensiveness is evident in Burton's treatments.

Peyser, Joan. *Bernstein: A Biography.* 1987. Revised ed. New York: Billboard Books, 1998. 510pp. Peyser's is a detailed analysis of Bernstein's psychological development that balances an appreciation of his considerable musical achievement with an exploration of his contradictions, personal conflicts, and character flaws. Based on extensive interviews with Bernstein associates, the book is rich in anecdotes that serve to present a complex portrait of a divided man.

Other Biographical Studies

Gradenwitz, Peter. *Leonard Bernstein: The Infinite Variety of a Musician.* New York: Saint Martin's, 1987. 310pp. Gradenwitz's thoroughly researched and well-illustrated study includes a biographical profile followed by a discussion of Bernstein's music by category. Includes a chronology, filmography, and discography. A friend of the composer, Gradenwitz rarely manages much objective criticism, and the book rarely penetrates Bernstein's reputation for a clear view of man and his personality.

Myers, Paul. *Leonard Bernstein.* London: Phaidon, 1998. 240pp. Myers's is a solid, readable biography and a useful introduction that details both Bernstein's achievements and failures, dealing honestly but not sensationally with his excesses, affairs, and tantrums.

Robinson, Paul. *Bernstein.* New York: Vanguard, 1982. 152pp. Useful as an introduction for the nonspecialist, Robinson offers a sketchy biographical profile followed by an assessment of Bernstein's career as a conductor.

Secrest, Meryle. *Leonard Bernstein: A Life.* New York: Knopf, 1994. 471pp. Denied cooperation by many Bernstein family and friends and access to his archives, Secrest was further limited by her own self-confessed inadequacy as a musical historian. The result is an uneven mix of gossip, insights, and trivial details struggling for coherence.

Biographical Films and Theatrical Adaptations

Leonard Bernstein: The Loves of Three Orchestras (1996). Producer: Humphrey Burton. This documentary investigates Bernstein's relationship to the New York Philharmonic, the Vienna Philharmonic, and the Israel Philharmonic, with performances spanning four decades. Video.

Leonard Bernstein: Reaching for the Note (1998). Producer: Susan Lacy. A film portrait featuring interviews with Bernstein's brother, children, collaborators, and fellow conductors. Video.

Teachers and Teaching: An Autobiographical Essay (1988). Producers: H. H. Hottlfeld and Harry J. Kraut. Bernstein recounts stories about key figures in his own musical education. Video.

Other Sources

Burton, William W., ed. *Conversations with Bernstein.* New York: Oxford University Press, 1995. 198pp. This volume collects the reminiscences of a wide assortment of friends, associates, and colleagues of the conductor for a multidimensional personal and professional portrait.

36. BILLY THE KID
1859–1881

American Western outlaw Billy the Kid was born in New York and lived in Kansas and New Mexico as a child. He became notorious in the Southwest as a gunslinger and cattle rustler, and in 1878 led a gang in the Johnson County cattle war. After killing two deputies he was captured and sentenced to hang. He escaped but was trapped and shot to death by Sheriff Pat Garrett. He was known as William H. Bonney, although his real name was probably Henry McCarty.

Recommended Biographies

Cline, Donald. *Alias Billy the Kid: The Man Behind the Legend.* Sante Fe, New Mexico: Sunstone Press, 1986. 145pp. For the reader who is looking for a clear-eyed, realistic assessment aided by solid scholarship, Cline's is a good choice. Little of the legend remains after Cline's puncturing. Billy the Kid is depicted as a rather ordinary outlaw whose character and "accomplishments" do not support his legend.

Tuska, Jon. *Billy the Kid: A Bio-Bibliography.* 1983. Revised as *Billy the Kid: His Life and Legend.* Albuquerque: University of New Mexico Press, 1997. 295pp. Tuska, a respected Western historian, supplies a factual biographical portrait based on modern scholarly findings before surveying the Kid's presentation in history, fiction, and film. The book has been called by one reviewer a "magnificent tour de force and a model for others who would study legendary heroes of the American West."

Utley, Robert M. *Billy the Kid: A Short and Violent Life.* Lincoln: University of Nebraska Press, 1989. 302pp. Impeccably researched using contemporaries' accounts, Utley presents a realistic portrait of Billy the Kid's character, career, and times, as well as the sources for the legends surrounding this charismatic outlaw. In Utley's view, Billy the Kid is a complex, cultural figure, shaped by the violence of the American frontier experience.

Other Biographical Studies

Adams, Ramon F. *A Fitting Death for Billy the Kid.* Norman: University of Oklahoma Press, 1960. 310pp. A narrative account that reviews the various sources of fact and fiction surrounding the Kid's life and career, Adams's is a reliable, lively, and scholarly biobibliographical study of the creation and development of the legend. Too exhaustive and convoluted in its minutiae for most general readers, the book is intended primarily for the specialist and Billy the Kid enthusiast.

Burns, Walter N. *The Saga of Billy the Kid.* 1926. Reprint ed. Albuquerque: University of New Mexico Press, 1999. 336pp. Along with Garrett's account, Burns's dramatic biography, mixing interviews with eyewitnesses and fabrications, is an important source in creating the Billy the Kid legend. Here the Kid takes on his more attractive trappings to support the view of him as a kind of Robin Hood of the Wild West figure. This edition includes a forward by Richard W. Etulain on the importance of Burns's book in the literature on Billy the Kid and the Lincoln County War.

Garrett, Pat F. *The Authentic Life of Billy the Kid, the Noted Desperado of the Southwest.* 1882. Reprint ed. Norman: University of Oklahoma Press, 1988. 156pp. Although factually unreliable and misleading, no other book has proven so important in shaping the Kid's posthumous career as a Western legend. Written by New Mexico journalist Ash Upson as narrated by Garrett, many of the leading elements of the myth are established, including the errors of naming him William H. Bonney and arming him at the time of his death.

Hunt, Frazier. *The Tragic Days of Billy the Kid.* New York: Hastings House, 1956. 316pp. As the title indicates, Hunt offers a more sympathetic view of Billy as a misunderstood, tragic victim of scheming politicians. More a refinement of the Billy the Kid legend than a reliable biography, the book nevertheless helps explain the persistence of the heroic myth of the Kid.

Jacobsen, Joel. *Such Men as Billy the Kid: The Lincoln County War Reconsidered.* Lincoln: University of Nebraska Press, 1994. 300pp. This factual, historical examination of the Lincoln County War serves to put Billy the Kid in a much wider context as a peripheral figure in an important event in Western history. Jacobsen makes a strong case that the central figures in the Lincoln County conflict are far more significant and interesting.

Nolan, Frederick W. *The West of Billy the Kid*. Norman: University of Oklahoma Press, 1998. 350pp. Nolan's illustrated biography does a fine job in placing Billy in his time and place. Context predominates here, but the reader looking for the authentic figure behind the legend should consult this volume.

Otero, Miguel A. *The Real Billy the Kid with New Light on the Lincoln County War*. New York: Rufus Rockwell Wilson, 1936. 200pp. The author, a former governor of New Mexico, has a solid and intimate regional knowledge to recommend this reinterpretation that exposes many of the inaccuracies in the Garrett account. However, a bias against Garrett produces an equal number of errors and misleading interpretations.

Tatum, Stephen. *Inventing Billy the Kid: Visions of the Outlaw in America, 1881–1891*. Albuquerque: University of New Mexico Press, 1982. 242pp. Although supplying a brief biographical summary that incorporates details that are controversial, the book is more a social-historical exploration of the creation of the Billy the Kid legend and its cultural significance.

Biographical Novels

Corle, Edwin. *Billy the Kid*. New York: Duell, Sloan and Pearce, 1953. 293pp. For the most part faithful to the known facts, the novel does invent some incidents, such as Billy's meeting with New Mexico governor Lew Wallace.

Everitt, David. *The Story of Pat Garrett and Billy the Kid*. New York: Knightsbridge, 1990. 389pp. Billy's career is seen from the perspective of lawman Pat Garrett who succeeds in bringing him down.

Fackler, Elizabeth. *Billy the Kid*. New York: Forge, 1995. 512pp. Billy is depicted as a scapegoat and a freedom fighter against corruption and big business in this biographical novel interweaving fact and legend.

Fictional Portraits

Bean, Amelia. *Time for Outrage*. New York: Doubleday, 1967. 287pp. The main narrative events are based on fact in this representation of Billy's career in 1878.

Lewis, Preston. *The Demise of Billy the Kid*. New York: Bantam Books,1995. 356pp. A fictional story is woven around the events of the Lincoln County War and Billy's battle with the Murphy-Dolan gang.

McMurtry, Larry. *Anything for Billy*. New York: Simon & Schuster, 1988. 382pp. The legend of Billy the Kid is submitted to a radical revisioning in which the outlaw is shown as a combination of holy fool and modern serial killer.

Momaday, N. Scott. *The Ancient Child*. New York: Doubleday, 1989. 313pp. The ghost of Billy the Kid converses with an American Indian woman in this meditation on the legacy of the western frontier experience.

Nye, Nelson Coral. *Pistols for Hire*. New York: Macmillan, 1941. 196pp. Billy is depicted as a killer rather than a hero in this authentic depiction of the Lincoln County War.

Ondaatje, Michael. *The Collected Works of Billy the Kid*. New York: W.W. Norton, 1984. 105pp. Billy's life and times are reconstructed in a mixture of period photos, illustration, poetry, and prose.

Savage, Douglas. *The Sons of Grady Rourke*. New York: Evans, 1967. 277pp. The framework for this western story is based on actual events, showing the Rourke brothers in the middle of the Lincoln County War and Billy's growing reputation.

Recommended Juvenile Biographies

Green, Carl R., and William R. Sanford. *Billy the Kid*. Hillside, New Jersey: Enslow, 1992. 48pp. MG. This is a factual, informative account of Billy's life, illustrated with photographs of the people and places associated with the outlaw.

Hamilton, John. *Billy the Kid*. Minneapolis: ABDO, 1996. 32pp. MG. Hamilton combines both the facts and the legends to form a life story of Billy that emphasizes his role in the Lincoln County War and his death.

Biographical Films and Theatrical Adaptations

Billy the Kid (1930). Director: King Vidor. John Mack Brown plays the title character in this realistic early western, featuring Wallace Beery as the pursuing marshal.

Billy the Kid (1941). Director: David Miller. Robert Taylor portrays Billy the Kid in this fictional version of his story, suggested by Walter Noble Burns's *The Saga of Billy the Kid*. With Brian Donlevy, Ian Hunter, and Mary Howard. Video.

Billy the Kid (1992). Director: Marino Amoruso. Part of the Legends of the American West series, this is a film profile using archival material. Video.

Billy the Kid (1998). Director: Kevin McCarey. An installment of the Gunfighters of the West series, the Kid's short, murderous life is profiled. Video.

The Left-Handed Gun (1958). Director: Arthur Penn. Based on a teleplay by Gore Vidal, this is an interesting take on the Billy the Kid legend as a maladjusted juvenile delinquent. Starring Paul Newman as the outlaw in a part originally intended for James Dean. Video.

The Outlaw (1943). Director: Howard Hughes. Hughes's famous star vehicle for Jane Russell offers a variation on Billy the Kid's story with an emphasis on his romantic relationship. With Jack Buetel as Billy and co-starring Walter Huston and Thomas Mitchell. Video.

Pat Garrett & Billy the Kid (1973). Director: Sam Peckinpah. James Coburn is Garrett and Kris Kristofferson portrays the Kid, with a soundtrack and appearance by Bob Dylan. Video.

37. OTTO VON BISMARCK
1815–1898

First chancellor of the German Empire, Bismarck is one of the towering figures of the nineteenth century. An advocate of German unification, Bismarck served as Prussian minister to the German diet at Frankfurt and as ambassador to Saint Petersburg and Paris. In 1862 he was appointed premier and helped expel Austria from the German Confederation and forge German unity under Prussian control. Under his system of alliances, Bismarck became Europe's leading statesman and powerbroker. The Bismarckian era ended in 1890 in a power struggle with Wilhelm II.

Autobiography and Primary Sources

Bismarck's autobiographical reflections, *Bismarck: The Man and Statesman* (1898), reprinted as *The Memoirs* (New York: H. Fertig, 1966. 2 vols.) and *Reflections and Reminiscences* (Theodore S. Hamgorov, ed. New York: Harper & Row, 1968. 274pp.), are very much the efforts of a defeated giant obsessed by his feud with Kaiser Wilhelm, justifying his legacy and should be read for the Iron Chancellor's voice and attitude rather than as revealing, trustworthy accounts.

Recommended Biographies

Crankshaw, Edward. *Bismarck*. New York: Viking, 1981. 451pp. In the author's psychological portrait, Bismarck emerges as a complex, brilliant, yet severely limited, rigid, and implacable man, who ruled by expedience and was almost wholly without scruples. Provocative in its interpretations and illuminating on the complex events leading up to the birth of the German nation, the book is a valuable, one-volume study.

Gall, Lothar. *Bismarck: The White Revolutionary*. Boston: Allen and Unwin, 1986. 2 vols. Comprehensive and insightful, Gall's monumental study concentrates on Bismarck's character and temperament. This authoritative book should prove to be the foundation text for all subsequent studies of Bismarck.

Other Biographical Studies

Eyck, Erich. *Bismarck and the German Empire*. Boston: Allen and Unwin, 1950. 327pp. Condensing a three-volume study into a single-volume political biography, Eyck presents Bismarck as a giant of statecraft with superior intellectual gifts who used every trick of deceit and disloyalty to further his aims. The book ignores Bismarck's final eight years after he left office. Eyck's liberalism provides an interesting challenge to the dominant German view of Bismarck's legacy, particularly in light of the Nazi debacle.

Kent, George O. *Bismarck and His Times*. Carbondale: Southern Illinois University Press, 1978. 184pp. Kent's study is best as an introduction to the period 1848 to 1890. Constricted by length, the highlights of Bismarck's career are glimpsed but with insufficient detail or much interpretation.

Medlicott, W.N. *Bismarck and Modern Germany*. New York: Harper, 1965. 200pp. Covering Bismarck's career from the 1860s until his death, this concise summary of Bismarck's role in the early German nation is an ideal introduction to the subject.

Palmer, Alan. *Bismarck.* New York: Scribner, 1976. 326pp. Aimed at a popular audience, Palmer's biography concentrates on Bismarck the man and statesman rather than the setting in which he operated, and by oversimplifying the nature of the problems Bismarck faced, the author obscures the nature of his accomplishments.

Pflanze, Otto. *Bismarck and the Development of Germany.* Princeton, New Jersey: Princeton University Press, 1963–1990. 3 vols. The author's massive, authoritative scholarly study is revealing both on Bismarck and his age and the complex relationship between the two.

Richter, Werner. *Bismarck.* New York: Putnam, 1965. 420pp. Richter's psychological study reinterprets most of the cherished legends about Bismarck, offering a darker side of his character in an analysis that concentrates on his political career.

Snyder, Louis L. *Blood and Iron Chancellor.* Princeton, New Jersey: Van Nostrand, 1967. 423pp. This is a documentary biography covering every aspect of Bismarck's life and career stringing together letters, articles, reports, news stories, and secondary sources. Readers must sort through a mass of material and draw their own conclusions.

Taylor, A.J.P. *Bismarck: The Man and the Statesman.* New York: Knopf, 1955. 286pp. Livened by an epigrammatic prose style and provocative judgments, Taylor's treatment focuses on the chancellor's rise to power in the 1860s and his removal from office in 1890, with a great deal of anecdotal information about Bismarck the man that helps humanize him. Many of Taylor's judgments about Bismarck's diplomacy are arguable, however.

Waller, Bruce. *Bismarck.* New York: Blackwell, 1985. 132pp. Waller's concise yet authoritative political biography provides a compact overview of Bismarck's personality, his achievement, and legacy, offering a fine introduction to the man and his period for the general reader.

Fictional Portraits

Collins, Norman. *The Quiet Lady.* New York: Harper, 1942. 432pp. The story of a fictional young woman's adventures during the Franco-Prussian War is interspersed with monologues from Napoleon III and Bismarck.

Fraser, George MacDonald. *Royal Flash.* New York: Knopf, 1970. 257pp. In this installment of Fraser's amusing series featuring bounder Harry Flashman, a young Bismarck at the beginning of his career is employed in a historical caper involving intrigue over German unification. Fraser's annotations balance Flashman's tendency to exaggerate and falsify history.

Rascovich, Mark. *Falkenhorst.* New York: Holt, 1974. 435pp. The novel provides the German perspective on the Franco-Prussian War in a fictional story that is framed by actual events and historical personages, such as Bismarck.

Recommended Juvenile Biographies

Rose, Jonathan. *Otto von Bismarck.* New York: Chelsea House, 1987. 112pp. MG. Part of the World Leaders Past & Present series, this is a solid biographical portrait that captures the high points of Bismarck's life and his era, sorting through the confusions of European alliances with skill.

Biographical Films and Theatrical Adaptations

Royal Flash (1975). Director: Richard Lester. This adaptation of Fraser's Flashman novel features the author's own screenplay and Oliver Reed in the role of Bismarck. History is turned into fast-paced farce and adventure with a refreshing debunking attitude toward heroic greatness. Bismarck has never been shown so sinister or as preposterous. Video.

Other Sources

Hollyday, Frederic B.M., ed. *Bismarck.* Englewood Cliffs, New Jersey: Prentice-Hall, 1970. 180pp. Part of the Great Lives Observed series, this collection of essays combines autobiographical material, eyewitness accounts, and modern scholarly evaluation to examine Bismarck from a variety of angles, placing his achievement and personality in a number of useful contexts.

38. WILLIAM BLAKE
1757–1827

English poet and artist, William Blake is one of the dominating figures in English Romanticism. Apprenticed as an engraver, Blake attended the Royal Academy but rebelled against its restrictions. Living almost his entire life in London, Blake engraved and published most of his works himself, combining text and illustrations. Blake was neither a commercial nor critical success until after his death; his works include *Songs of Innocence* (1789), *Songs of Experience* (1794), and the prophetic books, such as *The Marriage of Heaven and Hell* (1790), *Milton* (1804–1820), and *Jerusalem* (1804–1808).

Autobiography and Primary Sources

The Letters of William Blake. Geoffrey Keynes, ed. New York: Oxford University Press, 1957. 261pp. This scholarly collection of Blake's surviving letters is an indispensable source for the biographer in detailing the conditions of his life and his personality.

Bentley, G.E. Jr. *Blake Records.* Oxford: Clarendon Press, 1969. 678pp.; *Blake Records Supplement.* Oxford: Clarendon Press, 1988. 152pp. Bentley has meticulously and exhaustively collected all the known contemporary references and documents concerning Blake and his family. Essential for the scholar.

Recommended Biographies

Ackroyd, Peter. *Blake.* New York: Knopf, 1996. 399pp. An innovative and illuminating reassessment of Blake's life and career, Ackroyd's biography solidly situates Blake in his world as a work-

ing-class Londoner attuned to radical religious and philosophical ideas of the era. Blake is shown as anxiety-ridden and self-destructive, and his poetry and art reflect consistent themes in his character. Ackroyd celebrates Blake's enigmatic personality while locating his genius in understandable human and cultural terms.

Wilson, Mona. *The Life of William Blake.* 1927. 3rd ed. New York: Oxford University Press, 1971. 415pp. Long considered the authoritative, full-length study, Wilson's biography features previously unpublished material and has established the predominant modern view of Blake. Sympathetic yet balanced, Wilson's view of the poet does not neglect the social context that helped to shape Blake.

Other Biographical Studies

Davis, Michael. *William Blake: A New Kind of Man.* Berkeley: University of California Press, 1977. 181pp. Davis' critical biography is a lucid and coherent assessment of Blake's accomplishments both in poetry and art. Handsomely illustrated, the book lacks documentation to identify sources but is satisfactory as an introduction to Blake and his career.

Gilchrist, Alexander. *Life of William Blake.* 1863. Reprint ed. New York: Dover, 1998. 2 vols. Gilchrist's first, full-length biography resurrected Blake from virtual obscurity. The author's extensive research, including interviews with Blake's contemporaries, has proven to be essential for subsequent biographers.

King, James. *William Blake: His Life.* New York: Saint Martin's, 1991. 263pp. In King's objective and balanced appraisal, Blake is shown as a selfless, dedicated Christian prophet with a touch of the demonic artist. Synthesizing recent scholarship, King is content to locate Blake in his cultural context, making little attempt to probe his psyche beyond offering an Oedipal diagnosis for Blake's traumas.

Lindsay, Jack. *William Blake: His Life and Work.* New York: G. Braziller, 1979. 334pp. Breaking no new ground, Lindsay is best in portraying Blake in his daily life as a journeyman, husband, and zealot. The author is often harsh and unsympathetic in his treatment of Blake, seen not as a visionary genius but as a very limited individual beset by a recurring loss of nerve.

Lister, Raymond. *William Blake: An Introduction to the Man and His Work.* New York: Frederick Unger, 1970. 200pp. Lister's introductory study attempts to place Blake's works against a background of his life and times through the use of letters and comments by Blake's contemporaries. The book is particularly good on Blake's work as a printer, engraver, and artist with a generous selection of reproductions.

Margoliouth, Herschel M. *William Blake.* New York: Oxford University Press, 1951. 184pp. In a compact biographical and critical study, Margoliouth summarizes the major factual details of Blake's life with separate chapters on his art, lyrical poems, nature of his rebellion, and visionary works.

Fictional Portraits

Sherwood, Frances. *Vindication*. New York: Farrar, Straus, 1993. 435pp. In this fictionalized biography of Mary Wollstonecraft, literary and artistic London is glimpsed, with a plausible appearance by William Blake.

Biographical Films and Theatrical Adaptations

Shepherd, Jack. *In Lambeth*. London: Methuen, 1990. 52pp. Thomas Paine visits visionary poet William Blake in this dramatic confrontation of two different revolutionaries: the pragmatic Paine and the idealistic Blake.

William Blake: A Concise Biography (1993). Director: Malcolm Hossick. Part of the Famous Authors series, this film presents concise factual outlines of the writers' life along with a portrait of the social and historical background. Video.

39. GIOVANNI BOCCACCIO
1313–1375

An Italian poet and storyteller, Boccaccio's early works include the poems *Filostrato* and *Teseide*. He is best known for his famous *Decameron* (1348–1353), 100 witty and sometimes licentious tales set during the Black Death. The *Decameron* marks the first expression of Italian Renaissance humanist realism. Boccaccio also wrote the *Commento*, based on a series of lectures he gave in Florence on Dante's *Inferno* (1371).

Recommended Biographies

Bergin, Thomas G. *Boccaccio*. New York: Viking, 1981. 392pp. Although greatly indebted to Branca for its details, Bergin's is a reliable, sophisticated introduction to the man and his work more accessible for the nonspecialist. After chapters on Boccaccio's age and culture, the book proceeds chronologically with a exploration of the works, tracing the development of Boccaccio's ideas and artistry.

Branca, Vittore. *Boccaccio: The Man and His Works*. New York: New York University Press, 1976. 341pp. Branca is the acknowledged leading authority on Boccaccio, and his learned and scholarly biography shows the author's intimacy with the era and authoritative handling of the various controversies surrounding the record of Boccaccio's life. This is the preferred study for the serious student.

Serafini-Sauli, Judith P. *Giovanni Boccaccio*. Boston: Twayne, 1982. 173pp. This is a fine critical biography in the Twayne series that covers succinctly the leading elements in Boccaccio's life as well as a lucid analysis of many of his works. Featuring a detailed chronology, the book serves as an ideal introductory overview and summary of modern critical interpretations and research.

Other Biographical Studies

Carswell, Catherine. *The Tranquil Heart: Portrait of Giovanni Boccaccio*. New York: Harcourt, Brace, 1937. 352pp. The first biography of Boccaccio written by a woman, Carswell narrates the story of the writer's life against a background of the politics and literature of the period. Claiming that male biographers and critics have ignored "something of Boccaccio's essence," Carswell attempts a more rounded, sensitive portrait.

Chubb, Thomas C. *The Life of Giovanni Boccaccio*. New York: A. and C. Boni, 1930. 286pp. Closer to historical fiction than to more conventional biography, Chubb's entertaining life indulges in reconstructed conversations and imaginative conjecture, supplying a vivid, though unreliable, informal portrait of Boccaccio and his age.

Hutton, Edward. *Giovanni Boccaccio: A Biographical Study*. New York: J. Lane, 1910. 426pp. Hutton's erudite and scholarly study relates Boccaccio to his era and covers much of his writing, not just the *Decameron*. This is a pioneering biographical-critical study that still has much to offer the less-than-casual reader.

MacManus, Francis. *Boccaccio*. New York: Sheed & Ward, 1947. 267pp. MacManus's popular introductory study is outdated, particularly in its style that reads like the work of an early nineteenth-century antiquarian. Readers with patience and forbearance will be informed about Boccaccio's life and work; others will stumble over such archaisms as "what boots it" and "harsh to usward."

Symonds, John Addington. *Giovanni Boccaccio as Man and Author*. 1895. Reprint ed. New York: AMS Press, 1968. 100pp. Symonds's appreciative study of the man, his art, and influence helped to exalt Boccaccio's reputation, and the book retains its interest as an insightful critical text.

Biographical Films and Theatrical Adaptations

Decameron Nights (1952). Director: Hugo Fregonese. Louis Jourdan portrays the writer and characters from his stories in this film that interweaves an imagined scene from his life with some of his tales. With Joan Fontaine, Binnie Barnes, and Joan Collins. Video.

40. ANNE BOLEYN
ca. 1507–1536

Second wife of Henry VIII and the mother of Elizabeth I, Anne Boleyn was introduced to the English court in 1522 where she became the object of the king's passion. Refusing to become his mistress, Boleyn caused Henry to divorce Catherine of Aragon and set in motion the English Protestant Reformation. She delivered Elizabeth in 1533. Three years later, after she miscarried a son, charged with adultery and incest, Anne was beheaded.

Recommended Biographies

Bruce, Marie Louise. *Anne Boleyn*. New York: Coward-McCann, 1972. 380pp. The author's balanced and accessible biography challenges interpretations of Boleyn as a passive victim but argues against her guilt of adultery and incest. Meticulously documented, Bruce's account is a refreshing treatment that is also convincing in its interpretation.

Ives, E.W. *Anne Boleyn*. New York: Blackwell, 1986. 451pp. Ives adds considerably to the sources collected by Friedmann to become the most authoritative and comprehensive biography of Boleyn yet written. The author does an exceptional job in portraying Boleyn against her Tudor background, and, like Bruce, Ives shows her as more responsible for her downfall than previous interpretations have held. For a reader interested in a highly detailed and ultimately convincing view of the court intrigue that sealed Boleyn's fate, Ives's impressive study is the best source available.

Other Biographical Studies

Chapman, Hester W. *Anne Boleyn*. New York: Coward-McCann, 1974. 244pp. Challenging previous depictions of Boleyn as a wanton or witch, Chapman offers a sympathetic account of a woman of courage, intelligence, and energy who triumphed in a court as venomous as it was brilliant.

Friedmann, Paul. *Anne Boleyn: A Chapter of English History 1527–36*. New York: Blackwell, 1884. 2 vols. Friedmann's groundbreaking biographical study provided the authoritative documentary source for subsequent biographers of Boleyn. In Friedmann's view, Henry is morally despicable, and Anne is comparatively blameless.

Erickson, Carolly. *Mistress Anne*. New York: Summit Books, 1984. 288pp. In the author's interpretation, Anne is seen as a victim of sexual scandals, and her story is bathed in an aura of romantic doom. With imagined dialogue and interpretation of Boleyn's thoughts, this biography could also be classified as historical fiction.

Lofts, Norah. *Anne Boleyn*. New York: Coward-McCann, 1979. 192pp. Written by a popular and respected historical novelist, this illustrated biography draws on letters, diaries, and contemporary accounts to survey Boleyn's life and fate. She is depicted as a willful and ambitious woman who managed to dominate for a time an equally willful king.

Warnicke, Retha M. *The Rise and Fall of Anne Boleyn: Family Politics at the Court of Henry VIII*. New York: Cambridge University Press, 1989. 326pp. The author's radical reinterpretation of the factors that led to Boleyn's execution offers a number of fresh perspectives on Boleyn's personality and drama, challenging previous biographical accounts. Critics have questioned several of Warnicke's assertions and charged her with tailoring her evidence to fit her thesis.

Vercors. *Anne Boleyn*. Woodstock, New York: Overlook Press, 1989. 289pp. In the author's interpretation, Boleyn is a noble, brave, and intelligent queen and a victim of palace intrigue. The book captures the drama of Boleyn's rise and fall with historical conviction supplemented by imaginative surmises.

Readers may also consult the following group biographical studies of the wives of Henry VIII:

Fraser, Antonia. *The Wives of Henry VIII*. New York: Knopf, 1992. 479pp. The author delineates the cultural, familial, and political contexts for each of Henry's queens. Despite a lingering bias in favor of Catherine of Aragon and dislike for the king, Fraser animates the public and private events with a telling use of historical details and anecdotes.

Lindsey, Karen. *Divorced, Beheaded, Survived: A Feminist Reinterpretation of the Wives of Henry VIII.* Reading, Massachusetts: Addison-Wesley, 1995. 231pp. By applying the insights of feminist scholarship, the author shows Henry's six wives not as stereotypical victims but as lively, intelligent women struggling to survive in a treacherous court. Boleyn is portrayed not as a seductress but as politically savvy and sexually harassed. This is a revisionist approach with a number of fresh, amusing, and debatable perceptions on sixteenth-century English politics and its leading figures.

Weir, Alison. *The Six Wives of Henry VIII.* New York: Grove Weidenfeld, 1992. 645pp. The author contributes a vivid and full-blooded portrait of Henry's six queens that is sound in its scholarship and convincing. Weir's meticulous research supports a number of fresh observations that provides insights into the various forces that drove Henry VIII and his wives to their respective fates.

Biographical Novels

Anthony, Evelyn. *Anne Boleyn.* New York: Crowell, 1957. 310pp. Detailing the courtship and marriage of Henry VIII and Boleyn from 1526 when they first met until her execution, the novel provides a subtle portrait of both figures that treats history with respect.

Barnes, Margaret C. *Briefly Gaudy Hour.* Philadelphia: Macrae Smith, 1949. 335pp. This fictional biography chronicles Boleyn's life from age 18 to her execution in a portrait of Anne as compelling human figure, sympathetic but mixed.

Barrington, E. *Anne Boleyn.* New York: Doubleday, 1932. 396pp. This fictional treatment portrays Anne as hard and calculating against a solid period background and with fidelity to historical fact as evidenced by the use of a number of primary sources selected and arranged into a coherent artistic pattern.

Beck, L. Adams. *Anne Boleyn.* New York: Doubleday, 1934. 396pp. The courtship between Boleyn and Henry is depicted in this novel blending period details and imagined dialogue and situations.

Hackett, Francis. *Queen Anne Boleyn.* New York: Doubleday, 1939. 477pp. In this biographical account of Anne Boleyn's life and times, her early history is largely invented and the author admits to having built upon the existing historical facts with sheer imagination and provocative period details.

Hardwick, Mollie. *Blood Royal.* New York: Saint Martin's, 1989. 320pp. The author widens the focus here to consider the interlocked fate of the Boleyn family in a convincing depiction of the court world during the early Tudor period.

Lofts, Norah. *The Concubine.* Garden City, New York: Doubleday, 1963. 310pp. Following Boleyn from her arrival at court as a 16-year-old lady-in-waiting to her execution, this is a historically reliable, though impressionistic account. Each chapter begins with an excerpt from a historical source that is then augmented fictionally.

Maxwell, Robin *The Secret Diary of Anne Boleyn.* New York: Arcade, 1997. 288pp. The recently crowned Elizabeth finds her doomed mother's diary and learns its painful message: "Never relinquish control to any man." Anne's voice is plausible, and the narrative stays close to historical fact.

Plaidy, Jean. *The King's Pleasure.* New York: Appleton, 1949. 302pp. The novel describes the relationship between Anne Boleyn and the king from their first meeting. Anne is shown as a successful mistress but a disastrous queen who never truly loved the king and was no match for the complex, dominating Henry VIII; *Murder Most Royal* (New York: Putnam, 1972. 542pp.) dramatizes the history of Henry's marriages to Anne and Catherine Howard; *The Lady in the Tower* (New York: Ballantine, 1988. 402pp.) is a convincing autobiographical treatment of Boleyn's career; *The King's Secret Matter* (New York: Putnam, 1995. 284pp.) concerns Henry's secret negotiations to have his marriage annulled when Catherine of Aragon fails to produce a male heir. The novel depicts the ensuing power struggle that culminates in England's break with Rome.

Wiat, Philippa. *The Heir of Allington.* London: R. Hale, 1973. 319pp. Dramatizing the rumored relationship between Sir Thomas Wyatt, courtier, poet, and diplomat, and Anne Boleyn, the novel reconstructs the court world of Tudor England. It is by no mean certain that Wyatt was in fact Anne Boleyn's lover as the story suggests.

Fictional Portraits

Ainsworth, William Harrison. *Windsor Castle.* 1843. Reprint ed. New York: Dutton, 1952. 307pp. The author's popular historical romance interweaves details of the reign of Henry VIII with Gothic elements with a spectral figure who serves as a kind of vague symbol of conscience as Anne Boleyn is executed. Historically inaccurate for the most part, the novel is still interesting in employing historical figures in the role of romance heroes and heroines.

Peters, Maureen. *Henry VIII and His Six Wives.* New York: Saint Martin's, 1971. 222pp. As Henry lies dying, he relives his past and reviews his marital history. Since the novel covers so much ground there is obvious compression of details and simplification, though the chronology is accurate.

York, Robert. *My Lord the Fox.* New York: Vanguard, 1986. 152pp. The novel explores two of history's most vexing mysteries: was Elizabeth really the daughter of Henry VIII and who killed Amy Robsart, the wife of Elizabeth's supposed lover? Anthony Woodcourt, secret agent for Sir William Cecil, the Queen's powerful secretary, investigates both cases with some startling, though plausible, discoveries.

Biographical Films and Theatrical Adaptations

Anderson, Maxwell. *Anne of the Thousand Days.* New York: Dramatists Play Service, 1950. 75pp. Anderson traces Anne's relationship with Henry from their first encounters to the days before her execution. Rendered with dramatic intensity and with poetic prose, the play captures the human complexity of both protagonists.

Anna Bolena (1999). Director: Lofti Mansouri. A film of a live performance of Donizetti's opera with Joan Sutherland as Anne Boleyn and James Morris as Henry. Video.

Anne of the Thousand Days (1969). Director: Charles Jarrott. The relationship between Henry VIII (Richard Burton) and Anne (Genevieve Bujold) is given a lavish, though historically inaccurate treatment, in this Hollywood spectacle.

Fenton, Edward. *Anne of the Thousand Days* (New York: New American Library, 1970. 160pp.) This is the novelization based on the earlier screenplay. Video.

The Private Life of Henry VIII (1933). Director: Alexander Korda. Lavish historical chronicle with a stellar performance by Charles Laughton as the king, the film features Merle Oberon as Anne Boleyn. Video.

Six Wives of Henry VIII (1971). Director: Naomi Capon and John Glenister. In this acclaimed English television mini-series with installments on each of Henry's wives, Dorothy Tutin portrays Anne Boleyn with Keith Michell as a definitive Henry.

See also Elizabeth I; Henry VIII; Thomas Wolsey

41. SIMÓN BOLÍVAR
1783–1830

South American revolutionary leader who liberated Venezuela, Colombia, Panama, Ecuador, Peru, and Bolivia from Spanish rule, Simón Bolívar was born in Venezuela into a wealthy Creole family. When the revolution against Spain broke out in 1810, Bolívar joined the rebel forces and entered Caracas in 1813, hailed as "the liberator." His victory at Boyacá in 1819 was one of the greatest campaigns in military history. Made president of the Greater Colombia (present-day Colombia, Venezuela, Ecuador, and Panama), Bolívar freed Peru and pursued his quest for a united Spanish America, despite opposition to his control and high-handed methods. He died poor and bitterly hated, only later recognized throughout South America as a hero of independence.

Autobiography and Primary Sources

Selected Writings of Bolívar. Harold A. Bierck Jr., ed. New York: Colonial Press, 1951. 2 vols. A compilation of Bolívar's addresses, correspondence, and miscellaneous material. The best available source of Bolívar's works in English.

O'Leary, Daniel F. *Bolívar and the War of Independence.* Robert F. McNerney, ed. Austin, Texas: University of Texas Press, 1970. 386pp. This abridged translation of *Memorias del General Daniel Florencio O'Leary* is a valuable collection of contemporary records and eyewitness recollections by a colleague of Bolívar. The narrative account ends in 1826 so it does not provide the full picture, and O'Leary's partisan view limits its reliability.

Recommended Biographies

Masur, Gerhard. *Simón Bolívar.* Albuquerque: University of New Mexico Press, 1969. 572pp. Masur's thoughtful study of Bolívar's life and character remains the best available in English. The author balances Bolívar's strengths, failures, and contradictions into a believable human portrait in which his internal struggles are documented by excerpts from his writings.

Worcester, Donald E. *Bolívar.* Boston: Little, Brown, 1977. 243pp. Intended for a general audience, this is a solid, sympathetic, but balanced portrait that captures Bolívar the military leader and politician in a very readable narrative.

Other Biographical Studies

Angell, Hildegarde. *Simón Bolívar: South American Liberator.* New York: W.W. Norton, 1930. 296pp. This is a useful, though brief and somewhat simplified, popular biography. The author emphasizes Bolívar's historical background and, based on a fresh view of his letters and eyewitness accounts, supplies a credible personality profile.

Belaunde, Victor Andrés. *Bolívar and the Political Thought of the Spanish American Revolution.* Baltimore: Johns Hopkins University Press, 1938. 451pp. This is a careful and detailed analysis of the development of Bolívar's ideas in the context of the period.

Frank, Waldo. *Birth of a World: Bolívar in Terms of His People.* Boston: Houghton Mifflin, 1951. 432pp. Frank's study attempts a complex portrayal of a hero and human figure, but the book's emotional style and occasional distortions of the facts limit its usefulness.

Hagen, Victor Wolfgang von. *The Four Seasons of Manuela: The Love Story of Manuela Sáenz and Simón Bolívar.* New York: Duell, Sloan and Pearce, 1952. 320pp. This biography of the woman who became Bolívar's mistress from 1822 until his death offers an intimate look at their relationship recreated with some of the techniques of historical fiction.

Ludwig, Emil. *Bolívar: The Life of an Idealist.* New York: Alliance, 1942. 362pp. In the author's view, Bolívar should be viewed as an idealist struggling against the temptation of power in this full-scale biography, commissioned by the Venezuelan government. Although the portrait is intriguing and revealing, a good deal of idealization is evident in dramatizing the desired contrasts in Bolívar's character and career.

Madariaga, Salvador de. *Simón Bolívar.* 1952. Reprint ed. Coral Gables, Florida: University of Miami Press, 1967. 711pp. Massive and extensively documented, Madariaga's biography, written by a Spaniard in part to justify Spanish rule in the Americas, caused great offense when it was published in Central America. The author debunks the myths that have arisen around Bolívar to reveal his human side. Critics have complained that his book is more a malicious essay than an objective biography, but Madariaga argues his reading of Bolívar's character with a wealth of detail and skill in marshalling evidence.

Johnson, John J. *Simón Bolívar and Spanish American Independence 1783–1830.* Reprint ed. Princeton, New Jersey: Van Nostrand, 1968. 223pp. Johnson supplies a helpful introduction to Bolívar as a military and political leader, followed by a selection of important documents in which Bolívar expresses his political ideas.

Paine, Lauran. *Bolívar the Liberator.* New York: Roy, 1971. 207pp. A satisfying biography for the general reader, this short study makes extensive use of Spanish sources, though its interpretation of Latin American history should be read with skepticism.

Prieto, Luis B. *Simón Bolívar: Educator.* New York: Doubleday, 1970. 159pp. Synthesizing the various aspects of Bolívar's role as an educator and his philosophical influences, this critical study is well documented but at times uncritical.

Biographical Novels

Aguilera Malta, Demetrio. *Manuela, La Caballeresa Del Sol.* Carbondale: Southern Illinois University Press, 1967. 304pp. The novel depicts the relationship between Bolívar and his mistress Manuela Saenz, who comes to play an important role as his political adviser. Showing events on and off the battlefield and the unusual partnership of the great liberator and his unconventional mistress, the novel is faithful to history, and the characterization of Bolívar is convincing.

Boyd, William Y. *Bolívar: Liberator of a Continent: A Dramatized Biography.* SPI Books, 1998. 288pp. This novelized chronicle of Bolívar's life and times has a factual framework of the man and the era, but the emphasis is on a fast-moving adventure story with as much about the liberator's sexual conquests as his political ones. In Boyd's handling, Bolívar is a visionary hero, and the treatment highlights his greatness.

Garcia Marquez, Gabriel. *The General in His Labyrinth.* New York: Knopf, 1990. 285pp. In the last year of his life, Bolívar makes a final seven-month voyage down the Magdalena River from Bogota to the sea. The occasion is an opportunity for a self-assessment of his life, and the novel offers a remarkable blend of history and psychology with Bolívar presented as a great and complex individual in a life of triumph and disillusionment.

Recommended Juvenile Biographies

Goodnough, David. *Simón Bolívar: South American Liberator.* Springfield, New Jersey: Enslow, 1998. 128pp. MG. The author provides an informative summary of Bolívar's background, military and political career with his times helpfully explained.

Greene, Carol. *Simón Bolívar: South American Liberator.* Chicago: Childrens Press, 1989. 115pp. MG. This partially fictionalized biography with invented dialogue dramatizing the highlights of Bolívar's life includes a helpful timeline.

Wepman, Dennis. *Simón Bolívar.* New York: Chelsea House, 1985. 112pp. MG/YA. Dividing his life into six chronological phases: the playboy, the idealist, the firebrand, the soldier, the liberator, and the exile, this is a solid biographical account that portrays multiple sides of the South American leader. Helpfully illustrated with sidebar quotes and a chronology.

Biographical Films and Theatrical Adaptations

Simón Bolívar (1968). Director: Alessandro Blasetti. Maximilian Schell stars as Bolívar in this Italian film depicting scenes from the 1817–1823 rebellion in which Bolívar is shown attempting to unify rebel factions and, after winning independence for Venezuela, widening the struggle. Video.

Simón Bolívar: The Great Liberator (1993). Produced by German television, this documentary film discusses Bolívar's life, including his family background, education, military career, and role in the Wars of Independence, as well as the history of the American colonies under the Spanish. Video.

Other Sources

Bushnell, David, ed. *The Liberator Simón Bolívar: Man and Image.* New York: Knopf, 1970. 218pp. In a useful collection of primary and secondary materials, Bushnell provides a detailed chronology of Bolívar's life, a selection of his works, and excerpts from various interpretations of Bolívar from his own time to the present.

42. DANIEL BOONE
1734–1820

American frontiersman and one of the most mythologized American heroes, Daniel Boone was born near Reading, Pennsylvania. He served in Braddock's ill-fated expedition against Fort Duquesne in the French and Indian War. From 1769 to 1771 he explored the Kentucky region, blazing in 1775 the famous Wilderness Road, leading the first white settlers across the Appalachians into Kentucky and founding Boonesboro. During the American Revolution, he was captured by Shawnee Indians, escaped, and successfully defended Boonesboro from Indian attack. Charged with disloyalty, Boone was tried and acquitted. After several terms of service in the Virginia legislature, Boone headed west to Missouri, where he died.

Autobiography and Primary Sources

Filson, John. *The Discovery, Settlement, and Present State of Kentucke.* 1784. Reprint ed. New York: Corinth Books, 1962. 118pp. The author of Kentucky's first history presents as well Boone's alleged autobiography. Since the frontiersman was virtually illiterate, his words are actually the invention of Filson himself, based on interviews with Boone. Portraying Boone as a noble primitive in tune with nature, Filson helped form the Boone legend that subsequent writers and biographers have adapted or challenged.

Recommended Biographies

Bakeless, John. *Daniel Boone: Master of the Wilderness.* 1939. Reprint ed. Lincoln: University of Nebraska Press, 1989. 480pp. The standard life of Daniel Boone until the publication of Faragher's study, Bakeless's comprehensive account draws on the massive Draper manuscripts and both adds new information and corrects previous biographical distortions. The book is excellent as well as a cultural history of American frontier experience.

Faragher, John Mack. *Daniel Boone: The Life and Legend of an American Pioneer.* New York: Holt, 1992. 429pp. Based on the best eyewitness accounts of Boone's life and supplemented by extensive scholarship in Western history, the author fashions a remarkably balanced and detailed biography in which Boone is shown as complex and contradictory. Employing the methods of new social history, this is both a study of an American hero in his multiple dimensions and an analysis of the hero-making process.

Lofaro, Michael A. *The Life and Adventures of Daniel Boone.* Lexington: University of Kentucky Press, 1978. 150pp. Lofaro's scholarly interpretive study draws on primary sources to challenge previous accounts of Boone's life and accomplishments and is excellent in placing them in the context of the American frontier experience.

Other Biographical Studies

Draper, Lyman C. *The Life of Daniel Boone.* Ted F. Belue, ed. Mechanicsburg, Pennsylvania: Stackpole Books, 1998. 576pp. Draper collected more than 500 volumes of material on Boone, but his biography remained unfinished for 100 years until Belue, a scholar of early America, added his authoritative editing. The result is a revealing account with little-known information on Boone and his family, Indian life, the fur trade, and frontier life in general. Draper's notes from his 1851 interview with Boone's only surviving son have been published as *My Father, Daniel Boone: The Draper Interviews with Nathan Boone.* Neal O. Harmon, ed. (Lexington: University Press of Kentucky, 1999, 192pp.)

Elliott, Lawrence. *The Long Hunter: A New Life of Daniel Boone.* New York: Reader's Digest Press, 1976. 242pp. Looking beyond the legend, Elliott presents the frontiersman as a far more complex figure than previous accounts, and the book is recommended for its account of Boone's private side.

Houston, Peter. *A Sketch of the Life and Character of Daniel Boone.* Ted F. Belue, ed. Mechanicsburg, Pennsylvania: Stackpole Books, 1997. 96pp. Frontiersman Houston's reminiscences of Boone describes his initial explorations of Kentucky and Indian battles. Hard to follow for the uninitiated in Boone scholarship, the book is nonetheless interesting for its early eyewitness perspective.

Sweeney, J. Gray. *Columbus of the Woods: Daniel Boon and the Typology of Manifest Destiny.* Saint Louis: Washington University Gallery of Art, 1992. 83pp. This is a study of Boone as a visual symbol in American art, reflecting American views of the frontier, westward expansion, and heroism. The analysis adds much to an understanding of the Boone legacy and mythology that has persisted in books about him.

Biographical Novels

Eckert, Allen W. *The Court Martial of Daniel Boone.* Boston: Little, Brown, 1973. 309pp. Based on scrupulous review of the known sources with little invented material, the novel recreates the courtroom drama of Boone's charge of disloyalty and treason in conspiring to surrender Boonesboro to the British. Boone appears as well in several of the author's Narratives of America series, including *The Frontiersman* (1967), *Wilderness Empire* (1969), and *The Dark and Bloody River* (1995), in which Eckert supplements the facts with invented dialogue.

Judd, Cameron. *Boone: A Novel Based on the Life and Times of Daniel Boone.* New York: Bantam, 1995. 422pp. Although this fictional biography is based on Boone's actual experiences, there are several invented characters and incidents.

Seifert, Shirley. *Never No More: The Story of Rebecca Boone.* Philadelphia: Lippincott, 1964. 286pp. In this story of a year in the life of Daniel Boone and his wife Rebecca, it is 1773 and the Boone family and other settlers push through the wilderness to Kentucky, enduring an Indian attack in which the couple's son is killed. The author stays close to the known facts in telling the Boones' story.

Fictional Portraits

Daniel Boone appears as a character in countless novels depicting his own and others' frontier adventures. A few of the best include

Giles, Janice Holt. *The Kentuckians.* Boston: Houghton Mifflin, 1953. 272pp. Rendered with authenticity and conviction, the novel chronicles the struggles of the first pioneers in the Kentucky wilderness and the struggle for freedom from the authority of Virginia. The fictional characters and incidents connect with historical figures, such as Daniel Boone.

Henderson, Daniel. *Boone of the Wilderness.* New York: Dutton, 1921. 207pp. This adventure novel beginning in 1752 focuses on Boone's relationship with his nemesis in Kentucky, Anthony Arnold.

Receveur, Betty Layman. *Oh, Kentucky!* New York: Ballantine Books, 1990. 592pp. The story of the frontier settlement of Boonesboro is authentically chronicled through the fictional experiences of Kitty Gentry and her family.

Roberts, Elizabeth Madox. *The Great Meadow.* New York: Viking, 1930. 338pp. The daily concerns of a pioneer woman form the central drama of this novel of life in the Kentucky wilderness during the American Revolution. The novel provides an excellent treatment of ordinary life on the frontier, rendered poetically through the thoughts of the novel's central character, Diony Jarvis.

Wheelwright, Jere H. *Kentucky Stand.* New York: Scribner, 1951. 279pp. A young ex-schoolboy is the sole survivor of an Indian attack who makes it to Daniel Boone's settlement at Boonesboro and becomes a trapper and Indian fighter as the western settlement contends with hostile Indians and the British. The novel interweaves a fictional story with an authentic background of actual events, characters, like Boone, and a convincing frontier atmosphere.

Recommended Juvenile Biographies

Brown, John Mason. *Daniel Boone: The Opening of the Wilderness.* New York: Random House, 1952. 181pp. YA. A Landmark biography written by a celebrated author of children's books, Brown's dramatic account draws on Bakeless's biography for its sources and concentrates on capturing the frontier experience and its dangers to supply a context for an appreciation of Boone's achievements.

Cavan, Seamus. *Daniel Boone and the Opening of the Ohio Country.* New York: Chelsea House, 1991. 111pp. MG. With drawings, maps, and historic artwork, this handsome volume traces the career of Boone in war and pioneering, as well as his failures in land speculation and government so a believable human personality emerges.

Lawlor, Laurie. *Daniel Boone.* Niles, Illinois: Albert Whitman, 1989. 160pp. MG. Based on solid and extensive research, this chronicle of Boone's life dramatically and with novelistic touches captures the frontiersman from his youth in the Pennsylvania wilderness to his adventures exploring the "dark and bloody" western frontier. Throughout, Lawlor challenges the conventional myth of Boone as an inarticulate Indian fighter, asserting his heroism as a true leader in American westward expansion.

Biographical Films and Theatrical Adaptations

A&E Biography Video: The Adventures of Daniel Boone (1995). Producer: Peter Doyle. Intended to set the record straight, this documentary depicts Boone's career from boyhood, through his Indian fighting and pioneering, and his government service as an adviser to presidents. Despite challenging Boone's mythological treatment, the film casts Boone firmly in the heroic mold. Video.

Daniel Boone (1934). Director: David Howard. George O'Brien stars as the frontiersman in this romantic action-adventure tale illustrating Boone's leading settlers west from North Carolina into Kentucky. Video.

Daniel Boone: Trail Blazer (1956). Director: Ismael Rodriguez. Heroic but low-budget production depicts Daniel Boone's wilderness skills and Indian fighting as he leads a group of settlers to Boonesboro. Bruce Bennett stars as Boone. Video.

43. JOHN WILKES BOOTH
1838–1865

American actor and assassin of Abraham Lincoln, John Wilkes Booth was born in Maryland, the son of Junius Brutus Booth and brother of Edwin Booth, both celebrated Shakespearean actors. He made his stage debut at the age of 17 and was a popular stage performer. An ardent Confederate sympathizer, Booth conspired to kidnap President Lincoln and later to kill him and his cabinet with a group of conspirators. Booth shot the president on April 14, 1865. He was discovered two weeks later hiding in a Virginia barn where he died.

Autobiography and Primary Sources

Right or Wrong, God Judge Me: The Writings of John Wilkes Booth. John Rhodehamel and Louise Taper, eds. Urbana: University of Illinois Press, 1997. 171pp. Editors Rhodehamel and Taper have collected what remains of Booth's writings, more than doubling what had been previously published. The most important item is a 20-page manuscript written in 1860, modeled on Antony's funeral oration in Shakespeare's *Julius Caesar* showing that Booth's hatred for Lincoln was early and deeply rooted in his pro-slavery and pro-Southern ideology. Through their notes, the editors have put every document into context, and the result is a interesting narrative from Booth's perspective of the events leading up to Lincoln's assassination and insights into the personality of the assassin.

Recommended Biographies

Clarke, Asia Booth. *The Unlocked Book: A Memoir of John Wilkes Booth.* New York: Putnam, 1938. 205pp. Generally regarded as the single most important source for understanding Booth's personality, his sister's reminiscence, written in 1874, offers an intimate perspective on Booth, portraying him as an enigmatic figure, a mixture of romantic idealism and fanatical hatred.

Other Biographical Studies

Bishop, Jim. *The Day Lincoln Was Shot.* New York: Harper, 1955. 308pp. Bishop's detailed account of Abraham's Lincoln's last day is a riveting narrative, based on solid documentary evidence, of the movements of the president and Booth as they converge at Ford's Theatre.

Bryan, George S. *The Great American Myth.* New York: Carrick & Evans, 1940. 436pp. With its principal goal to correct misconceptions about the Lincoln assassination, Bryan's study is not a full-scale biography of Booth, but it does provide a summary of his life up to the assassination, correcting former errors.

Hanchett, William. *The Lincoln Murder Conspiracies.* Urbana: University of Illinois Press, 1983. 303pp. Hanchett's innovative study seeks to explain Booth's motives from the social factors that shaped him.

Kimmel, Stanley. *The Mad Booths of Maryland.* Indianapolis: Bobbs-Merrill, 1940. 400pp. Despite the book's lurid title, this is a detailed chronicle of the Booth family and theatrical history that establishes a helpful context for understanding Booth's motivation, joining a psychological and historical perspective.

Samples, Gordon. *Lust for Fame: The Stage Career of John Wilkes Booth.* Jefferson, North Carolina: McFarland, 1982. 238pp. This is the best and most authoritative study of Booth's theatrical career that offers considerable insights into Booth's development and personality.

Smith, Gene. *American Gothic: The Story of America's Legendary Theatrical Family: Junius, Edwin, and John Wilkes Booth.* New York: Simon & Schuster, 1992. 286pp. In this anecdotal group biography of the Booth family by the author of a number of popular historical and biographical books, nearly half the book is devoted to Lincoln's assassination, and it disappoints as a thorough theatrical or family history, weakened by the author's failure to probe or interpret and his willingness to accept evidence of dubious credibility.

Starkey, Larry. *Wilkes Booth Came to Washington.* New York: Random House, 1976. 209pp. The author's debatable thesis is that the Lincoln assassination was a Confederate plot to provoke war with England and that Booth was not a demented egomaniac but a foolish, trusting Confederate patriot and the dupe of the plot's true mastermind, John H. Surratt. Unconvincing and reflecting sloppy research, the book indulges in a number of idiosyncratic and farfetched interpretations.

Tidwell, William A., et al. *Come Retribution: The Confederate Secret Service and the Assassination of Lincoln.* Jackson: University Press of Mississippi, 1988. 510pp. This exhaustive analysis of the Lincoln conspiracy is the most authoritative, modern examination that provides sound evidence that Booth was an agent of the Confederate secret service.

Biographical Novels

Glasgow, Alice. *The Twisted Tendril: A Story of 1865.* New York: F.A. Stokes, 1928. 311pp. The novel dramatizes the stages of Booth's involvement in the conspiracy to kill the president and the events leading to his death in a believable version of Booth's story, weaving together factual details with some invented scenes and dialogue.

Jordan, Jan. *Dim the Flaring Lamps: A Novel of the Life of John Wilkes Booth.* Englewood Cliffs, New Jersey: Prentice-Hall, 1972. 282pp. This biographical novel attempts to provide a more personal motivation for Booth's assassination of Lincoln. Based on the actual events of Booth's life, the novel does resort to some speculation and surmises.

Kennelly, Ardyth. *The Spur.* New York: J. Messner, 1951. 304pp. Set during his last six days following the assassination, Booth reviews his 26 years and explains how he arrived at his decision to kill the president. The author uses her imagination freely, inventing thoughts and dialogue while balancing sympathy and censure.

Nottingham, Theodore J. *The Curse of Cain: The Untold Story of John Wilkes Booth.* Nicholasville, Kentucky: Appaloosa, 1991. 214pp. With so much fanciful speculation, the book is best categorized as biographical fiction instead of fact. Written by Booth's third great-grandson, the book dramatizes Booth's perceptions leading up to the assassination and offers the startling speculation that Booth escaped to Asia before returning to America in later life.

Robertson, David. *Booth: A Novel.* New York: Anchor Books, 1998. 326pp. Told from the perspective of John Surratt, the only conspirator in the plot to kill Abraham Lincoln who survived, the novel dramatically recreates the events of the conspiracy and the scene of wartime Washington, but is less successful in revealing Booth's enigmatic charac-

ter and motives. Much of the book is devoted to defending Surratt as an innocent victim of others' cunning.

Russell, Pamela R. *The Woman Who Loved John Wilkes Booth.* New York: Putnam, 1978. 379pp. The story of the conspiracy to assassinate Lincoln is told in the imagined diary of Mary Surratt, who becomes involved through her attraction to the charismatic Booth.

Stacton, David. *The Judges of the Secret Court.* New York: Pantheon, 1961. 255pp. Focusing on Booth from the morning before the assassination to the end of the conspirators' trial, the novel suggests that Booth committed suicide, a fact that remains debatable.

Stern, Philip Van Doren. *The Man Who Killed Lincoln: The Story of John Wilkes Booth and His Part in the Assassination.* New York: Random House, 1939. 376pp. Following carefully the actual sequence of events during the month of April, 1865, this semifictional account weaves facts into a continuous narrative in which Booth is portrayed as a captivating Byronic hero: pale, melancholy, and driven. The author lists the few deviations from the historical.

Fictional Portraits

Adicks, Richard. *A Court of Owls.* Sarasota, Florida: Pineapple Press, 1989. 269pp. The novel dramatizes the career of a Confederate soldier whose path crosses Booth's, leading to his involvement in the conspiracy to kill Lincoln.

Morrow, Honoré. *The Last Full Measure.* New York: Morrow, 1930. 340pp. The concluding volume of the author's trilogy on the events of the Lincoln presidency provides a full account of the Booth conspiracy and Lincoln's assassination.

King, Benjamin. *A Bullet for Lincoln.* Gretna, Louisiana: Pelican, 1993. 301pp. King's Civil War thriller constructs a realistic alternative account of the Lincoln assassination as a conspiracy among the nation's most powerful tycoons.

O'Toole, G.J.A. *The Cosgrove Report.* New York: Rawson, Wade, 1979. 424pp. This imaginative recreation of the Lincoln assassination traces the discoveries of a Pinkerton detective hired to prove that Booth is still alive. He uncovers an enormous political scandal, while the novel provides some ingenious solutions to questions that have dogged the Lincoln conspiracy in a devious, though entertaining, mixture of fact and fancy.

Steward, Barbara, and Dwight Steward. *The Lincoln Diddle.* New York: Morrow, 1979. 251pp. In this imaginative fantasy, Edgar Allan Poe, disguised as a detective, first fails to prevent Lincoln's murder then solves the mystery surrounding the conspiracy.

Wiegland, William. *The Chester A. Arthur Conspiracy.* New York: Dial Press, 1983. 446pp. The novel's intriguing fictional premise is that Booth did not perish in a Virginia barn and makes his way to New York where he gets involved in the political career of Chester A. Arthur.

Recommended Juvenile Biographies

Otfinoski, Steven. *John Wilkes Booth and the Civil War*. Woodbridge, Connecticut: Blackbirch Press, 1998. 80pp. MG. Relating the complex events of the era around the life story of Booth, the book follows his career from his youth, to his success as an actor, to an exploration of his motives for killing the president.

Biographical Films and Theatrical Adaptations

A&E Biography Video: John Wilkes Booth: Assassin in the Spotlight (1995). Producer: Kellie Flanagan. This documentary chronicling his entire career attempts to answer the question: who was John Wilkes Booth? Video.

Birth of a Nation (1915). Director: D.W. Griffith. In one of the most famous film depictions of the Lincoln assassination in Griffith's landmark Civil War epic, Booth is played by later film director Raoul Walsh. Video.

The Ordeal of Dr. Mudd (1980). Director: Paul Wendkos. Dramatizing the fate of the doctor who unwittingly aided Lincoln's assassin by setting Booth's broken leg and who was jailed as a conspirator, the aftermath of Booth's crime is seen from Mudd's perspectives as are his later heroics in prison during a yellow fever epidemic. Bill Grimble plays Booth; Dennis Weaver is Dr. Mudd. Video.

Prince of Players (1955). Director: Philip Dunne. In a screenplay by Moss Hart, Richard Burton portrays Edwin Booth in scenes dramatizing his stage career and offstage life, with John Derek as his notorious brother.

The Day Lincoln Was Shot (1988). Director: John Gray. Television film based on the Jim Bishop book, starring Lance Henricksen as Lincoln and Rob Morrow as John Wilkes Booth. Video.

See also Abraham Lincoln

44. JORGE LUIS BORGES
1897–1986

Argentine poet, critic, and short-story writer, Borges is generally recognized as the foremost modern Spanish American writer whose worldwide acclaim helped stimulate an interest in other Latin American writers. Born in Buenos Aires, Borges was educated in Switzerland and lived after World War I in Spain where he became associated with the Ultraist movement of avant-garde poets. Working at a Buenos Aires library, Borges perfected his characteristic fictional form, a hybrid of the short story and the essay with a strong metaphysical and fantasy component. His stories have been collected in such volumes as *Ficciones* and *Labyrinths*.

Autobiography and Primary Sources

Notoriously elusive and private, various sides of Borges's personality are revealed in a number of published interviews: *Conversations with Jorge Luis Borges* (New York: Holt, 1969. 144pp.); *Seven Conversations with Jorge Luis Borges* (Troy, New York: Whitson, 1982. 219pp.); *Borges at Eighty: Conversations.* (Bloomington: Indiana University Press, 1982. 176pp.); and *Twenty-Four Conversations with Borges* (New York: Grove Press, 1984. 157pp.).

Recommended Biographies

Rodriguez Monegal, Emir. *Jorge Luis Borges: A Literary Biography*. New York: Dutton, 1978. 502pp. Recognized as the standard biography of Borges before the publication of Woodhall's life, Rodriguez Monegal's study is based on personal contact with the author and firmly roots Borges's genius in the details of his surprisingly ordinary life.

Woodhall, James. *Borges: A Life*. New York: Basic Books, 1997. 333pp. The best general biography on Borges, Woodhall's study is competently researched and displays a familiarity with Argentine history and politics. The result is a convincing portrait of the artist and a sophisticated overview of his work.

Other Biographical Studies

Bell-Villada, Gene H. *Borges and His Fiction: A Guide to His Mind and Art*. Chapel Hill: University of North Carolina Press, 1981. 292pp. Bell-Villada's critical introduction to Borges's art provides two chapters on Borges's background tracing a tension between his Argentinean and international perspective.

Recommended Juvenile Biographies

Lennon, Adria. *Jorge Luis Borges*. New York: Chelsea House, 1992. 111pp. MG/YA. This well-researched life traces Borges's career from childhood, through his life under the Peron regime, to his eventual blindness and his years as a famous writer. The author includes as well a summary of Borges's artistic reputation and his unique artistic vision.

Biographical Films and Theatrical Adaptations

Borges and I (1983). Director: David Wheatley. This BBC documentary explores Borges's life and relates his works to his personal experiences, while attempting to reconcile his public and private selves. Video.

Other Sources

Di Giovanni, Norman T., ed. *In Memory of Borges*. London: Constable, 1988. 128pp. This tribute volume collects a number of interesting reflections from Borges's friends that offer an intimate glimpse of the often elusive Borges.

45–47. THE BORGIAS: RODRIGO BORGIA (POPE ALEXANDER VI CA.1431–1503); CESARE BORGIA (1476–1507); LUCREZIA BORGIA (1480–1519)

One of the most powerful and notorious families of the Italian Renaissance, the Borgias have become synonymous with political opportunism and corruption. Patriarch Rodrigo Borgia became Pope Alexander VI in 1492 and extended papal secular authority in Italy. He had a number of illegitimate children, including Cesare Borgia, widely regarded as the prototype of Machiavelli's *The Prince*, and Lucrezia Borgia, who became the Duchess of Ferrarra and whose alleged complicity in her family's poison plots and incestuous relations with her father and brother have fascinated later writers.

Recommended Biographies

Cloulas, Ivan. *The Borgias*. New York: F. Watts, 1989. 388pp. Cloulas, in an authoritative, captivating study, covers over two centuries in the lives of the Borgias, including such neglected figures as Alonso Borgia who maneuvered himself into the Italian aristocracy and eventually the papacy insuring that his nephew Rodrigo would succeed him, and Francis Borgia, Rodrigo's great-grandson, the Jesuit leader who became a saint.

Mallet, Michael E. *The Borgias: The Rise and Fall of a Renaissance Dynasty*. New York: Barnes and Noble, 1969. 351pp. Looking beyond scandal and villainy, Mallet provides an assessment of the political and social achievement of the Borgia family as a whole and helps to answer for a general reader why the family rose from relative obscurity to the highest position of Renaissance society as well as their historical and social significance.

Other Biographical Studies

Chamberlin, E.R. *The Fall of the House of Borgia*. New York: Dial Press, 1974. 347pp. Despite the title, only the last chapter concerns the Borgias's fall. Most of the book concentrates on the rise to power and the events that followed Rodrigo Borgia becoming pope in 1492. Based on standard sources, there is little here that is original or new, but the author considers the Borgias sympathetically without concealing or excusing their excesses.

Collison-Morley, Lacy. *The Story of the Borgias*. New York: Dutton, 1939. 329pp. Although no new facts of importance are uncovered, the author's account of the Borgia family compresses a great deal of information into a concise narrative, the thesis of which is that the Borgias were not very much worse than others during their time.

Corvo, Baron Frederick. *Chronicles of the House of Borgia*. 1901. Reprint ed. New York: Dover, 1962. 374pp. Teeming with Corvo's personal hypotheses, prejudices, and grudges, this eccentric but fascinating study examines multiple accusations that have been made against the Borgias and offers a provocative defense. Not to be regarded as objective, rigorously documented scholarship, the book, nevertheless, conjures up a vivid picture of the Renaissance and a subjective reflection of the author.

Fusero, Clemente. *The Borgias*. New York: Praeger, 1972. 352pp. The author examines the Borgia family in the context of Renaissance Europe, and, although he adds nothing new, he does provide a useful introduction based on contemporary and modern sources. The lack of documentation precludes the book's usefulness for scholars.

Johnson, Marion. *The Borgias.* London: Macdonald Futura, 1981. 232pp. This highly readable, beautifully illustrated biography offers no new insights but contradicts the popular image of a venomous Lucrezia and condemnation of the family as too simplistic, distorting an appreciation of their real talents and achievements.

Latour, Anny. *The Borgias.* New York: Abelard-Schuman, 1966. 184pp. Falling short of its claim of offering a reinterpretation of sources and an analysis of scholarly importance, this study provides a collection of quotes from contemporary writers with minimum connective explanations or interpretation and neither documentation of sources nor an index.

Lucas-Dubreton, Jean. *The Borgias.* New York: Dial Press, 1974. 347pp. This family study also provides a detailed picture of Rome and the Papal court during the Borgias' lifetime. The author debunks the notion that the Borgias were monsters of cruelty and corruption, and sees them as reflecting their times, conspicuous only in being more powerful than their contemporaries.

Cesare Borgia

Beuf, Maria Luigi. *Cesare Borgia: the Machiavellian Prince.* New York: Oxford University Press, 1942. 398pp. Trying to find a balance between castigating Cesare's character and overlooking his obvious vices, the author leans sentimentally toward the latter. Adding few new facts to the established record, this study does look at the evidence of Cesare's life and times with fresh eyes.

Bradford, Sarah. *Cesare Borgia: His Life and Times.* New York: Macmillan, 1976. 327pp. Intended to sort out the truth behind the Borgia legend and previous views of Cesare as the archetype of criminality, Bradford's study places him squarely in the context of political and social forces that shaped him, and he emerges as a contradictory and complex figure through her efforts.

Garner, John L. *Cesare Borgia: A Study of the Renaissance.* New York: McBride, Nast, 1912. 320pp. Placing Cesare in the context of his time, Garner's study, the first biography in English, shows him a product of the egoism of his age and a victim of unrestrained selfishness, a judgment reflecting the author's moral standards rather than an objective analysis of Borgia's own.

Woodward, William Harrison. *Cesare Borgia: A Biography.* New York: Dutton, 1914. 477pp. Solid and scholarly, based on extensive research, Woodward's study considers his subject from a wider context of the Borgia family as a whole and the history of papal Italy during their era.

Lucrezia Borgia

Bellonci, Maria. *The Life and Times of Lucrezia Borgia.* New York: Harcourt, Brace, 1953. 343pp. Bellonci's study relies on imaginative reconstruction based on evidence to animate Lucrezia's life and times. In her view, Lucrezia is a passionate, sometimes unwilling tool of her family's interests with little in common with the raven-haired pri-

soner of legend; her father is sympathetically treated as a fiercely devoted parent; and Cesare is portrayed as a ruthless powerseeker.

Erlanger, Rachel. *Lucrezia Borgia: A Biography.* New York: Hawthorn Books, 1978. 372pp. Finding a balance between interpretations of Lucrezia as a monster and a noble victim, Erlanger's study, based on thorough research, casts her in believable human terms and very much shaped by her times.

Gregorovius, Ferdinand. *Lucrezia Borgia: A Chapter from the Morals of the Italian Renaissance.* London: Phaidon Press, 1948. 362pp. First published in 1874, Gregorovius's study is a pioneering biographical work, the first serious account that relies on primary research synthesized novelistically into a dramatic narrative. Gregorovius begins the rehabilitation of Lucrezia's reputation, whom he views sympathetically.

Haslip, Joan. *Lucrezia Borgia: A Study.* Indianapolis: Bobbs-Merrill, 1953. 279pp. In an almost fictionalized account, the Borgias' story is dramatically narrated with undocumented quotations from a variety of contemporary sources. Colorful in its background painting, the book relies on a good deal of speculation to create a seamless and coherent narrative and psychological portrait.

Rodrigo Borgia (Alexander VI)

Ferrara, Orestes. *The Borgia Pope: Alexander VI.* New York: Sheed & Ward, 1940. 455pp. Attempting to rehabilitate the character of Alexander VI and refute the charges of his misdeeds, the book exposes the malice of previous interpretations; however, the author's special pleading puts in doubt his objective handling of the evidence.

Biographical Novels

Balchin, Nigel. *The Borgia Testament.* Boston: Houghton Mifflin, 1949. 212pp. Cast in the form of a journal written by Cesare Borgia while he awaits execution, the novel chronicles his career in flashbacks and reveals him to be a complex blend of guile and need.

Bennetts, Pamela. *The Borgia Prince.* New York: Saint Martin's, 1968. 254pp. Cesare Borgia is shown in war and love in a temperate portrait that resists portraying him as a monster.

Briggs, Jean. *The Flame of the Borgias.* New York: Harper & Row, 1975. 336pp. The novel describes the relationship between Lucrezia Borgia and Peitro Bembo, Venetian nobleman, poet, scholar, and later cardinal. Their doomed love affair is effectively set against the intrigues of the period.

Davis, Genevieve. *A Passion in the Blood.* New York: Simon & Schuster, 1977. 360pp. This sentimental account of Lucrezia Borgia shows her as an innocent victim of her politically driven father and the incestuous jealousy of her brother. Not reliable as history, the novel reinterprets the Borgias as a modern dysfunctional family.

Kenyon, Frank W. *The Naked Sword: The Story of Lucrezia Borgia.* New York: Dodd, Mead, 1968. 253pp. In this dramatization of Lucrezia Borgia's life, she is shown as a marriageable pawn in her father's and brother's ambitions, breaking away from their control only in her third marriage to the Duke of Ferrara. Rejecting previous characterization of

Lucrezia's villainy, the novel makes a plausible case that she should be regarded as a more blameless victim.

Plaidy, Jean. *Madonna of the Seven Hills.* New York: Putnam, 1958. 300pp. The story of the Borgias is told through the perspective of Lucrezia who is depicted not as the monster of legend but as the creation of her times in a controversial, speculative portrayal; *Light on Lucrezia.* New York: Putnam, 1976. 347pp. In arguing a more sympathetic view of Lucrezia Borgia, the novel shows her torn between her loyalty to her family and to her husband, the Duke of Ferrara. The interpretations of the historical figures are original, if debatable.

Seymour, Miranda. *Daughter of Shadows.* New York: Coward-McCann, 1977. 255pp. The novel dramatizes the Borgia family dynamics, concentrating on Lucrezia, a political pawn of her father and the victim of Cesare's amorous desires and jealousy. This is a authentic portrait of the age, with a credible interpretation of the Borgias.

Schirokauer, Alfred. *Lucrezia Borgia: A Dramatic Biography.* New York: Appleton, 1937. 377pp. This fictional biography emphasizes the sensational horror of the allegations against Lucrezia and her family.

Fictional Portraits

Challis, George. *The Bait and the Trap.* New York: Harper, 1951. 213pp. In this romanticized costume adventure set in Renaissance Italy, a fictional character enters the service of Cesare Borgia believing in his virtues. Events soon teach him otherwise.

Haasse, Hella S. *The Scarlet City: A Novel of 16th-Century Italy.* Chicago: Academy Chicago Publishers, 1990. 367pp. At the center of this novel describing the battle among French, Swiss, Spanish, and German armies for control of Italy in 1527 is Giovanni Borgia, who may be the son or brother of Cesare Borgia. There are few better historical novels that authentically reconstruct the era.

Herman, George. *Carnival of Saints.* New York: Ballantine Books, 1994. 419pp. In an ingenious novel describing the creation of commedia dell'-arte, a traveling acting company falls foul of the Borgias who are determined to suppress this new irreverent popular art form. This is a meticulous and vivid recreation of the period.

Holland, Cecelia. *City of God: A Novel of the Borgias.* New York: Knopf, 1979. 273pp. Set in sixteenth-century Rome as the Spanish, French, and Papal forces plot to divide and control the wealth of Italy, the novel details the intrigue of a Borgia spy and opportunist with a revealing perspective on the Borgia family and their era.

Maugham, W. Somerset. *Then and Now.* Garden City, New York: Doubleday, 1946. 278pp. Maugham depicts the political education of Niccolo Machiavelli through the actual career of Cesare Borgia, providing human and dramatic illustrations for the political wisdom of *The Prince.*

Samuel, Maurice. *Web of Fury: A Novel of the Borgia Fury.* New York: Knopf, 1947. 487pp. This tale of Renaissance Italy follows the adventures of a young peasant who vows vengeance on the murderers of his brother. Serving Cesare Borgia hoping for justice in a united Italy, he eventually discovers Borgia's true identity. The novel's fictional plot is interwoven with actual historical events for a brilliant close-up of life in the service of the Borgias.

Shellabarger, Samuel. *Prince of Foxes*. Boston: Little, Brown, 1947. 433pp. This swashbuckling adventure concerns a peasant who is taken in by Cesare Borgia's charms and is launched on a number of dangerous assignments on behalf of the Borgia cause. Shellabarger uses his considerable knowledge of Renaissance Italy to believably anchor the novel's nonstop romantic action.

Recommended Juvenile Biographies

Chamberlin, E.R. *Cesare Borgia*. London: International Textbook, 1969. 84pp. YA. Part of the International Profiles series, this brief, informative biography by a respected scholar is intended for the general adult and young adult reader.

Haney, John. *Cesare Borgia*. New York: Chelsea House, 1987. 112pp. MG/YA. Haney's is an informative, balanced portrait that covers the details of Borgia's life and career against a solid period background.

Biographical Films and Theatrical Adaptations

Bride of Vengeance (1949). Director: Mitchell Leisen. Paulette Goddard stars as Lucrezia Borgia and Macdonald Carey as Cesare Borgia in a romantic, costume drama in which Lucrezia is transformed from villainy by love.

Cesare Borgia (1923). Director: Richard Oswald. Conrad Veidt plays a bloodthirsty and determined Cesare in this tale of Renaissance ruthlessness. Video.

Prince of Foxes (1949). Director: Henry King. Hollywood's version of Shellabarger's costume adventure, filmed on location, features Orson Welles as Cesare Borgia.

See also Niccolo Machiavelli; Lorenzo de Medici

48. JAMES BOSWELL
1740–1795

Scottish author and lawyer, Boswell first achieved literary fame with *Account of Corsica* (1768), based on his visit to that island. His famous work, *The Life of Samuel Johnson, LL.D.* (1791), minutely records Johnson's brilliant conversations and is one of the greatest English biographies. In the twentieth century a large number of journals, letters, and other papers by Boswell were discovered in Ireland and elsewhere.

Autobiography and Primary Sources

The discovery of Boswell's letters and journals allows unprecedented access to the man and his activities. Several editions of the material housed at Yale have been published. See in particular, *General Correspondence of James Boswell* (New Haven, Connecticut: Yale University Press, 1993–1997. 2 vols.); *Private Papers of James*

Boswell (New York: McGraw-Hill, 1951–1955. 8 vols.). Selections from Boswell's journals are also available in

The Heart of Boswell: Six Journals in One Volume. Mark Harris, ed. (New York: McGraw-Hill, 1981. 407pp.); *The Journals of James Boswell, 1762–1795*. John Wain, ed. (New Haven, Connecticut: Yale University Press, 1991. 412pp.).

Recommended Biographies

Daiches, David. *James Boswell and His World*. New York: Scribner, 1976. 128pp. Despite its brevity, Daiches's illustrated study is thorough and competent, treating well the complexity of Boswell's character. Serves as a useful introduction.

Brady, Frank. *James Boswell: The Later Years 1769-95*. New York: McGraw-Hill, 1984. 609pp. Brady ably continues the biography begun by Pottle, picking up where the earlier book left off. Like Pottle's book, Brady's is a highly readable and comprehensive gathering of the essential facts of Boswell's life with a balanced assessment of his character.

Pottle, Frederick A. *James Boswell: The Earlier Years 1740-69*. New York: McGraw-Hill, 1966. 606pp. Pottle's is the most extensive and authoritative account of Boswell's formative years. Along with Brady's continuation, the biography is the standard source based on the extensive Yale archive of Boswell's papers.

Other Biographical Studies

Finlayson, Iain. *The Moth and the Candle: A Life of James Boswell*. New York: Saint Martin's, 1984. 273pp. Finlayson emphasizes Boswell the man rather than the writer in a readable, popular account.

Hutchinson, Roger. *All the Sweets of Being: A Life of James Boswell*. Edinburgh: Mainstream, 1995. 238pp. Hutchinson's is a well-written and often perceptive summary of Boswell's life relying mainly on Boswell's own words from his journals. The complexity and contradictions of Boswell's character as well as his artistic instincts come through clearly in Hutchinson's balanced presentation.

Lewis, D.B. Wyndham. *The Hooded Hawk: Or the Case of Mr. Boswell*. New York: Longmans, 1947. 312pp. Lewis's is an admiring biographical profile that attempts to defend Boswell's character against charges of his drunkenness and debauchery. To do so, Lewis glosses over the more unflattering aspects of Boswell's nature and behavior.

Pearson, Hesketh. *Johnson and Boswell: The Story of Their Lives*. New York: Harper, 1958. 390pp. This popular biography offers a dual portrait of Boswell and Johnson against their eighteenth-century background. A lively narrative of familiar anecdotes, Pearson's book rarely goes deeper than the surface.

Tinker, Chauncey B. *Young Boswell*. Boston: Atlantic Monthly Press, 1922. 266pp. Written before the discovery of Boswell's journals and more of his letters, Tinker's is a diligent, though now outdated, account of the writer's formative years.

Vulliamy, C.E. *James Boswell*. New York: Scribner, 1933. 276pp. Vulliamy's critical profile lacks either thoroughness or reliability in its factual details. Highly opinionated, a strong negative bias compromises the book's objectivity.

Biographical Novels

Muir, Marie. *Dear Mrs. Boswell*. New York: Saint Martin's, 1953. 310pp. Boswell is viewed from the perspective of his wife in a mixture of biographical fact and romance.

Other Sources

Newman, Donald J., ed. *James Boswell, Psychological Interpretations*. New York: Saint Martin's, 1995. 222pp. Boswell's personality contradictions are analyzed from an array of psychological perspectives in a fascinating and insightful examination of various stages of Boswell's development, work, and relationships.

See also Samuel Johnson

49. SANDRO BOTTICELLI
ca.1444–1510

Florentine painter of the Renaissance, Botticelli was born Alessandro di Mariano Filepepi. He apprenticed under Fra Filippo Lippi and became a favorite painter of the Medicis. His mythological allegories, *Spring*, *Birth of Venus*, *Mars and Venus*, and *Pallas Subduing a Centaur*, are his masterpieces. Botticelli's reputation was revived in the nineteenth century by the Pre-Raphaelites.

Recommended Biographies

Ettlinger, L.D., and Helen Ettlinger. *Botticelli*. New York: Oxford University Press, 1977. 216pp. This concise summary of Botticelli's life and critical assessment of his paintings is the best available short introduction to the subject.

Lightbown, Ronald. *Sandro Botticelli: Life and Work*. New York: Abbeville, 1989. 336pp. Lightbown's life is generally considered definitive, an authoritative account of what is known for sure about Botticelli's life and a balanced critical assessment of his artistry. Botticelli's entire oeuvre is reproduced in 224 color illustrations.

Other Biographical Studies

Horne, Herbert. *Botticelli: Painter of Florence*. 1908. Reprint ed. Princeton, New Jersey: Princeton University Press, 1980. 372pp. The first scholarly study of the painter relying exclusively on documentary evidence, Horne corrected a number of misconceptions and legends that had grown around Botticelli's life and art. The detailed sifting of the available evidence remains invaluable for the scholar, though the general reader will find his style and approach dry and his portrait somewhat lifeless.

Biographical Novels

Cleugh, James. *Tuscan Spring: A Novel about Sandro Botticelli*. New York: Reynal & Hitchcock,

1939. 328pp. This vivid but overcrowded pageant of Florence under the Medicis offers a great deal of information about Botticelli and the Renaissance with no overt anachronisms.

Fictional Portraits

Ripley, Alexandra. *The Time Returns*. New York: Avon, 1985. 423pp. Dramatizing a love affair involving Lorenzo de Medici, the novel colorfully and realistically captures the scene in fifteenth-century Florence with appearances by Botticelli and Michelangelo.

Shulman, Sandra. *The Florentine*. New York: Morrow, 1973. 314pp. In this romantic pageant of Florence under the Medicis, a young woman is forced to disguise herself as a boy and comes in contact with many of the leading figures of the time, including Botticelli, Leonardo da Vinci, and Savonarola.

Recommended Juvenile Biographies

Ripley, Elizabeth. *Botticelli: A Biography*. Philadelphia: Lippincott, 1960. 68pp. MG. Ripley's is a sympathetic, brief account of Botticelli's life and work with 32 reproductions that are critically examined to reveal the artist's techniques and achievement.

50. JOHANNES BRAHMS
1833–1897

German composer Brahms is regarded as one of the great musical figures of the romantic period. Born in Hamburg, the son of a musician, Brahms was a musical prodigy as a pianist and violinist and composed in almost every genre except opera. His four symphonies (1876, 1877, 1883, 1885) have been judged among the greatest in symphonic music. Brahms never married, although he had several love affairs and remained devoted to Clara Schumann after Richard Schumann's death.

Autobiography and Primary Sources

Johannes Brahms: Life and Letters. Styra Avins, ed. New York: Oxford University Press, 1998. 784pp. Based on selected letters with annotation that draws on the latest Brahms scholarship, this volume provides a fresh view of the composer's life, much of it in his own words. The result is the closest autobiographical view readers should expect of the very private Brahms who destroyed countless personal documents, letters, and musical scores he judged unworthy or compromising.

Recommended Biographies

Schauffler, Robert H. *The Unknown Brahms: His Life, Character, and Works, Based on New Material*. New York: Crown, 1933. 560pp. Setting out to uncover the influences behind Brahms's music, Schauffler's study presents the factual record and reveals the many sides of Brahms's character, with their influence on his works. Innovative and controversial, Schauffler's interpretation challenged previous conceptions and remains invaluable as a source for anecdotes and intimate details.

Swafford, Jan. *Johannes Brahms: A Biography*. New York: Knopf, 1998. 721pp. This exceptionally well-written chronicle of Brahms and his work may well prove to be the definitive life. Exhaustive in its research, Swafford's study traces the emotional and psychological trajectory of Brahms's genius and celebrates the composer's unique position in musical history. The author does not idealize his subject but exposes through the diaries and letters of his friends Brahms's testy, aloof genius. The author assumes the reader's familiarity with musical forms so some previous musical knowledge will enhance appreciation of Brahms's achievements.

Other Biographical Studies

Gál, Hans. *Johannes Brahms: His Work and Personality*. New York: Knopf, 1963. 245pp. Analysis of Brahms's music predominates in this study but does connect criticism with a biographical narrative and the social, political, and cultural climate of the times.

Geiringer, Karl. *Brahms: His Life and Work*. 1947. Revised ed. New York: Da Capo, 1982. 397pp. With more access to primary material than any previous biographer of Brahms, Geiringer's biography was a groundbreaking study, now somewhat superseded, that filled in numerous gaps in the Brahms record and filled out a more intimate and human portrait of the composer.

Holmes, Paul. *Brahms: His Life and Times*. Southborough, England: Baton Press, 1984. 163pp. Part of the Composers: Their Lives and Times illustrated series, Holmes's useful introduction traces the life of a complex and often paradoxical man who adopted a shell of indifference and rudeness for self-protection and control of over precarious emotions. Using letters and reminiscences of friends and colleagues and many black-and-white photographs, Holmes's life is a worthy starting place for an interested reader.

James, Burnett. *Brahms: A Critical Study*. New York: Praeger, 1972. 202pp. James approaches Brahms from a variety of standpoints offering a number of fresh insights about his early training and musical background, his influences, and relationships with Franz Liszt, the Schumanns, and Wagner. Challenging accepted ideas, James displays Brahms in his nineteenth-century context and discusses his twentieth-century relevance.

Latham, Peter. *Brahms*. London: Dent, 1948. 230pp. Part of the "Master Musician" series, Latham's concise study provides a helpful introduction with sound interpretation and a reliance on authoritative sources.

MacDonald, Malcolm. *Brahms*. New York: Schirmer Books, 1990. 490pp. MacDonald's informative, critical biography is firmly rooted in recent Brahms scholarship and features the author's balanced assessment of virtually all of Brahms's compositions.

May, Florence. *The Life of Johannes Brahms*. London: E. Arnold, 1905. 2 vols. As a student of Brahms, May provides an unprecedented intimate view of the master as musician and teacher. Although clearly devoted to Brahms, the author manages a balanced assessment that includes his flaws.

Niemann, Walter. *Brahms*. 1929. Reprint ed. New York: Cooper Square, 1969. 492pp. In one of the first modern critical studies of Brahms, Niemann divides his account into two parts with the first devoted to Brahms's life and the second to an analysis of his work. Both provide a great deal of information and critical synthesis that will appeal to a reader looking for a comprehensive single-volume study.

Recommended Juvenile Biographies

Goss, Madeleine. *Brahms the Master*. New York: Holt, 1943. 351pp. YA. This fictionalized biography covers all the facts of Brahms's life in a dramatic, though historically reliable, fashion.

Mirsky, Reba P. *Brahms*. Chicago: Follett, 1966. 160pp. MG. Mirsky achieves a useful balance between biographical and musical details. The book is particularly strong on the composer's long relationship with Robert and Clara Schumann.

Biographical Films and Theatrical Adaptations

Brahms (1984). Director: Herbert Chappell. BBC television production discusses the life of Brahms and his influence on the development of symphonic music. *Symphony No. 4* is performed by the Royal Philharmonic Orchestra, conducted by Andre Previn. Video.

Brahms (1987). Director: Nicholas Vazsonyi. Documentary film built around Brahms's music traces the composer's career from his youth and early tavern brawls, to his agony of writing his first symphony and his despair over his hopeless love for Clara Schumann. Video.

Johannes Brahms (1996). Director: Malcolm Hossick. Part of the Famous Composers series providing a concise biography and a musical overview. Video.

Other Sources

Frisch, Walter, ed. *Brahms and His World*. Princeton, New Jersey: Princeton University Press, 1990. 223pp. This collection by various scholars is divided into three useful sections: essays, reception and analysis, and memoirs (reprinted in English for the first time).

Musgrave, Michael, ed. *The Cambridge Companion to Brahms*. New York: Cambridge University Press, 1999. 325pp. Leading scholars and musicians reflect the latest scholarship in this comprehensive view of Brahms's life and works.

51. LOUIS D. BRANDEIS
1856–1941

A lawyer and Associate Justice of the U.S. Supreme Court, Brandeis established (1907) Massachusetts savings-bank insurance and successfully crusaded on behalf of labor, most notably in the case of *Muller vs. Oregon* (1908), in which he persuaded the U.S. Supreme Court to limit the working hours of women. He was appointed (1916) by President Woodrow Wilson to the Supreme Court despite anti-Semitic opposition and while there continued his advocacy of social and economic reforms, maintaining a position of judicial liberalism. He was one of the few justices who voted to uphold Rooseveldt's New Deal legislation. He retired from the bench in 1939.

Autobiography and Primary Sources

The Letters of Louis D. Brandeis. Melvin I. Urofsky and David W. Levy, eds. Albany: State University of New York Press, 1971–1978. 5 vols. This scholarly collection of Brandeis's letters provides the closest glimpse available of the justice's private opinions and personality.

Urofsky and Levy have also edited *"Half Brother, Half Son": The Letters of Louis D. Brandeis to Felix Frankfurter* (Norman: University of Oklahoma Press, 1989. 659pp.) that chronicles the two men's important relationship from Brandeis's perspective.

Recommended Biographies

Mason, Alpheus T. *Brandeis: A Free Man's Life.* Princeton, New Jersey: Princeton University Press, 1946. 713pp. The only biographer granted access to important private papers and to Brandeis himself through a series of interviews, Mason's has long been established as the standard, authoritative life. Best on the pre-Supreme Court years, the book is a vivid depiction of Brandeis's career and a balanced interpretive assessment.

Paper, Lewis. *Brandeis.* Englewood Cliffs, New Jersey: Prentice-Hall, 1983. 442pp. Paper's able, informative life is based on thorough research and interviews with former law clerks who provide numerous anecdotes illuminating Brandeis's personality. Different from other studies that have emphasized Brandeis's ideas or legal career, Paper's comprehensive account does not neglect Brandeis's private life and the complexity of his attitudes formed from his background and time.

Strum, Philippa. *Louis D. Brandeis: Justice for the People.* Cambridge, Massachusetts: Harvard University Press, 1984. 508pp. Strum's sympathetic but critical political and intellectual biography focuses mainly on Brandeis's life and career before 1916 and his nonjudicial activities while on the Supreme Court.

Urofsky, Melvin I. *A Mind of One Piece: Brandeis and American Reform.* New York: Scribner, 1971. 210pp. In a series of seven essays, Urofsky looks at different aspects of Brandeis's career, stressing the underlying unity of his ideas and interests; *Louis D. Brandeis and the Progressive Tradition.* Boston: Little, Brown, 1981. 183pp. Urofsky's concise and readable survey of Brandeis's life and career is a useful complement to his earlier interpretive essays and a fine general introduction to the man and his ideas.

Other Biographical Studies

Baker, Leonard. *Brandeis and Frankfurter: A Dual Biography.* New York: Harper & Row, 1984. 567pp. Pulitzer Prize–winning biographer and historian Baker has crafted two essentially separate biographical accounts that connect around the similarities in the two men's careers and their joint friendship. Adding little that is new to the portrait of either man, the book is nevertheless a good, readable account for the general reader.

Baskerville, Stephen W. *Of Laws and Limitations: An Intellectual Portrait of Louis Dembitz Brandeis.* Rutherford, New Jersey: Farleigh Dickinson University Press, 1994. 409pp. Baskerville's intellectual biography traces the evolution of Brandeis's social, economic, and political ideas. Although the key events of Brandeis's life and career are covered, the emphasis is on the intellectual themes that unite his activities.

Dawson, Nelson L. *Louis D. Brandeis, Felix Frankfurter, and the New Deal.* Hamden, Connecticut: Archon Books, 1980. 272pp. This is a well-researched and informative study of how Brandeis and Frankfurter's ideas and philosophies helped to shape New Deal policy. After brief chapters on the lives and ideas of both men, Dawson documents their personal relationships and their behind-the-scenes maneuverings during the 1930s.

Gal, Allon. *Brandeis of Boston.* Cambridge, Massachusetts: Harvard University Press, 1980. 271pp. Ending with Brandeis's accepting the leadership of the American Zionist movement in 1914, Gal's is the most detailed and illuminating study of Brandeis's early life and formative years. Set within a vividly depicted portrait of the Jewish intellectual circles of Boston during the early years of the twentieth century, Gal skillfully tracks the origin of Brandeis's Progressive political principles and his emergence as a Zionist leader.

Konefsky, Samuel J. *The Legacy of Holmes and Brandeis: A Study in the Influence of Ideas.* New York: Macmillan, 1956. 316pp. Konefsky's is a comparative study of the constitutional philosophy of Brandeis and Oliver Wendell Holmes and their relationship. The book does an excellent job characterizing the backgrounds and tempers of both men.

Murphy, Bruce A. *The Brandeis/Frankfurter Connection: The Secret Political Activities of Two Supreme Court Justices.* New York: Oxford University Press, 1982. 473pp. Murphy exposes the relationship between Brandeis and Frankfurter in which the former paid a retainer to the latter for 20 years so that Frankfurter could advocate causes Brandeis could not be involved with while on the Supreme Court. Although ably researched and revealing, the book has a sensationalist tone that overemphasizes the conspiratorial quality of the pair's extra-judicial activities.

Todd, A.L. *Justice on Trial: The Case of Louis D. Brandeis.* New York: McGraw-Hill, 1964. 275pp. Todd supplies a vivid and dramatic narrative account of Brandeis's confirmation hearing in 1916. The book makes clear that it was not simply Brandeis's Jewishness but the question of future role of the Supreme Court which turned the confirmation controversy into a significant event in American history.

Recommended Juvenile Biographies

Freedman, Suzanne. *Louis Brandeis: The People's Justice.* Springfield, New Jersey: Enslow, 1996. 104pp. YA. Freedman summarizes Brandeis's career as a progressive Boston lawyer and liberal dissenter on the Supreme Court, providing as well a selection of photographs and drawings and a chronology.

Gross, David C. *A Justice for All the People: Louis D. Brandeis.* New York: Lodestar Books, 1987. 116pp. MG. Although occasionally marred by excessive praise and oversimplification, Gross provides adequate coverage of Brandeis's upbringing, family life, and judicial career.

Biographical Films and Theatrical Adaptations

The Magnificent Yankee (1950). Director: John Sturges. Film adaptation of Emmet Lavery's play on the life of Supreme Court Justice Oliver Wendell Holmes (Louis Calhern) includes an appearance by Justice Brandeis (Eduard Franz). Video.

Other Sources

Dawson, Nelson L., ed. *Brandeis and America.* Lexington: University Press of Kentucky, 1989. 163pp. This collection of essays provides an overview of Brandeis's life, his political activities, and his relationships from some of the leading Brandeis specialists.

Frankfurter, Felix, ed. *Mr. Justice Brandeis.* New Haven, Connecticut: Yale University Press, 1932. 232pp. This collection of appreciations to commemorate Brandeis's seventy-fifth birthday supplies an interesting composite view of the man and his work from a number of vantage points.

52. BERTOLT BRECHT
1898–1956

German playwright and poet Bertolt Brecht and his experimental innovations helped to define the modern theater. In the 1920s, Brecht developed what he called epic theater in which narrative, montage, and argument were fused to shock the audience into deeper realization of his social and psychological themes. An avowed Marxist, Brecht went into exile when the Nazis came to power in 1933, settling in Denmark and later the United States. His plays include *The Threepenny Opera* (1928), *Mother Courage and Her Children* (1941), and *The Caucasian Chalk Circle* (1948).

Autobiography and Primary Sources

Bertolt Brecht Journals. John Willett, ed. New York: Routledge, 1993. 556pp. Covering the years 1938 through 1953, Brecht's journals offer a fascinating glimpse of the writer and his views on such topics as World War II, the Soviet Union, and socialist realism, as well as reflections on his works.

Diaries 1920–1922. Martha Ramthun, ed. New York: Saint Martin's, 1979. 182pp. In the only purely autobiographical record Brecht ever kept, this is a revealing portrait of the unknown writer struggling with his first works and developing his creative ideas and methods.

Recommended Biographies

Ewen, Frederic. *Bertolt Brecht: His Life, His Art, and His Times.* New York: Citadel Press, 1967. 573pp. Based on original research using unpublished material from the Brecht archives, Ewen demonstrates how Brecht's work is intimately bound up with the history of his time and shows how his political and dramatic views were shaped. Each of Brecht's major works is critically examined. Not as thorough as Völker's definitive study, Ewen's book remains useful as a critical integration of Brecht's life and work.

Völker, Klaus. *Brecht: A Biography.* New York: Seabury Press, 1978. 412pp. Völker's definitive study avoids ideological bias and preconceptions to embrace the objective approach of a biographical detective, uncovering new facts and reevaluating prior assumptions. Brecht the man is perceptively revealed with evidence to suggest that his art reflects his private life far more than he cared to admit and was consistent in certain basic political and philosophical concepts despite fluctuating ideological interests.

Other Biographical Studies

Esslin, Martin. *Brecht: The Man and His Work.* Garden City, New York: Doubleday, 1960. 360pp. Esslin's critical biography locates the vitality of Brecht's genius in his struggle to reconcile the Marxist dialectic with his artistic humanism. Delving deeply into psychological territory, the author at several points ventures into unsupported speculation, but his conjectures have the ring of possibility if not established fact. When it first appeared, the book's questioning of the depth of Brecht's political commitment was controversial, establishing the ground for a negative valuation of much of Brecht's life and ideology by subsequent writers.

Hayman, Ronald. *Brecht: A Biography.* New York: Oxford University Press, 1983. 423pp. Hayman's comprehensive life is weighted toward a psychological reading of Brecht's nature, supported by a number of anecdotal details that color his portrait. However, there are vital dimensions of Brecht's life, such as his poetry, that the book does not explore. Recommended for the author's insights into Brecht's contributions to experimental drama.

Lyons, James K. *Bertolt Brecht in America.* Princeton, New Jersey: Princeton University Press, 1982. 408pp. Providing the most detailed account of Brecht's life in America, Lyons's study documents the record with multiple interviews; government sources, including telephone wire taps; letters; and newspaper and magazine stories. The sources lead the author to revealing insights about Brecht's contradictory nature and inner conflicts.

Munsterer, Hans Otto. *The Young Brecht.* London: Libris, 1992. 195p. A member of an early group of Brecht's friends in Augsburg, the author supplements his recollection with those of other close associates for the first detailed portrait of the development of Brecht's personality during his formative years up to 1924.

Biographical Novels

Feinstein, Elaine. *Loving Brecht.* London: Hutchinson, 1992. 187pp. Brecht's private life is dramatized in this story of Freida Bloom, a Berlin cabaret singer, whose relationship with the writer is traced.

Fictional Portraits

Kaminsky, Stuart M. *The Howard Hughes Affair.* New York: Saint Martin's, 1979. 207pp. In the author's witty pastiche of the hard-boiled detective genre, 1940s Hollywood detective Toby Peters is hired to investigate a bizarre series of unexplained circumstances, assisted by Basil Rathbone for his Sherlock Holmesian expertise. The book includes an offbeat appearance by Brecht.

Biographical Films and Theatrical Adaptations

Bertolt Brecht (1989). Director: K. Tetzlaff. Originally produced in Germany in 1986, this documentary, part of the Film for the Humanities series, recounts the details of Brecht's life and relates them to his artistry, documented by photographs, newspaper clippings, correspondence, and other archival material.

Other Sources

Mews, Siegfried, et al, eds. *A Bertolt Brecht Reference Companion.* Westport, Connecticut: Greenwood, 1997. 448pp. This reference guide surveys Brecht's contribution to world drama, and is organized into five sections: theory and practice of theater, poetry and prose, film and music, Marxism and feminism, and Brecht's reputation in the United States, Latin America, and Asia.

Thomson, Peter, and Glendyr Sacks, eds. *The Cambridge Companion to Brecht.* New York: Cambridge University Press, 1994. 334pp. Individual essays place Brecht's art in its critical, biographical, and historical context.

53–57. THE BRONTËS: PATRICK BRONTË (1777–1861); CHARLOTTE BRONTË (1816–1855); BRANWELL BRONTË (1817–1848); EMILY BRONTË (1818–1848); ANNE BRONTË (1820–1849)

The family of Yorkshire clergyman Patrick Brontë, the four Brontë children formed a close emotional unit whose imaginary games became the basis for the poems and novels of Charlotte, Emily, and Anne. In 1847, Emily's *Wuthering Heights* and Anne's *Agnes Grey* were published and ignored, mistaken as the apprentice work of the author of *Jane Eyre*, Charlotte's masterpiece, which became a notorious bestseller. In 1848, Branwell, whose career as a painter was ruined by drink and drugs, died; Emily caught cold at his funeral and died of tuberculosis. Anne, whose *Tennant of Wildfell Hall* appeared in 1848, also died of tuberculosis in 1849. Charlotte published *Villette* in 1853, and married her father's curate, dying after only a year of marriage. Patrick survived all his children, living to the age of 84.

Autobiography and Primary Sources

While no autobiography exists, readers should consult Charlotte Brontë's influential reflections on Emily, written for the second edition of *Wuthering Heights*.

Barker, Juliet R. *The Brontës: A Life in Letters.* Woodstock, New York: Overlook, 1998. 414pp. Using selections from letters and diaries, as well as contemporary reviews, Barker allows the Brontës to tell their own story in an autobiographical supplement to her fine biographical study.

The Letters of Charlotte Brontë: With a Selection of Letters by Family and Friends. Margaret Smith, ed. Oxford: Clarendon Press, 1995. 627pp. Constitutes the scholarly edition of Brontë letters.

Recommended Biographies

Barker, Juliet R. *The Brontës.* New York: Saint Martin's, 1995. 1003pp. This definitive chronicle of the Brontës makes use of newly discovered letters and manuscripts and demolishes many myths. In Barker's contrary view, Patrick Brontë was not the cold patriarch of a family of victims. Charlotte is shown as ruthlessly self-willed who dominated her sisters; Emily is seen as psychologically and physically dependent on her fantasy world; Anne emerges as a more daring and revolutionary writer than Charlotte; and Branwell sheds his reputation as a wastrel whose talent and personality provided much of Charlotte's inspiration in her fiction. Daring in its viewpoint but anchored in solid scholarship, Barker's study is likely to remain the standard work for some time.

Gaskell, Elizabeth. *The Life of Charlotte Brontë.* 1857. Reprint ed. London: Oxford University Press, 1961. 476pp. Gaskell's classic literary biography, written shortly after Charlotte Brontë's death and drawing on the author's acquaintance with her subject during the final years of her life, as well as letters and reminiscences, is actually a study of the entire family. Gaskell's evocation of the Yorkshire scene is unsurpassed, and her own novelist perspective adds to her analysis, although Victorian discretion and a desire not to slander the still-living Patrick Brontë led to some self-censoring.

Other Biographical Studies

Bentley, Phyllis. *The Brontës and Their World.* New York: Scribner, 1969. 144pp. This illustrated biography locates the Brontës' story in the social and historical context of their times. Bentley, a Yorkshire native, draws on her considerable regional knowledge for her portrait of the family and their milieu.

Fraser, Rebecca. *The Brontës: Charlotte Brontë and Her Family.* New York: Crown, 1988. 543pp. Excellently documented, using recently uncovered sources, Fraser's biography vividly captures the close-knit Brontë family world, focusing on Charlotte as a woman of indomitable will often in conflict with the expectations of her times.

Hanson, Lawrence, and Elisabeth Hanson. *The Four Brontës: The Lives and Works of Charlotte, Branwell, Emily and Anne Brontë.* 1949. Reprint ed. Hamden, Connecticut: Archon Books, 1967. 414pp. Long regarded the standard reference volume on the Brontës, the book remains useful as a succinct, general account for the nonspecialist.

Knapp, Bettina L. *The Brontës: Branwell, Anne, Emily, Charlotte.* New York: Continuum, 1991. 204pp. This short, critical study relates the details of the Brontës' lives to the formation and expression of their art. A helpful introduction.

Lane, Margaret. *The Brontë Family: A Reconsideration of Mrs. Gaskell's Life of Charlotte Brontë.* 1953. Reprint ed. Westport, Connecticut: Greenwood, 1971. 368pp. Lane provides a revision of Elizabeth Gaskell's classic Victorian biography based on subsequent evidence.

Maurat, Charlotte. *The Brontës' Secret.* New York: Barnes and Noble, 1967. 271pp. Depending heavily on a small number of secondary sources, this mainly uncritical account concentrates on the Brontës' childhood and their "secret": the fantasy world of Angria and Gondal that preoccupied them for so long.

Morrison, Nancy B. *Haworth Harvest: The Lives of the Brontës.* London: Dent, 1969. 279pp. The Brontës' literary achievement is subordinated to the romance of their lives in an evocative but uncritical recounting of familiar details. The author's approach is closer to fiction than objective biography.

Willis, Irene C. *The Brontës.* New York: Macmillan, 1957. 143pp. Willis's short study is a balanced account with a strict regard for the truth and serves as a valuable introduction to the subject.

Wilks, Brian. *The Brontës.* New York: Viking, 1975. 144pp. Wilks's pictorial biography, intended for a general audience, provides a satisfying introduction to the Brontës.

Winnifrith, Tom. *The Brontës and Their Background: Romance and Reality.* New York: Barnes and Noble, 1973. 276pp. In a valuable introduction to the challenges facing a Brontë biographer, the author provides a survey of Brontëana, including contemporary reviews of their novels, the books they read, and attitudes toward religion, sex, and class in their lives and works.

Anne Brontë

Chitham, Edward. *A Life of Anne Brontë.* Cambridge, Massachusetts: Blackwell, 1991. 216pp. A solid study with a helpful survey of previous biographies and the challenges facing the Brontë interpreter, Chitham's examination offers a rounded portrait, despite scanty sources. Inevitably speculative at various points, Chitham supports his assumptions with the available evidence.

Gérin, Winifred. *Anne Brontë.* London: Nelson, 1959. 368pp. Like the other separate volumes in the author's study of each of the Brontë siblings, Gérin's life of Anne is detailed and thorough, restoring considerable interest to the often overshadowed sister. The book's strengths rest in its re-creation of the Yorkshire milieu through detailed study of the topography and local history.

Harrison, Ada M. and Derek Stanford. *Anne Brontë: Her Life and Work.* New York: J. Day, 1959. 259pp. In this two-part biography and critical study, Harrison treats the life with a strong bias toward Anne and against Charlotte, as well as an unprovable assumption of an important love affair.

Langland, Elizabeth. *Anne Brontë: The Other One.* New York: Barnes and Noble, 1989. 172pp. This brief critical study offers concise chapters on the life, influence, poems, and each of Anne Brontë's novels.

Branwell Brontë

Du Maurier, Daphne. *The Infernal World of Branwell Brontë.* Garden City, New York: Doubleday, 1961. 336pp. This sympathetic, impressionistic study portrays Branwell as a tragic figure whose descent into drugs and alcohol is presented not as the cause but the result of his failure to achieve artistic success. The author is at times guilty of claiming too much for her hero and filling gaps in the record with Freudian speculation.

Gérin, Winifred. *Branwell Brontë.* London: Nelson, 1961. 338pp. Gérin's study, based on the same evidence Du Maurier uses, reaches an opposite conclusion that challenges a number of myths concerning the family's artistic hope and eventual black sheep whose descent into failure and addiction is handled nonsensationally as a human and family tragedy rather than a romantic one. Critics have charged Gérin with ignoring and misreading evidence, however.

Law, Alice. *Patrick Branwell Brontë.* London: A.M. Philpot, 1923. 192pp. Law argues unconvincingly that Branwell had a large and influential role in the creation of *Wuthering Heights.*

Charlotte Brontë

Gérin, Winifred. *Charlotte Brontë: The Evolution of Genius.* New York: Oxford University Press, 1987. 617pp. The author's groundbreaking study, the first to document Charlotte's formative (and ultimately abortive) romance with her Belgian teacher Constantin Heger, is the fullest and most important of the author's separate volumes on each of the Brontë siblings. Although critics have cited the book's inattention to scholarly sources and documentation and critical superficiality, its considerable merits outweigh its faults.

Gordon, Lyndall. *Charlotte Brontë: A Passionate Life.* New York: W.W. Norton, 1994. 418pp. Winner of the 1994 Chiltenham Literary Prize, Gordon's biography adds little to the factual record but shapes familiar material into a cohesive psychological portrait. Gordon looks beyond the conventional image of Charlotte as a modest Victorian lady to reveal a strong and fierce individual who transformed her struggles into art and reexamines the autobiographical sources of her fiction.

Morgan, Helene. *Charlotte Brontë: The Self Concealed.* New York: W.W. Norton, 1976. 256. Interweaving biography and literary interpretation, this critical study traces the development of Charlotte Brontë's psyche and the ways she turned her female liabilities into artistic vision. The author's perspective uncovers a number of fresh but debatable interpretations.

Peters, Margot. *Unquiet Soul: A Biography of Charlotte Brontë.* Garden City, New York, 1975. 460pp. One of several feminist interpretations of the author, this study portrays Charlotte as an unofficial feminist in conflict with Victorian and male society. Her approach sometimes distorts by using the novels as biographical evidence.

Winnifrith, Tom. *A New Life of Charlotte Brontë.* New York: Saint Martin's, 1988. 136pp. This concise interpretive study concentrates on the connections between the novelist's life and art. Arranged topically with a chapter on each of the novels, Winnifrith's critical reading is a model of sound judgment and biographical discretion.

Emily Brontë

Chitham, Edward. *A Life of Emily Brontë.* New York: Blackwell, 1987. 284pp. Described as an investigative biography, Chitham's detailed study sifts through all the available evidence to reconstruct a detailed chronology of Emily's life and her intellectual and artistic development that carefully identifyies facts and speculations.

Frank, Katherine. *A Chainless Soul: A Life of Emily Brontë.* Boston: Houghton Mifflin, 1990. 302pp. From Frank's feminist perspective, backed by recent scholarship on the social and literary history of women in the nineteenth century, Emily Brontë is not the sentimentalized mystic oracle of previous interpretations but a self-willed, sometimes forbidding woman who was not simply a passive victim of Victorian patriarchy but made choices and boldly stuck to them. Her interpretation is dominated by a somewhat reductive thesis concerning Emily's struggle with anorexia.

Gérin, Winifred. *Emily Brontë: A Biography.* Oxford: Clarendon Press, 1971. 290pp. Gérin provides a straightforward account of the events of Emily Brontë's life, supported by the author's intimate knowledge about the Brontë family and environment. However, a lack of concrete evidence often leads her into unsupported speculation.

Hewish, John. *Emily Brontë: A Critical and Biographical Study.* New York: Saint Martin's, 1969. 204pp. Focusing mainly on ideas, Hewish's critical study turns to Emily's poetry and *Wuthering Heights* for fresh insights into her feelings and ideas.

Spark, Muriel, and Derek Stanford. *Emily Brontë: Her Life and Work.* New York: Coward-McCann, 1966. 271pp. Stanford provides a critical analysis of Emily's works, and Spark treats her life, attempting to explain how an unworldly spinster could have created such intensely real characters as Catherine and Heathcliff.

Patrick Brontë

Cannon, John. *The Road to Haworth.* New York: Viking, 1981. 138pp. Examining the Brontë patriarch and his Irish forebears, this study's thesis is that Patrick Brontë's stories of his past provided his daughters with material for their fiction. Cannon's rather thin angle for viewing the family is marred by overgeneralization, and the book shows little psychological or historical penetration.

Hopkins, Annette B. *The Father of the Brontës.* 1927. Reprint ed. New York: Greenwood, 1968. 179pp. Trying to bring the real man into better view and correct early injustices done to his reputation, Hopkins offers the first modern reassessment of Patrick Brontë. Drawing primarily on secondary sources, this study lacks sufficient background information to contribute much to a fuller understanding of the Brontës' patriarch.

Lock, John, and Canon W.T. Dixon. *A Man of Sorrow: The Life, Letters, and Times of Patrick Brontë.* London: Nelson, 1965. 566pp. Making use of his correspondence, the authors provide the fullest reconstruction of Patrick Brontë's life that humanizes him and contradicts previous depictions of his selfishness and tyranny. Unfortunately a lack of documentation and tendency to repeat traditional interpretations limit the book's scholarly usefulness.

Biographical Novels

Banks, Lynne Reid. *Dark Quartet: The Story of the Brontës.* New York: Delacorte, 1976. 432pp. Chronicling the short, tragic lives of the Brontë siblings, this fictionalized biography stays close to the sources but does resort to some speculation when the evidence is lacking; *Path to the Silent Country.* New York: Delacorte Press, 1977. 230pp. Banks continues her portrait of the Brontës plausibly recording Charlotte's years after the deaths of her sisters and brother.

Brindley, Louise. *In the Shadow of the Brontës.* New York: Saint Martin's, 1983. 272pp. This evocation of the Brontës' story is provided by a scullery maid with the ability to see into the sisters' futures and to discover the inspiration and sources for their writing. Faithful to what is known, the novel provides plausible suggestions about the factual basis of the Brontës' fiction.

Cornish, Dorothy Helen. *These Were the Brontës.* New York: Macmillan, 1940. 491pp. Centering on Charlotte Brontë's growth to maturity and literary genius, the novel observes the basic outlines of the Brontës' lives, with plausible surmises when facts fail.

Hughes, Glyn. *Brontë.* New York: Saint Martin's, 1996, 431pp. This fictional chronicle of the Brontë family contains much biographical fact and period details about Yorkshire life. Alternating chapters shift perspective among each of the siblings. Keeping close to the known facts, the author does speculate intelligently about certain aspects of the siblings' relationship and is more successful at depicting Anne and Branwell than capturing the literary genius of Emily and Charlotte.

Tully, James. *The Crimes of Charlotte Brontë.* New York: Carroll & Graf, 1999, 284pp. As if the Brontë family did not suffer enough, this highly speculative "solution" to the mysterious deaths of Anne, Emily, and Branwell involves the poisoning skill of the curate Charlotte eventually married. Based on evident research, Tully's premise is far more intriguing than convincing.

White, Hilda C. *Wild December: A Biographical Portrait of the Brontës.* New York: Dutton, 1957. 319pp. This fictionalized account of the Brontës' story relies mainly on Elizabeth Gaskell's biography for its scenes and interpretation. The novel begins after her siblings' deaths with Charlotte reflecting on their younger days.

Fictional Portraits

Haire-Sargeant, Lin. *H.—: The Story of Heathcliff's Journey Back to Wuthering Heights.* New York: Pocket Books, 1992. 292pp. In this inventive elaboration of *Wuthering Heights,* mixing fiction and fact, Charlotte Brontë in 1844 receives a long letter written by Heathcliff confessing his experiences that transformed him into a gentleman.

Recommended Juvenile Biographies

Guzzetti, Paula. *A Family Called Brontë.* New York: Dillon Press, 1994. 128pp. MG. A thoroughly researched account of the lives of the Brontës, this biography explores their literary genius and personal struggles with high-quality photographs and a lucid text.

Martin, Christopher. *The Brontës.* Vero Beach, Florida: Rourke, 1988. 112pp. YA. Illustrated by quotations from their works and letters, photographs and drawings, this useful introduction narrates the Brontës' story and examines the symbolism, structure, and themes of the sisters' major works.

Sellars, Jane. *Charlotte Brontë.* New York: Oxford University Press, 1998. 128pp. MG. This sophisticated, profusely illustrated biography is an ideal supplement for admirers of *Jane Eyre.* Countering a depiction as a saintly victim, Sellars portrays Charlotte Brontë as an intellectual, a rebel, and at times a manipulator.

Biographical Films and Theatrical Adaptations

The Brontë Sisters (1993). Director: Richard Spanswide. Part of the Films for the Humanities series, the documentary traces the lives and times of Charlotte, Emily, and Anne and illustrates sites associated with them. Video.

The Bronté Sisters (1997). Director: Peter Hort. Despite the misspelled title, this entry in the Famous Author series provides a factual outline of the sisters' lives and a visual picture of their social and historical background. Video.

Devotion (1946). Director: Curtis Bernhardt. Considerable liberties are taken in this Hollywood version of the Brontës story, featuring Olivia de Havilland as Charlotte, Ida Lupino as Emily, Nancy Coleman as Anne, and Arthur Kennedy as Branwell with an appearance by Sydney Greenstreet as novelist William Makepeace Thackeray.

Other Sources

Evans, Barbara, and Gareth Lloyd. *The Scribner Companion to the Brontës.* New York: Scribner, 1982. 400pp. This useful reference guide includes a calendar of events, full discussion of the juvenalia, critiques, synopses, glossaries of characters, places, and references, as well as a guide to Haworth and the environs.

58. JOHN BROWN
1800–1859

American abolitionist, John Brown was born in Connecticut and grew up in Ohio. After a succession of business failures, Brown settled in Kansas in 1855 to battle proslavery forces. The self-proclaimed instrument of God's wrath murdered, with his sons and followers, five in the Pottawatomie Massacre, initiating the violence of "Bleeding Kansas." Branded a criminal by the South and a hero by Northern abolitionists, Brown led an attack on the federal arsenal at Harpers Ferry in 1859 to incite a slave uprising. Compelled to surrender by troops commanded by Robert E. Lee, Brown was hanged on December 2, 1859.

Autobiography and Primary Sources

Primary material in the form of letters and speeches have been published in a number of useful sources. *The Life, Trial, and Execution of Capt. John Brown.* 1859. Reprint ed. New York: R.M. DeWitt, 1969. 100pp. Published soon after Brown's execution, this volume offers a contemporary view of the raid and trial with a number of primary sources.

Ruchames, Louis. *John Brown: The Making of a Revolutionary.* New York: Grosset & Dunlap, 1969. 315pp. First published in 1959 as *The John Brown Reader,* the volume tells John Brown's story both in his own words and from the perspectives of those who knew him.

Sanborn, Franklin B. *The Life and Letters of John Brown: Liberator of Kansas and Martyr of Virginia.* 1885. Reprint ed. New York: Negro University Press, 1969. 645pp. Although written by a staunch partisan and one of the "Secret Six" who aided Brown, this early biography offers a unique eyewitness view and remains an important source for letters and other primary documents.

Recommended Biographies

Boyer, Richard. *The Legend of John Brown: A Biography and a History.* New York: Knopf, 1973. 627pp. Boyer did not live to complete the second volume of his monumental study that would have considered John Brown's life after his arrival in Kansas and Harpers Ferry. This book remains the most detailed consideration of Brown's early life framed by the author's thesis that he was not a solitary fanatic but a man of his times. Brown is examined in relation to lengthy profiles of his contemporaries and attitudes toward slavery that help to explain his actions and beliefs.

Oates, Stephen B. *To Purge This Land with Blood: A Biography of John Brown.* New York: Harper & Row, 1970. 434pp. This full-scale study based on previously uncovered and neglected sources is a balanced view mainly concerned with Brown's activities in Kansas and the Harpers Ferry raid. Oates neither whitewashes Brown nor dismisses his impact or force of character, setting his actions solidly in their historical and cultural context.

Villard, Oswald G. *John Brown 1800–59: A Biography Fifty Years Later.* Boston: Houghton Mifflin, 1910. 738pp. Villard's minute and judicious biography has long remained the most comprehensive and authoritative study of Brown, covering every aspect of his life, career, and attitudes. Based on a painstaking collecting of documents and interviews with eyewitnesses, the book is an invaluable source for future interpreters of Brown's life and character.

Other Biographical Studies

Abels, Jules. *Man on Fire: John Brown and the Cause of Liberty.* New York: Macmillan, 1971. 428pp. Falling between a popular and a scholarly biography, the book's lack of documentation limits its usefulness, but it does include information on Brown's family after 1859 that other biographies neglect.

Du Bois, W.E.B. *John Brown.* 1909. Reprint ed. New York: International Publishers, 1962. 414pp. Du Bois's appreciative study grants Brown considerable respect for his stand against slavery and his unwavering commitment to the rights of African Americans. This biography is interesting not for any new light it sheds but on Du Bois's perspective on militancy in dealing with white supremacy.

Furnas, J.C. *The Road to Harpers Ferry.* New York: Sloane, 1959. 477pp. Another unsympathetic biographer, Furnas offers a psychological interpretation of Brown suggesting that childish fantasies led to deviant behavior. Failing to place Brown's mental and emotional make-up into any social and historical context limits the book's useful as a balanced analysis.

Keller, Allan. *Thunder at Harpers Ferry.* Englewood Cliffs, New Jersey: Prentice-Hall, 1958. 282pp. In an hour-by-hour account of the raid, the book recounts the incident in compelling dramatic fashion but glosses over Brown's early life. The book's lack of balance in portraying Brown limits its effectiveness as a biography.

Malin, James C. *John Brown and the Legend of Fifty-Six.* Philadelphia: American Philosophical Society, 1942. 794pp. This exhaustive critical study is restricted to Brown's activities in Kansas during 1856 and the Pottawatamie incident. It portrays Brown unsympathetically, providing documentation that tries to eliminate any grounds for Brown's heroism or altruism.

Stavis, Barrie. *John Brown: The Sword and the Word.* New York: A.S. Barnes, 1970. 191pp. In a defense of Brown's actions and character, Stavis sees him as a commanding autocrat with an intense but rational social concern. Uncritical of Brown's statements, Stavis can also be charged with reducing the enigma and contradictions of Brown's motives and behavior to simplistic solutions.

Warren, Robert Penn. *John Brown: The Making of a Martyr.* New York: Payson & Clark, 1929. 474pp. Warren is the most distinguished of the anti-Brown biographers who sets out to debunk the myths surrounding Brown. For Warren, Brown is an unheroic fanatic who needlessly shed blood motivated by a need for self-glorification.

Biographical Novels

Banks, Russell. *Cloudsplitter.* New York: HarperCollins, 1998. 768pp. Brown's son Owen narrates this haunting, though realistic and authentic, account of his father's life from a cabin in the Adirondacks, to service on the Underground Railroad, to the killings in Kansas and the Harpers Ferry revolt as the aged son obsessively circles around the impenetrable enigma of his father. Although history is at times reshaped thematically, a humanized portrait of Brown emerges, as well as a powerful animation of the antislavery movement of the 1840s and 1850s.

Ehrlich, Leonard. *God's Angry Man.* New York: Simon & Schuster, 1932. 400pp. In this free and vigorous adaptation of history, Brown's activities in Kansas and attack on Harpers Ferry are dramatized. Brown reaches near biblical stature in Ehrlich's passionate interpretation of him as a righteous fanatic.

Nelson, Truman. *The Surveyor.* Garden City, New York: Doubleday, 1960. 667pp. Covering John Brown's activities in Kansas, this is a sympathetic and detailed fictional account with a strong factual basis. Although the author deals with Brown objectively, his partiality causes him to overdraw the villainy of his opponents.

Olds, Bruce. *Raising Holy Hell.* New York: Holt, 1995. 333pp. Captured in a verbal collage of letters, diaries, newspaper articles, songs, poems, interviews, speeches, monologues, and eyewitness recollections, Brown's life and purpose are refracted in a symphony of multi-textured, contrapuntal voices and viewpoints to form a tour de force of imaginative, historical reconstruction.

Fictional Portraits

Allis, Marguerite. *Free Soil.* New York: Putnam, 1958. 288pp. The events of "Bleeding Kansas" are seen from the perspective of a family of settlers in this authentic re-creation of its era.

Benét, Stephen Vincent. *John Brown's Body.* New York: Farrar & Rinehart, 1928. 336pp. Benét's long narrative poem chronicling the Civil War locates the cause of the conflict in Brown's attack at Harpers Ferry, which is re-created in detail from the factual record.

Dixon, Thomas. *The Man in Gray: A Romance of North and South.* New York: Appleton, 1921. 427pp. The title refers to Robert E. Lee who is followed through the events leading up to the Civil War and through the war itself from a decidedly Southern perspective. A large portion of the book is devoted to John Brown who is depicted as a "criminal paranodiac" under the influence of religious fanaticism.

Fraser, George MacDonald. *Flashman and the Angel of the Lord.* New York: Knopf, 1995. 394pp. The cowardly bounder Harry Flashman becomes a triple secret agent as Brown's military adviser in an offbeat comic but factual treatment of the Harpers Ferry raid, with Brown surprisingly earning Flashy's grudging respect.

Lynn, Margaret. *Free Soil.* New York: Macmillan, 1920. 377pp. The Truman family journeys west to Kansas from New England and are plunged into the violence between free-soilers and proslavery advocates with a convincing appearance by John Brown.

Monfredo, Miriam Grace. *Through a Gold Eagle.* New York: Berkley, 1996. 336pp. In the author's ingenious and believable mystery series involving nineteenth-century librarian and feminist Glynis Tryon, she investigates several murders in a case tied to the funding of John Brown's raid and abolitionists' efforts to start the Civil War.

Stern, Philip Van Doren. *The Drums of Morning.* Garden City, New York: Doubleday, 1942. 625pp. In this fictional adventure tale, a young man becomes involved in Brown's activities in Kansas along with a painstaking re-creation of the abolitionist movement and the stages leading up to the Civil War.

Williams, Ben Ames. *House Divided.* Boston: Houghton Mifflin, 1947. 1514pp. In this massive panorama of the Civil War from the Southern perspective, many of the great events of the war are authentically depicted, including Brown's raid.

Recommended Juvenile Biographies

Cox, Clinton. *Fiery Vision: The Life and Death of John Brown.* New York: Scholastic, 1997. 230pp. MG/YA. Filled with quotes from eyewitnesses and scrupulously detailed accounts of events, this biography of Brown shows the human side of the historical icon. The book's length and particulars may be a deterrent to readers interested in a more general discussion of the issues or more analysis of the historical importance of the man and his cause.

Graham, Lorenz. *John Brown: A Cry for Freedom.* New York: Crowell, 1980. 180pp. MG/YA. The author portrays Brown against a fully developed background of the corrosive impact of slavery to help explain his actions and uses actual quotes by and about the abolitionist showing multiple sides of this controversial leader.

Rees, Douglas. *Lightning Time: A Novel.* 160pp. YA. In this fictional account, a 14-year-old boy runs away to join Brown's company and takes part in the raid on Harpers Ferry. Exploring the complexities of the abolitionist cause and the morality of killing for one's beliefs, the novel is an intriguing introduction to Brown and his cause.

Rinaldi, Ann. *Mine Eyes Have Seen.* New York: Scholastic, 1997. 288pp. YA. John Brown's daughter Annie recollects the summer of 1859 when she served as lookout at the farm near Harpers Ferry that served as her father's secret headquarters. From her vantage point, the novel provides a detailed, informative account of the raid and a unique human view of Brown.

Scott, John A., and Robert Alan. *John Brown of Harper's Ferry.* New York: Facts on File, 1988. 184pp. YA. Appropriate for general adult readers as well as young adults, this detailed account uses primary sources to highlight the dramatic episodes in Brown's life and shows how he was shaped by his era.

Biographical Films and Theatrical Adaptations

Stavis, Barrie. *Harpers Ferry: A Play about John Brown.* South Brunswick, New Jersey: A. S. Barnes, 1967. 94pp. A John Brown biographer dramatizes the Harpers Ferry raid.

Sante Fe Trail (1940). Director: Michael Curtiz. Not reliable as history, this adventure story set in

"Bloody Kansas" shows J.E.B. Stuart (Errol Flynn) teaming with George Armstrong Custer (Ronald Reagan) in pursuit of John Brown, portrayed with demonic intensity by Raymond Massey. Video.

59–60. THE BROWNINGS: ELIZABETH BARRETT BROWNING (1806–1861); ROBERT BROWNING (1812–1889)

English Victorian poets Elizabeth Barrett and Robert Browning had one of the most celebrated courtships and marriages of their era. Elizabeth Barrett was a semi-invalid in her family's London home when she began a correspondence with Robert Browning, who admired her poetry. Despite the opposition of Elizabeth Barrett's tyrannical father, the couple married in 1846 and moved to Florence where they spent the majority of their married life. There Elizabeth Barrett wrote her greatest poetry, *Sonnets from the Portuguese* (1850) and Robert Browning perfected his dramatic monologues, collected in such volumes as *Men and Women* (1855) and *Dramatis Personae* (1864).

Autobiography and Primary Sources

Diary of E.B.B. Philip Kelley and Ronald Hudson, eds. Athens: Ohio University Press, 1969. 358pp. Covering the period 1831 to 1832, this is a revealing reflection of Elizabeth Barrett Browning's daily routine and personal conflicts.

Letters of Robert Browning and Elizabeth Barrett Browning. Elvan Kintner, ed. Cambridge, Massachusetts: Harvard University Press, 1969. 2 vols. This collection of nearly 600 letters written between 1845 and the Brownings' departure for Italy 21 months later is the essential record of their courtship and early relationship. A briefer selection, *The Love Letters of Robert Browning and Elizabeth Barrett* (New York: Putnam, 1969. 230pp.) is also available.

Recommended Biographies

Forster, Margaret. *Elizabeth Barrett Browning.* Garden City, New York: Doubleday, 1989. 400pp. Taking full advantage of the Elizabeth Barrett Browning manuscripts discovered by Philip Kelley in 1961, Forster's biography is the most comprehensive and authoritative study of the poet's life yet published, and the fullest account of her early life. Unfortunately, the poetry is insufficiently discussed and analyzed, and without footnotes, it is difficult to judge when she departs from direct evidence for invention and speculation.

Irvine, William, and Park Honan. *The Book, the Ring, and the Poet: A Biography of Robert Browning.* New York: McGraw-Hill, 1974. 607pp. Irvine's death left the completion of the final chapters and editing to Honan. Together they have produced the most authoritative, meticulously researched account of the poet that supersedes earlier biographies in its comprehensiveness and objectivity. Their study integrates an analysis of Browning's poetry with his life, helpfully connecting a view of the artist and the man. Judicious in its

interpretations, the book provides many fresh and penetrating insights.

Karlin, Daniel. *The Courtship of Robert Browning and Elizabeth Barrett.* New York: Oxford University Press, 1987. 281pp. This is the most detailed, scholarly look at the famous romance that attempts to penetrate the various legends surrounding the pair and substitute a realistic depiction that also looks at the creative implication of their relationship.

Ryals, Clyde de L. *The Life of Robert Browning: A Critical Biography.* Cambridge, Massachusetts: Blackwell, 1996. 291pp. Recommended as the best first book to read on Browning, Ryals balances insightful commentary on the poet's life and work while examining the entire Browning corpus chronologically. Ryals also places Browning and his poetry in a clear cultural and historical context.

Other Biographical Studies

Burdett, Osbert. *The Brownings.* New York: Houghton Mifflin, 1929. 345pp. Adding little to the established story, Burdett's account is workmanlike and readable in chronicling the familiar Browning story.

Markus, Julia. *Dared and Done: The Marriage of Elizabeth Barrett and Robert Browning.* New York: Knopf, 1995. 382pp. Novelist Markus provides a dramatic psychological portrait of the couple that does not neglect the evident strain of their mutual dependency. The author asserts rather than effectively shows Barrett's stature as a major British poet, and she dominates the book as a fiercely confident poet but addicted to morphine and continually battling with depression.

Whiting, Lilian. *The Brownings: Their Life and Art.* Boston: Little, Brown, 1911. 304pp. With the assistance of the Brownings' son, the author collects a number of intimate anecdotes and previously unpublished letters in this portrait in which evident partisanship and sentimentality compromise its usefulness as a critical, objective study.

Winwar, Frances. *The Immortal Lovers: Elizabeth Barrett and Robert Browning: A Biography.* New York: Harper, 1950. 344pp. In this fictionalized treatment, the author adds nothing new to the record but dramatizes the couple's relationship often sentimentally with numerous inaccuracies.

Elizabeth Barrett Browning

Boas, Louise Schutz. *Elizabeth Barrett Browning.* New York: Longmans, 1930. 216pp. Focusing primarily on the famous courtship, Boas does provide additional information surrounding Elizabeth Barrett's life prior to Browning's wooing.

Clarke, Isabel C. *Elizabeth Barrett Browning: A Portrait.* 1929. Reprint ed. Port Washington, New York: Kennikat Press, 1970. 304pp. This narrative biography reconstructs Browning's life from letters and memoirs and is particularly strong on the Brownings' Italian residence. Romantic and unscholarly in its treatment, the book reconstructs some dialogue without documentation.

Hewlett, Margaret. *Elizabeth Barrett Browning: A Life.* New York: Knopf, 1952. 388pp. In one of the best introductions to the subject for the general reader, Hewlett provides a scrupulously re-

searched, sensitive but objective, analysis of Barrett and her relationship with Browning that does not gloss over their marriage difficulties and provides a more sympathetic portrait of Barrett's father. Unfortunately, there is little psychological or literary analysis.

Mander, Rosalie. *Mrs. Browning: The Story of Elizabeth Barrett Browning.* London: Weidenfeld and Nicolson, 1980. 162pp. Mander's short life will appeal to the general reader looking for a concise rendering of the basic facts, but for a more analytical and comprehensive treatment, readers should look elsewhere.

Mermin, Dorothy. *Elizabeth Barrett Browning: The Origins of a New Poetry.* Chicago: University of Chicago Press, 1989. 310. In this critical and biographical study, Mermin argues for Elizabeth Barrett's contribution both to the Victorian poetic tradition and the development of women's literature. Skillfully interweaving biography and a close reading of the poems, the author demonstrates how the poet's life as a woman writer is part of the essential meaning of her art.

Taplin, Gardner B. *The Life of Elizabeth Barrett Browning.* New Haven, Connecticut: Yale University Press, 1957. 482pp. Much more objective and scholarly than previous sentimental treatments, Taplin uncovers new information about Barrett's early life and factors that help to explain the opposition to her marriage. However, Taplin undervalues Barrett's poetry, and his lack of enthusiasm negatively affects the literary analysis.

Robert Browning

Griffin, William H., and Harry C. Minchin. *The Life of Robert Browning, with Notices of His Writing, His Family, and His Friends.* 1910. Reprint ed. Hamden, Connecticut: Archon Books, 1966. 344pp. Long regarded as the standard life of Browning, this exhaustive study draws upon friends' recollections, and though it does not offer sufficient interpretation and is reticent on certain aspects of Browning's life, it remains an invaluable source of Browning material.

Orr, Alexandra. *Life and Letters of Robert Browning.* Boston: Houghton Mifflin, 1891. 2 vols. A Browning acquaintance, Orr had access to unpublished letters which she used to advantage. Much of her treatment of the chronology and events, particularly the courtship, has been superseded and corrected by more recent scholarship.

Maynard, John. *Browning's Youth.* Cambridge, Massachusetts: Harvard University Press, 1977. 490pp. This informative, thoroughly researched and balanced account of Browning's early life up to his elopement traces the various cultural, family, and literary influences that shaped the poet.

Miller, Betty Bryson. *Robert Browning: A Portrait.* New York: Scribner, 1953. 317pp. Integrating Browning's life and work in a critical study, Miller brings to light a number of overlooked facts, new information, and a fresh interpretation of the poet's character and artistry from a decidedly Freudian orientation.

Thomas, Donald S. *Robert Browning: A Life within Life.* New York: Viking, 1983. 334pp. Thomas expands on Ward's thesis that Browning was a divided man in which a defensive wall of privacy protected complex hidden obsessions and feelings. Thomas does not attempt to reconcile the contradictions in Browning but displays them in a comprehensive and honest examination of his life and artistry.

Ward, Maisie. *Robert Browning and His World.* New York: Holt, 1967-69. 2 vols. Ward's exhaustive study uncovers a duality between the public Browning and a hidden intellectual and artist. Much of Ward's study attempts to place Browning in his milieu and his literary relationships, while challenging previous interpretations that have grown up around the poet.

Biographical Novels

Forster, Margaret. *Lady's Maid.* New York: Doubleday, 1991. 548pp. Elizabeth Barrett Browning's biographer retells the poet's story from the perspective of her maid, Elizabeth Wilson. Dramatically enlarging episodes found in primary sources, Forster offers a vivid picture of Victorian class and deference against the background of the Browning's courtship and married life.

Iremonger, Lucille. *How Do I Love Thee.* New York: Morrow, 1976. 359pp. This novelized biography describes the Browning romance from their courtship through their 15-year marriage in an idealized and somewhat saccharine treatment, full of gushy clichés.

Fictional Portraits

Woolf, Virginia. *Flush: A Biography.* New York: Harcourt, Brace, 1933. 185pp. Although neither strictly speaking fiction nor conventional biography, Woolf's often charming life of Elizabeth Barrett Browning's cocker spaniel becomes a means for providing the reader an unusual glimpse of life on Wimpole Street and in Italy with the Brownings.

Recommended Juvenile Biographies

Waite, Helen Elmira. *How Do I Love Thee: The Story of Elizabeth Barrett.* Philadelphia: Macrae Smith, 1953. 221pp. YA. The author dramatizes the familiar story of the Brownings' courtship in a fictional form appropriate for high school readers.

Biographical Films and Theatrical Adaptations

Besier, Rudolf. *The Barretts of Wimpole Street.* Boston: Little, Brown, 1932. 165pp. Besier's popular drama that continues to be performed and adapted set the standard interpretation of the couple's famous courtship and the triumph of the heart over a domineering Victorian patriarch. Recent biographers have been far more generous to Mr. Barrett.

The Barretts of Wimpole Street (1934). Director: Sidney Franklin. MGM's film version of Besier's stage play is well acted and entertaining, featuring Norma Shearer as Elizabeth Barrett, Frederic March as Robert Browning, and Charles Laughton as Mr. Barrett. Video.

The Barretts of Wimpole Street (1957). Director: Sidney Franklin. Franklin remade his 1934 film with Jennifer Jones as Elizabeth Barrett, Bill Travers as Browning, and John Gielgud as Mr. Barrett in this less successful, paler version of the famous love story. Video.

Other Sources

Garrett, Martin. *A Browning Chronology: Elizabeth Barrett and Robert Browning.* New York: Saint Martin's, 1999. 192pp. Garrett supplies an extensive log of the Brownings' activities in a useful reference guide.

61. WILLIAM JENNINGS BRYAN
1860–1925

U.S. political leader, orator, and lawyer, Bryan served (1891-1895) as a U.S. Congressman and in 1896 secured the Democratic presidential nomination after delivering his famous "cross of gold" speech at the Democratic convention. He lost the election to Republican William McKinley and ran unsuccessfully in the 1900 and 1908 presidential campaigns. He served (1913–1915) as Secretary of State under Woodrow Wilson. A fundamentalist, he successfully prosecuted at the 1925 Scopes trial concerning the teaching of evolution. Many of Bryan's reforms, including income tax, woman suffrage, and prohibition, were eventually adopted by the nation.

Autobiography and Primary Sources

The Memoirs of William Jennings Bryan. 1925. Reprint ed. New York: Haskell House, 1971. 560pp. Bryan lived to complete only two-fifths of his autobiography; the remainder was finished by his wife.

Recommended Biographies

Coletta, Paolo E. *William Jennings Bryan.* Lincoln: University of Nebraska Press, 1964–1969. 3 vols. Coletta's is the definitive life of Bryan. Admirably researched and documented, the three volumes provide an unequaled record of Bryan's activities, and the biography's tone of judicious sympathy allows a complex, human figure to emerge from the mountain of data Coletta has assembled.

Glad, Paul W. *The Trumpet Soundeth: William Jennings Bryan and His Democracy, 1896–1912.* Lincoln: University of Nebraska Press, 1960. 242pp. After tracing the cultural influences on Bryan's ideas and character, Glad closely examines his public career and leadership in the Democratic Party during the pivotal 12 years of his life; *William Jennings Bryan: A Profile* (New York: Hill & Wang, 1968. 251pp.) is a more general character study drawing on Bryan's entire life and serves as a fine general introduction to the man. See also the author's *McKinley, Bryan, and the People* (Philadelphia: Lippincott, 1964. 222pp.), a reassessment of the presidential election of 1896 that discusses the economic issues, the personalities of the candidates, and the political manuevering that led to McKinley's victory.

Koenig, Louis W. *Bryan: A Political Biography of William Jennings Bryan.* New York: Putnam, 1971. 736pp. Readers without the patience and endurance for Coletta's three volumes should consider Koenig as the best single-volume alternative. Koenig chronicles Bryan's public life in a lively, dramatic style, arguing that Bryan should be viewed as an effective political leader and a champion of social justice.

Other Biographical Studies

Anderson, David D. *William Jennings Bryan.* Boston: Twayne, 1981. 210pp. Anderson's critical biography looks at Bryan's writings and literary qualities to isolate his greatness as a visionary who helped prepare the political and intellectual ground for the U.S. in the twentieth century.

Ashby, LeRoy. *William Jennings Bryan: Champion of Democracy.* Boston: Twayne, 1987. 245pp. Ashby's is a thoughtful and well-balanced biography, particularly valuable for the social and political context in which Bryan lived as well as a skillful analysis of Bryan's numerous contradictions in his ideas and his actions.

Cherny, Robert. *A Righteous Cause: The Life of William Jennings Bryan.* Boston: Little, Brown, 1985. 225pp. A fact-filled, concise summary of Bryan's life and career, Cherny reduces many of the paradoxes and contradictions in Bryan's character and activities to the leading theme of Bryan as a zealous crusader.

Hibben, Paxton. *The Peerless Leader: William Jennings Bryan.* New York: Farrar and Rinehart, 1929. 446pp. Of all the early biographies, Hibben's is the most objective in its assessment and scholarly in its approach. Combining sympathy with accuracy and judiciousness, Hibben's study remains a highly readable, full-length portrait.

Levine, Lawrence W. *Defender of the Faith: William Jennings Bryan: The Last Decade, 1915–1925.* New York: Oxford University Press, 1965. 386pp. Levine's revisionist view of Bryan's last years suggests that his advocacy for prohibition and fundamentalism instead of a denial of his progressive views was consistent with his basic philosophy developed over his lifetime. This meticulously researched and highly readable account sheds considerable light on this period of Bryan's life and helps to solve the many paradoxes in Bryan's character and beliefs.

Long, John C. *Bryan: The Great Commoner.* New York: Appleton, 1928. 421pp. Written shortly after Bryan's death, this is a sympathetic portrait in which the political leader is described as "a cross between Saint George and Don Quixote."

Werner, Morris R. *Bryan.* New York: Harcourt, Brace, 1929. 374pp. The biographer of P.T. Barnum and Brigham Young provides an unsympathetic, hostile portrait that employs the caricaturist's skills in exaggerating his subject's flaws. The lack of sympathy and understanding is a distinct liability here, and the book has few answers to the question of Bryan's considerable popularity and successes.

Williams, Wayne C. *William Jennings Bryan.* New York: Putnam, 1936. 564pp. Described by a reviewer as a "cross between a good sermon and a campaign biography," this is an admiring portrait by a longtime friend and devoted follower. The book's lack of objectivity limits the book's interest in displaying a contemporary's vindication of Bryan's character and career.

Wilson, Charles M. *The Commoner: William Jennings Bryan.* Garden City, New York: Doubleday, 1970. 487pp. In a factual but unscholarly biography, Wilson attempts to explain the forces and events that shaped Bryan's career with only modest success, serving mainly the needs of the general reader looking for a simplified overview.

Fictional Portraits

Fast, Howard. *The American.* New York: Duell, Sloan, and Pearce, 1946. 337pp. This biographical novel on the life of John Peter Altgeld features scenes from Bryan's political career.

Vidal, Gore. *Empire.* New York: Random House, 1987. 486pp. Vidal's panoramic social chronicle set during the turn of the twentieth century features appearances by a number of historical figures, including Bryan.

Recommended Juvenile Biographies

Allen, Robert A. *William Jennings Bryan: Golden-Tongued Orator.* Milford, Michigan: Mott Media, 1992. 162pp. MG/YA. This is an informative biographical profile of Bryan's life and times.

Kosner, Alice. *The Voice of the People: William Jennings Bryan.* New York: J. Messner, 1970. 190pp. YA. Despite fictionalization, Kosner offers a rounded portrait with a full historical view of Bryan's era.

Biographical Films and Theatrical Adaptations

Lawrence, Jerome, and Robert E. Lee. *Inherit the Wind.* New York: Bantam, 1960. 129pp. This fictionalized version of Bryan's combat against Clarence Darrow in the Scopes "Monkey Trial" of 1925 was made into a memorable 1960 Stanley Kramer film starring Fredric March and Spencer Tracy. Video.

Wilson (1944). Director: Henry King. This film biography of Woodrow Wilson (Alexander Knox) features an appearance by Bryan, played by Edwin Maxwell. Video.

62. BUDDHA
ca. 563 BC–ca. 483 BC

Indian philosopher and founder of Buddhism, Buddha, whose name means "enlightened one," was born Siddhartha Gautama, the son of a king of a Sakya warrior clan. Expected to follow his father as a ruler, he left his exclusive palace life at the age of 29 to see more of the world and became a wandering ascetic, attaining enlightenment at the age of 35. For the rest of his life he preached and taught his disciples.

Recommended Biographies

Foucher, Alfred. *The Life of the Buddha According to the Ancient Texts and Monuments of India.* Middletown, Connecticut: Wesleyan University Press, 1963. 272pp. Foucher's scholarly examination of the various sources and treatments of Buddha is an essential reference source for a reader interested in the myriad complexities in uncovering Buddha's actual life.

Marshall, George N. *Buddha: The Quest for Serenity: A Biography.* Boston: Beacon Press, 1978. 239pp. Concentrating on Buddha the man rather than his teaching, Marshall approaches Buddha from a psychological perspective, attempting to understand his motivations and the social and behavioral forces that shaped him. Reconstructed from the recognized factual sources, Marshall helps humanize the image of Buddha.

Nelson, Walter H. *Buddha: His Life and His Teaching.* London: Luzac Oriental, 1996. 150pp. Nelson supplies an accessible and authoritative introductory overview of both the facts and the legends that became the foundation for a religion and a philosophy.

Thomas, Edward J. *The Life of Buddha as Legend and History.* New York: Knopf, 1927. 297pp. Thomas's sensible and scholarly approach sorts through the various versions of Buddha's life and significance to create an informative composite view that employs both a factual and mythological approach in capturing the essence of Buddha as a man and symbol.

Other Biographical Studies

Carrithers, Michael. *The Buddha.* New York: Oxford University Press, 1983. 102pp. Concentrating on Buddha's teaching and philosophy, this concise study offers a way into the biographical labyrinth through a better understanding of what we know for sure about his role and nature as a teacher.

Chodzin, Sherab. *The Awakened One: A Life of Buddha.* New York: Random House, 1994. 153pp. Blending legend and history, Buddha's life and teaching is recounted by a respected Buddhist teacher.

Kalupahana, David J., and Indrani Kalupahana. *The Way of Siddhartha: A Life of Buddha.* Boulder, Colorado: Shambhala, 1982. 238pp. This is an imaginative reconstruction of Buddha's life, written by two Buddhists, that blends fact and legend.

Ling, Trevor. *The Buddha: Buddhist Civilization in India and Ceylon.* New York: Scribner, 1973. 287pp. Lacking sufficient evidence to reconstruct fully a historical Buddha, Ling compensates by an informative presentation of his historical context, tracing the various conditions out of which Buddha emerged and his impact.

Mitchell, Robert A. *The Buddha: His Life Retold.* New York: Paragon, 1991. 274pp. Vividly incorporating material from Buddhist tradition not available in other books in English, Mitchell's simple, yet poetic rendering includes many of Buddha's more important discourses interspersed with historical and legendary narrative material. A good, nonscholarly resource for the general reader without a background in Buddhist studies.

Pye, Michael. *The Buddha.* Dallas, Texas: Duckworth, 1979. 148pp. Dealing straightforwardly with the challenge of deconstructing a factual life of Buddha from traditional sources, Pye divides his study into historical, legendary, and mythological versions, serving to isolate fact from fiction while still recognizing the considerable interest in the shaping of Buddha's identity and his meaning over time.

Saddhatissa, Hammalawa. *Before He Was Buddha: The Life of Siddhartha.* Berkeley, California: Seastone, 1998. 129pp. This imaginative reconstruction based on both fact and legend portrays the human side of Buddha's nature from childhood, through his years as a pilgrim, to his end as an elderly teacher.

Biographical Novels

Payne, Robert. *The Yellow Robe: A Novel of the Life of Buddha.* New York: Dodd, Mead, 1948. 308pp. This fictional account of Buddha's life is divided into two parts, showing the worldly life of the young prince and his years as a pilgrim and mendicant preacher. Blending fact and legend, the novel is a colorful, if overly reverential, biographical portrait.

Fictional Portraits

Barrett, William E. *Lady of the Lotus.* New York: Saint Martin's, 1989. 376pp. The novel focuses on Buddha's wife, Yasodhara, and their youthful romance and married life. Based on evident research into the period and the facts and legends surrounding Buddha, the novel provides plausible surmises of what might have been.

Hesse, Hermann. *Siddhartha.* New York: New Directions, 1951. 153pp. Based very loosely on Buddha's biography, Hesse presents a moral allegory of the search for enlightenment that reveals much of the author's own autobiographical longings.

Raina, Vimala. *Ambapali.* New York: Asia House, 1962. 439pp. The novel vividly recreates the life of the Indian court dancer who became the first woman to be accepted by Buddha as a disciple.

Recommended Juvenile Biographies

Cohen, Joan L. *Buddha.* New York: Delacorte Press, 1969. 86pp. MG. This is a simple, straightforward account of Buddha's life based on traditional sources, with a focus on his search for truth and enlightenment.

Kelen, Betty. *Gautama Buddha in Life and Legend.* New York: Lothrop, 1967. 192pp. YA. Combining archeological evidence and Buddhist theological legend, the life of Buddha is recorded from his childhood, his quest for wisdom, his years as a sage and teacher, to his death.

Serage, Nancy. *The Prince Who Gave Up a Throne.* New York: Crowell, 1966. 62pp. MG. Serage provides a sincere treatment of Buddha's life and teachings, enhanced with outstanding illustrations.

Biographical Films and Theatrical Adaptations

Little Buddha (1993). Director: Bernardo Bertolucci. The film alternates between the contemporary story of a Tibetan monk (Ying Ruocheng), who believes that a young boy in Seattle (Alex Wiesendanger) is the reincarnation of a holy man, and scenes from Buddha's life. Keanu Reeves portrays Buddha. Video.

63. JOHN BUNYAN
1628–1688

An English author, Bunyan was a tinker by trade and served (1644–1647) in the parliamentary army during the English Civil War. He became (1653) a Baptist lay preacher and during the Restoration was imprisoned (1660–1672) for unlicensed preaching. While in prison he wrote nine books, including the first part of his masterpiece *The Pilgrim's Progress* (published, 1678). The second part appeared in 1684. Other works by Bunyan include *Grace Abounding to the Chief of Sinners* (1666) and *The Life and Death of Mr. Badman* (1680).

Recommended Biographies

Brittain, Vera. *Valiant Pilgrim: The Story of John Bunyan and Puritan England.* New York: Macmillan, 1950. 440pp. Brittain includes both a reliable account of Bunyan's life and career and a remarkable recreation of his times. Based on the author's intimate knowledge of Bunyan's Bedfordshire countryside, the book achieves an immediacy of time and place that animates Bunyan's life and milieu.

Brown, John. *John Bunyan: His Life, Times, and Work.* 1885. Revised ed. Frank M. Harrison, ed. 1928. Reprint ed. Hamden, Connecticut: Archon Books, 1969. 515pp. All subsequent Bunyan biographers are indebted to Brown's exhaustively researched life that has long served as the standard reference source that amassed significant documentary evidence of Bunyan's life and work. To be consulted rather than read for its narrative account, the book remains an important biographical source.

Griffith, Gwilym O. *John Bunyan.* Garden City, New York: Doubleday, 1928. 327pp. Relying mainly on Brown for his facts, Griffith offers a more accessible narrative chronicle of Bunyan's life and times. For the general reader looking for a fast-paced, vivid account, Griffith's biography is a fine choice.

Winslow, Ola E. *John Bunyan.* New York: Macmillan, 1961. 242pp. Inslow, a Pulitzer Prize–winning biographer, provides an outstanding, highly readable reconstruction of Bunyan's life. The book manages a three-dimensional portrait of the man and his era and is one of the best choices for the general reader looking for an informed, sophisticated, and engaging overview.

Other Biographical Studies

Froude, J.A. *Bunyan.* 1880. Reprint ed. New York: AMS Press, 1968. 181pp. Outdated now in many of its factual details, Froude's was a pioneering critical biographical study that helped shift emphasis from Bunyan's religious views to his literary art.

Harrison, George B. *John Bunyan: Study in Personality.* Garden City, New York: Doubleday, 1928. 226pp. Harrison's is a short, informed account that traces the development of Bunyan's

thought and temperament through a reading of his works.

Hill, Christopher. *A Tinker and a Poor Man: John Bunyan and His Church.* New York: Knopf, 1989. 394pp. Hill's study is a provocative reassessment that stresses Bunyan's radicalism and fills in the considerable gaps in the biographical records with profiles of others with whom the author may or may not have been acquainted. Highly conjectural, the book works best as an animation of Bunyan's world and the cultural, economic, and religious issues that shaped his era.

Sharrock, Roger. *John Bunyan.* 1954. Revised ed. Westport, Connecticut: Greenwood, 1984. 163pp. Sharrock supplies a thoughtful critical assessment of all of Bunyan's works, related to their biographical and historical context.

Talon, Henri. *John Bunyan: The Man and His Works.* Cambridge, Massachusetts: Harvard University Press, 1951. 340pp. In a thorough, scholarly summary and interpretation from a French scholar, Talon places Bunyan's life and work in their social and religious contexts.

Biographical Novels

Barr, Gladys H. *The Pilgrim Prince.* New York: Holt, 1963. 288pp. Barr traces Bunyan's career from his difficult childhood through his days as an itinerant preacher and his imprisonment.

Recommended Juvenile Biographies

Wellman, Sam. *John Bunyan: Author of the Pilgrim's Progress.* Philadelphia: Chelsea House, 1998. 207pp. MG. Part of the Heroes of the Faith series, Wellman provides an informative summary of the major events in Bunyan's life with a good introduction to his era.

64. EDMUND BURKE
1729–1797

British political writer and statesman, Burke abandoned the study of law for writing and in 1765 entered Parliament. He advocated a more conciliatory policy toward the American colonies, opposed the Stamp Act, and promoted the impeachment (1787) of Warren Hastings, governor general of the British East India Company, in response to the company's aggressive behavior toward Indians. His works include *Vindication of Natural Society* (1756) and *Reflections on the Revolution in France* (1790), which supported rational rather than violent change and made him a spokesman for European conservatives.

Autobiography and Primary Sources

Selected Letters. Harvey C. Mansfield Jr., ed. Chicago: University of Chicago Press, 1984. 497pp. Based on the monumental edition, *The Correspondence of Edmund Burke* (Chicago: University of Chicago Press, 1958-78. 10 vols.), this is an excellent selection arranged by subject rather than chronologically, along with a compact sketch of Burke's life and career.

Recommended Biographies

Ayling, Stanley. *Edmund Burke: His Life and Opinions.* New York: Saint Martin's, 1988. 316pp. The best available single-volume biography, Ayling has taken advantage of the publication of Burke's complete correspondence to write an informed and balanced account that treats equally Burke's ideas, public career, and personal life.

Cone, Carl B. *Burke and the Nature of Politics.* Lexington: University of Kentucky Press, 1957–1964. 2 vols. In an excellent political biography, volume one covers Burke's life up to 1782; volume two, the remainder of his life and the impact on his views on the French Revolution. The first biography written since the bulk of Burke's papers became accessible, Cone's is a thorough narrative of Burke's public activities, speeches, and writings. The book is less useful in describing Burke's character and private life.

Kramnick, Isaac. *The Rage of Edmund Burke: Portrait of an Ambivalent Conservative.* New York: Basic Books, 1977. 225pp. Different from many other studies of Burke that concentrate on his public career, Kramnick provides a psychological profile of the inner man. Finding a divided man, Kramnick offers an ingenious reassessment that challenges conventional views of Burke's conservatism which the author sees as Burke's efforts to restrain his own radicalism and private emotional excesses.

Lock, F.P. *Edmund Burke: 1730–1784.* New York: Oxford University Press, 1998. 564pp. Lock's first installment of a projected two-volume life promises to become the standard modern biography. Ably researched and judicious in its interpretation, the book carefully relates the details of Burke's life, personality, and ideas to the wider cultural, historical, and political contexts.

O'Brien, Conor Cruise. *The Great Melody: A Thematic Biography and Commented Anthology of Edmund Burke.* Chicago: University of Chicago Press, 1992. 692pp. Tracing the development of Burke's thought through the Irish, American, Indian, and French controversies, O'Brien makes use of extensive excerpts from Burke's writings and speeches, allowing his subject to speak for himself. Readers should have a previous grasp of the main outlines of Burke's life and period to profit fully from O'Brien's celebration of the man and his genius.

Other Biographical Studies

Kirk, Russell. *Edmund Burke: A Genius Reconsidered.* New Rochelle, New York: Arlington House, 1967. 255pp. Kirk offers a reassessment based on new scholarship, concentrating on four significant issues with which Burke was associated: the American Revolution, parliamentary conflict with George III, the impeachment of Warren Hastings, and the French Revolution. Although clearly a Burke partisan, Kirk supplies a good, succinct introduction to Burke's life and thought.

MacPherson, C.B. *Burke.* New York: Oxford University Press, 1980. 83pp. Part of the Past Masters series, MacPherson offers a concise interpretation of Burke's political thought that stresses his consistency throughout his career.

Magnus, Philip. *Edmund Burke: A Life*. 1939. Reprint ed. New York: Russell & Russell, 1973. 367pp. Drawing on previously untapped archival material, Magnus extends and deepens the biographical record, although the more accomplished uses of the sources have been done by subsequent biographers.

Morley, John. *Burke*. 1888. Reprint ed. New York: AMS Press, 1968. 216pp. Morley's early critical biography, part of the English Men of Letters series, was an influential analysis, particularly on the influences that helped to shape Burke's ideas, which, along with Prior's biography, helped establish the view of Burke that modern biographers and historians would confirm and challenge.

Murray, Robert H. *Edmund Burke: A Biography*. New York: Oxford University Press, 1931. 423pp. Murray's is a dry, digressive, pedantic life-and-times approach whose scholarship has been superseded by later works drawing on archival sources not available to Murray.

Prior, James. *Memoir of the Life and Character of the Right Hon. Edmund Burke*. London: Baldwin Craddock, 1824. 2 vols. Prior's much-reprinted biography was the standard source during the nineteenth century. Highly sympathetic in its treatment, Prior's study contributed to the positive shaping of Burke's reputation.

Robinson, Nicholas K. *Edmund Burke: A Life in Caricature*. New Haven, Connecticut: Yale University Press, 1996. 240pp. Robinson provides an unusual approach, reviewing Burke's political career through his depiction by caricaturists. Beautifully illustrated, this is a fascinating look at Burke as seen by his contemporaries, as well as a window into his political and cultural world.

Fictional Portraits

Morrow, Honoré. *Let the King Beware*. New York: Morrow, 1936. 376pp. The events in England leading up to the American Revolution are dramatized in an unorthodox presentation, with characterizations of George III and Burke.

Biographical Films and Theatrical Adaptations

Liberty! The American Revolution (1997). Directors: Ellen Hovde and Muffie Meyer. This PBS documentary series features actors portraying the principals in dramatic readings from their letters and speeches. Edmund Burke is played by David Yelland. The companion volume is written by Thomas J. Fleming (New York: Viking, 1997. 394pp.) Video.

65. ROBERT BURNS
1759–1796

Scottish poet Robert Burns was raised on a farm, and after several unsuccessful agricultural ventures, he saw his first poems published in 1786. Excelling in depicting scenes of rural Scottish life and incorporating dialect that brought the rich freshness of the vernacular back into English poetry, Burns's most admired poems include "Auld Lang Syne," "Comin' thro' the Rye," "Tam o' Shanter,"

and "The Jolly Beggars." After a life of dissipation and financial setbacks as a farmer, Burns died at the age of 37.

Autobiography and Primary Sources

The Letters of Robert Burns. Ross Roy, ed. Oxford: Clarendon Press, 1985. 2 vols. The scholarly edition of the letters forms the essential basis for all biographical accounts.

Recommended Biographies

Fitzhugh, Robert T. *Robert Burns: The Man and the Poet*. Boston: Houghton Mifflin, 1970. 508pp. This honest reappraisal attempts to convey a believable human portrait freed from previous positive and negative misconception. Fitzhugh demolishes the notion that Burns was a near-illiterate field laborer. His balanced, though ultimately sympathetic, portrayal is of value to both the generalist and specialist.

Mackay, James A. *R.B.: A Biography of Robert Burns*. Edinburgh: Mainstream, 1992. 749pp. Burns scholar and editor of the complete works, the letters, and concordance, MacKay comes closest to writing a modern, definitive life. Countering every legend in the biographical tradition, MacKay sees Burns not as the simple, impoverished farmer who drank himself to death but a sober, pious, and driven man, supporting his contentions with irrefutable and weighty evidence.

McIntyre, Ian. *Dirt & Deity: A Life of Robert Burns*. London: HarperCollins, 1995. 465pp. Based on solid documentary and archival sources as well as firsthand testimony of those who knew Burns, McIntyre's competent biography places Burns squarely in his historical context and offers a fuller evaluation of Burns's songs and poems than other biographers. The result is a less idealized and more sharply appreciated figure than previous accounts.

Other Biographical Studies

Carswell, Catherine. *The Life of Robert Burns*. New York: Harcourt, Brace, 1931. 411pp. Carswell's candid though impressionistic interpretation roots Burns firmly as a product of country life in impoverished eighteenth-century Scotland. When it first appeared, the author's sexual candor produced a furious reaction from Burnsian idolaters. Few readers today, even the most devoted Burns sympathizers, will be troubled by the author's frankness.

Daiches, David. *Robert Burns*. New York: Rinehart, 1950. 376pp. This critical study of Burns's poetry supplies biographical contexts for their creation and is astute on Burns's education and influences.

Fowler, Richard H. *Robert Burns*. London: Routledge, 1988. 280pp. Fowler's concise study adds to the documentary record on Burns's career through his expert and technical treatment of the poet as a farmer and the conditions he faced earning a living off the land.

Ferguson, J. de Lancey. *Pride and Passion: Robert Burns 1759–96*. New York: Oxford University Press, 1939. 321pp. Discarding a chronological

narrative in favor of topical treatment in chapters devoted to "Scotland," "Education," "Men," "Women," "Livelihood," "Song," and "The Scot," Ferguson packs his study with revealing background information that would be hard to cover in a more traditional study.

Grimble, Ian. *Robert Burns: An Illustrated Biography*. New York: Bedrick, 1986. 128pp. Grimble's short illustrated life examines Burns's career and achievement in the context of Scottish life during the eighteenth century, providing an excellent introduction to the subject.

Hecht, Hans. *Robert Burns: The Man and His Work*. 1936. Revised ed. London: Hodge, 1950. 301pp. Hecht's generally accurate and informative biography is trustworthy and objective in its assessment but lacks much richness and color in capturing Burns's Scotland and his era.

Lindsay, Maurice. *Robert Burns: The Man, His Work, the Legend*. London: MacGibbon and Kee, 1954. 356pp. This biography written for the general reader integrates Burns's life with his poetry and places both in the context of his era. Written by a recognized Burns scholar, this account is both reliable and readable.

Lockhart, John G. *Life of Robert Burns*. 1831. Reprint ed. New York: Dutton, 1959. 322pp. Lockhart's popular early biography, highly regarded enough to be reprinted in the Everyman series, has been rejected by modern authorities as inaccurate and wrong-headed, perpetuating the myth that Burns's decline was a result of alcoholism.

Snyder, Franklyn B. *The Life of Robert Burns*. 1932. Reprint ed. Hamden, Connecticut: Archon Books, 1968. 524pp. Snyder's scholarly examination presents a radically different view of Burns compared to previous accounts. Burns is portrayed as a sober, industrious man, a sentimentalist but neither a rake nor a drunkard. Uncovering much new evidence and scrupulously documenting his findings, Snyder's analysis remains a valuable contribution to a fair, objective view of Burns.

Biographical Novels

Barke, James. *The Wind that Shakes the Barley*. New York: Macmillan, 1947. 384pp.; *Song in the Green Thorn Tree*. New York: Macmillan, 1948. 456pp.; *Wonder of All the Gay World*. New York: Macmillan, 1949. 671pp.; *Crest of the Broken Wave*. New York: Macmillan, 1953. 320pp.; *Well of the Silent Harp*. New York: Macmillan, 1954. 351pp. Barke's massive fictionalized biography chronicles Burns's entire life in a sensationalized rendering of the events in which the poet is often the target of the author's unobjective, devotional affection.

Biographical Films and Theatrical Adaptations

Drinkwater, John. *Robert Burns: A Play*. Boston: Houghton Mifflin, 1925. 121pp. Not so much a full dramatic rendering of Burns's life as a series of episodes in which the playwright has grouped some of the poet's most popular songs.

Other Sources

Bold, Alan N. *A Burns Companion*. New York: Saint Martin's, 1991. 447pp. Invaluable as a biographical and critical guide to the poet, this volume collects a great deal of essential information on Burns's life, social background, and poetic achievement.

Lindsay, Maurice. *The Burns Encyclopedia*. New York: Saint Martin's, 1980. 426pp. This exhaustive reference guide to the life and works of Burns includes the latest scholarship about the poet and his poetry as well as pertinent information on every person and place associated with Burns, including the full text of biographical accounts written by two of his contemporaries. The book is rightly regarded as one of the most useful volumes about Burns ever published.

66. AARON BURR
1756–1836

American statesman Aaron Burr was a distinguished soldier in the American Revolution. As a politician, he served in the New York assembly, as state attorney general, and as a U.S. senator. He was elected vice president under Thomas Jefferson, and in 1804 was defeated in his bid to become New York's governor largely through the opposition of Alexander Hamilton. Burr challenged Hamilton to a duel and mortally wounded him. Joining forces with James Wilkinson and Harman Blennerhassett in a plan to seize territory from the Spanish in the lower Mississippi valley, Burr was arrested and tried for treason, but was found not guilty. His remaining years were spent out of public life.

Autobiography and Primary Sources

The Political Correspondence and Public Papers of Aaron Burr. Mary Jo Kline and Joanne Wood Ryan, eds. Princeton, New Jersey: Princeton University Press, 1983. 2 vols. This is the fullest collection of Burr's personal writings, previously scattered in a number of earlier sources, including

Memoirs of Aaron Burr. 1837. Reprint ed. (Freeport, New York: Books for Libraries Press, 1970. 2 vols.); *The Private Journals of Aaron Burr* (New York: Harper & Brothers, 1838. 2 vols.); and *Correspondence of Aaron Burr and His Daughter Theodosia* (New York: Covici-Friede, 1929. 349pp.).

Recommended Biographies

Lomask, Milton. *Aaron Burr*. New York: Farrar, Straus, 1979–1982. 2 vols. Recognized as the definitive biography, Lomask's balanced and comprehensive study was the first written with the author's full access to the scholarly collection of Burr papers. In the author's view, Burr deserves neither the treason charge nor vilification. Instead he is shown as worthy, if limited and at times wrongheaded, individual.

Parmet, Herbert S., and Marie B. Hecht. *Aaron Burr: Portrait of an Ambitious Man*. New York: Macmillan, 1967. 399pp. Uncovering a number of new facts about Burr, this balanced, mainly politi-

cal biography reveals Burr as a complex and contradictory figure. The authors neglect neither his heroism during the Revolution nor his subsequent misdeeds and at times baffling behavior, though the real object of Burr's ambition remains obscure.

Other Biographical Studies

Fleming, Thomas. *Duel: Alexander Hamilton, Aaron Burr, and the Future of America*. New York: Perseus Books, 1999. 446pp. Fleming provides a fresh look at the often-told tale of the rivalry between Burr and Hamilton, relating their feud to the politics of their day and supplying a masterfully painted human view of both men's characters and careers as they moved irrevocably toward their fatal encounter.

Kennedy, Roger G. *Burr, Hamilton, and Jefferson: A Study in Character*. New York: Oxford University Press, 1999. 476pp. In Kennedy's provocative revisionist analysis of these three statesmen, he attempts to redeem Burr's reputation. Brimming with little-known facts, controversial interpretations, and intriguing speculation, the book offers a new look at the reputations of all three men with penetrating insights abounding.

Parton, James. *The Life and Times of Aaron Burr*. 1857. Revised edition. Boston: Osgood, 1877. 2 vols. The first scholarly study, Parton's biography drew on Burr's memoirs and journals, various papers of his associates and critics, as well as interviews with surviving eyewitnesses. Despite his documentary effort, Parton's account was widely criticized as too favorable to Burr.

Rogow, Arnold A. *A Fateful Friendship: Alexander Hamilton and Aaron Burr*. New York: Hill & Wang, 1998. 336pp. Rogow's detailed account of the relationship between Hamilton and Burr describes the context for their duel and the personal histories of both men. Although the true basis of their enmity will never be resolved, Rogow offers a number of intriguing possibilities that helps mitigate Burr's blame and reputation for villainy.

Schachner, Nathan. *Aaron Burr: A Biography*. New York: F.A. Stokes, 1937. 563pp. Drawing extensively on primary material and contemporary newspapers accounts, which are reprinted, Schachter's comprehensive biography sets out to solve the riddle of Burr and to defend him from the charge of deliberate murder, political opportunism, and treason.

Wandell, Samuel H., and Meade Minnigerode. *Aaron Burr: A Biography Compiled from Rare, and in Many Cases, Unpublished Sources*. New York: Putnam, 1925. 2 vols. An exhaustive study that takes advantage of a great deal of primary and secondary material by Burr, his relations, and associates, the authors' study attempts to present the facts surrounding Burr from his perspective without losing objectivity.

Vail, Philip. *The Great American Rascal: The Turbulent Life of Aaron Burr*. New York: Hawthorn, 1973. 243pp. Written by prolific historical novelist Noel B. Gerson, this is a highly colored biographical narrative that focuses on the dramatic highlights of Burr's career.

Biographical Novels

Harris, Cyril. *Street of Knives*. Boston: Little, Brown, 1950. 370pp. Beginning with Burr's trip west in 1806 and ending with his arrest for treason, the novel dramatizes the often shady, contradictory events of Burr's schemes to establish an independent republic in the west. In Harris's view, Burr is an immoral, selfish visionary and his book offers few insights into his qualities as a statesman or military leader.

Seton, Anya. *My Theodosia*. Boston: Houghton Mifflin, 1941. 422pp. Seton's focus is on Burr's beloved daughter from the age of 17 to her mysterious death 12 years later. The novel dramatizes scenes from Burr's life and captures his daring and bravado, as well as the politics of the period. Sticking close to the known facts, when accounts differ the author has chosen the interpretation that seems to be the most plausible.

Vidal, Gore. *Burr: A Novel*. New York: Random House, 1973. 430pp. Told partly by Burr himself at the end of his life, reflecting on the events of the Revolution and the early years of the Republic, Vidal's endlessly provocative, revisionist view, based on solid research, is at the expense of the other founders. Washington is shown as incompetent and Jefferson as a ruthless opportunist. Some of Vidal's assertions, such as Burr being the father of Martin Van Buren are more inventive than historically reliable.

Fictional Portraits

Beyea, Basil. *The Golden Mistress*. New York: Simon & Schuster, 1975. 380p; *Notorious Eliza*. New York: Simon & Schuster, 1978. 351pp. Beyea's two-volume fictionalized biography of Eliza Jumel traces her remarkable career as the most famous courtesan of her day, Burr's mistress, and later his wife. Features a dramatization of the Burr-Hamilton duel.

Falkner, Leonard. *Painted Lady: Eliza Jumel, Her Life and Times*. New York: Dutton, 1962. 252pp. Capturing the social life of New York during the early 1800s, this fictionalized biography of Eliza Jumel, spouse of Aaron Burr, traces her rise to prominence.

Pridgen, Tim. *West Goes the Road*. Garden City, New York: Doubleday, 1944. 226pp. Frontiersman Caesar Brown joins up with Aaron Burr but later opposes James Wilkinson and Burr's schemes. The novel's presentation of its historical background is uneven. Some of the scenes are mere sketches; others are plausible and authentic.

Stanley, Edward. *The Rock Cried Out*. New York: Duell, Sloan and Pearce, 1949. 311pp. The novel traces the curious career of Harman and Margaret Blennerhasset who become involved in Aaron Burr's scheme to establish a western republic. Although staying close to the historical record, the novel does make some rather glaring errors, and Burr never emerges in depth.

Recommended Juvenile Biographies

Nolan, Jeannette C. *Soldier, Statesman and Defendant Aaron Burr*. New York: J. Messner, 1972. 191pp. MG. This is a comprehensive treatment of

Burr's life and career that attempts to show him in the most positive light possible. Despite simplification and partisanship, the essential highlights and period are covered informatively.

Wise, William. *Aaron Burr*. New York: Putnam, 1968. 191pp. MG/YA. Insightful and detailed, this is a thorough and concise rendering of Burr's entire career.

Biographical Films and Theatrical Adaptations

Magnificent Doll (1946). Director: Frank Borzage. Hollywood historical romp features Ginger Rogers as Dolley Madison—in love with both James Madison (Burgess Meredith) and Aaron Burr (David Niven)—who helps Jefferson to win the presidency and secures her own eventual role as first lady. Not convincing either as history or drama, despite a screenplay by Irving Stone.

The Man Without a Country (1973). Director: Delbert Mann. In this adaptation of Everett Hale's classic tale starring Cliff Robertson as Philip Nolan, Aaron Burr is depicted in this intense character study. Video.

See also Alexander Hamilton; Thomas Jefferson

67. GEORGE GORDON, LORD BYRON
1788–1824

An English poet and his age's most sensational literary personality, Byron was the son of a notorious rake who abandoned his wife shortly after Byron's birth. At the age of 10, Byron succeeded to his great-uncle's title and was educated at Harrow and Trinity College, Cambridge, before embarking on a European grand tour. In 1811 he published to great acclaim the first two Cantos of *Childe Harold*, a melancholy, philosophical work. It was followed by a number of popular verse tales. After affairs with several women, including Lady Caroline Lamb, and a disastrous marriage, Byron left England for good in 1816. His later writings including the satiric epic *Don Juan*, his masterpiece. In 1824 he sailed to Greece to fight for Greek independence from the Turks but shortly died from fever.

Autobiography and Primary Sources

In one of the most notorious literary losses in history, Byron's memoirs were destroyed by his executor, John Cam Hobhouse, following his death, leaving biographers to speculate what his view of his life might have contained. Although he did not reveal all of himself in his letters and journals, readers can get their closest direct view of Byron there.

Byron's Letters and Journals. Leslie A. Marchand, ed. Cambridge, Massachusetts: Harvard University Press, 1973–1982. 12 vols. This is the monumental and skillfully edited scholarly edition of Byron's personal writings.

Selected Letters and Journals. Leslie A. Marchand, ed. Cambridge, Massachusetts: Harvard University Press, 1982. 400pp. Marchand has chosen 300 letters and some journal entries from the 12-volume edition to reflect the best writing rather than to give a biography through letters. He has included a helpful biographical summary.

Recommended Biographies

Grosskurth, Phyllis. *Byron: The Flawed Angel*. Boston: Houghton Mifflin, 1997. 510pp. Grosskurth's psychoanalytically oriented study is full of fresh insights as well as important new research into Byron's psyche and compulsions. She largely neglects Byron the poet, however, for a humane study of both the strengths and flaws of Byron, the man.

Marchand, Leslie A. *Byron: A Biography*. New York: Knopf, 1957. 3 vols. Towering over every other biography due to the depth of its scholarship and objectivity, Marchand's provides a minute day-to-day and, in recording Byron's end, a nearly hour-by-hour, fully documented account that remains definitive, though the less patient reader may crave more synthesis and interpretation.

Marchand, Leslie A. *Byron: A Portrait*. New York: Knopf, 1970. 518pp. Incorporating material uncovered since 1957 and any changed views, Marchand has distilled the essence of his massive three-volume study in the best one-volume study available.

Other Biographical Studies

Drinkwater, John. *The Pilgrim of Eternity: Byron: A Conflict*. 1925. Reprint ed. Port Washington, New York: Kennikat Press, 1969. 408pp. In an elaborate defense of Byron, Drinkwater carefully examines the available evidence but construes nearly every doubt in Byron's favor, limiting the book's usefulness as an objective critical account.

Eisler, Benita. *Byron: Child of Passion, Fool of Fame*. New York: Knopf, 1999. 800pp. Often overheated and highly conjectural, Eisler concentrates on the intimate details of Byron's often confused sexual identity and emotional make-up. The sensational at times overbalances the view here, but most readers will find it hard to resist the author's absorbing account of Byron's remarkable, scandal-rich career.

Grebanier, Bernard. *The Uninhibited Byron*. New York: Crown, 1970. 354pp. Grebanier's psychosexual analysis links the poet's paradoxical nature—his need for love and inability to accept it—to deep-seated sexual trauma. The author treats as facts assertions, such as Byron's incest, that others regard as unproven hypotheses.

Longford, Elizabeth. *The Life of Byron*. Boston: Little, Brown, 1976. 237pp. Longford's competent, short life of Byron is a useful introduction to the poet, his life, and era.

Maurois, André. *Byron*. New York: Appleton, 1930. 597pp. Maurois's biography examines Byron the man rather than the poet, fusing the known facts into a vivid portrait that falls short of the author's other literary studies of Shelley and Balzac.

Minta, Stephen. *On a Voiceless Shore: Byron in Greece*. New York: Holt, 1998. 288pp. Weaving a modern journey in the footsteps of Byron in Greece with biography and critical appreciation, Minta provides a moving, if at times idiosyncratic and impressionistic, portrait of Byron's times and his end.

Moore, Doris Langley. *The Late Lord Byron*. Philadelphia: Lippincott, 1961. 542pp. This interesting examination of the controversy surrounding the immediate aftermath of Byron's death offers fresh perspectives on Byron as well as new facts about his life based on the author's first use of the Lovelace papers, the archives of Byron's wife and descendents, the papers of Byron's publisher, and the journals of John Cam Hobhouse.

Quennell, Peter. *Byron: The Years of Fame*. New York: Viking, 1935. 255pp; *Byron in Italy*. New York: Viking, 1941. 274pp. Quennell retraces Byron's steps from 1811 to 1823, adding little new to the familiar story of Byron's years of celebrity and failing to resolve or effectively interpret the multiple contradictions in Byron's character and actions.

Raphael, Frederick. *Byron*. London: Thames and Hudson, 1982. 224pp. Raphael's lively and compressed biography is dominated with Byron's role as a sexual desperado. Full of gossip and sexual chit-chat, the book makes much of Byron's homosexual tendencies and is best in its account of Byron's youth and the events leading up to the breakdown of his marriage.

Biographical Novels

Aldanov, Mark. *For Thee the Best*. New York: Scribner, 1945. 215pp. The novel chronicles Byron's last five years as a springboard for dramatizing European politics in the 1820s.

Combüchen, Sigrid. *Byron: A Novel*. 1988. London: Heinemann, 1991. 518pp. In a fascinating biographical mosaic, Byron is presented from multiple viewpoints, including those of his half-sister, his wife, Mary Shelley, and his boon companion Hobhouse. Fashioned out of factual detail and invention, the novel's preface indicates some deliberate inaccuracies.

Dessau, Joanna. *Lord of the Ladies*. London: R. Hale, 1981. 171pp. Concentrating on Byron's many intimate affairs, the novel provides the perspectives of his lovers, including Lady Caroline Lamb, his wife, and mistresses Claire Clairmont and Teresa Guiccioli. The orientation is more romantic than biographical with the various narrative voices unconvincingly differentiated.

Iremonger, Lucille. *My Sister, My Love*. New York: Morrow, 1981. 312pp. Byron's love affair with his half-sister Augusta, an assertion that still is debated by Byron's biographers, is offered to explain the poet's exile from England. His life in Italy and Greece is also described. Solidly based on letters, diaries, and the historical record, and reading more like a biography than a novel, the book paints Byron as selfish, cruel, and lazy but mostly misses his genius.

Kenyon, Frank W. *The Absorbing Fire: The Byron Legend*. New York: Dodd, Mead, 1966. 382pp. This biographical portrait concentrates on Byron's personal relationships in scenes at various point of his notorious career. Slanted toward the best possible interpretation of Byron's behavior, the novel commits some errors in fact.

Marlowe, Derek. *A Single Summer with Lord B.* New York: Viking, 1970. 251pp. The summer is 1816; the scene Lake Geneva, and Lord B. is Byron in this dramatization of the poet's relationship with

Percy and Mary Shelley. Scenes and dialogue are supported by annotation and stay close to the sources. Marlowe's reverence for the facts and awe of Byron results in only a sketch of the outward man.

Nicole, Christopher. *The Secret Memoirs of Lord Byron.* Philadelphia: Lippincott, 1978. 416pp. Byron narrates his own story with an emphasis on his scandalous love life. Fact and fantasy are interwoven with notes added to distinguish the two.

Nye, Robert. *The Memoirs of Lord Byron.* London: Hamish Hamilton, 1989. 224pp. Imaginatively reconstructing Byron's memoirs, which were destroyed in 1824, Nye details Byron's final six years with references to his childhood, schooling, friendships, and love affairs in a remarkable impersonation of Byron's voice and psychological insight into his genius.

Prokosch, Frederic. *The Missolonghi Manuscript.* London: W.H. Allen, 1968. 338pp. The dying Byron recollects his past in a series of intimate notebook entries. Occasionally the author's imagination dominates the biographical fact.

West, Paul. *Lord Byron's Doctor.* New York: Doubleday, 1989. 277pp. Cast as the diary of John Polidori, Byron's physician and travelling companion, recording the poet's European tour of 1816, the novel offers a perspective on the Byron-Shelley relationship and a vivid case history on the cruelty of genius and the massive egotism of the Romantics.

Fictional Portraits

Aldiss, Brian. *Frankenstein Unbound.* New York: Random House, 1974. 212pp. In this intriguing science fiction/horror fantasy, a time traveler goes back to 1816 to discover that Frankenstein was not an invention of Mary Shelley but as real as his monster. Byron and the Shelleys appear as characters.

Edwards, Anne. *Haunted Summer.* New York: Coward-McCann, 1972. 278pp. The infamous summer holiday of 1816 in which Byron was joined in Switzerland by Percy and Mary Shelley forms the background for this fanciful Gothic tale narrated by Mary.

Gray, Austin K. *Teresa: Or Her Demon Lover.* New York: Scribner, 1945. 385pp. Chronicling the full and interesting life of Teresa Guiccioli, Byron's mistress in 1819, the novel offers an interesting and fresh slant on the poet with the basic outline of Guiccioli's history faithfully observed.

Holland, Tom. *Lord of the Dead: The Secret History of Byron.* New York: Pocket Books, 1995. 324pp. In this alternative version of Byron's biography, the poet's adventures as a vampire are dramatized. Although sensational fantasy predominates, the novel draws on the facts of Byron's life as well as clues from his poetry.

Powers, Tim. *The Stress of Her Regard.* New York: Ace Books, 1989. 392pp. In this historical fantasy, a Regency doctor flees England to avoid a charge of murder. Haunted by guilt, he is aided by Keats, Byron, and Shelley in understanding his torment.

Seymour, Miranda. *Count Manfred.* New York: Coward-McCann, 1977. 283pp. This Gothic tale includes in its cast Byron and Percy and Mary Shelley, with a reliable period background and actual details from Byron's life.

Biographical Films and Theatrical Adaptations

Bad Lord Byron (1949). Director: David MacDonald. On his deathbed, Byron (Dennis Price) dreams his last judgment, and a number of witnesses, including Lady Caroline Lamb (Joan Greenwood) and Annabella Milbanke (Sonia Holm) offer their perspectives, recounting the events of Byron's life that focus on his many romances. Peter Quennell, a Byron biographer, shares the writing credit. Video.

Bride of Frankenstein (1935). Director: James Whale. The prologue to this classic sequel to *Frankenstein* (1931) features Elsa Lancaster both as the bride and as Mary Shelley discussing the origin of her monster story before an audience of Shelley (Douglas Walton) and Byron (Gavin Gordon). Video.

Frankenstein Unbound (1990). Director: Roger Corman. Adapting Brian Aldiss's novel, Corman sends John Hurt back to the past to encounter Byron (Jason Patric), Percy and Mary Shelley (Michael Hutchence and Bridget Fonda) and their neighbor Dr. Frankenstein (Raul Julia) and his monster (Nick Brimble) in full B-movie splendor and wit. Video.

Gothic (1986). Director: Ken Russell. In Russell's phantasmagorical treatment of the night in 1816 when Mary Shelley (Natasha Richardson) conceived *Frankenstein*, Byron (Gabriel Byrne) is the evil genius behind their hallucinatory psychosexual experimentation, with Julian Sands as Shelley. Video.

Haunted Summer (1988). Director: Ivan Passer. Film version of Anne Edwards's novel of the relationship among Byron (Philip Anglim), Shelley (Eric Stoltz), Mary Shelley (Alice Krige), and Claire Clairmont (Laura Dern) during their famous 1816 summer together is atmospheric but ultimately unconvincing. Video.

Lady Caroline Lamb (1972). Director: Robert Bolt. Despite Bolt's script and an impressive cast, including Laurence Olivier as Wellington and Ralph Richardson as the Prince Regent, this is a flat and unconvincing treatment of the famous scandal of Lady Caroline Lamb's (Sarah Miles) highly public affair with Byron (Richard Chamberlain). Video.

See also Mary Shelley; Percy Bysshe Shelley

PELHAM LIBRARY

C

68. JOHN C. CALHOUN
1782–1850

A prominent U.S. statesman and lawyer, Calhoun was a congressman (1811–1817), a leading "war hawk" during the War of 1812, and secretary of war (1817–1825) under James Monroe. He twice served as vice president, under John Quincy Adams (1825–1829) and Andrew Jackson (1829–1832). An advocate of states' rights, he resigned (1832) the vice presidency after his election to the Senate and while there defended his states' rights principles in dramatic debates with Daniel Webster. From 1844 to 1845 he was secretary of state under John Tyler. Fiercely proslavery, Calhoun argued against the antislavery Wilmot Proviso (1846).

Autobiography and Primary Sources

The Papers of John C. Calhoun. Robert L. Meriwether, et al, eds. Columbia: University of South Carolina Press, 1959–1991. 21 vols. This scholarly edition of Calhoun's correspondence, speeches, and writings is arranged chronologically and includes helpful interpretative introductions to each volume.

Recommended Biographies

Bartlett, Irving H. *John C. Calhoun.* New York: W.W. Norton, 1993. 413pp. Regarded by many as the best single-volume biography available, Bartlett's is an elegantly written and argued summation of Calhoun's character and public career that makes his positions and the issues that prompted them understandable in the context of the history of the first half of the nineteenth century.

Coit, Margaret L. *John C. Calhoun: American Portrait.* Boston: Houghton Mifflin, 1950. 593pp. Winner of the Pulitzer Prize, Coit's biography is a well-written, vivid account of Calhoun's private and public life with an emphasis on his personal and intellectual growth and social and political background.

Niven, John. *John C. Calhoun and the Price of Union: A Biography.* Baton Rouge: Louisiana State University Press, 1988. 367pp. Niven's is one of the best compact lives of Calhoun available. He is shown as a complex blend of character traits and a flawed but impressive political figure.

Wiltse, Charles M. *John C. Calhoun.* Indianapolis: Bobbs-Merrill, 1944–1951. 3 vols. Still regarded as the definitive biography, Wiltse's is the most comprehensive treatment of Calhoun's life as well as an important interpretation of American history between 1782 and 1850. Although chargeable with partisanship, the volumes have been rightly called historical biography on the grand scale.

Other Biographical Studies

Holst, Hermann E. von. *John C. Calhoun.* 1881. Reprint ed. New York: AMS Press, 1972. 374pp. The first scholarly biography, the book's chief value today is historical, as an indicator of Calhoun's reputation during the post-Civil War period.

Hunt, Gaillard. *John C. Calhoun.* Philadelphia: George W. Jacobs, 1908. 335pp. Hunt covers the principal events of Calhoun's private and political life in a fair profile.

Meigs, William M. *The Life of John Caldwell Calhoun.* New York: Neale, 1917. 2 vols. Best on Calhoun's political career, this is a sound, well-documented study.

Peterson, Merrill D. *The Great Triumvirate: Webster, Clay, and Calhoun.* New York: Oxford University Press, 1987. 573pp. Peterson treats the collective political careers of the trio to characterize American history during the first half of the nineteenth century.

Styron, Arthur. *The Cast-Iron Man: John C. Calhoun and American Democracy.* New York: Longmans-Green, 1935. 428pp. Styron's interpretive biography casts Calhoun in the lead role of a personal and partisan view of American history during the first half of the nineteenth century.

Fictional Portraits

Hough, Emerson. *54-40 or Fight.* New York: Grosset & Dunlap, 1909. 402pp. This political novel set in a Washington drawing room concerns the dispute over the Northwest boundary as Calhoun faces down an English diplomat and a Russian baroness.

Recommended Juvenile Biographies

Brown, Warren. *John C. Calhoun.* New York: Chelsea House, 1993. 111pp. MG/YA. This is a workmanlike summary of Calhoun's life and career that attempts to make his positions understandable in relation to the wider social and historical issues of his era.

Celsi, Teresa N. *John C. Calhoun and the Roots of War.* Morristown, New Jersey: Silver Burdett, 1991. 135pp. MG/YA. Calhoun's role in the formation of the ideology that was used by the South to justify secession is ably and informatively traced.

Crane, William D. *Patriotic Rebel: John C. Calhoun.* New York: J. Messner, 1971. 189pp. YA. Interspersing anecdotes from Calhoun's private life with events from his political career, Crane's is a reliable portrait that is strong on the political and historical background.

Other Sources

Coit, Margaret L., ed. *John C. Calhoun.* Englewood Cliffs, New Jersey: Prentice-Hall, 1970. Part of the Great Lives Observed series, this volume brings together Calhoun's own writings, views from his contemporaries, and biographical and historical evaluation.

Thomas, John L., ed. *John C. Calhoun: A Profile.* New York: Hill & Wang, 1968. 228pp. This is an informative collection of views on Calhoun from his contemporaries and later critics and admirers.

69. MARIA CALLAS
1923–1977

Born Maria Kalogeropoulas in New York City, operatic soprano Maria Callas made her professional debut in 1947 at Verona. She married (1949) Italian industrialist Giovanni Batide Meneghini, separated from him (1959), and during the 1960s was romantically linked with Greek shipping magnate Aristotle Onassis. Callas first appeared at La Scala and at Covent Garden in 1950 and at the Metropolitan Opera House in 1952. She was known for her dramatic intensity and expressive phrasing in a wide variety of operatic roles. She received critical acclaim for her performance in Pier Pasolini's film, *Medea* (1970).

Autobiography and Primary Sources

Callas by Callas: The Secret Writings of "La Maria." Renzo and Roberto Allegri, eds. New York: Universe, 1998. 166pp. Interweaving photographs, diary entries, and letters, the book provides a version of Callas's life story, mainly in her own words. Readers will want to test Callas's perspective with more objective sources.

Recommended Biographies

Galatopoulos, Stelios. *Callas: Sacred Monster.* New York: Simon & Schuster, 1998. 564pp. Based on the author's intimate association with the singer from 1947 until her death, this is a comprehensive chronological narrative of both Callas's public career and private life. Making use of the singer's own reflections on her relationships and creative methods, the author tells Callas's story very much from her perspective, correcting a number of misleading speculations and slanders, and including a hundred pages of photographs, documenting Callas's performances.

Kesting, Jürgen. *Maria Callas.* Boston: Northeastern University Press, 1993. 416pp. The work of a German music critic, the book sets Callas's full career into a wider context and deals more with her vocal achievement than her private life.

Scott, Michael. *Maria Meneghini Callas.* Boston: Northeastern University Press, 1992. 312pp. Scott's exhaustively detailed review of Callas's career includes critical discussion of her recordings and firsthand accounts of many of her performances. More for the opera buff than the general reader, Scott's is the most thorough chronicle of Callas's career available.

Stassinopoulos, Arianna. *Maria Callas: The Woman Behind the Legend.* New York: Simon & Schuster, 1981. 383pp. In a thoroughly researched biography, the author emphasizes the private torments of Callas rather than her musical talents and achievements. The woman Stassinopoulos finds behind the legend is a self-divided, needy individual crushed by her celebrity.

Other Biographical Studies

Ardoin, John. *The Callas Legacy.* New York: Scribner, 1977. 240pp.; *Callas at Juilliard: The Master Classes.* New York: Knopf, 1987. 304pp. Both books supply a detailed look at the singer and her achievements in her recorded performances and as a teacher.

Bret, David. *Maria Callas: The Tigress and the Lamb.* London: Robson Books, 1997. 380pp. This is a cliché-ridden account of Callas's life story that relies on dramatic oversimplification to underscore the sensational contrasts in the diva's rise and fall.

Callas, Evangelia, with Lawrence G. Blochman. *My Daughter, Maria Callas.* New York: Fleet, 1960. 186pp. The singer's mother offers her perspectives on her daughter's childhood, family relationships, and career in a highly personal, self-pitying and partial account. Interesting revelations are

mixed with the author's often petty carping about her unfilial daughter.

Callas, Jackie. *Sisters.* New York: Saint Martin's, 1989. 249pp. Callas's sister offers a tiresome self-justification that adds little to what is already known about her famous sibling and the trial she represented to those who loved her.

Linakis, Steven. *Diva: The Life and Death of Maria Callas.* Englewood Cliffs, New Jersey: Prentice-Hall, 1980. 169pp. The singer's cousin who scarcely knew Callas in her later life offers a hostile memoir, long on gossip and sensational events but short on genuine insights into Callas's enigmatic personality. Poorly written, the summary of Callas's career is superficial and unreliable.

Meneghini, G.B., with Renzo Allegri. *My Wife Maria Callas.* New York: Farrar, Straus, 1983. 331pp. In a mostly straightforward account of their relationship from 1947 to 1959, Callas's husband sheds some light on the behind-the-scenes manuevering of her career while offering a defense of his own part in Callas's history and his perceived slanders against himself and Callas.

Moutsatsos, Kiki F. *The Onassis Women: An Eyewitness Account.* New York: Putnam, 1998. 368pp. An employee of the Onassis family for almost 30 years, the author offers an insider's account of Aristotle Onassis's affair with Callas.

Stancioff, Nadia. *Maria: Callas Remembered.* New York: Dutton, 1987. 258pp. The author, who served Callas as a secretary and became a close friend, offers her and others' reminiscences. Stancioff's intimacy provides often fascinating, behind-the-scenes, positive and negative glimpses of the diva.

Wisneski, Henry. *Maria Callas: The Art Behind the Legend.* Garden City, New York: Doubleday, 1975. 422pp. Documenting the stage career of the singer, the book includes photographs and a complete listing of Callas's appearances, as well as a description of her master classes at Juilliard in 1971 and 1972.

Biographical Novels

Bond, Alma H. *The Autobiography of Maria Callas.* Delhi, New York: Birch Book Press, 1998. 219pp. Extensively researched, this fictional autobiography, written by a psychoanalyst, offers a convincing personality portrait and impersonation of the singer's thoughts and feelings on stage and off.

Biographical Films and Theatrical Adaptations

McNally, Terence. *Master Class.* New York: Plume, 1996. 62pp. Callas's many sides are imaginatively displayed in this drama inspired by the series of master classes the singer conducted at Juilliard in the 1970s.

Maria (1987). Director: Tony Palmer. A prize-winning documentary of Callas's life and career with footage of her performances and interviews with family, friends, and professional associates. Video.

Maria Callas: Life and Art (1987). Directors: Alan Lewens and Alistair M. Long. This film portrait explores the woman behind the public figure. Video.

Onassis (1988). Director: Waris Hussein. Film biography of Aristotle Onasssis (Raul Julia) has Francesca Annis as Jacqueline Kennedy and Jane Seymour in the role of Maria Callas. Video.

Other Sources

Csampai, Attila, ed. *Callas: Images of a Legend.* New York: Stewart, Tabori & Chang, 1996. 264pp. This album of photographs chronicles Callas's life from childhood until her last year on stage and off. Serves as a visual supplement to other biographical and critical accounts.

Lowe, David A., ed. *Callas: As They Saw Her.* New York: Frederick Ungar, 1986. 264pp. This selection of Callas's own words and the reflections of those who knew the singer or heard her perform includes a listing of her performances.

70. JOHN CALVIN
1509–1564

French Protestant theologian of the Reformation, John Calvin was born Jean Chauvin in Picardy. Educated in theology and law, Calvin in 1533 experienced a "sudden conversion" that caused him to dedicate himself to the Reformation, formulating Protestant thought in the influential *Institutes of the Christian Religion* that set out his rejection of papal authority, the primacy of faith alone, and predestination. In 1536 he was invited to Geneva where in 1541 he established a government based on the subordination of the state to the church. Calvin's teachings spread widely throughout the western world, particularly to Scotland, England, and colonial America.

Autobiography and Primary Sources

Letters of John Calvin. Philadelphia: Presbyterian Board of Publications, 1854–1858. 2 vols. Providing the closest direct approach to Calvin's autobiographical reflections, his letters are useful reading for those who wish to supplement their appreciation with primary material.

Recommended Biographies

Bouwsma, William J. *John Calvin: A 16th-Century Portrait.* New York: Oxford University Press, 1987. 310pp. In a brilliant animation of a passionate and complex Calvin and his age, Bouwsma helps to place his subject back in his own time and re-interprets Calvin and the Reformation in their relationship to larger cultural movements of the Renaissance.

Wendel, François. *Calvin: The Origins and Development of His Religious Thought.* New York: Harper & Row, 1963. 383pp. Marked by a command of primary and secondary sources, Wendel's biographical study and critical examination of Calvin's intellectual development is still regarded as the most reliable biography available, though certain details have been corrected by subsequent scholarship.

Other Biographical Studies

Ganoczy, Alexandre. *The Young Calvin.* Philadelphia: Westminster, 1988. 408pp. Concentrating on Calvin's youth up to his 1538 exile in Strasbourg, Ganoczy's scholarly study is the best available on the subject and an essential aid to understanding Calvin's intellectual and spiritual development.

McGrath, Alister E. *A Life of John Calvin: A Study in the Shaping of Western Culture.* Cambridge, Massachusetts: Blackwell, 1990. 332pp. Placing Calvin's life and thought in the broadest context, McGrath's intellectual and cultural study traces the impact of sixteenth-century history and culture on Calvin and his influence on his own time and on later western culture.

Moura, Jean, and Paul Louvet. *Calvin: A Modern Biography.* Garden City, New York: Doubleday, 1932. 312pp. Seeking to humanize Calvin and extricate the man from his theological system, this study shows him with courage and sensitivity without glossing over his faults and failings. Unfortunately the lack of documentation or an index restricts its usefulness.

Parker, Thomas H.L. *John Calvin: A Biography.* Philadelphia: Westminster, 1975. 190pp. This compact full-life study intended for a general audience is reliable in its facts though its interpretations betray a strong pro-Calvin bias and should be appreciated with caution. Readers looking for a more objective assessment should look elsewhere.

Walker, Williston. *John Calvin: The Organizer of Reformed Protestantism 1509-64.* 1906. Reprint ed. New York: Shocken, 1969. 456pp. A straightforward, concise narrative of the essential facts about Calvin's life and career, Walker's trailblazing study that helped initiate modern Calvin studies remains a readable, temperate character sketch.

Biographical Novels

Barr, Gladys H. *The Master of Geneva: A Novel Based on the Life of John Calvin.* New York: Holt, 1961. 252pp. Following Calvin's life from 1521 to 1559, through his boyhood, conversion experience, and his becoming a citizen of Geneva, Barr is faithful to the facts of Calvin's life and the period.

Norton-Taylor, Duncan. *God's Man: A Novel on the Life of John Calvin.* Grand Rapids, Michigan: Baker Book House, 1979. 298pp. In a partially first-person account, the author attempts to humanize Calvin in a plausible and factual chronicle of his life and the issues that defined the period. If not made likeable, Calvin at least emerges as understandable.

Fictional Portraits

Macleod, Alison. *City of Light.* Boston: Houghton Mifflin, 1969. 287pp. In the sequel to the author's *The Heretic* (1966) and *The Hireling* (1968), an English secret agent journeys to Calvin's Geneva in the grips of spiritual fervor that involves him in a series of adventures. The author captures the era and its complexity with considerable insights.

Recommended Juvenile Biographies

Stepanek, Sally. *John Calvin.* New York: Chelsea House, 1987. 116pp. MG/YA. Skillful in orienting Calvin's life and ideas to his period, this is an informative and useful biographical and historical overview.

Other Sources

Potter, G.R., and M. Greengross. *John Calvin.* New York: Saint Martin's, 1983. 194pp. Part of the Documents of Modern History series, various documents by and about Calvin, his ideas, and activities are arranged chronologically.

71. ALBERT CAMUS
1913–1960

A French writer who, along with Jean-Paul Sartre, was one of the most famous proponents of existentialism, Albert Camus was born in Algiers and raised in grinding poverty by his mother after his father was killed in World War I. Educated at the University of Algiers, Camus wrote articles and organized, wrote, and acted in an theatrical company before going to Paris in 1939 to work as a journalist. During World War II, Camus joined the French resistance and edited the underground paper *Combat*. Such works as *The Myth of Sisyphus* (1942), *Caligula* (1944), *The Stranger* (1946), and *The Plague* (1948) established his reputation as one of the most important and influential writers of the twentieth century. Camus received the Nobel Prize for literature in 1957 before he was killed in an automobile accident.

Autobiography and Primary Sources

Notebooks. New York: Marlowe, 1995. 2 vols. Camus used his notebooks to sketch out ideas for future work and to record snatches of conversations, excerpts from his readings, and his general reflections, forming a fascinating, intimate intellectual diary.

Recommended Biographies

Lottman, Herbert. *Albert Camus: A Biography.* 1979. Revised edition. Corte Modera, California: Gingko Press, 1997. 805pp. Richly informative for the scholar as well as the general reader, Lottman's massive and authoritative biography corrects many errors in the record and is particularly adept in untangling the Sartre-Camus conflict and documenting Camus's resistance activities. Readers may feel overwhelmed by the minutiae Lottman has uncovered, but there is no better source of biographical information on Camus, nor a more convincing human portrait or a fuller treatment of the author's milieu or intellectual context.

McCarthy, Patrick. *Camus: A Critical Study of His Life and Work.* New York: Random House, 1982. 359pp. Less detailed than Lottman, but equally scrupulous in its research, McCarthy's study is more interpretive and at times highly critical of Camus as a philosopher and political thinker. Despite a tone of skeptical hostility, McCarthy's critical view serves to cut through the various myths surrounding Camus.

Todd, Oliver. *Albert Camus: A Life.* New York: Knopf, 1997. 434pp. Todd's exhaustive biography rivals Lottman in its details gained through interviewing hundreds of Camus's associates to form a meticulous, evenhanded reconstruction of Camus's life against a historical backdrop of North Africa and France. Camus emerges in all his complexity with his public and private lives fully revealed.

Other Biographical Studies

Brée, Germaine. *Camus.* 1959. Revised edition. New Brunswick, New Jersey: Rutgers University Press, 1972. 281pp. Drawing on her own personal acquaintance with Camus and firsthand knowledge of Algeria, the author provides a number of revealing biographical insights in this book in which three-quarters are devoted to a critical assessment of Camus's works.

Bronner, Stephen E. *Camus: Portrait of a Moralist.* Minneapolis: University of Minnesota Press, 1999. 176pp. Bronner's compact but thoughtful intellectual biography traces the central themes in Camus's art and work, providing fresh perspectives on his fiction, drama, and philosophical writings and his cultural, political, and historical contexts.

Lebesque, Morvan. *Portrait of Camus: An Illustrated Biography.* New York: Herder and Herder, 1971. 174pp. This collection of photographs is a useful complement to fuller biographical studies. The brief text provides the highlights of Camus's career and comments on his personality and literary achievement.

Parker, Emmett. *Albert Camus: The Artist in the Arena.* Madison: University of Wisconsin Press, 1965. 245pp. Parker concentrates on Camus's politics and journalistic career from the 1930s to 1960 and is revealing on Camus's political attitudes, which he defends against charges of impractical idealism.

Thody, Philip. *Albert Camus 1913–1960: A Biographical Study.* New York: Macmillan, 1962. 242pp. Thody's critical study traces Camus's life chronologically and examines the biographical connection in his works. His evident sympathy does not prevent him from dealing with Camus honestly. Although without access to the notebooks, manuscripts, and private papers, the book's usefulness as an authoritative scholarly assessment has been superseded by subsequent studies.

Recommended Juvenile Biographies

Bronner, Stephen E. *Albert Camus: The Thinker, the Artist, the Man.* New York: F. Watts, 1996. 142pp. YA. This densely written account of Camus's life and work presumes prior knowledge of terms and people, and some unmotivated readers will find Bronner's overview heavy going.

72. MICHELANGELO MERISI DA CARAVAGGIO
1573–1610

Italian painter, Caravaggio apprenticed in Milan before coming to Rome where he produced a number of important religious paintings for his patron Cardinal Francesco del Mont. His violent temper and erratic behavior resulted in a number of brawls, and in 1606 he fled Rome after killing a man in a duel. Considered an artistic revolutionary for his direct imitation of nature and his chiaroscuro technique of partially illuminating figures against a dark background, Caravaggio had an important influence on later painters.

Autobiography and Primary Sources

Friedlander, Walter F. *Caravaggio Studies*. Princeton, New Jersey: Princeton University Press, 1955. 320pp. In this invaluable sourcebook, Friedlander reprints virtually every contemporary and immediately posthumous source document on the artist.

Recommended Biographies

Hibbard, Howard. *Caravaggio*. New York: Harper & Row, 1983. 404pp. Using newly discovered documents and paintings and reflecting critical consensus that have revised many ideas about Caravaggio since Friedlander's collection, Hibbard's psychological assessment locates the painter and his works firmly in relation to his historical background. Although new material has emerged since publication, Hibbard's remains a must-read for anyone interested in a serious assessment of Caravaggio's life and works.

Langdon, Helen. *Caravaggio: A Life*. New York: Farrar, Straus, 1999. 436pp. In a balanced and compelling portrait of the artist, Langdon combines biographical and critical analysis in a reassessment of Caravaggio's life and work. The painter is shown both as a rebel and outsider, and as immersed in a fully displayed seventeenth-century Roman world of art, politics, and patronage.

Robb, Peter. *M: The Man Who Became Caravaggio*. New York: Holt, 2000. 570pp. A provocative, carefully researched fresh look at Caravaggio's life, work, and character, Robb presents a complex figure of a supremely talented and visionary artist with tragic human flaws, living in a dangerous and often cruel world. Each of these element are vividly portrayed.

Seward, Desmond. *Caravaggio: A Passionate Life*. New York: Morrow, 1998. 224pp. Although careful in its scholarship, Seward chronicles Caravaggio's life and era with the vivid intensity of a novel. The author's animation of sixteenth-century life helps the artist emerge fully in all his captivating contradiction. Few biographies are better in turning a life into a riveting drama.

Other Biographical Studies

Berenson, Bernard. *Caravaggio: His Incongruity and His Fame*. New York: Macmillan, 1953. 122pp. The first part of this critical study provides a detailed analysis of Caravaggio's important paintings; the second part discusses his style and influences. Opinionated but stimulating, the volume includes paintings now excluded from the canon.

Bersani, Leo, and Ulysse Dutoit. *Caravaggio's Secrets*. Cambridge, Massachusetts: MIT Press, 1998. 140pp. The authors offer a psychoanalytical reading of the artist. Jargon-heavy and complex,

the approach here is not for the general or casual reader, but the book does provide an ingenious reading of Caravaggio's temperament as revealed in a close analysis of his work.

Bonsanti, Giorgio. *Caravaggio*. Florence: SCALA, 1984. 80pp. This sumptuously illustrated volume traces Caravaggio's life and artistic development chronologically, analyzing his work and underscoring his achievement. Serves as a useful introduction to the artist.

Delogu, Giuseppe. *Caravaggio*. New York: Abrams, 1964. 163pp. This oversized art book with magnificent reproduction of Caravaggio's work includes a brief overview of the painter's life and assessment of his artistic genius.

Hinks, R.P. *Michelangelo Merisi da Caravaggio: His Life, His Legend, His Works*. New York: Beechhurst Press, 1953. 126pp. In the first full-length book about Caravaggio in English, the author gives a brief account of his life, based on the few known facts. Hinks then considers the testimony of Caravaggio's contemporaries and finally draws up a canon of his work in a probable historical sequence.

Moir, Alfred. *Caravaggio*. New York: Abrams, 1982. 168pp. In this illustrated introduction to the artist, a biographical essay accompanies a stunning reproduction of Caravaggio's works, of which 40 are in color. The succinct text shows a great deal of synthesis and reliable interpretation.

Biographical Novels

Calitri, Charles J. *The Goliath Head: A Novel about Caravaggio*. New York: Crown, 1972. 346pp. Calitri pieces together the few known facts with imaginary incidents, customs, and details of daily life to chronicle Caravaggio's troubled life beginning with his 1590 arrival in Rome.

Murray, Linda. *The Dark Fire*. New York: Morrow, 1977. 418pp. Tracing his career from his apprenticeship through his tragic end, the novel intermixes fact and fiction to capture the violent temperament of the artist.

Payne, Robert. *Caravaggio: A Novel*. Boston: Little, Brown, 1968. 329pp. Writing in exile to his patron, Caravaggio narrates his own story from his birth, through his apprenticeship in Milan, his Roman years, and tragic end as a fugitive. Often sensationalized, Payne's heightened style is appropriate given his subject, and the essential details of the painter's life are captured faithfully.

Biographical Films and Theatrical Adaptations

McGuinness, Frank. *Innocence: The Life and Death of Michelangelo Merisis, Caravaggio*. London: Faber and Faber, 1987. 62pp. As the playwright explains, "I pieced together a fiction of [Caravaggio's] life based on a reading of clues I imagined he'd left in his paintings.. .. I tried to make him a poet and in his poetry would be his painting."

Caravaggio (1987). Director: Derek Jarman. This controversial British film based on the life of Caravaggio depicts the painter's bisexuality, his relationship with prostitute models, and his violent

temperament, reproduced in a visual style that matches his paintings. Nigel Terry stars as the painter. Video.

Caravaggio (1991). Director: Claudio Stetta. Documentary film, part of the European video library arts series. Video.

73. THOMAS CARLYLE
1795–1881

English writer, historian, and social critic, Thomas Carlyle was born in Scotland. Strongly influenced by Goethe and transcendental philosophers, Carlyle first wrote several works interpreting German romantic thought. In 1826 he married Jane Welsh, who would prove to be a formidable assistant to Carlyle in his career. In 1833–1834 he published *Sartor Resartus* before moving to London to begin his monumental study of the French Revolution, which was completed in 1837 after the first draft was accidentally destroyed. Acclaimed as a Victorian sage and prophet, Carlyle continued to write prolifically and contentiously in such volumes as *On Heroes, Hero Worship, and the Heroic in History* (1841), *Past and Present* (1843), and a massive biography of Frederick the Great (1858–1865).

Autobiography and Primary Sources

The Collected Letters of Thomas and Jane Welsh Carlyle. Durham, North Carolina: Duke University Press, 1970–1995. 25vols. The monumental collection of letters is the essential source for biographical insights on Carlyle.

Reminiscences. K.J. Fielding and Ian Campbell, eds. New York: Oxford University Press, 1997. 481pp. Indispensable for Carlyle's insights into his life, career, and marriage, his memoir needs to be read alongside more critical sources for a balanced view.

Recommended Biographies

Froude, J.A. *Thomas Carlyle: A History of the First 40 Years of His Life, 1795–1835*. New York: Harper, 1882. 2 vols; *Thomas Carlyle, 1834–81: A History of His Life in London*. New York: Harper, 1884. 2 vols. Froude's monumental biography remains the starting point for all subsequent Carlyle biographers and initiated the controversies that have surrounded Carlyle ever since. Froude admired Carlyle as a misunderstood prophet but was determined to portray him honestly as he knew him: selfish, intolerant, and cruelly insensitive to his wife. His candor toppled a Victorian giant from his pedestal. Froude's work remains an invaluable source on Carlyle as well as one of the greatest examples of the art of biography; *My Relations with Carlyle* (New York: Scribner, 1903. 80pp.), published posthumously, is a justification of his assertions and of his most contentious claims of Carlyle's impotence; *Froude's Life of Carlyle*. John Clubbe, ed. (Columbus: Ohio State University Press, 1979. 725pp.) offers a one-volume abridged edition.

Kaplan, Fred. *Thomas Carlyle: A Biography*. Ithaca, New York: Cornell University Press, 1983.

614pp. The most important biography of Carlyle since Froude, Kaplan's detailed and balanced study places Carlyle squarely in his historical times and shows with skill the influence of Carlyle's Presbyterian boyhood throughout his life. Kaplan's life is likely to remain the definitive modern biography for some time to come.

Other Biographical Studies

Burdett, Osbert. *The Two Carlyles.* 1931. Reprint ed. New York: Haskell House, 1971. 309pp. Burdett's double biography avoids taking sides between Carlyle and his brilliant but frustrated wife. The author's character sketches challenge previous views, and the result is a more balanced account of Carlyle's greatness and his flaws.

Campbell, Ian. *Thomas Carlyle.* New York: Scribner, 1974. 210pp. In an succinct, knowledgeable introduction to Carlyle's life, drawn mainly from the correspondence, Campbell mounts a spirited defense of some of Carlyle's most indefensible political and moral positions.

Hanson, Lawrence, and Elizabeth Hanson. *Necessary Evil: The Life of Jane Welsh Carlyle.* London: Constable, 1952. 618pp. Composed almost entirely from the letters, this is the most detailed study of the Carlyles' marriage that does not take sides and allows both partners to speak for themselves.

Heffer, Simon. *Moral Desperado: A Life of Thomas Carlyle.* London: Weidenfeld and Nicolson, 1996. 420pp. Heffer attempts to rehabilitate Carlyle's reputation and achievement by setting both in context with only partial success. The book is best for its straightforward, readable account of Carlyle's life.

Holme, Thea. *The Carlyles at Home.* New York: Oxford University Press, 1965. 204pp. Written by the wife of the curator of the Carlyle home on Cheyne Row, this is an insider's look at their domestic life drawn primarily from the letters. As much a biography of the house as its residents, the book provides a unique vantage point on both Carlyle and his long-suffering wife.

Symons, Julian. *Thomas Carlyle: The Life and Ideas of a Prophet.* New York: Oxford University Press, 1952. 308pp. Based essentially on Froude, Symons's account of Carlyle's life adds nothing new to one's understanding, though its brevity might reward a reader impatient with more comprehensive treatments.

Wilson, David A. *Life of Carlyle.* London: K. Paul, 1923–1934. 6 vols. Wilson's massive multivolume study was intended to refute what he regarded as the calumnies committed by Froude. Painstaking in his scholarship, the volumes' usefulness does not survive their author's fierce partisanship.

Biographical Novels

Disch, Thomas M., and Charles Naylor. *Neighboring Lives.* New York: Scribner, 1981. 351pp. Portraying the literary life of Carlyle and his wife, the novel effectively captures the literary atmosphere of the period and Carlyle's wide circle of artists and writers.

Fictional Portraits

Kenyon, Frank W. *The Consuming Flame: The Story of George Eliot.* New York: Dodd, Mead, 1970. 223pp. In Kenyon's biographical novel on the life of George Eliot, Carlyle, as well as other great Victorian figures, is plausibly portrayed.

Michener, James A. *Caribbean.* New York: Random House, 1989. 672pp. Michener's panoramic fictional study of the Caribbean dramatizes the controversy surrounding Carlyle's defense of John Eyre's policies governing the treatment of the West Indies slave population.

74. ANDREW CARNEGIE
1835–1919

American industrialist and philanthropist, Andrew Carnegie was born in Scotland and in 1848 brought his family to Pittsburgh, Pennsylvania, where he worked in a cotton mill, as a telegrapher, and later as a superintendent of the Pennsylvania Railroad. In 1873 Carnegie concentrated on steel production, acquiring companies that were consolidated into the giant Carnegie Steel Company, which by 1900 produced a quarter of all the steel in the United States. Carnegie sold his interests in the company to the newly formed U.S. Steel Corporation in 1901 for a sum that made him one of the world's richest men. He retired from business to devote the rest of his life to his various philanthropic activities that included the founding of over 2,800 libraries.

Autobiography and Primary Sources

Autobiography of Andrew Carnegie. Boston: Houghton Mifflin, 1920. 385pp. While all of Carnegie's many books touch on his life and career, this final book is the fullest treatment of his life. It is most reliable for his account of his life before 1901. His version of the controversies is often self-serving, and he modestly de-emphasizes his philanthropic efforts during his retirement.

Recommended Biographies

Mackay, James A. *Andrew Carnegie: His Life and Times.* New York: J. Wiley, 1998. 320pp. MacKay departs significantly from previous biographies and resists the temptation to either lionize or denigrate his subject. Concise and balanced, MacKay's biography is the best available shorter life.

Wall, Joseph Frazier. *Andrew Carnegie.* New York: Oxford University Press, 1970. 1,137pp. Superseding Hendrick's uncritical study, Wall corrects many of the misconceptions surrounding Carnegie and offers a complex portrait and in-depth descriptions of the crucial events in Carnegie's life. Deservedly seen as the definitive biography.

Other Biographical Studies

Hacker, Louis. *The World of Andrew Carnegie.* Philadelphia: Lippincott, 1968. 473pp. Written by an economic historian, Hacker's study locates Carnegie solidly at the center of the transformation of American industry. Not for the casual reader, the book is one of the most detailed analyses of Carnegie's business dealings and impact on economic history.

Hendrick, Burton J. *The Life of Andrew Carnegie.* Garden City, New York: Doubleday, 1932. 2 vols. Hendrick's authorized biography based on correspondence, business records, and speeches supplied by Carnegie's family lacks any serious interpretation of his subject or his business practices, and the larger social background of Carnegie's career is largely ignored. Long considered the standard life, Hendrick's book remains valuable for the primary material it collects and its straightforward chronological narrative.

Livesay, Harold C. *Andrew Carnegie and the Rise of Big Business.* Boston: Little, Brown, 1975. 202pp. More accessible than Hacker's scholarly analysis, Livesay's concise survey similarly concentrates on Carnegie's business career and impact on the industrialization of America. Serves as a solid introduction to the subject.

Swetnam, George. *Andrew Carnegie.* Boston: Twayne, 1980. 186pp. Part of the United States Author series, this critical analysis considers Carnegie's development and importance as a writer.

Fictional Portraits

Clarke, William K. *The Robber Baroness.* New York: Saint Martin's, 1979. 437pp. Depicting the life of notorious miser and financier Hetty Green, the novel captures its era of the post-Civil War boom with plausible appearances by a number of important figures, including Carnegie, Melville, Twain, and Queen Victoria.

Jakes, John. *The Americans.* New York: Jove, 1980. 800pp. This installment of the Kent Family Chronicles depicts the robber baron era interweaving a fictional story around appearances of actual figures, such as Carnegie.

Schreiner, Samuel A. *Thine Is the Glory.* New York: Arbor House, 1975. 476pp. Covering the period from the Gilded Age through World War II from the fictional perspective of a family dynasty in America's Golden Triangle in Pittsburgh, the novel describes the growth of American industry with depictions of some of its great events, such as the Homestead Strike and Carnegie's involvement.

Recommended Juvenile Biographies

Meltzer, Milton. *The Many Lives of Andrew Carnegie.* New York: F. Watts, 1997. 160pp. MG. Tracing Carnegie's life in full from his impoverished immigrant childhood, through his business career and philanthropy, the book does present multiple contradictory sides of Carnegie's personality but does not try to reconcile them, leaving final judgments for the reader.

Shippen, Katherine B. *Andrew Carnegie and the Age of Steel.* New York: Random House, 1958. 183pp. YA. A Landmark book, this is a comprehensive biography and a worthy introduction to the subject for a high school reader.

Simon, Charlie M. *The Andrew Carnegie Story.* New York: Dutton, 1965. 224pp. MG. Detailed portrait of Carnegie's early years in Scotland and struggles in Pittsburgh, this readable account does not provide the full story but serves more as an aspiring rags-to-riches saga.

Biographical Films and Theatrical Adaptations

The Richest Man in the World: Andrew Carnegie (1997). Director: Austin Hoyt. Produced for the PBS American Experience series, this is a comprehensive and balanced look at Carnegie's life and career. Video.

75. LEWIS CARROLL
1832–1898

Lewis Carroll is the pseudonym for Charles Ludwidge Dodgson, English writer and mathematician. Educated at Oxford University where he remained his entire life on a clerical fellowship, Carroll was too shy and afflicted with a stammer to work as a minister but he lectured in mathematics from 1855 to 1881. Carroll could overcome his awkwardness only in the company of children and his classics of children's literature—*Alice's Adventures in Wonderland* (1865) and its sequel *Through the Looking Glass* (1872)—derived from stories he told friends' children.

Autobiography and Primary Sources

Diaries of Lewis Carroll. Roger L. Green, ed. 1954. Reprint ed. Westport, Connecticut: Greenwood, 1971. 2 vols. Carroll recorded his thoughts in his diaries from his becoming a fellow at Christ Church at the age of 23 until his death (with some breaks). Essential for tracking the author's activities, there are few clues about his writings.

Letters of Lewis Carroll. Morton N. Cohen, ed. New York: Oxford University Press, 1979. 2 vols. About a third of the extant letters are collected here, supplemented with Carroll's own drawings and photographs.

Selected Letters of Lewis Carroll. Morton N. Cohen, ed. (New York: Pantheon, 1982. 302pp.). A more compact selection of letters is presented here than in the earlier publication.

Recommended Biographies

Bakewell, Michael. *Lewis Carroll: A Biography.* New York: W.W. Norton, 1996. 381pp. In a fascinating depiction of Carroll's complex and contradictory character, Bakewell examines the writer's imagination for its biographical clues. In the author's view, Carroll reinvented reality in mathematics, photography, and his writing to make them serve his imaginative and emotional needs.

Cohen, Morton N. *Lewis Carroll: A Biography.* New York: Knopf, 1995. 557pp. Cohen's richly detailed portrait, written by the leading scholar on Carroll, is deservedly regarded as the definitive life. Drawing on the diaries and letters, Cohen offers new insights on Carroll's personality and ideas and the subtle and contradictory depths beneath an apparently placid existence. The darker aspect of Carroll's genius does not prevent Cohen from appreciating his achievement.

Hudson, Derek. *Lewis Carroll.* London: Constable, 1954. 354pp. Revised as *Lewis Carroll: An Illustrated Biography.* London: Constable, 1976. 272pp. Prior to Cohen's definitive study, Hudson's biography was the best available, the first to take full advantage of the diaries and newly discovered letters. Hudson is evenhanded in his treatment, balancing his appreciation for Carroll's genius with a willingness to deal with his flaws.

Leach, Karoline. *In the Shadow of the Dreamchild: A New Understanding of Lewis Carroll.* Chester, Pennsylvania: Dufour Editions, 1999. 294pp. In Leach's controversial reading of Carroll's life, the writer is cleared of the charge of pedophilia, but instead had a series of relationships with married women. Leach offers a convincing alternative to the dominate myth surrounding Carroll in which he emerges as a normal though less than perfect figure.

Thomas, Donald. *Lewis Carroll: A Portrait with Background.* London: J. Murray, 1998. 404pp. Thomas's psychological probing reveals a paradoxical Carroll, as fascinated with the underworld of crime, vice, and psychopathology as to his dream of Wonderland. Thomas's provocative character sketch challenges most established views of Carroll and helps establish an image of the writer very much part of his times and modern consciousness.

Other Biographical Studies

Clarke, Anne. *Lewis Carroll: A Biography.* New York: Schocken, 1979. 284pp. Written by the secretary of the Lewis Carroll Society and the editor of its journal, Clarke's biography draws on the diaries and much formerly unpublished material in a thorough and comprehensive life that locates him firmly as product of his times, resisting other's tendencies to dwell on darker and more perverse aspects of his temperament.

Collingwood, Stuart Dodgson. *The Life and Letters of Lewis Carroll.* 1898. Reprint ed. Detroit: Gale, 1967. 448pp. Written by Carroll's nephew immediately following his uncle's death as the official life; despite its lack of critical perspective, this early biography is still valuable for its firsthand insights.

Green, Roger L. *Lewis Carroll.* New York: H.Z. Walck, 1962. 84pp. Green's brief biographical essay by a recognized expert on the writer is insightful and provides a succinct critical introduction.

Lennon, Florence Becker. *Victoria Through the Looking-Glass: The Life of Lewis Carroll.* New York: Simon & Schuster, 1945. 387pp. Revised as *The Life of Lewis Carroll.* New York: Collier, 1962. 448pp. Lennon psychologically surveys Carroll's life from his early years, attempting to reveal the reasons behind his apparent split personality and finding answers in Carroll's temperament and the pressures of Victorian culture. Somewhat rambling and disorganized in its collection of materials, Lennon's interpretation that "Wonderland" was an escape from a convention-ridden life takes the reader only so far.

Pudney, John. *Lewis Carroll and His World.* New York: Scribner, 1976. 127pp. Pudney's brief illustrated biography is most valuable for its reproductions of Carroll's photographs and drawings and other rarely seen visual material.

Stoffel, Stephanie L. *Lewis Carroll in Wonderland: The Life and Times of Alice and Her Creator.* New York: Abrams, 1997. 176pp. Stoffel's short, beautifully illustrated overview of Carroll's life debunks many theories about the creator of Alice and restores a more positive view of his personality that has been increasingly dominated by a fascination with his darker side.

Fictional Portraits

Ducornet, Rikki. *The Jade Cabinet.* Normal, Illinois: Dalkey Archive Press, 1994. 158pp. Ducornet's poetic story of two blighted Victorian sisters features an appearance by Carroll as a near neighbor and the photographer of the girls.

Harries, Ann. *Manly Pursuits.* New York: Bloomsbury, 1999. 393pp. As Cecil Rhodes is close to death, an Oxford professor travels to South Africa to deliver hundreds of British songbirds to salve Rhodes's soul in this powerfully imagined tale with glimpses of Rhodes and such figures as Lewis Carroll, Oscar Wilde, and Rudyard Kipling.

Rogow, Roberta. *The Problem of the Missing Miss.* New York: Saint Martin's, 1998. 256pp. Sir Arthur Conan Doyle teams up with the Reverend Charles Dodgson to solve a mystery involving the disappearance of the daughter of a crusading politician in 1885 Brighton. The author's dark exploration of child prostitution in Victorian society is relieved by the amusing interplay between the two literary sleuths. See also the sequels, *The Problem of the Spiteful Spiritualist* (New York: St. Martin's, 1999. 282pp.) and *The Problem of the Evil Editor* (New York: St. Martin's, 2000. 298pp.).

Slavitt, David R. *Alice at 80: A Novel.* Garden City, New York: Doubleday, 1984. 257pp. Slavitt's angle on Carroll is the author's model for Alice, Alice Liddell, now 80 years old, reflecting on her life and her appropriation by the enigmatic author.

Thomas, Donald S. *Mad Hatter Summer.* New York: Viking, 1983. 310pp. This detective story with Lewis Carroll as both a suspect and sleuth involves a blackmail threat that results from the author's nude photographs of young girls. Thomas, a Carroll biographer and expert on the Victorian era, makes ingenious use of Carroll's writings and cast of mind to reflect Victorian life and literature.

Recommended Juvenile Biographies

Bessett, Lisa. *Very Truly Yours, Charles L. Dodgson, Alias Lewis Carroll: A Biography.* New York: Lothrop, Lee & Shepard, 1957. 118pp. MG. Authoritative, affectionate portrait of a complex man, this biography reprints many of Carroll's letters in creating his profile.

Richardson, Joanna. *The Young Lewis Carroll.* New York: Roy, 1963. 134pp. MG. This somewhat old-fashioned biographical look at Lewis Carroll's youth is written by a prolific and skilled biographer who weaves her research into a vivid narrative.

Wood, James P. *The Snark Was a Boojum: A Life of Lewis Carroll.* New York: Pantheon, 1966. 184pp. MG/YA. Presented in an amusing format and vividly written, Wood's biography treats Carroll frankly, balancing an appreciation for the writer's imaginative genius with an awareness of his sexual preoccupations.

Biographical Films and Theatrical Adaptations

Dreamchild: The True Story of Alice in Wonderland (1985). Director: Gavin Millar. Based on Donald Thomas's novel, *Alice at 80,*80-year-old Alice Hargreaves recalls her encounters with Lewis Carroll in the 1850s. Coral Brown stars as Carroll's inspiration for Alice. Video.

Other Sources

Gattégno, Jean. *Lewis Carroll: Fragments of a Looking-Glass.* New York: Crowell, 1974. 327pp. In a series of essays on multiple aspects of Carroll's character, activities, and attitudes, this collection treats such subjects as photography, religion, sexuality, trains, and girl-friendships in a helpful thematic organization.

76. KIT CARSON
1809–1868

American frontiersman, guide, soldier, and folk hero, Christopher "Kit" Carson worked as a cook, hunter, and guide, and during the 1840s joined explorer John C. Frémont as a guide in Frémont's Western expeditions. Carson served in the Mexican War, was appointed (1853) U.S. Indian agent, and during the Civil War commanded the First New Mexican Volunteers in campaigns against Native American tribes of the southwest. He was made a brigadier general and from 1866 to 1867 commanded Fort Garland, Colorado.

Autobiography and Primary Sources

"Dear Old Kit": The Historical Christopher Carson. Harvey L. Carter, ed. Norman: University of Oklahoma Press, 1968. 250pp. Carson's selective autobiographical reflections as dictated to DeWitt Peters around 1856 is reprinted in this scholarly edition that includes annotation and essays on Carson's life and the development of his legendary reputation.

The Expeditions of John Charles Frémont. Donald Jackson and Mary Lee Spence, eds. Urbana: University of Illinois Press, 1970-84. 3 vols. Carson's reputation as a frontiersman and American hero originates in this account of Frémont's Western expeditions.

Brewerton, George D. *Overland with Kit Carson: A Narrative of the Old Spanish Trail in 1848.* 1853. Reprint ed. Lincoln: University of Nebraska Press, 1993. 301pp. The author accompanied Carson on his second transcontinental journey as far as Sante Fe and features a vivid, firsthand account of Carson.

Recommended Biographies

Blackwelder, Bernice. *Great Westerner: The Story of Kit Carson.* Caldwell, Idaho: Caxton, 1962. 373pp. In a well-researched and highly readable factual account, the author concentrates on Carson's actual career rather than the many stories that contributed to his heroic legend.

Estergreen, M. Morgan. *Kit Carson: A Portrait in Courage.* Norman: University of Oklahoma Press, 1962. 320pp. Estergreen's is a vivid account of Carson's frontier career set clearly against the backdrop of the story of the West in the nineteenth century. For the author, Carson is the representative American frontiersman whose activities define a peculiarly American form of heroism.

Guild, Thelma S., and Harvey L. Carter. *Kit Carson: A Pattern for Heroes.* Lincoln: University of Nebraska Press, 1984. 367pp. The authors present Carson's life and career in a factual chronological narrative that places his achievements in the wider context of Western exploration and settlement. Sometimes the book's partisanship on behalf of Carson undermines objectivity, but still this is a far more realistic view than many other treatments.

Roberts, David. *A Newer World: Kit Carson, John C. Frémont, and the Claiming of the American West.* New York: Simon & Schuster, 2000. 320pp. Roberts provides a rousing narrative account of Frémont's career in the West from the early 1840s to the beginning of the Civil War. Frémont's more flamboyant, complicated nature is juxtaposed with that of Carson's in a human portrait of both men.

Other Biographical Studies

Abbott, John S. *Christopher Carson: Familiarly Known as Kit Carson.* 1873. Reprint ed. New York: Dorchester, 1977. 348pp. Not factually reliable, this early account recasts Carson into the archetypal virtuous Western hero. The book's chief interest is its contribution to the Carson legend.

Gerson, Noel B. *Kit Carson: Folk Hero and Man.* Garden City, New York: Doubleday, 1964. 255pp. A brief biographical sketch based on secondary sources that does little to alter the often misleading heroic inflation of Carson's life and achievement. Not reliable factually, the book is more folklore than an accurate portrait of the man.

Hough, Emerson. *The Way to the West and the Lives of These Early Americans: Boone, Crockett, Carson.* Indianapolis: Bobbs-Merrill, 1903. 430pp. Hough's group biographical portrait looks at the lives of the three men in the wider context of westward expansion.

Peters, DeWitt C. *The Life and Adventures of Kit Carson, the Nestor of the Rocky Mountains.* 1858–1874. Reprint ed. Freeport, New York: Books for Libraries Press, 1970. 534pp. Peters's biography collected facts derived from Carson himself and for the first time established the basic biographical record and the source for later legendary interpretations. Fictional embellishments and heroic distortions limit the book's reliability.

Sabin, Edwin L. *Kit Carson Days (1809–1868).* 1935. Reprint ed. Lincoln: University of Nebraska Press, 1995. 2 vols. Sabin adds considerably to the documentary record based on extensive research collecting firsthand views of Carson by associates. Although now superseded by more recent studies, Sabin's was for a long time the standard biographical source.

Trafzer, Clifford E. *The Kit Carson Campaign: The Last Great Navaho War.* Norman: University of Oklahoma Press, 1982. 277pp. This is a specialized study of the Carson-led military expedition to control the Navajos in the late 1860s. Sympathetic to both Carson and the Navajos, the book is an even-handed narrative account based on eyewitness sources and Navajo oral tradition.

Vestal, Stanley. *Kit Carson, the Happy Warrior of the Old West.* Boston: Houghton Mifflin, 1928. 297pp. Vestal exhalts Carson as "the greatest of the frontiersmen" in a romantic narrative closer to folklore than history.

Biographical Novels

Hogan, Ray. *Soldier in Buckskin.* Thorndike, Maine: Five Star Western, 1996. 296pp. Carson is shown in action against the Blackfoot and Ute and marrying an Arapaho and after her death a Spanish aristocrat. Blending fact and legend, Carson is idealized as a near-perfect Western hero.

Zollinger, Norman. *Meridian: A Novel of Kit Carson's West.* New York: Forge, 1997. 416pp. The events of Frémont's third expedition west of the 100th meridian is described from the perspective of a young cartographer and artist who is befriended by Carson.

Fictional Portraits

Holland, Cecelia. *The Bear Flag: A Novel of the Birth of California.* Boston: Houghton Mifflin, 1990. 422pp. The events of the Bear Flag Revolt are recounted with appearances by a number of historical figures including Carson.

O'Dell, Scott. *Hill of the Hawk.* Indianapolis: Bobbs-Merrill, 1947. 413pp. In an invented story, Carson appears with Kearney and Frémont during the events of the Bear Flag Revolt.

Truett, John A. *To Die in Dinetah: The Dark Legacy of Kit Carson.* Sante Fe, New Mexico: Sunstone Press, 1994. 179pp. Carson's involvement with the relocation of the Navajo during the "Long Walk" is recounted from the perspective of a young cavalry soldier.

Recommended Juvenile Biographies

Sanford, William R. *Kit Carson: Frontier Scout.* Springfield, New Jersey: Enslow, 1996. 48pp. MG. This is a lively, brief biographical portrait of Carson that emphasizes his wilderness skills and actual challenges.

Biographical Films and Theatrical Adaptations

Kit Carson (1940). Director: George B. Seitz. Carson is shown in action leading a wagon train to California. Starring Jon Hall, Ward Bond, and Dana Andrews as Frémont. Video.

See also John C. Frémont

77. RACHEL CARSON
1907–1964

American writer and marine biologist, Rachel Carson was born in Pennsylvania and received a graduate degree from Johns Hopkins University. Her naturalist's studies of the sea—*Under the Sea Wind* (1941), *The Sea Around Us* (1951), and *The Edge of the Sea* (1954)—were popular bestsellers, and her book *Silent Spring* (1962), warning of the danger from insecticides, is widely regarded as the foundation text that launched the modern environmental movement.

Autobiography and Primary Sources

Carson's many books, though not strictly speaking autobiographical, reveal interesting insights into the author's personality and attitudes, particularly *Under the Sea* (New York: Simon & Schuster, 1941. 314pp.) and *The Edge of the Sea* (Boston: Houghton Mifflin, 1955. 276pp.).

Always Rachel: The Letters of Rachel Carson and Dorothy Freeman, 1952–1964: The Story of a Remarkable Friendship. Boston: Beacon Press, 1994. 567pp. The private side of Carson emerges most clearly in this remarkably revealing collection from more than 750 letters written to her best friend of her later years.

Recommended Biographies

Lear, Linda J. *Rachel Carson: Witness for Nature.* New York: Holt, 1997. 634pp. The most exhaustive account yet written on Carson's private and public lives and influence. Lear's empathic biography serves as a detailed narrative chronology from an environmental historian well-placed to capture her subject in multiple dimensions. Although lacking hard-edged critical analysis, Lear still provides the roundest portrait available that should remain definitive for some time to come.

Other Biographical Studies

Brooks, Paul. *The House of Life: Rachel Carson at Work.* Boston: Houghton Mifflin, 1972. 350pp. Told mainly through Carson's own words from unpublished letters, pamphlets, speeches, and excerpts from her books, Brooks provides an account of Carson's development as a biologist and writer. Less detailed on Carson's personal life, Brooks's competent and insightful study is best on how her ideas and interests were formed into her books. Gartner, Carol B. *Rachel Carson.* New York: Frederick Ungar, 1983. 161pp. Including a yearly chronology and a brief biographical overview, the book is mainly a critical introduction to Carson as a writer and the literary qualities of her work. Graham, Frank Jr. *Since Silent Spring.* Boston: Houghton Mifflin, 1970. 333pp. Partially a sequel to *Silent Spring,* Graham considers the book in the context of Carson's life and development and summaries the controversies that surrounded its publication. McCay, Mary A. *Rachel Carson.* New York: Twayne, 1993. 122pp. This informative critical study that concentrates on Carson's literary skill does provide a succinct biographical overview and connects her experiences with her writing. Sterling, Philipp. *Sea and Earth: The Life of Rachel*

Carson. New York: Crowell, 1970. 213pp. Written for a general audience, including younger readers, Sterling fills in the details of Carson's life with reflections from her classmates and relatives and extracts from correspondence.

Recommended Juvenile Biographies

Harlan, Judith. *Sounding the Alarm: A Biography of Rachel Carson.* New York: Dillon Press, 1994. 128pp. MG. Tracing Carson's life and achievement, Harlan succeeds in placing her ideas in a wider context of the burgeoning ecological movement as well as the drama of Carson's advocacy and her opposition.

Jezer, Marty. *Rachel Carson.* New York: Chelsea House, 1988. 112pp. YA. Part of the American Women of Achievement series, this is a full and detailed biography of the biologist and author that captures her career and the impact of her writings on ecological awareness.

Wadsworth, Ginger. *Rachel Carson: Voice for the Earth.* Minneapolis: Lerner, 1992. 128pp. MG. Competently researched and enhanced by a liberal use of photographs, this is a lively survey of Carson's life, career, and influence.

Biographical Films and Theatrical Adaptations

Rachel Carson's Silent Spring (1993). Producer: Neil Goodwin. PBS documentary tells the story of the book, its author, and their impact on the environment. Readings by Meryl Streep. Video.

78. GEORGE WASHINGTON CARVER
ca.1864–1943

American botanist and agricultural chemist, Carver was born a slave and after a 15-year period of wandering Missouri, Kansas, and Iowa seeking an education while working in a laundry, as a cook, and as a homesteader, Carver earned his college degree in 1894. In 1896 he accepted an offer from Booker T. Washington to work at the Tuskegee Institute as director of agricultural research. Carver devoted himself to helping the lot of African American farmers by teaching the importance of soil improvement and crop diversification. He discovered hundreds of uses for the peanut, the sweet potato, and soybeans, stimulating their production, which helped transform Southern agriculture. Embraced as a powerful symbol of African American success and racial justice. Carver donated his life savings to create a foundation for research at Tuskegee.

Autobiography and Primary Sources

George Washington Carver in His Own Words. Gary R. Kremer, ed. Columbia: University of Missouri Press, 1987. 208pp. Using excerpts from his various writings, this collection approximates an autobiographical account of Carver's life, development, and attitudes.

Recommended Biographies

McMurry, Linda O. *George Washington Carver: Scientist and Symbol.* New York: Oxford Univer-

sity Press, 1981. 367pp. Easily the best biography available, definitive and authoritative, McMurry's provocative study serves to isolate the man from the myth, revealing his personal qualities, objectively assessing his contribution to science, and considering his wider symbolic influence.

Other Biographical Studies

Edwards, Ethel. *Carver of Tuskegee.* Cincinnati: Psyche Press, 1971. 237pp. Difficult to find, Edwards's study, based on personal interviews and the Tuskegee archive, provides a full account of Carver's scientific, academic, and interracial work.

Elliott, Lawrence. *George Washington Carver: The Man Who Overcame.* Englewood Cliffs, New Jersey: Prentice-Hall, 1966. 256pp. The author brings together a number of recollections to form a biographical portrait that chronicles Carver's remarkable career, very much in the heroic mode. The book is appropriate for younger readers, even though written for adults.

Holt, Rackham. *George Washington Carver: An American Biography.* Garden City, New York: Doubleday, 1943. 342pp. The earliest biography, written immediately after Carver's death and based on interviews with him and his associates, Holt's laudatory memorial, though lacking objectivity and committing some factual errors, remains valuable for its anecdotes unavailable in other sources.

Manber, David. *Wizard of Tuskegee: The Life of George Washington Carver.* New York: Crowell-Collier, 1967. 167pp. This short biographical sketch concentrates on Carver at Tuskegee, providing few original insights or objectivity but a succinct appreciation.

Neyland, James. *George Washington Carver.* Los Angeles: Melrose Square, 1991. 203pp. Neyland's is a popular biography that covers the highlights of Carver's career, although the book is rarely critical of the man.

Recommended Juvenile Biographies

Adair, Gene. *George Washington Carver.* New York: Chelsea House, 1989. 110pp. MG/YA. Part of the Black Americans of Achievement series, this is a solid narrative of Carver's life and career that frankly deals with his legend as distinct from the reality and his mixed legacy.

Bontemps, Arna. *The Story of George Washington Carver.* New York: Grosset & Dunlap, 1954. 181pp. YA. Concentrating on Carver's early life from 1896 to 1915, Bontemps's well-written account, though based on solid evidence, does indulge in fictional elements, blending what is known for sure with undocumentable surmises and fancy.

Rogers, Teresa. *George Washington Carver: Nature's Trailblazer.* Frederick, Maryland: Twenty-First Century Books, 1992. 72pp. MG. Concentrating on Carver's scientific achievement, this short though insightful book includes a listing of products he created from peanuts and sweet potatoes and his agricultural bulletins that capture the range of his accomplishments.

79. MARY CASSATT
1845–1926

American Impressionist painter, Cassatt studied and exhibited in Paris, where she spent most of her life. She was strongly influenced by the great French Impressionists, particularly Edgar Degas, who was a close friend. Cassatt is known for her domestic scenes, especially mother-and-child studies. Her works include several versions of *Mother and Child*, *Girl Arranging Her Hair* (1886), *The Bath* (1891–1892), *Lady at the Tea-Table* (1888), and *Modern Women*, a mural painted for the women's building of the 1893 Chicago exposition.

Autobiography and Primary Sources

Cassatt and Her Circle: Selected Letters. Nancy M. Mathews, ed. New York: Abbeville Press, 1984. 360pp. This selection of 208 letters from the artist, her friends, and family chronicles Cassatt's career from her student days in Philadelphia through her life in Paris. Best on the era and the practical side of an artist's life; private revelations are few.

Recommended Biographies

Hale, Nancy. *Mary Cassatt*. Garden City, New York: Doubleday, 1975. 333pp. Building on Sweet's pioneering research, Hale adds details to the biographical record as well as a vivid, novelistic ability to discover the animating, revealing detail. The book is particularly strong in showing Cassatt's creative process and artistic development.

Mathews, Nancy M. *Mary Cassatt: A Life*. New York: Villard Books, 1994. 383pp. In the most comprehensive and authoritative study yet published, Mathews fully documents Cassatt's childhood, family background, artistic training, professional relationships, and artistic development. The book provides new insights into Cassatt's personal life and artistic genius.

Sweet, Frederick A. *Miss Mary Cassatt, Impressionist from Pennsylvania*. Norman: University of Oklahoma Press, 1966. 242pp. One of the first serious, scholarly studies of the artist's life and career, Sweet's is a solidly researched factual record based on previously untapped primary material.

Other Biographical Studies

Carson, Julia. *Mary Cassatt*. New York: McKay, 1966. 193pp. Intended for the general reader, Carson's is a more modest, less scholarly biography, but will serve as an overview of Cassatt's life, artistic achievement, and era.

Dillon, Millicent. *After Egypt: Isadora Duncan and Mary Cassatt*. New York: Dutton, 1990. 403pp. This unusual dual biographical portrait looks at the life of these two American expatriates from the perspective of their visits a year apart in 1910 and 1911 to Egypt. More ambitious than ultimately convincing, the book does achieve some fresh perspectives from the uncovered parallels and contrasts between both women's lives and characters.

McKown, Robin. *The World of Mary Cassatt*. New York: Crowell, 1972. 253pp. Cassatt's life and artistic career is describe in the wider context of her relationships and connections with fellow artists in the Impressionist movement. Best on the cultural background, the book fails to penetrate the private side of Cassatt's identity and does require some prior familiarity with nineteenth-century art history for a full appreciation of the references and connections.

Wilson, Ellen. *American Painter in Paris: A Life of Mary Cassatt*. New York: Farrar, Straus, 1971. 205pp. In a brief, highly imaginative and speculative biography, Wilson approaches biographical fiction in the liberties taken recreating the artist's motivations, thoughts, and feelings.

Biographical Novels

King, Joan. *Impressionist: A Novel of Mary Cassatt*. New York: Beaufort Books, 1983. 320pp. This biographical novel stays close to the facts of Cassatt's life in an account of her career.

Recommended Juvenile Biographies

Cain, Michael. *Mary Cassatt*. New York: Chelsea House, 1989. 111pp. MG/YA. Cain's is a detailed summary of Cassatt's life and artistic career with an emphasis on the challenged faced by a woman artist during the period.

Meyer, Susan E. *Mary Cassatt*. New York: Abrams, 1990. 92pp. YA. Part of the First Impressions series, this book ably traces Cassatt's artistic career from the age of 21 as she prepares to leave Philadelphia for Paris to her death. Critical commentary on Cassatt's paintings is combined with details of Cassatt's life using quotes from her family, friends, and fellow artists.

Plain, Nancy. *Mary Cassatt: An Artist's Life*. New York: Dillon Press, 1994. 168pp. MG/YA. Extensively researched, this is a comprehensive portrait of the artist that places Cassatt's artistic and personal development in a wider social and historical context.

Biographical Films and Theatrical Adaptations

Mary Cassatt: Impressionist from Philadelphia (1975). Director: Perry M. Adato. Explores the painter's life and work with location footage of sites associated with Cassatt. Video.

80. WILLA CATHER
1873–1947

A novelist and short-story writer considered one of the greatest twentieth-century American authors, Cather first worked as a journalist and teacher in Pittsburgh. She went (1904) to New York City, where she published her first collection of short stories, *The Troll Garden* (1905), and was managing editor of *McClure's Magazine*. Her works include *O Pioneers* (1913), *My Antonia* (1918), *One of Ours* (1922; Pulitzer Prize), and *Death Comes for the Archbishop* (1927), widely regarded as her masterpiece.

Autobiography and Primary Sources

Willa Cather in Person: Interviews, Speeches, and Letters. L. Brent Bohlke, ed. Lincoln: University of Nebraska Press, 1986. 202pp. With many letters destroyed and surviving ones prevented by the conditions of Cather's will from publication, this collection of interviews, occasional pieces, and speeches offer the reader the best source of self-revelation from the excessively private writer.

Recommended Biographies

Lee, Hermione. *Willa Cather: Double Lives*. New York: Pantheon, 1989. 410pp. Lee's provocative critical biography offers a reassessment of Cather's achievement as a writer as well as a fascinating meditation on her psychological and emotional development. Her formative years are covered in detail before proceeding to a close reading of the works for what they reveal about the artist and the woman.

O'Brien, Sharon. *Willa Cather: The Emerging Voice*. New York: Oxford University Press, 1987. 464pp. Examining Cather's development up to 1915, O'Brien applies a feminist reading of Cather's early life, focusing on gender issues and the impact on her work of Cather's attempt to disguise her sexual identity. Sophisticated and well researched, O'Brien's study is a breakthrough reassessment of the private reaches of the writer's emotional and artistic life.

Woodress, James. *Willa Cather: A Literary Life*. Lincoln: University of Nebraska Press, 1987. 583pp. Woodress's study is by far the most comprehensive and detailed biographical record of Cather's life available, expanding on his earlier preliminary assessment, *Willa Cather: Her Life and Art* (New York: Pegasus, 1970. 288pp.). Avoiding psychological guesswork, Woodress is cautious and judicious in his interpretations, finding no evidence, for example, for Cather's lesbianism. Instead Woodress shifts the emphasis to Cather's achievements as a writer and her artistic development.

Other Biographical Studies

Bennett, Mildred R. *World of Willa Cather*. 1951. Revised ed. Lincoln: University of Nebraska Press, 1961. 226pp. Written by a Red Cloud, Nebraska, native, Bennett's collection of small-town anecdotes and family reminiscences presents the regional background for Cather's writing, based on interviews with individuals who knew the novelist.

Brown, E.K. *Willa Cather: A Critical Biography*. New York: Knopf, 1953. 351pp. This authorized critical biography, completed by Leon Edel, has been superseded by subsequent works that have drawn on important primary sources unavailable to Brown. Nevertheless, the book still offers a sensible assessment of Cather's literary achievement and an accurate overview of her career.

Lewis, Edith. *Willa Cather Living: A Personal Record*. New York: Knopf, 1953. 197pp. Cather's longtime companion supplies her personal recollections, originally produced as an aid to E.K. Brown's biographical research. The book offers interesting details of the pair's life together, the genesis of Cather's writings, and work habits.

Robinson, Phyllis. *Willa: The Life of Willa Cather.* Garden City, New York: Doubleday, 1983. 321pp. In a highly adulatory account, Robinson concentrates on the connection between Cather's writings and the people and places that she knew. The early half of Cather's life is most vividly delivered, with the mature years seen more indirectly and speculatively. Robinson is the first biographer that explicitly acknowledges that Cather was a lesbian.

Sergeant, Elizabeth S. *Willa Cather: A Memoir.* Philadelphia: Lippincott, 1953. 303pp. This is an informal portrait of the author by a friend of 40 years who first met Cather in 1910 when Sergeant was the managing editor at *McClure's* magazine. Filled with anecdotes, recollected conversations, and interesting sidelights, the book offers a believable, human portrait.

Wagenknecht, Edward. *Willa Cather.* New York: Continuum, 1994. 203pp. A brief summary of the significant events and influences in Cather's life is followed by an evaluation of her writing. A final chapter offers commentary on Cather's idiosyncrasies as a writer and her personality.

Woods, Lucia. *Willa Cather: A Pictorial Memoir.* Lincoln: University of Nebraska Press, 1986. 134pp. This is a richly detailed visual biography that documents Cather's varied career as journalist, editor, teacher, and novelist.

Recommended Juvenile Biographies

Keene, Ann T. *Willa Cather.* New York: J. Messner, 1994. 156pp. YA. Part of the Classic American Writers series, this is straightforward chronological account combining biographical insights and a description of Cather's major works. While it does not avoid questions of sexuality, the emphasis here is more on Cather the literary artist.

O'Brien, Sharon. *Willa Cather.* New York: Chelsea House, 1995. 143pp. YA. Part of the Lives of Notable Gay Men and Lesbians series, O'Brien, an acclaimed adult Cather biographer, engagingly explores the connections between Cather's artistic and psychological development while dealing openly and seriously with her lesbianism.

Wooten, Sara M. *Willa Cather.* Springfield, New Jersey: Enslow, 1998. 128pp. MG/YA. This is a somewhat dry but informative introduction to Cather's life and career with brief summaries of her novels and major stories and Cather's own views about particular works.

Biographical Films and Theatrical Adaptations

Into the Morning: Willa Cather's America (1988). Director: Richard Schickel. A film portrait of Cather's life, works, and times. Video.

81. CATHERINE DE' MEDICI
1519–1589

The daughter of Lorenzo de' Medici, Catherine married the duc d'Orleans who became Henry II of France and was the mother of Francis II, Charles IX, and Henry III. A strong defender of the power of the monarch against religious opposition from the Huguenots, Catherine helped plan the massacre of Saint Bartholomew's Day in 1572 in which Huguenot leader Coligny and hundreds of other Protestants were murdered.

Recommended Biographies

Knecht, R.J. *Catherine de' Medici.* New York: Longman, 1998. 288pp. Entry in the Profiles in Power series, this narrative account of Catherine's life also illuminates the complex social and political events of her time. With her flaws admitted, Knecht manages a good deal more sympathy for Catherine than other biographers, considering her a complex, modern figure whose superhuman efforts on behalf of her children gains his admiration.

Mahoney, Irene. *Madame Catherine.* New York: Coward-McCann, 1975. 381pp. Mahoney's single-volume sympathetic portrait is backed up with extensive research using primary sources and succeeds in penetrating the various legends surrounding Catherine to reveal a human though ultimately enigmatic portrait.

Van Dyke, Paul. *Catherine de' Medici.* New York: Scribner, 1922. 2 vols. Based on a decade of painstaking research in primary sources, Van Dyke's exhaustive, scholarly study is still the most detailed and reliable biography available. Neither an apologist nor a prosecutor, Van Dyke portrays Catherine clearly in the context of fully revealed public events seen through her perspective.

Other Biographical Studies

Heritier, Jean. *Catherine de' Medici.* New York: Saint Martin's, 1959. 480pp. Contrary to other portrayals of Catherine as a clever but unscrupulous politician, Heritier sees her as a great queen of France rivaling Isabella of Spain, Elizabeth I, and Catherine the Great. He makes his case in a chronological narrative of Catherine's entire life that assumes a certain knowledge of the period.

Neale, J.E. *The Age of Catherine de' Medici.* London: Cape, 1943. 114pp. Neale's succinct overview of Catherine's era is an ideal introduction to the often confusing social, political, and religious events that shaped the queen and were in turn shaped by her.

Roeder, Ralph. *Catherine de' Medici and the Lost Revolution.* New York: Viking, 1937. 629pp. Concentrating less on Catherine's personal history than the larger context of political, economic, and social forces at play during her time, Roeder's historical approach is an informative supplement to biographies with a more intimate focus on Catherine herself.

Ross Williamson, Hugh. *Catherine de' Medici.* New York: Viking, 1973. 288pp. This illustrated biography indulges in a good deal of psychological speculation and fictionalization and should be consulted with caution in looking for a reliable and carefully documented view.

Sichel, Edith. *Catherine de' Medici and the French Reformation.* New York: Dutton, 1905. 328pp. *The Later Years of Catherine de' Medici.* New York: Dutton, 1908. 445pp. Not a chronological narrative of events, Sichel's volumes offer instead a series of essays on aspects of Catherine's life and times.

Strage, Mark. *Women of Power: Catherine de' Medici.* New York: Harcourt, Brace, 1976. 368pp. Strage's group biography of Catherine, Diane de Poitiers, and Marguerite of Navarre traces their relationships and how they attempted to cope with events in sixteenth-century France. More a collection of dramatic incidents than a conventional biography.

Waldman, Milton. *Biography of a Family: Catherine de' Medici and Her Children.* Boston: Houghton Mifflin, 1936. 266pp. Waldman's account chronicles Catherine's life from the death of Henri II to the triumph of Henri IV, concentrating on her domination of her children. Each figure's story is described in detail, but events are arranged out of their chronological order, shaped by the demands of the drama. Waldman's treatment is closer to sensational fiction than reliable history.

Biographical Novels

Plaidy, Jean. *Madame Serpent.* New York: Putnam, 1975. 332pp.; *The Italian Woman.* New York: Putnam, 1976. 299pp.; *Queen Jezebel.* New York: Putnam, 1976. 380pp. Plaidy charts Catherine's career from her departure for France at the age of 14 to marry Henry of Orleans through her years as a formidable power behind the French throne and her war against the Huguenots. Vividly portrayed, the novels mix facts and speculation but follow history closely; *Evergreen Gallant* (New York: Putnam, 1973. 384pp.) looks at the reign of Henry II from his perspective.

Ross Williamson, Hugh. *The Florentine Woman.* New York: Saint Martin's, 1971. 253pp.; *Paris Is Worth a Mass.* New York: Saint Martin's, 1973. 223pp.; *The Last of the Valois.* New York: Saint Martin's, 1973. 246pp. Focusing on the French royal family from 1558 to 1589—from Catherine's rise to power to her death—this fictionalized trilogy strings a number of vivid anecdotes and historical details together to give life to his portraits. Catherine is portrayed as a devoted mother in a largely sympathetic view.

Fictional Portraits

Beach, Susan Hicks. *A Cardinal of the Medici.* New York: Macmillan, 1937. 411pp. Providing a look inside the Medici family, the novel follows the career of an illegitimate son of Giuliano de' Medici who rises to cardinal at the age of 19 but is poisoned by age 22. Well documented, and except for minor details, the novel is thoroughly accurate in its depiction of the period.

Dumas, Alexandre. *Queen Margot.* 1845. Reprint ed. New York: Hyperion, 1994. 542pp. Dumas's adventure tale is set against a background of the 1572 marriage between Marguerite de Valois and Henri IV that helps prompt the Saint Bartholomew's Day Massacre. Mixing fancy with history, Dumas offers an exciting, though unreliable, treatment of the period.

Dumas, Alexandre (fils). *Les Quarant Cing.* 1894. Reprint ed. London: Dent, 1968. 453pp. Dumas's exciting, invented story concerns the court intrigue during the reign of Henri III and the ambitions of his mother.

Dunnett, Dorothy. *Queen's Play.* New York: American House, 1964. Reprint ed. New York: Vintage, 432pp.; *Checkmate.* 1975. Reprint ed. New York: Vintage, 1997. 581pp. These installments of the author's Lymond Chronicles feature extensive views of Catherine and her court as Francis Crawford travels to France to protect the child-queen Mary from various conspiracies and becomes involved in later intrigues. Dunnett's novels are all exhaustively researched, with a solid grasp of the period and its historical figures, such as Catherine.

Haeger, Diane. *Courtesan.* New York: Pocket Star Books, 1993. 568pp. The love between France's Henry II and his mistress Diane de Poitiers is dramatized with revealing and believable details about the unhappy marriage between Henry and Catherine de' Medici.

Houston, Jane Dimmitt. *The Faith and the Flame.* New York: W. Sloane, 1958. 431pp. Court life is realistically dramatized through the perspective of a fictional lady-in-waiting to Catherine who is caught up in the religious conflict with the Protestants.

Lewis, Ada Cook. *The Longest Night.* New York: Einehardt, 1958. 334pp. The title refers to the infamous Saint Bartholomew's Day Massacre masterminded by Catherine. Historical events are plausibly interwoven with a fictional story of a young man recruited to kill Coligny.

Riley, Judith Merkle. *The Master of All Desires.* New York: Viking, 1999, 386pp. Catherine and Nostradamus are the historical figures who join the search for a magical object that can grant all wishes but at a considerable cost. Catherine is depicted as a ruthless tyrant, who must be stopped from acquiring absolute power.

Roessner, Michaela. *The Stars Dispose.* New York: Tor, 1997. 384pp. Set in Florence in the 1520s, this historical fantasy centers on an apprentice chef and sculptor who serves the Medicis and becomes linked through destiny and magic to Catherine. The historical events of the period are presented but with an occult flavoring.

Walder, Francis. *The Negotiators.* New York: McDowell, 1959. 166pp. The complex diplomatic manuevering between Catherine and Coligny are dramatized from the perspective of a fictional go-between in an authentic depiction of the historical background to the Huguenot conflict.

Biographical Films and Theatrical Adaptations

Queen Margot (1994). Director: Patrice Chereau. Based on the Dumas novel, this lavish historical drama pits Marguerite de Valois (Isabelle Adjani) against her mother, Catherine de' Medici (Virna Lisi), as the dowager queen plots to marry her to Henri de Navarre (Daniel Auteuil). The intrigue climaxes with the Saint Bartholomew's Day Massacre. The history is often confusing, but the details are lush and captivating. Video.

See also Lorenzo de' Medici; Mary Queen of Scots

82. CATHERINE OF SIENA
1347–1380

An Italian mystic and diplomat, Catherine began having visions in early childhood, and at 16 entered the Dominican order. She persuaded Pope Gregory XI to leave Avignon (1376) and return the papacy to Rome, thus ending the "Babylonian Captivity," and supported the claim of Pope Urban VI to the papal throne during the Great Schism. She also advocated a crusade against the Muslims. She was canonized in 1461 and although unlettered was made (1970) a Doctor of the Church.

Autobiography and Primary Sources

The Letters of Saint Catherine of Siena. Suzanne Noffke, ed. Binghampton, New York: Medieval & Renaissance Texts and Studies, 1988. 450pp. In the first volume of a projected four-volume collection, the first 88 of Catherine's surviving 382 letters are translated. The book is an essential source for insights into both her spirituality and political activities.

Recommended Biographies

Cavallini, Giulani. *Catherine of Siena.* New York: Geoffrey Chapman, 1998. 163pp. Part of the Outstanding Christian Thinkers series, Cavallini supplies a helpful and accessible survey of Catherine's writings and ideas along with an extensive chronology.

Gardner, Edmund G. *Saint Catherine of Siena: A Study in Religion, Literature, and History of the 14th Century in Italy.* New York: Dutton, 1907. 439pp. Gardner's is a scholarly account based on careful review of source material that provides a satisfactory factual chronology of Catherine's life and a judicious assessment of her personality and impact.

Noffke, Suzanne. *Catherine of Siena: Vision through a Distant Eye.* Collegeville, Minnesota: Liturgical Press, 1966. 267pp. Although not a chronological biography, Noffke, the recognized modern authority on Catherine's life and work, presents an authoritative examination of multiple aspects of Catherine's personality and thought.

Other Biographical Studies

Drane, Mrs. Augusta T. *The History of Saint Catherine of Siena and Her Companions.* London: Burnes and Oates, 1880. 2 vols. Drane's is a detailed and comprehensive gathering of materials to document Catherine's life, relationships, and times, superseded in its scholarship by Gardner.

Raymond of Capua. *The Life of Catherine of Siena.* New York: P.J. Kennedy, 1960. 385pp. First published in 1533, Raymond's firsthand account of Catherine's life is the main source for what we know about her. As Catherine's confessor, Raymond had unprecedented access, but he is neither a critical nor a detached observer.

Roberts, Margaret. *Saint Catherine of Siena and Her Times.* New York: Putnam, 1906. 300pp. Roberts's is an uneven account, alternating between informed social and historical background painting and romanticization. Reviewers have been equally divided, one calling the book a "readable, vivacious life," another "about the worst specimen of its class which we have seen."

Undset, Sigrid. *Catherine of Siena.* New York: Sheed & Ward, 1954. 293pp. The Scandinavian novelist shortly before her death produced this highly readable, though unscholarly, account of Catherine's life that attempts with some success to present her in her daily life as a recognizable human figure.

Biographical Novels

De Wohl, Louis. *Lay Siege to Heaven: A Novel of Saint Catherine of Siena.* New York: Lippincott, 1961. 315pp. The novel chronicles Catherine's career, including her upbringing, mystical experiences, and diplomatic service.

Unruh, Fritz von. *The Saint.* New York: Random House, 1950. 396pp. This fictional biography follows Catherine's career, although the novel's credibility is undercut by a persistent romantic idealization.

83. CATHERINE THE GREAT
1729–1796

Czarina of Russia, Catherine was born a relatively obscure German princess who in 1744 was chosen as the wife of the future Czar Peter III. When Peter succeeded to the throne, a group of conspirators, led by Grigori Orlov, Catherine's lover, deposed the Czar and installed Catherine as Czarina. Her early reign was marked by reform efforts, stimulated by her sympathy for such enlightened figures as Voltaire. She became increasingly conservative while increasing the power and prestige of Russia through savvy diplomacy and extending her country's western boundary.

Autobiography and Primary Sources

The Memoirs of Catherine the Great. Dominique Maroger, ed. New York: Macmillan, 1955. 400pp. Kept secret for more than a hundred years after her death and first published in full in 1907, Catherine's memoirs cover the period 1729 to 1759 and are fascinating in their revelations about her childhood. Catherine's memoirs have been an essential primary source for subsequent biographies, but should be read with skepticism.

Recommended Biographies

Alexander, John T. *Catherine the Great: Life and Legend.* New York: Oxford University Press, 1989. 418pp. Widely regarded as the best existing biography based on the most thorough use of primary sources in English, Alexander's sympathetic and intimate portrait concentrates on Catherine's reign and refutes many of the legends surrounding the empress, including the charge of nymphomania.

De Madariaga, Isabel. *Russia in the Age of Catherine the Great.* New Haven, Connecticut: Yale University Press, 1981. 698pp. In a comprehensive and minutely detailed scholarly analysis organized into sections on specific themes, the author emphasizes the political life of Catherine's age and provides a needed rehabilitation of the empress' reputation, destroying many myths that have distorted a balanced appreciation of her considerable achievements. De Madariaga's shortened version, *Catherine the Great: A Short History* (New Haven, Connecticut: Yale University Press, 1993. 244pp.) synthesizes her interpretation in one of the best available succinct studies of eighteenth-century Russia and an assessment of Catherine's reign.

Other Biographical Studies

Almedingen, Marthe Edith von. *Catherine: Empress of Russia.* New York: Dodd, Mead, 1961. 239pp. This is a highly partisan defense of Catherine's character and reign that mitigates nearly all the negatives based on the empress's genius as a political leader. The counterpoint to the author's uncritical appreciation can be found in Ian Grey's opposite assessment.

Anthony, Katharine. *Catherine the Great: Life and Legend.* Garden City, New York: Doubleday, 1925. 331pp. Applying a psychoanalytical method to Catherine based on the first extensive use of her diaries and letters, Anthony shows a keen eye for dramatic moments and a plausible psychological hypothesis, but much of her method and revelations have been superseded by more modern studies.

Cronin, Vincent. *Catherine: Empress of All the Russias.* New York: Morrow, 1978. 349pp. Cronin's popular biography uncovers no new material but does provide a detailed account of Catherine's personal habits and psychological surmises to explain her behavior.

Erickson, Carolly. *Great Catherine.* New York: Saint Martin's, 1995. 392pp. The author's popular account reads like a vivid historical novel capturing the drama of Catherine's life and emphasizing not her alleged personal immorality and her love life but her ambition to govern wisely and her considerable talents and achievements. Erickson shows the woman behind the image: indomitable, feisty, and often visionary, divided by her need for love and a reluctance to share her power.

Gooch, George P. *Catherine the Great and Other Studies.* New York: Longmans, 1954. 292pp. In a collection of essays, Gooch provides a context in intellectual and social history for Catherine's development and achievement.

Grey, Ian. *Catherine the Great: Autocrat and Empress of All Russia.* Philadelphia: Lippincott, 1962. 254pp. Grey's critical reappraisal denies Catherine almost any claim to greatness either in her rule or in her character. Grey's assessment provides a counterbalance to other uncritical appreciatory studies, but it seems clear that truth is likely to found somewhere between both extremes.

Haslip, Joan. *Catherine the Great: A Biography.* New York: Putnam, 1977. 382pp. Based on secondary sources and making no pretense to original scholarship, the author provides little new information and her lack of Russian and expertise in Russian history are distinct disadvantages. The book offers a character sketch for a general reader in which the author attempts to justify Catherine's behavior.

Kaus, Gina. *Catherine: Portrait of an Empress.* New York: Halcyon House, 1935. 384pp. Kaus's portrait concentrates on the formation of Catherine's character and her early years, largely neglecting her reign. Based on a close analysis of the memoirs, Kaus's view is markedly different from others, in part due to her uncritical acceptance of Catherine's own view of her past.

Oldenbourg, Zoë. *Catherine the Great.* New York: Pantheon, 1965. 378pp. Written by a respected historical novelist, this character study concentrates mainly on Catherine's life before she reached the throne and how Catherine the woman was shaped and matured. Only 100 pages are devoted to her long reign. Clearly written by a partisan, the book's lack of objectivity and surmises limits its usefulness as a reliable historical interpretation.

Raeff, Marc, ed. *Catherine the Great: A Profile.* New York: Hill & Wang, 1972. 331pp. This collection of essays by Russian and western historians on Catherine and her reign stresses her intellectual development and influence on Russian cultural and social life. More for the scholar and graduate student than the generalist.

Troyat, Henri. *Catherine the Great.* New York: Dutton, 1980. 377pp. Troyat's sympathetic portrait emphasizes the dramatic extremes in Catherine's character and reign to produce a fast-paced and riveting read that some readers will prefer to more minute and reliable scholarly accounts. The book commits a number of unsubstantiated and dubious generalizations about Russian history and repeats several misconceptions about Catherine that others have refuted.

Biographical Novels

Anthony, Evelyn. *Rebel Princess.* New York: Crowell, 1953. 249pp. Catherine's remarkable rise to power is depicted in a fictional treatment that faithfully portrays the essential facts of her life; *Royal Intrigue.* (New York: Crowell, 1954. 279pp.) continues Catherine's story into her reign, concentrating on her relationship with her son, Paul.

Lehr, Helene. *Star of the North: A Novel Based on the Life of Catherine the Great.* New York: Saint Martin's, 1990. 272pp. Following the outlines of Catherine's history this fictionalized biography treats the princess turned empress as the ultimate romantic heroine, from obscurity to power and from sexual neglect to mastery.

Fictional Portraits

Carnegie, Sacha. *Kasia and the Empress.* New York: Dodd, Mead, 1973. 246pp. Life in Catherine's court is described in this novel that offers believable characterizations and period details.

Pushkin, Alexander. *The Captain's Daughter.* 1837. Reprint ed. New York: Knopf, 1992. 369pp. Pushkin depicts army life during the reign of Catherine, supplementing the story with materials from the state archives and Catherine's private papers.

Rutherfurd, Edward. *Russka: The Novel of Russia.* New York: Crown, 1991. 760pp. The author's massive panoramic chronicle of Russian history

beginning in AD 180 through the twentieth century includes the impact of Catherine's reign.

Schoonover, Lawrence. *The Revolutionary.* Boston: Little, Brown, 1958. 495pp. This faithful biographical account of the life and career of American naval hero John Paul Jones follows his final service in Russia at the court of Catherine.

Recommended Juvenile Biographies

Almedingen, E.M. *The Young Catherine.* New York: Roy, 1966. 141pp. Recounting the childhood and marriage of Catherine, the novel concludes with the coup in 1762 that brings her to the Russian throne. The novel follows the basic outline of Catherine's life.

McGuire, Leslie. *Catherine the Great.* New York: Chelsea House, 1986. 112pp. MG. This comprehensive treatment of Catherine's life and reign portrays her as an inspired and energetic leader who helped transform Russia into a modern nation. Dealing frankly with the sexual side of Catherine's nature and experience, the book concentrates on her public life and policy decisions.

Noble, Iris. *Empress of all Russia.* New York: J. Messner, 1966. 191pp. MG/YA. Noble summarizes Catherine's achievement, emphasizing her strengths and minimizing her faults in a colorful dramatization of her life.

Biographical Films and Theatrical Adaptations

Shaw, George Bernard. *Great Catherine: A Thumbnail Sketch of Russian Court Life in the XVIII Century (Whom Glory Still Adores).* London: Constable, 1913. 266pp. In Shaw's amusing comedy, Catherine is presented as a sophisticated women of the world who flouts stifling court conventions.

Catherine the Great (1934). Director: Paul Czinner. Douglas Fairbanks Jr. and Elizabeth Bergner star in this lavish historical drama that concentrates on Catherine's unfortunate marriage and rise to power. Alternate title: *The Rise of Catherine the Great.* Video.

The Eagle (1925). Director: Clarence Brown. In this action/adventure Rudolph Valentino, a young Cossack, turns outlaw after rejecting the amorous advances of the empress (portrayed by Louise Dresser). Based on a Pushkin story. Video.

Great Catherine (1968). Director: Gordon Fleming. British film version of Shaw's comedy has Jeanne Moreau as Catherine, Peter O'Toole as a British officer, and Zero Mostel as Potemkin. Despite a fine cast, the drama is disappointing.

John Paul Jones (1959). Director: John Farrow. This adventure spectacle on the life of naval hero Jones (Robert Stack) features a cameo appearance by Bette Davis as Catherine. Video.

Royal Scandal (1945). Directors: Ernst Lubitsch and Otto Preminger. Tallulah Bankhead stars as Catherine in the remake of Lubitsch's 1924 *Forbidden Paradise*, finished by Preminger. This court drama concerns Catherine's promotion of a favorite (William Eyth) to high rank.

The Scarlet Empress (1934). Director: Josef von Sternberg. Marlene Dietrich plays Catherine in a strangely asexual, wooden performance; Sam Jaffe is Peter, and Louise Dresser plays the Empress Elizabeth against a stunning expressionist background that has made the film into a cult classic. Available on video as *Catherine the Great.* Video.

Shadow of the Eagle (1950). Director: Sidney Salkow. Binnie Barnes portrays Catherine in this court drama in scenes from her life.

Young Catherine (1991). Director: Michael Anderson. Television mini-series with Julia Ormond as Catherine; Vanessa Redgrave as Empress Elizabeth, and Maximillian Schell as Frederick the Great. Visually detailed with a fine cast but with questionable historical interpretations. Video.

84. MIGUEL DE CERVANTES
1547–1616

Spanish novelist, dramatist, and poet, Cervantes was born in Alcalá de Henares, but his youth and education are shrouded in mystery. In 1569 he went to Italy in the service of a cardinal, and in 1571 he fought in the naval battle of Lepanto where he received a wound that permanently crippled his left arm. While returning to Spain in 1575, he was captured by Barbary pirates and sold into slavery. Cervantes was ransomed in 1580 and returned to Spain where he struggled to support himself as a government purchasing agent that resulted in imprisonment. His first literary work was a pastoral romance published in 1585. Between 1582 and 1587 he wrote more than 20 plays, and in 1605, at the age of 58, published his masterpiece, Part 1 of *Don Quixote* (Part 2 followed in 1615). Cervantes's remarkable novel, which can be described as a satire on chivalrous romances and a moving tragic celebration of the power of illusion, has had an important impact on Western cultural history and the development of the novel.

Recommended Biographies

Canavaggio, Jean. *Cervantes*. New York: W.W. Norton, 1990. 348pp. The author, a renowned Cervantes scholar, provides as full a portrait of Cervantes as an exhaustive review of the archival record can supply. Accessible to the general reader as it is valuable for the specialist, Canavaggio draws on historical details to supplement the gaps in the life record, recognizing that the historical Cervantes is ultimately irrecoverable, and offers cogent and succinct literary criticism. This study won the 1987 Prix Goncourt for biography.

McKendrick, Melveena. *Cervantes*. Boston: Little, Brown, 1980. 310pp. Through masterful detective work from the scraps of surviving evidence, the author pieces together Cervantes's life in all its complexity with lucid appreciative criticism of his literary achievement.

Other Biographical Studies

Bell, Aubrey F.G. *Cervantes*. Norman: University of Oklahoma Press, 1947. 256pp. More a series of meditative and interpretative essays than a formal biography, the author draws on Cervantes's works to help reconstruct his life and places him securely in the context of his time.

Byron, William. *Cervantes: A Biography*. Garden City, New York: Doubleday, 1978. 583pp. More concerned with biographical data than literary criticism, Byron's exhaustive narrative is best in recreating the color and intensity of sixteenth-century Spain and Cervantes's presumed life as a prisoner in Algeria. Although he uncovers no new facts, he presents what is known vividly, though some may find the connections drawn between Cervantes's life and works farfetched.

Diaz-Plaja, Fernando. *Cervantes: The Life of a Genius*. New York: Scribner, 1970. 170pp. To fill in the gaps, the author incorporates many of the scenes from Cervantes's works that correspond to his personal life. The result is speculative but vivid.

Duran, Manuel. *Cervantes*. Boston: Twayne, 1974. 189pp. Mainly a work of literary criticism for the specialist, the book does include a brief biographical sketch and an account of the social and cultural factors that shaped his career.

Juan Arbo, Sebastian. *Cervantes: The Man and His Time*. New York: Thames and Hudson, 1955. 447pp. A good introduction for a general reader, the author fills in the blanks in the biographical record with speculations drawn from the works and historical details about 16th-century Spanish life.

Navarro Ledesma, Francisco. *Cervantes: The Man and the Genius*. New York: Charterhouse, 1973. 396pp. First published in Spain in 1905, this lively and reliable study captures the spirit of the man and his times. Still a useful introduction for undergraduates and general readers.

Predmore, Richard L. *Cervantes*. New York: Dodd, Mead, 1973. 224pp. Reliable and informative with every interpretation documented and every surmise identified as such, Predmore's beautifully illustrated volume reveals nothing new but brings Cervantes scholarship up to date for a general reader.

Schevill, Rudolph. *Cervantes*. 1919. Reprint ed. New York: Frederick Ungar, 1960. 388pp. Schevill's scholarly examination devotes its first five chapters to Cervantes's life with the remainder of the book an analysis of his literary achievement. More appropriate for an advanced student and specialist.

Biographical Novels

Frank, Bruno. *A Man Called Cervantes*. New York: Viking, 1935. 301pp. Presenting everything about Cervantes that is actually known with logical deductions in a imaginatively realized fictional biography, Frank weaves a credable story that does not seriously violate any known facts.

Marlowe, Stephen. *The Death and Life of Miguel de Cervantes: A Novel*. New York: Arcade, 1996. 495pp. Beginning with Cervantes's death, this fictional autobiography works its way back to his beginnings and the imaginative fermentation that eventually produced his classic novel. This book mixes the facts of Cervantes's life with fantasy, such as Cervantes's meeting with Shakespeare and Christopher Marlowe, and details from the period to form a sophisticated and exuberant meta-fiction.

Fictional Portraits

Chapman, Robin. *The Duchess's Diary*. Boston: Faber and Faber, 1985. 127pp. Taking an event from *Don Quixote* in which Quixote stays at a castle with an unnamed duke and duchess, this imaginative novel speculates that Cervantes himself stayed in the castle, and the duchess records her impressions of the visit as the appeal of the man and his art exerts its power on the noblewoman.

Rojas, Carlos. *The Garden of Janus*. Madison, New Jersey: Fairleigh Dickinson University Press, 1996. 218pp. Rojas's inventive probing of Cervantes's psyche supplies answers to the mysteries why the writer waited 10 years to write the second part of *Don Quixote* and who was Alonso Fernandez de Avellaneda, the plagiarist who wrote a sequel to Cervantes's novel. Answers are reached through the agency of the ghosts of the novelist's fictional characters.

Recommended Juvenile Biographies

Busoni, Rafaello. *The Man Who Was Don Quixote: The Story of Miguel Cervantes*. Englewood Cliffs, New Jersey: Prentice-Hall, 1958. 209pp. YA. In a sound historical and biographical work, Busoni presents the scanty facts about the writer's life against a fully realized period background.

Goldberg, Jake. *Miguel de Cervantes*. New York: Chelsea House, 1993. 111pp. MG. Part of the Hispanics of Achievement series, this informative biography describes both the life and career of Cervantes. Packed with information and helpful illustrations.

85. PAUL CÉZANNE
1839–1906

Considered by many the father of modern painting, Cézanne was born in Aix-en-Provence, France, where he remained throughout his life except for stays in Paris, where he was influenced by Pissaro, Manet, and others. Cézanne's development as an artist incorporated many themes and techniques of the impressionists, but he went beyond their ideas to anticipate twentieth-century expressionism and cubism.

Autobiography and Primary Sources

Paul Cézanne, Letters. John Rewald, ed. New York: Hacker, 1984. 339pp. The gradual collection and scholarly publication of Cézanne's correspondence transformed the biographies of the painter. There are few better sources in revealing the author in depth. Almost one-third of the collection are Cézanne's letters to his hometown friend, Emile Zola.

Recommended Biographies

Callow, Philip. *Lost Earth: A Life of Cezanne* Chicago: Ivan R. Dee, 1995. 395pp. Examining Cézanne's life within the context of his art in a boldly psychological interpretation, Callow stresses the more enigmatic aspects of the painter's personality and details of Cézanne's life and temperament often ignored by other biographers.

Based on contemporary accounts and on Joachim Gasquet's newly translated reminiscences, this is a revealing portrait of a very complex and thoroughly modern artistic genius.

Rewald, John. *Cézanne: A Biography.* New York: Abrams, 1986. 235pp. The most complete, fully illustrated survey of the artist's life available by the editor of Cézanne's letters who puts them to informative use in a classic biography. Scrupulous in its documentation and astute in its criticism, Rewald's study is deservedly ranked as the definitive life of the painter.

Other Biographical Studies

Beucken, Jean de. *Cézanne: A Pictorial Biography.* New York: Viking, 1962. 143pp. Written by a French art historian, this short illustrated biographical sketch offers a helpful visual supplement to more detailed biographies.

Fry, Roger. *Cézanne: A Study of His Development.* New York: Macmillan, 1927. 88pp. The first English study of Cézanne, Fry's breakthrough critical study helped create appreciation for post-impressionism beyond France. Fry is insightful on the development of Cézanne's artistic genius.

Hanson, Lawrence. *Mortal Victory: A Biography of Paul Cézanne.* New York: Holt, 1960, 222pp. Hanson's overly defensive portrait sets out to redeem what he perceives to be slights to Cézanne's moral character. Too partisan and speculative to be regarded as either objective or reliable.

Lindsay, Jack. *Cézanne: His Life and Art.* New York: New York Graphic Society, 1969. 360pp. Lindsay's psychological portrait follows Freudian concepts to interpret Cézanne, supported by details of the painter's social and artistic milieux. Very speculative, the book is nonetheless provocative and insightful. However, many critics have judged Lindsay's approach as highly romanticized and often contradictory.

Mack, Gerstle. *Paul Cézanne.* New York: Knopf, 1935. 437pp. The first comprehensive biography, containing previously unpublished material, including letters to Emile Zola and others, Mack's straightforward narrative corrects many previous errors and collects all the then-known facts, but rarely rises above the factual to offer an interpretation.

Venturi, Lionella. *Cézanne.* New York: Rizzoli, 1978. 175pp. Venturi's study is best on assessing the various influences that helped shape Cézanne's art and his influence on later artists. Artistic developments are located within the context of the painter's life. Includes many illustrations.

Vollard, Ambroise. *Paul Cézanne: His Life and Art.* New York: N.L. Brown, 1923. 126pp. Written by an early Cézanne advocate and art dealer, this is a gossipy and anecdotal collection that should be read with caution.

Biographical Novels

McLeave, Hugh. *A Man and His Mountain: The Life of Paul Cézanne.* New York: Macmillan, 1977. 365pp. Showing a great familiarity with the period and the man, this fictional biography traces Cézanne's career from boyhood convincingly.

Fictional Portraits

Poldermans, Joost. *Vincent: A Novel Based on the Life of Van Gogh.* New York: Holt, 1962. 317pp. Based on letters, diaries, and reminiscences, the novel recreates the life of Van Gogh and his associates, including Cézanne. Not reliable as strict biography, though based, at least in part, on recorded fact.

Stone, Irving. *Depths of Glory.* Garden City, New York: Doubleday, 1985. 652pp. In Stone's biographical novel on the life and times of Camille Pissarro, there is a full presentation of the Paris artist community and its principal figures, such as Cézanne.

Recommended Juvenile Biographies

Mason, Anthony. *Cézanne.* Hauppauge, New York: Barron's, 1994. 32pp. MG. Part biography and part art history and study guide, this useful, short account highlights a portion of Cézanne's life and his artistic development. Definitely for the artistically inclined rather than the beginner.

Sellier, Marie. *Cézanne from A to Z.* New York: Bedrick, 1996. 59pp. MG. Progressing both alphabetically and chronologically, each entry covers a particular aspect of Cézanne's life and work. Although the format may suggest a younger audience, the content is fairly sophisticated.

Biographical Films and Theatrical Adaptations

Cézanne: The Man and the Mountain (1985). Director: Jochen Richter. Focuses on Cézanne's fascination with nature, his love-hate relationship with his birthplace, and his obsession with Mount Sainte Victoire, his favorite subject, the documentary traces his career to his final recognition as a founder of modern painting. Video.

86. MARC CHAGALL
1887–1985

A Russian expressionist painter, whose lyrical, dreamlike style made him a forerunner of surrealism, Chagall studied under L.N. Bakst in Saint Petersburg. He left Russia in 1922 and settled in France. His works often depict pre-World War I Jewish life and folklore, and include *I and the Village* and *The Rabbi of Vitebsk.* Chagall also designed the sets and costumes for Stravinsky's ballet *Firebird* (1945), illustrated a number of books, created 12 stained-glass windows, symbolizing the tribes of Israel, and painted murals for New York's Metropolitan Opera House.

Autobiography and Primary Sources

Chagall by Chagall. Charles Sarlier, ed. New York: Abrams, 1980. 263pp. The painter arranges extracts from his earlier autobiography with additional material to provide a poetic, fragmentary commentary on his life and work.

My Life. New York: Orion Press, 1960. 173pp. Chagall's poetic memoirs cover the first 30 years of his life, written with a compelling nostalgia for his departed Russia. Less a factual account than rich,

dreamy meditation, the book provides an essential glimpse of the painter's emotional, artistic, and intellectual makeup.

Recommended Biographies

Alexander, Sidney. *Marc Chagall: A Biography.* New York: Putnam, 1978. 526pp. This is a lively life-and-times approach based on extensive interviews with the artist's associates. A full-length, three-dimensional, objective portrait, Alexander's biography both sheds new light on the artist and provides the general reader with an engaging, human portrait of Chagall.

Meyer, Franz. *Marc Chagall.* New York: Abrams, 1964. 775pp. Written by Chagall's son-in-law, this comprehensive and detailed study of the life and works has long served as the standard biography. Encyclopedic in its coverage, biographical insights derived from the artist himself and his family establish an authoritative chronological account and a record of Chagall's artistic development. A must for the serious student of the painter.

Other Biographical Studies

Bidermanas, Izis, and Roy McMullen. *The World of Marc Chagall.* Garden City, New York: Doubleday, 1968. 267pp. Bidermanas's photographs of Chagall at work and informal portraits from 1950s and 1960s are joined with some of Chagall's works, quotations from his writings, a chronology, and a biographical and critical essay by McMullen.

Chagall, Bella. *Burning Lights.* New York: Schocken, 1946. 268pp. Reissued as *First Encounter.* New York: Schocken Books, 1983. 348pp. Chagall's first wife provides her recollections of her life in Russia before the Revolution and with her husband through the 1940s. Along with Chagall's own memoir, this is an essential source of information on the artist, his background, and his artistic development.

Compton, Susan P. *Chagall.* New York: Abrams, 1985. 280pp. Compton's introduction to this catalog of a major retrospective exhibition supplies a sensible and thoughtful biographical and critical overview.

Crespelle, Jean-Paul. *Chagall.* New York: Coward-McCann, 1970. 287pp. Crespelle's lively, concise overview of Chagall's life and work serves as a worthwhile general introduction for the nonspecialist.

Haggard, Virginia. *My Life with Chagall.* New York: D.I. Fine, 1987. 190pp. Chagall's mistress provides her recollection of their life together from 1945 to 1952. A frank record of both the man and the artist, the book also documents Chagall's relationship with other artists, most notably Picasso.

Kagan, Andrew. *Marc Chagall.* New York: Abbeville Press, 1989. 128pp. Kagan supplies a brief overview of the significant stages of the artist's life, along with critical evaluation of Chagall's important work, a number of reproductions, and a chronology.

Kamensky, Aleksandr. *Chagall: The Russian Years 1907-22.* New York: Rizzoli, 1989. 376pp. The work of a leading Russian Chagall scholar, this study of the painter's Russian period sheds considerable fresh light on Chagall's work and relationships, setting his artistic development in the wider context of the Russian avant-garde of the period.

Recommended Juvenile Biographies

Greenfeld, Howard. *Marc Chagall*. New York: Abrams, 1989. 92pp. YA. Greenfield chronicles Chagall's life and career with an emphasis on how his childhood experience influenced his work.

Pozzi, Gianni. *Chagall*. New York: Bedrick, 1997. 64pp. MG/YA. This attractive oversized volume establishes the artist in his historical, social, cultural, and stylistic context.

Biographical Films and Theatrical Adaptations

Homage to Chagall (1987). Director: Harry Rasky. This film portrait includes interviews with the artist and his wife. Video.

Marc Chagall (1985). Director: Kim Evans. A documentary profile of Chagall's life and work. Video.

87. COCO CHANEL
1883–1971

Regarded as one of the most influential fashion designers in the twentieth century, French couturière Chanel freed women from corsets and long skirts and put them in simple, elegant outfits, inventing women's sportswear, the classic "little black dress," and costume jewelry. Chanel rose from obscurity to international fame and was intimate with Igor Stravinsky, Winston Churchill, and the Duke of Westminster.

Recommended Biographies

Galante, Pierre. *Mademoiselle Chanel*. Chicago: Regnery, 1973. 298pp. Presenting the designer against the social milieu of her times, this is an excellent perceptive account by a leading French journalist and long-time editor of *Paris-Match*. Despite clear admiration for Chanel's professional achievement, the author does not conceal her egocentricity or occasional nastiness.

Madsen, Axel. *Chanel: A Woman of Her Own*. New York: Holt, 1990. 388pp. Madsen's intimate portrait helpfully untangles the truth from the legend in Chanel's glamorous though bittersweet life. At times the account is thematically driven to show Chanel as the personification of postwar feminism, but for the most part this is the fullest and most reliable biography available in English.

Wallach, Janet. *Chanel: Her Style and Her Life*. New York: Doubleday, 1998. 192pp. In a visually stunning biographical treatment, the author intersperses large black-and-white photos of the designer, her clothes, and her homes with the story of her life based on attentive research into the Chanel archives and colleagues' anecdotes. Revealing and compelling.

Other Biographical Studies

Baudot, François. *Coco Chanel*. New York: Rizzoli, 1996. 80pp. This is a short biographical sketch that captures the highlights of Chanel's career and her personality. Serves as a useful introduction.

Charles-Roux, Edmonde. *Chanel*. New York: Knopf, 1975. 373pp. This distorted account fills in the obscure gaps in Chanel's life with supposition, circumstantial evidence, and gossip disguised as fact in an overall lifeless characterization.

De La Haye, Amy, and Shelley Tobin. *Chanel: The Couturiere at Work*. Woodstock, New York: Overlook Press, 1995. 136pp. Providing an inside look at the creations and the evolution of the House of Chanel, this gorgeously illustrated book provides a sympathetic and understanding view of its founder as well.

Haedrich, Marcel. *Coco Chanel: Her Life, Her Secrets*. Boston: Little, Brown, 1972. 272pp. Based on interviews with Chanel, Haedrich's account is sometimes unreliable since his subject's recollections are often fabrications, omitting the less flattering details of her life. Closer to an oral memoir than objective biography, the book is interesting in revealing the version of Chanel's life she wished published.

Mackrell, Alice. *Coco Chanel*. New York: Holmes & Meier, 1992. 95pp. Using photos and drawings, Chanel's achievement as a fashion designer is illustrated. The emphasis here is on Chanel's career rather than her private life.

Biographical Novels

Soliman, Patricia B. *Coco: The Novel*. New York: Putnam, 1990. 399pp. Chanel and her intimate friends narrate the highlights of the designer's career in a fictional recreation that is plausible.

Biographical Films and Theatrical Adaptations

Chanel, Chanel (1988). Directors: Eila Hershon and Roberto Guerra. Using rare archival footage, this documentary explores both Chanel's professional career and her personal life. Video.

Chanel Solitaire (1981). Director: George Kaczender. Uninspiring and cliché-heavy, the film looks at the designer's first 38 years, with an emphasis on her love life. Starring Marie-France Pisier, Timothy Dalton, and Rutger Hauer. Video.

88. CHARLIE CHAPLIN
1889–1977

Born in London, Charlie Chaplin began performing on the music hall stage and was recruited into the movies by Mack Sennett while on tour in America. His "Little Tramp" character became one of early film's most popular characters, making Chaplin one of the world's most famous individuals in the early twentieth century. In 1919 Chaplin co-founded United Artists, and his feature films include *The Kid* (1920), *The Gold Rush* (1924), *City Lights* (1931), *Modern Times* (1936), and *The Great Dictator* (1940). Chaplin's political sympa-

thies and personal scandals led to his exile from the United States after 1952.

Autobiography and Primary Sources

Chaplin's various autobiographical volumes are notoriously unreliable, revealing only what he wished the public to know and ignoring or disguising less flattering events. Still his version of his life and career possesses considerable interest for the reader who wishes a firsthand interpretation.

My Autobiography. New York: Simon & Schuster, 1964. 512pp. Written at the end of his film career, Chaplin's memory is untrustworthy, but his recollections are nonetheless fascinating and essential as a biographical source. Less an autobiography than a self-justification, the book is still filled with interesting information, though evasive. See also *My Life in Pictures* (New York: Grosset & Dunlop, 1975. 310pp.).

Geduld, Harry M., ed. *Charlie Chaplin's Own Story*. Bloomington: Indiana University Press, 1985. 175pp. Originally written in 1916 and later suppressed, this is an invaluable reflection of Chaplin's views at the height of his career. Geduld's notes document the discrepancies between this early autobiography and Chaplin's 1964 version.

Recommended Biographies

Lynn, Kenneth S. *Charlie Chaplin and His Times*. New York: Simon & Schuster, 1997. 604pp. Lynn's richly detailed and psychologically penetrating biography is dominated by a central thesis that Chaplin's drive was prompted by an unfulfilled wish to rescue his mother from poverty and madness. In addition to plumbing Chaplin's personal traumas, the book is excellent on the nature of Chaplin's genius and his era. In Lynn's skilled handling, a disturbing but complex Chaplin emerges in full.

Milton, Joyce. *Tramp: The Life of Charlie Chaplin*. New York: HarperCollins, 1996. 578pp. The author concentrates on Chaplin's political life, placing his career in its American historical context. Treating his various marriages and scandals, Mann makes a case that Chaplin may have suffered from manic depression, a diagnosis suited to this unsentimental portrait of a complicated man. The book is less assured in handling Chaplin's artistic achievements.

Robinson, Donald W. *Chaplin: His Life and Art*. New York: McGraw-Hill, 1985. 792pp. Robinson's exhaustive study details Chaplin's childhood in England, his film career, and his exile in Switzerland, along with a filmography, a list of theater tours, a summary of the FBI file on Chaplin, a detailed chronology, and a Chaplin who's who. Providing a great deal of new material, this is the essential reference source for any reader wishing to explore various aspects of Chaplin's remarkable career.

Other Biographical Studies

Bessy, Maurice. *Charlie Chaplin*. New York: Harper & Row, 1985. 438pp. This illustrated biography includes stills from Chaplin's films and other rare finds. Unfortunately, the text is often hyperbolic and uncritical, written by an acquaintance and clear admirer.

Chaplin, Charles Jr. *My Father: Charlie Chaplin.* New York: Random House, 1960. 369pp. Chaplin's son's biographical tribute to his father offers a treasure trove of previously unpublished information about the actor's working and living habits. Despite clear loyalty to his father's memory and occasional sentimentality, the book does not cover up faults and remains valuable for its intimate insights.

Cotes, Peter, and Thelma Niklaus. *The Little Fellow: The Life and Work of Charles Spencer Chaplin.* New York: Citadel Press, 1965. 181pp. The first half of the book provides a sketch of Chaplin's life; the second a study of his films, written by an admirer.

Epstein, Jerry. *Remembering Charlie: A Pictorial Biography.* New York: Doubleday, 1989. 228pp. This retrospective photographic record with text by a friend and colleague is best on the period after the late 1940s when firsthand memories deepen the portrait.

Huff, Theodore. *Charlie Chaplin.* New York: H. Schuman, 1951. 354pp. The first seriously researched biography on Chaplin's life up to 1950, this is a balanced account by neither a worshipper nor a detractor with little interpretation but an objective record of the actor's life and career. Still serves well as a useful reference volume.

Maland, Charles J. *Chaplin and American Culture: The Evolution of a Star Image.* Princeton, New Jersey: Princeton University Press, 1989. 442pp. Looking at Chaplin in the context of American culture and politics, Maland traces the actor's rise and fall from grace in a critical analysis of the perils of fame.

Manvell, Roger. *Charlie Chaplin.* Boston: Little, Brown, 1975. 240pp. Attempting to place Chaplin in a social and film context, this concise distillation of the most illuminating and revelatory data put into critical perspective is a useful introductory study.

McCabe, John. *Charlie Chaplin.* Garden City, New York: Doubleday, 1978. 297pp. Written by a respected film historian, McCabe updated Huff's account by incorporating more recent scholarship and recollections from members of Chaplin's family, as well as Stan Laurel's firsthand insights of the music hall years. Includes thumbnail synopses and evaluations of the films.

Robinson, Donald W. *Chaplin: The Mirror of Opinion.* Bloomington: Indiana University Press, 1983. 205pp. Robinson's first Chaplin study looks at the star from the perspective of his public appeal in a study that includes a filmography with the credits from all of Chaplin's feature films from 1923 to 1952.

Fictional Portraits

Fast, Howard. *Max.* Boston: Houghton Mifflin, 1982. 375pp. In the author's account of the fictional Max Britsky who struggles from poverty on the Lower East Side to help create the motion picture industry, actual film personalities, such as Douglas Fairbanks, Mary Pickford, and Chaplin are featured as characters.

Hall, Robert Lee. *Murder at San Simeon.* New York: Saint Martin's, 1988. 343pp. At one of his lavish parties, William Randolph Hearst must solve a murder, while a number of well-known personalities, including Marion Davies and Chaplin, are on hand for color.

Kaminsky, Stuart M. *The Man Who Shot Lewis Vance.* New York: Saint Martin's, 1986. 194pp. In this installment of the author's period detective series set in 1940s Los Angeles, John Wayne is being framed for murder, while Chaplin gets involved in the case.

Roosevelt, Elliott. *Murder in the East Room.* New York: Saint Martin's, 1993. 201pp. In yet another period mystery story, Chaplin puts in an appearance with Eleanor Roosevelt as the sleuth investigating the death of a senator at a state dinner in the White House.

Recommended Juvenile Biographies

Diamond, Arthur. *Charlie Chaplin.* San Diego: Lucent Books, 1995. 112pp. MG/YA. Diamond offers a balanced account of Chaplin's career that emphasizes his considerable achievement and impact.

Kamen, Gloria. *Charlie Chaplin.* New York: Atheneum, 1982. 70pp. MG. This lively, brief biographical portrait hits the high points of Chaplin's career and achievement. Vivid on the early days of Hollywood and Chaplin's comic genius.

Biographical Films and Theatrical Adaptations

Chaplin (1993). Director: Richard Attenborough. Based on Chaplin's *My Autobiography* and Robinson's life, this is a detailed chronicle of the actor's life from his early days in London, through his film triumphs, and scandals and exile. Robert Downey Jr. puts in a bravura performance in the title role, supported by a fine cast, including Geraldine Chaplin as her own grandmother. Slow moving at times and discursive, the film earns high marks for its effort to capture Chaplin's many sides. Video.

Unknown Chaplin (1982). Producers: Kevin Brownlow and David Gill. Narrated by James Mason, this documentary film presents interviews with Chaplin's family and associates and, using outtakes of filmed rehearsals, captures Chaplin's creative process. Video.

Young Charlie Chaplin (1989). Director: Baz Taylor. British television film depicts Chaplin's early struggle in poverty with a mother who is going mad. Ian McShane stars with Twiggy as Hannah Chaplin. Video.

Other Sources

Gehring, Wes D., ed. *Charlie Chaplin: A Bio-Bibliography.* Westport, Connecticut: Greenwood, 1985. 227pp. A bibliography of primary and secondary sources as well as discography and a Chaplin interview.

Lyons, Timothy J., ed. *Charlie Chaplin: A Guide to References and Resources.* Boston: G.K. Hall, 1979. 232pp. A comprehensive listing of material on Chaplin with synopses of the films and the locations of the primary archival sources.

89. CHARLEMAGNE
ca. 742–814

King of the Franks, Charlemagne, the son of Pepin the Short, ascended to the throne in 771. After battles against German tribes and the Moors, Charlemagne consolidated his power and extended his influence until he was crowned Emperor of the West by Pope Leo III in 800. During his reign, Europe experienced a revival of learning, which has been called the Carolingian renaissance. A Latin scholar and theologian as well as a brilliant military leader, Charlemagne became the first great monarch of medieval Europe and the first exponent of a united European community.

Recommended Biographies

Chamberlin, E.R. *The Emperor, Charlemagne.* New York: F. Watts, 1986. 245pp. This useful narrative account of Charlemagne's times presents a balanced view of his actual achievement and a human portrait that penetrates the various legends surrounding him. Recommended as a helpful introduction to the period and the man.

Winston, Richard. *Charlemagne: From the Hammer to the Cross.* Indianapolis: Bobbs-Merrill, 1954. 346pp. Depicting Charlemagne as a warrior, theologian, political reformer, and art patron, Winston's somewhat flattering portrait is still one of the most carefully written and readable biographies of Charlemagne available in English. Critics have suggested that Winston's treatment lacks depth and a three-dimensional quality; *Charlemagne* (New York: American Heritage, 1968. 153pp.) provides a brief overview in an illustrated format.

Other Biographical Studies

Almedingen, E.M. *Charlemagne: A Study.* London: Bodley Head, 1968. 252pp. This popular account concentrates on Charlemagne's times and cultural context, with only a single chapter on his character.

Boussard, Jacques. *The Civilization of Charlemagne.* New York: McGraw-Hill, 1968. 251pp. The times are predominant here, with separate chapters on the social, cultural, and historical life of Charlemagne's era.

Bullough, Donald A. *The Age of Charlemagne.* New York: Putnam, 1966. 212pp. Concentrating on Charlemagne's political career, this account follows him from king to emperor, reviewing the available evidence in its context, with chapters on religious history, art, and architect, aided by illustrations.

Einhard, and Notker the Stammerer. *Two Lives of Charlemagne.* Lewis Thorpe, ed. Baltimore: Penguin, 1969. 227pp. These are the earliest biographies of Charlemagne, written within a century of his death by ecclesiastics, and provide the basis for all subsequent biographies, supplying most of the scant information known about Charlemagne's early life, appearance, and personality.

Heer, Friedrich. *Charlemagne and His World*. New York: Macmillan, 1975. 272pp. In the author's dramatic, illustrated recreation of the life and times, Charlemagne is presented as an enlightened figure, a political innovator, and one of the great revolutionaries of the Middle Ages. Placing his achievement against its ninth century social, economic, and cultural background, Heer is as much concerned with Charlemagne's educational innovations and administrative genius as with his military exploits.

Hodgkin, Thomas. *Charles the Great*. 1899. Reprint ed. Port Washington, New York: Kennikat Press, 1970. 251pp. Hodgkin's scholarly analysis helpfully sorts through the various legendary materials that have competed with the facts in revealing the actual Charlemagne, and his study remains useful in piecing together a creditable portrait based on informed surmises.

Lamb, Harold. *Charlemagne: The Legend and the Man*. Garden City, New York: Doubleday, 1954. 320pp. In his dramatic reconsideration, Lamb seeks to penetrate the chivalrous and legendary to arrive at a human portrait. With a convincing historical background, Lamb succeeds in filling in the outlines of a creditable person with plausible guesswork anchored by historical sources and modern scholarship.

Fictional Portraits

Bulfinch, Thomas. *Bulfinch: The Legends of Charlemagne*. New York: Macmillan, 1997. 160pp. Writer and mythologist Thomas Bulfinch (1796–1867) was the first to create a popular compendium of ancient myths and legends drawing on a variety of sources. The legendary character of Charlemagne is superbly presented in this beautifully illustrated volume.

Johnson, Eyvind. *The Days of His Grace*. New York: Vanguard, 1970. 319pp. This adventure novel offers the perspective of Charlemagne's secretary on the emperor's life and times.

Pei, Mario. *Swords of Anjou*. New York: J. Day, 1953. 310pp. Pei's classic adventure tale is set during Charlemagne's reign and features a colorful presentation of his times.

The Song of Roland. Various editions. Written in the twelfth century, the first great narrative poem in French, *The Song of Roland* tells a story of a historical incident in the career of Charlemagne in which his army in 778 was attacked by the Gascons in the mountain passes of the Pyrenees. Charlemagne is elevated to almost supernatural heroic status and the incident modified to a battle against an enormous Saracen army with the survival of Christianity in the balance.

Recommended Juvenile Biographies

Banfield, Susan. *Charlemagne*. New York: Chelsea House, 1986. 112pp. MG. Part of the World Leaders Past & Present series, this is a clear and concise rendering of Charlemagne's life and times with helpful illustrations, a concise chronology, and quotes from a variety of sources.

Biel, Timothy L. *Charlemagne*. San Diego: Lucent Books, 1997. 127pp. MG. Attempting to separate facts from legend, this detailed biography recounts the life and achievements of Charlemagne with quotes from both primary and secondary sources, including an excerpt from *The Song of Roland*.

Stearns, Monroe. *Charlemagne: Monarch of the Middle Ages*. New York: F. Watts, 1971. 182pp. MG/YA. Stearns provides a life-and-times overview, filling in many of the details surrounding Charlemagne's life and reign with historical and cultural information.

Biographical Films and Theatrical Adaptations

Charlemagne (1994). Director: Clive Donner. French/Italian television mini-series depicts Charlemagne's ascension to the Frankish throne, his uniting of the nations of Western Europe, and his role in rebuilding Western civilization after the fall of the Roman empire. Christian Brendel portrays Charlemagne. Video.

Charlemagne and the Holy Roman Empire (1989). Part of the Films for the Humanities series, originally produced in association with the Spanish ministry of culture, the film looks at Charlemagne's life and reign. Video.

The Dark Ages: The Age of Charlemagne (1989). Producer: Fred Barzyk. Covering the new political and economic order that formed in the centuries after the fall of the Roman Empire, this documentary looks closely at Charlemagne's influential presence in the new world order. Video.

Other Sources

Loyn, H.R., and J. Percival, eds. *The Reign of Charlemagne*. New York: Saint Martin's, 1976. 164pp. This useful collection of documents, including monastic records, legislative material, and letters, some by Charlemagne himself, serves as an informative introduction to the reign and the age.

90. CHARLES I
1600–1649

King of England, Charles I became the heir of James I after the death of his older brother in 1612, succeeding to the throne in 1625. Offending his Protestant subjects by his marriage to the Catholic Henrietta Maria of France, Charles's disputes with Parliament escalated into civil war in 1641. Defeated at Marston Moor in 1644 and at Naseby in 1645, Charles was tried for treason and beheaded in 1649.

Autobiography and Primary Sources

The closest access to the private Charles comes largely through his letters, which are available in two useful collections: *The Letters, Speeches, and Proclamations*. Charles Petrie, ed. (New York: Funk & Wagnalls, 1968. 319pp.) and *Charles I in 1646: Letters of King Charles the First to Queen Henrietta Maria*. John Bruce, ed. (New York: AMS Press, 1968. 104pp.).

Recommended Biographies

Bowle, John. *Charles I: A Biography*. Boston: Little, Brown, 1975. 362pp. In the author's revisionist view, Charles is not a backward-looking despot but an enlightened blunderer, sensitive, steadfast in his convictions, and mistaken in his methods. In addition to providing a believable portrait of the king, backed up with an eye for revealing and entertaining details, the book is an excellent one-volume summary of the English Civil War.

Young, Michael B. *Charles I*. New York: Saint Martin's, 1997. 232pp. Young helpfully guides the reader through recent scholarship that has revised the view of early Stuart politics. Insightful and provocative, Young challenges a variety of misconceptions about the king and suggests where the truth can be found.

Other Biographical Studies

Ashley, Maurice. *Charles I and Oliver Cromwell: A Study in Contrasts and Comparisons*. New York: Methuen, 1987. 243pp. Ashley's dual biographical portrait is an insightful study that takes the full measure of both men. Ashley is recognized as the dean of Cromwellian studies, and it is interesting to have his reflections on Charles I.

Carlton, Charles. *Charles I: The Personal Monarch*. Boston: Routledge, 1983. 426pp. Using the findings of modern psychology to assess Charles's character, Carlton amasses an impressive assortment of facts to support his interpretation. Concentrating on Charles's personality, Carlton neglects the political world of early Stuart England and commits a number of factual errors, but there are few better intimate looks at court life and Charles's relationship with his wife.

Edwards, Graham. *The Last Days of Charles I*. Stroud, England: Sutton, 1999. 210pp. To mark the 350th anniversary of Charles I's execution, Edwards presents a compact yet thorough account of the events leading up to the king's death.

Gregg, Pauline. *King Charles I*. Berkeley: University of California Press, 1981. 196pp. Gregg's examination of the life and reign of the king is a worthy introduction for readers who need a solid grounding in the period.

Hibbert, Christopher. *Charles I*. New York: Harper & Row, 1968. 295pp. In Hibbert's view Charles is a victim who contrived his own doom, standing fast when compromise was essential and vacillating when decisiveness was needed. Unfortunately, the book lacks documentation to identify sources.

Higham, Florence. *Charles I: A Study*. 1932. Reprint ed. Westport, Connecticut: Greenwood, 1979. 315pp. In the first serious biographical study in the twentieth century, this is an authoritative and thorough work by an expert on seventeenth-century government and church policies, an expertise that helps put Charles I in the context of his times. A balanced account, Higham manages to synthesize complex events and personalities into a compelling drama.

John, Evan. *King Charles I*. New York: Roy, 1952. 314pp. In the author's sympathetic view, Charles is depicted as advanced in his attitudes and very different from his characterization by earlier proponents of the parliamentarian opposition. The book is less detailed and authoritative than other accounts, such as Bowle's.

Ollard, Richard. *The Image of the King: A Biography of Charles I and Charles II.* New York: Atheneum, 1979. 211pp. Concentrating mainly on the formation of the personality and temperament of Charles II, this psychological joint biographical study of father and son is arranged not into a chronological narrative but in a series of meditative essays.

Sharpe, Kevin. *The Personal Rule of Charles I.* New Haven, Connecticut: Yale University Press, 1993. 983pp. This massive historical study looks at the 1630s and attempts to decipher the king's motives and political actions. To explain Charles's break with Parliament, Sharpe shows the importance of his early years as prince and monarch in forming his ideas and character.

Biographical Novels

Anthony, Evelyn. *Charles the King.* Garden City, New York: Doubleday, 1961. 427pp. In this sympathetic portrait, the reign of Charles I is chronicled, with an emphasis on his relationship with his queen, Henrietta Maria. The often confusing events of the English Civil War are carefully delineated in this fictional interpretation that shows evidence of careful research.

Evans, Jean. *The Phoenix Rising.* New York: Saint Martin's, 1976. 205pp. Set during the months leading up to Charles's execution, the novel features the efforts of the king to retain control and the efforts of his son to gain support for his claim to the crown.

Gluyas, Constance. *My Lord Foxe.* New York: McKay, 1976. 490pp. The marriage between Charles and Henrietta Maria is the basis of this biographical novel that features a framework of fact and plausible, historical characterizations.

Lane, Jane. *The Young and Lonely King.* Leicester, England: Ulverscroft,1969. 452pp. This biographical account covers the life of Charles I from his early years to the birth of the future Charles II. Although dialogue and some situations are invented, the general outline of Charles's life is respected; *The Severed Crown.* New York: Simon & Schuster, 1972. 210pp. Narrated by a variety of witnesses, the novel details the final three years in the life of Charles I, through his imprisonment, trial, and execution. Often confusing and surprisingly slow moving despite the inherent drama.

Plaidy, Jean. *Myself, My Enemy.* New York: Putnam, 1983. 382pp. This autobiographical account of Queen Henrietta Maria chronicles her husband's reign and her fierce loyalty to him. The voice of the queen is authentic, and her perspective provides an interesting angle to view the royal household and the events of the English Civil War.

Fictional Portraits

Barnes, Margaret C. *Mary of Carisbrooke.* Philadelphia: Macrae Smith, 1956. 318pp. Concerning the captivity of Charles I in Carisbrooke Castle on the Isle of Wight during the months preceding his trial and execution, he is loyally served by the laundress Mary Floyd, who is caught up in the conflict between loyalists and Parliament. The services rendered by Floyd are authentic; the romance plot is, however, imaginary.

Irwin, Margaret. *The Proud Servant: The Story of Montrose.* New York: Harcourt, Brace, 1934. 441pp. Chronicling the career of James Graham, Marquess of Montrose, the faithful champion of Charles I in the battle with Parliament, the novel features authentic quotes from various letters and documents; *The Stranger Prince.* New York: Saint Martin's, 1937. 556pp. Looks at the actions of another of the king's champions, Prince Rupert.

Biographical Films and Theatrical Adaptations

Cromwell (1970). Director: Ken Hughes. A lavish historical epic with a miscast Richard Harris in the title role and a sympathetic view of Charles through Alec Guinness's compelling performance. Best for its battle scenes and period details. Video.

See also Oliver Cromwell

91. CHARLES II
1630–1685

Charles II was proclaimed king of Scotland and parts of Ireland and England after the execution in 1649 of his father, Charles I. He marched into England in 1651 but was defeated at the battle of Worcester, and he escaped to live in exile in France, Germany, and the Netherlands until 1660 when he was restored to the English throne. Charles's reign was marked by the gradual increase in the power of Parliament and the rise of the great political parties and England as a sea power. The pleasure-loving king also set the tone for the Restoration period in art and literature.

Autobiography and Primary Sources

The Letters, Speeches, and Declarations. Arthur Bryant, ed. New York: Funk & Wagnalls, 1968. 353pp. Brings together the largest collection of Charles II's primary source material.

My Dearest Minette. Ruth Norrington, ed. Chester Springs, Pennsylvania: Dufour Editions, 239pp. This collection of correspondence between Charles II and his sister with commentary placing the letters in context reveals details of court life among the royalty of both England and France between 1659 and 1670.

Recommended Biographies

Coote, Stephen. *Royal Survivor: The Life of Charles II.* New York: St. Martin's, 2000. 408pp. This is a sympathetic assessment of Charles that emphasizes his political wiles in a rousing popular, narrative biography that traces the king's career and character and makes sense of the complicated political maneuvering that shaped Charles's actions.

Fraser, Antonia. *Royal Charles: Charles II and the Restoration.* New York: Knopf, 1979. 524pp. Conceding the king's laziness and self-indulgence and meeting the various charges against the king with authority, Fraser insists on a charitable, affectionate view of Charles as an often courageous and effective monarch. Fraser's reinterpretation focuses on the king's personality and politics and is best in dramatizing the events of the civil war and his years in exile. She is less successful after 1660 when the facts are more complicated and the political context needs fuller exploration.

Hutton, Ronald. *Charles II: King of England, Scotland, and Ireland.* New York: Oxford University Press, 1989. 554pp. The most authoritative and definitive study of Charles II's reign, Hutton's work offers the fullest account of various aspects of Charles's life, including his years in exile. Although the public life is dominant here, there is no better source for its careful and detailed analysis.

Other Biographical Studies

Ashley, Maurice. *Charles II: The Man and the Statesman.* New York: Praeger, 1971. 358pp. Ashley's balanced assessment both praises and criticizes Charles's political skills and is particularly strong on the era's foreign affairs. Less revealing about the private life of the king.

Bryant, Arthur. *King Charles II.* New York: Longmans, 1931. 448pp. Bryant's minute narrative account begins with Charles's flight after the battle of Worcester through the years of his reign. Addressing the charges against Charles, Bryant insists that the king was a wise and loyal ruler, as well as a talented statesman. Very much a case for the defense, this is a full-bodied, dramatic vindication of Charles II.

Chapman, Hester W. *The Tragedy of Charles II in the Years 1630–1660.* Boston: Little, Brown, 1964. 415pp. Chapman's study of Charles's youth and years in exile is dominated by a central thesis that his early humiliations permanently scarred his character and influenced his conduct for the worse. Despite a degree of special pleading, Chapman manages a believable human portrait and a sound historical background.

Falkus, Christopher. *The Life and Times of Charles II.* Garden City, New York: Doubleday, 1972. 223pp. This visual biography chronicles the events of Charles's reign and offers some useful details to capture the king's personality. Serves as a solid introduction to Charles and his era.

Jones, James Rees. *Charles II: Royal Politician.* Boston: Allen and Unwin, 1987. 230pp. Jones's biographical/historical essay places the king in the context of the politics of the era. A succinct summary of the various forces that shaped the king by an recognized expert in the period.

Ollard, Richard. *The Image of the King: A Biography of Charles I and Charles II.* New York: Atheneum, 1979. 211pp. Ollard's double psychological biography of both kings is cast in a series of meditative essays that reveals how Charles II was haunted by the fate of his father, which explains many of his actions.

Palmer, Tony. *Charles II: Portrait of an Age.* London: Cassell, 1979. 311pp. Palmer's visual biography and history summarizes the highlights of Charles's reign and era with quotes from Charles and such contemporaries as John Evelyn and Samuel Pepys.

Pearson, Hesketh. *Merry Monarch: The Life and Likeness of Charles II.* New York: Harper, 1960. 274pp. Pearson's popular biography sets the king against the intellectual and cultural life of his time, broadening the portrait by a master of casual and witty biography. In Pearson's unorthodox view Charles is not the indolent weakling but a wise, tolerant, and personable ruler.

Biographical Novels

Evans, Jean. *The Phoenix Rising.* New York: Saint Martin's, 1976. 205pp. Set in the final months before the execution of Charles I, the novel dramatizes the efforts of the future Charles II to regain the throne before he is forced into exile. The story's framework is historical, but the characters lacks depth and specificity.

Goudge, Elizabeth. *The Child from the Sea.* New York: Coward-McCann, 1970. 736pp. Charles's relationship with Lucy Walter during his years before reaching the throne is the subject here in a blend of romance and history.

Heyer, Georgette. *Royal Escape.* New York: Doubleday, 1938. 386pp. Based on the historical events of Charles's attempt to regain the throne and his defeat at the battle of Worcester, this believable and well-researched adventure story details his daring escape to France; *The Great Roxhythe* (Boston: Small and Maynard, 1923. 418pp.) offers a character study of the closest political friend of Charles II, the Marquis of Roxhythe, and a close look at Restoration politics and the power behind Charles's throne.

Plaidy, Jean. *The Wandering Prince.* New York: Putnam, 1951. 318pp. The early years of Charles II are portrayed through the perspectives of two women in his life—his mistress Lucy Walter and his sister Henrietta Anne; *A Health Unto His Majesty* (New York: Putnam, 1956. 284pp.) looks at the middle years of Charles II from the perspective of his queen, Catherine of Braganza, and his mistress, Lady Castlemaine, who battle for dominance over Charles against a backdrop of the age's major events: the plague, the fire of London, and the conspiracy of Titus Oates; *Here Lies Our Sovereign Lord.* (New York: Putnam, 1957. 317pp.) is the story of the succession of mistresses in Charles II's life, vividly describing the court world of his reign; *The Three Crowns.* (New York: Putnam, 1965. 363pp.) dramatizes the succession struggle that grips England when Charles II is unable to produce an heir.

Sumner, Richard. *Mistress of the Boards.* New York: Random House, 1976. 332pp. A romanticized account of the liaison between English actress Nell Gwynne and Charles II with a vivid portrait of Restoration London and the events of the Great Fire.

A number of biographical novels look at the reign of Charles II and his character from the perspective of his queen, Catherine of Braganza.

Barnes, Margaret C. *With All My Heart.* Philadelphia: Macrae Smith, 1951. 284pp. Catherine of Braganza offers her perspective on the great events of the king's colorful reign. Does not violate history but draws heavily on romantic imagination to supplement the known facts.

Lewis, Hilda W. *Catherine.* New York: Putnam, 1966. 351pp. In this story of Charles II's queen, Catherine of Braganza, her perspective provides an angle on the important events of the the king's reign.

Macleod, Alison. *The Portingale.* London: Hodder and Stoughton, 1976. 381pp. In a fictional biography centered on her relationship with the king, Catherine of Braganza is shown as a sympathetic and complex individual.

Plaidy, Jean. *The Pleasures of Love.* New York: Putnam, 1992. 329pp. Catherine of Braganza narrates the story of her married life with Charles II.

Fictional Portraits

Barnes, Margaret C. *Lady on the Coin.* Philadelphia: Macrae Smith, 1963. 284pp. This story of Restoration court life describes the life of Frances Stuart, a distant cousin of Charles II who becomes the king's favorite and his choice for the model of Britannia on the coins of the realm. Filled with believable court politics and gossip.

Bates, H.C. *The Plot.* New York: Methuen, 1922. 250pp. Titus Oates and the Popish Plot of 1678 provides the occasion for a glimpse of Charles and his relationship with his wife.

Carr, Robyn. *Chelynne.* Boston: Little, Brown, 1980. 402pp.; *The Braeswood Tapestry.* Boston: Little, Brown, 1984. 297pp. Carr's convincing historical romances feature appearances by Charles during his exile and on his return to the throne.

Elsna, Hebe. *The King's Bastard.* London: Collins, 1971. 159pp. The novel focuses on the early life of James Scott, later the Duke of Monmouth, Charles's illegitimate son. Court life is vividly depicted, though events and details are simplified and idealized.

Goudge, Elizabeth. *The Child from the Sea.* New York: Coward-McCann, 1970. 598pp. Mixing fact and fancy, the novel dramatizes the story of the Welsh beauty Lucy Walters who bore Charles a son, later the Duke of Monmouth.

Irwin, Margaret. *Royal Flush: The Story of Minette.* New York: Harcourt, Brace, 1932. 405pp. Telling the story of Henrietta Stuart, the sister of Charles II and cousin of Louis XIV, the novel reveals the intimate details of two royal families and the motivations of Charles II and Louis XIV.

Scott, Walter. *Woodstock: Or the Cavalier.* 1826. Reprint ed. New York: Dutton, 1924. 461pp. The novel's romance revolves around Charles's famous escape from Cromwell at Woodstock. With a number of inaccuracies, the novel is history filtered through Scott's romantic imagination.

Tremain, Rose. *Restoration: A Novel of Seventeenth-Century England.* New York: Viking, 1990. 371pp. Set in the court world of Charles II, the novel describes the career of Robert Merivel who becomes the king's fool and doctor to the royal dogs and agrees to a marriage of convenience with one of the king's mistresses. A remarkable evocation of the period and atmosphere of the Restoration court.

Winsor, Kathleen. *Forever Amber.* New York: MacMillan, 1944. 722pp. Winsor's notorious bestselling novel follows the amorous adventures of beautiful tempestuous Amber Saint Clare to the highest reaches of Restoration England where she finds and loses favor with Charles II himself. Valid historical details, despite the often crude and superficial glorification of a courtesan's career and the dissolute life of the Restoration.

Biographical Films and Theatrical Adaptations

Forever Amber (1947). Director: Otto Preminger. Adapted from Kathleen Winsor's bestselling novel, Linda Darnell and Cornel Wilde star, with Charles II portrayed by a viperish George Sanders in a somewhat bowdlerized version of Winsor's Restoration sexual romp. Video.

The King's Thief (1955). Director: Robert Z. Leonard. George Sanders reprises his performance as Charles II from *Forever Amber* in this costume swashbuckler involving David Niven as a duke in a plot to steal the crown jewels. Video.

Restoration (1994). Director: Michael Hoffman. The film adaptation of Rose Tremain's novel casts Robert Downey Jr. in the role of the court physician contracted to marry the king's mistress. Sam Neill portrays Charles II and is part of an impressive cast including Meg Ryan, Hugh Grant, and Ian McKellen. Video.

92. CHARLES V
1500–1558

Holy Roman emperor and king of Spain as Charles V, Charles was the son of Philip I and the grandson of Ferdinand and Isabella. He was born in Ghent and raised by his aunt, Margaret of Austria. In 1519 he succeeded his grandfather Maximilian I as Holy Roman Emperor, controlling the largest European empire since Charlemagne. His reign was marked by continual conflict with France, the Ottoman Turks, and Protestants in Germany. Although his dream of a universal European empire was thwarted, Charles V has been widely respected for his integrity, strength of will, and sense of duty.

Autobiography and Primary Sources

Autobiography. London: Longmans, 1862. 161pp. Charles's memoir provides insights into his private as well as public life.

Correspondence of the Emperor Charles V. William Bradford, ed. 1850. Reprint ed. New York: AMS Press, 1971. 576pp. Charles's letters are an important source of biographical insights, particularly on his character and personality.

Recommended Biographies

Brandi, Karl. *The Emperor Charles V: The Growth and Destiny of a Man and of a World Empire.* New York: Knopf, 1939. 655pp. Brandt's interpretive study of Charles V's life and times is based on solid research by the greatest authority on Charles in his time. Considered the standard reference work and the best biography available.

Fernandez Alvarez, Manuel. *Charles V: Elected Emperor and Hereditary Ruler.* London: Thames and Hudson, 1975. 220pp. The author's cradle-to-grave comprehensive life offers a detailed chronological narrative that distills Charles the man from his policies and corrects misconceptions created by previous historians. Useful for the nonspecialist and expert alike.

Rady, Martyn. *Emperor Charles V.* New York: Longman, 1988. 136pp. The best available introduction to Charles's life and times. Rady carefully but succinctly untangles the complex political alignments of the period and the events of Charles's reign, along with a selection of primary documents and a chapter on how Charles has appeared to his biographers.

Other Biographical Studies

Armstrong, Edward. *The Emperor Charles V.* New York: Macmillan, 1902. 2 vols. Armstrong, with access to sources for the first time detailing aspects of Charles's private life, provides one of the first comprehensive and complex human portraits that challenged previous heroic depictions.

Habsburg, Otto von. *Charles V.* New York: Praeger, 1970. 258pp. Written by a descendent, this is a defensive vindication of his relative's reputation but still valuable in its psychological insights and Habsburg context and its accessibility for the general reader.

Schwarzenfeld, Gertrude von. *Charles V: Father of Europe.* Chicago: Regnery, 1957. 306pp. Organized thematically rather than chronologically, the book provides a far-ranging examination on Charles's impact on a number of events, places, and individuals. Useful as a supplement to a more traditional general biography.

Tyler, Royall. *The Emperor Charles V.* Fair Lawn, New Jersey: Essential Books, 1956. 375pp. Perceptive, particularly in capturing the era, Tyler's study is loaded with facts that help humanize his portrait. Based on a solid foundation of primary sources.

Biographical Novels

Hill, Pamela. *Here Lies Margot.* New York: Putnam, 1958. 254pp. The life of Margaret of Burgundy and her regency for her nephew, Charles V, are depicted in this novel that remains tied to the historical facts.

Zara, Louis. *Against This Rock.* New York: Creative Age Press, 1943. 635pp. In this fictionalized account of the life and reign of Charles V, he is depicted as a deeply religious man of justice and peace, continually struggling against various factions intent on splitting his kingdom. Often sentimental in its treatment, the novel nevertheless stays close to the facts of Charles's life and times.

Fictional Portraits

Clewes, Howard. *I, the King.* New York: Morrow, 1979. 287pp. The novel dramatizes the 1542 revolt lead by Gonzalo Pizarro against Charles V in protest for the treatment of the Incas. Colonial scenes are based on fact, but some liberties have been taken, particularly conversations that actually happened in letters.

De Wohl, Louis. *The Last Crusader.* Philadelphia: Lippincott, 1956. 448pp. This novel dramatizes the life of Spanish military hero, Don Juan of Austria, the son of Charles V, who rises from a childhood spent in a Spanish peasant's hut to play a pivotal role in the victory at Lepanto. The era is effectively and convincingly rendered.

Schoonover, Lawrence. *The Prisoner of Tordesillas.* Boston: Little, Brown, 1959. 309pp. Dramatizing the tragic life of Juana of Castille, the mother of Charles V, the novel shows her imprisoned for nearly 50 years in the fortress of Tordesillas, driven mad by her husband's infidelities and her son's indifference.

Recommended Juvenile Biographies

Grant, Neil. *Charles V: Holy Roman Emperor.* New York: F. Watts, 1970. 217pp. MG/YA. Grant's is a rich portrait of the king and his reign with an accurate period background.

93. GEOFFREY CHAUCER
ca. 1342–1400

England's first major writer who exploited the expressive power of the English vernacular, Geoffrey Chaucer was born in London, the son of a vintner. Historical records show that he was a page in the household of Prince Lionel, fought against the French, and was captured and ransomed by the king (Edward III). Employed on diplomatic missions, Chaucer visited Italy in 1372-1373 and in 1378, which greatly influenced his writing. His early work derived from French and Italian models. His masterpieces are *Troilus and Criseyde*, one of great love poems in English, and *The Canterbury Tales*, his unfinished story cycle told by pilgrims on their way to Canterbury. A master storyteller and craftsman, Chaucer extended the reach of literary expression to encompass a wide cross section of fourteenth-century English life. As Thomas Hoccleve observed soon after Chaucer's death in 1400, he was "the first findere of our faire langage."

Autobiography and Primary Sources

Chaucer Life-Records. Martin M. Crow and C.C. Olson, eds. Austin: University of Texas Press, 1967. 629pp. Brings together the 493 known documents pertaining to the poet and his family, arranged by subjects with a useful chronology, lengthy notes, and commentaries. Documents appear in their original Latin and French. Invaluable as a biographical source.

Recommended Biographies

Brewer, Derek. *Chaucer and His World.* New York: Dodd, Mead, 1978. 224pp. Anchoring the scanty factual record with a solid use of social, political, and economical history, as well as a critical reading of Chaucer's poetry, Brewer's integrative study brings together the life, times, and poetry, and is one of the best volumes available for the general reader.

Howard, Donald R. *Chaucer: His Life, His Work, His World.* New York: Dutton, 1987. 636pp.

Howard's comprehensive portrait of both the private man and his public context is accessible for the general reader, while useful to the scholar. Howard died before the final edit of his book was complete, which may explain some organizational problems and an excess of padding about the age to cover the thin areas of the factual record. Even so, Howard's achievement here is exceptional in bringing to the surface a complex and human portrait vividly seen against a believable period backdrop.

Pearsall, Derek. *The Life of Geoffrey Chaucer: A Critical Biography.* Cambridge, Massachusetts: Blackwell, 1992. 365pp. 336pp. Scrupulously relying on the *Life-Records* to guide his narrative, Pearsall rebuts what he considers popular but speculative biographies such as Howard's, but does believe that a close reading of the poems reveals that Chaucer indirectly transformed the events and concerns of his life into his art. Skeptical and informed, Pearsall's study is essential for the more advanced student interested in the state of current Chaucer scholarship.

Other Biographical Studies

Chute, Marchette. *Geoffrey Chaucer of England.* New York: Dutton, 1946. 346pp. In one of the first biographical studies written for a general audience, Chute incorporates the then-known facts about Chaucer's life and artistic career into a readable, informal, and often witty introductory account. Her conjectures are reasonable, and the man is set against a fully realized fourteenth-century backdrop.

Coulton, G.G. *Chaucer and His England.* 1908. Reprint ed. New York: Barnes and Noble, 1963. 321pp. Coulton supplements the few known facts about Chaucer with details about his era. The writer has well-defined convictions, several of which may seem overly conjectural, and there is a persistent diminution of medieval society that few writers today would commit.

Gardner, John. *The Life and Times of Chaucer.* New York: Knopf, 1977. 328pp. Gardner's novelistic impressionism may appall the scholarly but will likely delight a general audience. Weaving around the limited personal information historical and social detail, Gardner sets Chaucer clearly against a backdrop of his age. Readers who may be enthralled by Gardner's irreverent exuberance should be skeptical about several of his conjectures and surmises. Gardner's imagination is seductive and at times a delight, but much remains unverifiable and wrong, with invention filling in many of the gaps.

Lounsbury, Thomas R. *Studies in Chaucer: His Life and Writings.* New York: Harper, 1891–1892. 3 vols. Representing one of the earliest attempts to replace the Chaucer legends with what can be known for sure, Lounsbury evaluates all the previous biographical attempts from the sixteenth century in addition to offering a succinct biographical narrative based on the known facts. Today Lounsbury's critical study is interesting for a look at the ways Chaucer has been viewed since his death.

Wagenknecht, Edward. *The Personality of Chaucer.* Norman: University of Oklahoma Press, 1968.

155pp. Transcending the inherent limitations of the *Life-Records,* the author looks instead at Chaucer's works to assemble a psychological profile of personality and attitude revealed in his poetry. Useful mainly as a critical interpretation of his works.

Fictional Portraits

Crowley, Duane. *Riddle Me a Murder.* Manchala, Texas: Blue Bear Press, 1987. 231pp. This historical murder mystery employs Chaucer as sleuth as John of Gaunt's latest mistress is poisoned and a conspiracy is underway.

Darby, Catherine. *The Love Knot.* New York: Saint Martin's, 1989. 240pp. Philippa and Katherine de Roet are the subject of this fictional reconstruction. The former marries Chaucer; the latter's affair with John of Gaunt takes her to the center stage of the important events of the period.

Lindsay, Philip. *The Gentle Knight.* London: Hutchinson,1942. 207pp. This fictional retelling of Chaucer's *Canterbury Tales* presents the story of the Canterbury pilgrims as they set out from London with elements added to Chaucer's story. The emphasis here is not on their tales but the pilgrims themselves in this vivid reconstruction of medieval life and customs.

Rofheart, Martha. *Glendower Country.* New York: Putnam,1973. 381pp. Geoffrey Chaucer is one of the narrators who describes Welsh prince Owen Glendower in his rebellion against the English. The author admits to assembling from factual scraps a largely invented Glendower and his friendship with Chaucer.

Seton, Anya. *Katherine.* Boston: Houghton Mifflin, 1954. 588pp. This biographical novel depicts the life of Katherine Swynford, Chaucer's sister-in-law. Her love affair with John of Gaunt is portrayed against a fully realized background of medieval England.

Biographical Films and Theatrical Adaptations

The Canterbury Tales (1971). Director: Pier Paolo Pasolini. Four of Chaucer's tales, including the Wife of Bath's and the Merchant's tale, are presented with the director appearing as Chaucer. Video.

Other Sources

Boitani, Piero, and Jill Mann, eds. *The Cambridge Chaucer Companion.* New York: Cambridge University Press, 1986. 300pp. This collection of essays by international Chaucer experts establishes a context for Chaucer and provides analyses of his poetry.

Rossignol, Rosalyn. *Chaucer: A to Z: The Essential Reference to His Life and Works.* New York: Facts on File, 1999. 432pp. This rich reference volume organizes information on Chaucer, his works, and background into useful and accessible alphabetical entries.

94. ANTON CHEKHOV
1860–1904

Russian short-story writer, playwright, and physician, Chekhov was the son of a grocer and grandson of a serf. His early humorous sketches helped support his family while he studied medicine in Moscow. Chekhov's various collections of short stories mark him as one of the masters of the form. His dramatic masterpieces are *The Seagull* (1896), *Uncle Vanya* (1899), *The Three Sisters* (1901) and *The Cherry Orchard* (1904). Chekhov's focus on internal drama has had a profound influence on the development of the modern theater.

Autobiography and Primary Sources

Anton Chekhov's Life and Thought: Selected Letters and Commentary. Simon Karlinsky, ed. Chicago: Northwestern University Press, 1973. 494pp. This collection of Chekhov's correspondence is widely regarded as the best introduction to the writer, providing fascinating insights into his development as a writer. The introduction is a helpful capsule biography. An essential text for anyone interested in Chekhov.

Recommended Biographies

Callow, Philip. *Chekhov: The Hidden Ground.* Chicago: Ivan R. Dee, 1998. 416pp. Examining the life in the context of his art, Callow presents Chekhov as a peculiarly modern man, split between duty and pleasure, needing both solitude and society, an elusive ironist in which the love theme is central to understanding his life. Lacking the original scholarship of Rayfield, Callow's interpretive study offers very different conclusions and a synthesis that readers impatient with Rayfield's detachment may prefer.

Rayfield, Donald. *Anton Chekhov: A Life.* New York: Holt, 1998. 674pp. Rayfield, a noted Chekhov scholar whose *Chekhov: The Evolution of His Art* (New York: Barnes and Noble, 1975. 266pp.) is an important critical analysis of the relationship between Chekhov's life and art, provides a documentary biography that largely avoids interpretation in favor of the accumulation of tiny details. One of the strengths of Rayfield's approach is that he does not try to resolve the many contradictions in Chekhov's personality but displays his complexity in full. Includes a good deal of previously unpublished material.

Simmons, Ernest J. *Chekhov: A Biography.* New York: Little-Brown, 1962. 669pp. Simmons set out to document all the known facts about Chekhov's life, and his book is a richly documented, chronological narrative drawn from the various archival collections. Taking as its central theme the development of Chekhov as a writer, Simmons offers almost a day-by-day account with all the major and minor incidents faithfully reported.

Other Biographical Studies

Gillès, Daniel. *Chekhov: Observer without Illusion.* New York: Funk & Wagnalls, 1968. 436pp. The author challenges previous interpretations of Chekhov's personality and temperament but treats the life with considerable fictional license, lacking

the objectivity and skepticism of more scholarly approaches.

Hingley, Ronald. *A New Life of Anton Chekhov.* New York: Knopf, 1976. 352pp. Drawing on the full collection of Chekhov's letters and diaries and memoirs of his contemporaries, Hingley offers a revisionist view that dismisses the portrayal of Chekhov as a pessimist and claims that his short stories are greater achievements than his plays. Literary criticism is avoided except as a by-product of Chekhov's literary life, and Hingley's biography offers a more revealing look at the writer than many previous attempts, though several of his insights remain controversial.

Laffitte, Sophie. *Chekhov: 1860–1904.* New York: Scribner, 1973. 246pp. Lafitte's often laudatory appreciation of Chekhov can be read as a counterbalance to Hingley's more negative interpretation. Concentrating on Chekhov's theatrical career, his early writing is given short shrift.

Magarshack, David. *Chekhov: A Life.* New York: Grove Press, 1953. 431pp. A comprehensive biography based on the then recently published complete edition of his works and letters, Magarshack's is a useful factual survey that considers aspects of Chekhov's life that had not been given sufficient attention previously. He is less successful in his attempts at interpreting Chekhov's character and art.

Priestley, J.B. *Anton Chekhov.* London: International Textbook, 1970. 87pp. Priestly's appreciative essay sketches Chekhov's life and career with interest provided by the author's literary insights. Priestley largely ignores, however, less flattering views of the writer.

Pritchett, V.S. *Chekhov: A Spirit Set Free.* New York: Random House, 1988. 235pp. Despite the author's lack of Russian or firsthand knowledge of Russia and his reliance on previous biographers for details, Pritchett's study has considerable value for its opinions by a fellow fictional craftsman. Relating the life with the writing, Pritchett provides both a critical study of Chekhov's imagination and a sketch of the main outline of Chekhov's career.

Toumanova, Nina A. *Anton Chekhov: The Voice of Twilight Russia.* New York: Columbia University Press, 1937. 239pp. In the author's clear, balanced interpretation, Chekhov's career is seen in relation to social conditions and the historical atmosphere of his times. In Toumanova's view, Chekhov is a prophet of the fin de siècle collapse that preceded the Russian Revolution.

Troyat, Henri. *Chekhov.* New York: Dutton, 1986. 364pp. Reconstructing Chekhov's life in the spirit and methods of a novelist in dramatic scenes with dialogue, Troyat draws on his considerable acquaintance with the correspondence to justify his treatment. Eminently readable, Troyat's approach is neither scholarly nor thorough, but the general reader will find it difficult to resist the author's storytelling skill.

Other Sources

Clyman, Toby W., ed. *A Chekhov Companion.* Westport, Connecticut: Greenwood, 1985. 347pp. A collection of essays by well-known Chekhov and drama scholars, the writer and his works are placed in a variety of revealing contexts. Useful for a reader interested in current scholarly interpretations.

95. FRÉDÉRIC CHOPIN
1810–1849

Polish composer and pianist Frédéric Chopin was a child prodigy who performed in Warsaw, Vienna, and Munich before settling in Paris where he gave his first concert in 1831. Through Franz Liszt, Chopin met George Sand with whom he spent the winter of 1838-1839, when, despite declining health, he wrote the 24 preludes that are regarded as his masterpieces. His affair with George Sand lasted until 1847, and he died two years later of tuberculosis.

Autobiography and Primary Sources

Chopin's Letters. Henryk Opienski, ed. 1931. Reprint ed. New York: Vienna House, 1971. 420pp. An essential source for biographers, Opienski's collection of Chopin's letters includes some of the composer's diary entries.

Selected Correspondence of Fryderyk Chopin. Arthur Hedley, ed. New York: McGraw-Hill, 1963. 400pp. Hedley offers an additional selection from Chopin's complete correspondence, published in French and Polish, though he expurgated references to Chopin's homosexuality.

Chopin: A Self-Portrait in His Own Words. David Whitwell, ed. Northridge, California: Winds Press, 1986. 70pp. Extracts from Chopin's correspondence are here arranged by subject.

Recommended Biographies

Murdoch, William. *Chopin: His Life.* New York: Macmillan, 1935. 410pp. Still widely regarded as the best biography of Chopin in English, Murdoch's balanced account is supported by reliance on the correspondence and at the time newly discovered genealogical facts. Murdoch challenged most of the sentimental legends surrounding the composer and helped initiate the modern reevaluation of Chopin's life.

Hedley, Arthur. *Chopin.* 1949. Revised ed. London: Dent, 1974. 214pp. This entry in the Master Musician series is the work of an acknowledged Chopin authority, revised after Hedley's death by Maurice J.E. Brown. Based on original French and Polish sources, Hedley dispels numerous myths surrounding Chopin and counters the negative role played by George Sand in Chopin's life, as alleged by several biographers.

Siepmann, Jeremy. *Chopin: The Reluctant Romantic.* Boston: Northeastern University Press, 1995. 280pp. The author challenges the concept of Chopin as a romantic archetype to portray a man who felt largely out of sympathy with the age he came to personify. Based on the correspondence and diaries of the composer and his friends, Siepmann alternates between his biographical narrative and analysis of Chopin's music. The book includes appendixes that trace the trends in interpreting Chopin and a detailed calendar of his life.

Zamoyski, Adam. *Chopin: A New Biography.* Garden City, New York: Doubleday, 1980. 374pp. Zamoyski corrects earlier sentimental and false accounts of episodes in Chopin's life and stresses his Polish heritage and dependence on his fellow countrymen. Relying mainly on the correspondence, Zamoyski's narrative is reliable and includes an impressive bibliography of Chopin source material.

Other Biographical Studies

Atwood, William G. *The Lionness and the Little One: The Liaison of George Sand and Frédéric Chopin.* New York: Columbia University Press, 1980. 316pp. Focusing on the stormy relationship between Sand and Chopin, Atwood documents their affair relying almost entirely on their correspondence, journals, and other writings by the pair and their contemporaries. Falling short of its intention to be fair to both figures, this account repeats the conventional view of Sand as the powerful mother figure and Chopin the weak, sickly figure of legend.

Atwood, William G. *Fryderyk Chopin: Pianist from Warsaw.* New York: Columbia University Press, 1987. 305pp. Focusing exclusively on Chopin's career as a concert pianist, Atwood documents every known performance and includes English translations of contemporary reviews. Useful as a portrait of European concert life in the 1830s and 1840s, the book glimpses Chopin's development as a composer only indirectly.

Bidou, Henri. *Chopin.* New York: Knopf, 1927. 267pp. Bidou's brief critical study summarizes the events in Chopin's life, relating his chief compositions to them. The author's well-balanced biographical sketch is particularly valuable on Chopin's relationship with George Sand.

Boucourechliev, André. *Chopin: A Pictorial Biography.* New York: Viking, 1963. 144pp. With a selection of prints, drawings, paintings, and photographs, the book illustrates the places and people that formed an important part of Chopin's life.

Bourniquel, Camille. *Chopin.* New York: Grove Press, 1960. 192pp. Concise and carefully documented, this illustrated biography traces the salient features of Chopin's life and explodes various myths surrounding the composer, such as his constant physical and emotional agony. Chopin is shown enjoying life, honored and admired, never prevented by ill health from exploiting his talents. Serves as a useful introduction.

Gavoty, Benard. *Frédéric Chopin.* New York: Scribner, 1974. 452pp. The author sets out to dispel the sentimental legend that has distorted a clear view of Chopin in a critical biography that is strongest in its historical background. Too often, however, the author indulges in rhapsodic prose and fairly standard psychological speculations.

Huneker, James. *Chopin: The Man and His Music.* 1900. Revised ed. New York: Dover, 1966. 239pp. Critics are divided on Huneker's biography that has been praised for its sensitive and provocative analysis but criticized for its self-indulgent style and factual errors that are noted in the 1966 edition with corrections, footnotes, index, and bibliography by Herbert Weinstock.

Jordan, Ruth. *Nocturne: A Life of Chopin.* New York: Taplinger, 1978. 286pp. Based on secondary sources, Jordan's popular biography offers no new information or any fresh interpretations and is marred by quotes from letters scholars have deemed spurious and a cliché-ridden style. As a biographer of George Sand, Jordan details the couple's affair in depth.

Karasowski, Moritz. *Frédéric Chopin: His Life and Letters.* 1879. Revised ed. New York: Scribner, 1906. 2 vols. The first serious biography of Chopin, Karasowski's influential study was responsible for creating many of the myths surrounding the composers that later biographers have exposed as false.

Liszt, Franz. *Life of Chopin.* 1877. Reprint ed. New York: Vienna House, 1963. 184pp. Liszt's firsthand account of his friend is a fascinating character sketch by an admiring musical colleague. Scholars have challenged the truthfulness of many of the anecdotes that have contributed to the formation of the various Chopin legends that modern biographers have corrected.

Maine, Basil. *Chopin.* New York: Macmillan, 1933. 128pp. This brief biographical portrait stresses Chopin's Polish patriotism and provides a sympathetic account of his relationship with George Sand. However, the book is marred by several misstatements of fact and an uncritical acceptance of opinions and claims of earlier writers.

Marek, George, and Maria Gordon-Smith. *Chopin.* New York: Harper & Row, 1978. 289pp. In a strictly biographical study that largely ignores a discussion of Chopin's artistry, the authors attempt to prove that the composer was not a fragile, misty Romantic but a conscious musical innovator, conscientious craftsman, and intelligent, cultivated man.

Szulc, Tad. *Chopin in Paris: The Life and Times of the Romantic Composer.* New York: Scribner, 1998. 444pp. Emphasizing Chopin's life and times rather than his music, Szulc focuses on the composer's most creative period during his 18 years in Paris and places him squarely in the context of his artistic era and social setting. Largely neglecting Chopin's music, the book sheds considerable new light on the man and his milieu.

Weinstock, Herbert. *Chopin: The Man and His Music.* New York: Knopf, 1949. 336pp. Divided equally between biography and an analysis of Chopin's music, Weinstock's concise study is a valuable collection of data and sensible interpretation.

Wierzynski, Kazimierz. *The Life and Death of Chopin.* New York: Simon & Schuster, 1949. 441pp. Written by a Polish poet, this study, based on unpublished correspondence, counters the notion of Chopin as a frail solitary with an emphasis on the details of Chopin's youth, family, relations, and his Polish patriotism. The book is less successful in detailing Chopin's musical achievement.

Fictional Portraits

Kenyon, Frank W. *The Questing Heart: A Romantic Novel about George Sand.* New York: Dodd, Mead, 1964. 344pp. Based firmly on a framework of fact with fictional embellishments, this biographical novel describes the life story of George

Sand, with her relationship with Chopin prominently featured.

La Mure, Pierre. *Beyond Desire: A Novel Based on
the Life of Felix and Cécile Mendelssohn.* New
York: Random House, 1955. 404pp. In the novelist's convincing portrait of the composer and his
wife, Mendelssohn's era is also detailed, including
his relationship with Chopin.

Rousselot, Jean. *Hungarian Rhapsody: The Life of
Franz Liszt.* New York: Putnam, 1961. 248pp.
This fictional biography of Liszt traces his entire
career with an emphasis on his series of love affairs. His close friendship with Chopin is also featured in this rather romanticized version of Liszt's
life.

Recommended Juvenile Biographies

Chissell, Joan. *Chopin.* New York: Crowell, 1965.
94pp. MG. Written by a member of the music staff
of *The Times* of London, with photographs of the
places Chopin lived and worked as well as the music for 13 Chopin piano pieces, this volume ably
presents the highlights of Chopin's life and career.

Maurois, André. *Frédéric Chopin.* New York:
Harper, 1942. 91pp. MG. This is a short, illustrated
profile by the noted French literary biographer.

Murgia, Adelaide. *The Life and Times of Chopin.*
New York: Curtis, 1967. 75pp. YA. The highlights
of Chopin's career and times are presented in a lavishly illustrated picture biography.

Biographical Films and Theatrical Adaptations

Lisztomania (1975). Director: Ken Russell. In Russell's exuberant, excessive extravaganza of Franz
Liszt as the first rock star, Roger Daltrey portrays
Liszt with Kenneth Cole as Chopin. Biographical
accuracy seems beyond the point here. Video.

Impromptu (1991). Director: James Lapine.
George Sand, Chopin, and Liszt are on holiday as
proto-beatniks in this dynamic and inventive
drama, starring Judy Davis as the novelist, Hugh
Grant as a wan, ethereal Chopin, and Julian Sands
as Liszt. Video.

Notorious Woman (1974). Director: Waris
Hussien. Television mini-series on the life of
George Sand features Rosemary Harris in the title
role, George Chakiris as Chopin, and Alan Howard
as Mérimée. Video.

A Song to Remember (1945). Director: Charles
Vidor. Cornel Wilde stars as Chopin in this bio-pic
depicting the last years of the composer's life.
Merle Oberon portrays George Sand, and Stephen
Belcassy portrays Liszt. Redeemed mainly by its
music, the character portrayal here is superficial.
Video.

Other Sources

Samson, Jim, ed. *The Cambridge Companion to
Chopin.* New York: Cambridge University Press,
1992. 341pp. Modern scholarly views are represented in this useful collection of critical essays on
various aspects of the composer's life, character,
and works.

Samson, Jim, and John Rink, eds. *Chopin Studies.*
New York: Cambridge University Press,
1988–1994. 2 vols. These collections of critical essays reflect the latest scholarship on Chopin by
leading authorities.

Temperley, Nicholas. "Chopin," in *Early Romantic Masters I.* New York: W.W. Norton, 1985.
392pp. Extracted from *The New Grove Dictionary*
section on Chopin, Temperley updates the earlier
assessment with original research on Chopin's sexuality and provides a handy reference guide that reflects recent scholarship.

Walker, Alan. *The Chopin Companion: Profiles of
the Man and the Musician.* New York: W.W.
Norton, 1973. 312pp. The work of diverse hands,
various aspects of the composer's life and work are
covered in a well-organized and easily accessible
reference guide.

See also Franz Liszt; George Sand

96. AGATHA CHRISTIE
1890–1976

English writer of detective fiction and one of the
most popular authors of the twentieth century,
Christie produced over 80 books, many them featuring her famous detectives, Hercule Poirot and
Miss Jane Marple. Her mysteries are noted for their
skillful plots and include *The Mysterious Affair at
Styles* (1920), *The Murder at the Vicarage* (1930),
and *Murder on the Orient Express* (1934). Her
plays include the long-running *The Mousetrap*
(1952) and *Witness for the Prosecution* (1954).

Autobiography and Primary Sources

An Autobiography. New York: Dodd, Mead, 1977.
529pp. Begun in 1950 and completed 15 years
later, Christie reviews her life selectively in a series
of charming, beguiling recollections. Hardly a tell-
all, the book does provide glimpses of her creative
method and her personality.

Recommended Biographies

Gill, Gillian. *Agatha Christie: The Woman and Her
Mysteries.* New York: Free Press, 1990. 243pp.
Gill's is an astute probing of the sources of Christie's achievement as a writer and a plausible explanation of her personality. In the author's view,
Christie "used her writing as both catharsis and
therapy, translating into fiction her beliefs, fantasies, and personal anxieties, most of which
stemmed from childhood and youth." The book
skillfully draws the connection between those experiences and her later life and career.

Morgan, Janet. *Agatha Christie: A Biography.*
New York: Knopf, 1985. 393pp. The authorized
Christie biography is a sensible, comprehensive
narrative account of the writer's life, making use of
letters, diaries, and the author's notes. The book is
particularly strong on sources for Christie's characters and the autobiographical connections in her
books.

Other Biographical Studies

Cade, Jared. *Agatha Christie and the Eleven
Missing Days.* Chester Springs, Pennsylvania:
Dufour Editions, 1999. 258pp. Cade focuses on the
central mystery of Christie's life: her 11-day disappearance in 1926, which the author attributed to
amnesia. Cade concludes from a review of the evidence that Christie instead arranged her disappearance to punish her husband who had been unfaithful to her.

Murdoch, Derrick. *The Agatha Christie Mystery.*
New York: Publishers Marketing Group, 1976.
192pp. The first half of the book is devoted to a biographical summary, derived from secondary
sources; the second is a chronological account of
Christie's writings.

Osborne, Charles. *The Life and Crimes of Agatha
Christie.* New York: Holt, 1983. 256pp. Combining a biographical profile with a critical review
of all of Christie's writings, the book serves primarily a reference function for the reader needing
details of the author's publishing history.

Robyns, Gwen. *The Mystery of Agatha Christie.*
Garden City, New York: Doubleday, 1978. 320pp.
Rushed into publication following Christie's death,
this is an uneven mix of anecdotes and familiar details from previously published sources in which,
in the verdict of one reviewer, "errors, inconsistencies, and padding abound."

Fictional Portraits

Baxt, George. *The Bette Davis Murder Case.* New
York: Saint Martin's, 1994. 200pp. The movie star
recruits Christie to assist her in a murder investigation.

Larsen, Gaylord. *Dorothy and Agatha.* New York:
Dutton, 1990. 230pp. Dorothy Sayers enlists members of the Detective Club, including Agatha Christie, to help her solve a murder.

Tynan, Kathleen. *Agatha.* New York: Ballantine
Books, 1978. 247pp. The novel offers an inventive
solution to the mystery surrounding Christie's disappearance in 1926 that she attributed to amnesia.

Recommended Juvenile Biographies

Dommermuth-Costa, Carol. *Agatha Christie:
Writer of Mystery.* Minneapolis: Lerner, 1997.
112pp. YA. This informative biography blends details of Christie's personal life and writing career
into a full-length portrait, aided by photos and
sketches.

Biographical Films and Theatrical Adaptations

Agatha (1979). Director: Michael Apted. Vanessa
Redgrave portrays the writer in this speculative
drama concerning her 1926 disappearance, with
Dustin Hoffman as the American journalist who
tracks her down. Video.

Agatha Christie: How Did She Do It? (1986). Director: Toby Wallis. Explores Christie's character
and attempts to discover the secret of her appeal.
Includes archival footage of Christie and her family. Video.

Other Sources

Keating, H.R.F., ed. *Agatha Christie: First Lady of Crime.* New York: Holt, 1977. 224pp. In this useful collection, 14 mystery writers and literary critics analyze various aspects of Christie's career and achievement.

Sanders, Dennis, and Len Lovallo. *The Agatha Christie Companion: The Complete Guide to Agatha Christie's Life and Work.* New York: Delacorte, 1984. 523pp. This is an extensive reference volume, a delight for the browser and helpful for the reader needing easily accessible information on Christie's life and books.

Sova, Dawn B. *Agatha Christie A to Z: The Essential Reference to Her Life and Writings.* New York: Facts on File, 1996. 400pp. Although not including the solutions to Christie's murder mysteries, the book leaves out very little else in 2,500 alphabetically arranged entries on her books, characters, and relationships.

97. WINSTON S. CHURCHILL
1874–1965

One of the dominating public figures in the twentieth century, British statesman and writer Winston Churchill was educated at Harrow and Sandhurst. He served in India and fought in the Sudan. As a reporter during the Boer Wars, Churchill was captured and escaped. Elected to Parliament in 1900, he served as the first lord of the admiralty from 1911 to 1915. Disgraced by the failure of the Gallipoli invasion, Churchill volunteered for service on the Western Front. After World War I, he helped negotiate the treaty that established the Irish Free State. In 1940 he became prime minister and was Britain's inspirational and tactical war leader during World War II. He was knighted and awarded the Nobel Prize for literature in 1953.

Autobiography and Primary Sources

My Early Life: A Roving Commission. New York: Scribner, 1930. 372pp. The most directly autobiographical of his books, Churchill chronicles his life up to his marriage in 1908. Bathed in nostalgia, Churchill's reminiscences are more charming than self-perceptive. Nearly all of Churchill's many books have a strong autobiographical component as people and events are reported from his perspective. Volumes include *Lord Randolph Churchill* (New York: Macmillan, 1906. 2 vols); *The World Crisis 1911–18* (New York: Scribner, 1923–1931. 6 vols.); *Great Contemporaries* (New York: Putnam, 1937. 299pp.); and *The Second World War* (Boston: Houghton Mifflin, 1948–1954. 6 vols.).

Memoirs of the Second World War (Boston: Houghton Mifflin, 1959. 1,065pp.). An abridgment of Churchill's World War II volumes is available in this single volume.

Churchill & Roosevelt: The Complete Correspondence. Warren F. Kimball, ed. (Princeton, New Jersey: Princeton University Press, 1984. 3 vols.); *The Churchill Eisenhower Correspondence.* Peter G. Boyle, ed. (Chapel Hill: University of North Carolina Press, 1990. 230pp.); and *Winston and*

Clementine: The Personal Letters of the Churchills. Mary Soames, ed. (Boston: Houghton Mifflin, 1995. 702pp.). Churchill's correspondence is available in these useful collections.

Recommended Biographies

Gilbert, Martin. *Churchill: A Life.* New York: Holt, 1991. 1,066pp. In a single-volume reshaping of his massive, eight-volume official life, Gilbert compresses the public record and intimate private details for an animated portrait. More a synthesis and more interpretive than the longer biography, this volume is recommended for the reader looking for an authoritative single-volume study.

Manchester, William. *The Last Lion, Winston Spencer Churchill: Visions of Glory, 1874–1932.* Boston: Little, Brown, 1983. 973pp.; *The Last Lion, Winston Spencer Churchill: Alone 1932–1940.* Little, Brown, 1988. 756pp. Manchester's vivid, dramatic popular biography will be preferred by many readers over more staid and scholarly treatments. Critics have noted numerous factual errors and the jarring mixture of gossipy anecdote and stirring heroic appreciation. Most, however, have extravagantly praised Manchester's rich presentation of the historical and social contexts and his dramatic style and are impatiently awaiting the next installment.

Pelling, Henry. *Winston Churchill.* New York: Dutton, 1974. 724pp. Thoughtful, comprehensive, and scrupulous in its documentation, Pelling's study offers a useful, concise chronological narrative that depicts the highpoints of Churchill's life and political career. Pelling's book is ideal for the reader whose interest and patience does not extend to fuller treatments.

Other Biographical Studies

Bonham Carter, Violet. *Winston Churchill as I Knew Him.* New York: Harcourt, Brace, 1965. 495pp. Written by a close confidante of Churchill for nearly 60 years, Bonham Carter's appreciation offers invaluable personal insights and revealing dimensions of Churchill's temperament and character that have eluded other biographers.

Brendon, Piers. *Winston Churchill: A Biography.* New York: Harper & Row, 1984. 233pp. Making no claims to originality or prodigious research, Brendon aims instead to capture the essence of the man in a character profile. Driven, determined, and ambitious, Churchill is also shown as ill tempered, inconsistent, and often rude and cruel.

Charmley, John. *Churchill: The End of Glory: A Political Biography.* New York: Harcourt, Brace, 1994. 742pp. One of the more rabid of the revisionist writers on Churchill's career and legacy, Charmley argues against the view that the war against Hitler was justified or that Churchill was a great leader. Verifiable evidence often gives way to polemical outbursts and distortions. Churchill's career after 1945, for example, is dismissed in two and a half pages. Redresses the balance with a vengeance of more admiring Churchill apologists; however, Charmley's hypothesis will likely offend many.

Churchill, Randolph S. *Winston S. Churchill.* Boston: Houghton Mifflin, 1966–1969. 2 vols. Se-

lected by Churchill to write the authorized biography, his only son completed documenting his father's story only up to 1914. Boasting exclusive and unrestricted access to the massive Churchill archive for the first time, the volumes provide essential source material for subsequent biographers. Neither critical nor interpretive, this official life, like Gilbert's continuation, is valuable mainly for establishing the documentary record.

Gilbert, Martin. *Winston S. Churchill.* Boston: Houghton Mifflin, 1966–1988. 8 vols. A member of Randolph Churchill's research staff, Gilbert was selected to continue the authorized biography after Randolph's death, which he diligently completed after more than 20 years of labor. More discriminating than his predecessor, Gilbert still overwhelms rather than clarifies with his massive documentation and appreciation. Essential for the scholar and researcher, general readers will prefer Gilbert's one-volume synthesis.

Hough, Richard. *Winston and Clementine: The Triumphs and the Tragedies of the Churchills.* New York: Bantam, 1990. 528pp. The author provides an intimate portrait of a 57-year marriage, including the clashes of two strong-willed and often stubborn individualists.

Grant, R.G. *Winston Churchill: An Illustrated Biography.* New York: Gallery Books, 1989. 224pp. Grant's is a satisfying visual life with a competent text tracing the highpoints of Churchill's career.

Moran, Charles. *Churchill: The Struggle for Survival 1940-65.* Boston: Houghton Mifflin, 1966. 877pp. This account by Churchill's physician from 1940 provides essential biographical evidence as well as a unique view of his patient in the last years of Churchill's life.

Morgan, Ted. *Churchill: Young Man in a Hurry 1874–1915.* New York: Simon & Schuster, 1982. 607pp. Morgan traces the events of Churchill's first 41 years, the crucial formative years that help explain his later behavior. Vivid and highly readable, Morgan's well-crafted biography offers a useful lens to view Churchill's development.

Payne, Robert. *The Great Man: A Portrait of Winston Churchill.* New York: Coward-McCann, 1974. 416pp. The author of several popular biographies provides a largely hostile character sketch of a consummate ambitious man preoccupied with achieving greatness. Lacking scholarly authority, Payne's psychological treatment describes a very human rather than a heroic Churchill but without much penetration or balance.

Robbins, Keith. *Churchill.* New York: Longman, 1992. 186pp. An entry in the impressive Profiles in Power series, this succinct overview of Churchill's life and career is a study in failure, despite his determined genius. Seen as a pivotal modern figure, Churchill emerges as a complex figure in twentieth-century history.

Rose, Norman. *Churchill: The Unruly Giant.* New York: Free Press, 1995. 516pp. The first historian to be granted access to the Churchill archives since the publication of the authorized biography, Rose attempts to set the record straight in a largely balanced analysis of a great man with flaws and faults. Readers may find that negatives are given more prominence than the positives.

Sandys, Celia. *The Young Churchill: The Early Years of Winston Churchill.* New York: Dutton, 1995. 223pp. Written by Churchill's granddaughter, this affectionate look at Churchill's early years up to 1895 draws on private papers, letters, recollections, and photographs to tell the coming of age story; *Churchill Wanted Dead or Alive.* (New York: Carroll & Graf, 2000. 233pp.) continues Churchill's career through his journalist and military service during the Boer War.

Strawson, John. *Churchill and Hitler: In Victory and Defeat.* New York: Fromm International, 1998. 544pp. This dual biography of the adversaries chronicles the war years from a decidedly British perspective of an unabashed Churchillian admirer. Valuable in its contrasting treatment, Strawson presents a vivid portrait of the war leadership of both men.

Fictional Portraits

Churchill appears in many novels concerning both World Wars. Some of his more memorable fictional appearances occur in the following books.

Chaput, W.J. *The Man on the Train.* New York: Saint Martin's, 1986. 246pp. This thriller is based on the historic visit to the United States by Churchill in 1941. On a train through Vermont a German spy is determined to kill the prime minister.

Fitzgibbon, Constantine. *High Heroic.* New York: W.W. Norton, 1969. 176pp. The Irish struggle for independence is seen through the experiences of Michael Collins, one of the central figures in the drama, with scenes of his treaty negotiations with Churchill. The main events here are faithful to the facts.

Flanagan, Thomas. *The End of the Hunt.* New York: Dutton,1994. 627pp. Flanagan's impressive re-creation of the Irish Uprising and Civil War shows Churchill opposite Michael Collins in the negotiations that produced the Irish Free State.

Garfield, Brian. *The Paladin: A Novel Based on Fact.* New York: Simon & Schuster, 1979. 381pp. A fictional elaboration of Churchill's use of a schoolboy as a secret agent who plays a key role in the Dunkirk evacuation and the Normandy invasion, the novel shows Churchill in full warrior mode in a partially truthful story that stays close to the historical chronology.

Roosevelt, Elliott. *Murder at the Palace.* New York: Saint Martin's, 1987. 232pp. In this installment of the author's detective stories with Eleanor Roosevelt as sleuth, the first lady is in London and must solve a murder in Buckingham Palace; *The White House Pantry Murder.* (New York: Saint Martin's, 1987. 182pp. 1987.) is set in 1941 during Churchill's White House visit, and an intruder is found murdered. Eleanor suspects a wider Nazi assassination plot to destabilize the Allies.

Roosevelt, James, and Sam Toperoff. *A Family Matter.* New York: Scribner, 1980. 316pp. This is an insider's fictionalized view of the secret diplomatic maneuvering during World War II. Given Roosevelt's privileged position as his father's trusted assistant, the novel is convincing in its authenticity.

Smith, A.C.H. *Edward and Mrs. Simpson.* Bath, England: Firecrest1980. 300pp. The relationship between Edward, Prince of Wales, and Wallis Simpson is dramatized, with Churchill's role in the ensuing royal crisis plausibly shown.

Uris, Leon. *Redemption.* New York: HarperCollins, 1995. 827pp. In the author's sequel to *Trinity,* the author continues his Larkin family saga with scenes of the disastrous Gallipoli campaign in World War I based on Churchill secret memoranda.

Recommended Juvenile Biographies

Driemen, John E. *Winston Churchill: An Unbreakable Spirit.* Minneapolis: Dillon Press, 1990. 128pp. MG. In a flattering though realistic examination of the childhood, education, political career, and personal life of Churchill, Driemen is insightful in detailing the various difficulties Churchill faced and explaining the workings of the British government. Includes many photographs and a clear, detailed timeline.

Rodgers, Judith. *Winston Churchill.* New York: Chelsea House, 1986. 112pp. MG/YA. Part of the respected World Leaders Past & Present series, this is a comprehensive chronicle of Churchill's life that also fills in the social and historical context of his times.

Severance, John B. *Winston Churchill: Soldier, Statesman, Artist.* New York: Clarion Books, 1996. 144pp. YA. Carefully researched and organized, inclusive, and balanced, Severance's biography covers the high and low points of Churchill's personal and political life, quoting from his memoirs and correspondence. One of the best juvenile biographies available on the subject.

Biographical Films and Theatrical Adaptations

A&E Biography Video: Complete Churchill Set (1992). Director: Marisa Appugliese. With a script written by Churchill biographer Martin Gilbert, this four-part documentary traces Churchill's career with interviews and contemporary footage. Video.

Churchill and the Generals (1981). Director: Alan Gibson. Based on Churchill's war recollections, his leadership through the Battle of Britain is depicted with Timothy West as the prime minister, Arthur Hill as Franklin Roosevelt, and Richard A. Dysart as General Eisenhower. Video.

Edward and Mrs. Simpson (1981). Director: Waris Hussein. Emmy Award winning Thames Television series starring Edward Fox and Cynthia Harris in the title role, with Churchill's part in the abdication drama portrayed by Wensley Pithey. Video.

The Finest Hour (1981). Director: Peter Baylis. Based on Churchill's memoirs of World War II, his wartime leadership is the focus of this documentary with narration by Orson Welles. Video.

Gathering Storm (1974). Director: Herbert Wise. Richard Burton portrays Churchill in this film depiction of the pre-World War II years. Ian Bannen is Hitler, and Robin Bailey portrays Chamberlain. Video.

The Last Bastion (1984). Director: Chris Thomson. Timothy West portrays Churchill in this World War II television drama focusing on the political struggle among the prime minister, Roosevelt (Warren Mitchell), MacArthur (Robert Vaughn), and Australia's John Curtin (Michael Blakemore). Video.

The Warlords (1986). Producer: Lamancha Productions. This series of brief film biographies of World War II leaders, such as Hitler, De Gaulle, Mussolini, and Stalin, includes a portrait of Churchill. Video.

The Winds of War (1983). Director: Dan Curtis. In this television mini-series adaptation of Herman Wouk's novel, the lead up and early years of the World War II are seen through the experiences of the extended Henry family with Robert Mitchum as the patriarch. Howard Lang portrays Churchill. Video.

War and Remembrance (1988). Director: Dan Curtis. Continues the story of the Henry family to the end of the war. Robert Hardy plays Churchill. Video.

The Woman He Loved (1988). Director: Charles Jarrott. Anthony Andrews and Jane Seymour star as Edward VIII and Wallis Simpson in this made-for-television drama. Robert Hardy portrays Churchill. Video.

World War II: When Lions Roared (1994). Director: Joseph Sargent. The conduct of the war from the perspective of the Allied leaders is dramatized. Bob Hoskins portrays Churchill; Michael Caine is Stalin, and John Lithgow is Franklin Roosevelt. Video.

Young Winston (1972). Director: Richard Attenborough. Based on Churchill's *My Early Life,* this biographical film follows him through his schooling and his military and journalistic career to his election to Parliament at the age of 26. Simon Ward is utterly convincing in the title role. Others in the film's fine cast include Robert Shaw (Randolph Churchill), Anne Bancroft (Jenny Churchill), John Mills (Kitchener), and Anthony Hopkins (David Lloyd George). Video.

98. MARCUS TULLIUS CICERO
106 B.C.–43 B.C.

Commonly regarded as the greatest Roman orator, as well as a famous politician and philosopher, Cicero was a member of the senatorial party and held such political posts as curule aedile (69 B.C.), praetor (66 B.C.), and consul (63 B.C.). After crushing the Cataline conspiracy, he was accused of illegality and exiled but was recalled by Pompey, whom he joined against Julius Caesar. Cicero's tacit approval of Caesar's murder and defense of the republic in his *First Philippic* and *Second Philippic* led Octavian and Marc Antony to have him condemned and put to death. Cicero's orations became the standard of excellence in Latin prose.

Autobiography and Primary Sources

Cicero's letters are the essential primary sources for any biography. Translated editions include *Letters of Cicero: A Selection in Translation*. L.P. Wilkinson, ed. (New York: W.W. Norton, 1968. 207pp.) and *Letters to Atticus*. D.R. Shackleton Bailey, ed. (Cambridge, Massachusetts: Harvard University Press, 1999. 4 vols.).

Recommended Biographies

Lacey, W.K. *Cicero and the End of the Roman Republic*. New York: Barnes and Noble, 1978. 184pp. Intended for the general reader, Lacey summarizes all aspects of Cicero's career as a politician, orator, author, and philosopher and recounts the development of his character. The historical events and cultural details of his era are also fully explained.

Mitchell, Thomas. *Cicero*. New Haven, Connecticut: Yale University Press, 1979–1991. 2 vols. Mitchell's two-volume study is widely regarded as the standard reference for Cicero's political career. Thoroughly documented and comprehensive, the book explores both Cicero's political ideas and theories and the wider historical context that make sense of his shifting career.

Rawson, Elizabeth. *Cicero: A Portrait*. 1975. Revised ed. Ithaca, New York: Cornell University Press, 1983. 341pp. Aimed at the general reader, Rawson's is an informed and sensible chronicle of Cicero's life and personality that offers reasonable conjectures surrounding the largely undocumented majority of Cicero's life.

Shackleton Bailey, D.R. *Cicero*. New York: Scribner, 1972. 290pp. Cicero's public and private lives are explored in this highly readable account, based largely on Cicero's letters and writings that supply a remarkably intimate look at his daily activities and ideas.

Other Biographical Studies

Fuhrmann, Manfred. *Cicero and the Roman Republic*. Cambridge, Massachusetts: Blackwell, 1992. 249pp. Fuhrman combines biographical and historical material to bring Cicero vividly to life. The book offers a convincing psychological portrait in which Cicero's actions are seen clearly in their historical and cultural context.

Petersson, Torsten. *Cicero: A Biography*. Berkeley: University of California Press, 1920. 699pp. Petersson takes a life-and-times approach, filling in the considerable gaps in the biographical record with background information. The result is a vivid and credible portrait of the man and his era.

Stockton, David. *Cicero: A Political Biography*. London: Oxford University Press, 1971. 359pp. As the title indicates, Stockton's study concentrates exclusively on Cicero's political career. Written for British undergraduates, the book will serve the reader looking for a competent background study, though it does assume some prior knowledge.

Trollope, Anthony. *The Life of Cicero*. 1881. Reprint ed. New York: Arno Press, 1981. 2 vols. Trollope's biography has been both praised as a masterwork and dismissed as an indulgence. Cicero was unquestionably one of the Victorian novelist's great heroes, and the book attempts to make him recognizable as a human figure, as a sort of prototypical Victorian gentleman.

Wilkin, Robert N. *Eternal Lawyer: A Legal Biography of Cicero*. New York: Macmillan, 1947. 264pp. Cicero's career as a lawyer is compactly presented in relationship to the events and individuals of his times. The book features a clear analysis of the economic and political background of the period.

Biographical Novels

Benton, Kenneth. *Death on the Appian Way*. London: Chatto and Windus, 1974. 223pp. Cicero's feud with Clodius is dramatized.

Caldwell, Taylor. *A Pillar of Iron*. Garden City, New York: Doubleday, 1965. 649pp. This is a detailed and compelling biographical portrait of Cicero set against a vivid and authentic period backdrop.

Fictional Portraits

Burns, Ron. *Roman Shadows*. New York: Saint Martin's, 1992. 261pp. Burns's period mystery involves Cicero in a political dispute during the final days of the Roman Republic.

Saylor, Steven. *Roman Blood*. New York: Saint Martin's, 1991. 354pp.; *Catalina's Riddle*. New York: Saint Martin's, 1993. 430pp.; *The Venus Throw*. New York: Saint Martin's, 1995. 308pp.; *A Murder on the Appian Way*. New York: Saint Martin's, 1996. 304pp. Cicero appears regularly in Saylor's inventive period mysteries involving Gordianus the Finder.

Wagner, John, and Esther Wagner. *The Gift of Rome*. Boston: Little, Brown, 1961. 224pp. Cicero is shown defending a man against a charge of murdering his stepfather in a situation inspired by a real event.

See also Augustus; Julius Caesar

99. HENRY CLAY
1777–1852

An American statesman, called the "Great Compromiser" for his attempts to reconcile North and South, Clay practiced law in Kentucky and served both in the U.S. Senate and House of Representatives (1806-1852). He was one of the "war hawks" who supported the War of 1812 and in 1820 helped produced the Missouri Compromise on slavery. From 1825 to 1829, Clay served as secretary of state under John Quincy Adams. He was the Whig presidential candidate in 1844 but lost the election because of his position on the annexation of Texas. He was instrumental in shaping the Compromise of 1850, complex national provisions for "slave" and "free" states, which temporarily saved the nation from civil war.

Autobiography and Primary Sources

The Papers of Henry Clay. James F. Hopkin, et al., eds. Lexington: University of Press of Kentucky, 1959–1992. 11 vols. All Clay's extant letters are included as well as his speeches and writings in this monumental scholarly edition.

Recommended Biographies

Eaton, Clement. *Henry Clay and the Art of American Politics*. Boston: Little, Brown, 1957. 209pp. Based mainly on Clay's papers, this is a lucid, succinct, and well-written interpretive biography in which Clay's life and career are approached topically rather than chronologically. Eaton achieves a lifelike, engaging portrait of both the man and the politician.

Remini, Robert V. *Henry Clay: Statesman for the Union*. New York: W.W. Norton, 1991. 818pp. Remini's is a detailed account of Clay's personal and political life that also provides a balanced assessment of his strengths and weaknesses. Written by a leading expert of the era and its leading figures, Clay's life is shown clearly against a vivid social and historical background.

Schurz, Carl. *Life of Henry Clay*. Boston: Houghton Mifflin, 1887. 2 vols. The leading nineteenth-century biography, Schurz provides a scholarly, elegantly written account of Clay's political career and an insightful, balanced evaluation of his strengths and weaknesses.

Van Deusen, Glyndon G. *The Life of Henry Clay*. Boston: Little, Brown, 1937. 448pp. This is a scholarly, thorough, and readable political biography, still regarded as one of the best available. Carefully researched and balanced in its assessment, the book succeeds in locating Clay in the social and political context of his era.

Other Biographical Studies

Clay, Thomas Hart, and Ellis P. Oberholtzer. *Henry Clay*. Philadelphia: George W. Jacobs, 1910. 450pp. Begun by Clay's grandson, this admiring reassessment of Clay's reputation argues his importance both as a political leader and orator.

Mayo, Bernard. *Henry Clay: Spokesman of the New West*. Boston: Houghton Mifflin, 1937. 570pp. The first volume of a projected but uncompleted trilogy presents Clay's life up to the opening of the War of 1812. Minute in its details, this is the fullest presentation of Clay's formative years and the cultural and historical forces that shaped his ideas and character.

Poage, George R. *Henry Clay and the Whig Party*. Chapel Hill: University of North Carolina Press, 1936. 295pp. Poage's is a study of Clay's last decade with a brief summary of his career up to 1840. Mainly concerned with party politics, Clay is also viewed against the background of state and national issues during the period covered.

Peterson, Merrill D. *The Great Triumvirate: Webster, Clay, and Calhoun*. New York: Oxford University Press, 1987. 573pp. Peterson treats the collective political careers of the trio to characterize American history during the first half of the nineteenth century.

Biographical Novels

Crabb, Alfred L. *Home to Kentucky: A Novel of Henry Clay*. Indianapolis: Bobbs-Merrill, 1953. 339pp. Clay's life is dramatized from his days as a young lawyer through his career in Congress and unsuccessful presidential aspirations.

Fictional Portraits

Harper, Robert S. *The Road to Baltimore.* New York: M.S. Mill, 1942. 245pp. In this period romance, a young man shares a stagecoach with Henry Clay from Wheeling to Washington.

Recommended Juvenile Biographies

Peterson, Helen S. *Henry Clay: Leader in Congress.* New York: Chelsea House, 1991. 80pp. MG. Peterson supplies the necessary historical context to make Clay's political career understandable.

Biographical Films and Theatrical Adaptations

The Adams Chronicles (1975). Director: Paul Bogart. This popular PBS series dramatizes four generations of the Adams family in an entertaining and mostly reliable fashion. Henry Clay is portrayed by George Hearn. Video.

Shepherd, Jack. *The Adams Chronicles: Four Generations of Greatness* (Boston: Little, Brown, 1975. 448pp.). This is the companion book to the PBS series.

100. CLEOPATRA
69 B.C.–30 B.C.

The last queen of Egypt, Cleopatra was the daughter of Ptolemy XI and married her younger brother when she was 17. With the help of Julius Caesar, she led a successful revolt against her brother, wrestling control of the kingdom, but as a vassal state of Rome. Cleopatra became Caesar's mistress and bore him a son. Allied with Marc Antony after Caesar's assassination, the pair were defeated by Octavius (later Augustus) at the battle of Actium in 31 B.C. The lovers took their own lives, and the legend of Cleopatra as the archetypal temptress and romantic heroine has exerted a powerful influence in Western art ever since.

Recommended Biographies

Grant, Michael. *Cleopatra.* New York: Simon & Schuster, 1972. 301pp. Organized in four sections, Grant examines Cleopatra's first 21 years and her relationships with Caesar, Antony, and Octavius. In his view, Cleopatra should be seen as consumed by ambition to revive the former glory of her Greek ancestors. Provocative and crammed with detailed information, Grant's incisive study helps regain a credible historical Cleopatra, at odds with her legendary image.

Hughes-Hallet, Lucy. *Cleopatra: Histories, Dreams, and Distortions.* New York: Harper & Row, 1990. 338pp. The author, after summarizing the historical record, provides a fascinating feminist analysis of the ways in which succeeding generations have fashioned different views of the queen: as virtuous suicide, professional courtesan, scheming manipulator, and femme fatale. In Hughes-Hallet's view Cleopatra was in fact a

markedly abstemious lover whom each age has reinterpreted in its own erotic image.

Volkmann, Hans. *Cleopatra: A Study in Politics and Propaganda.* New York: Sagamore Press, 1958. 244pp. The author's political biography chronicles Cleopatra's life in the context of her efforts to remake the Ptolemaic empire in the midst of Roman expansionism. He shows clearly how later views of Cleopatra were the creation of her Roman enemies. Groundbreaking in its re-evaluation.

Other Biographical Studies

Bradford, Ernle. *Cleopatra.* New York: Harcourt, Brace, 1971. 279pp. Bradford's popular biography is lucid and lively but provides little to challenge the familiar interpretation of Cleopatra and her times.

Flamarion, Edith. *Cleopatra: The Life and Death of a Pharoah.* New York: Abrams, 1997. 159pp. Beautifully illustrated with period artifacts and later artistic representations, this concise description of Cleopatra's life includes a document section that assembles a number of contemporary and historical accounts.

Foss, Michael. *The Search for Cleopatra.* New York: Arcade, 1997. 192pp. Foss sets out to trace the factual basis for the various legends surrounding Cleopatra. Placing the Egyptian queen firmly in the context of her times, the book offers an explanation of why Cleopatra was such a formidable threat to Rome.

Lindsay, Jack. *Cleopatra.* New York: Coward-McCann, 1971. 560pp. Placing Cleopatra firmly in the context of her times with a revealing discussion of the Egyptian court system, dynastic rivalries, and religious beliefs, Lindsay supplements the known facts with sound speculation.

Ludwig, Emil. *Cleopatra: The Story of a Queen.* New York: Viking, 1937. 342pp. Ludwig's popular biography stresses the psychology of Cleopatra and her three Romans—Caesar, Antony, and Octavius. His dramatic narrative employs the technique of the historical novel and is lacking in the authority of other scholarly approaches.

Biographical Novels

Balderston, John L. *A Goddess to a God.* New York: Macmillan, 1948. 213pp. Narrated in a series of letters between Cleopatra and Julius Caesar, the novel covers the period from his invasion of Egypt to his assassination in a portrait of the pair's emotional side, along with vivid details of the period and its customs.

George, Margaret. *The Memoirs of Cleopatra.* New York: Saint Martin's, 1997. 964pp. Told in the first person from Cleopatra's earliest memories of her father's rule to her own reign and relationship with Julius Caesar and Marc Antony, this is an accurate reconstruction based on evident extensive research.

Gerson, Noel B. *That Egyptian Woman.* Garden City, New York: Doubleday, 1956. 317pp. Based on the lives of Julius Caesar and Cleopatra, the novel traces the Egyptian queen's meteoric rise. The author admits to having taken historical liber-

ties to create his vivid, though at times incredible, drama.

Lindsay, Kathleen. *Enchantress of the Nile.* London: Hurst and Blackett, 1965. 184pp. Lindsay offers a characterization that captures Cleopatra's political savvy as she plays one faction against another in order to consolidate her power and extend her control.

Mundy, Talbot. *Queen Cleopatra: A Novel.* Indianapolis: Bobbs-Merrill, 1929. 426pp. The novel dramatizes Cleopatra's life from her early struggles for the Egyptian throne to the end of her love affair with Julius Caesar. Vividly told, full of color and pageantry, considerable liberties have been taken with historical fact to vindicate Cleopatra's character.

Rofheart, Martha. *The Alexandrian.* New York: Crowell, 1976. 280pp. Cleopatra narrates her own story and her relationships with Julius Caeser and Marc Antony. The novel's basic outline is historically accurate.

Tarr, Judith. *Throne of Isis.* New York: Forge, 1994. 349pp. In this fictionalized version of Cleopatra's romances and reign, she emerges as a remarkably canny political leader who falls in love with the man she intended to use for her own purpose. The novel makes a concerted effort to stay close to actual historical facts and avoid the legendary pattern of previous treatments.

Fictional Portraits

Chase-Riboud, Barbara. *Portrait of a Nude Woman as Cleopatra.* New York: Morrow, 1987. 110pp. Based on Plutarch's history, this poetic sequence gives voice to Cleopatra and Antony and the various aspects of their passion and personalities.

Haggard, H. Rider. *Cleopatra.* 1889. Reprint ed. New York: Pocket Books, 1963. 290pp. In Haggard's historical romance, a conspiracy by Egyptian nobles to overthrow Cleopatra is done in by the queen's irresistibility. Despite the fanciful events, the novel is filled with many vivid and believable portraits of Egyptian life and culture.

Massie, Allan. *Augustus.* New York: Carroll & Graf, 1986. 381pp. First published in the United States as *Let the Emperor Speak,* this is a first-person narrative in which Augustus describes his career. Cleopatra is seen from a decidedly hostile perspective. Another view of the Egyptian queen is provided in the author's *Caesar* (New York: Carroll & Graf, 1994. 228pp.), a biographical novel of the life of Julius Caesar.

Wilder, Thornton. *The Ides of March* New York: Longmans, 1948. 198pp. Cleopatra is one of several witnesses to the last year of Julius Caesar's life in Wilder's fictional re-creation told in the form of letters exchanged by several of the principals.

Recommended Juvenile Biographies

Brooks, Polly S. *Cleopatra: Goddess of Egypt, Enemy of Rome.* New York: HarperCollins, 1995. 151pp. YA. As much an account of the Roman struggle for control in the Mediterranean as a life of Cleopatra, the author shows how her enemies played a role in demonizing her image. Brooks provides an alternative view that places Cleopatra in historical and cultural perspective.

Green, Robert. *Cleopatra*. New York: F. Watts, 1996. 63pp. MG. In an intriguing biography, Green traces how in a male-dominated world Cleopatra succeeded in challenging the power of the Roman Empire.

Hoobler, Dorothy. *Cleopatra*. New York: Chelsea House, 1986. 115pp. MG/YA. Hoobler restores a good deal of political savvy to the portrayal of Cleopatra, arguing that the Greco-Roman kingdom she dreamed of creating with Marc Antony might well have transformed Western history. Skeptical of past depictions, this is a fresh look at the most powerful woman in the ancient world.

Nardo, Don. *Cleopatra*. San Diego: Lucent Books, 1994. 112pp. MG/YA. A detailed, illustrated biography, Nardo discusses the life of Cleopatra in relation to the politics and power struggles of ancient Egypt and Rome. Contrary to previous views, Cleopatra is shown as a strong, intelligent, and caring ruler. Includes quotes from primary and secondary sources. Unfortunately, the many illustrations of Cleopatra the seductress is contrary to the thesis of the text.

Biographical Films and Theatrical Adaptations

Dryden, John. *All for Love* (1678). Various editions. In what is regarded as Dryden's finest play, he restricts the action to the last phase of Antony's career, when he is besieged in Alexandria. Cleopatra is reduced from Shakespeare's wider conception to that of a disappointed lover.

Shakespeare, William. *Antony and Cleopatra* (1607). Various editions. Although based mainly on Plutarch's negative assessment, Cleopatra attains tragic dignity and considerable savvy in Shakespeare's handling. There are several film versions of the play available on video.

Shaw, George Bernard. *Caesar and Cleopatra* (1901). Various editions. In Shaw's antiromantic interpretation, he declaws the temptress Cleopatra and presents her as a minor interlude for the pragmatic, unemotional Caesar. To achieve his realistic, unsentimental portrait, Shaw makes a number of changes in the historical record.

A&E Biography Video: Cleopatra: Destiny's Queen (1994). Director: Monte Markham. Ancient records combined with modern reenactments and computer-generated graphics bring to life the most powerful woman of the ancient world. This documentary look poses the question whether Cleopatra killed herself out of love for Antony or for her failure to seduce her conqueror, Octavius. Video.

Caesar and Cleopatra (1946). Director: Gabriel Pascal. Dull adaptation of Shaw's play with Claude Rains and Vivien Leigh in the title roles. Video.

Cleopatra (1934). Director: Cecil B. DeMille. Lavish Hollywood interpretation of Cleopatra as arch-temptress and Jazz Age bad girl with Claudette Colbert in the title role as history's wickedest women, Warren William as Caesar, and Henry Wilcoxon as Antony. Video.

Cleopatra (1963). Director: Joseph L. Mankiewicz. History takes a backseat to spectacle in this notorious, leaden, big-budget epic with the ultimate seducer played by Elizabeth Taylor whose offscreen affair with Richard Burton (Antony) provides much of the sizzle in an odd case of life imitating art. Rex Harrison portrays Caesar, and Roddy McDowall plays Octavius. Video.

Cleopatra (1999). Director: Fran Roddam. Based on Margaret George's novel, this made-for-television drama features Leonor Varela as the Egyptian queen, Billy Zane as Marc Antony, and Timothy Dalton as Julius Caesar. Video.

Serpent of the Nile (1953). Director: William Castle. Rhonda Fleming is the Egyptian queen in this B-movie production with Raymond Burr as Marc Antony.

See also Augustus; Julius Caesar

101. GROVER CLEVELAND
1837–1908

The twenty-second (1885-1889) and twenty-fourth (1893-1897) U.S. president, Cleveland practiced law in Buffalo, New York, and was elected (1882) mayor of the city and then governor of the state. His opposition to Tammany Hall graft and opportunism earned him a national following and election to the presidency as a Democrat. As president, Cleveland was conscientious, conservative, and a foe of political patronage. He implemented the Pendleton Civil Service Act (1883), repealed the 1890 Sherman Silver Purchase Act (1893), and used federal troops to break the 1894 Pullman Strike.

Autobiography and Primary Sources

The Letters of Grover Cleveland. Allan Nevins, ed. 1933. Reprint ed. New York: Da Capo Press, 1970. 640pp. Nevins has selected letters for their autobiographical and historical interests. Although there are no intimate revelations here, the depth of Cleveland's feelings and his character do emerge strongly.

Presidential Problems. New York: Century, 1904. 281pp. Cleveland reflects on some of the significant events of his presidencies such as the Venezuela boundary controversy and the Pullman strike in this series of essays written from the vantage point of his retirement from public life.

Recommended Biographies

Nevins, Allan. *Grover Cleveland: A Study in Courage*. New York: Dodd, Mead, 1932. 832pp. Nevins's monumental study is by far the most comprehensive treatment of Cleveland based on a wide array of primary and secondary sources. The man who emerges from Nevins's close attention is a complex figure, a "strong man of character," though with many human failings. When this biography was first published, one reviewer doubted that another would ever need be written, and no better life has been, to date.

Tugwell, Rexford G. *Grover Cleveland*. New York: Macmillan, 1968. 298pp. Readers without the stamina to take on Nevins may choose Tugwell's briefer, less-scholarly account of Cleveland's political career. In the author's candid view

Cleveland was a "plodder without flair but incorruptible in office." The book's chief strength is to make understandable and dramatic the various crises Cleveland dealt with to give his actions some understanding.

Welch, Richard E. *The Presidencies of Grover Cleveland*. Lawrence: University Press of Kansas, 1988. 268pp. In a well-argued reassessment of Cleveland's two administrations, Welch posits that despite modest achievements and an inflexibility that prevented compromise, Cleveland was an important president in the evolution of the presidency in the twentieth century. Welch makes his case by detailing Cleveland's challenges and the quality of his leadership.

Other Biographical Studies

Lynch, Denis T. *Grover Cleveland: A Man Four-Square*. New York: Liveright, 1932. 581pp. Lynch's is a popularly written, appreciative assessment that stresses Cleveland's role as a reformer. The essential details of Cleveland's life and career are arranged into a informative, if shallow, chronological narrative.

McElroy, Robert. *Grover Cleveland, the Man and Statesman: An Authorized Biography*. New York: Harper, 1923. 2 vols. More a campaign biography than an objective assessment, Cleveland's accomplishments as mayor of Buffalo, governor of New York, and president are dutifully chronicled with everything reflecting positively on Cleveland as a principled and independent leader.

Fictional Portraits

Belfer, Lauren. *City of Light*. New York: Dial Press, 1999. 518pp. Set in 1901 Buffalo, New York, this intriguing novel interweaves a murder investigation, the harnessing of Niagara Falls for hydroelectric power, and Grover Cleveland's personal involvement with the life of the novel's female protagonist.

Conroy, Sarah B. *Refinements of Love: A Novel about Clover and Henry Adams*. New York: Pantheon, 1993. 301pp. The relationship between Henry Adams and his wife, Clover, features appearances by a number of historical figures, including Cleveland.

Fast, Howard. *The American*. New York: Duell, Sloan, and Pearce, 1946. 337pp. This biographical novel on the life of John Peter Altgeld shows Cleveland during the Pullman Strike.

Recommended Juvenile Biographies

Collins, David R. *Grover Cleveland: 22nd and 24th President of the United States*. Ada, Oklahoma: Garrett, 1988. 119pp. MG. Cleveland's life and political career is adequately covered in this biographical portrait.

Kent, Zachary. *Grover Cleveland: Twenty-Second and Twenty-Fourth President of the United States*. Chicago: Childrens Press, 1988. 98pp. MG. Kent treats the basic details of Cleveland's private and public life.

Biographical Films and Theatrical Adaptations

Buffalo Bill & the Indians (1976). Director: Robert Altman. Altman's inventive and satiric take on the legends of the Wild West casts Paul Newman in the central role with a colorful supporting cast, including Pat McCormick as Grover Cleveland. Video.

Other Sources

Vexler, Robert I. *Grover Cleveland, 1837–1908: Chronology, Documents, Bibliographical Aids.* Dobbs Ferry, New York: Oceana, 1986. 118pp. Vexler supplies a useful reference guide with an extensive chronology, a sampling of primary documents, and an annotated bibliography.

102. SAMUEL TAYLOR COLERIDGE
1772–1834

A poet, critic, and essayist, Coleridge was one of the most brilliant, versatile, and influential literary figures of the English Romantic movement. He was educated at Cambridge, where he began his addiction to opium. With poet William Wordsworth, he published a volume of poetry *Lyrical Ballads* (1798), considered a landmark of early romanticism. The volume featured Coleridge's most famous poem "The Rime of the Ancient Mariner." Other well-known poems are "Kubla Khan" and "Christabel." Coleridge gave notable lectures on Shakespeare and in 1817 published *Biographia Literaria*, a collection of critical essays on philosophical and literary subjects.

Autobiography and Primary Sources

Readers have been well served in the scholarly editions of Coleridge's private papers and can consult the *Notebooks.* Kathleen Coburn, ed. (New York: Pantheon, 1957–1990. 4 vols.); *Collected Letters.* (Oxford: Clarendon Press, 1956-71. 6 vols.); and *Selected Letters.* H.J. Jackson, ed. (New York: Oxford University Press, 1987. 306pp.).

Recommended Biographies

Ashton, Rosemary. *The Life of Samuel Taylor Coleridge: A Critical Biography.* Cambridge, Massachusetts: Blackwell, 1996. 480pp. Ashton's is a thorough, lucid examination of Coleridge's complex personality and activities as a poet, critic, and philosopher. Coleridge's development is helpfully placed within a wider political and intellectual context of British and German Romanticism. Scholarly but not inaccessible for the nonspecialist, Ashton's is the best single-volume study available.

Bate, Walter Jackson. *Coleridge.* New York: Macmillan, 1969. 244pp. Bate's is a sensible, short critical study of Coleridge's life and work that retains its usefulness as a sophisticated overview that joins the various elements of Coleridge's career into a thematic and coherent whole.

Holmes, Richard. *Coleridge: Early Visions, 1772–1804.* New York: Viking, 1989. 409pp.; *Coleridge: Darker Reflections, 1804–1834.* New York: Pantheon, 1999. 622pp. Widely acclaimed as one of the finest literary biographies, Holmes's

scholarly yet highly readable life deserves such high praise. The portrait of Coleridge is nuanced, complex, and compelling, offering a fresh impression that makes other treatments seem distant and routine. Holmes probes the many facets of Coleridge's genius with all the energy and narrative power of a great novel. A monumental achievement.

Other Biographical Studies

Campbell, James D. *Samuel Taylor Coleridge: A Narrative of the Events of His Life.* 1894. Reprint ed. New York: Macmillan, 1970. 319pp. Campbell's full-length record of Coleridge's life and development has been superseded by later works that have drawn on wider primary sources.

Chambers, E.K. *Samuel Taylor Coleridge: A Biographical Study.* Oxford: Clarendon Press, 1938. 373pp. Long recognized as the standard biographical source, Chambers synthesizes primary and secondary sources into an exact, exhaustive compendium of dates and facts, but the book lacks an interpretive focus. The reader looking for a reliable chronicle of Coleridge's activities and relationships will find them here, but a deeper understanding of the man and the source of his genius is missing.

Charpentier, John. *Coleridge: The Sublime Somnambulist.* New York: Dodd, Mead, 1929. 332pp. The author, a French critic, traces the development of Coleridge's mind in this sympathetic portrait, too restrictive in its thematic focus to render a fully convincing multidimensional view.

Cornwell, John. *Coleridge: Poet and Revolutionary 1772–1804.* London: A. Lane, 1973. 430pp. Like Hanson, Cornwell concentrates on Coleridge's formative years but mainly from the perspective of his reaction to political events. The book serves to orient the reader to the wider social and historical contexts that make Coleridge's development comprehensible.

Doughty, Oswald. *Perturbed Spirit: The Life and Personality of Samuel Taylor Coleridge.* Rutherford, New Jersey: Fairleigh Dickinson University Press, 1981. 565pp. Focusing on Coleridge's relationships, this is a somewhat disjointed series of character sketches emphasizing the negative and darker aspects of Coleridge's temperament and genius. Mostly undocumented, the book indulges in a good deal of speculation about what Coleridge probably felt and how he might have reacted in given situations.

Fausset, Hugh I'Anson. *Samuel Taylor Coleridge.* 1926. Reprint ed. New York: Russell & Russell, 1967. 350pp. This is a highly romantic treatment of Coleridge's life that employs fictional elements to heighten the drama and characterization.

Hanson, Lawrence. *The Life of Samuel Taylor Coleridge: The Early Years.* New York: Oxford University Press, 1939. 575pp. Hanson's is a well-researched account of Coleridge's formative years, narrating his story up to the writer's move to the Lake District. Balanced in its assessment of Coleridge's character, Hanson relies extensively on quotations from letters and other documentary evidence, and the book continues to be a useful text

for the reader seeking to understand Coleridge's early development.

Traill, H.D. *Coleridge.* 1884. Reprint ed. New York: AMS Press, 1968. 211pp. Traill's early and influential study organized Coleridge's life and work into the major critical categories of poetry, criticism, and philosophy that have persisted.

Weissman, Stephen M. *His Brother's Keeper: A Psychobiography of Samuel Taylor Coleridge.* Madison: Connecticut: International Universities Press, 1989. 340pp. In this intriguing psychological analysis the author traces the source of Coleridge's unhappiness and torments to his early childhood experiences: the early death of his father and suicide of his brother. Weissman's confident, unverifiable assertions are potentially misleading for the reader without sufficient knowledge to counter the author's claims.

Fictional Portraits

Phillips, Jill M. *Walford's Oak.* New York: Carol, 1990. 218pp. Coleridge in Over Stowey is shown investigating a local ghost story.

Biographical Films and Theatrical Adaptations

The Strangest Voyage (1975). Director: Michael Twain. A biographical portrait and a reading of Coleridge's "The Rime of the Ancient Mariner." Video.

103. COLETTE
1873–1954

A French author famous for her popular, semiautobiographical novels characterized by sensitive observations, especially of women, Sidonie Gabrielle Colette's early series of novels were published in collaboration with the first of her three husbands and include *Claudine at School* (1900). Divorced in 1906, she worked as a music hall actress until 1914. Colette's other novels include *Chéri* (1920) and *Gigi* (1945). She was the first woman president of the Goncourt Academy and the second to be made a grand officer of the French Legion of Honor.

Autobiography and Primary Sources

Earthly Paradise: An Autobiography. Robert Phelps, ed. New York: Farrar, Straus, 1966. 505pp. Phelps has arranged selections of Colette's writings from her memoirs, novels, letters, and essays into a chronological record of the writer's life and views on people, places, and events.

Letters from Colette. Robert Phelps, ed. New York: Farrar, Straus, 1980. 214pp. Colette wrote, on average, a half-dozen letters a day, collected into five large volumes. This is a selection of some of the best that reveals her views on assorted topics.

Looking Backwards. Bloomington: Indiana University Press, 1975. 214pp. Bringing together two of Collette's reminiscences, *Journal à revours* (1941) and *De Ma Fentre* (1942), the volume includes her reflections on her childhood, her mother, and her origins as a writer and observations of wartime Paris.

Recommended Biographies

Francis, Claude, and Fernande Gontier. *Creating Colette*. South Royalton, Vermont: Steerforth Press, 1998–1999. 2 vols. Easily the most detailed collection of information on Colette, this is fascinating record of the writer's private and public lives with a vivid social and period background.

Richardson, Joanna. *Colette*. New York: F. Watts, 1984. 276pp. Thoroughly researched and comprehensive, this is a fine, balanced biographical portrait that supplies a detailed chronological record of Colette's private life and public career as well as a realistic assessment of Colette's character.

Sarde, Michèle. *Colette: Free and Unfettered*. New York: Morrow, 1980. 479pp. Based on some unpublished letters and manuscripts and interviews with Colette, this is an insightful biography that allows Colette to speak for herself as much as possible. From a feminist perspective, Colette's life is viewed as a long effort at liberation

Thurman, Judith. *Secrets of the Flesh: A Life of Colette*. New York: Knopf, 1999. 592pp. In a subtle, intelligent literary biography, Thurman manages to view Colette consistently through all her complexity and contradictions. While less personally detailed than Francis and Gontier's multivolume life, Thurman's is perhaps more successful in making psychological sense of Colette's character and the translation of her experiences into her works.

Other Biographical Studies

Crosland, Margaret. *Madame Colette: A Provincial in Paris*. London: P. Owen, 1953. 222pp. This is an appreciation rather than a critical, objective study, charming in its way of collecting interesting anecdotes to illustrate both the literary career and personality of Colette.

Crosland, Margaret. *Colette: The Difficulty of Loving: A Biography*. Indianapolis: Bobbs-Merrill, 1973. 284pp. Crosland's second treatment of Colette's life is a reinterpretation with some added facts to fill in the gap in the biographical record. More the highlights than a thorough record, the book serves mainly the general reader looking for a pleasing overview.

Davies, Margaret. *Colette*. New York: Grove Press, 1961. 120pp. Davies's is a compact introductory summary of the important events of Colette's life and a survey of her works.

Dormann, Genevieve. *Colette: A Passion for Life*. New York: Abbeville Press, 1985. 320pp. This pictorial biography contains 488 photographs of Colette, her husbands, lovers, family, and friends. The visual record is much stronger than the overgeneralized, superficial summary text.

Le Hardouin, Maria. *Colette: A Biographical Study*. London: Staples, 1958. 186pp. Le Hardouin emphasizes Colette's literary achievement rather than her personal drama in a sensible but undocumented overview.

Lottman, Herbert R. *Colette: A Life*. Boston: Little, Brown, 1991. 344pp. Lottman's is a careful, reliable summary of Colette's remarkable life, interweaving the story of her personal life with her evolution as a writer. The author shies away from offering an interpretation either of the author's life or work and fails to penetrates Colette's inner, imaginative life.

Marks, Elaine. *Colette*. New Brunswick, New Jersey: Rutgers University Press, 1960. 265pp. Although mainly concerned with a critical examination of the works, Marks's study includes a valuable, succinct account of Colette's life.

Massie, Allan. *Colette*. New York: Penguin, 1986. 152pp. Massie offers a well-written and informed introduction to Colette's life and works in this entry in the Lives of Modern Women series.

Mitchell, Yvonne. *Colette: A Taste for Life*. New York: Harcourt, Brace, 1975. 240pp. Beautifully illustrated, this is a competent biographical portrait more for the general reader than the scholar.

104. CHRISTOPHER COLUMBUS
1451–1506

Italian-born navigator and explorer, Columbus became a chart maker in Lisbon and a master mariner in the Portuguese merchant service. Convinced that a route to the East Indies could be discovered by going west, Columbus, after eight years of seeking royal support, gained approval for his voyage from Ferdinand and Isabella of Spain in 1492. After making landfall in San Salvador, Columbus returned to Spain and was made "admiral of the ocean sea." He undertook three subsequent voyages of discovery, exploring Puerto Rico, Cuba, Jamaica, Venezuela, and Honduras. As governor of the colony of Hispaniola, Columbus was charged with mismanagement and returned to Spain in chains in 1500. Heralded for initiating the beginning of continuous European efforts to explore and colonize the Americas, Columbus's "discoveries" have been qualified by previous claims of Viking colonization and charges of ruthless mistreatment of native populations. Few, however, would dispute that Columbus's voyages marked a turning point in world history.

Autobiography and Primary Sources

The Four Voyages. J.M. Cohen, ed. New York: Penguin, 1969. 320pp. Cohen weaves together Columbus's letters and log-book, the letters of the fleet physician and of a loyal lieutenant, the biography of Columbus's son, and Oviedo's official history into a narrative of the voyages.

Thacher, John B. *Christopher Columbus: His Life, His Work, His Remains as Revealed by Original Printed and Manuscript Records*. Cleveland: A.H. Clard, 1903. 3 vols. The author's reference volumes brings together documents, letters, and journals, and many portraits of Columbus.

Recommended Biographies

Davidson, Miles H. *Columbus Then and Now: A Life Reexamined*. Norman: University of Oklahoma Press, 1997. 609pp. Based on a fresh examination of manuscripts, diaries, letters, naval records, and shipping logs, Davidson supplies a comprehensive overview of Columbus's life, exposing a number of inaccuracies that have resulted from contemporary cultural biases toward the navigator.

Fernández-Armesto, Felipe. *Columbus*. New York: Oxford University Press, 1991. 218pp. This short, scholarly biographical study depicts a Columbus motivated by greed and the desire for social advancement whose anti-flat earth vision was not unique. Cutting through the legendary accretions that have distorted the truth, the author offers the unadorned facts within the context of the fifteenth century.

Morison, Samuel E. *Admiral of the Ocean Sea: A Life of Christopher Columbus*. Boston: Little, Brown, 1942. 680pp. Monumental in its scholarship and graceful in its prose, Morison's Pulitzer Prize–winning study remains authoritative on Columbus's achievements as a mariner and navigator. To prepare for his account Morison retraced Columbus's voyages in small sailing vessels, and the author's firsthand experience and mastery of nautical history makes this the preferred work on Columbus, centered not on his shadowy life on land but his greatness at sea; *Christopher Columbus, Mariner* (Boston: Little, Brown, 1955. 160pp.) provides a shorter assessment with many of the qualities of the longer work.

Phillips, William D., and Carla R. Phillips. *The Worlds of Christopher Columbus*. New York: Cambridge University Press, 1992. 322pp. Context predominates here in a readable, though scholarly account that corrects a number of misconceptions, such as a prevailing flat-earth view and the criminality of Columbus's crew. Excellent commonsense introduction for the context for Columbus's achievement and the history of European exploration before him.

Other Biographical Studies

Bradford, Ernle. *Christopher Columbus*. New York: Viking, 1973. 288pp. Bradford's readable, concise narrative biography shows Columbus as a great mariner but disastrous administrator. Filled with historical details, illustrations, and vivid anecdotes, the book rarely probes very deeply.

Collis, John S. *Christopher Columbus*. New York: Stein and Day, 1977. 208pp. Collis's brief biographical assessment balances a clear admiration for Columbus's determination and vision with a realistic view of his many failures. Dependent on other biographers for his facts, Collis contributes his own sailing trips aboard cargo ships to the West Indies to add color to his account.

Granzotto, Gianni. *Christopher Columbus*. Garden City, New York: Doubleday, 1985. 300pp. Written with the dramatic verve of a novelist, the author's popular life mixes fact with fancy and indulges in some sheer invention in imagining Columbus's private life and his relationship with Isabella.

Irving, Washington. *A History of the Life and Voyages of Christopher Columbus*. New York: Putnam, 1848. 3 vols. The first biography of Columbus in English, Irving's scholarly yet popular study casts Columbus firmly in the heroic mode: a visionary, wise and gentle in his dealings with the native population of the New World. Modern reassessments have reduced Irving's interpretation to quaint nostalgia.

Konig, Hans. *Columbus: His Enterprise.* New York: Monthly Review Press, 1976. 128pp. The author explodes the myth of Columbus as a courageous, visionary hero in an indictment of the greed, cruelty, and the beginning of European imperialism that he sees embodied in the man and his mission. A succinct prosecutorial account that is unapologetic in its polemicism.

Landström, Björn. *Columbus: The Story of Don Cristóbal Colón, Admiral of the Ocean.* New York: Macmillan, 1967. 207pp. This concise narrative life is documented with quotes from Columbus's own writing and dependent on research derived from Morison.

Madariaga, Salvador de. *Christopher Columbus.* New York: Macmillan, 1940. 524pp. The author's account is dominated by elaborate special pleading to prove his thesis that Columbus's ancestors were Spanish Jews. Few scholars today accept Madariaga's contentions, and the book remains a curious example of a discredited scholarly argument.

Sale, Kirkpatrick. *The Conquest of Paradise: Christopher Columbus and the Columbian Legacy.* New York: Knopf, 1990. 453pp. In perhaps the strongest example of modern revisionism of Columbus, Sale indicts the explorer as the archetypal western exploiter and destroyer of native cultures, motivated by greed and guilty of "ecohubris," the cause of many of our current ecological and cultural problems. Overblown in its vilification of Columbus, the book is nevertheless useful in providing the case for the prosecution.

Wilford, John Noble. *The Mysterious History of Columbus.* New York: Knopf, 1991. 318pp. Not a full-scale life but the "story of the story of Columbus," how the various versions of Columbus's character and story have been formed; Wilford provides a helpful general guide to what is known and not known about Columbus, synthesizing twentieth-century scholarship and summarizing various revisionist arguments.

Biographical Novels

Barreiro, José. *The Indian Chronicles.* Houston, Texas: Arte Público Press, 1993. 303pp. The historical figure of Columbus's Taino Indian translator narrates this recreation of the fatal European encounter with native American culture from the victims' perspective.

DiPerna, Paula. *The Discoveries of Mrs. Christopher Columbus: His Wife's Vision.* Sag Harbor, New York: Permanent Press, 1994. 287pp. DiPerna looks at the story of Columbus from the perspective of his wife and a feminist view, relying on a great deal of speculation and invention but based on a factual framework.

Forester, C.S. *To the Indies.* Boston: Little, Brown, 1940. 298pp. With a faithful account of Columbus's third voyage and the events that led to his disgrace and recall to Spain, Forester offers an aspect of Columbus's story that is rarely dealt with by novelists in such detail.

Johnston, Mary. *1492.* Boston: Little, Brown, 1922. 315pp. Following history closely, the novel chronicles Columbus's voyages of discovery—from his first crossing of the Atlantic to his death—from the perspective of a shipmate.

Sabatini, Rafael. *Columbus.* Boston: Houghton Mifflin, 1942. 430pp. Centered on the love story of Columbus and Beatriz Enriquez, the novel follows the mariner from his royal rebuff in Portugal through his tribulations at the Spanish court and first voyage. In Sabatini's distinctive colorful style, the novel offers a convincing picture of court life.

Street, James H. *The Velvet Doublet.* Garden City, New York: Doubleday, 1953. 317pp. The novel's fictional account of Columbus's first voyage is markedly hostile to the explorer and features a highly realistic look at fifteenth-century Spain.

Fictional Portraits

Belfrage, Cedric. *My Master Columbus.* Garden City, New York: Doubleday, 1961. 285pp. Columbus is seen from the perspective of a Native American who is "discovered" in 1492. More satire than an actual depiction of the historical Columbus, the details of the voyages are realistic. .

Card, Orson Scott. *Pastwatch: The Redemption of Christopher Columbus.* New York: Tor, 1996. 351pp. In this part-science fiction, part-historical drama the novel examines the devestating impact of Columbus's voyages and colonization with future scientists who intervene to alter the past. In a powerful portrait, Columbus is depicted as a religious and charismatic leader with both strengths and weaknesses.

Carpentier, Alejo. *The Harp and the Shadow.* San Francisco: Mercury House, 1990. 159pp. An imaginative inquiry into the character and myth of Columbus, the novel begins with Pius IX's canonization in the nineteenth century, followed by a confessional account by Columbus himself, and a final allegorical debate on his legacy by such figures as Jules Verne and Friedrich Schiller.

Cooper, James Fenimore. *Mercedes of Castille.* 1840. Reprint ed. New York: Appleton, 1873. 530pp. Cooper weaves a romance around the events of Columbus's first voyage. The author's own sea experience and reliance on Columbus's journals help the story's authenticity.

Frolich, Newton. *1492.* New York: Saint Martin's, 1990. 404pp. Ending with the start of Columbus's first voyage, the novel is mainly concerned with the years leading up to the voyage, with Columbus depicted as a Jewish convert trying to avoid persecution from the Inquisition. Implausible speculation undermines credibility.

Huntford, Roland. *Sea of Darkness.* New York: Scribner, 1975. 255pp. Columbus's early sailing career is dramatized, mixing actual accounts with a fanciful voyage to Newfoundland with a Norwegian explorer to learn the skills that will take him across the Atlantic on his own.

Marlowe, Stephen. *The Memoirs of Columbus.* New York: Scribner, 1987. 569pp. In the fanciful memoirs of Columbus, his life expands in a number of imaginative directions, including involvement with the Borgias in Italy, a voyage to Iceland, and

work for Isabella as a secret agent. Not intended as a factual treatment, the novel is nonetheless convincing in its period depiction.

Martin, Robert Stuart. *Accidental Indies.* Montreal: McGill-Queen's University Press, 2000. 128pp. Martin's poetic meditation on Columbus's discoveries uses details from his life to explore the ways in which we imaginatively possess the world and populate it with myths, language, and meaning.

Parini, Jay. *Bay of Arrows.* New York: Holt, 1992. 383pp. In parallel stories of visionary exploiters, a college professor obsesses over a long poem about Columbus, and the first voyage is recreated. Very much dependent on the modern perspective of Columbus as a rapacious imperialist, the novel exposes the hypocrisy of two like-minded egoists.

Posse, Abel. *The Dogs of Paradise.* New York: Atheneum, 1991. 301pp. In the author's second novel in a trilogy on the Spanish conquest of Latin America, Columbus's first voyage is imagined through the lens of magical realism with 1492 revealed as a lethal meeting of cultures.

Recommended Juvenile Biographies

Asimov, Isaac. *Christopher Columbus: Navigator to the New World.* Milwaukee: Gareth Stevens, 1991. 48pp. MG. Asimov's short survey of Columbus's life and voyages offers insight into the technology available to him in a beautifully illustrated book with a brief summary of the controversies surrounding the explorer and a useful glossary of terms.

Dodge, Stephen C. *Christopher Columbus and the First Voyages to the New World.* New York: Chelsea House, 1991. 128pp. MG/YA. Beautifully illustrated, this informative account of Columbus's voyages places his exploration firmly in their historical context.

Fritz, Jean. *Where Do You Think You're Going, Christopher Columbus?* New York: Putnam, 1980. 80pp. MG. Fritz's wry style and humorous approach is still accurate in its history, offering an amusing portrait of a determined Columbus who remained convinced he had found the way to the east and rejected the notion that he discovered a new world.

Meltzer, Milton. *Columbus and the World Around Him.* New York: F. Watts, 1990. 192pp. YA. This serious, well-documented, and perceptive history of Columbus and his four voyages stresses the terrible impact of Columbus and later Spanish explorers and settlers on native cultures.

Pelta, Kathy. *Discovering Columbus: How History Is Invented.* Minneapolis: Lerner, 1991. 192pp. MG/YA. Pelta summarizes the known facts about Columbus before describing how historians have investigated the mysteries surrounding him and how his image often has reflected the subjective aims of his biographers, providing an excellent introduction to historiography.

Biographical Films and Theatrical Adaptations

A&E Biography Video: Christopher Columbus: Explorer of the New World (1995). Producer: Martin Gillam. This is a visually attractive, generally reliable documentary portrait. Video.

Christopher Columbus (1949). Director: David MacDonald. Comprehensive biographical film treatment, stars Fredric March as Columbus in an earnest portrait with strong period flavor. Video.

Christopher Columbus (1985). Director: Alberto Lattuada. This television mini-series is a flaws-and-all treatment with Gabriel Byrne in the title role, an exact replica of the *Santa Maria*, and an impressive cast including Faye Dunaway as Isabella and Nicol Williamson as Ferdinand. Video.

Christopher Columbus: The Discovery (1992). Director: John Glen. Embarrassingly banal big-screen biography with a script credit for Mario Puzo shows Columbus (Georges Corraface) as an intrepid swashbuckler. Marlon Brando sleepwalks through a cameo as Torquemada, Rachel Ward portrays Isabella, and Tom Selleck implausibly impersonates Ferdinand. Video.

Columbus and the Age of Discovery (1991). Producer: Zvi Dor-Ner. In the definitive documentary commemorating the quincentennial, this PBS seven-part series explores the historical context, recreates Columbus's voyages, and analyzes the repercussions. Video. A companion volume by Dor-Ner is available (New York: Morrow, 1991. 370pp.) documenting Columbus's life and times and the author's own experiences sailing a replica of one of Columbus's ships.

1492: Conquest of Paradise (1992). Director: Ridley Scott. Political correctness dominates this big-screen treatment of Columbus's discovery of America with an emphasis on the disastrous effects on native inhabitants. More atmospheric than a reliable chronicle of events. Gérard Depardieu stars as Columbus, with Sigourney Weaver as Isabella. Video.

Other Sources

Bedini, Silvio, ed. *The Christopher Columbus Encyclopedia*. New York: Simon & Schuster, 1992. 2 vols. With more than 400 illustrations and in 350 alphabetically arranged entries, this reference source covers every aspect of Columbus' life and the age of exploration.

105. CONFUCIUS
551 B.C.–479 B.C.

Chinese philosopher and teacher, Confucius was born in what is now Shandong province in an era of great political violence. Troubled by the almost constant warfare among rival states, Confucius developed his own philosophy of morality and political reform that he taught to numerous students and disciples. Largely unknown during his lifetime, the efforts of his disciples, particularly Mencius, helped spread his fame and ideas. His teachings were passed down through the *Analects*, a collection of sayings and dialogues compiled by his disciples.

Autobiography and Primary Sources

The Analects of Confucius. Translated and annotated by Arthur Waley. New York: Vintage, 1970. 257pp. Almost all that we know about Confucius comes from this collection of his sayings, based on an earlier collection of his conversations, published a century or so after his death.

Recommended Biographies

Creel, H.G. *Confucius: The Man and the Myth*. New York: J. Day, 1949. 363pp. Rejecting the traditional sources on Confucius's life as unreliable, Creel uses his detailed knowledge of Chinese literature to fashion an authoritative reconstruction of Confucius the man, teacher, and philosopher in a well-documented, critical study. In Creel's view, Confucius should be seen as a revolutionary visionary and a forerunner of democratic ideals.

Liu, Wu-Chi. *Confucius, His Life and Time*. New York: Philosophical Library, 1955. 189pp. Liu incorporates and expands the earliest biography of Confucius into a helpful narrative to uncover the historical and human figure, along with a wider context of Confucius's times to help understand the forces that helped shape his ideas. Unlike Creel, who views Confucius as liberal and proto-democratic, Liu sees him as a conservative and preserver of feudal order.

Other Biographical Studies

Dawson, Raymond. *Confucius*. New York: Hill & Wang, 1982. 95pp. Part of the respected Past Masters series, this compact summary of Confucius's life, ideas, and influence is a useful introductory overview.

Lin, Yutang, ed. *The Wisdom of Confucius*. New York: Modern Library, 1938. 290pp. This useful compilation includes a translation of the earliest life of Confucius by Ssu-ma Ch'ien, written around 100 B.C.

Smith, D. Howard. *Confucius*. New York: Scribner, 1973. 240pp. With only a single chapter devoted to a biographical sketch of Confucius's life, the emphasis here is a reconstruction of the historical setting and the evolution of Confucius's teachings. Valuable as a introductory study, the book demonstrates detailed familiarity with early Chinese sources.

Wilhelm, Richard. *Confucius and Confucianism*. New York: Harcourt, Brace, 1931. 181pp. Written by a noted sinologist, this compact scholarly volume includes a translation of the oldest known biographical portrait of Confucius, a critical discussion of his teachings, and excerpts from some of his writings.

Biographical Novels

Chunli, Qu. *The Life of Confucius*. Beijing: Foreign Language Press, 1996. 645pp. This biographical novel depicts Confucius's life from birth to death, incorporating historical documents and folklore to create a rich portrait of the man and his time.

Inoue, Yashushi. *Confucius: A Novel*. Chester Springs, Pennsylvania: Dufour Editions, 1992. 168pp. Told from the perspective of one of his disciples in a series of lectures to students, Confucius is imaginatively captured in a series of vignettes, interwoven with documented dialogue taken from the *Analects*.

Fictional Portraits

Vidal, Gore. *Creation*. New York: Random House, 1981. 510pp. In Vidal's philosophical panorama, a diplomat from the Persian court undertakes a mission to India and China and his search for life's meaning brings him in contact with Buddha, Confucius, and Socrates.

Recommended Juvenile Biographies

Hoobler, Thomas, and Dorothy Hoobler. *Confucianism*. New York: Facts on File, 1993. 128pp. YA. Describes how Confucius's teachings evolved from principles of social order to a religion that has dominated Chinese culture.

Kelen, Betty. *Confucius: In Life and Legend*. New York: T. Nelson, 1971. 160pp. MG/YA. Kelen relates Confucius's ideas and development helpfully to his culture and era.

Sims, Bennett B. *Confucius*. New York: F. Watts, 1968. 139pp. MG/YA. This is a straightforward recounting of the factual and legendary sources on Confucius's background and the meaning of his precepts.

Biographical Films and Theatrical Adaptations

A&E Biography Video: Confucius: Words of Wisdom. Producer: Steven R. Talley. Traces Confucius's life from his impoverished childhood through his years as a revered teacher, using interviews with leading scholars, period illustrations, and location footage. Video.

The Life and Thought of Confucius (1980). Producer: Shan-Yuan Hsieh. A film profile of Confucius's life, times, and leading ideas. Video.

106. JOSEPH CONRAD
1857–1924

Born Jósef Teodor Konrad Walecz Korzeniowski of Polish parents, Joseph Conrad became one of the greatest novelists and prose stylists in English. He went to sea in 1874 and became a master mariner in the British merchant service in 1884. Conrad began his writing career in 1894 after his health declined following a stint as a riverboat captain in the Congo. His most notable works including *Lord Jim* (1900), *Heart of Darkness* (1902), *Nostromo* (1904), and *The Secret Agent* (1907).

Autobiography and Primary Sources

Conrad's most explicit autobiographical writings are *The Mirror of the Sea* (New York: Harper, 1906. 328pp.), which offers his reflections on the sea, and *A Personal Record* (Garden City, New York: Doubleday, 1925. 138pp.), in which Conrad supplies his own interpretation of several important events in his life, though his reliability should be checked with more objective sources.

Collected Letters. Frederick R. Karl and Laurence Davies, eds. New York: Cambridge University Press, 1983-90. 5 vols. Essential primary sources for Conrad's biographers and for the reader interested in a firsthand view of the author.

Recommended Biographies

Karl, Frederick R. *Joseph Conrad: The Three Lives.* New York: Farrar, Straus, 1979. 1,008pp. Karl, one of the editors of Conrad's letters, relies on them extensively in the most detailed biography available. More reliable than the earlier book by Jean-Aubry and more psychologically astute than Baines, Karl is particularly strong on Conrad's Polish years. Readers may find his dispensing with a more traditional chronological narrative for flashing back and forward somewhat confusing.

Meyers, Jeffrey. *Joseph Conrad: A Biography.* New York: Scribner, 1991. 428pp. Relying on a good deal of previously unpublished material, Meyers provides a lively and readable narrative that sheds new light on Conrad's seafaring career, his marriage, and literary friendships. Less daunting than Karl's massive study, Meyers is no less revealing in his psychological profile.

Najder, Zdzislaw. *Joseph Conrad: A Chronicle.* New Brunswick, New Jersey: Rutgers University Press, 1981. 647pp. A lucid, comprehensive account of Conrad's entire life and career with new, detailed, and authoritative information on Conrad's Polish background. With Conrad's various contradictions displayed, Najder offers a rounded portrait that does not reduce his subject to a single theory or interpretation.

Other Biographical Studies

Allen, Jerry. *The Thunder and the Sunshine: A Biography of Joseph Conrad.* New York: Putnam, 1958. 256pp. In Allen's somewhat fragmentary biography, some aspects of Conrad's life are given exhaustive treatment while others are ignored. A thesis dominates the book that the character Rita in Conrad's autobiographical novel *The Arrow of Gold* was actually Paula de Somoggy, mistress of Don Carlos, pretender to the Spanish throne, a contention that has been challenged by other scholars. In *The Sea Years of Joseph Conrad.* (Garden City, New York: Doubleday, 1965. 368pp.) Allen documents with encyclopedic thoroughness Conrad's life at sea and suggests prototypes for the novelist's fictional characters.

Baines, Jocelyn. *Joseph Conrad: A Critical Biography.* New York: McGraw-Hill, 1959. 523pp. In the first important scholarly biography, which has become a standard text in Conrad studies, Baines provides an analysis of the writer's works in relationship to the events of his life. A fuller and rounder portrait than its predecessors, Baines's book corrects several misconceptions advanced by Conrad himself, notably that he was shot in a duel. Instead Baines provides evidence that Conrad shot himself in despair over gambling loses. Information on Conrad's life is now more detailed and authoritative in later books, but Baines's critical analysis remains valuable.

Batchelor, John. *The Life of Joseph Conrad: A Critical Biography.* Cambridge, Massachusetts: Blackwell, 1996. 335pp. The author provides little new information but supplies a reliable compendium of facts from earlier biographers, augmented by a series of fresh critical readings of the works.

Coolidge, Olivia E. *The Three Lives of Joseph Conrad.* Boston: Houghton Mifflin, 1972. 230pp. Informative and perceptive, but now somewhat superseded by later biographies, Coolidge's comprehensive life includes a critical analysis of Conrad's stories and novels.

Conrad, Jessie. *Conrad and His Circle.* New York: Dutton, 1935. 162pp. Conrad's wife provides an intimate account of their life together from 1894 to his death. Valuable for its domestic details and information about Conrad's literary friendships.

Curle, Richard. *The Last Twelve Years of Joseph Conrad.* New York: Doubleday, 1928. 212pp. One of Conrad's intimate friends provides a loving tribute and meditation on their relationship.

Jean-Aubry, Georges. *The Sea Dreamer: A Definitive Biography of Joseph Conrad.* Garden City, New York: Doubleday, 1957. 321pp. Best regarded as a compendium of facts about Conrad's life and career rather than an interpretive synthesis of them.

Meyer, Bernard C. *Joseph Conrad: A Psychoanalytic Biography.* Princeton, New Jersey: Princeton University Press, 1967. 396pp. In Meyer's view Conrad's art served an important psychological function offering a corrective for painful personal trauma. Meyer provides a full-scale clinical analysis that is jargon-laden, with Conrad's elusive genius reduced to a number of fixations, fetishes, and complexes.

Sherry, Norman. *Conrad and His World.* London: Thames and Hudson, 1972. 128pp. This comprehensive illustrated biography includes a lucid chronological narrative by a recognized authority on Conrad's life and art.

Tennant, Roger. *Joseph Conrad: A Biography.* New York: Atheneum, 1981. 276pp. Providing no new facts about Conrad, the book instead disentangles them from the fiction surrounding Conrad, along with a psychologically credible portrait of the man from an admirer. Presents how and why Conrad's books were written rather than offering an assessment.

Watts, Cedric. *Joseph Conrad: A Literary Life.* New York: St. Martin's, 1989. 156pp. Part of the useful Literary Lives series, Watts looks comprehensively at Conrad's professional career, providing useful information on his writing practices, the publishing history of the books, and his literary relationships.

Biographical Films and Theatrical Adaptations

The Modern World: Ten Great Writers (1988). Director: David Thomas. An installment of the London Weekend Television series that looks at Conrad's life and literary career. Video.

Other Sources

Knowles, Owen, ed. *A Conrad Chronology.* Boston: G.K. Hall, 1990. 165pp. This is an extensive record of Conrad's activities based on a careful review of the available sources and a convenient reference aid.

Orr, Leonard, and Ted Billy, eds. *A Joseph Conrad Companion.* Westport, Connecticut: Greenwood, 1999. 346pp. This is thorough reference guide to both Conrad's writings and experiences.

Stape, J.H., ed. *The Cambridge Companion to Joseph Conrad.* New York: Cambridge University Press, 1996. 258pp. Various Conrad specialists offer insightful essays on a number of topics connected with the novelist's life, character, and works.

107. JOHN CONSTABLE
1776–1837

An English painter and, along with J.M.W. Turner, the most renowned nineteenth-century landscape painter, Constable began studying at the Royal Academy at the age of 23. His paintings were popular in France but were modestly received in England, and he was tardily admitted to the Royal Academy in 1829. His work influenced the Barbizon school and includes *The View on the Stour* (1819) and *The Hay Wain* (1821). Both paintings were exhibited at the Salon in Paris and won gold medals.

Autobiography and Primary Sources

Correspondence. R.B. Beckett, ed. London: H.M. Stationery Office, 1962-68. 6 vols. Constable's letters have been collected in this multivolume series, invaluable for their biographical details.

Recommended Biographies

Fraser, John L. *John Constable 1776–1837: The Man and His Mistress.* London: Hutchinson, 1976. 253pp. Fraser's is a scholarly, well-documented biography that synthesizes available sources into a thorough, balanced portrait of the artist.

Leslie, Charles R. *Memoirs of the Life of John Constable, Esq., R.A., Composed Chiefly of His Letters.* 1843. Revised ed. London: Phaidon, 1951. 423pp. The first biography of Constable remains one of the best. The book is based on selections from his letters and journals with a commentary by a longtime friend of the painter. The book remains an important biographical source of firsthand information. The 1951 edition, edited by Jonathan Mayne, points out the discrepancies between Leslie's versions and the original texts of the letters.

Reynolds, Graham. *Constable: The Natural Painter.* New York: McGraw-Hill, 1965. 238pp. The author, a keeper of the Constable collection in the Victoria and Albert Museum, provides a scholarly, well-written, brief but effective overview of Constable's life and artistic achievement.

Other Biographical Studies

Gadney, Reg. *Constable and His World.* New York: W.W. Norton, 1976. 128pp. Gadney's brief narrative account of Constable's life stresses his relationships with other painters, particularly Turner, along with some background on the art world of

Constable's era. Black-and-white illustrations of the painter's residences, friends, and works by the painter and his contemporaries supplement the text.

Shirley, Andrew. *The Rainbow: A Portrait of John Constable*. London: M. Joseph, 1949. 228pp. Shirley adds to the view of the painter insights from a number of previously untapped sources that give a more balanced and human sense of Constable with his flaws intact.

Windsor, Robert G.W.C. *John Constable I.R.A.* New York: Scribner, 1903. 231p. Windsor supplements Leslie's account with additional primary and secondary sources for a less partisan and more objective portrait of the painter.

108. CONSTANTINE THE GREAT
ca. AD 280–337

Roman emperor, Constantine was the son of Constantius I and Helena, who on the death of his father allied with Licinius for control of the empire. Constantine defeated Maxentius in 312 when Constantine, already sympathetic toward Christianity, adopted the cross as his symbol. In 312 the Edict of Milan removed the ban on Christianity throughout the empire. Constantine gained sole control over the empire in 324, and he began a program of administrative reforms to strengthen his regime's power. He moved his capital to Byzantium in 330, which was rebuilt as Constantinople. Constantine has been variously judged as a devout Christian convert or a political opportunist who used Christianity to unify his empire. What is uncontestable is that Constantine was one of the most influential rulers of antiquity during a turning point in Western history.

Recommended Biographies

Grant, Michael. *Constantine the Great: The Man and His Times*. New York: Scribner, 1994. 267pp. Embodying the latest scholarship, Grant's critical assessment of Constantine and his achievement is presented in a readable narrative that serves to untangle the political, religious, and cultural issues of his times. Recommended as the preferred introduction to Constantine and his age.

Kousoulas, D. George. *The Life and Times of Constantine the Great*. New York: Routledge, 1997. 511pp. In a vivid and dramatic reconstruction of Constantine's life written for the general reader, the author draws extensively on primary Latin and Greek sources to detail a complex figure enmeshed in an equally complex period of history that the book helpfully animates and clarifies.

Smith, John H. *Constantine the Great*. New York: Scribner, 1971. 359pp. Through careful use of primary sources, Smith provides a detailed yet readable attempt to get close to Constantine the man. He displays a not wholly admirable figure but a mixture of strengths and flaws. Smith is best on Constantine's involvement with Christianity and in his assessment of the ways legend and myth have distorted our view of Constantine.

Other Biographical Studies

Baker, George P. *Constantine the Great and the Christian Revolution*. New York: Dodd, Mead, 1930. 351pp. Baker's vivid and readable narrative of events in Constantine's reign emphasizes the role Constantine played in the evolution of modern Europe and the shift from paganism to Christianity. The book is particularly good on his family life, personal characteristics, religious experiences, and imperial policies.

Burckhardt, Jacob. *The Age of Constantine the Great*. 1853. Reprint ed. Berkeley: University of California Press, 1983. 400pp. Burckhardt's classic in historiography is not strictly speaking a biography but a close and detailed analysis of the period tracing the last phase of paganism and the rise of Christianity. Constantine's reign is masterfully portrayed by a distinguished Swiss historian who locates Constantine's motivation in his politic ambition rather than his religious fervor.

Dörries, Hermann. *Constantine the Great*. New York: Harper & Row, 1972. 250pp. In a concise but comprehensive portrait, Constantine emerges as a sympathetic figure as emperor and Christian champion. The emphasis here is theological, placing Constantine in the context of the religious beliefs of his time and his development as a Christian.

Firth, John B. *Constantine the Great: The Reorganization of the Empire and the Triumph of the Church*. New York: Putnam, 1905. 368pp. The first comprehensive biography in English, Firth's study has long been regarded as standard and a model of erudition by a classicist steeped in the period.

Gibbon, Edward. *The History of the Decline and Fall of the Roman Empire*. Reprint ed. New York: Modern Library, 1983. 3 vols. Gibbon devotes five chapters of his classic study to Constantine's life and reign.

Holsapple, Lloyd B. *Constantine the Great*. New York: Sheed & Ward, 1942. 475pp. In a solid recreation of Constantine's life and times, the author does not claim more than probability for many of his surmises. His approach is reasonable, but he betrays a strong Roman Catholic bias that limits objectivity.

Jones, Arnold H. *Constantine and the Conversion of Europe*. New York: Macmillan, 1948. 271pp. In a compact and readable account, Jones describes the chief political, military, economic, and religious events from Diocletian's accession to Constantine's death with an assessment of the emperor's character and achievement. Part of the Teach Yourself History series, Jones's introductory study is a marvel of clarity and compression.

MacMullen, Ramsay. *Constantine*. New York: Dial Press, 1969. 263pp. Describing the life, times, and achievements of Constantine in a balanced though overall sympathetic portrait, MacMullen provides one of the best general introductions for the nonspecialist. Without footnotes and with many quotes unattributed, MacMullen has less to offer the more expert reader.

Pohlsander, Hans A. *The Emperor Constantine*. New York: Routledge, 1996. 128pp. A compact and useful introduction to Constantine's life and times, Pohlsander's volume is intended for the un-

dergraduate but is also helpful for the general reader looking for more than the typical textbook coverage.

Biographical Novels

De Wohl, Louis. *The Living Wood*. Philadelphia: Lippincott, 1947. 318pp. In this romantic and reverential novel of the family history of Emperor Constantine and the search for the true cross, Helena is the central character. Her son is given a more balanced presentation.

Slaughter, Frank G. *Constantine: The Miracle of the Flaming Cross*. Garden City, New York: Doubleday, 1965. 430pp. Taking few liberties with history, the novel chronicles the career of Constantine, offering a clear background of the period and making the complex doctrinal battles of the early Christians understandable.

Recommended Juvenile Biographies

Killingray, Margaret. *Constantine*. Saint Paul, Minnesota: Greenhaven Press, 1980. 32pp. MG/YA. Part of the Greenhaven World History Program, this concise outline covers Constantine's life, reign, and era, supplemented with primary documents from a variety of historical sources.

Walworth, Nancy Z. *Constantine*. New York: Chelsea House, 1989. 111pp. MG/YA. This is a sensible and informative biographical and historical profile in which the events of Constantine's life are helpfully related to his times.

Biographical Films and Theatrical Adaptations

Sayers, Dorothy L. *The Emperor Constantine: A Chronicle*. London: Gollancz, 1951. 192pp. Sayers's chronicle play employs many scenes and a large cast to dramatize incidents in the life of Constantine from 305 to 307. Her history is sound while her religious sentiment is deep and sincere.

109. JAMES COOK
1728–1779

English explorer and navigator, Captain James Cook circumnavigated the earth two and a half times in a series of adventurous voyages that charted much of unknown Pacific. On his third voyage, he was killed by natives on the Hawaiian islands.

Autobiography and Primary Sources

The Journals of Captain James Cook on His Voyages of Discovery. J.C. Beaglehole, ed. Cambridge, Massachusetts: Cambridge University Press, 1955–1974. 4 vols. Cook's journals offer a version of his autobiography at least in regard to a chronology of his exploits, though the private man is studiously missing from his factual record.

Recommended Biographies

Beaglehole, J.C. *The Life of Captain Cook*. Stanford, California: Stanford University Press, 1974. 760pp. In this meticulous and exhaustive chronicle of Cook's life and career, the author accounts for Cook's every move, but curiously in such a massive study still mostly fails to capture Cook's human side. Essential for its documentation of the factual record.

Hough, Ralph. *Captain James Cook.* New York: W.W. Norton, 1994. 398pp. A more compact and readable account than Beaglehole's, this thoroughly researched biography provides new insights and interpretations based on the author's firsthand exploration of the sites associated with Cook's discoveries.

Other Biographical Studies

MacLean, Alistair. *Captain Cook.* Garden City, New York: Doubleday, 1972. 192pp. A popular and general account of Cook's early apprenticeship, his development as a navigator and cartographer, and his explorations. The text is workmanlike, but the real value here is in the book's illustrations.

Obeyesekere, Gananath. *The Apotheosis of Captain Cook: European Mythmaking in the Pacific.* Princeton, New Jersey: Princeton University Press, 1992. 251pp. In a provocative reassessment of Cook's death and the events leading up to it, the author, using journals and logs kept by Cook and his officers, debunks the commonly held notion that Cook was viewed as a god by the native population. Obeyesekere sees Cook's destructive side as responsible for his demise and challenges the presuppositions that go into writing history and anthropology.

Villiers, Alan. *Captain James Cook.* New York: Scribner, 1967. 307pp. The author, one of the world's foremost sailing masters, establishes an authenticity to his account of Cook's sea challenges and nautical genius. Adds a realistic dimension to the hazards Cook faced that is absent in other accounts.

Withey, Lynne. *Voyages of Discovery: Captain Cook and the Exploration of the Pacific.* New York: Morrow, 1987. 512pp. Withey's detailed chronicle of Cook's voyages sets his discoveries in the wider context of the impact of the European influence in the Pacific and Cook's ambivalent legacy.

Biographical Novels

Blunden, Godfrey. *Charco Harbour.* New York: Vanguard, 1968. 401pp. Cook's voyage to the South Seas and the first landfall in Australia are treated. Cook emerges as a complex individual, and the novel is scrupulously researched to produce believable scenes and characters.

Innes, Hammond. *The Last Voyage: Captain Cook's Lost Diary.* New York: Knopf, 1979. 253pp. The novel imagines what Cook might have reflected in a private journal of his fatal final voyage. The facts are accurately portrayed, but the attempt to arrive at the actual Cook beyond his legend is less successful.

Bushnell, Oswald Andrew. *The Return of Lono: A Novel of Captain Cook's Last Voyage.* Boston: Little, Brown, 1956. 290pp. Based on multiple journal accounts of Cook's end, the novel recreates the events that led to Cook's murder by natives who first regarded him as a god.

Recommended Juvenile Biographies

Blumberg, Rhoda. *The Remarkable Voyages of Captain Cook.* New York: Bradbury, 1991. 138pp. MG. This is a highly readable and superbly illustrated account by a Newbery Honor Book winner.

Kent, Zachary. *James Cook.* Chicago: Childrens Press, 1991. 128pp. MG. Part of the excellent World's Great Explorers series, this is a clear summary of Cook's career and introduction to the Pacific world.

Latham, Jean Lee. *Far Voyager: The Story of James Cook.* New York: Harper & Row, 1970. 242pp. YA. Recommended as an informative and reliable account.

110. CALVIN COOLIDGE
1872–1933

The thirtieth U.S. president, Coolidge practiced law in Northampton, Massachusetts, entered state politics as a Republican, and was mayor of Northampton (1910–1911), state senator (1912–1915), state lieutenant governor (1919–1921), and governor (1919–1920). Elected vice president with Warren G. Harding, he succeeded to the presidency after Harding's death (1923) and easily won a full term in 1924. His administration was marked by probusiness policies, and he encouraged the reckless stock market speculation of the late 1920s. He sponsored the Kellogg-Briand Pact (1927) outlawing war.

Autobiography and Primary Sources

The Autobiography of Calvin Coolidge. New York: Cosmopolitan, 1929. 246pp. Because he destroyed most of his private papers, Coolidge remains enigmatic in essential ways. His memoir, though as reserved and distant as the man, is the closest glimpse we get of his views.

Recommended Biographies

Ferrell, Robert H. *The Presidency of Calvin Coolidge.* Lawrence: University Press of Kansas, 1998. 244pp. Called the definitive account of the Coolidge era, Ferrell's is a well-researched study of American policy and society during the 1920s that succeeds in a balanced assessment of Coolidge's character and presidential leadership or lack thereof.

McCoy, Donald R. *Calvin Coolidge: The Quiet President.* New York: Macmillan, 1967. 472pp. McCoy's balanced assessment of the man and his public career is thorough and highly readable. In the author's view, Coolidge reflected his era and by blaming him for what he was, the critic is really faulting the America of his time.

Sobel, Robert. *Coolidge: An American Enigma.* Washington, DC: Regnery, 1998. 462pp. In Sobel's revisionist view, Coolidge is depicted very differently from his conventional image as a naive, do-nothing president and makes a strong case for his achievements. Even if the reader does not fully accept Sobel's often unverifiable assertions, the book presents a provocative reassessment that adds considerable depth and complexity to the previous simplistic view of the man and his leadership.

Other Biographical Studies

Fuess, Claude M. *Calvin Coolidge: The Man from Vermont.* Boston: Little, Brown, 1940. 522pp. An authorized biography that drew on family and domestic details supplied by his wife, Grace Anna Coolidge, Fuess's study is an extended, though modest, defense of the man and his actions. The book devotes considerable space to Coolidge's background and years before arriving on the national scene.

White, William A. *Calvin Coolidge: The Man Who Is President.* New York: Macmillan, 1925. 252pp.; *A Puritan in Babylon: The Story of Calvin Coolidge.* New York: Macmillan, 1938. 460pp. White's journalistic efforts attempt to penetrate Coolidge's famous reserve to find the man behind the persona. The 1938 book is the more detailed, drawing on interviews with Coolidge and those who knew him.

Recommended Juvenile Biographies

Kent, Zachary. *Calvin Coolidge: Thirtieth President of the United States.* Chicago: Childrens Press, 1988. 98pp. MG. A workmanlike summary of Coolidge's life and political career.

Stevens, Rita. *Calvin Coolidge: 30th President of the United States.* Ada, Oklahoma: Garrett, 1990. 122pp. MG. Stevens presents an informative biographical and historical portrait of Coolidge's career and his age.

Biographical Films and Theatrical Adaptations

The Court Martial of Billy Mitchell (1955). Director: Otto Preminger. This taut courtroom drama depicting the secret trial of Billy Mitchell (Gary Cooper) features an appearance by Calvin Coolidge played by Ian Wolfe. Video.

Other Sources

Moran, Philip R., ed. *Calvin Coolidge, 1872–1933: Chronology, Documents, Bibliographical Aids.* Dobbs Ferry, New York: Oceana, 1970. 144pp. This is a valuable collection of the most important presidential papers as well as a detailed chronology and annotated listing of source materials.

111. JAMES FENIMORE COOPER
1789–1851

Considered the first major U.S. novelist, Cooper is known for his stories about the American frontier. After his dismissal from Yale for disciplinary reasons, Cooper went to sea and was commissioned as a midshipman. He served until 1811 and then married and settled as a gentleman farmer. His first popular novel was *The Spy* (1821) but he became famous for his series of *Leatherstocking Tales* (1823-1841), which include *The Pioneers, The Last of the Mohicans, The Prairie, The Pathfinder,* and *The Deerslayer*. He also wrote sea novels and works of social criticism.

Autobiography and Primary Sources

The Letters and Journals of James Fenimore Cooper. James F. Beard, ed. Cambridge, Massachusetts: Harvard University Press, 1960–1968. 6 vols. This impressive scholarly collection features Beard's expert and extensive biographical comments and documentation. Essential for the scholar and serious student of Cooper and his era.

Recommended Biographies

Grossman, James. *James Fenimore Cooper.* Stanford, California: Stanford University Press, 1949. 292pp. Grossman's balanced and well-documented critical biography has long served as the standard modern life. Cooper's public career is carefully presented with the writer's many sides judiciously displayed.

Railton, Stephen. *Fenimore Cooper: A Study of His Life and Imagination.* Princeton, New Jersey: Princeton University Press, 1978. 282pp. Making fresh use of Beard's scholarly collection of Cooper's letters and journals, Railton provides a controversial psychological exploration of Cooper's complex identity. In the author's view, the writer's relationship with his father becomes the key to understanding many of the events in Cooper's life. The book's emphasis on Cooper's private life makes it an ideal complement to Grossman's insightful chronicle of the writer's public career.

Other Biographical Studies

Boynton, Henry W. *James Fenimore Cooper.* 1931. Reprint ed. New York: Frederick Ungar, 1966. 408pp. The first biographer with access to the Cooper family archives and the first published edition of Cooper's correspondence, Boynton's is a rousing defense of Cooper's character, though the writer's flaws are not glossed over. The result is a credible, human portrait.

Dekker, George. *James Fenimore Cooper: The American Scott.* New York: Barnes and Noble, 1967. 265pp. Dekker's is a solid critical study emphasizing Cooper's literary achievement. The book is particularly strong in relating Cooper's writings to his era, explaining both the novelist's popularity and influence.

Long, Robert E. *James Fenimore Cooper.* New York: Continuum, 1990. 213pp. Part of the Literature and Life series, Long's brief account provides coverage of Cooper's life and career before proceeding to a critical evaluation of his major works.

Lounsbury, Thomas R. *James Fenimore Cooper.* Boston: Houghton Mifflin, 1883. 306pp. The first full-length biography, Lounsbury provides a generally reliable account of Cooper's life, though without access to any family documents. Lack of sympathy for Cooper's personality and achievement contributes to a generally negative tone in the author's treatment.

Spiller, Robert E. *Fenimore Cooper: Critic of His Times.* New York: Minton Balch, 1931. 337pp. Less a biography than an intellectual history, Spiller emphasizes Cooper's role as a social critic,

tracing the origin of his ideas and their connections with his times.

Walker, Warren S. *James Fenimore Cooper: An Introduction and Interpretation.* New York: Barnes and Noble, 1962. 142pp. Walker's is an excellent concise overview of Cooper's life and artistic achievement, serving the general reader well.

Biographical Films and Theatrical Adaptations

Poe/Cooper/Irving (1987). Producer: January Productions. Part of the Meet the Classic Authors series, each of the three American writers is profiled. Video.

112. NICOLAS COPERNICUS
1473–1543

The Polish astronomer whose heliocentric hypothesis of the universe led to the Copernican Revolution and laid the foundations of modern astronomy, Copernicus was lay canon of the cathedral at Frauenburg, East Prussia, and practiced medicine. His towering work, *De revolutionibus orbium coelestium*, with its suggestion that the earth revolved around the sun, challenged Ptolemy's widely accepted geocentric theory of the universe. Copernicus's treatise was probably completed in 1530 and was published when its author lay on his deathbed.

Autobiography and Primary Sources

Birkenmajer, Ludwik A. *Nicolas Copernicus.* Ann Arbor, Michigan: UMI Research Press, 1975. 966pp. Including most of the known biographical material, Birkenmajer's is the most thorough scholarly reference source, despite its numerous translation errors.

Recommended Biographies

Rosen, Edward. *Copernicus and the Scientific Revolution.* Malabar, Florida: Krieger, 1984. 220pp. This is the most reliable, objective summary of what is known about Copernicus's life based on documentary evidence that is lucidly translated. Supplementing the considerable gaps in the biographical record, the book places Copernicus's challenges and achievements in their historical context.

Other Biographical Studies

Armitage, Angus. *Sun, Stand Thou Still: The Life and Work of Copernicus, Astronomer.* New York: Schuman, 1947. 210pp. Armitage, one of the twentieth-century's leading Copernicus scholars, offers an accessible and reliable summary of what is known about the astronomer's life and work. The book is an expansion of the author's earlier, *Copernicus: The Founder of Modern Astronomy* (New York: W.W. Norton, 1940. 183pp.).

Hoyle, Fred. *Nicholaus Copernicus: An Essay on His Life and Work.* New York: Harper & Row, 1973. 94pp. The work of an astronomer, Hoyle's is a brief summary more reliable on the work than the life, incorporating details that have been invali-

dated by modern scholarship or that are simply wrong. The book does serve to make accessible to a nonspecialist the challenges Copernicus faced and the progression of his ideas.

Koestler, Arthur. *The Sleepwalkers: A History of Man's Changing Vision of the Universe.* New York: Macmillan, 1959. 624pp. Koestler's often belittling look at Copernicus, Kepler, and Galileo is a popular but flawed account, marred by errors of fact and distortions to fit the book's thesis emphasizing the discrepancies between the achievements of these men and their personal limitations.

Biographical Novels

Banville, John. *Doctor Copernicus.* New York: W.W. Norton, 1976. 241pp. Banville's inventive fictional recreation of Copernicus's life and times stresses the high personal cost of his discovery that the Earth is not the center of the universe.

Recommended Juvenile Biographies

Veglahn, Nancy. *Dance of the Planets: The Universe of Nicolas Copernicus.* New York: Coward-McCann, 1979. 63pp. MG. This is a helpful and informative look at Copernicus, his achievement, and his era.

113. HERNÁN CORTÉS
1485–1547

A Spanish explorer and conquistador, Cortés went to Hispaniola (1504) and joined (1511) in the conquest of Cuba. In 1519 he led an expedition to explore the Yucatán and then marched on the Aztec capital, Tenochtitlán, where he took the Aztec emperor, Montezuma, prisoner. During an Aztec uprising against the Spaniards, Montezuma was killed and Cortés was forced to retreat. He returned in 1521 and conquered the capital, causing the fall of the Aztec empire. Cortés extended Spanish conquest into the rest of Mexico and North Central America, including Honduras.

Recommended Biographies

Madariaga, Salvador de. *Hernán Cortés: Conqueror of Mexico.* New York: Macmillan, 1941. 554pp. Combining a biography of Cortés with a history of the conquest of Mexico, this is a learned, accessible study, balanced in its approach, offering both the Spanish and the Aztec perspective.

Marks, Richard L. *Cortés: The Great Adventurer and the Fate of Aztec Mexico.* New York: Knopf, 1993. 347pp. Marks covers Cortés's early life in Spain and Cuba, as well as his postconquest years, though the book is mainly an extensive treatment of the invasion of Mexico.

Thomas, Hugh. *Conquest: Montezuma, Cortés, and the Fall of Old Mexico.* New York: Simon & Schuster, 1993. 812pp. Thomas supplies a highly detailed narrative history of the conquest with Cortés as the central figure in which his flaws as well as his achievements are acknowledged.

Other Biographical Studies

Collis, Maurice. *Cortés and Montezuma.* New York: Harcourt, Brace, 1955. 256pp. Collis's is a rousing narrative history of the conquest with a dual character study of the main antagonists. The book emphasizes the drama inherent in the story of the invasion and its cultural conflict with a perceptive analysis of both men's strengths and limitations.

Diaz del Castillo, Bernal. *The Discovery and Conquest of Mexico.* New York: Da Capo Press, 1996. 478pp. First published in Spain in 1632, the author supplements his own experience with Cortés's letters and contemporary documents to paint a highly critical portrait of the Spanish conqueror.

Gomara, Francesco Lopez de. *Cortés: The Life of the Conqueror by His Secretary.* Berkeley: University of California Press, 1964. 425pp. Cortés's secretary provides a far more sympathetic portrait than that of Diaz, and the book serves as an interesting contrast, stressing the heroic qualities of the conqueror.

Prescott, William H. *History of the Conquest of Mexico.* 1843. Reprint ed. New York: Dent, 1962. 2 vols. Prescott's highly influential and popular treatment of Cortés and the conquest is based on solid research but emphasizes the Spanish perspective in the confrontation with a barely understood primitive culture. The color and sweep of Prescott's narrative are hard to resist, despite its cultural limitations and Western bias.

White, Jon E.M. *Cortés and the Downfall of the Aztec Empire.* New York: Saint Martin's, 1971. 352pp. White's is a popular, though well-researched, account of Cortés and his times intended for the general reader. Although pro-Cortés in its sympathy, the book does not neglect Montezuma, and both men are viewed from the perspective of their cultures, with their strengths and weaknesses depicted equally.

Biographical Novels

Baron, Alexander. *The Golden Princess.* New York: Washburn, 1954. 378pp. Cortés's relationship with his Aztec interpreter is treated in a depiction of the two-year period from the establishment of Vera Cruz to the assault on Mexico City.

Marshall, Edison. *Cortez and Marina.* Garden City, New York: Doubleday, 1963. 461pp. Cortés narrates the events of the conquest of Mexico and his relationship with his Aztec mistress and interpreter.

Passuth, Laszlo. *Tialoc Weeps for Mexico.* San Francisco: Pacific, 1987. 487pp. Cortés is shown in action during the conquest of Mexico.

Portillo, José Lopez. *They Are Coming: The Conquest of Mexico.* 1987. Reprint ed. Denton: University of North Texas Press, 1992. 400pp. The alternate perspectives of Montezuma and Cortés are used to dramatize the clash of cultures and the eventual defeat of the Aztecs.

Shedd, Margaret C. *Malinche and Cortés.* Garden City, New York: Doubleday, 1971. 308pp. Malinche, Cortés's Aztec mistress, recounts her life with the Spanish conqueror.

Somerlott, Robert. *Death of the Fifth Sun.* New York: Viking, 1987. 504pp. Somerlott offers yet another take on Cortés's relationship with his Aztec mistress and an authentic depiction of Aztec customs and the details of the Spanish conquest.

Fictional Portraits

Highwater, Jamake. *The Sun, He Dies: A Novel about the End of the Aztec World.* Philadelphia: Lippincott, 1980. 319pp. The Spanish conquest is described from the perspective of the chief orator for Montezuma.

Jennings, Gary. *Aztec.* New York: Atheneum, 1980. 754pp. Jennings's panoramic look at Aztec culture features a detailed look at the arrival and eventual triumph of the Spanish under Cortés.

Shellabarger, Samuel. *Captain from Castile.* Boston: Little, Brown, 1945. 532pp. Shellabarger's adventure classic features a major role for Cortés during the conquest of Mexico.

Recommended Juvenile Biographies

Lilley, Stephen R. *Hernando Cortés.* San Diego: Lucent Books, 1996. 112pp. MG. Lilley's is a well-researched biographical and historical account that relies heavily on excerpts from contemporary sources.

Marrin, Albert. *Aztecs and Spaniards: Cortés and the Conquest of Mexico.* New York: Atheneum, 1986. 212pp. MG/YA. Using quotes from observers, Marrin offers a balanced perspective on the conquest that is fair to both sides.

Wepman, Dennis. *Hernán Cortés.* New York: Chelsea House, 1986. 115pp. MG/YA. Usefully illustrated with a clear and informative text, Wepman offers a helpful account that relates Cortés's life and career to the standards of his times.

Biographical Films and Theatrical Adaptations

Captain from Castile (1947). Director: Henry King. Film adaptation of Shellabarger's adventure classic has Tyrone Power in the starring role with Cortés played by Cesar Romero. Video.

114. STEPHEN CRANE
1871–1900

A novelist, poet, and short-story writer often considered the first modern American writer, Crane's first novel was *Maggie: A Girl of the Streets* (1893). He lived in poverty in New York City as a freelance writer until the publication of his next novel, *The Red Badge of Courage* (1895) brought him fame. Crane served as a foreign correspondent in Cuba and in Greece, and died of tuberculosis in Germany at the age of 28.

Autobiography and Primary Sources

The Correspondence of Stephen Crane. Stanley Wertheim and Paul Sorrentino, eds. New York: Columbia University Press, 1988. 2 vols. The 791 letters and book inscriptions collected here include all the known letters from and to Crane, as well as Cora Crane's correspondence relative to her husband's life and career.

Recommended Biographies

Benfey, Christopher E.G. *The Double Life of Stephen Crane.* New York: Knopf, 1992. 294pp. Benfey's interpretive biography is dominated by a thesis that Crane's life imitated his writing. Combining a close analysis of Crane's life and work, the book offers a plausible, though at times limiting, psychological explanation of the connection between the two.

Davis, Linda H. *Badge of Courage: The Life of Stephen Crane.* Boston: Houghton Mifflin, 1998. 414pp. Davis succeeds in revealing a believable human portrait beneath the legendary aura that has surrounded Crane's brief, dramatic life. Well researched and sensitive, Davis helps explain the often enigmatic core of Crane's genius.

Stallman, R.W. *Stephen Crane: A Biography.* New York: G. Braziller, 1968. 664pp. Stallman's is a highly detailed, objective biography that provides the clearest record of Crane's activities, correcting many errors and misleading interpretations of earlier biographers.

Other Biographical Studies

Beer, Thomas. *Stephen Crane: A Study in American Letters.* New York: Knopf, 1923. 248pp. The first book-length biography, Beer's is an anecdotally rich account that includes much unsubstantiated material based on an interview with the author conducted by Willis Clarke and testimony from Crane's contemporaries. Not always reliable in its judgments, the book is nonetheless an important biographical source on many details of Crane's life and personality.

Berryman, John. *Stephen Crane.* 1950. Revised ed. New York: Farrar, Straus, 1977. 347pp. Berryman's pioneering critical biography corrects a number of assertions made by Beer while also committing his own factual errors. Berryman's psychological interpretation, though ingenious, has been criticized by later scholars as overly conjectural and potentially misleading in the light of later discovery of important primary source material.

Cady, Edwin H. *Stephen Crane.* Boston: Twayne, 1962. 186pp. Cady's is a brief, reliable overview of Crane's life as well as a sensible critical assessment of his literary achievement.

Colvert, James B. *Stephen Crane.* New York: Harcourt, Brace, 1984. 186pp. Colvert supplies a reliable introductory summary of Crane's life and career serving the needs of the general reader seeking a basic orientation to the man and his work.

Gilkes, Lillian B. *Cora Crane: A Biography of Mrs. Stephen Crane.* Bloomington: Indiana University Press, 1960. 416pp. Gilkes's biography of Crane's common-law wife is solidly researched, using extensive primary sources, and sheds considerable light on the couple's relationship and the circle of the writer's final years.

Knapp, Bettina L. *Stephen Crane.* New York: Frederick Ungar, 1987. 198pp. Knapp supplies a basic biographical profile before proceeding to an analysis of Crane's major works.

Linson, Corwin K. *My Stephen Crane.* Edwin H. Cady, ed. Syracuse, New York: Syracuse University Press, 1958. 115pp. The author, an illustrator and friend of the writer from the 1890s, recorded his recollections of Crane in the 1920s. The book offers a believable portrait of Crane's struggles before the publication of *The Red Badge of Courage.*

Solomon, Eric. *Stephen Crane in England: A Portrait of the Artist.* Columbus: Ohio State University Press, 1964. 136pp. This is an informative study of Crane's move to England in 1897 and his association with such literary figures there as Henry James, H.G. Wells, Ford Madox Ford, and Joseph Conrad.

Biographical Novels

Zara, Louis. *Dark Rider: A Novel Based on the Life of Stephen Crane.* Cleveland: World, 1961. 505pp. This is faithful depiction of Crane's life and career based on solid research.

Fictional Portraits

Castor, Henry. *The Year of the Spaniard.* Garden City, New York: Doubleday, 1950. 274pp. Events of the Spanish-American War are seen through the perspectives of two college friends, one of whom covers the war as a journalist and meets Stephen Crane.

Recommended Juvenile Biographies

Franchere, Ruth. *Stephen Crane: The Story of an American Writer.* New York: Crowell, 1961. 216pp. MG/YA. This is perceptively written, serious literary biography that handles a difficult subject well.

Sufrin, Mark. *Stephen Crane.* New York: Maxwell Macmillan, 1992. 155pp. MG/YA. In a well-researched and authoritative study, Sufrin supplies a sensitive and informative life with every direct quote coming from a documented source.

Biographical Films and Theatrical Adaptations

Rough Riders (1997). Director: John Milius. This television miniseries on Teddy Roosevelt (Tom Berenger) and the Rough Riders during the Spanish-American War includes an appearance by Stephen Crane (Adam Storke) in his capacity as war correspondent. Video.

Other Sources

Wertheim, Stanley. *A Stephen Crane Encyclopedia.* Westport, Connecticut: Greenwood, 1997. 413pp. This reference volume covers Crane's works, characters, people, and places associated with the writer. The volume also includes a chronology and a bibliography of the most important studies on Crane.

Wertheim, Stanley. *The Crane Log: A Documentary Life of Stephen Crane, 1871–1900.* New York: G.K. Hall, 1994. 500pp. Organized chronologically, this is a detailed reference guide to Crane's life and associates with numerous illustrations and

brief biographies of the significant people in the author's life.

115. CRAZY HORSE
ca. 1841–1877

An Oglala chief considered the greatest leader of the Sioux, Crazy Horse inspired the resistance against white settlement in the Great Plains and with his people refused to agree to resettlement on a reservation. He was victorious against federal troops at Rosebud River (1876) and joined Sitting Bull and Gall in defeating General George Armstrong Custer at the Battle of Little Bighorn (1876). Arrested after surrendering, he was stabbed to death with a bayonet while allegedly trying to escape.

Recommended Biographies

Ambrose, Stephen E. *Crazy Horse and Custer: The Parallel Lives of Two American Warriors.* Garden City, New York: Doubleday, 1975. 527pp. Ambrose's dual biographical portraits of the two opponents are well researched and compellingly written with the comparison serving to elucidate both men in refreshing and original ways.

McMurtry, Larry. *Crazy Horse.* New York: Viking, 1999. 148pp. McMurtry substitutes a vivid evocation of Crazy Horse's times for the lack of precise data surrounding his life, which the author admits makes any biography on the warrior an "exercise in assumption, conjecture, and surmise." With the novelist's skill in entering imaginatively the life of the Plains Indian, the book is an excellent, succinct summary of both Crazy Horse's career and wider meaning.

Sandoz, Mari. *Crazy Horse: The Strange Man of the Oglalas: A Biography.* New York: Hastings House, 1942. 428pp. Described by Clifton Fadiman as "half history, half heroic epic... among the important records of the history of the American Indian" and by Wallace Stegner as written in the "spirit of the sagas, with a scrupulous regard to truth and history," Sandoz traces Crazy Horse's life from birth to death, using his life as a lens for a moving portrait of his people and his times.

Other Biographical Studies

Brown, Vinson. *Great Upon the Mountain: The Story of Crazy Horse, Legendary Mystic and Warrior.* New York: Macmillan, 1971. 169pp. Brown summarizes the highlights of Crazy Horse's life with an emphasis on his spiritual beliefs and values that directed his actions.

Kadlecek, Edward, and Mabell Kadlecek. *To Kill an Eagle: Indian Views on the Death of Crazy Horse.* Boulder, Colorado: Johnson Books, 1981. 170pp. The authors construct a portrait of Crazy Horse's life and death from contemporary Indian sources.

Biographical Novels

Blevins, Winfred. *Stone Song: A Novel of the Life of Crazy Horse.* New York: Forge, 1995. 400pp. Employing speculation and imagination on a fac-

tual framework, Blevins offers a fictional biography of Crazy Horse in which he is shown to be a faithful defender of Sioux values.

Dugan, Bill. *Crazy Horse.* New York: Harper Paperbacks, 1993. 309pp. Dugan dramatizes Crazy Horse's career as a warrior from his early teens in a combination of fact, imaginative conjecture, and invention.

Fictional Portraits

Virtually every dramatization of the Battle of the Little Bighorn includes a portrayal of Crazy Horse. Some of the most interesting and memorable fictional appearances are listed here:

Henry, Will. *No Survivors.* New York: Random House, 1950. 344pp. Henry's classic account of the Battle of the Little Bighorn features strong performances by Custer and Crazy Horse.

Heyen, William. *Crazy Horse in Stillness: Poems.* Brockport, New York: BOA Editions, 1996. 271pp. Informed by history, letters, and diaries, Heyen's lyrical sequence offers a wide-ranging meditation on Crazy Horse's life and meaning as well as a meditation on imagined lives of such figures as Custer and his wife Elizabeth.

O'Brien, Dan. *The Contract Surgeon.* New York: Lyons Press, 1999. 316pp. The details of Crazy Horse's end are dramatized in this novel about an army surgeon who befriends the Sioux leader and is drawn into conflicting loyalties when Crazy Horse is captured.

Pomerance, Bernard. *We Need to Dream All This Again.* New York: Viking, 1987. 101pp. Crazy Horse is seen in action against the whites in the Black Hills.

Sale, Richard. *The White Buffalo.* New York: Simon & Schuster, 1975. 253pp. This imaginary adventure yarn brings Crazy Horse and Wild Bill Hickok together in pursuit of a legendary white buffalo in an elegy to the close of the frontier.

Recommended Juvenile Biographies

Freedman, Russell. *The Life and Death of Crazy Horse.* New York: Holiday House, 1996. 166pp. YA. Freedman's balanced portrait of Crazy Horse's career is supplemented by pictographs sketched by a tribal historian and cousin of Crazy Horse. Named the ALA Best Book for Young Adults in 1997.

Goldman, Martin. *Crazy Horse: War Chief of the Oglala Sioux.* New York: F. Watts, 1996. 208pp. YA. This is an in-depth and scholarly biography that relates Crazy Horse's career against the wider backdrop of westward expansion and the relationship between the settlers and the Indians.

Guttmacher, Larry. *Crazy Horse: Sioux War Chief.* New York: Chelsea House, 1994. 119pp. MG/YA. Guttmacher's is a scholarly and authoritative treatment of Crazy Horse's life and times, with the informative text supplemented by high-quality period photographs and drawings.

St. George, Judith. *Crazy Horse.* New York: Putnam, 1994. 180pp. MG. St. George manages a balanced account, drawing on oral history records to provide a thoughtful character profile of Crazy

Horse and the mystique that surrounds him. Although the reconstruction of his early life is hypothetical, the account of his maturity and end is authentic.

Biographical Films and Theatrical Adaptations

A&E Biography Video: Crazy Horse: The Last Warrior (1995). Producer: Vann Debonne. A biographical profile featuring archival material and artistic representations, as well as expert testimony. Video.

Chief Crazy Horse (1955). Director: George Sherman. Victor Mature is surprisingly convincing as the Sioux warrior who is shown uniting his people for a stand against the white men.

Crazy Horse (1996). Director: John Irvin. Television dramatization of the Sioux warrior's life casts Michael Greyeyes in the central role with Peter Horton as Custer. Video.

Crazy Horse and Custer: The Untold Story (1990). This implausible adventure tale imagines a prior meeting between Crazy Horse and Custer as allies against the Blackfoot. Starring Slim Pickens, Wayne Maunder, and Michael Dante. Video.

Other Sources

Brininstool, E.A., ed. *Crazy Horse: The Invincible Oglala Sioux Chief: The "Inside Stories," by Actual Observers, of a Most Treacherous Deed Against a Great Indian Leader.* Los Angeles: Wetzel, 1949. 87pp. A collection of eyewitness accounts and documentary evidence describing Crazy Horse's end.

Clark, Robert A., ed. *The Killing of Chief Crazy Horse: Three Eyewitnesses.* Glendale, California: Arthur H. Clark, 1976. 152pp. A fascinating oral history of Crazy Horse's life and death from the perspective of his contemporaries.

Hardoff, Richard G., ed. *The Surrender and Death of Crazy Horse: A Source Book about a Tragic Episode in Lakota History.* Spokane, Washington: Arthur H. Clark, 1998. 288pp. This is a valuable collection of eyewitness and newspaper accounts, military reports, and photographs relating to the last four months of Crazy Horse's life.

See also George Armstrong Custer; Sitting Bull

116. DAVY CROCKETT
1786–1836

American frontiersman, politician, and folk hero, Crockett served (1813–1814) under Andrew Jackson against the Creek in the War of 1812, was elected (1821) to the Tennessee state legislature, and was a U.S. congressman (1827–1831, 1833–1835). He became known for his shrewd social and political comments and for his racy, backwoods humor. Defeated for reelection in 1835, he left Tennessee for Texas, where he lost his life in defense of the Alamo during Texas's struggle for independence from Mexico.

Autobiography and Primary Sources

Narrative of the Life of David Crockett of the State of Tennessee. 1834. Reprint ed. James A. Shackford and Stanley J. Falmsbee, eds. Knoxville: University of Tennessee Press, 1973. 211pp. Not always factually reliable, Crockett's recollections are nevertheless an essential source on the man and his experiences.

Recommended Biographies

Davis, William C. *Three Roads to the Alamo: The Lives and Fortunes of David Crockett, James Bowie, and William Barret Travis.* New York: HarperCollins, 1998. 791pp. Davis's group portrait is exhaustively researched and penetrates the myths surrounding Crockett's life and times to reveal a believable human figure whose motivations and behavior are related to the values and events of his era. The book's comparative approach is particularly useful in tracing the similarities and differences in the development of these three figures whose lives are resolved together at the Alamo.

Derr, Mark. *The Frontiersman: The Real Life and Many Legends of Davy Crockett.* New York: Morrow, 1993. 304pp. Derr offers a realistic portrait very different from that of the legends and myths surrounding the man. The book concentrates on what is known for sure, and Crockett is shown in relation to his era.

Shackford, James A. *David Crockett: The Man and the Legend.* Chapel Hill: University of North Carolina Press, 1956. 338pp. Shackford's is the definitive, scholarly examination of the facts of Crockett's life and career, as well as an evaluation of the literature that helped to create the Crockett legend. For more recent Crockett scholarship, readers should consult Lofaro.

Other Biographical Studies

Hauck, Richard B. *Crockett: A Bio-Bibliography.* Westport, Connecticut: Greenwood, 1982. 169pp. Hauck's is an excellent starting point for a succinct review of the biographical facts and to review the books and articles on Crockett.

Lofaro, Michael A. and Joe Cummings. *Crockett at Two Hundred: New Perspectives on the Man and the Myth.* Knoxville: University of Tennessee Press, 1989. 252pp. The authors update the biographical record based on recent scholarship.

Biographical Novels

Brown, Dee. *Wave High the Banner: A Novel Based on the Life of Davy Crockett.* Philadelphia: Macrae Smith, 1942. 367pp. Crockett's life from boyhood is depicted in which the various legends surrounding the frontiersman are joined to the known facts to produce a believable, heroic portrait.

Judd, Cameron. *Crockett of Tennessee: A Novel Based on the Life and Times of Davy Crockett.* New York: Bantam, 1994. 518pp. Crockett's career is traced from his youth, through his service in Congress, and his final heroic apotheosis at the Battle of the Alamo. While adhering to the basic facts, the novel supplements them with invention.

Fictional Portraits

Foreman, Leonard L. *The Road to San Jacinto.* New York: Dutton, 1943. 285pp. This historical romance dramatizes Crockett's end at the Battle of the Alamo, weaving together a fictional plot within an historical framework.

Harrigan, Steve. *The Gates of the Alamo.* New York: Knopf, 2000. 581pp. The events of the bloody siege at the Alamo are vividly captured in this novel that provides characterizations of the principal leaders, including Crockett, Travis, Houston, Bowie, and Santa Anna, but concentrates more on ordinary participants on both sides of the conflict.

Schechter, Harold. *Nevermore.* New York: Pocket Books, 1999. 322pp. In Schechter's ingenious period mystery, Crockett joins forces with Edgar Allen Poe to solve a series of murders in Baltimore.

Recommended Juvenile Biographies

Retan, Walter. *The Story of Davy Crockett.* New York: Dell, 1993. 102pp. MG. This is an informative summary of the highlights of Crockett's career.

Sanford, William R. *Davy Crockett: Defender of the Alamo.* Springfield, New Jersey: Enslow, 1996. 48pp. MG. Sanford is a basic, though fairly reliable, account of Crockett's career.

Biographical Films and Theatrical Adaptations

Paulding, James K. *The Lion of the West.* James N. Tidwell, ed. Stanford, California: Stanford University Press, 1954. 64pp. This influential early dramatization played an important role in spreading the Crockett legend.

The Alamo (1960). Director: John Wayne. Big-screen epic on the Battle of the Alamo casts Wayne in the Crockett role with a strong supporting cast of Richard Widmark, Laurence Harvey, and various John Ford alumni. Video.

Davy Crockett: King of the Wild Frontier (1955). Director: Norman Foster. In the film that helped make the coonskin cap a pop culture talisman, three episodes of the Disney television series are joined to approximate Crockett's life story. Fess Parker stars as Crockett with Buddy Ebsen. Video.

Davy Crockett and the River Pirates (1956), the sequel to *Davy Crockett: King of the Wild Frontier* unites Davy with the equally legendary Mike Fink. Video.

Other Sources

Lofaro, Michael A., ed. *Davy Crockett: The Man, The Legend, The Legacy 1786–1986.* Knoxville: University of Tennessee Press, 1986. 203pp. This collection of scholarly essays examines various aspects of Crockett's life and his representation in history, popular literature, and on film.

See also Sam Houston; Andrew Jackson

117. OLIVER CROMWELL
1599–1658

English statesman and lord protector of England, Oliver Cromwell entered Parliament in 1628, a staunch opponent of Charles I. During the ensuing civil war, he distinguished himself by his military skill and administrative abilities. At the king's trial, Cromwell led the demand for his execution. After a punitive expedition to Ireland and Scotland, Cromwell became a virtual dictator of the Commonwealth and was named lord protector in 1654.

Autobiography and Primary Sources

Primary source material is available in two important collections: *Memoirs of the Protector, Oliver Cromwell* (London: Longman, 1822. 2 vols.) and *The Writings and Speeches of Oliver Cromwell* (Cambridge, Massachusetts: Harvard University Press, 1937–1947. 4 vols.).

Recommended Biographies

Ashley, Maurice. *The Greatness of Oliver Cromwell.* New York: Macmillan, 1958. 382pp. In a spirited defense, Ashley challenges previous unfavorable judgments on Cromwell in a lucid and humane assessment by a expert in the era.

Coward, Barry. *Oliver Cromwell.* New York: Longman, 1991. 204pp. In the useful Profiles in Power series, Coward's chronological narrative draws on fresh interpretations based on modern scholarship to offer a number of answers to the many contradictions and puzzles surrounding Cromwell and his career. Balanced in its assessment, Coward's examination helps set Cromwell solidly in the context of his times and is an excellent choice for the reader in search of a concise study.

Fraser, Antonia. *Cromwell: The Lord Protector.* New York: Knopf, 1973. 774pp. Setting out to rescue Cromwell from obscurity and neglect by the general reader, Fraser provides a detailed portrait of Cromwell the man. Clearly not a Cromwell enthusiast, Fraser is nevertheless objective and fairminded in her assessment.

Gaunt, Peter. *Oliver Cromwell.* Cambridge, Massachusetts: Blackwell, 1996. 263pp. In a perceptive reexamination of Cromwell's life and career, Gaunt looks at the myths surrounding Cromwell and the shifting interpretations of him over the years. He then provides a chronological review, highlighting the key events and turning points in Cromwell's life.

Other Biographical Studies

Ashley, Maurice. *Charles I and Oliver Cromwell: A Study in Contrasts and Comparisons.* New York: Methuen, 1987. 243pp. Ashley's dual biographical portrait is an insightful study that takes the full measure of both men. Ashley is recognized as the dean of Cromwellian studies, and his interpretations are based on a lifetime of scholarship on the period.

Ashley, Maurice. *Oliver Cromwell and His World.* New York: Putnam, 1972. 128pp. Serving as a fine introduction and overview, Ashley summarizes the

major events of Cromwell's life along with a vivid period background.

Buchan, John. *Oliver Cromwell.* London: Hodder and Stoughton, 1934. 554pp. This straightforward popular biography is based chiefly on Gardiner but with some markedly different conclusions.

Gardiner, Samuel R. *Oliver Cromwell.* New York: Goupil, 1899. 216pp. Gardiner's early chronological narrative is a straightforward account of the events in Cromwell's life and a strong appreciation for his greatness in the struggle for political and religious reform.

Hill, Christopher. *God's Englishman: Oliver Cromwell and the English Revolution.* New York: Dial Press, 1970. 324pp. The author places Cromwell in the social and economic contexts of his times and assesses his impact on English history in a solid, political biography. In Hill's view, Cromwell was an unwitting revolutionary, not a willful desecrator or destroyer. Expects his readers to be already familiar with the outline of Cromwell's life.

Howell, Roger. *Cromwell.* Boston: Little, Brown, 1977. 269pp. In a competent, compact summary of existing knowledge based on leading secondary sources, Howell summarizes Cromwell's military and political career. While there is little here that is new, Howell's insights are reliable, if somewhat standard.

Roots, Ivan A., ed. *Cromwell: A Profile.* New York: Hill & Wang, 1973. 237pp. Written by recognized authorities, this collection of essays explores the religious, political, and economic aspects of Cromwell's career based on modern scholarship.

Wedgwood, C.V. *Oliver Cromwell.* 1939. Revised edition. New York: Macmillan, 1973. 128pp. The author's concise biographical profile is rich in detail and useful for the reader looking for a reliable, rounded portrait.

Fictional Portraits

Anthony, Evelyn. *Charles the King.* Garden City, New York: Doubleday, 1961. 427pp. Charles's conflict with his nemesis Cromwell is depicted, and the often confusing events of the English Civil War are carefully delineated in this fictional presentation that shows evidence of careful research.

Dumas, Alexandre. *Twenty Years After.* 1845. Reprint ed. New York: Oxford University Press, 1998. 845pp. The musketeers return for adventures that include an attempt to foil Cromwell's plot to capture and execute Charles I. Aiding Cromwell in his political machinations is the son of Milady who vows vengeance on the men who murdered his mother. Not reliable in historical events and dates.

Lane, Jane. *The Severed Crown.* New York: Simon & Schuster, 1972. 210pp. Narrated by a variety of witnesses, the novel details the final three years in the life of Charles I, through his imprisonment, trial, and execution. Often confusing and surprisingly slow moving despite the inherent drama.

Linington, Elizabeth. *The Kingbreaker.* Garden City, New York: Doubleday, 1958. 376pp. Set during the English Civil War and the conflict between Charles I and Cromwell, the novel's fictional story

depicts a Royalist who becomes a spy in Cromwell's household.

Scott, Walter. *Woodstock: Or the Cavalier.* 1826. Reprint ed. New York: Dutton, 1924. 461pp. The novel's romance revolves around Charles II's famous escape from Cromwell at Woodstock. With a number of inaccuracies, the novel is history filtered through Scott's romantic imagination.

Recommended Juvenile Biographies

Kaplan, Lawrence. *Oliver Cromwell.* New York: Chelsea House, 1986. 128pp. MG/YA. Balancing personal details with a comprehensive summary of Cromwell's political career, this is an accessible, informative presentation.

Levine, I.E. *Oliver Cromwell.* New York: J. Messner, 1966. 191pp. YA. Cromwell is portrayed as champion of religious and political freedom in this heroic account that stresses his achievements but largely ignores more troubling aspects of Cromwell's character and rule.

Young, Peter. *Oliver Cromwell.* Cranberry, New Jersey: A.S. Barnes, 1969. 92pp. YA. Part of the International Profiles series of brief illustrated biographies for general readers, Young's fact-filled account provides helpful background reading for students.

Biographical Films and Theatrical Adaptations

Drinkwater, John. *Oliver Cromwell: A Play.* New York: Houghton Mifflin, 1921. 96pp. Based on 15 years in Cromwell's life from 1639, the play is a succession of episodic glimpses of his development with an emphasis on his domestic life and his relationship to his mother, wife, and daughter.

Cromwell (1970). Director: Ken Hughes. British lavish historical epic with a miscast Richard Harris in the title role with unhistorical sympathies and motives. Best for its battle scenes and period details. Video.

Other Sources

Ashley, Maurice, ed. *Cromwell.* Englewood Cliffs, New Jersey: Prentice-Hall, 1969. 177pp. Part of the Great Lives Observed series, this useful volume brings together Cromwell's writings, contemporary views, and assessments by various writers.

See also Charles I; Charles II

118. MARIE CURIE
1867–1934

Chemist and physicist, Marie Curie was born in Warsaw, Poland. In 1891 she went to Paris to continue her studies and married Pierre Curie, working independently on her research in his laboratory. In 1898 they discovered polonium and radium, initiating the nuclear age. Marie Curie became the first women to receive a Nobel Prize for science in 1903; in 1911 she became the first scientist to receive a second Nobel Prize.

Autobiography and Primary Sources

Pierre Curie. 1923. Reprint ed. New York: Dover, 1963. 118pp. Marie Curie's biographical portrait of her husband includes her own autobiographical notes.

Recommended Biographies

Curie, Eve. *Madame Curie: A Biography.* New York: Doubleday, 1938. 393pp. Written by Curie's younger daughter, the book has long served as the standard life. An eyewitness to aspects of Curie's life closed to all other biographers and charged with cataloging Curie's papers, the author's intimate knowledge creates a moving tribute to her mother. Remarkably honest in its overall approach, the author does avoid any discussion of the scandal of the love affair with Paul Langevin.

Quinn, Susan. *Marie Curie: A Life.* New York: Simon & Schuster, 1995. 509pp. With access to archival material closed to researchers until 1990, Quinn's study provides new information on Curie's life in Poland, her marriage, her affair with Paul Langevin, and the challenges she faced as a woman scientist. The details help create a more human and far more complicated portrait than previous attempts that often cast Curie in the role of secular saint. Quinn's life is likely to remain the definitive biography for some time.

Other Biographical Studies

Giroud, Françoise. *Marie Curie: A Life.* New York: Holmes and Meier, 1986. 291pp. This highly personal study of Curie's private life and the challenges she faced as a woman scientist is based primarily on letters and published sources. Lacking footnotes or a bibliography, the book is intended for a general audience and serves as a useful introduction to Curie's character.

Pflaum, Rosalynd. *Grand Obsession: Madame Curie and Her World.* New York: Doubleday, 1989. 496pp. The author relates Curie's scientific achievement to the compelling backdrop of the human story of her family. Pflaum handles the various personalities with tact and fairness and provides a clear explanation of the technical aspect of Curie's work.

Reid, Robert. *Marie Curie.* New York: Saturday Review Press, 1974. 349pp. Based on cooperation with Curie's relatives, colleagues, and co-workers and unprecedented access to the archives of the Laboratoire Curie, the book provides a solid assessment of Curie's scientific achievement and a summary of the history of science during her era accessible for the general reader.

Woznicki, Robert. *Madame Curie: Daughter of Poland.* Miami, Florida: American Institute of Polish Culture, 1983. 175pp. Based on interviews with Eve Curie, this account of Marie Curie's life in Poland and France emphasizes her Polish roots and patriotism.

Recommended Juvenile Biographies

Pflaum, Rosalynd. *Marie Curie and Her Daughter Irene.* Minneapolis: Lerner, 1993. 144pp. MG. Concentrates on the professional lives of Marie Curie and her daughter, Irene Joliet-Curie, in a detailed account of Marie's discovery of radium, polonium, and natural radiation and her daughter's discovery of artificial radiation.

Greene, Carol. *Marie Curie: Pioneer Physicist.* Chicago: Childrens Press, 1984. 112pp. MG/YA. Solidly detailed highlights of Curie's life and contribution to science.

Steinke, Ann E. *Marie Curie and the Discovery of Radium.* Hauppauge, New York: Barron's, 1987. 123pp. YA. Part of Barron's Solutions series, this informative volume for readers aged 12 to 13 dramatizes the challenges Curie faced inside and outside the laboratory and includes supplementary aids, including a glossary and topics for essays.

Biographical Films and Theatrical Adaptations

Madame Curie (1943). Director: Mervyn LeRoy. Greer Garson and Walter Pidgeon star as Marie and Pierre Curie in a more convincing and truthful dramatization than other biographical film efforts. Video.

119. GEORGE ARMSTRONG CUSTER
1839–1876

American cavalry officer, George Armstrong Custer was born in Ohio and, after graduating from West Point in 1861, distinguished himself in battle during the Civil War, becoming in 1863 the youngest general in the Union army. After the war, Custer was the commander of the Seventh Cavalry. He proved himself as an Indian fighter at the battle of Washita in 1868. After leading the expedition into the Black Hills searching for gold, Custer participated in the 1876 campaign against the Sioux. On June 25 Custer came upon an immense Indian encampment on the Little Bighorn River. Despite the numerical superiority of the Indians, Custer divided his force and attacked. All his force of over 200 were massacred in one of the most famous events in American western history that turned Custer into an ambivalent American mythical figure.

Autobiography and Primary Sources

The Custer Story: The Life and Intimate Letters of General Custer and His Wife Elizabeth. Marguerite Merington, ed. New York: Devin-Adair, 1950. 339pp. Originally published in 1950, edited by a close friend of Elizabeth Custer with her approval, this collection of correspondence is an essential primary source to understand Custer and his wife, despite a bias in favor of supporting the heroic Custer legend.

My Life on the Plains. Milo M. Quaife, ed. Lincoln: University of Nebraska Press, 1972. 626pp. Originally published in 1874, Custer's memoirs offer a fascinating window on Custer's personality and his version of his story.

Nomad: George A. Custer in Turf, Field, and Farm. Brian W. Dippie, ed. Austin: University of Texas Press, 1980. 174pp. Under the pseudonym of "Nomad," Custer chronicled his experiences for a popular magazine and provides a number of revealing insights about his personality and temperament.

Following the Guidon. Norman: University of Oklahoma Press, 1966. 344pp.; *Tenting on the Plains.* Williamston, Massachusetts: Corner House, 1973. 403pp.; *Boots and Saddles.* Norman: University of Oklahoma Press, 1976. 276pp. Elizabeth Bacon Custer's three books portray her husband in adoring and hero-worshipping terms. Despite her obvious bias, the books offer her eyewitness perspective and the source for the positive Custer legend with which modern biographers have been forced to contend.

Recommended Biographies

Barnett, Louise K. *Touched by Fire: The Life, Death, and Mythic Afterlife of George Armstrong Custer.* New York: Holt, 1996. 540pp. Drawing on the latest historical research and battlefield archaeology, Barnett presents a detailed character study of Custer, his relationship with his wife, and his motivations behind his disastrous end. Looking beyond Custer's actual life, Barnett probes as well his mythical afterlife and the historical, social, and archetypal context that has grown around Custer's story and points to racial arrogance as one of the best keys to explain Custer's demise and history's continuing fascination with his character.

Connell, Evan S. *Son of the Morning Star: Custer and the Little Big Horn.* San Francisco: North Point, 1984. 441pp. Not strictly speaking a biography, Connell probes the meaning of the Custer massacre with the eye of storyteller interested in character and context. Connell demystifies the various legends surrounding Custer and the Last Stand, and while readers may challenge a number of his historical assertions, few will be able to resist his vivid reanimation of personalities and era.

Monaghan, Jay. *The Life of General George Armstrong Custer.* Boston: Little, Brown, 1959. 469pp. Making initial use of a larger body of primary evidence than any previous biography did, Monaghan's groundbreaking study clarifies various aspects of Custer's career and sees him as a victim of the poor generalship of his colleagues and ultimately a scapegoat of the military bureaucracy. Despite a partisan bias that flavors his otherwise balanced effort, Monaghan's life remains one of the most comprehensive and detailed biographies available.

Wert, Jeffrey D. *Custer: The Controversial Life of George Armstrong Custer.* New York: Simon & Schuster, 1996. 462pp. In a highly readable and objective account of Custer's life and character, Wert asserts that the Civil War, not the Little Bighorn, defined the man, and he concentrates on Custer's meteoric ascent during the war and his diminished effectiveness in its aftermath. Drawing on newly discovered material, Wert paints a balanced human and psychological portrait that avoids excessive claims of either his untarnished heroism or unmitigated villainy.

Other Biographical Studies

Ambrose, Stephen E. *Crazy Horse and Custer: The Parallel Lives of Two American Warriors.* Garden City, New York: Doubleday, 1975. 486pp.

Ambrose's dual biography provides a number of provocative parallels in the careers of the two famous opponents at the Little Bighorn that reveals a great deal about each man's personality and breathes fresh life into the familiar.

Dippie, Brian W. *Custer's Last Stand: The Anatomy of an American Myth.* Lincoln: University of Nebraska Press, 1994. 214pp. Restricting his focus to Custer's climax, Dippie looks closely at the massacre and its significance.

Frost, Lawrence A. *The Custer Album: A Pictorial Biography.* Seattle: Superior Publishing, 1964. 192pp. With more than 200 photographs and drawings of people, places, and artifacts associated with Custer, the author interweaves text that succinctly covers the highlights of Custer's career.

Hofling, Charles K. *Custer and the Little Big Horn: A Psychobiographical Inquiry.* Detroit: Wayne State University Press, 1981. 118pp. In Hofling's brief psychological character study, he reviews the main facts of the battle and Custer's life and offers a psychoanalytic interpretation of the decisions that led to Custer's disaster

Leckie, Shirley A. *Elizabeth Bacon Custer and the Making of a Myth.* Norman: University of Oklahoma Press, 1993. 419pp. The author's biographical study of Custer's wife provides an intimate portrait of their marriage and details Libbie's mythmaker role as the rewriter of history and the custodian of the Custer legend of the "boy hero," brilliant military commander, Christian patriot, and family man without faults.

Urwin, Gregory J. *Custer Victorious: The Civil War Battles of George A. Custer.* Toronto: Associated University Presses, 1983. 308pp. Urwin provides the fullest account of Custer's remarkable career during the Civil War with insights into his character under fire and as a commander of troops.

Utley, Robert M. *Cavalier in Buckskin: George Armstrong Custer.* Norman: University of Oklahoma Press, 1988. 216pp. Written by a respected expert in the post–Civil War western frontier, Utley's short life, though not as comprehensive as others available, is a valuable introduction both to Custer's life and his era by a meticulous scholar. In *Custer and the Great Controversy: The Origin and Development of a Legend.* (Los Angeles: Westernlore Press, 1962, 184pp.), Utley examines the debate over Custer's decisions at the Little Bighorn and the legacy of the event as American myth with sensible interpretation of Custer's character.

Van de Water, Frederick F. *Glory Hunter: A Life of General Custer.* Indianapolis: Bobbs-Merrill, 1934. 394pp. As its title indicates, Van de Water's study is harshly critical of Custer, portraying him as cruel, egotistical, and guided by an insatiable craving for glory. The author assembles a mountain of evidence for the prosecution, and though indulging in a good deal of unsubstantiated speculation, Van de Water's book has been influential in establishing the negative side of Custer's reputation.

Whittaker, Frederick. *A Complete Life of General George A. Custer: Through the Civil War.* 1876. Reprint ed. Lincoln: University of Nebraska Press, 1993. 648pp. Published only six months after Custer's death, Whittaker's biography traces his boyhood, his years at West Point, his Civil War exploits, and his transitions to the peacetime army. Although flawed by a lack of objectivity, the book offers revealing firsthand accounts and assessments as well as the beginning of the heroic mythmaking that formed the Custer legend.

Biographical Novels

Alter, Judy. *Libbie.* New York: Bantam, 1994. 404pp. In a first-person narrative, Elizabeth Custer tells the story of her courtship and married life with Custer and tries to deepen the realism of their life together with some deviations from history and some speculations about Custer's flaws and domestic conflict.

Blake, Michael. *Marching to Valhalla: A Novel of Custer's Last Days.* New York: Villard, 1996. 288pp. Cast in the form of a journal kept by Custer during the weeks leading up to the Little Bighorn, the novel presents a believable impersonation of Custer's voice and details about his character supported by evident research.

Chiaventone, Frederick J. *A Road We Do Not Know: A Novel of Custer at the Little Big Horn.* New York: Simon & Schuster, 1996. 333pp. Based on extensive research by a retired army officer, this is an hour-by-hour detailed account of the events leading up to the Battle of the Little Bighorn with an objective perspective of both sides in the conflict.

Hoyt, Edwin P. *The Last Stand: A Novel about George Armstrong Custer and the Indians of the Plains.* New York: Forge, 1995. 316pp. In his fictional recreation of Custer's military career, Hoyt provides a larger political and social context for the Little Bighorn and a detailed look at the personalities involved, particularly Custer, who is shown as a mass of contradictions and is neither romanticized nor condemned.

Jones, Douglas C. *The Court-Martial of George Armstrong Custer.* New York: Scribner, 1976. 291pp. This intriguing what-if novel imagines Custer's survival after the Little Bighorn and his trial for his role in the disaster. The novel takes the form of a taut psychological courtroom drama over the issue of Custer's character and military competence.

Skimin, Robert. *The River and the Horseman: A Novel of the Little Bighorn.* New York: Herodias, 1999. 364pp. This is a vivid recreation of the life and times of both Custer and Sitting Bull culminating in their confrontation on the battlefield.

Fictional Portraits

The most interesting of the many novels that offer a fictional view of Custer and the Battle of the Little Bighorn are listed here.

Berger, Thomas. *Little Big Man.* New York: Dial Press, 1964. 440pp. In Berger's darkly comic picaresque adventures of Jack Crabb, the only white survivor of Custer's Last Stand, the various myths of the American West are exploded, with Custer emerging as a self-absorbed neurotic.

Birney, Hoffman. *The Dice of God.* New York: Holt, 1956. 350pp. In b *roman à clef* , the novel chronicles the military career of Frederick Tuthill, standing in for Custer, leading up to the Indian massacre.

Garcia y Roberston, Rodrigo. *American Woman.* New York: Forge, 1998. 349pp. In a personalized version of the events leading up to the Little Bighorn, Sarah Kilroy arrives on the scene to Christianize the Indians, becomes the wife of a Cheyenne warrior, meets Custer and his wife, and records her conflict as the massacre unfolds.

Haycox, Ernest. *Bugles in the Afternoon.* Boston: Little, Brown, 1944. 306pp. The events leading up to Custer's Last Stand are believably seen from the perspective of a private in Custer's command.

Henry, Will. *No Survivors.* New York: Random House, 1950. 344pp. Henry's classic depiction of the Indian Wars and the Battle of the Little Bighorn is described fictionally through the story of Colonel Clayton, a stand-in for Custer who is shown as a brave but stupid man who sacrificed himself and his command for no valid purpose. Although cast in a fictional framework, the account of the period and its events are solidly based on fact.

Kaufman, Fred S. *Custer Passed Our Way.* Aberdeen, South Dakota: North Plains Press, 1971. 365pp. Based on a diary kept by the author's father, this documentary novel assembles a great deal of historical data about the Seventh Cavalry in the Dakota Territory during the years leading up to the Little Bighorn.

Mills, Charles K. *A Mighty Afternoon.* Garden City, New York: Doubleday, 1980. 183pp. In minute detail, this fictional recreation of the Battle of the Little Bighorn provides a convincing look at what happened and why.

Murray, Earl. *Flaming Sky.* New York: Forge, 1995. 382pp. A private investigator hired by Ulysses S. Grant to discredit Custer offers his findings on Custer's military leadership and the Battle of the Little Bighorn.

Recommended Juvenile Biographies

Razzi, Jim. *Custer and Crazy Horse: A Story of Two Warriors.* New York: Scholastic, 1989. 170pp. Razzi supplies a detailed dual biography that relates both men's stories against a fully realized historical background.

Biographical Films and Theatrical Adaptations

A&E Biography Video: George Armstrong Custer: America's Golden Cavalier (1997). Producer: Michael Cascio. Using archival photos and testimony by experts, this documentary film chronicles Custer's colorful life and military career. Video.

A&E Biography Video: George Custer: Showdown at Little Big Horn (1995). Producer: Robert Kirk. Profiles the life and military career of Custer and examines his psychology to determine what drove him to success and failure. Video.

Bugles in the Afternoon (1952). Director: Roy Rowland. Ray Milland plays a soldier branded a coward during the Civil War with action climaxing at the Little Bighorn. Sheb Wooley appears as Custer. Video.

Crazy Horse (1996). Director: John Irvin. Video. Television biographical film that traces the life of the Sioux warrior. Michael Greyeyes plays Crazy Horse, and Peter Horton appears as Custer. Fine revisionist drama from the Indian point of view with a strong cast. Video.

Custer of the West (1968). Director: Robert Siodmak. Video. Ambitious and detailed account of Custer's life with Robert Shaw in the title role and Mary Ure as Libbie Custer that swings uncertainly between Custer's heroism and human flaws. Video

Custer's Last Fight (1912). Director: Francis Ford. Silent reenactment of the Battle of the Little Bighorn with the heroic sacrifice of Custer to Indian savagery. Video.

Custer's Last Stand (1936). Director: Elmer Clifton. In a full-length version of a serial that features western adventure climaxing at the Little Bighorn, Frank McGlynn portrays Custer in this heroic version of the massacre. Video.

Last Stand at Little Bighorn (1992). Director: Paul Stekler. Documentary in PBS's American Experience series examines the Custer massacre from both opponents' points-of-view using journal and oral accounts, archival footage, film treatments, and Indian drawings. Video.

Little Big Man (1970). Director: Arthur Penn. Based on Thomas Berger's novel, Dustin Hoffman portrays Jack Crabb through his 121-year western odyssey, including his survival at the Little Bighorn. Richard Mulligan plays a demented Custer. Video.

The Plainsman (1936). Cecil B. DeMille. Western saga with Gary Cooper as Wild Bill Hickock and Jean Arthur as Calamity Jane in a series of implausible adventures, including an encounter with Custer (John Milgan). Video.

Sante Fe Trail (1940). Director: Michael Curtiz. Historically inaccurate western adventure teams Custer (Ronald Reagan) with J.E.B Stuart (Errol Flynn) in the fighting over Bleeding Kansas with Raymond Massey as John Brown. Custer was not yet a graduate of West Point at the time. Video.

Son of the Morning Star (1991). Director: Mike Robe. This television adaptation of Evan S. Connell's book follows the facts of Custer's career faithfully, straying from the truth only in suggesting that Custer had fathered an illegitimate Indian child, a persistent myth that has been disputed. Gary Cole portrays a complex Custer with Rosanna Arquette as his wife. Video.

They Died with Their Boots On (1942). Director: Raoul Walsh. Considerable liberties are taken with the Custer biography and the facts of the Battle of the Little Bighorn in this heroic interpretation, starring Errol Flynn as Custer and Olivia de Havilland as Libbie Custer. Video.

See also Crazy Horse; Sitting Bull

D

120. SALVADOR DALI
1904–1989

A Spanish surrealist painter, Dali was influenced by futurism and then by the work of Italian metaphysical painter Giorgio de Chirico. By 1929, Dali had become a surrealist, mixing images of dreams and hallucinations. One of his best-known works is *Persistence of Memory* (1931), and he made several studies of his wife, Gala. He also designed for movies such as Luis Buñuel's *Un Chien andalou* (1928), advertising, and the ballet.

Autobiography and Primary Sources

Diary of a Genius. Garden City, New York: Doubleday, 1965. 230pp. This is an autobiographical record of the painter's life between 1952 and 1963. Dali's random and erratic reflections display his scatalogical and religious obsessions and his often baffling temperament.

The Secret Life of Salvador Dali. New York: Dial Press, 1942. 400pp. Described by biographer Etherington-Smith as "a monstrous reinvention of his past," Dali offers an impressionistic version of his boyhood, schooling, courtships, Paris days, first exhibits, and involvement in the surrealist movement.

The Unspeakable Confessions of Salvador Dali. New York: Morrow, 1976. 300pp. In a series of recorded conversations with his friend André Perinaud, Dali records his often bizarre, intentionally shocking views on life, his art, and a wide gallery of modernist acquaintances, including Garcia Lorca, Breton, Miró, Picasso, Tzara, and Gaudi.

Recommended Biographies

Etherington-Smith, Meredith. *The Persistence of Memory: A Biography of Dali.* New York: Random House, 1992. 465pp. The author does an excellent job untangling the facts surrounding Dali's life from the legends and the artist's own inventions to create a believable human portrait and an insightful analysis of the relationship between Dali's eccentric life and his art.

Gibson, Ian. *The Shameful Life of Salvador Dali.* New York: W.W. Norton, 1998. 798pp. Gibson's is an intelligent, detailed summary of Dali's destruction of his artistic talent by commercialism

and exhibitionism. The book concentrates on Dali's early life, showing how his formative years prepared the ground for his subsequent behavior and his art. Despite the book's title, this is a balanced assessment equally strong on the details of Dali's life and his works.

Secrest, Meryle. *Salvador Dali.* New York: Dutton, 1986. 307pp. Secrest's interpretive study of Dali's life attempts to explain the emotional basis of his art and behavior. Well researched and argued, the book achieves a believable, human portrait in which the artist's artistic gifts and personal flaws are joined into a compelling, fascinating exploration of a complex figure.

Other Biographical Studies

Ades, Dawn. *Dali and Surrealism.* 1982. Revised as *Dali.* New York: Thames and Hudson, 1995. 216pp. Ades's is a critical survey of Dali's life and work with an emphasis on the 1930s and his connection with the surrealist movement. Insightful on Dali's artistic development, iconography, and appeal, Ades, as she admits in her preface, raises the important critical questions on Dali's achievement and appeal without necessarily answering all of them.

Cowles, Fleur. *The Case of Salvador Dali.* Boston: Little, Brown, 1960. 334pp. A grab bag of anecdotes, the book is divided into three sections: a chronological review of Dali's life, his achievement as a painter, writer, and mystic, and a final clinical analysis of his obsessions. Rarely critical, the book is more a compilation of material than an integrated study or an attempt to bring in a finding on the evidence presented.

Descharnes, Robert. *Salvador Dali, the Work, the Man.* New York: Abrams, 1984. 455pp. A chronological review of Dali's activities and works is supplemented by reproductions, excerpts from Dali's writings, and photographs of the artist and his circle. The writer, a longtime friend of the artist, rarely departs from his admiration for the "divine Dali" to offer any criticism. The book, however, is a comprehensive and complete assemblage of materials with 1,110 illustrations and 672 large color plates.

Lake, Carlton. *In Quest of Dali.* New York: Putnam, 1969. 316pp. Lake records his encounters with Dali in Paris and the United States during the

late 1960s on various self-promotion excursions. Featuring extended recorded conversations, the book offers a limited but vivid profile of the artist's temperament and life style.

Maddox, Conroy. *Dali.* New York: Crown, 1979. 96pp. The author, a British surrealist painter and art critic, supplies an intelligent, brief biographical essay that follows Dali's life and career mainly up to 1950. Serves as a basic introduction for the general reader.

Fictional Portraits

Kaminsky, Stuart M. *The Melting Clock.* New York: Mysterious Press,1991. 198pp. In this installment of the author's period detective series, Toby Peters is hired by Dali to recover a controversial painting that has been stolen.

Recommended Juvenile Biographies

Carter, David A. *Salvador Dali.* New York: Chelsea House, 1995. 119pp. YA. Dali the eccentric, the showman, and the gifted artist is treated in this biography that both relates Dali's artistic development to the details of his private life and to wider artistic and intellectual movements, such as surrealism and Freud's theories of the subconscious.

Biographical Films and Theatrical Adaptations

Soft Self-Portrait of Salvador Dali (1969). Director: Jean-Christope Averty. Filmed on location at Dali's villa in Port Lligat, Spain, this is an exploration of the painter's world, art, and philosophy. Video.

121. DANTE ALIGHIERI
1265–1321

An Italian poet and dominating literary artist of the Middle Ages, Dante was born in Florence and was active as a councilman, elector, and prior before being banished from the city in 1302 for his opposition to the temporal power of the pope. Dante's literary reputation is based mainly on the *Divine Comedy* (completed 1321), a long vernacular poem of the poet's journey through Hell, Purgatory, and Heaven composed during his exile. The poem is a remarkable synthesis of the medieval world view with a lyrical intensity derived from Dante's inspiration from Beatrice Portinari, the woman he loved.

Recommended Biographies

Barbi, Michele. *Life of Dante.* 1933. Reprint ed. Berkeley: University of California Press, 1954. 132pp. The definitive modern biography of Dante, Barbi's biography is authoritative and accessible, combining the facts of Dante's life with a sensible critical appraisal of his works by a lifetime Dante scholar.

Bergin, Thomas G. *Dante.* Boston: Houghton Mifflin, 1965. 326pp. Bergin's compact, informative critical guide to Dante combines chapters on the poet's age, life, and works and is one of the best available studies for the general reader and undergraduate.

Toynbee, Paget J. *Dante Alighieri: His Life and Work.* 1910. Revised ed. Charles Singleton, ed. New York: Harper & Row, 1965. 316pp. Toynbee's early scholarly biography has long been considered an authoritative work by a distinguished Dante scholar. Without resolving their veracity, Toynbee includes translations from early biographies and the first detailed genealogical table of Dante's family.

Other Biographical Studies

Biographies of Dante by Giovanni Boccaccio and Leonardo Bruni appeared shortly after his death and are available in *The Earliest Lives of Dante* (New York: Russell & Russell, 1968. 103pp.).

Moore, Edward. *Dante and His Early Biographers* (1889. Reprint ed. New York: Haskell House, 1970. 181pp.) provides a helpful analysis of these early works.

Anderson, William. *Dante the Maker.* London: Routledge, 1980. 497pp. Anderson's provocative critical study connects Dante's works with a speculative reconstruction of the mental process that created them based on modern psychological and neurophysiological studies of creativity. Challenging and daring in its concepts, this is an intriguing biography of Dante's mental development.

Chubb, Thomas C. *Dante and His World.* Boston: Little, Brown, 1967. 831pp. In a reconstruction of Dante's life from his works, contemporary writings, legends, gossip, and conjecture, Chubb is best on the political and intellectual background of Dante's times. Much is based on informed guesswork but does incorporate modern scholarship made accessible in a chatty, anecdotal style.

Dinsmore, Charles A. *Life of Dante Alighieri.* Boston: Houghton Mifflin, 1919. 306pp. Dinsmore's three-part organization provides the historical background, the known facts of Dante's life, and an analysis of his works.

Fergusson, Francis. *Dante.* New York: Macmillan, 1966. 214pp. In a critical biography intended for the general reader, Fergusson examines Dante's works chronologically, suggesting his mental and artistic development. However, the book lacks the specificity, completeness, and perceptiveness of Bergin's and Barbi's studies.

Grandgent, Charles H. *Dante.* New York: Duffield, 1916. 397pp. Grandgent's historical biography concentrates on tracing a portrait of the Middle Ages through the facts of Dante's life.

Leigh, Gertrude. *New Light on the Youth of Dante.* Boston: Houghton Mifflin, 1930. 278pp. Leigh's thesis is that insights into Dante's early years and references to actual political events and satire lie hidden beneath the allegory of the *Divine Comedy.* Her study was the result of 30 years of research, and what she uncovers considerably fills in the gaps in our knowledge of Dante's early years though surmises are inevitably dominant here.

Quinones, Ricardo J. *Dante Alighieri.* Boston: Twayne, 1979. 212pp. Quinones's compact critical biography provides a chronological analysis of Dante's works along with facts of his life in a scholarly though accessible treatment.

Biographical Novels

Schachner, Nathan. *The Wanderer: A Novel of Dante and Beatrice.* New York: Appleton-Century, 1944. 333pp. The author's fictional reconstruction of Dante's life focuses on his relationship with Beatrice, marred by an overly worshipful attitude toward the poet and a sentimental style, but partially redeemed by its colorful treatment of the period.

Recommended Juvenile Biographies

Rizzatti, Maria Luisa. *The Life and Times of Dante.* New York: Curtis, 1967. 75pp. YA. Beautifully illustrated, this visual biography sets Dante's life and artistic achievement clearly against the context of his times and Medieval world view.

Biographical Films and Theatrical Adaptations

Dante (1991). Director: Patrick H. Ryan. Filmed in Florence and throughout northern Italy, this documentary film provides a compelling introduction to Dante's life and work, with poet Galway Kinnell as the voice of Dante. Video.

Other Sources

Jacob, Rachel, ed. *The Cambridge Companion to Dante.* New York: Cambridge University Press, 1993. 270pp. Reflecting current scholarship, this collection of essays by noted scholars examines various aspects of Dante's life, age, and art.

122. CHARLES DARWIN
1809–1882

English naturalist Charles Darwin studied medicine in Edinburgh and for the ministry in Cambridge before turning to natural history. From 1831 to 1836 he sailed as the official naturalist aboard the *Beagle,* where Darwin began to accumulate data that resulted in his concept of evolution. In 1859 Darwin published his theory in *On the Origin of Species by Means of Natural Selection,* which he elaborated in later books, such as *The Descent of Man* (1871). A modest and self-effacing man who lived in quiet rural retirement, Darwin initiated one of the most profound revolutions in biological science.

Autobiography and Primary Sources

The Autobiography of Charles Darwin. 1879. Reprint ed. Nora Barlow, ed. New York: Harcourt, Brace, 1959. 253pp. Written at the end of his life, Darwin's reflections offer a history of his life and development leading up to the publication of *Origin of Species.* This edition, edited by his granddaughter, restores several passages previously suppressed by Darwin's family.

Charles Darwin's Letters: A Selection, 1825–1859. Frederick Burkhardt, ed. New York: Cambridge University Press, 1996. 249pp. This selection from the nine volumes of Darwin's collected correspondence (New York: Cambridge University Press, 1985–1991) spans his career from his university days to the publication of *Origin of Species* and provides unrivaled access to his daily life experience, scientific observations, personality, and friendships.

Charles Darwin's Notebooks. Paul H. Barrett, et al., eds. Ithaca, New York: Cornell University Press, 1987. 747pp. This collection of 11 notebooks and four related manuscripts written between 1836 and 1844 covers Darwin's most creative years and is a must for scholars. For all readers, however, they reveal the mind of man at work on a number of topics.

Recommended Biographies

Brent, Peter L. *Charles Darwin, "A Man of Enlarged Curiosity."* New York: Harper & Row, 1981. 536pp. Containing previously unpublished material from diaries and letters, Brent provides a portrait of Darwin's personality and psychological development that has been called by some critics the definitive private life of Darwin. Brent is excellent on Darwin's early years and in providing a convincing reassessment of his father.

Browne, Janet. *Charles Darwin: Voyager.* New York: Knopf, 1995. 591pp. In the first of a projected two-volume biography, Browne chronicles Darwin's childhood, education, voyages, family life, and early research up to 1856, offering a number of new insights in which Darwin is seen as more a product of his society than other biographies. With the completion of her life, Browne's biography promises to become the definitive modern life.

Desmond, Adrian, and James Moore. *Darwin: The Life of a Tormented Evolutionist.* New York: W.W. Norton, 1991. 808pp. Hailed as definitive by many critics, the authors' biography provides a detailed account of Darwin's life and time with a number of fresh insights and new material. Despite its size, readers will find this a captivating read with a remarkable synthesis of cultural, scientific, and personal data joined into a dramatic narrative.

Other Biographical Studies

Bowlby, John. *Charles Darwin: A New Life.* New York: W.W. Norton, 1990. 511pp. Drawing heavily on primary material, Bowlby, a British psychiatrist, focuses more on the man and his personality than on his works. Seen from a psychological perspective, Bowlby diagnoses Darwin's semi-invalidism as stemming from his repressed and prolonged bereavement for his mother.

Bowler, Peter J. *Charles Darwin: The Man and His Influence*. New York: Cambridge University Press, 1990. 250pp. Combining biography and cultural history, Bowler shows how Darwin's contemporaries were unable to appreciate those aspects of his thinking that are considered scientifically important today.

Clark, Ronald W. *The Survival of Charles Darwin: A Biography of a Man and an Idea*. New York: Random House, 1984. 449pp. Clark's useful dual biography of Darwin and Darwinism devotes the first half to a account of Darwin's life from his boyhood to his death before turning to a consideration of his evolutionary theories, including post-Darwinian developments. Clark makes the complexity of Darwin's ideas and scientific controversies accessible for the general reader.

Darwin, Francis. *The Life of Charles Darwin*. London: J. Murray, 1887. 3 vols. The standard life of Darwin by his son concentrates largely on examining his career. Providing essential information for later biographers, this life has largely been superseded by later treatments that have combined external events with internal views of Darwin's personality and development.

Gruber, Howard E. *Darwin on Man: A Psychological Study of Scientific Creativity, Together with Darwin's Early and Unpublished Notebooks*. 1974. Revised ed. Chicago: University of Chicago Press, 1981. 310pp. Drawing on the first transcription of unpublished notebooks, Gruber traces the growth of Darwin's theory of evolution from the point of view of developmental psychology. Gruber correlates Darwin's ideas about evolution with details from his family background and his religious and philosophical ideas.

Himmelfarb, Gertrude. *Darwin and the Darwinian Revolution*. Garden City, New York: Doubleday, 1959. 480pp. The author's bio-historical-philosophical study of the impact of Darwinism in the intellectual climate of the nineteenth century deals briefly with Darwin's early life and voyage to concentrate on the background of his theories and their repercussions. Himmelfarb challenges the conventional notion of Darwin's greatness and originality as a thinker, placing him squarely in the context of his times.

Huxley, Julian, and H.B.D. Kettlewell. *Charles Darwin and His World*. New York: Viking, 1965. 144pp. Included in the author's brief, though comprehensive, account of Darwin's life and works are illustrations including Darwin's sketches, contemporary cartoons, and portraits of the various figures in the controversy surrounding Darwin's ideas.

Irvine, William. *Apes, Angels, and Victorians: The Story of Darwin, Huxley, and Evolution*. New York: McGraw-Hill, 1955. 399pp. In a scholarly, lucid, and stylish account, Irvine offers a dual biography of Darwin and Huxley, the contrasting personalities at the center of the controversy that Darwin's theory produced.

Karp, Walter. *Charles Darwin and the Origin of Species*. New York: Harper & Row, 1968. 153pp. Karp provides a comprehensive portrait of Darwin useful for the general reader, tracing his intellectual development leading up to the publication of the *Origin of Species*. Darwin's concepts are presented carefully with the necessary background and context supplied.

Moore, Ruth. *Charles Darwin: A Great Life in Brief*. New York: Knopf, 1954. 206pp. Moore's concise account of Darwin's life, ideas, and writings is a useful introduction for the general reader.

Moorehead, Alan. *Darwin and the Beagle*. New York: Harper & Row, 1969. 280pp. Moorehead concentrates on Darwin's five-year voyage in a detailed account that develops an interesting contrast between Darwin and the captain of the *Beagle*, Robert Fitzroy. Includes paintings and watercolors by the artists who accompanied Darwin on the voyage.

White, Michael, and John Gribbon. *Darwin: A Life in Science*. New York: Dutton, 1995. 322pp. In alternating biographical and scientific chapters, the author provides both a succinct narrative life and an accessible account of the development of Darwin's ideas, the influences that shaped him, and his legacy to science and culture. Readers new to Darwin and his ideas may find this an ideal starting place.

Biographical Novels

Stone, Irving. *The Origin: A Biographical Novel of Charles Darwin*. Garden City, New York: Doubleday, 1980. 743pp. A fictional biography of vast research, Stone's novel weaves into a chronological narrative virtually everything that is known about Darwin's experiences, habits, attitudes, and manner of life. Best on Darwin the man, the novel is less successful in capturing Darwin the thinker, and his ideas are considerably simplified to the point of misrepresenting the issues surrounding the publication of *Origin of Species*.

Fictional Portraits

McDonald, Roger. *Mr. Darwin's Shooter*. New York: Atlantic Monthly Press, 1998. 365pp. The assistant that Darwin used to shoot his specimens provides his perspective on the voyage of the *Beagle* and the impact of Darwin's theories.

Steen, Thorvald. *Don Carlos*. Los Angeles: Sun and Moon, 1997. 160pp. Darwin is described in 1833 by an Italian laborer who meets the naturalist in Buenos Aires.

Subercaseaux, Benjamin. *Jemmy Button*. New York: Macmillan, 1954. 382pp. Based on the journals of Robert Fitzroy, captain of the *Beagle*, and Darwin, the novel chronicles the events of its first voyage in which four Fuegian natives are brought back to England. The natives' experiences in civilization and their eventual return, observed by Darwin, are intriguingly and plausibly detailed.

Recommended Juvenile Biographies

Nardo, Don. *Charles Darwin*. New York: Chelsea House, 1993. 111pp. MG. This is a well-written life of Darwin in which he is placed within a historical context and includes clear explanations of Darwin's theories.

Skelton, Renee. *Charles Darwin and the Theory of Natural Selection*. Hauppauge, New York: Barron's, 1987. 119pp. MA/YA. Part of Barron's informative Solutions series, Darwin's life and career are chronicled, with an emphasis on the origin and development of his theories. With a helpful glossary and topics for essays.

Stefoff, Rebecca. *Charles Darwin and the Evolution Revolution*. New York: Oxford University Press, 1996. 126pp. YA. In a thoroughly researched biography, the author emphasizes Darwin's scientific, social, and political influence with concise, helpful summaries of important concepts and extensive photographs of Darwin, his family, friends, and colleagues.

123. JEFFERSON DAVIS
1808–1889

American statesman and only president of the Confederate States of America, Jefferson Davis was born in Kentucky but moved to Mississippi when he was a boy. After graduating from West Point, Davis served in the Black Hawk War. In 1835 he married the daughter of Zachary Taylor; she died three months later. After a decade as a Mississippi planter, he married Varina Howell, was elected to Congress, and served with distinction in the Mexican War. As a U.S. senator, Davis was a champion of southern rights and the expansion of slavery. Elected president of the Confederacy in 1862, Davis closely managed the army and was involved in a number of arguments with his generals. After Lee surrendered without Davis's permission in 1865, Davis was captured in Georgia attempting to escape to the west. He was imprisoned for two years (1865-1867) then released.

Autobiography and Primary Sources

The Rise and Fall of the Confederate Government. 1881. Reprint ed. New York: Da Capo Press, 1990. 2 vols. Davis offers a defense of the Confederacy and most of his own actions as president. Rarely penetrating or self-revealing, Davis's account is incomplete and disappointing in its lack of candor.

The Papers of Jefferson Davis. Haskell M. Monroe, ed. Baton Rouge: Louisiana State University Press, 1971–1988. 9 vols. This collection covers documents from Davis's career through 1860. A projected 14-volume complete edition is underway at Rice University.

Davis, Varina H. *Jefferson Davis: Ex-President of the Confederate States of America: A Memoir by His Wife*. 1890. Reprint ed. Baltimore, Maryland: Nautical and Aviation Publishing Co., 1990. 2 vols. At the end of his life, Davis dictated his autobiographical reflections to his wife, concluding with his West Point experiences. These reflections are interwoven with letters, papers, and Varina Davis's own eyewitness account to form an essential source for Davis biographers and anyone interested in the Confederate president and the Confederacy's short history.

Recommended Biographies

Davis, William C. *Jefferson Davis: The Man and His Hour.* New York: HarperCollins, 1991. 784pp. Drawing on the extensive *Papers of Jefferson Davis* project at Rice University, Davis has produced the best biography of Jefferson Davis now available. In Davis's balanced view, the Confederate president was both dogged and courageous as well as politically inept and narrow-minded. Davis, a military historian, is most authoritative in his treatment of Davis as commander in chief. More than just a chronological narrative, the author manages a persuasive psychological interpretation of Davis's life.

Eaton, Clement. *Jefferson Davis.* New York: Free Press, 1977. 334pp. Based on hitherto unpublished material, Eaton corrects a number of factual errors in previous accounts and provides a reliable and balanced portrait. Davis is viewed as a man of high principles and character who nonetheless was a poor judge of men and a weak administrator. Eaton offers a number of new insights on Davis's early years, his relationship with the women in his life, his traits as a plantation owner, and the development of his ideas about the South. He devotes only a few pages, however, to the postwar years.

Other Biographical Studies

Allen, Felicity. *Jefferson Davis: Unconquerable Heart.* Columbia: University of Missouri Press, 2000. 808pp. As the title indicates, this is more hagiography than objective biography, emphasizing Davis's strengths and minimizing his flaws.

Chadwick, Bruce. *The Two American Presidents: A Dual Biography of Abraham Lincoln and Jefferson Davis.* Secaucus, New Jersey: Carol, 1999. 490pp. Chadwick's comparative study of Davis and Lincoln recapitulates conventional interpretations of the two men and offers little new to the view of either man.

Cutting, Elisabeth B. *Jefferson Davis, Political Soldier.* New York: Dodd Mead, 1930. 361pp. The author attempts to penetrate the various prejudices, pro and con, that have distorted Davis's portrait to discover the actual man. Based on hitherto unpublished materials of Davis's letters and his contemporaries' accounts, Davis emerges as a determined individual, responsible for his own downfall.

Dodd, William E. *Jefferson Davis.* 1907. Reprint ed. New York: Russell & Russell, 1966. 396pp. Dodd's limited and now dated account is nonetheless reliably based on primary sources. Dodd provides a favorably description of Davis's pre-Civil War achievements and exonerates Davis for sole responsibility in the Confederacy's defeat. He largely ignores Davis's last 25 years.

McElroy, Robert. *Jefferson Davis: The Unreal and the Real.* New York: Harper, 1937. 2 vols. McElroy's comprehensive life is based mainly on secondary sources and offers little that is new, and his work has been superseded by more recent efforts. The author identifies Davis's strict interpretation of the Constitution and belief in states' rights as keys to understanding his political and personal decisions.

Strode, Hudson. *Jefferson Davis.* New York: Harcourt, Brace, 1955–1964. 3 vols. Strode's exhaustive study is mostly useful today as a repository of family letters and interviews that fill in the details of Davis's life. Determined to explode previous characterizations of Davis as cold and aloof, Strode indulges in a great deal of special pleading to humanize Davis and exonerate him. Many current readers will be offended by Strode's decidedly southern viewpoint and justifications of southern attitudes, particularly his uncritical treatment of slavery, which often stresses slaves' loyalty and contentment.

Tate, Allen. *Jefferson Davis: His Rise and Fall.* 1929. Reprint ed. Nashville: J.S. Sanders, 1998. 293pp. Less a full biography than a polemical essay on Davis's role in the Confederacy's defeat, Tate ignores Davis's early life and concentrates on indicting him for the sin of pride, his obstinate refusal to acknowledge defeat, admit his errors, or conciliate his opponents.

Biographical Novels

Kane, Harnett T. *Bride of Fortune.* Garden City, New York: Doubleday, 1948. 301pp. In this fictional biography of Varina Howell Davis, her married life is dramatized from their first meeting to Davis's release from prison in 1867. Despite evident research and a factual framework, the novel is often superficial in its characterizations and often glamorizes the southern cause.

Olsen, Theodore V. *There Was a Season: A Biographical Novel of Jefferson Davis.* Garden City, New York: Doubleday, 1972. 444pp. Restricted to Davis's early years when he was a promising army officer, the novel dramatizes his courtship and brief marriage to Sarah Knox Taylor, the second daughter of Zachary Taylor, his commanding officer. Although based on fact, the novel invents some characters, events, and situations.

Seifert, Shirley. *The Proud Way.* Philadelphia: Lippincott, 1948. 316pp. Based on two years in the life of Varina Howell, the novel dramatizes the period when she first met Davis at age 17 until she married him. Seifert's romantic treatment does try to uncover character traits that help explain the Davises' development in later life.

Fictional Portraits

Agnew, James B. *Eggnog Riot.* San Rafael, California: Presidio Press, 1979. 211pp. Based on primary sources, the novel dramatizes an actual incident at West Point during Davis's years there.

Delmar, Vina. *Beloved.* New York: Harcourt, Brace, 1956. 382pp. This biographical novel dramatizes the career of Judah P. Benjamin, the Confederate secretary of war and state in Davis's cabinet, and provides an interesting angle for viewing the Confederate president.

Dixon, Thomas. *The Victim: A Romance of the Real Jefferson Davis.* New York: Appleton, 1914. 510pp. In a romanticized defense, Dixon chronicles Davis's heroism from his childhood and makes the case that Davis was a victim of both the North and the South.

Dowdey, Clifford. *The Proud Retreat.* Garden City, New York: Doubleday, 1953. 318pp. Depicting Davis's attempt to escape to the west with the Confederate treasury, which disappeared shortly after Lee's surrender, the novel depicts the events of Davis's retreat and speculation about the fate of the treasure.

Ryan, Edward J. *Comes an Echo on the Breeze.* New York: Exposition Press, 1949. 202pp. Dramatically re-creating Abraham Lincoln's military experience during the Black Hawk War, the novel includes appearances by both Jefferson Davis and Zachary Taylor.

Savage, Douglas. *The Court Martial of Robert E. Lee.* Conshohocken, Pennsylvania: Combined Books, 1993. 475pp. In an intriguing, convincing "what-if" scenario, the novel imagines what might have happened if Lee was court-martialed after the defeat at Gettysburg. Davis, like Lee, emerges as a complex figure.

Recommended Juvenile Biographies

Burch, Joann J. *Jefferson Davis: President of the Confederacy.* Springfield, New Jersey: Enslow, 1998. 128pp. MG. Burch supplies a balanced and comprehensive biographical portrait combining personal details with an informative summary of Davis's political career.

King, Perry Scott. *Jefferson Davis.* New York: Chelsea House, 1990. 111pp. MG. A somewhat disappointing entry in a distinguished biographical series, King's biography does provide a thorough and informative coverage of Davis's early life, but the account of the war years is a brief overview of the most important moments, and objectivity is sacrificed in consideration of Davis's legacy and importance.

Tate, Allen. *Jefferson Davis.* New York: Putnam, 1969. 189pp. YA. Tate's highly critical portrait of Davis supplies a controversial view on Davis's role in the Confederacy's defeat. For the sophisticated student ready to deal with complex issues.

Biographical Films and Theatrical Adaptations

Sante Fe Trail (1940). Director: Michael Curtiz. Not reliable as history, this adventure story set in "Bloody Kansas" shows J.E.B. Stuart (Errol Flynn) teaming with George Armstrong Custer (Ronald Reagan) in pursuit of John Brown. Jefferson Davis is plausibly portrayed by veteran character actor Erville Anderson. Video.

Tennessee Johnson (1942). Director: William Dieterle. In this drama depicting the political career of Andrew Johnson, played by Van Heflin, Jefferson Davis is portrayed by Morris Ankrum.

124. CHARLES DE GAULLE
1890–1970

French statesman and general and first president of the Fifth Republic, Charles De Gaulle served in combat during World War I until 1916 when he was captured. In 1940 he opposed the Franco-German armistice and fled to London where he organized the Free French forces. Unanimously elected provisional president of France in 1945, De Gaulle resigned in 1946 over disagreements with provisions in the new constitution. He came out of retirement in 1958 to help resolve the Algerian crisis, and in 1959 became president of France. De Gaulle's attempt to restore France to its former world stature brought him into conflict with Britain and the United States, and in 1966 he withdrew French troops from NATO and forced NATO troops out of France. In 1969 after defeat in a referendum decision on constitutional reform, De Gaulle resigned as president.

Autobiography and Primary Sources

The Complete War Memoirs of Charles de Gaulle. New York: Simon & Schuster, 1964. 1,048pp. De Gaulle's reflections on World War II offer insights into events, personalities, and his own personal idiosyncracies. Includes a selection of documents that allows the reader to evaluate the accuracy of his views.

Memoirs of Hope: Renewal and Endeavor. New York: Simon & Schuster, 1971. 392pp. This account of the years 1958 to 1962 is useful for light it sheds on De Gaulle's interpretation of events and his accounts of meetings with prominent contemporaries. However, his tone of unbending reserve and self-righteous defensiveness precludes much access to the inner man.

Recommended Biographies

Lacouture, Jean. *De Gaulle.* New York: W.W. Norton, 1990–1992. 2 vols. While no definitive biography is possible until De Gaulle's papers and letters are made available for scholarly examination, Lacouture's meticulous analysis is the fullest and most authoritative biography available. Sympathetic but evenhanded, Lacouture provides a comprehensive record of De Gaulle's life and a fair judgment of his place in history. The book in its subtle, complex, and dramatic skill has been hailed in France as one of the supreme works of contemporary biography.

Ledwidge, Sir Bernard. *De Gaulle.* New York: Saint Martin's, 1982. 418pp. Written by a British diplomat with access to hitherto unexamined official archives in Paris, London, and Washington, Ledwidge's comprehensive biography is sympathetic but not uncritical and is more accepting of De Gaulle's drive for establishing a Europe outside of Anglo-American control than other non-French biographers. Accessible for a general reader, Ledwidge largely succeeds in providing a balanced portrait of a complex man that acknowledges both his considerable achievements and limitations.

Williams, Charles. *The Last Great Frenchman: A Life of General De Gaulle.* New York: J. Wiley, 1995. 544pp. Williams details De Gaulle's relationship with the major leaders of the twentieth century and explores his complex, contradictory personal life. Based largely on secondary sources, Williams's biography does include interviews with a number of De Gaulle's associates woven into a lucid, readable account that depicts an affectionate, shy, and emotional private individual and a cold, ruthless, and proud public man.

Other Biographical Studies

Barrès, Philippe. *Charles de Gaulle.* New York: Doubleday, 1941. 260pp. In this first biography, Barrès introduces the leader of the Free French forces to a British and American audience, setting De Gaulle against a background of French politics and military policies in the prewar years. Discreet on certain points for purposes of military security, the author invests his subject in the role of hero and French savior.

Cogan, Charles G. *Charles de Gaulle: A Brief Biography with Documents.* New York: Saint Martin's, 1995. 256pp. This book combines a history of Gaullism, an examination of the three major stages of De Gaulle's career, and a collection of 25 primary sources, including government documents and excerpts from De Gaulle's memoirs, speeches, interviews, and press conferences.

Cook, Don. *Charles De Gaulle: A Biography.* New York: Putnam, 1983. 432pp. In a biography for the general reader, De Gaulle is seen from an American perspective that praises his war leadership and his role in extricating France from Algeria, but criticizes his stance toward NATO and opposition to Britain and the United States. De Gaulle's faults are predominant in Cook's portrait.

Crowley, Aidan. *De Gaulle: A Biography.* Indianapolis: Bobbs-Merrill, 1969. 510pp. Crowley provides an English perspective on De Gaulle and his legacy that synthesizes a number of secondary sources, including memoirs and critical studies, into a clear narrative. As a member of Parliament, Crowley has used his acquaintance with many of the prominent figures following World War II to add to the intimacy of his presentation.

Crozier, Brian. *De Gaulle.* New York: Scribner, 1973. 2 vols. Crozier's comprehensive study, the first in English, draws on a number of hitherto unavailable sources, documents, and reminiscences of contemporaries to support a largely unsympathetic interpretation in which De Gaulle's fame outstripped his more modest achievements and has ignored his substantial political failures. From an obvious hostile foreign perspective, Crozier fails to come to grips with De Gaulle's hold on the hearts and minds of the French.

Grinnell-Milne, Duncan. *The Triumph of Integrity: A Portrait of Charles de Gaulle.* New York: Macmillan, 1962. 334pp. Concentrating on the war years in an account written by someone who worked for De Gaulle as a liaison officer after the fall of France, this character sketch offers a good deal of firsthand information, but, overall, the book lacks objectivity. Rejecting the notion of De Gaulle's arrogance and pride, Grinnell-Milne takes De Gaulle's side on every point.

Mauriac, François. *De Gaulle.* Garden City, New York: Doubleday, 1966. 229pp. Mauriac sets out to show through De Gaulle's writings and speeches the consistency of his character in an appreciation that reads like a prose poem of praise. Useful for giving the reader a sense of De Gaulle's hold on the French imagination, the book fails to rise to the level of a critical assessment or a deep psychological analysis.

Schoenbrun, David. *The Three Lives of Charles de Gaulle.* New York: Atheneum, 1966. 373pp. Tracing De Gaulle's career as soldier, political leader in exile, and statesman, this is a skillfully written and carefully researched biographical study focused more on relating events in De Gaulle's life than in revealing his motivations.

Shennan, Andrew. *De Gaulle.* New York: Longman, 1993. 190pp. In this entry in the Profiles in Power series, Shennan follows closely De Gaulle's rise and fall in French politics providing the essential background information to see his actions in context and coherently. Covers the period 1940 to 1969 and is less concerned with the private De Gaulle than the politician.

Werth, Alexander. *De Gaulle: A Political Biography.* New York: Simon & Schuster, 1966. 416pp. Concentrating on De Gaulle's political career, Werth reveals the key to his ideas, actions, and quarrels in his rebellion from his opposition to the military establishment before the war to his defiance of Britain and America. With little original research and relying on rehashing the insights of others, Werth's interpretation is limited and lacks psychological depth to explain De Gaulle's political successes.

Fictional Portraits

Fabre-Luce, Alfred. *The Trial of Charles de Gaulle.* New York: Praeger, 1963. 270pp. Based on an invented political trial of De Gaulle for some of his policies, the author's anti-Gaullism is evident and colors the presentation of the man and his legacy.

Recommended Juvenile Biographies

Banfield, Susan. *Charles de Gaulle.* New York: Chelsea House, 1985. 111pp. MG/YA. Solid World Leaders Past & Present series entry that captures the highlights in De Gaulle's public career as war leader and French statesman.

Epstein, Sam. *Charles de Gaulle: Defender of France.* Champaign, Illinois: Garrard, 1973. 175pp. MG/YA. This is a full and informative chronicle of De Gaulle's life and career.

Whitelaw, Nancy. *Charles de Gaulle: I Am France.* New York: Dillon Press, 1991. 112pp. MG. Whitelaw summarizes the highlights of De Gaulle's life and impact on French and world history.

Biographical Films and Theatrical Adaptations

The Warlords (1986). Producer: Lamancha Productions. This series of brief film biographies of World War II leaders, such as Hitler, Mussolini, Stalin, and Churchill, includes a portrait of De Gaulle. Video.

125. THOMAS DE QUINCEY
1785–1859

An English essayist, De Quincey achieved literary fame with the publication of his *Confessions of an Opium Eater* (1822), which recounts his experiences as an opium addict. He contributed numerous essays to various journals, including *Blackwood's* magazine. His best work includes "On Murder Considered as One of the Fine Arts" and "Suspiria de Profundis."

Autobiography and Primary Sources

The Collected Writings of Thomas De Quincey. David Masson, ed. Edinburgh: A. and C. Black, 1889–1990. 14 vols. The first three volumes of De Quincey's collected works contain the most important of his autobiographical writings.

Recommended Biographies

Eaton, Horace A. *Thomas De Quincey: A Biography.* New York: Oxford University Press, 1936. 542pp. Eaton's painstakingly researched, comprehensive, and authoritative biography has long maintained its stature as the definitive, scholarly life. Establishing the chronological record, correcting previous errors, and filling in gaps, Eaton allows De Quincey to tell his own story as much as possible.

Lindop, Grevel. *The Opium Eater: A Life of Thomas De Quincey.* New York: Taplinger, 1981. 433pp. This reliable and sensitive biography emphasizes De Quincey's personality, his response to the traumas of his childhood, and the centrality of his opium addiction.

Other Biographical Studies

Barrell, John. *The Infection of Thomas De Quincey: A Psychopathology of Imperialism.* New Haven, Connecticut: Yale University Press, 1991. 235pp. In a demanding, challenging psychological examination, Barrell penetrates deeply into De Quincey's psyche to trace the origins and expressions of his obsessions.

Masson, David. *De Quincey.* 1881. Reprint ed. New York: AMS Press, 1968. 200pp. Masson, the editor of De Quincey's *Collected Writings* , draws on his extensive research into the writer's career to supply a concise and reliable account. The book is less successful in coming to grips with De Quincey's personality.

Page, H.A. *Thomas De Quincey: His Life and Writings with Unpublished Correspondence.* New York: Scribner, 1877. 2 vols. The first biography of De Quincey mainly organizes chronologically extracts from the writer's autobiographical writings and letters with commentary based on Page's own relationship with De Quincey.

Sackville-West, Edward. *A Flame in Sunlight: The Life and Work of Thomas De Quincey.* London: Cassell, 1936. 352pp. This sympathetic critical biography offers a coherent view of De Quincey's development and personality, identifying the important experiences that shaped him.

126. EUGENE V. DEBS
1855–1926

American labor organizer, socialist political leader, and pacifist, Debs was a national leader of the Brotherhood of Locomotive Firemen and founded (1893) the American Railway Union. He also cofounded (1898) the Socialist party and the

Industrial Workers of the World (1905). He was the Socialist candidate for president five times, conducting his last and most successful campaign in 1920, while serving a prison term under the World War I Espionage Act (1917). He was released in 1921.

Autobiography and Primary Sources

Eugene V. Debs Speaks. Jean Tussey, ed. New York: Pathfinder Press, 1970. 320pp. This selection of Debs's speeches and writings includes his essay "How I Became a Socialist."

Letters of Eugene V. Debs. J. Robert Constantine, ed. Urbana: University of Illinois Press, 1990. 3 vols. With a useful introductory biographical sketch, this scholarly edition of Debs's correspondence is an invaluable source on the man and the history of American radicalism.

Gentle Rebel: Letters of Eugene V. Debs. J. Robert Constantine, ed. Urbana: University of Illinois Press, 1995. 312pp. Constantine selects 500 of the most interesting and revealing of Debs's letters from his three-volume collection.

Walls and Bars. Chicago: Charles H. Kerr, 1973. 286pp. This series of articles written during Debs's incarceration in an Atlanta penitentiary is a searing indictment of prison life and his treatment.

Recommended Biographies

Ginger, Ray. *The Bending Cross: A Biography of Eugene Victor Debs.* New Brunswick, New Jersey: Rutgers University Press, 1949. 543pp. Ginger's is a lively, detailed, sympathetic biography that long served as the standard life until Salvatore. Based on extensive research using the accounts of Debs's associates, the book unfortunately lacks footnotes and a full disclosure of sources.

Salvatore, Nick. *Eugene V. Debs: Citizen and Socialist.* Urbana: University of Illinois Press, 1982. 437pp. Winner of the Dunning and Bancroft prizes, Salvatore's is currently the leading biography of Debs. Covering in detail Debs's personal and professional life, Salvatore probes Debs's psychological depths and development from conservative to socialist while placing his career in its wider historical and social context.

Young, Marguerite. *Harp Song for a Radical: The Life and Times of Eugene Victor Debs.* New York: Knopf, 1999. 599pp. Something of a biographical curiosity, this discursive, idiosyncratic, unfinished biographical portrait was the work of the novelist and poet author for the last 25 years of her life. Taking Debs's story only up to 1877, the book is as much about the age as the man with a vast cast animated imaginatively and impressionistically.

Other Biographical Studies

Brommel, Bernard. *Eugene V. Debs: Spokesman for Labor and Socialism.* Chicago: C.H. Kerr, 1978. 265pp. Brommel's is a solid, scholarly biography that adds to the biographical record, particularly on the role of Mabel Curry in Debs's life.

Coleman, McAlister. *Eugene V. Debs: A Man Unafraid.* New York: Greenberg, 1930. 345pp. Coleman's highly partisan and uncritical study of Debs's life concentrates on his rise to political lead-

ership and industrial actions. Lacking detachment, Coleman portrays a man far too wise and noble to be humanly believable.

Currie, Harold W. *Eugene V. Debs.* Boston: Twayne, 1976. 157pp. Serving the general reader as an introduction to the man and his ideas, this is a concise summary of Debs's views on labor, government, religion, war, and other topics.

Karsner, David. *Debs: His Authorized Life and Letters.* New York: Boni and Liveright, 1919. 244pp. The author, a journalist who covered Debs's trial in 1918, had access to Debs and his friends, as well as to important documentary sources, but the treatment is insufficiently objective to be fully effective and reliable as a critical biography.

Morgan, Howard W. *Eugene V. Debs: Socialist for President.* Syracuse, New York: Syracuse University Press, 1962. 257pp. As the author explains in his preface, this is "neither a biography of Debs nor a history of the American socialism" but an examination of the Socialists in national politics between 1900 and 1925. The result is a somewhat simplified portrait of Debs during his five campaigns for the presidency.

Biographical Novels

Nissenson, Aaron. *Song of Man: A Novel Based on the Life of Eugene V. Debs.* New Haven, Connecticut: Whittier Books, 1964. 200pp. The general outline of Debs's life is recreated in an admiring treatment, marred by unconvincing dialogue and a lack of penetration to reveal the man behind his ideas and activities.

Stone, Irving. *Adversary in the House.* Garden City, New York: Doubleday, 1947. 432pp. Stone depicts the career of Debs based on solid research and documentation.

Fictional Portraits

Fast, Howard. *The American.* New York: Duell, Sloan, and Pearce,1946. 337pp. Fast's biographical profile of the life of John Peter Altgeld involves appearances by a number of historical figures, including Debs.

Jakes, John. *Homeland.* New York: Doubleday, 1993. 785pp. Jakes's saga spans the period 1890 to 1900 and includes appearances by such historical figures as Thomas Edison, Clara Barton, Theodore Roosevelt, and Debs.

Mark, Grace. *The Dream Seekers.* New York: Morrow,1992. 412pp. Set during the 1893 Chicago World's Fair, the novel dramatizes the Pullman Strike and features appearances by such figures as Jane Addams, Clarence Darrow, and Debs.

Recommended Juvenile Biographies

Noble, Iris. *Labor's Advocate: Eugene V. Debs.* New York: J. Messner, 1966. 191pp. Noble's is a fictionalized account of Debs's life and career.

Selvin, David F. *Eugene Debs, Rebel, Labor Leader, Prophet: A Biography.* New York: Lothrop Lee, 1966. 192pp. YA. Selvin summarizes Debs's life and career in a rousing narrative account that is more carefully documented than Noble's treatment.

White, Anne T. *Eugene Debs: American Socialist.* New York: L. Hill, 1974. 137pp. MG/YA. White helpfully places Debs's career in the wider political and cultural context of his era.

Biographical Films and Theatrical Adaptations

Eugene Debs and the American Movement (1977). Directors: Renner Wunderlich and Margaret Lazarus. A documentary profile of Debs's public career and his impact on the labor movement. Video.

127. CLAUDE DEBUSSY
1862–1918

French composer and exponent of musical impressionism, Debussy greatly influenced the development of twentieth-century music with his use of harmony and dissonance, and his innovations in orchestration. His works include the famous tone poem *Prelude to the Afternoon of a Faun* (1894), the orchestral pieces *Nocturnes* (1899) and *The Sea* (1905), the popular piano piece *Clair de lune* (1903), the opera *Pelléas er Mélisande*, and many songs.

Autobiography and Primary Sources

Debussy Letters. François Lesure and Roger Nichols, eds. Cambridge, Massachusetts: Harvard University Press, 1987. 355pp. Comprising a quarter of Debussy's surviving correspondence, this is a rich collection revealing the composer's private and professional life as well as his astute observations of the cultural life of his time.

Recommended Biographies

Dietschy, Marcel. *A Portrait of Claude Debussy.* Oxford: Clarendon Press, 1990. 254pp. Dietschy's is an accomplished documentation of Debussy's background and development, and a psychological profile.

Lockspeiser, Edward. *Debussy: His Life and Mind.* New York: Macmillan, 1962–1965. 2 vols. Regarded as the standard life, this highly detailed study corrects previous efforts in the most comprehensive rendering of the composer's life, character, and musical development. *Debussy* (1936. Revised ed. London: Dent, 1980. 291pp.) is a more concise overview frequently updated to reflect more recent scholarship.

Nichols, Roger. *The Life of Debussy.* New York: Cambridge University Press, 1998. 184pp. Nichols is a concise though nuanced summary of Debussy's life and work that captures the complexity of the man and the impact of his work.

Other Biographical Studies

Brown, Jonathan. *Claude Debussy: An Essential Guide to His Life and Works.* London: Pavilion, 1996. 108pp. This is a basic critical overview of Debussy's life and music designed to enhance the nonspecialists listening enjoyment.

Dumesnil, Maurice. *Claude Debussy: Master of Dreams.* New York: Washburn, 1940. 326pp. Written by a pianist friend of the composer and based on personal notes of Debussy's widow who authorized the book, Dumesnil's appreciative, undocumented account is alternatively perceptive and lushly sentimental and idealized. Readers looking for precise information about the details of Debussy's life will be disappointed.

Holmes, Paul. *Debussy.* London: Omnibus, 1989. 136pp. Part of the Illustrated Lives of the Great Composers series, this is a lavishly illustrated biographical portrait that covers the essential events in the composer's life and connects his work to wider artistic and intellectual trends of his period.

Seroff, Victor. *Debussy: Musician of France.* New York: Putnam, 1956. 367pp. The emphasis here is on Debussy's personal life, love affairs, and scandals. Marred by factual errors, the book offers little analysis of Debussy's music other than the reviews of his contemporaries.

Vallas, Léon. *Claude Debussy: His Life and Works.* London: Oxford University Press, 1933. 275pp. Vallas, a French scholar, supplies an appreciative account of Debussy's life and music that has largely been superseded by later studies.

Biographical Novels

La Mure, Pierre. *Clair de Lune: A Novel About Claude Debussy.* New York: Random House, 1962. 467pp. Observing the basic facts of Debussy's biography, La Mure characterizes him as the archetypal suffering artist against an authentic period background.

Recommended Juvenile Biographies

Harvey, Harry B. *Claude of France: The Story of Debussy.* New York: Allen Towne, 1948. 190pp. YA. Including the observations of those who knew the composer personally, this is a colorful, informative biography that also paints an interesting picture of France in the last half of the nineteenth century.

Thompson, Wendy. *Claude Debussy.* New York: Viking, 1993. 48pp. YA. Debussy's life and work are discussed, along with simple keyboard arrangements and illustrations that capture the man and his music.

Young, Percy M. *Debussy.* New York: D. White, 1968. 76pp. MG. Young offers a full portrayal of Debussy's life, his music, and his background.

Biographical Films and Theatrical Adaptations

Camille Claudel (1989). Director: Bruno Nuytten. This screen depiction of the relationship between Claudel (Isabelle Adjani) and Rodin (Gerard Depardieu) includes an appearance by Maxime Leroux as Debussy. Video.

Other Sources

Nichols, Roger. *Debussy Remembered.* Portland, Oregon: Amadeus Press, 1992. 256pp. This informative volume brings together various views of the composer.

128. DANIEL DEFOE
1660–1731

One of the first English novelists, Defoe was an unsuccessful merchant before becoming a writer. He achieved fame with the poem *The True-Born Englishman* (1701) but did not begin writing novels until he was nearly 60. His works include the novels *Robinson Crusoe* (1719) and *Moll Flanders* (1722) and an account of the 1665 plague in London, *A Journal of the Plague Year* (1722). Called the father of modern journalism, Defoe was associated with 26 periodicals during his lifetime.

Autobiography and Primary Sources

The Letters of Daniel Defoe. G.H. Healey, ed. Oxford: Clarendon Press, 1955. 506pp. What little we know about Defoe's life is collected in this edition of his letters and various documents to and from the writer. Unfortunately, Defoe makes no reference to his fiction.

Recommended Biographies

Backscheider, Paula R. *Daniel Defoe: His Life.* Baltimore: Johns Hopkins University Press, 1989. 671pp. The author collects seemingly everything known about Defoe into a coherent, comprehensive narrative sequence. Adding to the record some new discoveries, correcting previous errors, and incorporating the best guesses, Backscheider offers the fullest treatment yet on the often maddeningly elusive writer.

Sutherland, James. *Defoe.* 1937. Reprint ed. New York: Barnes and Noble, 1971. 300pp. Sutherland's is a pioneering scholarly work that organizes the known facts about Defoe's life and career into a coherent and credible pattern that reveals much more of the personality and motives of the man than previous attempts and remains one of the best Defoe biographies available.

West, Richard. *Daniel Defoe: The Life and Strange, Surprising Adventures.* New York: Carroll & Graf, 1998. 427pp. West's is a rousing popular tour of Defoe's remarkable life and varied careers seen mainly from an assessment of his works and a vivid animation of his era.

Other Biographical Studies

Bastian, F. *Defoe's Early Life.* New York: Barnes and Noble, 1981. 377pp. Focusing on what little is known of Defoe's early life from his birth to his imprisonment in 1703, Bastian combs through Defoe's fiction, political and travel writing for autobiographical clues. Highly speculative, the book is often more ingenious than convincing.

Dottin, Paul. *The Life and Strange and Surprising Adventures of Daniel Defoe.* London: Paul, 1928. 322pp. The work of a French scholar, though now outdated by more recent scholarship, this is a generally reliable and sympathetic biographical narrative of Defoe's life, along with glimpses into the social and political history of his time.

FitzGerald, Brian. *Daniel Defoe: A Study in Conflict.* New York: Somerset, 1954. 248pp. The conflicts of the book's title refer to religious and political contradictions evident in Defoe's life, which this study attempts to explain and reconcile in terms of the writer's career and personality.

Moore, John R. *Daniel Defoe: Citizen of the Modern World*. Chicago: University of Chicago Press, 1958. 408pp. More for the specialist than the casual reader, Moore organizes his scholarly collection of materials and interpretations topically rather than chronologically with separate chapters on various aspects of Defoe's life and career.

Sutherland, James. *Daniel Defoe: A Critical Study*. Boston: Houghton Mifflin, 1971. 259pp. Sutherland followed his biography with a critical study of Defoe's works but includes here a succinct biographical profile as well as an evaluative chapter on Defoe's character and beliefs.

Watson, Francis. *Daniel Defoe*. New York: Longmans, 1952. 240pp. Watson's is a brief biographical portrait that synthesizes biographical and background material into a highly readable account suitable as an introduction for the general reader.

129. EDGAR DEGAS
1834–1917

An impressionist painter and sculptor, Degas ranks among the greatest of French artists. His favorite subjects were ballet dancers, women at their toilettes, café life, horses, and racetracks. His works include *Foyer of the Dance* (1872), *Absinthe* (1882), and *The Rehearsal* (1882), as well as pastels, drawings in charcoal, and many notable small sculptures of dancers and horses. Degas influenced such later artists as Toulouse-Lautrec and Picasso.

Autobiography and Primary Sources

Letters. Marcel Guérin, ed. Oxford: Bruno Cassirer, 1947. 270pp. Concerned mainly with practical matters, Degas's letters nevertheless give the flavor of the man and his personality.

Recommended Biographies

Dunlop, Ian. *Degas*. New York: Harper & Row, 1979. 240pp. Sumptuously illustrated, Dunlop's critical biography helpfully synthesizes recent research, placing the many contradictions in the painter's life in their wider social perspective, while relying on extensive quotations from Degas's own writings and those of his contemporaries and critics.

McMullen, Roy. *Degas: His Life, Times, and Work*. Boston: Houghton Mifflin, 1984. 517pp. Drawing on Degas's letters and notebooks, McMullen provides a complex and compelling portrait of the man who is shown as the product of his time and social class. Readable and accessible for the general reader, the book lacks sufficient illustrations of many of the works discussed and should be supplemented by the more extensive illustrated volumes by Dunlop, and Gordon and Forge.

Sutton, Denys. *Edgar Degas, Life and Work*. New York: Rizzoli, 1986. 343pp. Sutton's is a well-documented, insightful critical biography that places Degas against a solid social background. Both the painter's personality and his works are analyzed

through previously unpublished extracts from his correspondence.

Other Biographical Studies

Benfey, Christopher E.G. *Degas in New Orleans: Encounters in the Creole World of Kate Chopin and George Washington Cable*. New York: Knopf, 1998. 294pp. Benfey makes an ultimately unconvincing case that Degas's artistic development was significantly altered by his five-month 1872 stay in New Orleans. To capture the wider cultural scene, the book focuses on New Orleans writers Cable and Chopin, though there is no evidence that Degas encountered either of them.

Gordon, Robert, and Andrew Forge. *Degas*. New York: Abrams, 1988. 288pp. This handsome, large format includes more than 330 illustrations, a third of which are in color. The text consists of thematic chapters on various aspects of Degas's life, artistry, and relationships with his contemporaries.

Loyrette, Henri. *Degas: The Man and His Art*. New York: Abrams, 1993. 191pp. This beautifully illustrated volume explores Degas's often complex and contradictory character as revealed by his relationships and varied interests. The book serves as a solid introductory guide to both the artist and his work.

Fictional Portraits

La Mure, Pierre. *Moulin Rouge: A Novel Based on the Life of Henri de Toulouse-Lautrec*. New York: Random House,1950. 438pp. Degas is featured in this biographical portrait of Lautrec and his era.

Stone, Irving. *Depths of Glory*. Garden City, New York: Doubleday, 1985. 653pp. This fictional biography of Camille Pissarro features appearances by a number of his artist contemporaries, including Degas.

Weiss, David. *Naked Came I: A Novel of Rodin*. New York: Morrow, 1963. 660pp. Degas, as well as other period figures, round out the scene in this biographical novel on the life of sculptor Rodin.

Recommended Juvenile Biographies

Mannering, Douglas. *The Life and Works of Degas*. New York: Chelsea House, 1997. 80pp. MG. Mannering presents a useful critical analysis of Degas's artistic achievement and the essential features of his life and artistic career.

Meyer, Susan E. *Edgar Degas*. New York: Abrams, 1994. 92pp. YA. Part of the respected First Impressions series, this informative book explores the many contradictions in Degas's life and examines his major works in the context of the social and political milieu of his era.

Biographical Films and Theatrical Adaptations

Degas (1988). Director: Harry Rasky. A film portrait of Degas's life and work using the artist's own words and location footage of places associated with the painter. Video.

The Unquiet Spirit: The Life and Art of Edgar Degas, 1834–1917 (1980). Producer: Ann Turner. This is a biographical profile that attempts to con-

nect Degas's experiences with his artistic achievements. Video.

See also Mary Cassatt

130. EUGÈNE DELACROIX
1798–1863

The foremost painter of the French romantic movement, Delacroix studied with Géricault and was greatly influenced by him. Delacroix's dramatic, richly colored paintings feature themes from mythology, literature, and political, religious, and literary history and include *Greece Expiring on the Ruins of Missalonghi* (1827), *The Jewish Wedding* (1839), and *Entrance of the Crusaders into Constantinople* (1841). He also produced lithographs and outstanding murals for the Bourbon Palace, the Luxembourg Palace, and the Church of Saint-Sulpice in Paris.

Autobiography and Primary Sources

The Journal of Eugène Delacroix: A Selection. Hubert Wellington, ed. Ithaca, New York: Cornell University Press, 1980. 504pp. The painter's journal provides a remarkable insight into his creative process.

Selected Letters, 1813–63, of Eugène Delacroix. Jean Stewart, ed. New York: Saint Martin's, 1971. 414pp. This selection includes a valuable biographical-critical introduction by John Russell and reveals a great deal about the personality of the artist and his views on art and his era.

Recommended Biographies

Huyghe, René. *Delacroix*. New York: Abrams, 1963. 564pp. This critical biography is a thorough, well-documented, and well-illustrated study that lucidly explores the painter's artistic development and personality in the wider context of his period and its intellectual and artistic background.

Jobert, Barthelmy. *Delacroix*. Princeton, New Jersey: Princeton University Press, 1998. 336pp. This is detailed, comprehensive treatment of Delacroix's career that provides an important reassessment of the inner tensions and contradictions behind both his work and his life. Beautifully illustrated with 231 color plates, Jobert's is an informed, impeccably researched critical biography that helps to reshape the reader's view and appreciation of the painter.

Trapp, Frank A. *The Attainment of Delacroix*. Baltimore: Johns Hopkins University Press, 1970. 371pp. Trapp's is an excellent scholarly examination of Delacroix's artistry that considers his influences and the connection between the painter's personal experiences and the development of his art. Although highly readable, with the technical details mainly reserved for the notes, the book may overwhelm the casual reader and will most benefit readers with some art history background or prior knowledge.

Other Biographical Studies

Deslandres, Yvonne. *Delacroix: A Pictorial Biography*. New York: Viking, 1963. 144pp. An introduction to Delacroix's life and work, the book includes more than 100 illustrations and several color plates. The basic outline of the artist's life is covered, serving to orient the general reader.

Johnson, Lee. *Delacroix*. New York: W.W. Norton, 1963. 123pp. Johnson's succinct critical study of Delacroix's artistry is a penetrating summary that is applied far more extensively in the author's later definitive catalog.

Johnson, Lee. *The Paintings of Eugène Delacroix: A Critical Catalog*. Oxford: Clarendon Press, 1981-89. 6 vols. Johnson's definitive multi-volume catalog features extensive critical commentary on Delacroix's works that connect his life with his art.

Prideaux, Tom. *The World of Delacroix*. New York: Time-Life Books, 1966. 196pp. The illustrations are the standouts here, with a somewhat inflated and sentimentalized text summarizing the highlights of Delacroix's life and career.

Spector, Jack. *Delacroix: The Death of Sardanapalus*. New York: Viking, 1974. 135pp. The book focuses on the creation of Delacroix's masterpiece exploring both the technical challenges the painter faced and the psychological insights into the artist that can be gleaned from a close reading of the work.

Biographical Novels

Hersch, Virginia. *To Seize a Dream*. New York: Crown, 1948. 341pp. Hersch traces the painter's life, relying on quotations from his letters and diaries to provide authenticity.

Biographical Films and Theatrical Adaptations

Impromptu (1990). Director: James Lapine. This depiction of the 1830s Parisien bohemian art world centers on the complicated lives of George Sand, Chopin, and Liszt and includes an appearance by Ralph Brown as Delacroix. The impressive cast includes Judy Davis, Hugh Grant, Mandy Patinkin, Julian Sands, Bernadette Peters, and Emma Thompson. Video.

The Restless Eye: Eugène Delacroix (1980). Director: Colin Nears. This film portrait uses Delacroix's journals and paintings to tell the story of his life and work. Video.

131. RENÉ DESCARTES
1596-1650

A profoundly influential French mathematician, physicist, and philosopher, Descartes founded the rationalist school of philosophy known as Cartesianism. He initiated the study of analytic geometry, originating the use of Cartesian coordinates and the Cartesian curves, and expounded on his mathematical theories in his famous *Discourse on Method* (1637). Descartes introduced the concept of universal doubt, summed up in his famous phrase, *Cogito ergo sum* ("I think, therefore I am"), and considered the mind entirely separate from the body, a theory known as Cartesian dualism.

Autobiography and Primary Sources

Philosophical Letters. Anthony Kenny, ed. Oxford: Clarendon Press, 1970. 270pp. This collection of 100 letters have been selected for their philosophical rather than their historical interest. Brief commentary relates the letters to the events of Descartes's life.

Recommended Biographies

Gaukroger, Stephen. *Descartes: An Intellectual Biography*. New York: Oxford University Press, 1995. 499pp. In a fundamental reassessment of all aspects of Descartes's life and work, Gaukroger offers a subtle, penetrating portrait of the man and his thought, fully detailing how Descartes developed his ideas and the cultural and intellectual forces which shaped them.

Rodis-Lewis, Geneviève. *Descartes: His Life and Thought*. Ithaca, New York: Cornell University Press, 1998. 263pp. This is a detailed, scholarly biography by a distinguished French professor that attempts to correct the biographical record and establish a contrary view of the development of Descartes's personality compared to previous studies. Balanced and well-documented, the book does assume a solid grounding in the history of the period and its ideas.

Vrooman, Jack R. *René Descartes: A Biography*. New York: Putnam, 1970. 308pp. Generally regarded as the standard modern life, Vrooman focuses on six periods in Descartes's life that determined his development and collectively display different aspects of his genius. The book achieves a compellingly human and believable portrait of a complex figure.

Other Biographical Studies

Cottingham, John. *Descartes*. New York: Blackwell, 1986. 171pp. Cottingham's is an excellent introduction to Descartes's philosophy and writings with a helpful biographical chapter on his life and times.

Grene, Marjorie. *Descartes*. Minneapolis: University of Minnesota Press, 1985. 225pp. In a series of interrelated essays the book explores Descartes's ideas and the philosopher's relationship to his contemporaries and intellectual heritage. The book presupposes a degree of familiarity with analytical philosophy and the Cartesian system.

Pearl, Leon. *Descartes*. Boston: Twayne, 1977. 228pp. Pearl helpfully connects Descartes's ideas and intellectual development with his background and experiences in this succinct summary accessible for the general reader and student of philosophy.

Reith, Herman R. *René Descartes: The Story of a Soul*. Lanham, Maryland: University Press of America, 1986. 197pp. As the book's subtitle indicates, this is an internal, spiritual biography that traces the development of Descartes's character and theological ideas in relationship with his Catholic faith.

Sorell, Tom. *Descartes*. New York: Oxford University Press, 1987. 118pp. Part of the Past Masters series, Sorell's brief introductory study orients the general reader and nonspecialist to both the man and his ideas.

Recommended Juvenile Biographies

Hoyt, Edwin P. *He Freed the Minds of Men: René Descartes*. New York: J. Messner, 1969. 187pp. MG/YA. This is a carefully researched guide to Descartes's achievement, although the book does rely on some fictionalization.

Other Sources

Cottingham, John, ed. *The Cambridge Companion to Descartes*. New York: Cambridge University Press, 1992. 441pp. This is a collection of critical essays by the most eminent scholars of Descartes on various aspects of the philosopher's achievements as a scientist and philosopher.

132. JOHN DEWEY
1859-1952

American philosopher and influential educator, Dewey was a leading educational reformer of the early twentieth century. He founded a school of philosophy called "instrumentalism," related to the pragmatism of William James, which he applied to educational theory as a system of "learning by doing." Dewey's many writings include *The School and Society* (1899), *Democracy and Education* (1916), and *Experience and Education* (1938).

Autobiography and Primary Sources

"From Absolutism to Experimentalism" in Volume 2 of *Contemporary American Philosophy: Personal Statements*. George Plimpton Adams and William P. Montague, eds. New York: Macmillan, 1930. 2 vols. In the only autobiographical statement from Dewey, the philosopher comments on his intellectual development and influences.

Recommended Biographies

Dykhuizen, George. *The Life and Mind of John Dewey*. Carbondale: Southern Illinois University Press, 1973. 429pp. The only comprehensive biography, Dykhuizen's is a scholarly yet highly readable account of Dewey's career and intellectual life. Unlike most other studies, the book provides glimpses of Dewey's personal life and personality.

Other Biographical Studies

Campbell, Harry M. *John Dewey*. New York: Twayne, 1971. 161pp. Campbell's is a competent brief survey of the evolution of Dewey's ideas, organizing his career in an intellectually coherent fashion. The book is useful for the student and general reader interested in a concise overview.

Coughlain, Neil. *Young John Dewey: An Essay in American Intellectual History*. Chicago: University of Chicago Press, 1975. 187pp. Coughlain provides a concise and penetrating exploration of Dewey's early years and intellectual development, including those who helped shape his ideas and the young Dewey's evolving temperament.

Hook, Sidney. *John Dewey: An Intellectual Portrait.* New York: J. Day, 1939. 242pp. After a chapter on the man and his career, Hook, a student and friend of Dewey, summarizes the philosopher's views on such topics as philosophy and culture, truth, art, education, and society.

Nathanson, Jerome. *John Dewey: The Reconstruction of the Democratic Life.* New York: Scribner, 1951. 127pp. The emphasis here is on Dewey's ideas as a philosopher, psychologist, and educator, tracing his impact on American thought during the first half of the twentieth century. Although offering little on Dewey's life, the book is a solid introduction to his views and their influence.

Biographical Novels

Rosen, Norma. *John and Anzia: An American Romance.* New York: Dutton, 1989. 177pp. Based in part on clues in Dewey's poetry, Rosen dramatizes the 1917 affair between the philosopher and Polish immigrant and writer Anzia Yezierska.

Other Sources

Boydston, Jo Ann, ed. *Guide to the Works of John Dewey.* Carbondale: Southern Illinois University Press, 1970. 395pp. This collection of essays covers various topics on Dewey's ideas and achievements in philosophy, psychology, and education.

133. DIANA, PRINCESS OF WALES
1961–1997

Lady Diana Spencer became Princess of Wales after her 1981 marriage to Great Britain's Prince Charles. The couple's fairy-tale wedding, together with the princess's much-admired style and beauty and her efforts on behalf of such causes as AIDS victims and land mine removal, made Diana a popular public figure. The intimate details of her life, including her bitter separation and divorce from Charles, as well as her untimely death in a Paris car accident, were subjects of steady coverage by the news media worldwide.

Autobiography and Primary Sources

Diana: A Portrait in Her Own Words. Bill Adler, ed. New York: Morrow, 1999. 184pp. This volume presents a collection of Diana's significant quotes, approximating a kind of cut-and-paste autobiography.

Recommended Biographies

Edwards, Anne. *Ever After: Diana and the Life She Led.* New York: St. Martin's, 2000. 384pp. Edwards provides a restrained treatment of the essential details of Diana's life that resists sensationalism or partisanship, allowing the facts to speak for themselves.

Morton, Andrew. *Diana: Her True Story in Her Own Words.* New York: Simon & Schuster, 1997. 288pp. This is a revised edition of Morton's earlier *Diana: Her True Story* (New York: Simon & Schuster, 1992, 167pp.) that identifies Diana as his principal source and includes her personal recollections in her own words. The result is the version

of Diana's story that she wanted shared with the public. Morton describes the events surrounding her death to complete the story.

Smith, Sally Bedell. *Diana in Search of Herself: Portrait of a Troubled Princess.* New York: Time Books, 1999. 451pp. Smith's is one of the fullest and most substantive biographical accounts available that offers a credible and critical psychological portrait. Going considerably beyond the glamorous image, Smith offers a view of Diana that avoids painting her either as a victim or a heroine, offering a sophisticated understanding of her inner life and emotional needs.

Other Biographical Studies

Burchill, Julie. *Diana.* London: Weidenfeld and Nicolson, 1998. 240pp. This is an angry, partisan defense of Diana's life that casts the Royal Family as the main villains in Diana's sad end. It is too intemperate to be fully reliable in providing the whole story.

Buskin, Richard. *Princess Diana: Her Life Story 1961–1997.* New York: New American Library, 1997. 223pp. Originally published in 1992, this visual biography has been revised to cover the details of Diana's death and memorial service.

Holden, Anthony. *Diana: Her Life and Her Legacy.* New York: Random House, 1997. 189pp. Royal commentator Holden offers a photo essay with quotes from such figures as Nelson Mandela, Elton John, and Mother Teresa. The key moments of her life are covered but very much in the uncritical, tribute mode.

Seward, Ingrid. *Diana: An Intimate Portrait.* Contemporary Publishing, 1997. 256pp. One of many visual tributes.

Simmons, Simone. *Diana: The Secret Years.* New York: Ballantine Books, 1998. 192pp. An intimate of the princess following Diana's separation and divorce, Simmons offers her perspective of Diana's life on her own in a succession of behind-the-scenes details.

Spoto, Donald. *Diana: The Last Year.* New York: Harmony Books, 1997. 220pp. Less biography than hagiography, Spoto celebrates virtually every aspect of Diana during her final year. Lacking in objectivity or critical distance, the book's lone merit is to show Diana's final experiences through her eyes.

Biographical Novels

King, Norman. *The Prince and the Princess: The Love Story.* New York: Simon & Schuster, 1983. 253pp. Written before the fairy tales soured, this is a fictional treatment of Charles and Diana's relationship, which in retrospect seems quaint and beyond the sordid reach of reality.

Fictional Portraits

Lefcourt, Peter. *Di and I.* New York: Random House, 1994. 366pp. An amusing fantasy about an American who "rescues" Diana from her gilded prison and relocates her in suburban America.

Townsend, Sue. *The Queen and I.* New York: Soho Press, 1993. 239pp. In a satirical comic fantasy

Townsend imagines the lot of the royals if a socialist government abolished the monarchy and the Windsors took up residence in a run-down housing project.

Recommended Juvenile Biographies

Brennan, Kristine. *Diana, Princess of Wales.* Philadelphia: Chelsea House, 1999. 143pp. MG/YA. Part of the Women of Achievement series, this biographical profile traces the significant events in Diana's life with an emphasis on her influence and significance.

Cerasini, Marc. *Diana, Queen of Hearts.* New York: Random House, 1997. 94pp. MG. Cerasini offers an informative biographical profile covering Diana's background, rise to celebrity, and impact.

Whitelaw, Nancy. *Lady Diana Spencer: Princess of Wales.* Greensboro, North Carolina: Morgan Reynolds, 1998. 112pp. This is a thoughtful assessment of Diana's life, career in the public eye, and achievement.

Biographical Films and Theatrical Adaptations

A&E Biography Video: Diana: The True Story (1998). Producer: Tim Willcox. Diana's life story is chronicled in this film portrait. Video.

Charles & Diana: A Palace Divided (1993). Director: John Power. Roger Rees and Catherine Oxenberg portray the royal couple in a superficial dramatization of the collapse of their marriage. Video.

Diana 1961–1997 (1997). Producer: Gordon Carr. This is the official BBC commemorative video that celebrates the life of Diana using interviews, commentary, and film footage of her public appearances. Video.

Diana, A Celebration: The People's Princess Remembered (1997). Producer: Gordon Carr. BBC commemorative film recounts the events of her life and her charitable activities. Video.

Diana: A Tribute to the People's Princess (1998). Director: Gabrielle Beaumont. A dramatization of Diana's life from 1996 to her fatal accident, with Amy Seccombe as the Princess and George Jackos as Dodi Al Fayed. Suggests that Diana was about to accept Dodi's proposal of marriage before her death. Video.

Diana: Her True Story (1993). Director: Kevin Connor. This television adaptation of Andrew Morton's book stars Serena Scott Thomas as Diana and David Threlfall as Charles. Video.

134. CHARLES DICKENS
1812–1870

English novelist, Dickens was the son of an improvident naval clerk who was imprisoned for debt when Dickens was 12, compelling his son to labor in a blacking warehouse, a humiliation that permanently affected Dickens and helps explain his determined assault on fame and success as a novelist. After working as a court and parliamentary shorthand reporter, Dickens's first considerable success was *The Pickwick Papers* (1837). Among the most popular novelists of the Victorian age, Dickens published a string of popular and critical masterpieces, including *A Christmas Carol* (1843), *David Copperfield* (1850), *Bleak House* (1853), and *Great Expectations* (1861).

Autobiography and Primary Sources

An autobiographical fragment written while Dickens prepared to write *David Copperfield*, revealing the deep wound of his childhood humiliation for the first time to his friend and eventual biography John Forster, is reprinted in Forster's *Life*.

The Pilgrim Edition of the Letters of Charles Dickens. Madeline House and Graham Storey, eds. Oxford: Clarendon Press, 1965–1999. 11 vols. The unfinished definitive scholarly edition of Dickens's letters continues to move slowly toward completion, having reached the year 1867. A monumental task and invaluable for the biographer. A selection of Dickens's letters is available edited by David Paroissien (*Selected Letters*. London: Macmillan, 1985. 877pp.).

The Speeches of Charles Dickens. K.J. Fielding, ed. Atlantic Highlands, New Jersey: Humanities Press, 1988. 456pp. Dickens's many public pronouncements are insightful into his cast of mind and public persona.

Recommended Biographies

Ackroyd, Peter. *Dickens.* New York: HarperCollins, 1990. 1,195pp. Ackroyd's massive and provocative life and times study is best in its sensory apprehension of Dickens's world. His attempt to recreate Dickens's internal and external reality, however, is uneven, and readers may find the book's six dramatic interludes, in one of which Dickens debates T.S. Eliot and Thomas Chatterton, more daring than illuminating. Few other studies have produced a more complex, modern portrait of an insecure, driven, and ambitious man with all his intriguing oddities intact.

Forster, John. *The Life of Charles Dickens.* 1872-74. Reprint ed. New York: Dutton, 1928. 2 vols. Written by Dickens's intimate friend, Forster's life revealed for the first time the details of Dickens's early hardships and from his firsthand perspective invaluable details about the composition of the novels. However, Forster suppressed all references to Dickens's relationship with actress Ellen Ternan and other personal details. Ley's edition assesses Forster's strengths and weaknesses as a biographer and provides notes correcting details with facts learned since 1874.

Johnson, Edgar. *Charles Dickens: His Tragedy and Triumph.* New York: Simon & Schuster, 1952. 2 vols. Johnson's richly and meticulously documented and readable account remains the standard life in the absence of major new discoveries. Extending Forster's treatment with new information, objectivity, and candor, Johnson established the paradigm for viewing Dickens's life and career as a whole as well as a credible psychological profile of an often divided and complex figure.

Kaplan, Fred. *Dickens: A Biography.* New York: Morrow, 1988. 607pp. Ranking, along with Forster and Johnson, as the most comprehensive biography available, Kaplan synthesizes a vast amount of data into a coherent, readable account of Dickens's public and private selves and the relationship between the novelist's life and his writing. Kaplan exploits recent scholarship and access to unpublished letters and extends our view of Dickens in a number of aspects.

Other Biographical Studies

Langston, Robert. *The Childhood and Youth of Charles Dickens.* 1883. Revised ed. New York: Scribner, 1891. 260pp. Written out of dissatisfaction over Forster's cursory handling of Dickens's early years, Langston's study considerably extends the view of Dickens's childhood and youth with original research.

Leacock, Stephen. *Charles Dickens: His Life and Work.* Garden City, New York: Doubleday, 1936. 322pp. In this popular biography for the general reader Leacock offers a comprehensive survey of Dickens's life and literary career by an admirer who at times overly sentimentalizes Dickens's story.

Lindsay, Jack. *Charles Dickens: A Biographical and Critical Study.* New York: Philosophical Library, 1950. 459pp. Lindsay's critical biography set out to explode previous sentimental portraits, casting Dickens as a revolutionary who came to execrate the Victorian values he found necessary to celebrate in his books. Often distorted by a persistent Marxist-Freudian interpretative bias, Lindsay's study is nonetheless original, insightful, and provocative, grounded in a close reading of everything that Dickens wrote.

MacKenzie, Norman, and Jeanne MacKenzie. *Dickens: A Life.* New York: Oxford University Press, 1979. 434pp. Although adding nothing new to the established portrait, the MacKenzies have assembled all the relevant facts into a straightforward, balanced narrative, relating the novels to the events of Dickens's life and times that does not stress a particular view or bias and profiting from the details uncovered in the *Pilgrim Edition* of Dickens's letters.

Mankowitz, Wolf. *Dickens of London.* New York: Macmillan, 1977. 252pp. The companion volume to the BBC series of the same name, Mankowitz provides a beautifully illustrated introduction to Dickens for the general reader.

Murray, Brian. *Charles Dickens.* New York: Continuum, 1994. 198pp. In this entry in the Literature and Life series, Murray offers an accessible overview of Dickens's life and works with astute observations of the various paradoxes within Dickens's personality. A reliable introduction to the leading themes of Dickens's fiction and elements of his creative genius.

Pearson, Hesketh. *Dickens: His Character, Comedy, and Career.* New York: Harper, 1949. 361pp. Adding little new or original research, Pearson's lively narrative may still be preferred as a single-volume introduction with Pearson's theatrical expertise a distinct advantage in dealing with Dickens's debts to the stage.

Pope-Hennessy, Una. *Charles Dickens.* New York: Howell, Soskin, 1946. 488pp. The first biography to appear after the publication of the *Nonesuch Letters* and discoveries regarding Dickens's relationship with Ellen Ternan, Pope-Hennessy's life was the best available since Forster and prior to Edgar Johnson's definitive biography. It is unusual in its treatment of the often neglected role of Dickens's wife in his story.

Smith, Grahame. *Charles Dickens: A Literary Life.* New York: Saint Martin's, 1996. 190pp. Smith's critical study challenges the conventional view of Dickens's private creative impulse by examining the practical process of his literary production based on an analysis of his relationship with his publishers and his response to his readers and the demands of serialization.

Tomalin, Claire. *The Invisible Woman: The Story of Nelly Ternan and Charles Dickens.* New York: Knopf, 1991. 317pp. In the fullest account available of Dickens's secret 12-year relationship with the young actress Ellen Ternan, Tomalin portrays her as an intelligent woman who was both honored and trapped by Dickens's attention. Contrary to the opinion of Peter Ackroyd, Tomalin shares the view of Fred Kaplan that their relationship was consummated.

Wilson, Angus. *The World of Charles Dickens.* New York: Viking, 1970. 302pp. Wilson's critical appreciation examines how the novels derived from Dickens's public and private life. His approach produces a number of fresh insights and one of the subtlest interpretations of Dickens's life, mind, and art.

Biographical Novels

Bloom, Ursula. *The Romance of Charles Dickens.* London: R. Hall, 1960. 185pp. Dramatizes Dickens's first love for Maria Beadnell whose banker father disapproves of the young Dickens's lack of prospects. Years later Dickens reunites with the matronly Maria, again, to his disappointment. Based on facts, the novel employs invented dialogue.

Busch, Frederick. *The Mutual Friend.* New York: Harper & Row, 1978. 222pp. Busch's central narrative consciousness is George Dolby, Dickens's theatrical manager on his second American tour. On his deathbed in 1899 he recalls his relationship with the Inimitable, assuming a variety of perspectives, including a prostitute Dickens reclaimed, Kate Dickens, Ellen Ternan, and Dickens himself. Inventive imaginative tour of the man, his life, and his times.

Lincoln, Victoria. *Charles: A Novel.* Boston: Little, Brown, 1962. 403pp. Based on events in Dickens's early life, the novel dramatizes the stages of his becoming a novelist, including his humiliating personal life, his first love affair, his marriage, and the burden of his improvident father. An affectionate and at times overly sentimental portrait.

Fictional Portraits

Ackroyd, Peter. *English Music.* New York: Knopf, 1992. 399pp. Ackroyd's imaginative story tells of a boy who tours theaters as a spiritual healer. When he is transported into the creations of Dickens and other writers, he learns to hear the "English music" of the imagination throughout history.

Palmer, William J. *The Detective and Mr. Dickens.* New York: Saint Martin's, 1990. 290pp.; *The Highwayman and Mr. Dickens.* New York: Saint Martin's, 1992. 273pp.; *The Hoyden and Mr. Dickens.* New York: Saint Martin's, 1997. 241pp. Palmer's inventive historical mystery series employs Dickens and his friend Wilkie Collins in a number of ingenious and atmospheric Victorian intrigues with elements from Dickens's actual life.

Recommended Juvenile Biographies

Ayer, Eleanor H. *Charles Dickens.* San Diego: Lucent Books, 1997. 96pp. MG. In this brief, accessible biography, Ayer incorporates quotes from biographers and critics as well as selections from letters of Dickens and those who knew him.

Kyle, Elisabeth. *Great Ambitions: A Story of the Early Years of Charles Dickens.* New York: Holt, 1968. 217pp. YA. A fictionalized account of Dickens's life from the age of 12 to 27 when he had established himself as a successful novelist, the novel presents a convincing period background and offers insights into Dickens's thoughts and his creative process.

Martin, Christopher. *Charles Dickens.* Vero Beach, Florida: Rourke, 1990. 111pp. MG. Martin's is an informative look at Dickens's life, character, and literary career.

Biographical Films and Theatrical Adaptations

A&E Biography Video: Charles Dickens: A Tale of Ambition and Genius (1995). Producer: Melissa Jo Peltier. This is a relatively complete film portrait using archival photographs and location views. Video.

Charles Dickens, Novelist (1993). Director: Malcolm Hossick. Using portraits, contemporary drawings, photographs, and other archival material, this documentary film recounts Dickens's life and career. Video.

Other Sources

Collins, Philip, ed. *Dickens: Interviews and Recollections.* Totowa, New Jersey: Barnes and Noble, 1981. 2 vols. Collins collects a wide assortment of perspectives on the novelist from his friends, critics, and contemporary sources.

Davis, Paul. *Charles Dickens A to Z: The Essential Reference to His Life and Work.* New York: Facts on File, 1998. 423pp. Alphabetical reference guide to the full range of Dickens's biography, associates, and writing.

Epstein, Norrie. *Friendly Dickens.* New York: Viking, 1998. 576pp. A browser's delight, Epstein's reference guide to Dickens's life, works, and world is filled with odd and intriguing bits of information culled from a wide variety of sources, including Dickens's robust walking speed (4.8 mph) and the total number of characters he created (13,143). Includes interviews with Dickens experts and actors.

Hardwick, Michael, and Mollie Hardwick. *Dickens Encyclopedia.* New York: Holt, 1966. 250pp. A useful reference volume with a detailed chronol-

ogy and an alphabetical listing of information concerning Dickens's life, fiction, and associates.

Schlicke, Paul, ed. *Oxford Reader's Companion to Dickens.* New York: Oxford University Press, 1999. 654pp. An extensive reference guide to Dickens's life, relationships, works, and characters.

135. EMILY DICKINSON
1830–1886

American poet Emily Dickinson, the daughter of a prominent lawyer, was born in Amherst, Massachusetts, where she spent her entire life. Before she was 30, Dickinson began a gradual withdrawal from public activities, living as a recluse in her father's home, corresponding with but rarely seeing a number of friends and associates. Her creative peak as a poet occurred from 1858 to 1862, when she wrote intense, witty, and paradoxical personal investigations of emotions and existence. Dickinson published only seven poems during her lifetime. After her death, her sister discovered over 1,000 poems that established her reputation as one of the greatest poets in American literature.

Autobiography and Primary Sources

The Letters of Emily Dickinson. Thomas H. Johnson, ed. Cambridge, Masachusetts: Harvard University Press, 1958. 3 vols. More than 1,000 letters to more than 100 recipients are arranged chronologically with useful biographical links. The letters bring the reader as close to Dickinson as we can expect to get. An essential source for anyone seriously interested in the poet, her life, and work. A one-volume collection also edited by Johnson is available as *Selected Letters of Emily Dickenson* (Cambridge, Massachusetts: Harvard University Press, 1971. 364pp.).

Recommended Biographies

Farr, Judith. *The Passion of Emily Dickinson.* Cambridge, Massachusetts: Harvard University Press, 1992. 390pp. Setting the poet's work in the context of her life, literary tradition, and times, Farr's critical biography is one of the best available with a balanced and sensible interpretation based on solid research. Farr demonstrates the artistic influences on the poet's visual style and the influence of her sister-in-law and of Samuel Bowles on Dickinson's emotional makeup.

Johnson, Thomas H. *Emily Dickinson: An Interpretive Biography.* Cambridge, Massachusetts: Harvard University Press, 1955. 276pp. The editor of the standard edition of Dickinson's poetry and letters is an ideal candidate as her authoritative biography, and his scholarly and reliable critical biography is one of the best books available on both Dickinson's life and poetry. Placing Dickinson in her cultural background, Johnson sets out the growth of her emotional life and the structure and themes of her poetry. Johnson's interpretation reverses previous negative views of Dickinson's father who is seen as a positive influence, and establishes the significance of Thomas Wentworth

Higginson and Helen Hunt Jackson in Dickinson's development.

Sewall, Richard B. *The Life of Emily Dickinson.* New York: Farrar, Straus, 1974. 2 vols. Widely accepted as the closest to a definitive biography available, Sewall's thorough and meticulous study is the most comprehensive treatment with its first volume detailing her family background and historical and cultural background. Volume two turns from externals to Dickinson's growth and development. By carefully sifting through all the available facts and speculations, Sewall manages to shed considerable new light on both the poet and her poems.

Wolff, Cynthia G. *Emily Dickinson.* New York: Knopf, 1986. 641pp. Wolff's psychological biography concentrates largely on Dickinson's maturity, casting her as a toughminded visionary contending as a daughter and a woman in her family that is described as a "fortress of terrible loneliness." Provocative and insightful, Wolff's study connects Dickinson's life, times, and artistry in a revealing pattern, though some readers may find many of her conclusions as overly speculative and thesis bound.

Other Biographical Studies

Benfey, Christopher E.G. *Emily Dickinson: Lives of a Poet.* New York: G. Braziller, 1986. 141pp. Benfey's brief introduction to Dickinson's life and work is useful for the general reader though it repeats a number of views that have been corrected by fuller biographical accounts, for example, the blighting of his daughter's life by Dickinson's tyrannical Puritan father.

Bianchi, Martha D. *The Life and Letters of Emily Dickinson.* Boston: Houghton Mifflin, 1924. 386pp. Written by her niece, this is the first Dickinson biography and offers a number of firsthand reflections, despite a lack of objectivity and candor on certain topics.

Bingham, Millicent Todd. *Emily Dickinson: A Revelation.* New York: Harper, 1954. 109pp.; *Emily Dickinson's Home.* New York: Harper, 1955. 600pp. Bingham's revelation in her 1954 study of Dickinson's later years identifies Judge Otis P. Lord as a romantic attachment, which has been generally accepted by scholars. Her 1955 volume examines domestic life in the Dickinson household.

Cody, John. *After Great Pain: The Inner Life of Emily Dickinson.* Cambridge, Massachusetts: Harvard University Press, 1971. 538pp. Written by a psychiatrist, Cody's psychoanalytical study provides a Freudian explanation for Dickinson's odd behavior, based on her relationship with her mother whose early rejection of her daughter was the source of the poet's later psychotic episodes. Cody bases his analysis on a literal reading of the poems that other scholars have demonstrated is a risky business and potentially misleading.

Doriani, Beth M. *Emily Dickinson: Daughter of Prophecy.* Amherst: University of Massachusetts Press, 1996. 230pp. Tracing the development of Dickinson's distinctive and prophetic poetic voice, Doriani sets the poet in the context of patriarchal nineteenth-century New England to reveal her rhetorical strategies that result from being historically excluded from the role of preacher.

Higgins, David. *Portrait of Emily Dickinson: The Poet and Her Prose*. New Brunswick, New Jersey: Rutgers University Press, 1967. 266pp. Higgins's vantage point for uncovering Dickinson's interior life is through a close reading of her letters that reveal the influence of her family and friendships, as well as the stages of doubt, crisis, and grief reflecting in her poetry. Higgins documents a convincing case that the newspaper editor Samuel Bowles is the most likely candidate for Dickinson's crucial romantic attachment, which most current scholars now accept as plausible.

Jenkins, MacGregor. *Emily Dickinson: Friend and Neighbor*. Boston: Little, Brown, 1930. 150pp. Written by an Amherst native who was acquainted with the poet as a child, Jenkins's account offers a unique perspective on Dickinson family life and the poet's affection for children in an otherwise sentimental treatment.

Longsworth, Polly. *The World of Emily Dickinson*. New York: W.W. Norton, 1997. 144pp. This collection of photographs and drawings visually documents the poet's life, depicting all of the important people and places, along with a chronology of events. Better for a Dickinson enthusiast than as an introduction for the uninitiated because of its limited commentary.

McNeil, Helen. *Emily Dickinson*. New York: Pantheon, 1986. 208pp. Offering a Derridean reading of the poet, McNeil blends biography, history, feminism and poststructuralist literary criticism into an interpretation that identifies Dickinson's reclusiveness as a strategy for asking forbidden questions and allowed her to escape the normal constraints of a New England spinster. More for the specialist, the book assumes a great deal of familiarity with Dickinson's life, poetry, and the jargon of modern criticism.

Mossberg, Barbara Antonia Clarke. *Emily Dickinson: When a Writer Is a Daughter*. Bloomington: Indiana University Press, 1982. 214pp. Mossberg provides a penetrating psychological reconstruction of Dickinson's childhood and family background, emphasizing the impact of poet's relationship with her parents on her life and work.

Pollitt, Josephine. *Emily Dickinson: The Human Background of Her Poetry*. New York: Harper, 1930. 350pp. Pollitt's early interpretive biography stresses the importance of her New England background and offers a disputed candidate for Dickinson's central romantic detachment, based on plausible but inconclusive evidence that later biographers have rejected as fanciful.

Taggard, Genevieve. *The Life and Mind of Emily Dickinson*. New York: Knopf, 1930. 378pp. Taggard's early life is distinguished by its nominating the Reverend George H. Gould as the mysterious object of Dickinson's affection. Her candidate, as well as the dominating role played by Dickinson's father, have been largely rejected by subsequent scholars.

Walsh, John E. *The Hidden Life of Emily Dickinson*. New York: Scribner, 1971. 286pp. Walsh examines the factors that led Dickinson to become a recluse and offers an original analysis of the poet's various literary debts to Elizabeth Barrett Browning, Hawthorne, Emerson, and others in her creative process.

Ward, Theodora. *The Capsule of the Mind: Chapters in the Life of Emily Dickinson*. Cambridge, Massachusetts: Harvard University Press, 1961. 205pp. In a series of essays on various periods of Dickinson's life and her relationships, Ward shed new light on the poet's inner life, personality, and the development of her poetry. She succeeded in establishing the deep reliance Dickinson had for the writer's grandparents, Josiah and Elizabeth Holland.

Whicher, George F. *This Was a Poet: A Critical Biography of Emily Dickinson*. New York: Scribner, 1938. 337pp. In the first thorough critical study of Dickinson's life and poetry, Whicher corrects a number of previous misreadings in a careful analysis that is restricted to the provable and places the poet solidly in her New England and Puritan background. Now largely superseded by more recent studies, Whicher's account established the basic outline for seeing Dickinson's life undistorted by sentimentality.

Biographical Novels

Edwards, Anne. *The Hesitant Heart*. New York: Random House, 1974. 247pp. The author sets out to solve the various mysteries of Dickinson's emotional attachments in a series of imagined letters with only partial success. Best in its re-creation of the atmosphere of Dickinson's home and family.

Farr, Judith. *I Never Came to You in White*. Boston: Houghton Mifflin, 1996. 225pp. Dickinson biographer Farr dramatizes the poet's life in a series of imagined letters that span her life but focus on the her unhappy 10 month at Mount Holyoke Seminary in 1847. Although liberties are taken with the historical record, Farr is respectful of limits in fashioning a credible as well as responsible portrait and impersonation.

Fuller, Jamie. *The Diary of Emily Dickinson*. New York: Saint Martin's, 1996. 208pp. This fictionalized diary records the events and reflections of a single year from 1867 to 1868, mixing invented entries, editorial notes with biographical information, and a selection of imitative poetry to penetrate Dickinson's inner life. Fuller takes few major liberties with the basic facts in this sensitive reconstruction.

Fictional Portraits

Vernon, John. *Peter Doyle*. New York: Random House, 1991. 417pp. Vernon's picaresque fantasy concerning the search for Napoleon's dismembered penis includes an intriguing, fanciful meeting between nineteenth-century America's greatest poets, Dickinson and Walt Whitman. Vernon uses his strong sense of the past to subvert history comically.

Recommended Juvenile Biographies

Barth, Edna. *I'm Nobody! Who Are You?: The Story of Emily Dickinson*. New York: Seabury Press, 1971. 128pp. MG. This partially fictional-ized biography is based on actual incidents and conversations or derived from recorded facts of the poet's life. Includes a selection of more than 35 poems.

Fisher, Aileen and Olive Rabe. *We Dickinsons: The Life of Emily Dickinson as Seen through the Eyes of Her Brother Austin*. New York: Atheneum, 1965. 246pp. YA. This novel provides an intimate portrait of the poet from her brother's perspective that serves as an introduction to Dickinson and her poetry.

Longsworth, Polly. *Emily Dickinson: Her Letter to the World*. New York: Crowell, 1965. 169pp. YA. This sensitive biography explores the various forces—friends, family, reading, and New England background—that helped form Dickinson and direct her creative genius. The author presents a rich, complex inner current beneath the quiet surface of Dickinson's life.

Thayer, Bonita E. *Emily Dickinson*. New York: F. Watts, 1989. 144pp. MG. Providing extensive details of Dickinson's daily life, Thayer develops the theme of the conflict between the traditional expectations of women of the era and Dickinson's genius.

Biographical Films and Theatrical Adaptations

The Belle of Amherst (1976). Director: Charles S. Dubin. Adapted from the play by William Luce, Julie Harris portrays the poet with readings from her works and observations about her life and family. Video.

Emily Dickinson (1988). Director: Veronica Young. Tracing the events of Dickinson's life and criticism of her poetry, the film uses dramatizations and commentary by Adrienne Rich, Joyce Carol Oates, and others. Jane Alexander provides the voice of the poet. Video.

Other Sources

Eberwein, Jane D. *An Emily Dickinson Encyclopedia*. Westport, Connecticut: Greenwood, 1998. 395pp. This easy-to-use reference book covers a wide range of topics on Dickinson's life and poetry, including an entry for Carlo, Dickinson's dog. With a detailed chronology, recommendations for further reading following each entry, and a reprint of the surviving manuscript books of the poems. The study is both useful and a delight to read.

Grabher, Gudrun, Roland Hagenbuchle, and Cristanne Miller, eds. *The Emily Dickinson Handbook*. Amherst: University of Massachusetts Press, 1999. 512pp. The best of recent Dickinson scholarship is gathered together in a collection of essays that examines the poet's life and works from various useful perspectives.

Leyda, Jay. *The Years and Hours of Emily Dickinson*. 1960. Reprint ed. Hamden, Connecticut: Archon Books, 1970. 2 vols. Leyda meticulously gathers every known reference to the poet from a wide variety of sources, organizing the material chronologically in an invaluable documentary sourcebook.

136. DENIS DIDEROT
1713–1784

An influential French encyclopedist, philosopher, and literary figure, Diderot edited the famous *Encyclopédie* (1751-1771), which contained essays on various subjects written by nearly all the most important writers of the Enlightenment. The French government tried to suppress the 17-volume work, which presented the scientific advancements and advanced thought of the time. Diderot's other works include the play *La Père de famille* (1758), the character sketch *Le Neveu de Romeau* (1762), the novel *Jacques le fataliste* (1796), philosophical writings, and newspaper articles that pioneered modern art criticism.

Autobiography and Primary Sources

France, Peter. *Diderot*. New York: Oxford University Press, 1983. 116pp. France introduces a selection of Diderot's letters from his entire career that provides an insightful glimpse of the man, his character, and temperament.

Recommended Biographies

Furbank, P.N. *Diderot: A Critical Biography*. New York: Knopf, 1992. 524pp. Incorporating new scholarship since the publication of Wilson's two-volume life, Furbank's biography is intended more for the general reader, and the book succeeds admirably in tracing Diderot's life, works, and era with sympathy and perception.

Wilson, Arthur M. *Diderot*. New York: Oxford University Press, 1957–1972. 2 vols. Wilson's two-volume study is by far the most comprehensive critical biography on Diderot. Rich in detail and absorbing, Wilson's definitive account is both reliable and readable and should be the first choice for the serious reader.

Other Biographical Studies

Blum, Carol. *Diderot: The Virtue of a Philosopher*. New York: Viking, 1974. 182pp. Blum provides a biographical sketch joining evidence about Diderot's life, selections from his letters, and a reading of his major works. Focusing on Diderot's ethical values, the book offers an informed analysis of both the writer's private and public life.

Crocker, Lester. *The Embattled Philosopher: A Biography of Denis Diderot*. 1954. Revised ed. New York: Free Press, 1966. 420pp. Called by one reviewer, "a spirited, perhaps jazzed-up, life," Crocker chronicles Diderot's long and active public and private life closely, animated by novelistic touches and the former movie writer's flair for the dramatic.

Fellows, Otis E. *Diderot*. 1977. Revised ed. Boston: Twayne, 1989. 193pp. Following a biographical framework, Fellows supplies a useful introductory guide to Diderot's activities and intellectual development.

Fictional Portraits

Rebolledo, Francisco. *Rasero*. Baton Rouge: Louisiana State University Press, 1995. 552pp. This story of a young Spanish nobleman who comes to Paris during the ferment of the Enlightenment, shows the protagonist helping Diderot to edit the *Encyclopédie*.

137. MARLENE DIETRICH
1901–1992

German-born American movie actress and singer, Dietrich first gained fame as a femme fatale nightclub singer in the German film *The Blue Angel* (1930). Known for her on-screen glamour and sophistication, she was one of Hollywood's most popular and enduring stars. Her films include *Desire* (1936), *Destry Rides Again* (1939), *Foreign Affair* (1948), and *Witness for the Prosecution* (1957). In the 1950s and 1960s Dietrich appeared in cabarets, concerts, and on television in the United States and abroad.

Autobiography and Primary Sources

Marlene. New York: Grove Press, 1989. 273pp. Dietrich warns early on that "I have no interest in talking about my life.... Facts are unimportant" before supplying a less-than-forthcoming, though distinctively Dietrich-like, fiery memoir, often more revealing for what is not said than what is.

Recommended Biographies

Bach, Steven. *Marlene Dietrich: Life and Legend*. New York: Morrow, 1992. 626pp. Based on extensive interviews with the actress and associates, Bach's is a scholarly and authoritatively comprehensive biography that offers the fullest view of Dietrich's life, career, and personality. As the author observes, his book is "neither worship at the shrine nor autopsy: It is a celebration, and—very often—an act of wonder." To his credit Bach is able to maintain the reader's wonder throughout this candid tour of Dietrich's remarkable life.

Higham, Charles. *Marlene: The Life of Marlene Dietrich*. New York: W.W. Norton, 1977. 319pp. Neither sentimental nor sensational, Higham's portrait is a revealing, well-researched, and well-written account that offers a very different view of Dietrich than her film image.

Spoto, Donald. *Blue Angel: The Life of Marlene Dietrich*. New York: Doubleday, 1992. 335pp. Compared to other of Spoto's biographical efforts, this is a relatively restrained, sympathetic but balanced account that clearly shows the discrepancy between Dietrich's image and the reality of her life off screen.

Riva, Maria. *Marlene Dietrich: By Her Daughter*. New York: Knopf, 1993. 790pp. Dietrich's only child succeeds more than any other biographer in demystifying her mother's image. This intimate, often chilling insider's view, catalogs the succession of Dietrich's lovers, her odd battle with and acceptance of her screen image, and her often outrageous, often baffling behavior and personality.

Walker, Alexander. *Dietrich*. New York: Harper & Row, 1984. 207pp. Filled with excellent illustrations, Walker's is a balanced account of Dietrich's career. Walker's theme is that Dietrich's personality and career were shaped by her being a Prussian officer's daughter trained to follow orders.

Other Biographical Studies

Dickens, Homer. *The Films of Marlene Dietrich*. 1968. Revised ed. as *The Complete Films of Marlene Dietrich*. Secaucus, New Jersey: Carol, 1992. 224pp. Although detailed and reliable on Dietrich's film career, the book actually offers much more with revealing details about the actress's life and personality as well.

Frewin, Leslie. *Blonde Venus: A Life of Marlene Dietrich*. 1956. Revised ed. as *Dietrich: The Story of a Star*. New York: Stein and Day, 1967. 191pp. In a scathing review, Gilbert Seides wrote in the *New York Times*, "This is a remarkably consistent book. There is hardly a page without its commonplace, its echo of press-agent releases or fan magazine articles, its flat little anecdotes."

Kobal, John. *Marlene Dietrich*. London: Studio Vista, 1968. 160pp. The photographs in Kobal's tribute document the progress of the Dietrich legend, but the text rarely takes the reader beyond her persona.

Morley, Sheridan. *Marlene Dietrich*. New York: McGraw-Hill, 1976. 128pp. Morley concentrates on the creation of the Dietrich image and legend in a perceptive account.

O'Connor, Patrick. *Dietrich: Style and Substance*. New York: Dutton, 1991. 160pp. Featuring more than 150 informal, off-screen photographs, many never before published, the actress's career is chronicled from her cabaret days in the 1930s through her Hollywood triumphs.

Fictional Portraits

Baxt, George. *The Marlene Dietrich Murder Case*. New York: Saint Martin's, 1993. 218pp. In 1931 Marlene Dietrich is involved in a murder investigation in this period mystery.

Recommended Juvenile Biographies

Martin, Wednesday. *Marlene Dietrich*. New York: Chelsea House, 1995. 127pp. YA. Included in the Lives of Notable Gay Men and Lesbians series because of Dietrich's bisexual affairs, this is a candid and informative summary of the actress's career and private life.

Biographical Films and Theatrical Adaptations

Marlene (1983). Director: Maximillan Schell. A haunting film portrait from movie clips and interviews with Dietrich, who refused to let herself be filmed. Video.

138. WALT DISNEY
1901–1966

American movie producer and animation pioneer, Disney began his career as a cartoonist and in 1928 created the famous character Mickey Mouse in *Steamboat Willy*. Disney's studio produced the first feature-length cartoon, *Snow White and the Seven Dwarfs* (1938), which was followed by such animated films as *Pinnochio* (1940), *Bambi* (1942), *Alice in Wonderland* (1951), and *101*

Dalmations (1961). Disney also produced live action movies and television shows.

Recommended Biographies

Mosley, Leonard. *Disney's World: A Biography.* New York: Stein and Day, 1985. 330pp. A well-researched and comprehensive account, Mosley finds a credible balance between the often uncritical praise of Thomas's and Schickel's more disturbing portraits.

Schickel, Richard. *The Disney Version: The Life, Times, Art, and Commerce of Walt Disney.* New York: Simon & Schuster, 1968. 384pp. Schickel's is an engaging and provocative meditation on Disney's life, achievement, and cultural legacy. The book documents Disney's many contradictions, placing his career in a valuable, wider social context.

Thomas, Bob. *Walt Disney: An American Original.* New York: Simon & Schuster, 1976. 379pp. Although an authorized biography, Thomas makes use of the extensive Disney archive to provide a comprehensive, well-documented portrait of the man and his career. The book's lack of critical probing is, however, a liability.

Watts, Steven. *The Magic Kingdom: Walt Disney and the American Way of Life.* Boston: Houghton Mifflin, 1997. 526pp. A combination biography and cultural history, Watts's account is a coherent and nuanced portrait of the man, the growth and development of his empire, and a consideration of his achievement within a wider cultural and artistic context.

Other Biographical Studies

Eliot, Marc. *Walt Disney: Hollywood's Dark Prince.* Secaucus, New Jersey: Carol, 1993. 305pp. As the title indicates, the negative is overly accentuated in this often intemperate attack. No shred of the idealized myth of the benign "Uncle Walt" survives Eliot's scorn. Much conjecture is drawn from slim evidence. As Patrick McGilligan observes in his *New York Times* review, "The author's righteousness, the lack of empathy, the hammering away at Disney's mistakes and failures, the sniping at many of the famous films gets monotonous."

Green, Amy B., and Howard E. Green *Remembering Walt: Favorite Memories of Walt Disney.* New York: Hyperion, 1999. 212pp. This volume collects the recollections of more than 100 individuals who share their thoughts on Disney. The emphasis is on affectionate memories, but Disney's legendary temper and his challenging management style are glimpsed.

Jackson, Kathy M. *Walt Disney: A Bio-Bibliography.* Westport, Connecticut: Greenwood, 1993. 347pp. This is an excellent reference source, supplying a concise, factual summary of Disney's life and career with a survey of Disney's artistic and business accomplishments and a listing of resources.

Miller, Diane Disney. *The Story of Walt Disney.* As told to Peter Martin. New York: Holt, 1957. 247pp. Disney's oldest daughter supplies her affectionate recollections of her father as well as information about Disney's background, upbringing, and early

years in the movie business. Warm and intimate, if naive and uncritical, this is a version of the Disney story that Walt Disney Productions might have crafted.

Fictional Portraits

Apple, Max. *The Propheteers.* New York: Perennial Library, 1987. 306pp. In this imaginative, satiric critique of power and fame, Disney, Howard Johnson, and Margery Post are shown locked in a contest for control of their imagined Florida kingdoms. Disney comes out the worst by comparison, as a pop-culture tyrant.

Recommended Juvenile Biographies

Cole, Michael D. *Walt Disney: Creator of Mickey Mouse.* Springfield, New Jersey: Enslow, 1996. 112pp. MG/YA. This is a well-organized and informative account of Disney's childhood, family life, and eventual success in the movie business with a brief look at his company's achievements since the founder's death.

Fanning, Jim. *Walt Disney.* New York: Chelsea House, 1994. 127pp. MG/YA. Part of the Pop Culture Legends series, the biography traces Disney's career and emphasizes his contribution to American popular culture.

Ford, Barbara. *Walt Disney: A Biography.* New York: Walker, 1989. 160pp. MG/YA. An informative summary of Disney's life, career, and achievements.

Other Sources

Smith, Dave. *Disney A to Z: The Updated Official Encyclopedia.* New York: Hyperion, 1998. 633pp. With hundreds of illustrations and nearly 3,000 entries, this reference volume covers all aspects of Disney's life, work, and empire.

139. BENJAMIN DISRAELI
1804–1881

British statesman and novelist, Benjamin Disraeli was one of the dominant literary and political figures in Victorian England. Of Jewish ancestry, Disraeli was baptized in the Church of England in 1817. His first novel, *Vivian Grey*, was published in 1826, and he followed its success with other novels and political essays that displayed his advocacy of a romantic, aristocratic Toryism. Failing to win election to parliament four times, Disraeli finally was elected in 1837 and became in 1848 a prominent Tory leader. Having served as chancellor of the exchequer, Disraeli became prime minister in 1868, losing office to Gladstone the same year. He returned to power as prime minister (1874-1880) during which time he helped enact many domestic reforms and carried out an aggressive foreign policy that included the acquisition of the Suez Canal. Considered the founder of the modern Conservative party, Disraeli was created earl of Beaconsfield in 1876.

Autobiography and Primary Sources

Benjamin Disraeli Letters. J.A.W. Gunn, et al., eds. Toronto: University of Toronto Press, 1982–1998. 6 vols. Part of the Disraeli Project at Queen's University in Ontario, the collected letters have reached the year 1856 and contain revealing anecdotes of Disraeli's political adroitness and perceptions of his times.

Disraeli's Reminiscences. Helen W. and Marvin Swartz, eds. London: Hamilton, 1975. 166pp. A collection of Disraeli's witty but unreliable autobiographical notes, mostly from the period 1863 to 1865.

Recommended Biographies

Blake, Robert. *Disraeli.* New York: Saint Martin's, 1967. 819pp. Based on modern research and papers previously unavailable, Blake updates and corrects Monypenny and Buckle's standard biography with a fresh appraisal that keenly sets his political and literary career in critical and historical perspective. Blake's reliable and authoritative account is recommended as the best single-volume biography available.

Monypenny, William F., and G.E. Buckle. *The Life of Benjamin Disraeli, Earl of Beaconsfield.* New York: Macmillan, 1910-20. 6 vols. The monumental, thorough official biography remains the most useful source for information about Disraeli with its detailed narrative and its reprinting of innumerable primary documents. Discreetly silent on sexual and financial topics, the authors nevertheless offer sensible criticism and skillfully animate the historical context, though most readers will lack the patience or persistence to endure these often ponderous tomes.

Ridley, Jane. *Young Disraeli, 1804–1846.* New York: Crown, 1995. 406pp. The first of an anticipated comprehensive two-volume biography, Ridley provides a vivid and frank treatment of the first half of Disraeli's life that meticulously traces how he overcame his outsider status to become a force in British politics and formed his public and private personae.

Weintraub, Stanley. *Disraeli: A Biography.* New York: Dutton, 1993. 717pp. In Weintraub's view Disraeli is seen as the prototypical modern politician, driven only by ambition and endlessly reinventing himself. The reader may feel overwhelmed by the accumulation of details here that needs additional synthesis to make sense of Disraeli's many contradictions. Weintraub is particularly good, however, at analyzing Disraeli's fiction and describing Disraeli's relationship with Queen Victoria.

Other Biographical Studies

Bradford, Sarah. *Disraeli.* New York: Stein and Day, 1983. 432pp. Focusing mainly on Disraeli's personal life aided by material not previously available, Bradford manages a colorful, reliable account for the general reader that lacks the political detail provided by Blake. Nevertheless Bradford's is a nuanced and sensitive portrait of a complex man and a telling analysis of his personality.

Davis, Richard W. *Disraeli.* Boston: Little, Brown, 1976. 231pp. Davis, in what has been described as an "artless potboiler," supplies a highly critical portrait of Disraeli as an egotistical, ambitious opportunist with no fixed principles or policies. The book's thesis dominates the proceedings here and cannot be depended on for a balanced and objective view.

Froude, J.A. *Lord Beaconsfield.* 1890. Reprint ed. Freeport, New York: Books for Libraries Press, 1971. 267pp. The author of the standard biography of Carlyle provides a study of Disraeli from a largely Carlylean point of view with a staunch Tory bias that defends Disraeli's character and actions.

Hardwick, Mollie. *Mrs. Dizzy: The Life of Mary Anne Disraeli, Vicountess Beaconsfield.* New York: Saint Martin's, 1972. 218pp. Almost as much about Disraeli as his wife, Hardwick's anecdotal biography penetrates the public image to explore the human side of Disraeli focused on his domestic and marital relationship.

Hibbert, Christopher. *Disraeli and His World.* New York: Scribner, 1978. 128pp. In Hibbert's illustrated biographical sketch the personal not the political side of Disraeli predominates here. Hibbert's succinct and objective account will appeal to the generalist looking for a brief, adequate introduction.

Jerman, B.R. *The Young Disraeli.* Princeton, New Jersey: Princeton University Press, 1960. 327pp. Using various primary sources, including material from the Disraeli archives at Hughenden for the first time, Jerman sheds considerable new light on Disraeli's early private life through 1837. Connecting his financial and amorous entanglements to the creation of his novels, Jerman also documents for the first time the role played by Sara Austen in Disraeli's development.

Meynell, Wilfrid. *Benjamin Disraeli: An Unconventional Biography.* New York: Appleton, 1903. 520pp. Choosing to deemphasize Disraeli's political career for a detailed examination of his mind and character, Meynell stresses the important role played by his sister in Disraeli's life and was the first to emphasize Disraeli's precarious finances providing a decidedly human portrait of the Victorian icon.

Pearson, Hesketh. *Dizzy: The Life and Personality of Benjamin Disraeli.* New York: Harper, 1951. 310pp. Pearson's witty and highly readable interpretive biography uses dramatic vignettes to illuminate character. His political bias results in a number of simplifications, including reducing the Victorian period to an ideological duel between Pearson's hero Disraeli and his nemesis Gladstone.

Smith, Paul. *Disraeli: A Brief Life.* New York: Cambridge University Press, 1996. 246pp. A concise study aimed at the general reader and student, the book reflects the current scholarly reassessment of Disraeli's career and personality. Smith examines how Disraeli's Jewishness and romanticism affected his career and views.

Thane, Elswyth. *Young Disraeli.* New York: Harcourt, Brace, 1936. 337pp. Better categorized as biographical fiction, Thane's account of Disraeli's life from 1824 to 1839 employs imagined dialogue

and sets his actions against a vivid period backdrop.

Biographical Novels

Bonnet, Theodore. *The Mudlark.* Garden City, New York: Doubleday, 1949. 305pp. Concerning a street urchin whose encounter with Queen Victoria is used by Disraeli to persuade the queen to end her seclusion, the novel touches on almost the whole of Disraeli's life in a blending of historically accurate detail and fancy.

Edelman, Maurice. *Disraeli in Love.* New York: Stein and Day, 1972. 417pp.; *Disraeli Rising.* New York: Stein and Day, 1975. 348pp. Based on Blake's biography, Edelman dramatizes the more lurid chapters of Disraeli's life, including his love affair with Lady Sykes, up to 1852. Written by a former member of parliament, Edelman is best on the political scene.

Leslie, Doris. *The Prime Minister's Wife.* Garden City, New York: Doubleday, 1961. 319pp. The story of Mary Anne Evans, Disraeli's second wife, chronicles more than 50 years from the Regency period of her youth to Victorian London of her maturity, telling the Cinderella story of how a former milliner became a peer's wife. The framework is historical with considerable speculations about what might have been.

Fictional Portraits

Buruma, Ian. *Playing the Game.* New York: Farrar, Straus, 1991. 231pp. In a fictional autobiography of K.S. Ranjitsinghji, the great nineteenth-century Indian cricketer, invented conversations between Ranjitsinghji, Disraeli, and Oscar Wilde are imagined.

Macbeth, George. *Dizzy's Woman.* London: Cape, 1986. 171pp. Macbeth imagines the correspondence between Disraeli and his former mistress, the notorious Lady Londonberry, in a convincing impersonation of Disraeli's voice and a re-creation of the atmosphere of the era.

Recommended Juvenile Biographies

Grant, Neil. *Benjamin Disraeli: Prime Minister Extraordinary.* New York: F. Watts, 1969. 245pp. MG/YA. Grant supplies an entertaining and objective full-length portrait, covering in detail Disraeli's personal and public life.

Komroff, Manuel. *Disraeli.* New York: J. Messner, 1963. 191pp. MG. Komroff emphasizes Disraeli's public career and his age seen from the politician's perspective. Highly readable and informative.

McGuirk, Carol. *Benjamin Disraeli.* New York: Chelsea House, 1987. 112pp. MG/YA. Part of the World Leaders Past & Present series, this succinct and generously illustrated summary of the highlights of Disraeli's career establishes his unconventionality in his Jewish background and eccentricities as well as his rise to power and achievements as one of the most influential politicians in European history.

Biographical Films and Theatrical Adaptations

Housman, Laurence. *Angels & Ministers.* New York: Harcourt, Brace, 1922. 150pp. Housman portrays Disraeli in one of his brief dramatic vignettes on his deathbed reflecting on his life.

Disraeli (1929). Director: Alfred E. Green. George Arliss won the Best Actor Oscar for his performance as the British prime minister conniving to secure the Suez Canal for England against the Russians. Disraeli is portrayed as a devoted husband to his wife (Florence Anliss) and a matchmaker in a romance involving Lady Clarissa Pevensey (Joan Bennett). One of Hollywood's best biographical films, the movie is based on the play by Louis N. Parker (New York: J. Lane, 1911. 114pp.). Video.

Disraeli (1979). Director: Claude Whatham. Television mini-series written by David Butler (*Edward the King*), starring Ian McShane in the title role that chronicles Disraeli's career from 1832 to his death. Butler's book based on the series is available as *Disraeli, Portrait of a Romantic* (New York: Warner Books, 1980. 539pp.). Video.

Edward the King (1975). Director: John Gorrie. In this television mini-series chronicling the life of Edward VII, Timothy West plays the title character with Annette Crosbie as Queen Victoria and John Gielgud a standout as Disraeli. Video.

Mrs. Brown (1997). Director: John Madden. Antony Sher portrays Disraeli in this drama showing the relationship between Queen Victoria (Judi Dench) and her Scottish servant John Brown (Billy Connolly). Video.

The Mudlark (1950). Director: Jean Negulesco. Film version of the Bonnet novel, Alec Guinness portrays Disraeli in his scheme to convince Queen Victoria (Irene Dunne) to end her seclusion with the aid of a street urchin and the Queen's trusted servant John Brown (Finlay Currie).

Suez (1938). Director: Allan Dwan. Tyrone Power portrays French architect Ferdinand de Lesseps who pursues his goal of building the Suez Canal. Miles Mander portrays Disraeli and Loretta Young provides the love interest in a treatment that owes little to history.

Victoria Regina (1961). Director: George Schaefer. This made-for-television PBS film tells the story of Victoria's reign in a series of vignettes from her ascension to the throne in 1837 through the celebration of her Diamond Jubilee. Julie Harris stars as Victoria and James Donald as Prince Albert. Disraeli is played by veteran English actor Basil Rathbone. Video.

See also William Gladstone; Victoria

140. JOHN DONNE
1572–1631

English poet and clergyman, John Donne was raised a Catholic and, after education at Oxford, Cambridge and Lincoln's Inn and continental travel, became the secretary to Sir Thomas Egerton, lord keeper of the great seal. Donne achieved a reputation as a poet of witty, irreverent poems, collected in *Songs and Sonnets* (1633), including "The

Sun Rising," "The Flea," and "A Valediction: Forbidden Mourning." His marriage to Anne More, Egerton's niece, ruined his prospects as a courtier. After a long period of financial distress, Donne finally yielded to the wishes of James I and took orders in 1615, becoming famous for his sermons and religious poems and serving as royal chaplain and in 1621 dean of Saint Paul's, a position he held until his death. Donne's reputation as a poet was revived in the twentieth century through the advocacy of T.S. Eliot, who championed Donne's brilliant use of paradox and the conjunction of daring ideas and sensuous imagery, characteristics of the metaphysical poets.

Recommended Biographies

Carey, John. *John Donne: Life, Mind, and Art.* New York: Oxford University Press, 1981. 303pp. Carey's intellectual biography points toward an understanding of Donne's imagination and uses biographical details to help reveal the development of his artistry and consistency of his thought and character. Carey provides an unflattering though ultimately sympathetic portrait that challenges many preconceptions and constructs a psychological profile that is far less contradictory than other biographers have uncovered. Witty, sensitive, and provocative, Carey's is one of the foundation critical texts for understanding Donne as thinker and poet.

Bald, R.C. *John Donne: A Life.* New York: Oxford University Press, 1970. 627pp. Bald's meticulous and exhaustive research corrects errors and fancies committed by Walton and fills in the gaps of the biographical record with reliable factual details and avoids unsubstantiated psychological surmises. Bald deals expertly with the externals of Donne's life and his era, and readers wishing to penetrate Donne's inner life and growth and development of his artistry should consult Carey.

Walton, Izaak. *The Life of John Donne.* 1658. Reprint ed. London: Cambridge University Press, 1956. 426pp. The first biography of Donne has the advantage of Walton's acquaintance with the poet and his firsthand familiarity with his era. Later scholars have corrected many of Walton's facts and balanced Walton's partisanship with more objectivity, but Walton's account remains an important source for information on Donne and insightful for the way he was seen by a contemporary.

Other Biographical Studies

Clive, Mary. *Jack & the Doctor.* New York: Saint Martin's, 1966. 218pp. Clive's chatty, undocumented biography is chiefly relieved by its many fine illustrations. The text offers little that is new and is marred by errors and incessant conjecture.

Gosse, Edmund. *The Life and Letters of John Donne, Dean of Saint Paul's.* London: Heinemann, 1899. 2 vols. Gosse's enthusiasm for the poet and his poetry leads him into a number of dubious speculations, including reading his love lyrics as an autobiographical sequence. Untrustworthy in his handling of the facts, Gosse's impressionism achieves a vividness and drama that brings Donne and his age to life, but readers should be careful in accepting Gosse's version as reliable.

Jessop, Augustus. *John Donne, Sometime Dean of Saint Paul's.* Boston: Houghton Mifflin, 1897. Reprint ed. 1972. 238pp. Jessop participated in the revision of our understanding of Donne's life in the nineteenth century, and his study corrects many misconceptions created by Walton, but his book lacks the earlier writer's color and flare, and his treatment has been superseded by later scholars.

Le Comte, Edward. *Grace to a Witty Sinner: A Life of Donne.* New York: Walker, 1965. 307pp. Written for a general reader, Le Comte's factual study that avoids conjecture serves as an excellent introduction to the poet, his thought, and poetry, anchored firmly in his historical millieu.

Parfitt, George. *John Donne: A Literary Life.* New York: Saint Martin's, 1989. 140pp. Parfitt provides a close look at Donne's writing career and the impact of his experiences on it between his marriage at age 30 and his ordination at age 45. The book is particularly good on the period details that clarify the conditions under which Donne worked.

Parker, Derek. *John Donne and His World.* London: Thames and Hudson, 1975. 127pp. This attractive visual biography provides a brief summary of the highlights of Donne's career with a collection of contemporary illustrations and views of sites associated with the poet.

Biographical Novels

O'Connor, Garry. *Campion's Ghost.* London: Hodder and Stoughton, 1993. 246pp. Donne reflects back on his life and the events that led to his becoming a churchman in this fictionalized treatment of his story.

Vining, Elizabeth G. *Take Heed of Loving Me.* Philadelphia: Lippincott, 1963. 352pp. The novel focuses on Donne's relationship with his wife and reads more like a biography that keeps closely to the facts with a carefully researched historical background.

Fictional Portraits

Tourney, Leonard. *Knaves Templar.* New York: Saint Martin's, 1991. 282pp. In this installment of the author's historical mystery series, someone is killing the law students of Temple Bar. To solve the crime much of Elizabethan London must be sifted for clues, and Donne appears as a character.

Weiss, David. *Physician Extraordinary: A Novel of the Life and Times of William Harvey.* New York: Delacorte, 1975. 455pp. In this biographical novel on the career of doctor and scientist William Harvey many sixteenth- and seventeenth-century figures are depicted, including John Donne.

Other Sources

Ray, Robert. *A John Donne Companion.* New York: Garland, 1990. 414pp. In a collection of alphabetical entries, this reference source covers the major poems and prose works, as well as the persons and places in Donne's life.

141. FEODOR DOSTOEVSKY
1821–1881

Russian writer, Dostoevsky was born and raised in Moscow, the son of a military surgeon who was killed by his own serfs, an event that haunted Dostoevsky throughout his life. After attending engineering school, Dostoevsky abandoned government service for writing. His involvement with a radical group resulted in arrest and a four-year sentence to a Siberian labor camp. After his release, Dostoevsky struggled with financial hardships, a failed marriage, and compulsive gambling while producing his masterpieces, *Notes from the Underground* (1864), *Crime and Punishment* (1866), *The Idiot* (1868), and *The Brothers Karamazov* (1879–1880). Widely regarded as one of the greatest modern novelists, Dostoevsky contributed to the novel a profound psychological and philosophical complexity.

Autobiography and Primary Sources

The Diary of a Writer. David Magarshack, ed. New York: Scribner, 1949. 2 vols. In this remarkable collection of sketches, anecdotes, political polemics, and philosophical speculations, Dostoevsky offers a number of autobiographical revelations and his opinions on various matters.

The Complete Letters of Fyodor Doestoevsky. David A. Lowe, ed. Ann Arbor, Michigan: Ardis, 1995. 5 vols. Dostoevsky's many voices and obsessions are captured firsthand in these volumes, an essential biographical source. Dostoevsky's letters are also available in a single-volume collection, *Selected Letters of Fyodor Dostoevsky.* Joseph Frank and David I. Goldstein, eds. (New Brunswick, New Jersey: Rutgers University Press, 1987. 543pp.).

Notebooks. Edward Wasiolek, ed. Chicago: University of Chicago Press, 1967-71. 5 vols. Dostoevsky's fiction notebooks offer a unique view of the author's creative process.

The Unpublished Dostoevsky: Diaries and Notebooks (1860–1881). Carl R. Proffer, ed. Ann Arbor, Michigan: Ardis, 1973. 3 vols. The volumes present a fascinating array of material including the author's itineraries, daily reminders, list of epileptic attacks, and comments on literature.

Dostoevsky: A Self-Portrait. Jessie Coulson, ed. New York: Oxford University Press, 1962. 279pp. By assembling excerpts from Dostoevsky's letters and diaries with the necessary biographical links, Coulson offers a competent documentary biography. Because Dostoevsky was often guarded and reserved in his letters, the book's title is somewhat misleading, however.

Recommended Biographies

Frank, Joseph. *Dostoevsky.* Princeton, New Jersey: Princeton University Press, 1976–1997. 4 vols. Frank's monumental biography has reached the year 1871 with a final concluding volume needed to establish this multi-volume work as the definitive life. The most comprehensive resource available on Dostoevsky's life, the book is also the fullest recreation of the social and political context to establish and evaluate the writer's life and career. Frank's meticulous and detailed treatment is most useful for the informed reader. General readers might best start with either Kjetsaa or Yarmonlinsky's single-volume introductory studies before proceeding to Frank.

Hingley, Ronald. *Dostoyevsky: His Life and Work.* New York: Scribner, 1978. 222pp. Making use of Dostoevsky's complete works published in Russia in 1972 and sources unavailable to previous biographers, Hingley's study remains one of the most concise and accurate general biographies available in English. The author sticks to the facts, avoiding psychological speculation and novelistic reconstruction, in a sensible and thorough narrative and critical assessment.

Kjetsaa, Geir. *Fyodor Dostoevsky: A Writer's Life.* New York: Viking, 1987. 437pp. Written for the general reader, Kjetsaa's narrative follows Dostoevsky through his personal and artistic development and sets his inner contradictions and tortured obsessions against the history of his culture and times. Recommended for those who lack the patience for Frank's more comprehensive study.

Other Biographical Studies

Amoia, Alba. *Feodor Dostoevsky.* New York: Continuum, 1993. 312pp. Part of the Literature and Life: World Writers series, this critical study begins with a chronology and a succinct biographical essay, followed by a summary and critique of Dostoevsky's works. Based on Frank's multivolume study for its biographical details.

Berdyaev, Nicholas. *Dostoevsky: An Interpretation.* New York: Sheed & Ward, 1934. 227pp. Written by a Christian philosopher, Berdyaev's study is one of the best available works on Dostoevsky's spiritual side, although the author's contention that Dostoevsky was a great metaphysical thinker sometimes results in extravagant claims and critical obfuscation.

Carr, Edward H. *Dostoevsky (1821–1881): A New Biography.* Boston: Houghton Mifflin, 1931. 331pp. Using previously unavailable material, including letters, diaries by Dostoevsky's wife and daughter, Carr provides a reliable introduction to the novelist's life and career that replaces sentimental and romantic conceptions with a believable human portrait.

De Jonge, Alex. *Doestoevsky and the Age of Intensity.* New York: Saint Martin's, 1975. 244pp. De Jonge's intellectual biography traces the growth and development of Dostoevsky's thought and evolving philosophy.

Dostoevsky, Aimee. *Fyodor Dostoevsky.* 1922. Reprint ed. New York: Haskell House, 1972. 294pp. Written by Dostoevsky's daughter, despite distortions of fact, this biography is revealing on the novelist's domestic life and personal habits during his final decade.

Dostoevsky, Anna. *Dostoevsky: Reminiscences.* New York: Liveright, 1975. 448pp. In this translation of the diary of Dostoevsky's widow, the intimate domestic record of their 14-year marriage is insightful, despite her adoration that portrays the novelist as a doting, overprotective husband and a passionately devoted father whose epileptic condition was the sole cause for his irascibility.

Freud, Sigmund. *Dostoevsky and Parricide.* New York: Anchor Books, 1971. 84pp. In a psychological analysis of Dostoevsky's obsessions and the core of his genius, Freud establishes Dostoevsky's fascination with crime and criminality as the key to understanding his character and dilemmas.

Grossman, Leonid. *Dostoevsky: A Biography.* New York: Bobbs-Merrill, 1975. 647pp. In the best available biography by a Russian, Grossman's treatment is thorough and reliable with considerable original insights on Dostoevsky's Russian milieu.

Magarshack, David. *Dostoevsky.* New York: Harcourt, Brace, 1961. 399pp. The author concentrates on Dostoevsky's life prior to his 1867 marriage to his second wife, which is competently and skillfully narrated by a recognized Dostoevsky scholar.

Meier-Graefe, Julius. *Dostoevsky: The Man and His Work.* 1928. Reprint ed. New York: Haskell House, 1972. 406pp. In an enthusiastic appreciation by a German art critic, the author provides only a biographical sketch to concentrate on the inner man revealed in his writing. Though vividly impressionistic, the lack of documentation and Meier-Graefe's lack of knowledge of Russian renders this study not a reliable or scholarly work.

Mochulsky, Konstantin. *Dostoevsky: His Life and Work.* Princeton, New Jersey: Princeton University Press, 1967. 687pp. Mochulsky's insightful study is not a formal biography as much as a history of Dostoevsky's writings and a study of his creativity establishing a unified and comprehensible pattern of artistic and intellectual development.

Murry, John Middleton. *Fyodor Dostoevsky: A Critical Study.* 1916. Reprint ed. New York: Russell & Russell, 1966. 263pp. Murry's early study that portrays Dostoevsky as a mystic and prophet helped established an image of him in the West that later biographers have attempted to correct. The book is still valuable to establish the impact of Dostoevsky on European literary consciousness in the opening decades of the twentieth century.

Payne, Robert. *Dostoevsky: A Human Portrait.* New York: Knopf, 1961. 404pp. In this readable, popular biography, Payne rejects the portrayal of the novelist as a satanic, mystical figure for a more human portrait that records the inconsistencies in his behavior and a detailed chronology of his various relationships. Without uncovering much that is new, the book is serviceable as an introduction.

Rice, James L. *Dostoevsky and the Healing Art.* Ann Arbor, Michigan: Ardis, 1985. 352pp. Rice provides the most detailed account available on Dostoevsky's epilepsy. Appropriate primarily for the specialist.

Simmons, Ernest. *Dostoevski: The Making of a Novelist.* New York: Oxford University Press, 1940. 395pp. Restricted to an account of the development of Dostoevsky's creative process, Simmons makes use of biographical material only when it contributes to his central themes. Although exhaustively documented in certain respects, Simmons's study tones down or ignores many of the writer's traits, experiences, and conceptions.

Slonim, Marc. *The Three Loves of Dostoevsky.* New York: Rinehart, 1955. 300pp. Drawing on the

letters, diaries, and other primary and secondary sources, the author examines the writer's personal life as expressed by his relationships.

Troyat, Henri. *Firebrand: The Life of Dostoevsky.* New York: Roy Publishers, 1946. 438pp. Reading at times like a novel, Troyat provides a dramatic and often romantic narrative account stressing Dostoevsky's emotional development. A highly readable but partial biography, the book largely neglects the cultural and historical context that fixes the novelist in his milieu.

Yarmolinsky, Avrahm. *Dostoevsky: Works and Days.* 1934. Revised ed. New York: Funk and Wagnalls, 1971. 438pp. This critical biography remains one of the most readable and informative single-volume studies available. Yarmolinsky is especially good in showing how much of Dostoevsky's fiction is grounded in the experiences of his life.

Biographical Novels

Coulter, Stephen. *The Devil Inside: A Novel of Dostoevsky's Life.* Garden City, New York: Doubleday, 1960. 472pp. In a biographical profile that begins shortly before the death of Dostoevsky's father and ends with the writer's death in 1881, Coulter presents a sensational but highly readable account that stresses Dostoevsky's spiritual torment, sexual liaisons, and gambling obsession.

Fictional Portraits

Coetzee, J.M. *The Master of Petersburg.* New York: Viking, 1994. 250pp. Dostoevsky is the protagonist in this intense, brooding novel set in 1869 as the novelist returns to Saint Petersburg after his stepson's suspicious death. Plagued by seizures, tormented by an affair with his stepson's landlady, and involved with a revolutionary group, Dostoevsky struggles to resolve his responsibility to his family and society. Inventive in animating Dostoevsky's psyche and his demons, Coetzee violates biographical facts in this imaginative work, most notably the death of the writer's stepson who in fact outlived him.

Biographical Films and Theatrical Adaptations

The Modern World: Ten Great Writers (1988). Director: David Thomas. An installment of the London Weekend Television series looks at Dostoevsky's life and literary career. Video.

Other Sources

Sekirin, Peter. *Dostoevsky Archive: Firsthand Accounts of the Novelist from Contemporaries' Memoirs and Rare Periodicals, Most Translated into English for the First Time, with a Detailed Chronology and Annotated Bibliography.* Jefferson, North Carolina: McFarland, 1997. 370pp. Gathering memoirs, reviews, and personal recollections of almost everyone who came in contact with the author, the volume is arranged chronologically with biographical sketches of the people mentioned to form a revealing documentary account of how Dostoevsky was seen by those closest to him.

142. FREDERICK DOUGLASS
ca. 1817–1895

American abolitionist Frederick Douglass is considered by many to be the most influential black leader of the nineteenth century. Born a slave, Douglass escaped to freedom in 1838. As the editor of the *North Star*, Douglass became an important abolitionist leader who favored a political solution to slavery. During the Civil War, he helped organize black regiments. After the war, Douglass held a number of government posts and continued to speak out for equal rights.

Autobiography and Primary Sources

Autobiographies. New York: Library of America, 1994. 1,128pp. Collects Douglass's three progressively more detailed autobiographical works—*Narrative of the Life of Frederick Douglass* (1845), *My Bondage and My Freedom* (1855), and *Life and Times of Frederick Douglass* (1893).

Recommended Biographies

McFeely, William S. *Frederick Douglass*. New York: W.W. Norton, 1991. 465pp. The Pulitzer prize–winning biographer of Ulysses S. Grant offers a detailed and authoritative life that serves to reveal a complex figure against a solidly realized period background. The book is expected to stand as the definitive life for some time to come.

Quarles, Benjamin. *Frederick Douglass*. New York: Atheneum, 1948. 378pp. One of the finest and most original historians of his generation, Quarles explores Douglass's personal and family life, his impact on the antislavery movement, the Civil War, Reconstruction, women's suffrage, and the Republican party.

Other Biographical Studies

Bontemps, Arna. *Free at Last*. New York: Dodd, Mead, 1971. 310pp. A popular work with novelistic elements, this account largely ignores Douglass the writer, thinker, and political strategist.

Foner, Philip S. *Frederick Douglass*. New York: Citadel, 1964. 444pp. The author, an editor of the first major compilation of Douglass's writings, is skilled in placing Douglass's life and contributions in larger social and political contexts.

Martin, Waldo S. The Mind of *Frederick Douglass*. Chapel Hill: University of North Carolina Press, 1984. 333pp. This is an original approach with its emphasis on the development of Douglass's ideas, forming an interesting intellectual biography, best read as a complement to McFeely or Quarles.

Preston, Dickson J. *Young Frederick Douglass: The Maryland Years*. Baltimore, Maryland: Johns Hopkins University Press, 1980. 242pp. This study offers the most detailed account of Douglass's early years.

Washington, Booker T. *Frederick Douglass*. 1907. Reprint ed. New York: Greenwood, 1969. 365pp. Washington's 1907 study is chiefly interesting for its perspective by one important black leader of another.

Biographical Novels

Fuller, Edmund. *A Star Pointed North*. New York: Harper & Row, 1946. 361pp. The novel traces Douglass's career and is faithful to the facts of his life.

Recommended Juvenile Biographies

Banta, Melissa. *Frederick Douglass*. New York: Chelsea House, 1993. 76pp. MG. An informative account of Douglass's career.

Kerby, Mona. *Frederick Douglass*. New York: F. Watts, 1994. 63pp. MG. This illustrated biography offers a strong, dramatic sense of the great abolitionist and his influence.

Weiner, Eric. *The Story of Frederick Douglass*. Milwaukee, Wisconsin: G. Stevens, 1996. 108pp. YA. This is an informative and reliable account.

Biographical Films and Theatrical Adaptations

A&E Biography Video: Frederick Douglass (1997). Director: Craig Hoffner. Informative highlights of Douglass's life and times. Video.

Frederick Douglass: Abolitionist Editor (1992). Director: Rhonda Fabian. From the Black Americans Achievement Series, this 30-minute profile is appropriate for junior high and adult audiences. Video.

Frederick Douglass: When the Lion Wrote History (1994). Director: Orlando Bogwell. In this PBS series, Douglass's autobiographical writings and archival materials are used to present the story of his life. Video.

143. ARTHUR CONAN DOYLE
1859–1930

English author and physician, Doyle created the brilliant and eccentric Sherlock Holmes, literature's most famous fictional detective, in such novels as *A Study in Scarlet* (1887) and *The Hound of the Baskervilles* (1902) and in a series of short stories that appeared in the *Strand* magazine beginning in 1891. Conan Doyle's other works include the well-known science fiction novel, *The Lost World* (1912), historical romances, and political pamphlets.

Autobiography and Primary Sources

Memories and Adventures. Boston: Little, Brown, 1924. 410pp. Doyle's autobiographical account of his life and career is frank and revealing and serves as a valuable source of insights on the man, his background, and activities although it forms more a record of his external rather than internal life.

Recommended Biographies

Booth, Martin. *The Doctor, the Detective and Arthur Conan Doyle: A Biography of Arthur Conan Doyle*. New York: Saint Martin's, 2000. 371pp. Until Doyle's papers are finally opened to scholars, Booth's biography will likely stand as the standard life. The book achieves a skillful balance between the author and his work, taking Doyle at his own valuation as more than the creator of Sherlock Holmes.

Pearsall, Ronald. *Conan Doyle: A Biographical Solution*. New York: Saint Martin's, 1977. 208pp. Pearsall's popular critical biography covers the full range of Doyle's life and work in a sensible overview that links the author with his times.

Stashower, Daniel. *Teller of Tales: The Life of Arthur Conan Doyle*. New York: Holt, 1999. 472pp. This is an excellent biography that achieves a multidimensional portrayal of Doyle that covers the full range of his interests and activities.

Other Biographical Studies

Carr, John Dickson. *The Life of Arthur Conan Doyle*. New York: Harper, 1949. 304pp. Carr, a popular mystery writer, produced this authorized life with the cooperation of Doyle's children and made use of family letters and papers. Unfortunately, the biography is treated in a novelistic style with invented dialogue and an awestruck reverence for Doyle's every move and word.

Cox, Don R. *Arthur Conan Doyle*. New York: Frederick Ungar, 1985. 251pp. This critical study concentrates on the Holmes books and attempts to connect Doyle's life and writing only intermittently.

Doyle, Adrian M. Conan. *The True Conan Doyle*. New York: Coward-McCann, 1946. 30pp. Inspired by what the author felt was a false view of his father by Hesketh Pearson, this is a slim and not very helpful collection of recollections and defense of Doyle's spiritualism.

Edwards, Owen D. *The Quest for Sherlock Holmes: A Biographical Study of Arthur Conan Doyle*. New York: Barnes and Noble, 1983. 380pp. Edwards concentrates on Doyle's first 23 years in a psychologically penetrating, though highly conjectural, study that stresses the influences of Doyle's father, his Jesuit education, and his interest in Celtic lore.

Higham, Charles. *The Adventures of Conan Doyle: The Life of the Creator of Sherlock Holmes*. New York: W.W. Norton, 1976. 368pp. Higham has uncovered some new material in this popular biography that depends too much on a sifting of the autobiographical clues from Doyle's fiction. The section on spiritualism is the strongest part of the book.

Norden, Pierre. *Conan Doyle: A Biography*. New York: Holt, 1967. 370pp. Norden compresses the events of Doyle's first 40 years into a single chapter, and the sense of the writer's development suffers accordingly in this uneven critical biography.

Pearson, Hesketh. *Conan Doyle: His Life and Art*. 1943. Revised ed. London: Unwin, 1987. 193pp. Pearson's is a highly readable, entertaining overview that narrates the events of Doyle's career in a fast-moving, though rarely very penetrating, account.

Symons, Julian. *Conan Doyle: Portrait of an Artist*. New York: Mysterious Press, 1987. 137pp. Despite its limitations of supplying no discussion of Doyle's life prior to 1890, this still is one of the better short biographical portraits.

Fictional Portraits

Frost, Mark. *The List of 7.* New York: Morrow, 1993. 368pp; *The Six Messiahs.* New York: Morrow, 1995. 404pp. Frost employs Doyle as sleuth in this pair of period mysteries mixing fantasy and convincing period elements.

Hjortsberg, William. *Nevermore.* New York: Atlantic Monthly Press, 1994. 289pp. Hjortsberg's inventive novel links the living Doyle and Harry Houdini and the ghostly Edgar Allan Poe to solve collectively a series of baffling murders.

Michaels, Barbara. *Other Worlds.* New York: HarperCollins, 1999. 217pp. Set "outside of time and space, in the realm of the imagination," the novel brings together Doyle, Houdini, and other famous psychic researchers to consider two ghost tales in which they each attempt to explain away or justify the occult occurences.

Rogow, Roberta; *The Problem of the Missing Miss.* New York: St. Martin's, 1998. 259pp; *The Problem of the Spiteful Spiritualist.* New York: St. Martin's, 1999. 282pp; *The Problem of the Evil Editor.* New York: St. Martin's, 2000. 298pp. Rogow unhistorically but ingeniously teams Doyle up with Lewis Carroll to solve some period mysteries.

Satterthwait, Walter. *Escapade.* New York: Saint Martin's, 1995. 355pp. Doyle joins forces with Houdini to solve the ultimate locked-room mystery at an English country house.

Shatner, William, and Michael Tobias. *Believe.* New York: Berkley Books, 1992. 321pp. This is contest of wills and ideas between Doyle and Harry Houdini as they debate the question of life after death.

Recommended Juvenile Biographies

Adams, Cynthia. *The Mysterious Case of Sir Arthur Conan Doyle.* Greensboro, North Carolina: Morgan Reynolds, 1999. 112pp. MG. Adams covers both the private side and the public career of Doyle in a well-rounded, informative portrait.

Hoehling, Mary D. *The Real Sherlock Holmes: Arthur Conan Doyle.* New York: J. Messner, 1965. 191pp. MG. Relying on fictional dialogue, Hoehling dramatizes the story of Doyle's career and manages a convincing human portrait of the author.

Wood, James P. *The Man Who Hated Sherlock Holmes: A Life of Sir Arthur Conan Doyle.* New York: Pantheon, 1965. 180pp. MG. Despite some oversimplification, this is an absorbing narrative account of Doyle's life with a concentration on his struggles with his most famous creation.

Biographical Films and Theatrical Adaptations

FairyTale: A True Story (1997). Director: Charles Sturridge. Doyle (Peter O'Toole) and Houdini (Harvey Keitel) investigate the claim of two girls in 1917 that they have photographed fairies in their garden, giving the occasion for a spirited debate between the two over the questions of science versus spiritualism. Video.

Other Sources

Lellenberg, Jon L., ed. *The Quest for Sir Arthur Conan Doyle: Thirteen Biographers in Search of a Life.* Carbondale: Southern Illinois University Press, 1987. 217pp. This is an intriguing critical volume that looks at the various Doyle biographies to study the rise and fall of his reputation.

Orel, Harold, ed. *Sir Arthur Conan Doyle: Interviews and Recollections.* New York: Saint Martin's, 1991. 278pp. The editor presents a wide selection of views of the author by his contemporaries.

See also Harry Houdini

144. SIR FRANCIS DRAKE
ca. 1540–1596

English navigator and admiral, Sir Francis Drake was the first Englishman to circumnavigate the world (1577-1580). Born in Devonshire, Drake was apprenticed as a youth to a ship's captain. In 1572 he set out on the first of his marauding expeditions against the Spanish that culminated in his famous round-the-world voyage aboard the *Golden Hind.* On his return to England, Drake was knighted by Elizabeth I. A vice admiral in the fleet that defeated the Spanish Armada in 1588, Drake led an invasion of Portugal in 1589 that failed to capture Lisbon and a final unsuccessful venture against the Spanish in the West Indies. Dying of dysentery, Drake was buried at sea.

Autobiography and Primary Sources

The Last Voyage of Drake and Hawkins. Kenneth R. Andrews, ed. Cambridge, Massachusetts: Cambridge University Press, 1972. 283pp. Collects primary documents relating to Drake's failed mission to the West Indies.

The World Encompassed. 1628. Reprint ed. New York: Da Capo Press, 1969. 108pp. Assembled from Drake's own account and others' recollections, his epic circumnavigation is chronicled.

Recommended Biographies

Cummins, John G. *Francis Drake: The Lives of a Hero.* New York: Saint Martin's, 1995. 348pp. In a reexamination of the various myths surrounding Drake, the author presents a balanced assessment of a brilliant but flawed man whose meteoric rise was fueled by luck, talent, and ambition. Neither overly awed nor dismissive, Cummins finds a credible middle ground for an appreciation that takes full advantage of modern scholarship.

Sugden, John. *Sir Francis Drake.* New York: Holt, 1990. 355pp. Regarded as the standard, authoritative modern biography of Drake's life and legacy for a general reader, Sugden's study provides details of the admiral's private life on shore to humanize his legend. The book provides a packed chronology of Drake's progress against a background of Elizabethan politics that reveals a sympathetic yet mixed portrait of the man.

Other Biographical Studies

Andrews, Kenneth R. *Drake's Voyages.* New York: Scribner, 1967. 190pp. Andrews's authoritative assessment of Drake's naval accomplishments stresses their significance to the formation of British seapower.

Bradford, Ernle. *Drake.* London: Hodder and Stoughton, 1965. 251pp. Written by an assiduous scholar and veteran sailor, Bradford retraced many of Drake's steps adding considerably to his readable, straightforward account that misses little of importance. Although Bradford attempts to penetrate the mythical heroic aura of Drake with human details, this is still an admiring view in which most of Drake's motives and actions are defended.

Corbett, Sir Julian. *Sir Francis Drake.* 1890. Reprint ed. Westport, Connecticut: Greenwood, 1970. 209pp. Written by an authority on the Tudor navy, Corbett's early biography is written for a popular audience in which Drake is given the full hero's treatment with novelistic touches to emphasize drama and sentiment.

Kelsey, Harry. *Sir Francis Drake: The Queen's Pirate.* New Haven, Connecticut: Yale University Press, 1998. 566pp. In Kelsey's revisionist view, Drake is shown as a brave and resourceful seaman who was also a ruthless and frequently brutal man whose primary goal was self-enrichment. The book adds new details on Drake's early career but wastes little time on Drake's family history, childhood, or domestic life to concentrate on his sea career. Important in balancing earlier heroic interpretations, Kelsey's treatment is often guilty of judging Drake from a limiting modern standard.

Lloyd, Christopher. *Sir Francis Drake.* London: Faber and Faber, 1967. 144pp. In one of the first modern biographies to challenge previous hero-worship. Lloyd places a more complex and morally mixed Drake in his Elizabethan context and freely admits to the considerable gaps in our knowledge but refuses to fill them in with unsubstantiated speculations. A solid, serious, and reliable short life.

McKee, Alexander. *The Queen's Corsair: Drake's Journey of Circumnavigation.* New York: Stein and Day, 1979. 320pp. In a chronological narrative of Drake's circumnavigation based on primary sources such as the diaries and memoirs of the participants, McKee provides the most detailed account available. Drake's previous or subsequent career is beyond the scope of the book.

Thomson, George M. *Sir Francis Drake.* New York: Morrow, 1972. 358pp. In Thomson's dramatic, vivid, and well-illustrated biography written for the general reader, Drake's stature is emphasized, and his character and actions are defended, stressing his patriotic motivation over a desire for personal gain.

Williamson, James A. *Sir Francis Drake.* London: Collins, 1951. 160pp. Written by an acknowledged expert on Elizabethan explorers, Williamson's brief life is intended for a general audience and corrects many of the legends that have grown up around Drake and, while accepting a number of unflattering aspects of Drake's career and personality, the admiral remains a considerable heroic figure in this account.

Wilson, Derek. *The World Encompassed: Francis Drake and His Great Voyage.* New York: Harper & Row, 1977. 240pp. Concentrating on Drake's circumnavigation and based on primary sources, Wilson provides a perceptive analysis of Drake the man and the personal qualities that led to his success and near failure.

Biographical Novels

Fredman, John. *Does the Queen Still Live?* London: Allen, 1979. 321pp. The major events of Drake's life are covered in this fictionalized biography that features a generally reliable reflection of fact and an authentic period background.

Mason, F. van Wyck. *Golden Admiral.* Garden City, New York: Doubleday, 1953. 340pp. In the story of Drake and the defeat of the Spanish Armada, the novel covers only a single year in his life but provides multiple facts about Drake's earlier accomplishments, a sharp picture of English life and customs, and a display of the author's nautical knowledge.

Fictional Portraits

Chidsey, Donald Barr. *Reluctant Cavalier.* New York: Crown, 1960. 287pp. Chidsey's lively and colorful evocation of the Elizabethan period concerns a diplomat's secret negotiations with Spain who joins Drake for sea adventures culminating with the defeat of the Armada.

Fletcher, Inglis. *Roanoke Hundred.* Indianapolis: Bobbs-Merrill, 1948. 492pp. In this tale of the founding of the first English settlement in North America, Sir Richard Grenville is the central figure, but a great number of Elizabethan figures, including Drake, Sidney, Elizabeth I, and Hooker are portrayed.

Heyer, Georgette. *Beauvallet.* London: Heinemann, 1929. 330pp. Heyer's romantic adventure novel involves one of Drake's naval colleagues in action on the Spanish Main, in England and Spain with appearances by Drake, Frobisher, Elizabeth I, and Philip II. The historical background is plausibly reproduced.

Kingsley, Charles. *Westward Ho!* 1855. Reprint ed. New York: Dutton, 1967. 633pp. Kingsley's adventure story depicts a sailor who joins Drake's circumnavigation with a personal vendetta against a Spanish nobleman who captures the heart of his beloved.

Michener, James A. *Caribbean.* New York: Random House, 1989. 672pp. Michener's panoramic history of the Caribbean islands touches upon the age of the buccaneers, including Drake's exploits.

Recommended Juvenile Biographies

Duncan, Alice S. *Sir Francis Drake and the Struggle for an Ocean Empire.* New York: Chelsea House, 1993. 111pp. MG. Surveys the life and voyages of Drake as well as the expansion of the English navy in the sixteenth century.

Marrin, Albert. *The Sea King: Sir Francis Drake and His Times.* New York: Atheneum, 1995. 168pp. MG. In a lively, detailed, and meticulously researched account of Drake's life, this is not a romanticized biography but a gritty and often graphic

treatment of shipboard life and the brutality of the times. Justifiable praised as the definitive portrait of Drake, his career, and era for younger readers.

Sanderlin, George W. *The Sea-Dragon: Journals of Francis Drake's Voyage Around the World.* New York: Harper & Row, 1969. 243pp. MG/YA. Drake's journals are abbreviated and edited and supplemented with historical commentary to cover in detail his privateering career and circumnavigation.

Biographical Films and Theatrical Adaptations

Elizabeth R (1972). Directors: Claude Whatham, et al. Acclaimed PBS series chronicling the reign of Elizabeth I (Glenda Jackson) includes her relationship with Drake (John Woodvine). Video.

145. THEODORE DREISER
1871–1945

American novelist and pioneer of naturalistic fiction, Dreiser was a journalist for several midwestern newspapers before settling (1894) in New York City. There, he worked in publishing and eventually became president of Butterick Publications. His novels include *Sister Carrie* (1900) and *An American Tragedy* (1925), often considered his greatest work.

Autobiography and Primary Sources

Dreiser published two parts of a projected multivolume autobiography, *Dawn: A History of Myself* (New York: Liveright, 1931. 589pp.) and *Newspaper Days* (New York: Liveright, 1931. 502pp.). The first covers Dreiser's life up to his departure for Saint Louis to work as a reporter; the second chronicles his journalist career. Both volumes shocked reviewers with their frank personal revelations and honest depiction of sexual matters. In the unfinished account written in 1904, *An Amateur Laborer* (Richard W. Dowell, ed. Philadelphia: University of Pennsylvania Press, 1983. 207pp.), Dreiser recalls his three years of near suicidal depression following the publication of *Sister Carrie* in 1900.

Recommended Biographies

Lingeman, Richard R. *Theodore Dreiser.* New York: Putnam, 1986–1990. 2 vols. Lingeman's detailed and authoritative, award-winning two-volume life has established itself as the definitive biography. Dreiser's life and career are presented in a fascinating narrative treatment that reveals the writer in breadth and depth against a vivid social backdrop.

Moers, Ellen. *Two Dreisers.* New York: Viking, 1969. 404pp. Less a full-scale biography than a critical exploration of Dreiser's literary genius, Moers concentrates on *Sister Carrie* and *An American Tragedy* to take the measure of the writer, offering insightful analysis of his influences, cultural background, and legacy.

Swanberg, W.A. *Dreiser.* New York: Scribner, 1965. 614pp. Detailed and scrupulously re-

searched, Swanberg's life both extends and corrects Dreiser's biographical record, providing a comprehensive and coherent account of an often messy and confusing life.

Other Biographical Studies

Dreiser, Helen. *My Life with Dreiser.* Cleveland: World, 1941. 328pp. Dreiser's longtime companion whom he married two years before his death supplies an intimate view of their relationship, documented by the writer's letters to her.

Dreiser, Vera. *My Uncle Theodore.* New York: Nash, 1976. 238pp. The book describes Dreiser's family background and its influences on him while claiming to correct various misconceptions in previous biographies and the writer's own accounts, particularly in a less-than-favorable assessment of the role of Dreiser's mother.

Elias, Robert. *Theodore Dreiser: Apostle of Nature.* New York: Knopf, 1948. 354pp. The first full-length biography is based on important primary sources and on interviews with Dreiser before his death. The book's chief value lies in its detailed documenting of the writer's early, formative years.

Gerber, Philip. *Theodore Dreiser.* New York: Twayne, 1964. 220pp. Gerber's critical biography provides a useful summary of Dreiser's formative years and traces the autobiographical elements in his fictions.

Hakutani, Yoshinobu. *Young Dreiser.* Rutherford, New Jersey: Fairleigh Dickinson University Press, 1980. 228pp. The book details Dreiser's youth, journalism career, and early fiction writing up to *Sister Carrie,* contending that the writer's early work shows no conscious naturalist influence and that Dreiser primarily drew on his personal experiences for his plots, characterization, and philosophy.

Hussman, Lawrence Jr. *Dreiser and His Fiction.* Philadelphia: University of Pennsylvania Press, 1983. 215pp. The biographical connections between Dreiser's life and his work are explored in this insightful critical examination that stresses the impact of the writer's religious training on his values and relationships.

Lundquist, James. *Theodore Dreiser.* New York: Frederick Ungar, 1974. 150pp. This is a reliable, informative survey of Dreiser's life and works suitable as a introduction for the student and general reader.

Matthiessen, F.O. *Theodore Dreiser.* New York: W. Sloane, 1951. 267pp. Matthiessen, a distinguished American literary scholar, offers an interpretive examination of Dreiser's life and works. Valuable both as a critique and a social history, the book analyzes the sources of Dreiser's imaginative power and explores his influences and the wider social context that shaped him.

McAleer, John. *Theodore Dreiser.* New York: Barnes and Noble, 1968. 180pp. McAleer's biography is particularly strong on Dreiser's journalistic career and the writer's despair following the reception of *Sister Carrie.*

146. JOHN DRYDEN
1631–1700

English poet, dramatist, and critic considered by many to be the father of English literary criticism, Dryden's career flourished during the Restoration (1660). He became Poet Laureate in 1668 and Historiographer Royal in 1670. His works include the famous critical *Essay of Dramatic Poesy* (1668), the play *All For Love* (1677), and the brilliant satirical poems *Absalom and Achitophel* (1681, 1682) and *MacFlecknoe* (1682). After the accession of William of Orange, Dryden lost his laureate and court patronage and worked primarily on the translations from such Roman writers as Virgil.

Autobiography and Primary Sources

The Letters of John Dryden. Charles E. Ward, ed. Durham, North Carolina: Duke University Press, 1942. 196pp. Dryden's letters offer a helpful vantage point to viewing the writer's activities, relationships, character, and ideas.

Recommended Biographies

Hammond, Paul. *John Dryden: A Literary Life*. New York: Saint Martin's, 1991. 184pp. Concentrating on Dryden's literary career, Hammond provides a succinct exploration of the writer in the wider context of his age and literary heritage. The book serves as a valuable introduction for the reader before proceeding to Winn's monumental volume.

Ward, Charles E. *The Life of John Dryden*. Chapel Hill: University of North Carolina Press, 1961. 380pp. The editor of Dryden's letters produced the first scholarly biography based on extensive primary research. Ward's effort remains an important source of information on Dryden's life and career and an objective, informed assessment of the man and his achievement.

Wasserman, George. *John Dryden*. New York: Twayne, 1964. 174pp. Along with Hammond's short study of Dryden's writing career, Wasserman provides one of the best introductory studies, succinctly summarizing the highpoints of Dryden's life and career in the wider context of his times and literary and intellectual tradition.

Winn, James A. *John Dryden and His World*. New Haven, Connecticut: Yale University Press, 1987. 651pp. Winn's fully-documented lucid account of Dryden and his times has superseded all previous biographies in its depth, comprehensiveness, and authoritative synthesis of the latest scholarship. The book has legitimately been praised as the most important biography of Dryden ever written.

Other Biographical Studies

Bredvold, Louis J. *The Intellectual Milieu of John Dryden*. Ann Arbor: University of Michigan Press, 1934. 189pp. This collection of essays on seventeenth-century philosophic and religious topics are insightfully connected to the details of Dryden's life and writings to form a helpful context for the writer's intellectual development.

Johnson, Samuel. "Dryden" in *Lives of the English Poets*. 1781. Reprint ed. London: Oxford University Press, 1959. 2 vols. Johnson's is the first important critical assessment of Dryden's work and literary achievement with an incomplete sketch of the man and his personal life.

Osborn, James. *John Dryden: Some Biographical Facts and Problems*. 1940. Revised ed. Gainesville: University of Florida Press, 1965. 316pp. Osborn's scholarly account, more for the specialist and future biographers than the general reader, offers an insightful evaluation of Dryden's early biographers and an investigation into a number of shady areas of the writer's life and career.

Saintsbury, George. *Dryden*. 1881. Reprint ed. New York: AMS Press, 1968. 192pp. Saintsbury's critical assessment is chiefly interesting today for its view of Dryden's reputation in the nineteenth century when a strong Victorian bias against Dryden's sexual imagery limited a fully accurate appreciation.

Scott, Walter. *Life of John Dryden*. 1808. Reprint ed. Bernard Kreissman, ed. Lincoln: University of Nebraska Press, 1963. 471pp. Scott provided a biographical and critical introduction to his massive 18-volume edition of Dryden works.

Young, Kenneth. *John Dryden: A Critical Biography*. 1954. Reprint ed. New York: Russell & Russell, 1969. 240pp. Intended for the general reader rather than the specialist, Young's is a vivid portrait of the man and his age. The book's fictional elaboration of thoughts and dialogue aids interest though scholars may deplore Young's liberties.

147. W.E.B. DU BOIS
1868–1963

Influential African American civil rights leader, educator, and author, William Edward Burghardt Du Bois taught (1897–1910, 1934–1944) at Atlanta University, cofounded (1909) the National Association for the Advancement of Colored People (NAACP), and edited (1910–1934) the NAACP's influential magazine, *Crisis*. In 1919 he organized the first of several Pan African Congresses. Dubois became (1961) a member of the U. S. Communist party and spent the last two years of his life in Ghana. His writings include *The Souls of Black Folks* (1903), *Black Reconstruction in America* (1935), and *Color and Democracy* (1945).

Autobiography and Primary Sources

Du Bois published three versions of his autobiography at various points of his career: *Darkwater: Voices from Within the Veil*. 1920. Reprint ed. (New York: Dover, 1999. 162pp.); *Dusk of Dawn: An Essay Toward an Autobiography of a Race Concept*. 1940. Reprint ed. (New York: Schocken, 1968. 334pp.); and a final summary completed in 1960, *The Autobiography of W.E.B. Du Bois: A Soliloquy on Viewing My Life from the Last Decade of Its First Century*. Herbert Aptheker, ed. (New York: International, 1968. 448pp.). Each is essential reading for gauging the man and his ideas.

The Correspondence of W.E.B. Du Bois. Herbert Aptheker, ed. Amherst: University of Massachu-setts Press, 1973–1978. 3 vols. Du Bois's purely personal letters have been excluded from this collection that emphasizes his public career.

Recommended Biographies

Broderick, Francis L. *W.E.B. Du Bois: Negro Leader in a Time of Crisis*. Stanford, California: Stanford University Press, 1959. 259pp. This is a highly readable, thorough, and balanced intellectual biography that has long stood as one of the essential, standard sources on Du Bois's life and ideas.

Lewis, David C. *W.E.B. Du Bois: Biography of a Race, 1868–1919*. New York: Holt, 1993. 735pp. Skillfully covering the first half of Du Bois's life, this is a distinguished biography and cultural history in which Du Bois's life and ideas are related to wider historical, social, and cultural contexts. Lewis has penetrated more deeply than any other biographer the various contradictions of the man and produced a coherent and compelling human portrait.

Marable, Manning. *W.E.B. Du Bois: Black Radical Democrat*. Boston: Twayne, 1986. 285pp. Marable's thorough coverage of Du Bois's career relies mainly on his private papers and writings with a summary evaluation of Du Bois's shortcomings and errors in judgment. Many of Marable's assertions are controversial, but the book serves as a valuable, original reassessment.

Rudwick, Elliott. *W.E.B. Du Bois: Voice of the Black Protest Movement*. Urbana: University of Illinois Press, 1982. 400pp. First published in 1960 as *W.E.B. Du Bois: A Study in Minority Group Leadership*, Rudwick's is a pioneering study of Du Bois's career and an assessment of his leadership. One of the virtues of the book is the relating of Du Bois's life and ideas to their wider historical and cultural significance.

Other Biographical Studies

Du Bois, Shirley G. *His Day Is Marching On: A Memoir of W.E.B. Du Bois*. Philadelphia: Lippincott, 1971. 384pp.; *Du Bois: A Pictorial Biography*. Chicago: Johnson, 1978. 174pp. Du Bois's wife offers two views of their life together and a rarely glimpsed private, domestic side of Du Bois.

Horne, Gerald. *Black and Red: W.E.B. Du Bois and the Afro-American Response to the Cold War, 1944–1963*. Albany: State University of New York Press, 1986. 457pp. Contending that both Broderick and Rudwick have distorted Du Bois's later years, Horne attempts to set the record straight in a thoroughly researched and well-written study of this often confusing period of Du Bois's life.

Moore, Jack B. *W.E.B. Du Bois*. Boston: Twayne, 1981. 185pp. Moore's is a brief, interpretive biography that covers the highlights of Du Bois's life and career with attention to his many contradictions, as well as a helpful analysis of his writings.

Rampersad, Arnold. *The Art and Imagination of W.E.B. Du Bois*. Cambridge, Massachusetts: Harvard University Press, 1976. 325pp. With an emphasis on Du Bois's thought and character as reflected in his fiction, Rampersad's is a refreshing viewpoint on the man and his development.

Zamir, Shamoon. *Dark Voices: W.E.B. Du Bois and American Thought, 1888–1903.* Chicago: University of Chicago Press, 1995. 294pp. Zamir's is an illuminating examination of Du Bois's intellectual development, tracing the civil rights leader's career from his undergraduate days to the 1903 publication of *The Souls of Black Folk.*

Recommended Juvenile Biographies

Hamilton, Virginia. *W.E.B. Du Bois: A Biography.* New York: Crowell, 1972. 218pp. YA. Hamilton's book serves both a biographical and historical purpose in a meticulously annotated, comprehensive, and mainly objective treatment of Du Bois's life and times that allows him to speak for himself.

McKissack, Pat. *W.E.B. Du Bois.* New York: F. Watts, 1990. 143pp. MG. Carefully researched, McKissack's account balances historical and personal detail and is candid about Du Bois's weaknesses.

Stafford, Mark. *W.E.B. Du Bois.* New York: Chelsea House, 1989. 127pp. MG/YA. Stafford provides a generally sound portrait that captures both Du Bois's strengths and failings.

Biographical Films and Theatrical Adaptations

W.E.B. Du Bois: A Biography in Four Voices (1995). Director: Louis Massiah. Four black writers, Wesley Brown, Thulani Davis, Toni Banbara, and Amiri Baraka, describe different periods of Du Bois's life and his impact on their work. Video.

Other Sources

Logan, Rayford W., ed. *W.E.B. Du Bois: A Profile.* New York: Hill & Wang, 1971. 324pp. This collection of essays offers a group portrait of the man, his ideas, and his accomplishments by the leading Du Bois scholars.

Tuttle, W.M., ed. *W.E.B. Du Bois.* Englewood Cliffs, New Jersey: Prentice-Hall, 1973. 186pp. Part of the Great Lives Observed series, selections of Du Bois's writings are joined with views by his contemporaries and historical evaluations.

Weinberg, Meyer, ed. *The World of W.E.B. Du Bois.* Westport, Connecticut: Greenwood, 1992. 282pp.Du Bois's ideas, opinions, and judgments from his published and unpublished writings have been excerpted and grouped into 20 broad subject areas.

148. ALEXANDRE DUMAS
1802–1870

French novelist and dramatist known for his enduring romantic and historical adventures written alone or in collaboration, Dumas was largely self-educated. At 20 he obtained a minor post with the duc d'Orléans and later took part in the Revolution of 1830. The most popular of his works are *The Three Musketeers* (1844) and its two sequels, *The Count of Monte Cristo* (1845), *Queen Margot* (1845), and *The Black Tulip* (1850).

Autobiography and Primary Sources

My Memoirs. New York: Macmillan, 1907. 6 vols. From a writer who lived such an oversized life, one would expect nothing less in his autobiography of nearly 6,000 pages. Like his novels, Dumas's account of his life must be read with caution regarding its historical reliability. An abridgement is available (Westport, Connecticut: Greenwood, 1975. 257pp.).

Recommended Biographies

Maurois, André. *The Titans: A Three-Generation Biography of the Dumas.* 1957. Reprint ed. Westport, Connecticut: Greenwood, 1971. 508pp. Maurois's collective biography of Dumas, his father, and his son is both rich in anecdotes and fresh insights based on previously untapped sources. The book is particularly successful in animating the social scene of the period. *Alexandre Dumas: A Great Life in Brief* (New York: Knopf, 1954. 198pp.) is a reliable summary of the highlights of Dumas's life and writing career.

Ross, Michael. *Alexandre Dumas.* North Pomfret, Vermont: David and Charles, 1981. 293pp. Ross supplies a useful biographical profile, emphasizing the man rather than his works (though they are briefly but adequately covered) and helpfully sorting through the fact and the fiction surrounding Dumas's remarkable life story.

Schopp, Claude. *Alexandre Dumas: Genius of Life.* New York: F. Watts, 1988. 506pp. Drawing on previously unpublished letters, Schopp's is a fresh, spirited reassessment of the man and the writer that places Dumas squarely in his cultural and historical context. The book is particularly strong on Dumas's early years and formative experiences.

Other Biographical Studies

Bell, Craig A. *Alexandre Dumas: A Biography and Study.* London: Cassell, 1950. 420pp. Bell's is a sympathetic and reasonably complete survey of Dumas's career intended for the general reader.

Davidson, Arthur F. *Alexandre Dumas (père): His Life and Works.* Philadelphia: Lippincott, 1902. 426pp. Davidson's chronological account of Dumas's life and literary career is still valuable as a reference source although its old-fashioned, allusive style is a drawback.

Gribble, Francis. *Dumas: Father and Son.* New York: Dutton, 1930. 279pp. Gribble's is an anecdotally rich, gossipy look at both father and son that makes no effort to separate truth from fiction, and the evident lack of sympathy that the author has for his subject makes one wonder why Gribble took up their lives in the first place.

Hemmings, F.W.J. *King of Romance: A Portrait of Alexandre Dumas.* New York: Scribner, 1979. 231pp. As one disappointed reviewer observed, Hemmings's biography is "efficient but lightweight, not so much the story of Dumas's life as the stories of his life." Episodic in form, the biography rarely penetrates the colorful anecdote to reveal the motives and inner dynamics of the man.

Lucas-Dubreton, Jean. *Alexandre Dumas: The Fourth Musketeer.* New York: Coward-McCann, 1928. 276pp. The author presents a highly romanticized, dramatic account of Dumas's life that rivals the novelist's own fiction. Not reliable in many of its details, the book interweaves fact and fancy in a highly entertaining, if truthfully suspect, mix.

Spurr, Harry A. *The Life and Writings of Alexandre Dumas.* 1902. Revised ed. 1929. Reprint ed. New York: Haskell House, 1973. 321pp. This is a generally reliable summary of the highlights of Dumas's career addressed to the general reader.

Stowe, Richard S. *Alexandre Dumas Père.* Boston: Twayne, 1976. 164pp. More critical study than biography, Stowe reviews Dumas's remarkable literary production, relating the works to Dumas's life and their reception. An excellent starting point for the reader interested in surveying Dumas's creations.

Biographical Novels

Endore, S. Guy. *King of Paris.* New York: Simon & Schuster, 1956. 504pp. Endore treats Dumas's life as dramatically as a Dumas novel, capturing the essence, if not the letter of the writer's life.

Fictional Portraits

McConnor, Vincent. *I Am Vidocq.* New York: Dodd, Mead, 1985. 385pp. In a period mystery involving the renowned Parisian police chief, Eugene Vidocq, several crimes keep him busy in the summer of 1823. Both Dumas and Honoré de Balzac appear in the proceedings.

149. ALBRECHT DÜRER
1471–1528

The most influential artist of the German school, Dürer elevated graphic art to the realm of fine art and raised the status of the artist above that of other artisans. He produced a vast number of masterly, vivid woodcuts and engravings and was court painter to the emperors Maximilian and Charles V. His themes included religious subjects, plant and animal studies, and watercolor landscapes. Among his works are *Knight, Death, and the Devil* (1513), *Fall of Man* (1514), and *Saint Jerome in his Cell* (1514).

Autobiography and Primary Sources

Conway, William M. *The Literary Remains of Albrecht Dürer.* Cambridge, Massachusetts: Cambridge University Press, 1889. 288pp. Conway's collection of primary documentary evidence, including Dürer's travel diary and letters, is an essential biographical resource.

Recommended Biographies

Anzelewsky, Fedja. *Dürer: His Art and Life.* New York: Alpine Fine Arts Collection, 1980. 273pp. This is a well-documented and authoritative account of the artist's life and work, based on the best modern scholarship. Beautifully illustrated, the volume is an excellent resource to deepen an appreciation of Dürer's development as an artist.

Hutchinson, Jane C. *Albrecht Dürer: A Biography.* Princeton, New Jersey: Princeton University Press, 1990. 247pp. Hutchinson's is a masterly, meticulously documented life that links Dürer's artistic development with his personal life and the historical and intellectual background of pre-Reformation Europe. A standout biography by a leading scholar of German prints.

Biographical Novels

Fisher, Frances H. *Written in the Stars: A Novel about Albrecht Dürer.* New York: Harper, 1951. 304pp. Dürer's married life is dramatized against a full and authentic period backdrop.

Recommended Juvenile Biographies

Raboff, Ernest. *Albrecht Dürer.* Garden City, New York: Doubleday, 1970. 31pp. MG. This is a brief but informative introduction to the artist and his work.

Ripley, Elizabeth. *Dürer: A Biography.* Philadelphia: Lippincott, 1958. 68pp. MG. Ripley supplies a brief critical biography that includes the significant details of the artist's life plus commentary on his techniques.

150. ANTONÍN DVOŘÁK
1841–1904

A major Czech composer of richly lyrical music and brilliant instrumentation, Dvořák played viola in the National Theatre Orchestra (1861-1871) under Smetana and first attracted attention with the 1873 performance of his *Hymnus.* He composed his most famous work, *From the New World* (1893), while he was director of the National Conservatory in New York. Dvořák's works include nine symphonies, concertos, chamber music, and operas.

Autobiography and Primary Sources

Letters and Reminiscences. 1954. Reprint ed. New York: Da Capo Press, 1985. 243pp. Excerpts from the composer's letters and writings, as well as recollections by those who knew him, are collected here and arranged chronologically.

Recommended Biographies

Clapham, John. *Dvořák.* New York: W.W. Norton, 1979. 238pp. Despite its brevity, this is the top choice for an authoritative, scholarly treatment that balances details of the composer's private life, professional career, and critical assessment of his music.

Other Biographical Studies

Butterworth, Neil. *Dvořák: His Life and Times.* New York: Omnibus Press, 1984. 135pp. This entry in the Illustrated Lives of the Great Composers series supplies an informative overview of Dvořák's life and musical career with photographs chronicling his development and compositions.

Dvořák, Otakar. *Antonin Dvořák, My Father.* Paul J. Polansky, ed. Spillville, Iowa: Czech Historical Research Center,1993. 195pp. Dvořák's son supplies his affectionate recollections of his father, written when the author was 75 to feature "the events missing from the other books about my father." Intimate, firsthand personal details are supplemented by Polansky's own study of the composer's origins and early years.

Hughes, Gervase. *Dvořák: His Life and Music.* New York: Dodd, Mead, 1967. 247pp. The work of a British musicologist is directed to the general reader, providing a biographical summary and a simplified musical analysis.

Schönzeler, Hans H. *Dvořák.* New York: Scribner, 1984. 239pp. This is a popular biography that concentrates mainly on the composer's life and eschews much musical analysis. A chronological presentation is interrupted by thematic chapters on various aspects of Dvořák's compositions.

Stefan, Paul. *Anton Dvořák.* 1941. Reprint ed. New York: Da Capo Press, 1971. 336pp. Serving as a detailed reference source, the book proceeds year by year through Dvořák's career offering brief critical commentary on his compositions.

Biographical Novels

Skvorecky, Josef. *Dvořák in Love: A Light-Hearted Dream.* New York: Knopf, 1987. 322pp. This inventive novel chronicles Dvořák's three-year sojourn in America during the 1890s, told through vignettes of the lives of various people who briefly interact with the composer.

Fictional Portraits

Alexander, Lawrence. *The Big Stick.* Garden City, New York: Doubleday, 1986. 349pp. Dvořák is part of a large cast of historical figures, including William F. Cody, Edison, and Lillian Russell who appear in this period mystery with Theodore Roosevelt as the chief sleuth.

Recommended Juvenile Biographies

Young, Percy M. *Dvořák.* New York: David White, 1970. 80pp. MG. This is a highly informative biographical portrait that supplies a great deal of information on the composer's background and the personal influences on his life and music.

Other Sources

Beckerman, Michael, ed. *Dvořák and His World.* Princeton, New Jersey: Princeton University Press, 1993. 284pp. This volume combines interpretive essays with a selection of documentary evidence bearing on the composer's career and his works.

Tibbetts, John C., ed. *Dvořák in America, 1892–1895.* Portland, Oregon: Amadeus Press, 1993. 447pp. This collection of scholarly essays by various specialists offers a many-faceted view of Dvořák and his influence during his brief stay in America.

151. AMELIA EARHART
1897–1937

American aviator, Amelia Earhart became the first woman to cross the Atlantic by airplane (1928), and the first woman and second person to fly solo across the Atlantic (1932). She claimed a number of other aviation records following her transatlantic flight, including becoming the first person to fly solo from Honolulu to California (1935). In 1937, she attempted with copilot Frederick Noonan to fly around the world, but her plane disappeared without a trace on the long Pacific leg between New Guinea and Howland Island. One of the most famous and influential women of the twentieth century, Earhart challenged female stereotypes and helped open restricted professions in science and aviation to women. Her mysterious death remains shrouded in controversy.

Autobiography and Primary Sources

The Fun of It: Random Research of My Own Flying and of Women in Aviation. 1932. Reprint ed. Detroit, Michigan: Gale Research, 1975. 218pp. In this collection of essays, Earhart reflects on her transatlantic flight and the contributions of women to aviation.

Last Flight of Amelia Earhart. New York: Harcourt, Brace, 1937. 226pp. This posthumous volume includes details from Earhart's flights across the Pacific and her solo flight from Mexico City to New York as well as her notes describing the transworld flight around the equator prior to her disappearance.

Letters from Amelia: 1901-37. Jean L.Backus, ed. Boston: Beacon Press, 1982. 253pp.This selection of Earhart's letters to her mother form a documentary biography showing the aviator as a daughter, war nurse, bride, celebrity, and family provider and, based on Backus's extensive research, provides one of the fullest character studies of Earhart available that counters the idealized treatment the aviator has received.

20 hrs. 40 min.: Our Flight in the Friendship. New York: Putnam, 1928. 314pp. Describing her initial training and drawing on her log book from her transatlantic flight, Earhart provides her perspective and what she hoped would be accomplished by it.

Recommended Biographies

Butler, Susan. *East to the Dawn: The Life of Amelia Earhart.* Reading, Massachusetts: Addison-Wesley, 1997. 489pp. With a great deal of new, primary material, this is the single best, most comprehensive book available on Earhart's life. In a richly detailed, complex portrait, Butler penetrates the myths to arrive at Earhart's humanity and the personal cost of her considerable achievements.

Lovell, Mary S. *The Sounds of Wings: The Life of Amelia Earhart.* New York: St. Martin's, 1989. 420pp. Concentrating on Earhart's personality, character, and relationships with family and friends, Lovell devotes nearly equal attention to Earhart's husband, George Putnam, concluding this dual biography with his death in 1950. The author of a biography of Beryl Markham and a flyer herself is somewhat skeptical about Earhart's flying and navigational abilities and judges Earhart a willing collaborator in Putnam's campaign to make her the best-known woman flier in the world.

Rich, Doris L. *Amelia Earhart: A Biography.* Washington, DC: Smithsonian Institution, 1989. 321pp. A richly detailed portrait for general readers, Rich concentrates on Earhart's flying career but fails to expand on the popular perception of Earhart as a daring, heroic adventurer. In this version George Putnam assumes the human dimension as a scheming opportunist.

Other Biographical Studies

Briand, Paul Jr. *Daughter of the Sky: The Story of Amelia Earhart.* New York: Duell, Sloan and Pearce, 1960. 230pp. Beginning with Earhart's cross-Atlantic flight, Briand sketches in her early years as flashbacks in a well-documented though somewhat fictionalized narrative. Earhart's defects are largely ignored, and, although Briand rejects the spying mission theories concerning her final flight, he does contend that she and Noonan crash-landed near Saipan where they were executed by the Japanese.

Brink, Randall. *Lost Star: The Search for Amelia Earhart.* New York: W.W. Norton, 1995. 206pp.

Brink, an aviation industry journalist, alleges a vast government coverup of Earhart's espionage mission on her final flight with the strongest evidence and analysis ever offered that her plane was secretly equipped to take pictures of Japanese island installations. According to Brink, Earhart may have been one of several voices of "Tokyo Rose" and may have returned to the United States and assumed a new identity. Wild speculation is interspersed here with solid investigation and eyewitness accounts.

Burke, John. *Winged Legend: The Story of Amelia Earhart.* New York: Putnam, 1970. 255pp. Burke's psychobiographical study deemphasizes Earhart's final flight and attempts to place her entire career in context, showing how her motivation and character were rooted in her upbringing. Refreshing in its approach, Burke's study lacks documentation but serves as a useful introduction to the human side of Earhart's story.

Goerner, Fred G. *The Search for Amelia Earhart.* Garden City, New York: Doubleday, 1966. 336pp. Goerner mounts a detailed case that Earhart was on a spying mission on her final flight, was rescued by the Japanese, and died while imprisoned. This is a selective account with other conclusions left unexamined.

Goldstein, Donald M., and Katherine V. Dillon. *Amelia: The Centennial Biography of an Aviation Pioneer.* Washington, DC: Brassey's, 1997. 336pp. Depicting Earhart's life in depth, revealing the personality behind the publicity, this biography also presents a comprehensive review of all the conspiracy theories and asserts a definitive solution to what happened to Earhart.

Long, Elgen and Marie K. *Amelia Earhart: The Mystery Solved.* New York: Simon & Schuster, 1999. 320pp. This is a sensible investigation of the factors surrounding Earhart's disappearance that keeps to the facts and avoids flights of sensational fancy. For readers looking for a clear assessment of what can be known, this is a good choice.

Loomis, Vincent V., and Jeffrey L. Ethell. *Amelia Earhart: The Final Story.* New York: Random House, 1985. 159pp. After a brief summary of Earhart's life and flying career, the book concentrates on a detailed examination of the evidence from Earhart's final flight. The conclusion: Earhart was not on a spying mission but was a prisoner of the Japanese and died of dysentery sometime in 1938. Based on review of much technical data, the authors conclude that Earhart was neither an expert pilot nor a competent navigator.

Morrissey, Muriel. *Courage is the Price: The Biography of Amelia Earhart*. Wichita, Kansas: McCormick-Armstrong, 1963. 221pp. Written by Earhart's sister, this admiring biography does provide some intimate family details. See also *Amelia, My Courageous Sister* (Santa Clara, California: Osborne, 1987. 312pp.) that mounts a detailed analysis of Earhart's final flight with new information.

Pellegreno, Ann H. *World Flight: The Earhart Trial*. Ames: Iowa State University Press, 1971. 225pp. Pellegreno adds some technical specificity to her account of Earhart's fatal flight by following her route in a similar aircraft.

Putnam, George P. *Soaring Wings: A Biography of Amelia Earhart*. New York: Harcourt, Brace, 1939. 294pp. Emphasizing Earhart's achievements in aviation, in her writing, and in social activities, Putnam's account of his wife's life and career is more the work of the publicist than a candid and revealing insider's view.

Ware, Susan. *Still Missing: Amelia Earhart and the Search for Modern Feminism*. New York: W.W. Norton, 1993. 304pp. Ware's intriguing thematic interpretive biography serves as an examination of social and cultural life in the 1920s and 1930s. Through a feminist lens, Ware focuses on those aspects of Earhart's life and career that symbolized new opportunities for women and made her a powerful role model. Readers unfamiliar with many of the events and people associated with Earhart will need to consult more traditional biographical sources for identification.

Biographical Novels

Mendelsohn, Jane. *I Was Amelia Earhart*. New York: Knopf, 1996. 145pp. In a brilliantly imagined poetic meditation, Earhart provides her own version of her life and what happened when she and her navigator, Fred Noonan, disappeared in 1937, offering a rich psychological portrait of the flyer. This beautifully written novel stays close to the known facts for most of the story with Earhart's celebrity status dissected and the planning and execution of her final flight the central narrative action.

Fictional Portraits

Anderson, Alison. *Hidden Latitudes*. New York: Scribner, 1996. 223pp. Taking place 40 years after Earhart's disappearance, the novel imagines her life as the solitary inhabitant on a Pacific atoll whose solitude is broken by the arrival of a young couple in a damaged sailboat and with a damaged relationship. The reader learns one possible version of Earhart's fate when her plane went down.

Collins, Max Allan. *Flying Blind: A Novel of Amelia Earhart*. New York: Dutton, 1998. 343pp. Collins's historical mystery detective Nate Heller is hired by a jealous George Putnam in 1935 as a bodyguard and spy on his wife. After Earhart's disappearance, Heller searches for her on Saipan, dra-

matizing a possible solution of the persistent Earhart mystery.

Thayer, James S. *The Earhart Betrayal*. New York: Putnam, 1980. 324pp. In this intriguing thriller, it is 1946 as an American agent in Singapore, investigating the rumor that Earhart's bones have been found in a Japanese prisoner-of-war camp, begins to put together the puzzle of Earhart's disappearance and subsequent fate.

Recommended Juvenile Biographies

Pearce, Carol A. *Amelia Earhart*. New York: Facts on File, 1988. 169pp. MG/YA. Earhart's life and career are brought to life through vignettes in a well-told, absorbing narrative with a strong historical and sociological context.

Randolph, Blythe. *Amelia Earhart*. New York: F. Watts, 1987. 128pp. Randolph's biography is well balanced between factual background and personal details with her complex relationship with George Putnam dealt with honestly.

Shore, Nancy. *Amelia Earhart*. New York: Chelsea House, 1987. 111pp. MG/YA. Part of the American Women of Achievement series, this illustrated biography chronicles Earhart's life and flying career, as well as her legacy and impact on women's rights, identity, and professional and personal aspirations.

Woog, Adam. *Amelia Earhart*. San Diego: Lucent Books, 1997. 110pp. MG. Part of the Mysterious Deaths series, the book examines Earhart's final flight and the various evidence to suggest different conclusions. With primary source quotes, expert testimony, and recent evidence, readers are allowed to evaluate the facts and draw their own conclusions.

Biographical Films and Theatrical Adaptations

A&E Biography Video: Amelia Earhart: Queen of the Air (1996). Producer: Laura Verklan. Solid survey of Earhart's career using archival photos and film footage. Video.

Amelia Earhart (1988). Producer: Edward Mulhare. This documentary film looks at the facts and speculations surrounding the flyer's disappearance. Video.

Amelia Earhart (1993). Director: Nancy Porter. This installment in PBS's American Experience series chronicles Earhart's life and the publicity frenzy that surrounded her. Video.

Amelia Earhart: The Final Flight (1994). Director: Yves Simoneau. Diane Keaton stars as the aviator in a dramatization of her life climaxing in her last flight. Rutger Hauer portrays Fred Noonan and Bruce Dern is George Putnam. The script is based on Doris L. Rich's biography. Video.

Flight for Freedom (1943). Director: Lothar Mendes. Based loosely on Earhart's life and suggesting that Earhart's last flight was a spy mission, this RKO movie starring Rosalind Russell and Fred MacMurray is widely credited with inspiring later conspiracy theorists.

152. MARY BAKER EDDY
1821–1910

The American founder (1866) of the Christian Science movement, Eddy studied with mental healer Phineas Parkhurst Quimby and then published her own ideas on spiritual healing in *Science and Health* (1875). She founded the *Journal of Christian Science* (1883) and the *Christian Science Monitor* (1908). As pastor emeritus of the Mother Church in Boston, she continued to exert influence over all branches of the church even after her retirement.

Autobiography and Primary Sources

Prose Works Other than Science and Health with the Key to the Scriptures. Boston: First Church of Christ, Scientist, 1953. 13 vols. This is a compilation of Baker's letters, essays, sermons, and excerpts from her writings detailing her religious views.

Retrospection and Introspection. 1891. Reprint ed. Boston: First Church of Christ, Scientist, 1976. 95pp. Baker's autobiographical reflections are rarely penetrating and offer a rather simplified version of her life and development.

Recommended Biographies

Gill, Gillian. *Mary Baker Eddy*. Reading, Massachusetts: Perseus Books, 1998. 713pp. Gill supplies a balanced and insightful view of Eddy's life and development in the context of nineteenth-century American women's history. Based on access to the closely-guarded Christian Science archives, this is a fresh reevaluation of a complex human figure.

Peel, Robert. *Mary Baker Eddy*. New York: Putnam, 1971–1977. 3 vols. By far the most comprehensive and authoritative treatment of Eddy's life, Peel, with access to the Christian Science archives and the unpublished collection of Eddy's letters, documents Eddy's daily life fully and views her development in the context of her time. The author, a Christian Scientist, mostly achieves an objectivity that is neither excessively partisan nor debunking.

Thomas, Robert D. *"With Bleeding Footsteps": Mary Baker Eddy's Path to Religious Leadership*. New York: Knopf, 1994. 363pp. Thomas's is an intriguing psychological portrait of Eddy's formative years based on extensive primary research. Untangling the myth from the reality, the book deals extensively with Eddy's background, family relations, and the experiences that led to her conversion.

Other Biographical Studies

Bates, Ernest S., and John V. Dittemore. *Mary Baker Eddy: The Truth and the Tradition*. New York: Knopf, 1932. 476pp. Based on personal knowledge of Eddy and access to important primary sources, the authors present a realistic personal portrait that avoids the idealization of other accounts.

Beasley, Norman. *Mary Baker Eddy*. New York: Duell, Sloan and Pearce, 1963. 371pp. Very much the heroic portrait, Beasley's account is rarely critical or penetrating.

Dakin, Edwin F. *Mrs. Eddy: The Biography of a Virginal Mind.* New York: Scribner, 1929. 553pp. This is a complete, detailed account that achieves an objectivity rare in books about Eddy. Although now superseded by subsequent studies, Dakin helped establish the biographical record through diligent use of primary sources.

Milmine, Georgine. *The Life of Mary Baker G. Eddy and the History of Christian Science.* 1909. Reprint ed. Lincoln: University of Nebraska Press, 1993. 501pp. Originally a series of articles published in *McClure's* with Willa Cather as a researcher, this is an example of muckraking journalism that exploits a great deal of primary source information for a generally negative portrait of Eddy and Christian Science.

Nenneman, Richard A. *Persistent Pilgrim: The Life of Mary Baker Eddy.* Etna, New Hampshire: Nebbadoon Press, 1997, 366pp. The work of a Christian Scientist, Nenneman's is an accessible one-volume study. The author claims to be the only researcher beside Peel to have gone through all 10,000-plus of Eddy's letters. Eddy's perspective and the recollections of associates are woven into a narrative account of her personal development and leadership.

Silberger, Julius J. *Mary Baker Eddy: An Interpretive Biography of the Founder of Christian Science.* Boston: Little, Brown, 1980. 274pp. The author, a psychoanalyst, offers a coherent, though somewhat simplistic, psychological profile of Eddy based mainly on secondary sources. The book's strength resides in connecting the details of Eddy's character and experiences to the values of her era.

Wilbur, Sibyl. *The Life of Mary Baker Eddy.* Boston: Christian Science Publishing Society, 1907. 384pp. This authorized biography based on information supplied from Eddy herself represents the way she wished to be viewed by the public and the faithful.

Recommended Juvenile Biographies

Smith, Louise A. *Mary Baker Eddy.* New York: Chelsea House, 1991. 111pp. MG/YA. Smith's is an informative, well-organized biographical profile that relates Eddy's ideas and career to her era.

153. THOMAS ALVA EDISON
1847–1931

One of the most productive and well-known inventors of his time (over 1,300 U.S. and foreign patents), Edison received only three months of schooling in his youth and suffered from deafness throughout his life. He worked as a newsboy and telegraph operator, and his first inventions included the transmitter and receiver for the automatic telegraph. He invented the first successful phonograph, the first commercially practical incandescent lamp, and the Kinetoscope, and developed the synchronization of film with sound. His Pearl Street plant (New York City) was the first permanent central electric-light power plant in the

world; his workshops in Menlo Park and Orange, New Jersey, were forerunners of the modern research laboratory.

Autobiography and Primary Sources

Diary and Sundry Observations of Thomas Edison. Dagobert D. Runes, ed. New York: Philosophical Library, 1948. 181pp. Collects Edison's observations and opinions on a variety of subjects, including war, peace, education, spiritualism, and work.

The Papers of Thomas A. Edison. Reese V. Jenkins, et al., eds. Baltimore: Johns Hopkins University Press, 1989–. 4 vols. Drawing on the extensive Edison papers, notebooks, and letters held in the Edison Laboratory in West Orange, New Jersey, this multi-volume collection makes Edison's principal papers and essential primary resources available for readers and scholars.

Recommended Biographies

Baldwin, Neil. *Edison: Inventing the Century.* New York: Hyperion, 1995. 531pp. With access to Edison family papers and after years of research at the Edison corporate archives, Baldwin establishes a balanced, demythologized portrait that avoids conclusions but allows the reader unprecedented angles of viewing the man in full. Edison's achievements are set helpfully in the context of his time.

Israel, Paul. *Edison: A Life of Invention.* New York: Wiley, 1998. 552pp. The editor of Edison's papers concentrates on the details of his technical work and business dealings, his work methods, and achievements. Meticulously researched with assess to workshop diaries, letters, and the Edison archives, Israel sheds new light on previously unexamined aspects of the inventor's life and career.

Josephson, Matthew. *Edison.* New York: McGraw-Hill, 1959. 511pp. Josephson sifts fact from fable in an authoritative and widely regarded classic standard biography that tells Edison's full story as well as the beginnings of the telegraphic, electrical, record, motion picture, and auto industries and the sociological changes they caused. Taking pains to set Edison squarely within his historical context, Josephson misses few facts or anecdotes in describing his subject who emerges as a complex individual with great strengths and human failings.

Other Biographical Studies

Bryan, George S. *Edison: The Man and His Work.* New York: Knopf, 1926. 350pp. Reworking secondary sources into a competent factual summary of Edison's achievements, the book offers primarily a gathering of anecdotes without many attempts to penetrate beneath the surface.

Clark, Ronald W. *Edison: The Man Who Made the Future.* New York: Putnam, 1977. 256pp. Clark's lucid, coherent narrative is a good summary of Edison's career and how he was seen by others. Clark is best in his discussion of Edison's electrical and chemical interests and inventions but glosses over some unpleasant aspects of the inventor's personality, such as his alleged anti-Semitism and his dispute with inventor Nikola Tesla.

Conot, Robert. *A Streak of Luck.* New York: Seaview, 1978. 565pp. In Conot's revisionistic, iconoclastic treatment, Edison emerges with his hard edges intact. He is shown as a driven opportunist whose ambition for wealth was subverted by his passion for invention. Taking advantage of materials not available to Josephson, Conat provides details of the miseries of Edison's children and the inventor's uncouth and often unclean personal habits.

Dyer, Frank L., and Thomas C. Martin. *Edison: His Life and Inventions.* 1910. Expanded edition with the collaboration of William Meadowcroft. New York: Harper, 1929. 2 vols. Long regarded as the standard, authorized biography written by Dyer who was Edison's lawyer, Martin, an editor of *Electrical World*, and Meadowcroft, Edison's secretary, the book is a rich source of biographical details, particularly on Edison's early career. Relying on Edison's sometimes faulty recollections and bias, the biography is not reliable in all matters and steers clear of unflattering details.

Friedel, Robert D. *Edison's Electric Light: Biography of an Invention.* New Brunswick, New Jersey: Rutgers University Press, 1986. 263pp. Friedel provides a detailed examination of Edison's struggle to invent the electric light.

Frost, Lawrence A. *The Edison Album: A Pictorial Biography of Thomas Alva Edison.* Seattle: Superior Pub., 1969. 175pp. Arranges a selection of photographs chronologically to form a visual biography of Edison.

Jehl, Francis. *Menlo Park: Reminiscences.* Dearborn, Michigan: Edison Institute, 1937–1941. 3 vols. Written by an assistant in Edison's laboratory, Jehl's massive recollections offer a valuable eyewitness account of Edison in action, though not all of the details are accurate or reliable.

Jones, Francis A. *The Life Story of Thomas Alva Edison.* 1908. Revised ed. New York: Grosset and Dunlap, 1931. 405pp. This full-life biography concentrates on the two decades of 1870 to 1890 by an English writer based on interviews with Edison and materials from the Edison library. The first edition with the subtitle, "Sixty Years of an Inventor's Life," appeared in 1907.

Simonds, William A. *Edison: His Life, His Work, His Genius.* Indianapolis: Bobbs-Merrill, 1934. 349pp. Based on an intimate acquaintance as well as extensive research, Simonds's useful summary often lacks objectivity, and Simonds accepts Edison's own estimate of himself and his rivals.

Wachhorst, Wyn. *Thomas Alva Edison: An American Myth.* Cambridge, Massachusetts: MIT Press, 1981. 328pp. Not really a biography but an attempt to trace how Edison the man became Edison the myth and ultimately how his image as cultural hero reveals the American character. The author has read and digested virtually everything that had ever been written about Edison to establish his thesis that Edison helped bridge the gap between the rural nineteenth century and the urban twentieth century, between the age of steam and the age of electricity.

Fictional Portraits

Davis, Christopher. *A Peep into the 20th Century.* New York: Harper & Row, 1971. 200pp. Covering the last five months in the life of Rupert Weber in 1890, the first person to be executed in the electric chair, Davis uses the invention as a metaphor for the modern age with a look at Edison and his rivalry with George Westinghouse.

McCreary, Lew. *Mount's Mistake.* New York: Atlantic Monthly Press, 1987. 294pp. This picaresque tale follows the career of Jay Fielding Mount who after being struck by lightning as a boy crosses paths with Edison as he struggles to harness the power of electricity.

McMahon, Thomas. *Loving Little Egypt.* New York: Viking, 1987. 273pp. In a comic fantasy, the novel dramatizes the adventures of a scientific prodigy who creates an underground telephone network for blind people and must contend with the scientific establishment represented by Edison and Alexander Graham Bell, assisted by Nikola Tesla in a battle for the control of science.

Zagst, Michael. *"M.H." Meets President Harding.* New York: D.I. Fine, 1987. 247pp. This amusing caper novel involves a tentmaker who accompanies Edison on his camping trip with President Harding and finds himself involved with a woman who wants to kidnap the president.

Recommended Juvenile Biographies

Adair, Gene. *Thomas Alva Edison: Inventing the Electric Age.* New York: Oxford University Press, 1996. 141pp. YA. The author carefully explains the scientific principles on which Edison based his work in a full-length chronicle of his life. Focuses more on Edison's work than his personal life and character.

Buranelli, Vincent. *Thomas Alva Edison.* Englewood Cliffs, New Jersey: Silver Burdett, 1989. 133pp. MG. Traces the highlights of Edison's life and career with an emphasis on his invention of the phonograph, electric lighting, and motion pictures.

Cousins, Margaret. *The Story of Thomas Alva Edison.* New York: Random House, 1965. 185pp. MG. In a classic entry in the Landmark biographical series, this is a realistic guide to Edison's life that also considers how his inventions changed our world.

Egan, Louise. *Thomas Edison: The Great American Inventor.* Hauppauge, New York: Barron's, 1987. 160pp. MG. This entry in Barron's Solution series examines the life and achievements of Edison from his boyhood experiments through his search to harness electricity.

Biographical Films and Theatrical Adaptations

St. Germain, Mark. *Camping with Henry and Tom: A Play.* Garden City, New York: Fireside Theatre, 1995. 107pp. Based on the actual camping trip of Edison, Henry Ford, and President Warren Harding, this witty play imagines what might have transpired among the men as Ford vies to replace Harding as president, and Edison provides sharp commentary on human foibles.

A&E Biography Video: Thomas Edison: Father of Invention (1996). Features extensive photographic and film and sound footage of Edison and his laboratories in a solid chronological documentary look at the inventor's life and career. Video.

Edison's Miracle of Light (1995). Director: John Walter. In this segment from PBS' American Experience series, the story of the invention of the light bulb is described, including Edison's subsequent battle with George Westinghouse over the type of electric current to be used and the launching of Edison General Electric. Video.

Edison, the Man (1940). Director: Clarence Brown. Told in flashback by the 82-year-old inventor, the film chronicles Edison's life from his arrival in New York at 22. Spencer Tracy stars as Edison in a largely sentimental account. Video.

Young Tom Edison (1940). Director: Norman Taurog. Mickey Rooney stars in the story of Edison's boyhood showing the strained relationship with Edison's father (George Bancroft) and the support of his understanding mother (Faye Bainter). Video.

154. EDWARD VII
1841–1910

The eldest son of Queen Victoria and Prince Albert, Albert Edward, known as "Bertie," was created Prince of Wales soon after his birth. He traveled widely during his youth and in 1863 married Princess Alexandra of Denmark. After the death of his father (1861) and the subsequent seclusion of his mother, he represented the crown at ceremonial functions. He was a patron of the arts and sciences, an enthusiastic sportsman, and a leader of fashionable society, whose extravagance and many love affairs offended his mother. At 59 he succeeded to the throne and proved a popular king, who worked hard during his reign to maintain a stable foreign policy.

Autobiography and Primary Sources

Personal Letters of King Edward VII. J.P.C. Sewell, ed. London: Hutchinson, 1931. 254pp. Although most of Edward's correspondence was burned, this collection of surviving letters includes some from Queen Alexandra.

Recommended Biographies

Hibbert, Christopher. *The Royal Victorians: King Edward VII, His Family and Friends.* Philadelphia: Lippincott, 1976. 339pp. Hibbert's popular life acknowledges both Edward's virtues and faults in a clearly written and generously illustrated presentation. More readable and entertaining than Magnus's more scholarly treatment, Hibbert's life will likely appeal more to the general reader.

Magnus, Philip. *King Edward the Seventh.* New York: Dutton, 1964. 528pp. Concentrating on portraying Edward the man rather than his times, Magnus, through an exhaustive use of primary sources, provides a frank and fair view with new, vivid, and at times surprising details of his extravagant lifestyle and love life.

Plumbtre, George. *Edward VII.* London: Pavillion, 1995. 288pp. British historian Plumbtre provides a good summary of the life and reign of Edward. Despite his self-indulgence and infidelities, Edward emerges as a likable individual who made a considerable contribution to the power of the English monarchy.

Other Biographical Studies

Adams, William S. *Edwardian Portraits.* London: Secker and Warburg, 1956. 228pp. Adams's biographical sketch of Edward reveals his character traits and various indulgences, including women and gambling.

Brook-Shepherd, Gordon. *Uncle of Europe: The Social and Diplomatic Life of Edward VII.* New York: Harcourt, Brace, 1976. 384pp. The first quarter of the book provides an anecdotal survey of Edward's years as Prince of Wales with the majority devoted to his diplomatic career after 1901. In the author's view, Edward was a cool, calculating, and skilled diplomat.

Cowles, Virginia. *Gay Monarch: The Life and Pleasures of Edward VII.* New York: Harper, 1956. 378pp. Based on memoirs and letters, Cowles emphasizes Edward's social life in a gossipy, anecdotal treatment with the conclusion that Edward was a more useful and creative monarch than history has generally conceded.

Edwards, William H. *The Tragedy of Edward VII: A Psychological Study.* New York: Dodd, Mead, 1928. 355pp. According to the author, the source of Edward's behavior was his lack of a normal childhood, personal freedom, and opportunity to exercise his gifts. Often impressionistic with a number of dubious interpretations and misconceptions about Edward's foreign policy role, the book does work out its thesis against a vivid background of political, social, and family life.

Dangerfield, George. *Victoria's Heir: The Education of a Prince.* New York: Harcourt, Brace, 1941. 345pp. The author, himself an heir to the Strachey biographical tradition, offers an intimate often ironic portrait with only a brief discussion of the British political and historical context.

John, Pearson. *Edward the Rake: An Unwholesome Biography of Edward VII.* New York: Harcourt, Brace, 1975. 181pp. The emphasis here is on Edward's private life and the scandals that plagued his upbringing and maturity. The book pieces together fact, gossip, and surmises from a variety of secondary sources. Without documentation, it is not possible to evaluate the reliability of the book's assertions.

Jullian, Philippe. *Edward and the Edwardians.* New York: Viking, 1967. 312pp. In this readable look at Edward and his times by a Frenchman, Jullian combines gossip with astute political observation, but the book lacks coherence and is inaccurate in a number of details, particularly in attributing to Edward greater policy influence than he exerted.

Lee, Sir Sidney. *King Edward VII: A Biography.* New York: Macmillan, 1925–1927. 2 vols. The official life undertaken by Lee at the request of George V and based on documents in the royal archives is encyclopedic and often ponderous in its coverage. The first volume is devoted to Edward's long years as the Prince of Wales; the second to his reign. Still useful for its lengthy quotations from letters and the historical context, the book's discretion prevents a more intimate portrait with no mention of Edward's many mistresses.

Maurois, André. *King Edward and His Times.* London: Cassell, 1933. 312pp. In the author's study of European political and foreign policy during the first decade of the twentieth century, Edward is the central figure. The book clearly displays Maurois's gift for personal portraiture and character analysis.

Middlemas, Keith. *The Life and Times of Edward VII.* Garden City, New York: Doubleday, 1972. 224pp. Middlemas's is a fine illustrated biography that emphasizes Edward's personality and relationships rather than his political achievements.

St. Aubyn, Giles. *Edward VII: Prince and King.* New York: Atheneum, 1979. 555pp. Based on the papers of Francis Knollys, Edward's private secretary for nearly half a century, St. Aubyn's account provides a number of fresh perspectives, but Knollys's biases color the view, and this account should be read with some skepticism.

Wortham, Hugh E. *Edward VII: Man and King.* Boston: Little, Brown, 1931. 360pp. Wortham's full-length look at Edward and his epoch is marred by a lack of dates to pin down episodes and an insufficient identification of individuals involved in Edward's story.

Readers may be interested in several books concerning Edward's marriage, his queen, Alexandra of Denmark, and his extramarital relationships:

Aronson, Theo. *The King in Love: Edward VII's Mistresses.* New York: Harper & Row, 1988. 301pp. Chronicles the relationship between Edward and Lillie Langtry, Daisy Warwick, Alice Keppel, and others.

Battiscombe, Georgina. *Queen Alexandra.* Boston: Houghton Mifflin, 1969. 336pp. Battiscombe's vivid, sympathetic but realistic biography of Edward's wife reveals a good deal about their relationship.

Brough, James. *The Prince and the Lily.* New York: Coward-McCann, 1975. 312pp. In Brough's account of the relationship between Edward and Lillie Langtry, much is undocumented and based on informed speculation. There is considerable fictionalization and extraneous material to fill in details and make the story more readable. A lack of dates makes the narrative hard to follow at times.

Hough, Richard. *Edward and Alexandra: Their Private and Public Lives.* New York: St. Martin's, 1992. 369pp. In a dual biography, Hough delineates the symbiotic and even loving relationship between Edward and his wife, despite the friction caused by his philandering. Well researched and readable with numerous details of Edward's daily life, the book at times lacks depth and psychological subtlety.

Biographical Novels

Butler, David. *Edward VII: Prince of Hearts.* London: Weidenfeld and Nicolson, 1974. 327pp. Edward's rakish life before ascending to the throne is the focus here in a mix of invention and fact.

Tyler-Whittle, Michael. *Bertie, Albert Edward, Prince of Wales.* New York: St. Martin's, 1974.

327pp. *Edward: Edward the Seventh, King and Emperor.* New York: St. Martin's, 1975. 278pp. The author's two-volume chronicle of Edward's life is faithful to the known facts, though some liberties have been take to bridge the gap in the documentary record.

Fictional Portraits

Hall, Robert Lee. *The King Edward Plot.* New York: McGraw-Hill, 1980. 280pp. In 1906 a young actor and his genteel friend uncover a plot to kill the king. Invited to Sandringham for Edward's birthday celebration, the pair devise a means to foil the plot and expose the conspiracy.

Harrison, Ray. *A Season for Death.* New York: St. Martin's, 1987. 244pp. In this installment of the Sergeant Bragg historical mystery series, someone is blackmailing the Prince of Wales, and Bragg and Constable Morton are called in to protect the royal reputation.

Lovesey, Peter. *Bertie and the Tinman.* New York: Mysterious Press, 1987. 223pp.; *Bertie and the Seven Bodies.* New York: Mysterious Press, 1990. 196pp.; *Bertie and the Crime of Passion.* New York: Mysterious Press, 1995. 244pp. Lovesey's series of historical mysteries implausibly but entertainingly employs the Prince of Wales as sleuth in a rousing period reconstruction.

Perrin, Robert. *Jewels.* New York: Stein and Day, 1977. 269pp. Based on the theft of the Irish Crown Jewels in 1907, this is a tangled intrigue in which the theft is linked to a conspiracy to avoid a homosexual scandal involving Edward VII's brother-in-law. Drawing on contemporary records, there is a factual basis to a good deal of the story.

Selwyn, Francis. *Sergeant Verity and the Blood Royal.* New York: Stein and Day, 1979. 272pp. This Sergeant Verity historical mystery series entry has the policeman protecting the Prince of Wales on a trip to America in the 1860s.

Biographical Films and Theatrical Adaptations

The Duchess of Duke Street (1976). Directors: Bill Bain and Cyril Coke. The British television series created by John Hawksworth tells the story of Louisa Leyton who rises from the servant class to become the best cook in England, attracting the attention of the Prince of Wales. Gemma Jones stars. The novelization of the filmscript by Mollie Hardwick is available (New York: Holt, 1976. 307pp.). Video.

Edward the King (1975). Director: John Gorrie. The life and short reign of Edward VII are chronicled with his relationship with his parents detailed. Robert Hardy portrays Prince Albert; Annette Crosbie is Queen Victoria, and Timothy West is the Prince of Wales and later king. The book on which the screenplay was based is available by David E. Butler, *Edward the King* (New York: Pocket Books, 1974–1975. 2 vols.). Video.

Lillie (1990). Director: John Gorrie. Dramatizing the career of beauty and actress Lillie Langtry who becomes the mistress of Edward VII, Francesca Annis takes the title role with Dennis Lill as Edward, and Peter Egan as Oscar Wilde. The novel-

ization of the filmscript is available by David Butler (*Lillie.* New York: Warner Books, 1978. 435pp.). Both the film and the novel use invented dialogue and incidents within the framework of Langtry's life story.

See also Albert; Victoria

155. JONATHAN EDWARDS
1703–1758

American theologian and metaphysician, Edwards was a Calvinist preacher who furthered the Great Awakening religious revival movement in Puritan New England. His position on tests for church membership caused his dismissal (1750) from his Northampton, Massachusetts, congregation. He went to Stockbridge, where he oversaw the Native American mission and ministered to a small white congregation. From 1757 he was president of the College of New Jersey. His theological masterpiece is *Freedom of the Will* (1754).

Autobiography and Primary Sources

The Works of Jonathan Edwards. New Haven, Connecticut: Yale University Press, 1957–. 17 vols. This is the standard edition of Edwards's works and includes important letters and personal writings essential for establishing both Edwards's character and his interpretation of his life and development.

Recommended Biographies

Miller, Perry. *Jonathan Edwards.* 1949. Reprint ed. Cleveland: World, 1959. 348pp. Miller's interpretive, intellectual biography is a brilliant, groundbreaking study that intersperses commentary on Edwards's life and thought with criticism of his works.

Winslow, Ola E. *Jonathan Edwards, 1703–1758: A Biography.* New York: Macmillan, 1940. 406pp. Winslow's remains the best comprehensive treatment of Edwards's life and character. Scrupulously researched and well written, Winslow manages to turn the conventionally seen austere Edwards into a compelling, complex human figure.

Other Biographical Studies

Dwight, Sereno E. *Life of President Edwards.* New York: S. Converse, 1829. 776pp. This extensively researched work by Edwards's great grandson is an important source of primary material, collecting letters and other documentary evidence unavailable now from any other source.

Hopkins, Samuel. *The Life and Character of the Late Reverend Mr. Jonathan Edwards, President of the College of New Jersey.* 1765. Reprint ed. New York: AMS Press, 1976. 279pp. Hopkins's early appreciative study features extracts from Edwards's writings, including his "Personal Narrative," and has been an important biographical source for later studies.

Parkes, Henry B. *Jonathan Edwards: The Fiery Puritan.* New York: Minton Balch, 1930. 271pp. Written for the general reader, Parkes's interpretation of Edwards and his times is often far too dogmatic and misguided to be used as a reliable indicator of the man or his era. Too often Edwards slips into the background with his career used to launch an extended, negative assessment of Puritan society.

156. ALBERT EINSTEIN
1879–1955

Considered by many to be the greatest theoretical physicist of all time, Einstein received his doctorate from the University of Zurich and afterward worked as a patents examiner in Bern (1902–1909) and later as a professor of physics. In 1905 he published his special theory of relativity and by 1916 had completed a general theory of relativity; Einstein's theories would profoundly alter the way in which scientists viewed the structure of the universe and made possible the development of the atom bomb. Recipient of the 1921 Nobel Prize for physics, Einstein fled the Nazi regime in 1934 for the United States and worked at the Institute for Advanced Study, Princeton University, until his death.

Autobiography and Primary Sources

Ideas and Opinions. Carl Seelig, ed. New York: Bonanza Books, 1954. 377pp. Reprints many important passages from Einstein's previous books along with previously uncollected articles, revealing many facets of his mind and personality.

Out of My Later Years. 1950. Reprint ed. Westport, Connecticut: Greenwood, 1970. 282pp. Collects Einstein's essays, written during the last 15 years of his life, on such topics as relativity, the atom bomb, science and religion, and socialism, arranged by subject matter.

The World as I See It. New York: Philosophical Library, 1949. 112pp. Through selections of his addresses, letters, and writings, Einstein shares his opinions on such topics as education, peace, war, world politics, and being Jewish.

The Collected Papers of Albert Einstein. John Stachel, ed. Princeton, New Jersey: Princeton University Press, 1987–. 8 vols. Envisioned eventually to number as many as 30 volumes, this scholarly collection of Einstein's correspondence and writings has reached Einstein's Berlin years up to 1918, reprinting invaluable letters and other writings essential for clarifying the scientist's career and character.

Schlipp, Paul A., ed. *Albert Einstein: Philosopher-Scientist.* Evanston, Illinois: Library of Living Philosophers, 1949. 2 vols. Contains some of Einstein's most important writings and commentaries on the scientist, including Einstein's "Autobiographical Notes" that offer his views on his scientific work though not his personal life.

Recommended Biographies

Brian, Denis. *Einstein: A Life.* New York: Wiley, 1996. 509pp. Comprehensive and evenhanded, Brian's anecdotal biography draws on previously unavailable information to form a broad portrait integrating Einstein's genius with his public and private life. Without over-arguing a particular interpretation, Brian assembles an impressive array of perspectives on a deeply human, complex figure.

Frank, Philip. *Einstein: His Life and Times.* New York: Knopf, 1947. 298pp. Written by a friend and colleague, Frank, himself an eminent physicist, excels in re-creating the political, scientific, and philosophical background in which Einstein developed in a detailed and balanced account. Recommended both for its biographical details and its ability to communicate Einstein's physics to non-specialists.

Hoffman, Banesh, and Helen Dukas. *Albert Einstein: Creator and Rebel.* New York: Viking, 1972. 272pp. The work of Einstein's associates at Princeton, this is a sympathetic and competent account of the physicist's scientific impact. One of the best books available that helps readers understand Einstein's theories and influence; *Albert Einstein: The Human Side.* (Princeton, New Jersey: Princeton University Press, 1979. 167pp.) is a compilation of materials from the archives at the Institute of Advanced Study documenting Einstein's work habits and personal traits.

Pais, Abraham. *"Subtle is the Lord.. .": The Science and Life of Albert Einstein.* New York: Oxford University Press, 1982. 552pp. Written by a respected particle physicist, Pais's study is an authoritative assessment of Einstein's professional achievements. Hard-going at times for the nonscientist, Pais's two-track biography of Einstein as scientific thinker and human being provides one of the most accurate depictions of Einstein's life available.

Other Biographical Studies

Bernstein, Jeremy. *Einstein.* New York: Viking, 1973. 242pp. Organized around the three basic themes of Einstein's work—the special theory of relativity, the general theory of relativity and gravitation, and quantum theory—with biographical details within each section, Bernstein chronicles the essential progression of Einstein's professional career with revealing details on his personal traits.

Clark, Ronald W. *Einstein: The Life and Times.* New York: World Publishing, 1971. 718pp. Clark's popular, comprehensive biography, written by a nonscientist, excels in anecdotes illustrating Einstein's personal life. Clark is somewhat superficial in his treatment of Einstein's scientific theories and the controversies over them. *The Life and Times of Einstein: An Illustrated Biography.* (New York: Abrams, 1987. 368pp.) is a condensation of his longer study with photographs and artifacts arranged chronologically.

Folsing, Albrecht. *Albert Einstein: A Biography.* New York: Viking, 1997. 882pp. Exhaustively researched, this full-scale biography recasts the various elements in Einstein's life and career into a plausible human narrative. However, despite access to previously unpublished materials, Folsing does not resolve many of the controversies surrounding Einstein's private life, nor are his later years after 1933 treated in as much detail as his early development.

Highfield, Roger, and Paul Carter. *The Private Lives of Albert Einstein.* New York: St. Martin's, 1994. 353pp. In a revisionist exposé, the authors suggest that the physicist was a grandiose, patronizing tyrant with a fierce temper and manipulative arrogance. Intended as a corrective to more saintly treatments, the book comes close to character assassination and falls short of a fully rounded portrait in forcing its negative view. Ignoring Einstein's humanitarian and pacifist writings as well as his religious and philosophical outlook, the book also underplays Einstein's scientific contributions.

Lerner, Aaron B. *Einstein and Newton: A Comparison of Two Great Scientists.* New York: Lerner, 1973. 234pp. Lerner's dual biography contrasts the lives, characters, and contributions of the two scientists. Particularly useful in explaining Einstein's debt and challenge to Newtonian physics.

Sugimoto, Kenji. *Albert Einstein: A Photographic Biography.* New York: Schocken, 1989. 202pp. With some 400 photographs, extracts from letters, diaries, press clippings, and a brief connecting text, Sugimoto documents Einstein's life and scientific career.

White, Michael, and John Gribbon. *Einstein: A Life in Science.* New York: Dutton, 1994. 279pp. Einstein's work on relativity and quantum theory is put in perspective not only through the events of his life but also in its scientific and political context. Correcting a number of myths and mysteries surrounding Einstein, the book also offers new information, such as his FBI file and his possible schizophrenia.

Fictional Portraits

Gitlin, Todd. *The Murder of Albert Einstein.* New York: Farrar, Straus, 1992. 297pp. Social historian Gitlin in a ruminative thriller presents a trail of clues suggesting Einstein was murdered. By revealing who might have the motive Gitlin ingeniously places Einstein in the context of recent Cold War history.

Kaminsky, Stuart M. *Smart Moves.* New York: St. Martin's, 1986. 212pp. In this installment of the author's Toby Peters historical mystery series, Nazi assassins are trying to kill Einstein, and the private detective must foil the plot in an implausible but entertaining period thriller.

Lightman, Alan P. *Einstein's Dreams.* New York: Pantheon, 1993. 179pp. The author poetically reconstructs Einstein's dream life in 1905 while a patent clerk in Berne, Switzerland, as his relativity theory begins to take shape. More a meditation on the nature of time and an exploration of the workings of creative scientific mind than a biographical narrative.

McGrail, Anna. *Mrs. Einstein.* New York: W.W. Norton, 1998. 333pp. The novel imagines what might have become of Einstein's illegitimate daughter, Lieserl, who was given up for adoption in 1902. A frustrated scientist, Lieserl revenges herself on the father who refused to acknowledge her by discovering how to split the uranium atom that leads to the atomic bomb.

Recommended Juvenile Biographies

Bernstein, Jeremy. *Albert Einstein and the Frontiers of Physics.* New York: Oxford University Press, 1996. 189pp. YA. The author of one of the better general studies of Einstein's scientific career provides an illuminating biography for younger readers that describes in understandable language Einstein's theories and captures the quality of his imagination and intellect.

Cwiklik, Robert. *Albert Einstein and the Theory of Relativity.* Hauppauge, New York: Barron's, 1987. 184pp. MG/YA. This entry in Barron's Solution series traces the life and work of Einstein and explains his theory of relativity in comprehensible language.

Ireland, Karin. *Albert Einstein.* Englewood Cliffs, New Jersey: Silver Burdett, 1989. 108pp. MG. Part of the Pioneers in Change series that focuses on how individuals overcome obstacles to their achievement, Einstein's personal development and evolution of his scientific ideas are concisely explained with an emphasis on his political involvement in pacifism, Zionism, and the development of the atomic bomb.

Biographical Films and Theatrical Adaptations

Martin, Steve. *Picasso at the Lapin Agile.* New York: Grove Press, 1996. 150pp. Set in a Paris café in 1904, Picasso and Albert Einstein argue about physics and art.

A. Einstein (1979). Producer: Patrick Griffin. In an installment from the PBS Nova series, Einstein's life and times are documented through photographs, film clips, and readings from his writings. The documentary is particularly good on the social and political forces that dominated Einstein's personal life and professional career. Video.

A. Einstein: How I See the World (1991). Director: Richard Kroehling. Chronicles how Einstein became a peace advocate using news films, home movies, and excerpts from his diaries, letters, and published writing. Video.

Other Sources

French, A.P., ed. *Einstein: A Centenary Volume.* Cambridge, Massachusetts: Harvard University Press, 1979. 332pp. Critical essays by various scientist on the impact of Einstein's ideas along with excerpts from his writings form a useful reference volume.

Goldsmith, Marice, Alan McKay, and James Woudhuysen, eds. *Einstein: The First Hundred Years.* New York: Pergamon Press, 1980. 200pp. This essay collection written to honor the centennial of Einstein's birth covers various aspects of the physicist's life, career, and contribution.

Holton, Gerald and Yehuda Eikana, eds. *Albert Einstein: Historical and Cultural Perspectives.* Princeton, New Jersey: Princeton University Press, 1982. 439pp. A scholarly compilation that includes revealing personal reminiscences.

Kantha, Sachi Sri. *An Einstein Dictionary.* Westport, Connecticut: Greenwood, 1996. 298pp. Entries cover concepts and people that are connected to either Einstein's life or his contribution to science. Includes an extensive chronology, a genealogy chart of his family, and list of his patents.

Whitrow, G.J., ed. *Einstein: The Man and His Achievement.* New York: Dover, 1973. 94pp.

Based on BBC interviews, several scientists and philosophers, including Bertrand Russell and Karl Popper, reflect on Einstein's achievement and the impact of his theories.

157. DWIGHT D. EISENHOWER
1890–1969

Popularly known as "Ike," World War II's legendary general and the thirty-fourth U.S. president (1953–1961) was born in Denison, Texas, raised in Abilene, Kansas, and graduated from West Point (1915). As commander of the European theater of operations, he oversaw the North African campaign (1942–1943) and the invasion of Italy (1943); as supreme commander of the Allied Expeditionary Force, he supervised the D-Day offensive (1944). President during a prosperous, conservative postwar era, Eisenhower waged the Cold War against the Soviets, began a policy of intervention in Indochina, supported civil rights legislation, sent U.S. marines to Lebanon, and broke off diplomatic relations with Cuba in the wake of the Communist revolution there.

Autobiography and Primary Sources

At Ease: Stories I Tell to Friends. Garden City, New York: Doubleday, 1967. 400pp. Anecdotal reflections of Eisenhower's life from 1911, his first year at West Point, to 1952 with reminiscences about his childhood.

Crusade in Europe. Garden City, New York: Doubleday, 1948. 559pp. Eisenhower's personal narrative history of the war in Europe is an orderly, objective, well-documented account but not an autobiography in the conventional sense with few insights into the man behind the command decisions.

Mandate for Change. Garden City, New York: Doubleday, 1963. 650pp. The first volume of Eisenhower's presidential memoir covers his political career from 1943 and the first suggestion that he should run for office through his first term. Rarely reflective, Eisenhower does not reveal the process by which his political decisions were made.

Waging Peace. Garden City, New York: Doubleday, 1965. 741pp. Eisenhower provides his perspective on the events and decisions of his second term. Establishing the record fully and clearly, Eisenhower has few doubts about his decisions or second thoughts of the possibility that he should have acted differently.

The Eisenhower Diaries. Robert H. Ferrell, ed. New York: W.W. Norton, 1981. 445pp. Somewhat mislabeled as a diary of day-to-day activities, these reflections cover the period between 1935 and 1967 with lapses of months and years. At times revealing for their immediacy, the entries frustrate for what they omit: assessments of events, personalities, and Eisenhower's own emotional response. See also *Eisenhower: The Prewar Diaries and Selected Papers, 1905–1941.* Daniel D. Holt and James W. Leyerzapf, eds. (Baltimore, Maryland: Johns Hopkins University Press, 1998. 576pp.). This useful volume brings together primary material covering Eisenhower's early years.

The Papers of Dwight D. Eisenhower. Alfred D. Chandler Jr., ed. Baltimore: Johns Hopkins Press, 1970–1989. 13 vols. These collected papers are essential primary sources for the biographer.

Recommended Biographies

Ambrose, Stephen E. *Eisenhower.* New York: Simon & Schuster, 1983–1984. 2 vols. In the most thoroughly researched and comprehensive study available, Ambrose concentrates on the formation, development, and expression of Eisenhower's character through his military and political career. Clearly an admirer, Ambrose is not hesitant to criticize the general and the president on several occasions. Justifiably considered the definitive life. For a single-volume condensation, see *Eisenhower: Soldier and President* (New York: Simon & Schuster, 1990. 635pp.).

Pach, Chester J. *The Presidency of Dwight D. Eisenhower.* 1979. Revised edition. Lawrence, Kansas: University Press of Kansas, 1991. 283pp. Called by Stephen Ambrose the best single volume now available on the Eisenhower presidency, Pach's detailed study incorporates recent Eisenhower scholarship into a fair and balanced assessment of Eisenhower's leadership, successes, and shortcomings.

Perret, Geoffrey. *Eisenhower.* New York: Random House, 1999. 688pp. Perret's is a skillful chronological record of Eisenhower's military and political career that draws on newly available sources for a number of fresh perspectives. Balanced in his assessment, Perret offers a fully-rounded, credible human portrait.

Other Biographical Studies

Ambrose, Stephen E. *The Supreme Commander: The War Years of General Dwight D. Eisenhower.* Garden City, New York: Doubleday, 1970. 732pp. Ambrose's study of Eisenhower's military career prior to writing his comprehensive life treats Eisenhower's command decisions and relationships exhaustively in one of the most detailed accounts of the general's career.

Ambrose, Stephen E. *The Victors: Eisenhower and His Boys.* New York: Simon & Schuster, 1998. 396pp. Bringing together materials from several of his previous books, Ambrose documents Eisenhower's wartime leadership viewed from the vivid perspective of the men he commanded.

Beschloss, Michael R. *Eisenhower: A Centennial Life.* New York: HarperCollins, 1990. 253pp. Beschloss, a presidential historian, provides a biographical essay and assessment of Eisenhower's career with almost 300 photographs, many never previously published.

Brendon, Piers. *Ike: His Life and Times.* New York: Harper & Row, 1986. 478pp. Written by a British scholar, this account, focusing mainly on Eisenhower's presidency, disputes the notion that he was a strong and effective leader. Instead Eisenhower is shown as a bundle of contradictions who suffered from an infirmity of purpose and an avoidance of confrontation that served him well holding the Allies together during the war but failed him as president. Worthwhile as a effort in demythologizing Eisenhower, the book fall short of a truly balanced treatment.

David, Lester, and Irene David. *Ike and Mamie: The Story of the General and His Lady*. New York: Putnam, 1981. 288pp. Based on interviews, the book details the relationship between husband and wife with a number of fresh anecdotes about their private life together.

Davis, Kenneth S. *Soldier of Democracy: A Biography of Dwight Eisenhower*. New York: Doubleday, 1945. 577pp. This early biography remains useful for its many insights on Eisenhower's formative years in Kansas and his early military career.

Eisenhower, David. *Eisenhower: At War, 1943-45*. New York: Random House, 1986. 927pp. Eisenhower's grandson provides a nearly day-by-day treatment of the general's 19-month tenure as supreme Allied commander. A preliminary volume to the author's intended two-volume study of the Eisenhower presidency, David Eisenhower's political and diplomatic analysis attempts to show how Eisenhower's world view and political sense was forged by his war experience.

Eisenhower, Susan. *Mrs. Ike: Memories and Reflections on the Life of Mamie Eisenhower*. New York: Farrar, Straus, 1996. 392pp. Written by her granddaughter and based on unpublished letters, this tribute to Mamie Eisenhower portrays her as an independent, headstrong woman, showing her passionate relationship with a man who was her opposite. Highly sympathetic, this account does not skirt controversy and deals honestly with the various strains on the Eisenhowers' relationship.

Larson, Arthur. *Eisenhower: The President Nobody Knew*. New York: Scribner, 1968. 210pp. Written by a close friend and speech writer, this defense of the Eisenhower presidency makes a case for Eisenhower's decisive leadership and achievement in foreign policy. Larson's partisanship limits the book's reliability and balance.

Lee, R. Alton. *Dwight D. Eisenhower: Soldier and Statesman*. Chicago: Nelson-Hall, 1981. 379pp. Lee traces the highlights of Eisenhower's military and public career in a compact, judicious synthesis of modern historical judgment. However, little of Eisenhower's humanity is revealed, nor are his shortcomings fully investigated.

Longgood, William F. *Ike: A Pictorial Biography*. New York: Time-Life Books, 1969. 144pp. Produced immediately following Eisenhower's death, this visual tribute is chiefly useful for its many photographs arranged chronologically with connective text.

Lyon, Peter. *Eisenhower: Portrait of a Hero*. Boston: Little, Brown, 1974. 937pp. Lyons's exhaustive analysis of Eisenhower's character diagnoses the two sides of Eisenhower in a division between his public and private self, a disjunction that limited his effectiveness as a leader. Largely ignoring Eisenhower's early years, Lyon contrasts the general's considerable wartime successes with his presidential failures.

Miller, Merle. *Ike the Soldier: As They Knew Him*. New York: Putnam, 1987. 859pp. Beginning with Eisenhower's years at West Point, Miller exhaustively follows his career as junior officer, husband, father, and finally supreme commander in Europe, based on extensive interviews with those who knew him. Revealing unexpected human dimensions of Eisenhower's personality and character, Miller's adulation is somewhat wearying, however.

Morin, Relman. *Dwight D. Eisenhower: A Gauge of Greatness*. New York: Simon & Schuster, 1969. 256pp. Written as a tribute immediately following Eisenhower's death, this illustrated life underscores Eisenhower's achievements.

Neal, Steve. *The Eisenhowers: Reluctant Dynasty*. Garden City, New York: Doubleday, 1978. 493pp. Neal takes a wider perspective focusing on the Eisenhower family from the 1740s to the 1970s with the greatest emphasis on Eisenhower's military and political career and the life of his brother Milton.

Parmet, Herbert S. *Eisenhower and the American Crusades*. New York: Macmillan, 1972. 660pp. Following Eisenhower's political career from 1952 to his retirement nine years later, Parmet provides an objective assessment of Eisenhower's two terms as president and his character as an intuitive pragmatist.

Sixsmith, E.K.G. *Eisenhower as Military Commander*. New York: Stein and Day, 1973. 248pp. Written by a British army general, the book covers the whole of Eisenhower's military career from his West Point training. Of most value and interest to those who are already familiar with the details of the European operation during World War II, Sixsmith's British perspective is refreshing in a critical though ultimately favorable view of Eisenhower's generalship.

Fictional Portraits

Higgins, Jack. *Luciano's Luck*. New York: Stein and Day, 1981. 238pp. In this thriller, General Eisenhower assigns an agent to enlist gangster Lucky Luciano's assistance in gaining Mafia support for the Allied invasion of Sicily. The basis of the novel's circumstances are persistent rumors imagined as historical by the author.

Vaughan, Robert. *Over There*. New York: Bantam, 1992. 403pp. The events between 1912 and 1919 are experienced by a large cast of fictional characters whose paths cross those of historical figures, including a young Eisenhower.

Recommended Juvenile Biographies

Ambrose, Stephen E. *Ike: Abilene to Berlin*. New York: Harper & Row, 1973. 220pp. MG/YA. Eisenhower's acclaimed biography provides an account of the general's life from childhood through victory in Europe.

Brown, D. Clayton. *Dwight D. Eisenhower*. Springfield, New Jersey: Enslow, 1998. 128pp. MG. Sensible and informative biographical profile that balances personal information with Eisenhower's achievements.

Sandberg, Peter Lars. *Dwight D. Eisenhower*. New York: Chelsea House, 1986. 116pp. MG/YA. Sandberg presents a comprehensive summary of Eisenhower's life, personality, and military and political career.

Biographical Films and Theatrical Adaptations

A&E Biography Video: Dwight D. Eisenhower: Commander-in-Chief (1995). Director: Don Horan. Solid documentary look at Eisenhower's career. Video.

Churchill and the Generals (1981). Director: Alan Gibson. Based on Churchill's memoirs, the film details the prime minister's war leadership and his relationships with Franklin Roosevelt (Arthur Hill) and General Eisenhower (Richard A. Dysart). Timothy West portrays Churchill. Video.

Dwight D. Eisenhower (1991). Producer: Hearst Entertainment. Part of the Famous Americans of the 20th Century series, this is a biographical profile and an assessment of Eisenhower's achievements. Video.

Eisenhower (1993). Producer: Adriana Busch and Austin Hoyt. Installment of PBS's American Experience series. Thoughtful and detailed portrait of Eisenhower's life and career in the military and as president that captures his character as formed during his Kansas upbringing. Video.

Ike (1979). Director: Melville Shavelson. This made-for television biographical dramatization of Eisenhower's war years stars Robert Duvall as the general, with Bonnie Bartlett as Mamie and Lee Remick as Kay Summersby. Video.

158. GEORGE ELIOT
1819–1880

One of the great English novelists, Eliot (born Mary Ann Evans; later Marian Evans) wrote about life in small rural towns with deep insight into character and nineteenth-century culture, setting the course the novel would take in the twentieth century. Country-bred in a strict atmosphere of evangelical Protestantism, she eventually renounced organized religion entirely. An editor for the *Westminster Review*, she published a series of realistic sketches, *Scenes From Clerical Life* (1856), for *Blackwood's Magazine* under the name George Eliot, a pseudonym proposed by her life partner, literary critic George Lewes. Her novels include *Adam Bede* (1859), *The Mill on the Floss* (1860), *Silas Marner* (1861), and *Middlemarch* (1872), considered her masterpiece.

Autobiography and Primary Sources

Journals of George Eliot. Margaret Harris, ed. New York: Cambridge University Press, 1998. 500pp. Eliot's journals cover her life from 1854 and offers the reader an intimate look at the writer's personality, activities, and ideas.

Letters. Gordon S. Haight, ed. New Haven, Connecticut: Yale University Press, 1954–1974. 9 vols. Eliot's collected letters present a hitherto unavailable fully-rounded portrait of the author that is an essential source for biographers. Included are many letters to George Eliot allowing the reader to assess the responses of her intimates. Haight provides a one-volume collection of Eliot's correspondence as well as a number of newly discovered letters in *Selections from George Eliot's Letters* (New Haven, Connecticut: Yale University Press, 1985. 567pp.).

Recommended Biographies

Ashton, Rosemary. *George Eliot: A Life.* New York: Penguin, 1997. 465pp. Searching for the real George Eliot, Ashton's revisionist account of the novelist's life and work locates both in their social and intellectual milieu, suggesting that Eliot was more a product of her time than others have suggested. Ashton's is a skillful literary biography that paints a credible human portrait of the development of Eliot's character and artistry and the relation between the two.

Haight, Gordon S. *George Eliot: A Biography.* New York: Oxford University Press, 1968. 616pp. Written by the acknowledged leading expert on Eliot, Haight's exhaustive and scrupulously researched study establishes the factual record of Eliot's life, documenting the personal circumstances underlying the creation of her novels and weaving the various threads of Eliot's complex personality into a comprehensive pattern. The book avoids speculation and psychological interpretations so that it serves primarily as an authoritative reference source.

Hughes, Kathryn. *George Eliot: The Last Victorian.* New York: Farrar, Straus, 1999. 383pp. Hughes offers a convincing portrait of Eliot's emotional and artistic development in a well-researched and ably written account stressing the private person beneath the formidable public persona. Few studies have as credibly shown Eliot as intimately, connecting her personal conflicts and her social and intellectual milieu to show how they all contributed to forming her character and work.

Karl, Frederick R. *George Eliot: Voice of a Century.* New York: W.W. Norton, 1995. 708pp. Based on new material unavailable to Haight, Karl's dramatic, psychological study was written in part to expand the restrictive view of Haight's cautious account. In Karl's view, George Eliot's life and work encapsulated "the ambiguities, the anguish, and divisiveness of the Victorian era," and he uses Eliot's story to form a wider portrait of the Victorian era. With lucid critical commentary, Karl's biography supersedes all but Haight in its range and thoroughness.

Other Biographical Studies

Bellringer, Alan W. *George Eliot.* New York: St. Martin's, 1993. 166pp. Bellringer's critical study looks at both Eliot's life and work by establishing the intellectual climate of her time, including the social issues and religious questioning that shaped her life and fiction.

Bodenheimer, Rosemarie. *Real Life of Mary Ann Evans: George Eliot, Her Letters and Fiction.* Ithaca, New York: Cornell University Press, 1996. 320pp. In a full-scale study of George Eliot's correspondence, organized by topic and connected thematically to both her life and fiction, Bodenheimer fashions an analysis of some of the crises of Eliot's life that sheds light on the autobiographical context of her fiction and her textual strategies.

Bullett, Gerald. *George Eliot: Her Life and Her Books.* New Haven, Connecticut: Yale University Press, 1948. 273pp. This critical biography based on then recently discovered diaries and letters, Bullett offers an honest, readable assessment of Eliot's career as well as a stimulating analysis of her novels.

Crompton, Margaret. *George Eliot: The Woman.* New York: T. Yoseloff, 1960. 214pp. The first biography to take advantage of the publication of Eliot's collected letters, Crompton's book is a sensible treatment that offers few new insights or alteration of the basic paradigm for viewing Eliot's career previously established.

Cross, J.W. *George Eliot's Life as Related in Her Letters and Journals, Arranged and Edited by Her Husband.* New York: Harper, 1885. 3 vols. Written by Eliot's husband, Cross's massive appreciation, which was described by William Gladstone as "a Reticence in three volumes," is marred by suppression of compromising facts and alteration of the text of some of the letters. However, Cross's perspective remains a fascinating one.

Dodd, Valerie A. *George Eliot: An Intellectual Life.* New York: St. Martin's, 1990. 381pp. This study of Eliot's intellectual development from her childhood until she began her first fiction in 1856 combines biographical details and intellectual history, examining the many influences on her political, social, theological, moral, and literary positions.

Haight, Gordon S. *George Eliot and John Chapman, with Chapman's Diaries.* New Haven, Connecticut: Yale University Press, 1940. 261pp. Using Chapman's diaries for 1851 and 1860, Haight documents a crucial period of Eliot's life: her entry into the intellectual world of London when Chapman took her on as a reviewer for his liberal *Westminster Review.*

Hanson, Lawrence, and Elisabeth Hanson. *Marian Evans and George Eliot.* New York: Oxford University Press, 1952. 402pp. One of the most detailed general biographies available, the authors attempt to demythologize Eliot and substitute a clearer human portrait showing the transformation of Marian Evans into George Eliot. Their narrative is told clearly and sympathetically with no oversimplified psychological solutions to the various contradictions in Eliot's character.

Laski, Marghanita. *George Eliot and Her World.* New York: Scribner, 1978. 119pp. Laski's amply illustrated outline of the salient events of Eliot's life and social and historical background includes some original surmises suggesting the more negative influence of George Henry Lewes on Eliot as well as a possible explanation for George Eliot's sudden involvement with Johnnie Cross after Lewes's death.

McSweeney, Kerry. *George Eliot (Marian Evans): A Literary Life.* New York: St. Martin's, 1991. 156pp. Focusing on the events of her formative years, this concise literary biography places Eliot's works in the context of her life and her social and historical milieu.

Redinger, Ruby V. *George Eliot: The Emergent Self.* New York: Knopf, 1975. 515pp. Redinger's psychological study can be read as a companion to Haight's factual treatment, supplying the interpretation he studiously avoids. Redinger attempts to uncover the dynamics of Eliot's emotional and artistic development and her battle with her background to release her creativity. Some of Redinger's suggestions are less convincing than others, and she is sometimes guilty of inferring too many biographical details from the novels.

Taylor, Ina. *Woman of Contradictions: The Life of George Eliot.* New York: Morrow, 1989. 255pp. Taylor sets out to uncover the real George Eliot, concluding that she was everything a Victorian female was not supposed to be. Occasionally sketchy in the treatment of all aspects of Eliot's life and career, the book nevertheless sheds new light on Eliot's character and humanity.

Uglow, Jennifer. *George Eliot.* New York: Pantheon, 1987. 273pp. This feminist biography offering a candid and straightforward rereading of the novelist and her work focuses on Eliot's complex view of women, the radical departures she made in her life, and the moderate and even conservative stands she often took in her books. Uglow attempts to answer why Eliot denied her heroines the same opportunities for professional and personal fulfillment she struggled to achieve.

Biographical Novels

Kenyon, Frank W. *The Consuming Flame: The Story of George Eliot.* New York: Dodd, Mead, 1970. 223pp. Tracing the life of George Eliot up to her first great literary success, this biographical novel is based on Haight's edition of the *Letters* with fictional elaboration of dialogue and scene.

White, Terence De Vere. *Johnnie Cross.* New York: St. Martin's, 1983. 153pp. The novel reconstructs the story of Eliot's seven-month marriage at the age of 61 to Johnnie Cross, 20 years her junior. Cross in his 80s shares his recollections with the writer in a mixture of biographical details, psychological speculation, and literary gossip.

Fictional Portraits

Wilson, A.N. *Gentlemen in England.* New York: Viking, 1986. 311pp. Wilson's saga of Victorian life in an upper middle-class family includes appearances by several eminent Victorians, including George Eliot, Anthony Trollope, and Walter Pater.

Recommended Juvenile Biographies

Gaeddert, Louann B. *All-in-All: A Biography of George Eliot.* New York: Dutton, 1976. 138pp. MG. Based on the *Letters* and Haight's biography, this short account is a candid, sympathetic, and restrained portrait that follows Eliot's career from childhood.

Sprague, Rosemary. *George Eliot: A Biography.* New York: Chilton, 1968. 337pp. YA. Sprague's sympathetic portrait indulges in poetical license to dramatize Eliot's life and is closer to a fictional biography than a fully reliable, careful study.

Vipont, Elfrida. *Towards a High Attic: The Early Life of George Eliot.* New York: Holt, 1971. 145pp.

MG. This fictionalized biography draws heavily on Haight's edition of the *Letters* to produce a poetical and somewhat idealized portrait of Eliot's formative years.

Biographical Films and Theatrical Adaptations

George Eliot: A Concise Biography (1993). Director: Malcolm Hossick. Part of the Famous Authors series, this short documentary film gives a succinct factual outline of Eliot's life and the social and historical background to her writing. Video.

Other Sources

Hands, Timothy. *A George Eliot Chronology.* New York: Macmillan, 1988. 144pp. This excellent reference resource charts Eliot's activities in a detailed chronology.

Pinion, F.B. *A George Eliot Companion.* Totowa, New Jersey: Barnes and Noble, 1981. 277pp. Pinion provides a useful reference guide that supplies information on Eliot's works and life.

159. T.S. ELIOT
1888–1965

American-English poet and critic Thomas Stearns Eliot is considered one of the most influential and distinguished literary figures of the twentieth century. Born in Saint Louis, Missouri, he was educated at Harvard, the Sorbonne, and Oxford. After working as a teacher and bank clerk he edited literary magazines and eventually became director of Faber & Faber book publishers. Such early poetical works as *Prufrock and Other Observations* (1917) and *The Waste Land* (1922) express the anguish and desolation of modern life and the isolation of the individual. Eliot later turned from spiritual desolation to religious faith, embracing Anglo-Catholicism and exploring Christian themes in such dramatic works as *Murder in the Cathedral* (1935) and *The Cocktail Party* (1950). He was awarded the 1948 Nobel Prize in Literature.

Autobiography and Primary Sources

The Letters of T.S. Eliot. Valerie Eliot, ed. New York: Harcourt, Brace, 1988. 639pp. The first volume of Eliot's collected letters covers the period between 1898 and 1922. Included are not only Eliot's letters but material from his first wife, family, and friends that together reads like a documentary biography of his first 43 years.

Recommended Biographies

Ackroyd, Peter. *T.S. Eliot: A Life.* New York: Simon & Schuster, 1984. 400pp. Despite being prevented by Eliot's estate from quoting the poet's work, Ackroyd's well-researched and thoughtful narrative records the essential details of Eliot's personal life and internal development. Offering a number of new and surprising revelations, Ackroyd shows how Eliot's sense of drama shaped his works.

Gordon, Lyndall. *Eliot's Early Years.* New York: Oxford University Press, 1977. 174pp.; *Eliot's*

New Life. New York: Farrar, Straus, 1988. 356pp. In a groundbreaking two-volume inner biography Gordon demonstrates how Eliot's poetry was rooted in private aspects of his life. The first volume takes his story up to his Anglo-Catholic conversion at the age of 38. The second volume follows his last 38 years, structured by the internal logic of Eliot's personal and artistic development rather than being a strict chronology. Both volumes are based on unpublished papers revealing previously unknown details about Eliot's relationships with the various women in his life. In *T.S. Eliot: An Imperfect Life* (New York: W.W. Norton, 1999. 720pp.) the author incorporates a wealth of new materials and fresh insights to form a penetrating intellectual and psychologically astute biography, one of the best single-volume sources on the poet available.

Other Biographical Studies

Bergonzi, Bernard. *T.S. Eliot.* New York: Macmillan, 1972. 207pp. Tracing Eliot's life chronologically, this study describes Eliot's American roots, his literary friendships, and the cultural and historical context of Eliot's development and artistry.

Bush, Ronald. *T.S. Eliot: A Study in Character and Style.* New York: Oxford University Press, 1983. 287pp. Using the methods of psychoanalytic criticism, Bush traces the relationship between Eliot's writing and his psychic development. Bush, utilizing previous unexamined material, reveals a divided individual, split between thought and feeling.

Dale, Alzina S. *T.S. Eliot: The Philosopher Poet.* Wheaton, Illinois: Shaw, 1988. 209pp. Dale looks at the major events of Eliot's life and his development as a poet and thinker from the perspective of his spiritual growth, an often neglected side of the poet. The book is particularly strong on Eliot's Saint Louis and family background and his later years.

Kenner, Hugh. *The Invisible Poet: T.S. Eliot.* New York: McDowell, 1959. 346pp. Kenner's groundbreaking critical study connects Eliot's poetic development to the main currents of modernism.

Matthews, Thomas S. *Great Tom: Notes Toward the Definition of T.S. Eliot.* New York: Harper & Row, 1974. 219pp. Although not as grounded in primary material as subsequent studies, Matthews offers an interpretive account of Eliot's life and literary career shaped by his Unitarian upbringing and the sexual disorder that affected his first marriage and produced the nervous breakdown Eliot experienced while writing *The Waste Land.* Provocative and insightful, Matthews is overly dismissive of Eliot's drama and religious attitudes.

Miller, James E. *T.S. Eliot's Personal Waste Land: Exorcism of the Demons.* University Park: Pennsylvania State University Press, 1977. 176pp. Using Eliot's life to illuminate his poetry, Miller describes the personal torments that underlay his work. Revealing a number of new biographical insights, Miller's study is often speculative in its approach and should be read with some skepticism.

Sencourt, Robert. *T.S. Eliot: A Memoir.* Donald Adamson, ed. New York: Dodd Mead, 1971.

266pp. Sencourt's personal recollections of Eliot are supplemented with research on the poet's early life and work as a schoolmaster, banker, and editor. Filling in a number of gaps in the record, Sencourt's friendship for Eliot at times compromises his objectivity and without documentation it is unclear which of the author's observations are eyewitness views and which are hearsay, gossip, and surmises.

Sharpe, Tony. *T.S. Eliot: A Literary Life.* New York: St. Martin's, 1991. 189pp. Providing a solid introduction to Eliot's life and literary career, Sharpe sets both in their cultural and historical background.

Fictional Portraits

Cooley, Martha. *The Archivist.* Boston: Little, Brown, 1998. 328pp. Eliot's biography forms one of many contexts for this inventive, literate novel concerning a young poet's determination to unlock the secrets of Eliot's letters to Emily Hale (actually sealed from public view at Princeton until 2020). Her request to the custodian of the Eliot papers causes him to reexperience his relations with his wife that parallels Eliot's first marriage.

Recommended Juvenile Biographies

Asbee, Sue. *T.S. Eliot.* Vero Beach, Florida: Rourke. 1990. 111pp. YA. Provides a brief summary of Eliot's life and an in-depth analysis of some of his major poems.

Biographical Films and Theatrical Adaptations

Hastings, Michael. *Tom and Viv.* New York: Penguin, 1985. 126pp. Hastings dramatizes the relationship between Eliot and his first wife, Vivienne Haigh-Wood, and her misdiagnosed mental illness.

The Modern World: Ten Great Writers (1988). Director: David Thomas. An installment of the London Weekend Television series looks at Eliot's life and literary career. Video.

Tom & Viv (1994). Director: Brian Gilbert. Michael Hastings co-wrote the filmscript based on his play dramatizing Eliot's relationship with Vivienne Haigh-Wood. Willem Dafoe plays Eliot, and Miranda Richardson steals the show as the vivacious and troubled Vivienne. Video.

T.S. Eliot (1987). Director: Veronica Young. Part of the Voices and Visions series, incidents from Eliot's life are chronicled with filmed appearances by Eliot and critics who examine his character, artistry, and religious beliefs. Video.

Other Sources

Moody, A. David, ed. *The Cambridge Companion to T.S. Eliot.* New York: Cambridge University Press, 1994. 259pp. An international collection of Eliot scholars offers studies of different facets of the poet's life, work, and thought in historical perspective.

Pinion, F.B. *A T.S. Eliot Companion: Life and Works.* Totowa, New Jersey: Barnes and Noble, 1986. 304pp. This is an informative reference volume that covers details of Eliot's life and writings.

160. ELIZABETH I
1533–1603

The daughter of Henry VIII and Anne Boleyn, Elizabeth was declared illegitimate before her mother's execution (1536) but was restored to the succession (1544). The rallying point for discontented Protestants, she was imprisoned and her freedom later limited during the reign of her Catholic half-sister, Mary. At 25 she succeeded to the throne and proved a strong, courageous, and responsible ruler of unequaled popularity. Although marred by Catholic persecution, the Elizabethan period was a golden era in which a united England defeated the Spanish armada to emerge as a major European power with a strong navy, explored and settled the New World, and produced some of the greatest literary figures in history.

Autobiography and Primary Sources

Letters of Queen Elizabeth I. G.B. Harrison, ed. New York: Funk & Wagnalls, 1968. 323pp. This is an excellent collection of Elizabeth's writings that provides an invaluable window into her personality.

Recommended Biographies

Erickson, Carolly. *The First Elizabeth.* New York: Summit Books, 1983. 447pp. Blending psychological insight and solid research into the period, this vivid biography adds considerably to the portrait of Elizabeth. Unlike other biographies that have emphasized Elizabeth's chastity, Erickson's Elizabeth flaunts her sexual powers.

Neale, J.E. *Queen Elizabeth.* New York: Harcourt, Brace, 1934. 402pp. Even after more than 60 years, this remains the standard biography of Elizabeth I. Neale's study is a model of scholarship, elegant writing, and perceptive judgment. Some may find Neale's partisanship on behalf of the queen overly romanticized, and the author's biases are obvious, particularly a sexism that grates on modern readers.

Ridley, Jasper. *Elizabeth I: The Shrewdness of Virtue.* New York: Viking, 1989. 391pp. An award-winning biographer, the author offers a balanced portrait of Elizabeth that is both well researched and entertaining.

Somerset, Anne. *Elizabeth I.* New York: Knopf, 1992. 636pp. This has been called the fullest and best biography of the queen since Neale that focuses on both the ruler and the woman. Somerset's account of the queen brings her to life and places her in the context of the grand events of the times. This biography will appeal to those interested in the big picture rather than the minute details.

Other Biographical Studies

Bassnett, Susan. *Elizabeth I: A Feminist Perspective.* New York: Berg, 1988. 139pp. Despite its ideological subtitle, this is a shrewd, straightforward account and a useful, succinct introduction for the general reader.

Haigh, Christopher. *Elizabeth I.* New York: Longman, 1988. 198pp. This study takes a thematic approach with chapters on the queen's relationship with the church, Parliament, her nobles, council, and people in an iconoclastic and witty approach that is at times aimed to shock and is oversimplified.

Hibbert, Christopher. *The Virgin Queen: Elizabeth I, Genius of the Golden Age.* Reading, Massachusetts: Addison-Wesley, 1991. 287pp. This popular biography of Elizabeth provides an intimate portrait in a well-rounded and well-written study.

Jenkins, Elizabeth. *Elizabeth the Great.* New York: Coward-McCann, 1958. 336pp. This is a psychological biography, well grounded in research and details from contemporary sources.

Johnson, Paul. *Elizabeth I: A Biography.* New York: Holt, 1974. 480pp. A readable summary of scholarship since Neale's classic study, the emphasis here is the political dimension of Elizabeth's life.

MacCaffrey, Wallace T. *Elizabeth I.* New York: E. Arnold, 1993. 480pp. This account lacks the intimacy and color of other more personal studies of the monarch with its emphasis on Elizabethan politics.

Williams, Neville. *The Life and Times of Elizabeth I.* New York: Oxford University Press, 1972. 224pp. This lavishly illustrated volume complements Williams's earlier biography, *Elizabeth, Queen of England* (London: Weiderfeld & Nicolson, 1967. 388pp.). Both are good on the personal side of Elizabeth's character and the significance of her reign.

Biographical Novels

Anthony, Evelyn. *All the Queen's Men.* New York: Crowell, 1960. 307pp. The novel chronicles the first 30 years of Elizabeth's reign in which she must carefully negotiate through treacherous domestic and international politics. The novel's historical details are faithful to the facts.

Delves-Broughton, Josephine. *Heart of a Queen.* New York: Whittlesey House, 1950. 558pp. Elizabeth's relationships with the two principal men in her life—the earls of Leicester and Essex—are the focus here. The novel makes use of actual letters and recorded conversations and incidents that create an authentic portrait of the monarch and her era.

Dessau, Joanna. *The Red-Haired Brat.* New York: St. Martin's, 1978. 237pp.; *Absolute Elizabeth.* New York: St. Martin's, 1979. 192pp. The author provides two fictional versions of Elizabeth's story. The first is an autobiographical account that records Elizabeth's life from the age of three until she is crowned queen in 1558. *Absolute Elizabeth* juxtaposes Elizabeth in old age, a brilliant and formidable monarch, and her youth as a temperamental and giddy princess with an uncertain future. In both, Elizabeth's voice is convincing, and the sense of the period is authentic and reliable.

Ellis, Amanda Mae. *Elizabeth, the Woman.* New York: Dutton, 1951. 319pp. The novel dramatizes the life and reign of Elizabeth from age 10 to her death 60 years later, establishing both a psychological portrait of the queen and a vivid look at the period.

Harwood, Alice. *So Merciful a Queen, So Cruel a Woman.* Indianapolis: Bobbs-Merrill, 1958. 380pp. Elizabeth's rise to the throne and the consolidation of her power are traced. The court intrigue of the period is vividly reproduced, and the novel is faithful to the facts.

Irwin, Margaret. Princess Elizabeth trilogy. This trio of novels concentrates on Elizabeth's youth prior to her succession. In *Young Bess.* (New York: Harcourt, Brace, 1945, 274pp.), Elizabeth, at the age of 12, contends with the intrigues of her father's court. In *Elizabeth, Captive Princess.* (New York: Harcourt, Brace, 1948, 246pp.), during the reign of Mary I, Elizabeth is a virtual prisoner of her suspicious and temperamental half-sister; *Elizabeth and the Prince of Spain.* (New York: Harcourt, Brace, 1953, 251pp.) concludes Elizabeth's girlhood up to her succession as queen. The novels stay within the framework of history here, but with invented scenes and dialogue.

Kay, Susan. *Legacy.* New York: Crown, 1986. 648pp. The novel describes the remarkable career and reign of Elizabeth I and captures all the intrigue of court life while creating an intimate and astute portrait of the queen.

Kenyon, Frank W. *Shadow in the Sun: A Novel of Elizabeth I, the Virgin Queen.* New York: Crowell, 1958. 304pp. Covering Elizabeth I's life from childhood until her death, the novel is solidly researched and convincing, even though much of the dialogue and scenes are invented.

Letton, Jennette and Francis. *The Young Elizabeth.* New York: Harper, 1953. 277pp. During the years between the death of Henry VIII, and the ascension to the throne of her half-sister, Mary, the young princess is shown balancing the demands of the heart and the intrigue that surrounds her as a potential rival to Mary I. Captures the period and its intrigues with care and authenticity.

Miles, Rosalind. *I, Elizabeth: The Word of a Queen.* New York: Doubleday, 1994. 595pp. This autobiographical account shows Elizabeth perfecting her survival instincts with an emphasis on Elizabeth's emotional side.

Plaidy, Jean. *Queen of This Realm: The Story of Queen Elizabeth I.* New York: Putnam, 1984. 570pp. Elizabeth narrates her own life story. Wary of any sacrifice to her hard-won power and authority, Elizabeth resists marriage but not love. The novel is filled with telling period details.

Thorpe, Helen. *Elizabeth: Queen & Woman.* New York: Roy, 1971. 238pp. Focuses on Elizabeth's relationship with Sir Robert Dudley, purportedly her one true love. The queen is characterized with a blend of frailties and extraordinary self-possession. The historical elements are authentic and believable.

Fictional Portraits

Elizabeth I appears in dozens of historical novels, mysteries, and adventure stories as a character. The following offer interesting portraits of the queen:

Buckley, Fiona. *To Shield the Queen: A Mystery at Queen Elizabeth I's Court.* New York: Scribner, 1997. 278pp.; *The Doublet Affair.* New York: Scribner, 1998. 294pp.; *Queen's Ransom.* New York: Scribner, 2000. 348pp. This series of historical mysteries involves lady-in-waiting Ursula Blanchard in Elizabeth's court who is involved in intrigue derived in part from details of the queen's life and reign.

Eckerson, Olive. *My Lord Essex.* New York: Holt, 1955. 397pp. The novel dramatizes the tragic course of Elizabeth's romance with the Earl of Essex and his rise and fall.

Finney, Patricia. *The Firedrake's Eye.* New York: St. Martin's, 1992. 263pp. This concerns a conspiracy to assassinate Elizabeth during the festivities celebrating her ascension to the throne; *Unicorn's Blood.* (New York: Picador, 1998. 384pp.) features the pursuit of Elizabeth's youthful confession that she is not a virgin at all and naming Mary Queen of Scots as her heir.

Garrett, George. *Death of the Fox.* Garden City, New York: Doubleday, 1971. 739pp.; *The Succession: A Novel of Elizabeth and James.* Garden City, New York: Doubleday 1983. 538pp. Elizabeth I is at the center of the first two volumes of the author's acclaimed Elizabethan trilogy. Both novels achieve the effect of a grand choral orchestration of the age with insightful biographical portraits of many major players in the drama of Elizabeth's court.

Harper, Karen. *The Poyson Garden: A Bess Tudor Mystery.* New York: Delacorte Press, 1999. 288pp. In a historical mystery series, Elizabeth Tudor investigates the poisoning death of a number of her Boleyn relatives while she is watched suspiciously by her stepsister Queen Mary; *The Tidal Poole: An Elizabeth I Mystery* (New York: Delacorte, 2000. 288pp.) continues Elizabeth's career as a new queen whose coronation is marred by the brutal murder of a lady of the court.

Heaven, Constance. *The Queen and the Gypsy.* New York: Coward-McCann, 1977. 275pp. The novel explores the famous historical mystery of how Amy Robsart, the wife of Elizabeth's favorite, Robert Dudley, died.

Maxwell, Robin *The Secret Diary of Anne Boleyn.* New York: Arcade, 1997. 288pp. The recently crowned Elizabeth finds her doomed mother's diary and learns its painful message: "Never relinquish control to any man." *The Queen's Bastard* (New York: Arcade, 1999, 436pp.) imagines the survival of a son born to Elizabeth I and her lover Robert Dudley, Earl of Leicester. Arthur Dudley is switched at birth with a stillborn child and raised in ignorance as a country gentleman, with the queen believing he has died. Dudley narrates this story that includes a military career and excursions as a spy on the continent before his eventual climactic reunion with his father and mother. Dudley's story is juxtaposed with earlier scenes from Elizabeth's relationship with Leicester.

Schoonover, Lawrence L. *To Love a Queen.* Boston: Little, Brown, 1973. 383pp. The novel focuses on the relationship between Elizabeth and Walter Raleigh.

York, Robert. *My Lord the Fox.* New York: Vanguard, 1984. 152pp. This account takes up two of history's most persistent mysteries: Was Elizabeth Tudor's father really Henry VIII and what was the truth behind the death of Amy Robsart, the wife of Robert Dudley, the queen's supposed lover?

Recommended Juvenile Biographies

Bush, Catherine. *Elizabeth I.* New York: Chelsea House, 1987. 112pp. MG. This is an informative summary of Elizabeth's life and times.

Green, Robert. *Queen Elizabeth I.* New York: F. Watts, 1997. 64pp. MG. A good summary of Elizabeth's life, this biography is strongly flavored by details of contemporary life and customs.

Biographical Films and Theatrical Adaptations

A&E Biography Video: Elizabeth I: The Virgin Queen (1972). Director: Sue Hayes. Part of the popular television biography series, this informative account sets out to reveal the woman behind the myth. Video.

Elizabeth (1999). Director: Shekhar Kapur. Cate Blanchett is a standout as Elizabeth in this dark dramatization of the princess's rise to the throne and her steeling herself for the challenges that are thrust on her. Geoffrey Rush portrays Walsingham and Kathy Burke plays Mary I. Video.

Elizabeth R (1972). Directors: Claude Whatham, et al. This television dramatic series covers Elizabeth's life from age 17 to 70, anchored by a remarkable performance by Glenda Jackson. Both colorful and convincing. Video.

The Private Lives of Elizabeth and Essex (1939). Based on Maxwell Anderson's play, this is a lavish costume drama concerned with the relationship between Elizabeth and her favorite, the Earl of Essex, with an outstanding performance by Bette Davis as Elizabeth. Should not be regarded as authentic history, however. Video.

Shakespeare in Love (1998). Director: John Madden. This clever romantic comedy won the Academy Award for best picture of the year and an Oscar for Judi Dench for her portrayal of Elizabeth, the deus ex machina of the film's climax. Also starring Gwyneth Paltrow, Joseph Fiennes, and Geoffrey Rush. Video.

The Virgin Queen (1955). Davis repeats her portrayal of Elizabeth I in a drama concentrating on her conflicts with Walter Raleigh. Best for Davis's performance. Video.

161. DUKE ELLINGTON
1899–1974

One of the most celebrated figures of American jazz, Ellington was a pianist and composer whose orchestra performed in Harlem nightclubs, at jazz festivals, and in films, went on many European tours, and made hundreds of recordings. His numerous and varied compositions include *Mood Indigo*, *Sophisticated Lady*, and *Creole Rhapsody*. He was awarded the Presidential Medal of Freedom in 1969.

Autobiography and Primary Sources

Music Is My Mistress. Garden City, New York: Doubleday, 1973. 522pp. Ellington's collection of anecdotes is articulate, witty, and rarely critical, emphasizing exclusively the positive in his distinguished career and overlooking the obstacles he faced as a jazz musician and black man.

Recommended Biographies

Hasse, John E. *Beyond Category: The Life and Genius of Duke Ellington.* New York: Simon & Schuster, 1993. 479pp. Contrary to Collier's negative assessment, Hasse offers a well-written, spirited defense of Ellington's achievement as a great American composer in a carefully researched biography that chronicles Ellington's year-by-year musical growth and development.

Jewell, Derek. *Duke: A Portrait of Duke Ellington.* New York: W.W. Norton, 1977. 264pp. The first comprehensive biography following Ellington's death, Jewell's is a straightforward, accurate, well-written summary of Ellington's life and career.

Tucker, Mark. *Ellington: The Early Years.* Urbana: University of Illinois Press, 1991. 343pp. Tucker's is by far the most detailed and scholarly treatment of Ellington's early, formative years up to his debut at the Cotton Club in 1927. Based on extensive interviews with his early associates, Tucker sheds considerable fresh light on Ellington's background, education, musical development, and the cultural milieu of Washington, DC.

Other Biographical Studies

Collier, James L. *Duke Ellington.* New York: Oxford University Press, 1987. 340pp. Collier's judgmental, mainly negative, assessment of the man and his music is controversial. In Collier's view, Ellington was less a musical genius than an exploiter of others' talents. Although, Collier's interpretations are provocative and challenging, the book's lack of balance limits its overall effectiveness.

Dance, Stanley. *The World of Duke Ellington.* New York: Scribner, 1970. 311pp. Dance, a longtime friend of Ellington, offers his own recollections and those of the musician's associates in an oral history approach that is full of important, firsthand information.

Ellington, Mercer, with Stanley Dance. *Duke Ellington in Person: An Intimate Memoir.* Boston: Houghton Mifflin, 1978. 236pp. Ellington's son offers his reflections on his father's personal qualities and is more critical than Ellington's own benign recollections. The firsthand details supply a wealth of fresh insights into the personal dynamics of Ellington and his band.

George, Don. *Sweet Man: The Real Duke Ellington.* New York: Putnam, 1981. 272pp. This anecdotal account by Ellington's lyricist of various events in the musician's life from the 1940s to his death is an uneven mix of sentiment and the sensational with an emphasis on behind-the-scenes revelations.

Lawrence, Austin H. *Duke Ellington and His World.* New York: Schirmer Books, 1999. 500pp. This is a competent narrative biography of Ellington's performing career with capsule biographies of most of the musicians who worked in his orchestra. Ellington's personal life is only glimpsed in passing.

Steed, Janna T. *Duke Ellington: A Spiritual Biography*. New York: Crossrood, 1999. 192pp. This interpretive biographical profile focuses on Ellington's spirituality that the author attribute as the source of his genius. In the author's view Ellington's later Sacred Concerts were a natural expression of the spirituality that was a consistent force in the musician's make-up from his earliest days.

Travis, Dempsey J. *The Duke Ellington Primer*. Chicago: Urban Research Press, 1996. 202pp. Travis provides a straightforward, brief survey of Ellington's life and musical development with a full selection of illustrations.

Recommended Juvenile Biographies

Old, Wendie C. *Duke Ellington: Great of Jazz*. Springfield, New Jersey: Enslow, 1996. 128pp. MG. Old examines Ellington's life and career from his childhood through his struggles against racism, and eventual recognition in the musical world as an influential innovator.

Stwertka, Eve. *Duke Ellington: A Life in Music*. New York: F. Watts, 1994. 143pp. MG/YA. This is a detailed, comprehensive biography covering Ellington's entire career in a sympathetic but balanced treatment.

Woog, Adam. *Duke Ellington*. San Diego: Lucent Books, 1996. 112pp. MG/YA. Woog stresses Ellington's impact on the music world in this chronicle of his life and career.

Biographical Films and Theatrical Adaptations

Cotton Club (1984). Director: Francis Ford Coppola. Coppola's ambitious, uneven period love story features an impressive cast of Diane Lane, Richard Gere, and Bob Hoskins, fine performances, period atmosphere, and an appearance by Ellington, played by Zane Mark. Video.

Hoodlum (1996). Director: Bill Duke. In something of a spin-off of Coppola's *Cotton Club*, Laurence Fishburne reprises his role from the earlier film in a tale of his attempt to stop the mob from muscling into the Harlem numbers rackets. Starring Tim Roth, Andy Garcia, and Vanessa Williams. Ellington makes an appearance played by Tony Rich. Video.

Other Sources

Gammond, Peter, ed. *Duke Ellington: His Life and Music*. New York: Roy, 1958. 255pp. This compilation of articles by leading jazz critics focuses on particular aspects of Ellington's music or periods of his career, forming a group chronological portrait of his career.

Nicholson, Stuart, ed. *Reminiscing in Tempo: A Portrait of Duke Ellington*. Boston: Northeastern University Press, 1999. 320pp. Nicholson weaves Ellington's own words and those of his colleagues to form an oral history touching on every important aspect of Ellington's career.

Tucker, Mark, ed. *The Duke Ellington Reader*. New York: Oxford University Press, 1993. 536pp. This extensive collection of interviews, essays, re-

views, and memoirs cover Ellington's entire career and features important comments by Ellington on his music and creative method.

162. RALPH WALDO EMERSON
1803–1882

A poet, essayist, and lecturer who profoundly influenced American thought, Emerson was born in Boston and studied at Harvard, where he began his famous *Journal*. He was trained as a minister but retired from his pastorate and under the influence of Carlyle, Wordsworth, and Coleridge became interested in and a leading exponent of transcendentalism. His 1837 Harvard oration, "The American Scholar," called for independence from European cultural leadership and attracted wide attention. During the 1850s he became a strong supporter of abolitionism. His famous essays include "Nature" and "Self-Reliance."

Autobiography and Primary Sources

Emerson in His Journals. Joel Porte, ed. Cambridge, Massachusetts: Harvard University Press, 1982. 588pp. Porte selects from Emerson's massive journal material arranged into sections corresponding to periods of Emerson's life with a concise biographical introduction to each. This is an ideal starting point to examine Emerson's varied moods and revelations contained in his journals.

Journals and Miscellaneous Notebooks of Ralph Waldo Emerson. Cambridge, Massachusetts: Harvard University Press, 1960–1982. 16 vols. Brings together a wide range of materials from which autobiographical information can be gleaned.

The Letters of Ralph Waldo Emerson. New York: Columbia University Press, 1939–1995. 10 vols. Emerson's letters are essential for any biographical study and reveal the man in a number of guises.

Selected Letters of Ralph Waldo Emerson. Joel Myerson, ed. New York: Columbia University Press, 1997. 469pp. This one-volume collection assembles some of the most important and revealing of Emerson's letters.

Recommended Biographies

Allen, Gay Wilson. *Waldo Emerson: A Biography*. New York: Viking, 1981. 751pp. Allen probes the private depths and darker conflicts of Emerson's character more thoroughly than Rusk, making full use of new material uncovered since 1949. A lucid, sympathetic biography, Allen's study provides a comprehensive view of Emerson that locates him solidly in his cultural and intellectual milieu.

McAleer, John. *Ralph Waldo Emerson: Days of Encounter*. Boston: Little, Brown, 1984. 748pp. Looking at the significant events and people in Emerson's life in a series of brief, factually authoritative chapters, McAleer achieves an intimate portrait, bringing his reader closer to Emerson the man and thinker and his relationships than other biographical approaches.

Richardson, Robert D. *Emerson: The Mind on Fire*. Berkeley: University of California Press, 1995. 671pp. Richardson's clear and detailed intel-

lectual biography traces the development of Emerson's ideas and character and captures the varied aspects of Emerson's emotional life against a solid background of influences.

Rusk, Ralph L. *The Life of Ralph Waldo Emerson*. New York: Scribner, 1949. 592pp. Regarded as the standard source for details on Emerson's life by the editor of Emerson's letters. Without attempting a critical assessment of Emerson as a thinker or a writer, Rusk binds himself to the documented record, and readers interested in a more interpretive approach should supplement Rusk's study with those of Allen, McAleer, and Richardson.

Other Biographical Studies

Baker, Carlos. *Emerson Among the Eccentrics: A Group Portrait*. New York: Viking, 1996. 608pp. Baker's group portrait of the circle Emerson gathered around him in Concord from the 1830s to the 1870s. Vivid and rich in biographical detail, Baker's account fully illuminates Emerson's era and intellectual background.

Barish, Evelyn. *Emerson: The Roots of Prophecy*. Princeton, New Jersey: Princeton University Press, 1990. 267pp. Barish's intellectual biography examines Emerson's early years establishing a vivid portrait of American society of the period and the writer's family background while shedding new light on several aspects of Emerson's formative years.

Brooks, Van Wyck. *The Life of Emerson*. New York: Dutton, 1932. 315pp. Considered in its time a masterpiece of biographical writing, Brooks's devotional life sets Emerson fully against the backdrop of his times. Less critical than later treatments, Brooks's classic study helped establish Emerson's intellectual importance and remains a valuable cultural study.

Cabot, James E. *A Memoir of Ralph Waldo Emerson*. Boston: Houghton Mifflin, 1887. 2 vols. Cabot's authorized life remained the standard account until Rusk's biography, which superseded it.

Holmes, Oliver Wendall. *Ralph Waldo Emerson*. 1885. Reprint ed. New York: Chelsea House, 1980. 441pp. In the best of the early appreciative studies by an acquaintance, Holmes's book provides an insider's view on Emerson's background along with sensible insights on Emerson's ideas and impact.

Porte, Joel. *Representative Man: Ralph Waldo Emerson in His Time*. New York: Oxford University Press, 1979. 361pp. Less a biography of the man than of his ideas, Porte traces Emerson's development as a writer and thinker through a series of close textual analyses, collectively forming a narrative of Emerson's intellectual life.

Yannella, Donald. *Ralph Waldo Emerson*. Boston: Twayne, 1982. 147pp. This concise critical introduction to Emerson's life and ideas will be useful to undergraduates as well as general readers, particularly for its succinct analysis of the transcendentalist movement.

Fictional Portraits

Carlisle, Henry. *The Jonah Man*. New York: Knopf, 1984. 260pp. The captain of the whaling ship *Essex* narrates the story of his life as a survivor of a shipwreck when his ship is struck and sunk by a sperm whale in the Pacific. Based on an actual event, the novel speculates on the captain's subsequent life with an appearance by Emerson.

Colver, Anne. *Listen for the Voices.* New York: Farrar & Rinehart, 1939. 387pp. Life in Concord is depicted as a group of fictional characters interact with Emerson and Thoreau.

Fried, Albert. *The Prescott Chronicles.* New York: Putnam, 1976. 412pp. The panorama of American history is dramatized through the story of Prescott family from the American Revolution, through the Civil War, to modern times with appearances by a number of historical figures, including Emerson.

Recommended Juvenile Biographies

Derleth, August. *Emerson, Our Contemporary.* New York: Crowell-Collier, 1970. 168pp. YA. Using selections from Emerson's journals, essays, letters, and poetry, Derleth provides a solid critical introduction to the man and his ideas.

Wood, James P. *Trust Thyself: A Life of Ralph Waldo Emerson for the Young Reader.* New York: Pantheon, 1964. 182pp. YA. Wood's narrative biography captures the inner drama of Emerson's life, along with a detailed examination of his major works and the people and events that affected him.

Other Sources

Von Frank, Albert J. *An Emerson Chronology.* New York: Maxwell Macmillan, 1994. 569pp. This reference guide is a helpful tool to locate Emerson's activities on virtually a daily basis.

163. DESIDERIUS ERASMUS
ca. 1466–1536

Dutch Roman Catholic priest, humanist, and foremost scholar of his time. Erasmus was an advocate of church and social reform and an opponent of Scholastic theology. He produced the first critical edition of the Greek New Testament (1516) and paved the way for the Reformation with his famous *In Praise of Folly* (1509). Although eager for reform, he came into bitter conflict with Martin Lu-

ther, whose position on predestination he attacked in *On the Freedom of the Will* (1524).

Autobiography and Primary Sources

Erasmus's letters are a rich and invaluable source of biographical details and insights into Erasmus's character and ideas. *The Correspondence of Erasmus.* R.A.B. Mynors and D.F.S. Thomson, eds. (Toronto: University of Toronto Press, 1974–1999. 11 vols.) is the scholarly edition.

Erasmus and His Age: Selected Letters of Desiderius Erasmus. Hans J. Hillerbrand, ed. (New York: Harper & Row, 1970. 305pp.) provides a valuable selection of the most representative and revealing of his letters.

Recommended Biographies

Augustijn, Cornelius. *Erasmus: His Life, Works, and Influence.* Toronto: University of Toronto Press, 1991. 239pp. The author offers a reevaluation of Erasmus's life, writings, and impact drawing on recent scholarship. An informative intellectual biography, Erasmus's life and ideas are viewed in the wider context of his times.

Halkin, Léon-E. *Erasmus: A Critical Biography.* Cambridge, Massachusetts: Blackwell, 1993. 360pp. Both a biography and a study of Erasmus's works, the author relies on extensive excerpts from Erasmus's writings to present his ideas on philosophical, ethical, and theological topics. The book succeeds in providing a revealing portrait of Erasmus's personality in an accessible, reliable study.

Schoeck, Richard J. *Erasmus of Europe: The Making of a Humanist, 1467–1500.* New York: Barnes and Noble, 1990. 311pp. Schoeck's is the most detailed and authoritative study of Erasmus's formative years, describing his development through his schooling and first trip to England. This is the first part of a proposed two-volume life, which when completed, will likely become the modern definitive biography.

Other Biographical Studies

Bainton, Roland. *Erasmus of Christendom.* New York: Scribner, 1969. 308pp. An expansion of lectures delivered at the Princeton Theological Semi-

nary, Bainton's vivid and dramatic account helps to animate the man and his times in an accessible, though scholarly, reliable study.

Hyma, Albert. *The Life of Desiderius Erasmus.* Assen, The Netherlands: Van Gorcum, 1972. 140pp. Hyma's is a condensed overview of the highlights of Erasmus's life and works.

McConica, James. *Erasmus.* New York: Oxford University Press, 1991. 106pp. In a stimulating introduction to Erasmus's ideas and works, the author traces the major stages of Erasmus's career.

Smith, Preserved. *Erasmus: A Study of His Life, Ideals, and Place in History.* New York: Harper, 1923. 479pp. Smith's is a learned and still useful interpretive study that examines Erasmus's life, influences, ideas, and writings in his contemporary context and impact on the Reformation and humanism.

Sowards, J. Kelley. *Desiderius Erasmus.* Boston: Twayne, 1975. 152pp. More a literary study than a biographical account, Sowards deals with several categories of Erasmus's writings, including his satirical, devotional works, and philosophical and theological writings, touching on the events of Erasmus's life as they affected his literary career.

Fictional Portraits

Ozment, Steven. *The Bürgermeister's Daughter.* New York: St. Martin's, 1996. 227pp. The novel imagines an affair between a merchant's daughter and Erasmus.

Reade, Charles. *The Cloister and the Hearth.* 1861. Reprint ed. New York: Dutton, 1906. 703pp. Reade's classic historical romance blends invention with details from Erasmus's background and family life in a vivid presentation of fifteenth-century European life.

Recommended Juvenile Biographies

Mee, Charles L. *Erasmus: The Eye of the Hurricane.* New York: Coward-McCann, 1973. 128pp. YA. In a clear and readable account, Mee contrasts Erasmus's ideas with those of the established church and Luther's positions, setting Erasmus clearly in his historical and intellectual context.

F

164. WILLIAM FAULKNER
1897–1962

Recipient of the 1949 Nobel Prize in Literature, Faulkner is one of the great American writers of the twentieth century. Born in Mississippi, he trained as an RAF pilot in Canada (1918) and attended the University of Mississippi (1919–1920). His first book was *The Marble Faun* (1924), a collection of poems. Most of his novels are set in fictional Yoknapatawpha county, a microcosm of a decaying South in which traditional values and authority have slowly dissolved since the Civil War. His best-known novels include *The Sound and the Fury* (1929), *As I Lay Dying* (1930), *Sanctuary* (1931), *Light in August* (1932), *Absalom, Absalom!* (1936), and *Intruder in the Dust* (1948).

Autobiography and Primary Sources

Selected Letters of William Faulkner. Joseph Blotner, ed. New York: Random House, 1977. 488pp. This collection provides an intimate view of Faulkner's relationship with his family, his creative process, and his reflections on his craft.

Thinking of Home: William Faulkner's Letters to His Mother and Father, 1918–1925. James G. Watson, ed. New York: W.W. Norton, 1992. 253pp. Collects Faulkner's letters home during his formative years.

Recommended Biographies

Blotner, Joseph. *Faulkner: A Biography.* New York: Random House, 1974. 2 vols. Considered the definitive life, Blotner's exhaustive authorized study by a close friend of Faulkner attempts to demonstrate that the novelist's works derived from particular people, places, and events in his life, which he carefully documents. Faulkner emerges in full beneath a mountain of data that will likely remain the standard source for biographical details for some time to come. A condensed single-volume edition is available (New York: Random House, 1984. 777pp.).

Karl, Frederick R. *William Faulkner: American Writer.* New York: Weidenfeld and Nicolson, 1989. 1,131pp. Providing a more candid and more complex, psychologically richer portrait of Faulkner than Blotner's more circumspect, factual treat-

ment, Karl places the writer solidly in the modernist tradition and reveals a deeply conflicted man torn between innovation in his work and his love for the Southern past and tradition. Penetrating in its insights, Karl's biography offers the interpretation that Blotner often fails to provide.

Minter, David. *William Faulkner: His Life and Work.* Baltimore: Johns Hopkins University Press, 1980. 325pp. Regarded by many as the best-single volume critical study of Faulkner's life and works available, Minter's book provides no new information and depends on Blotner for its details, but the treatment is more tightly focused and will appeal to the reader without the patience for either Blotner or Karl's more exhaustive studies.

Other Biographical Studies

Coughlan, Robert. *The Private World of William Faulkner.* New York: Harper, 1954. 151pp. This journalistic account offers a sketch of the highlights of Faulkner's background, regional influences, and daily life for a general audience.

Faulkner, John. *My Brother Bill: An Affectionate Reminiscence.* New York: Trident Press, 1963. 277pp. His younger brother's reminiscences provides some firsthand views of Faulkner and his family but contains factual errors.

Gray, Richard. *The Life of William Faulkner: A Critical Biography.* Cambridge, Massachusetts: Blackwell. 1996. 448pp. Gray's critical study of the novelist features a substantial examination of his fiction from the perspective of Bakhtin's theories. Somewhat misnamed as a biography, the book looks chronologically at Faulkner's works and refers to his life to help illuminate them.

Oates, Stephen B. *William Faulkner: The Man and the Artist.* New York: Harper & Row, 1987. 363pp. Oates's comprehensive biography for a general reader is dependent on Blotner for his details and provides a sympathetic yet somewhat romanticized and sensationalized narrative of Faulkner's life with concise summaries of the major fiction, helpful for a new reader. Dramatic and highly readable, Oates will appeal to reader anxious for a narrative summary of Blotner's facts or a resolution of Karl's many revealed contradictions, but Oates sacrifices a good deal of complexity in pursuit of Faulkner's essence.

Singal, Daniel J. *William Faulkner: The Making of a Modernist.* Chapel Hill: University of North Carolina Press, 1997. 376pp. Singal's critical and intellectual biography focuses on the formation of Faulkner's ideas and artistry shaped by the cultural conflicts in his background. Providing a number of new insights and interpretations, Singal is persuasive in his handling of biographical details and criticism of the works.

Williamson, Joel. *William Faulkner and Southern History.* New York: Oxford University Press, 1993. 509pp. Connecting Faulkner's themes with his southern background, Williamson's critical study is useful in providing an intellectual and cultural context for viewing Faulkner's character formation and artistry.

Wittenberg, Judith B. *Faulkner: The Transfiguration of Biography.* Lincoln: University of Nebraska Press, 1979. 264pp. Wittenberg's literary and psychological biography chronologically analyzes Faulkner's fiction and their connection to his developing ideas and character. The book is useful in demonstrating the personal basis of his writing.

Fictional Portraits

Kaminsky, Stuart M. *Never Cross a Vampire.* New York: St. Martin's, 1980. 182pp. Faulkner in Hollywood is glimpsed in this installment of the author's period mystery series set in 1942 as private eye Toby Peters attempts to clear the novelist from a charge of murder.

Roosevelt, Elliott. *Murder in the Executive Mansion.* New York: St. Martin's,1995. 197pp. Faulkner makes an appearance in the author's historical mystery series with Eleanor Roosevelt as his principal sleuth.

Biographical Films and Theatrical Adaptations

William Faulkner (1979). Director: Robert Squier. Documentary film on Faulkner's life and works. Video.

Other Sources

Cox, Leland H. *William Faulkner: A Biographical and Reference Guide.* Detroit, Michigan: Gale Research, 1983. 308pp. Cox supplies a brief biographical profile, followed by a critical introduction to all of Faulkner's works.

Gresset, Michel. *A Faulkner Chronology.* Jackson: University Press of Mississippi, 1985. 120pp. Grosset tracks Faulkner's activities minutely based on a careful review of documentary sources. Interspersed are mini-essays on various aspects of Faulkner's character.

Hamblin, Robert W., and Charles A. Peek, eds. *A William Faulkner Encyclopedia.* Westport, Connecticut: Greenwood, 1999. 375pp. Alphabetical entries cover every aspect of Faulkner's works, characters, themes, and biographical details.

165. HENRY FIELDING
1707–1754

English novelist and dramatist, Fielding studied law and after settling (1729) in London began writing comedies, farces, and burlesques. He abandoned the stage and began writing novels after his *The Historical Register for 1736* (1737), which attacked the Walpole government, resulted in theatre censorship under the Licensing Act of 1737. His works include *Joseph Andrews* (1742) and *Tom Jones* (1749), one of the most renowned novels in English literature. Fielding became a magistrate in 1748 and helped organize the Bow Street Runners, an early police force.

Autobiography and Primary Sources

The Correspondence of Henry and Sarah Fielding. Martin C. Battestin and Clive T. Probyn, eds. New York: Oxford University Press, 1993. 207pp. What little survives of Fielding's personal writings is collected in this scholarly edition of the writer's 70 letters along with 30 letters from his favorite sister. In the words of its editors the volume allows the reader to come nearer to knowing both Fieldings "as their close friends and acquantances knew them." Readers can also get a sense of the man from his two travel narratives, *A Journey from This World to the Next* (1745) and *The Journal of a Voyage to Lisbon* (1755) (Reprint ed. New York: Oxford University Press, 1997. 242pp.).

Recommended Biographies

Battestin, Martin C., and Ruth Battestin. *Henry Fielding: A Life.* New York: Routledge, 1989. 738pp. Superseding all previous lives of Fielding and firmly established as the modern standard, this excellent biography offers a wealth of new information from previously untapped primary sources that creates a rounded and complex portrait of the private and public man.

Pagliaro, Harold E. *Henry Fielding: A Literary Life.* New York: St. Martin's, 1998. 237pp. This is a succinct, often revealing exploration of Fielding's professional and personal life that draws the connections between the two. Synthesizing modern scholarship, the book is an ideal introductory study for the general reader and undergraduate.

Thomas, Donald S. *Henry Fielding.* New York: St. Martin's, 1991. 436pp. Positioned between the Battestins' monumental life and Pagliaro's helpful

overview, Thomas's is a thorough, readable biography that is not as scholarly exact as the former nor as selective as the latter.

Other Biographical Studies

Cross, Wilbur L. *The History of Henry Fielding.* New Haven, Connecticut: Yale University Press, 1918. 3 vols. Cross's extensive multivolume life served until fairly recently as the standard biographical source on Fielding. Many of Cross's interpretations of the man and his era have been called into question by more recent scholarship.

Dobson, Austin. *Fielding.* 1883. Reprint ed. New York: AMS Press, 1968. 205pp. Dobson's is the first, generally reliable, full-length biography, serving today primarily a historical interest in displaying the view of the author during the Victorian period.

Dudden, F. Homes. *Henry Fielding: His Life, Works, and Times.* 1952. Reprint ed. Hamden, Connecticut: Archon Books, 1966. 2 vols. Attempting to do too much, covering the life, times, and works, Dudden's leisurely and discursive study winds up doing too little, offering few new insights and so wide a focus and a mountain of minutiae that the man eludes the author's grasp.

Hume, Robert D. *Henry Fielding and the London Theatre 1728-37.* New York: Oxford University Press, 1988. 304pp. Hume's is an important study of Fielding's career as a dramatist, supplying a year-by-year documentation of Fielding's stage successes before the Licensing Act of 1737. The author challenges the conventional wisdom that Fielding's turn from the stage to the novel was a gain rather than a loss for English literature.

Jenkins, Elizabeth. *Henry Fielding.* Denver: A. Swallow, 1948. 101pp. More a biographical sketch than a full portrait, Jenkins offers a readable, compressed, popular overview of the author's career as a playwright and novelist.

Jones, Benjamin M. *Henry Fielding, Novelist and Magistrate.* London: Allen and Unwin, 1933. 255pp. Jones supplied important new information about Fielding's career as a magistrate that has been integrated into later biographical studies.

Rogers, Pat. *Henry Fielding: A Biography.* New York: Scribner, 1979. 237pp. Rogers's often breezy and vivid dash through the highlights of Fielding's life and career is intended as a popular brief account for the general reader, and it succeeds on those terms. The unsatisfied reader will want to check the author's often unsupported opinions and sketchy historical background using more thorough accounts.

Fictional Portraits

Bosse, Malcolm J. *The Vast Memory of Love.* New York: Ticknor Fields, 1992. 482pp. The novel creates journal entries from 1753 by Fielding who records the plight of the poor and the criminal underworld.

Creasey, John. *The Masters of Bow Street.* New York: Simon & Schuster, 1974. 507pp. Fielding's involvement with the creation of the first professional police force in London is portrayed in a convincing portrait of the period.

166. F. SCOTT FITZGERALD
1896–1940

Fitzgerald is ranked among the great novelists and short-story writers of the twentieth century and is considered the literary explicator of the postwar 1920s "Jazz Age" era. Born of middle-class parents, he attended private schools and Princeton University before joining the army. He and his wife, Zelda, were notorious for their madcap lifestyle and after moving to Paris became part of a group of celebrated literary and artistic expatriates. His novels explore moral and financial dissipation, corruption, and disillusionment and include *This Side of Paradise* (1920), *The Beautiful and the Damned* (1922), *The Great Gatsby* (1925), and *Tender is the Night* (1934). His last years were spent as a Hollywood scriptwriter; he died leaving unfinished *The Last Tycoon*, a novel about the film industry, published in 1941.

Autobiography and Primary Sources

The Crack Up. Edmund Wilson, ed. New York: New Directions, 1945. 347pp. Collects a number of Fitzgerald's autobiographical essays written in the 1930s as well as his notebook of thoughts for future writing, and selected letters.

F. Scott Fitzgerald: A Life in Letters. Matthew J. Bruccoli, ed. New York: Scribner, 1994. 503pp. This collection of 428 letters grouped in chronological divisions from 1907 to 1940 with a brief biographical essay for each forms a revealing autobiographical portrait.

The Romantic Egoists: A Pictorial Autobiography from the Scrapbook and Album of F. Scott and Zelda Fitzgerald. New York: Scribner, 1974. 246pp. This oversized volume is made up of postcards, letters, clippings, and reviews from the seven scrapbooks and five photo albums kept by the Fitzgeralds, documenting their lives and travels. The result is a fascinating and often moving look at Scott and Zelda's lives from the mementoes that they preserved.

Recommended Biographies

Bruccoli, Matthew J. *Some Sort of Epic Grandeur.* New York: Harcourt, Brace, 1981. 624pp. Bruccoli, the recognized expert on Fitzgerald's texts, has written the most complete factual record with restrained and reliable interpretation based on solid documentation. Regarded as the standard reference source, though his method of accumulating data is at times tiresome and far more than the casual, general reader will want to know.

Meyers, Jeffrey. *Scott Fitzgerald: A Biography.* New York: HarperCollins, 1994. 400pp. Meyers's literary biography features some fresh material to form a brutally honest portrait of a genius forced by circumstances and temperament to squander his talent. Meyers provides evidence of Fitzgerald's weaknesses and strengths in a multi-dimensional character study.

Other Biographical Studies

Donaldson, Scott. *Fool for Love.* New York: Congdon and Weed, 1983. 262pp. In the author's view the key to understanding Fitzgerald is his lifelong inferiority complex, which led to an obsessive need to please and his disgust at his behavior. Donaldson traces this theme in Fitzgerald's various relationships in a credible personality portrait.

Latham, Aaron. *Crazy Sundays: F. Scott Fitzgerald in Hollywood.* New York: Viking, 1971. 308pp. Latham's sometimes disjointed examination of Fitzgerald's Hollywood years collects a number of anecdotes and analyzes the writer's work on various scripts.

Le Vot, André. *F. Scott Fitzgerald: A Biography.* Garden City, New York: Doubleday, 1983. 393pp. Written by a French scholar, the book is best on the French background to Fitzgerald's life and the connection between his personal experiences and his works.

Mayfield, Sara. *Exiles from Paradise: Zelda and Scott Fitzgerald.* New York: Delacorte, 1971. 309pp. Written by a lifelong friend of the couple who grew up with Zelda in Montgomery, Alabama, and based on personal recollections and research, this study of the couple's relationship contradicts previously published contentions, including the extent of Zelda's madness. In Mayfield's partisan view, Scott is mainly responsible for Zelda's decline.

Mellow, James R. *Invented Lives: F. Scott and Zelda Fitzgerald.* Boston: Houghton Mifflin, 1984. 569pp. In one of the most comprehensive studies of Fitzgerald's private life and relationship with Zelda, Mellow carefully documents the less attractive side of husband and wife with a penetrating psychological interpretation of both.

Milford, Nancy. *Zelda: A Biography.* New York: Harper & Row, 1970. 424pp. The most comprehensive and reliable full-length portrait of Zelda Fitzgerald based on extensive interviews. Milford challenges the glamour surrounding the Fitzgeralds to trace the progress of their self-destruction.

Mizener, Arthur. *The Far Side of Paradise: A Biography of F. Scott Fitzgerald.* Boston: Houghton Mifflin, 1951. 362pp. With access to significant Fitzgerald papers and interviews with his daughter and friends, this first full-length biography has now been superseded by later studies that better succeed in untangling the facts from the legends surrounding the writer. In *Scott Fitzgerald and His World* (New York: Putnam, 1972. 128pp.) photographs are supplemented by a brief biographical summary of the highlights of Fitzgerald's career.

Piper, Henry D. *F. Scott Fitzgerald: A Critical Portrait.* New York: Holt, 1965. 334pp. Piper's critical study is recommended for its factually reliable tracing of the sources for Fitzgerald's fiction and its portrait of the artist at work.

Sklar, Robert. *F. Scott Fitzgerald: The Last Laocoön.* New York: Oxford University Press, 1967. 376pp. This critical study of the man and the artist documents Fitzgerald's intellectual development and artistic process.

Turnbull, Andrew. *Scott Fitzgerald.* New York: Scribner, 1962. 364pp. Turnbull's biographical memoir based on the author's personal association with the author and interviews with others who knew him concentrates on Fitzgerald's personality

in a readable but incomplete narrative that at times represents Fitzgerald's questionable recollections as factual.

Biographical Novels

Zuckerman, George. *The Last Flapper.* Boston: Little, Brown, 1969. 439pp. The married life of Scott and Zelda is dramatized in this novel that relies on the biography but does invent dialogue and situations.

Fictional Portraits

Aldridge, James. *One Last Glimpse.* Boston: Little, Brown, 1977. 182pp. The Hemingway-Fitzgerald relationship is dramatized in this novel involving the pair on a motor tour of Brittany. The situation is invented but the dynamics of the writers' rivalry are based on fact.

Schulberg, Budd. *The Disenchanted.* New York: Knopf, 1950. 388pp. Schulberg's novel is based loosely on Fitzgerald's life in Hollywood.

Recommended Juvenile Biographies

Greenfeld, Howard. *F. Scott Fitzgerald.* New York: Crown, 1974. 136pp. YA. Greenfeld's is a useful critical introduction to Fitzgerald's writing that connects his works to his experiences.

Stewart, Gale B. *F.: The Importance of Scott Fitzgerald.* San Diego, California: Lucent Books, 1999. 128pp. Stewart summarizes the important events in Fitzgerald's life with an emphasis on his significance as a recorder of his era.

Biographical Films and Theatrical Adaptations

A&E Biography Video: F. Scott Fitzgerald: The Great American Dreamer (1997). Producer: Deirdre O'Hearn. Using interviews with family members and associates, this documentary chronicles Fitzgerald's life with literary appreciations by writers Tobias Wolff and Joseph Heller. Video.

Beloved Infidel (1959). Director: Henry King. Based on Sheilah Graham's romanticized account of her relationship with Fitzgerald, Gregory Peck portrays the novelist and Deborah Kerr plays a noble Graham coping with Fitzgerald's drinking and self-destruction. Neither star is convincing in their roles. Video.

F. Scott Fitzgerald: A Concise Biography (1995). Director: Malcolm Hossick. Brief but informative documentary look at Fitzgerald's life and career. Video.

F. Scott Fitzgerald and "The Last of the Belles" (1974). Director: George Schaeffer. Richard Chamberlain stars as the writer and Blythe Danner plays Zelda in the story of their courtship while Fitzgerald writes "The Last of the Belles," which is performed by Susan Sarandon and David Huffman. Video.

F. Scott Fitzgerald in Hollywood (1976). Director: Anthony Page. Made-for-television drama of Fitzgerald's Hollywood career. Jason Miller portrays Fitzgerald with Tuesday Weld as Zelda and Julia Foster as Sheilah Graham. Weld is the standout here for her performance as the fallen Zelda. Video.

F. Scott Fitzgerald: One Fine Morning (1995). Director: Sharon Leone. Presents a portrait of the writer, including critical comments and readings from several of his works and an interview with his granddaughter. Written by literary critic A. Walton Litz. Video.

Other Sources

Gale, Robert L. *An F. Scott Fitzgerald Encyclopedia.* Westport, Connecticut: Greenwood, 1998. 526pp. A reference source with alphabetically arranged entries for Fitzgerald's works, characters, family, and associates.

Tate, Mary Jo, and Matthew J. Bruccoli. *F. Scott Fitzgerald A to Z: The Essential Reference to His Life and Work.* New York: Facts on File, 1998. 340pp. Along with a detailed chronology, list of publications, and a full bibliography, the book alphabetically collects characters, people, and places in Fitzgerald's fiction and life.

167. GUSTAVE FLAUBERT
1821–1880

One of the best-known French novelists of all time and a master of the realistic novel, Flaubert was the son of a surgeon. Possessed of a sensitive and nervous disposition, he studied law unsuccessfully in Paris and returned home to devote himself to writing. For most of his life he lived with his mother and niece at Croisset, near Rouen. After five years of work, *Madame Bovary* was published in a Paris journal (1856). The novel, a masterpiece of controlled style, portrays the frustrations and love affairs of a romantic woman wed to a dull provincial doctor. The novel proved notorious, and Flaubert was prosecuted for immorality but won the case.

Autobiography and Primary Sources

The Letters of Gustave Flaubert. Francis Steegmuller, ed. Cambridge, Massachusetts: Harvard University Press, 1980–1982. 2 vols; *The Selected Letters of Gustave Flaubert.* Francis Steegmuller, ed. New York: Farrar, Straus, 1954. 281pp. Flaubert's remarkable letters are essential biographical sources and reveal various aspects of his character and artistic development.

Recommended Biographies

Bart, Benjamin F. *Flaubert.* Syracuse, New York: Syracuse University Press, 1967. 791pp. Fusing Flaubert's correspondence and new documentary sources into a unified, thorough narrative, Bart's reliable critical study comes closest to a definitive treatment of the novelist's life, career, and work. Scrupulously detailed to correct previous errors, Bart's book remains the authoritative source for biographical information.

Lottman, Herbert. *Flaubert: A Biography.* Boston: Little, Brown, 1989. 396pp. Lottman's sound, factual narrative will appeal more to the general reader than Bart's more scholarly examination. Richly informative and careful in setting the factual record straight, Lottman rarely ventures into interpretation, which results in a failure at times to connect the various sides of Flaubert's complex character.

Other Biographical Studies

Nadeau, Maurice. *The Greatness of Flaubert.* New York: Library Press, 1972. 307pp. Written by the editor of Flaubert's complete works, this is a descriptive rather than a critical biography with a factual, commonsensical viewpoint that achieves an intimate portrayal of Flaubert's life and character.

Sartre, Jean-Paul. *The Family Idiot: Gustave Flaubert 1821–1857.* Chicago: University of Chicago Press, 1981–1991. 4 vols. Sartre's remarkable, monumental 20-year effort to probe the enigma of Flaubert's character and the origins of his genius covers only half of Flaubert's life and was unfinished at the time of Sartre's death. Microscopic in its study of evidence, the conclusions Sartre reaches are often brilliant. More a meditation than a comprehensive biography, the book reveals as much about Sartre as Flaubert.

Shanks, Lewis P. *Flaubert's Youth, 1821–1845.* Baltimore: Johns Hopkins University Press, 1927. 250pp. Based on Flaubert's letters, juvenilia, and travel notes, Shanks documents the formative years of the novelist, though the book's scholarly usefulness has been superseded by later books drawing on more recently uncovered documentary sources.

Spencer, Philip. *Flaubert: A Biography.* New York: Grove Press, 1952. 268pp. Spencer's sympathetic and well-rounded portrait of Flaubert as a contradictory and tormented figure remains valid and insightful, despite many of its findings now superseded by new sources uncovered in the 1960s.

Starkie, Enid. *Flaubert: The Making of the Master.* New York: Atheneum, 1967. 403pp.; *Flaubert the Master: A Critical and Biographical Study.* New York: Atheneum, 1971. 390pp. Starkie, the masterful author of important biographical studies of Baudelaire, Rimbaud, and Gide, provides an excellent critical study of Flaubert's life and works, though ill health prevented this work from rising to the level of her earlier books. The first volume considers the novelist's life up to the publication of *Madame Bovary* ; the second his later career to his death. Sound in its judgments and rich in biographical details, the two volumes are important contributions to Flaubert studies.

Steegmuller, Francis. *Flaubert and Madame Bovary: A Double Portrait.* 1939. Revised ed. Chicago: University of Chicago Press, 1977. 374pp. Steegmuller's critical biography examines Flaubert's youth up to the inception and development of *Madame Bovary* and is recommended for its thorough analysis of the novelist's artistic process in producing his masterpiece.

Troyat, Henri. *Flaubert.* New York: Viking, 1992. 374pp. Troyat's readable, appreciative biography joins the various threads in Flaubert's life and character into a comprehensive, sensible pattern that will appeal to the general reader.

Fictional Portraits

Barnes, Julian. *Flaubert's Parrot.* New York: Vintage, 1990. 190pp. Part biography, part fiction and literary criticism, Barnes's novel concerns an English doctor's obsession with the novelist whose life converges with that of Flaubert.

Biographical Films and Theatrical Adaptations

Madame Bovary (1949). Director: Vincente Minnelli. The frame for this Hollywood version of Flaubert's classic novel is the novelist himself on trial for writing an indecent book. He narrates the story to prove his innocence. James Mason portrays Flaubert with Jennifer Jones and Van Heflin as Emma and Charles Bovary. Video.

168. HENRY FORD
1863–1947

America's pioneer automobile manufacturer, whose name became synonymous with mass production, Ford was born in Dearborn, Michigan, and left his father's farm to apprentice in a Detroit machine shop. He experimented on power-driven vehicles while working as a machinist and engineer with the Edison Company, and in 1892 completed his first car. After forming the Ford Motor Company in 1903, he adapted the conveyor belt and assembly line to automobile production, and in 1908 brought out the Model T, the first inexpensive, standardized car. Ford went on to produce vehicles and war materiel for the armed forces during both world wars. He was an advocate of employee profit-sharing, a staunch opponent of labor unions, an anti-Semite, and a poor company manager, who jeopardized his business and encouraged competition by failing to introduce new models in the face of consumer demand.

Autobiography and Primary Sources

My Life and Work. Garden City, New York: Doubleday, 1922. 289pp. Dictated to writer Samuel Crowther, Ford's autobiographical reflections cover the beginning of his career as a mechanic, his obsession with the concept of the automobile, and business principles. Factually unreliable, the book should be read with caution for biographical details. Two other volumes of memoirs allegedly the work of Ford himself—*Today and Tomorrow* (1926) and *Moving Forward* (1931)—are the creations of Crowther and offer few insights.

Recommended Biographies

Gelderman, Carol. *Henry Ford: The Wayward Capitalist.* New York: Dial Press, 1981. 463pp. Based on archival material uncovered since Nevins and Hill, this study of the development of the Ford Motor Company and the personality of its founder documents the inconsistencies in Ford's personality but allows the reader the final judgment on the questions of Ford's strengths and shortcomings.

Nevins, Allan, and Frank E. Hill. *Ford: The Times, the Man, the Company.* New York: Scribner, 1954. 688pp.; *Ford: Expansion and Challenge 1915-33.* New York: Scribner, 1957. 714pp; *Ford: Decline and Rebirth 1933-62.* New York: Scribner, 1963. 508pp. This three-volume study remains the most authoritative examination of Ford the man, the development of the automobile, and the Ford Motor Company. Based on extensive research, the authors set Ford's biography and the story of the company he founded against a clear cultural and historical background.

Other Biographical Studies

Brough, James. *The Ford Dynasty: An American Story.* Garden City, New York: Doubleday, 1977. 352pp. This popular, readable account centers on the lives of the three Fords who headed the Ford Motor Company—Henry, Edsel, and Henry Ford II. A loosely connected series of incidents chosen for their drama, the book veers toward sensationalism rather than careful documentation.

Burlingame, Roger. *Henry Ford: A Great Life in Brief.* New York: Knopf, 1955. 194pp. Written by an expert in mass production, this concise and balanced account of Ford's career avoids either adulation or debunking to form a reliable character study for a general audience.

Collier, Peter, and David Horowitz. *The Fords: An American Epic.* New York: Simon & Schuster, 1987. 496pp. This revisionist group biography of the Ford family focuses on the limits of power and the human weaknesses of the Fords. Told with a novelistic flair, anecdotes help raise Henry II while lowering Henry I.

Garrett, Garet. *The Wild Wheel: The World of Henry Ford.* New York: Pantheon, 1952. 220pp. Garrett's episodic account of Ford's business career is often repetitive and disorganized but serves as a character sketch of the personality behind the legend.

Herndon, Booton. *Ford: An Unconventional Biography of the Men and Their Times.* New York: Weybright and Talley, 1969. 408pp. Herndon's often gossipy account of Ford and his grandson was written with the cooperation of the Ford Motor Company and based on interviews with company officials and Ford associates. The emphases here are Ford's various roles as husband, father, and public figure.

Jardim, Anne. *The First Henry Ford: A Study in Personality and Business Leadership.* Cambridge, Massachusetts: MIT Press, 1970. 278pp. The author's psychobiography attempts to explain Ford's character and actions from a decidedly Freudian slant

Lacey, Robert. *Ford: The Men and the Machines.* Boston: Little, Brown, 1986. 778pp. The first half covers Ford's life and career; the second half considers the Ford family and their business. The Ford clan is depicted as strong-willed but emotionally suppressed in a vivid, dramatic portrait of family dynamics.

Marquis, Samuel S. *Henry Ford: An Interpretation.* Boston: Little, Brown, 1923. 206pp. Written by the one-time head of Ford's sociology department, Marquis offers a candid psychological sketch based on close observation of a contradictory and often baffling personality whose considerable strengths were offset by weaknesses.

Olsen, Sidney. *Young Henry Ford: A Picture History of the First 40 Years.* Detroit: Wayne State University Press, 1963. 188pp. This illustrated biography assembles a visual record of Ford's formative years.

Richards, William C. *The Last Billionaire*. New York: Scribner, 1948. 422pp. Richards's adulatory portrait features anecdotes based on interviews with Ford's associates not found in other biographies.

Simonds, William A. *Henry Ford: His Life, His Work, His Genius*. Indianapolis: Bobbs-Merrill, 1943. 365pp. This full account of Ford's life, career, and character, based on personal knowledge and unique source material is uncritical and undocumented but useful for its details, particularly on Ford's early years.

Sorenson, Charles E., with Samuel T. Williamson. *My Forty Years with Ford*. New York: W.W. Norton, 1956. 319pp. In an autobiography written by a Ford Motor Company vice president, Sorenson provides an intimate and knowledgeable view of the inner dynamics of the company between 1904 and 1944.

Sward, Keith. *The Legend of Henry Ford*. New York: Rinehart, 1948. 550pp. Regarded as the first scholarly study of Ford, this is a highly critical examination of the discrepancy between Ford's beliefs and business and labor practices by a former public relations employee of the Congress of Industrial Organizations. This is the most detailed and substantive of the hostile attacks on Ford and his legacy, which include E.G. Pipp, *The Real Henry Ford* (1922), Jonathan N. Leonard, *The Tragedy of Henry Ford* (1932), and Upton Sinclair, *The Flivver King* (1937).

Fictional Portraits

Doctorow, E.L. *Ragtime*. New York: Random House, 1975. 270pp. Ford makes a memorable appearance in the novel at an imagined dinner hosted by J.P. Morgan.

McMahon, Thomas. *Loving Little Egypt*. New York: Viking, 1987. 273pp. In a comic fantasy, the novel dramatizes the adventures of a scientific prodigy who creates an underground telephone network for the blind and must contend with the scientific establishment. Ford also makes an appearance here.

Recommended Juvenile Biographies

Aird, Hazel B. *Henry Ford: Young Man with Ideas*. Indianapolis: Bobbs-Merrill, 1960. 192pp. MG. Part of a respected and popular series on the childhood of famous figures, the book dramatizes Ford's early, formative years.

Gourley, Catherine. *Wheels of Time: A Biography of Henry Ford*. Brookfield, Connecticut: Millbrook Press, 1997. 47pp. MG. Written by an associate of the Henry Ford Museum, this account of Ford's life is both accurate and engaging, featuring archival photographs and Ford quotes.

Harris, Jacqueline L. *Henry Ford*. New York: F. Watts, 1984. 116pp. MG. Harris offers an informative survey of Ford's life, personality, and achievement.

Biographical Films and Theatrical Adaptations

St. Germain, Mark. *Camping with Henry and Tom: A Play*. Garden City, New York: Fireside Theatre, 1995. 107pp. Based on the actual camping trip of Edison, Henry Ford, and President Warren Harding, this witty play imagines what might have transpired among the men as Ford vies to replace Harding as president.

A&E Biography Video: Henry Ford (1994). Producer: Peter Tarshis. This documentary look at Ford's life and career features archival photographs and recollections by associates. Video.

Ford: The Man and the Machine (1987). Director: Allan Eastman. Cliff Robertson plays Ford in a biographical film that chronicles his life and career from the invention of his first combustion engine–powered wagon to his death. Hope Lange stars as Clara Ford. Video.

Other Sources

Rae, John B., ed. *Henry Ford*. Englewood Cliffs, New Jersey: Prentice-Hall, 1969. 180pp. Rae's useful volume includes primary documents, contemporary reminiscences, and historical accounts for a multiple perspective on Ford and his legacy.

169. E.M. FORSTER
1879–1970

One of the most important British novelists of the twentieth century, Forster served with the International Red Cross in Egypt during World War I and was made an honorary fellow of King's College, Cambridge, where he lived until his death. Many of his novels have been made into films and include *Where Angels Fear to Tread* (1905), *A Room With a View* (1908), *Howard's End* (1910), and *A Passage to India* (1924). He received the Order of Merit in 1968.

Autobiography and Primary Sources

Commonplace Book. Philip Gardner, ed. Stanford: Stanford University Press, 1985. 372pp. Begun in 1926, Forster recorded his stray thoughts, observations, and comments in a "commonplace book" that serves as a valuable complement to his letters in tracking his interests, attitudes, and ideas for novels never attempted during the last half of his life.

Selected Letters of E.M. Forster. Mary Lago and P.N. Furbank, eds. Cambridge, Massachusetts: Harvard University Press, 1983–1985. 2 vols. In an expertly edited and indexed scholarly collection, Forster's relationships, literary and personal, as well as his character are revealed in 446 of the 15,000 extant letters.

Recommended Biographies

Beauman, Nicole. *E.M. Forster: A Biography*. New York: Knopf, 1994. 404pp. Beauman chooses to focus on Forster the novelist rather than the man, detailing the experiences that helped shape his imagination and creative genius. By emphasizing the work rather than the life, the opposite of the ap-

proach taken by Furbank, Beauman offers an interesting complement to the earlier biography.

Furbank, P.N. *E.M. Forster: A Life*. New York: Harcourt, Brace, 1977–1978. 2 vols. Furbank's authorized biography drawing on all the available diaries and correspondence and interviews with the writer is one of the standout literary biographies. Thorough, excellently detailed, and judicious in its assessment, Furbank's biography should remain the definitive study for some time to come.

Lago, Mary. *E.M. Forster: A Literary Life*. New York: St. Martin's, 1995. 170pp. The co-editor with Furbank of Forster's letters presents a concise summary of Forster's literary career and the literary, publishing, and social contexts that shaped his writing. Ably serves the general reader and student.

Other Biographical Studies

King, Francis H. *E.M. Forster and His World*. New York: Scribner, 1978. 128pp. King, who knew the novelist, supplies a brisk, reliable, and sympathetic survey of Forster's life in this pictorial biography.

McDowell, Frederick P.W. *E.M. Forster*. Boston: Twayne, 1982. 174pp. McDowell's is a useful critical study of the works with a succinct biographical summary that serves the general reader and the undergraduate as a solid introduction and overview.

Stone, Wilfred. *The Cave and the Mountain: A Study of E.M. Forster*. Stanford, California: Stanford University Press, 1966. 436pp. This study of the writer and his works is divided into an initial consideration of Forster's cultural, historical, intellectual, and personal background followed by an thoughtful examination of his writings.

Trilling, Lionel. *E.M. Forster: A Study*. Norfolk, Connecticut: New Directions, 1943. 192pp. Trilling's was a groundbreaking critical analysis of Forster's novels and ideas with some biographical material included.

Biographical Films and Theatrical Adaptations

E.M. Forster (1997). Producer: Bob Portway. Friends, biographers, and literary critics discuss Forster's life, works, and views with an emphasis on the parallels between his experiences and those portrayed in his novels. Video.

Other Sources

Stape, J.H., ed. *E.M. Forster: Interviews and Recollections*. New York: St. Martin's, 1993. 235pp. Consisting mainly of contemporary views of Forster, this volume sheds considerable light on various aspects of the writer's activities and character.

170. ANATOLE FRANCE
1844–1924

Born Jacques Anatole Thibault, novelist and critic Anatole France has been celebrated as a renowned stylist and was probably the most prominent French man of letters of his time. Among his best-known works are *Penguin Island* (1909) and *The*

Revolt of the Angels (1914). He was awarded the 1921 Nobel Prize in Literature.

Recommended Biographies

Axelrad, Jacob. *Anatole France: A Life without Illusions.* New York: Harper, 1944. 480pp. Despite new scholarship and sources, Axelrad's biography remains both the first and best full-length study of France's life currently available. The author's sympathy with his subject sometimes overbalances critical objectivity. As Albert Guerard commented in his review, "it is penetrating—with blind spots; and sympathetic—with jarring undertones.... It is not 'definitive.'"

Dargan, Edwin P. *Anatole France: 1844–96.* New York: Oxford University Press, 1937. 729pp. Although Dargan did not live to complete his projected two-volume life, this first volume is by far the best and most detailed authoritative presentation of France's life through his fifty-first year.

Tylden-Wright, David. *Anatole France.* New York: Walker, 1967. 344pp. The author provides some new information in a reevaluation of France's life and career. Tylden-Wright attempts to penetrate France's personality with much conjecture that limits the book's reliability, but the book offers a provocative interpretive approach.

Other Biographical Studies

Jefferson, Alfred C. *Anatole France: The Politics of Skepticism.* New Brunswick, New Jersey: Rutgers University Press, 1965. 294pp. Jefferson's study of France's political ideas is an important supplement to any complete view of the writer.

Virtanen, Reino. *Anatole France.* New York: Twayne, 1968. 183pp. Virtanen provides a solid account of France's literary career with details of his life to help explain his artistic and intellectual development. The book is a fine introductory overview intended for the undergraduate and the general reader.

Biographical Films and Theatrical Adaptations

The Life of Emile Zola (1937). Director: William Dieterle. Well-crafted biographical film on Zola's life with an impressive Paul Muni in the title role and an appearance by France, played by Morris Carnovsky. Video.

171. FRANCIS OF ASSISI
1181–1226

One of the best-known Christian saints, Francis was the son of a wealthy merchant. After serving as a soldier, he underwent a religious conversion and renounced his worldly life in favor of poverty, humility, love of nature, and devotion to others and to the Roman church. While a lay preacher, he founded the Franciscan order of friars. He eventually gave up leadership of the order but continued his sponsorship of Franciscan endeavors. In 1224 he was afflicted with wounds from the crucifixion of Christ after experiencing a vision. His is the first known and attested appearance of stigmata and the only one celebrated liturgical by the Church. He was canonized in 1228 by Pope Gregory IX, his patron and friend.

Autobiography and Primary Sources

St. Francis of Assisi: Writings and Early Biographies: English Omnibus of the Sources for the Life of St. Francis. Marion A. Habig, ed. Chicago: Franciscan Herald Press, 1977. 1,808pp. The most complete compilation of source documents on St. Francis, the volume provides translations of the earliest biographies by Thomas of Celano and St. Bonaventure, as well as all of Francis's own writings.

Recommended Biographies

Frugoni, Chiari. *Francis of Assisi.* New York: Continuum, 1998. 168pp. Written by a professor of medieval history at the University of Rome, this brief biographical study concentrates on Francis's psychological development, analyzing his motivations within his historical context. A useful introduction, Frugoni's examination portrays the saint in human terms, including both his great strengths and weaknesses.

Green, Julien. *God's Fool: The Life and Times of Francis of Assisi.* New York: Harper & Row, 1985. 273pp. Told in a series of sharply drawn vignettes, Green presents and interprets the known facts and legends of Francis's life in a sympathetic inquiry into the saint's nature. Truthful to Francis's history, the book also serves as a useful introduction to the saint's spirituality.

Maynard, Theodore. *Richest of the Poor: The Life of St. Francis of Assisi.* Garden City, New York: Doubleday, 1948. 255pp. Maynard's balanced portrait avoids sentimentality and attempts to distinguish between legend and historical fact. His account differs markedly from Sabatier's in asserting that the Franciscan ideal and the values of the church were not irreconcilable.

Sabatier, Paul. *Life of Saint Francis of Assisi.* New York: Scribner, 1894. 448pp. Sabatier's groundbreaking scholarly study remains an invaluable source for subsequent treatments of Francis's life, character, and times. A French protestant, Sabatier's attack on the Catholic Church in its dealings with Francis has been controversial and caused the book to be condemned by Rome. Despite a strong polemical flavor, Sabatier's masterful scholarship on Francis's time has yet to be superseded by later historical or biographical efforts.

Other Biographical Studies

Almedingen, E.M. *St. Francis of Assisi: A Great Life in Brief.* New York: Knopf, 1967. 229pp. In this popular life for the general reader, Francis's life and personality are lyrically and dramatically captured with a carefully detailed historical and ecclesiastical background.

Boase, T.S.R. *St. Francis of Assisi.* 1936. Revised ed. Bloomington: Indiana University Press, 1968. 120pp. Boase's scholarly reliable biographical study accompanies a series of lithographs illustrating scenes from Francis's life.

Chesterton, G.K. *St. Francis of Assisi.* New York: Doubleday, 1924. 185pp. Chesterton's biographical essay is written from the perspective of a Catholic convert mediating on the religious experience for a skeptical reader while attempting to resolve the various contradictions and paradoxes in Francis's character. Serving as a brief introduction for the general reader, the author reveals as much about himself as his subject.

Cuthbert, Father. *Life of St. Francis of Assisi.* New York: Longmans, 1912. 453pp. In this well-documented account based on original sources, Cuthbert provides an orthodox reply to Sabatier's attack on the Catholic Church. The events of Francis's life are chronicled and placed in relation to the wider context of his times.

De La Bedoyère, Michael. *Francis: A Biography of the Saint of Assisi.* New York: Harper & Row, 1962. 288pp. The author achieves a useful critical perspective between hagiography and a strictly historical approach that captures the saint's humanity and spirituality.

Englebert, Omer. *Saint Francis of Assisi.* New York: Longmans, 1950. 352pp. The author constructs a detailed and reliable narrative account of Francis's life based on primary sources and modern scholarly discoveries with a good deal of ecclesiastical context to understand Francis's relationship with the Catholic Church.

Fortini, Arnaldo. *Francis of Assisi.* New York: Crossroad, 1981. 720pp. A translation of a 1926 work by Assisi's former mayor, the book is best on how the town and contemporary social values played a role in forming Francis's character. The book uncovers valuable primary sources to document Francis's background and milieu.

Goudge, Elizabeth. *My God and My All: The Life of St. Francis of Assisi.* New York: Coward-McCann, 1959. 317pp. Francis's life and times receive a novelistic treatment that vividly recreates Francis's character and world. Clearly a Francis partisan, Goudge does allow unflattering details about his personality to emerge.

Holl, Adolf. *The Last Christian.* Garden City, New York: Doubleday, 1980. 278pp. The author looks at Francis's life from a Marxist and Freudian perspective, arguing that he was the last Christian to take the biblical mandate of total voluntary poverty seriously. Thesis dominated, the study lacks a sufficiently firm historical context to support its claims.

Longford, Frank P. *Francis of Assisi: A Life for All Seasons.* London: Weidenfeld and Nicolson, 1978. 190pp. The author looks at Francis's spiritual development and helpfully reviews the various sources and previous biographical approaches. Longford looks at Francis's story from a contemporary orthodox Christian viewpoint and makes a case for the usefulness of Franciscan ideals to today's problems.

Matt, Leonard von. *St. Francis of Assisi: A Pictorial Biography.* Chicago: Regnery, 1956. 200pp. The author's biographical essay connects 200 photographs of artistic depictions of scenes illustrating Francis's life and teachings.

Mockler, Anthony. *Francis of Assisi: The Wandering Years.* Oxford: Phaidon, 1976. 256pp. Written by a military historian, the book locates the culminating event of Francis's life—his activities in the crusade of 1218. In Mockler's view Francis was a frustrated Christian warrior who translated his views of chivalry into religious terms. Provocative and admittedly speculative at various points, Mockler's study is an ingenious departure from other biographies.

Robson, Michael. *St. Francis of Assisi: The Legend and the Life.* London: G. Chapman, 1997. 294pp. The author traces the stages of the development of Francis's legend and his impact on his parents, various churchmen, and Saint Clare.

Smith, John H. *Francis of Assisi.* New York: Scribner, 1972. 210pp. Smith, a British novelist and historian, places Francis's life firmly against his historical and cultural background and creates a mixed portrait that stresses Francis's human weaknesses. Using Jungian analysis to unlock the secrets of Francis's personality, Smith's interpretations are fresh and insightful, but readers may find much of the book overly dominated by psychological speculation.

Biographical Novels

De Wohl, Louis. *The Joyful Beggar: A Novel of St. Francis of Assisi.* Philadelphia: Lippincott, 1958. 315pp. Traces the life of Francis from his realization of his religious calling with a convincing period background involving the political maneuvering of Frederick II over the fate of Italy.

Kazantzakis, Nikos. *Saint Francis.* New York: Simon & Schuster, 1962. 379pp. In the author's account, told from the perspective of one of Francis's closest disciples, the saint is seen as a symbol of man's struggle to achieve religious awareness. *God's Pauper.* Oxford: Cassirer, 1975. 390pp. Scenes from St. Francis's life among the poor of Italy are depicted.

Kossak, Zofia. *Blessed Are the Meek: A Novel About St. Francis of Assisi.* New York: Roy, 1944. 375pp. The novel chronicles the events of the early thirteenth century, including the Children's Crusade. In a crowded novel that mingles fact and fiction, Francis is a central figure whose activities conform to the broad outline of his history.

Lechner, Michael. *My Beautiful White Roses.* Lewistown, Pennsylvania: Smoketree Press, 1971. 257pp. This unusual account of Francis's life suggests that the saint was a Jew, and that his persecution is explained by this fact. Based on evident research, the novel's premise and contentions are highly speculative, but the period is authentically evoked.

Timmermans, Felix. *The Perfect Joy of St. Francis.* New York: Farrar, Straus, 1952. 344pp. More devotional than historical, the life of Francis is lyrically dramatized showing his transformation from callow youth to self-effacing monk as a morality play.

White, Helen Constance. *Bird of Fire: A Tale of St. Francis of Assisi.* New York: Macmillan, 1958. 281pp. White concentrates on Francis's transformation from his wayward youth to becoming a pious, self-effacing spiritual leader. Blending fact

and legend, the novel achieves a vivid portrait of Francis' age and psychology.

Williamson, Glen. *Repair My House.* Carol Stream, Illinois: Creation House, 1973. 173pp. This devotional novel dramatizes Francis's accepting his vocation and his ministry among the poor.

Fictional Portraits

Borden, Lucille P. *Sing to the Sun.* New York: Macmillan, 1933. 380pp. Francis is glimpsed through the perspective of two young lovers, and the novel captures the saint's impact on his contemporaries in a sentimental and often simplistic tribute.

Recommended Juvenile Biographies

Liversidge, Douglas. *St. Francis of Assisi.* New York: F. Watts, 1968. 164pp. MG. This is a highly detailed representation of Francis's life with authentic period details.

O'Dell, Scott. *The Road to Damietta.* Boston: Houghton Mifflin, 1985. 230pp. MG. Newbery and Hans Christian Andersen Medal winner, O'Dell fictionally dramatizes the transformation of St. Francis as seen through the eyes of the girl who loved him.

Biographical Films and Theatrical Adaptations

Brother Sun, Sister Moon (1972). Director: Franco Zeffirelli. A decidedly 1960s attitude dominates this dramatization of Francis's early years and spiritual struggles, starring Graham Faulkner, Judi Bowker, and Alec Guinness. Video.

Flowers of St. Francis (1950). Director: Roberto Rossellini. Rossellini dramatizes the story of St. Francis in a series of vignettes. Aldo Fabrizi stars as the saint. Video.

Francesco (1989). Director: Liliana Cavani. This treatment of Francis's transformation from self-indulgent youth to spiritual leader daringly casts tough guy Mickey Rourke as the saint with Helena Bonham Carter as a devoted disciple. Video.

172. FRANCISCO FRANCO
1892–1975

Spanish general and *caudillo* (leader) of Spain from 1939, Franco led right-wing Falangist troops to victory over the Republicans during the Spanish Civil War (1936–1939) and became head of state after the fall of Madrid. Although close to Germany and Italy, who had provided him with aid during the war, he kept Spain neutral in World War II. In the postwar years, Franco's rule became less totalitarian but he continued to maintain his grip on power. He was succeeded by King Juan Carlos, whom he had named as his successor in 1969.

Recommended Biographies

Fusi, Juan Pablo. *Franco: A Biography.* New York: Harper & Row, 1987. 202pp. The work of a Spanish historian, Fusi's brief but thorough biography provides one of the best overviews of Franco's life.

Balanced in its assessment, Fusi sets the man against the wider backdrop of modern Spanish history and politics.

Payne, Stanley G. *The Franco Regime.* Madison: University of Wisconsin Press, 1987. 677pp. Payne supplies a careful and thorough documentation of Franco's years in power that allows a reasonable and informed assessment of both the man and his regime. The book offers a clear view that helps explain how Franco maintained power in Spain for so long and why.

Preston, Paul. *Franco: A Biography.* New York: Basic Books, 1994. 1,002pp. Preston's biography is likely to remain definitive for some time to come. Massively documented and comprehensive, the book, despite the author's clear dislike for his subject, manages to fashion a complex human portrait that sheds new light on a variety of questions about Franco's life and regime.

Other Biographical Studies

Coles, Sydney F.A. *Franco of Spain: A Full-Length Biography.* Westminster, Maryland: Newman Press, 1956. 264pp. Despite its title, Coles's biography is far from complete and outdated by modern scholarship and documentation.

Crozier, Brian. *Franco.* Boston: Little, Brown, 1967. 589pp. In this journalistic reevaluation of Franco's life and career Crozier contends that "neither the Republican nor the Nationalist myth about Franco and about the Civil War stands up to scrutiny," and the book attempts a more balanced examination. Cautiously favorable to Franco, Crozier shares with his subject a hatred of communism that compromises his objectivity.

Ellwood, Sheelagh M. *Franco.* New York: Longman, 1994. 253pp. Part of the Profiles in Power series, this is a competent summary of Franco's political career in the wider political and historical context of his times. Serves as a useful overview for the undergraduate and the general reader looking for a helpful historical summary of Franco's role in shaping modern Spanish history.

Hills, George. *Franco: The Man and His Nation.* New York: Macmillan, 1967. 464pp. With access to family papers and Franco himself, Hills attempts a biographical profile and appraisal intended for the general reader with a slight knowledge of Spanish history or culture. Overly defensive of Franco's actions and more selective in its coverage than thorough, Hills is also chargeable with important factual errors.

Lloyd, Alan. *Franco.* Garden City, New York: Doubleday, 1969. 256pp. Lloyd's is a popular biography that attempts a balanced account of Franco. Following an episodic pattern that is sometimes hard to follow, the book lacks sufficient context and depth to provide more than a general introduction to its subject.

Tryhall, J.W.D. *El Caudillo: A Political Biography of Franco.* New York: McGraw-Hill, 1970. 304pp. Tryhall's scholarly and thorough account of Franco's political career looks at the events leading up to the Spanish Civil War and the political, social, and economic forces Franco contended with up to 1969. More a historical treatment than a biography, the book offers few details about Franco's private life, but the presentation of his relationship with his times is insightful and accomplished.

Recommended Juvenile Biographies

Garza, Hedda. *Francisco Franco.* New York: Chelsea House, 1987. 112pp. MG/YA. Garza supplies a detailed and informative biographical and historical account of Franco's rise to success and reign.

Biographical Films and Theatrical Adaptations

Franco, Caudillo of Spain (1978). Director: Jeremy Murray-Brown. Narrated by Henry Fonda, this film portrait traces Franco's career from his rise to power to his death. Video.

173. BENJAMIN FRANKLIN
1706–1790

Celebrated as one of the greatest American statesmen of all time, Franklin was the son of a tallow chandler and soapmaker. Born in Boston, he went to Philadelphia as a young man to work as a printer. He became owner and publisher of the *Pennsylvania Gazette* (1730) and later founded *Poor Richard's Almanack,* in which he articulated his common sense philosophy and which featured sayings that would become standard American proverbs. A man of diverse talents, he invented bifocals and the Franklin stove, and experimented with electricity. He served as delegate to the Continental Congress and was on the committee that drafted the Declaration of Independence, which he signed. His efforts during the Federal Constitutional Convention of 1787 helped bring the United States Constitution into being.

Autobiography and Primary Sources

The Autobiography of Benjamin Franklin. New Haven, Connecticut: Yale University Press, 1964. 357pp. An American literary classic, Franklin's reflections begun in 1771 as a letter to his son were never completed but chronicle his life to his 1757 arrival in London. For a helpful analysis of the *Autobiography* that separates the facts of Franklin's life from his inventions, see Ormond Seavey's *Becoming Benjamin Franklin: The Autobiography and the Life* (University Park: Pennsylvania State University Press, 1988. 266pp.).

Benjamin Franklin: A Biography in His Own Words. Thomas J. Fleming, ed. New York: Harper & Row, 1972. 416pp. Extracted from the *Papers,* historian and novelist Fleming allows Franklin to tell his own story, revealing many facets of his personality.

The Papers of Benjamin Franklin. Leonard W. Labaree, et al., eds. New Haven, Connecticut: Yale University Press, 1959–1996. 32 vols. This monumental scholarly edition of Franklin's writings is the essential starting point for biographers and allows access for the interested reader to Franklin's multiple interests and complex personality.

Recommended Biographies

Clark, Ronald W. *Benjamin Franklin: A Biography.* New York: Random House, 1983. 530pp. The most comprehensive and authoritative study of Franklin since Van Doren, Clark's exhaustive study makes full use of recent archival sources to reveal various aspects of Franklin's life and character that challenges other presentations. Clark's British perspective also contributes to an original and balanced assessment of Franklin's achievements and strengths and weaknesses.

Van Doren, Carl. *Benjamin Franklin.* New York: Viking, 1938. 845pp. The result of more than 10 years of research and based on much previously unused material, Van Doren's classic study has long been regarded as definitive, though more recent scholarship has revised many of the author's facts and interpretations. Franklin emerges in Van Doren's view as an unassailable hero; readers in search of a more balanced treatment should look elsewhere. Few biographies, however, are as well written as Van Doren's classic life.

Wright, Esmond. *Franklin of Philadelphia.* Cambridge, Massachusetts: Harvard University Press, 1986. 404pp. Wright's full-scale examination of Franklin's achievements and character is the best available in placing the man in the context of his times. The work of a British historian, the book's perspective is fresh and insightful in its study of the evolution of Franklin's political thought.

Other Biographical Studies

Aldridge, Alfred O. *Benjamin Franklin: Philosopher and Man.* Philadelphia: Lippincott, 1965. 438pp. The author provides a competent account of the events of Franklin's life with an emphasis on the development of his ideas.

Campbell, James. *Recovering Benjamin Franklin: An Exploration of a Life of Science and Service.* Chicago: Open Court Publishing, 1999. 302pp. Campbell's intellectual biographical portrait stresses Franklin's contributions to science, religion, philosophy, and politics.

Crane, Verner. *Benjamin Franklin and a Rising People.* Boston: Little, Brown, 1954. 219pp. An appreciative assessment of Franklin's life and achievement, Crane's undocumented study is balanced and includes details of Franklin's weaknesses as well as his strengths.

Currey, Cecil B. *Road to Revolution: Benjamin Franklin in England 1765–75.* Garden City, New York: Anchor Books, 1968. 422pp. The author provides one of the most detailed and reliable treatments of Franklin's years in England.

Fay, Bernard. *Franklin: The Apostle of Modern Times.* Boston: Little, Brown, 1929. 547pp. Fay's early biography draws on unpublished sources to document previously unknown relationships. The book largely concentrates on Franklin's years in France and remains valuable, despite several errors that have subsequently been corrected by later studies, for its political and cultural background.

Fleming, Thomas. *The Man Who Dared the Lightning: A New Look at Benjamin Franklin.* New York: Morrow, 1971. 532pp. Fleming concentrates on the mature Franklin during his years abroad, beginning his examination in 1752, five years before the *Autobiography* ends. A popular account that draws on the Yale edition of Franklin's papers, Fleming's study fleshes out Franklin's role in the birth of the American nation.

Jennings, Francis. *Benjamin Franklin, Politician.* New York: W.W. Norton, 1996. 240pp. Focusing on the pre-Revolutionary years, Jennings's title is somewhat misleading and is less a political biography than a polemical attack on the Penn family and the management of the Pennsylvania colony. Jennings offers evidence and provocative insights for readers looking for a counterpoint to more sympathetic views of Franklin.

Lopez, Claude-Anne. *Mon Cher Papa: Franklin and the Ladies of Paris.* New Haven, Connecticut: Yale University Press, 1966. 404pp. Examines Franklin's various friendships in France between 1777 and 1785 based on the *Papers* and documents an important period of Franklin's life.

Lopez, Claude-Anne, and Eugenia W. Herbert. *The Private Franklin: The Man and His Family.* New York: W.W. Norton, 1975. 366pp. The authors offer a detailed, intimate look at Franklin's home life and his role as husband, father, and grandfather. Balanced in its treatment, the book documents an important angle for viewing Franklin's character.

Middlekauff, Robert. *Benjamin Franklin and His Enemies.* Berkeley: University of California Press, 1996. 255pp. In a provocative reassessment, Middlekauff focuses on Franklin's relationships and what they reveal about Franklin's decidedly contradictory character. Not a comprehensive study, the book concentrates on key moments in Franklin's life that stress his humanity.

Morgan, David T. *The Devious Dr. Franklin, Colonial Agent: Benjamin Franklin's Years in London.* Macon, Georgia: Mercer University Press, 1996. 280pp. Focusing on Franklin's 15-and-a-half year career as a colonial agent in London, Morgan analyzes Franklin's skills as a diplomat and manipulator of his public image in a well-documented and balanced account that includes a clear-eyed view of both strengths and flaws in Franklin's character.

Parton, James. *Life and Times of Benjamin Franklin.* 1864. Reprint ed. New York: Da Capo, 1971. 2 vols. Long regarded as the standard life, Parton's biography has been superseded by later studies that have corrected many of Parton's factual errors.

Randall, Willard S. *A Little Revenge: Benjamin Franklin and His Son.* Boston: Little, Brown, 1984. 558pp. In a controversial interpretation of Franklin's relationship with his son, the father is shown as often overbearing and vindictive. Offers a rare look at Franklin's family life and a different conclusion of his character and temperament.

Skemp, Sheila L. *Benjamin and William Franklin: Father and Son, Patriot and Loyalist.* New York: St. Martin's, 1994. 205pp. This brief study looks at the personal background and political experiences of the two Franklins and the factors that divided them against the backdrop of events leading up to and during the Revolution. The book includes a selection of primary documents and a chronology.

Biographical Novels

Bowen, Catherine Drinker. *The Most Dangerous Man in America: Scenes from the Life of Benjamin Franklin*. Boston: Little, Brown, 1974. 274pp. Five scenes from Franklin's life are dramatized to reveal his true character.

Feuchtwanger, Lion. *Proud Destiny*. New York: Viking, 1947. 625pp. Deals with Franklin's Paris years and the maneuvering to get Louis XVI to assist the American cause. Meticulous in its historical reconstruction, the novel is somewhat ponderous as a drama and character study.

Banks, Polan. *The Gentleman from America*. New York: Jonathan Cape, 1930. 439pp. Dramatizing episodes from Franklin's life in Paris, the novel concentrates on the romantic adventures of Franklin's grandson. Inventing little regarding Franklin, the statesman's speeches and observations are drawn from his letters and writings.

Neilson, Winthrop, and Frances Winthrop. *Edge of Greatness*. New York: Putnam, 1951. 248pp. Dramatizes one day in the life of Franklin—July 18, 1755, the day of Braddock's infamous defeat—which begins his commitment to the cause of American independence.

Fictional Portraits

Bacheller, Irving. *In the Days of Poor Richard*. Indianapolis: Bobbs-Merrill, 1922. 414pp. In this panoramic account of the events of the American Revolution, Franklin is a central figure and his treatment is the strongest element of the book.

Fast, Howard. *Citizen Tom Paine*. New York: Duell, Sloan, and Pearce, 1943. 341pp. In this fictional biography of Tom Paine, Benjamin Franklin plays an important role in assisting the patriot in his writing career.

Hall, Robert Lee. *Benjamin Franklin and a Case of Christmas Murder*. New York: St. Martin's, 1991. 279pp.; *Murder at Drury Lane*. New York: St. Martin's, 1992. 279pp.; *Benjamin Franklin and a Case of Artful Murder*. New York: St. Martin's, 1994. 264pp.; *Murder by the Waters*. New York: St. Martin's, 1995. 261pp.; *London Blood*. New York: St. Martin's, 1997. 245pp. Hall's inventive and authentic period mysteries employ Franklin as sleuth in a series of adventures during his residence in England.

Levin, Benjamin H. *To Spit Against the Wind*. New York: Citadel Press, 1970. 569pp. Tracing the life and times of Tom Paine, Franklin appears as an important figure in Paine's development.

Mason, F. van Wyck. *Brimstone Club*. Boston: Little, Brown, 1971. 338pp. This adventure novel concerns the activities of London's Brimstone Club whose members include Franklin and Lord Sandwich.

Mathieson, Theodore. *The Devil and Ben Franklin*. New York, Simon & Schuster, 1961. 256pp. Set in colonial Philadelphia, this period mystery features a young Franklin who attempts to rationally explain a murderous curse.

Melville, Herman. *Israel Potter: His Fifty Years of Exile*. 1855. Reprint ed. Evanston, Illinois: Northwestern University Press, 1997. 235pp. Melville's

historical romance portrays Franklin as spymaster for the title character on secret missions in France.

O'Toole, G.J.A. *Poor Richard's Game*. New York: Delacorte, 1982. 309pp. This ingenious reworking of history involves an exiled Irish aristocrat who is sent to France to investigate a rumor that Franklin is a traitor to the American cause. The novel is largely invention but with a solid and authentic sense of personalities and historical events.

Wyckoff, Nicholas. *The Braintree Mission*. New York: Macmillan, 1957. 184pp. Franklin is one of many historical figures in this what-if drama in which George III is convinced to moderate his views on the American colonies.

Zochert, Donald. *Murder in the Hellfire Club*. New York: Holt, 1978. 240pp. Franklin in 1757 is called on to investigate a murder of a member of the notorious Hellfire Club.

Recommended Juvenile Biographies

Fleming, Thomas. *Benjamin Franklin*. New York: Four Winds Press, 1972. 116pp. MG. Novelist, historian, and Franklin biographer Fleming provides a solid and readable account of Franklin's life and achievement.

Fritz, Jean. *What's the Big Idea, Ben Franklin?* New York: Coward-McCann, 1976. 46pp. MG. Fritz' inimitable entertaining style dominates this readable summary of Franklin's life.

Looby, Chris. *Benjamin Franklin*. New York: Chelsea House, 1990. 120pp. MG/YA. A candid and honest assessment of Franklin's various accomplishments and human strengths and failings. Preferred for younger readers who are interested in a more unvarnished appreciation found in adult biographies.

Meltzer, Milton. *Benjamin Franklin: The New America?* New York: F. Watts, 1988. 287pp. MG/YA. Detailed and interesting comprehensive account of Franklin's career and character that also paints a vivid picture of the cultural and historical background.

Biographical Films and Theatrical Adaptations

A&E Biography Video: Benjamin Franklin: Citizen of the World (1994). Director: Adam Friedman. This documentary look at Franklin's character and career is thorough and balanced. Video.

Lafayette (1962). Director: Jean Dreville. French biography of Lafayette features Orson Welles's portrayal of Franklin. More color than substance. Video.

Liberty!: The American Revolution (1997). Directors: Ellen Hovde and Muffie Meyer. This PBS documentary series features actors portraying the principals in dramatic readings from their letters and speeches. Franklin is played by Philip Bosco. The companion volume is written by Thomas J. Fleming (New York: Viking, 1997), 394pp. Video.

1776 (1972). Director: Peter H. Hunt. The film version of the Broadway musical comedy by Sherman Edwards and Peter Stone that opened in 1969 concerns the first Continental Congress and the signing of the Declaration of Independence. Howard Da

Silva is a standout as Franklin, with William Daniels as John Adams and Ken Howard as Jefferson. Video

Other Sources

Foster, Leila M. *Benjamin Franklin: A Biographical Companion*. Santa Barbara, California: ABC-CLIO, 1997. 288pp. An encyclopedic reference volume on Franklin's writings, interests, and the people and events of his life. Includes a detailed chronology. An excellent resource for high school, college, and general readers.

174. FRANZ JOSEPH I
1830–1916

Emperor of Austria (1848–1916) and king of Hungary (1867–1916), Franz Joseph came to the throne during the revolutions of 1848. He suppressed a Hungarian revolt (1849) and lost Lombardy to Sardinia in the Italian War (1859). Austria's crushing defeat in the Austro-Prussian War (1866) resulted in the loss of Austrian influence over Germany and the rise of Prussia. In 1879 he joined Germany and Italy in the Triple Alliance. The emperor's harsh policies against Serbia contributed to the assassination of his nephew, Archduke Ferdinand, and the outbreak of World War I.

Recommended Biographies

Bled, Jean-Paul. *Franz Joseph*. Cambridge, Massachusetts: Blackwell, 1992. 359pp. This is a lively, dramatic biographical portrait of a man beset by personal tragedies whose rather ordinary qualities were insufficient to cope with the complexity of his empire's modernization. The book deals convincingly with the emperor's personality and the challenges he faced with his modest gifts as a leader.

Palmer, Alan W. *Twilight of the Habsburgs: The Life and Times of Emperor Franz Joseph*. New York: Grove Press, 1995. 388pp. Palmer's is a vivid, well-written biography that balances a presentation of Franz Joseph's public and private life with a wider consideration of his times and the historical events that shaped his reign. In Palmer's view, Franz Joseph emerges as a limited but decent man, not lacking in political or intellectual perception.

Other Biographical Studies

Beller, Steven. *Franz Joseph*. New York: Longman, 1996. 272pp. Part of the useful Profiles in Power series, Beller's is a competent interpretive summary of Franz Joseph's public career in the wider context of social, economic, and political events during his long reign.

Harding, Bertita. *Golden Fleece: The Story of Franz Joseph and Elizabeth of Austria*. Indianapolis: Bobbs-Merrill, 1937. 370pp. Harding's is a dramatic retelling of the story of the emperor and empress for a popular audience. With an emphasis on drama and romance, the wider significance of the royal couple's life is missed.

Marek, George. *The Eagles Die: Franz Joseph, Elizabeth, and Their Austria.* New York: Harper & Row, 1974. 532pp. The work of a noted musicologist, Marek concentrates on Franz Joseph's private and family life. The author's historical competence, however, is insufficient to set the Hapsburgs into a wider social and political focus.

Murad, Anatol. *Franz Joseph I of Austria and His Empire.* New York: Twayne, 1968. 259pp. Murad's is a more intimate look at Franz Joseph's private life and his relationships than other studies. The essential public activities are glimpsed with sufficient social and political context to make them comprehensible for the nonspecialist.

Redlich, Joseph. *Emperor Francis Joseph of Austria: A Biography.* 1929. Reprint ed. Hamden, Connecticut: Archon Books, 1965. 547pp. This is a sympathetic and revealing study of Franz Joseph and his long reign. With an emphasis on the emperor's public life, Redlich maintains his focus on Franz Joseph while giving sufficient historical context for the reader to follow his career clearly.

Biographical Novels

Abrahams, William M. *Imperial Waltz.* New York: Dial Press, 1954. 308pp. Based on the early life of the Empress Elizabeth of Austria, the novel dramatizes her years as a young Bavarian princess and includes the early years of her marriage to Franz Joseph.

Janetschek, Ottokar. *The Emperor Franz Joseph.* London: Laurie, 1953. 316pp. The novel recounts the 68-year reign of Franz Joseph in a generally faithful depiction of the emperor's life.

Fictional Portraits

Arnold, Michael. *The Archduke.* Garden City, New York: Doubleday, 1967. 297p. The tragic story of the Crown Prince Rudolf is dramatized in diary form with appearances by Franz Josef.

Dukthas, Ann. *The Time of Murder at Mayerling.* New York: St. Martin's, 1996. 217pp. This time-travel mystery takes up the actual murder-suicide of Crown Prince Rudolf and his mistress and features a revealing look at the decadent court of the Hapsburgs.

Biographical Films and Theatrical Adaptations

Mayerling (1936). Director: Anatole Litvak. The doomed relationship between Rudolf of Hapsburg (Charles Boyer) and Marie Vetsera (Danielle Darrieux) is dramatized with a depiction of Franz Josef, played by Jena Dax. Video.

Mayerling (1968). Director: Terence Young. Remake of the 1936 film with Omar Sharif as Prince Rudolf, Catherine Deneuve as his lover, and James Mason in the role of Franz Josef. Video.

175. FREDERICK THE GREAT (FREDERICK II OF PRUSSIA)
1712–1786

A brilliant military campaigner and in domestic affairs known historically as an "enlightened despot," Frederick was ill-treated and imprisoned by his tyrannical father as a youth. After succeeding to the throne in 1740, he secured Silesia during the War of the Austrian Succession (1740-1748) and his eventual victory in the Seven Years War (1756-1763) made Prussia the dominant military power in Europe. He instituted important legal and penal reforms, set up trade monopolies to encourage new industry, promoted education, strengthened the role of the nobility, and practiced religious tolerance.

Recommended Biographies

Asprey, Robert B. *Frederick the Great: Magnificent Enigma.* New York: Ticknor and Fields, 1986. 715pp. One of the most inviting re-creations of Frederick's life and times for the general reader, Asprey's comprehensive examination includes many insights into the contradictions of Frederick's personality and behavior. With an entertaining anecdotal style, Asprey shows his skill in presenting and interpreting the political and military events of the period.

Gooch, George P. *Frederick the Great: The Ruler, the Writer, the Man.* New York: Knopf, 1947. 376pp. Drawing on the entire range of Frederick's writings to illuminate his life and work, Gooch provides one of the best available assessments that locates Frederick's role in eighteenth-century politics and offers a moderate view that includes both his strengths and failings.

MacDonogh, Giles. *Frederick the Great: A Life in Deed and Letters.* New York: St. Martin's, 2000. 448pp. Drawing on the most recent scholarship, MacDonogh's is a well-written and insightful assessment of Frederick's life and times that substitutes a coherent and human portrait for the various appropriations of the man as a national and cultural symbol.

Mitford, Nancy. *Frederick the Great.* New York: Harper & Row, 1970. 291pp. Described with a novelist's eye for significant detail, Mitford supplies a rounded and coherent portrait of Frederick that focuses on the human dimension over the political and military aspect of his life and times.

Other Biographical Studies

Carlyle, Thomas. *The History of Friedrich II of Prussia.* New York: Scribner, 1858–1865. 10 vols. In Carlyle's monumental testimonial, Frederick is an unalloyed hero, and Carlyle's exhaustive celebration of the king's spirit and leadership allowed the author to present his theory of history and the great man.

Duffy, Christopher. *The Army of Frederick the Great.* New York: Hippocrene Books, 1974. 272pp.; *Frederick the Great: A Military Life.* New York: Atheneum, 1985. 407pp. Duffy's two important studies of Frederick's battles in the War of Austrian Succession and the Seven Years War pro-

vides an excellent reassessment of Frederick's military skills and the strategic problems he faced.

Dupuy, Trevor N. *The Military Life of Frederick the Great of Prussia.* New York: F. Watts, 1969. 172pp. Not as detailed or as scholarly as Duffy, the book is a reliable introduction to Frederick's military achievements and strengths as a military leader.

Gaxotte, Pierre. *Frederick the Great.* New Haven, Connecticut: Yale University Press, 1942. 420pp. Written by a French historian, this study emphasizes Frederick's Franco-Prussian temperament, his friendship with Voltaire, and the events of the Seven Years War. In Gaxotte's view, Frederick's flaws predominate over his greatness, and his examination provides a useful and entertaining introduction to its subject.

Hegemann, Werner. *Frederick the Great.* New York: Knopf, 1929. 541pp. This inventive indictment of Frederick's reputation is structured by the imagined conversation of an American millionaire scholar who prosecutes his case against a number of defenders.

Hubatsch, Walther. *Frederick the Great of Prussia: Absolutism and Administration.* London: Thames and Hudson, 1975. 303pp. In a systematic survey of Frederick's administrative accomplishments, Hubatsch provides a detailed assessment of the ruler's skills based on an extensive review of the archival record.

Johnson, Hubert C. *Frederick the Great and His Officials.* New Haven, Connecticut: Yale University Press, 1975. 318pp. Johnson locates Frederick's greatness in his leadership skill in this evaluation of his governmental policies.

Lavisse, Ernest. *The Youth of Frederick the Great.* 1892. Reprint ed. New York: AMS Press, 1972. 445pp. Lavisse offers a balanced treatment of Frederick's formative years up to his marriage in 1733 in a narrative account that emphasizes Frederick's relationship with his father, Frederick William.

Macaulay, Thomas Babington. *The Life of Frederick the Great.* New York: Delisser and Procter, 1859. 277pp. Macaulay's biographical sketch stands in marked contrast to Carlyle's unreserved adulation and balances Frederick's achievements with a view of his failings.

Paret, Peter. *Frederick the Great: A Profile.* New York: Hill & Wang, 1972. 249pp. Paret provides a short biographical profile, followed by extracts from the observations of other historians and eyewitnesses on specific aspects of the king's life and character.

Reddaway, William F. *Frederick the Great and the Rise of Prussia.* 1904. Reprint ed. New York: Haskell House, 1964. 368pp. The author places Frederick's achievements in the context of the creation of the Prussian state. In his view, Frederick falls short of greatness on a number of counts, and this study remains a useful, balanced assessment.

Reiners, Ludwig. *Frederick the Great.* New York: Putnam, 1960. 304pp. This portrait of Frederick is the work of a German businessman and enthusiast who recapitulates the events of Frederick's life accurately but provides no new insights or sources.

Ritter, Gerhard. *Frederick the Great: A Historical Profile.* Berkeley: University of California Press, 1974. 207pp. Ritter's is a scholarly, complex collection of essays on specific aspects of Frederick's life and policies. Should be read to supplement and enrich a more general biography.

Simon, Edith. *The Making of Frederick the Great.* Boston: Little, Brown, 1963. 296pp. In a well-written if somewhat romanticized account, Simon assesses the influence of King Frederick William I on the formation of his son's character up to 1745.

Wright, Constance. *A Royal Affinity: The Story of Frederick the Great and His Sister Wilhelmina von Bayreuth.* New York: Scribner, 1965. 309pp. Concentrating on the relationship of Frederick and his sister, this popular account mixes court gossip and invented dialogue and skirts the issue of Frederick's homosexuality.

Biographical Novels

Frank, Bruno. *The Days of the King.* New York: Readers Club, 1942. 235pp. Cast in the form of the Frederick's recollections of his past, the novel dramatizes three episodes from his life to reveal the human side of the Prussian ruler. The episodes have a factual basis, but they are supplemented with invention.

Sabatini, Rafael. *The Birth of Mischief.* Boston: Houghton Mifflin, 1945. 308pp. This is a straightforward fictionalized chronicle of the rise of Prussia from the reign of Frederick William I through the first years of Frederick's reign.

Recommended Juvenile Biographies

Kittredge, Mary. *Frederick the Great.* New York: Chelsea House, 1987. 112pp. MG/YA. This is a solid choice for an informative look at both the man and his era.

Snyder, Louis L., and Ida Mae Brown. *Frederick the Great: Prussian Warrior and Statesman.* New York: F. Watts, 1968. 177pp. MG. Snyder examines Frederick's talents as a military strategist, administrator, musician, and writer in a lucidly presented and entertaining portrait that includes his strengths and weaknesses.

Biographical Films and Theatrical Adaptations

Young Catherine (1991). Director: Michael Anderson. Maximilian Schell portrays Frederick the Great in this film treatment of the early years of Catherine the Great. Video.

Other Sources

Barker, Thomas M., ed. *Frederick the Great and the Making of Prussia.* New York: Holt, 1971. 103pp. This collection of essays explores various aspects of Frederick's personality and reign.

Snyder, Louis L., ed. *Frederick the Great.* Englewood Cliffs, New Jersey: Prentice-Hall, 1971. 182pp. Combining Frederick's own writings with contemporary and later historical views, this is a useful volume providing different perspectives on the man and his reign.

176. JOHN C. FRÉMONT
1813–1890

American explorer, soldier, and political leader, Frémont surveyed the Mississippi valley and explored the West during the early 1840s. He went (1845) to California, where he influenced the American settlers there to declare (1846) the Bear Flag Republic in defiance of Mexican rule. He was the first Republican presidential candidate (1856) and during the Civil War commanded the Department of the West. From 1878 to 1883 he was governor of Arizona Territory. Sometimes called the Pathfinder, Frémont helped open the West to settlement.

Autobiography and Primary Sources

Primary sources on Frémont's life and career come in a variety of forms, including Frémont's own unfinished *Memoirs of My Life* (Chicago: Belford, Clarke, 1886. 635pp.) that offers an account up to the war in California and the Mexican defeat. *The Letters of Jessie Benton Frémont.* Pamela Herr and Mary Lee Spence, eds. (Urbana: University of Illinois Press, 1993. 595pp.) is also a valuable source of firsthand information of the couple's life together, though without many intimate revelations.

Frémont's reports on his expeditions and correspondence can be found in *The Expeditions of John Charles Frémont.* Donald Jackson and Mary Lee Spence, eds. (Urbana: University of Illinois Press, 1970-84. 3 vols.). The participants' diaries of the 1848–1849 expedition are collected in *Frémont's Fourth Expedition: A Documentary Account of the Disaster of 1848–1849* (Glendale, California: Arthur H. Clark, 1960. 319pp.).

Recommended Biographies

Nevins, Allan. *Frémont: Pathmarker of the West.* New York: Longmans, 1955. 689pp. Nevins's sympathetic portrait of Frémont's life and career remains the most comprehensive treatment available. Despite a defensiveness that limits the book's objectivity, the range of Frémont's activities and accomplishments is vividly narrated.

Roberts, David. *A Newer World: Kit Carson, John C. Frémont, and the Claiming of the American West.* 2000. 320pp. Roberts provides a rousing narrative account of Frémont's career in the West from the early 1840s to the beginning of the Civil War. Frémont's more flamboyant, complicated nature is juxtaposed with that of Carson's in a human portrait of both men.

Rolle, Andrew F. *John Charles Frémont: Character as Destiny.* Norman: University of Oklahoma Press, 1991. 351pp. Rolle takes a psychobiographical approach for a thorough examination of Frémont's often contradictory, complex character. Sympathetic but balanced in its assessment of a flawed personality, Rolle offers many fresh interpretations of both the man and his activities that correct previous errors and omissions.

Other Biographical Studies

Brandon, William E. *The Men and the Mountain: Frémont's Fourth Expedition.* New York: Morrow, 1955. 337pp. This is a narrative account of Frémont's disastrous fourth expedition that attempted a winter crossing of the Rocky Mountains in 1848 in search of a pass that could be used for a railroad route across the Continental Divide. What began as exploration ended as a fight for survival.

Egan, Fero. *Frémont: Explorer for a Restless Nation.* Garden City, New York: Doubleday, 1977. 582pp. Egan provides a reliable, dramatic summary of Frémont's life through the 1830s and 1840s with an emphasis on the heroic years of exploration.

Herr, Pamela. *Jessie Benton Frémont: A Biography.* New York: F. Watts, 1987. 496pp. Herr's is a carefully researched, balanced biography of Frémont's wife that sheds considerable light on the couple's relationship and Frémont's demanding personality.

Biographical Novels

Alter, Judy. *Jessie: A Novel Based on the Life of Jessie Benton Frémont.* New York: Bantam Books, 1995. 436pp. Frémont's wife, Jessie, narrates her own story in a somewhat simplified version of the couple's life together.

Nevin, David. *Dream West.* New York: Putnam, 1983. 639pp. Nevin chronicles Frémont's career from the 1840s through the 1860s, following a basic factual framework with some surmises to fill in the gaps in the record.

Stone, Irving. *Immortal Wife.* Garden City, New York: Doubleday, 1944. 450pp. Frémont's career is seen from the perspective of his relationship with his wife Jessie Benton. Although the majority of the story is factual, there are invented dialogue and situations.

Fictional Portraits

Hawthorne, Hildegarde. *No Road Too Long.* New York: Longmans, 1940. 261pp. The novel dramatizes Frémont's third expedition in 1845 in a heroic portrait.

Holland, Cecelia. *The Bear Flag.* Boston: Houghton Mifflin, 1990. 422pp. The events of California's Bear Flag Revolt are depicted, with accurate appearances by Frémont.

Recommended Juvenile Biographies

Harris, Edward D. *John C. Frémont and the Great Western Reconnaissance.* New York: Chelsea House, 1990. 111pp. MG/YA. Harris documents Frémont's exploration and relates his activities to the wider theme of western expansion.

Biographical Films and Theatrical Adaptations

Dream West (1986). Director: Dick Lowry. Television miniseries adaptation of Nevin's novel casts Richard Chamberlain as Frémont, Alice Krige as Jessie, Rip Torn as Kit Carson, and F. Murray Abraham as Lincoln. Video.

See also Kit Carson

177. SIGMUND FREUD
1856–1939

Celebrated as the founder of psychoanalysis, Freud received his medical degree from the University of Vienna (1881) and served a medical apprenticeship in Paris. After returning to Vienna he began his famous collaboration with Josef Breuer on the use of hypnosis for hysteria. Freud later broke with Breuer and rejected hypnosis in favor of free association, a technique he devised to release repressed emotions from the subconscious. By 1913, his emphasis on infantile sexuality and the Oedipus complex had caused such disciples as C. C. Jung and Alfred Adler to break away and form their own schools. Although others would dispute aspects of his theories, the basic structure of analysis as the study of the unconscious has remained Freudian. Freud's works include *The Interpretation of Dreams* (1900), *Totem and Taboo* (1913), and *The Ego and the Id* (1923).

Autobiography and Primary Sources

An Autobiographical Study. New York: W.W. Norton, 1965. 141pp. Freud focuses almost exclusively on his professional career and the origin and growth of psychoanalysis and the public's reaction.

The Diary of Sigmund Freud, 1929–1939: A Record of the Final Decade. Michael Molnar, ed. New York: Simon & Schuster, 1997. 326pp. The diary records Freud's daily, private torment during his final decade, including his reaction to the rise of Nazism, his flight from Austria, relocation to London, and struggle with cancer. Freud's often laconic entries are helpfully annotated by Molnar.

Letters of Sigmund Freud. Ernst L. Freud, ed. New York: Basic Books, 1960. 470pp. Edited by Freud's youngest son, this selection of correspondence arranged chronologically from 1873 to 1939 provides a revealing personal portrait of the man and his personality.

Recommended Biographies

Clark, Ronald W. *Freud: The Man and the Cause.* New York: Random House, 1980. 652pp. Clark's balanced and reliable biography focuses on Freud's personal life and his role as the leader of the psychoanalysis movement. He is particularly strong on the cultural background from which Freud and the movement emerged. Clark demythologizes the heroic portrait created by Jones without undervaluing Freud's significance and achievement.

Gay, Peter. *Freud: A Life for Our Time.* New York: W.W. Norton, 1988. 810pp. Written by a distinguished historian who has also trained in psychoanalysis, Gay's comprehensive study deals directly with potentially embarrassing material that Jones glossed over or ignored to form a complex portrait of Freud's struggle to conquer his own inner demons as he formed a new theory of the mind. Freud's personality, his ideas, and the cultural background that help form both are captured in a coherent and revealing whole.

Jones, Ernest. *The Life and Work of Sigmund Freud.* New York: Basic Books, 1953–1957. 3 vols. Long regarded as the standard, authoritative

biography, Jones's comprehensive study cannot be regarded as definitive primarily because of its reluctance to damage Freud's reputation by unflattering material. However, Jones's partisanship does not outweigh his contribution in arranging the basic data of Freud's life and career into the accepted pattern with which all subsequent biographers have had to contend.

Wollheim, Richard. *Sigmund Freud.* New York: Viking, 1971. 292pp. The author's intellectual biography of Freud's career has been called by Peter Gay the best study of Freud's thought and serves as a useful introduction.

Other Biographical Studies

Balogh, Penelope. *Freud: A Biographical Introduction.* New York: Scribner, 1971. 144pp. An uncritical tribute from an ardent believer, Balogh's brief study derives most of its biographical details from Ernest Jones but still repeats a number of suspect anecdotes and legends as fact.

Brome, Vincent. *Freud and His Early Circle.* New York: Morrow, 1968. 275pp. Based on interviews and unpublished letters, Brome's study challenges a number of Jones's assertions on Freud's early career and followers with a solid presentation of Freud's Viennese milieu.

Costigan, Giovanni. *Sigmund Freud: A Short Biography.* New York: Macmillan, 1965. 306pp. Appropriate as an introduction for the general reader, Costigan's concise examination based on Freud's letters, writings, and Jones's standard biography sets out to dispel misconceptions and present a coherent portrait of the man and his ideas.

Ferris, Paul. *Dr. Freud, a Life.* Washington, DC: Counterpart Press, 1998. 480pp. Ferris looks at Freud's life and achievement from the perspective of his considerable influence on modern thought and culture. Neutral in the various debates over Freud's theories and leadership of the psychoanalytical movement, Ferris achieves a balanced and often irreverent human portrait.

Freud, Ernst, Lucie Freud, and Ilse Gribrich-Simitis, eds. *Sigmund Freud: His Life in Pictures and Words.* New York: Harcourt, Brace, 1978. 350pp. This pictorial biography includes important photographs of Freud, his family, and associates from family collections, as well as a biographical introduction by Kurt Eissler.

Isbister, J.N. *Freud: An Introduction to His Life and Work.* New York: Blackwell, 1985. 318pp. Claiming to have uncovered new facts about Freud's life, including the disputed revelation that Freud had an affair with his sister-in-law, Isbister focuses mainly on Freud's early and middle years and correlates his life with his works while applying a Freudian reading of his writings as the basis of many of his "revelations."

Krull, Marianne. *Freud and His Father.* New York: W.W. Norton, 1986. 294pp. Krull's thesis is that Freud's rejection of his seduction theory in favor of Oedipal conflict and infantile sexuality was based on his deep-rooted and unconscious fear of betraying the secret of his father's possible sexual misdeeds. Insightful in exploring Freud's inner conflicts during a seminal period in the development of psychoanalytic theory, the book is single-

minded in its approach and ultimately reductive in its interpretation.

McGrath, William J. *Freud's Discovery of the Psychoanalytic Movement.* Ithaca, New York: Cornell University Press, 1986. 336pp. Using newly available letters, McGrath documents Freud's imaginative and intellectual development in the context of historical and political events in Vienna at the turn of the century.

Newton, Peter M. *Freud: From Youthful Dream to Mid-Life Crisis.* New York: Guilford Press, 1995. 297pp. Newton's biographical study focuses on Freud's personal crisis that led to the breakthrough of the discovery of psychoanalysis. The book documents the stages of Freud's intellectual and personal development through an examination of newly discovered personal letters.

Roazen, Paul. *Freud and His Followers.* New York: Knopf, 1974. 602pp. Based on interviews with more that 70 individuals who knew Freud during the formative years of the psychoanalytic movement as well as previously untapped archival material, Roazen provides a detailed account of the inner politics of the movement in which Freud is portrayed as sometimes petty, grudging, and vengeful.

Robert, Marthe. *From Oedipus to Moses: Freud's Jewish Identity.* New York: Anchor Books, 1976. 229pp. Robert attributes Freud's desire to achieve recognition in Gentile society as a primary motivation as well as locates Freud's renunciation of his Jewishness to his guilt over his feelings about his father.

Sachs, Hanns. *Freud: Master and Friend.* Cambridge, Massachusetts: Harvard University Press, 1944. 195pp. This admiring memoir by a disciple and longtime friend has the advantage of firsthand intimacy. Although sometimes in error about factual details, Sachs presents a warmer, wittier, and livelier Freud than other studies.

Schur, Max. *Freud: Living and Dying.* New York: International Universities Press, 1972. 587pp. Written by Freud's physician, this account of his final decade corrects a number of factual errors in the record on Freud's illness and treatment as well as Freud's reflections on death and dying.

Storr, Anthony, and Anthony Stevens. *Freud & Jung: A Dual Introduction.* New York: Barnes and Noble, 1998. 138pp. Biographies of both figures in one volume are featured here. Storr introduces their personal and professional lives, providing an accessible summary of their leading ideas.

Wilson, Stephen. *Sigmund Freud.* Stroud, England: Sutton, 1997. 115pp. This is a concise and balanced introduction to Freud's life and ideas.

Biographical Novels

Daniels, Kathleen. *Minna's Story: The Secret Love of Doctor Sigmund Freud.* Sante Fe, New Mexico: Health Press, 1992. 177pp. Cast in the form of a diary kept by Freud's sister-in-law, Minna Bernay, the novel recounts her relationship with Freud and her influence on his theories. The nature of Freud's relationship with Minna remains controversial, and this interpretation, though employing carefully researched historical and biographical facts, still depends on considerable surmises and speculation.

Harrison, Carey. *Freud: A Novel*. London: Weidenfeld & Nicolson, 1984. 197pp. Freud narrates his own story looking back at the age of 82 and recalling scenes throughout his life.

Stone, Irving. *The Passions of the Mind*. Garden City, New York: Doubleday, 1971. 808pp. Stone's well-documented and earnest fictionalized biographical chronicle covers the entire range of Freud's life and career. Best on the surface details, Stone is less steady when attempting to dramatize Freud's thoughts and emotions.

Thomas, D.M. *Eating Pavlova*. New York: Carroll & Graf, 1994. 231pp. On his deathbed in 1939 Freud reflects on real and imaginary events in his life as he tries to come to terms with his impact on the world and his own personal sins.

Fictional Portraits

Baker, Kevin. *Dreamland*. New York: HarperCollins, 1999. 519pp. On his visit to America, Freud is depicted along with his troubled relationship with Jung.

Burgess, Anthony. *The End of the World News*. New York: McGraw-Hill, 1983. 388pp. Burgess's inventive fantasy weaves together three phenomena of the twentieth century: Freud, Trotsky, and the exploration of outer space. The section devoted to Freud forms a vivid, fictionalized life, showing Freud feuding with his associates and struggling with his own Oedipal complex.

Doctorow, E.L. *Ragtime*. New York: Random House, 1975. 270pp. Freud makes a brief but memorable cameo appearance in this imaginative repossession of the American scene in the early years of the twentieth century.

Hill, Carol DeChellis. *Henry James' Midnight Song*. New York: Poseidon Press, 1993. 445pp. Set in fin de siècle Vienna, this inventive and thoughtful historical novel involves the investigation of the death and disappearance of a woman discovered in Dr. Freud's study. Suspects include novelist Edith Wharton and her travelling companion Henry James. Brimming with ideas, the novel excels in reproducing the dark and menacing atmosphere of turn-of-the-century Vienna.

Korman, Keith. *Secret Dreams*. New York: Arcade, 1995. 435pp. Based loosely on the celebrated case of Sabrina Spielman, the novel dramatizes the efforts of Freud and Jung to treat Fraulein S. Jung is the central figure here in an imaginative reworking of Fraulein S.'s case history.

Meyer, Nicholas. *The Seven Per-Cent Solution*. New York: Ballantine Books, 1974. 237pp. Meyer's delightfully inventive period mystery has Sherlock Holmes joining forces with Freud to uncover a conspiracy, while the doctor assists the detective in treating his cocaine addiction.

Michalos, Peter. *Psyche*. New York: Doubleday, 1993. 257pp. Told through letters and diary entries, the novel dramatizes Freud's treatment of his first hysteria patient in 1886 whose revelations send him on an invented quest to Greece in search of the archetypes to embody his conception of the human mind and motivation.

Thomas, D.M. *The White Hotel*. New York: Viking, 1981. 274pp. Thomas's haunting novel tells the story of a fictitious patient of Freud's, which extends from her treatment to the Holocaust. The role played by Freud is fictional, though based on biographical details and relying in part on his actual words from his letters and works.

Trachtenberg, Inge. *An Arranged Marriage*. New York: W.W. Norton, 1975. 272pp. Freud is asked to use his psychoanalytical skills to aid a married couple in which the man is suffering from an affliction.

Thorne, Nicola. *Affairs of Love*. Garden City, New York: Doubleday, 1983. 400pp. The story of two sisters' late Victorian career in theater and medicine puts them in contact with leading figures, such as Ellen Terry and Freud.

Yalom, Irvin D. *When Nietzsche Wept: A Novel of Obsession*. New York: Basic Books, 1992. 306pp. The novel recreates the birth of psychotherapy in the imagined encounter between pioneering physician Josef Breuer and Friedrich Nietzsche. While most of the novel is invented, the essential details of the major characters' lives, including Freud's, are grounded in fact.

Recommended Juvenile Biographies

Mann, Barry. *Sigmund Freud*. Vero Beach, Florida: Rourke, 1993. 112pp. MG. Mann supplies the essential details of Freud's private and public life with a accessible examination of his ideas.

Muckenhoupt, Margaret. *Sigmund Freud: Explorer of the Unconscious*. New York: Oxford University Press, 1997. 160pp. YA. Part of the Oxford Portraits of Science series, this is less a full biographical treatment than a readable and clear explication of Freud's ideas. Psychoanalytic terms are defined and explained, and photographs enhance the presentation.

Neimark, Anne E. *Sigmund Freud: The World Within*. New York: Harcourt, Brace, 1976. 120pp. MG/YA. Neimark concentrates on the origins and development of Freud's theories in an informative biography.

Biographical Films and Theatrical Adaptations

Sartre, Jean-Paul. *The Freud Scenario*. Chicago: University of Chicago Press, 1986. 549pp. In an unfinished screenplay commissioned by John Huston, Sartre explores Freud's life as he is forming the basic tenets of psychoanalysis.

A&E Biography Video: Sigmund Freud: Analysis of the Mind (1996). A documentary film profile using archival material, location shots, and testimony by various experts. Video.

Freud (1962). Director: John Huston. Montgomery Clift stars as Freud in this darkly realistic portrait of Freud's early years and the development of his theories and personal battles. With Susannah York, Larry Parks, and David McCallum. Features inventive dream sequences.

Freud: The Hidden Nature of Man (1970). Director: George Kaczender. Dramatizes Freud's back-

ground, his personal struggles, and his ideas. Video.

Freud Under Analysis (1987). Director: Suzanne Simpson. This PBS Nova episode traces the development of Freud's ideas along with criticism of his thinking and psychoanalysis. Video.

The Interpretation of Dreams (1996). Producer: Eugenie Vink. A series of dream-sequence reenactments reveal the complexities of the human condition that Freud scrutinized. It also examines Freud's conceptions of the unconscious and his life story. Video.

Other Sources

Neu, Jerome, ed. *The Cambridge Companion to Freud*. New York: Cambridge University Press, 1991. 356pp. Leading scholars provide essays on various aspects of Freud's personality, career, and ideas.

Steadman, Ralph. *Sigmund Freud*. New York: Simon & Schuster, 1980. 118pp. In prose and drawings the author transforms the facts of Freud's life into an amusing, satiric, and intellectual exploration.

See also Carl Jung

178. ROBERT FROST
1874–1963

American poet whose work explored the character, people, and landscape of New England, Frost supported himself for much of his life by farming and by lecturing at several universities. His numerous volumes of poetry include *A Boy's Will* (1913), *New Hampshire* (1923), *Steeple Bush* (1947), and *In the Clearing* (1962). In 1961 he recited his poem, "The Gift Outright," at the inauguration of John F. Kennedy. Perhaps the most popular twentieth-century American poet, Frost received many honors, including four Pulitzer Prizes.

Autobiography and Primary Sources

Interviews with Robert Frost. Edward C. Lathem, ed. New York: Holt, 1966. 295pp. This compilation of mostly newspaper interviews is arranged chronologically from 1915 through 1962 and gives an interesting range of the poet's views on a wide range of topics.

Selected Letters of Robert Frost. Lawrance Thompson, ed. London: J. Cape, 1965. 645pp. More than 500 letters written from 1886 until the poet's death to and from 123 correspondents arranged in 10 sections with a biographical introduction to each. See also *Family Letters of Robert and Elinor Frost*. Arnold Grade, ed. (Albany: State University of New York Press, 1973. 293pp.), which collects nearly 200 letters to Frost's children, grandchildren, and members of his family and documents the poet's family tragedies.

Recommended Biographies

Meyers, Jeffrey. *Robert Frost: A Biography*. Boston: Houghton Mifflin, 1996. 424pp. Meyers's interpretation of Frost's life and personality concentrates on the poet's relationship with Kathleen Morrison, suggesting that the deteriorating relationship between Frost and Thompson, his biographer, can be explained by the pair's rivalry for her love. Besides this revelation, the book provides a more balanced assessment of Frost's strengths and weaknesses than Thompson, though Parini has argued that the biography is filled with sensationalist misinformation and misreadings of Frost's work.

Parini, Jay. *Robert Frost: A Life*. New York: Holt, 1999. 514pp. Like Pritchard and Meyers, Parini attempts to correct the negative portrait supplied by Thompson with a far more generous assessment, skillful in its exploration of the poetry and the poet, particularly of the inner conflict in Frost's sensibility. The book offers a helpful afterword, "Frost and His Biographers," that tracks presentations of the poet's life and character and explains Parini's intentions with his own study.

Pritchard, William. *Frost: A Literary Life Reconsidered*. New York: Oxford University Press, 1984. 286pp. Pritchard is an accomplished and sensitive guide to the poet and his works in this literary biography. Frost's poetry is examined in the context of his life with each shedding light on the other. Contrary to Thompson's harsher view, Pritchard grants Frost considerable integrity and achievement in the developing of his poetic voice.

Thompson, Lawrance. *Robert Frost*. New York: Holt Rinehart, 1966–1976. 3 vols. (Volume 3 with R.H. Winnick). By far the most comprehensive gathering of information about the poet, this authorized biography by a former mentor who developed a strong dislike for Frost reflects the author's emphasis on the darker side of Frost's personality. Not always subtle in its interpretation with leaden prose and a plodding method, the book nevertheless is indispensable for its facts even if it must be read, or endured, with some skepticism. A one-volume abridgement by E.C. Lathem is available as *Robert Frost: A Biography* (New York: Holt Rinehart, 1982. 543pp.).

Other Biographical Studies

Burnshaw, Stanley. *Robert Frost Himself*. New York: G. Braziller, 1986. 342pp. Frost's editor supplies his recollection of the poet directed at correcting the perceived inaccuracies in Lawrance Thompson's biography. In contrast to Thompson's "monster myth," Frost is depicted as humane and generous.

Mertins, Louis. *Robert Frost: Life and Talks-Walking*. Norman: University of Oklahoma Press, 1965. 450pp. The author has joined reminiscence, letters, and transcriptions of conversations with Frost from the early 1930s until his death. By far it is Frost's voice reflecting on various topics that is most interesting here, forming a kind of oral autobiography.

Morrison, Kathleen. *Robert Frost: A Pictorial Chronicle*. New York: Holt, 1974. 133pp. This pictorial biography was compiled by the housekeeper and business manager of the poet from 1938 until Frost's death. The book provides an intimate, first-hand glimpse of the poet's daily affairs for his last 25 years.

Sergeant, Elizabeth S. *Robert Frost: The Trial by Existence*. New York: Holt, 1960. 451pp. Drawing on the author's long acquaintance with the poet, the author presents "a selective record" of Frost's rise to fame from early poverty. The book's positives are its intimate details and allowing Frost to tell his own story as much as possible. The negative is an overly admiring perspective that lacks critical distance.

Sutton, William A., ed. *Newdick's Season of Frost: An Interrupted Biography of Robert Frost*. Albany: State University of New York Press, 1976. 454pp. Newdick was Frost's first authorized biographer whose work was edited by Sutton after the his death in 1939. Only Newdick's chapters on Frost's youth are intact; the rest of the book collects Newdick's research findings.

Walsh, John E. *Into My Own: The English Years of Robert Frost*. New York: Grove Press, 1988. 286pp. Walsh's is a detailed and illuminating account of Frost's literary development during his two-and-half-year stay in England from 1912 to 1915. Having left teaching, Frost attempted to prove himself as a poet. The story of this decision and its outcome is well told in this informed study.

Recommended Juvenile Biographies

Bober, Natalie. *A Restless Spirit: The Story of Robert Frost*. 1981. Revised ed.New York: Holt, 1991. 197pp. YA. Bober offers a frank assessment of Frost's struggles and triumphs in a human portrait that also gives a glimpse of the poet's darker side.

Biographical Films and Theatrical Adaptations

Robert Frost (1987). Director: Richard P. Rogers. A documentary portrait of Frost's life and work, includes narration by the poet and commentary by Richard Wilbur, Richard Poirier, and Joseph Brodsky. Video.

Robert Frost (1988). Director: Peter Hammer. This is a film profile with recitations from Frost's poetry. Video.

Robert Frost (1988). Director: Veronica Young. Part of the PBS Voices and Visions poetry series, Frost's life and works are explored through commentary by various writers and critics. Video.

Other Sources

Cramer, Jeffrey S. *Robert Frost Among His Poems: A Literary Companion to the Poet's Own Biographical Contexts and Associations*. Jefferson, North Carolina: McFarland, 1991. 296pp. Cramer places each of Frost's poems in relation to the context of Frost's life with composition and publication details.

Potter, James L. *Robert Frost Handbook*. University Park: Pennsylvania State University Press, 1980. 205pp. Potter presents a biographical summary followed by a close examination of representative poems.

179. ROBERT FULTON
1765–1815

The American inventor of the submarine and steamship, the multitalented Fulton was an expert gunsmith during the American Revolution and from 1782 to 1786 painted landscapes and portraits. His submarine, *Nautilus*, was launched (1800) in France and in 1807 he launched the *Clermont*, the first commercially successful steamboat. Fulton built several other vessels, including the first steam warship, the *Demologus*, launched in 1815.

Recommended Biographies

Dickinson, Henry W. *Robert Fulton: Engineer and Artist, His Life and Works*. 1913. Reprint ed. Freeport, New York: Books for Libraries Press, 1971. 333pp. Despite its age, Dickinson's biography is solidly researched based on primary sources and features reproductions of Fulton's drawings and plans.

Philip, Cynthia O. *Robert Fulton: A Biography*. New York: F. Watts, 1985. 371pp. Philip's is the best modern biography, well researched and written and drawing on a good deal of fresh material. The book substitutes for the often simplistic view of the inventor a complex, human portrait.

Other Biographical Studies

Flexner, James T. *Steamboats Come True: American Inventors in Action*. New York: Viking, 1944. 406pp. Flexner's study of the development of steam technology features an informative portrait of Fulton's achievement and character.

Morgan, John S. *Robert Fulton*. New York: Mason/Charter, 1977. 235pp. A synthesis of primary and secondary sources, Morgan's full-length biography solidly presents the essential facts of Fulton's life and his contributions as scientist and engineer in which technical issues are accessibly handled.

Parsons, William B. *Robert Fulton and the Submarine*. New York: Columbia University Press, 1922. 154pp. Parsons's specialized study of Fulton's efforts in submarine technology is authoritative and scholarly, filling in substantial details on this phase of the inventor's career.

Virginskii, V.S. *Robert Fulton 1765–1815*. New Delhi, India: Smithsonian Institution, 1976. 221pp. This is an outlandish, misleading interpretive account that supplies a Marxist interpretation of Fulton's life with the inventor presented as a proletarian hero.

Fictional Portraits

Forrest, Anthony. *The Pandora Secret*. New York: Farrar, Straus, 1982. 285pp. This thriller set during the Napoleonic Wars describes the attempt to protect Fulton's submarine design from falling into enemy hands.

Wilkins, William V. *Being Met Together*. New York: Macmillan, 1944. 510pp. Wilkins's historical panorama features an appearance by Fulton and a plot to rescue Napoleon from St. Helena by submarine.

Recommended Juvenile Biographies

Flammang, James M. *Robert Fulton: Inventor and Steamboat Builder*. Berkeley Heights, New Jersey: Enslow, 1999. 128pp. MG. Flammang focuses on Fulton's early work as an artist and his struggles to achieve success as an inventor, as well as his lesser-known work perfecting the submarine.

Henry, Joanne L. *Robert Fulton, Steamboat Builder*. New York: Chelsea House, 1991. 80pp. MG. Henry provides an informative portrait of Fulton and his inventions.

Landau, Elaine. *Robert Fulton*. New York: F. Watts, 1991. 62pp. MG. Treating both the personal story and the events of Fulton's career, Landau's is a reliable biography.

Biographical Films and Theatrical Adaptations

Little Old New York (1940) Director: Harry King. Richard Greene portrays Fulton in this romanticized treatment of the creation of his steamboat. Co-starring Alice Faye, Brenda Joyce, and Fred MacMurray. Video

G

180. THOMAS GAINSBOROUGH
1727–1788

An English painter, Gainsborough enjoyed great success as a society portraitist, although his favorite subject was landscapes. His portraits are celebrated for their elegance, vivacity, and refinement, and his landscapes influenced the work of Constable and English landscape painting in the nineteenth century. His paintings include *Perdita*, *The Blue Boy*, and *Lady Innes*.

Recommended Biographies

Hayes, John. *Gainsborough: Paintings and Drawings*. London: Phaidon Press, 1975. 232pp. Hayes is a recognized specialist in Gainsborough whose research is synthesized in a revealing assessment of the man and his work, featuring generous excerpts from the artist's letters.

Lindsay, Jack. *Thomas Gainsborough, His Life and Art*. New York: Universe, 1981. 244pp. Lindsay's critical biography is a full chronological account in which the artist and his work is set against a fully realized period backdrop. Gainsborough's letters help to present Gainsborough's personality and views.

Waterhouse, Ellis. *Gainsborough*. 1958. Revised ed. London: Spring Books, 1966. 296pp. Waterhouse's study remains the standard, authoritative source on Gainsborough's life and art. Gainsborough's paintings and drawings are beautifully reproduced, and Waterhouse's volume is preferred to give the reader the fullest exposure to the artist's achievement and development.

Other Biographical Studies

Whitley, William T. *Thomas Gainsborough*. New York: Scribner, 1915. 417pp. Whitley's detailed biography helped establish the factual record of Gainsborough's life, and the book remains an important reference source, though less flattering details of the artist have been omitted or de-emphasized.

Williamson, G.A. *The Ingenious Mr. Gainsborough: Thomas Gainsborough: A Biographical Study*. New York: St. Martin's, 1972. 224pp. Williamson's is a popular biography focused on Gainsborough the man rather than the artist. The book sketches his early life in a brief prologue, beginning in earnest with Gainsborough's arrival in Bath seeking his fortune as a portrait painter.

Woodall, Mary. *Thomas Gainsborough: His Life and Work*. New York: Chanticleer Press, 1949. 128pp. This is a brief summary of Gainsborough's work and life, interspersing the basic facts with excerpts from the artist's letters and a critical examination of his works. Serves as a reliable introduction and reference volume.

Recommended Juvenile Biographies

Glendinning, Sally. *Thomas Gainsborough: Artist of England*. Champaign, Illinois: Garrard, 1969. 154pp. MG. Glendinning's is a fictionalized biography that offers a skillful characterization of the artist and his era.

Ripley, Elizabeth. *Gainsborough: A Biography*. Philadelphia: Lippincott, 1964. 72pp. MG/YA. With a good selection of his works, unfortunately not in color, Ripley supplies a sensible overview of Gainsborough's artistic career and achievement.

181. GALILEO GALILEI
1564–1642

One of history's most important scientists, Galileo's work laid foundations for modern experimental science and greatly expanded human understanding of the universe. The young Galileo studied medicine at the University of Pisa but was soon drawn to mathematics and physics. In 1609 he constructed the first complete astronomical telescope and while exploring the heavens discovered several planetary satellites, studied Saturn, and confirmed the Copernican theory of the solar system, which stated that the sun rather than the earth is the center of our planetary system. Galileo's support of the banned theory marked a turning point in scientific and philosophical thought and resulted in a charge of heresy against him. He was tried by the Inquisition (1633), convicted, and forced to abjure his beliefs and writings concerning the theory.

Autobiography and Primary Sources

Discoveries and Opinions of Galileo. Garden City, New York: Doubleday, 1957. 302pp. A selection from Galileo's writings, the book provides his defense of the Copernican cosmology, the story of his development of a telescope, and his unorthodox opinions on science and philosophy.

Recommended Biographies

Drake, Stillman. *Galileo at Work: His Scientific Biography*. Chicago: University of Chicago Press, 1978. 536pp. Written by one of the most respected modern scholars on Galileo, this detailed and reliable examination of Galileo's scientific ideas and intellectual development challenges various misconceptions in a balanced and readable portrait. *Galileo* (New York: Hill & Wang, 1980. 100pp.) is a valuable, brief overview of Galileo's career, focusing on the issues surrounding his trial and the factors that caused it with a number of new and provocative insights.

Ronan, Colin A. *Galileo*. New York: Putnam, 1974. 264pp. In a lavishly illustrated, balanced account for the general reader, the author sets Galileo the man and scientist in the context of his times and reveals an individual who was fiery and pugnacious. The book may disappoint readers who desire a more detailed account of Galileo's scientific achievements.

Sobel, Dava. *Galileo's Daughter: A Historical Memoir of Science, Faith, and Love*. New York: Walker, 1999. 448pp. Sobel's fresh perspective on Galileo's life and personality comes from an examination of his relationship with his illegitimate daughter, Maria Celeste. The book features the first translation of her letters to her father, providing a rare, immediate glimpse of his conflict with the church and contemporary values. Galileo emerges as a fully understandable, human figure.

Other Biographical Studies

Allan-Olney, Mary. *The Private Life of Galileo*. London: Macmillan, 1870. 307pp. The author's source for her intimate look at Galileo are letters to and from his daughter which are quoted extensively, providing a human portrait often missing in other biographical treatments.

Brodrick, James. *Galileo: The Man, His Work, His Misfortunes.* New York: Harper & Row, 1964. 152pp. Written in defense of the Jesuits' role in Galileo's persecution, the author points to Galileo's own complicity, Pope Urban VIII's enmity, and the resentment of the academic establishment as the key factors in his fall.

De Santiliana, Giorgio. *The Crime of Galileo.* Chicago: University of Chicago Press, 1955. 339pp. Concentrating on Galileo's trial and its causes, the book examines the stages of Galileo's intellectual development and presents a character study against a clear cultural and historical background.

Fahie, John J. *Galileo: His Life and Work.* New York: J. Pott, 1903. 451pp. Fahie's early biography draws on the complete edition of Galileo's works in a treatment of the scientist's career that has been superseded by later more factually reliable accounts.

Geymonat, Ludovico. *Galileo Galilei: A Biography and Inquiry into His Philosophy of Science.* New York: McGraw-Hill, 1965. 260pp. Accessible for the nonspecialist, the book concentrates on Galileo's philosophical and scientific theories along with a biographical sketch.

Redondi, Pietro. *Galileo: Heretic.* Princeton, New Jersey: Princeton University Press, 1987. 356pp. In a new interpretation of Galileo's trial and the motives behind it, the author presents a meticulously documented examination of the historical and cultural forces at play with many original and controversial insights, although Galileo the man is not shown in as sharp a focus as his times.

Reston, James Jr. *Galileo: A Life.* New York: HarperCollins, 1995. 319pp. Reston emphasizes Galileo's personality and the politics of his era rather than his scientific achievements in this readable, popular account. The early, formative years are only sketched here, concentrating instead on those elements in Galileo's character which would make his later confrontation with the church inevitable.

Sharratt, Michael. *Galileo: Decisive Innovator.* Cambridge, Massachusetts: Blackwell, 1994. 247pp. In a short, readable summary of Galileo's life and work written by a Roman Catholic priest, the author emphasizes Galileo's relationship with the church and supplies a useful introduction for the nonscientist.

Biographical Novels

Harsányi, Zsolt. *The Star-Gazer.* New York: Putnam, 1939. 572pp. This fictional life of Galileo traces his career from boyhood through his scientific discoveries and his conflict with the church. The novel stays close to the facts of Galileo's life for its events and details.

Fictional Portraits

Weiss, David. *Physician Extraordinary: A Novel of the Life and Times of William Harvey.* New York: Delacorte, 1975. 455pp. In this biographical novel on the career of groundbreaking doctor and scientist William Harvey, his medical training in Padua is described, including his residence with Galileo.

Recommended Juvenile Biographies

Fisher, Leonard E. *Galileo.* New York: Atheneum, 1992. unpaged. MG. A beautifully illustrated biography that dramatically captures the complexity of Galileo's life and achievement in the context of his times.

Hightower, Paul N. *Galileo: Astronomer and Physicist.* Springfield, New Jersey: Enslow, 1997. 128pp. MG. Part of the Great Minds of Science series, this is a readable account of the key events of Galileo's life and his contributions to science. Includes several activities readers can do to illustrate the scientific discoveries.

MacLachlan, James H. *Galileo Galilei: First Physicist.* New York: Oxford University Press, 1997. 126pp. YA. This entry in the Oxford Portraits in Science series examines Galileo's personality, intellectual development, and scientific achievement, as well as the religious and political forces of his times.

Sis, Peter. *Starry Messenger.* New York: Farrar, Straus, 1996. unpaged. MG. A 1997 Caldecott Honor Book, this superbly illustrated biography traces Galileo's life from his childhood to his death, celebrating his capacity of observation and the impact of his discoveries on the science, philosophy, and art of Renaissance Italy.

Biographical Films and Theatrical Adaptations

Bentley, Eric. *The Recantation of Galileo Galilei: Scenes from History Perhaps.* New York: Harper & Row, 1972. 116pp. Bentley offers an original and controversial assessment of Galileo's nature in nine scenes from his life.

Brecht, Bertolt. *Galileo.* New York: Grove Press, 1966. 155pp. Brecht explores the question of a scientist's social and ethical responsibility in this dramatic characterization of Galileo who must choose between his survival and his life's work under the pressure of the church's persecution. See also the film version, *Galileo* (1975). Director: Joseph Losey. Topol takes the lead role with an impressive supporting cast, including Colin Blakely, Clive Revill, John Gielgud, Judy Parfitt, and Tom Conti. Video.

Goodwin, Richard. *The Hinge of the World.* New York: Farrar Straus, 1998. 209pp. Goodwin's play centers on the confrontation between Galileo and Pope Urban VIII.

Stavis, Barrie. *Lamp at Midnight: A Play about Galileo.* South Brunswick, New Jersey: A.S. Barnes, 1966. 107pp. See also the film version, *Lamp at Midnight* (1983). Director: George Schaefer. Both the play and film depict three events in Galileo's life: his invention of a telescope, his confrontation with the Inquisition, and the publication of *Dialogue on the Two Systems of the World.* The film stars Melvyn Douglas, David Wayne, Michael Hodern, and Kim Hunter. Video.

Galileo (1970). Director: Dennis Azzarella. After showing Galileo's experiments, the film dramatizes the conflict between his new scientific thinking and the church's authority. Video.

Other Sources

Finocchiaro, Maurice A., ed. *The Galileo Affair: A Documentary History.* Berkeley: University of California Press, 1989. 382pp. Translates some 50 key background documents surrounding Galileo's trial, along with an informative introduction, biographical descriptions of the main figures, and a chronology of events.

MacHamer, Peter K., ed. *The Cambridge Companion to Galileo.* New York: Cambridge University Press, 1998. 462pp. This collection of essays covers numerous facets of Galileo's life, ideas, and relationship with the church reflecting recent scholarship and modern interpretations of Galileo.

182. INDIRA GANDHI
1917–1984

The daughter of Jawaharlal Nehru, India's first prime minister, served as an aide to her father and as minister of information in the government of Shri Lal Bahadur Shastri, whom she succeeded in 1966. Under her leadership, India defeated Pakistan, which resulted in the formation of the state of Bangladesh. In 1975 she was found guilty of illegal political practices during the 1971 campaign, refused to resign, and declared a state of emergency during which opponents were arrested and the press censored. The conviction was overturned, but she and her Congress party were defeated in 1977. Elected again in 1980, she served until 1984, when she was assassinated by her Sikh security guards.

Autobiography and Primary Sources

Gandhi's personal writings and autobiographical reflections are available in several volumes, including *My Truth* (New York: Grove Press, 1982. 200pp.), her defensive retrospective of her principles and actions, and *Indira Gandhi on Herself and Her Times* (Calcutta: Ananda, 1987. 104pp.), one of the last interviews she conducted with Nemal S. Bose in which she discusses her life and political career. A selection of Gandhi's early letters to her father is also available in *Freedom's Daughter: Letters Between Indira Gandhi and Jawaharlal Nehru, 1922–1939.* Sonia Gandhi, ed. (Delhi: CBS Publishers, 1992. 483pp.).

Recommended Biographies

Gupte, Pranay. *Mother India: A Political Biography of Indira Gandhi.* New York: Scribner, 1992. 593pp. This is a lucid analysis of both Gandhi's political career and the factors that have affected the course of contemporary Indian history. Well written and documented, the book is critical but fair to Gandhi's leadership and personality.

Jayaker, Pupul. *Indira Gandhi: An Intimate Biography.* New York: Pantheon, 1993. 410pp. Based on extensive personal access to Gandhi at crucial points during her career, Jayaker's account includes details on Gandhi's childhood, schooling, marriage, political apprenticeship, and her career as prime minister, forming an often captivating portrait of a figure of great paradoxes.

Malhotra, Inder. *Indira Gandhi: A Personal and Political Biography.* London: Hodder and

Stoughton, 1989. 363pp. The leading comprehensive biography written by an eyewitness and confidante, Malhotra's assessment attempts to see Gandhi clearly as a complex and deeply flawed individual. What Malhotra uncovers is richer and more revealing than other treatments.

Other Biographical Studies

Adams, Jad, and Philip Whitehead. *The Dynasty: The Nehru-Gandhi Story.* New York: TV Books, 1997. 390pp. Based on letters, journalistic accounts, interviews, and original research, the authors trace the Nehru and Gandhi family fortunes from 1857 through the political careers of Indira and Rajiv Gandhi both in its public and private context.

Ali, Tariq. *An Indian Dynasty: The Story of the Nehru-Gandhi Family.* New York: Putnam, 1985. 318pp. In a dramatic exposé of the Nehru and Gandhi family, Indira Gandhi is given a hostile treatment, and Rajiv Gandhi is described as a pawn of Indira's dynastic ambitions. The book is flawed by factual errors.

Bhatia, Krishan. *Indira: A Biography of Prime Minister Gandhi.* New York: Praeger, 1974. 290pp. Written by one of India's most astute journalists, this biography chronicles Indira Gandhi's development and relationship with her father. Best on unraveling the complex Indian political scene.

Carras, Mary C. *Indira Gandhi in the Crucible of Leadership: A Political Biography.* Boston: Beacon Press, 1979. 289pp. Carras's analysis of Indira Gandhi's personality attempts to reveal the psychological factors in her rise to power and fall and is based on interviews with her subject conducted in 1975 and 1978. Highly speculative in certain interpretations, the book is nonetheless revealing and provocative.

Drieberg, Trevor. *Indira Gandhi: A Profile in Courage.* New York: Drake, 1973. 221pp. Drieberg's political biography describes Indira Gandhi's childhood, education, and political apprenticeship. The book concentrates on her 1966 election victory in an overly admiring portrait.

Hutheesing, Krishna. *Dear to Behold: An Intimate Portrait of Indira Gandhi.* New York: Macmillan, 1969. 221pp. Written by Indira Gandhi's aunt, this sympathetic account of her niece's early years and development provides invaluable firsthand information.

Masani, Zareer. *Indira Gandhi: A Biography.* New York: Crowell, 1976. 341pp. Completed before the declaration of the state of emergency in 1975, with a brief final chapter added dealing with it, Masani's biography is one of the most balanced and probing studies available on Gandhi's early life and political career that does not minimize either her accomplishments or weaknesses.

Mohan, Anand. *Indira Gandhi: A Personal and Political Biography.* New York: Meredith Press, 1967. 336pp. Written shortly after Gandhi's 1966 election as prime minister, Mohan's generally reliable account is based largely on interviews with Gandhi, her relatives, teachers, friends, and colleagues and documents her development leading up to her first national political challenge.

Moraes, Dom F. *Indira Gandhi.* Boston: Little, Brown, 1980. 336pp. Setting Gandhi's political career in its sociohistorical context, this political biography offers a number of interesting vignettes but is often sentimental and lacking in intellectual rigor and depth.

Sahgal, Nayantara. *Indira Gandhi: Her Road to Power.* New York: Frederick Ungar, 1982. 260pp. Written by Indira Gandhi's cousin, this highly partisan and hostile portrait originating in a family feud provides revealing firsthand information but lacks the objectivity and balance to serve as a fully reliable study.

Recommended Juvenile Biographies

Butler, Francelia. *Indira Gandhi.* New York: Chelsea House, 1987. 112pp. MG. This is a fair and honest assessment of Indira Gandhi's strengths and weaknesses that places her career in the wider context of India's history and challenges.

Currimbhoy, Nayana. *Indira Gandhi.* New York: F. Watts, 1985. 116pp. MG. Gandhi's personal and political career are competently handled in this generally objective assessment that depicts both the Indian leader's strengths and weaknesses.

Haskins, James. *India Under Indira and Rajiv Gandhi.* Hillside, New Jersey: Enslow, 1989. 104pp. MG. This dual portrait of mother and son delivers a good balance between personal and political details that includes the more controversial aspects of Gandhi's career.

Biographical Films and Theatrical Adaptations

The Dynasty (1997). Directors: Mark Anderson and Charles Bruce. Documents both the life of Mahatma Gandhi and the interlinked history of the Nehru-Gandhi families. Video.

See also Jawaharlal Nehru

183. MAHATMA GANDHI
1869–1948

One of history's great spiritual and political leaders, Mohandas Gandhi was born in Porbandar and educated in India and London. He became a lawyer and leader of the Indian community in South Africa (1893–1915), and it was there that he began to eschew Western ways and to develop his abstemious and celibate lifestyle. Upon his return to India, he worked toward Indian independence from Great Britain. He conducted campaigns of nonviolent civil disobedience, which included hunger strikes and marches and instituted a Quit India movement that resulted in his internment (1942–1944). He vigorously and unsuccessfully opposed the partition of a separate Muslim state (Pakistan). He was assassinated by a Hindu fanatic while holding a prayer and pacification meeting in New Delhi.

Autobiography and Primary Sources

An Autobiography: Or the Story of My Experience with Truth. Boston: Beacon Press, 1957. 528pp. Originally published in serialized form in the 1920s, Gandhi's recollections are remarkably sincere and self-critical in treating not only the details of his life but his feelings about them.

Recommended Biographies

Brown, Judith M. *Gandhi: Prisoner of Hope.* New Haven, Connecticut: Yale University Press, 1989. 440pp. By far the best available biography, Brown's scholarly though readable life relates Gandhi's personal life with his political career and succeeds in presenting a complex figure whose achievements are measured by their personal costs.

Chadha, Yogesh. *Gandhi: A Life.* New York: Wiley, 1998. 560pp. Chronicles Gandhi's life in a dramatic narrative focusing on the key events that formed his intellectual, spiritual, and political development. Respectful yet balanced, Chadha's treatment allows a fully rounded human portrait to emerge.

Fischer, Louis. *The Life of Mahatma Gandhi.* New York: Harper, 1950. 558pp. Fischer's affectionate biography based on interviews and an array of published and unpublished sources remains a valuable contribution to understanding the man and his movement. Although Fischer's partisanship is evident, he supplies the details and surmises that make Gandhi's motives and behavior clear, an element missing from other biographies.

Other Biographical Studies

Ashe, Geoffrey. *Gandhi.* New York: Stein and Day, 1968. 404pp. Ashe's reassessment of Gandhi's personality and his influence is strong on personal details and Gandhi's early years, but the book lacks documentation and serves mainly a general reader looking for a helpful introduction.

Clement, Catherine. *Gandhi: The Power of Pacifism.* New York: Abrams, 1996. 176pp. The author's angle for viewing Gandhi is his pacifism and relations with the British during the drive for Indian independence. The highlights of his career are presented with the impact of his personality on history detailed.

Easwaran, Eknath. *Gandhi, the Man: The Story of His Transformation.* Tomales, California: Nilgiri Press, 1997. 179pp. This biographical account concentrates on Gandhi's development from a shy, awkward young lawyer into the moral and political force of his country. Based on personal acquaintance, Easwaran's analysis illuminates the source of Gandhi's power and his leadership.

Gold, Gerald. *Gandhi: A Pictorial Biography.* New York: Newmarket Press, 1983. 192pp. Published as a companion to Richard Attenborough's 1982 film, the book provides an accurate outline of the events of Gandhi's life but omits a good deal of the complexity of his ideas and Indian politics.

Mehta, Ved. *Mahatma Gandhi and His Apostles.* New York: Viking, 1976. 260pp. Mehta's inquiry into the man behind the legend is based on extensive interviews with surviving relatives and disciples. Along with details of Gandhi's personal habits and daily routine the various sides of Gandhi's complex personality emerge clearly.

Nanda, B.R. *Mahatma Gandhi: A Biography.* Boston: Beacon Press, 1959. 542pp. This is a sympathetic but not sentimental account of Gandhi's life, career, and an accomplished history of India during the first half of the twentieth century. Nanda's interpretations of motivations and personalities are well balanced and insightful, and the book documents Gandhi's intellectual, moral, and political development.

Nehru, Jawaharlal. *Mahatma Gandhi.* 1949. Reprint ed. New York: Asia Publishing House, 1966. 171pp. Nehru's brief biographical sketch is valuable because of his perspective and firsthand account of important events in the independence effort from 1916 when Nehru first met Gandhi to the latter's death.

Payne, Robert. *The Life and Death of Mahatma Gandhi.* New York: Dutton, 1969. 703pp. Payne's sensitive, narrative account is at times over-reverent, but a complex personality does emerge with an evident "dark side." Inadequate in its political chronology, the book will appeal to readers in search of a dramatic portrayal of the man.

Pyarelai. *Mahatma Gandhi.* Ahmedabad: Navajivan Publishing, 1956–1986. 5 vols. The author's five volumes form a detailed narrative of the political events in Gandhi's life, but the man remains elusive. However, Pyarelai's exhaustive study is far more readable than Tendulkar's even more massive biography.

Rolland, Romain. *Mahatma Gandhi: The Man Who Became One with the Universal Being.* New York: Century, 1924. 250pp. The author's early appreciation of Gandhi significantly contributed to his worldwide reputation. Originally published as a series of articles for the journal *Europe,* the book has little value as biography but has historical interest showing how Gandhi was viewed in the West as the Gandhi phenomenon began.

Tendulkar, D.G. *Mahatma: Life of Mohandas Karamchand Gandhi.* Bombay: Publications Division, Government of India, 1951–1954. 8 vols. The author's mammoth multi-volume work is more a valuable repository of primary materials than a readable and carefully shaped, interpretive life. Despite the many volumes, the first half of Gandhi's life is cursorily treated.

Fictional Portraits

Narayan, R.K. *Waiting for the Mahatma.* East Lansing: Michigan State University Press, 1955. 241pp. A young Indian who falls in love with one of Gandhi's followers must wait months for the Mahatma's blessing in an intimate look at Gandhi's daily life and circle.

Wolpert, Stanley A. *Nine Hours to Rama.* New York: Random House, 1962. 376pp. Dramatizing the nine hours preceding Gandhi's assassination, the novel focuses on the assassin whose life is detailed in flashback, while the political issues swirling around Gandhi are traced.

Recommended Juvenile Biographies

Bush, Catherine. *Gandhi.* New York: Chelsea House, 1987. 111pp. MG/YA. Bush does an excellent job combining details of Gandhi's life with the complicated history of Indian independence.

Cheney, Glenn A. *Mahatma Gandhi.* New York: F. Watts, 1983. 114pp. MG. Informative and helpful

biography that traces Gandhi's development and impact.

Severance, John B. *Gandhi: Great Soul.* New York: Clarion Books, 1997. 144pp. MG/YA. The author relates the development of Gandhi's ideas with the personal evolution and historical context. Although positive in its appreciation, mention is also made of less flattering aspects of Gandhi's life, particularly his relationships with his wife and children.

Biographical Films and Theatrical Adaptations

A&E Biography Video: Gandhi: Pilgrim of Peace (1997). Producer: Noah Morowitz. This is an informative documentary profile using archival footage and interviews with experts. Video.

The Dynasty (1997). Directors: Mark Anderson and Charles Bruce. Documents both the life of Mahatma Gandhi and the interlinked history of the Nehru-Gandhi families. Video.

Gandhi (1982). Director: Richard Attenborough. This reverent and visually stunning biography traces Gandhi's life from his years as a young lawyer in South Africa through the struggle for Indian independence and the ensuing civil war. Ben Kingsley won the Best Actor Oscar for his compelling performance. The impressive supporting cast includes Edward Fox, John Gielgud, Candice Bergen, John Mills, Daniel Day-Lewis, and Trevor Howard. Video.

Gandhi (1990). Producer: Patricia Lagone. Written and narrated by James Cameron, this film biography uses archival footage to review Gandhi's life from his early manhood to his death. Video.

Lord Mountbatten: The Last Viceroy (1986). Director: Tom Clegg. A dramatization of the events leading up to and following Indian independence from the perspective of Lord Mountbatten and his wife. Starring Nicol Williamson, Janet Suzman, and Ian Richardson. Video.

Mahatma Gandhi: Soul Force (1978). Director: Don Thompson. Henry Fonda narrates this brief examination of Gandhi's philosophy of nonviolence and his quest for Indian independence using archival footage. Video.

Nine Hours to Rama (1963). Director: Mark Robson. Film version of Stanley A. Wolpert's novel, the film traces the forces leading up to Gandhi's assassination. Filmed on location, the film boasts a solid cast of Horst Buchholtz, Jose Ferrer, Robert Morley, Diane Baker, and Harry Andrews.

The Road to Indian Independence (1990). Directors: Marie-Louise Darien and Marc Ferro. Gandhi's nonviolent efforts to secure Indian independence and his attempt to halt the civil war that followed are chronicled. Video.

See also Jawaharlal Nehru

184. FEDERICO GARCÍA LORCA
1898–1936

Spanish poet and dramatist, García Lorca was inspired by the spirit and folklore of his native

Andalusia and became the most popular Spanish poet of his generation with the publication of his *Gypsy Ballads* (1928). Other works include *Lament for the Death of a Bullfighter* (1935), *The Poet in New York* (1955), and the plays *Blood Wedding* (1938) and *The House of Bernardo Alba* (1936). He was shot and killed by Nationalist soldiers at the outbreak of the Spanish Civil War.

Autobiography and Primary Sources

Selected Letters. David Gershator, ed. New York: New Directions, 1983. 172pp. Lorca's surviving letters are frustratingly free of personal revelations and private details.

Recommended Biographies

Gibson, Ian. *Federico García Lorca: A Life.* New York: Pantheon, 1989. 551pp. After a first book on Lorca's death, Gibson widens his investigatory method for a consideration of his life. Richly detailed and exhaustively researched through interviews and the Lorca archives, Gibson documents the religious, sexual, and social elements in the poet's sensibility, along with an insider's knowledge of Spanish culture.

Stainton, Leslie. *Lorca: A Dream of Life.* New York: Farrar, Straus, 1999. 579pp. Stainton's is a thorough, vivid biographical portrait that ably traces Lorca's psychological and artistic evolution. Realistically countering many of the myths that have surrounded the poet and playwright, the book does a remarkable job keeping the man in close and compelling focus.

Other Biographical Studies

Adams, Mildred. *García Lorca: Playwright and Poet.* New York: G. Braziller, 1977. 204pp. A friend of Lorca, Adams provides an affectionate, superficial appreciation of the man without reference to the poet's homosexuality or insight into his work. As one reviewer lamented, the book "accomplishes what had seemed impossible—to make the genius of Lorca seem trivial."

Barea, Arturo. *Lorca: The Poet and His People.* New York: Harcourt, Brace, 1949. 176pp. As the author, a Spanish poet, explains, his intention was "to bring Lorca's poetry nearer to readers, particularly non-Spanish readers, by showing how it reflects and transforms the world of the Spanish people to which it belongs." The social and political context of Lorca's development provides the primary focus here.

Cobb, Carl W. *Federico García Lorca.* New York: Twayne, 1967. 160pp. This is a reliable introductory overview of the poet's life and work aimed at the undergraduate and general reader.

García Lorca, Francisco. *In the Green Morning: Memories of Federico.* New York: New Directions, 1986. 256pp. Lorca's younger brother offers his recollections of Lorca's early life and family background. Despite the author's unique viewpoint, this is a selective memoir, curiously distant and often sketchy in details.

Gibson, Ian. *The Death of Lorca.* Chicago: J.P. O'Hara, 1973. 217pp. Gibson's initial study of García Lorca is a meticulously detailed investigation of the facts surrounding the poet's death. Based on eye-witness testimony, including the man who arrested Lorca, Gibson documents Nationalist repression in Granada and the broader political factors that led to the poet's execution.

Honig, Edwin. *Federico García Lorca.* Norfolk, Connecticut: New Directions, 1944. 242pp. The first detailed survey in English of Lorca's life and work, Honig establishes a workable chronology against which to view the poet and playwright's achievement. A number of Honig's details have been corrected by later accounts.

Biographical Films and Theatrical Adaptations

Federico García Lorca: A Murder in Granada (1976). Producer: Umberto López y Guerra. This is a film portrait of Lorca's life and the circumstances surrounding his death, featuring interviews with contemporaries and family members. Video.

185. JAMES A. GARFIELD
1831–1881

The twentieth U.S. president, Garfield was a teacher and principal (1857-1861) of Western Reserve Eclectic Institute in Hiram, Ohio, as well as a lay preacher of the Disciples of Christ. A major general of volunteers during the Civil War, he resigned in 1863 to take a seat in the House of Representatives, where he supported severe Reconstruction measures against the South. He was elected president in 1880 and the following July was shot and killed by Charles Guiteau, a disappointed office seeker.

Autobiography and Primary Sources

Crete and James: Personal Letters of Lucretia and James Garfield. John Shaw, ed. East Lansing: Michigan State University Press, 1994. 397pp. This collection of 300 letters exchanged between Garfield and his wife covers the years between 1853 and Garfield's death. Their courtship, Garfield's Ohio senate career, Civil War experience, and details of his presidency are discussed.

The Diary of James A. Garfield. Harry J. Brown and Frederick D. Williams, eds. East Lansing: Michigan State University Press, 1967-1981. 4 vols. Garfield's diary entries begin in 1848 and end in 1877, short of his presidency but still a revealing chronicle of Garfield's activities and views.

The Life and Letters of James Abram Garfield. Theodore Clark, ed. 1925. Reprint ed. Hamden, Connecticut: Archon Books, 1968. 2 vols. Clark documents this account of Garfield's life with extensive excerpts from the letters.

Recommended Biographies

Doenecke, Justus D. *The Presidencies of James A. Garfield and Chester A. Arthur.* Lawrence: University Press of Kansas, 1981. 229pp. Doenecke's assessment of the Garfield administration includes as well a consideration of Garfield's background, political and intellectual development, and strengths and weaknesses of his leadership.

Peskin, Allan. *Garfield.* Kent, Ohio: Kent State University Press, 1978. 716pp. Peskin's is the most thorough and reliable biography of Garfield available. The book replaces the various heroic myths surrounding Garfield with a balanced, realistic view of Garfield's background, development, and public career.

Other Biographical Studies

Caldwell, Robert G. *James A. Garfield: Party Chieftain.* New York: Dodd, Mead, 1931. 383pp. Although now outdated and superseded by later scholarship and interpretation, Caldwell's is a full-length account that captures both the details of Garfield's public career and his personality.

Clark, James C. *The Murder of James A. Garfield: The President's Last Days and the Trial and Execution of His Assassin.* Jefferson, North Carolina: McFarland, 1993. 185pp. Clark documents Garfield's assassination and its subsequent events in a narrative chronicle.

Leech, Margaret, and Harry J. Brown. *The Garfield Orbit.* New York: Harper & Row, 1978. 369pp. The portion of the book dealing with Garfield's eighteen-year congressional career and short-lived presidency is the work of Brown and far more reliable than Leech's often sentimentalized treatment of Garfield's early years and family life. The private Garfield and his love for the women in his life are the predominant interests here.

Taylor, John M. *Garfield of Ohio: The Available Man.* New York: W.W. Norton, 1970. 336pp. Taylor's narrative biography is a capable summary of Garfield's varied career. Useful for the general reader as an introductory overview of the man and his era.

Recommended Juvenile Biographies

Brown, Fern G. *James A. Garfield: 20th President of the United States.* Ada, Oklahoma: Garrett, 1990. 124pp. MG. A straightforward, factual summary of Garfield's life and presidency.

Lillegard, Dee. *James A. Garfield: Twentieth President of the United States.* Chicago: Childrens Press, 1987. 98pp. MG. The basic facts of Garfield's life, character, and career are covered in a competent overview.

186. GIUSEPPE GARIBALDI
1807–1882

Italian patriot and a major figure in the Risorgimento, Garibaldi first gained fame as a guerrilla leader in Brazilian and Uruguayan revolutions. On his return (1848) to Italy he fought brilliantly for Giuseppe Mazzini's Roman Republic and with his famous "red shirts" captured Sicily and Naples in a decisive guerrilla campaign against Austria. Garibaldi's surrender of these territories to King Victor Emmanuel I effectively unified Italy. He tried unsuccessfully to capture Rome from the pope in 1862 and 1867, and during the Franco-Prussian War (1870-1871) commanded a troop of French and Italian volunteers.

Autobiography and Primary Sources

Memoirs. New York: Appleton, 1931. 432pp. Although not always factually reliable, Garibaldi's account of his life provides a valuable glimpse of the man, his views, and temperament.

Recommended Biographies

Mack Smith, Denis. *Garibaldi: A Great Life in Brief.* New York: Knopf, 1956. 207pp. Mack Smith's compact biography is an excellent starting point to introduce the reader to Garibaldi and his times. Highly readable and informative, the book provides a balanced and credible portrait of the man within the wider context of his era.

Ridley, Jasper. *Garibaldi.* New York: Viking, 1976. 718pp. Ridley's is the most comprehensive, full-length biography of Garibaldi available. A synthesis of primary and secondary sources, the book provides new information on Garibaldi's career before 1848 and devotes considerable attention to his final twenty years. Readers interested in Garibaldi's military career should consult Trevelyan; on his political career Mack Smith is more assured, but Ridley is best on Garibaldi the man.

Trevelyan, George M. *Garibaldi.* New York: Longmans, 1907–1911. 3 vols. This is a classic historical narrative of Garibaldi's campaigns. Despite some errors of fact and interpretation, there are few better accounts of the era.

Other Biographical Studies

De Polnay, Peter. *Garibaldi: The Legend and the Man.* New York: T. Nelson, 1961. 255pp. This is a straightforward, factual narrative that uses letters and documents to illustrate Garibaldi's thoughts and activities. The book, however, offers little support for its interpretations, and a lack of clear documentation makes it difficult to evaluate their reliability.

Hibbert, Christopher. *Garibaldi and His Enemies: The Clash of Arms and Personalities in the Making of Italy.* Boston: Little, Brown, 1966. 423pp. Combining biographical and historical details, Hibbert concentrates on the most dramatic moments of Garibaldi's life. Very much the admirer, Hibbert sometimes glosses over Garibaldi's flaws, and neither the man nor his era is presented in depth.

Larg, David. *Giuseppe Garibaldi: A Biography.* 1934. Reprint ed. Port Washington, New York: Kennikat Press, 1970. 352pp. Larg's is a relatively brief and somewhat simplified account of Garibaldi's life and career that adds little to what is known about the man or his activities but does present the accepted view in a lively narrative.

LiPira, Benedict S. *Giuseppe Garibaldi: A Biography of the Father of Modern Italy.* Baltimore: Noble House, 1998. 121pp. LiPira's is an overview of Garibaldi's life and times that compresses a great deal of information into a brief account that will appeal primarily to the general reader.

Parris, John. *The Lion of Caprera: A Biography of Giuseppe Garibaldi.* New York: D. McKay, 1962. 352pp. The work of an English lawyer and amateur scholar, Parris recycles previous sources into a readable summary for the general reader.

Biographical Novels

Bryant, Dorothy. *Anita, Anita*. Berkeley, California: Ata, 1993. 300pp. The novel dramatizes Garibaldi's relationship with a Brazilian woman who joins his activities in South America and Italy and bears him four children.

Recommended Juvenile Biographies

Davenport, Marcia. *Garibaldi: Father of Modern Italy*. New York: Random House, 1957. 184pp. MG. This biography in the Landmark series is a fast-paced and informative narrative account of Garibaldi's life and career.

Viola, Herman J. *Giuseppe Garibaldi*. New York: Chelsea House, 1988. 112pp. MG/YA. Viola's biography is a solid introduction to both the man and his times that displays both his strengths and failings.

Other Sources

Mack Smith, Denis, ed. *Garibaldi*. Englewood Cliffs, New Jersey: Prentice-Hall, 1969. 182pp. Part of the Great Lives Observed series, the volume includes excerpts from Garibaldi's writings, views by his contemporaries, and modern critical assessments.

187. DAVID GARRICK
1717–1779

A renowned English actor of the eighteenth century, Garrick replaced the popular declamatory school with a more natural style of acting. A notably versatile actor, he excelled equally in contemporary drama as well as in Shakespearean roles. While manager of the Drury Lane Theatre (1747-1776) he instituted such reforms as the concealment of stage lighting from the audience. He also wrote several plays, including the farces *Miss in Her Teens* (1747) and *Bon Ton* (1775).

Autobiography and Primary Sources

Letters. David M. Little and George M. Kahrl, eds. Cambridge, Massachusetts: Harvard University, 1963. 3 vols. This scholarly collection of Garrick's letters is a fascinating and invaluable record of his activities, relationships, and personality.

Recommended Biographies

Kendall, Alan. *David Garrick: A Biography*. New York: St. Martin's, 1985. 224pp. Like Stone and Karhl's book, Kendall's biography is arranged topically and is more accessible and comprehensible for the nonspecialist. Garrick career is viewed from a variety of angles, taking full advantage of Garrick's own words from his letters, with many illustrations helping to capture the scene.

Oman, Carola. *David Garrick*. London: Hodder and Stoughton, 1958. 427pp. Oman's is a highly readable, vivid, life-and-times biography that offers a multidimensional portrait of Garrick in the wider context of his age.

Stone, George Winchester Jr., and George M. Karhl. *David Garrick: A Critical Biography*. Car-

bondale: Southern Illinois University Press, 1979. 771pp. In this scholarly and well-documented examination of the range of Garrick's activities and interests, the book is arranged not chronologically but topically with separate sections on Garrick as theatrical manager, playwright, actor, and social figure that include important documentary evidence. A basic resource for the specialist, student, and the general reader who already possesses a chronological sense of Garrick's career.

Other Biographical Studies

Barton, Margaret. *Garrick*. New York: Macmillan, 1948. 312pp. Barton's is a selective portrait, emphasizing Garrick's relationships and his social activities. Somewhat defensive in tone, the less flattering aspects of Garrick's character and behavior are minimized.

Fitzgerald, Percy H. *The Life of David Garrick*. 1868. Revised ed. London: Simpkin and Marshall, 1899. 480pp. Based on essential primary sources, Fitzgerald's authoritative documentation of Garrick's life and dealings remains an indispensable biographical source upon which all subsequent biographers have depended.

Knight, Joseph. *David Garrick*. 1894. Reprint ed. New York: B. Blom, 1969. 346pp. Knight offers little not covered more completely by Fitzgerald. To be consulted for its facts rather than read for pleasure.

Murphy, Arthur. *The Life of David Garrick*. 1801. Reprint ed. New York: B. Blom, 1969. 2 vols. The work of a contemporary playwright and associate of Garrick, Murphy provides a detailed record of Garrick's theatrical dealings and relationships and an important firsthand account of the man.

Fictional Portraits

Hall, Robert Lee. *Murder at Drury Lane*. New York: St. Martin's, 1992. 279pp. Garrick engages Benjamin Franklin to investigate a death during a performance at London's Drury Lane Theatre.

Recommended Juvenile Biographies

Stewart, Anna B. *Enter David Garrick*. Philadelphia: Lippincott, 1951. 278pp. YA. Stewart's fictionalized biography begins when Garrick, at age 10, sees his first play, and chronicles his career up to his death in a sympathetic and detailed presentation.

188. MARCUS GARVEY
1887–1940

The most influential African American leader of the 1920s and a proponent of black nationalism, Garvey founded (1914) the Universal Negro Improvement Association to foster worldwide unity among blacks and to promote the greatness of the African heritage in a "back to Africa" movement. He gained millions of followers with his brilliant oratory and his newspaper, *Negro World*, but his influence waned after he was jailed (1925) for mail fraud while attempting to establish the Black Star

Line, a shipping company for trade with Africa. He was deported (1927) to Jamaica.

Autobiography and Primary Sources

Philosophy and Opinions of Marcus Garvey. Amy Jacques Garvey, ed. 1923–1925. (Reprint ed. New York: Atheneum, 1969. 2 vols.) is the essential collection of Garvey's speeches and writings. A useful companion volume is *Marcus Garvey: Life and Lessons*. Robert A. Hill and Barbara Blair, eds. (Berkeley: University of California Press, 1987. 451pp.), which brings together a number of Garvey's writings from 1925 until his death, including his 1930 serialized autobiography.

Recommended Biographies

Cronon, Edward D. *Black Moses: The Story of Marcus Garvey and the Universal Negro Improvement Association*. Madison: University of Wisconsin Press, 1955. 278pp. The first full-length biography of Garvey is still one of the best available. Although Garvey's early life is sketchy, the book supplies an objective view, skillful in portraying the strength of Garvey's appeal as well as his limitations.

Stein, Judith. *The World of Marcus Garvey: Race and Class in Modern Society*. Baton Rouge: Louisiana State University Press, 1986. 294pp. Stein offers a reassessment of Garvey's career and Garveyism that substitutes a contrary class paradigm for understanding his appeal and the challenges he faced. Not for the casual reader, but those with sufficient background will be challenged by this absorbing analysis.

Other Biographical Studies

Fax, Elton C. *Garvey: The Story of a Pioneer Black Nationalist*. New York: Dodd, Mead, 1972. 305pp. Relying mainly on secondary sources and adding little to our knowledge of Garvey, besides some new details of his early years in Jamaica, Fax supplies a impassioned narrative account in which Garvey's personal strengths and weaknesses are fairly assessed.

Garvey, Amy Jacques. *Garvey and Garveyism*. 1963. Reprint ed. New York: Collier, 1976. 287pp. Garvey's second wife offers her perspective on the major events of Garvey's life with a uniquely personal view of Garvey's private side.

Lewis, Rupert. *Marcus Garvey: Anti-Colonial Champion*. Trenton, New Jersey: Africa World Press, 1988. 301pp. This is an extensive political biography and examination of Garvey's ideas that looks at his formative years, his early political activities in Jamaica, and his influence on national liberation movements in Africa, the Caribbean, and Central America.

Martin, Tony. *Race First: The Ideological and Organizational Struggle of Marcus Garvey and the Universal Negro Improvement Association*. Westport, Connecticut: Greenwood, 1976. 421pp. After a brief biographical introduction, Martin focuses on Garvey's ideological development and his public career. Thoroughly researched and organized topically, this is a major scholarly work serving scholars rather than the casual, general reader.

Nembhard, Lenford. *Trials and Triumphs of Marcus Garvey.* 1940. Reprint ed. Millbrook, New York: Kraus, 1978. 249pp. This early biographical account written by a fellow Jamaican concentrates movingly on Garvey's life after his deportation from the United States.

Recommended Juvenile Biographies

Davis, Daniel S. *Marcus Garvey.* New York: F. Watts, 1972. 179pp. MG/YA. This birth-to-death account is a balanced assessment that relates Garvey's career to the wider historical and cultural context.

Lawler, Mary. *Marcus Garvey.* New York: Chelsea House, 1988. 110pp. MG/YA. Lawler supplies a reliable, full treatment of Garvey's life and times.

Biographical Films and Theatrical Adaptations

Marcus Garvey: Toward Black Nationhood (1983). Producer: Werner Koch. Using archival photos, film footage, and excerpts from Garvey's writing, this film portrait features interviews with his relatives and contemporaries to present highlights of his career. Video.

Other Sources

Clarke, John H., ed. *Marcus Garvey and the Vision of Africa.* New York: Random House, 1974. 496pp. This is an important collections of writings by and about Garvey organized chronologically to follow his career, with concluding sections on Garvey and his critics and an examination of recent scholarship about him.

189. PAUL GAUGUIN
1848–1903

French artist whose work greatly influenced modern art, Gauguin was a sailor and stockbroker until his 30s, when he began to devote himself entirely to his art. He spent much time in the South Pacific, where he produced the brilliantly colored paintings of Polynesian life for which he is famous. His paintings include *La Orana Maria* (1891), *By the Sea* (1892), and *Where do we come from? What are we? Where are we going?* (1897). Gauguin also produced fine lithographs and pottery pieces.

Autobiography and Primary Sources

Gauguin's extensive writings are collected in a variety of editions, including *Gauguin: Letters from Brittany and the South Seas* (New York: Clarkson Potter, 1992. 160pp.); *The Intimate Journals of Paul Gauguin* (London: Heinemann, 1952. 138pp.); and *Noa Noa: The Tahiti Journal of Paul Gauguin.* (New York: Chronicle Books, 1994. 168pp.).

The Writings of a Savage. David Guérin, ed. (New York: Viking, 1978. 304pp.) and *Gauguin by Himself.* Belinda Thomson, ed. (Boston: Little, Brown, 1993. 320pp.). These are compilations of Gauguin's views from his letters, journals, and essays.

Recommended Biographies

Burnett, Robert. *The Life of Paul Gauguin.* New York: Oxford University Press, 1937. 294pp. Long regarded as the standard life, Burnett's is a well-researched, lucid account of Gauguin's life and personality that avoids either romanticization or condemnation. The basic facts of Gauguin's life are carefully assembled, allowing the painter to tell his own story as much as possible.

Perruchot, Henri. *Gauguin.* Cleveland: World, 1964. 398pp. Perruchot adds new details to the factual record supplied by Burnett and has superseded his biography as the standard source on the painter's life. Minutely documented, the author deals with the events of Gauguin's life with restraint, understanding, and sympathy.

Sweetman, David. *Paul Gauguin: A Life.* New York: Simon & Schuster, 1995. 600pp. Sweetman provides a highly readable, carefully documented reassessment that displays all the contradictions of Gauguin's life and character, free of the distortions of myth that have clouded a clear view of the artist. Realistic in its evaluation of the artist, the book succeeds in documenting Gauguin's development against a believable historical and cultural backdrop.

Other Biographical Studies

Becker, Beril. *Paul Gauguin: The Calm Madman.* New York: A. and C. Boni, 1931. 340pp. Although observing the basic factual outline of Gauguin's life, this is a highly fictionalized biography, about which one contemporary reviewer observed, "There is enough action here to supply plots for a dozen romantic biographies, but no valid explanation of how Gauguin found time to paint."

Danielsson, Bengt. *Gauguin in the South Seas.* Garden City, New York: Doubleday, 1965. 336pp. Limited to the events of Gauguin's final decade, this is a thorough, well-documented study of the painter's South Pacific period based on written sources and interviews with hundreds of individuals who actually knew the artist.

Gauguin, Pola. *My Father, Paul Gauguin.* New York: Knopf, 1937. 292pp. Gauguin's son supplies a corrective view of the various myths surrounding his father's behavior and experiences in the South Pacific, based on the painter's journals, letters, and his own childhood impressions and his mother's reminiscences. The book counters the notion that Gauguin's decision to abandon his business career and family was a rash decision or that the painter ever lost the affection of his wife and family.

Hanson, Lawrence, and Elisabeth Hanson. *Noble Savage: The Life of Paul Gauguin.* New York: Random House, 1955. 299pp. Intended for a popular audience, this is a detailed narrative biography emphasizing the dramatic aspect of Gauguin's story and personality that sometimes distorts the book's accuracy and objectivity.

Hoog, Michel. *Paul Gauguin: Life and Work.* New York: Rizzoli, 1987. 332pp. Hoog's critical biography concentrates on Gauguin's relationship with other artists and his artistic development. Countering the notion that Gauguin was an intuitive primitivist, Hoog suggests that Gauguin was a seri-

ous artist who approached his work deliberately with a strong theoretical basis.

Le Pinchon, Yann. *Gauguin: Life, Art, and Inspiration.* New York: Abrams, 1987. 268pp. Le Pinchon's is a brief critical summary of Gauguin's artistry with the essential outline of his life reliably summarized for the general reader.

Thomson, Belinda. *Gauguin.* New York: Thames and Hudson, 1987. 215pp. Serving as a solid introduction to the man and his art for the nonspecialist, Thomson is a fine choice for the reader looking for a reliable and accessible overview.

Biographical Novels

Gorham, Charles. *The Gold of Their Bodies.* New York: Dial Press, 1955. 276pp. This biographical account of the artist's life covers his career from his youth to his death in an account that adheres closely to the known biographical facts. The author's partisanship, however, often glosses over the less flattering sides of Gauguin's behavior.

Recommended Juvenile Biographies

Cachin, Françoise. *Gauguin: The Quest for Paradise.* New York: Abrams, 1992. 195pp. YA. Cachin's illustrated biography makes use of excerpts from the painter's letters and writings, as well as descriptions from his contemporaries.

Greenfeld, Howard. *Paul Gauguin.* New York: Abrams, 1993. 92pp. YA. Part of the First Impression series, this is a lucid critical survey of Gauguin's artistic development and achievement.

Spence, David. *Gauguin: Escape to Eden.* Hauppauge, New York: Barron's, 1998. 32pp. MG. This is a vividly illustrated, short survey of Gauguin's life and work.

Biographical Films and Theatrical Adaptations

Lust for Life (1956). Director: Vincente Minnelli. Film adaptation of Irving Stone novel with Kirk Douglas as the tortured Van Gogh and Anthony Quinn as Gauguin in an Oscar-winning performance. Video. See also the novel *Lust for Life* (New York: Doubleday, 1934. 489pp.).

The Wolf at the Door (1995). Director: Henning Carlsen. A believably biographical look at Gauguin's life after his return to Paris from Tahiti when he tries to raise the money to go back to the South Pacific. Donald Sutherland plays the artist. Video.

See also Vincent Van Gogh

190. GENGHIS KHAN
ca. 1167–1227

A brilliant and ruthless conqueror, and ruler of one of the largest land empires in history, Genghis Khan was born Temu-jin. After succeeding his father, Yekusai, as chieftain of a Mongol tribe, he began to consolidate his power by fighting to become ruler of a Mongol confederacy and subjugating many Mongolian tribes. He assumed the title Genghis Khan in 1206 after accepting leadership of the

Mongols during a meeting held in his capital, Karakorum. At his death, his empire stretched from the Pacific Ocean to the Caspian Sea and included northern China, Mongolia, southern Siberia, and central Asia.

Autobiography and Primary Sources

The History and the Life of Chinggis Khan: Secret History of the Mongols. New York: E.J. Brill, 1990. 183pp. Written by Mongol scholars during the thirteenth century, this remains the essential primary source for information on Genghis Khan's ancestors and successors, as well as details of his conquest. Clearly the work of devoted admirers, Genghis is celebrated as a flawless hero.

Recommended Biographies

Hartog, Leo de. *Genghis Khan: Conqueror of the World.* New York: St. Martin's, 1989. 230pp. The recommended popular biography, de Hartog's synthesizes earlier biographical and historical sources into a vivid and dramatic narrative that lacks interpretation or analysis but compensates with its animation of Genghis Khan's personality and times.

Hoàng, Michel. *Genghis Khan.* New York: New Amsterdam Books, 1991. 323pp. The author helpfully assembles most of the facts and legends surrounding Genghis without attempting to separate them all. The result is a full and colorful collection of details that brings his subject vividly to life.

Ratchnevsky, Paul. *Genghis Khan: His Life and Legacy.* Cambridge, Massachusetts: Blackwell, 1992. 313pp. Drawing on Mongolian, Chinese, Persian, and English sources, Ratchnevsky, a former British ambassador to Mongolia, has produced the definitive biography that supersedes all other studies in its research and documentation of Genghis Khan's life and times.

Other Biographical Studies

Brent, Peter L. *Genghis Khan.* New York: McGraw-Hill, 1976. 264pp. Brent's is an excellent account of the Mongol conquests and Genghis Khan's achievement and leadership, with a full treatment of Mongol customs and history.

Fox, Ralph. *Genghis Khan.* New York: Harcourt, Brace, 1936. 285pp. This is a sympathetic treatment that puts Genghis Khan's life story in the context of Mongolian history in a highly readable and lucid fashion.

Grousset, René. *Conqueror of the World.* New York: Orion, 1967. 300pp. Originally published in France in 1944 and long recognized as the standard, authoritative life, Grousset's careful and scholarly study was the most reliable and comprehensive biography available until Ratchnevsky's definitive life.

Lamb, Harold. *Genghis Khan: Emperor of All Men.* Garden City, New York: Doubleday, 1927. 268pp. In a popular biography with imagined dialogue and extensive speculation to fill the gaps in the factual record, Lamb provides a highly colorful and dramatic account of Genghis Khan's rise and conquests. Not reliable in many instances, Lamb's treatment is a readable introduction to Genghis and his times.

Liddell Hart, B.H. *Great Captains Unveiled.* 1928. Reprint ed. Freeport, New York: Books for Libraries Press, 1967. 274pp. Genghis Khan is one of the six military leaders that the author examines in a compact assessment of his strategic genius and impact.

Lister, R.P. *Genghis Khan.* New York: Stein and Day, 1969. 232pp. Lister, drawing on information from *The Secret History of the Mongols,* concentrates on Genghis Khan's early life and rise to power, placing him solidly in the context of his time and culture.

Martin, Henry Desmond. *The Rise of Chingis Khan and His Conquest of North China.* Baltimore, Maryland: Johns Hopkins University Press, 1950. 360pp. Providing a detailed and comprehensive depiction of the Mongol conquest between 1206 and 1227, the Mongol army, and its commander, the author's study is enriched by his own travels across the Mongolian steppes in the 1930s.

Vladimirtsov, B.Y. *The Life of Chingis Khan.* Boston: Houghton Mifflin, 1930. 172pp. The author provides a sociological examination of Mongol society to place Genghis Khan's life in sharper focus. An authority on Mongolian history and language, Vladimirtsov relies on primary sources in this character study accessible for the nonspecialist.

Biographical Novels

Baumann, Hans. *Sons of the Steppe: The Story of How the Conqueror Genghis Khan Was Overcome.* London: Oxford University Press, 1957. 273pp. This dramatization of Genghis Khan's conquest focuses on two of his grandsons: Arik-Buka who embraces the life of the Mongol warrior and Kublai Khan who yearns for peace. Their conflict, in which fact and legend is intertwined, is worked out against a vivid backdrop of camp life and in the campaign of Genghis Khan's hordes.

Caldwell, Taylor. *The Earth Is the Lord.* New York: Scribner, 1941. 550pp. Beginning with Genghis Khan's birth and ending with his first great victory, the novel is lushly dramatic, more operatic than historically accurate but captures its setting and customs effectively with a wealth of details.

Clou, John. *A Caravan to Camul.* Indianapolis: Bobbs-Merrill, 1954. 383pp. The novel deals with Genghis Khan's early years as seen through the perspective of a warrior and a philosopher in his service.

Sargent, Pamela. *Ruler of the Sky: A Novel of Genghis Khan.* New York: Crown, 1993. 703pp. This massive account of Genghis Khan's life is seen through the experiences of various women who loved him, including his mother and his various wives. Blending fact and fancy, the novel is somewhat plodding and repetitive in its approach, more atmospheric than revealing in capturing Genghis Khan's humanity and sources of greatness.

Fictional Portraits

Dandrea, Don. *Orlok.* Englewood, Florida: Pineapple Press, 1986. 319pp. The novel imagines the early life and military exploits of Subotai, Genghis Khan's brilliant lieutenant. The author admits that

he has departed from the generally accepted facts on historical characters and events.

Sproat, Robert. *Chinese Whispers.* London: Faber and Faber, 1988. 300pp. Ghenghis Khan and his hordes are depicted from a variety of witnesses, including enemies, allies, and victims.

Yarbro, Chelsea Quinn. *Path of the Eclipse.* New York: St. Martin's, 1983. 447pp. In this installment of Yarbro's historical vampire series, Count de Saint-Germain is pitted against Genghis Khan and his hordes as he comes to the aid of the daughter of a slain general.

Recommended Juvenile Biographies

Humphrey, Judy. *Genghis Khan.* New York: Chelsea House, 1988. 110pp. MG/YA. This is a competent account combining biographical details with a wider historical treatment of the Mongol conquest and its impact.

Lamb, Harold. *Genghis Khan and the Mongol Horde.* New York: Random House, 1954. 182pp. MG. Lamb, the author of a popular biography of Genghis Khan for adults, adapts his material and style for younger readers in an equally vivid account of the highlights of the conqueror's career.

Webb, Robert N. *Genghis Khan: Conqueror of the Medieval World.* New York: F. Watts, 1967. 120pp. MG. Webb supplies the essential information about Genghis Khan's life and times.

Biographical Films and Theatrical Adaptations

A&E Biography Video: Genghis Khan: Terror and Conquest (1995). Producer: Lionel Friedberg. With on-location footage in Mongolia, China, and the Middle East, this documentary looks at Genghis Khan's remarkable career with suggestions about the source of his powerful leadership. Video.

The Conqueror (1956). Director: Dick Powell. In what is widely regarded as one of the worst films ever made, John Wayne stars as Genghis Khan during his rise to power, with Susan Hayward, William Conrad, and Agnes Moorehead. Video.

Genghis Khan (1965). Director: Henry Lewin. Often inept, miscast epic loosely based on Genghis Khan's life and legend, starring Omar Sharif in the title role, supported by Stephen Boyd, James Mason, Eli Wallach, and Francoise Dorleac.

The Golden Horde (1951). Director: George Sherman. Set during the Mongol invasion, this historical romance shows Ann Blyth outwitting the invaders of her city. David Farrar, George Macready, Henry Brandon, and Richard Egan co-star.

Storm from the East (1994). Directors: Robert Marshall and Viviana Woodruff. This is a multipart film history of the Mongol empire from Genghis Khan to Kublai Khan. Video.

191. GEORGE III
1738–1820

The third Hanoverian king of Great Britain, George was the son of Frederick Louis, prince of Wales and grandson of George II, whom he succeeded to the throne in 1760. His insistence on maintaining royal leadership in government led to political instability and factionalism within Parliament. During his reign, the British lost their American colonies, trade was improved, Ireland and England united, philosophy, the arts, scientific thought, and exploration flourished, technology and transportation advanced, and the Industrial Revolution began. In 1810, after suffering the last in a series of mental breakdowns, possibly due to the hereditary disease porphyria, royal power devolved onto the prince regent.

Autobiography and Primary Sources

The Correspondence of King George III from 1760 to December 1783. Sir John Fortescue, ed. New York: Macmillan, 1927–1928. 6 vols. This edition of George's letters is marred by errors and misunderstandings and should be supplemented with Lewis Namier's *Additions and Corrections to Sir John Fortescue's Edition of the Correspondence of King George the Third* (Manchester: Manchester University Press, 1937. 86pp.).

The Later Correspondence of George III. A. Aspinall, ed. Cambridge, Massachusetts: Cambridge University Press, 1962–1970. 5 vols. Beginning when Fortescue stopped and succeeding where Fortescue failed in its meticulous editing, Aspinall assembles the remaining letters with scholarly precision and useful introductory essays.

The Letters of King George III. Bonamy Dobrée, ed. 1935. Reprint ed. New York: Funk and Wagnalls, 1968. 293pp. This selection of George's letters will appeal to the general reader interested in the high points and essential revelations contained in his correspondence.

Recommended Biographies

Ayling, Stanley. *George the Third.* New York: Knopf, 1972. 510pp. Ayling's competent and readable biography synthesizes primary and secondary sources and accumulates details that restores personality to the king, while balancing his view between the king's public and private life.

Brooke, John. *King George III.* New York: McGraw-Hill, 1972. 411pp. In the best available modern biography, Brooke sets George's life and political career solidly against the backdrop of his age. By an expert on the British political scene during the period, Brooke's balanced but sympathetic interpretation of George's character and influence is generally regarded as the standard, authoritative account.

Hibbert, Christopher. *George III: A Personal History.* New York: Basic Books, 1999. 400pp. Hibbert's clearly written and impressively researched biography concentrates on the complexities of George's personality and his private and family life. In a radical, fresh reassessment, Hibbert explodes a number of myths surrounding the king and reveals him as one of England's greatest kings: a competent ruler and patron of the arts and sciences who greatly enhanced the reputation of the monarchy.

Other Biographical Studies

Butterfield, Herbert. *George III and the Historians.* London: Collins, 1957. 304pp. Although not so much a biography as an examination of other biographies and studies of the king, Butterfield's assessment is illuminating in tracing the rise and fall of George III's reputation and the various biases of his critics and chroniclers.

Chenevix Trench, Charles. *The Royal Malady.* New York: Harcourt, Brace, 1965. 224pp. The first to make use of two unpublished diaries kept by royal physicians, Chenevix provides a detailed clinical account of the king's illness and the political maneuvering that compromised his treatment in 1788. The author also reveals a good deal about George III's personality.

Clarke, John. *The Life and Times of George III.* London: Weidenfeld and Nicolson, 1972. 223pp. Clarke's is a sound and sensible short biography that manages to compress a great deal of information into a coherent and accessible narrative.

Iremonger, Lucille. *Love and the Princesses.* New York: Crowell, 1958. 296pp. Iremonger supplies a biographical study of George and his relationship to his six daughters, concentrating on Princess Sophia and her illegitimate son.

Lloyd, Alan. *The King Who Lost America: A Portrait of the Life and Times of George III.* Garden City, New York: Doubleday, 1971. 369pp. In a biographical account intended for the general reader, the author assembles various anecdotes concerning George's reign that repeats conventional and disputed views and covers the king's last 30 years in a scanty 20 pages.

Long, John C. *George III: The Story of a Complex Man.* Boston: Little, Brown, 1961. 372pp. In a study devoted to the formation of George's character, Long mostly ignores much modern scholarship that has challenged the conventional and familiar view that is here expressed. The last half of the king's reign is barely sketched.

MacAlpine, Ida, and Richard Hunter. *George III and the Mad Business.* New York: Pantheon, 1970. 407pp. Written by two psychiatrists, this is deservedly regarded as the definitive, scholarly account of the king's illness that explodes numerous myths about George's madness.

Pain, Nesta. *George III at Home.* London: Eyre Methuen, 1975. 191pp. This account of George's private life concentrates on extensive accounts of his successive illnesses and of the scandals of his siblings and children.

Pares, Richard. *King George III and the Politicians.* Oxford: Clarendon Press, 1953. 214pp. Pares's political biography traces the king's transformation from his ineffectual youth to a self-confident and astute political leader.

Plumb, John H. *First Four Georges.* New York: Macmillan, 1956. 188pp. Plumb's composite biography of the four Georges is both lavishly illustrated and insightful in its character sketch of George III.

Biographical Novels

Maughan, A.M. *The King's Malady: The Young Pitt.* New York: J. Day, 1975. 270pp. British parliamentary politics during the reign of George III are dramatized in this fictionalized though reliable account of the career of William Pitt the Younger who remains loyal to the king in the sparring with Charles James Fox during the Regency crisis.

Morrow, Honoré. *Let the King Beware.* New York: Morrow, 1936. 376pp. The events leading up to the American Revolution are dramatized from the perspectives of a number of historical figures, including George III. The portrait of the king and the novel's interpretation of events are often at odds with more established views.

Plaidy, Jean. *The Prince and the Quakeress.* New York: Putnam, 1968. 318pp. The novel dramatizes one of the great royal mysteries: was the future George III secretly married to a young Quaker girl? The novel offers a speculative answer based on some evidence and George III's character, though historians have disputed most of the novel's suggestions; *The Third George* (New York: Putnam, 1987. 352pp.) concentrates on George III's marriage to Charlotte of Mecklenburg through political struggles, family troubles, and the onset of the king's illness; *Perdita's Prince* (New York: Putnam, 1987. 346pp.) describes the love affair of the young Prince of Wales (later George IV) and an actress, George III is presented as a stern obstacle to the couple's happiness.

Fictional Portraits

Ashton, Helen. *Footman in Powder.* New York: Dodd, Mead, 1954. 248pp. A behind-the-scenes look at the royal family is provided by a servant in the Prince of Wales' employ who is on hand for the various scandals and clashes of will between father and son.

Kenyon, Frank W. *The Duke's Mistress: The Story of Mary Ann Clarke.* New York: Dodd, Mead, 1969. 255pp. The novel tells the remarkable story of the cockney beauty who became the mistress of the second son of George III who survives the king's disapproval and causes one of the greatest royal scandals in English history.

Wheeler, Guy. *Cato's War.* New York: Macmillan, 1980. 320pp. The British perspective on the American Revolution is dramatized in the experiences of a British colonel sent to Carolina to recruit loyalists. A number of historical figures appear, including George III, Cornwallis, and Washington.

Recommended Juvenile Biographies

Fritz, Jean. *Can't You Make Them Behave, King George?* New York: Coward-McCann, 1977. 45pp. MG. Despite its facetious title and brevity, Fritz deals with a number of serious issues in this entertaining and informative biography, including the king's leadership, the effects of his illness, and the beginning of the American Revolution from the king's perspective.

Green, Robert. *King George III.* New York: F. Watts, 1977. 64pp. MG. Chronicling the important events of George III's life and reign in a readable text, supplemented by numerous illustrations, Green's is a suitable choice for a reliable overview.

Biographical Films and Theatrical Adaptations

Bennett, Alan. *The Madness of George III.* New York: Random House, 1992. 81pp. Bennett's thoughtful stage drama restores considerable humanity to George III whose illness occasions a brutal grab for power. Video.

A&E Biography Video: King George III: Mad or Maligned? (1995). Director: Sue Hayes. Filmed on location throughout England, the film examines George's life and reign in detail with the aid of historians to untangle the various contradictions surrounding the king. Video

The Adams Chronicles (1975). Director: Paul Bogart. George III is portrayed by John Tillinger in this dramatization of the life and times of the Adams family. Video.

Beau Brummell (1954). Director: Curtis Bernhardt. In this lavish period costume drama, Robert Morley portrays George III with Stewart Granger as Brummell and a supporting cast that includes Elizabeth Taylor and Peter Ustinov as the Prince Regent. Video.

Liberty! The American Revolution (1997). Directors: Ellen Hoyde and Muffie Meyer. Alex Jennings portrays George III in this documentary look at the Revolution with actors performing historical figures' words. Video.

The Madness of King George (1994). Director: Nicholas Hytner. In the film adaptation of Alan Bennett's play, Nigel Hawthorne reprises his critically acclaimed stage performance as a compellingly human George III whose illness becomes a battleground for political opportunists. With a solid supporting cast including Helen Mirren, Ian Holm, Rupert Everett, and Rupert Graves. Video.

See also George IV; William Pitt

193. GEORGE IV
1762–1830

The eldest son of George III and prince regent during his father's final illness, George was known for his extravagant and dissolute ways. He was illegally married to Maria Fitzherbert (1785) and in 1795, to secure parliamentary settlement of his enormous debts, married Caroline of Brunswick. His profligacy as well as his mistreatment of his wife, whom he unsuccessfully tried to divorce immediately after succeeding to the throne in 1820, aroused much public hostility and resulted in a loss of power and prestige for the monarchy.

Autobiography and Primary Sources

The Correspondence of George, Prince of Wales, 1770–1812. A. Aspinall, ed. New York: Oxford University Press, 1963–1978. 8 vols. Aspinall has produced the scholarly edition of George's letters prior to his coronation with solid documentation and helpful identifying notes.

The Letters of King George IV, 1812–1830. A. Aspinall, ed. Cambridge, Massachusetts: Cambridge University Press, 1938. 3 vols. The record of the king's correspondence is ably presented in this scholarly collection.

Recommended Biographies

David, Saul. *Prince of Pleasure: George IV and the Making of the Regency.* New York: Grove/Atlantic, 1999. 432pp. David's thoroughly researched and balanced study succeeds in placing George squarely in the historical milieu that he played a considerable role in shaping. Despite an often indulgent private life and public scandals, George is shown as a man of high intelligence, political ambition, and one of the central figures in the tumultuous changes the Regency produced.

Hibbert, Christopher. *George IV: Prince of Wales, 1762–1811.* New York: Harper & Row, 1974. 338pp; *George IV: Regent and King, 1811–1830.* New York: Harper & Row, 1975. 430pp. Hibbert's two-volume study is both highly readable and fully documented, based on extensive research in the royal archives at Windsor. More interested in George's personality and the formation of his character than the politics of his era, the book allows his achievements as a patron of the arts and his contribution to the transformation of London but does not gloss over his defects. Serves as the most comprehensive and authoritative full-length biography available.

Other Biographical Studies

Fitzgerald, Percy H. *The Life of George the Fourth: Including His Letters and Opinions.* New York: Harper, 1881. 921pp. Fitzgerald's is an old-fashioned historical biography, chiefly of use for its supply of letters documenting George's life and reign.

Fulford, Roger. *George the Fourth.* New York: Putnam, 1935. 301pp. The author attempts an accurate portrait of the king that includes his virtues as well as his failings and largely succeeds in animating his personality and era without the partisan bias of other treatments.

Leslie, Doris. *The Great Corinthian: A Portrait of the Prince Regent.* New York: Oxford University Press, 1953. 251pp. This defense of the prince overlooks his faults and is not reliable as an objective and unbiased portrait.

Leslie, Shane. *George IV.* Boston: Little, Brown, 1926. 209pp. Leslie's whitewashing of the king is marred by facetiousness and selectivity. As Leonard Woolf observed in a contemporary review, the book is "powered with epigrams and smart sayings and little stories and historical facts, but there is George IV exactly as he was before—a thoroughly bad king and a stupid, mean, treacherous, uneducated, unpleasant man."

Palmer, Alan W. *The Life and Times of George IV.* London: Weidenfeld and Nicolson, 1972. 224pp. This is an excellent illustrated biography with a sensible and well-written text that offers the high points of the king's life and personality.

Plumb, John H. *First Four Georges.* New York: Macmillan, 1956. 188pp. Plumb's composite biog-

raphy of the four Georges is both lavishly illustrated and insightful in its character sketch of the kings and their eras.

Priestley, J.B. *The Prince of Pleasure and His Regency.* New York: Harper & Row, 1969. 304pp. The emphasis here is on the Regency period rather than on the prince. Generously illustrated, the book offers a sympathetic character sketch that deals honestly with George's flaws.

Richardson, Joanna. *George the Magnificent: A Portrait of King George IV.* New York: Harcourt, Brace, 1966. 410pp. Largely ignoring the political dimension of George's reign, Richardson concentrates on George's creative achievements and a reassessment of his character. In a series of anecdotes, the author documents George's charms and generosity, though his flaws do not escape attention.

Smith, E.A. *George IV.* New Haven, Connecticut: Yale University Press, 1999. 306pp. Smith covers George's life from 1820 to 1830 in a revisionist assessment that contends that previous biographers and historians have overemphasized George's weaknesses and failures.

Readers interested in George IV's relationship with his wife Caroline and his various mistresses have a number of volumes from which to choose:

Fraser, Flora. *The Unruly Queen: The Life of Queen Caroline.* New York: Knopf, 1996. 537pp. Based on extensive research in the Royal Archives and other manuscript collections, this is the most complete and documented study of Caroline and her disastrous marriage.

Fulford, Roger. *The Trial of Queen Caroline.* New York: Stein and Day, 1968. 255pp. The most detailed account of Caroline's trial and the behind-the-scenes maneuvering. Particularly good on the public view of Caroline and George during the scandal.

Holme, Thea. *Caroline: A Biography of Caroline of Brunswick.* New York: Atheneum, 1980. 245pp. This is a lively, thought-provoking biography that is based on printed and unpublished sources.

Parry, Edward A. *Queen Caroline.* New York: Scribner, 1930. 353pp. Parry offers one of the best available defenses of Caroline's character and behavior.

Russell, Edward F. L. *Caroline, the Unhappy Queen.* South Brunswick, New Jersey: A. S. Barnes, 1968. 172pp. In a highly partisan defense of Caroline, George IV is depicted as a monster and his unfortunate wife as a misunderstood and innocent heroine.

Thompson, Grace E. *The Prince of Scandals: The Story of George the Fourth, of His Amours and Mistresses.* New York: Harper & Row, 1931. 316pp. This popular social biography based on diarist's accounts is mostly valuable for the manners and mores it displays. The view of George is largely hostile and simplistic.

Wilkins, William H. *Mrs. Fitzherbert and George IV.* London: Longmans, 1906. 2 vols. Wilkins's lengthy review of the relationship between George and Mrs. Fitzherbert is marred by the author's evident partisanship on behalf of the king's mistress.

Biographical Novels

Condon, Richard. *The Abandoned Woman.* New York: Dial Press, 1977. 317pp. Based loosely on historical facts, the novel follows Caroline's career from her marriage to her death. Condon distorts and invents to fit a modernist and satirical impulse.

Haeger, Diane. *The Secret Wife of King George IV.* New York: St. Martin's, 2000. 384pp. The Prince of Wales's relationship with Mrs. Fitzherbert is dramatized in a historically authentic account with cameo appearances by Charles Fox, Richard Sheridan, and a convincing portrait of George in conflict between love and duty.

Hardwick, Michael. *Regency Royal.* New York: Coward-McCann, 1978. 326pp. Chronicling George's career as prince, regent, and king, the novel is crammed with historical figures and stays close to history in its depiction of the era and its events.

Plaidy, Jean. *Perdita's Prince.* New York: Putnma, 1987. 346pp. Describing the love affair of the young Prince of Wales and Mary Robinson, a young actress, the novel dramatizes the widening rift between George III and his son and its political implications. In *Sweet Lass of Richmond.* (New York: Putnam, 1988. 381pp.), the Prince of Wales's scandalous affair with Mrs. Maria Fitzherbert is detailed with a vivid and authentic evocation of the period and the politics surrounding the affair; *Indiscretions of the Queen.* (New York: Putnam, 1988. 350pp.) deals with Caroline's life and relationship with George in a vivid and mainly accurate fictional account.

Fictional Portraits

The Prince Regent appears in countless historical novels and romances to lend atmosphere and glamour. Only a few of his more significant appearances are listed below.

Ashton, Helen. *Footman in Powder.* New York: Dodd, Mead, 1954. 248pp. A behind-the-scenes look at the royal family is provided by a servant in the Prince of Wales's employ who is on hand for the various scandals.

Laker, Rosalind. *The Sugar Pavilion.* New York: Doubleday, 1994. 370pp. The novel traces the career of a French émigré who enters the confectionery trade in Brighton and is embroiled in court intrigue surrounding the Regent and Mrs. Fitzherbert.

Main, Mary. *The Girl Who Was Never Queen: A Biographical Novel of Princess Charlotte of Wales.* Garden City, New York: Doubleday, 1962. 356pp. Princess Charlotte's life is dramatized with invention and surmises to fill in the gap in the factual record.

Orczy, Emma. *The Scarlet Pimpernel.* 1902. Various editions. In this classic adventure yarn, the Prince of Wales gets fashion advice from Sir Percy and the Carleton House scene is vividly captured.

Plaidy, Jean. *Goddess of the Green Room.* New York: Putnam, 1989. 351pp. The love affair between George's younger brother William, Duke of Clarence, and the actress Dorothy Jordon lasts for 23 years despite the royal family's efforts to separate the couple. The novel dramatizes their story

with an authentic look at the royals and the era. *The Regent's Daughter.* New York: Putnam, 1989. 389pp. The novel chronicles the short, unhappy life of Princess Charlotte, heir to the throne who is caught between her feuding parents but insists on marrying for love only to die during childbirth.

Biographical Films and Theatrical Adaptations

Beau Brummell (1954). Director: Curtis Bernhardt. In this lavish period costume drama, Stewart Granger stars as Brummell with a supporting cast that includes Elizabeth Taylor, Peter Ustinov as the Prince Regent and Rosemary Harris as Mrs. Fitzherbert. Video.

Lady Caroline Lamb (1972). Director: Robert Bolt. A distinguished cast is largely wasted in this disappointing drama based on the scandal surrounding Lady Lamb's affair with Byron. Sarah Miles and Richard Chamberlain are the lovers. Ralph Richardson appears as the Regent with Laurence Olivier as the Duke of Wellington. Video.

A Royal Scandal (1996). Director: Sheree Folkson. The relationship between the Prince and Caroline of Brunswick is dramatized with Richard E. Grant as George and Susan Lynch as his mismatched spouse. Neither is shown as blameless here in a vivid recreation of their lives and times. Video.

The Scarlet Pimpernel (1935). Director: Harold Young. Leslie Howard is the definitive Sir Percy in this classic film version of Baroness Orczy's Regency adventure novel. Merle Oberon plays Percy's wife and Raymond Massey is the villainous Chauvelin. Nigel Bruce appears as a foppish Prince Regent. Video.

The Scarlet Pimpernel (1982). Director: Clive Donner. In a television remake Anthony Andrews and Jane Seymour star as the Blakeneys with Ian McKellen as Chauvelin and Julian Fellowes as the Regent. Video.

See also George III

194. GERONIMO
1829–1909

Leader of the Chiricahua Apaches of Arizona, Geronimo led (1881-1886) a series of hit-and-run raids after the Apaches were forcibly removed (1876) to a barren reservation in New Mexico. He surrendered and escaped twice; after his third surrender in 1886, he was deported as a prisoner of war to Florida, imprisoned in Alabama for a time, and eventually settled in Oklahoma, where he became a prosperous farmer.

Autobiography and Primary Sources

Geronimo: His Own Story. 1906. New York: Dutton, 1970. 190pp. Geronimo spoke to S.M. Barrett through an Apache interpreter, narrating the story of his life. This edition of the autobiography considers several of Geronimo's statements in the light of recent scholarship.

Sonnichsen, C.L., ed. *Geronimo and the End of the Apache Wars.* Lincoln: University of Nebraska Press, 1986. 136pp. Collects important documen-

tary evidence written by participants and eyewitnesses on both sides related to Geronimo's pursuit and eventual capture.

Recommended Biographies

Adams, Alexander B. *Geronimo: A Biography.* New York: Putnam, 1971. 381pp. Adams's book is a carefully documented account of the Apache wars and Geronimo's life from the Indian viewpoint. Although with little information about Geronimo's personal life, the book is thorough in its historical and cultural context.

Debo, Angie. *Geronimo: The Man, His Time, His Place.* Norman: University of Oklahoma Press, 1976. 480pp. This is a sympathetic account of Geronimo's life and achievement that carefully evaluates the available evidence and questionable accounts, including Geronimo's own assertions found in his autobiography.

Other Biographical Studies

Aleshire, Peter. *The Fox and the Whirlwind: General George Crook and Geronimo: A Paired Biography.* New York: Wiley, 2000. 384pp. Aleshire explores the cultural differences and the linked similarities between Geronimo and his pursuer in this dual biography that uses personal memoirs and government reports and dispatches (as well as considerable conjecture to reconstruct Geronimo's early life) to capture both men in a web of historical and personal destiny.

Davis, Britton. *The Truth about Geronimo.* New Haven, Connecticut: Yale University Press, 1929. 253pp. The work of an officer who participated in the military operation to subdue Geronimo, the book supplies a balanced, objective look at the events and attempts to represent Geronimo's cause fairly.

Faulk, Odie B. *The Geronimo Campaign.* New York: Oxford University Press, 1969. 245pp. Faulk supplies a thorough, balanced reassessment of the military campaign to subdue Geronimo with a helpful summary of the known details of the warrior's life.

Biographical Novels

Carter, Forrest. *Watch for Me on the Mountain.* New York: Delacorte, 1978. 305pp. Geronimo is presented as a religious mystic in a somewhat idealized portrait that chronicles his life and times.

Conley, Robert J. *Geronimo: An American Legend.* New York: Pocket Books, 1994. 218pp. Conley concentrates on Geronimo's life from his escape from the reservation until his final surrender two years later, with a plausible, speculative account of his early years.

Dugan, Bill. *Geronimo.* New York: Harper & Row, 1994. 309pp. This is a fictional biography of the Apache chief, basing a reconstruction of his early years on oral tales and legends. For the later years, the novel stays close to the known facts.

Fictional Portraits

Alexander, Lawrence. *The Strenuous Life.* New York: Knightsbridge, 1991. 304pp. In this ingenious period mystery with Theodore Roosevelt as chief sleuth, a historical cast that includes John D. Rockefeller and Geronimo are connected to a wide-ranging conspiracy.

Fraser, George MacDonald. *Flashman and the Redskins*. New York: Penguin, 1983. 479pp. In this installment of Fraser's comic repossession of history, the bounder Harry Flashman is in the American West where he is captured by the Apaches and marries an Indian maiden with Geronimo serving as his best man.

Recommended Juvenile Biographies

Hermann, Spring. *Geronimo: A Freedom Fighter*. Springfield, New Jersey: Enslow, 1997. 128pp. MG. This is a well-documented account of Geronimo's life that covers his rise to leadership within his tribe to his death.

Schwarz, Melissa. *Geronimo: Apache Warrior*. New York: Chelsea House, 1992. 127pp. MG/YA. Schwarz presents a credible historical and psychological portrait of Geronimo that relates his actions against a clearly depicted historical background.

Shorto, Russell. *Geronimo and the Struggle for Apache Freedom*. Englewood Cliffs, New Jersey: Silver Burdett, 1989. 131pp. MG. Shorto places Geronimo's activities in the wider historical context of westward expansion.

Biographical Films and Theatrical Adaptations

A&E Biography Video: Geronimo: The Last Renegade (1993). Director: Donna E. Lusitana. Competent film profile using archival material and expert testimony. Video.

Apache (1954). Director: Robert Aldrich. Burt Lancaster is an Apache who refuses to surrender in this thoughtful western drama, with Geronimo played by Monte Blue. Video.

Geronimo (1962). Director: Arnold Laven. Chuck Connors is surprisingly convincing in this sympathetic treatment of Geronimo's clash with the army. Video.

Geronimo (1993). Director: Roger Young. Cable television drama looks at Geronimo at various stages of his career in a serious attempt to tell a truthful story based on Indian culture and historical records. Starring Joseph Runningfox, Jimmy Herman, and Michael Greyeyes. Video.

Geronimo: An American Legend (1994). Director: Walter Hill. The attempt to capture Geronimo is dramatized in this solid film portrait, featuring Wes Studi in the title role, Jason Patric as the film's narrator and central consciousness, and appearances by Robert Duvall as a scout and Gene Hackman as General Crook. Video.

Geronimo and the Apache Resistance (1988). Director: Neil Godwin. In an installment of PBS's American Experience series, the Apaches narrate their own story offering a very different portrait of Geronimo. Video.

195. GEORGE GERSHWIN
1898–1937

American composer George Gershwin was born in Brooklyn, New York, and at 16 worked as a song plugger in Tin Pan Alley and as a rehearsal pianist on Broadway. He began writing song revues and at 19 wrote his first successful song, "Swanee." In addition to many other popular songs, Gershwin wrote the scores for several musicals, including *Lady, Be Good!* (1924), *Girl Crazy* (1930), and *Of Thee I Sing* (1931). His compositions often combined traditional musical forms with jazz and folk themes and rhythms and include the symphonic *Rhapsody in Blue* (1924), the tone poem *An American in Paris* (1928), and the opera *Porgy and Bess* (1935).

Recommended Biographies

Jablonski, Edward. *Gershwin*. Garden City, New York: Doubleday, 1987. 436pp. Regarded by many as the definitive Gershwin biography, Jablonski's study is authoritative and detailed, based on extensive research. Indispensable for its facts, Jablonski's book rarely goes beyond them for speculative insights into the artist or his artistry, however.

Rosenberg, Deena. *Fascinating Rhythm: The Collaboration of George and Ira Gershwin*. New York: Dutton, 1991. 516pp. This study of the Gershwin brothers' collaboration makes the musical connection between George's music and Ira's lyrics accessible to the general reader. Packed with insights into the pair's personalities and development.

Other Biographical Studies

Armitage, Merle, ed. *George Gershwin*. New York: Longmans, 1938. 252pp. Appearing immediately after Gershwin's death, this memorial tribute includes reminiscences of the composer's friends and colleagues.

Armitage, Merle. *George Gershwin: Man and Legend*. New York: Duell, Sloan and Pearce, 1958. 188pp. Armitage, who managed Gershwin's final concerts and mounted critically acclaimed productions of *Porgy and Bess,* offers reminiscences of Gershwin's last years with a detailed history of the composition and staging of *Porgy and Bess,* as well as Ira Gershwin's biographical sketch of his brother.

De Santis, Florence. *Gershwin*. New York: Treves, 1987. 106pp. This short biographical sketch is intended for a general reader and features extensive photographs.

Ewen, David. *George Gershwin: His Journey to Greatness*. Englewood Cliffs, New Jersey: Prentice-Hall, 1970. 354pp. A popular biography that includes information from the Gershwin family, quotations from letters, and interviews with contemporaries. Concentrates on Gershwin's career rather than his private life. The book has been charged with misrepresentations and falsifications.

Goldberg, Isaac. *George Gershwin: A Study in American Music*. 1931. Revised ed. New York: Frederick Ungar, 1958. 387pp. Written with Gershwin's cooperation, Goldberg's study includes valuable information about the composer's childhood and early career. Not objective enough to be reliable in every aspect, the book remains an important biographical source.

Greenberg, Rodney. *George Gershwin*. London: Phaidon, 1998. 240pp. Part of the 20th Century Composers series, conductor Greenberg's biography serves as a useful critical introduction to the composer's life, artistry, and musical influence.

Jablonski, Edward, and Lawrence D. Stewart. *The Gershwin Years*. 1958. Revised ed. Garden City, New York: Doubleday, 1973. 416pp. This dual pictorial biography of the Gershwin brothers was written with the cooperation of Ira Gershwin and takes advantage of his extensive archives.

Kendall, Alan. *George Gershwin: A Biography*. New York: Universe Books, 1987. 192pp. In an often hostile reassessment of Gershwin's career and private life, Kendall omits important information while attending at considerable length to the composer's shortcomings.

Kimball, Robert, and Alfred Simon. *The Gershwins*. New York: Atheneum, 1973. 292pp. This sourcebook on George and Ira Gershwin includes a biographical sketch, tributes from family, friends, and admirers, and an impressive collection of photographs, diary and letter excerpts, and scores in an attractive coffee-table book format.

Payne, Robert. *Gershwin*. New York: Pyramid Books, 1960. 128pp. Payne's brief biographical sketch that relies on secondary sources is intended for a general audience and interestingly stresses the Jewish influences as the inspirational source for Gershwin's music.

Peyser, Joan. *The Memory of All That: The Life of George Gershwin*. New York: Simon & Schuster, 1993. 319pp. In an anecdotal, undocumented celebrity biography that lacks scholarly rigor and objectivity, Peyser makes a case that Gershwin fathered an illegitimate son with actress Mollie Charleston as well as other unflattering personal revelations that challenges the glamorous image of Gershwin that has persisted.

Schwartz, Charles M. *Gershwin: His Life and Music*. Indianapolis: Bobbs-Merrill, 1973. 428pp. Schwartz's scholarly examination is exhaustive in tracking down the sources for various legends surrounding Gershwin, along with a good deal of speculation concerning the composer's sexuality and relationships.

Recommended Juvenile Biographies

Rushmore, Robert. *The Life of George Gershwin*. New York: Crowell-Collier, 1966. 177pp. MG/YA. A critical study of Gershwin and his music.

Biographical Films and Theatrical Adaptations

Gershwin Remembered (1987). Producer: Peter Adams. This BBC television documentary tells Gershwin's story though the perspectives of his friends and colleagues, along with personal photos and rare home movies. Video.

Rhapsody in Blue (1945). Director: Irving Rapper. This Hollywood biopic mixes fiction with fact in a dramatization of Gershwin's career starring Robert Alda, Joan Leslie, and Alexis Smith. Video.

Other Sources

Carnovale, Norbert. *George Gershwin.* Westport, Connecticut: Greenwood, 2000. 632pp. This reference guide includes a brief biography, a discography, a filmography, and an extensive bibliography.

Hitchcock, H. Wiley and Stanley Sadie, eds. *The New Grove Dictionary of American Music.* London: Macmillan, 1986. 4 vols. The biographical essay summarizes Gershwin's life and provides a concise critical analysis of his music.

Suriano, Gregory R., ed. *Gershwin in His Time: A Biographical Scrapbook, 1919–1937.* New York: Gramercy, 1998. 140pp. With rare archival posters, newspaper and magazine articles, sheet music covers, movie stills, Broadway show photos, theater programs, and other memorabilia, Gershwin's entire career is arranged chronologically in scrapbook fashion. Includes articles by contemporary critics on Gershwin's contribution to popular and classical music, a critical biographical introduction, and a complete listing of Gershwin's works.

196. ANDRÉ GIDE
1869–1951

One of the foremost French literary figures of the first half of the twentieth century, Gide was a leader of French liberal thought and was a founder of the influential *New French Review* (1909). Among his best-known novels are *The Immoralist* (1902) and *The Counterfeiters* (1926). He also wrote plays, stories, and essays. In 1947 he was awarded the Nobel Prize in Literature.

Autobiography and Primary Sources

If I Die: An Autobiography. New York: Random House, 1935. 331pp. Gide describes his development up to the age of 25, dealing frankly with his homosexuality.

The Journals of André Gide. New York: Knopf, 1947–1951. 4 vols. The *Journals* cover 60 years of Gide's life and feature retrospective reflections of his earlier thoughts and activities. They have been described as "a record, unrivaled in its completeness, of the life and evolution of a contemporary artist."

Recommended Biographies

Delay, Jean. *The Youth of André Gide.* Chicago: University of Chicago Press, 1963. 498pp. The author, a psychiatrist and friend of the writer, supplies a detailed analysis of Gide's formative years up to 1895. With access to important unpublished sources as well as conversations with the writer in old age, Delay applies psychoanalytical theory tactfully in this accomplished literary biography.

O'Brien, Justin. *Portrait of André Gide: A Critical Biography.* New York: Knopf, 1953. 390pp. O'Brien's is a sympathetic but clear-eyed introduc-

tory overview of Gide's life and works. The basic events of Gide's life are mentioned but the majority of the book is devoted to Gide's thought and temperament as revealed in his principal works.

Sheridan, Alan. *André Gide: A Life in the Present.* Cambridge, Massachusetts: Harvard University Press, 1999. 709pp. The first full-scale life of Gide is a thorough, well-written and well-documented study that traces the ways in which the author transmuted the material of his life into his art. No other biography has dealt with the many complexities of Gide's personality and interests with such sympathetic understanding.

Other Biographical Studies

Fowlie, Wallace. *André Gide: His Life and Art.* New York: Macmillan, 1965. 217pp. The connection between the writer and his works is ably explored in this critical study of "the most persistently autobiographical of writers." The book discusses Gide's troubled childhood and adolescence, his religious and intellectual revolt, sexuality, and tortuous relationship with his cousin whom he eventually married.

Guerard, Albert. *André Gide.* Cambridge, Massachusetts: Harvard University Press, 1951. 287pp. This is a critical study of the writer's personality and works that assumes substantial familiarity with Gide and his works. Of particular interest is the author's treatment of Gide's autobiographical writings.

Martin du Gard, Roger. *Recollections of André Gide.* New York: Viking, 1953. 134pp. In an affectionate memoir Martin du Gard records his 30-year friendship with Gide from journal entries. Biographer and editor of Gide's *Journal* Justin O'Brien in his review said that "of all the personal memoirs devoted to André Gide, none depicts the man and his spirit more faithfully than these too few pages."

Painter, George D. *André Gide: A Critical Biography.* 1952. Revised ed. New York: Atheneum, 1968. 147pp. The biographer of Proust offers this introductory overview of Gide's life and works. The major events of the writer's life are mentioned along with a concise analysis of each of Gide's books.

Biographical Films and Theatrical Adaptations

Testimony (1987) Director: Tony Palmer. Biography of Russian composer Shostakovich casts Ben Kingsley in the central role. Gide makes an appearance played by Julian Stanley.

197–198. GILBERT & SULLIVAN: W.S. GILBERT (1836–1911); ARTHUR SULLIVAN (1842–1900)

The English creators of popular operettas, Sir William Gilbert wrote the libretto and Arthur Sullivan the music for *H. M. S. Pinafore* (1878), *The Pirates of Penzance* (1879), *Iolanthe* (1882), and *The Mikado* (1885), among many others. The Savoy Theatre in London was built to house their operettas. Gilbert also wrote plays and poetry; Sullivan com-

posed oratorios, the opera *Ivanhoe* (1891), songs such as "The Lost Chord," and the hymn, "Onward Christian Soldiers."

Recommended Biographies

Jacobs, Arthur. *Arthur Sullivan: A Victorian Musician.* New York: Oxford University Press, 1984. 470pp. In an excellent, well-researched biography, Jacobs corrects the record based on Sullivan's diaries and letters. Mixing biographical details with musical analysis, the book is both comprehensive and judicious in it assessment of Sullivan's character and achievement.

Pearson, Hesketh. *Gilbert: His Life and Strife.* 1957. Reprint ed. Westport, Connecticut: Greenwood, 1978. 276pp. Based on access to Gilbert's private papers and letters, Pearson fashions an intimate narrative account with a number of fresh insights.

Stedman, Jane W. *W.S. Gilbert: A Classic Victorian and His Theatre.* New York: Oxford University Press, 1996. 374pp. The author presents Gilbert as a complex figure often at odds with his times. In a well-researched and reasonable assessment, Stedman exposes a number of myths about Gilbert and his relationship with Sullivan, and offers insightful synopses of Gilbert's serious and comic works.

Other Biographical Studies

Baily, Leslie. *Gilbert and Sullivan.* New York: Viking, 1974. 119pp. The essential information about both men's lives and collaboration are covered in this highly readable, compact visual biography. Serves as a useful overview and introduction.

Dark, Sidney, and Rowland Grey. *W.S. Gilbert: His Life and Letters.* 1923. Reprint ed. New York: B. Blom, 1972. 269pp. This early biographical account is chiefly valuable for the many letters included and for its many intimate details concerning the productions of the various operas.

Eden, David. *Gilbert & Sullivan: The Creative Conflict.* Rutherford, New Jersey: Fairleigh Dickinson University Press, 1986. 224pp. This psychological study of Gilbert and Sullivan alone and together makes a number of provocative reassessments, including the suggestion that Gilbert's libretti reveal significant autobiographical details and the important role Sullivan played in keeping the partnership productive.

Ffinch, Michael. *Gilbert and Sullivan.* London: Weidenfeld and Nicolson, 1993. 294pp. This dual biography equally serves as an introduction to the world of the Victorian stage with a full account of the creation, production, plot, and reception of each of the operettas.

Hibbert, Christopher. *Gilbert & Sullivan and Their Victorian World.* New York: Putnam, 1976. 279pp. Hibbert presents the Gilbert and Sullivan collaboration against a background of the Victorian period in this lavishly illustrated volume that examines each of the operas in detail.

James, Alan. *Gilbert and Sullivan.* New York: Omnibus Press, 1989. 240pp. Part of the Illustrated Lives of Composers series, this is a workmanlike summary of the highlights of both men's lives and careers with a rich selection of visual material.

Sullivan, Herbert, and Newman Flower. *Sir Arthur Sullivan: His Life, Letters, and Diaries*. New York: Doran, 1927. 393pp. Herbert Sullivan was the composer's nephew and the first of his biographers to have had access to the Sullivan archive. Their study is chiefly valuable for the extensive use they make of this material in documenting Sullivan's career and his relationship with Gilbert.

Young, Percy M. *Sir Arthur Sullivan*. New York: W.W. Norton, 1972. 304pp. Young's critical biography carefully examines the composer's life and work in the context of his social and artistic background in a balanced account between biographical details and analysis of Sullivan's music.

Recommended Juvenile Biographies

Lavine, Sigmund A. *Wandering Minstrels We: The Story of Gilbert and Sullivan*. New York: Dodd, Mead, 1954. 303pp. YA. This is an entertaining anecdotal biography that serves as an informative introduction to the pair and their era.

Biographical Films and Theatrical Adaptations

The Great Gilbert and Sullivan (1953). Director: Sidney Gilliat. British film biography with Robert Morley and Maurice Evans as the collaborators with many highlights from their works.

Topsy-Turvey (1999). Director: Mike Leigh. A brilliant re-creation of the collaboration of Gilbert (Jim Broadbent) and Sullivan (Allan Corduner) centered around the production of "The Mikado." The film has been called one of the greatest movies ever made about the theater. Video.

Other Sources

Orel, Harold, ed. *Gilbert and Sullivan: Interviews and Recollections*. Iowa City: University of Iowa Press, 1994. 214pp. This is a valuable collection of perspectives on Gilbert and Sullivan from those who knew and worked with them, as well as contemporary critical views.

199. WILLIAM GLADSTONE
1809–1898

Prime Minister of Great Britain (1868-1894), a dominant figure in the Liberal party, and an able orator, Gladstone was deeply religious and brought a moralistic tone to politics that many represented the best qualities of the Victorian era, although he was deeply disliked by Queen Victoria. He introduced several reforms during his ministry, including competitive admission to the civil service, the secret ballot, parliamentary redistribution of seats in the House of Commons, and educational expansion. His advocacy of Irish home rule compromised his ministry, resulted in the slow decline of the Liberal party, and led to his retirement from office.

Autobiography and Primary Sources

The Gladstone Diaries. M.R.D. Foot and H.C.G. Matthew, eds. Oxford: Clarendon Press, 1968–1994. 14 vols. Gladstone's revealing daily account of his activities and thoughts is the essential primary source for the biographer and the reader interested in penetrating his public persona.

Recommended Biographies

Jenkins, Roy. *Gladstone: A Biography*. New York: Random House, 1997. 698pp. Jenkins's readable synthesis of established sources has the benefit of the author's own experience as a cabinet minister in the 1960s that helps to give shape and texture to Gladstone's political life. Recommended for the general reader.

Magnus, Philip. *Gladstone: A Biography*. New York: Dutton, 1954. 482pp. With access to the Gladstone diaries, Magnus focuses more on Gladstone's private side and areas of his life mostly ignored by Morley, including his relationship with Victoria and his wife, his lifelong efforts to save women from prostitution, and his attempt to rescue his sister from an opium addiction. Accordingly, Magnus's study is filled with private information and remains the best available single-volume biography that joins Gladstone's private and public lives.

Morley, John. *The Life of William Ewart Gladstone*. New York: Macmillan, 1903. 3 vols. Selected as the official biographer, Morley, a political colleague and former cabinet member, devoted five years to establishing and documenting the authoritative factual record, and his three-volume study remains the standard source for the external details of Gladstone's life. Readers interested more in the man than the public figure should consult Magnus instead.

Shannon, Richard. *Gladstone*. Chapel Hill: University of North Carolina Press, 1984–1999. 2 vols. In a revisionist study, Shannon provides an absorbing, almost day-to-day account of Gladstone's personal and political development that challenges previous views. The book challenges Morley for his comprehensiveness.

Other Biographical Studies

Bebbington, David W. *William Ewart Gladstone: Faith and Politics in Victorian Britain*. Grand Rapids, Michigan: Eerdmans, 1993. 270pp. Part of the Library of Religious Biography series, this concise narrative of Gladstone's public life is seen from the perspective of his religious faith and the conflict it caused with his political activity.

Collieu, E.G. *Gladstone*. London: Oxford University Press, 1968. 63pp. This is a brief, introductory overview of Gladstone's life and political career.

Crosby, Travis L. *The Two Mr. Gladstones: A Study in Psychology and History*. New Haven, Connecticut: Yale University Press, 1997. 320pp. In the author's psychoanalytic view, Gladstone is depicted as a passive-aggressive workaholic beset by stress. Often reductive in the extreme, Crosby's examination considers Gladstone's political accomplishments and personal obsessions as a form of stress management.

Feuchtwanger, E.J. *Gladstone*. New York: St. Martin's, 1975. 315pp. In a succinct chronological study of Gladstone's career, Feuchtwanger incorporates important research since Magnus. In the author's view, Gladstone is a complex blend of innocence and cunning whose first choice for his career was the church and not politics.

Jagger, Peter J. *Gladstone: The Making of a Christian Politician*. Allison Park, Pennsylvania: Pickwick, 1991. 326pp. Jagger looks at Gladstone's character and ideals from the perspective of his religious faith and the values of his era.

Marlow, Joyce. *The Oak and the Ivy: An Intimate Biography of William and Catherine Gladstone*. Garden City, New York: Doubleday, 1977. 324pp. This study of Gladstone's career is seen through the lens of his relationship with his wife. In Marlow's handling Catherine Gladstone's reputation is enhanced while her husband's is diminished in tracing Gladstone's motivation and contradictions.

Matthew, H.C.G. *Gladstone: 1809-74*. New York: Oxford University Press, 1986. 275pp. One of the editors of the Gladstone diaries, Matthew provides an introduction to them along with an insightful biographical essay on Gladstone's motives and character.

Reid, T. Wemyss, ed. *The Life of William Ewart Gladstone*. New York: Putnam, 1899. 2 vols. This collection of appreciative essays by various contemporaries and firsthand witnesses that appeared immediately following Gladstone's death is insightful and features an extensive selection of illustrations.

Stansky, Peter. *Gladstone: A Progress in Politics*. Boston: Little, Brown, 1979. 201pp. Relating several of Gladstone's key speeches to the formation of his ideas and policies, Stansky's study challenges the stereotype of the dour, moralizing, and hypocritical figure that has dominated the modern view of Gladstone.

Wilson, A.N. *Eminent Victorians*. New York: W.W. Norton, 1990. 240pp. Based on a BBC television series, this collection of brief biographical profiles includes a balanced assessment of Gladstone.

Fictional Portraits

Edelman, Maurice. *Disraeli Rising*. New York: Stein and Day, 1975. 348pp. Disraeli's relationship with his political nemesis Gladstone is dealt with in this biographical chronicle.

Mayerson, Evelyn W. *Princess in Amber*. Garden City, New York: Doubleday, 1985. 298pp. Gladstone is one of several historical personages who figure in this drama of Princess Beatrice's conflict with her mother, Queen Victoria, over her love for Prince Henry of Battenburg.

Plaidy, Jean. *The Widow of Windsor*. London: R. Hale, 1974. 351pp. Queen Victoria's years alone after the death of Prince Albert are dramatized, including her relationship with Gladstone; *Victoria Victorious*. New York: Putnam, 1985. 569pp. Victoria offers her perspectives on her various prime ministers, including Gladstone, in this autobiographical account.

Tyler-Whittle, Michael. *The Widow of Windsor.* New York: St. Martin's, 1973. 287pp. In the final volume of the author's trilogy on the life of Victoria, her widowhood is depicted, including her relationships with Disraeli and Gladstone.

Recommended Juvenile Biographies

Brand, Eric. *William Gladstone.* New York: Chelsea House, 1986. 115pp. MG/YA. Brand presents the essential details of both Gladstone's personal life, character, and political career.

Biographical Films and Theatrical Adaptations

Edward the King (1975). Director: John Gorrie. The life and short reign of Edward VII is chronicled. Robert Hardy portrays Prince Albert; Annette Crosbie is Queen Victoria, and Timothy West is the Prince of Wales and later king. Michael Holden portrays Gladstone. The book on which the screenplay was based is available by

David E. Butler, *Edward the King* (New York: Pocket Books, 1974–1975. 2 vols.). Video.

Khartoum (1966). Director: Basil Dearden. Ralph Richardson portrays Gladstone with Charlton Heston as Charles Gordon and Laurence Olivier as his nemesis, the Mahdi, in this often overly talky spectacle on the final days of Gordon at Khartoum. Video.

Other Sources

Jagger, Peter J., ed. *Gladstone.* Rio Grande, Ohio: Hambleton Press, 1998. 302pp. This collection of essays by leading historians examines Gladstone's life, character, and career from a number of interesting perspectives.

See also Benjamin Disraeli; Victoria

200. JOHANN WOLFGANG VON GOETHE
1749–1832

A German poet, dramatist, and novelist, and one of the most influential geniuses of world literature, Goethe was born in Frankfurt and studied law at Leipzig and Strasbourg. In 1774 he gained immediate fame with the publication of his epistolary novel *The Sorrows of Young Werther*, which was widely translated. From 1775 until his death, he lived at the court of Duke Charles Augustus of Saxe-Weimar. There he served as chief minister of state and director of the state theater and the scientific institutions. Among the best known of Goethe's immense body of work is the *Wilhelm Meister* series of novels (1796-1829) and the great dramatic poem *Faust*, the first part of which was published in 1808 and the second published shortly after his death.

Autobiography and Primary Sources

The Autobiography of Johann Wolfgang von Goethe. Chicago: University of Chicago Press, 1974. 2 vols. Goethe's retrospective account of his first 26 years was originally entitled *Dichtung und Wahrheit* (*Poetry and Truth*). Often unreliable as a factual record, his version of his youth and development is nevertheless a fascinating and essential biographical source.

Italian Journey. New York: Pantheon, 1962. 508pp. This is an interweaving of Goethe's letters and journal entries from his critical tour in 1786–1788.

Lewisohn, Ludwig, ed. *Goethe: The Story of a Man.* New York: Farrar, Straus, 1949. 2 vols. Chronologically arranging selections from Goethe's poems, autobiographical works, and letters, as well as contemporary accounts, Lewisohn fashions a biographical narrative mainly in Goethe's own words.

Recommended Biographies

Boyle, Nicholas. *Goethe: The Poet and the Age. Volume One: The Poetry of Desire (1749–1790). Volume Two: Revolution and Renunciation (1790–1803).* New York: Oxford University Press, 1991–1999. 2 vols. Boyle's exhaustive study promises to become the definitive modern life when completed. Covering the first half of Goethe's life, Boyle amasses all the details of his private and public development, placing him in the context of his age, and helpfully unravels Goethe's philosophy while providing a useful discussion of his major works.

Brown, Peter H. *Life of Goethe.* New York: Holt, 1920. 2 vols. Following Goethe's career from birth to death in an earnest and scholarly account, Brown's life lacks the liveliness of Lewes's classic study, but has long been considered a standard English source.

Fairley, Barker. *A Study of Goethe.* Oxford: Clarendon Press, 1947. 280pp. This study of Goethe's intellectual and emotional development concentrates on internal factors that constituted various conflicts that Goethe struggled to resolve throughout his life. The book serves as well to locate Goethe firmly in his cultural and historical context.

Friedenthal, Richard. *Goethe: His Life and Times.* Cleveland: World Publishing, 1965. 561pp. In a lively, informative life story and cultural history, Friedenthal makes Goethe accessible for a general reader with an emphasis on his human qualities, both positive and negative, so that he becomes a far more inviting and understandable figure than in more worshipful treatments.

Lewes, G.H. *The Life and Works of Goethe.* 1855. Reprint ed. New York: Frederick Ungar, 1965. 578pp. The first comprehensive and scholarly biography in English, Lewes's appreciative examination of Goethe's life and achievement remains an important starting point, although many details have been corrected in the light of more recent scholarship.

Other Biographical Studies

Bielschowsky, Albert. *Life of Goethe.* New York: Putnam, 1905–1908. 2 vols. The author's detailed critical and biographical study asserts that modern German identity would not have existed without Goethe's considerable influence. Bielschowsky's comprehensive study remains provocative and insightful.

Dieckmann, Liselotte. *Johann Wolfgang Goethe.* New York: Twayne, 1974. 202pp. In an objective assessment of Goethe's achievement, the author's critical study admits the poet's human flaws and attempts to demythologize Goethe and restore his humanity.

Eissler, Kurt R. *Goethe: A Psychoanalytical Study 1775-86.* Detroit: Wayne State University Press, 1963. 2 vols. Eissler's detailed Freudian interpretation of 10 critical years in Goethe's development reveals his unconscious conflict over his incestuous love for his sister. Controversial in its psychoanalytical approach and debatable in its conclusions, Eissler's provocative study is insightful and thorough in its method, though somewhat reductive in its thesis.

Haile, H.G. *Artist in Chrysalis: A Biographical Study of Goethe in Italy.* Urbana: University of Illinois Press, 1973. 201pp. With translations from passages of Goethe's letters and diaries, Haile provides a detailed account of the writer's important Italian visit that is shown to be crucial in his artistic development.

McCabe, Joseph. *Goethe: The Man and His Character.* Philadelphia: Lippincott, 1912. 378pp. Intended to supplement Lewes's portrait with new information, McCabe's study is detailed but often sentimental in its partisan viewpoint.

Nevinson, Henry W. *Goethe: Man and Poet.* New York: Harcourt, Brace, 1932. 264pp. This short, sympathetic biography serves as a succinct introduction for the general reader.

Reed, T.J. *Goethe.* New York: Oxford University Press, 1984. 114pp. Part of the Past Masters series, Reed supplies a succinct overview of the important details of Goethe's life and a critical introduction to his works.

Robertson, John G. *Goethe.* 1927. Revised ed. *The Life and Work of Goethe 1749–1832.* New York: Dutton, 1932. 350pp. Robertson's exhaustive study chronicles the known facts of Goethe's life and includes penetrating critical insights on the writer's literary achievements.

Thomas, Calvin. *Goethe.* New York: Holt, 1917. 368pp. Thomas's biographical and critical study is a solid appreciative examination divided equally between Goethe's life and work.

Williams, John R. *The Life of Goethe: A Critical Biography.* Malden, Massachusetts: Blackwell, 1998. 318pp. This chronological analysis of Goethe's works relates his literary achievement to the wide range of his public activities and contact with a wide range of public figures.

Biographical Novels

Mann, Thomas. *Lotte in Weimar.* New York: Knopf, 1940. 453pp. Also known as *The Beloved Returns,* Mann imagines Goethe's reunion with the model for the heroine of *The Sorrows of Young Werther* in 1816 in a convincing portrait of the artist.

Fictional Portraits

Gerson, Noel B. *The Anthem*. New York: M. Evans, 1967. 512pp. This ambitious novel dramatizes the struggle for religious freedom over a 300-year period and involves numerous historical figures, including Goethe.

Koch, Eric. *Icon in Love: A Novel of Goethe*. New York: Mosaic, 1998. 200pp. In this inventive fantasy that draws heavily on the facts of Goethe's life, the writer is reinvented as a twentieth-century poet whose love affair with a student allows him to complete the long-awaited *Faust, Part Two*.

Kundera, Milan. *Immortality*. New York: Grove Weidenfeld, 1991. 345pp. In a complex group portrait, Kundera imagines scenes from the relationship between Goethe and Bettina von Ârnim.

201. NIKOLAI GOGOL
1809–1852

A Russian short-story writer, novelist, and dramatist, Gogol is considered the father of Russian realism. He first gained literary success for his fanciful, romantic tales set in his native Ukraine. His masterpiece is the picaresque novel, *Dead Souls* (1842), of which only the first part survives. Other celebrated works by Gogol include the satirical play, *The Inspector-General* (1836), and *The Overcoat* (1842).

Recommended Biographies

Gippius, Vasilii. *Gogol*. Robert A. Maguire, ed. Ann Arbor, Michigan: Ardis, 1981. 216pp. First published in 1924 and widely regarded as a classic, Gippius's critical biography, despite an often difficult and poorly translated text, remains the best general study of Gogol's available.

Magarshack, David. *Gogol: A Life*. New York: Grove Press, 1957. 328pp. With much of its text extracts from Gogol's letters and testimony of those who knew him, Magarshack presents Gogol life and personality in detail. Sober and matter-of-fact in his presentation, Magarshack illustrates Gogol's development and religious search with a minimum of conjecture.

Setchkarev, Vsevolod. *Gogol: His Life and Works*. New York: New York University Press, 1965. 264pp. Divided between a biographical account of Gogol's life and a critical assessment of his works, Setchkarev's is a reliable, scholarly overview, recommended for the reader looking for a sensible orientation to the man and his art.

Other Biographical Studies

Karlinsky, Simon. *The Sexual Labyrinth of Nikolai Gogol*. Cambridge, Massachusetts: Harvard University Press, 1976. 333pp. Karlinsky's biographical profile is a psycho-sexual examination that locates the writer's homosexuality, which Gogol himself could neither accept nor forgive in himself, as the key to unlocking the mystery of the writer's personality.

Maguire, Robert A. *Exploring Gogol*. Stanford, California: Stanford University Press, 1994. 409pp. Maguire's is a valuable critical study that

relates Gogol's life with his works and his cultural and literary history.

Troyat, Henri. *Divided Soul: The Life of Gogol*. Garden City, New York: Doubleday, 1973. 489pp. Troyat's biography is a highly readable and dramatic account beneath a massive accumulation of details, both significant and trivial, documenting Gogol's life and character. Lacking in subtlety in its psychological analysis, Troyat's life is a mixed affair of colorful animation and simplification.

202. EMMA GOLDMAN
1869–1940

A Lithuanian-born anarchist and champion of free speech, Goldman immigrated (1886) to the United States, worked in the garment industry, and after 1889 was active in the anarchist movement. She was imprisoned in 1893, 1916, and 1917 for inciting riots, publicly advocating birth control, and for obstructing the draft. She was deported (1919) to Russia and later lived in England and Canada. She took an active part in the Spanish Civil War in 1936.

Autobiography and Primary Sources

Living My Life. New York: Knopf, 1931. 2 vols. Written during her exile from the U.S., Goldman's intense, compelling review of her remarkable life is one of the great autobiographies and an extremely valuable primary source on Goldman's life, career, and views.

Nowhere at Home: Letters from Exile of Emma Goldman and Alexander Berkman. Richard and Anna Maria Drinnon, eds. New York: Schocken, 1975. 282pp. A revealing supplement to Goldman's autobiography, these letters exchanged between Goldman and her longtime companion provide a useful indicator of Goldman's views during her years in exile.

Red Emma Speaks: An Emma Goldman Reader. Alix Kates Shulman, ed. New York: Schocken Books, 1983. 460pp. This is an important compilation of Goldman's writings and speeches.

Recommended Biographies

Drinnon, Richard. *Rebel in Paradise: A Biography of Emma Goldman*. Chicago: University of Chicago Press, 1961. 349pp. Thorough and clearly written, this first full-length biography is still one of the best available. Solidly researched, Drinnon's is a sympathetic but objective documentation of Goldman's public life in the context of her times.

Falk, Candace. *Love, Anarchy, and Emma Goldman*. New York: Holt, 1984. 603pp. More focused than Drinnon on Goldman's private life, Falk looks at Goldman's relationship with the several men in her life, particularly the doctor and former hobo Ben Reitman who became her lover and manager, to reveal the conflict between her private experience and political activities.

Wexler, Alice. *Emma Goldman: An Intimate Life*. New York: Pantheon, 1984. 339pp.; *Emma Goldman in Exile: From the Russian Revolution to the Spanish Civil War*. Boston: Beacon Press,

1989. 301pp. Taken together, Wexler's two volumes are the most thorough account of both her private and public life. The first book covers Goldman's life up to 1919; the second chronicles her years in exile.

Other Biographical Studies

Chalberg, John. *Emma Goldman: American Individualist*. New York: HarperCollins, 1991. 196pp. Chalberg's is a solid, compact biography that, although undocumented, makes considerable use of trustworthy primary and secondary sources.

Morton, Marian J. *Emma Goldman and the American Left: "Nowhere at Home."* New York: Twayne, 1992. 183pp. Combining biographical details with a useful survey of American leftist activism at the turn of the century, Morton's is an informative study that locates Goldman in the wider context of her time and radical thought.

Biographical Novels

Mannin, Ethel E. *Red Rose: A Novel Based on the Life of Emma Goldman*. New York: Jarrolds, 1941. 199pp. Although fictionalized, the novel follows Goldman's autobiography and uses imagination chiefly regarding the period not covered by Goldman herself.

Fictional Portraits

Bamford, Susannah. *The Gilded Cage*. New York: M. Evans, 1991. 424pp. In this period romance set in the 1890s, Goldman is depicted advocating her radical positions.

Doctorow, E.L. *Ragtime*. New York: Random House, 1975. 270pp. Goldman is shown playing a dual role in the public and private drama of Doctorow's inventive novel.

Glassgold, Peter. *The Angel Max*. New York: Harcourt, Brace, 1998. 450pp. The novel is a saga of the immigrant experience in America that includes views of Goldman and some of the important events at the turn of the century, including the McKinley assassination, the Triangle Shirtwaist Factory Fire, and anarchist and radical activities.

Recommended Juvenile Biographies

Gay, Kathlyn, and Martin K. Gay. *The Importance of Emma Goldman*. San Diego: Lucent Books, 1997. 128pp. MG/YA. Well written and documented, the Gays trace the stages of Goldman's development in her cultural and intellectual context.

Shulman, Alix. *To the Barricades: The Anarchist Life of Emma Goldman*. New York: Crowell, 1971. 255pp. YA. Well researched and written, Shulman traces Goldman's life in full with an informative chapter on anarchism and the various social causes with which Goldman was associated.

Waldstreicher, David. *Emma Goldman*. New York: Chelsea House, 1990. 111pp. MG/YA. In a clear and concise profile, Waldstreicher places Goldman's ideas in relationship with her experiences and treats her fairly without romanticizing her struggle.

Biographical Films and Theatrical Adaptations

Duberman, Martin B. *Mother Earth: An Epic Drama of Emma Goldman's Life.* New York: St. Martin's, 1991. 220pp. Duberman's drama, commissioned by PBS but never produced, traces Goldman's career in a mixture of history and invention.

E.G.: A Musical Portrait (1987). Producer: Joel Shatzky. Goldman's life and views are expressed in music in this filmed, mixed-media state performance starring Helene Williams in the title role. Video.

Red Emma, Queen of the Anarchists (1979). Director: Alan King. Written by Carol Bolt, the film dramatizes Goldman's first days in America and her early involvement with the anarchist movement during the years 1888 to 1892. Video.

Reds (1981). Director: Warren Beatty. Maureen Stapleton won an Academy Award for her portrayal of Goldman in Beatty's ode to American radicals John Reed (Beatty) and Louise Bryant (Diane Keaton). Jack Nicholson portrays Eugene O'Neill. Video.

203. OLIVER GOLDSMITH
1730–1774

An Anglo-Irish man of letters, Goldsmith was an unsuccessful physician before turning to literature. He achieved success in London literary circles as a contributor to periodicals and with his *The Citizen of the World* (1762), a series of satirical and whimsical essays. His most famous works are the comedies *The Good-Natur'd Man* (1768) and *She Stoops to Conquer* (1773), and the novel, *The Vicar of Wakefield* (1766).

Autobiography and Primary Sources

The Collected Letters of Oliver Goldsmith. Katharine C. Bolderston, ed. Cambridge, Massachusetts: Cambridge University Press, 1928. 189pp. The few surviving Goldsmith letters in this collection are of limited value in revealing details about Goldsmith's life or character.

Recommended Biographies

Freeman, William. *Oliver Goldsmith.* New York: Philosophical Society, 1952. 286pp. All that is known about Goldsmith's life is summarized in this succinct overview that largely avoids interpretation, allowing the events to speak for themselves.

Ginger, John. *The Notable Man: The Life and Times of Oliver Goldsmith.* London: Hamilton, 1977. 408pp. Ginger offers a decidedly counter-view of Goldsmith's character that differs from most other presentations. Drawing autobiographical revelations from Goldsmith's writings, the book makes a number of provocative psychological conjectures, anchored by a solid familiarity with the period.

Wardle, Ralph M. *Oliver Goldsmith.* Lawrence: University Press of Kansas, 1957. 330pp. Although Wardle offers no new details, his scholarly summary of existing sources is both thorough and au-

thoritative. Occasionally overly sympathetic and defensive, Wardle at least includes the unflattering information that infuriated his friends and enemies about Goldsmith's temperament and behavior.

Other Biographical Studies

Dobson, Austin. *Life of Oliver Goldsmith.* London: W.H. Scott, 1888. 214pp. Dobson's lively character portrait lacks the comprehensiveness of other studies but does offer a rich and multidimensional portrait.

Forster, John. *The Life and Times of Oliver Goldsmith.* 1854. Reprint ed. Westport, Connecticut: Greenwood, 1971. 460pp. Forster's continues to be an important source of information on Goldsmith's life that is found nowhere else.

Gwynn, Stephen. *Oliver Goldsmith.* New York: Holt, 1935. 287pp. Gwynn's is a sympathetic, popular biography which attempts to depict both sides of Goldsmith's character to show why he both charmed and exasperated his many friends and associates.

Irving, Washington. *Oliver Goldsmith: A Biography.* 1849. Reprint ed. Boston: Twayne, 1978. 654pp. More a tribute to Goldsmith's work and character, Irving supplies no new information, but his book is of interest primarily for Irving's perspective.

Prior, James. *The Life of Oliver Goldsmith.* London: J. Murray, 1837. 2 vols. The first full-length biography has the benefit of the author's firsthand knowledge, supplying important data that have been reworked by all subsequent biographers.

Sells, A. Lytton. *Oliver Goldsmith, His Life and Works.* New York: Barnes and Noble, 1974. 423pp. Sells divides his study between biographical and critical sections. Much of biographical information is outdated and selective, concentrating on long-resolved controversies while ignoring others.

Sherwin, Oscar. *Goldy: The Life and Times of Oliver Goldsmith.* New York: Twayne, 1961. 367pp. Sherwin's is a popular biography that features no new information but reworks the available sources into an entertaining but rarely penetrating account.

Wibberley, Leonard. *The Good-Natured Man: A Portrait of Oliver Goldsmith.* New York: Morrow, 1979. 255pp. Wibberley offers few fresh insights in what is mainly a rehash of the facts of Goldsmith's life and literary career.

Other Sources

Mikhail, E.H., ed. *Goldsmith: Interviews and Recollections.* New York: St. Martin's, 1993. 230pp. This useful volume brings together a wide selection of contemporary views of Goldsmith, covering both his charming and less flattering sides.

204. MAXIM GORKY
1868–1936

Born Aleksey Maximovich Pyeshkov, Gorky is considered the father of Soviet literature and the founder of the doctrine of socialist realism. His works are noted for their stark naturalism and in-

clude the most famous of his 15 plays, *The Lower Depths* (1902), the novel *The Mother* (1902), and the unfinished four-volume saga *The Life of Klim Samgin* (1927–1936), often considered his masterpiece. After the Russian Revolution, he headed the State Publishing House.

Autobiography and Primary Sources

Autobiography of Maxim Gorky. New York: Citadel Press, 1949. 616pp. Collecting Gorky's autobiographical trilogy—*My Childhood, In the World,* and *My Universities*—in a single volume, his recollections cover his formative years up to the beginnings of his literary career.

Fragments from My Diary. New York: Praeger, 1972. 265pp. The volume represents vignettes and anecdotes written from 1922 to 1924 in which Gorky comments on pre- and post-Revolutionary Russia. Little of Gorky's private life is conveyed.

Selected Letters. Andrew Barrett and Barry P. Schen, eds. New York: Oxford University Press, 1997. 391pp. This selection of 177 letters covers Gorky's life from 1899 until just before his death, organized into chronological sections, each with a helpful biographical introduction.

Recommended Biographies

Kaun, Alexander. *Maxim Gorky and His Russia.* London: Cape, 1931. 620pp. Kaun's is the first thorough documentation of Gorky's life and career, and it remains an important source of firsthand information from conversations with the author and recollections by his associates that have been relied upon by subsequent biographers.

Scherr, Barry P. *Maxim Gorky.* Boston: Twayne, 1988. 140pp. Readers in search of a reliable, succinct biographical and critical overview should consider Scherr's helpful volume. After considering Gorky's background and ideas, Scherr traces the writer's literary development in chapters devoted to Gorky's narrative and dramatic works.

Troyat, Henri. *Gorky.* New York: Crown, 1989. 216pp. Troyat's popular biography is full of the novelistic touches that can be found in his various literary biographies of Russian figures. Gorky emerges as an understandable human figure, seen against a vivid historical background. To achieve his desired narrative effects Troyat has reduced many complexities to clear patterns, and the interested reader will want to check many of Troyat's generalizations with more scholarly sources.

Yedlin, Tova. *Maxim Gorky: A Political Biography.* New York: Praeger, 1999. 260pp. Based on hitherto unavailable primary sources, Yedlin offers a refreshing assessment of Gorky's political beliefs and activities that contradicts many of the legends surrounding the writer. The book is particularly helpful in detailing Gorky's relationship with Lenin and Stalin.

Other Biographical Studies

Hare, Richard. *Maxim Gorky—Romantic Realist and Conservative Revolutionary.* New York: Oxford University Press, 1962. 156pp. Hare's interpretive study is a sophisticated reassessment that challenges a number of myths that have distorted a true portrait, providing sensible connections between Gorky's life, ideas, and works.

Holtzman, Filia. *The Young Maxim Gorky 1868–1902*. New York: Columbia University Press, 1948. 256pp. Holtzman's is a scholarly and reliable treatment of Gorky's early years that corrects many factual errors made by previous biographers and adds important details that helpfully locate the key to the mature writer in his formative experiences.

Levin, Dan. *Stormy Petrel: The Life and Work of Maxim Gorky*. 1965. Revised ed. New York: Schocken, 1986. 332pp. Close to biographical fiction, Levin's is a highly dramatized, idealized presentation that succeeds in animating the writer's life but at the cost of simplification and a lack of critical perspective.

Roskin, Alexander. *From the Banks of the Volga: The Life of Maxim Gorky*. New York: Philosophical Library, 1946. 126pp. As a contemporary reviewer observed, "This is a brilliant example of how contemporary Soviet writers treat complicated and controversial subjects: the long and turbulent career of the great Russian turns into a simple proletarian fable with a strict black-and-white approach to life and letters."

Wolfe, Bertram D. *The Bridge and the Abyss: The Troubled Friendship of Maxim Gorky and V.I. Lenin*. New York: Praeger, 1967. 180pp. Although limited to only a few years of Gorky's life and framed by his relationship with Lenin, Wolfe's is an often revealing look at the man and the artist during his most creative period.

Fictional Portraits

Gouzenko, Igor. *The Fall of a Titan*. New York: W.W. Norton, 1954. 629pp. Written by a Soviet defector, the novel offers a fictional version of Gorky's gradual downfall and death that is attributed to a sinister plot by the Politburo.

205. FRANCISCO JOSÉ DE GOYA Y LUCIENTES
1746–1828

A Spanish artist considered one of the the greatest painters of his century, Goya studied in Saragossa, Madrid, and Rome. He became painter to King Charles III (1786) and court painter to the court of Charles IV and Queen Maria Luisa (1789). He produced a number of portraits of royalty and other Madrid notables, and after 1793 began to create uncommissioned works, especially small cabinet paintings. Sometime during the years 1797 to 1805 he painted *Maja nude* and *Maja clothed*, two of his most celebrated paintings, and during this era also produced his *Caprichos*, etchings in the style of grotesque social satire. His etchings *Disastres de la Guerra* and paintings *May 2, 1808* and *May 3, 1808* depict the horrors and atrocities of the Napoleonic wars.

Autobiography and Primary Sources

Francisco Goya (1746–1828): Letters of Love and Friendship in Translation. Lewiston, Maine: Edwin Mellen Press, 1997. 145pp. Goya's letters helpfully reveal the man in his circle of relationships.

Recommended Biographies

Gassier, Pierre, and Juliet Wilson. *Life and Complete Works of Francisco Goya*. New York: Reynal, 1971. 400pp. Regarded as the standard reference source on Goya's life and works.

Hull, Anthony. *Goya: Man Among Kings*. New York: Hamilton Press, 1987. 242pp. This scholarly though readable biography concentrates on the man and his times rather than his art and serves as an adequate serious biography for the general reader.

Tomlinson, Janis A. *Francisco Goya y Lucientes 1746–1828*. New York: Chronicle Books, 1994. 320pp. In an authoritative and sumptuously illustrated survey of Goya's career, Tomlinson covers the full range of Goya's art and places him in the social and political context of his times, while not neglecting his inner life and the internal basis of his genius. See also the author's *Goya in the Twilight of the Enlightenment* (New Haven, Connecticut: Yale University Press, 1992. 240pp.) that helpfully sets Goya's life in the context of his era.

Other Biographical Studies

Baticle, Jeannine. *Goya: Painter of Terrible Splendor*. New York: Abrams, 1994. 175pp. Baticle provides a sound critical introduction to Goya's work and an overview of his career in this beautifully illustrated volume.

Gassier, Pierre. *Goya: A Witness of His Times*. Secaucus, New Jersey: Chartwell Books, 1983. 323pp. Gassier covers the highlights of Goya's life in a series of insightful chapters that locate Goya in the context of his cultural and historical era.

Glendinning, Nigel. *Goya and His Critics*. New Haven, Connecticut: Yale University Press, 1977. 340pp. After providing a brief biographical sketch, Glendinning examines Goya's relationship with his critics and the various approaches—political, psychological, romantic, and realistic—that have shaped our view of his achievements.

Holland, Vyvyan B. *Goya: A Pictorial Biography*. New York: Viking, 1962. 144pp. Holland's illustrated biography traces Goya's career helpfully with various photographs of his paintings and reproductions. A useful starting point, but readers more interested in the source of Goya's genius and inner turmoil should look elsewhere.

Licht, Fred. *Goya: The Origins of the Modern Temper in Art*. New York: Universe Books, 1979. 288pp. Arguing that Goya is a decisive figure in art history, Licht, through an analysis of individual works and comparison with other artists, provides a context for viewing Goya's enigmatic personality and vision. Assumes a good deal of expertise in art history and analysis.

Pérez Sanchez, Alfonso E., and Eleanor A. Sayre. *Goya and the Spirit of the Enlightenment*. Boston: Little, Brown, 1989. 407pp. This catalog from a major exhibit of Goya's works includes a number of introductory essays that summarize Goya's life and times. With a detailed chronology.

Salas, Xavier de. *Goya*. New York: Mayflower, 1979. 206pp. A useful, succinct biographical and critical study by a leading Goya scholar.

Vallentin, Antonina. *This I Saw: The Life and Times of Goya*. New York: Random House, 1949. 371pp. In a compact and informative study, the author sets Goya in his period and provides a detailed assessment of his paintings and drawings.

Waldmann, Susann. *Goya and the Duchess of Alba*. New York: Prestel, 1998. 108pp. The author concentrates on what can be known for sure about the relationship between the painter and the Duchess of Alba by examining contemporary documents, letters from Goya to his friends, and contemporary anecdotes.

Williams, Gwyn A. *Goya and the Impossible Revolution*. New York: Pantheon, 1976. 194pp. Relating Goya's works to his life and Spain's political and cultural context, Williams traces the source of Goya's development to his illness that turned him from idealism to a darker realism. Williams's thesis is provocative, if somewhat one-sided.

Biographical Novels

Braider, David. *Rage in Silence: A Novel Based on the Life of Goya*. New York: Putnam, 1969. 318pp. Concentrating on Goya's development from esteemed court painter to a great visionary artist, the novel provides a believable account of Goya's life and times.

Feuchtwanger, Lion. *This Is the Hour*. New York: Viking, 1951. 516pp. Based on Goya's life and focusing on his relationship with the Duchess of Alba, the novel often fails to convince in its often over excited and sentimental treatment.

Gerson, Noel B. *The Naked Maja*. New York: McGraw-Hill, 1959. 248pp. This biographical account follows Goya throughout his career and his relationship with the Duchess of Alba and stays close to the facts of Goya's life.

Marlowe, Stephen. *Colossus: A Novel about Goya and a World Gone Mad*. New York: Macmillan, 1972. 563pp. Following Goya's rise as a court painter, the novel treats his love affair with the Duchess of Alba and the growing darkening of his artistic vision. Built on a framework of facts, the novel supplements the historical record with surmises and speculation.

White, Max. *In the Blazing Light*. New York: Duell, Sloan and Pearce, 1946. 318pp. Setting Goya against a vivid background of the dissolute Bourbon court, the novel captures the complexity of the artist, though in pursuit of strong dramatic contrast biographical reliability is at times sacrificed.

Fictional Portraits

Larreta, Antonio. *The Last Portrait of the Duchess of Alba*. Bethesda, Maryland: Adler and Adler, 1988. 214pp. The novel speculates on the cause of the Duchess of Alba's death in 1802 from the perspective of one of her former lovers who is charged with investigating her death and Goya.

Rebolledo, Francisco. *Rasero*. New York: Penguin, 1996. 552pp. The novel records the progress of a young Spanish nobleman during the intellectual ferment of the Enlightenment, encountering many period figures, including Goya, Diderot, Voltaire, Rousseau, and Mozart.

Recommended Juvenile Biographies

Ripley, Elizabeth. *Goya: A Biography*. New York: Oxford University Press, 1956. 68pp. MG. Ripley provides a chronological account of Goya's personality and achievement with the more libertine aspects of his career de-emphasized but not to the point of dishonesty.

Richardson, Martha. *Francisco Goya*. New York: Chelsea House, 1994. 111pp. MG/YA. Richardson combines useful information about Goya's life, his artistic and court career, and the historical events that transformed his art.

Waldron, Ann. *Francisco Goya*. New York: Abrams, 1992. 92pp. YA. Tracing Goya's development from ambitious court painter to dark visionary, this is a useful introduction to Goya's life and artistic genius. Speculation fills in some of the gaps in the historical record and the author is less than candid in dealing with Goya's mistresses and simplistic in resolving his contradictions.

Wright, Patricia. *Goya*. New York: Dorling Kindersley, 1999. 64pp. MG. This oversized volume brings both the artist and his works to life in a beautifully illustrated guide.

Biographical Films and Theatrical Adaptations

Goya: His Life and Art (1981). Director: Jesús Fernández Santos. Produced by Spanish television, this documentary chronicles the life and times of Goya through his art. Video.

The Naked Maja (1959). Director: Henry Koster. Anthony Franciosa stars as Goya and Ava Gardner as the Duchess of Alba. Video.

206. ULYSSES S. GRANT
1822–1885

Born in Point Pleasant, Ohio, Grant graduated from West Point (1843), served in the Mexican War, but was forced to resign from the army (1854) because of heavy drinking. A failure at farming and in business, he clerked in the family leather store in Illinois until the Civil War began. He rose from the rank of colonel to major general, and in 1864 was named by President Lincoln commander-in-chief of the Union army. A skilled tactician and a courageous and organized military leader, Grant's Vicksburg campaign (1862-1863) was one of his greatest successes. He accepted the surrender of General Robert E. Lee at Appomattox Courthouse in April, 1865. Grant served as eighteenth U.S. president from 1869 to 1877.

Autobiography and Primary Sources

The Papers of Ulysses S. Grant. John Y. Simon, ed. Carbondale: Southern Illinois University Press, 1967–1995. 20 vols. This scholarly collection of Grant's significant writing throughout his career is the essential primary source on details of Grant's life.

Personal Memoirs. 1885–1886. Reprint ed. *Memoirs and Selected Letters: Personal Memoirs of U.S. Grant*. Mary Drake and William S. McFeely, eds. New York: Library of America, 1990. 1,199pp. An American autobiographical and literary classic, Grant's recollections are extraordinary given the circumstances of their composition. With Grant dying from throat cancer, he struggled to complete his memoirs to pay off extensive debts and secure his family's financial future. A third of Grant's narrative covers his life prior to the Civil War, and he offers no details of his postwar career.

The Personal Memoirs of Julia Dent Grant. John Y. Simon, ed. New York: Putnam, 1975. 346pp. Grant's wife offers a more intimate, personal, though not always reliable, account of her husband and their relationship.

Recommended Biographies

Catton, Bruce. *Grant Moves South*. Boston: Little, Brown, 1960. 564pp; *Grant Takes Command*. Boston: Little, Brown, 1969. 556pp. Catton takes up Grant's story where Lewis left off with a superbly realized account of Grant's military career. Challenging the contention of Grant as a drunkard and butcher, Catton establishes the positive portrait of Grant's military leadership that later historians and biographers have substantiated or qualified.

McFeely, William S. *Grant: A Biography*. New York: W.W. Norton, 1981. 592pp. McFeely's Pulitzer prize-winning biography is the best comprehensive modern study available. Countering the hero status of other accounts, Grant's flaws predominate here, and a considerable anti-war sentiment often negatively affects the assessment. McFeely's charge of Grant's racism has also been challenged by other experts. Despite much negativity, McFeely offers insightful interpretations that help to resolve the many enigmas in Grant's career and character.

Lewis, Lloyd. *Captain Sam Grant*. Boston: Little, Brown, 1950. 512pp. Regarded as the definitive treatment of Grant's early years, Lewis lived only long enough to publish one volume of a projected comprehensive life, with his research passed on to Bruce Catton for completion. Lewis tells Grant's story up to 1861 when Grant was named colonel of an Illinois regiment in a compassionate human portrait with every factual detail documented.

Perret, Geoffrey. *Ulysses S. Grant: Soldier and President*. New York: Random House, 1997. 542pp. Perret excels in describing Grant's military campaigns and offers a reassessment of Grant's political career that finds more to praise than most other treatments. In the author's sympathetic view, Grant should be best seen as a flawed, complex individual who overcame great personal and historical challenges. Based in part on documents recently released by the Grant family and the Grant papers.

Simpson, Brooks D. *Ulysses S. Grant: Triumph over Adversity*. Boston: Houghton Mifflin, 2000. 544pp. In a skillfully written, well-researched presentation, the first installment of a planned two-volume life, Simpson covers Grant's development and military career that does full justice to his personal life and complex psyche. Balanced in its assessments, Simpson's is an important reassessment of the man and his career.

Other Biographical Studies

Anderson, Nancy S., and Dwight Anderson. *The Generals: Ulysses S. Grant and Robert E. Lee*. New York: Knopf, 1988. 523pp. The Andersons' combined biography follows both generals from childhood through their West Point careers, during the war with Mexico and during the Civil War. The emphasis here is not military history but the personalities of both men, and the book is unfortunately marred by numerous factual errors

Badeau, Adam. *Military History of Ulysses S. Grant*. New York: Appleton, 1868–1881. 3 vols. Written by Grant's former military secretary with sections reviewed by Grant himself, Bandeau's dense and plodding narrative history still serves as an important authoritative source due to the author's unique access to Grant's own collection of military records.

Badeau, Adam. *Grant in Peace: From Appomattox to Mount McGregor: A Personal Record*. Hartford, Connecticut: S.S. Scranton, 1887. 591pp. Badeau continues his narrative account of Grant's postwar career in a gossipy, poorly organized account, redeemed primarily by the author's inconsistent first-hand information.

Caldwallader, Sylvanus. *Three Years with Grant*. Benjamin P. Thomas, ed. New York: Knopf, 1955. 353pp. War correspondent Caldwallader spent his three years with Grant in the field, and his recollections constitute a superior, vivid portrait of Grant as a military commander.

Carpenter, John A. *Ulysses S. Grant*. New York: Twayne, 1970. 217pp. A concise study of Grant's presidency, this is a superior treatment of the political background of the period and Grant's difficulties in office.

Catton, Bruce. *U.S. Grant and the American Military Tradition*. Boston: Little, Brown, 1954. 201pp. In a brief biographical sketch highlighting Grant's years as a soldier and president, Catton's thesis is that the very qualities that made Grant a brilliant general assured his ruin in politics. The book serves as a solid introductory study for the general reader.

Fuller, J.F.C. *The Generalship of Ulysses S. Grant*. New York: Dodd, Mead, 1929. 411pp; *Grant and Lee: A Study in Personality and Generalship*. Bloomington: Indiana University Press, 1957. 323pp. Fuller, a British military historian, challenges established notions in elevating Grant's generalship over that of his rival, Robert E. Lee. Both volumes make Fuller's case that Grant was the superior strategist and the war's supreme general.

Hesseltine, William B. *Ulysses S. Grant: Politician*. New York: Dodd, Mead, 1935. 480pp. Hesseltine mounts the prosecution's case for Grant's failures as a politician and character flaws that doomed his administration. Hesseltine's political biography is based on solid research and primary material, but there is little attempt to mask the author's contempt for his subject.

Pitkin, Thomas M. *The Captain Departs: Ulysses S. Grant's Last Campaign.* Carbondale: Southern Illinois University Press, 1973. 164pp. The book provides the fullest account of Grant's final days as he struggled to complete his memoirs.

Porter, Horace. *Campaigning with Grant.* New York: Century, 1897. 558pp. Porter, a staff officer, based his recollection of Grant during the final year of the war on his diary record and presents a vivid and immediate firsthand account.

Ross, Ishbel. *The General's Wife: The Life of Mrs. Ulysses S. Grant.* New York: Dodd, Mead, 1959. 372pp. In the first full-length biography of Grant's wife, the author assembles a carefully documented record with insights into the couple's relationship and Julia Grant's unwavering devotion for her husband.

Smith, Gene. *Lee and Grant: A Dual Biography.* New York: McGraw-Hill, 1984. 412pp. This popular biography is a workmanlike comparative study but offers little new in its assessment.

Williams, Kenneth P. *Lincoln Finds a General: A Military Study of the Civil War.* New York: Macmillan, 1949–1959. 5 vols. Williams's exhaustive and authoritative military history tells the story of Grant's military career up to 1864. Like Catton, the author challenges the notion that Grant was indifferent to the human cost in his campaigns or incapacitated by drink.

Biographical Novels

Jones, Ted. *Grant's War: A Novel of the Civil War.* Novato, California: Presidio Press, 1992. 314pp. A historian in 1910 interviews veterans for a study of General Grant. Their eyewitness accounts present a portrait of Grant as a commander.

Parry, Richard. *That Fateful Lightning: A Novel of Ulysses S. Grant.* New York: Ballantine Books, 2000. 368pp. This is an often moving, emotional account of Grant at the end of his life, struggling to complete his memoirs while afflicted with throat cancer. In a series of flashbacks, Grant reviews his life, offering speculative additions to the experiences and perspective offered in his actual memoirs.

Seifert, Shirley. *Captain Grant.* Philadelphia: Lippincott, 1946. 606pp. In a biographical novel covering Grant's early years, his career from childhood to the beginning of the Civil War concentrates on domestic details and Grant's relationship with his wife in an intensely sympathetic portrayal.

Skimin, Robert. *Ulysses: A Biographical Novel of U.S. Grant.* New York: St. Martin's, 1994. 448pp. This full-scale biographical account follows Grant from his West Point days through his presidency, offering a portrait of a driven individual wracked with self-doubt.

Todd, Helen. *A Man Named Grant.* Boston: Houghton Mifflin, 1940. 598pp. Faithful in the general outlines of Grant's life and career, the novel invents dialogue and Grant's thoughts to make a complex personality more human and understandable. Some simplification of situations has been committed to aid the novel's drama.

Fictional Portraits

Bannister, Don. *Long Day at Shiloh.* London: Routledge, 1981. 277pp. This authentic account of the first day of the bloody battle of Shiloh is told through the perspective of dozens of combatants, including Grant's role in the battle.

Churchill, Winston. *The Crisis.* New York: Macmillan, 1903. 522pp. In one of the best Civil War novels, a young lawyer is on hand for some of the pivotal events of the war and meets many of its major figures, including Lincoln, Grant, and Sherman.

Davis, Burke. *To Appomattox: Nine April Days, 1865.* New York: Rinehart, 1959. 433pp. Based on newspaper accounts, letters, and diaries, the novel reconstructs the final nine days of the Civil War culminating in the climactic meeting between Lee and Grant at Appomattox Court House.

Devon, Louis. *Aide to Glory.* New York: Crowell, 1952. 246pp. Based on the life story of John Rawlins, Grant's aide-de-camp and later secretary of war, this is a faithful historical account with interesting glimpses of Grant.

Ehrlich, Ev. *Grant Speaks.* New York: Warner, 2000. 400pp. Ehrlich embellishes the facts of Grant's life and military career with a number of bizarre fictions, including the central conceit that the man who became Ulysses S. Grant was an imposter, Hiram Grant, an underachieving misfit who appropriates the identity of his neighbor, Ulysses. This odd situation distorts the facts just enough to supply a comic, sardonic perspective on Grant's experiences at West Point, during the Mexican and Civil War, and in the White House.

Fast, Howard. *Freedom Road.* New York: Crown, 1944. 263pp. Fast's polemical look at racial conflict during Reconstruction follows the career of a freed slave who becomes a congressman. Grant's political career is glimpsed.

Foote, Shelby. *Shiloh.* New York: Random House, 1952. 226pp. Foote's recreation of the battle of Shiloh is rendered from the foot soldier's vantage point, but with appearances by the commanders including Grant whose words and actions are faithful to the facts.

Porter, Donald. *Jubilee Jim and the Wizard of Wall Street.* New York: Dutton, 1990. 568pp. Dramatizing the Railroad Wars of the 1860s that pitted Vanderbilt against Gould and Fisk, the novel shows how their competition affected the Grant administration and the crash of the gold market.

Schultz, Duane. *Glory Enough for All: The Battle of the Crater.* New York: St. Martin's, 1993. 360pp. The tragic scheme to blast through the Confederate trenches around Petersburg is dramatized with a convincingly damning look at the Union high command under Grant.

Shaara, Jeff. *The Last Full Measure.* New York: Ballantine, 1998. 560pp. The novel chronicles the Civil War from Lee's retreat from Gettysburg to his surrender through convincing recreation of the thoughts and feelings of Grant, Lee, Longstreet, and Joshua Lawrence Chamberlain. Remaining close to the historical record, the novel provides a convincing texture of the war's day-to-day reality and plausible interpretations of the war's leading

figures. In *Gone for Soldiers: A Novel of the Mexican War* (New York: Ballantine Books, 2000. 424pp.) the author looks back at the Mexican War, documenting the campaign mainly from the perspective of the American commander, Winfield Scott, and the young Captain Robert E. Lee. Lee's formative experiences on the battlefield and as a military leader are the main concern here, along with brief appearances by individuals destined to become generals in the Civil War: Grant, Jackson, Beauregard, Hancock, Johnston, and Longstreet, who learn their military craft against the Mexicans.

Recommended Juvenile Biographies

Marrin, Albert. *Unconditional Surrender: U.S. Grant and the Civil War.* New York: Atheneum, 1994. 200pp. MG. With chapters on Grant's earlier and later life, the book concentrates on his war career in a balanced assessment that admits Grant's failings as well as his strengths.

O'Brien, Steven. *Ulysses S. Grant.* New York: Chelsea House, 1991. 111pp. MG/YA. A solid, informative full-length portrait of Grant's childhood and military and political career.

Rickarby, Laura A. *Ulysses S. Grant and the Strategy of Victory.* Englewood Cliffs, New Jersey: Silver Burdett, 1991. 125pp. YA. Part of the publisher's informative History of the Civil War series, this is a readable assessment of Grant's leadership through the decisive campaigns of the war.

Biographical Films and Theatrical Adaptations

The Blue and the Gray (1982). Director: Andrew V. McLanglen. This television mini-series covers the events of the Civil War from the main perspective of a Pinkerton secret service agent played by Stacey Keach. Rip Torn portrays Grant. Video.

The Civil War (1989). Director: Ken Burns. Grant's early career as well as his military leadership are documented in Burns's acclaimed multipart film narrative of the Civil War. Video.

Civil War Legends (1989). Director: Gary DeMoss. A multipart series that documents the Civil War campaigns of Jackson, Lee, and Grant. Video.

The Day Lincoln Was Shot (1998). Director: John Gray. John Ashton portrays Grant in this dramatization of the Lincoln assassination. Video.

Gore Vidal's Lincoln (1988). Director: Lamont Johnson. Sam Waterston takes the title role with Mary Tyler Moore as his wife in this television adaptation of Gore Vidal's bestseller. Rod Steiger portrays Grant. Video.

Son of the Morning Star (1991). Director: Mike Robe. In the television adaptation of Evan S. Connell's book, Gary Cole is Custer and Stanley Anderson appears as Grant. Video.

See also Robert E. Lee; Abraham Lincoln

207. EL GRECO
1541–1614

Born Domenikos Theotokopoulos in Candia, Crete, El Greco trained first in the school of icon painting, studied in Venice under Titian, and painted in Rome before settling in Toledo, Spain. Famous for paintings that convey religious ecstasy and contain vivid highlights, elongated figures, and vibrant colors, El Greco's works include *Burial of Count Orgaz, Baptism, Crucifixion, and Assumption*. Relatively unknown outside of Spain for centuries, it was not until the mid-twentieth century that El Greco's work was widely celebrated.

Recommended Biographies

Wethey, Harold E. *El Greco and His School*. Princeton, New Jersey: Princeton University Press, 1962. 2 vols. Wethey's essential scholarly critical biography and catalogue of the works is the most conclusive study available of what is known for sure and what may be assumed about El Greco's life and artistic development.

Other Biographical Studies

Calvert, F., and C. Gascoine Hartley. *El Greco: An Account of His Life and Work*. New York: J. Lane, 1909. 188pp. The first important biography of the twentieth century, Calvert and Hartley reveal more details about El Greco's life and background based on archival research by Spanish scholar Manuel B. Cossio.

Gudiol, José. *Domenikos Theotokopoulos, El Greco, 1541–1614*. New York: Viking, 1973. 374pp. In a useful account meant for the general reader, Gudiol chronicles El Greco's development supported by a generous selection of reproductions.

Guinard, Paul. *El Greco: A Biographical and Critical Study*. Lausanne: Skira, 1956. 143pp. Guinard's study traces the major influences on the artist, based on modern scholarship.

Keleman, Pál. *El Greco Revisited*. New York: Macmillan, 1961. 176pp. This critical biographical assessment locates El Greco's artistic genius in the context of Byzantine art and the Greek colony in Venice, as well as through the influence of the Orthodox Church.

Lassaigne, Jacques. *El Greco*. London: Thames and Hudson, 1973. 264pp. Lassaigne's is a good, general survey of the painter's life and work that traces his development and incorporates new research to clear up old misconceptions. Recommended for the general reader and student.

Palomino, Antonio. *Lives of the Eminent Spanish Painters and Sculptors*. New York: Cambridge University Press, 1987. 405pp. Written in the eighteenth century by an eminent art historian, Palomino's survey of Spanish art includes all the then-known facts about El Greco's life in the first biographical portrait in English.

Stirling-Maxwell, William. *Annals of the Artists of Spain*. London: J. Ollivier, 1848. 2 vols. Reflecting the romantic sensibility of the nineteenth century, this study established an image of El Greco as an often mad genius whose paintings show the strain he felt. The biographical details are based on those established by Palomino in the eighteenth century.

Vallentin, Antonina. *El Greco*. Garden City, New York: Doubleday, 1955. 316pp. This study places the artist and the man in his era along with a critical assessment of the works. Vallentin stays close to the known facts and challenges many of the legends that have complicated an accurate view of the artist.

Biographical Novels

Borton, Elizabeth. *The Greek of Toledo: A Romantic Narrative about El Greco*. New York: Crowell, 1960. 295pp. In a narrative that dramatizes El Greco's life from his youth in Crete, through his apprenticeship in Venice and Rome, to Toledo, Borton suggests a plausible though speculative version of an unhappy romance based on a few available facts.

Braider, Donald. *Color from a Light Within: A Novel Based on the Life of El Greco*. New York: Putnam, 1967. 379pp. Following El Greco's life from Crete, to Italy, to Spain, the novel provides insights into the painter's genius and personal torments. Convincing in its recreation of time and place, Braider's presentation of the artist is plausible, if at times necessarily speculative.

Hersch, Virginia. *Bird of God: The Romance of El Greco*. New York: Harper, 1929. 332pp. Hersch's novelized biography is full of flights of fancy but is strong on the growth of El Greco as an artist.

Biographical Films and Theatrical Adaptations

El Greco (1963). Director: Luciano Salce. This Italian film dramatizes the life of El Greco with Mel Ferrer portraying the painter. Video.

El Greco (1983). Director: Michel Pinard. Part of the Films for the Humanities series, this documentary examines El Greco's artistic development. Video.

El Greco: Spirit of Toledo (1982). Director: Yvon Gerault. Filmed on location in Toledo and Venice at sites associated with the painter, the film traces El Greco's career from his beginning as an icon painter on Crete. Video.

208. JOHANN GUTENBERG
ca. 1397–1468

German inventor and printer credited with the invention of movable type, Gutenberg made his press in 1436 or 1437, formed a partnership with goldsmith Johann Furst, and began his famous bible, known variously as the *Gutenberg Bible*, the *Mazarin Bible*, and the *42-line Bible*, for the number of lines in each printed column. A financial debt to Furst forced Gutenberg to hand over his invention and the unfinished bible to Furst, who had the book completed. It is thought that Gutenberg later reestablished himself as a printer.

Autobiography and Primary Sources

The Beginning of the World of Books, with a Synopsis of the Gutenberg Documents. Margaret B. Stillwell, ed. New York: Bibliographical Soceity of America, 1972. 112pp. This volume summarizes the principal documents upon which our direct knowledge of Gutenberg's life is based.

Recommended Biographies

Kapr, Albert. *Johann Gutenberg: The Man and His Invention*. Brookfield, Vermont: Scolar Press, 1996. 316pp. Kapr's is by far the most exhaustive and authoritative gathering of evidence to document what can be known for sure about Gutenberg's life and career.

Other Biographical Studies

Ing, Janet. *Johann Gutenberg and His Bible: A Historical Study*. New York: Typophiles, 1988. 154pp. Although hard to find, Ing's specialist study provides a sound summary of the details surrounding Gutenberg's printing career and the Gutenberg Bible.

Scholderer, Victor. *Johann Gutenberg: The Inventor of Printing*. London: Trustees of the British Museum, 1963. 32pp. This short pamphlet offers a chronological narrative of Gutenberg's life and career with suggestions about his personality based on the available documentary evidence.

Recommended Juvenile Biographies

Burch, Joann J. *Fine Print: A Story about Johann Gutenberg*. Minneapolis: Carolrhoda Books, 1991. 64pp. MG. Burch compensates for the lack of hard evidence surrounding Gutenberg's life with a solid evocation of his time, together with some sensible deductions.

Harris, Brayton. *Johann Gutenberg and the Invention of Printing*. New York: F. Watts, 1972. 144pp. MG/YA. The few known facts are skillfully woven with a social and historical background. The mechanics of printing are made accessible.

209. ALEXANDER HAMILTON
1755–1804

A lawyer and banker, and one of America's great statesmen, Hamilton was born on Nevis in the West Indies and studied at King's College (now Columbia University) in New York (1773–1774). During the American Revolution he served in the Continental army and as George Washington's aide-de-camp and secretary. A New York delegate to the constitutional convention, he did much to get the constitution ratified, particularly through articles written for the Federalist Papers, a series he initiated. He served as Secretary of the Treasury under President Washington, supported trade with Great Britain, and opposed the French Revolution. An intense political feud with Aaron Burr, vice president to Thomas Jefferson, resulted in a duel between Burr and Hamilton, during which Hamilton was mortally wounded.

Autobiography and Primary Sources

The Papers of Alexander Hamilton. Harold Syrett and Jacob E. Cooke, eds. New York: Columbia University Press, 1961-87. 27 vols. This immense scholarly edition collects nearly all of Hamilton's papers and is an indispensable source for the biographer.

Alexander Hamilton: A Biography in His Own Words. Mary Jo Kline, ed. New York: Harper & Row, 1973. 416pp. Arranging Hamilton's writings to form a version of an autobiography, this volume helpfully chronicles Hamilton's life from his perspective.

Recommended Biographies

Brookhiser, Richard. *Alexander Hamilton, American.* New York: Simon & Schuster, 1999. 256pp. In a revealing, compact analysis, Brookhiser locates the source of Hamilton's greatness and failures in his origin and development. An admiring yet fair profile, the book ably captures the full range of Hamilton's complex character and offers an excellent introduction to the man, ideas, and era.

Cooke, Jacob E. *Alexander Hamilton.* New York: Scribner, 1982. 277pp. Written by one of the editors of Hamilton's papers, this brief, well-written biography is even-handed in its treatment of Ham-

ilton's public and private life. The book is particularly strong in analyzing Hamilton's political career and economic ideas. Recommended as one of the best concise studies available.

McDonald, Forrest. *Alexander Hamilton: A Biography.* New York: W.W. Norton, 1979. 464pp. In a strong defense of his ideas and motives, McDonald traces Hamilton's drive for acceptance from his earliest years, and, though admitting some character flaws, overall Hamilton is raised to hero status over Jefferson and Adams as the principal theorist of the American state.

Miller, John C. *Alexander Hamilton: Portrait in Paradox.* New York: Harper, 1959. 659pp. Miller's comprehensive and authoritative life remains one of the strongest and most insightful available, superior in its ability to locate Hamilton in his social, cultural, and historical context. According to Miller, Hamilton's preoccupation with the creation and maintenance of a strong union is the key to all of his ideas and policies. Shown as neither a hero nor a villain, Hamilton emerges as one of the complex and towering figures of his age.

Other Biographical Studies

Brown, Stuart G. *Alexander Hamilton.* New York: Washington Square Press, 1967. 183pp. This volume serves as an able, concise introduction to both Hamilton's life and ideas.

Emery, Noemie. *Alexander Hamilton: An Intimate Portrait.* New York: Putnam, 1982. 288pp. In an often romanticized, vivid treatment of Hamilton as tragic hero, the author is often highly speculative and questionable in some of his "intimate" conclusions.

Fleming, Thomas. *Duel: Alexander Hamilton, Aaron Burr, and the Future of America.* New York: Perseus Books, 1999. 446pp. Fleming provides a fresh look at the often-told tale of the rivalry between Burr and Hamilton, relating their feud to the politics of their day and supplying a masterly painted human view of both men's characters and careers as they moved irrevocably toward their fatal encounter.

Flexner, James T. *The Young Hamilton: A Biography.* Boston: Little, Brown, 1978. 497pp. Covering the first 26 years of Hamilton's life through his ex-

perience as Washington's young aide during the Revolution, this is a character study and rarely a flattering portrait of an immature youth that counters the notion that Washington was overly influenced by his aide.

Hacker, Louis M. *Alexander Hamilton in the American Tradition.* New York: McGraw-Hill, 1957. 273pp. In this vigorous and often polemical defense of his ideas, Hamilton is nearly canonized as the personification of the conservative capitalist tradition. Hacker's contentions have been equally vigorously denied by scholars who have challenged Hacker's denial of Hamilton's self-interest and personal ambition.

Hecht, Marie B. *Odd Destiny: The Life of Alexander Hamilton.* New York: Macmillan, 1982. 464pp. Hecht's admiring study examines Hamilton's personality as the key to understanding his motives and actions. More colorful than scholarly, the book is nonetheless entertaining in its animation of Hamilton's life and times and serves as a useful introduction.

Hendrickson, Robert A. *Hamilton.* New York: Mason/Charter, 1976. 2 vols. This is a highly romanticized, admiring portrait that despite its accumulation of details commits a number of factual errors. Hendrickson condensed his two volumes into one in *The Rise and Fall of Alexander Hamilton* (New York: Van Nostrand, 1981. 658p).

Lodge, Henry Cabot. *Alexander Hamilton.* 1882. Reprint ed. New York: Greenwood, 1969. 317pp. Lodge's partisan, adulatory tribute casts Hamilton as the preeminent genius in the creation of the American republic. Interesting today mainly for revealing Hamilton's status in the nineteenth century.

Kennedy, Roger G. *Burr, Hamilton, and Jefferson: A Study in Character.* New York: Oxford University Press, 1999. 476pp. In Kennedy's provocative revisionist analysis of these three statesmen, he attempts to redeem Burr's reputation. Brimming with little-known facts, controversial interpretations, and intriguing speculation, the book offers a new look at the reputations of all three men with penetrating insights abounding.

Mitchell, Broadus. *Alexander Hamilton.* New York: Macmillan, 1957-62. 2 vols. Mitchell's lengthy, detailed biography offers a strong defense of Hamilton's character and contribution. Often overly apologetic in tone and strongly anti-Jefferson, the book is strong on the historical and cultural background and deciphering Hamilton's economic programs.

Mitchell, Broadus. *Alexander Hamilton: A Concise Biography*. New York: Oxford University Press, 1976. 395pp. Written for the general reader, this is an informative biography that treats equally Hamilton's personal and public life.

Rogow, Arnold A. *A Fateful Friendship: Alexander Hamilton and Aaron Burr*. New York: Hill & Wang, 1998. 336pp. Rogow's detailed account of the relationship between Hamilton and Burr describes the context for their duel and the personal histories of both men.

Schachner, Nathan. *Alexander Hamilton*. New York: Appleton, 1946. 488pp. Now somewhat outdated by modern scholarship, Schachner's study is a balanced account that served to reverse Hamilton's falling reputation from biographers and historians in the 1920s and 1930s.

Stourzh, Gerald. *Alexander Hamilton and the Idea of Republican Government*. Ithaca, New York: Cornell University Press, 1970. 278pp. This developmental study of Hamilton's ideas and policies is informed and insightful in linking Hamilton's career and thought to contemporary cultural ideas.

Biographical Novels

Atherton, Gertrude. *The Conqueror: Being the True and Romantic Story of Alexander Hamilton*. New York: Macmillan, 1902. 546pp. A full-length biographical treatment, the novel presents a series of largely imagined portraits of historical figures and a not-always-reliable depiction of Hamilton's career.

Desmond, Alice. *Alexander Hamilton's Wife*. New York: Dodd, Mead, 1952. 273pp. Hamilton's political career is dramatized from the perspective of his relationship with his wife, Elizabeth Schuyler, the daughter of a famous Revolutionary War general. The details are trustworthy and the characterizations plausible.

Vidal, Gore. *Burr: A Novel*. New York: Random House, 1973. 430pp. Hamilton occupies a central position in Vidal's controversial but enthralling novel, partially narrated from Burr's perspective and expressing his self-justification. Included is Vidal's own unique solution to the mystery surrounding the fatal duel.

Fictional Portraits

Beyea, Basil. *Notorious Eliza*. New York: Simon & Schuster,1978. 351pp. This biographical account of Eliza Jumel, who becomes Aaron Burr's mistress, includes a dramatization of the famous Burr-Hamilton duel.

Fast, Howard. *The Unvanquished*. New York: Duell, Sloan and Pearce, 1942. 316pp. In the depictions of the American's largely disastrous military setbacks, all the key figures of the Revolution are authentically represented.

Flood, Charles B. *Monmouth*. Boston: Houghton Mifflin, 1961. 349pp. The events during the winter

of 1777 at Valley Forge are depicted through the experiences of an American officer and a female spy. The novel includes a plausible glimpse at the American command of Washington and his aide Hamilton.

Page, Elizabeth. *The Tree of Liberty*. New York: Farrar & Rinehart, 1939. 985pp. Page's historical pageant covers the period from the 1750s to the beginning of the nineteenth century with appearances by dozens of historical figures including Hamilton.

Safire, William. *Scandalmonger*. New York: Simon & Schuster, 2000. 496pp. In Safire's carefully researched presentation of the press treatment of the personal scandals of the founding fathers, the original tabloid journalist James Callendar is secretly in the employ of Thomas Jefferson to discredit Hamilton. The novel offers interesting looks at a wide cast of actual figures, including Washington, Jefferson, Madison, Burr, and Monroe.

Taylor, David. *Mistress of the Forge*. Philadelphia: Lippincott, 1964. 350pp. The events of 1798, including the Tory revolt, the Alien and Sedition Acts, and the creation of the American iron industry are dramatized with a revealing appearance by Hamilton throughout several crises.

Recommended Juvenile Biographies

Lomask, Milton. *Odd Destiny: A Life of Alexander Hamilton*. New York: Farrar, Straus, 1969. 180pp. MG/YA. Lomask's is a judicious and informative account of Hamilton's service during the Revolution and role in the formation of the American Republic.

O'Brien, Steven. *Alexander Hamilton*. New York: Chelsea House, 1989. 111pp. MG/YA. Comprehensive and well written, O'Brien provides sufficient background information to make Hamilton's actions and personality understandable in the context of his times.

Whitelaw, Nancy. *More Perfect Union: The Story of Alexander Hamilton*. Greensboro, North Carolina: Morgan Reynolds, 1997. 112pp. MG. Part of the Notable Americans series, the biography follows Hamilton from his birth in the West Indies to his duel with Aaron Burr and serves to present his talents and human frailties in an evenhanded portrait.

Biographical Films and Theatrical Adaptations

Alexander Hamilton (1931). Director: John G. Adolfi. George Arliss co-wrote and stars in this heroic tribute to Hamilton with Doris Kenyon as Mrs. Hamilton, Alan Mowbray as Washington, Montague Love as Thomas Jefferson, and Dudley Digges as Hamilton's political nemesis Senator Timothy Roberts.

Liberty!: The American Revolution (1997). Directors: Ellen Hovde and Muffie Meyer. This PBS documentary series features actors portraying the principals in dramatic readings from their letters and speeches. Hamilton is played by Colm Feore. The companion volume is written by Thomas J. Fleming (New York: Viking, 1997. 394pp.). Video.

George Washington (1984). Director: Buzz Kulik. Richard Schenkkan appears as Hamilton in this first part of a television mini-series chronicling the life of Washington, starring Barry Bostwick in the title role and Patty Duke as Martha Washington. Video.

George Washington: The Forging of a Nation (1986). Director: William A. Graham. The second half of the television mini-series on Washington's life concentrates on his presidency. With Richard Bekins in a principal role as Hamilton. Video.

Magnificent Doll (1946). Director: Frank Borzage. This historical dramatization of the Madisons features Ginger Rogers as Dolley and Burgess Meredith as John. Arthur Space and David Niven appear as Hamilton and Burr.

Other Sources

Cooke, Jacob E., ed. *Alexander Hamilton: A Profile*. New York: Hill & Wang, 1967. 259pp. This useful collection provides various historians' views of Hamilton.

See also Aaron Burr

210. GEORGE FRIDERIC HANDEL
1685–1759

A composer of operas, oratorios, and orchestral works, and one of the masters of Baroque music, Handel was born in Halle, Germany, the son of a barber-surgeon. He trained with organist and composer Friedrich Zachow for three years and then studied law. He composed four operas between 1705 and 1709, and in 1710 became music director to the elector of Hanover (later George I of England). He settled in England (1712), where he composed some of his most celebrated works, including *Water Music* (1717), *Israel in Egypt* (1737–1737), *Messiah* (presented, 1742), and *Judas Maccabeus* (1747).

Autobiography and Primary Sources

The Letters and Writings of George Frideric Handel. Erich H. Muller, ed. 1935. Reprint ed. Freeport, New York: Books for Libraries Press, 1970. 98pp. As one can see from the brevity of this volume, very few primary sources survive to assist the biographers or readers interested in autobiographical insights into Handel's personality or perspective.

Deutsch, Otto E. *Handel: A Documentary Biography*. New York: W.W. Norton, 1955. 942pp. Deutsch's exhaustive compendium of contemporary source documents arranged chronologically is the indispensable reference source for any interpretive biography or critical study of the composer.

Recommended Biographies

Burrows, Donald. *Handel*. New York: Schirmer Books, 1994. 491pp. The elusive personality of Handel is probed in this examination of the development of Handel's music and its relation to the details of his life. Sensible in its criticism and sensitive in its nuanced portrait of the artist and his age, Burrows's study uncovers new material and synthesizes existing scholarship for a solid biography of value to both the general reader and expert.

Hogwood, Christopher. *Handel*. London: Thames and Hudson, 1984. 312pp. Hogwood's sharply rendered account of Handel's life includes critical commentary on his music, incorporating modern scholarship on both. The book may be enjoyed more as a reference volume than a consistent biographical narrative, but the sensible handling of Handel and his achievement has a great deal to recommend it.

Keates, Jonathan. *Handel: The Man and His Music*. New York: St. Martin's, 1985. 346pp. Keates's critical biography may be too detailed and technical for the nonspecialist. The compensation is an informative examination of Handel's life and character stripped of romance and a sensible evaluation of his musical achievement.

Lang, Paul H. *George Frideric Handel*. New York: W. W. Norton, 1966. 731pp. Lang's reexamination of Handel's life and work is based on solid research and remains the fullest and most reliable interpretive study available. Lang challenges many of the myths that have grown about the composer and succeeds in presenting a believable human portrait.

Other Biographical Studies

Dean, Winton. *The New Grove Handel*. New York: W.W. Norton, 1983. 185pp. Dean's useful reference summary of the highlights of Handel's life includes an evaluation of his music and a detailed list of his compositions.

Dent, Edward J. *Handel*. London: Duckworth, 1934. 140pp. Dent's critical study is reliable and insightful, placing the man and his music solidly in the context of his time and revealing the various influences that helped shape his art.

Flower, Newman. *George Frideric Handel: His Personality and His Times*. New York: Cassell, 1923. 378pp. Long considered the standard biography, Flower's often romanticized account has been superseded by modern scholarship and treatments that are less willing to indulge in imaginative re-creations of Handel's thoughts and activities.

Landon, H.C.Robbins *Handel and His World*. Boston: Little, Brown, 1984. 256pp. Landon's pictorial biography synthesizes a great deal of archival data into a readable narrative that reveals both the man and his milieu.

Mainwaring, John. *Memoirs of the Life of George Frideric Handel*. 1760. Reprint ed. New York Da Capo Press, 1980. 208pp. Written soon after Handel's death, this first biography of the composer contains a number of details about his early and personal life, as well as a number of romantic anecdotes that have dominated the depiction of the composer and have been subsequently challenged.

Thompson, Wendy. *The Illustrated Lives of the Great Composers: Handel*. New York: Omnibus Press, 1994. 144pp. Thompson supplies a useful introduction to the man and music with a wide selection of illustrations documenting his life and career.

Weinstock, Herbert. *Handel*. 1946. Revised ed. New York: Knopf, 1959. 328pp. This detailed biography helpfully resolves discrepancies in the factual record of Handel's life and fills in the gaps with a sharply rendered historical background and a vivid depiction of Handel's London.

Recommended Juvenile Biographies

Ludwig, Charles. *George Frideric Handel: Composer of Messiah*. Milford, Michigan: Mott Media, 1987. 185pp. MG/YA. This is a highly detailed portrait of Handel and his era.

Sadie, Stanley. *Handel*. New York: Crowell, 1969. 95pp. MG. Mainly concerned with Handel's professional activities, Sadie places Handel among his peers and describes the circumstances surrounding his compositions with many examples of his music.

Biographical Films and Theatrical Adaptations

Farinelli (1994). Director: Gérard Corbiau. In this story of two brothers, one a composer and the other a castrato opera singer (Enrico Lo Verso and Stefano Dionisi), Jeroen Krabbé is memorable as Handel in a portrait that brings the composer to life vividly and accurately. Video.

Other Sources

Burrows, Donald, ed. *The Cambridge Companion to Handel*. New York: Cambridge University Press, 1997. 349pp. This compilation of essays by leading Handel experts looks at a wide range of issues surrounding the composer's life and work. Accessible for the general reader.

211. HANNIBAL
247 BC–ca. 183 BC

The son of Sicilian general Hamilcar Barca, who fought Rome during the First Punic War, Hannibal early learned to hate the Romans. After succeeding his brother-in-law as general and gaining the support of Carthage, he set out to invade Italy from Spain during the Second Punic War (218-201 BC). A tactical genius, Hannibal's crossing of the Alps with elephants is considered one of the most outstanding feats of military history. He advanced successfully toward Rome but was not able to take the city and was eventually forced to withdraw. He returned to Carthage, where he became chief magistrate. Sought by the Romans as an insurrectionist, he took poison as he was about to be captured.

Recommended Biographies

De Beer, Sir Gavin. *Hannibal: Challenging Rome's Supremacy*. New York: Viking, 1969 319pp. The author combines Polybius, Livy, Plutarch, and other sources, along with his own extensive research, to establish Hannibal's exact route across the Alps, presenting a detailed and authoritative narrative account. Overly meticulous at points for the casual reader, De Beer's study remains one of the most reliable studies available. For more on Hannibal's Alpine crossing, see the author's *Alps and Elephants* (New York: Dutton, 1956. 123pp.).

Lancel, Serge. *Hannibal*. Malden, Massachusetts: Blackwell, 1998. 243pp. Regarded as the definitive biography, Lancel's thorough and authoritative account by one of the leading authorities of Carthage portrays a complex man and military leader and provides details of every facet of Hannibal's campaigns and the political background of his times. Essential reading for any serious student of the subject.

Other Biographical Studies

Bradford, Ernle. *Hannibal*. New York: McGraw-Hill, 1981. 223pp. Bradford's narrative account is useful in establishing the cultural and historical background of the Carthaginians to make Hannibal's actions and the events of the Punic Wars comprehensible. He is also unusual in largely taking the Carthaginian side in the conflict and accordingly is willing to grant a great deal more humanity to Hannibal than other treatments that accepts the victors' valuation.

Cottrell, Leonard. *Hannibal: Enemy of Rome*. New York: Holt, 1961. 257pp. Cottrell's lively reconstruction of Hannibal's military achievement is based on his following the general's route into Italy. In a highly impressionistic account, the author begins with evident antipathy toward Hannibal and ends with admiration. For the generalist, Cottrell's approach comes close to fiction in reanimating scenes and events.

Dodge, Theodore A. *Hannibal*. 1891. Reprint ed. New York: Da Capo Press, 1995. 682pp. A decorated veteran of the U.S. Civil War, Dodge was one of the first scholars to retrace Hannibal's steps and visit all of the battlefields. His account is both a biography of Hannibal and a history of Carthage-Rome relations. Filled with useful details.

Lamb, Harold. *Hannibal: One Man Against Rome*. Garden City, New York: Doubleday, 1958. 310pp. Lamb has produced a fine historical narrative for the general reader, weaving together fact, scholarly conjecture and colorful period details.

Lazenby, J.F. *Hannibal's War: A Military History of the Second Punic War*. Norman: Oklahoma University Press, 1998. 340pp. Hannibal's military achievement and genius are central in this reliable and authoritative study of the various campaigns of the Second Punic War.

Livy. *The War with Hannibal: Books XXI–XXX of The History of Rome from Its Foundation*. Baltimore: Penguin, 1965. 711pp. Livy, writing more than a century after Hannibal's death and a determined Roman partisan, is much less reliable in his portrait of Hannibal than Polybius, but his account of the Second Punic War has remained an essential source for biographers of the Carthaginian general.

Peddie, John. *Hannibal's War*. Gloucestershire, England: Sutton, 1997. 232pp. Although not a biography in the strict sense, Peddie's study of Hannibal's campaign offers a number of insights into Hannibal's military genius and character.

Polybius. *The Histories*. Cambridge, Massachusetts: Harvard University Press, 1922–1927. 6 vols. This history of the Second Punic War by a contemporary of Hannibal is regarded as the most reliable early account and, along with Livy, is the essential source for information on Hannibal.

Prevas, John. *Hannibal Across the Alps: The Enigma Reexamined.* Rockville Centre, New York: Sarpedon, 1998. 232pp. Prevas re-engages the controversy of Hannibal's exact route across the Alps, along with a brief history of the Second Punic War and Hannibal's various battles.

Biographical Novels

Capps, Robert S. *Hannibal's Lieutenant.* Alexandria, Virginia: Manor House, 1994. 349pp. Hannibal is seen from the perspective of a fictional officer in his command in a reconstruction that follows the known facts closely.

Dolan, Mary. *Hannibal of Carthage.* New York: Macmillan, 1955. 308pp. Hannibal's character and military prowess are described from the perspective of a slave and eyewitness. The main events are historical though they are amplified by the author's speculation and imagination.

Leckie, Ross. *Hannibal.* Washington, DC: Regnery, 1996. 245pp. This autobiographical novel offers Hannibal's own account of his career in a convincing and realistic psychological profile and a vivid re-creation of the period. The author admits taking some liberties with history and inventing events and details.

Taleb, Mirza. *Hannibal: Man of Destiny.* Boston: Branden, 1974. 348pp. Scenes from Hannibal's campaigns during the Second Punic War are dramatized in this heroic and idealized portrayal.

Fictional Portraits

Baumann, Hans. *I Marched with Hannibal.* New York: Walck, 1962. 226pp. Hannibal's crossing of the Alps into Italy is seen from the perspective from a orphan who becomes a member of the invasion force.

Blasco-Ibanez, Vicente. *Sonnica.* New York: Duffield, 1912. 331pp. This adventure tale describes the bloody siege of Saguntum waged by Hannibal during the Punic Wars.

Gerard, Francis. *The Scarlet Beast.* New York: Longmans, 1935. 404pp. This fictional account of the events of the Second Punic War is written from a decidedly Roman perspective in which the Carthaginians are vilified. The book's partisanship undermines its objectivity and reliability as a balanced portrait of Hannibal and his achievements.

Recommended Juvenile Biographies

Green, Robert. *Hannibal.* New York: F. Watts, 1996. 63pp. MG. Concise and clearly written, this biography vividly re-creates Hannibal's military campaigns and establishes his achievements, surmounting almost impossible challenges presented by the Alps and the Romans.

Biographical Films and Theatrical Adaptations

Hannibal (1960). Director: Edgar G. Ulmer. Victor Mature stars as Hannibal in this costume epic depicting the general's famous crossing of the Alps. Also starring Rita Gam, Gabriele Ferzetti, and Milly Vitale.

212. WARREN G. HARDING
1865–1923

The twenty-ninth U.S. president, Harding served (1914–1920) as U.S. senator from Ohio before his nomination as Republican candidate for the presidency. Elected president by a wide majority, Harding worked for tariff revision and the repeal of high income taxes. His administration and his personal life were marked by scandal and corruption, the most well known of which was the Teapot Dome scandal involving the oil industry. Harding, who suffered from a serious heart condition, died while visiting San Francisco, before the scandals of his administration came to light.

Recommended Biographies

Russell, Francis. *The Shadow of Blooming Grove: Warren G. Harding and His Times.* New York: McGraw-Hill, 1968. 696pp. Russell's is a detailed chronological narrative of Harding's life with an emphasis on his background and the various scandals surrounding Harding's love life and political career.

Sinclair, Andrew. *The Available Man: The Life Behind the Masks of Warren Gamaliel Harding.* New York: Macmillan, 1965. 344pp. An English historian provides a sensible, well-balanced summary of Harding's background and political career. The book helps to explain why Harding was able to be elected president, despite his modest talents.

Trani, Eugene P., and David L. Wilson. *The Presidency of Warren Gamaliel Harding.* Lawrence: University Press of Kansas, 1977. 232pp. The authors present the best overall assessment of the Harding administration, recognizing both its failures and accomplishments.

Other Biographical Studies

Adams, Samuel H. *Incredible Era: The Life and Times of Warren Gamaliel Harding.* Boston: Houghton Mifflin, 1939. 456pp. Novelist Adams supplies a colorful, dramatic rendering of Harding's rise and fall with a focus on the scandal that plagued his career and his inability to rise to responsibilities of his office.

Anthony, Carl S. *Florence Harding: The First Lady, the Jazz Age, and the Death of America's Most Scandalous President.* New York: Morrow, 1998. 645pp. This is a comprehensively documented biography of Florence Kling Harding that sheds light on the couple's political marriage and relationship. Cleared of the suspected poisoning of her husband by the author, Florence Harding emerges as a strong and interesting figure and in the view of Anthony, "one of the greatest" first ladies.

Downes, Randolph C. *The Rise of Warren Gamaliel Harding, 1865–1920.* Columbus: Ohio State University Press, 1970. 734pp. Downes's is a detailed, scholarly political biography that chronicles Harding's career up to his election to the presidency. Downes grants Harding political ideals, but insufficient qualities for the task of national leadership.

Murray, Robert K. *The Harding Era: Warren G. Harding and His Administration.* Minneapolis: University of Minnesota Press, 1969. 626pp. Murray's is a detailed re-examination of Harding's rise to the presidency and his administration based on the previously restricted Harding papers. As one reviewer pointed out, Murray "has rescued an important period of American history from a morass of melodrama and low comedy, and made it both human and credible."

Biographical Novels

Blinder, Martin. *Fluke.* Sag Harbor, New York: Permanent Press, 1999. 213pp. Harding's mistress, Nan Britton, provides her perspective on her relationship with Harding from his days in Marion, Ohio, as a newspaper publisher, through his Senate career, and presidency.

Fictional Portraits

Zagst, Michael. *"M.H." Meets President Harding.* New York: D.I. Fine, 1987. 247pp. In 1923, Edison's camping trip with President Harding in West Virginia becomes the opportunity for a kidnapping plot by Mata Hari in disguise.

Vidal, Gore. *Hollywood: A Novel of America in the 1920s.* New York: Random House, 1990. 437pp. Vidal's social panorama depicts the corruption in the Harding administration, along with a large cast of historical figures.

Recommended Juvenile Biographies

Canadeo, Anne. *Warren G. Harding: 29th President of the United States.* Ada, Oklahoma: Garrett, 1990. 120pp. MG. This is a solid accounting of Harding's personality, career, and the events of his administration.

Wade, Linda R. *Warren G. Harding: Twenty-Ninth President of the United States.* Chicago: Childrens Press, 1989. 98pp. MG. Wade provides a straightforward, factual assessment of Harding's political career and presidential administration.

Biographical Films and Theatrical Adaptations

St. Germain, Mark. *Camping with Henry and Tom: A Play.* Garden City, New York: Fireside Theatre, 1995. 107pp. Based on the actual camping trip of Edison, Henry Ford, and President Warren Harding, this witty play imagines what might have transpired among the men as Ford vies to replace Harding as president.

Other Sources

Moran, Philip R., ed. *Warren G. Harding, 1865–1923: Chronology, Documents, Bibliographical Aids.* Dobbs Ferry, New York: Oceana, 1970. 120pp. This is a useful volume that includes a detailed chronology, all of the major speeches, and an annotated bibliography of works on Harding.

213. THOMAS HARDY
1840–1928

One of the great English writers of the nineteenth century, Hardy was born near Dorchester in Dorset,

England. The son of a stonemason, he could not afford to pursue a scholarly career and was apprenticed to a church architect. He continued to study Greek and Latin classics and to write, even while working for a London architect. His first novel to receive critical and popular acclaim was *Far From the Madding Crowd* (1874). His major works, set in the bleak and forbidding landscape of Dorset, are *The Return of the Native* (1878), *The Mayor of Casterbridge* (1886), *Tess of the D'Urbervilles* (1891), and *Jude the Obscure* (1896). A poet as well as a novelist, Hardy also authored a verse drama, *The Dynasts* (1903–1908), a historical epic of the Napoleonic era, considered one of his finest works.

Autobiography and Primary Sources

Hardy, Florence. *The Early Life of Thomas Hardy 1840-91*. London: Macmillan, 1928. 327pp.; *The Later Years of Thomas Hardy 1892–1928*. London: Macmillan, 1930. 289pp. Although credited to his second wife, Hardy himself wrote all but the last four chapters from his contemporary notes, letters, and diaries that he subsequently destroyed. In turn guarded, detached, candid, and revealing, this curious but indispensable semi-autobiography preserves primary materials that are available only here, but it should be read with caution for its overall reliability.; *The Life of Thomas Hardy* (New York: St. Martin's, 1962. 470pp.) is a one-volume condensation.

Collected Letters of Thomas Hardy. Richard L. Purdy and Michael Millgate, eds. New York: Oxford University Press, 1978–1988. 7 vols. This scholarly collection of Hardy's letters is an invaluable source of information on the writer's activities, ideas, and relationships.

Recommended Biographies

Gittings, Robert. *Young Thomas Hardy*. Boston: Little, Brown, 1975. 259pp.; *Thomas Hardy's Later Years*. Boston: Little, Brown, 1978. 244pp. In a detailed, often unflattering portrait, Gittings supplies a great deal of information about Hardy's family background and its influence on his development. A very human Hardy emerges here, a complex blend of weaknesses and strengths.

Millgate, Michael. *Thomas Hardy: A Biography*. New York: Random House, 1982. 637pp. Millgate has produced the most balanced and comprehensive biography available. More sympathetic to Hardy than Gittings, Millgate, however, does not avoid the less flattering aspects of the writer's character. Without resolving the various strands in Hardy's personality, the book fully displays Hardy in all his facets and sensitively reveals his works' biographical connections.

Other Biographical Studies

Blunden, Edmund. *Thomas Hardy*. New York: St. Martin's, 1942. 286pp. In a mainly literary study with Hardy's character glimpsed in passing, Blunden's study has the benefit of acquaintance with the author, a poet's sensibility, and a deep appreciation for rural life. On the negative side, as an ardent admirer, Blunden is rarely probing into the less flattering aspects of Hardy's personality or career.

Brennecke, Ernst. *The Life of Thomas Hardy*. New York: Greenberg, 1925. 259pp. Brennecke's early biography, which annoyed Hardy in its inaccuracy and speculation, helped stimulate him to produce the two-volume life allegedly by his wife. More a sketch than a fully-realized biography, Brennecke's book is inadequate in its details and too discreet to reproduce the man in full.

Deacon, Lois, and Terry Coleman. *Providence and Mr. Hardy*. London: Hutchinson, 1966. 244pp. The authors' controversial and dubious theory about Hardy's liaison with his cousin Tryphena Sparks dominates this study that locates Hardy's guilt over this relationship as a key to unlocking his attitudes.

Gibson, James. *Thomas Hardy: A Literary Life*. New York: St. Martin's, 1996. 206pp. Gibson's concise critical study chronicles the biographical, literary, and social contexts of Harding's writings and professional dealings and relationships.

Gittings, Robert, and Jo Manton. *The Second Mrs. Hardy*. Seattle, Washington: University of Washington Press, 1979. 150pp. This insightful portrait of Florence Hardy is a study in repression and domination by her genius husband. Illuminating in their relationship and in the domestic details of Hardy's final years.

Halliday, F.E. *Thomas Hardy: His Life and Work*. New York: Barnes and Noble, 1972. 206pp. This lively and well-illustrated volume offers the highlights of Hardy's life and career and serves as a useful introduction.

Hardy, Evelyn. *Thomas Hardy: A Critical Biography*. New York: St. Martin's, 1954. 342pp. Drawing on some unpublished material, Hardy's critical study is sketchy about the author's early years and often shallow in its insights.

Kay-Robinson, Denys. *The First Mrs. Thomas Hardy*. New York: St. Martin's, 1979. 278pp. In a study of Hardy's relationship with Emma Lavinia Gifford, she is shown as more sinned against than sinning, with the details of their marriage recounted largely through her eyes with a good deal of conjecture.

Orel, Harold. *The Final Years of Thomas Hardy, 1912–1928*. Lawrence: University Press of Kansas, 1976. 151pp. Orel's detailed study of Hardy's last years concentrates on his inner life as glimpsed through a critical analysis of his poems.

O'Sullivan, Timothy. *Thomas Hardy: An Illustrated Biography*. New York: St. Martin's, 1976. 192pp. With over 150 illustrations of personalities and topography this visual biography includes an adequate summary of Hardy's career with suggestions about the connection between the life and works.

Seymour-Smith, Martin. *Hardy*. New York: St. Martin's, 1994. 886pp. This exhaustive study is primarily a psychological and developmental biography that treats in full Hardy's complex psyche and relationships. Hardy's obsessions and dark fantasies are displayed in a provocative, brawling, interpretative study that is overly argumentative in its dismissal of previous biographical treatments.

At times Hardy is nearly forgotten in the wrangling over others' interpretations.

Stewart, J.I.M. *Thomas Hardy: A Critical Biography*. New York: Dodd, Mead, 1971. 249pp. Stewart sensibly connects Hardy's biography with his works in primarily a literary study with a standout chapter on Florence Hardy's *Life*.

Turner, Paul D.L. *The Life of Thomas Hardy: A Critical Biography*. Malden, Massachusetts: Blackwell, 1998. 326pp. Examining all of Hardy's works in separate chapters, Turner reveals the biographical and literary background for each.

Weber, Carl. *Hardy of Wessex*. 1940. Revised ed. New York: Columbia University Press, 1965. 342pp. Weber's well-written and comprehensive study focuses on Hardy's inner life and the biographical influences on his writings. Uneven overall in his coverage of Hardy's development, the book nonetheless makes a substantive contribution to understanding the author and his works.

Other Sources

Gibson, James, ed. *Thomas Hardy: Interviews and Recollections*. New York: St. Martin's, 1999. 268pp. Hardy's own recollections and those who knew him are arranged chronologically in this useful reference volume.

Kramer, Dale, ed. *The Cambridge Companion to Thomas Hardy*. New York: Cambridge University Press, 1999. 231pp. This collection of essays provides an overview of Hardy's works with useful details about the writer's life, ideas, and career.

214. WILLIAM HENRY HARRISON
1773–1841

The ninth U.S. president, Harrison served (1798) as secretary of the Northwest Territory, was the territorial delegate to Congress (1799), and served (1800–1812) as governor of Indiana Territory. He became a national hero after battling the Shawnees at the famous Battle of Tippecanoe (1811) and engaging the British at the Battle of the Thames (1813). Nominated (1840) as the Whig candidate for the presidency, Harrison waged a rousing campaign, using the slogan "Tippecanoe and Tyler too." He won the election but caught pneumonia during the inauguration and died a month later.

Autobiography and Primary Sources

Messages and Letters of William Henry Harrison. Logan Esarey, ed. Indianapolis: Indiana Historical Commission, 1922. 2 vols. Provides a sampling of Harrison's letters and writings.

Recommended Biographies

Goebel, Dorothy B. *William Henry Harrison: A Political Biography*. 1926. Reprint ed. Philadelphia: Porcupine Press, 1974. 456pp. Goebel's remains the strongest examination of Harrison's public career with both a portrait of his personality and his strengths and limitations as a leader.

Peterson, Norma L. *The Presidencies of William Henry Harrison and John Tyler*. Lawrence: University Press of Kansas, 1989. 329pp. Peterson's is a judicious, sensible assessment of the Harrison and Tyler administrations, presenting the policy decisions in the wider historical and political context.

Other Biographical Studies

Cleaves, Freeman. *Old Tippecanoe: William Henry Harrison and His Time.* 1939. Reprint ed. New York: Kennikat Press, 1969. 422pp. Cleaves's is a sympathetic assessment of Harrison's career, generally reliable and drawing on solid sources.

Gunderson, Robert G. *The Log Cabin Campaign.* Lexington: University Press of Kentucky, 1957. 292pp. Gunderson covers in detail the 1840 presidential election and Harrison's brief presidency based on an extensive review of contemporary sources.

Biographical Novels

Huston, James A. *Counterpoint.* Lawrenceville, Virginia: Brunswick, 1987. 629pp. The dual careers of Harrison and Tecumseh are contrasted in a chronicle of their lives leading us to the Battle of the Thames in 1813.

Recommended Juvenile Biographies

Fitz-Gerald, Christine M. *William Henry Harrison: Ninth President of the United States.* Chicago: Childrens Press, 1987. 98pp. MG. Straightforward, factual summary of the basic details of Harrison's life, character, and career.

Stefoff, Rebecca. *William Henry Harrison, 9th President of the United States.* Ada, Oklahoma: Garrett, 1990. 119pp. MG. Stefoff summarizes the important details in Harrison's career and his historical era.

Biographical Films and Theatrical Adaptations

Tecumseh: The Last Warrior (1995). Director: Larry Elikann. Television adaptation of Thom's novel, *Panther in the Sky,* dramatizes the life of Tecumseh (Jesse Borrego) with David Clennan portraying Harrison. Video.

Other Sources

Durfee, David A., ed. *William Henry Harrison, 1773–1841; John Tyler, 1790–1862: Chronology, Documents, Bibliographical Aids.* Dobbs Ferry, New York: Oceana, 1970. 144pp. Besides extensive chronologies, this useful volume collects representative documentary evidence as well as a listing of writings on Harrison and Tyler.

See also Tecumseh

215. NATHANIEL HAWTHORNE
1804–1864

An American novelist and short-story writer, Hawthorne is one of the great masters of American literature. Descended from a prominent Puritan family and born in Salem, Massachusetts, he was the son of a sea captain. After attending Bowdoin College (1821–1825), he devoted himself to writing and editing but could not support himself and took a job at a Boston customhouse. He also lived for a time at Brook Farm. After his marriage (1842), he worked as surveyor for the port of Salem (1846–1849). *The Scarlet Letter,* considered his masterpiece, was published in 1850. Hawthorne's other celebrated novels include *The House of Seven Gables* (1851), *The Blithedale Romance* (1852), and *The Marble Faun* (1860).

Autobiography and Primary Sources

The essential primary sources on Hawthorne's life and thoughts are available in the various scholarly editions of his correspondence and notebooks: *Letters.* Thomas Woodson, et al., eds. (Columbus: Ohio State University Press, 1984-88. 4 vols.); *The American Notebooks.* Claude M. Simpson, ed. (Columbus: Ohio State University Press, 1980. 604pp.); and *The English Notebooks.* Thomas Woodson and Bill Ellis, eds. (Columbus: Ohio State University Press, 1997. 2 vols.).

Recommended Biographies

Mellow, James R. *Nathaniel Hawthorne in His Times.* New York: Houghton Mifflin, 1980. 684pp. Winner of the National Book Award for biography, Mellow's excellent historical study serves to locate Hawthorne expertly in the intellectual, historical, and cultural context of his times. The Hawthorne that emerges in Mellow's vivid portrait contradicts the image of the brooding recluse. Instead, the author is shown as a determined artist in the midst of a rich circle of relationships that reveals the intellectual climate of pre-Civil War America.

Miller, Edwin H. *Salem Is My Dwelling Place: A Life of Nathaniel Hawthorne.* Iowa City: University of Iowa Press, 1991. 596pp. Miller's elegantly written psychological study is remarkably free of jargon and delicate in probing the inner drama of Hawthorne's life. Insightful particularly on the writer's relationship with his wife, Miller expertly suggests how Hawthorne's conflicts are reflected in his fiction.

Stewart, Randall. *Nathaniel Hawthorne: A Biography.* New Haven, Connecticut: Yale University Press, 1948. 279pp. Long regarded as the standard biography, Stewart's carefully researched examination repudiates the various legends of Hawthorne as a solitary figure haunted by the Puritan past. Instead Stewart documents Hawthorne's normal social life, happy marriage, and active political career. With only one chapter on Hawthorne the writer, Stewart's book serves chiefly for its addition to the factual knowledge of Hawthorne's life.

Turner, Arlin. *Nathaniel Hawthorne.* New York: Oxford University Press, 1980. 457pp. This superior critical biography is highly recommended for its sensible interpretation and its ability to join the inner world of Hawthorne's ideas and writing with the exterior world of his life and times. Turner replaces the image of a legendary Hawthorne with a moving human portrait.

Other Biographical Studies

Arvin, Newton. *Hawthorne.* Boston: Little, Brown, 1929. 303pp. This psychological and critical study uses the facts of Hawthorne's life as a framework for erecting an interpretation of the inner man. Arvin's portrait of an alienated Hawthorne, cut off from society, has been challenged by subsequent biographers.

Baym, Nina. *The Shape of Hawthorne's Career.* Ithaca, New York: Cornell University Press, 1976. 283pp. Tracing Hawthorne's intellectual and literary development, the book sets the writer in his cultural context, but the approach is thesis dominated with his life and works sometimes severely cut to fit the theme of the dilemma of the artist in nineteenth-century American society.

Cantwell, Robert. *Nathaniel Hawthorne: The American Years.* New York: Rinehart, 1948. 499pp. In the first volume of a projected but uncompleted two-volume life, Cantwell deals with Hawthorne's ancestry and life up to 1850. Hawthorne is shown not as a lonely recluse but as an active, engaged student, politician, and journalist.

Conway, Moncure. *The Life of Nathaniel Hawthorne.* 1890. Reprint ed. New York: Haskell House, 1968. 224pp. More reliable than Lathrop, Conway's study has the advantage of personal acquaintance with many in Hawthorne's circle.

Gorman, Herbert. *Hawthorne: A Study in Solitude.* New York: G. Doran, 1927. 179pp. Gorman's brief developmental and intellectual biographical study locates the source of Hawthorne's genius in his physical and intellectual isolation. In Gorman's handling, Hawthorne emerges as an overly romanticized and sentimental figure.

Hoeltje, Hubert. *Inward Sky: The Mind and Heart of Nathaniel Hawthorne.* Durham, North Carolina: Duke University Press, 1962. 579pp. Hoeltje's provocative and often highly speculative developmental biography sets out to uncover the pattern of Hawthorne's thoughts and to connect his inner, mental life with the facts of his career.

Hull, Raymona. *Nathaniel Hawthorne: The English Experience 1853–64.* Pittsburg, Pennsylvania: University of Pittsburg Press, 1980. 307pp. This is the fullest and most detailed year-by-year account of Hawthorne's extended stay in England and Europe to his death. Includes a biographical appendix of those who became part of Hawthorne's circle during the period.

James, Henry. *Hawthorne.* New York: Harper, 1879. 177pp. James's classic study has limited value as a biography since it is dependent on unreliable secondary sources. However, as a critical study it has lasting value for its interpretation of Hawthorne's fiction and its revelations of the young James working out his own aesthetic principles.

Lathrop, George P. *A Study in Hawthorne.* Boston: J.R. Osgood, 1876. 350pp. Written by Hawthorne's son-in-law, this early biographical portrait set the image of Hawthorne as the brooding, haunted isolate that subsequent biographies have modified in varying degrees. Not reliable as an objective or trustworthy profile.

Mather, Edward. *Nathaniel Hawthorne: A Modest Man.* New York: Crowell, 1940. 356pp. Written by an English biographer, this useful study helps set Hawthorne more solidly in his cultural and historical background and counters the notion of the writer as a loner. The book is strongest on Hawthorne's years abroad.

Normand, Jean. *Nathaniel Hawthorne: An Approach to an Analysis of Artistic Creation.* Cleveland: Case Western Reserve University Press, 1970. 474pp. Normand's provocative and insightful critical study of Hawthorne's artistic development is written for the literary expert and offers an original and fresh paradigm for viewing Hawthorne's creativity.

Van Doren, Mark. *Nathaniel Hawthorne.* New York: Viking, 1949. 285pp. Van Doren's brief critical biography is an admiring appreciation that served to dispel the image of the tortured recluse that had grown up around the writer. Van Doren grants Hawthorne more normalcy in his background and considerable more practicality in his genius.

Wagenknecht, Edward. *Nathaniel Hawthorne: Man and Writer.* New York: Oxford University Press, 1961. 233pp. Neither a chronological nor a critical study, Wagenknecht's "psychograph" is a character study that places the writer in the context of his times. Often gossipy and anecdotal, the book is uneven in its treatment with sensible interpretation mixed with shallow analysis.

Young, Philip. *Hawthorne's Secret: An Untold Tale.* Boston: Godine, 1984. 183pp. The title's secret refers to the author's revelation of Hawthorne's incestuous relationship with his sister. Admitting that the evidence is mainly conjectural and circumstantial, Young uses this ingenious speculation as a key to understanding Hawthorne's writing.

Recommended Juvenile Biographies

Whitelaw, Nancy. *Nathaniel Hawthorne: American Storyteller.* Greensboro, North Carolina: Morgan Reynolds, 1996. 112pp. MG/YA. This is a well-researched chronological biography that quotes frequently from Hawthorne's own words and sets his struggle to achieve artistic and financial success in the context of his times.

Wood, James P. *The Unpardonable Sin: A Life of Nathaniel Hawthorne.* New York: Pantheon, 1970. 180pp. MG/YA. In an informative and insightful description of Hawthorne's life and writing career, the essential facts are laid out with a concentration on the writer's human side and preoccupation with the question of evil.

Other Sources

Gale, Robert L. *A Nathaniel Hawthorne Encyclopedia.* New York: Greenwood, 1991. 509pp. Multiple alphabetically arranged entries identify Hawthorne's characters, summarize his literary works, and identify his family, friends, and associates. Included is an extensive chronology and useful appendixes on his background and circle.

216. FRANZ JOSEPH HAYDN
1732–1809

Austrian composer and one of history's greatest masters of classical music, Haydn became (1761) court musician to the Esterhazy family, a position he held for 29 years. Haydn's many works are notable for their liveliness, lyricism, and instrumental brilliance, and include over 100 symphonies, such as the *Surprise Symphony* (1791) and the *Clock Symphony* (1794), over 80 string quartets, more than 50 piano sonatas, two great oratorios, *The Creation* (1798) and *The Seasons* (1801), and numerous masses, operas, and songs.

Autobiography and Primary Sources

Collected Correspondence and London Notebooks of Joseph Haydn. H.C. Robbins Landon, ed. London: Barrie and Rockliff, 1959. 367pp. Containing some 300 letters and four diaries kept by the composer between 1791 and 1795, this volume adds immeasurably to our knowledge of Haydn the man and artist.

Recommended Biographies

Geiringer, Karl, and Irene Geiringer. *Haydn: A Creative Life in Music.* 1946. Revised ed. Berkeley: University of California Press, 1982. 434pp. Much revised in the light of developments in Haydn scholarship since it first appeared in 1946, this critical study has long been regarded as the standard single-volume life. Balanced and detailed, the book divides Haydn's career into five stylistic periods and discusses the compositions in each, connecting Haydn's life with his musical development.

Landon, H.C. Robbins. *Haydn: Chronicle and Works.* Bloomington: Indiana University Press, 1976–1980. 5 vols. The most comprehensive and authoritative study of Haydn, Landon's monumental study serves as a repository of essential primary sources that document the composer's life and times, placing each composition in its historical and cultural context. A nonconsecutive index makes it difficult to navigate easily through the five volumes. *Haydn: A Documentary Study* (New York: Rizzoli, 1981. 224pp.) includes over 200 illustrations, a chronology, and biographical narrative of the highlights of Haydn's career and serves as the best available visual introduction to the composer.

Other Biographical Studies

Barbaud, Pierre. *Haydn.* New York: Grove Press, 1959. 191pp. Barbaud's documentary and illustrated collection of materials on Haydn's life and times offers a fact-filled introduction.

Brenet, Michel. *Haydn.* London: Oxford University Press, 1926. 143pp. This concise assessment of the man and his music remains a useful introduction.

Butterworth, Neil. *Haydn.* New York: Omnibus, 1984. 144pp. Part of the Illustrated Lives of the Great Composers series, the author chronicles Haydn's life using contemporary documents, recollections of associates, and excerpts from Haydn's letters and diaries.

Hadden, J. Cuthbert. *Haydn.* New York: Dutton, 1902. 232pp. Hadden's life concentrates on the man rather than his music and is particularly detailed on Haydn's visits to London.

Hughes, Rosemary. *Haydn.* 1950. Revised ed. London: Dent, 1989. 271pp. In a workmanlike chronological narrative, this popular biography traces the outline of Haydn's life along with critical assessments of his composition.

Jacob, Heinrich E. *Joseph Haydn: His Art, Times, and Glory.* New York: Rinehart, 1950. 368pp. Jacob's popular biography is often sentimental and novelistic in its approach, creating a vivid but often distorted caricature of Haydn and his milieu. Should be read with caution as a reliable, factual account.

Landon, H.C. Robbins, and David Wyn Jones. *Haydn: His Life and Music.* Bloomington: Indiana University Press, 1988. 383pp. Synthesizing the massive material in Landon's five-volume definitive study, the book provides a useful overview in alternating chapters on Haydn's life and music.

Larsen, Jens Peter, and Georg Feder. *The New Grove Haydn.* New York: W.W. Norton, 1982. 237pp. This concise and useful reference source includes chapters on various aspects of Haydn's life and assessment of his music and personality based on recent scholarship.

Nohl, Ludwig. *Life of Haydn.* Chicago: Jansen McClurg, 1880. 195pp. Nohl's frequently reissued popular biography helped stimulate a positive reassessment of Haydn's music in the nineteenth century. His anecdotal appreciation considers Haydn's German characteristics and the relationship between his life and his music.

Somfai, László. *Joseph Haydn: His Life in Contemporary Pictures.* New York: Taplinger, 1969. 244pp. This illustrated biography documents Haydn's life, milieu, friends, patrons, and locations, along with excerpts from his correspondence and 26 portraits.

Wenborn, Neil. *Joseph Haydn: An Essential Guide to His Life and Works.* London: Trafalgar Square, 1997. 112pp. An entry in the Classic FM Lifelines series for British radio listeners, and the book serves as a readable introduction to Haydn's life and achievements.

Fictional Portraits

Weiss, David. *Sacred and Profane: A Novel of the Life and Times of Mozart.* New York: Morrow, 1968. 639pp. In this biographical account of Mozart's life, his era is vividly depicted with appearances by a number of historical figures, including Haydn.

Recommended Juvenile Biographies

Landon, H.C. Robbins, and Henry Raynor. *Haydn.* New York: Praeger, 1972. 107pp. MG. Co-written by the author of the definitive multivolume documentary life, this young person's guide to the composer's life and music makes use of contemporary sources and Haydn's diaries.

Mirsky, Reba P. *Haydn.* Chicago: Follett, 1963. 160pp. MG. In a highly readable narrative account, filled with anecdotes, Haydn's childhood and years as a court musician are covered. Does rely on invented dialogue for the early years but later uses quotes from the letters.

Thompson, Wendy. *Haydn*. New York: Viking, 1991. 48pp. MG. A chronological account of Haydn's life is supplemented with period art and extracts of keyboard arrangements. Useful for research, the book contains a number of interesting personal facts to enliven and dramatize its portrait of the composer and his era.

Biographical Films and Theatrical Adaptations

Haydn & Mozart (1984). Director: Herbert Chappell. Discusses the lives of the two composers and their influence on musical form and the development of the symphony orchestra with performances by the Royal Philharmonic Orchestra, conducted by André Previn, the film's narrator. Video.

Joseph Haydn (1996). Director: Malcolm Hossick. Part of the Famous Composers series, this is a concise biographical portrait and a musical overview. Video.

Other Sources

Sisman, Elaine R., ed. *Haydn and His World*. Princeton, New Jersey: Princeton University Press, 1997. 325pp. In this collection of essays by leading musicologists, various aspects of Haydn's life, artistic development, and compositions are discussed in relation to the aesthetic and cultural context of his time.

217. WILLIAM RANDOLPH HEARST
1863–1951

American journalist and publisher, Hearst created a vast publishing empire that included 18 newspapers and nine successful magazines. His success in "yellow journalism" resulted from his use of sensational, often lurid, stories and reached its peak after he purchased (1895) the New York *Morning Journal*. Hearst's epic circulation war with other New York papers whipped up anti-Spanish sentiment and contributed to the Spanish-American War (1898). Hearst also pursued a largely unsuccessful political career. His castle at San Simeon, California, won fame for its massive art collections and for its celebrity guests.

Autobiography and Primary Sources

William Randolph Hearst: A Portrait in His Own Words. Edmond Coblentz, ed. New York: Simon & Schuster, 1952. 309pp. A compilation of Hearst's letters, telegrams, memoranda, and editorial columns arranged chronologically to form a selective self-portrait and a collection of his views on many topics and his experiences.

Recommended Biographies

Nasaw, David. *The Chief: The Life of William Randolph Hearst*. Boston: Houghton Mifflin, 2000. 687pp. In an important reassessment based on access to the formerly closed Hearst archives,

Nasaw challenges many previous notions of Hearst's character, establishing a more sympathetic, human portrait than the one established by Orson Welles in *Citizen Kane*, offering not a defense but a fair hearing for this larger-than-life and complex figure.

Procter, Ben. *William Randolph Hearst: The Early Years, 1863–1910*. New York: Oxford University Press, 1998. 345pp. Procter's is a well-researched, highly detailed, and balanced account of Hearst's early life and the development and working of his journalistic empire. If the core of the inner man sometimes eludes Procter's grasp, the book is a remarkable full treatment of his activities in the wider context of his era.

Swanberg, W.A. *Citizen Hearst: A Biography of William Randolph Hearst*. New York: Scribner, 1961. 555pp. This Pulitzer Prize–winning account remains the best full-length study available. Objective and judicious in its assessment, Swanberg clearly displays both the strengths and weaknesses of the man, forming a complex, human portrait.

Other Biographical Studies

Carlisle, Rodney P. *Hearst and the New Deal: The Progressive as Reactionary*. New York: Garland, 1979. 228pp. Carlisle's intellectual biography can be read as a continuation of Littlefield's study of Hearst's progressive views up to 1920. Here Carlisle examines Hearst's views during the New Deal period, making the case for the consistency of Hearst's attitudes despite his apparent break with his earlier views.

Carlson, Oliver, and Ernest Sutherland Bates. *Hearst: Lord of San Simeon*. New York: Viking, 1936. 322pp. More balanced and reliable than either Lundberg or Older, the authors cover both Hearst's political activities and private life, particularly strong on Hearst's formative years and the sources of his personality.

Chaney, Lindsay, and Michael Cieply. *The Hearsts: Family and Empire: The Later Years*. New York: Simon & Schuster, 1981. 410pp. After a biographical section on Hearst, the book focuses on the Hearst heirs and the affairs of the Hearst Corporation since William Randolph's death.

Davies, Marion. *The Times We Had: Life with William Randolph Hearst*. Pamela Pfau and Kenneth S. Marx, eds. Indianapolis: Bobbs-Merrill, 1975. 276pp. In a series of taped recollections recorded just before Hearst's death in 1951, Davies offers her perspective on her relationship with Hearst. The editors help fill in the gaps and errors in Davies's memory.

Hearst, William Randolph Jr., with Jack Casserly. *The Hearsts: Father and Son*. Niwot, Colorado: Roberts Rinehart, 1991. 372pp. Hearst's son presents a memoir of his family. With a number of interesting firsthand details of his father, the author asserts that "critics never seemed to get it through their noodles that the old man loved us, and we cared about him. That was the bottom line."

Littlefield, Roy Everett, III. *William Randolph Hearst: His Role in American Progressivism*. Lanham, Maryland: University Press of America, 1980. 391pp. Littlefield's study is a scholarly analysis of Hearst's progressive views from 1895 to

1920, forming a revealing intellectual biographical portrait of Hearst during this period.

Lundberg, Ferdinand. *Imperial Hearst: A Social Biography*. New York: Equinox, 1936. 406pp. Lundberg's muckraking attack is a scathing critique of Hearst's character and career, particularly on Hearst's business empire. Too intemperate to be fully reliable, Lundberg's is the ideal complement with Older's book to display both sides of Hearst's reputation in the 1930s.

Older, Mrs. Fremont. *William Randolph Hearst: American*. New York: Appleton-Century, 1936. 581pp. Older's authorized biography is a highly sympathetic, superficial account, very much the picture Hearst wanted to appear to the public. As one contemporary review observed, "The whitewash is more remarkable in quantity than in quality for Mrs. Fremont Older has used a style as verbose as it is vulgar."

Tebbel, John. *The Life and Good Times of William Randolph Hearst*. New York: Dutton, 1952. 386pp. Hearst is examined in his various roles as a businessman, politician, parent, publisher, and ladies' man in a highly readable, generally favorable assessment, paying particular attention to the private man and his personality.

Winkler, John. *W.R. Hearst: An American Phenomenon*. New York: Simon & Schuster, 1928. 354pp.; *William Randolph Hearst: A New Appraisal*. New York: Hastings House, 1955. 325pp. Winkler's two biographical accounts, the latter an elaboration of the first based upon the confidential files made available to him by the Hearst trustees and corporation, lack sufficient critical objectivity to be trusted. Hearst is presented as a misunderstood man and is given the benefit of every doubt on his actions and character.

Fictional Portraits

Hall, Robert Lee. *Murder at San Simeon*. New York: St. Martin's, 1988. 343pp. While Hearst is hosting one of his lavish parties at San Simeon, an earthquake hits and then a murder occurs. Hearst takes up the investigation in a clever period mystery.

Hearst, Patricia, and Cordelia F. Biddle. *Murder at San Simeon*. New York: Scribner, 1996. 283pp. The book treats the actual event of Hollywood producer Thomas Ince's 1924 death aboard Hearst's yacht as a murder investigation with suspects including Hearst, Marion Davies, Charlie Chaplin, John Barrymore, and others.

Lynch, Daniel. *Yellow*. New York: Walker, 1992. 211pp. Hearst's role in the declaration of war against Spain is dramatized in this interesting period novel with appearances by a number of historical figures, including Ambrose Bierce, Frederic Remington, and Joseph Pulitzer.

McMahon, Thomas. *Loving Little Egypt*. New York: Viking, 1987. 273pp. In a comic fantasy, the novel dramatizes the adventures of a scientific prodigy who creates an underground telephone network for blind people and must contend with the scientific establishment represented by Hearst, Edison, and Alexander Graham Bell, assisted by Nikola Tesla in a battle for the control of science.

Vidal, Gore. *Empire*. New York: Random House, 1987. 486pp. Set in the aftermath of the Spanish-American War, Vidal's social panorama features a central role for Hearst in the novel's fictional story. He returns as a character in Vidal's *Hollywood: A Novel of America in the 1920s* (New York: Random House, 1990. 437pp.).

Recommended Juvenile Biographies

Frazier, Nancy. *William Randolph Hearst: Press Baron*. Englewood Cliffs, New Jersey: Silver Burdett, 1989. 128pp. MG/YA. Frazier manages a balanced portrait that serves to present both Hearst's achievements, as well as his less flattering qualities fairly.

Whitelaw, Nancy. *William Randolph Hearst and the American Century*. Greensboro, North Carolina: Morgan Reynolds,1999. 112pp. MG. Part of the Makers of the Media series, Whitelaw provides a fast-paced, anecdotally rich chronicle of Hearst's career. The book is balanced in its assessment, communicating Hearst's drive and determination as well as the less flattering side of his behavior and personality.

Biographical Films and Theatrical Adaptations

The Battle Over Citizen Kane (1996). Producer: Thomas Lennon. An installment of PBS's American Experience series, this documentary looks at Hearst's efforts to suppress Welles's film masterpiece. Video.

The Hearst and Davies Affair (1985). Director: David Lowell Rich. This made-for-television drama explores the relationship between Hearst (Robert Mitchum) and Marion Davies (Viginia Madsen) and Hearst's attempt to make her a movie star. Video.

Rough Riders (1997). Director: John Milius. Television miniseries on Teddy Roosevelt (Tom Berenger) and the Rough Riders during the Spanish-American War includes an appearance by Hearst (George Hamilton). Video.

Winchell (1998). Director: Bill Conti. Hearst is portrayed by Kevin Tighe in this biographical profile of journalist Walter Winchell (Stanley Tucci). Video.

218. HEINRICH HEINE
1797–1856

One of the greatest of the German lyric poets, Heine settled (1831) in Paris, where he supported the social ideals of the French Revolution and became the leading figure of the Young Germany literary movement to disseminate French revolutionary ideas into Germany. He later received a French government pension and worked as correspondent for German newspapers. His works include *Book of Songs* (1827) and *Travel Pictures* (1827–1831). His poems have been set to music by such composers as Schubert and Mendelssohn.

Recommended Biographies

Sammons, Jeffrey L. *Heinrich Heine: A Modern Biography*. Princeton, New Jersey: Princeton University Press, 1979. 425pp. Sammons's life is the best available. Meticulously researched and balanced in its assessment, the book succeeds better than any other in making human and realistic sense of Heine's many contradictions, while avoiding the sentimental distortions of other treatments.

Spencer, Hanna. *Heinrich Heine*. Boston: Twayne, 1982. 173pp. An excellent introductory study for the student and general reader, Spencer supplies a reliable, objective examination of the man and his work that serves as a useful starting point for an investigation of Heine.

Other Biographical Studies

Kossoff, Philip. *Valiant Heart: A Biography of Heinrich Heine*. New York: Cornwall Books, 1983. 217pp. In a well-written, factual account, Kossoff mainly avoids psychoanalysis to allow his readers to make up their own minds concerning Heine's temperament and behavior.

Pawel, Ernst. *The Poet Dying: Heinrich Heine's Last Year in Paris*. New York: Farrar, Straus, 1995. 277pp. The author, a respected biographer of Kafka, provides a moving chronicle of Heine's final years. Afflicted with a progressive paralysis of the spine, Heine continued to write despite his physical misery. The book is a close-up, intimate view of the poet's sad but heroic end.

Prawer, S.S. *Heine's Jewish Comedy*. New York: Oxford University Press, 1983. 841pp. Prawer's scholarly analysis of Heine's literary development is intended for the specialist but is an important source of information on the connection among the poet's life, views, and works.

Robertson, Ritchie. *Heine*. New York: Grove Press, 1988. 117pp. Robertson's intellectual biography serves as a useful, succinct overview, setting Heine in his wider cultural and historical context.

Untermeyer, Louis. *Heinrich Heine: Paradox and Poet: The Life*. New York: Harcourt, Brace, 1937. 403pp. Untermeyer, Heine's English translator, fully displays Heine's many contradictions in a suggestive critical biography. Although the poet's many paradoxes are unresolved, the book serves as sensitive analysis of the connections between Heine's life and works.

Vallentin, Antonina. *Poet in Exile: The Life of Heinrich Heine*. New York: Viking, 1934. 320pp. Vallentin's is a moving, dramatic, popular narrative account of Heine's tragic life. Although revealing little that is new or original, the book will appeal to the general reader looking for a compassionate rendering of the poet's sufferings and struggles.

219. ERNEST HEMINGWAY
1899–1961

One of the twentieth century's most prominent American literary figures, novelist and short-story writer Ernest Hemingway was born in Oak Park, Illinois, and was the son of a doctor. After graduating from high school (1917) he worked as a reporter for the Kansas City *Star* and during World War I served as an ambulance driver in Italy. During the 1920s, he became part of the Parisian expatriate circle surrounding Gertrude Stein and with the publication of *The Sun Also Rises* (1926) was recognized as a spokesman of what Stein termed the "lost generation." Hemingway served as a correspondent during the Spanish Civil War and later lived in Cuba, Key West, and Idaho. Awarded the Nobel Prize for literature in 1954, his many works include *A Farewell to Arms* (1929), *For Whom the Bell Tolls* (1940), the novella *The Old Man and the Sea* (1952), and the stories "The Snows of Kilimanjaro" and "The Killers." Hemingway committed suicide in 1961.

Autobiography and Primary Sources

A Moveable Feast. New York: Scribner, 1964. 211pp. Hemingway's evocative yet often mean-spirited memoir of his Paris days has been described as a work of fiction with real people as characters. Often factually unreliable, the work is nonetheless fascinating in reflecting Hemingway's view of his past.

Selected Letters 1917–1961. Carlos Baker, ed. New York: Scribner, 1981. 948pp. Documenting various stages of Hemingway's life and development, this collection of 600 letters reveals the many facets of the author's complex and often contradictory nature and temperament.

Recommended Biographies

Baker, Carlos. *Ernest Hemingway: A Life Story*. New York: Scribner, 1969. 697pp. Long regarded the standard life, Baker's exhaustive and minutely documented chronological account of Hemingway's life and career avoids either a critical assessment of the works or a interpretive thesis to frame the presentation. Instead, Baker assembles the factual record and allows the reader to judge Hemingway's motives. Indispensable as a reference source, Baker's study remains the one-volume book to turn to for its precision and objectivity.

Mellow, James R. *Hemingway: A Life Without Consequences*. Boston: Houghton Mifflin, 1992. 704pp. As the title indicates, Mellow offers a judgmental analysis that stresses the negative. The book looks at Hemingway's youth and career up to 1930 in minute detail and subsequently devotes only a fraction of his analysis to Hemingway's last 20 years. The book's strengths rest in Mellow's reassessment of Hemingway's development while correcting the record based on new research.

Meyers, Jeffrey. *Hemingway: A Biography*. New York: Harper & Row, 1986. 644pp. Meyers updates Baker's account with a number of new sources, including memoirs from intimates and Hemingway's FBI file, and weaves his material into a psychological analysis that reveals more of Hemingway's flaws than Baker. Although often focused on the writer's darker side, Meyers helpfully traces the biographical connections with the works and places Hemingway in a wider literary historical context.

Reynolds, Michael S. *The Young Hemingway*. New York: Blackwell, 1987. 291pp; *Hemingway: The*

Paris Years. New York: Blackwell, 1989. 402pp; *Hemingway: The 1930s.* New York: W.W. Norton, 1997. 360pp; *Hemingway: The Final Years.* New York: W.W. Norton, 1999. 416pp. Reynolds's multivolume life is widely regarded as the definitive modern biography. Synthesizing modern scholarship since Baker, Reynolds offers an objective yet sympathetic account that establishes the historical and cultural context for viewing Hemingway's life more expertly than any other biographical study.

Other Biographical Studies

Brian, Denis, ed. *The True Gen: An Intimate Portrait of Ernest Hemingway by Those Who Knew Him.* New York: Grove Press, 1988. 356pp. Based on interviews with 100 eyewitnesses whose reflections are placed in chronological order, the book serves as an uneven but often fascinating oral biography of Hemingway from a variety of perspectives.

Donaldson, Scott. *By Force of Will: The Life and Art of Ernest Hemingway.* New York: Viking, 1977. 367pp. By recording what Hemingway thought on a variety of subjects in thematic chapters, such as "Fame," "Money," "Sports," "Politics," "War," "Love," "Sex," "Art," and "Death," the book forms a fascinating intellectual biography that challenges many preconceptions and legends that have grown up around Hemingway.

Fenton, Charles A. *The Apprenticeship of Ernest Hemingway: The Early Years.* New York: Farrar, Straus, 1954. 302pp. Fenton's detailed and thorough treatment of Hemingway's life from 1916 to 1923 remains one of the most reliable sources on Hemingway's career as a journalism and his development as a writer.

Griffin, Peter. *Along With Youth: Hemingway, the Early Years.* New York: Oxford University Press, 1985. 258pp; *Less Than a Treason: Hemingway in Paris.* New York: Oxford University Press, 1990. 197pp. Griffin offers a number of previously unavailable sources in his detailed projected three-volume study. Supplementing but not replacing Baker, Griffin's account falls short of the equally detailed though more critically responsible and coherent multivolume treatment by Reynolds.

Hays, Peter L. *Ernest Hemingway.* New York: Continuum, 1991. 192pp. This is a lively and informative handbook that covers the essential biographical details and Hemingway's publishing history.

Hotchner, A.E. *Papa Hemingway: A Personal Memoir.* New York: Random House, 1966. 304pp. Revised ed. *Papa Hemingway: The Ecstasy and the Sorrow.* New York: Morrow, 1983. 322pp. Hotchner documents the last 13 years of Hemingway's life based on the author's extensive notes of his conversations with Hemingway during the period. Interesting in revealing Hemingway's opinions, the book is too gossipy and admiring to serve as a reliable, objective account, yet the positive side of Hemingway's character emerges here that has been underemphasized by subsequent biographers.

Kert, Bernice. *The Hemingway Women.* New York: W.W. Norton, 1983. 555pp. This biographical account looks at Hemingway from the perspective of his relationships with his mother, four wives, and several lovers. A fascinating angle for viewing both the man and writer.

Lynn, Kenneth S. *Hemingway.* New York: Simon & Schuster, 1987. 702pp. Lynn's psychosexual interpretive study locates the key to unlocking Hemingway's character and artistic preoccupations in a sexual identity conflict established from childhood. Lynn applies this reading of Hemingway to his work and career. Often insightful and provocative, Lynn's approach is ultimately reductive as the complexity of Hemingway's personality and artistry resists a single solution.

Sandison, David. *Ernest Hemingway: An Illustrated Biography.* Chicago: Chicago Review Press, 1999. 160pp. This is a visual record of Hemingway's life in which numerous photos are accompanied by a brief, basic text that covers the essential points.

Voss, Frederick. *Picturing Hemingway: A Writer in His Time.* New Haven, Connecticut: Yale University Press, 1999. 160pp. This collection of photos, drawings, and paintings to celebrate the Hemingway centennial chronicles the writer's life and features a essay by Hemingway biographer Michael S. Reynolds.

Biographical Novels

Carlile, Clancy. *The Paris Pilgrims.* New York: Carroll & Graf, 1999. 496pp. This documentary novel is set in Paris during Hemingway's first stay in Paris in 1922 and features appearances by virtually every figure associated with the expatriate scene and the Lost Generation, including Stein, Toklas, Pound, and Joyce.

Fictional Portraits

Aldridge, James. *One Last Glimpse.* Boston: Little, Brown, 1977. 182pp. The Hemingway-Fitzgerald relationship is dramatized in this novel involving the pair on a motor tour of Brittany. The situation is invented but the dynamics of the writers' rivalry are based on fact.

Alexander, Karl. *Papa and Fidel.* New York: T. Doherty, 1989. 310pp. Imagining what might have happened if, instead of a single meeting between Hemingway and Castro in 1961, the pair had met in 1957. As Castro plots his revolution, Hemingway is allowed a final reliving of his adventurous past in an idealized portrait of both figures.

Engel, Howard. *Murder in Montparnasse.* Woodstock, New York: Overlook Press, 1999. 304pp. Most will recognize Hemingway in the character of Jason Waddington in this inventive period mystery that interweaves details from Hemingway's life, actual figures such as Pound, Joyce, and Stein, and fictional characters from *The Sun Also Rises.*

Kaminsky, Stuart M. *High Midnight.* New York: St. Martin's, 1981. 188pp. In the author's amusing period detective series, Gary Cooper and Hemingway are victims of blackmail and violence in 1940s Hollywood.

Roosevelt, Elliott. *Murder in the Executive Mansion.* New York: St. Martin's, 1995. 197pp. In the author's series of White House mysteries with Eleanor Roosevelt as principal sleuth, a number of historical figures, including Hemingway and Faulkner, are involved in a murder plot that leads to a German spy ring in 1939.

Winegardner, Mark. *The Veracruz Blues.* New York: Viking, 1996. 251pp. Mexico in 1946 is the scene for this imaginary account of the first fully integrated baseball season in history. Hemingway and other historical figures, including Babe Ruth, Diego Rivera, and Frida Kahlo, make appearance to lend historical atmosphere.

Recommended Juvenile Biographies

Lyttle, Richard B. *Ernest Hemingway.* New York: Atheneum, 1992. 212pp. MG/YA. Lyttle supplies a competently researched and highly readable chronological narrative that provides the circumstances under which each of Hemingway's important books was written.

McDaniel, Melissa. *Ernest Hemingway.* New York: Chelsea House, 1997. 118pp. YA. In an objective account of Hemingway's life and work, McDaniel does not omit the various personal torments that led to Hemingway's often cruel and erratic behavior. This is a mature and sensible overview of the man and his genius.

Tessitore, John. *The Hunt and the Feast: A Life of Ernest Hemingway.* New York: F. Watts, 1996. 128pp. MG. In an often unflattering though balanced account, this biography stresses Hemingway's complexity as a man and writer.

Yannuzzi, Della A. *Ernest Hemingway: Writer and Adventurer.* Springfield, New Jersey: Enslow, 1998. 128pp. MG/YA. Part of the People to Know series, this biography begins with Hemingway's final triumphs as the author of *The Old Man and the Sea* and then reconstructs his earlier career. The book neither glosses over Hemingway's failures nor judges him, but provides a rich account of Hemingway's real life adventures and artistic habits and methods.

Biographical Films and Theatrical Adaptations

A&E Biography Video: Ernest Hemingway: Wrestling with Life (1997). Director: Stephen Crisman. Traces Hemingway's life from childhood using archival footage and interviews with family, friends, and associates. Video.

Ernest Hemingway (1996). Director: Malcolm Hossick. Part of the Famous Authors series, this is a compact look at Hemingway's life, writing, and times. Video.

Hemingway (1988). Director: Bernhard Sinkel. Stacey Keach portrays Hemingway in this television mini-series that dramatizes highlights of Hemingway's personal, professional, and celebrity life. Hemingway's four wives are played by Josephine Chaplin, Marisa Berenson, Lisa Banes, and Pamela Reed. Video.

Hemingway in Cuba (1995). Producer: Mark Woollen. A documentary portrait of Hemingway's years in Cuba with an emphasis on his private life. Video.

Hemingway's Adventures of a Young Man (1962). Director: Martin Ritt. Patched together from Hemingway's Nick Adams stories, this is an unconvincing and pretentious narrative that presents Hemingway's fiction as autobiographical confession. Starring Richard Beymer, Diane Baker, Paul Newman, Susan Strasberg, Jessica Tandy, and Eli Wallach.

In Love and War (1996). Director: Richard Attenborough. Adapted from *Hemingway in Love and War: The Lost Diary of Agnes Von Kurowsky*, this idealized and unreliable account of Hemingway's (Chris O'Donnell) affair with Red Cross nurse Kurowsky (Sandra Bullock) in Italy during World War I takes considerable liberties with the biographical facts. Video.

Michael Palin's Hemingway Adventure (2000). Director: David F. Turnbull. Palin retraces Hemingway's global travels with biographical and personality insights on the writer. A companion volume of photos and text is also available (New York: St. Martin's, 2000. 256pp.).

Waiting for the Moon (1987). Director: Jill Godmilow. A PBS Playhouse presentation dramatizing the relationship between Gertrude Stein (Linda Bassett) and Alice B. Toklas (Linda Hunt). Bruce McGill portrays Hemingway. Video.

Other Sources

Donaldson, Scott, ed. *The Cambridge Companion to Hemingway.* New York: Cambridge University Press, 1996. 321pp. This valuable collection of essays by recognized experts looks at various aspects of Hemingway's life and artistry.

Nelson, Gerald B., and Glory James. *Hemingway, Life and Works.* New York: Facts on File, 1984. 183pp. This is a detailed chronology that provides yearly, and in many cases monthly and daily, coverage of Hemingway's life. Serves as an excellent reference source.

Oliver, Charles M. *Ernest Hemingway A to Z: The Essential Reference to His Life and Work.* New York: Facts on File, 1998. 448pp. Exhaustive in its detailed identification of people and places associated with the author, this helpful alphabetical reference source includes a detailed chronology and suggestions for further reading on various points covered.

Plath, James, and Frank Simons, ed. *Remembering Ernest Hemingway.* Key West, Florida: Ketch & Yawl Press, 1999. 167pp. This is a collection of 13 interviews with people who knew Hemingway, including two of his sons.

220. HENRI IV
1553–1610

The first Bourbon king of France, Henri was raised as a Protestant but abjured his faith after the St. Bartholomew's Day Massacre (1572) of the Huguenots placed his life in danger. A prisoner of the court until his escape (1576), he returned to Protestantism and fought in the fifth of the Wars of Religion. His succession (1589) was challenged by Henri III and Henri, Duc de Guise, in the War of the Three Henrys, which resulted in Henri's conversion to Catholicism. A popular king, Henri encouraged agriculture, founded new industries, built roads and canals, expanded foreign trade, and supported the colonization of Canada. In 1598 he enacted the Edict of Nantes, which established political rights and some religious freedom for the Huguenots.

Recommended Biographies

Buisseret, David. *Henry IV.* Boston: Allen & Unwin, 1984. 235pp. Buisseret's carefully documented and reliable study is the recommended choice for the serious reader. Henri's reign is carefully chronicled, and his character is placed in the context of his time.

Mahoney, Irene. *Royal Cousin: The Life of Henri IV of France.* Garden City, New York: Doubleday, 1970. 451pp. In an impressive synthesis of primary and secondary sources, Mahoney's vivid narrative account is the best of the many popular biographies of Henri available.

Other Biographical Studies

Baird, Henry M. *The Huguenots and Henry of Navarre.* 1896. Reprint ed. New York: AMS Press, 1970. 2 vols. Long regarded as the standard life of Henri, Baird's study is well documented and generally reliable, though the author's partisanship on behalf of the Huguenots colors the presentation.

Hurst, Quentin. *Henry of Navarre.* New York: Appleton-Century, 1938. 319pp. In a judicious, straightforward account Henri is portrayed neither as a hero nor villain but as a human blend of both strengths and weaknesses. The book carefully sifts through the legends to present a factually believable monarch.

Mousnier, Roland. *The Assassination of Henry IV.* New York: Scribner, 1973. 428pp. In an intriguing reconstruction of the conditions surrounding Henri's murder in 1610, Mousnier traces the biographical and political details leading up to the assassination and its consequences.

Pearson, Hesketh. *Henry of Navarre: The King Who Dared.* New York: Harper & Row, 1963. 249pp. Pearson's popular account is marred by his evident hostility toward the Catholic church and the Jesuits and a partisan fondness for Henri that disassociates him from the shady intrigues of his age.

Russell of Liverpool (Edward F.L.). *Henry of Navarre: Henry IV of France.* New York: Praeger, 1970. 206pp. Based on secondary sources this simplistic chronological narrative portrays Henri as a great warrior and statesman but is vague on the source and nature of his greatness. The book also is vague about details of Henri's reign and concentrates on the Catholic-Protestant disputes.

Sedgwick, Henry D. *Henry of Navarre.* Indianapolis: Bobbs-Merrill, 1930. 324pp. This popular biography is balanced and historically reliable, relying extensively on quotations from Henri's letters to allow the king to tell his own story.

Seward, Desmond. *The First Bourbon: Henri IV, King of France and Navarre.* Boston: Gambit, 1971. 235pp. Concentrating on Henri the man rather than his reign, Seward's treatment makes extensive use of contemporary sources in portraying Henri.

Slocombe, George E. *The White Plumed Henry: King of France.* New York: Cosmopolitan, 1931. 378pp. In an overly romantic, undocumented popular biography written by a clear admirer, Slocombe's vivid narrative emphasizes Henri's humanity rather than the details of his reign.

Vioux, Marcelle. *Henry of Navarre: Le Vert-Galant.* New York: Dutton, 1937. 295pp. In an often oversimplified and gossipy portrait, Henri as womanizer predominates here with his role as monarch, statesman, and reformer omitted. Sensational court gossip forms the core of the book's appeal.

Willert, P.F. *Henry of Navarre and the Huguenots in France.* 1893. Reprint ed. New York: AMS Press, 1971. 478pp. More balanced and objective in its treatment than Baird, Willert's study reaches a high level in its depiction of the religious and political context of Henri's rise to power and reign.

Wolfe, Michael. *The Conversion of Henry IV.* Cambridge, Massachusetts: Harvard University Press, 1993. 253pp. Wolfe concentrates on the diplomatic, political, cultural, and theological meaning of the 1593 conversion of the Protestant Henri of Navarre and its implication for royal absolutism.

Biographical Novels

Mann, Heinrich. *Young Henry of Navarre.* New York: Knopf, 1937. 585pp.; *Henry, King of France.* New York: Knopf, 1939. 786pp. Mann's two-volume fictional biography traces Henri's life and reign in full. Although patterned with correspondences between sixteenth-century France and Nazi Germany and with a number of historical liberties, the book achieves a convincing vividness.

Plaidy, Jean. *Evergreen Gallant.* New York: Putnam, 1973. 384pp. Henri's reign is chronicled with the emphasis on his many amorous relations. In *Queen Jezebel.* (New York: Putnam, 1976. 417pp.) the intrigue of Catherine de' Medici against the Huguenots is featured with Henri's rise to power glimpsed.

Fictional Portraits

Davenat, Colette. *Deborah and the Siege of Paris.* New York: Morrow, 1976. 417pp. In third of the author's Elizabethan adventure trilogy, English secret agent Deborah, Countess of Norland, is in France in the thick of Henri IV's struggle to secure his throne.

Dumas, Alexandre. *Queen Margot: Or Marguerite de Valois.* New York: Hyperion, 1994. 542pp. The marriage of Marguerite, Charles IX's sister, and Henri of Navarre, which culminates in the infamous Saint Bartholomew's Day Massacre is the background for Dumas's rousing story of political intrigue and religious conflict.

Weyman, Stanley J. *From the Memoirs of a Minister of France.* 1895. Reprint ed. North Stratford, New Hampshire: Ayers, 1977. 325pp. The king, his wife, and mistresses are glimpsed from recollections of a minister in Henri's court.

Recommended Juvenile Biographies

Gross, Albert C. *Henry of Navarre.* New York: Chelsea House, 1988. 111pp. MG/YA. Gross supplies the essential personal and historical data to make Henri's life and reign understandable.

Biographical Films and Theatrical Adaptations

Queen Margot (1994). Director: Patrice Chéreau. In a film adaptation of Dumas's novel, Isabelle Adjani stars as the title character with Daniel Auteuil as Henri and Virna Lisi as Catherine de' Medici. Video.

See also Catherine de' Medici

221. HENRY VIII
1491–1547

Known for his ruthlessness and excesses, exemplified most notably by his many marriages, Henry VIII was nevertheless an active and charismatic ruler with considerable political insight. The second son of Henry VII, he became prince of Wales (1503) after the death of his brother, Arthur, and succeeded to the throne in 1509. He divorced his first wife, Catherine of Aragon, to marry Anne Boleyn, an act which led to a break with the Roman Catholic church, the establishment of the Church of England, the Act of Succession, and the dissolution of the monasteries. During Henry's reign, the royal treasury was severely depleted in wars against France and Scotland, Parliament became more powerful, and the British navy was strengthened and modernized.

Autobiography and Primary Sources

The Letters: A Selection. M. St. Clare Byrne, ed. New York: Funk & Wagnalls, 1968. 454pp. This interesting collection of the king's letters has been selected to follow the development of Henry's personality.

Recommended Biographies

Erickson, Carolly. *Great Harry.* New York: Summit, 1980. 428pp. In this popular biography, Henry's personal life dominates over issues of his reign and times. Judicious and carefully researched with an eye for the animating detail, the book will likely be preferred by readers fascinated by Henry the man and his domestic affairs.

Pollard, A.F. *Henry VIII.* New York: Longmans, 1905. 385pp. Long regarded as the preeminent chronological narrative of Henry's reign, Pollard's influential study examines Henry and his age sensibly, in the context of domestic and international affairs.

Ridley, Jasper. *Henry VIII.* New York: Viking, 1985. 473pp. Ridley's extraordinarily vivid account of Henry, his reign, and age replaces the characterization of former biographers with a fresh assessment in which the king is believably portrayed. Ridley expertly guides the reader through the various political complexities and is particularly strong on Tudor foreign affairs.

Scarisbrick, Jack J. *Henry VIII.* Berkeley: University of California Press, 1968. 561pp. Not a conventional chronological biography but a series of probing essays forming an intellectual and developmental biographical profile, Scarisbrick's analysis of Henry's character displays his many influences and contradictions, setting each in a lucidly presented historical perspective.

Smith, Lacey B. *Henry VIII: The Mask of Royalty.* Boston: Houghton Mifflin, 1971. 335pp. Smith's psychological profile looks at Henry at the end of his life and works backward in time to uncover the patterns in the king's development. Smith assumes a solid grasp of chronology and the details of Henry's reign, but the compensation is one of the best psychological character studies of a monarch ever written.

Other Biographical Studies

Bowle, John. *Henry VIII: A Biography.* Boston: Little, Brown, 1965. 316pp. Making extensive use of primary sources, Bowle portrays Henry against his Tudor and European background. Offering several interpretations that modern scholarship has questioned, the book is a highly readable orientation to the man and his times.

Bruce, Marie Louise. *The Making of Henry VIII.* New York: Coward-McCann, 1977. 254pp. Focusing on the years preceding Henry's accession to the throne and fleshing out his childhood from various primary sources, Bruce examines how the future king's development explains his behavior in maturity.

Hackett, Francis. *Henry the Eighth.* New York: Liveright, 1929. 452pp. In a vivid and colorful examination of Henry's life and times, Hackett succeeds in placing the king in a complex network of cultural and political relationships that helps to explain his character and behavior.

Lacey, Robert. *The Life and Times of Henry VIII.* New York: Praeger, 1974. 224pp. In a lavishly illustrated visual biography, the essential details of Henry's life and reign are capably depicted.

Morrison, Nancy B. *The Private Life of Henry VIII.* New York: Vanguard, 1964. 205pp. Morrison's biographical profile offers no new revelations but helpfully synthesizes information from a variety of sources suggesting how the popular and legendary image of Henry differs from the facts.

Starkey, David. *The Reign of Henry VIII: Personalities and Politics.* New York: F. Watts, 1986. 174pp. Although the author insists that his book is less about Henry than his court and political maneuvering, this revealing study does describe the king's character and sets him in the context of his times. Henry is shown as less a domineering presence than as one who was easily and often manipulated by those around him.

Williams, Neville. *Henry VIII and His Court.* New York: Macmillan, 1971. 271pp. In a beautifully illustrated biography of Henry's court, Williams helpfully supplies the cultural and political context for viewing Henry's actions.

Readers interested in Henry VIII and his wives have a number of books from which to choose:

Fraser, Antonia. *The Wives of Henry VIII.* New York: Knopf, 1992. 479pp. The author delineates the cultural, familial, and political contexts for each of Henry's queens. Despite a lingering bias in favor of Catherine of Aragon and disgust with the king, Fraser animates the public and private events of Henry's reign with a piquant use of historical details and anecdotes.

Lindsey, Karen. *Divorced, Beheaded, Survived: A Feminist Reinterpretation of the Wives of Henry VIII.* Reading, Massachusetts: Addison-Wesley, 1995. 231pp. By applying the insights of feminist scholarship, the author shows Henry's six wives not as stereotypical victims but as lively, intelligent women struggling to survive in a treacherous court. This is a revisionist approach with a number of fresh, amusing, and debatable perceptions on sixteenth-century English politics and its leading figures.

Weir, Alison. *The Six Wives of Henry VIII.* New York: Grove Weidenfeld, 1992. 645pp. The author contributes a vivid and full-blooded portrait of Henry's six queens that is sound in its scholarship and convincing. Weir's meticulous research supports a number of fresh observations that provide insights into the various forces that drove Henry VIII and his wives to their respective fates.

Biographical Novels

Barnes, Margaret C. *My Lady of Cleves.* Philadelphia: Macrae Smith, 1946. 351pp. The brief and disastrous fourth marriage of Henry and Anne of Cleves is dramatized. The novel imagines an infatuation between Anne and the painter Holbein, whose flattering portrait arouses the king's interest. In *The Tudor Rose* (Philadelphia: Macrae Smith, 1953. 313pp.) Henry's childhood is glimpsed in this story of the life of his mother, Elizabeth of York. In *King's Fool* (Philadelphia: Macrae Smith, 1959. 286pp.) Henry's reign is interestingly seen through the eyes of his jester, Will Somers.

Eady, Carol Maxwell. *Her Royal Destiny.* New York: Harmony Books, 1985. 387pp. The life of Catherine Parr, Henry's last wife, is dramatized in a convincing characterization and account of the period.

Ford, Ford Madox. *The Fifth Queen.* 1906. Reprint ed. New York: Oxford University Press, 1984. 592pp. In an expert historical reconstruction the brief, tragic marriage of Katherine Howard and Henry is dramatized.

George, Margaret. *The Autobiography of Henry VIII.* New York: St. Martin's, 1986. 932pp. In an oversized and brilliant reconstruction, the book imagines Henry's own account of his remarkable career. The result is partially a defense of his behavior that uses the irreverent comments of the king's jester, Will Somers, to balance Henry's self-justification.

Lewis, Hilda W. *I Am Mary Tudor.* New York: McKay, 1971. 422pp. Henry's reign is seen through the perspective of his first daughter, Mary. The novel captures the effects of the king's marriages on the young princess.

Lindsay, Philip. *Here Comes the King.* Boston: Little, Brown, 1933. 342pp. The relationship between Henry's fifth wife, Katherine Howard, and the king is chronicled from the wedding to her execution two years later.

Lofts, Norah. *The King's Pleasure*. Garden City, New York: Doubleday,1969. 318pp. The novel depicts the relationship between Henry and his first wife, Catherine of Aragon, in a vivid reconstruction of the era with careful attention to historical details.

Luke, Mary M. *The Ivy Crown: A Biographical Novel of Queen Katherine Parr*. Garden City, New York: Doubleday, 1984. 439pp. The story of Henry's last wife is dramatized, including her relationship with the declining Henry and her role in assisting Elizabeth Tudor.

Peters, Maureen. *Henry VIII and His Six Wives*. New York: St. Martin's, 1972. 222pp. As Henry lies dying, he relives his past and reviews his marital history. Since the novel covers so much ground there is obvious compression of details and simplification though the chronology is accurate.

Peters, Maureen. *Katheryn, the Wanton Queen*. London: R. Hale,1967. 224pp. In a dramatization that is faithful to historical facts though scenes and dialogue are invented, the story of Henry's fifth marriage to Katherine Howard is depicted.

Plaidy, Jean. *The Shadow of the Pomegranate*. London: R. Hale, 1962. 221pp. The novel explores the consequences of Catherine of Aragon's failure to provide Henry with a male heir. In *The Sixth Wife* (New York: Putnam, 1969. 252pp.) the story of Henry's final marriage with Catherine Parr is dramatized, showing how she survives her husband's unpredictability. *Murder Most Royal* (New York: Putnam, 1972. 542pp.) dramatizes Henry's marriages to Anne Boleyn and Catherine Howard, with the king shown as a complex amalgam of hypocrisy, shrewdness, sentimentality, and ruthlessness. *Uneasy Lies the Head* (New York: Putnam, 1984. 345pp.) is a fictionalized chronicle of the reign of Henry VII, with his son's childhood and youth described in a convincing re-creation of the period and its history. *In the Shadow of the Crown* (New York: Putnam, 1988. 438pp.) offers Mary Tudor's unique perspective on the events of her father's reign. *Katharine: The Virgin Widow* (New York: Putnam, 1993. 218pp.) is the story of Catherine of Aragon's first marriage to Henry VII's heir, Arthur, Prince of Wales. When he dies, Henry fatefully seizes on Catherine as his bride. In *The Rose without a Thorn* (New York: Putnam, 1994. 255pp.) Katherine Howard, Henry's fifth wife, narrates her life story in a convincing portrayal with authentic period details. *The King's Secret Matter* (New York: Putnam, 1995. 284pp.) depicts the ensuing power struggle that culminates with England's break with Rome after Henry's secret negotiations to have his marriage to Catherine of Aragon annulled break down.

Westcott, Jan. *The Queen's Grace*. New York: Crown, 1959. 444pp. The final years of Henry's reign are depicted in this account of the king's marriage to Catherine Parr. Her story is continued with her life as the Dowager Queen.

White, Beatrice. *Royal Nonesuch*. New York: Macmillan,1936. 256pp. At the center of this novel of Tudor court life is the relationship of Henry, his sister Mary, and her husband the Duke of Suffolk.

Fictional Portraits

Abbey, Anne Merton. *Kathryn: In the Court of Six Queens*. New York: Bantam, 1989. 454pp. The intrigue in Henry's court is described from the vantage point of a lady-in-waiting to the king's six wives. History is embellished here with imaginative speculation.

Ainsworth, William Harrison. *Windsor Castle*. 1843. Reprint ed. New York: Dutton, 1927. 307pp. The author's popular historical romance interweaves details of the reign of Henry VIII with Gothic elements with a spectral figure who serves as a kind of vague symbol of conscience as Anne Boleyn is executed. Historically inaccurate for the most part, the novel is still interesting in employing historical figures in the role of romance heroes and heroines.

Major, Charles. *When Knighthood Was in Flower*. 1898. Reprint ed. New York: AMS Press, 1970. 295pp. Major's bestselling historical romance concerns the love affair between Mary Tudor and commoner Charles Brandon.

Prescott, Hilda F.M. *The Man on a Donkey*. New York: Macmillan, 1952. 631pp. The novel describes the 1536 North Country rebellion against the king's suppression of the monastery from a variety of perspectives.

Riley, Judith Merkle. *The Serpent Garden*. New York: Viking, 1996. 467pp. The novel invents a fanciful plot by Henry and Cardinal Wolsey to put an English heir onto the throne of France in an evocative story filled with accurate period details.

Turton, Godfrey. *My Lord of Canterbury*. Garden City, New York: Doubleday, 1967. 316pp. In an autobiographical novel based on the life of Thomas Cranmer, one of the principal architects of the annulment of Henry's marriage to Catherine of Aragon, the tumultuous events of the king's reign are described from an interesting perspective that remains close to the known facts but fills in some gaps with plausible conjecture.

Recommended Juvenile Biographies

Dwyer, Frank. *Henry VIII*. New York: Chelsea House, 1988. 112pp. MG/YA. Dwyer's is a helpful introduction to Henry's personality, reign, and period.

Feuerlicht, Roberta S. *The Life and World of Henry VIII*. New York: Crowell, 1970. 161pp. MG/YA. This is a detailed look at the Tudor period along with the highlights of Henry's reign and influence.

Pittenger, W. Norman. *Henry VIII of England*. New York: F. Watts, 1970. 184pp. MG/YA. The king is presented clearly against an accurate and vivid period background.

Biographical Films and Theatrical Adaptations

Anderson, Maxwell. *Anne of the Thousand Days*. New York: Dramatists Play Service, 1950. 75pp. Anderson traces Anne's relationship with Henry from their first encounters to the days before her execution. Rendered with dramatic intensity and with poetic prose, the play captures the human complexity of both protagonists.

Bolt, Robert. *A Man for All Seasons*. New York: Random House, 1962. 163pp. Bolt's acclaimed dramatization of the conflict between Henry and Sir Thomas More present thoughtful portraits of the king and his friend and adviser who becomes his foe by opposing his divorce from Catherine of Aragon.

Shakespeare, William. *Henry VIII* (1613). Various editions. Shakespeare's historical drama concerns the execution of the duke of Buckingham, Catherine of Aragon's reaction to the king's hostility, Wolsey's fall from power, and the coronation of Anne Boleyn.

A&E Biography Video: Henry VIII: Scandals of a King (1996). Producer: Satel Doc. A documentary look at Henry VIII's life and reign through the art and documents of the period, locations associated with the king, and interviews with historians. Video.

Anna Bolena (1999). Director: Lofti Mansouri. A film of a live performance of Donizetti's opera with Joan Sutherland as Anne Boleyn and James Morris as Henry. Video.

Anne of the Thousand Days (1969). Director: Charles Jarrott. The relationship between Henry VIII (Richard Burton) and Anne Boleyn (Genevieve Bujold) is given a lavish, though historically inaccurate treatment, in this Hollywood spectacle. See Edward Fenton's *Anne of the Thousand Days* (New York: New American Library, 1970. 160pp.) for the novelization based on the screenplay. Video.

King Henry VIII (1999). Director: Steve Gillham. This is a brief film profile of Henry's life, personality, and reign. Video.

A Man for All Seasons (1966). Director: Fred Zinnemann. Standout adaptation of Robert Bolt's play casts Paul Scofield as Sir Thomas More with Wendy Hiller as his wife and Robert Shaw as a robust Henry. Video. See also the 1988 made-for-television adaptation of a London stage production, directed by and starring Charlton Heston as More with a supporting cast including Vanessa Redgrave and John Gielgud. Video.

The Private Life of Henry VIII (1933). Director: Alexander Korda. Lavish historical chronicle with a stellar performance by Charles Laughton as the king, with Merle Oberon as Anne Boleyn and Elsa Lancaster as Anne of Cleves. Video.

Six Wives of Henry VIII (1971). Directors: Naomi Capon and John Glenister. In this acclaimed English television mini-series with installments on each of Henry's wives, Keith Mitchell has been praised as the definitive Henry. The king's six wives are played by Annette Crosby, Dorothy Tutin, Elvi Hale, Anne Stallybrass, Angela Pleasence, and Rosalie Crutchley. Video.

The Sword and the Rose (1953). Director: Ken Annakin. Based on *When Knighthood Was in Flower* by Charles Major, the film dramatizes Mary Tudor's love of a commoner. James Robertson Justice stars as Henry with Glynis Johns and Richard Todd playing the leads. Video.

Young Bess (1953). Director: George Sidney. Based on Margaret Irwin's novel, the early years of Elizabeth Tudor are depicted with Charles

Laughton reprising his most famous role. Jean Simmons stars as the princess with Stewart Granger and Deborah Kerr. Video.

See also Anne Boleyn; Elizabeth I; Mary I; Thomas More; and Thomas Wolsey

222. PATRICK HENRY
1736–1799

The fiery, unequaled orator of the American Revolution, Henry was born in Virginia and although largely self-educated became a prominent trial lawyer. He bitterly denounced the Stamp Act (1765) and fervently encouraged revolt against the British in the southern colonies. He was a delegate to the House of Burgesses (1765–1774) and the Continental Congress (1774–1776), and as governor of Virginia (1776–1779, 1784–1786) led the fight for the Virginia Religious Freedom Act of 1785. An advocate of state sovereignty, he opposed ratification of the federal Constitution and worked to ensure the addition of the first 10 amendments (Bill of Rights) to the Constitution.

Autobiography and Primary Sources

Henry, William Wirt. *Patrick Henry: Life, Correspondence, and Speeches.* New York: Scribner, 1891. 3 vols. Since Henry preserved neither his speeches nor his thoughts, primary material for the biographer is scarce. The best source remains this defensive early biography written by Henry's grandson, which collects various documentary material, including a few letters, and reconstructions of Henry's speeches.

Recommended Biographies

Beeman, Richard R. *Patrick Henry: A Biography.* New York: McGraw-Hill, 1974. 229pp. Portraying Henry against his social and historical background, Beeman's succinct biographical profile penetrates the various legends surrounding the patriot for a sensible, balanced assessment. This is the book of choice for readers looking for a brief but comprehensive biography.

Mayer, Henry. *A Son of Thunder: Patrick Henry and the American Republic.* New York: F. Watts, 1986. 529pp. More interpretive than Meade's factual record, Mayer examines Henry in all his facets against a solid cultural and historical background. Both well researched and readable, Mayer's life combines the different strengths of both Beeman and Meade and restores a good deal of complexity to the image of Henry as American patriot.

Meade, Robert D. *Patrick Henry.* Philadelphia: Lippincott, 1957–1969. 2 vols. Meade's meticulously researched biography is the most comprehensive and detailed life available. Volume one covers Henry's life up to 1774, and volume two chronicles Henry's role in the Revolution and five terms as Virginia's governor. Countering previously established legends about Henry, Meade's authoritative study collects the essential facts for a balanced, objective view of Henry.

Other Biographical Studies

Axelrad, Jacob. *Patrick Henry: The Voice of Freedom.* New York: Random House, 1947. 318pp. This popular study of Henry's life and times has been superseded by later biographies that provide a richer portrait and a more informed social and historical context.

Morgan, George. *The True Patrick Henry.* Philadelphia: Lippincott, 1907. 493pp. Morgan's analytical study of Henry's character is balanced, solidly documented, and readable and remains a strong choice for the general reader.

Tyler, Moses C. *Patrick Henry.* 1887. Reprint ed. New York: AMS Press, 1972. 454pp. Tyler's early biography is more balanced than Wirt's account and defends Henry against attacks from the pro-Jefferson critics.

Vaughan, David J. *Give Me Liberty: The Uncompromising Statesmanship of Patrick Henry.* Nashville, Tennessee: Cumberland House, 1997. 285pp. Part of the Leaders in Action series, this admiring account looks at the source of Henry's beliefs and character.

Willison, George F. *Patrick Henry and His World.* Garden City, New York: Doubleday, 1969. 498pp. Willison provides a somewhat simplistic chronicle of Henry's life within the context of his times. Short on analysis and marred by occasional errors of fact, the book is undocumented and lacks familiarity with modern historical scholarship of the Revolutionary period.

Wirt, William. *Sketches of the Life and Character of Patrick Henry.* 1817. Reprint ed. Freeport, New York: Books for Libraries Press, 1970. 462pp. The first biography of Henry set the heroic model with which subsequent biographers have had to contend. The book remains valuable for its reconstruction of Henry's oratory based on various eyewitness recollections.

Biographical Novels

Gerson, Noel B. *Give Me Liberty: A Novel of Patrick Henry.* Garden City, New York: Doubleday, 1966. 347pp. This fictionalized biography follows Henry's career as a lawyer and orator and his pursuit, after the death of his first wife, of Dorothea Dandridge, also courted by John Paul Jones. The novel sticks to the basic facts of Henry's life with invented dialogue and situations.

Fictional Portraits

Bentley, Barbara. *Mistress Nancy.* New York: McGraw-Hill, 1980. 392pp. Based on the actual life of Nancy Randolph who faced a murder charge and was defended by Patrick Henry and John Marshall, the novel draws on journals and court documents to establish its authenticity.

Cooke, John Esten. *The Virginia Comedians.* New York: Appleton, 1854. 2 vols.; *Henry St. John, Gentleman.* New York: Harper, 1859. 503pp. In Cooke's historical romances set in Virginia at the outbreak of the Revolution, Patrick Henry figures prominently in the controversy over the Stamp Tax.

Erskine, John. *Give Me Liberty: The Story of an Innocent Man.* New York: F. A. Stokes, 1940. 313pp. Set in Virginia preceding the Revolution, the novel tells the story of a young admirer of Patrick Henry who, as Henry begins preaching rebellion more openly, finds himself in a conflict of loyalty and friendship.

Page, Elizabeth. *The Tree of Liberty.* New York: Holt, 1939. 985pp. In a vast historical panorama, the events of the birth of the American nation are depicted through their effects on three generations of several families. Most of the prominent historical figures make appearances, including Patrick Henry.

Ripley, Clements. *Clear for Action: A Novel about John Paul Jones.* New York: Appleton-Century, 1940. 310pp. This dramatic portrait of Jones that occasionally diverges from the historical record includes Jones's rivalry with Patrick Henry to win the hand of Dorothea Dandridge.

Recommended Juvenile Biographies

Fradin, Dennis B. *Patrick Henry: "Give Me Liberty or Give Me Death."* Hillside, New Jersey: Enslow, 1990. 48pp. Part of the Colonial Profiles series, this is a brief, though informative, biographical profile that relates Henry's activities to his era.

Fritz, Jean. *Where Was Patrick Henry on the 29th of May.* New York: Coward-McCann, 1975. 47pp. MG. Fritz's brief and entertaining biographical sketch looks at the stages of Henry's development as a patriot.

Sabin, Louis. *Patrick Henry: Voice of American Revolution.* Mahwah, New Jersey: Troll, 1982. 48pp. YA. This biographical portrait focuses on Henry's youth in colonial Virginia that helped determine his later life.

Biographical Films and Theatrical Adaptations

A&E Biography Video: Patrick Henry: Voice of Liberty (1995). This solid documentary profile looks at Henry's life from childhood. Video.

George Washington (1984) and *George Washington: The Forging of a Nation* (1986). Directors: Buzz Kulik and William A. Graham. In this two-part television mini-series chronicling the life of George Washington (Barry Bostwick) Patrick Henry is played by Henry Groenes and Daniel Davis. Video.

John Paul Jones (1959). Director: John Farrow. In this colorful spectacle on the life of the American naval hero, Maconald Carey appears as Patrick Henry as Jones's (Robert Stack) rival. Features a cameo appearance by Bette Davis as Catherine the Great. Video.

Liberty!: The American Revolution (1997). Directors: Ellen Hovde and Muffie Meyer. This PBS documentary series features actors portraying the principals in dramatic readings from their letters and speeches. Patrick Henry is played by James Naughton. The companion volume is written by Thomas J. Fleming (New York: Viking, 1997. 394pp.). Video.

223. ALFRED HITCHCOCK
1899–1980

An English-American director, writer, and producer of singular style, Hitchcock was born in London and began his directing career in 1925. His first popular films were *The Thirty-Nine Steps* (1935) and *The Lady Vanishes* (1938). He began working in the United States in 1940. Known for his suspense thrillers, his many celebrated films include *Shadow of a Doubt* (1943), *Notorious* (1946), *Strangers on a Train* (1951), *Rear Window* (1954), *Vertigo* (1958), *North by Northwest* (1959), *Psycho* (1960), *The Birds* (1963), and *Frenzy* (1972). He was often seen in humorous cameos in his films. During the 1950s and 1960s he produced and served as host for two successful television mystery-suspense series.

Autobiography and Primary Sources

Hitchcock's Notebooks: An Authorized and Illustrated Look Inside the Creative Mind of Alfred Hitchcock. Dan Auiler, ed. New York: Spike, 1999. 567pp. Auiler has sifted the Hitchcock archives to collect a rich variety of documents, including memos, script excerpts, stills, and storyboards to illustrate Hitchcock's creative method.

Hitchcock on Hitchcock: Selected Writings and Interviews. Sidney Gottlieb, ed. Los Angeles: University of California Press, 1995. 339pp. This collection of articles, essays, book introductions, and lectures offers Hitchcock's perspective on his films, filmmaking, and personal theories.

Recommended Biographies

Spoto, Donald. *The Dark Side of Genius: The Life of Alfred Hitchcock.* Boston: Little, Brown, 1983. 594pp. Spoto followed his fine critical study, *The Art of Alfred Hitchcock* (New York: Hopkinson and Blake, 1976. 523pp.), with this controversial biography and a negative portrait of a cruel, ungenerous, cowardly man. Written without the cooperation of Hitchcock's wife or daughter, the book relies on secondhand accounts and gossip from several suspect sources. Despite its weaknesses, Spoto's analysis is often skillful in placing the director in his cultural and artistic context.

Taylor, John Russell. *Hitch: The Life and Times of Alfred Hitchcock.* New York: Pantheon, 1978. 320pp. Regarded as the standard treatment of Hitchcock's life and career, Taylor's biography was written with the director's consent. Scrupulously researched, the book is particularly helpful in detailing Hitchcock's early life and career in Britain.

Other Biographical Studies

Freeman, David. *The Last Days of Alfred Hitchcock.* Woodstock, New York: Overlook Press, 1984. 281pp. Focusing on the last phase of Hitchcock's career when the director was in decline, this appreciative study dramatizes the severe challenges Hitchcock faced by a screenwriter who worked with the director on a film that was never made.

Leff, Leonard J. *Hitchcock and Selznick: The Rich and Strange Collaboration of Alfred Hitchcock and David O. Selznick in Hollywood.* New York: Weidenfeld and Nicolson, 1987. 383pp. Using interviews and unpublished archival material, Leff documents the collaboration between director and producer during the period 1939 to 1947 that resulted in four of Hitchcock's finest films.

Phillips, Gene D. *Alfred Hitchcock.* Boston: Twayne, 1984. 211pp. Combining critical analysis with biographical details, Phillips offers a succinct and sensible assessment.

Ryall, Tom. *Alfred Hitchcock and the British Cinema.* Urbana: University of Illinois Press, 1986. 193pp. Concentrating on Hitchcock's British years, Ryall is expert in establishing the cultural and cinema context out of which the director emerged.

Truffaut, François, and Helen G. Scott. *Hitchcock.* New York: Simon & Schuster, 1967. 256pp. This classic of film criticism is based on a series of interviews tracking Hitchcock's career film by film with the director's candid assessment.

Fictional Portraits

Baxt, George. *The Alfred Hitchcock Murder Case.* New York: St. Martin's, 1986. 277pp. Set in 1925 Munich and 1936 London, a murder on the set of one of Hitchcock's films results in the director being charged for a crime he did not commit. The novel's story is fictitious, but the references to Hitchcock's life and films are authentic.

Biographical Films and Theatrical Adaptations

Alfred Hitchcock (1985). Director: Richard Schickel. In this installment of the Men Who Made the Movies series, scenes from Hitchcock's films are combined with interviews with the director for a documentary profile of his life and artistry. Video.

Vintage Hitchcock (1970). Director: Saul J. Turell. This documentary looks at Hitchcock's early years in Britain, from his first job as a set designer in silent films and his first directorial efforts to his classic films of the 1930s. Video.

Other Sources

Deutelbaum, Marshall, and Leland Poague, eds. *A Hitchcock Reader.* Ames: Iowa State University Press, 1986. 355pp. Written by various film critics and Hitchcock experts, this is a useful collection that treats aspects of Hitchcock's life and films.

LaValley, Albert J., ed. *Focus on Hitchcock.* Englewood Cliffs, New Jersey: Prentice-Hall, 1972. 186pp. Brings together a number of essays on various aspects of Hitchcock's career and artistry.

224. ADOLF HITLER
1889–1945

Founder of National Socialism, German dictator, rabid anti-Semite, and architect of World War II, Hitler, with Joseph Stalin, is probably the most notorious public figure of the twentieth century. The son of an Austrian customs official, he dropped out of high school and after twice failing to gain admittance to the academy of arts in Vienna moved to Munich and joined the Bavarian army during World War I. He became the Nazi party chairman in 1921. In 1933 he was elected German chancellor. Under Hitler, Germany became one of the most brutally repressive and murderous societies in history; the media was state-controlled and censored, and Jews, other "non-Aryans," and dissidents were persecuted, imprisoned, and murdered with bureaucratic efficiency. Hitler's prosecution of the war (1938–1945) left millions dead and Germany in ruins. He committed suicide in his Berlin bunker as the Russian army was entering the city.

Autobiography and Primary Sources

Hitler's Letters and Notes. Werner Moser, ed. New York: Harper & Row, 1974. 390pp. This intriguing collection of primary materials includes letters written between 1906 and 1945, the notes Hitler wrote to clarify his thoughts as he prepared his speeches, and Eva Braun's 1935 diary.

Recommended Biographies

Bullock, Alan. *Hitler, a Study in Tyranny.* 1952. Revised ed. New York: Harper & Row, 1964. 848pp. Bullock's authoritative study of Hitler's character, career, and influence has long been regarded as the standard biography. Balanced and comprehensive, Bullock's study neglects Hitler's early days to concentrate on his years in power. Bullock's biography remains an essential source and excellent treatment of Hitler the man and modern German history.

Fest, Joachim C. *Hitler.* New York: Harcourt, Brace, 1974. 844pp. Fest's esteemed biographical treatment of Hitler's development offers much more information on his early years than Bullock and provides useful cultural analysis to help explain Hitler's rise and appeal.

Kershaw, Ian. *Hitler: 1889–1936: Hubris.* 1999. 845pp. In the first volume of a projected two-volume study, Kershaw emphasizes the historical forces that helped transform Hitler into a powerful dictator. Impressively documented and argued, Kershaw's study promises to become the definitive modern biography when completed.

Toland, John. *Adolf Hitler.* Garden City, New York: Doubleday, 1976. 1,035pp. Toland supplements previously published sources with multiple interviews from eyewitnesses and intimates. The author does not attempt to resolve the many contradictions he uncovers in Hitler's character and career but displays them objectively and vividly.

Other Biographical Studies

Bullock, Alan. *Hitler and Stalin: Parallel Lives.* New York: Knopf, 1992. 1,081pp. Bullock's fascinating dual biography offers a step-by-step progression of both leaders in gaining and using power. Both are chillingly shown as products of their time, not as unique monster figures.

Davidson, Eugene. *The Making of Hitler: The Birth and Rise of Nazism.* New York: Macmillan, 1977. 408pp.; *The Unmaking of Hitler.* Columbia: University of Missouri Press, 1996. 536pp. This narrative summary chronicles the events of Hitler's career from his rise to power to his death. However, the study offers very little to explain Hitler's personality or psychology and focuses exclusively on Hitler's political and military leadership.

Flood, Charles B. *Hitler: The Path to Power.* Boston: Houghton Mifflin, 1989. 686pp. Flood narrows his focus to the years between 1919 and 1923 to portray Hitler's character and early development. The events are dramatically rendered, and Hitler's supporting cast is vividly characterized.

Hamann, Brigitte. *Hitler's Vienna: A Dictator's Apprenticeship.* New York: Oxford University Press, 1999. 512pp. This is a careful, well-documented account of Hitler's life as a young man in Vienna before World War I that challenges a number of myths surrounding Hitler's early experiences and ideas.

Hayman, Ronald. *Hitler & Geli.* New York: Bloomsbury, 1998. 240pp. Hayman investigates the mystery surrounding the 1931 death by gunshot of Hitler's niece, Geli Raubal, as a potential clue to unlocking the secret of Hitler's destructiveness.

Heiden, Konrad. *Der Fuehrer: Hitler's Rise to Power.* Boston: Houghton Mifflin, 1944. 390pp. First published in 1936 by a bitter anti-Nazi émigré, Heiden traces Hitler's and the National Socialist Party's development up to 1934. Based on first-hand recollections, Heiden's examination of Hitler's early years is still respected by scholars for its insights.

Infield, Glenn B. *Eva and Adolf.* New York: Grosset & Dunlap, 1974. 330pp. The book provides a chronological and coherent account of the relationship based on previously unpublished archival material created in the investigation of Hitler's death.

Lukacs, John. *The Hitler of History.* New York: Knopf, 1997. 320pp. The book looks at what 100 biographers have made of Hitler and evaluates various interpretations for accuracy.

Maser, Werner. *Hitler: Legend, Myth, and Reality.* New York: Harper & Row, 1973. 433pp. In place of a chronological account, Maser organizes his treatment into thematic units to cover various aspects of Hitler's character and career. Incorporating new findings about his early life, Maser's psychological analysis dispels many of the legends that have grown up around the dictator.

Payne, Robert. *The Life and Death of Adolf Hitler.* New York: Praeger, 1973. 623pp. Payne's popular biography largely ignores social and political history to concentrate on Hitler the man in a narrative that reads like a novel. Lacking documentation, the book incorporates speculation as fact and should be read with caution, though few will be able to resist the book's narrative and imaginative power.

Redlich, Fritz. *Hitler: Diagnosis of a Destructive Prophet.* New York: Oxford University Press, 1998. 496pp. In a two-part study, the first summarizes the biography, and the second interprets Hitler's medical history to attempt to explain his personality and behavior.

Rosenbaum, Ron. *Explaining Hitler: The Search for the Origins of His Evil.* New York: Random House, 1998. 448pp. This journalistic investigation into Hitler's character takes the form of a series of encounters with historians, philosophers, filmmakers, and others who have tried to answer the Hitler enigma. Rosenbaum shows how Hitler has become a dark mirror in which we see aspects of ourselves.

Stone, Norman. *Hitler.* Boston: Little, Brown, 1980. 195pp. Stone's revisionist reassessment of Hitler's rise to power and political and military leadership is intended for the nonspecialist and incorporates a useful summary of modern research along with a good deal of unproven assertions and dubious interpretations.

Toland, John. *Hitler: The Pictorial Documentary of His Life.* Garden City, New York: Doubleday, 1978. 205pp. This useful visual biography arranges rare archival photographs to illustrate Hitler's life and time.

Trevor-Roper, Hugh. *The Last Days of Hitler.* New York: Macmillan, 1947. 254pp. Assigned by British intelligence to investigate Hitler's death, Trevor-Roper presents the essential facts that were uncovered as well as a character sketch of Hitler's mental and moral breakdown.

Waite, Robert. *The Psychopathic God, Adolf Hitler.* New York: Basic Books, 1971. 482pp. Waite's daring and controversial psychohistorical interpretation looks at the life for evidence to support the author's thesis concerning Hitler's private neuroses. Waite's method has been challenged by historians as suspect, but there is no denying the force and ingenuity of Waite's insights. See also *Kaiser and Führer: A Comparative Study of Personality and Politics* (Toronto: University of Toronto Press, 1998. 511pp.) for an interesting dual study of the personal lives and politics of Hitler and Wilhelm II.

Biographical Novels

Gold, Alison. *The Devil's Mistress: The Diary of Eva Braun.* Boston: Faber and Faber, 1997. 218pp. Based in part on Eva Braun's actual diary entries and embellished by the author's imagination, the novel offers an intriguing look at the couple's relationship and the banality of evil.

Hansen, Ron. *Hitler's Niece.* New York: HarperCollins, 1999. 310pp. Hansen probes Hitler's relationship with his niece, Geli Raubal, in a chilling and convincing psychological study that follows Hitler's rise to power and offers a plausible, though imaginative, solution to the mystery surrounding Geli's death.

Levine, Jacques. *Hitler's Secret Diaries.* Pittsburgh, Pennsylvania: Aiglon Press, 1988. 157pp. The novel imagines Hitler's reflections in a diary that he keeps from his youth in 1899.

West, Paul. *The Dry Danube: A Hitler Forgery.* New York: New Directions, 2000. 160pp. In a chillingly imagined stream-of-consciousness memoir, Hitler recounts his pre-World War I years in Vienna as a struggling, unsuccessful artist.

Fictional Portraits

Bainbridge, Beryl. *Young Adolf.* New York: G. Braziller, 1979. 219pp. Based on the spurious assertion that Hitler visited Liverpool in 1912, the novel imagines how this period of his life had an impact on Hitler's later development.

Dobbs, Michael. *Last Man to Die.* New York: HarperCollins, 1992. 288pp. In this World War II thriller a German prisoner in Britain escapes to become a hero of the Reich and is on hand for Hitler's end.

Gurr, David. *The Ring Master.* New York: Atheneum, 1987. 739pp. In a disturbing exploration of Naziism and Hitler's Germany concerning an obsessive love triangle involving Hitler, an English opera singer, and her brother, actuality provides a springboard for a presentation of myth and archetype.

Melchior, Ib. *Eva.* New York: Dodd, Mead, 1984. 218pp. This ingenious but implausible fantasy imagines what might have happened if Eva Braun had survived Hitler's death in the bunker.

Rusch, Kristine Katherine *Hitler's Angel.* New York: St. Martin's, 1988. 213pp. A historical mystery that takes up the circumstances surrounding the death of Hitler's niece and possible lover, Geli Raubal, in 1931.

Van Rjndt, Philippe. *The Trial of Adolf Hitler.* New York: Simon & Schuster, 1978. 334pp. In this fantasy, after Hitler's suicide attempt fails, he lives in a Bavarian village for the next 25 years before identifying himself and demanding to be tried as a moral test to expose the hypocrisy of the West.

West, Paul. *The Very Rich Hours of Count Von Stauffenberg.* New York: Harper & Row, 1980. 365pp. This imaginative reconstruction of the conspiracy to assassinate Hitler is well-researched and believable in its depiction of the era and its personalities.

Recommended Juvenile Biographies

Ayer, Eleanor H. *Adolf Hitler.* San Diego: Lucent Books, 1996. 128pp. MG/YA. Tracing Hitler's rise to power, leadership, and collapse with quotations from primary sources and recognized biographical studies, Ayer puts the Third Reich into historical perspective and challenges the interpretation of Hitler as a madman with a more complex consideration of his motives and personality traits.

Heyes, Eileen. *Adolf Hitler.* Brookfield, Connecticut: Millbrook Press, 1994. 160pp. MG/YA. Detailed and informative, the book looks at the biography to probe the question "How was the Hitler phenomenon possible?" Hitler's rise and fall are set against the economic and sociological contexts in Germany between the wars.

Wepman, Dennis. *Adolf Hitler.* New York: Chelsea House, 1987. 112pp. MG/YA. Sensible and workmanlike survey of Hitler's life and career from childhood to his death.

Biographical Films and Theatrical Adaptations

Antrobus, John. *Hitler in Liverpool.* New York: Riverrun Press, 1983. 139pp. As in Beryl Bainbridge's novel, *Young Adolf,* Antrobus imagines the dubious suggestion that Hitler visited England in 1912.

Hulme, George. *The Life and Death of Adolf Hitler.* Toronto: Macmillan, 1976. 246pp. This drama spans Hitler's entire career in scenes of repetitive horror that never fully bring the central character to life.

Rosenfeld, Alvin H. *Imagining Hitler.* Bloomington: Indiana University Press, 1985. 121pp. Rosenfeld surveys the portrayals of Hitler in American fiction and film following 1945.

Adolf Hitler: 1889–1945 (1976). Director: Walter McGhee. A documentary profile using still photography and film footage. Video.

The Bunker (1981). Director: George Schaefer. Anthony Hopkins won an Emmy for his performance as Hitler in this television film, co-starring Piper Laurie, Richard Jordan, Susan Blakely, and Cliff Gorman. Based on the James O'Donnell book. (Boston: Houghton Mifflin, 1978. 399pp.). Video.

The Democrat and the Dictator (1982). Producer: Betsy McCarthy. An installment of *A Walk Through the 20th Century with Bill Moyers* contrasting the different personalities of Roosevelt and Hitler. Video.

FDR and Hitler (1987). Producer: William T. Cartwright. This installment of the PBS *Between the Wars* series looks as the contrasting lives and political careers of Roosevelt and Hitler. Video.

The Gathering Storm (1974). Director: Herbert Wise. Based on Churchill's memoirs, this dramatization examines the buildup to war, with Richard Burton as Churchill and Ian Bannen as Hitler. Video.

Hitler (1962). Director: Stuart Heisler. Richard Basehart portrays Hitler in this dramatization of his rise to power and downfall. The supporting cast includes Cordula Trantow, Maria Emo, Martin Kosleck, and John Banner. Video.

Hitler (1996). Producer: ZDF. Six videocassette collection that presents various aspects of Hitler's life and character in a psychological profile that focuses on individual aspects of his personality and roles, such as "The Private Man," "The Seducer," "The Blackmailer," "The Dictator," "The Commander," and "The Criminal." Video.

Hitler: The Last Ten Days (1973). Director: Ennio de Concini. Alec Guinness portrays Hitler in his bunker during his final days, based on eyewitness testimony. Co-starring Simon Ward, Diane Cilento, and Adolfo Celi. Video.

Hitler: The Whole Story (1991). Director: Christian Herrendoerfer. Based on Joachim C. Fest's biography, the film follows Hitler's rise and fall. Previously released as *Hitler: A Career* (1984). Video.

Inside the Third Reich (1982). Director: Marvin J. Chomsky. Derek Jacobi stars as Hitler in this television mini-series based on Albert Speer's memoirs. Co-starring Rutger Hauer, John Gielgud, Blythe Danner, and Ian Holm. Video.

The Rise and Fall of the Third Reich (1968). Director: Jack Kaufman. Based on William L. Shirer's

book, the film traces Hitler's life and career from birth to death. Video.

The Warlords (1986). Producer: Lamancha Productions. This series of brief film biographies of World War II leaders, such as Mussolini, de Gaulle, Stalin, and Churchill, includes a portrait of Hitler. Video.

The Winds of War (1983); *War and Remembrance* (1989). Director: Dan Curtis. Hitler is portrayed by Steven Berkoff and Gunter Meisner in Herman Wouk's family saga, starring Robert Mitchum as Pug Henry, that covers two theaters of World War II. Video.

Other Sources

Hauner, Milan. *Hitler: A Chronology of His Life and Times.* New York: St. Martin's, 1983. 221pp. This detailed chronology traces Hitler's life in full along with the major historical events of his era.

225. THOMAS HOBBES
1588–1679

English political philosopher, Hobbes argued that human submission to sovereign authority is motivated by materialism and self-interest and that temporal power is superior to ecclesiastical power. Among his works are *Leviathan* (1651) and *De Homine* (1658). Hobbes's theories of the social contract were explored and reformulated by such later political theorists as Locke, Spinoza, and Rousseau.

Recommended Biographies

Martinich, Aloysius. *Hobbes: A Biography.* New York: Cambridge University Press, 1999. 390pp. Martinich's scholarly biography is likely to remain the standard life for some time to come. In a comprehensive account that traces Hobbes's personal and intellectual development in his historical context, Martinich synthesizes the available evidence and recent scholarship to present a striking, nuanced portrait.

Rogow, Arnold A. *Thomas Hobbes: Radical in the Service of Reaction.* New York: W.W. Norton, 1986. 287pp. Rogow suggests that Hobbes's pessimistic depiction of human nature has its psychological origin in the philosopher's character and his formative years. The book is an intriguing analysis based on limited sources that does supply a human context to an understanding of Hobbes's political philosophy.

Other Biographical Studies

Hinnant, Charles H. *Thomas Hobbes.* Boston: Twayne, 1977. 174pp. After an initial biographical summary, Hinnant provides a sensible introductory survey of Hobbes's work, suggesting his intellectual development from *The Elements of Law* (1640) to *The Leviathan* (1651).

Reik, Miriam M. *The Golden Lands of Thomas Hobbes.* Detroit: Wayne State University Press, 1977. 239pp. Treating in separate chapters Hobbes as humanist, scientist, political theorist, mathematician, Christian, and literary critic, Reik offers a

useful multidimensional portrait in this intellectual biography.

Robertson, George C. *Hobbes.* Philadelphia: Lippincott, 1886. 240pp. Robertson's is the first real scholarly biography, organizing the scanty details of Hobbes's life into a workable chronology. The considerable gaps in the record are filled in by background details and the intellectual climate that help shape Hobbes's ideas.

Tuck, Richard. *Hobbes.* New York: Oxford University Press, 1989. 127pp. Tuck's is a solid introductory overview that serves the general reader and the student well.

Other Sources

Sorell, Tom, ed. *The Cambridge Companion to Hobbes.* New York: Cambridge University Press, 1996. 404pp. This valuable collection of essays by recognized authorities cover various aspects of Hobbes's intellectual activities and works, with a biographical summary by Noel Malcolm.

226. WILLIAM HOGARTH
1697–1764

An English painter and engraver, Hogarth is famous for his series of morality and satirical engravings, *The Harlot's Progress* (1732), *The Rake's Progress* (1735), and *Marriage à la Mode* (1745), often considered his masterpiece. His paintings, *The Shrimp Girl* and *Captain Coran* (both 1740), are masterpieces of British painting. Hogarth also wrote a brilliant formal exposition on the Rococo aesthetic, titled *Analysis of Beauty* (1753).

Recommended Biographies

Bindman, David. *Hogarth.* New York: Oxford University Press, 1981. 216pp. Bindman's accessible yet learned interpretive study of the artist and his works is one of the most informative and useful single-volume studies available.

Paulson, Ronald. *Hogarth: His Life, Art, and Times.* 1971. Revised ed. New Brunswick: Rutgers University Press, 1991–1993. 3 vols. Paulson's is by far the most comprehensive and authoritative treatment of Hogarth's life interspersed with minute analyses of his paintings and prints. Extensively documented and illustrated, Paulson's study is likely to remain the standard source for some time to come.

Uglow, Jennifer. *Hogarth: A Life and a World.* New York: Farrar, Straus, 1997. 794pp. Uglow, a biographer of Elizabeth Gaskell and George Eliot, has written an able account of Hogarth's life and times that helps to make his artistry understandable by a clear depiction of the events and environment that inspired him. With 200 black-and-white illustrations and 14 color plates.

Other Biographical Studies

Dobson, Austin. *Hogarth.* 1879. Revised ed. as *William Hogarth.* London: Heinemann, 1907. 310pp. Dobson's version of Hogarth's life is a generally dependable, balanced portrait, excluding much of the previously unsubstantiated anecdotes about the artist.

Jarrett, Derek. *The Ingenious Mr. Hogarth*. London: M. Joseph, 1976. 223pp. Jarrett's critical biography lacks the comprehensiveness and authority of Paulson and Uglow but still has considerable merit as a reliable summary of Hogarth's life, personality, and artistry.

Lindsay, Jack. *Hogarth: His Art and His World*. New York: Taplinger, 1979. 277pp. Hogarth's life and work are discussed with skill and depth with 50 carefully selected illustrations. Lindsay is particularly strong on Hogarth's relationship to his age and his theory of art.

Quennell, Peter. *Hogarth's Progress*. New York: Viking, 1955. 318pp. As one contemporary reviewer observed, "If London is the major character... Hogarth himself, as observer and above all creative artist, is its focal point, and it is difficult to envisage a better balanced view of the artist—the man, his time, and his contribution—than the author gives us." Serves the general reader looking for a colorful orientation to the man and his era.

Fictional Portraits

Ackroyd, Peter. *English Music*. New York: Knopf, 1992. 399pp. Ackroyd's meditation on creativity includes appearances by such figures as Hogarth, Dickens, Blake, and Bunyan.

Hall, Robert Lee. *Benjamin Franklin and a Case of Artful Murder*. New York: St. Martin's, 1988. 279pp. Hogarth appears as a character in this installment of Hall's inventive historical mystery with Franklin as sleuth.

227. HERBERT HOOVER
1874–1964

The thirty-first U.S. president (1929–1932), Hoover was a mining engineer until 1914, when he began chairing several relief commissions, served as U.S. Food Administrator during World War I, and directed postwar European relief operations. He was Secretary of Commerce (1921–1929) under Presidents Harding and Coolidge. As president, Hoover established the Federal Farm Board and pressed for tariff revision. After the stock market crash (1929) and the start of the Great Depression, Hoover dealt severely with the Bonus Marchers (1932) and was reluctant to extend federal aid, although he did recommend a large public works program.

Autobiography and Primary Sources

Memoirs. New York: Macmillan, 1951–1952. 3 vols. Hoover's extensive recollections trace his life and career up to 1941.

Recommended Biographies

Fausold, Martin L. *The Presidency of Herbert C. Hoover*. Lawrence: University Press of Kansas, 1985. 288pp. Fausold's study is the most comprehensive treatment of the Hoover presidency, explicating his foreign and domestic policies and pro-

grams and providing a spirited reassessment of his leadership strengths and weaknesses.

Burner, David. *Herbert Hoover: A Public Life*. New York: Knopf, 1979. 433pp. This is the best single-volume full-length biography of Hoover available. Extensively researched and balanced in its assessment, the book joins an insightful analysis of the inner man with the details of his career. Readers with a preexisting conception of Hoover will have their view challenged by Burner's revealing portrait.

Nash, George N. *The Life of Herbert Hoover*. New York: W.W. Norton, 1983–1996. 3 vols. Nash's monumental multi-volume biography has only reached 1918. Painstakingly researched and well written, Nash's life is expected to become the definitive study when eventually completed. Until then, Nash provides the most comprehensive coverage of Hoover's background, upbringing, and pre-political career as an engineer and his humanitarian work during World War I.

Other Biographical Studies

Best, Gary D. *Herbert Hoover: The Post-presidential Years, 1933–1964*. Stanford, California: Hoover Institution Press, 1983. 2 vols. Best's extensively documented account of Hoover's 31 years after leaving the White House is the most comprehensive and reliable treatment of this often neglected period of Hoover's life. Although not uncritical, Best often provides only Hoover's side of things, and the book has little to say about Hoover's family and personal life.

Hoff Wilson, Joan. *Herbert Hoover: Forgotten Progressive*. Boston: Little, Brown, 1975. 367pp. The author's interpretive study looks at Hoover's Quaker background and early experiences that formed his progressive views, which Hoff Wilson contends shaped and unified Hoover's career to the end.

Lyons, Eugene. *Our Unknown Ex-President: A Portrait of Herbert Hoover*. 1948. Revised as *Herbert Hoover: A Biography*. Garden City, New York: Doubleday, 1964. 444pp. Both of Lyons's accounts of Hoover (the latter an update covering Hoover's activities up to his death) are highly laudatory and, although highly detailed and extensively researched, lack critical objectivity, falling as one reviewer pointed out "somewhere between campaign biography and hagiography."

Smith, Gene. *The Shattered Dream: Herbert Hoover and the Great Depression*. New York: Morrow, 1970. 278pp. Focusing on Hoover's presidency, Smith's is a highly readable, popular account aimed at the general reader. With Hoover's pre- and postpresidential life only sketched, the book serves primarily the reader looking for insight into Hoover's leadership failures.

Smith, Richard N. *An Uncommon Man: The Triumph of Herbert Hoover*. New York: Simon & Schuster, 1984. 488pp. Smith comes to Hoover's defense in a spirited revisionist, though objective, analysis that seeks to show how Hoover rebounded from his failures as president to reemerge as a valued statesman. Filled with insight into Hoover's character, the book will surprise readers whose

views of Hoover have been influenced by Democratic stereotypes.

Warren, Harris G. *Herbert Hoover and the Great Depression*. New York: Oxford University Press, 1959. 372pp. Warren provides a highly readable revisionist reassessment of Hoover's policies from 1928 to 1932 that seeks to rehabilitate his reputation without glossing over his errors and limitations.

Wilson, Carol G. *Herbert Hoover: A Challenge for Today*. New York: Evans, 1968. 338pp. Different from many treatments, Hoover's presidency is deemphasized here with a concentration on Hoover's personality, private life, and humanitarian activities, based on interviews with Hoover's friends and associates.

Recommended Juvenile Biographies

Clinton, Susan. *Herbert Hoover, Thirty-first President of the United States*. Chicago: Childrens Press, 1988. 96pp. MG. Clinton supplies the basic information about Hoover's life, character, and achievements.

Polikoff, Barbara G. *Herbert C. Hoover, 31st President of the United States*. Ada, Oklahoma: Garrett, 1990. 120pp. MG. The challenges of Hoover's presidency are chronicled in this informative biographical overview.

Terzian, James P. *The Many Worlds of Herbert Hoover*. New York: J. Messner, 1966. 191pp. MG/YA. The first half of this account describes Hoover's life; the second the history of his administration and political and cultural events up to his death.

Other Sources

Rice, Arnold S. *Herbert Hoover, 1874–1964: Chronological-Documents-Bibliographical Aids*. Dobbs Ferry, New York: Oceana, 1971. 114pp. Rice provides a extensive chronology, a sampling of primary documents, and a bibliography of important works on Hoover and his administration.

228. J. EDGAR HOOVER
1895–1972

American government administrator, John Edgar Hoover served in the Justice Department before becoming (1924) the first director of the Federal Bureau of Investigation. Under Hoover's direction, the FBI established a centralized fingerprint file, crime laboratory, and training school, fought organized crime, and during the 1950s and 1960s investigated and harassed alleged Communists, as well as protestors and political leaders. Hoover directed the FBI until his death.

Recommended Biographies

Gentry, Curt. *J. Edgar Hoover: The Man and His Secrets*. New York: W.W. Norton, 1991. 846pp. Drawing on hundreds of interviews and countless pages of previously classified documents, Gentry's is the most comprehensive gathering of evidence on Hoover's life and career. While avoiding the sensationalist approach of others, Gentry's findings are no less chilling in uncovering the abuses of power of a paranoid, sinister figure.

Powers, Richard G. *Secrecy and Power: The Life of J. Edgar Hoover.* New York: Free Press, 1987. 624pp. Equally thoroughly researched but more balanced in its assessment than Gentry, Powers keeps Hoover clearly in focus in a full-length, sensitive portrait. Unlike other works that simply accumulate charges against Hoover, Powers's biography helpfully explains why Hoover acted as he did, presenting him as a complex and significant figure.

Other Biographical Studies

Deloach, Cartha D. *Hoover's FBI: The Inside Story by Hoover's Trusted Lieutenant.* Washington, DC: Regnery, 1995. 440pp. The number three man in the FBI during the 1960s supplies his personal account of his boss and his actions that attempts to set the record straight on such controversies as the Kennedy and King assassinations and Hoover's alleged blackmailing of members of Congress.

De Toledano, Ralph. *J. Edgar Hoover: The Man in His Time.* New Rochelle, New York: Arlington House, 1973 384pp. The work of an unabashed Hoover apologist, De Toledano glosses over Hoover's shortcomings while attacking his critics with unsubstantiated accusations.

Demaris, Ovid. *The Director: An Oral Biography of J. Edgar Hoover.* New York: Harper's Magazine Press, 1975. 405pp. This is a useful collection of interviews with those who had personal and professional contact with Hoover throughout his career, offering different views of his character.

Messick, Hank. *John Edgar Hoover: An Inquiry into the Life and Times of John Edgar Hoover and the Continuing Partnership of Crime, Business, and Politics.* New York: D. McKay, 1972. 276pp. The polar opposite of De Toledano's paean of praise is this stinging indictment of Hoover's professional activities and personality, judging him'a hypocrite and an ideologue who was at least partially responsible for the rise of organized crime.

Nash, Jay R. *Citizen Hoover: A Critical Study of the Life and Times of J. Edgar Hoover and His FBI.* Chicago: Nelson-Hall, 1972. 298pp. Nash adds to the growing chorus of Hoover detractors in this reassessment of Hoover's career that finds little to praise and much to lament.

Summers, Anthony. *Official and Confidential: The Secret Life of J. Edgar Hoover.* New York: Putnam, 1993. 528pp. In the book that turned Hoover into a joke and worse, Summers reveals, among many allegations, that Hoover was a closet homosexual and transvestite and was indirectly responsible for the assassination of President Kennedy. Many of Summers's charges have been challenged, and the book is often so unsubstantiated and sensational that it must be read with skepticism.

Theoharis, Athan G. *The Boss: J. Edgar Hoover and the Great American Inquisition.* Philadelphia: Temple University Press, 1988. 489pp. Far more believable than Summers's sensational revelations is Theoharis's careful critical study of Hoover's life and career, based on previously untapped documentary evidence. The author allows the evidence to speak for itself in this portrait of the corruption of

power. In *J. Edgar Hoover, Sex, and Crime: An Historical Antidote* (Chicago: Ivan R. Dee, 1995. 175pp.) Theoharis takes on many of Summers's most startling allegations and offers a reasoned and documented rebuttal.

Fictional Portraits

Collins, Max Allan. *True Crime.* New York: St. Martin's, 1984. 304pp. The early years of the FBI in the 1930s and its pursuit of such criminals as Dillinger, Pretty Boy Floyd, Melvin Purvis, and the Barker gang is dramatized with a look at the ambitious and determined Hoover.

Gorman, Edward. *The Marilyn Tapes.* New York: Forge, 1995. 349pp. In an inventive thriller, various fictional and historical figures, including J. Edgar Hoover, Louella Parsons, the Kennedys, and the Mafia race to secure Monroe's secret recordings about her affairs. The action is periodically interrupted with excerpts from the tapes as Monroe tells her own story.

McMurtry, Larry, and Diana Ossana. *Pretty Boy Floyd.* New York: Simon & Schuster, 1994. 444pp. Floyd's career as a criminal celebrity provides an opportunity to portray the early FBI and Hoover's manipulation of its image.

Patterson, Harry. *Dillinger.* New York: Stein and Day,1983. 233pp. The pursuit of criminal John Dillinger forms the basis of this mainly fanciful story that does feature an authentic period background and a plausible portrait of the young Hoover.

Recommended Juvenile Biographies

Denenberg, Barry. *The True Story of J. Edgar Hoover and the FBI.* New York: Scholastic, 1993. 202pp. MG/YA. Denenberg combines biography and social history in a provocative, critical account of Hoover's rule of the FBI.

Biographical Films and Theatrical Adaptations

Blood Feud (1983). Director: Mike Newell. The conflict between Jimmy Hoffa (Robert Blake) and the Kennedys is dramatized. Sam Groom portrays John F. Kennedy, with Cotter Smith as Robert Kennedy, Forrest Tucker as Lyndon Johnson and Ernest Borgnine as Hoover. Video.

G-men: The Rise of J. Edgar Hoover (1991). Director: Irv Drasnin. An installment of PBS's American Experience series, this is a documentary look at the creation of the FBI and Hoover's career, mainly in the 1920s and 1930s. Video.

J. Edgar Hoover (1987). Director: Robert Collins. This made-for-television biography casts Treat Williams in the central role in scenes from Hoover's long career. Co-starring Rip Torn, David Ogden Stiers, Arndrew Duggan, and Louise Fletcher. Video.

Kennedy (1983). Director: Jim Goddard. Martin Sheen plays John F. Kennedy in this television mini-series with Blair Brown as Jackie, John Shea as Robert Kennedy, Nesbitt Blaisdell as Lyndon Johnson, and E.G. Marshall as Joseph Kennedy. Hoover is portrayed by Vincent Gardenia. Video.

The Private Files of J. Edgar Hoover (1977). Director: Larry Cohen. The emphasis here is on Hoover's seamy private life and sexual excesses. Broderick Crawford stars as the FBI head with a supporting cast of Jose Ferrer, Rip Torn, and Dan Dailey. Video.

Robert Kennedy and His Times (1985). Director: Marvin J. Chomsky. Based on Arthur M. Schlesinger's book, this television film traces Robert Kennedy's public career. With Brad Davis as Bobby, Cliff De Young as John F. Kennedy, Veronica Cartwright as Ethel Kennedy, and Juanin Clay as Jackie. Hoover is portrayed by Ned Beatty. Video.

See also John F. Kennedy; and Robert F. Kennedy

229. GERARD MANLEY HOPKINS
1844–1889

English poet and Jesuit priest, Hopkins composed verse noted for its intensity of language and experiments in prosody. Although he produced a small body of work, which did not appear in print until 1918, his work profoundly influenced twentieth-century poetry. His poems include "The Wreck of the *Deutschland*," "God's Grandeur," "The Windhover," "The Leaden Echo," and "The Golden Echo."

Autobiography and Primary Sources

Gerard Manley Hopkins: Selected Letters. Catherine Phillips, ed. New York: Oxford University Press, 1990. 343pp. This collection of 138 letters covers the years between 1861 to a month before Hopkins's death.

Recommended Biographies

Martin, Robert B. *Gerard Manley Hopkins: A Very Private Life.* New York: Putnam, 1991. 448pp. Martin supplies a full and convincing psychological portrait of the poet and the major struggles in Hopkins's life. Supplying new information from previously unpublished sources, the book helps penetrate the darker recesses of Hopkins's psyche and emotional life to form a consistent and comprehensible portrait.

Roberts, Gerald. *Gerard Manley Hopkins: A Literary Life.* New York: St. Martin's, 1993. 153pp. This is a useful, succinct account of Hopkins's poetic development tracing the connections between the poet's experiences and his work.

White, Norman. *Hopkins: A Literary Biography.* New York: Oxford University Press, 1992. 531pp. Thoroughly researched and sensitive, White's is one of the most complete biographies of Hopkins available. The book's reading of Hopkins's poetry is fresh and original, and the portrait of the man and the artist is credible and compelling.

Other Biographical Studies

Bergonzi, Bernard. *Gerard Manley Hopkins.* New York: Macmillan, 1977. 202pp. Bergonzi analyzes Hopkins's poems as they reflect the experiences of his life in this critical biography that places

Hopkins in his intellectual and cultural contexts. Drawing on letters and journals, the book documents Hopkins's conversion to Catholicism and his career as a priest and teacher.

Kitchen, Paddy. *Gerard Manley Hopkins.* New York: Atheneum, 1979. 243pp. The effect of Hopkins's vocation on his poetry is a central theme in this biographical portrait intended for the general reader that supplies a good overview. The author's emphasis on sexual themes somewhat overbalances the interpretation however.

Lahey, Gerald F. *Gerard Manley Hopkins.* 1930. Reprint ed. New York: Haskell House, 1969. 172pp. Lahey's brief biographical study still serves as an able introduction to the poet, covering the essential events in his life and their impact on his work.

Pick, John. *Gerard Manley Hopkins: Priest and Poet.* New York: Oxford University Press, 1942. 169pp. Pick helpfully connects the two major sides of Hopkins's vocation in a balanced account, particularly strong on the poet's stay in Dublin.

Ruggles, Eleanor. *Gerard Manley Hopkins: A Life.* 1944. Reprint ed. Port Washington, New York: Kennikat Press, 1969. 305pp. Highly readable, Ruggles is a competent popular biography, less detailed and scholarly than other treatments but vivid in its ability to capture Hopkins against a solid background of time and place.

Thomas, Alfred. *Hopkins the Jesuit: The Years of Training.* New York: Oxford University Press, 1969. 283pp. Thomas's is the most extensive treatment of Hopkins's daily life as a probationary Jesuit. Less an interpretation than a record of the available evidence, the book is essential for the scholar and specialist.

Biographical Films and Theatrical Adaptations

Gerard Manley Hopkins: Portrait of a Poet (1989). Director: Jeremy Hamp. Narrated by Anthony Hopkins, the poet's life is presented with dramatic performances by Peter Gale. Video.

230. HORACE
65 BC–8 BC

Roman lyric poet and satirist, Horace studied at Rome and Athens and fought with Brutus and the republicans at Philippi (42 BC). After returning to Rome, he was introduced to the wealthy statesman Maecanus, who became his patron. His work provides a vivid picture of Roman society during the Augustan age and includes the *Epodes*, two books of *Satires* and of *Epistles*, four books of *Odes*, and the *Ars Poetica*, all of which greatly influenced European poetry.

Autobiography and Primary Sources

Suetonius's *Life of Horace* written in the first century is the principal source, other than the autobiographical references in his poetry, for almost all the details about Horace's life and personality.

Recommended Biographies

Levi, Peter. *Horace: A Life.* New York: Routledge, 1998. 270pp. Lively and accessible for the nonspecialist, Levi's is a substantial biographical account that offers a vivid portrait of Horace's life and the world in which he lived. Based on a careful reading of the poetry, Levi reconstructs a consistent human portrait revealing both Horace's personality and beliefs.

Other Biographical Studies

D'Alton, John F. *Horace and His Age.* 1917. Reprint ed. New York: Russell & Russell, 1962. 296pp. D'Alton approaches Horace indirectly through a depiction of his era, assuming without evidence that the period's values reflect those of the poet.

Frank, Tenny. *Catullus and Horace: Two Poets in Their Environment.* New York: Holt, 1928. 291pp. Frank provides a balanced and reliable summary of what is known about the two Latin poets, avoiding in the case of Horace drawing unsubstantiated conclusions based on the opinions expressed in his work.

Noyes, Alfred. *Horace: A Portrait.* New York: Sheed & Ward, 1947. 292pp. Noyes's portrait is impressionistic, based on inferences drawn from the poetry to recreate imagined scenes from his life. The author's enthusiasm is contagious, and his critical insights are sensible, even though the biographical details are overly imaginative.

Sedgwick, Henry D. *Horace: A Biography.* Cambridge, Massachusetts: Harvard University Press, 1947. 182pp. Sedgwick's brief biographical account presents Horace as he appears in his poems as well as against a vivid historical background.

Shackleton Bailey, D.R. *Profile of Horace.* Cambridge, Massachusetts: Harvard University Press, 1982. 142pp. The author supplies a brief biographical sketch followed by a discussion of the poems in order of their publication. Meant for the scholar and specialist, the book is both learned and provocative in its insights.

Wilkinson, L.P. *Horace and His Lyric Poetry.* 1945. Revised ed. London: Cambridge University Press, 1968. 185pp. Wilkinson's is a solid critical study that provides a careful personality profile based on a informed reading of the poetry.

231. HARRY HOUDINI
1874–1926

American magician born Ehrich Weiss, Houdini took his name from the French magician, Robert Houdin. He became world famous for his escapes from such restraints as locks, handcuffs, straitjackets, and sealed chests under water. He was also noted for his pursuit of fraudulent spiritual mediums and their faked phenomena. He left his valuable library of magic to the Library of Congress.

Recommended Biographies

Brandon, Ruth. *The Life and Many Deaths of Harry Houdini.* New York: Random House, 1993. 355pp. Brandon supplies a fascinating, credible psycho-

logical profile that links Houdini's public career with his private obsessions.

Silverman, Kenneth. *Houdini!!! The Career of Ehrich Weiss.* New York: HarperCollins, 1996. 465pp. Uncovering previously untapped scrapbooks, diaries, court transcripts, and unpublished letters, Silverman provides a balanced, intimate look at Houdini's life and career that substitutes a living portrait in the context of his times for the many legends. A remarkable achievement.

Other Biographical Studies

Christopher, Milbourne. *Houdini: The Untold Story.* New York: Crowell, 1969. 281pp. The author, a past president of the Society of American Musicians, keeps Houdini's trade secrets but uncovers many little-known incidents of his life and aspects of his character, falling short of a fully developed portrait of the inner man. *Houdini: A Pictorial Biography.* (New York: Crowell, 1976. 218pp.) is a comprehensive pictorial biography using posters, photographs, and other Houdini memorabilia, including a facsimile of an autobiographical pamphlet published in 1917.

Fitzsimons, Raymond. *Death and the Magician: The Mystery of Houdini.* New York: Atheneum, 1981. 194pp. Written for the general reader, this is a brief summary of Houdini's stage career with an emphasis on his spiritualist activities.

Gresham, William L. *Houdini, the Man Who Walked through Walls.* New York: Holt, 1959. 306pp. The book reveals some of the Houdini's secrets while objectively presenting his transformation into an international celebrity and the discrepancy between his public persona and private identity.

Kelleck, Harold. *Houdini: His Life Story.* New York: Harcourt, Brace, 1928. 384pp. Kelleck's first full-length biography draws on Houdini's private papers and had the cooperation of Houdini's wife in its preparation. Discreet and selective in its view, the book still remains an important biographical source.

Meyer, Bernard C. *Houdini: A Mind in Chains: A Psychoanalytic Portrait.* New York: Dutton, 1976. 197pp. Meyer's is a detailed psychoanalytical analysis of Houdini's mental and emotional make-up. Much of the evidence cited is questionable and the unrelenting analysis is wearying, but the book does shed an interesting light on Houdini's internal conflicts.

Randi, James, and Bert R. Sugar. *Houdini: His Life and Art.* New York: Grosset & Dunlap, 1976. 191pp. This is a lavishly illustrated biography aimed at the general reader. Avoiding the how-to of Houdini's craft, the book concentrates on his public career, family life, and personality.

Fictional Portraits

Doctorow, E.L. *Ragtime.* New York: Random House, 1975. 270pp. Houdini is a pivotal recurring character in this imaginative repossession of the American scene in the early years of the twentieth century.

Hjortsberg, William. *Nevermore.* New York: Atlantic Monthly Press, 1994. 289pp. Houdini joins forces with Arthur Conan Doyle and the ghostly presence of Edgar Allan Poe to investigate a series of grisly murders.

Michaels, Barbara. *Other Worlds.* New York: HarperCollins, 1999. 217pp. Set "outside of time and space, in the realm of the imagination," the novel brings together Arthur Conan Doyle, Houdini, and other famous psychic researchers to consider two ghost tales in which they each attempt to explain away or justify the occult occurrences.

Satterthwait, Walter. *Escapade.* New York: St. Martin's, 1995. 355pp. An English houseparty murder tests the skills of guests Houdini and Arthur Conan Doyle in a locked-room mystery.

Shatner, William, and Michael Tobias. *Believe.* New York: Berkley Books, 1992. 321pp. Houdini and Arthur Conan Doyle match wits in a debate over the existence of the afterlife.

Stashower, Daniel. *The Adventure of the Ectoplasmic Man.* New York: Morrow, 1985. 203pp. Houdini is connected with Sherlock Holmes in this period mystery; *The Dime Museum Murders.* New York: Avon Books, 1999. 256pp. A young Houdini, assisted by his brother, investigates the bizarre murder of a wealthy New York toymaker in this lighthearted mystery.

Villars, Elizabeth. *One Night in Newport.* Garden City, New York: Doubleday, 1981. 360pp. Houdini is the guest of the rich and famous in 1912 Newport in this period novel concerning the social and financial dealings of the era's wealthiest figures.

Recommended Juvenile Biographies

Alden, Laura. *Houdini.* Chicago: Childrens Press, 1989. 98pp. MG. This is an informative biography focusing on Houdini's escapes, illusions, and crusade against spiritualism.

Kraske, Robert. *Harry Houdini: Master of Magic.* New York: Scholastic, 1989. 72pp. MG. Kraske's is a brief but informative overview of Houdini's career and time.

Woog, Adam. *The Importance of Harry Houdini.* San Diego: Lucent Books, 1995. 112pp. MG. Well researched and illustrated, Woog's biography covers Houdini's life, accomplishments, and significance.

Biographical Films and Theatrical Adaptations

A&E Biography Video: Houdini: The Great Escape (1994). Director: Alison Guss. Using photos, newsreel footage, and interviews with friends, family, and associates, Houdini's life and career is profiled. Video.

FairyTale: A True Story (1997). Director: Charles Sturridge. Arthur Conan Doyle (Peter O'Toole) and Houdini (Harvey Keitel) investigate the claim of two girls in 1917 that they have photographed fairies in their garden, giving the occasion for a spirited debate between the two over the questions of science versus spiritualism. Video.

Houdini (1953). Director: George Marshall. Tony Curtis stars as Houdini in this biographically inac-

curate but entertaining film drama. With Janet Leigh. Video.

Houdini (1986). Director: Elizabeth Koerner. A documentary look at Houdini's career, featuring interviews with the magician's niece and contemporary illusionists. Video.

Houdini (1998). Director: Pen Densham. Made-for-television biography following Houdini's life and career from his birth and immigration to America through his years of fame, with an emphasis on his relationship with his wife. Starring Johnathon Schaech, Stacy Edwards, Paul Sorvino, and David Warner as Arthur Conan Doyle. Video.

Houdini: The Life of the World's Greatest Escapologist (1993). Director: Anne B. Gyles. Originally broadcast by the BBC as part of the television series *Omnibus,* this is an informative biographical profile that chronicles Houdini's life and years in the public spotlight. Video.

Houdini Never Died (1987). Director: Pen Densham. Brief overview of Houdini's life and influences with demonstrations by contemporary magicians and rare footage of Houdini himself. Video.

232. SAM HOUSTON
1793–1863

Frontier hero and Texas statesman, Houston was born in Virginia and raised in Tennessee, where he lived with and was adopted by the Cherokee tribe. He was admitted to the bar (1818), practiced law, served as U.S. congressman (1823, 1825), and elected governor of Tennessee (1827). After moving to Texas (1833), he became a member of the conventions that set up the Texas provisional government and declared Texas independent, and was named commander-in-chief of the revolutionary troops fighting Mexico. At the battle of San Jacinto (1836) he defeated the Mexicans and captured General Santa Anna. Houston was elected the first president of the new Republic of Texas, represented the new state (1845) as senator, and served as governor. He was removed from the governorship (1861) after refusing to support the secession of Texas from the union.

Autobiography and Primary Sources

The Autobiography of Sam Houston. Donald Day and Harry H. Ullam, eds. Norman: University of Oklahoma Press, 1954. 298pp. Somewhat mistitled, this volume does include Houston's own story of his birth and childhood but draws on his letters to chronicle his career with biographical links to fill in the gaps.

The Writings of Sam Houston. Amelia W. Williams and Eugene C. Barker, eds. Austin: University of Texas Press, 1938–1943. 8 vols. With over 2,500 items, including Houston's letters and speeches, this scholarly collection covers his entire career and remains the most important source for primary material.

Recommended Biographies

De Bruhl, Marshall. *Sword of San Jacinto: A Life of Sam Houston.* New York: Random House, 1993. 446pp. Although undocumented, this is a well-researched and reliable account that provides a sympathetic but honest portrait of a complex Houston. Along with Marquis James's work, De Bruhl's biography is recommended for the reader interested in the exciting drama of Houston's life. For a weightier, more interpretively sophisticated treatment, Williams will be preferred.

Friend, Llerena. *Sam Houston: The Great Designer.* Austin: University of Texas Press, 1954. 394pp. Long regarded as one of the most scholarly authoritative studies of Houston, Friend's study draws on the evidence assembled in the eight volumes of Houston's papers. Objective in its assessment, the book concentrates on Houston's political career and provides minimal coverage of his early years, and frontier and military experiences.

James, Marquis. *The Raven: A Biography of Sam Houston.* Indianapolis: Bobbs-Merrill, 1929. 489pp. James's Pulitzer Prize–winning biography remains eminently readable in capturing the epic quality of Houston's life and achievements. Drawing on formerly unavailable family papers, James depicts Houston as a complex three-dimensional figure, but many of the author's interpretations have been challenged by more recent scholarship and sources.

Williams, John Hoyt. *Sam Houston: A Biography of the Father of Texas.* New York: Simon & Schuster, 1993. 448pp. Williams's scholarly assessment is perhaps the most critical of the available biographies. At times, Houston's flaws predominate, but a portrait emerges that places his achievements in their human context, and Houston is revealed as even more remarkable, given his limitations and the challenges he faced.

Other Biographical Studies

Braider, Donald. *Solitary Star: A Biography of Sam Houston.* New York: Putnam, 1974. 344pp. Written for the general reader, Braider's biography corrects some errors found in Marquis James, and is best in capturing the social and historical context for viewing Houston's career. Sometimes speculative with insufficient evidence to support contentions, Braider fails to resolve satisfactorily Houston's enigmatic character.

Creel, George. *Sam Houston: Colossus in Buckskin.* New York: Cosmopolitan, 1928. 340pp. Undocumented and intended for the general reader, this is a colorful, dramatic biographical account by an admirer who, to make a clear case for Houston's heroism, overlooks his many human failings and contradictions.

Gregory, Jack, and Rennard Strickland. *Sam Houston with the Cherokees, 1829–1833.* Austin: University of Texas Press, 1967. 206pp. Beginning in 1829 with Houston's resignation as governor of Tennessee, this is a detailed look at the four years Houston spent among the Cherokees. Based on a good deal of primary evidence, the book sifts through both the facts and the legends to show how Houston's years among the Indians help explain his later actions.

Williams, Alfred M. *Sam Houston and the War of Independence in Texas.* Boston: Houghton Mifflin, 1893. 405pp. The first scholarly assessment of Houston's life and career, Williams's study has long been superseded by later examinations that have more rigorously separated the facts from the legends surrounding Houston.

Wisehart, M.K. *Sam Houston: American Giant.* Washington, DC: Robert B. Luce, 1962. 712pp. This reassessment of Houston's character draws on the evidence of his collected writings and looks at Houston at various important points of his career. The book is sometimes confusing in its organization, but compensates with a sharper character focus than other treatments.

Biographical Novels

Crook, Elizabeth. *The Raven's Bride.* Dallas, Texas: Southern Methodist University Press, 1993. 418pp. The strange story of Houston's 11-week marriage in 1829 to Eliza Allen is dramatized, and the novel imaginatively speculates on the causes for the failure of their marriage; *Promised Lands.* New York: Doubleday, 1994. 511pp. Narrates the events of the Texas Revolution that culminates in the Goliad massacre from participants on both sides.

Gerson, Noel B. *Sam Houston: A Biographical Novel.* Garden City, New York: Doubleday, 1968. 297pp. In an admiring, heroic portrait, Gerson chronicles Houston's life from his early years in Tennessee through his leadership in the Texas Revolution and Republic, and his opposition to secession during the Civil War. Factual, if at times superficial, the novel commits the majority of its invention to depict Houston's early life.

Long, Jeff. *Empire of Bones: A Novel of Sam Houston and the Texas Revolution.* New York: Morrow, 1993. 256pp. Beginning with the Alamo, the novel dramatizes the events of the conflict culminating with the Battle of San Jacinto. Solidly researched, Houston's role in the decisive battle is vividly and reliably captured.

Michener, James A. *The Eagle and the Raven.* Austin, Texas: State House Press, 1990. 214pp. The novel provides the contrasting stories of Houston and Santa Anna. Both are depicted as larger than life but flawed. The book's climax is the decisive Battle of San Jacinto. Houston is also depicted in Michener's panoramic epic of Texas's history, *Texas* (New York: Random House, 1985. 1,096pp.).

Owen, Dean. *The Sam Houston Story.* Derby, Connecticut: Monarch Books, 1961. 210pp. From Houston's days as an Indian fighter through the Texas Revolution, this is a dramatic, fictional account of the highlights of Houston's career. Truthful to history, the novel covers too much territory to be considered thorough.

Robson, Luca St. Clair. *Walk in My Soul.* New York: Ballantine Books, 1985. 644pp. In a mostly invented story, life among the Cherokees in the first third of the nineteenth century is dramatized in a story of a young Cherokee woman's relationship with Sam Houston. The novel draws on Houston's actual four years living among the Indians.

Wellman, Paul I. *Magnificent Destiny: A Novel about the Great Secret Adventure of Andrew Jackson and Sam Houston.* Garden City, New York: Doubleday, 1962. 444pp. Seen largely through Andrew Jackson's perspective, the novel records his relationship with Houston who is shown from his first meeting with Jackson through his years as a congressman and during the struggle of Texas independence.

Fictional Portraits

Davis, J. Frank. *The Road to San Jacinto.* Indianapolis: Bobbs-Merrill, 1936. 334pp. In a faithful account of the events of Texas Revolution, the novel narrates the experiences of young man who finds himself in the center of the conflict.

Giles, Janice Holt. *Savanna.* Boston: Houghton Mifflin, 1961. 312pp. Set in 1830s in the Arkansas Territory, the novel offers an interesting, though mainly invented, look at Houston's pre-Texas life in an authentic re-creation of frontier life.

Harrigan, Steve. *The Gates of the Alamo.* New York: Knopf, 2000. 581pp. The events of the bloody siege at the Alamo is vividly captured in this novel that provides characterizations of the principal leaders, including Houston, Crockett, Travis, Bowie, and Santa Anna, but concentrates more on ordinary participants on both sides of the conflict.

Knaggs, John R. *The Bugles Are Silent: A Novel of the Texas Revolution.* Austin, Texas: Shoal Creek,1977. 287pp. The events and personalities of the conflict are depicted from the perspective of several combatants on both sides with interesting glimpses of Houston and others.

Michener, James A. *Texas.* New York: Random House,1985. 556pp. In Michener's massive historical panorama Houston figures prominently as one of many historical figures who interact with several fictional settlers.

Roark, Garland. *Hellfire Jackson.* Garden City, New York: Doubleday, 1966. 349pp. Set during the Texas Revolution, the novel describes the adventures of a disguised minister who encounters most of the prominent historical figures, including Houston.

Sanders, Leonard. *Star of Empire: A Novel of Old San Antonio.* New York: Delacorte Press, 1992. 437pp. This story of Texas history from the 1830s through the Civil War features the experiences of two brothers, one a protege of Houston who becomes his enemy.

Thompson, E.V. *Republic: A Novel of Texas.* New York: F. Watts, 1985. 436pp. Set in the early days of the Texas Republic, the novel describes the affairs of an Englishman dispatched to report on conditions who finds himself drawn into a series invented intrigues.

Venable, Clarke. *All the Brave Rifles.* Chicago: Reilly & Lee, 1929. 369pp. In this vivid reconstruction of the events in the Texas War of Independence most of the major figures, including Houston, are depicted in a fictional account that stays close to the facts with some embellishment.

Windle, Janice Woods. *True Women.* New York: Putnam, 1993. 451pp. Based on the lives of the au-

thor's ancestors, this historical saga chronicles the history of Texas from the Revolution through World War II.

Recommended Juvenile Biographies

Alter, Judy. *Sam Houston.* New York: Childrens Press, 1998. 42pp. MG. Alter, an adult historical and biographical novelist, provides a concise biography tracing the highlights of Houston's remarkable career.

Fritz, Jean. *Make Way for Sam Houston.* New York: Putnam, 1986. 109pp. MG. Fritz's engaging and candid account of Houston's life in the context of Texas's struggle for independence has all the virtues of the author's many biographies for younger readers: a lively, humorous style and a vivid historical reconstruction.

James, Bessie R., and Marquis James. *Six Feet Six: The Heroic Story of Sam Houston.* Indianapolis: Bobbs-Merrill, 1931. 251pp. YA. Marquis James, who wrote the Pulitzer Prize–winning adult biography of Houston, synthesizes his findings in an excellent version for younger readers.

Wade, Mary D. *I Am Houston.* Houston: Colophon House, 1993. 64pp. MG. This is a vivid, dramatic account of Houston's entire career.

Biographical Films and Theatrical Adaptations

The Alamo (1960). Director: John Wayne. Richard Boone appears on screen briefly as Houston in this heroic spectacle with Wayne as Davy Crockett, Richard Widmark as Jim Bowie, and Laurence Harvey as William Travis. Video.

Alamo: Thirteen Days to Glory (1987). Director: Peter Werner. In this television adaptation of J. Lon Tinkle's book, Lorne Greene appears as Houston with Brian Keith as Davy Crockett, James Arness as Jim Bowie, and Alan Baldwin as William Travis. Video.

The First Texan (1956). Director: Byron Hoskin. Joel McCrea stars as Houston in this biographical film that follows Houston's life from his early years through his presidency of the Republic of Texas.

Gone to Texas (1986). Director: Peter Levin. Sam Elliot portrays Houston in this television drama that depicts scenes from his life. Video.

The Last Command (1955). Director: Frank Lloyd. This depiction of the Alamo massacre focuses on Jim Bowie's role. Sterling Hayden takes the central role with Hugh Sanders as Houston. Video.

Lone Star (1951). Director: Vincent Sherman. In this fictional tale, Clark Gable is dispatched by Andrew Jackson (Lionel Barrymore) to convince Houston (Moroni Olsen) to settle the war with Mexico and lead Texas into the union. Ava Gardner provides the love interest. Video.

Man of Conquest (1939). Director: George Nichols Jr. Early biographical film stars Richard Dix as Houston and truthfully chronicles his career from Tennessee through the events of the Texas Revolution. Edward Ellis appears as Andrew Jackson.

Texas (1994). Director: Richard Long. television mini-series adapted from the Michener book casts

Stacy Keach as Houston, Patrick Duffy as Stephen Austin, and David Keith as Jim Bowie. Video.

True Women (1997). Director: Karen Arthur. An adaptation of the novel by Janice Woods Windle, starring Dana Delauney, Annabeth Gish, and Angelina Jolie. Houston is portrayed by John Schneider. Video.

See also Andrew Jackson

233. HOWARD HUGHES
1905–1976

An American business executive, Hughes inherited (1925) a fortune from his father, which he used to gain sole control of the lucrative Hughes Tool Company. He formed the Hughes Aircraft Company during the 1930s, designed planes, and as an aviator set numerous records. He also produced several motion pictures and during the 1960s purchased a number of Las Vegas casinos. A billionaire, he became a complete recluse in his later years.

Recommended Biographies

Bartlett, Donald L., and James B. Steele. *Empire! The Life, Legend, and Madness of Howard Hughes.* New York: W.W. Norton, 1976. 766pp. Meticulously detailed and well written, this is the best, most comprehensive and objective account of Hughes's life, career, and personality. Although the sensational details of Hughes's remarkable story are duly collected, they are handled without the shrill, tabloid approach of other treatments.

Other Biographical Studies

Brown, Peter H., and Pat H. Broeske. *Howard Hughes: The Untold Story.* New York: Dutton, 1996. 482pp. This is a highly personal account of Hughes's life with an emphasis on his womanizing, his relationship with his mother, and his descent into paranoia and drug addiction.

Drosnin, Michael. *Citizen Hughes.* New York: Holt, 1985. 532pp. Drosnin's is a detailed account of Hughes's life and business dealings during the years 1966 to 1970, based on Hughes's personal memoranda supplied by Hughes's insider, Robert A. Maheu.

Higham, Charles. *Howard Hughes: The Secret Life.* New York: Putnam, 1993. 368pp. The emphasis is on exposé here in a sensationalized approach in which research and interviews are joined with gossip and a good deal of speculation. As one reviewer observed, "It's a bit like reading an endless stream of tabloid headlines or attending a peepshow."

Keats, John. *Howard Hughes.* New York: Random House, 1966. 304pp. A potboiler that cuts and pastes details from back issues of gossip columns and magazines, the book supplies only an external, superficial, and sketchy portrait.

Maheu, Robert, and Richard Hack. *Next to Hughes: Behind the Power and Tragic Downfall of Howard Hughes by His Closest Advisor.* New York: HarperCollins, 1992. 289pp. Maheu presents an account of his association with Hughes from the 1950s to 1970, focusing on his business affairs rather than personal revelations about his character or private life. Maheu handled Hughes's Nevada affairs, speaking with him frequently by telephone, but never met Hughes face to face.

Mathison, Richard R. *His Weird and Wanton Ways: The Secret Life of Howard Hughes.* New York: Morrow, 1977. 247pp. Mathison supplies another sensational tell-all, focused mainly on Hughes's sex life.

Phelan, James. *Howard Hughes: The Hidden Years.* New York: Random House, 1976. 201pp. This is an account of Hughes's last years based on information supplied by Hughes's employees. The book supplies details of Hughes steady decline but few insights into why.

Fictional Portraits

Kaminsky, Stuart M. *The Howard Hughes Affair.* New York: St. Martin's, 1979. 207pp. In the 1940s, Hollywood private eye Toby Peters is hired by Hughes to investigate a series of unexplained occurrences, with Basil Rathbone offering his Sherlock Holmesian assistance.

Biographical Films and Theatrical Adaptations

The Amazing Howard Hughes (1977). Director: William A. Graham. Tommy Lee Jones is convincing in the title role of this made-for-television biography. Co-starring Ed Flanders, James Hampton, and Tovah Feldshuh. Video.

Hughes & Harlow: Angels in Hell (1977). Director: Larry Buchanan. The love affair between Hughes (Victor Holchak) and Jean Harlow (Lindsay Bloom) that occurred during the filming of *Hell's Angels* in 1930 is dramatized. Video.

Melvin and Howard (1984). Director: Jonathan Demme. Jason Robards portrays Hughes in this off-beat drama surrounding lovable loser Melvin Dummar (Paul LeMat) who gives the reclusive Hughes a ride and then figures in his will. Mary Steenburgen and Pamela Reed support. Video.

Tucker: The Man and His Dream (1988). Director: Francis Ford Coppola. Hughes is portrayed by Dean Stockwell in this portrait of industrialist Preston Tucker (Jeff Bridges). Video.

234. LANGSTON HUGHES
1902–1967

African American poet and central figure of the Harlem Renaissance, Hughes is known for his frequent use of dialect and jazz rhythms to depict urban African American life. His poetry volumes include *The Weary Blues* (1926), *Shakespeare in Harlem* (1942), and *One-Way Ticket* (1949). He also wrote plays, children's books, two autobiographies, newspaper sketches, and novels, including *Not Without Laughter* (1930).

Autobiography and Primary Sources

The Big Sea: An Autobiography. 1940. Reprint ed. New York: Hill & Wang, 1963. 335pp. Hughes offers a candid, anecdotal chronicle of his life up to the age of 27, including his freighter trip to Africa, living in Paris, his part in the Harlem Renaissance, his college days, and his early success as a poet.

I Wonder as I Wander: An Autobiography. 1956. Reprint ed. New York: Hill and Wang, 1993. 405pp. A personal narrative of Hughes's travels in Russia, Spain, China, and Japan, Hughes reflects on the period 1931 to 1937.

Arna Bontemps–Langston Hughes Letters, 1925–1967. Charles H. Nichols, ed. New York: Dodd, Mead, 1980. 529pp. From the more than 2,300 letters exchanged between the two writers, Nichols has selected 500 with an emphasis on what they reveal about each's personality and reflection of the cultural and social scene.

Recommended Biographies

Berry, Faith. *Langston Hughes: Before and Beyond Harlem.* Westport, Connecticut: L. Hill, 1983. 376pp. Without the same access as Rampersad to primary sources, Berry's study is still well researched and detailed in its account of Hughes's life up to his permanent move to Harlem in 1948. Berry's conclusion that Hughes was a homosexual is controversial. However, this remains the best single-volume account of the major influences that shaped his life and career.

Rampersad, Arnold. *The Life of Langston Hughes.* New York: Oxford University Press, 1986-88. 2 vols. Rampersad's is a highly acclaimed literary biography and is deservedly considered definitive. Based on full access to the monumental Hughes archive at Yale University and supplemented by extensive interviews, the book is a well-written, sensitive study that traces Hughes's public and private life against a clear cultural background.

Other Biographical Studies

Dickinson, Donald C. *A Bio-Bibliography of Langston Hughes, 1920-67.* 1967. Revised ed. Hamden, Connecticut: Archon Books, 1972. 267pp. Dickinson supplies a useful, detailed biographical essay as well as a bibliography of works by and about Hughes.

Emanuel, James A. *Langston Hughes.* New York: Twayne, 1967. 192pp. Emanuel's critical analysis of Hughes's poetic achievement begins with a brief biographical sketch before proceeding to a thematic analysis of Hughes's poetic development.

Recommended Juvenile Biographies

Hill, Christine M. *Langston Hughes: Poet of the Harlem Renaissance.* Springfield, New Jersey: Enslow, 1997. 128pp. MG/YA. Hill surveys the poet's life and accomplishments in profile that devotes attention to the often overlooked last third of Hughes's life.

Meltzer, Milton. *Langston Hughes: A Biography.* New York: Crowell, 1968. 268pp. YA. Meltzer was Hughes's friend and collaborator as well as a distinguished writer for younger readers. The book relies principally on Hughes's autobiographies, as well as interviews with the writer and by his friends and associates.

Rummel, Jack. *Langston Hughes.* New York: Chelsea House, 1988. 111pp. MG. Well illustrated, this is an informative, full-length portrait that covers the highlights of Hughes's public and private life.

Biographical Films and Theatrical Adaptations

Langston Hughes: The Dream Keeper (1988). Director: Veronica Young. An installment of the PBS Voices and Visions poetry series presents episodes from Hughes's life with recitations from his poetry. Video.

235. VICTOR HUGO
1802–1885

French poet, dramatist, and novelist, Hugo is recognized as a towering literary figure of the nineteenth century. The son of a general under Napoleon, he lived in Italy and Spain as a child and published his first book of poems at an early age. His plays include *Hernani* (1830), a poetic drama which broke with the conventions of the French theatre and caused a riot between the classicists and romanticists; *Le Roi s'amuse* (1832), the basis for Verdi's opera *Rigoletto*; and *Ruy Blas* (1838). His best-known novels are *Notre Dame de Paris* (1831) and *Les Misérables* (1862). Exiled from France because of his opposition to Napoleon III, he returned to Paris in 1870 and was elected to the National Assembly and the Senate. He was publicly venerated and acclaimed in his last years and was buried in the Panthéon.

Autobiography and Primary Sources

The Letters of Victor Hugo. Paul Meurice, ed. Boston: Houghton Mifflin, 1896–1898. 2 vols. Hugo's letters are an indispensable source for the biographer and the reader interested in a firsthand look at the writer.

Recommended Biographies

Maurois, André. *Olympio: The Life of Victor Hugo.* New York: Harper, 1956. 498pp. Using much unpublished material and a massive synthesis of much of the available evidence, Maurois's masterful biography is rich in personal detail and psychological interpretation, forming the most comprehensive portrait of Hugo available. One of the monuments of the biographer's art.

Richardson, Joanna. *Victor Hugo.* New York: St. Martin's, 1976. 334pp. Richardson's critical biography updates factual details based on scholarship in the 20 years since the appearance of Maurois's biography and reaches a very different conclusion. Hugo is shown as a self-centered and self-serving genius whose unflattering private life overshadows his heroic public image. Richardson's study serves as a concise and ultimately balanced critical assessment.

Robb, Graham. *Victor Hugo.* New York: W.W. Norton, 1997. 682pp. Winner of the 1997 Whitbread Biography Award, Robb's reassessment of Hugo's life penetrates the various myths surrounding the writer to present a believable human portrait of a self-invented artists and his complex web of motives and contradictions. Fully documented and making use of the latest research, Robb's life has been deservedly acclaimed as the best available study of the artist.

Other Biographical Studies

Duclaux, Mary. *Victor Hugo.* 1921. Reprint ed. Port Washington, New York: Kennikat Press, 1972. 268pp. Duclaux supplies the main facts surrounding Hugo's private, poetic, and political life in a mainly uncritical appreciation by a staunch admirer.

Edwards, Samuel. *Victor Hugo: A Tumultuous Life.* New York: McKay, 1971. 337pp. A nonscholarly popular study emphasizing Hugo the patriot over the literary artist, Edwards's dramatic account is stuffed with engaging anecdotes but is at times unreliable, cliché-ridden, and shallow in its criticism.

Grant, Elliott M. *The Career of Victor Hugo.* Cambridge, Massachusetts: Harvard University Press, 1945. 365pp. Not a full-scale biography, Grant's study concentrates on Hugo's public career as a writer and political figure. Sound and solidly based on the best primary and secondary sources then available, the book remains insightful and useful despite its being superseded at several places by more recent scholarship.

Houston, John Porter. *Victor Hugo.* 1974. Revised ed. New York: Twayne, 1988. 192pp. Houston supplies an extensive chronology and a survey of Hugo's life and work in a compact critical overview.

Josephson, Matthew. *Victor Hugo: A Realistic Biography of the Great Romantic.* Garden City, New York: Doubleday, 1942. 514pp. Josephson's comprehensive life, written for the nonspecialist, interprets Hugo's life as the search for artistic freedom, a theme of compelling relevance in the context of World War II when the book appeared. The book still serves as a readable, dramatic narrative that captures the epic and heroic sweep of Hugo's life.

Biographical Films and Theatrical Adaptations

Suez (1938). Director: Allan Dwan. Victor Varconi appears briefly as Hugo in this historically unreliable drama concerning Ferdinand de Lesseps's (Tyrone Power) drive to build the Suez Canal. Loretta Young and Annabella provide his conflicting love interests.

Other Sources

Frey, John A. *A Victor Hugo Encyclopedia.* Westport, Connecticut: Greenwood, 1999. 305pp. This reference tool supplies a brief biographical sketch followed by alphabetical entries on various aspects of Hugo's life and work.

236. ALDOUS HUXLEY
1894–1963

English author, Huxley came to the United States in the late 1930s and settled in California. His most famous novel is *Brave New World* (1932), which depicts a nightmarish twenty-fifth-century utopian civilization. Other novels by Huxley include *Point Counter Point* (1928), *Eyeless in Gaza* (1936), and *The Devils of Loudon* (1952). He also produced collections of short stories and essays such as *Brave New World Revisited* (1958).

Autobiography and Primary Sources

Letters of Aldous Huxley. Grover Smith, ed. New York: Harper & Row, 1970. 992pp. Beginning in 1899 and ending just before Huxley's death, this collection of letters is an invaluable gauge of the writer's observations, views of the intellectual scene, and his many interests through each stage of Huxley's career.

Recommended Biographies

Bedford, Sybille. *Aldous Huxley: A Biography.* New York: Knopf, 1974. 805pp. Bedford's remains the standout, definitive biography. Based on diaries, letters, interviews, and firsthand observations, the book provides a detailed chronological narrative of Huxley's life and career. The writer, herself a novelist, has captured the significant events vividly, constructing a multidimensional portrait of the writer by a close focus on his relationships.

Thody, Philip. *Huxley: A Biographical Introduction.* New York: Scribner, 1973. 144pp. More an inward analysis of Huxley's intellectual and artistic development, Thody examines the writer's ideas and the autobiographical elements in his novels. For the reader unwilling to tackle the more formidable, definitive life by Bedford, this is a useful, concise account of the author's life and work.

Other Biographical Studies

Dunaway, David K. *Huxley in Hollywood.* New York: Harper & Row, 1989. 458pp. Focused on Huxley's life in Hollywood from 1937 to his death, Dunaway provides a thorough documentation of Huxley's activities, relationships, and literary production during this period of his life.

Dunaway, David K. *Aldous Huxley Recollected: An Oral History.* New York: Carroll & Graf, 1995. 225pp. This collection of anecdotes from Huxley's family, friends, and colleagues concentrates on his years in Hollywood and his experimentation with meditation and mind-altering drugs.

Huxley, Laura Archera. *This Timeless Moment: A Personal View of Aldous Huxley.* New York: Farrar, Straus, 1968. 240pp. Huxley's second wife recollects her life with the writer from 1948 until his death based on reconstructed conversations and excerpts from Huxley's writings. This is an intimate, tender portrait that sheds considerable light on Huxley's personality and intellectual interests.

Biographical Films and Theatrical Adaptations

Priest of Love (1981). Director: Christopher Miles. Film portrait of the final years in the life of D.H. Lawrence (Ian McKellen) features an appearance by Huxley, played by James Faulkner. Video.

I

237. HENRIK IBSEN
1828–1906

No playwright has influenced twentieth-century drama as profoundly as Norwegian-born playwright Henrik Ibsen. His works, together with those of Swedish dramatist August Strindberg, explore character, gender, culture, and symbolism in ways that mark the advent of modern drama. Apprenticed to an apothecary at 16, Ibsen began writing poetry and by 1850 had published a verse play, *Catalina*. He next served an extended apprenticeship as stage manager and playwright with the National Stage in Bergen and as theatre director for Oslo's Norwegian Theatre. After his early plays were received with hostility and lack of critical understanding, he left Norway for Italy (1864); it was there and in Germany that he wrote the majority of his plays. He reached prominence as a dramatist with the first of his major works, *Brand* (1866). Among Ibsen's many notable dramas are *A Doll's House* (1879), *An Enemy of the People* (1882), *Hedda Gabler* (1890), and *The Master Builder* (1892).

Autobiography and Primary Sources

Letters of Henrik Ibsen. Mary Morrison, ed. New York: Duffield, 1908. 463pp. Ibsen's letters shed considerable light on his character, ideas, and creative method.

Recommended Biographies

Jorgenson, Theodore. *Henrik Ibsen: Life and Drama*. Northfield, Minnesota: St. Olaf College Press, 1945. 550pp. This critical biography provides separate chapters on each of the major plays and relates them to Ibsen's life and development as an artist and thinker.

Meyer, Michael. *Ibsen: A Biography*. Garden City, New York: Doubleday, 1971. 865pp. Meyer's reevaluation of Ibsen's life and work in the light of new material is commonly regarded as the definitive modern life, particularly strong on the theatrical world that Ibsen worked in and helped to transform.

Other Biographical Studies

Downs, Brian W. *Ibsen: The Intellectual Background*. Cambridge, Massachusetts: Cambridge University Press, 1946. 187pp. Downs traces Ibsen's relationship to his times, and his intellectual development is seen from the broader context of European thought.

Gosse, Edmund. *Henrik Ibsen*. New York: Scribner, 1907. 244pp. Gosse's biographical sketch is dominated by the author's definite viewpoint that later studies have challenged. Serves as a compact critical analysis connecting Ibsen's life, intellectual development, and artistry into a comprehensive, if debatable, pattern.

Heiberg, Hans. *Ibsen: A Portrait of the Artist*. Coral Gables, Florida: University of Miami Press, 1969. 319pp. Heiberg offers an interpretation of Ibsen's development to help explain his art and life. The book serves to locate Ibsen in the cultural context of European and Norwegian history.

Jaeger, Henrik B. *Henrik Ibsen, 1828-88: A Critical Biography*. 1890. Reprint ed. New York: B. Blom, 1972. 275pp. Jaeger's early study draws on the author's personal acquaintance and interviews, which provide original details on Ibsen's early life. However, the book cannot take advantage of the many facts and sources that emerged only after Ibsen's death.

Koht, Halvden. *Life of Ibsen*. 1931. Revised ed. New York: B. Blom, 1971. 507pp. Koht's comprehensive biography and interpretive study is fully documented and serves to connect details from Ibsen's plays with his life and intellectual development. Remains a valuable study of Ibsen's life and works.

Zucker, A.E. *Ibsen: The Master Builder*. New York: Holt, 1929. 319pp. This thorough, straightforward account helpfully captures Ibsen's humanity by drawing extensively on eyewitness testimony of those who knew him.

Biographical Films and Theatrical Adaptations

The Modern World: Ten Great Writers (1988). Director: David Thomas. An installment of the London Weekend Television series looks at Ibsen's life and literary career. Video.

Song of Norway (1970). Director: Andrew L. Stone. In this scenically stunning but biographically unreliable dramatization of the early life of composer Edvard Grieg (Toralv Maurstad), Frederick Jaeger appears briefly as Ibsen. Video.

Other Sources

Bryan, George B. *An Ibsen Companion*. Westport, Connecticut: Greenwood, 1984. 437pp. An alphabetical guide to Ibsen's life, work, and critical reception, this is an invaluable reference tool for students, scholars, and general readers.

McFarlane, James, ed. *The Cambridge Companion to Ibsen*. New York: Cambridge University Press, 1994. 271pp. This collection of critical essays touches on various aspects of Ibsen's thoughts, personality, and artistry and reflects the most recent scholarship and critical responses.

238. IGNATIUS OF LOYOLA
1491–1556

Spanish churchman, founder of the Society of Jesus (Jesuits), and the order's first general, Ignatius was of noble birth and was raised as a courtier. He joined the army (1517) and while convalescing from a wound (1521) converted to the religious life through reading a life of Christ. He was ordained in 1537. He formed the Society of Jesus with Francis Xavier and four others; in 1540 its constitutions, written by Ignatius, won papal acceptance. In addition to the *Constitutions*, by which the Jesuits have been governed since the order's founding, Ignatius wrote *Spiritual Exercises*, begun in 1522 and written over a number of years.

Autobiography and Primary Sources

The Autobiography of Saint Ignatius Loyola. John C. Olin, ed. New York: Fordham University Press, 1993. 113pp. Ignatius's reflections on his spiritual development were dictated to a disciple and are restricted to his inner life during his formative years.

Letters of Saint Ignatius of Loyola. William J. Young, ed. Chicago: Loyola University Press, 1959. 450pp. This is a selection of 228 letters taken from the 12-volume Spanish edition that offers a coherent view of Ignatius's life and personality in his own words.

Recommended Biographies

Caraman, Phillip. *Ignatius Loyola: A Biography of the Founder of the Jesuits.* San Francisco: Harper & Row, 1990. 222pp. Caraman presents an intimate portrait of Ignatius that incorporates recent scholarship. Particularly good on the Iberian background, this is the best introductory biography available.

Meissner, William W. *Ignatius of Loyola: The Psychology of a Saint.* New Haven, Connecticut: Yale University Press, 1992. 480pp. Written by a Jesuit and a psychoanalyst, Meissner's Freudian reading of Ignatius's life and development resists reductionism and largely succeeds in balancing the spiritual and the psychological. Although the non-specialist will likely be overwhelmed by the details Meissner assembles to present his analysis and his jargon, this is a provocative and rich portrait.

O'Malley, John W. *The First Jesuits.* Cambridge, Massachusetts: Harvard University Press, 1993. 457pp. O'Malley's scholarly account of the formative years of the Jesuit order, from 1540 to 1565, is the best book of its kind currently available. Candid and iconoclastic, O'Malley's authoritative study demolishes a number of myths that have distorted a factual view of both Ignatius and the order he founded.

Other Biographical Studies

Brodrick, James. *Saint Ignatius Loyola: The Pilgrim Years.* New York: Farrar, Straus, 1956. 372pp. The book restricts its view to the years of Ignatius's self-searching travels, and provides a meticulously researched reconstruction of his journeys and the resulting impact on his development.

Dudon, Paul. *St. Ignatius of Loyola.* Milwaukee: Bruce, 1949. 484pp. Dudon's is a reliable, objective, and well-documented summary of Ignatius's life and the formation and development of the Jesuit order.

Harvey, Robert. *Ignatius Loyola: A General in the Church Militant.* Milwaukee: Bruce, 1936. 273pp. Written by an non-Catholic enthusiast, Harvey's uncritical and frequently nonpenetrating examination at least considers Ignatius's achievement freed from the bias of dogma or devotion. This is a faithful record of Ignatius's activities, if an unsatisfactory explanation of his motives.

Hollis, Christopher. *Saint Ignatius.* New York: Harper, 1931. 287pp. Hollis's psychological study makes Ignatius's character and motives intelligible, but the historical background painting is inadequate and superficial.

Marcuse, Ludwig. *Soldier of the Church: A Life of Ignatius of Loyola.* New York: Simon & Schuster, 1939. 352pp. This somewhat fictionalized popular biography offers its speculation undistinguished from its facts, and is best on the background details that help frame Ignatius's story into a vivid, if unreliable, drama.

Matt, Leonard von, and Hugo Rahner. *St. Ignatius of Loyola: A Pictorial Biography.* Chicago: Regnery, 1956. 106pp. The book's many photo-

graphs are linked by a brief biographical text that serves as a useful introduction to the man and his era.

Maynard, Theodore. *Saint Ignatius and the Jesuits.* New York: Kennedy, 1956. 213pp. Maynard's is a reliable and thoughtful overview of Ignatius's life and work.

Purcell, Mary. *The First Jesuit: Saint Ignatius of Loyola.* 1957. Revised ed. Chicago: Loyola University Press, 1981. 294pp. Based on original sources, this is a readable popular account with a number of insights into Ignatius's character and behavior, though often idealized and devotional.

Tellechea Idígoras, J. Ignacio. *Ignatius of Loyola: The Pilgrim Saint.* Chicago: Loyola University Press, 1994. 628pp. Ignatius is allowed to tell his own story here through extensive excerpts from his autobiographical and spiritual writings and letters, supplemented by the author's period reconstruction.

Biographical Novels

De Wohl, Louis. *The Golden Thread.* Philadelphia: Lippincott, 1952. 254pp. Ignatius's transformation from worldly nobleman and soldier to religious leader is chronicled from 1521 to his death.

Fictional Portraits

De Wohl, Louis. *Set All Afire: A Novel of St. Francis Xavier.* Philadelphia: Lippincott, 1953. 280pp. Xavier's missionary work in Asia is depicted with an appearance by Ignatius as his prime motivator.

Recommended Juvenile Biographies

Janda, James. *Iñigo: The Life of St. Ignatius Loyola for Young Readers.* New York: Paulist Press, 1995. 85p YA. This is an inspiring, devotional look at Ignatius's life and work.

Biographical Films and Theatrical Adaptations

Pioneers of the Spirit: Ignatius Loyola (1998). Producer: Trinity Television. Part of a multipart series on significant men and women of faith. Video.

239. WASHINGTON IRVING
1783–1859

A literary idol in the United States, Irving was the first American author to achieve recognition in Europe. His first literary efforts were essays on New York society and the theater, and in 1809 he published his satirical *A History of New York*, considered the first example of American comic literature. His most famous stories, "Rip Van Winkle," and "The Legend of Sleepy Hollow," appeared in *The Sketch Book of Geoffrey Crayon* (1820). From 1842 to 1846 he served as the American minister to Spain.

Autobiography and Primary Sources

Readers interested in approaching Irving in his own words have a number of choices, including *Memoir of Washington Irving: With Selections from His*

Works and Criticism. Charles F. Adams, ed. 1810. Reprinted. (Freeport, New York: Books for Libraries Press, 1971. 299pp.); *Letters* (Boston: Twayne, 1978–1982. 4 vols.); and *Journals and Notebooks.* Wayne R. Klime, et al., eds. (Madison: University of Wisconsin Press, 1969–1986. 5 vols.).

Recommended Biographies

Rubin-Dorsky, Jeffrey. *Adrift in the Old World: The Psychological Pilgrimage of Washington Irving.* Chicago: University of Chicago Press, 1988. 328pp. This critical reevaluation of Irving's fiction from 1815 to 1832 traces the writer's development and American identity and delivers a coherent portrait despite occasional speculative leaps from scanty biographical and historical evidence.

Wagenknecht, Edward. *Washington Irving: Moderation Displayed.* New York: Oxford University Press, 1962. 223pp. The author concentrates on revealing Irving's personality and achieves a rounded picture that refuses to sentimentalize but does not neglect the writer's considerable charm.

Williams, Stanley T. *The Life of Washington Irving.* New York: Oxford University Press, 1935. 2 vols. Long considered the definitive life, Williams's comprehensive and authoritative study is scholarly but readable, synthesizing both primary and secondary sources into the standard factual record of Irving's life and character with both established in their historical context.

Other Biographical Studies

Bowers, Claude G. *The Spanish Adventures of Washington Irving.* Boston: Houghton Mifflin, 1940. 306pp. Bowers concentrates on Irving's stay in Spain in an anecdotal and often fictionalized narrative.

Cater, Harold D. *Washington Irving at Sunnyside.* Tarrytown, New York: Sleepy Hollow Restorations, 1957. 45pp. Written by the Executive Director of the Sleepy Hollow Restorations, this is a reliable account of Irving's life at Sunnyside in Tarrytown, New York.

Hedges, William. *Washington Irving: An American Study, 1802–1832.* Baltimore: Johns Hopkins University Press, 1965. 274pp. Hedges sets Irving in his American context as a participant in the development of an indigenous literature, providing as well a psychological profile based on a close reading of his works.

Hellman, George. *Washington Irving: Esquire, Ambassador at Large from the New World to the Old.* New York: Knopf, 1925. 355pp. Supplementing Pierre Irving's multivolume life with a good deal of original material, this is a solid, workmanlike effort that manages a more human and realistic portrait of the man and the artist than previous treatments.

Irving, Pierre M. *The Life and Letters of Washington Irving.* 1862–1864. Reprint ed. Detroit: Gale Research, 1967. 4 vols. The authorized initial biography by Irving's nephew established many of the romanticized legends surrounding Irving that subsequent biographers have challenged and corrected.

McClary, Ben H., ed. *Washington Irving and the House of Murray: Geoffrey Crayon Charms the British 1817–56.* Knoxville: University of Tennessee Press, 1969. 242pp. Irving's English reputation is solidly detailed in this scholarly collection that focuses on the writer's relationship with his English publisher, John Murray.

McFarland, Philip J. *Sojourners.* New York: Atheneum, 1979. 587pp. McFarland's unusual "multiple biography" approaches Irving through the people he knew. The result is a comprehensive group portrait of the man and his age.

Reichart, Walter A. *Washington Irving and Germany.* Ann Arbor: University of Michigan Press, 1957. 212pp. Irving's tour of Germany and Austria is the focus here in a scholarly, reliable sifting of extensive sources into an authoritative treatment.

Warner, Charles D. *Washington Irving.* Boston: Houghton Mifflin, 1881. 304pp. Warner's popular study draws on Pierre Irving's life for its facts and adds nothing new to the portrait of the writer beside an attempt to locate him in the context of an emerging American literary tradition.

Biographical Novels

Johnston, Johanna. *The Heart that Would Not Hold: A Biography of Washington Irving.* New York: M. Evans, 1971. 376pp. This fictionalized and romanticized narrative must be regarded as a biographical novel due to its inventions. The book concentrates on Irving's romantic sensibility and his relationships. The last 30 years of Irving's life are skimmed over in fewer than 50 pages.

Recommended Juvenile Biographies

Seton, Anya. *Washington Irving.* Boston: Houghton Mifflin, 1960. 184pp. MG/YA. In a well-written account, Seton covers Irving's full career, character, and relationships.

Wood, James P. *Sunnyside: A Life of Washington Irving.* New York: Pantheon, 1967. 182pp. YA. Wood concentrates on Irving's later life, combining literary criticism with biographical details to offer a sophisticated view of the author in his cultural context.

Biographical Films and Theatrical Adaptations

Little Old New York (1940). Director: Harry King. Theodore von Eltz portrays Irving in this romanticized treatment of Robert Fulton (Richard Greene) and his steamboat. Alice Faye, Brenda Joyce, and Fred MacMurray co-star. Video.

Poe/Cooper/Irving (1987). Producer: January Productions. Part of the Meet the Classic Authors series, each of the three American writers are profiled. Video.

240. ISABELLA I
1451–1504

The daughter of John II of Castile, Isabella married Ferdinand of Aragón in 1469. After the death of her half-brother (1474), she waged civil war against Juana la Beltraneja, who was supported by Alfonso V of Portugal, for the Castilian succession. She was victorious in 1479, the same year Ferdinand became king of Aragón. Known as the Catholic Kings, Isabella and Ferdinand ruled Castile and Aragón jointly, one result of which was a unified Spanish kingdom. During their reign, the Moors were driven out of Granada, and the arts and architecture flourished. Isabella revived the medieval Hermandad, an armed peacekeeping organization, to assert royal authority over the lawless Spanish nobles, limited the power of the religious military orders, established the Inquisition under royal control, expelled the Jews, forced the conversion of the Moors, and sponsored the explorations of Christopher Columbus.

Recommended Biographies

Liss, Peggy K. *Isabel the Queen: The Life and Times.* New York: Oxford University Press, 1992. 398pp. In a comprehensive and readable account, Liss places Isabella in her political and social context and makes a convincing case that she was a product of her environment. Dispelling many myths surrounding the queen, the book is particularly strong on Isabella's adolescence.

Rubin, Nancy. *Isabella of Castile: The First Renaissance Queen.* New York: St. Martin's, 1991. 468pp. Rubin provides a detailed and reliable account of Isabella's character and her reign with an emphasis on her considerable accomplishments. Apologetic of the queen's flaws and policy errors, the book is nonetheless a useful modern assessment of Isabella and her impact.

Other Biographical Studies

Fernández-Armesto, Felipe. *Ferdinand and Isabella.* New York: Taplinger, 1975. 209pp. This is reliable summary of the monarchs' lives together, along with a history of Castile during their reign. The book is strongest in its analysis of the interactions between the couples' personalities and their political activities.

McKendrick, Melveena. *Ferdinand and Isabella.* New York: American Heritage, 1968. 151pp. This is an informative historical review of Isabella's reign with solid details on the period background.

Miller, Townsend. *The Castle and the Crown: Spain 1451–1555.* New York: Coward-McCann, 1963. 379pp. In an undocumented, popular account, Isabella and the Spanish monarchy are viewed in a fully realized period context. A vivid and dramatic narrative history, the book also offers character analysis of the major figures.

Prescott, William H. *The History of the Reign of Ferdinand and Isabella.* New York: Harper, 1837. 3 vols. Prescott's is a classic historical account in which Isabella's reign is lit by the author's remarkable descriptive and narrative style.

Walsh, William T. *Isabella of Spain: The Last Crusader.* New York: McBride, 1930. 515pp. Isabella is seen sympathetically from a pro-Catholic perspective in her importance as a fighter for Christian civilization in Europe. Although carefully documented, Walsh's study is biased in its perspective and is interesting as an alternative view but not as a balanced assessment.

Biographical Novels

Kesten, Hermann. *Ferdinand and Isabella.* New York: A.A. Wyn, 1946. 373pp. In a biographical novel dramatizing Isabella's reign, the queen emerges as a complex blend of religious zeal and steely determination that formed a mixed legacy for Spain.

Lofts, Norah. *Crown of Aloes.* Boston: G.K. Hall, 1974. 612pp. On her deathbed Isabella reflects on her remarkable career. Based on fact, the author invents certain details to aid characterization.

Schoonover, Lawrence. *The Queen's Cross: A Biographical Romance of Queen Isabella of Spain.* New York: W. Sloane, 1955. 377pp. Combining factual material with fictional embellishment, the novel chronicles Isabella's reign, including the consolidation of power in Spain, the negotiation with Columbus, and the working of the Inquisition.

Fictional Portraits

Fast, Howard. *Torquemada.* Garden City, New York: Doubleday, 1966. 192pp. The novel captures the atmosphere of the Spanish Inquisition in a dramatic narrative centered on the relationship between Torquemada and a lifelong friend who is suspected of being a Jewish sympathizer.

Frolich, Newton. *1492.* New York: St. Martin's, 1990. 404pp. This dramatization of Columbus's life prior to his epic voyage concerns his negotiations with Isabella and the workings of the Inquisition.

Posse, Abel. *The Dogs of Paradise.* New York: Atheneum, 1987. 301pp. Columbus's voyage is viewed in a blend of fantasy and historical fact. Isabella and Ferdinand's court is vividly described.

Schoonover, Lawrence. *The Prisoner of Tordesillas.* Boston: Little, Brown, 1959. 309pp. The novel dramatizes the tragic life of Juana of Castile, the daughter of Ferdinand and Isabella, who spent nearly 50 years imprisoned in the fortress of Tordesillas.

Recommended Juvenile Biographies

Burch, Joann J. *Isabella of Castile: Queen on Horseback.* New York: F. Watts, 1991. 63pp. MG. A straightforward introduction to Isabella and her times, the book is illustrated with archival material.

Stevens, Paul. *Ferdinand and Isabella.* New York: Chelsea House, 1988. 111pp. MG. An informative summary of Isabella's life and reign that makes the complex politics of the period comprehensible.

Biographical Films and Theatrical Adaptations

Ferdinand and Isabella (1995). Directors: Jerry Baber and Rhonda Fabian. Adapted from the juvenile biography by Paul Stevens, this is a film portrait of the Spanish monarchs. Video.

See also Christopher Columbus

241. IVAN THE TERRIBLE
1533–1584

The first Russian ruler to formally assume the title of czar, Ivan IV succeeded (1533) his father Vasily III under the regency of his mother, which after her death (1538) alternated between several feuding Boyar families. After his coronation (1547), Ivan attempted to create a czarist autocracy by reducing the arbitrary governing powers of the Boyar nobles and establishing a general council with representatives of different social ranks. He reorganized the army, began Russia's eastward expansion, and encouraged trade with England. Peace treaties negotiated (1582, 1583) after an unsuccessful war against Poland and Sweden resulted in the loss of Russian territory. Paranoid and tyrannical in his later years, Ivan formed the *oprichnik* (1565), a special corps, to conduct a reign of terror against the Boyars. His cruelty is legendary. In one fit of rage, he killed his son and heir and dispatched unwanted wives by forcing them to take the veil or by having them murdered.

Recommended Biographies

Bobrick, Benson. *Fearful Majesty: The Life and Times of Ivan the Terrible.* New York: Putnam, 1987. 398pp. Based on up-to-date research, Bobrick focuses on Ivan's personality and political role and makes both comprehensible against a solid historical perspective. The book succeeds in transforming Ivan from a mad and villainous figure to a tragic one. Recommended as the best available modern interpretation of the man and his reign.

Grey, Ian. *Ivan the Terrible.* Philadelphia: Lippincott, 1964. 258pp. The book provides a realistic portrait of Ivan set against an authentic period background. Grey attempts to understand Ivan by the standards of his time. Clearly written and exhaustively researched, the book sets the factual record straight to form a believable profile of the man.

Troyat, Henri. *Ivan the Terrible.* New York: Dutton, 1984. 283pp. Troyat's detailed psychological portrait locates the key to Ivan's character in incidents from his early life. Concentrating on personality, the book neglects the historical perspective although there is a vivid depiction of sixteenth-century Moscow.

Other Biographical Studies

Carr, Francis. *Ivan the Terrible.* Totowa, New Jersey: Barnes and Noble, 1981. 220pp. Carr's history of Ivan's reign is marred by a simplistic thesis suggesting that the roots of Russia's aggressive imperialism can be traced back to the sixteenth century and a strained comparison between Ivan and Stalin.

Graham, Stephen. *Ivan the Terrible: The Life of Ivan IV of Russia.* New Haven, Connecticut: Yale University Press, 1933. 335pp. Graham's detailed account of Ivan's life and times, relying on contemporary sources, disputes the notion that the czar was mad, and offers a psychological assessment to explain his behavior.

Koslow, Jules. *Ivan the Terrible.* New York: Hill & Wang, 1962. 271pp. Although undocumented, this is a detailed narrative account that serves to capture both the era and the man in a vivid, dramatic presentation.

Payne, Robert, and Nikita Romanoff. *Ivan the Terrible.* New York: Crowell, 1975. 502pp. This popular biography that blends history, myth, and folklore is a lively, dramatic account of Ivan and his reign in which multiple grisly details are presented to support a depiction of the czar's madness and villainy.

Platonov, Sergei. *Ivan the Terrible.* Gulf Breeze, Florida: Academic International Press, 1974. 166pp. This straightforward analytical look at Ivan's reign by a Soviet historian is a balanced assessment that includes both a psychological profile based on the facts and a wider historical and cultural consideration of Ivan's rule. Includes a useful essay by Richard Hellie on Russian views of Ivan.

Skrynnikov, Ruslan G. *Ivan the Terrible.* Gulf Breeze, Florida: Academic International Press, 1981. 219pp. Contradicting many of the psychological interpretations of Ivan's character, Skrynnikov takes Ivan seriously as a strong ruler who made an important impact on the formation of the Russian state. A solid, objective account primarily for the history student.

Von Eckhardt, Hans. *Ivan the Terrible.* New York: Knopf, 1949. 421pp. This comprehensive biography based on extensive primary research serves more as a political biography that looks beyond Ivan's shocking behavior to place his actions in a wider historical context.

Waliszewski, Kazimierz. *Ivan the Terrible.* 1904. Reprint ed. Hamden, Connecticut: Archon Books, 1966. 431pp. This densely written but richly detailed biography remains valuable primarily for its anecdotal material that has been used by subsequent biographers for context and color to capture Ivan and his times.

Biographical Novels

Townsend, Larry. *Czar! A Novel of Ivan the Terrible.* Los Angeles: L.T. Publications, 1998. 650pp. Ivan's reign is depicted through the experiences of a fictional nobleman who remains loyal even as the czar's madness increases.

Fictional Portraits

Dunnett, Dorothy. *The Ringed Castle.* 1972. Reprint ed. New York: Vintage Books, 1997. 521pp. In this installment of the author's Lymond saga, Francis Crawford serves as Ivan's aide in administering rough justice to the czar's enemies. The period details are convincingly drawn.

Macleod, Alison. *The Muscovite.* Boston: Houghton Mifflin, 1971. 319pp. Based on the true story of an English trader to the court of Ivan the Terrible, the novel uses the trader's own accounts to re-create faithfully the period and its personalities at the Russian court.

Rutherfurd, Edward. *Russka: The Novel of Russia.* New York: Crown, 1991. 760pp. The novel's panoramic tableaux of 1,800 years of Russian history includes a depiction of Ivan the Terrible and his impact on Russian history.

Tolstoy, Aleksy. *Prince of Outlaws.* New York: Knopf, 1927. 406pp. The novel dramatizes the bloody reign of Ivan through the experiences of a Russian prince who opposes the czar and is forced to head a band of outlaws.

White, Leslie Turner. *Sir Rogue.* New York: Crown, 1954. 310pp. In a swashbuckling adventure tale an English nobleman must deliver a beautiful young girl to Ivan.

Yarbro, Chelsea Quinn. *Darker Jewels.* New York: Tor, 1993. 398pp. In this installment of Yarbro's historical vampire series, the court of Ivan the Terrible is the setting as the Comte de Saint-Germain helps assuage the czar's guilty conscience after his murder of his eldest son.

Recommended Juvenile Biographies

Apsler, Alfred. *Ivan the Terrible.* New York: J. Messner, 1971. 192pp. MG. Using some fictionalization, Apsler covers fully the historical period and provides insights into Ivan's complex character.

Butson, Thomas G. *Ivan the Terrible.* New York: Chelsea House, 1987. 112pp. MG/YA. In a balanced account, the book makes a case for Ivan's achievements as a ruler despite his cruelties.

Biographical Films and Theatrical Adaptations

Ivan the Terrible (1944–1946). Director: Sergei Eisenstein. Eisenstein's classic, lavish historical spectacle chronicles Ivan's reign from his coronation through several events of his reign. Nikolai Cherkassov plays Ivan in an intriguingly complex bravura performance. A planned third part was scripted but never filmed. Eisenstein's complete screenplay is available (New York: Simon & Schuster, 1970. 264pp.). Video.

242. ANDREW JACKSON
1767–1845

The seventh U.S. president (1829–1837), Jackson was born in a frontier region between North and South Carolina known as the Waxhaws. Orphaned at 14, he was a volunteer with the Revolutionary forces (1781). He was admitted to the bar in 1787, practiced law and served as public prosecutor in Tennessee Territory, member of the state House of Representatives, United States senator, and superior court judge. Jackson became a military hero of the War of 1812 after his army defeated the British at the Battle of New Orleans. A popular public figure affectionately nicknamed "Old Hickory," Jackson easily defeated John Quincy Adams in 1828 after losing to Adams in a hotly contested 1824 election decided by the House of Representatives. As president, he introduced the spoils system—rewarding Democratic party members with government posts—and caused controversy by depositing federal funds in Democratic banks rather than in the Bank of the United States.

Autobiography and Primary Sources

The Correspondence of Andrew Jackson. John S. Bassett, ed. Washington, DC: Carnegie Institute, 1926–1935. 7 vols. Until the completion of the *Papers,* this remains the largest available collection of Jackson's letters.

Narrative and Writings of Andrew Jackson. 1847. Reprint ed. Miami, Florida: Mnemosyne, 1969. 120pp. Jackson's autobiographical reflections were narrated to an unidentified writer who arranged them into a chronological sequence.

The Papers of Andrew Jackson. Harold D. Moser and Sharon MacPherson, eds. Knoxville: University of Tennessee Press, 1980–1991. 3 vols. This scholarly edition of Jackson's writings has now reached 1815 and when eventually completed will become an indispensable primary source for biographers and historians.

Recommended Biographies

Cole, Donald B. *The Presidency of Andrew Jackson.* Lawrence: University Press of Kansas, 1993. 342pp. This evenhanded and detailed look at Jackson's administration is widely regarded as the standard one-volume account of the Jackson presidency. Although granting Jackson's considerable leadership skills, Cole shows Jackson as often insecure and controlled by forces.

Parton, James. *Life of Andrew Jackson.* New York: Mason Brothers, 1860. 3 vols. Written by a distinguished nineteenth-century historian, Parton's biography served as the standard life until Remini's trilogy. Its chief value today rests in its source material based on the author's access to eyewitnesses.

Remini, Robert V. *Andrew Jackson and the Course of American Empire, 1767–1821.* New York: Harper & Row, 1977. 502pp.; *Andrew Jackson and the Course of American Freedom, 1822–1832.* New York: Harper & Row, 1981. 469pp.; *Andrew Jackson and the Course of American Democracy, 1833–1845.* New York: Harper & Row, 1984. 638pp. Remini's exhaustive, authoritative study is widely regarded as the definitive life. Wonderfully readable, the trilogy presents not only a complex portrait of Jackson, based on the best modern sources, but a superb recreation of the era. A one-volume condensation of Remini's study is also available as *The Life of Andrew Jackson* (New York: Harper & Row, 1988. 412pp.).

Other Biographical Studies

Bassett, John S. *The Life of Andrew Jackson.* 1911. Revised ed. New York: Macmillan, 1916. 2 vols. With a close and balanced focus on Jackson based on the letters and other manuscript sources, Bassett's workmanlike study is reliable but unsatisfying on the early years and the historical context.

Curtis, James C. *Andrew Jackson and the Search for Vindication.* Boston: Little, Brown, 1976. 194pp. In a strong revision of the heroic image, Curtis looks at Jackson's public career as a reflection of his tormented personality. His Jackson is a self-centered survivor dominated by a ruthless pursuit of power.

Davis, Burke. *Old Hickory: A Life of Andrew Jackson.* New York: Dial Press, 1977. 438pp. In Davis's popular biography Jackson's personality is the center of interest with his life and career presented in clear, dramatic lines. Somewhat old-fashioned in the light of modern scholarship, Davis's treatment restores the heroic image of Jackson that other historians and biographers have reassessed.

Eaton, John, and John Reid. *The Life of Andrew Jackson.* 1817. Reprint ed. Frank L. Owsley Jr., ed. University: University of Alabama Press, 1974. 424pp. The best of the early biographies by two of Jackson's intimates, the book is strongest on his military campaigns.

James, Marquis. *Andrew Jackson.* New York: Grosset & Dunlap, 1933–1937. 2 vols. Winner of the Pulitzer Prize in 1938, James's dramatic, popular biography is entertaining but marred by excessive partisanship and lack of objectivity. The book draws on much unpublished material, including a collection of over 1,200 letters.

Latner, Richard B. *The Presidency of Andrew Jackson: White House Politics 1829-37.* Athens: University of Georgia Press, 1979. 291pp. Latner's behind-the-scenes look at Jackson's administration stresses his relationship with his "Kitchen Cabinet" of unofficial advisers and the formation of his presidential policies.

Remini, Robert V. *Andrew Jackson.* New York: Twayne, 1966. 212pp. This concise treatment of Jackson's career by the author of the definitive life is a valuable, compact examination that challenges a number of myths about Jackson, including the legend of him as a reluctant politician.

Ward, John W. *Andrew Jackson: Symbol for an Age.* New York: Oxford University Press, 1955. 274pp. The author looks at the evolution and influence of Jackson as a popular cultural symbol. Intriguing in showing how the facts of Jackson's career and the force of his personality entered the American consciousness, Ward's examination is a provocative psycho-historical analysis.

Biographical Novels

Byrd, Max. *Jackson.* New York: Bantam, , 1997. 421pp. Set in 1828, this biographical account of Jackson's complex and contradictory character takes the form of research by an expatriate writer commissioned to pen a biography on the eve of the presidential campaign who uncovers facts that could undo Jackson.

Crabb, Alfred L. *Home to the Hermitage: A Novel of Andrew and Rachel Jackson.* Indianapolis:

Bobbs-Merrill, 1948. 318pp. The novel dramatizes Jackson's life from his return from the War of 1812 to his election as president in 1828. A highly partisan depiction, the novel offers the private side of Jackson's personality with an emphasis on his domestic affairs and relationship with his wife.

Gerson, Noel B. *Old Hickory*. Garden City, New York: Doubleday, 1964. 372pp. The novel traces Jackson's full life from his service in the Revolution through his death. This is a flattering portrait of the heroic Jackson with many of his rough edges and contradictions smoothed over.

Moore, John T. *Hearts of Hickory: A Story of Andrew Jackson and the War of 1812*. New York: Grosset & Dunlap, 1926. 450pp. The novel celebrates the lives of Tennessee's two most famous frontiersmen, Jackson and Davy Crockett in a romantic account of Indian fighting and warfare, culminating in the Battle of New Orleans. Not reliable as history or biography.

Nicholson, Meredith. *The Cavalier of Tennessee*. Indianapolis: Bobbs-Merrill, 1928. 402pp. In a highly romanticized version of Jackson's early life in Tennessee before his political career, the general is given the full heroic treatment as a man of honor in defense of his wife's reputation.

Stone, Irving. *The President's Lady: A Novel about Rachel and Andrew Jackson*. Garden City, New York: Doubleday, 1951. 278pp. Focusing on Jackson's married life and the scandal that dogged the couple, this is a reliable version of the facts with dialogue recreated from a variety of sources and plausible surmises about the speakers.

Wellman, Paul I. *Magnificent Destiny: A Novel about the Great Secret Adventure of Andrew Jackson and Sam Houston*. Garden City, New York: Doubleday, 1962. 479pp. The friendship between Jackson and Sam Houston is depicted from their Indian-fighting days through the Texas Revolution. The story is largely seen through Jackson's perspective.

Young, Stanley. *Young Hickory*. New York: Farrar & Rinehart, 1940. 271pp. Chronicling Jackson's early years, the novel traces his boyhood in North Carolina through his experiences in Tennessee, up to 1792 and the beginning of his military career. Since many of the details of Jackson's early years are scanty, a good deal of speculation is employed.

Fictional Portraits

Adams, Samuel H. *The Gorgeous Hussy*. New York: Grosset & Dunlap, 1934. 549pp. Washington politics from the 1810s to the Civil War are described from the perspective of Peggy Eaton, Jackson's famous protégé. Should not be regarded as reliable history.

Carlisle, Henry. *The Land Where the Sun Dies*. New York: Putnam, 1975. 347pp. Chronicling the effects of Jackson's Indian removal policy that results in the Seminole War, the novel is an accurate presentation of the period and its principals.

Jordan, Jan. *Give Me the Wind*. Englewood Cliffs, New Jersey: Prentice-Hall, 1973. 253pp. In this fictionalized life story of half-Cherokee John Ross, his relationship with Jackson during the War of 1812 and Jackson's Indian removal policy is treated.

Kent, Madeleine F. *The Corsair: A Biographical Novel of Jean Lafitte, Hero of the Battle of New Orleans*. Garden City, New York: Doubleday, 1955. 299pp. Jackson is shown in this partisan view of pirate Jean Lafitte who is offered as a genuine hero maligned by history.

Nevin, David. *1812*. New York: Forge, 1996. 445pp. This panoramic drama of the War of 1812 documents the principal events and leading figures, including Jackson, using the fictional frame of the experiences of a young woman war correspondent.

Palmer, Bruce. *Horseshoe Bend*. New York: Simon & Schuster, 1962. 572pp. Jackson's role in the Battle of Horseshoe Bend during the Creek Indian War is dramatized in a historically accurate but embellished story.

Slate, Sam J. *As Long as the Rivers Run*. Garden City, New York: Doubleday, 1972. 306pp. The novel looks at the battle against the Creek Indians in 1813 with a view of several of the historical figures of the period, including Jackson.

Recommended Juvenile Biographies

Judson, Karen. *Andrew Jackson*. Springfield, New Jersey: Enslow, 1997. 112pp. MG. Judson treats the major events of Jackson's personal and public life, relating his career to the history of the period.

Meltzer, Milton. *Andrew Jackson and His America*. New York: F. Watts, 1993. 207pp. MG/YA. Meltzer's highly critical portrait demolishes any lingering trace of Jackson's heroism. Jackson is shown as a product of his times, which the book vividly reconstructs with many concrete details.

Viola, Herman J. *Andrew Jackson*. New York: Chelsea House, 1986. 112pp. MG/YA. Excellent summary of Jackson's life and impact on American history during his lifetime.

Biographical Films and Theatrical Adaptations

A&E Biography Video: Andrew Jackson: A Man for the People (1995). Director: Adam Friedman. The documentary traces the various phases of Jackson's career with an emphasis on his heroism and leadership. Video.

Gorgeous Hussy (1936). Director: Clarence Brown. In the film adaptation of Samuel Adams's novel, a fictionalized biography of Jackson protégé Peggy Eaton (Joan Crawford), Lionel Barrymore portrays Jackson. Video.

The Buccaneer (1938). Director: Cecil B. DeMille. Colorful historical epic concerning pirate Jean Lafitte and the Battle of New Orleans. Fredric March is a standout in the title role, with Hugh Sothern as Jackson.

The Buccaneer (1953). Director: Anthony Quinn. Remake of the 1938 film, Charlton Heston stars as Jackson with Yul Brynner as Jean Lafitte torn between love interests played by Inger Stevens and Claire Bloom. Video.

The President's Lady (1953). Director: Henry Levin. Based on Irving Stone's novel, the relationship between Jackson and his wife Rachel is effec-

tively depicted, played by Charlton Heston and Susan Hayward. Video.

See also Sam Houston

243. THOMAS J. "STONEWALL" JACKSON
1824–1863

Confederate general and brilliant tactician, Jackson was born in Clarksburg, Virginia, and graduated from West Point (1846). After serving with distinction under Winfield Scott in the Mexican War, he taught at the Virginia Military Institute (1851–1861). During the Civil War, he earned his sobriquet at the first battle of Bull Run (1861), when he and his brigade were described as standing "like a stone wall." He led his troops to victories in the second battle of Bull Run (1862), the Antietam campaign (1862), and in the battles of Fredericksburg (1862), and Chancellorsville (1863). Mortally wounded by the fire of his own men during the Chancellorsville campaign, his death was a blow to the Confederate cause.

Autobiography and Primary Sources

Jackson's letters remain uncollected but some can be found quoted by Arnold, Cooke, Dabney, and especially in Anna Jackson's biographical portrait of her husband.

Recommended Biographies

Chambers, Lenoir. *Stonewall Jackson*. New York: Morrow, 1959. 2 vols. Chambers's comprehensive study remains one of the fullest treatments that provides the clearest account of Jackson's development and how his early years explain his military career. Setting the factual record straight, Chambers traces each phase of Jackson's life and, without attempting to resolve all the contradictions, shows them clearly.

Farwell, Byron. *Stonewall: A Biography of General Thomas J. Jackson*. New York: W.W. Norton, 1992. 560pp. Concluding that most of the legends surrounding Jackson, including his fabled eccentricities, lack a factual basis, Farwell sifts through the various sources to form a believable human portrait of a limited military genius and still fascinating personality.

Robertson, James I. Jr. *Stonewall Jackson: The Man, the Soldier, the Legend*. New York: Macmillan, 1997. 950pp. Like Farwell, Robertson explodes many of the Jackson myths and exhaustively reassembles a believable human portrait of a complex man. Combining the analytical ability of Vandiver with the details of Chambers, Robertson's authoritative examination can claim to be the closest to a definitive life of Jackson available.

Vandiver, Frank. *Mighty Stonewall*. New York: McGraw-Hill, 1957. 547pp. Long considered the definitive study, Vandiver's interpretive study is free of obvious partisanship, which allows Jackson's complex and contradictory character to emerge as a human figure and a product of his times. With his assessment fully grounded in scholarship, Vandiver's examination of Jackson's character remains one of the best and most believable assessments available.

Other Biographical Studies

Arnold, Thomas Jackson. *Early Life and Letters of General Thomas J. Jackson.* New York: Revell, 1916. 379pp. Written by Jackson's grandson, this filial appreciation provides valuable details about Jackson's early years and extracts from several letters unavailable elsewhere.

Bowers, John. *Stonewall Jackson: Portrait of a Soldier.* New York: Morrow, 1989. 367pp. Closer to biographical fiction than nonfiction, this is a vivid, entertaining animation of Jackson's career and character with imagined conversations and considerable invention.

Cooke, John Esten. *Stonewall Jackson: A Military Biography.* New York: Appleton, 1866. 587pp. Written by a Virginia novelist and Confederate staff officer who knew Jackson, the book is valuable chiefly for its insider's look at Confederate strategy, eyewitness testimony of the general in action, and dramatic battle recreation.

Dabney, Robert L. *Life and Campaigns of Lieut.-Gen. Thomas J. Jackson.* New York: Blelock, 1866. 742pp. Dabney, who served on Jackson's staff during the Valley Campaign, had the full cooperation of Jackson's widow, including access to letters, in producing this life. More a vindication than an objective presentation of fact, Dabney's tribute remains useful primarily as a reference source for quotations from the letters.

Davis, Burke. *They Called Him Stonewall: A Life of Lt. General T.J. Jackson, C.S.A.* New York: Holt, 1954. 470pp. Davis's popular biography is based on secondary sources, which are synthesized into an entertaining narrative that devotes more attention to Jackson's antebellum life than others and succeeds in recreating the drama of Jackson's campaigns and replacing legends with a believable human portrait.

Henderson, G.F.R. *Stonewall Jackson and the American Civil War.* 1898. Reprint ed. New York: Smithmark, 1994. 447pp. Written by a British soldier and military historian, Henderson's detailed military biography remains one of the best available tactical analysis of Jackson's campaigns. The book is less reliable as an objective consideration of Jackson's military genius and temperament.

Jackson, Anna Mary. *Life and Letters of General Thomas J. Jackson.* New York: Harper, 1892. 479pp. Mrs. Jackson's eloquent tribute to her husband relies on Dabney for the details of Jackson's military campaign and concentrates on his domestic and religious side. Indispensable as a source for information not found elsewhere, the book features long extracts from Jackson's correspondence.

Kostyal, K.M. *Stonewall Jackson: A Life Portrait.* Dallas: Taylor, 1999. 214pp. Using archival and contemporary portraits and drawings, this illustrated biography follows Jackson's career from boyhood, through West Point, the War with Mexico, his years at Virginia Military Institute, and the Civil War.

Tate, Allen. *Stonewall Jackson: The Good Soldier.* New York: Minton Balch, 1928. 322pp. The author, a distinguished poet and essayist, was also a clearly Southern partisan, but his character study does not gloss over Jackson's mistakes. Challenging many of the legends surrounding the general, Tate fashions alternatives in an undocumented narrative that is lively and imaginative, rather than reliable for its scholarship.

Biographical Novels

Dwyer, John. *Stonewall.* Nashville, Tennessee: Broadman & Holman, 1998. 640pp. Dwyer's is a panoramic epic woven around the events of Jackson's life with an emphasis on his spirituality and strength of character.

Herrin, Lamar. *The Unwritten Chronicles of Robert E. Lee.* New York: St. Martin's, 1991. 248pp. Through imagined letters and musings, the novel provides an impressionistic psychological character study of both Lee and his indispensable yet temperamental lieutenant, Stonewall Jackson.

Kane, Harnett T. *The Gallant Mrs. Stonewall.* Garden City, New York: Doubleday, 1957. 320pp. This biographical portrait of Anna Jackson describes her life with Jackson from their first meeting to his death. Carefully researched, this is a credible version of Jackson's personal, domestic story.

Slaughter, Frank G. *Stonewall Brigade.* Garden City, New York: Doubleday, 1975. 456pp. The history of Jackson's famous "foot cavalry" is recounted in a blend of fact and fiction through the perspective of a young Confederate medical officer.

Fictional Portraits

Jackson appears as a major or minor character in countless Civil War novels. Some of the most interesting portrayals are the following:

Johnston, Mary. *The Long Roll.* 1911. Reprint ed. Baltimore: Johns Hopkins University Press, 1996. 683pp. Johnston juggles Jackson's military campaigns with a romantic story of two Confederate volunteers vying for the love of the same woman. Jackson's eccentricities are fully displayed in a characterization that was criticized by the general's widow.

Keneally, Thomas. *Confederates.* New York: Harper & Row, 1979. 427pp. The Southern perspective on the Civil War is dramatized through the experiences of a member of the Stonewall Brigade, his wife, a widow who is also a Yankee spy, and a British journalist. The novel includes a strong portrait of Jackson and the military action that culminates at the Battle of Antietam.

King, Benjamin. *A Bullet for Stonewall.* Gretna, Louisiana: Pelican, 1990. 267pp. Jackson's death is the occasion for the author's conspiracy theorizing.

Robertson, Don. *The River and the Wilderness.* Garden City, New York: Doubleday, 1962. 764pp. Concentrating on the events of 1862, including Antietam and Fredericksburg, this panoramic recreation animates the experiences of combatants on both sides of the conflict, including Jackson's death.

Shaara, Jeff. *Gods and Generals.* New York: Ballantine Books, 1996. 498pp. In this "prequel" to his father's classic, *The Killer Angels,* Shaara looks at the events preceding Gettysburg, concentrating on the experiences and reflections of four participants: Lee, Chamberlain, Hancock, and Jackson.

Wicker, Tom. *Unto This Hour.* New York: Viking, 1984. 642pp. This authentic dramatization of the 1862 Battle of Manassas includes the actual experiences of a number of historical figures, such as Jackson.

Recommended Juvenile Biographies

Bennett, Barbara J. *Stonewall Jackson: Lee's Greatest Lieutenant.* Englewood Cliffs, New Jersey: Silver Burdett, 1991. MG. 135pp. Part of the History of the Civil War series, this is a solid, reliable account of Jackson's military career and skills as a battlefield commander.

Fritz, Jean. *Stonewall.* New York: Putnam, 1979. 152pp. MG. Although Jackson's eccentricities are fully displayed, Fritz also places Jackson firmly in the context of his times in this entertaining biography.

Gibboney, Douglas L. *Stonewall Jackson at Gettysburg.* Frederick, Virginia: Sergeant Kirkland's, 1997. 120pp. MG/YA. This intriguing what-if scenario imagines what might have happened had Jackson survived Fredericksburg and participated in the 1863 northern invasion. Solidly researched, the book's believability depends on a firm knowledge of Jackson's character and temperament that it communicates.

Biographical Films and Theatrical Adaptations

A&E Biography Video: Stonewall Jackson (1995). Director: Donna E. Lusitana. Explores the life and military skill of the Confederate general. Video.

Civil War Legends (1989). Director: Gary DeMoss. A multipart series that documents the Civil War campaigns of Jackson, Lee, and Grant. Video.

See also Robert E. Lee

244. JAMES I
1566–1625

The son of Mary, Queen of Scots, and Lord Darnley, James succeeded to the Scottish throne after the forced abdication of his mother (1567) and succeeded to the English crown (1603) on the strength of his descent from Margaret Tudor, daughter of Henry VII. His reign was marked by religious dissent between the established Church of England, Catholics, and Puritans. Anger at the increased severity of penal laws against the practice of Catholicism resulted in the Gunpowder Plot (1605), a failed attempt by Catholic conspirators to blow up Parliament and the king. James also faced conflicts with Parliament over his assertion of the divine right of monarchy and his inability to accept Parliament as a representative body of government. English colonization in North America and Scottish settlement in Ulster began during the reign of James I.

Autobiography and Primary Sources

King James and Letters of Homoerotic Desire. David M. Bergeron, ed. Iowa City: University of Iowa Press, 1999. 242pp. This is modern-spelling edition of letters exchanged between James and three male favorites—Lennox, Somerset, and Buckingham—with commentary that examines James's complex emotional life.

King James VI and I: Political Writings. Johann P. Sommerville, ed. New York: Cambridge University Press, 1994. 329pp. Bringing together all the early texts, this collection provides valuable insights into the king's ideas and intellectual qualities.

Letters of King James VI and I. G.P.V. Akrigg, ed. Berkeley: University of California Press, 1984. 546pp. This selection of 227 letters forms a revealing epistolary autobiography in an impeccably edited edition.

Recommended Biographies

Carrier, Irene. *James VI and I: King of Great Britain.* New York: Cambridge University Press, 1998. 153pp. Carrier explores the king's character from the perspective of various cultural and political contexts of his day, including the Anglo-Scottish union, church policy, financial difficulties, and James's relationship with Parliament. A valuable introductory study, the book includes a useful overview of historical treatments of James and evaluations of his reign.

Houston, S.J. *James I.* New York: Longman, 1995. 146pp. First published in 1973 but entirely rewritten in the light of recent scholarship on early Stuart government and politics, this is one of the best available short popular accounts of James's Scottish background, his reign, and the personalities and politics of the English court.

Willson, David H. *King James VI and I.* New York: Holt, 1956. 480pp. Long established as the standard, scholarly and most detailed biographical study, Willson emphasizes James's personal side over the political and documents the discrepancy between the king's aspirations and assertions in his writings and the less-flattering reality. Despite an overall hostility, Willson's examination remains one of the sharpest portraits of a complex and contradictory man and monarch.

Other Biographical Studies

Ashton, Robert, ed. *James I by His Contemporaries: An Account of His Career and Character as Seen by Some of His Contemporaries.* New York: Hutchinson, 1969. 290pp. This is a useful and revealing collection of recollections of James from a variety of perspectives, from his supporters and enemies.

Beavan, Bryan. *King James VI of Scotland and I of England.* London: Rubicon Press, 1996. 216pp. Beavan's is a reliable summary of James's reign and personality, informed by a sound political and cultural context.

Bergeron, David M. *Royal Family, Royal Lovers: King James of England and Scotland.* Columbia: University of Missouri Press, 1991. 222pp. Bergeron supplies a detailed, exhaustively documented, and well-written study of the interrelationships within the Stuart family, providing an intimate look at the personal life of James I.

Bingham, Caroline. *The Making of a King: The Early Years of James VI and I.* Garden City, New York: Doubleday, 1969. 199pp. The author submits James's childhood and youth up to the age of 17 to a predominantly Freudian interpretation of an emotionally deprived youth who grew up to become a mentally unstable adult. The book assumes the reader's familiarity with James's later history.

Durston, Christopher. *James I.* New York: Routledge, 1993. 69pp. This compact introduction offers brief chapters on James's character, his court, financial problems, and domestic, foreign, and church policies.

Lee, Maurice. *Government by Pen: Scotland Under James VI and I.* Urbana: University of Illinois Press, 1980. 232pp. Few other sources look at Scotland after James became king of England and Scotland. This thorough and reliable political history offers a chronological narrative account of Scottish politics from 1603 to 1625 and an important supplementary angle for viewing James's reign.

Lockyer, Roger. *James VI and I.* New York: Longman, 234. 240pp. The author's reappraisal of James uses historiography to reveal fresh perspectives on seventeenth-century British history and James's character and influence. While acknowledging James's limitations, Lockyer restores some stature to James's talents and achievements.

Mathew, David. *James I.* University: University of Alabama Press, 1968. 353pp. Complementing Willson's more descriptive approach with a more interpretive assessment, Mathew concentrates mainly on James's English years in a series of carefully drawn character sketches. Not attempting a comprehensive and chronological survey, Mathew's often brilliant analysis is for the reader who already has a firm sense of the king's life and the history of his reign.

McElwee, William. *The Wisest Fool in Christendom: The Reign of King James I and VI.* New York: Harcourt, Brace, 1958. 296pp. More balanced in its assessment than Willson, McElwee's accounts for James's virtues as well as his vices. Although the period background is carefully delineated, with a concentration on James's relationship with the English Parliament, the characterization lacks vividness, and the reader must endure a number of dull patches.

Scott, Otto J. *James I.* New York: Mason/Charter, 1976. 472pp. In a fast-paced and readable narrative history of the reign, the private side of James I is glimpsed through anecdotes and an often simplistic interpretation with greed and lust as his primary motives.

Williams, Charles. *James I.* 1934. Reprint ed. Freeport, New York: Books for Libraries Press, 1969. 310pp. Williams offers an intelligent and impartial analysis of the mind and character of the king. Because the background details are only sketched, this book would be an ideal complement to a more historically focused study.

Biographical Novels

Garrett, George. *Death of the Fox.* Garden City, New York: Doubleday, 1971. 739pp. In the first of the author's Elizabethan trilogy, Walter Raleigh's final hours before his execution are recreated using a variety of interior monologues, including Raleigh's, Francis Bacon's, and James I's; *The Succession: A Novel of Elizabeth and James.* Garden City, New York: Doubleday, 1983. 538pp. In Garrett's second volume of his trilogy the central political question who will succeed Elizabeth I is considered from multiple perspectives of actual and invented figures.

Harwood, Alice. *No Smoke Without Fire.* Indianapolis: Bobbs-Merrill, 1964. 530pp. The complex court politics in Scotland involving Mary, Queen of Scots, and her son, James VI, is detailed in a faithful historical account.

Oliver, Jane. *Mine Is the Kingdom.* Philadelphia: Lippincott, 1937. 452pp. The life and personality of James are chronicled in this biographical novel that suggests the king's complexity in a historical convincing portrait.

Fictional Portraits

Dexter, Charles. *The Street of Kings.* New York: Holt, 1957. 436pp. The scandal surrounding the death of Sir Thomas Overbury and the liaison between Frances Howard and Robert Carr is depicted in a mixture of fact and fancy but a colorful evocation of the Jacobean court.

Lewis, Hilda W. *Wife to Great Buckingham.* New York: Putnam, 1959. 331pp. The life and relationships of James's favorite, George Villiers, Duke of Buckingham, are shown from the perspective of his wife. In *Call Lady Purbeck* (New York: St. Martin's, 1961. 351pp.) life in the court of James I is depicted through the experiences of Frances Coke who is forced to marry the brother of the Duke of Buckingham.

Plaidy, Jean. *The Murder in the Tower.* New York: Putnam, 1964. 286pp. The scandal resulting from the liaison between Frances Howard and Robert Carr is vividly and faithfully dramatized.

Scott, Walter. *The Fortunes of Nigel.* 1823. Reprint ed. New York: Dutton, 1910. 457pp. Concerning the attempt by a Scottish nobleman to recover a debt from James I, Scott's novel features one of the finest fictional portraits of the monarch.

Shrimsley, Bernard. *Lion Rampant.* New York: Macmillan, 1984. 259pp. The novel offers a speculative solution to one of history's great royal mysteries: what became of Henry Frederick Stuart, Prince of Wales?

Stewart, Stanley N. *The King James Version.* New York: Random House, 1977. 335pp. Set in the court of James I, the novel authentically dramatizes the intrigue of Frances Howard to win Robert Carr, James I's favorite.

Tranter, Nigel. *Unicorn Rampant.* London: Hodder and Stoughton, 1984. 351pp. James's only return to Scotland after succeeding Elizabeth to the English throne in 1617 is dramatized from the perspective of a young courtier. *The Master of Gray Trilogy*. London: Coronet, 1996. 3 vols. The career of Patrick, Master of Gray, son and heir of the fifth Lord Gray, one of the most remarkable Scottish adventurers of his era, is chronicled with depictions of the intrigues of the Elizabethan and Jacobean courts.

Westcott, Jan. *The Border Lord*. New York: Crown, 1946. 464pp. In a dramatization of the career of Francis Hepburn, the Earl of Bothwell, the novel features Bothwell's conflict with James VI.

Woolf, Virginia. *Orlando*. New York: Harcourt, Brace, 1928. 333pp. In a brilliant historical fantasy, Woolf imagines a man who becomes a woman and must deal with court life in the time of Elizabeth, James I, Anne, and Victoria.

Recommended Juvenile Biographies

Dwyer, Frank. *James I*. New York: Chelsea House, 1988. 111pp. MG/YA. Dwyer's informative biography blends personal details and sufficient historical background to make James's actions and character understandable in the context of his era.

Biographical Films and Theatrical Adaptations

Orlando (1992). Director: Sally Potter. In a sumptuous adaptation of Virginia Woolf's historical fantasy, Tilda Swinton stars as the nobleman who becomes a woman and lives through 400 years of English history. Quentin Crisp appears as Queen Elizabeth and Dudley Sutton portrays James I. Video.

See also Charles I; Elizabeth I; Mary Queen of Scots; Walter Raleigh; William Shakespeare

245. HENRY JAMES
1843–1916

American novelist and critic born in New York City, James was the son of Henry James Sr., a Swedenborgian theologian, and brother of philosopher William James. Educated by private tutors in Europe and the United States, he attended Harvard Law School and during the 1860s wrote critical articles and reviews for the *Atlantic Monthly*. In 1876 he settled permanently in England and became a British subject in 1915. A master of the psychological novel and an explicator of the behavior of Americans abroad, James's many celebrated works include *Daisy Miller* (1879), *The Portrait of a Lady* (1881), *The Turn of the Screw* (1898), *The Wings of the Dove* (1902), and *The Golden Bowl* (1904).

Autobiography and Primary Sources

The Complete Notebooks of Henry James. Leon Edel and Lyall H. Powers, eds. New York: Oxford University Press, 1987. 633pp. Including nine notebooks James kept from 1878 to 1911, notes for his unfinished novels, and a scenario for a play, this invaluable collection reveals James's creative processes and a great deal of biographical information not available elsewhere from his pocket diaries.

Henry James: Autobiography. Frederick Dupee, ed. Princeton, New Jersey: Princeton University Press, 1983. 622pp. Brings together James's three autobiographical reminiscences: *A Small Boy and Others*, *Notes of a Son and Brother*, and *The Middle Years*.

Henry James: A Life in Letters. Philip Horne, ed. New York: Viking, 1999. 668pp. This chronologically arranged collection features nearly 150 unpublished letters. Each letter is ably introduced with its context supplied which, combined with James's own words, forms a revealing biographical narrative.

Letters. Leon Edel, ed. Cambridge, Massachusetts: Harvard University Press, 1974–1984. 4 vols. A literary treasure and indispensable as a biographical source, James's letters provide the closest vantage point for viewing the novelist directly. *Selected Letters* Cambridge, Massachusetts: Harvard University Press, 1990. 496pp. A useful one-volume compilation of letters chosen by Edel.

Recommended Biographies

Edel, Leon. *Henry James: The Untried Years, 1843-70*. Philadelphia: Lippincott, 1953. 350pp.; *Henry James: The Conquest of London, 1870-81*. Philadelphia: Lippincott, 1962. 465pp.; *Henry James: The Middle Years, 1882-95*. Philadelphia: Lippincott, 1962. 408pp.; *Henry James: The Treacherous Years, 1895–1901*. Philadelphia: Lippincott, 1969. 352pp.; *Henry James: The Master, 1901–16*. Philadelphia: Lippincott, 1972. 591pp. Edel's magisterial, definitive life has been justly praised as one of the highest expressions of the biographer's art. In its five detailed volumes, James has found his Boswell in Edel's sensitive, meticulously researched distillation of a lifelong of devotion to James's life and works. In *Henry James: A Life* (New York: Harper & Row, 1985. 740pp.) Edel provides a one-volume condensation and revision of his multivolume study reflecting modern scholarship since the books' first publication.

Kaplan, Fred. *Henry James: The Imagination of Genius*. New York: Morrow, 1992. 620pp. Kaplan's provocative and controversial critical biography depends mainly on Edel, the letters, and diaries and concentrates on interconnections between James's life and art in the light of modern attitudes toward feminism and homosexuality. The result is at times a relentless Freudian reading of the novelist, emphasizing his inner life and the displacement of James's complex sexual identity in his works.

Lewis, R.W.B. *The Jameses: A Family Narrative*. New York: Farrar, Straus, 1991. 696pp. In a worthy complement to Edel's closely focused examination, Lewis's group, family biography sets the James family squarely against their cultural background and shows how family interactions were central to the creative development of Henry and William James.

Other Biographical Studies

Edgar, Pelham. *Henry James: Man and Author*. Boston: Houghton Mifflin, 1927. 351pp. Devoting little attention to the man over the works, this biographical/critical study provides detailed plot summaries of James's stories and novels but few suggestions about the connection between James's art and his life.

Gordon, Lyndall. *A Private Life of Henry James: Two Women and His Art*. New York: W.W. Norton, 1999. 448pp. Gordon approaches her study of James's inner life from the perspectives of two women in his life who affected his development: his cousin Minny Temple and fellow expatriate novelist, Constance Woolson. By detailing their lives and relationship with the novelist, Gordon sheds a number of original insights on James's carefully guarded private nature.

Graham, Kenneth. *Henry James: A Literary Life*. New York: St. Martin's, 1994. 207pp. Graham's critical study follows James's writing life, placing his work in its literary and cultural context and tracing the connections between James's life and his art. Serves as one of the best introductory studies of both the man and his genius.

Hyde, H. Montgomery. *Henry James at Home*. New York: Farrar, Straus, 1969. 322pp. James's English years from 1876 to 1916 is the book's focus with an emphasis on the novelist's circle of friends and social and domestic affairs. There is little here about James's intellectual or artistic life during the period.

Le Clair, Robert C. *The Young Henry James: 1843-70*. New York: Bookman, 1955. 469pp. In a thoroughly researched and exhaustively documented account of James's early years, Le Clair places the novelist solidly in his family background and traces the influences of James's father and brother on the novelist's development. Avoiding psychological speculation, Le Clair's study is descriptive rather than analytical.

Novick, Sheldon M. *Henry James: The Young Master*. New York: Random House, 1996. 550pp. Chronicling James's experiences from birth to age 38, the book is richly detailed and attempts to offer a full and frank human portrait of the developing artist who is very different from the conventional view of the emotionally detached voyeur of other studies. The most controversial assertion of the book, James's passionate attachment to Oliver Wendell Holmes, is highly speculative.

Seymour, Miranda. *A Ring of Conspirators: Henry James and His Literary Circle, 1895–1915*. Boston: Houghton Mifflin, 1989. 327pp. The book's biographical portrait of James during his last two decades relies on anecdotes culled from the memoirs and biographies of the novelist's friends. James's humanity and vulnerability are detailed.

Fictional Portraits

Aiken, Joan. *The Haunting of Lamb House*. New York: St. Martin's, 1993. 200pp. Henry James's English home is the locale for this ghost story that features James and writer E.F. Benson making sense of the unexplainable.

Conroy, Sarah B. *Refinements of Love: A Novel about Clover and Henry Adams*. New York: Pantheon, 1993. 301pp. In this speculative account of 1885 death of Henry Adams's wife, Clover, James appears as a friend of the couple.

Hill, Carol DeChellis. *Henry James' Midnight Song.* New York: Poseidon Press, 1993. 445pp. Henry James is one of many historical suspects in an intriguing period murder mystery set in fin-de-siècle Vienna. The novel is a tour de force of historical animation with intriguing portraits of Edith Wharton, Freud, and Jung.

Vidal, Gore. *Empire.* New York: Random House, 1987. 486pp. In Vidal's panoramic novel set at the turn of the century concerning the emergence of America as a world power several historical figures, including Henry James, interact with imagined characters and a fictional story of political and social power hunters.

Biographical Films and Theatrical Adaptations

Henry James: American Writer, 1843–1916 (1995). Director: Malcolm Hossick. Part of the Famous Authors series, the documentary traces James's life and career using photographs and views of places associated with the author. Video.

Other Sources

Freedman, Jonathan, ed. *The Cambridge Companion to Henry James.* New York: Cambridge University Press, 1998. 256pp. This collection of essays by leading Jamesian scholars touches on various aspects of James's life and career, based on recent critical views.

Gale, Robert L. *A Henry James Encyclopedia.* New York: Greenwood, 1989. 791pp. An outstanding research tool, the book offers alphabetical entries on each of James's works, characters, friends, and relatives, with several appendixes listing entries under useful thematic categories.

Nowell-Smith, Simon, ed. *The Legend of the Master: Henry James.* 1947. Reprint ed. New York: Oxford University Press, 1985. 213pp. Collecting the reminiscences of more than 150 of James's acquaintances, this useful source of anecdotes arranged chronologically and reveals various facets of the novelist.

Page, Norman, ed. *Henry James: Interviews and Recollections.* New York: St. Martin's, 1984. 158pp. Based on the recollections of associates, Page documents James the conversationalist in vignettes arranged under broad subject areas.

246. JESSE JAMES
1847–1882

American outlaw, James was a member of Quantrill's raiders during the Civil War. In 1866 he and his brother, Frank, formed a band of outlaws that robbed banks and trains throughout the central states. After several members of the James Gang were caught following a failed bank robbery, the brothers lived quietly until 1879, when they robbed another train. Jesse James was later murdered for reward by gang member Robert Ford.

Recommended Biographies

Brant, Morley. *Jesse James: The Man and the Myth.* New York: Berkley Books, 1998. 312pp.

This is a well-written account that attempts to set the factual record straight and to produce a complex portrait of a man of intense loyalties and hatreds, as well as an irrepressible need to be known. Includes rare photos from the James family archives.

Settle, William A. Jr. *Jesse James Was His Name: Or, Fact and Fiction Concerning the Careers of the Notorious James Brothers of Missouri.* Columbia: University of Missouri Press, 1966. 263pp. Settle's is the most reliable, scholarly biography available in which the pertinent evidence is assembled and the legends are identified as such. Settle also is insightful in his explanation as to why the various myths surrounding James were created and why they have persisted.

Other Biographical Studies

Breihan, Carl W. *The Complete and Authentic Life of Jesse James.* New York: Frederick Fell, 1953. 287pp.; *The Day Jesse James Was Killed.* New York: Frederick Fell, 1961. 235pp.; *The Escapades of Frank and Jesse James.* New York: Frederick Fell, 1974. 288pp. Breihan's series of books on James is not trustworthy, mixing fact and legend, committing numerous errors, and inventing dialogue and situations.

Croy, Homer. *Jesse James Was My Neighbor.* New York: Duell, Sloan and Pearce, 1949. 313pp. Born a year after James's death, Croy collects a number of stories (both factual and legendary) from those who knew James. The book serves as a useful reference source, identifying all the outlaws that rode with James.

Love, Robertus. *The Rise and Fall of Jesse James.* New York: Putnam, 1926. 446pp. The first comprehensive, semi-objective biography, Love's chronological narrative is not error- or legend-free, but the book at least tries to penetrate beneath the myth to portray a realistic figure with understandable human motives.

Triplett, Frank. *The Life, Times, and Treacherous Death of Jesse James.* 1882. Reprint ed. Joseph Snell, ed. New York: Promontory Press, 1970. 344pp. Triplett attempted the first comprehensive telling of James's story based on contemporary newspaper accounts and, presumably, on interviews with James's mother and wife (who later claimed they had nothing to do with the book). Snell's 1970 edition provides a useful summary of the complicated history of the book and suggestions about its reliability.

Biographical Novels

Barry, Desmond. *The Chivalry of Crime.* Boston: Little, Brown, 2000. 384pp. Barry interweaves the story of an adolescent who dreams of becoming a "shootist" with a vivid retelling of James's life and career as a bank and train robber. James emerges as a plausible, complex blend of courtliness and pathological violence.

Dodd, Susan. *Mamaw.* New York: Viking, 1988. 350pp. The story of the James family is seen from the perspective of Zerelda Cole James, Jesse's mother, in an historically authentic biographical novel.

Hansen, Ron. *The Assassination of Jesse James by the Coward, Robert Ford.* New York: Knopf, 1983. 304pp. Hansen's retelling of the events surrounding James's death stays close to the known facts but adds a number of original insights.

Henry, Will. *Death of a Legend.* New York: Random House, 1954. 244pp. Henry provides a truthful portrait of James's murderous career stripped of any legendary glamour, based on a well-researched reconstruction of his life and background.

Ross, James R. *I, Jesse James.* Los Angeles: Dragon, 1989. 280pp. James offers his own defense for his life of crime in this fictional autobiographical account.

Fictional Portraits

Camp, Deborah. *Belle Starr.* New York: Harmony, 1987. 344pp. Outlaws James, Belle Starr, and Cole Younger are turned into romantic figures in this implausible drama that takes considerable liberties with the facts.

Taylor, Robert. *Loving Belle Starr.* Chapel Hill, North Carolina: Algonquin Books, 1984. 215pp. Compared to Camp, Taylor's depiction of western outlaw Belle Starr and the Youngers and James Gang is far more convincing, although the novel also blends facts and popular legends.

Recommended Juvenile Biographies

Bruns, Roger. *Jesse James: Legendary Outlaw.* Springfield, New Jersey: Enslow, 1998. 128pp. MG. Bruns's is an evenhanded account that helpfully places James's career in its historical context and shows how the facts have been distorted by popular culture.

Stiles, T.J. *Jesse James.* New York: Chelsea House, 1994. 111pp. MG/YA. Stiles supplies a factual account of James's development that isolates his criminal origin in his Civil War experience. Archival photographs aid the book's presentation.

Biographical Films and Theatrical Adaptations

A&E Biography Video: The James Gang: Outlaw Brothers (1995). Producers: Craig Haffner and Donna E. Lusitana. A film profile that attempts to replace the legend with a realistic depiction of the James Brothers and their brief, murderous career. Video.

Frank and Jesse (1994). Director: Robert Boris. This is a revisionist western with a brooding, sensitive Jesse played by Rob Lowe and his brother Frank portrayed by Bill Paxton. Video.

Great Missouri Raid (1951). Director: Gordon Douglas. Mainly fanciful depiction of how the James Brothers began their life of crime. Wendell Corey plays Jesse and Macdonald Carey plays Frank James. With Ward Bond, Bruce Bennett, and Bill Williams. Video. Corey reprises the role as James in the romantic comedy, *Alias Jesse James* (1959) (Director: Norman Z. McLeod), starring Bob Hope and Rhonda Fleming. Video.

The Great Northfield Minnesota Raid (1972). Director: Philip Kaufman. Robert Duvall portrays Jesse James in this interesting offbeat western about a bank robbery that goes wrong. Features Cliff Robertson in the role of Cole Younger. Video.

I Shot Jesse James (1949). Director: Samuel Fuller. This is an imaginative depiction of Bob Ford's (John Ireland) life after he shot Jesse James (Reed Hadley) in a sobering reassessment of Western myths by innovative director Fuller in his first film. Video.

Jesse James (1939). Director: Henry King. Western film classic with Tyrone Power as Jesse and Henry Fonda as Frank James with an impressive supporting cast, including Randolph Scott, Brian Donlevy, and John Carradine. Video. Remade in 1957 as *The True Story of Jesse James* (Director: Nicholas Ray) with Robert Wagner, Jeffrey Hunter, and Hope Lange. Video.

Last Days of Frank & Jesse James (1986). Director: William A. Graham. A reformed James Gang at the end of their murderous career is the focus here. Starring Johnny Cash, Kris Kristofferson, and Willie Nelson. Video.

The Long Riders (1980). Director: Walter Hill. Interesting, stylish western featuring the Younger and James families played by Hollywood brothers, including Stacy Keach, James Keach, Randy Quaid, Dennis Quaid, David Carradine, Keith Carradine, and Robert Carradine, Christopher Guest and Nicholas Guest. Video.

247. THOMAS JEFFERSON
1743–1826

Lawyer, planter, architect, scientist, diplomat, and third United States president (1801–1809), Jefferson is celebrated as one of the greatest statesmen in American history. Born in Albermarle County, Virginia, he attended (1760–1762) the College of William and Mary and in 1769 was elected to the Virginia House of Burgesses, where he was a leader of the patriot faction. A member of the Second Continental Congress, he drafted the Declaration of Independence (1776). He served as governor of Virginia (1779, 1780), Minister to France (1785–1789), and Secretary of State (1790–1793). Major events of Jefferson's presidency include the Louisiana Purchase (1803), the Lewis and Clark expedition (1804–1806), and passage of the Embargo Act (1807). He founded the University of Virginia (chartered 1819, opened 1825) and designed its first buildings.

Autobiography and Primary Sources

Jefferson Himself: A Personal Narrative of a Many-Sided American. Bernard Mayo, ed. Charlottesville: University Press of Virginia, 1942. 384pp. Selections from Jefferson's writings are arranged chronologically to form an autobiographical portrait.

The Life and Selected Writings of Thomas Jefferson. Adrienne Koch and William Peden, eds. New York: Random House, 1998. 691pp. Besides excerpts from Jefferson's published writings, biographical sketches of several prominent figures, and a selection of his letters, the volume includes his *Autobiography*, a brief biographical profile of his life from childhood until 1790.

The Papers of Thomas Jefferson. Julian P. Boyd, et al. eds. Princeton, New Jersey: Princeton University Press, 1950–1999. 27 vols. Available in chronological and topical formats, this monumental scholarly collection reprints every available letter by and to Jefferson, along with his major writings, journals, and speeches.

Recommended Biographies

Ellis, Joseph J. *American Sphinx: The Character of Thomas Jefferson*. New York: Knopf, 1997. 365pp. Not a comprehensive biographical treatment but a character study focused on various episodes in Jefferson's career, the book explores Jefferson's ideas and actions. Ellis's keen analysis penetrates the various layers that have obscured a direct view of Jefferson's true nature. The effect is a fresh appreciation that allows Jefferson to stand whole with his many contradictions in place but his significance undiminished.

Malone, Dumas. *Jefferson and His Time*. Boston: Little, Brown, 1948–1981. 6 vols. Malone's Pulitzer Prize–winning biography, the fruit of over 44 years of labor is the most comprehensive gathering of facts about Jefferson and is widely considered the definitive biography. Minutely detailed and authoritative, Malone's approach is more descriptive than interpretive, but critics have cited the author's clear sympathy toward his subject as a bar to objectivity. The study's enormous length makes it difficult at times to discover the important thematic paths through the thicket of facts, but the book remains an indispensable reference source for the serious student of Jefferson.

Peterson, Merrill D. *Thomas Jefferson and the New Nation: A Biography*. New York: Oxford University Press, 1970. 1,072pp. This interpretive study attempts to join Jefferson's life and ideas with his public career into a comprehensive whole and for the most part succeeds. Identifying the three major themes of democracy, nationalism, and the enlightenment running through Jefferson's entire career, the book, primarily intended for the general reader rather than the scholar, helpfully places Jefferson in a wider cultural and political context.

Randall, Willard S. *Thomas Jefferson: A Life*. New York: Holt, 1993. 708pp. In a fair, thoroughly researched study of Jefferson's life and times, Randall is particularly strong on Jefferson's early years and his life in Paris. Jefferson's public career is more cursorily handled. Based on new sources and a detailed reinterpretation of underexamined periods of Jefferson's life, particularly his years as a law student, Randall offers a fresh interpretation that helps to explain the contradictions many have noted in Jefferson's character and actions.

Other Biographical Studies

Adams, William H. *The Paris Years of Thomas Jefferson*. New Haven, Connecticut: Yale University Press, 1997. 320pp. Adams elegantly chronicles the five years, from 1784 to 1789, that Jefferson spent in Paris as American minister, vividly capturing the social and intellectual world that profoundly influenced Jefferson, according to the author, in this balanced and well-researched examination of Jefferson's life at a crucial period of his development.

Bowers, Claude G. *Jefferson and Hamilton: The Struggle for Democracy in America*. Boston: Houghton Mifflin, 1925. 531pp.; *Jefferson in Power: The Death Struggle of the Federalists*. Boston: Houghton Mifflin, 1936. 538pp.; *The Young Jefferson: 1743–1789*. Boston: Houghton Mifflin, 1945. 544pp. In a highly partisan study that takes Jefferson's side in the ideological debate against Alexander Hamilton over the soul of the American Republic, Jefferson is presented as the apostle of liberal democracy and the spiritual patron of the revivified Democratic Party. Not reliable as objective or accurate biography.

Brodie, Fawn M. *Thomas Jefferson: An Intimate History*. New York: W.W. Norton, 1974. 591pp. Brodie's controversial psychological study is a provocative mixture of vivid detail and speculation that attempts to build up a coherent inner portrait of the man to explain his many contradictions. By far the most debated contention is Brodie's assertion that Jefferson's sexual relationship with his slave Sally Hemings helps explain his ambiguity over slavery. Virginius Dabney's *The Jefferson Scandals: A Rebuttal* (New York: Dodd, Mead, 1981. 154pp.) offers a defense to several of Brodie's charges.

Burstein, Andrew. *The Inner Jefferson: Portrait of a Grieving Optimist*. Charlottesville: University Press of Virginia, 1996. 336pp. Burstein's intellectual biography recreates Jefferson's mental world based on what he read and how he responded to it. Jefferson's personality and private life are topically organized with many helpful insights into his complexity and contradictions.

Cunningham, Noble. *In Pursuit of Reason: The Life of Thomas Jefferson*. Baton Rouge: Louisiana State University Press, 1987. 414pp. This sensible intellectual biography sees Jefferson as the personification of the Enlightenment's faith in reason, progress, and education. Jefferson the thinker is predominant here with little on his passions and with his faults and mistakes downplayed or excused.

Gaustad, Edwin S. *Sworn on the Altar of God: A Religious Biography of Thomas Jefferson*. Grand Rapids, Michigan: William B. Eerdmans, 1996. 246pp. Looking at Jefferson's life and thoughts through his religious beliefs, this biography stresses a particular and important aspect of Jefferson's complex make-up. In a scholarly but readable analysis of Jefferson's personal theology and activities on behalf of religious freedom, the author supplies yet another context for judging the multifaceted Jefferson.

Kennedy, Roger G. *Burr, Hamilton, and Jefferson: A Study in Character*. New York: Oxford University Press, 1999. 476pp. In Kennedy's provocative revisionist analysis of these three statesmen, he attempts to redeem Burr's reputation. Brimming with little-known facts, controversial interpretations, and intriguing speculation, the book offers a new look at the reputations of all three men with penetrating insights abounding.

Kimball, Marie. *Jefferson*. New York: Coward-McCann, 1943–1950. 3 vols. Kimball's detailed and scholarly trilogy takes Jefferson's life from birth up to 1789 and his years in Europe. The volumes remain a mine of important and reliable information about Jefferson's formative years.

Mapp, Alf J. *Thomas Jefferson: A Strange Case of Mistaken Identity*. Lanham, Maryland: Madison Books, 487pp. This laudatory biography's subtitle establishes its thesis that modern biographers have misread Jefferson, and Mapp attempts to restore him to a more proper view stressing consistency rather than contradiction and achievement rather than failure to follow though on asserted ideals. A restorative reading particularly in the light of the debunkers, Mapp simplifies and smoothes over the rough edges in his attempt to reestablish Jefferson as a monument and an icon.

McDonald, Forrest. *The Presidency of Thomas Jefferson*. Lawrence: University Press of Kansas, 1976. 201pp. In a relentlessly realistic view, Jefferson's presidency is detailed. Highly critical of Jefferson's leadership, the book raises far more questions than it answers in its contracted space; the subject deserves a fuller and a more balanced treatment.

McLaughlin, Jack. *Jefferson and Monticello: The Biography of a Builder*. New York: Holt, 1988. 481pp. Focusing on Jefferson's domestic life and his involvement with his home, this scholarly yet readable study provides a number of original insights into Jefferson's personality through its detailed examination of the running of his estate.

Miller, John C. *The Wolf by the Ears: Thomas Jefferson and Slavery*. New York: Free Press, 1977. 319pp. Examining Jefferson's attitudes and actions regarding slavery from the 1760s to his death, Miller's is an objective and balanced assessment that dismisses many of Brodie's controversial assertions yet still depicts Jefferson as deeply flawed on this central contradiction in his ideas and behavior.

Randall, Henry S. *The Life of Thomas Jefferson*. New York: Derby & Jackson, 1858. 3 vols. The most valuable early biography of Jefferson, Randall's study made use of letters and papers that are now lost as well as interviews with Jefferson's descendants and acquaintances. Useful as a reference source for details not found elsewhere.

Risjord, Norman K. *Thomas Jefferson*. Madison, Wisconsin: Madison House, 1997. 210pp. In a brief biographical profile, the author attempts to reconcile the many contradictions Jefferson's life, thought, and career demonstrate and to place him in the context of his era. Serves as a useful introduction to the man and his ideas.

Schachner, Nathan. *Thomas Jefferson: A Biography*. New York: Appleton-Century, 1951. 2 vols. In a highly detailed compilation of facts, Jefferson's entire career is objectively presented, although lacking the scholarly penetration of Malone.

Smith, Page. *Jefferson: A Revealing Biography*. New York: McGraw-Hill, 1976. 310pp. In Smith's unusual view, Jefferson should be seen as essentially an artist whose political activities were contrary to his nature. A psychological interpretation that magnifies a single aspect of Jefferson's complex make-up, Jefferson emerges as an overly romanticized figure.

Biographical Novels

Byrd, Max. *Jefferson*. New York: Bantam, 1993. 424pp. Jefferson's years in France are dramatized through the perspective of his secretary in a convincing and compelling portrait of Jefferson. The focus is on Jefferson's personality and the crisis between his head and his heart.

Chase-Riboud, Barbara. *Sally Hemings*. New York: Viking, 1979. 372pp. Dramatizing the long-held, yet unproven, suspicion that Jefferson had an affair and a child with his slave, Sally Hemings, the novel details the affair over a 38-year period. The sequel, *The President's Daughter*. (New York: Crown, 1994. 467pp.) chronicles the imagined life of Jefferson's daughter with Sally Hemings, from 1822 to 1876.

Grimes, Roberta. *My Thomas: A Novel of Martha Jefferson's Life*. New York: Doubleday, 1993. 320pp. The novel takes the form of Martha Jefferson's journal from 1770 when she first meets Jefferson to her death in 1782. The novel's period research is scrupulous, and the impersonation of Martha Jefferson's voice and ideas is convincing.

Fictional Portraits

Burns, Ron. *Enslaved*. New York: St. Martin's, 1994. 262pp. Jefferson in retirement asks an army officer to investigate the disappearance of two slaves from his nephew's Kentucky plantation, which uncovers a complex tangle of corruption and discoveries. Based on an actual incident.

Delmar, Vina. *A Time for Titans*. New York: Harcourt, Brace, 1974. 366pp. The complicated diplomacy surrounding the Louisiana Purchase is depicted in the clash of three figures: Napoleon, Jefferson, and Toussaint L'Ouverture.

Erickson, Steve. *Arc d'X*. New York: Poseidon Press, 1993. 298pp. This fantasy novel has a strong biographical component as Sally Hemings's life with Jefferson in Paris is depicted, one of several stages of her reincarnation.

Page, Elizabeth. *The Tree of Liberty*. New York: Farrar & Rinehart, 1939. 985pp. In a vast panorama that traces American history from the 1750s to the early 1800s three fictional families interact with a number of actual figures, including Jefferson.

Safire, William. *Scandalmonger*. New York: Simon & Schuster, 2000. 496pp. In Safire's carefully researched presentation of the press treatment of the personal scandals of the founding fathers, the original tabloid journalist James Callendar supplies the first public airing of the president's relationship with his slave Sally Hemings. The novel offers interesting portraits of many important figures, including Washington, Hamilton, Madison, Burr, and Monroe.

Vidal, Gore. *Burr: A Novel*. New York: Random House, 1973. 430pp. Jefferson's vice president dominates Vidal's remarkably inventive depiction of the early American government and Burr's conflict with Jefferson.

Recommended Juvenile Biographies

Bober, Natalie. *Thomas Jefferson: Man on a Mountain*. New York: Atheneum, 1988. 274pp.

YA. In a carefully researched and detailed account using Jefferson's own writings Bober traces Jefferson's career and many facets. A balanced portrait, the examination does not omit Jefferson's weaknesses and paradoxes.

Fleming, Thomas. *Thomas Jefferson*. New York: Grosset & Dunlap, 1971. 182pp. MG/YA. In a vivid narrative loaded with personal details, Fleming surveys Jefferson's life, character, and contribution. His views on slavery and the personal controversies surrounding them are omitted, however.

Meltzer, Milton. *Thomas Jefferson*. New York: F. Watts, 1991. 255pp. MG/YA. In a chronological treatment of the major events in Jefferson's life, Meltzer emphasizes Jefferson's internal conflicts between his passions and his intellect and is particularly candid on Jefferson's views of slavery.

Old, Wendie C. *Thomas Jefferson*. Springfield, New Jersey: Enslow, 1997. 128pp. A concise narrative account of the highlights of Jefferson's life and career with useful quotations and illustrations.

Wibberley, Leonard. *Man of Liberty: A Life of Thomas Jefferson*. New York: Farrar, Straus, 1968. 404pp. MG. Originally published in four separate volumes, Wibberly's detailed treatment of Jefferson's life vividly recreates the period and background, along with reconstructed dialogue.

Biographical Films and Theatrical Adaptations

A&E Biography Video: Thomas Jefferson: Philosopher of Freedom (1995). Director: Adam Friedman. This documentary attempts a balanced view of both Jefferson's public and private life but stresses the latter. Video.

Jefferson in Paris (1995). Director: James Ivory. This mainly speculative account of Jefferson's years in France casts Nick Nolte as Jefferson in several crises of the heart with Sally Hemings (Thandie Newton) and Maria Cosway (Greta Scacchi). Video.

Lewis & Clark: The Journey of the Corps of Discovery (1997). Director: Ken Burns. Sam Waterston is the voice of Jefferson in this documentary reconstruction of Lewis & Clark's epic journey. Video.

Liberty!: The American Revolution (1997). Directors: Ellen Hovde and Muffie Meyer. This PBS documentary series features actors portraying the principals in dramatic readings from their letters and speeches. Campbell Scott portrays Jefferson. The companion volume is written by Thomas J. Fleming (New York: Viking, 1997. 394pp.) Video.

1776 (1972). Director: Peter H. Hunt. The film version of the Broadway musical comedy by Sherman Edwards and Peter Stone that opened in 1969 concerns the first Continental Congress and the signing of the Declaration of Independence. Ken Howard portrays Jefferson, and Blyth Danner is Martha Jefferson, with William Daniels as John Adams and Howard da Silva as Benjamin Franklin. Video.

Thomas Jefferson (1997). Director: Ken Burns. Jefferson receives Burns's characteristic documentary treatment with actors' readings from primary material and scholarly perspectives. Sam Waterston portrays Jefferson. Video.

Thomas Jefferson: A View from the Mountain (1995). Producer: Martin Doblmeier. Examines Jefferson's attitudes and actions toward slavery with an emphasis on the controversy over Sally Hemings. Video.

Other Sources

Brown, David S. *Thomas Jefferson: A Biographical Companion.* Santa Barbara, California: ABC-CLIO, 1998. 266pp. In a series of alphabetically arranged entries, Brown covers the significant topics in Jefferson's life and times, along with a selection of primary sources, including Jefferson's draft of the Declaration of Independence, letters, and his first inaugural address.

Koch, Adrienne, ed. *Jefferson.* Englewood Cliffs, New Jersey: Prentice-Hall, 1971. 180pp. Part of a useful series that brings together excerpts from Jefferson's writings and contemporary and scholarly views.

Peterson, Merrill D. *The Jefferson Image in the American Mind.* New York: Oxford University Press, 1960. 548pp. Peterson's fascinating study of the shifting views of Jefferson in the nineteenth and twentieth century helps to explain the approaches of Jefferson's many biographers.

Peterson, Merrill D., ed. *Thomas Jefferson: A Reference Biography.* New York: Scribner, 1986. 513pp. This compilation of essays on various themes in Jefferson's life, thought, and career, features a capsule biography by Dumas Malone.

248. JESUS CHRIST
ca. 6 BC–ca. AD 30

A first-century Jewish carpenter, prophet, and teacher, Jesus is considered the inspiration for Christianity and is looked upon by many as the Messiah and the Son of God. The Gospels of Matthew, Mark, Luke, and John provide the primary source of information about his life and death and report that he was miraculously conceived by Mary and born in Bethlehem in Judea. His father was Joseph, a carpenter. At 30 he was baptized by his cousin, John the Baptist, and shortly thereafter began his ministry. Accompanied by a group of disciples, he traveled throughout Judea preaching a doctrine of charity, universal love, repentance, and heavenly salvation, and is said to have performed numerous miracles. His teachings and assertion of divinity provoked skepticism and hostility on the part of Jewish and Roman leaders. He was convicted by Pontius Pilate, Roman prefect of Judea, of sedition and other crimes against the state and crucified. According to his followers, he rose from the dead on the third day, appeared to them, and ascended to heaven.

Autobiography and Primary Sources

Among the treatments of Jesus' life in the New Testament—the principal sources of information we have—it is generally believed that Mark's version is the closest to an eyewitness account with Matthew, Luke, and John depending on his account in varying degrees.

Recommended Biographies

Fredriksen, Paula. *Jesus of Nazareth, King of the Jews: A Jewish Life and the Emergence of Christianity.* New York: Knopf,1999. 320pp. Looking at the implication of Jesus' crucifixion, the one historical fact that we know for sure, Fredriksen posits a radical but plausible view of the historical Jesus, making accessible both the world of first-century Palestine and biblical scholarship.

Grant, Michael. *Jesus: An Historian's Review of the Gospels.* New York: Scribner, 1977. 261pp. Grant, an ancient historian, locates Jesus in the context of his times, setting forth a very human figure, shorn of the miraculous, whose ministry and apocalyptic message are given a comprehensible historical grounding.

Meier, John P. *A Marginal Jew.* New York: Doubleday, 1991–1994. 2 vols. One of the leading biblical scholars has attempted a "consensus document on who Jesus of Nazareth was" through a close examination of the fundamental facts of Jesus' life. Slow-going for the nonspecialist, Meier's study is nevertheless an impressive achievement and should not be missed by the reader looking for a definitive treatment of the historical Jesus.

Sanders, E.P. *The Historical Figure of Jesus.* New York: Penguin, 1993. 397pp. Sanders supplies a convincing view of Jesus as a human figure in his religious, cultural, and historical contexts. The book's chief value is to separate what can be known for sure about Jesus' life, using the evidence to supply a balanced picture of the historical Jesus.

Wilson, A.N. *Jesus.* New York: W.W. Norton, 1992. 269pp. Novelist and biographer Wilson provides a narrative account that overturns conventional wisdom on virtually every aspect of Jesus' life, including that he never set out to establish Christianity, was probably married, and the resurrection never happened. Although challenging to traditional belief, the book is well-researched and absorbing and serves to create a believable human portrait.

Other Biographical Studies

Bornkamm, Günther. *Jesus of Nazareth.* New York: Harper & Row, 1960. 239pp. Bornkamm, a German theologian manages a balanced view of Jesus between the twin extremes of history and faith. Free of scholarly jargon and accessible, Bornkamm offers a illuminating intellectual and spiritual history that maintains its footing in the verifiable.

Carpenter, Humphrey. *Jesus.* New York: Oxford University Press, 1980. 102pp. Part of the Past Masters series, Carpenter's concise study looks at Jesus as an important intellectual figure, examining his teachings and summarizing modern views on Jesus by historians and theologians.

Cross, Colin. *Who Was Jesus?* New York: Atheneum, 1970. 230pp. In Cross's view Jesus was a Jewish prophet, unoriginal theologically or morally, whose success came from his skills as a "brilliant propagandist." Scholarly superficial, Cross's is a journalistic effort that devotes most of its focus to a history of Israel and Christianity with Jesus the link between the two.

Crossan, John D. *Jesus: A Revolutionary Biography.* San Francisco: HarperSan Francisco, 1995. 209pp. Crossan's Jesus is a social revolutionary, and the book is primarily interesting for its depiction of the times and intellectual ferment from which Jesus developed.

Duquesne, Jacques. *Jesus: An Unconventional Biography.* Liquori, Missouri: Triumph Books, 1997. 304pp. Duquesne integrates modern scholarly research on the historical Jesus into a biographical narrative that comes close to biographical fiction in which the Gospel accounts are elaborated by both fact and imagination.

Enslin, Morton S. *The Prophet from Nazareth.* New York: McGraw-Hill, 1961. 221pp. Enslin concentrates on what we can know of Jesus by a close examination of his teachings. This intellectual biography depicts Jesus as a prophet in the Jewish tradition.

Renan, Ernest. *The Life of Jesus.* 1863. Reprint ed. New York: Modern Library, 1955. 393pp. Renan's narrative account of Jesus' life has been controversial by its insisting on Jesus' humanity and excluding the supernatural and miraculous from view. Instead a plausible human figure, fully integrated in his time and place is allowed to emerge.

Schweitzer, Albert. *The Quest of the Historical Jesus: A Critical Study of Its Progress from Reimarus to Wrede.* New York: Macmillan, 1922. 413pp. Like Strauss's book, Schweitzer's study is a critical assessment of the source material and previous biographical and historical attempts, which Schweitzer finds wanting in objectivity. The book is a classic of synthesis and reasoned argument.

Spoto, Donald. *The Hidden Jesus.* New York: St. Martin's, 1998. 312pp. The celebrity biographer and former monk turns his research skills on the life of Christ that challenges much of the conventional wisdom of Christianity's tradition. More devotional than sensational, Spoto offers a fresh look that attempts to balance both Jesus' divinity and his humanity.

Strauss, David F. *The Life of Jesus: Critically Examined.* 1846. Reprint ed. Philadelphia: Fortress Press, 1973. 812pp. Strauss's rationalistic examination of Jesus' life and the Gospels is the groundbreaking text in the search for the historical basis for understanding Jesus' activities and identity.

Biographical Novels

Asch, Sholem. *The Nazarene.* New York: Putnam, 1939. 698pp. Jesus' story is described from several points of view with an emphasis on his historical and cultural identity.

Bishop, Jim. *The Day Christ Died.* New York: Harper & Row, 1957. 336pp. Bishop's bestselling dramatization of Christ's passion is handled with a journalistic immediacy and vividness, elaborated by imagined dialogue and invention.

Burgess, Anthony. *Man of Nazareth.* New York: McGraw-Hill, 1979. 357pp. This is the novelization of Burgess's screenplay for the Franco Zefferelli television production, *Jesus of Nazareth* with Jesus' story told in a series of vividly described scenes.

Graves, Robert. *King Jesus.* New York: Minerva Press, 1946. 424pp. Graves retells the New Testament story with Jesus in the role of a political rather than spiritual leader, deemphasizing the miraculous, and playing up the historical context.

Holmes, Marjorie. *Two from Galilee.* New York: Bantam, 1974. 223pp.; *Three from Galilee.* New York: Harper & Row, 1985. 230pp.; *The Messiah.* New York: Harper & Row, 1987. 396pp. Holmes's fictional trilogy tells Jesus' life story from his birth, through his ministry, and crucifixion.

Kazantzakis, Nikos. *The Last Temptation of Christ.* New York: Simon & Schuster, 1960. 506pp. Kazantzakis's controversial depiction of Jesus is often at odds with the biblical sources to emphasize a believable all-too-human figure.

Mailer, Norman. *The Gospel According to the Son.* New York: Random House, 1997. 242pp. Mailer provides an autobiographical account of Jesus' life that gives Jesus' own account of his temptation by Satan, his three-year ministry, and his agony on the cross. This is a daring attempt to imagine Jesus' inner life.

Oursler, Fulton. *The Greatest Story Ever Told.* Garden City, New York: Doubleday, 1949. 299pp. Oursler's fictional account of the life of Jesus has been a perennial bestseller. The Gospel story is set against a richly described historical background.

Payne, Robert. *The Lord Jesus.* New York: Abelard-Schuman, 1964. 314pp. Describes Jesus' life from the calling of his first disciples to his ascension following his crucifixion with an emphasis on Jesus the man, conscious of both his responsibilities and full of doubts about his faith and abilities.

Saramago, José. *The Gospel According to Jesus Christ.* New York: Harcourt, Brace, 1994. 377pp. As controversial as Kazantzakis's novel, Saramago presents a fictional life of Jesus mixing magic, myth, and reality.

Fictional Portraits

Ashcroft, Mary E. *The Magdalene Gospel.* New York: Doubleday, 1995. 129pp. Mary Magdalene, Martha, and Mary offer their views of Jesus after he has been crucified.

Brod, Max. *The Master.* New York: Philosophical Library, 1951. 426pp. Attempting to explain the development of Christianity in the context of contemporary philosophical and religious ideas, the novel dramatizes Jesus' exposure to the ideas of a young Greek poet.

Callaghan, Morley. *A Time for Judas.* New York: St. Martin's, 1984. 247pp. Callaghan offers an alternative reading of Jesus' ministry and death, portraying Judas not as a villain but as a devoted friend.

Carse, James P. *The Gospel of the Beloved Disciple.* San Francisco: HarperSan Francisco, 1997. 144pp. Jesus' message is interpreted by a Samaritan woman who becomes Jesus' confidante during his ministry.

Costain, Thomas B. *The Silver Chalice.* Garden City, New York: Doubleday, 1952. 533pp. Costain's popular historical novel describes Jesus' ministry from the perspective of the silversmith commissioned to create the cup used by Jesus during the Last Supper.

Douglas, Lloyd C. *The Robe.* Boston: Houghton Mifflin, 1947. 472pp. Douglas's view of early Christianity features a dramatization of the crucifixion and its aftermath, focused on the life of the Roman tribune who acquires Jesus' robe.

Kinstler, Clysta. *The Moon under Her Feet.* New York: Harper & Row, 1989. 315pp. Kinstler's radically feminist version of Jesus' story combines the mythologies of paganism and Christianity in a story in which Mary Magdalene is a sorceress and lover of both Jesus and Judas.

Kossoff, David. *The Book of Witnesses.* New York: St. Martin's, 1972. 174pp.; *The Little Book of Sylvanus (Died 41 AD).* New York: St. Martin's, 1975. 144pp. Both of Kossoff's imaginative novels explores the enigma of Jesus' life. The first offers a chorus of eyewitnesses; in the second a skeptic in Herod's service investigates the implications of the recently crucified man.

Park, Paul. *The Gospel of Corax.* New York: Soho Press, 1996. 297pp. In a radical reinterpretation of the story of Jesus, Park imagines Jesus' trip to the east where he attains enlightenment.

Wibberley, Leonard. *The Testament of Theophilus: A Novel of Christ and Caesar.* New York: Morrow, 1973. 335pp. The story of Jesus and the early days of the Christian church are seen through the perspective of a former slave whose encounter with Jesus becomes a turning point in his life.

Recommended Juvenile Biographies

Dickens, Charles. *The Life of Our Lord.* Morristown, New Jersey: Silver Burdett, 1987. 93pp. Written for his children and based on Luke's Gospel account, Dickens's is a heartfelt version of Jesus' story.

Biographical Films and Theatrical Adaptations

A&E Biography Video: Jesus: His Life. Producer: Steven Talley. Scholars and theologians explore the myths and reality of Jesus' life and his legacy, along with location footage and dramatic re-creations. Video.

Day of Triumph (1986). Director: Irving Pichel. The story of Jesus' life is dramatized through flashbacks as seen from the eyes of the apostle Andrew and a leader of the Zealot underground movement in Judea (Lee J. Cobb). Robert Wilson portrays Christ, with Joanne Dru as Mary Magdalene and James Griffith as Judas. Video.

The Execution of Jesus (1995). Producer: William Kronick. Explores the facts and myths surrounding Jesus' death. Video.

From Jesus to Christ: The First Christians (1998). Director: William Cran. Documentary originally broadcast on PBS's Frontline series explores Jesus' life and the movement he started while challenging familiar assumptions and conventional notions about the origins of Christianity based on interviews with leading New Testament scholars. Video.

The Gospel According to St. Matthew (1964). Director: Pier Paolo Passolini. Passolini's masterwork retells the story of Christ in a neo-realistic tone emphasizing his role as a social revolutionary. Video.

The Greatest Story Ever Told (1965). Director: George Stevens. An all-star cast, including Max von Sydow, Charlton Heston, Sidney Poitier, and John Wayne, are featured in this epic panorama of scenes from Jesus' life. Video.

Jesus Christ, Superstar (1973). Director: Norman Jewison. Based on the rock opera by Tim Rice and Andrew Lloyd Webber, the last days of Christ's life are reenacted by a group of young tourists in Israel. Featuring Ted Neeley, Carl Anderson, Yvonne Elliman, and Josh Mostel. Video.

Jesus and His Times (1991). Director: Kaye Lavine. Depicts Jesus' life and era in a multipart series. Video.

Jesus of Nazareth (1977). Director: Franco Zefferelli. Television mini-series with a screenplay by Anthony Burgess portrays the life of Jesus with an all-star cast, including Robert Powell, Anne Bancroft, James Mason, Laurence Olivier, and Anthony Quinn. Video.

Last Temptation of Christ (1988). Director: Martin Scorsese. Controversial adaptation of Kanzantzakis's novel features a script by Paul Schrader and a Peter Gabriel score. With Willem Dafoe in the lead, supported by Harvey Keitel, Barbara Hershey, David Bowie, and Harry Dean Stanton. Video.

Where Jesus Walked (1988). Director: Rolf Forsberg. Depicting significant moments in Jesus' life using video footage of the actual places mentioned in the New Testament. Video.

Other Sources

Rousseau, John J., and Rami Arav. *Jesus and His World: An Archaeological and Cultural Dictionary.* Minneapolis: Fortress Press, 1995. 392pp. Alphabetical entries cover the important sites, persons, customs, and details surrounding Jesus' life and his cultural setting.

Theissen, Gerd, and Annette Merz. *The Historical Jesus: A Comprehensive Guide.* Minneapolis: Fortress Press, 1998. 624pp. This is a useful reference tool summarizing the scholarship that has developed to explain Jesus in his time and place.

249. JOAN OF ARC
ca. 1412–1431

French military leader, saint, and national heroine, Joan was the daughter of a farmer in the town of Domrémy. Born into a country devastated by the Hundred Years War, she was about 12 when she began to hear "voices" from St. Michael, St. Catherine, and St. Margaret telling her that her divine mission was to free France from the English and ensure that the dauphin was crowned king. She led her army to victory over the besieged city of Orleans (1429), took other English posts along the Loire, and routed the enemy at Patay. After unsuccessful attempts to besiege Paris (1429) and defend

Compiègne (1430), Joan was captured by the Burgundians and ransomed to the English. She was tried by an ecclesiastical court at Rouen on a charge of witchcraft, convicted, and burned at the stake. She was beatified in 1909 and canonized in 1920.

Autobiography and Primary Sources

Joan of Arc: In Her Own Words. Willard R. Trask, ed. New York: Turtle Point Press, 1996. 287pp. In a journal format with daily headings, the book arranges testimony from the trial that gives the impression of Joan's own personal memoirs. Occasionally, summaries of Joan's actions are rendered from her point of view.

The Trial of Joan of Arc. Westport, Connecticut: Associated Booksellers, 1956. 173pp. This translation of the full trial record of 1431 and the rehabilitation hearings in 1450 represents the major documentary record for any biographical view of Joan.

Recommended Biographies

Gies, Frances. *Joan of Arc: The Legend and the Reality.* New York: Harper & Row, 1981. 306pp. In a scholarly but sympathetic examination Gies restores a good deal of heroism to the view of Joan that has been diminished in historical and psychological studies of Joan and her legend. Joan is placed firmly in her historical context, and her achievements are fully supported.

Gordon, Mary. *Joan of Arc.* New York: Viking, 2000. 176pp. Gordon's compact "biographical meditation" on Joan's life and meaning summarizes the essential facts and offers a compelling interpretation that emphasizes Joan's vulnerability as well as her remarkable achievement. Gordon is particularly insightful in a chapter on later interpretations of Joan on stage and screen.

Pernoud, Régine. *Joan of Arc: By Herself and Her Witnesses.* New York: Stein and Day, 1966. 287pp. The author establishes the essential factual framework for an understanding of Joan's life and character based exclusively on contemporary sources. Interspersing Joan's own words and others' testimony from her trial with commentary, the authors refutes elements of the legend and historical and psychological speculation at odds with or unconnected with the facts.

Pernoud, Régine, and Marie-Veronique Clin. *Joan of Arc: Her Story.* New York: St. Martin's, 1999. 300pp. Supplementing Pernoud's earlier documentary history, the authors resift the available sources to present a detailed factual portrait that contradicts many of the myths that have surrounded Joan. Not a conventional chronological narrative, the book instead annotates the historical record out of which a plausible, human figure emerges.

Warner, Marina. *Joan of Arc: Image of Female Heroism.* New York: Knopf, 1981. 349pp. Although not a conventional biography, Warner considers first the historical Joan and her impact seen from the standards of her times and then treats her various depictions by the church, in history, art, and popular culture, showing how the values of each formed her image and interpreted her actions and character.

Other Biographical Studies

DeVries, Kelly. *Joan of Arc: A Military Leader.* Stroud, England: Sutton, 1999. 242pp. The author concentrates on Joan's military and leadership capabilities in a factual account that summarizes her campaigns and relates her achievement against a extensive review of contemporary military practices.

France, Anatole. *Life of Joan of Arc.* New York: J. Lane, 1909. 2 vols. France's skeptical revisionist study strips Joan of legendary and sacred elements to argue based on factual evidence that she was an ordinary peasant girl who became a pawn in a church and state battle for power.

Guillemin, Henri. *Joan, Maid of Orleans.* New York: Saturday Review Press, 1973. 280pp. In a popular biographical treatment based on primary sources, the author sees Joan as a simple, stubborn, and genuinely inspired peasant girl who became a political pawn of the French court to confuse the English and maintain peasant support for the French cause.

Lang, Andrew. *Maid of France.* New York: Longmans, 1908. 379pp. Lang counters Anatole France's skeptical and realistic view of Joan with a defense of Joan's heroic and inspirational identity.

Lucie-Smith, Edward. *Joan of Arc.* New York: W.W. Norton, 1977. 326pp. Using a factual reconstruction of Joan's career and character based on eyewitness and other accounts as a basis, the author presents a highly speculative Freudian reading of Joan's personality to solve the mystery of her voices and behavior. The result is a credible human portrait, but one in which conjecture plays a dominant role.

Michelet, Jules. *Joan of Arc: Or, the Maid of Orleans.* 1858. Reprint ed. Ann Arbor: Michigan University Press, 1967. 132pp. Although the first biographical study based mainly on the documentary record, Michelet's study is still highly colored by patriotism and legend.

Nash-Marshall. *Joan of Arc: A Spiritual Biography.* New York: Crossroad, 1999. 192pp. This is a narrative account and interpretation of Joan's story from a spiritual point of view, exploring the connection between Joan's spirituality and the nationalist cause she served.

Sackville-West, Vita. *Saint Joan of Arc.* New York: Doubleday, 1936. 395pp. In a dramatically vivid and psychologically convincing portrait, the author offers both a narrative account and an analysis based on the factual record. The author falls short, however, of offering a plausible rational explanation of Joan's voices.

Scott, W.S. *Jeanne d'Arc.* New York: Barnes and Noble, 1974. 239pp. Written by an English priest and literary scholar, Scott's appreciative tribute rejects the skeptical view of most modern biographers and allows the legend to stand unquestioned.

Smith, John H. *Joan of Arc.* New York: Scribner, 1973. 232pp. Placing Joan in her political, economic, and social context, this is a thoughtful, readable life for the general reader based mainly on primary sources that reevaluates the legend and offers a somewhat diminished character who was far greater as a mythical figure than as an actual military leader.

Biographical Novels

Fadiman, Edwin. *The Voice and the Light.* New York: Crown, 1949. 249pp. Describing Joan's early years before she comes to the aid of the dauphin, the novel provides a plausible human portrait as Joan listens to the voices that help her to accept her role as a warrior.

Keneally, Thomas. *Blood Red, Sister Rose.* New York: Viking, 1974. 384pp. Although employing deliberate anachronisms to aid accessibility, this fictional account of Joan's life supplies a shrewd psychological profile and a convincing period backdrop.

Marcantel, Pamela. *An Army of Angels: A Novel of Joan of Arc.* New York: St. Martin's, 1997. 578pp. Observing the basic facts surrounding Joan's life and career, this biographical novel fills in some gaps in her story with plausible inventions, while emphasizing Joan's humanity, self-doubt, and fears.

Plaidy, Jean. *Epitaph for Three Women.* New York: Putnam, 1981. 332pp. In a dramatic re-creation of the fifteenth century, Plaidy focuses on Joan, Catherine of Valois, and Eleanor of Gloucester as representatives of their age in scenes from their lives.

Twain, Mark. *The Personal Reflections of Joan of Arc.* New York: Harper, 1896. 461pp. Following the known facts of Joan's life, including her childhood, her military career, and her trial and execution, Twain presents Joan from the perspective of a fictional page and secretary.

Fictional Portraits

Doherty, P.C. *The Serpent Among the Lilies.* New York: St. Martin's, 1990. 189pp. Ingeniously mixing fact and fiction, an English war hero, rogue, and thief is detailed to investigate the true identity of Joan, and he becomes part of her campaign on and off the battlefield.

Haasse, Hella S. *In a Dark Wood Wandering.* Chicago: Academy, 1989. 574pp. Set during the Hundred Years War and centering on the career of Charles VI, Joan appears as an important figure.

Schoonover, Lawrence. *The Burnished Blade.* New York: Macmillan, 1948. 371pp. This adventure tale set in the fifteenth century involves a young armorer who is sent on a mission to unmask a smuggling ring and features appearances by Joan.

Recommended Juvenile Biographies

Banfield, Susan. *Joan of Arc.* New York: Chelsea House, 1985. 111pp. MG/YA. In a solid biographical summary of Joan's life and career her story is captured with helpful illustrations that bring the period to life.

Garden, Nancy. *Dove and Sword: A Novel of Joan of Arc.* New York: Farrar, Straus, 1995. 237pp. YA. Viewing Joan's life and career as a military leader from the perspective of a female companion, this detailed portrait supplements the factual evidence with a solid presentation of period details.

Stanley, Diane. *Joan of Arc.* New York: Morrow, 1998. 40pp. MG. In this picture-book biography, Stanley provides a compelling portrait of Joan in a carefully researched text and sumptuous illustrations inspired by medieval illuminated manuscripts.

Biographical Films and Theatrical Adaptations

Anouilh, Jean. *The Lark.* New York: Oxford University Press, 103pp. Anouilh arranges for Joan to act out her life story before her judges who provide a running commentary on her significance in this thoughtful and entertaining drama.

Schiller, Friedrich. *The Maiden of Orleans: A Romantic Tragedy.* 1801. Reprint ed. Chapel Hill: University of North Carolina Press, 1962. 130pp. Schiller emphasizes the epic and spiritual aspects of Joan's story in his drama.

Shakespeare, William. *Henry VI, part I.* (1592). Various editions. In Shakespeare's historical cycle concerning the conflict between the houses of York and Lancaster, the first play deals with the wars with France and the relief of Orleans by the French. Joan appears from a decidedly English perspective as a "minister of hell" and an ignoble witch.

Shaw, George Bernard. *Saint Joan.* (1924). Various editions. Shaw's popular and provocative drama chronicles Joan's rise, trial, and execution as a clash of irreconcilable moral goods with Shaw granting Joan's English judges far more fairness and conscientiousness than history has allowed.

A&E Biography Video: Joan of Arc (1998). Provocative interviews with leading scholars are interwoven with historical images and location views to present Joan's life and significance. Video.

Joan of Arc (1948). Director: Victor Fleming. Faithfully based on the Maxwell Anderson play (*Joan of Lorraine.* Washington: Anderson House, 1946. 138pp.), Ingrid Bergman stars as Joan with José Ferrer and John Ireland. Video.

Joan of Arc (1999). Director: Christian Duguay. Leelee Sobieski stars in this made-for-television dramatization, featuring an authentic look and an impressive supporting cast, including Peter O'Toole, Peter Strauss, Shirley MacLaine, and Maximillian Schell. Video.

Joan the Woman (1917). Director: Cecil B. DeMille. DeMille's first historical epic stars Geraldine Farrar in the title role. Video.

The Messenger: The Story of Joan of Arc (1999). Director: Luc Bresson. This visually stunning but often over-the-top and muddled version of Joan's story has Milla Jovovich in the central role and Dustin Hoffman as the voice of Joan's conscience questioning her sanity.

The Passion of Joan of Arc (1928). Director: Carl Dreyer. Joan's trial and execution are portrayed based on the actual court records but compressed into a single day in this silent film. Starring Maria Falconetti, Eugene Silvain, and Maurice Schutz. Video.

Saint Joan (1957). Director: Otto Preminger. Film adaptation of the Shaw play with an all-star cast, including Jean Seberg in her film debut as Joan, with Richard Widmark, John Gielgud, Richard Todd, and Anton Walbrook. Video.

250. POPE JOHN XXIII
1881–1963

Italian-born pope of the Roman Catholic church and one of the best-regarded popes of modern times, John was born Angelo Roncalli. He was made an archbishop in 1925, cardinal in 1953, and elected pope in 1958. He revolutionized the church, promoting cooperation with other Christian denominations and religions, and advocating social reform in developing countries. He convened (1962) the influential Vatican Second Council to promote ecumenical and liturgical reforms.

Autobiography and Primary Sources

In My Own Words: Pope John XXIII. Anthony F. Chiffolo, ed. Liquori, Missouri: Liquori Publications, 1999. 112pp. This is a collection of John's addresses, public statements, encyclical and personal letters, and other writings.

Journey of a Soul. New York: McGraw-Hill, 1965. 453pp. John offers an account of his inner life in a spiritual diary kept for his own use beginning at the age of 14 as a seminarian to 1962.

Letters to His Family (1901–1962). New York: McGraw-Hill, 1970. 833pp. This collection of 727 letters to his extensive family covers John's life from his seminary days to his ascent to the papal throne and shows him to be down-to-earth and practical, yet balanced by his spirituality.

Recommended Biographies

Hebblethwaite, Peter. *Pope John XXIII: Shepherd of the Modern World.* Garden City, New York: Doubleday, 1985. 550pp. Hebblethwaite's is the most scholarly, authoritative study of John that helps to explain the reasons behind his surprising transformation from a transitional pope to one who began a revolution in the Church. Demythologizing many of the legends surrounding John, the book portrays him with all his faults as well as his virtues.

Trevor, Meriol. *Pope John.* Garden City, New York: Doubleday, 1967. 312pp. Dealing exclusively with the man rather than his papacy, Trevor provides a believable portrait that challenges the conventional view of John as a benevolent but naive. Trevor concentrates on two aspects of John's early career, the Modernist crisis under Pius X in 1910 and John's struggles with the Vatican hierarchy during his service in Bulgaria, Greece, and Turkey.

Other Biographical Studies

Aradi, Zsolt, James Itucek, and James C. O'Neill. *Pope John XXIII: An Authoritative Biography.* New York: Farrar, Straus, 1959. 325pp. Covering John's life only up to his election and coronation as pope, this is the best written and most detailed of the early biographies, particularly strong on John's formative years, diplomatic career, and personality.

Elliott, Lawrence. *I Will Be Called John: A Biography of Pope John XXIII.* New York: Reader's Digest Press, 1973. 338pp. Elliott's is a highly sympathetic popular treatment of John's life and career that is at its best when it allows the man to reveal himself and shows him as he appeared to those who knew him well.

Hatch, Alden. *A Man Named John: The Life of Pope John XXIII.* New York: Hawthorn Books, 1963. 287pp. This is a lively popular narrative account of John's career consisting of anecdotal glimpses of the man that underscore his peasant roots and simplicity. A memorial chapter has been added dealing with his final days and death.

Pecher, Erich. *Pope John XXIII: A Pictorial Biography.* New York: McGraw-Hill, 1959. 143pp. This visual portrait contains photographs of John at various stages of his life with a basic biographical summary of the important events of his career up to his election as pope.

Perrotta, Paul C. *Pope John XXIII: His Life and Character.* New York: Nelson, 1959. 270pp. More historical than biographical, the author's study seeks to explain the reasons behind John's selection as pope and to view John's career in the wider context of the Church's modern history.

Recommended Juvenile Biographies

Walch, Timothy. *Pope John XXIII.* New York: Chelsea House, 1986. 115pp. MG/YA. Walch's is an informative summary of the life and times of John with an emphasis on his impact on Church history.

251. ANDREW JOHNSON
1808–1875

Johnson, the seventeenth United States president (1865–1869), was born in Raleigh, North Carolina. At 14 he was apprenticed to a tailor and later had his own prosperous tailor shop in Greenville, Tennessee. A man of no formal schooling, he was taught to write and to improve his reading and spelling through the efforts of his wife, Eliza McCardle. He was elected councilman and later mayor, was sent to the state general assembly (1835), and served as a United States congressman (1843–1853) and governor of Tennessee (1853–1857). Elected vice-president with Abraham Lincoln (1860), he succeeded to the presidency after Lincoln's assassination. His attempt to remove Secretary of War Edwin Stanton from office resulted in his impeachment (1868) by the House on a charge of violation of the Tenure of Offices Act. He was acquitted in the Senate. Although Johnson's presidency was dominated by the problems of Reconstruction, a highlight of his administration was the purchase (1867) of Alaska, negotiated by Secretary of State William Seward.

Autobiography and Primary Sources

The Papers of Andrew Johnson. LeRoy P. Graf and Ralph W. Haskins, eds. Knoxville: University of Tennessee Press, 1967–1992. 10 vols. The number of surviving Johnson letters is small, and this scholarly edition provides the fullest selection available of his correspondence and other writings, with detailed prefaces that provide significant biographical insights.

Recommended Biographies

Sefton, James E. *Andrew Johnson and the Uses of Constitutional Power.* Boston: Little, Brown, 1980. 218pp. The best available concise and balanced summary of Johnson's entire career, Sefton's critical biography is based on the Johnson Papers and other primary sources and is particularly strong on Johnson's antebellum years.

Trefousse, Hans L. *Andrew Johnson: A Biography.* New York: W.W. Norton, 1989. 463pp. In the most comprehensive, scrupulously documented account of Johnson's life and career, Trefousse's fair but ultimately negative assessment traces the flaws in Johnson's leadership, whose background made it impossible for him to keep pace with the changes emerging after the Civil War.

Other Biographical Studies

Brabson, Fay W. *Andrew Johnson: A Life in Pursuit of the Right Course, 1808–1875.* Durham, North Carolina: Seeman Printery, 1972. 306pp. The work of a career army officer and amateur historian, this is a strong defense of Johnson's career that emphasizes both the challenges and his successes as a leader during a critical period of American history.

Castel, Albert E. *The Presidency of Andrew Johnson.* Lawrence: University Press of Kansas, 1979. 262pp. Considered the standard short assessment of Johnson's presidency and Reconstruction activities, Castel's examination emphasizes Johnson's political ambitions, stubbornness, and short-sightedness.

Jones, James Sawyer. *The Life of Andrew Johnson: Seventeenth President of the United States.* 1901. Reprint ed. New York: AMS Press, 1975. 400pp. Using family papers, this is a balanced account of Johnson's life and career but incorporates some myths as facts. Most interesting for its contemporary evaluations of Johnson.

Lomask, Milton. *Andrew Johnson: President on Trial.* New York: Farrar, Straus, 1960. 376pp. Beginning on the night of Lincoln's assassination and taking Johnson's story through his impeachment trial, Lomask offers a carefully documented account, one of the best available on the trial.

McKitrick, Eric L. *Andrew Johnson and Reconstruction.* Chicago: University of Chicago Press, 1961. 533pp. Written for the specialist, this detailed assessment of Johnson's Reconstruction policies challenges the notion that his sensible plan was derailed by Republican radicals. In McKitrick's view, Johnson was the architect of his own failures who blocked reconciliation with the South.

Milton, George F. *The Age of Hate: Andrew Johnson and the Radicals.* 1930. Reprint ed. Hamden, Connecticut: Archon Books, 1965. 788pp. Not a comprehensive life but a carefully researched assessment of Johnson and Reconstruction, Milton's more sympathetic treatment should be read as a contrast to McKitrick's opposite conclusions.

Reece, B. Carroll. *The Courageous Commoner: A Biography of Andrew Johnson.* Charleston, West Virginia: Education Foundation. 1962. 168pp. Reece mounts a impassioned defense of Johnson in an often simplistic appreciation.

Royall, Margaret S. *Andrew Johnson—Presidential Scapegoat: A Biographical Re-evaluation.* New York: Exposition Press, 1958. 175pp. Patterned more like a biographical novel than a objective and reliable account, this is an anecdotal, gossipy treatment that cannot be trusted in all its details, and its partisan bias slants the presentation.

Stryker, Lloyd P. *Andrew Johnson: A Study in Courage.* New York: Macmillan, 1929. 881pp. Written by a defense attorney determined to retry Johnson's impeachment, this is a strongly partisan rehabilitation of Johnson's reputation. The focus is narrowed to the eight years of Johnson's political career beginning with the Civil War. Weak on the early years and often melodramatic and strident in its defensiveness.

Tappan, George L. *Andrew Johnson—Not Guilty.* New York: Comet Press, 1954. 139pp. Tappan's short biography is another defense, as its title indicates, of Johnson's character and leadership. Simplistic in its approach, its many assertions are insufficiently supported.

Thomas, Lately. *The First President Johnson: The Three Lives of the Seventeenth President of the United States of America.* New York: Morrow, 1968. 676pp. In a popular narrative account, Thomas concentrates on Johnson the man rather than his political role and policies through his career as congressman, governor, and president. Not reliable in all its details.

Winston, Robert W. *Andrew Johnson: Plebian and Patriot.* 1928. Reprint ed. New York: Barnes and Noble, 1969. 549pp. In a full-length biography, well documented by primary sources that is particularly strong on the early years, Winston's special pleading on behalf of Johnson's sincerity and bravery limits its usefulness as an objective account. Johnson's shortcomings are insufficiently described.

Biographical Novels

Gerson, Noel B. *The Yankee from Tennessee.* Garden City, New York: Doubleday, 1960. 382pp. Tracing Johnson's entire career, with considerable attention to the antebellum years and his relationship with his wife, Gerson takes some liberties with the facts as well and invents some scenes based on his interpretations.

McSpadden, J. Walker. *Storm Center: A Novel about Andy Johnson.* New York: Dodd, Mead, 1947. 393pp. Offering a simplified and error-ridden account of Johnson's life and political career, McSpadden's sympathetic treatment shows him as a loyal and capable leader facing enormous opposition.

Fictional Portraits

Crabb, Alfred L. *Supper at the Maxwell House.* Indianapolis: Bobbs-Merrill, 1943. 372pp. Nashville during Reconstruction is the novel's subject with appearances by several historical figures, including Nathan Bedford Forrest and Johnson.

Recommended Juvenile Biographies

Dubowski, Cathy E. *Andrew Johnson: Rebuilding the Union.* Englewood Cliffs, New Jersey: Silver Burdett, 1991. 125pp. MG. Part of the History of the Civil War series, the book informatively surveys Johnson's private life and political career.

Kent, Zachary. *Andrew Johnson: Seventeenth President of the United States.* Chicago: Childrens Press, 1989. 100pp. MG. Part of the Encyclopedia of Presidents series, this is a workmanlike survey of the details of Johnson's rise to political power and embattled presidency.

Biographical Films and Theatrical Adaptations

Andrew Johnson (1965). Director: Alexander Singer. Adapted from John F. Kennedy's *Profiles in Courage,* Walter Matthau portrays Johnson delivering his Union Speech in 1860. Video.

Tennessee Johnson (1942). Director: William Dieterle. Van Heflin stars as Johnson with Ruth Hussey as Eliza Johnson and Lionel Barrymore as Thaddeus Stevens in this film biography depicting Johnson's political rise and clash with Congress. Not reliable in all its historical details.

Other Sources

McKitrick, Eric L., ed. *Andrew Johnson: A Profile.* New York: Hill & Wang, 1969. 224pp. This is a collection of essays on various aspects of Jackson's life and career.

252. LYNDON B. JOHNSON
1908–1973

The thirty-sixth U.S. president (1963–1969), Lyndon Baines Johnson was born near Stonewall, Texas, and graduated from Southwest Texas State Teachers College (1930). He taught in a Houston high school and served as secretary to a Texas congressman before winning (1937) a vacant seat in the House of Representatives. He served in the Pacific during World War II and was elected to the U.S. Senate (1948, 1954). As John F. Kennedy's vice-president, Johnson became president after JFK's assassination (1963) and in 1964 was elected to a full term. His greatest accomplishment was to push forward a sweeping domestic "Great Society" program that included major civil rights, antipoverty, and healthcare (Medicare, Medicaid) legislation, and aid to education. However, his presidency was marred by heavy U.S. involvement in the Vietnam War and by riots in urban black ghettos. In 1968 he announced that he would not seek a second term as president.

Autobiography and Primary Sources

The Vantage Point: Perspectives of the Presidency. New York: Holt, 1971. 636pp. Johnson's presidential memoir is an uneven and rarely revealing recounting of the major efforts of his administration with almost no opinions expressed and almost nothing on Johnson's pre-presidential life. The book represents Johnson's story as he wanted it written in the voice and showing the personality of a thoughtful leader.

Taking Charge: The Johnson White House Tapes, 1963–1964. Michael R. Beschloss, ed. New York: Simon & Schuster, 1997. 591pp. Transcripts of recorded White House conversations display a remarkable firsthand view of Johnson's assumption of presidential power following the Kennedy assassination.

Recommended Biographies

Caro, Robert. *The Years of Lyndon Johnson: The Path to Power.* New York: Knopf, 1982. 786pp.; *Means of Ascent.* New York: Knopf, 1990. 432pp. Caro's exhaustively detailed and still unfinished multivolume biography has reached 1948 and promises to be the most comprehensive study available. Highly opinionated and harshly critical, Caro's judgmental analysis is a damning portrait of a political opportunist. The negatives that Caro so tirelessly assembles are unrelieved by any mitigation, but few will not admire Caro's thoroughness and persistence, despite his evident lack of sympathy for his subject. Equally admirable is Caro's excellence in detailing Johnson's Texas background.

Conkin, Paul. *Big Daddy from the Pedernales: Lyndon Baines Johnson.* Boston: Twayne, 1986. 324pp. In one of the most balanced and solidly researched examinations of Johnson's life and career Conkin presents LBJ as a complex blend of positives and negatives that produced a similarly mixed political record.

Dallek, Robert. *Lone Star Rising: Lyndon Johnson and His Times, 1908–1960.* New York: Oxford University Press, 1991. 721pp.; *Flawed Giant: Lyndon Johnson and His Times, 1961–1973.* New York: Oxford University Press, 1998. 754pp. Setting out to set the record straight and to resist the various biases that have slanted the view of LBJ, Dallek's impressive two-volume study provides a far more balanced assessment of Johnson's life and political career than Robert Caro's indictment, and has earned accolades as the definitive life.

Kearns, Doris. *Lyndon Johnson and the American Dream.* New York: Harper & Row, 1976. 432pp. In a psychological assessment based on conversations with Johnson, the author documents the behavior patterns, leadership style, and political beliefs that help to explain Johnson's achievements and failures. The book features extensive quotes from Johnson himself, revealing an often hidden human side.

Unger, Irwin, and Debi Unger. *LBJ: A Life.* New York: Wiley, 1999. 592pp. In a sympathetic account, the authors explore the political and personal influences that shaped Johnson into such a contradictory figure. While not glossing over Johnson's many flaws, the positives are emphasized here, showing the ways in which Johnson turned liabilities into assets.

Other Biographical Studies

Bernstein, Irving. *Guns or Butter: The Presidency of Lyndon Johnson.* New York: Oxford University Press, 1996. 606pp. This detailed chronicle of LBJ's presidency examines the interplay between Johnson's domestic agenda and disastrous Vietnam policy that proved to be the administration and the man's undoing.

Bornet, Vaughn D. *The Presidency of Lyndon B. Johnson.* Lawrence: University Press of Kansas, 1983. 415pp. In a scholarly and balanced assessment of the Johnson administration, Bornet defends Johnson's domestic policies and shows how foreign affairs derailed his presidency. The book, however, fails to animate the man behind the various policies.

Califano, Joseph A. *The Triumph and Tragedy of Lyndon Johnson: The White House Years.* New York: Simon & Schuster, 1991. 398pp. Califano, Johnson's top aide on domestic affairs from 1965 to 1969, offers his firsthand observation of the last three and a half years of the Johnson administration, capturing both the president's skills and flaws.

Dugger, Ronnie. *The Politician: The Life and Times of Lyndon Johnson: The Drive to Power from the Frontier to Master of the Senate.* New York: W.W. Norton, 1982. 514pp. In a hostile account of Johnson's life and political career up to his election as Senate majority leader, Dugger negatively traces the origin for Johnson's later behavior and presidential failures. Biographical chapters are interspersed with essays about Texas, Vietnam, and the danger of nuclear war.

Evans, Rowland, and Robert Novak. *Lyndon B. Johnson: The Exercise of Power.* New York: New American Library, 1966. 597pp. Evans and Novak provided the first serious political biography of Johnson's public career from 1931. Emphasizing Johnson's skill in political arm-twisting, the deeper mystery of Johnson's personality is unexamined.

Goldman, Eric F. *The Tragedy of Lyndon Johnson.* New York: Knopf, 1969. 531pp. As a special consultant to the president, Goldman offers his unflattering observation of Johnson's personality whose various flaws undid his legislative skills and domestic policy triumphs. Valuable for its eyewitness evidence.

Heren, Louis. *No Hail, No Farewell.* New York: Harper & Row, 1970. 275pp. This assessment of the Johnson administration by a British reporter provides a more sympathetic account free from the passionate bias Johnson stimulated in American writers.

Miller, Merle. *Lyndon: An Oral Biography.* New York: Putnam, 1980. 645pp. Weaving together the testimony of hundreds of individuals who observed Johnson at first hand, Miller fashions a multifaceted view that allows contradictions to stand.

Mooney, Booth. *LBJ: An Irreverent Chronicle.* New York: Crowell, 1976. 290pp. Written by Johnson's speech writer, this is an informal, anecdotal chronicle of Johnson's political career that offers a complex portrait of Johnson. The president's humanity is documented as well as his political skill.

Muslin, Hyman L., and Thomas H. Jobe. *Lyndon Johnson: The Tragic Self, a Psychohistorical Portrait.* New York: Insight Books, 1991. 234pp. The authors provide a psychological profile based on the psychoanalytic self-psychology model.

Reedy, George. *Lyndon B. Johnson: A Memoir.* New York: Andrews and McMeel, 1982. 159pp. The author, who worked for Johnson in the Senate and in the White House as press secretary, provides an assessment that balances Johnson's considerable personal flaws with his political skills.

Schulman, Bruce J. *Lyndon B. Johnson and American Liberalism: A Brief Biography with Documents.* New York: St. Martin's, 1995. 269pp. This is a brief but comprehensive account of the major events of Johnson's career with an emphasis on the role he played in the rise and fall of postwar American liberalism. Included are 15 documents, including Johnson's speeches and scholarly assessments, that help the reader evaluate both the man and his influence.

Steinberg, Alfred. *Sam Johnson's Boy: A Close-Up of the President from Texas.* New York: Macmillan, 1968. 871pp. Tracing Johnson's public career from childhood to early 1968, this is an anecdotally rich narrative drawn from interviews. Unscholarly, the book mixes truths, half-truths, and distortions and should be read with caution regarding its reliability.

Valenti, Jack. *A Very Human President.* New York: W.W. Norton, 1975. 402pp. Valenti, a long time Johnson friend and confidante, offers his eyewitness view in a series of anecdotes that clash with the admiring intention of the book to restore the luster to the Johnson presidency.

Fictional Portraits

Roosevelt, Elliott. *Murder and the First Lady.* New York: St. Martin's, 1984. 227pp.; *Murder in the Oval Office.* New York: St. Martin's, 1989. 170pp.; *Murder in the East Room.* New York: St. Martin's, 1993. 201pp. A young Lyndon Johnson in the 1940s appears as a character in the author's historical mystery series featuring Eleanor Roosevelt as sleuth.

Windle, Janice Woods. *Hill Country.* Marieta, Georgia: Longstreet Press, 1998. 474pp. Based on the actual experiences of the author's grandmother, the novel traces the life of an independent and resourceful Texan from the 1870s to the 1960s, and features a substantial appearance by LBJ.

Recommended Juvenile Biographies

Eskow, Dennis. *Lyndon Baines Johnson.* New York: F. Watts, 1993. 160pp. MG. In an overall sympathetic portrait, Johnson's life and political career is recounted with his contradictions acknowledged.

Kaye, Tony. *Lyndon B. Johnson.* New York: Chelsea House, 1988. 112pp. MG. An accurate and well-rounded portrait featuring newspaper photographs and sidebar quotes.

Schuman, Michael. *Lyndon B. Johnson.* Springfield, New Jersey: Enslow, 1998. 128pp. MG. Concentrating mainly on Johnson's public career, this objective account describes Johnson's accomplishments as well as his failures. Documented by Johnson's own words and excerpts from the recently published transcripts of audiotapes recorded during his presidency.

Biographical Films and Theatrical Adaptations

A&E Biography Video: Lyndon Johnson: Triumph and Tragedy (1997). Producer: Ron Steinman. This documentary assessment of Johnson's life and political career attempts a balanced view of both his achievements and failures. Video.

LBJ (1991). Producer: David Grubin. This detailed four-part acclaimed documentary look at Johnson's life and political career was originally broadcast on PBS in the American Experience series. Video.

LBJ: The Early Years (1988). Director: Peter Werner. Randy Quaid stars in the title role with Patti Lupone as Lady Bird in this dramatic treatment of Johnson's political career from his years as a congressman to his swearing in as president. Video.

The Right Stuff (1983). Director: Philip Kaufman. In the film version of Tom Wolfe's nonfiction book, Johnson (Donald Moffat) is shown as a cartoonish buffoon complete with temper tantrum after he is denied a publicity opportunity by Annie Glenn (Mary Jo Deschanel). Starring Ed Harris, Dennis Quaid, Sam Shepard, Scott Glenn, and Fred Ward. Video.

See also John F. Kennedy; Robert F. Kennedy

254. SAMUEL JOHNSON
1709–1784

Celebrated for his brilliance and wit, Johnson was the leading English literary scholar and critic of his day. The son of a bookseller, he grew up in poverty and suffered from the effects of scrofula throughout his life. He spent a year studying at Oxford and then worked as a bookseller and schoolmaster. After moving to London (1737), he began to write poetry and prose for *Gentleman's Magazine* and through his writings gained recognition in literary circles. England's first true man of letters, Johnson's works include *Life of Savage* (1744), *The Vanity of Human Wishes* (1749), a critically acclaimed edition of Shakespeare (1765), and *Lives of the Poets* (1779–1781). He is perhaps best known for his *Dictionary of the English Language* (1755), the first comprehensive English lexicon ever compiled and written.

Autobiography and Primary Sources

Dr. Johnson: His Life in Letters. David Littlejohn, ed. Englewood Cliffs, New Jersey: Prentice-Hall, 1965. 239pp. Interweaving over 200 letters with connective commentary, the volume forms a dramatic narrative of Johnson's career mainly in his words.

Johnson on Johnson: A Selection from the Personal and Autobiographical Writings of Samuel Johnson. John Wain, ed. New York: Dutton, 1976. 247pp. Using excerpts from his letters, diaries, and other writing, this volume fashions a version of Johnson's autobiography, along with a chronology and a who's who of individuals mentioned.

The Letters of Samuel Johnson. Bruce Redford, ed. Princeton, New Jersey: Princeton University Press, 1992–1994. 5 vols. The scholarly edition of Johnson's letters is indispensable as a biographical source and for insights into various aspects of Johnson's personality.

Recommended Biographies

Bate, Walter Jackson. *Samuel Johnson.* New York: Harcourt, Brace, 1977. 646pp. Bate's acclaimed psychological study connects Johnson's life, character, and work in an interpretive whole that stresses Johnson's modernity. The result is a darker, more complex portrayal than previous studies. Impressive in its scholarship and familiarity with the era, Bate's study is an extremely useful supplement to Boswell's treatment that deepens the view of Johnson's achievement and character.

Boswell, James. *Life of Samuel Johnson.* 1791. Reprint ed. New York: Oxford University Press, 1980. 1,492pp. A literary classic and at the apex of the biographer's art, Boswell's life is an enthralling narrative and generous, rounded character portrait. The emphasis is on Johnson's later years, taking full advantage of Boswell's eyewitness perspective and recorded conversations.

Clifford, James L. *Young Sam Johnson.* New York: McGraw-Hill, 1955. 377pp.; *Dictionary Johnson: Samuel Johnson's Middle Years.* New York: McGraw-Hill, 1979. 372pp. Clifford's two volumes trace Johnson's life up to 1763 and is one of the most detailed descriptive narratives on Johnson's life available. It is particularly strong on Johnson's first 40 years that Boswell insufficiently details.

Wain, John. *Samuel Johnson: A Biography.* New York: Viking, 1975. 388pp. Wain's unscholarly but sensitive and reliable examination portrays Johnson's humanity and does not overlook his defects as well as his character strengths. Recommended as a thoughtful introduction to the man and his era.

Other Biographical Studies

DeMaria, Robert. *The Life of Samuel Johnson: A Critical Biography.* Cambridge, Massachusetts: Blackwell, 1993. 356pp. Somewhat misleadingly titled, all but three of the book's chapters are devoted to an interpretive study of Johnson's works. A useful, though somewhat densely written introduction to Johnson's artistry.

Fussell, Paul. *Samuel Johnson and the Life of Writing.* New York: Harcourt, Brace, 1971. 303pp. Fussell's critical biography is the best book on Johnson the writer. In a refreshingly original portrait Fussell challenges the various legends and substitutes a realistic view of the writer at work.

Halliday, F.E. *Doctor Johnson and His World.* New York: Viking, 1968. 144pp. Halliday's is a useful visual biography that provides the highlights of Johnson's career in the context of his times.

Hibbert, Christopher. *The Personal History of Samuel Johnson.* New York: Harper & Row, 1971. 364pp. Hibbert concentrates on Johnson's inner life, including his loves and anxieties, in a well-documented and readable account that presents a darker, less attractive portrait of Johnson than Boswell's treatment.

Irwin, George. *Samuel Johnson: A Personality in Conflict.* Auckland, New Zealand: Auckland University Press, 1971. 168pp. Irwin offers a provocative psychological analysis of the causes for Johnson's periodic depressions, identifying them in the writer's guilt over his suppressed hatred for his mother and suggesting that Johnson's writings represent a heroic effort at self-analysis.

Kaminski, Thomas. *The Early Career of Samuel Johnson.* New York: Oxford University Press, 1987. 268pp. This is a detailed summary of Johnson's literary activities from his arrival in London in 1737 to his decision to begin his *Dictionary* in 1746. Enriching the picture of Johnson during the period, Kaminski challenges the legend of the desperate poverty Johnson experienced before his success.

Kingsmill, Hugh. *Johnson without Boswell: A Contemporary Portrait of Samuel Johnson.* New York: Knopf, 1941. 306pp. Offering a valuable supplement to Boswell, Kingsmill brings together other contemporary sources on Johnson's life.

Krutch, Joseph W. *Samuel Johnson.* New York: Holt, 1944. 599pp. Krutch provided the first modern scholarly biography of Johnson that covers his entire life with nearly half of the book devoted to the pre-Boswell years. Reliable and objective, Krutch's study remains a valuable assessment of Johnson, his work, and his times.

Lane, Margaret. *Samuel Johnson & His World.* New York: Harper & Row, 1975. 256pp. The highlights of Johnson's life and career are chronicled in this visual biography that is particularly useful in detailing Johnson's era.

Larsen, Lyle. *Dr. Johnson's Household.* Hamden, Connecticut: Archon Books, 1985. 155pp. Focusing on Johnson's family and domestic life during his middle and later years, Larsen uncovers some new facts and portrays several of the minor figures that formed Johnson's household.

Lipking, Lawrence I. *Samuel Johnson: The Life of an Author.* Cambridge, Massachusetts: Harvard University Press, 1998. 372pp. This critical biography focuses on Johnson's career as a writer and shows the relationship between Johnson's life and his works. With fresh readings of all the major works, Lipking charts the various conditions, both personal and cultural, that influenced Johnson's writing.

Pearson, Hesketh. *Johnson and Boswell: The Story of Their Lives.* New York: Harper, 1959. 390pp. In an opinionated dual biography, Pearson offers a colorful and readable but occasionally superficial portrait of the pair.

Stephen, Leslie. *Samuel Johnson.* 1878. Reprint ed. New York: AMS, 1968. 195pp. Stephen's brief character sketch remains a balanced appreciation of Johnson's mind and ideas.

Biographical Novels

Carter, Winifred. *Dr. Johnson's Dear Mistress.* New York: Philosophical Library, 1949. 319pp. Based on the life of Hester Thrale, the novel presents Johnson, his circle, and their times, but not with much penetration.

Norman, Charles. *Mr. Oddity: Samuel Johnson, LL.D.* London: J. Murray,1951. 348pp. This fictionalized biography of Johnson traces his life using some of the best conversations recorded in Boswell, and the novel serves as an entertaining and reasonably accurate introduction to Johnson, his circle, and his times.

Fictional Portraits

Annandale, Barbara. *The Bonnet Laird's Daughter.* New York: Coward-McCann,1977. 286pp. In this historical romance, a beautiful young Scot secretly marries a protégé of John Paul Jones, and Dr. Johnson rather implausibly helps her escape her father's wrath.

Buchan, John. *Midwinter.* New York: G. Doran,1923. 333pp. Buchan's romantic adventure tale set during the rebellion of Bonnie Prince Charlie employs Dr. Johnson as an important agent in the novel's intrigue plot.

De La Torre, Lillian. *Dr. Sam Johnson: Detector.* New York: Knopf, 1946. 257pp.; *The Detections of Dr. Sam Johnson.* Garden City, New York: Doubleday, 1960. 190pp.; *The Return of Dr. Sam Johnson, Detector.* New York: International Polygonics, 1985. 187pp.; *The Exploits of Dr. Sam Johnson, Detector.* New York: International Polygonics, 1987. 224pp. The author's series of period mysteries engagingly employs Johnson as a sleuth.

Recommended Juvenile Biographies

Brown, Ivor. *Dr. Johnson and His World.* New York: Walck, 1966, 47pp. YA. In a gracefully written and concise overview, Brown supplies an informative examination of Johnson and his age.

Biographical Films and Theatrical Adaptations

Newton, A. Edward. *Doctor Johnson: A Play.* Boston: Atlantic Monthly Press, 1923. 120pp. Newton's play dramatizes four scenes from Johnson's life with dialogue derived from Boswell, Johnson's letters, and other contemporary sources.

Lloyd's of London (1936). Director: Henry King. Yorke Sherwood portrays Dr. Johnson in this entertaining period adventure yarn concerning the British insurance firm and an employee's (Tyrone Power) competition with an English lord (George Sanders) for the love of a lady (Madeleine Carroll). Video.

Samuel Johnson: Writer, 1709–1784 (1996). Director: Malcolm Hossick. Traces Dr. Johnson's life and career using contemporary prints and views of places associated with his life. Video.

Other Sources

Clingham, Greg, ed. *The Cambridge Companion to Samuel Johnson.* New York: Cambridge University Press, 1997. 266pp. This reader's guide to Johnson's life and work by leading specialists includes a chronology and a guide for further reading.

Page, Norman, ed. *Dr. Johnson: Interviews and Recollections.* Totowa, New Jersey: Barnes and

Noble, 1986. 176pp. This is a useful collection of contemporary views of Johnson.

Page, Norman. *A Dr. Johnson Chronology.* Boston: G.K. Hall, 1990. 136pp. Johnson's activities are helpfully organized into an extensive chronology, extremely handy as a reference source.

Rogers, Pat. *The Samuel Johnson Encyclopedia.* Westport, Connecticut: Greenwood, 1996. 252pp. This useful reference volume covers various aspects of Johnson's life, circle, and writings.

See also See also James Boswell

255. JOHN PAUL JONES
1747–1792

America's Revolutionary War naval hero was born John Paul in Scotland and went to sea at age 12. While commanding the *Betsy* in 1773, he killed a mutinous crew member in self-defense and fled to avoid trial. By 1775 he was in Philadelphia and had added "Jones" to his name. After obtaining a commission in the Continental navy, he harried British ships off the coast of France and England and captured (1778) the British warship, *Drake.* As commander of the *Bonhomme Richard,* he successfully engaged (1779) the British in one of the most memorable battles in naval history. He received little recognition from the United States for his achievements. After serving in the Russian navy (1788–1789), he went to Paris, where he died. His grave was forgotten until 1905, when it was discovered by the U.S. ambassador to France. His remains were removed to the U.S. Naval Academy.

Autobiography and Primary Sources

Life and Correspondence of John Paul Jones, Including His Narrative of the Campaign of the Liman. Robert Sands, ed. New York: A. Chandler, 1830. 555pp. Published through an arrangement with Jones's niece who supplied a number of papers, Sands's volume, like Malcolm's, is a repository of important primary material.

Memoirs of Rear Admiral Paul Jones: Compiled from His Original Journals and Correspondence. Sir John Malcolm, ed. New York: Oliver and Boyd, 1830. 2 vols. This early collection reprints many of Jones's letters and other important primary material.

Recommended Biographies

Mackay, James A. *I Have Not Yet Begun to Fight: A Life of John Paul Jones.* New York: Atlantic Monthly Press, 1999. 320pp. In the first comprehensive reassessment of Jones's life in 40 years, MacKay has produced a vivid, well-researched and realistic dramatic account that locates both the source of Jones's achievements and his later downfall.

Morison, Samuel E. *John Paul Jones: A Sailor's Biography.* Boston: Little, Brown, 1959. 453pp. Winner of the 1959 Pulitzer Prize, Morison's exhaustively researched and authoritative character portrait and narrative of Jones's naval career is the most reliable treatment available. Morison's Jones is a far more complex, mixed figure than

other accounts, and the author excels in naval and period recreation. Included are appendixes that refute several of the legends that have distorted a factual view of Jones's life, personality, and accomplishments.

Other Biographical Studies

Abbott, John S. *The Life and Adventures of Rear-Admiral John Paul Jones, Commonly Called Paul Jones.* New York: Dodd, Mead, 1874. 359pp. Serves chiefly for its historical interest, sustaining the predominant nineteenth-century view of Jones's heroism.

Buell, Augustus C. *Paul Jones: Founder of the American Navy.* New York: Scribner, 1900. 2 vols. Buell's unreliable account mixes fact and fancy and was responsible for several fabrications that have distorted the factual record of Jones's life and career ever since.

DeKoven, Mrs. Reginald (Anna). *The Life and Letters of John Paul Jones.* New York: Scribner, 1913. 2 vols. Long considered the standard biographical account based on its restraint and solid documentation, primarily from Jones's letters, DeKoven nevertheless includes a number of anecdotes with little to no basis in fact and should be read with caution. It is also marred by an insufficient familiarity with naval matters and period details.

Golder, Frank A. *John Paul Jones in Russia.* Garden City, New York: Doubleday, 1927. 230pp. This book, based on discoveries in Russian archives, fills in a number of details of Jones's experiences in the Black Sea in the service of Catherine the Great.

Johnson, Gerald W. *The First Captain: The Story of John Paul Jones.* New York: Coward-McCann, 1947. 312pp. Johnson concentrates as much on the temperament and personality of Jones as his exploits, and occasionally imagines his thoughts and speculates on his motives, unsupported by evidence.

Lorenz, Lincoln. *John Paul Jones: Fighter for Freedom and Glory.* Annapolis, Maryland: United States Naval Institute, 1943. 846pp. Drawing on previously unavailable sources, Lorenz's narrative account is far more readable than DeKoven but shares with her biography the presentation of a number of legends without factual basis.

Mackenzie, Alexander S. *The Life of Paul Jones.* Boston: Hilliard Gray, 1841. 2 vols. Written by an American naval officer, Mackenzie's narrative account synthesizes limited documentary sources into a readable and colorful story describing Jones's various exploits.

Sherburne, John H. *The Life and Character of the Chevalier John Paul Jones, a Captain in the Navy of the United States during their Revolutionary War.* New York: Wilder and Campbell, 1825. 364pp. In the earliest serious biography, Sherburne provided the fullest, documented account of Jones's life available up to that time and set the heroic tone for subsequent views of Jones.

Thomson, Valentine. *Knight of the Seas: The Adventurous Life of John Paul Jones.* New York: Liveright, 1939. 608pp. This popular biography, though based on a number of previously untapped sources, fills in the gaps in the historical record with period details and imagination.

Walsh, John E. *Night on Fire: The First Complete Account of John Paul Jones' Greatest Battle.* New York: McGraw-Hill, 1978. 185pp. Using firsthand documents and contemporary accounts, Walsh devotes his book to a detailed account of Jones's naval engagement with the *Serapis.*

Biographical Novels

Ellsberg, Edward. *Captain Paul.* New York: Dodd, Mead, 1941. 607pp. Jones's life and adventures are described from the perspective of a Nantucket sailor. The novel climaxes with the battle between the *Bonhomme Richard* and the *Serapis.* The author notes the few instances in which he deviates from the facts.

Frye, Pearl. *Gallant Captain: A Biographical Novel Based on the Life of John Paul Jones.* Boston: Little, Brown, 1955. 324pp. Chronicling Jones's naval career, the novel, which climaxes with the battle with the *Serapis,* provides a mainly factual account with a convincing evocation of the period.

Haislip, Harvey. *Sailor Named Jones: A Novel of America's Greatest Captain.* Garden City, New York: Doubleday, 1957. 311pp. Supplementing Jones's actual activities during the American Revolution with a number of invented incidents, the novel culminates in the victory of the *Bonhomme Richard* over the *Serapis.*

Karig, Walter. *Don't Tread on Me.* New York: Rinehart, 1954. 442pp. A midshipman under Jones narrates this account of the captain's naval activities during the Revolution in a factually based account with a number of speculations and surmises.

McCulloch, John H. *The Splendid Renegade.* New York: Coward-McCann, 1928. 373pp. In a highly sentimental treatment, this fictionalized biography devotes its first half to Jones's early adventures before coming to America, with its climax the famous battle with the *Serapis.* Considerable invention limits the book's reliability as a factual account.

Ripley, Clements. *Clear for Action: A Novel about John Paul Jones.* New York: Appleton, 1940. 310pp. A fictional clerk chronicles Jones's naval career during the 1770s with invention and divergence from the historical record in the interest of drama.

Schoonover, Lawrence. *The Revolutionary.* Boston: Little, Brown, 1958. 495pp. In a largely faithful recounting of Jones's life and career, the novel follows him from his youth in Scotland, through his experience as a privateer in the fledgling American navy, to his final service in Russia.

Fictional Portraits

Churchill, Winston. *Richard Carvel.* New York: Macmillan, 1899. 540pp. Set during the American Revolution, the novel describes the experiences of a young man who is befriended by Jones and is wounded during the victory of the *Bonhomme Richard* over the *Serapis.*

Cooper, James Fenimore. *The Pilot.* 1823. Reprint ed. Albany: State University of New York Press, 1986. 479pp. The unnamed American naval pilot is based on Jones, and Cooper's nautical romance features adventures in England and America during the Revolution.

Boyd, James. *Drums.* New York: Grosset & Dunlap, 1925. 429pp. The American Revolution is presented from the perspective of a young North Carolina country gentleman who participates in Jones's naval actions against the British.

Gerson, Noel B. *Give Me Liberty: A Novel of Patrick Henry.* Garden City, New York: Doubleday, 1966. 347pp. This biographical novel based on the life of Patrick Henry features Jones as Henry's rival in love.

Jennings, John Edward. *The Sea Eagles.* Garden City, New York: Doubleday, 1950. 299pp. An adventure tale set at sea during the American Revolution, the novel depicts the experiences of two young men who take part in Jones's famous engagement with the *Serapis.*

McNamara, Tom. *Henry Lunt and the Ranger.* La Jolla, California: Nuventures, 1991. 348pp. Blending fact and fiction, this espionage and adventure novel concerns the naval engagements of Jones in the Irish Sea during 1778.

Melville, Herman. *Israel Potter.* 1855. Reprint ed. New York: Fordham University Press, 1991. 497pp. Melville's historical romance follows the adventures of a New Englander during the American Revolution who is on hand for the battle between the *Bonhomme Richard* and the *Serapis.* Based on an anonymous memoir that purports to be truthful.

Recommended Juvenile Biographies

Simmons, Clara Ann. *John Paul Jones: America's Sailor.* Annapolis, Maryland: Naval Institute Press, 1996. 112pp. MG. In a reliable account of Jones's life and career, the book includes illustrations, a useful chronology, glossary, and suggestions for further reading.

Syme, Ronald. *Captain John Paul Jones: America's Fighting Seaman.* New York: Morrow, 1968. 94pp. MG. Syme's account presents Jones as a complex figure, brave yet conceited and ruthless. The book relies on period documents to make its case.

Biographical Films and Theatrical Adaptations

A&E Biography Video: John Paul Jones: Captain of the High Seas (1995). Producers: Craig Haffner and Donna E. Lusitana. A documentary account of Jones's life and career. Video.

John Paul Jones (1959). Director: John Farrow. In this colorful and romanticized spectacle on the life of the American naval hero, Robert Stack is cast in the title role that shows Jones in love in Virginia (with Macdonald Carey as Patrick Henry and his rival), and at the French court (Jean-Pierre Aumont plays Louis XVI. Susana Canales portrays Marie Antoinette, and Charles Coburn appears as Ben Franklin). Features a cameo appearance by Bette Davis as Catherine the Great. Video.

256. BEN JONSON
1572–1637

A London-born dramatist and poet who strongly influenced the playwrights of his day, Jonson is considered one of the great playwrights of English literature. He worked as a bricklayer for a short time and after military service in Flanders joined Philip Henslowe's company as an actor and playwright. His first play, *Every Man in His Humour* (1598), featured William Shakespeare in the cast. Jonson's comedies are the most celebrated of his works and include *Volpone* (1606), *The Alchemist* (1610), and *Bartholomew Fair* (1614). He was a favorite of James I and wrote masques for the court; his popularity waned with the accession of Charles I (1625) and the failure of his final plays. Arrogant and quarrelsome, he was nevertheless a popular tavern companion, whose followers were known as the "sons of Ben."

Autobiography and Primary Sources

Ben Jonson. C.H. Herford and Percy Simpson, eds. Oxford: Clarendon Press, 1925–1963. 11 vols. This scholarly edition of Jonson's collected works includes the contemporary "interview" with the writer recorded in *Conversations* by Drummond of Hawthornden as well as other primary documentary material, and an extended biographical essay in volume one.

Recommended Biographies

Chute, Marchette. *Ben Jonson of Westminster.* New York: Dutton, 1953. 380pp. Chute's scholarly yet popular and readable portrait of Jonson and his times has the virtue of restoring Jonson's humanity judged by the standard of his day, yet Jonson's darker side and full complexity are sacrificed for a simpler, though sensible, view.

Miles, Rosalind. *Ben Jonson: His Life and Work.* New York: Routledge, 1986. 306pp. In a thorough and detailed narrative of Jonson's life, Miles assembles all the known facts and presents them without a strong interpretive bias. Despite the book's title, the view of Jonson's works is cursory with the connections between the life and the works largely undemonstrated.

Riggs, David. *Ben Jonson: A Life.* Cambridge, Massachusetts: Harvard University Press, 1989. 399pp. Deepening Chute's treatment by incorporating solid research and modern critical methodology, Riggs provides a psychological portrait that recognizes the various complex strands of Jonson's personality and traces their origins in Jonson's desire to conform, which was at odds with his compulsion to rebel. The result is a highly original and refreshing revision of previous views of Jonson that locates the man beneath the image and the erudition.

Other Biographical Studies

Kay, W. David. *Ben Jonson: A Literary Life.* New York: St. Martin's, 1995. 237pp. In this concise literary biography, the author places Jonson's career in its political and literary context to demonstrate the writer's various strategies to maintain his individual and artistic independence.

Linklater, Eric. *Ben Jonson and King James: Biography and Portrait.* New York: H. Smith, 1931. 328pp. Linklater's dual study is concerned mainly with Jonson in a readable, colorful, and highly fictionalized rendering, marked more by exuberance than penetration.

Palmer, John L. *Ben Jonson.* New York: Viking, 1934. 330pp. In Palmer's interpretive study, Jonson is depicted as representative of his age, and the book offers a coherent view of the man, his writings, and his times.

Smith, George. *Ben Jonson.* London: Macmillan, 1919. 310pp. In this critical biography only two chapters are devoted to the facts surrounding Jonson's life, with the rest of the book devoted to a study of his works.

Steegmuller, Francis. *O Rare Ben Jonson.* New York: Knopf, 1927. 158pp. This highly fictionalized biography maintains a factual framework but indulges in considerable invention to render Jonson's voice and thoughts.

Swinburne, Algernon C. *A Study of Ben Jonson.* 1889. Reprint ed. Lincoln: University of Nebraska Press, 1969. 212pp. Swinburne's highly original study of Jonson the man, literary artist, and his work remains an important critical text that shaped the modern view of the writer.

Symonds, John Addington. *Ben Jonson.* 1886. Reprint ed. New York: AMS, 1970. 202pp. This full-length critical portrait, along with Swinburne's study, helped solidify the view of Jonson in the nineteenth century.

Fictional Portraits

Fisher, Edward. *The Best House in Stratford.* New York: Abelard-Schuman,1965. 220pp. In the concluding volume of the author's fictional trilogy on the life of Shakespeare [preceded by *Shakespeare & Son* (1962) and *Love's Labour Won* (1963)] , his years as a playwright in London are depicted with his rivalry and friendship with Jonson a prominent feature. Although mostly invention, the novel features a plausible reconstruction of the era and the personalities of Shakespeare and Jonson.

Garrett, George. *Entered from the Sun.* New York: Doubleday, 1990. 349pp. The author explores the famous murder of Christopher Marlowe through detective work of a fictional actor and a retired soldier. Both Shakespeare and Jonson make appearances in this remarkable Elizabethan animation.

Malpass, Eric. *The Cleopatra Boy.* New York: St. Martin's,1974. 240pp. This second volume of the author's fictional trilogy on Shakespeare (in between *Sweet Will* and *A House of Women*) chronicles the playwright's mature career after the death of Elizabeth I. Shakespeare's relationship with Jonson is shown in this speculative but vivid interpretation of Shakespeare's life.

Other Sources

Brock, D. Hayward. *A Ben Jonson Companion.* Bloomington: Indiana University Press, 1983. 307pp. Brock supplies a helpful collection of information covering various aspects of Jonson's life, career, works, and times.

257. JAMES JOYCE
1882–1941

Irish novelist James Joyce is considered by many to be the most influential and significant novelist of 20th-century literature. One of ten children, he was born in a Dublin suburb and attended Jesuit schools and University College, Dublin (1899–1902), where he proved himself a brilliant though erratic student. Thereafter he lived with Nora Barnacle (m. 1931) and their children in Paris, Trieste, and Zurich. He returned to Ireland to open a chain of movie theaters in Dublin (1909), an enterprise that failed, and to oversee publication of his short-story collection, *Dubliners* (1912). Fears of prosecution on charges of obscenity and libel delayed publication until 1914. His *Ulysses* (1922), a novel chronicling the adventures of several characters during a single Dublin day in 1904, is a masterpiece of modern literature. Joyce's other celebrated works include *A Portrait of the Artist as a Young Man* (1916) and *Finnegans Wake* (1939).

Autobiography and Primary Sources

Letters of James Joyce. Stuart Gilbert and Richard Ellmann, eds. New York: Viking, 1957–1966. 3 vols. This scholarly edition collects both letters by and to Joyce and provides an essential window on the writer's personality.

Selected Letters of James Joyce. Richard Ellmann, ed. New York: Viking, 1975. 440pp. Ellmann provides a useful selection of Joyce's correspondence through the various stages of the writer's life and career.

Recommended Biographies

Beja, Morris. *James Joyce: A Literary Life.* Columbus: Ohio State University Press, 1992. 150pp. Beja's succinct critical biography traces the relationship between the author's life and works in one of the most accessible and satisfactory accounts for the general reader.

Ellmann, Richard. *James Joyce.* 1959. Revised ed. New York: Oxford University Press, 1982. 887pp. Ellman's definitive biography is a model of lucid and sensitive insight as well as exhaustive scholarship woven into a vivid and readable narrative. The book masterfully explores the interplay between Joyce's life and his fiction. Sympathetic but critical, Ellmann provides one of the finest biographical accounts ever written on a literary figure.

O'Brian, Edna. *James Joyce.* New York: Viking, 1999. 176pp. Lacking the comprehensiveness of Ellmann's magisterial portrait, O'Brian nevertheless supplies an insightful thumbnail sketch that is full of one Irish novelist's lively, sympathetic, but critical sense of a fellow colleague.

Other Biographical Studies

Anderson, Chester G. *James Joyce and His World.* New York: Viking, 1968. 144pp. This concise illustrated biography offers the highlights of Joyce's life and career accompanied by photographs that captures the era. Serves as a useful introduction to the man, his life, and works.

Bradley, Bruce. *James Joyce's Schooldays.* New York: St. Martin's, 1982. 179pp. Bradley's is a detailed, well-illustrated examination of Joyce's schooling prior to his entering University College. The book includes photographs and reproductions of Joyce's grades and disciplinary records.

Budgen, Frank. *James Joyce and the Making of Ulysses.* 1934. Reprint ed. Bloomington: Indiana University Press, 1960. 339pp. Written by a Joyce colleague during the writing of *Ulysses,* the book offers a helpful analysis of the novel accompanied by biographical details and recollections of Budgen's conversations with Joyce about his masterpiece.

Colum, Mary and Padraic. *Our Friend James Joyce.* Garden City, New York: Doubleday, 1958. 239pp. Longtime friends of Joyce present an affectionate anecdotal portrait of the artist as a young man in Dublin and through his exile in Paris. Not blind to Joyce's flaws, the Colums' recollections restore a good deal of Joyce's humanity and warmth to the dominant image of the cool, self-obsessed genius.

Costello, Peter. *James Joyce: The Years of Growth, 1882–1915.* New York: Pantheon, 1992. 374pp. Written for the general reader, Costello retraces Joyce's Irish and family background and offers additional details and some minor corrections of the chronology offered by Ellmann, which this book supplements but does not supersede.

Curran, Constantine P. *James Joyce Remembered.* New York: Oxford University Press, 1968. 129pp. Joyce's classmate and friend at University College provides a valuable account of Joyce's undergraduate years.

Davies, Stan G. *James Joyce: A Portrait of the Artist.* New York: Stein and Day, 1975. 328pp. Written by an Irish journalist, the book provides an unflattering portrait of Joyce that is overly simplified and sensational. Much about Joyce's drinking and relations with women, but little on his central preoccupations as a writer.

Gilbert, Stuart. *Reflections on James Joyce: Stuart Gilbert's Paris Journal.* Thomas F. Staley and Randolph Lewis, eds. Austin: University of Texas Press, 1993. 103pp. The author's friendship with Joyce from 1927 to 1941 made possible this collection of anecdotes and opinions regarding the writer's social life, relationship with his wife, and compositional techniques during the writing of *Finnegans Wake.* Also included are some of Joyce's previously unpublished letters to Gilbert and photographs.

Gorman, Herbert. *James Joyce.* New York: Farrar & Rinehart, 1939. 358pp. Joyce's authorized biography was written by a devout partisan with a reticence to disturb the master by unpleasant details. Although drawing on firsthand experience, Gorman's life has been superseded by Ellmann and other more objective, critical accounts.

Jackson, John W., and Peter Costello. *John Stanislaus Joyce: The Voluminous Life and Genius of James Joyce's Father.* New York: St. Martin's, 1998. 494pp. This biography of Joyce's father places his life in the context of his times and offers a revealing look at the family influences on Joyce's career and how memories of his father were reworked in his fiction.

Joyce, Stanislaus. *My Brother's Keeper*. New York: Viking, 1958. 257pp.; *The Complete Dublin Diary of Stanislaus Joyce*. Ithaca, New York: Cornell University Press, 1971. 188pp. Stanislaus Joyce's memoir and diary are essential source material for any biographer. Stanislaus was his brother's confidante and put-upon factotum, and his perspective is revealing and illuminating.

Maddox, Brenda. *Nora: The Real Life of Molly Bloom*. Boston: Houghton Mifflin, 1988. 472pp. This biographical portrait of Nora Barnacle, Joyce's longtime companion and later wife provides a detailed look at the couple's relationship and an interesting angle to view the domestic life of the writer.

Sullivan, Kevin. *Joyce Among the Jesuits*. New York: Columbia University Press, 1958. 259pp. Sullivan's detailed account of Joyce's Jesuit education is reliable and revealing, demonstrating the amount of invention Joyce used in *Stephen Hero* and *A Portrait of the Artist as a Young Man* and the mistake of regarding either work as autobiographical.

Fictional Portraits

Carlile, Clancy. *The Paris Pilgrims*. New York: Carroll & Graf, 1999. 496pp. This documentary novel is set in Paris during Hemingway's first stay there in 1922 and features appearances by virtually every figure associated with the expatriate scene and the Lost Generation, including Stein, Toklas, Pound, and Joyce.

Gold, Alison. *Clairvoyant: The Imagined Life of Lucia Joyce*. New York: Hyperion, 1992. 158pp. The novel looks at the relationship between Joyce and his mentally disturbed daughter narrated mainly in the form of Lucia's own words that offer an interesting glimpse of the Joyce household and circle.

Hays, Tony. *Murder in the Latin Quarter*. Bell Buckle, Tennessee: Iris Press, 1993. 215pp. In this period mystery, Sylvia Beach needs help when someone is murdered trying to burn copies of Joyce's newly published *Ulysses*.

Biographical Films and Theatrical Adaptations

Stoppard, Tom. *Travesties*. New York: Grove Press, 1975. 99pp. Stoppard's innovative biographical fantasy set in Zurich during World War I draws its inspiration from an actual event of Joyce's life: an amateur production of Wilde's *The Importance of Being Earnest*, connected with the birth of modernism and the Russian Revolution.

Is There One Who Understands Me? The World of James Joyce (1988). Director: Séan O Mórdhe. Shot on various locations at sites associated with the writer, this documentary look at his life and career received cooperation from Joyce's relatives and friends and used Richard Ellmann as a program consultant. Video.

James Joyce: Poet and Novelist, 1882–1941 (1996). Director: Malcolm Hossick. Joyce is pro-

filed using photos and views of places associated with his life. Video.

James Joyce's Ulysses (1987). Director: Nigel Walls. Focusing on the creation of his masterpiece, *Ulysses*, the film presents Joyce's personal experiences, background, and artistic philosophy. Video.

James Joyce's Women (1983). Director: Michael Pearce. Chris O'Neill portrays Joyce in this film version of the stage play adapted by Fionnula Flanagan from Joyce's works. Video.

The Modern World: Ten Great Writers (1988). Director: David Thomas. An installment of the London Weekend Television series looks at Joyce's life and literary career. Video.

Other Sources

Attridge, Derek, ed. *The Cambridge Companion to James Joyce*. New York: Cambridge University Press, 1990. 305pp. A collection of essays by leading Joyce scholars, the volume explores various aspects of the writer's life and art.

Fargnoli, A. Nicholas. *James Joyce A to Z: The Essential Reference to the Life and Work*. New York: Facts on File, 1995. 304pp. An alphabetical reference guide to Joyce's life and work, this useful volume offers a detailed chronology and entries on specific aspects of Joyce's writings, relationships, and background.

Mikhail, E.H., ed. *James Joyce: Interviews and Recollections*. London: Macmillan, 1990. 207pp. This volume collects a number of recollections of Joyce by friends, family, and associates.

258. JULIUS CAESAR
100 BC–44 BC

Caesar was born into the Julian gens, one of oldest Roman patrician families, and was a member of the democratic (popular) party. He began his political career after the death of the dictator, Sulla (78 BC), won several important government posts, and antagonized the senate by his reform initiatives, political alliances, popular support, and his organization (60 BC) of the First Triumvirate with Pompey (commander of the army) and the wealthy Crassus. With Caesar as consul (59 BC), the triumvirate controlled Roman politics. After the successful conquest of Gaul during the Gallic Wars (58-51 BC), Caesar waged (49 BC) civil war against the ambitious Pompey, crossed the Rubicon River from his province into Rome, and by 45 BC had defeated all the Pompeian forces. He was made dictator for life in 44 BC but was stabbed to death on the Ides of March by a group of senators angered by his dictatorial powers. He is viewed by historians as both an ambitious demagogue who destroyed the Roman Republic and a brilliant orator, statesman, politician, and military leader, as well as a gifted writer (*Commentaries*).

Autobiography and Primary Sources

Caesar's War Commentaries. John Warrington, ed. New York: Dutton, 1958. 304pp. Caesar provides his own account of his military campaigns in

Gaul and elsewhere, as well as a history of the Roman civil war.

Recommended Biographies

Duggan, Alfred. *Julius Caesar: A Great Life in Brief*. New York: Knopf, 1955. 205pp. Duggan, a distinguished historical novelist, provides a highly readable, concise biography that attempts to show Caesar as his contemporaries saw him. The book sets the stage for Caesar's career by detailing Roman politics in the year 100 BC

Gelzer, Matthias. *Caesar: Politician and Statesman*. Cambridge, Massachusetts: Harvard University Press, 1968. 359pp. In a detailed study based on contemporary sources, Gelzer thoroughly depicts the political background necessary for understanding Caesar's public career.

Grant, Michael. *Julius Caesar*. New York: McGraw-Hill, 1969. 271pp. An excellent general study that features lucid commentary and useful illustrations, this is a succinct synthesis of modern scholarship that serves as a strong introduction to the man and his times.

Other Biographical Studies

Balsdon, J.P.V.D. *Julius Caesar: A Political Biography*. New York: Atheneum, 1967. 184pp. In a careful synthesis of sources, Balsdon reassesses Caesar's political career that challenges many conventional interpretations. Serves as a readable introduction.

Bradford, Ernle. *Julius Caesar: The Pursuit of Power*. New York: Morrow, 1984. 312pp. Bradford's detailed character study concentrates on Caesar's ruthless ambitions and his corruption in pursuit of absolute power.

Buchan, John. *Julius Caesar*. New York: Appleton, 1932. 157pp. In this compact, scholarly biographical study, the author interprets Caesar's character in the context of his era, with an excellent treatment of Roman political, religious, and social life. Buchan assumes a certain amount of expertise beyond most general readers.

Dupuy, Trevor N. *The Military Life of Julius Caesar, Imperator*. New York: F. Watts, 1969. 195pp. Focusing on one important aspect of Caesar's life, the author explores his military career to reveal Caesar's qualities as a battlefield general and leader.

Ferrero, Guglielmo. *Julius Caesar*. 1933. Reprint ed. New York: W.W. Norton, 1962. 524pp. In an abridgment of the author's massive five-volume *The Greatness and the Decline of Rome*, Ferrero locates Caesar's greatness in his conquest of Gaul and neglects certain aspects of Caesar's more complex personality. This study is readable but somewhat romantic in its treatment with a number of debatable conclusions.

Fuller, J.F.C. *Julius Caesar: Man, Soldier, and Tyrant*. New Brunswick, New Jersey: Rutgers University Press, 1965. 336pp. Fuller's revisionist study restores considerable human failings to Caesar's portrait that balances his achievements with his mistakes and limitations.

Kahn, Arthur D. *The Education of Caesar: A Biography.* New York: Schocken, 1986. 514pp. Treating Caesar's development from 97 to 44 BC, Kahn's study provides a vivid, authentic period background to detail Caesar's interactions with his era. The author uses novelistic techniques to animate the scene and enter the psyche of Caesar.

Massie, Allan. *The Caesars.* New York: F. Watts, 1984. 233pp. Massie's collective study of Roman emperors from Julius Caesar to Domitian has the advantage of brevity and compression that does not neglect modern interpretation and scholarship, which fashions a fresh assessment that challenges a number of conventional views.

Meier, Christian. *Caesar.* New York: Basic Books, 1995. 513pp. An authoritative study of the political and social forces that formed Caesar and he transformed, this is a scholarly treatment of the man and his times, more useful for the specialist than for the general reader.

Walter, Gérard. *Caesar: A Biography.* New York: Scribner, 1952. 637pp. This comprehensive, heavily documented, and minutely detailed biography serves better as a factual reference source than a compelling and lively narrative. The book has many dull patches, and the author's lack of sympathy for his subject is intrusive.

Biographical Novels

Balderston, John L. *A Goddess to a God.* New York: Macmillan, 1948. 213pp. Told in the form of letters between Cleopatra and Caesar, the novel chronicles Caesar's life from his invasion of Egypt to his assassination with an emphasis on the emotional life of the pair.

Bentley, Phyllis. *Freedom, Farewell!* New York: Macmillan, 1936. 434pp. Tracing Caesar's career from his boyhood to his assassination, the novel offers a vivid and authentic portrait of his rise to power.

Jelusich, Mirko. *Caesar.* New York: R.R. Smith, 1930. 429pp. This is a full-length fictional biography tracing Caesar's life from boyhood through his military campaigns and political maneuvering in a believable portrait, occasionally marred by romance.

Mabie, Mary L. *Prepare Them for Caesar.* Boston: Little, Brown. 1949. 376pp. Consisting of episodes from Caesar's life from his youth to his death, the novel provides the highlights of his career with some plausible suggestions of Caesar's motivation and psychology.

Massie, Allan. *Caesar.* New York: Carroll & Graf, 1994. 228pp. Caesar's career from the crossing of the Rubicon to his assassination is chronicled from the perspective of one of his comrades-in-arms in a convincing and authentic account.

McCullough, Colleen. *Caesar's Women.* New York: Morrow, 1996. 696pp. McCullough traces Caesar's political rise after his return to Rome from his military conquests. The book's speculations and inventions are backed by evident research. In *Caesar: Let the Dice Fly* (New York: Morrow, 1997. 664pp.) the author chronicles Caesar's Gallic Wars and his fateful return to Rome from 54 to 48 BC. Caesar also appears as a character in the au-

thor's trilogy on the downfall of the Roman Republic (*The First Man in Rome, Fortune's Favorite,* and *The Grass Crown*).

Warner, Rex. *The Young Caesar.* Boston: Little, Brown, 1958. 353pp.; *Imperial Caesar.* Boston: Little, Brown, 1960. 343pp. In Warner's autobiographical novels, Caesar in maturity reflects on his youth and his rise to power in the first novel and in the second on his last fifteen years as he passes a sleepless night preceding his assassination. Although Caesar's thoughts are imagined, the novel stays close to the historical facts in a remarkable reconstruction and plausible portrait.

Wilder, Thornton. *The Ides of March.* New York: Harper, 1948. 246pp. Letters exchanged by several leading figures of Roman society in 44 BC capture the last year of Caesar's life. Wilder takes some liberties with history to give voice to figures who were already dead at the time.

Winn, Derek. *I Served Caesar.* London: Tom Stacey, 1972. 316pp. Caesar's early years and his climb to power are described from the vantage point of a trusted slave.

Fictional Portraits

Anderson, Paul L. *Swords in the North.* New York: Appleton, 1935. 270pp. Set during Caesar's invasion of Britain, the novel, based on solid scholarship, concerns a captured Roman aristocrat who is rescued by a British princess.

Brown, Esther. *Gaul Is Divided.* New York: William-Frederick Press, 1952. 263pp. Caesar's conquest of Gaul is seen from the perspective of Vercingetorix, the Arvernian chieftain and Caesar's great opponent.

Duggan, Alfred. *Winter Quarters.* New York: Coward-McCann, 1956. 284pp. The novel provides a foot soldier's perspective on the decline of the Roman Republic and Caesar's rise to political power.

Hardy, W.G. *The City of Libertines.* New York: Appleton, 1957. 437pp. Dramatizing the love affair between the poet Catullus and a prominent noblewoman, the novel captures the decline of the Roman Republic and its drift toward dictatorship with Caesar's rise to power depicted.

Jaro, Benita K. *The Door in the Wall.* Sag Harbor, New York: Permanent Press, 1994. 323pp. Caesar's ruthless pursuit of power and control are emphasized in this novel that sees his actions from the perspective of a gradually disillusioned supporter.

Taylor, Anna. *The Gods Are Not Mocked.* New York: Morrow, 1968. 312pp. The story of Caesar's invasion of Britain and political rise in Rome is described from the perspective of a Celtic girl and an ambitious Roman tribune.

Recommended Juvenile Biographies

Bruns, Roger. *Julius Caesar.* New York: Chelsea House, 1987. 112pp. MG/YA. This is a solid and sensible biographical and historical profile that considers Caesar's career in the political and cultural context of his times.

Coolidge, Olivia E. *Caesar's Gallic War.* Hamden, Connecticut: Linnet Books, 1991. 245pp. Narrated by a fictitious soldier in Caesar's army, the novel provides a vivid and readable companion to Caesar's *Commentaries on the Gallic War.*

Gunther, John. *Julius Caesar.* New York: Random House, 1959. 182pp. MG/YA. This Landmark biography offers a revealing portrait of Caesar's personal life and political and military career.

Nardo, Don. *The Importance of Julius Caesar.* San Diego, California: Lucent Books, 1996. 112pp. MG. The book helpfully sorts out Caesar's complex life and history in a readable narrative that covers both his achievements and less flattering behavior.

Tingay, Graham. *Julius Caesar.* New York: Cambridge University Press, 1991. 48pp. YA. This is a fully illustrated, brief but informative summary of Caesar's life, achievement, and impact.

Biographical Films and Theatrical Adaptations

Shakespeare, William. *Julius Caesar* (1599). Various editions. Based on Plutarch's *Lives*, the play concerns the events of 44 BC after Caesar's return to Rome from his successful campaign in Spain and the conspiracy that leads to his assassination and its aftermath.

Shaw, George Bernard. *Caesar and Cleopatra* (1901). Various editions. Caesar helps the young Cleopatra gain the throne and instructs her in the responsibilities of power in Shaw's historical drama of ideas. There is no suggestion of their actual love affair, which produced a son, and Caesar is the first of several superior practical moralists who appear in other of Shaw's plays.

White, Theodore. *Caesar at the Rubicon: A Play about Politics.* New York: Atheneum, 1968. 174pp. White attempts to dramatize the transformation in Caesar's character just before he seized control of the republic and became a dictator. Full of contemporary echoes, the play is naive in its understanding of Caesar and his times.

Caesar and Cleopatra (1946). Director: Gabriel Pascal. Claude Raines and Vivian Leigh star in this faithful adaptation of Shaw's play. Video.

Cleopatra (1963). Director: Joseph L. Mankiewicz. Rex Harrison is a standout here as Caesar in this otherwise dull historical pageant with Elizabeth Taylor as Cleopatra, Richard Burton as Antony, and Roddy McDowall as Octavius. Video.

Julius Caesar (1953). Director: Joseph L. Mankiewicz. This film adaptation of Shakespeare's play casts Louis Calhern in the title role, with Marlon Brando as Antony, James Mason as Brutus, and John Gielgud as Cassius. Video.

Julius Caesar (1970). Director: Stuart Burge. In this film version of Shakespeare's play John Gielgud portrays Caesar with Charlton Heston as Antony and Jason Robards as Brutus. Video.

See also Augustus; Cleopatra

259. CARL GUSTAV JUNG
1875–1961

Swiss psychiatrist and the founder of analytical psychology, Jung studied at Basel University (1895–1900) and received his MD at Zürich (1902). The publication of his book on the psychology of dementia praecox led to a meeting with Sigmund Freud (1907), whom he followed for several years. By 1914 he had completely broken with Freud over a disagreement with the Freudian belief in sexual trauma as the basis for neurosis and on interpretations of the Oedipus complex. Jung developed the concepts of introversion and extroversion, the theory of synchronicity, and theorized two dimensions in the unconscious, one of which is a personal unconscious and the other a collective unconscious containing universal symbols, or archetypes.

Autobiography and Primary Sources

Memories, Dreams, Reflections. Aniela Jaffé, ed. New York: Pantheon, 1963. 418pp. Four chapters of Jung's remarkable—and for the biographer indispensable—autobiography (although Jung rejected this term to describe them) were written by Jung beginning in 1957 when he was 81. The rest was based on conversation with Jaffé. Offering little on the outer events of his life, Jung presents instead an inner history of the development and landscape of his psyche.

Letters. Princeton, New Jersey: Princeton University Press, 1973-86. 2 vols. Jung's letters are essential source of insights into his activities, ideas, and character.

Recommended Biographies

Bennet, E.A. *C.G. Jung.* New York: Dutton, 1962. 165pp. With the assistance of Jung himself, who read the manuscript and suggested corrections, Bennet's biography has the advantage of being in agreement with Jung's own views on his past, and the book helps to set the record straight, as well as offering an alternate view of Jung's break with Freud and a defense of Jung's Nazi sympathies.

Brome, Vincent. *Jung.* New York: Atheneum, 1978. 327pp. In one of the best biographies of Jung available, Brome manages a balanced assessment that acknowledges the complexity and multiplicity of Jung's personality and thinking. Less reticent than Bennet, Brome helps clarify both the external details of Jung's life and the development of his ideas.

McLynn, Frank. *Carl Gustav Jung.* New York: St. Martin's, 1997. 623pp. Meticulously researched and readable, McLynn chronicles Jung's life, career, and development of his ideas, recognizing both Jung's genius and his considerable human failings. Without a particular ideological or psychological bias, McLynn's frank assessment serves as one of the most thorough biographies available that neither diminishes Jung's achievements nor overlooks his contradictions and flaws.

Stevens, Anthony. *On Jung.* Princeton, New Jersey: Princeton University Press, 1999. 312pp. Stevens provides a coherent explanation of the basic principles of Jungian psychology while examining every stage of Jung's personal and professional development. The book is particularly original and candid on the impact of Jung's family on his personality.

Other Biographical Studies

Brockway, Robert W. *Young Carl Jung.* Wilmette, Illinois: Chiron, 1996. 181pp. Based on information provided by Jung's son, this is an insightful account of Jung's childhood and formative years up to his completion of medical school and the start of his career as a psychiatrist. The book is valuable for revealing the impact of Jung's early experiences in forming his later theories.

Crowley, Vivianne. *Jung: A Journey of Transformation: Exploring His Life and Experiencing His Ideas.* Wheaton, Illinois: Quest Books, 1999. 160pp. This is a beautifully illustrated introduction to Jung's life and ideas that includes exercises that help integrate Jung's concepts to the reader's own psychological and spiritual investigations.

Donn, Linda. *Freud and Jung: Years of Friendship, Years of Loss.* New York: Scribner, 1988. 238pp. Concentrating on the years 1907 to 1913 of Jung's collaboration with Freud and the ensuing years of estrangement, this is a thoughtful double biography of both men that avoids partisanship and substitutes instead a humanized portrait of Freud and Jung.

Hannah, Barbara. *Jung: His Life and Work: A Biographical Memoir.* New York: Putnam, 1976. 376pp. Written by a longtime colleague and friend, this is a warm, personal reminiscence that provides a great deal of information on Jung's early life and fills in the external gaps in Jung's autobiography.

Homans, Peter. *Jung in Context: Modernity and the Making of a Psychology.* Chicago: University of Chicago Press, 1979. 234pp. In Homans's provocative psychological study, Jung becomes a paradigm for modern consciousness, and the book traces the psychological, religious, and sociological factors that shaped Jung's life and thought. Not for the uninitiated, the book is jargon-rich and assumes a good deal of technical expertise in-depth psychology.

Jaffé, Aniela. *From the Life and Work of C.G. Jung.* New York: Harper & Row, 1971.137pp. Providing an insider's view as Jung's secretary and pupil, Jaffé presents some of the best information available on Jung's work methods and daily routine during his final years.

Noll, Richard. *The Aryan Christ: The Secret Life of Carl Jung.* New York: Random House, 1997. 334pp. Noll's debunking study documents the sinister truth underlying Jung's ideas that he was offering not a psychological view or method but a religion with himself as the central deity. Not a full-scale biography, the book concentrates on the years between 1913 and 1930 in which Jung the charlatan, in the author's view, emerged.

Smith, Robert C. *The Wounded Jung: Effects of Jung's Relationships on His Life and Work.* Evanston, Illinois: Northwestern University Press, 1996. 208pp. Smith concentrates on the role played by the primary relationships in Jung's life, particularly those with women, on the formation of Jung's personality theory. Based on archival sources, interviews with Jung's associates, and correspondence, this book offers many valuable insights, particularly for readers already familiar with Jung's life and ideas.

Stern, Paul J. *C.G. Jung: The Haunted Prophet.* New York: G. Braziller, 1976. 267pp. In a provocative, lively, but sometimes reductionist case study, biographical material is linked with Jung's theories to form a character portrait in which Jung's battle with his own psychopathology achieves eventual transcendence. Stern can be charged with cutting Jung to fit a narrow thematic pattern, but the lesson the book draws from Jung's complex life and work is revealing and interesting.

Storr, Anthony, and Anthony Stevens. *Freud & Jung: A Dual Introduction.* New York: Barnes and Noble, 1998. 138pp. Biographies of both figures in one volume are featured here. Stevens introduces Jung's personal and professional life, providing an accessible summary of his leading ideas.

Van der Post, Laurens. *Jung and the Story of Our Time.* New York: Pantheon, 1975. 276pp. Based on his friendship during Jung's last 16 years, the author's affectionate assessment of Jung's ideas is viewed through van der Post's own development in South Africa that Jung's ideas help to explain. The book serves as an accessible general introduction to Jung, his ideas, and their contemporary relevance.

Wehr, Gerhard. *Portrait of Jung: An Illustrated Biography.* New York: Herder and Herder, 1971. 173pp. Serving as one of the most accessible introductions to the man and his ideas, Wehr's illustrated biography establishes the highlights of Jung's career and helpfully summarizes both the origin and the importance of Jung's work on the unconscious.

Wehr, Gerhard. *Jung: A Biography.* New York: Random House, 1987. 549pp. Greatly expanding his previous study, Wehr adds considerable details to this factual introduction to Jung's life and ideas. Comprehensive in scope, the book traces Jung's mystical development and establishes the various influences that shaped his thoughts.

Biographical Novels

Stone, Irving. *The Passions of the Mind.* Garden City, New York: Doubleday, 1971. 808pp. Freud's relationship with Jung is depicted in this accurate fictional biography of Freud.

Fictional Portraits

Burgess, Anthony. *The End of the World News.* New York: McGraw-Hill, 1983. 388pp. Weaving together the stories of Freud's life, Leon Trotsky's visit to New York, and the exploration of space, Burgess's inventive fantasy offers a meditation on the significance of all three. Jung appears as a character.

Findley, Timothy. *Pilgrim.* New York: HarperCollins, 2000. 486pp. Jung is shown in 1912 treating a patient who seems immortal and has been involved with such historical figures as Teresa of Avila, Leonardo da Vinci, Oscar Wilde, and Henry James. This intriguing novel connects the fantasy with authentic details of Jung's life and the development of his theories.

Hill, Carol DeChellis. *Henry James' Midnight Song.* New York: Poseidon Press, 1993. 445pp. Jung is one of many historical figures in this intriguing period murder mystery set in fin-de-siècle Vienna. Henry James, Edith Wharton, and Sigmund Freud are also featured.

Korman, Keith. *Secret Dreams.* New York: Arcade,1995. 435pp. Based loosely on an actual clinical case, the novel describes the efforts of Jung to treat Fraulein S.'s hysteria. Jung falls in love with his patient and finds himself travelling back in time to an earlier era of primitive ritual to unravel the mystery of the human psyche.

West, Morris L. *The World Is Made of Glass.* New York: Morrow, 1983. 322pp. West constructs a drama out of a brief reference in one of Jung's letters about a woman named Magda.

Biographical Films and Theatrical Adaptations

Carl Gustav Jung: An Introduction (1991). Director: Philip Engelen. This film profile explores Jung's exterior and interior life with visualization of his dreams and fantasies and the implication of his break with Freud. Video.

Carl Gustav Jung: Artist of the Soul (1997). Producer: Sheldon Rochlin. Examines Jung's life and work through interviews with his daughters and grandson. Video.

Face to Face: Professor Jung (1972). Producer: Hugh Burnett. In interviews Jung talks of his childhood, his life, work, views on death, and his friendship and later differences with Freud. Video.

Jung on Film (1957). Director: John W. Meaney. In an interview Jung discusses the major themes of his psychological research. Video.

Matter of Heart (1983). Director: Mark Whitney. Using rare home movies, archival material, and interviews, Jung's life, career, and ideas are treated. Includes conversations with Jung's friends, patients, and colleagues. Video.

The Story of Carl Gustav Jung (1972). Producer: Jonathan Stedell. Written by Laurens van der Post, this documentary portrait explores Jung's childhood, student years, development of his major theories, and later years. Video.

Other Sources

McGuire, William, and R.F.C. Hull. *C.G. Jung Speaking: Interviews and Encounters.* Princeton, New Jersey: Princeton University Press, 1977. 489pp. This collection of interviews and recollections of Jung and those who knew him at various points during his career serves as a valuable biographical reference as well as appreciation of the man.

Young-Eisendrath, Polly, and Terence Dawson, eds. *The Cambridge Companion to Jung.* New York: Cambridge University Press, 1997. 332pp. Various scholars provide insights into aspects of Jung's character, ideas, and writings.

See also Sigmund Freud

260–261. JUSTINIAN I (483–565) AND THEODORA (508–548)

The last Byzantine emperor to rule in the West, Justinian succeeded (527) his uncle, Justin I. He married Theodora, a former actress and prostitute, and ruled jointly with her. Theodora's decisiveness and political influence quelled the Nika riots (532), brought on by political rivalries in Constantinople as well as by Justinian's attempts to impose heavy taxation and religious orthodoxy on the diverse population of the empire, particularly the Christian Monophysites. Justinian's greatest accomplishment was the codification of Roman law, called the Corpus Juris Civilis. During his reign, North Africa and Italy were recaptured (533-548; 535-554) from the Vandals and the Ostrogoths, and the Hagia Sofia was built.

Recommended Biographies

Barker, John W. *Justinian and the Later Roman Empire.* Madison: University of Wisconsin Press, 1966. 318pp. Written as a succinct introduction to the man, his reign, and era, Barker provides a useful narrative history for the general reader.

Browning, Robert. *Justinian and Theodora.* New York: Praeger, 1971. 272pp. In this readable dual biography and history of their reign, Browning offers a detailed treatment that is solidly supported by modern scholarship. Beautifully illustrated, the book is recommended as the best starting point for the reader interested in the era and its central figures.

Other Biographical Studies

Baker, George P. *Justinian.* New York: Dodd, Mead, 1931. 340pp. Intended for the general reader, Baker's readable account of Justinian's character and achievement is fair and objective in a dramatic narrative with occasional anachronistic lapses. Baker's treatment will likely appeal to the nonspecialist looking for a colorful animation of the period.

Bridge, Antony. *Theodora: Portrait in a Byzantine Landscape.* Chicago: Academy Chicago, 1984. 193pp. Bridge provides an intricate human portrait and a plausible psychological interpretation of Theodora that grants her considerably more power and sympathy than most scholars have been willing to acknowledge.

Bury, John B. *A History of the Later Roman Empire from the Death of Theodosius to the Death of Justinian.* London: Macmillan, 1923. 2 vols. The second volume of Bury's respected and detailed history of the later Roman Empire treats Justinian's reign, with an emphasis on political and military history. Based on extensive research, Bury's portraits of the leading figures are vivid and compelling.

Diehl, Charles. *Theodora: Empress of Byzantium.* New York: Frederick Ungar, 1972. 204pp. Diehl's treatment places Theodora in her social, political, and religious context and shows her as she might have appeared to her contemporaries. The book assumes a more than general knowledge of Byzantine history.

Gerostergios, Asterios. *Justinian the Great: The Emperor and Saint.* Belmont, Massachusetts: Institute for Byzantine and Modern Greek Studies, 1982. Combining a history of Justinian's reign with a competent summary of his life and personality, the author provides a useful overview. 312pp.

Gibbon, Edward. *The History of the Decline and Fall of the Roman Empire.* 1776–1788. Reprint ed. John B. Bury, ed. New York: Macmillan, 1909–1914. 7 vols. Gibbon devotes five chapters of his monumental history to Justinian and his reign with details on Justinian's early years and an assessment of his achievements.

Holmes, William G. *The Age of Justinian and Theodora.* London: G. Bell, 1905–1907. 2 vols. Holmes's knowledge of primary sources considerably deepens Gibbon's earlier treatment of Justinian and the sixth century.

Moorhead, John. *Justinian.* New York: Longman, 1994. 202pp. Moorhead's is a scholarly reassessment of Justinian's reign in which the condition from which Justinian emerged are solidly detailed, as are his achievements, talents, and limitations.

Ure, Percy N. *Justinian and His Age.* London: Penguin, 1951. 262pp. Organized thematically around various historical and cultural aspects of Justinian's reign, this scholarly study provides an excellent introduction to the man and his times.

Biographical Novels

Bradshaw, Gillian. *The Bearkeeper's Daughter.* Boston: Houghton Mifflin, 1987. 310pp. The novel provides a convincing portrait of Theodora and her court from the perspective of a young man who gains the empress's favor. The details of court life and the customs of the era are convincingly rendered.

Gerson, Noel B. *Theodora.* Englewood Cliffs, New Jersey: Prentice-Hall, 1969. 275pp. Theodora's remarkable climb to power is dramatized in this colorful novel mixing fact with invention.

Lamb, Harold. *Theodora and the Emperor: The Drama of Justinian.* Garden City, New York: Doubleday, 1952. 336pp. The reign and relationship of Justinian and Theodora are depicted in this novel rich in historical detail, animated by invented incident and dialogue.

Wellman, Paul I. *The Female: A Novel of Another Time.* Garden City, New York: Doubleday, 1953. 492pp. Theodora's rise from humble origins to become a courtesan and empress is chronicled in a mixture of historical elements and fictional invention.

Fictional Portraits

Graves, Robert. *Count Belisarius.* New York: Random House,1938. 564pp. The novel centers on Justinian's great general and his campaigns in Persia, Africa, and against the Goths before the gates of Rome. For Graves, Belisarius is the last noble Roman and first chivalrous knight who becomes the nemesis of the emperor.

Masefield, John. *Basilissa: A Tale of the Empress Theodora.* New York: Macmillan, 1940. 307pp.

Masefield challenges the conventional portrait of Theodora as a callous opportunist to present her as a woman of rare talent and a good Christian. Although the framework is factual, the novel is mainly speculative.

Masefield, John. *Conquer: A Tale of the Nika Rebellion in Byzantium.* New York: Macmillan, 1941. 147pp. Based on an actual incident involving a rebellion in Byzantium in 532, the novel provides a convincing portrait of Justinian and Theodora, the latter treated far more sympathetically than most historians have done.

O'Connor, Richard. *The Vandal.* Garden City, New York: Doubleday,1960. 258pp. The conflict between Justinian and his general Belisarius is seen from the perspective of a young aide to the general in a fictional story with no basis in history but with a convincing period atmosphere.

Yarbro, Chelsea Quinn. *A Flame in Byzantium.* New York: Tor, 1987. 470pp. In this installment of the author's historical vampire series, Olivia Clemens must flee Rome, aided by Belisarius. Arriving in Byzantium, she is plunged into court intrigue. Historical figures, such as Belisarius and Justinian, are given parts in the invented story.

Biographical Films and Theatrical Adaptations

The Last Roman (1968). Director: Robert Sidmak. Film version of Felix Dann's German bestseller *Kampf um Rom* that stars Laurence Harvey as a Roman nobleman who journeys to Byzantium to elicit military support from Justinian. Orson Welles portrays the emperor with Sylvia Koscina as Theodora. Video.

262. FRANZ KAFKA
1883–1924

Kafka is widely considered one of the most influential twentieth-century writers. He was born into a middle-class Jewish family in Prague and studied law before securing a government position in the workman's compensation division. A master at portraying individuals trapped in a nightmare world of isolation and anxiety, his works include "The Metamorphosis" (1915) and "A Hunger Artist" (1922). Kafka died from tuberculosis at the age of 40. His novels *The Trial*, *The Castle*, and *Amerika* were published posthumously.

Autobiography and Primary Sources

The Diaries of Franz Kafka. Max Brod, ed. New York: Schocken, 1948–1949. 2 vols. Essential for understanding Kafka, his diaries, covering the period from 1910 to 1923, provide the closest direct access to the writer and deserve to be regarded as one of Kafka's greatest literary achievements.

I am Memory Come Alive: Autobiographical Writings. Nahum N. Glatzer, ed. New York: Schocken, 1974. 264pp. Using Kafka's letters, diary entries, as well as the memoirs of others, arranged chronologically, this collection forms a nearly continuous autobiography that traces the highlights of Kafka's development as an artist and thinker.

Letters to Friends, Family, and Editors. New York: Schocken, 1977. 509pp. This collection of Kafka's correspondence charts the writer's moods and relationships in an indispensable biographical source.

Recommended Biographies

Brod, Max. *Franz Kafka: A Biography*. 1947. Enlarged ed. New York: Schocken, 1960. 267pp. Written by Kafka's friend and literary executor who helped establish Kafka's literary reputation, Brod's close-up, human portrait draws on both his intimacy with the writer and many private letters. Rich in personal insights and factual material, Brod's book is an essential starting point for all subsequent biographers.

Hayman, Ronald. *Kafka: A Biography*. New York: Oxford University Press, 1982. 349pp. In a lucid, comprehensive biographical narrative, Hayman supplements his documentary research with interviews with Kafka's contemporaries. The book provides a clear view of Kafka's daily life and the pressure of family, relationships, and environment on his writing.

Karl, Frederick R. *Franz Kafka: Representative Man*. New York: Ticknor & Fields, 1991. 810pp. Karl places Kafka's life in the context of modernism, Freudianism, social history, and other topics. This is a critical, sometimes overly discursive, reflection of the writer as emblematic of his and our time. Serves as the leading critical biography currently available.

Pawel, Ernst. *The Nightmare of Reason: A Life of Franz Kafka*. New York: Farrar, Straus, 1984. 466pp. Pawel uses contemporary documents, letters, and reminiscences to present a balanced and coherent portrait of Kafka. Without minimizing the writer's neurotic conflicts, Pawel also demonstrates that Kafka was an efficient, highly regarded public servant.

Other Biographical Studies

Bauer, Johann. *Kafka and Prague*. New York: Praeger, 1971. 191pp. Linking atmospheric photographs of Prague with excerpts from Kafka's writings and a connecting text, Bauer captures the highlights of Kafka's life and works in a valuable introduction.

Citati, Pietro. *Kafka*. New York: Knopf, 1990. 320pp. Citati adds little that is new to a now-familiar psychobiographical portrait of the author. Densely written, selective in its emphasis, and finally incomplete, offering no insights about Kafka's Jewishness, his early life, or the formative political events of his times, the book can serve along with other texts as a critical introduction, but cannot stand alone.

Gilman, Sander L. *Franz Kafka: The Jewish Patient*. New York: Routledge, 1995. 328pp. Reproducing medical records for the first time, Gilman argues that the illness Kafka contracted in 1917 was the defining event of his life, which became a metaphor for his contemplation of his Jewishness. Provocative in its psychological interpretation, Gilman's analysis should be read as a supplement to more comprehensive, factual studies.

Glatzer, Nahum. *The Loves of Franz Kafka*. New York: Schocken, 1986. 85pp. Using letters and diary entries Glatzer focuses on Kafka's relationships with various women in his life.

Heller, Erich. *Franz Kafka*. New York: Viking, 1974. 128pp. Heller's critical study examines Kafka's works and their relationship to his life. Serves as a valuable introduction to the writer.

Mailloux, Peter. *A Hesitation Before Birth: The Life of Franz Kafka*. Newark: University of Delaware Press, 1989. 622pp. Although the author's lack of familiarity with German limits the book's scholarly usefulness, this is a highly readable study that combines psychological and literary analysis to make sense of Kafka's extraordinary self-tormenting personality. Weaving extracts from the letters and diaries into a narrative account, the book is strongest on delivering the day-to-day texture of the writer's life.

Robert, Marthe. *As Lonely as Franz Kafka*. New York: Harcourt, Brace, 1982. 250pp. In a sometimes densely written critical study, Robert's examination of Kafka's life and career is guided by her thesis that the writer's isolation, self-doubt, and alienation was a consequence of his conflicted attitudes toward his Jewishness.

Sharp, Daryl. *The Secret Raven: Conflict and Transformation in the Life of Franz Kafka*. Toronto: Inner City Books, 1980. 128pp. Applying the tenets of Jungian psychology, this is a detailed analysis of Kafka's life in terms of his neuroses. Sharp identifies conflicts between Kafka's desire to write and the demands of his job, his ambivalence toward women, and his alienation from his family. Sharp goes on to suggest why Kafka could neither give up his job nor marry.

Spann, Meno. *Franz Kafka*. Boston: Twayne, 1976. 205pp. This critical study attempts to trace the realistic and autobiographical basis for the guilt and anxiety expressed in Kafka's writings.

Unseld, Joachim. *Franz Kafka: A Writer's Life*. Riverside, California: Ariadne Press, 1994. 393pp. Unseld offers a fresh look at Kafka's literary dealings, examining his relationships and interactions with his publishers and his friend and literary executive Max Brod.

Wagenbach, Klaus. *Franz Kafka: Pictures of a Life*. New York: Pantheon, 1984. 221pp. In the best pictorial biography of Kafka, a clear and concise text is joined with photos of sites associated with the author, along with examples of documents and letters.

Biographical Novels

Ross, Maggie. *Milena*. London: HarperCollins, 1983. 280pp. The relationship between Kafka and Milena Jesenka Polak is explored.

Biographical Films and Theatrical Adaptations

Kafka (1991). Director: Steven Soderbergh. Using a number of elements from Kafka's writings, this expressionistic film follows the writer in 1919 as he discovers a friend's disappearance and conspiracy. Jeremy Irons portrays Kafka, with Theresa Russell, Ian Holm, Joel Grey, and Alec Guinness. Filmed on location in Prague. Video.

The Modern World: Ten Great Writers (1988). Director: David Thomas. An installment of the London Weekend Television series looks at Kafka's life and literary career. Video.

The Trials of Franz Kafka (1973). Producer: Harold Mantell. Narrated by Kurt Vonnegut, this film portrait examines Kafka's childhood, youth, and adulthood with scenes shot in Prague associated with the writer. Video.

Other Sources

Janouch, Gustav. *Conversations with Kafka*. New York: New Directions, 1971. 219pp. Based on the author's meetings with Kafka during his later years, the author reproduces the writer's views on a number of subjects.

Stern, J.P., ed. *The World of Franz Kafka*. New York: Holt, 1980. 263pp. This collection of essays features a detailed chronology of Kafka's life, critical essays by various specialists, and fictional and nonfictional pieces by writers, such as Philip Roth, inspired by Kafka.

263. WASSILY KANDINSKY
1866–1944

Russian painter usually regarded as the founder of abstract art, Kandinsky developed his style based upon his ideas concerning the dynamism of pure color and nonrepresentational art. He published (1912) an important theoretical study, *Concerning the Spiritual in Art*. Kandinsky exhibited with the Brücke group, cofounded the Blue Reiter group of artists, and during the 1920s taught at the Bauhaus design school.

Recommended Biographies

Grohmann, Will. *Wassily Kandinsky: Life and Work*. New York: Abrams, 1958. 428pp. Grohman's critical biography has remained the standard source on the artist's life and work. The book is lavishly illustrated with over 900 reproductions and is the best single source on the artist's de-

velopment and a comprehensive record of his career.

Hahl-Koch, Jelena. *Kandinsky*. New York: Rizzoli, 1994. 431pp. Hahl-Koch's is the most comprehensive treatment yet of Kandinsky's life and artistic development, informed by a careful reading of Kandinsky's writings and papers and modern scholarship. The book traces Kandinsky's artistic evolution stressing his Russian background and influences that offers a different emphasis from other art historians. Essential for the specialist, the book is a stimulating reassessment of the growth of the artist's genius.

Röthel, Hans Konrad, and Jean K. Benjamin. *Kandinsky*. New York: Hudson Hills Press, 1979. 172pp. This is a fine choice for a brief, accessible overview of the artist's life and career. A short introductory essay precedes a sampling of Kandinsky's works with critical commentary.

Other Biographical Studies

Derouet, Christian, and Vivian E. Barnett. *Kandinsky in Paris 1934-44*. New York: Solomon R. Guggenheim Museum, 1985. 268pp. This exhibition catalog, complementing Poling's, documents Kandinsky's final years in Paris with a text that covers the significant biographical details during this period in the artist's life, well-documented from archival evidence, letters, and the memoir of Nina Kandinsky.

Le Targat, François. *Kandinsky*. New York: Rizzoli, 1987. 128pp. The highlights of Kandinsky's life and career are summarized in this accessible introductory overview that includes a detailed chronology.

Poling, Clark V. *Kandinsky: Russian and Bauhaus Years*. New York: Solomon R. Guggenheim Museum, 1983. 360pp. Poling provides a scholarly, well-documented biographical overview of the artist's life from 1915 to 1933, which includes his life during the Russian Revolution and at the Bauhaus.

Volboudt, Pierre. *Kandinsky*. New York: Universe Books, 1986. 117pp. This is an insightful introduction to Kandinsky's life, artistic development, and works with excerpts from the painter's critical writings, excellent reproductions, and a chronology.

Weiss, Peg. *Kandinsky in Munich: The Formative Jugenstil Years*. Princeton, New Jersey: Princeton University Press, 1979. 268pp. Weiss's is a scholarly examination of Kandinsky's years in Munich from 1886 to 1914, locating the artist clearly in the city's cultural and artistic milieu and chronicling through extensive primary sources his training, private life, relationships, and influences.

264. IMMANUEL KANT
1724–1804

German metaphysician and one of the world's most renowned philosophers, Kant profoundly influenced nearly every area of thought. A private tutor, lecturer in science and philosophy, and professor of logic and metaphysics, Kant achieved wide renown through his teaching and his writings. His works include *Critique of Pure Reason* (1781), *Critique of*

Practical Reason (1788), and *Critique of Judgment* (1790).

Autobiography and Primary Sources

Correspondence. Arnulf Zweig, ed. New York: Cambridge University Press, 1999. 639pp. This is the most complete English edition of the philosopher's letters that chart Kant's intellectual development as well as shedding light on his personality and relationships.

Recommended Biographies

Cassirer, Ernst. *Kant's Life and Thought*. New Haven, Connecticut: Yale University Press, 1981. 429pp. Cassirer's is the best full-length portrait of Kant's life, personality, and the development of his ideas. To follow the book's discussion of Kant's philosophy considerable expertise is expected, but the general reader can still profit from the book's reliable and vivid biographical information and insights into Kant's personality.

Other Biographical Studies

Jaspers, Karl. *Kant*. New York: Harcourt, 1962. 159pp. Like Scruton's brief overview, Jaspers's compact study, the work of a well-known philosopher, supplies a basic introduction to Kant's life and ideas.

Paulsen, S. *Immanuel Kant: His Life and Doctrine*. New York: Scribner, 1902. 419pp. Paulsen documents Kant's life and teaching career with revealing personal details that locate him clearly against his period and intellectual background. The book presents the personal struggles of Kant's life compellingly.

Scruton, Roger. *Kant*. New York: Oxford University Press, 1982. 99pp. Part of the Past Masters series, Scruton provides a compact, introductory overview suitable for the general reader that includes a brief biographical summary.

Walker, Ralph. *Kant*. New York: Routledge, 1999. 64pp. Walker supplies a brief but useful and accessible introduction to Kant's life and ideas for the general reader.

Other Sources

Guyer, Paul, ed. *The Cambridge Companion to Kant*. New York: Cambridge University Press, 1992. 482pp. This collection of essays by noted Kant scholars treats different elements of Kant's ideas in the light of modern scholarship.

265. JOHN KEATS
1795–1821

One of the great English Romantic poets, the London-born Keats was the son of a livery stable keeper. He studied medicine and was apprenticed to a surgeon, but after befriending Leigh Hunt and his literary circle gave up surgery (1816) to devote himself to poetry. His first volume of poetry appeared in 1817 and received little attention; a long poem, *Endymion* (1818) was attacked in *Blackwood's Magazine* and *Quarterly Review*. He contracted tuberculosis, probably from nursing his brother, Tom, and remained in frail health until his early death from the disease. His works include the unfinished epic poem *Hyperion*, the ballad *La Belle Dame sans Merci*, and the great odes "To a Nightingale" and "On a Grecian Urn."

Autobiography and Primary Sources

Autobiography of Keats. Earle V. Weller, ed. London: Oxford University Press, 1933. 409pp. Arranging extracts from Keats's letters and recollections chronologically, the volume offers a approximation of Keats's autobiography in mostly his own words.

Letters of John Keats. Robert Gittings, ed. New York: Oxford University Press, 1970. 417pp. Invaluable as a biographical record, Keats's correspondence is one of the most revealing and moving records ever left by a writer.

Recommended Biographies

Bate, Walter Jackson. *John Keats.* Cambridge, Massachusetts: Harvard University Press, 1963. 732pp. Bate's Pulitzer Prize–winning biography is justifiably regarded as definitive. Meticulously researched and comprehensive, the biography traces in detail Keats's remarkable poetic development, even more evident by a clearly established sense of the various personal, economic, and cultural forces in opposition.

Gittings, Robert. *John Keats.* Boston: Little, Brown, 1968. 469pp. Gittings supplements the factual record with new details of Keats's family background, medical apprenticeship, illness, and relationship with Fanny Brawne. Scholarly and reliable, the book provides details of Keats's almost daily experience.

Motion, Andrew. *Keats.* New York: Farrar, Straus, 1998. 636pp. In the latest full-length biography, Motion emphasizes the social and political aspect of Keats's life and work that most critics have undervalued and neglected. In Motion's view, Keats was far from the sensuous aesthete and should be viewed as a more committed social radical. This perspective grounds the poets usefully in his era.

Ward, Aileen. *John Keats: The Making of a Poet.* New York: Viking, 1963. 450pp. Winner of the 1964 National Book Award for arts and letters, Ward's insightful examination of Keats's personal and artistic development traces various psychological patterns in the poet's personality, set firmly in a clear historical context. Less exhaustive and more synoptic and readable than Bate, Ward's study remains one of the finest critical biographies on Keats available.

Other Biographical Studies

Bush, Douglas. *John Keats: His Life and Writings.* New York: Macmillan, 1966. 224pp. Bush's concise critical biography serves as an excellent introduction to the poet and his poetry. Lacking the scope and detail of the recommended biographies, Bush's study is still a worthy starting point for the interested reader.

Colvin, Sidney. *Keats.* New York: Harper, 1887. 229pp.; *John Keats: His Life and Poetry, His Friends, Critics, and After-Fame.* 1917. Reprint ed. New York: Octagon Books, 1970. 598pp. Colvin expanded his earlier short life of Keats into the first fully detailed authoritative biography that remained the standard life until the 1960s. Now superseded, Colvin's study remains important for its inclusion of some original materials now destroyed.

Hewlett, Dorothy. *Adonais: A Life of John Keats.* 1937. Revised ed. New York: Barnes and Noble, 1970. 408pp. Hewlett provides a more concise treatment of Keats's life than Colvin and Lowell that helpfully connects the poets to his historical and cultural background. The 1970 revision includes a number of appendixes that reflects recent scholarship.

Houghton, Richard Monckton Milnes. *Life, Letters, and Literary Remains of John Keats.* 1848. Revised ed. New York: Putnam, 1867. 2 vols. This initial biography is chiefly useful for collecting a number of documentary sources and recollections of Keats's associates that have been exploited by subsequent biographers. The book fails to identify Fanny Brawne and her relationship with the poet and commits a number of errors in the factual record, so that the book now has mainly historical interest in charting Keats's image and reputation in the nineteenth century.

Hutton, Timothy. *Keats and His World.* New York: Viking, 1971. 144pp. This illustrated biography brings together a number of portraits, engravings, and reproductions of manuscripts.

Lowell, Amy. *John Keats.* Boston: Houghton Mifflin, 1925. 2 vols. Lowell's massive study follows Keats's life almost day-by-day and supplements the factual record with useful interpretation from a fellow poet. However, extracting significance from such a wealth of material is a labor for all but the most devoted and committed Keatsian.

Richardson, Joanna. *Fanny Brawne: A Biography.* New York: Vanguard, 1952. 190pp. Richardson brings together all the available information on the woman who played such a central role in Keats's life. Serves as a useful supplement for information concerning their relationship.

Rossetti, William Michael. *Life of John Keats.* 1887. Reprint ed. New York: AMS Press, 1971. 217pp. Rossetti's appreciation of Keats is less useful as a biography than as an indicator of Keats's literary reputation in the Victorian period.

Walsh, John E. *Darkling I Listen: The Last Days and Death of John Keats.* New York: St. Martin's, 1999. 208pp. This is a detailed account of the 100 days Keats spent in Italy leading up to his death, offering new insights on the poet's relationship with Fanny Brawne and the nature and progression of the illness that killed him.

Biographical Novels

Roberts, Cecil. *The Remarkable Young Man.* New York: Macmillan, 1954. 272pp. Dramatizing the friendship between Keats and the English painter Joseph Severn, the novel follows the pair to Rome where Keats succumbed to tuberculosis. Based on facts, the novel is reliable and convincing in evoking Keats's sad final days.

Fictional Portraits

Burgess, Anthony. *Abba Abba.* Boston: Little, Brown, 1977. 127pp. Burgess imagines a meeting between Keats and the Italian dialect poet Giuseppe Belli during the final months of Keats's life and how the encounter might have affected both men.

Clark, Tom. *Junkets on a Sad Planet: Scenes from the Life of John Keats.* Santa Rosa, California: Black Sparrow Press, 1994. 188pp. Clark's 127 poems and prose pieces reflect each significant event in Keats's life and each important poem in Keats's canon.

Powers, Tim. *The Stress of Her Regard.* New York: Ace Books, 1989. 392pp. In this historical fantasy, a Regency doctor flees England to avoid a charge of murder. Haunted by guilt, he is aided by Keats, Byron, and Shelley in understanding his torment.

Recommended Juvenile Biographies

Gittings, Robert, and Jo Manton. *The Story of John Keats.* New York: Dutton, 1962. 192pp. MG. Gittings, a respected Keats scholar, helps to assure a factual summary of Keats's life making use of the poet's letters and contemporary accounts, along with some fictionalization.

Biographical Films and Theatrical Adaptations

John Keats, Poet (1973). Director: John Barnes. James Mason narrates this film treatment of Keats's life with excerpts from his letters and works. Video.

John Keats: Poet, 1795–1821 (1997). Director: Malcolm Hossick. A concise look at Keats's life as well as the social and historical background to his poetry. Video.

Other Sources

Rollins, H.E. *The Keats Circle.* Cambridge, Massachusetts: Harvard University Press, 1965. 2 vols. Brings together an invaluable collection of letters and documents concerning Keats and his associates.

266. HELEN KELLER
1880–1968

American author and lecturer, Keller was blind and deaf from the age of two but after 1887 learned to read, write, and speak with the help of her teacher and companion, Anne Sullivan. She graduated with honors from Radcliffe College (1904), lectured throughout the United States and abroad, raised funds for the blind, and promoted other social causes. Her books include *The Story of My Life* (1903) and *The World I Live In* (1908).

Autobiography and Primary Sources

The Story of My Life. 1903. Reprint ed. Garden City, New York: Doubleday, 1954. 382pp. Written while she was in college, Keller's autobiographical reflections of her childhood and youth are a candid and revealing commentary on her life and how she experienced the world. *The World I Live In* (New York: Century, 1908. 195pp.) further elaborates on Keller's perception of the world. Keller discusses her religious views and how she discovered them through the teachings of Swedenborg in *My Religion* (Garden City, New York: Doubleday, 1927. 209pp.). *Midstream: My Later Life*. 1929. (Reprint ed. New York: Greenwood, 1968. 362pp.) Keller's story continues from her sophomore year at Radcliffe through her next 25 years in the wider world of work and public notoriety. Finally, Keller provides an affectionate recollection of her relationship with and debt to Anne Sullivan Macy in *Teacher: Anne Sullivan Macy: A Tribute by the Foster-Child of Her Mind* (Garden City, New York: Doubleday, 1956. 247pp.).

Recommended Biographies

Herrmann, Dorothy. *Helen Keller: A Life*. New York: Knopf, 1998. 394pp. Herrmann's full-length, complex portrait of Keller goes beyond the heroic legend to present a believable human figure. The complicated dynamics of Keller's relationship with Anne Sullivan are subtly examined, and the reader is given the most intimate, psychologically credible view of Keller yet attempted.

Lash, Joseph P. *Helen and Teacher: The Story of Helen Keller and Anne Sullivan Macy*. New York: Delacorte Press, 1980. 811pp. Lash's is a detailed dual biography, organized into sections on Keller's relationship with her teacher alone, with Sullivan and her husband, John Macy, and the 32 years following Sullivan Macy's death with her companion Polly Thomson. Full of telling information, the book takes a realistic view of the complex relationship between Keller and Sullivan and the human cost each imposed on the other.

Other Biographical Studies

Braddy, Nella. *Anne Sullivan Macy: The Story Behind Helen Keller*. Garden City, New York: Doubleday, 1933. 365pp. Braddy's view of Keller's story from the perspective of her teacher, Anne Sullivan Macy, is interesting and helps to broaden the context of Keller's story although the book is not as thorough and comprehensive as Lash's dual biography.

Brooks, Van Wyck. *Helen Keller: Sketch for a Portrait*. New York: Dutton, 1956. 166pp. Less a biography than a moving appreciation and a celebration of Keller's triumph and spirit based on the author's longtime friendship with Keller.

Recommended Juvenile Biographies

Davidson, Margaret. *Helen Keller*. New York: Scholastic, 1989. 96pp. MG. This is an informative, reliable account of Keller's relationship with Anne Sullivan Macy, her struggle to talk and read, and her later achievements.

Markham, Lois. *Helen Keller*. New York: F. Watts, 1993. 64pp. MG. In this well-written account, Markham puts Keller's life and achievement in believable human terms, less heroic but no less compelling than other more idealized treatments.

Wepman, Dennis. *Helen Keller*. New York: Chelsea House, 1987. 111pp. MG/YA. Chronicling the highlights of Keller's life through numerous quotes from her writings and from those who knew her, this is a capable biography with many useful photographs.

Biographical Films and Theatrical Adaptations

Gibson, William. *The Miracle Worker*. New York: Bantam, 1957. 122pp.; *Monday After the Miracle*. New York: Atheneum, 1983. 139pp. Gibson's pair of plays on Keller's life looks at the efforts of Anne Sullivan to teach the young Keller and scenes from the pair's later experiences.

Helen Keller in Her Story (1955). Director: Nancy Hamilton. Academy Award winning documentary using photographs, newsreels, and interviews to trace Keller's life. Video.

The Miracle Worker (1962). Director: Arthur Penn. Oscar-winning adaptation of Gibson's play with Patty Duke as Keller and Anne Bancroft as Anne Sullivan. Video. Remade for television in 1979 (Director: Paul Aaron) with Duke in the Sullivan role and Melissa Gilbert as Keller. Video.

267. JOHN F. KENNEDY
1917–1963

The youngest elected U.S. president and the first Roman Catholic president, Kennedy was born in Brookline, Massachusetts, the second son of businessman and diplomat Joseph P. Kennedy and Rose Fitzgerald Kennedy. After attending Harvard and serving in the U.S. Navy during World War II, he was elected to the U.S. House of Representatives and the U.S. Senate. After marrying Jacqueline Bouvier (1953), he won the 1957 Pulitzer Prize in biography for *Profiles in Courage*. JFK defeated Republican Richard Nixon for the presidency (1960) by a narrow popular margin and called for a "New Frontier," marked by sweeping domestic changes, including civil rights legislation, and space exploration. During his presidency, the Peace Corps was established, the Bay of Pigs invasion occurred, the Berlin Wall was erected, the Cuban Missile Crisis brought the United States to the brink of nuclear war with the Soviet Union, and the number of U.S. military advisors in South Vietnam was increased. JFK was assassinated in 1963 by Lee Harvey Oswald while riding in a motorcade in Dallas. His administration has been called "Camelot" in deference to the style, grace, intellectual atmosphere, and family life of the Kennedy White House and the enthusiasm inspired by the young president.

Recommended Biographies

Hamilton, Nigel. *JFK: Reckless Youth*. New York: Random House, 1992. 898pp. Hamilton supplies an account of Kennedy's life from his birth through his years in Europe when his father was ambassador to Great Britain, ending in 1946 (the first of a projected three-volume study). Exhaustively researched, Hamilton's study has uncovered fresh in-

formation and is the best book available on Kennedy's formative experiences.

Parmet, Herbert S. *Jack: The Struggles of John F. Kennedy*. New York: Dial Press, 1980. 586pp; *JFK: The Presidency of John F. Kennedy*. New York: Dial Press, 1983. 407pp. Parmet's two volumes constitute a full-length portrait, with the first book narrating Kennedy's career up to the 1960 presidential campaign and the second examining the essential themes of his administration. Despite a tendency toward vindication, Parmet allows a flawed and all-too-human figure to emerge.

Other Biographical Studies

Andersen, Christopher P. *Jack and Jackie: Portrait of an American Marriage*. New York: Morrow, 1996. 400pp. Filled with anecdotes and gossip, this treatment of the couple's relationship based on interviews provides few lurid details and manages an unexpectedly sympathetic view of both figures.

Blair, Joan, and Clay Blair. *The Search for JFK*. New York: Putnam, 1976. 608pp. In this account of Kennedy's formative years between his prep school graduation and his first election to Congress the emphasis is on his health, sexual relationships, and military career. The book suggests that Kennedy's performance as a naval commander was far less heroic than has been suggested and that his father was the dominant figure behind Kennedy's ambition and assault on power.

Brogan, Hugh. *Kennedy*. New York: Longman, 1996. 249pp. Part of the Profiles in Power series, this is an informative overview of Kennedy's political career and presidential leadership.

Davis, John H. *The Kennedys: Dynasty and Disaster*. New York: McGraw-Hill, 1984. 722pp. Tracing the history of four generations of the Kennedy family beginning in 1848, this often lurid indictment concentrates on Kennedy and collects a mass of gossip, innuendo, and evidence to please the most ardent Kennedy hater. Often rambling and diffuse, the book is dominated by its negative thesis and makes little pretense of offering an objective assessment.

Giglio, James N. *The Presidency of John F. Kennedy*. Lawrence: University Press of Kansas, 1991. 334pp. After supplying a useful introductory chapter on Kennedy's life and prepresidential career, Giglio offers a balanced assessment of the Kennedy presidency, making effective use of the oral histories collected in the JFK Library.

Hersh, Seymour M. *The Dark Side of Camelot*. Boston: Little, Brown, 1997. 498pp. Hersh's is a scathing exposé of Kennedy's reckless ambition and sexual promiscuity. The damning charges include the contention that Kennedy stole the 1960 election with the help of organized crime, that he personally directed assassination attempts on several foreign leaders, and that his Vietnam policy was largely dictated by the need to prove his manliness.

Klein, Edward. *All Too Human: The Love Story of Jack and Jackie Kennedy*. New York: Simon & Schuster, 1996. 406pp. In a somewhat breathless, journalistic account, the couple's relationship is detailed in a blend of fact, gossip, rumor, and conjecture with imagined conversations and dramatized episodes.

Mahoney, Richard D. *Sons and Brothers: The Days of Jack and Bobby Kennedy.* New York: Arcade, 1999. 441pp. This is a nuanced portrait of the relationship between the two brothers, tracing its evolution with an emphasis on the role their father played in both men's political lives.

Manchester, William. *One Brief Shining Moment: Remembering Kennedy.* Boston: Little, Brown, 1983. 280pp. Manchester in an elegiac and reverential appreciation supplements his own reminiscences with numerous other tributes and a lavish collection of photographs.

O'Donnell, Kenneth P., and David F. Powers. *"Johnny, We Hardly Knew Ye": Memories of John Fitzgerald Kennedy.* Boston: Little, Brown, 1972. 495pp. Focusing on Kennedy's political development from 1946 until his death, these anecdotes by devoted followers offer firsthand details on Kennedy's personality.

Reeves, Richard. *President Kennedy: Profile of Power.* New York: Simon & Schuster, 1994. 798pp. This account of Kennedy's three years as president focuses on his leadership in public policy. Each chapter features a different day in the administration that reveals how Kennedy responded to such crises as the Berlin Wall, Cuban Missile Crisis, Vietnam, and the arms race. Balanced in its interpretation, Reeve's analysis neither indicts Kennedy nor soft-pedals his limitations.

Reeves, Thomas C. *A Question of Character: A Life of John F. Kennedy.* New York: Free Press, 1991. 510pp. In a damning reassessment, Kennedy is portrayed as totally lacking in character, and the book serves as a synthesis of the revisionist assertions of Kennedy's flaws. Drawn exclusively from secondary sources, there is little attempt to separate fact from fiction in this bill of indictment against Kennedy.

Salinger, Pierre. *With Kennedy.* Garden City, New York: Doubleday, 1966. 391pp. Salinger, Kennedy's friend and press secretary, provides firsthand insights into Kennedy's decision-making and leadership style; *John F. Kennedy, Commander in Chief* (New York: Penguin, 1997. 150pp.) looks at Kennedy as a military leader.

Schlesinger, Arthur M. Jr. *A Thousand Days: John F. Kennedy in the White House.* Boston: Houghton Mifflin, 1965. 1,087pp. Schlesinger's personal account of his relationship with the president as a adviser is a partial view based on limited direct access on largely foreign affairs. In Schlesinger's view, Kennedy learned from his mistakes and grew as a leader, a position he supports with intimate details, though not concerning Kennedy's sexual activities, and an impressive reconstruction of the political context.

Sorenson, Theodore C. *Kennedy.* New York: Harper & Row, 1965. 783pp. Covering the decade Sorenson spent close to Kennedy from 1953 to 1963 as his aide and counsel, Sorenson was on hand for all the significant events of Kennedy's presidency, and his memoirs, though discreet on certain matters and admiring, serves as an invaluable eyewitness account and an invaluable biographical source.

White, Theodore H. *The Making of the President, 1960.* New York: Atheneum, 1961. 400pp. White's journalistic account of the 1960 election campaign is filled with revealing information that captures the drama and personalities on the campaign trail.

Wicker, Tom. *Kennedy without Tears: The Man Beneath the Myth.* New York: Morrow, 1964. 61pp. Wicker's brief character sketch attempts to reach the actual man behind the legend in a balanced profile that avoids either idolatry or condemnation.

Wills, Garry. *The Kennedy Imprisonment: A Meditation on Power.* Boston: Little, Brown, 1982. 310pp. Wills's provocative biographical essay speculates on the various forces and character traits that helped determine the behavior of Kennedy, his father, and his brothers. In Wills's speculative analysis, private flaws prevented Kennedy from achieving greatness as a leader.

Biographical Novels

Mayer, Robert. *I, J.F.K.* New York: Dutton, 1989. 262pp. The author imagines JFK in heaven 25 years after his death setting the record straight as he provides a version of his life while surrounded by Bobby Kennedy, Lyndon Johnson, Martin Luther King Jr., and Adlai Stevenson.

Fictional Portraits

Bernau, George. *Promises to Keep.* New York: Warner Books, 1988. 643pp. Bernau imagines what might have happened had Kennedy survived Dallas.

Rivers, Caryl. *Camelot.* Cambridge, Massachusetts: Zoland Books, 1998. 372pp. A young White House reporter provides an angle for viewing the Kennedy years with compellingly human views of a number of period figures, including JFK.

Delillo, Don. *Libra.* New York: Viking, 1988. 456pp. The central figures in the Kennedy assassination are imaginatively re-created in Delillo's literary version of the events, shown as a CIA conspiracy.

Korda, Michael. *The Immortals.* New York: Poseidon Press, 1992. 559pp. Fictionally re-creating the love affair between Kennedy and Marilyn Monroe, the novel offers a plausible but essentially speculative interpretation based on a factual framework.

Poyer, David. *The Only Thing to Fear.* New York: Forge, 1995. 429pp. In a fanciful thriller set in 1945, a convalescing Kennedy is transferred from the navy to Roosevelt's personal staff where he uncovers an assassination plot within the president's inner circle.

Thomas, D.M. *Flying in to Love.* New York: Scribner, 1992. 242pp. The Kennedy assassination is explored as the conjunction of history and myth in this blending of fact and fiction.

Recommended Juvenile Biographies

Cole, Michael D. *John F. Kennedy.* Springfield, New Jersey: Enslow, 1996. 128pp. MG. Cole presents Kennedy's family background, education, war record, and political career, as well as the main issues and events of his administration. Critical of Kennedy's failings, the book does not include sensational details of his personal life.

Goldman, Martin. *John F. Kennedy: Portrait of a President.* New York: Facts on File, 1995. 178pp. YA. This is an outstanding, well-researched presentation of Kennedy's character, record, and importance, with a sophisticated examination of the gap between the image and reality of Kennedy's life.

Randall, Marta. *John F. Kennedy.* New York: Chelsea House, 1988. 112pp. MG/YA. Randall offers a balanced and informed summary of Kennedy's life and career.

Biographical Films and Theatrical Adaptations

A&E Biography Video: John F. Kennedy: A Personal Story (1996). Producer: Rhys Thomas. Combining a visual portrait with testimony from those who knew Kennedy, as well as historians and critics, this film documentary manages a reasonably balanced look at the man behind the myth. Video.

Blood Feud (1983). Director: Mike Newell. The conflict between Jimmy Hoffa (Robert Blake) and the Kennedys is dramatized. Sam Groom portrays JFK, with Cotter Smith as Robert Kennedy, and Forrest Tucker as Lyndon Johnson.

J. Edgar Hoover (1987). Director: Robert E. Collins. In this film biography of the life and career of FBI long-time chief and powerbroker Hoover (Treat Williams), Art Hindle portrays Kennedy, with Rip Torn as Lyndon Johnson, David Ogden Stiers as Franklin D. Roosevelt, Walker Edmiston as Truman, and Andrew Duggan as Eisenhower. Video.

JFK (1991). Director: Oliver Stone. Based on the books *On the Trail of the Assassins* by Jim Garrison and *Crossfire: The Plot that Killed Kennedy* by Jim Marrs, the film dramatizes Jim Garrison's (Kevin Costner) investigation of the Kennedy assassination conspiracy. Video.

JFK: Reckless Youth (1993). Director: Harry Winer. Based on Nigel Hamilton's book, Patrick Dempsey portrays the young Kennedy, with Terry Kinney and Diana Scarwid as his parents. Video.

JFK Remembered (1988). Producer: ABC News. Using rare film footage and interviews with historians, politicians, and friends, the film provides a portrait of the man and the highlights of his life. Video.

John F. Kennedy (1981). Producer: CBS News. Covers the highlights of Kennedy's life and administration with an interview with Rose Kennedy on her son's childhood. Video.

John F. Kennedy: The Commemorative Video Album (1988). Producers: Hal Haley, et al. Issued to commemorate the twenty-fifth anniversary of Kennedy's death, the video includes three documentary films on different aspects of Kennedy's life. Video.

Kennedy (1983). Director: Jim Goddard. Martin Sheen plays JFK in this television mini-series with Blair Brown as Jackie, John Shea as Robert Kennedy, Nesbitt Blaisdell as Lyndon Johnson, and E.G. Marshall as Joseph Kennedy. Video.

The Kennedys of Massachusetts (1990). Director: Lamont Johnson. The film looks at the entire Kennedy clan with Steven Weber as JFK, Randle Mell as Robert Kennedy, and William L. Peterson as Joseph Kennedy. Video.

King (1978). Director: Abby Mann. William Jordan appears as JFK and Cliff De Young portrays Robert Kennedy in this film treatment of Martin Luther King's life. Paul Winfield portrays King. Video.

Life in Camelot: The Kennedy Years (1988). Producer: Peter W. Kunhardt. This is an informative pictorial history of the Kennedy presidency. Video.

The Missiles of October (1974). Director: Anthony Page. Dramatizing the Cuban Missile Crisis, William Devane portrays Kennedy, with Howard Da Silva as Khrushchev, and Martin Sheen as Robert Kennedy. Video.

Prince Jack (1983). Director: Bert Lovitt. This docudrama depicts Kennedy's political career with an intimate behind-the-scenes look at his presidency. Starring Lloyd Nolan, Dana Andrews, Robert Guillaume as Martin Luther King Jr., and Kenneth Mars as Lyndon Johnson. Video.

PT 109 (1963). Director: Leslie H. Martinson. Based on the book *PT 109: John F. Kennedy in World War II* (New York: Crest, 1963. 160pp.) by Robert J. Donovan, Cliff Robertson portrays Lieutenant Kennedy and his efforts to save his crew after his ship is sunk. Video.

Ruby (1992). Director: John Mackenzie. The story of the Kennedy assassination and its aftermath is dramatized from the perspective of Jack Ruby, the murderer of Lee Harvey Oswald. Danny Aiello takes the title role. Kevin Wiggins portrays JFK, with Mary Chris Wall as Jacqueline Kennedy, and Willie Garson as Oswald. Video.

See also Lyndon Johnson; Robert F. Kennedy; Jacqueline Kennedy Onassis

268. ROBERT F. KENNEDY
1925–1968

The younger brother of John F. Kennedy, Robert Kennedy was born in Brookline, Massachusetts, and graduated from Harvard and the University of Virginia Law School. He managed JFK's successful 1952 U.S. Senate race and from 1953 to 1956 was counsel to the Senate subcommittee chaired by Senator Joseph McCarthy. He then became chief counsel to the Senate subcommittee investigating labor rackets. He served as U.S. attorney general under JFK and in 1965 was elected U.S. senator from New York. A popular leader of the liberal Democrats, he ran as a presidential candidate in 1968. While giving a victory speech in Los Angeles after winning the California primary, he was gunned down by Sirhan Sirhan.

Autobiography and Primary Sources

Robert Kennedy in His Own Words: The Unpublished Recollections of the Kennedy Years. Edwin O. Guthman and Jeffrey Shulman, eds. New York: Bantam, 1988. 493pp. Part of the Kennedy Library's oral history project initiated by RFK, this is a candid collection of interviews conducted from 1964 to 1967 on the Kennedy administration.

Thirteen Days: A Memoir of the Cuban Missile Crisis. New York: W.W. Norton, 1963. 224pp. Kennedy renders his perspective of his brother's administration during the October 1962 confrontation with Russia over missiles in Cuba.

Recommended Biographies

Beren, Michael K. *The Last Patrician: Bobby Kennedy and the End of the American Aristocracy.* New York: St. Martin's, 1998. 275pp. Beren's provocative reassessment of Kennedy's character combines an intellectual biography with a cultural retrospective, placing Kennedy's career in a wider social context that challenges many accepted conceptions about the man and his ideals.

Heymann, C. David. *RFK: A Candid Biography of Robert F. Kennedy.* New York: Dutton, 1998. 596pp. Based on extensive research and new information from FBI, CIA, and Department of Justice records, Heymann provides a revealing full-scale biography for the general reader. The author of a number of celebrity biographies, Heymann details both Kennedy's public and private relationships with a strong emphasis on the latter.

Schlesinger, Arthur M. Jr. *Robert Kennedy and His Times.* New York: Houghton Mifflin, 1978. 1,066pp. Although written by an admitted partisan and chronologically incomplete (Kennedy's assassination is not described), the book is nevertheless one of the most comprehensive treatments of Kennedy's political career. Schlesinger excels in his narrative skill that animates the era.

Other Biographical Studies

David, Lester, and Irene David. *Bobby Kennedy: The Making of a Folk Hero.* New York: Dodd, Mead, 1986. 342pp. An anecdotal collection of stories about Kennedy from numerous interviews, not a straightforward narrative biography, this is a sympathetic appreciation rather than a critical assessment.

De Toledano, Ralph. *RFK: The Man Who Would Be President.* New York: Putnam, 1967. 381pp. In a scathing attack, the author presents a negative survey of Kennedy's political career. Mixing fact, hearsay, and innuendo, as well as distortion of the historical record, the book has been described as not a biography but a mugging.

Dooley, Brian. *Robert Kennedy: The Final Years.* New York: St. Martin's, 1996. 191pp. Dooley, a British journalist, offers a brief survey of Kennedy's career from 1965 to 1968, emphasizing his Senate experience and the transformation of his political ideas.

Guthman, Edwin O. *We Band of Brothers.* New York: Harper & Row, 1971. 339pp. Written by a special assistant to Kennedy at the Department of Justice and his first senatorial press secretary, this is an admiring recounting of Kennedy's public career with almost all of the blemishes omitted.

Halberstam, David. *The Unfinished Odyssey of Robert Kennedy.* New York: Random House, 1968. 211pp. A personal and impressionistic account of Kennedy's presidential campaign.

Hilty, James W. *Robert Kennedy: Brother Protector.* Philadelphia: Temple University Press, 1997. 642pp. Hilty's perceptive biography traces Kennedy's development as he gradually emerged from his elder brother's shadow. A second volume is projected to cover Kennedy's career after JFK's assassination.

Laing, Margaret I. *The Next Kennedy.* New York: Coward-McCann, 1968. 320pp. Written by a British journalist and serving as a campaign biography, the book is based on interviews with Kennedy's family and friends and portrays Kennedy as a strong, determined man with an almost maniacal energy.

Mahoney, Richard D. *Sons and Brothers: The Days of Jack and Bobby Kennedy.* New York: Arcade, 1999. 441pp. This is a nuanced portrait of the relationship between the two brothers, tracing its evolution with an emphasis on the role their father played in both men's political lives. The book is particularly strong on Robert's life following his older brother's death.

Navasky, Victor S. *Kennedy Justice.* New York: Atheneum, 1971. 482pp. Navasky examines in detail the operation of the U.S. Justice Department under Kennedy's leadership as attorney general. In a balanced assessment, the book grants both the department's achievements and shortcomings, as well as Kennedy's strengths and weaknesses.

Newfield, Jack. *Robert Kennedy: A Memoir.* New York: Dutton, 1969. 318pp. In a personal recollection by a reporter with a close association with Kennedy, Newfield surveys Kennedy's political career with an emphasis on his changes from JFK's assassination to his own death.

Shannon, William V. *The Heir Apparent: Robert Kennedy and the Struggle for Power.* New York: Macmillan, 1967. 309pp. Focusing on Kennedy's senate career, Shannon's political analysis treats Kennedy as more an idealist than an opportunist and is particularly insightful on the New York political scene.

Steel, Ronald. *In Love with Night: The American Romance with Robert Kennedy.* New York: Simon & Schuster, 2000. 222pp. Called a "study of character and circumstance" rather than a biography, Steel looks at the myths surrounding Robert Kennedy, their origins, and the considerable gap between the legend and the reality. In Steel's provocative rereading of Kennedy's character, he is depicted as a political opportunist whose admired advocacy for social justice had its roots in political necessity and self-interest.

Stein, Jean, and George Plimpton. *American Journey: The Times of Robert Kennedy.* New York: Harcourt, Brace, 1970. 372pp. In a moving, elegiac tribute, the book collects the reflections of the mourners on board the funeral train from New York to Washington following Kennedy's assassination.

Thompson, Robert E., and Hortense Myers. *Robert F. Kennedy: The Brother Within.* New York: Macmillan, 1962. 224pp. This early biography chronicles Kennedy's public career up to his early days as attorney general.

Vanden Heuvel, William J., and Milton Gwirtzman. *On His Own: Robert F. Kennedy 1964–1968*. Garden City, New York: Doubleday, 1970. 393pp. The authors, two of Kennedy's assistants, offer an insider's view of his last four years.

Witcover, Jules. *85 Days: The Last Campaign of Robert F. Kennedy*. New York: Putnam, 1969. 338pp. A journalistic account of Kennedy's presidential campaign.

Fictional Portraits

Hannibal, Edward. *Blood Feud*. New York: Ballantine Books, 1979. 310pp. Hannibal dramatizes the feud between Robert Kennedy and Jimmy Hoffa.

Rechy, John. *Marilyn's Daughter*. New York: Carroll & Graf, 1988. 531pp. The novel imagines a hypothetical daughter of Monroe and Bobby Kennedy who tries to uncover the truth about her parents.

Recommended Juvenile Biographies

Harrison, Barbara, and Daniel Terries. *A Ripple of Hope: The Life of Robert F. Kennedy*. New York: Lodestar, 1997. 133pp. YA. A solid survey of both the personal life and public career of Robert Kennedy, including many direct quotations from his speeches.

Petrillo, Daniel J. *Robert F. Kennedy*. New York: Chelsea House, 1989. 111pp. MG/YA. Balancing personal details with a full survey of Kennedy's political career, this is an informative biography that relates the man to his era.

Schulman, Arlene. *Robert F. Kennedy: Promise for the Future*. New York: Facts on File, 1997. 128pp. MG. This concise biography focuses on Kennedy's career as a social activist and politician.

Biographical Films and Theatrical Adaptations

Blood Feud (1983). Director: Mike Newell. The conflict between Jimmy Hoffa (Robert Blake) and the Kennedys is dramatized. Sam Groom portrays John F. Kennedy, with Cotter Smith as RFK, and Forrest Tucker as Lyndon Johnson. Video.

The Kennedys of Massachusetts (1990). Director: Lamont Johnson. The film looks at the entire Kennedy clan with Randle Mell as RFK, Steven Weber as John F. Kennedy, and William L. Peterson as Joseph Kennedy. Video.

The Kennedys: The Later Years 1962–1980 (1992). Director: Phillip Whitehead. An installment in the American Experience series, this documentary, using news clips, family photos, and rarely seen documentary material, looks at the Kennedy clan following the death of John F. Kennedy. Video.

Robert Kennedy and His Times (1985). Director: Marvin J. Chomsky. Based on Arthur M. Schlesinger's book, this television film traces Robert Kennedy's public career. With Brad Davis as Bobby, Cliff De Young as John F. Kennedy, Veronica Cartwright as Ethel Kennedy, and Juanin Clay as Jacqueline Kennedy. Video.

See also Lyndon Johnson; John F. Kennedy; Jacqueline Kennedy Onassis

269. JACK KEROUAC
1922–1969

A novelist and leading figure of the Beat Generation, Kerouac was born in Lowell, Massachusetts, and studied at Columbia University. His best-known novel *On the Road* (1957) is considered a testament to the Beat movement of the late 1950s and early 1960s, as well as a major twentieth-century literary work. Kerouac's other novels include *The Subterraneans* (1958), *The Dharma Bums* (1958), and *Big Sur* (1962).

Autobiography and Primary Sources

Almost all of Kerouac's fiction have a strong autobiographical element and offer the reader numerous insights into the writer's life and character, though a complete identification between the fiction and Kerouac's life is misleading. A more reliable source on the writer's actual attitudes and perspectives is his correspondence. *Selected Letters, 1940–1956*. Ann Charters, ed. New York: Viking, 1995. 629pp.; *Selected Letters: 1957–1969*. Ann Charters, ed. New York: Viking, 1999. 514pp. Charters's two-volume collection of Kerouac's letters chronicles his life from his college years to his later life. All sides of the writer's complex personality are displayed here in an invaluable record of Kerouac's development, relationships, and ideas.

Recommended Biographies

Charters, Ann. *Kerouac: A Biography*. San Francisco: Straight Arrow Books, 1973. 419pp. The first Kerouac biography remains an important, though not comprehensive, treatment of Kerouac, concentrating on the flowering of the Beats during the 1950s. With Kerouac himself as a primary source and access to valuable documentary evidence, Charters offers a year-by-year chronicle that traces how Kerouac processed the events of his life into his work.

McNally, Dennis. *Desolate Angel: Jack Kerouac, the Beat Generation, and America*. New York: Random House, 1979. 400pp. McNally extends Charter's focus by adding considerable details on Kerouac's early and later years as well as placing him and his writing in a wider sociological and artistic context.

Nicosia, Gerald. *Memory Babe: A Critical Biography of Jack Kerouac*. New York: Grove Press, 1983. 767pp. Nicosia's biography comes closest to a definitive study. Comprehensive, richly detailed, and authoritative, this critical biography includes a close consideration of Kerouac's books, establishing their relationship to Kerouac's life and their wider literary and cultural context.

Other Biographical Studies

Amburn, Ellis. *Subterranean Kerouac: The Hidden Life of Jack Kerouac*. New York: St. Martin's, 1998. 435pp. Based on his own relationship with the writer, the letters, and unpublished journals, Amburn traces Kerouac's personal torment to his repressed homoeroticism, and this detailed account of Kerouac's various demons provides a darker, psychological reading of the writer's character than is to be found in other treatments.

Cassady, Carolyn. *Off the Road: My Years with Cassady, Kerouac, and Ginsberg*. New York: Morrow, 1990. 436pp. This is an intimate look at the key Beat figures by a crucial eyewitness.

Christy, Jim. *The Long, Slow Death of Jack Kerouac*. Toronto: Echo Press, 1998. 110pp. Christy focuses on the last 10 years of Kerouac's life, a period largely dismissed by most biographers, to argue that this was a crucial period of the writer's spiritual development.

Clark, Tom. *Jack Kerouac*. New York: Harcourt, Brace, 1984. 254pp. Clark's balanced and concise study serves as a valuable introduction for readers without the patience for the fuller treatments by Charters, McNally, and Nicosia. The highlights of Kerouac's life are presented in a lively narrative that shows how the writer wove his life into his fiction.

Gifford, Barry, and Lawrence Lee. *Jack's Book: An Oral Biography of Jack Kerouac*. New York: St. Martin's, 1978. 339pp. Connecting excerpts from interviews with friends and acquaintances of Kerouac, the authors' oral history is a rich, informal storehouse of insights and biographical details.

Jarvis, Charles E. *Visions of Kerouac*. Lowell, Massachusetts: Ithaca Press, 1973. 220pp. The book's vision is filtered through the author's often intrusive subjective and speculative lens. Impressionistic rather than objective and critical, the book nevertheless contains some useful insights.

Johnson, Joyce. *Minor Characters*. Boston: Houghton Mifflin, 1983. 262pp. The author's recollection of her love affair with Kerouac in the 1950s provides an impressionistic but colorful portrait of the writer and the Beat scene.

Miles, Barry. *Jack Kerouac, King of the Beats: A Portrait*. New York: Holt, 1998. 332pp. Miles's character sketch captures Kerouac from a variety of perspectives that succeeds in establishing his complexity and contradictions. The book is less useful as a synthesis and coherent interpretation. Based on his close association with Kerouac's friends, Allen Ginsberg and William Burroughs, Miles offers some original observations, but often relies on familiar details derived from secondary sources.

Sandison, David. *Jack Kerouac: An Illustrated Biography*. Chicago: Chicago Review Press, 1999. 154pp. This is a visual record of Kerouac's life and times with a foreword by Carolyn Cassady.

Turner, Steve. *Angelheaded Hipster: A Life of Jack Kerouac*. New York: Viking, 1996. 224pp. This illustrated biography draws on interviews with Kerouac's friends, Allen Ginsberg and William Burroughs, for its portrait of the artist.

Biographical Films and Theatrical Adaptations

Duberman, Martin B. *Visions of Kerouac: A Play*. Boston: Little, Brown, 1977. 142pp. Using Kerouac's own words, the playwright dramatizes 13 scenes from Kerouac's life with an intriguing view of the man behind the artist.

Heart Beat (1980). Director: John Byrum. Based loosely on the memoir of Carolyn Cassady (Berkeley, California: Creative Arts Book, 1976. 93pp.),

John Heard stars as Kerouac, with Nick Nolte and Sissy Spacek as Neal and Carolyn Cassady. Video.

Kerouac (1985). Director: John Antonelli. Using rare documentary footage, this documentary portrait includes a performance by Jack Coulter as Kerouac. Video.

What Happened to Kerouac? (1987). Director: Richard Lerner. This film biography includes Kerouac's appearance on the Steve Allen and William F. Buckley television programs. Video.

Other Sources

Knight, Arthur, and Kit Knight. *Kerouac and the Beats: A Primary Sourcebook.* New York: Paragon House, 1988. 272pp. A selection of documentary materials on Kerouac and his circle.

270. JOHN MAYNARD KEYNES
1883–1946

English economist who greatly influenced the study of modern economics, Keynes taught at Cambridge, worked in the Treasury during World War I, and during World War II was consultant to the Exchequer and a director of the Bank of England. He was influential at the Bretton Woods Conference (1944) in proposals to establish a world bank. His theories, based on government planning to stimulate high levels of economic growth and employment, are expressed in his chief work, *The General Theory of Employment, Interest, and Money* (1936).

Autobiography and Primary Sources

The Letters of Lydia Lopokova and John Maynard Keynes. Polly Hill and Richard Keynes, eds. New York: Scribner, 1990. 367pp. Keynes's marriage to the Russian ballerina, Lydia Lopokova, shocked and dismayed his Bloomsbury circle, many of whom predicted wrongly that the marriage would fail. The story of the couple's attraction is recounted in their letters up to their marriage in 1925.

Recommended Biographies

Felix, David. *Keynes.* Westport, Connecticut: Greenwood, 1999. 322pp. Felix's critical biography is a balanced account tracing the connection between Keynes's personality and his ideas. The book weaves together a succinct presentation of Keynes's private and public life in a sympathetic but judicious assessment of his achievements and originality.

Moggridge, Donald E. *Keynes.* 1976. Revised ed. New York: Macmillan, 1980. 190pp.; *Maynard Keynes: An Economist's Biography.* New York: Routledge, 1992. 941pp. Moggridge, the editor of Keynes's collected works, supplies two excellent accounts. The first is a brief and excellent introduction to Keynes's intellect and economic ideas without much treatment of his personal life; the second a much more thorough, comprehensive portrait of the man and his career that has established the book as the best single-volume account and the standard academic biography.

Skidelsky, Robert. *John Maynard Keynes. Volume One: Hopes Betrayed 1883–1920.* New York: Viking, 1986. 447pp.; *Volume Two: The Economist as Savior 1920–1937.* New York: Penguin, 1994. 731pp. Skidelsky's as yet unfinished proposed three-volume biography is a masterful, full treatment of Keynes's public and private life and a far more candid and complex portrait than previous treatments.

Other Biographical Studies

Blaug, Mark. *John Maynard Keynes: Life, Ideas, Legacy.* New York: St. Martin's, 1990. 95pp. Blaug supplies an introduction to Keynes's life and ideas, supplemented through conversations with eight leading economists, including Paul Samuelson, James Tobin, and Milton Friedman.

Harrod, Roy F. *The Life of John Maynard Keynes.* New York: Harcourt, Brace, 1951. 674pp. This first Keynes biography by a former student is limited by a worshipful tone and a selective view that often distorts the full picture of Keynes's activities and interests. Keynes's homosexuality, for example, is discreetly ignored. Additionally, Harrod's interpretation of episodes is often idiosyncratic and controversial. Notable for its gathering of details into a workable chronology, the book has been superseded by later, more critical and authoritative studies.

Hession, Charles H. *John Maynard Keynes: A Personal Biography of the Man who Revolutionized Capitalism and the Way We Live.* New York: Macmillan, 1984. 400pp. Hession adds considerable personal details to Harrod's more guarded portrait, particularly on Keynes's formative years and his homosexuality. Although the analysis of the evolution of Keynes's economic ideas and professional activities is often insightful, as one contemporary review remarked, the author "is more earnest than illuminating."

Skidelsky, Robert. *Keynes.* New York: Oxford University Press, 1996. 136pp. An entry in the Past Masters series, this is a useful distillation of information on Keynes's life, career, and ideas that serves as an excellent overview for the nonspecialist.

Recommended Juvenile Biographies

Escoffier, Jeffrey. *John Maynard Keynes.* New York: Chelsea House, 1995. 135pp. YA. Part of the Lives of Notable Gay Men and Lesbians series, Escoffier's is a thoughtful and sensitive biographical portrait.

Biographical Films and Theatrical Adaptations

John Maynard Keynes: Life, Ideas, Legacy (1988). Director: Nigel Maslin. A film documentary, written by Mark Blaug, examining Keynes's life, public career, and writings. Video.

Wittgenstein (1993). Director: Derek Jarman. This experimental portrait of the Austrian philosopher Ludwig Wittgenstein (Karl Johnson) takes the form of a series of vignettes from his life, including his relationship with such figures as John Maynard Keynes (John Quentin) and Bertrand Russell (Michael Gough). Video.

271. NIKITA KHRUSHCHEV
1894–1971

First secretary of the Communist party of the Soviet Union and premier of the USSR, Khrushchev was a central figure in the destalinization program (1956) denouncing Joseph Stalin who replaced (1958) Nikolai Bulganin as premier. Khrushchev sought to ease Cold War tensions through "peaceful coexistence" with the West despite inflammatory rhetoric and such incidents as the downing of an American U2 spy plane (1960), the erecting of the Berlin Wall (1961), and the installment of Soviet missiles in Cuba (1962). During his rule, the USSR broke off friendly relations with China. He was removed from office in 1964.

Autobiography and Primary Sources

Khrushchev Remembers. Strobe Talbot, ed. Boston: Little, Brown, 1970 to 1974. 2 vols. Based on taped recollections made after Khrushchev's fall from power in 1964, this is a discursive, defensive memoir covering both the rise to power and years in command, and Khrushchev's views on many topics and version of his past.

Recommended Biographies

Crankshaw, Edward. *Khrushchev: A Career.* New York: Viking, 1966. 311pp. Crankshaw's interpretive biography on Khrushchev's political career is particularly interesting on his early years and rise to political power.

Khrushchev, Sergei. *Khrushchev on Khrushchev: An Inside Account of the Man and His Era.* Boston: Little, Brown, 1990. 423pp. While most biographies deal mainly with Khrushchev's public life, his son offers the most intimate view of the private man and his personality. Mainly covering the months leading up to Khrushchev's ouster and years up to his death, the book's lack of objectivity limits its usefulness, but the firsthand revelations are important in helping to get the man in focus.

Tompson, William J. *Khrushchev: A Political Life.* New York: St. Martin's, 1995. 341pp. Tompson's political biography is a thorough, detailed portrait of Khrushchev's life and career using newly released archival material. Although covering Khrushchev's peasant origins and rise to power, the book concentrates on his role in shaping Soviet society after Stalin and the causes for his removal from office.

Other Biographical Studies

Breslauer, George W. *Khrushchev and Brezhnev as Leaders.* Boston: Allen and Unwin, 1982. 318pp. Breslauer's dual biographical portrait concentrates on the leadership styles of both men while challenging the conventional wisdom of Khrushchev's lack of political savvy.

Medvedev, Roy A. *Khrushchev.* Garden City, New York: Anchor/Doubleday, 1983. 292pp. The work of a dissident Soviet historian attempts to restore

Khrushchev's reputation as a reformer of Stalinist injustices, concentrating mainly on his policy initiatives during the years in power. Medvedev offers few details on Khrushchev's private life but does provide interesting glimpses of his personality.

Werth, Alexander. *Russia under Khrushchev.* New York: Hill & Wang, 1962. 352pp. The author, a Russian-born British journalist, documents the social and political background that helps explain Khrushchev's rise to power and impact during his years in power. The biographical material is selective, devoted exclusively to his political career, trips abroad, and relations with the United States.

Fictional Portraits

Beal, John Robinson. *The Secret Speech: The Failure of Comrade Khrushchev's Leadership.* New York: Duell, Sloan, and Pearce, 1961. 138pp. This satiric political fantasy looks ahead to Khrushchev's downfall in a parody of the Soviet's own 1956 speech enumerating Stalin's errors. Khrushchev is portrayed as an inept leader.

Heywood, Joseph. *The Domino Conspiracy.* New York: Random House, 1998. 552pp. This espionage and political thriller shows the Soviets trying to protect Khrushchev from an assassin, while the CIA stalks someone trying to kill newly-elected President Kennedy.

Krotkov, Yuri. *The Nobel Prize.* New York: Simon & Schuster, 1980. 348pp. This is a fictionalized account of the events following Boris Pasternak's winning the 1958 Nobel Prize. Khrushchev is depicted as an intelligent party head and an interesting adversary for the artist Pasternak.

Recommended Juvenile Biographies

Ebon, Martin. *Nikita Khrushchev.* New York: Chelsea House, 1986. 112pp. MG/YA. Ebon's is a sensible, informative treatment of Khrushchev's career, shown in the wider context of Soviet history.

Kort, Michael. *Nikita Khrushchev.* New York: F. Watts, 1989. 160pp. MG. Kort is excellent on Khrushchev's political rise and the events that shaped Russian history from 1917 to 1964.

Biographical Films and Theatrical Adaptations

The Missiles of October (1974). Director: Anthony Page. Dramatizing the Cuban Missile Crisis, William Devane portrays John F. Kennedy, with Howard Da Silva as Khrushchev, and Martin Sheen as Robert F. Kennedy. Video.

Other Sources

McCauley, Martin, ed. *Khrushchev and Khrushchevism.* Bloomington: Indiana University Press, 1987. 243pp. This scholarly collection of critical assessments of Khrushchev's impact and influence on Soviet history offers various insights on Khruschchev's personality and leadership style.

272. SØREN KIERKEGAARD
1813–1855

Danish philosopher and religious thinker, Kierkegaard's theories profoundly influenced both twentieth-century Protestant theology and the existentialist movement. The dominant theme of Kierkegaard's writings is the individual's subjective relationship to truth and faith. Among his aesthetic works are *Either/Or* (1843) and *Philosophical Fragments* (1844); his religious writings include *Works of Love* (1847) and *Training in Christianity* (1850).

Autobiography and Primary Sources

Journals and Papers. Howard and Edna Hong, eds. Bloomington: University of Indiana Press, 1968–1979. 7 vols. Kierkegaard's private writings, collected here, provide an unprecedented access to the workings of the philosopher's mind and are an indispensable biographical source. See also *The Last Years: Journals 1853–1855.* Ronald G. Smith, ed. (New York: Harper & Row, 1965. 383pp.), a selection from Kierkegaard's journals that includes brief biographical notes documenting the philosopher's final years.

Letters and Documents. Princeton, New Jersey: Princeton University Press, 1978. 518pp. Consists of all the known correspondence to and from Kierkegaard as well as documents pertaining to his life and death.

Recommended Biographies

Lowrie, Walter. *Kierkegaard.* New York: Oxford University Press, 1938. 2 vols. Lowrie's remains the standard scholarly life. Lowrie's approach is to fashion a kind of autobiography from lengthy quotations from Kierkegaard's writings, allowing him as much as possible to narrate his own story. A distillation of his two-volume life that serves as a valuable introduction is available as *A Short Life of Kierkegaard* (Princeton, New Jersey: Princeton University Press, 1942. 271pp.).

Thompson, Josiah. *Kierkegaard.* New York: Knopf, 1973. 286pp. Focusing on Kierkegaard's life to reveal the sources and evolution of his philosophy, Thompson's account is more critical than Lowrie's, substituting a psychologically believable human portrait for the heroic and apologetic perspective that Lowrie often presents. Accessible to the nonspecialist, this is a skillful critical biography that helps the reader to see the philosopher clearly in the context of his background, influences, and development.

Other Biographical Studies

Gardiner, Patrick L. *Kierkegaard.* New York: Oxford University Press, 1988. 120pp. Part of the Past Masters series, Gardiner's compact study condenses the highlights of Kierkegaard's life and ideas into an accessible introduction for the general reader and student.

Grimsley, Ronald. *Søren Kierkegaard: A Biographical Introduction.* London: Studio Vista, 1973. 127pp. Part of the Leaders of Modern Thought series, this is a competent summary of the highlights of the philosopher's career with the con-

nections between Kierkegaard's experiences and his ideas underscored.

Biographical Novels

Anderson, Barbara. *Kierkegaard: A Fiction.* Syracuse, New York: Syracuse University Press, 1974. 155pp. Imagined journal entries from the philosopher's mother allows Anderson to meditate on the philosopher's character and ideas.

Other Sources

Hannay, Alastair, and Gordon D. Marino, eds. *The Cambridge Companion to Kierkegaard.* New York: Cambridge University Press, 1998. 428pp. This collection of critical essays by noted Kierkegaard scholars treats various aspects of the philosopher's ideas, attitudes, and experiences.

273. MARTIN LUTHER KING JR.
1929–1968

An American clergyman, eminent civil rights leader, and recipient of the 1964 Nobel Peace Prize, King was born in Atlanta, Georgia, the son of the pastor of the Ebenezer Baptist Church. He was ordained in 1947, graduated from Morehouse College (1948), and received his B.D. at Crozer Theological Seminary (1951) and Ph.D. from Boston University (1955). While serving as pastor of a Baptist church in Montgomery, Alabama, he led the boycott (1955 to 1956) against the segregated city bus companies in the wake of Rosa Parks's protest, and then organized the Southern Christian Leadership Conference. King's philosophy of civil disobedience and nonviolent protest led to frequent arrests. In 1963 he organized the massive March on Washington, where he delivered his eloquent "I have a dream" speech. King's methods were challenged in the mid–1960s by such militant civil rights leaders as Malcolm X. While on a trip to Memphis in support of striking sanitation workers, he was assassinated by James Earl Ray.

Autobiography and Primary Sources

The Autobiography of Martin Luther King Jr. Clayborne Carson, ed. New York: Warner Books, 1998. 400pp. The book arranges King's own words chronologically to approximate an autobiography. Serves as a useful compilation of King's reflections on his life and career.

The Papers of Martin Luther King Jr. Clayborne Carson, ed. Berkeley: University of California Press, 1992-. 3 vols. The first three volumes of a projected seven-volume series are a monumental collection of documents relating to King, including much previously unpublished material. Covers King's earliest writings to 1956. *Stride Toward Freedom: The Montgomery Story.* New York: Harper, 1958. 230pp.; *The Measure of a Man.* New York: Harper, 1959. 63pp.; *Strength to Love.* New York: Harper, 1963. 146pp.; *Why We Can't Wait.* New York: Harper, 1964. 178pp.; *Where Do We Go From Here?* New York: Harper, 1967. 209pp.; *The Trumpet of Conscience.* New York: Harper, 1968. 78pp. King's various books have an autobiographical basis, particularly his earlier books. All are significant in revealing King's analysis of the Civil Rights movement and racism in America.

Recommended Biographies

Branch, Taylor. *Parting the Waters: America in the King Years, 1954-63*. New York: Simon & Schuster, 1988. 1,064pp.; *Pillar of Fire: America in the King Years, 1963-65*. New York: Simon & Schuster, 1998. 746pp. With one further volume to come, Branch's impressive biographical study of King and his times promises to become the definitive life when completed. Volume one won the Pulitzer for history. Branch raises King's story to the epical, with an eye both for the details that animate the intimate and the dramatic as King's personal history is fit to the wider context of American political and cultural history.

Garrow, David J. *Bearing the Cross: Martin Luther King Jr. and the Southern Christian Leadership Conference*. New York: Morrow, 1986. 800pp. Garrow's Pulitzer Prize–winning study is one of the most informative and thorough examinations of the Civil Rights movement and King's leadership role. Based on hundreds of interviews with key figures and King's FBI and CIA files, this is a balanced assessment that treats King's strengths and weaknesses.

Lewis, David L. *King: A Biography*. Urbana: University of Illinois Press, 1978. 460pp. A revision of *King: A Critical Biography* (New York: Praeger, 1970. 460pp.). Scholarly, detailed, and critical, Lewis portrays King as a man of ability made great by a particular confluence of circumstances. Best on detailing the historical and cultural influences that helped shaped King's ideas and behavior.

Oates, Stephen B. *Let the Trumpet Sound: The Life of Martin Luther King Jr.* New York: Harper & Row, 1982. 560pp. Tracing King's religious, intellectual, and political development, Oates's readable, balanced study does not overlook King's shortcomings, and serves as one of the most comprehensive and compelling treatments of King available.

Other Biographical Studies

Baldwin, Lewis V. *There Is a Balm in Gilead: The Cultural Roots of Martin Luther King Jr.* Minneapolis: Fortress Press, 1991. 348pp. Baldwin examines the cultural context of King's development, identifying three major influences: the South, the idea of community, and Christian optimism that help explain King's philosophy and civil rights activism. Often reverential to his subject, Baldwin does provide a useful synthesis of King's cultural roots.

Bennett, Lerone. *What Manner of Man: A Biography of Martin Luther King Jr.* 1964. Revised ed. New York: Johnson, 1976. 251pp. Written by King's classmates at Morehouse College, this early admiring biography supplies useful information, particularly on King's early life and college years, but does not attempt a critical evaluation.

Bishop, Jim. *The Days of Martin Luther King Jr.* New York: Putnam, 1970. 516pp. Bishop dramatizes the assassination of King and through flashbacks the high points of his life. A vivid narrative for the general reader, the book provides little interpretation of King's personality or ideas.

Davis, Lenwood G. *I Have a Dream: The Life and Times of Martin Luther King Jr.* Westport, Connecticut: Negro Universities Press, 1969. 303pp. The first biographical study to suggest some criticism of King's leadership and character, Davis offers a carefully documented account of King's life and public career.

Downing, Frederick J. *To See the Promised Land: The Faith Pilgrimage of Martin Luther King Jr.* Macon, Georgia: Mercer University Press, 1986. 297pp. A psychohistorical study based on James Fowler's faith development theory, Downing traces the development of King's thought with an emphasis on his early childhood experience and his family background.

Dyson, Michael E. *I May Not Get There with You: The True Martin Luther King Jr.* New York: Free Press, 2000. 404pp. Dyson sets out to wrest the complex, human figure from the romanticized and sanitized image, to, in his words, "rescue King from his admirers and deliver him from his foes." While offering no new information, the book is chiefly important for its fresh approach that attempts to reveal the man in his own terms, flaws and all.

Fairclough, Adam. *To Redeem the Soul of America: The Southern Christian Leadership Conference and Martin Luther King Jr.* Athens: University of Georgia Press, 1987. 163pp. The work of a British scholar, this is a detailed study of the SCLC, the NAACP, and the development of King's ideas and leadership.

Franklin, V.P. *Martin Luther King Jr.* New York: Random House, 1998. 192pp. Franklin's biographical portrait emphasizes the role of African American churches and religious tradition in shaping King's ideas and actions.

King, Coretta Scott. *My Life with Martin Luther King Jr.* New York: Holt, 1969. 372pp. In a valuable reminiscence, King's widow describes their life together from their marriage in 1953 to King's death. The book is full of details of King's family and domestic life and the personal cost of King's social activism.

King, Martin Luther, Sr. *Daddy King: An Autobiography*. New York: Morrow, 1980. 215pp. In a heartbreaking account of the senior King's life and struggles, his son only appears two-thirds of the way through, but the King family history is essential for understanding the man and his development.

Miller, William R. *Martin Luther King Jr.: His Life, Martyrdom, and Meaning for the World*. New York: Weybright and Talley, 1968. 319pp. In an appreciation by a friend who traveled with King, Miller supplies a warm human portrait and details his personal torments but does not attempt a wider and critical assessment.

Peake, Thomas R. *Keeping the Dream Alive: A History of the Southern Christian Leadership Conference from King to the 1980s*. New York: P. Lang, 1987. 492pp. More a biography of the organization, the book does deal with King's ideas and

leadership. Garrow's similar study is more complete and revealing.

Biographical Novels

Johnson, Charles. *Dreamer*. New York: Scribner, 1998. 236pp. Johnson's multilayered novel explores both the character and implication of King's greatness in a story of a double who takes the job as King's stand-in and decoy. The novel presents King's private reflections based on actual details from his life and an insightful probing of his personality.

Fictional Portraits

Andrews, Robert. *Death in a Promised Land*. New York: Pocket Books, 1993. 305pp. In this provocative thriller, a CIA agent investigates evidence that links the FBI and the KGB to the King assassination.

Garrett, George. *The King of Babylon Shall Not Come Against You*. New York: Harcourt, Brace, 1996. 336pp. Garrett's poetic and challenging exploration of King's legacy involves an investigation in Florida of a murder committed on the same day as King's death. The novel includes biographical details from King's life as his martyrdom is probed for its ongoing relevance to American life.

Recommended Juvenile Biographies

Jakoubek, Robert E. *Martin Luther King Jr.* New York: Chelsea House, 1989. 143pp. MG/YA. Jakoubek presents the essential details of both King's personal and public life and connects his activities to the wider historical context of the civil rights movement.

Patterson, Lillie. *Martin Luther King Jr. and the Freedom Movement*. New York: Facts on File, 1989. 178pp. YA. This is a sophisticated political biography that also supplies a useful account of the civil rights movement.

Schuman, Michael. *Martin Luther King Jr.: Leader for Civil Rights*. Springfield, New Jersey: Enslow, 1996. 128pp. MG. Schuman covers the major events in King's life in a straightforward account.

Biographical Films and Theatrical Adaptations

A&E Biography Video: Martin Luther King Jr: The Man and the Dream (1997). Director: John Akomekah. Using archival footage and interviews with experts, the film provides a full-length biographical portrait. Video.

The Boy King (1986). Director: Billy James Parrott. Looks at King's early life and initial encounters with prejudice, his family life, and the influence of his parents on his ideas. Video.

King (1978). Director: Abby Mann. Television docudrama chronicling King's life, starring Paul Winfield in the title role, with Cicely Tyson and Ossie Davis. William Jordan and Cliff De Young portray John F. Kennedy and Robert Kennedy and Dick Anthony Williams appears as Malcolm X. A novelization of the screenplay by William

Johnston (New York: St. Martin's, 1978. 286pp.) is available. Video.

King: Montgomery to Memphis (1970). Producers: Ely Landau and Richard Kaplan. Follows King's career from 1955 to 1968 using newsreels and television coverage as well as excerpts from his speeches and interviews. Video.

Other Sources

Lincoln, C. Eric, ed. *Martin Luther King Jr.: A Profile.* New York: Hill & Wang, 1970. 232pp. A collection of essays by associates of King, arranged chronologically.

274. RUDYARD KIPLING
1865–1936

The first English writer awarded the Nobel Prize for Literature (1907), Kipling is famous for his verse, short stories, and novels of Anglo-Indian life, and children's stories. Born in Bombay, India, and educated in England, he worked as an editor in Lahore (1882–1889), where he composed his early poems and stories, returned to London (1889–1892), then lived in Vermont (1892–1896) and in England from 1900. His many works include *Plain Tales From the Hills* (1888), *The Light That Failed* (1890), *Barrack-Room Ballads* (1892), *The Jungle Book* (1894), *Captains Courageous* (1897), *Kim* (1901), *Just So Stories* (1902), and the poems "Gunga Din" (1897) and "If (1910)."

Autobiography and Primary Sources

Something of Myself and Other Autobiographical Writings. Thomas Pinney, ed. New York: Cambridge University Press, 1990. 294pp. Reprints Kipling's reticent autobiographical fragment and other reflections on his life and career.

The Letters of Rudyard Kipling. Thomas Pinney, ed. Iowa City: University of Iowa Press, 1990–. 4 vols. The first four volumes in an ongoing series collects Kipling's correspondence up to 1919 with the letters presented to form a coherent narrative, displaying the writer's many facets with confirmation both for his admirers and detractors.

Recommended Biographies

Carrington, Charles. *Rudyard Kipling: His Life and Work.* Garden City, New York: Doubleday, 1955. 433pp. The "official" biography, authorized and approved by Kipling's surviving daughter, Carrington's life is a full-scale, intimate, and knowledgeable account based on unpublished sources. Regarded as the standard source of facts concerning Kipling's life and career, Carrington's examination offers little interpretation of Kipling's character or more than a slight analysis of his works.

Ricketts, Harry. *Rudyard Kipling: A Life.* New York: Carroll & Graf, 2000. 448pp. Ricketts offers a fast-paced narrative account that helps to restore an appreciation for Kipling's literary achievement and personality. Without glossing over the unflattering aspects of Kipling's reactionary politics,

Ricketts traces their origin in the writer's grief over the deaths of his son in battle and his daughter.

Wilson, Angus. *The Strange Ride of Rudyard Kipling: His Life and Work.* New York: Viking, 1977. 370pp. Although its facts are mainly derived from Carrington, Wilson adds his own novelistic perspective to offer one of the best accounts of Kipling as a writer. Tracing the connections between Kipling's experiences and their transformation into his works, Wilson widens and deepens a view of Kipling's artistic temperament, personality, and the significance of his works.

Other Biographical Studies

Amis, Kingsley. *Rudyard Kipling and His World.* New York: Scribner, 1975. 128pp. This visual biography includes a brief, personal, and partisan commentary on Kipling's life with the facts based on Carrington's biography. Serves as a concise introduction, though the photographic record is stronger than the text.

Birkenhead, Frederick W.F.S. *Rudyard Kipling.* New York: Random House, 1978. 421pp. Birkenhead's biography in its first draft was banned from publication by Kipling's daughter after being commissioned by her. The author continued the project, however, and his revision was finally published after he and the daughter died. Based on the tightly protected family papers and interviews with surviving Kipling friends and associates, Birkenhead's portrait is less flattering to Kipling than Carrington's with details that suggests the writer's unpleasantness. Serves as a complement to Carrington's more balanced treatment.

Cross, Thomas N. *East and West: A Biography of Rudyard Kipling.* Ann Arbor, Michigan: Luckystone Press, 1992. 348pp. Cross emphasizes the impact of Kipling's early traumas as the key to his personality and the themes of his works in this biographical profile.

Fido, Martin. *Rudyard Kipling.* New York: Viking, 1974. 144pp. This illustrated biography serves as a lively introduction to Kipling's life and artistry.

Mason, Philip. *Kipling: The Glass, the Shadow, and the Fire.* New York: Harper & Row, 1975. 334pp. Not a full-scale biography, Mason's critical study concentrates on Kipling's works and their relationships with his life. Often insightful, Mason attempts to reconcile the considerable inconsistencies between Kipling the mature and compassionate artist and the jingoist imperialist.

Seymour-Smith, Martin. *Rudyard Kipling.* New York: St. Martin's, 1989. 375pp. This contentious, revisionist study challenges the perceived self-censorship in Carrington and Birkenhead's use of Kipling's papers for, in the author's own words, a "boldly speculative" interpretation suggesting that Kipling married to satisfy his homosexual longing for his wife's brother. Versus the 23 chapters devoted to Kipling's first 40 years, only two chapters cover his last 30 years.

Fictional Portraits

Harries, Ann. *Manly Pursuits.* New York: Bloomsbury, 1999. 339pp. As Cecil Rhodes is close to death, an Oxford professor travels to South Africa

to deliver hundreds of British songbirds to salve Rhodes's soul in this powerfully imagined tale with glimpses of Rhodes, and such figures as Lewis Carroll, Oscar Wilde, and Rudyard Kipling.

Recommended Juvenile Biographies

Kamen, Gloria. *Kipling: Storyteller of East and West.* New York: Atheneum, 1986. 72pp. MG. In a well-written and beautifully illustrated biography, Kamen covers Kipling's early years in India, his unhappy childhood in England, his development as a writer, and his family life. The book is particularly insightful in drawing the connections between Kipling's personal background and the themes in his works.

Biographical Films and Theatrical Adaptations

The Man Who Would Be King (1975). Director: John Huston. Christopher Plummer appears as the novelist who listens to the remarkable adventure of the story's two mercenary soldiers who journey to Kafiristan to establish a personal domain. Starring Sean Connery and Michael Caine. Video.

Other Sources

Orel, Harold. *A Kipling Chronology.* Boston: G.K. Hall, 1990. 127pp. This is a detailed chronology of Kipling's life.

Page, Norman. *A Kipling Companion.* New York: Macmillan, 1984. 202pp. Page supplies a chronology, a biographical profile organized by Kipling's life and travels, a who's who, and a critical survey of his creative works.

275. PAUL KLEE
1879–1940

Swiss painter, graphic artist, and art theorist, Klee exhibited with the Blue Reiter group (1911) and taught at the Bauhaus School (1922–1931) and the Düsseldorf academy (1931–1933), until the Nazis forced him to resign for producing what they designated "degenerate" art. His works are noted for their luminous and subtle color, texture, wit, and fantasy, and include *The Twittering Machine* (1922) and *Fish Magic* (1925). Klee produced more than 9,000 works during his lifetime and published an important textbook on painting.

Autobiography and Primary Sources

The Diaries of Paul Klee: 1898–1918. Felix Klee, ed. Berkeley: University of California Press, 1964. 434pp. The diaries cover Klee's early life and formative experiences and development from the age of 19 to 40, along with a brief autobiographical sketch written in 1940.

Paul Klee: His Life and Work in Documents. Felix Klee, ed. New York: G. Braziller, 1962. 212pp. The artist's son records his memories of his father and family life along with a collection of intimate family letters and photographs that cast light on Klee's personality and daily life.

Paul Klee: The Thinking Eye: The Notebooks of Paul Klee. Jurg Spiller, ed. 1961. 341pp. Written during his years as a teacher, Klee records his artistic theories and creative method.

Recommended Biographies

Grohmann, Will. *Paul Klee*. New York: Abrams, 1954. 448pp. Grohmann's remains the standard, scholarly biography and critical study. Highly detailed, based on the author's personal knowledge and access to Klee's extensive private papers, the book includes many reproductions of Klee's sketches and finished works, and documentary photographs, and reprints the artist's own brief autobiography.

San Lazzaro, Gualtieri di. *Klee: A Study of His Life and Work*. New York: Praeger, 1957. 304pp. With many reproductions of the artist's works and a sensitive biographical and critical analysis, this is a fine introduction to Klee's life and artistry. The author sheds light on Klee's personality and emotional life and the connections between his experiences and his development as an artist.

Other Biographical Studies

Giedion-Welker, Carola. *Paul Klee*. New York: Viking, 1952. 156pp. Devoted to Klee's growth and development as an artist, the book traces Klee's progress chronologically. Despite the author's personal acquaintance with Klee, there are few details here that help to explain the artist's temperament and private side.

Ponente, Nello. *Klee: Biographical and Critical Study*. Cleveland, Ohio: World, 1960. 140pp. This is a moderately useful introduction to Klee's life and artistic career in which the high points are covered with sufficient illustration to emphasis the artist's development and technical experiments.

Werckmeister, Otto K. *The Making of Paul Klee's Career, 1914–1920*. Chicago: University of Chicago Press, 1989. 335pp. Focused on the years of World War I in the formation of Klee's artistry and reputation, Werckmeister's is a scholarly examination of the economic and political factors that shaped Klee. Assuming a good deal of specialist knowledge, the book offers a challenging new assessment of the artist's conscious attempt to respond to shifting cultural values.

L

276. MARQUIS DE LAFAYETTE (MARIE JOSEPH PAUL YVES ROCH GILBERT DU MOTIER)
1757–1834

French general and political leader, Lafayette fought in the American Revolution under Washington and arranged for French troops and a fleet to aid the colonists. During the French Revolution, he was vice president of the National Assembly, drafted the *Declaration of the Rights of Man,* and commanded the National Guard. He was a member of the Chamber of Deputies in the Restoration and took part in the July Revolution of 1830.

Autobiography and Primary Sources

Lafayette in the Age of the American Revolution: Selected Letters and Documents, 1776–1790. Stanley J. Idzerda and Robert R. Crout, et al., eds. Ithaca, New York: Cornell University Press, 1977–1999. 5 vols. This scholarly collection of letters and documents to and from Lafayette is an indispensable source of biographical information during the period covered (currently up to 1785).

Recommended Biographies

Bernier, Olivier. *Lafayette: Hero of Two Worlds.* New York: Dutton, 1983. 356pp. In a popular, highly readable biography, Bernier manages a full-length portrait and a balanced assessment of Lafayette's strengths and weaknesses. Of the available single-volume studies, this is the most useful and accomplished.

Gottschalk, Louis R. *Lafayette.* Chicago: University of Chicago Press, 1935–73. 6 vols. Gottschalk's monumental study only covers Lafayette's life and career up to 1790 and is the most thorough biography of Lafayette's first 33 years. In addition to collecting important primary evidence, the author provides insights into Lafayette's motives based on psychological and family factors.

Other Biographical Studies

Buckman, Peter. *Lafayette: A Biography.* New York: Paddington Press, 1977. 288pp. Buckman's is a sympathetic overview intended for the general reader. Best on the French milieu in which Lafay-

ette moved, the treatment of his final 30 years is inadequate.

Gerson, Noel B. *Statue in Search of a Pedestal: A Biography of the Marquis de Lafayette.* New York: Dodd, Mead, 1976. 244pp. Gerson's anecdotal popular biography offers a mixed view of Lafayette, emphasizing both his virtues and failings, though the overall presentation lacks a sophisticated interpretive focus and is too often overly simplistic in its treatment.

La Fuye, Maurice de, and Emile A. Babeau. *Apostle of Liberty: A Life of La Fayette.* New York: T. Yoseloff, 1956. 344pp. The French perspective on Lafayette's character and career is interestingly reflected in this study. For those used to a heroic depiction the authors' scathing itemization of Lafayette's defects is sobering, if lacking in balance.

Latzko, Andreas. *Lafayette: A Life.* New York: Doubleday, 1936. 402pp. Latzko makes a valiant effort to comprehend Lafayette's life in full and falters, particularly on the details of the American Revolution. The book is strongest on the European context of Lafayette's life.

Loth, David G. *The People's General: The Personal Story of Lafayette.* New York: Scribner, 1951. 294pp. Focusing on Lafayette's private side, Loth's is a lively account that humanizes the reader's view of Lafayette, concentrating on his relationships with his wife, mistresses, and famous figures such as Washington, Franklin, Marie Antoinette, and Napoleon.

Sedgwick, Henry D. *La Fayette.* Indianapolis: Bobbs-Merrill, 1928. 433pp. Sedgwick's biographical profile concentrates on three important periods in Lafayette's life: his service in the American Revolution and involvement in the French revolutions of 1789 and 1830. The man is related to his times in a useful but somewhat old-fashioned and dull account.

Tower, Charlemagne Jr. *The Marquis de La Fayette in the American Revolution.* Philadelphia: Lippincott, 1895. 2 vols. Tower's early study of Lafayette's service in the American Revolution remains a significant source, though now mostly superseded by later scholarship.

Woodward, William E. *Lafayette.* New York: Farrar and Rinehart, 1938. 472pp. Woodward's

popular biography draws heavily on Gottschalk for its sources and offers a human portrait of a well-intentioned but limited idealist.

Biographical Novels

Wright, Constance. *A Chance for Glory.* New York: Holt, 1957. 255pp. Lafayette's activities during the French Revolution are depicted with an imagined rescue attempt when the American Revolutionary War hero becomes a captive of the Austrians.

Fictional Portraits

Mitchell, Silas W. *Hugh Wynne, Free Quaker.* 1897. Reprint ed. New York: Appleton-Century, 1924. 585pp. Mitchell's classic historical romance describes Revolutionary Philadelphia from the perspective of a Quaker merchant who serves as a spy for the Americans, becomes a prisoner of the British, and serves as a member of Lafayette's staff.

Taylor, David. *Farewell to Valley Forge.* Philadelphia: Lippincott, 1955. 378pp. Taylor's American Revolution adventure is set during the winter of 1778 and explores the attempt by General Charles Lee to replace Washington as head of the army and a trap set by the British to capture Lafayette.

Recommended Juvenile Biographies

Fritz, Jean. *Why Not, Lafayette?* New York: Putnam, 1999. 87pp. MG. Fritz's characteristic lively mix of animating details and an entertaining writing style is used to document Lafayette's career. Lafayette's early life is only briefly covered with his involvement in the American Revolution and his triumphal return at the end of his life emphasized.

Holbrook, Sabra. *Lafayette: Man in the Middle.* New York: Atheneum, 1977. 214pp. MG/YA. Holbrook's is a detailed portrait of the man and his times.

Horn, Pierre L. *Marquis de Lafayette.* New York: Chelsea House, 1989. 111pp. MG/YA. This is an informative biographical portrait that offers sufficient historical background to make Lafayette's actions and character clear.

Biographical Films and Theatrical Adaptations

Liberty!: The American Revolution (1997). Directors: Ellen Hovde and Muffie Meyer. This PBS documentary series features actors portraying the principals in dramatic readings from their letters and speeches. Lafayette is portrayed by Sebastian Roché. The companion volume is written by Thomas J. Fleming (New York: Viking, 1997. 394pp.) Video.

See also George Washington

277. D.H. LAWRENCE
1885–1930

English novelist, poet, short-story writer, and essayist, whose vivid prose style and deep insights into human nature helped to shape twentieth-century literature, David Herbert Lawrence was the sickly son of a Nottingham coal miner. After graduating from a two-year teacher-training course at University College (1905), he worked as a schoolmaster in a London suburb. An outspoken opponent of World War I, Lawrence and his German-born wife, Frieda, were suspected of espionage; after the war they left England and lived in various countries, including the United States, returning to England only for brief visits. Lawrence died of tuberculosis at 45. His greatest novels are *Sons and Lovers* (1913), *The Rainbow* (1915), and *Women in Love* (1921). *Lady Chatterley's Lover* (1928), controversial because of its explicit sexual content, was banned in England and the United States until 1959.

Autobiography and Primary Sources

The Letters of D.H. Lawrence. Keith Sagar and James T. Boulton, eds. New York: Cambridge University Press, 1979–1993. 7 vols. This scholarly edition of over 5,000 letters is an invaluable biographical resource and one of the best records of a modern literary figure.

Selected Letters. James T. Boulton, ed. New York: Cambridge University Press, 1997. 576pp. A collection of 300 letters from the Cambridge edition, this selection ranges across Lawrence's entire career and showcases one of English literature's finest correspondents.

Recommended Biographies

Cambridge Biography of D.H. Lawrence 1885–1930. This three-volume study written by preeminent Lawrence scholars and based on the most up-to-date scholarship is the most comprehensive and authoritative examination of Lawrence's life and career available and should remain the definitive account for some time to come:

Worthen, John. *D.H. Lawrence: The Early Years, 1885–1912.* New York: Cambridge University Press, 1991. 586pp. In this first volume of the *Cambridge Biography* chronicling Lawrence's formative years, Worthen's exhaustive sifting and interpretation of myriad details correct previous romanticizations, separating the facts from the fiction in Lawrence's autobiographical essays about his childhood and young manhood and the autobiographical basis of Lawrence's first three novels.

Kinkead-Weekes, Mark. *D.H. Lawrence: Triumph to Exile, 1912–1922.* New York: Cambridge University Press, 1996. 943pp. Covering the crucial decade in Lawrence's life and artistic career, this second volume of the *Cambridge Biography* scrupulously documents Lawrence's daily activities while shedding light on previously vague questions concerning Lawrence's sexuality, marriage, and relationships.

Ellis, David. *D.H. Lawrence: Dying Game, 1922–1930.* New York: Cambridge University Press, 1998. 780pp. Completing the *Cambridge Biography*'s comprehensive and minutely detailed examination of Lawrence's life, Ellis traces Lawrence's journeys from his leaving Europe in 1922 to his death in Venice in 1930 as Lawrence searched for an ideal community in Ceylon, Australia, the United States, and Mexico. More detailed than any previous account, Ellis's study corrects a number of misconceptions and provides a compelling portrait of the author's final struggles.

Maddox, Brenda. *D.H. Lawrence: The Story of a Marriage.* New York: Simon & Schuster, 1994. 620pp. Winner of the Whitbread Award for biography, Maddox's insightful and balanced account of Lawrence's tempestuous relationship with his wife supplies new information based on previously unpublished letters and challenges conventional views of Lawrence's sexuality, misogyny, anti-Semitism, and racism.

Meyers, Jeffrey. *D.H. Lawrence: A Biography.* New York: Knopf, 1990. 445pp. This is lucid, vivid, and comprehensive account of Lawrence's life and artistic career. Meyers's portrait of Lawrence is darker and more troubled than other versions and helps the reader understand the factors that impelled Lawrence to write and live as he did.

Moore, Harry T. *The Priest of Love: A Life of D.H. Lawrence.* New York: Farrar, Straus, 1974. 532pp. Long regarded as the standard biography, Moore's judicious yet sympathetic study of Lawrence's life is marked by its dispassionate objectivity, a refreshing anomaly in biographies of the writer. Remains the most useful, single-volume biography of Lawrence.

Nehls, Edward, ed. *D.H. Lawrence: A Composite Biography.* Madison: University of Wisconsin Press, 1957–1959. 3 vols. Nehls's monumental collection of published and unpublished accounts of Lawrence by various associates is arranged to form a chronological and thematical, multifaceted portrait. Includes recollections from Lawrence's sister, Frieda Lawrence, John Middleton Murry, Dorothy Brett, Mabel Dodge Luhan, and others.

Other Biographical Studies

Aldington, Richard. *D.H. Lawrence: Portrait of a Genius, But....* New York: Duell, Sloane and Pearce, 1950. 432pp. Novelist Aldington was the writer's friend from 1914 to Lawrence's death, and his recollections are supplemented by other's memoirs and an analysis of Lawrence's writings. Knowing Lawrence's faults at first hand, Aldington's is a sympathetic but balanced appreciation, as the book's title indicates.

Burgess, Anthony. *Flame into Being: The Life and Work of D.H. Lawrence.* New York: Arbor House, 1985. 276pp. Burgess's critical study is a warm-hearted appreciation that relates Lawrence's works to his life. The book, marked by Burgess's characteristic unorthodox views, provides a highly readable, though eccentric, introduction to the novelist.

Byrne, Janet. *A Genius for Living: The Life of Frieda Lawrence.* New York: HarperCollins, 1995. 504pp. In this full-scale biography of Frieda Lawrence and her marriage, Byrne counters other views of Lawrence's wife as selfish and unintelligent, showing her instead as a person who made an important contribution to Lawrence's creative efforts.

Callow, Philip. *Son and Lover: The Young Lawrence.* New York: Stein and Day, 1975. 316pp. Chronicling Lawrence's childhood and youth to 1919, Callow offers a novelistic treatment of the writer's developing consciousness.

Carswell, Catherine. *The Savage Pilgrimage: A Narrative of D.H. Lawrence.* New York: Harcourt, Brace, 1932. 296pp. Written by a friend during Lawrence's last 15 years, Carswell's recollections are supplemented by secondary sources to form a chronological narrative and balanced character portrait.

Chambers, Jessie. *D.H. Lawrence: A Personal Record.* New York: Barnes and Noble, 1965. 242pp. Chambers, Lawrence's adolescent sweetheart and the model for Miriam in *Sons and Lovers,* offers her emotional account of their relationship with valuable details on Lawrence's formative years.

Corke, Helen. *D.H. Lawrence: The Croyden Years.* Austin: University of Texas Press, 1965. 143pp. Corke provides a firsthand portrait of Lawrence as a young teacher based on her re-creation of her conversations with Lawrence.

Delany, Paul. *D.H. Lawrence's Nightmare: The Writer and His Circle in the Years of the Great War.* New York: Basic Books, 1979. 420pp. This is a thorough, scholarly reconstruction of Lawrence's day-to-day experiences during World War I, offering valuable insights into how the war affected Lawrence's ideas and writings.

Delavenay, Emile. *D.H. Lawrence: The Man and His Work: The Formative Years 1885–1919.* Carbondale: Southern Illinois University Press, 1972. 592pp. Described as an "environmental study," Delavenay's analysis charts the influences on Lawrence's development up to the writing of *Aaron's Rod.*

Moore, Harry T., and Warren Roberts. *D.H. Lawrence and His World.* New York: Viking, 1966. 143pp. This pictorial biography is chiefly valuable for its visual record of Lawrence's life, surroundings, and associates.

Murry, John Middleton. *Son of Woman: The Story of D.H. Lawrence.* New York: Cape and Smith, 1931. 367pp. Written by a one-time intimate, Murry provides an autobiographical reading of Lawrence's works and an uneven psychological portrait that alternates between adoration and attack.

Sagar, Keith M. *The Life of D.H. Lawrence.* New York: Pantheon, 1980. 256pp. Sagar's illustrated documentary life weaves together published and unpublished documents to form a reliable, concise biographical record.

Sagar, Keith M. *D.H. Lawrence: Life into Art.* Athens: University of Georgia Press, 1985. 372pp. This literary biography traces the transformation of Lawrence's experiences into his art and includes a sensitive and balanced reading of Lawrence's works in the context of his developing ideas and relationships.

Schneider, Daniel J. *The Consciousness of D.H. Lawrence: An Intellectual Biography.* Lawrence: University Press of Kansas, 1986. 207pp. Blending intellectual biography and psychology, Schneider traces the development of Lawrence's thoughts and feelings from the perspective of the writer's religious quest. The approach provides a fresh and stimulating, if sometimes reductionist, angle for viewing Lawrence's life and career.

Trease, Geoffrey. *The Phoenix and the Flame: D.H. Lawrence: A Biography.* New York: Viking, 1973. 177pp. Trease fictionally enhances Lawrence's story based on others' recollections. Not reliable in every detail, imagination is predominant here over careful scholarship and factual evidence.

Worthen, John. *D.H. Lawrence: A Literary Life.* New York: St. Martin's, 1989. 196pp. Worthen concentrates on the practical, professional considerations of Lawrence's writing career. This refreshing view of the writer shows how Lawrence dealt with censorship and finances while struggling to maintain the integrity of his art.

Fictional Portraits

White, Nelia G. *Daughter of Time.* New York: Macmillan, 1942. 272pp. In this fictionalized biography of Katherine Mansfield, D.H. Lawrence's friendship with the writer is depicted.

Biographical Films and Theatrical Adaptations

Coming Through (1993). Director: Peter Barber-Fleming. A dramatization of Lawrence's love affair with Frieda von Richthoven Weekley that led to their scandalous elopement in 1912. Kenneth Branagh portrays Lawrence and Helen Mirren stars as Frieda. Video.

D.H. Lawrence: As Son and Lover (1988). Director: Andrew Puddington. This dramatized biography uses Lawrence's letters, essays, and autobiographical sketches to document his life and ideas. Starring Sam Dale, Shona Morris, Yvonne Coulette, and Gordon Christie. Video.

D.H. Lawrence: Novelist, 1885–1930 (1995). Director: Peter Hoyt. Part of the Famous Authors series, this concise biography uses archival material and location photography to present the highlights of Lawrence's life and the social and historical background to his writing. Video.

Priest of Love (1981). Director: Christopher Miles. Ian McKellen portrays Lawrence in this drama concerning the furor surrounding the publication of *Lady Chatterley's Lover* and the novelist's final struggle with tuberculosis. Janet Suzman co-stars as Frieda Lawrence. Video.

Other Sources

Page, Norman, ed. *D.H. Lawrence: Interviews and Recollections.* New York: Barnes and Noble, 1981. 2 vols. Page helpfully collects Lawrence's own autobiographical comments with reminiscences by a number of individuals who knew him.

Pinion, F.B. *A D.H. Lawrence Companion.* New York: Barnes and Noble, 1979. 316pp. Pinion's is a useful reference guide, covering multiple aspects of the writer's life, work, and relationships.

Poplawski, Paul. *D.H. Lawrence: A Reference Companion.* Westport, Connecticut: Greenwood, 1996. 714pp. This handy reference guide to Lawrence's life, works, and criticism is usefully arranged to supply both a coherent overview and specific information about a single aspect of Lawrence's career.

Preston, Peter. *A D.H. Lawrence Chronology.* New York: St. Martin's, 1994. 208pp. This is a detailed, month-by-month listing of Lawrence's activities based on a careful review of the biographical record.

Sagar, Keith M. *A D.H. Lawrence Handbook.* Manchester, England: Manchester University Press, 1982. 454pp. Sagar's reference guide includes a chronology, a travel calendar, a glossary of Nottinghamshire dialect and mining terms, and a checklist of Lawrence's reading.

278. T.E. LAWRENCE
1888–1935

British soldier, scholar, and writer known as Lawrence of Arabia, Thomas Edward Lawrence became legendary as a guerrilla fighter with the Arabs against the Turks in World War I. After the war he worked to achieve independence for the Arabs. During the 1920s he joined the Royal Air Force and Royal Tank Corps under assumed names, eventually changing his name legally to T. E. Shaw. His best-known work is *Seven Pillars of Wisdom* (1926).

Autobiography and Primary Sources

The Letters of T.E. Lawrence. David Garrett, ed. New York: Doubleday, 1939. 896pp. Included are private letters, official reports, diary entries, and notes and memoranda, arranged by periods in Lawrence's life beginning with his early years as an archaeologist. Malcolm Brown has edited another collection of this material in *T.E. Lawrence: The Selected Letters.* (New York: W.W. Norton, 1989. 568pp.).

Seven Pillars of Wisdom. 1926. Reprint ed. New York: Anchor Books, 1991. 672pp. Lawrence's classic account of his experiences is also available in a reworked condensed version, *Revolt in the Desert* (New York: Barnes and Noble, 1993. 335pp.). Readers should refer to one of the biographies listed below to gauge the degree to which these are historical accounts or fabrications.

Recommended Biographies

Asher, Michael. *Lawrence: The Uncrowned King of Arabia.* Woodstock, New York: Overlook Press, 1999. 419pp. Based on retracing many of Lawrence's steps across the Arabian peninsula and sifting the record for inconsistencies, Asher provides a thoughtful narrative account of Lawrence's life as well as a plausible psychological profile to help explain his nature and actions.

Brown, Malcolm, and Julia Cave. *A Touch of Genius: The Life of T.E. Lawrence.* New York: Paragon House, 1989. 233pp. The authors provide a balanced and objective view of Lawrence's life and achievements that relies largely on his own words and allows the reader to decide how much to admire and how much to censure. Serves as a solid introduction to the subject.

Mack, John E. *A Prince of Our Disorder: The Life of T.E. Lawrence.* Boston: Little, Brown, 1976. 561pp. Mack's Pulitzer Prize–winning biography succeeds both in challenging the myth that has obscured a direct appreciation of the man and connecting Lawrence's inner life with his public actions. Thorough in its approach, well-researched, and judicious, Mack's study is the recommended first choice among Lawrence biographies.

Wilson, Jeremy. *Lawrence of Arabia: The Authorized Biography of T.E. Lawrence.* New York: Atheneum, 1990. 1,188pp. Easily the most comprehensive and detailed biography available, Wilson has devoted many years to trying to understand Lawrence's character and motives, and this is a fair assessment that is sympathetic but critical, avoiding undue adulation or debunking. For the reader with the stamina, this is a rewarding, multifaceted human portrait.

Other Biographical Studies

Aldington, Richard. *Lawrence of Arabia: A Biographical Enquiry.* Chicago: Regnery, 1955. 448pp. Aldington's is a harshly negative assessment of the man and his achievement, contending that Lawrence was largely a fraud who took in the public with cunning self-promotion. Liddell Hart, who has a very different view, complained that "the majority of the criticisms are superficial, and many are silly."

Brent, Peter L. *T.E. Lawrence.* New York: Putnam, 1975. 232pp. Concentrating primarily on the period 1916 to 1918, Brent offers a vivid narrative and a psychological analysis that suggests that Lawrence's identification with the Arabs sprang from his disgust at his illegitimacy.

Graves, Richard P. *Lawrence of Arabia and His World.* New York: Scribner, 1976. 127pp. In an attractive illustrated survey, Graves adds little to the understanding of Lawrence or the details of his remarkable adventures but does retell them competently, aided by the book's many photographs.

Graves, Robert. *Lawrence and the Arabs.* 1928. Reprint ed. New York: Paragon House, 1991. 454pp. Graves's narrative account, which was approved by Lawrence, of his Arabian adventures differs from Lowell Thomas's version. Graves, a Lawrence partisan and friend, does provide some interesting firsthand observations about Lawrence's complex character.

Hyde, H. Montgomery. *Solitary in the Ranks: Lawrence of Arabia as Airman and Private Soldier.* New York: Atheneum, 1978. 288pp. Hyde's sympathetic portrait of Lawrence after Arabia uses extensive documentation from Lawrence's correspondence and his air ministry records to present a sensitive and compelling portrait of a war casualty.

James, Lawrence. *The Golden Warrior: The Life and Legend of Lawrence of Arabia.* New York: Paragon House, 1993. 406pp. James offers a number of striking alternative views of Lawrence's character and motives, including assertions that Lawrence fabricated his rape and torture by the Turks, exaggerated his account of the capture of Damascus, and was an active homosexual.

Knightley, Phillip, and Colin Simpson. *The Secret Lives of Lawrence of Arabia.* New York: McGraw-Hill, 1970. 333pp. This presentation of details from Lawrence's life by a British journalistic team has a distinct sensationalistic tone and is something of a guilty pleasure, mixing colorful details and significant insights with conjecture and errors in a highly readable and entertaining fashion.

Liddell Hart, B.H. *Colonel Lawrence: The Man Behind the Legend.* New York: Dodd, Mead, 1934. 382pp. This is both a history of the Arab revolt and a biographical profile that corrects aspects of the Lawrence legend and is the ideal accompaniment to Lawrence's own account of his Arabian experiences.

Nutting, Anthony. *Lawrence of Arabia: The Man and the Motives.* New York: C.N. Potter, 1961. 256pp. The author, a former British Foreign Office minister, offers a mainly balanced account of Lawrence's background, development, and activities. Best on the political background, the attempts at psychological analysis lack subtlety.

Stewart, Desmond. *T.E. Lawrence.* New York: Harper & Row, 1977. 352pp. Stewart presents a provocative view of Lawrence that is far from the heroic portrayal of the legend. In Stewart's view, Lawrence exaggerated his Arabic experiences to expiate guilt feelings about his military and political failures. Lawrence is very much a scaled-down, human figure in Stewart's handling, and the book offers an interesting challenge to the conventional view.

Thomas, Lowell. *With Lawrence in Arabia.* New York: Century, 1924. 408pp. Thomas more than any other "invented" Lawrence of Arabia and provided the initial burnishing of his legend in this journalistic account.

Weintraub, Stanley. *Private Shaw and Public Shaw: A Dual Portrait of Lawrence of Arabia and George Bernard Shaw.* New York: G. Braziller, 1963. 302pp. Weintraub concentrates here on the friendship between Lawrence and Shaw and the role the latter played in shaping Lawrence's literary career.

Weintraub, Stanley, and Rodelle Weintraub. *Lawrence of Arabia: The Literary Impulse.* Baton Rouge: Louisiana State University Press, 1975. 175pp. The first full-length study of Lawrence the writer, the book has many insightful things to say

about Lawrence's personality and temperament. Should be taken up after the reader is familiar with both Lawrence's life and works.

Yardley, Michael. *T. E. Lawrence: A Biography.* New York: Stein and Day, 1987. 267pp. Yardley is equally concerned here with the development of the Lawrence legend as the man himself in this factually sound recounting of the essential events and details of Lawrence's life.

Biographical Novels

Stevens, David. *The Waters of Babylon: A Novel about Lawrence After Arabia.* New York: Simon & Schuster, 2000. 320pp. Based on the known facts, the novel imagines Lawrence's life in the ranks of the Royal Air Force during his post-World War I career. Lawrence confronts his past in this evocative impersonation of a man unable to live up to his own heroic ideals.

Fictional Portraits

Aldridge, James. *Heroes of the Empty View.* New York: Knopf, 1954. 428pp. In a fictional reflection of Lawrence's life, Aldridge's protagonist mirrors Lawrence in a number of ways, both in his experiences and attitudes.

Blankfort, Michael. *Behold the Fire.* New York: New American Library, 1965. 397pp. Lawrence is one of several historical figures who appear in this novel about a group of Palestinian Jews who act as spies for the British during World War I.

Booth, Martin. *Dreaming of Samarkand.* New York Morrow, 1990. 452pp. Elaborating on an early event in Lawrence's life, the novel describes the love triangle involving Lawrence, English poet James Elroy Flecker and his wife, set in the years leading up to World War I.

Eden, Matthew. *The Murder of Lawrence of Arabia.* New York: Crowell, 1979. 271pp. This mystery novel looks at the facts surrounding Lawrence's death, concluding that his motorcycle crash was no accident. Lawrence's last weeks are described in a mainly fanciful speculation supplemented by actual details from his biography.

Hastings, Michael. *The Devil's Spy.* New York: Scribner, 1988. 326pp. Like Blankfort's novel, this espionage novel is based on the actual Jewish spy network that worked for the British during World War I. A fictional account of the activities of a spy and her British contact is connected with the actual events and such figures as General Allenby and Lawrence.

Irving, Clive. *Promise the Earth.* New York: Harper & Row, 1982. 402pp. This solid and authentic historical novel dramatizes the struggle to establish a Jewish Palestine state during the years 1916 to 1919 with appearances of a number of historical figures, including Lawrence.

Recommended Juvenile Biographies

MacLean, Alastair. *Lawrence of Arabia.* New York: Random House, 1962. 177pp. MG/YA. A Landmark biography, MacLean provides an often gripping account of Lawrence's adventures derived mainly from Lawrence's own accounts.

Thomas, John. *The True Story of Lawrence of Arabia.* Chicago: Childrens Press, 1964. 141pp. MG. Separating truth from the legend is by no means an easy task and Thomas offers a generally reliable version of the events based on primary and secondary sources.

Biographical Films and Theatrical Adaptations

A Dangerous Man: Lawrence After Arabia (1998). Director: Christopher Menaul. This interesting historical and biographical film picks up Lawrence's story in 1919, exploring the diplomatic negotiation at the Versailles Conference. Ralph Fiennes portrays Lawrence. Video.

Lawrence of Arabia (1962). Director: David Lean. Lean's stunning biographical film features a remarkable performance by Peter O'Toole in the title role with an impressive supporting cast, including Omar Sharif, Anthony Quinn, Alec Guinness. Claude Raines, and Anthony Quayle. Video.

Lawrence of Arabia (1996). This is a brief overview of Lawrence's life that emphasizes facts over the legend, with dramatic, low-budget reenactments. Video.

279. ROBERT E. LEE
1807–1870

A brilliant Civil War general and commander of the Confederate forces, Lee was the son of Revolutionary War cavalry officer Henry "Light-Horse Harry" Lee. He was born in Stratford, Virginia, and graduated second in his class from West Point (1829). He was captain of engineers during the Mexican War (1846–1848), served as superintendent of West Point (1852–1855), and led the company of marines that captured abolitionist John Brown at Harpers Ferry (1859). Although opposed to slavery and secession, his loyalty to Virginia caused him to decline field command of the Union forces and resign from the army (1861). After becoming a full Confederate general, he gained command of the Army of Northern Virginia. He successfully defended Richmond during the Seven Days Battle (1862) and subsequently scored victories at the second battle of Bull Run (1862), Fredericksburg (1862), and Chancellorsville (1863). Lee's forces never recovered from the defeat at the Battle of Gettysburg (1863) and on April 9, 1865, Lee surrendered to General Ulysses S. Grant at Appomattox Courthouse. After the war, he served as president of Washington College (now Washington and Lee University).

Autobiography and Primary Sources

Horn, Stanley F., ed. *The Robert E. Lee Reader.* Indianapolis: Bobbs-Merrill, 1949. 542pp. Weaving extracts from Lee's own words, recollections, and biographical sources, Horn presents a composite, documentary life that serves as a useful introduction to the man and his reputation.

Jones, J. William. *Personal Reminiscences, Anecdotes and Letters of General Robert E. Lee.* 1874. Reprint ed., Harrisburg, Pennsylvania: Archive Society, 1996. 509pp. Jones's early biographical portrait is chiefly useful as a repository of recollections and primary materials, including extracts from Lee's correspondence. Arranged topically, Jones's analysis is unreliable in all its details. Jones's *Life and Letters of Robert Edward Lee* (New York: Neale, 1906. 480pp.) is a later distillation of his sources that includes several antebellum letters, some of which have been edited and altered by Jones.

Lee, Robert E. Jr. *Recollections and Letters of General Robert E. Lee*. New York: Doubleday, 1904. 461pp. Written by Lee's youngest son, this remains an important source of family information about Lee, with edited excerpts from unpublished letters. Lee's narrative begins in 1846, but the majority of the book is devoted to the postwar years.

Long, Armistead L. *Memoirs of Robert E. Lee*. New York: Stoddart, 1886. 707pp. Long, a Confederate general and colleague of Lee, includes a number of important letters and firsthand evidence of the general.

Recommended Biographies

Dowdey, Clifford. *Lee*. Boston: Little, Brown, 1965. 781pp. Based on some previously untapped sources, Dowdey's is a readable, one-volume account that offers a convincing psychological portrait of Lee and an integrated study that unites his personal and military history. Relatively free from partisanship, Dowdey attempts to place Lee in a wider context as a true American hero, rather than as a saint of the lost Southern cause.

Freeman, Douglas S. *R.E. Lee: A Biography*. New York: Scribner, 1934–1935. 4 vols. The result of 20 years of labor, Freeman produced the definitive study of Lee that remains the most comprehensive treatment of Lee's life and career. Meticulous in its research and its ability to synthesize a mountain of source material into a skilled narrative, Freeman's Pulitzer Prize–winning life is not without flaws through its defensive bias in Lee's favor. Despite its limitations, Freeman's biography is the study against which all subsequent biographers must measure their own work.

Thomas, Emory M. *Robert E. Lee: A Biography*. New York: W.W. Norton, 1995. 472pp. Serving as a corrective to the saintly, heroic portrait created by Freeman and other biographers, Thomas offers a believable human portrait of a complex Lee. In a balanced, full-scale examination in which the Civil War represents only a third of the book, Thomas penetrates the various legends surrounding Lee and demonstrates the human core and personal relationships that formed his character and directed his behavior.

Other Biographical Studies

Anderson, Nancy S., and Dwight Anderson. *The Generals: Ulysses S. Grant and Robert E. Lee*. New York: Knopf, 1988. 523pp. This dual biography emphasizes the personal over the military in an account that follows both men from childhood through the Civil War, with their postwar careers given scant attention. Unfortunately, the book is marred by a number of factual errors and fictionalized elements that reduce the book's reliability.

Bradford, Gamaliel. *Lee the American*. 1912. Revised ed. Boston: Houghton Mifflin, 1940. 324pp. Bradford takes a psychological approach to detail the significant stages of Lee's development, though Lee's extreme reserve and privacy proved to be an insurmountable challenge in this early attempt at uncovering a fully satisfying, coherent portrait.

Brown, Robert R. *"And One Was a Soldier": The Spiritual Pilgrimage of Robert E. Lee*. Shippenburg, Pennsylvania: White Mane, 1998. 125pp. Spanning Lee's entire life, Brown focuses on Lee's spiritual life to help explain how his religious values formed his character and determined his behavior.

Connelly, Thomas L. *The Marble Man: Robert E. Lee and His Image in American Society*. New York: Knopf, 1977. 249pp. Tracing the evolution of Lee's image and reputation, Connelly challenges many conclusions that have become standard in viewing Lee. Showing that Lee's flawless heroic image was formed only after his death, Connelly argues that Lee should be seen as far more complex and mixed than many have suggested. The book provides a useful analysis of all the principal books on Lee from the 1860s to the 1960s.

Cooke, John Esten. *A Life of General Robert E. Lee*. New York: Appleton, 1871. 577pp. Cooke, a Confederate staff officer and postwar novelist, draws on his own observations of Lee in action during the war in this critical but ultimately admiring early biography.

Davis, Burke. *Gray Fox: Robert E. Lee and the Civil War*. New York: Rinehart, 1956. 466pp. Limited to the war years, Davis's popular, dramatic narrative account is an intimate daily treatment of Lee's military activities that grants a number of personal and strategic shortcomings in an attempt to free the man from the legend.

Fishwick, Marshall W. *Lee After the War*. New York: Dodd, Mead, 1963. 242pp. In an often impressionistic meditation on Lee's greatness, the author shifts the focus from Lee the general to his years as college president and his attempts to reconcile North and South by his example.

Flood, Charles B. *Lee: The Last Years*. Boston: Houghton Mifflin, 1981. 308pp. Flood presents a detailed account of Lee's last five years that does not overlook Lee's flaws in an overall sympathetic portrait of Lee's magnanimity in defeat.

Fuller, J.F.C. *Grant and Lee: A Study in Personality and Generalship*. Bloomington: Indiana University Press, 1957. 323pp. Fuller, a British military historian, challenges established notions in elevating Grant's generalship over that of his rival, Robert E. Lee.

Hendrick, Burton J. *The Lees of Virginia: Biography of a Family*. Boston: Little, Brown, 1935. 455pp. Covering two centuries of family history, Hendrick's group biography somewhat shortchanges Robert and his father for other less well-known members of the distinguished American family.

Miers, Earl S. *Robert E. Lee: A Great Life in Brief*. New York: Knopf, 1958. 203pp. Serving as useful, concise introduction, Miers concentrates on Lee's Civil War activities to the neglect of the antebellum and postwar years.

Nagel, Paul C. *The Lees of Virginia: Seven Generations of an American Family*. New York: Oxford University Press, 1990. 332pp. Chronicling the Lee family from its descendants' arrival in Virginia in 1640 to the death of Robert E. Lee, Nagel's study focuses on the family relationships rather than historical events and background. The last four chapters are devoted to Lee, who is shown not as a soldier but as a son, brother, husband, father, and cousin.

Nolan, Alan T. *Lee Considered: Robert E. Lee and Civil War History*. Chapel Hill: University of North Carolina Press, 1991. 231pp. Nolan's revisionist study debunks Lee's reputation as a man and commander. Refuting accepted wisdom, the emphasis here is with Lee's strategic blunders and shortcomings. A welcomed, if biased and intemperate, challenge to Lee idolatry.

Page, Thomas N. *Robert E. Lee: Man and Soldier*. New York: Scribner, 1911. 734pp. Page's biography is more comprehensive than most other early biographies but is still limited by the author's presentation of Lee's greatness with few reservations.

Sanborn, Margaret. *Robert E. Lee*. Philadelphia: Lippincott, 1966–1967. 2 vols. Sanborn's full-scale reassessment draws on some fresh sources and treats in detail Lee's entire life, but the book is marred by a weakness in military matters and an uncritical tone that identifies closely with Lee at the expense of others who are blamed for Lee's failures. Chiefly serving as an anthology of anecdotes and trivia, the book lacks sufficient objectivity and synthesis to produce a satisfactorily coherent and trustworthy portrait.

Smith, Gene. *Lee and Grant: A Dual Biography*. New York: McGraw-Hill, 1984. 412pp. This popular biography is a workmanlike comparative study but offers little that is new in its assessment.

Stern, Philip Van Doren. *Robert E. Lee: The Man and the Soldier*. New York: McGraw-Hill, 1963. 256pp. This pictorial biography is chiefly valuable for its illustrations rather than its text, which provides an admiring profile of Lee.

Winston, Robert W. *Robert E. Lee: A Biography*. New York: Morrow, 1934. 428pp. Winston's concise yet comprehensive biography has been unjustifiably overshadowed by Freeman's definitive and more authoritative life that appeared at the same time.

Young, James C. *Marse Robert: Knight of the Confederacy*. New York: Henkle, 1929. 362pp. As its title indicates, Young's partisan and adoring portrait of Lee presents an appraisal of the general's military genius and the character traits that made it possible. More hagiography than biography.

Biographical Novels

Adams, Richard. *Traveller*. New York: Knopf, 1988. 269pp. The military career and personality of Lee are originally captured from the perspective of his beloved horse, Traveller. The horse's unique angle of vision supplies a fresh and moving portrait of its master.

Altsheler, Joseph A. *The Shades of the Wilderness: A Story of Lee's Great Stand.* New York: Appleton, 1916. 311pp. Altsheler paints a noble portrait of Lee from the Gettysburg retreat to the Battle of the Wilderness.

Davis, Burke. *To Appomattox: Nine April Days.* New York: Rinehart,1959. 433pp. This documentary novel dramatizes the events leading up to Lee's surrender, based on contemporary accounts, letters, and diaries.

Herrin, Lamar. *The Unwritten Chronicles of Robert E. Lee.* New York: St. Martin's, 1989. 245pp. In a montage of letters and musings of both Robert E. Lee and Stonewall Jackson, the novel offers an impressionistic and psychological portrait of both men.

Kane, Harnett T. *The Lady of Arlington.* Garden City, New York: Doubleday,1953. 288pp. Lee's married life is dramatized from the perspective of his wife, Mary Custis Lee. The book has a solid basis in fact.

Shaara, Jeff. *Gods and Generals.* New York: Ballantine, 1996. 498pp. The novel, a prequel to his father's *The Killer Angels,* dramatizes the events leading up to the Battle of Gettysburg through the experiences of Lee, Joshua Lawrence Chamberlain, Winfield Scott Hancock, and Stonewall Jackson. Shaara's *The Last Full Measure* (New York: Ballantine Books, 1998. 560pp.) deals with the period from Lee's retreat from Gettysburg to his surrender through convincing recreation of the thoughts and feelings of Grant, Lee, Longstreet, and Joshua Lawrence Chamberlain. In *Gone for Soldiers: A Novel of the Mexican War* (New York: Ballantine Books, 2000. 424pp.), the author looks back at the Mexican War, documenting the campaign mainly from the perspective of the American commander, Winfield Scott, and the young Captain Robert E. Lee. Lee's formative experiences on the battlefield and as a military leader are the main concern here, along with brief appearances by individuals destined to become generals in the Civil War, such as Grant, Jackson, Beauregard, Hancock, Johnston, and Longstreet, who learn their military craft against the Mexicans.

Shaara, Michael. *The Killer Angels.* New York: McKay,1974. 374pp. Shaara's Pulitzer Prize–winning dramatization of the Battle of Gettysburg captures the conflict from multiple perspectives, including Lee's, Longstreet's, and Chamberlain's. Meticulous in its research, Shaara's interpretation of the commanders is authentic and compelling.

Wicker, Tom. *Unto This Hour.* New York: Viking, 1984. 642pp. The 1862 second battle of Bull Run or Manassas is recounted from the perspective of the commanders and the common soldier. Lee's strategic genius is captured, with every remark by a historical figure authenticated.

Fictional Portraits

Robert E. Lee appears in countless Civil War novels. A few of his most interesting depictions can be found in the following:

Dixon, Thomas. *The Man in Gray.* New York: Appleton, 1921. 427pp. Lee is the central character in this romanticized portrayal of his Civil War generalship from a decidedly Southern perspective.

Harper, M.A. *For the Love of Robert E. Lee.* New York: Soho, 1992. 325pp. A young woman in the 1960s fantasizes about Lee's life in a moving portrait based on history, family legends, and her own imagination.

Hart, Scott. *Eight April Days.* New York: Coward-McCann,1949. 188pp. The novel dramatizes the Confederate army's retreat from Petersburg and the events leading up to Lee's surrender at Appomattox.

Johnston, Mary. *Cease Firing.* Boston: Houghton Mifflin, 1912. 457pp. The Confederate point of view on the events of the Civil War is dramatized in a fictional story that features a depiction of Lee.

Leekley, John. *The Blue and the Gray.* New York: Dell,1982. 303pp. The events of the Civil War are reflected by the contrasting experiences of cousins on opposite sides of the conflict. The events and historical figures are accurately described, aided by historian Bruce Catton who served as the book's historical consultant.

Masters, Edgar Lee. *Lee: A Dramatic Poem.* New York: Macmillan, 1926. 139pp. Masters's narrative poem represents several scenes from Lee's life, with his wife, at Gettysburg, and at his funeral.

Savage, Douglas. *The Court Martial of Robert E. Lee.* New York: Warner Books, 1993. 475pp. The novel speculates about what might have happened had Lee been court-martialed following the Gettysburg defeat. On trial, Lee must review and justify his strategy. Most of the novel's dialogue is based on actual comments.

Seifert, Shirley. *Farewell, My General.* Philadelphia: Lippincott,1954. 315pp. In a fictionalized account of cavalry officer J.E.B. Stuart from his Indian fighting days in Kansas in the 1850s through the Civil War, Lee, as Stuart's commander is convincingly portrayed.

Skimin, Robert. *Gray Victory.* New York: St. Martin's,1988. 378pp. In a fascinating what-if speculation, the novel imagines a Confederate victory and J.E.B. Stuart's court-martial for the defeat at Gettysburg. Lee must face the politics of the new nation his victory has created.

Recommended Juvenile Biographies

Archer, Jules. *A House Divided: The Lives of Ulysses S. Grant and Robert E. Lee.* New York: Scholastic, 1995. 184pp. MG/YA. In alternating chapters this dual biography follows the lives of both generals with sufficient historical background to establish a context to view both heroic but human commanders that does not gloss over their failings.

Brown, Warren. *Robert E. Lee.* New York: Chelsea House, 1992. 111pp. MG. In an accurate and balanced biography, Lee's military career predominates over his personal life, but Brown attributes both Lee's achievements and his failures to his character traits.

Freeman, Douglas S. *Lee of Virginia.* New York: Scribner, 1958. 243pp. YA. Freeman, the distinguished Lee biographer offers his insights for younger readers in a compact but thorough portrait.

Biographical Films and Theatrical Adaptations

Drinkwater, John. *Robert E. Lee: A Play.* Boston: Houghton Mifflin, 1923. 128pp. Drinkwater's drama of the Civil War is built around the personality of Lee, whom one contemporary reviewer described as a "wooden tragedian."

A&E Biography Video: Robert E. Lee (1996). Director: Craig Haffner. Chronicles Lee's life and military career highlighting the origin of his greatness in command and character. Video.

The Blue and the Gray (1982). Director: Andrew V. McLaglen. Robert Symonds portrays Lee, with Rip Torn as Grant and Gregory Peck as Lincoln in this television mini-series. Video.

Civil War Legends (1989). Director: Gary DeMoss. This documentary portrait looks at the highlights of Lee's military career to illustrate his skills as a battlefield commander and leadership. Video.

Gettysburg (1993). Director: Ronald F. Maxwell. In the film adaptation of Michael Shaara's *The Killer Angels,* Martin Sheen portrays Lee. Video.

Other Sources

Gallagher, Gary W., ed. *Lee the Soldier.* Lincoln: University of Nebraska Press, 1996. 620pp. Detailing Lee's Civil War career and probing the question of his military leadership, this anthology brings together postwar remarks by Lee, essays by his contemporaries, biographical excerpts, and new articles evaluating Lee's decisions, character, and reputation.

See also Jefferson Davis; Ulysses S. Grant; Thomas "Stonewall" Jackson

280. VLADIMIR ILYICH LENIN
1870–1924

Founder of Bolshevism, leader of the Russian Revolution (1917), and founder of the Soviet state, Lenin was born Vladimir Ilyich Ulyanov in Simbirsk, the son of a school and civil service official. He became a revolutionary after his elder brother was executed (1887) for plotting to assassinate the czar. A law student, he was banished from the University of Kazan for his revolutionary activities and exiled to Siberia (1895–1900). He continued his activities abroad, publishing a pamphlet *What is to be Done* (1902), which detailed his method for bringing the Marxist revolution to Russia. Factional disputes between Bolsheviks and the less radical Mensheviks were interrupted by the abortive 1905 revolution, when Lenin and his followers briefly returned to Russia. After the 1917 Bolshevik victory, Lenin consolidated power. He established the Comintern to promote world revolution, founded the Cheka secret police to eliminate all organized opposition, and set up a dictatorship of the Communist party to control the hierarchy of all local, regional, and central soviet political units.

Autobiography and Primary Sources

The Letters of Lenin. Elizabeth Hill and Doris Mudie, eds. Westport, Connecticut: Hyperion

Press, 1973. 499pp. This selection of 340 letters emphasizes both Lenin's personal and political activities from 1896 to 1922 and are the most intimate and revealing of all his writings.

Recommended Biographies

Clark, Ronald W. *Lenin*. New York: Harper & Row, 1988. 564pp. Despite a number of drawbacks, including the author's lack of Russian that puts essential primary sources out of his direct reach and a tendency to uncritically accept Lenin's own justification for his behavior, this is a useful biography for the general reader that successfully connects the man with the theorist and revolutionary leader.

Fischer, Louis. *The Life of Lenin*. New York: Harper & Row, 1964. 703pp. In a careful, thorough, and nonjudgmental account, Fischer's biography devotes less than a quarter of the book to Lenin's life before seizing power in 1917, with the bulk of his examination devoted to Lenin's last five years. More a study of Lenin's political activities, Fischer's presentation does not attempt intimate close-ups of the man.

Shub, David. *Lenin: A Biography*. Garden City, New York: Doubleday, 1948. 438pp. Written by someone who knew and worked with Lenin, Shub's useful and readable account of Lenin's life and the Russian revolutionary movement from the nineteenth century to Lenin's death is not sympathetic but fair and adds to our knowledge of Lenin's personality and private life.

Volkogonov, Dmitrii A. *Lenin: A New Biography*. New York: Free Press, 1994. 529pp. In the first biography based on recently published secret archival material, Volkogonov, a special assistant to Boris Yeltsin, presents a damning political portrait of Lenin that demystifies him and demolishes the notion that, had Lenin survived, the perversion of the revolution by Stalin would have been prevented. In the author's insightful, though often intemperate, view, Lenin is portrayed as a totalitarian megalomaniac and state terrorist who initiated what would later be described as the characteristics of Stalinism.

Other Biographical Studies

Balabanoff, Angelica. *Impressions of Lenin*. Ann Arbor: University of Michigan Press, 1964. 152pp. These recollections by an early leader of Soviet Russia who broke with Lenin in the 1920s are valuable as a primary source for intimate insights into Lenin's character and behavior. While condemning his actions, Balabanoff avoids condemning the man.

Carrère d'Encausse, Hélène. *Lenin: Revolution and Power*. New York: Longman, 1982. 279pp. The author's analysis of the man and his career is helpfully placed in a Russian and historical context that both widens and deepens the standard view of Lenin.

Cliff, Tony. *Lenin*. London: Pluto Press, 1975–1979. 4 vols. Cliff's massive study of Lenin and the Russian Revolution is sympathetic without being uncritical and manages to find a useful balance between excessive admiration and censure.

Serves as a valuable reference source for information on the man and era.

Conquest, Robert. *V.I. Lenin*. New York: Viking, 1972. 152pp. Serves as a concise, critical introduction to the man, his career, and his times.

Deutscher, Isaac. *Lenin's Childhood*. New York: Oxford University Press, 1970. 67pp. Originally the opening chapter for an intended full-length biography that the author did not live to complete, Deutscher's authoritative and revealing study covers the period from Lenin's birth to his elder brother's execution, and is one of the best treatments of Lenin's early life and family background.

Fox, Ralph. *Lenin: A Biography*. New York: Harcourt, Brace, 1934. 320pp. This popular biography written by a member of the Soviet Communist party sets out the basic facts of Lenin's life based on recognized Russian sources. Best on the period before 1917.

Gourfinkel, Nina. *Lenin*. New York: Grove Press, 1961. 189pp. Reissued as *Portrait of Lenin: An Illustrated Biography* (New York: Herder and Herder, 1972. 175pp.). The highlights of Lenin's life and career are covered to accompany a valuable collection of photographs. Serves as a useful introduction to the subject.

Hill, Christopher. *Lenin and the Russian Revolution*. New York: Macmillan, 1950. 245pp. In a scholarly though readable presentation of Lenin and the course of the revolution, the Russian leader is shown in his roles as theoretician, organizer, and leader rather than as an individual.

Hollis, Christopher. *Lenin*. Milwaukee: Bruce Publishing, 1938. 277pp. Reissued as *Lenin: Portrait of a Professional Revolutionary* (New York: Longman, 1938. 285pp.). Written from a Catholic perspective, Hollis views Lenin as a mistaken visionary whose lack of Christian belief insured his failure. Best on Lenin's pre-1917 background, Hollis's is an original, though limited examination.

Krupskaya, Nadezhda. *Reminiscences of Lenin*. Moscow: Foreign Language Publishing, 1959. 552pp. These memoirs by Lenin's wife are uniformly laudatory, but despite the lack of critical objectivity, her reflections remain a valuable source of information on Lenin's private and domestic life.

Lewin, Moshe. *Lenin's Last Struggle*. New York: Pantheon, 1968. 193pp. In a sympathetic account of Lenin's final years, he is portrayed as a disillusioned figure struggling to hang on to power and to control the state that he helped to create. Unfortunately, Lewin's analysis does not fit Lenin's compelling end into a wider pattern of his entire life.

Page, Stanley W. *Lenin and World Revolution*. New York: New York University Press, 1959. 252pp. In a psychological analysis based on Lenin's writings and behavior, Page identifies Lenin's compulsive need to dominate at the core of his cold, revolutionary fanaticism.

Payne, Robert. *The Life and Death of Lenin*. New York: Simon & Schuster, 1964. 672pp. This popular biographical study covers mainly Lenin's years in power in an often superficial and cliché-ridden treatment. The book concludes with the sensational conjecture that Lenin was poisoned by Stalin.

Possony, S.T. *Lenin: The Compulsive Revolutionary*. New York: Regnery, 1964. 418pp. In a balanced account in which one-half of the book is devoted to Lenin's life prior to 1917, Possony provides a psychological profile dominated by his thesis that Lenin possessed a destructive inner compulsion that helps explain his conspiratorial politics. Based in part on various police records, the book is best in unraveling the complex underground political world that Lenin inhabited before coming to power.

Service, Robert. *Lenin: A Political Life*. Bloomington: Indiana University Press, 1985–1995. 3 vols. Service's exhaustive political biography is a masterful account of Lenin's strategies and tactics but is marred by a clear emotional identification with his subject, in which Lenin is depicted as a self-confident visionary who is staunchly defended against all his critics.

Shukman, Harold. *Lenin and the Russian Revolution*. New York: Putnam, 1967. 224pp. Shukman's clear and concise historical biography is dependable and attempts to integrate his study of Lenin with an equal focus on the man and the leader, showing how Lenin's character flaws helped determine his actions.

Theen, Rolf H. W. *Lenin: Genesis and Development of a Revolutionary*. Philadelphia: Lippincott, 1973. 194pp. Covering Lenin's entire life but focusing more than half of the book on Lenin's formative years up to 1900, Theen provides useful information about Lenin's development and the origin of his ideas and behavior.

Treadgold, Donald W. *Lenin and His Rivals: The Struggle for Russia's Future 1898–1906*. New York: Praeger, 1955. 291pp. Offering details of Lenin's critical years before launching the Russian Revolution, Lenin is criticized as manipulative and misrepresenting his aims to conceal a personal drive for power.

Trotsky, Leon. *The Young Lenin*. Garden City, New York: Doubleday, 1972. 224pp. Chronicling Lenin's formative years up to age 23, Trotsky, who observed Lenin at close range, attempts to demolish the Lenin cult engineered by Stalin by providing Lenin with a more human, believable character.

Valentinov, Nikolay. *Encounters with Lenin*. New York: Oxford University Press, 1968. 273pp.; *The Early Years of Lenin*. Ann Arbor: University of Michigan Press, 1969. 302pp. The author, a brief associate of Lenin in Switzerland, presents in *Encounters* a detailed portrait of Lenin in 1904. His 1969 volume is a negative view of Lenin's development, in which he is shown as a spoiled child of the middle class, an exploitative landlord, and a stubborn fanatic.

Williams, Beryl. *Lenin*. New York: Longman, 2000. 232pp. Part of the Profiles in Power series, this is a concise study of Lenin and his role in the Russian Revolution and the early years of Communist rule, concentrating on the years between 1917 and 1924. Williams draws on recent scholarship and newly available documentary evidence.

Biographical Novels

Brien, Alan. *Lenin*. New York: Morrow, 1987. 735pp. Told in the form of an invented diary, Lenin narrates his life in a fiction that sticks close to main events, with an emphasis on Lenin's human side in a personality portrait that blends the historical and the imaginary.

Casey, Jane B. *I, Krupskaya: My Life with Lenin.* Boston: Houghton Mifflin, 1974. 327pp. This fictional autobiographical account by Lenin's wife documents her relationship that deteriorates as Lenin gains power.

Solzhenitsyn, Aleksandr. *Lenin in Zurich.* New York: Farrar, Straus, 1976. 309pp. This is an unflattering, day-to-day account of Lenin and his circle in Switzerland following the failed 1905 Russian Revolution. Although the events and situations are mainly historical, the book is dominated by the author's theme, tracing Russia's collapse during World War I and under the Communists.

Fictional Portraits

Appel, Allen. *Time after Time.* New York: Carroll & Graf, 1985. 372pp. In a time-travelling fantasy, a young history professor imaginatively goes back in time to the Russian Revolution and encounters major historical figures, such as Lenin, and gets involved in the fate of Nicholas II and his family.

Carlisle, Henry, and Olga Carlisle. *The Idealists.* New York: Thomas Dunne, 1999. 290pp. This family drama is played out against the events leading up to Russian Revolution and features appearances by such historical figures as Lenin, Kerensky, Trotsky, Gorky, and Pasternak.

Elliott, John. *Blood on the Snow.* London: Souvenir Press, 1977. 334pp. Chronicling the early stages of the Russian Revolution, including the 1905 Bloody Sunday procession to the Winter Palace, the mutiny of the *Potemkin*, and the struggle between the Bolsheviks and the Czar's secret police, this fictional story is set against an authentic historical background.

Herlin, Hans. *Grishin.* Garden City, New York: Doubleday, 1987. 324pp. A political thriller set during the early years of Lenin's reign, an assassin is given the assignment of killing Lenin should secret negotiations with the British fail. A number of liberties are taken with history to facilitate the novel's suspense.

Hyman, Tom. *Seven Days to Petrograd.* New York: Viking, 1988. 412pp. In a thriller whose background is Lenin's famous train journey to the Finland Station to ignite the Revolution, an American intelligence agent is detailed to infiltrate Lenin's circle and kill him before he arrives in Russia.

Littell, Robert. *The Revolutionist: A Novel of Russia.* New York: Bantam, 1988. 467pp. Dramatizing the Russian Revolution and the formation of the Soviet state up to the death of Stalin, the novel, blending fact and fiction, follows a fictional idealist who sees his dreams betrayed by Lenin and Stalin.

Sela, Owen. *The Petrograd Consignment.* New York: Dial Press, 1979. 312pp. The mainly true story of how the Germans encouraged the Russian Revolution to get Russia out of World War I is the background for this political thriller that follows Lenin on his sealed railway car to the Finland Station to ignite the Revolution.

Recommended Juvenile Biographies

Haney, John. *Vladimir Ilich Lenin.* New York: Chelsea House, 1988. 112pp. MG/YA. Haney's is a solid, reliable historical and biographical account of Lenin's life, career, and impact on Russian history.

Levine, I.E. *Lenin: The Man Who Made a Revolution.* New York: J. Messner, 1969. 189pp. MG/YA. Levine covers Lenin's life in full in a detailed portrait that relates his life and development against the historical events of his period.

Topalian, Elyse. *V.I. Lenin.* New York: F. Watts, 1983. 122pp. MG. This is a straightforward, generally reliable account of Lenin's public career with some details on his private life and personality.

Biographical Films and Theatrical Adaptations

Bolt, Robert. *State of Revolution.* New York: S. French, 1977. 66pp. Bolt dramatizes the story of the Russian Revolution as seen through the events of Lenin's life from 1910 to his death with characterizations of Gorky, Stalin, and Trotsky.

Stoppard, Tom. *Travesties.* New York: Grove Press, 1975. 99pp. In Stoppard's inventive comedy of ideas, Lenin appears along with James Joyce in Switzerland during World War I where the trivial and the profound do battle with one another.

A&E Biography Video: Vladimir Ilyich Lenin: Voice of Revolution (1996). Producer: Bob Niemade. A thorough and reliable documentary portrait using archival footage and expert testimony. Video.

Lenin (1990). Producer: Patricia Lagone. This documentary study chronicles Lenin's life and times using archival footage and observation by eyewitnesses. Video.

Nicholas and Alexandra (1971). Director: Franklin Schaffner. Michael Bryant appears as Lenin in this lavish film depiction of the fall of the Romanovs. The fine cast includes Michael Jayston, Janet Suzman, Jack Hawkins, and Laurence Olivier. Video.

Stalin (1992). Director: Ivan Posser. In this film biography of the life and career of Stalin, Robert Duvall plays the Russian leader, with Maximilian Schell as Lenin, Daniel Massey as Trotsky, and Murray Ewan as Khrushchev. Video.

Other Sources

Silverman, Saul N., ed. *Lenin.* Englewood Cliffs, New Jersey: Prentice-Hall, 1972. 213pp. Part of the Great Lives Observed series, this useful volume reprints selections of Lenin's writings, and contemporary and critical views of him; Weber, Gerda. *Lenin: Life and Works.* New York: Facts on File, 1980. 224pp. Useful as a reference tool, this is a detailed day-to-day account of Lenin's activities, including his works, personal relationships, travels, and speeches.

See also Joseph Stalin; Leon Trotsky

281. JOHN LENNON
1940–1980

A British singer, songwriter, and member of the Beatles, a group that dominated rock music in the 1960s, Lennon was born in Liverpool and at 14 began playing with a rock/skiffle group, the Quarrymen. He wrote songs with Paul McCartney and the two occasionally appeared as a duo. After George Harrison joined the Quarrymen, the group changed its name to Johnny and the Moondogs, then the Silver Beatles, and finally, the Beatles. Popular in Europe from 1961, "Beatlemania" swept the United States in 1963 with the group's first hits "She Loves You" and "I Want to Hold Your Hand." Most of the Beatles' lyrics and music were written by Lennon and McCartney. In 1969 Lennon formed the Plastic Ono Band with his second wife, Yoko Ono. The Beatles disbanded (1970) after producing 18 albums and appearing in four films. Lennon was shot to death in front of his New York apartment building by a fan, Mark Chapman.

Autobiography and Primary Sources

Lennon Remembers. San Francisco: Straight Arrow Books, 1971. 189pp. This collection of interviews Lennon conducted with *Rolling Stone* in 1970 offers irreverent and revealing insights about his life, career, and the meaning of the Beatles phenomenon.

The Playboy Interviews with John Lennon & Yoko Ono. G. Barry Golson, ed. Chicago: Playboy Press, 1981. 193pp. In another series of interviews with Lennon and Ono, their life together, social causes, and private and public attitudes are displayed.

Recommended Biographies

Coleman, Ray. *John Winston Lennon.* 1985. Revised ed. as *John Lennon: The Definitive Biography.* New York: Harper & Row, 1992. 767pp. Written by a trusted friend and with the cooperation of many intimates, Coleman's biography is the most comprehensive and factually reliable account. Sometimes overly sentimental and admiring, Coleman is biased in favor of Lennon's post-Beatles career, but the book is the best and most complete biography of Lennon available.

Norman, Philip. *Shout! The Beatles in Their Generation.* New York: Simon & Schuster, 1981. 414pp. Exhaustively researched and reliable, Norman's collective biography of the four Beatles is particularly strong on their early lives, concert tours, recording sessions, and financial affairs. Ending in 1970, Norman's study is one of the best available on the Beatles years.

Schaffner, Nicholas. *Beatles Forever.* New York: McGraw-Hill, 1978. 222pp. Treating each Beatle individually, Schaffner's readable account provides useful biographical material arranged chronologically from 1964.

Other Biographical Studies

Baird, Julia. *John Lennon, My Brother.* New York: Holt, 1988. 156pp. Lennon's sister corrects the factual record about the artist's family background and early years.

Blake, John. *All You Needed Was Love: The Beatles After the Beatles.* New York: Perigree Books, 1981. 286pp. The bitter personal wrangling and financial squabbling of the Beatles at the end are the focus here. Lennon and Yoko Ono receive the most attention, but the solo careers of each of the four former Beatles through Lennon's murder are covered.

Davies, Hunter. *The Beatles: The Authorized Biography.* 1968. Revised ed. New York: McGraw-Hill, 1978. 381pp. Along with the other Beatles, Davies chronicles Lennon's life through 1967, but he is reticent and discreet on various aspects of their history.

Elliott, Anthony. *The Mourning of John Lennon.* Berkeley: University of California Press, 1999. 235pp. Presenting a psychoanalysis of Lennon's life and music, this self-described "metabiography" explores the personal and cultural implication of Lennon's career from a number of intriguing angles, but the book is jargon-heavy and marred by some factual errors and significant omissions.

Fawcett, Anthony. *John Lennon: One Day at a Time.* New York: Grove Press, 1981. 192pp. Fawcett supplies an account of Lennon's activities after the dissolution of the Beatles during the 1970s in a mix of realistic details and questionable generalizations.

Giuliano, Geoffrey. *Two of Us: John Lennon & Paul McCartney Behind the Myth.* New York: Penguin, 1999. 256pp. The Lennon/McCartney collaboration is detailed with the conventional view of Lennon as the rebel and McCartney as the sentimentalist, but the book does provide useful day-to-day specifics on their relationships and the blending of two very different personalities to produce remarkable popular music.

Goldman, Albert. *The Lives of John Lennon.* New York: Morrow, 1988. 719pp. Goldman's controversial biographical exposé devotes half its coverage to Lennon's post-Beatles period, and the artist is shown at his worst: an often drunk, heroin-addicted depressive under the control of a manipulative wife. Denied the right to quote from Lennon's songs, Goldman's portrait is often undocumented, hostile, and sensationalistic.

Green, John. *Dakota Days.* New York: St. Martin's, 1983. 260pp. Lennon's final years as a recluse and house-husband in New York's Dakota apartments are the focus here with numerous details from Lennon's mostly hidden last years.

Lennon, Cynthia. *A Twist of Lennon.* New York: Avon, 1980. 190pp. Lennon's first wife weighs in with her recollections of their relationship and the early Beatles years.

Pang, May. *Loving John.* New York: Warner Books, 1983. 336pp. This tell-all by Lennon's mistress is confined to her brief relationship with the musician in the mid–1970s.

Seaman, Frederic. *The Last Days of John Lennon: A Personal Memoir.* New York: Carol, 1991. 262pp. Based on the diary of Lennon's personal assistant from 1979 to 1980 and employing reconstructed dialogue, Seaman's firsthand account presents Lennon's contradictory and complex character in his final year: insecure, self-doubting, and obsessed with food, sex, and the occult.

Shotton, Pete. *John Lennon in My Life.* New York: Stein and Day, 1983. 208pp. Written by Lennon's boyhood friend, Shotton's personal recollections provide some valuable firsthand details of Lennon's early Liverpool days.

Wiener, Jon. *Come Together: John Lennon in His Time.* New York: Random House, 1984. 379pp. Drawing in part on Lennon's FBI and Immigration and Naturalization Service files, Weiner traces Lennon's personal and political growth from the 1960s through the 1970s as an avant-garde artist, antiwar activist, and feminist father. Wiener's *Gimme Some Truth: John Lennon and the FBI* (Berkeley: University of California Press, 1999. 313pp.) details his 14-year court battle to win release of the Lennon file and reproduces the documents in facsimile.

Recommended Juvenile Biographies

Conord, Bruce W. *John Lennon.* New York: Chelsea House, 1994. 127pp. MG/YA. Part of the Pop Culture Legends series, this concise, well-researched biography deals honestly with the negative aspects of Lennon's life, including drug use, struggles with depression, and troubled relationships.

Glassman, Bruce S. *John Lennon and Paul McCartney: Their Magic and Their Muse.* Woodbridge, Connecticut: Blackbirch Press, 1995. 112pp. MG. Beginning with brief biographies of the pair, the book focuses on their collaboration and their unique chemistry that produced their music.

Wright, David K. *John Lennon: The Beatles and Beyond.* Springfield, New Jersey: Enslow, 1996. 112pp. MG. This competent survey of Lennon's background, development, eccentricities, and scandals includes a chronology and a selected discography.

Biographical Films and Theatrical Adaptations

Backbeat (1994). Director: Iain Softley. The Beatles' beginning in the Hamburg underground music scene is dramatized. John Lennon (Ian Hart) and the band's original bass player, Stu Sutcliffe (Stephen Dorff), are romantically involved with the same woman, Astrid Kircherr (Kai Wiesinger). Gary Bakewell and Chris O'Neill portray Paul McCartney and George Harrison. Video.

The Beatles Anthology (1996). Director: Geoff Wonfor. A documentary look at the story of the Beatles using archival footage and interviews with the surviving band members. Video.

The Hours and Times (1992). Director: Christopher Münch. Ian Hart, who would repeat his uncanny impersonation in *Backbeat* portrays John Lennon in this dramatic speculation of what might have happened when Lennon and Beatles' manager Brian Epstein (David Angus) went on holiday to Spain in 1963. Video.

Imagine: John Lennon (1988). Director: Andrew Solt. This documentary look at Lennon's life story is narrated by the artist himself with excerpts from more than 240 hours of film and videotape. Video.

John & Yoko: A Love Story (1985). Director: Sandor Stern. Television movie unconvincingly presents Lennon and Ono's relationship from their first meeting through their marriage. Mark McGann and Kim Miyori play the couple. Video.

Other Sources

Cott, Jonathan, and Christine Doudna, eds. *The Ballad of John and Yoko.* New York: Doubleday, 1982. 317pp. Bringing together interviews and biographical sketches, this volume serves as a useful reference source.

Castleman, Harry, and Walter J. Podrazik. *All Together Now.* Ann Arbor, Michigan: Pierian Press, 1975. 379pp.; *The Beatles Again?* Ann Arbor, Michigan: Pierian Press, 1977. 280pp.; *The End of the Beatles?* Ann Arbor, Michigan: Pierian Press, 1985. 553pp. This series of discographies includes valuable biographical chapters.

Solt, Andrew, and Sam Egan. *Imagine: John Lennon.* New York: Macmillan, 1988. 255pp. A companion volume to the 1988 film biography based on Lennon's personal archives, this is a revealing visual portrait but underrepresents the Beatles period.

Thomson, Elizabeth, and David Gutman, eds. *The Lennon Companion: 25 Years of Comment.* New York: Shirmer Books, 1988. 273pp. This collection of reprinted and original critical articles covers Lennon's entire career with separate section on the biographical, artistic, and political aspects of his life.

282. LEONARDO DA VINCI
1452–1519

Italian painter, sculptor, architect, musician, engineer, and scientist, Leonardo is acknowledged as a genius and celebrated as history's outstanding "Renaissance Man." He was born in the Tuscan village of Vinci, the illegitimate son of a Florentine notary and a peasant girl. He early showed artistic talent, moved to Florence (1466) to study painting with Verrocchio, and was registered in the painters' guild (1472). From c.1482 to 1498 he worked at the Milanese court of Ludovico Sforza as an architect, military engineer, inventor, theatrical designer, sculptor, musician, scientist, art theorist, and painter. After Sforza's downfall, Leonardo studied mathematics, anatomy, botany, and geology, remained active as a painter and sculptor, and briefly served as a military engineer for Cesare Borgia. His last years were spent in France at the invitation of Francis I. Leonardo's most famous works are the fresco *Last Supper* (c.1495–1498) and *Mona Lisa* (c. 1514); he left numerous notebooks containing drawings of scientific precision and unequalled artistry, which included such subjects as flying machines and intricate anatomical studies of people, plants, and animals.

Autobiography and Primary Sources

The Notebooks of Leonardo da Vinci. Jean Paul Richter, ed. 1883. Reprint ed. New York: Dover, 1970. 2 vols. Leonardo's remarkable notebooks are the essential sources for investigating the many facets of the artist's interests and genius.

Treatise on Painting. Princeton, New Jersey: Princeton University Press, 1956. 2 vols. Leonardo's reflections on art are invaluable for his view of the role of the artist and his methods.

Recommended Biographies

Bramly, Serge. *Leonardo: Discovering the Life of Leonardo da Vinci.* New York: HarperCollins, 1991. 493pp. Bramly's acclaimed biography is the result of extensive research sifting through the evidence to reconstruct the artist's life in one of most authoritative and comprehensive studies available.

Clark, Kenneth. *Leonardo da Vinci.* 1939. Revised ed. New York: Viking, 1988. 274pp. Clark's insightful presentation of Leonardo's artistic development remains one of the best studies of the man and the artist.

Kemp, Martin. *Leonardo da Vinci: The Marvellous Works of Nature and Man.* Cambridge, Massachusetts: Harvard University Press, 1982. 384pp. The strength of Kemp's narrative of Leonardo's life and inner development is that it looks at him not exclusively as an artist but as a whole man in which all his diverse interests converge to reflect his remarkable genius. Kemp masterfully places Leonardo in his historical and intellectual context.

Other Biographical Studies

Brown, David A. *Leonardo da Vinci: Origins of a Genius.* New Haven, Connecticut: Yale University Press, 1998. 248pp. In the first full-length study of the young Leonardo, Brown explores the early experiences and developmental processes that culminated in the artist's mature works.

Douglas, R. Langston. *Leonardo da Vinci: His Life and His Pictures.* Chicago: University of Chicago Press, 1944. 127pp. Douglas provides a brief biographical sketch followed by a chronological examination of Leonardo's drawings, writings, and paintings. Valuable in its succinctness, Douglas's study is opinionated and slightly debunking, arguing that Leonardo was not a great painter but still one of the greatest of men.

Eissler, Kurt R. *Leonardo da Vinci: Psychoanalytic Notes on the Enigma.* New York: International Universities Press, 1961. 375pp. Like Freud, Eissler takes up the various psychological enigmas of Leonardo's genius in a series of biographical essays without the chronological arrangement of a conventional biography.

Freud, Sigmund. *Leonardo da Vinci and a Memory of His Childhood.* New York: W.W. Norton, 1964. 116pp. In what may be termed the world's first psychobiography, Freud explores Leonardo from the perspective of sexual repression. Unreliable in many of its facts, Freud's groundbreaking study remains insightful and a significant refinement of the biographer's art.

Friedenthal, Richard. *Leonardo da Vinci: A Pictorial Biography.* New York: Viking, 1959. 143pp. In a brief, comprehensive survey of Leonardo's life and art, reproductions of his works are arranged chronologically with commentary on his personal-

ity and genius that sets his career against the background of his age.

Gould, Cecil. *Leonardo: The Artist and the Non-Artist.* New York: Graphic Society. 1975. 192pp. This is a succinct account of Leonardo's career as an artist with the evolution of his artistry and influence traced. Leonardo's non-artistic side is only briefly covered.

Heydenreich, Ludwig H. *Leonardo da Vinci.* New York: Macmillan, 1954. 2 vols. Heydenreich's first volume is a biographical assessment in which the author attempts to portray Leonardo as a complex but unified personality. The book traces how his ideas were expressed in his works.

McCurdy, Edward. *The Mind of Leonardo da Vinci.* New York: Dodd, Mead, 1928. 360pp. Despite the book's title, McCurdy's concern is more with the scope of Leonardo's learning and his various interests in music, engineering, and experimental aviation, as well as painting. Based on solid research of Leonardo's writings, this examination offers a careful and detailed portrait of the artist in his cultural and historical context.

Payne, Robert. *Leonardo.* Garden City, New York: Doubleday, 1978. 344pp. Payne's readable narrative portrait covers the basic facts of Leonardo's life and artistic career but is weakened by an oversimplified historical context and several dubious interpretations.

Taylor, Rachel A. *Leonardo da Vinci the Florentine: A Study in Personality.* New York: Harper, 1928. 580pp. This poetic and often imaginative reconstruction provides a vivid portrait of Leonardo's Italian background and his inner, psychic life, mixing fact and fancy.

Turner, Richard A. *Inventing Leonardo.* New York: Knopf, 1993. 268pp. Turner's provocative, illustrated cultural historical study compares the known facts about Leonardo with their presentation and interpretation by subsequent biographers and critics. Turner shows how each era has remade Leonardo in its own image.

Vallentin, Antonina. *Leonardo da Vinci: The Tragic Pursuit of Perfection.* New York: Viking, 1938. 561pp. Vallentin's narrative biography is solidly researched and based on a careful review of Leonardo's writings. The essential known facts are presented, supplemented by an imaginative and entertaining reconstruction of Renaissance life.

Zubov, V.P. *Leonardo da Vinci.* Cambridge, Massachusetts: Harvard University Press, 1968. 335pp. Zubov's interpretive biography focuses on Leonardo in the context of the history of scientific thought, an aspect of Leonardo that receives insufficient attention by most biographers. Zubov's learned and sensible examination is a valuable supplement to supply a full picture of Leonardo's greatness and achievements.

Biographical Novels

Berry, R.M. *Leonardo's Horse.* Normal, Illinois: FC2, 1997. 317pp. Based on an actual event in Leonardo's life, the artist struggles unsuccessfully to complete an immense bronze horse for Duke Ludovico Sforza.

Merezhkovsky, Dmitry. *The Romance of Leonardo da Vinci.* New York: Putnam, 1902. 463. In an impressive fictionalized biography, Leonardo's artistic development is traced against a vivid background of his age's religious and political struggles.

Fictional Portraits

Dann, Jack. *The Memory Cathedral: A Secret History of Leonardo da Vinci.* New York: Bantam, 1995. 485pp. This imaginative historical fantasy speculates what might have happened had Leonardo actually built his flying machine. Co-opted by the Medicis, Leonardo's invention results in a moral quandary.

De'Firenze, Rina. *Mystery of the Mona Lisa.* Mamaronek, New York: Hastings, 1996. 353pp. In a well-researched but ultimately speculative investigation into the source of Leonardo's genius, the novelist explores the influence of his mother on his development.

Herman, George. *Carnival of Saints.* New York: Ballantine Books, 1994. 419pp.; *A Comedy of Murders.* New York: Carroll & Graf, 1994. 355pp.; *Tears of the Madonna.* New York: Carroll & Graf, 1996. 274pp. In the author's meticulously historical adventure and mystery novels, Leonardo is the central figure who turns his considerable genius to solving Renaissance-era intrigue and murder.

La Mure, Pierre. *The Private Life of Mona Lisa.* Boston: Little, Brown, 1976. 406pp. In a detailed and convincing recreation of Renaissance Italy, the novel imagines the life of Leonardo's model for the *Mona Lisa,* while speculating why he painted the portrait and for whom.

Mayfield, Sara. *Mona Lisa: the Woman in the Portrait: A Fictional Biography.* New York: Grossett & Dunlap, 1974. 356pp. The novel reconstructs a partly factual, mainly speculative life story for Leonardo's model, Lisa Gherardini Giaconda.

Perutz, Leo. *Leonardo's Judas.* New York: Arcade, 1989. 154pp. In an imaginative recreation of Leonardo's artistic process, the painter finds his model for Judas for his *Last Supper* in a German merchant.

Woodhouse, Martin, and Robert Ross. *The Medici Guns.* New York: Dutton, 1975. 277pp.; *The Medici Emerald.* New York: Dutton, 1976. 223pp.; *The Medici Hawks.* New York: Dutton, 1978. 202pp. The authors' fanciful series of Renaissance adventures all employ Leonardo, who faces a series of historical challenges with inventions, based in part on details from his notebooks.

Recommended Juvenile Biographies

McLanathan, Richard B.K. *Leonardo da Vinci.* New York: Abrams, 1990. 92pp. MG/YA. This well-organized and highly readable introduction to the artist and his works features high-quality reproductions and photographs of various locales that Leonardo lived in or visited.

Stanley, Diane. *Leonardo da Vinci.* New York: Morrow, 1996. 48pp. MG. In an acccessible overview, Stanley presents Leonardo's considerable achievements but also acknowledges his limitations, cultural background, and artistic techniques.

One of the best books this writer/artist has produced.

Vezzosi, Alessandro. *Leonardo da Vinci: The Mind of the Renaissance.* New York: Abrams, 1997. 160pp. YA. A succinct survey of Leonardo's life and work, the author sets the artist's career in its cultural context and his place in intellectual and art history.

Biographical Films and Theatrical Adaptations

A&E Biography Video: Leonardo da Vinci: Renaissance Master (1997). Director: Molly Thompson. Chronicles Leonardo's life and art using film of locales associated with the artist, views of his works and writings, and critical commentary by experts. Video.

The Life of Leonardo da Vinci (1972). Director: Renato Castellani. Italian television production that dramatizes Leonardo's life and career. Video.

283. C.S. LEWIS
1898–1963

English author, Clive Staples Lewis taught at Oxford and Cambridge. His works include *The Allegory of Love* (1936), *The Screwtape Letters* (1942), and *English Literature in the Sixteenth Century* (1954), as well as literary essays and poems. He is perhaps most famous for his celebrated series of allegorical fantasies for children, *The Chronicles of Narnia.*

Autobiography and Primary Sources

All My Road Before Me: The Diary of C.S. Lewis, 1922–1927. Walter Hooper, ed. San Diego: Harcourt, Brace, 1991. 508pp. Lewis's private and emotional life during his years as a student and teacher at Oxford are covered here with important details of his relationship with Janie King Moore.

Letters of C.S. Lewis. 1966. Revised ed. Walter Hooper, ed. San Diego: Harcourt, Brace, 1993. 528pp. Covering Lewis's life from 1916 to his death, this collection is a valuable supplement to Lewis's diary and autobiography to give a full and rounded picture of the man, his temperament, and ideas.

Surprised by Joy: The Shape of My Early Life. New York: Harcourt, Brace, 1955. 238pp. Lewis provides an autobiographical account of his spiritual development from childhood through his schooling and his evolving Christian faith.

Recommended Biographies

Green, Roger L., and Walter Hooper. *C.S. Lewis: A Biography.* New York: Harcourt, Brace, 1974. 320pp. This first comprehensive biography remains a major source of information about Lewis's life based on family papers and Lewis's diaries, letters, and autobiographical writings. Often too reverential to provide much critical interpretation of Lewis's motives and personality, the book is nevertheless filled with firsthand information unavailable from any other source.

Sayer, George. *Jack: C.S. Lewis and His Times.* San Francisco: Harper & Row, 1988. 278pp. Sayer's portrait is more critical than Green and Hooper and succeeds in covering in detail aspects of Lewis's personality as well as the wider cultural and intellectual context out of which his life and work can be better understood.

Wilson, A.N. *C.S. Lewis: A Biography.* New York: W.W. Norton, 1990. 334pp. Wilson's is by far the best-written and most engaging biographical portrait of Lewis. Rejecting the saintly depiction of others, Wilson offers instead a complex figure cast in realistic and believable human terms.

Other Biographical Studies

Gresham, Douglas. *Lenten Lands: My Childhood with Joy Davidman and C.S. Lewis.* New York: Macmillan, 1988. 225pp. Lewis's stepson offers his recollections that have been called by one critic "overwritten, repetitious, and shallow." While another suggests that the book gives a "splendid impression of what the household was like at the Kilns during the 1950s."

Griffin, Henry W. *Clive Staples Lewis: A Dramatic Life.* San Francisco: Harper & Row, 1986. 507pp. The book's subtitle indicates the fictionalized method here in which various scenes from Lewis's life are reconstructed based on both sources and conjecture.

Hooper, Walter. *Through Joy and Beyond: A Pictorial Biography of C.S. Lewis.* New York: Macmillan, 1982. 176pp. This is a visual record of Lewis's life, supplemented by his own words and reminiscences by the writer's acquaintances.

Lawlor, John. *C.S. Lewis: Memories and Reflections.* Spence, 1998. 132pp. The author, Lewis's student and friend, supplies his recollections as well as previously unpublished personal correspondence, along with a critical assessment of Lewis's works.

Recommended Juvenile Biographies

Arnott, Anne. *The Secret Country of C.S. Lewis.* Grand Rapids, Michigan: William B. Eerdmans, 1975. 127pp. This is a sensitive, devotional tribute to Lewis as a Christian thinker that covers the significant events in his life and his important books.

Wellman, Sam. *C.S. Lewis: Author of Mere Christianity.* Philadelphia: Chelsea House, 1999. 207pp. YA. Part of the Heroes of the faith series, this is a detailed presentation of Lewis's life and times with critical commentary on his works and ideas.

Biographical Films and Theatrical Adaptations

Nicholson, William. *Shadowlands.* New York: Plume, 1990. 100pp. Nicholson's stageplay is an adaptation of his screenplay for the 1985 film that was remade in 1993. The play dramatizes the late romance between Lewis and Joy Gresham.

Shadowlands (1985). Director: Norman Stone. Joss Ackland portrays Lewis in this moving story of the writer's late-life romance with and marriage to American Joy Gresham (Claire Bloom). Video.

Shadowlands (1993). Director: Richard Attenborough. This film version of Nicholson's play casts Anthony Hopkins as Lewis with Debra Winger as Gresham. A novelization by Leonore Fleischer is available (New York: Penguin, 1993. 263pp.). Video.

Other Sources

Como, Jame T., ed. *C.S. Lewis at the Breakfast Table and Other Reminiscences.* New York: Macmillan, 1979. 299pp. A collection of reminiscences, including profiles from two of Lewis's biographers.

Hooper, Walter, ed. *C.S. Lewis: A Companion and Guide.* San Francisco: HarperSan Francisco, 1996. 940pp. This is an award-winning reference compendium by the eminent Lewis scholar that includes a complete chronological biography, a Who's Who listing of Lewis's family, friends, and associates, and a What's What guide, identifying significant places and things in the writer's life and works.

284. ABRAHAM LINCOLN
1809–1865

The sixteenth U.S. president and one of America's best-known leaders, Lincoln was born in a log cabin in Kentucky and raised in poverty. After the death (1818) of his mother, Nancy Hanks, his father married (1819) Mrs. Sarah Johnston and in 1830 the family moved to Illinois. Largely self-taught, Lincoln studied law on his own while working at various jobs, including rail splitter, in New Salem, Illinois. He was elected (1834) to the state legislature, in which he served four terms, and a year after receiving (1836) his attorney's license moved to Springfield, where he became a partner in a law firm. He married (1842) Mary Todd. Lincoln was elected (1847) to the House of Representatives as a Whig, but his opposition to the Mexican War lost him a second term. In 1858 he ran as a Republican for the Senate against Stephen Douglas, lost the election, but gained national recognition from his debates with Douglas. Soon after Lincoln's election to the presidency (1860), South Carolina seceded from the union; the Civil War began the following April. In 1863 Lincoln issued the Emancipation Proclamation, which abolished slavery, and gave the Gettysburg Address, a masterpiece of oratory that upheld preservation of the union and expressed grief for the war dead. Lincoln was reelected in 1864; on April 14, 1865, he was shot to death by actor John Wilkes Booth while attending a play at Ford's Theatre.

Autobiography and Primary Sources

Abraham Lincoln: A Documentary Portrait Through His Speeches and Writings. Don E. Fehrenbacher, ed. New York: New American Library, 1964. 288pp. This selection of Lincoln's writings is arranged chronologically to approximate an autobiography.

Abraham Lincoln: Speeches and Writings 1832–1858. New York: The Library of America. 898pp.; *Abraham Lincoln: Speeches and Writings*

1859–1865. New York: The Library of America. 787pp. This useful collection of Lincoln's letters, speeches, and miscellaneous writings is flawlessly edited with helpful notes and an extensive chronology.

The Collected Works of Abraham Lincoln. Roy P. Basler, Marion D. Pratt, and Lloyd A. Dunlap, eds. New Brunswick, New Jersey: Rutgers University Press, 1953–1955. 9 vols. The standard, scholarly edition of Lincoln's letters, government papers, and miscellaneous writings. The volumes' annotations provide considerable biographical insights.

Recommended Biographies

Donald, David H. *Lincoln*. New York: Simon & Schuster, 1995. 715pp. Donald's acclaimed biography sheds new light on many aspects of Lincoln's life and development, especially on his prewar legal career. The book illuminates the connections between Lincoln's private life and public career and presents him as an ambitious, unprepared, and indecisive leader who was often a tormented and defeated individual with remarkable resources and capacity for personal growth.

Neely, Mark E. Jr. *The Last Best Hope of Earth: Abraham Lincoln and the Promise of America*. Cambridge, Massachusetts: Harvard University Press, 1993. 214pp. Focusing on the adult Lincoln during his years as a politician and his presidency, Neely emphasizes the public rather than the private man and shows him as a consummate politician.

Oates, Stephen B. *With Malice Toward None: The Life of Lincoln*. New York: Harper & Row, 1977. 492pp. Oates sets out to rescue Lincoln from his legend, showing him as neither saintly nor superhuman. Lincoln is instead depicted as proud, determined, and haunted with recurrent bouts of melancholy. Synthesizing modern scholarship, Oates provides an objective, understated, and believable narrative portrait. Oates's *Abraham Lincoln: The Man Behind the Myth* (New York: HarperCollins, 1993. 224pp.) separates the historical truth from the legends that have surrounded and obscured the humanity of the icon.

Randall, James G. *Lincoln: The President*. New York: Dodd, Mead, 1945–1955. 4 vols. Left unfinished at the time of the author's death, the final volume was completed by Richard N. Current. Detailed, authoritative, and dispassionate, Randall's study has been praised as a model of scholarship and the most comprehensive treatment of the Lincoln presidency.

Thomas, Benjamin P. *Abraham Lincoln: A Biography*. New York: Knopf, 1952. 548pp. An authoritative and highly readable critical study has long been considered the best one-volume biography available. Drawing on the author's vast knowledge of primary and secondary sources and firsthand intimacy with Lincoln's Springfield, Illinois, Thomas's is a valuable synthesis and balanced treatment.

Other Biographical Studies

Anastaplo, George. *Abraham Lincoln: A Constitutional Biography*. Lanham, Maryland: Rowman & Littlefield, 1999. 373pp. The author's intellectual biography centers on the development of his legal and constitutional thought. The book helps answer how and why Lincoln acted the way he did when faced with the constitutional challenges that the Civil War represented.

Barton, William E. *The Life of Abraham Lincoln*. Indianapolis: Bobbs-Merrill, 1925. 2 vols. Based on interviews and primary research, Barton's biography is strongest on Lincoln's early years, family background, and development.

Beveridge, Albert J. *Abraham Lincoln: 1809–1858*. Boston: Houghton Mifflin, 1928. 2 vols. The author lived to complete only half of a projected four-volume study but managed to supply one of the most comprehensive factual accounts of Lincoln's youth, law career, and early political life.

Burlingame, Michael. *The Inner World of Abraham Lincoln*. Urbana: University of Illinois Press, 1994. 416pp. This psychobiography is based on manuscript and newspaper sources as well as reminiscences of people who knew Lincoln. Using both Freudian and Jungian theory, Burlingame offers a fresh and provocative interpretation of Lincoln's psyche.

Chadwick, Bruce. *The Two American Presidents: A Dual Biography of Abraham Lincoln and Jefferson Davis*. Secaucus, New Jersey: Carol, 1999. 490pp. Chadwick's comparative study of Davis and Lincoln recapitulates conventional interpretations of the two men and offers little new to a portrait of either man.

Charnwood, Godfrey R.B. *Abraham Lincoln*. New York: Holt, 1916. 479pp. Long respected as one of the best-written single-volume accounts and balanced appreciations of Lincoln, Charnwood's life retains its appeal, but is not reliable in all its facts and includes material of dubious authenticity.

Clark, Leon P. *Lincoln: A Psycho-Biography*. New York: Scribner, 1933. 570pp. Clark's psychoanalytical study shapes an understanding of Lincoln's life and personality from a strongly Freudian pattern, employing novelistic techniques to animate considerable speculation.

Duff, John J. *A. Lincoln: Prairie Lawyer*. New York: Rinehart, 1960. 433pp. Detailing Lincoln's legal career from 1837 to 1858, this is the most comprehensive account available about this important period in Lincoln's life. Poorly organized and disjointed, the book, however, reads more like a compendium of facts than a narrative or thematic synthesis.

Guelzo, Allen C. *Abraham Lincoln: Redeemer President*. Grand Rapids, Michigan: William B. Eerdmans, 1999. 516pp. This intellectual biography explores Lincoln's ideas, particularly his religious views in the context of the values of his era. In Guelzo's provocative view, Lincoln emerges as a complex and paradoxical thinker.

Hanchett, William. *Out of the Wilderness: The Life of Abraham Lincoln*. Urbana: University of Illinois Press, 1994. 151pp. A brief, straightforward, authoritative biography for the nonspecialist general reader, Hanchett presents the highlights of Lincoln's career and a plausible portrait of Lincoln the man.

Herndon, William H., and Jesse W. Weik. *Herndon's Lincoln: The True Story of a Great Life*. Chicago: Belford Clarke, 1889. 3 vols. Herndon, Lincoln's law partner, supplies invaluable firsthand information about Lincoln's life, particularly before his presidency, but the biography includes some dubious anecdotes and interpretations that have been challenged by others.

Kunhardt, Philip B. Jr., Philip B. Kunhardt, III, and Peter W. Kunhardt. *Lincoln: An Illustrated Biography*. New York: Random House, 1992. 415pp. In 900 pictures, this handsome volume describes Lincoln's life mainly through images. The text features many of Lincoln's own words and those of eyewitnesses. Each month of the Lincoln presidency is given a double-page spread illustrating the prominent events and figures.

Luthin, Reinhard H. *The Real Abraham Lincoln: A Complete One-Volume History of His Life and Times*. Englewood Cliffs, New Jersey: Prentice-Hall, 1960. 778pp. In a scholarly, factual narrative emphasizing Lincoln's political life, two-thirds of Luthin's study is devoted to Lincoln's presidency.

Masters, Edgar Lee. *Lincoln the Man*. New York: Dodd, Mead, 1931. 520pp. Based on Herndon and Beveridge, Masters's angry, hostile interpretation belittles Lincoln the man and denigrates his achievements. Serves as an unflattering counterpoint to other adoring appreciations.

McPherson, James M. *Abraham Lincoln and the Second American Revolution*. New York: Oxford University Press, 1990. 173pp. McPherson's collection of essays on Lincoln during the Civil War offers an insightful analysis of his personality and political philosophy.

Morris, Jan. *Lincoln: A Foreigner's Quest*. New York: Simon & Schuster, 2000. 205pp. Morris's is a personal investigation of Lincoln's life and meaning that includes a tour of sites associated with him. Morris reconstructs the public and private man in a fresh and original portrait.

Nicolay, John G., and John Hay. *Abraham Lincoln: A History*. New York: Century, 1890. 10 vols. This massive study produced by Lincoln's private secretaries is chiefly valuable today as an important reference source for scholars.

Paludan, Phillip S. *The Presidency of Abraham Lincoln*. Lawrence: University Press of Kansas, 1994. 384pp. This scholarly analysis of the Lincoln administration has been praised as the best single-volume study of the Lincoln presidency. Clearly written and carefully argued, the book manages to synthesize a great deal of material and complexity into an insightful account.

Sandburg, Carl. *Abraham Lincoln: The Prairie Years*. New York: Harcourt, Brace, 1926. 2 vols.; *Abraham Lincoln: The War Years*. New York: Harcourt, Brace, 1939. 4 vols. Sandburg's six volumes have been excessively praised and censured. The first two volumes, covering Lincoln's first 51 years, are a kind of prose poem, impressionistic and evocative in its reconstructed atmosphere. The four volumes on Lincoln's presidency are more factually grounded. A one-volume condensation is also available as *Abraham Lincoln: The Prairie Years and the War Years* (New York: Harcourt, Brace, 1974. 762pp.).

Stephenson, Nathaniel W. *Lincoln: An Account of His Personal Life.* Indianapolis: Bobbs-Merrill, 1922. 474pp. Stephenson's psychohistorical study focuses on the inner Lincoln, his thoughts and emotional private side. The result is an often compelling and convincing character study and one of the first psychobiographies ever attempted.

Strozier, Charles B. *Lincoln's Quest for Union: Public and Private Meanings.* New York: Basic Books, 1982. 271pp. In a psychobiography, Strozier portrays Lincoln as a divided man in which his private life and public actions are joined in a plausible character portrait. The book is particularly strong on Lincoln's relationship with his wife and sons.

Tarbell, Ida M. *The Early Life of Abraham Lincoln.* New York: McClure, 1896. 240pp; *The Life of Abraham Lincoln.* New York: Doubleday, 1900. 2 vols. Tarbell, the famous muckraking journalist, produced two popular biographies based on extensive primary research.

Thomas, Benjamin P. *Portrait for Posterity: Lincoln and His Biographers.* New Brunswick, New Jersey: Rutgers University Press, 1947. 329pp. This is a valuable critical survey and analysis of the various versions of Lincoln that biographers have produced, revealing as much about the writers and their times as their subject.

Williams, Thomas H. *Lincoln and His Generals.* New York: Grosset & Dunlap, 1952. 363pp. The book concentrates on Lincoln's skills and challenges as a commander in chief. Opinionated and provocative, if not always convincing, Williams mounts a strong case for Lincoln's superior strategic ability.

Wilson, Douglas L. *Honor's Voice: The Transformation of Abraham Lincoln.* New York: Knopf, 1998. 383pp. This is an inner portrait of Lincoln's formative years between 1831 and 1842. In Wilson's refreshing and believable view, Lincoln is shown in his search for identity and a vocation in law and politics.

Several biographical studies on Mary Todd Lincoln also contain valuable information on Lincoln and the couple's relationship and married life:

Baker, Jean H. *Mary Todd Lincoln: A Biography.* New York: W.W. Norton, 1987. 429pp. Drawing extensively on Turner's volume of letters and the historical, cultural, and feminist context for understanding Mary Todd Lincoln, Baker's is the best available biography that provocatively reassesses Mary's relationship with her husband.

Evans, William A. *Mrs. Abraham Lincoln: A Study of Her Personality and Her Influence on Lincoln.* New York: Knopf, 1932. 377pp. This psychological study by a medical doctor of Mary Todd Lincoln's life and personality is based on a careful examination of medical evidence. The book details her health, her influence on her husband, and an overall vindication of her reputation.

Neely, Mark E. Jr., and R. Gerald McMurtry. *The Insanity File: The Case of Mary Todd Lincoln.* Carbondale: Southern Illinois University Press, 1986. 203pp. In a detailed examination of the available

evidence, the book addresses several areas of controversy surrounding Mary Todd Lincoln's insanity trial, including the nature and extent of her illness, the fairness of her trial, and the motives of her son, who had her committed in 1875.

Randall, Ruth P. *Mary Lincoln: Biography of a Marriage.* Boston: Little, Brown, 1953. 555pp. Written by the wife of Lincoln scholar James G. Randall, this scholarly double biography of Abraham and Mary Todd Lincoln is a defense of their happy marriage and Mary Todd's character.

Sandburg, Carl, and Paul M. Angle. *Mary Lincoln: Wife and Widow.* New York: Harcourt, Brace, 1932. 357pp. The first part of the book tells the story of the couple's marriage; the second collects documents, including letters and newspaper accounts.

Turner, Justin G., and Linda L. *Mary Todd Lincoln: Her Life and Letters.* New York: Knopf, 1972. 750pp. An invaluable factual source, the volume collects more than 600 letters interwoven with a biographical narrative beginning in 1840.

Biographical Novels

Bacheller, Irving. *A Man for the Ages.* New York: Grosset & Dunlap, 1919. 416pp. Mixing both fact and fancy, the novel constructs Lincoln's youth and pioneer experiences, concluding with his courtship of Mary Todd. In *Father Abraham* (Indianapolis: Bobbs-Merrill, 1925. 419pp.) the author explores Lincoln's influence on several characters.

Bishop, Jim. *The Day Lincoln Was Shot.* New York: Harper, 1955. 308pp. Although factually based, the book offers a number of fictionalized reconstructions of the events leading up to Lincoln's assassination.

Carnahan, Walter. *Hoffman's Row.* Indianapolis: Bobbs-Merrill, 1963. 223pp. Based on an actual incident during Lincoln's courtship of Mary Todd, the future president is challenged to a duel by a rival. A romantic story involving a runaway slave augments the factual incidents.

Colver, Anne. *Lincoln's Wife.* New York: Farrar & Rinehart, 1943. 406pp. Mary Todd Lincoln narrates her own story from her courtship to her husband's assassination. Though marred by several factual errors, the novel presents a fair portrait of Mary Todd.

Dixon, Thomas. *The Southerner: A Romance of the Real Lincoln.* New York: Appleton, 1913. 543pp. Lincoln is the central character in this historical romance that mixes idealization and a lifelike presentation.

DuGarm, Henry K. *When Lilacs Bloom Again: A Novel Based on the Life and Times of Abraham Lincoln.* Monot, North Dakota: North American Heritage Press, 1988. 358pp. Lincoln's life is viewed from the perspective of an invented character, based on actual events with dialogue based on his actual writings.

Lancaster, Bruce. *For Us the Living.* New York: F. A. Stokes, 1940. 556pp. Lincoln's early years in Indiana and Illinois during the 1820s and 1830s are described; what is known is supplemented with plausible surmises and period details.

Morrow, Honoré. *Great Captain.* New York: Morrow, 1930. 668pp. The author's biographical trilogy made up of the separate volumes *Forever Free* (1927), *With Malice Toward None* (1928), and *The Last Full Measure* (1930) details Lincoln's life during his presidency.

Ryan, Edward J. *Comes an Echo on the Breeze.* New York: Exposition Press, 1949. 202pp. Lincoln's military experiences during the Black Hawk War is described, with appearances by other historical figures, such as Zachary Taylor and Jefferson Davis. Although accurate in its historical elements, situations and dialogue are invented.

Safire, William. *Freedom.* Garden City, New York: Doubleday, 1987. 1,125pp. Safire's massive, panoramic novel treats the first two years of the Civil War and focuses on the complex political forces that Lincoln attempts to control as he moves towards issuing the Emancipation Proclamation.

Slotkin, Richard. *Abe: A Novel of the Young Lincoln.* New York: Holt, 2000. 478pp. Slotkin dramatizes the formation of Lincoln's character in his early experiences in a brilliant reconstruction of Lincoln's era and environment, imaginatively embellishing the facts of Lincoln's youth and inventing plausible circumstances to reflect a believable, human figure.

Stone, Irving. *Love Is Eternal: A Novel About Mary Todd Lincoln and Abraham Lincoln.* Garden City, New York: Doubleday, 1954. 468pp. Stone dramatizes Lincoln's married life employing actual events from Lincoln's family and public history.

Vidal, Gore. *Lincoln.* New York: Random House, 1984. 657pp. Vidal provides a three-dimensional portrait of Lincoln during his presidency, supplied from a variety of sources and vantage points. The author's interpretation is fresh, original, debatable, and never dull.

Wilson, Dorothy C. *Lincoln's Mothers.* Garden City, New York: Doubleday, 1981. 423pp. The novel looks at Lincoln's childhood and youth from the perspective of his natural mother, Nancy Hanks, and his stepmother Sally Bush. Keeping close to the known facts, the novel does invent a friendship between Lincoln's two mothers.

Wilson, William E. *Abe Lincoln of Pigeon Creek.* New York: Whittlesey House, 1949. 288pp. Using a factual framework but with considerable invention, Lincoln's youth in Indiana is dramatized from the arrival of his stepmother in 1817 to a riverboat trip in 1830.

Fictional Portraits

Only a few of the almost countless fictional appearances of Lincoln can be mentioned here, books of exceptional literary quality or with unusual or significant portrayals of Lincoln.

Babcock, Bernice. *The Soul of Ann Rutledge: Abraham Lincoln's Romance.* Philadelphia: Lippincott, 1919. 322pp. In an idealized treatment of Lincoln's first romance with Ann Rutledge, the majority of the story is invented rather than factual; *Soul of Abe Lincoln.* Philadelphia: Lippincott, 1923. 328pp. Set during the Civil War, the novel traces the influence of Lincoln on a young Southern couple with a realistic presentation of the Lincoln assassination.

Brown, Katharine. *The Father*. New York: John Day, 1928. 368pp. The abolition movement during the 1850s is the novel's subject as a young abolitionist attracts the attention of a Springfield lawyer, Abraham Lincoln.

Churchill, Winston. *The Crisis*. New York: Macmillan,1901. 522pp. Churchill's classic Civil War novel includes depictions of such historical figures as Lincoln, Grant, and Sherman.

Fraser, George MacDonald. *Flash for Freedom*. London: Barrie and Jenkins,1971. 295pp. In this installment of the author's historical comic series involving the braggart and bully Harry Flashman, Flashy is in America during the 1840s where he encounters Congressman Lincoln, who sees through the Englishman's deceptions and rescues him from slavehunters.

Lewis, Oscar. *The Lost Years: A Biographical Fantasy*. New York: Knopf, 1951. 121pp. In an intriguing historical fantasy, the novel imagines what might have happened had Lincoln survived Booth's assassination attempt. After finishing his second term, Lincoln, unpopular and disappointed, journeys to California for a final contribution to American history.

King, Benjamin. *A Bullet for Lincoln*. Gretna, Louisiana: Pelican, 1993. 301pp. King's Civil War thriller constructs a realistic alternative account of the Lincoln assassination as a conspiracy among the nation's most powerful tycoons.

Mallon, Thomas. *Henry and Clara*. New York: Ticknor & Fields, 1994. 358pp. This inventive and historically authentic re-creation depicts the lives of Henry and Clara Rathbone, the young couple seated in the president's box at Ford's Theatre on the night of the assassination.

Seifert, Shirley. *The Senator's Lady*. Philadelphia: Lippincott,1967. 377pp. This biographical novel about the romance between Stephen Douglas and Addie Cutts includes scenes from the Lincoln-Douglas debates.

Steward, Barbara, and Dwight Steward. *The Lincoln Diddle*. New York: Morrow, 1979. 251pp. In this imaginative fantasy, Edgar Allan Poe, disguised as a detective, first fails to prevent Lincoln's murder then solves the mystery surrounding the conspiracy.

Whitney, Janet. *Intrigue in Baltimore*. Boston: Little, Brown,1951. 296pp. The novel recreates the events and atmosphere immediately following Lincoln's election in 1860. As Lincoln heads to Washington, the question is whether Maryland will stay loyal to the Union.

Williams, Ben Ames. *House Divided*. Boston: Houghton Mifflin, 1947. 1,514pp. Describing the events of the Civil War from the Southern perspective, the novel explores divided loyalties when a proud Southern family learns that their patriarch was also the grandfather of Abraham Lincoln.

Recommended Juvenile Biographies

Freedman, Russell. *Lincoln: A Photobiography*. New York: Ticknor & Fields, 1987. 150pp. MA.

1988 Newbery Medal winner for the most distinguished contribution to American literature, the first nonfiction book selected in over 30 years, Freedman's well-balanced photobiography contrasts the legend with the facts and relies on quotes from original sources.

Meltzer, Milton, ed. *Lincoln: In His Own Words*. New York: Harcourt, Brace, 1993. 226pp. MG/YA. Background commentary and quotations from Lincoln's letters and speeches provide a personal view of his life, thoughts, and actions.

North, Sterling. *Abe Lincoln: Log Cabin to White House*. 1956. Reprint ed.New York: Random House, 1987. 184pp. MG/YA. Part of the Landmark Books series, North's factual biography remains one of the best books on Lincoln for younger readers.

Biographical Films and Theatrical Adaptations

A&E Biography Video: Abraham Lincoln: Preserving the USA (1997). Producers: Craig Haffner and Donna E. Lusitana. A documentary look at Lincoln's life through archival material and testimony of experts. Video.

Abraham Lincoln (1930). Director: D.W. Griffith. Walter Huston portrays Lincoln in Griffith's first talky in a biographical film that follows his career from birth to death. The supporting cast includes Una Merkel, Kay Hammond, and Hobart Bosworth. Video.

Abraham Lincoln (1990). Producer: Peter Edwards. Concise documentary on Lincoln's life narrated by historian James M. McPherson. Video.

Abe Lincoln in Illinois (1940). Director: John Cromwell. Raymond Massey is a standout as the lead in this film biography that chronicles Lincoln's life from youth through his election as president. The screenplay was written by Robert Sherwood based on his Pulitzer Prize–winning play. Ruth Gordon plays Mary Todd. Video.

The Blue and the Gray (1982). Director: Andrew V. McLaglen. Gregory Peck portrays Lincoln in this television mini-series centering on the adventures of a Pinkerton agent (Stacy Keach). Janice Carroll appears as Mary Todd Lincoln and Rip Torn depicts Grant. Video.

The Civil War (1990). Director: Ken Burns. Lincoln is a central figure in Burns's acclaimed documentary. His words are read by Sam Watterson. Video.

The Day Lincoln Was Shot (1988). Director: John Gray. Television film based on Jim Bishop's book, starring Lance Henricksen as Lincoln, John Ashton as Ulysses S. Grant, and Rob Morrow as John Wilkes Booth. Video.

Gore Vidal's Lincoln (1988). Director: Lamont Johnson. In this television adaptation of Vidal's novel, Sam Waterson is convincing as Lincoln with Mary Tyler Moore as Mary Todd. Video.

Lincoln (1992). Director: Peter W. Kunhardt. Using excerpts from Lincoln's letters, speeches, and diaries read by Jason Robards, this four-cassette documentary chronicles the Lincoln presidency and conduct of the Civil War. Video.

North and South (1985–1986). Director: Richard T. Heffron. In this television mini-series based on John Jakes's novels, Hal Holbrook portrays Lincoln during the turmoil of the Civil War that splits apart the Hazard family. Video.

Of Human Hearts (1938). Director: Clarence Brown. Adapted from the story "Benefits Forgot," by Honoré Morrow, this sentimental drama set just before the Civil War concerns a stern preacher (Walter Huston) who receives a lesson in human compassion from Abraham Lincoln (John Carradine). Video.

The Perfect Tribute (1991). Director: Jack Bender. In a television adaptation of Mary Raymond Shipman Andrews's classic historical romance, a Southern teenager searching for his wounded brother encounters Lincoln (Jason Robards) in Washington following the Gettysburg Address.

Young Mr. Lincoln (1939). Director: John Ford. Acclaimed film biography of Lincoln's early years stars Henry Fonda in the title role, with Alice Brady, Marjorie Weaver, and Ward Bond. Video.

Other Sources

Holzer, Harold, ed. *Lincoln as I Knew Him: Gossip, Tributes, and Revelations from His Best Friends and Worst Enemies*. Chapel Hill, North Carolina: Algonquin Books,1999. 269pp. This is a handy and lively compilation of anecdotes on Lincoln from a wide variety of observers, including members of his family, colleagues, and critics (including his assassin), selected to bring out elements of his character and how he appeared to his contemporaries.

Miers, Earl S., ed. *Lincoln Day by Day: A Chronology 1809–1865*. Washington: Lincoln Sesquicentennial Commission, 1960. 3 vols. In a remarkable scholarly work, Lincoln's daily activities are carefully annotated.

Neely, Mark E. Jr. *The Abraham Lincoln Encyclopedia*. New York: McGraw-Hill, 1982. 356pp. Arranging information on Lincoln's life, thought, family, friends, associates, speeches, and biographers into a accessible reference tool, this is a browser's delight.

Shaw, Archer H. *The Lincoln Encyclopedia: The Spoken and Written Words of A. Lincoln Arranged for Ready Reference*. New York: Macmillan, 1950. 395pp. Biographical details and autobiographical reflections are included in this helpful arrangement of Lincoln's writings and speeches. The reader should be careful, however, because some spurious material is also included.

Stern, Philip Van Doren, ed. *The Life and Writings of Abraham Lincoln*. New York: Modern Library, 1999. 912pp. First published in 1940, this useful volume includes a 200-page biographical essay by Stern, a chronology of Lincoln's life, and a selection of 275 documents, addresses, speeches, and letters, placed in their historical context.

See also John Wilkes Booth; Ulysses S. Grant; Andrew Johnson

285. CHARLES A. LINDBERGH JR.
1902–1974

The first aviator to make a solo, nonstop transatlantic flight, Lindbergh was born in Detroit and attended the University of Wisconsin. He left school (1922) to study flying, served as a flying cadet, was commissioned (1925) in the air force reserve, and then worked as an airmail pilot. On May 20, 1927, Lindbergh set off across the Atlantic in *The Spirit of St. Louis*, arriving in Paris the next day. His flight astounded the world and made him an overnight hero. He made numerous goodwill flights to promote interest in aviation. Lindbergh married (1929) Anne Morrow; the kidnapping and murder of their son (1932) led to a federal law on kidnapping. Criticized for his pro-German isolationist stance prior to World War II, he later flew combat missions in the Pacific theater. His later years were devoted to conservation issues. His autobiography *The Spirit of St. Louis* was awarded a Pulitzer Prize.

Autobiography and Primary Sources

Autobiography of Values. William A. Jovanovich and Judith A. Schiff, eds. New York: Harcourt, Brace, 1978. 423pp. Extracted from a 2,000-page manuscript Lindbergh left at his death, Lindbergh records his opinions on a variety of topics, as well as his reflections about his youth, sudden fame, and his later activities and interests.

Boyhood on the Upper Mississippi. St. Paul: Minnesota Historical Society, 1972. 50pp. Lindbergh's early years in Minnesota are the subject of this charming reminiscence.

The Spirit of St. Louis. New York: Scribner, 1953. 562pp. Lindbergh provides a detailed account of his 1927 flight, as well as reminiscences of his boyhood and early flying and reflections on his subsequent career.

The Wartime Journals of Charles A. Lindbergh. New York: Harcourt, Brace, 1970. 1,038pp. Lindbergh's journals written from 1937 to 1945 are filled with the minutiae of his everyday life, candid opinions, and often self-serving vindications of his prewar politics and wartime activities.

We. New York: Putnam, 1927. 318pp. Lindbergh's autobiographical reflections, published only a few months after his historic flight, presents the story of his youth and barnstorming days, as well as an account of the transatlantic flight that is less polished and accomplished but more immediate than his later account in *The Spirit of St. Louis.*

Recommended Biographies

Berg, A. Scott. *Lindbergh.* New York: Putnam, 1998. 628pp. Berg's Pulitzer Prize–winning biography is the first to take advantage of unfettered access to Lindbergh's private papers. The result is a fresh, penetrating, balanced narrative account with a close focus on the private man and the complex inner forces that produced both his achievements and controversy. Deservedly considered the definitive life.

Milton, Joyce. *Loss of Eden: A Biography of Charles and Anne Morrow Lindbergh.* New York: HarperCollins, 1993. 520pp. Milton's dual biography based on new documentary evidence is the authoritative treatment of the couple's relationship. The book serves as both biography and cultural history as the Lindberghs are seen against a fully developed historical context.

Other Biographical Studies

Cole, Wayne S. *Charles A. Lindbergh and the Battle Against American Intervention in World War II.* New York: Harcourt, Brace, 1974. 298pp. Cole's thesis in reviewing Lindbergh's prewar beliefs and activities is that he acted out of genuine patriotic concern that it would be a mistake for the United States to enter the war on the Allied side. Cole insists that there is no evidence that Lindbergh desired to aid the Nazi war effort, and that charges of Lindbergh's anti-Semitism, racism, and fascism are unfair.

Davis, Kenneth S. *The Hero: Charles A. Lindbergh and the American Dream.* Garden City, New York: Doubleday, 1959. 527pp. Davis, in a scholarly and authoritative examination of Lindbergh's life and career, looks at the flyer as he conformed to and fell from the archetypal pattern of the hero as formulated by Joseph Campbell in *The Hero with a Thousand Faces.* Davis narrates in detail Lindbergh's story up to America's entry into World War II.

Gill, Brendan. *Lindbergh Alone.* New York: Harcourt, Brace, 1977. 216pp. In a tribute published to commemorate the fiftieth anniversary of Lindbergh's flight, Gill attempts to re-create the flyer's personality at the time of his greatest achievement.

Larson, Bruce L. *Lindbergh of Minnesota: A Political Biography.* New York: Harcourt, Brace, 1973. 363pp. This biography of Lindbergh's father features details of his son's childhood and the pressures that helped formed the flyer.

Lindbergh, Anne Morrow. *Diaries and Letters of Anne Morrow Lindbergh.* New York: Harcourt, Brace, 1972–1980. 5 vols. Anne Morrow Lindbergh's multi-volumed collection of letters and diaries are often poetic and moving concerning her life with Lindbergh and his personal qualities.

Luckett, Perry D. *Charles A. Lindbergh: A Bio-Bibliography.* New York: Greenwood, 1986. 147pp. This bibliography lists the many writings devoted to various aspects of Lindbergh's life and career, along with a detailed chronology and a concise biographical profile.

Mosley, Leonard. *Lindbergh: A Biography.* Garden City, New York: Doubleday, 1976. 446pp. The first full-scale biography written after Lindbergh's death stresses the private, human side of Lindbergh, supported by strong use of Lindbergh's own writings and other intimate sources. Informal rather than scholarly, the book commits some factual errors and its breezy style may be disconcerting at times.

Ross, Walter S. *The Last Hero: Charles A. Lindbergh.* 1968. Revised ed. New York: Harper & Row, 1976. 400pp. The value of Ross's life is its dispassionate, factual approach that sets the record straight. A Lindbergh admirer, Ross makes a strong case for the aviator's heroism, as well as a well-documented treatment of Lindbergh's years of exile and controversy.

Fictional Portraits

Coburn, Andrew. *Birthright.* New York: Simon & Schuster, 1997. 316pp. Mixing fact and fancy, the novel imagines the fate of the Lindbergh baby who, now grown and running for high political office, learns the truth of his parentage.

Collins, Max Allan. *Stolen Away.* New York: Bantam, 1991. 514pp. The novel offers a highly original and speculative unraveling of the Lindbergh kidnapping.

Kilian, Michael. *Dance on a Sinking Ship.* New York: St. Martin's, 1988. 419pp. Set on board an ocean liner in 1935 this espionage thriller features a cast of historical figures, including Charles Lindbergh, who is revealed as one of America's greatest spies in an ingenious, though fanciful, explanation of Lindbergh's apparent Nazi sympathies.

Lindbergh, Reeve. *The Names of the Mountains.* New York: Simon & Schuster, 1992. 237pp. In a thinly veiled autobiographical account, Lindbergh offers insights into the home life of Charles and Anne Lindbergh and their children.

Roosevelt, Elliott. *A First Class Murder.* New York: St. Martin's, 1991. 261pp. In another shipboard mystery, Eleanor Roosevelt investigates poisoning aboard the *Normandie* in 1938 with a passenger list including Lindbergh, Jack Benny, Josephine Baker, and a teenaged John F. Kennedy.

Recommended Juvenile Biographies

Denenberg, Barry. *An American Hero: The True Story of Charles A. Lindbergh.* New York: Scholastic, 1996. 255pp. MG/YA. In a carefully researched, in-depth and candid assessment of Lindbergh's career, the public achievement and private torments of the aviator invite the reader to contemplate the complexity of modern heroism.

Giblin, James. *Charles A. Lindbergh: A Human Hero.* New York: Clarion Books, 1997. 212pp. MG/YA. Meticulously researched, this detailed, sympathetic yet balanced biography tells the full story of Lindbergh's controversial career largely through his own words and archival photos.

Randolph, Blythe. *Charles Lindbergh.* New York: F. Watts, 1990. 160pp. MG/YA. This is a well-written but mostly unsympathetic portrait with frequent quotes from Lindbergh's autobiographies and the highlights of his career presented objectively.

Biographical Films and Theatrical Adaptations

A&E Biography Video: Lucky: The Story of Charles Lindberg (1995). Looks at the years of Lindbergh's achievement, celebrity, and controversy using archival footage and expert testimony. Video.

Crime of the Century (1990). Director: Mark Rydell. Based on Ludovic Kennedy's *The Airman and the Carpenter* (New York: Viking, 1985. 438pp.), the events of the Lindbergh kidnapping and the trial and execution of Bruno Hauptmann are dramatized. Stephen Rea and Isabella

Rossellini portray the Hauptmanns and Scott N. Stevens appears as Lindbergh. Video.

Lindbergh (1990). Director: Stephen Ives. An award-winning installment of the American Experience series on PBS, the documentary faithfully traces Lindbergh's life using rarely seen archival footage, new scholarship, and interviews with family members. Video.

The Lindbergh Kidnapping Case (1976). Director: Buzz Kulik. Anthony Hopkins portrays Bruno Hauptmann in this fact-based television drama of the kidnapping. Charles and Anne Morrow Lindbergh are played by Cliff De Young and Sian Barbara Allen. Video.

The Spirit of St. Louis (1957). Director: Billy Wilder. Jimmy Stewart is compelling and convincing in the role of the flyer in this film based on Lindbergh's autobiography. Video.

286. FRANZ LISZT
1811–1886

Hungarian revolutionary figure and composer of romantic music, Liszt was considered one of the greatest pianists of his time. He made his debut at nine, then studied in Vienna with Czerny and Salieri. During his years as a popular piano virtuoso in Paris (1823–1825), he was influenced by Chopin, Berlioz, and Paganini. He began composing while musical director (1848–1859) to the Duke of Weimar and later moved to Rome, where he became an abbé (1865). He spent the years 1880 to 1885 in Rome, Weimer, and Budapest, teaching the next generation of famous pianists. His works include 13 symphonic poems, a form he invented, the B minor piano sonata, the Faust Symphony, and 20 Hungarian rhapsodies. His daughter, Cosima, married composer Richard Wagner.

Autobiography and Primary Sources

Portrait of Liszt: By Himself and His Contemporaries. Adrian Williams, ed.New York: Oxford University Press, 1990. 746pp. Liszt's biography is told through his own words and those of his contemporaries with a connective narrative text. This is one of the best sources of eyewitness information about Liszt's activities and character.

Selected Letters. Adrian Williams, ed. New York: Oxford University Press, 1998. 1,064pp. This extensive selection of Liszt's letters includes biographical sketches to identify correspondents.

Recommended Biographies

Taylor, Ronald. *Franz Liszt: The Man and the Musician*. New York: Universe Books, 1986. 285pp. In a clearly written, compact, and sensible factual portrait that is both accessible to the nonspecialist and useful for the specialist, Taylor reassesses the various legends surrounding Liszt and substitutes a plausible character study.

Walker, Alan. *Franz Liszt*. New York: Knopf, 1983–1996. 3 vols. The result of more than a quarter century of labor, Walker has produced the most detailed and authoritative study of Liszt, equally strong on Liszt's life and music. Scholarly yet accessible to the nonspecialist and lively, despite its monumental length and careful documentation, Walker's trilogy is at times overly defensive to preserve Liszt's reputation, but Walker's extraordinary research to reconstruct Liszt's almost daily activities compensates in his study's thoroughness and lucidity.

Watson, Derek. *Liszt*. New York: Macmillan, 1989. 404pp. In the best available one-volume critical study, half of Watson's book is devoted to Liszt's biography with the second half concerned with a critical assessment of Liszt's work as a musician and composer. Balanced in his approach, Watson reveals a convincing individual who is obscured by neither his glamour nor his shortcomings.

Other Biographical Studies

Allsobrook, David I. *Liszt: My Traveling Circus Life*. Carbondale: Southern Illinois University Press, 1991. 215pp. The author documents the six months Liszt spent in England during 1840 and 1841, drawing heavily on the diaries kept by one of Liszt's traveling companions.

Beckett, Walter. *Liszt*. 1956. Revised ed. London: Dent, 1963. 185pp. This brief introductory study considers both Liszt's private and public lives but adds little new to Liszt's depiction and repeats several errors from his secondary sources.

Burger, Ernst. *Franz Liszt: A Chronicle of His Life in Pictures and Documents*. Princeton, New Jersey: Princeton University Press, 1989. 358pp. With 650 illustrations this is the most comprehensive and richest visual biography with a year-by-year account of Liszt's activities and compositions.

Corder, Frederick. *Ferenz Liszt*. New York: Harper, 1925. 178pp. Corder's brief biographical portrait focuses on Liszt's professional activities and offers few details about his personal life. Corder met Liszt, and he does provide some interesting firsthand observations.

Hamburger, Klára. *Liszt*. Budapest: Corvina, 1980. 242pp. Written by a fellow Hungarian, Hamburger's study provides a fresh perspective on Liszt's background and some new material for viewing the musician in his contemporary and nationalistic context.

Huneker, James. *Franz Liszt*. 1911. Reprint ed. New York: AMS, 1971. 458pp. Huneker's exhaustive early biography mixes fact as well as gossip, cannot be trusted, and has been superseded by later studies.

László, Zsigmond, and Béla Mátéka. *Franz Liszt: A Biography in Pictures*. Budapest: Corvina, 1968. 247pp. Superseded by Burger's more comprehensive and authoritative collection of portraits, photographs, and miscellaneous manuscripts, this volume still serves as a brief, visual orientation to the man and his music.

Newman, Ernest. *The Man Liszt*. New York: Scribner, 1935. 313pp. Setting out to demolish the Liszt legend, Newman offers a full-length psychological study focusing mainly on his relationship with women, offering few insights about Liszt as a pianist or musician. Factually suspect and incorrect in many instances, Newman's debunking thesis of Liszt as a social climber drives his arrangement and interpretation of the musician's character and career.

Perényi, Eleanor. *Liszt: The Artist as Romantic Hero*. Boston: Little, Brown, 1974. 466pp. Perenyi's often brilliant but uneven study of Liszt as a man, musician, and phenomenon corrects many misconceptions and is successful in placing the musician in his historical and cultural context. However, scandals predominate here, and her attempt to draw larger interpretations from scanty evidence makes the book read at times like biographical fiction.

Sitwell, Sacheverell. *Liszt*. 1934. Revised ed. New York: Philosophical Library, 1967. 400pp. Sitwell's readable appreciation is undocumented and untrustworthy in its facts but does provide an evocative recreation of Liszt's era and artistic milieu.

Biographical Novels

Harsányi, Zsolt. *Immortal Franz: The Life and Loves of a Genius*. New York: F. A. Stokes, 1937. 486pp. This is an idealized biographical portrait mixing actual details with invented scenes and dialogue.

Rousselot, Jean. *Hungarian Rhapsody: The Life of Franz Liszt*. New York: Putnam, 1961. 248pp. In a romanticized version of Liszt's life that emphasizes his love affairs, the novel chronicles the musician's career from childhood within a factual framework, though with some of the dates incorrect.

Winwar, Frances. *The Last Love of Camille*. New York: Harper, 1954. 272pp. The novel dramatizes Liszt's relationship with Marie Duplessis in a vivid reconstruction of the period and an emphasis on Liszt's romantic glamour.

Fictional Portraits

Kenyon, Frank W. *Passionate Rebel: The Story of Hector Berlioz*. New York: Dodd, Mead, 1972. 255pp. In this fictional account of the musical career of Berlioz, Liszt appears as a character, as does such other historical figures as Dumas and Paganini. *The Questing Heart: A Romantic Novel about George Sand*. New York: Dodd, Mead, 1964. 344pp. Liszt's relationship with George Sand and Chopin is depicted in this well-researched and mainly factual account of the life of the French writer.

Recommended Juvenile Biographies

Walker, Alan. *Liszt*. New York: Crowell, 1973. 108pp. MG. Walker supplies a wealth of factual information on Liszt's life, personality, and musical achievements.

Biographical Films and Theatrical Adaptations

Impromptu (1991). Director: James Lapine. Bohemian Paris during the 1830s is the scene for this evocative drama concerning George Sand (Judy Davis) and her relationship with Chopin (Hugh Grant). Julian Sands appears as Liszt. Video.

Liszt at Weimar (1988). Director: A documentary look at Liszt's music in relation to the historical and cultural forces surrounding its composition and performance. Video.

Lisztomania (1975). Director: Ken Russell. Russell's outlandish extravaganza looks at Liszt as the first rock star. Roger Daltry plays the musician with Sara Kestelman as Princess Carolyne, Imogene Claire as George Sand, and Paul Nicholas as Richard Wagner. Video.

Song of Love (1947). Director: Clarence Brown. Biographical film dramatizing the relationship of Clara and Robert Schumann (Katharine Hepburn and Paul Henreid) and Johannes Brahms (Robert Walker). Liszt appears as a character played by Henry Daniell. Video.

Song of Norway (1970). Director: Andrew L. Stone. In this film biography of Norwegian composer Edvard Grieg (Toraly Maustad). Liszt is depicted by Henry Gilbert. Video.

Song Without End: The Story of Franz Liszt (1960). Directors: Charles Vidor and George Cukor. Hollywood treatment of Liszt's life emphasizes his scandalous love affairs. Dirk Bogarde plays the musician with Capucine as Princess Carolyne, Patricia Morison as Geoge Sand, Alexander Davion as Chopin, and Lyndon Brook as Wagner. Video.

See also Frédéric Chopin; George Sand

287. DAVID LIVINGSTONE
1813–1873

Scottish explorer and missionary in Africa, Livingstone hoped to abolish the slave trade by opening the continent to Christian commerce and missionary stations. He explored much of Africa, discovered the Zambezi River and Victoria Falls, and sought the source of the Nile. While recovering from an illness in Ujiji on Lake Tanganyika, his historic meeting with Anglo-American journalist Henry Stanley took place. He died in central Africa and is buried in Westminster Abbey.

Autobiography and Primary Sources

Readers interested in the numerous primary sources can consult the many volumes of Livingstone's own published accounts of his expeditions, several collections of his correspondence, and his lectures and journals. One of the most recent collections is *David Livingstone: Letters and Documents, 1841–1872*. Timothy Holmes, ed. (Bloomington: Indiana University Press, 1990. 202pp.), which makes available many items for the first time. Among the more important editions of his journals are *Livingstone's African Journal 1853–1856*. I. Schapera, ed. (Berkeley: University of California Press, 1963. 2 vols.) and *The Last Journals of David Livingstone in Central Africa, from 1865 to His Death*. Horace Waller, ed. (London: Murray, 1874. 2 vols.).

Recommended Biographies

Jeal, Tim. *Livingstone*. New York: Putnam, 1973. 427pp. Politically and historically sophisticated, Jeal's is the best modern life of Livingstone. Re-

jecting the sentimental depiction of previous writers, Jeal presents a far more human and complex figure. Livingstone's achievements are duly noted but placed in their wider context and compared to other equally deserving but less lionized figures. Well researched and judicious in its assessment, the book offers the reader the clearest and most believable picture of the man and his career.

Seaver, George. *David Livingstone: His Life and Letters*. New York: Harper, 1957. 650pp. Seaver provides a scholarly, detailed biography largely made up of Livingstone's own words, allowing the explorer and missionary to tell his own story.

Simmons, Jack. *Livingstone and Africa*. New York: Macmillan, 1954. 160pp. Simmons's is a compact, factually reliable summary of Livingstone's life and career that ably serves as an introduction for the general reader.

Other Biographical Studies

Blaikie, William G. *The Personal Life of David Livingstone*. New York: F.H. Revell, 1880. 508pp. Livingstone's authorized biography had full access to the explorer's private papers and the full cooperation of his wife and family to produce this solid account that remained the standard source for many years before being superseded by more recent, more critically objective treatments.

Campbell, Reginald J. *Livingstone*. New York: Dodd, Mead, 1930. 295pp. Campbell's is the first modern reassessment of Livingstone's life and career that attempted a more balanced portrait of the man with his human flaws more honestly revealed.

Coupland, Sir Reginald. *Livingstone's Last Journey*. New York: Macmillan, 1946. 271pp. Based on previously untapped primary sources, Coupland provides a straightforward, factual account of Livingstone's last expedition and Stanley's attempt to find the explorer with a comparison of the characters of the two men.

Debenham, Frank. *Way to Ilala: David Livingstone's Pilgrimage*. New York: Longman, 1955. 336pp. Of the more specialized studies, Debenham concentrates on Livingstone's achievements as a geographer in an objective assessment filled with valuable illustrations.

Gelfand, Michael. *Livingstone the Doctor: His Life and Travels: A Study in Medical History*. London: Blackwell, 1957. 333pp. As the title indicates, this is a focused study of Livingstone's medical achievements, shedding considerable light on this neglected aspect of Livingstone's career.

Hughes, Thomas. *David Livingstone*. New York: Macmillan, 1889. 208pp. Of the many popular accounts published in the nineteenth century, Hughes's is one of the best. Although dependent on Blaikie for its research, the book offers a more compressed account that is still generally reliable though sharing in the period's uncritical promulgation of Livingstone's heroic image.

Huxley, Elspeth. *Livingstone and His African Journeys*. New York: Saturday Review Press, 1974. 224pp. Huxley's profusely illustrated biography is a lively and reliable narrative account of the high points of Livingstone's career but leaves

untouched the deeper sources of Livingstone's ideas and motivation.

Listowel, Judith. *The Other Livingstone*. New York: Scribner, 1974. 292pp. Listowel's provocative reassessment places Livingstone's achievement in the wider context of African exploration and demonstrates how Livingstone took credit for the achievement of others. The book offers a corrective view missing in many accounts that deserves attention.

Martelli, George. *Livingstone's River: A History of the Zambezi Expedition 1858-64*. New York: Simon & Schuster, 1970. 286pp. Martelli offers a revisionist character portrait based on a careful review of the facts surrounding the ill-fated Zambezi Expedition and the accounts of its participants. Although the evidence emphasizes Livingstone's human failures, the book is fair in its assessment, and the explorer's courage and resourcefulness are enhanced rather than diminished by looking at him clearly.

Ransford, Oliver. *David Livingstone: The Dark Interior*. New York: St. Martin's, 1978. 332pp. Ransford explains Livingstone's many contradictions by diagnosing a manic depressive disorder called cyclothymia. With his diagnosis in hand, Ransford follows Livingstone's career to confirm it. Although the dark side of Livingstone's personality is emphasized here, the book nevertheless supplies an intriguing exploration of Livingstone's behavior that makes considerable sense.

Fictional Portraits

Hagerfors, Lennart. *The Whales of Lake Tanganyika*. New York: Grove Press, 1989. 172pp. This is a fictional retelling of Stanley's 1871 expedition to find Livingstone from the perspective of a British sailor who offers a realistic view of both men.

Recommended Juvenile Biographies

Clinton, Susan. *Henry Stanley and David Livingstone*. Chicago: Childrens Press, 1990. 128pp. MG. Clinton's dual biography tracks their accomplishments in the context of African exploration.

Humble, Richard. *The Travels of Livingstone*. New York: F. Watts, 1991. 32pp. MG. This brief account follows Livingstone's African journeys and the difficulties he faced.

Wellman, Sam. *David Livingstone: Missionary and Explorer*. Philadelphia: Chelsea House, 1999. MG/YA. 207pp. Part of the Heroes of the Faith series, this is detailed biography emphasizing Livingstone's missionary career. The book uses some fictionalization about his childhood but otherwise relies on extensive quotations from Livingstone's diaries.

Biographical Films and Theatrical Adaptations

Stanley and Livingstone (1939). Director: Henry King. Heroic interpretation of Stanley's search for Livingstone is more legendary than reliable. Spencer Tracy is the pursuer, and Cedric Hardwicke is the pursued Livingstone. Video.

See also Henry Stanley

288. DAVID LLOYD GEORGE
1863–1945

Welsh statesman, prime minister (1916–1922), and one of Britain's greatest war leaders, Lloyd George was elected (1890) a Liberal member of Parliament and served his Welsh constituency for over 54 years. As Chancellor of the Exchequer (1908–1915) he implemented a "people's budget" calling for a system of social insurance, which became the Parliament Act of 1911. He was munitions minister and war minister (1915–1916) before becoming Prime Minister of a coalition government. His bold, aggressive war policy set him at odds with the military leadership, but he was effective in unifying military command under Marshal Foch. He advocated a moderate course concerning war reparations at the Paris Peace Conference (1919). His later policies, particularly over Irish independence, and lack of Conservative support resulted in the downfall of his ministry. In the 1930s he was critical of appeasement policies toward Nazi Germany. He was raised to the peerage a few months before his death.

Autobiography and Primary Sources

Lloyd George: Family Letters 1885–1936. Kenneth O. Morgan, ed. Cardiff: University of Wales Press, 1973. 227pp. This selection of personal letters includes Lloyd George's diary kept as a youth.

My Darling Pussy: The Letters of Lloyd George and Frances Stevenson 1913–1941. A.J.P. Taylor, ed. London: Weidenfeld and Nicolson, 1975. 258pp. Lloyd George's correspondence with his secretary, mistress, and second wife provides a human look at the man and their relationship.

*War Memoirs of David Lloyd George.*c Boston: Little, Brown, 1933–1937. 6 vols. Lloyd George's monumental account of his perspectives on the events of World War I is an elaborate but only partially convincing justification of his own and British policy during the war. A dispassionate and exact defense, the volumes reveal little of Lloyd George's emotional side.

Recommended Biographies

Gilbert, Bentley B. *David Lloyd George: A Political Life.* Columbus: Ohio State University Press, 1987–1992. 2 vols. Taking the story up to 1916, this is a clear, fully documented examination of Lloyd George's political formation, development, and exercise of power. Gilbert's study lucidly integrates complex events and influences into an accessible, balanced analysis with a number of fresh insights from previously untapped primary sources.

Grigg, John. *The Young Lloyd George.* Berkeley: University of California Press, 1974. 320pp.; *Lloyd George: The People's Champion, 1902–11.* Berkeley: University of California Press, 1978. 391pp.; *Lloyd George: From Peace to War, 1912–16.* Berkeley: University of California Press, 1985. 527pp. Although denied access to Lloyd George's private papers, Grigg's is a superbly researched, monumental biography that sets the record straight on many episodes and is the most intimate and subtly drawn portrait available on the years covered.

Owen, Frank. *Tempestuous Journey: Lloyd George, His Life and Times.* New York: McGraw-Hill, 1955. 784pp. Based on the extensive Lloyd George archives, Owen presents a dramatic, comprehensive narrative account that deals with both Lloyd George's public and private lives, both of which are firmly connected to a vivid historical and cultural background.

Rowland, Peter. *David Lloyd George: A Biography.* New York: Macmillan, 1976. 872pp. Rowland's comprehensive biography with more than 200 pages devoted to Lloyd George's life after 1922 begins with a chronological narrative and shifts to a topical approach to handle the complex events following World War I. The book is more balanced than many other studies with extensive archival research that is allowed to speak for itself.

Other Biographical Studies

Beaverbrook, Max A. *The Decline and Fall of Lloyd George: And Great Was the Fall Thereof.* New York: Duell, Sloan and Pearce, 1963. 320pp. In a gossipy account backed up by important documentation acquired from Lloyd George's estate, Beaverbrook gives the insider's view of Lloyd George's failure to hold together his coalition government in 1922. Provides an intriguing perspective on this defining event in Lloyd George's political career.

Campbell, John. *Lloyd George: The Goat in the Wilderness 1922–31.* London: Cape, 1977. 383pp. In a study of Lloyd George after he stepped down as Prime Minister in 1922, Campbell makes a strong case that despite being out of office Lloyd George remained one of the most important British political figures between the wars. Supplies a detailed perspective on this neglected, underrated chapter of Lloyd George's life.

Cregler, Don M. *Bounder from Wales: Lloyd George's Career Before the First World War.* Columbia: University of Missouri Press, 1976. 292pp. The focus here is on Lloyd George's early political development in a scholarly and well-documented study.

Edwards, John H. *David Lloyd George: The Man and the Statesman.* New York: J.H. Sears, 1929. 2 vols. This authorized biography by a staunch admirer records largely what Lloyd George wanted to be presented publicly. Factual errors and exaggeration mars Edwards's examination, which is stronger on Lloyd George's personal side than on his political career.

George, William. *My Brother and I.* London: Eyre and Spottiswoode, 1958. 323pp. Lloyd George's younger brother's account is a study in sibling rivalry and a resentful recollection of his elder brother's slights.

George, W.R.P. *The Making of Lloyd George.* Hamden, Connecticut: Archon Books, 1976. 184pp. Lloyd George's nephew covers his uncle's family background and early life up to his entry into Parliament in 1890, making use of previously unavailable diaries, notes, and letters.

Jones, Thomas. *Lloyd George.* Cambridge, Massachusetts: Harvard University Press, 1951. 330pp. Chiefly concerned with Lloyd George's political career, this is a compact, objective assessment that is ultimately sympathetic but without illusions regarding Lloyd George's failings.

Kinnear, Michael. *The Fall of Lloyd George: The Political Crisis of 1922.* Toronto: Toronto University Press, 1973. 317pp. Based on an analysis of contemporary sources, Kinnear analyzes the factors leading up to Lloyd George's resignation from the prime ministership in 1922.

Lloyd George, Frances. *The Years That Are Past.* London: Hutchinson, 1967. 296pp. This memoir by Lloyd George's former secretary, mistress, and second wife is an affectionate tribute with valuable firsthand insights into Lloyd George's postwar years.

Lloyd George, Richard. *My Father, Lloyd George.* New York: Crown, 1961. 248pp. The personal memories of Lloyd George's eldest son deals frankly with his father's marital problems and character frailties, making public for the first time some of his father's infidelities and his son's resentment.

Mallet, Charles. *Mr. Lloyd George: A Study.* New York: Dutton, 1930. 313pp. In an extremely negative assessment, Mallet mounts an often intemperate prosecution that depicts Lloyd George as a self-seeking opportunist, lacking in both personal stability and sincerity.

McCormick, Donald. *The Mask of Merlin: A Critical Story of David Lloyd George.* New York: Holt, 1964. 343pp. In another distinctly hostile review of Lloyd George's personality and career, he is held responsible for the defeat of British liberalism. The book's polemical approach limits its usefulness as a balanced assessment.

Morgan, Kenneth O. *Lloyd George.* London: Weidenfeld and Nicolson, 1974. 224pp. Morgan concentrates on Lloyd George's Welsh background and its influence on his political development.

Packer, Ian. *Lloyd George.* New York: St. Martin's, 1998. 144pp. A compact, sensible overview of Lloyd George's life and political career, the book serves as a useful introduction to its subject.

Pugh, Martin. *Lloyd George.* New York: Longman, 1988. 206pp. Part of the Profiles in Power series, this is a concise and sensible overview of Lloyd George's public career and impact on his era.

Sylvester, A.J. *The Real Lloyd George.* London: Cassell, 1947. 322pp. A member of Lloyd George's staff, Sylvester provides a firsthand look at his aging chief but lacks the critical objectivity and distance to serve as a totally reliable account.

Thomson, Malcolm. *David Lloyd George: The Official Biography.* New York: Hutchinson, 1948. 470pp. Authorized by Lloyd George's widow, this is an often dull and uninspired biography in which reticence limits revelations.

Wrigley, Chris. *Lloyd George.* Cambridge, Massachusetts: Blackwell, 1992. 170pp. Wrigley, an authority on Lloyd George's relationship with the British labor movement, looks at the politician's entire career in a compact study that summarizes current thinking regarding Lloyd George's role in English politics in the twentieth century.

Biographical Novels

Benedictus, David. *Lloyd George.* London: Weidenfeld and Nicolson, 1981. 222pp. In a blend of fact and fantasy Benedictus presents a version of Lloyd George's life up to the end of World War I that merely skims a distorted surface.

Jones, Jack. *The Man David: An Imaginative Presentation Based on Fact of the Life of David Lloyd George from 1880 to 1914.* London: Hamilton, 1944. 248pp. Jones dramatizes Lloyd George's formative years and rise to political power in a blend of actual facts, imaginative embellishments, and invented situations and dialogue.

Fictional Portraits

FitzGibbon, Constantine. *High Heroic.* 1969. New York: W.W. Norton, 1969. 176pp. Centering on Irish leader Michael Collins, the novel dramatizes the events of the Irish struggle for independence based on a framework of history and appearances by a number of historical figures, such as Lloyd George, Churchill, and Yeats.

Flanagan, Thomas. *The End of the Hunt.* New York: Dutton, 1994. 627pp. Flanagan's impressive re-creation of the Irish Uprising and the Irish Civil War features the treaty negotiations as Michael Collins must contend with the political wiles of Churchill and Lloyd George.

Linscott, Gillian. *Dance on Blood.* New York: St. Martin's, 1998. 250pp. Nell Bray, the author's suffragette, here in her series of atmospheric historical mysteries is blackmailed by Lloyd George to prevent a cache of compromising letters from falling into the hands of the Germans.

Recommended Juvenile Biographies

Shearman, Deirdre. *David Lloyd George.* New York: Chelsea House, 1988. 112pp. MG/YA. Shearman supplies a straightforward, factual review of Lloyd George's rise to power and political career, as well as a helpful historical context to understand his actions.

Biographical Films and Theatrical Adaptations

A Dangerous Man: Lawrence After Arabia (1990). Director: Christopher Menaul. Ralph Fiennes portrays T.E. Lawrence in a drama set during the 1919 Paris Peace Conference as he tries to secure Arab independence. Bernard Lloyd portrays Lloyd George. Video.

Nancy Astor (1984). Director: Richard Stroud. Lisa Harrow portrays the American-born woman who became a member of the British Parliament. Brian Hawksley appears as Lloyd George with James Fox and Dan O'Herlihy. Video.

Wilson (1944). Director: Henry King. In an exceptional biographical treatment of the life of Woodrow Wilson from his days as president of Princeton to his unsuccessful attempt to persuade the United States to join the League of Nations. Alexander Knox stars in the title role. Clifford Brooke plays Lloyd George. Video.

Young Winston (1972). Director: Richard Attenborough. Based on Churchill's *My Early Life,* this biographical film follows him through his schooling, and his military and journalistic career to his election to Parliament at the age of 26. Simon Ward is utterly convincing in the title role. Others in the film's fine cast include Robert Shaw (Randolph Churchill), Anne Bancroft (Jenny Churchill), John Mills (Kitchener), and Anthony Hopkins (David Lloyd George). Video.

Other Sources

Gilbert, Martin, ed. *Lloyd George.* Englewood Cliffs, New Jersey: Prentice Hall, 1968. 182pp. Part of the Great Lives Observed series, this useful volume collects Lloyd George's own words and various views of him from contemporaries and scholars.

289. JOHN LOCKE
1632–1704

English philosopher and founder of British empiricism, Locke greatly influenced philosophy and political theory through his writings. Accused of radicalism by the government, he went to Holland until the accession of William and Mary after the Glorious Revolution of 1688. His works include *Two Treatises on Civil Government* (1689), his famous *Essay Concerning Human Understanding* (1690), and *The Reasonableness of Christianity* (1695).

Autobiography and Primary Sources

The Correspondence of John Locke. E.S. DeBeer, ed. Oxford: Clarendon Press, 1976–1989. 8 vols. The scholarly collection of Locke's correspondence, recently completed, should help the production of a modern definitive biography.

Recommended Biographies

Cranston, Maurice. *John Locke: A Biography.* New York: Macmillan, 1957. 496pp. Drawing on Locke's personal papers at Oxford, Cranston has written the standard scholarly life, which manages to arranged the essential facts of Locke's life impartially, setting the philosopher firmly against his historical and cultural background.

Other Biographical Studies

Aaron, Richard I. *John Locke.* New York: Oxford University Press, 1937. 328pp. After an initial, compact summary of Locke's life, Aaron provides an analysis of Locke's theory of knowledge and his views on ethics, political theory, and religion.

Ayers, Michael. *Locke.* New York: Routledge, 1999. 64pp. Part of the excellent Great Philosophers series, Ayers offers a compact biographical summary of Locke's life and thought that serves as useful introduction for the general reader.

Cope, Kevin L. *John Locke Revisited.* New York: Twayne, 1999. 147pp. Cope's succinct introductory study supplies a chronology and a brief biographical chapter before proceeding to a review of Locke's ideas and works.

Bourne, Henry R.F. *The Life of John Locke.* New York: Harper, 1876. 2 vols. The first scholarly biography, Bourne's study is out of date in the light of more recent scholarship and the availability of Locke's manuscripts, journals, and notebooks.

Biographical Films and Theatrical Adaptations

Citizen Locke (1995). Director: Agieszka Piotrowska. This is a dramatic presentation of the man and his ideas. Video.

Other Sources

Chappell, Vere, ed. *The Cambridge Companion to Locke.* New York: Cambridge University Press, 1994. 329pp. This wide-ranging collection of scholarly essays by various Locke experts includes an overview by Chappell on the philosopher's life and times.

290. JACK LONDON
1876–1916

American author, London was a gold seeker during the first Klondike gold rush and a war correspondent in Mexico during World War I. His novels were highly popular in their day and include *The Call of the Wild* (1903), *The Sea Wolf* (1904), *White Fang* (1905), and *Martin Eden* (1909). A socialist, London considered his social tracts, *The People of the Abyss* (1903) and *The Iron Heel* (1907), as his most important works. He committed suicide at age 40.

Autobiography and Primary Sources

John Barleycorn: Alcoholic Memoirs. 1913. Reprint ed. New York: Oxford University Press, 1989. 237pp. London's frank confession about his alcoholism is also a plea for prohibition.

The Letters of Jack London. Earle Labor, Robert C. Leitz, III and I. Milo Shepard, eds. Stanford, California: Stanford University Press, 1988. 3 vols. In nearly 1,500 letters, London's life is covered from his youth to just before his death. This important scholarly collection allows the reader to correct a number of faulty impressions about London's character and activities made by biographers prior to its availability.

Recommended Biographies

London, Joan D. *Jack London and His Times: An Unconventional Biography.* 1939. Revised ed. Seattle: University of Washington Press, 1968. 385pp. The writer's daughter offers a informed look at London's early surroundings and personal life. Her reconstruction of West Coast events and personalities brings London into sharp focus, providing fresh insights into his influences and motivations.

Sinclair, Andrew. *Jack: A Biography of Jack London.* New York: Harper & Row, 1977. 297pp. Sinclair's is essentially an investigation to separate the various myths surrounding London from the facts, paying particular attention to the contradictory theories surrounding the writer's death. Provocative in many regards, the psychological speculation is often overly pat and reductive.

Other Biographical Studies

Barltrop, Robert. *Jack London: The Man, the Writer, the Rebel.* London: Pluto Press, 1976. 206pp. In a strong overview of London's life, the author provides an interesting analysis of London's political ideas from a socialist perspective.

Hedrick, Joan. *Solitary Comrade: Jack London and His Work.* Chapel Hill: University of North Carolina Press, 1982. 265pp. Hedrick's critical biography attempts to explain London's life and art in terms of his psychological and social conflicts. Often illuminating, Hedrick's study succeeds in offering a helpful analysis that connects London's experiences, personality, and his works.

Kershaw, Alex. *Jack London.* New York: St. Martin's, 1998. 335pp. Kershaw's is a rousing narrative summary of London's life and career that offers no original research but a competent synthesis of sources to fashion a fast-paced but not very penetrating account. Good on the what and the when; the book falls short on the why.

Labor, Earle. *Jack London.* New York: Twayne, 1974. 179pp. Although mainly a critical study of London's works, Labor traces the connection between London's experiences and his writing.

O'Connor, Richard. *Jack London: A Biography.* Boston: Little, Brown, 1964. 430pp. O'Connor's is a competent, though somewhat plodding, summary of the essential facts of London's life without much psychological or interpretive penetration.

Stone, Irving. *Sailor on Horseback.* Boston: Houghton Mifflin, 1938. 338pp. Stone's early biography based on previously unavailable papers and family documents allows London to tell his own story. Not always objective or critical, this is a vivid account but hard to tell what is imagined and what is verifiable.

Walker, Franklin. *Jack London and the Klondike: The Genesis of an American Writer.* San Marino, California: Huntington Library, 1966. 288pp. Walker's is a useful study of London's Klondike experiences that helps to set the factual record straight, as well as offering insights into London's reworking of his experiences into his art.

Biographical Novels

Fenady, Andrew J. *The Summer of Jack London.* New York: Walker, 1985. 173pp. It's the summer of 1896 and London has just returned to San Francisco after a disastrous sea voyage. The novel recreates events in his life including his beginning his first novel and his affair with a society beauty. Often more fictional than factual, the novel does provide a believable character portrait of the young writer.

Recommended Juvenile Biographies

Dyer, Daniel. *Jack London: A Biography.* New York: Scholastic, 1997. 221pp. YA. Dyer's is a balanced and exhaustive biography that emphasizes London's early struggles and spirit of adventure and determination. The book is particularly strong on the historical context of London's life and work.

Schroeder, Alan. *Jack London.* New York: Chelsea House, 1992. 127pp. YA. This is an informative

and candid treatment of London's adventurous, turbulent life that shows how London's experiences are reflected in his novels and stories.

Biographical Films and Theatrical Adaptations

Jack London (1943). Director: Alfred Santell. Not biographically reliable, this treatment of London's activities stars Michael O'Shea in the title role, supported by Susan Hayward and Virginia Mayo. Video.

Jack London (1976). Director: Michel Viotte. A film portrait that presents the author in the context of his times. Video.

Klondike Fever (1979). Director: Peter Carter. This fictional adventure yarn sends a young Jack London (Jeff East) from San Francisco to the Klondike goldfields in 1898. With Rod Steiger, Angie Dickinson, and Lorne Greene. Video.

My Jack London: A Daughter Remembers (1984). Director: Geoffrey Bell. A documentary using reminiscences of London's daughter Becky along with family photos and film footage. Video.

291. HENRY WADSWORTH LONGFELLOW
1807–1882

One of the most popular Americans poet of his time, Longfellow created a new body of romantic American legends with such poems as *Evangeline* (1847), *The Song of Hiawatha* (1855), and *The Courtship of Miles Standish* (1858). Other well-known poems by Longfellow include "The Ride of Paul Revere," "The Village Blacksmith," "Excelsior," and "The Wreck of the Hesperus."

Autobiography and Primary Sources

The Letters of Henry Wadsworth Longfellow. Andrew Hilen, ed. Cambridge, Massachusetts: Harvard University Press, 1966–1982. 6 vols. Hilen brings together all the extant letters in an impeccably edited scholarly collection that shows the writer in his many relationships.

Recommended Biographies

Arvin, Newton. *Longfellow: His Life and Work.* Boston: Little, Brown, 1963. 338pp. Arvin's biographical and critical study is a model of discriminating assessment. The essential details of Longfellow's life are presented, with the more specialized work of scholars on various aspects of the poet's career synthesized into a coherent view.

Thompson, Lawrance. *Young Longfellow 1807-43.* New York: Macmillan, 1938. 443pp. Offering a scholarly reassessment of Longfellow's youth and early years up to his second marriage, Thompson's study sheds considerable light on the poet's development with details that add substance and dimension to less probing, earlier treatments.

Wagenknecht, Edward. *Longfellow: A Full-Length Portrait.* New York: Longmans, 1955. 370pp.; *Henry Wadsworth Longfellow: Portrait of an American Humanist.* New York: Oxford Univer-

sity Press, 1966. 252pp. Both of Wagenknecht's critical biographies, the latter a more compact revision of the first, present portraits strikingly at odds with previous studies. Bent on a balanced reassessment, the books have a strong defensive and argumentative quality as the author takes on previous misconceptions made by earlier biographers and the scorn of modern critics concerning Longfellow's poetry.

Williams, Cecil B. *Henry Wadsworth Longfellow.* New York: Twayne, 1964. 221pp. Part of the compact Twayne series, Williams's is an excellent starting point with its succinct biographical overview and sensible criticism of Longfellow's work.

Other Biographical Studies

Gorman, Herbert. *Victorian American: Henry Wadsworth Longfellow.* New York: G.H. Doran, 1926. 363pp. Gorman's interpretive biographical portrait serves to locate the poet against his cultural milieu and his European influences that the author argues formed Longfellow's character more than his American background.

Kennedy, W. Sloane. *Henry W. Longfellow: Biography, Anecdotes, Letters, Criticism.* Boston: D. Lothrop, 1882. 368pp. Kennedy's is an early collection of materials, including primary documents and tributes from Longfellow's contemporaries.

Longfellow, Samuel. *The Life of Henry Wadsworth Longfellow with Extracts from His Journals and Correspondence.* 1886-87. Reprint ed. New York: Greenwood, 1969. 3 vols. The authorized biography written by the poet's brother includes extensive extracts from Longfellow's letters and journals with its third volume devoted to reminiscences and anecdotes by friends and associates. The volumes remain an important scholarly source.

Norton, Charles Eliot. *Henry Wadsworth Longfellow: A Sketch of His Life Together with Longfellow's Chief Autobiographical Poems.* New York: Houghton Mifflin, 1907. 120pp. Norton's brief biographical sketch is supplemented with a convenient selection of the poet's autobiographical verses.

Underwood, Francis H. *Henry Wadsworth Longfellow: A Biographical Sketch.* 1882. Reprint ed. New York: Haskell House, 1973. 303pp. Longfellow's first biographer had the assistance of the poet himself and incorporates the recollections of his associates.

Fictional Portraits

Forbes, Esther. *O, Genteel Lady!* Boston: Houghton Mifflin, 1926. 296pp. The novel offers a portrait of the literary and philosophical circles of Concord and Boston with depictions of Longfellow, Emerson, and Thoreau.

Recommended Juvenile Biographies

Lukes, Bonnie L. *Henry Wadsworth Longfellow: America's Beloved Poet.* Greensboro, North Carolina: Morgan Reynolds, 1998. 128pp. MG/YA. Lukes makes full use of Longfellow's own words from his journals and letters in this informative and well-written biographical and critical study.

Peare, Catherine O. *Henry Wadsworth Longfellow: His Life*. New York: Holt, 1953. 116pp. MG. Highly fictionalized, Peare's is a somewhat idealized portrait, more inspiring than careful in its documentation of Longfellow's life and personality.

Biographical Films and Theatrical Adaptations

The Adventures of Mark Twain (1944). Director: Irving Rapper. Fredric March is convincing as Twain from his years on the Mississippi, out west, and as a celebrated literary figure. Alexis Smith portrays Twain's wife, and Davison Clark appears as Longfellow. Video.

292. LOUIS IX
1214–1270

King of France, Louis succeeded (1226) his father, Louis VIII, and was influenced during much of his reign by his mother, Blanche of Castile. He led the sixth Crusade but was captured in Egypt and ransomed. He died of plague while leading the eighth Crusade. An able administrator and diplomat, Louis curbed private feudal warfare, encouraged the use of Roman law, and negotiated favorable treaties with England and Aragón. He was canonized in 1297.

Recommended Biographies

Labarge, Margaret W. *Saint Louis: Louis IX, Most Christian King of France*. Boston: Little, Brown, 1968. 303pp . This is a skillful, accessible biography for the nonspecialist that treats Louis's life and reign as well and the social, political, and religious context of his time.

Richard, Jean. *Saint Louis: Crusader King of France*. New York: Cambridge University Press, 1992. 354pp. Richard's is an excellent narrative account of Louis's life and reign that manages to make the king and saint a credible human figure. Richard carefully sifts through archival evidence, contemporary accounts, and later hagiographies to fashion a coherent and comprehensive portrait.

Other Biographical Studies

Joinville, Jean, Sire de. *Life of St. Louis*. New York: Sheed & Ward, 1955. 306pp. This first biography was the work of Louis's contemporary and friend, and Joinville's account is an important source for anecdotal information.

Jordan, William C. *Louis IX and the Challenge of the Crusade: A Study in Rulership*. Princeton, New Jersey: Princeton University Press, 1979. 291pp. Considered required reading for any serious student of the thirteenth century, Jordan's is a scholarly account of Louis's reign and the impact of his first crusade on his life and leadership.

Perry, Frederick. *St. Louis (Louis IX of France): The Most Christian King*. New York: Putnam, 1900. 303pp. Perry's is a solid historical account of Louis's reign, strong on the cultural and political background, with few insights about Louis's personal life.

Fictional Portraits

Connell, Evan S. *Deus lo Volt! Chronicle of the Crusades*. Washington, DC: Counterpoint, 2000. 462pp. Connell's fictional approximation of a medieval chronicle presents an account of the Crusades from Pope Urban II's call to action through Louis IX's final personal crusade from the perspective of a knight in Louis's service. The novel offers portraits of such historical figures as Richard the Lionheart and Saladin as well as Louis.

De Wohl, Louis. *The Quiet Light*. Philadelphia: Lippincott,1950. 317pp. This biographical novel on the life of Thomas Aquinas features portraits of both Frederick II and Louis IX.

293. LOUIS XIV
1638–1715

Nicknamed the "Sun King" because of the brilliance of his court, Louis XIV became king of France after the death (1643) of his father, Louis XIII, but real power was wielded by his mother, Anne of Austria, named regent, and the Prime Minister, Cardinal Mazarin. Louis married (1660) Maria Theresa of Spain. When he took control of the government after Mazarin's death (1661), France was economically depleted by the Thirty Years War, the Fronde-uprisings (1648–1653) fomented by *parlements* and discontented nobles against the crown and fiscal abuses. He strengthened France financially through the use of such able ministers as Jean-Baptist Colbert and discouraged discontent among the aristocracy by keeping the nobility at court. His persecution of the Huguenots led to revocation (1685) of the Edict of Nantes. Such military escapades as the War of the Spanish Succession (1701–1714) squandered fiscal resources. Louis built the great palace at Versailles and stimulated art and literature. An archetypal absolute monarch, he is credited with saying, "L'état c'est moi" ("I am the state").

Recommended Biographies

Bernier, Olivier. *Louis XIV: A Royal Life*. Garden City, New York: Doubleday, 1987. 373pp. A lively and accurate account of Louis's life and reign that relies heavily on printed primary sources, Bernier deals equally with Louis as man, icon, and politician in a generally admiring portrait that is lucid in its historical analysis and convincing in its interpretation of the king.

Erlanger, Philippe. *Louis XIV*. New York: Praeger, 1970. 412pp. In one of the best character portraits of Louis, Erlanger surveys the king's entire life and reign in an intimate, personal history. In the author's view, Louis emerges as a shrewd, icy egoist whose drive for absolutism stemmed from a motive of self-defense and an obsession with his own greatness. Erlanger attributes many of the shortcomings of the king and his rule to his persistent bouts of ill health and debilitating medical treatment.

Wolf, John B. *Louis XIV*. New York: W.W. Norton, 1968. 678pp. Wolf covers every aspect of Louis's life and reign using his own words from his diaries, decrees, and letters to form a portrait of the king as he appeared to his ministers, generals, and subjects. Redressing the balance of more critical assessments, Wolf extends a sympathetic yet convincing view of the king that challenges previous negative views.

Other Biographical Studies

Bertrand, Louis. *The Private Life of Louis XIV*. New York: L. Carrier, 1929. 189pp. An accessible, scholarly biography, Bertrand provides a number of impressionistic sketches to animate this study that attempts to look beneath the allure of Louis's court and reputation to the actual man. The assessment is far more generous and flattering than many other accounts.

Bluche, François. *Louis XIV*. New York: F. Watts, 1990. 702pp. Bluche's is a revisionist assessment of Louis's reign that considers him a powerful cultural influence and a great statesman who shaped a colonial empire, expanded French territory, and founded the modern French state. The original French edition won the 1986 Grand Prix de l'Histoire Moet-Hennessy.

Cronin, Vincent. *Louis XIV*. Boston: Houghton Mifflin, 1965. 384pp. In a highly sympathetic assessment, Cronin focuses on the king's human side, with his various romances occupying a large portion of the text, but treated with restraint. Louis emerges as a complex individual beset by the contradiction between his private desires and public responsibilities.

Forester, C.S. *Louis XIV: King of France and Navarre*. New York: Dodd, Mead, 1928. 246pp. Historical novelist Forester provides a brief, readable narrative history of Louis's reign in which personal details are joined with historical coverage.

Hatton, Ragnhild M. *Louis XIV and His World*. New York: Putnam, 1972. 128pp. In an illustrated biography that compresses a great deal of material into a straightforward narrative, Hatton reevaluates the various myths surrounding the Sun King and his relationships with his family and various mistresses. Serves as a useful introduction to the subject of Louis's personality and his age.

Lewis, W.H. *Louis XIV: An Informal Portrait*. New York: Harcourt, Brace, 1959. 224pp. In an impressionistic psychological portrait rather than a thorough biography, Lewis traces the development of the king's character and provides a defense of Louis's greatness against many of the charges leveled against him by other biographers and historians.

Michel, Prince of Greece. *Louis XIV: The Other Side of the Sun*. New York: Harper & Row, 1983. 447pp. In a sharply negative portrait of Louis's court and the king's shortcomings, this appraisal finds little to suggest the glamour or greatness of Louis or his reign.

Mitford, Nancy. *The Sun King*. 1966. Reprint ed. New York: Penguin, 1994. 255pp. Mitford looks closely at the king's daily routine and personal characteristics in a balanced, though overall negative, assessment. Louis is depicted as a coldly detached and self-absorbed monarch, surrounded by self-serving and scheming courtiers. The book's strength is an animated re-creation of aristocratic society and Louis's court world. It is lavishly illustrated.

Norton, Lucy. *The Sun King and His Loves.* London: Hamilton, 1983. 156pp. Norton concentrates on the four women in Louis's life and his passion for his palace and his garden. In an intimate personal portrait there is little to suggest the factors that established Louis's greatness as a king.

Ogg, David. *Louis XIV.* New York: Oxford University Press, 1959. 224pp. In a solid analysis of Louis's reign, Ogg looks closely at the political and cultural factors that help to explain the king's motives and behavior. More a study of Louis's policies than his private life, the book presents a strong context for judging his rule.

Biographical Novels

Acland, Alice. *The Secret Wife.* New York: St. Martin's, 1975. 203pp. Françoise d'Aubigne, Madame de Maintenon, tells her own story of her rise to prominence as Louis's mistress and eventually his second wife.

Auchincloss, Louis. *The Cat and the King.* Boston: Houghton Mifflin, 1981. 183pp. The novel provides a convincing glimpse of daily life at Versailles during Louis's reign from the perspective of the Duc de Saint-Simon.

Chandernagor, Françoise d'Aubigne. *The King's Way.* San Diego, California: Harcourt, Brace, 1984. 497pp. This autobiographical novel traces the remarkable rise to power of Françoise d'Aubigne who becomes Louis's mistress and second wife as the powerful Madame de Maintenon. Relying on Madame de Maintenon's own words from her letters and diaries, the novel presents her as a complex mixture of ambition and self-doubt.

Doyle, Arthur Conan. *The Refugees.* New York: Harper, 1893. 366p. The novel depicts the rivalry between two of Louis's mistresses, Madame de Maintenon and the Marquise de Montespan, as well as the persecution of the Huguenots.

Hill, Pamela. *The Crown and the Shadow.* New York: Putnam, 1955. 314pp. Based on the life of Françoise d'Aubigne, Madame de Maintenon, the second wife of Louis XIV, the novel stays close to the historical facts with a modern interpretation of Madame de Maintenon as a proto-feminist.

Irwin, Margaret. *Royal Flush: The Story of Minette.* New York: St. Martin's, 1932. 352pp. The life of Henrietta Stuart, daughter of Charles I and cousin of Louis XIV is dramatized in a vivid and revealing intimate look at both royal families and the personalities and motivations of Louis and Charles II.

Law, Janice. *All the King's Ladies.* New York: St. Martin's, 1986. 310pp. Blending actual events and figures with invention, the novel describes the rise to power of Athenais de Montespan, who becomes Louis's mistress and attempts to control him with the aid of a sorceress.

Pell, Sylvia. *The Shadow of the Sun.* New York: Coward-McCann, 1978. 343pp. Louis's tangled relationship with various women is dramatized from 1660 to 1673. Married to Maria Theresa, he is romantically involved with Louise de la Valliere,

Athénais de Montespan, and Madame de Maintenon.

Plaidy, Jean. *Louis the Well-Beloved.* London: R. Hale, 1959. 251pp. In an biographical portrait of the early life of Louis XV who succeeds his father to the throne at the age of five, the novel depicts Louis XIV's final years and the intrigue for control of the infant king that followed his death.

Sanders, Joan. *The Marquis.* Boston: Houghton Mifflin, 1963. 405pp. The novel looks at the relationship between Louis XIV and Madame de Montespan from the perspective of her husband who defies the king and asserts his ill treatment when the king makes his wife his mistress.

Fictional Portraits

Butler, Mildred A. *Ward of the Sun King.* New York: Funk and Wagnalls, 1970. 156pp. In an atmospheric and historically convincing story, a young girl brought up in a school for the impoverished children of the nobility resists her harsh treatment and flees to England and New France.

Coryn, Marjorie. *Sorrow by Day.* New York: Appleton-Century, 1950. 312pp. In an adroit use of historical elements, the novel describes the pursuit by the king's cousin of a Gascon nobleman who succeeds in court circles by blackmailing the king's mistress.

Dumas, Alexandre. *The Man in the Iron Mask.* 1850. Reprint ed. New York: Oxford University Press, 1991. 626pp. Dumas's classic tale of adventure and intrigue in the court of Louis XIV turns on the imprisoned man whose identity can alter French history. The Four Musketeers are divided by the implications of their discovery. In *The Vicomte de Bragelonne* (1857. Reprint ed. New York: Oxford University Press, 1998. 738pp.), Dumas's Four Musketeers are featured dealing with intrigue during the Fronde, the uprising of nobles against Cardinal Mazarin's control over the infant Louis XIV. Alternative title: *Twenty Years After.*

Fuller, Iola. *All the Golden Gifts.* New York: Putnam, 1966. 252pp. In this historical romance set in the court of Louis XIV, a young woman becomes the king's favorite but resists his attentions in favor of a young musketeer and a young gentleman. The period details and atmosphere of the French court are convincing.

Golon, Sergeanne. *Angelique.* New York: Bantam, 1971. 820pp.; *Angelique and the King.* New York: Bantam, 1971. 505pp.; *Angelique in Revolt.* New York: Bantam, 1971. 470pp. This series of historical romances follows the career of a beautiful and resourceful French woman who becomes a favorite of Louis before joining the Huguenot cause. The novels display a remarkably detailed and convincing period mastery with plausible appearances of several historical figures, including Louis XIV.

Lewis, Janet. *The Ghost of Monsieur Scarron.* Garden City, New York: Doubleday, 1959. 378pp. Based on an authentic event, the novel concerns the search and prosecution of those responsible for writing a critical pamphlet about the Sun King as a innocent bookbinder is unjustly implicated in the crime.

McIntyre, Vonda N. *The Moon and the Sun.* New York: Pocket Books, 1997. 421pp. In an alternative-history fable, Louis hopes to ensure his immortality by devouring the entrails of a sea-woman trapped by a Jesuit explorer. Despite the fantasy, the novel is carefully researched to recreate Versailles and Louis's court.

Riley, Judith Merkle. *The Oracle Glass.* New York: Viking, 1994. 510pp. Based on the actual existence of a coven of Paris witches during the reign of Louis XIV, the novel provides a fascinating look at the dark side of Louis's court from the perspective of a young girl with prophetic powers who exerts her control over the king and his court.

Recommended Juvenile Biographies

Horn, Pierre L. *King Louis XIV.* New York: Chelsea House, 1986. 116pp. MG/YA. Horn orients the reader well to the events of Louis's reign and his activities.

Smith, David L. *Louis XIV.* New York: Cambridge University Press, 1992. 132pp. YA. Smith displays through primary and secondary sources a detailed view of the political and social context of Louis's reign and the man who set the tone for his age.

Stearns, Monroe. *Louis XIV of France: Pattern of Majesty.* New York: F. Watts, 1971. 183pp. YA. Stearns offers a less flattering portrait than can be found elsewhere in a critical scrutiny of the king and his era.

Biographical Films and Theatrical Adaptations

The Fifth Musketeer (1979). Director: Ken Annakin. Another remake of Dumas's *The Man in the Iron Mask* features an outstanding cast, including Beau Bridges as Louis and his twin, Ursula Andress, José Ferrer, Cornel Wilde, Lloyd Bridges, Alan Hale Jr., Rex Harrison, and Olivia de Havilland. Video.

The Iron Mask (1929). Director: Allan Dwan. Douglas Fairbanks's final swashbuckling turn casts him as D'Artaganan is this lavish adaptation of Dumas's novel. William Blackwell appears as Louis and his twin. A silent film with some talking segments, the 1940 reissue features a narration by Douglas Fairbanks Jr. Video.

The Man in the Iron Mask (1939). Director: James Whale. In this version of Dumas's swashbuckling classic, Louis Howard portrays Louis XIV with the musketeers played by Alan Hale, Warren William, Joseph Schildkraut, and Walter Kingsford. Video.

The Man in the Iron Mask (1977). Director: Mike Newell. Richard Chamberlain attempts the dual role of Louis and the mysterious prisoner in this television adaptation of Dumas's classic musketeer adventure. He is supported by an outstanding cast of Patrick McGoohan, Louis Jourdan, Jenny Agutter, Ian Holm, and Ralph Richardson. Video.

The Man in the Iron Mask (1998). Director: Randall Wallace. The most recent adaptation of Dumas's novel casts Leonardo DiCaprio in the dual role of Louis and lookalike with the musketeers played by Jeremy Irons, John Malkovich, Gabriel Byrne, and Gérard Depardieu. Video.

The Man in the Iron Mask (1998). Director: William Rickert. This overlooked version of Dumas's novel released in the same year as the Leonardo DiCaprio bigger-budget version features a number of unknown actors in a smaller scale, budget drama. Nick Rickert stars as Louis with Edward Albert, Dennis Hayden, William Rickert (the film's director), and Rex Ryon as the musketeers. Video.

The Return of the Musketeers (1989). Director: Richard Lester. Based loosely on Dumas's *Twenty Years After*, Lester reassembles his well-cast musketeers—Oliver Reed, Richard Chamberlain, Frank Finlay, and Michael York—for more adventures and intrigues caused by Milady's devious daughter. David Birkin appears as the youthful Louis and Alan Howard portrays Cromwell. Video.

The Rise of Louis XIV (1966). Director: Roberto Rossellini. Made for French television, this docudrama captures the atmosphere and events of the Sun King's court as well as a human portrait of the king. Starring Jean-Marie Patte, Raymond Jourdan, and Dominique Vincent. Video.

Star of India (1953). Director: Arthur Lubin. Cornel Wilde stars in this costume drama concerning a French nobleman trying to regain his inheritance during the reign of Louis XIV, with John Slater portraying the Sun King.

Other Sources

Rule, John C., ed. *Louis XIV.* Englewood Cliffs, New Jersey: Prentice-Hall, 1973. 181pp. Part of the Great Lives Observed series, the book provides Louis's own works, the views of his contemporaries, and current critical assessments of the man and his reign.

Wolf, John B., ed. *Louis XIV: A Profile.* New York: W.W. Norton, 1972. 265pp. This is useful volume that includes a brief biographical profile and essays by various scholars on aspects of the king's life, personality, and reign.

294. ROBERT LOWELL
1917–1977

American poet, playwright, and translator, Lowell won the Pulitzer Prize in 1947 for his poetry collection *Lord Weary's Castle* (1946) and again in 1974 for *The Dolphin* (1973). His autobiographical volume in verse and prose, *Life Studies* (1959), is one of the most influential recent examples of confessional poetry. Lowell won acclaim for his translations of Greek tragedy and various European poets. His other works include a trilogy of plays, *The Old Glory* (1968).

Autobiography and Primary Sources

Life Studies. New York: Farrar, Straus,1959. 90pp. Lowell's collection of confessional poems includes an autobiographical fragment. Another section appears in his *Collected Prose* (New York: Farrar, Straus,1987. 377pp.).

Recommended Biographies

Hamilton, Ian. *Robert Lowell: A Biography.* New York: Random House, 1982. 527pp. Based on extensive use of Lowell's correspondence and interviews with many of the poet's associates, Hamilton's is a detailed, comprehensive biography that keeps Lowell's often harrowing personal battles in clear focus with considerable sensitivity and understanding.

Mariani, Paul. *Lost Puritan: A Life of Robert Lowell.* New York: W.W. Norton, 1994. 527pp. Complementing Hamilton with newly available sources, including the author's interviews with friends and relatives and Lowell's unpublished letters, Mariani traces the various crises of Lowell's life, examining their impact on his work. While not superseding Hamilton's biography, Mariani adds details and perspective not found in the earlier account and a closer examination of Lowell's poetry and artistic development.

Other Biographical Studies

Axelrod, Stephen. *Robert Lowell: Life and Art.* Princeton, New Jersey: Princeton University Press, 1978. 286pp. Using the poetry as an ongoing autobiographical meditation and moral and psychological journey, Axelrod's is a readable account with many insights on Lowell's influences, friendships, and formative experiences.

Heymann, C. David. *American Aristocracy: The Lives and Times of James Russell, Amy, and Robert Lowell.* New York: Dodd, Mead, 1980. 561pp. Heymann's group biography is particularly useful in its depiction of Lowell's family and cultural background and the distance he went in rejecting many of its values, while retaining others. Nearly half of the book is devoted to Robert.

Meyers, Jeffrey. *Manic Power: Robert Lowell and His Circle.* New York: Arbor House, 1987. 228pp. Meyers supplies a group portrait and cultural history focused on Lowell's relationship with poets Randall Jarrell, John Berryman, and Theodore Roethke. Based on previously published biographies and memoirs, this is an anecdotally rich account of the four poets' self-destructive tendencies and mutual dependencies.

Biographical Films and Theatrical Adaptations

Robert Lowell: A Mania for Phrases (1988). Director: Veronica Young. Part of PBS's Voices and Visions poetry series, Lowell's life and works are presented and discussed by such commentators as Derek Walcott, Frank Bidart, and Anthony Hecht. Video.

Other Sources

Meyers, Jeffrey, ed. *Robert Lowell: Interviews and Memoirs.* Ann Arbor: University of Michigan Press, 1988. 369pp. This useful volume reprints 20 interviews with the poet as well as recollections by such writers as Norman Mailer, Seamus Heaney, Alfred Kazin, and Helen Vendler.

295. MARTIN LUTHER
1483–1546

The leader of the Protestant Reformation was born in Eisleben, Saxony, into a family of small landholders. He abandoned his law studies after undergoing a religious experience, entered an Augustinian monastery in Erfurt, and was ordained in 1507. While professor of Scripture at Wittenburg University (from 1512), Luther denounced the practice of selling indulgences in his 95 theses, which he posted on the church door. His *Address to the Christian Nobility of the German Nation* (1520) advocated German control of ecclesiastical matters and called for such religious reforms as clerical marriage. He was excommunicated after publicly burning a papal bull and summoned before Emperor Charles V to renounce his heresies at the Diet of Worms (1521). He refused, was outlawed, and retired to Wartburg castle, where he translated the New Testament into German and began work on the Old. Luther wrote two catechisms (1529) that formed the basis of Lutheranism. He returned to Wittenburg to direct the reform movement and to try to contain extremism. The evangelical doctrine he advocated spread throughout the Western world and marked the first challenge to the authority of the Roman Catholic church.

Autobiography and Primary Sources

Luther's letters are reprinted in volumes 48–50 of his *Works.* Jaroslav Pelikán, ed. (St. Louis: Concordia, 1955–1986. 55 vols.). They are also available in the *Letters of Martin Luther.* Margaret A. Currie, ed. (London: Macmillan, 1908. 482pp.).

Recommended Biographies

Bainton, Roland. *Here I Stand: A Life of Martin Luther.* Nashville, Tennessee: Abingdon Press, 1950. 336pp. Bainton's popular biography, which has been called the most readable Luther biography in English, makes Luther's ideas and milieu accessible for a general reader that does not neglect the findings of modern scholarship. Luther's life and times are arranged into a series of vivid and dramatic scenes that recreates the spiritual setting of the sixteenth century.

Brecht, Martin. *Martin Luther..* Philadelphia: Fortress Press, 1985-93. 3 vols. Written by a Protestant church historian and incorporating the most up-to-date theological scholarship on the Reformation, Brecht's detailed study is equally strong on Luther the man, his times, and the theological context.

Marius, Richard. *Martin Luther: The Christian Between God and Death.* Cambridge, Massachusetts: Belknap Press, 1999. 592pp. Relying on a close reading of Luther's writings and contemporary documents, Marius's critical biography is often harsh in its assessment of the man and his legacy. However, this is a provocative, well-written account that challenges previous views with a compelling, though debatable, comprehensive view of Luther's personality and ambivalent influence.

Oberman, Heiko A. *Luther: Man Between God and the Devil.* New Haven, Connecticut: Yale University Press, 1989. 380pp. This highly acclaimed biographical study, regarded by many as the definitive modern biography, features a brilliant account of Luther's evolution as a man, thinker, and Christian in the context of his times. Oberman stresses a darker Luther who is shown beset by depression and emotional violence. The book is equally strong on cultural, intellectual, and theological history.

Todd, John M. *Luther: A Life.* New York: Crossroad, 1982. 396pp. Todd's study of Luther's personality depicts him as a coarse, angry man with severe psychological problems. Although undocumented, the book is rich in quotes of Luther's own words and offers a compelling human portrait of the man, as well as a clear presentation of the complex theological context of his development.

Other Biographical Studies

Boehmer, Heinrich. *Martin Luther: Road to Reformation.* Philadelphia: Muhlenberg Press, 1957. 449pp. Boehmer's is an informative study that traces Luther's formative experiences up to 1521, allowing him to speak for himself as much as possible.

Dickens, A.G. *Martin Luther and the Reformation.* Mystic, Connecticut: L. Verry, 1967. 184pp. This is a concise historical overview that locates Luther's ideas and actions in their wider historical, religious, and cultural contexts. Serves as a solid, compact introduction to both the man and his era.

Edwards, Mark U. Jr. *Luther's Last Battles: Politics and Polemics 1531-46.* Ithaca, New York: Cornell University Press, 1983. 254pp. As its title indicates, Edwards focuses on Luther's later embattled career. Reliable and detailed, Edwards is expert in establishing the theological and historical context of Luther's final years.

Erikson, Erik H. *Young Man Luther: A Study in Psychoanalysis and History.* New York: W.W. Norton, 1960. 288pp. Erikson's controversial psychohistory applies his development theories of adolescence to Luther, revealing an identity crisis and a difficult relationship with his father. Criticized for its limited evidence on which to base its interpretations, Erikson's study is nonetheless fascinating and challenging in its concepts of Luther's youthful development.

Fife, Robert. *The Revolt of Martin Luther.* New York: Columbia University Press, 1957. 726pp. Fife's scholarly biography traces Luther's life in detail up to 1521 and sets him clearly in the context of his times.

Friedenthal, Richard. *Luther: His Life and Times.* New York: Harcourt, Brace, 1970. 566pp. In an often sprawling, discursive account, Friedenthal connects Luther's life and career to his historical and cultural background. Relying on contemporary documents, the book allows readers to draw their own conclusions about Luther's character and impact.

Haile, H.G. *Luther: An Experiment in Biography.* Garden City, New York: Doubleday, 1980. 422pp. Relying almost exclusively on Luther's own writings, the book concentrates on his relationships and creates a believable character portrait that does not overlook Luther's vulgarities and prejudices.

Lohse, Bernhard. *Martin Luther: An Introduction to His Life and Work.* Philadelphia: Fortress Press, 1986. 288pp. One of the best available single-volume guides to Luther and his ideas, the book records the current state of modern research on Luther and is free from a particular ideological bias, allowing the reader to form his own judgments.

Mackinnon, James. *Martin Luther and the Reformation.* New York: Longmans, 1925–1930. 4 vols. This is a scholarly yet readable historical biography that still serves as one of the most comprehensive and authoritative treatments of the man and his times.

Manns, Peter. *Martin Luther: An Illustrated Biography.* New York: Crossroad, 1982. 223pp. A useful but incomplete sympathetic account of Luther's life and thought by a Catholic priest, the book is especially good at explaining the historical and religious context of Luther's development.

Marius, Richard. *Luther.* Philadelphia: Lippincott, 1974. 269pp. Written for the general reader, Marius re-examines and reinterprets commonly accepted facts about Luther and his times and provides a valuable introduction to the subject.

Ritter, Gerhard. *Luther: His Life and Work.* New York: Harper & Row, 1963. 256pp. In a compact, candid assessment of the man and his achievements for a general audience Ritter provides a balanced treatment that grants both Luther's greatness and his limitations.

Rupp, Gordon. *Luther's Progress to the Diet of Worms.* Chicago: Wilcox and Follett, 1951. 109pp. Rupp helpfully and authoritatively traces the development of Luther's intellectual and theological development prior to 1517 and the posting of his Ninety-Five Theses in Wittenberg.

Schwiebert, E.C. *Luther and His Times.* St. Louis: Concordia, 1950. 892pp. An excellent orientation to Luther's personality, career, and historical context, Schwiebert's study serves as a solid introduction to the leading issues surrounding Luther's life and times.

Thiel, Rudolf. *Luther.* Philadelphia: Muhlenberg Press, 1955. 492pp. In a developmental biography Thiel traces the various aspects of Luther's character and his relationship with the Catholic Church. Serves as well as a helpful account of Luther's times.

Todd, John M. *Martin Luther: A Biographical Study.* Westminster, Maryland: Newman Press, 1964. 290pp. Written from a Roman Catholic perspective for the specialist, this is a succinct and concise account of Luther's life and career, particularly strong on Luther's Catholic context.

Biographical Novels

Barr, Gladys H. *Monk in Armour.* New York: Abingdon, 1950. 256pp. Martin Luther's life is depicted in this fictionalized biography from his boyhood to his marriage. Often oversimplified, the novel provides an idealized version of Luther's development and the events of the beginnings of the Protestant Reformation.

Davis, William S. *The Friar of Wittenburg.* New York: Macmillan, 1912. 433pp. The novel covers the years between 1517 and 1521 and is narrated by

a nobleman who is won over to Luther's side and becomes involved in some of the striking scenes from his life. Luther is sympathetically treated and sugar-coated.

Ludwig, Charles. *Queen of the Reformation.* Minneapolis: Bethany House, 1986. 224pp. In a romantic, idealized devotional novel, Luther's relationship with his wife, Katharina von Bora, is depicted, as well as the couple's opposition to Catholic orthodoxy.

Fictional Portraits

Hocking, Joseph. *The Sword of the Lord: A Romance of the Time of Martin Luther.* New York: Dutton, 1909. 334pp. In a fictional story, an Englishman is sent to escort a lady back to England during the Reformation, and Luther is portrayed in a historically reliable fashion.

Oliver, Jane. *Flame of Fire.* New York: Putnam, 1961. 288pp. In a fictionalized biography of William Tyndale who produced the first English translation of the Bible, Luther appears as a character with a major impact on Tyndale's life mission in an authentic depiction of the religious issues of the period.

Reade, Charles. *The Cloister and the Hearth.* 1861. Reprint ed. New York: Dutton, 1906. 703pp. In a picaresque adventure tale, Reade imagines the life of Erasmus's parents in a series of exciting scenes set in fifteenth-century Europe and featuring an appearance by Luther.

Waltari, Mika. *The Adventurer.* New York: Putnam, 1950. 377pp. Set during the turmoil of the Reformation, the novel dramatizes the adventures of the young Finnish student and later doctor who encounters some of the central figures of the period, including Paracelsus and Luther.

Recommended Juvenile Biographies

Cowie, Leonard W. *Martin Luther: Leader of the Reformation.* New York: Praeger, 1969. 122pp. MG/YA. Luther's public and private life is objectively depicted in an account that follows him from his school days to his last years. The text is interspersed with quotations from Luther and others.

O'Neill, Judith. *Martin Luther.* London: Cambridge University Press, 1975. 48pp. MG. This is a sensible historical/biographical overview that relates Luther's life and the high points of his career with his historical and cultural context.

Stepanek, Sally. *Martin Luther.* New York: Chelsea House, 1986. 120pp. MG/YA. Stepanek provides a reliable guide to Luther and his times in an objective and fair assessment of the man and his movement.

Biographical Films and Theatrical Adaptations

Osborne, John. *Luther.* New York: Criterion Books, 1962. 102pp. The play traces Luther's life from 1506 to 1530 as the archetypal rebel in conflict with his father, God, the church, and ultimately with himself in a sixteenth-century world full of modern correspondences.

Luther (1974). Director: Guy Green. In an adaptation of John Osborne's play, 29 years in the life of Luther are chronicled, including his clashes with Rome, the Peasant's Revolt, the Diet of Worms, and the launching of the Reformation. Stacy Keach stars in the tile role, with Patrick Magee, Judi Dench, and Robert Stephens. Video.

Martin Luther (1953). Director: Irving Pichel. French-made biography of Luther, starring Niall MacGinnis in the title role, with Annette Carell as Katherine von Bora, Hans Lefebre as Charles V, and Phillip Leaver as Pope Leo X. Video.

Martin Luther (1983). Producer: Rainer Wolfhardt. In this German television presentation, Lambert Habeck portrays Luther in scenes from his life. Video.

296. ROSA LUXEMBURG
1871–1919

German revolutionary born in Russian Poland, Luxemburg was influenced in her youth by the patriotic idealism of Polish poet and playwright Adam Mickiewicz and the first Polish socialists, whose group she joined in 1887. Forced to flee Poland because of her revolutionary activities, she settled in Zürich, where she became a Marxist and founder (1892) of the Polish Socialist Party and the Social Democratic Party of Poland (1894). After acquiring German citizenship through marriage (1898), she organized workers in the German Social Democratic Party (SPD), participated in the Polish revolution of 1905, and published her most famous work, *The Accumulation of Capital* (1914). While in prison during World War I, she formed with Karl Liebknecht and Clara Zetkin the Spartacus League, which became the German Communist Party (1918). In 1919 Luxemburg and Liebknecht were arrested for taking part in a Sparticist uprising and murdered by soldiers while on their way to prison.

Autobiography and Primary Sources

The Letters of Rosa Luxemburg. Stephen E. Bonner, ed. Atlantic Highlands, New Jersey: Humanities Press, 1993. 307pp. An essential source for the biographer and a supplement for anyone interested in encountering Luxemburg directly, her correspondence is collected in this scholarly edition.

Rosa Luxemburg Speaks. Mary-Alice Waters, ed.New York: Pathfinder Press, 1970. 473pp. Drawing on excerpts from Luxemburg's writings,

this informative volume offers the reader a useful introduction to the woman through her own words.

Recommended Biographies

Bronner, Stephen E. *Rosa Luxemburg: A Revolutionary for Our Times.* University Park: Pennsylvania State University Press, 1997. 130pp. Bronner provides a succinct introduction to Luxemburg's political views by placing her intellectual development in the context of Marxism and the international socialist movement.

Nettl, J.P. *Rosa Luxemburg.* London: Oxford University Press, 1966. 2 vols. The first truly scholarly analysis of Luxemburg's life and career, Nettl's lengthy, but readable, study remains definitive, drawing extensively on Luxemburg's correspondence to trace the development of her ideas and her place in the history of socialism. A one-volume abridgement is also available (New York: Oxford University Press, 1969. 557pp.).

Ettinger, Elzbieta. *Rosa Luxemburg: A Life.* Boston: Beacon Press, 1986. 286pp. Concentrating more on Luxemburg's private life and personality than Nettl's more integrated study, Ettinger's book is a useful supplement but, because Luxemburg's ideas are not considered in-depth and the historical context is sketchy, is unsatisfying as a single source. Drawing on recently uncovered Polish material, Ettinger supplies a vivid portrait of Luxemburg's passionate and contradictory nature.

Other Biographical Studies

Abraham, Richard. *Rosa Luxemburg: A Life for the International.* New York: Berg, 1989. 178pp. In a concise introduction to Luxemburg's life, theories, and achievements for the general reader, Abraham's narrative and interpretive synthesis is sometimes confusing for readers unfamiliar with Marxist ideology, and his treatment of Luxemburg's Jewishness and femininity is superficial. Does serve as an overview of Luxemburg's public life for those unfamiliar with the subject.

Basso, Lelio. *Rosa Luxemburg: A Reappraisal.* New York: Praeger, 1975. 183pp. Basso's intellectual biography traces the development of Luxemburg's ideas and her impact on Marxist theory. Passionate in its advocacy of Luxemburg's importance as a thinker, the book is recommended as a sensible assessment of her intellectual achievement.

Cliff, Tony. *Rosa Luxemburg.* London: Bookmarks, 1959. 83pp. Cliff's succinct political biography focuses on Luxemburg's teachings and place

in the international socialist movement. An outstanding introduction that makes accessible to the nonspecialist complex political theory and socialist ideology.

Frölich, Paul. *Rosa Luxemburg: Ideas in Action.* London: Pluto Press, 1972. 329pp. The work of one of Luxemburg's colleagues, Frölich's is an insider's view with all the emotional immediacy and bias of a devoted admirer.

Geras, Norman. *The Legacy of Rosa Luxemburg.* London: NLB, 1976. 210pp. In a reinterpretation of several major aspects of Luxemburg's works and impact, Geras focuses more on her revolutionary ideas than her personality and life.

Biographical Novels

Döblin, Alfred. *A People Betrayed.* New York: Fromm International, 1983. 642pp. In a cinematic panorama that weaves fictional and historical characters and events, the novel captures Berlin in 1918 with details of Rosa Luxemburg's wartime activities. In the sequel, *Karl and Rosa* (New York: Fromm International, 1983. 547pp.) Döblin narrates the tragic fate of Rosa Luxemburg and Karl Liebknecht who lead the proletarian revolution in Germany that erupts following World War I. Their story, told in a symphony of fictional and historical voices, becomes a moving personal tragedy as well as a political epic of Germany between the wars.

Biographical Films and Theatrical Adaptations

The Great War and the Shaping of the 20th Century (1996). Director: Carl Byker. In this acclaimed PBS documentary series Nasassia Kinski provides the voice of Rosa Luxemburg in a moving segment depicting her war activities and tragic death. Video.

Rosa Luxemburg (1985). Director: Margarethe Von Trotta. Based on Luxemburg's own writings, this German film thoughtfully dramatizes her political and personal life. Barbara Sukova is impressive as Luxemburg, with Otto Sander as Karl Liebknecht. Video.

Other Sources

Le Blanc, Paul, ed. *Rosa Luxemburg: Reflections and Writings.* Amherst, New York:Humanity Books, 1999. 272pp. This volume combines recollections, critical views, and excerpts from Luxemburg's writings and speeches.

297. DOUGLAS MACARTHUR
1880–1964

American general and hero of World War II, MacArthur was born in Little Rock, Arkansas, was reared on army posts, and attended military school and West Point. He commanded the 42nd (Rainbow) Division and the 84th Infantry Brigade during World War I, and as superintendent of West Point (1919–1922) helped modernize the academy's military training program. He held various commands in the Philippines (1922–1925), was department commander of the Philippines (1928), and served as U.S. Army chief of staff (1930–1935). He retired from the army (1937) but was recalled (1941) to command U.S. forces in East Asia, eventually directing the campaign to liberate the Philippines. He led the postwar reconstruction of Japan as Allied supreme commander and commanded U.N. forces during the Korean conflict. His unwillingness to obey President Truman's order to limit the war to Korea led to his removal from command (1951). He retired from active service and in 1952 became the chairman of the board of the Remington Rand Corporation.

Autobiography and Primary Sources

Reminiscences. New York: McGraw-Hill, 1964. 438pp. Defensive and self-serving, MacArthur's recollections were written in the last two years of his life and because of the overall tone of the author's infallibility provide an often inadvertent, unflattering illumination of MacArthur's character.

Reports of General MacArthur. Charles A. Willoughby, ed. Washington, DC: Department of the Army, 1966. 4 vols. Covering the events between 1941 and 1948 this collection of MacArthur's reports offers the general's own assessment of his wartime and postwar activities, although the army issued a disclaimer challenging the accuracy of many of MacArthur's findings.

A Soldier Speaks: Public Papers and Speeches of General of the Army Douglas MacArthur. Vorin E. Whan, ed. New York: Praeger, 1965. 367pp. This useful compilation of MacArthur's speeches, letters, and public writings is arranged chronologically from 1908 to his 1964 birthday address. Includes photographs from his entire career.

Recommended Biographies

James, D. Clayton. *The Years of MacArthur.* Boston: Houghton Mifflin, 1970–1985. 3 vols. Universally regarded as the definitive biography and acclaimed as one of the finest military biographies ever written, James's scholarly, exhaustively documented, enormously detailed treatment of MacArthur's entire career is balanced, comprehensive, and extremely readable, despite its length. However, even James, who devoted over two decades to his subject, admits that MacArthur the man remains for him a bewildering figure.

Manchester, William. *American Caesar: Douglas MacArthur, 1880–1964.* Boston: Little, Brown, 1978. 793pp. Based largely on James, Manchester's bestselling biography concentrates on MacArthur's character and personality and allows his many paradoxes to stand unresolved.

Perret, Geoffrey. *Old Soldiers Never Die: The Life of Douglas MacArthur.* New York: Random House, 1996. 663pp. This is the best one-volume biography available. Perret supplies a comprehensive, well-written, and believable human portrait of MacArthur that avoids the distortion of either undue adulation or vilification. Granting MacArthur high marks as a military commander, Perret does not avoid criticizing him for his shortcomings.

Other Biographical Studies

Blair, Clay Jr. *MacArthur.* Garden City, New York: Doubleday, 1977. 346pp. Written as a companion to the 1977 film, Blair concentrates on the World War II years with less fully developed sections on MacArthur's early and later career. More balanced than many books on the subject, Blair allows MacArthur's achievements to stand but is critical as well.

Gunther, John. *The Riddle of MacArthur: Japan, Korea, and the Far East.* New York: Harper, 1951. 240pp. Gunther's character study, though marred by factual errors and selectivity, is the first more complex treatment of MacArthur's complicated psyche.

Kelley, Frank R., and Cornelius Ryan. *MacArthur: Man of Action.* Garden City, New York: Doubleday, 1950. 191pp. Written before MacArthur's dismissal in 1951, the authors provide a

mainly heroic portrait of the general, more as a paragon than a man. The book is undocumented and error-filled. In *Star-Spangled Mikado* (New York: R.M. McBride, 1947. 282pp.), the same team offers a more critical assessment of MacArthur's administration of Japan following the war.

Lee, Clark, and Richard Henschel. *Douglas MacArthur.* New York: Holt, 1952. 370pp. This brief, informal biographical portrait that covers MacArthur's life from his birth to 1951 includes some interesting facts about the general's early years, but is chiefly valuable for its extensive pictorial record.

Long, Gavin. *MacArthur as Military Commander.* Princeton, New Jersey: Van Nostrand, 1969. 243pp. Written by the general editor of the official Australian history of World War II, this military biography covers MacArthur's career from his days at West Point to the end of the Philippine campaign in a balanced, objective assessment of MacArthur's skill as a commander.

Miller, Francis T. *General Douglas MacArthur: Soldier-Statesman.* Philadelphia: Winston, 1951. 313pp. Revision of *General Douglas MacArthur: Fighter for Freedom* (1942). Miller's 1942 biographical tribute was the first in the field, and the revision serves primarily as a historical document reflecting MacArthur's public reputation both during the war and following his dismissal by Truman.

Petillo, Carol M. *Douglas MacArthur: The Philippine Years.* Bloomington: Indiana University Press, 1981. 301pp. This highly speculative psychobiography examines MacArthur's years in the Philippines to provide a key for understanding his motives and subsequent behavior.

Schaller, Michael. *Douglas MacArthur: The Far Eastern General.* New York: Oxford University Press, 1989. 320pp. In a political profile rather than a full-scale biography, Schaller argues that MacArthur was an unscrupulous, self-serving soldier whose own manipulation of his image gave him an undeserved reputation. In one of the strongest negative assessments yet written, the book de-emphasizes anything in MacArthur's favor and is far too polemical to be reliable as a full and trustworthy portrait.

Schoor, Gene. *General Douglas MacArthur: A Pictorial Biography.* New York: Field, 1951. 46pp. This brief illustrated biography includes over 125 photographs arranged chronologically, documenting MacArthur's life and military career up to 1951.

Scott, Robert A. *Douglas MacArthur and the Century of War*. New York: Facts on File, 1997. 160pp. In a useful, casebook approach, MacArthur's life and political and military career are traced using photographs, primary sources, and historical assessments.

Smith, Robert. *MacArthur in Korea: The Naked Emperor*. New York: Simon & Schuster, 1982. 256pp. In a misleading title, Smith's ranges over MacArthur's entire career, assembling evidence to discredit the general and justify his dismissal by Truman. The book's negative bias is as distorting as the more adulatory studies by MacArthur partisans.

Whitney, Courtney. *MacArthur: His Rendezvous with Destiny*. New York: Knopf, 1955. 542pp. A close associate of MacArthur throughout the war years, Whitney has the advantage of firsthand access that few others can claim, but the overall assessment of the general is as a flawless commander, and the lack of critical balance limits the book's believability.

Willoughby, Charles A., and John Chamberlain. *MacArthur, 1941–51*. New York: McGraw-Hill, 1954. 441pp. Although featuring a firsthand look at MacArthur's command decisions by Willoughby, the general's intelligence chief during the war, this is a highly partisan defense of MacArthur's military career and is very much the version of events that MacArthur himself supported.

Fictional Portraits

Conroy, Robert. *1901*. Novato, California: Lyford Books, 1995. 374pp. In this alternate history, the novel imagines a German invasion of the United States in 1901 with a huge cast of historical figures, including Douglas MacArthur, forced to respond to events consistently with their personalities.

Kaminsky, Stuart M. *Buried Caesars*. New York: Mysterious Press, 1989. 179pp. In this installment of the author's clever historical mystery series, private eye Toby Peters is hired by General MacArthur in 1942 to find one of his aides who has absconded with papers that could destroy his political aspirations.

Slater, Ian. *MacArthur Must Die*. New York: D.I. Fine, 1994. 296pp. In a historical thriller, MacArthur's life in Brisbane after his retreat from the Philippines is described, as a plot to assassinate him is launched by the Japanese.

Weaver, John D. *Another Such Victory*. New York: Viking, 1948. 250pp. This story of a family spending a summer in the Washington encampment of the Bonus Army features an interesting sketch of MacArthur.

Webb, James H. *The Emperor's General*. New York: Broadway Books, 1999. 401pp. Webb offers a speculative inquiry into MacArthur's postwar dealings with the Japanese. The general's enormous ego and human failings are viewed from the perspective of a fictional aide-de-camp.

Recommended Juvenile Biographies

Devaney, John. *Douglas MacArthur: Something of a Hero*. New York: Putnam, 1979. 191pp. YA. As its title indicates, this is a balanced assessment of both sides of MacArthur's character and achievement that does not gloss over the less-flattering aspects of the general.

Feinberg, Barbara S. *Douglas MacArthur: American Hero*. New York: F. Watts, 1999. 128pp. MG. Provides a full-scale chronological account of MacArthur's life and career from childhood.

Finkelstein, Norman H. *The Emperor General: A Biography of Douglas MacArthur*. Minneapolis: Dillon Press, 1989. 128pp. MG. Capturing the high points of MacArthur's life in an accessible style and with useful illustrations, this is an adequate introduction to the man and his achievements.

Biographical Films and Theatrical Adaptations

A&E Biography Video: General Douglas MacArthur (1995). Producer: Lou Reda. In a full-length biographical portrait, MacArthur's remarkable career is documented as well as his considerable personality paradoxes. Video.

American Caesar (1985). Director: John McGreevy. Based on Manchester's book, this documentary, narrated by John Huston, chronicles MacArthur's entire career. Video.

An American Guerrilla in the Philippines (1950). Director: Fritz Lang. Tyrone Power leads a solid cast in a heroic depiction of the resistance to the Japanese after the fall of the Philippines. Robert Barrat reprises his portrayal as General MacArthur from *They Were Expendable*.

The Court Martial of Billy Mitchell (1955). Director: Otto Preminger. A taut courtroom drama based on the secret 1925 trial of Billy Mitchell, who condemned America's lack of readiness for a coming war with Japan. Gary Cooper stars as Billy Mitchell, Dayton Lummis appears as MacArthur, and Rod Steiger is a standout as an attorney. Video.

Inchon! (1982). Director: Terence Young. Produced by Sung Myung Moon's Unification Church, this is a laughable heroic epic depicting MacArthur's triumph during the Korean War, with an odd, bravura performance by Laurence Olivier as MacArthur.

In Pursuit of Honor (1995). Director: Ken Olin. Based on a true story, the film depicts five cavalry soldiers ordered by MacArthur (James Sikking) in 1935 to destroy their mounts as part of the army's modernization. Instead they attempt to drive 400 horses to safety in Canada. Starring Don Johnson, Craig Sheffer, and Bob Gunton. Video.

The Last Bastion (1984). Director: Chris Thomson. Robert Vaughn portrays MacArthur in this World War II television drama focusing on the political struggles among Churchill (Timothy West), Roosevelt (Warren Mitchell), and Australia's John Curtin (Michael Blakemore). Video.

MacArthur (1977). Director: Joseph Sargent. Gregory Peck portrays MacArthur from the fall of Corregidor to his dismissal by Truman. Dan

O'Herlihy plays Franklin D. Roosevelt and Ed Flanders is Truman. Video.

MacArthur: The Defiant General (1981). Producer: Arthur Holch. This is a personality profile that examines the controversies that dogged MacArthur's career. Video.

They Were Expendable (1945). Director: John Ford. Based on the true story of a PT boat squadron in the Philippines during the Japanese invasion, Robert Barrat portrays MacArthur with a strong cast including Robert Montgomery, John Wayne, and Donna Reed. Video.

Truman (1995). Director: Frank Pierson. Based on David McCullough's Pulitzer Prize–winning biography, Gary Sinise portrays Truman from 1917 to 1968. The film features the president's stormy relationship with MacArthur (Daniel von Bargen). Video.

Other Sources

Wittner, Lawrence S., ed. *MacArthur*. Englewood Cliffs, New Jersey: Prentice-Hall, 1971. 186pp. Part of the Great Lives Observed series, this useful volume includes excerpts from MacArthur's own writings, contemporaries recollections, and scholar's assessments.

298. NICCOLÒ MACHIAVELLI
1469–1527

Italian statesman and political theorist, Machiavelli was one of the outstanding figures of the Renaissance. He served the Republic of Florence as defense secretary and diplomat but lost his position when the Medicis came to power. His famous work is *The Prince* (1532), a treatise on Italian politics and the attainment of political power. Among his other works are the play, *Mandragola* (1524), and the brilliant *History of Florence* (1532).

Autobiography and Primary Sources

The Letters of Machiavelli. Allan Gilbert, ed. Chicago: University of Chicago Press, 1988. 252pp. This collection of letters is an invaluable source of information on Machiavelli's activities, relationships, and ideas.

Recommended Biographies

De Grazia, Sebastian. *Machiavelli in Hell*. Princeton, New Jersey: Princeton University Press, 1989. 497pp. De Grazia's intellectual biography is a well-written reassessment that argues that Machiavelli should be evaluated in political rather than moral terms and in the context of his times. However, as one reviewer argues, the book "creates an appealing and familiar Machiavelli, but it does so at the price of neutralizing many of the toughest challenges he continues to offer us."

Ridolfi, Roberto. *The Life of Machiavelli*. Chicago: University of Chicago Press, 1963. 337pp. This is the fullest and most authoritative guide to Machiavelli's life with the first half of the book devoted to his political career and the second to his years in exile. The book helps to animate Machiavelli's public and private life against a vivid background of historical events and politics of his era.

Other Biographical Studies

Curry, Patrick. *Introducing Machiavelli.* New York: Totem Books, 1996. 175pp. This is a lively overview of Machiavelli's life and ideas intended for the generalist and student.

Prezzolini, Giuseppe. *Machiavelli.* New York: Farrar, Straus, 1967. 372pp. Looking first at Machiavelli's ideas, the author devotes most of his efforts on Machiavelli's influences with a brief overview of his experiences.

Ruffo-Fiore, Silvia. *Niccolò Machiavelli.* Boston: Twayne, 1982. 179pp. This critical study provides a useful summary of Machiavelli's life and the connection between his experiences and his ideas. Suitable for the undergraduate and the general reader.

Skinner, Quentin. *Machiavelli.* New York: Hill & Wang, 1981. 102pp. Skinner provides a brief biographical overview as well as a helpful introduction to Machiavelli's works and philosophy geared to the general reader.

Tarlton, Charles D. *Fortune's Circle: A Biographical Interpretation of Niccolò Machiavelli.* Chicago: Quadrangle Press, 1970. 159pp. Tarlton defends Machiavelli from the charge of immorality by focusing on his ideas, his environment, and relationships. Too selective to be useful as a comprehensive overview, the book is nevertheless a stimulating analysis aimed at the general reader rather than the specialist.

Biographical Novels

Maugham, W. Somerset. *Then and Now.* Garden City, New York: Doubleday, 1946. 278pp. Maugham dramatizes the political education of Machiavelli, linking his theories from *The Prince* to period events.

Fictional Portraits

Bennetts, Pamela. *The Borgia Prince.* New York: St. Martin's, 1968. 254pp. Cesare Borgia is shown in war and love in a temperate portrait that resists portraying him as a monster. Machiavelli is on hand to observe the prince and develop his notion of political power.

Eliot, George. *Romola.* 1863. Reprint ed. New York: Oxford University Press, 1998. 622pp. Eliot's historical novel set in fifteenth-century Florence weaves a fictional story around actual events and appearances by such historical figures as Lorenzo de'Medici, Charles VIII, Savonarola, and Machiavelli.

Haasse, Hella S. *The Scarlet City: A Novel of 16th-Century Italy.* Chicago: Academy Chicago Publishers, 1990. 367pp. In Haase's masterful recreation of the Italian Wars during the sixteenth century, a large cast of historical figures are featured, including Alexander VI, Cesare Borgia, Michelangelo, and Machiavelli.

See also The Borgias and Lorenzo de'Medici

299–300. JAMES MADISON (1751–1836); DOLLEY MADISON (1768–1849)

The fourth U.S. president (1809–1817), Madison was born in Port Conway, Virginia, and graduated (1771) from the College of New Jersey (now Princeton). He served in the Continental Congress (1780–1783, 1787) and in the Virginia State Legislature (1784–1786). Known as the "father of the Constitution," Madison promoted the Annapolis Convention which led to the Constitutional Convention (1787) and co-authored the *Federalist Papers*, political essays supporting the Constitution. As congressman from Virginia (1789–1797) he strongly advocated the Bill of Rights. During the 1790s he helped found the Democratic-Republican Party, later the Democratic Party, and fought against passage of the Alien and Sedition Acts (1798). Madison served as Jefferson's secretary of state (1801–1808). A trade embargo against Great Britain in his first presidential term led to the War of 1812; British troops burned the White House (1814). Madison's postwar term was marked by a period of new prosperity and national expansion. He retired to his plantation, Montpelier, in 1817 and served as Rector of the University of Virginia from 1826.

Born to Quaker parents in Guilford County, North Carolina, Dolley Madison was raised in simplicity and married (1790) Quaker John Todd, who died in a yellow fever epidemic (1793). She left the Friends to marry (1794) James Madison and served as official White House hostess for widower Thomas Jefferson. She was known as a lavish hostess and noted for her wit, charm, and tact.

Autobiography and Primary Sources

James Madison: A Biography in His Own Words. Merrill D. Peterson, ed. New York: Harper & Row, 1974. 416pp. Using extracts from Madison's writings, explanatory notes, and connecting text, Madison provides his own version of his life experience and ideas.

Memoirs and Letters of Dolley Madison. Lucia B. Cutts, ed. 1886. Reprint ed. Port Washington, New York: Kennikat Press, 1971. 210pp. This compilation of Dolley Madison's writings was collected by her grandniece and serves as an indispensable primary biographical source and revealing look at her character and wit.

The Papers of James Madison. William T. Hutchinson, ed. Chicago: University of Chicago Press, 1962–1987. 14 vols. This still unfinished scholarly edition of Madison's writings has replaced in accuracy and comprehensibility two previous collections: *Letters and Other Writings of James Madison.* William C. Rives, ed. (Philadelphia: Lippincott, 1865. 4 vols.) and *The Writings of James Madison.* Gaillard Hunt, ed. (New York: Putnam, 1900–1910. 9 vols.).

Recommended Biographies

Brant, Irving. *James Madison.* Indianapolis: Bobbs-Merrill, 1941–1961. 6 vols. Brant's monumental biography remains the most comprehensive gathering of facts concerning Madison's life and is regarded as definitive, despite the author's inability to admit his subject's shortcomings. Exhaustively detailed on every aspect of Madison's personal and private life, Brant's treatment is at times ponderous. General readers may prefer Brant's one-volume condensation, *The Fourth President: A Life of James Madison* (Indianapolis: Bobbs-Merrill, 1970. 681pp.), which eliminates the original endnotes and the author's rebuttal of other historians' views, but still manages to capture the spirit of the man, and includes all the important details of Madison's life.

Ketcham, Ralph. *James Madison: A Biography.* New York: Macmillan, 1971. 753pp. The best available one-volume biography, Ketcham's analysis of Madison's life and thought is judicious and balanced and frequently at odds with Brant's more sympathetic treatment of Madison's personal strengths and achievements.

Moore, Virginia. *The Madisons: A Biography.* New York: McGraw-Hill, 1979. 568pp. This well-researched, highly readable chronological account of the Madisons' relationship is based on the writings of both James and Dolley Madison. The pragmatic and intellectual James is contrasted with the passionate Dolley, both of whose personalities begin to merge in the later stages of their relationship.

Rutland, Robert A. *James Madison: The Founding Father.* New York: Macmillan, 1987. 287pp. Far less detailed than Ketcham and written for a more popular audience, Rutland's is a succinct and balanced assessment that serves both to underscore Madison's influence and talents but does not shy away from criticism of his leadership and capabilities.

Other Biographical Studies

Adams, John Quincy. *The Lives of James Madison and James Monroe, the Fourth and Fifth Presidents of the United States.* Boston: Phillips/Sampson, 1850. 432pp. This first biography of Madison is an informal portrait based on Adams's personal acquaintance. The book retains historical significance, considering its author and his perspective on the historical era.

Anthony, Katharine. *Dolley Madison, Her Life and Times.* Garden City, New York: Doubleday, 1949. 426pp. In an undocumented, vivid account for the general reader, Dolley Madison's life is helpfully placed in her historical and cultural context.

Banning, Lance. *The Sacred Fire of Liberty: James Madison and the Founding of the Federal Republic.* Ithaca, New York: Cornell University Press, 1995. 543pp. Banning's brilliant and original intellectual biography chronicles the development of Madison's thought from 1780 to 1792 and challenges many of the assumptions of previous biographers and historians and alters the paradigm for viewing Madison's ideological role in the founding.

Gay, Sydney H. *James Madison.* 1884. Reprint ed. New York: AMS Press, 1972. 342pp. Gay's hostile account of Madison's character and achievement surveys the highlights of his career and finds him wanting as a man, president, and war leader. The book serves as an example of the negative, pro-Federalist view of Madison that subsequent biographers have been forced to address.

Hunt, Gaillard. *The Life of James Madison.* 1902. Reprint ed. New York: Russell & Russell, 1968. 402pp. Written by an early editor of Madison's writings, this is a scholarly biography that draws on the author's familiarity with the primary material. More generous to Madison than Gay, Hunt provides a more balanced assessment but still with a strong anti-Jefferson and pro-Hamilton bias.

McCoy, Drew R. *The Last of the Fathers: James Madison and the Republican Legacy.* New York: Cambridge University Press, 1989. 386pp. The focus here is on the neglected period in Madison's life, between his retirement in 1817 and his death. In a beautifully written and richly detailed topical account, McCoy broadens the intellectual portrait of Madison by showing his persistent effort to realize the founders' vision in the development of the young nation.

Miller, William L. *The Business of May Next: James Madison and the Founding.* Charlottesville: University Press of Press, 1992, 296pp. In an intellectual and political biography, Miller concentrates on the critical years between 1784 and 1791 and the shaping of the Constitution and the debate over its ratification. Madison's intellectual development is used to illuminate the moral and ideological basis for the American government.

Rives, William C. *History of the Life and Times of James Madison.* Boston: Little, Brown, 1859–1868. 3 vols. Rives's early scholarly treatment of Madison's life drew on primary sources, which he quotes from extensively. However, Rives takes Madison's story only up to 1797, and the author's historical and political interests cause him to lose the biographical focus for significant stretches. Clearly the work of an admirer, Rives's bias limits his objectivity and his facts are not always reliable.

Rutland, Robert A. *The Presidency of James Madison.* Lawrence: University Press of Kansas, 1990. 233pp. Written by an acknowledged expert on Madison and the early years of the United States, Rutland's succinct examination of Madison's presidency balances praise and criticism in an overall sympathetic assessment of his administration.

Schultz, Harold S. *James Madison.* New York: Twayne, 1970. 241pp. This political biography offers a succinct and balanced assessment of Madison's public career that is often at odds with Brant's interpretation but lacks details on his personal life and cultural history.

Biographical Novels

Brown, Rita Mae. *Dolley: A Novel of Dolley Madison in Love and War.* New York: Bantam, 1994. 382pp. Dolley Madison tells her own story through her diary and emerges as a complex, savvy politician who must contend with a male-dominated political world in a remarkable historical reconstruction of the era and its leading figures.

Wilson, Dorothy C. *Queen Dolley: The Life and Times of Dolley Madison.* Garden City, New York: Doubleday, 1987. 373pp. In a largely faithful account of Dolley Madison's life and times, her

youth, first marriage, and her relationship with James Madison is depicted.

Fictional Portraits

Hoffmann, Peggy. *My Dear Cousin.* New York: Harcourt, Brace, 1970. 435pp. This story of the War of 1812 describes the tragic romance between a Baltimore belle and the British ambassador, with appearances by a number of historical figures, including James and Dolley Madison.

Martin, William. *Back Bay.* New York: Crown, 1979. 437pp. The mysterious disappearance of a valuable tea set fashioned by Paul Revere and presented to George Washington in 1789 forms the situation to this historical novel that features appearances by a number of historical figures, including Dolley Madison.

Nevin, David. *1812.* New York: Forge, 1996. 445pp. Interweaving a fictional story with an accurate historical account of the events of the War of 1812, the Madisons' White House experiences are described.

Vidal, Gore. *Burr: A Novel.* New York: Random House, 1973. 430p. Told partly by Burr himself at the end of his life reflecting on the events of the Revolution and the early years of the Republic, Vidal's endlessly provocative revisionist view, based on solid research, is often highly critical of the founding fathers. Both James and Dolley Madison are depicted.

Recommended Juvenile Biographies

Davidson, Mary R. *Dolley Madison: Famous First Lady.* New York: Chelsea House, 1992. 80pp. MG. The highlights of Dolley Madison's life and role as first lady are chronicled in this adequate chronological narrative.

Fritz, Jean. *The Great Little Madison.* New York: Putnam, 1989. 149pp. MG. Blending details about Madison's private life, his partnership with his wife, and the historical context, Fritz animates Madison's life and era with her characteristic vividness and invitingly light, comic tone.

Leavell, J. Perry. *James Madison.* New York: Chelsea House, 1988. 111pp. MG/YA. Leavell's is a solid, informative survey of Madison's life in the context of the historical events of his era.

Malone, Mary. *James Madison.* Springfield, New Jersey: Enslow, 1997. 128pp. MA/YA. Although some personal information about Madison's childhood, education, and marriage is included, the emphasis here is on Madison's public career and intellectual contributions in a sympathetic profile.

Quakenbush, Robert M. *James Madison and Dolley Madison and Their Times.* New York: Pippin Press, 1992. 36pp. MG. In a humorous approach that allows both Madisons to reflect on their lives together during the creation of the Constitution and the War of 1812, the major events of their lives are presented with the author's customary cartoonlike drawings.

Biographical Films and Theatrical Adaptations

Liberty!: The American Revolution (1997). Directors: Ellen Hovde and Muffie Meyer. This PBS documentary series features actors portraying the principals in dramatic readings from their letters and speeches. James Madison is played by Jefferson Mays. The companion volume is written by Thomas J. Fleming (New York: Viking, 1997. 394pp.). Video.

Magnificent Doll (1946). Director: Frank Borzage. Hollywood historical romp features Ginger Rogers as Dolley Madison—in love with both James Madison (Burgess Meredith) and Aaron Burr (David Niven)—who helps Jefferson to win the presidency and secures her own eventual role as first lady. Not convincing either as history or drama, despite a screenplay by Irving Stone.

Other Sources

Rutland, Robert A., ed. *James Madison and the American Nation 1751–1836: An Encyclopedia.* New York: Simon & Schuster, 1994. 509pp. This alphabetically arranged reference volume focuses on Madison's life and times, covering most of the key events and personalities.

301. FERDINAND MAGELLAN
ca. 1480–1521

Portuguese navigator who commanded the first expedition around the world, Magellan sailed from Spain with five ships to look for a western route to the East Indies. He explored the east coast of South America and discovered and entered the strait that bears his name. He continued across the Pacific and reached the Philippines, where he was killed in a skirmish with natives. Only one ship returned to Spain, thus completing the voyage around the world.

Autobiography and Primary Sources

Magellan's Voyage around the World: Three Contemporary Accounts. Charles E. Nowell, ed. Evanston, Illinois: Northwestern University Press, 1962. 351pp. This useful volume brings together the eyewitness accounts of Antonio Pigafetta, the recollections of survivors of the circumnavigation after their return to Spain, and an account by a contemporary Portuguese historian.

Recommended Biographies

Guillemard, Francis H.H. *The Life of Ferdinand Magellan and the First Circumnavigation of the Globe 1480–1521.* 1890. Reprint ed. New York: AMS Press, 1971. 353pp. Guillemard's study of Magellan's life and the circumnavigation remains one of the most reliable and compelling treatments available. The essential evidence of Magellan's life is collected, with documentary evidence supplied in useful appendixes. The highpoint, however, is the author's rousing, unsurpassed narrative account of the voyage.

Parr, Charles M. *So Noble a Captain: The Life and Times of Ferdinand Magellan.* New York:

Crowell, 1953. 423pp. The emphasis here is on the times over Magellan's life, but there are few better or more authoritative accounts of the background to Magellan's voyage. Once Magellan takes center stage, the narration of his leadership during the voyage is dramatic and revealing.

Roditi, Edouard. *Magellan of the Pacific.* New York: McGraw-Hill, 1973. 271pp. Regarded by many as the best popular biography of Magellan in English, Roditi's is a well-written narrative account mostly devoted to events of the voyage but with insight into Magellan's motives and the reasons for his shift of allegiance from Portugal to Spain.

Other Biographical Studies

Joyner, Tim. *Magellan.* Camden, Maine: International Marine, 1992. 365pp. The work of a fisheries biologist, this is a straightforward account that relates Magellan's achievement in the wider context of the European search for a sea route to India and draws on the author's own sailing experiences along the coast of South America.

Zweig, Stefan. *Conqueror of the Seas.* New York: Viking, 1938. 335pp. Zweig's is an impressionistic account of Magellan's voyage with an emphasis on its challenges and drama, not always reliable or very penetrating, but still entertaining.

Fictional Portraits

Ponce de Leon, N. Baccino. *Five Black Ships.* New York: Harcourt, Brace, 1994. 347pp. Magellan's circumnavigation is recounted from the imagined perspective of the expedition's jester in a narrative that stays close to the actual dates and events of the voyage.

Recommended Juvenile Biographies

Brewster, Scott. *Ferdinand Magellan.* Englewood Cliffs, New Jersey: Silver Burdett, 1990. 104pp. MG. An installment in the What Made Them Great series, this is a vivid account of Magellan's voyage around the world and the events leading up to his death.

Hargrove, Jim. *Ferdinand Magellan.* Chicago: Childrens Press, 1990. 128pp. MG. Hargrove sets the man and his accomplishments in the political, economic, and cultural contexts of his period in a highly readable account that makes use of primary sources to add immediacy.

Stefoff, Rebecca. *Ferdinand Magellan and the Discovery of the World Oceans.* New York: Chelsea House, 1990. 127pp. YA. In a detailed biography, what little is known of Magellan's early life is covered, and the voyage is vividly chronicled.

302. GUSTAV MAHLER
1860–1911

A composer and conductor born in Austrian Bohemia, Mahler studied at the University of Vienna and the Vienna Conservatory. He was conductor of the Budapest Imperial Opera (1888–1890), the Hamburg Municipal Theater (1891–1897), the Vi-

enna State Opera (1897–1907), the New York Philharmonic (1909–1911), and the Metropolitan Opera (1908–1910). He composed his nine symphonies in the off seasons (an unfinished tenth was completed by Deryck Cooke) and wrote numerous song cycles. His later works influenced the next generation of Austrian composers, particularly Arthur Schoenberg and Alban Berg. Mahler's symphonies are known for their startling harmonic and orchestral effects and for their use of solo and choral voices.

Autobiography and Primary Sources

Blaukopf, Kurt, and Herta Blaukopf. *Mahler: His Life, Work, and World.* London: Thames and Hudson, 1991. 255pp. The authors collect a variety of contemporary materials, including letters, reviews, concert programs, and diary extracts, to create a view of Mahler in his own words and those of his friends, colleagues, and critics.

Selected Letters. Knud Marner, ed. New York: Farrar, Straus, 1979. 480pp. This rich sampling of Mahler's correspondence provides invaluable insights into the composer's character and the milieu in which he worked.

Recommended Biographies

Carr, Jonathan. *Mahler: A Biography.* Woodstock, New York: Overlook Press, 1998. 254pp. The most insightful and provocative single-volume study of the composer, Carr's examination draws on source material unavailable in English and challenges many of the widely held assumptions about Mahler in a lucid and balanced account. An excellent initial choice for the student and nonspecialist.

La Grange, Henry-Louis de. *Mahler.* Garden City, New York: Doubleday, 1973. 982pp.; *Gustav Mahler: Vienna: The Years of Challenge 1897–1904.* New York: Oxford University Press, 1994. 892pp.; *Gustav Mahler: Vienna, Triumph and Disillusion 1904–1907.* New York: Oxford University Press, 2000. 1,024pp. La Grange's tireless research has produced the most comprehensive gathering of facts surrounding every aspect of Mahler's life and career up to 1907, with additional volumes to come. Almost microscopic in its attention to detail, La Grange provides a nearly day-by-day account. All subsequent biographers will be indebted to his efforts, though the casual reader will likely use La Grange's monumental volumes as a reference source rather than a sustained narrative.

Mitchell, Donald. *Gustav Mahler: The Early Years.* 1958. Revised ed. Berkeley: University of California Press, 1980. 338pp.; *Gustav Mahler: The Wunderhorn Years.* Boulder, Colorado: Westview Press, 1976. 461pp.; *Gustav Mahler: Songs and Symphonies of Life and Death.* Berkeley: University of California Press, 1985. 659pp. Mitchell's first volume of his multivolume study provides an exceptional, thorough, and revealing treatment of Mahler's youth and development. His subsequent volumes are increasingly devoted less to biography than to a critical analysis of Mahler's artistic development and musical genius.

Other Biographical Studies

Bauer-Lechner, Natalie. *Recollections of Gustav Mahler.* New York: Cambridge University Press, 1980. 250pp. The author, a close friend and confidante of Mahler during his early years in Vienna, provides an affectionate and believable intimate, anecdotal portrait of the composer in a series of vignettes with re-created conversations.

Blaukopf, Kurt. *Gustav Mahler.* New York: Praeger, 1973. 279pp. A valuable single-volume approach to Mahler's character and artistry, and critical the reception of his work, Blaukopf emphasizes the interplay between the composer and his society with a number of provocative psychological insights on various aspects of Mahler's personality.

Cardus, Neville. *Gustav Mahler: His Mind and His Music.* New York: St. Martin's, 1965. 191pp. Largely focused on Mahler's music rather than his life, Cardus analyses each of Mahler's compositions chronologically, with a brief biographical context. The result presents a valuable intellectual and artistic portrait of the evolution of Mahler's musical and imaginative genius.

Engel, Gabriel. *Gustav Mahler: Song-Symphonist.* New York: Bruckner Society of America, 1932. 132pp. Engel's early biography is based on Mahler's letters, many of which were not available when the book was written; therefore, the book's biographical portrait is limited and incomplete, and superseded by later works.

Franklin, Peter. *The Life of Mahler.* New York: Cambridge University Press, 1997. 228pp. Written by a leading European conductor, this sensible critical biography helps separate the myth from the facts surrounding the composer but does presuppose some prior knowledge about Mahler's life, circle, and music.

Gartenberg, Egon. *Mahler: The Man and His Music.* New York: Schirmer Books, 1978. 406pp. Dividing his study between Mahler's life and a chronological critical analysis of his compositions, Gartenberg's study is suitable for a wide audience, including those without a technical musical background. The book is particularly revealing on Mahler's Viennese background.

Haylock, Julian. *Gustav Mahler: An Essential Guide to His Life and Works.* London: Pavilion, 1996. 106pp. Part of the Classic FM Lifelines series, this is a succinct and useful introduction to the man and his music.

Holbrook, David. *Gustav Mahler and the Courage to Be.* London: Vision Press, 1975. 270pp. The author examines Mahler's Ninth Symphony and his final years as the point of entry to consider the composer's psychological make-up and artistic genius. The book presupposes prior knowledge of Mahler's life and music.

Kennedy, Michael. *Mahler.* London: Dent, 1974. 196pp. Serving as a useful brief introduction to the man, his music, and his times, Kennedy's approach is accessible and useful to the uninitiated, general reader.

Loschnigg, Franz. *The Cultural Education of Gustav Mahler.* Madison: University of Wisconsin Press, 1976. 2 vols. Examining Mahler's youth and development, Loschnigg provides an insightful survey of the cultural and intellectual context out of which the composer emerged, particularly strong on Mahler's Jewish heritage.

Walter, Bruno. *Gustav Mahler.* 1937. Revised ed. New York: Greystone Press, 1941. 236pp. The recollections of Mahler's assistant provide a unique firsthand account of Mahler's professional life as a composer-conductor. At times self-serving, Walter glosses over certain details of his relationship with Mahler's family circle.

Books by and about Mahler's wife document the couple's life together and the personal and domestic aspect of the composer's life.

Giroud, Françoise. *Alma Mahler: Or, the Art of Being Loved.* New York: Oxford University Press, 1991. 162pp. Giroud's critical biography of Alma Mahler portrays her in an unsympathetic light as a man-hungry beauty rather than the muse of other treatments. Her relationship with Mahler is the chief focus.

Keegan, Suzanne. *The Bride of the Wind: The Life and Times of Alma Mahler-Werfel.* New York: Viking, 1992. 346pp. In a well-organized, readable, and vivid portrait of the woman and her times, Keegan draws on a variety of factual sources to create a sympathetic but critical psychological portrait of Alma Mahler and her relationship with the several men in her life.

Mahler, Alma. *Gustav Mahler: Memories and Letters.* 1946. Revised ed. Donald Mitchell, ed. Seattle: University of Washington Press, 1968. 369pp. Offering her unique perspective of her 10-year marriage, Alma Mahler is often protective of her own and her husband's reputation but includes personal details not available anywhere else.

Monson, Karen. *Alma Mahler: Muse to Genius: From Fin-de-siècle Vienna to Hollywood's Heyday.* Boston: Houghton Mifflin, 1983. 348pp. Monson's chronological narrative of Alma Mahler's life and relationships depends strongly on her subject's own recollections of her life with Mahler and makes little attempt at interpretation to solve the mystery of her appeal to so many creative figures.

Biographical Films and Theatrical Adaptations

Mahler (1974). Director: Ken Russell. Biographical fantasy based on Mahler's life and his relationship with his wife. The couple is portrayed by Robert Powell and Georgina Hale. Video.

Other Sources

Blaukopf, Kurt, ed. *Mahler: A Documentary Study.* New York: Oxford University Press, 1976. 280pp. This fascinating collection of contemporary pictures and written documents are arranged in chronological order with valuable notes, presenting a unique look at Mahler's milieu and career.

Lebrecht, Norman, ed. *Mahler Remembered.* New York: W.W. Norton, 1988. 322pp. Drawing on books, articles, memoirs, and letters of Mahler's contemporaries, Lebrecht arranges his material chronologically to document Mahler's life, person-

ality, and musical accomplishment as seen through friends and associates.

303. MOSES MAIMONIDES
1135–1204

A Spanish scholar and physician, Maimonides was the foremost Jewish thinker of the Middle Ages. Forced to flee Muslim Spain because of persecution, his family fled to Egypt, where Maimonides became court physician to Saladin. His works include the *Mishneh Torah*, a codification of Jewish doctrine, *Guide for the Perplexed*, and the *Moreh Nevukhim*. Maimonides's work has influenced Jewish and Christian scholars.

Autobiography and Primary Sources

Letters of Maimonides. Leon D. Stitskin, ed. New York: Yeshiva University Press, 1977. 199pp. Maimonides's collected letters are a rich source of insights into his mind and ideas. See also *Epistles of Maimonides: Crisis of Leadership* (Philadelphia: Jewish Publication Society, 1985. 292pp.), which reprints his most important epistles on religious persecution, the claims of Christianity and Islam, and the rational challenge to faith.

Recommended Biographies

Heschel, Abraham J. *Maimonides: A Biography.* New York: Farrar, Straus, 1982. 273pp. Originally published in Germany in 1935, Heschel supplies a popular introduction to Maimonides's life and ideas in a lyrical style for which the philosopher-theologian was well known. Legends are incorporated into the account but they are identified as such. The book is particularly strong on the Muslim milieu of the period.

Zeitlin, Solomon. *Maimonides: A Biography.* 1935. Revised ed. New York: Bloch, 1955. 234pp. Zeitlin is more thorough than Heschel in collecting the existing evidence, supplying plausible conjectures to fill the gaps in the record. The book, however, assumes considerable familiarity with Jewish history.

Other Biographical Studies

Yellin, David. *Maimonides: His Life and Works.* 1903. Reprint ed. New York: Hermon Press, 1972. 193pp. Now out of date due to modern scholarship, this volume was written before new primary material helped redefine insights into Maimonides's life and career.

Biographical Novels

Le Porrier, Herbert. *The Doctor from Cordova: A Biographical Novel about the Great Philosopher Maimonides.* Garden City, New York: Doubleday, 1979. 280pp. Maimonides narrates the story of his life in this fictional autobiography that chronicles his boyhood in Cordova, exile from Spain, travels in the Islamic world, and final service as court physician to Saladin.

Morrison, Lester M. *Trial and Triumph: A Novel about Maimonides.* New York: Crown, 1965. 469pp. The known events of Maimonides's life and

career are chronicled in this biographical novel that offers plausible surmises for gaps in the record.

Recommended Juvenile Biographies

Marcus, Rebecca B. *Moses Maimonides: Rabbi, Philosopher, and Physician.* New York: F. Watts, 1989. 114pp. MG. Marcus presents Maimonides's life and ideas in a helpful summary with a solid historical background.

304. MALCOLM X
1925–1965

Born Malcolm Little in Omaha, Nebraska, militant African American leader Malcolm X was converted to the Nation of Islam while serving a prison sentence (1946–1952) and upon his release became a Muslim minister. His following in the movement equaled and even surpassed that of Muslim leader Elijah Mohammed. Malcolm formed a rival organization, the Muslim Mosque, Inc., and after a pilgrimage to Mecca, he converted to orthodox Islam and began to eschew separatism in favor of a policy supporting racial coexistence. He founded (1964) the Organization for Afro-American Unity (OAAU) and was assassinated during an OAAU meeting in a New York City auditorium.

Autobiography and Primary Sources

The Autobiography of Malcolm X. As told to Alex Haley. New York: Grove Press, 1965. 455pp. Dictated to Alex Haley, Malcolm X narrates his development from street criminal to Civil Rights leader. The book is regarded as a classic work on the African American experience and a revealing look at a fascinating figure. Bruce Perry has challenged several facts recorded here, and his book should be consulted as a useful complement for biographical details.

Malcolm X's correspondence and speeches are collected in several collections. The best are the following: *By Any Means Necessary: Speeches, Interviews, and a Letter by Malcolm X* (New York: Pathfinder Press, 1970. 184pp.); *Malcolm Speaks: Selected Speeches and Statements.* George Breitman, ed. (New York: Merit Publishers, 1965. 232pp.); and *The Speeches of Malcolm X.* Archie Epps, ed. (London: Owen, 1969. 191pp.).

Recommended Biographies

Goldman, Peter. *The Death and Life of Malcolm X.* New York: Harper & Row, 1973. 438pp. Contrary to other presentations of a heroic, idealized Malcolm X, Goldman reveals a far more human, limited individual. Uneven in its presentation of certain aspects of Malcolm X's life, Goldman's study is nevertheless provocative and challenging in attempting to answer how Malcolm X both influenced his era and was in turn shaped by his times.

Lomax, Louis E. *To Kill a Black Man.* Los Angeles: Holloway House, 1968. 256pp. Although undocumented and impressionistic, Lomax's biographical comparative portrait of Malcolm X and Martin Luther King Jr. is based on firsthand knowledge of both men and is insightful as well as provocative in its interpretations. Lomax's earlier book, *When the Word is Given* (Cleveland, Ohio: World, 1963. 223pp.), includes a portrait of Malcolm X during his days as a Muslim minister.

Perry, Bruce. *Malcolm: The Life of a Man Who Changed Black America*. New York: Talman, 1991. 542pp. Exhaustively researched, based on more than 400 interviews and Malcolm X's FBI file, Perry's psychohistorical analysis traces Malcolm X's development, beginning with his abused childhood. Controversial in many of its findings and at odds with the facts recorded in the *Autobiography,* Perry's examination challenges the conventional view of Malcolm X and replaces the legend that has surrounded him with a believable human portrait.

Other Biographical Studies

Breitman, George. *The Last Year of Malcolm X: The Evolution of a Revolutionary*. New York: Merit, 1967. 169pp. Breitman considers Malcolm X's intellectual and political development in his final year and serves as an important supplement to the *Autobiography*. Drawing mainly on the speeches, Breitman chronicles the important period when Malcolm left the Nation of Islam and began to evolve a new political and moral ideology, becoming, from Breitman's Marxist perspective, a social revolutionary.

Breitman, George, Herman Porter, and Baxter Smith. *The Assassination of Malcolm X*. New York: Pathfinder Press, 1976. 190pp. In a detailed look at the controversies surrounding Malcolm X's death, the book challenges the official verdict and suggests a different interpretation of the event, while correcting several misconceptions about Malcolm's development and ideas.

Cone, James H. *Martin and Malcolm and America*. Maryknoll, New York: Orbis Books, 1991. 358pp. This comparative study of the ideas of Malcolm X and Martin Luther King Jr. suggests how each man moved toward the other's viewpoint by the time of their deaths, and makes the case that Malcolm X's legacy is equal in importance to King's.

Curtis, Richard. *The Life of Malcolm X*. Philadelphia: Macrae Smith, 1971. 164pp. This brief summary of Malcolm X's life and thought serves as a succinct and sensitive introduction for both the general and the younger reader.

DeCaro, Louis A. *On the Side of My People: A Religious Life of Malcolm X*. New York: New York University Press, 1996. 363pp. In a scholarly but accessible analysis, DeCaro focuses on Malcolm's spiritual development from his early years to his spiritual awakening, relationship with Elijah Muhammad, and his pilgrimage to Mecca. Correcting many previous interpretations, the book shows how family factors and his experiences helped determine his pro-African ideas and Sunni orthodoxy.

Dyson, Michael E. *Making Malcolm: The Myth and Meaning of Malcolm X*. New York: Oxford University Press, 1995. 215pp. In a series of essays, Dyson chronicles Malcolm X's legacy, including his achievements and failures, and his influence on American popular culture. Dyson critiques every important biography of Malcolm X to show how

interpretations of his life reveal as much about the biographers as they do about the man.

Wolfenstein, Eugene V. *The Victims of Democracy: Malcolm X and the Black Revolution*. Los Angeles: University of California Press, 1981. 422pp. The book provides a Marxist and Freudian psychoanalytical reading of Malcolm X's life and career. Jargon-heavy and highly speculative, this examination is not for readers without a previous background in political theory and psychoanalysis, as well as a knowledge of Malcolm X's life and ideas.

Recommended Juvenile Biographies

Brown, Kevin. *Malcolm X: His Life and Legacy.* Brookfield, Connecticut: Millbrook Press, 1995. 112pp. YA. Brown's political biography provides useful information about the history of the Nation of Islam and the civil rights movement to help explain Malcolm X's development. The book deals candidly with both the Black leader's strengths and weaknesses.

Myers, Walter D. *Malcolm X: By Any Means Necessary*. New York: Scholastic, 1993. 210pp. YA. In a frank, often impassioned, sympathetic portrait of Malcolm X and his evolution, Myers places the Black leader's development in clear moral and personal terms in the search for self-respect that dictated his ideas.

Rummel, Jack. *Malcolm X*. New York: Chelsea House, 1989. 110pp. MG/YA. This is a solid account of the highlights of Malcolm X's life and ideas set firmly in their historical and cultural context.

Biographical Films and Theatrical Adaptations

Baldwin, James. *One Day When I Was Lost: A Scenario*. New York: Dial Press, 1973. 280pp. Baldwin's filmscript based on Alex Haley's *Autobiography* dramatizes the highlights of Malcolm's life.

A&E Biography Video: Malcolm X (1995). Producer: Ron Steinman. This installment of the Biography series presents a film portrait of Malcolm X, tracing his development as a civil rights and Black Muslim leader through excerpts from his speeches, interviews, a secret recording of an FBI agent trying to bribe Malcolm, and a never-before-seen confession of one of his assassins. Video.

The Greatest (1977). Director: Tom Gries. Muhammad Ali plays himself in this film autobiography, with James Earl Jones portraying Malcolm X. Video.

King (1978). Director: Abby Mann. Television docudrama chronicling King's life, starring Paul Winfield in the title role, with Cicely Tyson as Coretta King and Ossie Davis as Martin Luther King Sr. Dick Anthony Williams appears as Malcolm X. Video.

Malcolm X (1972). Producer: Marvin Worth and Arnold Perl. Adapted from the *Autobiography,* this Oscar-nominated documentary chronicles Malcolm's life and career with his words spoken by James Earl Jones. Video.

Malcolm X (1991). Director: Woodie King Jr. Malcolm X's life and leadership of the Black Muslim movement is chronicled in a documentary narrated by Ossie Davis. Video.

Malcolm X (1992). Director: Spike Lee. Based on the *Autobiography,* Lee's powerful biographical film is animated by strong performances by Denzel Washington as Malcolm, Angela Bassett as his wife Betty Shabazz, and Al Freeman Jr. as Elijah Muhammad. Video.

Malcolm X: Make It Plain (1994). Director: Orlando Bagwell. In this installment of PBS's American Experience series Malcolm's life and legacy are depicted through interviews and archival footage in a definitive film biographical portrait. A companion volume, *Malcolm X: Make It Plain* (New York: Viking, 1994. 245pp.), by William Strickland and Cheryll Greene is also available. Video.

The Real Malcolm X (1992). Producer: CBS News. Hosted by Dan Rather, this documentary examines Malcolm X's life through interviews with Betty Shabazz, Dick Gregory, Andrew Young, and others and contains exclusive footage from some of his speeches. Video.

Roots: The Next Generation (1979). Directors: Georg Stanford Brown and Charles S. Dubin. In the sequel to the 1977 television mini-series, the story of Alex Haley's ancestors is continued from the 1880s to 1967 with Haley's (James Earl Jones) relationship with Malcolm X (Al Freeman Jr.) depicted. Video.

Other Sources

Clarke, John H., ed. *Malcolm X: The Man and His Times.* New York: Macmillan, 1969. 360pp. A valuable reference source, this volume collects both Malcolm's own writings and speeches and the perspective of journalists, critics, and those who knew him to form a revealing chronological portrait.

Randall, Dudley, and Margaret G. Burroughs, eds. *For Malcolm: Poems on the Life and Death of Malcolm X*. Detroit: Broadside Press, 1969. 127pp. This moving collection of poems is organized topically on Malcolm X's life, death, and legacy.

305. STÉPHANE MALLARMÉ
1842–1898

Influential French poet who taught English for a living, Mallarmé was the chief forebear of the Symbolists, a group of French poets and writers who rejected realism in favor of the metaphysical and mysterious. His best-known poems include *The Afternoon of a Faun* (1876), which inspired a composition by Claude Debussy, and *A Throw of the Dice Will Never Eliminate Chance* (1897). A selection of prose, *Divagations,* was published in 1897.

Autobiography and Primary Sources

Selected Letters of Stéphane Mallarmé. Rosemary Lloyd, ed. Chicago: University of Chicago Press, 1988. 238pp. Lloyd's introduction to this collection of the poet's letters provides a useful overview of Mallarmé's life and relationships. The letters concentrate on those that reveal the poet's artistic ideas and thoughts on his life.

Recommended Biographies

Gill, Austin. *The Early Mallarmé.* Oxford: Clarendon Press, 1979–1986. 2 vols. Gill's detailed account of Mallarmé's life up to 1864 is by far the most authoritative examination of the poet's formative years. Meticulously researched, Gill's book is aimed at the specialist and scholar.

Lloyd, Rosemary. *Mallarmé: The Poet and His Circle.* Ithaca, New York: Cornell University Press, 1999. 258pp. Focused by a close reading of Mallarmé's correspondence, Lloyd presents a fascinating literary biography that traces the poet's development, his cultural background, and his literary relationships with such figures as Gide, Valéry, and Morisot.

Millan, Gordon. *A Throw of the Dice: The Life of Stéphane Mallarmé.* New York: Farrar, Straus, 1994. 389pp. Millan's is a well-researched portrait that makes accessible to the general reader the man and his poetry. Synthesizing modern scholarship and making use of new documentary evidence, the book traces Mallarmé's artistic development and the connections with his personal experience that reveal a complex human figure, handled with understanding and sympathy.

Other Biographical Studies

Fowlie, Wallace. *Mallarmé.* Chicago: University of Chicago Press, 1953. 299pp. Fowlie devotes only a small fraction of his critical study to a consideration of Mallarmé's biography before moving on to a detailed study of individual poems.

Mauron, Charles. *Introduction to the Psychoanalysis of Mallarmé.* Berkeley: University of California Press, 1963. 280pp. The work of the founder of the French school of psychocriticism locates the key to understanding the poet in his early loss of his mother and sister. These traumatic experiences are then used as the lens to view his work and mature experiences.

Michaud, Guy. *Mallarmé.* New York: New York University Press, 1965. 180pp. Michaud's critical study of Mallarmé's poetry includes useful summary commentary on his life and experiences.

St. Aubyn, Frederic C. *Stéphane Mallarmé.* 1969. Revised ed. New York: Twayne, 1989. 170pp. St. Aubyn's biographical section is brief but covers the essential points before supplying a critical overview of his major poetry and prose. Serves as a valuable introduction for the student and motivated general reader.

306. EDOUARD MANET
1832–1883

A celebrated French painter who profoundly influenced the Impressionists, Manet was born in Paris and went to sea to avoid studying law. On his return, he studied art with painter Thomas Couture. Partly influenced by Goya and Velázquez, Manet introduced a new pictorial language, and his works, particularly *Déjuner sur l'herbe* and *Olympia* (both 1863), were often severely attacked by both critics and the public. However, he commanded a strong following among fellow painters and was defended by Emile Zola. By 1900 his techniques were understood and appreciated, and his works were hung in the Louvre.

Autobiography and Primary Sources

Manet by Himself. Juliet Wilson-Boreau, ed. Boston: Little, Brown, 1991. 320pp. This useful volume collects letters, Manet's comments on art, and recorded recollections of his contemporaries, grouped by time periods.

Manet by Himself and His Contemporaries. Pierre Courthion and Pierre Cailler, eds. New York: Roy, 1960. 238pp. This valuable collection brings together many primary documents, a selection of Manet's correspondence as well as reminiscences from his contemporaries, such as Baudelaire, Zola, and Mallarmé. The various materials are arranged chronologically with connecting extracts from a number of biographies and critical studies, many unavailable in English.

Recommended Biographies

Brombert, Beth A. *Edouard Manet: Rebel in a Frock Coat.* Boston: Little, Brown, 1996. 505pp. Brombert supplies a provocative, richly detailed portrait of the artist and his age with a number of fresh and stimulating insights into Manet's complexity and social milieu, tracing the sources of the painter's contradictions and the duality between his public and private personas.

Perutz, Vivien. *Edouard Manet.* Lewisburg, Pennsylvania: Bucknell University Press, 1993. 237pp. Written for the nonspecialist, the book features a brief account of Manet's life and times followed by a chapter on the painter's aesthetics and a detailed critical analysis of his works that incorporates recent research and the various controversies surrounding the artist and his creations.

Other Biographical Studies

Bataille, Georges. *Manet.* New York: Skira, 1955. 135pp. A succinct biographical and critical study, Bataille's slim volume serves as a reliable and useful introduction to the man and his artistry.

Cachin, Françoise, and Charles S. Moffett. *Manet: 1832–83.* New York: Abrams, 1983. 160pp. This exhibition catalogue includes a critical analysis of Manet's oeuvre and a portrait of the artist's personality and temperament, as well as a detailed chronology, biographical details reflecting recent research, and unpublished letters to Zola.

Cachin, Françoise. *Manet.* New York: Holt, 1991. 160pp. Designed for nonspecialists, Cachin locates Manet in his social, political, and artistic contexts with numerous photos of principal works, followed by a detailed chronology.

Duret, Théodore. *Manet and the French Impressionists.* Philadelphia: Lippincott, 1912. 256pp. The first detailed biography of Manet presents a chronological survey of his career and a firsthand portrait of the artist, making use of letters exchanged between Manet and the author. Duret provides a valuable vantage point for seeing the artist clearly, though the facts are not all reliable, and Duret's interpretation of his friend has been qualified by later, more scholarly accounts.

Perruchot, Henri. *Manet.* Cleveland: World, 1962. 296pp. Featuring new material and reflecting modern scholarship, Perruchot adds considerable details concerning Manet's early years. In Perruchot's view, Manet should be regarded as the true father of modern art, a revolutionary despite his facade of upper-class propriety. The book presents a credible picture of the complex make up of Manet's personality.

Fictional Portraits

Stone, Irving. *Depths of Glory.* Garden City, New York: Doubleday, 1955. 653pp. This biographical novel on the life of Camille Pissarro features the appearance of a number of contemporary artists, including Monet, Cézanne, Gauguin, Degas, Seurat, Cassatt, and Manet.

Recommended Juvenile Biographies

Harris, Nathaniel. *The Life and Works of Manet.* New York: Shooting Star Press, 1994. 79pp. MG. Harris covers the highlights of Manet's life and artistic career and relates his artistry to his era and influences.

Spence, David. *Manet: A New Realism.* Hauppauge, New York: Barron's, 1997. 32pp. MG. Part of Barron's Great Artists series, this is sensible introduction to both the man and his art.

Wright, Patricia. *Manet.* New York: Dorling Kindersley, 1993. 64pp. MG. One of the innovatively designed Eyewitness Books, this informative visual guide to Manet's life and art includes reproductions of the paintings and sketches with extensive information in captions and sidebars.

Biographical Films and Theatrical Adaptations

Edouard Manet: Painter of Modern Life (1983). Director: Judith Wechsler. Examines Manet's life and works and interprets his major paintings using the artist's own words and those of friends, including Zola, Baudelaire, Mallarmé, and others. Video.

307. THOMAS MANN
1875–1955

An outstanding German novelist of the twentieth century, Mann was born in Lübeck and was the younger brother of novelist Heinrich Mann. An outspoken critic of fascism, Mann left Hitler's Germany for Switzerland (1933), was deprived of his German citizenship by the Nazis (1936), settled in the United States. (1938), and became a U.S. citizen (1944). He returned to Switzerland in 1953. His works include *Buddenbrooks* (1901), *Death in Venice* (1912), *The Magic Mountain* (1924), and the tetralogy *Joseph and His Brothers* (1933–1944). He was awarded the 1929 Nobel Prize in Literature.

Autobiography and Primary Sources

Diaries. New York: Abrams, 1982. 471pp. The publication of Mann's surviving diaries from the periods 1918–1921 and 1933–1955 have resulted in a radical reassessment of Mann's life and character and new interpretations by biographers and critics. No other primary source gets closer to the man and his complex emotional and intellectual makeup.

Letters of Thomas Mann, 1889–1955. Richard and Clara Winston, eds. New York: Knopf, 1970. 690pp. Mann's letters offer the reader a strong sense of immediacy on the personal, political, social, and cultural issues that shaped the writer.

A Sketch of My Life. New York: Knopf, 1961. 87pp. Written after receiving the Nobel Prize in 1929, Mann's autobiographical account chronicles his life up to that point, including important details on the genesis of his books, his working methods, and views on various private and public matters.

Story of a Novel: The Genesis of Doctor Faustus. New York: Knopf, 1961. 242pp. Mann's activities during the writing of *Doctor Faustus* in the 1940s are recounted with insights about the book's composition and Mann's relationship with the German émigré community between 1943 and 1947.

Recommended Biographies

Hayman, Ronald. *Thomas Mann: A Biography*. New York: Scribner, 1995. 672pp. Making use of Mann's diaries and papers unsealed 20 years after his death, this is a detailed, comprehensive, almost daily account of Mann's life. Hayman penetrates the writer's various public and protective masks and demonstrates how his often tormented inner life was reflected through his fictional characters.

Prater, Donald A. *Thomas Mann: A Life*. New York: Oxford University Press, 1995. 554pp. Prater stresses the development of Mann's political ideas in a comprehensive, intimate study that details Mann's shift from a German nationalist during World War I to an opponent of Hitler and proponent of international humanism. The book largely ignores Mann's fiction and, therefore, interestingly supplements more literary biographies such as Hayman's and Winston's.

Winston, Richard. *Thomas Mann: The Making of an Artist 1875–1911*. New York: Knopf, 1981. 325pp. Written by the translator of Mann's *Letters* and *Diaries* this excellently written and documented account traces Mann's life and development up to the year he wrote *Death in Venice*. Expertly detailing the autobiographical basis of Mann's fiction and his intellectual influences, Winston's critical biography is one of the best available on the early years and Mann's development as an artist.

Other Biographical Studies

Hamilton, Nigel. *The Brothers Mann: The Lives of Heinrich and Thomas Mann, 1871–1950*. New Haven, Connecticut: Yale University Press, 1979. 422pp. This dual biographical study of Thomas and his elder brother relies mainly on their correspondence to chronicle their often stormy relationship

and the various artistic and political issues that united and divided them.

Heilbut, Anthony. *Thomas Mann: Eros and Literature*. New York: Knopf, 1996. 636pp. Drawing extensively on the suggestions of homosexual desires revealed in Mann's diaries, Heibut offers a psychosexual interpretation of Mann's life. At times confusingly organized and free-ranging in pursuit of his theme, Heilbut's study is also witty and well documented with a consistent, though somewhat reductive, view of Mann's psychological complexes and their relation to his works.

Léser, Esther H. *Thomas Mann's Short Fiction: An Intellectual Biography*. Cranbury, New Jersey: Associated University Presses, 1989. 349pp. Léser approaches Mann's emotional and intellectual development through a close critical reading of all his short fiction, drawing heavily on Mann's letters and diaries.

Mann, Erika. *The Last Year of Thomas Mann*. New York: Farrar, Straus, 1958. 119pp. This tribute to the author's father provides invaluable firsthand data on Mann's final year of life.

Mann, Katia. *Unwritten Memories*. Elisabeth Plessen and Michael Mann, eds. New York: Knopf, 1975. 165pp. In a transcription of television interviews with Mann's wife at the age of 90, these recollections supply interesting details on the sources for *Death in Venice* and *The Magic Mountain* and sketches of the Mann family and circle of friends.

Reich-Ranicki, Marcel. *Thomas Mann and His Family*. London: Collins, 1989. 230pp. The author supplies a family portrait, with profiles of Thomas, Heinrich, Erika, Klaus, Golo, and Katia Mann.

Biographical Films and Theatrical Adaptations

Thomas Mann (1987). Producer: David Thomas and Nigel Wattis. Mann is one of 10 modern writers profiled in this documentary series originally shown on British television. Video.

Other Sources

Bürgin, Hans, and Hans-Otto Mayer. *Thomas Mann: A Chronicle of His Life*. University: University of Alabama Press, 1969. 290pp. Detailing the main facts of Mann's life and literary career in an extensive monthly and even daily chronology utilizing quotes from Mann himself, this work serves as a valuable reference source.

308. KATHERINE MANSFIELD
1888–1923

New Zealand-born British author, Mansfield is considered a master of the short-story form. She first achieved recognition with the story collections, *Bliss* (1920) and *The Garden Party* (1922). *Novels and Novelists* (1930) is a compilation of Mansfield's critical essays. Her collected stories were published in 1937.

Autobiography and Primary Sources

Collected Letters of Katherine Mansfield. Vincent O'Sullivan and Margaret Scott, eds. New York: Oxford University Press, 1984–1996. 4 vols. A one-volume collection of Mansfield's correspondence is available in *Selected Letters*. Vincent O'Sullivan, ed. (New York: Oxford University Press, 1989. 320pp.). Mansfield's letters are indispensable as a biographical source, providing revealing insights into her relationships and personal struggles.

Journal of Katherine Mansfield. J. Middleton Murry, ed. New York: Knopf, 1927. 255pp. Scholars have demonstrated that the journal is a contrivance put together by Murry from a variety of sources and cannot be trusted as the autobiographical source it purports to be. However, with its unreliability in mind, the journal provides a fragmentary record of Mansfield's impressions and self-analysis, and a heartbreaking history of personal suffering.

Recommended Biographies

Alpers, Antony. *The Life of Katherine Mansfield*. New York: Viking, 1980. 466pp. Drawing on "20 times more material" than his earlier biography, Alpers has written the fullest account of Mansfield's life available. The book is a judicious, detailed account of both the woman and the writer. His earlier *Katherine Mansfield: A Biography* (New York: Knopf, 1953. 376pp.) is less authoritative, and, as the author admits in his later study, was written to spare the feelings of those still living who were associated with the writer.

Tomalin, Claire. *Katherine Mansfield: A Secret Life*. New York: Knopf, 1988. 292pp. Tomalin's more selective feminist view of the writer is less detailed than Alpers but emphasizes certain aspects of Mansfield's life, such as her medical history and her relationship with Ida Constance Baker and D.H. Lawrence, that Tomalin suggests Alpers underestimated. In Tomalin's view, Mansfield is shown as an emblematic suffering artist and woman.

Other Biographical Studies

Baker, Ida, and Georgina Joysmith. *Katherine Mansfield: The Memories of L.M.* Taplinger. London: Joseph, 1971. 240pp. The recollections of a close companion of Mansfield provide a valuable firsthand, though limited, account of the writer.

Berkman, Sylvia. *Katherine Mansfield: A Critical Study*. New Haven, Connecticut: Yale University Press, 1951. 246pp. Concentrating on Mansfield's artistic development, this critical biography demonstrates the relationship between the author's life and her use of it in her works.

Boddy, Gillian. *Katherine Mansfield: The Woman and the Writer*. New York: Penguin, 1988. 323pp. Boddy's solid introduction to the writer and her work includes a biographical portrait, extracts from Mansfield's letters and journals, a critical essay, and a collection of representative works. Boddy helps demystify Mansfield, revealing a fully recognizable, human figure.

Daly, Saralyn R. *Katherine Mansfield.* New York: Macmillan, 1994. 168pp. Daly supplies a brief but insightful critical biography that challenges conventional wisdom about Mansfield's literary development, based on the author's close study of the early drafts of her major stories.

Fullbrook, Kate. *Katherine Mansfield.* Bloomington: Indiana University Press, 1986. 146pp. Part of the Key Women Writers series, Fullbrook offers mainly a critical study of Mansfield's artistic development from a feminist perspective.

Hanson, Claire, and Andrew Gurr. *Katherine Mansfield.* New York: St. Martin's, 1981. 146pp. In a brief critical study, Mansfield's life is used chiefly as a background to her stories and for an understanding of her literary personality and the development of her aesthetic principles.

Mantz, R.E., and J. Middleton Murry. *The Life of Katherine Mansfield.* London: Constable, 1933. 349pp. The earliest biography of the writer, Mantz helped form Mansfield's image that later biographers have challenged. Based in part on interviews with Mansfield's contemporaries, Mantz also relied on Murry's selective and expurgated editions of Mansfield's letters and journals.

Meyers, Jeffrey. *Katherine Mansfield: A Biography.* New York: New Directions, 1980. 306pp. Meyers's scholarly study focuses on Mansfield's personal relationships in a psychological portrait that presents a darker, more complex, and less attractive view of the writer than other studies. The book is less detailed on the cultural background of Mansfield's times.

Biographical Novels

White, Nelia G. *Daughter of Time.* New York: Macmillan, 1942. 272pp. A vivid, convincing, mainly faithful portrait of the artist in a fictionalized biography that chronicles Mansfield's life from her childhood in New Zealand to her death. White is less successful in creating believable portraits of the men in Mansfield's life.

Recommended Juvenile Biographies

Phillimore, Jane. *Katherine Mansfield.* Vero Beach, Florida: Rourke, 1990. 110pp. MG. Phillimore provides a helpful overview of Mansfield's life and writing career, with a critical introduction that stresses her originality as a short story writer.

Steinbauer, Janine. *Katherine Mansfield.* Mankato, Minnesota: Creative Company, 1995. 64pp. MG. This is a brief introduction to Mansfield's career and artistry, with excerpts from her works.

Biographical Films and Theatrical Adaptations

Priest of Love (1981). Director: Christopher Miles. Ian McKellen portrays D.H. Lawrence in this drama concerning the furor surrounding the publication of *Lady Chatterley's Lover* and the novelist's struggle with tuberculosis. Janet Suzman co-stars as Frieda Lawrence and Adrienne Burgess appears as Katherine Mansfield. Video.

309. MAO ZEDONG (MAO TSE-TUNG)
1893–1976

The founder and leader of the People's Republic of China, Mao was the son of an educated Hunanese peasant. He was trained in Chinese classics and received a modern education. One of the original members of the Chinese Communist Party, Mao was ousted from the party's central committee after leading the "Autumn Harvest Uprising" (1927), which was crushed by the Kuomintang. Mao led the Red Army on the Long March (1934–1935) to Shaanxi province to escape encirclement by Chiang Kai-shek's Kuomintang forces. The Communists allied themselves with the Kuomintang against the Japanese during the Second Sino-Japanese War (1937–1945). The post-World War II civil war resulted in victory for the Communists, and Mao became chairman of the newly established People's Republic. He launched the Great Leap Forward (1958), a failed economic program, and the Cultural Revolution (1966–1976) to solidify his ideological line and rid the party of revisionists. During the 1970s he favored a measure of détente with the West. His meeting with President Nixon (1972) signaled improved relations with the United States.

Autobiography and Primary Sources

Mao's writings, including articles, speeches, and letters, are available in a number of volumes, including *Selected Works* (Peking: Foreign Language Press, 1961–1967. 5 vols.); *Mao Papers: Anthology and Bibliography.* Jerome Ch'en, ed. (New York: Oxford University Press, 1970. 221pp.); and *Chairman Mao Talks to the People.* Stuart Schram, ed. (New York: Pantheon, 1975. 352pp.), a collection of Mao's speeches and letters that covers the period 1956 to 1971.

The Secret Speeches of Chairman Mao. Roderick MacFarquhar, et al, eds. Cambridge, Massachusetts: Harvard University Press, 1989. 561pp. This collection of Mao's speeches offers insights into both the Chinese leader's political ideas and public persona.

Recommended Biographies

Ch'en, Jerome. *Mao and the Chinese Revolution.* New York: Oxford University Press, 1965. 419pp. In an outstanding, well-documented analysis of Mao's life and times, Ch'en places the Chinese leader in the context of other Chinese revolutionaries and traces how he was able to put his ideas into practice. Correcting a number of factual errors and misjudgments about Mao, the book provides a balanced portrait and one of the fullest appreciations of Mao's achievements and complex character.

Rice, Edward E. *Mao's Way.* Berkeley: University of California Press, 1972. 596pp. In a detailed chronological narrative of Mao's career from his birth through 1971, Rice allows the facts to speak for themselves instead of providing analysis or interpretation. The result is one of the most comprehensively documented histories available.

Schram, Stuart. *Mao Tse-tung.* New York: Simon & Schuster, 1966. 351pp. Schram's political biography has long maintained its standing as the most

perceptive and judicious full-length biography. Considered a classic, the book provides an outstanding short history of Mao and the Chinese Revolution. Readers interested in the development of Mao's political ideology should consult Schram's *The Political Thought of Mao Tse-tung* (New York: Praeger, 1963. 479pp.) that includes translations of excerpts from Mao's writings.

Short, Philip. *Mao: A Life.* New York: Holt, 2000. 782pp. Short's is a masterful biography, incorporating revealing, recently available Chinese sources to shed considerable light on Mao's early life and his complex personality. Vivid as well as judicious in its assessment, Short makes a strong bid for having written the definitive Mao biography.

Spence, Jonathan D. *Mao Zedong.* New York: Viking, 1999. 160pp. Spence's compact biographical profile incorporates a good deal of modern scholarship to form an excellent, accessible account of Mao's development against a vivid historical and cultural background.

Other Biographical Studies

Breslin, Shaun. *Mao.* New York: Longman, 1998. 224pp. Part of the Profiles in Power series, this is a brief overview of Mao's life and political career. Sometimes overly compressed with assertions unproven, the book serves as a solid introduction to modern Chinese history and Mao's considerable role in shaping it.

Chou, Eric. *Mao Tse-tung: The Man and the Myth.* New York: Stein and Day, 1982. 289pp. In an overall hostile assessment, Chou, a Chinese journalist who broke with Mao in the 1960s, stresses the shortcomings of the man and his leadership.

Cohen, Arthur A. *The Communism of Mao Tse-tung.* Chicago: University of Chicago Press, 1964. 210pp. In a well-documented, judicious account of Mao's intellectual development, Cohen usefully separates the myths from the facts surrounding the Chinese leader, locating his greatness in his pragmatic talents and tactical brilliance rather than the originality of his ideas.

Devillers, Philippe. *Mao.* New York: Schocken, 1969. 317pp. This useful volume collects excerpts from Mao's writings, with a succinct portrait of the man and political leader.

Fitzgerald, C. P. *Mao Tse-tung and China.* New York: Holmes and Meier, 1976. 166pp. Less interested in Mao the man than his achievements as a political leader, Fitzgerald's study is a succinct history of the Chinese Communist Party from 1949 to 1975. The author's contention that Mao was one of the greatest figures in the twentieth century lacks objectivity, making no distinction between Mao's early and later career.

Han, Suyin. *The Morning Deluge: Mao Tse-tung and the Chinese Revolution 1893–1954.* Boston: Little, Brown, 1972. 571pp.; *Wind in the Tower: Mao Tse-tung and the Chinese Revolution 1949–1975.* Boston: Little, Brown, 1976. 404pp. Portraying Mao alternately as a sage and a saint, Han's two-volume popular biography lacks critical perspective and documentation, reading more like biographical fiction with a dramatic vividness but with a selection of details to support her positive thesis, ignoring less flattering evidence.

Hsiao, Yü. *Mao Tse-tung and I Were Beggars*. Syracuse, New York: Syracuse University Press, 1959. 266pp. Supplying virtually everything we know about Mao as a young man between the ages of 19 and 28, Hsiao, Mao's schoolmate, offers his recollections, particularly the pair's travels as itinerant beggars in 1917.

Karnow, Stanley. *Mao and China*. 1972. Revised ed. New York: Penguin, 1990. 573pp. Karnow focuses on the Cultural Revolution and Mao's central role in it with a revealing portrait of Mao at the end of his long career.

Leys, Simon. *The Chairman's New Clothes: Mao and the Cultural Revolution*. New York: St. Martin's, 1977. 261pp. Like Karnow, Leys's focus is on the Cultural Revolution, seen as a tragic climax of Mao's limited vision of revolutionary reform.

Li, Zhizui. *The Private Life of Chairman Mao*. New York: Random House, 1994. 682pp. Written by Mao's personal physician from 1954 to the Chinese leader's death, the book provides an unprecedented firsthand, intimate portrait of Mao at the height of his power. Li includes a number of recorded conversations with Mao on political and personal matters and details of his growing paranoia and secretive personal life.

Lifton, Robert J. *Revolutionary Immortality: Mao Tse-tung and the Chinese Cultural Revolution*. New York: Random House, 1968. 178pp. Although not a full-scale psychobiography, Lifton examines the psychological basis for the Cultural Revolution, understandable as a form of Mao's survivor paranoia and grandiosity.

MacGregor-Hastie, Roy. *The Red Barbarians: The Life and Times of Mao Tse-tung*. New York: T.V. Boardman, 1961. 224pp. This assessment of the Chinese Revolution and Mao is marred by a lack of objectivity and errors of fact. The book is not reliable as a biographical or historical reference.

Meisner, Maurice. *Mao's China*. New York: Free Press, 1977. 416pp. This is a detailed, scholarly account of Mao's activities as Chinese leader after the Communist victory in 1949. Different from accounts that stress Mao's years in opposition, Meisner presents one of the fullest analyses of Mao's achievements and shortcomings in power.

Pálóczi-Horváth, Gyorgy. *Mao Tse-tung: Emperor of the Blue Ants*. Garden City, New York: Doubleday, 1963. 343pp. This political biography chronicles Mao's development from his peasant beginning to 1962, finding much to admire in the guerilla leader and much to censure once Mao had gained control. The book features new details from previously unavailable Russian documents.

Payne, Robert. *Mao Tse-tung: Ruler of Red China*. New York: Schuman, 1950. 303pp. Revised as *Portrait of a Revolutionary: Mao Tse-tung* (New York: Abelard-Schuman, 1961. 343pp.) and *Mao Tse-tung* (New York: Weybright & Talle, 1969. 343pp.). Drawing on an interview with Mao in 1946, Payne locates Mao in the context of Chinese history but occasionally indulges in imaginative flights of fancy in a literary rather than a factual interpretation of Mao's character and career.

Pye, Lucian W. *Mao Tse-tung: The Man in the Leader*. New York: Basic Books, 1976. 346pp. Pye's provocative psychological examination attempts to join the private man and revolutionary leader, uncovering the roots of his behavior and motivation in his early childhood experiences. Since the details of Mao's private life are so scanty, they provide a very weak foundation for many of Pye's interpretations. However, the book does display Mao's emotional complexities better than most other biographical accounts.

Salisbury, Harrison E. *The Long March: The Untold Story*. New York: Harper & Row, 1985. 419pp. Based on interviews with survivors, Chinese historians, and the author's own retracing of portions of the Long March route in 1984, Salisbury supplies the fullest account of the military retreat that helped formed Mao's heroic reputation.

Snow, Edgar. *Red Star over China*. 1938. Revised ed. New York: Grove Press, 1968. 543pp. Snow's early and highly regarded portrait of Mao features extracts from his interviews with the Chinese leader and provides indispensable autobiographical details of Mao's early life. Snow issued three later reports on Mao and the course of the Chinese revolution based on visits to China in 1960 and 1970, which includes interviews with Chairman Mao: *The Other Side of the River: Red China Today* (New York: Random House, 1962. 810pp.), revised as *Red China Today* (New York: Random House, 1970. 749pp.), and *The Long Revolution* (New York: Random House, 1972. 269pp.).

Terrill, Ross. *Mao: A Biography*. New York: Harper & Row, 1980. 481pp. Painstakingly researched and intended for the general reader, this reliable, comprehensive account of Mao's life and political career balances both his achievements and failures. In a clear-eyed assessment, Terrill admires the early revolutionary but not the ruler of the People's Republic, a role that, according to the author, ran counter to Mao's strengths as a man and political leader.

Terrill, Ross. *The White-Boned Demon: A Biography of Madame Mao Zedong*. New York: Morrow, 1984. 446pp. Terrill's anecdotal biography paints a harshly critical portrait of Mao's fourth wife and the couple's relationship. In the author's view, the Cultural Revolution was largely attributed to Jiang Ching's vindictiveness and retribution for the wrongs she felt she received from party officials in the 1930s. Although many of the book's sources are clearly Jiang's enemies, Terrill's overall characterization of her seems consistent and convincing, if individual details are questionable.

Uhalley, Stephen Jr. *Mao Tse-tung: A Critical Biography*. New York: F. Watts, 1975. 233pp. Treating Mao's life from his boyhood, Uhalley's biography is best on the details of Mao's career prior to 1949. Following the Communists' victory, the author loses his critical focus, glossing over the shortcomings of Mao's years in power.

Wilson, Dick. *The People's Emperor, Mao: A Biography of Mao Tse-tung*. Garden City, New York: Doubleday, 1980. 530pp. In an anecdotal biography, the author attempts to humanize Mao and to join his personal and political lives using excerpts from his writings, speeches, conversations, and the views of associates. An earthy figure with clear peasant roots emerges, but the book is only partially successful in integrating all facets of Mao's personality and beliefs into a coherent whole.

Biographical Novels

Min, Anchee. *Becoming Madame Mao*. Boston: Houghton Mifflin, 2000. 337pp. Mao's wife, Jiang Ching, tells the story of her life from her childhood, through her career as an actress, meeting Mao and accompanying him to the pinnacle of power in the Communist victory, and gaining her reputation as the "White-Boned Demon" of the Cultural Revolution to be reviled by the Chinese people in her unsuccessful drive to succeed her husband. The novel offers a fascinating look at the couple's life together and a human portrait of a figure who has often been seen as a monster.

Shih, Benjamin. *Mao: A Young Man from the Yangtze Valley*. Port Washington, New York: Ashley Books, 1974. 320pp. This fictionalized account is told from the perspective of an imagined daughter born in 1935 after the Long March in a mixture of fact and imagination.

Fictional Portraits

Bosse, Malcolm J. *Fire in Heaven*. New York: Simon & Schuster, 1985. 654pp. In the author's sequel to *The Warlord* (1985), Mao's rise to power is dramatized as the background to this fictional story.

Cordell, Alexander. *The Dream and the Destiny*. Garden City, New York: Doubleday, 1975. 368pp. Mao's leadership on the Long March is seen from the perspective of a young medical student.

Grant, Maxwell. *Blood Red Rose*. New York: Macmillan, 1986. 418pp. Set in China during the 1930s, a young American doctor must flee Shanghai and finds herself accompanying Mao on the Long March.

Tuten, Frederic. *The Adventures of Mao on the Long March*. New York: Marion Boyars, 1997. 121pp. Tuten's poetic, meditative novel presents Mao's thoughts and doubts on the revolution he tries to manage and its implication for the people he is leading on the Long March.

Recommended Juvenile Biographies

Garza, Hedda. *Mao Zedong*. New York: Chelsea House, 1988. 112pp. MG/YA. A solid historical biography that relates Mao's career in the context of modern Chinese history.

Marrin, Albert. *Mao Tse-tung and His China*. New York: Viking, 1989. 282pp. MG/YA. The two sides of Mao's complex character—heroic revolutionary and cruel ideologue—fail to coalesce satisfactorily, but the book serves as a readable overview of modern Chinese history.

Stefoff, Rebecca. *Mao Zedong: Founder of the People's Republic of China*. Brookfield, Connecticut: Millbrook Press, 1996. 128pp. MG. In a well-written biography of Mao's life and career, Stefoff covers the highlights in a balanced assessment.

Biographical Films and Theatrical Adaptations

Kundun (1997). Director: Martin Scorsese. Robert Lin portrays Mao in Scorsese's lyrical film of the fourteenth Dalai Lama culminating in his confrontation with the Chinese government. Video.

Mao: Long March to Power (1979). Director: Don Thompson. A film look at Mao's struggle for power, culminating in the 1949 Communist victory. Video.

Mao: Organized Chaos (1978). Director: Don Thompson. Based on archival footage, this is a documentary look at Mao's years as Chinese ruler. Video.

Mao Tse-tung (1979). Producer: David L. Wolper. Narrated by Mike Wallace, Mao's life is described with an emphasis on his military and political struggles. Video.

Nixon (1995). Director: Oliver Stone. In Stone's controversial biographical portrait of Richard Nixon, Anthony Hopkins stars and Mao is played by Ric Young during the historic Nixon visit to China. Video.

Other Sources

Wilson, Dick, ed. *Mao Tse-tung in the Scales of History: A Preliminary Assessment.* New York: Cambridge University Press, 1977. 331pp. This valuable collection of critical essays by a number of leading Mao scholars presents views on various aspects of Mao's life and thought.

310. MARIE ANTOINETTE
1755–1793

The daughter of Austrian Archduchess Maria Theresa and the Holy Roman Emperor Francis I, Marie Antoinette was married (1770) to the French dauphin, who became Louis XVI (1774). She was unhappy in the marriage, which remained unconsummated for seven years. Unpopular for her attempts to influence French foreign policy in favor of Austria, Marie Antoinette also became notorious for her extravagance, most notably in the scandal known as the Affair of the Diamond Necklace, and aroused hostility for her indifference to economic problems. During the French Revolution, she and the royal family tried to escape but were apprehended (1791) at Varennes. She attempted negotiations with revolutionary leaders and at the same time secretly tried to arrange Austrian intervention. She was convicted of treason by the Revolutionary Tribunal and guillotined (1793).

Autobiography and Primary Sources

Secrets of Marie Antoinette: A Collection of Letters. Olivier Bernier, ed. New York: Doubleday, 1986. 326pp. Marie Antoinette's correspondence with her mother Maria Theresa, Empress of Austria, from the former's departure for France in 1770 until her mother's death in 1780 reveals Marie Antoinette's lack of true friends, her flaunting of court etiquette at Versailles, and her meddling in politics.

Recommended Biographies

Cronin, Vincent. *Louis and Antoinette.* New York: Morrow, 1974. 445pp. Cronin's dual biography of the king and queen provides a revisionist interpretation in which both Louis XVI and Marie Antoinette are sympathetically depicted as innocent victims and Antoinette a kind, sincere queen with a genuine concern for the welfare of her people. A study with considerable psychological depth and believability, Cronin's examination is nevertheless guilty of one-sidedness in its presentation, emphasizing the positive and hurrying over the less flattering evidence.

Erickson, Carolly. *To the Scaffold: The Life of Marie Antoinette.* New York: Morrow, 1991. 384pp. Beautifully written and thoroughly researched, Erickson's book offers a balanced, detailed account of Marie Antoinette's life with an emphasis on the personal aspects of her everyday activities.

Haslip, Joan. *Marie Antoinette.* New York: Weidenfeld and Nicolson, 1988. 306pp. A lively and mostly accurate portrait of the queen, Haslip's qualified sympathy avoids either excessive praise or blame. The book serves as a good introduction to the personality of the queen but is not as strong on the historical and cultural context that shaped her life.

Lever, Evelyne. *Marie Antoinette: The Last Queen of France.* New York: Farrar, Straus, 2000. 352pp. Lever, drawing on diaries, letters, and firsthand accounts, has crafted a fast-paced, historical-biographical narrative that captures with skill Marie Antoinette's personality, relationships, and the events that shaped her destiny.

Zweig, Stefan. *Marie Antoinette: The Portrait of an Average Woman.* New York: Viking, 1933. 476pp. In a detailed, psychological study, Zweig challenges the conventional view of Marie Antoinette depicting her as an ordinary woman forced by the French Revolution into playing a heroic role. Emphasizing her human qualities, Zweig restores a good deal of sympathy to his subject, though many of his more romantic interpretations have been challenged by later biographers.

Other Biographical Studies

Asquith, Annunziata. *Marie Antoinette.* New York: Taplinger, 1976. 232pp. A highly readable, illustrated life, the author chronicles the events of Marie Antoinette's life from her childhood to her execution in a succinct narrative that vividly captures the highlights.

Castelot, André. *Queen of France.* New York: Harper, 1957. 434pp. In a documentary study that largely eschews interpretation, Castelot provides a nearly day-by-day account of Marie Antoinette's life from age 14 to her death, interweaving recollections and reconstructed conversations from a variety of contemporary sources.

Farr, Evelyn. *Marie-Antoinette and Count Axel Fersen: The Untold Love Story.* Chester Springs, Pennsylvania: Dufour Editions, 1995. 256pp. Farr, like Loomis, attempts to untangle the mysteries surrounding the relationship between Marie Antoinette and Count Fersen with contrary interpretations. Although Loomis concludes that there is no

evidence that the couple were in fact lovers, Farr asserts that theirs was a deeply passionate love affair.

Hearsey, John. *Marie Antoinette.* New York: Dutton, 1972. 296pp. Written for the general reader, Hearsey supplies a personal history of the queen, including reconstructed conversations from a variety of undocumented sources. A reliable introduction, the book includes a historical appendix listing the events of Antoinette's life along with corresponding historical and cultural events.

Huisman, Philippe, and Marguerite Jallut. *Marie Antoinette.* New York: Viking, 1971. 249pp. In a lavishly illustrated biography, the authors set the events of Marie Antoinette's life and her personality in the context of the cultural values of her times.

Loomis, Stanley. *The Fatal Friendship: Marie Antoinette, Count Fersen, and the Flight to Varennes.* Garden City, New York: Doubleday, 1972. 367pp. Focusing on the various questions surrounding Antoinette's relationship with the Swedish nobleman, Fersen, Loomis addresses whether the pair were in fact lovers, whether Louis was aware of their relationship, and what part Fersen played in the royal family's flight. A vivid and convincing reconstruction of events with some invented dialogue, the book provides considerable psychological depth to a portrait of the queen.

Mayer, Dorothy. *Marie Antoinette: The Tragic Queen.* New York: Coward-McCann, 1969. 385pp. Mayer offers a sympathetic portrait of the queen in an enjoyable, full-length biography. Without overstressing the scandalous aspects of Marie Antoinette's life, Mayer keeps her sharply in focus through the events of the French Revolution.

Seward, Desmond. *Marie Antoinette.* New York: St. Martin's, 1981. 297pp. Although more willing than Cronin to consider Marie Antoinette's flaws, Seward argues that instead of being an incompetent meddler in state affairs she was the only important female political figure to emerge during the French Revolution and stresses her political savvy, forced by a weak husband to save the throne for her son.

Thomas, Chantal. *The Wicked Queen: The Origins of the Myth of Marie-Antoinette.* New York: Zone Books, 1999. 224pp. In a revealing analysis, Thomas traces the various stages in the formation of the negative myths surrounding Marie Antoinette. Separating the facts from the legends, Thomas exposes the motives of the pamphleteers' campaign to discredit the foreign-born queen.

Biographical Novels

Beck, L. Adams. *The Empress of Hearts.* New York: Dodd, Mead, 1928. 300pp. Beck's is a loving depiction of Marie Antoinette's life and character, too idealized to be useful to the reader looking for more than a glamorous, romantic treatment.

Chapman, Hester W. *Fear No More.* New York: Reynal, 1968. 349pp. The fall of the king and queen are seen from the limited, though intimate, perceptions of their young son, the dauphin.

Dumas, Alexandre. *Chevalier de Maison-Rouge.* Boston: Little, Brown, 1894. 512pp. Marie Antoinette's end is dramatized in this blend of historical fact and swashbuckling adventure as efforts to rescue the queen fail, and she meets her fate on the guillotine.

Dumas, Alexandre. *The Countess de Charny: Or, the Fall of the French Monarchy.* New York: T.B. Peterson, 1853. 392pp. The royal family's flight to Varennes is depicted in this exciting narrative account of their failed attempt to reach freedom.

Dumas, Alexandre. *The Queen's Necklace.* 1848. Reprint ed. New York: Collier, 1902. 426pp. In a fictional retelling of the diamond necklace scandal that helped discredit the queen in the public view, Dumas embroiders the historical facts with his characteristic entertaining invention.

Harding, Bertita. *Farewell 'Toinette: A Footnote to History.* Indianapolis: Bobbs-Merrill, 1938. 261pp. Harding offers a fictional reconstruction of Marie Antoinette's wedding journey from Vienna to Versailles in a mixture of fantasy, farce, and history.

Holt, Victoria. *The Queen's Confession.* Garden City, New York: Doubleday, 1968. 430pp. Marie Antoinette tells her own story in the form of her memoirs. Solidly researched, the novel remains close to history and provides a remarkable recreation of the period and a convincing, human portrait of the queen.

Kenyon, Frank W. *Marie Antoinette.* New York: Crowell, 1956. 371pp. Marie Antoinette's life is dramatized from her arrival in France at the age of 14 to her execution. Blending the actual with the imaginary, Kenyon offers a sympathetic view of the passionate queen in the grip of historical forces she cannot control.

Prole, Lozania. *Sweet Marie Antoinette.* London: R. Hale, 1969. 190pp. In an often simplified and idealized biographical portrait, Marie Antoinette's life is dramatized from her betrothal to her execution.

Fictional Portraits

Dukthas, Ann. *The Prince Lost to Time.* New York: St. Martin's, 1995. 229pp. In a time-travelling adventure, the novel attempts a speculative but plausible solution to the historical mystery of the lost dauphin.

Dumas, Alexandre. *The Memoirs of a Physician.* 1950. Reprint ed. New York: Collier, 1902. 534pp. The decline of Louis XV and the early reign of Louis XVI are described from the perspective of a swindler who penetrates to the center of court power.

Feuchtwanger, Lion. *Proud Destiny.* New York: Viking, 1947. 625p. Deals with Benjamin Franklin's Paris years and the maneuvering to get Louis XVI to assist the American cause. Meticulous in its historical reconstruction, the novel is somewhat ponderous as a drama and character study.

John, Evan. *King's Masque.* New York: Dutton, 1941. 477pp. Focusing on the relationship between Marie Antoinette and Count Fersen, this panoramic historical novel covers the events of the American and French Revolution as well as the emergence of Sweden under Gustav III.

Jolis, Alan. *Love and Terror.* New York: Atlantic Monthly Press, 1998. 288pp. The pursuit and cap-

ture of Marie Antoinette are dramatized in this historical thriller setting the queen and Count Fersen against one of Robespierre's agents.

Jordan, Mildred. *Asylum for the Queen.* New York: Knopf, 1948. 409pp. In a fanciful tale concerning a plan to free Louis XVI and Marie Antoinette from imprisonment and relocate them in the Pennsylvania wilderness, the novel provides an authentic look at the events and atmosphere in France and America during the period.

Laker, Rosalind. *To Dance with Kings.* New York: Doubleday, 1988. 564pp. Three generations of a French family are involved in court life during the reigns of Louis XIV, XV, and XVI until the Revolution.

Mackin, Jeanne. *The Frenchwoman.* New York: St. Martin's, 1989. 387pp. In a blend of fact and fiction, Marie Antoinette's favorite dressmaker provides the focus on this historical adventure that sends her to the log-cabin colony in America intended as a royalist refuge.

Piercy, Marge. *City of Darkness, City of Light.* New York: Fawcett, 1996. 479pp. The events of the French Revolution are described from the perspectives of a number of actual women participants and includes a look at the royal family.

Wheatley, Dennis. *The Man Who Killed the King.* New York: Putnam, 1965. 568pp. This swashbuckling adventure tale features a British agent sent to save the French royal family, which brings him into contact with the royals, the inner revolutionary circle, and a young Napoleon. The novel offers an ingenious solution to the disappearance of the dauphin.

Recommended Juvenile Biographies

Kielty, Bernadine. *Marie Antoinette.* New York: Random House, 1955. 184pp. MG. Part of the Landmark series, this is an informative, though fictionalized, account of Marie Antoinette's life and character.

Komroff, Manuel. *Marie Antoinette.* New York: J. Messner, 1967. 191pp. MG/YA. Komroff's is a generally reliable and detailed treatment of Marie Antoinette's life and times.

MacDonald, Fiona. *The World in the Time of Marie Antoinette.* Parsippany, New Jersey: Dillon Press, 1998. 48pp. MG. This is a brief overview with an emphasis on the era.

Biographical Films and Theatrical Adaptations

Sinclair, Upton. *Marie Antoinette: A Play.* New York: Vanguard, 1939. 200pp. Sinclair presents Marie Antoinette's entire life in a series of brief, significant glimpses.

A&E Biography Video: Marie Antoinette: The Tragic Queen (1996). Director: Chris Lethbridge. The documentary traces the events of Marie Antoinette's life and the course of the French Revolution that shaped her end. Video.

Marie Antoinette (1938). Director: W.S. Van Dyke. Based on Stefan Zweig's biography, this is a lavish Hollywood film biography, with F. Scott Fitzgerald receiving writing credit, casting Norma

Shearer as Marie Antoinette, Robert Morley as Louis, and Tyrone Power as Count Fersen. Video.

Marie Antoinette (1955). Director: Jean Delannoy. Michèle Morgan portrays Marie Antoinette in this French film version of her life. Co-starring Richard Todd as Count Fersen and Jean Morel as Louis XVI.

La Marseillaise (1938). Director: Jean Renoir. Lise Delamare portrays Marie Antoinette and Pierre Renoir plays Louis XVI in Renoir's dramatization of the French Revolution told as a human story.

311. CHRISTOPHER MARLOWE
1564–1593

Considered by many to be the greatest English pre-Shakespearean dramatist, Marlowe was born in Canterbury and educated at Cambridge. He went to London in 1587 and became an actor and playwright for the Lord Admiral's Company. His most significant works are *Tamburlaine the Great* (1587), *The Jew of Malta* (1588), *Edward II* (1593), *Dr. Faustus* (1601), and the long poem *Hero and Leander* (1598). His dramas have heroic and tragic themes and are thought to have influenced Shakespeare's work. Marlowe was stabbed to death during a tavern brawl, the result of what some scholars believe to be a murder plot stemming from his activities as a government agent.

Recommended Biographies

Bakeless, John. *The Tragicall History of Christopher Marlowe.* Cambridge, Massachusetts: Harvard University Press, 1942. 2 vols. The author's two decades of research sifting the fragmentary evidence are reflected in this exhaustive, scholarly account. The study is less to be enjoyed as a narrative than consulted as a reference. Bakeless's earlier study, *Christopher Marlowe: The Man in His Time* (New York: Morrow, 1937. 404pp.), distills his preliminary findings in a more accessible and readable fashion.

Kocher, Paul H. *Christopher Marlowe: A Study of His Thought, Learning, and Character.* Chapel Hill: University of North Carolina Press, 1946. 344pp. This intellectual and critical biography remains close to the known facts and avoids sensational speculation in one of the finest accounts available, exploring Marlowe's mind, character, and the intellectual and cultural milieu that shaped him.

Wraight, A.D. *In Search of Christopher Marlowe: A Pictorial Biography.* New York: Vanguard, 1965. 376pp. This visual biography intended for the general reader reviews Marlowe's life and works against the background of his times, which is ably captured in the book's many illustrations.

Other Biographical Studies

Boas, F.S. *Marlowe and His Circle: A Biographical Survey.* Oxford: Clarendon Press, 1929. 159pp. The focus here is an indirect view of Marlowe as reflected in the author's detailed research into the lives of the men with whom the writer associated.

Boas, F.S. *Christopher Marlowe: A Biographical and Critical Study.* Oxford: Clarendon Press, 1940. 336pp. The author assembles through contemporary documents the factual details of Marlowe's life that is both sensible and reliable, if not as adventuresome as other biographers.

Eccles, Mark. *Christopher Marlowe in London.* Cambridge, Massachusetts: Harvard University Press, 1934. 185pp. Based on previously unexamined archival sources, the book focuses on Marlowe's London circle, particularly his relationship with the poet Thomas Watson.

Henderson, Philip. *And Morning in His Eyes.* London: Boriswood, 1937. 352pp. Henderson's is a thorough popular biographical portrait that fills in the gaps in the record with period details and shows Marlowe indirectly through the experiences of others. In *Christopher Marlowe,* (New York: Longmans, 1952, 162pp.) half of the book is devoted to Marlowe's life and the other to his works in a solid critical examination.

Hilton, Della. *Who Was Kit Marlowe?* New York: Taplinger, 1977. 163pp. The answer to the book's title is far from definitive and relies on considerable speculation in attempting to sort through the various controversies surrounding the writer's characters, beliefs, and roles.

Hotson, Leslie. *The Death of Christopher Marlowe.* Cambridge, Massachusetts: Harvard University Press, 1925. 76pp. Hotson's brief monograph shows the result of his tireless scholarly detective work, shedding light on both Marlowe's life and death by discovering the inquest record following Marlowe's demise.

Levin, Harry. *The Overreacher: A Study of Christopher Marlowe.* Cambridge, Massachusetts: Harvard University Press, 1952. 231pp. Although more a critical than a biographical study, Levin's provocative assessment of Marlowe's writings provides a coherent character portrait.

Nicholl, Charles. *The Reckoning: The Murder of Christopher Marlowe.* New York: Harcourt, Brace, 1994. 413pp. The book enters the shady controversy over Marlowe's "murder" with the intriguing, though highly speculative, conspiracy theory that the writer was murdered with governmental complicity in a plot against Sir Walter Raleigh.

Norman, Charles. *The Muses' Darling: The Life of Christopher Marlowe.* New York: Rinehart, 1946. 272pp. In a partially fictionalized account leaning heavily towards the sentimental and idealized, Marlowe's life is vividly, if unreliably, dramatized.

Poirier, Michel. *Christopher Marlowe.* London: Chatto and Windus, 1951. 215pp. Poirier offers chapters on Marlowe's life, his personality and ideas, individual works, and qualities as a poet.

Ross Williamson, Hugh. *Kind Kit: An Informal Biography of Christopher Marlowe.* New York: St. Martin's, 1973. 269pp. Closer to biographical fiction than fact, the book employs imaginary dialogue and speculation disguised as fact in a eminently readable but factually unreliable account.

Rowse, A.L. *Christopher Marlowe: His Life and Work.* New York: Harper & Row, 1964. 219pp. Rowse fashions a literary portrait of the man and

appreciation of his works in the context of the Elizabethan world view. In the absence of evidence, Rowse is forced to rely on the questionable practice of using the works as a source for speculations about Marlowe's life.

Biographical Novels

Burgess, Anthony. *A Dead Man in Deptford.* New York: Carroll & Graf, 1995. 272pp. Burgess recreates the life and times of Christopher Marlowe in a brilliant evocation of the Elizabethan age. Although he asserts that all the historical facts are verifiable, inevitably the book's speculation concerning Marlowe's end is open to question and controversial.

Cronyn, George W. *Mermaid Tavern.* New York: Knight,1937. 416pp. In a colorful rather than strictly accurate account of Marlowe's life, the novel invents a romantic explanation for the writer's shady activities and demise.

De Maria, Robert. *To Be a King: A Novel about Christopher Marlowe.* Indianapolis: Bobbs-Merrill, 1976. 356pp. Chronicling Marlowe's life from childhood to Cambridge, literary London, and the Elizabethan court, the novel speculatively asserts the writer's espionage activities as fact.

Wichelns, Lee. *The Shadow of the Earth.* New York: Elysian Press,1987. 293pp. This biographical novel traces Marlowe's life and career from his university days through his literary triumphs and his shady death in a tavern brawl. With some imaginative embellishments, the novel stays close to the known biographical facts.

Fictional Portraits

Barker, Shirley. *Liza Bowe.* New York: Random House,1956. 245pp. Literary London during the Elizabethan period is the subject of this colorful portrait of the Mermaid Tavern and a young barmaid who becomes associated with virtually every important literary figure, including Shakespeare and Marlowe, and plays a role in providing Marlowe with his subject in *Doctor Faustus.*

Cook, Judith. *The Slicing Edge of Death.* New York: St. Martin's, 1993. 234pp. Offering a credible, fictional solution to the mystery surrounding Marlowe's death, the novel identifies the motives of several individuals for murder in a speculative conspiracy theory involving Marlowe's espionage activities on behalf of Elizabeth and Sir Walter Raleigh.

Cowell, Stephanie. *Nicholas Cooke.* New York: W.W. Norton, 1993. 448pp. In the first-person account of a young boy who in 1593 runs off to London, the protagonist meets and is seduced by Marlowe who employs him as an actor. The novel is a detailed and convincing recreation of Elizabethan times and personalities.

Dhondy, Farrukh. *Black Swan.* Boston: Houghton Mifflin, 1993. 217pp. In this Elizabethan intrigue, the diaries of a physician reveals the secret life of Marlowe in an atmospheric but fanciful solution to the many mysteries surrounding the writer.

Garrett, George. *Entered from the Sun.* Garden City, New York: Doubleday, 1990. 349pp. An ac-

tor and an army veteran investigate the mystery of Marlowe's end at a Deptford tavern, uncovering a great deal about Elizabethan life and intriguing speculations about the writer.

Goldstein, Lisa. *Strange Devices of the Sun and Moon.* New York: St. Martin's, 1993. 384pp. In a historical fantasy, a young widow becomes involved in Marlowe's espionage activities while searching for her missing son.

Biographical Films and Theatrical Adaptations

Life of Shakespeare (1978). Director: Mark Cunningham. In a dramatic speculation about Shakespeare's life, Ian McShane appears as Marlowe, with Tim Curry as Shakespeare, Meg Wynn Owen as Ann Hathaway, and Patience Collier as Elizabeth. Video.

Shakespeare in Love (1998). Director: John Madden. In a delightful fantasy, the origin of two of Shakespeare's greatest plays are imagined in the bard's (Ralph Fiennes) passion for a young noblewoman (Gwyneth Paltrow). Rupert Everett appears as Marlowe whose death is here attributed to Shakespeare's dangerous liaison. Video.

Other Sources

Maclure, Millar, ed. *Marlowe: The Critical Heritage.* Boston: Routledge,1976. 207pp. This useful volume brings together the shifting and contrary views of Marlowe the man and the artist since his death.

312. ANDREW MARVELL
1621–1678

English metaphysical poet, Marvell was assistant to John Milton and a member of Parliament. A Puritan, he was known as one of the chief wits and satirists of his time. His brilliant lyric poetry includes "The Garden," "The Definition of Love," "To His Coy Mistress," and "Horation Ode."

Recommended Biographies

Hunt, John Dixon. *Andrew Marvell: His Life and Writings.* Ithaca, New York: Cornell University Press, 1978. 206pp. Hunt's critical biography is a comprehensive, well-illustrated survey of Marvell's life, times, and works. Accessible for the general reader, the book serves as a reliable introduction.

Legouis, Pierre. *Andrew Marvell: Poet, Puritan, Patriot.* Oxford: Clarendon Press, 1965. 262pp. Still the most reliable and authoritative scholarly critical biography, the essential biographical details are carefully recounted in Legouis's abridgement of his much longer French text, first published in 1928, that incorporates subsequent scholarly findings.

Murray, Nicholas. *World Enough and Time: The Life of Andrew Marvell.* New York: St. Martin's, 2000. 294pp. Murray uses the results of modern scholarship to shape a fresh assessment of Marvell that adds details to the biographical record. The author shows a strong grasp of the period and offers a solid popular biography.

Other Biographical Studies

Birrell, Augustine. *Andrew Marvell.* New York: Macmillan, 1905. 241pp. Despite its age, this sensible, historically based study is still useful, relying on Marvell's own words and those of his contemporaries to animate the poet's life against a vivid period background.

Bradbrook, M.C., and M.G. Lloyd Thomas. *Andrew Marvell.* Cambridge, Massachusetts: Cambridge University Press, 1940. 161pp. Surveying Marvell's works, this critical study illuminates Marvell's personality and career indirectly as reflected in his writing. Comprehensive in scope and rich in insight, this study retains its usefulness for the more-than-casual reader with some prior familiarity with Marvell's period.

Craze, Michael. *The Life and Lyrics of Andrew Marvell.* New York: Barnes and Noble, 1979. 333pp. This collection of Marvell's lyrics includes a brief biographical summary of the known facts about the poet's life.

Other Sources

Ray, Robert. *An Andrew Marvell Companion.* New York: Garland, 1998. 214pp. Ray includes a chronology, a biographical profile, and a dictionary of people, places, and terms associated with the poet and his work in this useful, accessible reference guide.

313. KARL MARX
1818–1883

German social philosopher and the founder of modern socialism, Marx was born in Trier, the son of a Jewish lawyer who converted to Lutheranism. He studied law at Bonn and Berlin but turned to philosophy and received his Ph.D. at Jena (1841). At first a proponent of materialism, Marx demanded radical reforms while editing the magazine *Reinische Zeitung*. After the magazine was suppressed (1843), he moved with his wife to Paris, Brussels, and finally to London, where he spent the rest of his life in great poverty. He became a socialist, joined (1847) the Communist League, and with his lifelong friend and collaborator, Friedrich Engels, published (1848) *The Communist Manifesto*, which summarizes Marx's social philosophy. In London, Marx cofounded (1864) and led the International Workingman's Association. His theories gained primacy in Europe, especially with the publication (1867–1894) of his monumental three-volume work, *Das Kapital*. Marxist theory argues that as feudalism gave way to capitalism, so capitalism would inevitably be replaced by socialism and eventually, communism.

Autobiography and Primary Sources

Karl Marx/Friedrich Engels: Selected Letters. The Personal Correspondence, 1844-77. Fritz J. Raddatz, ed. Boston: Little, Brown, 1982. 194pp. In a selection of only 150 of the 4,000 existing letters, Marx's poverty and financial dependence on Engels are revealed as are the personalities of both men.

The Letters of Karl Marx. Saul K. Padover, ed. Englewood Cliffs, New Jersey: Prentice-Hall, 1979. 576pp. Covering Marx's life from his youth as a college student to shortly before his death, this comprehensive selection of his correspondence is an invaluable primary source on Marx's thought and character.

Selected Correspondence: 1845–1895/Karl Marx and Friedrich Engels. New York: International Publishers, 1942. 551pp. Marx's human trials and character can be glimpsed in this record of his relationship with Engels.

Recommended Biographies

McLellan, David. *Karl Marx: His Life and Thought.* New York: Harper & Row, 1973. 498pp. A full-length personal and intellectual biography, McLellan's examination is both lucid and balanced in its presentation and achieves a remarkable integration of the various facets of Marx's life; *Karl Marx* (New York: Viking, 1975. 110pp.) is a condensation of McLellan's longer work and serves as a useful introduction for the general reader to the man and his ideas.

Manuel, Frank E. *A Requiem for Karl Marx.* Cambridge, Massachusetts: Harvard University Press, 1995. 255pp. Part biography and part meditation on Marx's reputation and influence, this is a clear-eyed, lucidly written dissection of Marx's character and ideas, which are shown originating in violent hatred. Crafted with a novelistic vividness and supported by evident expertise in political and intellectual history, Manuel's study is a challenging reassessment and penetrating psychological portrait.

Padover, Saul K. *Karl Marx: An Intimate Biography.* New York: McGraw-Hill, 1978. 667pp. Focusing on Marx's private life and intimate relationships with his parents, wife, and children and the personal forces that shaped him, Padover creates a detailed human portrait of a divided man and a complex blend of personal strengths and flaws.

Wheen, Francis. *Karl Marx: A Life.* New York: W.W. Norton, 2000. 448pp. In a convincing as well as entertaining account, Wheen helps to humanize Marx while disposing of a number of myths that have obscured the view of his character and development. Without an ideological bias, Wheen focuses on the whole man, not just his ideas, in an insightful and fresh reappraisal.

Other Biographical Studies

Berlin, Isaiah. *Karl Marx: His Life and Environment.* 1939. Reprint ed. New York: Oxford University Press, 1963. 295pp. Despite a clear anti-Communist bias, Berlin provides a succinct summary of the highlights of Marx's life and the development of his ideas. The study is particularly strong on the social and political atmosphere in which Marx worked.

Blumenberg, Werner. *Karl Marx: An Illustrated Biography.* New York: Verso, 1998. 175pp. Including virtually every photograph of Marx and his associates, this visual biography considers both Marx's private and public lives and the interconnections between the two. Serves as an excellent introduction to the man and his ideas for the nonspecialist.

Liebknecht, Wilhelm. *Karl Marx: Biographical Memoirs.* 1901. Reprint ed. New York: Greenwood, 1968. 181pp. Written by a close associate, Liebknecht's recollections form a partial portrait rather than a full-scale biography, enlivened by many anecdotes that humanize the formidable and often remote thinker.

Mehring, Franz. *Karl Marx: The Story of His Life.* 1918. Reprint ed. New York: Covici Friede, 1935. 608pp. Long regarded as the definitive life until more recent scholarship offered new findings and altered interpretations, Mehring's study still serves, despite its sycophantic tone, as one of the most comprehensive accounts of Marx's career, his relationship with his family and friends, and the wider historical and cultural context for viewing Marx's ideas.

Nicolaevsky, Boris, and Otto Maenchen-Helfen. *Karl Marx: Man and Fighter.* Philadelphia: Lippincott, 1936. 391pp. The authors supply a detailed account of Marx's family background and early years.

Payne, Robert. *Marx.* New York: Simon & Schuster, 1968. 582pp. In a hostile account, Payne details how Marx's family, friends, and environment shaped him. Grudgingly acknowledging Marx's successes, the book emphasizes his failures and flaws and scores low marks on objectivity and balance.

Raddatz, Fritz. *Karl Marx: A Political Biography.* Boston: Little, Brown, 1978. 335pp. Raddatz adds few fresh or original insights or revelation to a fairly standard account of Marx's life. Unfortunately the book provides scant coverage of Marx's early life and the development of his ideas.

Rühle, Otto. *Karl Marx: His Life and Work.* New York: Viking, 1929. 419pp. At times excessively psychoanalytical in its approach, the book offers a coherent, though limited, view of Marx's character and the development of his ideas.

Schwarzschild, Leopold. *The Red Prussian: The Life and Legend of Karl Marx.* New York: Scribner, 1947. 422pp. Based mainly on the Marx-Engels correspondence, the author debunks any greatness associated with Marx, showing him as a petty, dishonest, and unscrupulous opportunist, a loose thinker, and a bad prophet. The book's lack of objectivity limits its overall usefulness.

Seigel, Jerrold E. *Marx's Fate: The Shape of a Life.* Princeton, New Jersey: Princeton University Press, 1978. 451pp. In a psychohistorical approach, Seigel offers a number of new interpretations on various aspects of Marx's life and thought framed by what the author reveals was the ultimately unsuccessful attempt by Marx to resolve his intellectual abstractions in the face of experience.

Fictional Portraits

Ackroyd, Peter. *The Trial of Elizabeth Cree.* New York: Doubleday, 1995. 288pp. The search for a serial killer in London's Limehouse in 1880 is connected with the trial of a young actress accused of murdering her husband. Karl Marx, novelist George Gissing, and music hall comedian Dan Leno get involved in the investigation.

Chernaik, Judith. *The Daughter: A Novel Based on the Life of Eleanor Marx.* New York: Harper & Row, 1979. 216pp. Mixing fact and invention, the novel explores the life of Marx's youngest daughter, Eleanor, a member of London's socialist and intellectual set who committed suicide when her actor husband deserted her.

Feuer, Lewis S. *The Case of the Revolutionist's Daughter: Sherlock Holmes Meets Karl Marx.* Buffalo, New York: Prometheus Books, 1983. 159pp. In an inventive historical mystery with a biographical basis, featuring a convincing period atmosphere, Sherlock Holmes is hired by Marx to find his missing daughter.

Thorne, Nicola. *Sisters and Lovers.* Garden City, New York: Doubleday, 1981. 589pp. Three Victorian sisters arrive in London in the 1850s in search of husbands, and their stories are linked to a number of historical figures, including Florence Nightingale, John Ruskin, and Karl Marx.

Recommended Juvenile Biographies

Alexander, Albert. *Karl Marx: The Father of Modern Socialism.* New York: F. Watts, 1969. 147pp. MG/YA. Alexander provides the highlights of Marx's career, glimpses of his personality, and a solid discussion of his influence and legacy.

Feinberg, Barbara S. *Marx and Marxism.* New York: F. Watts, 1985. 122pp. MG. This is a useful and informative overview that makes Marx's views accessible in the context of his times.

Kettle, Arnold. *Karl Marx: Founder of Modern Communism.* New York: Roy, 1964. 120pp. YA. After a succinct account of Marx's life, Kettle, a distinguished literary critic, discusses Marx's ideas on economics, history, and revolution in a sincere and concise appreciation, now somewhat dated by historical events.

Biographical Films and Theatrical Adaptations

Zinn, Howard. *Marx in Soho: A Play on History.* Cambridge, Massachusetts: South End Press, 1999. 55pp. Zinn's one-man play imagines Marx coming back to life in present-day New York to see how his economic theories have fared. The play also sheds some light on Marx's relationships with his wife and daughter.

Karl Marx and Marxism (1993). Director: Alan Horrox. This documentary looks at the man, his life, and roots of his philosophy and the development of his thinking. Video.

Other Sources

Carver, Terrell, ed. *The Cambridge Companion to Marx.* New York: Cambridge University Press, 1991. 357pp. This collection of essays by respected scholars begins with an overview by Carver on Marx's life and works, followed by critiques on Marx's philosophy.

Draper, Hal. *The Marx-Engles Chronicle: A Day-to-Day Chronicle of Marx and Engels' Life*

and Activity. New York: Schocken, 1985. 297pp. This is a meticulously researched, detailed chronology that records everything that is known about both men's activities.

Foner, Philip S., ed. *When Karl Marx Died: Comments in 1883.* New York: International Publishers, 1973. 272pp. A collection of articles and tributes following Marx's death in 1883, this useful volume provides the reader with a clear sense of how Marx variously appeared to his contemporaries.

McLellan, David. *Karl Marx: Interviews and Recollections.* Totowa, New Jersey: Barnes and Noble, 1981. 186pp. Marx's own words and those of his contemporaries are gathered together to form an interesting multi-angled profile.

Rubel, Maximilien and Margaret Manale. *Marx without Myth: A Chronological Study of His Life and Work.* New York: Blackwell, 1975. 368pp. In an invaluable reference tool, the authors have divided Marx's life into distinct periods and supplied a year-by-year chronology of Marx and his family for each period. The book is particularly helpful when read in conjunction with other biographies.

314. MARY I
1516–1558

The daughter of Henry VIII and Catherine of Aragon and the half-sister of Elizabeth I, Mary became queen (1553) after the death of her half-brother, Edward VI, and the nine-day usurpation of the throne by Lady Jane Grey. A devout Roman Catholic, she endeavored to restore Catholicism in England, and her subsequent persecution of Protestants, hundreds of whom were burnt as heretics, earned her the sobriquet "Bloody Mary." Her alliance with and marriage to Philip II of Spain (1554) led to war with France, the loss of Calais (1558), and the hostility of the English people toward the queen. The childless Mary was succeeded by Elizabeth I.

Recommended Biographies

Erickson, Carolly. *Bloody Mary.* Garden City, New York: Doubleday, 1978. 533pp. Focusing on Mary's personal life, Erickson portrays the queen as neither a monster nor a misunderstood heroine but a consistent woman of her times shaped by events beyond her control. Erickson's sympathetic but balanced study refutes many myths surrounding Mary and supplies valuable cultural and historical contexts to understand her.

Loades, David M. *Mary Tudor: A Life.* New York: Blackwell, 1989. 410pp. Featuring new evidence from archival sources, Loades's balanced, scholarly biography supersedes Prescott in its scholarship and interpretations. Presenting a far more complex, respected figure than previous studies, the author's emphasis on the gender challenges Mary faced as a ruler helps to explain her successes and failures as queen and restores considerable sympathy for the queen.

Prescott, Hilda F.M. *Spanish Tudor: Life of Bloody Mary.* New York: Columbia University Press, 1940. 562pp.; reissued as *Mary Tudor.* (New York:

Macmillan, 1953). In a balanced, scholarly study that has long served as the standard life, Prescott neither condones nor ignores Mary's failures as a queen and her character flaws. Written with a dramatic, novelistic skill, the book vividly captures Mary's compelling human story and the personal and public influences that shaped her life.

Other Biographical Studies

Loach, Jennifer. *Parliament and the Crown in the Reign of Mary Tudor.* New York: Oxford University Press, 1986. 262pp. This specialized study of Mary's relationship with Parliament offers a revisionist view of Mary as a remarkably successful monarch.

Loades, David M. *The Reign of Mary Tudor.* New York: St. Martin's, 1979. 444pp. In the most detailed, scholarly study of Mary's five-and-a-half year reign, Loades examines the structure of the state, and its finances, and foreign and religious affairs, as well as includes three chapters on Mary's personal and political affairs. Loades's convincing evidence challenges more negative views of Mary's reign and character and complements his later biography with essential political and historical context for a balanced view of the queen.

Maynard, Theodore. *Bloody Mary.* Milwaukee: Bruce, 1955. 297pp. Written from a Catholic perspective, Maynard counters the verdict of history with a defense of Mary's reputation, asserting that she should be regarded as one of the holiest of English monarchs: a pure, courageous, pious, and honest individual whose crimes were no worse than her contemporaries'. Considerable uncritical special pleading is necessary to support this positive view.

Ridley, Jasper. *The Life and Times of Mary Tudor.* London: Weidenfeld and Nicolson, 1973. 224pp. Ridley's illustrated biography serves as a solid introduction to Mary's life and era for the nonspecialist.

Tittler, Robert. *The Reign of Mary I.* New York: Longman, 1983. 117pp. In a revisionist assessment, Tittler counters standard views of Mary's failures as a person and ruler and offers evidence to support a contrary view of the queen's successes.

Waldman, Milton. *The Lady Mary: A Biography of Mary Tudor.* New York: Scribner, 1972. 224pp. Only a small portion of Waldman's biography is devoted to Mary's reign, concentrating instead on her childhood and the difficult years of the 1530s and 1540s. Well written but undocumented, Waldman's handling of complex events and figures is clear, if at times overly simplified.

Weir, Alison. *The Children of Henry VIII.* New York: Ballantine Books, 1996. 385pp. In a group portrait of Henry VIII's children, the emphasis is on the personal over political history. The book features a detailed look at Mary's relationship with her half-sister Elizabeth. All the Tudors are shown as complex humans with both strengths and weaknesses.

Biographical Novels

Elsna, Hebe. *Prelude for Two Queens.* London: Collins, 1972. 160pp. The childhood and youth of both Mary and Elizabeth Tudor are dramatized in a credible, though somewhat idealized account.

Lewis, Hilda W. *I Am Mary Tudor.* New York: McKay, 1972. 422pp. The reign of her father is described from the first-person perspective of Mary through her ascension to the throne in a convincing depiction of the age and an intriguing animation of Mary's psyche.

Plaidy, Jean. *The Spanish Bridegroom.* New York: Putnam, 1971. 301pp. This biographical novel dramatizes the personal and political life of Spain's Philip II through his relationship with a number of women, including his marriage to Mary Tudor. The author's *In the Shadow of the Crown* (New York: Putnam, 1988. 381pp.) is an autobiographical account of Queen Mary's life and reign.

Zara, Louis. *In the House of the King.* New York: Crown, 1952. 306pp. Tracing the life of Mary's husband, Spain's Philip II, the novel dramatizes his career from boyhood to death, with an emphasis on the king's amorous relationships. Invention mars the novel's reliability as either biography or history.

Fictional Portraits

Ainsworth, William Harrison. *The Tower of London.* 1840. Reprint ed. New York: Dutton, 1928. 455pp. The novel offers a fictionalized account of the various claimants to the English throne on the death of Edward VI, including Mary and Elizabeth Tudor and Lady Jane Grey. With only a framework of history, the novel features mainly romantic embellishments.

Dukthas, Ann. *In the Time of the Poisoned Queen.* New York: St. Martin's, 1998. 273pp. In an ingenious historical mystery, time-traveler Nicholas Segalla uncovers a elaborate plot to poison Mary.

Harper, Karen. *The Poyson Garden: A Bess Tudor Mystery.* New York: Delacorte, 1999. 288pp. In a historical mystery series, Elizabeth Tudor investigates the poisoning deaths of a number of her Boleyn relatives while she is watched suspiciously by her half-sister Queen Mary.

Harwood, Alice. *The Lily and the Leopards.* Indianapolis: Bobbs-Merrill, 1949. 508pp. The tragically brief life of Lady Jane Grey is faithfully depicted. A companion to both Mary and Elizabeth Tudor, Lady Jane is swept up in the coup d'etat that puts her on the throne for nine days before she is executed.

Major, Charles. *When Knighthood Was in Flower.* New York: Grosset & Dunlap,1898. 358pp. Major's popular historical romance recounts Mary's affair with the commoner, Charles Brandon.

Ross Williamson, Hugh. *The Cardinal in Exile.* London: Joseph, 1969. 217pp. In the sequel to *The Cardinal in England* (1970), Henry VIII's cousin, who has become a cardinal, goes first to Rome where he almost becomes Pope before returning to England when Mary comes to the throne.

Wheelwright, Jere H. *The Strong Room.* New York: Scribner, 1948. 302pp. In a fictional intrigue plot, an English aristocrat works to prevent Mary from wedding Philip II of Spain, ingeniously connecting invention with actual historical events of the period.

Recommended Juvenile Biographies

Roll, Winifred. *Mary I: The History of an Unhappy Tudor Queen.* Englewood Cliffs, New Jersey: Prentice-Hall, 1980. 266pp. MA/YA. Roll's is an extensive, well-researched, balanced, and detailed account of Mary's childhood, rise to the throne, and reign that indulges in a minimum of speculation and is intended for the serious student of the period.

Biographical Films and Theatrical Adaptations

Tennyson, Alfred. *Queen Mary.* Boston: Osgood, 1875. 263pp. Tennyson's historical drama presents the principal events of Mary's reign, including Wyatt's rebellion, her marriage to Philip II, the death of Cranmer, and the loss of Calais.

Elizabeth (1998). Director: Shekhar Kapur. In a darkly evocative portrait of Elizabeth's succession, Kathy Burke portrays Queen Mary, with Cate Blanchett as Elizabeth and Joseph Fiennes as Robert Dudley. Video.

Elizabeth R (1972). Director: Claude Whatham, et al. Covering Elizabeth's life from age 17 to age 70, this acclaimed series is anchored by a remarkable performance by Glenda Jackson in the title role, Daphne Slater portrays Mary, with Peter Jeffrey as Philip II. Video.

The Sword and the Rose (1953). Director: Ken Annakin. Based on Charles Mayor's *When Knighthood Was in Flower,* Mary's early romantic life is invented as she (Glynis Johns) prefers a commoner (Richard Todd) over the advances of a nobleman (Michael Gough). Features a fine performance by James Robertson Justice as Henry VIII. Video.

See also Anne Boleyn; Elizabeth I; Henry VIII; Philip II

315. MARY QUEEN OF SCOTS
1542–1587

The daughter of James V of Scotland and Mary of Guise, Mary was born at Linlithgow and became the Scottish queen six days later, upon the death of her father. She was brought up in France and married (1558) the dauphin, crowned Francis I (1559). Francis died in 1560 and Mary returned (1561) to Scotland, where she married (1565) her Catholic cousin, Henry Stuart, Lord Darnley. Their son, James (later James I of England), was born in 1566. Power struggles between the queen and the scheming, unpopular Darnley led to Darnley's murder (1567) on the orders of the Earl of Bothwell, whom Mary later married. Public outrage and Protestant opposition to the marriage forced her to abdicate and flee to England, where, as heir presumptive of Elizabeth I, she became the focus of Catholic plots against the English throne. Imprisoned for 19 years while Parliament and Elizabeth debated her fate, Mary was finally tried and then beheaded at Fotheringay castle after evidence implicated her in a plot led by Anthony Babington.

Recommended Biographies

Donaldson, Gordon. *Mary Queen of Scots.* London: English Universities Press, 1974. 200pp. In a sympathetic reassessment, Donaldson provides convincing evidence to support an altered view of Mary as a savvy politician and neither the victim of her passions nor of circumstance. In Donaldson's view, the queen's strengths add to the complexity of her story, which this book freshly presents.

Fraser, Antonia. *Mary Queen of Scots.* New York: Delacorte Press, 1969. 613pp. In a convincing rehabilitation of Mary's reputation, Fraser looks at the personal history of the queen against a vivid backdrop of sixteenth-century attitudes and politics. In Fraser's revisionist view, Mary is presented as a sympathetically tragic figure, betrayed by those closest to her.

Henderson, T.F. *Mary Queen of Scots: Her Environment and Tragedy.* New York: Scribner, 1905. 2 vols. This narrative, critical biography, despite its age, has long established itself as the standard life by its judiciousness, balance, and comprehensiveness. Henderson is particularly strong on the cultural and historical conditions underlying Mary's career and the influence of foreign affairs on her development.

Wormald, Jenny. *Mary Queen of Scots: A Study in Failure.* London: G. Philip, 1988. 206pp. In contrast to Donaldson's defense of Mary, Wormald provides the prosecution's view, impressively assembling the evidence of her character flaws, mismanagement, and misjudgments.

Other Biographical Studies

Cowan, Ian B. *The Enigma of Mary Stuart.* New York: St. Martin's, 1971. 222pp. This useful book employs biographical and historical attitudes toward Mary through selected excerpts from various accounts of crucial moments of her reign and captivity. Offering no judgments, Cowan instead arranges both favorable and negative interpretations, allowing the reader to reach his or her own conclusion.

Gorman, Herbert. *The Scottish Queen.* New York: Farrar & Rinehart, 1932. 605pp. A highly readable, dramatic narrative biography, Gorman's account presents Mary as the unhappy victim of circumstances that resisted her control and conspired to produce her downfall. What is missing here is a more balanced view that grants more responsibility to Mary herself for her fate.

Lewis, Jayne E. *Mary Queen of Scots: Romance and Nation.* New York: Routledge, 1998. 256pp. Lewis looks at the contradictory and changing image of Mary through the century, from the Scottish and English perspectives and the points of view of the Elizabethan, Jacobean, Georgian, Victorian, and Modern periods. The result is a fascinating account of how the queen reflects each era's values.

Morrison, Nancy B. *Mary Queen of Scots.* New York: Vanguard, 1960. 286pp. This is a vivid but undocumented narrative history of the queen's life and reign in a series of dramatized scenes in which it is difficult to separate fact from the imagination.

Strickland, Agnes. *Lives of the Queens of Scotland.* New York: Harper, 1851–1859. 8 vols. Strickland's quaint Victorian study of Mary is striking in its positive depiction. Although the book's interpretations are dated and chiefly interesting from a historical perspective, this examination does ably employ primary documents and supplies some well-founded details.

Zweig, Stefan. *Mary, Queen of Scotland and the Isles.* New York: Viking, 1935. 366pp. In a psychological biography written for the general reader, Zweig concentrates his attention on Mary's passionate relationship with the Earl of Bothwell to dramatize his characterization of the queen as a victim of her intense feelings. Provocative rather than reliable, Zweig's vivid account is nevertheless a fascinating character portrait.

Biographical Novels

Balin, Beverly. *King in Hell.* New York: Coward-McCann, 1971. 568pp. With a number of controversial interpretations, the novel explores the relationship between Mary and her third husband, James Hepburn, Earl of Bothwell. Contrary to historical consensus, the novel pleads Bothwell's innocence in the death of Mary's second husband, Lord Darnley, and accepts the validity of the Casket Letters that suggest Bothwell and Mary's affair before Darnley's death.

Bowen, Marjorie. *Double Dallilaly.* London: Cassell, 1933. 383pp. The various intrigues surrounding Mary's tenuous grasp on the Scottish throne and her rivalry with Elizabeth I are dramatized. In *Queen's Caprice* (London: Cassell, 1933. 287pp.), the crucial years of Mary's reign are dramatized from her first meeting with Lord Darnley in 1565 to her imprisonment in Lochleven Castle in 1567. The novel's interpretation of events fits the historical facts, although some liberties have been taken regarding motivation.

Byrd, Elizabeth. *Immortal Queen.* New York: Ballantine Books, 1956. 591pp. As Mary awaits her execution in 1587, her entire life is reviewed. She emerges as a complex figure shaped by her age, imperious but needy and no match for Elizabeth.

Fallon, Frederic. *The White Queen.* Garden City, New York: Doubleday, 1972. 322pp. With some liberties taken with the historical facts, the novel chronicles Mary's troubled reign from her return to France through her relationships with Darnley and Bothwell.

George, Margaret. *Mary Queen of Scotland and the Isles.* New York: St. Martin's, 1992. 870pp. In a remarkable effort of historical recreation, Mary's life and character are convincingly examined from a variety of vantage points to arrive at a multidimensional, complex portrait.

Harwood, Alice. *Seats of the Mighty: A Novel of James Stuart, brother of Mary Queen of Scots.* Indianapolis: Bobbs-Merrill, 1956. 469pp.; *No Smoke without Fire.* Indianapolis: Bobbs-Merrill, 1964. 530pp. The author's two novels look at life in Mary's court from the perspective of her half-brother, James Stuart, Earl of Moray. The historical events before and after Mary's fall from power are faithfully presented.

Irwin, Margaret. *The Gay Galliard.* New York: Harcourt, Brace, 1942. 543pp. With incidents and dialogue partially drawn from contemporary records, the novel dramatizes the love affair between Mary and Bothwell and the mysterious death of Mary's second husband, Darnley. The novel fea-

tures a more sympathetic portrayal of Bothwell than most historical accounts.

Kenyon, Frank W. *Mary of Scotland.* New York: Crowell, 1957. 344pp. Mary's reign, from her return to Scotland to her execution, is dramatized in a consistent but debatable interpretation of events and motives.

Kurlbaum, Margarete S. *Mary, Queen of Scots.* New York: Harcourt, Brace, 1929. 504pp. Beginning with Mary's arrival in Scotland, the novel provides a highly romanticized and often inaccurate account of events, full of ingenious conjectures about what people felt and thought.

Lane, Jane. *Parcel of Rogues.* New York: Rinehart, 1948. 448pp. Mary's Scottish reign is chronicled from 1542 to 1581. The novel is faithful to the spirit of the times if not to every factual detail, with a plausible interpretation concerning the disputed Casket Letters.

Oliver, Jane. *The Lion and the Rose.* New York: Putnam, 1958. 382pp. Mary's career from her return to Scotland to her execution is dramatized. The novel reflects the author's conviction that Mary and Bothwell were innocent in the death of Lord Darnley.

Plaidy, Jean. *Royal Road to Fotheringay.* New York: Putnam, 1968. 349pp. The novel traces Mary's entire career in France, Scotland, and England, sticking close to the historical facts with some speculation concerning motive. In *The Captive Queen of Scotland* (New York: Putnam, 1970. 410pp.) Mary's captivity in England is dramatized. After the Battle of Longside, Mary flees to England for protection and is offered a succession of royal prison cells until her end at Fotheringay.

Tannahill, Reay. *Fatal Majesty: A Novel of Mary Queen of Scots.* New York: St. Martin's, 1999. 466pp. Mary's story after her return to Scotland from France is dramatized with an emphasis on the political intrigue that she faced. Mary herself is somewhat lost in the shuffle here in the rush of events.

Fictional Portraits

Byrd, Elizabeth. *Maid of Honor: A Novel Set in the Court of Mary Queen of Scots.* New York: St. Martin's, 1979. 313pp. Court intrigue during Mary's reign is described from the perspective of the queen's maid of honor.

Dukthas, Ann. *A Time for the Death of a King.* New York: St. Martin's, 1994. 226pp. In an inventive time-travel investigation, the mystery surrounding the murder of Lord Darnley is explored. Grounded in fact, the novel's solutions to a number of mysteries involving Mary are highly speculative.

Dunnett, Dorothy. *The Game of Kings.* New York: Putnam, 1961. 543pp. The initial novel of the Lymond Saga is set in 1547 as Mary is spirited to France from Scotland; *Queen's Play.* New York: Putnam, 1964. 432pp. Francis Crawford protects the young Mary in France during the reign of Henri II; *Checkmate.* New York: Putnam, 1975. 581pp. In the final installment of the author's Lymond Saga, high court politics between France and England involves Mary Queen of Scots as Francis

Crawford attempts to resolve crises with his identity and marriage.

Hill, Pamela. *The Green Salamander.* New York: St. Martin's, 1977. 288pp. The story of Margaret Douglas, mother of Mary's second husband, Darnley, is depicted as she plays a dangerous political game against rivals and conspirators in Scotland and England to secure her family's fortune. In *The Sword and the Flame* (New York: St. Martin's, 1992. 316pp.) the life of Mary of Guise, wife of Scottish King James V and mother of Mary Queen of Scots, is narrated from the perspective of a noblewoman attendant.

Oliver, Jane. *Mine Is the Kingdom.* Philadelphia: Lippincott, 1937. 452pp. This biographical novel chronicling the life of Scotland's James VI and England's James I includes a look at the future king's early life in Mary's court.

Scott, Walter. *The Abbot.* 1820. Reprint ed. New York: Dutton, 1936. 470pp. In an exciting blend of romance and history, the story concerns Mary's imprisonment at Lochleven Castle, her escape, and her supporters' defeat at the Battle of Longside.

Westcott, Jan. *The Tower and the Dream.* New York: Putnam, 1974. 322pp. The rivalry between Elizabeth I and Mary is dramatized from the perspective of the actual Elizabeth Talbot, Countess of Shrewsbury, one of the most fascinating figures of the Elizabethan period.

Recommended Juvenile Biographies

Hahn, Emily. *Mary Queen of Scots.* New York: Random House, 1953. 184pp. MG. Part of the Landmark series, this is a vivid and mainly objective account of the highlights of Mary's life and reign.

Plaidy, Jean. *The Young Mary Queen of Scots.* New York: Roy, 1963. 144pp. MG. Plaidy, the prolific historical novelist, documents Mary's early years through her return to Scotland as a widow at the age of 18.

Stepanek, Sally. *Mary Queen of Scots.* New York: Chelsea House, 1987. 111pp. MG/YA. Part of the publisher's World Leaders series, the highlights of Mary's life are summarized, with some oversimplification of the complex political and cultural context and some fictionalization.

Biographical Films and Theatrical Adaptations

Anderson, Maxwell. *Mary of Scotland.* 1934. Anderson's blank-verse drama presents episodes from Mary's life, from her arrival in Scotland in 1561 to her imprisonment in Lochleven Castle. Anderson exalts Mary's honor, chastity, and integrity more than history has granted and blames the unflattering events, such as Darnley's end, the murder of Rizzio, and the betrayal of Bothwell, to the machinations of Elizabeth I.

Bolt, Robert. *Vivat! Vivat Regina: A Play in Two Acts.* London: Heineman, 1971. 96pp. Bolt's study of the effects of power is focused on the clash between Mary and Elizabeth I, elaborating on the events leading up to Mary's execution.

Drinkwater, John. *Mary Stuart.* Boston: Houghton Mifflin, 1921. 73pp. In Drinkwater's interpretation, Mary is a noble and loving woman done in by her poor choices of men.

Masefield, John. *End and Beginning.* New York: Macmillan, 1933. 50pp. Masefield's poetic drama memorializes the last few hours of Mary's life.

Schiller, Friedrich. *Mary Stuart.* New York: Penguin, 1998. 150pp. Schiller's verse drama first published in 1800 treats the conflict between Elizabeth I and Mary while the latter is in prison awaiting execution. In Schiller's interpretation, Mary is depicted as a warm and loving woman who gains moral transcendence through suffering and accepting her fate.

Mary of Scotland (1936). Director: John Ford. In the film adaptation of Maxwell Anderson's play, Katharine Hepburn stars as Mary, with Fredric March as Bothwell, Douglas Walton as Darnley, and Florence Eldridge as Elizabeth I. Video.

Mary, Queen of Scots (1971). Director: Charles Jarrot. More colorful than historically accurate, this period drama features strong performances by Vanessa Redgrave in the title role and Glenda Jackson as Elizabeth I. With Patrick McGoohan, Timothy Dalton, Trevor Howard, Ian Holm, and Daniel Massey. Video.

Mary Stuart (1982). Director: Peter Butler. Performance by the English National Opera of Donizetti's 1835 opera based on Schiller's tragedy. Video.

See also Catherine de' Medici; Elizabeth I; James I

316. COTTON MATHER
1663–1728

American Puritan clergyman and author, Mather was an advisor in Sir William Phips's government, and helped to found Yale University. His wide scientific interest made him the first native-born American elected to London's Royal Society. His works include *Memorable Providences Relating to Witchcraft and Possessions* (1689), which helped to stir up the hysteria that led to the Salem witch trials, and *Magnalia Christi Americana* (1702), a brilliant religious history of the colonies.

Autobiography and Primary Sources

Diary of Cotton Mather. Worthington C. Ford. 1911–1912. Reprint ed. New York: Frederick Ungar, 1957. 2 vols. Mather's private reflections are an essential source for information on his activities, ideas, and personality.

Paterna: The Autobiography of Cotton Mather. Ronald A. Bosco, ed. Delmar, New York: Scholars' Facsimiles and Reprints, 1976. 432pp. Published in 1702, Mather's devotional recollections were originally written as an inspirational lesson for his son.

Selected Letters of Cotton Mather. Kenneth Silverman, ed. Baton Rouge: Louisiana State University Press, 1971. 446pp. Four-fifths of the extant letters are included in this collection, arranged in a chronological and thematic scheme.

Recommended Biographies

Levin, David. *Cotton Mather: The Young Life of the Lord's Remembrancer 1663–1703.* Cambridge, Massachusetts: Harvard University Press, 1978. 360pp. Levin's is a well-written and -researched account of Mather's formative experiences, ideas, and background. Balanced in its assessment, the book helps to humanize Mather, describing his shortcomings as well as his strengths.

Silverman, Kenneth. *The Life and Times of Cotton Mather.* New York: Harper & Row, 1984. 479pp. Silverman's Pulitzer Prize–winning biography is deservedly regarded as the definitive life. Based on extensive archival research, the book converts its considerable scholarship into an accessible, compelling narrative that manages a balanced portrait of a figure far more complex and interesting than conventional wisdom has suggested.

Middlekauff, Robert. *The Mathers: Three Generations of Puritan Intellectuals 1596–1728.* New York: Oxford University Press, 1971. 440pp. Winner of the Bancroft Prize, Middlekauff's scholarly account of the evolution of Puritan thought in America is centered on the intellectual and spiritual lives of Richard, Increase, and Cotton Mather, drawing on their private papers, unpublished writings, sermons, and works.

Other Biographical Studies

Boas, Ralph, and Louise Boas. *Cotton Mather: Keeper of the Puritan Conscience.* 1928. Reprint ed. Hamden, Connecticut: Archon Books, 1964. 271pp. This is a well-written overview using frequent quotations from Mather's writings and from his contemporaries to present a selective portrait of the man and his era.

Lovelace, Richard F. *The American Pietism of Cotton Mather: Origins of American Evangelicalism.* Grand Rapids, Michigan: William B. Eerdmans, 1979. 350pp. Lovelace's intellectual and spiritual profile places Mather in his Puritan context and depicts his influence on the Evangelical movement.

Mather, Samuel. *The Life of the Very Reverend and Learned Cotton Mather.* 1729. Reprint ed. New York: Garrett Press, 1970. 186pp. Mather's son offers a brief, admiring portrait of his father. The book's perspective makes this an important source for authentic details.

Wendell, Barrett. *Cotton Mather: The Puritan Priest.* 1891. Reprint ed. New York: Chelsea House, 1980. 321pp. Wendell supplies a still valuable biographical profile. Although selective in its approach, the book provides insights into Mather's private and public life against a background of New England intellectual life.

Fictional Portraits

Barker, Shirley. *Peace, My Daughters.* New York: Crown, 1949. 248pp. Barker's romantic treatment of the Salem witchcraft trials features a portrait of Mather.

Breslin, Howard. *The Silver Oar.* New York: Crowell, 1954. 310pp. A condemned pirate narrates his perspective on the 1689 Boston Revolution against Governor Andros, with an appearance by Mather.

Elliott, Edward E. *The Devil and the Mathers.* San Francisco: Strawberry Hill, 1989. 375pp. This is a generally accurate version of the events of 1692 in Salem as witchcraft hysteria is fueled by the religious zeal of Cotton Mather to produce a number of executions.

Winwar, Frances. *Gallows Hill.* New York: Holt, 1937. 292pp. Mather is shown investigating the claims that the devil has infected townspeople in colonial Salem in a convincing depiction of period customs.

Recommended Juvenile Biographies

Wood, James P. *The Admirable Cotton Mather.* New York: Seabury Press, 1971. 164pp. MG/YA. Wood attempts to view Mather in his own terms based on contemporary values in a balanced appraisal. Some previous knowledge of colonial history will help readers' comprehension.

317. HENRI MATISSE
1869–1954

Prolific French painter, sculptor, and lithographer, Matisse is considered, with Pablo Picasso, one of the two foremost artists of the modern period. He gave up the study of law after taking up painting during an illness in 1890 and studied with academician Bouguereau and with Gustave Moreau. Influenced by the Impressionists, Matisse's vivid, exuberant use of color caused his style and that of his circle to be dubbed "Fauvism." After the demise of Fauvism, Matisse continued to use color expressively. By 1909, his fame had spread worldwide. He exhibited in Russia and the United States, and in 1917 settled in Nice. Matisse designed for the ballet and illustrated the works of such authors as Baudelaire. His works include *Woman with a Hat* (1905), *Joy of Life* (1906), and *The Blue Nude* (1907). At age 80, he decorated the Dominican Nunnery chapel at Venice, France, and in his last years, produced brilliant paper cutouts and stencils.

Autobiography and Primary Sources

Matisse on Art. Jack D. Flam, ed. New York: Phaidon, 1973. 199pp. Flam collects a number of important documents by the artist that reveal Matisse's development in his own words.

Recommended Biographies

Barr, Alfred H. Jr. *Matisse: His Art and His Public.* New York: Museum of Modern Art, 1951. 591pp. The first full-scale scholarly treatment of Matisse's life and work remains one of the best and includes indispensable source materials, including several important statements by the painter on his art. The biographical details are based in part on information obtained directly from Matisse and several close associates.

Flam, Jack D. *Matisse: The Man and His Art 1869–1918.* Ithaca, New York: Cornell University Press, 1986. 523pp. In the first volume of a proposed two-volume study, Flam's biography is a worthy successor to Barr, updating the earlier book with subsequent scholarship that substantially revises Barr's interpretation of Matisse's life, character, and stylistic development.

Spurling, Hilary. *The Unknown Matisse: A Life of Henri Matisse: The Early Years, 1869–1908.* New York: Knopf, 1998. 480pp. Spurling's groundbreaking biography based on extensive research fills in a number of gaps in the factual record and provides the most detailed account of Matisse's early years and artistic development. Replacing previous speculation with convincing biographical evidence, Spurling's nuanced portrait is both insightful and coherent and alters several important assumptions about the painter.

Other Biographical Studies

Herrera, Hayden. *Matisse: A Portrait.* New York: Harcourt, Brace, 1993. 223pp. In an excellent introduction to Matisse's life and works, Herrera's sensible text is complemented by a number of well-chosen illustrations.

Lassaigne, Jacques. *Matisse: Biographical and Critical Study.* New York: Crown, 1972. 138pp. This is a concise, though mainly derivative and uncritical summary of Matisse's career, along with selections from his work.

Russell, John. *Matisse: Father & Son.* New York: Abrams, 1999. 415pp. Based on recently available unpublished correspondence between Henri Matisse and his art-dealer son Pierre, Russell crafts an intimate portrait of both men's lives.

Schneider, Pierre. *Matisse.* New York: Rizzoli, 1984. 752pp. This authoritative study of Matisse's artistic development includes new biographical material, including previously unpublished letters. Schneider's often discursive text and thematic organization makes it difficult to assemble a clear and consecutive biographical portrait of the artist, but the book is invaluable for demonstrating Matisse's artistic evolution in its cultural context.

Watkins, Nicholas. *Matisse.* New York: Oxford University Press, 1985. 240pp. In a sensible, concise, chronological narrative, Watkins surveys Matisse's career while summarizing various critical interpretations of his artistic development. Serves as an excellent introduction to the man and his genius.

Fictional Portraits

Longstreet, Stephen. *The Burning Man.* New York: Random House, 1958. 428pp. In an account of a young Spanish painter's career, the novel observes the basic outline of Picasso's life with liberal invention. Such figures as Gertrude Stein and Henri Matisse appear as named characters.

Longstreet, Stephen. *The Young Men of Paris.* New York: Delacorte, 1967. 275pp. In a biographical novel on the life of the artist Modigliani in bohemian Paris in the years before World War I, a number of other artists, including Picasso, Matisse, Chagall, and Utrillo, are also depicted.

Recommended Juvenile Biographies

Kostenevich, A.G. *Henri Matisse.* New York: Abrams, 1997. 92pp. MG/YA. Part of the acclaimed First Impressions series, the book orients the reader to the main details of Matisse's career

and an appreciation of his artistry, impact, and influences.

Mason, Anthony. *Matisse.* Hauppauge, New York: Barron's, 1995. 32pp. MG. Mason supplies a brief introduction to Matisse's life and development as an artist as well as his influences and impact.

Biographical Films and Theatrical Adaptations

Matisse (1987). Director: Didier Baussy. The film provides a portrait of the artist through archival footage and critical examinations of his art. Video.

Matisse in Nice (1986). Director: Michael Gill. This documentary follows Matisse's career and his artistic influences when in 1917 he left Paris to live for 13 years in Nice. Video.

318. W. SOMERSET MAUGHAM
1874–1965

British author, William Somerset Maugham studied medicine and completed his internship but never practiced. In World War II he served as a secret agent for the British. He first achieved success as a popular playwright, but he is most famous for his short stories and novels, including *Of Human Bondage* (1915), *The Moon and Sixpence* (1919), and *The Razor's Edge* (1944). During his later years Maugham primarily wrote essays.

Autobiography and Primary Sources

Strictly Personal. 1941. Reprint ed. New York: Arno Press, 1977. 272pp. As the author explains, "This is not an account of great events, but of the small things that happened to me during the first 15 months of the war." The book details Maugham's stay in France until its fall.

The Summing Up. 1938. Reprint ed. New York: Arno Press, 1977. 310pp. Described as an autobiography not of his life but his mind, Maugham offers insights into his introduction to literature, his writings, and his philosophical musings.

A Writer's Notebook. 1949. Reprint ed. Westport, Connecticut: Greenwood, 1970. 367pp. Maugham has extracted portions of the notebook he kept since 1892. Although there is little revealed about his private and personal life, this is a indispensable guide to the writer's literary views and creative methods.

Recommended Biographies

Calder, Robert L. *Willie: The Life of W. Somerset Maugham.* New York: St. Martin's, 1989. 429pp. The confidences of Maugham's companion, Alan Searle, lends insights to the private life of the writer in this biography that contrasts with Morgan's darker-toned portrait. Calder traces the author's development as well as the discrepancy between his public persona and his often hidden private side.

Morgan, Ted. *Somerset Maugham.* New York: Simon & Schuster, 1980. 711pp. Morgan's candid, extensively researched and detailed biography is, along with Calder's, the best choice for a sophisticated, nuanced portrait of the writer. The use of previously restricted archival material and inter-

views with those who knew the writer helps the presentation of a credible psychological profile of Maugham's often unflattering character and behavior.

Raphael, Frederic. *Somerset Maugham and His World.* New York: Scribner, 1977. 128pp. Raphael's is a compact critical biography in which more than 100 photographs complement a shrewd and stylish overview of Maugham's life and work. Serves as a valuable introduction.

Other Biographical Studies

Cordell, Richard A. *Somerset Maugham: A Biographical and Critical Study.* Bloomington: Indiana University Press, 1961. 274pp. Too admiring to be fully useful, Cordell's biographical sketch that precedes a critical review of his works is further compromised by Maugham's participation in the book's production that resulted in some misinformation.

Curtis, Anthony. *The Pattern of Maugham: A Critical Portrait.* New York: Taplinger, 1974. 278pp. Curtis's book is a solid critical introduction to Maugham's work that includes details about the writer's life and times in its critique.

Kanin, Garson. *Remembering Mr. Maugham.* New York: Atheneum, 1966. 240pp. Kanin's journal entries reconstruct meetings and conversations with Maugham during a 25-year friendship.

Maugham, Robin. *Somerset and All the Maughams.* New York: New American Library, 1966. 270pp.; *Escape from the Shadows.* London: Hodder and Stoughton, 1972. 273pp.; *Conversations with Willie.* New York: Simon & Schuster, 1978. 188pp. Maugham's nephew supplies a number of anecdotal glimpses of his famous uncle in three volumes, mixing family background, firsthand observations, and reconstructed conversations.

Pfeiffer, K.G. *W. Somerset Maugham: A Candid Portrait.* New York: W.W. Norton, 1959. 222pp. Less a full-length biography than a sketch by a former friend of the writer and bridge companion. As one reviewer acidly observed, the book "bears about the same relationship to biography or criticism as the Emperor's clothes bore to Saville Row suiting."

Other Sources

Rogal, Samuel J. *A William Somerset Maugham Encyclopedia.* Westport, Connecticut: Greenwood, 1997. 376pp. Rogal covers every aspect of Maugham's life and works in this useful reference guide.

319. JOSEPH R. MCCARTHY
1908–1957

U.S. Republican Senator from Wisconsin, McCarthy was responsible for the dubbed "McCarthy era" in the mid–1950s because of his sensational investigations into alleged American communist subversion. His Senate subcommittee investigated federal departments, the army, prominent citizens, and Hollywood personalities. McCarthy's influence declined when he was formally censured by the Senate following the national publicity generated by the Army-McCarthy hearings. The term "McCarthyism" came to denote indiscriminate attacks made publicly and without proof.

Recommended Biographies

Herman, Arthur. *Joseph McCarthy: Reexamining the Life and Legacy of America's Most Hated Senator.* New York: Free Press, 1999. 404pp. Herman's revisionist interpretation argues that McCarthy "was making a good point badly," and uses previously unavailable Soviet, FBI, Pentagon, National Security Agency, and Congressional archival sources to help buttress his case. Controversial in many of its views, the book nevertheless deserves a hearing if only for its provocative dissenting opinions.

Oshinsky, David M. *A Conspiracy So Immense: The World of Joe McCarthy.* New York: Free Press, 1983. 597pp. Although not as detailed as Reeves's biography, Oshinsky's is a more forceful narrative portrait that draws more convincing interpretive conclusions about the man and his era. For the reader looking for a single, well-written, researched, and argued account, this is the first choice.

Reeves, Thomas C. *The Life and Times of Joe McCarthy: A Biography.* New York: Stein and Day, 1982. 819pp. Reeves is the most detailed, comprehensive treatment of McCarthy's life available. In a balanced, objective assessment, the book meticulously traces the steps in the fall of a complex man of intelligence and formidable energy.

Rovere, Richard H. *Senator Joe McCarthy.* New York: Harcourt, Brace, 1959. 280pp. Rovere's journalistic account is the best of the early biographers. Devoted almost exclusively to McCarthy's Washington career, the book is knowledgeable about its milieu and the means by which McCarthy rose to power. Walter Lippmann called this portrait of McCarthy "the definitive job, and I can't imagine what else there is to say about him."

Other Biographical Studies

Anderson, Jackson, and Ronald May. *McCarthy: The Man, the Senator, the "Ism."* Boston: Beacon Press, 1952. 416pp. This investigative report, written at the height of McCarthy's notoriety, traces his career from his early days in Wisconsin with a strong muckraking intention to expose the man's flaws and tactics.

Buckley, William F., and L. Brent Bozell. *McCarthy and His Enemies: The Record and Its Meaning.* Chicago: Regnery, 1954. 413pp. The pro-McCarthy perspective is displayed in this early defense that praises McCarthy as a courageous fighter of communism. Acknowledging McCarthy's mistakes, the authors contend that the ends justify the means, concluding that "as long as McCarthyism fixes its goal with its present precision, it is a movement around which men of good will and stern morality can close ranks."

Cook, Fred J. *The Nightmare Decade: The Life and Times of Senator Joseph McCarthy.* New York: Random House, 1971. 626pp. Cook's polemical documentation of McCarthy's deceptions and abuses of power lacks depth and scholarly objectivity, but as a litany of malfeasance and complicity it is a powerful indictment.

Feuerlicht, Roberta S. *Joe McCarthy and McCarthyism: The Hate that Haunts America.* New York: McGraw-Hill, 1972. 160pp. More concerned with the roots and legacy of McCarthyism than with the man, Feuerlicht's is an impassioned case for the prosecution and a warning about McCarthyism's lingering influence.

Griffith, Robert. *The Politics of Fear: Joseph R. McCarthy and the Senate.* Amherst: University of Massachusetts Press, 1987. 362pp. Winner of the Turner Award in American history, Griffith's is an astute, scholarly account of the political dynamics that allowed McCarthy to operate for so long without censure. Best on the era that shaped and supported McCarthy.

Landis, Mark. *Joseph McCarthy: The Politics of Chaos.* Selingsgrove, Pennsylvania: Suquehanna University Press, 1987. 171pp. Landis analyzes McCarthy's behavior using psychoanalytical and social science theories of personality development. Based on secondary sources, Landis provides an intriguing, if not always convincing, interdisciplinary approach to McCarthy's make-up.

O'Brien, Michael. *McCarthy and McCarthyism in Wisconsin.* Columbia: University of Missouri Press, 1980. 269pp. O'Brien corrects the flaws in many previous biographies of McCarthy by fully treating his pre-Washington experience, helpfully illustrating that the key to understanding the man is to be found in his formative upbringing and early career in Wisconsin.

Thomas, Lately. *When Even Angels Wept: The Senator Joseph McCarthy Affair—A Story without a Hero.* New York: Morrow, 1973. 654pp. Thomas's popular biography lacks documentation but attempts firsthand reconstruction of events in a series of descriptive rather than analytical vignettes. As one reviewer pointed out about the author's "absurdly objective approach," it is "like being objective about acne."

Biographical Novels

Buckley, William F. *The Redhunter: A Novel Based on the Life and Times of Senator Joe McCarthy.* Boston: Little, Brown, 1999. 421pp. Buckley supplies a surprisingly balanced view of McCarthy's life and times with his strengths and weaknesses equally depicted.

Fictional Portraits

Vidal, Gore. *Washington, D.C.* Boston: Little, Brown, 1967. 377pp. Vidal's social chronicle follows the careers of two politicians from the 1930s to the 1950s with portrayals by several historical figures, including Franklin Roosevelt and McCarthy.

Recommended Juvenile Biographies

Cohen, Daniel. *Joseph McCarthy: The Misuse of Political Power.* Brookfield, Connecticut: Millbrook Press, 1996. 128pp. MG/YA. Cohen presents a vivid account of McCarthy's career and

era that attempts a fair assessment, quoting from both McCarthy's supporters and detractors.

Ingalls, Robert P. *Point of Order: A Profile of Senator Joe McCarthy.* New York: Putnam, 1981. 159pp. YA. This is an objective review of McCarthy's career that quotes directly from his speeches and the reactions of his opponents. The reader should have a solid understanding of the American political system to follow this treatment.

Sherrow, Victoria. *Joseph McCarthy and the Cold War.* Woodbridge, Connecticut: Blackbirch Press, 1998. 79pp. MG. Part of the Notorious Americans and Their Times series, the book documents McCarthy's actions and probes his motives, providing a clear account of his historical era.

Biographical Films and Theatrical Adaptations

A&E Biography Video: Joseph McCarthy: An American Inquisitor (1995). Directors: Richard O'Regan and Rebecca Haggarty. A film portrait tracing McCarthy's background, political rise, and years of notoriety. Video.

Citizen Cohn (1992). Director: Frank Pierson. This chilling look at the life of Roy Cohn (James Woods), chief counsel for McCarthy, is based on Nicholas von Hoffman's biography and dramatizes Cohn's relationship with McCarthy (Joe Don Baker). Video.

Joseph McCarthy (1962). Director: Alan Landsberg. McCarthy's life and political career are examined with excerpts from the U.S. Army–McCarthy hearings. Video.

McCarthy: Death of a Witchhunter (1986). Director: Emile de Antonio. Originally released as the motion picture, *Point of Order*, in 1964, the film, with an introduction by Paul Newman, examines McCarthy's political rise and subsequent fall. Video.

Tail Gunner Joe (1977). Director: Jud Taylor. McCarthy's rise to national prominence and fall is dramatized in this biographical film with Peter Boyle starring in the title role, supported by John Forsythe, Burgess Meredith, Patricia Neal, and Jean Stapleton.

Other Sources

Klingaman, William K. *Encyclopedia of the McCarthy Era.* New York: Facts on File, 1996. 502pp. This useful reference volume provides biographical profiles of leading personalities of the era, including an extensive chronology from 1919 to 1960 and appendixes of important documents.

320. WILLIAM MCKINLEY
1843–1901

The twenty-fifth U.S. president, McKinley was a Republican congressman and governor of Ohio before defeating (1896) Democrat William Jennings Bryan for the presidency. During his term in office, the United States fought the Spanish-American War, the Philippines revolted against American rule, Cuba became a U.S. protectorate, and the United States annexed Hawaii and fostered the

Open Door policy with China. Reelected in 1900, McKinley was shot to death by an anarchist while attending the 1901 Pan-American Exposition at Buffalo, New York.

Recommended Biographies

Leech, Margaret. *In the Days of McKinley.* New York: Harper, 1959. 686pp. Leech, a Pulitzer Prize–winning historian, combines a biographical portrait with a vivid depiction of the period. Sympathetic but not uncritical, Leech's book provides a revealing treatment of McKinley's private life, particularly regarding his relationship with his wife.

Morgan, H. Wayne. *William McKinley and His America.* Syracuse, New York: Syracuse University Press, 1963. 595pp. Morgan's study is the most detailed and thorough assessment of McKinley's public career. McKinley is presented in human terms in the context of his times in a way that challenges previous treatments of his personality, leadership, and impact.

Gould, Lewis L. *The Presidency of William McKinley.* Lawrence: University Press of Kansas, 1980. 294pp. Gould argues that McKinley should be regarded as the first modern president and supplies a positive reassessment of his leadership and the achievements of his administration.

Other Biographical Studies

Glad, Paul W. *McKinley, Bryan, and the People.* Philadelphia: Lippincott, 1964. 222pp. Glad's is a reassessment of the presidential election of 1896 that discusses the economic issues, the personalities of the candidates, and the political maneuvering that led to McKinley's victory.

Olcott, Charles S. *The Life of William McKinley.* Boston: Houghton Mifflin, 1916. 2 vols. This first biography lacks much penetration and is out of date although it is a convenient repository of useful documentary evidence.

Fictional Portraits

Conroy, Robert. *1901.* Novato, California: Lyford Books, 1995. 374pp. This inventive alternative history imagines a German invasion of the United States in 1901 and includes plausible depictions of a score of historical figures, including McKinley.

Saunders, Raymond M. *Fenwick Travers and the Years of Empire.* Novato, California: Lyford Books, 1993. 360pp. This installment of Saunders's comic historical series features events during the Spanish-American War and the Boxer Rebellion in China, with cameos by McKinley, "Black Jack" Pershing, and Theodore Roosevelt.

Vidal, Gore. *Empire.* New York: Random House, 1987. 486pp. Vidal's depiction of America's rise as a world power in the aftermath of the Spanish-American War features a large cast of historical figures, including McKinley, William Jennings, Bryan, Randolph Hearst, and Theodore Roosevelt.

Recommended Juvenile Biographies

Collins, David R. *William McKinley: 25th President of the United States.* Ada, Oklahoma: Garrett,

1990. 122pp. MG. This is a straightforward summary of McKinley's career and accomplishments.

Hoyt, Edwin P. *William McKinley.* Chicago: Reilly & Lee, 1967. 138pp. MG. This is a first-rate introduction to the period that helps make McKinley's career comprehensible.

Kent, Zachary. *William McKinley: Twenty-fifth President of the United States.* Chicago: Childrens Press, 1988. 98pp. MG. Kent, like Collins, offers a competent overview of McKinley's political career, with some details on his personality and private life.

Biographical Films and Theatrical Adaptations

The Rough Riders (1997). Director: John Milius. Tom Berenger portrays the young Theodore Roosevelt during his military experience in Cuba, with Brian Keith as McKinley and a supporting cast that includes Sam Eliott, Gary Busey, Chris Noth, and George Hamilton. Video.

321. MARGARET MEAD
1901–1978

Cultural anthropologist Margaret Mead was born in Philadelphia and graduated from Barnard College (1923) and Columbia University (Ph.D. 1929), having studied with anthropologists Franz Boas and Ruth Benedict. Mead's extensive fieldwork focused on child rearing, personality, and culture, and was primarily carried out among the peoples of the South Pacific. Her many works helped to popularize anthropology and include *Coming of Age in Samoa* (1928), *Growing Up in New Guinea* (1930), and her autobiography *Blackberry Winter* (1972). From 1926 until her death she was associated with the New York Museum of Natural History and after 1954 was an adjunct professor of anthropology at Columbia.

Autobiography and Primary Sources

Blackberry Winter: My Earlier Years. New York: Morrow, 1972. 305pp. A lucid, witty record of her life, Mead narrates her development from the perspective of her early family life, college years, marriages, and early field work. Despite the book's subtitle, Mead does briefly touch on her later experiences, although not in the detail that she anticipated would be provided in a second volume that she never completed.

Letters from the Field: 1925–1975. New York: Harper & Row, 1977. 343pp. In a collection of letters written from each of her major field expeditions, prefaced by introductions explaining relevant personal and scientific circumstances, Mead's changes and growth can be glimpsed as well as her immediate impressions that would be later shaped into her scholarship.

Margaret Mead: Some Personal Views. Rhoda Metraux, ed. New York: Walker, 1979. 286pp. Collects Mead's question-and-answer columns published in *Redbook* from 1963 to 1979. Additional essays from *Redbook* are collected in *Aspects of the Present* (New York: Morrow, 1980. 319pp), which records Mead's observations on such topics

as women's rights, peace, education, and the American family.

Recommended Biographies

Cassidy, Robert. *Margaret Mead: A Voice for the Century.* New York: Universe Books, 1982. 176pp. Written with Mead's cooperation in 1977 when she realized that she would not be able to write the sequel to *Blackberry Winter,* Cassidy's biography supplements Mead's personal insights with a chronological account of her career, in which each chapter looks at some aspect of Mead's work, showing how her life developed as a result.

Howard, Jane. *Margaret Mead: A Life.* New York: Simon & Schuster, 1984. 527pp. Based on extensive interviews with associates, Howard forms a composite portrait, concentrating more on Mead's personal rather than public life, providing a detailed account of the anthropologist's relationships. Cassidy's biography is a better choice for those interested in Mead's professional development, but Howard presents more data on Mead's character and personality.

Other Biographical Studies

Bateson, Mary C. *With a Daughter's Eye: A Memoir of Margaret Mead and Gregory Bateson.* New York: Morrow, 1984. 242pp. In an intimate, candid account of her parents, Mead's daughter provides details about the relationship between her mother and Gregory Bateson and Ruth Benedict in an affectionate but honest recollection.

Freeman, Derek. *Margaret Mead and Samoa: The Making and Unmaking of an Anthropological Myth.* Cambridge, Massachusetts: Harvard University Press, 1983. 379pp. Freeman's controversial attack on Mead's research in Samoa challenges the anthropologist's methods and findings. The weakness of Freeman's argument has been exposed by many Mead supporters, but the book has become unavoidable in examining Mead's groundbreaking *Coming of Age in Samoa.*

Holmes, Lowell D. *Quest for the Real Samoa: The Mead/Freeman Controversy and Beyond.* South Hadley, Massachusetts: Bergin and Harvey, 1987. 209pp. The author's own research in Samoa during the 1950s largely substantiates Mead's earlier findings. Holmes's judicious criticism of Freeman's attack deserves to be read as a more measured, balanced account of the controversy.

Lapsley, Hilary. *Margaret Mead and Ruth Benedict: The Kinship of Women.* Amherst: University of Massachusetts Press, 1999. 416pp. Lapsley offers a sensitive account of the relationship between Mead and Ruth Benedict from their first meeting at Columbia University in the early 1920s to Benedict's death in 1948.

Recommended Juvenile Biographies

Mark, Joan T. *Margaret Mead, Anthropologist: Coming of Age in America.* New York: Oxford University Press, 1998. 144pp. MG. Part of the Oxford Portrait in Science series, this is a lively, well-researched profile of Mead's life and achievements that makes her work understandable for a younger reader.

Tilton, Rafael. *Margaret Mead.* San Diego: Lucent Books, 1994. 112pp. MG. A readable, informative, well-illustrated biography, Tilton discusses Mead's contributions to anthropology, the controversy surrounding her reputation, as well as her three marriages and divorces.

Ziesk, Edra. *Margaret Mead.* New York: Chelsea House, 1990. 109pp. MG/YA. In a balanced portrait of Mead's life and career, Ziesk traces the anthropologist's development and her contributions to science, women's history, and feminism.

Biographical Films and Theatrical Adaptations

Margaret Mead: American Anthropologist (1988). Producer: Films for the Humanities. In a film profile, Mead's career as a scientist and thinker is documented. Video.

Margaret Mead and Samoa (1988). Director: Frank Heimans. A documentary look at the Mead/Freeman controversy. Video.

Margaret Mead: Taking Notice (1980). Director: Ann Peck. This PBS documentary uses newsreel footage, photographs, and interviews with Mead and her colleagues to trace her career and ideas. Video.

322. LORENZO DE' MEDICI
1449–1492

Italian merchant prince called "the Magnificent," Lorenzo is one of the towering figures of the Renaissance. He was virtual ruler of Florence and eventually gained control of the city's public funds. He was an astute politician and diplomat, a patron of the arts, literature, and learning, and a scholar and poet.

Autobiography and Primary Sources

Lives of the Early Medici: As Told in Their Correspondence. Janet Ross, ed. Boston: Badger, 1911. 351pp. This still useful volume weaves together letters to cover the lives of Cosimo, Piero, and Lorenzo.

Recommended Biographies

Hook, Judith. *Lorenzo de' Medici: An Historical Biography.* London: Hamilton, 1984. 206pp. Drawing on recent scholarship in Florentine economy, politics, and family histories, Hook places de' Medici in the context of his times. Accessible for the general reader and student, Hook's is a concise, balanced historical biography.

Ross Williamson, Hugh. *Lorenzo the Magnificent.* New York: Putnam, 1974. 288pp. The book takes a colorful popular life-and-times approach featuring extensive illustrations that serves as a capable introduction, though many of Ross Williamson's characterizations and interpretations should be accepted with caution.

Other Biographical Studies

Rubinstein, Nicolai. *Lorenzo de' Medici: The Formation of His Statecraft.* Oxford: Oxford University Press, 1977. 94pp. Rubinstein's is a highly detailed, scholarly account of the politics of de' Medici's era and his leadership.

Sturm-Maddox, Sarah. *Lorenzo de' Medici.* New York: Twayne, 1974. 173pp. This critical study examines de' Medici as a writer, providing a close focus on his character and personality as viewed through his works.

Fictional Portraits

Eliot, George. *Romola.* 1863. Reprint ed. New York: Oxford University Press, 1998. 622pp. Eliot's historical novel set in fifteenth-century Florence weaves a fictional story around actual events and appearances by such historical figures as Lorenzo, Charles VIII, Savonarola, and Machiavelli.

La Mure, Pierre. *The Private Life of Mona Lisa.* Boston: Little, Brown, 1976. 406pp. In a detailed and convincing recreation of Renaissance Italy, the novel imagines the life of Leonardo's model for the *Mona Lisa,* while speculating why he painted the portrait and for whom. Several historical figures are featured, including Charles VIII, Savonarola, and Lorenzo de' Medici.

Ripley, Alexandra. *The Time Returns.* Garden City, New York: Doubleday, 1985. 334pp. The novel, based on accurate details from Lorenzo's life, imagines a love affair between the Florentine nobleman and a gentlewoman.

Stone, Irving. *The Agony and the Ecstasy.* Garden City, New York: Doubleday, 1961. 664pp. Stone's convincing portrait of Michelangelo's career from boyhood features his relationship with his Florentine patron, Lorenzo de' Medici.

Shulman, Sandra. *The Florentine.* New York: Morrow, 1973. 314pp. Lorenzo de' Medici's hold on power in Florence during the 1480s is dramatized from the perspective of a young woman who disguises herself as a boy and comes into contact with several historical figures, including Leonardo da Vinci, Savonarola, Botticelli, Pico della Mirandola, and Ghirlandajo.

Woodhouse, Martin, and Robert Ross. *The Medici Guns.* New York: Dutton, 1975. 277pp.; *The Medici Emerald.* New York: Dutton, 1976. 223pp.; 17 b *The Medici Hawks.* New York: Dutton, 1978. 202pp. This intriguing historical series features Leonardo da Vinci in a number of fanciful adventures and portrayals of a number of period figures, including Lorenzo and Pope Sixtus IV.

Recommended Juvenile Biographies

Mee, Charles L. *Lorenzo de' Medici and the Renaissance.* New York: American Heritage, 1969. 153pp. YA. This sound, visual biography and overview of the period serves both young adult and general readers.

See also Catherine de' Medici

323. GOLDA MEIR
1898–1978

Israeli prime minister Golda Meir was born Golda Mabovitch in Kiev, Russia, and immigrated (1906) to Milwaukee with her family. She became a schoolteacher, involved herself with the Zionist labor movement, and in 1921 moved to Palestine with her husband, Morris Meyerson. She was head of the Histadrut (1936) and after Israeli independence (1948) served as minister to Moscow. Meir was elected to the Knesset (1949), served as minister of labor (1949–1956) and foreign minister (1956–1966), and in 1966 became secretary general of the dominant Mapai party, later the Labor Party. She succeeded (1969) Levi Eshkol as prime minister and formed a broad coalition government. Meir (the name was Hebraized from Meyerson in 1956) faced criticism for negotiating with hostile Arab nations but nevertheless retained enormous personal popularity. During her ministry, Israel fought the Yom Kippur War (1973) against Egypt and Syria. She resigned from office in 1974.

Autobiography and Primary Sources

A Land of Our Own: An Oral Autobiography. Marie Syrkin, ed. New York: Putnam, 1973. 251pp. In a collection of interviews, articles, and speeches, the first two chapters gather together a number of Meir's biographical reflections.

My Life. New York: Putnam, 1975. 480pp. In a remarkably candid account of her life from her early days in Russia through her adolescence in America, her immigration to Palestine in the 1920s to her political career as labor and foreign minister and finally prime minister, Meir reveals the personal cost of her public service and her unflagging convictions on behalf of Israel. One of the most revealing and fascinating autobiographies of any political figure.

Recommended Biographies

Martin, Ralph G. *Golda: The Romantic Years.* New York: Scribner, 1988. 422pp. In the most comprehensive and authoritative account of Meir's early years from childhood through the establishment of Israel in 1948, Martin, through interviews and archival research, establishes a detailed factual record of Meir's development and a convincing human portrait.

Other Biographical Studies

Mann, Peggy. *Golda: The Life of Israel's Prime Minister.* New York: Coward-McCann, 1971. 287pp. Written by a long time associate, this is an honest, balanced assessment of Meir's private and public lives.

Meir, Menahem. *My Mother, Golda Meir: A Son's Evocation of Life with Golda Meir.* New York: Arbor House, 1983. 254pp. The emphasis here is an intimate portrait of the woman and mother rather than the political figure. Rich in anecdotes, the book expresses a son's moving tribute to his mother.

Slater, Robert. *Golda: the Uncrowned Queen of Israel: A Pictorial Biography.* New York: J. David, 1981. 277pp. This visual biography is chiefly valuable for its photographic record rather than for its text, which tends more to flattery than a balanced, objective assessment.

Syrkin, Marie. *Golda Meir: Israel's Leader.* New York: Putnam, 1969. 366pp. Revised ed. of *Golda Meir: Woman with a Cause* (New York: Putnam, 1963. 320pp.). In this early political biography written by a close associate, Syrkin attempts to isolate the character traits that account for Meir's political successes, though covering mainly her rise to power.

Fictional Portraits

Wouk, Herman. *The Glory.* Boston: Little, Brown, 1994. 685pp. Wouk's family saga interweaves a fictional story around such events as the Yom Kippur War, the Entebbe rescue, and the signing of the Camp David accord, with appearances by a number of historical figures, including Meir.

Recommended Juvenile Biographies

Amdur, Richard. *Golda Meir: A Leader in Peace and War.* New York: Fawcett Columbine, 1990. 117pp. MG. Meir's life and character are set against a clear background of the founding of the state of Israel and its conflict with the Arab world.

Hitzeroth, Deborah. *Golda Meir.* San Diego: Lucent Books, 1998. 111pp. MG. Using quotes from primary and secondary sources, this informative biography chronicles the highlights of Meir's eventful life from childhood through the heroic struggle to create and sustain Israel.

McAuley, Karen. *Golda Meir.* New York: Chelsea House, 1985. 112pp. MG/YA. McAuley offers a straightforward and informative summary of Meir's public and private life with a clearly outlined historical background.

Biographical Films and Theatrical Adaptations

Gibson, William. *Notes on How to Turn a Phoenix into Ashes: The Story of the Stage Production, with the Text of Golda.* New York: Atheneum, 1978. 149pp. Told in flashbacks, Gibson dramatizes the significant events in Meir's life in a multilayered portrait of her public and private life.

Sword of Gideon (1989). Director: Michael Anderson. A made-for-cable film depiction of the hunt for the terrorists who murdered the Israeli athletes at the 1972 Munich Olympics. Starring Steven Bauer, Michael York, Rod Steiger, and Colleen Dewhurst as Golda Meir. Video.

A Woman Called Golda (1982). Director: Alan Gibson. Judy Davis portrays the young Meir and Ingrid Bergman depicts her in maturity in an excellent made-for-television biographical drama. Leonard Nimoy, Anne Jackson, Ned Beatty, and Robert Loggia co-star. A novelization by Michael Avallone (New York: Leisure Books, 1982. 265pp.) is also available. Video.

324. HERMAN MELVILLE
1819–1891

One of world literature's best-known writers, Melville was born in New York City into an impoverished family of distinguished Dutch and English colonial ancestry. At 15 he left school and worked at a variety of jobs before signing on as a cabin boy (1839) on a whaling ship. From 1841 to 1844 he worked on whalers and spent time in Tahiti and other Pacific islands, the literary result of which was the popular romantic novels *Typee* (1846), *Omoo* (1847), and *Redburn* (1849). His masterpiece, *Moby Dick* (1851), was not successful. By 1866, mounting debts, ill health, and the failure to win an audience for his work forced Melville to sell the Pittsfield, Massachusetts farm where he had lived since 1850. He obtained a poorly paid position as a customs inspector in New York City, a job he held for 19 years. He died in poverty and obscurity. Melville's other well-known works include the short stories "Benito Cereno" and "Bartleby the Scrivener," and the novella *Billy Budd*, published posthumously in 1924.

Autobiography and Primary Sources

The Letters of Herman Melville. Merrell R. Davis and William H. Gilman, eds. New Haven, Connecticut: Yale University Press, 1960. 398pp. This scholarly edition collects the 271 known Melville letters.

Recommended Biographies

Howard, Leon. *Herman Melville: A Biography.* Berkeley: University of California Press, 1951. 354pp. Based on new source material and modern scholarship, Howard's critical biography has long served as the standard source for a reliable and comprehensive narrative account of Melville's life. Scrupulously factual in its approach, Howard resists any speculation that exceeds the evidence. Trustworthy but limited by a lack of details, particularly on Melville's years of obscurity.

Miller, Edwin H. *Melville.* New York: G. Braziller, 1975. 382pp. Miller's psychobiography probes Melville's psyche in a provocative, insightful interpretation that sees Melville as his own Ishmael, a psychological orphan with an unresolved Oedipal conflict. The book is excellent on Melville's relationship with Hawthorne.

Parker, Hershel. *Herman Melville: A Biography. Volume I, 1819–1851.* Baltimore: Johns Hopkins University Press, 1996. 941pp. In the first volume of what promises to be the definitive biography, Parker in minute detail synthesizes the results of others' and his own extensive research into the most comprehensive and authoritative treatment of Melville's life to date. Taking Melville's story up to 1851 with the publication of *Moby Dick*, Melville is securely rooted in his family, social, and intellectual milieu.

Robertson-Lorant, Laurie. *Melville: A Biography.* New York: Clarkson Potter, 1995. 710pp. Drawing on a substantial cache of recently discovered family letters, Robertson-Lorant presents a comprehensive and consistent portrait of the artist and a speculative, though plausible, account of how the

events of his life were refined into his fiction. Readers impatient with the minutiae of Parker's more documentary examination may prefer this vivid and dramatic rendering of Melville's life in which the author's private and public lives are sensitively portrayed.

Other Biographical Studies

Allen, Gay Wilson. *Melville and His World.* New York: Viking, 1971. 144pp. This pictorial biography includes a concise factual account of Melville's life that serves the general reader as a succinct orientation to the author's career.

Anderson, Charles R. *Melville in the South Seas.* New York: Columbia University Press, 1939. 522pp. In a detailed, factual record of Melville's years at sea, based on previously unpublished sources, Anderson corrects the factual record and provides the means to evaluate the autobiographical basis for Melville's first fiction.

Arvin, Newton. *Herman Melville.* New York: W. Sloane, 1950. 316pp. In an often brilliant, finely written critical biography, Arvin offers a psychological interpretation of Melville's personality from a consistent Freudian perspective. Arvin shapes the biographical facts to fit his thesis of Melville's torment, ignoring biographical details that do not contribute to his portrait.

Garner, Stanton. *The Civil War World of Herman Melville.* Lawrence: University Press of Kansas, 1993. 560pp. Focusing on Melville's shifting moods and attitudes during the period 1859 to 1866, Garner deals with a lack of direct evidence by examining Melville indirectly through the views and circumstances of Melville's friends, family, and neighbors and a close reading of Melville's *Battle-Pieces.*

Gilman, William H. *Melville's Early Life and Redburn.* New York: New York University Press, 1951. 378pp. Focusing on the period 1819 to 1841, Gilman supplies a number of new sources on Melville's family background and documents how Melville's voyage to Liverpool as an ordinary seaman in 1839 was considerably reworked imaginatively for his fourth novel, *Redburn.*

Hardwick, Elizabeth. *Herman Melville.* New York: Viking, 2000. 159pp. Part of the Penguin Lives series, this brief critical biography concentrates on the essence of the man and his writing in a critically perceptive overview and distillation.

Kirby, David K. *Herman Melville.* New York: Continuum, 1993. 192pp. Kirby presents a helpful overview of Melville's life and works, concentrating on the external events of Melville's career, the sequence of his work, and the writer's internal development.

Metcalf, Eleanor Melville. *Herman Melville: Cycle and Epicycle.* Cambridge, Massachusetts: Harvard University Press, 1953. 311pp. Melville's granddaughter assembles her collection of family papers and letters by, to, and about her grandfather to form a biographical record with connecting commentary.

Mumford, Lewis. *Herman Melville.* 1929. Revised ed. New York: Harcourt, Brace, 1962. 256pp. A critical biography that is particularly good on the period background, Mumford's study is strongest on its interpretation of Melville's works than its presentation of the facts of his life. Relying mainly on Melville's own writings as principal sources, Mumford adds little to the factual record.

Sealts, Merton M. Jr. *The Early Lives of Melville: Nineteenth-Century Biographical Sketches and Their Authors.* Madison: University of Wisconsin Press, 1974. 280pp. This volume collects all the 19th-century biographical writings on Melville from reference works, newspaper articles, reminiscences requested by Melville's granddaughter, and a fragmentary memoranda book by Melville's wife. Sealts's earlier book, *Melville as Lecturer.* (Cambridge, Massachusetts: Harvard University Press, 1957. 202pp.) documents Melville's life between 1858 and 1861 when he abandoned his writing career for the lecture circuit, Sealts provides reviews and partial texts of these lectures reconstructed from newspaper accounts.

Weaver, Raymond. *Herman Melville: Mariner and Mystic.* New York: G.H. Doran, 1921. 399pp. The first Melville biography is mostly reliant on Melville's fiction as a factual record of his life, a method that later biographers have demonstrated is problematic. With little else to go on, Weaver covers the author's last 37 years in a single brief chapter.

Fictional Portraits

Aronin, Ben. *Walt Whitman's Secret.* Chicago, Angus Books, 1955. 374pp. Whitman's early life from the 1840s to 1860s is depicted with appearances by several literary figures, including Emerson, Thoreau, and Melville.

Busch, Frederick. *The Night Inspector.* New York: Harmony Books, 1999. 278pp. Busch's darkly evocative recreation of post-Civil War New York City centers on a disillusioned Union sharpshooter whose path crosses that of Melville, working in bitter anonymity as a customs inspector.

Clarke, William K. *The Robber Baroness.* New York: St. Martin's, 1979. 347pp. The early years of the notorious miser and financier Hetty Green is depicted as well as New York City in the 1850s and 1860s with appearances by several historical figures, including Herman Melville.

Duberstein, Larry. *The Handsome Sailor.* Sag Harbor, New York: Permanent Press, 1998. 267pp. In a fictionalized account of Melville's largely unknown later years of silence, the author speculates that Melville's depression was a result of a failed love affair with an actual Sarah Morewood (although no evidence exists to suggest they were lovers) and his regeneration from his relationship with a fictional widow. Duberstein's fancy is anchored by a remarkable period reconstruction.

Recommended Juvenile Biographies

Bixby, William. *Rebel Genius: The Life of Herman Melville.* New York: McKay, 1970. 133pp. MG. Informative, if somewhat idealized, Bixby relates the highpoints of Melville's life and literary career with an emphasis on the writer's temperament that shaped his writing and disappointments.

Keyes, Charlotte E. *High on the Mainmast: A Biography of Herman Melville.* New Haven, Connecticut: College & University Press, 1966. 158pp. MG/YA. Keyes's is a well-written, well-researched biography that connects Melville's experiences with the themes of his writings.

Stefoff, Rebecca. *Herman Melville.* New York: J. Messner, 1994. 156pp. YA. In an exceptional biography, the author connects Melville's life and works in a sensitive account that serves as an ideal complement to a student's exposure to Melville's novels.

Biographical Films and Theatrical Adaptations

Herman Melville: American Writer, 1819–1891 (1993). Director: Malcolm Hossick. The film traces Melville's life and writing career, using photographs and views of places associated with him. Video.

Herman Melville: Consider the Sea (1995). Director: Charles Olin. Poet Richard Wilbur narrates this film portrait of Melville, focusing on his personality and his obsession with the sea. Video.

Herman Melville: Damned in Paradise (1985). Director: Robert D. Squier. Narrated by John Huston, this documentary blends photographs with interviews with critics and biographers to examine Melville's life and works. Video.

Other Sources

Gale, Robert L. *A Herman Melville Encyclopedia.* Westport, Connecticut: Greenwood, 1995. 536pp. In a comprehensive reference guide to Melville's life and works, individual entries cover the author's characters, family members, friends, and acquaintances.

Leyda, Jay. *The Melville Log: A Documentary Life of Herman Melville, 1819–1891.* 1951. Revised ed. New York: Harcourt, Brace, 1969. 2 vols. Leyda's massive assemblage of every existent fact about Melville, arranged chronologically, is the indispensable reference source for any biographer and allows, in Leyda's words, "each reader the opportunity to be his own biographer of Herman Melville."

325. H.L. MENCKEN
1880–1956

American journalist, editor, and author, Henry Louis Mencken became famous as an iconoclastic critic of American society. He wrote for the Baltimore *Sun* and cofounded and edited the *American Mercury.* Among his works are *Prejudices* (1919–1927), a six-volume collection of essays, and an authoritative study, *The American Language* (1919).

Autobiography and Primary Sources

Mencken left extensive autobiographical materials. Published during his lifetime, his trilogy, *Happy Days.* 1940. Reprint ed. (Baltimore, Maryland: Johns Hopkins University Press, 1996. 313pp.), *Newspaper Days.* 1941. Reprint ed. (New York: Knopf, 1963. 313pp.), and *Heathen Days.* 1943. (Reprint ed. New York: AMS Press, 1987. 299pp.), constitutes an entertaining but not always factually reliable series of anecdotes ranging over significant segments of Mencken's life. More candid are the two book-length memoirs recently published in abridged form after the 35 years following his death stipulated in Mencken's will:

My Life as Author and Editor. Jonathan Yardley, ed. (New York: Knopf, 1993. 449pp.) covers Mencken's career up to 1923.

Thirty-Five Years of Newspaper Work: A Memoir. Fred C. Hobson, ed. (Baltimore: Johns Hopkins University Press, 1994. 390pp.) treats his early years with the Baltimore *Evening Sun*, his brief stint as a war correspondent, his travels to Cuba, and his coverage of presidential candidates.

The Diaries of H.L. Mencken. Charles A. Fecher, ed. New York: Knopf, 1989. 476pp. Covering the years 1930 to 1948, Mencken's diaries include both astute literary and social observations, candid assessment of important figures, and unsettling examples of the writer's slurs on Jews and African Americans.

Mencken's letters are also an important source of insight on his activities and temperament. The fullest collection is the *Letters of H.L. Mencken.* Guy J. Forque, ed. (Boston: Northeastern University Press, 1961. 506pp.). An additional valuable collection documenting Mencken's relationship with the young writer he later married is *Mencken and Sara: A Life in Letters: The Private Correspondence of H.L. Mencken and Sara Haardt.* Marion Elizabeth Rodgers, ed. (New York: McGraw-Hill, 1987. 551pp.).

Recommended Biographies

Bode, Carl. *Mencken.* Carbondale: Southern Illinois University Press, 1969. 452pp. Bode's is a strong critical biography, carefully researched and judicious in its assessment of Mencken's public and private life, his flaws, and his literary achievements.

Hobson, Fred C. *Mencken: A Life.* New York: Random House, 1994. 650pp. Based on the posthumously released personal papers, Hobson's biography looks closely at the discrepancy between the myths promulgated by Mencken and the reality. No other biography has fixed the writer with such clear and detailed focus. The book should remain the definitive life for some time to come.

Manchester, William. *Disturber of the Peace: The Life of H.L. Mencken.* New York: Harper, 1950. 348pp. Manchester's authorized biography lacks critical objectivity and is as one reviewer remarked "almost painfully adulatory," but few are better at crafting an entertaining, vivid narrative.

Other Biographical Studies

Goldberg, Isaac. *The Man Mencken: A Biographical and Critical Survey.* 1925. Reprint ed. New York: AMS Press, 1968. 388pp. Based on information (and misinformation) supplied by Mencken, Goldberg's account represents the way in which the writer wanted to be seen. Not reliable due to both what it includes and what it omits.

Kemler, Edgar. *The Irreverent Mr. Mencken.* Boston: Little, Brown, 1950. 317pp. Like Goldberg, Kemler received assistance from Mencken in the biographical details provided, so the same caution applied to Goldberg applies here. The book concentrates on Mencken's public career as a battle with American public opinion.

Mayfield, Sara. *The Constant Circle: H.L. Mencken and His Friends.* New York: Delacorte, 1968. 307pp. Often blinded by her loyalties, Mayfield, a hometown friend of Mencken's wife, supplies a highly laudatory series of recollections of limited usefulness.

Stenerson, Douglas C. *H.L. Mencken: Iconoclast from Baltimore.* Chicago: University of Chicago Press, 1971. 287pp. Stenerson's is an intellectual history of Mencken's ideas and development. By no means a comprehensive biographical portrait, the book does deal closely with Mencken's personality and prejudices in the context of his era.

Williams, William H.A. *H.L. Mencken Revisited.* New York:Twayne, 1999. 195pp. This is a critical introduction to Mencken's life and works, based on a close reading of his books, articles, letters, and memoirs.

Fictional Portraits

Swaim, Don. *The H.L. Mencken Murder Case.* New York: St. Martin's, 1988. 174pp. Mencken is featured as a sleuth in this period mystery set during the 1940s.

315. FELIX MENDELSSOHN-BARTHOLDY
1809–1847

German Romantic composer Mendelssohn is a major figure of nineteenth-century music. He wrote his famous overture to *A Midsummer Night's Dream* at age 17. Among his other works are the *Reformation* (1832), *Italian* (1833), and *Scottish* (1842) symphonies, and the *Fingal's Cave* overture (1832). Mendelssohn was also a celebrated conductor, who revived interest in Bach's work. He helped found the Leipzig Conservatory (1843).

Autobiography and Primary Sources

Felix Mendelssohn: Letters. Gisella Selden-Goth, ed. New York: Putnam, 1945. 373pp. A collection of Mendelssohn's letters from 1821 to his death, with an emphasis on his correspondence with musical colleagues revealing his musical opinions.

Felix Mendelssohn: A Life in Letters. Rudolf Elvers, ed. New York: Fromm International, 1986. 334pp. In a selection of 125 of the more than 4,000 known letters that spans the composer's life from age 12, the emphasis is on Mendelssohn's private, family relationships. Includes biographical notes and a detailed chronology.

The Mendelssohns on Honeymoon: The 1837 Diary of Felix and Cécile Mendelssohn-Bartholdy Together with Letters to Their Families. Peter Ward Jones, ed. New York: Oxford University Press, 1997. 225pp. This daily record of the newly-weds offers a unique view on the composer's activities and impressions.

Recommended Biographies

Marek, George. *Gentle Genius: The Story of Felix Mendelssohn.* New York: Funk & Wagnalls, 1973. 365pp. Written for the general reader, Marek's biographical account serves as a fine introduction to the man and his music.

Warrack, John H. *The New Grove Early Romantic Masters 2.* New York: W.W. Norton, 1985. 314pp. This succinct profile incorporates modern research and is the first choice for the reader interested in a brief but authoritative biographical and critical account of the composer's life and works.

Werner, Eric. *Mendelssohn: A New Image of the Composer and His Age.* New York: Free Press, 1963. 545pp. Based on a close examination of more than 8,000 unpublished letters written by and to the composer, Werner provides new details and corrects the factual record in the most authoritative and comprehensive study available.

Other Biographical Studies

Blunt, Wilfrid. *On Wings of Song: A Biography of Felix Mendelssohn.* New York: Scribner, 1974. 288pp. In an anecdotal account, Blunt examines Mendelssohn's life against the background of nineteenth-century life. Relying on the composer's letters and diaries, the book avoids interpretation and does not treat Mendelssohn's music critically.

Hensel, Sebastian. *The Mendelssohn Family (1729–1847) from Letters and Journals.* New York: Harper, 1881. 2 vols. Hensel's group biography includes details on the composer's grandfather, parents, and siblings. Based on an extensive collection of family papers, Hensel's has long served as a useful source book on Mendelssohn's life and background.

Hiller, Ferdinand. *Mendelssohn: Letters and Recollections.* 1874. Revised ed. New York: Vienna House, 1972. 223pp. Hiller, a contemporary of the composer, offers a number of firsthand impressions of Mendelssohn and his relationships with Chopin and Liszt.

Jacob, Heinrich E. *Felix Mendelssohn and His Times.* Englewood Cliffs, New Jersey: Prentice-Hall, 1963. 356pp. In a nonchronological account, Jacob examines various aspects of Mendelssohn's personality in terms of his era, setting his compositions firmly in their cultural context.

Kupferberg, Herbert. *The Mendelssohns: Three Generations of Genius.* New York: Scribner, 1972. 272pp. In a group biography of Mendelssohn's distinguished family, two-thirds of the book centers on the composer's life and is particularly strong on his Jewish background.

Lampadius, W.A. *The Life of Felix Mendelssohn-Bartholdy.* 1865. Revised ed. Boston: D. Ditson, 1887. 333pp. Originally published in Germany in 1848, this early biography includes a number of contemporary recollections of the composer.

Petitpierre, Jacques. *The Romance of the Mendelssohns.* London: Dobson, 1947. 251pp. The author focuses on the composer's married life.

Polko, Elise. *Reminiscences of Felix Mendelssohn-Bartholdy: A Social and Artistic Biography.* 1869. Reprint ed. Macomb, Illinois: Glenbridge, 1987. 232pp. The author, who studied singing under Mendelssohn, provides a contemporary first-hand recollection and assessment of the composer, including opinions and testimonies of many other contemporaries. Not always reliable in its use of primary sources, Polko's account is nevertheless a touching, personal tribute.

Radcliffe, Philip. *Mendelssohn.* New York: Dent, 1954. 208pp. In a balanced, reliable assessment, part of the Master Musician series, Radcliffe presents a chronological account of the composer's life and career, followed by chapters on his personality and influences, and a critique of his music by genre.

Biographical Novels

La Mure, Pierre. *Beyond Desire: A Novel Based on the Life of Felix and Cécile Mendelssohn.* New York: Random House, 1955. 310pp. The composer's life is dramatized with an emphasis on Mendelssohn's relationship with the opera singer Maria Sala and his married life. The novel also offers a convincing portrait of its era with appearances by a number of historical figures, including Chopin, Schumann, and Wagner.

Recommended Juvenile Biographies

Hurd, Michael. *Mendelssohn.* New York: Crowell, 1971. 87pp. MG. This is brief but informative and balanced introduction to the composer's life and accomplishments.

Kupferberg, Herbert. *Felix Mendelssohn: His Life, His Family, His Music.* New York: Scribner, 1972. 176pp. YA. A standout profile of Mendelssohn's life and times, this is both a highly readable and vivid presentation that integrates the details of the composer's life with his genius and achievements.

Moshansky, Mozelle. *Mendelssohn: His Life and Times.* Neptune, New Jersey: Paganiniana, 1981. 144pp. YA. Like Kupferberg, Moshansky places the composer in a wider historical and cultural context that helps to make his accomplishments understandable.

327. KLEMENS VON METTERNICH
1773–1859

Austrian statesman who brokered post-Napoleonic stability in Europe, Metternich was born in Koblenz of a noble Rhenish family. He pursued a diplomatic career in Saxony, Prussia, and France, and in 1809 became Austrian foreign minister. Committed to Austrian interests, he negotiated the 1810 marriage of Archduchess Marie Louise to Napoleon and in 1812 forged a temporary alliance with France. He then allied Austria, Russia, and Prussia against Napoleon and at the Congress of Vienna (1814–1815) reinstituted a system in which a balance of power was maintained between European nations. The period between 1815–1848 is often called the "Age of Metternich." His system relied upon political and religious censorship, espionage, and the suppression of revolutionary and nationalist movements. His power waned after 1826 and he was overthrown during the revolutions of 1848. He was forced to flee to England but returned to Austria in 1851.

Autobiography and Primary Sources

Memoirs of Prince Metternich. New York: Scribner, 1880–1882. 5 vols. Prepared by Metternich's son, this collection of autobiographical notes and primary documents is an indispensable source for all subsequent biographers. The casual reader should come to the *Memoirs* with prior acquaintance with the highlights of Metternich's life and career.

Recommended Biographies

Palmer, Alan W. *Metternich.* New York: Harper & Row, 1972. 405pp. In an excellent critical biography, Palmer presents Metternich not as a stereotypical reactionary but as a complex individual whose policies are traced through their political and social context. Well-researched and readable, Palmer reveals both the private and public aspects of Metternich's life.

Seward, Desmond. *Metternich: The First European.* New York: Viking, 1991. 300pp. This lively, highly sympathetic, interpretive biography views Metternich as the consummate statesman of his age. Relying heavily on Metternich's personal and state papers, Seward covers Metternich's private and family life as well as his public career.

Other Biographical Studies

Cecil, Algernon. *Metternich 1773–1859: A Study of His Period and His Personality.* New York: Macmillan, 1933. 344pp. In a vigorous defense of Metternich's ideals and integrity, Cecil concentrates on Metternick's public career and the historical forces that shaped it.

Du Coudray, Helene. *Metternich.* New Haven, Connecticut: Yale University Press, 1936. 415pp. In a readable account of Metternich's entire life with an emphasis on his years in power, Du Coudray presents an often witty and colorful synthesis of primary and secondary source materials.

Herman, Arthur. *Metternich.* New York: Century, 1932. 370pp. Herman combines an account of Metternich's diplomatic career with a brief history of European politics during his lifetime. Although attacked by Heinrich Srbik, the author of the standard biography of Metternich in German, for its interpretation and facts, Herman's account serves the general reader as a succinct introduction to the man and his era.

Malleson, George B. *The Life of Prince Metternich.* Philadelphia: Lippincott, 1888. 209pp. Written by an English military historian, the book makes use of Metternich's *Memoirs* for most of its details supporting an interpretation of the statesman as a reactionary opponent of nationalism.

Milne, Andrew. *Metternich.* Totowa, New Jersey: Rowman and Littlefield, 1975. 189pp. Milne's is a brief, sympathetic overview of Metternich's diplomatic career that also provides a discussion of the modern trends in viewing Metternich's life and achievement.

Sandeman, George A. C. *Metternich.* New York: Brentano's, 1911. 358pp. Based on German sources, the book offers no new facts or more than a conventional interpretation, marred by several inaccuracies and an annoyingly flippant style.

Fictional Portraits

Anthony, Evelyn. *Far Flies the Eagle.* New York: Crowell, 1955. 208pp. European history from 1807 to 1820 is dramatized in the conflict between Napoleon and Russia's Alexander I. The complexity of history is reduced here to dramatic simplifications with appearances by a wide range of historical figures, including Metternich.

Waldeck, R.G. *Lustre in the Sky.* Garden City, New York: Doubleday, 1946. 434pp. The scene is the Congress of Vienna as the map of Europe is redrawn after Napoleon's defeat. The novel focuses on the Talleyrand's public and private affairs with appearances by Alexander I and Metternich.

Zilahy, Lajos. *Century in Scarlet.* New York: McGraw-Hill, 1965. 411pp. Chronicling European history in the nineteenth century from the Congress of Vienna from the perspective of twin Hungarian aristocrats, Metternich is one of several historical figures who are glimpsed.

Recommended Juvenile Biographies

Archer, Jules. *Colossus of Europe: Metternich.* New York: J. Messner, 1970. 191pp. YA. This is a complete and authentic look at Metternich's life and the social, political, and diplomatic contexts of his era. Although fictionalized, the dialogue is derived from Metternich's memoirs.

Von der Heide, John T. *Klemens von Metternich.* New York: Chelsea House, 1988. 112pp. YA. Ably serves as a clear introduction to the man and the complex historical and diplomatic issues of his era.

Biographical Films and Theatrical Adaptations

Conquest (1937). Director: Clarence Brown. Napoleon's relationship with the Polish Countess Walewska is depicted with Charles Boyer and Greta Garbo as the lovers. Ian Wolfe depicts Metternich. Video.

Immortal Beloved (1994). Director: Bernard Rose. In this intriguing and visually stunning film, the mystery of who is the "immortal beloved" referred to in a letter found after Beethoven's death leads to flashbacks dramatizing the composer's life and loves. Considerable liberties with the facts prevent the film from being viewed as a faithful account, but Gary Oldman as Beethoven is well cast as the tortured genius. Isabella Rossellini co-stars, and Barry Humphries appears as Metternich. Video.

328. MICHELANGELO BUONARROTI
1475–1564

Italian painter, sculptor, and architect, Michelangelo is celebrated as the greatest artistic genius of the Renaissance. He was born in Tuscany and as a child studied with Florentine painter Ghirlandaio and Bertoldo di Giovanni, a sculptor employed by

the Medici family. Michelangelo lived with the Medicis from 1490 to 1492. In Rome he sculpted the marble *Pieta* (1498–1499) and sculpted *David* (1501–1504) in Florence. He was commissioned (1505) to design and sculpt a tomb for Pope Julius II in Rome and while there painted the ceiling of the Sistine Chapel, considered one of the most influential works in art history. After living in Florence (1515–1534), he returned to Rome to paint *The Last Judgment* in the Sistine Chapel (1534). His last great work was the redesign of St. Peter's Basilica in Rome (1540–1550).

Autobiography and Primary Sources

I, Michelangelo, Sculptor: An Autobiography Through Letters. Irving and Jean Stone, eds. New York: New American Library, 1964. 256pp. The Stones use Michelangelo's own words with connectives to approximate an autobiographical account.

Michelangelo: Life, Letters, and Poetry. New York: Oxford University Press, 1987. 182pp. This collection of the artist's writings includes the biography of Ascanio Condivi, Michelangelo's pupil for eleven years before the master's death. Intended by the artist to correct errors made by Vasari with many facts supplied by Michelangelo, Condivi's life represents what Michelangelo wished to be known and is close to an autobiography.

The Letters of Michelangelo. E.H. Ramsden, ed. Stanford, California: Stanford University Press, 1964. 2 vols. This scholarly edition of Michelangelo's letters features a biographical introduction and chronology and appendixes identifying events, people, and places mentioned.

Recommended Biographies

Bull, George Anthony. *Michelangelo: A Biography.* New York: St. Martin's, 1996. 504pp. Incorporating recent research, Bull's comprehensive study emphasizes Michelangelo's times, and is particularly strong on the complex politics of the period. Avoiding art criticism, Bull concentrates instead on the factual circumstances surrounding Michelangelo's creations. Bull is also strong on the artist's family relationships and everyday life.

Einem, Herbert von. *Michelangelo.* London: Methuen, 1973. 329pp. Originally published in Germany in 1959, this is a distinguished scholarly study that surveys Michelangelo's entire career. It is particularly strong on the Renaissance context and the factual circumstances surrounding each of the artist's commissions. Meant for a sophisticated reader with considerable prior knowledge of the artist and art history.

Hibbard, Howard. *Michelangelo.* New York: Harper & Row, 1974. 347pp. A short, reliable introduction to Michelangelo's life and artistic achievements, Hibbard's is an excellent choice for the general reader.

Murray, Linda. *Michelangelo.* New York: Oxford University Press, 1980. 216pp. Murray's chronological survey of Michelangelo's works aimed at a broad, nonscholarly audience, is particularly strong on the political and economic background of the period.

Other Biographical Studies

Beck, James H. *Three Worlds of Michelangelo.* New York: W.W. Norton, 1999. 269pp. Beck examines the artist from the perspective of his relationship with the three individuals who had the largest impact on his career and development: his father, Lorenzo de' Medici, and Pope Julius II. Ending when Julius dies in 1513, when Michelangelo is only 38, Beck's approach is limited to the artist's early development.

Brandes, Georg. *Michelangelo: His Life, His Times, His Era.* New York: Frederick Ungar, 1963. 428pp. First published in Danish in 1921, Brandes's anecdotal narrative is imaginative and lively, though it lacks documentation and an index. Often provocative in its assertions, Brandes can still be read with pleasure and benefits.

De Tolnay, Charles. *Michelangelo.* Princeton, New Jersey: Princeton University Press, 1943–1960. 5 vols. Massive in its documentation, De Tolnay's five volumes cover virtually every aspect of Michelangelo's life and work. To be consulted rather than read through, De Tolnay's examination provides thoughtful suggestions about the artist's motives, character, and times, though the reader must assemble a coherent portrait beneath a mass of data.

Finlayson, Donald. *Michelangelo the Man.* New York: Crowell, 1935. 356pp. Although adding nothing new to the factual record, Finlayson attempts a human portrait of the artist based on a close reading of his letters and poetry. Unfortunately, the book is weakest on context, with an inaccurate and incomplete historical background.

Liebert, Robert. *Michelangelo: A Psychoanalytic Study of His Life and Images.* New Haven, Connecticut: Yale University Press, 1983. 447pp. The author, a psychoanalyst, offers a Freudian perspective in a fascinating and believable approach. Although hampered by the paucity of known facts about Michelangelo's early life, Liebert traces how the artist's conscious and unconscious preoccupations relate to the events of his life and his art.

Morgan, Charles H. *The Life of Michelangelo.* New York: Reynal, 1960. 253pp. In a narrative account drawing on contemporary sources and modern scholarship, Morgan avoids psychological surmises for a consideration of the artist in the context of his times. The book is excellent on detailing Michelangelo's artistic methods.

Murray, Linda. *Michelangelo: His Life, Work, and Times.* London: Thames and Hudson, 1984. 240pp. This illustrated biography serves as a useful introduction, particularly to Michelangelo's cultural and historical milieu.

Rizzatti, Maria Luisa. *The Life and Times of Michelangelo.* Philadelphia: Curtis, 1967. 75pp. This pleasing illustrated biography includes a brief sketch outlining the essential details of Michelangelo's life and career.

Rolland, Romain. *The Life of Michel Angelo.* New York: Dutton, 1912. 208pp. Neither a full-scale biography nor critical study but a series of essays on the personality of the artist, Rolland's examination veered steadily toward the sensational and hyperbolic in its psychological surmises.

Salvini, Roberto. *The Hidden Michelangelo.* Oxford: Phaidon Press, 1978. 191pp. In a provocative interpretation of Michelangelo's inner conflicts based on a close analysis of his works, Salvini's examination is often marred by subjectivity and a dense prose style. The book is inappropriate as an introduction for the uninitiated reader.

Schott, Rudolf. *Michelangelo.* New York: Tudor, 1963. 254pp. Schott's probing inquiry into Michelangelo's psyche and artistic temperament is full of interesting insights, but the book is often too far removed from the artist's historical and cultural context to anchor its conclusions reliably. Michelangelo is seen more as a universal artistic archetype than a creation of his age.

Symonds, John Addington. *The Life of Michelangelo Buonarroti.* New York: Scribner, 1893. 2 vols. Long established as the standard life, Symonds's factual investigation is based on a close study of primary and secondary sources. Although now superseded by modern scholarship, Symonds's account retains more than historical importance for its insights into the artist's personality and genius.

Vasari, Giorgio. *Lives of the Artists.* New York: Penguin, 1965. 478pp. Originally published in 1550 with a second edition in 1568, Vasari's biographical account of Michelangelo is the first and, along with Condivi's *Life,* the only contemporary account of the artist's life. Michelangelo himself criticized the inexactitude and misrepresentations, but Vasari retains a historical interest, presenting a contemporary's view of the artist.

Wilson, Charles. *Life and Works of Michelangelo Buonarroti.* London: J. Murray, 1876. 567pp. The first modern biography based primarily on documents from the Buonarroti archives, Wilson corrects many of the errors made by Vasari and Condivi in a detailed and reliable account, although the artist is often judged by a Victorian rather than a Renaissance standard, and the homosexual element in Michelangelo's life is ignored.

Biographical Novels

Alexander, Sidney. *Michelangelo, the Florentine.* New York: Random House, 1957. 464pp.; *The Hand of Michelangelo.* Athens: Ohio University Press, 1977. 693pp.; *Nicodemus: The Roman Years of Michelangelo Buonarroti.* Athens: Ohio University Press, 1984. 293pp. Alexander's trilogy chronicles Michelangelo's entire life from his early career in Florence through his troubled years in Rome. The books supplement a portrait of Michelangelo with a history of his era in general and Renaissance Jewish history in particular through a number of fictional characters.

Stone, Irving. *The Agony and the Ecstasy.* Garden City, New York: Doubleday, 1961. 664pp. Tracing Michelangelo's life and career from his apprenticeship at the age of 13, Stone offers a moving portrait of the artist's torment and his age in this entertaining work based on extensive research that supports certain imaginative liberties.

Fictional Portraits

Haasse, Hella S. *The Scarlet City.* Chicago: Academy, 1990. 367pp. The novel dramatizes the Italian Wars during the sixteenth century in which French, Swiss, Spanish, and German armies vie for control of Italy. The Borgias, Machiavelli, Vitoria Colonna, and Michelangelo are all depicted as they are shaped by historical forces.

Otto, Whitney. *The Passion Dream Book.* New York: HarperCollins, 1998. 276pp. In this fanciful story, a young female artist frustrated by a lack of recognition agrees to spy on Michelangelo. Her story is connected with a descendant in the twentieth century.

Ripley, Alexandra. *The Time Returns.* Garden City, New York: Doubleday, 1985. 334pp. The life of Lorenzo de' Medici, one of Michelangelo's early patrons, is dramatized in a fictional story involving his relationship with a young gentlewoman. Botticelli and Michelangelo are both depicted.

Weiss, David. *The Venetian.* New York: Morrow, 1976. 366pp. In a biographical novel on the life of Renaissance painter Titian, the aging artist recalls his life and his relationship with a number of historical figures, including Michelangelo.

Recommended Juvenile Biographies

Lace, William W. *Michelangelo.* San Diego: Lucent Books, 1993. 112pp. MG. Lace surveys the major events of Michelangelo's life against a convincing historical and cultural backdrop.

McLanathan, Richard B.K. *Michelangelo.* New York: Abrams, 1993. 92pp. MG/YA. This full-length biographical portrait links the artist firmly to his era and provides a sober but insightful appreciation of Michelangelo's genius and achievement.

Petit, Jayne. *Michelangelo: Genius of the Renaissance.* New York: F. Watts, 1998. 128pp. MG. This is an informative overview of the artist's life, achievement, and era.

Biographical Films and Theatrical Adaptations

A&E Biography Video: Michelangelo: Artist and Man (1994). Director: Adam Freedman. In a documentary portrait, Michelangelo's private and public lives are described against a solid historical background. Video.

The Agony and the Ecstasy (1965). Director: Carol Reed. In a sumptuous Hollywood adaptation of Irving Stone's novel, Charlton Heston portrays Michelangelo in conflict with Pope Julius II (Rex Harrsion) over the completion of the Sistine Chapel's ceiling. The drama is introduced by a short documentary account of the artist's career. Video.

Michelangelo: Self-Portrait (1990). Director: Richard Lyford. An autobiographical portrait from the artist's own writings and comtemporaries' accounts. Video.

Michelangelo: The Last Giant (1967). Director: Tom Priestley. Michelangelo's life is described using quotes from his biographers and excerpts from his writings. Video.

329. JOHN STUART MILL
1806–1873

An influential British philosopher and economist, Mill was a precocious child, who was educated privately by his father, philosopher, economist, and historian James Mill. After abandoning the study of law, Mill worked for the East India company (1823–1858), eventually rising to the position of head of the examiner's office. During this time he wrote for periodicals and published *A System of Logic* (1843) and *Principles of Political Economy* (1848), which affected English radical thought. His famous essay, *On Liberty* (1859), was written with his wife, Harriet Taylor (d.1858), and was dedicated to her. His essay, *Utilitarianism*, was published in 1863. Mill served as a member of Parliament from 1865 to 1868. After his retirement, he spent much time in Avignon, France, where his wife was buried and where he died. His celebrated *Autobiography* was published the year of his death.

Autobiography and Primary Sources

Autobiography and Other Writing. Jack Stillinger, ed. Boston: Houghton Mifflin, 1969. 477pp. Mill's *Autobiography* is a literary classic, chronicling Mill's education and development under the strict intellectual regime of his father. Dealing mainly with his early life, Mill devotes less than a third of the book to his last thirty years.

Letters of John Stuart Mill. Hugh S.R. Elliot, ed. New York: Longmans, 1910. 2 vols. Unlike his *Autobiography*, Mill's letters are free from self-consciousness and afford a rare glimpse of the man and his character that contrasts with the view presented in his essays.

Recommended Biographies

Borchard, Ruth. *John Stuart Mill: The Man*. London: Watts, 1957. 156pp. Borchard's brief account of Mill's life serves as a reliable introduction to the man and his ideas.

Packe, Michael St. John. *The Life of John Stuart Mill*. New York: Macmillan, 1954. 567pp. Rich in detail and documentation, Packe's definitive life draws on the existing sources to fashion a full and comprehensive portrait of the man and his intellectual development. Eminently readable, Packe's assessment is lucid and sensitive, synthesizing the various facts about Mill's life into a vivid human narrative.

Other Biographical Studies

Bain, Alexander. *John Stuart Mill: A Criticism with Personal Recollections*. New York: Holt, 1882. 201pp. Written by a close friend, Bain's appreciation is informed by firsthand impressions that present a believable human portrait, though many of Bain's contentions have been subject to scholarly debate ever since they appeared, particularly the degree to which Harriet Taylor contributed to Mill's writing and ideas.

Carlisle, Janice. *John Stuart Mill and the Writing of Character*. Athens: University of Georgia Press, 1991. 333pp. In Carlisle's study of Mill's life and work, the emphasis is on his internal conflicts and the personal sources for the contradictions in his ideas and writings.

Courtney, W.L. *Life of John Stuart Mill*. New York: F. Whittaker, 1889. 194pp. Courtney's early biography is based mainly on the *Autobiography* and accepts most of Bain's interpretations, adding little to the record of Mill's life and a view of his personality.

Ellery, John B. *John Stuart Mill*. New York: Twayne, 1964. 134pp. Ellery's concise critical study of Mill's life and ideas is a useful introduction.

Glassman, Peter. *J.S. Mill: The Evolution of a Genius*. Gainesville: University of Florida Press, 1985. 188pp. This psychological study of Mill's development relates his writings to the circumstances of his life to demonstrate how Mill's intellectual activities should be seen as the philosopher's attempt to compensate for his damaged childhood.

Hayek, F.A. *John Stuart Mill and Harriet Taylor*. Chicago: University of Chicago Press, 1951. 320pp. Hayek's annotated collection of letters and assessment of previously unavailable documentary evidence revised the view of Mill and his relationship with Harriet Taylor established by Bain and others.

Kamm, Josephine. *John Stuart Mill in Love*. London: Gordon and Cremonesi, 1977. 253pp. Kamm focuses on the various women in Mill's life to trace their impact on his ideas and development.

Mazlish, Bruce. *James and John Stuart Mill: Father and Son in the 19th Century*. New York: Basic Books, 1975. 484pp. In a double biographical portrait of father and son, Mazlish argues the importance of generational conflict in the evolution of modern ideas. The Mills are made to serve as an archetypal role in a cultural Oedipal conflict. Despite the provocativeness of its assertion, Mazlish's study is thesis-driven in which biographical evidence is made to fit a psychohistorical model.

Pappe, H.O. *John Stuart Mill and the Harriet Taylor Myth*. London: Cambridge University Press, 1960. 51pp. The book focuses on the controversy surrounding Mill's reliance upon and debt to Harriet Taylor, the central critical controversy surrounding Mill. In Pappe's view, the degree to which Taylor served as Mill's collaborator has been overestimated.

Fictional Portraits

Disch, Thomas M., and Charles Naylor. *Neighboring Lives*. New York: Scribner, 1981. 294pp. Literary London during the Victorian period is depicted in the story of Thomas and Jane Carlyle but with appearances by a number of figures, including, Robert Browning, William Morris, and Mill.

Other Sources

Spencer, Herbert, et al. *John Stuart Mill: His Life and Works*. Boston: Osgood, 1873. 96pp. Prepared shortly after Mill's death, this tribute volume consists of a dozen sketches by the philosopher's contemporaries on various aspects of Mill's character and career.

330. JOHN MILTON
1608–1674

One of the great English poets, Milton was born in London, the son of a wealthy scrivener, and was educated at St. Paul's School and Cambridge. His early works include the poem "Il Penseroso" and the masque *Comus* (1634). During the English Civil War, Milton wrote *Areopagitica* (1644), a prose piece in defense of freedom of the press, provoked by the condemnation of his essays in favor of divorce. A pamphlet, *The Tenure of Kings and Magistrates* (1649), supported the Puritan cause against Charles I and secured him a position as Latin secretary for foreign affairs in Cromwell's government. By the 1650s his already weak sight had failed; he became totally blind and had to dictate his work to secretaries. He was forced into hiding after the Restoration (1660) and some of his books were burned, but he was included in the general amnesty. His blank-verse epic poem, *Paradise Lost*, one of the masterpieces of English literature, appeared in 1667. His final great works were *Paradise Regained* and *Samson Agonistes* (1671).

Autobiography and Primary Sources

Milton on Himself. John S. Diekhoff, ed. New York: Oxford University Press, 1939. 307pp. This useful volume gathers together the passages from Milton's writings in which the poet comments on his life, ideas, and works.

Recommended Biographies

Brown, Cedric. *John Milton: A Literary Life*. New York: St. Martin's, 1995. 212pp. Brown supplies a concise introduction to Milton's entire literary career with a sensible reading of his works in the context of their times.

Parker, William R. *Milton: A Biography*. Oxford: Clarendon Press, 1968. 2 vols. Parker's 30 years of study and research has produced the standard, scholarly biography. The first volume is a chronological narrative of Milton's life, with the second volume Parker's scholarly notes. The arrangement allows the reader not to get bogged down in critical debates.

Shawcross, John T. *John Milton: The Self and the World*. Lexington: University of Kentucky Press, 1992. 358pp. Shawcross's psychological study complements Parker's factual study with a series of thought-provoking interpretations, including gender conflict and the homoerotic element in Milton's life and work. The author's probings of Milton's psyche are anchored by chapters supplying biographical and literary overviews.

Wilson, A.N. *The Life of John Milton*. New York: Oxford University Press, 1983. 278pp. With a novelist's eye for animating detail, Wilson supplies a boldly opinionated narrative that serves as well as an excellent guide to the seventeenth century. Synthesizing often dry scholarship into a believable human portrait, Wilson rescues Milton from the specialist and convincingly argues his relevance and importance for the general reader.

Other Biographical Studies

Darbishire, Helen, ed. *The Early Lives of Milton.* 1932. Revised ed. New York: Barnes and Noble, 1965. 353pp. This volume presents modernized texts of six biographies of Milton written in the seventeenth century.

Hill, Christopher. *Milton and the English Revolution.* New York: Viking, 1978. 541pp. Like Saurat's earlier portrait, Hill stresses the revolutionary character of Milton's thoughts and connects him with the radical elements of the English Revolution. Stimulating and fresh in its views, Hill's revisionist focus is a worthy supplement to the more conventional interpretations offered by Parker and others.

Levi, Peter. *Eden Renewed: The Public and Private Life of John Milton.* New York: St. Martin's, 1997. 332pp. In an affectionate, witty, opinionated, and entertaining popular account written by an English poet and biographer, Levi's critical biography chooses to ignore certain elements of Milton's life and concentrate on Milton's artistry. Best used as a supplement to more comprehensive treatments of Milton's life, such as Parker's and Wilson's.

Masson, David. *The Life of John Milton.* London: Macmillan, 1881–1896. 7 vols. Masson's massive study encompasses Milton's life as well as a detailed political, religious, and literary history of his period. More a Milton reference sourcebook Masson's factual compilation collects useful as well as trivial data that most readers will prefer to have synthesized.

Pattison, Mark. *Milton.* 1879. Reprint ed. New York: AMS Press, 1968. 220pp. Pattison's Victorian biography has the virtue of brevity compared to Masson, with some challenging interpretations if no new facts to add to the record.

Saurat, Denis. *Milton: Man and Thinker.* New York: Dial Press, 1925. 363pp. Saurat's interpretative study sets out to demolish the conservative, Puritan image of Milton for a more dynamic portrait of a complex thinker and revolutionary who should be seen as one of the greatest of all philosophical poets.

Thorpe, James E. *John Milton: The Inner Life.* San Marino, California: Huntington Library, 1983. 191pp. Thorpe's appreciative study chronicles Milton's intellectual and artistic development that stresses his considerable achievements and greatness as a man and artist. There is no doubting Thorpe's admiration, and the book's enthusiasm is contagious.

Tillyard, E.M.W. *Milton.* New York: Barnes and Noble, 1930. 396pp. This critical biography stresses Milton's early development, devoting considerably less attention to his later years. Sensible in its evocation of the intellectual underpinnings of Milton's age, Tillyard's examination is coherent if uninspired.

Wagenknecht, Edward. *The Personality of Milton.* Norman: University of Oklahoma Press, 1970. 170pp.This is a popular account of Milton's life and work that delivers a personality profile based on the author's close reading of primary and secondary sources. Serves the general reader as a lively, informal introduction.

Biographical Novels

Figes, Eva. *The Tree of Knowledge.* New York: Pantheon, 1990. 154pp. In an extended monologue narrated by one of Milton's daughters, Milton is depicted as a cruel misogynist who is insensitive and intolerant to his daughters in a negative feminist reading of Milton and his times.

Fuller, Edmund. *John Milton.* 1944. Reprint ed. New York: Seabury Press, 1967. 242pp. In a fictionalized account of Milton's life, the novel stays close to the facts of the poet's life and is reliable, despite a fiercely Protestant viewpoint.

Graves, Robert. *Wife to Mr. Milton.* London: Cassell, 1944. 372pp. In a first-person narrative of Milton's first wife, the story of their troubled relationship is told against a backdrop of the English Civil War. Audacious in its recreation of Milton's intimate, private life, Graves anchors his fancies with convincing period details.

Fictional Portraits

Ackroyd, Peter. *Milton in America.* New York: Doubleday, 1997. 307pp. The novel imagines Milton's 1660 journey to America in search of moral purity in Puritan New England. This inventive fantasy provides an occasion for an exploration of Milton's psyche and a man who becomes a destroyer of paradise in the name of goodness.

Macaulay, Rose. *The Shadow Flies.* New York: Harper, 1932. 476pp. Set during the English Civil War, a young women visits poet Robert Herrick in Cambridge where she interacts with a number of literary figures, including Abraham Cowley, Richard Crashaw, and Milton.

West, Paul. *Sporting with Amaryllis.* Woodstock, New York: Overlook Press, 1996. 160pp. West imagines a 17-year-old Milton introduced to his muse and sexuality through the agency of an unworldly London streetwalker. This is an exhilarating evocation of the era and a fanciful but intriguing portrait of the artist as a young man.

Biographical Films and Theatrical Adaptations

Milton: 1608–1674 (1987). Producer: Anthony Thwaite. This film profile covers the highlights of Milton's career with commentary on his works and personality. Video.

Milton and His Times (1985). Producer: Stephen Mantell. Milton's development and achievement is profiled against a wider historical, political, and cultural background. Video.

Other Sources

Campbell, Gordon. *A Milton Chronology.* New York: St. Martin's, 1997. 255pp. This detailed chronological record is a valuable reference source of the poet's almost daily activities.

French, J. Milton, ed. *The Life Records of John Milton.* New York: Godian Press. 1966. 5 vols. In an indispensable scholarly collection of all the existent documents concerning the poet's life, the series assembles the essential raw materials for a biographical study of Milton.

331. MOLIÈRE (JEAN-BAPTISTE POQUELIN)
1622–1673

France's great comic dramatist was born in Paris, the son of a merchant who was upholsterer to Louis XIII. As a young man, he joined the Béjart troupe of actors and toured for 13 years with the company as actor-manager and playwright. Molière's first success was *Le Docteur Amoreuse*, performed in 1658 for Louis XIV. The troupe performed under royal patronage at the Palais Royal and is the ancestor of the Comédie Francaise. Molière's satires on hypocrisy and pointed characterizations, although popular, were castigated as impious and slanderous by some critics and authors. He also wrote farces, comedies, masks, and ballets for the court. His plays include *Les Précieuses Ridicules* (1659), often called the first comedy of manners, *Le Tartuffe* (1664), *Le Misanthrope* (1666), *Le Bourgeois Gentilhomme* (1670), and *Le Malade Imaginaire* (1673). Molière became fatally ill on stage while acting the lead role of the hypochondriac in the latter play.

Recommended Biographies

Fernandez, Ramon. *Molière: The Man Seen Through the Plays.* New York: Hill & Wang, 1958. 212pp. As the book's title indicates, Fernandez fills in the considerable gaps in Molière's biography with informed speculation based on a close reading of the plays. Filled with intriguing insights into Molière's character and comic vision, Fernandez may annoy biographical purists but few other books offer such a stimulating portrait of Molière.

Howarth, W.D. *Molière: A Playwright and His Audience.* New York: Cambridge University Press, 1982. 325pp. Howarth's focus is mainly historical, establishing the connection between Molière's career and works and the cultural, historical, and artistic world in which he lived. In the absence of direct evidence, the book creates a believable social milieu that builds up an indirect portrait of the artist.

Palmer, John. *Molière: His Life and Works.* New York: Brewer and Warren, 1930. 518pp. Penetrating the various legends to extract the probable truths, Palmer places Molière squarely in his period, and this study remains the most reliable and comprehensive biography available in English. Palmer deals credibly with the playwright's marriage and family relations.

Other Biographical Studies

Lewis, D.B. Wyndham. *Molière: The Comic Mask.* New York: Coward-McCann, 1959. 214pp. Describing Molière's early life before proceeding through his plays and relating them to the events in Molière's life, Lewis enlivens his narrative with fictionalized elements and accepts several debatable anecdotes as facts. The result is a highly readable but not always reliable account that portrays both the man and the artist.

Matthews, Brander. *Molière: His Life and Works.* New York: Scribner, 1910. 385pp. Matthew's critical biography summarizes the details of Molière's early life followed by a study of the works.

Tilley, Arthur A. *Molière*. Cambridge, England: University Press, 1921. 363pp. More a study of the playwright's genius, the facts of Molière's life are condensed into its first chapter, followed by a critical reading of the works.

Biographical Novels

Arnott, Peter D. *Ballet of Comedians: A Novel Based on the Life of J.B.P. Molière*. New York: Macmillan, 1971. 320pp. Molière is convincingly shown rebelling against his family for a life in the theater, first as an actor and later as a playwright.

Bulgakov, Mikhail. *The Life of Monsieur de Molière*. New York: Funk & Wagnalls, 1970. 259pp. Combining nonfictional and fictional elements but with enough fancy to be treated as a novel, Bulgakov provides an account of Molière's life and career that alternates between the superficial and the sensational.

Dussane, Béatrix. *An Actor Named Molière*. New York: Scribner, 1937. 304pp. Molière is depicted running his troupe, writing, and rehearsing prior to a command performance before Louis XIV at Versailles in an evocative presentation of the man and his age.

O'Shaughnessy, Michael. *Monsieur Molière, a Novel*. New York: Crowell, 1959. 280pp. Stringing together a number of colorful anecdotes, the novel documents Molière's stage career in a combination of factual material and fancy based on the playwright's writing and historical sources.

Biographical Films and Theatrical Adaptations

Moeller, Philip. *Molière: A Romantic Play in Three Acts*. New York: Knopf, 1919. 237pp. Moeller's play shows the playwright at various stages of his career with biographical facts distorted to fit the exigency of the drama.

Molière (1984). Director: Bill Alexander. Based on Mikhail Bulgakov's book, the Royal Shakespeare Company follows Molière's life as he changes from a confident theater director to a broken-down sycophant after being beset by both church and state. Starring Antony Sher. Video.

332. CLAUDE MONET
1840–1926

French landscape painter and the founder of Impressionism, Monet was encouraged in his youth to paint in the open air by the marine painter Boudin. After serving with the army in Algeria (1860–1862), he studied painting in Paris despite parental objections. His friends included such future major impressionists as Pissaro, Cézanne, Renoir, and Sisley. The term "Impressionism" was coined after Monet's painting *Impression: Sunrise* (1872). Fascinated by the effects of light, Monet began in 1889 to paint series of subjects, such as Rouen Cathedral, at different times of day. His last great series were pictures of water lilies, which he painted at his home in Giverny.

Autobiography and Primary Sources

Monet by Himself. Richard Kendell, ed. Boston: Little, Brown, 1990. 328pp. In a chronologically arranged selection of letters along with reproductions from his works, Monet reveals himself in many different moods and circumstances, illuminating both his work methods and financial woes.

Recommended Biographies

Mount, Charles M. *Monet: A Biography*. New York: Simon & Schuster, 1966. 444pp. Synthesizing valuable original research and evidence only available from French sources, Mount's useful scholarly study is marred by a partisan defense of Monet's first wife and a disapproval of the painter's private life. Despite a negative assessment of the man, Mount's documentation fills in a number of gaps in the biographical record and serves as a challenging contrast to more reverent admiring portraits.

Spate, Virginia. *Claude Monet: Life and Work*. New York: Rizzoli, 1992. 348pp. In a critical biography based on a careful study of over 3,000 surviving letters, Spate portrays Monet as a far more complex individual than is conventionally presented. Monet is shown clearly in his social, historical, and artistic context.

Tucker, Paul H. *Claude Monet: Life and Art*. New Haven, Connecticut: Yale University Press, 1995. 250pp. Tucker's narrative biography supplies a realistic life story that is both honest and objective. Tucker challenges the widely held notion of Monet's financial constraints and relates his works to the social and political circumstances of his times.

Other Biographical Studies

Gordon, Robert, and Andrew Forge. *Monet*. New York: Abrams, 1983. 304pp. In a thorough record of Monet's artistic production and his internal struggles, this critical study includes previously unpublished documents and letters.

Gwynn, Stephen. *Claude Monet and His Garden: The Story of an Artist's Paradise*. New York: Macmillan, 1934. 170pp. This is an impressionistic, undocumented look at the last half of Monet's life and his years at Giverny, including his creation of his garden and his relationship with Georges Clemenceau.

Joyce, Claire. *Monet at Giverny*. New York: Mayflower, 1973. 144pp. In contrast to Gwynn's more romantic treatment, Joyce looks at Monet during the Giverny period from a more solidly documented perspective, using a number of published and unpublished sources.

Mauclair, Camille. *Claude Monet*. New York: Dodd, Mead, 1924. 62pp. In the first biographical profile in English, Mauclair provides a biographical sketch of the highlights of Monet's career and aesthetic principles.

Rachman, Carla. *Monet*. London: Phaidon Press, 1997. 351pp. This is a handsome entry in the Art and Ideas series that reproduces the artist's works with a text by a respected scholar, which covers both biographical and technical details about the artist.

Taylor, John Russell. *The Life and Art of Claude Monet: Impressions of France*. New York: Crescent Books, 1995. 160pp. With more than 150 reproductions of paintings, drawings, sketches, and rare photos, Taylor offers an informative overview of Monet's life and work

Weeks, C.P.P. *Camille: A Study of Claude Monet*. London: Sidgwick and Jackson, 1962. 204pp. Based on the standard French sources, this is a highly readable portrait of the artist in the context of the Impressionist movement.

Biographical Novels

Figes, Eva. *Light*. New York: Pantheon, 1983. 91pp. Describing a day in the life of Monet in 1900 as he completes his "Water Lilies," the novel employs details from the painter's life and career as the starting point for a lyrical and meditative exploration of various themes.

Fictional Portraits

Stone, Irving. *Depths of Glory*. Garden City, New York: Doubleday, 1985. 653pp. This biographical novel chronicles the life of Camille Pissarro and Paris during the Impressionist heyday with appearances by a number of artists, including Monet, Courbet, Corot, Cézanne, Gauguin, Degas, Seurat, Cassatt, and Manet.

Weiss, David. *Naked Came I: A Novel of Rodin*. New York: Morrow, 1963. 660pp. The life and times of French sculptor Auguste Rodin are reliably depicted with some invented dialogue and scenes, including portraits of a number of historical figures, including Monet, Degas, Bernard Shaw, Renoir, Victor Hugo, Emile Zola, and Rainer Maria Rilke.

Recommended Juvenile Biographies

Patin, Sylvie. *Monet: The Ultimate Impressionist*. New York: Abrams, 1993. 175pp. YA. Patin includes excerpts from Monet's letters and other writings and 236 illustrations to document Monet's life and artistic achievement.

Waldron, Ann. *Claude Monet*. New York: Abrams, 1981. 92pp. YA. Part of the First Impressions series, this is an excellent introduction to Monet's life and art, chronicling his career from his boyhood through his studies in Paris and eventual achievement as a recognized master.

Welton, Jude. *Monet*. New York: Dorling Kindersley, 1999. 64pp. MG. This entry in the Eyewitness Books series is a visually exciting and informative treatment of Monet's life, art, and techniques.

Biographical Films and Theatrical Adaptations

Monet (1989). Director: Michael Gill. Using letters, journals, interviews, and archival film footage of Monet himself, this film profile traces the painter's lifelong quest to capture on canvas the effects of light and color seen in nature. Video.

333. JAMES MONROE
1758–1831

The fifth U.S. president (1817–1825), Monroe was born in Westmoreland County, Virginia. He dropped out of the College of William and Mary to fight in the American Revolution and after the war studied law (1780–1783) under Thomas Jefferson. He served (1782) in the Virginia legislature, in the Continental Congress under the Articles of Confederation (1783–1786), in the U.S. Senate (1790–1794), and as minister to France (1794–1796). While governor of Virginia (1799–1802), he was named special envoy to France and helped negotiate the Louisiana Purchase (1803). He served in James Madison's cabinet as secretary of state and secretary of war during the War of 1812. Elected to the presidency as a Democratic-Republican, Monroe's administration became known as the Era of Good Feeling because of postwar prosperity and expansion. The Rush-Bagot agreement (1817) settled Canadian boundary disputes with Great Britain, Florida was purchased from Spain (1819), the Santa Fe Trail was opened (1821), the Missouri Compromise was enacted, and the Monroe Doctrine, which opposed European intervention in the Americas, became a cornerstone of U.S. foreign policy.

Autobiography and Primary Sources

The Autobiography of James Monroe. Stuart G. Brown, ed. Syracuse, New York: Syracuse University Press, 1959. 236pp. Monroe's autobiographical fragments, written at the end of his life to relieve his financial distress, were intended to convince an ungrateful nation how much it owed him.

The Writings of James Monroe. Stanislaus M. Hamilton, ed. New York: Putnam, 1898–1903. 7 vols. Monroe's papers are collected in this multivolume scholarly edition, which is an indispensable primary source of insights into Monroe's character and ideas.

Recommended Biographies

Ammon, Harry. *James Monroe: The Quest for National Identity.* New York: McGraw-Hill, 1971. 706pp. Rightfully regarded as the standard scholarly life, Ammon's meticulously documented study deals expertly with the complex issues that shaped Monroe's career as well as his relationships. The book is particularly strong on American diplomatic history during the era. Balanced and reliable, Ammon presents a multidimensional Monroe with both his qualities and his flaws displayed.

Cresson, W.P.P. *James Monroe.* Chapel Hill: University of North Carolina Press, 1946. 577pp. Completed by others after the author's death in 1932, Cresson's study is a thorough, scholarly yet readable reevaluation of Monroe's character and career. At times overly defensive on Monroe's behalf, Cresson's is a reliable and comprehensive examination of the full course of Monroe's life.

Cunningham, Noble. *The Presidency of James Monroe.* Lawrence: University Press of Kansas, 1996. 246pp. Cunningham's is the best available examination of Monroe's two-term presidential administration, chronicling the major domestic and

foreign policy issues and Monroe's leadership and political beliefs.

Other Biographical Studies

Adams, John Quincy. *The Lives of James Madison and James Monroe: Fourth and Fifth Presidents of the United States.* Boston: Phillips, Sampson, 1850. 432pp. Adams's dual biographical sketch of Madison and Monroe treats each man separately. Adams includes his 1831 eulogy in which he pays tribute to Monroe and surveys his career as well as provides an account of Monroe's presidency.

Morgan, George. *The Life of James Monroe.* 1921. Reprint ed. New York: AMS Press, 1969. 484pp. Morgan's somewhat uneven and limited life concentrates on Monroe's early life and diplomatic career, failing to treat his presidency in detail. Highly partisan, the book lacks a critical edge and has been superseded by later studies.

Styron, Arthur. *The Last of the Cocked Hats: James Monroe and the Virginia Dynasty.* Norman: University of Oklahoma Press, 1945. 480pp. In a life-and-times approach, the latter predominates, and Monroe's personality and private life are obscured under a mass of details concerning his era.

Fictional Portraits

Carlisle, Henry. *The Land Where the Sun Dies.* New York: Putnam, 1975. 318pp. Chronicling the Indian removal policy masterminded by Andrew Jackson, which led to the Seminole War, Monroe appears as an ineffectual political leader.

Delmar, Vina. *A Time for Titans.* San Diego, California: Harcourt, Brace, 1974. 336pp. The complicated diplomatic maneuverings that led to the Louisiana Purchase are dramatized in the clash between three historical titans: Napoleon, Jefferson, and Haiti's Toussaint L'Ouverture. Other secondary figures, such as Madison, Monroe, and Henri Christophe also are described.

Fast, Howard. *Citizen Tom Paine.* New York: Duell, Sloan and Pearce, 1943. 341pp. In this fictionalized biography of Thomas Paine, numerous historical figures are depicted, including Monroe, Jefferson, Washington, Napoleon, and Franklin.

West, Jessamyn. *The Massacre at Fall Creek.* New York: Harcourt, Brace, 1975. 373pp. Based on an actual 1824 murder of Seneca Indians on the frontier of Indiana, the novel dramatizes the massacre and the subsequent trial of the men charged in the crime, with appearances by Monroe and John C. Calhoun.

Recommended Juvenile Biographies

Old, Wendie C. *James Monroe.* Springfield, New Jersey: Enslow, 1998. 128pp. MG. Old's is a well-written account of Monroe that relates his life to the major historical events and allows his contributions to emerge.

Stefoff, Rebecca. *James Monroe: 5th President of the United States.* Ada, Oklahoma: Garrett, 1988. 121pp. MG. This is a reliable summary of the high points of Monroe's life and presidential administration, emphasizing the challenges he faced.

Wetzel, Charles. *James Monroe.* New York: Chelsea House, 1989. 111pp. MG/YA. Monroe's life and career are usefully summarized in this informative and well-illustrated biography.

334. MARILYN MONROE
1926–1962

Movie actress and world-famous sex symbol, Monroe was born Norma Jean Baker in Los Angeles and was raised in orphanages. She worked as a model and began to win movie roles in the 1940s. By the 1950s she had gained fame for her breathy singing voice and seductive film roles. In 1953 she posed for the first issue of *Playboy* magazine. Her films include *The Seven-Year Itch* (1955), *Bus Stop* (1956), *Some Like It Hot* (1959), and *The Misfits* (1960). Married for a brief time as a teenager, her second husband was baseball player Joe DiMaggio and her third was playwright Arthur Miller. After her death at 36, she became a Hollywood legend.

Autobiography and Primary Sources

My Story. New York: Stein and Day, 1974. 143pp. In a partially autobiographical account of Monroe's life up to 1954, the book, co-written with novelist and playwright Ben Hecht, shatters the actress's "dumb blonde" image in an honest, witty, and intelligent account that provides insight into her character.

Conversations with Marilyn. William J. Weatherby, ed. New York: Mason/Charter, 1976. 229pp. Based on the author's 1960 talks with Monroe and observations on the set of her last film, *The Misfits*, Weatherby offers a number of firsthand anecdotes and reconstructions of interviews.

Marilyn: Her Life in Her Own Words: Marilyn Monroe's Revealing Last Words and Photographs. George Barris, ed. Secaucus, New Jersey: Birch Lane Press, 1995. 163pp. Culled from conversation with Monroe in 1962 shortly before her death as the actress intended to complete her autobiographical reflections begun in *My Story*, Barris offers his experiences with the actress and his reconstruction of the actress's personal reflections.

Marilyn Monroe: In Her Own Words. Roger G. Taylor, ed. New York: Putnam, 1983. 122pp. This is a compilation of various statements by Monroe from a variety of published and unpublished sources.

Recommended Biographies

Guiles, Fred L. *Legend: The Life and Death of Marilyn Monroe.* New York: Stein and Day, 1984. 501pp. Commonly regarded as the standard biographical treatment, Guiles updates and alters many of his conclusions in his earlier *Norma Jean: The Life of Marilyn Monroe* (New York: McGraw-Hill, 1969. 341pp.) with new material, interviews with friends and associates, and a more candid treatment of the actress's death based on subsequent research.

Spoto, Donald. *Marilyn Monroe: The Biography.* New York: HarperCollins, 1993. 698pp. Spoto's is an exhaustive portrait of Monroe that draws on previously unavailable sources, including previously sealed letters, diaries, and other papers. In a surprising revisionist view, Spoto dismisses the Kennedy connection in Monroe's life and contentions that she was murdered or committed suicide, and takes the actress far more seriously and more compassionately than have other treatments.

Summers, Anthony. *Goddess: The Secret Lives of Marilyn Monroe.* New York: Macmillan, 1985. 415pp. Based on hundreds of interviews and extensive research, this is an absorbing, convincing biography that sheds considerable light on the circumstances surrounding Monroe's death and Robert Kennedy's effort to cover up his relationship with the actress. Sensible rather than sensational, Summers adds numerous factual details to a portrait of a short, tormented life.

Other Biographical Studies

Freeman, Lucy. *Why Norma Jean Killed Marilyn Monroe.* Chicago: Global Rights, 1992. 191pp. In a psychological analysis, Freeman looks at the factors that caused Monroe to take her own life.

Haspiel, James. *Marilyn: The Ultimate Look at the Legend.* New York: Holt, 1991. 207pp. Haspiel, a close friend of the star, relies on his collections of photos and letters for a intimate and personal portrait of Monroe.

Hoyt, Edwin P. *Marilyn: The Tragic Venus.* Radnor, Pennsylvania: Chilton, 1973. 279pp. Hoyt, who admits to never having seen any of Monroe's films, supplies a journalistic and superficial account that arranges the details of Monroe's biography to dramatize how money, power, and fame produced the tragedy of her life.

Kahn, Roger. *Joe and Marilyn: A Memory of Love.* New York: Morrow, 1986. 269pp. Chronicling the lives of DiMaggio and Monroe before, during, and after their brief marriage, Kahn debunks many myths surrounding the couple and exposes a number of unsubstantiated rumors in a balanced treatment of their relationship.

Leaming, Barbara. *Marilyn Monroe.* New York: Crown, 1998. 464pp. Prolific celebrity biographer Leaming provides a detailed psychological portrait of the actress beginning in 1951 with her early life sketchily presented in flashback. Livened by novelistic technique, the book animates a human portrait in a series of dramatic episodes that reveals Monroe as an intelligent, self-destructive perfectionist.

Mailer, Norman. *Marilyn: A Biography.* New York: Grossett & Dunlap, 1973. 270pp. Mailer's "novel biography" has been described as a metaphysical coffee-table book, a sumptuously illustrated book with the author's meditation on Monroe's life and career including the daring Mailer touches of animation and self-obsession. Mailer continues his fascination with the actress in *Of Women and Their Elegance* (New York: Simon & Schuster, 1981. 288pp.), a series of imagined interviews to accompany a portfolio of photographs.

McCann, Graham. *Marilyn Monroe.* New Brunswick, New Jersey: Rutgers University Press, 1988. 241pp. Drawing on critical theory, feminism, and film studies, McCann's "anti-biography" looks at Monroe's film career from 1947 onward to examine how her image was manufactured and its per-

sonal cost, integrating Monroe's own comments in his depiction. Often jargon-heavy and self-indulgent, the book is less a study of the person than a meditation on her public persona.

Miller, Arthur. *Timebends: A Life.* New York: Grove Press, 1987. 614pp. The playwright provides his view of the couple's marriage in his autobiography.

Miracle, Berniece Baker, and Mona Rae. *My Sister Marilyn: A Memoir of Marilyn Monroe.* New York: Workman, 1994. 238pp. Monroe's half-sister, whom the actress learned about when she was 12, and niece offer their recollections of their relationships. The emphasis is on the intimate private person seen in her family relations, along with photographs and letters, most of which are published here for the first time.

Rollyson, Carl E. Jr. *Marilyn Monroe: A Life of the Actress.* Ann Arbor, Michigan: UMI Research Press, 1986. 255pp. The author focuses on Monroe's acting career and the relationship between her growth as an actress and her film roles in shaping her identity. Though marred by stylistic excesses and dependent on other sources for its biographical details, the book does offer an in-depth analysis of each of Monroe's films and a rare appreciation of her acting methods.

Shevey, Sandra. *The Marilyn Scandal: Her True Life Revealed by Those Who Knew Her.* New York: Morrow, 1987. 326pp. This is mainly a rehash of previously peddled revelations, featuring the comments of a few associates who have broken their silence, but it offers little that is new or different. Factual errors and dubious assertions limit the book's reliability and usefulness.

Slatzer, Robert F. *The Life and Curious Death of Marilyn Monroe.* New York: Pinnacle House, 1974. 348pp. The author claims to have been briefly married to Monroe in 1952, and Slatzer's controversial account was one of the first books to challenge the finding that Monroe's death was suicide. The book's chief value is the reprinting of a number of documents, including Monroe's autopsy report and will.

Spada, James. *Monroe: Her Life in Pictures.* Garden City, New York: Doubleday, 1982. 194pp. In a scrapbook approach bringing together a wide collection of photographs, Spada includes an excellent brief biographical profile.

Speriglio, Milo, and Adele Gregory. *Crypt 33: The Saga of Marilyn Monroe: The Final Word.* New York: Carol, 1992. 380pp. The subtitle here might be viewed as wishful thinking in yet another sensational account of Monroe's rise to stardom with an emphasis on the actress' underworld ties. In the authors' version of Monroe's end, the actress was murdered by Mafia hit men.

Steinem, Gloria. *Marilyn.* Photographs by George Barris. New York: Holt, 1986. 182pp. In a thoughtful series of biographical essays, Steinem concentrates on Monroe's personality in a feminist and archetypal context. Written to accompany George Barris's photographs and unpublished interview with the actress shortly before her death, Steinem manages a multidimensional portrait that avoids either the hyperbole or sensationalism of other accounts.

Wolfe, Donald H. *The Last Days of Marilyn Monroe.* New York: Morrow, 1998. 464pp. With sensational revelations concerning Monroe's "murder" predominant here, Wolfe offers a brief account of the actress's life before focusing on the period leading up to her death. According to Wolfe, Monroe was killed in the name of national security.

Zolotow, Maurice. *Marilyn Monroe.* New York: Harcourt, Brace, 1960. 340pp. Although appearing too early to consider her life in full, Zolotow's was the first scholarly biography based in part on interviews with the actress and helpfully sets the factual record straight. Attempting to reconcile Monroe's public image with her private self, the book offers a number of psychological conjectures as well as lively animation of the actress's career.

Biographical Novels

Korda, Michael. *The Immortals.* New York: Poseidon Press, 1992. 559pp. Monroe's relationship with John F. and Robert Kennedy is dramatized in a fictional celebrity tell-all, blending actual facts with imagined pillow talk.

Oates, Joyce Carol. *Blonde.* New York: Ecco Press, 2000. 768pp. Oates imaginatively reconstructs the significant events in Monroe's life and speculates on her subject's thoughts and feelings in this impressive meditation on a wasted life.

Toperoff, Sam. *Queen of Desire.* New York: HarperCollins, 1992. 276pp. In a series of imagined scenes from various stages of Monroe's life, the novel sticks to the biographical chronology and a plausible portrait of the actress as the basis for the novel's ingenious fancy.

Fictional Portraits

Douglas, Carole Nelson, ed. *Marilyn: Shades of Blonde.* New York: Forge, 1997. 352pp. This is a collection of 21 short stories by various genre authors involving Monroe as a character in various realistic and fanciful guises.

Gorman, Edward. *The Marilyn Tapes.* New York: Forge, 1995. 349pp. In an inventive thriller, various fictional and historical figures, including J. Edgar Hoover, Louella Parsons, the Kennedys, and the Mafia, race to secure Monroe's secret recordings about her affairs. The action is periodically interrupted with excerpts from the tapes as Monroe tells her own story.

Rechy, John. *Marilyn's Daughter.* New York: Carroll & Graf, 1988. 531pp. The novel imagines a hypothetical daughter of Monroe and Robert Kennedy who tries to uncover the truth about her parents.

Recommended Juvenile Biographies

Krohn, Katherine E. *Marilyn Monroe: Norma Jean's Dream.* Minneapolis: Lerner, 1997. 128pp. YA. This is a reliable and balanced account of the actress's rise to stardom and her personal struggles despite her fame.

Lefkowitz, Frances. *Marilyn Monroe.* New York: Chelsea House, 1995. 120pp. MG/YA. In a detailed, well-written biographical account the book offers a sympathetic view of Monroe's talent, determination, and personal sacrifices to achieve stardom, candidly acknowledging the less flattering aspects of the actress's life and career.

Woog, Adam. *Marilyn Monroe.* San Diego: Lucent Books, 1997. 96pp. MG. After a brief overview of Monroe's life and career, the author provides a detailed account of the actress's death and discusses the various theories that have been offered to explain it.

Biographical Films and Theatrical Adaptations

A&E Biography Video: Marilyn Monroe: The Mortal Goddess (1996). Director: Donatello Baglivo. Chronicles Monroe's life and career using early family photos, home movies, and outtakes from her films, along with interviews with family, friends, and co-workers. Video.

Goodbye, Norma Jean (1976). Director: Larry Buchanan. Tawdry dramatization of Monroe's early years and early Hollywood career. Starring Misty Rowe as Monroe. Video.

Goodnight, Sweet Marilyn (1989). Director: Larry Buchanan. In an equally sleazy sequel to *Goodbye, Norma Jean,* Paula Lane portrays Monroe in a ludicrous interpretation of the actress's death. Video.

Marilyn (1963). Documentary tribute narrated by Rock Hudson uses film clips to narrate the story of Monroe's life and career. Video.

Marilyn and Bobby: Her Final Affair (1994). Director: Bradford May. A made-for-cable-television film sensationalizing the controversial details surrounding Monroe's relationship with Robert Kennedy. The film's sordid climax is the scramble to cover up details following her death. Melody Anderson stars as the actress and James F. Kelly portrays Kennedy. Video.

Marilyn Monroe (1964). Producer: Art Lieberman. Narrated by Mike Wallace, this compilation of interviews, photographs, film footage, and news clips chronicles Monroe's life from birth to death. Video.

Marilyn Monroe: Beyond the Legend (1986). Director: Gene Feldman. This documentary features interviews with Monroe's co-stars and friends. Video.

Marilyn: The Last Word (1993). Directors: Paul Nichols, Joe Tobin. Featuring dramatic re-creations, the film deals with the controversy surrounding Monroe's death. Video.

Marilyn: The Untold Story (1980). Directors: Jack Arnold, John Flynn, and Lawrence Schiller. Based on Norman Mailer's biography of Monroe, Catherine Hicks delivers an Emmy-nominated performance as Monroe, with Tracey Gold as the young Norma Jean. Video.

Norma Jean & Marilyn (1996). Director: Tim Fywell. The actress portrayed by Mira Sorvino is haunted by her younger self (Ashley Judd) in this cable drama offering a psychological profile of a clashing alter ego, dramatizing the personal cost of Monroe's stardom. Video.

Other Sources

Cunningham, Ernest W. *The Ultimate Marilyn.* Los Angeles: Renaissance Books, 1998. 383pp. A collection of facts about Monroe's life and career to appeal to the trivia buff and the Monroe enthusiast.

Riese, Randall, and Neal Hitchens. *The Unabridged Marilyn: Her Life from A to Z.* New York: Congden and Weed, 1987. 578pp. This fascinating reference collection of various materials regarding Monroe's life and career ranges from the trivial to the substantial, including an extensive bibliography and discography, contemporary reviews of her films, quotes about her, and three short studio biographies.

Victor, Adam. *The Marilyn Encyclopedia.* Woodstock, New York: Overlook Press,1999. 341pp. Arranged into alphabetical entries, this is a detailed coverage of virtually every aspect of Monroe's life and associations. Important information is mixed with trivia. A fan and buff's delight; others will be overwhelmed by the minutiae.

Wagenknecht, Edward, ed. *Marilyn Monroe: A Composite View.* Philadelphia: Chilton, 1983. 200pp. The book reprints interviews with Monroe along with reminiscences by friends and critics.

335. MICHEL DE MONTAIGNE
1533–1592

French essayist Montaigne is regarded as one of the great masters of the essay form. He was a magistrate and mayor of Bordeaux, and engaged in diplomacy during the French religious civil wars. He published three books of essays; a fourth appeared posthumously in 1595. His essays greatly influenced French and English literature.

Autobiography and Primary Sources

The Autobiography of Michel de Montaigne. New York: Random House, 1935. 328pp. Montaigne's autobiographical statements from his essays, travel writings, and letters are arranged chronologically and linked with sufficient explanatory material to approximate a life story in mainly Montaigne's own words.

Recommended Biographies

Frame, Donald M. *Montaigne: A Biography.* New York: Harcourt, Brace, 1965. 408pp. Frame's definitive biography is a remarkable achievement in which a lifetime of research and work on Montaigne have been skillfully synthesized into a lucid, readable, and accessible portrait of Montaigne in his cultural and historical context.

Other Biographical Studies

Hoffmann, George. *Montaigne's Career.* New York: Oxford University Press, 1998. 188pp. Hoffmann's is a specialized but informative look at Montaigne's creative process that emphasizes his writing practices and the details of his daily life that shaped his ideas and career.

Sichel, Edith. *Michel de Montaigne.* New York: Dutton, 1911. 271pp. The author allows Montaigne to speak for himself in a solid overview of his life, character, and works.

Tetel, Marcel. *Montaigne.* New York: Twayne, 1974. 138pp. Part of the useful Twayne series directed at undergraduates and the general reader, Tetel supplies a chronology and brief biographical comments while concentrating on Montaigne's literary and philosophical development.

Willis, Irene C. *Montaigne.* New York: Knopf, 1927. 135pp. Relying on extensive extracts from Montaigne's writings, this is less a biography than a critique of his writing and thought. Serves the general reader as a starting point for further investigation.

336. SIR THOMAS MORE
1478–1535

English statesman, writer, and Roman Catholic saint, More was educated in the household of Cardinal Morton and at Oxford, and became a successful lawyer in London. Celebrated for his brilliance, subtlety, and wit, he was a favorite of Henry VIII. He entered the king's service in 1518, was knighted in 1521, and despite his disapproval over Henry's divorce of Catherine of Aragon in defiance of the pope succeeded (1529) Cardinal Wolsey as lord chancellor. He resigned (1532) because of ill health and because of disagreements over the king's policies. He refused to accept the Act of Supremacy making Henry head of the of the English church, was imprisoned (1534) in the Tower, condemned for high treason, and beheaded. He was canonized in 1935. His best-known work is *Utopia* (1516).

Autobiography and Primary Sources

Correspondence. Elizabeth F. Rogers, ed. Princeton, New Jersey: Princeton University Press, 1947. 584pp. This scholarly collection of the extant letters offers the most complete personal record of More's life available.

Recommended Biographies

Ackroyd, Peter. *The Life of Thomas More.* New York: Nan A. Talese, 1998. 447pp. Ackroyd deepens and humanizes our view of More, challenging the conventional, simplified depiction of his sanctity and heroism of conscience. More, however, is not diminished but made credible and sympathetic in the context of a vibrantly painted Tudor background. Ackroyd's empathy with More's values and his age sharpens the presentation and convinces the reader of More's uniqueness and heroism, not by ignoring the unflattering but by embracing his complexity.

Fox, Alistair. *Thomas More: History and Providence.* New Haven, Connecticut: Yale University Press, 1982. 271pp. In a fascinating intellectual biography, Fox provides a comprehensive account of the progress and evolution of More's ideas. In a fresh and original perspective, the many contradictions and inconsistencies in More's character and thoughts are coherently blended in a persuasive portrait.

Guy, John. *The Public Career of Sir Thomas More.* New Haven, Connecticut: Yale University Press, 1980. 220pp. In a detailed, admirably researched assessment of More's public career from his early legal career to his resignation as Henry VIII's lord chancellor in 1532, Guy assembles a great deal of new information about More as a state official. The book is revealing about More's administrative achievements and the political forces that shaped his career.

Marius, Richard. *Thomas More: A Biography.* New York: Knopf, 1984. 562pp. In a first-rate popular biography that combines a narrative history with a novelist's flair in imagining what More might have thought and felt, Marius darkens the conventional portrait of More, dealing harshly with the ambiguities and contradictions of his character and his private and sexual life. Marius's interpretations are stimulating and supported by careful research and represent a contrary human portrait very different from that of the saintly and heroic image of previous studies.

Other Biographical Studies

Chambers, R.W. *Thomas More.* New York: Harcourt, Brace, 1935. 416pp. Long held as the standard life, Chambers's literary biography presents a masterful synthesis of sources that counters previous hagiographies with a religiously neutral account in which More is presented as a great scholar and humanist. The author's evident loathing for Henry VIII intrudes, but the book remains a valuable study of More and his milieu.

Kenny, Anthony. *Thomas More.* New York: Oxford University Press, 1983. 111pp. Kenny's concise biography serves as an excellent introduction to the man and his era.

Martz, Louis M. *Thomas More: The Search for the Inner Man.* New Haven, Connecticut: Yale University Press, 1990. 112pp. Martz's short biographical study was written to counter the more negative portrait by Marius and restore the luster to More's greatness. The book offers a defense of the various charges against More that attributes his flaws to the values of his day.

Monti, James. *The King's Good Servant but God's First: The Life and Writings of Saint Thomas More.* San Francisco: Ignatius Press, 1997. 490pp. More is viewed from an unabashed Roman Catholic perspective that finds evidence for his sainthood in his devotion to his family, his spiritual development, and his final persecution in which More's conscience overcame his allegiance to the crown. More sophisticated and objective than earlier hagiographies, the book nevertheless serves as more a tribute to More's faith than an investigation into his humanity.

Reynolds, Ernest E. *The Field Is Won: The Life and Death of Saint Thomas More.* Milwaukee: Bruce, 1968. 396pp. In a revision and expansion of the author's earlier *Trial of St. Thomas More* (1964), based on new research with recent scholarship summarized, Reynolds concentrates on the religious aspect of More's career. More's beliefs are studied against their historical background along with a close analysis of his writings.

Ridley, Jasper. *Statesman and Saint: Cardinal Wolsey, Sir Thomas More, and the Politics of Henry VIII.* New York: Viking, 1983. 338pp. This dual biography of Thomas Wolsey and Sir Thomas More takes the measure of both men and concludes

that the former was the better minister, while the latter was an intolerant fanatic and impractical idealist.

Roper, William. *The Life of Sir Thomas More.* 1626. Reprinted. Springfield, Illinois: Templegate, 1992. 125pp. Roper's tribute to his father-in-law, written in 1535, offers a sketch of More's life that is valuable for its perspective but not always factually reliable.

Biographical Novels

Beahn, John E. *A Man Born Again: Saint Thomas More.* Milwaukee: Bruce, 1954. 208pp. More's rise to power and fall from favor are dramatized in this often idealized portrait of the Tudor saint.

Brady, Charles A. *Stage of Fools.* New York: Dutton, 1953. 381pp. Blending facts and imaginative speculation, the novel dramatizes More's rise to political power and the ensuing break with Henry VIII. More is depicted as the lone man of principles in a corrupt and self-serving Tudor court.

Plaidy, Jean. *St. Thomas Eve.* New York: Putnam, 1970. 284pp. In a fully realized historical dramatization of the conflict between Henry VIII and More, the novel provides a reliable account of the events and a credible portrait of the contenders.

White, Olive B. *The King's Good Servant.* New York: Macmillan, 1936. 521pp. Chronicling the last six years in More's life, the novel dramatizes the king's effort to convince More to support his divorce in a historically accurate presentation with believable portraits of the major and minor figures of the era.

Fictional Portraits

Benson, Robert H. *The King's Achievement.* New York: P.J. Kennedy, 1905. 377pp. In a sweeping, panoramic novel dramatizing the destruction caused by the Protestant Reformation in England, numerous historical characters, including More, are presented in a faithful reconstruction of the religious and political atmosphere of the era.

Matthew, Anne I. *Warm Wind, West Wind.* New York: Crown, 1956. 310pp. This intriguing and convincing family saga set during the reign of Henry VIII shows the impact of the new Humanist learning of Erasmus and More, who are both plausibly depicted.

Biographical Films and Theatrical Adaptations

Bolt, Robert. *A Man for All Seasons.* New York: Random House, 1962. 186pp. Bolt depicts the conflict between Henry VIII and More in a moving drama that anachronistically presents More as an early individualist and proponent of civil disobedience, while ignoring the unflattering, unheroic details of More's character and behavior.

A Man for All Seasons (1966). Director: Fred Zimmerman. An Oscar-winning film version of Robert Bolt's play features masterful performances by Paul Scofield as More, Robert Shaw as Henry VIII, and Wendy Hiller as More's wife. Video.

A Man for All Seasons (1988). Director: Charlton Heston. Heston's cable television adaptation of the London stage production of Bolt's play has Heston in the lead as More with a strong supporting cast, including Vanessa Redgrave as More's wife and Martin Chamberlain as Henry. Video.

See also Anne Boleyn; Henry VIII; Thomas Wolsey

337. J. PIERPONT MORGAN
1837–1913

The son of financier Junius Spencer Morgan (1813–1890), John Pierpont Morgan built the family fortune into a vast financial and industrial empire. He was born in Hartford, Connecticut, studied abroad, and after working in a New York City banking house became the New York agent and then sole manager for J. S. Morgan & Company. He developed a railroad empire, financed manufacturing and mining, controlled banks, insurance companies, shipping lines, and communications systems. In 1901 he formed U.S. Steel, the world's first billion-dollar corporation. Many of his commercial ventures, including gold speculation during the Civil War and the sale of obsolete carbines to the Union and his lending practices and financial dominance during the panics of 1895 and 1897, aroused controversy. In 1912 he defended his activities before a congressional committee investigating the "money trust." An avid sportsman, yachtsman, and art collector, Morgan financed many philanthropies and left legacies to the Metropolitan Museum of Art and the Pierpont Morgan Library.

Recommended Biographies

Chernow, Ron. *The House of Morgan: An American Banking Dynasty and the Rise of Modern Finance.* New York: Atlantic Monthly Press, 1990. 812pp. Of the several books examining the Morgan family and its business ventures, Chernow's is the best, providing a lucid, balanced, and revealing account that penetrates the inner workings of the Morgans, and their companies, power, and legacy.

Sinclair, Andrew. *Corsair: The Life of J. Pierpont Morgan.* Boston: Little, Brown, 1981. 269pp. Although offering little new information or original research, Sinclair tells the familiar details of Morgan's life and career in a highly readable and entertaining style that manages a coherent psychological interpretation of the financier's personality traits.

Strouse, Jean. *Morgan: American Financier.* New York: Random House, 1999. 796pp. Drawing on previous untapped archival sources, Strouse constructs an insightful, fresh portrait of Morgan that differs considerably from the views presented by apologists and detractors. Looking at Morgan's dealings and character afresh in the context of his times, the book manages a nuanced, revealing study of a complex, believable human rather than a monster or paragon.

Other Biographical Studies

Allen, Frederick L. *The Great Pierpont Morgan.* New York: Harper, 1949. 306pp. More a character study than a fully detailed narrative account, Allen attempts to answer the question what kind of man Morgan was. He achieves a balanced, objective answer, avoiding the distortions of Morgan advocates and enemies, focused mainly on Morgan's public career rather than his private life.

Canfield, Cass. *The Incredible Pierpont Morgan: Financier and Art Collector.* New York: Harper & Row, 1974. 176pp. In a sympathetic account, Canfield summarizes the highlights of Morgan's career before proceeding to his main focus: Morgan as art collector. The book's many photographs support Canfield's contention that Morgan was a formidable and talented art critic.

Carosso, Vincent P. *The Morgans: Private International Bankers, 1854–1913.* Cambridge, Massachusetts: Harvard University Press, 1987. 888pp. In a scholarly analysis based on access to the Morgan business archives, Carosso traces in detail the development of Morgan's business dealings and their financial and governmental influence. Exhaustive and revealing, the book is an objective and factual account that resists taking an interpretive position on Morgan and his legacy.

Corey, Lewis. *The House of Morgan: A Social Biography of the Masters of Money.* 1930. Reprint ed. New York: AMS Press, 1969. 479pp. In one of the best histories of Morgan's business dealings based on official records, Corey does provide a highly critical verdict on Morgan's financial decisions that attributes his success to a ruthless drive for power and control.

Hovey, Carl. *The Life Story of J. Pierpont Morgan.* New York: Sturgis and Walton, 1912. 352pp. In a eulogistic tribute, Hovey's early biographical sketch presents Morgan as a serious and intelligent shaper of vital financial issues. Although including valuable insider's anecdotal details, the book neglects Morgan's private life and has little to offer about Morgan's personality.

Hoyt, Edwin P. *The House of Morgan.* New York: Dodd, Mead, 1966. 428pp. Hoyt begins his study of the Morgan family dynasty in 1636, tracing the growth of American business as reflected in the Morgans' fortunes. Sympathetic to Morgan, Hoyt differentiates him from others like Jay Gould and Jim Fisk. Based mainly on Satterlee and Corey for its details, the book is marred by factual errors and an often overly partisan perspective.

Jackson, Stanley. *J. P. Morgan: A Biography.* New York: Stein and Day, 1983. 332pp. Jackson concentrates on Morgan's personal life and family relationships in an undocumented and highly speculative account.

Satterlee, Herbert L. *J. Pierpont Morgan: An Intimate Portrait.* New York: Macmillan, 1939. 595pp. Written by Morgan's son-in-law, this defensive appreciation does claim serious attention because of Satterlee's unique access to important documents denied other biographers. The book manages to collect its data into a detailed chronological narrative that is one of the fullest and most comprehensive accounts of Morgan's doings, but without much criticism or interpretive coherence.

Wheeler, George. *Pierpont Morgan and Friends: The Anatomy of a Myth.* Englewood Cliffs, New Jersey: Prentice-Hall, 1973. 338pp. In a debunking of conventional views of Morgan's importance as a financial power and shaper, Wheeler offers evidence and conjecture that Morgan's financial acumen is overrated and much of his success was reactive to circumstances, compelled more by arrogance and greed than a larger vision. Lacking balance and objectivity, Wheeler rarely rises above polemical attack.

Winkler, John. *Morgan the Magnificent: The Life of J. Pierpont Morgan: 1837–1913.* New York: Vanguard, 1930. 313pp. Winkler's popular biography opens with a summary chapter on the man followed by chapters on the highlights of his career. More a presentation of the facts than an interpretation, this is a useful collection of anecdotes, gossip, and facts but without needed synthesis and historical and economic context.

Fictional Portraits

Carr, Caleb. *The Alienist.* New York: Random House, 1994. 496pp. Carr's inventive historical mystery is set in 1896 New York City as a psychologist attempts to find a serial killer. Several historical figures, including Theodore Roosevelt, Franz Boas, Lincoln Steffens, and Morgan, appear.

Doctorow, E.L. *Ragtime.* New York: Random House, 1975. 270pp. The climax of Doctorow's groundbreaking historical fiction is set in Morgan's New York City home, and the novel includes an unforgettable meeting between Morgan and Henry Ford.

Kruger, Mary. *No Honeymoon for Death.* New York: Kensington, 1995. 288pp. In this installment of the author's historical mystery series, Morgan enlists the help of husband and wife sleuths to solve the mysterious disappearance of a fellow financier.

Longstreet, Stephen. *The Bank.* New York: Putnam, 1976. 377pp. The rise of a great American banking family is dramatized with appearances by a number of the leading financial figures of the Gilded Age, including Jay Gould, James Fisk, Cornelius Vanderbilt, and Morgan.

Villars, Elizabeth. *One Night in Newport.* Garden City, New York: Doubleday, 1981. 360pp. Newport, Rhode Island, in 1912 is the scene for this social drama as a mother tries to find husbands for her three daughters, and Morgan and his fellow financiers attempt to outwit each other.

Biographical Films and Theatrical Adaptations

Jones, Jeffrey M. *J. P. Morgan Saves the Nation.* Los Angeles: Sun & Moon Press, 1996. 120pp. Jones's musical, set during the financial panic of 1907 in which Morgan battles to control the American economy, serves as the occasion for a consideration of the clash of American values.

A&E Biography Video: J. Pierpont Morgan: Emperor of Wall Street (1996). Director: Bill Harris. Using archival photographs, this documentary portrait covers the highlights of Morgan's life and career. Video.

338. WILLIAM MORRIS
1834–1896

English author, artist, designer, and social reformer, Morris was a member of the pre-Raphaelite Brotherhood who sought to counteract the effects of industrialization by a return to the artistic aesthetic of the Medieval era. He set up Morris and Co. to make carvings, stained glass, tapestries, carpets, wallpaper, and furniture. His founding of Kelmscott Press influenced typographical and book design. He was a founder of the Socialist League. Morris's writings include *The Defense of Guenevere and Other Poems* (1858) and *The Dream of John Ball* (1888).

Autobiography and Primary Sources

The Collected Letters of William Morris. Norman Kelvin, ed. Princeton, New Jersey: Princeton University Press, 1984–1996. 4 vols. Morris's letters are mainly business records of his continual frenzy of activities without much time for reflections or self-revelations. However, Morris does provide glimpses of his troubled marriage and his often confused political and artistic positions.

Morris, May, ed. *William Morris: Artist, Writer, Socialist.* 1936. Reprint ed. New York: B. Blom, 1971. 2 vols. Morris's daughter provides an important miscellaneous collection of documents, including family records, reviews, articles, and opinions of those who knew the artist.

Recommended Biographies

Henderson, Philip. *William Morris: His Life, Work, and Friends.* New York: McGraw-Hill, 1967. 388pp. Profiting by new materials, Henderson provides an insightful narrative that traces the connections among Morris's private, public, and artistic life against the context of his times. Detailing Morris's relationship with the many important figures from various disciplines, Henderson demonstrates Morris's centrality in the critical issues of his day.

Lindsay, Jack. *William Morris: His Life and Work.* New York: Taplinger, 1979. 432pp. While offering no new revelations, Lindsay's is a respectable synthesis of scholarship that attempts to weave Morris's complicated life and many interests and achievements into a coherent whole. The book is recommended to the reader looking for a sensible overview before proceeding to the longer treatments.

Mackail, J.W. *The Life of William Morris.* New York: Longmans, 1899. 2 vols. Mackail's authorized biography has long established itself as the standard life based on the author's access to unpublished materials, much of which has been lost, and conversations with Morris's intimates. Mackail weaves his sources into a detailed, comprehensive chronological narrative that remains one of the most important sources of information about Morris's activities. Reticence prevents a frank discussion of Morris's marital and extramarital affairs, and Mackail should be supplemented by more recent biographies.

MacCarthy, Fiona. *William Morris: A Life for Our Time.* New York: Knopf, 1995. 780pp.

MaCarthy's fresh evaluation of Morris, his achievements, and influence is the first choice for a single volume study. Well documented and provocative, MacCarthy's revisionist study takes on previous biographers and, with the aid of modern scholarship, presents an engaging, complex portrait that does full credit to a complex and multidimensional genius whose private and public lives are connected coherently.

Other Biographical Studies

Arnot, Robert P. *William Morris: The Man and the Myth*. New York: Monthly Review Press, 1964. 131pp. Arnot's important revisionist study of Morris as a political thinker challenges the conventional view of his ideas as muddleheaded and irrelevant, with a view of Morris as a coherent and committed revolutionary socialist.

Bradley, Ian C. *William Morris and His World*. New York: Scribner, 1978. 127pp. Bradley's pictorial biography has a competently written and accessible text that summarizes the high points of Morris's career. Serves the general reader well.

Cary, Elisabeth. *William Morris: Poet, Craftsman, Socialist*. New York: Putnam, 1902. 296pp. The first full-scale biography since Mackail, Cary's brief life offers a competent review of the highlights of Morris's career, marred by the author's hostility to Morris's socialism.

Clutton-Brock, Arthur. *William Morris: His Work and Influence*. New York: Holt, 1914. 256pp. This appreciative study asserts Morris's importance in the formation of modernism and serves as a competent introduction to the man and his work.

Compton-Rickett, Arthur. *William Morris: A Study in Personality*. 1913. Reprint ed. Port Washington, New York: Kennikat Press, 1972. 325pp. Based in part on interviews with Morris's associates, this is a study of Morris's character as he appeared to his contemporaries. An ardent admirer, the author provides some fresh insights and anecdotes, but his sympathy does not extend sufficiently to take Morris's political ideas seriously.

Coote, Stephen. *William Morris: His Life and Work*. New York: Smithmark, 1995. 224pp. Coote manages to cover in brief Morris's life and diverse achievements with detailed coverage of Morris as designer and his leadership in the Arts and Crafts movement.

Eshleman, Lloyd W. *A Victorian Rebel: The Life of William Morris*. New York: Scribner, 1940. 386pp. Eshleman presents the chief facts of Morris's life in a developmental biography emphasizing the evolution of his ideas. The book is constrained by its scholarship, and readers interested in a clearer narrative of Morris's life and times should look elsewhere.

Faulkner, Peter. *Against the Age: An Introduction to William Morris*. Boston: Allen and Unwin, 1980. 193pp. Tracing Morris's life though his achievements as a poet, craftsman, designer, and socialist, Faulkner's is an excellent introduction to the man and his importance. The book quotes extensively from Morris's writings and letters.

Jackson, Holbrook. *William Morris: Craftsman, Socialist*. 1908. Reprint ed. Westport, Connecticut:

Greenwood, 1971. 160pp. Contrary to many views of Morris's political ideas as either negative or irrelevant, Jackson argues their centrality and connection with Morris's art. The book is particularly insightful in providing the intellectual context for Morris's development.

Noyes, Alfred. *William Morris*. London: Macmillan, 1908. 156pp. This short critical biography focuses mainly on Morris's poetry and is inadequate on the other aspects of Morris's remarkably diverse creative life and dismissive of his political ideas.

Shaw, George Bernard. *William Morris As I Knew Him*. New York: Dodd, Mead, 1936. 52pp. Shaw as a young man in the 1880s was befriended by Morris, and Shaw offers his reminiscences with a focus on Morris's political and socialist convictions. Fascinating for what Shaw reveals about both Morris and himself during this period.

Stansky, Peter. *William Morris*. New York: Oxford University Press, 1983. 96pp. Stansky's concise introduction to Morris's life and achievement is an ideal first choice for readers beginning their exploration.

Thompson, E.P. *William Morris: Romantic to Revolutionary*. 1955. Revised ed. New York: Pantheon, 1977. 829pp. This is the most thorough account of Morris's political development. Challenging previous writers hostile to Morris's evolving socialism who have described his political ideas as confused and a distraction, Thompson shows how central and coherent Morris's revolutionary ideas were.

Thompson, Paul. *The Work of William Morris*. 1967. Revised ed. New York: Oxford University Press, 1991. 318pp. Thompson provides a brief biographical portrait before proceeding to an examination of Morris's various activities. Taking advantage of recent scholarship, the book considers Morris in relationship to his era.

Fictional Portraits

Cameron, William. *Day Is Coming*. New York: Macmillan, 1944. 573pp. Tracing the development of the socialist and craft movements in England from 1887 to 1939, the novel's fictional hero joins Morris and features a detailed discussion of the latter's ideals.

Savage, Elizabeth. *Willowwood*. Boston: Little, Brown, 1978. 214pp. Recreating the artistic world of Dante Gabriel Rossetti and the Pre-Raphaelite Brotherhood, the novel dramatizes Rossetti's complicated emotional life and includes appearances by notable figures of his circle, including John Ruskin and Morris and his wife.

Other Sources

Salmon, Nicholas, and Derek Baker. *William Morris Chronology*. Boston: Thoemmes Press, 1996. 292pp. Based on letters, diaries, and memoirs, the book provides the most detailed and comprehensive account of Morris's daily activities, along with appreciations and anecdotes by associates.

339. MOTHER TERESA
1910–1997

The founder of the Missionaries of Charity and recipient of the 1979 Nobel Peace Prize, Mother Teresa was born Agnes Gonxha Bejaxhiu in Skopje, Macedonia, of Albanian parents. She joined the Loreto order of nuns and took her vows in 1937. In 1948 she began her work with the destitute and dying of Calcutta and the following year became an Indian citizen. In 1950 she became the mother superior of the Missionaries of Charity, which founded such establishments as the Nirmal Hriday, or Home for the Dying, and a home for abandoned children and teenage girls. The order has organized food-distribution and medical treatment programs, set up clinics and a community for lepers, and provided hospices for AIDS victims. Mother Teresa received many awards during her lifetime. After her death, her body lay in state in Calcutta, and her funeral was televised internationally.

Autobiography and Primary Sources

My Life for the Poor: Mother Teresa of Calcutta. Balado Gonzalo and Jane Playfoot, eds. New York: Ballantine Books, 1987. 114pp. Collected from various interviews, Mother Teresa's own words are arranged to approximate an autobiographical account of her childhood, family, early years in Albania, religious training, years teaching in India, her call to leave her order to serve the poor, and the growth and development of the Missionaries of Charity.

A Simple Path. New York: Ballantine Books, 1995. 202pp. Compiled with the assistance of writer Lucinda Vardey before her death, Mother Teresa's autobiographical reflections explain her spiritual beliefs and the experiences that led her to undertake her charitable works. The book offers a candid look at Mother Teresa's everyday life and her religious and humane values.

Recommended Biographies

Egan, Eileen. *Such a Vision of the Street: Mother Teresa: The Spirit and the Work*. Garden City, New York: Doubleday, 1985. 448pp. A detailed record of Mother Teresa's achievements, Egan's biography is a sympathetic though balanced appreciation that includes the author's objections to some of Mother Teresa's policies and actions. Based on extensive interviews and firsthand knowledge, Egan's account is much more thorough than other tributes.

Sebba, Anne. *Mother Teresa: Beyond the Image*. New York: Doubleday, 1997. 297pp. Based on extensive interviews with many associates, several of whom are critical of Mother Teresa's methods, the author achieves a balanced and evenhanded portrait that deals honestly and fairly with her subject, stressing her human qualities and the practical challenges of her ministry. The result is not to diminish Mother Teresa's achievements but to understand them and her in human rather than saintly terms.

Spink, Kathryn. *Mother Teresa: A Complete Authorized Biography*. San Francisco: Harper &

Row, 1997. 306pp. Based on the author's intimacy with Mother Teresa for more than 18 years, Spink chronicles her life from her youth to her winning the Nobel Peace Prize in 1979. The book achieves a believable, sympathetic portrait of an austere, determined woman, whose development is captured through many private and public incidents, carefully presented.

Other Biographical Studies

Allegri, Renzo. *Teresa of the Poor: The Story of Her Life.* Ann Arbor, Michigan: Charis Books, 1996. 175pp. Based on conversations with Mother Teresa and original research, the author provides a series of biographical sketches to illuminate Mother Teresa's character and accomplishments, with a number of previously unpublished details.

Chawla, Navin. *Mother Teresa.* 1992. Reprint ed. Rockport, Massachusetts: Element, 1996. 231pp. In an uncritical appreciation, Chawla presents the background, development, and achievement of Mother Teresa, using many letters and rare photographs to tell her story, framed by the author's struggle to comprehend Mother Teresa's life of devotion and self-sacrifice.

Doig, Desmond. *Mother Teresa: Her People and Her Work.* New York: Harper & Row, 1976. 175pp. Doig's impressionistic journalistic account of Mother Teresa in Calcutta was the first book to spread the story of her charitable work among the city's poor. Based on interviews and firsthand observations, Doig supplies a believable portrait, but offers little on Mother Teresa's life before her arrival in India.

Gonzalez-Balado, José Luis. *Mother Teresa: Her Life, Her Work, Her Message: 1910–1997: A Memoir.* Liquori, Missouri: Liquori, 1997. 192pp. Written by one of her co-workers, the book draws mainly on secondary sources for its review of Mother Teresa's life and development, enlivened by firsthand insights and an insider's knowledge of the workings of Mother Teresa's many charities.

Le Joly, Edward, S.J. *Mother Teresa of Calcutta: A Biography.* San Francisco: Harper & Row, 1985. 345pp. Written by the spiritual director to the Missionaries of Charity, Le Joly's informed and insider's perspective provides a reliable portrait of Mother Teresa's achievements, character, and spiritual development. The book, however, supplies few details about Mother Teresa's life before Calcutta.

Muggeridge, Malcolm. *Something Beautiful for God: Mother Teresa of Calcutta.* New York: Harper & Row, 1971. 156pp. Based on a television interview, Muggeridge's highly subjective biographical sketch and appreciation of Mother Teresa's life and work feature her responses to a number of provocative questions.

Porter, David. *Mother Teresa: The Early Years.* Grand Rapids, Michigan: William B. Eerdmans, 1986. 100pp. Porter's is a valuable look at Mother Teresa's Albanian background and early life in Yugoslavia with useful primary sources, including those provided by Mother Teresa's brother.

Rai, Raghu, and Navin Chawla. *Faith and Compassion: The Life and Work of Mother Teresa.* Rockport, Massachusetts: Element, 1996. 192pp.

Written by two Hindu authors using powerful photographs, letters, and interviews, the book chronicles Mother Teresa's spiritual development, beliefs, and achievement in a moving tribute.

Royle, Roger. *Mother Teresa: A Life in Pictures.* San Francisco: Harper & Row, 1992. 159pp. Royle's is a moving visual record of Mother Teresa's life and work with the poor.

Serrou, Robert. *Teresa of Calcutta: A Pictorial Biography.* New York: McGraw-Hill, 1980. 127pp. This illustrated biography concentrates on Mother Teresa's years in India but does provide informed information on her early development.

Spink, Kathryn. *The Miracle of Love: Mother Teresa of Calcutta.* San Francisco: Harper & Row, 1981. 256pp. In a conversational and anecdote-rich account, Spink concentrates on the activities of the Missionaries of Charity, particularly the Co-Workers, an international layperson organization founded by Mother Teresa. Using Mother Teresa's own words and those of individual co-workers, the book provides a detailed chronicle of Mother Teresa's mission to the poor and suffering.

Recommended Juvenile Biographies

Clucas, Joan. *Mother Teresa.* New York: Chelsea House, 1989. 111pp. MG/YA. This is an informative, clearly written chronicle of Mother Teresa's life that covers her early years as well as her work in India.

Greene, Carol. *Mother Teresa: Friend of the Friendless.* Chicago: Childrens Press, 1983. 31pp. Greene supplies a brief, appreciatory account that covers the significant events of Mother Teresa's life.

Johnson, Linda C. *Mother Teresa: Protector of the Sick.* Woodbridge, Connecticut: Blackbirch Press, 1991. 64pp. MG. Part of the Library of Famous Women series, this is a full-length portrait of Mother Teresa, emphasizing her challenges and accomplishments.

Biographical Films and Theatrical Adaptations

A&E Biography Video: Mother Teresa: A Life of Devotion (1997). Producer: Helen Bullough. A film tribute that features interviews with those who knew and worked with Mother Teresa and extensive footage of her work in Calcutta, covering her early years in Macedonia to her winning of the Nobel Peace Prize. Video.

Mother Teresa (1986). Directors: Ann and Jeanette Petrie. Mother Teresa's life and achievement are celebrated in this documentary portrait. Video.

The World of Mother Teresa (1981). Producer: Ann Petrie. This documentary opens with the 1979 Nobel Prize award ceremony and follows Mother Teresa as she tours the facilities she founded in Calcutta. Includes an interview. Video.

340. WOLFGANG AMADEUS MOZART
1756–1791

Austrian composer who produced some of the world's greatest music, Mozart was born in Salzburg and was taught by his father to play the harpsichord, violin, and organ. A child prodigy, he began composing before the age of five and by six was touring European courts. By the age of 13 he had written concertos, sonatas, symphonies, a German operetta, and an Italian opera. He was concert-master to the Archbishop of Salzburg from 1771 to 1781 and in 1787 became court composer to Emperor Joseph II in Vienna. He wrote three of his greatest symphonies, 39, 40, and 41 (the Jupiter Symphony), within a three-month period in 1788. His more than 600 works show great expressive beauty and technical perfection, and include *Eine Kleine Nachtmusik* (1787); the operas *Don Giovanni* (1787), *Cosi Fan Tutte* (1790), and *The Magic Flute* (1791); and the uncompleted *Requiem* (1791).

Autobiography and Primary Sources

The Letters of Mozart and His Family. Emily Anderson, ed. New York: St. Martin's, 1966. 2 vols. Other collections include *Mozart's Letters.* Eric Blom, ed. (Baltimore, Maryland: Penguin, 1956. 277pp.) and *Mozart's Letters: An Illustrated Selection.* (Boston: Little, Brown, 1990. 254pp.).

Mozart Speaks: Views on Music, Musicians, and the World. Robert L. Marshall, ed. New York: Shirmer Books, 1995. 446pp. Passages from Mozart's letters and contemporaries' accounts are arranged topically so the reader can easily discover the composer's thoughts on a variety of subjects.

Deutsch, Otto E. *Mozart: A Documentary Biography, 1765–1891.* Stanford, California: Stanford University Press, 1965. 680pp. An invaluable sourcebook, all the relevant documents of Mozart's life, excluding his letters, are collected with annotations.

Recommended Biographies

Gay, Peter. *Mozart.* New York: Viking, 1999. 177pp. Despite its brevity, Gay's is a lucidly written and insightful biographical profile that traces Mozart's life in a series of developmental stages that make sense of the composer's artistry and psychological temperament, while challenging a number of legends that have obscured a clear view.

Kuster, Konrad. *Mozart: A Musical Biography.* New York: Oxford University Press, 1996. 428pp. Kuster treats Mozart's creative life through his works, chronologically examining many of his compositions while pointing out the events and relationships that affected Mozart's development. Full of original and provocative commentary, Kuster's study does assume a certain degree of technical expertise.

Rosselli, John. *The Life of Mozart.* New York: Cambridge University Press, 1998. 225pp. Rosselli's useful, concise life places Mozart in the context of his times and uses reliable sources to explore the composer's various relationships. The book's musical criticism is within reach of the non-specialist without technical knowledge.

Schenk, Erich. *Mozart and His Times.* New York: Knopf, 1959. 452pp. Without providing any musical criticism, Schenk presents a solid factual chronology that challenges many misconceptions committed by other biographers. Schenk's study relies on original and extensive research to substitute a realistic view for more conventional idealized and sentimental presentations.

Solomon, Maynard. *Mozart: A Life.* New York: HarperCollins, 1995. 640pp. Solomon's psychobiography attempts a coherent and integrated portrait of Mozart's artistic and personal development based on a careful review of existing evidence. At the center of the author's analysis is Mozart's troubled relationship with his father that is used to explain the composer's behavioral peculiarities and one of the important sources of Mozart's genius. Exhilarating in its interpretive energy, Solomon's examination does not resolve all the paradoxes and mysteries in Mozart's career but does help the reader to see him whole, in plausible human terms.

Other Biographical Studies

Blom, Eric. *Mozart.* London: Dent, 1935. 388pp. Blom's concise critical biography combines a reliable treatment of Mozart's personality, the sequence of events that shaped him, and a valuable critique of the composer's music.

Braunbehrens, Volkmar. *Mozart in Vienna, 1781–1791.* New York: Grove Weidenfeld, 1990. 481pp. This revisionist study looks at Mozart's last 11 years, placing his musical life in its social, political, and artistic context. With new evidence, Braunbehrens challenges the notion that Mozart was uninterested in politics, unhappy in his marriage, and financially unsuccessful. Often densely written and argumentative, the book's sociological approach adds a fresh dimension for understanding Mozart's life and works.

Burk, John N. *Mozart and His Music.* New York: Random House, 1959. 453p. Devoting half the book to a consideration of Mozart's life and half to a chronological listing of his works, this concise, readable reference tool is intended for the nonspecialist and serves as a worthwhile introduction and overview.

Davenport, Marcia. *Mozart.* New York: Scribner, 1932. 400pp. A lively and entertaining narrative life, Davenport's presentation, though carefully documented, features imaginary conversations with Mozart and his associates. Scholars may challenge Davenport's inventions and interpretations, but the general reader will enjoy the book's vividness and drama.

Davies, Peter J. *Mozart in Person: His Character and Health.* New York: Greenwood, 1989. 299pp. Mozart's life is studied clinically by a physician who looks at Mozart's psychological and physical symptoms to help explain his life and his behavioral peculiarities, including an informed diagnosis about the causes of the composer's death.

Einstein, Alfred. *Mozart: His Character, His Work.* New York: Oxford University Press, 1945. 492pp. Not a chronological biography but a series of essays on Mozart's life, personality, and works,

Einstein's thoughtful and informed analysis provides a multidimensional approach that does assume some prior knowledge of Mozart's life and works.

Elias, Robert. *Mozart: Portrait of a Genius.* Los Angeles: University of California Press, 1993. 152pp. This brief psychological and sociological study is valuable on the connections between Mozart and his cultural and historical context. Dependant on unreliable secondary sources for biographical details, Elias accepts several Mozart legends as fact.

Fischer, Hans Conrad, and Lutz Besch. *The Life of Mozart: An Account in Text and Pictures.* New York: St. Martin's, 1969. 203pp. This compact visual biography integrates text and illustrations into a chronological depiction of Mozart's life and musical career.

Ghéon, Henri. *In Search of Mozart.* New York: Sheed & Ward, 1934. 366pp. In a highly poetic, lyrical meditation on the source of Mozart's genius, this intriguing book is unreliable in some of its factual details and veers toward the sentimental but does stimulate interesting consideration of the composer's uniqueness and achievement.

Gutman, Robert W. *Mozart: A Cultural Biography.* New York: Harcourt, Brace,1999. 839pp. By concentrating on the connections between Mozart's life and his cultural background, Gutman offers a fresh assessment that challenges previous versions that have characterized the composer as an outsider and vulgarian. Gutman's Mozart is an "austere moralist of vital force, incisiveness, and strength of purpose." The book is equally adept and provocative in analyzing Mozart's music and how it evolved in his milieu.

Hildesheimer, Wolfgang. *Mozart.* New York: Farrar, Straus, 1982. 408pp. Neither a systematic nor a chronological examination, the book offers instead an extended psychological analysis interweaving biographical details, Mozart's own words, and a critical discussion of the composer's works. Provocative and argumentative, Hildesheimer's observations attempt to reveal Mozart's psyche and the sources of his genius, but the book presupposes familiarity with the man and his works.

Holmes, Edward. *The Life of Mozart.* 1845. Reprint ed. Da Capo Press, 1995. 364pp. One of the strongest early biographies, Holmes's is a reliable chronicle of the composer's life, the first to be based on Mozart's letters and contemporary memoirs.

Hussey, Dyneley. *Wolfgang Amade Mozart.* 1928. Reprint ed. Freeport, New York: Books for Libraries Press, 1969. 368pp. In a highly readable and informative introductory study intended for the general reader, Hussey traces the interconnections between Mozart's life and works.

Hutchings, Arthur. *Mozart: The Man, The Musician.* New York: Shirmer Books, 1976. 113pp. In a beautifully illustrated pictorial biography, Hutchings's text divides its attention between the man and the musician with a reliable and informed assessment of the composer's personality, development, and relationships.

Jahn, Otto. *Life of Mozart.* London: Novello, 1882. 3 vols. Jahn's massive, authoritative biography is one of the landmarks of Mozart studies. Meticulously researched and documented, Jahn's objective collection of biographical details remains an important reference source for details on Mozart's life.

Keys, Ivor. *Mozart: His Music and His Life.* New York: Holmes and Meier, 1980. 248pp. Inviting and useful for the general reader, Keys chronicles the connections between Mozart's life and works in a concise, well-written narrative biography.

Landon, H.C. Robbins. *1791: Mozart's Last Year.* New York: Schirmer Books, 1988. 240pp. Written to set the record straight on the details of Mozart's death in response to Peter Shaffer's controversial presentation in *Amadeus,* Landon presents a thorough and informed account.

Landon, H.C. Robbins. *Mozart: The Golden Years, 1789-91.* New York: Schirmer Books, 1989. 271pp. Broadening his early work on Mozart's final year, Landon similarly chronicles Mozart's last decade through the composer's letters and a detailed reconstruction of the musical and social scene.

Levey, Michael. *The Life and Death of Mozart.* New York: Stein and Day, 1971. 278pp. This is a chronological description of Mozart's life and works written for the nonspecialist. Levey focuses his attention on Mozart's operas and their reflection on the composer's personality and genius.

Niemetschek, Franz. *Life of Mozart.* 1798. Reprint ed. London: L. Hyman, 1956. 87pp. This early biography includes valuable firsthand impressions from a number of contemporaries, supplemented by primary sources. The book's somewhat sentimentalized portrait of Mozart is not as reliable as its vivid milieu.

Ottaway, Hugh. *Mozart.* Detroit: Wayne State University Press, 1980. 208pp. Ottaway's is a lucidly written, well-illustrated overview intended for the general reader that does its job of making the man and his music accessible.

Sadie, Stanley. *Mozart.* New York: Vienna House, 1965. 192pp. Sadie's is a useful, concise handbook on the man and his music with a great deal of information admirably synthesized into comprehensible tables and appendixes.

Sadie, Stanley. *The New Grove Mozart.* New York: W.W. Norton, 1983. 247pp. In one of the best condensed studies of Mozart's life and his works, Sadie synthesizes recent scholarship in a helpful reference format. The book's factual orientation does not allow for conjecture or interpretation, but the reader looking for the uncontested facts should consult this valuable source.

Sitwell, Sacheverell. *Mozart.* New York: Appleton, 1932. 184pp. Sitwell's brief biographical essay compresses the highlights of Mozart's career and genius in an evocative appreciation.

Stafford, William. *The Mozart Myth: A Critical Reassessment.* Stanford, California: Stanford University Press, 1991. 285pp. In an objective review of the various myths surrounding the composer, Stafford traces them back to their origin and assesses their relative plausibility and accuracy.

Steptoe, Andrew. *Mozart*. New York: Knopf, 1997. 208pp. The author uses extracts from the correspondence of Mozart's family to narrate the composer's life story against his social, cultural, and musical background of the late eighteenth century.

Turner, W.J. *Mozart: The Man and His Works*. 1938. Revised ed. London: Methuen, 1965. 376pp. Turner anchors his presentation of Mozart and his career through extensive use of the composer's letters. Mozart is allowed, for the most part, to tell his own story.

Valentin, Erich. *Mozart: A Pictorial Biography*. New York: Viking, 1960. 143pp. A wide selection of illustrations is connected by a serviceable, uninspired text.

Biographical Novels

Grun, Bernard. *The Golden Quill: A Novel Based on the Life of Mozart*. New York: Putnam, 1956. 377pp. Told in the form of a diary written by Mozart's sister, this fictional life of the composer follows Mozart's career from child prodigy through his triumphs and premature death. Some liberties with the facts have been taken.

Neider, Charles. *Mozart and the Archboody*. New York: Penguin, 1991. 87pp. In a first-person account, Mozart writes to his father about his career frustrations and aspirations in a believable impersonation of the composer's voice.

Weiss, David. *Sacred and Profane: A Novel of the Life and Times of Mozart*. New York: Morrow, 1968. 639pp. Weiss's fictional biography follows the course of Mozart's life and career in a chronologically reliable sequence with invented situations and conversations and a plausible, if speculative, interpretation of motives.

Weiss, David. *The Assassination of Mozart*. New York: Morrow, 1970. 232pp. A young American couple in 1823 set out to investigate the circumstances of Mozart's death. Their inquiry takes them throughout Europe and encounters with individuals who help them develop a possible, though highly speculative solution to the mystery.

Fictional Portraits

Burgess, Anthony. *On Mozart: A Paean for Wolfgang, Being a Celestial Colloquy, an Opera Libretto, a Film Script, a Schizophrenic Dialogue, a Bewildered Rumination, a Stendhalian Transcription, and a Heartfelt Homage Upon the Bicentenary of the Death of Wolfgang Amadeus Mozart*. New York: Ticknor & Fields, 1992. 160pp. As Burgess's subtitle indicates, this is a fascinating miscellany combining fictional elements, imaginative speculation, and criticism. Set in heaven as the Persian Gulf War is waged, a collection of departed composers debate about music, while the author wrangles with his alter ego about the meaning of Mozart and his music.

Bastable, Bernard. *Dead, Mr. Mozart*. New York: St. Martin's, 1995. 183pp.; *Too Many Notes, Mr. Mozart*. New York: Carroll & Graf, 1996. 183pp. Bastable's amusing historical mystery series imagines the composer's life if he had not died in 1791.

Hersey, John. *Antonietta*. New York: Knopf, 1991. 304pp. This is the story of a Stradivarius violin that is possessed by a variety of owners, including Mozart, Berlioz, Stravinsky, and others.

Jacob, Naomi. *The Irish Boy: A Romantic Biography*. London: Hutchinson,1955. 288pp. In a fictionalized account of the life and career of Irish opera singer Michael Kelly, the novel describes Kelly's relationship with Mozart. Details of Kelly's early years are invented, and some liberties have been taken with the facts.

Mörike, Eduard F. *Mozart on the Way to Prague*. New York: Pantheon, 1947. 124pp. The novel imagines an incident in Mozart's life connected with his composition of *Don Giovanni*. On his way to Prague, Mozart is inspired by the country life around him. The novel is knowledgeable about the details of Mozart's life and the atmosphere of his times.

Recommended Juvenile Biographies

Loewen, Nancy. *Mozart*. Vero Beach, Florida: Rourke, 1989. 111pp. MG. This solid, straightforward biography chronicles Mozart's entire life.

Parouty, Michel. *Mozart: From Child Prodigy to Tragic Hero*. New York: Abrams, 1993. 191pp. MG/YA. Part of Abrams's Discoveries series, this visually rich biography with 187 illustrations, most in color, traces Mozart's life from early childhood through his triumphs in Vienna and premature death.

Thompson, Wendy. *Wolfgang Amadeus Mozart*. New York: Viking, 1991. 48pp. MG/YA. Although brief, this is a serious and attractive biography. Mozart's story is described with useful historical and sociological background.

Biographical Films and Theatrical Adaptations

A&E Biography Video: Mozart (1995). Director: Molly Thompson. This is an informative documentary profile using archival material, location footage, and commentary by a variety of experts to capture the composer's personality, achievement, and era. Video.

Amadeus (1984). Director: Milos Forman. Forman's visually stunning and Oscar-winning adaptation of Peter Shaffer's drama casts Tom Hulce as a buffoonish Mozart whose genius haunts his nemesis Antonio Salieri (F. Murrary Abraham). Shaffer's play is also available (New York: Harper & Row, 1981. 109pp.). Video.

Mozart (1987). Director: Nicholas Vazsonyi. Narrated by Sir Anthony Quayle, this film biography features shots of Mozart's Salzburg home and locations associated with the composer. Video.

The Mozart Story (1937). Director: Karl Hartl. A dramatized biography from Antonio Salieri's perspective, starring Hans Holt, William Vedder, Rene Deltgen. Video.

Wolfgang Amadeus Mozart (1996). Director: Malcolm Hossick. A concise visual biography and musical overview of Mozart's genius and his times. Video.

Other Sources

Biancolli, Louis L., ed. *The Mozart Handbook: A Guide to the Man and His Music*. Cleveland: World, 1954. 629pp. A collection of musical and biographical material on Mozart, including contemporary accounts and coverage of such topics as Mozart's childhood and the women in his life.

Clive, Peter. *Mozart and His Circle: A Biographical Dictionary*. New Haven, Connecticut: Yale University Press, 1994. 242pp. Made up of several hundred biographical entries on individuals associated with the life and career of the composer.

Dimond, Peter, ed. *A Mozart Diary: A Chronological Reconstruction of the Composer's Life, 1761–1791*. Westport, Connecticut: Greenwood, 1997. 231pp. Dimond compiles a daily log of Mozart's activities based on various biographical sources.

King, Alec H. *Mozart: A Biography, with a Survey of Books, Editions, and Recordings*. Hamden, Connecticut: Archon Books, 1970. 114pp. Along with a brief biographical sketch, this reference tool surveys books on Mozart and recordings of his compositions.

Landon, H.C. Robbins, ed. *The Mozart Compendium: A Guide to Mozart's Life and Music*. New York: W.W. Norton, 1990. 452pp. A useful reference tool with a detailed chronology, list of compositions by genre and essays on the composer's personal life and work habits.

341. MUHAMMAD
ca. 570–632

The founder of Islam, Muhammad was born in Mecca and was a member of the ruling Kuraish tribal federation. Orphaned soon after birth, he was brought up by an uncle and became a wealthy merchant. At 40 he declared himself selected by God to be the Arab prophet of true religion. He began to preach as God's messenger and called upon the Meccans to accept Allah as the only god. As his influence grew, hostility toward his teachings increased, and in 622 he was forced to flee Mecca to escape a murder plot. He and some of his followers settled in Yathrib, which Muhammad renamed Medina ("City of the Prophet"). This event is known as the Hegira (departure). In Medina, Muhammad founded an Islamic community and extended his territory through conquest and conversion. In 630, he captured Mecca without bloodshed and made the city the political and spiritual capital of Islam. His revelations are collected in the Muslim sacred book, the *Qur'an*.

Recommended Biographies

Armstrong, Karen. *Muhammad: A Biography of the Prophet*. San Francisco: HarperSan Francisco, 1992. 290pp. In one of the finest biographies available, Armstrong's life is readable and sympathetic but objective in which Muhammad is treated as a complex, understandable human being seen from the perspective of his family and tribal relationships.

Cook, Michael. *Muhammad.* New York: Oxford University Press, 1983. 94pp. Cook's is the best choice for the reader looking for a succinct, straightforward introduction to Muhammad's life and ideas. The book helpfully separates the historical from the legendary in the various sources and offers a plausible synthesis.

Lings, Martin. *Muhammad: His Life Based on the Earliest Sources.* New York: Inner Traditions International, 1983. 359pp. This straightforward, objective chronological narrative is based on eighth- and ninth-century Arabic biographical sources and, although the book does not attempt to extricate the historical from the legendary, it does offer a convenient synthesis of important source material.

Rodinson, Maxime. *Mohammed.* New York: Pantheon, 1971. 360pp. Written by a French Islamicist, Rodinson's penetrating study examines Muhammad's development in personal and social terms as the product of his times, evolving as one of the world's greatest thinkers and inspiring leaders. Rodinson's Muhammad is shorn of much of his spiritual dimension, but the book is persuasive in its ability to recreate his era and the social factors that shaped his ideas and actions.

Watt, William M. *Muhammad at Mecca.* Oxford: Clarendon Press, 1953. 418pp.; *Muhammad at Medina.* Oxford: Clarendon Press, 1956. 418pp.; *Muhammad's Mecca: History in the Quran.* Edinburgh: Edinburgh University Press, 1988. 113pp. Watt's authoritative series of books are all painstakingly researched and objective. The first details Muhammad's early life; the second continues his story to his death. The third probes the Qur'an for historical details on Muhammad's life and times. An abridged version of Watt's first two volumes is available as *Muhammad: Prophet and Statesman* (London: Oxford University Press, 1961. 250pp.).

Other Biographical Studies

Andrae, Tor. *Mohammed: The Man and His Faith.* New York: Scribner, 1936. 274pp. Based on extensive research, Andrae's valuable study creates a believable psychological portrait of Muhammad against a solidly constructed period background.

Bennett, Clinton. *In Search of Muhammad.* New York: Cassell, 1998. 276pp. Bennett supplies a review of the historical and the biographical sources from the seventh century to the present, with a timeline of the main events in Muhammad's life.

Bodley, Ronald V. *The Messenger: The Life of Mohammed.* New York: Doubleday, 1946. 368pp. Written for the nonspecialist and inspired by the author's firsthand immersion in Islamic culture, Bodley corrects a number of Western misconceptions but offers his own highly fictionalized account that views Muhammad as a contemporary.

Dermenghem, Emile. *The Life of Mahomet.* New York: Dial Press, 1930. 352pp. A thorough and informed reconstruction of Muhammad, Dermenghem's study employs fictional techniques to dramatize his story in which coherence and analysis are sometimes sacrificed for colorful details. Although the book presupposes some prior knowledge of Islam, the book will appeal to the general reader searching for an involving and entertaining narrative biography.

Forward, Matin. *Muhammad: A Short Biography.* Oxford: One World, 1997. 131pp. This is a concise though informative account of Muhammad's life and exploration of his role in the development of Islam.

Glubb, John B. *The Life and Times of Muhammad.* New York: Stein and Day, 1970. 446pp. Glubb concentrates on Muhammad's military career, and in his detailed reconstruction of his campaigns the book adds an important dimension to an appreciation of Muhammad's career. For Glubb, Muhammad is seen not as a spiritual ascetic but as a man of his times, shown against his social, political, and religious background.

Haykal, Muhammad. *The Life of Muhammad.* Philadelphia: North American Trust, 1976. 639pp. First published in 1935, this biography by an Islamic scholar integrates traditional views of Muhammad with modern western historico-critical scholarship. The result is only partially successful as Haykal fails to extricate a fully realized historical Muhammad from his spiritual legend.

Ibn Ishaq, Muhammad. *The Life of Muhammad.* Abd al-Malik Ibn Hisham, ed. New York: Oxford University Press, 1955. 813pp. The most important early Arab biography, written in the eighth century, Ibn Ishaq's devotional account includes Muhammad's sayings, activities, and military campaign. Not always reliable as history, the book is the foundation text for Muslim interpretations of the prophet's life and career.

Margoliouth, David S. *Mohammed and the Rise of Islam.* New York: Putnam, 1905. 481pp. This early popular study is a solid and respectable overview of Muhammad's military and political career, accessible to the general reader.

Muir, William. *The Life of Mohammed from Original Sources.* 1861. Revised ed. T.H. Weir, ed. Edinburgh: J. Grant, 1923. 4 vols. Muir's monumental study, one of the earliest scholarly treatments in English, collects and synthesizes details of Muhammad's life and times from important Arab sources, still retains its importance as a reference source, though Weir's interpretation is far less useful.

Newby, Gordon D. *The Making of the Last Prophet: A Reconstruction of the Earliest Biography of Muhammad.* Columbia: University of South Carolina Press, 1989. 265pp. The author supplements the version of Muhammad's life offered by the 8th century chronicler Ibn Ishaq with additional details from various sources that fills in many of the gaps in Ibn Ishaq's early account.

Biographical Novels

Hoyt, Edwin P. *The Voice of Allah.* New York: John Day, 1970. 468pp. Drawing from both historical and traditional sources, this sympathetic fictional biography covers the highlights of Muhammad's career and features a wealth of information about period Arab customs.

Recommended Juvenile Biographies

Kelen, Betty. *Muhammad: The Messenger of God.* Nashville: Nelson, 1975. 278pp. MG/YA. Kelen's is a detailed account of Muhammad's life with a

helpful period and cultural background that help make his ideas and impact understandable.

Pike, Royston. *Mohammed: Prophet of the Religion of Islam.* New York: Praeger, 1969. 117pp. MG. Pike helps to make Muhammad's beliefs accessible in a fine summary of the significant events of his life and the development of his philosophy.

Biographical Films and Theatrical Adaptations

Mohammad: Messenger of God (1977). Also titled *The Message.* Director: Moustapha Akkad. Although Muhammad is not portrayed, this sincere and controversial historical epic on the founding of the Moslem religion focuses on Muhammad's uncle, portrayed by Anthony Quinn, and the unification of Arab tribes around Muhammad's message. Also starring Irene Papas, Michael Ansara, and Michael Forrest. Video.

342. EDVARD MUNCH
1863–1944

Norwegian painter and graphic artist, Munch's work foreshadowed expressionism and influenced the development of modern art. He abandoned impressionism to portray themes of death, fear, and anxiety. Munch is perhaps best known for his powerful and shocking woodcuts, including the famous *The Shriek* (1893) and *The Kiss* (1895). Negative reaction to his fearsome images caused the closing of an exhibition of his works in Berlin.

Recommended Biographies

Eggum, Arne. *Edvard Munch: Paintings, Sketches, and Studies.* New York: C.N. Potter, 1984. 305pp. The author, the chief curator of the Munch Museum, supplies an authoritative survey of Munch's life, career, and artistic achievement based on access to important primary sources.

Heller, Reinhold. *Munch, His Life and Work.* Chicago: University of Chicago Press, 1984. 240pp. Scholarly, well researched, and illustrated, Heller's account of the main episodes in Munch's life and the development of his art is enriched by placing him in the wider cultural context of his times and the network of relationships which helped frame his ideas and feelings.

Stang, Ragna T. *Edvard Munch: The Man and His Art.* New York: Abbeville Press, 1979. 319pp. Stang, the longtime director of the Oslo Municipal Collection and the Munch Museum and Archives, published this scholarly account shortly before her death. The story of Munch's life is presented in a highly readable narrative that sheds considerable light on the artist's personality and development.

Other Biographical Studies

Benesch, Otto. *Edvard Munch.* London: Phaidon, 1960. 143pp. The text to this beautifully illustrated collection of Munch's works is a succinct summary of the artist's life and development, and the book is an excellent starting point to see the range of the artist's achievement with reliable critical and biographical commentary.

Deknatel, Frederick B. *Edvard Munch.* New York: Chanticleer, 1950. 120pp. This early study and catalog provides a brief essay describing Munch's life and work based on reliable sources.

Hodin, J.P. *Edvard Munch.* New York: Praeger, 1972. 216pp. Based partly on the author's interview with the artist in 1938, the book offers an analysis of Munch's personality and artistic development with an extensive selection of reproductions. The critic Peter Gay called the book "an instructive failure" that "is too timid in the private dimension."

Langaard, Johan H., and R.A. Revold. *Edvard Munch: Masterpieces from the Artist's Collection in the Munch Museum in Oslo.* New York: Universe, 1972. 62pp. This useful volume offers a comprehensive survey of Munch's artistic career and insights into his personality drawn from such primary sources as Munch's diary.

Selz, Jean. *E. Munch.* New York: Crown, 1974. 96pp. Selz's is a useful overview of Munch's life and art, with many reproductions used to chronicle his career, technique, and accomplishments.

Biographical Films and Theatrical Adaptations

Edvard Munch (1974). Director: Peter Watkins. Based on the artist's memoirs, this biographical film focuses on Munch's early years. With Geir Westby, Gro Fraas, and Eli Ryg. Video.

343. BENITO MUSSOLINI
1883–1945

Dictator of Italy and leader of the Italian Fascist movement, Mussolini was the son of a blacksmith who was an ardent socialist. He was editor (1912–1914) of the socialist party newspaper and gained prominence as a leader of the revolutionary left wing of the party. When World War I broke out, he turned to nationalism and after serving in the army formed (1919) a fascist group in Milan. In 1921 the Fascist Party was organized and Mussolini elected to parliament. The Fascist militia marched (1922) on Rome, leading the king to make Mussolini premier. Called *Il Duce,* Mussolini formed a dictatorship, eliminating opponents, restricting the press, and ending parliamentary government. The Lateran Treaty acknowledging Vatican independence and sovereignty was signed (1929). Italy brutally conquered Ethiopia during the Italo-Ethiopian War (1935–1936), joined Hitler (1939), and declared war on the Allies (1940). After Italian defeats in Greece, Africa, and at home, Mussolini lost Fascist support and was arrested (1943). He was rescued by the Germans and made head of a Fascist puppet government in northern Italy. After the German defeat (1945), Mussolini was captured, court-martialed, and shot.

Autobiography and Primary Sources

My Autobiography. New York: Scribner, 1928. 318pp. Dictated at the height of his power and full of rhetorical flourishes and ranting, Mussolini's selective account of his career is an unapologetic, arrogant defense of his actions but does capture his public persona and personality.

My Rise and Fall. 1948. Reprinted. Max Ascoli, ed. New York: Da Capo Press, 1998. 590pp. This autobiographical account adds to Mussolini's earlier treatment of his own rise to power with this perspective of his defeat, written between his rescue by the Nazis and his execution, in which he attempts to justify his actions and evade personal responsibility for Italy's collapse.

Recommended Biographies

Kirkpatrick, Ivone. *Mussolini: A Study in Power.* New York: Hawthorn, 1964. 701pp. Written by a British diplomat stationed in Berlin and Rome during much of Mussolini's rule and based on interviews with him as well as extensive documentary evidence, Kirkpatrick supplies a balanced, informed analysis of the Italian leader's personality and motives. In Kirkpatrick's view, Mussolini was an unprincipled leader, more controlled by events than in charge of them, whose public life is connected with his private needs.

Mack Smith, Denis. *Mussolini.* New York: Knopf, 1982. 429pp. This political biography is generally held as the best in the field: subtle, meticulously documented, and balanced, Mack Smith's careful, authoritative explication of Mussollini's public career is buttressed by an insightful psychological profile. Few other studies so ably resolve Mussolini's many contradictions into a coherent and consistent portrait.

Ridley, Jasper. *Mussolini.* New York: St. Martin's, 1998. 430pp. The most recent full-length biography treats Mussolini as a far more complex individual than previous treatments. Acknowledging the sincerity of his political beliefs, Ridley traces Mussolini's betrayal of his ideals by his grandiose dreams inextricably bound to his own ambitions and needs. Ridley achieves an admirable balance that helps explain both Mussolini's talents and flaws.

Other Biographical Studies

Collier, Richard. *Duce!: A Biography of Benito Mussolini.* New York: Viking, 1971. 447pp. Collier's journalistic narrative based on extensive interviews with eyewitnesses is packed with anecdotes that produce a varied and detailed portrait of the man. However, the book's lack of context distorts the view, with Collier substituting drama for criticism and assessment.

Fermi, Laura. *Mussolini.* Chicago: University of Chicago Press, 1961. 477pp. Written by the wife of exiled physicist Enrico Fermi who lived under Mussolini's rule until 1938, the book offers a psychological interpretation of the Fascist leader and a theory about his rise to power, neither of which are fully satisfying. The book does however provide a rich supply of anecdotes and an informed atmosphere of life under Mussolini.

Gallo, Max. *Mussolini's Italy.* New York: Macmillan, 1973. 452pp. Despite its title, this is a biography of Mussolini constructed out of dramatized episodes in the Italian leader's life with an emphasis on the factors that shaped him. The book's main benefit is a view of Mussolini from his cultural and historical context, but the interpretation does not add very much to the conventional

view, and the essential motivations remain shadowy.

Gregor, A. James. *Young Mussolini and the Intellectual Origins of Fascism.* Berkeley: University of California Press, 1979. 271pp. In Gregor's controversial assessment of Mussolini's early intellectual and political development, the conventional notion that Mussolini was little more than a power-hungry opportunist is challenged. Gregor sees instead a sophisticated and coherent politician whose shift from socialism to Fascism is explained in the context of other modern revolutionary movements.

Halperin, Samuel W. *Mussolini and Italian Fascism.* Princeton, New Jersey: Van Nostrand, 1964. 191pp. Halperin offers a brief analysis of Mussolini and modern Italian history with a coherent, though debatable, interpretation of the man and his times. The book is useful as an introduction to both.

Hibbert, Christopher. *Il Duce: The Life of Benito Mussolini.* Boston: Little, Brown, 1962. 367pp. Setting out to solve the enigma of Mussolini's personality and appeal, Hibbert is only partially successful, choosing to concentrate on the Italian leader's end and foreign policy rather than his background and rise to power. Not reliable or penetrating on the bulk of Mussolini's life, the book is absorbing on his fall, but the reader is no closer in understanding the man in full.

Hoyt, Edwin P. *Mussolini's Empire: The Rise and Fall of the Fascist Vision.* New York: Wiley, 1994. 298pp. Hoyt, in a curious defense of Mussolini's character and achievements, paints him as an intelligent, dynamic, and courageous leader whose failings were more political than moral. To sustain sympathy, Hoyt must gloss over a number of Mussolini's obvious character flaws. Redressing the balance of views of Mussolini as either a buffoon or a monster, Hoyt fails to convince that he was underrated and misunderstood.

Joes, Anthony J. *Mussolini.* New York: F. Watts, 1982. 405pp. Reflecting more recent revisionist scholarly views on the Fascists in Italy and Mussolini's rise to power and performance, Joes grants considerable credit to Mussolini for rescuing Italy from the chaos following World War I and analyzes the factors that caused his revolutionary leadership to flounder and self-destruct. The book's thesis is controversial, and to make his case Joes is forced to accept many Fascist assertions while ignoring contrary evidence.

MacGregor-Hastie, Roy. *The Day of the Lion: The Life and Death of Fascist Italy.* New York: Coward-McCann, 1964. 395pp. Based on Italian sources, many unpublished interviews, and Mussolini's letters, the book is anecdotal and better on its details than in its attempt to explain Mussolini and his wider implications, which is often confused and uncritical.

Megaro, Gaudens. *Mussolini in the Making.* Boston: Houghton Mifflin, 1938. 347pp. Written too soon to consider the full range of Mussolini's career, Megaro's study of Mussolini's intellectual development and political apprenticeship before he became the leader of the Italian Socialist Party remains a valuable source of information on the leader's influences and his shift from socialism to fascism.

Monelli, Paolo. *Mussolini: The Intimate Life of a Demagogue*. New York: Vanguard, 1954. 304pp. Not a full-length historical biography, the emphasis here, as its subtitle indicates, is the private life of Mussolini. Captured with seamy details are Mussolini's many affairs and evidence of his deterioration leading up to his sordid end.

Mussolini, Rachele G. *Mussolini: An Intimate Biography*. New York: Morrow, 1974. 308pp. Mussolini's widow's recollection of the life and career of her husband is chiefly interesting for its details of Mussolini's private life and habits. Her unapologetic defense of her husband's attitudes and actions requires a historical reconstruction that falsifies facts and is out of touch with reality.

Pini, Giorgio. *The Official Life of Benito Mussolini*. London: Hutchinson, 1939. 270pp. Written by a Fascist sympathizer and editor of Mussolini's newspaper, Pini's laudatory tribute is chiefly interesting not for its biographical details, which are unreliable, but in exposing the heroic glorification of Mussolini's supporters.

Sarfatti, Margherita. *The Life of Benito Mussolini*. New York: F.A. Stokes, 1925. 352pp. Like Pini, Sarfatti was an intimate of Mussolini and a staff member of his newspaper and similar to Pini's later treatment the book is a propagandistic exercise in hero-worship, combining inaccuracy with partisanship.

Seldes, George. *Sawdust Caesar: The Untold Story of Mussolini and Fascism*. New York: Harper, 1935. 459pp. Compared with the early hagiographies of Pini and Sarfatti, Seldes's is a scathing attack on Mussolini and his regime. As a litany of Fascist abuses the book is compelling; it is less satisfactory in understanding Mussolini's rise to power and popularity among his countrymen.

Biographical Novels

Gelb, Alan. *Mussolini*. New York: Pocket Book, 1985. 313pp. This fictional biography traces Mussolini's rise to power and the events of World War II showing both the Italian leader's public and private sides. Although essentially faithful to history, the novel does invent scenes and conversations.

Recommended Juvenile Biographies

Hartenian, Lawrence R. *Benito Mussolini*. New York: Chelsea House, 1988. 112pp. MG/YA. This is a balanced and informative treatment of Mussolini's life, character, and times.

Lyttle, Richard B. *Il Duce: The Rise and Fall of Benito Mussolini*. New York: Atheneum, 1987. 213pp. YA. In a detailed, chronological narrative that traces Mussolini's life from childhood, Lyttle takes a nonjudgmental approach that lets the political and moral context speak for itself. The effect is a masterful presentation of a complex individual.

Mulvihill, Margaret. *Mussolini and Italian Fascism*. New York: F. Watts, 1990. 62pp. MG. Mulvihill emphasizes the conditions from which Mussolini rose to power and the political philosophy of the Fascists.

Biographical Films and Theatrical Adaptations

A&E Biography Video: Mussolini: Italy's Nightmare (1995). Director: Molly Thompson. Using newsreel footage and historical analysis, Mussolini's career is chronicled. Video.

Lion of the Desert (1981). Director: Moustapha Akkad. Dramatizes the true story of Libyan guerilla leader Omar Mukhtar (Anthony Quinn) who led his Bedouin horsemen to battle Mussolini (Rod Steiger) and his mechanized army to a standstill between 1911 and 1931. Also starring John Gielgud, Oliver Reed, and Irene Papas. Video.

Benito Mussolini (1962). Producer: David L. Wolper. This documentary portrait uses archival footage to depict Mussolini's life, character, and rise and fall. Video.

Mussolini (1986). Producer: David C. Rea. A documentary portrait of Mussolini's life and political career in which Sir F. W. Deakins served as historical adviser. Video.

Mussolini: The Decline and Fall of Il Duce (1985). Director: Alberto Negrin. Originally made for cable television this docudrama features Bob Hoskins as Mussolini, seen from the perspective of his daughter (Susan Sarandon) and focusing on his relationship with his son-in-law (Anthony Hopkins). Video.

Tea with Mussolini (1999). Director: Franco Zeffirelli. Claudio Spadaro appears as Mussolini in this semiautobiographical account of the director's early life during the war years. With Cher, Judi Dench, Joan Plowright, and Maggie Smith. Video.

The Warlords (1986). Producer: Lamancha Productions. This series of brief film biographies of World War II leaders, such as Hitler, De Gaulle, Stalin, and Churchill, includes a portrait of Mussolini. Video.

344. VLADIMIR NABOKOV
1899–1977

One of the great 20th-century novelists and a writer of extraordinary imagination, originality, and wit, Nabokov was born in St. Petersburg, Russia, immigrated to England after the Russian Revolution (1917), and graduated from Cambridge (1922). He moved to the United States (1940), was professor of Russian literature at Cornell (1948–1959), and then settled in Switzerland. He wrote in Russian under the name V. Sirin before 1940. His most famous novel is *Lolita* (1958), the story of a middle-aged man's passion for a 12-year-old girl. Nabokov's other works include *Pnin* (1957), *Pale Fire* (1962), and *Ada* (1969). Nabokov also wrote short stories, poems, and essays, and developed an international reputation as a lepidopterist.

Autobiography and Primary Sources

Selected Letters, 1940–1977. Dmitri Nabokov and Matthew J. Bruccoli, eds. San Diego, California: Harcourt, Brace, 1989. 582pp. Chronicling his life from his arrival in America to his death, Nabokov's correspondence, mainly letters to his editors, reveals little about his creative process, family relationships, or private thoughts, but the writer's twin passions: lepidoptera and literature come through clearly.

Speak Memory. New York: Putnam, 1979. 316pp. First published as *Conclusive Evidence* in 1947 and subsequently revised, Nabokov's autobiographical recollections mainly concern his life in Russia before the revolution, his undergraduate years at Cambridge University, and his life as a writer in Europe between 1922 and 1940 before arriving in America. One of the finest literary autobiographies ever written and an essential source to view Nabokov's own version of his developing sensibility.

Strong Opinions. New York: McGraw-Hill, 1973. 335pp. A collection of interviews and articles presents Nabokov's idiosyncratic views on various topics, including art, literature, politics, and education.

Recommended Biographies

Boyd, Brian. *Vladimir Nabokov: The Russian Years.* Princeton, New Jersey: Princeton University Press, 1990. 607pp.; *Vladimir Nabokov: The American Years.* Princeton, New Jersey: Princeton University Press, 1991. 783pp. Rightly regarded as the standard, authoritative life, Boyd's subtle and sympathetic two-volume study is impressively researched, based on interviews with associates and Nabokov's private files. Expertly blending a chronological narrative with a revealing cultural context and insightful criticism, Boyd portrays Nabokov in the round as a complex figure defined by his rootlessness.

Field, Andrew. *VN: The Life and Art of Vladimir Nabokov.* New York: Crown, 1986. 417pp. Field incorporates a good deal of his previous books, much of it verbatim, before carrying Nabokov's story forward to his death. Like his other books, Field adds to the biographical record from unpublished sources, but here he treats Nabokov with considerably more hostility, presenting the writer as narcissistic who in his later career betrays his genius through self-indulgence and arrogance.

Schiff, Stacy. *Véra (Mrs. Vladimir Nabokov): Portrait of a Marriage.* New York: Random House, 1999. 456pp. In a superb account of Nabokov's 52-year marriage and a nuanced portrait of the artist's wife, Schiff details the couples' literary and emotional partnership while shedding considerable light on the private, intimate side of the elusive and protective writer.

Other Biographical Studies

Field, Andrew. *Nabokov: His Life in Art: A Critical Narrative.* Boston: Little, Brown, 1967. 397pp. Field's first of three books on the writer is a critical study of Nabokov's artistic development. Conversational in tone and often discursive, Field provides a glimpse of the artist's many personas and a comprehensive analysis of his works, including their dominant themes and autobiographical elements. In *Nabokov: His Life in Part.* (New York: Viking, 1977. 285pp.) Field benefited from Nabokov's cooperation in granting access to his private papers and interviews before quarreling with Field over the final draft. The book adds considerable information about the writer, mainly on his early life and writing career prior to his coming to America. Field includes Nabokov's own words from his conversations as a form of running commentary to the chronological narrative.

Hyde, George M. *Vladimir Nabokov: America's Russian Novelist.* Atlantic Highlands, New Jersey: Humanities Press, 1977. 230pp. This critical survey of Nabokov's entire artistic career is particularly valuable for demonstrating the autobiographical elements in the works and the biographical factors that helped shaped Nabokov's creative method and artistic preoccupations.

Johnson, Kurt, and Steven L. Coates. *Nabokov's Blues: The Scientific Odyssey of a Literary Genius.* Cambridge, Massachusetts: Zoland Books, 1999. 372pp. The authors examine the role lepidopterology played in Nabokov's life and his contributions to science. This is a lively and informative look at an important aspect of the writer's life.

Lee, Lawrence. *Vladimir Nabokov.* Boston: Twayne, 1976. 168pp. Lee's sensible critical survey of Nabokov's art includes a concise biographical overview.

Levy, Alan. *Vladimir Nabokov: The Velvet Butterfly.* Sag Harbor, New York: Permanent Press, 1984. 160pp. Reprinting interviews with Nabokov in 1970, this book is a collection of quotes by and about the novelist. Insights are mixed with factual errors, omissions, and questionable interpretations.

Ross, Charles S. *Vladimir Nabokov: Life, Work, and Criticism.* Fredericton, New Brunswick: York Press, 1985. 47pp. Ross's critical overview includes a brief biographical sketch and serves as a useful introduction to the man and his works for the uninitiated.

Other Sources

Alexandrov, Vladimir, ed. *The Garland Companion to Vladimir Nabokov.* New York: Garland, 1995. 798pp. This collection of 74 critical articles covers all aspects of Nabokov's life and works. Includes a chronology and a bibliography.

Quennell, Peter, ed. *Vladimir Nabokov: His Life, His Work, His World: A Tribute.* New York: Morrow, 1980. 139pp. This memorial volume offers a number of reflections about the man and his work from admirers.

345. NAPOLEON BONAPARTE
1769–1821

French general and emperor, Napoleon was born in Corsica and sent to military schools at Brienne and Paris. He became an artillery officer (1785) and won the rank of brigadier general after successfully dislodging the British from Toulon (1793). His career advanced dramatically after he dispersed a royalist Parisian uprising (1795). He was victorious against Austria in the Italian campaign (1796–1797) and became a national hero, but his attempt to crush the British empire by striking Egypt ultimately failed when the French fleet was destroyed by Nelson's forces in Aboukis Bay (1798). Returning to Paris, Napoleon engineered the 1799 coup that made him first consul and virtual dictator. He reorganized the government, established the Code Napoléon, and in 1804 crowned himself emperor. He extended French territory during the Napoleonic Wars, lost the Battle of Trafalgar against the British navy (1805), and instituted (1806) the Continental System to cut off European trade with England. Napoleon's disastrous Russian campaign resulted in the retreat and destruction (1812) of his grand army. An alliance of European nations defeated the French at the Battle of Leipzig (1813), and France was invaded (1814). Napoleon abdicated and was exiled to the island of Elba. He escaped, returned to France, and ruled for the Hundred Days. He was defeated at the Battle of Waterloo (1815) and exiled to St. Helena, where he died. He was married to Josephine de Beauharnais (1796–1809), whom he divorced to wed the Archduchess Marie Louise of Austria.

Autobiography and Primary Sources

Letters and Documents. John E. Howard. Oxford: Oxford University Press, 1962. 540pp. This is a collection mainly of letters on military affairs and official state documents.

Memoirs. Somerset de Chain, ed. New York: Harper, 1950. 605pp. While in exile on St. Helena, Napoleon dictated an account of his career to his staff. The seven volumes have been condensed and reshaped into a chronological narrative here that is hardly objective but revealing in Napoleon's defense of his actions.

Mind of Napoleon: A Selection of His Written and Spoken Words. J. Christopher Herold, ed. New York: Columbia University Press, 1955. 322pp. This useful collection of Napoleon's writing and remarks offers a close look at the man's thought process, personality, and self-assessment.

Napoleon Self-Revealed. J.M. Thompson, ed. Boston: Houghton Mifflin, 1934. 383pp. This is a selection of Napoleon's letters arranged chronologically from 1784 to 1815. See also the same editor's *Napoleon's Letters*. (New York: Dutton, 1954. 312pp.).

Recommended Biographies

Chandler, David G. *The Campaigns of Napoleon*. New York: Macmillan, 1966. 1,172pp.; *Napoleon*. New York: Saturday Review Press, 1973. 224pp. The distinguished British military historian has followed his monumental authoritative and compre-hensive history of Napoleon's military campaigns with a shorter assessment of Napoleon's military genius and character. Although neglecting the domestic side of Napoleon's achievement, Chandler's studies are the best choices for the reader primarily interested in Napoleon's battlefield experience.

Cronin, Vincent. *Napoleon Bonaparte: An Intimate Biography*. New York: Morrow, 1971. 480pp. Based on previously unavailable material, including the notebooks of Napoleon's closest childhood friend, the letters of an early lover, the memoirs of Napoleon's valet, and General Bertrand's St. Helena diary, Cronin portrays Napoleon's personal life with an emphasis on private and civil rather than military matters. The result is a fascinating collection of intimate glimpses of Napoleon's daily life, love affairs, and personality quirks that brings the monument or monster to believable human life.

Markham, Felix M. *Napoleon and the Awakening of Europe*. New York: Macmillan, 1954. 184pp.; *Napoleon*. New York: New American Library, 1963. 293pp. Both of Markham's studies serve as useful compact introductions to the man and his accomplishments. The earlier book compresses Napoleon's career to its essentials with a sensible assessment; the later examination provides a balanced and comprehensive survey of Napoleon's military and political accomplishments.

Schom, Alan. *Napoleon Bonaparte*. New York: HarperCollins, 1997. 888pp. Schom's vivid narrative history traces Napoleon's rise and fall, his military and domestic accomplishments, and his private life in an impressive synthesis of primary and secondary sources. Any reader coming to the book with a sense of Napoleon's greatness will come away with a much more sobered, realistic view. Schom penetrates the Napoleonic legend to reveal a limited and flawed figure.

Thompson, J.M. *Napoleon Bonaparte*. New York: Barnes and Noble, 1996. 463pp. Avoiding either undue admiration or censure, Thompson manages a detailed, objective portrait that follows Napoleon from his childhood through his country-by-country conquests until his final defeat. Based on Napoleon's own words and a superbly realized historical background, Thompson achieves a multidimensional psychological and human portrait.

Other Biographical Studies

Aubry, Octave. *Napoleon: Soldier and Emperor*. Philadelphia: Lippincott, 1938. 454pp. A popular life by a French scholar, Aubry's summary of Napoleon's life from his student days to his death is vigorously presented and helpfully organized. Still a valid and useful introduction for the general reader.

Barnett, Corelli. *Bonaparte*. New York: Hill & Wang, 1978. 224pp. Barnett, a distinguished English military historian, provides a highly critical assessment of Napoleon's military genius. Debunking the notion of Napoleon's greatness as a commander and strategist, Barnett attributes his successes to accident, while offering a damning catalog of his blunders. The book offers little on Napoleon's domestic leadership, administrative, legal, and educational reforms.

Bergeron, Louis. *France under Napoleon*. Princeton, New Jersey: Princeton University Press, 1981. 230pp. More strictly speaking a social history than a biography, Bergeron's expert and concise survey of the political, administrative, social, economic, and cultural life under Napoleon is a valuable supplement to studies more narrowly focused on the man instead of his times.

Bruce, Evangeline. *Napoleon and Josephine: An Improbable Marriage*. New York: Scribner, 1995. 555pp. In an extremely readable account of Napoleon's relationship with his first wife for the general reader, Bruce provides an entertaining introduction to Napoleon's private life, based mainly on Napoleon and Josephine's own letters and journals.

Castelot, André. *Napoleon*. New York: Harper & Row, 1971. 627pp. Following Napoleon's career from childhood to his death, Castelot is objective in his assessment while animating his detailed account with fictional elements and a sometimes confusing narrative style. Undocumented, Castelot integrates his primary and secondary sources cleverly into his text. Serves as an entertaining initial source for the general reader.

Ellis, Geoffry J. *Napoleon*. New York: Longman, 1997. 290pp. Part of the Profiles in Power series, Ellis takes a thematic rather than a chronological approach to Napoleon's career in an able assessment of his leadership and accomplishments. It is not intended as a first look at Napoleon, but the reader who is already familiar with the basics will profit from Ellis's lucid examination.

Erickson, Carolly. *Josephine: A Life of the Empress*. New York: St. Martin's, 1999. 432pp. Extensively researched and richly detailed, Erickson's dramatic portrait of Josephine achieves a psychological and intimate presentation along with an accomplished background painting that brings both wife and husband to vivid life.

Fisher, H.A.L. *Napoleon*. New York: Holt, 1913. 256pp. Fisher's biographical essay offers little more than an outline of Napoleon's career and few details on his military campaigns, concentrating instead on an analysis of his character and personality. Although not free from British bias, Fisher's brief account deliveries more lucid and interesting insights than other much longer examinations.

Fournier, August. *Napoleon I: A Biography*. New York: Holt, 1911. 836pp. In a respected early biography that reprints valuable documentary sources Fournier portrays an ambitious Napoleon consumed by dreams of personal glory. The author's Austrian partisanship results in some distortion of fact, and Fournier's hostility causes him to emphasize Napoleon's defects over his strengths.

Guerard, Albert. *Napoleon I: A Great Life in Brief*. New York: Knopf, 1956. 199pp. Guerard is skillful in compressing a great deal of information about Napoleon and his times in a slim volume that will appeal to the general reader looking for a concise introduction that neither exalts nor diminishes.

Holtman, Robert B. *The Napoleonic Revolution*. Philadelphia: Lippincott, 1967. 225pp. Napoleon is depicted as a revolutionary innovator in military, government, economics, law, and diplomacy in an objective assessment of his ideas and achievements as well as their origins and wider social context. A thematic rather than a narrative account, Holtman's is a worthy complement to other studies of Napoleon focused on his military genius.

Horne, Alistair. *How Far from Austerlitz?: Napoleon 1805–1815*. New York: St. Martin's, 1997. 429pp. Horne's assessment of Napoleon as military commander, despite the book's title, chronicles his entire career with side glances at his private life and personality, along with vivid sketches of his associates.

Jones, R. Ben. *Napoleon: Man and Myth*. New York: Holmes and Meier, 1977. 221pp. Jones's penetrating concise study attempts to explain Napoleon's rise to power and achievement based on a fuller understanding of the cultural, historical, and political conditions that helped make his career possible. The result challenges notions of Napoleon's greatness and destiny, substituting a realistic human assessment.

Kircheisen, Friedrich M. *Napoleon*. New York: Harcourt, Brace, 1932. 761pp. An abridgement of the author's nine-volume German study adapted for the general reader, Kirscheisen's treatment is balanced and extremely readable. The book has been described as the most accurate and complete "short" biography.

Korngold, Ralph. *Last Years of Napoleon: His Captivity on St. Helena*. New York: Harcourt, Brace, 1959. 429pp. This is an account of the daily life of Napoleon and his household during his six years' exile, based on eyewitness accounts.

Laing, Margaret I. *Josephine and Napoleon*. New York: Mason/Charter, 1974. 196pp. In an attractively illustrated volume, Laing chronicles the relationship between Josephine and Napoleon, using their letters to chart their emotionally turbulent marriage.

Lefebvre, Georges. *Napoleon*. New York: Columbia University Press, 1969. 2 vols. Not as much a biography but a detailed historical survey of the Napoleonic period, Lefebvre's often dense, scholarly analysis is one of the most comprehensive and insightful examinations of the social, economic, and political context needed for an understanding of Napoleon's rise, fall, and achievements.

Maurois, André. *Napoleon and His World*. New York: Viking, 1964. 160pp. In a vividly written short text to accompany a varied collection of illustrations, Maurois excludes a great deal and glosses over important topics. Napoleon is idealized as a projection of values and characteristics that Maurois admires.

Rose, J. Holland. *The Life of Napoleon I*. New York: Macmillan, 1902. 2 vols. Long regarded as one of the best overall historical studies, Rose's life is balanced and scrupulously documented, drawing extensively on official British records.

Seward, Desmond. *Napoleon and Hitler: A Comparative Biography*. New York: Viking, 1989. 319pp. Seward's dual biography emphasizes the parallels and similarities in the two leaders' careers and characters. To make his case, obvious differences are glossed over, and the book has errors of

fact and interpretation that may mislead the general reader.

Thompson, James M. *Napoleon Bonaparte: His Rise and Fall*. New York: Oxford University Press, 1951. 411pp. Written by an authority on the French Revolution, Thompson's scholarly, though readable, biography serves better than any other book available to connect Napoleon's early career with his times. Less concerned with Napoleon's military affairs, Thompson concentrates on his domestic achievement in a lively and original reassessment.

Tulard, Jean. *Napoleon: The Myth of a Saviour*. London: Weidenfeld and Nicolson, 1984. 470pp. Tulard, an acknowledged French expert on the period, surveys Napoleon's career with a revisionist view of the factors that account for Napoleon's rise to power and the bourgeoisie who supported and abandoned him based on their self-interest. Tulard's analysis provides a sensible alternative to the great-man thesis of other Napoleonic studies.

Biographical Novels

Austin, Frederick B. *Forty Centuries Look Down*. New York: F. A. Stokes, 1937. 373pp. Adapting Napoleon's correspondence for much of its dialogue, the novel dramatizes the Egyptian campaign and his troubled relationship with Josephine. *The Road to Glory*. (New York: grosset & Dunlap, 1935. 349pp.) is told from Napoleon's perspective and imagined thoughts. The novel describes his first Italian campaign and the beginning of his legendary reputation.

Beck, L. Adams. *The Thunderer: A Romance of Napoleon and Josephine*. New York: Dodd, Mead, 1927. 333pp. Napoleon is depicted as a lover and husband in this fictionalized and idealized view of his relationship with Josephine.

Burgess, Anthony. *Napoleon Symphony*. New York: Knopf, 1974. 365pp. Burgess's inventive novel interprets Napoleon's career as a comic opera or symphony in four movements, from his first campaigns through his marriage, triumphs, and defeat.

Coryn, M.S. *Goodbye, My Son*. New York: Appleton-Century, 1943. 582pp. Tracing the history of the Bonaparte family from the perspective of Napoleon's mother, this is an accurate, though somewhat romanticized, treatment of the facts. The author's *The Marriage of Josephine*. (New York: Appleton-Century, 1945. 312pp.) in an idealized version of history and a debatable interpretation of Josephine, dramatizing her life from her imprisonment during the French Revolution through the first few years of her married life. *Alone Among Men*. (New York: Appleton-Century, 1947. 313pp.) is set in 1799 during the coup d'etat that made Napoleon First Consul of France, concentrating on Napoleon's relationship with Josephine and the intrigue that brings him to supreme power.

Costain, Thomas B. *The Last Love*. Garden City, New York: Doubleday, 1963. 434pp. Based on some historical fact but with invention and liberties taken, the novel dramatizes Napoleon's life in exile on St. Helena through his relationship with a young Englishwoman and includes flashback to his youth and campaigns.

Gerson, Noel B. *The Emperor's Ladies*. Garden City, New York: Doubleday, 1959. 356pp. Gerson looks at Napoleon's private and married life in a somewhat selective and sanitized version of the facts, focusing on Napoleon as husband and father.

Gibbs, Willa. *Tell Your Sons: A Novel of the Napoleonic Era*. New York: Farrar, Straus, 1946. 525pp. Napoleon's career is described from the perspective of a young admirer. Despite the romantic lens of hero worship, a strong impression of Napoleon is presented.

Gulland, Sandra. *The Many Lives and Secret Sorrows of Josephine B*. New York: Scribner, 1999. 436pp; *Tales of Passion, Tales of Woe*. New York: Scribner, 1999. 370pp. The first two volumes of a projected trilogy follows Josephine's career before meeting Napoleon and during their married life together.

Herbert, A.P. *Why Waterloo?* Garden City, New York: Doubleday, 1953. 352pp. Based on considerable historical research, the novel tells the story of Napoleon's exile on Elba, his escape, and the events leading up to his final defeat at Waterloo.

Kenyon, Frank W. *The Emperor's Lady: A Novel Based on the Life of the Empress Josephine*. New York: Crowell, 1952. 501pp. Blending facts and invention, the novel dramatizes the life of Josephine from her life on Martinique, her imprisonment during the Revolution, and marriage to Napoleon. The author's *My Brother Napoleon: The Confessions of Caroline Bonaparte* (New York: Dodd, Mead, 1971. 253pp.) is a first-person narrative by Napoleon's sister that dramatizes Napoleon's rise to power and years of triumph.

Krasnov, Peter N. *Napoleon and the Cossacks*. New York: Duffield & Green, 1931. 593pp. The disastrous 1812 Russian campaign is dramatized with authentic period flavor from the perspective of two fictional figures as well as Napoleon and Alexander I.

Lancaster, Sheila. *Mistress of Fortune*. London: Hodder and Stoughton, 1982. 318pp. The novel chronicles the early years of Josephine from her childhood on Martinique, through her marriage to a French aristocrat, her affair with a leader of the Revolution, and her first meeting and relationship with Napoleon. Faithful to facts, the author does invent some plausible scenes and dialogue.

Lofts, Norah. *A Rose for Virtue*. Garden City, New York: Doubleday, 1971. 348pp. Josephine's daughter and Napoleon's stepdaughter tells her story and her perspective on the relationship between her parents. Blending facts and speculation, the novel features an authentic period atmosphere.

Maass, Edgar. *Imperial Venus: A Novel of Napoleon's Favorite Sister*. Indianapolis: Bobbs-Merrill, 1946. 421pp. In a thorough and authentic portrait of Napoleon's family and background, this biographical novel dramatizes the life of Maria Paolina Bonaparte, who rises in the world with her brother's success in Haiti and Italy, and despite disfavor remains loyal to her brother in defeat.

Nezelof, Pierre. *Napoleon and His Son*. New York: Liveright, 1936. 474pp. Covering events from Napoleon's second marriage to his son's death at the age of 22, the novel observes the historical facts but does not penetrate the surface details with much insight.

Pilgrim, David. *So Great a Man.* New York: Harper,1937. 463pp. Covering the period 1808 to 1809 when Napoleon is at the zenith of his career, the novel employs a fictional young Frenchman who accompanies Napoleon's mistress, Countess Walewska, from Warsaw to Paris. As a page in the emperor's household, he becomes an observer of the leading figures of the period.

Powers, Anne. *The Thousand Fires.* Indianapolis: Bobbs-Merrill, 1957. 434pp. Napoleon's rise and fall is dramatized from the perspective of a fictional officer who joins the general staff. Events rush by in this dramatic rendering.

Rambaud, Patrick. *The Battle.* New York: Grove Press, 2000. 256pp. Rambaud's acclaimed reconstruction of the bloody Battle of Essling in 1809 features a strong portrait of Napoleon, as well as characterizations of Marshalls Berthier, Lannes, and Massena, and writer Stendhal.

Schönthan, Gaby von. *The Roses of Malmaison: The Turbulent Life of the Beautiful Josephine.* London: Cassell,1966. 309pp. Josephine narrates her own story in a fictional recreation that quotes directly from Napoleon's correspondence to aid authenticity.

Winwar, Frances. *The Eagle and the Rock.* New York: Harper, 1963. 371pp. In a fictionalization of Napoleon's life that stays close to the biographical sources, Winwar chronicles his career from his early military service through his triumphs and defeats.

Fictional Portraits

Only a small fraction of the countless novels in which Napoleon appears can be listed here. Selected are those books that treat Napoleon in significant or original ways.

Aragon, Louis. *Holy Week.* New York: Putnam, 1961. 541pp. This impressive historical panorama is set during the beginning of Napoleon's Hundred Days, shown through its effects on a huge cast of historical figures.

Delmar, Vina. *A Time for Titans.* New York: Harcourt, Brace, 1974. 366pp. The diplomatic maneuverings surrounding the Louisiana Purchase are dramatized in this inventive novel that centers on Napoleon, Jefferson, and Haiti's Toussaint L'Ouverture.

Kane, Harnett T. *The Amazing Mrs. Bonaparte.* Garden City, New York: Doubleday, 1963. 301pp. Based on the true story of Baltimore's Betsy Patterson who marries Jerome Bonaparte, Napoleon's younger brother, before he is recalled to France alone, the novel dramatizes her life convincingly and authentically.

Komroff, Manuel. *Waterloo.* New York: Coward-McCann,1936. 307pp. The Hundred Days and the climactic Battle of Waterloo are ironically and unheroically treated from the perspectives of many of the participants.

Leys, Simon. *The Death of Napoleon.* New York: Farrar, Straus, 1992. 129pp. This intriguing what-if historical fable explores the possibility that Napo-

leon does not die on St. Helena in 1821 but escapes and returns to France to confront his legacy.

Manceron, Claude. *So Brief a Spring.* New York: Putnam,1958. 452pp. Based on extensive research, the events of the Hundred Days are described from the perspective of a young Frenchman with an emphasis on the political forces that sweep Napoleon back to power.

McDonough, James. *The Limits of Glory: A Novel of Waterloo.* Novato, California: Presidio, 1991. 300pp. In a historical faithful depiction of the famous battle, the novel offers the perspectives of the generals, combatants, and onlookers on both sides.

McKenney, Ruth. *Mirage.* New York: Farrar, Straus, 1956. 726pp. In a panoramic historical novel concerning Napoleon's Egyptian campaign, fictional characters interact with historical figures and participate in actual events, and the novel includes vivid depictions of the Battle of the Pyramids and Nelson's naval triumph at the Battle of the Nile.

Selinko, Annemarie. *Desiree.* New York: Morrow, 1953. 594pp. With a strong basis in fact, this historical romance dramatizes the real-life story of Desiree Clary, an early love of Napoleon. Covering Napoleon's rise to his defeat at Waterloo, Desiree marries one of Napoleon's generals and becomes the Queen of Sweden.

Tolstoy, Leo. *War and Peace.* 1872. Various editions. Napoleon emerges as the novel's principal villain in Tolstoy's epic treatment of the Napoleonic era from 1805 to 1820. For Tolstoy, Napoleon is the blind egoist with his soft white hands, twitching leg, and eau de cologne, incapable of recognizing his own limitations and dependency.

Wilkins, William V. *Being Met Together.* New York: Macmillan, 1944. 510pp. A young American comes to Europe to serve Napoleon and participates in a fictional rescue attempt at St. Helena by submarine.

Recommended Juvenile Biographies

Marrin, Albert. *Napoleon and the Napoleonic Wars.* New York: Viking, 1993. 276pp. MG/YA. Marrin interprets Napoleon's life and career in the context of his times in what has been called "the definitive work on this period of French history" for younger readers.

McGuire, Leslie. *Napoleon.* New York: Chelsea House, 1986. 111pp. MG/YA. A solid biographical/historical summary of Napoleon's career and character that emphasizes his military genius and the impact of his rule in France and throughout Europe during the period.

Weidhorn, Manfred. *Napoleon.* New York: Atheneum, 1986. 212pp. YA. Weidhorn emphasizes the military and political aspects of Napoleon's life in a sophisticated treatment that does assume prior knowledge of European history.

Biographical Films and Theatrical Adaptations

Hardy, Thomas. *The Dynasts.* London: Macmillan, 1924. 325pp. Napoleon is the central figure in

Hardy's remarkable poetic drama that covers the major events between 1805 and 1812.

Trench, Herbert. *Napoleon: A Play.* New York: Oxford University Press, 1919. 102pp. Set during the period of the threatened French invasion of England, the play dramatizes the attempt by an Englishman to convince Napoleon of the error of his ways.

Battle of Waterloo, 1815 (1990). Producer: Henri de Turenne. Using live-action reenactments and drawings, Napoleon's career up to the battle is illustrated. Video.

The Campaigns of Napoleon: The Story of the Napoleonic Wars (1996). Three of Napoleon's greatest battles, Austerlitz, Borodino, and Waterloo are depicted using high-tech graphics and live-action sequences. Video.

Conquerors (1997). Directors: Nigel Maslin and Robert Marshall. Film profiles of four great leaders: Peter the Great, Napoleon, Alexander the Great, and Suleyman. Video.

Conquest (1937). Director: Clarence Brown. Charles Boyer depicts Napoleon from 1807 to 1815 and his romantic involvement with the Polish Countess Marie Walewska (Greta Garbo). Video.

Desiree (1954). Director: Henry Koster. This film version of the Selinko novel features a "method" Napoleon played by Marlon Brando with Merle Oberon as Josephine, and Jean Simmons as the seamstress who rejects the emperor for another. Video.

Eagle in a Cage (1971). Director: Fielder Cook. Napoleon in exile on St. Helena is the subject of this fine British drama with Kenneth Haigh in the title role and a stellar supporting cast of John Gielgud, Ralph Richardson, and Billie Whitelaw.

Napoleon (1927). Director: Abel Gance. Gance's silent masterwork traces Napoleon's life from his youth through the Italian campaign, with Albert Dieudonné in the title role. Video.

Napoleon (1955). Director: Sacha Guitry. Napoleon's youth as a soldier through his final exile is dramatized. With an impressive cast, including Orson Welles, Maria Schell, Yves Montand, and Erich von Stroheim. Video.

War and Peace (1956). Director: King Vidor. Disappointing Hollywood version of Tolstoy's novel casts Herbert Lom as Napoleon. With Henry Fonda, Mel Ferrer, and Audrey Hepburn. Video.

War and Peace (1968) Director: Sergei Bondarchuk. This classic Russian production of the Tolstoy novel offers painstaking period recreation and impressive battle scenes. With Bondarchuk also starring as Pierre. Video.

War and Peace (1973). Director: John Davies. Multi-part BBC production features Anthony Hopkins as Pierre, Alan Dobie as Andre, and Morag Hood as Natasha. Napoleon is portrayed by David Swift. Video.

Waterloo (1970). Director: Sergei Bondarchuk. This historical account of the Battle of Waterloo features an unusual interpretation of Napoleon by Rod Steiger. Wellington is more convincingly portrayed by Christopher Plummer. A novelization of the screenplay by Frederick E. Smith (London: H. Baker, 1970. 157pp.) is available. Video.

Young Mr. Pitt (1942). Director: Carol Reed. Herbert Lom portrays Napoleon in this biographical drama on the life of William Pitt, starring Robert Donat, Robert Morley, and John Mills.

Other Sources

Haythornthwaite, Philip J. *The Napoleonic Source Book.* New York: Facts on File, 1990. 414pp. This is a useful handbook to the era from the French Revolution to Waterloo with a selective biographical section on the prominent figures.

Hutt, Maurice, ed. *Napoleon.* Englewood Cliffs, New Jersey: Prentice-Hall, 1972. 180pp. This useful reference source includes Napoleon's own reflections, the recollection of his contemporaries, and historians' interpretation and assessment.

Nicholls, David. *Napoleon: A Biographical Companion.* Santa Barbara, California: ABC-CLIO, 1999. 318pp. This reference guide covers Napoleon's life, achievement, rise and fall from power, and influences.

See also Horatio Nelson; Wellington, Duke of

346–347. NAPOLEON III (1808–1873); EMPRESS EUGÉNIE (1826–1920)

Emperor of the French from 1852 to 1870, Louis Napoleon Bonaparte was the son of Louis Bonaparte and Hortense de Beauharnais, and the nephew of Napoleon I. He spent his youth in Switzerland and Germany, and became a captain in the Swiss army. After attempting several military coups against King Louis Philippe of France, he was jailed but escaped to England (1846). He was elected President of France after the Revolution of 1848 and in 1852 dissolved the legislature and made himself emperor. His regime promoted domestic prosperity, successfully fought the Russians in the Crimean War (1854–1856), improved Franco-British relations, expanded French territory, and built the Suez Canal. However French intervention (1861–1867) in Mexico and the installation of Maximilian as Mexican emperor proved a failure. By the 1860s, opposition to Napoleon III's repressive, corrupt government had grown. His ill-conceived war with Prussia (1870) ended with his defeat, capture, and the collapse of his empire. He was exiled to England, where he died.

Empress of the French (1853–1870) and consort of Napoleon III, Eugénie actively participated in the politics of the Second Empire, acting as regent when her husband was at war. She strongly supported the measures that led to the Franco-Prussian War, was deposed with her husband after the French defeat, and fled to England, where she settled. She was celebrated for her exceptional beauty and charm.

Recommended Biographies

Bresler, Fenton. *Napoleon III: A Life.* New York: Carroll & Graf, 1999. 438pp. Written for the general reader, Bresler's fresh look at Napoleon III and his era emphasizes personalities over events. Bresler paints a complex portrait of Napoleon III, arguing that his achievement is far greater than most have been willing to grant, and the reader gets an intimate look at the man in this well-written and argued presentation.

Guerard, Albert. *Napoleon III: A Great Life in Brief.* New York: Knopf, 1955. 207pp. Guerard's is the first choice for the reader looking for a concise introductory study of Louis Napoleon and his times. Lucid and balanced, Guerard ably summarizes the essential events of Napoleon's career along with a reliable treatment of his character.

Kurtz, Harold. *The Empress Eugénie.* Boston: Houghton, Mifflin, 1965. 407pp. Scholarly yet readable, Kurtz's is an authoritative study of the empress which challenges the conventional view of her as an interfering schemer who pushed her husband to disastrous decisions. Instead, Kurtz provides an objective assessment that grants to Eugénie more positives than negatives.

Ridley, Jasper. *Napoleon III and Eugénie.* New York: Viking, 1980. 768pp. Ridley's is the finest joint biography of the pair available. Covering their entire lives from Louis Napoleon's birth to Eugénie's death in 1920, Ridley is also reliable on French history, particularly on the events between 1850 and 1870. Based on valuable primary and secondary sources, Ridley tells the personal story of the royal couple in a compelling, reliable, and extremely readable fashion.

Simpson, Frederick A. *The Rise of Louis Napoleon.* 1909. Revised ed. London: Cass, 1968. 400pp.; *Louis Napoleon and the Recovery of France.* 1923. Reprint ed. Westport, Connecticut: Greenwood, 1975. 400pp. Simpson's scholarly and authoritative historical biography remains one of the finest comprehensive treatments of Louis Napoleon's life and reign. The first volume covers his first 40 years in a balanced assessment based on primary and historical sources. The second volume surveys the period from 1848 to 1856 with an emphasis on the history of France during the period but with an intimate and personal view of Napoleon III.

Other Biographical Studies

Aronson, Theo. *The Fall of the Third Napoleon.* Indianapolis: Bobbs-Merrill, 1970. 271pp. This is a detailed, popular account of the final six weeks of Napoleon's reign in which objectivity is sometimes sacrificed by partisanship and for the demands of a compelling human drama.

Aubry, Octave. *Eugénie: Empress of the French.* Philadelphia: Lippincott, 1931. 356pp. This is a highly romanticized and melodramatic look at the empress's life and character in which Eugénie is cast in the role of a tragic heroine and victim of circumstances rather than the cause of her own failures.

Barschak, Erna. *The Innocent Empress: An Intimate Study of Eugénie.* New York: Dutton, 1943. 346pp. Covering her life from her adolescence to her death, Barschak provides a psychological view of the empress in a series of revealing anecdotes that are used to interpret her character. Best on Eugénie's childhood, youth, and widowhood,

Barschak is less convincing in capturing her years in power.

Bierman, John. *Napoleon III and His Carnival Empire.* New York: St. Martin's, 1988. 416pp. Although offering no new information or original research, Bierman's is a highly readable, journalistic account of the events of the Second Empire and its ruler. Lively and entertaining, the book occasionally lapses into imaginative conjecture about the figures' motives and feelings.

Brodsky, Alyn. *Imperial Charade: A Biography of Emperor Napoleon III and Empress Eugénie.* Indianapolis: Bobbs-Merrill, 1978. 330pp. Dramatizing the story of "Europe's most successful adventurers," Brodsky chronicles Napoleon's rise and marriage to the equally ambitious Spanish countess through their fall from power in an unscholarly anecdotal account, marred by clichés and melodrama.

Cheetham, F.H. *Louis Napoleon and the Genesis of the Second Empire.* New York: J. Lane, 1909. 394pp. Cheetham's life-and-times study is readable and detailed but incomplete and with a strong partisanship that limits its objectivity and reliability.

Corley, T.A.B. *Democratic Despot: A Life of Napoleon III.* New York: C.N. Potter, 1961. 402pp. Corley's is a richly detailed, sympathetic but critical biography that focuses on the key questions of Napoleon III's career: how he rose to power in 1848 and managed to hold onto power for two decades.

D'Auvergne, Edmund B. F. *Napoleon the Third: A Biography.* New York: Dodd, Mead, 1929. 255pp. In a brief, readable introduction to Napoleon III and his career, D'Auvergne concentrates on his private life with the details of his times only lightly sketched. D'Auvergne's study would be a good choice as a first book on the subject before proceeding to more thorough and comprehensive studies.

Duff, David. *Eugenie and Napoleon III.* New York: Morrow, 1978. 308pp. Based entirely on secondary sources, this joint biography, written for a general reader, is a collection of colorful anecdotes but lacks objectivity and balance. The book also assumes considerable prior knowledge of the period and French culture.

Guedalla, Philip. *Second Empire.* New York: Putnam, 1922. 360pp. Written with wit and irony in the manner of Lytton Strachey, Guedalla's historical survey covers the fortunes of the Bonaparte family and provides a personal narrative of Napoleon III from his birth through his career as prince, president, and emperor. Amusing and often brilliant, Guedalla's epigrammatic style is entertaining but often impressionistic, neglecting facts in pursuit of the *bon mot* and amusing oddity.

McMillan, James F. *Napoleon III.* New York: Longman, 1991. 188pp. Part of the Profiles in Power series, this is a model of economy and clarity that takes advantage of modern scholarship to offer a balanced assessment of Napoleon's reign and character. The book is an excellent overview of the period and sensible in its judgments.

Rheinhardt, Emil A. *Napoleon and Eugénie: The Tragicomedy of an Empire.* New York: Knopf,

1931. 363pp. In a fair, sympathetic psychological portrait by a Viennese poet and portrait painter, Rheinhardt supplies a reasonably accurate and believable narrative that captures the royal couple and their era.

Sencourt, Robert. *The Life of the Empress Eugénie.* New York: Scribner, 1931. 387pp. Sencourt's authorized biography makes use of private family papers and archival sources previously unavailable for a comprehensive, detailed treatment of the empress's life and the significant events of the Second Empire. Written with undiluted sympathy for the empress, little of Eugénie's less flattering elements are dealt with, but the book, despite its lack of objectivity, does provide a compelling human portrait.

Sencourt, Robert. *Napoleon III: The Modern Emperor.* New York: Appleton-Century, 1933. 383pp. Drawing on a good deal of unpublished source material, Sencourt's historical biography looks at Napoleon III as a forerunner of the modern political figure. The book's partisanship, particularly concerning the Empress Eugénie, occasionally distorts, but Sencourt does deliver a multidimensional portrait of Louis Napoleon.

Smith, W.H.C. *Napoleon III.* New York: St. Martin's, 1973. 296pp. Concentrating on the domestic and foreign policy of the Second Empire, Smith virtually ignores Louis Napoleon's life before 1830; however, using Napoleon's own writings, the book offers a sympathetic though balanced portrait of the man as a figure of his times. The book is an excellent choice for the reader interested primarily in the political dimension of Louis Napoleon's life.

Thompson, James M. *Louis Napoleon and the Second Empire.* New York: Noonday, 1955. 342pp. Written by a recognized expert on the French Revolution, Thompson's solid and informed examination of Louis Napoleon's life and times is a fair assessment that grants Napoleon III his achievements as well as his human failings.

Wellman, Rita. *Eugénie: Star-crossed Empress of the French.* New York: Scribner, 1941. 326pp. Covering the details of Eugénie's life from her arrival in France to her death in a series of dramatic episodes, this is a popular, entertaining treatment, more idealized than realistic in its view of the Empress and her career.

Williams, Roger L. *The Mortal Napoleon III.* Princeton, New Jersey: Princeton University Press, 1972. 226pp. This specialized medical analysis examines in detail Napoleon's illnesses with a new suggestion that he died of kidney failure rather than bladder stones as commonly assumed. Williams suggests that Napoleon's high-serum uric acid may have contributed to his drive and obstinacy.

Biographical Novels

Aubry, Octave. *The Phantom Emperor: The Romance and Tragedy of Napoleon III.* New York: Harper, 1929. 351pp. In a romantically fictionalized portrait, Napoleon III is depicted as a kindly figure with the Empress Eugénie cast in the melodramatic role of the regime's evil genius. The book's historical details are accurate, but the interpretation is suspect.

Chapman, Hester W. *Eugénie.* Boston: Little, Brown, 1961. 469pp. The Empress Eugénie's life from her childhood in Spain through her years on the French throne is dramatized from the perspective of her English governess and later companion and an eyewitness to the events of the Second Empire.

Kenyon, Frank W. *That Spanish Woman.* New York: Dodd, Mead, 1963. 342pp. Eugénie tells her own story with an emphasis on the glamour of the French court during the Second Empire. *Imperial Courtesan.* New York: Dodd, Mead, 1967. 255pp. Based on the true story of English woman Elizabeth Ann Haryett who becomes Louis Napoleon's mistress and participates in his scheming to take the French throne as Napoleon III, the novel is a blend of fact and fancy with a believable period atmosphere.

Neumann, Alfred. *Another Caesar.* New York: Knopf, 1935. 589pp.; *The Gaudy Empire.* New York: Knopf, 1937. 552pp. Louis Napoleon's reign during France's Second Empire between 1856 and 1870 is dramatized, although the chronicle of events is marred by factual errors.

Fictional Portraits

Collins, Norman. *Quiet Lady.* New York: Harper, 1942. 432pp. Events during the Siege of Paris and the Commune are dramatized from the perspective of a young woman whose story is interspersed with monologues from both Bismarck and Napoleon III.

Costain, Thomas B. *The Tontine.* Garden City, New York: Doubleday, 1955. 2 vols. Costain's immense historical panorama concerns the fate of two English families and a lottery-insurance scheme during the first half of the nineteenth century. In addition to following the stories of several fictional characters, the novel offers glimpses of the Bonaparte family as it falls with Napoleon I and attempts to reassert its influence through Louis Napoleon.

Moore, Brian. *The Magician's Wife.* New York: Dutton, 1998. 229pp. Moore's atmospheric and thoughtful novel features a French illusionist and his wife who are recruited by Napoleon III to further France's interests in Algeria.

Powers, Anne. *Rachel.* New York: Pinnacle, 1973. 320pp. The legendary French actress Elisa Felix, known as Rachel, tells her own story of her stage career and many love affairs with such figures as Alfred de Musset and Louis Napoleon.

Saunders, Diana. *The Passion of Letty Fox.* New York: D.I. Fine, 1987. 305pp. In a fanciful tale set during the Franco-Prussian War, a vaudeville performer is recruited as the public stand-in for the Empress Eugénie and becomes a target for an assassination attempt.

Biographical Films and Theatrical Adaptations

Juarez (1939). Director: William Dieterle. Claude Raines is impressive in the role of Napoleon III in this interesting historical film of the conflict between Juarez (Paul Muni) and the Emperor Maximilian (Brian Aherne) and the Empress Carlotta (Bette Davis). With Gale Sondergaard as Eugénie. Video.

Suez (1938). Director: Allan Dwan. This historically unreliable drama concerns Ferdinand de Lesseps's (Tyrone Power) drive to build the Suez Canal. Loretta Young and Annabella provide his conflicting love interests. Leon Ames portrays a Napoleon III.

348. JAWAHARLAL NEHRU
1889–1964

The first prime minister of independent India and a highly skillful politician and statesman, Nehru was educated at Harrow and Cambridge. He was admitted to the English bar (1912) and for several years practiced law in India. After the British massacre of Indian nationalists at Amritsar (1919), he devoted himself to the struggle for Indian independence. He was elected president of the Indian National Congress (1929) and spent most of the years from 1930 to 1936 in prison for taking part in civil disobedience campaigns. During World War II, Nehru opposed aiding the British unless India was immediately freed, and he was imprisoned (1942–1945). After his release, Nehru negotiated the creation (1947) of two independent states: India and Pakistan. Prime minister until his death, Nehru guided India through the difficult early years of independence and despite some criticism over his foreign policy retained enormous popularity in India.

Autobiography and Primary Sources

Autobiography of Jawaharlal Nehru. New York: Oxford University Press, 1990. 640pp. First published in 1936 and written by Nehru almost entirely during his imprisonment in 1934 to 1935, these autobiographical reflections provide insights into Nehru's background, influences, and early political and intellectual development.

Freedom's Daughter: Letters Between Indira Gandhi and Jawaharlal Nehru, 1922-39. Sonia Gandhi, ed. Delhi: CBS Publishers, 1992. 483pp. Nehru's correspondence with his daughter provides interesting insights into his thoughts during the period and his role as a father.

Letters to Chief Ministers: 1947-64. G. Parthasarathi, ed. Delhi: Oxford University Press, 1985–1989. 5 vols. This multivolume series is an important record of Nehru's concerns and interpretations of events throughout his years in power.

Recommended Biographies

Brecher, Michael. *Nehru: A Political Biography.* New York: Oxford University Press, 1959. 682pp. Based on extensive interviews with Nehru and his associates, this is a meticulously researched and sound analysis of Indian politics during the Nehru era. The book is particularly strong on Nehru's relationship with his father and Mahatma Gandhi and offers a convincing human portrait of a complex individual. One of the best and most comprehensive single-volume studies available.

Gopal, Sarvepalli. *Jawharlal Nehru: A Biography.* Cambridge, Massachusetts: Harvard University Press, 1976–1984. 3 vols. Gopal's monumental biographical/historical study leads the field as the most comprehensive and detailed examination available. Based on exclusive access to private papers and government archives, Gopal, a former senior Foreign Affairs official, provides an intimate look at decision making and Nehru's development, nationalist leadership, and years in power. A one-volume abridged edition is available (New York: Oxford University Press, 1993. 516pp.).

Wolpert, Stanley A. *Nehru: A Tryst with Destiny.* New York: Oxford University Press, 1996. 546pp. In a psychological analysis, Wolpert creates a nuanced portrait of the Indian leader, tracing his intellectual and political development, and his complex relationships with his father, Mahatma Gandhi, and Lady Edwina Mountbatten. Drawing heavily on Nehru's own writings, contemporaries' views, and official documents, Wolpert's well-documented, balanced, and readable narrative is an excellent choice as a thorough, provocative single-volume study.

Other Biographical Studies

Adams, Jad, and Philip Whitehead. *The Dynasty: The Nehru-Gandhi Story.* New York: TV Books, 1997. 390pp. Based on letters, journalistic accounts, interviews, and original research, the authors trace the Nehru and Gandhi family fortunes from 1857 through the political careers of Indira and Rajiv Gandhi both in their public and private contexts.

Akbar, M.J. *Nehru: The Making of India.* New York: Viking, 1988. 609pp. This journalistic account by a Moslem nationalist is filled with interesting anecdotes but is often superficial in its interpretations and selective in its approach and theme, which attempts to explain the breakdown of Indian unity into religious factionalism.

Brown, Judith M. *Nehru.* New York: Longman, 1999. 209pp. Part of the Profiles in Power series, Brown's study of Nehru's political career is not a full-scale biography but a thematic look at a number of related issues regarding modern Indian history and Nehru's role in shaping it. Written for the nonspecialist, the book is a solid introduction to twentieth-century Indian society and politics.

Crocker, W.R. *Nehru: A Contemporary's Estimate.* New York: Oxford University Press, 1969. 186pp. Written by an Australian diplomat who served in India during Nehru's premiership, the book offers a realistic portrait of Nehru's development, leadership, and political management during his years in power in a challenge to many of the heroic myths surrounding the Indian leader.

Edwardes, Michael. *Nehru: A Political Biography.* New York: Praeger, 1972. 351pp. A lucid chronicle of Nehru's political development, Edwardes's examination details the Indian leader's influences, achievements, and failures, which, though offering little that is new, does synthesize a variety of sources into a readable narrative. Edwardes's earlier *Nehru: A Pictorial Biography* (New York: Viking, 1962. 143pp.) presents the highlights of Nehru's career in a useful illustrated biography.

Judd, Denis. *Jawaharlal Nehru.* Cardiff: 6PC, 1993. 97pp. Judd presents a brief political portrait of Nehru, including a sketch of his early life, politi-

cal development, and career as nationalist leader and prime minister, with a concluding chapter on his legacy.

Moraes, F.R. *Jawaharlal Nehru: A Biography.* New York: Macmillan, 1956. 511pp. Written by the Indian editor of the *Times* of India, Moraes's political biography is objective and not uncritical and based on interviews with many of Nehru's contemporaries. Two-thirds of the book is devoted to pre-independence, and the study ends before Nehru's entire political career could be assessed in full.

Mukerjee, H. *The Gentle Colossus: A Study of Jawaharlal Nehru.* New York: Oxford University Press, 1986. 239pp. Written by a Hindu Nationalist, Mukerjee's study is largely an admiring apology for an Indian national hero. Lacking objectivity and critical distance, the book is unreliable in its interpretations and serves mainly to inform readers how Nehru is seen by many of his countrymen.

Nanda, B.R. *Jawaharlal Nehru: Rebel and Statesman.* New York: Oxford University Press, 1995. 312pp. In a collection of 16 essays on various aspect of Nehru's life, career, and achievements, Nanda presents a reevaluation by placing Nehru in the social and political context of his times. As the founder of India's Nehru Memorial Museum, the author shows his evident admiration for Nehru, but does raise important questions regarding his leadership, questioning whether Nehru might have prevented partition and whether his pursuit of nonalignment was a mistake.

Sheean, Vincent. *Nehru: The Years of Power.* New York: Random House, 1960. 306pp. This is a readable but mainly uncritical examination that does serve to make Indian politics accessible to a Western reader. Not chronologically arranged, the book is more an appreciative discursive essay on Nehru's achievements, published before the more serious charges against Nehru's leadership could be considered.

Shorter, B. *Nehru: A Voice for Mankind.* New York: J. Day, 1970. 312pp. Although selective and often superficial in its treatment of Nehru's career, Shorter's sympathetic tribute is enlivened by the author's conversations with Nehru and his relatives, which features their own words on several topics.

Tyson, Geoffrey. *Nehru: The Years of Power.* New York: Praeger, 1966. 206pp. Divided into an initial section that lists Nehru's domestic and foreign policy accomplishments and a second section on his influences and personal characteristics, this is a brief and reliable account of post-independence Indian politics and Nehru's leadership.

Fictional Portraits

Murari, T.N. *The Last Victory.* New York: St. Martin's, 1988. 335pp. In a sequel to the author's *The Imperial Agent,* (1987) a continuation of Kipling's adventure classic, *Kim,* Kimball O'Hara's story is continued into the 1910s with appearances by Nehru and Mahatma Gandhi.

Tharoor, Shashi. *The Great Indian Novel.* New York: Viking, 1989. 423pp. Tharoor offers an ingenious retelling of the ancient Indian epic, the *Mahabharata,* to reflect twentieth-century Indian

political history, with appearances by the major figures, including Nehru.

Recommended Juvenile Biographies

Apsler, Alfred. *Fighter for Independence: Jawaharlal Nehru.* New York: J. Messner, 1963. 191pp. YA. Apsler reveals a complex figure in this biographical profile that traces Nehru's development under Gandhi and offers an accessible and informative summary of the major events in modern Indian history.

Finck, Lila. *Jawaharlal Nehru.* New York: Chelsea House, 1987. 112pp. MG/YA. Finck's is a reliable account of Nehru's life, political career, and character against a clear historical and cultural background of India's drive for independence and the aftermath.

Lamb, Beatrice P. *The Nehrus of India: Three Generations of Leadership.* Chicago: Reilly & Lee, 1961. 214pp. YA. Lamb's group biography proceeds from the birth of Nehru's father to the political career of his daughter, Indira, up to 1967. Well written, this approach helps to make Nehru's ideas and actions understandable in a wider historical context.

Biographical Films and Theatrical Adaptations

The Dynasty (1997). Directors: Mark Anderson and Charles Bruce. Documents both the life of Mahatma Gandhi and the interlinked history of the Nehru and Gandhi families. Video.

Gandhi (1982). Director: Richard Attenborough. The Oscar-winning film biography of Gandhi (Ben Kingsley) features Roshan Seth as Nehru in a compelling, grand spectacle of India's fight for independence. Video.

Lord Mountbatten: The Last Viceroy (1986). Director: Tony Clegg This television mini-series looks at the events leading up to Indian independence from the perspective of Mountbatten's (Nicol Williamson) efforts to transfer British power to the new nation. Ian Richardson portrays Nehru, with Janet Suzman as Lady Mountbatten and Sam Dastor as Gandhi. A novelization by David Butler is available (New York: Pocket Books, 1986. 295pp.). Video.

See also Indira Gandhi; Mahatma Gandhi

349. HORATIO NELSON
1758–1805

British admiral and the most famous of Britain's naval heroes, Nelson entered the navy at 12, became a captain at 20, and saw service in the West Indies, in the Baltic, and in Canada. When the British entered (1793) the French Revolutionary Wars, he was given command of the *Agamemnon*, was instrumental in defeating the Spanish fleet off Cape St. Vincent (1797), and won fame and honors after defeating the French fleet at the Battle of Aboukir (1798). Soon afterwards he began his scandalous affair with Lady Emma Hamilton. When the war with France was renewed (1803), Nelson blockaded the French fleet at Toulon for 22 months. The naval war culminated in the Battle of Trafalgar (1805), before which Nelson gave his famous signal, "England expects that every man will do his duty." Nelson was fatally wounded during the battle. His spectacular victory at Trafalgar ensured British naval supremacy for the rest of the century.

Autobiography and Primary Sources

Nelson's letters and dispatches are available in a number of volumes, including *The Nelson Touch: An Anthology of Lord Nelson's Letters.* Clemence Dane, ed. (London: Heinemann, 1942. 285pp.); *Nelson's Letters to His Wife and Other Documents, 1785–1831* (London: Routledge, 1958. 630pp.); *Nelson's Letters.* Geoffrey Rawson, ed. (New York: Dutton, 1960. 486pp.); and *The Dispatches and Letters of Vice Admiral Viscount Nelson* (London: Colburn, 1845–1846. 7 vols.).

Recommended Biographies

Oman, Carola. *Nelson.* Garden City, New York: Doubleday, 1946. 748pp. Oman's meticulously researched examination of Nelson's life and times remains the most comprehensive work on Nelson. Filling in a number of factual details and challenging prior interpretation, Oman's is a rich character study in a year-by-year narrative, with all the essential facts included and both the man and the era considered in depth.

Pocock, Tom. *Horatio Nelson.* New York: Knopf, 1988. 367pp. Richly detailed and well documented from Nelson's papers and other manuscript sources, along with a solidly presented social background, Pocock's readable narrative account for the general reader offers a balanced, nuanced portrait of a far more complex figure than other more admiring studies. Nelson is displayed with all his contradictions intact, a believable, human figure.

Warner, Oliver. *Victory: The Life of Lord Nelson.* Boston: Little, Brown, 1958. 393pp. Finding a balance between Nelson, naval commander, and his private life ashore, Warner's is an unbiased, penetrating, and authoritative chronological life. The book is particularly strong on naval history as well as on Nelson's professional skills and often troubled relationships with his superiors and subordinates.

Other Biographical Studies

Bradford, Ernle. *Nelson: The Essential Hero.* New York: Harcourt, Brace, 1977. 368pp. Written by a British sailor-historian, Bradford covers Nelson's entire life with an emphasis on his naval engagements at the Nile, Copenhagen, and Trafalgar. A compact, highly entertaining introduction by an unabashed admirer whose sea experience brings Nelson's story to vivid life.

Browne, G. Lathom. *Nelson: The Public and Private Life of Horatio Viscount Nelson.* London: Unwin, 1891. 472pp. Weaving together Nelson's own reflections and recollections by his family and friends Browne covers Nelson's life in full in a readable biography.

Clarke, J.S., and J. MacArthur. *The Life of Admiral Lord Nelson.* London: Bensley, 1809. 2 vols. The earliest, official biography remains an indispensable biographical source of factual details from contemporary sources, as well as Nelson's own autobiographical reflections of his life up to 1799. Mainly the story of Nelson's naval achievements, the book offers only scant references to his relationship with Emma Hamilton.

Forester, C.S. *Lord Nelson.* Indianapolis: Bobbs-Merrill, 1929. 353pp. The author of the Hornblower novels presents a highly readable portrait of Nelson and account of British naval history during his era. Without offering much that is new or original, Forester's is a reliable synthesis of sources turned into a vivid, dramatic narrative history.

Hattersley, Roy. *Nelson.* New York: Saturday Review Press, 1974. 223pp. This abundantly illustrated biography has a lively text that treats Nelson as a rounded, human figure who was a brilliant tactical commander, loved and respected by his men but also vain and egotistical. His career is traced chronologically.

Hibbert, Christopher. *Nelson: A Personal History.* Reading, Massachusetts: Addison-Wesley, 1994. 472pp. In a lively, highly readable account of Nelson's private life, particularly his liaison with Lady Hamilton, Hibbert deemphasizes Nelson's naval career but does fashion an entertaining narrative based on primary and reliable secondary sources. By excluding much concerning Nelson's naval temperament and achievement, Hibbert's is a limited view of an irascible, vain, self-deceiving figure enthralled by a woman.

Howarth, David A., and Stephen Howarth. *Lord Nelson: The Immortal Memory.* New York: Viking, 1989. 390pp. Written by a father and son, both respected military historians, this anecdote-rich popular biography is enthusiastically appreciative and glosses over many of Nelson's flaws. To be enjoyed less for its critique or analysis but for its vivid, dramatic narrative approach written with flair and an eye for colorful detail.

Mahan, Alfred T. *The Life of Nelson.* Boston: Little, Brown, 1897. 2 vols. Abridged ed. New York: Penguin, 1942. 253pp. Mahan's American perspective helps him approach Nelson in a much less patriotic and more balanced fashion, offering detailed, critical accounts of his naval battles and an inquiry into the depths and complexity of Nelson's personality and leadership.

Pocock, Tom. *Nelson and His World.* New York: Viking, 1968. 142pp. This visual biography is an excellent first encounter with the man and his era. Pocock's text is particularly good on Nelson's youth and naval achievements.

Southey, Robert. *The Life of Nelson.* 1813. Reprint ed. Annapolis, Maryland: Naval Institute Press, 1990. 306pp. Southey's popular treatment of Nelson's life depends on the facts derived from Clarke and MacArthur and is a tribute to a national hero with only glimpses of a more complex, human figure, with a critical view of Nelson's involvement with the Hamiltons.

Walder, David. *Nelson: A Biography.* New York: Dial Press, 1978. 538pp. Concentrating on Nelson's private life, Walder traces the admiral's rise and puts his affair with Lady Hamilton in its proper context. Unfortunately, the book is weakest on the source of Nelson's naval achievements. Balanced in its interpretation, Walder presents both Nelson's greatness and weaknesses.

Biographies of Emma Hamilton and accounts of Nelson's relationship with the Hamiltons are available that shed light on Nelson's private, domestic life.

Fraser, Flora. *Emma, Lady Hamilton.* New York: Knopf, 1987. 356pp. Regarded as the standard biography of Lady Hamilton, Fraser's well-written portrait reveals a complex woman with far more than her beauty to recommend her to Nelson.

Hardwick, Mollie. *Emma, Lady Hamilton.* New York: Holt, 1970. 312pp. Carefully researched and with some new information, Hardwick's is a sympathetic and rounded portrait of Emma Hamilton that puts her affair with Nelson in the wider context of her life and times.

Lofts, Norah. *Emma Hamilton.* New York: Coward-McCann, 1978. 192pp. This attractive illustrated biography offers a sympathetic but somewhat superficial portrait of Lady Hamilton.

Russell, Jack. *Nelson and the Hamiltons.* New York: Simon & Schuster, 1969. 448pp. Russell's account of Nelson's affair with Emma Hamilton is overbalanced by historical detail that breaks the book's focus. Written for the general reader, Russell's account does provide a convenient collection of extracts from Nelson and the Hamiltons' letters, journals, and private papers.

Biographical Novels

Dessau, Joanna. *The Blacksmith's Daughter.* London: R. Hale, 1983. 191pp. In a biographical novel that is faithful to the basic outline of Emma Hamilton's life, her rise from humble origins, her marriage to the British diplomat Sir William Hamilton, and her affair with Lord Nelson are depicted, with a number of invented scenes and imagined dialogue.

Field, Bradda. *Bride of Glory.* New York: Greystone Press, 1942. 963pp. Emma Hamilton's career is depicted, including her affair with Nelson in a biographical novel that is packed with historical and political details.

Foxell, Nigel. *Loving Emma.* Brighton, England: Harvester, 1986. 201pp. Climaxing with the beginning of Nelson's affair with Lady Hamilton, the majority of this biographical novel concerns the events in the admiral's life leading up to their first meeting. Factually reliable in part, certain liberties have been taken in the interest of the drama.

Frye, Pearl. *A Game for Empire.* Boston: Little, Brown, 1950. 471pp. Nelson's naval career is dramatized from 1793 to 1798 and his triumph at the Battle of the Nile, using the admiral's letters to aid authenticity. In *The Sleeping Sword* (Boston: Little, Brown, 1952. 400pp.) Frye continues her biographical account of Nelson's career from 1799, through his affair with Lady Hamilton, to his death at Trafalgar.

Hodge, Jane Aiken. *Shadow of a Lady.* New York: Putnam, 1973. 317pp. In a blend of fact and fiction, the court world of Naples and Nelson's relationship with Lady Hamilton are dramatized from the perspective of one of Emma's friends.

Kenyon, Frank W. *Emma*. New York: Crowell, 1935. 314pp. Lady Hamilton's marriage and affair with Nelson is depicted from Emma's perspective in an often speculative interpretation of the motives and characters of the lovers.

Lewis, Paul. *The Nelson Touch*. New York: Holt, 1960. 267pp. Tracing Nelson's personal and professional career from 1787 to his death, this is more an idealized treatment than a dependable biographical account.

Sontag, Susan. *The Volcano Lover*. New York: Farrar, Straus, 1992. 419pp. Sontag's inventive repossession of history dramatizes the odd triangular relationship of Nelson and the Hamiltons, whose story is used as the occasion for a consideration of the causes of revolution, the condition of women, and the nature of love.

Stacton, David. *Sir William: Or A Lesson in Love*. New York: Putnam, 1963. 352pp. In a realistic alternative to the romantic idealization of the Nelson-Hamilton affair, Stacton looks at the couple from the perspective of Sir William Hamilton.

Styles, Showell. *A Kiss for Captain Hardy*. Boston: Faber and Faber, 1979. 188pp. Nelson's naval career during his affair with Lady Hamilton is depicted, culminating in his final triumph at Trafalgar and his death.

Fictional Portraits

Kent, Alexander. *The In-Shore Squadron*. New York: Putnam, 1979. 256pp. The author's naval series featuring the British captain Richard Bolitho concerns his challenges as a squadron commander and his relationship with Nelson in action that climaxes with the Battle of Copenhagen.

Lambdin, Dewey. *A King's Commander*. New York: D.I. Fine,1997. 374pp. Set during the 1790s, this installment of Lambdin's historical naval series features Alan Lewrie in action against the French during the Battle of the Glorious First of June and alongside Nelson in a several engagements.

Pope, Dudley. *Ramage at Trafalgar*. London: Secker & Warburg,1986. 214pp. Nicholas Ramage, Pope's naval series hero, joins Nelson's command in the blockade of the French and Spanish off Cadiz, culminating at Trafalgar. The details concerning Nelson and the battle are truthful to history.

Shannon, Dell. *The Scalpel and the Sword*. New York: Morrow, 1987. 392pp. An Irish surgeon goes to sea with the Royal Navy and is on hand at the death of Nelson in an accurately described dramatization of Trafalgar and Nelson's mortal wounding.

Styles, Showell. *The Sea Officer*. New York: Macmillan, 1962. 272pp. One of England's greatest naval officers, Edward Pellew, is shown in action during the American Revolution and the French wars with appearances by a number of other historical figures, including Nelson, in a factually accurate biographical novel.

Unsworth, Barry. *Losing Nelson*. New York: Nan A. Talese, 1999. 338pp. Unsworth's ingenious meditation on the life of Nelson and the power of his legend takes the form of a contemporary Lon-

doner's obsession with the military hero who imaginatively relives the events of Nelson's life.

Woodman, Richard. *The Bomb Vessel*. New York: Walker, 1986. 215pp. In this installment of the naval series involving Nathaniel Drinkwater, the Baltic campaign against Napoleon is depicted, climaxing in the Battle of Copenhagen. In *Decision at Trafalgar* (New York: Walker, 1986. 209pp.), the events leading up to Trafalgar are portrayed in a historically reliable account based in part on the recorded words of the combatants like Nelson and the French Admiral Villeneuve.

Recommended Juvenile Biographies

Gimpel, Herbert J. *Lord Nelson*. New York: F. Watts, 1966. 228pp. MG. This is a careful chronicle of Nelson's career that is better on the events and historical background than on Nelson's private side and character. His relationship with Lady Hamilton is glossed over.

Russell, Jack. *Nelson: Hero of Trafalgar*. New York: Putnam, 1968. 224pp. YA. Russell, a noted expert on Nelson and his era, supplies a highly detailed and informative summary of the man, his career, and the important historical events.

Whipple, A.B.C. *Hero of Trafalgar*. New York: Random House, 1963. 186pp. MG/YA. Whipple traces Nelson's life from his twelfth year to his death in this Landmark biography that emphasizes Nelson the naval hero, with Emma Hamilton left out almost entirely.

Biographical Films and Theatrical Adaptations

Horatio Nelson and the Battle of Trafalgar (1993). Producer: Phil Grabsky. Segment of the British television Great Commanders series that covers Nelson's career leading up to its climax at Trafalgar. Video.

I Remember Nelson (1998). Director: Simon Langston. Multi-part British television account of Nelson's career as seen from the perspectives of his wife, a friend, his First Officer, and a young sailor at his final battle, starring Kenneth Colley, Anna Massey, Geraldine James, Raf Vallone, and Daniel Massey. Video.

The Nelson Affair (1973). Director: James C. Jones. This British drama of the Nelson-Hamilton affair features Peter Finch in the role of Nelson, with Glenda Jackson as Emma. Solid supporting cast of Michael Jayston, Anthony Quayle, and Nigel Stock. Alternative British title: *A Bequest to the Nation*.

That Hamilton Woman (1941). Director: Alexander Korda. Wartime film brings together Laurence Olivier as Nelson and Vivien Leigh as Lady Hamilton in this rousing drama of their love against a backdrop of war. Video.

Other Sources

Harris, David, ed. *The Nelson Almanac: A Book of Days Recording Nelson's Life and the Events that Shaped His Era*. Annapolis, Maryland: Naval Institute Press, 1998. 192pp. In a collection of biographical essays and letters arranged in diary form,

each month features an article on aspects of Nelson's life and career followed by a detailed chronology.

350. NERO
AD 37–68

Born Lucius Domitius Ahenobarbus, the infamous Roman emperor Nero was the son of Agrippina, the great-granddaughter of the emperor Augustus. He was adopted by his stepfather, Claudius I, whom he succeeded as emperor in AD 54. Nero had Claudius's son, Britannicus, murdered (AD 55) and killed his mother (AD 59) and his wife, Octavia (AD 62). He later married his mistress, Poppaea. Nero accused the Christians of starting the fire (AD 64) that burned half of Rome, and he began the first Christian persecutions. Beginning in AD 68, Nero's cruelty, instability, and imposition of heavy taxes led to a series of revolts, including one by his Praetorian Guard. The revolts caused Nero to commit suicide.

Recommended Biographies

Grant, Michael. *Nero: Emperor in Revolt*. New York: American Heritage, 1970. 272pp. Grant's biographical profile complements a selection of illustrations that serve as a compact, lucid, introductory study by a master in the field. Grant offers a sympathetic portrait that attempts to understand Nero in the context of his times, portraying him as no more eccentric or monstrous than his contemporaries.

Griffin, Miriam. *Nero: The End of a Dynasty*. New Haven, Connecticut: Yale University Press, 1985. 320pp. Based on ancient sources, Griffin supplies a psychological analysis of Nero's development and character that sheds light on the emperor's background and motivation during his reign. Not for the uninitiated general reader, Griffin's study presupposes understanding of Roman culture and terminology.

Warmington, B.H. *Nero: Reality and Legend*. New York: W.W. Norton, 1970. 180pp. In a critical reassessment of Nero and his reign, Warmington presents the Roman emperor stripped of his sensational legend as an understandable figure of his times who was a talented administrator and positive ruler.

Other Biographical Studies

Bishop, John. *Nero: The Man and the Legend*. San Diego: A.S. Barnes, 1965. 208pp. Based exclusively on the major ancient sources, in particular Tacitus, Suetonius, and Dio Cassius, Bishop's is a highly readable introductory study for the general reader that serves to detail contemporary views of Nero with an attempt to understand the man within his historical and cultural context.

Grabsky, Phil. *I, Caesar: Ruling the Roman Empire*. Parkwest, New York: BBC Books, 1998. 256p. Written for the curious general reader, this companion book for an A&E television history series traces the rise and fall of the Roman Empire through the lives of several emperors, including Nero. Sweeping generalizations sometimes lead the author into errors of fact and some long-outmoded interpretations.

Henderson, Bernard W. *The Life and Principate of the Emperor Nero*. Philadelphia: Lippincott, 1903. 529pp. In a solid, historical study, Henderson synthesizes ancient sources and modern research into a balanced narrative combining information on Nero's life with a study of his reign and times.

Shotter, David. *Nero*. New York: Routledge, 1997. 104pp. Shotter's compact overview includes a chronology and chapters on Nero's early life and the events of his reign, as well as a critical assessment of previous studies of the emperor.

Suetonius. *Nero*. Bristol, England: Bristol Classical Press, 1977. 118pp. Published about A.D. 121 in *The Lives of the Caesars*, Suetonius's biographical profile is one of the principal ancient sources of information on Nero. His colorful depiction emphasizing the sensational should be read with skepticism for its reliability, but few texts are better in showing how the image of Nero in the conventional view was created.

Weigall, Arthur. *Nero: The Singing Emperor of Rome*. Garden City, New York: Doubleday, 1930. 425pp. Challenging popular conceptions of Nero's character, Weigall rehabilitates Nero's reputation, presenting him as a lover of music and poetry and a patron of the arts who did not cause the fire to Rome and made a concerted effort to relieve the suffering it caused. Weigall is not successful in vindicating Nero of all the charges against him, and the book's defensiveness compromises objectivity.

Biographical Novels

Comfort, Alex. *Imperial Patient*. London: Duckworth, 1987. 206pp. Nero is glimpsed from the perspective of a physician who, brought to Rome to treat the emperor's wife Octavia for infertility, becomes caught up in court intrigue.

Graves, Robert. *Claudius the God*. New York: H. Smith and R. Haas, 1935. 538pp. In the sequel to *I, Claudius*, Claudius chronicles his reign as emperor with a depiction of the young Nero who will succeed him.

Kosztolanyi, Deszo. *Bloody Poet*. New York: Macy-Masius, 1928. 344pp. Nero is depicted as an artistic figure driven mad by his frustrated genius. Nero's excesses are primary here in a historically unreliable presentation.

Maier, Paul L. *The Flames of Rome*. Garden City, New York: Doubleday, 1981. 443pp. The persecution of the early Christians during Nero's reign is the book's subject with a carefully observed historical framework for its fictional drama.

Pargeter, Edith. *Hortensius, Friend of Nero*. New York: Greystone Press, 1937. 232pp. Set during the period after the fire of Rome when Nero is rebuilding the city, the novel, written in the form of a diary kept by the emperor's friend, details Nero's growing madness and excesses. Neither convincing nor accurate in its depiction, the novel simplifies and takes a number of liberties with the facts.

Ronalds, Mary T. *Nero*. Garden City, New York: Doubleday, 1969. 360pp. Nero tells his own story in a defense of his actions and character. Not reliable as history nor psychologically convincing, this one-sided special pleading offers a number of dubious biographical interpretations.

Sheean, Vincent. *Beware of Caesar*. New York: Random House, 1965. 244pp. Carefully based on actual events and historical details, the novel chronicles the political intrigues of Nero's rule in which the emperor's former tutor, Seneca, is implicated in a conspiracy.

Van Santvoord, Seymour. *Octavia: A Tale of Ancient Rome*. New York: Dutton, 1923. 458pp. In a tale that follows historical facts closely and includes a detailed depiction of Roman customs, the reigns of Caligula, Claudius, and Nero are described from the perspective of Nero's virtuous wife.

Fictional Portraits

Gillespie, Donna. *The Light Bearer*. New York: Berkley, 1994. 788pp. Spanning the years between AD 52 and 96, the excesses of two Roman tyrants, Nero and Domitian, are used as a backdrop for a fictional story involving a pagan warrior priestess and a Roman nobleman in a vigorous historical romance.

Hersey, John. *The Conspiracy*. New York: Knopf, 1972. 274pp. Told through the secret communiqués of Nero's agents, the repression of men of letters by their former patron is presented, suggesting many contemporary parallels. The author has relied upon historical sources, but admits that this version is not meant to be taken as historically accurate.

Mason, Anita. *The Illusionist*. New York: Holt, 1984. 309pp. This fanciful story concerns the famous magician Simon Magus who journeys to Rome for a climactic test of his powers before Nero.

Mitchison, Naomi. *The Blood of the Martyrs*. New York: Whittlesey House,1948. 499pp. The story of Nero's persecution of the Christians is depicted from the perspective of a Roman senator's family in a vivid portrait of the period following the Piso conspiracy to assassinate the emperor.

Sienkiewicz, Henryk. *Quo Vadis?* 1896. Reprint ed. New York: Hippocrene, 1992. 493pp. Set during the reign of Nero and the early years of the Christian church, this panoramic novel includes scenes of Nero's excesses and the burning of Rome.

Waltari, Mika. *The Roman*. New York: Putnam, 1966. 637pp. In a fictional tale with an authentic period background, a young Roman nobleman serves Nero in the persecution of Christians after the burning of Rome before converting to the new faith.

White, Leslie Turner. *Scorpus the Moor*. Garden City, New York: Doubleday, 1962. 288pp. Nero's Rome is portrayed from the perspective of an Arab who is forced to live by his wits and comes to the attention of the emperor in a colorful rather than historically believable period drama.

Yarbro, Chelsea Quinn. *Blood Games*. New York: St. Martin's, 1979. 458pp. This installment of the author's historical vampire series is set in Rome during Nero's reign in which the Gothic details pale before Roman excesses.

Recommended Juvenile Biographies

Powers, Elizabeth. *Nero*. New York: Chelsea House, 1988. 112pp. MG/YA. This is an informative biography that relates Nero's life and reign against a fully realized cultural and historical background.

Biographical Films and Theatrical Adaptations

I, Claudius (1980). Director: Herbert Wise. The acclaimed BBC series based on Robert Graves's novels is remarkably faithful to his intimate portrait of a dysfunctional first family of Imperial Rome, absolutely corrupted by power. Christopher Biggins appears as a young Nero who will succeed the aging Claudius (Derek Jacobi). Video.

Quo Vadis? (1951). Director: Mervyn LeRoy. Massive adaptation of Sienkiewicz's novel about Christian persecution during Nero's reign features Peter Ustinov as the emperor and Robert Taylor and Deborah Kerr as the leads. Remade for television in 1985 with Klaus Maria Brandauer as Nero. Video.

The Silver Chalice (1954). Director: Victor Saville. Film version of Thomas Costain's novel (Garden City, New York: Doubleday, 1952. 533pp.) about a young Greek sculptor who makes the cup Jesus uses at the Last Supper features the screen debut of Paul Newman and a portrayal of Nero by Jacques Aubuchon. Video.

Other Sources

Eisner, Jas, and Jamie Masters, eds. *Reflections of Nero: Culture, History, and Representation*. Chapel Hill: University of North Carolina Press, 1994. 239pp. Through chapters on various presentations of Nero, this useful volume illustrates the ways in which the various myths surrounding the emperor have been shaped in popular consciousness.

See also Saint Paul; Saint Peter

351. PABLO NERUDA
1904–1973

Chilean poet, diplomat, and Communist leader, Neruda was awarded the 1971 Nobel Prize in Literature during his service as Chilean ambassador to France. He died in Chile the week of the military coup that overthrew the government. Neruda's many volumes of poetry include *Twenty Love Poems and One Song of Despair* (1924), *Canto General* (1950), and *Elementary Odes* (1954).

Autobiography and Primary Sources

Isla Negra: A Notebook. New York: Farrar, Straus, 1982. 416pp. This is a collection of autobiographical poems written during the 1960s and represents a kind of summing up of Neruda's life and his intentions.

Memoirs. New York: Farrar, Straus, 1977. 370pp. Called by one reviewer a "book of lapses, of airy interstices," but still "a sort of distilled essence" of the poet and "the starting point for all future biographers," Neruda's recollections fail to reveal much about his private life and are far too fragmentary and selective to give the reader more than the flavor of the man.

Passions and Impressions. Matilde Neruda, ed. New York: Farrar, Straus, 1983. 396pp. This is a compilation of Neruda's speeches and writings during the 1960s that document this period in the writer's life.

Recommended Biographies

Teitelboim, Volodia. *Neruda: An Intimate Biography.* Austin: University of Texas Press, 1991. 506pp. The work of the poet's close friend and political colleague, Teitelboim's biography is currently the only comprehensive study of Neruda's life available in English. The author's firsthand view is useful and helpful, although the lack of objectivity and distance limit the book's reliability.

Duran, Manuel, and Margery Safir. *Earth Tones: The Poetry of Pablo Neruda.* Bloomington: Indiana University Press, 1981. 200pp. The author surveys the life of Neruda through his work, proceeding chronologically, tracing the relationship between Neruda's experiences and his writing. Serves as a useful introductory overview.

Other Biographical Studies

Agosín, Marjorie. *Pablo Neruda.* New York: Twayne, 1986. 157pp. The author prefaces her critical study with a brief biographical summary derived from the untranslated biography written by Neruda's niece.

Bizzarro, Salvatore. *Pablo Neruda: All Poets the Poet.* Metuchen, New Jersey: Scarecrow Press, 1979. 192pp. The second half of the author's critical study includes biographical information provided by Delia Del Carril and Matilde Urrutia on Neruda's time in Spain, the years of hiding, and the poet's last days.

Fictional Portraits

Skármeta, Antonio. *Burning Patience.* New York: Putnam, 1987. 118pp. Also available as *The Postman: Il Postino.* Set in Chile during the 1970s, the novel explores the relationship between the poet and the young man who delivers his mail on Isla Negra as Neruda tutors the postman in love and poetry.

Recommended Juvenile Biographies

Goodnough, David. *Pablo Neruda: Nobel Prize-Winning Poet.* Springfield, New Jersey: Enslow, 1998. 128pp. MG. Clearly written and well-documented, Goodnough's is a fine introduction and overview of the man, his works, and times.

Roman, Joseph. *Pablo Neruda.* New York: Chelsea House, 1992. 111pp. MG/YA. Serves as a solid, basic source of information about the poet, his times, and political activities. Includes English translations of some of Neruda's poetry.

Biographical Films and Theatrical Adaptations

Il Postino (1994). Director: Michael Radford. In a film adaptation of Skármeta's novel, Philippe Noiret portrays Neruda who is fancifully exiled to Italy in 1952 to explore his relationship with the Italian postman played by Massimo Troisi. Video.

352. JOHN HENRY NEWMAN
1801–1890

English clergyman and founder of the Oxford Movement, Newman was a Church of England vicar and tutor at Oxford until his conversion to Roman Catholicism (1845). He entered the Oratorians and was eventually created a cardinal. He wrote several hymns, including "Lead Kindly Light," as well as popular and inspiring essays, poetry, religious novels, and *Apologia pro Vita Sua* (1864), considered a masterpiece of religious autobiography.

Autobiography and Primary Sources

Letters and Diaries. Oxford: Clarendon Press, 1961–1995. 31 vols. This scholarly edition of Newman's personal writings is indispensable for biographical insights. A one-volume collection is also available in *Letters of John Henry Newman: A Selection.* Derek Stanford and Muriel Spark, eds. (London: P. Owen, 1957. 251pp.).

Apologia pro Vita Sua: Being a History of His Religious Opinions. Martin J. Svaglic, ed. Oxford: Clarendon Press, 1967. 604pp. Newman's classic autobiography remains the starting point for biographers and readers interested in Newman's perspective on his spiritual progress.

Autobiographical Writings. Henry Tristram, ed. New York: Sheed and Ward, 1957. 338pp. Includes all of Newman's autobiographical writings besides the *Apologia* and is an invaluable aid to the study of Newman's life.

Recommended Biographies

Ker, Ian. *John Henry Newman: A Biography.* New York: Oxford University Press, 1988. 762pp. Ker's biography remains the best available single-volume study that skillfully combines Newman's complex personality, public career, intellectual development, and artistry into a full-length, convincing portrait.

Trevor, Meriol. *Newman.* Garden City, New York: Doubleday, 1962–1963. 2 vols. Supplementing Ward's life with new source material and providing a more balanced account between Newman's Anglican and Catholic life, Trevor's is an exhaustive portrait of Newman's personal life. A useful abridgment of Trevor's massive study is available as *Newman's Journey* (Huntington, Indiana: Our Sunday Visitor Press, 1985. 271pp.).

Ward, Wilfrid. *The Life of John Henry Cardinal Newman.* New York: Longmans, 1912. 2 vols. Long serving as the standard account of Newman's life and times, Ward's comprehensive study retains its usefulness as a important source, primarily on Newman's postconversion career.

Other Biographical Studies

Atkins, Gaius G. *Life of Cardinal Newman.* New York: Harper, 1931. 338pp. Superseded by later scholarship, Atkins's is a sober profile that attempts to encapsulate Newman's personality, development, and impact in a short, focused account. The book is often simplistic and as one contemporary reviewer pointed out, Atkins "failed not merely to construct in his own imagination the authentic Newman but even a coherent, vital, convincing Newman."

Dessain, Charles S. *John Henry Newman.* 1966. Revised ed. New York: Oxford University Press, 1980. 178pp. The work of the archivist of Newman's Birmingham Oratory, this is an intellectual biography with a strong Catholic bias, often far too polemical to be fully satisfying.

Lapati, Americo D. *John Henry Newman.* New York: Twayne, 1972. 161pp. This is compact, focused critical study of Newman's intellectual development, connecting important details about the writer's life and character with his work. Serves as a valuable supplement to other biographies more concerned with narrating Newman's personal story.

Martin, Brian. *John Henry Newman: His Life and Work.* New York: Oxford University Press, 1982. 160pp. Martin's is a brief but full account of Newman's life and work, suitable as a solid and sound introductory overview.

O'Faolin, Sean. *Newman's Way: The Odyssey of John Henry Newman.* New York: Devin-Adair, 1952. 335pp. The author concentrates on Newman's development up to his conversion in an often eccentric, impressionistic, and highly critical profile.

Ruggles, Eleanor. *Journey into Faith: The Anglican Life of John Henry Newman.* New York: W.W. Norton, 1948. 336pp. Focused on the years leading up to Newman's conversion to Catholicism, Ruggles adds useful background information to the *Apologia,* and the study serves as a useful complement to Newman's autobiographical masterpiece.

Sencourt, Robert. *The Life of Newman.* London: Dacre Press, 1948. 314pp. Sencourt relates Newman's intellectual and spiritual progress in terms of its wider cultural and historical contexts in a learned and useful study that sheds light on the influences that shaped Newman's ideas and writings.

Ward, Maisie. *Young Mr. Newman.* New York: Sheed & Ward, 1948. 477pp. Wilfrid Ward's daughter complements her father's two-volume life with an objective study of Newman's preconversion life, based on his diary and family letters. Newly available primary material has made Ward's account out of date.

Biographical Novels

Trevor, Meriol. *Shadows and Images.* New York: McKay, 1960. 273pp. Newman's conversion to Roman Catholicism is dramatized around a fictional story of a daughter of an Anglican clergyman who becomes engaged to a Roman Catholic. Trevor, a respected Newman biographer, uses Newman's own letters and autobiographical writings to support this treatment.

353. ISAAC NEWTON
1642–1727

A mathematician and physicist who is considered by many to be the greatest and most influential scientist who ever lived, Newton entered Cambridge University in 1661. When the university closed (1664–1666) during the years of the great plague, Newton went home to Woolsthorpe, Lincolnshire, where he made his most important discoveries. From 1669 to 1701 he taught mathematics at Cambridge, was his university's representative in Parliament (1689–1690, 1701–1702), served as president of the Royal Society from 1703 until his death, and was knighted in 1705. His achievements include the theory of universal gravitation, the development of calculus, the derivation of Kepler's Law of planetary motion, the binomial theorem, and theories of optics. His theories are explained in his *Philosophiae Naturalis Principia Mathematica* (1687).

Autobiography and Primary Sources

Correspondence. H.W. Turnbull, ed. Cambridge, Massachusetts: Cambridge University Press, 1959–1977. 7 vols. Newton's collected letters are invaluable in reconstructing his ideas, personality, and relationships, and this is an excellent scholarly edition with useful annotations.

Stukeley, William. *Memoirs of Sir Isaac Newton's Life: Being Some Account of His Family and Chiefly of the Junior Part of his Life.* A. Hastings White, ed. London: Taylor and Francis, 1936. 86pp. Virtually all of the information we have about Newton's early life has been collected from eyewitness accounts in the 1750s by the antiquarian William Stukeley. His biographical anecdotes and own recollections remain the indispensable source for all future biographers.

Recommended Biographies

Christianson, Gale E. *In the Presence of the Creator: Isaac Newton and His Times.* New York: Free Press, 1984. 623pp. Without the thoroughness and authority of Westfall, Christianson's comprehensive biography is more accessible, particularly for the nonscientist. Solidly based on primary sources and modern scholarship, the book presents Newton's life in the context of his era.

Hall, A. Rupert. *Isaac Newton: Adventurer in Thought.* Cambridge, Massachusetts: Blackwell, 1992. 468pp. Summarizing modern scholarship on Newton's life and scientific methods, Hall presents a straightforward, accessible overview of a complex figure who is displayed in his various roles as historian, theologian, chemist, civil servant, and natural philosopher. Hall argues that no single intellectual key, neither Platonism nor mysticism, serves to unlock the secrets of Newton's genius, and that Hall's eclectic intellectual approach does more justice to Newton's multiplicity.

Manuel, Frank E. *A Portrait of Isaac Newton.* Cambridge, Massachusetts: Harvard University Press, 1968. 478pp. In a psychological analysis Manuel traces Newton's development and personality, piecing together clues provided from Newton's own writings. Offering a number of revealing and provocative insights, most notably the trauma of his father's early death and his mother's remarriage on Newton's make-up, Manuel's is a convincing and well-documented, though ultimately in many cases hypothetical, interpretation of the scientist's life and career.

Westfall, Richard S. *Never at Rest: A Biography of Isaac Newton.* New York: Cambridge University Press, 1980. 908pp. Justifiably considered the definitive modern biography, Westfall's meticulously documented examination synthesizes past and present scholarship into a richly detailed portrait of a complex man seen through his remarkable scientific work. In Westfall's capable handling, Newton the man, the scientist, philosopher, and public figure emerges clearly. *The Life of Isaac Newton* (New York: Cambridge University Press, 1993. 328pp.) is an abridged edition.

Other Biographical Studies

Andrade, Edward. *Sir Isaac Newton.* Garden City, New York: Doubleday, 1958. 140pp. With the virtue of brevity, Andrade offers a informed overview of Newton's life and scientific career in which his contributions are placed in historical context. For the reader looking for a succinct introduction, this is a first-rate choice.

Brewster, Sir David. *Life of Sir Isaac Newton.* New York: Harper, 1831. 366pp.; *Memoirs of the Life, Writings, and Discoveries of Sir Isaac Newton.* Edinburgh: Constable, 1855. 2 vols. Brewster's early popular life of Newton did much to establish his heroic reputation. Brewster continued gathering material on Newton from the scientist's manuscripts and Stukeley's materials, which was not published until 1936, organized into his monumental two-volume study from which most subsequent biographers have drawn materials and against which they have measured their own interpretation.

De Morgan, Augustus. *Newton: His Friend and His Niece.* 1855. Reprint ed. London: Dawsons, 1968. 161pp.; *Essays on the Life and Work of Newton.* Chicago: Open Court, 1914. 198pp. Contrary to the heroic portrait of Newton offered by Brewster, De Morgan's examination is a more realistic depiction, critical of the flaws of Newton's character and behavior, particularly to his niece. De Morgan helped to initiate a more human and complex view of Newton that has dominated many treatments of his life ever since De Morgan's books were published.

Lerner, Aaron B. *Einstein and Newton: A Comparison of Two Great Scientists.* New York: Lerner, 1973. 234pp. Lerner's dual biography contrasts the lives, characters, and contributions of the two scientists. Particularly useful in explaining Einstein's debt and challenge to Newtonian physics.

More, Louis T. *Isaac Newton: A Biography.* New York: Scribner, 1934. 675pp. More's lengthy and detailed critical study is based on extensive research in the Portsmouth collection of Newton's personal and unpublished papers and is broadened by the author's expertise in the history of science. Cogently and lucidly presented, More's is an insightful and balanced portrait, now superseded by later studies incorporating more recent research.

White, Michael. *Isaac Newton: The Last Sorcerer.* Reading, Massachusetts: Addison-Wesley, 1997. 402pp. White's revisionist intellectual biography widens the view of Newton by attending to elements in his character and work that challenge the popular conception of the pure scientist. White shows that Newton was a practicing alchemist and a student of biblical prophecy, astrology, numerology, and natural magic. The book traces the connections between the occult and Newton's scientific achievements and personal eccentricities.

Recommended Juvenile Biographies

Anderson, Margaret J. *Isaac Newton: The Greatest Scientist of All Time.* Springfield, New Jersey: Enslow, 1996. 128pp. MG/YA. Newton the man is presented with extensive details about his personal habits and human eccentricities and flaws. His scientific discoveries, however, receive less satisfactory attention. The book does includes a number of experiments that help readers understand the scientific principles Newton studied.

Christianson, Gale E. *Isaac Newton and the Scientific Revolution.* New York: Oxford University Press, 1996. 155pp. YA. Christianson, the author of a valuable adult biography of Newton, animates the scientist's personality and work by concentrating on the pivotal events in his life, including his upbringing, education, discoveries, and setbacks. Newton's achievement is placed in its scientific and historical context.

Maury, Jean-Pierre. *Newton: The Father of Modern Astronomy.* New York: Abrams, 1992. 143pp. MG/YA. In a lively summary of Newton's life and work, the scientist's achievement as a physicist and astronomer is discussed, with many useful illustrations.

Biographical Films and Theatrical Adaptations

A&E Biography Video: Sir Isaac Newton: The Gravity of Genius (1996). Producer: Peter Doyle. Newton's life, ideas, and achievements are presented in this documentary portrait. Video.

Peter the Great (1986). Directors: Marvin Chomsky and Lawrence Schiller. Television miniseries on the life of Peter the Great (Maximillian Schell) features an appearance by Trevor Howard as Isaac Newton. Video.

Other Sources

Gjertsen, Derek. *The Newton Handbook.* New York: Routledge, 1986. 665pp. More than 500 short entries alphabetically arranged on various aspects of Newton's life and times, including scientific topics, historical background, influences, and contemporaries.

354. NICHOLAS II
1868–1918

The last Russian czar, Nicholas succeeded (1894) his father, Alexander III. An ineffective and autocratic ruler, his suppression of opposition and persecution of religious minorities gave rise to revolutionary movements, including the Social Democratic Labor Party (1898), later divided into the Mensheviks and Bolsheviks. The humiliating Russian defeat in the Russo-Japanese War (1904–1905) led to further revolts and strikes. After the Revolution of 1905, Nicholas granted limited civil rights and called the first elective Duma (parliament), but these reforms were not upheld. The military defeats of World War I, discontent at home, food shortages, and the increasing unpopularity of the czarina, who had filled the court with irresponsible favorites such as the monk, Rasputin, resulted in the 1917 Russian Revolution and the czar's abdication and arrest. In July, 1918, Nicholas and his family were shot to death in a cellar in Ekaterinburg and their bodies burned.

Autobiography and Primary Sources

The Complete Wartime Correspondence of Tsar Nicholas II and the Empress Alexandra: April 1914-March 1917. Joseph T. Fuhrmann, ed. Westport, Connecticut: Greenwood, 1999. 773pp. This is the first complete edition of Nicholas and Alexandra's letters and telegrams written during World War I that offer insights on their relationship and the events that led to the collapse of the czarist regime.

A Lifelong Passion: Nicholas and Alexandra: Their Own Story. Sergei Mironenko and Andrei Maylunas, eds. New York: Doubleday, 1997. 667pp. A selection of letters and private papers of Nicholas, Alexandra, their children, relatives, and confidants, including Nicholas's diary, are arranged chronologically to approximate an autobiographical reflection from 1881 to 1918.

Recommended Biographies

Kurth, Peter. *Tsar: The Lost World of Nicholas and Alexandra.* Boston: Little, Brown, 1995. 229pp. Kurth's beautifully illustrated biography presents a comprehensive overview of the reign and private life of Nicholas, Alexandra, and their family. Evenhanded in its assessment, Kurth's biographical essay is well documented and sensitively written.

Lieven, D.C.B. *Nicholas II: Twilight of the Empire.* New York: St. Martin's, 1994. 292pp. The work of a renowned expert on imperial Russian history, Lieven's authoritative biography emphasizes Nicholas's dual role as emperor and politician. Nicholas's character and motives are fully explained in the context of his times and the various social and political forces he tried unsuccessfully to master.

Massie, Robert. *Nicholas and Alexandra: An Intimate Account of the Last of the Romanovs and the Fall of Imperial Russia.* New York: Atheneum, 1967. 584pp. Massie's intimate history of the royal family focuses on Nicholas and Alexandra's concern over their hemophiliac son as the key for understanding their actions, including the rise to prominence of Rasputin. The book is a marvel of research and historical synthesis that is shaped into an entertaining compelling human drama. In *The Romanovs: The Final Chapter* (New York: Random House, 1995. 308pp.) Massie follows the Romanovs' story beyond 1918 in a gripping historical and forensic search for truth surrounding the

execution and the exposure of the claims of several reputed royal survivors, most notably Anna Anderson, whose assertion that she was their daughter Anastasia was invalidated by DNA testing.

Warth, Robert D. *Nicholas II: The Life and Reign of Russia's Last Monarch.* New York: Greenwood, 1997. 344pp. In a comprehensive political biography, Warth makes use of the 1992 opening of the State Archive of the Russian Federation to present a fresh reassessment of Nicholas's public life. In Warth's view, Nicholas was a conscientious and intelligent ruler whose mistakes stemmed from his stubborn determination to uphold the autocratic tradition.

Other Biographical Studies

Botkin, Gleb. *The Real Romanovs.* New York: F.H. Revell, 1931. 336pp. The author, the son of Nicholas's physician, who was raised in the Romanov court world, provides an intimate, personal view of the royal family and court life. Much of the book's final section is devoted to supporting the claim that Anna Anderson was indeed Anastasia, Nicholas's youngest daughter.

Cowles, Virginia. *The Last Tsar.* New York: Putnam, 1977. 232pp. Cowles's biographical text to accompany a selection of photographs offers little that is new or original but instead is a straightforward account of the court world of the Romanovs, repeating the conventional wisdom of Nicholas's weakness and Alexandra's character flaws.

Ferro, Marc. *Nicholas II: Last of the Tsars.* New York: Oxford University Press, 1993. 305pp. Ferro, a French historian and expert on the Russian Revolution, in a fluently written study, captures Nicholas's personality through letters, diaries, and contemporary accounts. Ferro's apparent acceptance of one of the wilder theories that Nicholas and his family escaped execution and lived out their remaining years in the West undermines the book's overall credibility.

King, Greg. *The Last Empress: Life and Times of Alexandra Feodorovna, Empress of Russia.* Secaucus, New Jersey: Carol, 1994. 431pp. In a popular, sympathetic biography of the consort of Nicholas II, King helps to explain Alexandra's mature behavior by considering in depth her girlhood and early development. Quoting extensively from diaries, letters, and contemporary accounts, King offers a believable portrait of a flawed but compelling human figure.

Lyons, Marvin. *Nicholas II: The Last Tsar.* New York: St. Martin's, 1974. 224pp. With many previous unpublished photographs, Lyons documents Nicholas's life from birth to his captivity and execution. With a minimal text, the illustrations are allowed to tell their own compelling story of a lost royal world.

Perry, John Curtis, and Constantine V. Pleshakov. *The Flight of the Romanovs: A Family Saga.* New York: Basic Books, 1999. 427pp. This group portrait and history of the Romanov family follows members from the 1860s to the 1960s. The book concentrates on the final three czars: Alexander II, Alexander III, and Nicholas II in a balanced and revealing account.

Radzinsky, Edvard. *The Last Tsar: The Life and Death of Nicholas II.* New York: Doubleday, 1992. 475pp. Written by a prominent Russian playwright, Radzinsky devotes two-thirds of the book to an investigation into the events leading up to the execution of Nicholas II and his family, uncovering new details from previously unavailable Soviet sources while employing a dramatist's sense of narrative tension and suspense. The book is less sure-footed on the political and social background of Nicholas's reign.

Richards, Guy. *The Hunt for the Czar.* Garden City, New York: Doubleday, 1970. 265pp. Richards's journalistic account focuses on the final year of Nicholas's reign and the controversy over his and his family's execution. Treated as a real-life intrigue drama, the book asserts that the royal family was rescued by two American secret agents for a life of exile in the West in a dubious version of the facts.

Biographical Novels

Bowen, True. *And the Stars Shall Fall.* New York: Wyn, 1951. 377pp. The life of the last Russian royal family is seen through the experiences of Alexandra who is depicted sympathetically in a reasonably accurate historical account of events.

Gavin, Catherine. *The Snow Mountain.* New York: Pantheon, 1974. 509pp. The final years of the Romanovs are seen from the perspective of Nicholas's eldest daughter in a convincing view with a reliable historical framework.

Hoe, Susanna. *God Save the Tsar.* New York: St. Martin's, 1978. 223pp. Although imagining the escape of the Romanovs from Ekaterinburg, the novel begins with a scrupulously accurate account of what is known of the final days of Nicholas and his family and a plausible reconstruction of their relationships with one another.

Lambton, Antony. *Elizabeth and Alexandra.* New York: Dutton, 1986. 415pp. In a scrupulously researched, factually based account, the novel tells the story of Alexandra's younger sister Elizabeth, who marries Nicholas II's uncle.

Fictional Portraits

Appel, Allen. *Time after Time.* New York: Carroll & Graf, 1985. 377pp. In an inventive time travel story, a young history professor journeys to Russia during the revolution and becomes involved with the fate of the Romanovs.

Borovsky, Natasha. *A Daughter of the Nobility.* New York: Holt, 1985. 500pp. A young Russian woman becomes a friend of Nicholas's children as the events of the Russian Revolution destroy the family.

Butler, Gwendoline. *The Red Staircase.* New York: Coward-McCann, 1979. 431pp. A young woman is hired as a companion to a Russian child, but she is employed to help break the power of Rasputin over the czar's family.

Haskin, Gretchen. *An Imperial Affair.* New York: Dial Press, 1980. 312pp. A Russian prince attempts to rescue the Romanovs from Ekaterinburg in 1917.

Lescroart, John T. *Rasputin's Revenge*. New York: D.I. Fine, 1987. 285pp. In an inventive mystery with authentic period touches, Sherlock Holmes's son is summoned to Russia by Alexandra to root out an assassin who is eliminating the czar's advisers.

Pazzi, Roberto. *Search for the Emperor*. New York: Knopf, 1988. 195pp. This is a fanciful story about an attempt to rescue Nicholas and his family. In *The Princess and the Dragon* (New York: Knopf, 1990. 162pp.) the collapse of Romanov control is glimpsed from the perspective of the Grand Duke George, Nicholas's younger brother.

Solzhenitsyn, Aleksandr. *November 1916: The Red Wheel/Knot II*. New York: Farrar, Straus, 1998. 1,014pp. In the second volume of the author's immense historical panorama, following *August 1914* (1972), Solzhenitsyn chronicles Russia at the outbreak of the revolution with an immense cast of fictional and historical characters, including Nicholas II.

Stevens, R.T. *The Summer Day Is Gone*. Garden City, New York: Doubleday, 1976. 424pp. In this invented tale, a British secret agent ingratiates himself with the Russian royal family in 1911.

Recommended Juvenile Biographies

Vogt, George. *Nicholas II*. New York: Chelsea House, 1987. 116pp. MG/YA. Vogt traces Nicholas's reign and his relationship with his family in this competent biography with a strong historical component.

Biographical Films and Theatrical Adaptations

A&E Biography Video: Rasputin: The Mad Monk (1997). Producer: Thomas Fuchs. This profile of Rasputin traces his relationship with Nicholas II and his family. Video.

A&E Biography Video: Secrets of the Romanovs (1997). Producer: FilmRoos. Producer: Based on previously unavailable archival sources, the story of the final days of Nicholas and his family are depicted using rare footage and interviews. Video.

Anastasia: The Mystery of Anna (1986). Director: Marvin J. Chomsky. Amy Irving portrays the woman who claimed to be the Grand Duchess Anastasia, the sole surviving daughter of Nicholas (Omar Sharif) who relives her experience of her family's murder. Video.

The Last Days of the Last Tsar (1992). Director: Anatoly Ivanov. Mixing dramatic re-creations and newsreel footage, the film documents the exile and execution of Nicholas II and his family. Video.

Last of the Czars (1996). Directors: Mark Anderson and Teresa Cherfas. Featuring never-before-seen film footage and survivor interviews, the end of the Romanov dynasty is presented. Video.

Nicholas and Alexandra (1971). Director: Franklin J. Schaffner. Based on Robert Massie's book, this is an elaborate film chronicle of the final years of Nicholas's reign, with fine performances by Michael Jayston and Janet Suzman in the title roles and an all-star supporting cast, including Laurence

Olivier, Michael Redgrave, Jack Hawkins, and Curt Jurgens. Video.

Rasputin (1985). Director: Elem Klimov. Russian version of Rasputin's relationship with the Romanovs. Video.

Rasputin and the Empress (1933). Director: Richard Boleslawski. Ethel, John, and Lionel Barrymore are together for the first and only time on film in this early film treatment of the Romanovs and the influence of Rasputin. Ralph Morgan depicts Nicholas II. Video.

Rasputin: Dark Servant of Destiny (1996). Director: Uli Edel. Ian McKellen portrays Nicholas and Greta Scacchi is Alexandra in this impressive production filmed in St. Petersburg. The film is dominated by Alan Rickman's haunting portrait of Rasputin. Video.

Rasputin the Mad Monk (1966). Director: Don Sharp. Christopher Lee attempts Rasputin in this version of the Romanovs' story. With Barbara Shelley, Richard Pasco, and Francis Matthews. Video.

Russia's Last Tsar (1994). Director: Robert Kenner. In a National Geographic television special, Nicholas's life and reign are documented using newly discovered photographs and archival film. Video.

Other Sources

Mironenko, Sergei, et al. *Nicholas and Alexandra: The Last Imperial Family of Tsarist Russia*. New York: Abrams, 1998. 400pp. The story of Nicholas and Alexandra is glimpsed through their possessions in a beautifully illustrated display of the imperial family treasures along with chapters on various aspects of their lives and society.

355. FRIEDRICH NIETZSCHE
1844–1900

Influential German philosopher, Nietzsche was born in Prussia, the son of a clergyman. He studied Greek and Latin at Bonn and Leipzig and was appointed (1869) to the chair of classical philology at Basel. He was forced to leave his post (1879) because of nervous disturbances and eye trouble. By 1889, he had suffered a complete mental breakdown. Nietzsche introduced the concept of the "superman," who transcends slavish Christianity and creates a new, heroic morality through his creative "will to power." This concept was misappropriated by the Nazi party in the 1930s and 1940s, who used it to justify their idea of Aryan supremacy. Nietzsche's most famous works include *Thus Spake Zarathustra* (1893–1891) and *Beyond Good and Evil* (1886).

Autobiography and Primary Sources

Ecce Homo: How One Becomes What One Is. New York: Penguin, 1993. 141pp. Written in 1888, only a month before his final collapse into madness, Nietzsche wrote this assessment of his own development. He details the heroes he identified with and struggled against, including Schopenhauer, Wagner, and Christ and clarifies the main tenets of

his beliefs. All is expressed in a mixture of styles and moods.

Nietzsche: A Self-Portrait from His Letters. Peter Fuss and Henry Shapiro, eds. Cambridge, Massachusetts: Harvard University Press, 1971. 196pp. Using excerpts from Nietzsche's letters from 1866 to 1889, the editors arrange a autobiographical profile of the philosopher.

Selected Letters of Friedrich Nietzsche. Christopher Middleton, ed. Chicago: University of Chicago Press, 1969. 370pp. This selection of more than 200 letters emphasizes multiple sides of the philosopher and is a good introduction to many of his ideas and themes that his writings develop.

Recommended Biographies

Hayman, Ronald. *Nietzsche: A Critical Life*. New York: Oxford University Press, 1980. 424pp. Hayman's developmental biography relates the details of Nietzsche's life with his ideas and works in a dramatic, balanced narrative portrait. Hayman makes the often confusing multiplicity of Nietzsche's life and philosophy into an accessible and compelling pattern.

Hollingdale, R.J. *Nietzsche: The Man and His Philosophy*. Baton Rouge: Louisiana State University Press, 1965. 326pp. Written in part to rescue Nietzsche from both his Nazi admirers and detractors, Hollingdale attempts to see the philosopher in the context of his ideas, considering each of his works in relation to his biography and his intellectual development. Well written and balanced, the book helps the reader appreciate Nietzsche in his own terms, allowing him to speak for himself without a distorting agenda from the author.

Kaufman, Walter. *Nietzsche: Philosopher, Psychologist, Antichrist*. Princeton, New Jersey: Princeton University Press, 1950. 409pp. Kaufman, the translator of Nietzsche's works into English, presents a seminal reappraisal of the philosopher's life and work that corrects previous misinterpretations of both. Nietzsche's development is insightfully traced, showing his influences, consistency, and coherence as a thinker.

Other Biographical Studies

Andreas-Salomé, Lou. *Nietzsche*. 1894. Redding Ridge, Connecticut: Black Swan Books, 1988. 168pp. The work of a close companion of Nietzsche during the 1880s, the book offers a number of interesting firsthand observations but is unreliable as a completely factual account of the philosopher's life.

Brinton, Crane. *Nietzsche*. Cambridge, Massachusetts: Harvard University Press, 1941. 266pp. In a short biographical study marred by factual errors and bias, Brinton fails to extract Nietzsche from Naziism, in which he is seen as a inspiration and a symptom of a peculiarly German madness.

Chamberlain, Lesley. *Nietzsche in Turin: An Intimate Biography*. New York: St. Martin's, 1997. 272pp. Limited to Nietzsche's 1888 year in Turin, the last year before his descent into madness, Chamberlain details the philosopher's relationship with Wagner and his private torments in which despair was resisted by an explosive creative energy.

Sympathetic and insightful, Chamberlain's portrait serves to connect Nietzsche's personal experiences with his ideas.

Copleston, Frederick. *Friedrich Nietzsche: Philosopher of Culture.* 1942. Reprint ed. New York: Barnes and Noble, 1975. 273pp. Combining a biographical profile and a critical treatment of Nietzsche's ideas, Copleston achieves a balanced and sympathetic portrait considering the general hostility to the man and his ideas when the book first appeared.

Danto, Arthur C. *Nietzsche as Philosopher.* New York: Macmillan, 1965. 250pp. Viewing Nietzsche's life primarily through his works, Danto attempts to connect all of the philosopher's thinking into a coherent system, resolving contradictions and inconsistencies. Often provocative, Danto makes a strong case for Nietzsche's modern relevance.

Halévy, Daniel. *The Life of Friedrich Nietzsche.* New York: Macmillan, 1911. 368pp. In a clear and balanced early biographical study that is sympathetic to Nietzsche, Halévy does not gloss over the disagreeable aspects of his character.

Mügge, Maximilian A. *Friedrich Nietzsche: His Life and Work.* New York: Brentano's, 1908. 458pp. This early biographical study is one of the first rigorously scholarly works that helped establish the factual record, correcting misconceptions and errors committed by Andreas-Salomé and Nietzsche's sisters.

Nehamas, Alexander. *Nietzsche: Life as Literature.* Cambridge, Massachusetts: Harvard University Press, 1985. 261pp. In an original and challenging interpretation of Nietzsche's ideas and development Nehamas focuses on several paradoxes in the philosopher's view and offers the means to resolve them in a consistent approach to Nietzsche's outlook and temperament.

Pletsch, Carl. *Young Nietzsche Becoming a Genius.* New York: Free Press, 1991. 261pp. Pletsch focuses on Nietzsche's early life and writing and the forces that shaped his development, relying heavily on Freudian analysis. After the trauma of his father's death when Nietzsche was five, the philosopher, in Pletsch's view, sought and rebelled against a series of actual and intellectual fathers. The book is particularly strong on Nietzsche's relationship with Wagner.

Reyburn, H.A. *Nietzsche: The Story of a Human Philosopher.* London: Macmillan, 1946. 499pp. Reyburn's psychological analysis of Nietzsche's life and philosophy traces the sources of his ideas to his personal torments, relying on considerable speculation and conjecture to make his case.

Taylor, Quentin P. *The Republic of Genius: A Reconstruction of Nietzsche's Early Thought.* Rochester, New York: University of Rochester Press, 1997. 288pp. Taylor looks at Nietzsche's early life and writing and the personal, social, cultural, and political influences that shaped his early philosophy.

Biographical Novels

Krell, David F. *Nietzsche: A Novel.* Albany: State University of New York Press, 1996. 364pp. This fictionalized portrait of the philosopher focuses on his sad end after being institutionalized in 1889.

Fictional Portraits

Yalom, Irvin D. *When Nietzsche Wept: A Novel of Obsession* New York: Basic Books, 1992. 306pp. After the breakup of Nietzsche's affair with Lou Salomé, his suicidal despair leads him to a fanciful meeting with pioneering psychiatrist Josef Breuer. As their relationship grows into friendship, the pair discovers that they share much in common. The meeting is invented, but the essential details of the lives of each figure have a strong factual basis.

Biographical Films and Theatrical Adaptations

Wagner (1983). Director: Tony Palmer. Originally a nine-hour British television mini-series, Richard Burton's last film release is a visually stunning but overlong and confusing biographical depiction of the composer's life with Burton in the lead and Vanessa Redgrave as Cosima Wagner. Ronald Pickup portrays Nietzsche. Video.

Other Sources

Magnum, Bernard, and Kathleen M. Higgins, eds. *The Cambridge Companion to Nietzsche.* New York: Cambridge University Press, 1996. 403pp. Useful for the first-time reader and specialist, this collection of critical essays explores various aspects of Nietzsche's life, ideas, and works.

356. FLORENCE NIGHTINGALE
1823–1910

English nurse and the founder of modern nursing, Nightingale studied with the nursing sisters of St. Vincent de Paul and at the institute for Protestant deaconesses in Kaiserswirth, Germany. In 1854, during the Crimean War, she was asked by the British government to recruit and train nurses to tend wounded soldiers. She sailed with 38 nurses to Scutari, where she improved sanitary conditions and discipline in two large army hospitals. Known as "The Lady with the Lamp," Nightingale had become a legend by the war's end. She established (1860) the Nightingale School and Home for training nurses in London and was the first woman awarded the British Order of Merit (1907).

Autobiography and Primary Sources

Ever Yours, Florence Nightingale: Selected Letters. Martha Vicinus and Bea Nergaard, eds. Cambridge, Massachusetts: Harvard University Press, 1990. 461pp. This selection of Nightingale's correspondence includes thoughtful, linking biographical essays that put her letters in the context of her activities and achievements. The woman behind the legend emerges clearly and instructively.

Florence Nightingale: Letters and Reflections. Rosemary Hartill, ed. Harrisberg, Pennsylvania: Morehouse, 1997. 160pp. In a useful collection of Nightingale's letters and writings a very different impression of the reformer emerges that serves to humanize her and challenges the conventional wisdom of her saintliness.

"I Have Done My Duty": Florence Nightingale in the Crimean War, 1854-56. Sue M. Goldie, ed. Iowa City: University of Iowa Press, 1987. 326pp. This collection of Nightingale's correspondence from the Crimea offers a fascinating self-portrait during her most challenging period and an alternative view of Nightingale that strongly contrasts with the mythical figure she became in popular imagination.

Letters from Egypt. Anthony Sattin, ed. London: Weidenfeld & Nicolson, 1987. 223pp. Nightingale's letters home during her five-month tour of Egypt in 1849–1950 has been described as the "best personal travel account of Egypt ever written."

Nightingale's writings are available in several volumes that illuminate her experiences, ideas, and attitudes. See particularly *Notes on Nursing: What It Is and What It Is Not.* 1860. (Reprint ed. New York: Dover, 1969. 140pp.); *"Cassandra" and Other Selections from Suggestions for Thought.* Mary Poovey, ed. (New York: New York University Press, 1993. 244pp.); and *Suggestions for Thought: Selections and Commentaries.* Janet A. MacRae, ed. (Philadelphia: University of Pennsylvania Press, 1994. 218pp.).

Recommended Biographies

Cook, Sir Edward. *The Life of Florence Nightingale.* London: Macmillan, 1913. 2 vols. Cook's official biography remains the most comprehensive, authoritative source on Nightingale's life, making full use of the extensive private archive that he had access to for the first time. Her Crimean experience is rightly regarded as the starting point for more valuable contributions. Well balanced and critical, Cook details Nightingale's achievements without glossing over her contradictions and failings.

Hobbs, Colleen A. *Florence Nightingale.* New York: Twayne, 1997. 110pp. Hobbs's insightful critical study of Nightingale's writings, including both her published and unpublished works on travel and nursing, her letters, and spiritual autobiography captures the complexity of her ideas and relates them to her life and accomplishments.

Small, Hugh. *Florence Nightingale: Avenging Angel.* New York: St. Martin's, 1999. 221pp. Drawing on previously unavailable sources, Small presents a revisionist view of Nightingale that challenges many conventional depictions of her life and her achievement. Arguing that Nightingale's breakdown following the Crimean War was not neurosis but guilt over the death of so many in wartime hospitals, Small adds depth to our view of Nightingale as a person and her relationships.

Woodham-Smith, Mrs. Cecil. *Florence Nightingale 1820–1910.* New York: McGraw-Hill, 1951. 372pp. Based on extensive research in primary material, Woodham-Smith delivers a lively, well-balanced, and readable narrative synthesis of multiple sources. Not as authoritative or as detailed as Cook, Woodham-Smith's more succinct account will appeal to the general reader.

Other Biographical Studies

Andrews, Mary R.S. *A Lost Commander: Florence Nightingale*. Garden City, New York: Doubleday, 1929. 299pp. Andrews's sentimental account of Nightingale's life is written to contrast with Strachey's more realistic portrait that underscores her saintly achievements. Indulging in a number of imaginary conversations and scenes, the book is not fully reliable but does provide many quotations from Nightingale's letters and contemporaries' recollections.

Dossey, Barbara M. *Florence Nightingale: Mystic, Visionary, Reformer*. Springhouse, Pennsylvania: Springhouse Corp., 1999. 350pp. Serves as an authoritative reference source on Nightingale's life, her family background, her war service, and health care theories and practices.

Goldsmith, Margaret L. *Florence Nightingale: The Woman and the Legend*. London: Hodder and Stoughton, 1937. 320pp. In an undocumented popular account based mainly on Cook, Goldsmith provides a balanced, unsentimental portrait that serves the general reader well as a reliable introduction to the woman and her era.

Huxley, Elspeth. *Florence Nightingale*. New York: Putnam, 1975. 254pp. Drawing mainly on Cook and Woodham-Smith for her sources, Huxley offers little that is new or original in a straightforward narrative account that serves to make clear the considerable obstacles Nightingale faced from her family and medical profession. Usefully illustrated, the book is a serviceable introduction for the general reader.

Smith, F.B. *Florence Nightingale: Reputation and Power*. New York: St. Martin's, 1982. 216pp. In a carefully researched reassessment, Smith concentrates on Nightingale's methods and relationship with politicians, civil servants, and philanthropists to expose many unflattering aspects of the Nightingale legend and her own self-promotion. Not a full-scale biography, Smith's is a valuable reevaluation of Nightingale's reforms based on a thorough reading of the various Nightingale papers.

Strachey, Lytton. *Eminent Victorians*. New York: Modern Library, 1999. 267pp. Strachey's essay, first published in 1918, attempts to penetrate the various levels of the Nightingale myth to offer a more human, complex, but compelling portrait of the reformer who seems far more believable as an individual than as a saint.

Biographical Novels

Gordon, Richard. *The Private Life of Florence Nightingale*. New York: Atheneum, 1979. 232pp. The discrepancy between Nightingale's public persona and her true character is exposed by a muckraking journalist who manages an unsympathetic and diminished human portrait.

Terrot, Charles. *The Passionate Pilgrim*. New York: Harper,1949. 231pp. The story of Nightingale's efforts to introduce women as nurses in military hospitals during the Crimean War is dramatized in a simplified and idealized presentation within a framework of historical fact.

Fictional Portraits

Holt, Victoria. *Secret for a Nightingale*. Garden City, New York: Doubleday, 1986. 371pp. This historical romance tells the story of a widow who begins a nursing career and works alongside Nightingale in the Crimea.

Perry, Anne. *A Sudden Fearful Death*. New York: Fawcett, 1993. 383pp. In this installment of the author's historical mystery series, William Monk investigates the strangling death of one of Nightingale's nurses in London.

Rayner, Claire. *Bedford Row*. New York: Putnam, 1977. 278pp. In the seventh installment of the author's Performers series, Martha Lackland travels to Scutari during the Crimean War where she encounters Nightingale in her nursing work.

Thorne, Nicola. *Sisters & Lovers*. Garden City, New York: Doubleday, 1981. 589pp. Events and personalities during the Victorian period are seen from the perspectives of three sisters, including a glimpse of Nightingale's work during the Crimean War.

Recommended Juvenile Biographies

Shor, Donnali. *Florence Nightingale*. Englewood Cliffs, New Jersey: Silver Burdett, 1990. 104pp. MG. Part of the What Made Them Great series, this is a clear and straightforward account of Nightingale's life and career.

Siegel, Beatrice. *Faithful Friend: The Story of Florence Nightingale*. New York: Scholastic, 1991. 128pp. MG. Siegel offers a balanced account of Nightingale's career, with an emphasis on the adversity that she faced in trying to improve health care.

Woodham-Smith, Mrs. Cecil. *Lonely Crusader: The Life of Florence Nightingale*. New York: McGraw-Hill, 1951. 255pp. YA. This abridged edition of the author's highly acclaimed adult biography eliminates some of the social and political details and treats Nightingale's later years less fully.

Biographical Films and Theatrical Adaptations

Reid, Edith G. *Florence Nightingale*. New York: Macmillan, 1922. 118pp. Reid's drama treats the significant events of Nightingale's life in a sentimental and lifeless fashion.

Florence Nightingale (1990). Producer: David Wallace. Nightingale's life and work is chronicled through photographs, drawings, and her own words, as well as interviews with authorities on her career and nursing theory. Video.

The Lady of the Lamp (1951). Director: Herbert Wilcox. This heroic biographical film portrays Nightingale's (Anna Neagle) nursing career. Helena Pachard portrays Victoria, with Arthur Young as Gladstone.

The White Angel (1936). Director: William Dieterle. Not reliable as either biography or history, Nightingale's career is dramatized by a miscast Kay Francis in the title role, supported by Halliwell Hobbes as Lord Raglan.

357. RICHARD M. NIXON
1913–1994

The thirty-seventh U.S. president (1969–1974), Nixon was born into a Quaker family in Yorba Linda, California. He graduated from Whittier College (1934) and received his law degree from Duke University (1937). After serving in World War II, he was elected to the House of Representatives (1946, 1948) and the Senate (1950). He first achieved prominence as a member of the House Un-American Activities Committee investigating alleged communists. Nixon was elected vice president (1952, 1956) in the Eisenhower administration but lost the 1960 presidential election to John F. Kennedy and failed to win the governorship of California (1963). He defeated (1968) Hubert Humphrey for the presidency and was reelected in 1972. He began a gradual withdrawal from Vietnam but ordered invasions of Cambodia and Laos (1970), the bombing of Hanoi, and the mining of Haiphong Harbor (1972). He pursued détente with the USSR and was the first president to visit China (1972). The Watergate scandal and the resulting impeachment hearings led to his resignation from office. He was pardoned by his successor, Gerald Ford. He retired to write his memoirs and other books, and in his later years emerged as an elder statesman.

Autobiography and Primary Sources

In the Arena: A Memoir of Victory, Defeat, and Renewal. New York: Simon & Schuster, 1990. 384pp. Nixon's final retrospective on his career in which he settles old scores and refights old battles is an often rambling but revealing look at the man and his preoccupations. Admirers and opponents will each find much to sustain their positions.

Leaders. New York: Warner Books, 1982. 371pp. Biographical profiles of a wide selection of world leaders, including De Gaulle, MacArthur, Khrushchev, Zhou Enlai, Anwar el-Sadat, and Golda Meir, enlivened by Nixon's description of his personal encounters with them.

RN: The Memoirs of Richard Nixon. New York: Grosset & Dunlap, 1978. 1,120pp. Informative, though selective and rarely self-revealing, Nixon's account is mostly based on his appointment diary, in which he provides his version of the events during his presidency.

Six Crises. Garden City, Garden City, New York: Doubleday, 1962. 460pp. Nixon reveals his thoughts on such personal and professional challenges as the Hiss case, the 1952 fund scandal, Eisenhower's 1955 heart attack, Nixon's 1958 trip to Caracas, his 1959 meetings with Khrushchev, and the 1960 election campaign.

Recommended Biographies

Ambrose, Stephen E. *Nixon*. New York: Simon & Schuster, 1987–1991. 3 vols. Ambrose's absorbing, straightforward narrative chronology is the most comprehensive factual record of Nixon's life and career. The book fairly displays both sides of Nixon, the personality details that brought about his downfall as well as his domestic and foreign policy successes, but Ambrose devotes less attention to analysis and interpretation than to set the basic record straight in an unbiased, objective manner and allows readers to reach their own conclusions.

Brodie, Fawn M. *Richard Nixon: The Shaping of His Character*. New York: W.W. Norton, 1981. 574pp. Brodie's is the most factually reliable of the several psychological studies of Nixon. As its subtitle indicates, the author investigates Nixon's development, particularly strong on his early years and political career. The study takes Nixon's story to 1963 with only a chapter on his later years.

Morris, Roger. *Richard Milhous Nixon: The Rise of an American Politician*. New York: Holt, 1990. 1,005 pp. In the first of a projected three-volume biography, Morris narrates Nixon's development and early political career up to the 1952 election. Excellently researched, authoritative in its details, and fresh in its insights, Morris amasses impressive data into a compelling, human story that brings the reader closer than any other study to an understanding of a complex individual's formative years.

Parmet, Herbert S. *Richard Nixon and His America*. Boston: Little, Brown, 1990. 775pp. Parmet places Nixon's life and career in the context of social and intellectual history in a sympathetic reappraisal. The book follows the suggestion of the author that history will be kinder to Nixon's strengths and achievements. While critical of Nixon's early campaigns and mixed presidential record, Parmet offers a less shadowy, less complicated, and tormented figure, stressing his rise over his fall (Watergate is covered in only six pages at the book's close).

Other Biographical Studies

Abrahamsen, David. *Nixon vs. Nixon: An Emotional Tragedy*. New York: Simon & Schuster, 1977. 267pp. The author, a psychoanalyst, provides a clinical evaluation of Nixon whose self-destructive contradictions reveal a severe character disorder. Based on an analysis of Nixon's writings, public statements, and interviews, Abrahamsen offers a number of interesting insights into Nixon's behavior and motivation, and is far less strident and sensational than other psychohistories of the man, but the author is too far removed from his patient to offer a fully reliable, believable diagnosis.

Aitken, Jonathan. *Nixon: A Life*. Washington, DC: Regnery, 1993. 633pp. The first biography written with Nixon's full cooperation, Aitken's study features access to previously sealed private papers and extensive interviews that shed considerable fresh light on Nixon's personality and career development, even as the core of the man eludes him.

Anson, Robert S. *Exile: The Unquiet Oblivion of Richard M. Nixon*. New York: Simon & Schuster, 1984. 360pp. This objective journalistic account of Nixon's life from his resignation to his seventieth birthday in 1983 chronicles the process of Nixon's rehabilitation based on extensive interviews, though not with Nixon himself. Scrupulous in its research, this is a valuable summary of the decade following Nixon's fall from power.

Cavan, Sherri. *20th Century Gothic: America's Nixon*. San Francisco: Wigan Pier Press, 1979. 330pp. The author seeks a sociohistorical explanation of Nixon's character and career as expressed in his dichotomous, gothic outlook of the struggle between the forces of good and evil. Like Wills, Cavan uses her portrait of Nixon to explore wider themes concerning the American character and the Nixonian era.

Costello, William. *The Facts about Nixon: An Unauthorized Biography*. New York: Viking, 1960. 306pp. Based on a careful examination of the public record, Costello concentrates on Nixon's campaigns while vice president to present a devastating indictment of Nixon's deceit and ruthlessness. Objective yet critical without hostility, Costello adds to the biographical record essential details of Nixon's strengths and flaws as a politician, even as the core of his personality remains elusive.

De Toledano, Ralph. *Nixon*. 1956. Revised ed. New York: Duell, Sloan and Pearce, 1960. 250pp.; *One Man Alone: Richard Nixon*. New York: Funk & Wagnalls, 1969. 386pp. Both of the author's biographical studies are unapologetic defenses of Nixon's character and public career. Preaching mainly to the converted among Nixon's supporters, De Toledano rewrites history at several important stages in Nixon's career to diminish the negatives that a more objective, critical study must acknowledge.

Gellman, Irwin F. *The Contender: Richard Nixon: The Congress Years, 1946–1952*. New York: Free Press, 1999. 590pp. Focusing on Nixon's first congressional race to his vice presidential nomination in 1952, the author refutes the charges against him as an unprincipled opportunist and the non-factually supported tenets of the conventional anti-Nixon myth. Avoiding consideration of Nixon's personality, the book concentrates on his public career in a challenging revision of accepted wisdom regarding Nixon's political beginnings, drawing exclusively on primary, archival sources.

Henderson, Charles P. *The Nixon Theology*. New York: Harper & Row, 1972. 210pp. Henderson's psychological and moral analysis of Nixon's beliefs and development attempts to solve the enigma of his character by demonstrating his attempt to reconcile his religious faith with his contradictory personal experience. In Henderson's view Nixon misappropriated religious values into a strident patriotism and defense of his own political ends.

Hoyt, Edwin P. *The Nixons: An American Family*. New York: Random House, 1972. 307pp. This admiring genealogical study traces Nixon's ancestors through critical periods of American history such as the American Revolution and Civil War. Nixon's own life is presented in glowing terms from his childhood to the presidency.

Keogh, James. *This Is Nixon*. New York: Putnam, 1956. 191pp. This early complimentary campaign biography was intended to address the charges of Nixon's opponents that he lacked principles and convictions. Using Nixon's own words to complement a review of his political record, Keogh presents a portrait of the man too perfect to be credible.

Kornitzer, Bela. *The Real Nixon: An Intimate Biography*. Chicago: Rand McNally, 1960. 352pp. The book focuses on Nixon's family background and early influences on his development. Ignoring the more unflattering and controversial aspects of Nixon's character and career, Kornitzer's highly burnished heroic portrait is chiefly valuable for the domestic details of Nixon's personal life.

Lurie, Leonard. *The Running of Richard Nixon*. New York: Coward-McCann, 1972. 409pp. In a highly critical examination, Lurie traces Nixon's development from childhood through his first term, accumulating damning evidence that supports the book's thesis that Nixon was completely lacking in principles and honesty, driven by political expediency and a lust for power. Confirmed Nixon opponents will no doubt agree, but the book's lack of objectivity limits its reliability and thoroughness.

Mazlish, Bruce. *In Search of Nixon: A Psychohistorical Inquiry*. New York: Basic Books, 1972. 187pp. Mazlish's brief psychological sketch by a history professor serves to unite the private and public sides of Nixon's character in a restrained but still thesis-dominated Freudian reading, drawn from Nixon's own writings and speeches as well as secondary sources. Without more intimate access, Mazlish's interpretation is intriguing but unverifiable.

Mazo, Earl. *Richard Nixon: A Political and Personal Portrait*. New York: Harper, 1959. 309pp. Based on numerous interviews with Nixon and his friends and enemies, Mazo offers a psychological portrait and an examination of his political career. Although ultimately fair and sympathetic, Mazo does not gloss over the less flattering and damning charges and concludes that Nixon lacked core political convictions.

Mazo, Earl, and Stephen Hess. *Nixon: A Political Portrait*. New York: Harper & Row, 1968. 326pp. This is an update of Mazo's earlier book, adding eight new chapters bringing Nixon's story up to his second presidential campaign. Like the previous book, the authors are balanced in their assessment, granting both Nixon's achievements and strengths as well as his failures and flaws.

Small, Melvin. *The Presidency of Richard Nixon*. Lawrence: University Press of Kansas, 1999. 387pp. Arranged topically, Small's evaluative study of the Nixon administration is a balanced assessment based on fresh archival sources.

Spalding, Henry D. *The Nixon Nobody Knows*. Middle Village, New York: J. David, 1972. 456pp. A flattering appreciation that stresses a warm and sympathetic man misunderstood by his critics. Nixon's childhood and early political career, particularly the Alger Hiss case, are covered but with an emphasis on Nixon's unblemished heroic qualities as befits a campaign biography.

Sulzberger, C.L. *The World and Richard Nixon*. New York: Prentice-Hall, 1987. 269pp. Nixon's foreign policy achievements are the focus in this assessment of the Nixon presidency based on extensive interviews with the former president and world leaders. Sulzberger concludes that Nixon should be seen as an adept and farsighted statesman who made an important historical contribution to American foreign policy.

Volkan, Vamik, Norman Itzkowitz, and Andrew Dod. *Richard Nixon: A Psychobiography*. New York: Columbia University Press, 1997. 190pp. Based on extensive interviews with Nixon intimates, the authors explore the development of Nixon's complex psyche in a psychobiography that draws useful connections between his unconscious and emotional make-up and his leadership style and actions.

Voorhis, Horace J. *The Strange Case of Richard Nixon*. New York: P.S. Ericksson, 1972. 341pp. Nixon's congressional opponent in 1946 offers his own assessment of the man who defeated him by carefully presenting Nixon's record on a number of political issues as well as a litany of Nixon's campaign abuses and presidential failures.

White, Theodore H. *Breach of Faith: The Fall of Richard Nixon*. New York: Atheneum, 1975. 373pp. In a highly readable journalistic account, White describes the end of the Nixon presidency from Nixon's first reaction to the news of the Watergate burglary to his resignation. Both Nixon admirers and detractors will find their conceptions challenged in this solid reporting effort. Unfortunately White's analysis draws few connections between Nixon's fall and earlier behavior, and his defense of Nixon's men in the White House seems overly generous.

Wicker, Tom. *One of Us: Richard Nixon and the American Dream*. New York: Random House, 1991. 731pp. In an impressionist reassessment of Nixon's life and career and its larger significance, Wicker, a former member of Nixon's "enemies list," rates Nixon as one of the greatest presidents and a representative, compellingly tragic figure. Wicker offers perspectives on both Nixon's underappreciated achievements and his transgressions.

Wills, Garry. *Nixon Agonistes: The Crisis of the Self-Made Man*. Boston: Houghton Mifflin, 1970. 617pp. Wills treats Nixon as symbol in this discursive meditation on American politics and character. In the author's view Nixon is a personification of American "classical liberalism," self-created and ever-adaptive to the expediency of popular opinion. Frequently insightful, Wills uses his interpretation of Nixon's personality and character to examine American values.

Woodstone, Arthur. *Nixon's Head*. New York: St. Martin's, 1972. 248pp. In a savage psychological analysis by a British journalist, selective evidence is arranged with considerable speculation to support a view of Nixon as an unstable, reactionary anal compulsive beset by a punishing self-anger. No attempt has been made here to balance his attack with any mitigation.

Woodward, Bob, and Carl Bernstein. *The Final Days*. New York: Simon & Schuster, 1976. 476pp. Based on extensive unnamed sources, the authors provide a behind-the-scenes look at the final weeks of the Nixon presidency. Lacking the perspective of distance and scholarly thoroughness, the book is at times a riveting narrative of hearsay evidence from unattributed sources and striking vignettes.

Fictional Portraits

Coover, Robert. *The Public Burning*. New York: Viking, 1977. 534pp. Set during the first year of the Eisenhower administration, Coover's political fantasy dealing with the Rosenbergs, features a prominent role for Nixon who reminisces about his early years and is one of the most interesting figures in this dark satire.

Ehrlichman, John. *The China Card*. New York: Simon & Schuster, 1986. 523pp. Ehrlichman's political thriller is woven around the events of Nixon's visit to China and offers an interesting portrait of the author's former boss.

Maxwell, Mark. *Nixoncarver*. New York: St. Martin's, 1998. 178pp. This ingenious fantasy speculates on what might have happened had Nixon met writer Raymond Carver while walking along a California beach and became friends. The inner compulsions of both men are explored.

Roth, Philip. *Our Gang*. New York: Bantam, 1973. 237pp. Roth's acid political satire involves President Nixon in a deadly contest with the Boy Scouts over the abortion issue in which the author flays Nixon, his leadership, and the contemporary political scene.

Recommended Juvenile Biographies

Goldman, Martin S. and John A. Scott. *Richard M. Nixon: The Complex President*. New York: Facts on File, 1998. 146pp. MG/YA. This is an in-depth examination of Nixon's personality and career that manages a sophisticated view of the man and his motivations, and uses Nixon's own words and contemporary sources to make its case.

Larsen, Rebecca. *Richard Nixon: Rise and Fall of a President*. New York: F. Watts, 1991. 189pp. MG. Following the trend among recent adult biography, Larsen puts Watergate in perspective in assessing Nixon's mixed record, emphasizing the positives as well as the negatives. Sympathetic but evenhanded, the book concentrates on the public Nixon but does include some information about his private life.

Nadel, Laurie. *The Great Stream of History: A Biography of Richard M. Nixon*. New York: Atheneum, 1991. 220pp. MG/YA. In a less than objective profile of Nixon's life and political career, Nadel, a producer for *ABC News,* emphasizes the dark side of Nixon's character in a sometimes discursive review of the former president's flaws and failures.

Biographical Films and Theatrical Adaptations

Monsell, Thomas. *Nixon on Stage and Screen: The Thirty-Seventh President as Depicted in Films, Television, Plays, and Opera*. Jefferson, North Carolina: McFarland, 1998. 239pp. Monsell lists the various dramatic presentations that feature Nixon as a character.

Vidal, Gore. *An Evening with Richard Nixon*. New York: Random House, 1972. 157pp. In Vidal's "essay-play," Nixon's own words are used in counterpoint to fictionalized characterizations of Kennedy, Eisenhower, and George Washington as Nixon tells the story of his life.

A&E Biography Video: Richard Nixon: Man and President (1996). Producer: Alan Goldberg. Using rare photographs and interviews with close friends and observers, this is a fresh documentary portrait of Nixon's private and public lives. Video.

Dick (1999). Director: Andrew Fleming. This is a broad but occasionally clever comedy of a pair of high school girls (Kirsten Dunst and Michelle Wil-

liams) who wander away from their White House tour for an encounter with President Nixon (Dan Hedaya) in the midst of the Watergate investigation. Video.

Elvis Meets Nixon (1997). Director: Allan Arkush. Bob Gunton portrays Nixon and Rick Peters is Elvis Presley in this dramatization of the real-life meeting of Elvis with the president. Video.

The Final Days (1989). Director: Richard Pearce. Based on the book by Woodward and Bernstein, this teleplay written by Hugh Whitemore stars Lane Smith as Nixon, Theodore Bikel as Kissinger, David Ogden Stiers, and Ed Flanders. Video.

Kissinger and Nixon (1995). Director: Daniel Petrie. This film, based on Walter Isaacson's *Kissinger: A Biography,* stars Ron Silver and Beau Bridges in the title roles. Video.

Milhous: A White Comedy (1971). Director: Emile de Antonio. A compilation of newsreel and television footage with interviews with various political critics, Nixon's public career is presented from a hostile perspective. Video.

Nixon (1990). Producer: Elizabeth Deane. Originally broadcast as a two-part segment of PBS's American Experience series, this definitive film portrait covers Nixon's life from childhood through his political career up to his resignation from the presidency. Video.

Nixon (1996). Director: Oliver Stone. Although it takes some creative license and incurred the wrath of Nixon's daughters, Stone's biographical portrait is surprisingly sympathetic with a convincing depiction of Nixon by Anthony Hopkins. Also starring Joan Allen as Pat Nixon and Mary Steenburgen as Nixon's mother. Video.

Nixon about Nixon (1994). Producers: Ronald M. Miller and Montgomery G. Jarmain. In a series of filmed interviews, Nixon offers a number of reflections on his career and motives. Video.

Nixon: Checkers to Watergate (1976). Directors: Charles Braverman and Ken Rudolph. In a compilation of archival stills, speeches, interviews, and press conferences, Nixon's public career is documented. Video.

President Richard M. Nixon (1991). Director: Anthony R. Potter. In a taped interview, Nixon discusses his presidency from the perspective of his long political career. Video.

President Richard Nixon—Talking with David Frost (1994). Director: Jorn Winther. In excerpts from 28 hours of recorded interviews taped in 1977, Nixon reflects on his career. Video.

The Real Richard Nixon (1995). Director: Jesse Raiford. A candid, objective film portrait. Video.

Richard Nixon Reflects (1990). Producers: MPI Home Video. In a candid 90-minute interview, Nixon reflects on John F. Kennedy, Bush, Reagan, and Gorbachev, as well as his handling of Watergate. Video.

Secret Honor (1984). Director: Robert Altman. This film version of Philip Baker Hall's one-man stage show features a devastating portrait of a petty tyrant railing against the world and Nixon's perceived betrayal by all. Video.

Other Sources

Bremer, Howard F. *Richard M. Nixon: Chronology, Documents, and Bibliographical Aids.* Dobbs Ferry, New York: Oceana, 1975. 252pp. Bremer supplies a useful chronology of the important events in Nixon's life, along with a selection of documents and an annotated listing of works about him.

Strober, Gerald S., and Deborah H. *Nixon: An Oral History of His Presidency.* New York: HarperCollins, 1994. 576pp. Interviews with many individuals involved in the Nixon administration and with critics are topically arranged to form a balanced portrait of Nixon the man and politician during his presidency.

358. GEORGIA O'KEEFFE
1887–1986

American painter, O'Keeffe was born in Sun Prairie, Wisconsin, and worked as a commercial artist in Chicago before studying abstract design with A. W. Dow in New York. She then taught art in a Texas school. Her first exhibition (1916) was at a New York gallery, 291, owned by photographer Alfred Stieglitz, whom she married (1924). She lived much of her life in New Mexico. Known for her flower paintings and Southwestern motifs, O'Keeffe turned to abstract designs in her later years. Her works include *Black Iris* (1926) and *Cow's Skull: Red, White, and Blue* (1931).

Autobiography and Primary Sources

Georgia O'Keeffe. New York: Viking, 1976. 250pp. Although not an autobiography, the artist offers a selection of her works with commentary. Guarded in her personal revelations (there is no mention made to her marriage to Stieglitz for example), O'Keeffe nevertheless is direct, witty, and at times acerbic in detailing the inspiration for her work, her artistic progress, and her attitudes.

Georgia O'Keeffe: Art and Letters. Jack Cowart, Juan Hamilton, and Sarah Greenough, eds. Boston: Little, Brown, 1989. 306pp. The catalog for the National Gallery of Art's retrospective following O'Keeffe's death includes many color reproductions, a chronology, and critical commentary on aspects of the artist's life and work, as well as a selection of 125 letters.

Lovingly, Georgia: The Complete Correspondence of Georgia O'Keeffe and Anita Pollitzer. New York: Simon & Schuster, 1990. 365pp. This record of O'Keeffe's friendship with Pollitzer covers most of the artist's life from her student days and includes revealing insights about her character and ideas not available in any other source.

Recommended Biographies

Lisle, Laurie. *Portrait of an Artist: A Biography of Georgia O'Keeffe*. 1980. Revised ed. Albuquerque: University of New Mexico Press, 1986. 408pp. O'Keeffe's first biographer, Lisle revised and expanded her earlier life to bring the artist's story to her death in 1986. Competent and work-

manlike, Lisle corrects the factual record, and her account remains one of the most comprehensive documentations of O'Keeffe's personal life and artistic development.

Robinson, Roxana. *Georgia O'Keeffe: A Life*. New York: Harper & Row, 1989. 639pp. Making full use of extensive primary sources unavailable during O'Keeffe's lifetime and interviews, Robinson's life has established itself as the definitive study. The complexity of the artist's character is displayed from a decidedly feminist perspective that traces her influences and originality with skill and perceptiveness.

Other Biographical Studies

Castro, Jan G. *The Art and Life of Georgia O'Keeffe*. New York: Crown, 1985. 192pp. With reproductions of more than 100 paintings and photographs by the artist, this handsome visual study features a critical and biographical text documented with letters and interviews that introduces the general reader to the artist's genius and personality.

Eisler, Benita. *O'Keeffe and Stieglitz: An American Romance*. New York: Doubleday, 1991. 546pp. Using unpublished letters and papers as well as interviews with associates, Eisler chronicles in intimate detail the 26-year relationship between O'Keeffe and photographer Alfred Stieglitz. The interlocking careers of both figures are displayed with revelations about their troubled life together.

Hoffman, Katherine. *An Enduring Spirit: The Art of Georgia O'Keeffe*. Metuchen, New Jersey: Scarecrow Press, 1984. 185pp. In a critical study of O'Keeffe's artistry, Hoffman's analysis is arranged chronologically, with the connection between her life and her art established, based mainly on secondary sources. Offering little that is fresh and original, Hoffman's brief examination serves as a basic introduction to the artist and her work.

Hogrefe, Jeffrey. *O'Keeffe: The Life of an American Legend*. New York: Bantam, 1992. 376pp. Hogrefe's anecdote-rich biography focuses on O'Keeffe's intimate, private life, alleging early sexual abuse as the key to understanding her later relationships. Less thorough than selective, with an emphasis on the sensational, the book offers a pro-

vocative perspective on the artist's life, but should be read as an adjunct to the more authoritative efforts of Lisle and Robinson.

Patten, Christine T., and Alvaro Cardona-Hine. *Miss O'Keeffe*. Albuquerque: University of New Mexico Press, 1992. 201pp. Patten, a nurse and companion to the artist during her final years, offers a glimpse of O'Keeffe's daily life when she could no longer see well enough to paint.

Peters, Sarah W. *Becoming O'Keeffe: The Early Years*. New York: Abbeville Press, 1991. 397pp. Limited to the period between 1915 and 1930, Peters's study is strong on the artist's influences, development, and essential artistic beliefs and style. Meticulously researched, the book serves to place O'Keeffe within her larger artistic context. It is less satisfactory in its speculation about O'Keeffe's personal motivations and feelings.

Pollitzer, Anita. *A Woman on Paper: Georgia O'Keeffe*. New York: Simon & Schuster, 1988. 290pp. Originally begun with O'Keeffe's cooperation, which she later withdrew, charging the author with romanticizing her life, Pollitzer's biography is primarily an anecdotal memoir of their friendship and an appreciation of the artist's talent rather than a thorough, factual record of O'Keeffe's life. Best on their early friendship between 1914 and 1917.

Recommended Juvenile Biographies

Berry, Michael. *Georgia O'Keeffe*. New York: Chelsea House, 1988. 111pp. MG/YA. Part of the American Women of Achievement series, this is a candid summary of O'Keeffe's life and artistry that deals honestly with the artist's relationships.

Gherman, Beverly. *Georgia O'Keeffe: The Wildness and Wonder of Her World*. New York: Atheneum, 1986. 131pp. MG/YA. Gherman's intimate appreciation of O'Keeffe's genius includes a basic summary of the highlights of the artist's life.

Nicolson, Lois. *Georgia O'Keeffe*. San Diego: Lucent Books, 1995. 112pp. MG. Well documented and organized, Nicolson's biography includes quotations from a variety of primary sources. Unfortunately, the reproductions of her works are not in color.

Biographical Films and Theatrical Adaptations

Georgia O'Keeffe (1977). Director: Perry M. Adato. This PBS broadcast explores O'Keeffe's life and works through an examination of her paintings, environment, and philosophy. Video.

Susan B. Anthony Slept Here (1995). Director: Alvin Cooperman. Written by Lynn Sherr this documentary looks at the lives and places associated with seven famous American women, including O'Keeffe. Video.

Other Sources

Merrill, Christopher, and Ellen Bradbury, eds. *From the Faraway Nearby: Georgia O'Keeffe As Icon.* Reading, Massachusetts: Addison-Wesley, 1992. 293pp. This collection considers O'Keeffe's art and life from the perspective of her public image through memoirs, poetry, photographs, and essays.

359. JACQUELINE BOUVIER KENNEDY ONASSIS
1929–1994

One of the most stylish and idolized of American first ladies, Onassis was born into a socially prominent family in Southampton, New York. She attended Vassar and the Sorbonne, and worked (1951–1953) as a journalist and photographer before marrying (1953) John F. Kennedy. As first lady, she planned and directed the restoration of the White House and had Congress declare the building a national museum. She retired from public life after President Kennedy's assassination and in 1968 married Greek shipping tycoon Aristotle Onassis. After his death (1975), she lived mainly in New York and worked as a book editor.

Autobiography and Primary Sources

The Uncommon Wisdom of Jacqueline Kennedy Onassis: A Portrait in Her Own Words. Bill Adler, ed. New York: Carol, 1994. 156pp. Adler collects quotes from Onassis in a helpful volume that gives voice to the often elusive and private figure.

Recommended Biographies

Birmingham, Stephen. *Jacqueline Bouvier Kennedy Onassis.* New York: Grosset & Dunlap, 1978. 242pp. In a credible psychological analysis of Onassis's character and development, Birmingham traces her life from childhood with an emphasis on the major events that shaped her: her parents' divorce, her schooling, and her two marriages. Admiring but restrained in its handling of Onassis's private life, Birmingham's study is far from authoritative and scholarly but a distinct improvement over the typical celebrity tell-all.

Ladowsky, Ellen. *Jacqueline Kennedy Onassis.* New York: Random House, 1997. 208pp. This is a fresh appreciation of Jacqueline Onassis that locates her uniqueness in her ambition, intelligence, and determined fight for the safety and security of her family and herself. Regarded as important in her own right, not just as a spouse and mother, Onassis is revealed in compelling human terms.

Spoto, Donald. *Jacqueline Bouvier Kennedy Onassis: A Life.* New York: St. Martin's, 2000. 348pp. Spoto is skeptical of the more lurid revelations of other biographies and offers a more restrained, complex, and human portrait that is far more believable than most other treatments, despite an occasional lack of critical distance and objectivity.

Other Biographical Studies

Andersen, Christopher P. *Jack and Jackie: Portrait of an American Marriage.* New York: Morrow, 1996. 400p. Filled with anecdotes and gossip, this treatment of the couple's relationship based on interviews provides few lurid details and manages an unexpectedly sympathetic view of both figures. The lives of both prior to their marriage are briefly sketched. In *Jackie After Jack: Portrait of the Lady.* (New York: Morrow, 1998. 472pp.) the author continues Onassis's story during the three decades following JFK's assassination in a tell-all that mixes documented fact and a great deal of unattributed assertions.

David, Lester. *Jacqueline Kennedy Onassis: A Portrait of Her Private Years.* Secaucus, New Jersey: Carol, 1994. 242pp. Davis's chronicle of Onassis's years after her marriage to Aristotle Onassis includes a number of revisionist revelations about her relationship with John Kennedy, most notably that she possessed a deep interest in politics and edited the president's speeches. The book's primary value rests in its many details of Onassis's daily routine and personal habits.

Davis, John H. *Jacqueline Bouvier: An Intimate Memoir.* New York: Wiley, 1996. 208pp. Written by Onassis's cousin, Davis's account covers Onassis's life up to her marriage to John Kennedy. Davis's many anecdotes and personal details are narrated with an evident bias against Onassis's mother.

Heymann, C. David. *A Woman Named Jackie.* Secaucus, New Jersey: Carol, 1989. 715pp. This book is rarely much more than a superficial catalog of Onassis's personal failings in a jumble of insignificant, reheated gossip, intimate details from dubious sources, and farfetched conjecture.

Kelley, Kitty. *Jackie Oh!* Secaucus, New Jersey: L. Stuart, 1978. 352pp. Very much a sensational tell-all in a heap of facts, gossip, and rumors, Kelley dishes the dirt on Onassis's marriages in a tabloid style with no effort to separate the real from the invented, with imagined dialogue and characterizations that carry little believability.

Klein, Edward. *All Too Human: The Love Story of Jack and Jackie Kennedy.* New York: Simon & Schuster, 1996. 406pp. In a somewhat breathless, journalistic account, the couple's relationship is detailed in a blend of fact, gossip, rumor, and conjecture with imagined conversations and dramatized episodes. In *Just Jackie: Her Private Years* (New York: Ballantine Books, 1998. 399pp.) Klein supplies an anecdotal mix of alleged intimate facts and quotes from a wide assortment of friends and associates.

Koestenbaum, Wayne. *Jackie Under My Skin: Interpreting an Icon.* New York: Farrar, Straus, 1995. 291pp. The author treats Onassis as a symbol and complex "text" to be deconstructed. The result is a mixed bag of meditations of Onassis's significance as a cultural icon. Although not a chronological biographical study, events and details of Onassis's life are probed for their deeper significance. Less illuminating than reflective of the author's own obsessions and pretensions.

Leamer, Laurence. *The Kennedy Women: The Saga of an American Family.* New York: Villard Books, 1994. 933pp. Leamer's group portrait of the Kennedy daughters and spouses is a thorough and reasonably restrained series of character sketches that provides an important context for viewing Onassis's relationship with the Kennedy clan.

Lowe, Jacques. *Jacqueline Kennedy Onassis: The Making of a First Lady.* Los Angeles: General Publishing Group, 1999. 128pp. This book of photographs accompanied by a brief text provides a stunning visual record of Onassis's married life to John Kennedy.

Osborne, Claire G. *Jackie: A Legend Defined.* New York: Avon, 1997. 181pp. This is a largely sympathetic collection of facts about the life of Jacqueline Kennedy Onassis covering her private and public life but without the sensational revelations of other tell-alls.

Taraborrelli, J. Randy. *Jackie, Ethel, Joan: Women of Camelot.* New York: Warner Books, 2000. 528pp. This group portrait of the Kennedy wives looks at the private lives of the three women, their relationships, and the burden of being members of the Kennedy clan.

Thayer, Mary Van Rensselaer. *Jacqueline Bouvier Kennedy.* Garden City, New York: Doubleday, 1962. 127pp. A brief, anecdotal early biographical portrait, Thayer's treatment is excessively admiring with an emphasis on her subject's glamorous image. *Jacqueline Kennedy: The White House Years.* Boston: Little, Brown, 1971. 362pp. Covers Onassis's life as the First Lady in a factual chronicle that enjoyed the subject's cooperation and the use of some of her personal files. Not personally revealing, the book is more the record of Onassis's career as White House hostess and redecorator.

Fictional Portraits

Preston, Caroline. *Jackie by Josie.* New York: Scribner, 1997. 314pp. This comic novel concerns a young woman who takes a job as a research assistant for a celebrity biographer rushing out an Onassis book shortly after her death. As the heroine deals with her own unfaithful husband, she learns important lessons from Onassis on dealing with a charming philandering spouse.

Recommended Juvenile Biographies

Anderson, Catherine C. *Jacqueline Kennedy Onassis: Woman of Courage.* Minneapolis: Lerner, 1995. 88pp. MG. Often excessively admiring, Anderson makes a strong case for Onassis's courage, grace, and strength in the face of adversity in this recounting of her life story, although the true dimension of her adversity is not revealed in full.

Capeci, Anne. *Meet Jacqueline Kennedy Onassis.* New York: Random House, 1995. 93pp. MG. This is an easy-to-read profile that covers Onassis's

White House years, publishing career, and relationship with her children.

Santow, Dan. *Jacqueline Bouvier Kennedy Onassis, 1929–1994.* Danbury, Connecticut: Childrens Press, 1998. 118pp. MG. Sanlow's is an informative profile of Jacqueline Kennedy Onassis that helps to explain the nature of her mystique and hold on people's imagination.

Biographical Films and Theatrical Adaptations

A&E Biography Video: Jacqueline Kennedy Onassis (1995). Director: Maurice Paleau. In a full-length film portrait, Onassis's private life is the focus, from her days as the First Lady through her marriage to Aristotle Onassis and career as a book editor. Video.

The Greek Tycoon (1978). Director: J. Lee Thompson. In a fictionalization clearly based on the Onassis/Kennedy marriage, Jacqueline Bisset and Anthony Quinn portray the famous pair. Video.

Jackie (1995). Director: Charles Furneaux. Onassis's life is traced using rare archival footage, home movies, and interviews with family and friends. Video.

Jackie Onassis: An Intimate Portrait (1993). Producer: Louise M. Gallup. A detailed personality profile focused on Onassis's out-of-the-spotlight life. Video.

Jacqueline Bouvier Kennedy (1981). Director: Steve Gethers. Made-for-television biographical portrait from Onassis's childhood through the White House years. Starring Jaclyn Smith in the title role, with James Franciscus as JFK and James F. Kelly as Robert Kennedy. Video.

Jacqueline Kennedy Onassis (1991). Director: Maurice Paleau. A documentary examination of Onassis's life using archival sources, home movies, and interviews with associates. Video.

Jacqueline Kennedy Onassis Remembered (1994). Producer: CBS News. A commemorative video featuring Onassis in various CBS broadcasts, including a 1960 Person to Person interview and her famous tour of the White House. Video.

Onassis: The Richest Man in the World (1988). Director: Waris Hussein. Based on the novel by Peter Evans, Aristotle Onassis's rise from poverty is depicted with Raul Julia in the title role, Jane Seymour as Maria Callas, and Francesca Annis as Jacqueline Kennedy. Video.

A Woman Named Jackie (1994). Director: Larry Peerle. Based on Heymann's book, this television mini-series casts Roma Downey in the title role, with Stephen Collins as JFK, Tim Ransom as Robert Kennedy, and Joss Ackland as Aristotle Onassis. Video.

Other Sources

Anthony, Carl S. *As We Remember Her: Jacqueline Kennedy Onassis in the Words of Her Family and Friends.* New York: HarperCollins, 1998. 288pp. Based on interviews with Onassis's friends, family, and colleagues, including previously sealed accounts from the Kennedy Library Oral Histories, this collection of reminiscences provides a varied and multidimensional portrait.

See also John F. Kennedy; Robert F. Kennedy

360. EUGENE O'NEILL
1888–1953

Widely considered to be one of America's greatest dramatists, O'Neill was the younger son of a popular actor. After attending Princeton for a year, he worked at a variety of jobs and in 1912 contracted tuberculosis. He began to write plays while convalescing from the disease and from 1914 to 1915 studied playwriting at Harvard. O'Neill's one-act plays were produced by the Provincetown Players in New York. His first full-length play to be produced was *Beyond the Horizon* (1920). O'Neill's body of work is stylistically varied and ambitious in scope and except for the comedy, *Ah, Wilderness!* (1935), inexorably tragic. His plays include *Anna Christie* (1921), *Strange Interlude* (1928), the trilogy *Mourning Becomes Electra* (1931), *The Iceman Cometh* (1946), and his autobiographical masterpiece *Long Day's Journey Into Night* (1956). He received the Nobel Prize in Literature (1936).

Autobiography and Primary Sources

As Ever, Gene: The Letters of Eugene O'Neill to George Jean Nathan. Nancy L. and Eugene L. Roberts, eds. Rutherford, New Jersey: Fairleigh Dickinson University Press, 1987. 248pp. O'Neill's correspondence with the celebrated dramatic critic covers the period from 1919 to 1949 with many revelations about the playwright's creative methods and composition of his plays.

"Love and Admiration and Respect": The O'Neill-Commins Correspondence. Durham, North Carolina: Duke University Press, 1986. 248pp. O'Neill's letters to and from his editor, Saxe Commins, cover the period between 1920 and 1951 and include Commins's memoir of the playwright, which supplies useful biographical information as well as insights into O'Neill's personality and creative method.

Selected Letters of Eugene O'Neill. Travis Bogard and Jackson R. Bryer, eds. New Haven, Connecticut: Yale University Press, 602pp. Essential to understanding O'Neill, this selection of nearly 600 letters, many published for the first time, covers a 50-year period, arranged in chronological sections with a biographical introduction, and provides the closest view a reader can expect to get of the intensely private O'Neill, while contradicting much of the conventional wisdom about the playwright, particularly his intellectual unsophistication and artistic aloofness.

Recommended Biographies

Alexander, Doris. *The Tempering of Eugene O'Neill.* New York: Harcourt, Brace, 1962. 300pp. In a psychological study of O'Neill's family, influences, and intellectual development, separate chapters are devoted to individual family members and figures who had a major impact on O'Neill. Alexander's careful presentation serves as an insightful analysis of the playwright's character and development up to his first success in 1920. In *Eugene O'Neill's Creative Struggle: The Decisive Decade, 1924–1933.* (University Park: Pennsylvania State University Press, 1992. 339pp.), Alexander continues her examination of O'Neill's life from the perspective of his plays. The book shows how O'Neill both consciously and unconsciously incorporated autobiographical experience into his art.

Black, Stephen A. *Eugene O'Neill: Beyond Mourning and Tragedy.* New Haven, Connecticut: Yale University Press, 1999. 543pp. The author, an English professor and a trained psychoanalyst, has crafted a meticulously researched and intelligently written biography that supplies fresh insights into O'Neill's life and work. In the author's view, O'Neill worked through his personal torments by recasting them in his plays, and the book traces the connections between the playwright's experiences and his works.

Gelb, Arthur, and Barbara Gelb. *O'Neill.* 1962. Revised ed. New York: Harper & Row, 1974. 990pp. Based on extensive interviews and archival research, the Gelbs' biography is a detailed and comprehensive gathering of factual material into a readable narrative chronology that relates the dramatist's life to his work and is particularly strong on the literary and theatrical world of O'Neill's time. The authors have begun a complete rewrite and reinterpretation of their earlier biography based on previously unknown or withheld material. The first volume, *O'Neill: Life with Monte Cristo* (New York: Applause, 2000. 758pp.) covers O'Neill's childhood and self-destructive youth and family relations through his first Broadway triumph in 1920.

Sheaffer, Louis. *O'Neill: Son and Playwright.* Boston: Little, Brown, 1968. 543pp.; *O'Neill: Son and Artist.* Boston: Little, Brown, 1973. 750pp. Sheaffer's monumental two-volume biography is scrupulously researched, based on interviews and the fullest use of documentary evidence that has yet been unearthed. Judicious in its interpretation, thoroughly presenting all sides to controversial points, this is biography by accumulation rather than interpretation and synthesis. One controlling theme, however, is contained in the word "son" of Sheaffer's titles, which serves to connect the dramatist's art and life through his attempt to come to terms with his parents and family background.

Other Biographical Studies

Boulton, Agnes. *Part of a Long Story.* Garden City, New York: Doubleday, 1958. 331pp. O'Neill's second wife offers her view of her life with the playwright from 1917 to 1919. By no means a comprehensive treatment of these important years in O'Neill's development, as its title reflects, Boulton's is an uneven, impressionistic recreation of her past with occasionally illuminating immediacy.

Bowen, Croswell. *The Curse of the Misbegotten.* New York: McGraw-Hill, 1959. 384pp. Bowen's group portrait of the O'Neill clan is ruled by his thesis that the family was beset by the curse of emotional coldness. Well documented, with a great deal of family evidence to bolster its somewhat narrow thematic focus, Bowen's study features a number of insights supplied by O'Neill's son, Shane.

Carpenter, Frederic I. *Eugene O'Neill*. New York: Twayne, 1964. 191pp. As an entry in the Twayne Author series, Carpenter's compact critical study supplies a brief biographical sketch and chronology before concentrating on the playwright's artistry.

Clark, Barrett H. *Eugene O'Neill*. New York: McBride, 1926. 110pp.; *Eugene O'Neill: The Man and His Plays*. New York: Dover, 1967. 183pp. Clark, O'Neill's first biographer, supplies an anecdote-rich examination that has an immediacy lacking in more comprehensive and authoritative studies. Clark's 1947 expansion of his first book relies on O'Neill's own letters to him to document O'Neill's years of public silence.

Frenz, Horst. *Eugene O'Neill*. New York: Frederick Ungar, 1971. 121pp. Part of the Modern Literature Monograph series, Frenz's brief presentation of O'Neill's life and critical study of his works serves as a useful introduction.

Leech, Clifford. *Eugene O'Neill*. New York: Grove Press, 1963. 120pp. A compact introductory study, Leech provides the highlights of O'Neill's life and career, as well as a criticism of his works.

Skinner, Richard Dana. *Eugene O'Neill: A Poet's Quest*. New York: Longmans, 1935. 242pp. Skinner's critical study of O'Neill's works is presented as a developmental study of his evolving genius. While establishing a moral and intellectual continuity in O'Neill's works, Skinner's treatment features O'Neill's own compositional chronology, produced at the author's request, that sheds light on his creative method.

Recommended Juvenile Biographies

Coolidge, Olivia E. *Eugene O'Neill*. New York: Scribner, 1966. 223pp. YA. In a compact and informative biographical study, Coolidge assembles the basic facts of O'Neill's life and career along with a summary of his plays and critical attitudes toward the playwright.

Gassner, John. *Eugene O'Neill*. Minneapolis: University of Minnesota Press, 1965. 48pp. YA. Part of the University of Minnesota American Writers pamphlet series written for high school students, Gassner provides a brief summary of O'Neill's life and career and criticism of his works.

Biographical Films and Theatrical Adaptations

Entertaining Angels: The Dorothy Day Story (1996). Director: Michael Ray Rhodes. Moira Kelly portrays Dorothy Day in this film biography, with Martin Sheen as Peter Maurin and James Lancaster as O'Neill. Video.

Eugene O'Neill: 1888–1953 (1996). Director: Malcolm Hossick. The film traces O'Neill's life and literary career using archival photographs and views of places associated with the playwright. Video.

Reds (1981). Director: Warren Beatty. Beatty's romantic epic on the lives of John Reed (Beatty) and Louise Bryant (Diane Keaton) features a striking performance by Jack Nicholson as O'Neill. Video.

Other Sources

Manheim, Michael, ed. *The Cambridge Companion to Eugene O'Neill*. New York: Cambridge University Press, 1998. 256pp. The book presents a collection of essays dealing with various aspects of O'Neill's life and work and his influences and relationship with the theater of his time.

Ranald, Margaret L. *The Eugene O'Neill Companion*. Westport, Connecticut: Greenwood, 1984. 827pp. Along with synopses of the plays and character analyses, this useful reference source features alphabetical biographical entries on many of O'Neill's associates and family members, as well as a detailed chronology.

361. J. ROBERT OPPENHEIMER
1904–1967

American physicist, Julius Robert Oppenheimer headed the Manhattan Project, which developed the first atomic bomb. He strongly opposed construction of the hydrogen bomb on technical and moral grounds but was overruled by President Truman. Chair of the general advisory committee of the U.S. Atomic Energy Commission, he was charged in 1953 with sharing atomic secrets with Soviets and his security clearance was suspended by President Eisenhower. In 1954, a special panel and the AEC judged him innocent of disloyalty but a security risk. In 1963, Oppenheimer received the Atomic Energy Commission's Fermi award for his work in theoretical physics.

Autobiography and Primary Sources

Robert Oppenheimer: Letters and Recollections. Alice K. Smith and Charles Weinar, eds. Cambridge, Massachusetts: Harvard University Press, 1980. 376pp. Combining personal letters with reminiscences of those who knew and worked with Oppenheimer into a coherent narrative, this is an important source of insights into the scientist's complex character.

Recommended Biographies

Goodchild, Peter. *J. Robert Oppenheimer: Shatterer of Worlds*. Boston: Houghton Mifflin, 1980. 301pp. The companion volume for a BBC documentary on Oppenheimer's life, Goodchild's is an excellent overview, well researched and balanced in its assessment.

Other Biographical Studies

Chevalier, Haakron. *Oppenheimer: The Story of a Friendship*. New York: G. Braziller, 1965. 219pp. The author's account of his ambiguous relationship with Oppenheimer reads, in the view of one reviewer "like a rejected lover whose patience, after years of being scorned, has turned to fury." By another, that the portrait "lacks depth and roundness and poses some questions about how well Chevalier really knew Oppenheimer."

Davis, Nuel P. *Lawrence and Oppenheimer*. New York: Simon & Schuster, 1968. 384pp. This is a comparison of the characters, motives, and relationship of Oppenheimer and Ernest Lawrence, the inventor of the cyclotron, culled from interviews with scientists who worked with both men. Lacking in objectivity, Davis is clearly pro-Oppenheimer at the expense of Lawrence.

Kunetka, James W. *Oppenheimer: The Years of Risk*. Englewood Cliffs, New Jersey: Prentice-Hall, 1982. 292pp. Focusing exclusively on the years from 1942 to 1954, this is a thorough review of Oppenheimer's activities during this important period. However, as a reviewer observes, "there is little analysis or reflection on the significance of Oppenheimer's achievements, and no attempt is made to understand Oppenheimer's inner life."

Michelmore, Peter. *The Swift Years: The Robert Oppenheimer Story*. New York: Dodd, Mead, 1969. 273pp. A highly sympathetic, lively and anecdotally rich account, the book is neither comprehensive nor analytically strong. One reviewer called the book "more an exploitation of the Oppenheimer story than a contribution to it."

Rouzé, Michel. *Robert Oppenheimer: The Man and His Theories*. New York: Taplinger, 1965. 192pp. In a well-illustrated summary, the book traces the backgrounds of the scientists who contributed to the development of the atomic bomb with Oppenheimer at the center.

Stern, Philip M., with Harold Green. *The Oppenheimer Case: Security on Trial*. New York: Harper & Row, 1969. 591pp. This is the most detailed account of the 1954 investigation by the Atomic Energy Commission on Oppenheimer's private life and reliability as a security risk.

Biographical Novels

Thackara, James. *America's Children*. London: Chatto & Windus, 1984. 330pp. Oppenheimer's personality and career are portrayed in this novel that imaginatively explores both actual and invented situations from his life between 1929 and 1954.

Fictional Portraits

Silman, Roberta. *Beginning the World Again*. New York: Viking, 1990. 410pp. This is a behind-the-scenes account of the creation of the atomic bomb as seen from the perspective of a wife of one of the Manhattan Project's scientists.

Smith, Martin Cruz. *Stallion Gate*. New York: Random House, 1986. 321pp. The events at Los Alamos are described in this thriller from the perspective of a Native American guard who is ordered to find evidence that Oppenheimer is a communist spy.

Recommended Juvenile Biographies

Drieman, J.E. *Atomic Dawn: A Biography of Robert Oppenheimer*. Minneapolis: Dillon Press, 1989. 160pp. MG. Oppenheimer and his achievements are brought into focus in this straightforward account that concentrates on his early years and his leadership of the Manhattan Project and features more on Oppenheimer's personality than other treatments.

Larsen, Rebecca. *Oppenheimer and the Atomic Bomb*. New York: F. Watts, 1988. 192pp. YA.

Larsen does an excellent job of introducing the man, his work, and times. Well researched and well written, the book supplies a fascinating portrait of life at Los Alamos, based on primary sources.

Royal, Denise. *The Story of J. Robert Oppenheimer.* New York: St. Martin's, 1969. 196pp. YA. This is an informative profile using excerpts from Oppenheimer's writings and the views of scientists who knew him.

Rummel, Jack. *Robert Oppenheimer: Dark Prince.* New York: Facts on File, 1992. 140pp. MG/YA. In a sympathetic and objective account, Rummel emphasizes the science behind Oppenheimer's work that made the atomic bomb possible.

Biographical Films and Theatrical Adaptations

Kipphardt, Heinar. *In the Matter of J. Robert Oppenheimer.* New York: Hill & Wang, 1968. 141pp. A play based on the transcript of the 1954 hearing of the Atomic Energy Commission on the question of Oppenheimer's security clearance.

A&E Biography Video: J. Robert Oppenheimer: Father of the Atomic Bomb (1995). Director: Mary Dore. This is an informative film profile based on archival footage and testimony from eyewitnesses and experts. Video.

The Beginning of the End (1947). Director: Norman Taurog. Hume Cronyn portrays Oppenheimer in this drama of the development of the bomb.

The Day after Trinity (1980). Director: Jon Else. A documentary account describing Oppenheimer's role in developing the atomic bomb and his fall during the McCarthy era, using the words of people who worked with him. Video.

Day One (1989). Director: Joseph Sargent. The race to build the atom bomb and the decision to use it is dramatized in this television drama with Richard Dysart as Truman, Brian Dennehy as General Leslie Groves, and David Strathain as J. Robert Oppenheimer. Video.

Enola Gay: The Men, the Mission, the Atomic Bomb (1980). Director: David L. Rich. The events leading up to the dropping of the atomic bomb and its aftereffects on the airmen are explored. Robert Waldren plays Oppenheimer. Video.

Fat Man and Little Boy (1989). Director: Roland Joffe. This partially fictionalized account of the atomic bomb development focuses on the human conflict between General Leslie Groves (Paul Newman) and Oppenheimer (Dwight Schultz). Video.

Hiroshima (1995). Director: Roger Spottiswoode. This innovative, semidocumentary drama of the events leading up to the dropping of the atomic bomb mixes re-creation of scenes with newsreels and archival material. The drama focuses on Truman (Kenneth Welsh), with Jeffrey DeMunn as Oppenheimer. Video.

362. GEORGE ORWELL
1903–1950

British novelist, essayist, and critic, Orwell was born Eric Arthur Blair in India. He attended Eton and from 1922 to 1927 served with the Indian imperial police in Burma. He then lived penuriously in Paris and London. In 1936 he fought in the Spanish Civil War on the Republican side and was seriously wounded. *Homage to Catalonia* (1938) relates his experiences during the war. Orwell's most famous novels are *Animal Farm* (1946), a satirical and savage fable about communism, and *Nineteen Eighty-Four* (1949), which depicts a totalitarian society of the future. Other works include the autobiographical *The Road to Wigan Pier* (1937) and many excellent literary essays.

Autobiography and Primary Sources

Collected Essays, Journalism, and Letters of George Orwell. Sonia Orwell and Ian Angus, eds. New York: Harcourt, Brace, 1968. 4 vols. Arranged chronologically, this important collection of mostly previously unpublished material forms an essential documentary record for the biographer, with considerable autobiographical insights.

Down and Out in Paris and London. New York: Harper, 1933. 292pp. Orwell supplies an account of his youth trying to survive in poverty as a dishwasher in Paris and as a tramp in London.

Homage to Catalonia. London: Secker and Warburg, 1938. 313pp. One of Orwell's best books, the writer chronicles his experiences during the Spanish Civil War that reveals a great deal about the kind of man Orwell was personally and the evolution of his political ideas.

The Road to Wigan Pier. London: Gollancz, 1937. 264pp. Orwell's documentary report on conditions in the north of England during the 1930s includes his reflections on socialism and its limitations as well as insights into the writer's moral development.

Recommended Biographies

Crick, Bernard. *George Orwell: A Life.* Boston: Little, Brown, 1980. 473pp. The first biographer given unfettered access by Orwell's widow to the substantial holdings of documents she controlled, supplemented with interviews of surviving eyewitnesses, Crick does a solid, judicious job of authoritatively filling in the factual record and offering a credible portrait of the man. Avoiding the discretion and partisanship of other authorized biographies, Crick's study is fair and balanced but offers little on Orwell's works and literary qualities.

Davidson, Peter H. *George Orwell: A Literary Life.* New York: St. Martin's, 1996. 175pp. This concise but comprehensive account of Orwell's influences, creative development, and literary career is arranged around a series of events in the author's life that shaped his experience and work. The book is an excellent choice for the reader looking for an introduction to the man and his works or to read before tackling the much longer studies by Crick and Shelden.

Shelden, Michael. *Orwell: The Authorized Biography.* New York: HarperCollins, 1991. 497pp. Like Crick, Shelden had the cooperation of the Orwell estate for his biography and access to the important documentary sources among the writer's papers. The book's research is put to good use in an accurate, fair, chronological account that allows the writer to emerge in all his complexity and contradictions. For Shelden, Orwell is first and foremost a literary figure, and his politics take a secondary position to his literary qualities. The emphasis serves as a valuable complement to Crick's equally exhaustive account of Orwell's private life.

Other Biographical Studies

Atkins, John A. *George Orwell: A Literary and Biographical Study.* New York: Frederick Ungar, 1954. 348pp. The author, a newspaper co-worker of Orwell supplies his recollections and appreciation. Without access to the Orwell archive, Atkins's biographical treatment is selective and often superficial on details that go beyond the author's personal experience.

Fyvel, T.R. *George Orwell: A Personal Memoir.* New York: Macmillan, 1982. 221pp. The author's recollections of his 10-year friendship with Orwell are supplemented with an appreciation of Orwell's works and a section on the writer's years before they met. The book serves as a useful short, general introduction to the life and work for the general reader.

Hollis, Christopher. *A Study of George Orwell: The Man and His Works.* Chicago: Regnery, 1956. 212pp. Hollis, a schoolmate of Orwell at Eton who also knew the author in Burma, provides a critical study of the writer's works with valuable reminiscences. Hollis's criticism is useful and sensible, but the biographical information is not error-free.

Ingle, Stephen. *George Orwell: A Political Life.* New York: St. Martin's, 1993. 146pp. Ingle's compact study focuses on the development and expression of Orwell's political ideas. Treating his background and attempt to distance himself from it, his contact with the working class, and political conversion during the Spanish Civil War, Ingle makes Orwell's sometimes contradictory ideas coherent and understandable.

Rees, Richard. *George Orwell: Fugitive from the Camp of Victory.* Carbondale: Southern Illinois University Press, 1961. 151pp. Written by an associate, Rees's brief, balanced critical study of Orwell's works includes his personal reminiscences that help create a human portrait of the man with his strengths and weaknesses presented.

Stansky, Peter, and William Abraham. *The Unknown Orwell.* New York: Knopf, 1972. 316pp. Portraying his youth up to 1933 as Eric Blair transformed himself into George Orwell, the authors offer a psychological analysis of Orwell's formative years that is sensible and perceptive, although hampered by a lack of full access to the Orwell archive. In *Orwell: The Transformation* (New York: Knopf, 1980. 304pp.) the authors cover the years 1933 to 1938, showing Orwell's political conversion through the effects of poverty and the Spanish Civil War, as well as the influence of the writer's first wife, Eileen O'Shaughnessy. The authors supply a valuable biographical portrait and a coherent view of the connection between Orwell's life, ideas, and art.

Woodcock, George. *The Crystal Spirit: A Study of George Orwell.* Boston: Little, Brown, 1966. 366pp. The author, a friend of Orwell during the writer's final decade, begins with personal memories before proceeding with a critical study of the works that draws biographical parallels. Attempting to abide by Orwell's wish that no biography be written of his life, Woodcock falls short of a fully realized life study but does give fascinating glimpses of the man and artist.

Recommended Juvenile Biographies

Ferrell, Keith. *George Orwell: The Political Pen.* New York: M. Evans, 1985. 180pp. YA. This is an astute and informative examination of Orwell's life and political philosophy, sympathetic but even-handed in its approach. Readers should have some prior familiarity with Orwell's works.

Flynn, Nigel. *George Orwell.* Vero Beach, Florida: Rourke, 1990. 112pp. MG. The details of Orwell's life are ably and informatively presented, along with critical interpretations of his works.

Biographical Films and Theatrical Adaptations

George Orwell (1983). Director: Nigel Williams. A film introduction to the writer's life and works, using archival material, interviews, and views of the places where he lived. Video.

George Orwell: Journalist and Novelist, 1903–1950 (1996). Director: Peter Hort. Using photographs, archival material, and views of places associated with the author, the film traces Orwell's life and literary career. Video.

Other Sources

Coppard, Audrey and Bernard Crick. *Orwell Remembered.* New York: Facts on File, 1984. 287pp. This is a useful collection of reminiscences and appreciations from a variety of witnesses and critics of Orwell's life and works.

Gross, Miriam, ed. *The World of George Orwell.* New York: Simon & Schuster, 1971. 182pp. This collection of essays by friends, associates, and critics forms a kind of composite biographical portrait that captures the complexity and contradictions of the man in a somewhat disjointed though still useful volume.

363. THOMAS PAINE
1737–1809

English-born writer and political theorist, Paine was the son of a Quaker. An excise officer, he was dismissed from his post for agitating on behalf of higher salaries and immigrated to America (1774). His popular and highly influential pamphlet, *Common Sense* (1776), urged American independence from England. *The Crisis* (1776–1783), a series of patriotic pamphlets, was a source of inspiration during the American Revolution. Paine returned to England (1787), where he wrote (1791, 1792) *The Rights of Man*, which attacked English institutions and defended the French Revolution. Prosecuted for treason, he was forced to flee to France and was elected to the French National Convention. While imprisoned (1793–1794) during the Reign of Terror, he wrote his controversial *The Age of Reason*, an antibiblical work. He returned to America (1802) and died in poverty.

Autobiography and Primary Sources

The Collected Writings of Thomas Paine. Eric Foner, ed. New York: Library of America, 1995. 905pp. This useful single-volume collection brings together Paine's best-known works, along with a reliable chronology as well as letters, articles, and pamphlets.

The Complete Writings of Thomas Paine. Philip S. Foner, ed. New York: Citadel Press, 1945. 2 vols. Despite its title, this is not a complete edition of Paine's writings, and the reader should still consult the Conway edition for reliability in textual details.

The Writings of Thomas Paine. Moncure Conway, ed. 1894. Revised ed. London: Routledge, 1996. 4 vols. Conway's scholarly edition of Paine's writing has long served as the most complete and reliable edition, supplemented by Philip S. Foner's edition.

Recommended Biographies

Aldridge, Alfred O. *Man of Reason: The Life of Thomas Paine*. Philadelphia: Lippincott, 1959. 348pp. The author's balanced and carefully researched study, based on much previously unpublished material, is the definitive, scholarly record of Paine's career. Few other studies have displayed as well the many sides of Paine's interests and charac-

ter, nor offer as judicious an assessment of his strengths and weaknesses as a man and thinker. The author's *Thomas Paine's American Ideology* (Newark: University of Delaware Press, 1984. 327pp.) is an intellectual biography that examines Paine's writings between 1775 and 1786, Aldridge draws parallels between the writer's experiences and his works, as well as the intellectual climate that he reflected and help to shape.

Fruchtman, Jack. *Thomas Paine: Apostle of Freedom*. New York: Four Walls Eight Windows, 1994. 557pp. Fruchtman's critical biography covers both Paine's life and works and corrects a number of misunderstandings concerning the man and his ideas. Strongly sympathetic, Fruchtman presents a solid case for Paine's achievements while capturing the drama of his struggles.

Hawke, David F. *Paine*. New York: Harper & Row, 1974. 500pp. Painstakingly researched, Hawke's sensitive and sensible survey of Paine's career and character is balanced in its display of the writer's achievements and shortcomings. Paine is shown not as an original thinker but as one who reflected the temper of his times, which the book presents clearly.

Keane, John. *Tom Paine: A Political Life*. Boston: Little, Brown, 1995. 644pp. Richly detailed and solidly researched, this is a balanced assessment of Paine's life and public career, particularly revealing concerning his early years in England and his decade in France. In a striking reappraisal of Paine's political theories and influences, Keane offers an insightful perspective on Paine as well his intellectual and social context.

Other Biographical Studies

Ayer, A.J. *Thomas Paine*. New York: Atheneum, 1988. 195pp. In an introductory study for the general reader, Ayer compactly covers the highlights of Paine's life and critically examines his political ideas and writings. Often the focus shifts from Paine to larger historical and political issues with Ayer's trenchant views on a number of topics. Readers will be better prepared by coming to Ayer after first reading Paine's writings.

Conway, Moncure. *The Life of Thomas Paine*. New York: Putnam, 1892. 2 vols. Although based on a careful examination of primary material,

Conway's biography is marred by the author's partisanship that distorts the record in an otherwise comprehensive and detailed treatment.

Edwards, Samuel. *Rebel: A Biography of Thomas Paine*. New York: Praeger, 1974. 304pp. Edwards, a novelist as well as biographer, presents an entertaining popular account of Paine's life from birth to death, including the writer's tangled personal life. Relying on extensive quotations from Paine's writings, the man is vividly portrayed, but not all of the details are reliable.

Foner, Eric. *Tom Paine and Revolutionary America*. New York: Oxford University Press, 1976. 326pp. With only a brief sketch of Paine's life before and after 1774–1787, Foner's intellectual biography asserts a controversial thesis of the class origins of Paine's revolutionary ideas. The book serves mainly a historical purpose in detailing the Philadelphia of Paine's time and the intellectual and cultural ferment of his era, placing Paine's ideas in their social context.

Pearson, Hesketh. *Tom Paine, Friend of Mankind*. New York: Harper, 1937. 293pp. Beginning with Paine's arrival in America at the age of 37, Pearson's is a straightforward, sympathetic narrative biography with an emphasis on Paine the man, who is displayed through ample quotations from his writing. Often uncritical and uninformed by modern scholarship, Pearson's study for the most part allows his subject to speak for himself in a balanced, if limited, assessment.

Philip, Mark. *Paine*. New York: Oxford University Press, 1989. 130pp. Mainly a critical survey of Paine's major writings, biographical details here are limited to a brief introductory chapter.

Powell, David. *Tom Paine: The Greatest Exile*. New York: St. Martin's, 1985. 303pp. Often highly speculative, Powell imagines Paine's responses to his experiences. Taking the liberties of fictional biographers, Powell's work achieves an animated vividness, but the reliability of the account is undermined by the imagination.

Williamson, Audrey. *Thomas Paine: His Life, Work and Times*. New York: St. Martin's, 1973. 296pp. Incorporating a great deal of new information, particularly on Paine's early life in England and later period in France, Williamson's comprehensive life is weakest on the American years and annoyingly uses Paine as an excuse to digress on a variety of modern matters.

Biographical Novels

Fast, Howard. *Citizen Tom Paine*. New York: Duell, Sloan and Pearce, 1943. 341pp. Fast's highly-regarded fictionalized biography of Paine follows him from poverty in England through his years in Revolutionary America and France. Generally reliable in its biographical and historical details, Paine is presented at times more an inspiring symbol than credible human figure.

Levin, Benjamin H. *To Spit Against the Wind*. New York: Citadel Press, 1970. 569pp. In this full-length fictionalized biography, Paine is depicted as an uncompromising idealist whose advanced ideas bring him little respect or success.

Fictional Portraits

Eastlake, William. *The Long Naked Descent into Boston*. New York: Viking, 1977. 291pp. Paine, as well as a large cast of historical figures, appear in Boston on the eve of the Revolution in this comic fantasy that emphasizes the founders' human frailties over their virtues.

Piercy, Marge. *City of Darkness, City of Light*. New York: Fawcett, 1996. 479pp. Blending historical figures and fictional characters, the novel depicts the events of the French Revolution with an authentic appearance by Tom Paine.

Recommended Juvenile Biographies

Coolidge, Olivia E. *Tom Paine, Revolutionary*. New York: Scribner, 1969. 213pp. YA. This is a well-balanced and unbiased account of Paine's career with a full depiction of the historical background.

Meltzer, Milton. *Tom Paine: Voice of a Revolution*. New York: F. Watts, 1996. 175pp. MG/YA. Excellent, well-researched and well-written biography that captures the man, his eventful life, and the era in France, England, and America.

Vail, John J. *Thomas Paine*. New York: Chelsea House, 1990. 111pp. MG/YA. Paine's life is placed in its political and social context in an objective assessment of mainly the writer's public career.

Biographical Films and Theatrical Adaptations

Fast, Howard. *Citizen Tom Paine*. Boston: Houghton Mifflin, 1986. 119pp. The author adapts his own novel for the stage.

Foster, Paul. *Tom Paine: A Play in Two Parts*. New York: Grove Press, 1968. 112pp. Foster's is an experimental drama that offers a portrait of the enigmatic Paine in scenes from his life and testimony by those who knew him.

Shepherd, Jack. *In Lambeth*. London: Methuen, 1990. 52pp. Paine visits visionary poet William Blake in this dramatic confrontation of two different revolutionaries: the pragmatist Paine and the idealistic Blake.

Liberty!: The American Revolution (1997). Directors: Ellen Hovde and Muffie Meyer. This PBS documentary series features actors portraying the principals in dramatic readings from their letters and speeches. Paine is depicted by Roger Rees. The companion volume is written by Thomas J. Fleming (New York: Viking, 1997. 394pp.). Video.

364. CHARLES STEWART PARNELL
1846–1891

Irish nationalist leader, Parnell was the son of a Protestant landowner. He was elected to the British Parliament (1875) and through his filibusters obstructed parliamentary business to make the Irish question a priority topic. He united moderates and militant Fenians in the struggle for land reform and encouraged the use of boycotts to bring pressure on landlords and their agents. His efforts helped persuade Prime Minister William Gladstone to introduce the first Home Rule Bill (1866). Parnell's political career ended after he was named (1889) correspondent in a divorce case.

Autobiography and Primary Sources

Parnell: A Documentary History. Noel Kissane, ed. Dublin: National Library of Ireland, 1991. 118pp. Parnell's life and political career are chronicled using a variety of contemporary sources in this illustrated study.

Recommended Biographies

Kee, Robert. *The Laurel and the Ivy: The Story of Charles Stewart Parnell and Irish Nationalism*. New York: Viking, 1994. 659pp. An Irish journalist and popular historian, Kee presents a readable, well-researched narrative in which nearly two-thirds of the book is devoted to Parnell's formative years as a politician up to 1881. The final third focuses on his relationship with Katherine O'Shea, which is impressively handled.

Lyons, F.S.L. *Charles Stewart Parnell*. New York: Oxford University Press, 1977. 704pp. One of the fullest, scholarly treatments of Parnell's character, life, and public career, Lyons examines the various myths surrounding Parnell realistically. Judicious in his assessment, Lyons supplies a masterful synthesis of various primary sources from Parnell and his associates and demonstrates an expert knowledge of the period.

Other Biographical Studies

Abels, Jules. *The Parnell Tragedy*. New York: Macmillan, 1966. 408pp. This readable popular life is weakened by sweeping generalizations and a lack of documentation, but the story of Parnell's rise and fall is rendered dramatically with human immediacy.

Foster, R.F. *Charles Stewart Parnell: The Man and His Family*. Atlantic Highlands, New Jersey: Humanities Press, 1976. 403pp. In a fresh look at both Parnell and nineteenth-century Ireland, Foster examines Parnell's family background and social milieu to demonstrate their influence on his personal development. The book does not examine Parnell's wider political career, suggesting that indeed all politics is local and that to understand the man you must understand his region and family.

Haslip, Joan. *Parnell: A Biography*. New York: F.A. Stokes, 1937. 405pp. A solid, well-researched, and vivid narrative that focuses on Parnell's political career after treating his family background and youth. Haslip neither glosses over the Irish leader's weaknesses nor diminishes his achievements. The book clearly displays Parnell's appeal to his countrymen and the pathos of his fall.

O'Brian, R. Barry. *The Life of Charles Stewart Parnell, 1846–1891*. 1898. Reprint ed. New York: Greenwood, 1969. 2 vols. O'Brian's early heroic portrait of the Irish leader is highly partisan but does supply a great deal of information about Parnell's life and times.

Parnell, John H. *Charles Stewart Parnell: A Memoir*. New York: Holt, 1914. 312pp. Parnell's brother supplies his admiring recollections and a valuable insider's view of the Irish leader's family background and his mental state during several critical periods of his public career.

Parnell, Katherine. *Charles Stewart Parnell: His Love Story and Political Life*. New York: Doran, 1914. 2 vols. The woman behind the Parnell scandal, whom he married in 1891 after her divorce, offers her side of their relationship, told mainly from the Irish leader's letters. Frank in many of its intimate details, the book is less reliable in all its fact and dates and does not pretend to offer an objective view.

Biographical Novels

Eden, Dorothy. *Never Call It Loving*. New York: Coward-McCann, 1966. 319pp. Parnell's relationship with Kitty O'Shea is dramatized with an emphasis on his private life rather than a wider examination of Parnell's political career.

Leonard, Hugh. *Parnell and the Englishwoman*. New York: Atheneum, 1991. 265pp. Precise and reliable in its historical details, the novel depicts the affair between Parnell and Mrs. O'Shea and the resulting scandal.

Fictional Portraits

Flanagan, Thomas. *The Tenants of Time*. New York: Dutton, 1988. 824pp. Flanagan's massive and masterful recreation of Irish events in 1867 features appearances by a large cast of historical figures, including Parnell.

Recommended Juvenile Biographies

Haney, John. *Charles Stewart Parnell*. New York: Chelsea House, 1989. 111pp. MG/YA. Haney makes Parnell's story understandable in the context of his times and the issues surrounding Irish independence.

Biographical Films and Theatrical Adaptations

Captain Boycott (1947). Director: Frank Launder. Set in the 1880s, the movie dramatizes the origin of the word "boycott" in Irish resistance to the harsh treatment of an English landlord (Cecil Parker). Stewart Granger and Kathleen Ryan star as two young lovers, and Parnell is depicted by Robert Donat. Video.

Parnell (1937). Director: John M. Stahl. In the film version of Elsi Schauffler's play (New York: S. French, 1936. 150pp.), Clark Gable unconvincingly stars in the title role with Myrna Loy as Kitty O'Shea in this disappointing treatment of Parnell's rise and fall.

Other Sources

Boyce, D. George and Alan O'Day, eds. *Parnell in Perspective.* New York: Routledge, 1991. 319pp. This is a collection of essays by various scholars on Parnell's life, his ideas, and his treatment in literature and biographies.

365. BLAISE PASCAL
1623–1662

French mathematician, physicist, and religious philosopher, Pascal was a precocious child who was taught by his father, a civil servant. During his adolescence, he wrote a well-received paper on conic sections and invented a calculating machine. His experiments greatly added to the knowledge of atmospheric pressure. He pioneered hydrodynamics and fluid mechanics, discovering the basis of hydraulics, now known as Pascal's Law. He is also credited with founding the modern theory of probability. His *Provincial Letters* (1656) and the posthumously published *Pensées* (1670) express his religious philosophy.

Recommended Biographies

Cole, John R. *Pascal: The Man and His Two Loves.* New York: New York University Press, 1995. 349pp. The two sides of Pascal's life and development, the scientific and religious, are integrated into a complete portrait of a complex human figure. Treating his upbringing and family relationships, Cole offers a plausible explanation for Pascal's midlife spiritual conversion that establishes the links connecting the contradictions in his life and career.

Mesnard, Jean. *Pascal, His Life and Works.* New York: Philosophical Library, 1952. 211pp. Written as an introductory study, Mesnard's informed analysis integrates the many sides of Pascal into a credible and consistent unity and challenges previous views. Mesnard rejects the notion that Pascal's life divides between science and religion, arguing that his scientific inquiry did not decrease as his devotion grew. Pascal is portrayed as being excessively proud, merciless to his rivals, and anxious to gain full credit for his achievements. Mesnard's more realistic view does not diminish the man's genius or achievement but makes him more human and believable.

Mortimer, Ernest. *Blaise Pascal: The Life and Work of a Realist.* New York: Harper, 1959. 249pp. In a sympathetic yet balanced account, Mortimer places Pascal firmly in his times, detailing his relationships with Montaigne and Descartes and discussing the various intellectual and religious controversies that influenced Pascal's development. Mortimer serves to orient the reader so that a full appreciation of Pascal's genius is possible.

Other Biographical Studies

Bishop, Morris. *Pascal, the Life of Genius.* New York: Reynal and Hitchcock, 1936. 398pp. In a solid, detailed portrait, Bishop excels in depicting Pascal's achievements as a scientist, inventor, and mathematician. The book is less satisfying on Pascal's religious development, which is unsympathetically treated. Pascal is shown in his many parts, but Bishop falls short of adequately unifying them.

Cailliet, Emile. *Pascal: The Emergence of Genius.* New York: Harper, 1961. 383pp. Focusing on Pascal's intellectual development up to 1656, Cailliet supplies an accurate and detailed portrait, incorporating modern scholarship on Pascal's life and times. His presentation of Pascal's religious ideas is seen from a decidedly Protestant perspective that often shifts his analysis to advocacy.

O'Connell, Marvin R. *Blaise Pascal: Reasons of the Heart.* Grand Rapids, Michigan: William B. Eerdmans, 1997. 210pp. Part of the Library of Religious Biography series, this is a chronological narrative of Pascal's life and times that emphasizes the forces that compelled Pascal toward spirituality. O'Connell is particularly insightful on the Jansenist controversy that influenced Pascal's development.

Rogers, Ben. *Pascal.* New York: Routledge, 1999. 64pp. This entry in the distinguished Great Philosophers series is an informative and accessible introduction to Pascal's life and thought aimed at the general reader.

Steinmann, Jean. *Pascal.* New York: Harcourt, Brace, 1966. 304pp. Covering adequately the many sides of Pascal's interests, the book concentrates on his religious thinking. Often emotional in its presentation, Steinmann's narrative is based mainly on primary sources, and his critical study of Pascal's writings is both detailed and insightful.

Biographical Films and Theatrical Adaptations

Blaise Pascal (1971). Director: Roberto Rossellini. In an Italian made-for-television production, Pascal (Pierre Arditi) is shown struggling to understand the natural world while pursuing an inner quest for religious faith. Video.

366. LOUIS PASTEUR
1822–1895

French chemist and developer of pasteurization, Pasteur taught at the Sorbonne from 1867 to 1889. He researched stereochemistry and fermentation and experimented with bacteria. He developed the pasteurization process while working to keep wine, vinegar, and beer from souring. Pasteur discovered how to control silkworm disease, studied chicken cholera, and developed a vaccination technique against anthrax, which was successfully used (1885) against rabies. The Pasteur Institute, a teaching and research center on virulent and contagious diseases, was founded (1888) in Paris with Pasteur as its director.

Recommended Biographies

Debré, Patrice. *Louis Pasteur.* Baltimore:, Johns Hopkins University Press, 1998. 552pp. Written by a French immunologist and physician, Debré's balanced reassessment of Pasteur's life and accomplishments relies on Pasteur's notebooks and writings in a well-documented narrative account. Pasteur is placed in his historical, political, and cultural context and shown in his relationship with his scientific colleagues.

Dubos, René. *Louis Pasteur: Freelance of Science.* Boston: Little, Brown, 1950. 418pp. The author, a distinguished scientist, provides both an excellent biography of Pasteur and a history of science in the nineteenth century. Chronicling both with a wealth of intimate detail and excerpts from Pasteur's own work, the book's quality stems from its ability to make the complexity of Pasteur's work and ideas understandable for the nonscientist. In *Pasteur and Modern Science* (Garden City, New York: Anchor Books, 1960. 159pp.) the author condenses the essential details of Pasteur's life and career in a brief but remarkably rich and authoritative account. This is the best choice for the reader interested in an introduction to Pasteur and his scientific era.

Duclaux, Emile. *Pasteur: The History of a Mind.* Philadelphia: W.B. Saunders, 1920. 363pp. Written by Pasteur's former pupil, friend, and successor at the Pasteur Institute, Duclaux offers an invaluable insider's view of Pasteur's scientific discoveries and methods. The book is consciously restricted to Pasteur's scientific life and offers few details about his private life or attitudes or relationships beyond his laboratory.

Geison, Gerald L. *The Private Science of Louis Pasteur.* Princeton, New Jersey: Princeton University Press, 1995. 378pp. Geison's controversial revisionist study by a close examination of Pasteur's laboratory notebooks and unpublished correspondence reassesses many of Pasteur's important discoveries with evidence of scientific misconduct. Without diminishing the scientist's considerable strengths and genius, his flaws are exposed as the book demonstrates the discrepancy between the public view of the man and his work and a darker reality.

Vallery-Radot, René. *The Life of Pasteur.* Garden City, New York: Doubleday, 1919. 484pp. Pasteur's son-in-law presents one of the most comprehensive records of Pasteur's life with extensive quotations from the scientist's letters, notes, and lectures. Although clearly a partisan view, the book's reliance on documentary evidence of both Pasteur's personal and scientific life makes it one of the most important and valuable sources of information on the scientist.

Other Biographical Studies

Compton, Piers. *The Genius of Louis Pasteur.* New York: Macmillan, 1932. 361pp. Arranged topically based on Pasteur's work rather than chronologically, Compton enthusiastically and clearly presents the highlights of the scientist's achievement, although he adds little that is new or original. This book serves the general reader in search of a competent introduction to the man and his genius.

Cuny, Hilaire. *Louis Pasteur: The Man and His Theories.* New York: P.S. Eriksson, 1963. 192pp. Cuny's useful introductory study includes a succinct biographical account, chronology, and excerpts from Pasteur's writings.

Dolan, Edward F. *Pasteur and the Invisible Giants.* New York: Dodd, Mead, 1958. 214pp. In a simplified, dramatic narrative, Dolan provides an immediate appreciation of Pasteur's character and career, suitable for the general reader and students.

Holmes, Samuel J. *Louis Pasteur.* New York: Harcourt, Brace, 1924. 149pp. This highly condensed yet clear summary of Pasteur's life and scientific career is suited for the general reader and students looking for a serviceable introduction.

Nicolle, Jacques. *Louis Pasteur: The Story of His Major Discoveries.* New York: Basic Books, 1961. 252pp. Each of the 10 chapters deals with one of Pasteur's discoveries, and the book makes accessible for the nonscientist Pasteur's scientific method and genius. Although biographical details are presented incidentally rather than chronologically and in full, Nicolle does offer a useful glimpse of Pasteur's personality and temperament.

Reynolds, Moira D. *How Pasteur Changed History: The Story of Louis Pasteur and the Pasteur Institute.* Bradenton, Florida: McGuinn & McGuire, 1994. 151pp. With only a little more than half of the book devoted to Pasteur's life and achievement, Reynolds informatively surveys the activities of the Pasteur Institute, founded in 1888. Written for the nonscientist, this is a serviceable, brief introduction to Pasteur's scientific activities, influences, and legacy, though not his personal life.

Vallery-Radot, Pasteur. *Louis Pasteur: A Great Life in Brief.* New York: Knopf, 1958. 199pp. The author, Pasteur's grandson, supplies an intimate, though reverent biographical sketch.

Recommended Juvenile Biographies

Birch, Beverley. *Pasteur's Fight Against Microbes.* Hauppauge, New York: Barron's, 1996. 48pp. MG. Birch's is an informative view of Pasteur's career and scientific contribution that helps to make his discoveries accessible.

Smith, Linda W. *Louis Pasteur: Disease Fighter.* Springfield, New Jersey: Enslow, 1997. 128pp. MG/YA. Well-written biography that makes Pasteur's discoveries comprehensible without losing the impact and drama of his achievement. An activity section allows readers to explore techniques and principles.

Yount, Lisa. *The Importance of Louis Pasteur.* San Diego: Lucent Books, 1994. 96pp. MG/YA. Although supplying some information about Pasteur's personal life, the focus is clearly on his scientific work, using valuable primary sources to help tell Pasteur's story.

Biographical Films and Theatrical Adaptations

The Story of Louis Pasteur (1936). Director: William Dieterle. Paul Muni is a standout as the scientist in this excellent Hollywood biographical film tracing Pasteur's life and his most famous discoveries. Josephine Hutchinson co-stars as Mrs. Pasteur, with Holliwell Hobbes as Lister and Iphigenie Castiglioni as the Empress Eugénie. Video.

367. SAINT PATRICK
ca. 389–461

A missionary bishop said to have been born in Britain to a Christian family of Roman citizenship, Patrick is the patron saint of Ireland. He entered a monastery in Gaul and was consecrated a missionary bishop. Sent to convert Ireland to Christianity, he was especially successful in Ulster and Tara. He founded his see at Armagh. His writings include "Letter to Coroticus" and the autobiographical *Confessio,* written during his last years.

Autobiography and Primary Sources

St. Patrick: His Writings and Muirchu's Life. A.B.E. Hood, ed. Totowa, New Jersey: Rowman and Littlefield, 1978. 101pp. This slim volume collects the few works attributed to Patrick as well as an early life written in seventh century.

Recommended Biographies

Bury, John B. *The Life of St. Patrick and His Place in History.* 1905. Reprint ed. New York: Dover, 1998. 405pp. Bury established the historical framework by which Patrick has continued to be subsequently understood, cutting through the various legends to arrive at a historical figure, placed in the context of the spread of Christianity in the later Roman empire. Bury's meticulous scholarly review of the scant sources is masterful, and his expertise helps fashion a credible biographical narrative.

Hanson, Richard P.C. *Saint Patrick: His Origins and Career.* New York: Oxford University Press, 1968. 248pp.; *Life and Writings of the Historical St. Patrick.* New York: Seabury Press, 1983. 138pp. Hanson's two scholarly books on Patrick provide a solid historical outline of his times, close analysis of the existing sources, and a critical study of Patrick's writings. Both help to separate the various legends surrounding the saint from the historical figure that can be known.

Thompson, E.A. *Who Was St. Patrick?* New York: St. Martin's, 1985. 190pp. Limiting himself to what is known for sure about Patrick from his writings, Thompson assembles the few facts into a credible portrait in the context of his times. Debunking earlier lives and legends, Thompson argues that Patrick was not Ireland's first bishop, did not work miracles, and did not drive the snakes from Ireland.

Other Biographical Studies

Bercot, David W. *Let Me Die in Ireland, the True Story of Patrick.* Tyler, Texas: Scroll, 1999. 192pp. Rejecting many of the traditional views of Patrick, Bercot offers an alternative view, based on research of early Christianity and plausible conjecture, in a highly fictionalized narrative account with imagined dialogue. Although it reads more like a fictional biography, Bercot's presentation incorporates a realistic and fresh approach that serves to animate the era and Patrick in believable human terms.

Bieler, Ludwig. *The Life and Legend of St. Patrick: Problems of Modern Scholarship.* Dublin: Clonmore and Reynolds, 1949. 146pp. Bieler helpfully surveys scholarship on Patrick and his era as well as the validity of previous biographies.

Concannon, Mrs. Thomas. *Saint Patrick.* New York: Longmans, 1931. 260pp. In a readable account based on historical sources that are first assessed, Concannon synthesizes a good deal of scholarship into dramatic account emphasizing Patrick's saintly character.

Gallico, Paul. *The Steadfast Man: A Biography of St. Patrick.* Garden City, New York: Doubleday, 1958. 238pp. Presenting the known data along with plausible conjecture, Gallico supplies a readable narrative portrait for the general reader. Included is a translation of the *Confessio,* rejection of most of the legends surrounding the saint, and a more realistic view of the man. Unfortunately, Gallico's scholarship is inadequate, and the presentation of Patrick, though lively and compelling, is more hypothetical than factual.

Hopkins, Alannah. *The Living Legend of St. Patrick.* New York: St. Martin's, 1989. 191pp. After a brief summary of the known facts about Patrick, the book examines the origin of the legends about Patrick and the scholarly debate over him, as well as the impact of the St. Patrick image in Ireland and the United States.

MacNeill, Eoin. *St. Patrick, Apostle of Ireland.* 1934. Revised ed. Dublin: Clonmore and Reynolds, 1964. 121pp. Based on a study of Patrick's writings and historical records, MacNeill's is a simply written devotional presentation of Patrick's achievements as a missionary.

Simms, George O. *St. Patrick: The Real Story of Patrick Who Became Ireland's Patron Saint.* Dublin: O'Brien Press, 1991. 93pp. Simms's brief account focuses on Patrick's writings to present a credible portrait of the man as an alternative to the many traditional legends surrounding the Irish saint.

Biographical Novels

Beahn, John E. *A Man Cleansed by God.* Westminster, Maryland: Newman Press, 1959. 175pp. Using Patrick's *Confessio* as a guide, the novel reconstructs the saint's experiences, filling in the gaps with plausible surmises.

Hamilton, Joan L. *The Lion and the Cross.* Garden City, New York: Doubleday, 1979. 372pp. Weaving what little is known about Patrick in fact and legend with imagined incidents and dialogue, the novel tells Patrick's story of his enslavement in Ireland, his escape, and missionary activities.

Schofield, William G. *The Deer Cry: A Novel of Patrick of Eirinn.* New York: Longmans, 1948. 307pp. Based in part on Patrick's own writings but including a number of legends, the novel constructs a biographical narrative from the saint's youth in England, his capture by Irish marauders, life as a herdsman, escape, and his eventual return to Ireland as a missionary.

Fictional Portraits

Osborne-McKnight, Julienne. *I Am of Irelaunde: A Novel of Patrick and Osian.* New York: Forge, 2000. 301pp. The author connects the life of Patrick with the ancient myths of Ireland in a humanized portrait.

Parke, Godwin. *The Last Rainbow.* New York: Bantam, 1985. 421pp. In a fictional tale, Patrick suffers hardships and torture in preaching to the Picts. Fantasy and fact are blended together in an atmospheric novel.

Ragosta, Millie J. *Druid's Enchantment.* Garden City, New York: Doubleday, 1985. 183pp. In a fanciful story, the daughter of the High King of Ireland meets Patrick, whose preaching challenges the power of the Druids. The novel features convincing fifth-century period details.

Recommended Juvenile Biographies

Corfe, Tom. *St. Patrick and Irish Christianity.* Minneapolis: Lerner, 1979. 51pp. MG. Corfe helpfully relates what is known about Patrick against the wider historical and religious context of his era.

Roquette, Ruth. *Saint Patrick, the Irish Saint.* Minneapolis: Dillon Press, 1981. 48pp. MG. This is summary of information about Patrick, both factual and legendary.

Biographical Films and Theatrical Adaptations

A&E Biography Video: Saint Patrick: The Man and the Myth (1996). Director: Patricia Phillips. Both what is known and the various legends surrounding Patrick are explored in this film portrait. Video.

St. Patrick: The Irish Legend (2000). Director: Robert Hughes. Patrick Bergen portrays St. Patrick in imagined scenes from his life, including his captivity, escape, and return to Ireland to convert the island to Christianity. Malcolm McDowell plays a British cardinal with whom Patrick battles. Alan Bates and Susannah York also appear. Video.

368. GEORGE S. PATTON JR.
1885–1945

U.S. general whose ruthlessness and tactical brilliance as a tank commander earned him the nickname "Old Blood and Guts," Patton was born in San Gabriel, California, and graduated (1909) from West Point. He served in World War I as commander of a tank brigade and later in the cavalry and tank corps. During World War II he commanded (1942–1943) a corps in North Africa and the Seventh Army in Sicily. As commander of the Third Army in 1944, he swept through northern France and relieved Bastogne during the Battle of the Bulge (1945). Patton's troops crossed the Rhine and cut a swath across Germany into Czechoslovakia. After serving as military governor of Bavaria, he was given command of the Fifteenth Army. He was fatally injured in an automobile accident in Germany.

Autobiography and Primary Sources

The Patton Papers. Martin Blumenson, ed. Boston: Houghton Mifflin, 1972-74. 2 vols. This essential collection of Patton's writings includes his diary and letters, as well as correspondence from others. A rich documentary resource, the various paradoxes of Patton's complex character are amply displayed.

War as I Knew It. Boston: Houghton Mifflin, 1947. 425pp. Patton's World War II reflections are collected in a series of "open" letters to his wife during the African and Sicilian campaigns, as well as a terse and technical account of the Third Army's activities written by the general after the war.

Recommended Biographies

D'Este, Carlo. *Patton: A Genius for War.* New York: HarperCollins, 1995. 977pp. Making full use of *The Patton Papers,* D'Este does supply an alternative view of Patton often at odds with the depiction by both Blumenson and Farago. Unlike the fearless win-at-any-cost warrior, D'Este portrays a deeply religious, literate romantic who cared deeply for his soldiers and who consciously created the Patton persona with which he has been identified. Half the book is devoted to Patton's life prior to World War II, establishing a strong context for viewing his development. The book is also particularly insightful on Patton's relationship with Eisenhower, Bradley, and Montgomery.

Farago, Ladislas. *Patton: Ordeal and Triumph..* New York: Obolensky, 1963. 865pp. Farago's comprehensive and detailed life has long established itself as the standard biography. Sympathetic yet objective, Farago incorporates anecdotal material and Patton's own words into a multidimensional portrait. Justly praised for its accuracy and believability, the 1970 film and George C. Scott's Oscar-winning performance were based on Farago's biography. The author's *The Last Days of Patton* (New York: McGraw-Hill, 1981. 319pp.) describes Patton's life from the Allied victory over Germany until his death nine months later, treating the sad end of the general in an uneven account that does not meet the authoritative standard of the author's complete life.

Other Biographical Studies

Allen, Robert S. *Lucky Forward: The History of Patton's Third U.S. Army.* New York: Vanguard Press, 1947. 424pp. Written by a member of Patton's staff, this is a detailed history of the Third Army during World War II as well as a biographical sketch of Patton. Allen is excessively partisan on behalf of his unit and its commander but does offer a vivid, firsthand operational view of Patton's command decisions.

Anders, Curt. *Warrior: The Story of General George S. Patton.* New York: Putnam, 1967. 223pp. Serviceable as a brief introduction to Patton's life and military career, Anders adds little to the established view of Patton's character and his many paradoxes. His story is better treated in the longer, critical studies.

Ayers, Fred. *Before the Colors Fade: Portrait of a Soldier.* Boston: Houghton Mifflin, 1964. 266pp. Written by Patton's nephew who served on the general's staff, Ayers's affectionate tribute, though lacking in objectivity and often inept in its military history, still has much to recommend it. The book is a valuable source of intimate, family details of Patton's upbringing and career before World War II available nowhere else, has an insightful foreword by General Omar Bradley, and adds a number of personal details to the record, most notably correcting the oft-repeated assertion that Patton's ivory-handled pistols were pearl-handled.

Blumenson, Martin. *Patton, the Man Behind the Legend.* New York: Morrow, 1985. 320pp. The editor of *The Patton Papers* quotes extensively from this material in a short popular biography by an undisguised Patton partisan. Readers will profit from the author's evident expertise in military history and the source material. However, the book falls short in delivering either a new slant or a last word on the often-paradoxical Patton.

Codman, Charles R. *Drive.* Boston: Little, Brown, 1957. 335pp. Another of Patton's staff officers provides his account of Patton's military campaign based on letters Codman wrote home to his wife at the time. The result is an effective, informal, behind-the-scenes account that captures a number of sides of Patton as military commander and man, and offers a valuable collection of colorful anecdotes.

Essame, H. *Patton: A Study in Command.* New York: Scribner, 1974. 280pp. Essame assesses Patton's military performance, concluding that he ranks with the greatest military commanders. To back up his assertion, Essame offers the testimony of generals he fought against and alongside (whose views of Patton's skill are considerably more qualified). While perceptive on the details of modern warfare and Patton's command decisions, the author is at times overly dismissive and apologetic concerning Patton's blunders.

Hogg, Ian V. *The Biography of General George S. Patton.* New York: Galley Press, 1982. 160pp. The author, an expert on infantry warfare and weaponry, provides a sympathetic portrait of Patton's career with only a brief sketch of his pre-World War II activities. The book features more than 200 illustrations.

Patton, Robert H. *The Pattons: A Personal History of an American Family.* New York: Crown, 1994. 320pp. Written by Patton's grandson, this group portrait of the Pattons, based on family papers and anecdotes, covers the general's ancestors since the sixteenth century. Patton himself is treated in detail with an emphasis on his private life and character.

Province, Charles M. *The Unknown Patton.* New York: Hippocrene Books, 1983. 261pp. The work of an unabashed admirer, Province's book is less a full-scale biography than a collection of facts and anecdotes ranging over Patton's life and military career. Most of the material offered is far from unknown.

Sobel, Brian. *The Fighting Pattons.* Westport, Connecticut: Praeger, 1997. 248pp. Based on extensive interviews, Sobel delivers a dual biography of Patton and his only son who followed in his father's footstep as a general and battle commander. The book includes intimate details supplied by Patton's son and daughter.

Fictional Portraits

Charyn, Jerome. *Captain Kidd*. New York: St. Martin's, 1999. 207pp. In a satiric, black comedy, an officer in Patton's Third Army exploits his opportunities while serving his commander in a number of official and unofficial capacities.

Irving, Clifford. *Tom Mix and Pancho Villa*. New York: St. Martin's, 1982. 568pp. This historical fantasy imagines what might have happened had cowboy actor Tom Mix joined Pancho Villa's guerilla band. The story includes Mix and Villa's confrontation with Patton as a young army lieutenant.

Leopold, Christopher. *Blood and Guts Is Going Nuts*. Garden City, New York: Doubleday, 1977. 245pp. This novel offers an alternative version of Patton's final days after his dismissal as commander of the Third Army in 1945 in this mixture of mystery and political/military satire.

Recommended Juvenile Biographies

Carpenter, Allan. *George Smith Patton Jr.: The Last Romantic*. Vero Beach, Florida: Rourke, 1987. 112pp. MG. With an emphasis on Patton's character and contradictions, the biography serves to capture skillfully the spirit of man.

Peck, Ira. *Patton*. New York: Scholastic, 1970. 142pp. MG/YA. Peck's is a full account of Patton's military career and personality that provides a balanced assessment, allowing a more complex figure to emerge.

Peifer, Charles. *Soldier of Destiny: A Biography of George Patton*. Minneapolis, Minnesota: Dillon Press, 1989. 126pp. MG. Peifer is accurate on the details of Patton's career and in describing the historical events though this account is slightly fictionalized.

Biographical Films and Theatrical Adaptations

A&E Biography Video: General George Patton: A Genius for War. Director: Don Horan. Through archival footage, recollections of associates, and criticism by historians, this documentary profile captures the many sides of Patton, including his excesses and eccentricities. Video.

Brass Target (1978). Director: John Hough. Fanciful thriller involving a plot to kill Patton (George Kennedy) and steal millions in Nazi gold. Starring Sophia Loren, Max von Sydow, and John Cassavettes. Video.

Famous Generals (1984). Producer: Calvin Productions. This is a dual biographical portrait of Patton and Eisenhower. Video.

Ike (1979). Director: Melville Shavelson. In this made-for-television biography of Eisenhower's war career, Robert Duvall portrays the general with Lee Remick as Kaye Summersby and Darrin McGavin as Patton. Video.

Is Paris Burning? (1966). Director: Rene Clement. The story of the liberation of Paris is told in a screenplay written by Gore Vidal and Francis Ford Coppola with a star-studded cast, including Jean-Paul Belmondo, Alain Delon, Simone Signoret, and with Kirk Douglas as Patton. Video.

The Last Days of Patton (1986). Director: Delbert Mann. George C. Scott reprises his portrayal of Patton in a made-for-television drama concerning the general's controversial final days, based on Farago's book. With Eva Marie Saint as Mrs. Patton and Richard A. Dysart as Eisenhower. Video.

Patton (1970). Director: Franklin J. Schaffner. Based on the Farago biography, this screenplay by Francis Ford Coppola and Edmund H. North is an acclaimed biographical portrait of Patton's World War II years. The film features an Oscar-winning performance by George C. Scott in the title role with a strong performance by Karl Malden as Omar Bradley. Video.

Patton: Old Blood and Guts (1986). Producer: Army Pictorial Center. Documents Patton's leadership through his military campaigns of World War II. Video.

Patton: The Man Behind the Myth (1980). Producer: Arthur Holch. This is a character study that presents both the public figure and the inner man behind the image. Video.

369. SAINT PAUL
ca. AD 10–ca. AD 65

An apostle to the Gentiles and a major figure in the early Christian church, Paul was born a Jew in Tarsus and was the son of a Roman citizen. His Jewish name was Saul. He was educated in Jerusalem, became a zealous nationalist, and was active in the persecution of Christians until AD 33, when biblical text records that he was temporarily blinded by a vision of Jesus while traveling on the road to Damascus. He converted to Christianity, was baptized, and set out on a series of missionary journeys throughout the region. He was imprisoned (AD 60) in Rome but allowed to carry on his ministry. According to tradition, he was beheaded during Emperor Nero's persecution of Christians. Paul's epistles greatly influenced Christian belief and practice.

Autobiography and Primary Sources

Perhaps the most famous letters ever written are Paul's epistles, collected in the New Testament. The epistles offer a number of tantalizing autobiographical insights. Luke provides the initial biographical information about Paul in the Acts of the Apostles in the New Testament.

Recommended Biographies

Grant, Michael. *Saint Paul*. New York: Scribner, 1976. 250pp. This is a solid introductory study based on the autobiographical details derived from Paul's letters and an account of his four evangelical journeys. By widening the historical and cultural context to consider the Jews, Greeks, and Romans, Grant helps to make comprehensible Paul's life, work, and character.

Murphy-O'Connor, Jerome. *Paul: A Critical Life*. New York: Oxford University Press, 1996. 416pp. With the assumption that Luke's account of Paul in the Acts is historically unreliable, the author turns to the evidence in Paul's letters for its biographical,

historical, and chronological deductions. Supplementing the source material is the author's exhaustive cultural context that treats Paul from a number of intriguing viewpoints. The author conjectures that Paul was a widower who had lost his family tragically and suggests that Ephesus, not Rome, was the likely site of Paul's imprisonment.

Roetzel, Calvin J. *Paul: The Man and the Myth*. Columbia: University of South Carolina Press, 1998. 245pp. Part of the Studies on Personalities of the New Testament series, Roetzel examines Paul and his theology in its cultural context. In contrast to the heroic figure of the Acts, Roetzel's Paul is a physically weak literary artist, rather than a compelling preacher, who retained his sympathy toward Judaism and the Hellenistic culture of his childhood.

Sanders, E.P. *Paul*. New York: Oxford University Press, 1991. 138pp. This is a solid introductory study of Paul's life and thought by one of the preeminent scholars on the subject whose research has substantially influenced recent scholarship.

Wilson, A.N. *Paul: The Mind of the Apostle*. New York: W.W. Norton, 1997. 273pp. Novelist and biographer Wilson summarizes all that is known about Paul's life and puts it in its historical and cultural context. Often insightful and provocative, Wilson's imaginative reconstruction of Paul's character and his times is delightfully entertaining and instructive.

Other Biographical Studies

Bornkamm, Günther. *Paul, Paulus*. New York: Harper & Row, 1971. 259pp. The first half of this study reconstructs the life of Paul based on the seven epistles the author considers genuine; the second half is an interpretation of Paul's thought, in particular the doctrine of justification by faith.

Bradford, Ernle. *Paul the Traveller*. New York: Macmillan, 1976. 246pp. Bradford's treatment is closer to historical fiction than biography. As one contemporary reviewer remarked, the book will please those "who like historical distortions depicted vividly."

Glover, Terrot R. *Paul of Tarsus*. New York: G.H. Doran, 1925. 256pp. Based on a series of lectures, Glover's interpretation of Paul's life, character, and ideas is informed by the author's wide knowledge of the Mediterranean background of the early Christian era.

Goodspeed, Edgar J. *Paul: A Biography Drawn from Evidence in the Apostle's Writing*. Nashville, Tennessee: Abingdon Press, 1947. 246pp. Goodspeed, a distinguished biblical scholar, presents a judicious narrative biography based on Paul's writings and New Testament scholarship.

Hengel, Martin, and Anna Maria Schwemer. *Paul Between Damascus and Antioch: The Unknown Years*. Louisville, Kentucky: Westminster Press, 1997. 530pp. The authors provide an informed speculation based on the available sources concerning one of the most obscure periods of Paul's career between his conversion to Christianity in AD 33 and his first missionary journey in AD 46.

Hock, Ronald F. *The Social Context of Paul's Ministry: Tent-Making and Apostleship*. Philadelphia:

Fortress Press, 1980. 112pp. Hock considers Paul as artisan in an effort to understand his life and travels. A solid presentation of Paul's cultural and social background supports this often revealing inquiry into the practical details of Paul's life.

Jewett, Robert. *A Chronology of Paul's Life*. Philadelphia: Fortress Press, 1979. 160pp. Through a close examination of the evidence from Paul's letters and passages in the Acts, as well as modern scholarship, Jewett establishes a plausible chronology of Paul's life.

Knox, Wilfred L. *St. Paul*. New York: Appleton, 1932. 153pp. A vividly written, popular biography, the life of Paul is presented in the context of his role in organizing and unifying the early Christian church from a historical rather than a devotional perspective.

Luedemann, Gerd. *Paul, Apostle to the Gentiles: Studies in Chronology*. Philadelphia: Fortress Press, 1984. 311pp. The author subjects the conventional reconstruction of Paul's life to a series of critical objections based on a variety of sources to point out the flaws in the accepted accounts and to offer alternative possibilities.

Morton, Henry C.V. *In the Steps of St. Paul*. New York: Dodd, Mead, 1936. 499pp. Using the Acts of the Apostles as a guide, Morton retraces Paul's journeys in a vivid travelogue and animated recreation of Paul's life and times.

Nock, Arthur D. *St. Paul*. New York: Harper, 1937. 255pp. This short biography is conservative in its approach, keeping as close as possible to the known sources. The book includes chapters on Paul's environment and the cultural and historical setting.

Pollock, J.C. *The Apostle: A Life of Paul*. Garden City, New York: Doubleday, 1969. 244pp. Ignoring modern critical scholarship, Pollock's biography is based on a literal reading of biblical materials. Facts derived from the New Testament are reworked into a dramatic narrative.

Riesner, Rainer. *Paul's Early Period: Chronology, Mission Strategy, Theology*. Grand Rapids, Michigan: William B. Eerdmans, 1998. 512pp. In an exhaustive, scholarly work, Riesner sifts through biblical and historical sources to reach an understanding of Paul in his cultural context and a plausible chronology of his life and ministry.

Schweitzer, Albert. *Paul and His Interpreters: A Critical History*. New York: Macmillan, 1912. 252pp. The author assesses the various sources and versions of Paul's life and underscores the impossibility of establishing a fully-realized historical Paul. In *The Mysticism of Paul the Apostle* (New York: Holt, 1931. 411pp.) Schweitzer provides a context for understanding the man and his ideas in a study of Paul's thought, work, and influence.

Spencer, Floyd A. *Beyond Damascus: A Biography of Paul the Tarsian*. New York: Harper, 1934. 466pp. In a semi-fictionalized biography, Spencer combines the events of Paul's life recorded in the Acts and Paul's letters with an authentic period background based on ancient sources and archaeological research.

Wallace, Richard, and Wynne Williams. *The Three Worlds of Paul of Tarsus*. New York: Routledge,

1998. 239pp. Through an exploration of the life of Paul, the book examines the three fundamental cultural layers—regional, Hellenistic, and Roman—that shaped Paul and the early Christian church.

Biographical Novels

Asch, Sholem. *The Apostle*. New York: Putnam, 1943. 804pp. In a chronicle of Paul's life and the early years of Christianity, Asch supplements the scanty biographical record derived from biblical sources with a carefully presented historical background.

Ball, Charles F. *The Life and Times of the Apostle Paul*. Wheaton, Illinois: Tyndale House, 1996. 200pp. This fictionalized account of Paul's life and religious career covers his life from his conversion to Christianity to his death. The existing sources are embellished with imagined details.

Berstl, Julius. *The Tentmaker*. New York: Rinehart, 1952. 312pp. Paul's early life is the dramatic focus here, depicted as a complex blend of three different cultures: Jewish, Greek, and Roman. The novel's climax is Paul's conversion experience on the road to Damascus.

Blythe, LeGette. *Man on Fire: A Novel of the Life of St. Paul*. New York: Funk & Wagnalls, 1964. 376pp. In a blend of fact, legend, and invention, Paul's life is dramatized in a account of the early Christian church up to his martyrdom.

Buckmaster, Henrietta. *And Walk in Love: A Novel Based on the Life of the Apostle Paul*. New York: Random House, 1956. 404pp. The known facts are interwoven with fictional elaboration to form a believable biography of Paul from Christ's crucifixion to Paul's death.

Caldwell, Taylor. *Great Lion of God*. Garden City, New York: Doubleday, 1970. 629pp. Paul's early life as the intellectual son of a wealthy Roman-Jewish family is dramatized through his conversion, travels, and martyrdom. Rich in historical material, the novel has a factual framework derived from extensive sources.

Cash, Johnny. *Man in White*. San Francisco: Harper & Row, 1986. 226pp. The stages of Paul's conversion are dramatized in this fictional and devotional meditation on the apostle's spiritual development.

De Wohl, Louis. *Glorious Folly: A Novel of the Time of St. Paul*. Philadelphia: Lippincott, 1957. 384pp. Paul's life is depicted from his early years as a virulent anti-Christian, through his conversion, and ministry in a fictional elaboration based on biblical fact, supposition, and conjecture.

Miller, Rex. *I, Paul*. New York: Duell, Sloan and Pearce, 1940. 210pp. Paul is presented as the narrator for the events of his life, including his conversion and ministry, in a novel that stays close to what is known about Paul's life from biblical sources.

Poirier, Leon. *Saint Paul: A Historical Novel of His Life*. St. Louis: B. Herder, 1961. 213pp. In a devotional rendering of Paul's life drawn from biblical sources, his experiences from his conversion to his death are depicted.

Slaughter, Frank G. *God's Warrior*. Garden City, New York: Doubleday, 1967. 371pp. Following Paul's career from his early years in Tarsus through his conversion and travels throughout the Mediterranean world. The facts are supplemented with plausible surmises.

Fictional Portraits

Chinn, Laurene. *The Soothsayer*. New York: Morrow, 1972. 240pp. Paul converts Timothy, who accompanies him in his missionary work, in a fictional tale with an authentic period atmosphere.

Maier, Paul L. *The Flames of Rome*. Garden City, New York: Doubleday, 1981. 443pp. Rome under the emperors Claudius and Nero and the early Christian church is depicted, with appearances by both Peter and Paul.

Neilson, Winthrop, and Frances Neilson. *The Woman Who Loved Paul*. Garden City, New York: Doubleday, 1978. 255pp. The novel imagines a woman who helps Paul in his mission to Corinth, Ephesus, and Rome.

Steen, John W. *Barnabas*. Nashville, Tennessee: Broadman, 1971. 127pp. Paul is joined by Barnabas to convert the people of Tarsus; this is a mainly fictional account.

Recommended Juvenile Biographies

Luce, Harry K. *St. Paul*. New York: Putnam, 1958. 118pp. MG. This is a straightforward presentation of Paul's life as he reveals himself in his letters.

Pittenger, W. Norman. *The Life of Saint Paul*. New York: F. Watts, 1968. 141pp. MG. This book discusses the world Paul lived in, other religions of his time, sources of information about him, and his teachings and influence.

Thompson, Blanche J. *Peter and Paul: The Rock and the Sword*. New York: Farrar, Straus, 1964. 174pp. MG. Without relying on fictional devices, Thompson summarizes the known events and allows the participants to speak for themselves in this informative look at the founding and the early years of Christianity.

See also Saint Peter

370. WILLIAM PENN
1644–1718

English Quaker and founder of Pennsylvania, Penn wrote numerous tracts on Quaker beliefs and was briefly imprisoned for his religious nonconformity. While acting as trustee for a Quaker proprietor of West Jersey in the American colonies, Penn obtained a charter for Pennsylvania (named for Penn's father) from Charles II and received a grant from the Duke of York (later James II), which extended the colony's boundaries. Thousands of European Quakers immigrated to Pennsylvania in search of religious and political freedom.

Autobiography and Primary Sources

The Papers of William Penn. Mary M. Dunn and Richard S. Dunn, eds. Philadelphia: University of Pennsylvania Press, 1981–1987. 5 vols. This scholarly collection of Penn's writings is an invaluable biographical and historical source.

William Penn and the Founding of Pennsylvania: A Documentary History. Jean R. Soderlund and Richard S. Dunn, eds. Philadelphia: University of Pennsylvania Press, 1983. 416pp. Published to mark the tercentenary of the founding of Pennsylvania, this useful volume brings together essential primary documents on Penn and the Pennsylvania colony.

Recommended Biographies

Dunn, Mary M. *William Penn, Politics and Conscience.* Princeton, New Jersey: Princeton University Press, 1967. 206pp. Dunn's intellectual and political biography draws the connection between Penn's ideas and actions as reflected by a careful reading of his writings. Though often viewed as politically inconsistent, Dunn makes a strong case for the unity of Penn's ideas and behavior based on his determined efforts on behalf of religious toleration. Few works are better at analyzing the inner dynamics of Penn's mental make-up.

Peare, Catherine O. *William Penn: A Biography.* Philadelphia: Lippincott, 1957. 448pp. Widely considered the definitive life, this scholarly treatment sets Penn's personal and public life against the background of his times. Balanced in its assessment, Peare's presentation reveals a complex individual whose many sides and paradoxes are joined in a lively and compelling human portrait.

Wildes, Harry E. *William Penn.* New York: Macmillan, 1974. 469pp. In a realistic and scrupulously researched biography that integrates Penn's private and public lives, Wildes's is a distinguished effort in which plausible and judicious deductions are offered to fill gaps in the factual record. Despite some errors of fact and documentation, the full, human story of Penn emerges in a well-written account.

Other Biographical Studies

Brailsford, Mabel R. *The Making of William Penn.* New York: Longmans, 1930. 367pp. Brailsford focuses on Penn's background and development from his boyhood in Ireland, his education, and the important individuals in his life up to 1681. Well documented, Brailsford supplies a vivid recreation of the Quaker world Penn moved in and the formation of his essential character.

Endy, Melvin B. *William Penn and Early Quakerism.* Princeton, New Jersey: Princeton University Press, 1973. 410pp. Penn is examined from the context of Quakerism and the religious movement he helped to shape. Endy's interpretive study is based on solid research and serves both as an excellent summary of Penn's religious thought and a history of early Quakerism.

Fantel, Hans. *William Penn: Apostle of Dissent.* New York: Morrow, 1974. 298pp. In a readable, sympathetic, popular biography, Fantel summarizes Penn's transition from cavalier to Quaker and his political and social beliefs. In his enthusiasm for Penn's achievement, Fantel sometimes allows speculation to exceed the evidence, and his historical judgments are occasionally superficial and misleading.

Graham, John W. *William Penn, Founder of Pennsylvania.* New York: F.A. Stokes, 1917. 332pp. A well-written, sympathetic biography, Graham weaves extracts from Penn's writings and historical documents into a reliable narrative life, allowing Penn to speak for himself as much as possible with judicious surmises when primary evidence is lacking.

Hull, William I. *Eight First Biographies of William Penn in Seven Languages and Seven Lands.* Swarthmore, Pennsylvania: Swarthmore College Press, 1936. 136pp. Hull helpfully collects the earliest Penn biographies and provides a critical assessment.

Hull, William I. *William Penn: A Topical Biography.* New York: Oxford University Press, 1937. 362pp. Arranged topically rather than chronologically, Hull deals with multiple aspects of Penn's life and character, including his homes, family, boyhood, conversion, theology, imprisonment, and statesmanship. Serves as an excellent reference tool.

Illick, Joseph E. *William Penn, the Politician: His Relations with the English Government.* Ithaca, New York: Cornell University Press, 1965. 267pp. Choosing to concentrate on Penn's political rather than spiritual context, Illick summarizes the often-complicated negotiating that Penn was forced to undertake to protect his colony from government interference, and an appreciation of Penn's political skills is clearly established.

Janney, Samuel M. *The Life of William Penn: With Selections from His Correspondence and Autobiography.* Philadelphia: Friends Book Association, 1851. 560pp. Long regarded as the standard life, Janney's biography features extensive quotations from Penn's writings and historical documents.

Vulliamy, C.E. *William Penn.* New York: Scribner, 1984. 302pp. This is a reliable, well-researched account of Penn's life that sets him firmly in his historical context.

Fictional Portraits

Hoffman, Daniel. *Brotherly Love.* New York: Random House, 1981. 176pp. This historical verse narrative concerning Penn's life and the rise and fall of his Pennsylvania colony is based solidly on historical fact and incorporates excerpts from colonial laws and contemporary letters.

Recommended Juvenile Biographies

Doherty, Kiernan. *William Penn: Quaker Colonist.* Brookfield, Connecticut: Millbrook Press, 1998. 192pp. MG/YA. This is an excellent account of Penn's life and times that is both well-documented and vivid in its characterization of a believable and human Penn.

Foster, Genevieve. *The World of William Penn.* New York: Scribner, 1973. 192pp. MG. Details of Penn's life are interspersed with the activities of others from his era, including Marquette, Joliet, La Salle, Newton, Halley, and Peter the Great.

Stefoff, Rebecca. *William Penn.* New York: Chelsea House, 1998. 112pp. MG/YA. A solid and informative life of Penn that locates his values and

activities in the wider cultural and historical context.

Biographical Films and Theatrical Adaptations

The Courageous Mr. Penn (1941). Director: Lance Comfort. A British biographical film that depicts Penn's achievements as a Quaker and political leader. Starring Clifford Evans in the title role with Deborah Kerr as Gugliema Springett, Dennis Arundel as Charles II, and Henry Oscar as Samuel Pepys. Video.

Other Sources

Dunn, Mary M., and Richard S. Dunn, eds. *The World of William Penn.* Philadelphia: University of Pennsylvania Press, 1986. 421pp. In a valuable collection of critical essays, various aspects of Penn's life and times are treated by leading specialists.

371. SAMUEL PEPYS
1633–1703

An English public official and celebrated diarist, Pepys was a successful naval administrator and served as president of the Royal Society. His fame rests with his diary, which provides an intimate record of his life and a graphic picture of society during the early Restoration period. Written in code from 1660–1669, Pepys's diary was first deciphered and published in 1825.

Autobiography and Primary Sources

The Diary of Samuel Pepys. Robert Latham and William Matthews, ed. Berkeley: University of California Press, 1970. 1970-83. 10 vols. Pepys's diary is one of the literary treasures of the seventeenth century, allowing us to know far more about him than any other figure during the period. Various abridgements are available; one of the best is *The Shorter Pepys* (Berkeley: University of California Press, 1985. 1,096pp.).

The Letters of Samuel Pepys and His Family Circle. Helen T. Health, ed. Oxford: Clarendon Press, 1956. 253pp. Pepys's letters are an excellent complement to his diary, filling in areas of his life not covered by the diary and providing an interesting contrast to the private personality revealed there.

Recommended Biographies

Bryant, Arthur. *Samuel Pepys.* New York: Macmillan, 1933-39. 3 vols. In the most detailed, comprehensive life of the diarist, Pepys's private and public life are integrated in an objective portrait that allows Pepys to speak for himself whenever appropriate and supplies a fully realized social and historical background to understand the man and his era. The author unfortunately ends his narrative in 1689, neglecting the last decade of Pepys's life.

Ollard, Richard. *Pepys: A Biography.* New York: Holt, 1974. 374pp. Ollard's full-length life is a worthy successor to Bryant and is informed by modern scholarship and the author's own expertise on the seventeenth-century navy. Pepys is displayed as having a mixture of admirable and less flattering qualities in a fair, balanced portrait in which his ideas and motives are fully detailed in their period context.

Other Biographical Studies

Barber, Richard. *Samuel Pepys, Esquire*. Berkeley: University of California Press, 1970. 64pp. In an exhibition catalog, Barber's text, accompanied by many illustrations, presents a workmanlike narrative of Pepys's life.

Bradford, Gamaliel. *The Soul of Samuel Pepys*. Boston: Houghton Mifflin, 1924. 261pp. Based on a close reading of the *Diary*, Bradford attempts a profile of the diarist's "soul" in a topically arranged psychological study that examines the man from a variety of interesting angles.

Cleugh, James. *The Amorous Master Pepys*. London: Frederick Muller, 1958. 186pp. Drawing on excerpts from the *Diary*, Cleugh collects the intimate, human evidence of the diarist in a limited, one-sided portrait, written for the general reader.

Drinkwater, John. *Pepys: His Life and Character*. New York: Doubleday, 1930. 374pp. Concentrating on Pepys's public life, Drinkwater's popular account serves as an excellent complement to the view offered by the *Diary*. Covering not just the decade of the *Diary*, Drinkwater spans Pepys's entire life and connects both the private man and his public activities into a credible, sympathetic portrait.

Emden, Cecil S. *Pepys Himself*. New York: Oxford University Press, 1963. 146pp. The author's character study of Pepys is derived from a close study of the *Diary* and letters and includes a number of credible interpretations of the diarist's motives and personality.

Hearsey, John. *Young Mr. Pepys*. New York: Scribner, 1973. 306pp. Despite its title, the book's first two chapters alone cover Pepys's early life and times before proceeding to a more detailed summary of the years of the *Diary* with extensive quotes but an inadequate substitute for the work itself.

Hunt, Percival. *Samuel Pepys in the Diary*. Pittsburgh: University of Pittsburgh Press, 1958. 178pp. The author supplies a critical reading of Pepys's character as it is revealed through a close examination of the *Diary*.

Lubbock, Percy. *Samuel Pepys*. New York: Scribner, 1909. 284pp. In a biographical sketch based on previously published material, mainly Wheatley, Lubbock presents the highlights of Pepys's life and career with details surrounding the writing of the *Diary*.

Lucas-Dubreton, Jean. *Samuel Pepys: A Portrait in Miniature*. New York: Putnam, 1925. 280pp. Confined to Pepys's life during the years recorded in the *Diary*, this is a highly fictionalized recreation that uses the facts as a launching pad for a highly imaginative, literary, and speculative presentation.

Moorhouse, Esther H. *Samuel Pepys, Administrator, Observer, Gossip*. New York: Dutton, 1909. 327pp. Based on a careful reading of the *Diary* and the writings of Pepys's contemporaries,

Moorhouse offers a balanced introduction to Pepys's personality, private, and public life.

Ponsonby, Arthur. *Samuel Pepys*. New York: Macmillan, 1928. 160pp. An English authority on seventeenth-century diaries and diarists extends his considerable expertise to a consideration of Pepys, showing him as his contemporaries saw him and in relation to other chroniclers of his times.

Tanner, J.R. *Mr. Pepys: An Introduction to the Diary, Together with a Sketch of His Later Life*. New York: Harcourt, Brace, 1924. 308pp. In a topical arrangement under such headings as family, books, food, music, and plays, Tanner offers a sampler of excerpts from the *Diary* as well as a detailed biographical portrait with an full analysis of Pepys's career as Secretary of the Admiralty.

Taylor, Ivan E. *Samuel Pepys*. New York: Macmillan, 1989. 152pp. Taylor's fine critical study of Pepys's writings is an excellent introduction to the man, his works, and his era.

Trease, Geoffrey. *Samuel Pepys and His World*. New York: Scribner, 1972. 128pp. This illustrated life and times serves as a useful introduction to Pepys and the *Diary* for the general reader before proceeding to fuller acquaintance with both.

Wheatley, Henry B. *Samuel Pepys and the World He Lived In*. New York: Scribner, 1880. 311pp. Wheatley's early biography places Pepys's life in a wider social context and supplies details of Pepys's life before and after the *Diary* decade.

Wilson, John H. *The Private Life of Mr. Pepys*. New York: Farrar, Straus, 1959. 249pp. Pepys as libertine, as revealed in the *Diary*, is the book's focus that deals only sketchily with the years before and after the decade covered in the *Diary*. Out of context, Pepys's amorous relations tend to distort the wider view of his character and career, which the author does remind his reader, but the book still provides an entertaining summary for the reader unwilling to tackle the *Diary* in full.

Biographical Novels

Abernethy, Cecil. *Mr. Pepys of Seething Lane*. New York: McGraw-Hill, 1957. 384pp. Using the *Diary* as its fundamental source, this novel constructs a lively and vivid narrative of Pepys's life with only occasional invented scenes and dialogue.

Delaforce, Patrick. *Pepys in Love: Elizabeth's Story*. London: Bishopgate, 1986. 248pp. This fictional account concentrates on Pepys's domestic life as seen from the perspective of his wife.

George, Sara. *The Journal of Mrs. Pepys: Portrait of a Marriage*. New York: St. Martin's, 1999. 340pp. This ingenious imaginative creation based on a careful reading of the *Diary* provides Elizabeth Pepys own journal entries as she reflects on her often troubled marriage and her era before her early death at the age of 29.

Fictional Portraits

Mount, Ferdinand. *Jem (and Sam)*. New York: Carroll & Graf, 1999. 425pp. The novel provides a fictional alternative to Pepys's famous *Diary* in the imagined memoir of Jem Mount, a real-life drinking companion of the diarist, who becomes his

friend's rival as their very different fortunes are compared from Mount's envious perspective.

Biographical Films and Theatrical Adaptations

The Courageous Mr. Penn (1941). Director: Lance Comfort. In this biographical portrait of William Penn (Clifford Evans) as Quaker and colonial leader, Pepys makes an appearance, played by Henry Oscar. Deborah Kerr co-stars. Video.

372–373. JUAN PERÓN (1895–1974); EVA DUARTE PERÓN (1919–1952)

President of Argentina, Perón led an army clique that helped overthrow (1943) the government of Ramón Castillo. He served as secretary of labor and social welfare, and as minister of war and vice president. Popular with the unions and the workers, he was elected president in 1946. He began a program of industrialization and social reform, and maintained a position of anti-imperialism and hostility toward the United States. After the death of his wife, Eva, with whom he co-governed, his popularity declined. Religious and military opposition to Peronist corruption and repression led to a military takeover (1955) and Perón was forced into exile. After living in Paraguay and Spain, he returned (1973) to Argentina and was reelected president. After his death, he was succeeded in office by his third wife, Isabel.

Argentine political leader born Eva Duarte, Perón was an actress before her marriage (1945) to Juan Perón. After his election as president, she ran the ministries of labor and health and formed the Eva Perón Social Aid Foundation for the needy. Known as Evita, she was a popular public figure and a fiery orator, who championed the causes of women, labor, and the poor.

Autobiography and Primary Sources

In My Own Words: Evita. New York: New Press, 1996. 119pp. Although its authenticity is disputed, these reflections, purportedly dictated by Eva Perón shortly before her death, are a series of often rambling assertions of her beliefs and opinions. In his introduction, Joseph A. Page argues for the book's authenticity and supplies a useful summary of Evita's life and work.

My Mission in Life. New York: Vantage Press, 1953. 216pp. Also available as *Evita by Evita: Eva Duarte Perón Tells Her Own Story*. (New York: Two Continents, 1978. 245pp.). Notorious for her fabrication of her own history, Eva Perón supplies a highly subjective and self-serving version of her history. Not always reliable for its facts, the book does provide a rare glimpse of her thoughts and character.

Recommended Biographies

Barnes, John. *Evita: First Lady: A Biography of Eva Perón*. New York: Grove Press, 1978. 195pp. Serving as a readable introduction, Barnes offers a sympathetic though balanced account of Evita's life and career, with an emphasis on her personal life in a year-by-year narrative.

Crassweller, Robert D. *Perón and the Enigmas of Argentina*. New York: W.W. Norton, 1987. 432pp. This is a thoughtful and skillful biography that serves to sift through the facts, gossip, and legend to present a clear picture of Perón's personality. The book is particularly good on Perón's early life and the cultural and historical forces that shaped him.

Fraser, Nicholas, and Marysa Navarro. *Eva Perón*. New York: W.W. Norton, 1980. 192pp. Well researched using important documentary evidence and interviews, this is the most objective, historically accurate biography of Eva Perón currently available. Evita is displayed in a believable human portrait, remarkably free from bias, reverence, or censure.

Page, Joseph A. *Perón: A Biography*. New York: Random House, 1983. 594pp. In a full-scale, exhaustive study of the Argentine president, Page covers Perón's political and private life and debunks a number of myths surrounding him. The book supplies a detailed chronology of Perón's career, informed by an extensive knowledge of Argentine politics. While not totally resolving all the various paradoxes of Perón and Argentina, this is the fullest and most authoritative account of the details of his life and regime.

Other Biographical Studies

Alexander, Robert J. *Juan Domingo Perón: A History*. Boulder, Colorado: Westview Press, 1970. 177pp. As its subtitle indicates, Alexander attempts to place Perón's political career in its Argentine social and political context. The interpretation and details of Perón's life and career have been largely superseded by Page's more authoritative study.

Dujovne Ortiz, Alicia. *Eva Perón: A Biography*. New York: St. Martin's, 1996. 325pp. In a popular biography with a strong emphasis on gossip and sensation, this often disjointed and overwritten impressionistic account mixes newly declassified sources from the Perón government with rumor and conjecture. The book's major weakness, however, is an inadequate treatment of Argentine social and political history necessary to make Evita's story understandable.

Elia, Tomás de. *Evita: An Intimate Portrait of Eva Perón*. New York: Rizzoli, 1997. 191pp. This lavishly illustrated biographical chronicle of Evita's private and public life makes use of private family photographs, magazine covers, and publicity stills, as well as pictures of her jewelry and wardrobe.

Harbinson, W.A. *Evita!: Saint or Sinner?* New York: St. Martin's, 1996. 216pp. As the book's title indicates, a melodramatic quality of sensational extremes predominates in this account. Based on secondary sources, the author recycles most of the well-known stories about Evita, turning her into a one-dimensional figure. Almost a third of the book concerns Madonna and the film version of the Andrew Lloyd Webber musical.

Main, Mary. *The Woman with the Whip: Eva Perón*. 1952. Revised ed. as *Evita: The Woman With the Whip*. New York: Dodd, Mead, 1980.

268pp. Although somewhat moderated in the revision with a more sympathetic acknowledgement of her accomplishments, this is a highly critical assessment that reveals the distrust and dislike of the Argentine establishment for the woman and her influence.

Taylor, Julie M. *Eva Perón: The Myths of a Woman*. Chicago: University of Chicago Press, 1979. 175pp. Less a full-scale biography than a consideration of the Evita myth and her transformation into a popular cultural icon, Taylor examines, after a brief biographical sketch and analysis of her political milieu, the origin and expression of the various legends and images of Perón that reflect Argentine culture and political history.

Biographical Novels

Martínez, Tomás Eloy. *The Peron Novel*. New York: Pantheon, 1988. 357pp. In an exhilarating fictional portrait of Juan Perón, the ailing dictator is studied, from his return to Argentina after his 18 years of exile to his death. Fantasy helps penetrate the man's public image to reveal a hollow, accidental leader.

Martínez, Tomás Eloy. *Santa Evita*. New York: Knopf, 1996. 371pp. The author's inventive modernist fiction concentrates on Evita's posthumous career as a preserved corpse battled over by her supporters and enemies. Retelling episodes from her life, Martínez's novel is a thoughtful and artful meditation on modern mythmaking.

Fictional Portraits

Pridgen, William. *Night of the Dragon's Blood*. Plataka, Florida: Hodge & Braddock, 1997. 192pp. This comic horror novel is set in 1952 as one of Evita's former lovers discovers that she is not dead but undead and a prisoner of a cabal of Nazi vampires, led by Adolf Hitler.

Recommended Juvenile Biographies

DeChancie, John. *Juan Perón*. New York: Chelsea House, 1987. 111pp. MG/YA. DeChancie does an excellent job of chronicling Perón's life and career, while informing the reader about the historical and cultural factors that help make his actions understandable.

Biographical Films and Theatrical Adaptations

Lloyd Webber, Andrew, and Tim Rice. *Evita: The Legend of Eva Perón* (1919–1952). New York: Avon, 1975. 123pp. With a brief biographical sketch by Rice, the book reprints the libretto of the popular musical.

A&E Biography Video: Evita: The Woman Behind the Myth (1996). Producer: Deirdre O'Hearn. Using archival footage and testimony from a number of associates and experts, this is solid documentary portrait. Video.

Evita (1997). Director: Alan Parker. In the much-anticipated film version of the Lloyd Webber/Rice musical with a screenplay by Parker and Oliver Stone, Madonna stars in a lavish paean to a popular heroine. With Jonathan Pryce as Juan

Perón and Antonio Banderas as the chorus figure Che. Video.

Evita Peron (1981). Director: Marvin J. Chomsky. Based on the Barnes biography, Faye Dunaway depicts Evita, with James Farentino as Juan Perón, in a television drama written by Ronald Harwood.

374. SAINT PETER
Died ca. AD 65

The leader of the 12 disciples and the first bishop of Rome, Peter was a native of Bethsaida, where he and his brother, Andrew, another disciple, were fishermen. His given name was Simon, and Jesus gave him the nickname Cepha (an Aramaic word meaning rock), which was translated into Greek as Petros, or Peter. His association with Jesus, denial of him after the Last Supper, and subsequent ministry and deliverance from prison are recorded in the Gospels and other books of the New Testament; some facts of his life have been gleaned from second-century sources. At the time of his martyrdom, he headed the local church in Rome and is believed to have been crucified upside down on Vatican hill.

Autobiography and Primary Sources

What little is known of Peter's early life and relationship with Jesus Christ is contained in the New Testament, with Peter's activities among the earliest Christians chronicled by Luke in the Acts of the Apostles, in the epistles attributed to Peter himself, and in a few references in Paul's epistles.

Recommended Biographies

Grant, Michael. *Saint Peter: A Biography*. New York: Scribner, 1995. 212pp. Grant provides a helpful summary of the scant historical evidence available to form a biographical profile with the various legendary material labeled as such. Grant's insistence on historical objectivity and synthesis of modern scholarship makes this an excellent choice for the reader interested in what can be known for sure about the apostle.

O'Connor, Daniel W. *Peter in Rome: The Literary, Liturgical, and Archaeological Evidence*. New York: Columbia University Press, 1969. 242pp. In the most extensive scholarly treatment of the various evidence on Peter's residence, martyrdom, and burial in Rome, O'Connor exhaustively sifts through historical and liturgical sources as well as recent archaeological evidence to present a number of plausible insights concerning Peter's Roman experiences and his death.

Walsh, William T. *Saint Peter, the Apostle*. New York: Macmillan, 1948. 307pp. In a highly readable popular study from a clearly devotional viewpoint, Walsh combines biblical evidence, traditional and legendary material, and fictional conjecture to present a sensitive and believable human portrait of Peter's psychological and spiritual development.

Other Biographical Studies

Cullmann, Oscar. *Peter: Disciple, Apostle, Martyr: A Historical and Theological Study*. 1953. Revised ed. Philadelphia: Westminster Press, 1962. 252pp. In a scholarly attempt to locate Peter's career in the context of the early Christian church, Cullman first examines the evidence to support the apostle's preeminence and authority before looking critically at the theological implications of scriptural texts on the primacy of Peter.

Elton, Godfrey. *Simon Peter.* Garden City, New York: Doubleday, 1966. 236pp. Relying on biblical sources, Elton provides a fictionalized, devotional retelling of Jesus' ministry from Peter's perspective and the development of his spiritual faith. Although his sources are documented, Elton's reconstruction of Peter's consciousness and personality depends mainly on the imagination.

Findlay, James A. *A Portrait of Peter.* New York: Abingdon Press, 1935. 214pp. Findlay's portrait is notable primarily in contrast to the conventional view of the apostle who is not shown as an impulsive and simple fisherman but a straightforward and incisive disciple and leader of the early Christians.

Foakes-Jackson, Frederick J. *Peter, Prince of Apostles: A Study in the History and Tradition of Christianity.* New York: G.H. Doran, 1927. 320pp. As its subtitle indicates, the author constructs a biography of Peter combining both historical fact and traditional material. Fact and legend are helpfully distinguished.

Perkins, Pheme. *Peter: Apostle for the Whole Church.* Columbia: University of South Carolina Press, 1994. 209pp. Perkins surveys the various sources that have formed the popular view of Peter, supplementing New Testament sources with information drawn from archaeological research.

Robertson, Archibald T. *Epochs in the Life of Simon Peter.* New York: Scribner, 1933. 342pp. In a competent scholarly interpretation of the New Testament sources, the author presents a biographical study of Peter that is informed by an evident grasp of the various controversies surrounding Peter's life and role in the early church.

Biographical Novels

Douglas, Lloyd C. *The Big Fisherman.* Boston: Houghton Mifflin, 1948. 581pp. Peter's life following the death of Jesus is narrated from a variety of perspectives, including Peter's, in Douglas's bestseller that combines biblical sources, traditional, fictional, and historical material, and the author's own interpretation of various historical figures.

Frieberger, Kurt. *Fisher of Men: A Novel of Simon Peter.* New York: Appleton-Century, 1954. 368pp. Relying on a number of invented details to fill in the gaps in Peter's biography, the novel follows his career from his youth in Galilee to his martyrdom in Rome, creating a believable, if highly conjectural, human portrait.

Murphy, Walter F. *Upon This Rock: The Life of St. Peter.* New York: Macmillan, 1987. 538pp. Narrated by a fictional follower of Jesus, Peter's life story is presented against a vivid backdrop of the early Christian community and life during the first century. The novel's extensive speculation beyond the canonical sources is at least plausible historically.

Slaughter, Frank G. *Upon This Rock: A Novel of Simon Peter, Prince of Apostles.* New York: Coward-McCann, 1963. 352pp. Peter's life is narrated from his days as a humble fisherman, through his years with Jesus, and his leadership among the apostles and early Christians in a blend of scriptural, historical, archaeological, and imaginative sources.

Fictional Portraits

Chinn, Laurene. *Marcus.* New York: Morrow, 1965. 370pp. The life of the apostle Mark is dramatized, first as Jesus' disciple and later with Paul on Cyprus and Peter in Rome in a blend of fact, tradition, and speculation.

Costain, Thomas B. *The Silver Chalice.* Garden City, New York: Doubleday, 1952. 533pp. Basil, a silversmith who fashions a vessel to house the cup used by Jesus at the Last Supper, wanders throughout the ancient world among the early Christians, including Luke, Paul, and Peter.

Douglas, Lloyd C. *The Robe.* Boston: Houghton Mifflin, 1942. 695pp. The story of the Roman soldier who wins the robe Jesus wore at the time of his death shows him on a quest to understand his own growing faith that leads to Peter and the lot of the early Christians.

Mason, Anita. *The Illusionist.* New York: Holt, 1983. 309pp. In this fanciful tale about Simon Magus, the famous magician meets Peter and must compete with the new Christian faith in a test of powers before the Emperor Nero.

Sienkiewicz, Henryk. *Quo Vadis?* 1896. Reprint ed. New York: Hippocrene, 1992. 493pp. The author connects a fictional story of a Roman patrician's love for a captured Christian princess with a historical recreation of Rome during Nero's reign and a view of Peter and the early Christian church.

Slaughter, Frank G. *The Sins of Herod: A Novel of Rome and the Early Church.* Garden City, New York: Doubleday, 1968. 370pp. The early years of Christianity are described from the perspective of a Roman citizen of Judea who must choose between Roman law and his growing Christian faith. A number of historical figures are presented, including Caligula, Herod, John, James, and Peter.

Recommended Juvenile Biographies

Pittenger, W. Norman. *The Life of Saint Peter.* New York: F. Watts, 1971. 116pp. MG/YA. Pittenger's is a vivid, historically reliable account of Peter's life, with an emphasis on early church history.

Thompson, Blanche J. *Peter and Paul: The Rock and the Sword.* New York: Farrar, Straus, 1964. 174pp. MG. Without recourse to fictional devices, Thompson summarizes the known events and allows the participants to speak for themselves in this informative look at the founding and the early years of Christianity.

Williams, Albert N. *Simon Peter, Fisher of Men: A Fictionalized Autobiography of the Apostle Peter.* New York: Association Press, 1954. 159pp. MG/YA. Although fictionalized, the book does succeed in humanizing Peter and bringing his era to life with vivid details.

Biographical Films and Theatrical Adaptations

The Big Fisherman (1959). Director: Frank Borzage. Film version of Lloyd C. Douglas's novel, starring Howard Keel, John Saxon, Herbert Lom, and Susan Kohner.

The Silver Chalice (1954). Director: Victor Saville. This film version of Thomas Costain's novel about a young Greek sculptor who makes the cup Jesus uses at the Last Supper features the screen debut of Paul Newman and a portrayal of Nero by Jacques Aubuchon and Saint Peter by Lorne Greene. Video.

See also Jesus Christ; Saint Paul

375. PETER THE GREAT
1672–1725

A major figure in the westernization of Russia and the development of imperial Russia, Peter I became joint czar in 1682 with his half-brother, Ivan, and ruled solely beginning in 1696. He traveled in Europe (1697–1698) to learn techniques of war and industry, and hired numerous European craftsmen to work in Russia. He initiated domestic and administrative reforms, modernized the armed forces, and concluded (1700) peace with the Ottoman Empire. From 1700 to 1721, Russia and an alliance consisting of Denmark and Saxony-Poland waged the Northern War against Sweden. The war resulted in Russian domination of the Baltic Sea, where Peter built his new capital, St. Petersburg. Credited with modernizing and strengthening Russia, Peter was nevertheless brutal in his exercise of power and remains a controversial figure in Russian history.

Recommended Biographies

Anderson, M.S. *Peter the Great.* New York: Longman, 1995. 234pp. Part of the Profiles in Power series, Anderson gives Peter full credit for his many achievements but creates a realistic character profile in which his energy and vision are intermixed with the coarseness of his personal behavior, a lack of human affection in his private relationships, and a brutality in public affairs.

Grey, Ian. *Peter the Great: Emperor of All Russia.* Philadelphia: Lippincott, 1960. 505pp. In an eclectic mixture of history, scholarship, and imaginative reconstruction, Grey depicts a different Peter, not the dynamic barbarian of previous views, but a dedicated and selfless Russian leader. Grey supports his interpretation with a wealth of primary source materials. Grey's believable human portrait of the man is set against a masterful re-creation of place and time.

Klyuchevsky, Vasili. *Peter the Great.* New York: St. Martin's, 1958. 282pp. First published in 1910, the work of a leading Russian expert on Peter and Russian history, Klyuchevsky's influential historical biography remains one of the best assessments of Peter's life, development, character, and accomplishments.

Massie, Robert. *Peter the Great: His Life and World.* New York: Knopf, 1980. 909pp. Massie's award-winning narrative biography of Peter's life and times is absorbing in its ability to dramatize Peter's story so that it reads like a suspense novel. Peter is portrayed with nearly superhuman qualities and failings. The book offers little interpretation of events, but Massie's compensation in narrative interest is impressive.

Other Biographical Studies

De Jonge, Alex. *Fire and Water: A Life of Peter the Great.* New York: Coward-McCann, 1980. 278pp. Written for the general reader, this is a anecdote-rich recapitulation of Peter's life and times that attempts to show him as his contemporaries saw him, based largely on the diaries of foreign observers.

Graham, Stephen. *Peter the Great: A Life of Peter I of Russia, Called the Great.* Westport, Connecticut: Greenwood, 1971. 376pp. The emphasis in Graham's biography is the personal side of Peter with sufficient historical details to see him in context.

Lee, Stephen J. *Peter the Great.* New York: Routledge, 1993. 78pp. Part of the Lancaster Pamphlet series, this topically arranged survey of various aspects of Peter's life and reign is a useful, concise summary and assessment.

Marshall, William. *Peter the Great.* New York: Longman, 1996. 149pp. Marshall's topical rather than chronological study of Peter includes chapters on the Russian background, Peter's early life and character, warfare, and reforms. Includes some documentary records, glossaries of terms, and a genealogy of the Romanovs.

Schuyler, Eugene. *Peter the Great, Emperor of Russia: A Study in Historical Biography.* 1884. Reprint ed. New York: Russell & Russell, 1967. 2 vols. Despite its age, Schuyler's remains the most detailed narrative history of Peter's life and reign in English, though his approach is dated and his coverage uneven, with most of the attention devoted to the early years of Peter's rule.

Summer, Benedict H. *Peter the Great and the Emergence of Russia.* New York: Macmillan, 1951. 216pp. After an opening chapter devoted to biographical details, Summer focuses on Peter's achievement in modernizing Russia in a succinct and reliable assessment.

Troyat, Henri. *Peter the Great.* New York: Dutton, 1987. 392pp. Troyat's popularized biography stresses Peter's larger-than-life appetites and excesses, which are depicted in a wealth of colorful details and anecdotes. Not always reliable as history, Troyat's approach comes close to biographical fiction by its degree of imaginative conjecture.

Biographical Novels

Hill, Pamela. *Tsar's Woman.* New York: St. Martin's, 1985. 207pp. This is the implausible but true story of the peasant woman who became Peter's mistress, wife, and finally Catherine I, Empress of Russia.

Jones, Maurice B. *Peter Called the Great.* New York: F.A. Stokes, 1936. 379pp. Jones's narrative begins with Peter's return to Russia in 1698 after his first journey abroad and closes with his death,

stressing Peter's relationships with his wives and mistresses and his years of madness. The facts are interspersed with conjecture, and there are too many errors for the account to be fully reliable.

Markish, David. *Jesters.* New York: Holt, 1988. 246pp. Peter's life and times are reflected from the perspective of three Jews who become his trusted advisers but who live at his pleasure as his "jesters." This imaginative novel offers a believable interpretation of Peter's reign and character.

Merezhkovsky, Dmitry. *Peter and Alexis.* New York: Putnam, 1906. 556pp. This massive historical reconstruction concentrates on Peter's relationship with his son in an often moving account in which factual details are imaginatively embellished.

Price, Jeramie. *Katrina.* New York: Farrar, Straus, 1955. 305pp. Focusing on the relationship between Peter and his second wife, Catherine, who, though born a peasant, is raised to the throne as Catherine I. Not always reliable as history, some liberties have been taken in telling the couple's story.

Tolstoy, Aleksy. *Peter the Great.* New York: Covici, 1932. 387pp. Blending historical events with invented scenes and characters, this is an epic re-creation of Peter's reign and the transformation of Russia into a great European power. Peter's dominating personality centers this atmospheric novel.

Fictional Portraits

Nicholson, Christina. *The Power and the Passion.* New York: Coward-McCann, 1977. 320pp. In a fanciful tale, the novel tracks the romantic adventures of a young woman who becomes the mistress of three monarchs: William III of England, Augustus II of Poland, and Peter the Great.

Rutherfurd, Edward. *Russka: The Novel of Russia.* New York: Crown, 1991. 760pp. This immense family saga covers more than 1,800 years of Russian history with a view of the impact of its rulers, including Ivan the Terrible, Peter, and Catherine the Great.

Recommended Juvenile Biographies

McDermott, Kathleen. *Peter the Great.* New York: Chelsea House, 1991. 109pp. MG/YA. This biography is particularly helpful in delivering a reliable overview of Russian history, making Peter's achievements comprehensible.

Putnam, Peter. *Peter: The Revolutionary Tsar.* New York: Harper & Row, 1973. 269pp. YA. Putnam emphasizes the complexity of Peter's character in a generally accurate, objective, and anecdotally rich narrative account.

Biographical Films and Theatrical Adaptations

Conquerors (1997). Directors: Nigel Maslin and Robert Marshall. The film profiles four great leaders: Peter the Great, Napoleon, Alexander the Great, and Suleyman. Video.

Peter the First (1937). Director: Vladimir Petrov. A lavish Russian film biography tracing Peter's life

from the early years of his reign to his final days. Video.

Peter the Great (1992). Directors: Marvin J. Chomsky and Lawrence Schiller. Based on Massie's book, this television miniseries stars Maximilian Schell in the title role with Laurence Olivier, Vanessa Redgrave, and Omar Sharif. Video.

Other Sources

Oliva, L. Jay, ed. *Peter the Great.* Englewood Cliffs, New Jersey: Prentice-Hall, 1970. 181pp. Part of the Great Lives Observed series, this useful collection brings together Peter's own writings, contemporaries' views, and modern historian's interpretations of the czar's character, achievement, and influence.

376. PETRARCH
1304–1374

Born Francesco Petrarca, Petrarch is a major figure of Italian as well as world literature. Supported by such patrons as Cardinal Colonna and the Visconti of Milan, he spent his life in study, travel, and writing poetry, epistles, and other prose works, mainly in Latin. He helped to spread the Renaissance viewpoint through his criticism of medieval scholasticism and through his correspondence and considerable influence. He perfected the sonnet form and was one of the earliest poetic masters of the Italian vernacular. Petrarch's inspiration for his great love lyrics was a woman referred to as "Laura," whom he first saw in 1327, and who died of the plague in 1348.

Autobiography and Primary Sources

Petrarch's poetry provides one of the most autobiographically revealing glimpses of any creative artist. The poet is also helpfully viewed in his letters. Editions include *Letters.* Morris Bishop, ed. (Bloomington: Indiana University Press, 1966. 306pp.) and *Letters of Old Age* (Baltimore, Maryland: Johns Hopkins University Press, 1992. 2 vols.).

Recommended Biographies

Bergin, Thomas G. *Petrarch.* New York: Twayne, 1970. 213pp. Bergin's critical study connects Petrarch's works with the details of his life and a consideration of his cultural and intellectual context. Serves as an excellent introduction to the man and his art.

Mann, Nicholas. *Petrarch.* New York: Oxford University Press, 1984. 121pp. Like Bergin, Mann's concise critical study is a useful introduction that makes full use of modern scholarship regarding Petrarch and his era.

Other Biographical Studies

Bishop, Morris. *Petrarch and His World.* Bloomington: Indiana University Press, 1963. 399pp. Bishop's readable overview of the poet and his times is an uneven mix of useful criticism and distorting simplification. Petrarch is affectionately but realistically shown with his shortcomings intact, even as his achievements are highlighted.

Foster, Kenelm. *Petrarch: Poet and Humanist.* Edinburgh: Edinburgh University Press, 1984. 241pp. Foster combines biographical details with a critical reading of Petrarch's works and influence to form a useful introduction to the writer.

Tatham, Edward H.R. *Francesco Petrarca: The First Modern Man of Letters: His Life and Correspondence.* New York: Macmillan, 1925–1926. 2 vols. Tatham's exhaustive but discursive biography contains much matter but is marred by a moralistic tone and imprecision of fact and interpretation.

Trinkaus, Charles. *The Poet as Philosopher: Petrarch and the Formation of Renaissance Consciousness.* New Haven, Connecticut: Yale University Press, 1979. 147pp. Written as a lecture series, this critical study examines Petrarch's works and their influence on Renaissance humanism. Petrarch is seen as emblematic of a profound transformation in human consciousness and individuality.

Whitfield, John H. *Petrarch and the Renascence.* 1943. Reprint ed. New York: Russell & Russell, 1965. 170pp. This is a valuable, brief survey of the historical background essential for an understanding of Petrarch's impact and influence. In Whitfield's view, Petrarch is a bridge figure between the ancients and the moderns.

Wilkins, Ernest H. *Life of Petrarch.* Chicago: University of Chicago Press, 1961. 275pp. Based on Petrarch's letters, this log of Petrarch's chronological activities emphasizes his character traits and interests beyond his literary work. Unfortunately, the book rarely achieves sufficient distance to blend Petrarch's many aspects into a coherent and convincing whole or to demonstrate how his experiences formed his ideas and personality.

377. PHILIP II
1527–1598

Crowned (1556) king of Spain after the abdication of his father, Holy Roman Emperor, Charles V, Philip ruled an empire consisting of Milan, Naples, Sicily, the Netherlands, the Franche-Comté, large areas of the New World, and the Philippine Islands. A devout Catholic, Philip used the Spanish Inquisition and religious persecution to centralize power under an absolute monarchy. His absolutist policies resulted in the revolt of the Protestant Netherlands, which was only partly subdued. He was recognized King Philip I of Portugal in 1580. English attacks on Spanish shipping and their support of the Dutch rebels led to an attempted invasion by Spain's invincible Armada. The ignominious defeat (1588) of the Armada by the English destroyed Spanish naval supremacy. Among Philip's four wives was Mary I of England (m. 1554).

Recommended Biographies

Kamen, Henry A.F. *Philip of Spain.* New Haven, Connecticut: Yale University Press, 1997. 384pp. Reversing the judgments of many pro-Protestant writers, Kamen presents a well-researched and -argued defense of Philip's reign and character that treats him as a believable human being in the context of his times. Kamen's special pleading at times undermines the credibility of his portrait, but the book's scholarship and perceptiveness are first rate.

Parker, Geoffrey. *Philip II.* Boston: Little, Brown, 1978. 234pp. Based in part on Philip's letters and administrative papers that serve to humanize him, Parker challenges the view of the Spanish monarch as a malevolent tyrant. Instead he is depicted as a hardworking, self-doubting yet competent administrator and a credible, complex individual by presenting both his strengths and weaknesses objectively.

Pierson, Peter. *Philip II of Spain.* London: Thames and Hudson, 1975. 240pp. The author's provocative character profile of Philip traces the sources and influence of his conservatism and caution from his early experiences through the events of his reign. The result is one of the closest views yet attempted of Philip's personality and temperament.

Other Biographical Studies

Grierson, Edward. *The Fatal Inheritance: Philip II and the Spanish Netherlands.* Garden City, New York: Doubleday, 1969. 390pp. Grierson focuses on a crucial event during Philip's reign, the rebellion of the Netherlands against Spanish rule, re-creating the complex events of the period for the nonspecialist with psychological insights into Philip's leadership, motivations, and character. In *King of Two Worlds: Philip II of Spain* (New York: Putnam, 1974. 240pp.) the author attempts to explain the motives of a mixed figure seen in a series of revealing glimpses in which Philip is shown as a cautious, paranoid, and bigoted man.

Parker, Geoffrey. *The Grand Strategy of Philip II.* New Haven, Connecticut: Yale University Press, 1998. 446pp. Parker's investigation of Philip's policy decisions focuses on three important aspects of his reign: his dealing with the Netherlands, his foreign relations with Scotland and England, and the military campaign of the Armada. The book clarifies the factors that contributed to Philip's failures, including the king's own idiosyncrasies.

Petrie, Charles. *Philip II of Spain.* New York: W.W. Norton, 1963. 318pp. Philip remains the central focus in this life and times biography aimed at the general reader. Vivid and dramatic, Petrie succeeds in animating Philip's times but his pro-Philip interpretations are often superficial, inadequately dealing with many of the more controversial aspects of Philip's rule and character.

Walsh, William T. *Philip II.* New York: Sheed & Ward, 1937. 770pp. Philip's life story is told against a rich background of sixteenth-century history. Viewed with a strong pro-Catholic bias, Philip is sympathetically treated.

Woodward, Geoffrey. *Philip II.* New York: Longman, 1992. 135pp. Woodward's is a useful, brief overview of the highlights of Philip's reign and an assessment of his leadership and personality. Sections cover Philip's character, governmental and economic issues, and foreign and domestic affairs. There is also a brief selection of documents.

Biographical Novels

Irwin, Margaret. *Elizabeth and the Prince of Spain.* London: Chatto & Windus, 1953. 255pp. In this depiction of Elizabeth of Valois's girlhood and her interaction with Philip II, first as his lover, and, after Mary I's death, as his wife, history forms the novel's basic framework with a number of invented scenes and imagined dialogue.

Kesten, Hermann. *I, the King.* London: Routledge, 1940. 538pp. In a fictional account of Philip's reign and personality, the novel covers the king's life from his mid-20s to his death, with the major events of the period accurately described.

Plaidy, Jean. *The Spanish Bridegroom.* Philadelphia: Macrae, 1956. 288pp. In an attempt to arrive at a realistic and truthful portrait, Philip's life is depicted through his four marriages. In *The Scarlet Cloak.* (London: Hale, 1969. 335pp.), the intrigue surrounding Philip's plot to invade England and restore Catholicism is dramatized through the experiences of two Spanish brothers swept up in the events of the Armada.

Wilbur, Marguerite K. *The Unquenchable Flame: The Life of Philip II.* New York: Hastings House, 1952. 342pp. This is a fictionalized retelling of Philip's life story against an authentic but simplified period background, which includes appearances by most of the important figures of Philip's era.

Zara, Louis. *In the House of the King.* New York: Crown, 1952. 306pp. Tracing Philip's life from his boyhood to his death, the novel emphasizes the king's amorous relations and political intrigues in a vivid depiction of the era.

Fictional Portraits

Benitez Rojo, Antonio. *Sea of Lentils.* Amherst: University of Massachusetts Press, 1990. 201pp. This inventive modernist novel offers a number of perspectives on Spain's colonization of America, including the deathbed reflections of Philip II.

De Wohl, Louis. *The Last Crusader.* Philadelphia: Lippincott, 1956. 448pp. The remarkable life and times of the Spanish military hero Don Juan of Austria are dramatized in this book. The son of the Emperor Charles V, Juan spent his childhood with peasants before being recognized by Philip II as his half brother.

O'Brien, Kate. *For One Sweet Grape.* Garden City, New York: Doubleday, 1946. 340pp. Set in the court of Philip II, the novel dramatizes the relationship between the king and the Castilian princess Ana de Mendoza. Based on a historical incident, the author's drama is mainly invented.

Ross Williamson, Hugh. *The Princess a Nun.* London: Joseph, 1978. 192pp. The novel retells the story of Ana de Mendoza whose loss of Philip's favor results in her banishment.

Biographical Films and Theatrical Adaptations

O'Brien, Kate. *That Lady: A Romantic Drama.* New York: Harper, 1949. 143pp. This is the author's dramatic version of her novel, *For One Sweet Grape.*

Elizabeth (1998). Director: Shekhar Kapur. George Yiasoumi appears briefly as Philip II in this dark period drama of Elizabeth's rise to the throne. Video.

Elizabeth R (1972). Director: Roderick Graham. This television dramatic series covers Elizabeth's life from age 17 to 70, anchored by a remarkable performance by Glenda Jackson. Both colorful and convincing, with an portrayal of Philip II by Peter Jeffrey. Video.

Fire Over England (1937). Director: William K. Howard. In the first film pairing of Laurence Olivier and Vivien Leigh, this adventure drama depicts an English naval officer's espionage work in the Spanish court on the eve of the Armada's sailing. Raymond Massey depicts Philip, with Flora Robson as Elizabeth I. Video.

That Lady (1955). Director: Terrence Young. In the film version of the O'Brien novel and play, Paul Scofield depicts Philip and Olivia de Havilland plays the Spanish princess who loses the king's favor.

Other Sources

Rule, J.C., and J. TePaske, eds. *The Character of Philip II: The Problem of Moral Judgments in History.* Boston: Heath, 1963. 103pp. This useful volume brings together various historical and biographical evaluations of Philip II.

See also Elizabeth I; Mary I

378. PABLO PICASSO
1881–1973

Spanish-born painter, sculptor, graphic artist, and ceramist of exceptional virtuosity, versatility, and originality, Picasso is considered one of the greatest artists of the twentieth century. At 15 he studied at the Royal Academy of Art in Barcelona and lived and worked in France from 1904. During his "blue period" (1901–1904), he produced such paintings as *The Old Guitarist* (1903). The works of his lyrical "rose period" (1905–1906) often depict scenes from circus life. With Braque and Gris, Picasso developed Cubism; his *Les Demoiselles d'Avignon* (1907) is an important early cubist work. His works of the 1920s include the cubist *Three Musicians* (1921) and the classical *Three Women at the Fountain* (1921). His large canvas, *Guernica* (1937), depicts the agonies of the Spanish Civil War. Notable later works include *Rape of the Sabines* (1963) and *Young Bather with Sand Shovel* (1971). He produced a brilliant series of etchings toward the end of his life.

Recommended Biographies

O'Brian, Patrick. *Pablo Ruiz Picasso: A Biography.* New York: Putnam, 1976. 511pp. Written for the nonspecialist, O'Brian devotes half of his comprehensive study to Picasso's Spanish background in the years before World War I. Offering few critical insights into Picasso's genius or art, the book's strength comes from the author's evident expertise with the Spanish and Catalan milieu that shaped the young artist's development.

Penrose, Roland. *Picasso: His Life and Work.* New York: Harper & Row, 1959. 517pp. A well-researched, sympathetic, and penetrating biography by an English artist who knew Picasso for many years, Penrose's study offers a year-by-year detailed account of Picasso's life and artistic career.

Richardson, John. *A Life of Picasso.* New York: Random House, 1991–1996. 2 vols. With two of a projected four-volume study now complete, Richardson's masterful biography promises to be definitive for a long time to come. The painter's works, not his private life, are the chief focus here, though his daily activities are minutely displayed. The author supplies a meticulously researched and objective assessment of Picasso's overall development, seen from the wider context of modern art and culture. No other study supplies such a clear-eyed perspective on the nature of Picasso's genius and his world.

Other Biographical Studies

Boeck, Wilhelm, and Jaime Sabartés. *Picasso.* New York: Abrams, 1955. 524pp. Boeck's critical survey of Picasso's development as an artist from his beginnings is prefaced by a 60-page reminiscence of the artist by Sabartés, Picasso's secretary and longtime companion.

Brassai. *Picasso and Company.* Garden City, New York: Doubleday, 1966. 289pp. Told in the form of a journal recording the celebrated photographer's relationship with his friend from the period 1932 to 1947 and 1960 to 1962, Brassai's reminiscences feature reconstructions of conversations with the artist as well as valuable photographs of the artist at work. Also available as *Conversations with Picasso* (Chicago: University of Chicago Press, 1999. 400pp.).

Cabanne, Pierre. *Pablo Picasso: His Life and Times.* New York: Morrow, 1977. 606pp. Cabanne's detailed, comprehensive account of both the man and the artist is an often-unflattering portrait, marred by errors of fact, undocumented assertions, and simplistic art criticism and history.

Cirlot, Juan-Eduardo. *Picasso: Birth of a Genius.* New York: Praeger, 1972. 288pp. In the text accompanying a catalog of Picasso's donation of his early work to the city of Barcelona, Cirlot traces Picasso's artistic development from childhood up to 1917.

Crespelle, Jean-Paul. *Picasso and His Women.* New York: Coward-McCann, 1969. 223pp. Picasso is viewed in relation to his two wives and many companions who influenced his life and work. At times superficial and voyeuristic, the book's details are mostly based on previously published sources and offers little that is original.

Duncan, David D. *The Private World of Pablo Picasso.* New York: Harper, 1958. 171pp. Duncan's book of photographs with short background text records Picasso throughout the process of producing two paintings. The artist's creative process is documented.

Elgar, Frank, and Robert Maillard. *Picasso.* 1956. Revised ed. New York: Tudor, 1972. 247pp. The book combines a critical survey of Picasso's art as well as a biographical chronology in which the pro-

duction of the artist's major works is connected to his experiences.

Gedo, Mary. *Picasso: Art as Autobiography.* Chicago: University of Chicago Press, 1980. 304pp. Developing a psychological profile of the artist, drawing connections between his life and his work, Gedo identifies Picasso's dependency on others in his personal and professional life. Picasso's youth, family, and sexual relationships are considered in combination with biographical insights, art criticism, and conjecture.

Gilot, Françoise, and Carlton Lake. *Life with Picasso.* New York: McGraw-HIll, 1964. 373pp. Picasso's mistress, model, and mother of two of his children provides her frank and often painful recollections of her time with the artist, covering the period 1943 to 1953. Through reconstructed conversations, Picasso's personality and views on art are displayed. Although Gilot clearly respects Picasso's genius, she reveals his difficult, unflattering human limitations.

Huffington, Arianna S. *Picasso: Creator and Destroyer.* New York: Simon & Schuster, 1988. 558pp. Picasso's destructive private life rather than his creative genius is the focus in this bestselling biography. Based on conversations with Françoise Gilot and Picasso's daughter, the artist is depicted as a manipulative sadist in an often one-sided portrait.

Levy, Lorraine. *Picasso.* New York: Holt, 1991. 160pp. This is a brief, illustrated survey of Picasso's career. Photographs of the artist and his world and reproductions of his most famous and lesser known works make this a worthy overview for the general reader.

Mailer, Norman. *Portrait of Picasso as a Young Man: An Interpretive Biography.* New York: Atlantic Monthly Press, 1995. 400pp. Covering the years between Picasso's birth and 1914, Mailer assembles a number of eyewitness accounts to balance his novelistic freedom of psychological speculation and opinion. Although it adds nothing new to the biographical record, Mailer's impressionistic interpretation is interesting, particularly on Picasso's sexual obsessions, even though the young Picasso begins to resemble the young Mailer.

Olivier, Fernande. *Picasso and His Friends.* New York: Appleton-Century, 1965. 186pp. Picasso's early companion provides her recollections on their relationship from 1903 to 1912, shedding light on the pre-World War I life of the artist while he was still an unknown painter but at the center of the avant-garde art movement in the Bateau-Lavoir in Paris's Montmartre.

Palau i Fabre, Joseph. *Picasso: The Early Years, 1881–1907.* New York: Rizzoli, 1981. 560pp. Written by a Catalan friend of Picasso, this fascinating collection of more than 1,500 drawings, sketches, paintings, and documents is linked with background information on the artist's life up to the age of 26. Particularly useful for the social and family context of the young artist.

Sabartés, Jaime. *Picasso: An Intimate Portrait.* New York: Prentice-Hall, 1948. 230pp. Picasso's longtime secretary and companion, whose association with the painter spanned the period from 1899 and 1904 and from 1935 to 1940, provides his recollections of the artist's personality, habits, and creative process, as well as useful details about Picasso's early years in Spain.

Warncke, Carsten-Peter. *Picasso.* Köln: Taschen, 1991. 740pp. With more than 900 full-color and hundreds of black-and-white illustrations, this is an in-depth, comprehensive survey of Picasso and his works that serves as a valuable introduction to the full range of the artist's accomplishments.

Fictional Portraits

Longstreet, Stephen. *The Burning Man.* New York: Random House, 1958. 428pp. The story of Julio Diaz Navarro is based in part on the facts of Picasso's life as the young Spanish artist rises from poverty to become one of the world's most controversial artists; *The Young Men of Paris.* (New York: Delacorte, 1967. 275pp.) is a biographical novel about the artist Modigliani and the Paris art world before World War I, with appearances by such figures as Picasso, Matisse, Chagall, Utrillo, and Apollinaire.

Recommended Juvenile Biographies

Beardsley, John. *Pablo Picasso.* New York: Abrams, 1991. 92pp. YA. By interweaving biographical detail with criticism, Picasso's immense talent, dominating personality, and influence are lucidly summarized. The book also treats honestly Picasso's difficult side, particularly his relationships with women.

Bernadac, Marie-Laure, and Paule Dubouchet. *Picasso: Master of the New Idea.* New York: Abrams, 1993. 191pp. YA. Filled with many illustrations, Picasso's career is traced from his early days in Spain through his years of renown, relying on firsthand accounts of the artist by friends and associates, as well as excerpts from Picasso's own writings.

Lyttle, Richard B. *Pablo Picasso: The Man and the Image.* New York: Atheneum, 1989. 246pp. YA. Integrating details on the artist's life, work, and times into a thorough biography, Lyttle deals frankly with the less flattering side of Picasso's personality.

Selfridge, John W. *Pablo Picasso.* New York: Chelsea House, 1994. 111pp. MG/YA. Part of the Hispanics of Achievement series, the author's competent presentation of Picasso's life and work connects his works with his early years in Spain and historical events that help shape his artistic vision.

Biographical Films and Theatrical Adaptations

Martin, Steve. *Picasso at the Lapin Agile.* New York: Grove Press, 1996. 150pp. Set in a Paris café in 1904, Picasso and Albert Einstein argue about physics and art.

A&E Biography Video: Pablo Picasso: A Primitive Soul (1999). Producer: Molly Thompson. The documentary traces the painter's life and artistic career with location footage and presentation of a wide selection of his work. Video.

Mystery of Picasso (1956). Director: H.G. Clouzot. Exploring the man and his artistic method, this unusual film portrait shows Picasso creating several works before the camera. Video.

Pablo Picasso (1988). Producer: Films for the Humanities. This film portrait shows how the artist shaped the modern aesthetic vision and how his career spanned the great artistic movements of the twentieth century. Video.

Picasso (1985). Director: Didier Baussy. Part of the Portrait of the Artist series, this is a film profile of Picasso's life displaying some of his most famous works in the process. Video.

Picasso: The Man and His Work (1986). Director: Edward Quinn. This film chronicle of Picasso's life and career reveals many hitherto unknown aspects of his work and personality. Video.

Surviving Picasso (1996). Director: James Ivory. Anthony Hopkins depicts the painter as an ego-driven exploiter of women in this drama based on Arianna Huffington's book. The film concentrates on Picasso's 10-year affair with Françoise Gilot (Natascha McElhone). Joss Ackland appears as Matisse. Video.

Other Sources

McCully, Marilyn, ed. *A Picasso Anthology: Documents, Criticism, Reminiscences.* Princeton, New Jersey: Princeton University Press, 1982. 288pp. Picasso's creative process and attitudes toward art are revealed in a variety of source documents and statements from friends and associates on the man and his art.

McCully, Marilyn, ed. *Picasso: The Early Years, 1892–1906.* Washington, DC: National Gallery of Art, 1997. 430pp. This collection of essays focuses on Picasso's formative years between the ages of 11 and 24 and the evolution of his artistic talent, historical and social background, and the influences of friends and family.

379. WILLIAM PITT
1759–1806

British statesman known as "Pitt the Younger," Pitt was the second son of the Earl of Chatham ("Pitt the Elder"). He trained as a lawyer, entered Parliament in 1781, and became Chancellor of the Exchequer (1792). At the invitation of George III, he became prime minister—at age 24, the youngest in British history. In his first ministry (1783–1801), Pitt strengthened national finances and British interests in India and managed to stave off establishment of an unlimited regency when the king became temporarily insane (1788–1789), in order to stay in office. War with France and discontent in England forced his resignation (1801). His second ministry (1804–1806) was marked by the great British naval victory at Trafalgar (1805) and the allied defeat at Austerlitz (1805).

Recommended Biographies

Ehrman, John. *The Younger Pitt: The Years of Acclaim.* New York: Dutton, 1969. 710pp.; *The Younger Pitt: The Reluctant Transition.* Stanford, California: Stanford University Press, 1983. 689pp. With two volumes of a planned trilogy completed, bringing Pitt's career up to 1796, Ehrman's is a monumental scholarly study of Pitt's public life and the complex domestic and foreign policy issues of his era. The book is less successful in animating Pitt's private human side, and the biographical focus often gives way to a wider historical perspective.

Reilly, Robin. *William Pitt the Younger.* New York: Putnam, 1979. 502pp. Written for the general reader, Reilly's treatment of Pitt's personal life concentrates on those episodes that reveal his character and personality. As such, this well-written life serves as a valuable complement to Ehrman's more comprehensive treatment of Pitt's public career.

Other Biographical Studies

Evans, Eric J. *William Pitt the Younger.* New York: Routledge, 1997. 96pp. Evans's succinct examination of Pitt's career looks at the economic, domestic, and foreign policy context, as well as the political and governmental issues that shaped his public life.

Jarrett, Derek. *Pitt the Younger.* New York: Scribner, 1974. 224pp. In a brief, attractively illustrated biography, Jarrett concentrates almost exclusively on Pitt's public life, with few details about his private side. While adding little new to the conventional view, Jarrett's treatment serves as a useful introduction to Pitt's career and era.

Mackesy, Piers. *War without Victory: The Downfall of Pitt, 1799–1802.* New York: Oxford University Press, 1984. 248pp. This is a study of the political struggle that brought about the fall of the Pitt ministry in 1801 and the acceptance of the Treaty of Amien in 1802. A brilliantly written narrative history for the nonspecialist, Mackesy's study sheds considerable light on the later years of Pitt's political career.

Rosebery, Archibald. *Pitt.* New York: Macmillan, 1891. 298pp. Rosebery's interpretive biography relies on Stanhope for its details and is primarily interesting for its assessment of Pitt's character. In Rosebery's view, Pitt was overmatched by circumstances, and his premature prominence explains much about his subsequent failures.

Stanhope, Philip H. *Life of the Right Honourable William Pitt.* London: J. Murray, 1861–1862. 4 vols. The standard Victorian life is monumental in its detail, though now superseded by the authoritative, modern political biography by Ehrman.

Wilson, Philip W. *William Pitt, the Younger.* Garden City, New York: Doubleday, 1930. 347pp. In this political biography, Wilson, a former member of Parliament, writes a dramatic narrative that animates Pitt's life and times, though he can be charged with simplification in pursuit of a clear and compelling story and vivid characterization.

Biographical Novels

Maughan, A.M. *Young Pitt.* New York: J. Day, 1974. 270pp. Pitt's political career is dramatized in this biographical novel that concentrates on English parliamentary politics and Pitt's conflict with Charles James Fox.

Recommended Juvenile Biographies

Noble, Iris. *Rivals in Parliament: William Pitt and Charles Fox.* New York: J. Messner, 1970. 191pp. MG. This is a fictionalized biography more sympathetic to Fox than Pitt, who is portrayed as a cold, stiff, and austere figure.

Biographical Films and Theatrical Adaptations

Beau Brummell (1954). Director: Curtis Bernhardt. In this lavish period costume drama, Robert Morley portrays George III with Stewart Granger as Brummell and a supporting cast that includes Elizabeth Taylor, Peter Ustinov as the Prince Regent, and Paul Rogers as Pitt. Video.

The Madness of King George (1994). Director: Nicholas Hytner. In the film adaptation of Alan Bennett's play, Nigel Hawthorne reprises his critically acclaimed stage performance as a compelling human George III whose illness becomes a battleground for political opportunists. A solid supporting cast includes Helen Mirren, Ian Holm, and Julian Wadman as Pitt and Jim Carter as Fox. Video.

The Young Mr. Pitt (1942). Director: Carol Reed. Robert Donat stars as the young prime minister in a depiction of Pitt's political career. With Ramond Lovell as George III, Herbert Lom as Napoleon, and Robert Morley as Fox.

See also George III; George IV

380. EDGAR ALLAN POE
1809–1849

A poet and short-story writer famous for his compelling tales of the mysterious and the macabre, Poe is acknowledged as one of the most original writers in American literature. Born in Boston, he was orphaned at a young age and raised by his wealthy stepfather in Richmond, Virginia. He briefly attended the University of Virginia and West Point, but was expelled (1831) from the academy for numerous infractions. During the 1830s and 1840s he edited and wrote for various publications in Richmond, Philadelphia, and New York. An alleged alcoholic, he is reported to have died after a drinking binge in Baltimore. His works include the poems "The Raven" (1845) and "Annabel Lee" (1849), and the stories "The Fall of the House of Usher" (1839), "Murders in the Rue Morgue" (1841), and "The Purloined Letter" (1844).

Autobiography and Primary Sources

The Letters of Edgar Allan Poe. John Ward Ostrom, ed. Cambridge, MA: Harvard University Press, 1948. 2 vols. This scholarly edition of Poe's letters is invaluable to chart the writer's activities, relationships, and temperament.

Thomas, Dwight, and David K. Jackson. *The Poe Log: A Documentary Life of Edgar Allan Poe.* Boston: G.K. Hall, 1987. 919pp. Not a biography in the traditional sense, the book provides the verifiable facts of Poe's life as they were recorded in contemporary documents to form the basic raw data of Poe's life and reputation.

Recommended Biographies

Quinn, Arthur Hobson. *Edgar Allan Poe: A Critical Biography.* New York: Appleton-Century, 1941. 804pp. This was regarded as the standard life of Poe until Silverman's more recent biography. Still a useful study both of the life and the works.

Silverman, Kenneth. *Edgar A. Poe: Mournful and Never-Ending Remembrance.* New York: HarperCollins, 1991. 564pp. The first comprehensive life of Poe since Quinn, Silverman's account has the advantage of a vast amount of scholarship since the earlier book and a more modern sensibility to deal with the various contradictions implied in Poe's works and life. An insightful and judicious account that neither neglects the facts nor overwhelms them with an interpretative bias, the book has been called "a lasting monument among Poe studies."

Other Biographical Studies

Allen, Hervey. *Israfel: The Life and Times of Edgar Allan Poe.* New York: G.H. Doran, 1926. 748pp. This is the best of the early biographies of Poe, still important for its view of Poe's human side, though the book is marred by romanticizing and accepts speculation as fact and repeats rumors to support its psychological theories.

Bonaparte, Marie. *The Life and Works of Edgar Allan Poe: A Psychoanalytical Interpretation.* New York: Humanities Press, 1949. 749pp. With an introduction by Freud, this study offers a full-scale, provocative treatment from a psychoanalytical perspective.

Krutch, Joseph W. *Edgar Allan Poe: A Study in Genius.* New York: Knopf, 1926. 224pp. This interesting and still useful psychological study helped reestablish Poe's reputation as one of nineteenth-century America's leading literary figures.

Mankowitz, Wolf. *The Extraordinary Mr. Poe: A Biography of Edgar Allan Poe.* New York: Summit Books, 1978. 248pp. A workmanlike summary of the facts that emphasizes the unrelieved misery of Poe's life as the key to understanding his genius.

Sinclair, David. *Edgar Allan Poe.* London: J.M. Dent, 1977. 272pp. This somewhat uneven account for the nonspecialist adds little new to the established portrait of Poe. Sinclair relies on analyses of the works to explain the writer's life, quoting extensively, if at times unconvincingly, to prove his points.

Symons, Julian. *The Tell-Tale Heart: A Biography of Edgar Allan Poe.* New York: Harper & Row, 1978. 259pp. A respected author of mysteries as well as a critic, Symons provides a unique vantage point on the inventor of the detective story. Best for his discussion of Poe's craftsmanship and milieu.

Wagenknecht, Edward. *Edgar Allan Poe: The Man Behind the Legend.* New York: Oxford University Press, 1963. 276pp. This popular, judiciously balanced life for the nonspecialist considers Poe's works primarily in the context of his life, intending to arrive at a plausible portrait of the character and personality of the writer.

Biographical Novels

Hurwood, Bernhardt. *My Savage Muse: The Story of My Life: Edgar Allan Poe, An Imaginative Work.* New York: Everest House, 1980. 336pp. In this first-person novel, the author presents a plausible impersonation of Poe's voice and memories of childhood as well as his struggle and anguish to produce his works while dealing with sizable personal demons.

Madsen, David. *Black Plume: The Suppressed Memoirs of Edgar Allan Poe.* New York: Simon & Schuster, 1980. 318pp. In this first-person account, Poe emerges as a prisoner of his sensual nature, indulging his passion in experiences that include opium and murder. In a fictional episode, Poe finds himself on the trail of a killer in an exercise in terror and detection that rivals those in his stories.

Marlowe, Stephen. *The Lighthouse at the End of the World.* New York: Dutton, 1995. 320pp. Beginning as a straightforward biographical account based on the known facts about Poe's last days, the novel moves into the realm of surrealistic fiction. The imaginative story fills in the gap of Poe's disappearance before his death in a Baltimore hospital with an eerie tale in which characters from Poe's books appear.

Moore, Barbara. *The Fever Called Living.* Garden City, New York: Doubleday, 1976. 350pp. Tracing the last five years of Poe's life, the novel attempts to penetrate the various myths surrounding Poe to create a plausible portrait of the man.

O'Neal, Cothburn. *Very Young Mrs. Poe.* New York: Crown, 1956. 247pp. Poe is reflected in the story of his young wife Virginia and her role in helping Poe develop his literary genius. Although faithful to the known facts, this is a somewhat idealized and romanticized portrait.

Fictional Portraits

It is not surprising that the inventor of the modern detective story whose own life presents a number of unsolved mysteries should appear in several suspense and detection novels.

Hatvary, George Egon. *The Murder of Edgar Allan Poe.* New York: Carroll & Graf, 1997. 211pp. This ingenious novel treats Poe's death as a mystery in which Poe's own creation, Auguste Dupin, travels to Baltimore to discover who in fact killed Poe.

Meyers, Manny. *The Last Mystery of Edgar Allan Poe.* Philadelphia: Lippincott, 1978. 202pp. In 1846 a destitute Poe is recruited by New York's superintendent of police to assist in the search for a brutal killer of two young society heiresses.

Perowne, Barry. *A Singular Conspiracy.* Indianapolis: Bobbs-Merrill, 1974. 209pp. The novel speculates on what might have happened to Poe during the first four months of 1844, a blank in his history that has puzzled biographers. Here Poe journeys to Paris where he meets his champion, French poet Charles Baudelaire.

Schechter, Harold. *Nevermore.* New York: Pocket Books, 1999. 322pp. In Schechter's ingenious period mystery, Davy Crockett joins forces with Edgar Allan Poe to solve a series of murders in Baltimore.

Steward, Barbara, and Dwight Steward. *Evermore.* New York: Morrow, 1978. 202pp. ; *The Lincoln Diddle.* New York: Morrow, 1979. 251pp. The premise for these historical mysteries is that Poe did not die in 1849. He instead stages his own death and reemerges as Henri Le Rennet, detective.

Recommended Juvenile Biographies

Anderson, Madelyn Klein. *Edgar Allan Poe: A Mystery.* New York: F. Watts, 1993. 156pp. MG. Anderson's able biographical account presents a complex portrait of a brilliant critic, gifted poet, and writer who was fiercely opinionated, romantic, and wildly impractical.

LeVert, Suzanne. *Edgar Allan Poe.* New York: Chelsea House, 1992. 111pp. YA. This interesting and informative life of Poe focuses on the writer's long struggle for literary success.

Biographical Films and Theatrical Adaptations

A&E Biography Video: The Mystery of Edgar Allan Poe (1997). Producer: Noah Morowitz. This is a straightforward documentary account of Poe's life and career. Video.

Edgar Allan Poe, 1809–1849 (1996). Director: Malcolm Hossick. This brief documentary portrait traces Poes life and career using drawings, photographs, and film footage of places associated with the writer. Video.

Edgar Allan Poe: Architect of Dreams (1995). Director: Jean M. McClure. A brief examination of Poe's life that features location shots, dramatizations from his works, and an appreciation by poet and Poe scholar Dave Smith. Video.

Edgar Allan Poe: Terror of the Soul (1994). Producer: Karen Thomas. PBS-produced biography includes interviews with Poe scholars and dramatic re-creations from his life and his works. Video.

The Loves of Edgar Allan Poe (1942). Director: Harry Lockman A bland biographical drama of Poe's life and the women who influenced him. Shepperd Strudwick stars as the writer with Linda Darnell as Virginia Clemm.

Poe/Cooper/Irving (1987). Producer: January Productions. Part of the Meet the Classic Authors series, each of the three American writers are profiled. Video.

The Spectre of Edgar Allan Poe (1973). Director: Mohry Quandour. Based loosely on Poe's own torments, this horror film recounts Poe's visit to an asylum where his love Lenore is being held in the midst of murder and torture. Robert Walker Jr. stars. Video

381. MARCO POLO
ca. 1254–1324

Venetian traveler famous for his overland journey to China (1271–1275) with his father and uncle, Polo became a favorite of Kublai Khan, whom he served as an envoy throughout China and in the states of southeast Asia. Polo was appointed governor of Yangchow for three years, and in 1295 re-

turned to Venice. He commanded a galley in the Venetian war against Genoa and was taken prisoner (1296) by the Genoese. During his two-year imprisonment, he dictated an account of his travels, which later inspired explorers to seek a sea passage to the Far East.

Autobiography and Primary Sources

Marco Polo: The Description of the World. Arthur Moule and Paul Pelliot, eds. London: Routledge, 1938. 2 vols. Marco Polo's account of his travels is also the chief source for information concerning his life. This scholarly edition also includes a genealogy of the traveler's family, a useful chronology, and helpful notes identifying historical figures, events, and customs. For a modernized English translation see *The Travels of Marco Polo.* Milton Rugoff, ed. (New York: Modern Library, 1953. 302pp.).

Recommended Biographies

Hart, Henry. *Marco Polo: Venetian Adventurer.* 1942. Revised ed. Norman: University of Oklahoma Press, 1967. 306pp. In a chronological narrative account, Polo's life from birth to death is presented in a scholarly though highly readable fashion; the book is particularly strong on Polo's European background.

Humble, Richard. *Marco Polo.* New York: Putnam, 1975. 232pp. In a vivid retelling of Polo's journey to China, Humble stresses the human drama involved and the aspects of Polo's character revealed in his writings. Humble also presents a clear and absorbing account of the period background that helps explain Polo's motives and reactions. The book's many illustrations are an added bonus.

Larner, John. *Marco Polo and the Discovery of the World.* New Haven, Connecticut: Yale University Press, 1999. 250pp. This is a well-researched examination of Polo's impact in which his journeys are related to the wider context of the age of European discovery. The author relies on a close reading of Polo's writings to unlock some aspects of his personality.

Other Biographical Studies

Collis, Maurice. *Marco Polo.* London: Faber and Faber, 1950. 190pp. Collis offers a critical commentary of Polo's account of his journeys, setting Polo's words in the wider context of what history and scholarship have revealed, a method that helps to explain the discoverer's character and creativity.

Olschki, Leonardo. *Marco Polo's Asia.* Berkeley: University of California Press, 1960. 459pp. Polo's journeys are put in the context of earlier travelers and accounts based on the author's considerable scholarship concerning Medieval Europe and Asia. Olschki's wide-ranging notes on Polo's account serve as a valuable companion reference volume with helpful information on many aspects of Polo's life and times.

Biographical Novels

Jennings, Gary. *The Journeyer.* New York: Atheneum, 1984. 782pp. Based in part on his actual

journey with considerable embellishment, Marco Polo narrates his adventures throughout Asia.

Marshall, Edison. *Caravan to Xanadu: A Novel of Marco Polo.* New York: Farrar, Straus, 1953. 371pp. Marco Polo narrates his travels in a fictionalized version of the traveler's account, emphasizing the human drama with a credible portrait of the adventurer.

Fictional Portraits

Byrne, Donn. *Messer Marco Polo.* New York: Century, 1921. 147pp. Only loosely based on fact, Polo's adventures in China are treated as an exotic, romantic tale of the traveler's love of Kublai Khan's daughter.

Calvino, Italo. *Invisible Cities.* New York: Harcourt, Brace, 1974. 165pp. In a blend of fact and fantasy, the novel constructs an imagined conversation between Polo and Kublai Khan as the former entertains and instructs the latter in a tour of a symbolic landscape.

Griffiths, Paul. *Myself and Marco Polo: A Novel of Changes.* New York: Random House, 1990. 274pp. Griffiths's novel imagines what Rustichello, the writer to whom Polo dictated his adventures while in prison, might have added to the manuscript.

Recommended Juvenile Biographies

Greene, Carol. *Marco Polo: Voyager to the Orient.* Chicago: Childrens Press, 1987. 109pp. MG. Greene's is a competent evocation of Polo's journey and the challenges he faced.

Hull, Mary. *The Travels of Marco Polo.* San Diego: Lucent Books, 1995. 96pp. MG. This informative narrative history of Polo's journeys is documented with numerous quotations from primary sources.

Stefoff, Rebecca. *Marco Polo and the Medieval Explorers.* New York: Chelsea House, 1992. 111pp. MG/YA. Polo's achievements are placed in their historical context in this well-written and well-researched biography/history.

Biographical Films and Theatrical Adaptations

O'Neill, Eugene. *Marco's Millions.* New York: Boni & Liveright, 1927. 218pp. Polo is presented as a swaggering traveling salesman who is loved in vain by Kublai Khan's daughter in this satiric fantasy.

A&E Biography Video: Marco Polo: Journey to the East (1995). Director: Bill Harris. Polo's background and journeys are chronicled in this informative documentary portrait. Video.

Adventures of Marco Polo (1938). Director: Archie Mayo. In a screenplay by Robert Sherwood, Gary Cooper portrays Polo in a fictional elaboration of his Asian journey. George Baber appears as Kublai Khan. Video.

Marco (1973). Director: Seymour Robbie. Musical adventure with Desi Arnaz Jr. as Polo and Zero Mostel as Kublai Khan. Video.

Marco Polo (1961). Director: Hugo Fregonese. Italian version of Polo's life and journey with Rory

Calhoun in the title role and Camillo Pilotto as Kublai Khan.

Marco Polo (1982). Diretor: Guiliano Montaldo. Television miniseries starring Ken Marshall as Polo, Ruocheng Ying as Kublai Khan, and Burt Lancaster as Pope Gregory X.

Marco Polo (1997). Director: George Erschbamer. Don Diamont portrays Marco Polo in this film version of his travels and adventures with a strong supporting cast, including Herbert Lom, Jack Palance, and Oliver Reed. Video.

Marco the Magnificent (1965). Director: Noel Howard. This is an episodic, mostly fictional treatment of Polo's life and adventures with Horst Buchholz in the title role and Anthony Quinn as Kublai Khan.

382. ALEXANDER POPE
1688–1744

Pope is acknowledged by many as one of the greatest poets of the eighteenth century and the greatest English verse satirist. He was born in London and suffered from a childhood tubercular condition, which left him with poor health and a spinal curvature; he never grew taller than 4 feet, 6 inches. As a Roman Catholic, he could not receive a Protestant education and after the age of 12 was largely self-taught. A prodigy in his teens, he became a fixture in London literary society by the age of 17. His works include *Essay on Criticism* (1711), written in heroic couplets, the mock-epic *The Rape of the Lock* (1714), the satirical poem *The Dunciad* (1728–1743), and translations of *The Iliad* and *The Odyssey*. He also wrote *An Essay on Man* (1734) and *Moral Essays* (1731–1735).

Autobiography and Primary Sources

Correspondence. George Sherburn, ed. Oxford: Clarendon Press, 1956. 5 vols. This scholarly edition of Pope's correspondence is a monument of modern scholarship that reveals the many sides of the writer and his relationships with a wide artistic and social circle. A selection is also available in *Letters* (New York: Oxford University Press, 1960. 384pp.).

Recommended Biographies

Mack, Maynard. *Alexander Pope: A Life.* New Haven, Connecticut: Yale University Press, 1985. 975pp. Painstakingly researched by the leading Pope authority, Mack's definitive life is a richly detailed biography as well as a literary and cultural history that brings Pope's intellectual and poetic development into close and compelling focus.

Rosslyn, Felicity. *Alexander Pope: A Literary Life.* New York: St. Martin's, 1990. 176pp. For the reader desiring a more compact treatment of Pope's life and works than Mack's monumental study, Rosslyn's is a fine choice. Sympathetic but balanced in its approach, Pope's remarkable rise to prominence is described against the compelling background of his physical and cultural challenges.

Other Biographical Studies

Ault, N. *New Light on Pope.* London: Methuen, 1949. 379pp. Ault takes a thematic approach, offering not a comprehensive biography but an examination of various aspects of the writer's life, work, and relationships.

Dobrée, Bonamy. *Alexander Pope.* 1951. Reprint ed. New York: Greenwood, 1969. 125pp. This is a brief survey of Pope's life and works that provides the essential details in a balanced appreciation.

Johnson, Samuel. "Pope" in *Lives of the English Poets.* 1781. Reprint ed. London, Oxford University Press, 1959, 2 vols. Johnson's brief introduction to Pope's life and poetry features astute critical assessment and remains one of the best early treatments of Pope's characteristics as a poet.

Quennell, Peter. *Alexander Pope: The Education of Genius, 1688–1728.* New York: Stein and Day, 1968. 278pp. Quennell's biography covers the first 40 years of Pope's life, up to the publication of *The Dunciad.* Informed by the author's familiarity with Pope's social and cultural context, the book casts light on his development as a man and poet, relating Pope's work to his experiences.

Sherburn, George. *The Early Career of Alexander Pope.* Oxford: Clarendon Press, 1934. 326pp. Like the author's scholarly edition of Pope's letters, this is a scrupulously documented and authoritative account of Pope's formative years as a writer.

Sitwell, Edith. *Alexander Pope.* 1930. Reprint ed. New York: W.W. Norton, 1962. 256pp. In an enthusiastic appreciation, Sitwell contributed to the revival of interest in Pope's life and work in the twentieth century. Although offering little in the way of original research, Sitwell's is an enthusiastic vindication of the poet that sets out to challenge conventional notions about the man and his work. Although overly defensive and biased in Pope's favor, Sitwell helps to redress the balance in the view of Pope's nature and achievement that had suffered from comparison with the Romantics.

Stephen, Leslie. *Alexander Pope.* 1880. Reprint ed. New York: AMS, 1958. 210pp. Written by the famous eighteenth-century specialist and editor of the *Dictionary of National Biography,* Stephen's elegant and succinct biographical profile is a sensitive and lucid appreciation informed by the author's considerable expertise.

Other Sources

Berry, Reginald. *A Pope Chronology.* Boston: G.K. Hall, 1988. 221pp. Berry supplies a detailed chronology of Pope's activities and publications.

383. EZRA POUND
1885–1972

Influential twentieth-century poet, and a critic and translator, Pound was one of the century's most famous and controversial literary figures. He was born in Idaho and graduated from Hamilton College (1905) and the University of Pennsylvania (M.A., 1906). He went to Europe in 1907 and during the early 1920s lived in Paris, where he was associated with the literary circle surrounding Ger-

trude Stein. He settled (1925) in Italy and during World War II broadcast pro-fascist and anti-Semitic propaganda to the United States for the Italians. He was tried for treason in the United States and confined (1946–1958) to a mental institution. He returned to Italy after his release. A champion of the imagist and vorticist movements, he influenced such poets as T. S. Eliot and W. B. Yeats. His major works are *Homage to Sextus Propertius* (1918), *Hugh Selwyn Mauberley* (1920), and the epic *Cantos* (1925–1960).

Autobiography and Primary Sources

Ezra and Dorothy Pound: Letters in Captivity, 1945–46. Robert Spoo and Omar Pound, ed. New York: Oxford University Press, 1998. 448pp. When he was incarcerated in Italy at the end of World War II, Pound was allowed to write only to his wife, and the record of his correspondence affords a unique look at this troubled yet remarkably productive period of the poet's life. The collection also includes military and FBI documents.

Selected Letters of Ezra Pound, 1907–1941. D.D. Paige, ed. New York: New Directions, 1971. 358pp. Pound's letters offer a running commentary on the creation of literary modernism and his contact with virtually everyone of significance in literature during the period. The letters show the man in all his contradictions, full of charm, arrogance, wit, and vulgarity.

Recommended Biographies

Carpenter, Humphrey. *A Serious Character: The Life of Ezra Pound.* Boston: Houghton Mifflin, 1988. 1,005pp. Despite hostility to Pound's artistry, Carpenter's biography provides one of the fullest depictions of the poet's life and one of the liveliest narratives available. Pound's many masks are penetrated to reveal an arrogant egoist with a mixture of pretension and vulgarity whose personal, human failures dominate Carpenter's portrayal.

Flory, Wendy S. *The American Ezra Pound.* New Haven, Connecticut: Yale University Press, 1989. 246pp. A convincing brief biography, Flory's depiction of the poet's motivations and inner conflicts is credible and judicious in that the poet is convincingly connected to the complex and contradictory public figure.

Tytell, John. *Ezra Pound: The Solitary Volcano.* New York: Anchor Press, 1987. 368pp. This is a well-researched, highly readable full-length account of a self-destructive genius. Tytell captures Pound's many moods but is less successful in explaining the motivation behind the writer's often erratic behavior.

Wilhelm, James J. *The American Roots of Ezra Pound.* Garland, 1986. 230pp.; *Ezra Pound in London and Paris, 1908–1925.* University Park: Pennsylvania State University Press, 1990. 360pp.; *Ezra Pound: The Tragic Years, 1925–1972.* University Park: Pennsylvania State University Press, 1994. 390pp. Wilhelm's three-volume study is painstakingly researched and balanced, correcting the factual record and shedding considerable light on Pound's character and development.

Other Biographical Studies

Ackroyd, Peter. *Ezra Pound and His World.* New York: Scribner, 1980. 127pp. The author's concise and lively text accompanying a series of photographs summarizes the essential details of Pound's life and career with occasional literary judgments on his significance as a poet and critic.

Cornell, Julien. *The Trial of Ezra Pound.* New York: J. Day, 1966. 215pp. Pound's lawyer provides his view of the complicated legal maneuvering surrounding the treason charges against the poet. The book includes a transcript of the hearing to determine Pound's competence to stand trial.

Heymann, C. David. *Ezra Pound: The Last Rower: A Political Profile.* New York: Viking, 1976. 372pp. The first scholar granted access to Pound's massive FBI file, Heymann documents the writer's growing preoccupation in the 1930s with economic issues, his increasingly violent anti-Semitic views, and support of Italy's fascist regime during World War II. Less useful for its biographical interpretation to explain Pound's behavior, the book provides the fullest record available of his political activities.

Levy, Alan. *Ezra Pound: The Voice of Silence.* Sag Harbor, New York: Permanent Press, 1983. 149pp. Written for the general reader, Levy sketches Pound's life with a chronology, excerpts by and about the writer, and a critical treatment of selected poetry.

Meacham, Henry M. *The Caged Panther: Ezra Pound at Saint Elizabeths.* New York: Twayne, 1967. 222pp. After a brief sketch of the poet's early life and activities during World War II that led to his being confined in a mental hospital, the book chronicles the 13 years Pound spent in St. Elizabeths and the efforts to secure his release in a documentary account.

Norman, Charles. *Ezra Pound.* 1960. Revised ed. New York: Funk and Wagnalls, 1969. 493pp. Pound's life story up to the date of its writing is told chiefly through letters and the recollections of those who knew the poet. More a patchwork than an interpretive synthesis, the book is chiefly valuable for the multiple views of Pound offered, even if he eludes the author's ability to bring him to comprehensible terms.

Stock, Noel. *The Life of Ezra Pound.* New York: Pantheon, 1970. 472pp. With access to Pound's own collection of books and papers, Stock provides a well-documented and reliable biography that replaces the various myths and legends about the poet with fact. Often discreet about Pound's private life and incomplete on many details, however, the book falls short of providing a fully satisfying study.

Torrey, E. Fuller. *The Roots of Treason: Ezra Pound and the Secret of St. Elizabeths.* New York: McGraw-Hill, 1983. 339pp. This psychological examination of Pound's wartime activities and subsequent years confined to a mental hospital offers the assertion that Pound avoided a trial for treason by feigning madness assisted by a conspiracy among the team of psychiatrists who evaluated him. Along with unsupported charges and surmises, Torrey clarifies some obscure aspects of Pound's years at St. Elizabeths, but the sensational and unproven undermine the book's reliability.

Biographical Films and Theatrical Adaptations

Findley, Timothy. *The Trials of Ezra Pound.* Winnipeg: Blizzard, 1995. 78pp. In Findley's dramatic interpretation of Pound's treason and sanity hearings, the poet offers his own revealing analysis of his self-destruction.

Ezra Pound (1987). Director: Richard P. Rodgers. A film exploration of the poet's life and work with commentary by Basil Bunting, James Laughlin, Alfred Kazin, and Hugh Kenner. Video.

Ezra Pound: American Odyssey (1988). Director: Lawrence Pitkethly. This film portrait explores both Pound's artistic achievements and the controversies that surround him. Video.

Hemingway (1988). Director: Bernhard Sinkel. Stacey Keach portrays Hemingway in this television mini-series that dramatizes highlights of Hemingway's personal, professional, and celebrity life. Pound is depicted by Geoffrey Corey. Video.

Other Sources

Nadel, Ira B., ed. *The Cambridge Companion to Ezra Pound.* New York: Cambridge University Press, 1999. 300pp. This useful collection of critical essays covers various aspects of Pound's work and life, including chapters on politics, anti-Semitism, and gender issues.

384. ELVIS PRESLEY
1935–1977

The first major rock and roll star, Presley was born in Tupelo, Mississippi, and began recording in 1953. He dominated rock music during the 1950s and early 1960s with such hits as "Love Me Tender," "Heartbreak Hotel," "Hound Dog," "Blue Suede Shoes," and "Don't Be Cruel." A popular movie star, his many films include *Jailhouse Rock* (1957), *Blue Hawaii* (1961), and *Viva Las Vegas* (1964). After his death he became a cult hero and his Memphis home, Graceland, became a national shrine for his many fans.

Autobiography and Primary Sources

Elvis in His Own Words. Mike Farren and Pearce Marchbank, ed. New York: Omnibus, 1977. 128pp. Extracts from the few interviews Presley granted are collected here.

Recommended Biographies

Brown, Peter H., and Pat H. Broeske. *Down at the End of Lonely Street: The Life and Death of Elvis Presley.* New York: Dutton, 1997. 524pp. Based on extensive interviews with associates and new documentary material, this is a comprehensive, realistic treatment of Presley's life and career that achieves a balance between sympathy and demythologizing. A well-researched synthesis of new and previously revealed details that allows a complex portrait to emerge.

Guralnick, Peter. *The Last Train to Memphis.* Boston: Little, Brown, 1994. 560pp; *Careless Love: The Unmaking of Elvis Presley.* Boston: Little, Brown, 1999. 767pp. Praised as the finest rock-and-roll biography ever written and among the most ambitious biographical undertakings yet devoted to a major American figure of the second half of the twentieth century, Guralnick's impressively researched, objective, and utterly engrossing life can rightfully claim to be the definitive study for some time to come. Presley is seen up close in captivating detail as well as from a wider historical and cultural context.

Hammontree, Patsy. *Elvis Presley: A Bio-Bibliography.* Westport, Connecticut: Greenwood, 1985. 301pp. Scholarly and reliable, Hammontree avoids both the excesses of the fan and the debunker in this helpful reference source that covers Presley's life and career with precision and insight.

Hopkins, Jerry. *Elvis: A Biography.* New York: Simon & Schuster, 1971. 448pp. The first attempt at a comprehensive, objective biography, Hopkins's treatment is short on interpretation but factually reliable with Presley's southern, religious, and family background fully described; *Elvis: The Final Years.* New York: St. Martin's, 1980. 258pp. Completing Presley's story, Hopkins details the singer's sad end that manages to avoid the excesses of either the pathos of his admirers or the bathos of his detractors.

Jorgensen, Ernst. *Elvis Presley: A Life in Music.* New York: St. Martin's, 1998. 454pp. The author, the director of RCA's Elvis recordings catalog, views Presley's working life as a singer through a detailed and anecdote-rich narrative account of his studio and concert career. The result is revelatory and valuable, going beyond the image of Elvis as cultural myth and flawed icon to reveal the source and development of his musical talent.

Other Biographical Studies

Dundy, Elaine. *Elvis and Gladys.* New York: Macmillan, 1985. 350pp. Dundy's psychological portrait of Presley and his mother is one of the most insightful and objective attempts to penetrate the Elvis myth and to substitute a credible human profile. Judicious in its analysis, conjectures are identified as such, taking Presley's story only up to his mother's death in 1958.

Frew, Tim. *Elvis: His Life and Music.* New York: Barnes and Noble, 1997. 176pp. This pictorial biography traces Elvis's rise from humble beginnings in Tupelo, Mississippi, into a rock and cultural icon.

Geller, Larry. *If I Can Dream: Elvis's Own Story.* New York: Simon & Schuster, 1989. 331pp. The work of Presley's hairdresser and spiritual adviser, the biography claims to provide Elvis's story as the "King" himself would have written it. Offbeat and lacking objectivity, the book contrasts with others in which the sordid is predominant by viewing Presley's life as an almost mystical quest for enlightenment.

Giuliano, Geoffrey, and Deborah Lynn Black. *The Illustrated Elvis Presley.* Edison, New Jersey: Chartwell Books, 1994. 96pp. A photo-biography in which the illustrations provide the major illumination.

Goldman, Albert. *Elvis.* New York: McGraw-Hill, 1981. 598pp. In a debunking assault on the Presley myth, this is Elvis's warts and little else: the singer as a crass, rednecked narcissist, besotted by drugs and fame, in a one-sided, condescending caricature to rival the worst and best Elvis impersonators. Goldman's tabloid revelations are undocumented and unverifiable although the book uses a former Presley bodyguard as one of its chief sources.

Greenwood, Earl, and Kathleen Tracy. *The Boy Who Would Be King.* New York: Dutton, 1990. 310pp. Written by Elvis's cousin and press agent, the first eyewitness account by a blood relative, the book chronicles the singer's childhood in Mississippi and his youth in Memphis and offers a believable, balanced treatment of Elvis's formative years and important family background.

Harbinson, W.A. *The Illustrated Elvis.* New York: Grosset & Dunlap, 1976. 160pp. One of many illustrated biographies in which the photographs make more impact than the serviceable text connecting them.

Juanico, June. *Elvis: In the Twilight of Memory.* New York: Arcade, 1997. 319pp. Elvis's early girlfriend recalls their relationship from 1955 to 1957 in an intimate diary-like account that alternates between treacly sweet, cliché-ridden, refreshing, and moving.

Lichter, Paul. *The Boy Who Dared to Rock: The Definitive Elvis.* Garden City, New York: Doubleday, 1978. 304pp. Compiled by an avid fan, the facts of Elvis's life and career are summarized with little analysis other than admiration. The details concerning Presley's drug dependency are overlooked. The book does include a useful discography, complete up to 1978, and a listing of live performances.

Marsh, Dave. *Elvis.* New York: Times Books, 1982. 245pp. Marsh's critical illustrated biography keeps the music in the foreground as he objectively surveys the singer's career, his impact, influence, and long decline after the exuberant energy of his early recordings. Includes a discography and filmography.

Presley, Priscilla Beaulieu. *Elvis and Me.* As told to Sandra Jarmon. New York: Putnam, 1985. 320pp. Priscilla Presley recounts her relationship with the singer from their first meeting in 1959 when she was 14 through their marriage, and divorce in 1973. A strong defensive tone is evident as others' versions of their life together are rebutted.

West, Red, Sonny West, and Dave Hebler. As told to Steve Dunleavy. *Elvis: What Happened?* New York: Ballantine Books, 1977. 332pp. The first of Elvis's inner circle to break their silence on Presley's drug use and misbehavior, West and company offer their eyewitness testimony filtered through an evident bias that compromises the book's reliability.

Whitmer, Peter O. *The Inner Elvis: A Psychological Biography of Elvis Aaron Presley.* New York: Hyperion, 1996. 480pp. Whitmer, a clinical psychologist, probes Presley's psyche guided by a central theme that the death of his twin brother at childbirth offers the key to explain the singer's eating disorders, dependency, sexual abnormalities, and singing talent.

Biographical Novels

Charters, Samuel B. *Elvis Presley Calls His Mother After the Ed Sullivan Show.* Minneapolis: Coffee House Press, 1992. 128pp. The novel captures the innocent, shy, and sensitive Elvis after his 1957 appearance on the Ed Sullivan Show in an extended monologue by the singer on the telephone to his mother.

Fictional Portraits

Baty, Keith, and Robert Graham. *Elvis: The Novel.* Chester Springs, Pennsylvania: Dufour Editions, 1984. 222pp. This is an alternative version of Elvis's life with differences and similarities presented to offer an indirect, reflected portrait of the actual Presley.

Childress, Mark. *Tender.* New York: Harmony Books, 566pp. Elvis alter-ego, Leroy Kirby, follows the same route to stardom and destruction in this fictional take on the Elvis phenomenon.

Duff, Gerald. *That's All Right, Mama.* Dallas: Baskerville, 1995. 278pp. The novel takes the form of the autobiography of Jesse Presley, Elvis's stillborn twin brother. Serving his famous brother as a personal and professional stand-in, Elvis's career is glimpsed through the lens of sibling rivalry.

Womack, Jack. *Elvissey.* New York: Tor, 1993. 319pp. This futuristic tale describes the efforts of a troubled couple who journey back in time to 1954 to kidnap the young Elvis to have him save what is left of humanity.

Recommended Juvenile Biographies

Daily, Robert. *Elvis Presley: The King of Rock 'n' Roll.* New York: F. Watts, 1996. 144pp. MG. Presley's contributions and influence are stressed in this candid narrative account of his rise to fame, success, and sudden death.

Gentry, Tony. *Elvis Presley.* New York: Chelsea House, 1994. 127pp. MG. Sympathetic but realistic in noting the controversies in Presley's life and career, this is a clearly written chronological account.

Wootton, Richard. *Elvis!* New York: Random House, 1985. 127pp. MG. Wootton covers Elvis's life and career from his early days to his death in a well-balanced evaluation. Clearly a fan, Wootton does not glorify the aspects of Presley's personality that eventually ruined him.

Biographical Films and Theatrical Adaptations

A&E Biography Video: Elvis Presley: Story of a Legend (1993). Producer: Melanie Blythe. This profile includes interviews with members of Elvis's inner circle and rare home movies. Video.

Elvis (1979). Director: John Carpenter. Kurt Russell stars as Elvis in this made-for-television biography tracing his life from high school to his 1969 comeback. Shelley Winters appears as Gladys Presley, with Pat Hingle as Colonel Tom Parker, and Season Hubley as Priscilla. Video.

Elvis (1990). Director: James Gordon. A biographical portrait using rare newsreel footage and film clips. Video.

Elvis and Me (1990). Director: Larry Peerce. Based on the book by Priscilla Beaulieu Presley, Elvis is portrayed by Dale Midkiff (with his singing voice supplied by country star Ronnie McDowell) in this television mini-series. Susan Walters portrays Priscilla. Video.

Elvis: That's the Way It Is (1970). Director: Denis Sanders. Informal, admiring documentary on Elvis's preparing for his Las Vegas opening in 1969. Video.

Elvis: The Beginning (1993). Director: Steve Bassett. Interviews with Elvis's oldest friends and first band members reconstruct the events of his first road tour. Video.

Elvis: The Complete Story (1997). Using Presley's own words about his rise to fame, the film concentrates on his film career with interviews with many of his co-stars. Video.

Elvis in Hollywood (1993). Director: Frank Martin. Documentary look at Elvis's film career with his 1956 screen test, production stills, outtakes, and interviews with co-stars, directors, and friends. Video.

Elvis Memories (1986). Producers: George Klein and Jerry L. Williams. With interviews, performances, and home movies, this film tribute is presented by fellow musicians, entertainers, relatives, and friends. Video.

Elvis on Tour (1972). Directors: Pierre Adidge and Robert Abel. Concert performances. Video.

Heartbreak Hotel (1988). Director: Chris Columbus. Unconvincing comedy in which Elvis (David Keith) is kidnapped and taken to the home of an avid fan (Tuesday Weld). Video.

This Is Elvis (1981). Directors: Andrew Solt and Malcolm Lee. Documentary footage is combined with dramatic recreations of events in Presley's life. Video.

Touched by Love (1980). Director: Gus Trikonis. Based on the book *To Elvis with Love* by Lena Canada, this sentimental drama records a person with cerebral palsy's pen-pal relationship with Elvis. Starring Diane Lane and Deborah Raffin. Video.

Other Sources

Coffey, Frank. *The Complete Idiot's Guide to Elvis.* New York: Macmillan, 1997. 352pp. A compendium of background information, details on Presley's performances, recordings, and films.

Cotten, Lee. *All Shook Up: Elvis Day-by-Day, 1954–1977.* Ann Arbor, Michigan: Pierian Press, 1985. 580pp. A daily calendar of Elvis's activities from the beginning of his musical career to his death.

Evans, Mike. *The King on the Road: Elvis on Tour, 1954–1971.* New York: St. Martin's, 1996. 208pp. This is a comprehensive guide to Elvis's days on the road from his earliest performances to the end of his career.

Guralnick, Peter, and Ernst Jorgensen. *Elvis Day by Day.* New York: Ballantine Books, 1999. 384pp. The leading authorities on Presley's life and music provide a complete account of the singer's life using previously unavailable materials collected by Elvis Presley Enterprises.

Latham, Caroline, and Jeannie Sakol. *E Is for Elvis: An A-to-Z Illustrated Guide to the King of Rock and Roll.* New York: New American Library, 1990. 301pp. Topically arranged reference guide to many aspects of Presley's life and career.

Pierce, Patricia J. *The Ultimate Elvis: Elvis Presley Day by Day.* New York: Simon & Schuster, 1994. 560pp. One of several chronologies detailing Presley's public and private life in a daily calendar of his life from birth to death, along with posthumous sightings.

Quain, Kevin, ed. *The Elvis Reader: Texts and Sources on the King of Rock 'n' Roll.* New York: St. Martin's, 1992. 344pp. This is a rich collection of various writers' views of Elvis the man and the myth.

Stanley, David, and Frank Coffey. *The Elvis Encyclopedia.* Los Angeles: General Pub. Group, 1994. 287pp. This reference compendium includes a day-by-day chronology, first-person anecdotes from friends and family, photos, letters, and private papers, as well as an Elvis quiz for the serious devotee.

Wroth, Fred L. *Elvis: His Life from A to Z.* Chicago: Contemporary Books, 1988. 618pp. Yet another mixture of trivial and essential data on the performer.

385. MARCEL PROUST
1871–1922

French novelist and one of the major figures of modern literature, Proust was born in Paris to wealthy bourgeois parents and was plagued by asthma as a child and neuroses as an adult. By 1907 he had retired from Parisian society and lived as a recluse in a cork-lined room, where at night he worked on the seven-part, semi-autobiographical *Remembrance of Things Past* (1907–1919), regarded as one of the greatest novels of the twentieth century.

Autobiography and Primary Sources

Marcel Proust on Art and Literature, 1896–1919. Sylvia Townsend Warner, ed. New York: Carroll & Graf, 1984. 416pp. This critical collection presents Proust's view on writing, art, and such literary masters as Tolstoy, Goethe, and Stendhal.

Selected Letters. Philip Kolb, ed. New York: Oxford University Press, 1983–1989. 2 vols. Kolb's scholarly edition of Proust's voluminous correspondence clearly shows the various guises of the writer as well as his dominant preoccupation with health. Indispensable as a biographical source with insights into the outer and inner dynamics of his genius.

Recommended Biographies

Carter, William C. *Marcel Proust: A Life.* New Haven, Connecticut: Yale University Press, 2000. 946pp. Taking into account newly available correspondence and memoirs, Carter supplies a full-scale reassessment of Proust's life that offers fresh insights into many aspects of the writer's ac-

tivities, work, relationships, and temperament. The book is particularly strong in its careful tracing of the slow evolution of Proust's creativity.

Hayman, Ronald. *Proust: A Biography.* New York: HarperCollins, 1990. 564pp. Taking advantage of Proust's correspondence, edited by Philip Kolb, Hayman's biography adds new details to the life record provided by Painter and draws a convincing, nuanced portrait of a complex, multisided Proust in search of a unifying identity.

Painter, George. *Proust.* 1959-65. Revised ed. New York: Random House, 1978. 2 vols. Regarded as the standard life, Painter's is an exhaustive study of Proust's life and the connections between his experiences and his writing. No other source is so packed with details or exploits as fully the primary and secondary sources. Painter is particularly strong on Proust's creative method and the origin of his genius in his family background, upbringing, and milieu.

White, Edmund. *Marcel Proust.* New York: Viking, 1999. 165pp. White, a novelist, supplies a biographical overview that serves to distill Proust's essence in a concise succession of memorable scenes from his life told with the fiction writer's eye for detail. Elegantly written and insightful, White's critical introduction to the man and his works is recommended for the reader looking for a good place to start on Proust.

Other Biographical Studies

Albaret, Céleste. *Monsieur Proust.* New York: McGraw-Hill, 1976. 387pp. Proust's housekeeper and confidante offers her recollections of the writer from 1914 to his death. An adoring portrait, Albaret's view passes over less flattering aspects of Proust's personality and private life, but still definitively documents his unusual domestic routine.

Barker, Richard H. *Marcel Proust: A Biography.* New York: Criterion, 1958. 373pp. Based chiefly on Proust's letters, contemporary accounts, and memoirs written by his friends, Barker supplies a nearly day-by-day chronological narrative. There is little attempt at sorting out the accuracy of the assembled facts or going beyond the facts to reach interpretive conclusions.

Bersani, Leo. *Marcel Proust: The Fictions of Life and Art.* New York: Oxford University Press, 1965. 269pp. Bersani's monograph is useful in drawing convincing distinctions between Proust's life and his works. As opposed to many others who regard Proust's fiction as autobiography, Bersani suggests the ways in which his fiction does not necessarily reflect but responds to unresolved psychological tensions.

Brée, Germaine. *The World of Marcel Proust.* Boston: Houghton Mifflin, 1966. 295pp. This is an excellent companion volume to Proust's life and work and is one of the better general introductions to his work in English, featuring a sketch of his life, a survey of all his published writings, and critical chapters on his masterpiece.

Cattaui, Georges. *Marcel Proust.* New York: Funk & Wagnalls, 1968. 125pp. This is a good popular account of Proust's life and work that ably serves the general reader as a solid introduction.

Maurois, André. *The World of Marcel Proust.* New York: Harper & Row, 1974. 288pp. First published in France in 1960, this pictorial biography still serves as a useful introduction for the general reader, identifying the highlights of Proust's career and the people and places associated with his life and work.

May, Derwent. *Proust.* New York: Oxford University Press, 1983. 85pp. Part of the Past Masters series, May supplies a succinct critical introduction that traces the relationship between Proust's life and his work.

Miller, Milton L. *Nostalgia: A Psychoanalytic Study of Marcel Proust.* Boston: Houghton Mifflin, 1956. 306pp. Miller's psychological analysis of the man and the artist puts his emotional life and his work in a Freudian psychoanalytic context. Not intended for the casual, general reader, the book presumes considerable familiarity with psychoanalysis and its terminology.

Rivers, J.E. *Proust and the Art of Love.* New York: Columbia University Press, 1980. 327pp. Rivers mounts a convincing attack on the homosexual stereotypes that have distorted views of Proust's life and work. Instead he asserts a view of Proust that connects his ideas on sexuality and behavior with contemporary views and modern gender research.

Sawsom, William. *Proust and His World.* London: Thames and Hudson, 1973. 128pp. Sawsom's is a pictorial biography that covers the major events of Proust's life and captures the sites associated with the author.

Shattuck, Roger. *Proust.* New York: Viking, 1974. 180pp. Part of the Modern Masters series, Shattuck's is a lucid and provocative critical study that offers insights on Proust's personality, temperament, and creative method.

Biographical Films and Theatrical Adaptations

Céleste (1981). Director: Percy Adlon. Based on the book by Céleste Albaret, Proust is seen through the eyes of the woman who for nine years before his death served him as cook, companion, secretary, and surrogate mother. Video.

Marcel Proust (1988). Director: David Thomas. In this installment of the London Weekend Television series, *Ten Great Writers,* Proust's life and works are examined. Video.

102 Boulevard Haussman (1991). Director: Vdayan Prasad. Alan Bates interprets the writer in an extended monologue. Video.

Other Sources

Quennell, Peter, ed. *Marcel Proust, 1871–1922: A Centennial Volume.* New York: Simon & Schuster, 1971. 216pp. A valuable collection of critical essays on various aspects of Proust's life, work, and world.

386. GIACOMO PUCCINI
1858–1924

Italian opera composer whose works are among the most popular in the operatic repertory, Puccini first achieved recognition with a one-act opera, *Le Villi* (1884). Other well-known operas by Puccini include *Manon Lescaut* (1893), *La Bohème* (1896), *Tosca* (1900), *Madame Butterfly* (1904), and *Gianni Schicchi* (1918).

Autobiography and Primary Sources

Letters of Giacomo Puccini. Giuseppe Adami, ed. 1931. Reprint ed. New York: Vienna House, 1973. 335pp. A collection dealing with the composition and production of his operas, the letters provide insights into Puccini's creative method as well as his views of other composers and the various singers who interpreted his works.

Recommended Biographies

Carner, Mosco. *Puccini: A Critical Biography.* 1959. Revised ed. New York: Holmes and Meier, 1974. 520pp. Regarded as the standard source on Puccini's life and operas, Carner offers a Freudian perspective on the composer's personality; however, the book's strength is a chronological analysis of Puccini's compositions.

Marek, George. *Puccini: A Biography.* New York: Simon & Schuster, 1951. 412pp. Marek's is a highly readable, well-documented life that is based on previously unpublished evidence, which the author uses to fill in many gaps in the biographical record. The book is less successful in its criticism of the operas.

Other Biographical Studies

Dry, Wakeling. *Giacomo Puccini.* New York: J. Lane, 1906. 114pp. This first biographical profile features the author's recollected conversations with the composer.

Fiorentino, Dante del. *Immortal Bohemian: An Intimate Memoir of Giacomo Puccini.* New York: Prentice-Hall, 1952. 232pp. Based on the author's personal acquaintance with the composer when Puccini was 50, the book is a charming portrait, particularly valuable for the author's firsthand glimpses.

Greenfeld, Howard. *Puccini: A Biography.* New York: Putnam, 1980. 299pp. The author provides a generally reliable summary of the main events of Puccini's life but fails to penetrate very deeply to an understanding of the inner man or his creative methods.

Greenfield, Edward. *Puccini: Keeper of the Seal.* London: Arrow Books, 1958. 255pp. Greenfield's is a compact overview of the main highlights of Puccini's life joined with a sensible analysis of his work.

Jackson, Stanley. *Monsieur Butterfly: The Story of Giacomo Puccini.* New York: Stein and Day, 1974. 267pp. With enough novelization to be categorized as biographical fiction, Jackson offers an entertaining but not always reliable treatment of Puccini's life, with a major emphasis on his many loves and

the intrigues surrounding the writing and staging of the operas.

Seligman, Vincent. *Puccini Among Friends.* New York: Macmillan, 1938. 373pp. The book consists of a series of letters written by the composer to the author's mother from 1905 with commentary, offering an interesting view of Puccini.

Specht, Richard. *Giacomo Puccini: The Man, His Life, His Work.* New York: Knopf, 1933. 256pp. Highly idealized and selective in its presentation, Specht's account of Puccini's life is not reliable.

Weaver, William. *Puccini: The Man and His Music.* New York: Dutton, 1977. 147pp. Weaver's capsulated text is too abbreviated to provide more than the essentials. The book's many illustrations, however, make up for the somewhat superficial coverage.

Wilson, Conrad. *Giacomo Puccini.* London: Phaidon, 1997. 239pp. Wilson puts the composer's life and work in perspective, and this well-illustrated volume serves as a good starting place for those captivated by Puccini's music looking for more information about the operas and their composers before moving on to more scholarly and thorough treatments.

Fictional Portraits

Paul, Barbara. *A Cadenza for Caruso.* New York: St. Martin's, 1984. 146pp. Puccini is charged with murder in this mystery set in 1910. Enrico Caruso attempts to clear his friend by discovering the real killer. Despite the fanciful story, the novel does offer an authentic depiction of the New York opera world of the period.

Biographical Films and Theatrical Adaptations

Giacomo Puccini, 1858–1924 (1996). Director: Malcolm Hossick. A film profile touching on the main events of Puccini's life, his work, and cultural background. Video.

Puccini (1984). Director: Tony Palmer. A dramatic presentation of a scandal that nearly ruined Puccini's career. Starring Robert Stephens, Virginia McKenna, and Judith Howarth. Video.

Other Sources

Weaver, William, and Simonetta Puccini, eds. *The Puccini Companion.* New York: W.W. Norton, 1994. 436pp. This excellent reference source is an accessible collection of information about the composer's life and work.

387. ALEKSANDR PUSHKIN
1799–1837

Russian poet and prose writer, Pushkin ranked among the foremost figures in Russian literature. Pushkin's poetic works include *Ruslan and Ludmilla* (1820), *The Prisoner of the Caucasus* (1820), and his masterpiece, *Eugene Onegin* (1833). Among his other major works are the dramas *The Stone Guest* (1830) and *Boris Godunov* (1831),

and the short story "The Queen of Spades" (1834). Pushkin was killed by his wife's lover in a duel.

Autobiography and Primary Sources

Pushkin on Literature. Tatiana Wolff, ed. Stanford, California: Stanford University Press, 1986. 554pp. This collection of the writer's comments on his own writing and others takes the reader, in the words of V.S. Pritchett, "straight into the writer's workshop."

The Letters of Alexander Pushkin. J. Thomas Shaw, ed. Bloomington: Indiana University Press, 1963. 3 vols. The notable letters that shed light on the man and his life are included here in an invaluable collection.

Recommended Biographies

Edmonds, Robin. *Pushkin: The Man and His Age.* New York: St. Martin's, 1995. 303pp. Edmonds focuses on Pushkin's life in its historical context that makes clear the ways in which history, politics, and culture contributed to forming his genius and affecting his career.

Feinstein, Elaine. *Pushkin: A Biography.* Hopewell, New Jersey: Ecco Press, 1999. 309pp. The author, an English poet and novelist, presents a well-written narrative account of Pushkin's life that serves as a fine accessible introduction for the general reader. The book documents the many contradictions in Pushkin's personality, aided by recently uncovered sources that challenge previous assumptions and deepen our view of the man and his relationships.

Simmons, E. J. *Pushkin.* Cambridge, Massachusetts: Harvard University Press, 1937. 485pp. Pushkin's life and work are traced against a fully realized period background, synthesizing primary and secondary sources into a clear and thorough narrative of Pushkin's activities and relationships.

Other Biographical Studies

Bethea, David M. *Realizing Metaphors: Alexander Pushkin and the Life of the Poet.* Madison: University of Wisconsin Press, 1998. 244pp. Bethea's interesting literary biography is an effort to trace the connections between the poet's life and his work.

Magarshack, David. *Pushkin: A Biography.* New York: Grove Press, 1967. 320pp. Relying mainly on translated excerpts from Pushkin's letters and diaries, as well as quotes from friends and associates, Magarshack assembles the poet's life in a serviceable, introductory biography, illustrated with portraits and Pushkin's own pen sketches.

Mirsky, D.S. *Pushkin.* 1926. Reprint ed. New York: Haskell House, 1974. 266pp. Mirsky's early biography has been superseded by later research.

Troyat, Henri. *Pushkin.* New York: Pantheon, 1950. 508pp. Troyat's is a highly entertaining, vivid depiction of Pushkin's life that includes a panoramic portrait of Russian life between 1799 and 1837. The emphasis here is on Pushkin the man rather than his works, and the deeper reaches of the poet's character and motivation eludes Troyat's grasp.

Vitale, Serena. *Pushkin's Button*. New York: Farrar, Straus, 1999. 355pp. Vitale's is a vivid, meticulous account of Pushkin's last few months and death, chronicling the events and the personalities that led to the poet's fatal duel.

Biographical Novels

Killens, John Oliver. *Great Black Russian*. Detroit, Michigan: Wayne State University Press, 1989. 393pp. Killens provides a full-length dramatization of Pushkin's life with an emphasis on his African ancestry that is suggested as the reason for the poet's unique perspective and various social conflicts.

Lambert, Lydia. *Pushkin: Poet and Lover*. Garden City, New York: Doubleday, 1946. 276pp. This is a fictionalized biography that Pushkin biographer E.J. Simmons called "Strachey strained through Maurois to emerge as the *reducio ad absurdum* of all impressionistic romanticized biographies."

Petrie, Glen. *The Fourth King*. New York: Atheneum, 433pp. Pushkin's life is chronicled from 1826 to his death with an emphasis on his marriage and its tragic consequences.

Recommended Juvenile Biographies

Chaney, J.R. *Aleksandr Pushkin: Poet for the People*. Minneapolis: Lerner, 1992. 112pp. MG/YA. This is a useful, informative appreciatory study that helps orient the reader to the main events of Pushkin's life, his most important works, and his achievement and legacy.

388. FRANÇOIS RABELAIS
ca. 1483–1553

French writer, physician, and monk, Rabelais is considered one of the comic geniuses of world literature. A humanist, he left the Franciscans to enter the more scholarly Benedictine order and practiced medicine in Lyons, where he also edited Latin works and composed burlesque almanacs. In Lyons, Rabelais wrote his celebrated *Gargantua* (1532) and *Pantagruel* (1532 or 1533), a robust and ribald collection of humorous tales about two legendary giants.

Recommended Biographies

Frame, Donald M. *François Rabelais: A Study.* New York: Harcourt, Brace, 1977. 238pp. Frame's critical study of Rabelais's life, genius, and works, though demanding, is the best single source on the writer available. The book chronicles the essential facts that are known about Rabelais's life then takes the reader on a skillful tour of what can be learned from a close analysis of his works.

Plattard, Jean. *Life of François Rabelais.* New York: Knopf, 1931. 308pp. Although partially dated by subsequent research and modern critical views, Plattard remains the standard source for the essential facts of Rabelais's life. Readers of Plattard will want to supplement their reading by consulting Frame, Febvre, and Krailsheimer for alternative views on several points.

Other Biographical Studies

Febvre, Lucien. *The Problem of Unbelief in the 16th Century: The Religion of Rabelais.* Cambridge, Massachusetts: Harvard University Press, 1982. 516pp. Febvre's intellectual history challenges the notion of Rabelais's atheism and anti-Christian views. The book has been praised as one of the seminal works of history published in the twentieth century. Challenging for the nonspecialist, the book is indispensable for the scholar of the period.

Krailsheimer, A.J. *Rabelais and the Franciscans.* Oxford: Clarendon Press, 1963. 334pp. Krailsheimer's is a solid critical study that elucidates Rabelais's Franciscan training and its influence on his thinking and his work.

Lewis, D.B. Wyndham. *Doctor Rabelais.* New York: Sheed & Ward, 1957. 274pp. The author's enthusiasm for Rabelais leads him astray historically, filling in imaginative details when evidence fails. As one reviewer remarked, Lewis pays Rabelais "the supreme compliment of trying to imitate his style, with the consequence that many pages of this study are of impenetrable opacity and confusion."

Powys, John Cowper. *Rabelais: His Life.* New York: Philosophical Library, 1948. 424pp. Powys's life is a dense prose tangle with impressionistic glimpses, some factual, some farfetched, and the book cannot be relied on for its overall accuracy.

Putnam, Samuel. *François Rabelais: Man of the Renaissance: A Spiritual Biography.* New York: H. Smith, 1929. 530pp. Putnam fills in the considerable gaps in the biographical record with the background of his times and questionable interpretations.

Tilley, Arthur. *François Rabelais.* 1907. Reprint ed. Port Washington, New York: Kennikat Press, 1970. 388pp. Tilley's collection of biographical data, forming part of this study, was in its day an essential source, now out of date due to subsequent scholarship.

389. SIR WALTER RALEIGH
1554–1618

English soldier, explorer, courtier, and poet, the young Raleigh served (1569) with the Huguenot army in France and may have studied at Oxford and at the Middle Temple. After suppressing (1580) a rebellion in Ireland, he went to court, where he became a favorite of Elizabeth I. He was knighted (1585) and appointed captain (1587) of the queen's guard. He organized the colonization expeditions to America that ended with the tragedy of the "lost colony" on Roanoke Island. He was imprisoned by James I (1603) for suspected treason, and lived in the Tower of London until 1616. He was later executed on the same charge.

Autobiography and Primary Sources

The Letters of Sir Walter Ralegh. Agnes Latham and Joyce Youings, eds. Exeter: University of Exeter Press, 1999. 403pp. This scholarly collection of letters features excellent documentation that forms a sensible biography in its own right.

Recommended Biographies

Adamson, J.H., and H.F. Folland. *The Shepherd of the Ocean: An Account of Sir Walter Ralegh and His Times.* Boston: Gambit, 1969. 464pp. In a very detailed biography, the complexity of Raleigh is ably demonstrated. Quoting extensively from Raleigh's writings helps establish a rounded portrait, measured by the standards of his times.

Greenblatt, Stephen J. *Sir Walter Ralegh: The Renaissance Man and His Role.* New Haven, Connecticut: Yale University Press, 1973. 209pp. Greenblatt helpfully connects Raleigh the man of action with the writer and philosopher in a richly nuanced portrait. The book demonstrates how Raleigh was fundamentally a role-player and how his writings became a way to reconcile frustrations and conflicts in his life

Lacey, Robert. *Sir Walter Ralegh.* New York: Atheneum, 1974. 415pp. Written for the general reader, this is a useful, balanced assessment of Raleigh's life, character, and career. Well illustrated and organized, the book follows Raleigh's actions and exposes a credible human being in the context of his era.

Wallace, Willard M. *Sir Walter Raleigh.* Princeton, New Jersey: Princeton University Press, 1959. 327pp. In a balanced, judicious life, Raleigh's many-faceted character and interests are fully displayed against a solidly realized period background. Based on the leading authorities as well as new sources, Wallace's is an excellent choice for a concise but authoritative account.

Other Biographical Studies

Anthony, Irvin. *Ralegh and His World.* New York: Scribner, 1934. 339pp. Based on original sources, Anthony supplies a readable account of Raleigh's life and times in a series of vivid, dramatic vignettes. Clearly a Raleigh partisan, Anthony shows his hero as a adventurous plunger and daring opportunist.

Irwin, Margaret. *That Great Lucifer: A Portrait of Sir Walter Ralegh*. New York: Harcourt, Brace, 1960. 320pp. Raleigh is portrayed mainly through his own words in a series of impressions rather than a full-scale chronological account. He is shown as a complicated mixture of virtues and stubbornness, against a colorful Elizabethan background.

Oakeshott, Walter F. *The Queen and the Poet*. New York: Barnes and Noble, 1962. 232pp. The book uses Raleigh's poetry as the key for understanding his complicated relationship with Elizabeth I. It provides a number of valuable details concerning Raleigh's life at court and his shifting fortune as a royal favorite.

Ross Williamson, Hugh. *Sir Walter Raleigh*. London: Faber and Faber, 1951. 215pp. A brief but balanced biographical portrait that covers Raleigh's multiple careers as a poet, historian, scientist, philosopher, as well as sailor, soldier, and courtier.

Rowse, A.L. *Sir Walter Ralegh: His Family and Private Life*. New York: Harper, 1962. 348pp. Based on a discovered diary, Rowse reconstructs the history of the family of Raleigh's wife, the Throckmortons. Rowse uses the revelations the diary suggests to provide a reassessment of Raleigh's personality and history.

Strathmann, Ernest A. *Sir Walter Ralegh: A Study in Elizabethan Skepticism*. New York: Columbia University Press, 1951. 293pp. This intellectual biography considers the background and development of Raleigh's religious and philosophical beliefs, particularly the charge of atheism leveled against him by his contemporaries. Raleigh is shown instead as a skeptic and advocate of intellectual freedom.

Thompson, Edwin J. *Sir Walter Ralegh: The Last of the Elizabethans*. New Haven, Connecticut: Yale University Press, 1936. 416pp. Thompson's highly sympathetic biography judges Raleigh from the ethical standards of his day and displays the Elizabethan in a rounded portrait with his inconsistencies and paradoxes intact. At times overly defensive, Thompson gives short shrift to Raleigh's enemies and fails to explain the considerable hostility that Raleigh inspired in many.

Williams, Norman L. *Sir Walter Raleigh*. London: Eyre and Spottiswoode, 1962. 295pp. Raleigh's own words and those of his contemporaries are woven together along with official records, anecdotes, and eyewitness reports into a coherent narrative of Raleigh's life.

Biographical Novels

Garrett, George. *Death of the Fox*. New York: Harcourt, Brace, 1971. 739pp. On his final day before his execution, Raleigh recalls the events of his life in this imaginative evocation rooted in fact.

Lofts, Norah. *Here Was a Man*. New York: Knopf, 1936. 304pp. This is an episodic retelling of Raleigh's life in a humanized portrait that mixes the facts with idealization.

Nye, Robert. *The Voyage of the Destiny*. New York: Putnam, 1982. 387pp. Raleigh narrates his final voyage in 1616 while recalling his relationship with Elizabeth as he awaits his execution on a treason charge.

Schoonover, Lawrence L. *To Love a Queen*. Boston: Little, Brown, 1973. 383pp. The rise and fall of Raleigh's career are dramatized from his early obscurity through his success as the queen's favorite and his end as a traitor, executed on the block by James I.

Sutcliff, Rosemary. *Lady in Waiting*. New York: Coward-McCann, 1957. 253pp. Bess Throckmorton, lady-in-waiting to the queen, becomes Raleigh's secret bride. Their relationship endures Elizabeth's disfavor and a treason charge from James I.

Turner, Judy. *Ralegh's Fair Bess*. New York: St. Martin's, 1974. 192pp. This book describes the marriage of Raleigh and Bess Throckmorton in a blend of fact and invention that observes the basic outline of their history and relationship with both Elizabeth I and James I.

Fictional Portraits

Burgess, Anthony. *A Dead Man in Deptford*. New York: Carroll & Graf, 1995. 272pp. Raleigh introduces Christopher Marlowe to the seductive pleasures of tobacco in this imaginative recounting of the playwright's shady career as a spy.

Fletcher, Inglis. *Roanoke Hundred*. Indianapolis: Bobbs-Merrill, 1948. 492pp. The founding of the first English settlement in North America on Roanoke Island is dramatized with a large cast of historical figures, including Raleigh, Sir Richard Grenville, and Sir Francis Drake.

Graham, Winston. *The Grove of Eagles*. 1964. Garden City, New York: Doubleday, 1964. 498p. In 1597 a second Spanish Armada threatens England, and the event is seen from the perspective of the son of the governor of the most vital fortress on the Cornish coast. Raleigh acts his historical part in the crisis.

Kingsley, Charles. *Westward Ho!* 1855. Reprint ed. New York: Dutton, 1923. 489pp. Kingsley's classic adventure tale records the Elizabethan voyages of exploration and military engagement against the Spanish with appearances by Sir Francis Drake and Raleigh.

Marshall, Edison. *The Lost Colony*. Garden City, New York: Doubleday, 1964. 1964. 438pp. The novel speculates on the fate of the colony founded by Raleigh at Roanoke Island in North Carolina in an imaginative but plausible interpretation.

Wilson, Derek. *Her Majesty's Captain*. Boston: Little, Brown, 1978. 311pp. Sir Robert Dudley, the son of Elizabeth's favorite, the Earl of Leicester, narrates his voyage with Raleigh in action against the Spanish on the raid of Cadiz.

Recommended Juvenile Biographies

Aronson, Marc. *Sir Walter Ralegh and the Quest for El Dorado*. Boston: Houghton Mifflin, 2000. 240pp. YA. This is a well-researched and insightful biography tracing Raleigh's successes and failures, allowing a complex portrait of the man and his age to emerge.

Norman, Charles. *The Shepherd of the Oceans: Sir Walter Raleigh*. New York: McKay, 1952. 179pp. YA. Avoiding fictionalization and relying on frequent quotations from contemporary documents, this is a well-written and solidly documented biography that skillfully captures Raleigh's life and times.

Trease, Geoffrey. *Sir Walter Ralegh, Captain and Adventurer*. New York: Vanguard Press, 1950. 248pp. YA. Trease chronicles Raleigh's life from 1558 to his death in a vivid portrait that allows a complex, human figure to emerge against a clear historical background.

Biographical Films and Theatrical Adaptations

Elizabeth R (1972). Directors: Claude Whatham, et al. Both colorful and convincing, this dramatic television series covers Elizabeth's life from age 17 to 70, anchored by a remarkable performance by Glenda Jackson. Raleigh is portrayed by Nicholas Selby. Video.

The Private Lives of Elizabeth and Essex (1939). Director: Michael Curtiz. Based on Maxwell Anderson's play, this is a lavish costume drama concerned with the relationship between Elizabeth and one of her favorites, the Earl of Essex, with an outstanding performance by Bette Davis as Elizabeth. Should not be regarded as authentic history, however. Raleigh appears played by Vincent Price. Video.

Roanoak (1986). Director: Jan Egleson. PBS American Playhouse production dramatizing the fate of the Lost Colony. J. Kenneth Campbell portrays Raleigh. Video.

The Virgin Queen (1955). Director: Henry Koster. Bette Davis repeats her portrayal of Elizabeth I in a drama concentrating on her conflicts with Walter Raleigh (Richard Todd). Joan Collins plays Bess Throckmorton. Best for Davis's performance. Video.

Other Sources

Mills, Jerry L. *Sir Walter Raleigh: A Reference Guide*. New York: Macmillan, 1986. 116pp. Mills provides an accessible guide to the details of Raleigh's life and times, useful for the general reader and period specialist.

See also Elizabeth I; James I

390. RAPHAEL
1483–1520

One of the great Italian Renaissance painters, Raphael was influenced by Perugino, whose workshop he entered in 1494, and by Leonardo Da Vinci, Michelangelo, Masaccio, and Fra Bartolomeo. Among his many works are his famous Madonna paintings (1504–1508), the Stanza della Segnatura (1511) in the Vatican, which include the *School of Athens* and the *Triumph of Religion*, and the Sistine Chapel tapestries (1515–1516). Raphael was chief architect of the Vatican and also designed churches, palaces, and mansions.

Recommended Biographies

Cuzin, Jean Pierre. *Raphael: His Life and Works.* Secaucus, New Jersey: Chartwell Books, 1985. 259pp. This is a handsome collection of Raphael's works that helps document his life and artistic achievement in a chronological survey.

Jones, Roger, and Nicholas Penny. *Raphael.* New Haven, Connecticut: Yale University Press, 1983. 256pp. Looking at Raphael's achievements as a painter, architect, and archaeologist, the authors locate the artist's activities in the context of his times and supply a thorough and coherent survey of the artist's career.

Thompson, David. *Raphael: The Life and Legacy.* London: BBC, 1983. 256pp. Thompson's illustrated biography serves as a valuable introduction to the man, his times, and achievement for the general reader.

Other Biographical Studies

Beck, James H. *Raphael.* New York: Abrams, 1994. 126pp. This is a beautifully illustrated volume of reproductions with a serviceable text that provides an introductory overview of the artist and his works.

Crowe, J.A., and G.B. Cavalcaselle. *Raphael: His Life and Works.* London: J. Murray, 1882–1885. 2 vols. An exhaustive collection of the available documentary evidence upon which Raphael's biography can be based. Remains a valuable reference tool.

Fischel, Oskar. *Raphael.* London: K. Paul, 1948. 2 vols. Fischel's substantial, scholarly examination traces Raphael's artistic development through a close analysis of his work and frames his discussion by a detailed consideration of his cultural, social, and artistic context.

McCurdy, Edward. *Raphael Santi.* New York: Hodder and Stoughton, 1917. 206pp. Written for the general reader and nonspecialist, McCurdy's is a useful life-and-times account that draws on the appropriate primary and secondary sources.

Oppé, Adolf P. *Raphael.* 1909. Revised ed. Charles Mitchell, ed. New York: Praeger, 1970. 130pp. Thoroughly researched and sensible in its conclusions, this solid, concise treatment of Raphael's life and works remains within the bounds of the existing evidence and avoids the idealization and embellishment of many previous accounts.

Passavant, J.D. *Raphael of Urbino and His Father Giovanni Santi.* New York: Macmillan, 1872. 313pp. Passavant's early research into the details of Raphael's life and background remains an important reference source for biographers who are indebted to his findings.

Pope-Hennessy, John. *Raphael.* New York: New York University Press, 1970. 303pp. This series of lectures, although supplying a chronology, is topically arranged to explain Raphael's creative method and the circumstances surrounding his commissions. A distillation of a lifetime of work on the artist, Pope-Hennessy is able to supply considerable insights into Raphael's working methods and the character of his ideas.

Vasari, Giorgio. *Lives of the Artists.* 1550. Reprint ed. New York: Penguin, 1965. 2 vols. Vasari's biographical sketch provides the only information on Raphael's early life, although the writer had no firsthand knowledge of the painter, and the veracity of his anecdotes is suspect.

Fictional Portraits

Briggs, Jean. *The Flame of the Borgias.* New York: Harper & Row, 1975. 336pp. This dramatization of the relationship between Pietro Bembo and Lucrezia Borgia features an appearance by Raphael.

Recommended Juvenile Biographies

Ripley, Elizabeth. *Raphael.* Philadelphia: Lippincott, 1961. 68pp. MG. Ripley's is an informative critical introduction to Raphael's life and art.

Biographical Films and Theatrical Adaptations

Raphael (1982). Director: Ann Turner. A three-tape collection that traces Raphael's life and artistic career, shot on location in Italy at sites associated with the artist and in museums displaying his works. Video.

391. REMBRANDT
1606–1669

Dutch painter, etcher, and draftsman considered the greatest master of the Dutch school, Rembrandt Harmenszoon van Rijn first achieved distinction as a portrait painter. An influential teacher as well as an artist, Rembrandt produced more than 600 paintings, some 300 etchings, and about 2,000 drawings. Two of his most famous paintings are *The Night Watch* (1642) and *Aristotle Contemplating the Bust of Homer* (1653).

Autobiography and Primary Sources

Strauss, Walter L., and Marjon van der Meulen. *The Rembrandt Documents.* New York: Abaris Books, 1979. 668pp. This important scholarly collection brings together the relevant documentary sources on Rembrandt's life.

Recommended Biographies

Schama, Simon. *Rembrandt's Eyes.* New York: Knopf, 1999. 640pp. Schama constructs a nuanced biographical profile compensating for the paucity of historical evidence through a close critical reading of his paintings and a superb recreation of the world in which Rembrandt moved. The book attempts to penetrate the artist's thought processes and perspective through plausible conjecture, scholarship, and art criticism.

Schwartz, Gary. *Rembrandt: His Life, His Paintings.* New York: Viking, 1985. 380pp. Schwartz's well-documented survey of Rembrandt's life and art reveals the painter indirectly through his relations to his patrons and the ways in which the artist interpreted their literary, cultural, and religious ideas in his works. In stark contrast with previous portrayals, Rembrandt is shown in realistic, human terms as vain, unsociable, and greedy. Provocative and original, Schwartz's reassessment presents a major challenge to the conventional view of the artist.

White, Christopher. *Rembrandt and His World.* New York: Viking, 1964, 144pp. In an accessible popular account, White orients the general reader to the essential details of Rembrandt's life, art, and times. Serves as an ideal introduction.

Other Biographical Studies

Alpers, Svetlana. *Rembrandt's Enterprise: The Studio and the Market.* Chicago: University of Chicago Press, 1988. 160pp. Alpers provides a fresh look at the artist and his milieu, examining the ways in which his relationship to his materials, his studio procedures, and the marketplace helped to shape his art.

Benesch, Otto. *Rembrandt: A Biographical and Critical Study.* 1957. Reprint ed. as *Rembrandt.* New York: Rizzoli, 1990. 139pp. In a beautifully illustrated critical biography, Benesch traces Rembrandt's artistic development, his personality, and relationships in a judicious treatment for the general reader that avoids sentimentality and incorporates modern scholarship.

Mee, Charles L. *Rembrandt's Portrait: A Biography.* New York: Simon & Schuster, 1988. 336pp. Written for a popular audience, this is a vivid narrative account of Rembrandt's life that synthesizes other secondary sources into a realistic portrait of Rembrandt as flawed genius. Best in conveying a sense of place and time, the book is unfortunately overloaded with conjectures and a debatable emphasis on Rembrandt's personal shortcomings.

Rosenberg, Jakob. *Rembrandt: Life and Work.* 1948. Revised ed. Ithaca, New York: Cornell University Press, 1980. 386pp. Lucid and comprehensive, Rosenberg provides a brief biographical portrait before proceeding to a critical survey of the paintings, grouped topically with chapters on portraiture, biblical subjects, landscape, genre, mythology, and history.

Biographical Novels

Schmitt, Gladys. *Rembrandt.* New York: Random House, 1961. 657pp. Rembrandt's career is dramatized from 1623 until his death in a novel that stays close to the known facts.

Weiss, David. *I, Rembrandt.* New York: St. Martin's, 1979. 342pp. Rembrandt narrates the story of his life at the age of 48 in 1654 as he undertakes some of his greatest work. The novel features a speculative friendship between the painter and the Dutch philosopher Spinoza.

Fictional Portraits

Heller, Joseph. *Picture This.* New York: Putnam, 1988. 352pp. Heller imagines the artist as he is working on the painting *Aristotle Contemplating the Bust of Homer* as a vehicle for a discursive meditation on multiple themes.

Recommended Juvenile Biographies

Bonafoux, Pascal. *Rembrandt: Master of the Portrait*. New York: Abrams, 1992. 175pp. YA. Traces the life and career along with an analysis of Rembrandt's masterpieces and his influence.

Pescio, Claudio. *Rembrandt and Seventeenth-Century Holland*. New York: Bedrick, 1995. 64pp. MG. Part of the Masters of Art series, this is an excellent art book for younger readers that brings Rembrandt into sharp focus against a vivid period background.

Schwartz, Gary. *Rembrandt*. New York: Abrams, 1992. 92pp. YA. An excellent entry in the First Impressions series by a Rembrandt authority and biographer, the highlights of the painter's life are chronicled with sufficient political and social history to provide a context. The book is handsomely designed and beautifully illustrated.

Biographical Films and Theatrical Adaptations

Rembrandt (1936). Director: Alexander Korda. Charles Laughton is a standout as the painter in this film biography. The talented supporting cast includes Gertrude Lawrence and Elsa Lancaster. Video.

Rembrandt–1669 (1977). Director: Jos Stelling. A Dutch film that re-creates Rembrandt's final year. Starring Frans Stelling, Tom de Koff, and Aye Fil. Video.

392. PIERRE-AUGUSTE RENOIR
1841–1919

French impressionist painter known for works of shimmering, vibrant color and richness, Renoir began to earn his living in the 1870s with such portraits as *Madame Charpentier and Her Children* (1876). His outdoor scenes of the period include *The Swing* and *Moulin Galette* (both 1876). After traveling in Algeria and Italy, Renoir mounted an exhibition (1883), which guaranteed him financial success. Crippled by arthritis from 1903, he nevertheless produced some of his greatest paintings as well as major works of sculpture. His most celebrated paintings include *Luncheon of the Boating Party* (1881) and *Bather* (1917–1918).

Recommended Biographies

Renoir, Jean. *Renoir, My Father*. Boston: Little, Brown, 1962. 465pp. The second son of the painter, Jean Renoir, the renowned film director, offers his affectionate reflections on his father in a rich series of vignettes describing Renoir's family, work habits, and circle of friends. Not precise on dates, Renoir's impressions are nevertheless an invaluable source of information on the painter.

Vollard, Ambroise. *Renoir: An Intimate Record*. New York: Knopf, 1925. 248pp. The author, one of Renoir's dealers and longtime associate, presents not a formal biography but an anecdotal reflection based on conversations with the painter on various events in his life and the author's own firsthand observations. Vollard's lively insider's view suc-

ceeds in animating Renoir's personality and character.

White, Barbara E. *Renoir: His Life, Art, and Letters*. New York: Abrams, 1984. 311pp. Meticulous and thorough, White supplies the clearest and most complete factual record of Renoir's life that documents the painter's experience with an exactitude missing from the more impressionistic accounts by the painter's son and by Vollard. White shows a considerably darker side to Renoir's life and temperament, displayed in letters published here for the first time that trace his artistic development and relationship to other members of the Impressionist circle.

Other Biographical Studies

Distal, Anne. *Renoir: A Sensuous Vision*. New York: Abrams, 1995. 175pp. Distal's lively and insightful account of Renior's life is enlivened by quotations from the artist himself, his friends, and family, and includes a wide selection of reproductions.

Hanson, Lawrence. *Renoir: The Man, the Painter, and His World*. New York: Dodd, Mead, 1968. 332pp. Suited for general readers and students, Hanson's biography is an informed, chronological account of Renoir's life and artistic development, concentrating on his impressionist and early postimpressionist period.

Monneret, Sophie. *Renoir*. New York: Holt, 1990. 160pp. Accompanying over 200 reproductions of Renoir's painting and contemporary photographs, the text surveys Renoir's life and work in the context of the artistic and cultural developments of his time.

Fictional Portraits

Weiss, David. *Naked Came I: A Novel of Rodin*. New York: Morrow, 1963. 660pp. This biographical novel on the life of French sculptor Auguste Rodin recreates his era with appearances by a number of historical figures, include Renoir, Degas, Monet, Victor Hugo, and Emile Zola.

Recommended Juvenile Biographies

Rayfield, Susan. *Pierre-Auguste Renoir*. New York: Abrams, 1998. 92pp. MG. Part of the informative First Impressions series, Rayfield chronicles Renoir's life and career from his youth through his success, and his physically afflicted years before his death. Includes commentary from Jean Renoir and recollections from the painter himself and his friends.

393. CECIL RHODES
1853–1902

British business magnate, colonialist, and imperialist, Rhodes staked a claim in Africa's Kimberley diamond fields and in 1880 founded the De Beers Mining Company at Kimberley. He then formed the British South Africa Company to develop the area that is now Zimbabwe. He was premier of the Cape Colony until his complicity in the Jameson Raid (1896) into the Transvaal forced his resigna-

tion. He then developed the country called Rhodesia in his honor and served as a commander during the Boer War. The Rhodes scholarships were founded with much of his £6 million fortune.

Recommended Biographies

Lockhart, J.G., and C.M. Woodhouse. *Cecil Rhodes: The Colossus of Southern Africa*. New York: Macmillan, 1963. 525pp. Given unrestricted access to previously unavailable material, the authors have used their primary sources to produce a fair and thorough biography that served as the standard life until the publication of the monumental study by Rotberg and Shore. Cautious in their assessment, the book fails to convincingly unite Rhodes's considerable strengths with his weaknesses.

Roberts, Brian. *Cecil Rhodes: Flawed Colossus*. New York: W.W. Norton, 1988. 319pp. This is a brilliantly argued and well-researched portrait of the demythologized private man based on hitherto unused sources that deals frankly with Rhodes's homosexuality and misogyny. Fair in his analysis of Rhodes's character and development, Roberts's is a superbly written, thoughtful reassessment.

Rotberg, Robert I., and Miles F. Shore. *The Founder: Cecil Rhodes and the Pursuit of Power*. New York: Oxford University Press, 1988. 800pp. Meticulously researched, this is the fullest and most comprehensive survey of Rhodes's career that replaces Lockhart and Woodhouse as the definitive life. The book covers every aspect of Rhodes's private and public life with fresh insights based on original research.

Thomas, Antony. *Rhodes: Race for Africa*. New York: St. Martin's, 1997. 368pp. Thomas, who wrote the 1997 television dram b *Rhodes*, presents a balanced portrait that acknowledges Rhodes's talents and drive but also traces the corruption of his idealism by power and the connection between Rhodes and the Boer War and the apartheid system. Relying for the most part on primary sources to tell Rhodes's story, Thomas offers plausible surmises, labeled as such, for the gaps in the factual record.

Other Biographical Studies

Baker, Sir Herbert. *Cecil Rhodes: By His Architect*. London: Oxford University Press, 1934. 182pp. Closely associated with Rhodes from 1892 until his death, Baker was in a unique position to understand Rhodes's aspirations in artistic and architectural matters as he attempted to realize them. The result is a different, tempered view of the empire builder than other accounts.

Flint, John E. *Cecil Rhodes*. Boston: Little, Brown, 1974. 268pp. Flint's largely negative assessment of Rhodes's ambitions and abilities serves as a valuable alternative view from the African perspective to other more heroic treatments of Rhodes's achievements and character.

Fuller, Thomas E. *The Right Honourable Cecil John Rhodes: A Monograph and Reminiscence*. New York: Longmans, 1910. 276pp. Incomplete and limited in his perspective, the author, a former agent general for the Cape, offers his recollections on his association with Rhodes in an anecdotal, uncritical account that sheds light on Rhodes's personality.

Gross, Felix. *Rhodes of Africa*. New York: Praeger, 1957. 433pp. The work of a South African journalist, Gross's detailed biography draws on extensive source material to provide new insights on Rhodes's career. Lack of documentation, however, limits the book's usefulness, and Gross's scholarship has largely been superseded by later studies.

Jourdan, Philip. *Cecil Rhodes: His Private Life by His Private Secretary*. New York: J. Lane, 1911. 292pp. Based on the author's recollections of the eight-year period preceding Rhodes's death, Jourdan supplies a biographical portrait filled with anecdotes and reconstructed conversations. Not always reliable in its historical facts, the book is, however, a useful complement to other accounts for its intimate view of Rhodes's personality.

Le Sueur, Gordon. *Cecil Rhodes: The Man and His Work*. London: J. Murray, 1913. 345pp. Sketchy and limited in its perspective, this work by one of Rhodes's private secretaries nevertheless offers a stock of intimate personal details to the supply.

Marlowe, John. *Cecil Rhodes: The Anatomy of Empire*. New York: Mason & Lipscomb, 1972. 304pp. Rhodes is presented as the embodiment of British imperialism in this often-superficial review of his life that offers little that is new and is selective in its coverage to emphasize a negative judgment.

McDonald, James G. *Rhodes: A Life*. New York: McBride, 1928. 428pp. An associate of Rhodes during the last 12 years, McDonald provides a partisan's view that fails to achieve much distance on Rhodes's accomplishments or character, but does offers firsthand views of significant episodes of Rhodes's career.

Michell, Sir Lewis. *Life and Times of the Right Honourable Cecil John Rhodes*. New York: Kennerley, 1910. 2 vols. The first full-scale life by Rhodes's friend, executor, and trustee under his will, Michell's biography draws on his access to private and official papers to supply significant details on Rhodes's career. However, the book finds little to criticize in the portrayal of Rhodes's greatness, and current readers will likely prefer the more critical balance of subsequent biographies.

Millin, Sarah G. *Cecil Rhodes*. 1933. Revised ed. as *Rhodes*. London: Chatto and Windus, 1953. 406pp. Millin, a novelist, handles this biography with dramatic flair in documenting Rhodes's career from his experiences in the mines of South Africa until his death. At times impressionistic, Millin is fair in her assessment and achieves a highly readable animation of a rounded and believable human figure.

Plomer, William. *Cecil Rhodes*. New York: Appleton, 1933. 179pp. Versus the hero-worship of earlier accounts, Plomer is harshly critical of Rhodes's character and accomplishments. Granting Rhodes's talents, he is portrayed as an exemplar of imperialism. Plomer supports his assertions with compelling evidence, and his view complements more benign verdicts on Rhodes's legacy.

Williams, Basil. *Cecil Rhodes*. New York: Holt, 1921. 353pp. Based on the author's acquaintance with Rhodes, the book supplies a character sketch and an overview of Rhodes's career. A Rhodes apologist, Williams does not defend all of his actions, but the reader will be better served by more complete and objective treatments.

Fictional Portraits

Fish, Robert L. *Rough Diamond*. Garden City, New York: Doubleday, 1981. 356pp. Barney Barnet is an English adventurer who seeks his fortune in South Africa's diamond fields where he meets Rhodes and participates in some of the events of the period.

Harries, Ann. *Manly Pursuits*. New York: Bloomsbury, 1999. 339pp. As Rhodes is close to death, an Oxford professor travels to South Africa to deliver hundreds of British songbirds to save Rhodes's soul in this powerfully imagined tale with glimpses of Rhodes and such figures as Lewis Carroll, Oscar Wilde, and Rudyard Kipling.

Michener, James A. *The Covenant*. New York: Random House, 1980. 877pp. Michener's massive panoramic portrayal of South Africa's history interweaves a multiple family saga with actual events and appearances by many historical figures, including Rhodes, Kruger, Buller, and Shakka.

Samkange, Stanlake. *On Trial for My Country*. London: Heinemann, 1967. 160pp. The novel dramatizes the conflict between Rhodes and Lobengula, king of the Matabele and the maneuvering that resulted in the seizure of Matebele territory.

Smith, Wilbur. *Men of Men*. Garden City, New York: Doubleday, 1983. 518pp. The fictional Ballantyne family fortune is linked to the commercial and territorial empire founded by Rhodes.

Young, Francis Brett. *The City of Gold*. New York: Reynal & Hitchcock, 1939. 658pp. Southern African history is dramatized in this novel that mixes a fictional story with accurate depictions of the founding of Johannesburg, the Jameson Raid, and the events leading up to the Boer War, with appearances by Rhodes and Paul Kruger.

Recommended Juvenile Biographies

Gibbs, Peter. *The True Story of Cecil Rhodes in Africa*. Chicago: Childrens Press, 1964. 139pp. MG. This is a helpful review of Rhodes's career, character, and the history of the region that he played an important role in shaping.

Biographical Films and Theatrical Adaptations

Rhodes (1997). Director: David Drury. Joe Shaw plays the young Rhodes and his father, Martin Shaw, portrays the elder in this biographical film written by biographer Antony Thomas. Filmed on location. Video.

394. RICHARD I
1157–1199

English king known as Richard Coeur de Leon (the Lionheart), Richard was the third son of Henry II and Eleanor of Aquitaine. He succeeded to the throne upon the death of his father and spent all but six months of his reign out of England, primarily on the Third Crusade. He captured Messina and Cyprus and stormed Acre, but was unable to seize Jerusalem. On the journey home, he was captured by Leopold V of Austria, handed over to Holy Roman Emperor Henry VI, and released only after paying a large ransom. He returned to England to suppress a revolt against him led by his brother, John, and to raise funds. He was killed while fighting against Philip II in France.

Recommended Biographies

Bridge, Antony. *Richard the Lionheart*. New York: M. Evans, 1989. 259pp. Finding a balance between the heroic image and its opposite realistic diminishment of earlier studies, Bridge supplies a sensible reevaluation of Richard's life and career that insists on his being regarded as a complex individual, not just a brutal adventurer.

Gillingham, John. *The Life and Times of Richard I*. 1973. Revised ed. as *Richard I*. New Haven, Connecticut: Yale University Press, 1999. 336pp. In this reassessment of Richard's reign and personality, the author considers the reasons for Richard's fluctuating reputation over the centuries and offers a new interpretation of the significance of his reign in which Richard is shown as a masterful ruler. In *Richard Coeur de Lion: Kingship, Chivalry and War in the Twelfth Century*. (Rio Grande, Ohio: Hambleton Press, 1994. 266pp.), Gillingham places Richard's career in the context of his times, shown in his various roles as king and military leader.

Henderson, Philip. *Richard, Coeur de Lion: A Biography*. New York: W.W. Norton, 1959. 256pp. Out of contemporary chronicles and modern historical research the author goes beyond Richard's heroic image to portray a complex human figure and a man thoroughly a part of his time. Written for a general reader, this is a reliable, sensible, and absorbing narrative account of Richard's life, character, and times.

Other Biographical Studies

Brundage, James A. *Richard Lion Heart*. New York: Scribner, 1974. 278pp. Brundage's biographical study concentrates on Richard's activities as leader of the Third Crusade in a straightforward narrative account with a final chapter offering an evaluation of his character and career. In the author's realistic but balanced view, Richard is shown as often vain, arrogant, tyrannical, and greedy, yet also the towering hero of his age.

Howser, Harry S. *Richard I in England*. Garland: Tangelwüld, 1986. 109pp. Limited to the six-month period in 1194 in which Richard lived in England as king, Howser provides a damning assessment of the king's reign, which is shown as one of the worst in English history, sparking the barons' revolt that led to their confrontation with King John and the signing of the Magna Carta in 1215.

Norgate, Kate. *Richard the Lion Heart*. London: Macmillan, 1924. 349pp. Although superseded by later treatments and modern research, Norgate's early biography is still a valuable full-length portrait of Richard's career, personality, and time that balances acknowledgment of his achievement with a fair assessment of his character flaws and missteps.

Regan, Geoffrey. *Lionhearts: Saladin and Richard I and the Era of the Third Crusade*. New York: Walker, 1999. 288pp. Regan's narrative account of the Third Crusade is focused by the dual careers of the opposing commanders, Richard and Saladin. The early lives and rise to power of both men are summarized before describing the conflict and their military decisions. Strong on the details of the combat, Regan is not always reliable as a judge of Richard's character. Richard's homosexuality is strongly resisted, and the author accepts much of his barbarous treatment of his enemy with little protest.

Biographical Novels

Barnes, Margaret C. *The Passionate Brood*. Philadelphia: Macrae Smith, 1945. 308pp. Beginning with the minstrel Blondel's joining Richard's service, this fictionalized account chronicles the highlights of Richard's life through his death in a mix of facts, conjecture, and invention.

Challis, George. *The Golden Knight*. New York: Greystone Press, 1937. 297pp. Joining the facts with legends and invention, the novel dramatizes Richard's imprisonment in Austria and his eventual rescue by his troubadour Blondel.

Charques, Dorothy. *Men Like Shadows*. New York: Coward-McCann, 1953. 343pp. In a believable recreation of the events of the Third Crusade, the novel's perspective is that of an invented knight in Richard's service.

Haycraft, Molly. *My Lord Brother the Lion Heart*. Philadelphia: Lippincott, 1968. 320pp. Richard's favorite sister Joan narrates the story of her life that includes her accompanying Richard on the Third Crusade and her attempts to find her brother when he is imprisoned in Austria.

Lofts, Norah. *The Lute Player*. Garden City, New York: Doubleday, 1951. 465pp. The story of Richard during the Third Crusade is told from the perspective of the musician Blondel, who is on hand during the sacking of Cyprus, the siege of Acre, and the battle of Arsouf, in a blend of the actual, the legendary, and the imaginary. See also *Eleanor the Queen* (Garden City, New York: Doubleday, 1955. 249pp.) in which the story of Richard's mother is dramatized.

Plaidy, Jean. *Heart of the Lion*. New York: Putnam, 1980. 331pp. The highlights of Richard's career when he ascends to the throne are dramatized in a convincing and reliable treatment. In *The Courts of Love* New York: Putnam, 1988. 383pp.), Eleanor of Aquitaine, Richard's mother, narrates the story of his life, her marriages, and the fate of her children in an authentic portrayal.

Rofheart, Martha. *Lionheart! A Novel of Richard I, King of England*. New York: Simon & Schuster, 1981. 410pp. Richard's life, reign, and times are chronicled from a variety of real and imagined witnesses that stay close to the historical and biographical sources.

Shelby, Graham. *The Devil Is Loose*. Garden City, New York: Doubleday, 1974. 261pp. The dynastic conflict between Richard and his brother John is dramatized from the death of Henry II to Richard's death with the historical incidents accurately presented. In *The Kings of Vain Intent*. (New York: McKay, 1971. 320pp.) the events of the Third Crusade are presented in a historically faithful dramatization.

Williams, Jay. *Tomorrow's Fire*. New York: Atheneum, 1964. 364pp. Told in the form of a journal account of a troubadour in Richard's service during the Third Crusade, the novel offers a portrait of the king as insecure and unstable.

Fictional Portraits

Adams, Doris Sutcliffe. *No Man's Son*. London: R. Hale, 1961. 240pp. Set during the siege of Acre during the Third Crusade, this is a fanciful story of a poor knight's efforts to find a husband for his daughter, in which the details of the conflict and its era are authentically presented.

Balling. L. Christian. *Champion*. New York: Atlantic Monthly Press, 1988. 309pp. Scenes from the life of William Marshal, Earl of Pembroke, and England's greatest knight, are dramatized as the chivalric Marshal finds himself caught up in the dynastic struggle between Richard and his Prince John.

Bennetts, Pamela. *Richard and the Knights of God*. New York: St. Martin's, 1973. 253pp. In an invented adventure tale set during the Third Crusade, supported by evident research and accurate period details, a knight saves the life of Saladin's nephew and wins as a reward a French hostage, Latisse de Vaudemont.

Kaufman, Pamela. *Shield of Three Lions*. New York: Crown, 1983. 474pp.; *Banners of Gold*. New York: Crown, 1986. 436pp. The novels follow the adventures of Lady Alix of Wanthwaite who, disguised as a boy, becomes Richard's page and amorous love interest during the Third Crusade and later is a hostage in Austria during Richard's imprisonment.

Penman, Sharon K. *The Queen's Man*. New York: Holt, 1996. 291pp.; *Cruel as the Grave*. New York: Holt, 1998. 242pp. Set in the 1190s, Penman's historical mysteries features a young bastard son of the bishop of Chester as its detective in several detective missions for Eleanor of Aquitaine who sits on the English throne as regent in Richard's absence while he is a prisoner in Austria.

Phillips, Jill M. *The Rain Maiden*. Secaucus, New Jersey: Citadel Press, 1987. 593pp. Set in the world of France's Philip II, the novel tells the story of Isabel of Haunnault who marries the king but who is also loved by Richard.

Prescott, Hilda F.M. *The Unhurrying Chase*. New York: Dodd, Mead, 1925. 360pp. Prescott's impressive historical reconstruction concerns the adventures of a young Frenchman whose lands are seized by the young Richard of Poitou, later to become king.

Scott, Walter. *Ivanhoe*. 1819. Reprint ed. New York: Bantam, 1997. 686pp.; *The Talisman*. 1825. Reprint ed. New York: Dutton, 1907. 319pp.

Scott's classic historical novels set during Richard's reign offer a glimpse of the historical Richard and actual events around a core of fictional characters and imagined adventures.

Vidal, Gore. *A Search for the King: A 12th-Century Legend*. New York: Dutton, 1950. 255pp. Vidal's first novel dramatizes the legendary activities of Blondel, Richard's faithful minstrel, who searches for the king after he is imprisoned.

Recommended Juvenile Biographies

Gibbs, Christopher. *Richard the Lionheart and the Crusades*. New York: Bookwright Press, 1985. 60pp. MG. This is an informative account of the crusades with a strong focus on Richard's role.

Pittenger, W. Norman. *Richard the Lion-Hearted: The Crusader King*. New York: F. Watts, 1970. 149pp. MG/YA. Pittenger's is a competent life-and-times view of Richard's reign.

Suskind, Richard. *The Crusader King: Richard the Lionhearted*. Boston: Little, Brown, 1973. 120pp. MG. Suskind treats fully the man and his era in an informative summary.

Biographical Films and Theatrical Adaptations

Ivanhoe (1952). Director: Richard Thorpe. Norman Wooland portrays Richard in this Hollywood version of Scott's classic. Starring Robert Taylor, Elizabeth Taylor, Joan Fontaine, and George Sanders. Video.

Ivanhoe (1982). Director: Douglas Camfield. Television adaptation of the Scott novel, starring Anthony Andrews, James Mason, Sam Neill, Michael Hodern, and Julian Glover. Video.

Ivanhoe (1997). Director: Stuart Orme. Rory Edwards portrays Richard in yet another adaptation of Scott's novel as a television miniseries starring Steven Waddington, Christopher Lee, Victoria Smurfit, and Susan Lynch. Video.

King Richard and the Crusades (1954). Director: David Butler. Based on Scott's *The Talisman*, George Sanders is Richard in this plodding film treatment of the Third Crusade, with Rex Harrison as Saladin and Paula Raymond as Berengeria. Laurence Harvey plays a loyal knight determined to protect the king from assassins, and Virginia Mayo is his love interest. Video.

The Lion in Winter (1968). Director: Anthony Harvey. Acclaimed film version of James Goldman's play (New York: Random House, 1966. 110pp.) looks at the dysfunctional royal family life of Henry II (Peter O'Toole) and Eleanor of Aquitaine (Katharine Hepburn) as they battle over the succession. Anthony Hopkins makes his film debut as Richard, and Nigel Terry portrays his brother John. Video.

395. RICHARD III
1452–1485

English king Richard III was created Duke of Gloucester at the coronation of his elder brother, Edward IV (1461), and after Edward's death was protector of his 12-year-old nephew, Edward V. After Edward V and his brother were murdered. Richard had himself crowned king (1483). Historical evidence pointing to Richard as instigator of the murders of the two young princes is inconclusive. He instituted reforms and encouraged trade but could not defeat the forces who supported Henry Tudor's claim to the throne. Richard was killed at Bosworth Field, after which Henry Tudor ascended the throne as Henry VII.

Autobiography and Primary Sources

Richard III: A Source Book. Keith Dockray, ed. Gloucestershire, England: Sutton, 1997. 141pp. This collection of contemporary source material allows the reader to penetrate the various myths surrounding Richard to reach a more direct view of the man and the origin of his reputation.

Recommended Biographies

Kendall, Paul M. *Richard the Third.* New York: W.W. Norton, 1956. 602pp. Kendall's well-researched, full-length biography sets in order the facts about Richard's career, with particular attention to the years before his accession. Sympathetic to his subject, Kendall manages an objective view that avoids either excessive vilification or admiration or the bias of a prosecutor or defender. A brilliantly written scholarly biography, Richard is presented as a product of his times with a complex blend of strengths and flaws.

Potter, Jeremy. *Good King Richard?: An Account of Richard III and His Reputation 1483–1983.* London: Constable, 1983. 287pp. Potter supplies a helpful survey of past historical and biographical treatments of Richard that clearly establishes the terms of the Great Debate over one of England's most controversial and enigmatic kings. Potter, a chairman of the Richard III Society, is an unabashed Richard apologist, but he offers both sides in the debate.

Ross, Charles. *Richard III.* Berkeley: University of California Press, 1983. 265pp. Ross helpfully places Richard's behavior in the context of his times and reveals a man who was neither especially admirable nor wicked, and Ross's analysis clearly reveals Richard's many paradoxes. The book is noteworthy for not taking sides and allowing the reader to decide how to judge the man.

Other Biographical Studies

Cheetham, Anthony. *The Life and Times of Richard III.* London: Weidenfeld and Nicolson, 1972. 224pp. This illustrated biography traces Richard's career through contemporary illustrations and a sound text that offers a balanced portrait.

Fields, Bertram. *Royal Blood: Richard III and the Mystery of the Princes.* New York: HarperCollins, 1998. 335pp. The author, an entertainment lawyer, applies his legal skills to the case of Richard III versus the princes and related charges against Richard and Edward IV. Weighing the evidence on both sides, the book supplies a colorful, fresh look at Richard's career and his times for the general reader.

Gairdner, James. *History of the Life and Reign of Richard the Third.* 1898. Revised ed. Cambridge, Massachusetts: Cambridge University Press, 1968. 388pp. Long considered the standard life, Gairdner's is a balanced and largely objective assessment that confirms much of the negative views presented first by Sir Thomas More and established as conventional wisdom by Shakespeare. The author was a master of the period and supports his presentation with primary sources.

Horrox, Rosemary. *Richard III: A Study in Service.* New York: Cambridge University Press, 1989. 358pp. The book attempts to explain why Richard failed to retain the kingship after his accession by examining the exercise of political power in the fifteenth century. Based on primary sources and modern scholarship, Horrox's study that focuses on Richard's policies rather than his personality offers a fresh and insightful approach for evaluating Richard's reign and leadership.

Kendall, Paul M., ed. *Richard III: The Great Debate.* New York: W.W. Norton, 1992. 239pp. This volume brings together two influential source documents that helped to shape Richard's reputation and view of his character: Sir Thomas More's *History of King Richard III* and Horace Walpole's *The Life and Reign of King Richard III.*

Lamb, V.B. *The Betrayal of Richard III: An Introduction to the Controversy.* Gloucestershire, England: Sutton, 1990. 112pp. In a survey of the life and times of Richard, Lamb examines the contemporary evidence and the development of his reputation since his death.

More, Thomas. *The History of King Richard III.* Richard S. Sylvester, ed. New Haven, Connecticut: Yale University Press, 1976. 168pp. More's openly hostile and biased history shaped Shakespeare's portrayal of Richard and helped establish the view of his monstrousness and villainy.

Pollard, A.J. *Richard III and the Princes in the Tower.* New York: St. Martin's, 1991. 260pp. In a lavishly illustrated biography, Pollard summarizes Richard's early life, rise to power, and the tangled facts concerning the mysterious death of his nephews. A collection of contemporary documents is included.

Rowse, A.L. *Bosworth Field and the Wars of the Roses.* Garden City, New York: Doubleday, 1966. 317pp. This popular account of the dynastic struggle between the Lancastrians and the Yorkists from 1399 to 1485 attempts to validate Shakespeare's interpretation of the period and the personality and actions of Richard. Rowse's evident Tudor sympathies dominate his assessment of the villainous Yorkists.

Seward, Desmond. *Richard III: England's Black Legend.* New York: F. Watts, 1984. 220pp. The author recycles the major charges against Richard in a ringing denunciation of the man and his career, calling him "the most terrifying man ever to occupy the English throne." Well researched and well written, Seward adds little new to the Great Debate but makes a strong case for the prosecution.

Weir, Alison. *The Princes in the Tower.* New York: Ballantine Books, 1993. 287pp. In a careful sifting of the available evidence, a reconstruction of the period, and character analysis of the leading figures

(particularly Richard's), the author concludes that Richard indeed was responsible for the death of his nephews. Solidly presented and argued, Weir offers a fresh examination of one of history's greatest mysteries.

Biographical Novels

Anand, Valerie. *Crown of Roses.* New York: St. Martin's, 1989. 404pp. In a markedly contrarian portrait of Richard, the events leading up to Richard's accession are dramatized in a convincing portrayal of the confusing allegiances and personalities of the leading figures.

Belle, Pamela. *The Lodestar.* New York: St. Martin's, 1989. 533pp. Richard's rise to power is glimpsed through a courtier who becomes a trusted member of the Duke's retinue, with the historical facts forming the basis of the story and conjecture filling out gaps in the record.

Bowen, Marjorie. *Dickon.* New York: Beagle, 1971. 255pp. Richard's brief reign after seizing power is depicted.

Carleton, Patrick. *Under the Hog.* New York: Dutton, 1938. 514pp. Carleton offers a fictionalized interpretation of how Richard came to power and who he was.

Eckerson, Olive. *The Golden Yoke: A Novel of the War of the Roses.* New York: Coward-McCann, 1961. 415pp. In a sympathetic portrait of Richard, his relationship with Anne Neville is the focus as the lovers find themselves on opposite sides in the dynastic struggle of the Wars of the Roses.

Edwards, Rhoda. *The Broken Swords.* Garden City, New York: Doubleday, 1976. 295pp. Richard's brief reign is depicted from a variety of eye-witnesses, including the king himself, in a credible, balanced portrait. In *Fortune's Wheel* (Garden City, New York: Doubleday, 1979. 273pp.), contrary to other depictions of Richard as villainous monster, he is shown here as an earnest man torn between his loyalty to his brother and the Earl of Warwick, whose daughter he loves.

Gellis, Roberta. *The Dragon and the Rose.* Chicago: Playboy Press, 1977. 363pp. The dynastic struggle of the Wars of the Roses is dramatized with the basic outlines of history observed.

Jarman, Rosemary H. *We Speak No Treason.* Boston: Little, Brown, 1971. 575pp. Richard's enigmatic personality is captured through a series of witnesses: a woman who loves him, his jester, and a loyal man-at-arms. Written by an unapologetic Richard partisan, the novel shows Richard as sensitive, honest, and just.

Leary, Francis W. *Fire and Morning.* New York: Putnam, 1957. 297pp. Scenes from Richard's reign are dramatized from the perspective of a fictional gentleman and soldier who attempts to uncover the mystery surrounding the murdered princes.

Nickell, Lesley J. *The White Queen.* New York: St. Martin's, 1978. 349pp. Richard's character and career are portrayed from the perspective of Anne Neville, daughter of Warwick the Kingmaker, who becomes a pawn in the political intrigue of the period. The author fills in the historical facts with plausible surmises.

Oman, Carola. *Crouchback*. New York: Holt, 1929. 327pp. Richard's personality and reign are seen mainly through the perspective of Anne Neville, Richard's queen. Faithful to the historical record, the novel traces Richard's rise to power, the fate of the princes in the tower, and the test of loyalty that Anne, the daughter of Richard's enemy, Warwick, must face.

Palmer, Marian. *The White Boar*. Garden City, New York: Doubleday, 1968. 373pp. Seen through the biased perspective of two devoted friends, Richard is sympathetically portrayed as a victim brought down by court intrigue and the ambition of his rivals.

Penman, Sharon K. *The Sunne in Splendour*. New York: Holt, 1982. 1982. 936pp. Penman's massive revisionist view of Richard portrays him as a stalwart supporter of his brother, Edward IV, and tragically in love with Anne Neville, a woman whom he is forbidden to marry. The book's interpretation is debatable, but the scrupulousness of its historical and period details is beyond reproach.

Plaidy, Jean. *The Sun in Splendour*. New York: Putnam, 1982. 365pp. This historically reliable account of the Yorkist triumph and collapse during the Wars of the Roses chronicles the reigns of Edward IV and Richard III. In *The Reluctant Queen: The Story of Anne of York* (New York: Putnam, 1990. 299pp.), Anne Neville, Richard's queen and the daughter of his political enemy, narrates her story and the events of Richard's troubled career. See also *The Goldsmith's Wife* (New York: Putnam, 1974. 318pp.) for the story of Jane Shore, Edward IV's mistress, who offers a sympathetic portrait of Richard.

Tyler-Whittle, Michael. *Richard III: The Last Plantagenet*. Philadelphia: Chilton Books, 1970. 292pp. Richard's life and career are chronicled from age seven to his death in a documentary approach that attempts to portray the real Richard, somewhere between the monster of Tudor partisans and the misunderstood hero of later apologists.

Vance, Marguerite. *Song for a Lute*. New York: Dutton, 1958. 160pp. Vance offers a positive reevaluation of Richard's character through the perspective of Anne Neville. Richard is shown as a devoted husband who was determined to rule justly. To support this defense, many unflattering events and actions are excluded from view.

Fictional Portraits

Abbey, Margaret. *The Son of York*. London: New English Library, 1971. 144pp. The novel's fictional story is connected to the political intrigue that brings Richard to the throne. In *The Heart Is a Traitor*. (London: R. Hale, 1978. 192pp.) and *Blood of the Boar* (London: R. Hale, 1979. 189pp.) the adventures of Catherine Newberry and her love for Richard are chronicled.

Barnes, Margaret C. *The King's Bed*. Philadelphia: Macrae Smith, 1962. 286pp. A young woman is thrust onto the center stage of history when Richard spends the night before the battle of Bosworth Field at her father's inn, and she is given the dangerous task of delivering the king's final message. Legend, fact, and fiction are blended here.

Doherty, P.C. *The Fate of Princes*. New York: St. Martin's, 1991. 192pp. Offering an intriguing solution to the fate of the princes in the Tower, this historical mystery displays the bloody politics and personalities of the Wars of the Roses and Richard's rise to the throne.

Farrington, Robert. *The Killing of Richard III*. London: Chatto & Windus, 1971. 287pp. Richard's privy clerk undertakes a series of secret missions, including an attempted kidnapping of Henry Tudor, during the rush of events leading up to the Battle of Bosworth Field.

Potter, Jeremy. *A Trail of Blood*. New York: McCall, 1971. 281pp. Set during the 1550s, the novel features a pair of Tudor investigators who uncover evidence about the murder of the princes in the Tower that exonerates Richard and could topple Henry VIII.

Sedley, Kate. *Death and the Chapman*. New York: St. Martin's, 1992. 190pp; *The Plymouth Cloak*. New York: St. Martin's, 1993. 192pp. Sedley's historical mystery series set during the fifteenth century involves an itinerant peddler as sleuth with appearances by Richard.

Stevenson, Robert Louis. *The Black Arrow*. 1888. Reprint ed. New York: Scribner, 1987. 328pp. Set during the Wars of the Roses, Stevenson's classic tale of conspiracy and revenge features an appearance by Richard, Duke of Gloucester.

Tey, Josephine. *The Daughter of Time*. New York: Macmillan, 1952. 204pp. Tey's classic mystery has an incapacitated Scotland Yard detective take up the case against Richard in the murder of his nephews.

Biographical Films and Theatrical Adaptations

Shakespeare, William. *Richard III*. (1594). Multiple editions. Influenced by Sir Thomas More and other Tudor apologists, Shakespeare's portrait of Richard as a seductive, Machiavellian monster set the type for the view of Richard that has dominated, despite the concerted efforts of those who have attempted to restore his reputation.

Looking for Richard (1996). Director: Al Pacino. This semi-documentary meditation on Richard's character as presented by Shakespeare follows Pacino's struggles to come to grips with the part. Key scenes in the play are presented with such actors as Alec Baldwin, Winona Ryder, Kevin Spacey, and F. Murray Abraham. Video.

Richard III (1955). Director: Laurence Olivier. Acclaimed film production of Shakespeare's play featuring a gripping performance by Olivier and an exceptional supporting cast, including Cedric Hardwicke, Ralph Richardson, John Gielgud, and Claire Bloom. Video.

Richard III (1995). Director: Richard Loncraine. Shakespeare is relocated in an English fascist state during the 1930s in this inventive interpretation based on Richard Eyre's stage adaptation. Starring Ian McKellen in a bravura performance, supported by Annette Bening, Nigel Hawthorne, Kristin Scott Thomas, Maggie Smith, and Jon Wood. Video.

Tower of London (1939). Director: Rowland V. Lee. Basil Rathbone portrays Richard on his murderous climb to power in this historical melodrama. The cast includes Boris Karloff, Barbara O'Neill, Vincent Price, and Leo G. Carroll. Video.

Tower of London (1962). Director: Roger Corman. Remake of the 1939 film with Vincent Price taking the role of Richard. Also starring Michael Pate, Joan Freeman, and Robert Brown. Video.

The Tragedy of Richard the Third (1983). Director: Jane Howell. This production from the BBC Shakespeare plays features an ensemble cast who perform the entire Wars of the Roses play cycle in a playscape set with Ron Cook as Richard and Brian Protheroe as Edward IV. Video.

Other Sources

Gillingham, John, ed. *Richard III: A Medieval Kingship*. New York: St. Martin's, 1993. 154pp. Seven specialists present their views on Richard's life and reign, covering his youth, usurpation of the crown, foreign affairs, military skill, and reputations.

Petre, James. *Richard III: Crown and People*. London: Richard III Society, 1985. 446pp. Reprinting articles from *The Ricardian*, the journal of the Richard III Society, this useful volume looks at various aspects of Richard's life, career, and times.

396. ARMANDE-JEAN DU PLESSIS, DUC DE RICHELIEU
1585–1642

The chief minister of Louis XIII, statesman, and cardinal of the Roman Church, Richelieu became minister in 1624. A master of diplomacy and ruthlessness, he made France a great power and secured the monarchy against internal revolt. He successfully mounted the siege of the Huguenot stronghold of La Rochelle, which destroyed Huguenot political power, suppressed conspiracies of the nobles, and allied France with Sweden and Saxe-Weimar against the Holy Roman Emperor during the Thirty Years War. He strengthened the navy, encouraged colonial trade and expansion, and was a patron of the arts.

Autobiography and Primary Sources

Political Testament of Cardinal Richelieu: The Significant Chapters and Supporting Selections. Madison: University of Wisconsin Press, 1964. 148pp. This useful collection of Richelieu's writing helps the reader get a direct feel for the man and his ideas.

Recommended Biographies

Bergin, Joseph. *Cardinal Richelieu: Power and the Pursuit of Wealth*. New Haven, Connecticut: Yale University Press, 1985. 341pp.; *The Rise of Richelieu*. New Haven, Connecticut: Yale University Press, 1991. 282pp. Bergin's two important studies concerning Richelieu's fortune and apprenticeship are both meticulously researched and rich in original insights that challenge conventional views of the cardinal's character and career. Both books are firmly grounded in the values of the period that help to explain the source of Richelieu's power and genius, which the author insists was not uniquely innate but typical of his cultural and social milieu.

Treasure, G.R.R. *Cardinal Richelieu and the Development of Absolutism.* New York: St. Martin's, 1972. 316pp. This scholarly political biography authoritatively explores Richelieu's motives and character as it surveys his career, from his rise to power, his relationship to the king, the administrative and fiscal reforms he instituted, to his diplomacy during the Thirty Years War. Richelieu the man, the theologian, and the patron of the arts is also examined. See also *Richelieu and Mazarin* (New York: Routledge, 1998. 96pp.) for a succinct, comparative assessment of both men's careers, characters, and achievements.

Wedgwood, C.V. *Richelieu and the French Monarchy.* 1949. Revised ed. New York: Collier, 1962. 155pp. Wedgewood's carefully researched and sensible study of Richelieu's career is a preferred introduction for the general reader looking for a competent orientation to the period and the man.

Other Biographical Studies

Auchincloss, Louis. *Richelieu.* New York: Viking, 1973. 263pp. This illustrated biography with a biographical profile by novelist Auchincloss concentrates on Richelieu's character and personal details rather than his policies and statecraft, presented topically rather than chronologically. Appropriate as a useful introduction for the general reader.

Burckhardt, Carl. *Richelieu and His Age.* New York: Harcourt, Brace, 1970. 3 vols. Burckhardt's monumental study, originally published in four volumes in German between 1933 and 1967 is extremely detailed, though not free of error and has been superseded by subsequent research.

Church, William. *Richelieu and Reason of State.* Princeton, New Jersey: Princeton University Press, 1972. 554pp. Rather than a chronological survey of Richelieu's life and career, Church examines the political, religious, and moral values that help explain his ideas and actions. The result is a masterful, intellectual biographical portrait that serves to locate Richelieu's motives and perspective in the context of his times.

Federn, Karl. *Richelieu.* Reprint ed. New York: Haskell House, 1970. 253pp. Federn's survey of Richelieu's career helps to reveal the man behind his multiple roles as well as the cultural, social, and historical contexts that help to explain his actions, values, and accomplishments.

Knecht, R.J. *Richelieu.* New York: Longman, 1991. 259pp. Part of the Profiles in Power series, this insightful examination of Richelieu's character and career summarizes the highpoints and the contexts to help explain his motivations and policies.

Lodge, Richard. *Richelieu.* 1896. Reprint ed. Port Washington, New York: Kennikat Press, 1970. 235pp. Lodge's early life-and-times study is factually reliable but dated in its interpretation of Richelieu's achievement and influence.

Marvick, Elizabeth W. *The Young Richelieu: A Psychoanalytic Approach to Leadership.* Chicago: University of Chicago Press, 1983. 276pp. Tracing

the origins of Richelieu's leadership and behavior through a psychoanalytical examination of his childhood experiences, family background, and early relationships, Marvick provides a number of provocative but ultimately speculative insights into Richelieu's psychic makeup and development.

O'Connell, D.P. *Richelieu.* Cleveland: World, 1968. 509pp. O'Connell's vivid, dramatic narrative history focuses almost exclusively on Richelieu the diplomatist and politician, offering few details about his private life.

Tapié, Victor-Lucien. *France in the Age of Louis XIII and Richelieu.* New York: Praeger, 1975. 622pp. The author's dual study of the French king and his chief minister remains one of the best one-volume studies of the period available. Less a biography of either man than a solid treatment of their times, the book does provide a keen analysis of both men and their motivations.

Fictional Portraits

Anthony, Evelyn. *The Cardinal and the Queen.* New York: Coward-McCann, 1968. 221pp. Based on the rumors that Richelieu was the lover of Anne of Austria, the father of Louis XIV, and was responsible for the murder of the Duke of Buckingham, the novel captures the intrigue and romance of the court of Louis XIII.

Dumas, Alexandre. *The Three Musketeers.* 1844. Various editions. Dumas's classic swashbuckler casts Richelieu as the wily manipulator and adversary for D'Artagnan and his colleagues.

Mallet-Joris, Françoise. *The Favourite.* New York: Farrar, Straus, 1962. 282pp. Louis XIII's relationship with a maid of honor prompts Richelieu's enmity in a period psychological study.

Vigny, Alfred de. *Cinq-Mars.* 1826. Reprint ed. Boston: Little, Brown, 1907. 2 vols. This exciting historical adventure tale depicts the Marquis of Cinq-Mars's attempt to overthrow the cardinal and a convincing portrait of Richelieu's wiles.

Yarbro, Chelsea Quinn. *A Candle for D'Artagnan.* New York: Tor, 1989. 485pp. In the author's inventive historical vampire series, this installment depicts the intrigues of Cardinal Richelieu as he struggles to hold onto power against the rising force of Mazarin.

Recommended Juvenile Biographies

Glossop, Pat. *Cardinal Richelieu.* New York: Chelsea House, 1990. 111pp. MG/YA. A solid overview of Richelieu's life and times that serves equally well as biography and history of the period.

Biographical Films and Theatrical Adaptations

Bulwer Lytton, Edward. *Richelieu; or The Conspiracy.* 1839. Reprint ed. New York: Appleton, 1930. 263pp. Concerning the events between 1630 and 1642 in which Richelieu foils an attempt to overthrow and assassinate him, Bulwer Lytton's verse drama shows the cardinal as courageous and adroit in matching wits with his opponents.

Cardinal Richelieu (1935). Director: Rowland V. Lee. George Arliss portrays the cardinal, and Edward Arnold is Louis VIII. Video.

The Devils (1971). Director: Ken Russell. Christopher Logue and Graham Armitage appear respectively as Richelieu and Louis XIII in Russell's macabre, excessive interpretation of Aldous Huxley's *The Devils of Loudon.* Starring Vanessa Redgrave and Oliver Reed. Video.

The Three Musketeers (1948). Director: George Sidney. Vincent Price plays Richelieu in this version of the Dumas novel with Lana Turner, Gene Kelly, June Allyson, Van Heflin, Keenan Wynn, Gig Young, and Angela Lansbury. Video.

The Three Musketeers (1973) and *The Four Musketeers* (1974). Director: Richard Lester. Charlton Heston is a standout as the cardinal in Lester's witty and inventive adaptation of Dumas's classic. Starring Micheal York, Oliver Reed, Richard Chamberlain, Frank Finlay, Christopher Lee, Faye Dunaway, and Raquel Welch. Video.

The Three Musketeers (1993). Director: Stephen Herek. Generation-X version of Dumas starring Kiefer Sutherland, Charlie Sheen, Chris O'Donnell, and Oliver Platt, with Tim Curry as Richelieu. Video.

Other Sources

Bergin, Joseph, and Laurence Brockliss, eds. *Richelieu and His Age.* Oxford: Clarendon Press, 1992. 288pp. This collection of the research of a number of experts looks at Richelieu's career from several different angles. Collectively, the portrait that emerges is a rounded, human view that connects his religious life and his statesmanship.

397. RAINER MARIA RILKE
1875–1926

German poet and one of the greatest lyric poets of modern German literature, Rilke attended the University of Prague, then married briefly and traveled extensively. During World War I he returned to Germany, where war service and chronic ill health compromised his work. After the war he settled in Switzerland. He died from blood poisoning after pricking his finger on a rose thorn. His poems are complex and symbolic, rich and mystical, and works include *Stories of God* (1904), *Poems From the Book of Hours* (1905), and *The Duino Elegies* (1923).

Autobiography and Primary Sources

Letters of Rainer Maria Rilke. New York: W.W. Norton, 1969. 2 vols. Rilke's correspondence is an indispensable biographical source, offering the reader a direct view of the poet's personality, ideas, and creative method.

Rilke and Benvenuta: An Intimate Correspondence. Magda von Hattingberg, ed. New York: Fromm International, 1987. 148pp. Rilke's correspondence with an admirer whom he had never met, Viennese concert pianist Magda von Hattinberg, is collected in a series of letters which the poet referred to as "the testament of my whole past and future existence."

Recommended Biographies

Freedman, Ralph. *Life of a Poet: Rainer Maria Rilke*. New York: Farrar, Straus, 1996. 640pp. Combining the strength of Leppmann's critical acumen with Prater's objectivity, Freedman has produced a superior biographical study. With a clarity and fullness missing in most treatments, the book narrates the essential episodes in Rilke's life, meticulously revealing the relationship between his experiences and his art. Freedman's approach is level-headed and judicious.

Leppmann, Wolfgang. *Rilke: A Life*. New York: Fromm International, 1984. 421pp. Extremely valuable as a reference source, Leppmann's meticulous collection of every factual detail available on the poet and its connection with his work is impressive, yet the approach is daunting for the casual reader despite its excellence as a character analysis. Others may be put off by the author's jaunty style and sweeping generalizations, but the book excels in its critical acumen and psychological penetration.

Prater, Donald. *A Ringing Glass: The Life of Rainer Maria Rilke*. New York: Oxford University Press, 1986. 472pp. Although the author himself disclaims producing a definitive study since important documentation remains unavailable, Prater's is a very detailed, three-dimensional portrait outlined against the chronological background out of which his writing and ideas developed. Relying mainly on direct quotation to tell Rilke's story, Prater is an objective chronicler, primarily of the external facts of the poet's life.

Other Biographical Studies

Butler, E.M. *Rainer Maria Rilke*. New York: Macmillan, 1941. 437pp. In her attempt to shed the myths to reveal the man, Butler finds little to admire about the poet or his work. A persistent hostility distorts this assessment, but the book does serve to replace the visionary image of Rilke promulgated by his admirers with a more realistic, human portrait.

Heerikhuizen, F.W. van. *Rainer Maria Rilke: His Life and Work*. New York: Philosophical Library, 1952. 396pp. The author narrates the story of Rilke's life from a critical analysis of his poetry, letters, and relationships. Alternately well-documented and overly impressionistic, Heerikhuizen's study is hard going for the nonspecialist.

Hendry, J.F. *The Sacred Threshold: A Life of Rainer Maria Rilke*. New York: Carcanet, 1984. 184pp. Hendry's brief critical life draws the connections between the poet's experiences and his work, concentrating in particular on Rilke's affair with the pianist Magda von Hattingberg as a lens to explore the man and his creative method.

Holthusen, Hans E. *Portrait of Rilke: An Illustrated Biography*. New York: Herder and Herder, 1971. 175pp. The photographs are the major appeal in this visual biography that documents the highlights of Rilke's career and surroundings.

Kleinbard, David. *The Beginning of Terror: A Psychological Study of Rainer Maria Rilke's Life and Work*. New York: New York University Press, 1993. 275pp. Kleinbard traces Rilke's development through a psychoanalytical examination of his relationships with his parents and the connection between his illness and creative genius. Not all the quotations in German are translated, which will be a source of frustration for the non-German reader.

Peters, H.F. *Rainer Maria Rilke: Masks and the Man*. Seattle: University of Washington Press, 1960. 226pp. Peters traces the influence of Rilke's experience on his writings in a sensible introduction to both the man and his poetry.

Purtscher, Nora von Wydenbruck. *Rilke, Man and Poet: A Biographical Study*. New York: Appleton-Century, 1950. 373pp. Written by the niece of the poet's friend and patron, Princess Marie Thurn und Taxis, to whom the *Duino Elegies* were dedicated, the author surveys Rilke's entire life and supplements the conventional view with a number of revealing details.

Salis, Jean Randolphe de. *Rainer Maria Rilke: The Years in Switzerland*. Berkeley: University of California Press, 1964. 321pp. In a study originally published in Germany in 1936, Salis, an acquaintance of the poet, describes Rilke's last seven years while attempting to correct the image of Rilke as a delicate and overly sensitive visionary but indulges in his own sentimental impressions of the poet's final agonies.

Schoolfield, George C. *Rilke's Last Year*. Lawrence: University of Kansas Libraries, 1969. 73pp. In examining Rilke's death, Schoolfield broadens his biographical focus to consider the making and influence of Rilke's reputation among his admirers.

Fictional Portraits

Weiss, David. *Naked Came I: A Novel of Rodin*. New York: Morrow, 1963. 660pp. Rilke served for a time as Rodin's assistant, and he is depicted in this biographical novel on Rodin's life and career.

398. ARTHUR RIMBAUD
1854–1891

French poet who influenced the symbolists and subsequent modern poets, Rimbaud lived with poet Paul Verlaine in London and Brussels, until Verlaine shot and wounded Rimbaud in a drunken brawl, thus ending the relationship. His works include *A Season in Hell* (1873) a confessional autobiography, and *Les Illuminations* (published 1886), a collection of prose poems.

Autobiography and Primary Sources

Selected Letters. Wallace Fowlie, ed. Chicago: University of Chicago Press, 1966. 370pp. This selection of Rimbaud's letters has been chosen to emphasize biographical details and his poetic beliefs.

Recommended Biographies

Nicholl, Charles. *Somebody Else: Arthur Rimbaud in Africa 1880–91*. Chicago: University of Chicago

Press, 1998. 352pp. In a vivid depiction, the book assembles the fragmentary documentary evidence with a reenactment of the poet's travels to portray Rimbaud's wandering life in East Africa after he abandoned poetry. Winner of Britain's 1998 Hawthornden Prize.

Petitfils, Pierre. *Rimbaud*. Charlottesville: University Press of Viginia, 1987. 388pp. Written by the preeminent Rimbaud scholar, Petitfils's exhaustive and meticulous sifting of the evidence results in a detailed factual record of the poet's experiences and activities. Preferred as the most comprehensive and accurate reference source, the book does not attempt an interpretation but presents the facts objectively.

Starkie, Enid. *Arthur Rimbaud*. 1938. Revised ed. New York: New Directions, 1961. 491pp. Revised three times in the light of new documentary evidence, Starkie's detailed, scholarly life has long served as the standard authoritative source of information on Rimbaud's life and career as well as a penetrating character analysis.

Steinmetz, Jean-Luc. *Arthur Rimbaud: Presence of an Enigma*. New York: Welcome Rain, 2000. 486pp. Winner of the 1991 Grand Prix de L'Academie Française, Steinmetz manages to connect the two halves of Rimbaud's life, joining his artistic career with his wandering by an underlying consistent spiritual quest. The biography is likely to remain the standard life for some time to come.

Other Biographical Studies

Bonnefoy, Yves. *Rimbaud*. New York: Harper & Row, 1973. 145pp. The book is a sustained meditation on the poet through his works and life rather than a sustained biographical account. Uncovering no new biographical information, Bonnefoy does synthesize standard sources into an interesting interpretation.

Carré, Jean-Marie. *A Season in Hell: The Life of Rimbaud*. New York: Macaulay, 1931. 312pp. This account is divided into three parts: Rimbaud's intellectual development, relating his early experiences to his writing up to age 19; his wanderings in Europe and Africa; and his return home and death. Establishing the basic chronology of Rimbaud's life, Carré's version has been superseded by subsequent scholarship.

Chadwick, C. *Rimbaud*. Atlantic Heights, New Jersey: Humanities Press, 1979. 151pp. In a reliable introduction to the life and work, Chadwick examines Rimbaud's poetry after a brief biographical chapter. The book is particularly acute on Rimbaud's personal and poetic relationship with Verlaine. Unfortunately, for the non-French reader, the extensive quotations from Rimbaud's works are not translated.

Fowlie, Wallace. *Rimbaud*. Chicago: University of Chicago Press, 1965. 280pp. This critical study of Rimbaud's writings includes a short and straightforward account of the poet's short life.

Hanson, Elisabeth. *My Poor Arthur: An Illumination of Arthur Rimbaud*. New York: Holt, 1960. 307pp. Hanson's biography is chiefly useful for its treatment of the known facts of Rimbaud's life, but fails to achieve much illumination of motives, psychology, or the connection between the poet's experiences and his works. Dominated by its thesis of Rimbaud's mother complex, Hanson's view is often simplistic and distorting.

Ivry, Benjamin. *Arthur Rimbaud.* New York: Stewart, Tabori and Chang, 1998. 136pp. Part of the short biographical outline series on significant gay and lesbian writers, artists, and performers, Ivry relates Rimbaud's sexuality to his experiences and writing. Extremely detailed, though condensed, the book treats Rimbaud's homosexuality not as peripheral but as the defining aspect of Rimbaud's life and genius.

Rickword, Edgell. *Rimbaud: The Boy and the Poet.* New York: Knopf, 1924. 234pp. The first biography in English collects the then-known facts about Rimbaud's life into a complete account, now superseded by subsequent scholarship.

St. Aubyn, Frederic C. *Arthur Rimbaud.* 1975. Revised ed. New York: Twayne, 1988. 176pp. The author's critical introduction provides a competent orientation both to the man and his works for general readers and students.

Biographical Novels

Bercovici, Konrad. *Savage Prodigal.* New York: Beechhurst Press, 1948. 255pp. The novel recounts the events of Rimbaud's life, including his relationship with Verlaine and his years of wandering in Africa and the Middle East, constructing some of the dialogue from the poet's own words.

Reed, Jeremy. *Delirium: An Interpretation of Arthur Rimbaud.* San Francisco: City Lights Books, 1994. 136pp. The novel chiefly focuses on Rimbaud's life around 1873 when he left school to begin his brief, intense poetic career.

Ullman, James R. *The Day on Fire: A Novel Suggested by the Life of Arthur Rimbaud.* Cleveland, Ohio: World, 1958. 701pp. Mixing fact and invention, the novel traces Rimbaud's story from his childhood with an emphasis on the nature of the personal torments that Rimbaud reflected in his poetry.

Biographical Films and Theatrical Adaptations

Total Eclipse (1996). Director: Agnieszka Holland. The film version of Christopher Hampton's play (London: Faber and Faber, 1995. 120pp.) dramatizes the destructive relationship between Rimbaud (Leonardo DiCaprio) and Paul Verlaine (David Thewlis). Video.

399. DIEGO RIVERA
1886–1957

Mexican mural painter, Rivera and his assistants produced large murals on public buildings that dealt with the life, history, and social problems of Mexico. In the United States, Rivera painted murals for buildings in San Francisco, Detroit, and New York, including a mural for Rockefeller Center that was moved to Mexico City because of the inclusion of a portrait of Lenin. A Marxist, Rivera was successful in gaining permission for Trotsky to

come to Mexico. Rivera was married to the Mexican painter, Frida Kahlo.

Autobiography and Primary Sources

My Art, My Life. With Gladys March. New York: Citadel Press, 1960. 197pp. This version of Rivera's autobiography was compiled by March from interviews, with Rivera's comments arranged chronologically. The appendix contains recollections from the artist's four wives.

Recommended Biographies

Hamill, Pete. *Diego Rivera.* New York: Abrams, 1999. 207pp. Hamill's is a sound introduction to Rivera's life and achievement. Without adding any new details, Hamill is able to craft a full and rounded portrait of the man, his artistry, and the complex relationships, both personal and political, that shaped him.

Marnham, Patrick. *Dreaming with His Eyes Open: A Life of Diego Rivera.* New York: Knopf, 1998. 350pp. Marnham continues the effort begun by Wolfe of untangling the myths from the reality surrounding Rivera's life. Based on extensive research and providing a rich evocation of the period and place, Marnham's study skillfully shows how the artist's personality and culture shaped his art and substitutes a believable human figure for the often oversized legend.

Wolfe, Bertram D. *The Fabulous Life of Diego Rivera.* New York: Stein and Day, 1963. 457pp. Wolfe updates his earlier study to describe Rivera's entire life, attempting to correct the "tall tales for which Diego was famous." The book remains the standard source and the most comprehensive treatment of Rivera's life available.

Other Biographical Studies

Arquin, Florence. *Diego Rivera: The Shaping of an Artist, 1889–1921.* Norman: University of Oklahoma Press, 1971. 150pp. The author, a painter and a friend of Rivera's family, presents the artist's early years and development in Mexico, Spain, France, and Italy in a valuable assessment of the years up to 1921.

Wolfe, Bertram D. *Diego Rivera: His Life and Times.* New York: Knopf, 1939. 420pp. Wolfe's first attempt to summarize Rivera's life and achievement, based on the author's personal acquaintance with the painter, was substantially reworked to form the full-length, more critical view of Rivera in Wolfe's 1963 biography.

Fictional Portraits

Poniatowska, Elena. *Dear Diego.* New York: Putnam, 1986. 86pp. This novella is composed of 12 letters sent to Rivera by Angelina Beloff, the painter's abandoned common-law wife, pleading to be reunited with the artist. Although Rivera is a missing presence here, his considerable powers of attraction are compellingly registered on the imagined Angelina.

Winegardner, Mark. *The Veracruz Blues.* New York: Viking, 1996. 251pp. In 1946 a number of prominent major leaguers are induced to join the Mexican league for the first fully integrated base-

ball season in this fanciful but atmospheric tale with a number of actual figures, including Rivera, Frida Kahlo, Ernest Hemingway, and Babe Ruth.

Recommended Juvenile Biographies

Cockcroft, James D. *Diego Rivera.* New York: Chelsea House, 1991. 119pp. MG/YA. Cockcroft's is a packed source of information on the painter's life, work, and times that deals frankly with the personal details and the controversies surrounding Rivera.

Gonzales, Doreen. *Diego Rivera: His Art, His Life.* Springfield, New Jersey: Enslow, 1996. 128pp. MG/YA. While concentrating on his artistic achievement, Gonzales supplies an unflattering portrait of the artist as a self-absorbed man who damaged his relationships with his family, wives, and children.

Hargrove, Jim. *Diego Rivera: Mexican Muralist.* Chicago: Childrens Press, 1990. 122pp. MG. This is a thoroughly documented and well-written introduction to the artist and his work although the black-and-white photos do not do justice to the latter.

Biographical Films and Theatrical Adaptations

The Cradle Will Rock (1999). Director: Tim Robbins. This account of Orson Welles's attempt to mount a musical about a steel strike in the 1930s features Rubén Blades as Diego Rivera at work on his mural for Rockefeller (John Cusack). With Angus MacFadyen as Welles and Cary Elwes as John Housman. Video.

Diego Rivera: I Paint What I See (1989). Director: M. Lance. A film portrait of Rivera's life and work with location shots of his murals. Video.

400. PAUL ROBESON
1898–1976

Celebrated African American actor and bass singer, Robeson won acclaim for his performances in such plays as Eugene O'Neill's *Emperor Jones,* DuBose Hayward's *Porgy,* Shakespeare's *Othello,* and the Jerome Kern musical, *Show Boat,* as well as for his concert performances and interpretations of spirituals. His communist affiliations and his winning of the Stalin Peace Prize made him a controversial figure in the United States. He lived and worked in Europe and the Soviet Union during the 1950s, returning to the United States in 1963.

Autobiography and Primary Sources

Here I Stand. Boston: Beacon Press, 1958. 121pp. Robeson justifies his beliefs and actions in an impassioned, accessible, and simplified version of his life story.

Paul Robeson Speaks: Writings, Speeches, Interviews, 1918–1974. Philip S. Foner, ed. New York: Brunner/Mazel, 1978. 623pp. This is an important and useful collection of Robeson's views from a variety of sources.

Recommended Biographies

Duberman, Martin B. *Paul Robeson*. New York: Knopf, 1988. 804pp. Duberman's is the standout, definitive biography, extensively researched, comprehensive in its approach, and judicious in its assessments. A reviewer from the *Nation* predicted that the book "will rank among the finest biographies of any twentieth-century American figure."

Other Biographical Studies

Gilliam, Dorothy B. *Paul Robeson: All American*. Washington, DC: New Republic, 1976. 216pp. Lacking much penetration, Gilliam presents the highlights of Robeson's public career. This book serves primarily as a starting point or an accessible overview.

Graham, Shirley. *Paul Robeson: Citizen of the World*. New York: J. Messner, 1946. 264pp. The work of the wife of W.E.B. DuBois, this highly flattering portrait lacks objectivity and cannot be trusted in all its details.

Hoyt, Edwin P. *Paul Robeson: The American Othello*. Cleveland: World, 1967. 228pp. Hoyt's is a sympathetic but critical account of Robeson's career that deals candidly with his strengths and weaknesses, particularly, in the view of Hoyt, his political naivete.

Robeson, Eslanda G. *Paul Robeson, Negro*. New York: Harper, 1930. 178pp. Langston Hughes observed that this early account by Robeson's wife was a "naively intimate book that couldn't have been bettered by the best press agent." Frank confession alternates with puffery, but the first-hand insights are nevertheless useful on Robeson's private life.

Robeson, Susan. *The Whole World in His Hands: A Pictorial Biography of Paul Robeson*. Secaucus, New Jersey: Citadel Press, 1981. 254pp. Robeson's granddaughter offers an affectionate testimonial, chiefly useful for the many photographs that chronicle Robeson's career.

Fictional Portraits

Kaminsky, Stuart M. *Smart Moves*. New York: St. Martin's, 1986. 212pp. In this installment of Kaminsky's clever period mystery series, private eye Toby Peters tracks down a Nazi assassination squad bent on killing Albert Einstein, and he crosses paths with Paul Robeson who is appearing in *Othello*.

Recommended Juvenile Biographies

Ehrlich, Scott. *Paul Robeson*. New York: Chelsea House, 1988. 111pp. MG/YA. Ehrlich offers an informative account of Robeson's impact and achievement in this biographical profile that mainly focuses on his public life.

Larsen, Rebecca. *Paul Robeson: Hero Before His Time*. New York: F. Watts, 1989. 158pp. MG/YA. Larsen summarizes the important information on Robeson's personal life and career, with quotes from the actor and his contemporaries, and deals frankly with the controversies. Readers should have some knowledge of the history of the period.

Wright, David K. *Paul Robeson: Actor, Singer, Political Activist*. Springfield, New Jersey: Enslow, 1998. 128pp. MG/YA. This is an engaging, well-written introduction to Robeson's life that relies upon telling quotes and photographs to tell its story.

Biographical Films and Theatrical Adaptations

Paul Robeson (1979). Director: Lloyd Richards. A dramatic presentation of Robeson's life, starring James Earl Jones and Burt Wallace. Video

Paul Robeson: Here I Stand (1999). Director: St. Clair Bourne. Robeson's life and achievements are presented, narrated by Ossie Davis. Video.

Paul Robeson: The Tallest Tree in the Forest (1977). Producer: Gil Noble. A film portrait using archival footage and interviews with friends and associates. Video.

Paul Robeson—Tribute to an Artist (1982). Director: Saul J. Turell. A short documentary portrait originally released as a motion picture in 1979, narrated by Sidney Poitier. Video.

A Profile of Paul Robeson (1975). Robert N. Zagone. A documentary account of Robeson's public career and personality using interviews with eyewitnesses and associates and archival footage. Video.

Other Sources

Stewart, Jeffrey, ed. *Paul Robeson: Artist and Citizen*. New Brunswick, New Jersey: Rutgers University Press, 1998. 331pp. This collection of scholarly essays touches on various aspects of Robeson's personality and career. Includes 240 illustrations.

401. MAXIMILIEN ROBESPIERRE
1758–1794

French politician and leading figure of the French Revolution, Robespierre served on the States-General of 1789, became leader of the Jacobins, and was elected to the Commune of Paris. As deputy from Paris in the National Convention, he purged the rival moderate Girondists and was elected to the Committee of Public Safety, from which he initiated the Reign of Terror. Opposition to Robespierre's abuse of power grew, resulting in his arrest, summary trial, and execution.

Recommended Biographies

Hardman, John. *Robespierre*. New York: Longman, 1999. 248pp. This entry in the Profiles in Power series, supplies a reliable, succinct survey of Robespierre's life and revolutionary career. Serving as an excellent introduction, Hardman's analysis traces Robespierre's rise to power and his policies, displaying the discrepancy between his words and actions.

Jordan, David P. *The Revolutionary Career of Maximilien Robespierre*. New York: Free Press, 1985. 308pp. Jordan's intellectual biography emphasizes Robespierre's career rather than his private life. In Jordan's well-researched and plausible analysis of the crucial events of Robespierre's public life, he is sympathetically treated as a committed idealist. Accepting Robespierre's own words in his defense, Jordan ultimately fails to resolve the central paradox of Robespierre's ideals and his actions during the Reign of Terror.

Thompson, James M. *Robespierre*. New York: Appleton, 1936. 2 vols. Thompson's scholarly biography remains the most comprehensive study available. Based on years of research in France and a meticulous sifting of documentary evidence, the book collects all the available evidence and uses the author's considerable expertise in the period to reach cautious but judicious, objective conclusions about Robespierre's motivations and psychology.

Other Biographical Studies

Gallo, Max. *Robespierre the Incorruptible: A Psycho-Biography*. New York: Herder & Herder, 1971. 336pp. Gallo supplies a Freudian reading of Robespierre's character and development, locating the basis for understanding his later behavior in the traumas of his childhood.

Hampson, Norman. *The Life and Opinions of Maximilien Robespierre*. London: Duckworth, 1974. 313pp. Hampson's innovative approach on viewing Robespierre's character and career takes the form of a dialogue between a university tutor and three students—a Marxist, a civil servant, and a clergyman. The approach displays Robespierre's many contradictions without arriving at any definitive conclusions.

Lewes, G.H. *The Life of Maximilien Robespierre*. London: Routledge, 1849. 328pp. The first serious biography of Robespierre in English includes letters published here for the first time. Without succeeding to reconcile the various contradictions in Robespierre's character and career, Lewes does display his various sides in a generally objective view.

Mathiez, Albert. *The Fall of Robespierre and Other Essays*. New York: Knopf, 1927. 249pp. The author died before attempting the full-scale biography that his lifetime of research anticipated; however, this collection of 12 essays, based on Robespierre's speeches, letters, and contemporary records considers various aspects of his career.

Rudé, George. *Robespierre: Portrait of a Revolutionary Democrat*. New York: Viking, 1975. 254pp. The author's sympathetic political portrait depicts Robespierre as "the outstanding leader of the French Revolution who was the first great champion of democracy and people's rights." Rudé's contention is supported in a series of essays that look at various aspects of Robespierre's career. While plausible, the book's interpretation does not satisfactorily square the image of Robespierre as democratic hero and leader of the Reign of Terror.

Biographical Novels

Coryn, M.S. *The Incorruptible*. New York: Appleton-Century, 1943. 247pp. Robespierre is seen from a variety of perspectives, including those of both his friends and enemies, during his last five months.

Mantel, Hilary. *A Place of Greater Safety*. New York: Atheneum, 1993. 749pp. Robespierre, Danton, and Desmoulins provide narrative focus in this account of the French Revolution. All are shown in their rise to power and in conflict with one another as they attempt to control the rush of events that leads to the Reign of Terror. A remarkable achievement of historical reconstruction.

Piercy, Marge. *City of Darkness, City of Light*. New York: Fawcett, 1996. 479pp. The events of the French Revolution are depicted from the perspectives of several fictional and historical figures, including Danton and Robespierre, in a factual, faithful reconstruction of the period.

Fictional Portraits

De Bois, Helma. *The Incorruptible: A Tale of Revolution and Royalty*. New York: Crown, 1965. 402pp. In a faithful chronology of the events of the French Revolution, a fictional character's journal believably records his connections with many of the important figures, including Robespierre.

Lee, Tanith. *The Gods Are Thirsty*. Woodstock, New York: Overlook Press, 1996. 514pp. Camille Desmoulins, called the voice of the Revolution, is the focus for this fictionalized history that interweaves actual events with the imaginary and includes a portrayal of several central figures including Robespierre.

Recommended Juvenile Biographies

Carson, S.L. *Maximilien Robespierre*. New York: Chelsea House, 1988. 112pp. MG/YA. Carson supplies the essential information needed to understand Robespierre's character and actions, as well as a clear depiction of the events leading up to the French Revolution and its aftermath.

Biographical Films and Theatrical Adaptations

Danton (1982). Director: Andrzej Wajda. The Reign of Terror is viewed through the conflict between Danton (Gerard Depardieu) and Robespierre (Wojciech Pszoniak) as they attempt to control the forces they have helped to unleash. Echoes of modern Polish history can be detected in this provocative historical film with intriguing character studies of both men. Video.

The French Revolution (1971). Producer: Learning Corp. A brief video history of the French Revolution that focuses on the enigmatic figure of Robespierre to trace how the ideals of the Revolution were compromised. Video.

Marie Antoinette (1938). Director: W.S. Van Dyke. This Hollywood biography of Marie Antoinette cast Norma Shearer in the title role, with Tyrone Power as Count Ferson and Robert Morley as Louis XVI. George Meeker appears as Robespierre. Video.

Napoleon (1927). Director: Abel Gance. Gance's masterwork on the life of Napoleon depicts the events of the French Revolution and the Reign of Terror with portraits of Robespierre (Edmond Van Dyke), Desmoulins (Robert Vidalm), and Louis XVI (Louis Sance). Video.

The Reign of Terror (1949). Director: Anthony Mann. Historical melodrama concerning the scramble to possess the black book that records the names of Robespierre's victims during the Terror. Richard Basehart portrays Robespierre, with Wade Crosby as Danton and Jess Barker as St. Just. The fictional characters are portrayed by Robert Cummings and Arlene Dahl. Video.

Other Sources

Haydon, Colin, and William Doyle, eds. *Robespierre*. New York: Cambridge University Press, 1999. 295pp. A collection of critical essays that attempt to explain the various contradictory views of Robespierre, including his representation in history, drama, and fiction.

Rudé, George, ed. *Robespierre*. Englewood Cliffs, New Jersey: Prentice-Hall, 1967. 181pp. Part of the useful Great Lives Observed series, this collection brings together Robespierre's own words, views by contemporaries, and modern critical commentary.

402. JACKIE ROBINSON
1919–1972

The first African American baseball player to play in the major leagues, Robinson was signed by Brooklyn Dodgers president Branch Rickey to play for the Montreal Royals, a Brooklyn farm club. He was brought up to the Brooklyn Dodgers in 1947 and played until 1956. A formidable player, Robinson set batting and fielding records. He became the first African American admitted to the Baseball Hall of Fame.

Autobiography and Primary Sources

Baseball Has Done It. Charles Dexter, ed. Philadelphia: Lippincott, 1964. 216pp. A chronological account of the integration of baseball based on Robinson's own recollections and interviews with others. Robinson's optimism that baseball's success could be duplicated in society would later darken as his experience showed otherwise.

I Never Had It Made. As told to Alfred Duckett. New York: Putnam, 1972. 287pp. Based on interviews with Robinson before his death, only a quarter of the book is devoted to his baseball career and includes his realistic, sometimes bitter, recollections of his struggles against racism.

Jackie Robinson: My Own Story. As told to Wendell Smith. New York: Greenberg, 1948. 170pp. Written shortly after Robinson's rookie season, the book records Robinson's own assessment of his early life and the significance of his breaking the color barrier in baseball.

Rowan, Carl T., with Jackie Robinson. *Wait Till Next Year: The Life Story of Jackie Robinson*. New York: Random House, 1960. 339pp. Rowan, a respected African American journalist, collaborated with Robinson on an account of his life that emphasizes not his baseball career but his civil rights activities and continuing struggles after baseball.

Recommended Biographies

Falkner, David. *Great Time Coming: The Life of Jackie Robinson from Baseball to Birmingham*. New York: Simon & Schuster, 1995. 382pp. The first full-length biography is a balanced and objective assessment of Robinson's life and character that includes details of his early life and the years following his retirement. Falkner offers a sensible interpretation concerning Robinson's own understanding of his significance and an explanation of his political decisions connected to his civil rights activism.

Rampersad, Arnold. *Jackie Robinson: A Biography*. New York: Random House, 1997. 512pp. Granted access to Robinson's personal papers and synthesizing journalistic, archival, and oral evidence, Rampersad has produced what should likely be the definitive biography of Robinson for some time to come. The result of the author's diligent research is a revealing, comprehensive portrait of Robinson that puts his life and character in a wider cultural and social context. Both the man and his times are displayed more clearly than any other book on the subject.

Tygiel, Jules. *Baseball's Great Experiment: Jackie Robinson and His Legacy*. New York: Oxford University Press, 1983. 392pp. Considered the definitive account of the integration of baseball, the book focuses on Robinson's experiences but widens the perspective to include those of other black players, establishing a revealing cultural context to view Robinson's achievement.

Other Biographical Studies

Allen, Maury. *Jackie Robinson: A Life Remembered*. New York: F. Watts, 1987. 260pp. Drawing on the recollections of former teammates, coaches, umpires, opponents, owners, and family members, Allen supplies a sensitive tribute and character profile. Appropriate for both adult and young adult readers.

Frommer, Harvey. *Rickey & Robinson: The Men Who Broke Baseball's Color Barrier*. New York: Macmillan, 1982. 240pp. Frommer's dual biography of Robinson and the Dodgers' general manager traces their lives and careers up to their meeting that changed baseball and society and their relationship following Robinson's retirement.

Mann, Arthur. *The Jackie Robinson Story*. New York: Grosset & Dunlap, 1956. 224pp. Written by a former sportswriter and Branch Rickey assistant, this popular account offers an uncritical summary of Robinson's life up to his rookie season and his subsequent baseball achievements.

Robinson, Rachel. With Lee Daniels. *Jackie Robinson: An Intimate Portrait*. New York: Abrams, 1996. 240pp. Robinson's wife supplies a personal account of her husband's rise to stardom, his baseball career, and later civil rights activities. Almost half the book is devoted to Robinson's life off the field and after his retirement. The high point of the volume is its many photographs from the family's album.

Robinson, Sharon. *Stealing Home: An Intimate Family Portrait by the Daughter of Jackie Robinson*. New York: HarperCollins, 1996. 213pp. The author presents a tribute to her father that has little to say about his early struggles or his controversial break with black leaders like Malcolm X and Martin Luther King Jr. or his controversial support of Richard Nixon in 1960. Instead, Robinson as family man is emphasized with the difficulty of living in his shadow the major insight.

Roeder, William. *Jackie Robinson*. New York: A.S. Barnes, 1950. 183pp. In a popular factual account, Roeder chronicles Robinson's struggles to reach the major leagues, his relationship with Branch Rickey, and some details of Robinson's private, domestic life.

Recommended Juvenile Biographies

Coombs, Karen M. *Jackie Robinson: Baseball's Civil Rights Legend*. Springfield, New Jersey: Enslow, 1997. 128pp. YA. Named by the San Diego Book Awards Association as the best children's book of 1997, Coombs's biography narrates the events of Robinson's life and achieves a human portrait of the man, with an emphasis on his civil rights activities.

Denenberg, Barry. *Stealing Home: The Story of Jackie Robinson*. New York: Scholastic, 1997. 116pp. MG. This is a straightforward account of Robinson's life on and off the baseball diamond.

Robinson, Jackie, and Alfred Duckett. *Breakthrough to the Big League*. New York: Harper, 1965. 168pp. MG. Robinson offers his own story that emphasizes his 1949 rookie season and the steps that led up to it. Unfortunately, the book includes little on Robinson's life after baseball.

Weidhorn, Manfred. *Jackie Robinson*. New York: Atheneum, 1993. 207pp. MG/YA. This is a thorough, sympathetic biography that features a vivid picture of the social milieu of his period.

Biographical Films and Theatrical Adaptations

A&E Biography Video: Jackie Robinson (1991). Director: Alfred E. Green. Photos, archival footage, and interviews combine to present a reliable documentary portrait of the man and his achievements. Video.

The Court Martial of Jackie Robinson (1990). Director: Larry Peerce. André Braugher stars as Robinson in this dramatization of an episode from his army service. With Daniel Stern, Ruby Dee, and Bruce Dern. Video.

Jackie Robinson: Breaking Barriers (1997). Producer: Heather Mitchell. A video tribute that includes interviews with family members, rare photographs, and game and newsreel footage. Video.

The Jackie Robinson Story (1950). Director: Alfred E. Green. Robinson plays himself in this film biography tracing his life from college to the big leagues. Ruby Dee portrays Rachel Robinson, and Minor Watson plays Branch Rickey. Video.

Soul of the Game (1996). Director: Kevin R. Sullivan. Television film depicting the lives of Sachel Paige (Delroy Lindo), Josh Gibson (Mykel Williamson), and Jackie Robinson (Blair Underwood) in the Negro League during 1954 as they compete to become the first black player in the big leagues. Edward Herrmann portrays Branch Rickey, the man who will choose among them. Video.

Other Sources

Kahn, Roger, and Jules Tygiel, eds. *The Jackie Robinson Reader: Perspectives on an American Hero*. New York: Dutton, 1997. 278pp. This valuable collection of writings documents the cultural impact of the man and his achievements.

Stout, Glenn, ed. *Jackie Robinson Between the Baselines*. San Francisco: Woodford Press, 1997. 204pp. This collection of essays accesses Robinson's baseball career from his college days through the majors.

403. JOHN D. ROCKEFELLER
1839–1937

American industrialist, financier, and philanthropist, Rockefeller established the Standard Oil Company. He ruthlessly unified the oil industry into the Standard Oil Trust, a holding company and monopoly dissolved by a famous antitrust decision (1911) of the U.S. Supreme Court. Rockefeller was a director of the United States Steel Corporation, financed railroads and banks, and used his considerable fortune to found numerous organizations and philanthropies.

Autobiography and Primary Sources

Dear Father/Dear Son: Correspondence of John D. Rockefeller and John D. Rockefeller Jr. New York: Fordham University Press, 1994. 237pp. A collection of previously unpublished letters between John D. Rockefeller senior and junior helps document the Rockefeller family fortune over the course of 50 years.

John D. Rockefeller Interviews, 1917–1920, Conducted by William O. Inglis. David F. Hawke, ed. Westport, Connecticut: Meckler, 1984. 2 vols. In the absence of a more formal autobiography, Rockefeller's own words, collected here in a series of interviews, show his assessment of his career and his views on a variety of topics.

Random Reminiscences of Men and Events. Tarrytown, New York: Sleepy Hollow Press, 1984. 124pp. Based on interviews conducted by Frank N. Doubleday and printed in the magazine *World's Work* in 1908–1909, Rockefeller's recollections touch on his business practices, philanthropy, and philosophy.

Recommended Biographies

Chernow, Ron. *Titan: The Life of John D. Rockefeller*. New York: Random House, 1998. 774pp. The first biography written following the availability of an important archive of Rockefeller's papers, Chernow's is a masterful synthesis of research and analysis that is the most complete, credible portrait of the man and his career yet written. Both positives and negatives are fully displayed in Chernow's sympathetic but balanced assessment that has been described as a "triumph of the art of biography."

Hawke, David F. *John D.: The Founding Father of the Rockefellers*. New York: Harper & Row, 1980. 260pp. Hawke's objective and detailed portrait presents the many sides of a complex Rockefeller that does not gloss over his flaws, even as he acknowledges his achievements and human qualities. Serves as the best brief study that connects the industrialist with the private individual.

Nevins, Allan. *John D. Rockefeller: The Heroic Age of American Enterprise*. New York: Scribner, 1940. 2 vols. Nevins's impressive biography, long regarded as the standard life, was in the author's view "an effort to illuminate without fear or favor all aspects of the work of a remarkable innovator who left a deep imprint upon both the industry and the philanthropy of his nation." With free access to the private papers of the Rockefeller family, Nevins supplies an objective account of Rockefeller's business career.

Nevins, Allan. *Study in Power: John D. Rockefeller, Industrialist and Philanthropist*. New York: Scribner, 1953. 2 vols. Retaining all the essential data of his earlier study, Nevins supplements it with subsequently available letters from Rockefeller and Standard Oil executives and revises other interpretations for a more complete account of Rockefeller's life.

Other Biographical Studies

Flynn, John T. *God's Gold: The Story of Rockefeller and His Times*. New York: Harcourt, Brace, 1932. 520pp. In Flynn's sympathetic assessment, Rockefeller's fortune was "not only the most honestly acquired but was amassed in the building of a great constructive business and in the development of a new system of industry." The facts of Rockefeller's life are carefully set out as well as the background and environment that help explain his actions and character.

Tarbell, Ida M. *History of the Standard Oil Company*. New York: McClure, 1904. 2 vols. Tarbell's classic muckraking study of the origin, growth, and influence of Standard Oil is an impressive achievement and still required reading. Tarbell's Rockefeller remains enigmatic even after her realistic portrayal of a manipulative and miserly figure.

Fictional Portraits

Alexander, Lawrence. *The Strenuous Life*. New York: Knightsbridge, 1991. 304pp. New York City Police Commissioner Theodore Roosevelt must deal with a conspiracy that connects him with such disparate historical figures as Geronimo and John D. Rockefeller.

Ferrell, Elizabeth. *Full of Thy Riches*. New York: M.S. Mill, 1944. 315pp. In an unconvincing romantic tale of a young wife and her elderly husband in West Virginia's oil country during the Civil War, a young Rockefeller is portrayed.

Longstreet, Stephen. *The Bank*. New York: Putnam, 1976. 377pp. The novel portrays the rise of a great American banking family from the Civil War through the 1929 Wall Street crash with appearances by a number of historical figures, including Rockefeller, Morgan, Fisk, Vanderbilt, and Gould.

Schreiner, Samuel A. *Thine Is the Glory*. New York: Arbor House, 1975. 470pp. The story of America's Golden Triangle in Pittsburgh from the Gilded Age through World War II is chronicled in this family saga with appearances by Rockefeller, Carnegie, and Frick.

Recommended Juvenile Biographies

Coffey, Ellen G. *John D. Rockefeller: Empire Builder*. Englewood Cliffs, New Jersey: Silver Burdett, 1989. 112pp. MG. Rockefeller's business and private life are displayed in this balanced biography that presents his sometimes ruthless business practices along with his happy family life and philanthropy.

Biographical Films and Theatrical Adaptations

A&E Biography Video: The Rockefellers (1994). Director: Alison Guss. This family portrait covers John D. Rockefeller's life before moving on to the next generation. Video.

404. AUGUSTE RODIN
1840–1917

French sculptor whose works are characterized by great vitality and emotional intensity, Rodin first gained recognition with *The Age of Bronze* (1876), exhibited at the Salon in 1877 and purchased for the Luxembourg Gardens. Thereafter, Rodin lived and worked in a government-subsidized apartment in Paris. Among his other works are *The Thinker* (1879) and *Adam and Eve* (1881), two works originally sculpted for Rodin's massive unfinished *Gate of Hell*; *The Kiss* (1886); and *The Burghers of Calais* (1894).

Autobiography and Primary Sources

Rodin on Art. New York: Horizon Press, 1971. 259pp. This is a valuable collection of Rodin's comments on his art and his fellow artists.

Recommended Biographies

Butler, Ruth. *Rodin: The Shape of Genius*. New Haven, Connecticut: Yale University Press, 1993. 591pp. Butler's thoughtful and skillful biographical portrait is based on extensive use of Rodin's letters and is particularly perceptive on the sculptor's relationships and their connections to his art. More selective and interpretively focused than Grunfeld's life, the book clarifies important aspects of Rodin's life so that his personality and achievement become far more understandable and coherent.

Champigneulle, Bernard. *Rodin*. New York: Abrams, 1967. 287pp. Champigneulle's is a useful critical overview for the nonspecialist that includes a sensible appreciation of Rodin's achievements as an artistic innovator as well as a revealing account of the artist's personality and private life.

Grunfeld, Frederic V. *Rodin: A Biography*. New York: Holt, 1987. 738pp. Regarded as the definitive study, Grunfeld's is a remarkably detailed and meticulously researched study that integrates Ro-

din's artistic development, personality, and relationships, as well as his historical and cultural contexts into a sensitive and judicious portrait. Essential for the specialist, the general reader can still enjoy and profit from this well-written and accomplished biography.

Other Biographical Studies

Cladel, Judith. *Rodin*. New York: Harcourt, Brace, 1937. 342pp. The author, a close friend and Rodin's secretary, supplies a respectful, influential appreciation of the sculptor, informed by letters and firsthand observations. Cladel's earlier book, *Rodin: The Man and His Art* (New York: Century, 1917. 357pp.), is a more limited, selective treatment but still possesses interesting observations that have been of service to later biographers.

Descharnes, Robert, and Jean-François Chabrun. *Auguste Rodin*. New York: Viking, 1967. 277pp. Serving as an excellent introduction to the man, his life and times, and his works, this volume is principally valuable for its many photographs, an extensive chronology, and some new information based on previously untapped documentary sources.

Laurent, Monique. *Rodin*. New York: Holt, 1990. 160pp. This collection of reproductions of Rodin's works features a brief biographical and critical overview useful for the general reader and student.

Rilke, Rainer Maria. *Rodin*. New York: Fine Editions Press, 1954. 75pp. Rilke served as Rodin's secretary, and this brief essay is an important source of insights into the sculptor's creative process, personality, and artistic development.

Biographical Novels

Delbée, Anne. *Camille Claudel, une Femme*. San Francisco: Mercury, 1992. 373pp. Rodin's relationship with his longtime model and mistress Camille Claudel is dramatized in a moving account of their life together.

Weiss, David. *Naked Came I: A Novel of Rodin*. New York: Morrow, 1963. 660pp. Rodin's full life is chronicled in this fictional biography that stays close to the actual details of his career, with some invented dialogue and scenes.

Recommended Juvenile Biographies

Pinet, Helene. *Rodin: The Hands of Genius*. New York: Abrams, 1992. 143pp. YA. This informative critical study with 210 illustrations, mostly in color, helpfully analyzes the evolution of Rodin's art, his sculptural techniques, and his personality and private life.

Ripley, Elizabeth. *Rodin: A Biography*. Philadelphia: Lippincott, 1966. 72pp. MG. Ripley covers both the main events of Rodin's life and his evolving artistic development.

Biographical Films and Theatrical Adaptations

Camille Claudel (1989). Director: Bruno Nuytten. Gerarde Depardieu stars as Rodin in this intense film look at the sculptor's relationship with his model and mistress Claudel (Isabelle Adjani). Video.

405. ELEANOR ROOSEVELT
1884–1962

Influential American first lady and humanitarian, Roosevelt was married to thirty-second president, Franklin D. Roosevelt. She encouraged youth movements and worked for minority rights and combated poverty and unemployment. She held the first press conference by a first lady and wrote a daily column titled "My Day." Roosevelt served as U.S. delegate to the United Nations, chaired the U.N. Commission on Human Rights, and co-authored the Universal Declaration of Human Rights.

Autobiography and Primary Sources

Autobiography. New York: Harper, 1961. 454pp. This volume is composed of material selected from Roosevelt's three previous volumes of memoirs— *This Is My Story, This I Remember*, and *On My Own* —with added chapters covering the years between 1958 and 1961.

Empty Without You: The Intimate Letters of Eleanor Roosevelt and Lorena Hickok. Roger Streitmother, ed. New York: Free Press, 1998. 307pp. Challenging the conventional view of Eleanor Roosevelt, her intense and passionate relationship during a 30-year friendship with Associated Press reporter Lorena Hickok is revealed in this collection of their correspondence. More intriguing than the question of whether their relationship was physical as the editor asserts is a portrait of Roosevelt that is remarkably human, showing a vulnerable side rarely glimpsed in public.

Love, Eleanor: Eleanor Roosevelt and Her Friends. Joseph P. Lash, ed. Garden City, New York: Doubleday, 1982. 534pp; *A World of Love: Eleanor Roosevelt and her friends, 1943–1962*. Joseph P. Lash, ed. Garden City, New York: Doubleday, 1985. 610pp. These volumes of Roosevelt's letters to and from her circle of friends are arranged chronologically with Lash's commentary.

Mother and Daughter: The Letters of Eleanor Roosevelt and Anna Roosevelt. Bernard Asbell, ed. New York: Coward-McCann, 1982. 366pp. This collection of correspondence between Roosevelt and her oldest child provides interesting sidelights on the Roosevelt family life as well as displaying a warmer mother-daughter relationship than has been portrayed by many.

On My Own. New York: Harper, 1958. 241pp. Roosevelt chronicles her life after her husband's death, with comments on the figures and events she witnessed since 1945.

This I Remember. New York: Harper, 1949. 387pp. Roosevelt continues her account of her life from 1924 to 1945, with personal yet objective insights and an intimate account of the Roosevelts' years in power.

This Is My Story. New York: Harper, 1937. 365pp. This autobiographical account covers the years from early childhood to the 1924 Democratic election and Franklin D. Roosevelt's election as governor of New York. Roosevelt is discreet on the painful details of her marriage.

Recommended Biographies

Cook, Blanche W. *Eleanor Roosevelt*. New York: Viking, 1992-99. 2 vols. Taking Eleanor Roosevelt's story up to 1938, Cook's controversial, highly praised reassessment of Roosevelt's private and public lives has a strong feminist interpretation in which Eleanor is a figure of fierce strength and determination who overcame considerable obstacles to emerge in her own right as one of the greatest figures of the twentieth century. Cook achieves a nuanced human portrait that has helped to redefine the popular and critical view of Roosevelt and her influence.

Goodwin, Doris Kearns. *No Ordinary Time: Franklin and Eleanor Roosevelt: The Homefront in World War II*. New York: Simon & Schuster, 1994. 759pp. Goodwin's Pulitzer Prize–winning work describes the homefront during World War II from the perspectives of Franklin and Eleanor Roosevelt and their associates in the White House. Based on diaries, interviews, and White House records, the book offers an unprecedented glimpse inside the first family and the Roosevelt administration during a turning point in American history. With an evident preference for Franklin, Goodwin is able to show the heroism of both figures in a humanly compelling fashion.

Lash, Joseph P. *Eleanor and Franklin: The Story of Their Relationship Based on Eleanor Roosevelt's Private Papers*. New York: W.W. Norton, 1971. 765pp. Lash's splendidly written, popular account still dominates the field. Drawing on the author's own recollections and primary sources, Lash compassionately portrays Eleanor's troubled childhood and her complex relationship with her husband.

Lash, Joseph P. *Eleanor: The Years Alone*. New York: W.W. Norton, 1972. 368pp. Lash continues the story of Roosevelt's private and public life following the death of Franklin D. Roosevelt. Her global activities and strong influence on Democratic party politics are well documented, although Lash's evident partisanship prevents a fully objective analysis of motives and the psychological causes for her actions.

Youngs, J. William. *Eleanor Roosevelt: A Personal and Public Life*. Boston: Little, Brown, 1985. 246pp. Youngs's well-written study has the virtue of succinctness and compression. Drawing on recent scholarship and access to primary sources, the book deals frankly with Roosevelt's private life that predominates over details about her public life.

Other Biographical Studies

Berger, Jason. *A New Deal for the World: Eleanor Roosevelt and American Foreign Policy, 1920–1962*. New York: Columbia University Press, 1981. 240pp. Berger's scholarly intellectual biography traces the development of Roosevelt's intellectual and political development and its wider policy impact over almost half a century of American history.

Black, Allida M. *Casting Her Own Shadow: Eleanor Roosevelt and the Shaping of Postwar Liberalism*. New York: Columbia University Press, 1996. 298pp. Focusing on Roosevelt's political career after her husband's death, this well-researched assessment documents her emergence as a major influence on the Democratic party and civil rights in the postwar era.

Caroli, Betty B. *The Roosevelt Women*. New York: Basic Books, 1998. 528pp. In a vivid group portrait of the wives, mothers, sisters, and daughters of the two Roosevelt presidents, Caroli supplies a brief biographical profile of Eleanor in the context of her membership in a fascinating family clan.

Hareven, Tamara K. *Eleanor Roosevelt: An American Conscience*. Chicago: Quadrangle, 1968. 326pp. Written by an Israeli, Hareven's assessment of Roosevelt's public career, achievement, and influence has the advantage of impartiality and distance but is hampered by the unavailability of significant primary sources at the time of its writing.

Hickok, Lorena A. *Eleanor Roosevelt: Reluctant First Lady*. New York: Dodd, Mead, 1962. 176pp. Journalist and close friend and suspected lover of Roosevelt offers her recollections primarily of the early White House years and her friend's emergence as a public figure.

Lash, Joseph P. *Life Was Meant to Be Lived: A Centenary Portrait of Eleanor Roosevelt*. New York: W.W. Norton, 1984. 197pp. Lash's tribute to Roosevelt achievement and influence is captured in this illustrated volume that offers a succinct biographical sketch and overview of her private and public life.

Roosevelt, Elliott, and James Brough. *An Untold Story: The Roosevelts of Hyde Park*. New York: Putnam, 1973. 366pp.; *A Rendezvous with Destiny: The Roosevelts of the White House*. New York: Putnam, 1975. 446pp.; *Mother R: Eleanor Roosevelt's Untold Story*. New York: Putnam, 1977. 288pp. Elliott Roosevelt's memoir trilogy chronicles his recollections of his parents in a narrative history from his childhood in 1916 to Eleanor's death and challenges many assertions about Eleanor and Franklin that are contrary to his firsthand, though restricted and often biased, view.

Roosevelt, James. *My Parents: A Differing View*. Chicago: Playboy Press, 1970. 369pp. The eldest son of the Roosevelts provides his own recollections of his parents and family, differing mainly from the interpretations of his brother Elliott. Readers with time and interest can compare the two contrasting views. Both provide intimate firsthand glimpses, interesting anecdotes, and their own subjective biases.

Steinberg, Alfred. *Mrs. R: The Life of Eleanor Roosevelt*. New York: Putnam, 1958. 384pp. Before the publication of Lash's two volumes Steinberg's was the reigning popular, straightforward account of Eleanor's public and private life. Lacking in penetration, the book knits together Eleanor's story supplementing her autobiographical reflections from other undocumented sources.

Biographical Novels

Lerman, Rhoda. *Eleanor*. New York: Holt, 1979. 297pp. The married life of Eleanor and Franklin between 1918 and 1921 is dramatized in a well-researched credible portrayal.

Fictional Portraits

Kaminsky, Stuart M. *The Fala Factor*. New York: St. Martin's, 1985. 174pp. Eleanor Roosevelt hires private eye Toby Peters in 1942 when she is convinced that her husband's prized Scottie has been kidnapped and replaced by an imposter.

Roosevelt, Elliott. Eleanor Roosevelt Mystery Series. (1984–). Set during the White House years, Eleanor Roosevelt is the principal sleuth in this entertaining historical mystery series with appearances by a number of historical figures in unexpected situations.

Recommended Juvenile Biographies

Friedman, Russell. *Eleanor Roosevelt: A Life of Discovery*. New York: Clarion Books, 1993. 198pp. MG/YA. Ably researched and highly readable, Freedman's photobiography covers Roosevelt's private and public lives and deals frankly with her married life. A standout biography for younger readers.

Spangenburg, Ray, and Diane K. Moser. *Eleanor Roosevelt: A Passion to Improve*. New York: Facts on File, 1997. 114pp. MG. This appreciation of Roosevelt's accomplishments traces her struggles from an unhappy childhood to her emergence as a world leader with an emphasis on her personal qualities that contributed to her achievements.

Toor, Rachel. *Eleanor Roosevelt*. New York: Chelsea House, 1989. 112pp. YA. Part of the American Women of Achievement series, this well-written, generally objective biography summarizes Roosevelt's early years and private life but focuses attention on her public career.

Biographical Films and Theatrical Adaptations

A&E Biography Video: Eleanor Roosevelt: A Restless Spirit. Director: Harry Rasky. Both the public and private lives of Roosevelt are shown in this film portrait based on photographs, film footage, and expert testimony. Video.

Eleanor and Franklin (1976). Director: Daniel Petrie. Television miniseries based on Lash's Pulitzer Prize-winning book features exceptional performances by Jane Alexander as Eleanor and Edward Herrmann as Franklin. Video.

Eleanor and Franklin: The White House Years (1977). Director: Daniel Petrie. Sequel to the 1976 television miniseries in which Alexander and Herrmann reprise their portrayals in scenes from the White House years. Video.

Eleanor: First Lady of the World (1982). Director: John Erman. Jean Stapleton stars as Eleanor in a made-for-television portrait of her years following her husband's death. Richard McKenzie appears as Truman. Video.

The Eleanor Roosevelt Story (1965). Director: Richard Kaplan. Academy Award–winning documentary describing Eleanor Roosevelt's life from childhood. Video.

Sunrise at Campobello (1960). Director: Vincent J. Donehue. Film version of the Tony Award–winning play by Dory Schary (New York: Random House, 1958. 109pp.) stars Greer Garson as Eleanor and Ralph Bellamy as Franklin in a moving dramatization of Franklin's battle with polio from when he is first stricken.

Other Sources

Flemion, Jess, and Colleen M. O'Connor, eds. *Eleanor Roosevelt: An American Journey.* San Diego: San Diego State University Press, 1987. 392pp. This collection of essays on various aspects of Roosevelt's career and influence includes a series of political cartoons and a tribute by John F. Kennedy.

Hoff, Joan, and Marjorie Lightman, eds. *Without Precedent: The Life and Career of Eleanor Roosevelt.* Bloomington: Indiana University Press, 1984. 266pp. These scholarly essays consider Roosevelt's life and career critically, challenging conventional wisdom, and granting to Eleanor Roosevelt the wider, serious consideration of her significance often missing in other accounts.

See also Franklin D. Roosevelt

406. FRANKLIN D. ROOSEVELT
1882–1945

The thirty-second U.S. president and the longest-serving commander in chief in U.S. history, Roosevelt served in the New York state senate and as assistant secretary of the Navy, and ran unsuccessfully as the Democratic vice presidential candidate (1920). After recuperating from a severe attack of polio, which left him partially paralyzed, Roosevelt returned to politics and was elected governor of New York and then president of the United States (1932). During his 12 years in office, sweeping social legislation, collectively known as the New Deal, was passed to alleviate the devastating effects of the Great Depression. During World War II, Roosevelt led the United States as part of the Allied effort against Germany and Japan.

Autobiography and Primary Sources

F.D.R.: His Personal Letters. Elliott Roosevelt, ed. New York: Duell, Sloan and Pearce, 1950. 2 vols. Covering the years 1928 to 1945, beginning with Roosevelt's term as governor of New York to shortly before his death, this collection offers a fascinating glimpse of the man and his development in office.

Recommended Biographies

Davis, Kenneth S. *FDR.* New York: Putnam (vol. 1) and Random House, 1972–1986. 3 vols. Less scholarly than Friedel's study, Davis's three-volume biography tells Roosevelt's story up to the completion of his first term in 1937 in a valuable life and times approach for the general reader. Although clearly an admirer, Davis is not uncritical, providing a believable human portrait against a richly detailed historical background.

Friedel, Frank B. *Franklin D. Roosevelt.* Boston: Little, Brown, 1952–1973. 4 vols. Long established as the standard life, Friedel's massive study is an authoritative and exhaustive synthesis of archival and printed sources that establishes a reli-able factual record and a judicious assessment of Roosevelt's character and motives. In *Franklin D. Roosevelt: A Rendezvous With Destiny* (Boston: Little, Brown, 1990. 710pp.) Friedel distills the essence of the man in a fine one-volume survey of Roosevelt's life and career.

Goodwin, Doris Kearns. *No Ordinary Time: Franklin and Eleanor Roosevelt: The Homefront in World War II.* New York: Simon & Schuster, 1994. 759pp. Goodwin's Pulitzer Prize–winning work describes the homefront during World War II from the perspectives of Franklin and Eleanor Roosevelt and their associates in the White House. Based on diaries, interviews, and White House records, the book offers an unprecedented glimpse inside the first family and the Roosevelt administration during a turning point in American history. With an evident preference for Franklin, Goodwin is able to show the heroism of both figures in a humanly compelling fashion.

Morgan, Ted. *F.D.R.: A Biography.* New York: Simon & Schuster, 1985. 830pp. Morgan's well-written and well-researched popular biography concentrates on the man rather than his political career. Although careful to record the important events of Roosevelt's life and times, Morgan keeps a firm focus on the man for a nuanced, balanced portrait of a complex individual.

Ward, Geoffrey. *Before the Trumpet: Young Franklin Roosevelt, 1882–1905.* New York: Harper & Row, 1985. 390pp.; *A First Class Temperament: The Emergence of Franklin Roosevelt.* New York: Harper & Row, 1989. 889pp. Ward's excellent biography narrates Roosevelt's history up to his election as governor of New York in 1928. His early years and development are traced against a vivid family and social background. Ward helps clarify how the mature Roosevelt was formed and developed.

Other Biographical Studies

Burns, James M. *Roosevelt.* New York: Harcourt, Brace, 1956–1970. 2 vols. Burns's political biography covers Roosevelt's entire career and is excellent in discovering the animating detail that brings history and character to life. Despite respect for Roosevelt's accomplishment, Burns is often harshly critical of the leader, who is depicted as a complex and deeply divided man whose many contradictions are documented.

Ferrell, Robert H. *The Dying President: Franklin D. Roosevelt 1944–1945.* Columbia: University of Missouri Press, 1998. 185pp. In a concise, intimate account of Roosevelt's last year, presidential historian Ferrell supplies an authoritative analysis of Roosevelt's medical condition and the political cover-up that kept the truth from the electorate.

Hatch, Alden. *Franklin D. Roosevelt: An Informal Biography.* New York: Holt, 1947. 413pp. Hatch's novelized biography is a one-sided heroic treatment of a great leader and lovable personality. Simplistic and impressionistic, the book adds little new information, nor does it penetrate the aura of reverence that surrounded Roosevelt after his death.

Larrabee, Eric. *Commander in Chief: Franklin Delano Roosevelt, His Lieutenants, and Their War.* New York: Harper & Row, 1987. 723pp. The book's focus is Roosevelt's wartime leadership in a comprehensive group portrait of the individuals that directed America's war effort. Larrabee demonstrates Roosevelt's strategic skills and extraordinary ability to overcome clashing egos to preserve the Allied coalition.

Lash, Joseph P. *Eleanor and Franklin: The Story of Their Relationship Based on Eleanor Roosevelt's Private Papers.* New York: W.W. Norton, 1971. 765pp. More Eleanor's than Franklin's story, Lash's popular and highly readable, compelling account of their relationship follows the pair from their early years to Franklin's death, mainly reported from Eleanor's perspective.

Maney, Patrick J. *The Roosevelt Presence: The Life and Legacy of FDR.* Berkeley: University of California Press, 1998. 270pp. Maney's concise and balanced reassessment of Roosevelt's life and influence explores the various myths surrounding him and their reality, while arguing Roosevelt's wider impact on modern American history. A first-rate, compact biography and critical interpretation.

McJimsey, George T. *The Presidency of Franklin Delano Roosevelt.* Lawrence: University Press of Kansas, 2000. 376pp. Part of the American Presidency series, this is a synthesis of the best modern scholarship for a reassessment of the Roosevelt administration. Concise and balanced, McJimsey deals with Roosevelt's leadership style and includes a separate chapter on Eleanor Roosevelt and her emergence as a public figure and advocate of social causes.

Miller, Nathan. *F.D.R.: An Intimate History.* Garden City, New York: Doubleday, 1983. 563pp. Miller's compact summary of Roosevelt's life based on secondary sources is informative but limited in the interest of compression. Half the book deals with Franklin's life before the presidency, and the war years are summarized in a mere 40 pages.

Roosevelt, Elliott, and James Brough. *An Untold Story: The Roosevelts of Hyde Park.* New York: Putnam, 1973. 366pp.; *A Rendezvous with Destiny: The Roosevelts of the White House.* New York: Putnam, 1975. 446pp. Elliott Roosevelt's recollections of his parents form a narrative history from his childhood in 1916 to his father's death. An additional volume deals with Eleanor's life after the White House.

Roosevelt, James. *My Parents: A Differing View.* Chicago: Playboy Press, 1970. 369pp. The eldest son of the Roosevelts provides his own recollections of his parents and family, differing mainly from the interpretations of his brother Elliott. Readers with time and interest can compare the two contrasting views. Both provide intimate firsthand glimpses, interesting anecdotes, and their own subjective biases.

Schlesinger, Arthur M. Jr. *The Age of Roosevelt.* Boston: Houghton Mifflin, 1957–1960. 3 vols. The author's masterful historical biography follows Roosevelt's career up to 1936 with an emphasis on his leadership during the Depression.

Tugwell, Rexford G. *The Democratic Roosevelt: A Biography of Franklin D. Roosevelt.* Garden City, New York: Doubleday, 1957. 712pp. The author, a member of Roosevelt's original "brain trust," offers a detailed objective biography connecting Roosevelt's political and private life based on the author's own firsthand views.

Fictional Portraits

Charyn, Jerome. *The Franklin Scare*. New York: Arbor House, 1977. 326pp. The Roosevelt White House is glimpsed from the perspective of the president's barber.

Meade, Glenn. *The Sands of Sakkara*. New York: St. Martin's, 1999. 436pp. In a suspenseful thriller set in 1943, based on some facts, Hitler plots to assassinate Roosevelt and Churchill as they meet in Cairo to plan the Allied invasion of Europe.

Poyer, David. *The Only Thing to Fear*. New York: Forge, 1995. 429pp. In a fanciful thriller set in 1945, John F. Kennedy is transferred to Roosevelt's presidential staff and helps foil an assassination attempt.

Roosevelt, Elliott. *The President's Man*. New York: St. Martin's, 1991. 245pp.; *New Deal for Death*. New York: St. Martin's, 1993. 251pp. Roosevelt in the early 1930s uses the services of Jack "Blackjack" Endicott to foil several conspiracies designed to deny Roosevelt the presidency.

Roosevelt, James, and Sam Toperoff. *A Family Matter*. New York: Simon & Schuster, 1980. 316pp. James Roosevelt, his father's assistant, provides a convincing insider's view of the secret diplomatic maneuvering of the Allies during World War II.

Spike, Paul. *The Night Letter*. New York: Putnam, 1979. 380pp. This political thriller blends a credible reconstruction of 1940 Washington with a plot about compromising photos of Roosevelt embracing Missy LeHand.

Recommended Juvenile Biographies

Friedman, Russell. *Franklin Delano Roosevelt*. New York: Clarion Books, 1990. 200pp. MG. Newbery Award–winning biography offers a compelling, accessible personal portrait of Roosevelt in which his personal struggles put his achievements into a human context. Informative photographs are included.

Israel, Fred L. *Franklin Delano Roosevelt*. New York: Chelsea House, 1985. 112pp. MG/YA. Israel supplies a straightforward, reliable summary of the highlights of Roosevelt's life and career, emphasizing the challenges he faced and his leadership skills.

Larsen, Rebecca. *Franklin D. Roosevelt: Man of Destiny*. New York: F. Watts, 1991. 208pp. YA. This is an in-depth and detailed look at Roosevelt's life, career, and character. Although the tone is admiring, Larsen deals honestly with Roosevelt's faults, including his affair with Lucy Mercer and some of his less flattering political dealings.

Biographical Films and Theatrical Adaptations

A&E Biography Video: FDR (1994). Director: John Alan Kane. Two-part biographical portrait covering the Depression and the war years. Video.

The Democrat and the Dictator (1987). Producer: Betsy McCarthy. Bill Moyers presents a contrasting portrait of Roosevelt and Hitler, focusing on their youth, personalities, leadership styles, and political goals. Video.

Eleanor and Franklin (1976). Director: Daniel Petrie. Television miniseries based on Lash's Pulitzer Prize–winning book features exceptional performances by Jane Alexander as Eleanor and Edward Herrmann as Franklin. Video.

Eleanor and Franklin: The White House Years (1977). Director: Daniel Petrie. Sequel to the 1976 television miniseries in which Alexander and Herrmann reprise their portrayals in scenes from the White House years. Video.

FDR (1994). Producer: David Grubin. An installment in the American Experience series, this is an exceptional film portrait that covers Roosevelt's entire life and political career using photographs, archival footage, and expert testimony. Video.

Franklin D. Roosevelt (1982). Producer: David L. Wolper. Film profile based on archival footage. Video.

The Last Bastion (1984). Director: Chris Thomson. Warren Mitchell portrays Roosevelt in this World War II television drama focusing on the political struggle among the president, Churchill (Timothy West), MacArthur (Robert Vaughn), and Australia's John Curtin (Michael Blakemore). Video.

Sunrise at Campobello (1960). Director: Vincent J. Donehue. Film version of the Tony Award–winning play by Dory Schary (New York: Random House, 1958. 109pp.) stars Greer Garson as Eleanor and Ralph Bellamy as Franklin in a moving dramatization of Franklin's battle with polio, from when he is first stricken.

World War II: When Lions Roared (1994). Director: Joseph Sargent. The conduct of the war from the perspective of the Allied leaders is dramatized. Bob Hoskins portrays Churchill; Michael Caine is Stalin, and John Lithgow is Roosevelt. Video.

Other Sources

Bremer, Howard F., ed. *Franklin Delano Roosevelt, 1882–1945*. Dobbs Ferry, New York: Oceana, 1971. 220pp. Part of the Presidential Chronologies series, this is a detailed calendar of Roosevelt's activities.

Graham, Otis L., and Meghan R. Wander. *Franklin D. Roosevelt: His Life and Times: An Encyclopedic View*. Boston: G.K. Hall, 1985. 483pp. The book's 321 brief articles, arranged alphabetically, cover a wide range of topics on Roosevelt's life and times.

Nash, Gerald D., ed. *Franklin Delano Roosevelt*. Englewood Cliffs, New Jersey: Prentice-Hall, 1967. 182pp. Part of the Great Lives Observed series, excerpts from Roosevelt's writings and speeches are collected, along with contemporaries' recollections, and historians' assessments.

Rosenbaum, Herbert D. *Franklin D. Roosevelt: The Man, the Myth, the Era, 1882–1945*. New York: Greenwood, 1987. 426pp. This collection of critical essays explores multiple aspects of Roosevelt's life and times.

See also Eleanor Roosevelt; Harry S Truman

407. THEODORE ROOSEVELT
1858–1919

The twenty-sixth U.S. president, Roosevelt won fame leading a volunteer regiment, the Rough Riders, during the Spanish-American War. He served as William McKinley's vice president and took over the presidency after McKinley's assassination (1901), becoming the youngest president in U.S. history. A progressive Republican, Roosevelt tried to regulate business and financial monopolies, oversaw passage of the Pure Food and Drug Act, initiated conservation programs, and began work on the Panama Canal. He was awarded the 1906 Nobel Peace Prize for mediating in the Russo-Japanese War. He served two terms in office and unsuccessfully ran again in 1912 as a Progressive Party candidate.

Autobiography and Primary Sources

Autobiography. New York: Macmillan, 1913. 615pp. Roosevelt's selective recollections (his first wife, for example, is never mentioned) are often historically unreliable, constituting the author's defense of his actions. Yet despite its limitations, Roosevelt's unique voice and personality are evident.

The Letters of Theodore Roosevelt. Elting E. Morrison, ed. Cambridge, Massachusetts: Harvard University Press, 1951–1954. 8 vols. More reliable than his autobiography in terms of both history and biography is this scholarly collection of Roosevelt's correspondence that provides invaluable insights into the man, his ideas, and policies.

Recommended Biographies

Brands, H.W. *T.R.: The Last Romantic*. New York: Basic Books, 1997. 897pp. In a meticulously researched and readable single-volume study, Brands successfully connects both the private and public aspects of Roosevelt's life and career, relying on Roosevelt's own words from his letters to tell his story directly. In Brands's view, Roosevelt's heroic public image masked private imperfections that he struggled with throughout his life.

Harbaugh, William H. *The Life and Times of Theodore Roosevelt*. New York: Farrar, Straus, 1961. 540pp. Avoiding the excesses of both Roosevelt's admirers and detractors, Harbaugh's balanced and well-researched biography and interpretation set a new critical standard in portraying Roosevelt and remains a solid choice for a thorough full-length, single-volume study.

Jeffers, H. Paul. *Commissioner Roosevelt: The Story of Theodore Roosevelt and the New York City Police, 1895–1897*. New York: Wiley, 1994. 285pp.; *Colonel Roosevelt: Theodore Roosevelt Goes to War, 1897–1898*. New York: J. Wiley, 1996. 301pp. Jeffers's two completed volumes of a proposed multivolume popular biography cover only four years in Roosevelt's life, but their significance in forming his character and political career is effectively argued in these well-researched, readable narratives that animate both the man and his era.

Miller, Nathan. *Theodore Roosevelt*. New York: Morrow, 1992. 624pp. Miller's comprehensive one-volume biography concentrates less on the public Roosevelt than on his relations with his family, associates, and particularly his first and second wives. The result is a lucid, plausible character study in which the details of his career are given an understandable human context.

Morris, Edmund. *The Rise of Theodore Roosevelt*. New York: Coward-McCann, 1979. 886pp. Morris's Pulitzer Prize–winning biography authoritatively documents Roosevelt's life from his birth to 1901 when he assumes the presidency. The book excels in shrewdly capturing Roosevelt's personality and development and fully integrating the private man and his many public poses.

Other Biographical Studies

Bishop, Joseph B. *Theodore Roosevelt and His Time*. New York: Scribner, 1920. 2 vols. Bishop's biography tells Roosevelt's story mainly in his subject's own words, using excerpts from his letters. This serves as a readable narrative for the reader without the time to contend with the eight volumes of Roosevelt's published correspondence.

Blum, John M. *The Republican Roosevelt*. Cambridge, Massachusetts: Harvard University Press, 1954. 170pp. Blum's compact political biography arranges the details of Roosevelt's career as the basis for a lively and provocative interpretation that challenges conventional wisdom.

Burton, David H. *Theodore Roosevelt*. New York: Twayne, 1972. 236pp. Burton's intellectual biography traces the development of his ideas and policies. In *Theodore Roosevelt, American Politician: An Assessment* (Madison, New Jersey: Fairleigh Dickinson University Press, 1997. 171pp.), Burton provides a political profile of Roosevelt's principles and practices, applying the theory of decision making to his career.

Busch, Noel F. *T.R.: The Story of Theodore Roosevelt and His Influence on Our Time*. New York: Reynal, 1963. 346pp. Busch's compact life offers little that is new but synthesizes the available sources into an accessible narrative. Anecdotes predominate here, and Busch's presentation of political matters is often simplistic and misleading.

Charnwood, Godfrey R. B. *Theodore Roosevelt*. Boston: Atlantic Monthly Press, 1923. 232pp. Lord Charnwood admits to hero worship for his subject, but he is able to deal dispassionately with the man and his accomplishments in a series of impressionistic glimpses that simplify Roosevelt's life into a series of clear moral choices.

Chessman, G. Wallace. *Theodore Roosevelt and the Politics of Power*. Boston: Little, Brown, 1969. 214pp. Chessman's political biography offers little on Roosevelt's private life and no new interpretations but a solid summary of his public life, suitable as an introduction for the general reader.

Cooper, John M. Jr. *The Warrior and the Priest: Woodrow Wilson and Theodore Roosevelt*. Cambridge, Massachusetts: Harvard University Press, 1983. 442pp. Cooper's dual biography is a well-written comparative study, alternating between incisive views and characterizations of both men at turning points of their careers. In Cooper's view Roosevelt and Wilson are "the principal architects of modern American politics," and the book offers a cogent case in support of his assertion.

Gardner, Joseph L. *Departing Glory: Theodore Roosevelt as Ex-President*. New York: Scribner, 1973. 432pp. In a well-written, moving account Gardner focuses on Roosevelt's sad final years and political disappointments after 1908. The book offers a compelling look at Roosevelt's frustrations in which his seemingly boundless energy was dispersed in a number of unproductive channels.

Gould, Lewis L. *The Presidency of Theodore Roosevelt*. Lawrence: University Press of Kansas, 1991. 355pp. In Gould's judicious and balanced assessment, Roosevelt stands in the second rank of presidents in the category of near great. The book supports Gould's view in an analytical narrative of Roosevelt's administrations in their historical and political context. This book is regarded as the standard work on the subject.

Hagedorn, Hermann. *Roosevelt in the Badlands*. Boston: Houghton Mifflin, 1921. 475pp.; *The Roosevelt Family of Sagemore Hill*. New York: Macmillan, 1954. 435pp. Written by a devoted admirer and longtime friend, Hagedorn supplies details on Roosevelt's ranching days in Dakota from 1883 to 1887 and his family life from his second marriage to his death. Both books collect anecdotes from a variety of sources to paint a colorful look at the nonpolitical side of Roosevelt's life.

Lorant, Stefan. *The Life and Times of Theodore Roosevelt*. Garden City, New York: Doubleday, 1959. 640pp. Lorant's visual biography is a standout in the genre. The 750 photographs are wisely chosen and the accompanying text is balanced, straightforward, and accurate. An excellent starting point for the reader interested in Roosevelt and his era.

McCullough, David. *Mornings on Horseback*. New York: Simon & Schuster, 1981. 445pp. McCullough vividly describes Roosevelt's life from age 10 to 28, expertly and compellingly telling the fascinating story of Roosevelt's family background, his childhood illness, and his development under the important influence of his father and mother. The book is particularly strong in the social background that helps explain Roosevelt's values.

Pringle, Henry E. *Theodore Roosevelt, a Biography*. New York: Harcourt, Brace, 1931. 627pp. Pringle's Pulitzer Prize–winning biography is the work of a muckraking journalist who shocked his audience with a highly critical assessment that challenged the heroic image of Roosevelt. Pringle's work retains a historical interest for helping to initiate a view of Roosevelt that accounts for his flaws as well as his virtues.

Putnam, Carleton. *Theodore Roosevelt: The Formative Years, 1858–1884*. New York: Scribner, 1958. 616pp. Putnam only completed one volume of a projected four, chronicling Roosevelt's story up to his twenty-eighth year. Exhaustive in its factual details, the book is useful as a reference tool rather than a compelling narrative or interpretive synthesis.

Renehan, Edward J. Jr. *The Lion's Pride: Theodore Roosevelt and His Family in Peace and War*. New York: Oxford University Press, 1998. 320pp. In an anecdotally rich group portrait of the Roosevelt family, Renehan explores Roosevelt's principles of service and martial spirit as they are tested by the experiences of his sons in World War I. Based on previously unpublished family letters, papers, and interviews, the book shows a moving human side of Roosevelt's nature in his relationship with his children.

Robinson, Corinne Roosevelt. *My Brother Theodore Roosevelt*. New York: Scribner, 1921. 365pp. Roosevelt's sister offers a heartfelt tribute to her brother that is valuable for its intimate details of the pair's childhood. Her later views of her admired older brother are wreathed in sentiment and hero-worship.

Roosevelt, Nicholas. *Theodore Roosevelt: The Man as I Knew Him*. New York: Dodd, Mead, 1967. 205pp. Roosevelt's cousin provides a biographical account based on his recollections, family letters, and diaries and adds a number of intimate glimpses of the man and politician.

Thayer, William R. *Theodore Roosevelt*. Boston: Houghton Mifflin, 1919. 474pp. Thayer's early biography draws on his intimacy with his subject, but the lack of objectivity is evident in his concluding comment that "Those of us who knew him, knew him as the most astonishing human expression of the creative spirit we had ever seen."

Wagenknecht, Edward. *The Seven Worlds of Theodore Roosevelt*. New York: Longmans, 1958. 325pp. The author's psychological character study looks at Roosevelt's many roles, interests, and ideas to arrive at a credible profile. Lively and packed with anecdotes, Wagenknecht's analysis is thoughtful and provocative. Readers should come prepared with a prior familiarity of the chronology of Roosevelt's career.

Biographical Novels

Garfield, Brian. *Manifest Destiny*. New York: Penzler Books, 1989. 408pp. In a novel based partly on fact, Roosevelt's ranching experiences in the Badlands following the deaths of his mother and wife are dramatized.

Gerson, Noel B. *TR*. Garden City, New York: Doubleday, 1970. 441pp. Supported by solid research and an authentic period recreation, Roosevelt's life and times are dramatized at full length.

Wilson, Dorothy C. *Alice and Edith: A Biographical Novel of the Two Wives of Theodore Roosevelt*. New York: Doubleday, 1989. 400pp. Chronicling the life of Roosevelt from the perspective of his wives, the novel dramatizes the trauma of Alice's sudden death and Roosevelt's slow recovery before marrying a childhood friend who rejected an earlier proposal.

Fictional Portraits

Alexander, Lawrence. *The Big Stick*. Garden City, New York: Doubleday, 1986. 349pp.; *Speak Softly*. Garden City, New York: Doubleday, 1987. 250pp.; *The Strenuous Life*. Garden City, New York: Knightsbridge, 1991. 304pp. This inventive and entertaining historical mystery series shows Roosevelt as New York's police commissioner investigating crimes and rubbing elbows with a diverse group of historical figures such as Geronimo, Dvořák, Lillian Russell, Edison, and Rockefeller.

Bowen, Peter. *Yellowstone Kelly.* Ottawa, Illinois: Jameson, 1987. 282pp.; *Imperial Kelly.* New York: Crown, 1992. 210pp. Bowen's irreverent historical series featuring adventurer Luther Kelly shows him in offbeat action alongside a number of historical figures, including Roosevelt.

Carr, Caleb. *The Alienist.* New York: Random House, 1994. 496pp. Carr's atmospheric and authentic historical crime novel shows Roosevelt as New York's police commissioner interacting with the novel's main characters as they work to solve a series of baffling murders. See also the sequel *The Angel of Darkness* (New York: Random House, 1997. 400pp.)

Henry, Will. *San Juan Hill.* New York: Random House, 1962. 276pp. Henry's classic historical adventure novel describes the fighting of the Rough Riders during the Cuban campaign in a version that is faithful to the basic historical outline and features a convincing portrayal of Roosevelt's leadership under fire.

Jeffers, H. Paul. *The Adventure of the Stalwart Companions.* New York: Harper & Row, 1978. 190pp. Roosevelt biographer Jeffers arranges an 1880 meeting between Roosevelt and Sherlock Holmes as the latter tutors the future police commissioner in detective work.

Jones, Douglas C. *Remember Santiago.* New York: Holt, 1988. 354pp. The Cuban invasion of 1898 is depicted from a series of eyewitness accounts in a convincing historical recreation.

Schorr, Mark. *Bully!* New York: St. Martin's, 1985. 196pp. In a fanciful tale, Roosevelt seeks the assistance of a former Rough Rider to thwart a conspiracy aimed at blocking Roosevelt's presidential election.

Vidal, Gore. *Empire.* New York: Random House, 1987. 486pp. Vidal's panoramic political novel is set in the aftermath of the Spanish American War and dramatizes the United States' emergence as a world power. A large cast of historical figures, including Roosevelt, is featured.

Williams, Gordon. *Pomeroy.* New York: Arbor House, 1982. 299pp. This espionage novel set during the Roosevelt presidency sends an American hustler and adventurer as the president's personal undercover agent on a dangerous mission to Edwardian London with the control of Europe hanging in the balance.

Recommended Juvenile Biographies

Fritz, Jean. *Bully for You, Teddy Roosevelt.* New York: Scholastic, 1992. 127pp. MG. Fritz's exuberant, witty, demystifying approach to historical icons is applied to Roosevelt whose personality is dramatically displayed in a highly entertaining biography. A *School Library Journal* best book of the year.

Markham, Lois. *Theodore Roosevelt.* New York: Chelsea House, 1985. 111pp. MG. A reliable summary of the highlights of Roosevelt's life and career.

Meltzer, Milton. *Theodore Roosevelt and His America.* New York: F. Watts, 1994. 191pp. YA. Meltzer provides a detailed critical appreciation of Roosevelt's personality and accomplishments that does not gloss over his complexities and contradictions. A thoughtful and revealing biographical portrait.

Whitelaw, Nancy. *Theodore Roosevelt Takes Charge.* Morton Grove, Illinois: A. Whitman, 1992. 192pp. YA. In a readable account of Roosevelt's life, the emphasis is on an appreciation of his accomplishments in the context of his era and personal challenges. Although sympathetic, Whitelaw does not ignore her subject's shortcomings.

Biographical Films and Theatrical Adaptations

A&E Biography Video: Theodore Roosevelt: Roughrider to Rushmore (1995). Director: Bill Harris. This is a documentary portrait using archival footage and family interviews. Video.

The Indomitable Teddy Roosevelt (1983). Director: Harrison Engle. Mixing newsreel footage with dramatized scenes, Roosevelt's career and character are presented. Narrated by George C. Scott, with Roosevelt portrayed by Bob Boyd. Video.

The Rough Riders (1997). Director: John Milius. Tom Berenger portrays the young Roosevelt during his military experience in Cuba. With Brian Keith as McKinley and a supporting cast that includes Sam Eliott, Gary Busey, Chris Noth, and George Hamilton. Video.

TR and His Times (1984). Producer: Janet Roach. An installment of A Walk Through the 20th Century with Bill Moyers, this is a film portrait with an emphasis on Roosevelt's public career and era. Video.

TR: The Story of Theodore Roosevelt (1996). Producer: David Grubin. Excellent film portrait, part of the American Experience series on PBS. Video.

The Wind and the Lion (1975). Director: John Milius. Brian Keith portrays President Roosevelt who sends out the marines when a Moroccan sheik (Sean Connery) kidnaps an American woman (Candice Bergen). Loosely based on an actual incident. Video.

Other Sources

Black, Gilbert J., ed. *Theodore Roosevelt, 1858–1919: Chronology, Documents, Bibliographical Aids.* Dobbs Ferry, New York: Oceana, 1969. 120pp. This is a useful reference tool with an extensive chronology, a selection of important documents, and an annotated bibliography of secondary sources.

Gable, John A. *Theodore Roosevelt Cyclopedia.* 1941. Revised ed. New York: Greenwood, 1989. 680pp. Along with a detailed chronology, this compendium of Roosevelt's statements is classified by subject matter.

Grantham, Dewey, ed. *Theodore Roosevelt.* Englewood Cliffs, New Jersey; Prentice-Hall, 1971. 181pp. Part of the Great Lives Observed series, this useful collection brings together Roosevelt's own writings, contemporaries' observations, and modern historical views.

408. DANTE GABRIEL ROSSETTI
1828–1882

English poet and painter, Rossetti was the son of poet and critic Gabriele Rossetti and the brother of poet Christina Rossetti. He was a founder of the Pre-Raphaelites, a brotherhood of artists formed in reaction against the prevailing academic style. At age 19, Rossetti published "The Blessed Damozel," considered by many to be his best poem. A master of the sonnet form, one of his finest works is the sonnet sequence "The House of Life." His collected works appeared in 1870. Although he produced paintings and drawings, his reputation rests primarily upon his poetry.

Autobiography and Primary Sources

Letters of Dante Gabriel Rossetti. Oswald Doughty and John R. Wahl, eds. Oxford: Clarendon Press, 1965–1967. 4 vols. The scholarly collection of Rossetti's correspondence is an invaluable research source for the biographer, but overall the autobiographical revelations revealed are limited, and the artist rarely comments on his inner life, feelings, or his works in any detail.

Recommended Biographies

Dobbs, Brian, and Judy Dobbs. *Dante Gabriel Rossetti: An Alien Victorian.* London: Macdonald and Jane's, 1977. 257pp. Like Riede's study, this is a valuable, reliable overview of Rossetti's life and career that is an excellent choice for the reader looking for a informed orientation to the subject.

Doughty, Oswald. *Dante Gabriel Rossetti: A Victorian Romantic.* New Haven, Connecticut: Yale University Press, 1949. 712pp. Doughty's authoritative, scholarly biography still leads the field as the most comprehensive available, setting Rossetti securely against his background. Several of Doughty's interpretations have proven controversial, but on the whole this is a balanced view that establishes the basic factual record of the artist's life and career.

Grylls, R. Glynn. *Portrait of Rossetti.* Carbondale: Southern Illinois University Press, 1964. 258pp. Grylls's study can be profitably read as a companion to Doughty for her different interpretations of several of his conclusions regarding Rossetti's character and relationships. Based on original research, Grylls sheds light on areas of Rossetti's life that remained shadowy in Doughty's handling.

Riede, David. *Dante Gabriel Rossetti.* New York: Macmillan, 1992. 186pp. Riede's penetrating reassessment of Rossetti's life, art, and influence serves as an excellent compact introduction that covers the full range of the artist's career and relationships. Riede is particularly insightful on how Rossetti helped to create his own legend with a clear eye on his market even as he espoused the concept of art for art's sake.

Other Biographical Studies

Angeli, Helen Rossetti. *Dante Gabriel Rossetti: His Friends and Enemies.* 1949. Reprint ed. New York: B. Blom, 1972. 291pp. Angeli looks at Rossetti's relationships with separate chapters devoted to each of the significant figures in his life. Written for the reader already well acquainted with Rossetti's background and the art movement with which he is associated.

Ash, Russell. *Dante Gabriel Rossetti.* New York: Abrams, 1995. unpaged. This elegant volume reproduces 40 of Rossetti's finest works in large, full-color plates and includes an illustrated introductory text that outlines the artist's life and career and sets his art in the context of his time.

Faxon, Alicia C. *Dante Gabriel Rossetti.* New York: Abbeville Press, 1989. 255pp. In a beautifully illustrated biography by an art historian, Faxon concentrates on Rossetti's paintings and their intellectual themes, his techniques, and the development of his style. The book's art criticism includes a brief biographical summary.

Waugh, Evelyn. *Rossetti: His Life and Works.* New York: Dodd, Mead, 1928. 232pp. Waugh's critical biography is an elegantly written defense of Rossetti's artistry that includes a restrained summary of his life. A pleasure to read, Waugh's rather idiosyncratic approach is often revealing if limited by the author's discretion and refusal to come to a conclusion about the implications he generates.

Winwar, Frances. *Poor Splendid Wings: The Rossettis and Their Circle.* Boston: Little, Brown, 1933. 413pp. Rossetti is the central figure in Winwar's group portrait of the Pre-Raphaelite Brotherhood. Constructed like a novel with an eye toward drama and character, Winwar's florid style is a distraction and often the distinction between documentation and invention is blurred.

Biographical Novels

Kitchen, Paddy. *The Golden Veil.* London: Hamilton, 1981. 286pp. Based on the life of Elizabeth Siddal, Rossetti's model and mistress, the novel traces her career from her youth and her involvement in the bohemian circle that included Rossetti, Millais, Swinburne, Morris, and Holman Hunt.

Savage, Elizabeth. *Willowwood.* Boston: Little, Brown, 1978. 214pp. Rossetti's complicated emotional life is the focus of this novel that portrays the artist's relationship with Elizabeth Siddal and his circle that includes Ruskin and Morris.

Biographical Films and Theatrical Adaptations

Dante's Inferno: Life of Dante Gabriel Rossetti (1969). Director: Ken Russell. Oliver Reed stars as the artist and poet whose scandalous life style is presented with Russell's characteristic exuberance and excess. Video.

409. JEAN-JACQUES ROUSSEAU
1712–1778

Swiss-French philosopher, political theorist, and author, Rousseau wrote music articles for philoso- pher and critic Denis Diderot's *Encyclopédie* and won fame with an essay on the corruption of human nature by the arts and sciences. Other important essays are *Origin of the Inequality of Man* (1754), *The Social Contract* (1762), influential during the French Revolution, and *Confessions* (1782). His novels include *Héloïse* (1761) and *Émile* (1762). Rousseau's primary philosophy was that humans are by nature good but are corrupted by society. He advocated a humanistic and enlightened educational system that would enhance the natural interests and potential of the child.

Autobiography and Primary Sources

Confessions. New York: Knopf, 1992. 306pp. Begun in 1766 and published posthumously, Rousseau's *Confessions* is arguably the most famous and influential autobiography ever written. The book is a fundamental though problematic text for Rousseau's biographers who must contend with the degree of invention employed in the author's memories and self-assessment.

Recommended Biographies

Cranston, Maurice. *Jean-Jacques: The Early Life and Work of Jean-Jacques Rousseau, 1712–1754.* New York: W.W. Norton, 1983. 382pp.; *The Noble Savage: Jean-Jacques Rousseau, 1754–1762.* Chicago: University of Chicago Press, 1991. 399pp.; *The Solitary Self: Jean-Jacques Rousseau in Exile and Adversity.* Chicago: University of Chicago Press, 1997. 260pp. This is a masterful biographical trilogy that is both judicious and thorough in using all the available sources to view Rousseau clearly in a subtle, human portrait.

Green, F.C. *Jean-Jacques Rousseau: A Critical Study of His Life and Writings.* Cambridge, Massachusetts: Cambridge University Press, 1955. 376pp. Carefully documented and based on modern scholarship, Green's critical biography is an excellent, learned tour of Rousseau's mental landscape and his achievement.

Guélhenno, Jean. *Jean-Jacques Rousseau.* New York: Columbia University Press, 1966. 2 vols. Regarded as the standard life and a masterpiece of the biographer's art, Guélhenno supplies one of the most comprehensive chronological studies of Rousseau's life and development available. The author explains that his aim was to "study Rousseau's thought in its process of development and not as a series of results....I resolved to relive it day by day." A marvel of scholarship, the book animates Rousseau and his ideas in a superior biographical treatment.

Other Biographical Studies

Blanchard, William H. *Rousseau and the Spirit of Revolt: A Psychological Study.* Ann Arbor: University of Michigan Press, 1967. 300pp. Blanchard's psychological examination locates the origin and development of Rousseau's ideas in his early experiences and emotional make-up. The book presupposes prior familiarity with psychoanalytic theory and terminology.

Conroy, Peter V. *Jean-Jacques Rousseau.* New York: Simon & Schuster, 1998. 171pp. Conroy's succinct overview of Rousseau's life and work pro- vides a brief biographical sketch before proceeding to a critical reading of his writings and a final chapter on Rousseau's legacy and influence. Recommended as a starting point for a reader's introduction to the man and his impact.

Crocker, Lester. *Jean-Jacques Rousseau.* New York: Macmillan, 1968–1973. 2 vols. This provocative intellectual biography attempts to integrate Rousseau's morals, politics, pedagogy, and social theory into a coherent psychological response stemming from his distrust of human nature, personal insecurities, and yearning for social order. Rousseau is also viewed in the context of his times.

Grimsley, Ronald. *Jean-Jacques Rousseau: A Study in Self-Awareness.* Cardiff: University of Wales Press, 1961. 338pp. This developmental biography traces the formation of Rousseau's conception of self through a critical reading of his works.

Grimsley, Ronald. *Rousseau and the Religious Quest.* Oxford: Clarendon Press, 1968. 148pp. Grimsley's analysis of Rousseau's religious ideas are presented looking first at the biographical details that explain his intellectual and moral development before considering the principal documents and his various notions on God, hell, and paradise.

Wokler, Robert. *Rousseau.* New York: Oxford University Press, 1995. 132pp. Part of the Past Masters series, this is a solid introduction to the man, his works, and ideas.

Biographical Novels

Endore, S. Guy. *Voltaire! Voltaire!* New York: Simon & Schuster, 1961. 507pp. The novel presents the parallel and contrasting lives of the eighteenth-century's towering intellectual forces—Rousseau and Voltaire. With a strong basis in fact, the novel portrays the personalities of both men.

Fictional Portraits

Feuchtwanger, Lion. *'Tis Folly to Be Wise.* New York: J. Messner, 1953. 367pp. The novel looks at Rousseau's death and its connection to a fictional story.

Rebolledo, Francisco. *Rasero.* Baton Rouge: Louisiana State University Press, 1995. 552pp. A young Spanish nobleman visits France during the intellectual ferment of the Enlightenment where he meets such figures as Diderot, Lavoisier, Mozart, Voltaire, and Rousseau.

Recommended Juvenile Biographies

Webb, Robert N. *Jean-Jacques Rousseau: The Father of Romanticism.* New York: F. Watts, 1970. 116pp. MG/YA. This is a competent introduction to the man and his ideas, relating Rousseau to the wider historical and cultural context.

Biographical Films and Theatrical Adaptations

Jean-Jacques Rousseau (1997). Producer: Films for the Humanities. Rousseau's life, personality, and thought is examined in this film portrait. Video.

410. PETER PAUL RUBENS
1577–1640

The foremost seventeenth-century Flemish painter and one of the greatest Baroque painters, Rubens lived and worked in Italy, Antwerp, Spain, England, and Brussels. From 1622 to 1625 he carried out numerous commissions for the French court. A painter celebrated for his exuberant style, rich colors, and sensuous effects, Rubens's many works include *History of Marie de Médici* and *Judgment of Paris*, *Three Graces*, and *Venus and Adonis*, commissioned for the Spanish court. He influenced many artists, including Van Dyck and Renoir.

Autobiography and Primary Sources

The Letters of Peter Paul Rubens. Evanston, Illinois: Northwestern University Press, 1991. 528pp. Invaluable as a biographical source, Rubens's collected correspondence provides insights into the man and his creative method.

Recommended Biographies

Belkin, Kristen L. *Rubens*. London: Phaidon, 1998. 351pp. Written by one of the editors of Rubens's letters, Belkin provides a chronological narrative of the artist's life that explores such themes as his artistic techniques, the role of women in his life and art, and his involvement in contemporary political and religious issues. The various threads of Rubens's career are usefully joined here in a credible human portrait.

Lescourret, Marie-Anne. *Rubens: A Double Life*. Chicago: I.R. Dee, 1993. 289pp. Lescourret's is a vivid portrait of the artist against a clear background of his times. The book helps to connect the private and public aspects of Rubens's life and his artistic and diplomatic careers, into a coherent, psychological portrait.

White, Christopher. *Rubens and His World*. New York: Viking, 1968. 144pp.; *Peter Paul Rubens, Man and Artist*. New Haven, Connecticut: Yale University Press, 1987. 310pp. Both of White's fine studies are recommended as comprehensive overviews for the general reader. White, the director of the Ashmolean Museum in Oxford, sensibly covers all aspects of Rubens's remarkable career and his period background.

Other Biographical Studies

Avermaete, Roger. *Rubens and His Times*. New York: A.S. Barnes, 1968. 218pp. Contrary to most biographical interpretations, Avermaete presents Rubens's personality and career in a decidedly negative light. According to the author, Rubens was far from the admirable individual recorded by his contemporaries and later biographers. Unfortunately, the evidence supporting Avermaete's contentions is undocumented, making it difficult to sort out fact from speculation.

Baudouin, Frans. *Pietro Paulo Rubens*. New York: Abrams, 1977. 405pp. This collection of essays by the former curator of the Rubens House covers various aspects of Rubens's career, along with nearly 300 illustrations.

Burckhardt, Jacob. *Recollections of Rubens*. New York: Phaidon, 1950. 374pp. Originally published in 1898, the last work of the great nineteenth-century Swiss historian, this series of critical essays examines various aspects of Rubens's life and works. Besides analyses of Rubens's paintings and their connection with his career, the book includes a selection from the artist's correspondence.

Cabanne, Pierre. *Rubens*. New York: Tudor, 1967. 286pp. Cabanne's critical examination of Rubens's art and the evolution of his style and technique provides helpful information on the connection between Rubens's life, creative method, and artistic achievement.

Cammaerts, Emile. *Rubens: Painter and Diplomat*. London: Faber and Faber, 1932. 293pp. This sympathetic assessment of Rubens's multiple achievements in art and diplomacy is chiefly valuable for establishing a recognizable historical background for viewing the artist's career.

Edwards, Samuel. *Peter Paul Rubens: A Biography of a Giant*. New York: McKay, 1973. 250pp. Edwards's readable nonscholarly biography displays both the man and the artist but is marred by conjecture and limited scholarship.

Fletcher, Jennifer. *Peter Paul Rubens*. New York: Praeger, 1968. 90pp. This compact visual introduction to the man and his work is arranged into short chapters on Rubens's life, diplomatic career, and artistry. Useful as an introduction for the general reader and student.

Held, Julius S. *Rubens and His Circle*. Princeton, New Jersey: Princeton University Press, 1982. 207pp. This collection of 15 scholarly articles with Rubens as their focus by the premier scholar in the field of seventeenth-century Flemish art covers such topics as Rubens's book illustrations and the iconography of his paintings.

Michel, Emile. *Rubens: His Life, His Work, and His Time*. New York: Scribner, 1899. 2 vols. Michel's early comprehensive study has retained its value as a reference source, but many of the author's contentions are unsupported, and the book should be read alongside subsequent treatments to judge reliability.

Wedgwood, C.V. *The World of Rubens: 1577–1640*. New York: Time-Life Books, 1967. 192pp. Directed at the general reader, the volume provides a chronological examination of Rubens's life and works. Serves as a popular introduction to Rubens and the political events of his times.

Biographical Novels

Braider, Donald. *An Epic Joy: A Novel Based on the Life of Rubens*. New York: Putnam, 1971. 352pp. A convincing and biographicaly accurate depiction of Rubens's life that connects his artistic achievement with his diplomatic career.

Harsányi, Zsolt. *Lover of Life*. New York: Putnam, 1942. 678pp. The novel traces Rubens's artistic development, diplomatic career, and personal life from his youth to his death in a thorough, believable account.

Wallach, Ira J. *The Horn and the Roses: A Novel Based on the Life of Peter Paul Rubens*. New York: Boni and Gaer, 1947. 347pp. In a fictionalized bi-

ography that tracks Rubens's rise to success in art and diplomacy, Wallach endorses the controversial theory that many of Rubens's masterpieces were done not by him but by others in his workshop.

Recommended Juvenile Biographies

McLanathan, Richard B.K. *Peter Paul Rubens*. New York: Abrams, 1995. 92pp. YA. Part of the impressive First Impressions series, McLanathan presents Rubens's life and artistry through comparisons with his contemporaries and an analysis of the sources of his inspiration.

Ripley, Elizabeth. *Rubens: A Biography*. New York: Walck, 1957. 68pp. MG. This is a highly idealized portrait of the artist, celebrating his genius and achievement.

411. JOHN RUSKIN
1819–1900

English art critic and social theorist, Ruskin was educated by his wealthy, evangelical parents. The first of his five-volume *Modern Painters* appeared in 1843 and championed J.W.M. Turner. Other volumes of art criticism include *The Seven Lamps of Architecture* (1849) and *The Stones of Venice* (1851–1853). As a social theorist, his suggestions for reform included old-age pensions, nationalized education, and organized labor. Ruskin supported the Pre-Raphaelite movement and was England's first professor of art. His autobiography *Praeterita* (1885–1889) was unfinished.

Autobiography and Primary Sources

Praeterita. Kent, England: G. Allen, 1886–1889. 3 vols. One of the greatest literary autobiographies, *Praeterita* has both helped and hindered a clear assessment of Ruskin and his life. Often unreliable and misleading, Ruskin's account of his upbringing should be read alongside an objective biographical study. An abridged edition is available as *Praeterita: The Autobiography of John Ruskin* (New York: Oxford University Press, 1990. 592pp.).

Recommended Biographies

Abse, Joan. *John Ruskin: The Passionate Moralist*. New York: Knopf, 1981. 363pp. Drawing on considerable new material, Abse supplies a richly detailed, nuanced account of Ruskin's character and career. Connecting the various strands of Ruskin's life and work, Abse's is a sympathetic though objective and highly readable narrative.

Evans, Joan. *John Ruskin*. New York: Oxford University Press, 1954. 447pp. A superior biography by an eminent art historian who edited Ruskin's diaries, Evans's study balances both Ruskin's public and private life, his work, and his personality in a fair-minded assessment.

Hilton, Tim. *John Ruskin*. New Haven, Connecticut: Yale University Press, 1985-2000. 2 vols. Hilton's two-volume study is the modern authoritative life and the fullest account available of Ruskin's background, development, and relationships. Hilton is particularly insightful on Ruskin's formative years, and the author's sympathetic approach extends beyond Ruskin to his parents and his wife, avoiding the caricatures of other treatments.

Hunt, John Dixon. *The Wider Sea: A Life of John Ruskin.*. New York: Viking, 1982. 512pp. Hunt's biography excels in tracing the relationship between Ruskin's life and work, showing the origin and connections of his ideas to his experiences. Ruskin's career is also placed in the wider context of his times.

Other Biographical Studies

Benson, Arthur C. *Ruskin: A Study in Personality.* New York: Putnam, 1911. 323pp. This series of university lectures ranges over the events of Ruskin's life, his work, and character to form an interpretation of the man that is sympathetic, discursive, and at times evasive.

Collingwood, W.G. *The Life and Work of John Ruskin.* London: Methuen, 1893. 2 vols. Written by Ruskin's private secretary and completed before his subject's death, Collingwood's sympathetic account is uneven, with debatable interpretations, yet it does include a number of firsthand details that are not available elsewhere.

Cook, Edward T. *The Life of John Ruskin.* New York: Macmillan, 1911. 2 vols. Long established as the standard life, the work of Ruskin's lifelong friend who had access to the writer's diaries, notebooks, and letters, though superseded by modern scholarship, still retains its value as a reference source. Cook's sympathy and discretion in certain areas prevent the volumes from achieving complete objectivity and comprehensiveness.

Kemp, Wolfgang. *The Desire of My Eyes: The Life and Work of John Ruskin.* New York: Farrar, Straus, 1990. 513pp. Originally published in Germany in 1983, this is more a critical study than a full-scale biography in the form of a series of idiosyncratic essays on particular aspects of Ruskin's writings. Introducing Ruskin to readers unfamiliar with the man or his ideas, The author presents Ruskin as an influential reformer, educator, and ecologist.

Larg, David. *John Ruskin.* 1933. Reprint ed. New York: Haskell House, 1974. 151pp. This brief psychological sketch relies on Cook for its biographical details, which are submitted to a Freudian interpretation, centered around Ruskin's overpowering mother, his disastrous marriage, and failed relationships.

Leon, Derrick. *Ruskin: The Great Victorian.* London: Routledge, 1949. 595pp. The author died before completing intended revisions of this overview of Ruskin's life, works, and times. The book serves more as a reference source collecting details about Ruskin than a polished interpretation.

Quennell, Peter. *John Ruskin: The Portrait of a Prophet.* New York: Viking, 1949. 289pp. In a largely compassionate analysis of Ruskin's personality, Quennell emphasizes the private man in a sensible, balanced assessment. Ruskin's neurotic egotism is a tempting target for ridicule, which Quennell avoids, substituting instead a credible human portrait.

Rosenberg, John D. *The Darkening Glass: A Portrait of Ruskin's Genius.* New York: Columbia University Press, 1961. 274pp. Rosenberg's is a thoughtful intellectual biography, organized into thematic sections on art, architecture, society, wilderness, and peace.

Williams-Elis, Amabel. *The Exquisite Tragedy: An Intimate Life of John Ruskin.* Garden City, New York: Doubleday, 1929. 371pp. A popular biography relying on Cook for its biographical facts that the author synthesizes into a dramatic narrative that attempts to explain the causes of Ruskin's frustrations and personal failures in his parents' overbearing influence.

Biographical Novels

McDonald, Eva. *John Ruskin's Wife.* London: R. Hale, 1979. 219pp. The novel dramatizes the strange marriage between Ruskin and Effie Gray and the scandal that ensues when she becomes the model for artist John Everett Millais.

Williams, Lawrence. *I, James McNeill Whistler.* New York: Simon & Schuster, 1972. 383pp. This fictional autobiography of the artist features the notorious lawsuit Whistler brought against Ruskin for defamation of character.

Fictional Portraits

Kitchen, Paddy. *The Golden Veil.* London: Hamilton, 1981. 286pp. Based on the life of Elizabeth Siddal, Rossetti's model and mistress, the novel traces her career from her youth and her involvement in the bohemian circle that included Ruskin, Millais, Swinburne, Morris, and Holman Hunt.

Morazzoni, Martin. *The Invention of Truth.* New York: Knopf, 1993. 112pp. This inventive novel links the creation of the Bayeaux tapestry in the eleventh century with the visit of Ruskin to Amiens where he reflects on his life and art.

Savage, Elizabeth. *Willowwood.* Boston: Little, Brown, 1978. 214pp. Rossetti's complicated emotional life is the focus of this novel that portrays the artist's relationship with Elizabeth Siddal and his circle that includes Ruskin and Morris.

Thorne, Nicola. *Sisters and Lovers.* Garden City, New York: Doubleday, 1981. 589pp. Three Victorian sisters arrive in London in the 1850s in search of husbands, and their stories are linked to a number of historical figures, including Florence Nightingale, Karl Marx, and John Ruskin.

Other Sources

Bradley, John L. *A Ruskin Chronology.* New York: St. Martin's, 1997. 129pp. Bradley supplies an extensive chronology of Ruskin's activities, works, and the principal historical events during his lifetime.

412. BERTRAND RUSSELL
1872–1970

British philosopher, mathematician, and social reformer, Russell related logic and mathematics in his most important works, *The Principals of Math-* ematics (1903) and the three-volume *Principia Mathematica* (1910–1913), written with Alfred North Whitehead. He cofounded the experimental Beacon Hill School, which influenced the founding of schools in Britain and America, and taught at various institutions in the United States. His other works include *Marriage and Morals* (1929), *Education and the Social Order* (1932), and *An Inquiry into Meaning and Truth* (1940). He received the Nobel Prize for Literature (1950).

Autobiography and Primary Sources

The Autobiography of Bertrand Russell. Boston: Little, Brown, 1967–1969. 3 vols. Russell's voluminous autobiography mixes narrative with letters. Often selective in his recollections, Russell provides few insights into his feeling about individuals and events, concentrating instead largely on public affairs.

The Selected Letters of Bertrand Russell. Volume One: The Private Years, 1884–1914. Nicholas Griffin, ed. Boston: Houghton Mifflin, 1992. 553pp. Although each of the chapters of Russell's autobiography includes a collection of letters, this is a far more revealing selection of his correspondence, covering his private and scholarly years prior to his years as a public figure beginning in World War I.

Recommended Biographies

Clark, Ronald W. *The Life of Bertrand Russell.* New York: Knopf, 1975. 766pp. Clark's authoritative and comprehensive biography is the best source for data on Russell's public and private life as well as his political, philosophical, and personal development. Based on the best available primary and secondary sources, this is likely to remain the definitive life at least until the completion of Monk's proposed two-volume biography. In *Bertrand Russell and His World* (New York: Thames and Hudson, 1981. 127pp.), Clark provides a brief overview in this illustrated biography that documents Russell's life in the context of his times.

Monk, Ray. *Bertrand Russell: The Spirit of Solitude, 1872–1921.* New York: Free Press, 1996. 695pp. The acclaimed biographer of Wittgenstein has begun a detailed account of Russell's life. In an admirable integration of private and public sides, emotional and intellectual development, Monk offers a nuanced portrait of a complex and often paradoxical figure. Accessible, despite some highly technical passages on Russell's philosophical work, Monk's interpretive and critical treatment is lively and sensible in its judgments, and Russell emerges as a believable human figure.

Moorehead, Caroline. *Bertrand Russell: A Life.* New York: Viking, 1993. 596pp. In a solid, detailed overview of Russell's life and work, Moorehead clearly displays both Russell's achievements and flaws. Given Russell's long life, multiple activities, and relationships, the book is a marvel of compression in which the many patterns of Russell's complex life are followed, resulting in a vivid and compelling portrait.

Other Biographical Studies

Ayer, A.J. *Bertrand Russell*. New York: Viking, 1972. 168pp. Ayer's compact entry in the Modern Masters series provides a brief biographical overview of the major incidents in Russell's life, but the book's chief value is to make the philosopher's ideas accessible for the general reader.

Brink, Andrew. *Bertrand Russell: A Psychobiography of a Moralist*. Atlantic Highlands, New Jersey: Humanities Press, 1989. 174pp. Brink's detailed psychological analysis is particularly good on Russell's early development but is uneven in tracing the connections between the philosopher's personal traumas and his ideas and works.

Crawshay-Williams, Rupert. *Russell Remembered*. New York: Oxford University Press, 1970. 163pp. Written by a close friend of Russell during his last 25 years, these recollections concentrate on Russell's personality and character, his private side among friends, and the details of everyday life. Contrary to other views, Russell is displayed as a warm, outgoing, and affectionate friend.

Gottshalk, Herbert. *Bertrand Russell: A Life*. New York: Roy, 1965. 128pp. The book is an inadequate introduction to Russell's life and work. Assertions are unsupported, and the book fails to communicate the basis for the author's evident reverence for his subject.

Grayling, A.C. *Russell*. New York: Oxford University Press, 1996. 115pp. An entry in the Past Masters series, this is a concise survey of Russell's thought, with a biographical first chapter that summarizes the important events in his life. Serves as a fine starting point for viewing the man and his ideas.

Kuntz, Paul G. *Bertrand Russell*. Boston: Twayne, 1986. 186pp. Kuntz's intellectual biography follows the significant events in both Russell's life and his philosophical development with an emphasis on the latter in a succinct and learned overview.

Russell, Dora. *The Tamarisk Tree: My Quest for Liberty and Love*. New York: Dutton, 1975. 304pp. Russell's second wife supplies her recollections of their open marriage. Her version of their relationship, which ended in 1932, differs from Russell's own account and serves as an alternative perspective to their life together.

Ryan, Alan. *Bertrand Russell: A Political Life*. New York: Hill & Wang, 1988. 226pp. Concentrating exclusively on Russell's public career, as well as his ideas on society, war, and peace, Ryan's is a lucid, balanced assessment. As well as detailing Russell's altruism and passionate commitment to certain causes, Ryan exposes his inconsistencies.

Tait, Katherine. *My Father, Bertrand Russell*. New York: Harcourt, Brace, 1975. 211pp. Written by Russell's daughter by his second wife, the book vividly and candidly recollects her life with her father. Russell's flaws, his egotism, and insensitivity, are honestly detailed in the discrepancy between Russell's theory of education and morals and their effect on his daughter.

Vellacott, Jo. *Bertrand Russell and the Pacifists in the First World War*. New York: St. Martin's, 1981. 326pp. This specialized study focuses on Russell's opposition to World War I and the circle of conscientious objectors and pacifists with whom he was associated. Exhaustively researched, well-written, and insightful, this is the best account available of Russell's wartime activities.

Wood, Alan. *Bertrand Russell: The Passionate Skeptic: A Biography*. New York: Simon & Schuster, 1958. 249pp. Wood's affectionate portrait is based on much firsthand evidence as one of Russell's students and colleagues. The book is on solid ground on the details of Russell's public life and the development of his philosophical ideas, but rarely intrudes beyond the surface of the philosopher's complicated private life.

Fictional Portraits

Duffy, Bruce. *The World as I Found It*. New York: Ticknor and Fields, 1987. 546pp. This inventive biographical fiction on the life of philosopher Ludwig Wittgenstein details his relationship with G.E. Moore and Russell.

Biographical Films and Theatrical Adaptations

Tom & Viv (1994). Director: Brian Gilbert. Michael Hastings co-wrote the filmscript based on his play (New York: Penguin, 1985. 126pp.) dramatizing T.S. Eliot's relationship with Vivienne Haigh-Wood. Willem Dafoe plays Eliot, and Miranda Richardson steals the show as the vivacious and troubled Vivienne. Nicholas Grace portrays Russell, a complicating factor in the couple's marriage. Video.

Wittgenstein (1993). Director: Derek Jarman. This experimental portrait of the Austrian philosopher Ludwig Wittgenstein (Karl Johnson) takes the form of a series of vignettes from his life, including his relationship with such figures as John Maynard Keynes (John Quentin) and Russell (Michael Gough). Video.

413. ANWAR EL-SADAT
1918–1981

Egyptian political leader, Sadat took part in the bloodless coup that deposed King Farouk (1952) and during the 1950s and 1960s held various government posts. Chosen as President Nasser's vice president, he became president after Nasser's death (1970). Sadat expelled Soviet military advisors, supported the Arab oil boycott against the West, and waged the Yom Kippur war with Syria against Israel (1973). During the 1970s he established closer ties with the United States and began peace negotiations with Israel, which resulted in the Camp David peace accords (1977). He shared the 1978 Nobel Peace Prize with Israeli prime minister Menachem Begin. He was assassinated by extremist army officers opposed to his peace initiatives.

Autobiography and Primary Sources

In Search of Identity: An Autobiography. New York: Harper & Row, 1978. 360pp. Sadat offers impressions and anecdotes of his life and his public career. Revealing the character of the man and his views on important historical events, the book shows evidence of haste with inaccuracies and factual errors and should be read alongside a more reliable history or biography.

Those I Have Known. New York: Continuum, 1984. 140pp. Based on taped interviews for publication in his political party's newspaper, Sadat muses on the world leaders with whom he had contact and recalls great events, including the Egyptian revolution of 1952 and the Middle East wars of 1967 and 1973, concluding with his view on the Arab-Israeli conflict and the peace initiative.

Recommended Biographies

Finkelstone, Joseph. *Anwar Sadat: Visionary Who Dared.* Portland, Oregon: Frank Cass, 1996. 297pp. The work of a journalist who knew Sadat in the last years of his life, Finkelstone traces Sadat's background and rise to power, as well as providing an intriguing insider's view of the complex political and diplomatic maneuvering that characterized Sadat's rule.

Israeli, Raphael, with Carol Bardenstein. *Man of Defiance: A Political Biography of Anwar Sadat.*
New York: Barnes and Noble, 1985. 314pp. Written by a professor at Hebrew University, this political biography traces the evolution of Sadat's life and character from the traditional values he was imbued with in the village life of his boyhood through the various stages of his rise to power and his leadership years.

Other Biographical Studies

Fernández-Armesto, Felipe. *Sadat and His Statecraft.* London: Kensal Press, 1982. 196pp. After placing Sadat in a wider Egyptian historical context, the author provides a reliable assessment of his rule and peace efforts.

Heikal, Mohamed. *Autumn of Fury: The Assassination of Sadat.* New York: Random House, 1983. 290pp. Heikal's controversial analysis of the forces that ended Sadat's reign is the work of a former confidant and prominent Egyptian journalist who broke with Sadat over policy issues. As a proponent of Nasser's policies, particularly Pan-Arabism and nonalignment, Heikal judges Sadat's leadership as a failure, resulting in his isolation from the Arab world and his own people, which played a role in his death. Despite the author's clearly polemical bias, the book supplies a remarkably detailed history of the conspiracy that brought Sadat down and a provocative assessment of its origin.

Hirst, David, and Irene Beeson. *Sadat.* London: Faber and Faber, 1981. 203pp. This reevaluation of Sadat is harshly critical of the man and his leadership, contending that his public image as a great statesman was in stark contrast with the reality. Sadat is shown as a venal, hypocritical megalomaniac, concealing a deeply rooted inferiority complex. Although solidly documented from Sadat's own words, the book lacks balance but serves as a challenge to other presentations of a heroic Sadat.

Narayan, B.K. *Anwar el Sadat: Man with a Mission.* New Delhi: Vikas, 1977. 162pp. In a useful overview, Narayan supplies a personal and political portrait that attempts a balanced, although limited, account in the wider context of his times.

Sadat, Camelia. *My Father and I.* New York: Macmillan, 1985. 203pp. Sadat's daughter offers her account of her relationship with her father. More personally revealing than her mother's memoir, the book supplies intimate details of Sadat's
private life and character as a father rather than a political figure.

Sadat, Jehan. *A Woman of Egypt.* New York: Simon & Schuster, 1987. 478pp. Sadat's wife weaves her recollections of her husband's political life with her own activities as a social activist on behalf of Egyptian women. Often an unreliable and selective view, the book does supply some firsthand details on the negotiations leading to the Camp David agreement.

Shoukra, Ghali. *Egypt: Portrait of a President 1971-81: The Counter-Revolution in Egypt: Sadat's Road to Jerusalem.* London: Zed, 1981. 465pp. In a critical assessment, Shoukra, an exiled Egyptian sociologist and intellectual, argues that Sadat betrayed the progressive goals of Nasser. In making his argument, the author provides insightful glimpses of Sadat's character, placing his actions in their socioeconomic context.

Sullivan, George. *Sadat: The Man Who Changed Mid-East History.* New York: Walker, 1981. 124pp. A visual biography that links a series of photographs with a serviceable, though basic, text.

Fictional Portraits

Wouk, Herman. *The Glory.* Boston: Little, Brown, 1994. 685pp. Wouk's panoramic chronicle of modern Israel's history includes the Six Day War, the Yom Kippur War, the Entebbe rescue, and the signing of the Camp David accords with portrayals of Sadat, Begin, and others.

Recommended Juvenile Biographies

Aufderheide, Patricia. *Anwar Sadat.* New York: Chelsea House, 1985. 112pp. MG/YA. This is a workmanlike overview of the highlights of Sadat's life seen in their wider historical and cultural contexts.

Diamond, Arthur. *The Importance of Anwar Sadat.* San Diego: Lucent Books, 1994. 112pp. MG/YA. An informative survey of Sadat's life and political career, concentrating on his role in the Middle East peace process.

Rosen, Deborah N. *Anwar el-Sadat: Middle East Peacemaker.* Chicago: Childrens Press, 1986. 152pp. MG. Rosen offers a detailed account of

Sadat's life, covering his rise to power and his achievements.

Biographical Films and Theatrical Adaptations

Death on the Nile: The Struggle for Peace and the Assassination of Anwar Sadat (1989). Producer: Ted Jessup. *ABC News* profile of Sadat's career, his peace settlement with Israel, and the events surrounding his assassination. Video.

Sadat (1983). Director: Richard Michaels. Lou Gossett Jr. portrays Sadat in scenes from his life from the beginning of his political career to his assassination. Video.

414. GEORGE SAND
1804–1876

Born Amandine Aurore Lucie Dupin, French novelist George Sand became notorious for her unconventional lifestyle, which included a preference for wearing men's clothing, the use of her chosen pseudonym, and open liaisons with such notable figures as Chopin and De Musset. She wrote some 80 novels, which were widely popular and include *La Mare au diable* (1846), *Les Matres sonneurs* (1853), and *Indiana* (1853).

Autobiography and Primary Sources

The Intimate Journals of George Sand. Marie Jenny Howe, ed. Chicago: Academy Chicago, 1990. 198pp. This collection brings together Sand's journal to Alfred de Musset, the Piffoel journal of her composed conversations between her masculine and feminine selves, and letters and reflections. Sand's journal writing is considered by many as her most expressive and natural self-exploration.

Letters of George Sand. Raphael L. de Beaufort, ed. 1886. Reprint ed. New York: AMS Press, 3 vols. Sand's voluminous correspondence records her many moods, roles, and wide circle of friends and associates in an essential biographical source.

Story of My Life: The Autobiography of George Sand. Thelma Jurgrau, ed. Albany: State University Press of New York, 1991. 1,184pp. Mainly covering the years 1847 to 1854, Sand recounts the story of her career with unflagging energy and honesty. One of the classic literary autobiographies.

Recommended Biographies

Barry, Joseph. *Infamous Woman: The Life of George Sand.* Garden City, New York: Doubleday, 1976. 461pp. Relying primarily on Sand's letters and autobiography, the book traces the stages of her evolving self-awareness with an emphasis on her intimate relationships rather than her writings.

Cate, Curtis. *George Sand: A Biography.* Boston: Houghton Mifflin, 1975. 812pp. Cate's skilled and detailed account of Sand's life and career is based on previously unpublished correspondence. Strongest on the writer's artistic evolution and the careful untangling of the human figure behind the various legends.

Dickenson, Donna. *George Sand: A Brave Man, the Most Womanly Woman.* New York: St. Martin's, 1988. 190pp. This excellent, brief biographical profile is arranged not chronologically but topically, examining Sand from a variety of perspectives. Incorporating modern scholarship, Dickenson provides a helpful analysis of the rise and fall of Sand's reputation, penetrating the various legends and biases that have obscured the view of Sand as a person and as a literary figure.

Maurois, André. *Lélia: The Life of George Sand.* New York: Harper, 1953. 482pp. Maurois's psychological, critical biography is one of the classics of the biographer's art, rivaling the author's other literary biographies. Although the book's interpretation of Sand's emotional and intellectual development is debatable and in many ways has been superseded by later studies, Maurois's treatment is still lively, readable, and provocative.

Winegarten, Renee. *The Double Life of George Sand, Woman and Writer: A Critical Biography.* New York: Basic Books, 1978. 339pp. Winegarten emphasizes gender issues explaining Sand's motives and behavior as a search to counter sexual stereotypes "to be a total person in harmony with herself." Provocative and insightful, Winegarten's feminist perspective serves as a useful complement to Cate's more gender-neutral study.

Other Biographical Studies

Atwood, William G. *The Lionness and the Little One: The Liaison of George Sand and Frédéric Chopin.* New York: Columbia University Press, 1980. 316pp. Focusing on the stormy relationship between Sand and Chopin, Atwood documents their affair, relying almost entirely on correspondence, journals, and other writings by the pair and their contemporaries. Falling short of its intention to be fair to both figures, this account repeats the conventional view of Sand as the powerful mother figure and Chopin the weak, sickly figure of legend.

Edwards, Samuel. *George Sand: A Biography of the First Modern, Liberated Woman.* New York: McKay, 1972. 271pp. This popular biography emphasizes Sand the eccentric rather than the literary figure in a highly colored, cliché-ridden account of Sand's liaisons, scandals, and oddities. It adds nothing to the biographical record.

Howe, Marie J. *George Sand: The Search for Love.* New York: J. Day, 1927. 351pp. Calling Sand "the most misunderstood woman in the history of literature," Howe attempts an appreciative reassessment from an early feminist perspective. Redressing the balance of previous negative views, Howe is guilty of idealization and excessive partisanship.

Jordan, Ruth. *George Sand: A Biographical Portrait.* New York: Taplinger, 1976. 367pp. Less detailed than other full-length studies, Jordan places Sand in the context of her times and delivers a plausible psychological profile to help explain her motives and behavior. The book concentrates on Sand's private life and offers few insights on her literary work.

Naginski, Isabell H. *George Sand: Writing for Her Life.* New Brunswick: Rutgers University Press, 1991. 281pp. This critical study of Sand's writing

life and works shifts the focus from her eccentric lifestyle and love affairs to her career that produced nearly 80 novels and 25 plays. Examining in detail Sand's principal works, Naginski traces her artistic development and literary themes.

Schermerhorn, Elizabeth W. *The Seven Strings of the Lyre: The Romantic Life of George Sand, 1804–1876.* Boston: Houghton Mifflin, 1927. 327pp. The title refers to the seven significant lovers in Sand's life, who are the focus of this account of her career and personality. Avoiding sensationalism and sentimentality, the book provides a sympathetic and credible narrative portrait.

Seyd, Felizia. *Romantic Rebel: The Life and Times of George Sand.* New York: Viking, 1940. 286pp. Seyd's study is chiefly valuable for its historical content, relating Sand's life and writing to the intellectual, social, and political context of her times between 1830 and 1870.

Winwar, Frances. *The Life of the Heart: George Sand and Her Times.* New York: Harper, 1945. 312pp. Winwar's idealized and sentimental account takes considerable novelistic liberties to penetrate Sand's thoughts and feelings. Factual errors also undermine the book's reliability.

Biographical Novels

Kenyon, Frank W. *The Questing Heart: A Romantic Novel about George Sand.* New York: Dodd, Mead, 1964. 344pp. Based on a framework of fact with fictional embellishments, this biographical novel traces Sand's life, career, and relationships from childhood until 1849.

Recommended Juvenile Biographies

Hovey, Tamara. *A Mind of Her Own: The Life of the Writer George Sand.* New York: Harper & Row, 1977. 211pp. MG/YA. This is a detailed account of Sand's life and career that emphasizes her individuality and challenge of conventions.

Biographical Films and Theatrical Adaptations

Impromptu (1991). Director: James Lapine. George Sand, Chopin, and Liszt are on holiday as proto-beatniks in this dynamic and inventive drama, starring Judy Davis as the novelist, Hugh Grant as a wan, ethereal Chopin, and Julian Sands as Liszt. Video.

Notorious Woman (1974). Director: Waris Hussien. Television mini-series on the life of George Sand features Rosemary Harris in the title role, George Chakiris as Chopin, and Alan Howard as Prosper Mérimée.

A Song to Remember (1945). Director: Charles Vidor. Cornel Wilde stars as Chopin in this bio-pic depicting the last years of the composer's life. Merle Oberon portrays George Sand, and Stephen Belcassy plays Liszt. The film is redeemed mainly by its music; the character portrayal here is superficial. Video.

See also Frédéric Chopin; Franz Liszt

415. MARGARET SANGER
1883–1966

Leader of the birth-control movement in the United States, Sanger attended nursing school and was active for a time in the labor movement. Her work with the poor as a public-health nurse on the Lower East Side of Manhattan convinced her of the necessity of birth control. She studied in London with Havelock Ellis, and on her return to the United States was indicted for sending contraceptive information through the mail and arrested for conducting a birth-control clinic. Sanger gradually won support from the public and the courts for the legalization of birth control. She organized the American Birth Control League and was president of the International Planned Parenthood Federation.

Autobiography and Primary Sources

Margaret Sanger: An Autobiography. New York: W.W. Norton, 1938. 504pp. Sanger's second attempt to recollect her life and career shares with her earlier book a selectivity that emphasizes her cause over full disclosure of her personal life and motives. Despite limitations and unreliability, Sanger's assessment of her actions is still a valuable biographical source.

My Fight for Birth Control. New York: Farrar & Rinehart, 1931. 360pp. Sanger provides a selective and not always reliable account of her 17-year struggle to change birth control policies with preliminary chapters on her childhood, upbringing, marriage, and family life.

Recommended Biographies

Chesler, Ellen. *Woman of Valor: Margaret Sanger and the Birth Control Movement in America.* New York: Simon & Schuster, 1992. 639pp. Neither excessively admiring nor critical, Chesler's is a balanced, well-researched biography that allows a complex human portrait to emerge. Sanger's personal history is joined to a history of the movement that she led to form the clearest and most sensible view available of the woman and her achievement.

Kennedy, David M. *Birth Control in America: The Career of Margaret Sanger.* New Haven, Connecticut: Yale University Press, 1971. 320pp. Winner of the Bancroft Prize in American history, Kennedy's biographical profile and social history demonstrate how Sanger's energy and determination, as well as her foibles and vanities contributed to and hindered the birth-control movement in America. Although Sanger's character is central to his analysis, Kennedy provides few details on her private life, concentrating instead on the challenges she faced and the social and historical background up to the beginning of World War II.

Other Biographical Studies

Douglas, Emily Taft. *Pioneer of the Future.* New York: Holt, 1970. 274pp. Written by a longtime birth-control advocate, Douglas's biographical tribute to Sanger's life and achievement provides only limited details of her personal life, her two marriages, and association with Havelock Ellis. Sanger's leadership of the birth-control movement and her public life are predominant here in a largely uncritical appreciation.

Gray, Madeline. *Margaret Sanger: A Biography of the Champion of Birth Control.* New York: R. Marek, 1979. 494pp. Based on interviews and previously restricted letters and diaries, Gray sheds light on Sanger's private life. Lacking balance, however, the book's emphasis on Sanger's flaws and weaknesses and the trivial details of her relationships fails to integrate satisfactorily her human side and public achievements.

Lader, Lawrence. *The Margaret Sanger Story and the Fight for Birth Control.* Garden City, New York: Doubleday, 1955. 352pp. Based on interviews with Sanger and her associates, this is a reverent account that had Sanger's cooperation in its production (including her editing of the final manuscript). Like Sanger's autobiographies, the book commits several inaccuracies and misrepresentations in a version of Sanger's life and career that she wanted presented.

Biographical Novels

Gerson, Noel B. *The Crusader: A Novel on the Life of Margaret Sanger.* Boston: Little, Brown, 1970. 375pp. This biographical novel follows Sanger's life and activism from the early years of the twentieth century to 1930 in a factually reliable account.

Recommended Juvenile Biographies

Bachrach, Deborah. *Margaret Sanger.* San Diego: Lucent Books, 1993. 112pp. MG/YA. Bachrach identifies Sanger's achievement against a clearly defined social backdrop that emphasizes the challenges she faced over the issue of the reproductive rights of women.

Lader, Lawrence, and Milton Meltzer. *Margaret Sanger: Pioneer of Birth Control.* New York: Crowell, 1969. 174pp. YA. This is an inspiring, heroic portrayal of Sanger's life and achievement incorporating details from Lader's 1955 adult biography and indirectly expressing Sanger's own view of her story.

Whitelaw, Nancy. *Margaret Sanger: "Every Child a Wanted Child."* New York: Dillon Press, 1994. 160pp. YA. A well-balanced, sensitive account that covers both Sanger's private and public lives, Whitelaw identifies the thoughtful and impulsive sides of Sanger's character that help to explain her sometimes contradictory actions.

Biographical Films and Theatrical Adaptations

Margaret Sanger: A Public Nuisance (1992). Directors: Terese Svoboda and Steve Bull. Using original photographs, film footage, sound recordings, and staged events, Sanger's public and private career is portrayed. Video.

Portrait of a Rebel: Margaret Sanger (1982). Director: Virgil W. Vogel. Sanger is depicted attempting to repeal the Comstock Act in this television drama starring Bonnie Franklin as Sanger, David Duke as William Sanger, and Richard Johnson as Havelock Ellis. Video.

416. JEAN-PAUL SARTRE
1905–1980

French philosopher, playwright, and novelist, Sartre was the leading exponent of existentialism. He served in the army during World War II and was taken prisoner but escaped and joined the resistance. His works include his monumental treatise *Being and Nothingness* (1943); the plays *No Exit* (1944) and *The Condemned of Altona* (1956); the novel *Nausea* (1938); and a trilogy of novels, *The Age of Reason, The Reprieve* (both 1945), and *Troubled Sleep* (1949). He also wrote major studies of literary figures and many essays. He refused the 1964 Nobel Prize in Literature.

Autobiography and Primary Sources

War Diaries of Jean-Paul Sartre: November 1939–March 1940. New York: Pantheon, 1984. 366pp. Sartre's surviving diaries provide insight into his complex personality when he was 34, in one of the most human portraits of the man in which much of his later work is anticipated.

Witness to My Life: The Letters of Jean-Paul Sartre to Simone de Beauvoir, 1926–1939. Simone de Beauvoir, ed. New York: Macmillan, 1992. 448pp. This collection of correspondence between Sartre and de Beauvoir and others sheds considerable light on the pair's relationship and Sartre's private side.

The Words. New York: G. Braziller, 1964. 255pp. Sartre's autobiography up to the age of 10 confesses the impact of his father's death on his development in a partly psychological, partly ideological reconstruction of his past that has been exposed by biographer Cohen-Solal as biographically unreliable.

Recommended Biographies

Cohen-Solal, Annie. *Sartre: A Life.* New York: Pantheon, 1987. 591pp. Although the author decided to concentrate on Sartre's life at the expense of his works, this is the fullest investigation of the writer's activities, based on original research using family archives and interviews with many of the writer's associates. Cohen-Solal's portrait is often contrary to the version of his life and character that Sartre and his admirers have presented.

Gerassi, John. *Jean-Paul Sartre: Hated Conscience of His Century. Volume One: Protestant or Protester?* Chicago: University of Chicago Press, 1989. 213pp. Gerassi abandoned his intention to produce a multivolume biography on the publication of Cohen-Solal's authoritative study. In the single volume he completed, Gerassi chronicles Sartre's life and intellectual development through the end of World War II in an intellectual biography that is candid about Sartre's inconsistencies and shortcomings.

Hayman, Ronald. *Sartre: A Life.* New York: Simon & Schuster, 1987. 572pp. In a richly detailed, in-depth look at Sartre's life and times, Hayman integrates the philosopher's personal, literary, and political development into a full-length, credible human portrait. Sartre's many personal shortcomings are displayed, as well as the consistency of his political and intellectual values through his many activities and relationships.

Other Biographical Studies

Beauvoir, Simone de. *Adieux: A Farewell to Sartre.* New York: Pantheon, 1984. 453pp. De Beauvoir's reflections of her life with Sartre take the form of a diary she kept from 1970 to 1980 and a number of conversations with Sartre she recorded in 1974. The book captures the nature of their relationship (also discussed in de Beauvoir's multivolume autobiography) and Sartre's views on a number of subjects, including himself, his work, and his career as a writer.

Brée, Germaine. *Camus and Sartre: Crisis and Commitments.* New York: Dell, 1972. 287pp. This dual biographical profile of Sartre's relationship with Camus is convincing in its meticulous documentation. The author concludes that Sartre was "the last of the great system-builders" who set out to rethink the world to reform it.

Fullbrook, Kate, and Edward Fullbrook. *Simone de Beauvoir and Jean-Paul Sartre: The Remaking of a Twentieth-Century Legend.* New York: Basic Books, 1994. 214pp. This revisionist view of the Sartre-de Beauvoir relationship challenges conventional wisdom arguing that de Beauvoir, not Sartre, "was always the driving intellectual power in the joint development of the couple's most influential ideas."

Thody, Philip. *Jean-Paul Sartre: A Literary and Political Study.* New York: Macmillan, 1960. 269pp. Thody's critical survey of Sartre's works connects his literary production with his experiences and traces his development from an imaginative writer to a polemicist.

Thody, Philip. *Sartre: A Biographical Introduction.* New York: Scribner, 1971. 160pp. Derived mainly from Sartre's autobiographical writings, Thody's study is best on the writer's later years.

Thompson, Kenneth, and Margaret Thompson. *Sartre: Life and Works.* New York: Facts on File, 1984. 227pp. This is a straightforward, year-by-year account of Sartre's life and work and his personal and political relations.

Wardman, Harold W. *Jean-Paul Sartre: The Evolution of His Thought and Art.* Lewiston, New York: Edwin Mellen Press, 1992. 439pp. Wardman's critical literary biography traces Sartre's intellectual and artistic development chronologically, integrating his literary production and his political and philosophical activities with his experiences and historical events.

Biographical Films and Theatrical Adaptations

Sartre by Himself (1984). Directors: Alexandre Astruc and Michel Contat. Made in Paris in 1976, Sartre reflects on various aspects of his life and ideas. Video.

417. FRIEDRICH SCHILLER
1759–1805

German dramatist and poet, Schiller is a major literary figure who ranks second only to Goethe as the founder of modern German literature. His major works include "Ode to Joy" (1785), the dramatic trilogy *Wallenstein* (1798-1799) and the plays *Mary Stuart* (1800) and *Wilhelm Tell* (1804). Schiller also produced translations of dramatic works and notable ballads and philosophical lyrics.

Recommended Biographies

Düntzer, Heinrich. *The Life of Schiller.* London: Macmillan, 1883. 455pp. Despite its age and often quaint, literary style, this is still one of the most authoritative and comprehensive treatments of Schiller's life and career, following both in minute detail.

Garland, Henry B. *Schiller.* New York: McBride, 1950. 280pp. Garland supplies a human portrait of Schiller, dealing fully with his early struggles and the experiences that formed his character and are reflected in his works. Well written and accessible for the nonspecialist, Garland's is a sensitive and sensible appreciation of Schiller's genius and nature.

Other Biographical Studies

Carlyle, Thomas. *Life of Schiller.* 1825. Reprint ed. Columbia, South Carolina: Camden House, 1992. 288pp. Carlyle's idiosyncratic portrait is chiefly interesting for its reflections of its author's views on German Romanticism. The biographical details lack depth and authority.

Nevinson, Henry W. *Life of Friedrich Schiller.* London: Scott, 1889. 203pp. Nevinson is far more willing than Carlyle to view Schiller as a mixture of human traits, which helps create a more rounded, credible portrait. Not all aspects of Schiller's life are covered with the same degree of care, however.

Passage, Charles E. *Friedrich Schiller.* New York: Frederick Ungar, 1975. 203pp. Mostly a critical study of the works, the biographical section focuses on Schiller's personality and his relationship with Goethe. A good choice for the reader needing a competent overview.

Thomas, Calvin. *The Life and Works of Friedrich Schiller.* New York: Holt, 1901. 481pp. Thomas's is a solid, scholarly study that sheds light on Schiller's personality and his literary gifts.

Fictional Portraits

Carpentier, Alejo. *The Harp and the Shadow.* San Francisco: Mercury, 1990. 159pp. In this imaginative inquiry into the character and achievement of Christopher Columbus, Pius IX considers his canonization and Jules Verne and Schiller conduct a debate over his legacy.

418. ARNOLD SCHOENBERG
1874–1951

An Austrian composer and music teacher who immigrated to the United States, Schoenberg revolutionized music by introducing a 12-tone technique of composition. He founded a famous private seminar in composition and the Society for Musical Performances, at which neither critics nor applause were allowed. His many works include *Transfigured Night* (1899), *Pierrot Lunaire* (1912), and the unfinished opera, *Moses and Aaron* (1932–1951), considered his masterpiece.

Autobiography and Primary Sources

Arnold Schoenberg Letters. Erwin Stern, ed. Berkeley: University of California Press, 1987. 309pp. Schoenberg's letters are remarkably revealing and offer the best glimpse of the complexity of the composer's personality, his intellect, and temperament. Readers can gain additional insights from *The Berg-Schoenberg Correspondence.* Juliane Brand, Christopher Hailey, and Donald Harris, eds. (New York: W.W. Norton, 1988. 497pp.), the letters between two of the most influential figures in twentieth-century music, which span the years 1911 to 1935.

Recommended Biographies

Neighbor, Oliver. "Arnold Schoenberg" in *The New Grove Second Viennese School.* New York: W.W. Norton, 1983. 201pp. Neighbor provides a valuable synthesis of current scholarship in an insightful critical essay that includes a succinct biographical summary.

Stuckenschmidt, Hans H. *Schoenberg: His Life, World, and Work.* New York: Schirmer Books, 1977. 581pp. The most comprehensive account of Schoenberg's life and career, Stuckenschmidt employs a wealth of primary sources to present an authoritative study. The casual reader may be overwhelmed by the details, but the motivated reader will profit from the book's extensive documentation.

Other Biographical Studies

MacDonald, Malcolm. *Schoenberg.* London: Dent, 1976. 289pp. Part of the Master Musicians series, this useful handbook serves as a solid, if selective, introduction and overview.

Newlin, Dika. *Schoenberg Remembered: Diaries and Recollections.* New York: Pendragon Press, 1980. 369pp. The book is taken from a diary kept during the years 1939 to 1941 when the author was studying with Schoenberg at the University of California, Los Angeles, and includes an account of their later relationship. An intimate glimpse of the man, the book also presents an informed account of Schoenberg's American period.

Reich, Willi. *Schoenberg: A Critical Biography.* New York: Praeger, 1971. 268pp. Reich weaves documentary sources into a chronological survey of the composer's life and works. The book provides a lucid account of Schoenberg's stylistic development and a vivid portrait of the composer's personality, although the organization is often confusing.

Smith, Joan A. *Schoenberg and His Circle: A Viennese Portrait.* New York: Schirmer Books, 1986. 319pp. This is a revealing collection of views of the composer from many individuals who knew and worked with Schoenberg.

Wellesz, Egon. *Arnold Schoenberg: The Formative Years*. 1925. Revised ed. New York: Galaxy, 1971. 156pp. The first biography of the composer traces Schoenberg's life and career up to the 1920s and draws on the author's friendship with Schoenberg and his cooperation. Remains an important source on the man and his musical development.

Biographical Films and Theatrical Adaptations

Arnold Schoenberg: My Evolution (1991). Director: Bill Wolfe. A biographical portrait using Schoenberg's own words from a lecture delivered at the University of California, Los Angeles, in 1949. Video.

Other Sources

Bailey, Walter B. *The Arnold Schoenberg Companion*. Westport, Connecticut: Greenwood, 1998. 335pp. Bringing together insightful critical views and documents, this is a valuable collection based on the latest scholarship.

Frisch, Walter, ed. *Schoenberg and His World*. Princeton, New Jersey: Princeton University Press, 1999. 350pp. This accessible reference volume includes biographical essays, surveys of Schoenberg's music from different periods in his career, and critical examinations of his development and musical theory.

419. FRANZ SCHUBERT
1797–1828

Austrian composer Schubert studied with Salieri at the Royal Seminary and then taught at his father's elementary school and composed in his spare time. His only musical appointment was as a teacher to the children of a Hungarian nobleman. Among Schubert's symphonies, his *Fifth* (1816), *Eighth* (1822), and *Ninth* (the *Unfinished*, 1828) rank as some of the greatest in music history. He is also famous for his piano pieces and string quartets and especially for his more than 600 *lieder*.

Autobiography and Primary Sources

Letters and Other Writings. Otto E. Deutsch, ed. 1928. Reprint ed. Freeport, New York: Books for Libraries Press, 1970. 143pp. A collection of mainly brief letters, the first written when Schubert was 15, the last shortly before his death. Included as well are extracts from his diary and a short allegorical story.

Deutsch, Otto E. *The Schubert Reader: A Life of Franz Schubert in Letters and Documents*. New York: W.W. Norton, 1947. 1.039pp. More than 1,200 documents–excerpts from letters, diaries, reviews, and programs–bearing on Schubert's life and work are arranged chronologically and form an indispensable biographical source. The author's *Schubert: Memoirs by His Friends* (New York: Macmillan, 1958. 501pp.) serves as a supplement to *The Schubert Reader* with a collection of memoirs by Schubert's friends and associates and additional documents.

Recommended Biographies

Brown, Maurice J.E. *Schubert: A Critical Biography*. New York: St. Martin's, 1958. 414pp. Drawing on Deutsch's collection of primary and secondary sources, Brown's is a comprehensive chronological account of Schubert's career, focusing on the sequence of his compositions and their connections with Schubert's experiences. Brown's study is still regarded as the standard critical biography.

Brown, Maurice J.E. *The New Grove Schubert*. New York: W.W. Norton, 1983. 186pp. Along with a detailed authoritative chronicle of Schubert's music arranged by type and date of composition, this useful reference source includes a succinct biographical profile, serving as a fine starting point for the reader interested in the composer's life, music, and background.

McKay, Elizabeth N. *Franz Schubert: A Biography*. New York: Oxford University Press, 1996. 362pp. Incorporating new research in Germany, Austria, and the United States, McKay's concise account of Schubert's life, times, and music for the general reader is skillfully presented with revealing insights into Schubert's sexuality, opium use, manic-depression, and his physical decline after he contracted syphilis. Challenging less critical views of Schubert in previous biographies, McKay makes accessible the findings that have greatly altered Schubert studies.

Other Biographical Studies

Fischer-Dieskau, Dietrich. *Schubert's Songs: A Biographical Study*. New York: Knopf, 1977. 333pp. Setting Schubert's songs against the background of his life in Vienna, the author, an expert on German *lieder*, traces Schubert's musical development.

Flower, Newman. *Franz Schubert: The Man and His Circle*. New York: F.A. Stokes, 1928. 369pp. Without attempting any analysis of Schubert's music, Flower focuses on the composer's life and relationships in a well-documented and profusely illustrated account. The book includes anecdotes and details not mentioned anywhere else, based on the author's meticulous research.

Gibbs, Christopher H. *The Life of Schubert*. New York: Cambridge University Press, 2000. 210pp. Gibbs traces the connections between the composer's life and music, laying out the key biographical evidence objectively and giving sufficient information to allow readers to make their own interpretations. The result is a fair and balanced portrait.

Hilmar, Ernst. *Franz Schubert in His Time*. Portland, Oregon: Amadeus Press, 1988. 157pp. Hilmar's collection of essays covers various aspects of Schubert's life and background, though not his music. The book's chief value rests in its skepticism of conventional wisdom regarding Schubert which Hilmar challenges, offering instead a number of fresh and provocative insights.

Hutchings, Arthur. *Schubert*. New York: Dutton, 1945. 233pp. Part of the Master Musicians series, this useful introductory study includes a reliable biographical overview, a critical examination of Schubert's music, and appendixes with a detailed chronology and biographical comments by the composer's contemporaries.

Jackson, Stephen. *Franz Schubert: An Essential Guide to His Life and Works*. London: Pavilion, 1996. 110pp. In a popular introduction for the nonexpert, Jackson supplies the highlights of Schubert's life and a critical appreciation of his music.

Kobald, Karl. *Franz Schubert and His Times*. New York: Knopf, 1928. 277pp. Arranged topically instead of chronologically, this biographical portrait sets the composer against the background of Viennese life and his circle of friends in a series of useful essays. It is illuminating on several aspects of the composer's private life, work method, and relationships.

Marek, George. *Schubert*. New York: Viking, 1986. 254pp. Marek critically reviews the existing biographical treatments of Schubert's life and career before offering a contrary view by underscoring aspects of the composer's life, such as his sexuality, his criminal record, and his relationship with Beethoven. The book presupposes prior knowledge of the composer's life and work.

Osborne, Charles. *Schubert and His Vienna*. New York: Knopf, 1985. 209pp. Schubert's Viennese background is the focus in this study that captures the composer indirectly through a vivid recreation of his society, culture, and time.

Reed, John. *Schubert*. New York: Schirmer Books, 1997. 270pp. This brief critical biography by a respected Schubert expert is an excellent choice to serve as an introduction to the man, his music, and his era. The author's earlier book, *Schubert: The Final Years* (New York: St. Martin's, 1972. 280pp.) covers the years 1825 to 1828.

Schauffler, Robert H. *Franz Schubert: The Ariel of Music*. New York: Putnam, 1949. 427pp. In a popular, critical biography, Schauffler's study is divided into a section on the man and one on his music. Although relying on extensive quotations from Schubert's letters and contemporary accounts, the book is marred by a distracting informal style and digressive, psychoanalytical speculation.

Wechsberg, Josef. *Schubert: His Life, His Work, His Time*. New York: Rizzoli, 1977. 224pp. In a handsomely produced illustrated biography, Wechsberg places Schubert in the political and cultural context of nineteenth-century Vienna and challenges the many myths surrounding the composer's life and works.

Woodford, Peggy. *Schubert: His Life and Times*. New York: Two Continents, 1978. 159pp. In a valuable illustrated biography, Woodford summarizes Schubert's life and career against the political and social background of his times. Includes excerpts from Schubert's letters and recollections from friends and associates.

Biographical Novels

Härtling, Peter. *Schubert: Twelve Moments Musicaux and a Novel*. New York: Holmes & Meier, 1995. 248pp. Using Schubert's *lieder* as a key to understanding the composer's emotional state, this inventive novel draws the connection between Schubert's work and his life.

Recommended Juvenile Biographies

Thompson, Wendy. *Franz Schubert*. New York: Viking, 1991. 48pp. MG. Thompson's is a brief introduction to Schubert's life, career, and works that serves to stimulate interest in the composer.

Biographical Films and Theatrical Adaptations

Franz Schubert (1996). Director: Malcolm Hossick. A brief film profile of the composer, part of the Famous Composers series. Video.

Other Sources

Clive, H.P. *Schubert and His World: A Biographical Dictionary*. New York: Oxford University Press, 1997. 310pp. In a series of informative entries, this useful reference volume covers multiple aspects of Schubert's life, milieu, and associates.

Erickson, Raymond, ed. *Schubert's Vienna*. New Haven, Connecticut: Yale University Press, 1997. 283pp. With chapters by various scholars, this book details life in Vienna during Schubert's period, illuminating Viennese culture, society, and politics.

Gibbs, Christopher, ed. *The Cambridge Companion to Schubert*. New York: Cambridge University Press, 1997. 340pp. This collection of critical essays examines various aspects of the composer's life and music.

420. ROBERT SCHUMANN
1810–1856

German composer, influential music critic, and leader of the romantic movement, Schumann's articles championed such composers as Chopin and Brahms. He wrote brilliant piano compositions and composed songs and orchestral music. He died in a sanitarium, which he had entered after suffering a nervous breakdown in 1854. He was married to the outstanding pianist and composer, Clara Schumann. Robert Schumann's works include the 1840 song cycles *Frauenliebe und-Leben* and *Dichterliebe*, *Spring Symphony* (1841), *Piano Concerto in A Minor* (1846), and the *Rhenish Symphony* (1850).

Autobiography and Primary Sources

The Complete Correspondence of Clara and Robert Schumann. Eva Weissweiler, ed. New York: P. Lang, 1994–1996. 2 vols. This collection of letters offers the reader insights into the couple's private and professional lives as well as their relationship with several musical associates, including Liszt, Chopin, and Mendelssohn.

The Marriage Diaries of Robert and Clara Schumann. Gerd Nauhaus, ed. Boston: Northeastern University Press, 1993. 416pp. Covering the period 1840 to 1844, these joint diary entries illuminate the couple's relationship and their views on intimate as well as professional matters. It includes

their candid comments on musical associates, such as Liszt and Mendelssohn.

Recommended Biographies

Daverio, John. *Robert Schumann: Herald of a New Poetic Age*. New York: Oxford University Press, 1997. 607pp. In the most comprehensive study that incorporates new documentary evidence, Daverio supplies a judicious and nuanced portrait of a complex figure that reexamines conventional wisdom regarding the composer's genius, career, and details of his private life. Full of fresh and original insight, Daverio's is likely to remain the definitive life for some time to come.

Niecks, Frederick. *Robert Schumann*. Christina Niecks, ed. New York: Dutton, 1925. 336pp. Niecks's reliable, balanced biographical account remains one of the best studies available on the composer. Based on the author's own acquaintance with Schumann and interviews with his associates, the book provides a richly detailed account of every period of Schumann's career. The author did not complete a planned second critical volume on the composer's music, so the musical commentary here is only related to Schumann's biographical experiences and creative method.

Taylor, Ronald. *Robert Schumann: His Life and Work*. New York: Universe Books, 1982. 354pp. In a well-written narrative biography for the general reader, Taylor concentrates on Schumann's life and sets his story against the cultural and intellectual background of his time. Sensible and balanced, Taylor avoids the sentimental excesses of previous biographical treatments for a credible, human portrait.

Other Biographical Studies

Bedford, Herbert. *Robert Schumann: His Life and Work*. New York: Harper, 1925. 267pp. Bedford's biographical profile sets Schumann in the context of the romantic movement, tracing the developments of his life and genius as an expression of the values of his era.

Brion, Marcel. *Schumann and the Romantic Age*. New York: Macmillan, 1956. 375pp. Brion's study places Schumann in the context of German romanticism and offers not a full biography but a character sketch with musical judgments that are not always reliable.

Chissell, Joan. *Schumann*. London: Dent, 1948. 275pp. Chissell provides a reliable summary of Schumann's life along with a critical appreciation of his music.

Fuller-Maitland, J.A. *Schumann*. 1884. Reprint ed. Port Washington, New York: Kennikat Press, 1970. 150pp. This early critical biography includes both a section on Schumann's life and a critical analysis of his works.

Litzmann, Berthold. *Clara Schumann: An Artist's Life*. London: Macmillan, 1913. 2 vols. An abridged translation of the three-volume German study published in 1902, this is an important reference source for information on both Clara and Robert Schumann with excerpts from the couple's diaries and correspondence. Not a critical biography,

Litzmann's study allows Clara Schumann to tell her story mainly in her own words.

Ostwald, Peter. *Schumann: The Inner Voices of a Musical Genius*. Boston: Northeastern University Press, 1985. 390pp. The author, a practicing psychiatrist and amateur musician, traces the details of Schumann's life with an emphasis on the composer's medical and psychiatric history, offering an exact diagnosis of Schumann's physical and mental condition based on primary sources. Although highly speculative, Ostwald's view is provocative and daring, offering many revealing insights into Schumann's personality and the origins of his many torments.

Plantings, Leon B. *Schumann as Critic*. New Haven, Connecticut: Yale University Press, 1967. 354pp. Plantings's specialized scholarly study focuses on Schumann as editor and musical critic. By carefully documenting Schumann's literary activities, the book provides many insights into the composer's aesthetics, his views on contemporary music and musicians, and his mental and philosophical approach to his art.

Reich, Nancy B. *Clara Schumann: The Artist and the Woman*. Ithaca, New York: Cornell University Press, 1985. 346pp. The best modern study of Clara Schumann available in English, Reich's carefully documented study sheds considerable light on her relationship with Schumann and the wider musical and literary circle of the couple.

Schauffler, Robert H. *Florestan: The Life and Work of Robert Schumann*. New York: Holt, 1945. 574pp. Divided into biographical and critical sections, Schauffler's analysis of Schumann's personality and genius is an uneven mix of primary sources, anecdotes, and psychological speculation. Written in an informal, popular style, Schauffler animates the drama of Schumann's life, but much of the book's interpretations are highly questionable.

Walker, Alan. *Schumann*. London: Faber and Faber, 1976. 128pp. This is an extremely useful succinct account of the significant details and controversies surrounding Schumann's life and career based on modern research, and serves as an excellent starting point or synthesis for the reader looking for an orientation to the issues that continue to be debated by Schumann scholars.

Wasielewski, Joseph Wilhelm von. *Life of Robert Schumann*. Boston: O. Ditson, 1871. 275pp. The first Schumann biography is based on the author's firsthand knowledge of the composer and interviews with his associates. The book also collects a number of important primary sources.

Biographical Novels

Painter, Eleanor. *Spring Symphony*. New York: Harper, 1941. 362pp. Drawing on Clara and Robert Schumann's correspondence, this biographical novel focuses on their relationship in a partly factual, partly sentimental handling.

White, Hilda. *Song Without End: The Love Story of Clara and Robert Schumann*. New York: Dutton, 1959. 300pp. White's fictional biography begins in 1832 and covers the years of the couple's marriage in a romanticized treatment with invented dialogue and situations.

Fictional Portraits

La Mure, Pierre. *Beyond Desire: A Novel Based on the Life of Felix and Cécile Mendelssohn.* New York: Random House, 1955. 310pp. Mendelssohn's life is dramatized with an emphasis on his relationship with the opera singer Maria Sala and his married life. The novel also offers a convincing portrait of its era with appearances by a number of historical figures, including Chopin, Schumann, and Wagner.

Recommended Juvenile Biographies

Dowley, Tim. *Schumann: His Life and Time.* New York: Hipprocrene Books, 1982. 144pp. MG/YA. Dowley's is a reliable and detailed account of the composer's life in his wider cultural contexts that serves younger and general readers as a useful introduction.

Kyle, Elisabeth. *Duet: The Story of Clara and Robert Schumann.* New York: Dutton, 1959. 300pp. YA. This fictionalized biography concentrates on the early years of the Schumanns' relationship.

Biographical Films and Theatrical Adaptations

Song of Love (1947). Director: Clarence Brown. Paul Henreid and Katharine Hepburn portray the Schumanns in this film portrait with Robert Walker as Johannes Brahms and Henry Daniell as Liszt. Video.

Other Sources

Todd, R. Larry, ed. *Schumann and His World.* Princeton, New Jersey: Princeton University Press, 1994. 395pp. This collection of critical essays by a variety of scholars explores various aspects of Schumann's life and music, as well as unpublished correspondence between Clara Schumann and Felix and Paul Mendelssohn.

421. ALBERT SCHWEITZER
1875–1965

Alsatian medical missionary, theologian, and musician, Schweitzer established (1913) a hospital at Lambaréné, Gabon (then French Equatorial Africa), to which he devoted his life. He was an authority on Bach and a noted performer of Bach's organ music. Frequently honored for his inspiring humanitarian work, he was awarded the 1952 Nobel Peace Prize. His many writings include *The Quest of the Historical Jesus* (1906), *Philosophy of Civilization* (1923), *From My African Notebook* (1936), and *Reverence for Life* (tr. 1969).

Autobiography and Primary Sources

Letters, 1905–1965. Hans W. Bähr, ed. New York: Macmillan, 1992. 420pp. In a rich selection of Schweitzer's voluminous correspondence, each stage of his varied career is represented allowing a view of the man that humanizes the Schweitzer of legend.

Out of My Life and Thought: An Autobiography. New York: Holt, 1933. 274pp. This is an intimate, unsentimental self-assessment of Schweitzer's life, career, and the process that led to his African mission. Essential for getting a sense of the man and his ideas.

Recommended Biographies

Marshall, George, and David Poling. *Schweitzer: A Biography.* Garden City, New York: Doubleday, 1971. 392pp. Confirmed in its reliability by Schweitzer's daughter in its foreword, this is a detailed, illustrated biography that surveys Schweitzer's many careers as philosopher, theologian, musician, and doctor. Although sympathetic, the book looks at Schweitzer clearly with his decision to work in Africa shown as a understandable human decision based on his character and past experiences.

Seaver, George. *Albert Schweitzer: The Man and His Mind.* 1947. Revised ed. New York: Harper, 1955. 370pp. Seaver's well-documented, intellectual biography traces the stages of Schweitzer's life and thought as well as his accomplishments in his various careers in Europe and Africa.

Other Biographical Studies

Augustiny, Waldemar. *The Road to Lambaréné: A Biography of Albert Schweitzer.* London: F. Muller, 1956. 228pp. This biography was edited and approved by Schweitzer and represents the version of Schweitzer's story that he wanted published.

Berman, Edgar Dr. *In Africa with Schweitzer.* New York: New Horizon Press, 1986. 308pp. Based on the author's 1960 stay with Schweitzer in Africa, this memoir offers details of the challenges faced as well as recollections of philosophical discussions with Schweitzer.

Brabazon, James. *Albert Schweitzer: A Biography.* New York: Putnam, 1975. 509pp. Staying close to the documentary sources of Schweitzer's own writing, supplemented by interviews with associates and secondary sources, this comprehensive biography summarizes Schweitzer's career, his philosophical and theological ideas, and his personality. Written to redress the balance after McKnight's vitriolic attack on Schweitzer's reputation, this is a far more sympathetic, heroic portrait.

Franck, Frederick. *Days with Albert Schweitzer.* New York: Holt, 1959. 178pp. A New York dentist who went to Schweitzer's jungle hospital in 1958 to set up a dental clinic reports his impressions of Schweitzer, supplying a number of vivid details to a portrait of a dedicated humanitarian.

McKnight, Gerald. *Verdict on Schweitzer: The Man Behind the Legend of Lambaréné.* New York: J. Day, 1964. 254pp. Posing the opening question, "Is Schweitzer a saint or a fraud?" this debunking indictment concludes the latter in an often intemperate, biased attack. McKnight's polemical demythologizing falls short of a balanced, realistic assessment.

Payne, Robert. *The Three Worlds of Albert Schweitzer.* New York: T. Nelson, 1957. 252pp. Schweitzer's life and achievement are measured against the background of his activities in music, theology, and medicine. Sympathetic but not reverent, Payne's account is a useful introduction to the man and his accomplishments.

Recommended Juvenile Biographies

Cranford, Gail. *Albert Schweitzer.* Englewood Cliffs, New Jersey: Silver Burdett, 1990. 104pp. MG. Schweitzer's entire life is covered in a lively, readable summary that includes direct quotes from Schweitzer's writings.

Greene, Carol. *Albert Schweitzer: Friend of All Life.* Chicago: Childrens Press, 1993. 45pp. MG. Greene's is a basic overview and appreciatory tribute that stresses Schweitzer's achievement and benevolence.

Robles, Harold E. *Albert Schweitzer: An Adventurer for Humanity.* Brookfield, Connecticut: Millbrook Press, 1994. 64pp. MG. This is a straightforward, accessible biographical portrait that successfully animates Schweitzer's life and accomplishments.

Biographical Films and Theatrical Adaptations

The Spirit of Albert Schweitzer (1988). Producer: John Scudder. This film tribute features reminiscences by those who knew Schweitzer. Video.

422. SIR WALTER SCOTT
1771–1832

Scottish novelist and poet considered the inventor of the regional and historical novel, Scott published translations of German ballads and narrative poems, including *The Lay of the Last Minstrel* (1805) and *The Lady of the Lake* (1810). His first novel, *Waverley* (1814), was an immediate success and was followed by such equally popular works as *Guy Mannering* (1815), *Rob Roy* (1818), and *The Heart of Midlothian* (1818). His most famous work is *Ivanhoe* (1820).

Autobiography and Primary Sources

The Journal of Sir Walter Scott. W.E.K. Anderson, ed. Oxford: Clarendon Press, 1972. 812pp. Scott's diary gives a day-to-day account of his last six years of financial ruin and increasing ill health, as well as heroic fortitude.

The Letters of Sir Walter Scott. H.J.C. Grierson, ed. 1932-37. Reprint ed. New York: AMS Press, 1971. 12 vols. The publication of Scott's massive correspondence helped reshape and correct the impression of the writer popularized by Lockhart.

Recommended Biographies

Johnson, Edgar. *Sir Walter Scott: The Great Unknown.* New York: Macmillan, 1970. 2 vols. Johnson's excellent scholarly biography corrects the factual record and the fabrications of Lockhart. Included are sensible critical appreciations of Scott's writings. Johnson's enthusiasm for the man and his writing is infectious, and the reader will have a renewed appreciation for both with the aid of this impressive biography, still regarded as the standard life.

Sutherland, John. *The Life of Walter Scott: A Critical Biography.* Cambridge, Massachusetts: Blackwell, 1995. 386pp. Sutherland modulates Johnson's enthusiasm for Scott and his writing with a more critical assessment that does not ignore the less favorable aspects of both. The book is particularly strong in drawing the connection between Scott's creations and his experience and historical elements.

Wilson, A.N. *The Laird of Abbotsford: A View of Sir Walter Scott.* New York: Oxford University Press, 1980. 197pp. Wilson's sympathetic reassessment of the writer whom the author contends was "the greatest single imaginative genius of the nineteenth century" takes the form of a series of topical essays exploring and relating various aspects of Scott's life, career, and artistry.

Other Biographical Studies

Buchan, John. *Sir Walter Scott.* New York: Coward-McCann, 1932. 384pp. Buchan corrects some of Lockhart's mistakes, but this lively and vivid biographical portrait is chiefly valuable as an entertaining narrative that animates Scott's life and character against a fully realized historical and regional background.

Carswell, Donald. *Scott and His Circle: With Four Portrait Studies.* New York: Doubleday, 1930. 299pp. After an initial study of Scott as businessman, solicitor, sheriff, politician, and author, Carswell turns his attention to three of Scott's friends: James Hogg, John Lockhart, and Joanna Baillie. Written to counter excessive admiration of Scott, Carswell emphasizes the writer's human frailties and the mundane details of his life.

Clark, Arthur M. *Sir Walter Scott: The Formative Years.* New York: Barnes and Noble, 1970. 322pp. Clark's study covers Scott's early years before he wrote his novels, correcting a number of misconceptions and errors made by Lockhart and illuminating Scott's early reading and his developing personality.

Daiches, David. *Sir Walter Scott and His World.* New York: Viking, 1971. 143pp. The illustrations overwhelm a brief but sensible text in which Scott's life and literary activities are placed in the wider historical and cultural context.

Grierson, H.J.C. *Sir Walter Scott.* New York: Columbia University Press, 1938. 320pp. The editor of Scott's letters offers a supplement and corrective to Lockhart's life. Solid in its fact but dry, Grierson's book is less to be read for pleasure than consulted as a reference source.

Gwynn, Stephen. *The Life of Sir Walter Scott.* Boston: Little, Brown, 1930. 384pp. This is a straightforward synthesis of Scott's life based on Lockhart and Scott's journals, along with critical chapters on Scott's novels.

Lockhart, J.G. *Memoirs of the Life of Sir Walter Scott, Bart.* 1837. Reprint ed. New York: Dutton, 1969. 675pp. Lockhart's much-admired biography lost considerable luster with the arrival of Edgar Johnson's definitive study that pointed out the earlier book's factual errors and inventions. Although it must be read with caution, Lockhart's affectionate tribute still has the value of insights based on the author's personal knowledge of the writer.

Pearson, Hesketh. *Walter Scott: His Life and Personality.* New York: Harper & Row, 1954. 295pp. Pearson's popular biography is a highly colored and entertaining narrative, the first to draw on the scholarly editions of Scott's letters and journal.

Pope-Hennessy, Una. *The Laird of Abbotsford.* New York: Putnam, 1932. 310pp. Depending largely on Lockhart for its facts, Pope-Hennessy's biographical profile is a lively, informal presentation of Scott's writing career and character, underscoring a number of aspects of Scott's life, particularly the hospitality of Abbotsford and the writer's financial collapse.

Wagenknecht, Edward. *Sir Walter Scott.* New York: Continuum, 1991. 239pp. The first part of Wagenknecht's study is a brief biographical portrait, followed by a chronological survey of his works, and ending with a final section devoted to the writer's personality, interests, and habits.

Biographical Novels

Oliver, Jane. *The Blue Heaven Bends over All.* London: Collins, 1971. 384pp. Scott's life and writing career are dramatized from childhood with authentic period and regional customs.

Fictional Portraits

Price, Eugenia. *Bright Captivity.* Garden City, New York: Doubleday, 1991. 631pp. The first book of the author's Georgia trilogy is set during and following the War of 1812 and tells the story of an American woman who falls in love with and marries a British officer. They journey to England and Scotland where they meet Scott.

Scarborough, Elizabeth A. *The Lady in the Loch.* New York: Ace Books, 1998. 258pp. In this imaginative fantasy mystery, Scott is the newly appointed sheriff of Edinburgh who must investigate a series of grisly murders in an "alternative" Edinburgh.

423. WILLIAM SHAKESPEARE
1564–1616

English dramatist, poet, and actor-manager, Shakespeare is considered by many to be the greatest playwright in world literature. He was born and educated in Stratford-on-Avon and married Anne Hathaway, by whom he had three children. He moved to London, where he wrote and acted for the Lord Chamberlain's Men and was a director and later part owner of the Globe and Blackfriars theatres. His first published works were the narrative poems *Venus and Adonis* (1593) and *The Rape of Lucrece* (1594). He composed 154 sonnets and 37 plays, the first of which was *Henry VI* (ca.1590). His last play was *Two Noble Kinsmen* (ca.1612).

Autobiography and Primary Sources

Chambers, E.K. *William Shakespeare: A Study of Facts and Problems.* Oxford: Clarendon Press, 1930. 2 vols. Chambers's exhaustive scholarly collection of relevant documentary evidence concerning Shakespeare's life is joined by the author's analysis of the factual evidence, including a chronology of the plays. In *A Short Life of Shakespeare* (Oxford: Clarendon Press, 1963. 260pp.) Chambers synthesizes his documentary research into a factually reliable account of Shakespeare's life and career.

Schoenbaum, S. *Shakespeare: A Documentary Life.* New York: Oxford University Press, 1975. 273pp; *William Shakespeare: A Compact Documentary Life.* New York: Oxford University Press, 1987. 384pp. Schoenbaum's scholarly volumes collect the essential documentary evidence, which is woven into a factual, reliable narrative account. These are the volumes to consult to examine the sources and what reasonable biographical conclusions can be drawn from them.

Recommended Biographies

Chute, Marchette. *Shakespeare of London.* New York: Dutton, 1949. 397pp. Chute provides an entertaining, popular reconstruction of Shakespeare's life and times based on contemporary source materials, which are woven into a vivid narrative animated with novelistic skill. Still an excellent choice for the general reader.

Honan, Park. *Shakespeare: A Life.* New York: Oxford University Press, 1998. 479pp. This is a comprehensive, well-written biographical portrait that incorporates modern scholarship into a reasonably argued, meticulously researched study. Honan sticks to the facts, filling the gaps with illuminating background details.

Schoenbaum, S. *Shakespeare's Lives.* New York: Oxford University Press, 1970. 838pp. The book exhaustively and expertly surveys the various "Shakespeares," factual, legendary, and fictional, as well the alternative Shakespeares, such as Marlowe, Bacon, and the Earl of Oxford, who have been offered as the real authors of the plays. Serving as a kind of biography of biographies, Schoenbaum's lucid review of the existing evidence, conjecture, and fantasy is an essential summary of the controversy surrounding the repossession of the historical Shakespeare.

Wells, Stanley. *Shakespeare: A Life in Drama.* New York: W.W. Norton, 1995. 403pp. The author, the director of the Shakespeare Institute in England and the general editor of the "Oxford Shakespeare," summarizes what is known about Shakespeare's life and career in the theater before chronologically examining his plays and poems.

Other Biographical Studies

Adams, Joseph Quincy. *A Life of William Shakespeare.* Boston: Houghton Mifflin, 1923. 560pp. In Adams's scholarly account, the Elizabethan and theatrical background is brought to the foreground in order to view Shakespeare in his cultural context. The effect is to replace a mythical figure with a believable human one seen from the values and details of his time.

Bradbrook, M.C. *Shakespeare: The Poet in His World.* New York: Columbia University Press, 1980. 272pp. Described as an "applied biography," Bradbrook's study relates the known details of Shakespeare's life and the development of English theatrical history to the wider context of the times. Full of fresh insights, the book offers plausible surmises based on a careful study of documentary sources.

Brown, Ivor. *Shakespeare*. Garden City, New York: Doubleday, 1949. 306pp. Written by a respected British drama critic and scholar, Brown presents the ascertainable facts and opinions of Shakespeare's life along with a vivid recreation of the playwright's times.

Burgess, Anthony. *Shakespeare*. New York: Knopf, 1970. 272pp. In an informal account of the main facts about Shakespeare's life, along with a good deal of speculation, Burgess provides an entertaining, eccentric, informative narrative treatment.

Dowden, Edward. *Shakespeare: A Critical Study of His Mind and Art*. New York: Barnes and Noble, 1875. 434pp. One of the earliest full-scale biographical profiles, Dowden compensates for the paucity of factual evidence by arguing that the plays and poetry reveal the man, and the author constructs a subjective, speculative inner history of the stages of the playwright's growth to maturity.

Dutton, Richard. *William Shakespeare: A Literary Life*. New York: St. Martin's, 1994. 180pp. Not a conventional biography, Dutton instead traces Shakespeare's literary career through a close examination of the works and what they reveal to us about the playwright's creative method.

Eccles, Mark. *Shakespeare in Warwickshire*. Madison: University of Wisconsin Press, 1961. 182pp. Eccles focuses on Shakespeare's background and roots in Stratford to help explain the man and his values. Careful in its documentation, the book sheds considerable light on Shakespeare's development.

Fraser, Russell A. *Young Shakespeare*. New York: Columbia University Press, 1988. 247pp. Tracing the connection between Shakespeare's life and art, Fraser interprets how the playwright lived, worked, and created in a unified, coherent portrait of his first 30 years. Full of fresh and original insights the book attempts to show how Shakespeare's background and early memories played a key role in his developing genius.

Halliday, F.E. *Shakespeare: A Pictorial Biography*. New York: Viking, 1956. 147pp. A simple, straightforward summary text of what we know about Shakespeare's life, along with conjecture, is joined to handsome illustrations of sites associated with the playwright and facsimiles of records.

Kay, Dennis. *William Shakespeare: His Life and Times*. New York: Twayne, 1995. 186pp. Kay presents a concise summary of Shakespeare's life against a solid period background, tracing the context out of which the writer's works were created.

Laroque, François. *The Age of Shakespeare*. New York: Abrams, 1993. 191pp. This richly detailed, lavishly illustrated biographical portrait integrates the known facts of Shakespeare's life with his political, social, and artistic background.

Lee, Sir Sidney. *Life of William Shakespeare*. 1898. Reprint ed. New York: Dover, 1968. 792pp. Lee attempted to reign in the subjective excesses of Dowden and others by refocusing on what is known rather than what the plays and poems sug-

gest about Shakespeare. Unfortunately, reliable evidence is still intermixed with the legendary.

O'Connor, Garry. *William Shakespeare: A Popular Life*. New York: Applause Books, 1999. 377pp. O'Connor's impressionistic, informal biography takes a psychosexual approach, attempting to humanize the bard, setting the man clearly in his era, while freely speculating about Shakespeare's thoughts and motives. Lists and tables at the end of the book helpfully outline facts and conjecture about Shakespeare.

Pohl, Frederick J. *Like to the Lark: The Early Years of Shakespeare*. New York: C.N. Potter, 1972. 195pp. Pohl raises the many questions that remain unanswered surrounding Shakespeare's early life and offers his own intriguing but highly speculative solutions. Although conclusive answers are impossible in the absence of more factual evidence, Pohl's energetic assurance that an authentic Shakespeare can be known is refreshing.

Quennell, Peter. *Shakespeare: A Biography*. Cleveland: World, 1963. 352pp. Combining documentary evidence with what can be gleaned from Shakespeare's works and through his times, Quennell supplies a credible, nuanced portrait of the man that is more judicious and balanced than most.

Rowse, A.L. *Shakespeare: A Biography*. New York: Harper & Row, 1963. 484pp. Rowse concentrates on Shakespeare's sonnets, which are mined for biographical details. Highly speculative, Rowse's findings should be read with caution as they are more provocative than provable; *Shakespeare the Man* (New York: St. Martin's, 1988. 253pp.) restates his earlier contentions and confidently identifies the dark lady of the sonnets.

Wagenknecht, Edward. *The Personality of Shakespeare*. Norman: University of Oklahoma Press, 1972. 190pp. Wagenknecht applies his "psychographic method" to what can be learned about Shakespeare's character and temperament by the known facts and a close reading of the work. Highly speculative and unprovable, this is more a lively exercise in the imagination than a reliable study.

Wilson, Ian. *Shakespeare: The Evidence: Unlocking the Mysteries of the Man and His Works*. New York: St. Martin's, 1995. 498pp. Wilson takes up most of the controversies surrounding Shakespeare's life and authorship, which are addressed by reference to the documentary and historical evidence. Includes a Shakespeare family tree, chronology, and selection of documents.

Biographical Novels

Brophy, John. *Gentleman of Stratford*. New York: Harper, 1940. 348pp. Staying close to the known facts and drawing conclusions about Shakespeare's character from his writing, the novel dramatizes the playwright's career with a convincing period background.

Buckmaster, Henrietta. *All the Living: A Novel of One Year in the Life of William Shakespeare*. New York: Random House, 1962. 523pp. The year is 1600 in this dramatic recreation of Shakespeare's involvement with the Dark Lady of the sonnets and his participation in the Essex conspiracy. The his-

torical background is reliable, but Shakespeare's activities are based on plausible conjectures.

Burgess, Anthony. *Nothing Like the Sun: A Story of Shakespeare's Love Life*. New York: W.W. Norton, 1964. 234pp. Shakespeare in love is Burgess's focus in this inventive recreation of the playwright's life in Stratford and London, speculating about the inspiration for his poetry and the personal basis for the plays. Burgess interweaves invention, facts, and an impressive period animation.

Burton, Philip. *You, My Brother: A Novel Based on the Lives of Edmund and William Shakespeare*. New York: Random House, 1973. 561pp. Richly textured and solidly researched, the novel follows the activities of Shakespeare's younger brother who, at the peak of his elder brother's career, becomes an apprentice at the Globe and is plunged into the world of his famous sibling.

Chambrun, Clara Longworth de. *Two Loves Have I*. Philadelphia: Lippincott, 1934. 366pp. Filling in the biographical gaps with intriguing speculation, the novel supplies a portrait of Shakespeare that answers several intriguing mysteries with plausible and dubious conjecture.

Cowell, Stephanie. *The Players*. New York: W.W. Norton, 1997. 353pp. Shakespeare's apprenticeship in London is dramatized as he begins his career as an actor and playwright in the center of a lively circle that includes Marlowe and Jonson.

Fisher, Edward. *Shakespeare & Son*. New York: Abelard-Schuman, 1962. 214pp.; *Love's Labour's Won*. New York: Abelard-Schuman, 1963. 224pp.; *The Best House in Stratford*. New York: Abelard-Schuman, 1965. 220pp. Fisher's trilogy on Shakespeare's life and literary career follows him from the age of 15, through the lost years, until his retirement to Stratford. Although mostly speculative, the novels provide a convincing period atmosphere and a credible psychological profile.

Malpass, Eric. *Sweet Will*. New York: St. Martin's, 1974. 287pp.; *The Cleopatra Boy*. New York: St. Martin's, 1974. 240pp.; *A House of Women*. New York: St. Martin's, 1975. 224pp. Malpass's trilogy chronicles Shakespeare's life from his early years in Stratford, his London theatrical success, through his retirement. What is known for certain is present, supplemented with invention and plausible surmises.

Mortimer, John. *Will Shakespeare: The Untold Story*. New York: Delacorte, 1977. 256pp. Blending fact, legend, and invention, the novel, told from the perspective of a one-time boy actor, chronicles Shakespeare's rise to success.

Fictional Portraits

Barker, Shirley. *Liza Bowe*. New York: Random House, 1956. 245pp. In a colorful depiction of the Mermaid Tavern's personalities and activities, many actual figures, including Marlowe, Nash, Kyd, and Shakespeare, intermingle with the novel's fictional story of a young tavern maid and a Thames boatman.

Brahms, Caryl. *No Bed for Bacon*. London: M. Joseph, 1941. 224pp. History is repossessed as farce with Shakespeare depicted as a commercial hack and Francis Bacon as an ineffectual dandy.

Burgess, Anthony. *A Dead Man in Deptford.* New York: Carroll & Graf, 1995. 272pp. Burgess's imaginative reconstruction of Christopher Marlowe's life includes a brief appearance by the up-and-coming newcomer from Stratford.

Garrett, George. *Entered from the Sun.* Garden City, New York: Doubleday, 1990. 349pp. This imaginative investigation of the facts surrounding Marlowe's death by an actor and aging army veteran includes testimony from Shakespeare and Ben Jonson.

Hayes, Tony. *Murder on the Twelfth Night.* Bell Buckle, Tennessee: Iris Press, 1993. 155pp. In this inventive period mystery, Shakespeare joins forces with Ben Jonson to find a murderer before Puritans can close down the theaters.

Jong, Erica. *Serenissima: A Novel of Venice.* Boston: Houghton Mifflin, 1987. 225pp. In an inventive time-travel novel, a Hollywood actress is transported back to sixteenth-century Venice where she meets Shakespeare as he is writing *The Merchant of Venice.*

Kellerman, Faye. *The Quality of Mercy.* New York: Morrow, 1989. 607pp. In this intriguing period mystery, Shakespeare is shown investigating the murder of a fellow actor and joining forces with a young Jewish woman for an excursion to Spain to help release Jews from the Inquisition.

MacInnes, Colin. *Three Years to Play.* New York: Farrar, Straus, 1970. 365pp. This fanciful story offers the source for Shakespeare's *As You Like It* as a young actor's experiences are transformed.

Nye, Robert. *Mrs. Shakespeare: The Complete Works.* London: Sinclair-Stevenson, 1993. 216pp. This comic treatment of Shakespeare's life and times takes the form of an account written by Anne Hathaway of a week she spends with her husband in London in which she reveals that she is the Dark Lady of the sonnets and confirms her husband's bisexuality. In *The Late Mr. Shakespeare* (New York: Arcade, 1999. 398pp.) Shakespeare's life and times are narrated by an octogenarian former actor who mixes fact, fantasy, anecdotes, and gossip in an often outrageous, original treatment.

Rooke, Leon. *Shakespeare's Dog.* New York: Knopf, 1983. 157pp. In a dog's eye view of Shakespeare, the playwright's dog, Mr. Hooker, provides a unique perspective on his master.

Recommended Juvenile Biographies

Shellard, Dominic. *William Shakespeare.* New York: Oxford University Press, 1998. 128pp. MG. Shellard covers what is known about Shakespeare's life with a view of the political and social background of Elizabethan England.

Stanley, Diane, and Peter Vennema. *Bard of Avon: The Story of William Shakespeare.* New York: Morrow, 1992. 46pp. MG. A brief, reliable biography using only historically sound evidence.

Thrasher, Thomas. *William Shakespeare.* San Diego: Lucent Books, 1999. 108pp. MG. Thrasher's is an informative biographical profile that connects the known facts with period details to animate the writer and his times.

Biographical Films and Theatrical Adaptations

A&E Biography Video: William Shakespeare: A Life of Drama (1996). Director: Rebecca Jones. A film portrait using dramatic readings, film excerpts, and location footage. Video.

Life of Shakespeare (1978). Director: Mark Cunningham. In a dramatic speculation about Shakespeare's life, Tim Curry portrays Shakespeare, Meg Wynn Owen is Anne Hathaway, Ian McShane appears as Marlowe, and Patience Collier is Elizabeth I. Video.

Shakespeare in Love (1998). Director: John Madden. In an inventive screenplay by Marc Norman and Tom Stoppard, this lushly evocative fantasy about the origin of *Romeo and Juliet* features standout performances by Joseph Fiennes as the bard with inky fingernails, Gwyneth Paltrow, Geoffrey Rush, Ruppert Everett as Marlowe, and Judi Dench as Elizabeth I. Video.

William Shakespeare: Poet and Dramatist, 1564–1616 (1993). Director: Malcolm Hossick. Using contemporary drawings, paintings, and portraits, Shakespeare's life is chronicled, including a portrait of his social and historical background. Video.

Other Sources

Bentley, Gerald E. *Shakespeare: A Biographical Handbook.* New Haven, Connecticut: Yale University Press, 1961. 256pp. This scholarly reference tool collects and comments on the relevant documentary evidence.

Boyce, Charles. *Shakespeare A to Z.* New York: Facts on File, 1990. 742pp. Alphabetical listings of people, places, and events associated with Shakespeare's life and career.

Campbell, Oscar J., ed. *The Reader's Encyclopedia of Shakespeare.* New York: Crowell, 1966. 1,014pp. Campbell's detailed collection of articles covers virtually every aspect of Shakespeare's life, writings, and reputation. Each play is covered in detail with commentary on performance history.

Fox, Levi. *The Shakespeare Handbook.* Boston: G.K. Hall, 1987. 264pp. Along with a chronology, the book provides chapters on Shakespeare's life, Elizabethan and theatrical background, and a summary of the plays, films, and performances.

Kasten, David S., ed. *A Companion to Shakespeare.* Malden, Massachusetts: Blackwell, 1999. 523pp. A collection of essays that examines aspects of Shakespeare's theatrical, political, intellectual, and social background.

Martin, Michael R., and Richard C. Harrier. *The Concise Encyclopedic Guide to Shakespeare.* New York: Horizon Press, 1971. 450pp. Intended for the general reader, this volume offers a rich collection of background information, synopses of the plays, listings of characters, and biographical sketches of those associated with Shakespeare.

Rosenblum, Joseph, ed. *Shakespeare.* Pasadena, California: Salem Press, 1998. 482pp. Includes a brief biographical summary along with analytical surveys of the plays and poetry.

Wells, Stanley. *A Dictionary of Shakespeare.* New York: Oxford University Press, 1998. 234pp. This concise, illustrated reference source covers all aspects of Shakespeare, his time, impact, and influence.

424. GEORGE BERNARD SHAW
1856–1950

Irish playwright and critic who invigorated the Victorian theatre with his witty, ironic plays of serious philosophical and social content, Shaw also worked as a journalist and music critic in London. As a drama critic, he promoted the plays of Henrik Ibsen. A dedicated socialist, Shaw became a leader of the Fabian Society and a popular public speaker on behalf of socialism. His plays include *Mrs. Warren's Profession* (1893), *Caesar and Cleopatra* (1899), *Major Barbara* (1905), *Man and Superman* (1905), *Pygmalion* (1913), and *Saint Joan* (1923). He received the 1925 Nobel Prize for Literature.

Autobiography and Primary Sources

Bernard Shaw: The Diaries, 1885–1897. Stanley Weintraub, ed. University Park: Pennsylvania State University Press, 1986. 2 vols. Shaw's diaries are indispensable sources for revealing his formative years and the evolution of his genius.

Collected Letters. Dan H. Laurence, ed. New York: Viking, 1985-88. 4 vols. Shaw's correspondence makes up a fascinating record of his energy, relationships, and multiple sides. The letters cover everything from his comments on his plays and their production and business matters, to his ongoing dialogue with a wide circle of friends and associates.

Shaw: An Autobiography. Stanley Weintraub, ed. New York: Weybright and Talley, 1969–1970. 2 vols. A variety of sources are arranged chronologically by Weintraub to simulate a full-scale reflection of Shaw's life in his own words.

Recommended Biographies

Dervin, Daniel. *Bernard Shaw: A Psychological Study.* Lewisburg, Pennsylvania: Bucknell University Press, 1975. 350pp. Dervin traces the effects of Shaw's early family relationships and other influences on his development in a Freudian reading that provides a useful analysis of the connections between Shaw's experiences and his works.

Holroyd, Michael. *Bernard Shaw.* New York: Random House, 1988–1992. 4 vols. Holroyd's monumental life is one of the classic literary biographies. Authoritative, perceptive as well as exhaustive, requiring more than 15 years to research and write, Holroyd synthesizes all the relevant source material into a full-length portrait that makes the man and his remarkable career comprehensible in human, artistic, and social terms. Holroyd's single-volume abridgment, *Bernard Shaw: The One-Volume Definitive Edition* (New York: Random House, 1998. 704pp.) eliminates the documentation and concentrates on Shaw's literary career and the significant moments in Shaw's long life.

Hugo, Leon. *Edwardian Shaw: The Writer and His Age*. New York: St. Martin's, 1999. 320pp. Chronicling Shaw's life and career during Edward VII's reign from 1901 to 1910, this is a sensible, detailed presentation of Shaw's various interests, activities, and artistic development in the context of his times.

Peters, Sally. *Bernard Shaw: The Ascent of the Superman*. New Haven, Connecticut: Yale University Press, 1996. 328pp. Peters's insightful, controversial interpretation of Shaw's emotional and intellectual development focuses on the often repressed and disguised core of his makeup, including gender ambivalence and homosexuality. Many of Peters's conclusions are highly speculative, if not extravagant, fitting Shaw's life to the concealed pattern she has uncovered, but the book is never dull and provides a different paradigm to view Shaw's temperament and development.

Other Biographical Studies

Brown, Ivor. *Shaw in His Time*. London: Nelson, 1965. 212pp. Shaw's character, ideas, and works are reviewed against the political, social, intellectual, and artistic context of his era. Provides a useful overview in breadth rather than depth.

Chappelow, Allan. *Shaw the Villager and Human Being: A Biographical Symposium*. New York: Macmillan, 1962. 354pp.; *"The Chucker-Out": A Biographical Exposition and Critique*. New York: AMS Press, 1969. 558pp. The author's two volumes collect Shaw's own words from letters, speeches, lectures, and conversations with the author as well as comments from Shaw's neighbors at Ayot St. Lawrence.

Colbourne, Maurice. *The Real Bernard Shaw*. New York: Dodd, Mead, 1940. 342pp. Colbourne, a producer, actor, and admirer, attempts to synthesize Shaw's many ideas and works into a unified philosophy. The first portion of the book provides a biographical portrait; the rest is critical commentary and interpretation.

DuCann, Charles G.L. *The Loves of George Bernard Shaw*. New York: Funk & Wagnalls, 1963. 300pp. This is a journalistic, arch, gossipy, and mainly hostile review of Shaw's relationships with women. Readers looking to learn anything substantive about Shaw's relationships with the women in his life should turn to Peters.

Ervine, St. John. *Bernard Shaw: His Life, Work, and Friends*. New York: Morrow, 1956. 628pp. Written by an Anglo-Irish playwright and a friend of Shaw for more than 40 years, Ervine's biographical portrait is based on his own knowledge and the memories of others. Despite his friendship, Ervine is not uncritical, and his readable account is packed with anecdotes and personal insights.

Harris, Frank. *Bernard Shaw: An Unauthorized Biography Based on Firsthand Information*. New York: Simon & Schuster, 1931. 430pp. Although billed as unauthorized, the book had Shaw's input in the form of corrections to the proofs and a postscript. Less a full-scale biography than a sketchy series of impressions based on the author's association with the playwright.

Henderson, Archibald. *George Bernard Shaw, His Life and Works: A Critical Biography*. New York: Boni and Liveright, 1918. 528pp.; *Bernard Shaw:*

Playboy and Prophet. New York: Appleton, 1932. 871pp.; *George Bernard Shaw: Man of the Century*. New York: Appleton-Century, 1956. 969pp. Henderson's successively longer biographical and critical tomes in which each subsequent volume revises and supersedes the previous one draw on the author's intimacy with Shaw and received his cooperation. The result is often a disorderly compilation of facts, naive assessment, and extravagant praise.

Irvine, William. *The Universe of G.B.S.* New York: Whittlesey House, 1949. 439pp. Irvine's intellectual biography traces Shaw's artistic and philosophical development in a sympathetic yet critical assessment. The book's biographical coverage is sporadic and limited, but the book does provide a valuable summary of the range and nature of Shaw's intellect.

Pearson, Hesketh. *George Bernard Shaw: His Life and Personality*. 1942. Revised ed. New York: Atheneum, 1963. 480pp.; *G.B.S.: A Full-Length Portrait*. New York: Harper, 1942. 390pp.; *G.B.S.: A Postscript*. New York: Harper, 1950. 191pp. Pearson's sequence of anecdotal biographical portraits is packed with vivid glimpses of Shaw's personality but lacks critical distance and objectivity.

Rosset, B.C. *Shaw of Dublin: The Formative Years*. University Park: Pennsylvania State University Press, 1964. 388pp. Rosset's intriguing study of the impact of Shaw's Irish childhood on his development centers on the question of the playwright's paternity and Shaw's fear that his mother's adulterous relationship would be uncovered.

Shenfield, Margaret. *Bernard Shaw: A Pictorial Biography*. New York: Viking, 1962. 144pp. A chronological arrangement of photographs of Shaw and his milieu is connected by a straightforward, though compact summary of his life and times. This book will serve to orient general readers.

Silver, Arnold J. *Bernard Shaw: The Darker Side*. Stanford, California: Stanford University Press, 1982. 353pp. In a psychological profile from a Freudian perspective, Silver identifies a conflict between Shaw's humane impulses and darker destructive passions. Their origins are traced from his childhood, his problematic relationships with his parents, and the various women in his life.

Smith, J. Percy. *The Unrepentant Pilgrim: A Study of the Development of Bernard Shaw*. Boston: Houghton Mifflin, 1965. 274pp. This documentary examination of Shaw's literary development during his 20s and 30s relies on the playwright's diaries, letters, and writings to trace his evolution as a writer and thinker.

Weintraub, Stanley. *Private Shaw and Public Shaw: A Dual Biography of Lawrence of Arabia and George Bernard Shaw*. New York: G. Braziller, 1963. 302pp. This detailed and fascinating account of Shaw's friendship with T.E. Lawrence is based on previously unpublished material from the Shaw and Lawrence estates and sheds considerable light on Shaw's friendship with Lawrence from the early 1920s to Lawrence's death on a motorcycle, a gift from the Shaws, in 1935.

Weintraub, Stanley. *Journey to Heartbreak: The Crucible Years of Bernard Shaw 1914–1918*. New York: Weybright and Talley, 1971. 368pp. Weintraub focuses on the war years in which Shaw's vocal opposition to the carnage created a heated debate between Shaw and his prowar opponents. Weintraub documents the many stages in their battle, as well as the intellectual and artistic impact on Shaw of his wartime attitudes.

Weintraub, Stanley. *The Unexpected Shaw: Biographical Approaches to George Bernard Shaw and His Work*. New York": Frederick Ungar, 1982. 254pp. In a collection of essays and introductions, Weintraub provides biographical and critical portraits of Shaw in unfamiliar guises: as prizefighting enthusiast, art critic, actor, and Irish patriot. The book also uncovers sources for many of the plays from Shaw's experiences, reading, and acquaintances.

Winsten, Stephen. *Days with Bernard Shaw*. New York: Vanguard, 1949. 327pp.; *Shaw's Corner*. New York: Roy, 1952. 238pp.; *Jesting Apostle: The Private Life of Bernard Shaw*. New York: Dutton, 1957. 231pp. Winsten, Shaw's neighbor at Ayot St. Lawrence, provides his perspective in a series of volumes featuring recorded conversations. The 1957 book offers a more analytical and less admiring synthesis of the author's impressions of Shaw's personality and attitudes.

Fictional Portraits

Linscott, Gillian. *Stage Fright*. New York: St. Martin's, 1993. 188pp. In this installment of the author's entertaining historical mystery series, suffragette Nell Bray is called in by Shaw when one of his leading ladies begins to receive threats.

Meyer, Nicholas. *The West End Horror*. New York: Dutton, 1976. 222pp. An 1895 murder of a theater critic launches Sherlock Holmes into a complex mystery that involves such historical figures as George Bernard Shaw and Oscar Wilde.

Recommended Juvenile Biographies

Coolidge, Olivia E. *George Bernard Shaw*. Boston: Houghton Mifflin, 1968. 226pp. YA. This is a skillfully written biography that covers the major events of Shaw's life and provides a critical assessment of his works and ideas. Recommended for the general adult reader as well.

Biographical Films and Theatrical Adaptations

George Bernard Shaw: A Concise Biography (1993). Director: Malcolm Hossick. This film portrait illustrates the highlights of Shaw's life and career against the background of his times. Video.

Other Sources

Gibbs, A.M. *Shaw: Interviews and Recollections*. Iowa City: University of Iowa Press, 1990. 560pp. Collects multiple glimpses of Shaw from friends and associates excerpted from other works, as well as interviews with the playwright.

Hardwick, Michael, and Mollie Hardwick. *The Bernard Shaw Companion*. London: J. Murray, 1973. 193pp. This reference volume features a chronology of the works, plot summaries, a who's who, a sampling of quotes, and a brief biographical profile.

Innes, Christopher D., ed. *The Cambridge Companion to George Bernard Shaw.* New York: Cambridge University Press, 1998. 320pp. In essays by scholars and critics, this useful collection surveys multiple aspects of Shaw's drama, ideas, and character.

Rattray, Robert F. *Bernard Shaw: A Chronicle.* New York: Roy, 1951. 347pp. Details about Shaw's life, activities, and work are arranged to form an extensive chronology from 1865 to Shaw's death.

425. MARY SHELLEY
1797–1851

The daughter of feminist writer Mary Wollstonecraft and political philosopher William Godwin, and the wife of Romantic poet Percy Bysshe Shelley, Mary Shelley is famous for her Gothic horror novel *Frankenstein* (1818). She wrote other novels, including the partly autobiographical *Lodore* (1835), and edited her husband's works.

Autobiography and Primary Sources

The Journals of Mary Wollstonecraft Shelley. Paula R. Feldman and Diane Scott-Kilvert, eds. New York: Oxford University Press, 1987. 2 vols. The journals cover the years 1814, when Mary eloped with Shelley, to 1844, seven years before her death, and along with the volumes' notes form a coherent chronicle of the author's life. Includes a chronology, maps of the Shelleys's travels, and portraits and biographical profiles of the members of the Shelleys' social circle.

The Letters of Mary Wollstonecraft Shelley. Betty T. Bennett, ed. Baltimore: Johns Hopkins University Press, 1980–1988. 3 vols. Mary Shelley's 1,276 extant letters illuminate her personality and intellectual and artistic interests, as well as her relationship with a wide circle of famous individuals, including Byron, Keats, Scott, Washington Irving, Charles and Mary Lamb, and Disraeli.

Selected Letters of Mary Wollstonecraft Shelley. Betty T. Bennett, ed. Baltimore: Johns Hopkins University Press, 1994. 480pp. This selection of 230 of Shelley's letters cover the period 1814, shortly after her elopement, through 1850, a few months before her death. Also includes the editor's introductory biographical and critical portrait of the author.

Recommended Biographies

Mellor, Anne K. *Mary Shelley: Her Life, Her Fiction, Her Monsters.* New York: Methuen, 1988. 275pp. Mellor perceptively draws the connections between Mary Shelley's life and her work, focusing on the origin and biographical insights contained in her most famous book. In Mellor's view, *Frankenstein* reveals Shelley's refusal to provide Mary with a normal family life as well as her unhappy childhood. The book uses Marxist and feminist theory for fresh elucidation of aspects of Shelley's temperament and genius.

Spark, Muriel. *Child of Light.* 1951. Revised as *Mary Shelley: A Biography.* New York: Dutton, 1987. 248pp. Novelist Spark supplies an accessible account of Shelley's life and works designed for the general reader. Dividing her book into biographical and critical sections, Spark presents an entertaining overview that summarizes the important events in Shelley's life and development, along with a reasonable appreciation of her works.

Sunstein, Emily W. *Mary Shelley: Romance and Reality.* Boston: Little, Brown, 1989. 478pp. Sunstein's is the leading scholarly biography that makes full use of primary sources and modern scholarship. The book looks clearly at Shelley's entire life, succeeding where many other treatments fall short in demonstrating Shelley's importance in her own right. Her years with Shelley are put in perspective after a clear examination of her upbringing, followed by a full discussion of her years after her husband's death.

Other Biographical Studies

Dunn, Jane. *Moon in Eclipse: A Life of Mary Shelley.* New York: St. Martin's, 1978. 374pp. In a popular, straightforward, though somewhat superficial biographical portrait, Dunn attempts with only limited success to draw Mary Shelley out of the shadow of her famous husband to reveal a complex woman. Her treatment of the social, literary, and political aspect of her life is cursory and simplistic.

Gerson, Noel B. *Daughter of Earth and Water.* New York: Morrow, 1973. 280pp. Gerson's straightforward, popular chronological narrative of Mary Shelley's life centers on the years up to her husband's death, paying little attention to her years alone.

Gittings, Robert, and Jo Manton. *Claire Clairmont and the Shelleys.* New York: Oxford University Press, 1992. 281pp. Gittings provides the book's account of the Shelleys' circle of family and friends, followed by Manton's presentation of the last 57 years of Mary Shelley's stepsister, Claire Clairmont.

Grylls, R. Glynn. *Mary Shelley: A Biography.* New York: Oxford University Press, 1938. 345pp. A full-length, competent scholarly biography, Grylls's examination helped to present Mary Shelley on her own beyond the long shadow cast by her husband. With access to previously unpublished sources, the book illuminates many aspects of the author's life, particularly the 29 years following Shelley's death.

Hill-Miller, Katherine. *"My Hideous Progeny": Mary Shelley, William Godwin, and the Father-Daughter Relationship.* Newark: University of Delaware Press, 1995. 249pp. The author uses Shelley's relationship with her father as the key for understanding her development and works in a psychological and critical study.

Leighton, Margaret C. *Shelley's Mary: A Life of Mary Godwin Shelley.* New York: Farrar, Straus, 1973. 234pp. Leighton's popular account of Shelley's life and times draws on her journal and letters and is intended to lead to a fuller appreciation of the author and her work.

Marshall, Florence A. *The Life and Letters of Mary Wollstonecraft Shelley.* London: R. Bentley, 1889.

2 vols. In the first official biography, Marshall narrates the events of Mary Shelley's life through long excerpts from her letters. The book, in a partisan and idealized presentation, attempts to redress previous negative or slighting assessments by Percy Shelley's advocates, such as Trelawney, who undervalued and falsified Mary Shelley's significance.

Neumann, Bonnie R. *The Lonely Muse: A Critical Biography of Mary Wollstonecraft Shelley.* Salzburg: University of Salzburg, 1979. 283pp. Neumann's cogent reassessment allows Mary Shelley to emerge from her husband's shadow, treating her work and development as a consistent search to transcend a dominating sense of alienation.

Nitchie, Elizabeth. *Mary Shelley: Author of "Frankenstein."* New Brunswick, New Jersey: Rutgers University Press, 1953. 255pp. This compact biographical assessment looks closely at Shelley's works to reveal features of her thought and personality. In Nitchie's view, her later fiction represents an effort to re-explore the emotional landscape of her earlier days.

St. Clair, William. *The Godwins and the Shelleys: The Biography of a Family.* New York: W.W. Norton, 1989. 572pp. Despite the book's title, the focus here is almost exclusively on William Godwin, and its discussion of the Shelleys is largely restricted to the details of the elopement and its impact on the Godwin family. The insights on Mary Shelley come largely from a fuller understanding of her upbringing by her two remarkable parents.

Walling, William A. *Mary Shelley.* New York: Twayne, 1972. 173pp. Walling provides no new biographical facts to the familiar record of events but does offer extended critical examination of Shelley's works after *Frankenstein* to supply a fuller portrait of the artist and her achievement.

Williams, John. *Mary Shelley: A Literary Life.* New York: St. Martin's, 1999. 210pp. Williams's is a careful review of Shelley's literary career with an emphasis on her professional relationships and the growth of her skills as a writer.

Biographical Novels

Bolton, Guy. *The Olympians.* Cleveland, Ohio: World, 1961. 301pp. Bolton dramatizes the events leading up to Percy Shelley's elopement with Mary Godwin and its impact on the Godwin family.

Chernaik, Judith. *Love's Children.* New York: Knopf, 1992. 229pp. This group portrait of the women connected with Percy Shelley takes the shape of journal entries by Harriet Westbrook, Fanny Godwin, Claire Clairmont, and Mary Godwin.

Fictional Portraits

Aldiss, Brian. *Frankenstein Unbound.* New York: Random House, 1973. 212pp. In this intriguing science fiction/horror/fantasy, a time traveler goes back to 1816 to discover that Frankenstein was not an invention of Mary Shelley but as real as his monster. Byron and the Shelleys appear as characters.

Carrere, Emmanuel. *Gothic Romance.* New York: Scribner, 1990. 307pp. Interweaving actual with imagined events, the novel dramatizes the events leading up to Shelley's composition of *Franken-stein.*

Edwards, Anne. *Haunted Summer.* New York: Coward-McCann, 1972. 278p. The infamous summer holiday of 1816 in which Byron was joined in Switzerland by Percy and Mary Shelley forms the background for this fanciful gothic tale narrated by Mary.

Seymour, Miranda. *Count Manfred.* New York: Coward-McCann, 1977. 283p. This gothic tale includes in its cast Byron and Percy and Mary Shelley with a reliable period background and actual details from Byron's life.

Recommended Juvenile Biographies

Harris, Janet. *The Woman Who Created Franken-stein: A Portrait of Mary Shelley.* New York: Harper & Row, 1979. 216pp. MG/YA. Mostly concerned with the creation of Shelley's famous novel, this is a candid, well-written biography and critical study that traces the genesis of the novel, Shelley's influences, and her themes.

Miller, Calvin C. *Spirit Like a Storm: The Story of Mary Shelley.* Greensboro, North Carolina: Morgan Reynolds, 1996. 122pp. YA. In a well-written biographical portrait, Miller summarizes the main events of Shelley's life with an emphasis on the creation of *Frankenstein.*

Nichols, Joan K. *Mary Shelley: Frankenstein's Creator.* Berkeley, California: Conari Press, 1998. 150pp. YA. Nichols deals honestly with the circumstances of Shelley's life and vividly portrays her social and intellectual background.

Biographical Films and Theatrical Adaptations

Gothic (1986). Director: Ken Russell. In Russell's phantasmagoric treatment of the night in 1816 when Mary Shelley (Natasha Richardson) conceived *Frankenstein*, Byron (Gabriel Byrne) is the evil genius behind their hallucinatory psychosexual experimentation. Julian Sands portays Percy Shelley. Video.

Haunted Summer (1988). Director: Ivan Passer. Film version of Anne Edwards's novel of the relationships among Byron (Philip Anglim), Shelley (Eric Stoltz), Mary Shelley (Alice Krige), and Claire Clairmont (Laura Dern) during their famous 1816 summer together is atmospheric but ultimately unconvincing. Video.

See also George Gordon, Lord Byron; Percy Bysshe Shelley; Mary Wollstonecraft

426. PERCY BYSSHE SHELLEY
1792–1822

One of the great English Romantic poets, Shelley was expelled from Oxford after co-publishing a pamphlet entitled *The Necessity of Atheism.* Dedicated to social and political reform, his first important poem, *Queen Mab* (1813), advocated the destruction of established institutions as a cure for so-

cial ills. His other works include *Prometheus Un-bound* (1820) and *Adonais* (1821), as well as the shorter poems "Ode to the West Wind," "To a Sky-lark," and "Ozymandias." He was drowned in a boating accident in Italy.

Autobiography and Primary Sources

The Letters of Percy Bysshe Shelley. Frederick L. Jones, ed. Oxford: Clarendon Press, 1964. 2 vols. This scholarly collection of the 700 extant letters cover Shelley's life from 1803 to his final note written four days before his death and reveals multiple sides of the poet as well as his relationships.

Shelley and His Circle. Kenneth N. Cameron and Donald H. Reiman, eds. Cambridge, Massachusetts: Harvard University Press, 1961–1986. 8 vols. Indispensable for the scholar and specialist these volumes collect all the existing documentary evidence on Shelley and his associates.

Recommended Biographies

Cameron, Kenneth N. *The Young Shelley: Genesis of a Radical.* New York: Macmillan, 1950. 437pp.; *Shelley: The Golden Years.* Cambridge, Massachusetts: Harvard University Press, 1974. 669pp. Cameron's heavily documented and scholarly critical biography traces clearly Shelley's intellectual and artistic development and the connection between his life and his work. One of the many excellencies in Cameron's achievement is its historical reconstruction that helps to make Shelley's life and activities clear, based on his reaction to the values and standards of his times.

Holmes, Richard. *Shelley: The Pursuit.* New York: Dutton, 1975. 829pp. Holmes's lively narrative will appeal to the general reader in search of an entertaining treatment of Shelley's remarkable life. Holmes offers a believable human portrait of a complex figure who is neither bathed in an admiring glow nor vilified for his shortcomings. The author's reflections on his efforts to uncover Shelley's personality and spirit are discussed in his interesting meditation on the biographer's art, *Footsteps: Adventures of a Romantic Biographer* (New York: Viking Press, 1985. 288pp.).

White, Newman I. *Shelley.* New York: Knopf, 1940. 2 vols. White's judicious and authoritative factual narrative remains the standard, scholarly life. The result of more than 20 years of labor and access to the poet's private papers, White documents clearly Shelley's activities and replaces the ineffectual angel image with a believable portrait of a working poet in the context of his times. A one-volume abridgement is also available as *A Portrait of Shelley* (New York: Knopf, 1945. 482pp.).

Other Biographical Studies

Blunden, Edmund. *Shelley: A Life Story.* New York: Viking, 1947. 388pp. Blunden, himself a highly regarded poet, supplies a succinct overview of the man and his works designed for the general reader. Often highly opinionated and informal, Blunden's insights retain their value in orienting the reader to an appreciation of Shelley's genius.

Dowden, Edward. *The Life of Percy Bysshe Shelley.* 1886. Reprint ed. New York: Barnes and No-

ble, 1966. 602pp. Dowden's biography, the first scholarly, full-length life, was authorized by Lady Jane Shelley and both profited from and was limited by his patron's involvement in the project. The book provides insights based on primary material and interviews with those who knew Shelley, but the interpretation lacks critical balance and sufficient candor to challenge the prevailing conception of the ethereal tragic poet.

Fuller, Jean O. *Shelley: A Biography.* London: Cape, 1968. 336pp. Fuller's is a highly opinionated review of the poet's life and significance. Not a good first book on the subject, it is, however, a lively and provocative reassessment with many insights from its original perspective.

Gittings, Robert, and Jo Manton. *Claire Clairmont and the Shelleys.* New York: Oxford University Press, 1992. 281pp. Gittings provides the book's account of the Shelleys' circle of family and friends, followed by Manton's presentation of the last 57 years of Mary Shelley's stepsister, Claire Clairmont.

Hogg, Thomas J. *The Life of Percy Bysshe Shelley.* 1858. Reprint ed. New York: Dutton, 1906. 585pp. Hogg, Shelley's Oxford classmate who was expelled along with the poet for atheistic views, portrays his former friend from the distance of his own eventual conventionality. Initially authorized by Shelley's heirs, their approval was withdrawn due to the unflattering light Hogg casts on their relationship.

Maurois, André. *Ariel: The Life of Shelley.* New York: Appleton, 1924. 334pp. Maurois's life could be classified as biographical fiction in its idealized, dramatic presentation that indulges in a great deal of imaginative conjecture supporting a view of Shelley that later critics and biographers have worked hard to correct.

Medwin, Thomas. *The Life of Percy Bysshe Shelley.* 1847. Revised ed. New York: Oxford University Press, 1913. 542pp. One of the earliest biographical accounts by Shelley's cousin and classmate at Eton, Medwin's recollections and reconstruction of the episodes in Shelley's life are not to be trusted and should be read with skepticism.

O'Neill, Michael. *Percy Bysshe Shelley: A Literary Life.* New York: St. Martin's, 1990. 176pp. O'Neill's book serves as a compact record of the major events of Shelley's life and the publication information on his works. Without venturing too deeply into Shelley's private life, this is more an account of the working poet and the intellectual, political, and social factors that shaped his art and ideas.

Peacock, Thomas Love. *Peacock's Memoirs of Shelley with Shelley's Letters to Peacock.* H.F.B. Brett-Smith, ed. London: H. Frowde, 1909. 219pp. Peacock's recollections are selective and chiefly valuable for their alternative view of Shelley's English activities.

Tomalin, Claire. *Shelley and His World.* New York: Scribner, 1980. 128pp. This compact illustrated biography includes a detailed chronology and a sensible overview of Shelley's life and times with excerpts from the poet's notebooks, letters, and poetry.

Trelawney, Edward J. *Recollections of the Last Days of Shelley and Byron.* 1858. Reprint ed. Williamstown, Massachusetts: Corner House, 1975. 304pp. Even though the author was on the scene during Shelley's final days, Trelawney's account is not trustworthy in its facts, interpretation of Shelley's character, or his portrayal of Mary Shelley during this period.

Biographical Novels

Bolton, Guy. *The Olympians.* Cleveland: World, 1961. 301pp. Bolton dramatizes the events leading up to Percy Shelley's elopement with Mary Godwin and its impact on the Godwin family.

Chernaik, Judith. *Love's Children.* New York: Knopf, 1992. 229pp. This group portrait of the women connected with Percy Shelley takes the shape of journal entries by Harriet Westbrook, Fanny Godwin, Claire Clairmont, and Mary Godwin.

Kenyon, Frank W. *The Golden Years: A Novel Based on the Life and Loves of Percy Bysshe Shelley.* New York: Crowell, 1959. 312pp. Shelley's life is dramatized from his college days, through his marriage to Harriet Westbrook and his elopement with Mary Godwin, to his death.

Fictional Portraits

Edwards, Anne. *Haunted Summer.* New York: Coward-McCann, 1972. 278p. The infamous summer holiday of 1816 in which Byron was joined in Switzerland by Percy and Mary Shelley forms the background for this fanciful gothic tale narrated by Mary.

Powers, Tim. *The Stress of Her Regard.* New York: Ace Books, 1989. 392pp. In this historical fantasy, a Regency-era doctor flees England to avoid a charge of murder. Haunted by guilt, he is aided by Keats, Byron, and Shelley in understanding his torment.

Seymour, Miranda. *Count Manfred.* New York: Coward-McCann & Geohegan, 1977. 283p. This gothic tale includes in its cast Byron and Percy and Mary Shelley with a reliable period background and actual details from Byron's life.

Recommended Juvenile Biographies

Rush, Philip. *The Young Shelley.* New York: Roy, 1962. 135pp. MG. Dealing with Shelley's schooldays, this brief biographical profile offers a summary of the poet's adult career in an epilogue.

Biographical Films and Theatrical Adaptations

Gothic (1986). Director: Ken Russell. In Russell's phantasmagoric treatment of the night in 1816 when Mary Shelley (Natasha Richardson) conceived *Frankenstein*, Byron (Gabriel Byrne) is the evil genius behind their hallucinatory psychosexual experimentation. Julian Sands portrays Shelley. Video.

Haunted Summer (1988). Director: Ivan Passer. Film version of Anne Edwards's novel of the relationships between Byron (Philip Anglim), Shelley (Eric Stoltz), Mary Shelley (Alice Krige), and

Claire Clairmont (Laura Dern) during their famous 1816 summer together is atmospheric but ultimately unconvincing. Video.

Percy Bysshe Shelley: Poet, 1792–1822 (1993). Director: Malcolm Hossick. A film portrait that chronicles Shelley's life through images of the poet, his times, and places associated with him. Video.

See also George Gordon, Lord Byron; John Keats; Mary Shelley

427. RICHARD BRINSLEY SHERIDAN
1751–1816

Irish-born dramatist and politician, Sheridan is famous for his witty comedies of manners, including *The Rivals* (1775), *The School for Scandal* (1777), and *The Critic* (1779). He was a Whig member of Parliament and served as secretary of the treasury, treasurer of the navy, and member of the Privy Council. He was a close friend of George IV when he was the prince regent and was part-owner and director of the new Drury Lane Theatre.

Autobiography and Primary Sources

The Letters of Richard Brinsley Sheridan. Cecil Prince, ed. Oxford: Clarendon Press, 1966. 3 vols. Essential for establishing the biographical record, Sheridan's letters are a rich source of insights into his nature and relationships.

Recommended Biographies

O'Toole, Fintan. *A Traitor's Kiss: The Life of Richard Brinsley Sheridan.* New York: Farrar, Straus, 1998. 519pp. O'Toole's recent biography leads the field in an excellent narrative life. Unlike other treatments that emphasize Sheridan's climb to literary fame and his rake's progress, O'Toole concentrates more on Sheridan's political and business career. The book succeeds in drawing a portrait of a complex man, shaped by his Irish background and reformist views, while struggling for London success. The book is particularly strong on Sheridan's complex romantic relationships and the social and political background that makes his actions comprehensible.

Other Biographical Studies

Bingham, Madeleine. *Sheridan: The Track of a Comet.* New York: St. Martin's, 1972. 383pp. Bingham's narrative account of Sheridan's life and career is connected by the suggestion that Sheridan was essentially an actor, able to play many roles and driven by social ambition. Somewhat oversimplified in its interpretation, the book manages a coherent portrait against a clear family and social background that makes Sheridan's motive and behavior understandable.

Butler, E.M. *Sheridan: A Ghost Story.* London: Constable, 1931. 312pp. Butler's interpretive study of Sheridan's life and work seeks to identify his character through his various roles and guises as playwright, politician, and wit. The first section of the book reviews previous biographies and studies

of Sheridan, illuminating their contradictions and failures to reveal the man fully.

Darlington, W.A. *Sheridan.* New York: Macmillan, 1933. 144pp. Darlington's brief, readable biographical portrait is intended as an objective assessment based only on reliable sources. The book largely succeeds in its aim and serves as a useful introduction that balances its attention equally between Sheridan's dramatic and political activities.

Foss, Kenelm. *Here Lies Richard Brinsley Sheridan.* New York: Dutton, 1940. 390pp. Foregoing a strict chronological approach for a topical one, Foss arranges his discussion of Sheridan in broad categories of his activities and interests. The book does not distinguish between hard evidence and debatable surmise, and the reader should look elsewhere for a succinct summary of Sheridan's activities.

Gibbs, Lewis. *Sheridan: His Life and His Theatre.* New York: Morrow, 1948. 280pp. In a sympathetic account, Gibbs presents Sheridan in his public roles as theater manager, playwright, and politician, with an emphasis on the latter. The book is more circumspect and discreet on Sheridan's private life.

Glasgow, Alice. *Sheridan of Drury Lane: A Biography.* New York: F.A. Stokes, 1940. 310pp. Closer to biographical fiction than nonfiction, Glasgow treats Sheridan as the colorful hero of a period romance. Since it is often impossible to separate fact from gossip, the reader looking for more than an entertaining narrative should approach the book with caution.

Moore, Thomas. *Memoirs of the Life of the Right Honourable Richard Brinsley Sheridan.* 1825. Reprint ed. Freeport, New York: Books for Libraries Press, 1971. 2 vols. Commissioned by Sheridan's second wife, Moore's biography makes use of the surviving papers and the author's own personal recollection of his subject. Despite this, Moore's treatment fails to penetrate very deeply the surface of Sheridan's career or to reveal the man in full.

Rhodes, R. Crompton. *Harlequin Sheridan: The Man and the Legends.* Oxford: Blackwell, 1933. 305pp. As the book's title indicates, Rhodes presents the various myths and masks disguising Sheridan's true identity. Although unable to resolve all Sheridan's contradictions, the book does clarify how he was viewed by his contemporaries.

Sherwin, Oscar. *Uncorking Old Sherry: The Life and Times of Richard Brinsley Sheridan.* New York: Twayne, 1960. 352pp. An informal biography that emphasizes his social milieu, Sherwin gathers the many anecdotes Sheridan prompted into an entertaining, discursive collection. The book provides little of substance on Sheridan's career as a playwright or politician.

Biographical Novels

Walker, Joan. *Marriage of Harlequin: A Biographical Novel of the Important Years in the Life of Richard Brinsley Sheridan.* Toronto: McClelland & Stewart, 1962. 256pp. Walker's fictionalized account is reasonably reliable in keeping to the biographical facts.

Fictional Portraits

Hardwick, Michael. *Regency Royal.* New York: Coward-McCann, 1978. 326pp. The career of George IV is presented with appearances by Sheridan as the Prince of Wales's companion.

Plaidy, Jean. *Perdita's Prince.* London: R. Hale, 1969. 346pp. Sheridan's relationship with the Prince of Wales is shown in this novel that centers on the future George IV's love affair with actress Mary Robinson. In *Goddess of the Green Room* (London: R. Hale, 1971. 351pp.), the longtime affair between William, Duke of Clarence, and actress Dorothy Jordon is dramatized, featuring a depiction of Sheridan.

Other Sources

Mikhail, E.H., ed. *Sheridan: Interviews and Recollections.* New York: St. Martin's, 1989. 152pp. This collection of contemporary views of Sheridan and his own words provides interesting glimpses of the man.

See also George IV

428. WILLIAM TECUMSEH SHERMAN
1820–1891

American Union general in the Civil War, Sherman was given command of the army of Tennessee and, with Ulysses S. Grant, took part in the Chattanooga Campaign. As supreme commander in the west, Sherman invaded Georgia, captured and burned Atlanta, and marched on Savannah. He pushed the Confederate army north, eventually accepting General Joseph Johnston's surrender at Durham, North Carolina. He later served as commander of the U.S. Army and refused the Republican nomination for president.

Autobiography and Primary Sources

Memoirs of General William T. Sherman. 1875. Reprint ed. New York: Library of America, 2 vols. An excellent starting point and an essential biographical source is Sherman's own vivid, controversial account of his life.

Sherman's Civil War: Selected Correspondence of William T. Sherman, 1860–1865. Brooks D. Simpson and Jean V. Berlin, eds. Chapel Hill: University of North Carolina Press, 1999. 948pp. This is a collection of more than 400 letters that reveal Sherman's thoughts on his battles and campaigns, much about his complex personality, and thoughts on such subjects as race relations, military strategy, the press, and Reconstruction.

Recommended Biographies

Fellman, Michael. *Citizen Sherman: A Life of William Tecumseh Sherman.* New York: Random House, 1995. 486pp. Fellman, in a well-documented interpretive study that emphasizes the private Sherman and his psychological makeup, produces a provocative portrait of a complex figure.

Hirshson, Stanley P. *The White Tecumseh: A Biography of General William T. Sherman.* New York:

Wiley, 1997. 475pp. Hirshson takes issue with the psychological speculation of Fellman and the interpretations of other historians and biographers in this strongly argued, opinionated reassessment in which the author defends Sherman against charges of racism and bad generalship. Not the ideal first Sherman biography, the book nevertheless provides a stimulating view on some of the central controversies surrounding the general's personality and career.

Lewis, Lloyd. *Sherman: Fighting Prophet.* New York: Harcourt, Brace, 1932. 690pp. Long serving as the standard biography, Lewis's account remains one of the best sources available, particularly on Sherman's life prior to 1861.

Other Biographical Studies

Athearn, Robert G. *William Tecumseh Sherman and the Settlement of the West.* Norman: University of Oklahoma Press, 1956. 371pp. A thorough and well-documented account of Sherman's career in the west, Athearn's meticulous study is the best reference source on this period of Sherman's life.

Coburn, Mark. *Terrible Innocence: General Sherman at War.* New York: Hippocrene Books, 1993. 248pp. Coburn covers Sherman's military activities from 1864 through 1865 in an informal account that displays both the general's personality and strategies.

Liddell Hart, B.H. *Sherman: Soldier, Realist, American.* New York: Dodd, Mead, 1929. 456pp. Sherman the strategist of modern warfare is the focus here in a biographical portrait that attempts to reveal Sherman's personality and achievement as a battlefield commander.

Marszalek, John F. *Sherman: A Soldier's Passion for Order.* New York: Free Press, 1993. 635pp. In an insightful, though at times reductive reassessment, Marszalek offers a controversial analysis of the sources for Sherman's ideas about warfare and his battlefield behavior in his early family background.

Merrill, James M. *William Tecumseh Sherman.* Chicago: Rand McNally, 1971. 445pp. Sherman's life, character, and military career is viewed against the background of his times. Based on extensive use of Sherman's letters, Merrill's popular biography humanizes the view of the stern commander with an emphasis on his family relationships and private side.

Miers, Earl S. *The General Who Marched to Hell.* New York: Knopf, 1951. 349pp. Focused on Sherman's 1864 campaign, this is a vividly written, objective assessment of his strategy and leadership, presenting both sides on the question of Sherman's performance of his duties.

Vetter, Charles E. *Sherman: Merchant of Terror, Advocate of Peace.* Gretna, Louisiana: Pelican, 1992. 347pp. Vetter supplies an account of Sherman's career and an intellectual profile of his ideas.

Fictional Portraits

Bass, Cynthia. *Sherman's March.* New York: Villard Books, 1994. 228pp. Sherman's campaign across Georgia in 1864 is depicted from three vantage points: Sherman's own, that of a captain in the

Union army, and that of a widowed southern farmwife and refugee.

Brick, John. *Jubilee.* Garden City, New York: Doubleday, 1956. 320pp. A New York Union officer sees action at Gettysburg before joining Sherman's army for the battles at Lookout Mountain and Atlanta and the march to the sea in this vivid fictional account.

Churchill, Winston. *The Crisis.* New York: Macmillan, 1903. 522pp. In one of the best Civil War novels, a young lawyer is on hand for some of the pivotal events of the war and meets many of its major figures, including Lincoln, Grant, and Sherman.

Johnston, Terry C. *The Shadow Riders.* New York: St. Martin's, 1991. 379pp. Sherman is in command of the U.S. army for the last great Indian uprising of the southern Plains tribes that culminates in the Battle of Adobe Walls.

Jones, Douglas C. *The Court-Martial of George Armstrong Custer.* New York: Scribner, 1976. 291pp. This intriguing what-if novel imagines Custer's survival after the Little Bighorn and the trial for his role in the disaster. The novel takes the form of a taut, psychological courtroom drama over the issue of Custer's character and military competence with a prominent role by Sherman.

Rawl, Miriam Freeman. *From the Ashes of Ruin.* Columbia, South Carolina: Summerhouse Press, 1999. 371pp. This novel exploring the devastation of Sherman's campaign in South Carolina features the actual correspondence between Sherman and Confederate general Hampton over the rules of engagement.

Recommended Juvenile Biographies

Blassingame, Wyatt. *William Tecumseh Sherman: Defender of the Union.* Englewood Cliffs, New Jersey: Prentice-Hall, 1970. 143pp. MG. Despite a heroic depiction, this is a detailed account of Sherman's military career.

Whitelaw, Nancy. *William Tecumseh Sherman: Defender and Destroyer.* Greensboro, North Carolina: Morgan Reynolds, 1996. 111pp. MG. Both the personal and military sides of Sherman, his strengths and weaknesses, are presented in this informative, sophisticated assessment that allows readers to draw their own conclusions.

Biographical Films and Theatrical Adaptations

Grant and Sherman (1997). Director: Tom DiPerna. The Union generals' careers are covered in this useful documentary profile. Video.

Other Sources

Wheeler, Richard, ed. *We Knew William Tecumseh Sherman.* New York: Crowell, 1977. 130pp. Wheeler has arranged a number of firsthand accounts of Sherman chronologically.

See also Ulysses S. Grant

429. SIR PHILIP SIDNEY
1554–1586

English author and courtier, Sidney was a favorite of Elizabeth I and a model of Renaissance chivalry. He strongly influenced English poetry through such works as *Arcadia* (1590), *Astrophel and Stella* (1591), and *The Defense of Poesie* (1595). He served in several diplomatic missions abroad and was fatally wounded at the battle of Zutphen.

Recommended Biographies

Duncan-Jones, Katherine. *Sir Philip Sidney: Courtier Poet.* New Haven, Connecticut: Yale University Press, 1991. 350pp. This is a fresh, carefully documented and generously illustrated study that relates the events and people in the author's life to his literary creation. Provocative in its psychological exploration, the author's analysis challenges conventional wisdom and offers a number of intriguing, revisionist interpretations. 13 Howell, Roger. *Sir Philip Sidney: The Shepherd Knight.* Boston: Little, Brown, 1968. 308pp. Divided into three main sections chronicling the phases of Sidney's career as courtier and diplomat, man of letters, and man of action, this succinct and sensible overview of the details of Sidney's various careers creates a rounded portrait of the man and his times. 13 Wallace, Malcolm W. *The Life of Sir Philip Sidney.* Cambridge: Cambridge University Press, 1915. 428pp. Long established as the standard, scholarly life, Wallace's is a straightforward, authoritative narrative of Sidney's career, with important insights into his family background and schooling.

Other Biographical Studies

Addleshaw, Percy. *Sir Philip Sidney.* 1909. Reprint ed. Port Washington, New York: Kennikat Press, 1970. 381pp. Addleshaw's critical assessment of Sidney's reputation is far more negative than other interpreters, stressing his human failings and his antipathy toward Catholics.

Berry, Edward. *The Making of Sir Philip Sidney.* Toronto: University of Toronto Press, 1999. 256pp. Combining biography, social history, and literary criticism, Berry explores how Sidney "made" or created himself as a poet by casting representations of himself in his literary creations.

Bill, Alfred H. *Astrophel: Or the Life and Death of the Renowned Sir Philip Sidney.* New York: Farrar & Rinehart, 1937. 372pp. The author narrates the story of Sidney's life set against a fully presented background of sixteenth-century history. The book is better on the times than the life.

Boas, F.S. *Sir Philip Sidney, Representative Elizabethan: His Life and Writings.* London: Staples Press, 1955. 204pp. Boas's succinct critical introduction is balanced in its approach and judicious in its interpretation and serves its purpose to highlight the full range of Sidney's ideas, works, and activities.

Bourne, Henry R.F. *Sir Philip Sidney: Type of English Chivalry in the Elizabethan Age.* New York: Putnam, 1891. 384pp. Bourne's influential nineteenth-century study helped expand the factual record based on important archival and documentary

sources, and his biography remained the standard source until Wallace.

Buxton, John. *Sir Philip Sidney and the English Renaissance.* New York: St. Martin's, 1954. 284pp. In a realistic assessment, Buxton examines Sidney's role as a literary patron, arguing his considerable influence on English poetry and drama. Reliable in its scholarship and sensible in its judgment, this is a valuable analysis of the literary aspects of Sidney's career.

Connell, Dorothy. *Sir Philip Sidney: The Maker's Mind.* Oxford: Clarendon Press, 1977. 163pp. Connell's brief critical study analyzes Sidney's style, critical theory, and creative method to suggest his "habit of mind," which is both unique to the man and representative of his age.

Denkinger, Emma M. *Immortal Sidney.* New York: Brentano's, 1931. 317pp. Denkinger's popular biography serves to orient the general reader to Sidney's life, work, and career against a vividly depicted period background.

Greville, Fulke. *Life of the Renowned Sir Philip Sidney.* 1652. Revised ed. as *Sir Fulke Greville's Life of Sir Philip Sidney.* Nowell Smith, ed. Oxford: Clarendon Press, 1907. 279pp. The earliest biography, Greville's highly laudatory tribute to his friend is not always factually trustworthy but remains important for its firsthand information and insights into Sidney's character, despite its lack of objectivity.

Hamilton, A.C. *Sir Philip Sidney: A Study of His Life and Work.* New York: Cambridge University Press, 1977. 216pp. The book argues that Sidney deserves to be regarded as the central figure of the English Renaissance and that his political and literary activities reveal the age's defining values. Hamilton's biographical summary is limited by its uncritical acceptance of many of the details concerning Sidney that have been called into question.

Kimbrough, Robert. *Sir Philip Sidney.* New York: Twayne, 1971. 162pp. Kimbrough's is a sensible and helpful critical introduction to Sidney's life and artistic career and the connection between the two.

Myrick, Kenneth. *Sir Philip Sidney as a Literary Craftsman.* Cambridge, Massachusetts: Harvard University Press, 1935. 362pp. Although chiefly a literary study, Myrick's analysis of Sidney's artistry does draw connections between his work and his life.

Osborn, James M. *Young Philip Sidney 1572–1577.* New Haven, Connecticut: Yale University Press, 1972. 565pp. This specialized study covers, in-depth, Sidney's European travels in the 1570s, based on previously unpublished letters. Osborn fills in the gaps in the biographical record with a vivid portrait of the historical background.

Warren, C. Henry. *Sir Philip Sidney: A Study in Conflict.* New York: T. Nelson, 1936. 246pp. Warren's interpretive biography looks at Sidney's role as a poet as the defining aspect of his identity, subjecting the known facts about Sidney's life to an interesting emphasis.

Wilson, Mona. *Sir Philip Sidney.* New York: Oxford University Press, 1932. 328pp. Although based mainly on Wallace for its facts, Wilson de-

votes more attention to Sidney's literary career and fashions a competent portrait based on the quality of thought and values his works reveal. Without sentimentality or idealization, Wilson allows the documentary evidence to speak for itself.

Fictional Portraits

Birkhead, Margaret. *Trust and Treason.* New York: St. Martin's, 1991. 384pp. This look at Elizabethan intrigue focuses on the prominent Woodfall family. Several prominent figures appear including Sidney, Robert Cecil, Christopher Hatton, and Frances Walsingham.

Finney, Patricia. *The Firedrake's Eye.* New York: St. Martin's, 1992. 263pp. This suspenseful Elizabethan thriller concerning a plot to assassinate Elizabeth I features appearances by a number of historical figures, such as Sidney, Raleigh, and Walsingham.

Fletcher, Inglis. *Roanoke Hundred.* Indianapolis: Bobbs-Merrill, 1948. 492pp. The founding of the first English settlement in North America on Roanoke Island off the coast of Virginia features a large cast of Elizabethan figures, including Sidney, Richard Grenville, Thomas Hariot, Richard Hooker, and Drake.

Foote, Dorothy N. *The Constant Star.* New York: Scribner, 1959. 340pp. Not reliable as history, the novel dramatizes the life of Frances Walsingham who marries two of Elizabethan England's most famous men, Sidney and the Earl of Essex.

Goudge, Elizabeth. *Towers in the Mist.* New York: Coward-McCann, 1938. 386pp. Elizabethan Oxford is the scene of this atmospheric novel that features Sidney and Raleigh as young scholars and a royal visit by Elizabeth I.

430. FRANK SINATRA
1915–1998

A popular and enduring American singer and film actor, Sinatra gained fame as a band singer with the Harry James and Tommy Dorsey bands before becoming a teenage idol as a solo performer. He made several musical films and distinguished himself as a fine dramatic actor in such movies as *From Here to Eternity* (1953), *The Manchurian Candidate* (1960), and *The Detective* (1968). Sinatra made concert tours during the last three decades of his life.

Recommended Biographies

Clarke, Donald. *All or Nothing at All: A Life of Frank Sinatra.* New York: Fromm International, 1997. 290pp. Clarke, an expert on popular music, does not avoid the tabloid or darker, private side of Sinatra's career but emphasizes his musical talents and development in a highly opinionated but sensible assessment. Clarke's focus on Sinatra's music helps to anchor this biography to the essential details of the singer's appeal and interest.

Freedland, Michael. *All the Way: A Biography of Frank Sinatra.* New York: St. Martin's, 1997. 438pp. Freedland's comprehensive biography offers a balanced and fair portrait, avoiding the excesses of either undue admiration or vilification. Sinatra's entire career is chronicled, with his various scandals not overwhelming a detailed examination of his musical and movie career and the source of Sinatra's talent and achievement.

Friedwald, Will. *Sinatra! The Song is You: The Singer's Art.* New York: Scribner, 1995. 557pp. Friedwald has chosen to emphasize the main reason anyone should be interested in Sinatra: his music. The book provides a meticulously detailed chronological assessment of Sinatra's musical career based on interviews with arrangers and musicians who worked with the singer. Friedwald clearly admires Sinatra's talent, but he is not reluctant to point out his occasional artistic mistakes.

Other Biographical Studies

Britt, Stan. *Frank Sinatra: A Celebration.* New York: Schirmer Books, 1995. 160pp. This illustrated tribute is organized by time periods and concludes each section with details on Sinatra's recordings, movies, and performances. Unfortunately, alongside a good deal of Sinatra facts and trivia are a number of errors in dates and details.

Coleman, Ray. *Sinatra: A Portrait of the Artist.* Atlanta: Turner, 1995. 192pp. This album of photographs is linked with a serviceable text that traces the highlights of Sinatra's long career.

Granata, Charles L. *Sessions with Sinatra: Frank Sinatra and the Art of Recording.* Chicago: A Cappella, 1999. 238pp. Instead of focusing on Sinatra's personalities and relationships, Granata looks closely at Sinatra as a singer and recording artist, drawing on all the extant unedited tapes of the performer's studio sessions. The book provides a unique history of Sinatra's life and the evolution of his art.

Hamill, Pete. *Why Sinatra Matters.* Boston: Little, Brown, 1998. 185pp. Hamill's biographical essay and cultural meditation traces Sinatra's career through the mid–1950s. In Hamill's view Sinatra's life represents the fulfillment of the American dream and his significance in creating a new sound, the "urban American voice." The book is intriguing in its focus on the larger cultural aspect of Sinatra's talent and success.

Holder, Deborah. *Completely Frank: The Life of Frank Sinatra.* Bloomsbury, 1997. 191pp. This is a workmanlike summary of Sinatra's childhood, crooning days, comeback as a movie star, and his public and private battles. Serves to orient the reader to the facts, if readers need reminding of such an overexposed life.

Kelley, Kitty. *His Way: The Unauthorized Biography of Frank Sinatra.* New York: Bantam, 1986. 575pp. Kelley confirms in detail the unflattering reputation of Sinatra for bad temper, errors of judgment, and excesses. Although full of matter, based on hundreds of interviews, providing a comprehensive chronicle of Sinatra's background, his rise to fame, and the turbulent holding onto the spotlight, the book is overly slanted toward the negative so that even his good deeds and virtues are given a sinister spin. The book confirms the tabloid headlines rather than introduces any new or startling revelations.

Lahr, John. *Sinatra: The Artist and the Man.* New York: Random House, 1997. 156pp. Lahr, the drama critic for *The New Yorker*, attempts to reconcile the contradictions between the sensitive musical interpreter and the insensitive bully but succeeds mainly in accentuating the paradoxes. More penetrating and revealing are the book's many behind-the-scenes photographs by Bob Willoughby and William Read Woodfield.

Rockwell, John. *Sinatra: An American Classic.* New York: Random House, 1984. 251pp. This illustrated biography features a brief text that highlights Sinatra's climb to fame and his various romances, alleged underworld ties, and brawls. Rockwell is best when focused on Sinatra the artist, the evolution of his musical style, and his groundbreaking 1950s recordings.

Shaw, Arnold. *Sinatra: Twentieth Century Romantic.* New York: Holt, 1968. 371pp. Shaw's flattering portrait chronicles Sinatra's career from his beginning in the 1930s up to the end of his marriage to Mia Farrow. The various scandals are put into perspective, and Shaw allows readers to form their own opinions of the inner man based on the facts supplied. Called a "retrospective cameo," *Sinatra: The Entertainer* (New York: Delilah Books, 1982. 155pp.) supplies a discursive appreciation of the man and his music.

Sinatra, Nancy. *Frank Sinatra: My Father.* Garden City, New York: Doubleday, 1985. 334pp.; *Frank Sinatra: An American Legend.* Los Angeles: General, 1998. 383pp. Nancy Sinatra's two tribute volumes (the second a revision and update of the first) accentuates the positive in rebuttal to the various negative charges against Sinatra that you would expect from an adoring daughter. Includes equally glowing recollections from individuals such as Doris Day, Bing Crosby, and Richard Nixon.

Sullivan, Robert. *Remembering Sinatra: A Life in Pictures.* New York: Time, Inc., 1998. 128pp. This tribute volume published immediately following Sinatra's death provides a visual record of Sinatra's life and career from the photo archives of Time-Life.

Taraborrelli, J. Randy. *Sinatra: Behind the Legend.* Secaucus, New Jersey: Carol, 1997. 547pp. Celebrity biographer Taraborelli rehashes the well-worn scandals and adds a few new charges, such as Sinatra's alleged affair with Jackie Kennedy. Taraborelli's advantage over Kitty Kelley's exposé is that he continues Sinatra's story into the 1990s. Readers fascinated with the private life of the pop icon will be intrigued; others will likely feel they have heard this all before.

Wilson, Earl. *Sinatra: An Unauthorized Biography.* New York: Macmillan, 1976. 357pp. Sinatra sued Wilson, calling his biography "false, fictionalized, boring, and uninteresting." Actually, the book is rarely boring as it is filled with anecdotes that reveal both sides of Sinatra: the charming and generous friend as well as the arrogant, vindictive enemy. Wilson fails to blend the two into a coherent development or interpretation.

Zehme, Bill. *The Way You Wear Your Hat.* New York: Macmillan, 1998. 385pp. Written with Sinatra's cooperation, this selective, informal biographical profile combines extensive personal details of Sinatra's likes and dislikes, photographs, and recollections from intimates such as Angie Dickinson, Tony Curtis, Robert Wagner, Joey Bishop, Tony Bennett, and Sinatra's daughters Nancy and Tina Sinatra. The emphasis is on the glamorous image, not the darker side of Sinatra's behavior and fame.

Recommended Juvenile Biographies

Hawes, Esme. *The Life and Times of Frank Sinatra.* New York: Chelsea House, 1997. 48pp. MG. Hawes covers the high points of Sinatra's career and his impact as a singer, actor, and popular icon.

Biographical Films and Theatrical Adaptations

A&E Biography Video: The Rat Pack: The True Stories of the Original Kings of Cool: Frank Sinatra, Dean Martin, Sammy Davis Jr., Peter Lawford, Joey Bishop (1999). A four-part video series that offers a group portrait of the entertainers in the 1950s and 1960s. Video.

Frank Sinatra: A Passionate Life. (1998). Producer: Rick Beeman. Sinatra's life and career are captured through songs, news and film clips, and interviews. Video.

Frank Sinatra: They Were Very Good Years (1997). Director: Ted Newsom. Multi-part video series covers Sinatra's career in depth. Video.

The Rat Pack (1996). Director: Rob Cohen. Sinatra during the Vegas years of the 1950s and early 1960s is the focus here that deals with the singer's support for Kennedy (William L. Petersen) that is complicated by Sinatra's mob ties. Ray Liotta stars as Sinatra, with Joe Mantegna as Dean Martin and Don Cheadle as Sammy Davis Jr. Video.

Sinatra (1992). Director: James Sadwith. This made-for-television biopic tracks Sinatra's life from childhood through his crooner days, movie career, and his three marriages. Philip Casnoff is convincing in the title role, supported by Olympia Dukakis, Joe Santos, Gina Gershon, and Rod Steiger. Video.

Sinatra: The Best is Yet to Come. (1999). Director: Jeff Margolis. This is a documentary film portrait covering the singer's career from interviews, film clips, archival photos, and performance footage. Video.

Other Sources

Mustazza, Leonard. *Ol' Blue Eyes: A Frank Sinatra Encyclopedia.* Westport, Connecticut: Greenwood, 1998. 436pp. Arranged alphabetically in sections on Sinatra's music, film, radio, and television appearances, this extensive reference source includes the first published listing of Internet resources.

Peters, Richard. *The Frank Sinatra Scrapbook: His Life and Times in Words and Pictures.* New York: St. Martin's, 1982. 158pp. The essential facts of Sinatra's life and career are covered in this miscellaneous collection of photos, reprinted magazine articles, and lists of recording sessions and movies.

Petkov, Steven, and Leonard Mustazza, eds. *The Frank Sinatra Reader.* New York: Oxford University Press, 1995. 297pp. In a collection of magazine articles and book excerpts by music critics and journalists, various aspects of Sinatra's career, musical development, and cultural appeal are explored.

Vare, Ethlie A., ed. *Legend: Frank Sinatra and the American Dream.* New York: Berkley Books, 1995. 222pp. This collection of journalistic articles and reflections by such individuals as Christopher Buckley, Harry Connick Jr., John Rockwell, Louella Parsons, and Rosalind Russell provides various perspectives on Sinatra's life and career.

431. SITTING BULL
ca. 1831–1890

A Sioux chief, Sitting Bull led the Indian forces that defeated and massacred General Custer's troops at the Battle of the Little Bighorn. He was later pardoned by the U.S. government and settled on a reservation. He appeared for a time in Buffalo Bill's Wild West Show. Accused of encouraging the Sioux to refuse sale of their lands and of practicing the ghost dance religion, he was killed while allegedly resisting arrest.

Recommended Biographies

Utley, Robert M. *The Lance and the Shield: The Life and Times of Sitting Bull.* New York: Holt, 1993. 413pp. Using Vestal's original notes, Utley supplements them with his own research into Sioux culture and the period to offer a fresh assessment viewing the man largely from the Lakota perspective, which has been described as the new standard against which all future lives of Sitting Bull will be measured.

Vestal, Stanley. *Sitting Bull, Champion of the Sioux: A Biography.* 1932. Revised ed. Norman: University of Oklahoma Press, 1980. 349pp. Vestal's highly readable, meticulously researched biography has long served as the definitive life. The book is based on many firsthand accounts by Sitting Bull's relatives and friends as well as a rich collection of contemporary sources.

Other Biographical Studies

Adams, Alexander B. *Sitting Bull: An Epic of the Plains.* New York: Putnam, 1973. 446pp. Supplementing his biographical profile of Sitting Bull with events in the history of the Sioux, Adams provides a fast-paced, popular narrative account, based on a judicious selection of primary and secondary sources.

Anderson, Gary C. *Sitting Bull and the Paradox of Lakota Nationhood.* New York: HarperCollins, 1996. 194pp. This is a stimulating historical study that relates Sitting Bull's career and leadership in the wider context of westward expansion and tribal affairs during the period.

Manzione, Joseph A. *"I Am Looking to the North for My Life"—Sitting Bull, 1876–1881.* Salt Lake City: University of Utah Press, 1991. 172pp. Manzione supplies a carefully documented account of Sitting Bull's activities during the five-year period following Little Bighorn up to his surrender. The book deals with the pursuit of Little

Bighorn refugees and the political wrangling over what should be done with them.

Biographical Novels

Dugan, Bill. *Sitting Bull.* New York: Harper, 1994. 308pp. In an account that is faithful to the known facts, Sitting Bull's career is dramatized from the 1830s to his death.

Jones, Douglas C. *Arresting Sitting Bull.* New York: Scribner, 1977. 249pp. Sitting Bull's sad end and the Indian unrest that culminates in the tragedy of Wounded Knee is dramatized in this convincing and compelling reconstruction and embellishment of actual events.

Skimin, Robert. *The River and the Horseman: A Novel of the Little Bighorn.* New York: Herodias, 1999. 364pp. This is a vivid recreation of the life and times of both Custer and Sitting Bull culminating in their confrontation on the battlefield.

Fictional Portraits

Berger, Thomas. *The Return of Little Big Man.* Boston: Little, Brown, 1999. 432pp. In this sequel to Berger's comic western classic, Jack Crabb continues his account of his eventful life after Little Bighorn with appearances by such western icons as Sitting Bull, Buffalo Bill, Wild Bill Hickok, Annie Oakley, and Wyatt Earp, all shown in Berger's patented revisionist, demythologizing style.

Blackburn, Thomas W. *A Good Day to Die.* New York: Leisure Books, 1996. 269pp. The events leading up to the Battle of Wounded Knee are dramatized, including Sitting Bull's last days, recorded by a newspaper reporter sent to the Dakota reservation to interview him.

Every, Dale Van. *The Day the Sun Died.* Boston: Little, Brown, 1971. 320pp. Indian affairs on the Great Plains from 1889 to Wounded Knee in 1891 are chronicled with a look at the dying Sitting Bull.

Haines, Edwin. *The Winter War.* Boston: Little, Brown, 1961. 247pp. The campaign against Sitting Bull after Little Bighorn is dramatized in this account of the army's pursuit of the Sioux and the Cheyenne during the winter of 1876.

McMurtry, Larry. *Buffalo Girls.* New York: Simon & Schuster, 1990. 351pp. Set in 1887 when Buffalo Bill's Wild West Show toured Europe, Sitting Bull is glimpsed in his role as traveling western icon.

Recommended Juvenile Biographies

Bernotas, Bob. *Sitting Bull: Chief of the Sioux.* New York: Chelsea House, 1992. 111pp. MG/YA. In a well-written account, Bernotas provides a great deal of information on tribal history and U.S. Indian policy while summarizing what we know about Sitting Bull's background and the main events of his life.

Marrin, Albert. *Sitting Bull and His World.* New York: Dutton, 2000. 256pp. YA. Marrin's informative, detailed portrait of Sitting Bull relates his career against a solidly developed period and cultural background.

St. George, Judith. *To See with the Heart: The Life of Sitting Bull.* New York: Putnam, 1996. 182pp.

MG. This is a compelling, readable, and detailed study of Sitting Bull's character, times, and culture.

Biographical Films and Theatrical Adaptations

A&E Biography Video: Sitting Bull: Chief of the Lakota Nation (1995). Director: Yann Debonne. Sitting Bull's career is depicted using archival material and expert testimony. Video.

Buffalo Bill & the Indians, or Sitting Bull's History Lesson (1976). Director: Robert Altman. Altman's comic take on western legend Buffalo Bill Cody (Paul Newman) shows him as a huckster and exploiter of the west and his own past. Sitting Bull appears played by Frank Kaquitts. An impressive ensemble cast includes Geraldine Chaplin, Joel Grey, Harvey Keitel, Burt Lancaster, and Kevin McCarthy. Video.

Buffalo Girls (1995). Director: Rod Hardy. This film adaptation of Larry McMurtry's novel concerning Calamity Jane (Anjelica Huston) and Wild Bill Hickok (Sam Elliott) includes a depiction of Sitting Bull, played by Russell Means. Video.

Son of the Morning Star (1991). Director: Mike Robe. This television adaptation of Evan S. Connell's book follows the facts of Custer's career faithfully, straying from the truth only in suggesting that Custer had fathered an illegitimate Indian child, a persistent myth that has been disputed. Gary Cole portrays a complex Custer with Rosanna Arquette as his wife. Sitting Bull is played by Floyd "Red Crow" Westerman. Video.

See also Crazy Horse; George Armstrong Custer

432. ADAM SMITH
1723–1790

Scottish economist, Smith is famous for his *The Wealth of Nations* (1776), a treatise advocating the free market that came to be regarded as the classic system of economics. Although some of his theories were negated by the Industrial Revolution, Smith's influence on later economics has never been surpassed. An earlier philosophical work, *Theory of Moral Sentiments* (1759), was written while Smith was a professor at the University of Glasgow.

Autobiography and Primary Sources

The Correspondence of Adam Smith. Ernest Campbell Mossner and Ian S. Ross, eds. Oxford: Clarendon Press, 1977. 441pp. Smith's letters are rarely revealing about his inner feelings, ideas, or work, but they do document his activities and relationships.

Recommended Biographies

Campbell, R.H., and A.S. Skinner. *Adam Smith.* New York: St. Martin's, 1982. 231pp. The authors supply a valuable introduction to the man and his works. Smith is shown as a student, teacher, and administrator, with highlights of his life in London, relationship with David Hume, and his European travels. Each of Smith's works is analyzed succinctly to trace the relationship between Smith's ethical and economic theories and his influence.

Ross, Ian Simpson. *The Life of Adam Smith*. New York: Oxford University Press, 1995. 495pp. Written by the co-editor of Smith's correspondence, Ross's exhaustive, authoritative full-scale biography supplies as much information as modern research and scholarship has discovered. Ross's thoroughness establishes this as the definitive biography.

Other Biographical Studies

Fay, Charles R. *Adam Smith and the Scotland of His Day*. Cambridge, Massachusetts: Cambridge University Press, 1956. 174pp. Fay compensates for a paucity of details on Smith's life by focusing on his Scottish background. Not chronologically but topically arranged, the book is an excellent presentation of the intellectual and social milieu that helps to explain Smith's development and achievement.

Haldane, R.B. *Life of Adam Smith*. London: W. Scott, 1887. 161pp. One of the first biographical portraits, Haldane adds certain details to the record from primary sources before proceeding to an evaluation of Smith's ideas and works.

Hirst, Francis W. *Adam Smith*. New York: Macmillan, 1904. 240pp. Adding little new to the biographical record established by Rae, Hirst's more compact study has mainly the virtue of its brevity to recommend it.

Rae, John. *Life of Adam Smith*. 1895. Expanded ed. New York: A.M. Kelley, 1965. 449pp. The first comprehensive biography, Rae's exhaustive assemblage of facts and anecdotes has long served as the standard source. A book more to refer to than to enjoy, the 1965 expanded edition features an essay by Jacob Viner summarizing biographical research since 1985.

Scott, William R. *Adam Smith as Student and Professor*. New York: A.M. Kelley, 1965. 445pp. Scott's scholarly examination of Smith's university career up to 1764 provides previously unpublished documents from university records at Glasgow and Edinburgh that the book reprints. Essential for readers interested in this period of Smith's career but overly specialized for the general reader.

West, E.G. *Adam Smith: The Man and His Works*. Indianapolis: Liberty Press, 1976. 254pp. West's uncritical appreciation of Smith's ideas and contribution does provide an accessible introduction but adds little to the biographical record. Good as a starting point.

433. JOHN SMITH
ca. 1580–1631

English adventurer and American colonist, Smith sailed (1606) to America, where he helped establish Jamestown in Virginia, England's first permanent North American colony. He explored the area and developed trade relations with the Native Americans. He was captured by Chief Powhatan and was probably saved from death by the chief's daughter, Pocahontas. Smith wrote several books

on his explorations, including *A Description of New England* (1616) and *The Generall Historie of Virginia, New-England, and the Summer Isles* (1624).

Autobiography and Primary Sources

The Complete Works of Captain John Smith 1580–1631. Philip L. Barbour, ed. Chapel Hill: University of North Carolina Press, 1986. 3 vols. The basis of almost all information about Smith's life and activities is contained in his accounts of his travels, the accuracy of which have continued to be debated by his biographers. Full of inaccuracies and inconsistencies, his collected works provide a fascinating personal record of his journeys and adventures.

Recommended Biographies

Barbour, Philip L. *The Three Worlds of Captain John Smith*. Boston: Houghton Mifflin, 1964. 553pp. Barbour's authoritative synthesis of modern scholarship establishes this as the definitive treatment of Smith's life and career. Careful in its surmises and enthusiastic yet balanced in its approach, Barbour's study locates Smith in the context of his age and submits Smith's own accounts to the proper test of credibility based on the careful sifting of primary and secondary sources.

Smith, Bradford. *Captain John Smith: His Life and Legend*. Philadelphia: Lippincott, 1953. 375pp. In a readable, scholarly biography the author scrupulously reviews the evidence concerning the trustworthiness of Smith's accounts, relying on the research of Laura Polyani Striker for the verification of much of Smith's Hungarian and Transylvanian adventures. Although largely superseded in its scholarship by Barbour, Smith's treatment retains its appeal and usefulness as a fair-minded and balanced account.

Vaughan, Alden T. *American Genesis: Captain John Smith as the Founder of Virginia*. Boston: Little, Brown, 1975. 207pp. Vaughan's fascinating study of Smith's life in Virginia considers the man "as a symbol of England's early imperial impulse... a man whose career illustrates a formative stage in our national identity." In Vaughan's view, Smith was transformed in Virginia from a self-seeking soldier of fortune into an American prototype.

Other Biographical Studies

Bradley, Arthur G. *Captain John Smith*. London: Macmillan, 1905. 226pp. Relying chiefly on Smith's own account this is a readable, though uncritical, summary of the chief events in his life.

Chatterton, E.K. *Captain John Smith*. New York: Harper, 1927. 286pp. Chatterton devotes a third of his biography to Smith's experiences in eastern Europe to help substantiate his overall truthfulness, arguing that he must have relied on his personal experiences since other accounts were unavailable to him. Chatterton then goes on to consider Smith's Jamestown experiences, accepting as authentic Smith's account of Pocahontas.

Emerson, Everett. *Captain John Smith*. New York: Twayne, 1971. 143pp. Emerson's critical biogra-

phy derives its data from Barbour but does make its own contribution by seeking to discover the essence of the man from a close reading of his writings. Serves as a useful overview and introduction.

Fletcher, John G. *John Smith—Also Pocahontas*. New York: Brentano's, 1928. 303pp. Fletcher presents a version of the human and realistic truth behind the various legends surrounding Smith. The result is a revisionist portrait of a considerably diminished adventurer, shown as brave, ambitious, daring, unscrupulous, and short-sighted.

Gerson, Noel B. *The Great Rogue: A Biography of Captain John Smith*. New York: McKay, 1966. 306pp. Gerson's straightforward, popular biography for the general reader is a mixture of fact and legend with little effort to distinguish the two. As the title indicates, the book features a partially debunking approach.

Hillard, George S. *Captain John Smith*. New York: Harper, 1902. 223pp. Like Woods, Hillard's review of Smith's career is a sympathetic treatment that corroborates the essential details of Smith's own account.

Lewis, Paul. *The Glorious Scoundrel: A Biography of Captain John Smith*. New York: Dodd, Mead, 1978. 251pp. Paul Lewis is one of many pseudonyms for the prolific popular writer Noel B. Gerson and this is an abridged rewrite of the author's 1966 popular biography.

Simms, William G. *The Life of Captain John Smith, the Founder of Virginia*. New York: A.L. Burt, 1846. 374pp. Simms's early biographical portrait closely follows Smith's own account, supplementing the adventurer's own words with imaginative and dramatic elaboration.

Woods, Katharine P. *The True Story of Captain John Smith*. New York: Doubleday, 1901. 382pp. Woods attempts to solve the issue of Smith's veracity by comparing his account to what is known from other sources. Concluding that Smith is believable, her book helped resuscitate Smith's reputation.

Biographical Novels

Bowman, John C. *Powhatan's Daughter*. New York: Viking, 1973. 336pp. Bowman's treatment of Smith's relationship with Pocahontas and her subsequent life in England is a blend of fact, legend, and imaginative elaboration.

Garnett, David. *Pocahontas; or, The Nonpareil of Virginia*. New York: Harcourt, Brace, 1933. 344pp. In a realistic portrait of life in Virginia during the era of its earliest European settlement, Pocahontas's life is depicted, with recorded facts supplemented with romantic invention.

Gerson, Noel B. *Daughter of Eve*. Garden City, New York: Doubleday, 1958. 320pp. Smith biographer Gerson dramatizes the relationship between Smith and Pocahontas, including scenes from the early life in the Jamestown settlement and Pocahontas's career in England as a curiosity. Considerable liberties have been taken with the biographical facts here.

Wohl, Burton. *Soldier in Paradise*. New York: Putnam, 1977. 345pp. Wohl gives a full-length, fictionalized portrait of Smith's remarkable career based on his own accounts but treated from a realistic perspective in which the adventurer is portrayed as a human mix of virtues and flaws.

Fictional Portraits

Barth, John. *The Sot-Weed Factor*. Garden City, New York: Doubleday, 1967. 756pp. Barth's wildly inventive comic treatment of colonial times features appearances by John Smith and Pocahontas with the author's unconventional spin on history.

Bernhard, Virginia. *A Durable Fire*. New York: Morrow, 1990. 384pp. Impressive re-creation of life in the Jamestown settlement includes depictions of Smith, Pocahontas, and John Rolfe.

Bourne, Peter. *Soldiers of Fortune*. London: Hutchinson, 1962. 256pp. This group portrait of the first colonists of Virginia combines Smith's story with those of a number of settlers from different stratas of English society during the period.

Donnell, Susan. *Pocahontas*. New York: Berkley, 1991. 456pp. In a speculative elaboration of Pocahontas's relationship with Smith and her later life in England with John Rolfe, Donnell emphasizes romance over historical accuracy.

Mason, F. van Wyck. *The Sea Venture*. Garden City, New York: Doubleday, 1961. 349pp. The story of the first settlement in Bermuda founded by George Somers is connected with the details of Somers's relief effort to aid Jamestown. Smith, Pocahontas, and Rolfe are depicted.

Recommended Juvenile Biographies

Fritz, Jean. *The Double Life of Pocahontas*. New York: Putnam, 1983. 96pp. MG. Fritz's is an engagingly written and well-researched biographical and historical narrative that covers both Pocahontas's life in America and England and Smith's adventures.

Syme, Ronald. *John Smith of Virginia*. New York: Morrow, 1954. 192pp. MG. This is a comprehensive account of Smith's activities as a soldier, navigator, and colonizer, with his character revealed through quotes from Smith's own writings.

Biographical Films and Theatrical Adaptations

A&E Biography Video: Pocahontas: Her True Story (1995). Director: Monte Markham. Pocahontas's relationship with John Smith is covered in this film biography of her life in America and England. Video.

Captain John Smith and Pocahontas (1953). Director: Lew Landers. Anthony Dexter stars as Smith in this predictable romantic version of the famous story, with Jody Lawrence as Pocahontas.

Pocahontas: The Legend (1995). Director: Daniele Suissa. Miles O'Keeffe portrays Smith in this live-action version of the story of his relationship with Pocahontas (Sandrine Holt). Video.

434. JOSEPH SMITH
1805–1844

The American founder of the Church of Jesus Christ of Latter-Day Saints, Smith claimed to have had a vision of golden tablets inscribed with sacred writings. He published the writings as the *Book of Mormon* (1829) and founded the Mormon church after he said an angel conferred priesthood upon him. Repeated persecutions forced Smith and his followers to settle in Nauvoo, Illinois, after obtaining a favorable state charter. After declaring himself a candidate for the U.S. presidency, anti-Mormons contrived his arrest on charges of treason and conspiracy. He was murdered by a mob while in jail.

Autobiography and Primary Sources

History of the Church of Jesus Christ of Latter-day Saints, Period 1. History of Joseph Smith, the Prophet, by Himself. Brigham H. Roberts, ed. Salt Lake City: Deseret Book Company, 1902–1912. 6 vols. Collects primary documents, the essential writings of Smith, excerpts from his diaries, and reminiscences by associates.

Joseph Smith: Selected Sermons and Writings. Robert L. Millet, ed. New York: Paulist Press, 1989. 266pp. Includes a selection of his letters and Smith's autobiographical reflections written in 1838 to explain himself and his principles.

Recommended Biographies

Brodie, Fawn M. *No Man Knows My History: The Life of Joseph Smith, the Mormon Prophet*. 1945. Revised ed. New York: Knopf, 1971. 499pp. Brodie's groundbreaking psychobiography is a thoroughly researched, objective exploration of Smith's character and psyche. Brodie, a former Mormon, offers credible suggestions about the cultural and psychological origin of Smith's religious experience and his development. Brodie's revision adds documentary evidence and additional support from psychological research to her controversial findings. Readers can also consult the volume, *Reconsidering No Man Knows My History: Fawn M. Brodie and Joseph Smith in Retrospect*. Newell G. Bringhust, ed. (Utah State University Press, 1996. 192pp.), for a collection of critical essays on Brodie's approach, her book, and its continuing importance.

Bushman, Richard L. *Joseph Smith and the Beginnings of Mormonism*. Urbana: University of Illinois Press, 1984. 262pp. This is the most detailed and perceptive portrait of Smith's family background and early life up to 1831. Bushman, a Mormon and a respected historian of colonial America, traces Smith's cultural background as well as his developing ideas that launched Mormonism. Smith is seen not as a collection of phobias but as a sincere visionary who "outgrew his culture," and the events of Smith's formative years are chronicled "as the participants themselves experienced them, using their own words where possible."

Hill, Donna. *Joseph Smith: The First Mormon*. Garden City, New York: Doubleday, 1977. 527pp. Hill's sympathetic though critical account of Smith's life and times is well-written and documented and treats fairly, if without resolution, the controversies surrounding Smith and his teachings. The book includes an appendix of short biographical sketches of Smith's adversaries, dissenters, and supporters.

Other Biographical Studies

Anderson, Robert D. *Inside the Mind of Joseph Smith: Psychobiography and the Book of Mormon*. Salt Lake City: Signature Books, 1999. 263pp. The work of a psychiatrist, Anderson's systematic psychobiographic study traces the record of Smith's psyche from the evidence contained in *The Book of Mormon*. With a solid grasp on early Mormon history Anderson provides a naturalistic explanation for the factors that possibly motivated Smith in his visionary conceptions.

Beardsley, Harry M. *Joseph Smith and His Mormon Empire*. Boston: Houghton Mifflin, 1931. 421pp. Like Riley, Beardsley supplies a psychological analysis of Smith, diagnosing him as either paranoid, schizophrenic, or a victim of dementia praecox. The book's strength is its solid historical background with which to view Smith.

Cannon, George O. *Life of Joseph Smith: The Prophet*. 1888. Reprint ed. Salt Lake City: Deseret, 1986. 562pp. Although the work of a devout disciple, Cannon's early hagiography is the first comprehensive portrait with details not reported elsewhere, drawn from firsthand accounts.

Evans, John H. *Joseph Smith: An American Prophet*. New York: Macmillan, 1933. 447pp. More sympathetic than other psychological and skeptical studies, Evans grants Smith's sincerity while placing his development in its cultural and historical context and demonstrating Smith's charismatic impact on his disciples. The book is arranged not chronologically but topically and is full of insights, although the reader should have a sense of Smith's history before reading.

Gibbons, Francis M. *Joseph Smith: Martyr: Prophet of God*. Salt Lake City: Deseret, 1977. 377pp. This partisan portrait offers little criticism but does provide a useful, though biased, summary of the major events in Smith's life.

Riley, I. Woodbridge. *The Founder of Mormonism: A Psychological Study of Joseph Smith*. New York: Dodd, Mead, 1902. 446pp. Riley offers a historical and psychological analysis for Smith's ideas and behavior, tracing the roots of Mormonism to the cultural attitudes of the times, identifying possible contemporary sources of *The Book of Mormon*, and attributing Smith's religious experience to epilepsy.

Smith, Lucy Mack. *Biographical Sketches of Joseph Smith, the Prophet*. 1853. Reprint ed. New York: Arno Press, 1969. 282pp. This memoir by Smith's mother is one of the essential sources for his family background and activities before 1830.

Stewart, John J. *Joseph Smith: The Mormon Prophet*. Salt Lake City: Mercury, 1966. 257pp. Stewart's defense of Smith's life and teaching is chiefly interesting for its perspective on the roots of Smith's negative reputation in his challenge to religious, political, and moral orthodoxy.

Taves, Ernest H. *Trouble Enough: Joseph Smith and the Book of Mormon.* Buffalo, New York: Prometheus Books, 1984. 280pp. Taves's specialized study focuses on the origins and authorship controversy over *The Book of Mormon.* Based on careful stylistic analysis, Taves concludes that Smith was likely its sole author.

Biographical Novels

Card, Orson Scott. *A Woman of Destiny.* New York: Berkley Books, 1984. 713pp. Card provides a sympathetic view of Smith in the fictionalized account of one of his wives.

Fisher, Vardis. *Children of God: An American Epic.* New York: Harper, 1939. 769pp. Fisher's panoramic narrative chronicles the founding of Mormonism from Smith's first visions through the religious persecution in the Midwest and the epic trek west led by Brigham Young.

Furnas, Joseph C. *The Devil's Rainbow.* New York: Harper, 1962. 341pp. Smith is portrayed from the perspective of a fictional protégé who records Smith's life from his first revelation to his murder. Somewhat oversimplified, Smith is presented as a paranoiac who helps bring about his own destruction.

Fictional Portraits

Lauritzen, Jonreed. *The Everlasting Fire.* Garden City, New York: Doubleday, 1962. 474pp. Focusing on the events of the Mormon migration west through the perspective of a fictional family who endure hostility and prejudice, the novel depicts the events leading up to Smith's murder and Brigham Young's rise to leadership.

Lund, Gerald N. *The Work and the Glory.* Salt Lake City: Bookcraft, 1990–1999 . 9 vols. Lund's multivolume family saga follows the lives and fortunes of the Steed family who meet Smith in Palmyra, New York, and become linked with Mormon history.

Pryor, Elinor. *And Never Yield.* New York: Macmillan, 1942. 520pp. Life among the Mormons in Missouri and Illinois during the 1830s and 1840s is portrayed through the experiences of a fictional couple. The major events are faithful to the historical record.

Biographical Films and Theatrical Adaptations

Brigham Young: Frontiersman (1940). Director: Henry Hathaway. Vincent Price portrays Smith with Dean Jagger in the title role in this dramatization of the history of the Mormons through the founding of Salt Lake City. Tyrone Power and Linda Darnell carry the nonhistorical load. Video.

Trail of Hope (1997). Director: Lee Groberg. This insightful PBS documentary traces the history of the Mormons and their trek west. The companion volume by Heidi S. Swinton, *American Prophet: The Story of Joseph Smith* (Salt Lake City: Shadow Mountain, 1999. 160pp.), reprints the film's commentary by leading historians, including Robert Remini. Video.

Other Sources

Conkling, J. Christopher. *A Joseph Smith Chronology.* Salt Lake City, Utah: Deseret, 1979. 276pp. This useful reference guide collects the basic facts of Smith's life without interpretation, in chronological order.

See also Brigham Young

435. BENEDICT DE SPINOZA
1623–1677

Dutch philosopher, Spinoza was expelled from the Jewish community of his native Amsterdam for his independence of thought. A rationalist and pantheist, he was influenced by Descartes but rejected Descartes's mind-body duality theory. Spinoza's most famous work is *Ethics* (1677).

Autobiography and Primary Sources

Letters. Steve Barbone, Lee Rice, and Jacop Adler, eds. Indianapolis: Hackett, 1995. 404pp. Spinoza's letters provide the essential biographical details and insights into his character.

Recommended Biographies

Gullan-Whur, Margaret. *Within Reason: A Life of Spinoza.* Chester Springs, Pennsylvania: Dufour Editions, 1998. 320pp. This scholarly examination traces how Spinoza's life is reflected in his writings and carefully describes his intellectual circle and the historical and cultural context of his age.

Nadler, Steven M. *Spinoza: A Life.* New York: Cambridge University Press, 1999. 407pp. Based on detailed period archival research, Nadler's well-written and authoritative life is aimed at the general reader and features a remarkable animation of seventeenth-century Dutch culture and politics and Jewish Amsterdam. Nadler explores Spinoza's relationship to his Jewish community and the possible reasons for his excommunication in 1656. The book also supplies an accessible introduction to Spinoza's philosophy.

Pollock, Frederick. *Spinoza: His Life and Philosophy.* New York: Macmillan, 1899. 427pp. Still considered one of the finest biographies of Spinoza, Pollock adds to the factual record through his use of Spinoza's letters. It includes the earliest biographical profile of Spinoza, written by Johannes Köhler, based on firsthand knowledge of the philosopher.

Wolfson, Abraham. *Spinoza: A Life of Reason.* 1932. Reprint ed. New York: Philosophical Library, 1969. 347pp. Wolfson weaves the little that is known about Spinoza into an effective narrative account. Beginning with the philosopher's ancestry, the book traces the development of his ideas and their connections with his experience and character.

Other Biographical Studies

Browne, Lewis. *Blessed Spinoza: A Biography of the Philosopher.* New York: Macmillan, 1932. 334pp. Offering little on his philosophy, this narrative biography emphasizes Spinoza's hardships and persecution and overall goodness, relying on surmises for most of the details on the philosopher's youth and personality.

Martineau, James. *A Study of Spinoza.* London: Macmillan, 1882. 371pp. Martineau's study includes a compact biographical survey along with a vivid depiction of his background in the *marranos* community, development as a thinker, and Spinoza's scientific interests.

Roth, Leon. *Spinoza.* Boston: Little, Brown, 1929. 250pp. In a workmanlike general account of Spinoza's life, character, and ideas, Roth allows the philosopher to speak for himself through extensive quotations from his works and letters connected by a running commentary.

Scruton, Roger. *Spinoza.* New York: Oxford University Press, 1986. 122pp. This brief introductory study synthesizes a number of secondary sources to present Spinoza's life and ideas in an accessible but at times oversimplified fashion.

Fictional Portraits

Weiss, David. *I, Rembrandt.* New York: St. Martin's, 1979. 342pp. Rembrandt narrates the story of his life at the age of 48 in 1654 as he undertakes some of his greatest work. The novel features a speculative friendship between the painter and Spinoza.

Other Sources

Garrett, Don, ed. *The Cambridge Companion to Spinoza.* New York: Cambridge University Press, 1996. 433pp. This useful collection of critical essays explores different aspects of Spinoza's life and character, and the emergence of his philosophical system.

436. JOSEPH STALIN
1879–1953

Soviet dictator, Stalin was born Josif Dzhugashvili, the son of a Georgian shoemaker. He studied for the priesthood but was expelled from divinity school and became a committed Marxist and a disciple of Lenin. He changed his name to Stalin ("man of steel") about 1913. He took power after Lenin's death (1924) and proved equally ruthless in domestic and foreign affairs. Stalin's mass purges during the 1930s resulted in the imprisonment, exile, and execution of millions of Soviet citizens. He invaded eastern Poland and Finland, imposed communism on the Baltic states, expanded Soviet influence into the countries of eastern Europe after World War II, and pursued hardline Cold War policies abroad.

Recommended Biographies

McNeal, Robert H. *Stalin: Man and Ruler.* New York: New York University Press, 1988. 389pp. In a challenging reexamination, McNeal uses the new materials that have emerged since Stalin's death to produce a strikingly different human portrait. Without whitewashing his considerable crimes, McNeal adds dimension to the conventional portrayal of Stalin's monstrousness, granting him political skills and understandable human traits.

Radzinsky, Edvard. *Stalin: The First In-Depth Biography Based on Explosive New Documents from Russia's Secret Archives.* New York: Doubleday, 1996. 607pp. This gripping narrative biography, drawing on newly available sources, traces the consistency in Stalin's development and behavior that challenges the accumulated myths that have obscured Stalin's character, motives, and behavior.

Tucker, Robert C. *Stalin as Revolutionary: 1878–1929.* New York: W.W. Norton, 1973. 519pp.; *Stalin in Power: The Revolution from Above: 1928–1941.* New York: W.W. Norton, 1990. 707pp. Tucker's two completed volumes of a projected narrative and interpretive trilogy are impressive achievements, solidly researched and argued, connecting Stalin's personal story with its wider historical, political, and cultural context.

Ulam, Adam B. *Stalin: The Man and His Era.* New York: Viking, 1973. 760pp. Ulam's comprehensive biography and history of the Russian Revolution and the Soviet regime up to Stalin's death supplies one of the fullest portraits available of Stalin's political development, his relationship with Lenin, the reasons for the Great Purge, and Stalin's wartime leadership. In Ulam's view, it is the banality of Stalin's evil that predominates over a more complex explanation of the man and his career.

Other Biographical Studies

Bullock, Alan. *Hitler and Stalin: Parallel Lives.* New York: Knopf, 1992. 1,081pp. Bullock's fascinating dual biography offers a step-by-step progression of both leaders in gaining and using power. Both are chillingly shown as products of their time, not as unique monster figures.

Carrère d'Encausse, Hélène. *Stalin: Order through Terror.* New York: Longman, 1981. 269pp. The author's interpretive biographical portrait offers plausible suggestions to explain Stalin's often contradictory behavior and motives.

Conquest, Robert. *Stalin: Breaker of Nations.* New York: Viking, 1991. 346pp. Intended for the general reader, this carefully researched and well-written portrait of the man and history of his career places Stalin in a broad historical and cultural perspective. Conquest is less successful in dealing with Stalin's ascent to power, but the book is loaded with fascinating incidents and anecdotes of Stalin's rule.

Deutscher, Isaac. *Stalin: A Political Biography.* 1949. Revised ed. New York: Oxford University Press, 1967. 661pp. In this massive, lucid, and highly readable political biography, Deutscher objectively assesses Stalin's part in the Russian Revolution and his subsequent leadership with psychological insight and a firm historical perspective. The emphasis here is Stalin the ruler rather than the man.

Fischer, Louis. *The Life and Death of Stalin.* New York: Harper, 1952. 272pp. Fischer's journalistic account based on extended stays in Russia in the 1920s and 1930s is best in its vivid depiction of the Soviet leadership circles. Stalin is shown in his political role, and the private figure remains shadowy with attempts at psychoanalytical interpretation of his personality inadequate.

Hingley, Ronald. *Joseph Stalin: Man and Legend.* New York: McGraw-Hill, 1974. 482pp. Hingley's revisionist study sets out to redress the balance by granting Stalin's achievement as a leader who consolidated Lenin's faltering Bolshevik state into a great world power. However, the author is as severe in dismissing the positive legends as the negative ones, substituting a realistic, fair assessment in their place.

Laqueur, Walter. *Stalin: The Glasnost Revelations.* New York: Scribner, 1990. 382pp. This reassessment based on previously unavailable Russian sources captures Stalin and his career from a variety of angles. The book is less successful as a sustained biographical portrait. Rather it collects a series of new and old impressions that need a fuller and more systematic interpretive unity.

Lewis, Jonathan, and Phillip Whitehead. *Stalin: A Time for Judgement.* New York: Pantheon, 1990. 254pp. A companion volume to a British television documentary series on Stalin's reign, the book includes excerpts from survivors of the purges.

Medvedev, Roy A. *On Stalin and Stalinism.* New York: Oxford University Press, 1979. 205pp. Medvedev, a Soviet historian, provides new information based on interviews of Stalin's associates and formerly restricted archival material. In the author's view, Stalin subverted the goals of the revolution, and his crimes overwhelm his achievements.

Payne, Robert. *The Rise and Fall of Stalin.* New York: Simon & Schuster, 1965. 767pp. Payne's overstuffed biography collects facts and legends and reaches a number of questionable conclusions based on scanty or suspect evidence. In need of editing, the book gives similar emphasis to important and unimportant details, along with repetition and contradictions.

Slusser, Robert M. *Stalin in October: The Man Who Missed the Revolution.* Baltimore: Johns Hopkins University Press, 1987. 281pp. Slusser's specialized study is devoted to Stalin's role in the Bolshevik Revolution between March and October 1917 and his relationship with Lenin and Trotsky. Contrary to Soviet propaganda and Stalin's own contentions, Slusser convincingly argues that Stalin's role was insignificant, a fact that prompted his purge of those that knew this to be the case.

Smith, Edward. *The Young Stalin: The Early Years of an Elusive Revolutionary.* New York: Farrar, Straus, 1967. 470pp. Smith reconstructs the details of Stalin's life up to the age of 37, based partly on his czarist police file. Smith hypothesizes that Stalin had contacts with and was possibly employed by the secret police. Other revelations include Stalin's early anti-Semitism and the importance of the death of Stalin's first wife in 1907 as a turning point in his career. Although much evidence has been suppressed by Stalin himself, Smith provides interesting and plausible conjectures for gaps in the record that locate the basis of Stalin's character and political successes in his earliest experiences.

Trotsky, Leon. *Stalin: An Appraisal of the Man and His Influence.* 1941. Revised ed. New York: Stein and Day, 1967. 516pp. Written by Stalin's great enemy whose death Stalin ordered, Trotsky's assessment of Stalin's career and character has fascinat-

ing behind-the-scenes and personal views unavailable from any other source.

Volkogonov, Dmitrii A. *Stalin: Triumph and Tragedy.* New York: Grove Weidenfeld, 1991. 642pp. The author eliminates any doubt about Stalin's responsibility in countless deaths, based on an examination of his personal papers with his marginal comments or initials on mass execution lists. Valuable for its unique archival material, the book is less successful as a fully realized biographical study.

Warth, Robert D. *Joseph Stalin.* New York: Twayne, 1969. 176pp. Serving as a concise introduction to Stalin's life and political career, Warth's is an objective and thoughtful assessment that avoids speculation and remains close to the documented evidence.

Biographical Novels

Jones, Mervyn. *Joseph.* New York: Atheneum, 1970. 506pp. Stalin's life is dramatized from his days as a poor seminary student through the events of the Russian Revolution, civil war, and party intrigue that makes him one of history's most powerful dictators. Blending the known and the imagined, the novel attempts to trace the psychological factors that explain Stalin's motives and behavior.

Krotkov, Yuri. *The Red Monarch: Scenes from the Life of Stalin.* New York: W.W. Norton, 1979. 253pp. In a chronological account of Stalin's life through a series of real and imagined vignettes, scenes include Mao's visit to the Soviet Union in 1949, the Teheran Conference, Stalin's wife's suicide, and his death.

Lourie, Richard. *The Autobiography of Joseph Stalin.* Washington, DC: Counterpoint, 1999. 261pp. In the 1930s as Stalin obsesses over Trotsky's rumored biography of him, the Soviet dictator offers his own version of his life story in a convincing portrayal of a man consumed by a need for power and control and devoid of any principles or humanity.

Fictional Portraits

Aksyonov, Vassily. *Generations of Winter.* New York: Random House, 1994. 656pp.; *The Winter's Hero.* Random House, 1996. 496pp. This family saga offers a convincing panoramic view of Stalin's growing power and oppression.

Littell, Robert. *The Revolutionist: A Novel of Russia.* New York: Bantam Books, 1988. 467pp. In a blend of fact and fiction the events of the Russian Revolution and the creation of the Soviet state are detailed up to the death of Stalin.

Meade, Glenn. *Snow Wolf.* New York: St. Martin's, 1996. 432pp. This inventive thriller concerns the shadowy rumors surrounding Stalin's death.

Rkybakov, Anatoli. *Children of the Arbat.* Boston: Little, Brown, 1988. 685pp.; *Fear.* Boston: Little, Brown, 1992. 686pp.; *Dust and Ashes.* Boston: Little, Brown, 1996. 480pp. Rybakov's remarkable Arbat Trilogy provides a detailed examination of life in Russia during Stalin's rule.

Trifonov, Yuri. *Disappearance.* Ann Arbor, Michigan: Ardis, 1991. 181pp. The events of the Great Terror and Stalin's purges in the 1930s are depicted through the experiences of a Russian family.

Wright, Patricia. *Journey into Fire*. Garden City, New York: Doubleday, 1977. 391pp. The survival of a Russian musician and his wife during the Russian Revolution and its aftermath is dramatized.

Recommended Juvenile Biographies

Caulkins, Janet. *Joseph Stalin*. New York: F. Watts, 1990. 160pp. MG/YA. Caulkins's is a lucid account of Stalin's life and Soviet history that emphasizes Stalin's role as an agent of change.

Marrin, Albert. *Stalin*. New York: Viking Kestral, 1988. 244pp. MG/YA. Marrin's is the most detailed biographical and historical account of Stalin's life and times available for younger readers. Balanced and informative, the book manages a sophisticated view of Stalin's character and times.

Otfinoski, Steven. *Joseph Stalin: Russia's Last Czar*. Brookfield, Connecticut: Millbrook Press, 1993. 128pp. MG/YA. Covering Stalin's entire life, this is a balanced and skillful account that allows the human side of Stalin's character to emerge.

Biographical Films and Theatrical Adaptations

A&E Biography Video: Joseph Stalin: Red Terror (1996). Producer: Alison Guss. This film portrait covers both Stalin's career and his impact through archival footage and testimony by experts. Video.

Children of the Revolution (1996). Director: Peter Duncan. This satirical Australian film imagines a passionate Stalinist (Judy Davis) who becomes the dictator's lover and bears him a son who grows up reflecting his father's behavior. F. Murray Abraham portrays Stalin. Video.

Hitler and Stalin (1993). Producer: CBS News. Using film clips and interviews with experts, this is a film overview of the life, relationship, and impact of the two leaders, co-hosted by Charles Kuralt and Norman Schwarzkopf. Video.

The Inner Circle (1991). Director: Andrei Konchalovsky. Based on the life of the actual projectionist who ran movies for Stalin from 1935 to the dictator's death, this interesting film captures life within the Kremlin during Stalin's reign. With Bob Hoskins, Tom Hulce, and Lolita Davidovich. Video.

Joseph Stalin (1963). Director: Jack Haley. In this installment of television's *Biography* series hosted by Mike Wallace, Stalin's ruthlessness is emphasized in this profile. Video.

Red Tsar (1984). Director: Julia Spark. Segment of the television program, *History in Action*. Video.

Stalin (1991). Director: Ivan Passer. Featuring actual Russian locations, this biographical film covers Stalin's public and private life with a convincing portrayal by Robert Duvall in the lead role. Video.

Stalin: Man and Image (1975). Producer: Nielson-Ferns International. Canadian television production narrated by Henry Fonda. Video.

Testimony (1987). Director: Tony Palmer. This biographical portrait of composer Dmitri Shostakovich (Ben Kingsley) treats his political conflicts, with Terence Rigby as Stalin.

The Warlords (1986). Producer: Lamancha Productions. This series of brief film biographies of World War II leaders, such as Hitler, DeGaulle, Mussolini, and Churchill, includes a portrait of Stalin. Video.

World War II: When Lions Roared (1994). Director: Joseph Sargent. The conduct of the war from the perspective of the Allied leaders is dramatized. Bob Hoskins portrays Churchill; Michael Caine is Stalin, and John Lithgow is Franklin Roosevelt. Video.

Other Sources

Rappaport, Helen. *Joseph Stalin: A Biographical Companion*. Santa Barbara, California: ABC-CLIO, 1999. 372pp. This reference source features alphabetically arranged entries on the many figures associated with Stalin and his era.

See also Vladimir Lenin; Leon Trotsky

437. SIR HENRY M. STANLEY
1841–1904

An Anglo-American journalist and explorer, Stanley fought in the Civil War for both Union and Confederate armies and afterwards worked for the New York *Herald*. The newspaper sent him to Africa to find the missionary and explorer, David Livingstone. Their famous meeting took place on the shores of Lake Tanganyika. He later led several African expeditions, organized the future Independent State of the Congo, and helped to ensure British influence in Uganda.

Autobiography and Primary Sources

Autobiography of Henry Morton Stanley. 1909. Reprint ed. Boston: Houghton Mifflin, 1970. 551pp. Stanley's unfinished memoir was published posthumously, edited and sanitized by Stanley's wife who helped to preserve the positive self-image that Stanley worked hard to foster while concealing details about his background and activities. Stanley's own accounts of his African experiences— *How I Found Livingstone* (New York: Scribner, 1874. 736pp.); *Through the Dark Continent*. (1878. Reprint ed. New York: Greenwood, 1969. 2 vols.); and *In Darkest Africa* (New York: Scribner, 1890. 2 vols.)—are equally slanted and should be read alongside more objective accounts.

Recommended Biographies

Farwell, Byron. *The Man Who Presumed: A Biography of Henry M. Stanley*. New York: Holt, 1957. 334pp. This is a full-length biography that reveals the details of Stanley's life that he concealed, including his bitter childhood, his service in the American Civil War, and his relationships. The result is a sympathetic though realistic and balanced assessment.

Hall, Richard S. *Stanley: An Adventurer Explored*. Boston: Houghton Mifflin, 1975. 400pp. Drawing on the important manuscript sources, Hall's is the most comprehensive and authoritative biography available. As one reviewer pointed out, Hall "grasps the essence of Stanley's heretofore elusive

personality and for the first time the great explorer and journalist becomes an understandable, human figure."

Other Biographical Studies

Anstruther, Ian. *Dr. Livingstone, I Presume?* New York: Dutton, 1957. 207pp. Anstruther sheds some light on Stanley's character and does not disguise his flaws, but the account only covers in full Stanley's life up to 1874.

Busoni, Rafaello. *Stanley's Africa*. New York: Viking, 1944. 288pp. Busoni's highly fictionalized, impressionistic narrative of Stanley's African travels is chiefly redeemed by its illustrations.

Hird, Frank. *H.M. Stanley: The Authorized Life*. London: Stanley Paul, 1935. 320pp. Hird adds some documentary evidence to the picture of Stanley, but his account falls short of a fully authoritative humanized view. The book is still more a memorial than an objective study.

Sterling, Thomas. *Stanley's Way: A Sentimental Journey Through Central Africa*. New York: Atheneum, 1960. 258pp. The author retraces Stanley's steps through Africa, offering an unorthodox travelogue with often-deflating comments on Stanley's heroics.

Wassermann, Jakob. *Bula Matari: Stanley, Conqueror of a Continent*. New York: Liveright, 1933. 351pp. Although depending on Stanley's accounts for its facts, this is an often-intriguing but highly speculative early psychological profile that reveals a mixed figure.

Biographical Novels

Forbath, Peter. *The Last Hero*. New York: Simon & Schuster, 1988. 729pp. Scrupulous in its faithfulness to the facts, the novel dramatizes the expedition led by Stanley up the Congo to Emir Pasha's beleaguered garrison after the fall of Khartoum in 1885.

Fictional Portraits

Hagerfors, Lennart. *The Whales of Lake Tanganyika*. New York: Grove Press, 1989. 172pp. This is a fictional retelling of Stanley's 1871 expedition to find Livingstone from the perspective of a British sailor who offers a realistic view of both men.

Recommended Juvenile Biographies

Cohen, Daniel. *Henry Stanley and the Quest for the Source of the Nile*. New York: Evans, 1985. 175pp. MG. Cohen summarizes Stanley's explorations in a vivid, dramatic narrative account.

Clinton, Susan. *Henry Stanley and David Livingstone*. Chicago: Childrens Press, 1990. 128pp. MG. Clinton's dual biography tracks the accomplishments of both men in the context of African exploration.

Sherman, Steven. *Henry Stanley and the European Explorers of Africa*. New York: Chelsea House, 1993. 111pp. MG/YA. Stanley's explorations are described along with the discoveries of Mungo Park and David Livingstone.

Biographical Films and Theatrical Adaptations

Henry Morton Stanley (1976). Director: Fred Burnley. Dramatizes Stanley's expedition in search of the headwaters of the Lualaba River, narrated by Anthony Quinn. Video.

Stanley and Livingstone (1939). Director: Henry King. This heroic interpretation of Stanley's search for Livingstone is more legendary than reliable. Spencer Tracy is the pursuer, and Cedric Hardwicke is the pursued Livingstone. Video.

See also David Livingstone

438. GERTRUDE STEIN
1874–1946

American author and patron of the arts, Stein lived chiefly in Paris, where she encouraged, aided, and influenced such literary and artistic figures as Ernest Hemingway, F. Scott Fitzgerald, Pablo Picasso, and Henri Matisse. It was Stein who coined the phrase the "lost generation" to describe post–World War I American expatriate writers. Her longtime secretary and lover was Alice B. Toklas. Stein's innovative writings were known for experimental syntax and include *Three Lives* (1909) and *The Autobiography of Alice B. Toklas* (1933).

Autobiography and Primary Sources

The Autobiography of Alice B. Toklas. 1933. New York: Modern Library, 1980. 252pp. Stein's most popular work is her recollections and observations on expatriate life in Paris, modern art, and a number of prominent figures rendered from the perspective of her longtime companion and lover.

Everybody's Autobiography. New York: Random House, 1937. 318pp. Stein's sequel to *The Autobiography of Alice B. Toklas* is concerned chiefly with her visit to America after the success of her earlier book.

Stein's personal writings are collected in several volumes, including *Dear Sammy: Letters from Gertrude Stein and Alice B. Toklas.* M. Steward, ed. (Boston: Houghton Mifflin, 1977. 260 pp.); *The Letters of Gertrude Stein and Carl Van Vechten: 1913–1946.* Edward Burns, ed. (New York: Columbia University Press, 1986. 2 vols.); and *The Letters of Gertrude Stein and Thornton Wilder.* Edward Burns and Ulla E. Dydo, eds. (New Haven, Connecticut: Yale University Press, 1996. 452 pp.).

Recommended Biographies

Hobhouse, Janet. *Everybody Who Was Anybody: A Biography of Gertrude Stein.* New York: Putnam, 1975. 244pp. Hobhouse's compact, excellently illustrated, critical biography tells the story of Stein's life and artistic development largely through an examination of the writer's various relationships: with her brother, Toklas, Picasso and the cubists, Hemingway, and other artists of the Lost Generation.

Mellow, James R. *Charmed Circle: Gertrude Stein and Company.* New York: Praeger, 1974. 528pp. Mellow's is the most thorough and authoritative bi-

ography of Stein. As its title indicates, the book relates Stein's life and work to the wider context of her artistic and cultural milieu. The connection helps to explain Stein's interests and activities in the wider currents of modernism.

Wagner-Martin, Linda. *"Favored Strangers": Gertrude Stein and Her Family.* New Brunswick, New Jersey: Rutgers University Press, 1995. 346pp. Drawing on previously unavailable family papers, Wagner-Martin emphasizes Stein's German-Jewish family background, her relationship with her older brothers, Michael and Leo, and her early feminist and lesbian experiences to trace her personal and artistic development. Full of fresh anecdotes and details, the book offers an original, nuanced portrait that stands in marked contrast with previous biographical treatments.

Wineapple, Brenda. *Sister Brother: Gertrude and Leo Stein.* New York: Putnam, 1996. 514pp. Wineapple's impressive biographical study of Stein's relationship with her brother is particularly strong on the pair's upbringing in Oakland, California, and the years up to 1910 when the formerly symbiotic pair began their long estrangement.

Other Biographical Studies

Bridgman, Richard. *Gertrude Stein in Pieces.* New York: Oxford University Press, 1970. 411pp. Bridgman's critical study of Stein's published and unpublished works traces her artistic development and relates her production to the events of her life. Although not a full-scale literary biography, the book remains one of the finest critical studies available that succeeds in providing a valuable framework for appreciating her achievement and connecting the various stages of her career.

Brinnin, John M. *The Third Rose: Gertrude Stein and Her World.* Boston: Little, Brown, 1959. 427pp. Brinnin's influential critical biography is detailed and thorough, although its scholarship and reliability has been superseded by later, more careful studies that have better separated the legendary and self-serving details of Stein's own account from the facts and offer a more acute critical assessment of her literary achievement.

Knapp, Bettina L. *Gertrude Stein.* New York: Continuum, 1990. 201pp. Knapp supplies a good introduction of Stein's life and works with a succinct biographical section (mainly the years in France) followed by a survey of the writer's important works.

Rogers, William G. *When This You See Remember Me: Gertrude Stein in Person.* New York: Rinehart, 1948. 247pp. Based on the author's affectionate recollections of time spent with Stein and their correspondence that is included, Rogers supplies an intimate biographical portrait concerned mainly with the author's personal qualities and characteristics.

Souhami, Diana. *Gertrude and Alice.* New York: HarperCollins, 1991. 300pp. In a balanced, dual biography that focuses on the relationship between Stein and Toklas, Souhami supplies a useful synthesis of source materials that serves as an informative, anecdotally rich introduction to the pair for the general reader.

Sprigge, Elizabeth. *Gertrude Stein: Her Life and Work.* New York: Harper, 1957. 277pp. The first full-scale critical biography, Sprigge's life does provide significant factual details from archival research, but often relies uncritically on Stein's own account to trace her subject's development.

Stewart, Allegra. *Gertrude Stein and the Present.* Cambridge, Massachusetts: Harvard University Press, 1967. 223pp. Stewart's critical analysis of Stein's writing includes a valuable biographical chapter that considers the writer's family background, education, and scientific and philosophical interests.

Toklas, Alice B. *What Is Remembered.* New York: Holt, 1963. 186pp. Toklas's autobiography is rarely analytical or revelatory but supplies interesting details on the couple's relationship and life together, as well as the many important figures that they hosted.

Fictional Portraits

Carlile, Clancy. *The Paris Pilgrims.* New York: Carroll & Graf, 1999. 496pp. This documentary novel is set in Paris during Hemingway's first stay there in 1922 and features appearances by virtually every figure associated with the expatriate scene and the Lost Generation, including Stein and Toklas.

Engel, Howard. *Murder in Montparnasse.* Woodstock, New York: Overlook Press, 1999. 304pp. This inventive period mystery mixes such real figures as James Joyce, Ezra Pound, Stein, and Toklas with a Hemingway-esque figure and fictional characters from *The Sun Also Rises* in a witty literary thriller.

Longstreet, Stephen. *The Burning Man.* New York: Random House, 1958. 428pp. Longstreet's fictionalized life of a Spanish artist who closely resembles Picasso offers glimpses of a number of actual figures, including Apollinaire, Matisse, and Stein.

Roosevelt, Elliott. *Murder in the Chateau.* New York: St. Martin's, 1996. 200pp. In this installment of the Eleanor Roosevelt mystery series, the first lady is in occupied France where she meets Erwin Rommel and Stein in a far-fetched period mystery.

Steward, Samuel M. *Murder Is Murder Is Murder.* Boston: Alyson, 1985. 189pp.; *The Caravaggio Shawl.* Boston: Alyson, 1989. 209pp. Steward's mystery series employs Stein and Toklas as sleuths during the 1930s.

Recommended Juvenile Biographies

Greenfeld, Howard. *Gertrude Stein: A Biography.* New York: Crown, 1973. 151pp. YA. Greenfield supplies a workmanlike summary of the highlights of Stein's career with an emphasis on her early Paris years and her relationship with Alice B. Toklas.

La Farge, Ann. *Gertrude Stein.* New York: Chelsea House, 1988. 111pp. MG/YA. Part of the American Women of Achievement series, this is an informative biographical profile of Stein's life and artistic impact.

Rogers, William G. *Gertrude Stein Is Gertrude Stein Is Gertrude Stein.* New York: Crowell, 1973.

237pp. YA. Stein's life and work are set in their wider historical and cultural contexts, and the book includes firsthand recollections by the author who maintained a friendship with the writer from World War I until her death.

Biographical Films and Theatrical Adaptations

Martin, Marty. *Gertrude Stein, Gertrude Stein, Gertrude Stein: A One-character Play.* New York: Vintage Books, 1980. 60pp. The text of the popular one-person stage show starring Pat Carroll.

Gertrude Stein: When You See This, Remember Me (1970). Director: Perry M. Adato. This is a film version of Stein's autobiography with passages from her writings, photographs, film footage, and interviews with those who knew the writer, including Virgil Thomson and Jean Genet. Video.

The Moderns (1988). Director: Alan Rudolph. Both Hemingway (Kevin O'Connor) and Stein (Elsa Raven) are portrayed in this romanticized period drama of expatriate life in 1926 Paris. Starring Keith Carradine, Linda Fiorentino, and Geraldine Chaplin. Video.

Waiting for the Moon (1986). Director: Jill Godmilow. This PBS production dramatizes the relationship between Stein (Linda Bassett) and Alice B. Toklas (Linda Hunt). Video.

Other Sources

Kellner, Bruce, ed. *A Gertrude Stein Companion: Content with the Example.* New York: Greenwood, 1988. 352pp. This reference volume of critical essays on Stein includes an extensive biographical dictionary of her circle, and a selection of her remarks on a variety of topics.

Simon, Linda, ed. *Gertrude Stein Remembered.* Lincoln: University of Nebraska Press, 1994. 195pp. Collects reminiscences from individuals who knew Stein at various points in her career from her student days in the United States to her final years in Paris.

Stendhal, Renate, ed. *Gertrude Stein in Words and Pictures: A Photobiography.* Chapel Hill, North Carolina: Algonquin Books, 1994. 286pp. This handsome collection of photographs is connected by selections from Stein's own writings and others' recollections of her.

See also Ernest Hemingway

439. STENDHAL (MARIE HENRI BEYLE)
1783–1842

French novelist and a pioneer of the psychological novel, Stendahl's youth in Grenoble was marked by hatred of his father and of the Jesuit, Royalist atmosphere in his home. He went to Paris, where he obtained a position at the ministry of war and served as a dragoon in Napoleon's army. During the reign of Louis Philippe he served as consul in Trieste and Civitavecchia, returning to Paris a few months before his death. His works include *The*

Red and the Black (1830) and *The Charterhouse of Parma* (1839).

Autobiography and Primary Sources

The Life of Henry Brulard. Chicago: University of Chicago Press, 1986. 347pp. Stendhal's unfinished autobiography was begun in November 1835 and abandoned the following March. The work provides valuable glimpses of the writer's self-assessment.

The Private Diaries of Stendhal. Robert Sage, ed. New York: W.W. Norton, 1962. 556pp. Indispensable as a biographical source, Stendhal's diaries show him to be one of the most persistently self-analytical writers.

To the Happy Few: Selected Letters. E. Boudot-Lamotte, ed. New York: Grove Press, 1955. 384pp. As with his fragmentary autobiography and diaries, Stendhal's letters are essential sources for biographical insight into the multiple personas of the man.

Recommended Biographies

Alter, Robert, with Carol Cosman. *A Lion for Love: A Critical Biography of Stendhal.* New York: Basic Books, 1979. 285pp. Alter's study, conducted with the assistance of his wife, is a superior effort of compression and judicious interpretation. Stendhal is examined in his various guises and in his careers as critic, journalist, travel writer, and novelist. Without undue simplification, the book offers a reliable means to see Stendhal whole, with his complexity intact.

Keates, Jonathan. *Stendhal.* New York: Carroll & Graf, 1997. 477pp. Keates, both a novelist and biographer, supplies a highly readable, richly detailed narrative biography that relates Stendhal's development to his political and cultural background. Keates shows the connections as well as the differences between Stendhal's life and character and his fiction. Readers already familiar with *The Red and the Black* and *The Charterhouse of Parma* will be best served by Keates's study.

Other Biographical Studies

Fowlie, Wallace. *Stendhal.* New York: Macmillan, 1969. 240pp. Part of the Masters of World Literature series, this introductory critical biography is a useful synthesis of prevailing critical views that stresses the influence of Stendhal's life and personality on his writing and philosophy.

Green, F.C. *Stendhal.* Cambridge, Massachusetts: Cambridge University Press, 1939. 336pp. Green's biography is the first in English to examine the full range of Stendhal's works and begin to draw the appropriate connections between their creation and the writer's experiences. Conjecture is identified as such, and if the book falls short of a fully satisfying scholarly approach, it does still serve as an accessible, perceptive, and readable overview of Stendhal's career.

Hemmings, F.W.J. *Stendhal: A Study of His Novels.* Oxford: Clarendon Press, 1964. 232pp. Hemmings's important critical study of Stendhal's four great novels supplies a good deal of information about the writer's creative process, personal-

ity, and what the novels reveal about Stendhal's biography.

Josephson, Matthew. *Stendhal: Or the Pursuit of Happiness.* Garden City, New York: Doubleday, 1946. 489pp. Josephson's thorough account displays the writer from various angles in a readable narrative, skillfully assembling appropriate primary material that does justice to Stendhal's full career.

Kayser, Rudolf. *Stendhal: The Life of an Egoist.* New York: Holt, 1930. 278pp. Kayser's mainly novelized biography attempts to animate Stendhal's personality against a vivid depiction of the crucial events of his life. Selective, and with insufficient attention to Stendhal's writing, Kayser's treatment is more entertaining than useful in supplying a complete and reliable portrait.

May, Gita. *Stendhal and the Age of Napoleon.* New York: Columbia University Press, 1977. 332pp. The complex interplay between Stendhal's personality and history is the book's focus. May is strongest on background elements, although the core of Stendhal's identity eludes her grasp, and the discussion of his works repeats familiar views.

Richardson, Joanna. *Stendhal.* New York: Coward-McCann, 1974. 344pp. Richardson stresses not Stendhal the literary figure but Stendhal the man, offering glimpses of his personality from his letters and diaries. This limited approach leaves a number of questions concerning Stendhal's development unaddressed.

Strickland, Geoffrey. *Stendhal: The Education of a Novelist.* New York: Cambridge University Press, 1974. 302pp. Strickland's intellectual biography traces the stages of Stendhal's development as a critic, moral philosopher, and imaginative artist. Objective, concise, and lucid, Strickland's study sets Stendhal in a broad intellectual context and supplies a provocative and coherent means to understand his development.

Tillett, Margaret G. *Stendhal: The Background to the Novels.* New York: Oxford University Press, 1971. 157pp. Addressed to the general reader, Tillett's compact critical introduction supplies the necessary background for an appreciation of Stendhal's novels, examining each in their political, social, and personal context.

Wood, Michael. *Stendhal.* Ithaca, New York: Cornell University Press, 1971. 208pp. Like Tillett's study, Wood's is a valuable introductory study that serves to orient the reader to Stendhal's literary work, career, and life.

Fictional Portraits

Rambaud, Patrick. *The Battle.* New York: Grove Press, 2000. 256pp. In Rambaud's acclaimed reconstruction of the bloody Battle of Essling in 1809, Stendhal is featured in a subplot, waiting in Vienna for news of the battle while consumed by passion for a beautiful Austrian woman, Anna Krauss.

440. LAURENCE STERNE
1713–1768

English novelist Sterne became an Anglican clergyman, served in a Yorkshire parish, and then went to London, where he was a great social success. The first volume of his masterpiece *Tristram Shandy* (1760) was denounced by such celebrated literary figures as Samuel Johnson and Horace Walpole but was widely read. Eight more volumes followed (1781-1767). After leading a rather dissolute life, during which he frequently suffered from ill health, Sterne died of tuberculosis.

Autobiography and Primary Sources

Letters. L.P. Curtis, ed. Oxford: Clarendon Press, 1935. 495pp. Sterne's 222 surviving letters are reprinted in this scholarly edition.

Recommended Biographies

Cash, Arthur H. *Laurence Sterne.* London: Methuen, 1975–1986. 2 vols. Cash's authoritative, comprehensive life is widely regarded as the definitive modern biography. Cash's Sterne is considerably darker and more realistic than the version offered by Cross and most other interpreters. Judicious in its views and balanced, Sterne becomes a multidimensional, complex figure in Cash's competent presentation.

Cross, Wilbur L. *The Life and Times of Laurence Sterne.* 1909. Revised ed. New Haven, Connecticut: Yale University Press, 1929. 670pp. Before Cash, Cross's study was the standard biography and the fullest and most authoritative presentation of Sterne's life, career, and relationships.

Hartley, Lodwick. *This is Lorence: A Narrative of the Reverend Laurence Sterne.* 1943. Revised ed. as *Laurence Sterne: A Biographical Essay.* Chapel Hill: University of North Carolina Press, 1968. 302pp. Hartley's informal and lively overview of Sterne's life and works is recommended for general readers looking for an entertaining introduction.

Thomson, David. *Wild Excursions: The Life and Fiction of Laurence Sterne.* New York: McGraw-Hill, 1972. 325pp. Thomson's lively and provocative critical biography attempts to resuscitate Sterne's relevance for a modern reader even as he portrays him as an unreliable, evasive man. Many of Thomson's views are debatable, but he is rarely dull, and the book is a good choice to sample the flavor of the man and his achievement.

Other Biographical Studies

Connely, Willard. *Laurence Sterne as Yorick.* London: Bodley Head, 1958. 240pp. Restricted to the last nine years of Sterne's life, Connely provides a reliable summary for the general reader against a solid social and cultural background.

Fitzgerald, Percy H. *The Life of Laurence Sterne.* 1864. Revised ed. London: Downey, 1896. 2 vols. Despite some useful information about Sterne's travels in France, Fitzgerald's early study is marred by errors of fact and a lack of critical balance in its interpretation.

Melville, Lewis. *The Life and Letters of Laurence Sterne.* London: S. Paul, 1911. 2 vols. Melville's extensive reliance on Sterne's letters allows the author to tell his own story.

Sichel, Walter S. *Sterne: A Study.* Philadelphia: Lippincott, 1910. 360pp. Providing little that is new or original, besides two new letters and making Sterne's *Journal to Eliza* more accessible to readers, Sichel recycles familiar views of the man and an overly hostile critical estimation.

Traill, H.D. *The Life of Laurence Sterne.* 1882. Reprint ed. New York: AMS Press, 1968. 176pp. Traill's brief biographical profile is incomplete, focused almost exclusively on Sterne's years as an author.

Yoseloff, Thomas. *A Fellow of Infinite Jest.* New York: Prentice-Hall, 1945. 232pp. This popular biography adds nothing to the record besides evidence of the author's own enthusiasm. While rarely very subtle or profound, Yoseloff's straightforward narrative at least has the merits of liveliness.

Biographical Novels

Bill, Alfred H. *Alas, Poor Yorick!* Boston: Little, Brown, 1927. 263pp. The novel imagines three episodes from Sterne's life.

441. WALLACE STEVENS
1879–1955

American poet whose verse is rich in imagery and ideas, Stevens worked for a Hartford insurance company from 1916 until his death. He achieved literary recognition only after winning the 1955 Pulitzer Prize for his *Collected Poems.* Other poetry volumes include *Harmonium* (1923) and *Transport to Summer* (1947).

Autobiography and Primary Sources

Letters of Wallace Stevens. Holly Stevens, ed. New York: Knopf, 1966. 890pp. A collection of 800 letters covers 60 years of Stevens's life from 1895 to his death, along with extracts from the poet's unpublished journal. The letters touch on Stevens's poetic practices, the development of his ideas on truth, imagination, and reality, and his reflections on the events of his life.

Recommended Biographies

Bates, Milton. *Wallace Stevens: A Mythology of Self.* Berkeley: University of California Press, 1985. 319pp. Bates's comprehensive biographical study portrays Stevens as a man of multiple identities, a role player whose many sides were refracted in the parts he scrupulously performed throughout his life. Drawing mainly on Stevens's letters, Bates's study is a fascinating, plausible attempt to penetrate the psyche of a closely guarded, private sensibility.

Brazeau, Peter. *Parts of a World: Wallace Stevens Remembered: An Oral Biography.* New York: Random House, 1983. 330pp. Stevens is portrayed from a variety of angles in this collection of reminiscences from more than 150 scholars, family members, neighbors, business associates, and friends. Rich in anecdotes and details of Stevens's professional life and character, Stevens's public persona rather than his private, creative life is interestingly displayed.

Richardson, Joan. *Wallace Stevens.* New York: Beech Tree, 1986–1988. 2 vols. By far the most comprehensive and authoritative biography, Richardson's study shows in great detail the evolution of Stevens's genius, his poetic development, and his often guarded and concealed multiple identities. Volume one covers Stevens's formative years up to 1923; volume two, the years of his maturity from the publication of *Harmonium* in 1923 to his death. Richardson challenges a number of popular notions concerning the poet and displays with considerable skill and judiciousness his complex and often contradictory nature.

Other Biographical Studies

Lensing, George A. *Wallace Stevens: A Poet's Growth.* Baton Rouge: Louisiana State University Press, 1986. 313pp. In a series of thematic chapters, Lensing traces Stevens's development in an intellectual biography that presents the sources of the poet's inspiration and compositional method derived from his letters, journals, notebooks, and his annotations in his books.

Morse, Samuel French. *Wallace Stevens: Poetry as Life.* New York: Pegasus, 1970. 232pp. Morse relates the events of Stevens's life to his poetic development in this brief critical introduction to the poet's ideas and creative method, authorized by Stevens's widow and daughter. The details of Stevens's life are exclusively those that shed light on his poetic career.

Sharpe, Tony. *Wallace Stevens: A Literary Life.* New York: St. Martin's, 1999. 240pp. Sharpe's critical intellectual biography challenges the conventional portrait of Stevens as a conservative, detached, poetry-writing insurance executive, substituting instead a man in turmoil and an important American intellectual. This scholarly work assembles a great number of anecdotes and details of Stevens's life that are then used to help explain the significance of his ideas and his poetry. A solid grounding in Stevens's works is essential for a full appreciation of Sharpe's study.

Stevens, Holly. *Souvenirs and Prophecies: The Young Wallace Stevens.* New York: Knopf, 1977. 288pp. Stevens's daughter supplies a revealing portrait of the poet's formative years based largely on his journals that he began as a Harvard sophomore in 1898 to 1914 and his first published poetry. Despite heavy editing of the most personal portions of Stevens's letters and journals, the book supplies a fascinating look at the poet's artistic and professional development.

Biographical Films and Theatrical Adaptations

Wallace Stevens: Man Made Out of Words (1987). Director: Richard P. Rogers. This segment of the Voices and Visions poetry series explores Stevens's life and work with commentary by Helen Vendler, Mark Strand, James Merrill, Joan Richardson, and Harold Bloom. Video.

Other Sources

Doggett, Frank, and Robert Battel, ed. *Wallace Stevens: A Celebration*. Princeton, New Jersey: Princeton University Press, 1980. 361pp. Honoring the centennial of the poet's birth, this valuable collection of essays focuses on Stevens's personality and life as well as his poetry.

442. ROBERT LOUIS STEVENSON
1850–1894

Scottish novelist, poet, and essayist, Stevenson was admitted to the bar but never practiced. He published essays and stories, such as "A Lodging for the Night," in various periodicals, but his first popular success came with publication of the novels *Treasure Island* (1883) and the fantasy *Prince Otto* (1885). In 1889 Stevenson settled in Samoa with his family. Other well-known works by Stevenson include *A Child's Garden of Verses* (1885), *Kidnapped* (1886), and *The Strange Case of Dr. Jekyll and Mr. Hyde* (1886).

Autobiography and Primary Sources

The Letters of Robert Louis Stevenson. Bradford A. Booth and Ernest Mehew, eds. New Haven, Connecticut: Yale University Press, 1994–1995. 8 vols. This impressive definitive edition of Stevenson's letters includes substantial commentary that constitutes a full biographical portrait, anchored by the writer's own words and views of his constantly shifting moods.

Selected Letters of Robert Louis Stevenson. Ernest Mehew, ed. New Haven, Connecticut: Yale University Press, 1997. 626pp. Containing 317 of Stevenson's most interesting and revealing letters, this is the recommended book for the reader unable or unwilling to tackle the more than 2,800 letters contained in the eight-volume scholarly edition.

Recommended Biographies

Bell, Ian. *Dream of Exile: Robert Louis Stevenson: A Biography*. New York: Holt, 1993. 296pp. Bell's brief, sympathetic but balanced biography is the work of a Scottish journalist, and, although it does not attempt scholarly thoroughness or documentation, it does provide a sensible, judicious assessment of the writer's personality, his circle, and literary career.

Calder, Jenni. *Robert Louis Stevenson: A Life Study*. New York: Oxford University Press, 1980. 362pp. Calder's is an extremely competent, well-written account of the relationship between Stevenson's life and work, particularly strong on the writer's Scottish background and the biographical sources for his stories and fictional characters.

Furnas, J.C. *Voyage to Windward: The Life of Robert Louis Stevenson*. New York: Simon & Schuster, 1951. 478pp. Furnas's interpretive chronological account is thorough, balanced, and unsentimental, and is one of the most readable chronicles of Stevenson's life. Drawing on much unpublished material, and particularly strong on Stevenson's American and Pacific activities, the book is a masterful three-dimensional portrait of a complex figure.

McLynn, F.J. *Robert Louis Stevenson: A Biography*. New York: Random House, 1994. 587pp. Thoroughly detailed and controversial in its insights into Stevenson's relationship with his wife, McLynn presents a complex portrait of a divided man.

Other Biographical Studies

Balfour, Sir Graham. *Life of Robert Louis Stevenson*. New York: Scribner, 1901. 2 vols. The official biography contracted by Stevenson's wife, Balfour's is a solid, if uninspired, account by one of the writer's cousins. More reverent than candid, particularly on the writer's less-respectable behavior, Balfour's life still includes useful information not available elsewhere.

Bevan, Bryan. *Robert Louis Stevenson: Poet and Teller of Tales*. New York: St. Martin's, 1992. 197pp. Bevan's compact biography is a fine choice for a sensible, balanced overview of the writer's life and literary career for the general reader.

Carré, Jean-Marie. *The Frail Warrior: A Life of Robert Louis Stevenson*. New York: Coward-McCann, 1930. 297pp. The author attempts an intermediate portrait somewhere between the angelic figure presented by Balfour and the more realistic view of Steuart. Readable and thorough, at least concerning Stevenson's maturity, the book occasionally falters into melodrama, and, as its title indicates, Stevenson is shown as more pathetic than heroic.

Daiches, David. *Robert Louis Stevenson and His World*. London: Thames and Hudson, 1973. 128pp. Daiches's illustrated biography links a series of photographs and drawings of the author, his associates, haunts, and travel destinations with a sensible biographical overview.

Davies, Hunter. *The Teller of Tales: In Search of Robert Louis Stevenson*. New York: Interlink Books, 1996. 321pp. Recounting Stevenson's life as well as the author's own visits to places where the writer lived, biographical chapters alternate with "letters" to Stevenson, informing him "what's been happening to some of the places you once knew so well."

Mackay, Margaret. *The Violent Friend: The Story of Mrs. Robert Louis Stevenson*. Garden City, New York: Doubleday, 1968. 566pp. The book's biographical portrait of Stevenson's wife is loaded with details of the writer's private life, his travels, and illness. Long resented by Stevenson's admirers, Fanny Stevenson emerges from the writer's shadow, and Mackay offers a very different view of the couple's relationship than previous treatments.

Masson, Rosaline O. *I Can Remember Robert Louis Stevenson*. New York: F.A. Stokes, 1922. 369pp. This collection of personal memories of the writer's relatives, schoolmates, friends, and acquaintances supplies a number of interesting, though rarely critical or penetrating views of the writer at various stages of his development. In *Life of Robert Louis Stevenson* (New York: F.A. Stokes, 1923. 358pp.) Masson followed her compilation of reminiscences with a full-length biography that reinforces the romantic image of Stevenson that he helped to fashion and later biographers have challenged. The book is mainly valu-

able for its details of the writer's boyhood and Edinburgh period.

Osbourne, Lloyd. *An Intimate Portrait of R.L.S.* New York: Scribner, 1924. 155pp. Stevenson's stepson provides his recollection of life in the writer's household and the family's travels. Impressionistic and affectionate with no attempt at completeness, the book supplies an interesting collection of episodes and details of Stevenson's personality and private life.

Pope-Hennessy, John. *Robert Louis Stevenson*. New York: Simon & Schuster, 1974. 320pp. The author did not live to rewrite his manuscript as intended, and the book's unevenness is evident, particularly in the weakness of the Scottish background. However, this is still an engaging, informal biographical reassessment geared to the general reader.

Rice, Edward. *Journey to Upolu: Robert Louis Stevenson, Victorian Rebel*. New York: Dodd, Mead, 1974. 145pp. Rice challenges the conventional view of Stevenson as a proper Victorian with an emphasis on his rebellious side.

Saposnik, Irving S. *Robert Louis Stevenson*. New York: Twayne, 1974. 164pp. This critical study of Stevenson's literary career connects his writing life with his experiences in a sensible introduction.

Steuart, J.A. *Robert Louis Stevenson: Man and Writer: A Critical Biography*. Boston: Little, Brown, 1924. 2 vols. Steuart's life is one of the first that directly challenged the romantic, legendary image of Stevenson and substituted a much more realistic, frank, and rounded portrait. Stevenson's is far more interesting and believable with his weaknesses and flaws displayed as well as his virtues, and Steuart helped to fashion a more complex view that subsequent biographers and critics have shared.

Fictional Portraits

Stern, G.B. *No Son of Mine*. New York: Macmillan, 1948. 327pp. A tramp is taken for Stevenson's son, which causes him to investigate the life of his "father," with a biographical portrait emerging indirectly using extracts from the letters and works.

Recommended Juvenile Biographies

Carpenter, Angelica S. *Robert Louis Stevenson: Finding Treasure Island*. Minneapolis: Lerner, 1997. 144pp. MG. A readable, full-length biographical portrait, Carpenter includes quotations from the letters and the writer's observations of his travels and the events that shaped his life.

Gherman, Beverly. *Robert Louis Stevenson: Teller of Tales*. New York: Atheneum, 1996. 136pp. MG. This is a straightforward narrative account that emphasizes Stevenson as author, husband, world traveler, invalid, and celebrity.

Wood, James P. *The Lantern Bearer: A Life of Robert Louis Stevenson*. New York: Pantheon, 1965. 182pp. MG/YA. This is a colorful, well-written, and well-documented account in which the writer's strengths and weaknesses are treated equally.

Other Sources

Hammond, J.R. *A Robert Louis Stevenson Chronology*. New York: St. Martin's, 1997. 150pp. An essay on Stevenson's family and biographical sketches of his circle are combined with a detailed chronology for quick reference to the writer's activities.

Terry, R.C., ed. *Robert Louis Stevenson: Interviews and Recollections*. Iowa City: University of Iowa Press, 1996. 216pp. Terry supplies a biographical portrait from the recollections of the central figures in his life, including his wife, his mother, stepson, and literary associates, such as Henry Adams and Andrew Lang. Includes a Stevenson chronology.

443. HARRIET BEECHER STOWE
1811–1896

American author, Stowe was the sister of clergyman, abolitionist, and lecturer Henry Ward Beecher. She taught in her sister Catherine's school in Hartford, Connecticut, and moved with her family to Cincinnati, Ohio. There, Harriet began writing and married Professor Calvin Ellis Stowe. Her widely read anti-slavery novel *Uncle Tom's Cabin* (1852) stirred the conscience of Americans regarding slavery, influenced the abolitionist debate, and contributed to the outbreak of the Civil War. Stowe's other popular works include *The Minister's Wooing* (1859) and *Old Town Folks* (1869).

Autobiography and Primary Sources

Life and Letters of Harriet Beecher Stowe. A.A. Fields, ed. Cambridge, Massachusetts: Harvard University Press, 1897. 406pp. Fields, a close friend of the author, collects a wide assortment of letters and other primary documents, along with a reverent biographical commentary.

Stowe, Charles E. *The Life of Harriet Beecher Stowe Compiled from Her Journals and Letters*. Boston: Houghton Mifflin, 1889. 530pp. Stowe's son produced this biography under the close supervision of his mother. It can be regarded as something of an autobiography, a discreet, restricted view of the writer's life as she wished to be remembered. Chiefly valuable for its firsthand insights and selection of family letters and personal writings.

Recommended Biographies

Foster, Charles H. *The Rungless Ladder: Harriet Beecher Stowe and New England Puritanism*. 1954. Reprint ed. Totowa, New Jersey: Cooper Square, 1970. 278pp. Foster's critical and intellectual biography provides a detailed account of the genesis of *Uncle Tom's Cabin* and Stowe's literary career from the perspective of her religious background.

Hedrick, Joan. *Harriet Beecher Stowe: A Life*. New York: Oxford University Press, 1994. 507pp. Hedrick's well-written and thoroughly researched biography using previously unavailable materials looks at Stowe's life and times from a feminist perspective. Her emphasis on the challenges faced by women in the nineteenth century provides a fresh assessment of Stowe's development and achievement.

Wilson, Forrest. *Crusader in Crinoline: The Life of Harriet Beecher Stowe*. Philadelphia: Lippincott, 1941. 706pp. Wilson's full-length, thorough, well-documented biography has long established itself as the standard, modern life. Balanced, well written, and perceptive, the book is particularly strong in its animation of Stowe's historical and cultural era.

Other Biographical Studies

Gerson, Noel B. *Harriet Beecher Stowe: A Biography*. New York: Praeger, 1976. 218pp. Gerson recounts the well-known facts of Stowe's life without providing much insight to reveal the writer's personality or character.

Gilbertson, Cathrene. *Harriet Beecher Stowe*. New York: Appleton-Century, 1937. 330pp. Gilbertson's is one of the first balanced and objective assessments of Stowe's life in the context of her time. Without documentation, the book is intended for the general reader and still serves as a discerning overview, particularly strong on Stowe's religious development.

Johnston, Johanna. *Runaway to Heaven: The Story of Harriet Beecher Stowe*. Garden City, New York: Doubleday, 1963. 490pp. Based on secondary sources, Johnston supplies no new information but synthesizes existing sources into a workmanlike, if uninspired, account in which Stowe as a woman predominates over her role as an author.

Stowe, Charles E., and Lyman Beecher Stowe. *Harriet Beecher Stowe: The Story of Her Life*. Boston: Houghton Mifflin, 1911. 313pp. Reworking Charles Stowe's 1889 work, the writer's son and grandson collaborated on this centennial volume, which is less a full-length biography than a character study. The book explores in a number of intimate details Stowe's development as teacher, writer, wife, mother, and public figure.

Stowe, Lyman Beecher. *Saints, Sinners, and Beechers*. Indianapolis: Bobbs-Merrill, 1934. 450pp. Stowe's grandson provides a group portrait of the father, grandfather, and 10 children of Lyman Beecher in a series of lively, revealing biographical sketches.

Wagenknecht, Edward. *Harriet Beecher Stowe: The Known and the Unknown*. New York: Oxford University Press, 1965. 267pp. This insightful character study examines Stowe as daughter, wife, and mother over her role as author and reformer through a close examination of her letters and writings.

Biographical Novels

Brown, Karl. *The Cup Trembling*. New York: Duell, Sloan, and Pearce, 1953. 312pp. Stowe's relationship with her son, Frederick, and his Civil War service are dramatized in this character portrait that observes the basic biographical facts but offers a decidedly modern interpretation of mother and son.

Fictional Portraits

McCall, Dan. *Beecher*. New York: Dutton, 1979. 214pp. The scandal that surrounded Stowe's brother, Henry Ward Beecher when he was accused of seducing one of his parishioners is dramatized with a large cast of historical figures, including his sister, Susan B. Anthony, and Victoria Woodhull.

Recommended Juvenile Biographies

Coil, Suzanne M. *Harriet Beecher Stowe*. New York: F. Watts, 1993. 173pp. MG. A richly detailed biography that is animated by excerpts from Stowe's letters and works, the book stresses Stowe's struggle to balance her writing career and her family responsibilities. *Uncle Tom's Cabin* is not the sole focus here, with Stowe's lesser-known works and shifting literary reputation discussed.

Fritz, Jean. *Harriet Beecher Stowe and the Beecher Preachers*. New York: Putnam, 1994. 144pp. MG. Fritz's well-written, informative biography chronicles Stowe's life in the context of her family, era, and the social movements with which she was associated. Both the strengths and weaknesses of the eccentric Beecher family are presented.

Johnston, Norma. *Harriet: The Life and World of Harriet Beecher Stowe*. New York: Simon & Schuster, 1994. 242pp. MG/YA. An in-depth biography, Johnston's well-documented, balanced narrative explores Stowe's life as well as American society during the period, and touches on aspects of Stowe's life that are rarely mentioned in other Stowe biographies for younger readers.

444. RICHARD STRAUSS
1864–1949

German composer and conductor, Strauss was the last great Romantic composer. His first major work, the D minor symphony, was first performed in 1880. He was conductor at Meiningen and for the Berlin Philharmonic, and co-directed the Vienna State Opera. He served for a time as head of musical affairs under the Nazis but was officially exonerated of collaboration after World War II. His works include *Death and Transfiguration* (1889) and *Thus Spake Zarathustra* (1895) and the operas *Der Rosenkavalier* (1911) and *Ariadne auf Naxos* (1912).

Autobiography and Primary Sources

Recollections and Reflections. Willi Schuh, ed. London: Boosey & Hawkes, 1953. 173pp. This collection of occasional pieces written from 1903 to 1948 offers glimpses of Strauss's complex character and his creative process.

Recommended Biographies

Boyden, Matthew. *Richard Strauss*. Boston: Northeastern University Press, 1999. 448pp. Boyden's chronological portrait deals frankly with Strauss's flaws while displaying his musical genius. In the author's view, Strauss should be seen as the last of the great nineteenth-century Romantics, not as a groundbreaking modernist, guided not by musical principles but by ego and pragmatism. This is a challenging revisionist view that offers a provocative, coherent approach to Strauss's life as a whole.

Del Mar, Norman. *Richard Strauss: A Critical Commentary on His Life and Works*. Philadelphia: Chilton, 1962–1972. 3 vols. Del Mar's monumental three-volume study is considered the definitive critical biography. Daunting in its comprehensiveness and dense in its technical analysis for the nonspecialist, the book serves more as a useful reference and critical guide than a narrative to be read from cover to cover.

Gilliam, Bryan. *The Life of Richard Strauss*. New York: Cambridge University Press, 1998. 202pp. Gilliam's reliable, succinct biography covers Strauss's early musical development and achievement, as well as the turbulent personal and professional years between the wars. Serves as an excellent introductory overview by one of the leading modern authorities on the composer.

Kennedy, Michael. *Richard Strauss: Man, Musician, Enigma*. New York: Cambridge University Press, 1999. 451pp. Kennedy's comprehensive reassessment of Strauss's life and career, drawing on diaries, letters, and interviews with surviving family members, explores the disparity between the man and the musician, between his personal aloofness and reserve and the passion of his music. In seeking answers for the discrepancies, Kennedy looks closely at Strauss's family background, relationships, and the influence of German culture while challenging many previous interpretations.

Schuh, Willi. *Richard Strauss: A Chronicle of the Early Years 1864–98*. New York: Cambridge University Press, 1982. 555pp. The author, a prominent Swiss musicologist and critic, supplies the most comprehensive, authoritative biographical study of Strauss's life and development up to his move to Berlin in 1898. Quoting extensively from letters to and from the composer, the book offers an unparalleled display of Strauss as a working musician and of his influence.

Other Biographical Studies

Ashley, Tim. *Richard Strauss*. London: Phaidon Press, 1999. 240pp. Ashley's compact biographical profile emphasizes the political context of Strauss's life and the connection between his experiences and his compositions. In a balanced assessment, Ashley deals frankly with the composer's anti-Semitism and his allegiance to Hitler's Third Reich.

Finck, Henry T. *Richard Strauss: The Man and His Works*. Boston: Little, Brown, 1917. 328pp. Finck's early profile and assessment is a factual summary of the basic facts of Strauss's life up to 1916, animated by a number of interesting anecdotes, and critical commentary on Strauss's music.

Jefferson, Alan. *The Life of Richard Strauss*. Newton Abbot, England: David and Charles, 1973. 240pp. Based mainly on secondary sources and aimed at the nonspecialist, Jefferson treats the composer's life sympathetically, but not uncritically, and the book is a good starting point for the general reader looking for a solid introduction to Strauss's life. In *Richard Strauss* (London:

Macmillan, 1975. 112pp.) the author provides a brief illustrated biography that is chiefly valuable for its many photographs of the composer, places he was associated with, and stagings of his operas.

Kennedy, Michael. *Richard Strauss*. 1976. Revised ed. London: Dent, 1988. 237pp. This relatively brief survey of Strauss's life and work, part of the Master Musician series, is a useful and reliable introduction. In Kennedy's view Strauss "remains the most misunderstood and misrepresented of the great composers of the last hundred years," and the book presents the controversies, paradoxes in Strauss's character, and his shifting reputation. Biographical chapters are followed by a critical appreciation of Strauss's music.

Krause, Ernst. *Richard Strauss: The Man and His Work*. London: Collet's, 1964. 587pp. This translation of Krause's important scholarly study, originally published in Germany in 1955 and revised in 1963, remains a valuable analysis that connects Strauss's aesthetic development to his cultural, political, and historical background.

Marek, George. *Richard Strauss: The Life of a Non-Hero*. New York: Simon & Schuster, 1967. 350pp. As the book's subtitle indicates, Marek's is a provocative, mainly negative, assessment of Strauss's character and private life. In the author's view, Strauss's great promise in youth was unfulfilled, and the book attempts to trace the reasons why.

Newman, Ernest. *Richard Strauss*. London: J. Lane, 1908. 144pp. The first critical biographical study of Strauss and his musical career that appeared when the composer was only 44 includes a character sketch by Alfred Kalisch based on his own direct observations of Strauss.

Nice, David. *Richard Strauss*. London: Omnibus Press, 1994. 160pp. Part of the Illustrated Lives of the Great Composers series, this is basic illustrated overview of Strauss's life and musical career.

Biographical Films and Theatrical Adaptations

Richard Strauss (1996). Director: Malcolm Hossick. A concise biographical and musical overview. Video.

Other Sources

Gilliam, Bryan, ed. *Richard Strauss: New Perspectives on the Composer and His Work*. Duke University Press, 1992. 289pp. Strauss's life and works are examined and evaluated from a variety of perspectives by leading scholars.

Gilliam, Bryan, ed. *Richard Strauss and His World*. Princeton, New Jersey: Princeton University Press, 1992. 425pp. This useful collection is divided into four parts: original essays by musicologists, selected Strauss correspondence, four memoirs of the composer, and critical reviews of the music and its reception.

445. IGOR STRAVINSKY
1882–1971

Russian-born composer considered by many to be the greatest twentieth-century composer, Stravinsky abandoned a career in law after meeting the composer Rimsky-Korsakov, with whom he studied. Stravinsky's *The Firebird* (1910) and *Petrouchka* (1911) were composed for impresario Sergei Diaghilev's Ballets Russe. *The Rite of Spring*, a landmark in modern music, was first performed as a ballet in 1913. He immigrated to the United States in 1939 and became an American citizen. Other works by Stravinsky include *The Soldier's Tale* (1918) and *Orpheus* (1948).

Autobiography and Primary Sources

Dearest Bubushkin: The Correspondence of Vera and Igor Stravinsky, 1921–1954. Robert Craft, ed. New York: Thames and Hudson, 1985. 239pp. This collection of letters between husband is wife are mostly from the 1930s and includes excerpts from Vera Stravinsky's diaries, 1922–1971.

Stravinsky: An Autobiography. 1936. Reprint ed. New York: W.W. Norton, 1962. 176pp. The English translation of *Chroniques de ma vie*. As Stravinsky wrote in the foreword, "The aim of this volume is to set down a few recollections connected with various periods of my life...a simple account of important events side by side with facts of minor consequence." Selective but factually reliable on the details mentioned, the book is alternately candid and guarded, often a dry chronicle of outward events.

Stravinsky: Selected Correspondence. Robert Craft, ed. New York: Knopf, 1982–1985. 3 vols. Close to three-quarters of the content are letters to Stravinsky rather than from him, with revealing and inconsequential letters linked with extensive narrative commentary by Craft. There are few major musical or personal revelations.

Recommended Biographies

Craft, Robert. *Stravinsky: Chronicle of a Friendship*. 1972. Revised ed. Nashville, Tennessee: Vanderbilt University Press, 1994. 608pp. Stravinsky's longtime friend, collaborator, and editor, described as Stravinsky's Boswell, supplies a detailed record of the two men's relationship, and the book is the standard biographical source for the last decades of Stravinsky's life. Factual details have been corrected from the earlier version with postscripts added that provide a rounded personal portrait. Craft's *Stravinsky: Glimpses of a Life* (New York: St. Martin's, 1993. 416pp.) is a collection of biographical and critical essays written about the composer from 1948 to 1971.

Griffiths, Paul. *Stravinsky*. New York: Schirmer Books, 1993. 253pp. Organized chronologically with a brief sketch of Stravinsky's activities during the period under consideration followed by an analysis of that period's compositions, this is an excellent overview with a sensible critical focus.

Taruskin, Richard. *Stravinsky and the Russian Traditions: A Biography of the Works through "Mavra."* Berkeley: University of California Press, 1996. 2 vols. Taruskin's remarkable scholarly assessment of Stravinsky's works focuses on the connection between his music and Russian culture. The volumes skillfully locate the sources of the composer's works and alter the ways we have previously understood the man and his music.

Walsh, Stephen. *Stravinsky: A Creative Spring: Russia and France, 1882–1934*. New York: Knopf, 1999. 698pp. In the first installment of a projected two-volume life, Walsh covers the composer's formative years and the creation of his most famous works. Correcting many factual errors in the biographical record, Walsh emphasizes the importance of Stravinsky's Russian roots and musical training in shaping his career.

Other Biographical Studies

Boucourechliev, André. *Stravinsky*. New York: Holmes and Meier, 1987. 335pp. Biographical details alternate with highly technical discussions of Stravinsky's compositions. Daunting for the nonspecialist, Bourcourechliev's analysis is packed with lucid and discriminating judgments and revelations about Stravinsky's private life.

Druskin, Mikhail. *Igor Stavinsky: His Life, Works, and Views*. New York: Cambridge University Press, 1983. 194pp. Druskin, a Russian musicologist, provides a brief overview of the composer and his work. The book's chief interest and usefulness is its emphasis on Stravinsky's Russian background and influences.

Oliver, Michael. *Igor Stravinsky*. London: Phaidon Press, 1995. 240pp. Part of the 20th Century Composers series, this is a profile of Stravinsky's life and musical career organized in chronological units representing various stages of the composer's work. It serves as a solid, accessible orientation to the shape and nature of Stravinsky's achievement.

Routh, Francis. *Stravinsky*. London: Dent, 1975. 202pp. Part of the Master Musicians series, Routh's study is a useful reference guide with a catalogue of the composer's work, a chronology with a side-by-side listing of contemporary events, and a factual, rather than interpretive, summary of the major events of Stravinsky's life.

Stravinsky, Vera, and Robert Craft. *Stravinsky in Pictures and Documents*. New York: Simon & Schuster, 1978. 688pp. This is a somewhat disjointed and incomplete documentary biography assembled from excerpts of various materials. The volume requires prior knowledge of the composer's career.

Tansman, Alexandre. *Igor Stravinsky: The Man and His Music*. New York: Putnam, 1949. 295pp. Tansman's early biographical and critical assessment, the work of a friend and composer, mainly considers Stravinsky's creative methods and compositions. Both the man and his music are extensively praised, and neither receive much objective criticism.

Tierney, Neil. *The Unknown Country: A Life of Igor Stravinsky*. London: R. Hale, 1977. 272pp. This is an accomplished and comprehensive biography, rich in insights from the composer's associates, but occasionally the surmises approach the level of biographical fiction. The latitude taken to fill in the gaps in the record succeeds in animating Stravinsky's life and time, but readers should be cautious about accepting all the details as fully reliable.

Vlad, Roman. *Stravinsky*. New York: Oxford University Press, 1960. 232pp. The work of one of Italy's foremost composers, Vlad's chronological presentation of Stravinsky's compositions is chiefly interesting for the emphasis placed on the composer's later serial works. The biographical element is largely reserved to Stravinsky's creative method and the experiences that impacted his creativity.

White, Eric W. *Stravinsky: The Composer and His Works*. Berkeley: University of California Press, 1979. 656pp. The majority of White's scholarly examination is devoted to criticism of Stravinsky's compositions. The biographical material is restricted mainly to the composer's public career.

Recommended Juvenile Biographies

Dobrin, Arnold. *Igor Stravinsky: His Life and Times*. New York: Crowell, 1970. 197pp. MG. Stravinsky's life is chronicled from his childhood in a lively portrait that illuminates both the composer's works and the cultural background that he helped to shape.

Biographical Films and Theatrical Adaptations

Nijinsky (1980). Director: Herbert Ross. Stravinsky is portrayed by Ronald Pickup in this biographical film on the relationship between the Russian dancer (George De La Pena) and impresario Sergei Diaghilev (Alan Bates). Video.

"Once, at a Border. . .": Aspects of Stravinsky (1986). Director: Tony Palmer. Includes interviews with the composer, friends, family, and musical contemporaries. Video.

Stravinsky (1965). Directors: Roman Kroiter and Wolf Koenig. At the age of 80, Stravinsky reminisces about his life and career during a trip to Hamburg and a recording session of his *Symphony of Psalms*. Video.

Stravinsky (1996). Director: Malcolm Hossick. Part of the Famous Composers series, this is brief film profile that presents the basic outline of Stravinsky's life, work, and achievement. Video.

446. AUGUST STRINDBERG
1849–1912

Swedish playwright and novelist whose innovative dramas influenced the modern theater, Strindberg attended the University of Uppsala until poverty forced him to abandon his studies and to take work as a tutor, journalist, and librarian. He achieved renown with the publication of *The Red Room* (1879), a novel that helped initiate Swedish realism. His dramas include *Miss Julie* (1888), *The Dream Play* (1902), and *The Ghost Sonata* (1907).

Autobiography and Primary Sources

Strindberg's Letters. Michael Robinson, ed. Chicago: University of Chicago Press, 1992. 2 vols. In a selection of 679 letters from the nearly 10,000 extant correspondences, Strindberg's autobiographical reflections evident here are revealing and reflect his many moods and internal as well as external conflicts.

Recommended Biographies

Lagercrantz, Olof. *August Strindberg*. New York: Farrar, Straus, 1984. 398pp. The work of a Swedish poet, critic, and editor, Lagercrantz's full-length portrait is a marvel of compression and judicious interpretation. Strindberg is examined frankly with his many flaws and mental instability noted and explained as the basis for his creative achievement.

Meyer, Michael. *Strindberg: A Biography*. New York: Random House, 1985. 651pp. Meyer, the respected biographer of Ibsen, supplies an equally exhaustive and authoritative study of the Swedish writer. Drawing on a good deal of previously unpublished material, the book offers the fullest and most complete portrait available that revises and refines the accepted view of many aspects of the playwright's life and art.

Other Biographical Studies

Brandell, Gunnar. *Strindberg in Inferno*. Cambridge, Massachusetts: Harvard University Press, 1974. 223pp. Restricted to Strindberg's activities and development in the 1890s, Brandell's is a scholarly, meticulous documentation of the crucial, formative years of the playwright's life by one of Sweden's foremost authorities on Strindberg.

Carlson, Harry G. *Out of Inferno: Strindberg's Reawakening as an Artist*. Seattle: University of Washington Press, 1996. 390pp. In a highly readable and accessible analysis Carlson traces the factors that led to Strindberg's psychic despair in the 1890s and his creative reemergence in 1897 through his personal renewal.

Johnson, Walter G. *August Strindberg*. Boston: Twayne, 1976. 221pp. One of America's most important Strindberg experts provides a compact introductory overview of the playwright's life and career in a series of topical chapters on Strindberg as autobiographer, poet, storyteller, dramatist, scientist, and scholar.

McGill, Vivian J. *August Strindberg: The Bedeviled Viking*. New York: Brentano's, 1930. 459pp. McGill's narrative and interpretive biography is constructed out of a close reading of Strindberg's works for their autobiographical revelations. The result is a vivid, coherent, but questionable external and internal portrait of the playwright's life and psyche.

Sprigge, Elizabeth. *The Strange Life of August Strindberg*. New York: Macmillan, 1949. 246pp. Sprigge's is a thorough, reliable biography drawing on the playwright's letters, his and others' works, and interviews with his children. The book's main achievement is to avoid a reductionism that limits Strindberg to restrictive classification. Instead, Sprigge allows the playwright's complexity and paradoxes full display.

Strindberg, Freda Uhl. *Marriage with Genius*. London: Cape, 1937. 453pp. The playwright's second wife records her view of their brief time together (1893–1897) as well as an analysis of Strindberg's personality during a crucial period in his life. Subjective and selective in her view, the book is nonetheless a fascinating glimpse of the couple's mutual torment.

Waal, Carla. *Harriet Bosse: Strindberg's Muse and Interpreter.* Carbondale: Southern Illinois University Press, 1990. 298pp. This informative biography of Strindberg's third wife (1901–1904) and actress who performed in many of his plays draws on previously inaccessible archival sources to document her life and relationship with the playwright.

Biographical Films and Theatrical Adaptations

Enquist, Per Olov. *The Night of the Tribades: A Play for 1889.* New York: Hill & Wang, 1977. 81pp. Enquist's drama looks at the playwright during the rehearsal of his play, *The Stranger.*

Wilson, Colin. *Strindberg: A Play in Two Scenes.* New York: Random House, 1972. 94pp. Strindberg is captured in a series of monologues in which the playwright works over his inner life and torments.

447. SUN YAT-SEN
1866–1925

Chinese revolutionary, Sun is revered as the ideological father of modern China. He founded a revolutionary movement against the Manchus and after the Chinese revolution served as provisional president of the new republic. He later directed the Kuomintang political party. Sun's opposition to the government of Yüan Shih-k'ai led to his exile; after his return he headed a self-proclaimed national government and in the ensuing struggle against Beijing cooperated with the Communists and organized a military academy with Chiang Kai-shek, who succeeded him on his death.

Recommended Biographies

Bergère, Marie-Claire. *Sun Yat-Sen.* Stanford, California: Stanford University Press, 1998. 480pp. In a fresh evaluation of the man and the principal events of his life and times, Bergère manages a balanced portrait of a far more complex figure than others have suggested.

Schiffrin, Harold Z. *Sun Yat-Sen, Reluctant Revolutionary.* Boston: Little, Brown, 1980. 290pp. Schiffrin has produced the standard biography, a compact summary of the author's considerable research on Sun's writings and synthesis of modern scholarship, including Schiffrin's own earlier study, *Sun Yat-Sen and the Origins of the Chinese Revolution* (Berkeley: University of California Press, 1968. 412pp.), which exhaustively covers Sun's development during his first 40 years.

Sharman, Lyon. *Sun Yat-Sen: His Life and Its Meaning: A Critical Biography.* 1934. Reprint ed. Hamden, Connecticut: Archon Books, 1965. 418pp. Sharman's was the first reliable critical survey of Sun's character and career, and it remains a useful, conscientious sifting of the facts from the legends and hero worship that have distorted a clear view of the man.

Other Biographical Studies

Bruce, Robert. *Sun Yat-Sen.* London: Oxford University Press, 1969. 64pp. Despite its brevity, this is an excellent, succinct overview that serves to orient the reader both to the highlights of Sun's life and career and the political and historical issues that help to explain his development and activities.

Martin, Bernard. *Strange Vigor: A Biography of Sun Yat-Sen.* London: Heinemann, 1944. 250pp. Martin's is a reliable and highly readable account of Sun's political career that is informed by a solid sense of the era and the complex forces that shaped Sun.

Restarick, Henry B. *Sun Yat-Sen: Liberator of China.* New Haven, Connecticut: Yale University Press, 1931. 167pp. This short account concentrates on Sun's early life and career up to 1911 from information gained from those who knew him in Hawaii.

Fictional Portraits

Elegant, Robert S. *Dynasty.* New York: McGraw-Hill, 1977. 625pp. This family saga reflects Chinese history during the first 70 years of the twentieth century, with appearances by Sun Yat-Sen, Chiang Kai-Shek, and Mao Zedong.

Recommended Juvenile Biographies

Barlow, Jeffrey G. *Sun Yat-Sen.* New York: Chelsea House, 1987. 112pp. MG/YA. This is a fine, straightforward account of Sun Yat-Sen's life and impact on modern Chinese history.

448. JONATHAN SWIFT
1667–1745

Considered the greatest prose satirist in English literature, the Irish-born Swift was ordained an Anglican priest in Ireland and left a small living to settle in England. Two satires, *The Battle of the Books* and *A Tale of a Tub,* appeared in 1704. He was made Dean of Saint Patrick's Cathedral in Dublin (1713) and retired in Ireland (1715). He deplored the plight of the Irish poor, expressing his dismay in *Drapier Letters* (1724) and the later, bitterly ironic "A Modest Proposal" (1729). He satirized English society in his masterpiece *Gulliver's Travels* (1726), his best-known work. Toward the end of his life he developed a brain disorder and by 1742 was declared insane.

Autobiography and Primary Sources

The Correspondence of Jonathan Swift. Harold Williams, ed. Oxford: Clarendon Press, 1965–1972. 5 vols. The modern scholarly edition of Swift's voluminous correspondence is an essential source of biographical details and glimpses of the various sides of Swift's personality.

Recommended Biographies

Ehrenpreis, Irvin. *Swift: The Man, His Works, and the Age.* Cambridge, Massachusetts: Harvard University Press, 1962–1983. 3 vols. Ehrenpreis's monumental study has been widely acclaimed as the definitive life that should maintain its authorita-

tiveness for some time to come. The volumes combine scrupulous scholarship and judicious interpretation in a detailed presentation of Swift's life and social milieu, as well as a masterful analysis of his writings. Ranks with Richard Ellmann's biography of James Joyce and Leon Edel's biography of Henry James as one of the greatest literary biographies.

Glendinning, Victoria. *Jonathan Swift: A Portrait.* New York: Holt, 1999. 324pp. Foregoing a chronological approach for a discursive character portrait that surveys Swift's many personal and professional contradictions and peculiarities, the book, though lacking the thoroughness and completeness of other accounts, compensates with close attention to the main events and relationships that defined Swift's public persona, private life, and personality.

McMinn, Joseph. *Jonathan Swift: A Literary Life.* New York: St. Martin's, 1991. 172pp. McMinn's compact introductory account examines the full range of Swift's writing and literary achievements with succinct commentary on the social, political, theological, and personal context to his literary career.

Nokes, David. *Jonathan Swift: A Hypocrite Reversed: A Critical Biography.* New York: Oxford University Press, 1985. 427pp. Nokes provides the best, up-to-date, single-volume study for the general reader. Judicious and scholarly, without sacrificing readability, Nokes's assessment of Swift's character and context is nuanced and insightful and serves the reader without the patience to tackle Ehrenpreis.

Other Biographical Studies

Craik, Henry. *The Life of Jonathan Swift.* 1882. Revised ed. London: Macmillan, 1894. 2 vols. Craik's lengthy, scholarly biography remained the standard life until Ehrenpreis. Although superseded by modern scholarship, the book still retains its usefulness as a reference source on details on Swift's life and personality.

Ehrenpreis, Irvin. *The Personality of Jonathan Swift.* Cambridge, Massachusetts: Harvard University Press, 1958. 179pp. The author of the definitive life supplies a succinct preview of Swift's character and temperament that is useful as a starting point for the reader interested in a cogent summary of the essential elements in Swift's life.

Ewald, William B. *The Masks of Jonathan Swift.* Cambridge, Massachusetts: Harvard University Press, 1954. 203pp. Ewald approaches Swift as the master of impersonation and role playing, and this critical study offers a perceptive analysis of Swift's many guises in his life and his writing.

Forster, John. *The Life of Jonathan Swift.* New York: Harper, 1876. 477pp. Forster, Dickens's close friend and biographer, completed only one volume, covering Swift's life up to the year 1711. His balanced assessment is chiefly important for moderating the intemperate attacks on Swift's life and work by such Victorian stalwarts as Macaulay and Thackeray.

Johnston, Denis. *In Search of Swift.* New York: Barnes and Noble, 1959. 240pp. Johnston's provocative study attempts to separate the facts from fiction and legend surrounding various aspects of Swift's life. His "solutions" to the various Swiftian puzzles include debatable assertions about his parentage and his relationships with Stella and Vanessa. Although supported with considerable evidence, Johnston's controversial assertions remain hypothetical but absorbing.

Murry, John Middleton. *Jonathan Swift: A Critical Biography*. New York: Farrar, Straus, 1955. 508pp. Murry's biographical profile is vivid and opinionated. Although representing no original research, the book is a sensible and lively summary of Swift's writing, his political and social background, and the various contradictions of his private life.

Quintana, Ricardo. *The Mind and Art of Jonathan Swift*. 1936. Revised ed. New York: Oxford University Press, 1953. 400pp. Quintana's sensible critical biography is carefully researched, avoids undue conjecture, and is best on Swift's influences, his development, and his public career. The author's *Swift: An Introduction* (New York: Oxford University Press, 1955. 204pp.) is a brief critical survey of the man, his personality, and works and represents the author's reassessment based on later Swiftian research. Serves as a balanced, cautious introductory study.

Rowse, A.L. *Jonathan Swift*. New York: Scribner, 1975. 240pp. Although it adds little that is new or original, Rowse's popular biography is a well-written, entertaining narrative that excels in capturing the political milieu of Swift's era. The book is less convincing in dealing with Swift's writing and private life.

Biographical Novels

Clewes, Winston. *The Violent Friends*. New York: Appleton-Century, 1945. 225pp. Swift's relationships with the "Vanessa" and "Stella" of his writings are portrayed, from the time of his return to Ireland as Dean of St. Patrick's in Dublin to Stella's death. The central facts are consistent with Swift's biography, though some liberties have been taken.

Fictional Portraits

Auchincloss, Louis. *Exit Lady Masham*. Boston: Houghton Mifflin, 1983. 169pp. Auchincloss's portrait of court life during the reign of Queen Anne features portrayals of a number of historical figures, including Jonathan Swift.

Jong, Erica. *Fanny*. New York: New American Library, 1980. 505pp. Jong's picaresque comedy features a female "Tom Jones" who meets, while working in a brothel, a number of historical figures, including Swift, Hogarth, and John Cleland.

Thackeray, William Makepeace. *The History of Henry Esmond*. 1852. Reprint ed. New York: Penguin, 1985. 544pp. Thackeray's historical novel set in the early eighteenth century offers glimpses of such figures as Richard Steele, Joseph Addison, and Swift.

449. ALGERNON CHARLES SWINBURNE
1837–1909

English lyric poet with a close association with the Pre-Raphaelites, including Rossetti, Swinburne achieved fame with *Atalanta in Calydon* (1865), a poetic drama based on Greek tragedy. His other works include *Poems and Ballads* (1866), *A Song of Italy* (1867), and *Tristram of Lyonesse* (1882). An epileptic and alcoholic, Swinburne lived in virtual seclusion from 1878. His critical work helped stimulate appreciation of older English dramatists and of William Blake.

Autobiography and Primary Sources

The Swinburne Letters. Cecil Y. Lang, ed. New Haven, Connecticut: Yale University Press, 1959–1962. 6 vols. This scholarly edition of the writer's letters has been crucial in shaping modern assessments of Swinburne's biography and development.

Recommended Biographies

Gosse, Edmund. *The Life of Algernon Charles Swinburne*. New York: Macmillan, 1917. 363pp. The first significant biography of the poet and still one of the most important, Gosse's life is a carefully researched, vivid account drawing on the author's personal knowledge of Swinburne and the recollections of those who knew him. Gosse suppresses some of the less flattering aspects of Swinburne's life and character, and his account needs to be supplemented with more frank, later studies.

Henderson, Philip. *Swinburne: Portrait of a Poet*. New York: Macmillan, 1974. 305pp. Henderson's critical biography is a balanced attempt to measure both Swinburne's deviance and his achievement, offering a closely focused view of the poet's personal development and its impact on his literary work.

Lafourcade, Georges. *Swinburne: A Literary Biography*. 1932. Reprint ed. New York: Russell & Russell, 1967. 314pp. More candid than Gosse, Lafourcade's is an accomplished biography that adds to the biographical record and corrects many misconceptions. Balanced, sympathetic but critical, the biography offers a believable multidimensional human view of Swinburne.

Other Biographical Studies

Fuller, Jean O. *Swinburne: A Critical Biography*. London: Chatto & Windus, 1968. 319pp. Fuller's account of Swinburne's life is dominated by its contention that the writer's relationship with his cousin Mary Leeth is the fundamental experience of his life. The approach is selective and reductive, showing the man exclusively in the context of his sexuality.

Thomas, Donald S. *Swinburne: The Poet in His World*. New York: Oxford University Press, 1979. 256pp. This short, lively biography provides a compact overview that serves as a useful introduction to the poet, his career, and his times.

Watts-Dunton, Clara. *The Home Life of Swinburne*. New York: F.A. Stokes, 1922. 288pp. This is a valuable reminiscence, despite its reverent and defensive tone, based on the author's firsthand observation of Swinburne's domestic life and personal habits.

450. JOHN MILLINGTON SYNGE
1871–1909

Irish dramatist and poet, Synge was a central figure in the Irish Literary Renaissance of the late nineteenth and early twentieth centuries. His plays reflect his experience in the Aran Islands and include *In the Shadow of the Glen* (1903), *Riders to the Sea* (1904), *The Playboy of the Western World* (1907), and *The Tinker's Wedding* (1908). He organized the Abbey Theatre in Dublin with W.B. Yeats and others.

Autobiography and Primary Sources

The Autobiography of J.M. Synge. Alan Price, ed. London: Oxford University Press, 1965. 46pp. Written mainly when the playwright was 25 and before his period of literary creativity, this autobiographical fragment is interesting for the light it sheds on Synge's view of his formative years.

The Collected Letters of John Millington Synge: 1907–1909. Ann Saddlemyer, ed. Oxford: Clarendon Press, 1983–1984. 2 vols. Synge's letters are essential sources for the biographer to gain a clearer view of his personality and development. This scholarly collection has useful introductions and annotations.

Recommended Biographies

Greene, David H., and Edward M. Stephens. *J.M. Synge 1871–1909*. 1959. Revised ed. New York: New York University Press, 1989. 372pp. Making full use of Edward M. Stephens's voluminous family memoir, Greene provides a lucid, vivid account of the writer's development and the connection between his experiences and his writing.

Kiely, David M. *John Millington Synge: A Biography*. New York: St. Martin's, 1995. 305pp. This is a rich, exhaustively researched, absorbing biography that follows Synge's development from childhood, relating his experiences and artistic achievement to the wider cultural context of his period.

Other Biographical Studies

Gerstenberger, Donna L. *John Millington Synge*. 1964. Revised ed. Boston: Twayne, 1990. 144pp. Gerstenberger's mainly critical introduction has a brief biographical summary and touches on the impact of Synge's experiences, relationships, and milieu on his compositions.

Skelton, Robin. *J.M. Synge and His World*. New York: Viking, 1971. 144pp. Skelton's visual biography is an excellent introduction to the writer, his life, and background. The author's *The Writings of J.M. Synge* (Indianapolis: Bobbs-Merrill, 1971. 190pp.) is a more scholarly, analytical study of Synge's plays, essays, and poems with fresh interpretations of their evolution and the connection between the works and Synge's experiences and artistic development.

Stephens, Edward. *My Uncle John: Edward Stephens's Life of J.M. Synge.* Andrew Carpenter, ed. London: Oxford University Press, 1974. 222pp. On his death, Synge's nephew left a 14-volume biographical manuscript of his uncle. This condensation presents selections with the editor's paraphrases. Stephens's insights are chiefly useful for the information they provide on Synge's background and family relations.

Other Sources

Kopper, Edward A. Jr., ed. *A J.M. Synge Literary Companion.* Westport, Connecticut: Greenwood, 1988. 268pp. Along with a brief biography and chronology, this valuable reference source has chapters by various specialists on Synge's prose, poems, each of his six plays, and topical coverage of Synge's relationship to the Irish Literary Renaissance and his use of language.

Mikhail, E.H., ed. *J.M. Synge: Interviews and Recollections.* London: Macmillan, 1977. 138pp. This useful volume collects the observations of many who knew Synge, including Yeats, Lady Gregory, George Moore, James Stephens, and Padraic Colum.

451. RABINDRANATH TAGORE
1861–1941

A celebrated Bengali Indian author and recipient of the 1913 Nobel Prize in Literature, Tagore produced an enormous amount of literary work, including some 50 dramas, 100 books of verse, 40 volumes of novels and short fiction, and books of essays and philosophy. His best-known work in the western world is the poetry volume, *Gitanjali* (1912).

Autobiography and Primary Sources

My Reminiscences. London: Macmillan, 1917. 272pp. Most of these "memory pictures" are drawn from Tagore's boyhood and early youth. The book is purposely selective with more literary than biographical significance, and the author warns that "to take them as an attempt at autobiography would be a mistake."

Selected Letters of Rabindranath Tagore. Krishna Dutta and Andrew Robinson, eds. New York: Cambridge University Press, 1997. 561pp. This useful collection of letters covers the years 1879 to 1941 and is arranged topically as well as chronologically, reflecting Tagore's principal activities and concerns in each period.

Recommended Biographies

Dutta, Krishna, and Andrew Robinson. *Rabindranath Tagore: The Myriad-Minded Man.* New York: St. Martin's, 1995. 493pp. Drawing on previously unpublished material, the authors supply a detailed and reliable chronicle of Tagore's life and a nuanced, complex portrait of his personality and background that helps to explain his complicated reputation in the West and in India.

Kripalani, Krishna. *Rabindranath Tagore: A Life.* New York: Oxford University Press, 1962. 417pp. Based on firsthand knowledge, Kripalani's intimate account emphasizes Tagore the man, his family life, childhood, emotional development, travel, and educational experiments. Not intended as a critical survey of the literary work, the book is, however, rich in personal details.

Other Biographical Studies

Rhys, Ernest. *Rabindranath Tagore: A Biographical Study.* New York: Macmillan, 1915. 157pp. Rhys's early critical biography is the work of an evident admirer that offers a sympathetic interpretation of Tagore's writing and his reception in the West.

Roy, Basanta K. *Rabindranath Tagore: The Man and His Poetry.* New York: Dodd, Mead, 1915. 223pp. This early biography intended to introduce the recent Nobel Prize winner to an American audience is sketchy in its details and superficial in its critical interpretation. Roy's uncritical appreciation is partially redeemed by the author's personal acquaintance with his subject.

Thompson, Edward J. *Rabindranath Tagore: His Life and Work.* London: Oxford University Press, 1921. 112pp.; *Rabindranath Tagore: Poet and Dramatist.* Oxford: Oxford University Press, 1926. 327pp. Thompson's critical biographical studies are still useful analyses for their appreciation of the Bengali context of Tagore's work and the connection between the writer's life and his writing.

452. ZACHARY TAYLOR
1784–1850

The twelfth U.S. president, Taylor was a bold and resourceful military commander during the Black Hawk and Mexican Wars, and was known as "Old Rough and Ready." His decisive defeat of Santa Anna at the battle of Buena Vista made him a national hero. Elected president as a Whig, he proved popular, although his term (1849-1850) was brief. He supported the Wilmot Proviso, which excluded slavery from territories gained as a result of the Mexican War. His death from cholera temporarily postponed a compromise between slave and free states.

Recommended Biographies

Bauer, K. Jack. *Zachary Taylor: Soldier, Planter, Statesman of the Old Southwest.* Baton Rouge: Louisiana State University Press, 1985. 348pp. Bauer offers reliable and serious coverage of Taylor's full career in sections on his early years, service during the Mexican War, and presidency.

Dyer, Brainerd. *Zachary Taylor.* Baton Rouge: Louisiana State University Press, 1946. 455pp. Dyer's is an excellent scholarly biography and historical study that evaluates Taylor's personality, public career, and times, supplying a realistic, credible view of the colorful Taylor.

Hamilton, Holman. *Zachary Taylor.* Indianapolis: Bobbs-Merrill, 1941–1951. 2 vols. Hamilton's is among the most comprehensive treatment of Taylor's life and character. Volume one takes Taylor's story through the Mexican War; volume two treats his presidential term. Exhaustively researched and balanced in its assessment, Hamilton's study has long served as the definitive and best biography available.

Other Biographical Studies

Howard, Oliver O. *General Taylor.* New York: Appleton, 1892. 386pp. This early uncritical biography focuses exclusively on Taylor's military career with only a few pages devoted to his presidency.

McKinley, Silas B., and Silas Bent. *Old Rough and Ready: The Life and Times of Zachary Taylor.* New York: Vanguard Press, 1946. 329pp. This popular biography provides a competent overview of Taylor's full career, though errors mar the book's reliability.

Smith, Elbert B. *The Presidencies of Zachary Taylor and Millard Fillmore.* Lawrence: University Press of Kansas, 1988. 302pp. Smith's is the most comprehensive, scholarly treatment of Taylor's presidency. Based on extensive research using primary and secondary sources, the book treats Taylor's leadership and various policies in detail.

Fictional Portraits

Eckert, Allen W. *Twilight of Empire.* Boston: Little, Brown, 1988. 587pp. Eckert's "narrative history" covers the opening decades of the nineteenth century and the settlement of the American frontier with depictions of Taylor, Andrew Jackson, Lincoln, and John Reynolds.

Olsen, Theodore V. *There Was a Season: A Biographical Novel of Jefferson Davis.* Garden City, New York: Doubleday, 1972. 444pp. Restricted to Davis's early years when he was a promising army officer, the novel dramatizes his courtship and brief marriage to Sarah Knox Taylor, the second daughter of Zachary Taylor, his commanding officer. Although based on fact, the novel invents some characters, events, and situations.

Ryan, Edward J. *Comes an Echo on the Breeze.* New York: Exposition Press, 1949. 202pp. Abraham Lincoln's military experience during the 1832 Black Hawk War is featured in this novel that also displays such historical figures as Taylor and Jefferson Davis.

Recommended Juvenile Biographies

Collins, David R. *Zachary Taylor: 12th President of the United States.* Ada, Oklahoma: Garrett, 1989. 121pp. MG. Collins's is a workmanlike account of Taylor's life, emphasizing his military accomplishments and the presidential years.

Kent, Zachary. *Zachary Taylor: Twelfth President of the United States.* Chicago: Childrens Press, 1988. 98pp. MG. This is a straightforward summary of Taylor's life and career.

Young, Bob. *Old Rough and Ready: Zachary Taylor.* New York: J. Messner, 1970. 191pp. MG. In an objective and unromantic treatment, Young offers a reliable account of Taylor's family background, early years, and military and political careers.

Biographical Films and Theatrical Adaptations

Distant Drums (1951). Director: Raoul Walsh. Adventure yarn set during the Seminole War features a depiction of Taylor (Robert Barrat) and a cast that includes Gary Cooper and Mari Aldon. Video.

Seminole (1953). Director: Budd Boetticher. Rock Hudson plays an earnest soldier trying to help an Indian tribe during the Seminole War, with an appearance by Taylor (Fay Roope).

Other Sources

Farrell, John J. *Zachary Taylor: 1784–1850 and Millard Filmore, 1800–1874: Chronology, Documents, Bibliographical Aids.* Dobbs Ferry, New York: Oceana, 1971. 118pp. Farrell supplies a useful reference source, linking an extensive chronology of both men with a selection of primary sources and an annotated bibliography.

453. PETER ILYICH TCHAIKOVSKY
1840–1893

Russian composer and one of the most popular composers in history, Tchaikovsky is known for the drama and emotional intensity of his music. His many famous works include the symphony *Romeo and Juliet* (1869); the ballets *Swan Lake* (1877), *The Sleeping Beauty* (1890), and *The Nutcracker* (1892); the *Pathétique Symphony* (No. 6, 1893); and operas, concertos, songs, piano pieces, string quartets, and numerous other compositions.

Autobiography and Primary Sources

The Diaries of Tchaikovsky. New York: W.W. Norton, 1945. 365pp. Tchaikovsky kept his diaries from age 33 to two years before his death. They represent a frank account of his daily experience through the most important period, biographically and musically, in the composer's life.

Letters to His Family: An Autobiography. New York: Stein and Day, 1981. 577pp. This collection of letters covers the period from 1861, when the composer was 21, to the year of his death, and provides a unique insight into the Tchaikovsky's life and character.

Tchaikovsky: A Self-Portrait. Aleksandra A. Orlova, ed. New York: Oxford University Press, 1990. 436pp. Compiled from letters, diaries, and articles and arranged chronologically, this is a profile of the composer and his times in his own words.

Recommended Biographies

Brown, David. *Tchaikovsky.* New York: W.W. Norton, 1978–1992. 4 vols. Brown's is the leading biography both in terms of its comprehensiveness and the lucidity of its interpretation. The portrait of the composer is balanced and fair with Tchaikovsky's career, personality, and relationships presented in detail. Well written, with a minimum of technical jargon used to analyze the music, Brown's impressive study is essential for scholars but should not prevent a general reader's enjoyment.

Poznansky, Alexander. *Tchaikovsky: The Quest for the Inner Man.* New York: Schirmer Books, 1991. 679pp. Describing his work as "historical psychology," Poznansky's is a provocative and fresh portrait that changes the paradigm in the conventional view of the composer in a number of essential ways. Poznansky argues that Tchaikovsky was neither a tormented homosexual nor a suicide victim, and the quest to unlock the inner man rests on a more complete understanding of nineteenth-century Russian culture that the book helps to supply. In *Tchaikovsky's Last Days: A Documentary Study* (Oxford: Clarendon Press, 1997. 236pp.) Poznansky collects the relevant evidence, including a good deal of newly unrestricted material, to document the composer's last months, helping to support the author's contention that cholera, not suicide, was the cause of Tchaikovsky's death.

Weinstock, Herbert. *Tchaikovsky.* New York: Knopf, 1943. 386pp. Weinstock's is a sober, restrained assessment of the composer's life and career that clears away much of the glamour and sentimentality that have clung to Tchaikovsky. In its place Weinstock substitutes a reliable chronology and a well-documented portrait in which the connections between the composer's life and his music are made clear.

Other Biographical Studies

Abraham, Gerald E. *Tchaikovsky: A Short Biography.* 1945. Reprint ed. Westport, Connecticut: Hyperion Press, 1993. 144pp. Although superseded by more recent scholarship, Abraham's is still a useful biographical profile that covers the essential facts of the composer's life.

Evans, Edwin. *Tchaikovsky.* New York: Dutton, 1906. 207pp. The biographical details are derived from Modest Tchaikovsky with the majority of the book devoted to a critical survey of the composer's work.

Garden, Edward. *Tchaikovsky.* New York: Octagon Books, 1973. 194pp. Part of the Master Musicians series, Garden's introductory overview emphasizes Tchaikovsky's musical development with sufficient biographical details to show the connection between the composer's life and his music.

Gee, John, and Elliott Selby. *The Triumph of Tchaikovsky: A Biography.* New York: Vanguard, 1960. 206pp. This study explores Tchaikovsky the man rather than the musician, with an emphasis on his emotional life and homosexuality. With an immediacy derived from diaries and letters, the authors supply a mainly judicious psychological analysis to explain both the composer's torment and achievement.

Hanson, Lawrence, and Elisabeth Hanson. *Tchaikovsky: The Man Behind the Music.* New York: Dodd, Mead, 1966. 385pp. The Hansons' popular biography attempts to rehabilitate Tchaikovsky's reputation. The book's emphasis is biographical with little musical analysis and a certain degree of special pleading in insisting that the composer is worthy of the reader's sympathy.

Holden, Anthony. *Tchaikovsky: A Biography.* New York: Random House, 1995. 490pp. Holden focuses on Tchaikovsky's homosexuality as the key to understanding the man and his genius. The book makes a case that the composer did not die of cholera but poisoned himself on account of indiscretions with the czar's nephew. Well written and documented, Holden offers a credible explanation for the conflict between Tchaikovsky's private and public personas.

Kendall, Alan. *Tchaikovsky: A Biography.* London: Bodley Head, 1988. 257pp. Kendall's sensible and highly readable biography explores at length the circumstances of Tchaikovsky's death and the question whether it was self-inflicted.

Nice, David. *Tchaikovsky.* New York: Simon & Schuster, 1995. 192pp. Part of the Classic FM Lifelines series, this is a lively introduction to the composer's life and music for the interested generalist with more biography than musical analysis.

Tchaikovsky, Modest. *The Life and Letters of Peter Ilich Tchaikovsky.* Rosa Newmarch, ed. New York: Dodd, Mead, 1924. 782pp. The composer's brother supplies a series of biographical views and letters from various stages of Tchaikovsky's life. Neither complete nor objective, the book's perspective distorts a clear and balanced view of the composer's personality.

Warrack, John H. *Tchaikovsky.* New York: Scribner, 1973. 287pp. This illustrated biography aimed at the general reader provides nontechnical summaries of Tchaikovsky's major works as well as a generally reliable account of the composer's career, relationships, creative method, and development. The author deals frankly with Tchaikovsky's homosexuality and helpfully places him in his Russian and musical context.

Yoffe, Elkhonon. *Tchaikovsky in America.* New York: Oxford University Press, 1986. 216pp. Yoffe's specialized documentary study of Tchaikovsky's visit to America in 1891 makes use of the composer's diaries and letters as well as contemporary newspaper accounts, supplying an interesting view of the composer's final years.

Biographical Novels

Mann, Klaus. *Pathetic Symphony: A Novel about Tchaikovsky.* New York: Allen, Towne & Heath, 1948. 346pp. The composer's life and career are dramatized through interior monologues giving the impression of what Tchaikovsky might have been thinking when composing and performing.

Recommended Juvenile Biographies

Clark, Elizabeth. *Tchaikovsky.* New York: Bookwright, 1988. 32pp. MG. This is a simple, though informative, biographical profile of the composer and an appreciatory introduction to his achievement.

Tames, Richard. *Peter Ilyich Tchaikovsky.* New York: F. Watts, 1991. 32pp. MG. Tames offers a brief overview of the essential details of Tchaikovsky's career.

Thompson, Wendy. *Pyotr Ilyich Tchaikovsky.* New York: Viking, 1993. 48pp. YA. Thompson's presentation of Tchaikovsky's life and career joins an explanation of the historical and social context with critical commentary of his compositions. Tchaikovsky's personal torments are dealt with frankly.

Biographical Films and Theatrical Adaptations

The Life, Times, and Music of Peter Ilyich Tchaikovsky (1992). Director: Graham Holloway. Interweaving dramatizations and images, this is a film portrait of the composer that considers his life and art in the context of his times. Video.

The Music Lovers (1971). Director: Ken Russell. Tchaikovsky receives the notorious Russell treatment in this controversial and biographically unreliable film portrait of the composer's torments. With Richard Chamberlain as Tchaikovsky, supported by Glenda Jackson. Video.

Peter Ilyich Tchaikovsky (1997). Director: Simon Broughton. Tchaikovsky's life and work are presented through performance sequences, interviews, and commentary. Video.

Tchaikovsky (1984). Director: Herbert Chappell. Andre Previn conducts the Royal Philharmonic Orchestra and narrates this discussion of the composer's life and work with a performance of his *Symphony No. 6.* Video.

Tchaikovsky (1996). Director: Malcolm Hossick. This is a brief biographical overview and appreciation of the composer's achievement. Video.

Other Sources

Brown, David, ed. *Tchaikovsky Remembered.* Portland, Oregon: Amadeus Press, 1994. 248pp. After supplying a chronology of the composer's life and work, Brown selects reminiscences by over 80 of Tchaikovsky's friends, colleagues, and acquaintances who provide a wealth of material about the man and his music.

Kearney, Leslie, ed. *Tchaikovsky and His World.* Princeton, New Jersey: Princeton University Press, 1998. 350pp. Scholars from several disciplines explore various aspects of Tchaikovsky's music and biography with an emphasis on his later life and influence. Includes for the first time in English some of the composer's own writings about music.

Poznansky, Alexander, ed. *Tchaikovsky through Others' Eyes.* Bloomington: Indiana University Press, 1999. 311pp. This collection of views of Tchaikovsky by his contemporaries, arranged chronologically, serves as an informative collection of biographical materials.

454. TECUMSEH
ca. 1768–1813

A Shawnee Indian chief and warrior, Tecumseh sought to unite various Native American tribes against encroachment of their lands. The effort failed despite British and widespread Indian support after the defeat of Tecumseh's brother, Tenskwatawa, at the battle of Tippecanoe (1811). Tecumseh allied himself with the British during the War of 1812 and was made a brigadier general. He died while fighting troops under command of William Henry Harrison in the Battle of the Thames.

Autobiography and Primary Sources

Tecumseh: Fact and Fiction in Early Records. Carl F. Klinck, ed. Englewood Cliffs, New Jersey: Prentice-Hall, 1961. 246pp. This collection of excerpts from early accounts is an excellent starting point to survey the sources available.

Recommended Biographies

Edmunds, R. David. *Tecumseh and the Quest for Indian Leadership.* Boston: Little, Brown, 1984. 246pp. Edmunds's biography of Tecumseh, along with his companion volume on his brother, Tenskwatawa, *The Shawnee Prophet* (Lincoln: University of Nebraska Press, 1984. 260pp.), are sound, scholarly accounts that cut through the mythology to reveal credible personalities in the context of their times and culture.

Gilbert, Bil. *God Gave Us This Country: Tekamthi and the First American Civil War.* New York: Atheneum, 1989. 369pp. Gilbert's is a fascinating historical account of Indian-colonial affairs, fully documenting the Indian perspective on the settlers' expansion westward and the resistance efforts of the Shawnee from the mid-eighteenth century to 1811. At the center of the narrative is Tecumseh, or Tekamthi, as he was known to his fellow tribesmen, who emerges as a rounded, believable figure.

Sugden, John. *Tecumseh: A Life.* New York: Holt, 1998. 492pp. Expanding the scope of his earlier *Tecumseh's Last Stand* (Norman: University of Oklahoma Press, 1985. 298pp.), which dealt exclusively with his final battle, Sugden presents an intimately focused, full-length authoritative account of Tecumseh's life and times. Scrupulous in its research and richly detailed, the book has been widely praised as the definitive study that is unlikely to be surpassed.

Other Biographical Studies

Drake, Benjamin. *Life of Tecumseh and His Brother The Prophet with a Historical Sketch of the Shawanoe Indians.* 1841. Reprint ed. New York: Arno Press, 1969. 235pp. The earliest full biography, Drake's discriminating study remains an important source of generally reliable evidence, drawing on information from Tecumseh's acquaintances.

Eckert, Allen W. *A Sorrow in Our Heart: The Life of Tecumseh.* New York: Konecky & Konecky, 1992. 862pp. Describing his effort as a "narrative biography," Eckert mixes considerable research with imaginative reconstructions to characterize Tecumseh and his times. Despite questionable interpretations and embellishments that could qualify the book as historical fiction, Eckert achieves an epic magnification through the accumulation of his data.

Oskinson, John M. *Tecumseh and His Times.* New York: Putnam, 1938. 244pp. A popular sympathetic biography that takes Tecumseh's and the Indian side. Poor writing and superficial distinctions make this book only marginally useful.

Tucker, Glenn. *Tecumseh: Vision of Glory.* Indianapolis: Bobbs-Merrill, 1956. 399pp. Arguing that Tecumseh was "the most extraordinary Indian that has appeared in history," Tucker alternates between reliable historical reporting and excessive adulation, allowing too many of the legends surrounding the Shawnee chief to go unquestioned.

Biographical Novels

Huston, James A. *Counterpoint.* Lawrenceville, Virginia: Brunswick, 1987. 629pp. The dual careers of William Henry Harrison and Tecumseh are contrasted in a chronicle of their lives leading us to the Battle of the Thames in 1813.

Thom, James Alexander. *Panther in the Sky.* New York: Ballantine Books, 1989. 655pp. Thom's fictional biography of Tecumseh is an accurate and mostly reliable version of Tecumseh's life from the Indian perspective.

Fictional Portraits

Anness, Milford E. *Song of Metamoris.* Caldwell, Idaho: Caxton Printers, 1964. 509pp. The novel tells the story of a young Delaware chief who works with Tecumseh to unite the tribes to fight against further encroachment by the white settlers.

Eckert, Allen W. *The Frontiersmen.* Boston: Little, Brown, 1967. 626pp. The first of the author's Narratives of America series describes frontier life in the old Northwest Territory with an authentic portrayal of Tecumseh. Eckert's *Johnny Logan: Shawnee Spy* (Boston: Little, Brown, 1983. 217pp.) also includes a portrait of Tecumseh.

Fuller, Iola. *The Loon Feather.* New York: Harcourt, Brace, 1940. 419pp. Indian life in Michigan during the opening decades of the nineteenth century is depicted from the perspective of Tecumseh's daughter in a fictional tale with realistic background elements.

Recommended Juvenile Biographies

Cwiklik, Robert. *Tecumseh, Shawnee Rebel.* New York: Chelsea House, 1992. 110pp. MG/YA. Despite an overly heroic presentation of Tecumseh's character, this is an informative presentation that relates his activities against a solid period background.

Immell, Myra, and William H. *Tecumseh.* San Diego: Lucent Books, 1997. 112pp. MG/YA. This is a thorough account featuring numerous boxed quotes from primary and secondary sources.

Stefoff, Rebecca. *Tecumseh and the Shawnee Confederation.* New York: Facts on File, 1998. 138pp. MG/YA. Stefoff combines a biographical portrait with narrative history of Tecumseh's times and interesting coverage of Shawnee life.

Biographical Films and Theatrical Adaptations

Brave Warrior (1952). Director: Spencer G. Bennet. Jay Silverheels portrays Tecumseh in this fanciful and forgettable drama with Jon Hall, Michael Ansara, and Christine Larson.

Tecumseh: The Last Warrior (1995). Director: Larry Elikann. Based on Thom's fictional biography, Jesse Borrego portrays the noble Tecumseh in this earnest tribute. Video.

See also William Henry Harrison

455. PIERRE TEILHARD DE CHARDIN
1881–1955

French Jesuit, paleontologist, and philosopher, Teilhard spent the years 1926 to 1946 in China, where he discovered and studied Peking Man, a Pleistocene hominid. His *The Phenomenon of Man*, published posthumously in 1955, attempts to reconcile evolution and Christianity. Among Teilhard's other works, all published posthumously, are *The Divine Milieu* (1956) and *Hymn of the Universe* (1964).

Autobiography and Primary Sources

Several useful collections of Teilhard's letters chronicle important stages of his carer: *Letters from Egypt, 1905–1908* (New York: Herder and Herder, 1965, 256pp.); *Letters from Hastings, 1908–1912* (New York: Herder and Herder, 1968. 206pp.); *Letters from Paris, 1912–1914* (New York: Herder and Herder, 1967. 157pp.); *The Making of a Mind: Letters from a Soldier-Priest, 1914–1919* (New York: Harper & Row, 1961. 315pp.); and *Letters from a Traveller.* (New York: Harper, 1962. 380pp.).

Recommended Biographies

Cuénot, Claude. *Teilhard de Chardin: A Biographical Study.* Baltimore: Helicon, 1965. 492pp. This is the most comprehensive and authoritative presentation of Teilhard's life that both establishes the essential chronology and lucidly interprets his spiritual and intellectual development. As a reference tool documenting Teilhard's activities, Cuénot's is

still unsurpassed; the book is less helpful in capturing Teilhard's personality and private side.

Lukas, Mary, and Ellen Lukas. *Teilhard.* Garden City, New York: Doubleday, 1977. 360pp. If Cuénot stresses the public life and activities of Teilhard, the Lukases offer a more intimate glimpse of his personality, relationships, and emotional life. Their journalistic approach lacks full documentation, but the treatment is overall objective and fair.

Speaight, Robert. *The Life of Teilhard de Chardin.* New York: Harper & Row, 1967. 360pp. In many ways Speight combines the intellectual approach taken by Cuénot and the personal stressed by the Lukases, providing the best choice for the general reader in which Teilhard the man and the thinker is made accessible and understandable.

Other Biographical Studies

Barbour, George B. *In the Field with Teilhard de Chardin.* New York: Herder and Herder, 1965. 160pp. Barbour worked closely with Teilhard for more than 20 years during expeditions in China, the United States, and South Africa, and these recollections are valuable for the information they provide on Teilhard's character and the background from which his ideas were developed.

Cristiani, Léon. *Pierre Teilhard de Chardin: His Life and Spirit.* New York: Macmillan, 1960. 120pp. One of the first studies of Teilhard's life and work, Cristiani provides a bare-bones biographical summary, devoting most of the attention to Teilhard's philosophy. The book does include quotations from Teilhard's journals and letters.

De Terra, Helmut. *Memories of Teilhard de Chardin.* New York: Harper & Row, 1964. 141pp. The work of a German geologist who met with Teilhard frequently, this collection of reminiscences sheds light mainly on Teilhard the scientist.

Grenet, Paul. *Teilhard de Chardin: The Man and His Theories.* New York: Eriksson, 1966. 176pp. This is a compact overview, combining a biographical summary, photos, essays by Teilhard, and an analysis of his theories and philosophy.

King, Ursula. *Spirit of Fire: The Life and Vision of Teilhard de Chardin.* Maryknoll, New York: Orbis Books, 1996. 245pp. A fine introduction to the man and his ideas, this is a lavishly illustrated biographical portrait that includes selections from Teilhard's writings.

Lubac, Henri de. *Teilhard de Chardin: The Man and His Meaning.* New York: Hawthorn Books, 1965. 203pp. Lubac's is a lucid, intellectual and spiritual portrait based on the author's personal acquaintance with Teilhard and unpublished correspondence and notes.

Raven, Charles E. *Teilhard de Chardin: Scientist and Seer.* New York: Harper & Row, 1962. 221pp. With a compact summary of Teilhard's experiences, Raven concentrates on tracing the development of his philosophy and his influences.

Fictional Portraits

Marks, Peter. *Skullduggery.* New York: Carroll & Graf, 1987. 284pp. This inventive novel is a specu-

lative examination of the 1953 revelation that the Piltdown Man was a fake and the question of who was responsible for the hoax. A number of historical figures are presented, including Teilhard.

Recommended Juvenile Biographies

Simon, Charlie M. *Faith Has Need of All the Truth: A Life of Pierre de Chardin.* New York: Dutton, 1974. 180pp. YA. Simon describes Teilhard's early life, his vocation as a Jesuit, and his career as a paleontologist giving the reader a vivid account of his life.

456. ALFRED LORD TENNYSON
1809–1892

Among the most famous English poets of the Victorian era, Tennyson was appointed poet laureate in 1850 and created a peer in 1883. His *Poems* (1832) include the famous "The Lotus-Eaters" and "The Lady of Shalott." His next published volume, *Poems* (1842), established his reputation as a great poet and include the pieces "Locksley Hall" and "Morte d'Arthur." Among his other works are *In Memorium* (1850), *The Charge of the Light Brigade* (1855), and *Idylls of the King* (1859-1885).

Autobiography and Primary Sources

The Letters of Alfred Lord Tennyson. Cecil Y. Lang and Edgar F. Shannon, eds. Cambridge, Massachusetts: Harvard University Press, 1981–1990. 3 vols. Although Tennyson remarked that he would "as soon kill a pig as write a letter," this is an often fascinating, meticulously edited collection of the poet's letters, helpful in understanding the man, his relationships, and the mundane as well as substantive details of his professional life.

Recommended Biographies

Buckley, Jerome H. *Tennyson: The Growth of a Poet.* Cambridge, Massachusetts: Harvard University Press, 1960. 289pp. Buckley's critical biography is a judicious, readable account of Tennyson's poetic and intellectual development. Buckley traces the various patterns linking Tennyson's long public and poetic career and offers convincing critical evidence to support the author's contention that Tennyson was the greatest English poet between Wordsworth and Yeats.

Martin, Robert B. *Tennyson: The Unquiet Heart.* New York: Oxford University Press, 1980. 643pp. In the fullest and frankest biography available, regarded by many as definitive, Martin challenges both the idealized and debunking portraits of previous studies to portray a flawed but still admirable figure who is captured against a vividly re-created Victorian background.

Ricks, Christopher. *Tennyson.* 1972. Revised ed. Berkeley: University of California Press, 1989. 390pp. The editor of Tennyson's works, Ricks achieves his intention to show "the making of Tennyson the man; to establish the distinct power, subtlety, and variety of his poems along with the artistic principles and preoccupations that shaped his work; and to suggest the relationships between the man and the poet." Shrewd in its critical judgments and highly readable, Ricks's is a foundation text in the modern understanding of the man and his work.

Other Biographical Studies

Fausset, Hugh I'Anson. *Tennyson: A Modern Portrait.* New York: Appleton, 1923. 309pp. In one of the earliest modern reassessments, Fausset attempts "to disengage the man's reality from his appearance, his spiritual significance from the sentimental picture before which for so long men and women prostrated themselves." Fausset grants the poet's craftsmanship and lyrical gifts but finds him wanting from a post-Victorian standard.

Henderson, Philip. *Tennyson: Poet and Prophet.* London: Routledge, 1978. 225pp. This critical biography is a highly readable and sympathetic portrait that asserts Tennyson's modern relevance by his prophetic anticipation of modern anxiety and doubt. Includes an informative selection of photographs of the poet, his manuscripts, his associates, and places linked with Tennyson.

Levi, Peter. *Tennyson.* New York: Scribner, 1993. 370pp. Discursive and erudite, Levi's critical biography will appeal mainly to the specialist or Tennyson enthusiast with the general reader having a much harder time untangling Levi's impressive but often frustrating display of learning and insight. For the recondite reader, Levi has a great many insights about Tennyson's development and achievement as a man and poet.

Nicolson, Harold. *Tennyson: Aspects of His Life, Character, and Poetry.* Boston: Houghton Mifflin, 1923. 308pp. Nicolson's influential, revisionist interpretive biography concludes that Tennyson was "an extremely good emotional poet, but a very second-rate instructional bard...of shallow intelligence." Nicolson's study established the modern conventional view of the poet divided between his private and public poetic roles.

Ormond, Leonée. *Alfred Tennyson: A Literary Life.* New York: St. Martin's, 1993. 221pp. Ormond surveys Tennyson's life and career with an emphasis on his professional life and the history of his publications.

Page, Norman. *Tennyson: An Illustrated Life.* New York: New Amsterdam, 1993. 192pp. A short biographical account accompanies over 70 photographs and portraits of the poet at various stages of his life, and his family, friends, residences, and manuscripts.

Richardson, Joanna. *The Pre-eminent Victorian: A Study of Tennyson.* London: Cape, 1962. 313pp. Richardson's study shows the revival in interest and sympathy for the Victorian period. In her view, Tennyson is seen positively in the context of his age, and the author attempts to rejoin Tennyson the lyric poet and the public spokesman.

Tennyson, Charles. *Alfred Tennyson.* New York: Macmillan, 1949. 580pp. Tennyson's grandson adds to the biographical record important, previously unavailable biographical material related to the poet's early life and details missing from Hallam Tennyson's earlier book. A straightforward narrative account, the book emphasizes Tennyson's personal rather than literary side.

Tennyson, Hallam. *Alfred Lord Tennyson: A Memoir by His Son.* New York: Macmillan, 1897. 2 vols. Tennyson's first biography by his son arranges letters to and from the poet along with reminiscences by associates. Rarely critical or candid about Tennyson's private life, the book retains its usefulness, not for its completeness or interpretation, but as an important source of biographical details.

Thorn, Michael. *Tennyson.* New York: St. Martin's, 1993. 566pp. In a popular and at times simplified presentation, Thorn gathers many anecdotes to form a vivid and colorful view of the poet's personality and career. The author's interpretations are often out of step with current scholarly views that have challenged seeing Tennyson, as Thorn does, as a representative Victorian figure.

Fictional Portraits

Fleming, H.K. *The Day They Kidnapped Queen Victoria.* New York: St. Martin's, 1978. 191pp. Fleming's inventive, amusing historical thriller explores what happens when Queen Victoria's train to Balmoral is highjacked and Disraeli heads up the rescue, implausibly recruiting Tennyson to assist.

Other Sources

Page, Norman, ed. *Tennyson: Interviews and Recollections.* Totawa, New Jersey: Barnes and Noble, 1983. 202pp. Page collects Tennyson's own words as well as reminiscences by associates in a useful volume that offers interesting glimpses of various aspects of Tennyson's life and poetic career.

Pinion, F.B. *A Tennyson Companion: Life and Works.* New York: St. Martin's, 1984. 267pp. This is a useful reference volume that provides accessible information about the poet's life and work.

457. TERESA OF AVILA
1515–1582

Spanish nun and mystic, Teresa was a leading figure in the Counter-Reformation and is a patron saint of Spain. She founded a house of reformed Carmelites—the Discalced, or Barefoot, Carmelites—and founded convents of nuns and friars. She was canonized in 1622 and was the first woman named a Doctor of the Catholic Church. Her writings include *Life* (1562-1565), a spiritual autobiography, and *Interior Castle* (1577), a discourse on the contemplative life.

Autobiography and Primary Sources

The Life of Saint Teresa of Avila by Herself. New York: Viking/Penguin, 1987. 316pp. Regarded as a classic spiritual autobiography, Teresa's own account of her life is the essential starting point for any serious appreciation of her nature and impact.

The Letters of St. Teresa of Jesus. E. Allison Peers, ed. London: Sheed and Ward, 1980. 2 vols. This is a complete, scholarly edition of Teresa's letters, an indispensable source to reveal her character and relationships.

Recommended Biographies

Lincoln, Victoria. *Teresa: A Woman.* Albany: State University of New York Press, 1984. 440pp. Closer to fiction than to a scholarly biography, Lincoln's is nonetheless an often-revealing portrait of Teresa as a proto-feminist. Imaginative without violating the essential facts, Lincoln's account offers a fresh and original human portrait.

Medwick, Cathleen. *Teresa of Avila: The Progress of a Soul.* New York: Knopf, 1999. 282pp. Medwick's popular biography is a refreshing, modern reconsideration. Solid scholarship is woven into a compelling narrative account that treats Teresa as a fascinating, complex figure, more realistically grounded than in previous treatments.

Walsh, William T. *St. Teresa of Avila: A Biography.* Milwaukee: Bruce Publishing, 1943. 592pp. The first scholarly biography, Walsh's study remains one of the best and most trustworthy available. Based on careful research using primary and contemporary sources, Walsh presents a credible human figure against a fully realized period background.

Other Biographical Studies

Clissold, Stephen. *St. Teresa of Avila.* New York: Seabury Press, 1982. 272pp. Clissold takes a psychological approach to identify the sources of Teresa's development, examining her mysticism against the background of her family, milieu, and emotional needs.

Gross, Francis L. *The Making of a Mystic: Seasons in the Life of Teresa of Avila.* Albany: State University of New York Press, 1993. 285pp. Applying the concepts of developmental psychology to Teresa's life and formative experiences, this is a provocative reassessment.

Papasogli, Giorgio. *St. Teresa of Avila.* New York: Society of Saint Paul, 1959. 408pp. Approved by the Catholic hierarchy, this is a generally reliable account of Teresa's life and ideas that, despite an uncritical tone, is full of useful details about her career and era.

Fictional Portraits

Rohrbach, Peter-Thomas. *Bold Encounter: A Novel Based on the Life of St. John of the Cross.* Milwaukee: Bruce, 1960. 224pp. John's life is chronicled from his student days to his meeting with Teresa and his founding of the first Discalced monastery.

458. WILLIAM MAKEPEACE THACKERAY
1811–1863

Thackeray was, along with Dickens, the preeminent novelist of the early Victorian era. His most famous work, *Vanity Fair* (1848), had a major impact in establishing a realistic standard for the novel. His other works include *Pendennis* (1850), *Henry Esmond* (1852), and *The Newcomes* (1853-1855).

Autobiography and Primary Sources

The Letters and Private Papers of William Makepeace Thackeray. Gordon N. Ray, ed. Cambridge, Massachusetts: Harvard University Press, 1945–1946. 4 vols. Ray's scholarly collection of Thackeray's letters and papers is invaluable as a biographical source. One reviewer suggested that the volumes form the equivalent of a new Thackeray novel with the author as the central figure.

The Letters and Private Papers of William Makepeace Thackeray. Edgar F. Harden, ed. New York: Garland, 1994. 2 vols. Harden supplements Ray's collection with new letters and papers uncovered since the earlier volumes first appeared that cast fresh light on virtually every stage of the writer's career. In *Selected Letters of William Makepeace Thackeray* (New York: New York University Press, 1996. 416pp.), Harden selects the most revealing of Thackeray's letters to his family and friends. Includes extracts from his diaries as well as 75 of Thackeray's comic illustrations.

Recommended Biographies

Monsarrat, Ann. *An Uneasy Victorian: Thackeray the Man 1811–1863.* New York: Dodd, Mead, 1980. 461pp. Concentrating mainly on Thackeray's career as a novelist, Monsarrat's lively study, the only one specifically aimed at the general reader, is particularly useful on Victorian publishing practices and the novelist's relations with his times and with Mrs. Brookfield.

Ray, Gordon N. *Thackeray.* New York: McGraw-Hill, 1955–1958. 2 vols. Ray's monumental biography has long served as the definitive life. Solidly grounded by an intimate familiarity with the Thackeray canon, Ray's detailed study serves as well as an absorbing cultural history with Thackeray's development shown clearly against a vivid period background. Literary critic Jacob Korg has called Ray's achievement "one of the most finished critical biographies ever written."

Other Biographical Studies

Carey, John. *Thackeray: Prodigal Genius.* London: Faber and Faber, 1977. 208pp. Carey's critical study begins with a biographical summary before proceeding topically through an examination of Thackeray's works to identify characteristics of his personality.

Peters, Catherine. *Thackeray's Universe: Shifting Worlds of Imagination and Reality.* New York: Oxford University Press, 1987. 292pp. This is a highly readable summary of Thackeray's life and some of his works, part biography and part literary criticism, in which the autobiographical connections to the fiction are explored.

Ray, Gordon N. *The Buried Life: A Study of the Relation between Thackeray's Fiction and His Personal History.* Cambridge, Massachusetts: Harvard University Press, 1952. 148pp. Ray's preliminary findings before completing his two-volume life should not be overlooked. It is a revealing study of the biographical sources in the fiction. A marvel of critical distillation and judicious analysis, the study is informed by the author's impressive familiarity with Thackeray's life, works, and era.

Stevenson, Lionel. *The Showman of Vanity Fair: The Life of William Makepeace Thackeray.* 1947. Revised ed. New York: Russell & Russell, 1968. 405pp. The first full-length, scholarly biography, Stevenson's study covers the essential details of the writer's life with several factual details corrected in his revision after the appearance of Ray's edition of Thackeray's letters and his more authoritative biography. This single volume has the virtue of compression and is still one of the best shorter biographies available.

Biographical Novels

Forster, Margaret. *Memoirs of a Victorian Gentleman: William Makepeace Thackeray.* New York: Morrow, 1979. 391pp. This book imagines Thackeray's own account of his life and career, based on his letters and private papers and his recorded reflections. The novel is faithful to the biographical facts.

Fictional Portraits

Banks, Lynne Reid. *Path to the Silent Country.* New York: Delacorte, 1977. 230pp. Banks's biographical novel concerns Charlotte Brontë's years alone and her fame in London following the publication of *Jane Eyre.* Charlotte meets Thackeray, to whom she dedicated her novel.

459. THOMAS À BECKET
ca. 1118–1170

English martyr and archbishop of Canterbury, Becket first served as chancellor under Henry II. As archbishop, he supported the church against the monarchy and was increasingly at odds with the king. The rift culminated in Becket's refusal to support the Constitutions of Clarendon, which limited church authority. A threatened papal interdict brought a temporary reconciliation; however, Henry's expression of anger following Becket's excommunication of several bishops inspired four knights of the king's household to waylay and murder the archbishop at Canterbury Cathedral. He was canonized in 1173.

Autobiography and Primary Sources

Materials for the History of Thomas Becket, Archbishop of Canterbury. J.C. Roberston, ed. 1875–1885. Reprint ed. Wiesbaden: Kraus Reprint, 1965. 7 vols. Contains an assortment of documentary evidence as well as contemporary accounts by those who knew Becket.

Recommended Biographies

Barlow, Frank. *Thomas Becket.* Berkeley: University of California Press, 1986. 334pp. Concentrating on Becket's quarrel with Henry II, this is a scholarly, reliable account that carefully reviews contemporary sources but resists taking sides. The book skillfully illuminates each phase of Becket's life and provides credible insights into his personality. Along with Knowles, Barlow's study is the most trustworthy available.

Knowles, David. *Thomas Becket.* Stanford, California: Stanford University Press, 1971. 183pp. This is a brief but informative and lucidly presented study, backed up by extensive scholarship. Objectively and accessibly, Knowles sets Becket's life and his clash with Henry in the context of twelfth-century Britain.

Winston, Richard. *Thomas Becket.* New York: Knopf, 1967. 413pp. Winston supplies a full-length, objective account of Becket's life. Although not as scholarly or original as either Barlow or Knowles, the book serves as a solid, generally reliable overview for the general reader.

Other Biographical Studies

Duggan, Alfred. *My Life for My Sheep.* New York: Coward-McCann, 1955. 341pp. Highly fictionalized, Duggan's account lacks documentation but delivers a sharply focused narrative framed by the duel between Becket and Henry II and a masterful reconstruction of the period background.

Speaight, Robert. *St. Thomas of Canterbury.* New York: Longmans, 1938. 220pp. The author, a member of the original company to perform T.S. Eliot's *Murder in the Cathedral,* and who appeared in the role of Becket nearly 700 times, offers a psychological interpretation from a decidedly pro-Becket viewpoint.

Biographical Novels

Butler, Margaret. *The Lion of England.* New York: Coward-McCann, 1973. 344pp.; *The Lion of Justice.* New York: Coward-McCann, 1975. 280pp.; *The Lion of Christ.* New York: Coward-McCann, 1977. 334pp. The relationship between Becket and Henry II is chronicled from 1152 to Becket's murder in a mixture of authentic details, history, and conjecture.

Meyer, Conrad F. *The Saint: A Fictional Biography of Thomas Becket.* Providence, Rhode Island: Brown University Press, 1977. 129pp. Meyer offers a generally reliable account of Becket's life, concentrating on his troubled friendship with Henry II.

Mydans, Shelley. *Thomas: A Novel of the Life, Passions, and Miracles of Becket.* Garden City, New York: Doubleday, 1965. 439pp. This is a full-length fictionalized portrait of Becket's life and career with invented dialogue but a trustworthy sequence of events.

Plaidy, Jean. *The Plantagenet Prelude.* New York: Putnam, 1976. 335pp. Plaidy chronicles the beginning of the Plantagenet dynasty with the relationship between Eleanor of Aquitaine and Henry II and the king's friendship with Becket.

Fictional Portraits

York, Robert. *The Swords of December.* New York: Scribner, 1978. 216pp. This ingenious alternative interpretation of Henry II and Becket portrays both men as heretics and Becket's murder as a ritual sacrifice. York's thesis is more entertaining than credible, but the book offers a fresh look at Henry, Eleanor of Aquitaine, and Becket.

Recommended Juvenile Biographies

Corfe, Tom. *Archbishop Thomas and King Henry II*. New York: Cambridge University Press, 1975. 48pp. MG. This is a brief dual portrait that relates the conflict between the two men to its wider historical significance.

Duggan, Alfred. *The Falcon and the Dove: A Life of Thomas Becket of Canterbury*. New York: Pantheon Books, 1966. 217pp. YA. Duggan supplies a vivid evocation of the period that places the dispute between Henry and Becket in the context of the times.

Biographical Films and Theatrical Adaptations

Anouilh, Jean. *Becket: Or the Honor of God*. New York: Coward-McCann, 1960. 128pp. Although committing a number of historical inaccuracies, Anouilh's drama offers an arresting psychological profile of both Becket and Henry.

Eliot, T.S. *Murder in the Cathedral*. New York: Harcourt, Brace, 1935. 88pp. Eliot's poetic drama looks at the last few weeks of Becket's life in a highly stylized but often compelling treatment.

Fry, Christopher. *Curtmantle*. New York: Oxford University Press, 1961. 99pp. Fry's verse drama covers nearly all the years of the reign of Henry II and his relationship with Becket.

Tennyson, Alfred. *Becket*. London: Macmillan, 1884. 213pp. Tennyson's verse tragedy deals with the quarrel between Henry II and Becket, culminating in the latter's murder.

Becket (1964). Director: Peter Glanville. Based on Anouilh's play, Richard Burton portrays Becket and Peter O'Toole is Henry II in this impressive period drama. Video.

460. DYLAN THOMAS
1914–1953

Welsh poet ranked among the great twentieth-century poets, Thomas first achieved recognition with his controversial volume, *Eighteen Poems* (1934). His prose works include *Portrait of the Artist as a Young Dog* (1940) and *Adventures in the Skin Trade* (1955). Among his other works are *A Child's Christmas in Wales* (1955) and the dramatic work, *Under Milk Wood* (1954), both written for the radio.

Autobiography and Primary Sources

The Collected Letters of Dylan Thomas. Paul Ferris, ed. London: Dent, 1985. 982pp. Ferris's edition of Thomas's letters replaces the earlier *Selected Letters*. Constantine Fitzgibbon, ed. (New York: New Directions, 1966. 420pp.) in terms of comprehensiveness and autobiographical insights. The letters show the poet's various sides and complexity, very different from his public persona.

Portrait of the Artist as a Young Dog. Norfolk, Connecticut: New Directions, 1940. 186pp. Prose sketches describing the childhood and adolescence of a young Welshman with close correspondences to Thomas's own experiences.

Recommended Biographies

Ferris, Paul. *Dylan Thomas*. New York: Dial Press, 1977. 399pp. Regarded as a classic literary biography, Ferris's highly detailed, balanced study takes advantage of material which has become available since Fitzgibbon's biography, supplemented by interviews with hundreds of the poet's friends and associates. The result is a sensible, sympathetic but candid assessment of the poet and his development, and the standard source for a reliable chronological account of his life.

Fitzgibbon, Constantine. *The Life of Dylan Thomas*. Boston: Little, Brown, 1965. 370pp. The author was chosen by the trustees of the Dylan Thomas estate to write the official biography, and Fitzgibbon's account is based on the author's own association with the poet and the first full access to the letters and personal papers. Best on Thomas's London career, the book establishes the basic biographical record, while challenging a number of conventional views of the poet regarding his drinking and carousing.

Other Biographical Studies

Ackerman, John. *Dylan Thomas: His Life and Work*. New York: Oxford University Press, 1964. 201pp. Ackerman's mainly critical study of Thomas's poetry is chiefly useful for the Welsh context offered to help explain his development. The biographical details are limited, and the coverage of Thomas's Welsh background has been superseded by Ferris and Fitzgibbon.

Brinnin, John M. *Dylan Thomas in America*. Boston: Little, Brown, 1955. 245pp. The author, the organizer of Thomas's reading tour of America, features a frank, firsthand account of the poet's sad end in the first book-length biographical study. Brinnin is less capable in dealing with Thomas's earlier life and the sources of his unhappiness and compulsive drinking.

Perkins, Derek C. *Dylan Thomas and His World*. Swansea: Domino Books, 1995. 147pp. Blending biographical and literary insights this well-illustrated volume traces the connection between Thomas's Welsh background and his works.

Read, Bill. *The Days of Dylan Thomas*. New York: McGraw-Hill, 1964. 184pp. Read's brief chronological presentation mainly of Thomas's early life and career before he came to America is based on Thomas's letters and interviews with associates. The highlights of the poet's life are vividly summarized with anecdotes and photographs. Serves as a reliable introduction.

Sinclair, Andrew. *Dylan Thomas: No Man More Magical*. New York: Holt, 1975. 240pp. Sinclair's illustrated biography features little that is fresh or original in terms of biographical insights, more an appreciation than a detailed critical biography, redeemed chiefly by its photographic record.

Thomas, Caitlin. *Leftover Life to Kill*. Boston: Little, Brown, 1957. 239pp. The first attempt by Thomas's wife to come to terms with her husband and their relationship offers few personal glimpses of the poet and mainly concerns her painfully over-dramatized attempt to emerge from her husband's long shadow.

Thomas, Caitlin, with George Tremlett. *Caitlin: Life with Dylan Thomas*. New York: Holt, 1987. 212pp. Based on a series of recorded interviews, Caitlin Thomas's often-harrowing recollections of her life with the poet are arranged into a vivid narrative that sheds considerable light on the poet's personality and private life.

Tremlett, George. *Dylan Thomas: In the Mercy of His Means*. New York: St. Martin's, 1992. 206pp. Tremlett's discursive meditation on the poet, derived from his work with Thomas's widow, adds little to the understanding of a poet about whom the author admits that "much of his writing does not appeal to me."

Biographical Novels

Summers, John. *Dylan*. London: New English Library, 1970. 253pp. The novel dramatizes the poet's life after leaving University College, Wales, and his travels before beginning his literary career.

Biographical Films and Theatrical Adaptations

Michaels, Sidney. *Dylan*. New York: Random House, 1964. 116pp. Michaels's play is based on incidents from the poet's life derived from Brinnin and Caitlin Thomas's books.

Dylan Thomas (1988). Director: Alan Torjussen. Thomas's life is examined through photographs, his readings from his work, and film footage of places associated with the poet. Video.

Other Sources

Davies, James A. *A Reference Companion to Dylan Thomas*. New York: Greenwood, 1998. 392pp. This useful reference volume begins with a biographical overview before proceeding to a systematic examination of his work, with a final section on critical responses

461. HENRY DAVID THOREAU
1817–1862

American writer and Transcendentalist, Thoreau is a major figure in American thought and literature. His most celebrated work is *Walden* (1854), a discourse on his life in harmony with nature at Walden Pond. Thoreau's influential essay, "Civil Disobedience" (1849), was written after he was imprisoned overnight for refusing to pay a poll tax supporting the Mexican War that to him represented an extension of slavery.

Autobiography and Primary Sources

All of Thoreau's writings have a strong autobiographical basis in that they record his own travels and activities. However, the degree to which they can be read strictly as self-revelation has been an ongoing critical debate.

The Correspondence of Henry David Thoreau. Walter Hardin and Carl Bode, eds. New York: New York University Press, 1958. 665pp. Collects letters written by and to Thoreau from 1836 to 1862, arranged chronologically. With introductory commentary for each year summarizing historical events and the writer's activities, the volume forms a fragmentary but vivid biographical portrait.

Journal. John C. Broderick, ed. Princeton, New Jersey: Princeton University Press, 1981–1992. 5 vols. Thoreau's massive *Journal* has been widely praised as his greatest literary and intellectual accomplishment and is an indispensable source in gauging the man, his personality, and his ideas.

Recommended Biographies

Canby, Henry S. *Thoreau.* Boston: Houghton Mifflin, 1939. 508pp. The first truly scholarly biography, Canby's study remained the standard source until Harding. Based on solid research, Canby's assessment reveals a coherent pattern linking Thoreau's various interests and many-sided personality in which the conventional view of Thoreau's misogyny and misanthropy is challenged. Literary historian Robert Spiller called the book not only "the sanest biography of Thoreau, but it is one of the sanest I have read of anyone."

Harding, Walter R. *The Days of Henry Thoreau.* New York: Knopf, 1965. 498pp. In the most detailed account of Thoreau's life, Harding establishes the definitive record. Based on solid research, the book allows the facts to speak for themselves, although Harding's occasional interpretations are convincing and judicious. Because the author has purposefully avoided analysis of Thoreau's writing, the reader might want to consult Richardson for a supplemental portrait of the writer, his ideas, and his works.

Richardson, Robert D. *Henry Thoreau: A Life of the Mind.* Berkeley: University of California Press, 1986. 455pp. Richardson's acclaimed intellectual biography covers Thoreau's life from 1837 to his death and explores his development "as a writer, naturalist, and a reader." Richardson's internal approach represents an ideal complement to Harding's chronicle of the external details of Thoreau's life and public activities.

Other Biographical Studies

Bazalgette, Léon. *Henry Thoreau: Bachelor of Nature.* New York: Harcourt, Brace, 1924. 357pp. The work of a French writer, this is a popularization of Thoreau's life in which it is often difficult deciphering where Thoreau ends and Bazalgette begins, and vice versa. Grandiloquent and heroic in style, in marked contrast to the man celebrated, the book retains little usefulness today.

Bridgman, Richard. *Dark Thoreau.* Lincoln: University of Nebraska Press, 1982. 306pp. Bridgman's exploration of Thoreau's personality and its impact on his writing stresses his underlying pessimism and morbidity and often relies on a reductive and occasionally distorting psychoanalytic method to make its case.

Channing, William E. *Thoreau, the Poet-Naturalist.* 1873. Enlarged ed. F.B. Sanborn, ed. Boston: Goodspeed, 1902. 357pp. The author, a friend of the writer and a member of the Concord circle, offered this early tribute of recollections that features valuable firsthand observations, as well as an extended imaginary conversation between Thoreau, Emerson, and the author.

Derleth, August. *Concord Rebel: A Life of Henry David Thoreau.* Philadelphia: Chilton, 1962. 206pp. The work of a popular historical novelist, Derleth's presentation of Thoreau's life is based on secondary sources and represents an entertaining, though rarely penetrating, synthesis and overview for the general reader.

Hough, Henry B. *Thoreau of Walden.* New York: Simon & Schuster, 1956. 275pp. This is a readable introduction that reviews the highlights of Thoreau's life with anecdotes and quotations from his works. Serves to orient the nonspecialist to the man and his writing.

Lebeaux, Richard. *Young Man Thoreau.* Amherst: University of Massachusetts Press, 1977. 262pp.; *Thoreau's Seasons.* Amherst: University of Massachusetts Press, 1984. 410pp. Together, Lebeaux's two volumes complete a full-scale psycho-biography that applies the psychoanalytic-sociological identity theory of Erik Erickson. Controversial in its thesis of Thoreau's identity crisis originating in oedipal conflict, the book is loaded with insights of interest to anyone looking for possible sources for Thoreau's intellectual and emotional development.

Milder, Robert. *Reimagining Thoreau.* New York: Cambridge University Press, 1994. 237pp. Combining biographical and manuscript evidence, Milder presents a reconsideration of Thoreau's career from 1837 to his death. Milder's interesting focus is the impact of Thoreau's efforts to resolve the conflict between himself and his community.

Salt, Henry S. *Life of Henry David Thoreau.* 1890. Revised ed. London: W. Scott, 1896. 153pp. The first true biography of Thoreau is by a British writer, and Salt's undocumented account organizes fact and conjecture into a chronological and thematic account, now of mainly historical interest on nineteenth-century attitudes toward the writer.

Sanborn, Franklin B. *The Life of Henry David Thoreau.* 1917. Reprint ed. Boston: Houghton Mifflin, 1976. 541pp. Sanborn's biography is important for the testimony he records of those who knew the writer, as well as the author's own knowledge of Thoreau at Harvard. The book also supplies a catalog of Thoreau's library.

Schneider, Richard J. *Henry David Thoreau.* Boston: Twayne, 1987. 176pp. Schneider connects Thoreau's life and work in a reliable critical overview for the student.

Fictional Portraits

Aronin, Ben. *Walt Whitman's Secret.* Chicago: Argus Books, 1955. 374pp. Thoreau's association with Whitman is included in this biographical novel tracing the poet's career from the 1840s to the 1860s.

Colver, Anne. *Listen for the Voices.* New York: Farrar & Rinehart, 1939. 387pp. Concord, Massachusetts, is the setting for this novel that connects a number of fictional characters with such actual figures as Emerson and Thoreau to capture the period and its intellectual and artistic ferment.

Ehrlich, Leonard. *God's Angry Man.* New York: Simon & Schuster, 1932. 401pp. Thoreau's meeting with the abolitionist John Brown is dramatized

in this partly factual, partly imaginary account of Brown's incendiary career.

Forbes, Esther. *O, Genteel Lady!* Chicago: Academy, 1986. 296pp. Longfellow, Emerson, Thoreau, and other literary celebrities meet in Concord and Boston in a series of discussions of their works and ideas.

Longstreth, Thomas M. *Two Rivers Meet in Concord.* Philadelphia: Westminster Press, 1946. 286pp. This novel concerns period cultural life in Concord with appearances by such figures as Emerson and Margaret Fuller. The fictional character's relationship with Thoreau is central here.

Recommended Juvenile Biographies

Anderson, Peter. *Henry David Thoreau: American Naturalist.* New York: F. Watts, 1995. 63pp. MG. Part of the highly praised First Book series, this basic presentation of the facts of Thoreau's life and career features a lively text and an attractive format with interesting illustrations.

Burleigh, Robert. *A Man Named Thoreau.* New York: Atheneum, 1985. 31pp. MG. Although in a picture book format, this is a surprisingly substantive guide to Thoreau's life and ideas. Although concepts are simplified, there is no serious distortion.

Miller, Douglas T. *Henry David Thoreau.* New York: Facts on File, 1991. 114pp. YA. Arranged topically rather than chronologically, Miller's examination of Thoreau's personality is balanced, informative, and well written.

Biographical Films and Theatrical Adaptations

Lawrence, Jerome, and Robert E. Lee. *The Night Thoreau Spent in Jail.* New York: Hill & Wang, 1990. 104pp. This dramatization of Thoreau's act of civil disobedience in opposition to the Mexican War is a stimulating evocation of Thoreau's personality and ideas.

Other Sources

Borst, Raymond R., ed. *The Thoreau Log: A Documentary Log.* Boston: G.K. Hall, 1991. 654pp. A remarkable reference tool, Thoreau's daily activities, those he saw and wrote to, and what he was reading are carefully recorded, challenging the conception that the writer led an isolated life. Includes brief biographies of significant people in Thoreau's life.

Myerson, Joel, ed. *The Cambridge Companion to Henry David Thoreau.* New York: Cambridge University Press, 1995. 247pp. This collection of essays by a distinguished array of Thoreau specialists and critics sheds light on various aspects of the writer's life and work, particularly how his biography informed his writing and how personal and historical influences shaped his career.

462. TITIAN
ca. 1488–1576

Born Tiziano Vecellio, Venitian painter Titian is one of the greatest Renaissance artists. Renowned for his originality, composition, and rich use of color, he received numerous commissions during his lifetime and greatly influenced later generations of painters. His works include altarpieces such as the celebrated *Assumption of the Virgin* (1518) and many portraits as well as mythological and historical scenes.

Recommended Biographies

Crowe, J.A., and G.B. Cavalcaselle. *Titian: His Life and Times.* London: J. Murrary, 1877. 2 vols. The authors established the accepted documentary record on Titian's life and career, arranging all the existing sources chronologically and using them as the basis for an authoritative biographical summary. Although additional documents have been uncovered since the book's publication, this remains the indispensable biographical source upon which subsequent critical and biographical studies have depended.

Hope, Charles. *Titian.* New York: Harper & Row, 1980. 170pp. Hope's revisionist assessment of Titian and his work is lively and insightful. Challenging accepted wisdom, including the date of Titian's birth, Hope offers a fresh look at the painter's development, character, influence, and the significance of his paintings. Some prior knowledge of Titian and his work will assist the reader in assessing his controversial assertions.

Rosand, David. *Titian.* New York: Abrams, 1978. 158pp. In an introduction to Titian's work by the acknowledged Titian expert, the paintings are examined within a chronological framework that sheds light on the painter's life and intellectual and artistic development. Recommended as an excellent introduction.

Other Biographical Studies

Cole, Bruce. *Titian and Venetian Painting, 1450–1590.* New York: HarperCollins, 1998. 272pp. In a well-illustrated, sensitive introduction to Titian's life and work, Cole examines the painter's development chronologically from various points of view, including his cultural, historical, and artistic background.

Gronau, Georg. *Titian.* New York: Scribner, 1904. 322pp. Gronau, a recognized authority on the painter, provides a critical assessment that includes biographical information as it relates to Titian's creative method and production of his works.

Morassi, Antonio. *Titian.* Greenwich, Connecticut: Graphic Society, 1964. 69pp. This brief illustrated volume surveys Titian's artistic development and career for the general reader.

Ridolfi, Carlo. *The Life of Titian.* Bruce Cole, Julia C. and Peter Bondanella, eds. University Park: Pennsylvania State University Press, 1996. 146pp. Written by a seventeenth-century Venetian artist and writer, Ridolfi's life is translated into English for the first time in a critical edition that considers questions of reliability and the importance of the biography for the study of Titian and Renaissance art.

Riggs, Arthur S. *Titian the Magnificent and the Venice of His Day.* Indianapolis: Bobbs-Merrill, 1946. 390pp. Riggs's enthusiastic celebration of Titian's genius and character takes the form of a somewhat over simplified and often uncritical chronological survey of his life aimed at the general reader.

Vasari, Giorgio. *Lives of the Artists.* 1550. Reprint ed. New York: Penguin, 1965. 2 vols. Vasari's portrait of the painter is the principal source of biographical and anecdotal information on Titian and is less speculative than other profiles in Vasari's monumental collection because of the author's acquaintance with the painter.

Biographical Novels

Cecchi, Dario. *Titian.* New York: Farrar, Straus, 1958. 232pp. The details of Titian's life and career are enhanced with invented dialogue and period details.

Weiss, David. *The Venetian.* New York: Morrow, 1976. 366pp. An elderly Titian recalls his long career in this fictional autobiography that is reliable in its summary of the painter's life and work and the period background.

Fictional Portraits

Borton, Elizabeth. *The Greek of Toledo: A Romantic Narrative about El Greco.* New York: Crowell, 1959. 277pp. El Greco's apprenticeship years in Italy under Titian and Tintoretto are depicted in this imaginative embellishment of the facts about the painter's life.

Braider, Donald. *Color from a Light Within: A Novel Based on the Life of El Greco.* New York: Putnam, 1967. 379pp. El Greco's apprenticeship under Titian is included in this biographical portrait of the Cretian artist.

Recommended Juvenile Biographies

Ripley, Elizabeth. *Titian: A Biography.* New York: Oxford University Press, 1962. 68pp. MG. Titian's life story is narrated along with a representative sampling of his works that are critically analyzed.

Biographical Films and Theatrical Adaptations

Titian (1989). Director: Didier Baussy. This is an informative film profile that covers both the major events of the painter's life and a critique of his works. Video.

Other Sources

Rostand, David, ed. *Titian: His World and His Legacy.* New York: Columbia University Press, 1982. 349pp. This collection of critical essays by leading experts touches on various aspects of Titian's life, art, and times.

463. LEO TOLSTOY
1828–1910

Russian novelist Tolstoy is often regarded as one of the world's greatest writers. His masterpiece is *War and Peace* (1862–1869), an epic novel of five families set against the background of the Napoleonic Wars. Another celebrated novel is *Anna Karenina* (1873–1876), the tragic story of an adulterous affair. Tolstoy's other works include the short story, "The Death of Ivan Ilyich," and the novels *The Kreutzer Sonata* (1889) and *Resurrection* (1899–1900).

Autobiography and Primary Sources

Childhood, Boyhood, Youth. New York: Knopf, 1991. 314pp. Tolstoy's fictionalized recollections of his early years are revealing even though readers should be cautious in assuming a total autobiographical account.

Confession. New York: W.W. Norton, 1996. 95pp. Tolstoy's recounting of his psychological crisis and religious conversion following the completion of *Anna Karenina* is crucial for an understanding of the man and particularly his later ideas and activities.

Tolstoy's Diaries. R.F. Christian, ed. New York: Scribner, 1985. 2 vols. Tolstoy kept a diary from the age of 18 until shortly before his death; this selection reprints the most interesting passages that best reveal Tolstoy as a writer, moralist, social thinker, and private family man.

Tolstoy's Letters. R.F. Christian, ed. Cambridge, Massachusetts: Harvard University Press, 1978. 2 vols. This collection of 608 letters arranged chronologically covers the years 1845 to 1910. Although only a small portion of Tolstoy's extant correspondence, the volumes are indispensable, providing a great deal of biographical material hitherto unavailable to non-Russian readers.

Recommended Biographies

Maude, Aylmer. *The Life of Tolstoy.* New York: Dodd, Mead, 1910. 2 vols. Maude's early biography remains an important achievement. The author, an intimate of the writer and translator of his works, possessed unique familiarity with and access to his subject, which is put to good use in a comprehensive and detailed account.

Simmons, Ernest. *Leo Tolstoy.* Boston: Little, Brown, 1936. 790pp. The most scholarly of the available Tolstoy biographies. Simmons's objective and factual approach is reliable, serving better as a reference source than to be enjoyed as an entertaining narrative.

Troyat, Henri. *Tolstoy.* Garden City, New York: Doubleday, 1967. 762pp. Troyat's entertaining and vivid biography pushes the limit of imaginative conjecture in which Tolstoy's life is treated like a novel with the writer as its central character. Troyat's facts are reliable, however, and the book attempts to reconcile the various paradoxes that the writer's life suggests with skill.

Wilson, A.N. *Tolstoy.* New York: W.W. Norton, 1988. 572pp. Wilson's is an opinionated and lively intellectual biography that traces the development of Tolstoy's artistry and ideas. Well researched and impressive in its ability to establish the essential patterns in Tolstoy's character, Wilson's biography is a remarkable achievement, ranking with the best literary biographies.

Other Biographical Studies

Asquith, Cynthia. *Married to Tolstoy*. Boston: Houghton Mifflin, 1961. 288pp. Asquith sees herself as "a self-appointed Counsel for the Defense" in the case against Sonya in the Tolstoy marriage battle. The book covers mostly familiar territory for the general reader, relieved by a willingness to grant that both parties shared responsibility for the misery in their marriage.

Bulgakov, V.F. *The Last Year of Leo Tolstoy*. New York: Dial Press, 1971. 235pp. Tolstoy's personal secretary kept an extensive diary recording the events leading up to the writer's death. Bulgakov's objectivity in the conflict and strife surrounding Tolstoy's break with his family makes this one of the most important sources for reliable information on the end of Tolstoy's life.

Courcel, Martine de. *Tolstoy: The Ultimate Reconciliation*. New York: Scribner, 1988. 458pp. Offering little that is new except the questionable contention that Tolstoy's final departure from his family represented "the ultimate reconciliation" of his contradictions and his decision to return to artistic literature, this is a psychologically oriented biography based mainly on a close reading of Tolstoy's diaries and letters.

Crankshaw, Edward. *Tolstoy: The Making of a Novelist*. New York: Viking, 1974. 276pp. This illustrated biography helpfully documents Tolstoy's life in pictures; the text, however, is remarkably hostile to the man, particularly in his later stage as a religious and moral sage.

Edwards, Anne. *The Life of Countess Tolstoy*. New York: Simon & Schuster, 1981. 512pp. Edwards is a strong advocate for Sonya over the novelist in their marital battle. The book offers little that is new on one of the most publicized marriages in history other than its feminist perspective.

Gustafson, Richard F. *Leo Tolstoy: Resident and Stranger*. Princeton, New Jersey: Princeton University Press, 1986. 480pp. Gustafson's critical analysis of Tolstoy's metaphysics and ethics tracks the consistency in his thinking, countering the widely held view that Tolstoy was divided between the preconversion artist and the postconversion reformer and prophet.

Hofmann, Modest, and André Pierre. *By Deeds of Truth: The Life of Leo Tolstoy*. New York: Crown, 1958. 268pp. This brief overview concentrates on capturing Tolstoy's personality and the cultural and moral atmosphere in which he developed. While offering little that is new, the book is a lively, readable summary of the highlights of Tolstoy's life and character.

Kuzminskaya, Tatyana A. *Tolstoy as I Knew Him*. New York: Macmillan, 1948. 439pp. Written by Tolstoy's sister-in-law, this account of the author's life during the 1860s and 1870s has been called by biographer Ernest Simmons, "a veritable treasure-trove" of revealing glimpses of Tolstoy's domestic affairs.

Nazaroff, Alexander I. *Tolstoy: The Inconstant Genius*. New York: F.A. Stokes, 1929. 332pp. Nazaroff fashions a dramatic narrative account of Tolstoy's life for the general reader. The author prefers Tolstoy the artist rather than Tolstoy the prophet and holy man, and the division between the two is not adequately reconciled.

Rolland, Romain. *Tolstoy*. New York: Dutton, 1911. 312pp. Rolland's appreciative study of Tolstoy is based on firsthand knowledge and concentrates on the writer's later career.

Shirer, William L. *Love and Hatred: The Troubled Marriage of Leo and Sonya Tolstoy*. New York: Simon & Schuster, 1994. 400pp. Shirer focuses mainly on the last decades of Tolstoy's 48-year marriage with a third of the book concerned with Tolstoy's final year. The book attempts to be fair to both parties, but is rarely very penetrating beyond the sad details of the couple's relationship.

Smoluchowski, Louise. *Lev and Sonya: The Story of the Tolstoy Marriage*. New York: Putnam, 1987. 288pp. This is credible, even-handed account of the Tolstoys's 48-year marriage based on primary sources.

Tolstoy, Alexandra. *Tolstoy: A Life of My Father*. New York: Harper, 1953. 543pp. Tolstoy's youngest daughter supplies her recollections. Alexandra was the writer's closest companion and amanuensis during his final years, and her perspective is revealing on Tolstoy's last phase, even though there is a lack of critical detachment, and the partisan battles over control of Tolstoy are still being waged.

Tolstoy, Sergei. *Tolstoy Remembered by His Son*. New York: Atheneum, 1962. 234pp. Tolstoy's eldest son presents his memories of his father written before Sergei's death in 1947. While his perspective is interesting, there is little here that is particularly striking or original.

Tolstoy, Tatyana. *Tolstoy Remembered*. New York: McGraw-Hill, 1977. 312pp. These recollections by Tolstoy's daughter portray the writer as an affectionate if demanding father and generous, likable man whose passion for social justice alienated his wife and some of his children. The portrait offers an interesting, festive side to Tolstoy's family life that is mostly obscured by the grim details of the contest of wills between husband and wife.

Biographical Novels

Parini, Jay. *The Last Station: A Novel of Tolstoy's Last Year*. New York: Holt, 1990. 290pp. The novel follows Tolstoy's last days from a variety of perspectives. Factually accurate as to events, the novel freely imagines the central figures' conversations and thoughts.

Fictional Portraits

Okudzhava, Bulat S. *The Extraordinary Adventures of Secret Agent Shipov*. London: Abelard-Schuman, 1973. 214pp. Based on an actual incident in Tolstoy's life, the novel dramatizes the czarist secret police's investigation of the novelist's life in 1862.

Recommended Juvenile Biographies

Carroll, Sara N. *The Search: A Biography of Leo Tolstoy*. New York: Harper & Row, 1973. 158pp. MG/YA. This is an accurate, well-written biography that documents Tolstoy's story through excerpts from his diaries and other primary sources.

Biographical Films and Theatrical Adaptations

Stevens, Henry B. *Tolstoy: A Play in Seven Scenes*. New York: Crowell, 1928. 155pp. Stevens dramatizes a series of episodes from Tolstoy's life from 1878 to his death that follow the biographical record and uses much of the writer's own words.

Leo Tolstoy (1988). Director: S. Sivachenko. This Russian film biographical portrait features narration by English actors Alan Dobie and Anna Massey. Video.

Leo Tolstoy: A Brilliant Look at the Life of Leo Tolstoy (1984). Director: Sergei Gerasimov. This Russian film documents Tolstoy's life with archival material and footage of places associated with the writer. Video.

464. ARTURO TOSCANINI
1867–1957

Italian conductor Toscanini was a cellist with minor European orchestras before achieving international recognition as one of the world's greatest conductors. He was musical director at La Scala in Milan and conducted the New York Metropolitan and Philharmonic orchestras. The NBC Symphony Orchestra was created for him. He was known for his tempestuous personality and the electrifying performances he elicited from his musicians.

Recommended Biographies

Sachs, Harvey. *Toscanini*. Philadelphia: Lippincott, 1978. 380pp. The book's documentation of Toscanini's private and public life takes advantage of all the significant sources and is the most comprehensive and balanced account of the conductor's life available. Sachs revisits and updates aspects of Toscanini's career and personality in *Reflections on Toscanini* (New York: Grove, Weidenfeld, 1991. 191pp.), a collection of essays and reviews.

Other Biographical Studies

Chotzinoff, Samuel. *Toscanini: An Intimate Portrait*. New York: Knopf, 1956. 148pp. This personal memoir, based on the author's relationship with Toscanini since 1926, is a series of anecdotes mainly documenting the conductor's idiosyncrasies. The author's pursuit of a good story often results in falsification, and the book should be read with caution with regard to its overall truthfulness.

Haggin, B.H. *Arturo Toscanini: Contemporary Recollections of the Maestro*. New York: Da Capo, 1989. 297pp. This interesting volumes brings together two previous books by the author, *Conversations with Toscanini* (Garden City, New York: Doubleday, 1959. 261pp.) and *The Toscanini Musicians Knew* (New York: Horizon Press, 1967.

245pp.). Both supply useful insights from Toscanini's own perspective and by musicians who knew him.

Horowitz, Joseph. *Understanding Toscanini.* New York: Knopf, 1987. 492pp. Less the story of Toscanini than America's response to him, Horowitz's study, combining biography, cultural history, and musical criticism, has been scathingly attacked by such Toscanini experts as Harvey Sachs. Horowitz's focus is wider than an attempt to understand Toscanini, offering a socioeconomic study of the classical music industry in which Toscanini serves as a springboard.

Marek, George. *Toscanini.* New York: Atheneum, 1975. 321pp. Marek's is a readable, anecdotal survey of Toscanini's career and character. Neither a scholarly nor a complete biography and often highly conjectural, the book is an uneven and disorganized account but can still be enjoyed though not always trusted.

Matthews, Denis. *Arturo Toscanini.* New York: Hippocrene Books, 1982. 176pp. This brief overview ably serves as a useful introduction for the general reader. The book features numerous illustrations and a reliable discography.

Sacchi, Filippo. *The Magic Baton.* New York: Putnam, 1957. 224pp. The work of an Italian journalist and a friend of the conductor, Sacchi's account combines firsthand details and familiarity with the Italian musical scene. This is the best of the several biographical portraits by Toscanini's friends and associates. Others include Nicotra, Tobia. *Arturo Toscanini* (New York: Knopf, 1929. 235pp.); Stefan, Paul. *Arturo Toscanini* (New York: Viking, 1936. 126pp.); and Taubman, Howard. *The Maestro: The Life of Arturo Toscanini* (New York: Simon & Schuster, 1951. 342pp.).

Fictional Portraits

Paul, Barbara. *A Cadenza for Caruso.* New York: St. Martin's, 1984. 146pp. Puccini is charged with murder in this mystery set in 1910. Enrico Caruso attempts to clear his friend by discovering the real killer. Despite the fanciful story, the novel does offer an authentic depiction of the New York opera world of the period and an appearance by Toscanini.

Biographical Films and Theatrical Adaptations

Toscanini: The Maestro (1985). Director: Peter Rosen. A documentary profile using rare home movies and interviews with those who knew and worked with the conductor. Video.

465. HENRI DE TOULOUSE-LAUTREC
1864–1901

French painter and lithographer Toulouse-Lautrec is famous for his depictions of Parisian nightlife. The son of a wealthy nobleman, Lautrec fell and broke both his legs as a child, and his growth was permanently stunted. He studied in Paris and set-tled in the Montmartre district, where he painted popular entertainers such as the dancers and personalities of the Moulin Rouge cabaret. Influenced by Degas and by Japanese prints, his work did much to popularize the lithographic poster. His works include *At the Moulin de la Galette* (1892) and *Seated Female Clown* (1896).

Autobiography and Primary Sources

The Letters of Henri de Toulouse-Lautrec. Herbert D. Schimmel, ed. New York: Oxford University Press, 1991. 444pp. This collection of more than 600 letters is the most complete record of the artist's correspondence available. The letters fill in many gaps in the record of his life and artistic development.

Recommended Biographies

Hanson, Lawrence, and Elisabeth Hanson. *The Tragic Life of Toulouse-Lautrec.* New York: Random House, 1956. 277pp. More a psychological than an artistic study, the Hansons supply a vivid character study that, despite the book's title, is far from sentimental in its approach. With an eye for the telling detail, the book tracks the various stages of Lautrec's career and his many personal disappointments.

Frey, Julia. *Toulouse-Lautrec: A Life.* New York: Viking, 1994. 595pp. Written by the leading expert on the painter and his work, Frey's is among the most comprehensive and detailed biographies available, based on meticulous research and aided by previously unavailable family letters. An in-depth analysis of the environmental, family, and psychological factors that formed the artist, the book substitutes a credible, human portrait for the various distortions of previous views of his life and character.

Other Biographical Studies

Adriani, Götz. *Toulouse-Lautrec.* New York: Thames and Hudson, 1987. 336pp. Adriani's text for a West German exhibition includes previously unpublished photographs and an extensive narrative chronology.

Huisman, Philippe, and M.G. Dortu. *Lautrec by Lautrec.* New York: Galahad Books, 1964. 274pp. The text is a straightforward account of Lautrec's life with a number of intimate details. The bulk of the book, however, is a collection of the pictures, photographs, and correspondence the artist left to his friend and art dealer, Maurice Joyant. Particularly interesting in documenting the artist's early years, the portrait of the man that emerges from this private material contradicts the image of the debauched rebel of conventional wisdom.

Mack, Gerstle. *Toulouse-Lautrec.* New York: Knopf, 1938. 370pp. The first full-length biography, Mack's study continues to serve the scholar and general reader alike in its thoroughness and meticulous research. Mack surveys the artist's life, his work, and his milieu.

Perruchot, Henri. *Toulouse-Lautrec.* New York: Collier, 1962. 350pp. Perruchot's is a lively, anecdotally rich study that captures the man from a number of perspectives, informed by a solid sense of the cultural setting of the artist's era.

Biographical Novels

La Mure, Pierre. *Moulin Rouge: A Novel Based on the Life of Henri de Toulouse-Lautrec.* New York: Random House, 1950. 438pp. Tracing Lautrec's life from his boyhood to his death, La Mure's is a sympathetic and somewhat sentimentalized treatment with an authentic period background.

Fictional Portraits

Berkman, Ted. *To Seize the Passing Dream: A Novel of Whistler, His Women, and His World.* Garden City, New York: Doubleday, 1972. 491pp. Berkman's fictionalized biography of painter James McNeill Whistler portrays many of the literary and artistic figures of the period, including Lautrec.

Longstreet, Stephen, and Ethel Longstreet. *Man of Montmarte: A Novel Based on the Life of Maurice Utrillo.* New York: Funk & Wagnalls, 1958. 403pp. This fictional biography of French painter Utrillo vividly presents his life and times with appearances by figures from the artistic world, including Degas and Lautrec.

Lovesey, Peter. *Bertie and the Crime of Passion.* New York: Mysterious Press, 1995. 244pp. In this installment of the author's amusing period mysteries involving the future Edward VII as an unlikely sleuth, Bertie is in Paris investigating a murder at the Moulin Rouge with Sarah Bernhardt as his assistant and Lautrec as his crime-scene sketch artist.

Stone, Irving. *Lust for Life.* Garden City, New York: Doubleday, 1934. 500pp. Stone's remarkable fictional biography of Van Gogh includes appearances by a number of period figures, including Lautrec, Gauguin, Cezanne, Henri Rousseau, and Zola.

Recommended Juvenile Biographies

Bryant, Jennifer. *Henri de Toulouse-Lautrec, Artist.* New York: Chelsea House, 1994. 127pp. MG/YA. Part of the Great Achievers series, this informative biography emphasizes the challenges Lautrec faced from his disability.

Horwitz, Sylvia L. *Toulouse-Lautrec: His World.* New York: Harper & Row, 1973. 215pp. YA. Lautrec's life and artistic career are candidly and sensitively treated, supplemented by a wide selection of the painter's works and photographs of the artist.

Biographical Films and Theatrical Adaptations

Moulin Rouge (1954). Director: John Huston. Jose Ferrar is convincing as the painter in this rich evocation of period Paris. Co-starring Zsa Zsa Gabor, Eric Pohlmann, Christopher Lee, and Peter Cushing. Video.

Toulouse-Lautrec (1988). Director: Hilary Chadwick. Lautrec's life, career, and paintings are covered in an informative film portrait of the man and his age. Video.

466. ANTHONY TROLLOPE
1815–1882

Acknowledged as one of the great English Victorian novelists, Trollope worked for the British postal service until 1867. He achieved fame with *The Warden* (1855), the first in a popular series of Barsetshire novels. A sharp but sympathetic observer of Victorian social and political life, Trollope is also famous for his Palliser series, which include the novels *Phineas Finn* (1869), *The Eustace Diamonds* (1873), and *The Prime Minister* (1876).

Autobiography and Primary Sources

An Autobiography. David Skilton, ed. New York: Penguin, 1996. 285pp. Trollope's frank account of his writing life helped set back his reputation among his contemporaries, who were looking for inspiration rather than perspiration among their creative writers. Along with the *Letters*, Trollope's memoir is indispensable in gaining the measure of the man.

The Letters of Anthony Trollope. N. John Hall, ed. Stanford, California: Stanford University Press, 1983. 2 vols. More than 1,800 letters show Trollope's relations with his publishers, his work for the post office, and his extended trips abroad. Also included are many letters to and about Trollope by associates.

Recommended Biographies

Glendinning, Victoria. *Anthony Trollope*. New York: Knopf, 1993. 551pp. This is a richly detailed, shrewd assessment of the man and the novelist. Glendinning is effective in establishing the connections between Trollope's experiences and his writing and the private man beneath his public image. The book is excellent on the social history that animates the novelist's era and values.

Hall, N. John. *Trollope: A Biography*. New York: Oxford University Press, 1991. 581pp. As editor of the collected works and the letters, Hall is the recognized Trollope authority, and his biography has been hailed as definitive. Both highly readable and informative, Hall's portrait of Trollope is one of the fullest and richest that has yet been written.

Mullen, Richard. *Anthony Trollope: A Victorian in His World*. London: Duckworth, 1990. 767pp. Mullen argues that Trollope embodied Victorian values, and this critical biography draws connections among his personal experiences, his era, and his works. The book is useful in calling attention to the personal issues that the novelist continued to deal with in his fiction.

Super, R.H. *The Chronicler of Barsetshire: A Life of Anthony Trollope*. Ann Arbor: University of Michigan Press, 1988. 528pp. Arranged into a year-by-year account, this detailed, comprehensive study emphasizes fact over interpretation and character analysis. Super adds considerably to the view of Trollope's school days and professional life, and the book is an impressive achievement in authoritatively establishing the biographical record of the novelist.

Other Biographical Studies

Booth, Bradford. *Anthony Trollope: Aspects of His Life and Work*. Bloomington: Indiana University Press, 1958. 258pp. Neither a complete survey of the man nor of his works, Booth's study attempts to establish how Trollope's view of the world shaped his fiction, while placing his novels in the context of Victorian novel-writing and publishing practices.

Pope-Hennessey, James. *Anthony Trollope*. Boston: Little, Brown, 1971. 400pp. Written to help justify the revival of interest in Trollope's work, the book is a mixture of plot summaries, critical analysis, and biographical data. More an appreciation than an analysis or interpretation with little that goes beyond what can be gleaned from *An Autobiography*.

Sadleir, Michael. *Anthony Trollope: A Commentary*. New York: Houghton Mifflin, 1927. 423pp. Sadleir's pioneering biographical portrait and critical study helped begin the modern revival of interest in Trollope and the restoration of his reputation as a novelist. His chapter, "The Portrait of Anthony," remains one of the best character sketches of the novelist.

Snow, C.P. *Trollope: His Life and Work*. New York: Scribner, 1975. 191pp. This lavishly illustrated biography records Snow's admiration for both the man and the novelist. The text forms a useful introduction, particularly strong on Trollope's childhood and civil service career.

Super, Robert H. *Trollope in the Post Office*. Ann Arbor: University of Michigan Press, 1981. 135pp. Drawing on the Post Office Records Department and Trollope's own traveling journal, Super details the novelist's 34-year career, in which he rose from a teenage junior clerk to a senior official. The book makes clear how important Trollope's professional career was to his life and how his work experiences permeate his writing.

Walpole, Horace. *Anthony Trollope*. New York: Macmillan, 1928. 205pp. A compact, limited view of Trollope and his work, part of the English Men of Letters series, Walpole's study is the work of an enthusiast for other converts.

Fictional Portraits

Russell, Ray. *Princess Pamela*. Boston: Houghton Mifflin, 1979. 428pp. Written in the form of a diary kept by a young Englishwoman in 1837, the year of Victoria's succession, the novel features characterizations of a number of historical figures, including a young Anthony Trollope.

Wilson, A.N. *Gentlemen in England*. New York: Viking, 1986. 311pp. Wilson's portrait of Victorian London in the 1880s features appearances by a number of actual figures, including Trollope, George Eliot, and Walter Pater.

Other Sources

Terry, R.C. *A Trollope Chronology*. Basinstoke, England: Macmillan, 1989. 167pp. This is a convenient reference guide to Trollope's activities and the publication of his many works.

Terry, R.C. *Oxford Reader's Companion to Trollope*. New York: Oxford University Press, 1999. 408pp. This extensive reference guide covers Trollope's 47 novels and characters as well as details of the novelist's private and public life in a series of alphabetically arranged entries.

Terry, R.C., ed. *Trollope: Interviews and Recollections*. New York: St. Martin's, 1987. 257pp. This compendium collects a wide variety of comments on the novelist from his contemporaries.

467. LEON TROTSKY
1879–1940

Russian Communist revolutionary and a founder of the Soviet Union, Trotsky was born Lev Davidovich Bronstein. He was a chief organizer of the 1917 October Revolution, served as Lenin's commissar for foreign affairs, and while commissar of war organized the Red Army. When Stalin came to power, he was deported and during his exile advocated international revolution and attacked Stalinism. He settled in Mexico City, where he was murdered by an alleged Stalinist agent.

Autobiography and Primary Sources

Diary in Exile, 1935. Cambridge, Massachusetts: Harvard University Press, 1958. 218pp. This diary kept by Trotsky during his period of exile in France and Norway is a revealing look at the private man.

My Life. New York: Grosset & Dunlap, 1966. 599pp. Trotsky narrates his own story up to 1929 in a fascinating and surprisingly candid reflection of the events and key figures of the Russian Revolution and the formation of the Soviet state. Essential reading for an understanding of Trotsky's self-conception and understanding of history.

Writings of Leon Trotsky. George Breitman and Sarah Lovell, eds. New York: Pathfinder Press, 1973–1975. 12 vols. This enormous collection of Trotsky's pamphlets, articles, letters, and interviews is an important source for information about the man and his ideas.

Recommended Biographies

Carmichael, Joel. *Trotsky: An Appreciation of His Life*. New York: St. Martin's, 1975. 512pp. Blending a narrative account of Trotsky's life with an insightful psychological analysis, Carmichael is successful in providing a balanced examination of the man and his historical role. Trotsky the man, orator, and writer predominates here, as the book helps to disentangle his character from his public persona.

Deutscher, Isaac. *The Prophet Armed: Trotsky 1879–1921*. New York: Oxford University Press, 1954. 540pp.; *The Prophet Unarmed: Trotsky 1921–1929*. New York: Oxford University Press, 1959. 490pp.; *The Prophet Outcast: Trotsky 1919–1940*. New York: Oxford University Press, 1963. 543pp. In by far the fullest, most detailed account of Trotsky's life, Deutscher's sympathy (both ideological and personal) for his subject helps humanize the man without unduly disguising his flaws. Well written, drawing on czarist and Bolshevik records, interviews with eyewitnesses, and Trotsky's intimate correspondence with his wife and family, Deutscher's account creates a complex portrait in which Trotsky's ideas, development, and human strengths and weaknesses are drawn in compelling detail.

Howe, Irving. *Leon Trotsky.* New York: Viking, 1978. 214pp. Howe's is a tough-minded, though fair, introductory study of Trotsky's life and thought in which his development as a revolutionary philosopher is examined chiefly through his writing and speeches.

Volkogonov, Dmitri. *Trotsky: The Eternal Revolutionary.* New York: Free Press, 1996. 524pp. Serving as a more realistic counterpoint to Deutscher's overall adulatory account, Volkogonov draws on formerly restricted Soviet archives for a sobering human portrait in which Trotsky's revolutionary greatness and tragic shortcomings are kept in clear focus in a full-length study. The book challenges the notion that had Trotsky been successful in the battle with Stalin for control of the revolution, the outcome would have been considerably different.

Other Biographical Studies

Eastman, Max. *Leon Trotsky: The Portrait of a Youth.* New York: Greenberg, 1925. 181pp. Eastman, an intimate of Trotsky, supplies this portrait of his friend's early years in a sentimental account, chiefly valuable for the anecdotes that Trotsky supplied the author.

Glotzer, Albert. *Trotsky: Memoir & Critique.* Buffalo, New York: Pathfinder Books, 1990. 343pp. This is an account of the author's personal contacts with Trotsky during his exile as well as an appraisal of his character and ideas. The book supplements the biographical record with a detailed account of Trotsky's conflict with Stalin during the 1930s.

King, David. *Trotsky: A Photographic Biography.* New York: Blackwell, 1986. 214pp. King's illustrated biography is chiefly useful for its photographic record with a serviceable, though rarely penetrating text.

Payne, Robert. *The Life and Death of Trotsky.* New York: McGraw-Hill, 1977. 498pp. Often superficial, Payne's entertaining presentation of Trotsky's life and times takes the form of a series of highly colored dramatic vignettes that illuminate the man, though offering few clues to locate the source of the man's power or weaknesses.

Serge, Victor, and Natalia Sedova-Trotsky. *The Life and Death of Leon Trotsky.* New York: Basic Books, 1975. 296pp. The joint work of a committed supporter and Trotsky's second wife is a partisan study of Trotsky's career as a political leader and Marxist theoretician in which Trotsky and Lenin's dictatorial abuses are excused with only Stalin's crimes censured, supplemented by intimate, personal recollections.

Van Heijenoort, Jan. *With Trotsky in Exile.* Cambridge, Massachusetts: Harvard University Press, 1978. 164pp. Serving as Trotsky's secretary, translator, and bodyguard during his exile, the author supplies his recollections of those years, based on notes he kept at the time. The book is a valuable corrective to other accounts of Trotsky's final days.

Warth, Robert D. *Leon Trotsky.* Boston: Twayne, 1977. 215pp. This is an incisive, detailed introductory study of the man and his ideas, appropriate for the student and general reader looking for a concise, reliable orientation.

Wistrich, Robert S. *Trotsky: Fate of a Revolutionary.* New York: Stein and Day, 1982. 235pp. This is a well-documented, full-length biography that offers a balanced assessment of the man and his times, with an emphasis on the reasons for Trotsky's fall from power.

Wyndham, Francis and David King. *Trotsky: A Documentary.* New York: Praeger, 1972. 204pp. The authors add to this collection of pictures, photographs, and drawings chronicling Trotsky's life from his childhood to his death with a brief, sympathetic prose profile mainly constructed out of Trotsky's own words.

Biographical Novels

Wolfe, Bernard. *Trotsky Dead.* Los Angeles: Wollstonecraft, 1975. 372pp. The author, who served as one of Trotsky's secretaries in Mexico, provides an accurate fictional account of Trotsky's last days.

Fictional Portraits

Burgess, Anthony. *The End of the World News.* New York: McGraw-Hill, 1983. 388pp. Burgess's inventive historical fantasy interweaves the events from the lives of Freud and Trotsky into a meditation on the greatest events of the twentieth century.

Elliott, John. *Blood on the Snow.* New York: St. Martin's, 1977. 334pp. The early stages of the Russian Revolution are dramatized in the events of 1905 with appearances by Trotsky, Gorky, and Lenin.

Hanlon, Emily. *Petersburg.* New York: Putnam, 1988. 541pp. Weaving a fictional story around the events in Russia during 1905, the novel portrays Nicholas II, Gorky, Trotsky, and other historical figures.

Recommended Juvenile Biographies

Archer, Jules. *Trotsky: World Revolutionary.* New York: J. Messner, 1973. 191pp. MG/YA. Archer presents Trotsky with both his strengths and faults and clarifies without oversimplifying the political circumstances of the Russian Revolution and its aftermath.

Garza, Hedda. *Leon Trotsky.* New York: Chelsea House, 1986. 112pp. MG/YA. This is a full-length, informative portrait that helps establish Trotsky's historical significance, as well as his personal strengths and weaknesses.

Biographical Films and Theatrical Adaptations

Weiss, Peter. *Trotsky in Exile.* New York: Atheneum, 1972. 123pp. Weiss chronicles Trotsky's last years and death in an often preachy drama.

The Assassination of Trotsky (1972). Director: Joseph Losey. Richard Burton portrays Trotsky in the days leading up to his murder. Alain Delon and Romy Schneider co-star. Video.

Zina (1985). Director: Ken McMullen. This dark, cerebral film explores the psychological traumas experienced by Trotsky's daughter (Domiziana Giordano). Philip Madoc portrays Trotsky.

See also Vladimir Lenin; Joseph Stalin

468. HARRY S TRUMAN
1884–1972

The thirty-third U. S. president, Truman was active in Kansas City politics before serving as vice president under Franklin D. Roosevelt. He became president upon Roosevelt's death (1945). Truman accepted the German surrender, made the controversial decision to drop the atomic bomb on Japan to end the Pacific war, was involved in the establishment of the United Nations, instituted the Truman Doctrine and the Marshall Plan, and supported the establishment of NATO. His second term (1949–1953) was marked by the Korean conflict and the anti-Communist hysteria generated by Senator Joseph McCarthy.

Autobiography and Primary Sources

The Autobiography of Harry S. Truman. Robert H. Ferrell, ed. Boulder: Colorado Associated University Press, 1980. 153pp. Fragmentary reminiscences of Truman's childhood, military service, and early political career written during several periods of his life are pieced together in a continuous narrative.

Memoirs. Garden City, New York: Doubleday, 1955–1956. 2 vols. Volume one covers Truman's first year as president; volume two covers the remainder of the presidential years. Truman's recollections have been called the most candid self-assessment of any former president in which his mind and character are frankly depicted in the story of these years as he saw them.

Off the Record: The Private Papers of Harry S. Truman. Robert H. Ferrell, ed. New York: Harper & Row, 1980. 448pp. Two-thirds of the book deal with Turman's presidency and include letters sent to family and friends, a diary, and several letters written in the heat of the moment but never sent. Ferrell's text puts the writings in their historical context.

Where the Buck Stops: The Personal and Private Writings of Harry S. Truman. Margaret Truman, ed. New York: Warner Books, 1989. 388pp. This is a potpourri of anecdotes and opinions by Truman, chiefly about the presidency and occupants of the White House.

There are several valuable collections of Truman's letters, including *Letters from Father: The Truman Family's Personal Correspondence.* Margaret Truman, ed. (New York: Arbor House, 1981. 255pp.); *Dear Bess: The Letters from Harry to Bess Truman, 1910–1959.* Robert H. Ferrell, ed. (New York: W.W. Norton, 1983. 593pp.); and *Letters Home.* Monte M. Poen, ed. (New York: Putnam, 1984. 303pp.).

Recommended Biographies

Ferrell, Robert H. *Harry S. Truman: A Life*. Columbia: University of Missouri Press, 1994. 501pp. Recognized as the leading scholarly expert on Truman, Ferrell has written an exhaustively researched reinterpretation of the life and political career that draws contrary conclusions to the accepted view on both. By exploiting little-known sources, Ferrell sheds considerable new light on many of the key episodes in Truman's career.

Hamby, Alonzo L. *Man of the People: A Life of Harry S. Truman*. New York: Oxford University Press, 1995. 760pp. Hamby takes a psychological approach to penetrate the public image and reveal a more complex personality: insecure, ambitious, divided by conflicted ideological principles, and trapped by a changing cultural ethos. Hamby's dispassionate, coherent portrait may lack the warmth and narrative grace of other Truman biographers, but his interpretation is credible and paradigm-changing.

Jenkins, Roy. *Truman*. New York: Harper & Row, 1986. 232pp. Written from the perspective of an experienced political leader, Jenkins's is a well-done and insightful, admiring but not uncritical, short biography. Although based entirely on secondary sources, the book is a valuable synthesis that humanizes Truman and animates his challenges as a world leader.

McCullough, David. *Truman*. New York: Simon & Schuster, 1992. 1,117pp. Winner of the Pulitzer Prize, McCullough's masterful narrative biography is both well researched and a highly entertaining, absorbing examination of the values that shaped Truman and those he showed throughout his career. The book has been legitimately hailed as a classic presidential biography.

Miller, Richard L. *Truman: The Rise to Power*. New York: McGraw-Hill, 1986. 536pp. Devoted exclusively to Truman's prepresidential political career, this is a challenging, well-documented, and well-argued reinterpretation that contradicts the conventional wisdom about Truman's political naiveté. Miller documents Truman's accommodations with the strategies and tactics of Kansas City's Pendergast machine and his treading a fine line between principles and corruption.

Other Biographical Studies

Daniels, Jonathan. *The Man from Independence*. Philadelphia: Lippincott, 1950. 384pp. The best of the early biographies, Daniels's assessment is highly adulatory but filled with realistic details on Truman's background, family, and development, gained from interviews with Truman and his associates.

Dayton, Eldorous L. *Give 'Em Hell Harry: An Informal Biography of the Terrible Tempered Mr. T*. New York: Devin-Adair, 1956. 250pp. Not to be trusted in its details, gossipy, and hostile, Dayton's hack job trades on its "no-holds barred" approach, but the effect is an undocumented character assassination.

Donovan, Robert J. *Conflict and Crisis, the Presidency of Harry S. Truman, 1945–1948*. New York: W.W. Norton, 1977. 473pp.; *Tumultuous Years:*

The Presidency of Harry S. Truman, 1949–1953. New York: W.W. Norton, 1982. 444pp. A detailed, chronological account of the Truman presidency, Donovan's study is a must for a close look at Truman's leadership and decision making. Donovan shows no evident bias, allowing the reader to assess Truman's presidency based on the record that the books ably supply.

Ferrell, Robert H. *Harry S. Truman and the Modern American Presidency*. Boston: Little, Brown, 1983. 220pp. Ferrell's preliminary study of Truman's political career from his first elected post to his retirement is a brief selective survey emphasizing Truman's leadership qualities. The book falls short as a critically balanced, thorough, concise summary.

Gosnell, Harold F. *Truman's Crises: A Political Biography of Harry S. Truman*. Westport, Connecticut: Greenwood, 1980. 656pp. Gosnell challenges the notion of Truman's "accidental" genius, depicting instead a thoughtful political leader. Thoroughly researched from primary sources, this is a detailed examination of Truman's decision-making processes, relationships with administrators and legislators, and use of the media in a balanced view of his political career.

Helm, William P. *Harry Truman: A Political Biography*. New York: Duell, Sloan and Pearce, 1947. 241pp. This early political profile covers Truman's career from his first senate nomination in 1934 to his succession to the presidency, written by a friend "with the President's knowledge, consent, and co-operation." Helm manages a candid portrait of a practical politician rather than a celebration of the farm boy's rise to success.

McCoy, Donald R. *The Presidency of Harry S. Truman*. Lawrence, Kansas: University Press of Kansas, 1984. 351pp. A highly regarded factual survey of the Truman presidency, McCoy's is a balanced view, avoiding either revisionist debunking or excessive praise. The biographical details are first rate.

Miller, Merle. *Plain Speaking: An Oral Biography of Harry S. Truman*. New York: Putnam, 1974. 448pp. Based on a series of extensive interviews with the former president in the early 1960s, supplemented by oral testimony from eyewitnesses at various stages of Truman's career, Miller's is a highly entertaining presentation in which the man is honestly displayed. However, Miller is rarely probing in his questions and his commentary can be annoying and intrusive.

Pemberton, William E. *Harry S. Truman: Fair Dealer and Cold Warrior*. Boston: Twayne, 1989. 227pp. Pemberton's is a sensible biographical profile and assessment of the Truman presidency. A model of lucid succinctness, this is an excellent choice for the reader looking for a brief interpretive overview of the man and his effectiveness as a leader.

Robbins, Charles. *Last of His Kind: An Informal Portrait of Harry S. Truman*. New York: Morrow, 1979. 159pp. Based on interviews with Truman in 1953, supplemented by archival material, such as Truman's autobiographical notes, and the reflections of others, Robbins's is an affectionate, rarely critical, oral portrait.

Robbins, Jhan. *Bess & Harry: An American Love Story*. New York: Putnam, 1980. 194pp. This is an uncritical tribute to the Trumans's relationship, based on secondary sources.

Steinberg, Alfred. *The Man from Missouri: The Life and Times of Harry S. Truman*. New York: Putnam, 1962. 447pp. With a look at Truman's forebears, Steinberg admiringly narrates the Missourian's life and career up to his political retirement. Best on the pre-Washington years of Truman's early family life and World War I combat service.

Truman, Margaret. *Harry S. Truman*. New York: Morrow, 1972. 602pp. Truman is described through the loving and loyal eyes of his daughter. Despite a lack of critical objectivity, the book provides a series of intimate glimpses of Truman, the family man, his temperament, and private side.

Fictional Portraits

Maxwell, A.E. *Steal the Sun*. New York: Richard Marek, 1981. 288pp. This historical thriller concerns the events leading up to the first atomic bomb tests and Truman's decision to use the bomb to help end World War II.

Recommended Juvenile Biographies

Feinberg, Barbara S. *Harry S. Truman*. New York: F. Watts, 1994. 144pp. YA. Based on contemporary accounts, Truman's writings, and recent analysis of the Truman administration, Feinberg supplies a balanced, insightful portrait of the man and his career that is considerably more sophisticated in its presentation than is usual in books for younger readers.

Fleming, Thomas. *Harry S. Truman, President*. New York: Walker, 1993. 136pp. MG. This is a lively, informative biography, chiefly focused on Truman's presidency and the issues he had to face.

Leavell, J. Perry. *Harry S. Truman*. New York: Chelsea House, 1988. 111pp. MG. Workmanlike and informative, this is a solid choice for an introduction to the man and his career.

Biographical Films and Theatrical Adaptations

A&E Biography Video: Harry S. Truman (1994). Director: Deidre O'Hearn. This documentary portrait features archival footage and comments by a variety of witnesses of Truman's career and assessments of the man and his legacy. Video.

Day One (1989). Director: Joseph Sargent. The race to build the atom bomb and the decision to use it is dramatized in this television film with Richard Dysart as Truman, Brian Dennehy as General Leslie Groves, and David Stratharn as J. Robert Oppenheimer. Video.

Give 'Em Hell, Harry! (1975). Director: Steve Binder. James Whitmore stars in a film version of his one-man show as Truman who narrates events in his life as well as his strong opinions. Video.

Harry S. Truman (1962). Director: Jack Haley Jr. This is a film profile covering Truman's political career using archival footage. Video.

Hiroshima (1995). Director: Roger Spottiswoode. This innovative, semidocumentary drama of the events leading up to the dropping of the atom bomb mixes re-creation of scenes with newsreels and archival material. The drama focuses on Truman (Kenneth Welsh), with Jeffrey DeMunn as Oppenheimer. Video.

Truman (1995). Director: Frank Pierson. Based on David McCullough's book, this biographical portrait follows Truman's life from 1917 to 1968, starring Gary Sinise in the title role and Diana Scarwid as Bess Truman. Video.

Truman (1997). Producer: David Grubin. This impressive installment of the American Experience series supplies a full film portrait of Truman's life, with commentary by his contemporaries and historians. Video.

Other Sources

Kirkendall, Richard S., ed. *The Harry S. Truman Encyclopedia.* Boston: G.K. Hall, 1989. 404pp. A collection of alphabetically arranged biographical and topical articles by a number of scholars and specialists covering various aspects of the man, his associates, and his political career.

See also Franklin D. Roosevelt

469. SOJOURNER TRUTH
1797–1883

An American abolitionist and a former slave, Truth left domestic employment in New York to preach emancipation and women's rights. Although she remained illiterate, she was a highly compelling speaker. After the Civil War she worked to resettle freed slaves.

Autobiography and Primary Sources

Narrative of Sojourner Truth. As told to Olive Gilbert. 1850. Reprint ed. New York: Penguin, 1998. 352pp. Truth was illiterate, and this "as-told-to" autobiography is the principal documentary record of her life. Gilbert standardized Truth's dialectal speech and was at times an unsympathetic witness to her life story, but Truth's personality and oratorical skills are still evident in this important record of slavery and the years immediately following emancipation.

Recommended Biographies

Mabee, Carleton, and Susan Mabee Newhouse. *Sojourner Truth—Slave, Prophet, Legend.* New York: New York University Press, 1993. 293pp. Uncovering neglected sources, the book provides valuable new insights on Truth's life and the origin and credibility of many of the legends that have surrounded her. This is the first biography that has attempted to discover the best available sources about Truth's life and to remain close to those sources in telling her story.

Painter, Nell Irvin. *Sojourner Truth: A Life, a Symbol.* New York: W.W. Norton, 1996. 370pp. Painter's is a sophisticated untangling of the various levels of myth, self-invention, and distortion surrounding Truth, revealing a much more complex and compelling figure than in any previous biography. The book traces how Truth emerged from slavery fashioning new identities to serve her independent life and how her life has been subsumed by her symbolic significance for blacks and women.

Other Biographical Studies

Bernard, Jacqueline. *Journey Toward Freedom: The Story of Sojourner Truth.* 1967. Reprint ed. New York: Feminist Press, 1990. 267pp. Originally written for young adult readers, Bernard's recounting of Truth's life can serve the general adult reader as well. Blending primary source material and some fictionalization, Bernard's narrative is generally accurate and highly engaging, aided by created dialogue and interior monologues, at some cost, however, to the book's overall reliability.

Fauset, Arthur H. *Sojourner Truth: God's Faithful Pilgrim.* 1938. Reprint ed. New York: Russell and Russell, 1971. 187pp. In a modern retelling of Truth's autobiography, Fauset embellishes with background material and speculation concerning Truth's thoughts and feelings while observing the essential facts as she recalled them.

Pauli, Hertha. *Her Name Was Sojourner Truth.* New York: Avon, 1962. 250pp. A somewhat disjointed blend of scholarship and fictionalization, Pauli seems unclear about her audience and intention. The book submits some of the legends surrounding Truth to the test of fact, while creating others through speculative leaps.

Stetson, Erlene, and Linda David. *Glorying in Tribulation: The Lifework of Sojourner Truth.* East Lansing: Michigan State University Press, 1994. 242pp. The authors carefully examine all the evidence surrounding Truth's life and helpfully analyze the perspective of Truth herself, her supporters, and opponents who have fashioned our view of the person and her significance.

Recommended Juvenile Biographies

Krass, Peter. *Sojourner Truth.* New York: Chelsea House, 1988. 110pp. MG/YA. Krass provides a thoughtful and informative account of Truth's life and achievement.

McKissack, Patricia, and Frederick L. McKissack. *Sojourner Truth: Ain't I a Woman?* New York: Scholastic, 1993. 178pp. MG. The authors supply an informative narrative describing the principle events of Truth's life, brief biographical sketches of the many people she knew and worked with, and the conditions for African Americans and women during her lifetime.

Whalin, Terry. *Sojourner Truth: American Abolitionist.* New York: Chelsea House, 1999. 201pp. MG/YA. This a detailed and comprehensive treatment of Truth's life in the wider context of her times. Serves both as a fine biographical profile and history.

Biographical Films and Theatrical Adaptations

Sojourner Truth: "Ain't I a Woman?" (1989). Director: Judy Chaiken. A dramatization in her own words and from those who knew her, including Frederick Douglass, Harriet Beecher Stowe, and Abraham Lincoln. Performances by Valeria Parker, Julie Harris, Roscoe Lee Browne, Rose Marie Perfect, and James Gosa. Video.

Sojourner Truth: Antislavery Activist (1992). Director: Rhonda Fabian. Adapted from the book by Peter Krass, this is a film profile that looks at Truth's life and work in the wider historical and cultural background. Video.

470. HARRIET TUBMAN
1826–1913

American abolitionist and escaped slave, Tubman became one of the most successful "conductors" on the Underground Railroad. Nicknamed "Moses," she helped more than 300 slaves to freedom. During the Civil War, she was a nurse, laundress, scout, and spy for the Union forces.

Recommended Biographies

Conrad, Earl. *Harriet Tubman.* Washington, DC: Associated Publishers, 1943. 248pp. Conrad's life remains the standard biographical source, based on a careful gathering of documentary evidence that helpfully separates the actual woman from her considerable legend.

Other Biographical Studies

Bradford, Sarah H. *Scenes in the Life of Harriet Tubman.* 1869. Revised as *Harriet: The Moses of Her People.* New York: Lockwood, 1886. 149pp. Bradford's was the first biographical profile of Tubman, written to gain funds to help her pay for her farm and based on Tubman's own account. The revision is an expanded version supplemented by recollections of Tubman's friends and family.

Franklin, John Hope. "Harriet Tubman" in *Notable American Women.* Cambridge, Massachusetts: Harvard University Press, 1971. vol. 3. Franklin provides an extensive biographical profile that is reliable, relating her activities to the historical context.

Biographical Novels

Heidish, Marcy M. *A Woman Called Moses.* Boston: Houghton Mifflin, 1976. 308pp. Tubman narrates her own story in this fictional memoir based on facts but with some imaginative embellishment of her early years.

Fictional Portraits

Olds, Bruce. *Raising Holy Hell.* New York: Holt, 1995. 335pp. Abolitionist John Brown is captured from a variety of perspectives, including Tubman's.

Parrish, Anne. *A Clouded Star.* New York: Harper, 1948. 242pp. The novel, based on the recollections of a participant, recreates a journey north by a group of fugitive slaves led by Tubman.

Recommended Juvenile Biographies

McClard, Megan. *Harriet Tubman: Slavery and the Underground Railroad.* Englewood Cliffs,

New Jersey: Silver Burdett, 1991. YA. 247pp. An installment of the History of the Civil War series, this informative biography places Tubman's abolitionist activities in their wider historical and cultural context.

Petry, Ann. *Harriet Tubman: Conductor on the Underground Railroad*. New York: Crowell, 1955. 247pp. MG. Considered a classic fictional biography for young people, Petry's is a vivid narrative that underscores Tubman's courage and challenges in conducting slaves to freedom.

Taylor, M.W. *Harriet Tubman: Antislavery Activist*. New York: Chelsea House, 1991. 111pp. MG/YA. This is a substantial portrait of Tubman that goes beyond the usual details of her role as a leader of the Underground Railroad to look at her activities in a wider historical context.

Biographical Films and Theatrical Adaptations

Harriet Tubman: Antislavery Activist (1992). Director: Rhonda Fabian. Adapted from M.W. Taylor's biography, Tubman's role before, during, and after the Civil War is depicted. Video.

A Woman Called Moses (1979). Director: Paul Wendkos. Based on Marcy Heidish's novel, Cicely Tyson portrays Tubman in this made-for-television film. Video.

471. IVAN TURGENEV
1818–1883

Russian novelist, dramatist, and short-story writer, Turgenev is one of the foremost figures of Russian literature. His first success was "Khor and Kalinch," a story of peasant life later included in the collection, *A Sportsman's Sketches* (1852). The book, which attacks serfdom, is thought to have influenced Alexander II to emancipate the serfs. Among Turgenev's other works are the play *A Month in the Country* (1850), the novel *Fathers and Sons* (1862), considered his masterpiece, and the short story "First Love" (1870).

Autobiography and Primary Sources

Letters. David Lowe, ed. Ann Arbor, Michigan: Ardis, 1983. 2 vols. Reproducing 334 of the author's more than 6,000 extant letters, this collection has been selected to provide a picture of the man and the artist from 1831 until his death. A one-volume selection of 236 letters is also available in

Turgenev's Letters. A.V. Knowles, ed. (New York: Scribner, 1983. 299pp.), geared to reveal Turgenev's biography.

Recommended Biographies

Magarshack, David. *Turgenev: A Life*. New York: Grove Press, 1954. 328pp. Magarshack's interpretive biography is more thematically arranged than strictly chronological. The book draws sensible conclusions based on a careful sifting of the record. This is probably not the best first book to read on Turgenev, but it does offer sound and original views of its subject.

Schapiro, Leonard. *Turgenev: His Life and Times*. New York: Random House, 1978. 382pp. Drawing on extensive and previously untapped primary sources, Schapiro's is a detailed chronological life that animates a human Turgenev based on his own words and the view of those who knew him.

Yarmolinsky, Avrahm. *Turgenev: The Man, His Art and His Age*. 1926. Revised ed. New York: Collier, 1961. 384pp. The author's Russian sources and his attempt to place Turgenev clearly in his historical and cultural contexts make this a still-valuable biographical and critical study.

Other Biographical Studies

Lloyd, John A.T. *Ivan Turgenev*. 1942. Reprint ed. Port Washington, New York: Kennikat Press, 1972. 227pp. Lloyd's biographical profile depends mainly on Turgenev's works to help clarify aspects of his background and personality. Such an approach is fraught with errors and omissions, and Lloyd's study has been superseded by more comprehensive and well-documented biographies.

Pritchett, V.S. *The Gentle Barbarian: The Life and Work of Turgenev*. New York: Random House, 1977. 243pp. Based mainly on secondary sources, Pritchett presents a lively account of the writer's life and works for the general reader that is particularly strong on Turgenev's writing techniques.

Troyat, Henri. *Turgenev*. New York: Dutton, 1988. 184pp. Troyat's is an enjoyable, often vivid, biographical portrait that will appeal primarily to the general reader looking for a succinct, fast-paced treatment that sympathetically displays a credible human figure.

472. J.M.W. TURNER
1775–1851

English painter Joseph Mallard William Turner is considered one of the foremost English romantic painters and among the most original of the landscape artists. His work is famous for its richness of light and atmosphere and includes *Sun Rising through Vapor* (1807), *The Fighting Téméraire* (1839), and *Rain, Steam, and Speed: The Great Western Railway* (1844).

Autobiography and Primary Sources

Collected Correspondence of J.M.W. Turner with an Early Diary and a Memoir by George Jones. John Gage, ed. New York: Oxford University Press, 1980. 315pp. Although little of Turner's correspondence has survived, this scholarly edition of his extant letters is supplemented by a personal recollection by his friend and fellow artist George Jones and the "Diary of a Tour in Wales in 1792," which has been shown not to be the work of Turner.

Recommended Biographies

Bailey, Anthony. *Standing in the Sun: A Life of J.M.W. Turner*. New York: HarperCollins, 1998. 478pp. In a thorough, balanced assessment of the artist, Bailey sheds considerable new light on the highly secretive Turner based on extensive primary and secondary sources. Not the hero of previous

treatments, Bailey's Turner is a complex mixture of character traits, fully illuminated in his social and cultural setting.

Finberg, A.J. *The Life of J.M.W. Turner, R.A.* 1939. Revised ed. Oxford: Clarendon Press, 1961. 543pp. Regarded as the standard, factual life, Finberg's "chronicle-biography" is a meticulously researched, almost daily account of the painter's life based on a close examination of the painter's sketchbooks and notebooks that form a diary kept between his fourteenth and seventy-first years. To be consulted rather than enjoyed as a compelling narrative.

Gage, John. *J.M.W. Turner: A Wonderful Range of Mind*. New Haven, Connecticut: Yale University Press, 1991. 262pp. Organized thematically rather than chronologically, Gage's study is a sophisticated general introduction to both the artist and his works, particularly valuable in presenting the intellectual and artistic milieu of Turner's times.

Hamilton, James. *Turner: A Life*. London: Hodder & Stoughton, 1997. 363pp. Hamilton's is a solid, scholarly review of Turner's life and work that synthesizes modern scholarship and makes rich use of contemporary memoirs of the painter. Hamilton joins the artist's public and private sides into a coherent human whole.

Other Biographical Studies

Hamerton, Philip G. *The Life of J.M.W. Turner, R.A.* Boston: Roberts, 1882. 404pp. More factually reliable than Thornbury, Hamerton's critical biography repeats many of the unsubstantiated anecdotes in the earlier book, but still serves a historical purpose reflecting Turner's reputation by a sensitive and insightful Victorian artist and critic.

Lindsay, Jack. *J.M.W. Turner: His Life and Work: A Critical Biography*. Greenwich, Connecticut: New York Graphic Society, 1966. 275pp. Lindsay attempts to assemble a coherent portrait of the man and the artist seen through a Freudian and Marxist lens. The book emphasizes Turner's inner life as revealed in his writings and paintings, in the context of Romanticism.

Reynolds, Graham. *Turner*. New York: Abrams, 1969. 216pp. Reynolds's critical biography is a sensible and informed introduction that gives an overview of Turner's artistic methods and techniques, the influences on his work, his artistic circle, and personality.

Thornbury, Walter. *The Life of J.M.W. Turner, R.A., Founded on Letters and Papers Furnished by His Friends and Fellow Academicians*. 1862. Revised ed. New York: Holt, 1877. 636pp. Although discursive and error-filled, this earliest biography does include a number of firsthand observations of the painter's friends and associates as well as excerpts from Turner's correspondence that have survived only in Thornbury's transcriptions.

Wilton, Andrew. *J.M.W. Turner: His Art and Life*. New York: Rizzoli, 1979. 527pp. Supplementing a catalog of Turner's paintings and watercolors, Wilton supplies an extensive critical survey of the painter's life and works addressed to a more scholarly audience than his later book, *Turner in His Time*.

Wilton, Andrew. *Turner in His Time*. New York: Abrams, 1987. 256pp. Wilton covers the essential facts of Turner's life relying as much as possible on the painter's own words and those of his contemporaries. The book serves as an excellent introductory study for the general reader.

Biographical Novels

Noonan, Michael. *The Sun Is God*. New York: Delacorte, 1973. 217pp. Noonan's fictional biography emphasizes the gap between the artist's public and private life. The external events are factual, but they are joined with invention based on interpretive leaps.

Recommended Juvenile Biographies

Kenner, Robert. *J.M.W. Turner*. New York: Abrams, 1995. 92pp. MG. Part of the respected First Impressions series, this is a lucid study of Turner's life and work that captures his achievement and impact on later artists.

473. MARK TWAIN
1835–1910

American author and humorist originally named Samuel Langhorne Clemens, Twain worked for a time as a riverboat pilot and took his pseudonym from the river call marking a water depth of two fathoms. While working as a journalist, he first won fame with his comic story, "The Celebrated Jumping Frog of Calaveras County" (1865). His novel, *The Adventures of Huckleberry Finn* (1884), is a masterpiece that influenced many subsequent American writers. Among Twain's other works are *Innocents Abroad* (1869), *The Adventures of Tom Sawyer* (1876) and *The Prince and the Pauper* (1882).

Autobiography and Primary Sources

The Autobiography of Mark Twain. Charles Neider, ed. New York: Harperperennial, 1990. 432pp. Twain's collection of anecdotes ranges over his entire life and is an essential biographical source, though critics have long debated the degree of invention represented here.

Mark Twain's Notebooks and Journals. Frederick Anderson, et al., eds. Berkeley: University of California Press, 1975–1979. 3 vols. Twain's notebooks and journals are essential for the scholar, though mainly cryptic and impenetrable for the general reader.

The Selected Letters of Mark Twain. Charles Neider, ed. New York: Harper & Row, 1982. 328pp. This selection of Twain's letters spans his life from the age of 18 to a few months before his death and shows his development into a comic writer and satirist. It does not include his courtship letters or passages revealing aspects of Twain's character that the editor found objectionable.

Recommended Biographies

Emerson, Everett. *The Authentic Mark Twain: A Literary Biography of Samuel L. Clemens*. Philadelphia: University of Pennsylvania Press, 1984.

330pp. Emerson supplies a biographical overview of Twain's literary career based on recent scholarship. In the author's view Twain's career went into a steady decline following *Huckleberry Finn* as the novelist drifted further and further from his "authentic" self. In *Mark Twain: A Literary Life* (Philadelphia: University of Pennsylvania Press, 1999. 344pp.) Emerson sticks close to the works themselves to reveal the man in a well-researched, informative, and sensible assessment that allows Twain to tell his own story as much as possible.

Ferguson, J. de Lancey. *Mark Twain: Man and Legend*. Indianapolis: Bobbs-Merrill, 1943. 352pp. Although focusing exclusively on Twain's literary career, Ferguson's study is well regarded as an overview in which the author attempts to trace "the forces which made him a writer, to tell how he wrote his books and why he wrote them as he did," relying on Twain's own words to tell his story.

Hoffman, Andrew. *Inventing Mark Twain: The Lives of Samuel Langhorne Clemens*. New York: Morrow, 1997. 572pp. Hoffman provocatively examines the relationship between the man and his persona, suggesting that the public figure we identify as Mark Twain hid an insecure, brooding figure who could be a reactionary and a racist. The book's psychological insight is challenging and helpful in replacing a simple view of the man with a much more complex one.

Kaplan, Justin. *Mr. Clemens and Mark Twain: A Biography*. New York: Simon & Schuster, 1966. 424pp. Kaplan's Pulitzer Prize–winning biography is highly detailed and well written. Beginning in 1866 when Twain was 31, Kaplan chronicles the writer's maturity, tracing the split between the man and his mask, between the social satirist and the Gilded Age success hunter. Sophisticated and provocative in its interpretation, Kaplan's is a justifiably admired literary biography.

Lauber, John. *The Inventions of Mark Twain*. New York: Hill & Wang, 1990. 340pp. Lauber's lively, accessible survey of Twain's life and career looks at the man and his work against his social and cultural background. Twain is seen as an Edison-like inventor, not the divided artist, but a man very much tapping into the spirit of the age.

Sanborn, Margaret. *Mark Twain: The Bachelor Years*. New York: Doubleday, 1990. 508pp. Sanborn's study of Twain's early life is the ideal complement to Kaplan's account of the mature writer. Readable and vivid, the book relies heavily on archival sources and is very helpful in sorting through the discrepancies between the facts and Twain's own version of his past.

Wagenknecht, Edward. *Mark Twain: The Man and His Work*. 1935. Revised ed. Norman: University of Oklahoma Press, 1967. 272pp. This is a fair, sensible interpretive biography that finds a middle ground between Brooks's tragic portrait and DeVoto's comic celebration of Twain's genius and achievement. Wagenknecht's moderate approach makes this one of the most reliable critical biographies and is recommended for the reader looking for a coherent overview of Twain's entire career.

Other Biographical Studies

Benson, Ivan. *Mark Twain's Western Years*. Stanford, California: Stanford University Press, 1938. 218pp. This is an extensive study of Twain's life during the years 1861 to 1866, when he lived in Nevada and California. Benson's account is regarded as the standard source on the beginnings and early development of Twain's writing career.

Brashear, Minnie. *Mark Twain: Son of Missouri*. Chapel Hill: University of North Carolina Press, 1934. 294pp. This critical study of Twain's early years deepens an appreciation for the cultural setting of Hannibal and its impact on the writer's development. Brashear counters the notion that Twain was a natural talent blooming in the wilderness, suggesting instead his systematic development by absorbing European cultural models as well as vernacular ones.

Brooks, Van Wyck. *The Ordeal of Mark Twain*. 1920. New York: Dutton, 1933. 325pp. Brooks's groundbreaking psychological assessment of Twain's character and career helped form the pattern for viewing the author that has dominated the subsequent biographical and critical debate. As Brooks explains, "The main idea in the book is that Mark Twain's career was a tragedy—a tragedy for himself and a tragedy for mankind." In his view, Twain was damaged by events of his childhood and ruined by respectability, resulting in a division between the comic performer and the pessimist.

Budd, Louis J. *Our Mark Twain: The Making of His Public Personality*. Philadelphia: University of Pennsylvania Press, 1983. 266pp. Supplementing the several literary biographies, Budd approaches Twain from the perspective of his public career as lecturer, newspaperman, humorist, businessman, and social commentator. Budd shows how Twain carefully crafted his public persona and was in turn shaped by his public image.

DeVoto, Bernard. *Mark Twain's America*. Boston: Little, Brown, 1932. 353pp. DeVoto challenges Brooks's argument that Twain was a frustrated, limited writer, asserting his achievement as a frontier humorist who opened up American life for literature. The book concentrates on Twain's early life and development to celebrate his unique gift for vernacular realism.

Gabrilowitsch, Clara Clemens. *My Father, Mark Twain*. 1931. Reprint ed. New York: AMS Press, 1976. 292pp. Twain's daughter offers her memories of her father as his family knew him, based in part on private letters not previously published.

Harris, Susan K. *The Courtship of Olivia Langdon and Mark Twain*. New York: Cambridge University Press, 1996. 202pp. Harris presents a challenging, revisionist interpretation of Twain's much debated relationship with his wife, based on diaries and letters. Olivia Langdon Clemens is revealed as a vibrant, intellectual figure who challenged her husband in important ways.

Hill, Hamlin. *Mark Twain: God's Fool*. New York: Harper, 1973. 308pp. Hill's detailed treatment of Twain's last decade is a sobering, unflattering portrait of the disintegration of his family and talent. Based largely on notebooks kept by Twain's secretary, Hill's examination offers a very different view of Twain's happy family life established by Paine.

Howells, William Dean. *My Mark Twain: Reminiscences and Criticisms*. New York: Harper, 1910. 189pp. Novelist Howells's friendship with Twain extended for more than 45 years, and his reminiscences include a number of intimate, generous, and affectionate glimpses. The second half of the book reprints criticism of Twain's works that previously appeared in the *Atlantic Monthly*.

Kaplan, Justin. *Mark Twain and His World*. New York: Simon & Schuster, 1974. 224pp. This illustrated biography allows Kaplan to comment briefly on Twain's entire life, particularly his early years and formative influences excluded from his Pulitzer Prize–winning biography. Highly rated as an introduction for the general reader.

Lauber, John. *The Making of Mark Twain: A Biography*. New York: American Heritage Press, 1985. 298pp. Covering much the same ground that Sanborn does in more detail, Lauber treats Twain's formative years up to 1870 and helpfully separates the various legends, inventions, and facts surrounding Twain's early life.

Lennon, Nigey. *The Sagebrush Bohemian: Mark Twain in California*. New York: Paragon House, 1991. 203pp. Focusing on Twain's life during the 1860s, this is a lighthearted, anecdotal chronicle by an unapologetic partisan. Entertaining rather than penetrative or original, the book occasionally indulges in a number of questionable speculations but maintains its interest with the richness of the material presented from Twain's early journalism.

MacNaughton, William R. *Mark Twain's Last Years as a Writer*. Columbia: University of Missouri Press, 1979. 254pp. The author's carefully researched study of Twain's final decade challenges the view argued by Brooks and Hill of the author's artistic failure brought on by personal despair. In MacNaughton's view, Twain's later work has been undervalued, his personal distress overstated, and the period rather than being atypical was a logical continuation of long-established patterns.

Meltzer, Milton. *Mark Twain Himself: A Pictorial Biography*. New York: Crowell, 1960. 303pp. This is a fascinating selection of photographs, drawings, and cartoons with a text composed mainly of selections from Twain's autobiography, letters, speeches, notebooks, journalistic pieces, and fiction.

Paine, Albert B. *Mark Twain: A Biography: The Personal and Literary Life of Samuel Langhorne Clemens*. 1912. Reprint ed. New York: Chelsea House, 1980. 3 vols. Paine, the authorized biographer and one of the literary executors of the writer, crafted this monumental biography, which long served as the standard source and began the debate over Twain's character and career. The author's unequalled access to Twain and his papers gives his study its importance, while the lack of critical objectivity and slighting of Twain's literary career are drawbacks. An abridged version of Paine's multivolume work is available as *A Short Life of Mark Twain* (New York: Harper, 1920. 343pp.).

Powers, Ron. *Dangerous Water: A Biography of the Boy Who Became Mark Twain*. New York: Basic Books, 1999. 328pp. Written by a native of

Hannibal, Missouri, Powers, a Pulitzer Prize–winning author, provides a considerably darker view of Twain's early life up to 1858, emphasizing the author's tragic background. Although it assumes prior knowledge of Twain's career and work, the book is an illuminating exploration of Twain's psyche and family and cultural influences.

Steinbrink, Jeffrey. *Getting to Be Mark Twain*. Berkeley: University of California Press, 1991. 221pp. This biographical portrait covers the years 1867 to 1871, from Twain's move east to his completion of *Roughing It*, focusing on the writer's relationship with his wife and father-in-law and arguing that these were the pivotal years in defining the writer. Steinbrink allows Twain to speak for himself through excerpts from his letters.

Wecter, Dixon. *Sam Clemens of Hannibal*. Boston: Houghton Mifflin, 1952. 335pp. Wecter did not live to complete a planned multivolume biography, taking Twain's story only up to his eighteenth year and Twain's departure from Hannibal in 1853. As one of Twain's literary executors, Wecter had unprecedented access to unpublished Twain papers and his portrait of the writer's formative years is still one of the most thorough and authoritative available.

Willis, Resa. *Mark and Livy: The Love Story of Mark Twain and the Woman Who Almost Tamed Him*. New York: Atheneum, 1992. 334pp. Focusing on Twain's domestic life, Willis insightfully examines the role of his wife as a personal influence and editor of his work, as well as Twain's important relationship with his children.

Biographical Novels

Hauser, Thomas. *Mark Twain Remembers*. New York: Barricuda Books, 1999. 207pp. Set in 1910, Mark Twain on his deathbed reflects back on a six-week period in 1856 when he was 20 years old. Mingling Twain's own words with invention, the novel offers a version of the future novelist's coming-of-age experience in his encounter with slavery.

Fictional Portraits

Appel, Allen. *Twice Upon a Time*. New York: Carroll & Graf, 1988. 351pp. In this amusing time travel fantasy, a historian is transported back to 1876 to discuss Twain's work with the author while attempting to stop Custer's Last Stand from happening.

Brock, Darryl. *If I Never Get Back*. New York: Crown, 1990. 424pp. A modern journalist is transported back in time to 1869 to join the Cincinnati Red Stockings for their legendary 64-0 season, "inventing" the bunt, hot dog, and Cracker Jack and getting a tour of New York by Mark Twain.

Carkeet, David. *I Been There Before*. New York: Harper & Row, 1985. 314pp. Twain is resurrected to return to his old haunts in contemporary Carson City, Nevada, and elsewhere in this inventive novel that animates the writer's spirit, humor, and voice.

Heck, Peter J. *Death on the Mississippi*. New York: Berkley, 1995. 290pp.; *A Connecticut Yankee in Criminal Court*. New York: Berkley, 1996. 311pp.; *The Prince and the Prosecutor*. New York: Berkley, 1997. 336pp. Heck's amusing series of

period mysteries, based loosely on details from Twain's life, employs the famous writer as a sleuth.

Oates, Joyce Carol. *A Bloodsmoor Romance*. New York: Dutton, 1982. 615pp. The remarkable Zinn daughters are the subject of this modernist romance, which the author describes as "the other side of *Little Women*." One becomes the mistress of Mark Twain.

Vidal, Gore. *1876*. New York: Random House, 1976. 364pp. Twain is one of several historical figures appearing in the novel's social portrait of the Gilded Age.

Recommended Juvenile Biographies

Cox, Clinton. *Mark Twain: America's Humorist, Dreamer, Prophet*. New York: Scholastic, 1995. 234pp. MG. This is a sophisticated presentation of Twain's life and ideas that emphasizes his evolving views on race and personal freedom, including archival photographs and extensive quotes from Twain's writing.

Lyttle, Richard B. *Mark Twain-The Man and His Adventures*. New York: Atheneum, 1994. 230pp. MG/YA. This is the most detailed account of Twain's life available for younger readers, enlivened by many quotes from the author and illustrations.

Meltzer, Milton. *Mark Twain: A Writer's Life*. New York: F. Watts, 1985. 120pp. MG/YA. Meltzer's informative survey of Twain's life is a readable account with good integration of background information. Older readers may prefer the author's *Mark Twain Himself: A Pictorial Biography*.

Biographical Films and Theatrical Adaptations

A&E Biography Video: Mark Twain: His Amazing Adventures (1995). Producer: Noah Horowitz. A film profile of Twain's life from boyhood, with archival photographs, interviews with biographers and critics, and excerpts from his writings. Video.

The Adventures of Mark Twain (1944). Director: Irving Rapper. Fredric March is convincing as Twain from his years on the Mississippi, out west, and as a celebrated literary figure. Alexis Smith portrays Twain's wife. Video.

The Innocents Abroad (1983). Director: Luciano Salce. This PBS adaptation of Twain's book has Craig Wasson as the writer and a strong ensemble cast, including Brooke Adams and David Ogden Stiers. Video.

Mark Twain, American Writer, 1835–1910 (1993). Director: Malcolm Hossick. Twain's life and literary career is documented using photographs and footage of places associated with the author. Video.

Mark Twain and Me (1991). Director: Daniel Petrie. Jason Robards portrays the aging writer and presents his relationship with his daughter and her friend. With Talia Shire, Amy Stewart, and Chris Wiggins. Video.

Mark Twain's America (1993). Director: Donald B. Hyatt. Period photographs chronicle Twain's life and times. Video.

Mark Twain Tonight (1967). Director: Paul Bogart. Hal Holbrook's celebrated one-man show animates the man and his opinions. Video.

Other Sources

Horn, Jason G. *Mark Twain: A Descriptive Guide to Biographical Sources.* Lonhom, Maryland: Scarecrow Press, 1999. 144pp. An annotated bibliography of 250 biographical sources from the earliest known to current works.

Kaplan, Justin, ed. *Mark Twain, a Profile.* New York: Hill & Wang, 1967. 232pp. This is a useful compendium of views on the man and his works.

LeMaster, J.R., and John D. Wilson, eds. *The Mark Twain Encyclopedia.* New York: Garland, 1993. 848pp. Alphabetically arranged entries cover topics related to Twain's life and times, with most of the author's novels, short stories, and other writing treated in separate articles, along with entries for characters and fictional locales, aspects of Twain's literary style, and views on social, political, and moral issues.

Rasmussen, R. Kent. *Mark Twain A to Z: The Essential Reference to His Life and Writings.* New York: Facts on File, 1995. 552pp. An alphabetical compilation of entries on various aspects of Twain's life and works, along with numerous photographs and a chronological chart listing personal and professional activities alongside major historical and literary events.

Robinson, Forrest G., ed. *The Cambridge Companion to Mark Twain.* New York: Cambridge University Press, 1995. 282pp. This book features cutting-edge critical essays from prominent Twain scholars on a wide variety of biographical and literary topics and includes a Twain chronology.

474. MARTIN VAN BUREN
1782–1862

The eighth U.S. president (1837–1841), Van Buren served in the Senate and as governor of New York. He was Andrew Jackson's secretary of state and vice president before easily winning the presidency. Van Buren's term in office was marked by the financial Panic of 1837, implementation of the independent treasury system, and attempts to conciliate differences with Great Britain arising out of the Caroline Affair (1837) and the Aroostook War (1839). Van Buren lost a second term to William Henry Harrison and failed in two later presidential bids. A Democrat, he nevertheless supported Abraham Lincoln at the outbreak of the Civil War.

Autobiography and Primary Sources

The Autobiography of Martin Van Buren. John C. Fitzpatrick. 1920. Reprint ed. New York: Da Capo Press, 1973. 2 vols. Van Buren's memoirs are the major source of information on his early life up to 1834.

Recommended Biographies

Cole, Donald B. *Martin Van Buren and the American Political System.* Princeton, New Jersey: Princeton University Press, 1984. 477pp. Cole focuses exclusively on Van Buren's political career in a reliable and objective study that is particularly lucid on his prepresidential activities.

Niven, John. *Martin Van Buren: The Romantic Age of American Politics.* New York: Oxford University Press, 1983. 715pp. Niven's meticulously researched and perceptive analysis of the man and his era makes this the leading Van Buren biography in its balanced assessment.

Other Biographical Studies

Alexander, Holmes. *The American Talleyrand: The Career and Contemporaries of Martin Van Buren, Eighth President.* 1935. Reprint ed. New York: Russell & Russell, 1968. 430pp. This is an unsympathetic profile of Van Buren, who is credited with originating many of the corrupt practices of American political life.

Curtis, James C. *The Fox at Bay: Martin Van Buren and the Presidency.* Lexington: University of Kentucky Press, 1970. 233pp. Prior to the publication of Wilson's book, this was the standard source on Van Buren's presidency, the first scholarly assessment of Van Buren's overall performance as chief executive.

Lynch, Denis T. *An Epoch and a Man: Martin Van Buren and His Times.* 1929. Reprint ed. Millwood, New York: Kennikat Press, 1971. 2 vols. Combining biography with social and political history, this is an exhaustive account in which the man and his accomplishments get lost in the accumulated details.

Mushkat, Jerome, and Joseph G. Rayback. *Martin Van Buren: Law, Politics, and the Shaping of Republican Ideology.* DeKalb: Northern Illinois University Press, 1997. 261pp. Using a biographical approach, the authors provide a reassessment of the development of Van Buren's political and legal ideas that challenges conventional wisdom with fresh insights.

Remini, Robert V. *Martin Van Buren and the Making of the Democratic Party.* New York: Columbia University Press, 1959. 271pp. Remini examines the contributions made by Van Buren to the formation of the Democratic party from 1821 to 1828, offering fresh details on Van Buren's activities and a positive take on his personality and political principles.

Wilson, Major L. *The Presidency of Martin Van Buren.* Lawrence: University Press of Kansas, 1984. 252pp. Wilson's analysis of the Van Buren presidency is one of the most thoughtful and accomplished books on the subject. Van Buren is depicted as a skillful leader who was occasionally indecisive and passive, but whose presidency was a qualified success.

Fictional Portraits

Chase-Riboud, Barbara. *Echo of Lions.* New York: Morrow, 1989. 416pp. The author's dramatization of the *Amistad* case features characterizations of Van Buren and John Quincy Adams.

Gerson, Noel B. *The Slender Reed.* Garden City, New York: Doubleday, 1965. 394pp. This bio-

graphical novel on the life of James Knox Polk features a depiction of Van Buren.

Pesci, David. *Amistad.* New York: Marlowe, 1997. 240pp. Van Buren's role in the controversy surrounding what should be done with the slaves aboard the *Amistad* is characterized in Pesci's compelling account.

Vidal, Gore. *Burr: A Novel.* New York: Random House, 1973. 430pp. Told partly by Burr himself at the end of his life reflecting on the events of the American Revolution and the early years of the Republic, Vidal's endlessly provocative, revisionist view, based on solid research, is at the expense of the other founders. Washington is shown as incompetent and Jefferson as a ruthless opportunist. Some of Vidal's assertions, such as Burr being the father of Martin Van Buren, are more inventive than historically reliable.

Recommended Juvenile Biographies

Ellis, Rafaela. *Martin Van Buren: 8th President of the United States.* Ada, Oklahoma: Garrett, 1989. 120pp. MG. Ellis's is a competent overview of Van Buren's life, personality, and presidential career.

Hargrove, Jim. *Martin Van Buren: Eighth President of the United States.* Chicago: Childrens Press, 1987. 98pp. MG. Hargrove presents the major highlights of Van Buren's life and career in a straightforward factual account.

Biographical Films and Theatrical Adaptations

Amistad (1997). Director: Steven Spielberg. Spielberg's dramatization of the controversy surrounding the slave ship *Amistad* that reaches the Supreme Court features Nigel Hawthorne as an opportunistic Van Buren mostly concerned with re-election in contrast with the noble, principled John Quincy Adams (Anthony Hopkins). Video.

475. VINCENT VAN GOGH
1853–1890

Dutch postimpressionist painter and one of history's most celebrated artists, Van Gogh lived and worked in Holland and France. Famous for his richly colored and textured still lifes, café scenes, and scenes from peasant life, Van Gogh's works include *The Potato Eaters* (1885), *Starry Night* (1889), and an incomparable series of sunflowers. Plagued by attacks of dementia, he committed suicide.

Autobiography and Primary Sources

The Letters of Vincent Van Gogh. Ronald de Leeuw, ed. New York: Penguin, 1998. 509pp. The artist's letters present a remarkable, moving record of Van Gogh's life and self-assessment. This edition is based on the expanded four-volume Dutch edition of the letters and covers an 18-year period from 1872 to 1890.

Recommended Biographies

Callow, Philip. *Vincent Van Gogh: A Life.* Chicago: I.R. Dee, 1990. 295pp. In a highly readable narrative account, Callow explores the development of Van Gogh's genius and his emergence as an artist based on recent scholarship. By placing the artist's life in its historical context, the book traces how the artist struggled to find his vocation and self-expression in the cultural milieu of his day.

Sweetman, David. *Van Gogh: His Life and Art.* New York: Crown, 1990. 391pp. This is a sensible and sensitive, highly detailed account of Van Gogh's life and career that strips away the encrusted legends surrounding the artist to see him realistically against a solid social and artistic background.

Tralbaut, Marc Edo. *Vincent Van Gogh.* New York: Viking, 1969. 350pp. The founder and director of the International Van Gogh Archives has written the preeminent psychological biography. Connecting the letters and the works with a balanced assessment of the artist in an accomplished narrative, Tralbaut's study remains one of the best available.

Other Biographical Studies

Barrielle, Jean-François. *The Life and Work of Vincent van Gogh.* Secaucus, New Jersey: Chartwell Books, 1984. 255pp. Combining biographical details with a critical assessment of Van Gogh's artistic development and achievement, Barrielle's is a sensitive, reliable critical biography.

Burra, Peter J.S. *Van Gogh.* New York: Macmillan, 1934. 142pp. Part of the Great Lives series, this is a workmanlike introductory study of the artist and his work aimed at the general reader.

Cabanne, Pierre. *Van Gogh.* Englewood Cliffs, New Jersey: Prentice-Hall, 1963. 288pp. Weaving extensive passages from the letters, Cabanne presents a succinct overview of the artist's development and character.

Du Quesne-Van Gogh, Elisabeth H. *Personal Recollections of Vincent Van Gogh.* Boston: Houghton Mifflin, 1913. 58pp. The artist's younger sister provides her memories of the artist in the first published account of Van Gogh's life, supplying important firsthand details of the artist's relations with his family.

Elgar, Frank. *Van Gogh: A Study of His Life and Work.* New York: Praeger, 1958. 239pp. A rich selection of the artist's works is joined with an astute appraisal of Van Gogh's life and work that attempts to dispel the myth of the artist-martyr for a more sophisticated appreciation of his achievement.

Hammacher, A.M., and Renilde Hammacher. *Van Gogh: A Documentary Biography.* London: Thames and Hudson, 1982. 240pp. Excerpts from Van Gogh's correspondence are linked with photographs and reproductions from the artist's works to present a detailed chronicle.

Hanson, Lawrence, and Elisabeth Hanson. *Passionate Pilgrim: The Life of Vincent Van Gogh.* New York: Random House, 1955. 300pp. The Hansons provide a frank yet sympathetic treatment of Van Gogh's life for the general reader. With almost no art criticism, the book concentrates on the man, who is portrayed realistically with his flaws honestly displayed.

Hulsker, Jan. *Vincent and Theo Van Gogh: A Dual Biography.* Ann Arbor, Michigan: Fuller, 1990. 470pp. Hulsker's informative dual biography of the artist and his brother is marked by solid scholarship that sheds new light on Van Gogh and his family relationships and corrects many of the myths. The book is divided into four major stages of the brothers' lives: their early years, first interest in art, artistic dealings, and deaths.

Leymarie, Jean. *Who Was Van Gogh?* Cleveland: World, 1968. 210pp. The details of Van Gogh's life are reliably documented, along with a valuable selection of his work and an analysis of his artistry.

Lubin, A.J. *Stranger on the Earth: A Psychological Biography of Vincent Van Gogh.* New York: Holt, 1972. 265pp. The work of a clinical psychologist and practicing psychoanalyst, Lubin's is a complete psychological reading of the man that examines the familial, historical, cultural, religious, literary, and artistic forces that formed his personal conflicts.

Meier-Graefe, Julius. *Vincent Van Gogh: A Biographical Study.* Boston: Medici Society, 1926. 2 vols. The first full-length biography of the artist is a powerful narrative synthesis depending mainly on the letters for its depiction of the conflict in Van Gogh's life and the paradoxes in his character.

Piérard, Louis. *The Tragic Life of Vincent Van Gogh.* Boston: Houghton Mifflin, 1925. 125pp. A native of Borinage, the mining district in Belgium where Van Gogh worked as a lay preacher, the author supplies some firsthand information from those who knew the artist during this important period in his life.

Pollock, Griselda, and Fred Orton. *Vincent van Gogh: Artist of His Time.* New York: Dutton, 1978. 80pp. This is an exceptionally well-handled, concise overview of Van Gogh's life and artistic achievement that serves to orient the general reader to the essential issues surrounding the artist and his development.

Wallace, Robert. *The World of Van Gogh: 1853–1890.* New York: Time-Life Books, 1969. 192pp. Beautifully illustrated, this is a useful introduction to the man, his times, and his art.

Zurcher, Bernard. *Vincent van Gogh: Art, Life, and Letters.* New York: Rizzoli, 1985. 325pp. This beautifully illustrated critical biography supplies a sensible, balanced chronicle of Van Gogh's life and artistic development. Although repeating a good deal of familiar information, the book also adds some interesting details to the life story, while challenging a number of previously accepted notions.

Biographical Novels

Cooperstein, Claire. *Johanna: A Novel of the Van Gogh Family.* New York: Scribner, 1995. 270pp. The role of Van Gogh's sister-in-law in saving his paintings is recorded in this imagined diary of the young widow of Van Gogh's brother Theo.

Poldermans, Joost. *Vincent: A Novel Based on the Life of Van Gogh.* New York: Holt, 1962. 317pp. In a version of Van Gogh's story that is stripped of romance, the painter is depicted as a misfit and an enigma to his friends and family. Based on fact, the novel does employ invented letters and dialogue.

Stone, Irving. *Lust for Life.* New York: Doubleday, 1934. 489pp. Although the novel uses invented dialogue, the major details of Van Gogh's life and career are accurate in this meticulously researched, comprehensive biographical novel.

Fictional Portraits

Tuten, Frederic. *Van Gogh's Bad Café.* New York: Morrow, 1997. 163pp. This inventive fantasy parallels Van Gogh's final days leading up to his suicide with the experience of the artist's morphine-addicted lover who is transported to the East Village a hundred years later.

Recommended Juvenile Biographies

Dobrin, Arnold. *I Am a Stranger on Earth: The Story of Vincent Van Gogh.* New York: F. Warne, 1975. 95pp. MG/YA. With extensive use of quotes from the artist's letters and illustrated with his drawings and paintings, this is a substantial and thoughtful biographical portrait.

Hughes, Andrew. *Van Gogh.* Hauppauge, New York: Barron's, 1994. 32pp. MG. Van Gogh's life and career are summarized with a useful discussion of his artistic method, influences, and impact.

Tyson, Peter. *Vincent Van Gogh: Artist.* New York: Chelsea House, 1996. 127pp. MG/YA. Part of the Great Achievers: Lives of the Physically Challenged series, drawn exclusively from archival material, this is a sophisticated, thorough biography, despite the oddity of including Van Gogh in the "physically challenged" category.

Biographical Films and Theatrical Adaptations

A&E Biography Video: Vincent Van Gogh: A Stroke of Genius (1997). Producer: Kathleen Callan. A film profile that covers the details of the painter's life, personality, and artistic achievement with location footage and expert testimony. Video.

Lust for Life (1956). Director: Vincent Minelli. Kirk Douglas's intense convincing portrait of the painter is remarkable in this filmed version of

Irving Stone's novel. Anthony Quinn portrays Paul Gauguin. Video.

Van Gogh (1992). Director: Maurice Pialat. Award-winning film portrait of Van Gogh's final days that offers a fresh view of the painter that largely steers clear of the sensational for a more internal inner portrait. Jacques Dutronc is impressive in the lead role, with Alexandra London and Bernard Le Coq. Video.

Vincent and Theo (1990). Director: Robert Altman. Altman's is a stunning and compelling look at the tortured relationship between the artist (Tim Roth) and his brother (Paul Rhys). Video.

Vincent: The Life and Death of Vincent Van Gogh (1987). Director: Paul Cox. John Hurt reads passages of the artist's letters and diaries in a sensitive and informative documentary portrait. Video.

See also Paul Gauguin

476. DIEGO VELÁZQUEZ
1599–1660

Spanish painter Velázquez was court painter to Philip IV, beginning in 1623. His style was influenced by Rubens and by the Italian artists of the High Renaissance, and he, in turn had great influence on artists of the nineteenth century, from Goya to the impressionists. His masterpieces include *The Drunkards, Christ on the Cross, Surrender of Breda* (ca. 1635), and *Maids of Honor* (1656–1657). Shortly before his death, he organized the marriage ceremonies of the Spanish princess Maria Theresa and Louis XIV of France.

Recommended Biographies

Brown, Jonathan. *Velázquez: Painter and Courtier*. New Haven, Connecticut: Yale University Press, 1986. 322pp. Brown's is the best overview of the painter's life and works that shows the connection between Velázquez's artistic career and his life as a courtier. The gaps in the biographical record are filled with logical assumptions, and the book is excellent on the social history that helps explain the painter's milieu and the forces that shaped his career. In *Velázquez: The Technique of Genius*. With Carmen Garrido. (New Haven, Connecticut: Yale University Press, 1998. 224pp.), the authors, after a brief introduction to the painter's life and career and a discussion of his materials and techniques, focus on 30 works that span Velázquez's career to trace his artistic development.

Harris, Enriqueta. *Velázquez*. Ithaca, New York: Cornell University Press, 1982. 240pp. Harris includes translations of the primary early sources for details on the artist's life by Antonio Palomino and Francisco Pacheco and uses a close analysis of the works to clarify and correct details suggested by these works. The result is a reliable assessment of both the life and artistry based on sound scholarship.

Other Biographical Studies

Gudiol, José. *Velázquez*. New York: Viking, 1974. 325pp. Gudiol's study quotes extensively from the principal documentary sources to establish a bio-

graphical chronology while analyzing the painter's masterpieces to trace his artistic evolution.

Justi, Karl. *Diego Velázquez and His Times*. Philadelphia: Lippincott, 1889. 506pp. Justi's is an informative volume that makes up for the scarcity of hard evidence on the artist's life with social and cultural background and a close analysis of the works for their revelations about Velázquez's creative method and genius.

Stevenson, Robert A.M. *Velázquez*. 1895. Reprint ed. London: G. Bell, 1962. 182pp. Stevenson's critical study of Velázquez's works attempts to reach conclusions on the artist's achievement and temperament based on formal considerations.

Trapier, Elizabeth du Gué. *Velázquez*. New York: Hispanic Society of America, 1948. 434pp. Trapier synthesizes the available sources to reconstruct a narrative account of the artist's life, supplemented by historical and cultural details and an examination of influences and artistic techniques.

Recommended Juvenile Biographies

Ripley, Elizabeth. *Velázquez*. Philadelphia: Lippincott, 1965. 72pp. MG. Ripley summarizes the essential facts of the painter's life and includes reproductions from different periods of his career.

Treviño, Elizabeth Borton de. *I, Juan de Parega*. New York: Farrar, Straus, 1965. 192pp. This Newbery Award–winning novel looks at Velázquez from the perspective of his slave, who learns to paint in secret.

Biographical Films and Theatrical Adaptations

Velázquez (1989). Director: José Antonio Páramo. Discusses the artist's life and work. Video.

Velázquez (1991). Director: Didier Baussy. The painter's character is revealed through examining his work in chronological order. Included are various aspects of his life and times and his relationship with Philip IV. Video.

477. GIUSEPPE VERDI
1813–1901

One of the foremost Italian opera composers, Verdi is celebrated for such enduring works as *Ernani* (1844), *Rigoletto* (1851), considered his masterpiece, *Il Trovatore* (1853), *La Traviata* (1853), *La Forza del destino* (1862), *Aïda* (1871), and his great *Requiem* (1874). A master of dramatic composition, he produced operas of great power, subtlety, and brilliance even during his later years, including *Otello* (1887) and *Falstaff* (1893).

Autobiography and Primary Sources

Letters of Giuseppe Verdi. Charles Osborne, ed. New York: Holt, 1972. 280pp. This collection of nearly 300 letters covers the composer's life from age 30 to 87. Most are day-to-day exchanges with those connected with his work, including comments on his operas and artistic approach. However, they rarely display Verdi's thoughts on his contemporaries or much self-assessment.

Verdi: A Documentary Study. William Weaver, ed. London: Thames and Hudson, 1977. 256pp. This useful collection of documentary sources include Verdi's often inaccurate autobiographical narrative and a number of contemporaries' recollections.

Verdi: The Man in His Letters. Franz Werfel and Paul Stefan, eds. New York: L.B. Fischer, 1942. 469pp. This selection of Verdi's letters includes a copy of his will and the autobiographical narrative the composer wrote at the age of 65.

Recommended Biographies

Budden, Julian. *Verdi*. New York: Vintage Press, 1987. 404pp. Divided between an examination of Verdi's life and work, Budden's is a distinguished study that synthesizes up-to-date scholarship in a reliable and insightful presentation by the leading expert on Verdi and his operas.

Phillips-Matz, Mary Jane. *Verdi: A Biography*. New York: Oxford University Press, 1993. 941pp. Drawing on a wide range of sources, many previously overlooked, this is a remarkably detailed, authoritative reexamination of Verdi's life. More complex than previously shown, the composer is portrayed frankly with his flaws clearly displayed. The book should remain the standard biography for some time to come.

Walker, Frank. *The Man Verdi*. New York: Knopf, 1962. 526pp. Excluding all discussion of Verdi's music, Walker concentrates on "Verdi the man through the stories of his relationships with some of those who knew him best." The result is an indispensable reference source, a meticulously documented, authoritative collection of facts about the composer.

Other Biographical Studies

Gatti, Carlo. *Verdi: The Man and His Music*. New York: Putnam, 1955. 371pp. Gatti's is a highly detailed gathering of factual details surrounding Verdi's life and his compositions. Mostly valuable as a reference source, the book is insufficiently objective to provide a reliable interpretative assessment of the man or his music.

Hume, Paul. *Verdi: The Man and His Music*. New York: Dutton, 1977. 173pp. Divided into three sections—the composer's life, plot summaries of his operas, and cast lists of important performances—Hume's popular study aimed at a general audience is chiefly redeemed by its illustrations. Otherwise, the analysis is undistinguished and not fully reliable.

Hussey, Dyneley. *Verdi*. New York: Dutton, 1940. 355pp. Hussey's critical biography is based mainly on Verdi's letters and includes an in-depth analysis of the works.

Martin, George. *Verdi: His Music, Life and Times*. New York: Dodd, Mead, 1963. 633pp. This immense collection of material on the composer ranges widely over biographical details, Verdi's social and political background, and musical criticism. More selectivity and focus would have made the book stronger, but the motivated reader will find much matter in Martin's comprehensive survey.

Osborne, Charles. *Verdi: A Life in the Theatre.* New York: Knopf, 1987. 360pp. An accessible biography for the generalist, Osborne's provides little original research but synthesizes familiar details into a narrative overview that is rarely penetrating.

Sheean, Vincent. *Orpheus at Eighty.* New York: Random House, 1958. 372pp. Sheean narrates the story of Verdi's life in flashbacks from the perspective of his final year. The device helps to connect the various aspects of the man and his development into a coherent and comprehensible pattern. The book's musical criticism is not as strong as the historical and cultural background.

Southwell-Sander, Peter S. *Verdi: His Life and Times.* Neptune, New Jersey: Paganiniana, 1980. 160pp. Part of the Illustrated Lives of the Great Composers series, this is a brief overview through text and photographs that serves its purpose as a popular introduction for the general reader.

Toye, Francis. *Giuseppe Verdi: His Life and Works.* New York: Knopf, 1931. 467pp. The first comprehensive and scholarly biographical study includes an overview of Verdi's life and a detailed analysis of each of his 27 operas.

Wechsberg, Josef. *Verdi.* New York: Putnam, 1974. 255pp. Offering no new research or original insights and an often simplistic and misleading presentation, this is a popular biography of limited value beyond a basic introduction that will need to be corrected by more sophisticated treatments.

Ybarra, T.R. *Verdi: Miracle Man of Opera.* New York: Harcourt, Brace, 1955. 312pp. This is a popular biography written by an enthusiast and is not reliable in all its details, indulging in a good deal of fictionalization to enhance the author's own operatic style.

Fictional Portraits

Werfel, Franz. *Verdi: A Novel of the Opera.* New York: Simon & Schuster, 1926. 438pp. Werfel deals mainly with Verdi's relationship with Wagner; the book mixes biographical details with romantic elements.

Recommended Juvenile Biographies

Malvern, Gladys. *On Golden Wings.* Philadelphia: Macrae Smith, 1960. 192pp. MG. This is a highly fictionalized though intimate portrait of the composer's life and music. Although it often reads like a libretto from one of Verdi's operas, it does adhere fairly closely to the biographical facts.

Tames, Richard. *Giuseppe Verdi.* New York: F. Watts, 1991. 32pp. MG. Tames offers a brief but competent life-and-times overview that covers the highlights of Verdi's career and achievement.

Vernon, Roland. *Introducing Verdi.* Parsippany, New Jersey: Silver Burdett, 1997. 32pp. MG. This is a well-written appreciation of Verdi's music that touches on some details of his life and career.

Biographical Films and Theatrical Adaptations

Giuseppe Verdi (1996). Director: Malcolm Hossick. Part of the Famous Composer series, this

is a brief biographical and musical overview of Verdi's life and accomplishments. Video.

Verdi (1982). Director: Renato Castellani. This television miniseries traces Verdi's career with Ronald Pickup in the title role, with Carla Fracci and interpretations of Verdi's works by Luciano Pavarotti and Maria Callas. Video.

Other Sources

Conati, Marcello, ed. *Encounters with Verdi.* Ithaca, New York: Cornell University Press, 1984. 417pp. The volume gathers together recollections of Verdi by a wide circle of his contemporaries.

Weaver, William, and Martin Chusid, eds. *The Verdi Companion.* New York: W.W. Norton, 1979. 366pp. This is a useful collection of critical essays on various aspects of the composer's life and works, with a chronology, a glossary of people associated with Verding, and a listing of his major works by the date of their first performance.

478. JAN VERMEER
1632–1675

Dutch painter ranked among the greatest Durch masters and celebrated for his use of light and color, Vermeer spent his entire life in Delft, where he was twice dean of the painters' guild. Fewer than 35 paintings can be attributed to him and forgeries of his work are frequent. His paintings include *The Milkmaid* (1658–1660), *Girl Asleep* (1657), and *Young Woman With a Water Jug* (1664–1665).

Recommended Biographies

Blankert, Albert. *Vermeer of Delft.* New York: Dutton, 1978. 176pp. Blankert includes a section of important documents related to Vermeer's life and career along with an idiosyncratic but provocative and revealing examination of the man and his work.

Blankert, Albert, John M. Montias, and Gilles Aillaud. *Vermeer.* New York: Rizzoli, 1988. 231pp. This useful volume is an ideal introductory overview for the non-expert, collecting concisely the known biographical details, a critical analysis of the works, and a catalog of the paintings.

Montias, John M. *Vermeer and His Milieu: A Web of Social History.* Princeton, New Jersey: Princeton University Press, 1989. 407pp. Through exhaustive archival research, Montias has added considerably to the social, historical, and biographical record of Vermeer's life and time. Reconstructing the social and economic context of seventeenth-century Delft, the book presents a vivid portrait of the events that would have affected the painter and influenced his art. An indispensable reference source for the scholar and more-than-casual student of Vermeer.

Other Biographical Studies

Gowing, Lawrence. *Vermeer.* 1953. Revised ed. New York: Harper & Row, 1970. 160pp. Through a careful analysis of Vermeer's paintings, Gowing intuits a portrait of the man and artist, concluding

that he was a far more complex figure than has been previously believed.

Koningsberger, Hans. *The World of Vermeer 1632–1675.* New York: Time-Life Books, 1967. 192pp. In a visually appealing introduction to the artist and his times, the book is divided into an essay on the painter and his place in Dutch seventeenth-century art and reproductions of Vermeer's paintings and those of his period. The factual information is reliable, and the book serves as a useful overview for the non-expert.

Slatkes, Leonard J. *Vermeer and His Contemporaries.* New York: Abbeville Press, 1981. 158pp. Preceded by a brief introduction outlining recent scholarship, the book offers more than 70 pages of color reproductions, as well as a close analysis of the paintings, tracing the painter's achievement and development through comparisons with the other artists of the 1650s and 1660s who were influenced by Vermeer.

Snow, Edward A. *A Study of Vermeer.* Berkeley: University of California Press, 1979. 183pp. Snow offers a psychological interpretation of the artist and his paintings. A fresh and provocative approach, Snow's study is ingenious guesswork given the lack of solid evidence, but it is nevertheless an important scholarly treatment that goes further than most in penetrating the shadowy and enigmatic Vermeer.

Swillens, P.T.A. *Johannes Vermeer, Painter of Delft: 1632–1675.* New York: Studio Vista, 1950. 221pp. This scholarly reference volume supplies a biographical outline in addition to a close reading of the paintings for what they may reveal about the artist's interests and values.

Thienen, Frithjof van. *Jan Vermeer of Delft.* New York: Harper, 1949. 24pp. Reproductions of all of Vermeer's paintings are joined to a compact introductory essay that gives all the known facts of the painter's life.

Fictional Portraits

Chevalier, Tracy. *Girl with a Pearl Earring.* New York: Dutton, 2000. 233pp. Chevalier imaginatively enters Vermeer's household during the 1660s as seen from the perspective of a teenaged servant who becomes the painter's assistant and ultimately the model for one of his most famous paintings.

Laker, Rosalind. *The Golden Tulip.* New York: Doubleday, 1991. 585pp. This historical romance involving a woman artist in the Netherlands during the seventeenth century includes a depiction of Vermeer.

479. VICTORIA
1819–1901

Queen of Great Britain and Ireland and empress of India, Victoria succeeded (1837) to the throne after the death of William IV and reigned during the height of the British Empire. She married Albert of Saxe-Coburg-Gotha (1840), who became the dominant influence in her life. Their domestic life, as well as Victoria's conscientiousness and strict morals, helped restore the prestige of the monarchy and establish it as a symbol of public service. Victoria's active role in government and her sometimes adversarial relations with a succession of prime ministers affected the political life of her reign.

Autobiography and Primary Sources

Queen Victoria in Her Letters and Journals: A Selection. Christopher Hibbert, ed. New York: Viking, 1985. 374pp. This selection of Victoria's writings offers a strikingly different view of the stolid, humorless Victorian icon, revealing her humanity and animation, while tracing the evolution of a shy young princess into the powerful symbol of her era.

Recommended Biographies

Charlot, Monica. *Victoria: The Young Queen.* Cambridge, Massachusetts: Blackwell, 1991. 492pp. Ending her coverage with the death of Prince Albert in 1861, Charlot, in the first volume of a projected full-length study, provides a fresh and fully documented view of Victoria, with an emphasis on her personality and relationships. Her Victoria is a complex figure, flawed but granted considerably more political acumen than have previous historians.

Longford, Elizabeth. *Queen Victoria: Born to Succeed.* New York: Harper & Row, 1965. 635pp. Longford includes both the personal and political sides of Victoria in a full-length, psychologically based portrait. The book is particularly interesting in its gender discussion that attempts to relate the queen's life in the context of the social history of women during the period.

St. Aubyn, Giles. *Queen Victoria.* New York: Atheneum, 1992. 669pp. In an admirable summary of what is known about Victoria's life based on new information that has emerged from the full opening of the Royal Archives, the book supplies a sympathetic yet balanced portrait of the woman and her reign.

Strachey, Lytton. *Queen Victoria.* New York: Harcourt, Brace, 1921. 423pp. In a full-scale workup of the biographical method developed in *Eminent Victorians* (1918), Strachey's portrait is significant both in establishing a dominating view of the queen and by its influence on the modern biographer's art. Looking beyond the history of her reign, Strachey concentrates on Victoria's personality and foibles, replacing respectful reverence with a critical, though convincingly human, portrayal.

Weintraub, Stanley. *Victoria: an Intimate Biography.* New York: Dutton, 1987. 700pp. Weintraub's account is well-written and impeccably researched with an emphasis on Victoria's personal, not political, life but with sufficient historical and cultural context to make the queen's public activities and personal values understandable. Based on a number of hitherto unavailable sources, the portrait Weintraub offers is both candid and convincing.

Woodham-Smith, Cecil. *Queen Victoria: From Her Birth to the Death of the Prince Consort.* New York: Knopf, 1972. 495pp. The author lived to complete only a partial study ending in the year 1861, but the details he assembled represent one of the fullest and most authoritative treatments of Victoria's childhood, early reign, and married life.

Other Biographical Studies

Benson, E.F. *Queen Victoria.* New York: Longmans, 1935. 406pp. Benson combines an examination of Victoria's personal life and character with an account of the principal events of her reign and the queen's attitudes toward domestic and international affairs. More balanced and carefully documented than Strachey's groundbreaking biography, Benson's study remains an important biographical source, reliably synthesizing previously unexamined archival sources.

Bolitho, Hector. *The Reign of Queen Victoria.* New York: Macmillan, 1948. 437pp. Synthesizing material from his previous books, *Albert the Good* (1932), *Victoria: The Widow and Her Son* (1934), and *Victoria and Albert* (1938), Bolitho narrates Victoria's life story with an emphasis on the personal rather than the political.

Cullen, Tom. *The Empress Brown: The True Story of a Victorian Scandal.* Boston: Houghton Mifflin, 1969. 250pp. Cullen focuses on the relationship between Victoria and her Scottish servant, John Brown, based on Victoria's letters, the papers of the queen's private secretary, and contemporary accounts. Cullen concludes that the alleged scandal is unfounded, and the book offers its own reasoned assessment of the curious dependency Victoria had on Brown.

Epton, Nina. *Victoria and Her Daughters.* New York: W.W. Norton, 1971. 252pp. Tracing the lives of Victoria's five daughters, Epton examines Victoria's qualities as a mother, relating her public image as a domestic paragon with the reality. Unscholarly and undocumented, the book is chiefly interesting for its many anecdotes, and its extensive quotations from the unpublished papers of the queen's private secretary.

Erickson, Carolly. *Her Little Majesty: The Life of Queen Victoria.* New York: Simon & Schuster, 1997. 304pp. Despite an engaging, entertaining novelistic style, this brief biography falls short in its penetration and comprehensiveness. What Erickson chooses to cover is done so with a flourish and often with the omniscient power of the fiction writer.

Hibbert, Christopher. *Queen Victoria: A Personal History.* New York: Basic Books, 2000. 464pp. Hibbert's is a lively reassessment that challenges conventional wisdom, presenting Victoria as shy and vulnerable as well as formidable. In a series of colorful anecdotes the book helps present a complex, human figure.

Marshall, Dorothy. *The Life and Times of Victoria.* New York: Praeger, 1974. 224pp. In a beautifully illustrated biography, Marshall connects the public and private life of Victoria with a carefully constructed period background. A good, brief biographical introduction for the general reader.

Sitwell, Edith. *Victoria of England.* Boston: Houghton Mifflin, 1936. 349pp. Not attempting a full history of the reign, this is a portrait of the woman and her relationships. Influenced by Strachey's approach, Sitwell presents a series of dramatic scenes with many imaginative surmises but with few new insights.

Biographical Novels

Anthony, Evelyn. *Victoria and Albert.* New York: Crowell, 1958. 312pp. The novel looks at the famous royal marriage with a controversial portrait of Albert who does not claim Victoria's blind allegiance to him. The historical background is well developed.

Harrod-Eagles, Cynthia. *I, Victoria.* New York: St. Martin's, 1996. 415pp. At the end of her life, Victoria reflects back on her long reign in this fictional autobiography that attempts to humanize the portrait of the formidable queen.

Ludwig, Charles. *Defender of the Faith.* Minneapolis: Bethany House, 1988. 202pp. This devotional novel dramatizes Victoria's spiritual life in scenes from her life in which her faith is tested.

Plaidy, Jean. *Victoria in the Wings.* London: R. Hale, 1972. 349pp.; *Captive of Kensington Palace.* New York: Putnam, 1976. 288pp.; *The Queen and Lord M.* New York: Putnam, 1977. 268pp.; *The Queen's Husband.* New York: Putnam, 1978. 382pp.; *The Widow of Windsor.* New York: Putnam, 1974. 351pp. Plaidy's biographical series follows Victoria's life and times from her childhood. With *Victoria Victorious* (New York: Putnam, 1986. 569pp.), Plaidy offers Victoria's own version of her life in an imagined autobiography.

Prole, Lozania. *The Little Victoria.* Bath, England: Chivers, 1957. 278pp. Victoria's childhood and youth up to her marriage is dramatized in this mainly factual account with imaginary embellishments.

Whittle, Tyler. *The Young Victoria.* New York: St. Martin's, 1971. 246pp.; *Albert's Victoria.* New York: St. Martin's, 1972. 263pp.; *The Widow of Windsor.* New York: St. Martin's, 1973. 287pp. Whittle's biographical trilogy follows Victoria's entire life in a faithful account rooted in the known facts.

Fictional Portraits

Bonnet, Theodore. *The Mudlark.* Garden City, New York: Doubleday, 1949. 305pp. This inventive tale dramatizes the roles played by a London urchin and Disraeli in convincing the queen to end her 14 years of seclusion following the death of Albert.

Byrd, Elizabeth. *The Long Enchantment.* London: Macmillan, 1973. 250pp. A maid at Balmoral describes the relationship between Victoria and John Brown.

Fleming, H.K. *The Day They Kidnapped Queen Victoria.* New York: St. Martin's, 1978. 170pp. In an amusing fanciful story, Victoria's train is hijacked, and she is kidnapped. The rescue effort is led by Disraeli with implausible assistance from Tennyson.

Mayerson, Evelyn W. *Princess in Amber.* Garden City, New York: Doubleday, 1985. 298pp. Princess Beatrice, the youngest daughter of Queen Victoria is the focus here for an interesting perspective on Victoria's family relationships.

Prole, Lozania. *The Queen's Daughters.* London: R. Hale, 1973. 206pp. This is a group fictional portrait of Victoria's five daughters, depicting their relationships with their mother.

Routh, Jonathan. *The Secret Life of Queen Victoria.* Garden City, New York: Doubleday, 1980. 110pp. In an imagined diary, the novel records Victoria's attempt to break free from her public responsibilities during a secret visit to Jamaica.

Recommended Juvenile Biographies

Grant, Neil. *Victoria, Queen and Empress.* New York: F. Watts, 1970. 233pp. MG/YA. Grant stresses Victoria's relationship with the central male figures in her life, including Melbourne, Albert, Disraeli, and John Brown.

Green, Robert. *Queen Victoria.* New York: F. Watts, 1998. 64pp. MG. This is an informative, well-written biographical overview with suggestions for additional reading, Internet resources, and a genealogical family tree.

Shearman, Deirdre. *Queen Victoria.* New York: Chelsea House, 1986. 115pp. MG/YA. Shearman orients the reader well to the historical and cultural aspects of Victoria's reign in this informative biographical and historical account.

Biographical Films and Theatrical Adaptations

Carb, David, and Walter P. Eaton. *Queen Victoria.* New York: Dutton, 1922. 213pp. This dramatic account of Victoria's life from her girlhood to her Jubilee has been described as a good dramatization of Lytton Strachey's biography.

Housman, Laurence. *Victoria Regina.* New York: Scribners, 1935. 469pp. This volume brings together the author's Palace Plays that look at Victoria's reign and marriage. In the playwright's view, Victoria is the irresistible headstrong force meeting the immovable scholarly and reserved Prince. However, Albert emerges with a refreshing sense of humor.

Norris, Kathleen. *Victoria: A Play in Four Acts and Twelve Scenes.* Garden City, New York: Doubleday, 1934. 140pp. This closet drama of dramatic episodes from Queen Victoria's life lacks a unifying dramatic principle and fails to rise much beyond a sketch.

Edward the King (1975). Director: John Garrie. The life and short reign of Edward VII is chronicled with his relationship with his parents detailed. Robert Hardy portrays Prince Albert; Annette Crosbie is Queen Victoria, and Timothy West is the Prince of Wales and later king. Video.

Evening at Osborne: A Portrait of Queen Victoria in Her Own Words (1991). Director: Richard Stroud. British actress Prunella Scales depicts the queen in this film version of the one-person stage play by Katrina Hendrey in which Victoria's comments on her life and times are taken from her letters and journals. Video.

Mrs. Brown (1997). Director: John Madden. This is a believable, restrained look at Victoria's relationship with Scottish servant John Brown. Judi Dench is convincing as the queen, with an equally strong performance by Billy Connolly as Brown. Video.

Sixty Glorious Years (1938). Director: Herbert Wilcox. Anna Neagle reprises her portrayal of Victoria in this sequel to *Victoria the Great* (1937).

Victoria Regina (1961). Director: George Schaefer. This made-for-television film tells the story of Victoria's reign in a series of vignettes from her ascension to the throne in 1837 through the celebration of her Diamond Jubilee. Julie Harris stars as Victoria with James Donald as Prince Albert. Video.

Victoria the Great (1937). Director: Herbert Wilcox. Anna Neagle puts in a fine performance as Victoria in this biographical film that emphasizes the queen's relationship with Prince Albert (Anton Walbrook).

Other Sources

Homans, Margaret, and Adrienne Munich, eds. *Remaking Queen Victoria.* New York: Cambridge University Press, 1997. 294pp. A collection of essays by scholars in a number of disciplines explores the cultural significance of Victoria.

Munich, Adrienne. *Queen Victoria's Secrets.* New York: Columbia University Press, 1998. 272pp. This meditation on Victoria as cultural symbol is often fascinating and daring in its generalizing leaps, weaving together feminist, anthropological, and postcolonial approaches to the portrait of the queen and her era.

See also Albert; Benjamin Disraeli; Edward VII; William Gladstone

480. VOLTAIRE
1694–1778

Born François-Marie Arouet, French philosopher and author, Voltaire ranks among the greatest literary and historical geniuses. A towering figure of the Enlightenment, he advocated political and religious tolerance and supported the ideas of Newton and Locke. An enemy of the tyrannical French nobility, he spent much of his life in exile. His works include *Letters Concerning the English Nation* (1733) and *Candide* (1759). He also contributed to Diderot's *Encyclopedia* and wrote his own *Philosophical Dictionary* (1764).

Autobiography and Primary Sources

Correspondence and Related Documents. Theodore Besterman, ed. Toronto: University of Toronto Press, 1968–1977. 51 vols. This monumental scholarly collection of Voltaire's 20,000 known letters is far too daunting for most general readers who may prefer to sample Voltaire's letters in smaller doses in such volumes as *Voltaire in His Letters* (New York: Putnam, 1919. 270pp.) and *Selected Letters of Voltaire.* Richard A. Brooks, ed. (New York: New York University Press, 349pp.).

Recommended Biographies

Aldridge, A. Owen. *Voltaire and the Century of Light.* Princeton, New Jersey: Princeton University Press, 1975. 443pp. Less individualistic and more accessible than Besterman, Aldridge's is a measured, clear, and economical survey of Voltaire's life and writings that serves as a good introduction.

Besterman, Theodore. *Voltaire.* New York: Harcourt, Brace, 1969. 637pp. For Besterman, the editor of his letters, Voltaire is simply "the greatest of French writers," and the book attempts to justify this view, often with a condescension and scorn for the unconvinced that is distracting. Despite Besterman's bias, this remains an important source for information on Voltaire by one of the leading authorities on the writer.

Wade, Ira O. *The Intellectual Development of Voltaire.* Princeton, New Jersey: Princeton University Press, 1969. 807pp. Tracing Voltaire's life from birth to the 1750s, Wade's is a comprehensive, accessible examination of the philosopher's training and his relationship to other eighteenth-century thinkers.

Other Biographical Studies

Aldington, Richard. *Voltaire.* New York: Dutton, 1925. 278pp. Divided into two equal sections on Voltaire's life and works, Aldington's study is often brilliant, always entertaining, and serves as a stimulating introduction, although the author's own clear prejudices compromise his judgment at various points.

Gray, John. *Voltaire.* New York: Routledge, 1999. 64pp. Gray's brief biographical summary is a useful sketch by an expert but written for those with no special background in philosophy.

Hearsey, John. *Voltaire.* New York: Barnes and Noble, 1976. 367pp. Written for the general reader, Hearsey's is a readable introductory account that attempts to uncover the elements and activities that helped form Voltaire's genius. Hearsey's reach exceeds his grasp at several points, defeated by the lack of expertise needed to cover adequately the full range of Voltaire's achievements.

Lanson, Gustave. *Voltaire.* New York: Wiley, 1966. 258pp. Originally published in 1906, Lanson's is a wide-ranging account of Voltaire's intellectual and creative development, as well as a critical assessment of Voltaire's imaginative work.

Morley, John. *Voltaire.* New York: Appleton, 1872. 263pp. An important nineteenth-century biography, Morley's study is a balanced assessment and a careful assembling of the significant factual record.

Noyes, Alfred. *Voltaire.* New York: Sheed & Ward, 1936. 643pp. Noyes's study of Voltaire's life and work is dominated by its central thesis that the philosopher was not an enemy of the Catholic church and was in fact a deeply religious man. Noyes's evident bias limits the reliability of his interpretation, but his portrait does serve as an interesting alternative to the rationalist view of Voltaire.

Torrey, Norman L. *The Spirit of Voltaire.* New York: Columbia University Press, 1938. 314pp. Not a full-length portrait, Torrey selects from the telling details and events to reveal the man and his philosophy. Although not recommended as a first book on the subject, Torrey's study is a challenging and learned analysis for the reader with a basic grasp of Voltaire's life and work.

Biographical Novels

Endore, S. Guy. *Voltaire! Voltaire!* New York: Simon & Schuster, 1961. 507pp. This is a dual biographical profile of Voltaire and his rival Jean-Jacques Rousseau.

Fictional Portraits

Rebolledo, Francisco. *Rasero.* Baton Rouge: Louisiana State University Press, 1995. 552pp. A young Spanish nobleman comes to Paris during the 17th century to interact with a number of historical figures, and he is on hand for Voltaire's death.

Biographical Films and Theatrical Adaptations

Voltaire (1933). Director: John G. Adolfi. George Arliss is a standout in this biographical portrait of the writer. With Margaret Lindsay, Doris Kenyon, Reginald Owen, and Alan Mowbray.

481. RICHARD WAGNER
1813–1883

German composer, whose influential works represent the height of musical Romanticism, Wagner first achieved success with *Rienzi* (1840). His other early works include *Tannhäuser* (1844) and *Lohengrin* (1848). He was active in the Revolution of 1848 and forced to flee for eight years to Switzerland. Wagner settled in Bayreuth, where he built a theater and completed his famous *Ring* myth-cycle: *Das Rheingold* (1854), *Die Walküre* (1856), *Siegfried* (1869), and *Die Götterdämmerung* (1874). His last opera was *Parsifal* (1882).

Autobiography and Primary Sources

Art, Life, and Theories of Richard Wagner Selected from His Writings. E.L. Burlingame, ed. New York: Holt, 1875. 305pp. Burlingame's excellent selection of Wagner's writings includes the composer's "Autobiographical Sketch" that covers his life up to 1842.

The Diary of Richard Wagner 1865–1882: The Brown Book. New York: Cambridge University Press, 1980. 218pp. Wagner's reflections cover his life from 1846 to 1882. See also *Cosima Wagner's Diaries.* Martin Gregor-Dallin and Dietrich Mack, eds. (New York: Harcourt, Brace, 1978–1980. 2 vols.), a detailed account of the composer's life from 1869 to Wagner's death.

My Life. 1911. Mary Whittall, ed. New York: Cambridge University Press, 1983. 786pp. Wagner's memoir was begun in 1864 at the request of King Ludwig II and completed in 1880. This edition restores personal details left out of prior editions. Other autobiographical reflections can be found in *Wagner's Prose Works.* William Ashton Ellis, ed. (London: Kegan Paul, 1893–1899. 8 vols.).

Selected Letters of Richard Wagner. Stewart Spencer and Barry Millington, eds. New York: W.W. Norton, 1987. 858pp. Arranged chronologically in sections preceded by a biographical and historical introductory essay, this is a collection of some 500 letters that provides a rare glimpse of the composer's development, creative process, and changing attitudes on various subjects.

Recommended Biographies

Deathridge, John, and Carl Dahlhaus. *The New Grove Wagner.* New York: W.W. Norton, 1984. 226pp. A model of succinct scholarship and interpretation, this slim volume offers the best general introduction to Wagner's life and work. This is the standout reference source for the general reader.

Gál, Hans. *Richard Wagner.* New York: Stein and Day, 1976. 236pp. A highly readable biography, Gál's critical study includes a compact overview of Wagner's life and a learned, though accessible, analysis of his works. Dealing frankly with the contradictions of Wagner's character, the book is a sophisticated assessment and a valuable guide to the man and his music.

Newman, Ernest. *The Life of Richard Wagner.* New York: Knopf, 1933–1946. 4 vols. Newman's monumental biography is still regarded as the standard source. Painstakingly researched and extremely well written, Newman's multivolumes may intimidate the general reader, but the energy expended is ably repaid by the fullest views of the composer ever attempted.

Watson, Derek. *Richard Wagner: A Biography.* London: Dent, 1979. 352pp. A readable and authoritative biography for both the serious student and the casual reader, Watson's life is a synthesis of primary and secondary sources with an emphasis on Wagner's life, personality, and social context rather than his music.

Other Biographical Studies

Anderson, Robert. *Wagner: A Biography: With a Survey of Books, Editions, and Recordings.* Hamden, Connecticut: Linnet Books, 1980. 154pp. Anderson's brief biography is a useful overview, but the book's chief importance is a thoughtful survey of biographical and critical works on the composer.

Barth, Herbert, Dietrich Mack, and Egon Voss. *Wagner: A Documentary Study.* New York: Oxford University Press, 1975. 256pp. This is an excellent and comprehensive collection of documents, illustrations, and photographs.

Bekker, Paul. *Richard Wagner: His Life and Work.* New York: W.W. Norton, 1931. 522pp. Bekker's critical biography attempts to connect Wagner's life with his work in which both are united in the composer's pursuit of an emotional engagement with experience. Often dense and overly elaborate, the book is not for the uninitiated.

Chancellor, John. *Wagner.* Boston: Little, Brown, 1978. 308pp. Fiercely partisan, this uncritical, adulatory synthesis of others' research is too unbalanced to offer a fully reliable assessment and provides no new information, other than the depth of the author's devotion.

Ellis, William A. *Life of Richard Wagner.* London: K. Paul, 1900–1908. 6 vols. Ellis's massive biographical study only reached the year 1859 before he abandoned the project. Although limited in its scholarship and lacking access to a number of important primary sources, the volumes are still regarded as an important factual guide to the years covered.

Gutman, Robert W. *Richard Wagner: The Man, His Mind, and His Music.* New York: Harcourt, Brace, 1968. 490pp. Gutman's is a highly critical biographical study that emphasizes the composer's character flaws and anti-Semitism.

Kapp, Julius. *The Women in Wagner's Life.* New York: Knopf, 1931. 284pp. The author concentrates on Wagner's relationships with the significant women in his life, based on a careful sifting of primary source material.

Katz, Jacob. *The Darker Side of Genius: Richard Wagner's Anti-Semitism.* Hanover, New Hampshire: University Press of New England, 1986. 158pp. Katz supplies an examination of the development of Wagner's anti-Semitism with scholarly attention to detail but remaining accessible for the general reader. Wagner's attitudes are placed in their wider social and historical context.

Mayer, Hans. *Portrait of Wagner: An Illustrated Biography.* New York: Herder and Herder, 1972. 175pp. Wagner's personality is described against the social and political background of his times with more than 50 illustrations and photographs. Useful for the general reader looking for a biographical introduction.

Millington, Barry. *Wagner.* 1984. Revised ed. Princeton, New Jersey: Princeton University Press, 1992. 342pp. Part of the Master Musicians series, Millington attempts to separate the facts from the various myths surrounding Wagner and fashions a compact, balanced assessment that neither downplays nor overemphasizes the various controversies surrounding the composer.

Newman, Ernest. *Wagner as Man and Artist*. New York: Knopf, 1924. 399pp. Newman's first biographical study preceded his monumental life and is chiefly instructive as a compact synthesis of interpretations developed more elaborately in his four-volume study. The book is particularly incisive in pointing out the discrepancies between Wagner's autobiographical remarks and the biographical facts.

Osborne, Charles. *Wagner and His World*. New York: Scribner, 1977. 128pp. Osborne's is a basic visual introduction to the composer and his background.

Panofsky, Walter. *Wagner: A Pictorial Biography*. New York: Viking, 1963. 144pp. A sketchy biographical overview accompanies a selection of illustrations and photographs. Neither complete nor sophisticated enough to serve as a basic introduction, the book is chiefly a picture book.

Sabor, Rudolph. *The Real Wagner*. London: A. Deutsch, 1987. 312pp. Arranged topically rather than chronologically, Sabor's is a sophisticated examination of the many controversies surrounding Wagner's life and career and the complexity of his character. The reader who already has a clear view of the composer's history will find many provocative and challenging insights.

Taylor, Ronald. *Richard Wagner: His Life, Art, and Thought*. New York: Taplinger, 1979. 285pp. This is a sensible, concise, well-researched, and well-written biography that is particularly strong on the wider historical and cultural background of Wagner's career. The relatively simplistic musical analysis is supplemented by an appendix with excerpts from various individuals such as Shaw, Tolstoy, Debussy, Stravinsky, and Boulez on Wagner's music.

Westernhagen, Curt von. *Wagner: A Biography*. 1968. Revised ed. New York: Cambridge University Press, 1978. 2 vols. Drawing on new documentary sources published since Newman's study, Westernhagen's biography synthesizes new insights into a straightforward narrative account. Although the author purports to "display the personality complete with its inner contradictions... and to leave judgment to the reader," critics have complained that evidence is slanted in Wagner's favor, with the more unflattering aspects of the composer's character and anti-Semitic attitudes downplayed.

White, Chappell. *An Introduction to the Life and Work of Richard Wagner*. Englewood Cliffs, New Jersey: Prentice-Hall, 1967. 186pp. White's is a sensible, compact survey of Wagner's life and work for the general reader seeking a basic overview.

Biographical Novels

Harding, Bertita. *Magic Fire: Scenes around Richard Wagner*. Indianapolis: Bobbs-Merrill, 1953. 457pp. The novel strings together a series of episodes from Wagner's life using invented dialogue to present a multidimensional portrait of the composer and his times.

Richardson, Henry H. *The Young Cosima*. New York: W.W. Norton, 1939. 390pp. The novel tells the story of 12 years in the life of Cosima and her first marriage, ending with her decision to live with Wagner.

Fictional Portraits

Gurr, David. *The Ring Master*. New York: Atheneum, 1987. 739pp. Gurr's exploration of Nazism and Hitler's Germany uses Wagner and his Ring cycle as a touchstone to explain Hitler's evil.

Werfel, Franz. *Verdi: A Novel of the Opera*. New York: Simon & Schuster, 1926. 438pp. Werfel deals mainly with Verdi's relationship with Wagner in a fictional account that mixes biographical details with romantic elements.

Recommended Juvenile Biographies

Padmore, Elaine. *Wagner*. New York: Crowell, 1973. 100pp. MG. Padmore captures both the man and his music in an account suitable for students with some musical background.

Stearns, Monroe. *Richard Wagner: Titan of Music*. New York: F. Watts, 1964. 306pp. MG/YA. This is a well-researched, objective biography that deals frankly with Wagner's character flaws and questionable behavior.

Tames, Richard. *Richard Wagner*. New York: F. Watts, 1991. 132pp. Examines the composer's life and achievements in the context of his era.

Biographical Films and Theatrical Adaptations

Lisztomania (1975). Director: Ken Russell. Russell's outlandish extravaganza looks at Franz Liszt as the first rock star. Roger Daltry plays the musician with Sara Kestelman as Princess Carolyn, Imogene Claire as George Sand, and Paul Nicholas as Wagner. Video.

Ludwig (1972). Director: Luchino Visconti. The story of the relationship between Ludwig II (Helmut Berger) and Wagner (Trevor Howard) is dramatized in this lavish depiction of the king's madness and obsession with the composer. Video.

Song Without End (1960). Director: King Vidor. This musical biography of Franz Liszt (Dirk Borgarde) features an appearance by Lyndon Brook in the role of Wagner. Video.

Wagner (1983). Director: Tony Palmer. Originally a nine-hour British television miniseries, Richard Burton's last film release is a visually stunning but overly long and confusing biographical depiction of the composer's life, with Burton in the lead and Vanessa Redgrave as Cosima Wagner. Ronald Pickup portrays Nietzsche. Video.

Other Sources

Bunbridge, Peter, and Richard Sutter. *The Wagner Companion*. New York: Cambridge University Press, 1979. 462pp. This collection of critical essays from various scholars covers many broad categories of the composer's career and works.

Hodson, Phillip. *Who's Who in Wagner: An A-to-Z Look at His Life and Work*. New York: Macmillan, 1984. 182pp. As the title indicates, this is a series of alphabetically arranged entries covering multiple aspects of the composer's life, work, and associates.

Millington, Barry, ed. *The Wagner Compendium*. New York: Schirmer Books, 1992. 431pp. This is a collection of 18 essays by noted scholars on the composer's life, character, intellectual and musical background, opinions, creative method, and influences.

Muller, Ulrich, ed. *Wagner Handbook*. Cambridge, Massachusetts: Harvard University Press, 1992. 711pp. An extensive collection of essays by many of the world's leading Wagner experts. The composer's career, cultural relationships, psychology, and influence are covered.

482. ANDY WARHOL
1927–1987

American artist and filmmaker famous for his pop art works featuring such commonplace objects as soup cans and dollar bills, Warhol also produced multi-image, silkscreen paintings of Marilyn Monroe and Jacqueline Kennedy. He and his assistants worked out of a large New York loft space known as The Factory. Warhol's films include *Chelsea Girls* (1966) and *Trash* (1971). He also founded the celebrity magazine, *Interview* (1973).

Autobiography and Primary Sources

The Andy Warhol Diaries. Pat Hackett, ed. New York: Warner Books, 1989. 807pp. These are a series of daily telephone interviews recorded from 1976 until only five days before Warhol's death. What began as an expense account diary grew into a shorthand continual sketch of Warhol's world, forming often fascinating, often endlessly repetitive and self-absorbed glimpses into the life of the artist and his preoccupations.

The Philosophy of Andy Warhol: From A to B and Back Again. New York: Harcourt, Brace, 1988. 241pp. Covering a variety of topics, Warhol records his views on such subjects as love, beauty, and fame. Alternately insightful, rambling, slyly candid, and aphoristic.

Recommended Biographies

Bockris, Victor. *The Life and Death of Andy Warhol*. New York: Bantam, 1989. 392pp. Bockris's comprehensive life is the standard biography, well-documented and balanced, based on the author's personal knowledge and extensive interviews with Warhol's family, friends, and associates. Sympathetic in its handling of the artist's personality and career, the book succeeds in presenting a complex portrait often at odds with the public persona.

Bourdon, David. *Warhol*. New York: Abrams, 1989. 432pp. The work of an art critic, Bourdon's assessment of Warhol's life and career emphasizes his artistry over his long service as a professional celebrity. With over 300 reproductions, Bourdon's critical biography is the ideal overview of Warhol's artistic development from commercial illustrator to one of the most significant figures in modern art.

Other Biographical Studies

Colacello, Bob. *Holy Terror: Andy Warhol Close Up.* New York: St. Martin's, 1989. 514pp. Colacello's is an intimate look at Warhol in the 1970s, the years of the author's association with the artist during the early years of *Interview* magazine. The author's close-up method reveals Warhol's flaws but also distorts, emphasizing Warhol the celebrity to the exclusion of other considerations.

Koch, Stephen. *Stargazer: Andy Warhol's World and His Films.* New York: Praeger, 1973. 155pp. Koch's book is the definitive critical treatment of Warhol's career as a filmmaker, tracing his development in the context of the underground, independent film circle of the period.

Biographical Films and Theatrical Adaptations

A&E Biography Video: Andy Warhol: A Life at the Edge (1998). Producer: Jeff Swimmer. Warhol's artistic career and celebrityhood are both chronicled in this film profile featuring the perspectives of numerous friends and associates. Video.

Andy Warhol (1987). Director: Kim Evans. A film profile originally produced for London Weekend Television. Video.

Basquiat (1996). Director: Julian Schnabel. David Bowie depicts Warhol in this film study of artist Jean Michel Basquiat (Jeffrey Wright) in an authentic look at the New York art scene in the 1980s. Video.

I Shot Andy Warhol (1996). Director: Mary Harron. This film focuses on the actual event of Valerie Solanas's attack on Warhol in 1968. Lili Taylor is convincing as Solanas and Jared Harris portrays Warhol. Harron's screenplay is also available (New York: Grove Press, 1996. 224pp.). Video.

Portrait of an Artist: Andy Warhol (1987). Director: Kim Evans. British television profile looks at Warhol's activities in art and film. Video.

Superstar: The Life and Times of Andy Warhol (1991). Director: Chuck Workman. A visual and oral biographical portrait, recording the recollections of Warhol's friends and family. Video.

483. BOOKER T. WASHINGTON
1856–1915

An African American educator, born into slavery, Washington founded Tuskeege Institute, which, under his direction, became one of the leading black schools in the United States. His position that economic equality for African Americans must be attained before the achievement of social equality was opposed by black activist W.E.B. DuBois. Washington organized the National Negro Business League, a group committed to black economic independence. His many writings include his autobiography, *Up From Slavery* (1901), and *The Story of the Negro* (1909).

Autobiography and Primary Sources

The Booker T. Washington Papers. Louis R. Harlan, ed. Urbana: University of Illinois Press, 1972–1989. 14 vols. This scholarly collection of Washington's papers is invaluable for the scholar and the biographer, collecting the essential documentary evidence.

Up from Slavery. New York: Doubleday, 1901. 330pp. Washington's much reprinted and admired autobiography is an essential source on the educator's early life. Washington's version of his life story was written to inspire, and the details support the book's positivist theme of the struggle for success.

My Larger Education: Being Chapters from My Experience (New York: Doubleday, 1911. 313pp.), Washington adds to his reflections on his early life his years of success, with views of the many famous individuals with whom he had contact.

Recommended Biographies

Harlan, Louis R. *Booker T. Washington: The Making of a Black Leader 1856–1901.* New York: Oxford University Press, 1972. 379pp.; *Booker T. Washington: The Wizard of Tuskegee 1901–1915.* New York: Oxford University Press, 1983. 548pp. This Pulitzer Prize–winning study is generally regarded as the definitive life, far more critical and sophisticated in its interpretation than earlier biographies. In Harlan's treatment, Washington is shown as a complex figure, very different from his admired public image.

Other Biographical Studies

Bontemps, Arna. *Young Booker: Booker T. Washington's Early Days.* New York: Dodd, Mead, 1972. 196pp. Chronicling Washington's life from his birth to his 1895 Atlanta Compromise speech, the book is a popular, dramatic account lacking much sophistication in interpreting Washington's development and legacy, staying close to Washington's own account.

Mathews, Basil. *Booker T. Washington: Educator and Interracial Interpreter.* Cambridge, Massachusetts: Harvard University Press, 1948. 350pp. Although often an uncritical admirer, Mathews documents his study with important primary materials, including letters, interviews, and archival records.

Scott, Emmett, and Lyman Beecher Stowe. *Booker T. Washington: Builder of a Civilization.* New York: Doubleday, 1916. 331pp. Although not a comprehensive life, the book provides a full treatment of Washington's career as an educator, relying on his own writings and the cooperation of the Tuskegee Institute.

Spencer, Samuel R. Jr. *Booker T. Washington and the Negro's Place in American Life.* Boston: Little, Brown, 1955. 212pp. Spencer's compact and highly readable portrait, although sympathetic, does suggest a more complex view of the man and his ideas. The book's brevity, however, prevents a fully sophisticated interpretation and reassessment.

Fictional Portraits

Doctorow, E.L. *Ragtime.* New York: Random House, 1975. 270pp. Washington makes a memorable appearance in a confrontation with the novel's militant Coalhouse Walker.

Recommended Juvenile Biographies

McKissack, Patricia, and Frederick L. McKissack. *The Story of Booker T. Washington.* Chicago: Childrens Press, 1991. 31pp. MG. The book concentrates on Washington's Tuskegee years and is fair both on his contributions and his controversial views.

Schroeder, Alan. *Booker T. Washington.* New York: Chelsea House, 1992. 143pp. MG/YA. Part of the Black Americans of Achievement series, this is an informative, respective, but not uncritical portrait of Washington's rise to prominence and his ideas in the context of his times.

Troy, Don. *Booker T. Washington.* Chanhassen, Minnesota: Child's World, 1999. 39pp. MG. In magazine style, this brief, illustrated biography introduces Washington's life and accomplishments.

Biographical Films and Theatrical Adaptations

Booker T. Washington (1983). Director: William Greaves. Winner of the CINE Golden Eagle Award, this candid docudrama traces Washington's life in a series of scenes. Video.

Ragtime (1981). Director: Milos Forman. In this disappointing film adaptation of E.L. Doctorow's novel, Moses Gunn appears as Washington who tries to mediate between Coalhouse Walker (Howard E. Rollins Jr.) and the authorities when the latter occupies J.P. Morgan's mansion. Video.

Other Sources

Thornbrough, Emma Lou, ed. *Booker T. Washington.* Englewood Cliffs, New Jersey: Prentice-Hall, 1969. 184pp. Part of the Great Lives Observed series, this useful collection brings together excerpts from Washington's own writings, contemporaries' accounts, and modern critical assessments.

484. GEORGE WASHINGTON
1732–1799

The commander-in-chief of the Continental Army during the American Revolution and the first U.S. president, Washington is often called the "Father of His Country." He presided over the Constitutional Convention and played a major role in the adoption of the Constitution. Chosen president in 1789, Washington created a federal judiciary and a national bank. During his second term, Washington endeavored to keep the nation neutral in Britain's war with France, implemented Jay's Treaty with England (1794), and faced the Whiskey Rebellion (1794). He declined a third term in office.

Autobiography and Primary Sources

The Diaries of George Washington. Donald Jackson, ed. Charlottesville: University Press of Virginia, 1977–1979. 6 vols. Washington's diaries lack personal revelations and his thoughts on people and events, but do supply essential information about his daily activities.

George Washington's Diaries: An Abridgement. Dorothy Twohig, ed. (Charlottesville: University Press of Virginia, 1999. 453pp.). A one-volume selection of his diaries.

George Washington: A Biography in His Own Words. Ralph K. Andrist, ed. New York: Newsweek, 1972. 2 vols. Based on the Washington papers, Andrist arranges Washington's own words to approximate an autobiographical account.

George Washington: In His Own Words. Maureen Harrison and Steve Gilbert, eds. New York: Barnes and Noble, 1997. 372pp. A selection for the general reader of Washington's writings, including extracts from his 1753 journal, a selection of presidential papers, and his will.

Writings of George Washington. John Rhodehamel, ed. New York: Library of America, 1997. 1,149pp. A splendidly edited collection of Washington's letters, speeches, diary entries, and military and presidential papers offers the reader a glimpse of the man and his character as revealed in his writings.

Writings of George Washington. Washington, DC: Government Printing Office, 1931–1944. 39 vols. This multivolume series includes only the letters from Washington. The ongoing multivolume Papers of George Washington series (Charlottesville: University of Virginia Press, 1983–1999. 9 vols.) when completed (the series has reached the year 1777) will form a more complete scholarly record of all the correspondence.

Recommended Biographies

Alden, John R. *George Washington: A Biography.* Baton Rouge: Louisiana State University Press, 1984. 326pp. One of the best single-volume biographies available, Alden synthesizes considerable research into an accessible, lively narrative account recommended for the general reader looking for a concise, sensible summation of the man and his career.

Cunliffe, Marcus. *George Washington: Man and Monument.* Boston: Little, Brown, 1958. 234pp. Cunliffe's groundbreaking interpretive study set the standard for subsequent assessments of Washington, the man and the icon. A personality study, Cunliffe takes neither a debunking nor eulogizing approach. Instead he attempts to uncover the human figure beneath the legend.

Flexner, James T. *George Washington.* Boston: Little, Brown, 1965–1972. 4 vols. Along with Freeman's monumental life, Flexner's multivolume study is exhaustive and is regarded the definitive personal biography of Washington. Less useful for the scholar by its lack of full documentation, the account is more geared to the general reader, placing a complex, human figure in his wider social and historical context. Flexner's one-volume abridgment, *Washington: The Indispensable Man* (Boston: Little, Brown, 1974. 423pp.), is a useful condensation.

Freeman, Douglas S. *George Washington: A Biography.* New York: Scribner, 1948–1957. 7 vols. Like his equally massive and groundbreaking biography of Robert E. Lee, Freeman's study is a triumph of the biographer's art. Based on unsurpassed research, the volumes recreate Washington's daily life. It remains the definitive factual treatment to which all subsequent studies owe a considerable debt. An abridgement of Freeman's seven volumes by Richard Harwell is available as *Washington* (New York: Scribner, 1968. 780pp.).

Other Biographical Studies

Brookhiser, Richard. *Founding Father: Rediscovering George Washington.* New York: Free Press, 1996. 230pp. Described by the author as a "moral biography," in the tradition of Plutarch, Brookhiser's brief, interpretive study looks at the nature of Washington's leadership and his character traits in his public and private lives.

Clark, E. Harrison. *All Cloudless Glory: The Life of George Washington.* Washington, DC: Regnery, 1996. 2 vols. Closer to autobiography, this is a documentary-based chronicle from his letters, diaries, and papers that allows Washington to narrate his own story, revealing the human figure beneath the myth.

Davis, Burke. *George Washington and the American Revolution.* New York: Random House, 1975. 497pp. Davis's popular account of Washington's military leadership during the Revolutionary War emphasizes the human cost and challenge that he faced, aided by eyewitness accounts.

Emery, Noemie. *Washington: A Biography.* New York: Putnam, 1976. 432pp. A popular biography, Emery's life attempts to set Washington into a believable psychological and vivid historical context. Only partially successful, the book settles for sketches over more sophisticated analysis, and the interpretation is often more provocative than credible.

Ferling, John E. *The First of Men: A Life of George Washington.* Knoxville: The University of Tennessee Press, 1988. 598pp. Ferling emphasizes the complex, conflicted man in this demythologized study. Balanced, well documented, and readable, the book exploits significant primary research, but does occasionally enter the uncertain realm of psychological speculation.

Hughes, Rupert. *George Washington.* New York: Morrow, 1926–1930. 3 vols. Left unfinished by the author's death, Hughes's study takes Washington's story up to 1781. The book is a highly critical, often intemperate, assault on Washington's reputation. Hughes's emphasis on the disagreeable, unsavory, and scandalous skews the picture of the man and his era, but the book is the most vivid of the iconoclastic studies.

Irving, Washington. *The Life of George Washington.* New York: Putnam, 1855–1859. 5 vols. Irving's monumental life has chiefly a literary value although the author does attempt to see Washington as a credible human figure.

Marshall, John. *Life of George Washington.* Philadelphia: C.P. Wayne, 1804. 5 vols. Written by the Supreme Court Chief Justice, Marshall's multivolume biography is more accurate than

Weems's hagiographic and mythological treatment, but Marshall's admiration causes him to miss the man behind the monument.

McDonald, Forrest. *The Presidency of George Washington.* Lawrence: University Press of Kansas, 1974. 210pp. McDonald's study of Washington's presidency includes appropriate biographical details, but focuses on Washington's leadership and the social, political, and economic issues faced by his administration.

Nettels, Curtis P. *George Washington and American Independence.* Boston: Little, Brown, 1951. 333pp. Nettels's stimulating account of the Revolutionary War years revises a number of commonly accepted views and is an excellent, informative source on Washington's military leadership.

Randall, Willard S. *George Washington: A Life.* New York: Holt, 1997. 548pp. Randall adds to the already extensive coverage of Washington's life with an emphasis on his family background and frontier activities before the Revolutionary War, attempting to reveal a recognizable human figure from the details of his formative years.

Schwartz, Barry. *George Washington: The Making of an American Symbol.* New York: Free Press, 1987. 250pp. Schwartz examines how the image of Washington was shaped by his contemporaries. Although not a full-scale biography, the book is nevertheless an important supplemental source that shows how Washington the icon was formed and why.

Stephenson, Nathaniel W., and Waldo H. Dunn. *George Washington.* New York: Oxford University Press, 1940. 2 vols. The authors' narrative biography presents Washington realistically against a solid period background. Drawing extensively on primary documentary evidence, the book shows how Washington's strengths and achievements can still emerge as the focus shifts from the myth to the reality.

Wall, Charles C. *George Washington: Citizen-Soldier.* Charlottesville: University Press of Virginia, 1980. 217pp. Wall deals primarily with the years between Washington's military expedition to Ohio in 1754 and his resignation from command in 1783. Written by the longtime director of Mount Vernon, the book offers a unique perspective on the man as he is rarely seen.

Weems, Mason L. *The Life of Washington.* 1800. Reprint ed. Cambridge, Massachusetts: Harvard University Press, 1967. 226pp. Published shortly after Washington's death, Weems's popular and influential laudatory and didactic treatment of Washington's life retains a historical and cultural significance as the source of the many of the legends, such as the cherry tree story.

Woodward, William E. *George Washington: The Images and the Man.* New York: Boni and Liveright, 1926. 460pp. Woodward's is the first of a number of revisionist, debunking reassessments of Washington that attempt to connect Washington to his cultural milieu, showing him as an opportunist whose motives were far from selfless.

Wright, Esmond. *Washington and the American Revolution.* New York: Collier, 1962. 222pp. Despite what the title suggests, this is a full-length biography covering both Washington's private side and public activities. The book serves the reader looking for a competent, concise overview.

Biographical Novels

Bowen, Marjorie. *The Soldier of Virginia: A Novel of George Washington.* 1912. Reprint ed. New York: Kensington, 1975. 283pp. Bowen's is an idealized, romanticized view of Washington using scenes from the French and Indian War and the Revolutionary War.

Boyce, Burke. *Man from Mt. Vernon.* New York: Harper & Row, 1961. 338pp.; *Morning of a Hero.* New York: Harper & Row, 1963. 340pp. Boyce's novels dramatize significant portions of Washington's life. The first book chronicles the crucial events of the American Revolution; the second, Washington's early years in the 1750s. Both books provide a rounded, realistic alternative to the idealized legend.

Clark, Mary Higgins. *Aspire to the Heavens: A Portrait of George Washington.* Cutchogue, New York: Buccaneer Books, 1991. 213pp. Mystery writer Clark attempts a biographical novel here that covers Washington's career from his youth to his end, emphasizing his humanity in imaginative elaboration of the facts.

Fast, Howard. *The Unvanquished.* New York: Duell, Sloan and Pearce, 1942. 316pp. Washington's string of defeats during 1776 in New York are dramatized, culminating with the general's crucial victory at Trenton.

Grey, Zane. *George Washington, Frontiersman.* Reprint ed. Lexington: University Press of Kentucky, 1994. 268pp. Written near the end of Grey's career, the novel dramatizes the life of Washington from his birth to his taking command of the Continental Army in 1775. This edition includes editorial notes comparing the historical record with Grey's treatment.

Kilian, Michael. *Major Washington.* New York: St. Martin's, 1998. 353pp. Kilian covers the years 1753 to 1755 in Washington's early military career against the French in the Ohio Valley in a mixture of sound research, authentic period details, and imaginative embellishments, conjecture, and invention.

Martin, William. *Citizen Washington.* New York: Warren Books, 1999. 583pp. A variety of perspectives from fictional and historical figures are collected for a multidimensional portrait of Washington as a man, slave owner, military leader, and political figure.

Pier, Anthony S. *The Young Man from Mount Vernon.* New York: F.A. Stokes, 1940. 364pp. Covering Washington's formative years during the 1740s and 1750s, the novel awkwardly employs two imagined historians to offer commentary on Washington's story, assessing its truthfulness.

Wilson, Dorothy Clarke. *Lady Washington.* Garden City, New York: Doubleday, 1984. 376pp. This biographical portrait of Martha Washington dramatizes her life and times from her childhood through her 40-year marriage.

Fictional Portraits

Cooper, James Fenimore. *The Spy.* 1821. Reprint ed. New York: Scribner, 1931. 463pp. Washington appears in disguise behind enemy lines in this espionage novel set in Westchester County during the American Revolution.

Davis, Burke. *Yorktown.* New York: Rinehart, 1952. 306pp. The events leading up to the decisive battle at Yorktown are glimpsed from the perspective of a soldier active in the campaign.

Flood, Charles B. *Monmouth.* Boston: Houghton Mifflin, 1961. 349pp. This action/adventure novel is set during the fateful winter of 1777–1778 and depicts Washington at Valley Forge and on the battlefield, climaxing at the Battle of Monmouth.

Frey, Ruby F. *Red Morning.* New York: Putnam, 1946. 380pp. This historical romance set in the Ohio Valley during the French and Indian War features appearances by several historical figures, including Washington.

Kantor, MacKinlay. *Valley Forge.* New York: M. Evans, 1975. 339pp. Scrupulously researched, the novel blends fact and fiction to chronicle the winter of 1777–1778 and Washington's attempt to keep his army together.

Kurtz, Katherine. *Two Crowns for America.* New York: Bantam Books, 1996. 375pp. Kurtz's intriguing fantasy portrays a secret cabal of Freemasons that attempts to control the outcome of the Revolution. The events are in part viewed from a member of Washington's personal staff.

Sterne, Emma G. *The Drums of Monmouth.* New York: Court Book Co., 1935. 287pp. Seen from the perspective of poet Philip Freneau, the novel provides a look at Washington's leadership during the decisive Battle of Monmouth.

Recommended Juvenile Biographies

Bruns, Roger. *George Washington.* New York: Chelsea House, 1987. 116pp. MG/YA. A readable, visually appealing biography that emphasizes Washington's humanity with his flaws and private side intact.

Fleming, Thomas. *First in the Hearts: A Biography of George Washington.* New York: W.W. Norton, 1968. 136pp. MG/YA. Novelist and historian Fleming offers an accomplished portrait of the man and his era.

Meltzer, Milton. *George Washington and the Birth of Our Country.* New York: F. Watts, 1986. 188pp. MG/YA. Meltzer has produced another fine biographical/historical presentation of Washington's life in the context of the events surrounding the founding of the United States.

Biographical Films and Theatrical Adaptations

Anderson, Maxwell. *Valley Forge: A Play in Three Acts.* Washington, DC: Anderson, 1934. 152pp. Washington during the winter of 1776 is the focus of Anderson's drama that imagines the general being tempted to make peace with the British.

A&E Biography Video: George Washington: Founding Father (1994). Director: Monte Markham. This film portrait traces Washington's entire life from his early years, through the Revolutionary War and his presidency. Video.

The Crossing (2000). Director: Robert Harmon. Based on Howard Fast's book, this drama about Washington's daring attack on Trenton features Jeff Daniels as Washington, Roger Rees as General Hugh Mercer, and Steven McCarthy as Alexander Hamilton. Video.

George Washington (1984). Director: Buzz Kukik. Barry Bostwick stars in the title role in this made-for-television miniseries, adapted from James T. Flexner's biography, co-starring Patty Duke as Martha Washington and Philip Casnoff as Lafayette. Video.

George Washington: The Forging of a Nation (1986), directed by William A. Graham, covers Washington's post-Revolutionary War career. This is the sequel to the 1984 miniseries. Video.

George Washington: The Man Who Wouldn't Be King (1992). Producer: David Sutherland. A segment of PBS's American Experience series, this profile was written by fictional biographer William Martin. Video.

Liberty! The American Revolution (1997). Directors: Ellen Hovde and Muffie Meyer. This PBS documentary series features actors portraying the principals in dramatic readings from their letters and speeches. Washington is played by Stephen Lang. The companion volume is written by Thomas J. Fleming (New York: Viking, 1997. 394pp.) Video.

See also Benedict Arnold; Alexander Hamilton; Thomas Paine

485. DANIEL WEBSTER
1782–1852

An American statesman, lawyer, and one of the greatest orators of his time, Webster served in the House of Representative (1813–1817 and 1823–1827), where he was renowned for his brilliant speeches and public addresses. As a U.S. senator from Massachusetts (1827–1841), he became a national political figure. He supported protective tariffs, was a strong pro-Union advocate, and supported the Compromise of 1850 as a means toward preserving the Union. A leader of the Whig Party, Webster unsuccessfully ran for president in 1836. He served as secretary of state under presidents Harrison and Tyler.

Autobiography and Primary Sources

The Letters of Daniel Webster. C.H. Van Tyne, ed. 1902. Reprint ed. New York: Greenwood, 1969. 789pp. This selection of Webster's letters to his family and intimates is arranged topically.

The Papers of Daniel Webster. Charles M. Witse, ed. Hanover, New Hampshire: University Press of New England, 1974–1989. 14 vols. Webster's full correspondence is collected in the first seven volumes of this scholarly edition of his papers.

Speak for Yourself, Daniel: A Life of Webster in His Own Words. Walker Lewis, ed. Boston: Houghton Mifflin, 1969. 505pp. The editor has arranged

Webster's letters chronologically to approximate an autobiography, emphasizing his human side and character, including his flaws.

Recommended Biographies

Bartlett, Irving H. *Daniel Webster.* New York: W.W. Norton, 1978. 333pp. In a fair assessment, Bartlett looks closely at Webster's private side and reveals both his achievements and his human failings. Bartlett's analysis of Webster's character and temperament is well documented and sensibly argued, and the book is a solid choice for the reader looking for more than the details of Webster's political career.

Baxter, Maurice G. *One and Inseparable: Daniel Webster and the Union.* Cambridge, Massachusetts: Harvard University Press, 1984. 646pp. Baxter's is a standout scholarly biography that treats Webster's life, both public and private, in full, based on extensive primary research. Not as compellingly written as Rimini's equally extensive treatment, Baxter's study is nevertheless an impressive achievement, a judicious and insightful presentation of Webster's life and times.

Remini, Robert V. *Daniel Webster: The Man and His Times.* New York: W.W. Norton, 1997. 796pp. Along with Baxter's biography, Remini's is one of the most comprehensive interpretive studies available. The book looks closely and realistically at both Webster's political career and private life and vividly animates the era in American politics between the War of 1812 and the beginning of the Civil War that Webster dominated. This is a major work by a respected historian and biographer.

Other Biographical Studies

Current, Richard N. *Daniel Webster and the Rise of National Conservatism.* Boston: Little, Brown, 1955. 215pp. The emphasis of Current's succinct interpretive study is the relationship between Webster's political career and developing conservative ideas between 1820 and 1850 in the context of his times and the wider pattern of American history prior to the Civil War. This is a provocative analysis that looks at Webster clearly and knowledgeably.

Curtis, George T. *Life of Daniel Webster.* New York: Appleton, 1869. 2 vols. Written by one of Webster's literary executors, this early biography features important firsthand details, as well as letters and recollections to be found nowhere else.

Dalzell, Robert F. Jr. *Daniel Webster and the Trial of American Nationalism 1843–1852.* Boston: Houghton Mifflin, 1973. 363pp. Focusing on the last decade of Webster's life, Dalzell examines in detail his presidential quest and offers an insightful analysis of why he failed to attain the presidency.

Fuess, Claude M. *Daniel Webster.* Boston: Little, Brown, 1930. 2 vols. Long regarded as the standard biography, Fuess's two-volume study is highly detailed and readable but insufficiently critical to be completely reliable on all aspects of Webster's life, particularly his shortcomings, which are downplayed.

Nathans, Sydney. *Daniel Webster and Jacksonian Democracy.* Baltimore: Johns Hopkins University Press, 1973. 249pp. Nathans provides a study of Webster's role in presidential politics, including his opposition to Andrew Jackson and his unsuccessful pursuit of the presidency.

Peterson, Merrill D. *The Great Triumvirate: Webster, Clay, and Calhoun.* New York: Oxford University Press, 1987. 573pp. Peterson treats the collective political careers of the trio to characterize American history during the first half of the nineteenth century.

Biographical Novels

Morrow, Honoré. *Black Daniel: The Love Story of a Great Man.* New York: Morrow, 1931. 370pp. Morrow relates the love story between Webster and his second wife, Caroline LeRoy, in a sentimentalized account.

Fictional Portraits

Breslin, Howard. *The Tamarack Tree.* New York: Whittlesey, 1947. 438pp. An 1840 political convention on top of Mount Stratton in Vermont with Webster as the featured speaker is the dramatic occasion for this novel of small-town life.

Recommended Juvenile Biographies

Allen, Robert A. *Daniel Webster: Defender of the Union.* Milford, Michigan: Mott Media, 1989. 166pp. MG. Webster's life as an orator and statesman is informatively chronicled with the historical context of his career examined.

Biographical Films and Theatrical Adaptations

Benét, Stephen Vincent, and Douglas Moore. *The Devil and Daniel Webster: An Opera in One Act.* New York: Farrar & Rinehart, 1939. 78pp. In the dramatic version of Benét's story, Webster defends a New Hampshire farmer who has sold his soul to the devil.

Macleish, Archibald. *Scratch.* Boston: Houghton Mifflin, 1971. 116pp. In Macleish's innovative alternative to Benét's story and drama, Webster himself is put on trial for selling his soul to the devil for his 1850 vote in favor of the Fugitive Slave Law.

The Devil & Daniel Webster (1941). Director: William Dieterle. Edward Arnold plays Webster in this film adaptation of Benét's story, with James Craig, Walter Huston, Gene Lockhart, and Jane Darwell. Video.

Gorgeous Hussy (1936). Director: Clarence Brown. In the film adaptation of Samuel Adams's novel (New York: Grosset & Dunlap, 1934. 549pp.), a fictionalized biography of Jackson protégé Peggy Eaton (Joan Crawford), Lionel Barrymore portrays Jackson, and Sidney Toler plays Webster. Video.

Other Sources

Shewmaker, Kenneth E., ed. *Daniel Webster, "The Completest Man": Essays and Documents.* Hanover, New Hampshire: University Press of New England, 1990. 311pp. Four distinguished scholars provide critical essays on different aspects of Webster's career, along with a sampling of relevant documentary evidence.

486. ARTHUR WELLESLEY, DUKE OF WELLINGTON
1769–1852

A British general and statesman known as "the Iron Duke," Wellington began his military career in Flanders and India. During the Napoleonic Wars, he drove the French from Spain and Portugal in the Peninsular War (1808-1814) and was victorious against Napoleon at the Battle of Waterloo (1815). He served in the Tory government and as Prime Minister (1828-1830) and passed the Catholic Emancipation Act (1829). His opposition to parliamentary reforms caused the downfall of his ministry. In 1842 he was made commander-in-chief for life.

Autobiography and Primary Sources

There are several collections of Wellington's letters and personal public writings available: *Despatches, Correspondence, and Memoranda of Field Marshal Arthur, Duke of Wellington.* Arthur Richard Wellesley, ed. (London: J. Murray, 1867, 2 vols.); *The Words of Wellington: Collected from His Dispatches, Letters, and Speeches.* Edith Walford, ed. (New York: Scribner, 1869. 207pp.); and *Wellington at War, 1794–1815: A Selection of His Wartime Letters.* Antony Brett-James, ed. (New York: St. Martin's, 1961. 337pp.).

Recommended Biographies

Hibbert, Christopher. *Wellington: A Personal History.* Reading, Massachusetts: Addison-Wesley, 1997. 460pp. The best single-volume biography available, Hibbert's study chronicles both Wellington's achievements as a military commander and political figure and presents a believable psychological profile of Wellington's personality.

Longford, Elizabeth. *Wellington.* New York: Harper & Row, 1970–1973. 2 vols. Longford adds considerably to our view of the intimate, domestic side of Wellington's life in this detailed, and carefully researched study. Sympathetic, but not uncritical, Longford's is the most comprehensive and accomplished biography currently available.

Other Biographical Studies

Aldington, Richard. *Wellington.* London: Heinemann, 1946. 378pp. Aldington's is a straightforward factual account of Wellington's career set against a vivid period background.

Cooper, Leonard. *The Age of Wellington: The Life and Times of the Duke of Wellington, 1769–1852.* New York: Dodd, Mead, 1963. 308pp. The times predominate over the life in Cooper's anecdotal study that can be charged at several places with misleading oversimplification.

Fortescue, Sir J.W. *Wellington.* New York: Dodd, Mead, 1925. 313pp. The work of a distinguished British military historian, Fortescue devotes his attention almost exclusively to Wellington's military career and virtually ignores the British general's life after Waterloo. What the book does well is provide an informed assessment of Wellington's military leadership and strategic decisions during his 28-year army life.

Gleig, G.R. *Life of Arthur, Duke of Wellington.* 1865. Reprint ed. New York: Dutton, 1909. 438pp. Based on the author's close relationship with his subject, Gleig's life is an important source for anecdotal information about Wellington's life and military career, despite its respectful tone and lack of critical objectivity.

Guedalla, Philip. *Wellington.* New York: Harper, 1931. 536pp. The book covers Wellington's life in full, but devotes most of its attention to his political career after Waterloo. Less assured on the military details, Guedalla is accomplished on the social and cultural background with which to view a convincingly human figure. The book's focus is, however, sometimes diffused by the author's highly mannered style.

Maxwell, Sir Herbert. *The Life of Wellington.* Boston: Little, Brown, 1899. 2 vols. The first truly objective account of Wellington's character and career, Maxwell's is a highly detailed and impressively researched biography.

Weller, Jac. *Wellington at Waterloo.* New York: Crowell, 1967. 264pp.; *Wellington in India.* 1972. Reprint ed. Harrisburg, Pennsylvania: Stackpole Books, 1993. 338pp.; *Wellington in the Peninsula.* Harrisburg, Pennsylvania: Stackpole Books, 1999. 392pp. This series of military historical studies provides a full and detailed summary of Wellington's military career from his initial commands in India through his triumph at Waterloo.

Fictional Portraits

Cornwell, Bernard. The Sharpe series. 1981–. Cornwell's acclaimed adventure series features the exploits of British officer Richard Sharpe during the Napoleonic Wars includes frequent appearances by Wellington, who was responsible for promoting Sharpe from the ranks.

Heyer, Georgette. *An Infamous Army.* Garden City, New York: Doubleday, 1938. 415pp. Heyer's classic period novel looks at the events of the Hundred Days culminating at Waterloo from the perspective of a group of English aristocrats, including an officer on Wellington's staff.

Fraser, George MacDonald. *Flashman.* New York: Signet, 1969. 252pp. An aging Wellington conducts Flashman to a royal audience with Victoria and Albert to accept the undeserved thanks of a grateful nation for Flashy's apparent heroism during the Afghan War in this first installment of Fraser's delightfully inventive historical series.

Komroff, Manuel. *Waterloo.* New York: Coward-McCann, 1936. 307pp. The novel offers a realistic and credible portrayal of the events during Napoleon's Hundred Days, culminating at Waterloo.

McDonough, James. *The Limits of Glory: A Novel of Waterloo.* Novato, California: Presidio, 1991. 300pp. The generals—Wellington, Napoleon, and Blücher—offer their perspectives on the strategies on the battlefield of Waterloo, supplemented by the view of other combatants in a truthful reconstruction.

Biographical Films and Theatrical Adaptations

The Iron Duke (1934). Director: Victor Saville. George Arliss puts in another of his famous historical portrayals in this biographical account of Wellington's life. Co-starring Gladys Cooper, Emlyn Williams, and Felix Aylmer. Video.

Lady Caroline Lamb (1972). Director: Robert Bolt. Despite Bolt's script and an impressive cast, including Laurence Olivier as Wellington and Ralph Richardson as the Prince Regent, this is a flat and unconvincing treatment of the famous scandal of Lady Caroline Lamb's (Sarah Miles) highly public affair with Byron (Richard Chamberlain). Video.

Waterloo (1970). Director: Sergei Bondarchuk. This historical account of the Battle of Waterloo features an unusual interpretation of Napoleon by Rod Steiger. Wellington is more convincingly portrayed by Christopher Plummer. A novelization of the screenplay by Frederick E. Smith (London: Pan Books, 1970. 189pp.) is available. Video.

See also Napoleon Bonaparte; Horatio Nelson

487. H.G. WELLS
1866–1946

English author and social thinker, Herbert George Wells was a biology teacher before becoming a novelist. He is famous for such enduring science fiction classics as *The Time Machine* (1895), *The Invisible Man* (1897), and *The War of the Worlds* (1898). His realistic novels, considered his finest achievement, include *Tono-Bungay* (1909) and *The History of Mr. Polly* (1910). Among his other works are *A Modern Utopia* (1905) and *The Outline of History* (1920).

Autobiography and Primary Sources

The Correspondence of H.G. Wells. David C. Smith, ed. Brookfield, Vermont: Pickering & Chatto, 1998. 4 vols. Wells's extensive correspondence is a detailed record of his activities and his relationship with a wide literary and social circle. Indispensable as a biographical source.

Experiment in Autobiography: Discoveries and Conclusions of a Very Ordinary Brain (Since 1866). New York: Macmillan, 1934. 218pp. Wells's candid autobiographical reflections trace his development, views of his contemporaries, and his political and social views at various periods of his life.

Recommended Biographies

MacKenzie, Norman, and Jeanne MacKenzie. *H.G. Wells: A Biography.* New York: Simon & Schuster, 1973. 487pp. The authors present a balanced, detailed assessment that offers a credible psychological portrait of the contradictions in Wells's nature that help to explain his literary career as well as his relationships.

Smith, David C. *H.G. Wells, Desperately Mortal: A Biography.* New Haven, Connecticut: Yale University Press, 1986. 634pp. Smith's well-documented, balanced study is among the most comprehensive, full-length treatments of Wells's life based on extensive primary research. More a topical analysis than a chronological narrative, the book serves as a valuable reference tool.

West, Anthony. *H.G. Wells: Aspects of a Life.* New York: Random House, 1984. 404pp. Written by Wells's son from his liaison with Rebecca West, the book is a memoir-biography that, unlike Gordon Ray's study of the Wells-West relationship, takes his father's side in the couple's conflict and the writer's quarrels with Henry James, Bernard Shaw, the Fabians, and others. Despite an often intemperate tone and bias, the book includes valuable details on Wells's early life and personality.

Other Biographical Studies

Brome, Vincent. *H.G. Wells: A Biography.* New York: Longmans, 1951. 255pp. The first full-length biography, Brome's is an anecdotal, secondhand, journalistic account, and more an impressionist sketch based on others' recollections.

Coren, Michael. *The Invisible Man: The Life and Liberties of H.G. Wells.* New York: Atheneum, 1993. 240pp. Coren focuses on the dark side of Wells's ideas and behavior, including his callous treatment of the women in his life, his alleged anti-Semitism, and his connection to fascism. The book is more an indictment than an attempt at a rounded, objective assessment.

Dickson, Lovat. *H.G. Wells: His Turbulent Life and Times.* New York: Atheneum, 1969. 330pp. An informal and selective biographical portrait, Dickson offers fewer than 50 pages to Wells's last three decades, concentrating instead on the writer's youth, and his literary success, scandalous sexual life, and literary and intellectual relationships. Dickson dismisses Wells's social and political writing and sees his career as largely a failure, based on a lack of what he labels "moral muscle."

Foot, Michael. *H.G.: The History of Mr. Wells.* Washington, DC: Counterpoint, 1995. 318pp. The author, the former leader of the British Labour Party, presents a sympathetic reassessment of Well's life, works, and ideas in the context of social developments that the writer anticipated. In the interest of his thesis, Foot glosses over many unflattering aspects of Wells's notions and personality.

Kagarlitski, J. *The Life and Thought of H.G. Wells.* New York: Barnes and Noble, 1966. 210pp. This critical study by a Russian scholar is a brief survey of Wells's career and the connections between his life and work.

Ray, Gordon N. *H.G. Wells and Rebecca West.* New Haven, Connecticut: Yale University Press, 1974. 215pp. Ray focuses on the relationship between Wells and West in an examination written with the latter's cooperation and with access to Wells's 800 letters to her. West's side of their turbulent affair and breakup is prominent here, but the book does offer an intimate portrait of Wells during a crucial period of his career.

Fictional Portraits

Alexander, Karl. *Time after Time*. New York: Delacorte, 1979. 341pp. Wells chases Jack the Ripper in his time machine to 1979 San Francisco in this inventive fantasy.

Hughes, David. *The Man Who Invented Tomorrow*. London: Constable, 1968. 191pp. 213pp. The production of a television film on Wells is the occasion for this often-funny meditation on the writer's identity and modern relevance.

Recommended Juvenile Biographies

Ferrell, Keith. *H.G. Wells: First Citizen of the Future*. New York: M. Evans, 1983. 192pp. YA. This is thoughtful, sympathetic biography that does not slight the scandals of Wells's private life and offers a balanced, well-researched, fact-filled account.

Nardo, Don. *H.G. Wells*. San Diego: Lucent Books, 1992. 111pp. MG/YA. Nardo explores the life of the author with extensive quotations from primary sources and background information.

Wood, James P. *I Told You So!: A Life of H.G. Wells*. New York: Pantheon, 1969. 182pp. MG/YA. Wood traces how Wells's personal experiences were transformed into his writings.

Biographical Films and Theatrical Adaptations

A&E Biography Video: H.G. Wells: Time Traveler (1995). Producer: Craig Haffner. Wells's literary career and private life are both profiled in this film biography. Video.

Time after Time (1979). Director: Nicholas Meyer. This film version of Karl Alexander's novel casts Malcolm McDowell as Wells, Mary Steenburgen as his modern love interest, and David Warner as Jack the Ripper, whom he chases to contemporary San Francisco. Video.

Other Sources

Hammond, J.R. *An H.G. Wells Chronology*. New York: St. Martin's, 1999. 192pp. This is a useful reference tool, documenting Wells's activities in detail.

Hammond, J.R., ed. *H.G. Wells: Interviews and Recollections*. Totowa, New Jersey: Barnes and Noble, 1980. 121pp. Wells's own comments on his life and work are joined with the views of his contemporaries.

488. JOHN WESLEY
1703–1791

English evangelical preacher and founder of Methodism, Wesley was greatly influenced by Martin Luther's preface to the Epistle to the Romans, and from that derived the message of salvation that informed his preaching. He is said to have preached 40,000 sermons and to have traveled 250,000 miles. The Methodist church became a sect separate from the Anglican church, although that was not Wesley's original intention.

Autobiography and Primary Sources

The Journal of John Wesley. Elizabeth Jay, ed. New York: Oxford University Press, 1987. 290pp. This is a convenient, carefully edited selection from Wesley's journal covering the years 1735 through 1790.

Letters of John Wesley. John Telford, ed. London: Epworth, 1931. 8 vols. This is the most comprehensive collection of Wesley's letters. A one-volume edition, *Selected Letters*. Frederick C. Gill, ed. (London: Epworth, 1956. 244pp.) is also available.

Recommended Biographies

Ayling, Stanley. *John Wesley*. Nashville, Tennessee: Abingdon, 1979. 350pp. Ayling synthesizes his sources from Wesley's journal and letters into an objective, fair, and surprisingly irreverent overview of Wesley's life and career, accessible and entertaining for the general reader.

Pudney, John. *John Wesley and His World*. New York: Scribner, 1978. 128pp. Pudney captures Wesley in the context of his culture and environment in this fully illustrated biography that is both highly readable and carefully researched from contemporary sources. Pudney challenges the usual presentation of Wesley as dour and stern.

Rack, Henry D. *Reasonable Enthusiast: John Wesley and the Rise of Methodism*. Philadelphia: Trinity Press, 1989. 656pp. Based on extensive scholarship that has substantially altered our view of Wesley, Rack presents a fresh assessment of a contradictory man, set firmly in the context of his times.

Other Biographical Studies

Heitzenrater, Richard P. *John Wesley: His Own Biographer*. Nashville, Tennessee: Abington Press, 1984. 220pp. Rather than producing an interpretive study, the author assembles materials that allow readers to draw their own conclusions about the man and his beliefs based on the many facets he presented to his age.

Piette, Maximin. *John Wesley in the Evolution of Protestantism*. New York: Sheed & Ward, 1937. 569pp. The work of a French Franciscan friar, the book locates Wesley's achievement in the broadest possible context of Protestant thought from the sixteenth to the eighteenth centuries. Beginning with Luther and Zwingli, Piette turns in the second half of his survey to Wesley's personality and theological beliefs. Although limited in its biographical focus to Wesley as religious leader, the portrait provided is insightful and solidly grounded by historical and primary research.

Southey, Robert. *Life of John Wesley*. 1820. Reprint ed. New York: F.A. Stokes, 1903. 374pp. Although Southey's life of Wesley is highly critical and inaccurate in many of its details, this early assessment has considerable historical interest of a near contemporary view of the man and his times.

Biographical Novels

Drakeford, John W. *Take Her, Mr. Wesley*. Waco, Texas: Word Books, 1973. 142pp. Based on Wesley's diaries and eyewitness accounts, the novel supplies a journal account of a year in Wesley's life in the Georgia colony and his relationship with Sophia Hopkey.

Oemler, Marie C. *The Holy Lover*. New York: Boni & Liveright, 1927. 315pp. Based on the time he spent in Georgia, this novel portrays Wesley in unflattering terms during his first and last love affair.

Williamson, Glen. *Sons of Susanna*. Wheaton, Illinois: Tyndale House, 1991. 236pp. Wesley, his mother, Susanna, and brother Charles are depicted in this devotional novel that depicts Wesley's background and the early years of Methodism.

Fictional Portraits

Andrew, Prudence. *A New Creature*. New York: Putnam, 1968. 331pp. Wesley is shown preaching and spreading the message of Methodism in this novel that portrays the effects of his conversion on a Bristol merchant.

Crow, Donna F. *A Gentle Calling*. Wheaton, Illinois: Victor Books, 1987. 199pp. Set in 1749, a British school teacher seeks her spiritual way and encounters Wesley, who provides some of her answers.

Morris, Gilbert. *The Ramparts of Heaven*. Wheaton, Illinois: Tyndale House, 1997. 400pp. Wesley and the Methodist movement are the subject of this devotional historical novel.

Shellabarger, Samuel. *Lord Vanity*. Boston: Little, Brown, 1953. 473pp. Shellabarger's panoramic view of eighteenth-century life features appearances by a number of historical figures, including James Wolfe, Beau Nash, and Wesley.

Yerby, Frank. *Jarrett's Jade*. New York: Dial Press, 1959. 342pp. This historical romance set in colonial Savannah, Georgia, features an appearance by Wesley during his service to James Oglethorpe.

Recommended Juvenile Biographies

Wellman, Sam. *John Wesley: Founder of the Methodist Church*. New York: Chelsea House, 1998. 207pp. MG/YA. Part of the Heroes of Faith series, this is a fast-paced, informative life of the founder of Methodism, emphasizing Wesley's determination to spread his message to all classes of society.

489. EDITH WHARTON
1862–1937

American novelist and short-story writer, Wharton is noted for her subtle, ironic, and superbly crafted fictional accounts of New York society. Her most famous novels are *The House of Mirth* (1905), *Ethan Frome* (1911), and *The Age of Innocence* (1920; Pulitzer Prize). She also wrote travel books, literary criticism, and poetry. She was awarded the French Legion of Honor for her service during World War I.

Autobiography and Primary Sources

A Backward Glance: An Autobiography. 1934. Reprint ed. New York: Scribner, 1964. 385pp. The novelist reflects discreetly on her life, background, and relationships. Included is a fascinating and revealing chapter in which Wharton discusses her artistic methods.

The Letters of Edith Wharton. R.W.B. Lewis, ed. New York: Scribner, 1988. 654pp. Of her 4,000 existing letters, Lewis has chosen nearly 400 that show the novelist "at her epistolary best and most characteristic." The selections illuminate Wharton's daily life, writing career, and her relationship with an extensive circle of friends, including Henry James, Bernard Berenson, and Kenneth Clark.

Recommended Biographies

Benstock, Shari. *No Gifts for Chance: A Biography of Edith Wharton.* New York: Scribner, 1994. 546pp. In a feminist reading of Wharton's life and character, Benstock challenges the conception of the writer as an emotionally withdrawn observer, arguing that the novelist instead should be viewed as an ambitious, determined individual who consciously fashioned both her own identity and her art. Based on previously untapped archival material, Benstock both adds to the biographical record and uses her data for a fresh, insightful portrait.

Lewis, R.W.B. *Edith Wharton: A Biography.* New York: Harper & Row, 1975. 592pp. Lewis's Pulitzer Prize–winning biography is the first and still one of the best scholarly biographies based on personal papers not available to previous writers. Lewis fills in the record of a multifaceted woman along with a vivid evocation of her social background and circle.

Wolff, Cynthia G. *A Feast of Words: The Triumph of Edith Wharton.* New York: Oxford University Press, 1976. 453pp. Interpreting the material that Lewis uncovered in his study, Wolff presents a coherent psychological profile of Wharton's personality and development. Wolff's feminist perspective sheds considerable light on the challenges Wharton faced to achieve a wider identity and status as a serious writer.

Other Biographical Studies

Auchincloss, Louis. *Edith Wharton: A Woman in Her Time.* New York: Viking, 1971. 191pp. Auchincloss's text to accompany a series of evocative illustrations provides a character sketch as well as brief coverage of her social background, her era, relationships, and a critique of her writing. Serves as a basic overview for the general reader.

Dwight, Eleanor. *Edith Wharton: An Extraordinary Life.* New York: Abrams, 1994. 296pp. With more than 300 illustrations, Dwight supplies a visual tour of Wharton's life and world, finding in the various settings a revealing key to understanding the author's personality and artistic method.

Kellogg, Grace. *The Two Lives of Edith Wharton: The Woman and Her Work.* New York: Appleton-Century, 1965. 332pp. Kellogg's imaginative rather than scholarly biography should be read with caution. In the absence of fact the author fills in the gaps with surmises to reconstruct the inner life of her subject. The result is a provocative appreciation of Wharton's life, personality, and work but lacking in scholarly precision and reliability.

Lawson, Richard. *Edith Wharton.* New York: Frederick Ungar, 1977. 118pp. Lawson's critical

introduction to some of Wharton's works sketches the connections between the novelist's writing and her life in a useful, though limited study.

Lubbock, Percy. *Portrait of Edith Wharton.* New York: Appleton-Century, 1947. 249pp. Lubbock creates his portrait from his own and others' reminiscences. Dismissive of Wharton's literary achievement, Lubbock's view is incomplete, with interesting details on her social life and relationship but little on her genius and identity as a writer.

McDowell, Margaret B. *Edith Wharton.* Boston: Twayne, 1976. 186pp. McDowell's compact critical study of Wharton's fiction includes a concise overview of her life in its opening chapter, summarizing Wharton's career and her relationship with Henry James and others.

Price, Alan. *The End of the Age of Innocence: Edith Wharton and the First World War.* New York: St. Martin's, 1996. 238pp. Price supplies a detailed account of Wharton's wartime activities, exploring the writer's motive in devoting herself to the war effort.

Fictional Portraits

Aiken, Joan. *The Haunting of Lamb House.* New York: St. Martin's, 1993. 200pp. Henry James's English home is the locale for this ghost story that features James and writer E.F. Benson making sense of the unexplainable. Wharton, writer Hugh Walpole, and James's brother William make appearances.

Hill, Carol DeChellis. *Henry James' Midnight Song.* New York: Poseidon Press, 1993. 445pp. Wharton is one of many historical suspects in an intriguing period murder mystery set in fin-de-siècle Vienna. The novel is a tour de force of historical animation with intriguing portraits of James, Freud, and Jung.

Recommended Juvenile Biographies

Leach, William. *Edith Wharton.* New York: Chelsea House, 1987. 111pp. MG/YA. Leach's is an accomplished treatment of Wharton's life and her literary achievement.

Turk, Ruth. *Edith Wharton: Beyond the Age of Innocence.* Greensboro, North Carolina: Tudor, 1998. 72pp. MG/YA. This is an engaging, though somewhat simplified, portrait of the author that stresses the obstacles to Wharton's literary career.

Worth, Richard. *Edith Wharton.* New York: J. Messner, 1994. 154pp. MG/YA. Part of the Classic American Writers series, Worth outlines the major events of Wharton's life with critical commentary on some of her most famous works and a discussion of how the values of society of her day were reflected in her writing.

Other Sources

Wright, Sarah B. *Edith Wharton A to Z: The Essential Guide to the Life and Work.* New York: Facts on File, 1998. 330pp. Wharton's life, work, and associates are extensively covered through alphabetically arranged entries.

See also Henry James

490. JAMES MCNEILL WHISTLER
1834–1903

American painter, etcher, and wit, Whistler lived and worked mainly in London. He is perhaps best known for the famous portrait of his mother, *Arrangement in Black and Gray* (1872). He first achieved success with *The Little White Girl* (1863). His other works include *Old Battersea Bridge* (1872-1875) and a famous portrait of Thomas Carlyle (1873). Whistler designed interiors that foreshadowed the Art Nouveau movement and published critical essays and aphorisms. His published lecture, *Ten O'clock* (1888) greatly influenced art theory.

Autobiography and Primary Sources

Whistler on Art: Selected Letters and Writings of James McNeill Whistler. Nigel Thorp, ed. Washington, DC: Smithsonian Institution Press, 1994. 184pp. In a collection of documents arranged chronologically, Whistler comments on art to his family, friends, and colleagues.

Recommended Biographies

Anderson, Ronald, and Anne Koval. *James McNeill Whistler: Beyond the Myth.* New York: Carroll & Graf, 1995. 544pp. Anderson's is a major reassessment of the artist that challenges the conventional notion of Whistler as an irascible dandy at war with critics and his fellow artists. Anderson's Whistler is a far more complex figure, and the book does an excellent job exploring his private as well as public side.

Weintraub, Stanley. *Whistler: A Biography.* New York: Weybright and Talley, 1974. 498pp. Weintraub's is the standout Whistler biography. It is vividly written and carefully documented, making good use of primary sources. The author is at home with the era, and Whistler is realistically presented against a solid period background.

Other Biographical Studies

Fleming, Gordon H. *The Young Whistler 1834–1866.* London: Allen and Unwin, 1978. 264pp. Covering the first 32 years of the artist's life, Fleming attempts to document the record, separating the facts from Whistler's misrepresentations of his past. The author, however, provides few insights about the meaning of the facts he has unearthed related to Whistler's formative years. In *James Abbott McNeill Whistler* (New York: St. Martin's, 1991. 367pp.), an expansion and continuation of his earlier book, Fleming treats Whistler's life in full with the same cautious reliance on facts rather than an interpretation of their meaning on Whistler's development as a man and an artist.

Gregory, Horace. *The World of James McNeill Whistler.* New York: T. Nelson, 1959. 255pp. Gregory's critical biography is a gossipy, undocumented chronicle, marred by inaccuracies and imaginative flights of fancy.

Laver, James. *Whistler.* 1930. Revised ed. London: Faber and Faber, 1951. 318pp. Superseded by later biographies in terms of sources and factual details, Laver's is a compact interpretive survey of Whistler's career and character that tries to redress the realistic balance compared to the Pennells' extravagant admiration.

McMullen, Roy. *Victorian Outsider: A Biography of J.A.M. Whistler.* New York: Dutton, 1973. 307pp. Describing his biography as a "descriptive evaluation," McMullen offers a psychological interpretation of Whistler's personality in a study intended for the general reader. Highly speculative and impressionistic, the book is more lively than reliable and is poorly documented.

Pearson, Hesketh. *The Man Whistler.* New York: Harper, 1952. 276pp. Pearson's is an enjoyable, lively biographical sketch that is more a collection of anecdotes than a true biography and that rarely penetrates very deeply behind Whistler's entertaining public persona. As the title indicates, Whistler the artist is left to others to analyze, and the result is a selective and disjointed presentation of Whistler the wit.

Pennell, Elizabeth R., and Joseph Pennell. *The Life of James McNeill Whistler.* 1908. Reprint ed. New York: AMS Press, 1973. 2 vols. Whistler provided the authors with anecdotes, reminiscences, and correspondence shortly before his death and, accordingly, this is an important source, but should be used with care. Details unflattering to the artist are simply omitted, and Whistler was a notoriously unreliable witness; *Whistler Journal* (Philadelphia: Lippincott, 1921. 339pp.) is a diary record of the authors' meetings with Whistler, supplemented by interviews and letters from his acquaintants.

Prideaux, Tom. *The World of Whistler: 1834–1903.* New York: Time-Life Books, 1970. 191pp. A brief biographical sketch serves as an introduction to reproductions of Whistler's works. The painter's milieu and the works of his colleagues and rivals are also represented.

Spalding, Frances. *Whistler.* Oxford: Phaidon, 1979. 80pp. Spalding offers little on Whistler's life but does critique his artistic method as a preliminary for a presentation of a number of his works.

Sutton, Denys. *Nocturne: The Art of James McNeill Whistler.* Philadelphia: Lippincott, 1964. 153pp. Although not a biography, Sutton does attempt to trace Whistler's artistic development and consider his ideas against his cultural background.

Walker, John. *James McNeill Whistler.* New York: Abrams, 1987. 160pp. This collection of reproductions supplies only a brief text that sketches an overview of Whistler's career.

Biographical Novels

Berkman, Ted. *To Seize the Passing Dream: A Novel of Whistler, His Women, and His World.* Garden City, New York: Doubleday, 1972. 431pp. In a convincing portrait of Whistler and his times, the artist is displayed as a far more complex and troubled figure than is usual, with his cynical, witty public persona a mask disguising self-doubt.

Williams, Lawrence. *I, James McNeill Whistler: An Autobiography.* New York: Simon & Schuster, 1972. 383pp. Whistler narrates his own story from the 1850s to the 1890s in a generally reliable chronicle of his activities, including his notorious lawsuit against John Ruskin for defamation of character.

Fictional Portraits

Butler, David. *Lillie.* New York: Warner, 1978. 435pp. This biographical novel on the life of English beauty and actress Lillie Langtry features appearances by Whistler, Oscar Wilde, Randolph Churchill, Leopold of Belgium, Millais, and Edward, Prince of Wales.

Fitzgerald, Nancy. *Chelsea.* Garden City, New York: Doubleday, 1979. 231pp. This period romance features an authentic depiction of the Victorian art scene with appearances by Whistler and Oscar Wilde.

Recommended Juvenile Biographies

Berman, Avis. *James McNeill Whistler.* New York: Abrams, 1993. 92pp. YA. Part of the acclaimed First Impressions series, this is an informative biographical profile and introduction to Whistler's art and times.

Biographical Films and Theatrical Adaptations

Lillie (1990). Director: John Gorrie. Dramatizing the career of beauty and actress Lillie Langtry who becomes the mistress of Edward VII, Francesca Annis takes the title role with Dennis Lill as Edward, Don Fellows as Whistler, and Peter Egan as Oscar Wilde.

491. WALT WHITMAN
1819–1892

Considered by many to be one of the the greatest American poets, Whitman worked as a printer, journalist, and carpenter, and during the Civil War served as a volunteer nurse in Washington. His first volume of poetry was *Leaves of Grass* (1855), published at his own expense. Whitman's unorthodox style, realistic depiction of contemporary life, and sexual candor shocked his contemporaries, but the poet's genius was recognized by such figures as Ralph Waldo Emerson and Henry David Thoreau. Among Whitman's other volumes are *Drum-Taps* (1865) and the prose collection, *Democratic Vistas* (1871).

Autobiography and Primary Sources

The Correspondence of Walt Whitman. Edwin H. Miller, ed. New York: New York University Press, 1961–1977. 6 vols. This is the scholarly comprehensive collection of Whitman's letters. Miller in *Selected Letters of Walt Whitman* (Iowa City: University of Iowa Press, 1990. 320pp.) has selected 250 of the 2,800 letters in the multivolume set to form "an autobiography, but an admittedly limited one."

Daybooks and Notebooks. William White, ed. New York: New York University Press, 1978. 3 vols. This collection reprints Whitman's business and personal records kept between 1876 and 1891. Whitman's *Notebooks and Unpublished Prose Manuscripts.* Edward F. Grier, ed. (New York: New York University Press, 1984. 6 vols.) is an essential scholarly edition of personal writings that illuminates the poet's creative method and ideas.

The Sacrificial Years: A Chronicle of Walt Whitman's Experiences in the Civil War. John H. McElroy, ed. 1999. McElroy collects for the first time all of Whitman's letters, articles, and other writings that record his reactions to the war, arranging them into a chronological sequence that approximates a diary of the poet's war experiences.

Recommended Biographies

Allen, Gay Wilson. *The Solitary Singer: A Critical Biography of Walt Whitman.* 1955. Revised ed. New York: New York University Press, 1967. 616pp. Long established as the standard biography, Allen's account is reliable, carefully documented, and balanced in its assessment. In *Walt Whitman* (New York: Grove Press, 1961. 192pp.} Allen supplies a concise, introductory study consisting of a succinct overview of Whitman's life as well as excerpts from his work.

Kaplan, Justin. *Walt Whitman: A Life.* New York: Simon & Schuster, 1980. 432pp. In a richly detailed, acute psychological profile, Kaplan focuses on Whitman's thoughts, works, and relationships, avoiding either undue adulation or denigration. Kaplan's is a fine choice for the general reader who wishes a competent and insightful look at the poet's life and times.

Loving, Jerome. *Walt Whitman: The Song of Himself.* Berkeley: University of California Press, 1999. 568pp. Loving, one of the preeminent Whitman scholars, sheds new light on the poet's early background and his teaching and journalistic careers, identifies the sources for many of the anecdotes on Whitman, and corrects and extends the biographical record in an authoritative and illuminating critical biography.

Miller, Edwin H. *Walt Whitman's Poetry: A Psychological Journey.* Boston: Houghton Mifflin, 1968. 245pp. Miller, the editor of Whitman's correspondence, is a knowledgeable and skillful interpreter of the poet's development who uses the poetry as an autobiographical mirror.

Zweig, Paul. *Walt Whitman: The Making of the Poet.* New York: Basic Books, 1984. 372pp. Zweig concentrates on the central question surrounding Whitman: how he transformed himself into an influential poet. Beginning his examination in 1848 and continuing until the end of the Civil War, Zweig brilliantly analyzes Whitman's achievement and the cultural and intellectual background that helps to explain his progress.

Other Biographical Studies

Asselineau, Roger. *The Evolution of Walt Whitman.* Cambridge, Massachusetts: Harvard University Press, 1960–1962. 2 vols. Asselineau's groundbreaking biographical and critical study anticipated the continuing modern debates over Whitman's life and work. Volume one is devoted to Whitman's biography; volume two offers a thoughtful critical reading of his works.

Binns, Henry B. *A Life of Walt Whitman.* New York: Dutton, 1905. 369pp. Widely recognized as the first truly objective account of Whitman's life, Binns's study is more suggestive than conclusive, with some speculation that has not been sustained by later research.

Black, Stephen A. *Whitman's Journeys into Chaos: A Psychoanalytic Study of the Poetic Process*. Princeton, New Jersey: Princeton University Press, 1975. 255pp. Black's psychoanalytic study of Whitman's imagination concentrates on his poetic development in the years between 1855 and 1865. Highly speculative but penetrating, the analysis emphasizes the autoerotic over the homoerotic as a key to understanding Whitman's poetry and creativity.

Callow, Philip. *From Noon to Starry Night: A Life of Walt Whitman*. Chicago: I.R. Dee, 1992. 394pp. In Callow's portrait, Whitman is a man of massive contradictions and masks obscuring his true identity. The book retraces familiar ground in the story of the poet's remarkable progress that is documented more expertly and fully by Allen, Kaplan, Loving, and Zweig.

Canby, Henry S. *Walt Whitman: An American*. Boston: Houghton Mifflin, 1943. 381pp. Canby's is an intellectual biography, tracing the development of Whitman's ideas and evolving personality. Not concerned with the external events of Whitman's life but the interior conflicts, Canby provides a stimulating and plausible psychological profile.

Carpenter, Edward. *Days with Walt Whitman: With Some Notes on His Life and Works*. New York: Macmillan, 1906. 186pp. Carpenter's is the most critical treatment of the several biographies written by Whitman's disciples. Based on interviews with the poet, the book calls attention to the conflicts in Whitman's nature, a theme that has been explored more fully in subsequent biographies.

Cavitch, David. *My Soul and I: The Inner Life of Walt Whitman*. Boston: Beacon Press, 1985. 193pp. Cavitch's psychological reading of Whitman's life and work sheds light on various relationship conflicts evident in his writings, locating the source of the poet's ego assertion his attempt to resolve his feelings about his parents. Lacking the literary-historical breadth of other works, the book is nevertheless an insightful study for the reader who already has a firm grasp on Whitman's life and poetry.

Holloway, Emory. *Whitman: An Interpretation in Narrative*. New York: Knopf, 1926. 330pp. Holloway's Pulitzer Prize–winning biography is a full-length, well-researched interpretive study that delivers a credible psychological portrait of the poet, centered on the author's insistence on Whitman's heterosexuality.

Knapp, Bettina L. *Walt Whitman*. New York: Continuum, 1993. 240pp. Knapp supplies a brief biographical profile, followed by a critical analysis of Whitman's poetry and prose that serves the general reader and undergraduate well in orienting them to the man and his works.

Miller, James E. *Walt Whitman*. New York: Twayne, 1962. 188pp. This entry in the Twayne Author series is a sensible critical introduction tracing the connection between Whitman's life and his works and is an excellent overview for the student and the general reader.

Morris, Roy Jr. *The Better Angel: Walt Whitman in the Civil War*. New York: Oxford University Press, 2000. 288pp. This is the first complete account of the poet's Civil War years that documents the importance of Whitman's war experiences in shaping his life and work.

Perry, Bliss. *Walt Whitman, His Life and Work*. Boston: Houghton Mifflin, 1906. 318pp. Along with Binns, Perry's is one of the strongest early interpretive studies of the poet. Well written and well researched, the book sets out to fashion an objective portrait of the man and his work that has retained its value as an sensible and informed assessment.

Reynolds, David S. *Walt Whitman's America: A Cultural Biography*. New York: Knopf, 1995. 671pp. This is a detailed and often brilliant analysis that locates Whitman in the complex context of his times. By taking a wider, cultural view of Whitman's development, the book offers fresh insights that illuminate both the man and his era.

Rubin, Joseph J. *The Historical Whitman*. University Park: Pennsylvania State University Press, 1973. 406pp. Concentrating on Whitman's early career as a journalist before 1855, Rubin establishes a colorful background to view the poet's formative years that includes both documentary evidence and imaginative reconstructions.

Schmidgall, Gary. *Walt Whitman: A Gay Life*. New York: Dutton, 1997. 428pp. Schmidgall's is a reductive homoerotic reading of Whitman's life and work that sees the poet only in terms of his homosexual longing and conflict.

Schyberg, Frederik. *Walt Whitman*. New York: Columbia University Press, 1951. 387pp. The work of a Danish literary critic, the book offers a Freudian reading of Whitman's life and work in which he is shown, not as a prophet or reformer, but principally as a great lyric poet and a lonely and often bewildered searcher.

Traubel, Horace. *With Walt Whitman in Camden*. 1906–1996. Multiple publishers, 9 vols. Traubel's exhaustive transcriptions of his daily encounters with the poet during his final four years are an essential biographical source on Whitman's views during his last years. A single-volume selection of the key passages, *Walt Whitman's Camden Conversations*. Walter Teller, ed. (New Brunswick, New Jersey: Rutgers University Press, 1973. 215pp.), is also available.

Biographical Novels

Aronin, Ben. *Walt Whitman's Secret*. Chicago: Argus Books, 1955. 374pp. This biographical novel traces Whitman's career and personal life from his early years to his initial literary success following the publication of *Leaves of Grass* in a generally faithful account.

Erskine, John. *The Start of the Road*. New York: F.A. Stokes, 1938. 344pp. Erskine's fictionalized account is based on Whitman's life from 1848 to 1865 and speculates on an affair with a woman in New Orleans who bore the poet a son.

Overton, Grant M. *The Answerers*. New York: Harcourt, Brace, 1921. 373pp. Overton's fictional biography follows the main events of Whitman's life but often lapses into sentimentality and melodrama.

Fictional Portraits

Vernon, John. *Peter Doyle*. New York: Random House, 1991. 417pp. Vernon's picaresque fantasy concerning the search for Napoleon's dismembered penis includes an intriguing, fanciful meeting between two of nineteenth-century America's greatest poets, Emily Dickinson and Walt Whitman. Vernon uses his strong sense of the past to subvert history comically.

Recommended Juvenile Biographies

Loewen, Nancy. *Walt Whitman*. Mankato, Minnesota: Creative Editions, 1994. 45pp. MG. Combining biographical information with brief selections from his works, Loewen helps the reader appreciate Whitman and his poetry.

Reef, Catherine. *Walt Whitman*. New York: Clarion Books, 1995. 148pp. MG/YA. This is an honest, informative exploration of Whitman's life with numerous excerpts from his writings. Reef deals with the writer's homosexuality openly, though briefly.

Stoutenburg, Adrien, and Laura N. Baker. *Listen America: A Life of Walt Whitman*. New York: Scribner, 1968. 182pp. YA. This is a well-documented, objective account in which Whitman is presented in the context of his times with liberal excerpts from the poet's writings.

Biographical Films and Theatrical Adaptations

Beautiful Dreamers (1992). Director: John Kent Harrison. Based on Whitman's visit to Canada in 1880, the film dramatizes the poet's relationship with a young Canadian physician who wishes to apply the poet's sense of human compassion on the mentally ill. Rip Torn portrays Whitman. With Colm Feore. Video.

Walt Whitman (1988). Director: Jock Smithie. Scenes from Whitman's life are recreated with recitations from his poetry. Video.

Walt Whitman (1988). Director: Veronica Young. Part of the PBS Voices and Visions poetry series, this film exploration of Whitman's life and work features commentary from Allen Ginsberg, Galway Kinnell, and Donald Hall. Video.

Walt Whitman: Sweet Bird of Freedom (1997). Director: Philip Schmidt. Dramatic monologue performed by Dallas McKennan filmed in Camden, New Jersey. Video.

Other Sources

Allen, Gay Wilson. *The New Walt Whitman Handbook*. New York: New York University Press, 1975. 423pp. This is an extremely useful reference guide to many aspects of Whitman's work and life, particularly recommended for its analysis of the many biographies available and of the shaping of Whitman's reputation.

Krieg, Joann P. *A Whitman Chronology*. Iowa City: University of Iowa Press, 1998. 207pp. Krieg supplies a detailed chronology of Whitman's activities and publishing history.

LeMaster, J.R., and Donald D. Kummings, eds. *Walt Whitman: An Encyclopedia*. New York: Garland, 1998. 847pp. This extensive reference volume covers more than 750 topics on multiple aspects of Whitman's life, attitudes, literary career, and works.

492. OSCAR WILDE
1854–1900

Irish-born author and wit, Wilde was the most famous figure in the Aesthetic Movement of the 1880s and 1890s that emphasized "art for art's sake." He achieved literary success and fame for his novel, *The Picture of Dorian Gray* (1891), poetry, children's stories, and such sophisticated, brilliantly witty plays as *Lady Windemere's Fan* (1892), *A Woman of No Importance* (1893), and his masterpiece, *The Importance of Being Earnest* (1895). Married and a devoted father of two sons, Wilde was charge with homosexual offenses, stemming from his intimacy with Lord Alfred Douglas, and sentenced to prison for two years. There he wrote his most famous poem, *The Ballad of Reading Gaol* (published, 1898). On his release in 1897, Wilde moved to France where ill health and bankruptcy affected his final years.

Autobiography and Primary Sources

Letters of Oscar Wilde. Rupert Hart-Davis, ed. New York: Harcourt, Brace, 1962. 958pp. Beginning with his years at Oxford, this collection of more than 1,000 letters to Wilde's family, friends, and acquaintances includes the writer's remarkable survey of his career and defense, *De Profundis*. In *More Letters of Oscar Wilde.* Rupert Hart-Davis, ed. (New York: Vanguard, 1985. 215pp.) Hart-Davis adds a supplement of 164 letters to the record of Wilde's correspondence, which has been called Wilde's most impressive achievement after *The Importance of Being Earnest.*

Selected Letters of Oscar Wilde. New York: Oxford University Press, 1979. 406pp. This selection of Wilde's letters cover his entire career and provide the reader unwilling to tackle the letters in full an excellent sampling.

Recommended Biographies

Ellmann, Richard. *Oscar Wilde.* New York: Knopf, 1988. 680pp. Ellmann's definitive biography is a masterpiece of the biographer's art. Meticulously researched, sympathetic to Wilde's achievements and sensitive to the writer's flaws, this is a brilliantly written and unsurpassed narrative account that manages to present Wilde's well-known story with a focus and freshness that tower over other versions.

Knox, Melissa. *Oscar Wilde: A Long and Lovely Suicide.* New Haven, Connecticut: Yale University Press, 1994. 185pp. Knox provides a full-length psychoanalytic biography that explores the links among Wilde's formative years, his relationships, and his psychological development to reveal both his creativity and self-destructive behavior. The book offers a number of original, provocative (and debatable) insights that challenge conventional interpretations.

Schmidgall, Gary. *The Stranger Wilde: Interpreting Oscar.* New York: Dutton, 1994. 494pp. The author stresses the importance of Wilde's homosexuality and his era's homophobia in shaping his life and career in a well-researched and persuasive critical biography. Schmidgall's vantage point is a useful one that offers a number of fresh and original insights.

Other Biographical Studies

Douglas, Alfred. *Oscar Wilde and Myself.* New York: Duffield, 1914. 306pp.; *Oscar Wilde: A Summing Up.* London: Richards Press, 1961. 140pp. The author's two biographical accounts, the latter published after his death, offer Douglas's self-defense in his relationship with Wilde. The books reveal little about their friendship but much about the disillusionment and betrayal Douglas felt.

Gide, André. *Oscar Wilde.* London: W. Kimber, 1951. 96pp. Gide's recollections serve as a more critical corrective to the largely sympathetic portraits of Wilde in exile written by his admirers. Gide is considerably less flattering in his view.

Harris, Frank. *Oscar Wilde: His Life and Confessions.* Garden City, New York: Garden City Publishing, 1930. 470pp. Harris's book is as much about the author as Wilde. Harris casts himself in the role of the writer's staunch defender while lesser figures abandoned him. This imaginative version of Wilde's career is not trustworthy and should be read with caution by those more interested in Wilde than Harris.

Holland, Vyvyan B. *Oscar Wilde: A Pictorial Biography.* New York: Viking, 1960. 144pp. Wilde's son supplies a brief, straightforward overview accompanying nearly 150 illustrations.

Housman, Laurence. *Echo de Paris: A Study from Life.* New York: Appleton, 1924. 71pp. This brief recollection reconstructs a conversation with Wilde in 1899 in dramatic form, capturing both the brilliance of Wilde the conversationalist and the pathos of his final days in exile.

Hyde, H. Montgomery. *Oscar Wilde: A Biography.* New York: Farrar, Straus, 1975. 410pp. Hyde, an English barrister, collects his extensive research to treat mainly the events leading up to Wilde's trials, the court cases, the imprisonment, and the last years. Hyde's earlier books, *The Trials of Oscar Wilde* (1948. Reprint ed. New York: Dover, 1973. 366pp.) and *Oscar Wilde: The Aftermath* (New York: Farrar, Straus, 1963. 221pp.) are the preliminary findings, reworked and combined into his biographical study.

Jullian, Philippe. *Oscar Wilde.* New York: Viking, 1968. 420pp. A lively but unscholarly biography by a French writer, Jullian's study draws on previously untapped resources to display the multiplicity of Wilde's personality and a vivid portrait of the fin-de-siècle aesthetic movement. In the author's view, Wilde's downfall was self-inflicted through self-indulgence.

O'Sullivan, Vincent. *Aspects of Wilde.* New York: Holt, 1936. 231pp. This is a sympathetic character study based largely on remarks made by Wilde to the author during the years of their friendship in Paris after the writer's release from prison.

Pearson, Hesketh. *Oscar Wilde: His Life and Wit.* New York: Harper, 1946. 345pp. Pearson's popular biography is sympathetic and objective, resisting the sensationalism of previous accounts but occasionally indulging in sentimentality. The book's chief success is its series of colorful anecdotes that help display Wilde in the round. Pearson's attempts at psychological analysis are less persuasive.

Sherard, Robert H. *Life of Oscar Wilde.* New York: Dodd, Mead, 1906. 403pp. This first biography of Wilde is the work of a friend and is admittedly an apology and defense intended to clear the writer's name. The result is a selective, uncritical eulogy.

Stokes, John. *Oscar Wilde: Myths, Miracles, and Imitations.* New York: Cambridge University Press, 1996. 216pp. Taking a thematic rather than a conventional chronological approach, Stokes explores Wilde in his biographical, literary, and historical contexts with an emphasis on his shifting image in the popular imagination. Includes an interesting chapter on Wilde's portrayal in plays and films based on his life.

Winwar, Frances. *Oscar Wilde and the Yellow Nineties.* New York: Harper, 1940. 381pp. Winwar began the series of more objective biographies of Wilde with this attempt to trace his life against the background of his times and its intellectual and social background.

Biographical Novels

Ackroyd, Peter. *The Last Testament of Oscar Wilde.* New York: Harper & Row, 1983. 185pp. During his final year, Wilde reflects on his life in this convincing first-person narrative that is both moving and insightful.

Elfman, Claire. *The Case of the Pederast's Wife.* Chester Springs, Pennsylvania: Dufour Editions, 2000. 188pp. The novel looks at Wilde's life and era from the perspective of his wife Constance who comes under the treatment of a young doctor with new ideas derived from Freud to explore the trauma of Wilde's trial on his wife.

Hall, Desmond. *I Give You Oscar Wilde: A Biographical Novel.* New York: New American Library, 1965. 343pp. Wilde's career from the 1880s is depicted in a balanced, sympathetic portrait that mixes fact and fancy with invented details and conversations.

Reilly, Robert. *The God of Mirrors.* Boston: Atlantic Monthly Press, 1986. 403pp. Focused on Wilde's relationship with Lord Alfred Douglas and the famous trials, Reilly supplements the facts with imagination and conjecture to capture the emotional contours of Wilde's experiences.

Fictional Portraits

Berkman, Ted. *To Seize the Passing Dream: A Novel of Whistler, His Women, and His World.* Garden City, New York: Doubleday, 1972. 431pp. Berkman's biographical portrait of Whistler features a convincing depiction of his artistic circle and personalities, including Wilde, Beardsley, Rossetti, Swinburne, Degas, and Proust.

Brown, Russell. *Sherlock Holmes and the Mysterious Friend of Oscar Wilde.* New York: St. Martin's, 1988. 176pp. Sherlock Holmes comes to the aid of Wilde in helping a Swedish inventor avoid blackmailers in this Victorian-era mystery that ingeniously connects the famous detective with figures and circumstances out of Wilde's life.

Buruma, Ian. *Playing the Game*. New York: Farrar, Straus, 1991. 234pp. This inventive biographical portrait of the great Indian cricketer, K.S. Ranjitsinhji, features imagined conversations with such figures as Wilde and Benjamin Disraeli.

Butler, David. *Lillie*. New York: Warner, 1978. 435pp. This biographical novel on the life of English beauty and actress Lillie Langtry features appearances by Whistler, Wilde, Randolph Churchill, Leopold of Belgium, Millais, and the Prince of Wales.

Fitzgerald, Nancy. *Chelsea*. Garden City, New York: Doubleday, 1979. 231pp. This period romance features an authentic depiction of the Victorian art scene with appearances by Whistler and Wilde.

Harries, Ann. *Manly Pursuits*. New York: Bloomsbury, 1999. 339pp. As Cecil Rhodes is close to death, an Oxford professor travels to South Africa to deliver hundreds of British songbirds to salve Rhodes's soul in this powerfully imagined tale with glimpses of Rhodes and such figures as Lewis Carroll, Oscar Wilde, and Rudyard Kipling.

Meyer, Nicholas. *The West End Horror*. New York: Dutton, 1976. 222pp. An 1895 murder of a theater critic launches Sherlock Holmes on a complex mystery that involves such historical figures as George Bernard Shaw and Wilde.

Satterthwait, Walter. *Wilde West*. New York: St. Martin's, 1991. 374pp. While on his American lecture tour, Wilde is charged in a series of murders in an inventive, comic mystery combining actual details of Wilde's life with considerable fancy.

Vernon, John. *All for Love: Baby Doe and the Silver Dollar*. New York: Simon & Schuster, 1995. 235pp. The story of Baby Doe Tabor's remarkable career is depicted with an appearance by Wilde on his American tour.

Recommended Juvenile Biographies

Nunokawa, Jeff. *Oscar Wilde*. New York: Chelsea House, 1995. 119pp. YA. Part of the Lives of Notable Gay Men and Lesbian series, this scholarly biographical profile begins with Wilde's conviction and imprisonment, followed by flashbacks to the process that led to the writer's downfall.

Biographical Films and Theatrical Adaptations

Bentley, Eric. *Lord Alfred's Lover*. Toronto: Personal Library, 1981. 127pp. Alfred Douglas in the last months of his life in 1945 looks back on his relationship with Wilde in this dramatization that combines facts about the writer's life with imagined conversations.

Eagleton, Terry. *Saint Oscar*. Cambridge, Massachusetts: Blackwell, 1997. 225pp. Eagleton presents Wilde as a "hero of modernism" with his Irish background emphasized in this dramatization of actual and imagined scenes from his life.

Hare, David. *The Judas Kiss*. New York: Grove Press, 1998. 115pp. Hare places Wilde's trial for "acts of gross indecency" in both its personal and political context and deepens the view of the author as a man of firmly held principles.

Kaufman, Moises. *Gross Indecency: The Three Trials of Oscar Wilde*. New York: Vintage Books, 1998. 143pp. Fashioning the trial transcripts into a concise drama, Kaufman explores how social forces, homophobia, and Wilde's personality combined to affect the outcome.

Forbidden Passion: The Oscar Wilde Movie (1987). Director: Henry Herbert. Michael Gambon portrays Wilde during his sad final days in this British film. Video.

Lillie (1990). Director: John Gorrie. Dramatizing the career of beauty and actress Lillie Langtry who becomes the mistress of Edward VII, Francesca Annis takes the title role with Dennis Lill as Edward, Don Fellows as Whistler, and Peter Egan as Wilde.

Oscar Wilde (1960). Director: Gregory Ratoff. Robert Morley is convincing as the writer in this drama that focuses on Wilde's trials. With John Neville, Ralph Richardson, Dennis Price, and Alexander Knox.

Oscar Wilde: Spendthrift of Genius (1986). Director: Sean O'Mordha. With a script by Richard Ellmann, this film portrait includes the only known recording of Wilde reading from "The Ballad of Reading Gaol." Video.

Salame's Last Dance (1989). Director: Ken Russell. Russell's flamboyant depiction of Wilde's play features Nicholas Grace as the writer and performances by Glenda Jackson, Stratford Johns, and Douglas Hodge. Video.

The Trials of Oscar Wilde (1960). Director: Ken Hughes. Based on Montgomery Hyde's book and John Furnell's play, *The Stringed Lute* (New York: Rider, 1955. 198pp.), Peter Finch portrays Wilde in his suit against the Marquis of Queensbury and his subsequent trial for indecency. Also starring John Fraser, Lionel Jeffries, Nigel Patrick, and James Mason. Video.

Wilde (1998). Director: Brian Gilbert. Adapted from Richard Ellmann's book, the film dramatizes scenes from the writer's life with Stephen Fry as Wilde, Jude Law as Bosie Douglas, Tom Wilkinson as the Marquess of Queensbury, and Jennifer Ehle as Constance Wilde. Stefan Rudnick's *Wilde: A Novel* (Los Angeles, California: Dove Books, 1998. 179pp.) is a novelization inspired by the screenplay by Julian Mitchell. Video.

Other Sources

Beckson, Karl E. *The Oscar Wilde Encyclopedia*. New York: AMS Press, 1998. 456pp. Alphabetically arranged entries cover Wilde's art, biography, historical events, and social mores in a rich and accessible reference work.

Holland, Merlin. *The Wilde Album*. New York: Holt, 1998. 192pp. Wilde's grandson assembles press clippings, cartoons, photographs, and theater programs to document the writer's emergence as a media celebrity. The accompanying text examines

Wilde's life with an emphasis on his background and relationships.

Mikhail, E.H. *Oscar Wilde: Interviews and Recollections*. New York: Barnes and Noble, 1979. 2 vols. Wilde is captured from a variety of angles and perspectives from both his friends, foes, and contemporary accounts.

Page, Norman. *An Oscar Wilde Chronology*. Boston: G.K. Hall, 1991. 105pp. Page supplies a monthly and often daily account of Wilde's activities as well as a biographical glossary of his circle.

493. WILHELM II
1859–1941

Emperor of Germany and king of Prussia, Wilhelm was the grandson of Queen Victoria of England. His determination to maintain and extend the royal prerogative in governing German affairs resulted in the resignation of his chancellor, Otto von Bismarck. Wilhelm strengthened the Triple Alliance and promoted the nationalistic imperialism that contributed to World War I. Forced to abdicate after the war, he found asylum in Holland.

Autobiography and Primary Sources

The Kaiser's Memoirs/Wilhelm II. New York: Harper, 1922. 365pp. Wilhelm's self-serving account of his life should be read alongside a more objective account to measure the discrepancies and judge Wilhelm's perspective.

Recommended Biographies

Balfour, Michael. *The Kaiser and His Times*. Boston: Houghton Mifflin, 1964. 524pp. Balfour sets Wilhelm in the context of German history and his family background in an highly readable, reliable account by an expert in the period. The book successfully balances the presentation of Wilhelm's character and personality with a revealing portrait of his age and the political, social, economic, and diplomatic forces that the kaiser was ultimately unable to control.

Cecil, Lamar. *Wilhelm II: Prince and Emperor*. Chapel Hill: University of North Carolina Press, 1989–1996, 2 vols. Based on meticulous archival research, Cecil supplies a comprehensive psychological and political profile that is exceptionally detailed and incisive in its interpretive analysis.

Palmer, Alan. *The Kaiser: Warlord of the Second Reich*. New York: Scribner, 1978. 276pp. Although written for the generalist, Palmer's readable narrative portrait is solidly documented using the standard published and manuscript sources that are synthesized and compressed into a believable, fair portrait of the man. Although Wilhelm's considerable character deficiencies predominate, Palmer is able to suggest his depth and complexity that are lacking in several other biographies.

Röhl, John C.G. *Young Wilhelm: The Kaiser's Early Life, 1859–1888*. New York: Cambridge University Press, 1998. 979pp. Röhl's is by far the most scholarly and comprehensive treatment of Wilhelm's boyhood, youth, and formative years. Röhl's earlier historical study, *Germany without*

Bismarck: The Crisis of Government in the Second Reich 1890–1900 (Berkeley: University of California Press, 1967. 304pp.) explores Wilhelm's early reign and his dispute with Bismarck.

Other Biographical Studies

Cowles, Virginia. *The Kaiser.* New York: Harper & Row, 1963. 445pp. This biography is so riddled with errors that even the date of Wilhelm's death is incorrect. Offering little more than a recycled synthesis of borrowed sources, Cowles's Wilhelm lacks depth and believability.

Davis, A.N. *The Kaiser I Knew: My 14 Years with the Kaiser.* New York: Harper, 1918. 300pp. The Kaiser's American dentist offers this early biographical portrait. Gossipy and constructed from fragmentary conversations, the book, despite its jingoistic tone, does provide some illumination of Wilhelm's complex personality.

Kohut, Thomas A. *Wilhelm II and the Germans: A Study in Leadership.* New York: Oxford University Press, 1991. 331pp. In a psychoanalytic approach Kohut focuses on the relationship between Wilhelm and his parents as the source for his policies and behavior.

Kürenberg, Joachim von. *The Kaiser: A Life of Wilhelm II, Last Emperor of Germany.* New York: Simon & Schuster, 1955. 461pp. The author, a German nobleman who was a confidant of the kaiser, supplies a number of firsthand glimpses of Wilhelm in old age and records conversations revealing the former kaiser's views on men and events.

Ludwig, Emil. *Kaiser Wilhelm II.* New York: Putnam, 1926. 459pp. Ludwig constructs from memoirs and documentary evidence a credible psychological profile of Wilhelm, a young man of considerable promise who came to power too soon and never fully matured and whose character flaws helped determine German and world history.

Müller, George A. von. *The Kaiser and His Court.* New York: Harcourt, Brace, 1964. 430pp. The author as chief of the naval cabinet had frequent contact with Wilhelm, and his recollections and assessments are recorded in diary entries from the assassination of Franz Ferdinand to Wilhelm's abdication. The book graphically presents Wilhelm's unsteadiness as a leader and growing isolation and irrelevance during the war years.

Nowak, Karl F. *Kaiser and Chancellor: The Opening Years of the Reign of Kaiser Wilhelm II.* New York: Macmillan, 1930. 290pp. This is a detailed look at the first two years of Wilhelm's reign and the widening breach between the kaiser and Bismarck, which culminated in the dismissal of the chancellor. Based on official documents and conversatons with the kaiser, Nowak supplies a convincing character study of a man dominated by his mother and ill-prepared to rule.

Van der Kiste, John. *Kaiser Wilhelm II: Germany's Last Emperor.* New York: Sutton, 1999. 272pp. This is a concise biographical profile written for the general reader and serving as a reliable overview that attempts to capture the complexity of Wilhelm's character and the era that he unsuccessfully attempted to dominate.

Waite, Robert. *Kaiser and Führer: A Comparative Study of Personality and Politics.* Toronto: University of Toronto Press, 1998. 511pp. Waite takes a psychological approach in this comparative study of the personal lives and politics of Wilhelm II and Adolf Hitler, contrasting their intellectual worlds, wartime strategies, and their crucial early developments.

Whittle, Tyler. *The Last Kaiser: A Biography of Wilhelm II, German Emperor and King of Prussia.* New York: Times Books, 1977. 368pp. This popular biography is written from the English royal family's point of view with a great deal on Wilhelm's youth and his admiration for his grandmother, Queen Victoria. The book is far less assured dealing with Wilhelm in his mature years and the complex events leading up to World War I.

Wilson, Lawrence. *The Incredible Kaiser: A Portrait of William II.* New York: A.S. Barnes, 1965. 196pp. Wilson's study lacks penetration and depth, substituting instead a facile and often-melodramatic presentation that is too one-dimensional to be believable.

Fictional Portraits

Butler, David. *Lusitania.* New York: Random House, 1982. 578pp. The sinking of the *Lusitania* in 1915 is described from a variety of perspectives in Germany, England, and America, including Wilhelm's.

Conroy, Robert. *1901.* Novato, California: Lyford Books, 1995. 374pp. This inventive alternative history imagines a German invasion of the United States in 1901 and plausible depictions of a score of historical figures, including Wilhelm.

Fagyas, Maria. *Court of Honor.* New York: Simon & Schuster, 1978. 377pp. Life in Wilhelm's court prior to World War I is the subject of this novel involving a scandal among the Prussian military.

Biographical Films and Theatrical Adaptations

Edward the King (1975). Director: John Gorrie. Video. The life and short reign of Edward VII are chronicled with his relationship with his parents detailed. Robert Hardy portrays Prince Albert; Annette Crosbie is Queen Victoria, and Timothy West is the Prince of Wales and later king. Wilhelm appears played by Christopher Neame. The book on which the screenplay was based is available by David E. Butler, *Edward the King* (New York: Pocket Books, 1974–1975. 2 vols.). Video.

Other Sources

Röhl, John C.G., and N. Sombart, eds. *Kaiser Wilhelm II: New Interpretations.* New York: Cambridge University Press, 1982. 319pp. This collection of scholarly views based on recent research provides a collective portrait on Wilhelm's character and reign.

494. WILLIAM THE CONQUEROR
ca. 1028–1087

English king William I was duke of Normandy when, in 1066, he invaded England and defeated King Harold at Hastings in what is often referred to as the Norman Conquest. William harshly suppressed rebellions that broke out after his coronation and created a strong feudal government. The Domesday Book was compiled by his order (1086). Considered one of the greatest English monarchs, William I is a pivotal figure in world history.

Recommended Biographies

Douglas, David. *William the Conqueror: The Norman Impact upon England.* Berkeley: University of California Press, 1964. 476pp. Douglas ably explores William's administrative, military, and diplomatic achievements in a scholarly and thorough assessment by a leading historian of the period. The work is both a study of Anglo-Norman history and a reliable biographical portrait.

Russell, Phillips. *William the Conqueror.* New York: Scribner, 1933. 334pp. In Russell's reassessment, William's greatest achievement was not the conquest of England but his earlier subjugation of Normandy. William's early years are connected to the leading incidents of his later life in a lively, accurate narrative account.

Other Biographical Studies

Ashley, Maurice. *The Life and Times of William I.* London: Weidenfeld and Nicolson, 1973. 224pp. This is a handsomely illustrated biography with Ashley's biographical essay that covers the important details of William's life and reign. Useful as an introduction to the subject.

Barlow, Frank. *William I and the Norman Conquest.* Mystic, Connecticut: L. Verry, 1965. 206pp. Barlow's is a helpful overview of William's life and time suited for the general reader. The book is particularly strong on social historical details.

Benton, Sarah H. *The Life of William the Conqueror from the Early Chronicles.* New York: Dial Press, 1927. 298pp. William's life is retold largely from French sources, illustrated with prints and photographs. Little attempt is made to sort out the facts from the legends, including both with an emphasis on the colorful and the picturesque.

Freeman, Edward. *William the Conqueror.* New York: Macmillan, 1894. 200pp. This is a heroic portrait of William, celebrating his greatness as he ascends to the English throne. Despite uncritical partisanship in William's favor, the book provides extensive coverage of William's life before 1066 and the details of the invasion and conquest.

Lloyd, Alan. *The Making of the King, 1066.* New York: Holt, 1966. 243pp. Drawing on the Anglo-Saxon Chronicles, early English histories, and modern research, Lloyd fashions a competent narrative history of the Norman Conquest focused on the lives of William, Harold II, and Harald III of Norway.

Slocombe, George. *William, the Conqueror.* New York: Putnam, 1961. 271pp. Although undocumented and unscholarly, this is an accurate and straightforward synthesis of the facts derived from the chronicles and modern authorities, with the gaps in the record filled in with assumptions of feelings and motivations.

Biographical Novels

Anand, Valerie. *The Norman Pretender.* New York: Scribner, 1979. 410pp. The novel dramatizes the final years of Saxon England that climaxes with William's victory at Hastings in a convincing portrait of the era and its central figures, including William, Edward the Confessor, and Harold II. In *The Disputed Crown* (New York: Scribner, 1982. 297pp.), Anand describes the two decades following William's victory and the continuing conflict between Saxons and Normans.

Heyer, Georgette. *The Conqueror.* London: Heinemann, 1931. 405pp. Heyer's fictional biography reconstructs William's life from birth through his victory in 1066, depicting him as a shrewd and driven man who inspires a loyal following.

Lewis, Hilda W. *Wife to the Bastard.* New York: D. McKay, 1967. 352pp. Matilda, the first woman to be crowned queen of England, is portrayed in this novel that presents her relationship with William. Lewis's *Harold Was My King* (New York: D. McKay, 1970. 246pp.) looks at the events of the Norman Conquest and its aftermath from the perspective of a knight loyal to Harold.

Lide, Mary. *Fortune's Knave: The Making of William the Conqueror.* New York: St. Martin's, 1993. 269pp. William's formative years from 1035 to 1054 are covered in this carefully researched novel that manages a plausible and human drama out of William's rise to power.

Muntz, Hope. *The Golden Warrior: The Story of Harold and William.* New York: Scribner, 1949. 354pp. This is a dual fictional portrait of Harold and William and the events leading up to the Battle of Hastings, based on contemporary sources.

Plaidy, Jean. *The Bastard King.* New York: Putnam, 1979. 319pp. William's rise to the English throne is dramatized with a concentration on his relationship with Matilda of Flanders and the fate of his children.

Todd, Catherine. *Bond of Honour.* New York: St. Martin's, 1981. 223pp. William's life and career are captured through letters, diaries, and imagined conversations in a believable portrait with a vivid re-creation of the era and the battles that climaxes with William gaining the English throne.

Wingate, John. *William, the Conqueror: An Historical Novel.* New York: F. Watts, 1983. 355pp. Wingate's is a detailed recreation of William's progress to the English throne that is generally reliable in its history and convincing in its interpretation of personalities and motives.

Fictional Portraits

Gerson, Noel B. *The Conqueror's Wife.* Garden City, New York: Doubleday, 1957. 285pp. Gerson's focus is on William's wife, Matilda of Flanders, in an admittedly fictional version of their life together.

Holland, Cecelia. *The Firedrake.* New York: Atheneum, 1966. 243pp. William and the events of the Norman invasion and conquest are authentically described from the perspective of an itinerant Irish knight who serves the Norman cause.

Lytton, Edward Bulwer. *Harold: The Last of the Saxon Kings.* New York: Dutton, 1970. 456pp. Although focused on the final days of Edward the Confessor and the scramble for power that brings Harold to the throne, this classic historical novel provides a portrait of William and his victory at Hastings.

Prescott, Hilda F.M. *Son of Dust.* London: Constable, 1932. 364pp. Prescott's classic historical novel is set in William's Norman court before the conquest.

Sprague, Rosemary. *Red Lion and Gold Dragon.* Philadelphia: Chilton Books, 1967. 264pp. Events of the Norman Conquest are seen from the perspective of a Saxon who fights with Harold at Hastings and wins the respect of William after the battle.

Recommended Juvenile Biographies

Green, Robert. *William the Conqueror.* New York: F. Watts, 1998. 64pp. MG. This is an informative profile of William and the forces that led to his conquest in 1066 and the impact of his victory on Anglo-Saxon culture.

495. TENNESSEE WILLIAMS
1911–1983

One of America's foremost dramatists whose plays have become classics of the American theater, Williams first gained success with the productions of *The Glass Menagerie* (1945) and *A Streetcar Named Desire* (1947; Pulitzer Prize). Other plays include *Summer and Smoke* (1948), *Cat on a Hot Tin Roof* (1955; Pulitzer Prize), and *Night of the Iguana* (1961).

Autobiography and Primary Sources

Conversations with Tennessee Williams. Albert J. Devlin, ed. Jackson: University Press of Mississippi, 1986. 369pp. Devlin has collected dozens of interviews with Williams recorded from 1940 to 1981, filled with insights about his life and work, as well as contradictions and misleading information.

Memoirs. Garden City, New York: Doubleday, 1975. 264pp. Ranging over his past and present, the playwright releases a deluge of anecdotes and opinions. Often coy and discrete on personal details, Williams offers some insights about the influences that shaped his life and his plays.

Recommended Biographies

Hayman, Ronald. *Tennessee Williams: Everyone Else Is an Audience.* New Haven, Connecticut: Yale University Press, 1993. 286pp. Hayman's critical biography traces the relationship between Williams's life and his art. The book is insightful on the autobiographical sources and the thematic interconnections of Williams's plays, stories, and films.

Leverich, Lyle. *Tom: The Unknown Tennessee Williams.* New York: Crown, 1995. 644pp. The first book in a projected two-volume biography traces Williams's life from his birth to the opening of *The Glass Menagerie* in 1945. Leverich amasses a remarkable factual record, more detailed and authoritative than any previous account. Although sympathetic, the author does not skirt the less-flattering side of his subject's character and behavior, and the result is a balanced, thorough, and convincing partial portrait. If the second volume can achieve the same high standard, Leverich's will certainly become the definitive biography for some time to come.

Other Biographical Studies

Maxwell, Gilbert. *Tennessee Williams and Friends: An Informal Biography.* Cleveland: World, 1965. 333pp. The book is a series of recollections by a friend who knew Williams from the beginning of his career. Rich in anecdotes, Maxwell's presentation shows a believable human figure very different from the public and legendary figure of other treatments.

Rader, Dotson. *Tennessee: Cry of the Heart.* New York: Doubleday, 1985. 348pp. One of Williams's loyal friends during his last decade presents a tormented, frustrated artist. Rader's suggestion that Williams was a disappointed political radical is unconvincing, and the book is overly thesis-dominated to be fully reliable.

Smith, Bruce. *Costly Performances: Tennessee Williams: The Last Stage.* New York: Paragon House, 1990. 262pp. Smith's is a journalistic, exploitative tell-all concerning the playwright's sad end, full of accounts of drug and alcohol abuse and the wastage of a great literary talent.

Spoto, Donald. *The Kindness of Strangers: The Life of Tennessee Williams.* Boston: Little, Brown, 1985. 409pp. Spoto's popular biography is comprehensive, arranging the facts into a reliable sequence, but the book fails to penetrate convincingly the surface details to reveal a credible psychological portrait. Too often the book relies uncritically on Williams's own version of his past.

Tischler, Nancy. *Tennessee Williams: Rebellious Puritan.* New York: Citadel Press, 1961. 319pp. This early critical biography of the playwright's first 50 years is still one of the better studies available. The book is a critically astute attempt to connect the man and his work, unified by the central conflict indicated by the book's subtitle.

Williams, Dakin, and Shepherd Mead. *Tennessee Williams: An Intimate Biography.* New York: Arbor House, 1983. 352pp. Williams's younger brother supplies his recollections, supplemented by letters, interviews, and his mother's and brother's own memoirs. The chief importance of the book is the author's intimate knowledge of Williams's family background. On the playwright's life outside the family circle, the book is much less reliable and comprehensive.

Williams, Edwina Dakin. *Remember Me to Tom.* As told to Lucy Freeman. New York: Putnam, 1963. 255pp. Williams's mother provides her defensive recollections of the playwright's childhood, adolescence, and eventual success as a writer. Full of anecdote and sentiment, the author draws on letters and journals as well as her often unreliable memory.

Biographical Films and Theatrical Adaptations

A&E Biography Video: Tennessee Williams: Wounded Genius (1998). Producer: Paul Budline. This film portrait documents how Williams's early experiences gave him the material for his work but also provided the source for the personal problems that would be his downfall. Williams's brother, biographers, and friends offer their perspectives, and the playwright is seen in excerpts from television interviews. Video.

Tennessee Williams: Orpheus of the American Stage (1994). Director: Merrill Brockway. This film study of the playwright's life and work includes excerpts from his most celebrated scenes, footage from interviews, as well as reminiscences from Gore Vidal and Edward Albee. Video.

Other Sources

Leavitt, Richard F., ed. *The World of Tennessee Williams*. New York: Putnam, 1978. 168pp. A varied selection of illustrations, including previously unpublished photographs, letters, rehearsal notes, manuscripts, review clippings, and memorabilia. The biographical text is the work of a longtime friend of the playwright.

Roudane, Matthew C., ed. *The Cambridge Companion to Tennessee Williams*. New York: Cambridge University Press, 1998. 275pp. This collection of 13 original essays from leading scholars covers Williams's work from his early apprentice years through his last play, with additional coverage of biographical issues, his short stories, and poems.

496. WILLIAM CARLOS WILLIAMS
1883–1963

Considered one of the twentieth century's most important and original American poets, Williams was also a physician who practiced medicine in New Jersey for over 40 years. His works include *Poems* (1909), *Sour Grapes* (1921), *Paterson* (1946–1958), and *Pictures from Breughel* (1963; Pulitzer Prize). He also wrote essays, including "In the American Grain" (1925), short stories, and novels.

Autobiography and Primary Sources

Autobiography. New York: Random House, 1951. 402pp. Williams's informal and honest reflections cover his childhood and youth, his training as a doctor, and his efforts to succeed as a writer. A fascinating glimpse of a multifaceted man and an indispensable biographical source.

Interviews with William Carlos Williams: "Speaking Straight Ahead" Linda Welshimer, ed. New York: New Directions, 1976. 108pp. Williams discusses his theories of poetic meter and diction, as well as his contemporaries Pound and Eliot, and his comments on a variety of topics are arranged alphabetically by subject.

I Wanted to Write a Poem: The Autobiography of the Works of a Poet. Edith Head, ed. Boston: Beacon Press, 1958. 99pp. This original and unusual "descriptive bibliography" includes Williams's recollections of his discovery of poetry and his first attempts to write poems.

The Selected Letters of William Carlos Williams. John C. Thirwall, ed. New York: New Directions, 1984. 352pp. Spanning 54 years of the poet's life, this remarkably candid collection of letters reveals a great deal about the nature of the man, his conception of poetry, and his fellow poets.

Recommended Biographies

Mariani, Paul. *William Carlos Williams: A New World Naked*. New York: McGraw-Hill, 1981. 874pp. Exhaustively researched, Mariani's authoritative study assembles from a mountain of facts the essential record of Williams's life. Less successful as an interpretation of those facts, Mariani's account is the fullest treatment of the man and his career available.

Whittemore, Reed. *William Carlos Williams: Poet from Jersey*. Boston: Houghton Mifflin, 1975. 404pp. Although far less detailed than Mariani, Whittemore's account reads more like a series of sketches than a finished portrait, but the book does attempt to shape the various facts by a controlling theme: Williams's Americanism and the conflict between his service to medicine and modernism. The book's reach exceeds its grasp but still is an important critical work that attempts to draw essential connections between the man and his work.

Other Biographical Studies

Fischer-Wirth, Ann W. *William Carlos Williams and Autobiography: The Woods of His Own Nature*. University Park: Pennsylvania State University Press, 1989. 216pp. The author treats Williams's works in their autobiographical context and attempts to explore the identity of the private poet through them. The result is a fascinating and revealing analysis that sheds considerable light on the inner tensions that shaped both Williams's personality and his work.

Whitaker, Thomas R. *William Carlos Williams*. New York: Twayne, 1968. 183pp. Whitaker's is a fine critical introduction to Williams's work that considers the poet's development and influences.

Recommended Juvenile Biographies

Baldwin, Neil. *To All Gentleness: William Carlos Williams, the Doctor-Poet*. New York: Atheneum, 1984. 223pp. YA. Although using some invented scenes and reconstructed dialogue, this is a full and compelling documentation of the poet's life, achievement, and personality.

Biographical Films and Theatrical Adaptations

William Carlos Williams (1988). Director: Richard P. Rogers. An installment of the PBS Voices and Vision series this is a film profile of the poet's life and works. Video.

497. WOODROW WILSON
1856–1924

Wilson was president of Princeton and governor of New Jersey before his election in 1912 as the twenty-eighth U.S. president. Wilson's achievements during his two terms in office include the Underwood Tariff (1913), establishment of the Federal Reserve System and the Federal Trade Commission (both in 1914), the Clayton Anti-Trust Act (1914), the Federal Child Labor Law (1916), and the Federal Farm Loans Act. The seventeenth (1913), eighteenth (1919), and nineteenth (1920) amendments were also passed, and the United States entered World War I. Wilson's Fourteen Points set forth provisions for postwar peace, and he secured adoption of the League of Nations (1918). He was awarded the Nobel Peace Prize in 1919.

Autobiography and Primary Sources

A President in Love: The Courtship Letters of Woodrow Wilson and Edith Bolling Galt. Edwin Tribble, ed. Boston: Little, Brown, 1981. 225pp. This is a excellently edited collection of Wilson's intimate correspondence with his second wife from their first meeting in 1915 to their wedding eight months later. Remarkable for their candor and passion, the collection is a revealing look at the human side of the otherwise austere and seemingly distant Wilson.

The Papers of Woodrow Wilson. Arthur S. Link, et. al., eds. Princeton, New Jersey: Princeton University Press, 1966-94. 69 vols. This monumental scholarly series is the repository of all of Wilson's important personal and governmental papers and is invaluable for the scholar and biographer.

Recommended Biographies

Cooper, John M. Jr. *The Warrior and the Priest: Woodrow Wilson and Theodore Roosevelt*. Cambridge, Massachusetts: Harvard University Press, 1983. 442pp. Cooper's dual biography is a well-written comparative study, alternating between incisive views and characterizations of both men at turning points of their careers. In Cooper's view, Roosevelt and Wilson are "the principal architects of modern American politics," and the book offers a cogent case in support of his assertion.

Heckscher, August. *Woodrow Wilson*. New York: Scribner, 1991. 743pp. Heckscher's is the most thorough and accurate single volume biography available. Covering Wilson's personality, political philosophy, and public career, Heckscher's account is both detailed and persuasive, thoroughly documented and judicious in its conclusions.

Link, Arthur S. *Wilson*. Princeton, New Jersey: Princeton University Press, 1947-65. 5 vols. Link's multivolume study takes an account of Wilson's life and career up to 1917 and the United States's entry into World War I. Meticulously researched by a scholar who has devoted his career to the subject, Link's biography is regarded as the standard, authoritative source on the years covered. A one-volume overview by the author, *Woodrow*

Wilson: A Profile (New York: Hill & Wang, 1968. 197pp.), is an excellent introductory study.

Walworth, Arthur. *Woodrow Wilson.* 1958. Reprint ed. New York: W.W. Norton, 1978. 438pp. This Pulitzer Prize–winning biography is a thorough and comprehensive assessment of the man and his career, emphasizing the private and intellectual sides of Wilson's personality. For the author, Wilson's religious background helps to define both the man and his values, and the image of Wilson the prophet serves as the thematic link to connect his entire career.

Weinstein, Edwin A. *Woodrow Wilson: A Medical and Psychological Study.* Princeton, New Jersey: Princeton University Press, 1981. 399pp. Offering a revaluation of Wilson's life from a medical and psychological viewpoint, Weinstein examines through extensive primary research the impact of Wilson's health on events during his political career. The book has been called a must-read for anyone wishing to understand Wilson's character.

Other Biographical Studies

Auchincloss, Louis. *Woodrow Wilson.* New York: Viking, 2000. 176pp. In the author's view, Wilson was "the greatest idealist who ever occupied the White House," and this succinct biographical portrait shows the private man, his ideas, and public challenges in a series of vividly realized character sketches.

Baker, Ray S. *Woodrow Wilson: Life and Letters.* New York: Doubleday, 1927–1939. 8 vols. The work of Wilson's press secretary at the Versailles Peace Conference, Baker's massive documentary study is a rich sourcebook of diaries, letters, and papers arranged into a detailed chronology to be consulted rather than read through for pleasure.

Blum, John M. *Woodrow Wilson and the Politics of Morality.* Boston: Little, Brown, 1956. 215pp. Blum's brief interpretive study finds much to criticize in Wilson's temperament and leadership. Provocative and controversial in its analysis, the book serves as a valuable complement to other studies that choose to cast Wilson in a more tragic and heroic role.

Bragdon, Henry W. *Woodrow Wilson: The Academic Years.* Cambridge, Massachusetts: Harvard University Press, 1967. 579pp. This is a scholarly and authoritative treatment of Wilson's student days and career as a teacher and administrator. The bulk of the book is devoted to Wilson's presidency of Princeton and his gaining a national reputation for educational innovation. The book makes a convincing argument on how Wilson's academic career influenced his later political career.

Clements, Kendrick A. *The Presidency of Woodrow Wilson.* Lawrence: University Press of Kansas, 1992. 303pp. Synthesizing recent scholarship, Clements's is an excellent account of the Wilson presidency and an analysis of reasons for the successes and failures of his domestic and foreign policy initiatives.

Ferrell, Robert H. *Woodrow Wilson and World War I, 1917–1921.* New York: Harper & Row, 1985. 346pp. Ferrell's is a masterful survey of Wilson as a war leader and peacemaker. Balanced but critical of Wilson's achievement, the book praises

Wilson's ability to mobilize the nation to contribute to the Allied victory but criticizes his performance as a statesman and postwar politician.

Freud, Sigmund, and William C. Bullitt. *Thomas Woodrow Wilson: A Psychological Study.* Boston: Houghton Mifflin, 1967. 307pp. This curious combination of psychoanalysis and political criticism attempts to connect Wilson's inner neuroses and public actions in a often cruel and reductive attack.

Garraty, John A. *Woodrow Wilson: A Great Life in Brief.* New York: Knopf, 1956. 206pp. This concise, objective overview summarizes the outstanding events in Wilson's life and presents a believable psychological portrait.

Osborn, George C. *Woodrow Wilson: The Early Years.* Baton Rouge: Louisiana State University Press, 1968. 345pp. Ending with Wilson's appointment to the presidency of Princeton, Osborn's is a thorough, scholarly chronicle of Wilson's formative, prepolitical years. Osborn examines the influences of family, teachers, and friends upon the young man, as well as the nature and origin of his character strengths and weaknesses that will be evident in his political career.

Schulte Nordholt, J.W. *Woodrow Wilson: A Life for World Peace.* Berkeley: University of California Press, 1991. 495pp. The work of a Dutch historian, Schulte's study traces the development of Wilson's political philosophy and its application during his presidency. Although offering a refreshing European perspective, the book is marred at several places by a lack of general knowledge of American history.

Shachtman, Tom. *Edith & Woodrow: A Presidential Romance.* New York: Putnam, 1981. 299pp. An unscholarly but lively story of Wilson's relationship with his second wife, Shachtman supplies a personal portrait of the president supported by extensive excerpts from the letters and diaries.

Smith, Gene. *When the Cheering Stopped: The Last Years of Woodrow Wilson.* New York: Morrow, 1964. 307pp. Smith chronicles Wilson's illness during the final two years of his presidency and his unsuccessful attempt to gain support for the League of Nations. Scholars have criticized Smith's characterizations and treatment of complex issues, but the general reader will find the poignancy of the human drama compelling and satisfying.

Fictional Portraits

Butler, David. *Lusitania.* New York: Random House, 1982. 578pp. The sinking of the *Lusitania* in 1915 is described from a variety of perspectives in Germany, England, and America, including Wilson's.

Pilpel, Robert H. *To the Honor of the Fleet.* New York: Atheneum, 1979. 459pp. Wilson appears as a character in this historical thriller involving a secret plan to help keep America out of World War I, culminating in the Battle of Jutland.

Shellabarger, Samuel. *Tolbecken.* Boston: Little, Brown, 1956. 370pp. Shellabarger's family saga set in the nineteenth century and during World War I includes scenes of period undergraduate life at Princeton with Wilson as its president.

Vidal, Gore. *Hollywood.* New York: Random House, 1990. 437pp. Wilson is only one of several historical figures used to portray America life during the 1920s in Vidal's social panorama.

Recommended Juvenile Biographies

Leavell, J. Perry. *Woodrow Wilson.* New York: Chelsea House, 1987. 116pp. MG/YA. Leavell's is a straightforward factual and informative review of Wilson's life and times.

Randolph, Sallie G. *Woodrow Wilson: President.* New York: Walker, 1992. 124pp. MG/YA. Randolph covers Wilson's entire life in this sophisticated and informative biography that emphasizes his personal side with sufficient historical background to make his challenges and actions understandable.

Rogers, James T. *Woodrow Wilson: Visionary for Peace.* New York: Facts on File, 1997. 96pp. YA. Usable by young adults and general readers, this entry in the Makers of America series presents a succinct, reliable overview of Wilson's life, personality, and career.

Biographical Films and Theatrical Adaptations

A&E Biography Video: Woodrow Wilson: Reluctant Warrior (1996). Director: Paul Budline. This is an informative full-length biographical profile. Video.

Wilson (1944). Director: Henry King. Alexander Knox is a standout in the title role in this film biography dramatizing Wilson's life from his days as president of Princeton through the White House years. Co-starring Charles Coburn, Geraldine Fitzgerald, Cedric Hardwicke, and Vincent Price. Video.

Woodrow Wilson (1962). Installment of the Biography television program hosted by Mike Wallace. Video.

Other Sources

Vexler, Robert I., ed. *Woodrow Wilson, 1856–1924: Chronology, Documents, Bibliographical Aids.* Dobbs Ferry, New York: Oceana, 1969. 123pp. Vexler provides a detailed chronology, a sample of important documentary evidence, and an annotated bibliography on sources.

498. LUDWIG WITTGENSTEIN
1889–1951

Austrian philosopher Wittgenstein profoundly influenced recent British and American philosophy with his two chief works, *Tractatus Logico-Philosophicus* (1921) and *Philisophical Investigations* (1953). His work focuses on the philosophy of logical positivism and language philosophy. Wittgenstein was professor of philosophy at Cambridge from 1929 to 1947.

Autobiography and Primary Sources

Ludwig Wittgenstein, Cambridge Letters. Brian McGuinness and G.H. Von Wright, eds. Cambridge, Massachusetts: Blackwell, 1995. 349pp. Wittgenstein's correspondence with members of his Cambridge circle, such as Bertrand Russell, G.E. Moore, and John Maynard Keynes, offers an intriguing look at the philosopher's character and his relationships.

Recommended Biographies

McGuinness, Brian. *Wittgenstein: A Life: Young Ludwig 1889–1921.* Berkeley: University of California Press, 1988. 322pp. The first volume of an anticipated two-volume life is an authoritative and exhaustive survey of Wittgenstein's early years up to 1921, based on previously untapped sources. Although highly detailed in terms of the facts uncovered, the book is somewhat restrained in interpreting Wittgenstein's personality.

Monk, Ray. *Ludwig Wittgenstein: The Duty of Genius.* New York: Free Press, 1990. 645pp. Monk's is a impressive biography that uses Wittgenstein's private papers, his diaries, and letters to provide insights into his personality and ideas. Judicious and balanced, Monk creates a highly sympathetic portrait of a compelling human figure.

Other Biographical Studies

Bartley, William W. *Wittgenstein.* 1973. Revised ed. LaSalle, Illinois: Open Court, 1985. 218pp. Concentrating on the "mystery years" of Wittgenstein's life, the decade after the end of World War I, Bartley both provides a corrective to the factual record and a good deal of speculation based on slender evidence. In Bartley's view, Wittgenstein's homosexuality led to intense guilt and suffering over his sexual desires, which explains his mood of self-hatred and suicidal despair during the period.

Hacker, P.M.S. *Wittgenstein.* New York: Routledge, 1999. 64pp. Hacker, a recognized expert on the philosopher, supplies an accessible, compact biographical summary of Wittgenstein's life and thought in this helpful introduction for the general reader.

Biographical Novels

Duffy, Bruce. *The World as I Found It.* New York: Ticknor & Fields, 1987. 546pp. Duffy traces Wittgenstein's career from the years before World War I through 1951. The novel is faithful to the facts of the philosopher's life and offers a believable portrait of Wittgenstein and his relationships with the English philosophers Bertrand Russell and G.E. Moore.

Fictional Portraits

Collins, Randall. *The Case of the Philosopher's Ring.* New York: Crown, 1978. 152pp. Sherlock Holmes is dispatched to Cambridge to deal with a threat to Wittgenstein's life in this evocative period mystery with portraits of the members of the philosopher's university circle, including Bertrand Russell and John Maynard Keynes.

Eagleton, Terry. *Saints and Scholars.* New York: Verso, 1987. 145pp. Eagleton's novel imagines a fanciful meeting in 1916 with Wittgenstein, Irish revolutionary James Connolly, Marxist philosopher Nikolai Bakhtin, and Leopold Bloom, the fictional hero of James Joyce's *Ulysses,* for philosophical debate on political and social issues.

Biographical Films and Theatrical Adaptations

Wittgenstein (1993). Director: Derek Jarman. This experimental portrait of Wittgenstein (Karl Johnson) takes the form of a series of vignettes from his life, including his relationship with such figures as John Maynard Keynes (John Quentin) and Bertrand Russell (Michael Gough). Video.

Other Sources

Rhees, Rush, ed. *Recollections of Wittgenstein.* New York: Oxford University Press, 1984. 236pp. This collection of reminiscences by Wittgenstein's students and friends includes revealing insights not available in any other source.

Sluga, Hans and David G. Stern, eds. *The Cambridge Companion to Wittgenstein.* New York: Cambridge University Press, 1996. 509pp. This collection of original essays by an international team of scholars sheds light on the development of Wittgenstein's ideas and work.

499. MARY WOLLSTONECRAFT
1759–1797

English writer and champion of women's rights, Wollstonecraft was an early proponent of educational equality for women. Her famous tract, *Vindication of the Rights of Women* (1792), is the first great feminist document. Her daughter was Mary Godwin Shelley, the author of *Frankenstein.*

Autobiography and Primary Sources

Collected Letters of Mary Wollstonecraft. Ralph M. Wardle, ed. Ithaca, New York: Cornell University Press, 1979. 439pp. Wollstonecraft's 346 surviving letters are mainly to Gordon Imlay and her husband, William Godwin, and record the details of her daily life and private feelings.

Recommended Biographies

Flexner, Eleanor. *Mary Wollstonecraft: A Biography.* New York: Coward-McCann, 1972. 307pp. Flexner's is a carefully documented critical biography that portrays an emotionally and intellectually complex woman, examining in detail the development of her ideas and the biographical connections between her life and her works.

Sunstein, Emily W. *A Different Face: The Life of Mary Wollstonecraft.* New York: Harper & Row, 1975. 383pp. Sunstein emphasizes the darker side of Wollstonecraft's life and temperament, supplying a credible psychological portrait based on the letters and an autobiographical reading of her works.

Tomalin, Claire. *The Life and Death of Mary Wollstonecraft.* New York: Harcourt, Brace, 1975. 216pp. Tomalin offers a sympathetic, though critical, assessment of Wollstonecraft's life and works that adds new details and corrections to the biographical record. Far from being a feminist saint, Tomalin's Wollstonecraft is a complex blend of strengths and weaknesses, as well as a compellingly human figure.

Other Biographical Studies

George, Margaret. *One Woman's "Situation": A Study of Mary Wollstonecraft.* Urbana: University of Illinois Press, 1970. 174pp. George offers the first sustained feminist reading of Wollstonecraft's life and ideas. Based on a close reading of Wollstonecraft's writing, George traces their autobiographical connections and offers a psychological interpretation to explain her motives for rebelling against the standards of the times.

Godwin, William. *Memoirs of Mary Wollstonecraft.* 1927. Reprint ed. New York: Haskell House, 1969. 351pp. This critical edition of Godwin's memoirs of his wife, written shortly after Wollstonecraft's death, supplements Godwin's text with hitherto unpublished letters and extensive notes assessing Godwin's account and identifying many of its references.

Lorch, Jennifer. *Mary Wollstonecraft: The Making of a Radical Feminist.* New York: St. Martin's, 1990. 127pp. Including a brief biographical overview, Lorch concentrates on Wollstonecraft's development as a thinker, her influences, and modern relevance.

Nixon, Edna. *Mary Wollstonecraft: Her Life and Times.* London: Dent, 1971. 271pp. Nixon's is a straightforward, reliable account of Wollstonecraft's life with an emphasis on her personality as glimpsed both from her works and her relationships.

Pennell, Elizabeth R. *Life of Mary Wollstonecraft.* Boston: Roberts, 1884. 360pp. The first full-length biography, Pennell's is a pioneering reassessment that helped to rehabilitate Wollstonecraft's reputation and importance. Drawing mainly on William Godwin's memoirs, the book is incomplete and limited in its sources but retains an historical interest as an early feminist reading of Wollstonecraft's career.

St. Clair, William. *The Godwins and the Shelleys: The Biography of a Family.* New York: W.W. Norton, 1989. 572pp. Despite the book's title, the focus here is almost exclusively on William Godwin, and its discussion of the Shelleys is largely restricted to the details of Mary Godwin's elopement with Percy Shelley and its impact on the Godwin family.

Wardle, Ralph M. *Mary Wollstonecraft: A Critical Biography.* 1951. Revised ed. Lincoln: University of Nebraska Press, 1966. 366pp. In the first scholarly biography based on hitherto untapped printed and manuscript sources, Wardle's critical study constructs a mainly reliable chronological narrative that relates Wollstonecraft's life and ideas to her work and the context of her times.

Biographical Novels

Detre, Jean. *A Most Extraordinary Pair.* Garden City, New York: Doubleday, 1975. 328pp. Mixing actual and invented letters and journal entries, the novel dramatizes Wollstonecraft's romance with

William Godwin up to her death in childbirth in a blend of accurate reporting and speculative fancy.

Sherwood, Frances. *Vindication*. New York: Farrar, Straus, 1993. 435pp. Sherwood offers a fictionalized biographical portrait of Wollstonecraft with many deviations from the facts in a modern repossession of Wollstonecraft's history and circle.

Recommended Juvenile Biographies

Miller, Calvin C. *Mary Wollstonecraft and the Rights of Women*. Greensboro, North Carolina: Morgan Reynolds, 1999. 112pp. This is an informative biography that relates Wollstonecraft's experiences with her developing political and feminist beliefs.

See also Mary Shelley

500. THOMAS WOLSEY
ca. 1475–1530

English statesman and cardinal, Wolsey was the lord chancellor to Henry VIII. He negotiated a treaty of universal peace between England and the principal European states and was twice a candidate for the papacy. Wolsey's failure to quickly secure Henry's divorce from Catherine of Aragon incurred the king's anger and his urging of a French marriage on the king aroused the enmity of Anne Boleyn. He lost the chancellorship, was arrested on a false charge, and died en route to London.

Recommended Biographies

Ferguson, Charles W. *Naked to Mine Enemies: The Life of Cardinal Wolsey*. Boston: Little, Brown, 1958. 543pp. Aimed at the general reader, though based on scholarly research, Ferguson sets Wolsey's personal history against a vivid period background and a social history of the early Tudor era.

Harvey, Nancy L. *Thomas Cardinal Wolsey*. New York: Macmillan, 1980. 238pp. Serving as a reliable introductory study for the general reader, Harvey's account follows the trajectory of Wolsey's career quoting extensively from primary sources.

Pollard, A.F. *Wolsey*. New York: Longmans, 1929. 393pp. Pollard covers Wolsey's political career and makes a balanced and judicious case for his place in English history by a great authority on the subject. The book traces both Wolsey's achievements and depicts the less attractive sides of his character.

Other Biographical Studies

Cavendish, George. *The Life and Death of Cardinal Wolsey*. Richard S. Sylvester, ed. New York: Oxford University Press, 1959. 304pp. This biographical profile by Wolsey's contemporary, first published in 1557, is sympathetic, granting him considerable loyalty to Henry VIII and strength of character.

Guy, John. *The Cardinal's Court: The Impact of Thomas Wolsey in Star Chamber*. Totowa, New Jersey: Rowman and Littlefield, 1977. 191pp.

Guy's specialized study examines in detail Wolsey's court relations based on a careful review of archival sources. The book gives the reader already familiar with the general outlines of Wolsey's career an authoritative view of his skills as a politician and the challenges he faced.

Gwyn, Peter. *The King's Cardinal: The Rise and Fall of Thomas Wolsey*. London: Barrie & Jenkins, 1990. 666pp. Gwyn's is a controversial revisionist portrait that, in the words of one reviewer, "tells us what Wolsey was not, not what he did." The book constructs a new model for viewing the chancellor with a selective presentation of details that challenges conventional views.

Ridley, Jasper. *Statesman and Saint: Cardinal Wolsey, Sir Thomas More, and the Politics of Henry VIII*. New York: Viking, 1983. 338pp. This dual biography of Wolsey and Sir Thomas More takes the measure of both men and concludes that the former was the better minister, while the latter was an intolerant fanatic and impractical idealist.

Taunton, Ethereal L. *Thomas Wolsey: Legate and Reformer*. New York: J. Lane, 1902. 253pp. The author, a Catholic priest, offers an extremely positive assessment of Wolsey's strength of character and effectiveness as a political leader, based on a careful review of government documents.

Williams, Neville. *The Cardinal and the Secretary*. New York: Macmillan, 1976. 278pp. Williams's book is a dual biography of Wolsey and Thomas Cromwell, his successor as chief minister to Henry VIII. The rise to power of both men is chronicled with their comparative strengths and limitations examined.

Fictional Portraits

Clynes, Michael. The Roger Shallot mystery series. 1991– . Wolsey appears frequently in Clynes's series of Tudor period mysteries involving Sir Roger Shallot and his employer Benjamin Daunbey. Titles include *The White Rose Murders* (1991), *The Grail Murders* (1993), *A Brood of Vipers* (1994), and *The Gallows Murder* (1996).

Lide, Mary. *Command of the King*. London: Grafton Books, 1990. 287pp. This tale, set during the early 1500s, offers a convincing look at Wolsey, Tudor life, and the court intrigues of the period.

Plaidy, Jean. *The King's Secret Matter*. New York: Putnam, 1995. 284pp. Wolsey figures prominently in this fictional depiction of the secret negotiations to arrange Henry's divorce from Catherine of Aragon.

Riley, Judith Merkle. *The Serpent Garden*. New York: Viking, 1996. 467pp. Henry VIII and Wolsey hatch a plot to put an English heir onto the French throne in this fanciful story involving a woman painter with a convincing period flavor.

Biographical Films and Theatrical Adaptations

Anne of the Thousand Days (1969). Director: Charles Jarrott. The relationship between Henry VIII (Richard Burton) and Anne Boleyn (Genevieve Bujold) is given a lavish, though historically inaccurate treatment, in this Hollywood

spectacle. Anthony Quayle portrays Wolsey. See Edward Fenton's *Anne of the Thousand Days* (New York: New American Library, 1970. 160pp.) for the novelization based on the screenplay. Video.

A Man for All Seasons (1966). Director: Fred Zimmerman. An Oscar-winning film version of Robert Bolt's play features masterful performances by Paul Scofield as More, Robert Shaw as Henry VIII, and Wendy Hiller as More's wife. Orson Welles appears briefly as Wolsey. Video.

A Man for All Seasons (1988). Director: Charlton Heston. Heston's cable television adaptation of the London stage production of Bolt's play has Heston in the lead as More with a strong supporting cast, including Vanessa Redgrave as More's wife, Martin Chamberlain as Henry, and John Gielgud as Wolsey. Video.

Six Wives of Henry VIII (1971). Directors: Naomi Capon and John Glenister. In this acclaimed English television miniseries with installments on each of Henry's wives, Keith Mitchell has been praised as the definitive Henry. The king's six wives are played by Annette Crosby, Dorothy Tutin, Elvi Hale, Anne Stallybrass, Angela Pleasence, and Rosalie Crutchley. Wolsey is portrayed by John Baskombe. Video.

See also Anne Boleyn; Henry VIII; Sir Thomas More

501. VIRGINIA WOOLF
1882–1941

English novelist and essayist considered a major innovator in twentieth-century fiction, Woolf belonged to a circle of writers, artists, and critics known as the Bloomsbury Group. Known for her use of stream-of-consciousness, Woolf's novels include *Mrs. Dalloway* (1925), *To the Lighthouse* (1927), and *The Waves* (1931). *The Common Reader* (1925) and *The Second Common Reader* (1933) are among the collections of her brilliant critical essays. Woolf is also celebrated for her published lecture, "A Room of One's Own" (1929). After battling mental illness, she committed suicide by drowning.

Autobiography and Primary Sources

The Diary of Virginia Woolf. Anne O. Bell, ed. New York: Harcourt, Brace, 1977–1984. 5 vols. Woolf's daily record of her life and feelings is an indispensable biographical source and a literary treasure, legitimately regarded as one of the very greatest diaries ever produced.

A Moment's Liberty: The Shorter Diary. Anne O. Bell, ed. (San Diego: Harcourt, Brace, 1990. 516pp.). This is an abridged edition of the earlier published diary.

The Letters of Virginia Woolf. Nigel Nicolson, ed. New York: Harcourt, Brace, 1975–1980. 6 vols. Woolf's letters provide a remarkable access to Woolf's personality, relationships, and genius. One of the great letter collections.

Congenial Spirits: The Selected Letters of Virginia Woolf. Joanne T. Banks, ed. (San Diego: Harcourt,

Brace, 1989. 472pp.). This collection includes some newly discovered letters.

Moments of Being: Unpublished Autobiographical Writings. Jeanne Schnikind, ed. New York: Harcourt, Brace, 1976. 207pp. This volume supplements Woolf's autobiographical volumes, *A Room of One's Own* (1929) and *Three Guineas* (1938) with five fragmentary memoirs written between 1907 and 1940, mostly dealing with the writer's first 30 years.

A Passionate Apprentice: The Early Journals, 1897–1909. Mitchell A. Leaska, ed. San Diego: Harcourt, Brace, 1990. 444pp. These seven notebooks written before Woolf launched her career as a writer illuminates the future artist's daily routine, family background, and developing sensibility.

Recommended Biographies

Bell, Quentin. *Virginia Woolf: A Biography.* New York: Harcourt, Brace, 1972. 2 vols. Bell's monumental biography stands above all others in terms of its comprehensiveness and authoritative insider's view. The work of Woolf's nephew, Bell's study takes full advantage of his intimacy with his aunt and access to important family papers.

Gordon, Lyndall. *Virginia Woolf: A Writer's Life.* New York: W.W. Norton, 1984. 341pp. Gordon's innovative study applies Woolf's own narrative technique to her life by focusing on a series of epiphanic moments that shaped her sensibility and art. The result is a revealing analysis of Woolf's inner life and the process she used to help transform the modern novel.

King, James. *Virginia Woolf.* New York: W.W. Norton, 1995. 699pp. King's is an insightful literary biography that explores the relationship between her life and her writings. An excellent, sophisticated introduction to Woolf's character and writing for the beginner and a refreshing reassessment for the specialist.

Lee, Hermione. *Virginia Woolf.* New York: Knopf, 1997. 893pp. This is a discerning and thoroughly absorbing account of Woolf's life and development. Although Lee has uncovered few new facts, she synthesizes her sources into a sensitive and penetrating examination that succeeds in allowing Woolf's human story and complexity to emerge. Lee replaces the image of the frail victim with a credible figure full of vitality and contradictions.

Other Biographical Studies

Dally, Peter. *The Marriage of Heaven and Hell: Manic Depression and the Life of Virginia Woolf.* New York: St. Martin's, 1999. 225pp. British psychiatrist Dally offers a psychobiographical diagnosis that suggests that Woolf suffered from cyclothymic disorder, a seasonal manic depression. This condition is applied to a simplified summary of the events of Woolf's life.

Dunn, Jane. *A Very Close Conspiracy: Vanessa Bell and Virginia Woolf.* Boston: Little, Brown, 1990. 338pp. Dunn's look at the Stephen sisters sheds light on both women's personality, their family background, and relationship. In a thematically arranged analysis the author demonstrates how their kinship and sibling rivalries illuminate possi-

ble explanations for Woolf's interests and temperament.

Leaska, Mitchell A. *Granite and Rainbow: The Hidden Life of Virginia Woolf.* New York: Farrar, Straus, 1998. 513pp. Less a biography than a series of critical observations on various aspects of Woolf's life and work, Leaska, a recognized authority on the writer, has many perceptive things to say particularly about the author's emotional and sexual life and its relation to the creative process.

Lehman, John. *Virginia Woolf and Her World.* New York: Harcourt, Brace, 1977. 128pp. This is an illustrated biography with a brief text that provides a workmanlike overview of the highlights of Woolf's life and literary career.

Mepham, John. *Virginia Woolf: A Literary Life.* New York: St. Martin's, 1991. 222pp. Mepham's brief critical biography narrates the story of Woolf's writing career as a series of experiments reflecting the writer's developing sensibility and quest for a meaningful view of her life.

Pippett, Aileen. *The Moth and the Star: A Biography of Virginia Woolf.* Boston: Little, Brown, 1955. 368pp. Pippett's early biography is comprehensive but limited in its sources and therefore more impressionistic than subsequent studies, more an accomplished sketch than a complete portrait.

Poole, Roger. *The Unknown Virginia Woolf.* New York: Cambridge University Press, 1995. 289pp. Poole offers a new interpretation of Woolf's mental history based on a close reading of Woolf's diaries, letters, and novels, as well as how Woolf's sexuality helps to inform her works.

Reid, Panthea. *Art and Affection: A Life of Virginia Woolf.* New York: Oxford University Press, 1996. 570pp. Reid's is an in-depth psychological reading of Woolf's life and career that locates the source of her torment in a lack of maternal love and a lifelong rivalry with her sister, Vanessa Bell. Correcting a number of misconceptions about Woolf's childhood and relationships, particularly with her husband, the book challenges many preconceptions and substitutes a fresh and coherent interpretation.

Rose, Phyllis. *Woman of Letters: A Life of Virginia Woolf.* New York: Oxford University Press, 1978. 298pp. Rose connects the details of Woolf's life with her works in a critical biography that empathetically follows the writer's considerable psychic distress and the personal challenges she faced to create her art from a feminist perspective.

Spater, George, and Ian Parsons. *A Marriage of True Minds: An Intimate Portrait of Leonard and Virginia Woolf.* New York: Harcourt, Brace, 1977. 210pp. Drawing mainly on Leonard Woolf's private papers and autobiography, the authors chronicle the Woolfs' 28-year marriage with a great deal of domestic details and a number of previously unpublished photographs from the family album.

Fictional Portraits

Cunningham, Michael. *The Hours.* New York: Farrar, Straus, 1998. 229pp. Woolf's suicide is movingly narrated in Cunningham's Pulitzer Prize–winning novel that mixes a number of interlinked stories in a modern repossession of Woolf's *Mrs. Dalloway.*

Hawkes, Ellen. *The Shadow and the Moth: A Novel of Espionage with Virginia Woolf.* New York: St. Martin's, 1983. 279pp. Virginia Woolf in 1917 recovering from a mental breakdown and suicide attempt gets involved in a complex mystery prompted by the downing death of a Belgian refugee. Other members of the Bloomsbury circle, including Leonard Woolf, Roger Fry, and Clive and Vanessa Bell are also involved.

Nunez, Sigrid. *Mitz: The Marmoset of Bloomsbury.* New York: HarperCollins, 1998. 116pp. The domestic life of Virginia and Leonard Woolf in the 1930s is imaginatively reflected through their pet marmoset.

Recommended Juvenile Biographies

Asbee, Sue. *Virginia Woolf.* Vero Beach, Florida: Rourke, 1990. 110pp. MG/YA. This is a brief survey of Woolf's life and a critical analysis of her major works.

Biographical Films and Theatrical Adaptations

Tom & Viv (1994). Director: Brian Gilbert. Michael Hastings co-wrote the filmscript based on his play (New York: Penguin, 1985. 126pp.) dramatizing Eliot's relationship with Vivienne Haigh-Wood. Willem Dafoe plays Eliot, and Miranda Richardson steals the show as the vivacious and troubled Vivienne. Joanna McCollum appears as Woolf. Video.

Virginia Woolf (1997). Producer: Bob Portway. A look at Woolf's life and writing techniques through excerpts from her works. Video.

Virginia Woolf (1988). Director: David Thomas. Eileen Aitkins portrays the author in a dramatized reading from her works with commentary on the writer's life and achievement. Video.

Other Sources

Bishop, Edward. *A Virginia Woolf Chronology.* Boston: G.K. Hall, 1989. 268pp. A valuable reference source, this is an extensive chronology that allows the reader to follow with ease the development of Woolf's writing, related to her reading and domestic and social life.

Hussey, Mark. *Virginia Woolf A to Z.* New York: Facts on File, 1995. 452pp. Alphabetical entries cover every aspect of Woolf's work and her life.

Noble, Joan R., ed. *Recollections of Virginia Woolf.* 1972. Reprint ed. Athens: Ohio University Press, 1994. 207pp. Noble collects a rich assortment of firsthand views of the writer.

Stape, J.H., ed. *Virginia Woolf: Interviews and Recollections.* Iowa City: University of Iowa Press, 1995. 195pp. Multiple perspectives on Virginia Woolf are collected from 42 relatives, close friends, acquaintances, and fellow writers.

502. WILLIAM WORDSWORTH
1770–1850

One of the greatest English poets of the Romantic movement and England's poet laureate, Wordsworth spent much of his life in the Lake District, about which he wrote. He collaborated with Samuel Taylor Coleridge on *Lyrical Ballads* (1798), which includes Wordsworth's famous "Tintern Abbey." Among his other works are the autobiographical *The Prelude* (1805) and *Poems in Two Volumes* (1807), which includes "Ode: Intimations of Immortality," the poem "Daffodils," and the sonnet "The World is Too Much with Us."

Autobiography and Primary Sources

Wordsworth can be usefully viewed through several collections of his letters including *The Letters of William and Dorothy Wordsworth*. Ernest de Selincourt, ed. (Oxford: Clarendon Press, 1967–1993. 8 vols.); *The Love Letters of William and Mary Wordsworth*. Beth Darlington, ed. (Ithaca, New York: Cornell University Press, 1981. 265pp.); and *Letters of William Wordsworth: A New Selection*. Alan G. Hill, ed. (New York: Oxford University Press, 1984. 330pp.).

Reed, Mark L. *Wordsworth: The Chronology of the Early Years 1770–99*. Cambridge, Massachusetts: Harvard University Press, 1967. 369pp.; *Wordsworth: The Chronology of the Middle Years 1800–15*. Cambridge, Massachusetts: Harvard University Press, 1975. 782pp. Reed's remarkable collection of all the documented facts of Wordsworth's activities up to the year 1815 is fashioned into a daily log giving the reader unprecedented access to the poet's personal experiences and making available the data of his life story.

Recommended Biographies

Gill, Stephen. *William Wordsworth: A Life*. New York: Oxford University Press, 1989. 525pp. Incorporating modern interpretations and scholarship, Gill's is the preferred single-volume critical biography. Extending if not fully superseding the view of the poet provided by Moorman, Gill is masterful in relating the details of Wordsworth's life with his work in a sophisticated but highly readable narrative account.

Moorman, Mary. *William Wordsworth: A Biography*. Oxford: Clarendon Press, 1957–1965. 2 vols. Moorman's detailed, comprehensive, and scholarly study remains the most complete record of Wordsworth's life. Avoiding the tendency of other biographies, Moorman balances her study with equal attention to the poet's years of great acclaim but poetic decline, finding not a radical break between the young poet of the revolution and the Tory apologist of the establishment but a coherence and unity.

Williams, John. *William Wordsworth: A Literary Life*. New York: St. Martin's, 1996. 208pp. Williams's brief biographical and critical study traces Wordsworth's artistic development, while challenging a number of commonly held views, particularly the notion that the poet's youth was untroubled. Williams looks closely at the dominant patterns in the poet's entire career, and the book provides a fresh assessment of both the man and his works.

Other Biographical Studies

Davies, Hunter. *William Wordsworth: A Biography*. New York: Atheneum, 1980. 367pp. In a popular condensation of the poet's life, Davies manages an accessible guided tour for the general reader. Based mainly on Moorman, the standard modern biography, this is a lively, informal summary of the highlights with a breezy, irreverent style that some may find infectious, others annoying.

Halliday, F.E. *Wordsworth and His World*. London: Thames and Hudson, 1970. 143pp. This visual biography blends a brief text with pictures of Wordsworth and the people and places associated with him. The highlights of the poet's life are covered with the poetry related to the places illustrated.

Harper, George M. *William Wordsworth: His Life, Works and Influence*. New York: Scribner, 1916. 2 vols. The first comprehensive, scholarly biography, Harper's is a diligently researched chronological study. Praised as "the finest critical presentment of Wordsworth's personality, period, work, and influence that has appeared," Harper's study was the standard biography throughout the first half of the twentieth century.

Legouis, Emile. *The Early Life of William Wordsworth, 1770-98*. 1897. Reprint ed. New York: Russell & Russell, 1965. 480pp. Legouis's study of Wordsworth's formative years and the autobiographical connection to *The Prelude* began the critical debate over the degree that the poem can be read as a accurate reflection of the poet's life, an issue that has dogged Wordsworth studies ever since.

Mahoney, John L. *William Wordsworth: A Poetic Life*. New York: Fordham University Press, 1997. 375pp. Mahoney's biographical study examines Wordworth's literary achievement and life through a close reading of several key and representative poems. Mahoney finds an underlying unity connecting Wordsworth's entire career, while drawing attention to the key transformative moments in his private and creative life.

Meyer, George W. *Wordsworth's Formative Years*. Ann Arbor: University of Michigan Press, 1943. 265pp. Focusing on the poet's life up to 1798, Meyer turned not to *The Prelude* but to the letters and Wordsworth's early poetry as a more accurate gauge of the poet's actual development.

Wordsworth, Christopher. *Memoirs of William Wordsworth*. Boston: Ticknor Reed, 1851. 2 vols. This tribute written by Wordsworth's nephew shortly after the poet's death is a partial portrait, primarily celebrating Wordsworth's Victorian laureate status. Discreet on the poet's years in France and initial sympathy toward the revolution, the book seeks out to burnish a reputation rather than reveal a life.

Recommended Juvenile Biographies

Bober, Natalie. *William Wordsworth: The Wandering Poet*. Nashville, Tennessee: T. Nelson, 1975. 191pp. MG/YA. Bober's is an extensive presentation of Wordsworth's life that captures his poetic method and impact.

Biographical Films and Theatrical Adaptations

Clouds of Glory (1988). Director: Ken Russell. David Warner portrays the poet, with David Hemmings as Coleridge and Felicity Kendall as Dorothy in this multipart British television series on the life of the poet. Video.

Wordsworth, 1770–1850 (1988). Director: Richard Mervyn. Wordsworth's life is briefly chronicled with readings from his works. Narrated by John Gielgud. Video.

Other Sources

Pinion, F.B. *A Wordsworth Chronology*. Boston: G.K. Hall, 1988. 255pp. Not as detailed or as thorough as Reed's two volumes, Pinion's is a useful reference source on Wordsworth's activities and compositions after 1815.

See also Samuel Taylor Coleridge

503. SIR CHRISTOPHER WREN
1623–1723

English architect Wren had an early career as a professor of astronomy and brilliant mathematician. He designed many new buildings after the Great Fire of London (1666), including St. Paul's Cathedral. His other buildings include Oxford's Sheldonian Theatre, London's Chelsea Hospital, and the Temple Bar in London. He also designed residences. Wren's work had great influence on church architecture in England and abroad.

Autobiography and Primary Sources

Wren, Christopher Jr. *Life and Works of Sir Christopher Wren from the Parentalia, or Memoirs by His Son Christopher*. Ernest J. Enthoven. New York: S. Buckley, 1903. 368pp. Assembled by Wren's son, this is an essential collection of documentary evidence on the architect and his family, including transcriptions of original sources now lost. The accompanying biographical account is untrustworthy, however, written to commemorate rather than reveal.

Recommended Biographies

Beard, Geoffrey W. *The Work of Christopher Wren*. London: Bloomsbury Books, 1987. 240pp. Aimed at the general reader, this is a highly readable, accessible illustrated presentation of the biographical facts and an introduction to Wren's accomplishments.

Little, Bryan D. G. *Sir Christopher Wren: A Historical Biography*. London: R. Hale, 1975. 288pp. Little's is a fascinating chronological narrative account of Wren's life that compensates for the lack of hard evidence about Wren's life by attempting to demonstrate the ways in which social and political events shaped his career and his art.

Summerson, John. *Sir Christopher Wren*. New York: Macmillan, 1951. 159pp. Part of the Brief Lives series, Summerson supplies for the general reader a concise biographical and critical introduction that adequately presents Wren's achievements in an accessible fashion.

Whinney, Margaret. *Christopher Wren*. New York: Praeger, 1971. 216pp. This is a major evaluation of the man and his work, equally accomplished in its presentation of Wren's character and temperament as his achievement. Accessible for the general reader, the book has something to offer the specialist as well.

Other Biographical Studies

Bennett, J.A. *The Mathematical Science of Christopher Wren*. New York: Cambridge University Press, 1982. 148pp. Bennett's is a specialized, scholarly study that looks closely at Wren's scientific activities, an area of Wren's life that has not received appropriate attention.

Chambers, James. *Christopher Wren*. New York: Sutton, 1998. 128pp. Part of the Pocket Biographies series, this is a good, basic overview of Wren's life and achievements that serves to orient the general reader in a concise summary.

Downes, Kerry. *The Architecture of Wren*. New York: Universe Books, 1982. 139pp. Although the book does not pretend to offer a comprehensive coverage of Wren's architectural development, this is a major study that has been called "the best single book on Wren." More an interpretation than a biography, Downes's study does offer insights on the man as well as his genius.

Hutchinson, Harold F. *Sir Christopher Wren: A Biography*. New York: Stein and Day, 1976. 191pp. Too brief to serve as more than an introduction, Hutchinson does attend to Wren's early scientific career before shifting to his architectural accomplishments.

Sekler, Eduard F. *Wren and His Place in European Architecture*. New York: Macmillan, 1956. 217pp. The biographical details presented serve mainly to place Wren's achievement in a chronological sequence. A quarter of this specialized study is devoted to reproductions of original plans and drawings and photographs of his buildings.

Weaver, Lawrence. *Sir Christopher Wren, Scientist, Scholar and Architect*. New York: Scribner, 1923. 173pp. Although brief, Weaver's is a reliable overview of the few documented facts concerning Wren's life, contemporary sources on his personality, and a competent review of his achievements.

Whitaker-Wilson, Cecil. *Sir Christopher Wren: His Life and Times*. New York: McBride, 1932. 268pp. Written to honor the tercentenary of his birth, this is a tribute volume that pads the meager biographical details with an evocation of life in London during the architect's lifetime.

Biographical Novels

Weiss, David. *Myself, Christopher Wren*. New York: Coward-McCann, 1974. 922pp. Weiss's massive biographical novel traces Wren's career from 1636 to 1708, following him through the English Civil War, the Restoration, the rebuilding of London after the Great Fire, and his struggle to complete St. Paul's Cathedral. With invented scenes and dialogue, the novel remains close to the facts of Wren's life and the events of the period.

Fictional Portraits

Laker, Rosalind. *Circle of Pearls*. Garden City, New York: Doubleday, 1990. 519pp. Wren's career as an architect is tied with this tale of a Royalist gentlewoman during the English Civil War.

Recommended Juvenile Biographies

Gould, Heywood. *Sir Christopher Wren: Renaissance Architect, Philosopher, and Scientist*. New York: F. Watts, 1970. 216pp. MG/YA. This is a substantial and informative biography that covers the full range of Wren's achievements, while relating his development to the wider historical and political context.

Weir, Rosemary. *The Man Who Built a City: A Life of Sir Christopher Wren*. New York: Farrar, Straus, 1971. 208pp. MG/YA. Although fictionalized, this is a detailed portrait of the man, his genius, and his times.

504. FRANK LLOYD WRIGHT
1867–1959

Widely considered the greatest American architect, Wright became known for his "prairie style," featuring strong, horizontal lines, low roofs, and open floorplans. Famous examples of this style are located in the Chicago and Phoenix areas. He was the first U.S. architect to introduce open planning in houses. Other buildings designed by Wright include the Larkin Office Building (Buffalo, 1904), the "Falling Water" house (Pennsylvania, 1936–1937), and the Guggenheim Museum (New York, 1946–1959).

Autobiography and Primary Sources

An Autobiography. New York: Duell, Sloan and Pearce, 1943. 561pp. Wright's often self-serving and unreliable recollections presented here are nevertheless a rich source of information on the man's perspective on his career, his taste, personality, and architectural views. Wright's biographer, Robert Twombly, has called the book "difficult, revealing, inaccurate, but compelling."

Letters to Apprentices. Fresno: Press at California State University, 1982. 211pp.; *Letters to Architects*. Fresno: Press at California State University, 1984. 227pp.; *Letters to Clients*. Fresno: Press at California State University, 1986. 320pp. Wright's letters arranged by recipients are an important reference source for the architect's strong views and remarkable and maddening personality traits.

Recommended Biographies

Gill, Brendan. *Many Masks: A Life of Frank Lloyd Wright*. New York: Putnam, 1987. 544pp. Gill, in a witty, irreverent, and candid assessment, alternates between admiration for the architect and disapproval of the man. As the book's title indicates, the focus is on Wright's various invented selves, contradictions, and paradoxes. Includes 300 photographs and drawings, as well as previously unpublished letters.

Secrest, Meryle. *Frank Lloyd Wright*. New York: Knopf, 1992. 634pp. Secrest narrates Wright's life

in full with a particular attention to detailing the architect's private side and family relationships that is strongest on the women in Wright's life, particularly the architect's life with his third wife, Olgivanna, and their working partnership. Extensively researched and drawing on the archives of the Wright Memorial Foundation, the book provides fresh insights into Wright's turbulent career and often contradictory personality.

Twombly, Robert C. *Frank Lloyd Wright: His Life and His Architecture*. New York: Wiley, 1979. 444pp. The author has reworked and expanded his earlier book, *Frank Lloyd Wright: An Interpretive Biography* (New York: Harper & Row, 1973. 373pp.), to present a sensible, balanced examination of the architect and his work that relates the various private crises and public scandals in Wright's life to his projects and artistic development.

Other Biographical Studies

Blake, Peter. *The Master Builders: Le Corbusier, Mies Van der Rohe, Frank Lloyd Wright*. New York: W.W. Norton, 1976. 399pp. Blake's multiple portraits of the leading figures of modern architecture are sensible and objective accounts that relate the career of each to the intellectual and artistic ideas that they helped to define.

Brooks, H. Allen. *Frank Lloyd Wright and the Prairie School*. New York: G. Braziller, 1984. 120pp. Brooks's text for a catalog exhibition of drawings and photographs summarizes Wright's early breakthrough contributions to domestic architecture.

Farr, Finis. *Frank Lloyd Wright: A Biography*. New York: Scribner, 1961. 293pp. The first full-length biography is a compact and chronological, popular study that emphasizes Wright the man throughout a career filled with both triumphs and setbacks.

Johnson, Donald L. *Frank Lloyd Wright Versus America: The 1930s*. Cambridge, Massachusetts: MIT Press, 1990. 436pp. Johnson provides extensive coverage of Wright's life and work between 1928 and 1941, offering one of the most detailed accounts available of the architect's "second golden age."

Muschamp, Herbert. *Man about Town: Frank Lloyd Wright in New York City*. Cambridge, Massachusetts: MIT Press, 1983. 214pp. Limited to Wright's final period between 1935 and 1959, Muschamp chronicles the impact of New York on the architect's development. Muschamp's thesis about the importance New York played in Wright's career challenges accepted views.

Scully, Vincent J. *Frank Lloyd Wright*. New York: G. Braziller, 1960. 125pp. Scully's informed, concise assessment of Wright's career offers suggestions about the various influences that shaped his ideas and the contexts out of which his work evolved, with affinities as diverse as Whitman and Nietzsche.

Smith, Norris K. *Frank Lloyd Wright: A Study in Architectural Content*. Englewood Cliffs, New Jersey: Prentice-Hall, 1966. 178pp. In Smith's revisionist appraisal of Wright's career and achievement, the architect is seen not as a modernist but as a romantic conservative, a utopian deeply rooted in American mythology.

Tafel, Edgar. *Apprentice to Genius: Years with Frank Lloyd Wright.* New York: McGraw-Hill, 1979. 228pp. Tafel, an architect and Wright associate, shares his reminiscences mainly about the Depression era that grants the architect genius but exposes his unpleasant personality as an arrogant, blustering braggart.

Wright, John Lloyd. *My Father Who Is on Earth.* New York: Putnam, 1946. 231pp. Wright's son supplies anecdotal reminiscences as an "unconventional portrait of an unconventional man." Although the book details Wright's shortcomings as a family man, a fully believable Wright eludes the grasp of his son.

Wright, Olgivanna Lloyd. *The Shining Brow: Frank Lloyd Wright.* New York: Horizon, 1966. 300pp. Wright's third wife offers her recollections of their relationship from the 1920s with an emphasis on Wright's private rather than public life. *Frank Lloyd Wright: His Life, His Works, His Words* (New York: Horizon, 1966. 224pp.) focuses on her husband's work in a chronological account of the various projects Wright undertook during the years of their marriage.

Biographical Novels

Levin, Meyer. *The Architect.* New York: Simon & Schuster, 1981. 413pp. Based on the early life of the architect, Levin's novel traces Wright's development of his art, his main passion that dominates an unconventional private life.

Fictional Portraits

Miles, Keith. *Murder in Perspective: An Architectural Mystery.* New York: Walker, 1997. 250pp. This murder mystery features an appearance by Wright during the building of the Arizona Biltmore in Phoenix in the 1920s.

Recommended Juvenile Biographies

Boulton, Alexander O. *Frank Lloyd Wright: An Illustrated Biography.* New York: Rizzoli, 1993. 128pp. YA. This handsomely designed, large volume is an excellent introduction to Wright's life and work that deals frankly with the architect's private life.

McDonough, Yona Z. *Frank Lloyd Wright.* New York: Chelsea House, 1992. 111pp. MG/YA. This is a competent, informative overview of Wright's life and art.

Rubin, Susan G. *Frank Lloyd Wright.* New York: Abrams, 1994. 92pp. MG/YA. Part of the acclaimed First Impressions series, Rubin covers both the significant events of Wright's life and his development as an architect, with numerous photographs of his most famous projects.

Biographical Films and Theatrical Adaptations

Muldoon, Paul. *Shining Brow.* Boston: Faber and Faber, 1993. 86pp. Commissioned by the Madison Opera as a libretto for American composer Daron Aric Hagen, Muldoon's dramatic poem tells the story of Wright's genius and his affair with the wife of a wealthy client.

Frank Lloyd Wright (1998). Director: Ken Burns. This is an impressive film treatment of Wright's life and achievement that covers both his private life, personality, and public career with views of many of his most famous buildings. Video.

Frank Lloyd Wright: American Architect (1988). Producer: Films for the Humanities. A documentary film portrait that covers Wright's life, career, and accomplishments. Video.

Frank Lloyd Wright: Portrait of an Artist (1983). Director: Murray Grigor. This film portrait traces the development of Wright's architectural vision and includes recordings of the architect's reflections. Video.

Frank Lloyd Wright: The Mike Wallace Interviews (1994). Director: Bob Eisenhardt. These interviews were filmed in 1957 with a taped introduction and conclusion by Wallace in 1994. Video.

Other Sources

Brooks, H. Allen. *Writings on Wright: Selected Comment on Frank Lloyd Wright.* Cambridge, Massachusetts: MIT Press, 1981. 229pp. Various clients, critics, and associates offer their recollections of Wright's genius, achievement, and legacy.

Tafel, Edgar. *About Wright: An Album of Recollections by Those Who Knew Him.* New York: J. Wiley, 1993. 326pp. This is a rich collection of reminiscences from clients, builders, apprentices, and family members forming an intimate portrait of the architect. With letters and photographs never before published.

505–506. WILBUR WRIGHT (1867–1912); ORVILLE WRIGHT (1871–1948)

American aeronautical engineers Wilbur and Orville Wright are renowned for building and flying the first successful powered heavier-than-air aircraft, flown at Kitty Hawk, North Carolina, in 1903. They initially experimented with gliders, for which Wilbur invented the first aileron, and built and experimented with a wind tunnel. After Kitty Hawk, the Wrights built several biplanes and won fame with record-breaking flights in the United States and France.

Autobiography and Primary Sources

Miracle at Kitty Hawk: The Letters of Wilbur and Orville Wright. Fred C. Kelly, ed. New York: Farrar, Straus, 1951. 482pp. This collection of some 500 letters has extensive biographical interest, focusing less on the technical side of the Wrights's aviation work contained in *The Papers* and more on their collaboration, daily activities, and personalities.

The Papers of Wilbur and Orville Wright. Marvin W. McFarland, ed. New York: McGraw-Hill, 1953. 2 vols. Containing some 1,200 letters, notes, diagrams, and rare photographs, this important collection of primary materials documents the Wrights's progress and relationship, essential for the biographer and the historian of aviation.

How We Invented the Airplane. Fred C. Kelly, ed. New York: McKay, 1953. 78pp. Testimony written by Orville Wright for a governmental lawsuit provides a brief, detailed account of the stages leading up to the first airplane flight from his perspective.

Recommended Biographies

Crouch, Tom D. *The Bishop's Boys: A Life of Wilbur and Orville Wright.* New York: W.W. Norton, 1989. 606pp. Balancing both the story of the Wrights' technical achievement with the most sophisticated and credible look at their background, temperament, and development, Crouch's well-researched study is a compelling biography of both men and their family and as a history of early aviation.

Howard, Fred. *Wilbur and Orville: A Biography of the Wright Brothers.* New York: Knopf, 1987. 530pp. Howard's is a thorough, well-documented account that places the Wrights' achievement in a wide historical context and continues their story beyond 1909 and the legal wrangling that followed their triumphant flight. Sensible in its interpretations of the brothers and detailed in documenting their story, the biography is an excellent portrait of the men and their times.

Kelly, Fred C. *The Wright Brothers: A Biography Authorized by Orville Wright.* New York: Harcourt, Brace, 1943. 340pp. Reflecting both information gained from Orville Wright and his editorial input, Kelly's undocumented narrative account comes close to an autobiography and as such continues to claim interest. Readers looking for the full story behind the winning of lawsuits against aviaton pioneer Glenn Hammond Curtiss for patent disputes and Orville's perspective should look elsewhere.

Other Biographical Studies

Combs, Harry, with Martin Caidin. *Kill Devil Hill: Discovering the Secret of the Wright Brothers.* Boston: Houghton Mifflin, 1979. 389pp. Combs, an experienced pilot and aeronautical engineer, supplies an accessible summary of the technical achievements of the Wright brothers for the nonspecialist. The book is less useful as a critical and realistic evaluation of the Wrights' personalities and development.

Freudenthal, Elsbeth E. *Flight into History: The Wright Brothers and the Air Age.* Norman: University of Oklahoma Press, 1949. 268pp. Fred C. Kelly's review of Freudenthal's effort to reassess the Wrights' achievement in the wider context of aviation history stated that "For persistent inaccuracy, basic misconceptions, and distortions, this book should set some kind of record." In the author's view, the Wrights are seen less as innovators than in practical exploiters of the work of others, and this thesis dominants the book's somewhat slanted presentation of the facts.

McMahon, John R. *The Wright Brothers: Fathers of Flight.* Boston: Little, Brown, 1930. 308pp. More myth than a reliable biography, McMahon's treatment imagines conversations and reduces the actual story of the Wrights' achievement to a romanticized pleasing pattern of the eventual rewards of pluck and native ingenuity. Orville Wright attempted to suppress its publication.

Walsh, John E. *One Day at Kitty Hawk: The Untold Story of the Wright Brothers and the Airplane.* New York: Crowell, 1975. 305pp. Surveying the Wrights' activities up to 1909, Walsh argues that Wilbur was the preeminent force behind the brothers' efforts, a fact that has been obscured by his early death and Orville's self-serving manipulation of the facts through Kelly's biography, a thesis that later biographers have disputed.

Recommended Juvenile Biographies

Freedman, Russell. *The Wright Brothers: How They Invented the Airplane.* New York: Holiday House, 1991. 129pp. MG/YA. Profusely illustrated, this is a lively and informative account of the Wright brothers' background and technical achievements. A 1992 Newbery Honor Book.

Haynes, Richard M. *The Wright Brothers.* Englewood Cliffs, New Jersey: Silver Burdett, 1991. 143pp. MG. This biography relies on extensive quotes from the Wrights' letters and writings to trace their lives and demonstrate their accomplishments.

Welch, Becky. *The Wright Brothers: Conquering the Sky.* New York: Fawcett Columbine, 1992. 120pp. MG. Welch's is a competent narrative account of the Wrights' achievement.

Biographical Films and Theatrical Adaptations

A&E Biography Video: Wilbur & Orville: Dreams of Flying (1994). Producer: Gino Del Guercio. The Wrights' background and achievement are profiled using archival material and rare photos and film footage. Video.

The Winds of Kitty Hawk (1978). Director: E.W. Swackhamer. David Huffman plays Orville and Michael Moriarty is Wilbur in this dramatization of the brothers' attempt to be the first into the air. Video.

The Wright Stuff (1996). Producer: Nancy Porter. In an installment of PBS's American Experience series, the Wrights are viewed in a full-length biographical portrait. Video.

Other Sources

Renstrom, Arthur G. *Wilbur & Orville Wright: A Chronology.* Washington, DC: Library of Congress, 1975. 234pp. Renstrom supplies a detailed chronology of the Wrights' activities based on a careful review of all the relevant source material.

507. WILLIAM BUTLER YEATS
1865–1939

Irish poet and playwright, Yeats is considered one of the world's greatest lyric poets and a major figure of twentieth-century literature. Irish nationalism is an important element of his early works, such as *The Wanderings of Oisin* (1889). Among his other poems are "The Lake Isle of Innisfree," "The Second Coming," "The Tower," and "Sailing to Byzantium." Yeats was a cofounder of the Abbey Theatre and his dramatic works include *The Hour Glass* (1904) and *Deirdre* (1907). Yeats was a member of the Irish senate and winner of the 1923 Nobel Prize in Literature.

Autobiography and Primary Sources

Autobiographies. William H. O'Donnell and Douglas N. Archibald, eds. New York: Simon & Schuster, 1999. 560pp. Consisting of six autobiographical works that Yeats combined into a single memoir of his first 58 years, this is a fascinating, though selective and creative, series of recollections. The editors provide useful explanatory notes to help clarify the discrepancy between Yeats's version and the facts.

The Collected Letters of W.B. Yeats. John Kelly, ed. New York: Oxford University Press, 1986–. 3 vols. This collection has substantially expanded our view and altered many assumptions about Yeats's life, personality, and ideas, reflected in the first volume of R.F. Foster's impressive new biography of the poet's formative years. While awaiting the completion of this scholarly collection, which has reached the year 1904, the reader can still rely on the *Letters of W.B. Yeats.* Allan Wade, ed. (London: R. Hart-Davis, 1954. 938pp.).

Memoirs. Denis Donoghue, ed. New York: Macmillan, 1973. 318pp. This work reprints the first draft of Yeats's autobiography written in 1915 and 1916 and his journal from 1908 to 1930. More immediate and less artistically reworked than his *Autobiographies,* this is, like Yeats's letters, an indispensable source of biographical details.

Recommended Biographies

Alldritt, Keith. *W.B. Yeats: The Man and the Milieu.* New York: Clarkson Potter, 1997. 388pp.
More concerned with Yeats's public life and relationships, Alldritt succinctly covers the writer's entire life in the context of his times. Rejecting the notion of Yeats as a mystic dreamer, the book portrays him as ambitious and preoccupied with status and money.

Ellmann, Richard. *Yeats: The Man and the Masks.* New York: Macmillan, 1948. 331pp. Ellmann's book has long been regarded as the finest critical biography available. Emphasizing Yeats's intellectual and literary development through his many identity shifts, Ellmann ably tracks the inner drama of Yeats's life. The author's *The Identity of Yeats* (New York: Oxford University Press, 1954. 343pp.) is an equally impressive critical study of Yeats's poetic development.

Foster, R.F. *W.B. Yeats: A Life.* New York: Oxford University Press, 1997. 640pp. The first volume of Foster's masterful, authoritative study narrates the story of Yeats's life up to 1914. Drawing on modern scholarship, particularly John Kelly's scholarly edition of Yeats's letters, Foster's meticulously detailed account is the fullest and most comprehensive portrait of the artist that has been produced and promises when completed to become the standard biographical source for some time to come.

Jeffares, A. Norman. *W.B. Yeats: A New Biography.* New York: Farrar, Straus, 1989. 374pp. Revising his 1949 biography in the light of new sources and scholarship, Jeffares's is a reliable, well-documented, comprehensive, and intimate narrative treatment of Yeats's life that would well serve the reader as an excellent general introduction. One particular merit is the collection of photographs provided.

Other Biographical Studies

Brown, Terence. *The Life of W.B. Yeats: A Critical Biography.* Malden, Massachusetts: Blackwell, 1999. 410pp. Brown's is an able, judicious account of the relationship among Yeats's life, personality, and artistic career. The book is particularly insightful on Yeats's poetry and his evolving sensibility and cultural background.

Hone, Joseph. *W.B. Yeats: 1865–1939.* 1943. Revised ed. New York: Macmillan, 1962. 535pp. The first comprehensive biography, Hone's factual record has been long superseded, but the book does
draw on the author's 30-year friendship with his subject and a firsthand view of Irish intellectual life from the 1880s.

Jeffares, A. Norman. *W.B. Yeats: Man and Poet.* New Haven, Connecticut: Yale University Press, 1949. 365pp. More objective and critically astute than Hone's authorized biography, Jeffares provides a more complete and thoroughly documented account of Yeats's career with an emphasis on his development as a poet and the relationship between his life and his work. The author's 1989 revision, discussed above, incorporates more recent scholarship.

Mac Liammóir, Micheál, and Eavan Boland. *W.B. Yeats and His World.* New York: Scribner, 1978. 144pp. This is a fine illustrated biography combining photographs of the poet, his associates, and sites with a sensible text that covers the highpoints of Yeats's career and accomplishments.

Macrae, Alasdair. *W.B. Yeats: A Literary Life.* New York: St. Martin's, 1995. 204pp. Macrae's literary biography stresses Yeats's public activities; relationship with family, friends, and colleagues; and publishing history with a discussion of his works and politics in their historical context.

Maddox, Brenda. *Yeats's Ghosts: The Secret Life of W.B. Yeats.* New York: HarperCollins, 1999. 474pp. Maddox begins her study in 1917, when the poet was 51, and concentrates on his relationship with his wife, Georgie Hyde-Lees, and their mutual fascination with automatic writing and the occult. In the author's view, Yeats's wife used her husband's fascination with her as a medium to control him and make him dependent on her.

Murphy, William M. *Family Secrets: W.B. Yeats and His Relatives.* Syracuse, New York: Syracuse University Press, 1995. 534pp. In a sequel to the author's acclaimed biography of John Butler Yeats, *Prodigal Father* (1978). Murphy provides one of the most detailed and revealing studies of Yeats's family background and his relationship with his parents and his siblings, based on previously untapped primary sources.

Tuohy, Frank. *Yeats.* New York: Macmillan, 1976. 232pp. Tuohy approaches Yeats from his historical, social, and intellectual context with a wealth of background detail to help explain the writer's activities and interests. Written for the nonspecialist, the book succeeds in providing the general reader with a solid introduction to the man, the writer, and his times.

Fictional Portraits

Fitzgibbon, Constantine. *High Heroic*. New York: W.W. Norton, 1969. 176pp. Irish revolutionary leader Michael Collins's life is the subject here with portrayals by a number of historical figures, including Yeats.

Spellman, Cathy C. *An Excess of Love*. New York: Delacorte, 1985. 526pp. Two sisters get involved in the Irish independence movement in this novel featuring appearances by a large cast of historical figures, including Michael Collins, James Connolly, Sean O'Casey, Eamon De Valera, Constance Markievicz, and Yeats.

Recommended Juvenile Biographies

Spivak, Gayatri. *Myself Must I Remake: The Life and Poetry of W.B. Yeats*. New York: Crowell, 1974. 201pp. YA. This is a sophisticated portrait of the poet's development that presupposes a background in Irish and English literary history.

Biographical Films and Theatrical Adaptations

Young Cassidy (1965). Director: Jack Cardiff. This colorful look at Dublin life during 1910 features Rod Taylor as playwright Sean O'Casey and an appearance by Yeats, played by Michael Redgrave. A fine supporting cast includes Julie Christie, Maggie Smith, Edith Evans, and Jack MacGowran.

Other Sources

McCready, Sam. *A William Butler Yeats Encyclopedia*. Westport, Connecticut: Greenwood, 1997. 484pp. This valuable reference volume is a comprehensive record of Yeats's life and work through 1,000 alphabetically arranged entries on his writings, allusions, and people and places with whom he was associated.

Mikhail, E.H. *W.B. Yeats: Interviews and Recollections*. New York: Barnes and Noble, 1977. 2 vols. This is a rich and varied collection of views on the poet by friends, associates, and contemporaries.

508. BRIGHAM YOUNG
1801–1877

American Mormon leader Brigham Young spent three years as a missionary in England before assuming the Mormon leadership after the death of founder Joseph Smith (1844). Young led the great Mormon migration west from Nauvoo, Illinois, to Utah, where he directed the settlement of Salt Lake City. Under his direction, the city became a prosperous community. Young was the first governor of Utah but lost his post after the U.S. military expedition against the Mormons, known as the Utah War.

Autobiography and Primary Sources

Diary of Brigham Young, 1857. Ernest L. Cooley, ed. Salt Lake City, Utah: Tanner Trust Fund, 1980. 105pp. This is the only one of Young's diaries and journals to be published, covering several months in 1857.

Letters of Brigham Young to His Sons. Dean C. Jessee, ed. Salt City, Utah: Deseret, 1974. 375pp. This collection of letters offers a revealing personal portrait of the man.

Manuscript History of Brigham Young. Elden J. Watson, ed. Salt Lake City, Utah: Elden J. Watson, 1968–1971. 2 vols. Contemporary documents from the 1850s have been assembled to record Young's public career.

Recommended Biographies

Arrington, Leonard J. *Brigham Young: American Moses*. New York: Knopf, 1985. 522pp. The author, a Mormon historian, has used unprecedented access to archival sources to produce the most detailed, authoritative study of Young. In the author's provocative assessment, Young embodied the "supreme American paradox," uniting "the business genius of a Rockefeller with the spiritual sensitivities of an Emerson, the lusty enjoyment of the pleasures of good living with the tenderness of a Florence Nightingale."

Bringhurst, Newell G. *Brigham Young and the Expanding American Frontier*. Boston: Little, Brown, 1986. 246pp. Bringhurst's narrative biography traces the steps by which Young became a Mormon and his rise to leadership in the aftermath of Joseph Smith's murder. Young's achievements are placed in the context of frontier history. Serves as a solid introductory study for the general reader and student.

Other Biographical Studies

Gates, Susa Young, with Leah D. Widtsoe. *The Life Story of Brigham Young*. New York: Macmillan, 1930. 388pp. Young's daughter organizes her recollections into a biographical profile of her father, dealing with his character and family life. Although intended as a vindication of her father's memory, the book is a rich source of unique, anecdotal details of Young's domestic life.

Hirshson, Stanley P. *The Lion of the Lord: A Biography of Brigham Young*. New York: Knopf, 1969. 391pp. Lack of objectivity mars this debunking study that portrays Young as a charlatan and a liar. The author's attack on polygamy dominates this treatment that never fully resolves the contradictions in Young's character or his multiple roles into a plausible psychological portrait.

Nibley, Preston. *Brigham Young: The Man and His Work*. Salt Lake City, Utah: Deseret, 1936. 551pp. Nibley's documentary chronicle covers Young's life, using extensive excerpts from his sermons and letters.

Werner, Morris R. *Brigham Young*. New York: Harcourt, Brace, 1925. 487pp. The author offers an entertaining, dramatic narrative account of Young's life and Mormon history that goes back to Joseph Smith and the founding of Mormonism. All

sides of Young's enigmatic character are well depicted with extensive quotations from his sermons.

Biographical Novels

Fisher, Vardis. *Children of God: An American Epic*. New York: Harper, 1939. 769pp. Fisher's panoramic narrative chronicles the founding of Mormonism from Smith's first visions through the religious persecution in the Midwest and the epic trek west led by Brigham Young.

Furnas, Joseph C. *The Devil's Rainbow*. New York: Harper, 1962. 341pp. Young's rise to leadership of the Mormons is portrayed in this fictional account of Joseph Smith's life from his first revelation to his murder.

Fictional Portraits

Bailey, Paul. *For Time and All Eternity*. Garden City, New York: Doubleday, 1964. 400pp. The government's campaign against the Mormon practice of polygamy is dramatized in this story of Mormon woman. Young is depicted.

Bowen, Peter. *Kelly Blue*. New York: Crown, 1991. 264pp. This humorous western tale concerns the adventures of an army scout, Indian fighter, and adventurer who is pursued by Brigham Young and is in the thick of the fighting during the Indian wars of the 1870s.

Jones, Cleo. *Sister Wives*. New York: St. Martin's, 1984. 474pp. Mormon practices during the 1850s are dramatized from the perspective of a woman who rebels from her fate as her husband's third wife. Actual events and appearances by several historical figures, including Young, Mark Twain, and James Buchanan, are blended with the novel's invented story.

Lauritzen, Jonreed. *The Everlasting Fire*. Garden City, New York: Doubleday, 1962. 474pp. Focusing on the events of the Mormon migration west through the perspective of a fictional family who endure hostility and prejudice, the novel depicts the events leading up to Smith's murder and Brigham Young's rise to leadership.

Reife, A.R. *Salt Lake City*. New York: New American Library, 1989. 351pp. The founding of Salt Lake City and the early years of the Mormons in Utah are depicted from the perspective of a Young follower who must contend with Indians, hostile settlers, an unforgiving landscape, and the government's determination to suppress the Mormons.

Recommended Juvenile Biographies

Bernotas, Bob. *Brigham Young*. New York: Chelsea House, 1992. 111pp. MG/YA. Bernotas's is an informative biographical/historical overview that traces the major events of Young's career in their wider historical context.

Simon, Charnan. *Brigham Young: Mormon and Pioneer*. New York: Childrens Press, 1998. 42pp. MG. This is a brief, though helpful, objective account of Young's life, that deals frankly with polygamy and religious intolerance.

Biographical Films and Theatrical Adaptations

A&E Biography Video: Brigham Young: Architect of Faith (1995). Young's life is profiled in a balanced, objective view. Video.

Brigham Young: Frontiersman (1940). Director: Henry Hathaway. Vincent Price portrays Smith with Dean Jagger in the title role in this dramatization of the history of the Mormons through the founding of Salt Lake City. Tyrone Power and Linda Darnell carry the nonhistorical load. Video.

Trail of Hope (1997). Director: Lee Groberg. This insightful PBS documentary traces the history of the Mormons and their trek west. The companion volume by Heidi S. Swinton, *American Prophet: The Story of Joseph Smith* (Salt Lake City: Shadow Mountain, 1999. 160pp.), reprints the film's commentary by leading historians, including Robert Remini. Video.

See also Joseph Smith

Z

509. EMILE ZOLA
1840–1902

French novelist Emile Zola was a major exponent of literary naturalism. He first won success with the novel *Thérèse Racquin* (1867). His series of 20 novels, *Les Rougon-Macquart* (1871–1893), includes *The Dram-Shop* (1877), *Nana* (1880), and *Germinal* (1885). An ardent advocate of social reform and an anti-Catholic, Zola wrote numerous diatribes against the clergy and the church. His pamphlet, *J'accuse* (1898), attacked the army in the Dreyfus affair, in which documents had been forged to imprison an army officer for treason.

Recommended Biographies

Brown, Frederick. *Zola: A Life*. New York: Farrar, Straus, 1995. 888pp. Brown's monumental study matches the man, capturing both the private and public lives of a complex figure as well as his social, political, and intellectual world. Based on new research and documentary evidence, Brown's adds both breadth and depth to our view of the writer, and the book is likely to remain the standard life for some time to come.

Hemmings, F.W.J. *The Life and Times of Emile Zola*. New York: Scribner, 1977. 192pp. Hemmings's is an excellent, brief scholarly biography that relates aspects of Zola's life to their sociohistorical context and their reflection in his works. The book is a wonder of critical and scholarly compression, achieving a full and convincing human portrait.

Richardson, Joanna. *Zola*. New York: St. Martin's, 1978. 283pp. Richardson's readable critical biography traces the evolution of Zola's creativity and the connection between his life and his works. Recommended for the general reader looking for a good introduction.

Schom, Alan. *Emile Zola: A Biography*. New York: Holt, 1988. 303pp. For readers without the patience and persistence needed to tackle Brown's massive study, Schom's full-length portrait is an excellent alternative. Judicious in its treatment and informed by a solid presentation of time and place, the book skillfully presents Zola's remarkable progress from obscurity to the center of his age's controversies.

Other Biographical Studies

Josephson, Matthew. *Zola and His Times*. Garden City, New York: Garden City Pub. Co., 1928. 558pp. Although now superseded by subsequent scholarship and biographies, Josephson's massively documented study can still serve as an useful biographical presentation that shows the various sides of Zola's character set against a solid period background.

Lapp, John S. *Zola Before the Rougon-Macquart*. Toronto: University of Toronto Press, 1964. 171pp. The author limits his focus to Zola's formative years, ably chronicling the experiences that led to his first creative work and evolution of his creative ideas that shaped his first masterpieces.

Nelson, Brian. *Zola and the Bourgeoisie*. New York: Barnes and Noble, 1983. 230pp. Nelson's mainly critical study presents an interesting and revealing portrait of Zola's relationship to his times, showing that despite the novelist's attack on bourgeois values, his relationship to them is far more complicated. The social theme that the book traces is used as means of seeing Zola's career as a logical progression and unified whole.

Walker, Philip. *Emile Zola*. New York: Humanities Press, 1968. 118pp. Walker's brief biographical and critical profile is an informed and concise overview intended for the student and the generalist.

Walker, Philip. *Zola*. Boston: Routledge, 1985. 257pp. This is an admiring though critical biographical portrait that is not exhaustive but readable and informative. Serves mainly the general reader looking for a solid introduction.

Wilson, Angus. *Emile Zola: An Introductory Study of His Novels*. 1952. Revised ed. London: Secker and Warburg, 1964. 148pp. Wilson's lively introduction to Zola's life and work began an important reevaluation of the novelist and his achievement. This compact study retains its usefulness as a sensible critical overview of one novelist's view of another.

Biographical Films and Theatrical Adaptations

I Accuse! (1958). Director: Jose Ferrer. With a screenplay written by Gore Vidal, this dramatic account of the Dreyfus affair features Jose Ferrer as Dreyfus and Emlyn Williams as Zola, his defender.

The Life of Emile Zola (1937). Director: William Dieterle. Paul Muni puts in a stellar performance as the writer in a biographical portait focused on the Dreyfus scandal. A strong supporting cast includes Gale Sondergaard, Gloria Holden, and Joseph Schildkraut. Video.

Prisoner of Honor (1991). Director: Ken Russell. Russell's unique treatment of the Dreyfus affair is unreliable historically but still fascinating. A strong cast includes Richard Dreyfuss, Oliver Reed, Peter Firth, Brian Blessed, and a portrayal of Zola by Martin Friend. Video.

Indexes

Author Index

Numbers refer to entry numbers.

Index of Books and Other Works by Title

Numbers refer to entry numbers. Author or authors appear in parantheses following the title. Titles without authors are either films or television series, or else letters, memoirs, diaries, or autobiographies by the historical figure.

Index of Figures by Nationality

Numbers refer to entry numbers. This index is sorted by region, then by time period rather than alphabetically. Countries within regions are listed alphabetically following entries for the general region.

Index of Figures by Occupation

Numbers refer to entry numbers.

Index of Figures by Time, Period, and Place

Numbers refer to entry numbers.

Subject Index

Numbers refer to entry numbers.